*The Consumer Credit and Sales
Legal Practice Series*

FAIR CREDIT REPORTING

Sixth Edition

With CD-Rom

Chi Chi Wu
Elizabeth De Armond

Contributing Authors: Carolyn L. Carter, Richard Rubin, Ian B. Lyngklip, Leonard A. Bennett, Charles Delbaum, Lauren K. Saunders, Jonathan Sheldon, Joanne Faulkner

National Consumer Law Center

77 Summer Street, 10th Floor   Boston, MA 02110

www.consumerlaw.org

About NCLC	The National Consumer Law Center, a nonprofit corporation founded in 1969, assists consumers, advocates, and public policy makers nationwide who use the powerful and complex tools of consumer law to ensure justice and fair treatment for all, particularly those whose poverty renders them powerless to demand accountability from the economic marketplace. For more information, go to www.consumerlaw.org.
Ordering NCLC Publications	Order securely online at www.consumerlaw.org, or contact Publications Department, National Consumer Law Center, 77 Summer Street, Boston, MA 02110, (617) 542-9595, FAX: (617) 542-8028, e-mail: publications@nclc.org.
Training and Conferences	NCLC participates in numerous national, regional, and local consumer law trainings. Its annual fall conference is a forum for consumer rights attorneys from legal services programs, private practice, government, and nonprofit organizations to share insights into common problems and explore novel and tested approaches that promote consumer justice in the marketplace. Contact NCLC for more information or see our web site.
Case Consulting	Case analysis, consulting and co-counseling for lawyers representing vulnerable consumers are among NCLC's important activities. Administration on Aging funds allow us to provide free consulting to legal services advocates representing elderly consumers on many types of cases. Massachusetts Legal Assistance Corporation funds permit case assistance to advocates representing low-income Massachusetts consumers. Other funding may allow NCLC to provide very brief consultations to other advocates without charge. More comprehensive case analysis and research is available for a reasonable fee. See our web site for more information at www.consumerlaw.org.
Charitable Donations and Cy Pres Awards	NCLC's work depends in part on the support of private donors. Tax-deductible donations should be made payable to National Consumer Law Center, Inc. For more information, contact Suzanne Cutler of NCLC's Development Office at (617) 542-8010 or scutler@nclc.org. NCLC has also received generous court-approved *cy pres* awards arising from consumer class actions to advance the interests of class members. For more information, contact Robert Hobbs (rhobbs@nclc.org) or Rich Dubois (rdubois@nclc.org) at (617) 542-8010.
Comments and Corrections	Write to the above address to the attention of the Editorial Department or e-mail consumerlaw@nclc.org.
About This Volume	This is the Sixth Edition of *Fair Credit Reporting* with a 2006 companion CD-Rom. The Sixth Edition and 2006 CD-Rom supersede all prior editions, supplements, and CDs, which should all be discarded. Continuing developments can be found in periodic updates to this volume and in NCLC REPORTS, *Consumer Credit & Usury Edition*.
Cite This Volume As	National Consumer Law Center, Fair Credit Reporting (6th ed. 2006).
Attention	*This publication is designed to provide authoritative information concerning the subject matter covered. Always use the most current edition and supplement, and use other sources for more recent developments or for special rules for individual jurisdictions. This publication cannot substitute for the independent judgment and skills of an attorney or other professional. Non-attorneys are cautioned against using these materials to conduct a lawsuit without advice from an attorney and are cautioned against engaging in the unauthorized practice of law.*
Copyright	© 2006 by National Consumer Law Center, Inc. All Rights Reserved ISBN-13 978-1-60248-000-1 (this volume) ISBN-10 1-60248-000-1 (this volume) ISBN 0-943116-10-4 (Series) Library of Congress Control Number 2006937720

About the Authors

Chi Chi Wu is an NCLC staff attorney focusing on consumer credit issues, including fair credit reporting, credit cards, refund anticipation loans, and medical debt. She is the co-author of *Credit Discrimination* (4th ed. 2005) and contributing author to the prior edition of this volume, *Truth in Lending* (5th ed. 2003), and *The Cost of Credit* (3d ed. 2005). She was formerly an assistant attorney general with the Consumer Protection Division of the Massachusetts Attorney General's Office, and an attorney with the Asian Outreach Unit of Greater Boston Legal Services.

Elizabeth De Armond is on the faculty of Chicago-Kent College of Law. She has been a frequent contributor to NCLC publications and is a contributing author to *Fair Credit Reporting* (5th ed. 2002), *Consumer Warranty Law* (3d ed. 2006), *Unfair and Deceptive Acts and Practices* (6th ed. 2004), and *Automobile Fraud* (2d ed. 2003). She was in private practice in Texas and a clerk for the Hon. Cornelia Kennedy of the United States Court of Appeals for the Sixth Circuit. She is a member of the Illinois, Massachusetts and Texas bars.

Leonard A. Bennett has been in private practice in Newport News, Virginia, focusing on the representation of consumers and litigating cases throughout the country, since 1988. He is a member of the National Association of Consumer Advocates (NACA), Virginia State Bar Association, Virginia Trial Lawyers Association, and the Newport News Bar Association. Over the years he has been a speaker at numerous conferences and workshops, including several of NACA's Fair Credit Reporting Act national conferences.

Carolyn L. Carter is NCLC's deputy director for advocacy and was formerly co-director of Legal Services, Inc., in Gettysburg, Pennsylvania, and director of the Law Reform Office of the Cleveland Legal Aid Society. Her numerous publications include *Consumer Warranty Law* (3d ed. 2006), *Unfair and Deceptive Acts and Practices* (6th ed. 2004), *Repossessions* (6th ed. 2005), and *Automobile Fraud* (2d ed. 2003). She is a member of the Federal Reserve Board Consumer Advisory Council and was the 1992 recipient of the Vern Countryman Consumer Award.

Charles Delbaum is a staff attorney at NCLC focusing on class action litigation and is the co-author of *Consumer Class Actions* (6th ed. 2006). Immediately prior to joining NCLC in 2005, he was the director of litigation and advocacy at New Orleans Legal Assistance for thirteen years. He also supervised the Tulane Law School consumer/foreclosure clinic, co-authored a chapter on Louisiana Consumer Law for the 2001 and 2005 Louisiana Legal Services Desk books, and presented on consumer and other Louisiana topics at numerous CLEs. In 2000, he was the recipient of the Louisiana State Bar Association Pro Bono Publico Career Service Award. He has been a plaintiff's attorney for over thirty years.

Joanne S. Faulkner has a private consumer law practice in New Haven, Connecticut. Previously, she was an attorney at New Haven Legal Assistance for many years and has served as chair of the Consumer Law Section of the Connecticut Bar Association and as a member of the FRB's Consumer Advisory Council. She has contributed to a number of NCLC publications, including *Fair Credit Reporting* (5th ed. 2002). She is the 2002 recipient of the Vern Countryman Consumer Law Award.

Ian B. Lyngklip is a partner at Lyngklip & Taub Consumer Law Group PLC. He is a State Bar of Michigan Consumer Law Section Counsel chairperson and is currently serving on the National Association of Consumer Advocates board of directors. His recent honors include the Oakland County Bar Association Pro Bono Service Award (2005) and the Frank Kelly

Award, Michigan State Bar Association Consumer Law Section (2004). In 2003, he was named the Consumer Advocate of the Year by the National Association of Consumer Advocates. He participates regularly in the training of consumer law around the country.

Richard Rubin is a private attorney in Santa Fe, New Mexico whose practice is limited to representing consumers and consulting for other consumer rights specialists. He is a past co-chair of the National Association of Consumer Advocates, has taught consumer law at the University of New Mexico School of Law, and presents continuing legal education and attorney training programs throughout the country. He is the 2000 recipient of the Vern Countryman Consumer Law Award.

Lauren K. Saunders is the managing attorney of NCLC's Washington, DC, office. She has long been involved in public interest work including as directing attorney of the Federal Rights Project of the National Senior Citizens Law Center; deputy litigation director and housing conditions directing attorney at Bet Tzedek Legal Services in Los Angeles; and an associate in the public interest law firm Hall & Phillips. She is co-author of *Combating Foreclosure Rescue Scams* (2006), and a contributing author to *Foreclosures* (2006 Supplement).

Jonathan Sheldon has been an NCLC staff attorney writing on deceptive practices law, automobile fraud, leasing, and other consumer law topics since 1976. Previously he was a staff attorney with the Federal Trade Commission. His publications include *Unfair and Deceptive Acts and Practices* (1982, 1988, 1991, 1997, 2001, 2004), *Consumer Warranty Law* (1997, 2001, 2006), *Automobile Fraud* (1998, 2003), *Consumer Arbitration Agreements* (2001, 2002, 2003, 2004), *Credit Discrimination* (1st ed. 1993), and *Fair Credit Reporting* (2d ed. 1988).

Acknowledgements: We are particularly grateful to Denise Lisio for editorial supervision; Nathan Day for editorial assistance; Shirlron Williams for assistance with cite checking; Ariel Patterson, Mary Kingsley, Gillian Feiner, and Allen Agnitti for research assistance; Shannon Halbrook for production assistance; Mary McLean for indexing; Xylutions for typesetting services; and Neil Fogarty of Law Disks for developing the CD-Rom. Special thanks to Evan Hendricks, Deanne Loonin, Charlie Harak, Tom Domonoske, and Matt Erausquin for their substantive contributions. In addition, thanks also to Jim Francis, Tom Stubbs, Rick Feferman, Jamie Fishman, David Szwak, David Mour, Chris Green, and Robert Sola for contributing pleadings. We also appreciate all those who contributed to the prior five editions of this volume, especially Anthony Rodriguez, Willard Ogburn, and Mark Budnitz.

What Your Library Should Contain

The Consumer Credit and Sales Legal Practice Series contains 17 titles, updated annually, arranged into four libraries, and designed to be an attorney's primary practice guide and legal resource in all 50 states. Each manual includes a CD-Rom allowing pinpoint searches and the pasting of text into a word processor.

Debtor Rights Library

2006 Eighth Edition (Two Volumes) with CD-Rom, Including Law Disks' 2006 Bankruptcy Forms

Consumer Bankruptcy Law and Practice: the definitive personal bankruptcy manual, from the initial interview to final discharge, including consumer rights as creditors when a company files for bankruptcy. This revised edition fully incorporates the 2005 Act in the text and includes such practice aids as a redlined Code, Interim Rules, a date calculator, over 150 pleadings and forms, initial forms software, means test data, and a client questionnaire and handout.

2004 Fifth Edition, 2006 Supplement, and 2006 CD-Rom

Fair Debt Collection: the basic reference, covering the Fair Debt Collection Practices Act and common law, state statutory and other federal debt collection protections. Appendices and companion CD-Rom contain sample pleadings and discovery, the FTC Commentary, *all* FTC staff opinion letters, and summaries of reported and unreported cases.

2005 First Edition, 2006 Supplement, and 2006 CD-Rom

Foreclosures: a new volume covering VA, FHA and other types of home foreclosures, workout agreements, servicer obligations, and tax liens. The CD-Rom reprints key federal statutes, regulations, interpretations, and handbooks, and contains numerous pleadings.

2005 Sixth Edition, 2005 Supplement, and 2006 CD-Rom

Repossessions: a unique guide to motor vehicle and mobile home repossessions, threatened seizures of household goods, statutory liens, and automobile lease and rent-to-own default remedies. The CD-Rom reprints relevant UCC provisions, summarizes many other state statutes, and includes many pleadings covering a wide variety of cases.

2006 Third Edition with CD-Rom

Student Loan Law: student loan debt collection; closed school, false certification, disability, and other discharges; tax intercepts, wage garnishment, and offset of social security benefits; and repayment plans, consolidation loans, deferments, and non-payment of loan based on school fraud. CD-Rom and appendices contain numerous forms, pleadings, letters and regulations.

2004 Third Edition, 2006 Supplement, and 2006 CD-Rom

Access to Utility Service: the only examination of consumer rights when dealing with regulated, de-regulated, and unregulated utilities, including telecommunications, terminations, billing errors, low-income payment plans, utility allowances in subsidized housing, LIHEAP, and weatherization. Includes summaries of state utility regulations.

Credit and Banking Library

2003 Fifth Edition, 2006 Supplement, and 2006 CD-Rom

Truth in Lending: detailed analysis of *all* aspects of TILA, the Consumer Leasing Act, and the Home Ownership and Equity Protection Act (HOEPA). Appendices and the CD-Rom contain the Acts, Reg. Z, Reg. M, and their Official Staff Commentaries, numerous sample pleadings, rescission notices, and two programs to compute APRs.

National Consumer Law Center ■ 77 Summer Street ■ 10th Floor ■ Boston MA ■ 02110
(617) 542-9595 ■ FAX (617) 542-8028 ■ publications@nclc.org
Order securely online at www.consumerlaw.org

2006 Sixth Edition with CD-Rom	**Fair Credit Reporting:** the key resource for handling any type of credit reporting issue, from cleaning up blemished credit records to suing reporting agencies and creditors for inaccurate reports. Covers credit scoring, privacy issues, identity theft, the FCRA, the new FACT Act, the Credit Repair Organizations Act, state credit reporting and repair statutes, and common law claims.
2005 Third Edition, 2006 Supplement, and 2006 CD-Rom	**Consumer Banking and Payments Law:** unique analysis of consumer law (and NACHA rules) as to checks, money orders, credit, debit, and stored value cards, and banker's right of setoff. Also extensive treatment of electronic records and signatures, electronic transfer of food stamps, and direct deposits of federal payments. The CD-Rom and appendices reprint relevant agency interpretations and pleadings.
2005 Third Edition, 2006 Supplement, and 2006 CD-Rom	**The Cost of Credit: Regulation, Preemption, and Industry Abuses:** a one-of-a-kind resource detailing state and federal regulation of consumer credit in all fifty states, federal usury preemption, explaining credit math, and how to challenge excessive credit charges and credit insurance. The CD-Rom includes a credit math program and hard-to-find agency interpretations.
2005 Fourth Edition, 2006 Supplement, and 2006 CD-Rom	**Credit Discrimination:** analysis of the Equal Credit Opportunity Act, Fair Housing Act, Civil Rights Acts, and state credit discrimination statutes, including reprints of all relevant federal interpretations, government enforcement actions, and numerous sample pleadings.

Consumer Litigation Library

2004 Fourth Edition, 2006 Supplement, and 2006 CD-Rom	**Consumer Arbitration Agreements:** numerous successful approaches to challenge the enforceability of a binding arbitration agreement, the interrelation of the Federal Arbitration Act and state law, class actions in arbitration, collections via arbitration, the right to discovery, and other topics. Appendices and CD-Rom include sample discovery, numerous briefs, arbitration service provider rules and affidavits as to arbitrator costs and bias.
2006 Sixth Edition with CD-Rom	**Consumer Class Actions:** makes class action litigation manageable even for small offices, including numerous sample pleadings, class certification memoranda, discovery, class notices, settlement materials, and much more. Includes a detailed analysis of the Class Action Fairness Act of 2005, recent changes to Rule 23, class arbitration, and other contributions from experienced consumer class action litigators around the country.
2006 CD-Rom with Index Guide: ALL pleadings from ALL NCLC Manuals, including Consumer Law Pleadings Numbers One through Twelve	**Consumer Law Pleadings on CD-Rom:** Over 1200 notable recent pleadings from all types of consumer cases, including predatory lending, foreclosures, automobile fraud, lemon laws, debt collection, fair credit reporting, home improvement fraud, rent to own, student loans, and lender liability. Finding aids pinpoint the desired pleading in seconds, ready to paste into a word processing program.

Deception and Warranties Library

2004 Sixth Edition, 2006 Supplement, and 2006 CD-Rom	**Unfair and Deceptive Acts and Practices:** the only practice manual covering all aspects of a deceptive practices case in every state. Special sections on automobile sales, the federal racketeering (RICO) statute, unfair insurance practices, and the FTC Holder Rule.
2003 Second Edition, 2006 Supplement, and 2006 CD-Rom	**Automobile Fraud:** examination of title law, odometer tampering, lemon laundering, sale of salvage and wrecked cars, undisclosed prior use, prior damage to new cars, numerous sample pleadings, and title search techniques.
2006 Third Edition with CD-Rom	**Consumer Warranty Law:** comprehensive treatment of new and used car lemon laws, the Magnuson-Moss Warranty Act, UCC Articles 2 and 2A, mobile home, new home, and assistive device warranty laws, FTC Used Car Rule, tort theories, car repair and home improvement statutes, service contract and lease laws, with numerous sample pleadings.

National Consumer Law Center ■ 77 Summer Street ■ 10th Floor ■ Boston MA ■ 02110
(617) 542-9595 ■ FAX (617) 542-8028 ■ publications@nclc.org
Order securely online at www.consumerlaw.org

NCLC's CD-Roms

Every NCLC manual comes with a companion CD-Rom featuring pop-up menus, PDF-format, Internet-style navigation of appendices, indices, and bonus pleadings, hard-to-find agency interpretations and other practice aids. Documents can be copied into a word processing program. Of special note is *Consumer Law in a Box*:

December 2006 CD-Rom — **Consumer Law in a Box:** a double CD-Rom combining *all* documents and software from 17 other NCLC CD-Roms. Quickly pinpoint a document from thousands found on the CD through keyword searches and Internet-style navigation, links, bookmarks, and other finding aids.

Other NCLC Publications for Lawyers

issued 24 times a year — **NCLC REPORTS** covers the latest developments and ideas in the practice of consumer law.

2006 Second Edition with CD-Rom — **The Practice of Consumer Law: Seeking Economic Justice:** contains an essential overview to consumer law and explains how to get started in a private or legal services consumer practice. Packed with invaluable sample pleadings and practice pointers for even experienced consumer attorneys.

First Edition with CD-Rom — **STOP Predatory Lending: A Guide for Legal Advocates:** provides a roadmap and practical legal strategy for litigating predatory lending abuses, from small loans to mortgage loans. The CD-Rom contains a credit math program, pleadings, legislative and administrative materials, and underwriting guidelines.

National Consumer Law Center Guide Series are books designed for consumers, counselors, and attorneys new to consumer law:

2006 Edition — **NCLC Guide to Surviving Debt:** a great overview of consumer law. Everything a paralegal, new attorney, or client needs to know about debt collectors, managing credit card debt, whether to refinance, credit card problems, home foreclosures, evictions, repossessions, credit reporting, utility terminations, student loans, budgeting, and bankruptcy.

2006 Edition — **NCLC Guide to the Rights of Utility Consumers:** explains consumer rights concerning electric, gas, and other utility services: shut off protections, rights to restore terminated service, bill payment options, weatherization tips, rights to government assistance, and much more.

2006 Edition — **NCLC Guide to the Consumer Rights for Domestic Violence Survivors:** provides practical advice to help survivors get back on their feet financially and safely establish their economic independence.

First Edition — **NCLC Guide to Mobile Homes:** what consumers and their advocates need to know about mobile home dealer sales practices and an in-depth look at mobile home quality and defects, with 35 photographs and construction details.

First Edition — **Return to Sender: Getting a Refund or Replacement for Your Lemon Car:** find how lemon laws work, what consumers and their lawyers should know to evaluate each other, investigative techniques and discovery tips, how to handle both informal dispute resolution and trials, and more.

Visit **www.consumerlaw.org** to order securely online or for more information on all NCLC manuals and CD-Roms, including the full tables of contents, indices, listings of CD-Rom contents, and **web-based searches of the manuals' full text**.

National Consumer Law Center ■ 77 Summer Street ■ 10th Floor ■ Boston MA ■ 02110
(617) 542-9595 ■ FAX (617) 542-8028 ■ publications@nclc.org
Order securely online at www.consumerlaw.org

Finding Aids and Search Tips

The Consumer Credit and Sales Legal Practice Series presently contains seventeen volumes, twelve supplements, and seventeen companion CD-Roms—all constantly being updated. The Series includes over 10,000 pages, 100 chapters, 100 appendices, and over 1000 pleadings, as well as hundreds of documents found on the CD-Roms, but not found in the books. Here are a number of ways to pinpoint in seconds what you need from this array of materials.

Internet-Based Searches

www.consumerlaw.org — **Electronically search every chapter and appendix of all seventeen manuals and their supplements:** go to www.consumerlaw.org/keyword and enter a case name, regulation cite, or other search term. You are instantly given the book names and page numbers of any of the NCLC manuals containing that term, with those hits shown in context.

www.consumerlaw.org — **Current indexes, tables of contents, and CD-Rom contents for all seventeen volumes** are found at www.consumerlaw.org. Just click on *The Consumer Credit and Sales Legal Practice Series* and scroll down to the book you want. Then click on that volume's index, contents, or CD-Rom contents.

Finding Material on NCLC's CD-Roms

Consumer Law in a Box CD-Rom — **Electronically search all seventeen NCLC CD-Roms,** including thousands of agency interpretations, all NCLC appendices and over 1000 pleadings: use Acrobat's search button* in NCLC's *Consumer Law in a Box CD-Rom* (this CD-Rom is free to set subscribers) to find every instance that a keyword appears on any of our seventeen CD-Roms. Then, with one click, go to that location to see the full text of the document.

CD-Rom accompanying this volume — **Electronically search the CD-Rom accompanying this volume,** including pleadings, agency interpretations, and regulations. Use Acrobat's search button* to find every instance that a keyword appears on the CD-Rom, and then, with one click, go to that location on the CD-Rom. Or just click on subject buttons until you navigate to the document you need.

Finding Pleadings

Consumer Law Pleadings on CD-Rom and Index Guide — **Search five different ways for the right pleading from over 1000 choices:** use the *Index Guide* accompanying *Consumer Law Pleadings on CD-Rom* to search for pleadings by type, subject, publication title, name of contributor, or contributor's jurisdiction. The guide also provides a summary of the pleading once the right pleading is located. *Consumer Law Pleadings on CD-Rom* and the *Consumer Law in a Box CD-Rom* also let you search for all pleadings electronically by subject, type of pleading, and by publication title, giving you instant access to the full pleading in Word and/or PDF format once you find the pleading you need.

Using This Volume to Find Material in All Seventeen Volumes

This volume — **The Quick Reference** at the back of this volume lets you pinpoint manual sections or appendices where over 1000 different subject areas are covered.

---

* Users of NCLC CD-Roms should become familiar with "search," a powerful Acrobat tool, distinguished from "find," another Acrobat feature that is less powerful than "search." The Acrobat 5 "search" icon is a pair of binoculars with paper in the background, while the "find" icon is a pair of binoculars without the paper. Acrobat 6 and 7 use one icon, a pair of binoculars labeled "Search," that opens a dialog box with search options.

Summary Contents

Contents xi

CD-Rom Contents xxxvii

Chapter 1	Introduction	1
Chapter 2	Scope: Consumer Reports and Consumer Reporting Agencies	25
Chapter 3	Obtaining and Examining a Report of the Consumer's File	65
Chapter 4	Accuracy in Consumer Reports	87
Chapter 5	Restrictions on Information in Consumer Reports	151
Chapter 6	Activities and Duties of Furnishers of Information to Consumer Reporting Agencies	173
Chapter 7	Permissible Releases and Uses of Consumer Reports	203
Chapter 8	Notices Concerning Consumer Reports	245
Chapter 9	Identity Theft	285
Chapter 10	Available Claims for Consumer Reporting Disputes	299
Chapter 11	Private Remedies and Public Enforcement	337
Chapter 12	Consumer Self-Help: Advising Consumers Concerning Their Credit History and Rating	387
Chapter 13	Investigative Consumer Reports	411
Chapter 14	Credit Scoring	427

ix

Chapter 15	Credit Repair Legislation	447
Chapter 16	Privacy Protection	473
Appendix A	Fair Credit Reporting Act	495
Appendix B	FCRA Regulations, Interpretations, and Guidelines	535
Appendix C	FTC and FRB Model Forms	581
Appendix D	FTC Official Staff Commentary	627
Appendix E	Index to Federal Trade Commission Informal Staff Opinion Letters with FCRA Sections	647
Appendix F	Credit Repair Organizations Act	667
Appendix G	Gramm-Leach-Bliley	673
Appendix H	Summary of State Laws on Consumer Reporting, Identity Theft, Credit Repair, and Security Freezes	727
Appendix I	Sample Credit Reports and Industry Forms	775
Appendix J	Sample Pleadings and Other Litigation Documents	787
Appendix K	Government Enforcement Orders	847
Appendix L	Consumer Guides to Credit Reporting and Credit Scores (Appropriate for General Distribution)	851
Appendix M	Fair Credit Reporting Related Websites	857
	Index	859
	Quick Reference to Consumer Credit and Sales Legal Practice Series	907
	About the Companion CD-Rom	927

Contents

CD-Rom Contents xxxvii

Chapter 1 Introduction

1.1 About This Manual. 1
   1.1.1 Introduction 1
   1.1.2 Structure of the Manual 2
   1.1.3 Clearinghouse and Other Citations 3
   1.1.4 Updates 3
1.2 About Credit Reporting 4
   1.2.1 Terminology and Convention 4
   1.2.2 About the Industry 4
1.3 About the FCRA 6
   1.3.1 Overview 6
   1.3.2 FCRA Litigation 7
   1.3.3 Federal Agency Interpretations of the FCRA 7
      1.3.3.1 FCRA Regulations 7
      1.3.3.2 FTC Official Staff Commentary and Informal Opinion Letters 9
1.4 FCRA Legislative History 10
   1.4.1 Introduction. 10
   1.4.2 Early Legislative History. 10
   1.4.3 Senate Bill 823 11
   1.4.4 Passage of the Fair Credit Reporting Act 15
   1.4.5 FCRA Amendments Before the Consumer Credit Reporting Act of 1996 . . 15
   1.4.6 The Consumer Credit Reporting Reform Act of 1996 16
   1.4.7 1997 and 1999 Amendments 20
   1.4.8 The USA PATRIOT Act 21
   1.4.9 The Fair and Accurate Credit Transactions Act of 2003 21
      1.4.9.1 Legislative History 21
      1.4.9.2 Key Provisions 22
   1.4.10 Legislation Since FACTA. 24

Chapter 2 Scope: Consumer Reports and Consumer Reporting Agencies

2.1 Introduction 25
   2.1.1 Definitions Analyzed in This Chapter 25
   2.1.2 Concepts Analyzed in Other Chapters 25
2.2 FCRA Applies to "Consumers" 26
2.3 Is a "Consumer Report" Involved?. 26
   2.3.1 Overview 26
      2.3.1.1 General 26
      2.3.1.2 A Consumer Report Compared to a Consumer's File 26
   2.3.2 Information Must Be Communicated by a "Consumer Reporting Agency". 27

Fair Credit Reporting

- 2.3.3 Report Must Bear On and Identify a Consumer. 27
  - 2.3.3.1 General 27
  - 2.3.3.2 Coded Lists 27
  - 2.3.3.3 Reports on Businesses Are Not Consumer Reports 27
- 2.3.4 Information Must Bear On a Consumer's Creditworthiness, Credit Standing or Capacity, Character, Reputation, Personal Characteristics, or Mode of Living 28
  - 2.3.4.1 General 28
  - 2.3.4.2 Identifying Information and Credit Header Information 28
    - 2.3.4.2.1 General 28
    - 2.3.4.2.2 Gramm-Leach Bliley Act restrictions on disclosure of "credit header" information 29
    - 2.3.4.2.3 Prescreening lists 30
    - 2.3.4.2.4 Inquiry Reports and trigger lists 30
- 2.3.5 Information Must Be Used, Expected to Be Used, or Collected for Certain Purposes 30
  - 2.3.5.1 General 30
  - 2.3.5.2 Partial Use of a Prior Consumer Report Makes New Report a Consumer Report. 31
  - 2.3.5.3 Expected Use of Information. 32
  - 2.3.5.4 Purpose for Collecting Information. 33
- 2.3.6 Purposes That Make Information a Consumer Report. 34
  - 2.3.6.1 General 34
  - 2.3.6.2 Reports on Individuals for Business, Not Consumer, Purposes Are Not Consumer Reports. 34
  - 2.3.6.3 Credit Purposes. 36
    - 2.3.6.3.1 General 36
    - 2.3.6.3.2 Check writing, check approval and similar lists 37
    - 2.3.6.3.3 Reports on tenants 38
  - 2.3.6.4 Employment Reports 39
    - 2.3.6.4.1 General 39
    - 2.3.6.4.2 Employment agency and employee misconduct investigation report exceptions 40
  - 2.3.6.5 Insurance Reports 40
    - 2.3.6.5.1 Insurance underwriting purposes. 40
    - 2.3.6.5.2 Insurance claims reports 40
  - 2.3.6.6 Governmental Licenses and Benefits. 41
  - 2.3.6.7 Risk Assessment of Current Obligations 42
  - 2.3.6.8 Legitimate Business Need for Information. 42
  - 2.3.6.9 Government Determination of Child Support Payment Levels. 44
- 2.4 Statutory Exemptions to Definition of Consumer Report 44
  - 2.4.1 Overview 44
  - 2.4.2 Where Report Based on First-Hand Experience. 44
  - 2.4.3 Information Shared by Affiliates 46
    - 2.4.3.1 Types of Affiliate Sharing Excluded from Definition of Consumer Report. 46
    - 2.4.3.2 Right to Opt Out from Affiliate Sharing 46
      - 2.4.3.2.1 Two opt-out rights for affiliate sharing. 46
      - 2.4.3.2.2 Opt-out right for affiliate sharing of third party information 47
      - 2.4.3.2.3 Opt-out right for affiliate sharing for marketing purposes . . 47
      - 2.4.3.2.4 Preemption of state regulation of affiliate sharing 48
  - 2.4.4 Certain Employment Reports 48
    - 2.4.4.1 Employee Misconduct Investigation Reports 48
    - 2.4.4.2 Employment Agency Communications 48

Contents

      2.4.4.2.1 Overview.. 48
      2.4.4.2.2 Investigative report................................. 49
      2.4.4.2.3 Made for purposes of employment procurement 49
      2.4.4.2.4 Regularly performs employment procurement services... 49
      2.4.4.2.5 Consumer consent and required disclosures 49
  2.4.5 Credit Card Issuer's Authorization to Extend Credit................. 49
  2.4.6 Conveying Decision to Party Who Requested That Creditor Extend Credit to Consumer 50
 2.5 The Consumer Reporting Agency 51
  2.5.1 General.. 51
  2.5.2 "Any Person Which, For Monetary Fees, Dues, or on a Cooperative Nonprofit Basis" 51
  2.5.3 "Regularly Engages ... in the Practice of Assembling or Evaluating ... Information on Consumers"... 51
    2.5.3.1 Regularly Engages... 51
    2.5.3.2 Assemble or Evaluate.. 52
  2.5.4 Furnishing Consumer Reports to Third Party 53
  2.5.5 Exception for Joint Lenders and Users............................... 53
  2.5.6 Exception for Federal Government Agencies 54
  2.5.7 State and Local Government Agencies................................ 55
 2.6 The FCRA Distinguishes Special Types of Consumer Reporting Agencies...... 56
  2.6.1 "Nationwide" Consumer Reporting Agencies........................ 56
    2.6.1.1 General... 56
    2.6.1.2 Responsibilities of Nationwide Consumer Reporting Agencies 56
    2.6.1.3 FTC Circumvention Rule 57
  2.6.2 Nationwide Specialty Consumer Reporting Agencies 58
    2.6.2.1 General... 58
    2.6.2.2 Types of Nationwide Specialty Consumer Reporting Agencies: Medical Information, Tenant Screening, and Check Writing Agencies.. 58
  2.6.3 Resellers of Consumer Reports.. 58
    2.6.3.1 Overview 58
    2.6.3.2 FCRA Coverage of Resellers................................. 58
    2.6.3.3 Duties of Resellers 59
  2.6.4 Trucker Database Services... 60
 2.7 Examples of Consumer Reporting Agencies 60
  2.7.1 Credit Bureaus, Inspection Bureaus, and Consumer Reporting Agencies Collecting Public Record Data 60
  2.7.2 Creditors As Consumer Reporting Agencies.......................... 60
  2.7.3 Collection Agencies and Credit Bureau Collection Departments....... 61
  2.7.4 Data Brokers.. 61
  2.7.5 Detective and Employment Agencies, Employers 62
  2.7.6 College Placement Offices 63
  2.7.7 Attorneys 63
  2.7.8 Accident Reporting Bureaus and Compilers of Insurance Claim Lists..... 63
  2.7.9 Telephone Companies.. 64
  2.7.10 Alternative Credit Bureaus.. 64
  2.7.11 Retailer Database Services.. 64

Chapter 3   **Obtaining and Examining a Report of the Consumer's File**

 3.1 Introduction.. 65
 3.2 What Is Contained in a Consumer Reporting File 66
  3.2.1 Investigative Reports Distinguished from Consumer Reports........... 66
  3.2.2 Few Limits on Information That May Be Gathered and Filed on Consumers.. 66
  3.2.3 Information Found in Files with the "Big Three" Credit Bureaus 66

    3.2.3.1 Introduction 66
    3.2.3.2 Information Found in the File 66
    3.2.3.3 Sources of Information in the File 67
  3.2.4 Information Found in Files at More Specialized Reporting Agencies 68
 3.3 Consumer's Right to Access the Consumer's File 69
  3.3.1 Access from a User 69
    3.3.1.1 Advantages 69
    3.3.1.2 Can a CRA Prevent Users from Providing Reports to Consumers? .. 69
    3.3.1.3 Mortgage Lenders Must Supply Credit Scores 69
    3.3.1.4 User Disclosure Where Report Will Lead to Adverse Employment Action 69
    3.3.1.5 User Disclosure Where Information Obtained From a Person Other Than a Reporting Agency Leads to Credit Denial or an Increase in Credit Charges 69
    3.3.1.6 User Disclosure of Adverse Information Obtained from an Affiliate ... 70
  3.3.2 Right to a Free Annual Disclosure 70
  3.3.3 "Free" Reports That Are Not Free 71
  3.3.4 Right to Obtain a Credit Score 72
  3.3.5 Right to Free Reports Following a Fraud Alert or Other Fraud 72
  3.3.6 Free Report Following Adverse Action or After Certain Communications from Affiliated Debt Collection Agencies 73
  3.3.7 Free Report for the Unemployed and for Public Assistance Recipients 74
  3.3.8 State Law Right to Additional Free Reports 74
  3.3.9 Right to Obtain a Report for a Fee at Any Time from Any Type of Reporting Agency 74
    3.3.9.1 General 74
    3.3.9.2 Legal Limits on the Price of a Report 75
    3.3.9.3 Time Within Which Report Must Be Provided 75
 3.4 Mechanics of Obtaining a Consumer Report 75
  3.4.1 Deciding from Which CRA to Seek a Report 75
  3.4.2 How to Request a Consumer Report 76
    3.4.2.1 Free Annual Reports from the "Big Three" National Credit Bureaus 76
    3.4.2.2 Other Reports from the "Big Three" National Credit Bureaus 76
    3.4.2.3 Obtaining Reports from Specialized CRAs, Local CRAs 77
  3.4.3 Requirement of Proper Consumer Identification 78
  3.4.4 Ability of a Consumer's Representative to Receive a Report 78
  3.4.5 Unreasonable Preconditions to Disclosure 79
 3.5 File Information That Must Be Disclosed 80
  3.5.1 General 80
  3.5.2 Credit Scores 80
  3.5.3 Disclosure of Sources of Reporting Information 81
  3.5.4 Identification of Users Receiving Reports 81
    3.5.4.1 General 81
    3.5.4.2 Exception for FBI Counter-Intelligence and Government Security Clearance Usage 82
  3.5.5 Identification of Checks upon Which Adverse Characterizations of the Consumer Are Based 82
  3.5.6 Disclosure of Previously Reported Information 82
  3.5.7 Disclosure of Other Persons in Consumer's File 82
  3.5.8 Audit Trail and Other Ancillary Information 82
 3.6 The Form of the Disclosure 83
  3.6.1 Electronic and Mail Disclosures 83
  3.6.2 In-Person and Telephone Disclosures 83
  3.6.3 CRA Oral Assistance to Help Consumers Understand the Report 84

Contents

3.7 Examining the Consumer Report	84
3.7.1 The Consumer's Identity	84
3.7.2 Substance of the Report	84
3.7.2.1 A Report Is Just One Snapshot in Time	84
3.7.2.2 Differences in Reports Provided to the Consumer and to Users	85
3.7.2.3 Reading the Report	85
3.7.2.4 Errors to Look For	85
3.7.3 Information on Those Requesting Reports on the Consumer	86

Chapter 4 Accuracy in Consumer Reports

4.1 First Considerations	87
4.1.1 FCRA Places Two Separate Accuracy Obligations on Consumer Reporting Agencies	87
4.1.2 Congressional Intent to Combat Inaccurate Consumer Reports	87
4.1.3 Prevalence of Inaccurate Consumer Reports	88
4.1.3.1 Studies and Reports Show Consumer Reports Prone to Errors	88
4.1.3.2 FACTA Requires FTC to Study the Accuracy of Consumer Reports	90
4.2 What Is Accuracy?	91
4.2.1 Consumer Reporting Agency Must Do More Than Just Pass Along Information Provided by the Furnisher	91
4.2.2 Accuracy Standard Applies to Report Actually Supplied to User, Not to Consumer Reporting Agency's Later Explanation of That Information	92
4.2.3 Technically Accurate Reports Can Be Misleading and Inaccurate	92
4.2.4 Information Must Relate to the Consumer	94
4.2.5 Consumer Reporting Agency May Not Report Unverifiable Information	95
4.3 Types of Inaccurate Information	95
4.3.1 Introduction	95
4.3.2 Inaccuracies Caused by Furnishers	95
4.3.2.1 Furnisher Provision of Inaccurate Data	95
4.3.2.2 Failure of Many Creditors to Furnish Data to Consumer Reporting Agencies	96
4.3.2.3 Furnishers That Withhold Data	96
4.3.2.4 Furnisher Failure to Update Debts Discharged in Bankruptcy	97
4.3.2.5 Errors in Collection of Public Record Information	98
4.3.2.5.1 How public record information is collected	98
4.3.2.5.2 How errors occur in public record information	99
4.3.3 Consumer Reporting Agency Errors in Matching Data to Consumer Files	99
4.3.3.1 Mixed or Merged Files	99
4.3.3.2 How Consumer Reporting Agencies "Build" Their Files	100
4.3.3.3 Studies on Mixed Files	100
4.3.3.4 Mixed Public Records Information	101
4.3.3.5 Mixed Files Resulting from Subscriber Inquiries	101
4.3.3.6 Consumer Source of Information Used for Matching	102
4.3.3.7 Mixed Files and Identity Theft	102
4.3.3.8 Fixing a Mixed File	102
4.3.4 Consumer Reporting Agency Errors in Retrieving Consumer Files	103
4.3.5 Identity Theft	104
4.3.6 Consumer Reporting Agency's Refusal to Provide Reports on Targeted Consumers	104
4.4 CRA Liability for Reporting Inaccurate Information	105
4.4.1 Introduction	105
4.4.2 The Consumer Report Must Be Inaccurate	106
4.4.3 The CRA Must Furnish a Consumer Report	106
4.4.4 Resellers Must Follow Reasonable Procedures	106

Fair Credit Reporting

  4.4.5 The CRA Must Follow Reasonable Procedures 107
    4.4.5.1 Determining Reasonableness 107
      4.4.5.1.1 No strict liability 107
      4.4.5.1.2 Standard of reasonableness and the balancing test 107
      4.4.5.1.3 Establishing the availability and minimal burden of corrective measures 107
      4.4.5.1.4 Factors bearing on reasonableness. 108
      4.4.5.1.5 Consumer reporting agency must actually follow procedures that it establishes 109
    4.4.5.2 Proof Issues 110
      4.4.5.2.1 Burden of proof 110
      4.4.5.2.2 Sources of proof. 112
    4.4.5.3 Damages As an Element of a Reasonable Procedures Claim 112
  4.4.6 Reasonableness of Specific Consumer Reporting Agency Procedures 113
    4.4.6.1 Management Policies Encouraging Unfavorable or Inaccurate Information. 113
    4.4.6.2 Illogical Files and Internal Inconsistencies 113
    4.4.6.3 Inaccurate Sources 114
    4.4.6.4 Public Record Information. 115
    4.4.6.5 Mismerged Information and Wrong Consumer Identification. 117
    4.4.6.6 Identity Theft 118
    4.4.6.7 Transcription, Data Communication, and Interpretation 119
    4.4.6.8 Incomplete and Outdated Items in the File 119
      4.4.6.8.1 General 119
      4.4.6.8.2 Missing accounts and other items not covered in a consumer's file 120
      4.4.6.8.3 Incomplete reporting of existing accounts 121
      4.4.6.8.4 Reasonable methods to acquire updated information . . . 122
      4.4.6.8.5 Reporting of significant updated information that is furnished to a consumer reporting agency 122
    4.4.6.9 Bankruptcy Reporting 123
      4.4.6.9.1 General 123
      4.4.6.9.2 Reporting a debt discharged in bankruptcy 123
      4.4.6.9.3 Included in bankruptcy 124
      4.4.6.9.4 Other bankruptcy issues 124
  4.4.7 Procedures for Reports of Adverse Public Record Information for Employment Purposes 125
    4.4.7.1 General 125
    4.4.7.2 Election to Notify Consumer of Release of Public Record Information 125
    4.4.7.3 Election to Establish Strict Procedures for Complete and Up-to-Date Public Record Information 125
    4.4.7.4 Exemption for National Security Investigations 126
4.5 Consumer Reporting Agency Reinvestigation and Correction of Disputed Information 126
  4.5.1 Introduction 126
  4.5.2 The Consumer's Request for a Reinvestigation 128
    4.5.2.1 When a Consumer Reporting Agency Must Reinvestigate 128
    4.5.2.2 The Consumer Must Make the Request to the Consumer Reporting Agency 129
    4.5.2.3 Resellers and Affiliates 130
    4.5.2.4 Frivolous or Irrelevant Disputes 131
    4.5.2.5 Practical Tips in Making a Dispute 132
  4.5.3 Nature of the Reinvestigation 135
    4.5.3.1 Introduction 135

Contents

      4.5.3.2 Heightened Standard and Balancing Test 135
      4.5.3.3 Nature of the Required Reinvestigation 136
   4.5.4 Agency's Reinvestigation Must Involve the Person Who Furnished the Disputed Information to the Reporting Agency 138
      4.5.4.1 General 138
      4.5.4.2 Consumer Reporting Agency Must Notify the Furnisher of the Disputed Information 139
   4.5.5 Deadline for Reporting Agency to Respond 140
      4.5.5.1 Generally Applicable Deadlines 140
      4.5.5.2 Expedited Resolution of Disputes 141
   4.5.6 E-OSCAR and Other Aspects of the "Big Three's" Reinvestigation Procedures 141
      4.5.6.1 E-OSCAR 141
      4.5.6.2 The Processing of Consumer Disputes 142
      4.5.6.3 Deposing the "Big Three" As to Reinvestigation Procedures 143
 4.6 Corrections as a Result of Reinvestigations of Disputed Information 143
   4.6.1 Notice to Consumer of Results of Reinvestigation 143
   4.6.2 Correction or Deletion of Disputed Information 143
   4.6.3 Consumer Follow-Up Steps Where Corrections Made 144
 4.7 Reinsertion of Information Previously Deleted from Consumer's File 145
   4.7.1 The Problem of Reinsertion 145
   4.7.2 Consumer Reporting Agency Must Maintain Procedures to Prevent Reinsertion 146
   4.7.3 Furnisher Certification of Reinserted Information 146
   4.7.4 Notice of Reinsertion 146
 4.8 Inclusion of Additional Information in Consumer's File 146
   4.8.1 Consumer's Right to File Statement of Dispute 146
      4.8.1.1 Overview 146
      4.8.1.2 Consumer Reporting Agency Must Include Statement of Dispute in Subsequent Reports 147
   4.8.2 Other Notations of Dispute; Fraud and Military Alerts 148
   4.8.3 Consumer Explanations for Adverse Information 148
   4.8.4 Consumer Offers of New Information 148
 4.9 Notification to Previous Users Who Received Disputed Information 149
   4.9.1 Consumer Request for Notification 149
   4.9.2 Agency Disclosure to Consumer of Right to Request Notification 149
   4.9.3 Payment for Notification 150

Chapter 5 **Restrictions on Information in Consumer Reports**

 5.1 Introduction 151
 5.2 Restrictions on the Obsolete Information 151
   5.2.1 Overview 151
   5.2.2 General Principles 151
      5.2.2.1 No Restriction on Use of Favorable Information 151
      5.2.2.2 Deletion of Information Before It Is Obsolete 152
      5.2.2.3 Consumer Reporting Agency Cannot Report Even Existence of Obsolete Information 152
   5.2.3 Maximum Time Periods to Retain Adverse Information 153
      5.2.3.1 Structure of the FCRA 153
      5.2.3.2 Any Other Adverse Item 153
      5.2.3.3 Accounts Placed for Collection or Charged Off 154
          5.2.3.3.1 The 180-day rule 154
          5.2.3.3.2 Nature of charge-offs 155

Fair Credit Reporting

	5.2.3.3.3 Furnisher's duty to provide the date of delinquency, charge-off, collection or other event	155
	5.2.3.3.4 Effect of subsequent events	155
	5.2.3.3.5 Debt collectors and "re-aging"	156
	5.2.3.3.6 Debt collectors must use creditor's date of account delinquency	157
5.2.3.4	Suits and Judgments	157
5.2.3.5	Tax Liens	158
5.2.3.6	Criminal Records	158
5.2.3.7	Bankruptcy Reports Considered Obsolete After Ten Years	158
5.2.3.8	Prescreening Inquiries	159
5.2.3.9	Student Loans	159
5.2.4 Transactions Exceeding Monetary Thresholds		160
5.2.5 Reasonable Procedures Concerning Obsolete Information		160
5.2.5.1	General	160
5.2.5.2	What Are "Reasonable" Procedures?	161
5.2.5.3	Specific Procedural Requirements Regarding Obsolete Information	161
5.2.5.4	Procedures Determining Whether an Exemption Applies	161
5.2.6 Preemption of State Obsolescence Laws		161
5.3 Restrictions for Disputed Information		161
5.3.1 General		161
5.3.2 FCRA Restrictions on Disputed Information		162
5.3.2.1	Restrictions on Consumer Reporting Agencies	162
5.3.2.2	Restrictions on the Furnishing of Disputed Information	162
5.3.3 Fair Debt Collection Practices Act Restrictions		162
5.3.4 Limits on Furnishing Information on Disputed Credit Card and Open-End Accounts		163
5.3.5 Real Estate Settlement Procedures Act Restrictions		164
5.4 Other FCRA Restrictions		164
5.4.1 Medical Information Restrictions		164
5.4.1.1	Medical Information Definition	164
5.4.1.2	Consumer Reporting Agencies Required to Obtain Consent to Report Medical Information	165
5.4.1.3	Restrictions on Reporting the Identifying Information of Medical Information Furnishers	165
5.4.1.4	Affiliate Sharing Exception Not Applicable to Medical Information	166
5.4.1.5	Medical Information Creditor Restrictions	166
	5.4.1.5.1 Creditors may not discriminate against applicants on the basis of medical information	166
	5.4.1.5.2 Scope of prohibition	167
	5.4.1.5.3 Medical financial information exception	167
	5.4.1.5.4 Special purpose credit assistance and medical financing programs	168
	5.4.1.5.5 Other exceptions	168
5.4.2 Information from Personal Interviews		169
5.5 Other Federal Laws Restricting Information in Credit Records		169
5.5.1 Protection for Servicemembers		169
5.5.2 Discrimination and Retaliation for Exercising Rights Is Prohibited		169
5.5.3 Federal Agencies Are Restricted in Information They May Furnish		170
5.6 Information About Another		170
5.6.1 Spouse or Former Spouse		170
5.6.2 Cosigners and Authorized Users		170
5.6.3 State Law Restrictions Regarding Cosigners		171

Contents

    5.7 State Law Restrictions 171
           5.7.1 Restrictions on Child Support Debts 171
           5.7.2 State Law Restrictions in General 171

Chapter 6   Activities and Duties of Furnishers of Information to Consumer Reporting Agencies

    6.1 Introduction 173
        6.1.1 Overview 173
        6.1.2 Congress Eliminated Private Enforcement of the Duties to Furnish Accurate and Complete Information or to Prevent and Investigate Identity Theft 174
    6.2 Creditors and Others Who Furnish Information to Consumer Reporting Agencies 175
        6.2.1 Furnishers Provide Information to Consumer Reporting Agencies. 175
        6.2.2 Limitations on Who Is a Furnisher 175
                6.2.2.1 Special Rules for Affiliate Sharing 175
                6.2.2.2 Direct Selling of Information Not Covered 176
                6.2.2.3 Certain State Laws Regarding Furnishers Are Preempted 176
    6.3 Furnishing Information to Consumer Reporting Agencies 176
        6.3.1 Information Is Usually Furnished Electronically 176
        6.3.2 Metro 2: The Standard Automated Format for Furnishing Information to Consumer Reporting Agencies 177
        6.3.3 The Metro 2 Format Used by Creditors 178
                6.3.3.1 Overview 178
                6.3.3.2 Objective Standard 178
                6.3.3.3 Base Segment Contains Information About the Consumer and the Debt 179
                6.3.3.4 Associated Consumers Segment Has Information on Joint Debtors and Other Authorized Users of Credit 180
                6.3.3.5 Transfers of Accounts Segment Tracks Holders of Debt 180
                6.3.3.6 Other Metro 2 Segments Serve Specialized Purposes 181
                6.3.3.7 Common Errors 181
                6.3.3.8 Metro 2 and Debt Collectors 182
                6.3.3.9 Metro 2 and Student Loans 182
                6.3.3.10 Metro 2 and Utility Bills 183
                6.3.3.11 Metro 2 and Dishonored Checks 183
                6.3.3.12 Metro 2 and Bankruptcy 183
    6.4 Standards of Accuracy for Furnishers 184
        6.4.1 Introduction 184
        6.4.2 General Duty to Report Accurately 184
        6.4.3 Accuracy and Integrity Regulations for Furnishers 185
        6.4.4 Accuracy When Creditor Clearly and Conspicuously Maintains a Special Address for the Consumer to Give Notification of Inaccurate Information .. 186
        6.4.5 Duty of Accuracy When Creditor Furnishes Information to an Affiliate ... 187
    6.5 Furnishers Have Duty to Correct and Update Furnished Information 187
        6.5.1 Creditors Must Promptly Correct and Update Information 187
        6.5.2 Disputing Inaccurate Information with the Creditor 188
        6.5.3 Sometimes Adverse Information May Not Be Furnished During a Dispute .. 189
        6.5.4 Universal Data Form May Be Used to Make Corrections 189
    6.6 Furnisher Must Note Disputes 190
    6.7 Furnisher Must Furnish Dates of Delinquency 191
    6.8 Furnishers Must Provide Notice of Closed Account 191
    6.9 "Financial Institution" As Defined by Gramm-Leach-Bliley Must Notify Customers of Negative Information Furnished to Reporting Agencies 191

Fair Credit Reporting

 6.10 Formal Consumer Reporting Agency Dispute Process Subjects the Furnisher to Obligations That Are Enforceable by the Consumer 192
  6.10.1 Overview. 192
  6.10.2 Furnishers Are Liable to Consumers in Private Suits for Breach of the Formal Investigation Responsibilities 193
  6.10.3 Consumer Reporting Agency Investigation Must Involve the Furnisher . . 196
  6.10.4 Furnisher's Duty upon Notification of Dispute by the Reporting Agency to Conduct a Reasonable Investigation 197
  6.10.5 Furnishers Must Permanently Delete, Modify, or Block Inaccurate, Incomplete, or Unverifiable Information 198
  6.10.6 Furnisher Must Report Investigation Results 199
   6.10.6.1 Furnisher Must Report the Results of Its Investigation to the Reporting Agency That Provided Notice of the Dispute 199
   6.10.6.2 Corrected Information Must Be Reported to Other Agencies As Well 199
   6.10.6.3 Time for Investigation and Reporting Results Is Limited 199
   6.10.6.4 Report of Investigation Results May Be Electronic 199
  6.10.7 Private Enforcement Is Subject to the FCRA's Hybrid Two-Year Statute of Limitations. 200
 6.11 Furnisher Liability for Discrimination, Including Retaliating Against a Consumer for Exercising Federal Statutory Rights 200
 6.12 Furnisher Liability for Related Torts. 201
 6.13 Reinvestigation Requirements Applicable to Resellers. 202
 6.14 Furnishers Subject to Identity Theft Duties and Responsibilities 202

Chapter 7 **Permissible Releases and Uses of Consumer Reports**

 7.1 General 203
  7.1.1 Background 203
  7.1.2 Reports May Be Released Only for Permissible Purposes 203
  7.1.3 Can a Consumer Deny Permission for a Release of a Consumer Report?. . 204
  7.1.4 Reports May Be Used Only for Permissible Purposes. 205
  7.1.5 Users Must Be Informed of FCRA Requirements 205
  7.1.6 Agents of the User 206
  7.1.7 Release by One Reporting Agency to Another 206
  7.1.8 Is Information a Consumer Report If Released for Impermissible Purposes? 207
  7.1.9 Discovering an Impermissible Use. 207
 7.2 Permissible Uses. 207
  7.2.1 In Response to a Court Order. 207
  7.2.2 Consumer's Written Instructions 209
  7.2.3 Permissible Use in Connection with Credit. 209
   7.2.3.1 General 209
    7.2.3.1.1 Overview 209
    7.2.3.1.2 Definition of "credit transaction" 210
    7.2.3.1.3 Must credit be for personal, family, or household purposes? 210
   7.2.3.2 Extension of Credit 211
   7.2.3.3 Account Review 211
   7.2.3.4 Collection of Credit Accounts and Judgment Debts. 212
  7.2.4 Permissible Use in Connection with Employment 214
   7.2.4.1 Overview. 214
   7.2.4.2 Employment Purposes 214
   7.2.4.3 Employer Must Provide Prior Certification. 215
    7.2.4.3.1 General. 215

Contents

- 7.2.4.3.2 Employer must obtain employee's consent 215
- 7.2.4.3.3 Employer must make disclosures in case of adverse action 215
- 7.2.4.4 Agency Must Enclose Summary of Consumer Rights 216
- 7.2.4.5 Employee Misconduct Investigations Not Considered Consumer Reports 216
- 7.2.5 Permissible Use in Connection with Insurance 216
- 7.2.6 Permissible Use in Connection with Government Licenses or Other Benefits. 217
- 7.2.7 Risk Assessment of Existing Credit Obligations 218
- 7.2.8 Legitimate Business Need 218
  - 7.2.8.1 Overview 218
  - 7.2.8.2 Business Transaction Initiated by the Consumer 218
    - 7.2.8.2.1 General. 218
    - 7.2.8.2.2 Business transaction 218
      - 7.2.8.2.2.1 Business transaction for personal, family, or household purposes. 218
      - 7.2.8.2.2.2 Business transaction must relate to eligibility . . 220
    - 7.2.8.2.3 Initiated by the consumer 220
    - 7.2.8.2.4 Legitimate business need. 221
  - 7.2.8.3 Business Need to Review a Consumer's Account 221
- 7.2.9 Use by Officials to Determine Child Support Payment Levels 222
- 7.2.10 Other Permissible Uses by Government Agencies 222
  - 7.2.10.1 Introduction. 222
  - 7.2.10.2 Identifying Information Furnished to the Government 222
  - 7.2.10.3 Investigation of FCRA Violations. 223
  - 7.2.10.4 Permissible Use by FBI for Counterintelligence Purposes. 223
  - 7.2.10.5 Disclosures to Governmental Agencies for Counterterrorism Purposes 224
- 7.3 Permissible Uses of Consumer Lists. 224
  - 7.3.1 General. 224
  - 7.3.2 When a List Is a Consumer Report Requiring a Permissible Purpose 224
    - 7.3.2.1 General 224
    - 7.3.2.2 Credit Guides 225
    - 7.3.2.3 Coded Lists 225
    - 7.3.2.4 Target Marketing Lists 225
  - 7.3.3 No FCRA Restriction Where List Not Collected or Used for FCRA Purpose. 226
  - 7.3.4 Lists for Prescreening "Firm Offers" of Credit or Insurance 227
    - 7.3.4.1 General 227
    - 7.3.4.2 Prescreened Lists Are a Type of Consumer Report 227
    - 7.3.4.3 A "Firm Offer" Is Required 228
    - 7.3.4.4 Consumers Can Elect to Be Excluded from Prescreening Lists . . . 229
- 7.4 Potentially Impermissible Purposes 230
  - 7.4.1 General. 230
  - 7.4.2 Use in Divorce, Child Support, or Paternity Proceedings. 230
  - 7.4.3 Use in Tax Collection Proceedings 230
  - 7.4.4 Use in Civil or Criminal Litigation 231
  - 7.4.5 Use by Investigators 232
  - 7.4.6 Use of Reports on the Consumer's Spouse, Relatives, or Other Third Parties 233
    - 7.4.6.1 General Rule. 233
    - 7.4.6.2 Exceptions for Credit Transactions 233
    - 7.4.6.3 Other Types of Transactions 234
    - 7.4.6.4 Joint Information 235

    7.4.7 Use in Connection with Insurance Claims. 235
    7.4.8 Marketing 236
    7.4.9 Other Impermissible Uses 236
7.5 Agency Procedures Insuring That Only Users with Permissible Purposes Obtain Reports 237
    7.5.1 General 237
    7.5.2 User Identification and Certifications 238
        7.5.2.1 Nature of Certification 238
        7.5.2.2 Blanket Certifications 238
        7.5.2.3 Follow-Up and Continuing Reports. 239
    7.5.3 Agency Verification Procedures. 239
    7.5.4 Electronic Communication of Reports 240
    7.5.5 Retention of Request Records. 240
7.6 Liability of Reporting Agency Employees for Impermissible Uses 240
7.7 User Liability for Impermissible Purposes. 241
    7.7.1 General 241
    7.7.2 Uncertified Uses of a Consumer Report 242
    7.7.3 Willful Noncompliance of User. 242
    7.7.4 User's Liability for Criminal False Pretenses. 243
    7.7.5 Vicarious Liability of User for Acts of Employees. 244

Chapter 8 Notices Concerning Consumer Reports

8.1 Introduction and Structure of Chapter. 245
8.2 Notices to Consumers 245
    8.2.1 Overview 245
    8.2.2 Notice of Summary of Consumers Rights Under the FCRA: "The Summary of Consumer Rights Notice" 246
        8.2.2.1 Content of Notice 246
        8.2.2.2 Time and Manner of Notice. 247
        8.2.2.3 Enforcement of Notice Rights 247
    8.2.3 Summary of Consumer Rights for Identity Theft Victims: "The Summary of Consumer Identity Theft Rights Notice" 247
        8.2.3.1 Content of Notice 247
        8.2.3.2 Time and Manner of Notice. 247
        8.2.3.3 Enforcement of Notice Rights 247
    8.2.4 Notices of Preparation of Credit Score and Scoring Model: "The Credit Score Notice" 248
        8.2.4.1 Nature and Content of Notice 248
        8.2.4.2 Time and Manner of Notice. 248
        8.2.4.3 Enforcement of Right 248
    8.2.5 Notices of Use of Credit Score and Scoring Model Relating to Mortgage Transactions: "The Mortgage Scoring Notice" 248
        8.2.5.1 Content of Notice 248
            8.2.5.1.1 Overview 248
            8.2.5.1.2 Credit score information from consumer reporting agencies 249
            8.2.5.1.3 Home loan notice. 250
        8.2.5.2 Time and Manner of Notice. 250
        8.2.5.3 Enforcement of Right 250
    8.2.6 Adverse Action Based upon Consumer Report: "The Adverse Action Notice". 250
        8.2.6.1 Nature and Importance of Adverse Action Notice 250
        8.2.6.2 Content of Notice 251
            8.2.6.2.1 General. 251

Contents

        8.2.6.2.2 Content of notice: identification of action and actor 251
        8.2.6.2.3 Content of notice: identity of the consumer reporting agency 251
        8.2.6.2.4 Content of notice: other mandatory information 252
        8.2.6.2.5 Content of notice: copy of report for adverse action relating to employment 252
     8.2.6.3 Manner of Giving Notice 252
        8.2.6.3.1 Who must provide notice 252
        8.2.6.3.2 Oral, electronic, or written 253
     8.2.6.4 When Notice Required 253
        8.2.6.4.1 General requirements 253
        8.2.6.4.2 Overview and summary of what is an "adverse action"?... 254
        8.2.6.4.3 When notice required: following adverse action on credit 255
            8.2.6.4.3.1 General requirement 255
            8.2.6.4.3.2 Definition of "credit" 255
            8.2.6.4.3.3 "Denial" of credit defined 256
            8.2.6.4.3.4 Special situation: risk-based pricing 257
            8.2.6.4.3.5 Special situation: accepted counteroffers 258
            8.2.6.4.3.6 Special situation: price quotes 258
            8.2.6.4.3.7 Special situation: cosigners 258
            8.2.6.4.3.8 Special situation: prescreening offers 259
            8.2.6.4.3.9 Special situation: account reviews 259
            8.2.6.4.3.10 Other situations constituting credit 259
        8.2.6.4.4 Time for notice: following adverse action on employment 259
            8.2.6.4.4.1 Overview 259
            8.2.6.4.4.2 Employee misconduct investigations 260
            8.2.6.4.4.3 Notice requirements for employment adverse actions 260
        8.2.6.4.5 Time for notice: following adverse action on insurance .. 261
        8.2.6.4.6 Time for notice: following adverse action on government benefits 262
        8.2.6.4.7 Other situations 262
            8.2.6.4.7.1 Transactions initiated by the consumer 262
            8.2.6.4.7.2 Check writing or approval services 263
            8.2.6.4.7.3 Leases 263
            8.2.6.4.7.4 Sale of property 263
     8.2.6.5 Enforcement of Right 264
     8.2.6.6 Comparison to ECOA Notice 264
  8.2.7 Notice of Adverse Use of Information Other Than Consumer Report 266
     8.2.7.1 Nature and Content of Notice 266
     8.2.7.2 Residential Lease As Credit 266
     8.2.7.3 Time and Manner of Notice 267
     8.2.7.4 Application to Particular Transactions 267
        8.2.7.4.1 Example: car financing transactions 267
        8.2.7.4.2 Example: verification of loan information 267
        8.2.7.4.3 Example: accommodation parties 267
        8.2.7.4.4 Example: investigation of information in a consumer report 267
     8.2.7.5 Special Rules for Information Shared by Affiliates 268
        8.2.7.5.1 Overview 268
        8.2.7.5.2 Enforcement of right 268
  8.2.8 Increased Price Based Upon Use of Consumer Report: "The Risk-Based Pricing Notice" 268

Fair Credit Reporting

    8.2.8.1 General 268
    8.2.8.2 Nature and Content of Notice 269
    8.2.8.3 Time and Manner of Notice. 269
    8.2.8.4 Enforcement of Notice Rights 270
  8.2.9 Notice When Information Is Used for Prescreening Purposes: "The Prescreening Use Notice" 270
    8.2.9.1 Content and Nature of Notice 270
    8.2.9.2 Time and Manner of Notice. 270
    8.2.9.3 Enforcement of Right. 271
  8.2.10 Notice When Negative Information Provided by Financial Institutions: "The Negative Information Reporting Notice" 271
  8.2.11 Notice Required Before Federal Agency May Disclose Debtor Information: "The Governmental Agency Reporting Notice". 272
    8.2.11.1 Introduction. 272
    8.2.11.2 Content of Notice. 272
    8.2.11.3 Time and Manner of Notice. 272
  8.2.12 Notice of Results of Consumer Reporting Agency Reinvestigation: "The Reinvestigation Results Notice" 272
    8.2.12.1 General. 272
    8.2.12.2 Nature and Content of Notice. 272
    8.2.12.3 Time and Manner of Notice. 273
    8.2.12.4 Enforcement 273
  8.2.13 Notice That Deleted Information Has Been Reinserted Into a Consumer Report File: "The Reinsertion Notice". 273
    8.2.13.1 General. 273
    8.2.13.2 Nature and Content of Notice. 273
    8.2.13.3 Time and Manner of Notice. 274
    8.2.13.4 Enforcement of Notice Rights 274
    8.2.13.5 Bringing Reinsertion Cases 274
      8.2.13.5.1 What constitutes reinsertion 274
      8.2.13.5.2 Strategies for litigating reinsertion cases. 274
  8.2.14 Notice of Frivolous Dispute 275
    8.2.14.1 Nature and Content of Notice. 275
    8.2.14.2 Time and Manner of Notice. 275
    8.2.14.3 Enforcement of Notice Rights 275
  8.2.15 Notice in Cases of Fraud Alert That Consumer May Request a Free Copy of the File. 276
    8.2.15.1 Nature and Content of Notice. 276
    8.2.15.2 Time and Manner of Notice. 276
    8.2.15.3 Enforcement of Notice Rights 276
  8.2.16 Notice to Consumer If Agency Refuses to Block Alleged Identity Theft Information 276
  8.2.17 Notice from an Employer That It May Obtain a Consumer Report: "The Employment Use Notice" 276
    8.2.17.1 Nature and Content of Notice. 276
    8.2.17.2 Time and Manner of Notice. 276
      8.2.17.2.1 General. 276
      8.2.17.2.2 Exception: investigation of employee misconduct 277
      8.2.17.2.3 Exception: truckers 277
    8.2.17.3 Enforcement of Right 277
  8.2.18 Notice When Credit Information May Be Used by Affiliates: "The Affiliate Sharing Notice" 278
    8.2.18.1 Content and Nature of Notice. 278
    8.2.18.2 Time and Manner of Notice. 278
      8.2.18.2.1 General. 278

Contents

8.2.18.2.1.1 Affiliate sharing marketing notice	278
8.2.18.2.1.2 Affiliate sharing exclusion notice	279
8.2.18.2.2 Relation to the Gramm-Leach-Bliley Act	279
8.2.18.3 Enforcement of Right	279
8.2.19 Notice That Government Official Plans to Obtain a Consumer Report for Child Support Purposes: "The Child Support Use Notice"	279
8.2.19.1 Content and Nature of Notice	279
8.2.19.2 Time and Manner of Notice	280
8.2.19.3 Enforcement of Right	280
8.2.20 Public Record Information for Employment Purposes	280
8.2.20.1 Content and Nature of Notice	280
8.2.20.2 Time and Manner of Notice	281
8.2.20.2.1 General	281
8.2.20.2.2 Exception for government agencies	281
8.2.20.3 Enforcement of Right	281
8.2.21 Notice of Preparation of Investigative Consumer Reports: "The Investigative Report Notice"	281
8.2.22 Notice of Right to Opt Out of Prescreening	281
8.2.22.1 Content of Notice	281
8.2.22.2 Time and Manner of Notice	281
8.2.22.3 Enforcement of Right	282
8.2.23 Special State Law Requirements	282
8.2.24 Other Notices	282
8.3 Notices to Consumer Reporting Agencies	282
8.4 Notices to Furnishers of Credit Information	282
8.4.1 Notices of Furnisher's Duties Under the Act	282
8.4.2 Other Notices	283
8.5 Notices to Users of Consumer Reports	283
8.5.1 Overview	283
8.5.2 Notices of User's Duties Under the Act	283
8.5.3 Notices of Address Discrepancy	283
8.5.3.1 Nature and Content of Notice	283
8.5.3.2 Time and Manner of Notice	284
8.5.3.3 Enforcement of Notice Rights	284
8.5.4 Notices of Deletion or Dispute	284
8.5.4.1 Nature and Content of Notice	284
8.5.4.2 Time and Manner of Notice	284
8.5.4.3 Enforcement of Notice Rights	284

Chapter 9 Identity Theft

9.1 General	285
9.2 The FCRA's Identity Theft Prevention and Credit History Restoration Provisions	285
9.2.1 Overview	285
9.2.2 Fraud Alerts and Active Military Duty Alerts	287
9.2.2.1 General	287
9.2.2.1.1 Overview	287
9.2.2.1.2 Appropriate proof of identity	287
9.2.2.2 Initial Fraud Alerts	287
9.2.2.3 Extended Fraud Alerts	288
9.2.2.3.1 Overview	288
9.2.2.3.2 Identity theft report	288
9.2.2.3.3 Effects of the extended fraud alert	288
9.2.2.4 Active Military Duty Alerts	289

		9.2.2.5 Effects of Alerts	289
	9.2.3	Identity Theft Victim's Access to Information About the Theft	289
		9.2.3.1 Access to Thief's Transaction Information	289
		9.2.3.2 Debt Collectors Must Provide Information to Victims and Notify Creditors	290
	9.2.4	Blocking of Fraudulent Information	291
		9.2.4.1 Agency Responsibilities	291
		9.2.4.2 Furnisher Responsibilities	291
	9.2.5	Preventing Theft of Consumer's Identification Information	292
		9.2.5.1 Card Number and Social Security Number Truncation	292
		9.2.5.2 Address Discrepancies	293
		9.2.5.3 Disposal of Consumer Information	293
	9.2.6	Creditor Implementation of Red Flag Guidelines	293
9.3	Identity Theft and Assumption Deterrence Act		294
9.4	State Identity Theft Statutes		295
9.5	Filing Suit Under the FCRA and Other Laws to Rectify Identity Theft		297

Chapter 10 — Available Claims for Consumer Reporting Disputes

10.1	Introduction		299
10.2	FCRA Claims		299
	10.2.1 General		299
	10.2.2 FCRA Claims Against Reporting Agencies		300
		10.2.2.1 Claims Relating to Inaccurate Reports	300
		10.2.2.1.1 General	300
		10.2.2.1.2 Reasonable procedures	300
		10.2.2.1.3 The report must in fact be inaccurate	301
		10.2.2.1.4 Injury and causation	302
		10.2.2.1.5 Relation of claim to one based on the failure to reinvestigate	302
		10.2.2.2 Claims for Failure to Properly Handle Consumer Disputes, Reinvestigations	302
		10.2.2.3 Claims Relating to Obsolete Reports	303
		10.2.2.4 Claims Relating to Consumer Reporting Agencies Furnishing Reports for Impermissible Purposes	303
		10.2.2.5 Claims Relating to Medical Information Reported Without Consumer Consent	304
		10.2.2.6 Claims Relating to Investigative Reports	305
		10.2.2.7 Claims Relating to Adverse Public Record Information for Employment Purposes	305
		10.2.2.8 Claims for Failure to Disclose the Content of a Consumer's File	305
	10.2.3 Claims Against Resellers		305
	10.2.4 FCRA Claims Against Creditors and Others Furnishing Information to Consumer Reporting Agencies		306
		10.2.4.1 Private FCRA Right of Action Not Available for Many Furnisher Violations	306
		10.2.4.2 Claims Relating to Furnisher's Reinvestigation in Response to a Consumer Reporting Agency Request	306
	10.2.5 FCRA Claims Against Users of Consumer Reports		308
		10.2.5.1 Claims Against Those Obtaining Reports Without a Permissible Purpose or Under False Pretenses	308
		10.2.5.2 Claims Against Users for Failure to Provide Required Notices	309
		10.2.5.3 Claims Against Users for Failing to Comply with Requirements for Investigative Reports	310
		10.2.5.4 Claims Relating to Prescreening Lists	310

Contents

10.3 Other Federal Statutory Claims 310
10.4 The FCRA's Qualified Immunity for Tort Claims 311
    10.4.1 Background 311
    10.4.2 Immunity Only Applies to the "Reporting" of Information 312
    10.4.3 Immunity Applies Only to Information Discovered Exclusively Through FCRA-Required Disclosure 313
    10.4.4 Immunity Applies Only to Enumerated Tort Claims 314
    10.4.5 A Furnisher of Information to a Non-Reporting Agency Is Not Immunized. . 315
    10.4.6 No Immunity Where Malice or Willful Intent 316
10.5 Common Law Tort Claims Where Immunity Does Not Apply 317
    10.5.1 Advantages of a Tort Claim 317
    10.5.2 Elements of a Defamation Claim. 318
    10.5.3 Elements of Invasion of Privacy Claim. 319
    10.5.4 Elements of Negligence Claim 319
10.6 State Statutory Claims 320
    10.6.1 State Credit Reporting Statutes 320
    10.6.2 State Deceptive Practices Statutes 320
    10.6.3 State Identity Theft Laws 321
10.7 FCRA's Preemption of State Law Claims 321
    10.7.1 No "Field" Preemption 321
    10.7.2 When Is State Law Inconsistent with the FCRA?. 321
    10.7.3 Overview Concerning Explicit FCRA Preemption Language 323
        10.7.3.1 A Roadmap. 323
        10.7.3.2 General Principles of Interpretation. 324
        10.7.3.3 Applicability of Pre-FACTA Case Law to Current FCRA Preemption Provisions. 324
    10.7.4 Interpretations of "With Respect to the Subject Matter Regulated" 324
        10.7.4.1 Overview of Case Law Interpreting § 1681t(b)(1) 324
        10.7.4.2 Minority Cases Find Statutory and Common Law Claims Generally Preempted. 325
        10.7.4.3 Only Statutory, Not Common Law Claims Are Preempted 325
        10.7.4.4 Preemption Only Where State Statute Closely Resembles FCRA Provision 326
        10.7.4.5 Preemption Applies Only to Claims Based on Conduct Occurring *After* FCRA Liability Is Triggered 327
    10.7.5 Section 1681t(b)(1) Preemption Language Applies to Eleven FCRA Provisions 328
        10.7.5.1 Introduction. 328
        10.7.5.2 Provisions Regarding Furnishers. 328
        10.7.5.3 Provisions Regarding Consumer Reporting Agencies 329
        10.7.5.4 Provisions Regarding Users 330
        10.7.5.5 Provision Regarding Businesses and Identity Theft 330
    10.7.6 Affiliate Exchange Preemption—§ 1681t(b)(2). 330
    10.7.7 Disclosure Preemption—§ 1681t(b)(3) 331
    10.7.8 Preemption Related to Frequency of Free Consumer Report Disclosures—§ 1681t(b)(4). 332
    10.7.9 Preemption Related to "Conduct Required by" Twelve FCRA Provisions—§ 1681t(b)(5) 332
        10.7.9.1 Narrow Construction. 332
        10.7.9.2 Reporting Agency Provisions That Preempt State Law. 332
        10.7.9.3 User Provisions That Preempt State Law 333
        10.7.9.4 Furnisher Provisions That Preempt State Law. 334
        10.7.9.5 Debt Collector Provisions That Preempt State Law 335
        10.7.9.6 Preemption by Provision Relating to Those Accepting Credit or Debit Cards. 335

Fair Credit Reporting

Chapter 11	Private Remedies and Public Enforcement	
	11.1 Introduction	337
	11.2 Selecting the Parties	337
	11.2.1 Plaintiffs	337
	11.2.2 Class Actions	338
	11.2.3 Defendants	339
	11.3 Case Selection	340
	11.4 Selecting the Court	340
	11.4.1 FCRA Claims May Be Brought in Federal or State Court	340
	11.4.2 Bringing Related State Law Claims in Federal Court	341
	11.4.3 Personal Jurisdiction	341
	11.4.4 Selecting the Appropriate Court	343
	11.4.5 Removal	343
	11.5 Statute of Limitations	344
	11.5.1 FCRA Limitations Period	344
	11.5.2 Limitations Period for Other Legal Claims	344
	11.6 Discovery and Litigation Strategies	345
	11.6.1 General	345
	11.6.2 Informal Discovery	345
	11.6.3 Formal Discovery	346
	11.6.3.1 General	346
	11.6.3.2 Electronic Discovery	348
	11.6.3.3 Company Information About Defendants	348
	11.6.3.4 Confidentiality Agreements and Protective Orders	348
	11.6.3.5 Consumer Reports and Evidentiary Issues	349
	11.6.3.6 Subpoenas	350
	11.6.3.7 Insurance Coverage for FCRA Liability	350
	11.6.4 Record Retention	350
	11.7 Right to Jury Trial; Jury Instructions	351
	11.8 Defenses, Counterclaims, and Third Party Claims	351
	11.9 Enforceability of Arbitration Agreements	353
	11.10 Damages	354
	11.10.1 Damages Generally	354
	11.10.2 Actual Damages	355
	11.10.2.1 General	355
	11.10.2.2 Damages for Pecuniary Loss	355
	11.10.2.3 Intangible Damages	358
	11.10.2.3.1 Are intangible damages available?	358
	11.10.2.3.2 Proving intangible damages	359
	11.10.2.4 Nominal Damages	361
	11.11 Statutory Damages	363
	11.12 Punitive Damages	364
	11.12.1 Prerequisites for Punitive Damages	364
	11.12.1.1 Relation to Common Law Standards	364
	11.12.1.2 Proving Willfulness	364
	11.12.1.3 No Need to Prove Actual Damages	368
	11.12.2 Determining the Amount of Punitive Damages	369
	11.12.2.1 No Fixed Upper Limit on Size of Award	369
	11.12.2.2 Determining the Size of the Award	369
	11.12.3 Punitive Damages: Decided by Judge or Jury?	370
	11.13 Injunctive and Declaratory Relief	371
	11.14 Attorney Fees and Costs	373
	11.14.1 When Are Fees and Costs Awarded?	373
	11.14.2 Calculating the Size of the Attorney Fee Award	374

Contents

     11.14.2.1 FCRA Awards Will Be Based on Standards Enunciated in Other Federal Fee-Shifting Statutes 374
     11.14.2.2 Current Federal Fee-Shifting Standards 375
   11.14.3 Maximizing the Chances of an Adequate Fee Award 375
   11.14.4 Preserving Fee Entitlement When Case Is Settled 376
   11.14.5 Rule 68 and Attorney Fee Awards 377
   11.14.6 Interest on Judgments 378
  11.15 Quick Reference to Published Awards 378
  11.16 Public Enforcement 379
   11.16.1 Administrative Enforcement Agencies 379
   11.16.2 Federal Trade Commission Enforcement 380
     11.16.2.1 General FTC Enforcement Powers 380
     11.16.2.2 FTC Enforcement Powers Against Information Furnishers Are Limited 382
     11.16.2.3 FTC and Federal Banking Agencies Rulemaking, FTC Staff Commentary and Opinion Letters 383
   11.16.3 Criminal Enforcement 383
   11.16.4 State Enforcement 384
     11.16.4.1 General State Enforcement Powers 384
     11.16.4.2 State Enforcement Powers Against Information Furnishers Are Extremely Limited 384
     11.16.4.3 State Notification of Federal Regulators 384
     11.16.4.4 State Investigatory Powers 385
     11.16.4.5 Limitation on State Action While Federal Action Is Pending ... 385

Chapter 12 **Consumer Self-Help: Advising Consumers Concerning Their Credit History and Rating**

  12.1 Introduction 387
  12.2 Impermissible Uses of Consumer Reports 387
   12.2.1 Introduction 387
   12.2.2 User's Curiosity; General Publication in the Community 387
   12.2.3 Publication of Bad Debt Lists 388
   12.2.4 Divorce and Custody Proceedings, Tort Suits, Criminal Actions, Immigration Matters, and Other Litigation 388
   12.2.5 Using a Consumer's Credit History to Evaluate Other Family Members and Associates 388
  12.3 Consumers Should Not Fear a Collector's Threats to Report a Debt to a Consumer Reporting Agency 389
  12.4 Does Withholding Payment As Part of a Dispute Ruin a Consumer's Credit Record? 390
   12.4.1 Introduction 390
   12.4.2 Disputes Relating to Credit Card Charges 390
   12.4.3 Telephone and Other Utility Charges 391
   12.4.4 Home Mortgages and Home Equity Lines of Credit 391
   12.4.5 Student Loans and Other Government Debts 391
   12.4.6 Debt Being Collected by a Debt Collector 391
   12.4.7 FCRA Protections Where Consumer Disputes a Debt 392
   12.4.8 ECOA Protections When Raising Federal Statutory Rights 392
  12.5 The Wrong Way to Improve a Credit Record 392
   12.5.1 Credit Repair 392
   12.5.2 Debt Elimination, Debt Settlement, and Debt Adjustment 392
   12.5.3 Making Payments on Old Defaults 392
   12.5.4 Taking on New Debt 393
   12.5.5 File Segregation Is Not Recommended 393

Fair Credit Reporting

12.6 Ways to Improve a Credit Record 393
    12.6.1 First Considerations 393
    12.6.2 Correcting Inaccurate Information 394
        12.6.2.1 Disputing the Information 394
        12.6.2.2 Steps the Consumer Reporting Agency and Creditor Must Take in Response to the Consumer's Dispute 395
        12.6.2.3 Contacting the Creditor 395
    12.6.3 Dealing with Public Record Information 395
    12.6.4 Dealing with Negative Information When Settling Non-FCRA Litigation ... 396
        12.6.4.1 Importance of Resolving Credit Reporting Issues 396
        12.6.4.2 Negotiating Settlement Covering Credit Reporting 396
        12.6.4.3 Selecting the Correct Settlement Language 397
        12.6.4.4 Obtaining Court Approval 398
        12.6.4.5 Court Orders Should Cover Consumer Reporting Issues 398
        12.6.4.6 Cleaning Up the Consumer's File Where Dispute Settlement Does Not Deal with Consumer Reporting 399
        12.6.4.7 Monitoring the Consumer's File After Resolution of a Dispute ... 399
    12.6.5 Cleaning Up Student Loan Defaults 399
    12.6.6 Identity Theft 400
        12.6.6.1 Cleaning Up After Identity Theft 400
        12.6.6.2 Heading Off New Identity Theft Problems 401
    12.6.7 Removing Recent Delinquencies 401
        12.6.7.1 Introduction 401
        12.6.7.2 New Loans, Refinancing, and Shifting Payment Priorities ... 401
        12.6.7.3 Negotiating Repayment Schedules 402
    12.6.8 Discharging Obligations in Bankruptcy 403
    12.6.9 Providing Additional Information to the Creditor 404
12.7 Coping with a Substandard Credit Record 405
    12.7.1 Automobile Loans and Leases 405
    12.7.2 Home Mortgage Applications 406
    12.7.3 Residential Lease Applications 407
    12.7.4 Utility Service 407
    12.7.5 Insurance 408
    12.7.6 Access to a Credit Card 408
    12.7.7 Banking and Check Cashing 409
    12.7.8 Student Loans and Grants 409
    12.7.9 Eligibility for Public Assistance 409
12.8 Consumer Reporting Issues for Immigrants 410

Chapter 13   Investigative Consumer Reports

13.1 Introduction 411
    13.1.1 What Is an Investigative Consumer Report? 411
    13.1.2 Overview of Additional Obligations Required for an Investigative Consumer Report 411
13.2 FCRA Definition 412
    13.2.1 General 412
    13.2.2 Report Must Concern Character, General Reputation, Personal Characteristics, or Mode of Living 412
    13.2.3 Information Must Be Obtained from Third Party Personal Interviews ... 413
    13.2.4 Reports Excluded from the Definition 413
        13.2.4.1 General 413
        13.2.4.2 Employee Misconduct Investigation Reports 414
13.3 Types of Investigative Reports 414
    13.3.1 Reports for Insurance Purposes 414

Contents

  13.3.2 Reports for Employment Purposes................................ 415
  13.3.3 Reports for Landlords.. 416
  13.3.4 Other Types of Investigative Reports............................ 417
 13.4 Disclosure to Consumer of Investigative Report's Existence............... 417
  13.4.1 Notice That User Has Requested an Investigative Report........... 417
   13.4.1.1 General... 417
   13.4.1.2 When Notice Must Be Sent........................... 417
   13.4.1.3 Content of Notice................................... 418
   13.4.1.4 Form of Notice..................................... 418
   13.4.1.5 Certification to Consumer Reporting Agency of Notice to Consumer... 419
   13.4.1.6 Relationship to Notice of Adverse Action Based on Consumer Report... 419
  13.4.2 Consumer's Right to Additional Disclosures...................... 419
   13.4.2.1 General... 419
   13.4.2.2 User Must Disclose Questions Asked, Not Answers Given..... 420
   13.4.2.3 Disclosure of Names of Sources Interviewed Not Required..... 420
   13.4.2.4 Form of Disclosure.................................. 421
  13.4.3 Consumer Reporting Agency Must Disclose Consumer Report........ 421
  13.4.4 Users' Reasonable Procedures Defense........................... 422
  13.4.5 Waiver of Consumer Rights.................................... 422
 13.5 Consumer Utilization of Investigative Report Notices.................... 422
  13.5.1 Consumer's Permission Necessary for Employee Investigation Report, Except for Employee Misconduct Investigation Reports............. 422
  13.5.2 Steps the Consumer Can Take upon Notice of Request for an Investigative Report... 423
 13.6 Consumer Reporting Agency Procedures for Investigative Reports.......... 424
  13.6.1 Procedures Required for Any Consumer Report................... 424
  13.6.2 Special Procedures for Investigative Consumer Reports............. 424
   13.6.2.1 General... 424
   13.6.2.2 Information from Personal Interviews................... 424
   13.6.2.3 Adverse Information Based on Public Records........... 425
   13.6.2.4 Verification of Information for Re-Use in Subsequent Investigative Report................................. 425
 13.7 State Laws on Investigative Reports................................... 426

Chapter 14 **Credit Scoring**

 14.1 Introduction.. 427
 14.2 What Is Credit Scoring?.. 427
  14.2.1 The Basics.. 427
  14.2.2 The Variations... 428
   14.2.2.1 Credit Risk Scores.................................. 428
   14.2.2.2 Custom Versus Generic Scores....................... 428
   14.2.2.3 Specialty Scores.................................... 428
   14.2.2.4 Credit Application Scores........................... 429
  14.2.3 Definition of Credit Score..................................... 429
   14.2.3.1 FCRA Definition................................... 429
   14.2.3.2 Regulation B Definition............................. 429
 14.3 Widespread Use of Credit Scores..................................... 430
 14.4 Disclosure to Consumers of Credit Score............................... 431
  14.4.1 FCRA Disclosure Requirements................................ 431
  14.4.2 How to Obtain a Credit Score.................................. 432
  14.4.3 Variations in Credit Score by Consumer Reporting Agencies........ 432
 14.5 How a Credit Score Is Calculated..................................... 433

14.5.1 The Black Box 433
14.5.2 How Fair Isaac Scores Are Developed 433
    14.5.2.1 Fair Isaac's Scoring Factors 433
    14.5.2.2 FICO Scorecards 435
14.5.3 Factors in Freddie Mac's Automated Underwriting System 435
14.5.4 Ideas on How to Peek into the Black Box. 435
14.6 How Consumers Can Improve Their Credit Scores 436
  14.6.1 Industry's Advice 436
  14.6.2 Additional Advice. 436
  14.6.3 Re-Scoring. 437
14.7 Policy Concerns with Credit Scoring Systems 437
  14.7.1 Lack of Transparency 437
  14.7.2 Lack of Flexibility 437
  14.7.3 Credit Scores, Risk-based Pricing, and Subprime Loans 438
14.8 Concerns About the Accuracy of Credit Scores 439
  14.8.1 Garbage In, Garbage Out: The Effect of Consumer Reporting
       Inaccuracies on Credit Scores 439
  14.8.2 Credit Scores Do Not Allow the FCRA's Dispute Mechanisms to Work
       As Intended 439
  14.8.3 The Effect of Inaccurate, Non-derogatory Information. 440
    14.8.3.1 General. 440
    14.8.3.2 Missing Limits. 440
    14.8.3.3 Unreported Information. 441
    14.8.3.4 Student Loan Deferments 441
    14.8.3.5 Duplicate Accounts 442
    14.8.3.6 Wrong Account Type 442
    14.8.3.7 Too Many Accounts 442
  14.8.4 Lack of Validation and Re-Validation. 442
  14.8.5 Lender Misuse of Credit Scoring Models 443
14.9 Do Credit Scores Discriminate? 443
  14.9.1 Credit Scoring's Disparate Impact 443
  14.9.2 The Growing Credit Scoring Gap 444
14.10 Credit Scores and Insurance 445
14.11 Credit Scores and Utility Service 446

Chapter 15   Credit Repair Legislation

15.1 General 447
  15.1.1 Nature of Credit Repair Organizations 447
  15.1.2 Overview of Credit Repair Laws. 447
  15.1.3 The Surprising Reach of Credit Repair Laws. 448
15.2 Federal Credit Repair Organizations Act 448
  15.2.1 Introduction 448
  15.2.2 Scope 449
    15.2.2.1 Some CROA Restrictions Apply to "Credit Repair
          Organizations" While Others Apply to Any Person. 449
    15.2.2.2 Definition of "Credit Repair Organization" 449
       15.2.2.2.1 Broad Definition Covers Wide Array of Entities 449
       15.2.2.2.2 "In return for the payment of money or other valuable
              consideration" 450
       15.2.2.2.3 Types of advertisements and services that meet the
              definition. 451
       15.2.2.2.4 Other Definitions 451
    15.2.2.3 Exceptions to Definition of "Credit Repair Organization" 451
       15.2.2.3.1 Introduction. 451

                15.2.2.3.2 Non-Profit Organizations 452
                15.2.2.3.3 Creditors who are restructuring a consumer's debt 452
                15.2.2.3.4 Depository institutions and credit unions 453
        15.2.2.4 Credit Repair Services That Are Ancillary to Another Activity .. 453
        15.2.2.5 Attorneys 454
        15.2.2.6 Debt Collectors 454
        15.2.2.7 Sellers Who Advertise Credit Repair................... 455
  15.2.3 Credit Repair Organizations Must Make Specific Disclosures........ 456
  15.2.4 Requirements for Credit Repair Contracts...................... 457
  15.2.5 Three-Day Right to Cancel................................ 457
  15.2.6 Prohibition of Advance Payment to Credit Repair Organization 457
  15.2.7 Prohibitions of Deceptive Practices, Applicable to Any Person......... 458
        15.2.7.1 Overview 458
        15.2.7.2 Misstatements to Consumer Reporting Agencies or Creditors ... 458
        15.2.7.3 Concealment of the Consumer's Identity 459
        15.2.7.4 Misrepresentations Regarding the Services of a Credit Repair
                  Organization 459
        15.2.7.5 Fraud and Deception............................. 459
  15.2.8 Private Remedies 460
        15.2.8.1 Noncomplying Contract Is Void 460
        15.2.8.2 Who May Sue 460
        15.2.8.3 Liability Not Limited to Credit Repair Organizations.......... 461
        15.2.8.4 Does an Arbitration Clause Apply to CROA Claims? 461
        15.2.8.5 Damages...................................... 462
                15.2.8.5.1 Statutory formula for damages 462
                15.2.8.5.2 Actual damages 462
                15.2.8.5.3 Punitive damages 462
        15.2.8.6 Class Actions 463
        15.2.8.7 Jurisdiction 463
        15.2.8.8 Pleading...................................... 463
        15.2.8.9 Statute of Limitations 463
        15.2.8.10 Jury Trial 464
  15.2.9 Relation to State Laws................................... 464
  15.2.10 Federal and State Enforcement of the Federal Act 464
15.3 State Credit Repair Laws 464
  15.3.1 Introduction 464
  15.3.2 Coverage... 465
  15.3.3 Exemptions 466
  15.3.4 Do State Credit Repair Laws Apply to Retailers Who Arrange Credit for
          Customers?.. 466
        15.3.4.1 Introduction.................................... 466
        15.3.4.2 Requirement of Payment of Fee for the Credit Services 466
        15.3.4.3 Do Retailers Fall Within a Specific Statutory Exemption?...... 468
        15.3.4.4 Legislative Intent 468
  15.3.5 Substantive Prohibitions................................... 468
  15.3.6 Private Causes of Action 469
  15.3.7 State Remedies... 470
  15.3.8 Federal Preemption 470
15.4 Federal Telemarketing Statutes and Regulations 470
  15.4.1 Federal Telemarketing and Consumer Fraud and Abuse Prevention Act.. 470
  15.4.2 Federal Telephone Consumer Protection Act..................... 472
  15.4.3 State Telemarketing Statutes 472

Fair Credit Reporting

Chapter 16   Privacy Protection

16.1 Overview 473
16.2 Privacy from Governmental Intrusion 475
16.3 Tort of Invasion of Privacy 475
16.4 Statutory Protection of Financial Information 479
    16.4.1 The Gramm-Leach-Bliley Act 479
        16.4.1.1 Overview 479
        16.4.1.2 "Financial Institutions"—Entities That Must Comply with Gramm-Leach-Bliley 480
        16.4.1.3 "Customers" and "Consumers"—Those Protected by Gramm-Leach-Bliley 480
        16.4.1.4 "Nonpublic Personal Information"—the Information Covered by Gramm-Leach-Bliley 481
        16.4.1.5 Exempt Disclosures 481
            16.4.1.5.1 Overview 481
            16.4.1.5.2 Disclosures to affiliates 481
            16.4.1.5.3 Categories of exempted disclosures 482
            16.4.1.5.4 Gramm-Leach-Bliley's limits on redisclosure and reuse of the information 483
        16.4.1.6 Gramm-Leach-Bliley's Privacy Notices Requirement 483
        16.4.1.7 Opting Out 484
            16.4.1.7.1 General 484
            16.4.1.7.2 The opt-out notice 484
            16.4.1.7.3 Exercise of the opt-out right 486
        16.4.1.8 Limits on Sharing Account Number Information for Marketing Purposes 486
        16.4.1.9 Impact on Fair Credit Reporting Act 486
        16.4.1.10 Implementation and Enforcement of Gramm-Leach Bliley 486
        16.4.1.11 No Private Right of Action under Gramm-Leach-Bliley 487
        16.4.1.12 Limited Preemption of State Law 488
        16.4.1.13 Weaknesses of Gramm-Leach-Bliley 488
    16.4.2 Other State and Federal Protections 489
        16.4.2.1 Protections Related to Computers and the Internet 489
        16.4.2.2 The Financial Information Privacy Act 490
        16.4.2.3 The Federal Trade Commission Act 490
        16.4.2.4 State Statutes 490
16.5 Common Law Protection of Financial Information 492
16.6 Interests Impeding Legislative Protection of Financial Information 493

Appendix A   Fair Credit Reporting Act

A.1 Cross-Reference Table of 15 U.S.C. Section Numbers with Fair Credit Reporting Act Section Numbers 495
A.2 The Fair Credit Reporting Act 496

Appendix B   FCRA Regulations, Interpretations, and Guidelines

B.1 Federal Trade Commission Regulations 535
B.2 Federal Reserve System Regulations 547
B.3 Banking Agency Regulations 551
    B.3.1 Office of the Comptroller of the Currency Regulations 551
    B.3.2 Federal Reserve System Regulations 556
    B.3.3 Federal Deposit Insurance Corporation Regulations 562
    B.3.4 Office of Thrift Supervision Regulations 567

Contents

	B.3.5 National Credit Union Administration Regulations	572
	B.3.6 Security and Exchange Commission Regulations	578

Appendix C   **FTC and FRB Model Forms**

C.1 Standardized Form for Requesting Annual File Disclosures (Requesting a Free Credit Report) ... 581
C.2 General Summary of Consumer Rights ... 584
C.3 Summary of Consumer Identity Theft Rights ... 587
C.4 FTC Identity Theft Affidavit ... 590
C.5 Notice of Furnisher Responsibilities ... 598
C.6 Notice to Users of Consumer Reports ... 603
C.7 Model Prescreen Opt-Out Notices ... 613
C.8 Model Notices of Furnishing Negative Information ... 618
C.9 ECOA Adverse Action Forms (Regulation B, 12 C.F.R. Part 202, Appendix C) . 619

Appendix D   **FTC Official Staff Commentary** ... 627

Appendix E   **Index to Federal Trade Commission Informal Staff Opinion Letters with FCRA Sections** ... 647

Appendix F   **Credit Repair Organizations Act** ... 667

Appendix G   **Gramm-Leach-Bliley**

G.1 Gramm-Leach-Bliley Act ... 673
G.2 FTC Rules—Selected Provisions ... 678
G.3 Banking Agency Regulations ... 693
    G.3.1 Office of the Comptroller of the Currency Regulations ... 693
    G.3.2 Federal Reserve System Regulations ... 698
    G.3.3 Federal Deposit Insurance Corporation Regulations ... 709
    G.3.4 Office of Thrift Supervision Regulations ... 715
    G.3.5 National Credit Union Administration Regulations ... 720
G.4 Sample Opt-Out Notices ... 725

Appendix H   **Summary of State Laws on Consumer Reporting, Identity Theft, Credit Repair, and Security Freezes**

H.1 Introduction ... 727
H.2 State-by-State Summaries of Laws on Credit Reports, Identity Theft, and Security Freezes ... 727

Appendix I   **Sample Credit Reports and Industry Forms**

I.1 Sample Credit Reports ... 775
    I.1.1 Equifax ... 775
    I.1.2 Experian ... 778
    I.1.3 TransUnion ... 782
I.2 Universal Data Form ... 785
I.3 Automated Consumer Dispute Verification Form ... 786

Appendix J   **Sample Pleadings and Other Litigation Documents**

J.1 Introduction ... 787
J.2 Complaints ... 788

Fair Credit Reporting

J.2.1 Complaint—Failure to Reinvestigate	788
J.2.2 Complaint—Impermissible Purposes	789
J.2.3 Complaint—Mixed File	791
J.2.4 Complaint—Accuracy; Specialty Reporting Agency	793
J.3 Sample Interrogatories	799
J.3.1 Interrogatories—Reinvestigation (to CRA)	799
J.3.2 Interrogatories—Impermissible Purpose	803
J.3.3 Interrogatories—Reinvestigation (to Furnisher)	806
J.4 Sample Requests for Production	808
J.4.1 Request for Production of Documents (to Furnisher)	808
J.4.2 Request for Production of Documents (to CRA)	811
J.5 Sample Requests for Admissions	814
J.5.1 Sample Requests for Admissions (to Furnisher)	814
J.5.2 Sample Requests for Admissions (to CRA)	816
J.6 Sample Notices of Deposition	818
J.6.1 Sample Notice of Deposition (to Furnisher)—Fed. R. Civ. P. 30(b)(6)	818
J.6.2 Sample Notice of Deposition (to Furnisher)—Video Deposition	820
J.7 Sample Confidentiality Order	821
J.8 Sample Litigation Documents	822
J.8.1 Sample Closing Argument	822
J.8.2 Jury Instructions—Reinvestigation	832
J.8.3 Jury Instructions—Mixed File	836
J.8.4 Jury Instructions—Impermissible Purpose	838
J.9 Sample Settlement Language to Address Credit Reporting	844
J.9.1 Introduction	844
J.9.2 Alternative I: Deleting All Mention of the Debt	844
J.9.3 Alterative II: Correcting the Status of an Account, But Retaining Information About the Account	845

Appendix K Government Enforcement Orders

K.1 Introduction	847
K.2 Orders Against Experian (Formerly TRW)	847
K.3 Equifax	847
K.4 Trans Union	848
K.5 ChoicePoint	848
K.6 Resellers of Consumer Reports	849
K.7 Users of Consumer Reports	849
K.8 Furnishers	850
K.9 Identity Thief	850

Appendix L Consumer Guides to Credit Reporting and Credit Scores (Appropriate for General Distribution) ... 851

Appendix M Fair Credit Reporting Related Websites ... 857

Index ... 859

Quick Reference to Consumer Credit and Sales Legal Practice Series ... 907

About the Companion CD-Rom ... 927

CD-Rom Contents

How to Use/Help
CD-Rom Text Search (Adobe Acrobat 5 and 6)
Searching NCLC Manuals
Ten-Second Tutorial on Adobe Acrobat 5
Two-Minute Tutorials on Adobe Acrobat 5 and 6
    Navigation: Bookmarks
    Disappearing Bookmarks?
    Navigation Links
    Navigation Arrows
    Navigation: "Back" Arrow
    Adobe Acrobat Articles
    View-Zoom-Magnification: Making Text Larger
    Full Screen vs. Bookmark View
    Copying Text in Adobe Acrobat
    How to Copy Only One Column
    Printing
    Other Sources of Help
Microsoft Word Files
About This CD-Rom
How to Install Adobe Acrobat Reader, with Search
Finding Aids for NCLC Manuals: What Is Available in the Books

Map of CD-Rom Contents

Acrobat 6.0 Problem

Federal, State Statutes
Fair Credit Reporting Act
    Cross Reference Table: U.S.C. and FCRA Section Numbers (Appendix A.1)
    Current FCRA (Appendix A.2)
    Redlined Version of FCRA Showing FACTA Amendments (Appendix A.2.2, 2005 Supplement)
    FACTA (Appendix A.2.3, 2005 Supplement)
    Pre-FACTA Fair Credit Reporting Act (Appendix A.2 and A.2.1, 2005 Supplement)
    1996 Amendments to FCRA
    FCRA Pre-1996 Amendments (*Fair Credit Reporting* (5th ed. 2002), Appendix A.3)
    Summary of FCRA (Appendix B.2.1, 2005 Supplement)
FACTA Legislative History
    House

Fair Credit Reporting

"The Importance of the National Credit Reporting System to Consumers and the US Economy," No. 108-26, May 8, 2003

"The Fair Credit Reporting Act: How it Functions For Consumers and the Economy," No. 108-33, June 4, 2003

"The Role of the FCRA in the Credit Granting Process," No. 108-33, June 12, 2003

"Role of FCRA in Employee Background Checks and the Collection of Medical Information," June 17, 2003

"Fighting Identity Theft," June 24, 2003

H.R. 2622: The Fair and Accurate Credit Transactions Act of 2003, Committee on Financial Services, No. 108-47 (July 9, 2003)

Fair and Accurate Credit Transactions Act of 2003: H.R. Rep. 108-263, Committee on Financial Services (Sept 4, 2003)

Fair and Accurate Credit Transactions Act of 2003: H.R. Rep. 108-263 (Supplemental Report), House Committee on Financial Services (Sept. 9, 2003)

Senate

Addressing Measures to Enhance the Operation of the Fair Credit Reporting Act (July 31, 2003)

Consumer Awareness and Understanding of the Credit Granting Process (July 29, 2003)

The Accuracy of Credit Report Information and the Fair Credit Reporting Act (July 10, 2003)

Affiliate Sharing Practices and Their Relationship to the Fair Credit Reporting Act (June 26, 2003)

The Growing Problem of Identity Theft and Its Relationship to the Fair Credit Reporting Act (June 19, 2003)

An Overview of the Fair Credit Reporting Act (May 20, 2003)

Amending the Fair Credit Reporting Act, S. Rep. 108-166 (Oct. 17, 2003)

Manager's Package on S. 1753 (With Explanations and S. 1753): Senate's Proposed Bill in Response to H.R. 2622 (Sept. 22, 2003)

Sen. Bunning's Statement, Cong. Rec. S. 14172 (Nov. 6, 2003)

Conference Report on H.R. 2622 (Nov. 21, 2003)

Sen. Sarbanes' Statement, Cong. Rec. S.15806–15807 (Nov. 24, 2003)

FACTA Regulations

Regulations on Effective Date of FACTA Amendments (Appendix L, 2005 Supplement)

FTC (Appendix B.1)

FRB (Appendix B.2)

Other Agencies (Appendix B.3)

FACTA Supplemental Federal Register Material (22 Fed. Reg. Notices)

New Proposed FACTA Regulations

Fair Credit Reporting Affiliate Marketing Regulations; Proposed Rule

Prescreen Opt-Out Disclosure; Proposed Rule

Medical Information Privacy Regulations; Proposed Rule

Proposed Standards as to FCRA's Applicability to Affiliate Information Sharing

Proposed FTC Interpretations (*Fair Credit Reporting* (5th ed. 2002), Appendix A.6.1)

Note—FACTA relationship to Affiliate Information Sharing (Appendix A.6.1, 2005 Supplement)

Proposed OCC Regulations (*Fair Credit Reporting* (5th ed. 2002), Appendix A.6.2)

FTC Official Staff Commentary, Opinion Letter

CD-Rom Contents

    FTC Official Staff Commentary (Appendix D)
    Supplementary Information to FTC Official Staff Commentary (Superceded by FACTA) (*Fair Credit Reporting* (5th ed. 2002), Appendix C.2)
    FTC Official Opinion Letter (Superceded by FACTA) (*Fair Credit Reporting* (5th ed. 2002), Appendix C.4)
FTC Staff Opinion Letters
    Sectional Index to FTC Staff Opinion Letters on FCRA (Appendix E)
Full Text of FTC Staff Opinion Letters on FCRA (1971–2001)

Other Statutes

Credit Repair Organizations Act
    Federal Act (Appendix F)
    1996 Amendments to CROA
Gramm-Leach-Bliley
    Selected Statutory Provisions (Appendix G.1)
    Selected FTC Rules (Appendix G.2)
    Banking Agency Regulations
        OCC (Appendix G.3.1)
        Federal Reserve (Appendix G.3.2)
        FDIC (Appendix G.3.3)
        OTS (Appendix G.3.4)
        NCUA (Appendix G.3.5)
    Sample Opt-Out Notices (Appendix G.4)
Miscellaneous Federal Interagency Regs on Data Security (12 Fed. Reg. Notices)
State-by-State Summaries of Laws on Credit Reports and Identity Theft (Appendix H)

Model, Sample Forms

Sample Credit Reports
    Equifax (Appendix I.1.1)
    Experian (Appendix I.1.2)
    Trans Union (Appendix I.1.3)
    Sample Merged Report from TrueCredit
    Sample Credit Report for Creditor Use
Summary of Rights
    General Summary of Consumer Rights (Appendix C.2)
    Summary of Consumer Identity Theft Rights (Appendix C.3)
Standardized Form for Requesting Annual File Disclosures (Requesting a Free Credit Report) (Appendix C.1)
FRB Model Forms: Adverse Action and ECOA (Appendix C.9)
FTC Model Form: User Responsibilities (Appendix C.6)
FTC Model Form: Responsibilities of Furnishers (Appendix C.5)
Model Prescreen Opt-Out Notices (Appendix C.7)
Model Notices of Furnishing Negative Information (Appendix C.8)
Sample Opt-Out Notices (Appendix G.4)
Sample FTC Identity Theft Affidavit and Instructions for Filling Out Affidavit (Appendix C.4)
Sample Credit Bureau Contracts and Sales Brochure
    Sample Credit Bureau Agreement for Services (Equifax) (Appendix I.2)
    Sample Credit Bureau Agreement for Services (Experian)
    Sample Credit Bureau Agreement for Services (Credit Bureau Connection)
    Sample Credit Bureau Agreement for Online Credit Scoring Services (Equifax BEACON)
    Experian and Freddie Mac Agreement for Services

Fair Credit Reporting

    Factual Data Corp. and Freddie Mac Agreement for Services (*Fair Credit Reporting* (5th ed. 2002), Appendix G.1.2)
    Factual Data Corp. and Equifax Reseller Service Agreement (*Fair Credit Reporting* (5th ed. 2002), Appendix G.1.3)
    Sales Brochure for Experian Credit Profile Report
  Universal Data Form (Appendix G.2)
  Univeral Data Form (Alternate)
  Automated Consumer Dispute Verification Form (Appendix I.4)

Government Enforcement Orders, Reports, Briefs

Federal Agency Reports
  FTC Tabulation of Consumer Complaints Against Credit Bureaus
  FTC Report to Congress Under FACTA
  FRB Report: Credit Report Accuracy and Access to Credit
  An Overview of Consumer Data and Credit Data, Federal Reserve Board Bulletin (February 2003)
  FTC and FRB Report to Congress on the Fair Credit Reporting Act Dispute Process (August, 2006)
  GAO Report to Congress on Credit Reporting Literacy (March, 2005)

Government Enforcement Orders
  Experian (TRW) (Appendix K.2)
  Equifax (Appendix K.3)
  Trans Union (Appendix K.4)
  ChoicePoint (Appendix K.5)
  Resellers (Appendix K.6)
  Users (Appendix K.7)
  Furnishers (Appendix K.8)
  ID Thief (Appendix K.9)
  Complaint by State Attorney General Against Insurance Company for Improper Use of Credit Scoring
  FTC Settlement with Credit Repair Organization
  FTC v. Consumerinfo.com, Inc. (C.D. Cal. Aug. 15, 2005), Stipulated Final Judgment and Order for Permanent Injunction

FTC Amicus Briefs
  Ashby v. Farmers Group: Adverse Action by Insurance Company
  Willes v. State Farm Casualty Co.: Adverse Action by Insurance Company
  Cole v. U.S. Capital: Sham Offer of Credit Is Not a Firm Offer Under FCRA
  Whitfield v. Radian Guaranty: FCRA Adverse Action Requirements Apply to Insurance Provider

Consumer, General Information

  FCRA-Related Web Links (Appendix M)
  NCLC's Consumer Guides to Credit Reporting and Credit Scoring (Appendix L)
  Know Your Score—A Brochure from Consumers Federation of America on Credit Scoring
  Credit Scores and Implications for Consumers, Consumer Federation of America and NCRA

Pleadings

  Sample Request for Consumer's Credit Report
  Client Retainer Forms
  Demand Letter—Claim for Unauthorized Access to Consumer's Credit Report

CD-Rom Contents

Sample Letter—Explaining Damages to Opposing Counsel and the Theories for Asserting Such Damages
Expert Witness Report and Analysis Regarding Credit Reporting
Complaints
    Credit Reporting Agencies
        Complaint—Mixed Credit Files (Appendix J.2.3)
        Complaint—Accuracy; Specialty Reporting Agency (Appendix J.2.4)
        Complaint—Identity Theft Case, Violations of the FCRA and FDCPA, and Defamation
        Complaint—Identity Theft Case, Violations of the Federal and California Fair Credit Reporting and Fair Debt Collection Statutes
        Complaint—Identity Theft Case, Violations of the FCRA and FDCPA, and Defamation
        Complaint—Identity Theft Case, Violations of the FDCPA, FCRA, Truth in Lending Act and California Debt Collection Statute
        Class Action Complaint and Demand for Jury Trial, Oklahoma Consumer Reporting Agency
        Complaint and Demand for Jury Trial—Failure to Correct Inaccurate Credit Reports That Result from Mixing Credit Data of Different People in an Individual's Credit Reports
        Complaint—Failure to Correct Inaccurate Credit Reports That Result from Mixing Credit Data of Different People in an Individual's Credit Reports
        Complaint and Demand for Jury Trial—Failure to Correct Inaccurate Credit Reports After Learning of an Identity Theft
        Complaint—Claim for Unauthorized Access to Consumer's Credit Report
        FCRA Complaint Against Multiple Reporting Agencies
        Complaint—Unauthorized Release of Credit Report After Imposter Applied for Credit
        Punitive Damage Complaint Against Credit Reporting Agencies and Creditors—Identity Theft
        Complaint Against Reporting Agency Under Federal and State Law—Reporting Default on Nonexistent Student Loan
        Complaint Against Credit Reporting Agency and Furnisher—Failure to Have Reasonable Procedures to Ensure Accuracy and Failure to Reinvestigate Accuracy of Information Furnished to Credit Reporting Agency (Appendix J.2.1)
        Sample Complaint—Accuracy (*Fair Credit Reporting* (5th ed. 2002), Appendix I.1.3)
    Creditors, Furnishers of Information
        Complaint Against Furnisher for Failure to Conduct Proper Reinvestigation of Disputed Information
        Original Complaint and Request for Trial by Jury—Continuously Reporting Inaccurate Information to a Credit Reporting Agency After Being Notified of the Error
        Complaint and Demand for Jury Trial—Continuously Reporting Inaccurate Information to a Credit Reporting Agency After Being Notified of the Error
        First Amended and Restated Complaint and Demand for Jury Trial—Denying Low-Cost Car Insurance Premium on Basis of Credit Report Without Telling the Customer
        Complaint Against Information Furnishers—Mistaken Identity (Prior to FCRA 1996 Amendments)

Fair Credit Reporting

        Complaint Against Information Suppliers and Multiple Reporting Agencies (Prior to FCRA 1996 Amendments)

        Sample Complaint—Failure to Reinvestigate (*Fair Credit Reporting* (5th ed. 2002), Appendix I.1.1)

    Impermissible Use

        Sample Complaint—Impermissible Purposes (*Fair Credit Reporting* (5th ed. 2002), Appendix I.1.2)

        Complaint—Unauthorized Use of a Credit Report

        Class Action Complaint—Insurance Company Obtains Credit Reports with Impermissible Purposes, Under False Pretenses and Fails to Provide Adverse Action Notice (Appendix J.2.2)

        Class Action Complaint—Impermissible Access

    Investigative Reports

        Sample Complaint—Investigative Report (*Fair Credit Reporting* (5th ed. 2002), Appendix I.1.4)

    Credit Repair

        Complaint—Violation of Credit Repair Organization Statute Against Car Dealer

        Complaint—FCRA Violations in Connection with Home Improvement Scam

    Use of Credit Score

        Class Action Complaint Against Insurance Company—Improper Use of Credit Scoring

        Complaint Against FNMA—Improper Use of Credit Scoring

    Consumer Notice

        Complaint—Failure of Car Dealer to Provide Adverse Action Notice

        Class Action Complaint—Adverse Action Notice Violation (Appendix I.1.5, 2005 Supplement)

        Complaint Against Provider of Wireless Phone Services for Failing to Provide Adverse Action Notice

        Complaint Against Financing Company—"Spot Delivery" Case for Failure to Provide Adverse Action Notice

    Order of Sanctions Against Plaintiff's Attorney for Bringing Frivolous Claims

Discovery

    Interrogatories

        Sample Interrogatories—Accuracy (*Fair Credit Reporting* (5th ed. 2002), Appendix I.2.1)

        Sample Interrogatories—Metro 2 Format (*Fair Credit Reporting* (5th ed. 2002), Appendix I.2.2)

        Sample Interrogatories—Impermissible Purposes (Appendix J.3.2)

        Interrogatories—Reinvestigation (to CRA) (Appendix J.3.1)

        Interrogatories—Reinvestigation (to Furnisher) (Appendix J.3.3)

        Interrogatories to CRA re Accuracy of Credit File

        Interrogatories to CRA re Accuracy of Credit File

        Plaintiff's Interrogatories to Creditors

        Plaintiff's Interrogatories to Creditors; Affidavit

        Interrogatories to Credit Reporting Agency; Affidavit

        Interrogatories and Document Requests—Unauthorized Use of Credit Report

        Interrogatories to Multiple Reporting Agencies

        Interrogatories and Document Requests—Case Alleging Car Dealer Violates Credit Repair Organization Statute

        Interrogatories to Home Improvement Contractor—FCRA Violations

        Interrogatories to Home Improvement Contractor's Assignee—FCRA Violations

CD-Rom Contents

        Interrogatories—Identity Theft Case
        Interrogatories and Document Requests—Identity Theft Case
        Interrogatories and Document Requests—Case Against Reporting Agency Under Federal and State Law for Reporting Default on Nonexistent Student Loan
        Interrogatories and Document Requests—Metro 2B Duty to Investigate
        Interrogatories to User—Permissible Purposes
        Interrogatories to Reporting Agency—Permissible Purposes

Document Requests
        Sample Document Requests—Users (*Fair Credit Reporting* (5th ed. 2002), Appendix I.3.1)
        Sample Document Requests—Metro 2 (*Fair Credit Reporting* (5th ed. 2002), Appendix I.3.2)
        Request for Production of Documents to Furnisher (Appendix I.3.3, 2005 Supplement)
        Request for Production of Documents (to Furnisher) (Appendix J.4.1)
        Request for Production of Documents (to CRA) (Appendix J.4.2)
        Request for Production of Documents to Furnisher re Reinvestigation
        Request for Production of Documents to CRAs
        Request for Production of Documents to CRA—Accuracy of Credit File
        Motion for Production of Documents; Affidavit; Letter—Continuously Reporting Inaccurate Information to a Credit Reporting Agency After Being Notified of the Error
        Requests for Production of Documents to First Defendant; Affidavit
        Requests for Production of Documents to Second Defendant; Affidavit
        Requests for Production of Documents to Credit Reporting Agency; Affidavit
        Document Requests—Multiple Reporting Agencies
        Document Requests, Interrogatories, and Requests for Admissions—Multiple Reporting Agencies and Furnishers of Information (in Case Before 1996 FCRA Amendments)
        Document Requests—Home Improvement Contractor in Case Involving FCRA Violations
        Document Requests—Home Improvement Contractor's Assignee in Case Involving FCRA Violations
        Document Requests—Identity Theft Case
        Document Request—Permissible Purpose

Subpoenas
        Sample Subpoena of Custodian of Records (*Fair Credit Reporting* (5th ed. 2002), Appendix I.4.1)
        Federal Subpoena Commanding Production of Documents
        Subpoena Commanding Production of Documents
        Subpoena *Duces Tecum* Issued to Non-Party

Requests for Admissions
        Sample Requests for Admissions (to Furnisher) (Appendix J.5.1)
        Sample Requests for Admissions (to CRA) (Appendix J.5.2)
        Requests for Admissions to Furnisher
        Requests for Admissions to Furnisher—Accuracy of Credit File
        Plaintiff's First Set of Requests for Admissions
        Requests for Admissions—Home Improvement Contractor in Case Involving FCRA Violations
        Requests for Admissions—Home Improvement Contractor's Assignee in Case Involving FCRA Violations
        Requests for Admissions

Notices of Depositions

Fair Credit Reporting

> > > Sample Notice of Deposition (to Furnisher)—Fed. R. Civ. P. 30(b)(6) (Appendix J.6.1)
> > > Sample Notice of Deposition (to Furnisher)—Video Deposition (Appendix J.6.2)
> > > Sample Notice of Deposition (*Fair Credit Reporting* (5th ed. 2002), Appendix I.4.2)
> > > Sample Notice of Deposition—Fed. R. Civ. Pro. 30(b)(6) (*Fair Credit Reporting* (5th ed. 2002), Appendix I.4.3)
> > > Notice of Deposition
> > *Motions to Compel*
> > > Opposition to Motion to Compel Arbitration and to Stay Discovery; Affidavit—Continuously Reporting Inaccurate Information to a Credit Reporting Agency After Being Notified of the Error
> > > Motion to Compel Defendant's Responses to Requests for Production
> > > Memorandum in Support of Motion to Compel Defendants' Responses to Requests for Production
> > > Motion to Compel Defendant's Responses
> > > Memorandum in Support of Motion to Compel Defendant's Responses; Affidavit
> > > Motion to Compel Discovery and Brief in Support
> > > Memorandum Opposing Defendant's Discovery Objections—Identity Theft
> > > Decision in *Zahran v. Trans Union*—Denial of Protective Order for Discovery Material
> > *Deposition Transcripts*
> > > Deposition of Trans Union Employee Regarding Changes in Information in the CRA File
> > > Deposition of Equifax Employee About Correcting Errors in a Credit File
> > > Three Depositions of Trans Union Employees Regarding Reinvestigation Process and Procedures, Including Use of Quotas for Reinvestigating Disputes
> > *Trial Transcripts*
> > > Trial Transcript—Furnisher Reinvestigation
> > > Cross-Examination of Trans Union Employee in Case Involving Accuracy and Reinvestigation, Pt. 1
> > > Cross-Examination of Trans Union Employee in Case Involving Accuracy and Reinvestigation, Pt. 2
> > > Sample Direct Testimony—Damages (*Fair Credit Reporting* (5th ed. 2002), Appendix I.5.1)
> > > Closing Argument, Case Involving Accuracy and Reinvestigation (Appendix J.8.1)
> > > Plaintiff's Closing Arguments to the Jury (*Fair Credit Reporting* (5th ed. 2002), Appendix I.5.2)
> > > *Trial Transcripts—Reinvestigation and Accuracy Claims Against Equifax*
> > > > Opening Statement
> > > > Closing Arguments
> > > > Testimony of Equifax Chief Privacy Officer
> > > > Testimony of Equifax Director of Consumer Care
> > > > Testimony of Identity Theft Victim—Day One
> > > > Testimony of Identity Theft Victim—Day Two
> > > > Testimony of Editor of *Privacy Times* Newsletter
> > > > Testimony of Equifax Database Manager
> > *Motions, Briefs and Memoranda*
> > > Opposition to Motion to Exclude Expert's Testimony in Case Involving Mixed Credit

CD-Rom Contents

- Opposition to Partial Summary Judgment in Case Involving Mixed Credit Files
- Plaintiff's Request for Leave to Respond to Defendants' Motion to Strike and Reply Brief, Adverse Action Case Against Provider of Wireless Phone Services
- Plaintiff's Opposition to Defendants' Motion to Dismiss, Adverse Action Case Against Provider of Wireless Phone Services
- Defendant's (Alltel) Reply Brief in Support of Its Motion to Dismiss, Adverse Action Case Against Provider of Wireless Phone Services
- Defendant's (Alltel) Motion to Dismiss And Incorporated Memorandum in Support, Adverse Action Case Against Provider of Wireless Phone Services
- Plaintiff's Response and Opposition to Motion to Dismiss Claims Against Furnisher
- Plaintiff's Response and Opposition to Motion to Dismiss
- Motion to Exclude Evidence of Statements Made by Creditors as Hearsay
- Opposition to Motion to Dismiss, Failure by Credit Union to Investigate Inaccurate Information
- Memo Opposing Defendant's Motion for Summary Judgment—§ 1681s-2(b) (Failure to Conduct Reasonable Reinvestigation) Case
- Memo Opposing Motion for Judgment as Matter of Law—§ 1681s-2(b) (Failure to Conduct Reasonable Reinvestigation) Case
- Memo Opposing Motion to Dismiss—"Spot Delivery" Case
- Plaintiff's Motion for Summary Judgment—"Spot Delivery" Case
- Furnisher Liability Brief, Failure to Investigate
- Furnisher Liability Brief, Statute of Limitations
- Furnisher Liability Reply, Statute of Limitations
- Memo Opposing Motion to Dismiss, Order—Continuously Reporting Inaccurate Information to a Credit Reporting Agency After Being Notified of the Error
- Motion for Leave to File; Order—Denying Low-Cost Car Insurance Premium on Basis of Credit Report Without Telling the Customer
- Motion to Strike the Defendant's Answer; Affidavit
- Memo in Support of Motion to Strike Answer
- Opposition to Implead and Join Imposter; Order
- Opposition to Motion to Dismissal
- Response and Opposition to Motion to Dismiss
- Memo in Opposition to Motion to Dismiss; Order
- Memo in Opposition to Partial Motion to Dismiss; Affidavit
- Response and Opposition to Motion for Partial Summary Judgment
- Statement of Material Fact in Opposition to Motion for Summary Judgment
- Motion for Summary Judgment in Merged Case; Order
- Motion for Summary Judgment on the Issue of Liability
- Memo in Support of Motion for Summary Judgment on the Issue of Liability
- Reply to Defendant's Opposition to Motion for Summary Judgment
- Consumer's Proposal for Joint Pre-Trial Order
- Brief—Unauthorized Release of Credit Report After Imposter Applied for Credit
- Appellant's Reply Brief—Unauthorized Release of Credit Report After Imposter Applied for Credit
- Memo—Applicability of Credit Repair Organization Statute to Car Dealer
- Memo Opposing Alleged Settlement of Credit Reporting Claims
- Response to Motion to Dismiss—Unauthorized Use of Credit Report
- Memo Opposing Motion to Dismiss—Multiple Reporting Agencies
- Post-Trial Motion—Opposition to Motion for JMOL, New Trial and Remittitur

FTC Amicus Briefs

- *Ashby v. Farmers Group*: Adverse Action by Insurance Company

Fair Credit Reporting

Willes v. State Farm Casualty Co.: Adverse Action by Insurance Company
Cole v. U.S. Capital: Sham Offer of Credit Is Not a Firm Offer Under FCRA
Whitfield v. Radian Guaranty: FCRA Adverse Action Requirements Apply to Insurance Provider

Other Trial Documents
Pretrial Order in FCRA Accuracy and Impermissible Access Case
Pretrial Order, Trial Brief, Motion in *Limine* and Memorandum—Identity Theft Case
Jury Instructions for FCRA Claims Based on Accuracy and Reinvestigation Violations
Jury Instructions for State Defamation Claim
Sample Jury Instructions—*Bryant* (*Fair Credit Reporting* (5th ed. 2002), Appendix I.5.3)
Sample Jury Instructions—*Jones* (*Fair Credit Reporting* (5th ed. 2002), Appendix I.5.4)
Sample Jury Instructions—Furnisher Reinvestigation and Impermissible Purpose (Appendix J.8.4)
Transcript of Jury Instructions (Appendix J.8.2)
Sample Jury Instructions—Furnisher Reinvestigation
Jury Instructions—Punitive Damage Claims Against Credit Reporting Agencies and Creditors for Identity Theft
Jury Instruction—Obtaining Credit Report Without Permissible Purpose (False Pretenses)
Jury Instructions—Maximum Possible Accuracy, Defamation
Jury Instructions—Accuracy (Appendix J.8.3)
Plaintiff's Brief on Defendant's Motion for Post-Trial Relief—Identity Theft Case
Special Interrogatories to the Jury—Identity Theft Case
Sample Confidentiality Order (Appendix J.7)
Attorney Fee Motion and Memorandum—Punitive Damage Claims Against Credit Reporting Agencies and Creditors for Identity Theft

Settlement Agreement And Release
Sample Settlement Language to Address Credit Reporting (Appendix J.9)
Class Action Settlement Where Consumer Who Did Not File Bankruptcy Was Reported as "Included" in Bankruptcy
Mutual Settlement Agreement

Fair Credit Reporting Appendices on CD-Rom

Table of Contents
Appendix A, Fair Credit Reporting Act
Appendix B, FCRA Regulations, Interpretations, and Guidelines
Appendix C, FTC and FRB Model Forms
Appendix D, FTC Official Staff Commentary
Appendix E, Index to Federal Trade Commission Informal Staff Opinion Letters with FCRA Sections
Appendix F, Credit Repair Organizations Act
Appendix G, Gramm-Leach-Bliley
Appendix H, Summary of State Laws on Consumer Reporting, Identity Theft, Credit Repair, and Security Freezes
Appendix I, Sample Credit Reports and Industry Forms
Appendix J, Sample Pleadings and Other Litigation Documents
Appendix K, Government Enforcement Orders
Appendix L, Consumer Guides to Credit Reporting and Credit Scores
Appendix M, Fair Credit Reporting Related Websites

CD-Rom Contents

    Index
    Quick Reference to *Consumer Credit and Sales Legal Practice Series*
    What Your Library Should Contain

Word Pleadings on CD-Rom

    Sample Request for Consumer's Credit Report
    Client Retainer Forms
    Demand Letter—Claim for Unauthorized Access to Consumer's Credit Report
    Sample Letter Explaining Damages to Opposing Counsel and the Theories for Asserting Such Damages
    Expert Witness Report and Analysis Regarding Credit Reporting
    Complaints
    Discovery
    Motions, Briefs, and Memoranda
    Other Trial Documents
    Settlement Agreement and Release

Contents of NCLC Publications

    Internet-Based Keyword Search of All NCLC Manuals
    Detailed and Summary Tables of Contents for Each Manual
    Short Description of Each Manual's Features with Link to Manual's Detailed Index
    Short Index to Major Topics Covered in the 17-Volume Series
    Descriptions of Other NCLC Books for Lawyers and Consumers
    Features of *Consumer Law in a Box* (17 CD-Roms Combined into Two-CD-Rom Set)
    Printer-Friendly 3-Page Description of All NCLC Publications, Latest Supplements
    Printer-Friendly 25-Page Brochure Describing All NCLC Publications
    Printer-Friendly Order Form for All NCLC Publications
    Order Securely On-line

Consumer Education Brochures, Books

    Legal and General Audience Books Available to Order from NCLC
        The Practice of Consumer Law, Seeking Economic Justice
        STOP Predatory Lending, A Guide for Legal Advocates, with CD-Rom
        Return to Sender: Getting a Refund or Replacement for Your Lemon Car
        The NCLC Guide to Surviving Debt (2006 ed.)
        The NCLC Guide to the Rights of Utility Consumers
        The NCLC Guide to Consumer Rights for Domestic Violence Survivors
        The NCLC Guide to Consumer Rights for Immigrants
        The NCLC Guide to Mobile Homes
        Printer-Friendly Order Form
        Order Securely On-line
    Brochures for Consumers on This CD-Rom
        General Consumer Education Brochures
        Consumer Concerns for Older Americans
        Immigrant Justice in the Consumer Marketplace

Order NCLC Publications, CD-Roms

    NCLC Manuals and CD-Roms
    Order Publications On-line
    Printer-Friendly Order Form
    Consumer Law in a Box CD-Rom
    Credit Math, *Bankruptcy Forms* Software

Fair Credit Reporting

    Printer-Friendly Publications Brochure
    NCLC Newsletters
    Case Assistance
    Conferences, Training
    Books for Lawyers, Consumers
    Consumer Education Pamphlets
    Consumer Web Links

About NCLC, About This CD-Rom
National Consumer Law Center
    Mission Statement
    Contact Information: Boston, Washington Offices
    Go to NCLC Website
    What Your Library Should Contain
    Order NCLC Publications On-line
    Learn More About NCLC Manuals, CD-Roms,
    Order Form: Order NCLC Publications via Mail, Phone, Fax
About This CD-Rom
    What Is Contained on This CD-Rom
    Finding Aids for NCLC Manuals: What Is Available in the Books?
    Disclaimers—Need to Adapt Pleadings; Unauthorized Practice of Law
License Agreement, Copyrights, Trademarks: Please Read
Law Disks: CD-Rom Producer, Publisher of *Bankruptcy Forms* Software

Acrobat Reader 5.0.5 and 7.0.7

Chapter 1 Introduction

1.1 About This Manual

1.1.1 Introduction

This manual provides information and advice to attorneys and other consumer advocates on various consumer credit reporting issues. Subjects covered by this manual include the following: the consumer credit reporting industry and how it affects consumers' access to credit; inaccurate consumer credit reports and how to correct them; restrictions on information in credit reports; the legal obligations of those who furnish information to consumer reporting agencies; litigation under the Fair Credit Reporting Act (FCRA); the credit reporting implications of disputing debts with creditors; counseling consumers with blemished or incomplete credit histories; credit repair organizations; credit scores; identity theft; and privacy issues relating to credit reports. There are invariably consumer reporting implications for most consumer problems; this manual attempts to cover the most significant of these.

The growth of the credit reporting industry has paralleled the exponential growth in the availability of credit and personal information about consumers. Data brokers, check approval service companies, tenant screening agencies, employment reporting companies, mortgage reporting agencies, collection service companies, and others all maintain consumer files that creditors and others use to make decisions about access to credit or employment for consumers. More than four billion pieces of information data are entered monthly into computer records.[1] This growth in the availability and sharing of credit and personal information on consumers has also resulted in problems like theft of identity and reduced consumer privacy for financial and other information.

Consumers face many challenges in managing their credit information, including finding out: who has received their information, how those users have employed the information to determine their access to credit or employment; what consumers can do to correct any errors and mistakes; and how to handle resistance by consumer reporting agencies or others to clearing inaccuracies contained in their reports. In addition, consumers face numerous risks to the security of their credit information, including identity theft.[2] Finally consumers must deal with the increasing use of credit scores and the effect such scores have on access to—and cost of—credit, financial services, and products.

A good credit history is a significant asset for many consumers. Information contained in a consumer's credit reporting file affects their access to home mortgages, car loans, utility services, residential tenancies, employment, and even insurance. In addition, it can control the rate at which consumers may obtain credit. Many consumers misunderstand the data that is included in their credit history and the effect of an adverse credit history. This manual clarifies many of these issues. For example, a debt collector's threat to ruin someone's credit rating often is taken quite seriously by consumers, but rarely should have any effect on when the consumer pays a bill. Moreover, consumers often have valid defenses to a debt that would justify withholding payment from creditors. They nevertheless fail to do so because they fear hurting their credit record. The best strategy may run counter to a consumer's instinctive response: disputing a credit obligation may be the best way to clear up an adverse credit record.

Consumers often have no idea what information about themselves is in a reporting agency's files. They should be encouraged to examine their files because credit files frequently contain errors, some of them sufficiently significant to cause credit to be denied. This manual explains how consumers can determine if their credit history is adversely affecting them, which items in their reports are not permitted to be there because they are outdated or fail to meet some restriction for information, and which approaches will most effectively correct inaccurate or incomplete information. This manual also explains the protections that consumers can invoke under the FCRA when they have been the victims of identity theft.

---

1 Consumer Data Industry Association (CDIA), About CDIA, www.cdiaonline.org/about.cfm. *See also* Federal Trade Commission and Federal Reserve Board, Report to Congress on the Fair Credit Reporting Act Dispute Process (Aug. 2006), *available at* www.ftc.gov/os/comments/fcradispute/P044808fcradisputeprocessreporttocongress.pdf.

2 *Prepared Statement of the Federal Trade Commission Before the Subcommittee on Commerce, Trade, and Consumer Protection Committee on Energy and Commerce, on Protecting Consumers' Data: Policy Issues Raised by ChoicePoint, U.S. H.R.* (Mar. 15, 2005), *available at* www.ftc.gov/os/2005/03/050315protectingconsumerdata.pdf.

Correcting inaccurate or otherwise prohibited information can be accomplished short of litigation, but the manual explains consumer litigation rights where errors are not corrected or where a consumer has already incurred an injury. Litigation opportunities also arise where parties use a consumer's credit report without a permissible purpose or fail to adequately notify consumers of the adverse use of a report. This manual also explains the claims available (and not available) against those who furnish inaccurate information to consumer reporting agencies and fail to properly reinvestigate disputes from consumers. These claims and litigation strategies are discussed in detail in this manual.

This manual also explores methods of cleaning up a consumer's credit record. This involves consumer strategies targeted at reporting agencies, users of the reports, and those who furnish information about the consumer to reporting agencies. Cleaning up a credit record also involves, as an essential part of any settlement of a dispute with a creditor, resolving with that creditor how the creditor will report the dispute to a reporting agency. This manual also discusses credit repair organizations and the general federal and state laws governing these entities that promise to clear or repair consumers' bad credit.

Increasingly, creditors and others who use credit reporting information rely on credit scores or other risk assessments to make credit decisions. Use of credit scores is not a new phenomenon; however the increase in use raises many questions about its fairness, accuracy, and potential adverse effect on consumers. This manual discusses how credit scores are developed and used, and how consumers can both learn about and improve their credit scores.

Protecting consumer privacy is a longstanding goal for policymakers and it is one of the primary purposes of the FCRA. This manual includes a general discussion of consumer financial privacy and how it is affected by the credit reporting industry. Also included in this manual are discussions of applicable federal and state statutes, common law tort claims, and identity theft laws that consumers may utilize to protect their privacy. In addition to consumer reporting agencies, other "data brokers" have developed highly sophisticated databases of consumer information, much of which falls outside the scope of the FCRA, the Gramm-Leach-Bliley Act, or other laws and regulations intended to protect consumer data. Data brokers typically provide information services to a variety of businesses and government entities, usually to detect fraudulent transactions or to assist in locating individuals.[3] The issues of consumer privacy, identity theft, and accountability raised by "data broker" activities are discussed in Chapter 16, *infra*.

---

3 *Prepared Statement of the Federal Trade Commission on Protecting Consumers' Data: Policy Issues Raised by ChoicePoint, Before the House Subcommittee on Commerce, Trade, Consumer Protection Committee on Energy and Commerce* (Mar. 15, 2005), *available at* www.ftc.gov/os/2005/03/050315protectingconsumerdata.pdf.

1.1.2 Structure of the Manual

Chapter 1 provides an introduction to the manual, the credit reporting industry, the Fair Credit Reporting Act (FCRA), the two major amendments to the FCRA (the Consumer Credit Reporting Reform Act of 1996 (1996 Reform Act)[4] and the Fair and Accurate Credit Transactions Act of 2003 (FACTA)[5]), and legislative histories of all of these Acts. Chapter 2 discusses the scope of the Fair Credit Reporting Act, including what is and is not a consumer report or consumer reporting agency.

Chapters 3, 4, and 5 address the contents of consumer reports. Chapter 3 discusses the process of obtaining and analyzing a credit report, and provides an overview of the contents of a report. It examines one of the more important FCRA rights, i.e., the ability of consumers to obtain a copy of the contents of their reporting agency file. Chapter 4 discusses the accuracy and completeness of a report's contents, explaining why reports contain inaccuracies, what accuracy standards apply to consumer reporting agencies, and what a consumer can do to correct inaccuracies. Chapter 5 looks at information that is subject to specific reporting restrictions, including obsolete information, medical information, and disputed information. Chapter 6 addresses the standards and obligations of creditors and others who furnish information to consumer reporting agencies. This chapter also discusses furnisher liability for failing to conduct appropriate investigations when consumers dispute the accuracy of information furnished to consumer reporting agencies.

Chapters 7, 8, and 9 discuss consumers' affirmative rights under the Act. Consumer reports may only be used for certain purposes. These purposes and the agencies' obligations to release reports only for those purposes are treated in Chapter 7. Chapter 8 addresses the notices and disclosures that the Act requires various parties to provide to consumers concerning their credit records. Most of these disclosures are mandated by the FCRA, but some flow from the federal Equal Credit Opportunity Act or from state law. Chapter 9 discusses the rights that consumers have with respect to identity theft under both the FCRA and state law, including the right to include various alerts in the credit files and to block information resulting from identity theft.

Chapters 10 and 11 pertain to various sorts of remedies that consumers can pursue with respect to their rights under the Fair Credit Reporting Act and otherwise. Chapter 10 analyzes remedies under the Act and under state credit reporting laws. It also discusses the ever critical issue of when the FCRA preempts (and does not preempt) state laws on credit reporting. Chapter 11 discusses considerations in litigation an FCRA case, as well as public enforcement of the Act. Chapter 12 provides a discussion of non-litigation

---

4 Pub. L. No. 104-208 (Sept. 30, 1996).
5 Pub. L. No. 108-159 (2003).

remedies and resources that consumers can use to correct and improve their credit files.

The remaining chapters in the manual address particular specialized issues. Chapter 13 discusses a special kind of report called an "investigative consumer report." Typically consumer reports are based on objective information obtained from creditors, public records, and similar sources. Investigative consumer reports, however, are a special type of consumer report where more subjective information is obtained from personal interviews. Chapter 14 focuses on creditors' increasing use of credit scores in determining access to credit and the terms of such credit. This chapter describes credit scores, how creditors develop and use them, how consumers can improve their credit scores, and some of the policy implications of using these scores to determine access to credit. Chapter 15 addresses credit repair organizations, including the definition of a credit repair organization, how state laws govern such organizations, federal and state enforcement actions against credit repair organizations, and how federal telemarketing statutes and regulations apply to credit repair organizations. Lastly, Chapter 16 discusses privacy issues that arise in the context of the credit reporting industry. Compliance with the Gramm-Leach-Bliley Act and other privacy related subjects are covered in this chapter.

Considerable attention has been given in this manual to reprinting significant FCRA materials in the appendices and on the accompanying CD-Rom. Appendix A reprints the FCRA in its current form as amended by the Fair and Accurate Credit Transactions Act of 2003 (FACTA). The accompanying CD-Rom includes the public law version of FACTA, a version of the FCRA that displays the FACTA amendments in redline, the FCRA prior to FACTA and the 1996 Reform Act. Appendix B has the collection of regulations issued pursuant to the FCRA and the FACTA amendments. Appendix C provides the model forms that the Federal Trade Commission (FTC) and other agencies have issued to concerning the FCRA, along with a copy of the adverse action notice to be issued pursuant to the Equal Credit Opportunity Act. Appendix D reprints the FTC's Official Staff Commentary on the FCRA. An index to the FTC's informal staff opinion letters, organized by FCRA section, is provided in Appendix E; the letters themselves are provided in the CD-Rom accompanying this manual.

Appendix F reproduces the Credit Repair Organizations Act. Appendix G contains the Gramm-Leach-Bliley Act, its regulations, and examples of model notices that comply with that act. Appendix H provides a state-by-state summary of state laws that affect consumer credit reports, including credit reporting statutes, identity theft statutes, credit repair organization statutes, security freeze laws, and similar legislation. Appendix I contains sample credit reports and other consumer reporting agency documents. Appendix J provides sample FCRA complaints and discovery requests, and contains various sample excerpts from a jury trial, including closing statements and jury instructions. Appendix K summarizes enforcement orders from the FTC against violators; the actual orders are reproduced on the CD-Rom.

Appendix L gives guidance to understanding consumer reports and credit scores, while Appendix M lists helpful fair credit reporting websites.

This manual also includes a CD-Rom containing all of the appendices found in the manual, plus extra materials. These extra materials include prior versions of the FCRA; full versions of the FTC staff opinion letters; full reproductions of FTC enforcement orders; additional sample pleadings; and additional documents used by the credit reporting industry. The CD-Rom also contains all of the *Federal Register* notices for FCRA regulations and interpretations, including the proposed and final rules for regulations that have already been issued as well as current outstanding proposals.

This manual also contains two indices. The first is a detailed index for this manual. The second, a "Quick Reference," is an index not only for to this manual, but also for the other manuals in NCLC's *Consumer Credit and Sales Legal Practice Series*. The detailed table of contents at the beginning of the book also facilitates reference to the appropriate manual subsections. Finally, there is a keyword search function for this and all other NCLC manuals at www.nclc.org.

1.1.3 Clearinghouse and Other Citations

Certain documents referenced in this manual are cited by a "Clearinghouse" number. The Sargent Shriver National Center on Poverty Law (formerly known as the National Clearinghouse for Legal Services) retains copies of cases of special interest to low-income advocates, including unpublished cases. Many of these cases are available on the organization's website, www.povertylaw.org. Website access is free; but there is a $10 per copy plus shipping fee for hard copies. For older pleadings unavailable on the website, call the Shriver Center at 312-263-3830.

Other unreported cases cited in this manual are maintained on NCLC's website at www.consumerlaw.org/unreported. Access to these cases is available for free.

This manual also cites to certain federal agency materials interpreting the Equal Credit Opportunity Act, the Fair Debt Collection Practices Act, and other titles in the Consumer Credit Protection Act. The easiest way to have interpretations of these statutes at your fingertips is to consult NCLC's *Credit Discrimination* (4th ed. 2005 and Supp.), *Fair Debt Collection* (5th ed. 2004 and Supp.) or other manuals in this series.

1.1.4 Updates

This manual will be supplemented, usually on an annual basis. Between supplements, new developments are reported in NCLC REPORTS, *Consumer Credit and Usury Edition*, published bimonthly. For more information contact Publications Department, National Consumer Law Center, 77 Summer St., 10th Fl., Boston MA 02110-1006, 617-542-9595.

1.2 About Credit Reporting

1.2.1 Terminology and Convention

The FCRA regulates primarily "consumer reporting agencies" and "consumer reports."[6] A consumer reporting agency includes "credit bureaus," but it also includes many other entities such as check approval services, tenant screening bureaus, and employment screening agencies.[7] A consumer report includes credit reports, but it also includes tenant reports, employment reports, and many other types of reports.

This manual primarily uses the term "consumer reporting agencies" or CRAs to refer to those entities regulated by the FCRA. It will also occasionally use the term "credit bureau" to refer to CRAs that primarily focus on consumer credit information, most particularly the three major nationwide CRAs agencies (Experian, Equifax, and TransUnion, which are popularly known as the "Big Three"). This manual will refer to both "consumer reports" as regulated by the FCRA and "credit reports," particularly when referring to consumer reports issued by credit bureaus.

1.2.2 About the Industry

The consumer reporting industry is big business. Information about consumers is often sought by lenders, credit sellers, insurance companies, employers, and others who use the information to minimize the risk of extending credit, selling insurance, or hiring a new employee. The applicant provides some of this information. However, companies called consumer reporting agencies (CRAs) aggregate and store information on individuals and sell it to those who need it, such as potential creditors—banks, retailers and other lenders. They also sell information to prospective employers, landlords, and insurers.

According to the Consumer Data Industry Association (CDIA), the trade association for CRAs, there are 500 American CRAs, mortgage reporting companies, collection servicing companies, check services companies, tenant screening companies, and employment reporting companies.[8] One billion credit cards are in use in the United States and a similar number of consumer reports are issued annually in the United States.[9] CRAs play an integral and expansive role in the United States economy, as they can facilitate, or in many cases frustrate, a consumer's access to credit, and determine the speed of credit transactions (credit grantors can now receive consumer reports almost instantaneously).

The consumer credit reporting industry highly profitable and busy. Nationally, CRAs generate $2.8 billion in sales annually, an amount that has increased since 1972 at twice the rate of the economy or of consumer credit.[10] CRAs receive from data furnishers approximately 4 billion updates on about 1.5 billion accounts for more than 210 million consumer files each month.[11] CRAs also issue close to 3 million consumer credit reports every day.[12] The three nationwide agencies, Equifax, TransUnion, and Experian (formerly TRW), generate more than one billion consumer reports each year.[13] Only about 57.4 million of these consumer reports go to consumers.[14]

In addition to the "Big Three," there are other specialized national firms[15] and also many smaller CRAs throughout the United States. Some of these CRAs keep records only on consumers living within limited geographic areas. Of these CRAs, most are either affiliated with or fully owned by one of the "Big Three" nationwide CRAs. This means that they store and distribute consumer reports through either Equifax, TransUnion or Experian. The remaining smaller CRAs gather their own information.

---

6 See Ch. 2, *infra*.

7 See Prepared Statement of the Federal Trade Commission on Protecting Consumers' Data: Policy Issues Raised by ChoicePoint, Before the House Subcommittee on Commerce, Trade, Consumer Protection Committee on Energy and Commerce (Mar. 15, 2005), *available at* www.ftc.gov/os/2005/03/050315protectingconsumerdata.pdf.

8 About CDIA, www.cdiaonline.com/about.cfm.

9 *Id*. *See also* Federal Trade Commission and Federal Reserve Board, Report to Congress on the Fair Credit Reporting Act Dispute Process (Aug. 2006), *available at* www.ftc.gov/os/comments/fcradispute/P044808fcradisputeprocessreporttocongress.pdf.

10 Robert M. Hunt, *What's in the File? The Economics and Law of Consumer Credit Bureaus*, Bus. Rev. Q2 17, 18 (2002).

11 Federal Trade Commission and Federal Reserve Board, Report to Congress on the Fair Credit Reporting Act Dispute Process (Aug. 2006), *available at* www.ftc.gov/os/comments/fcradispute/P044808fcradisputeprocessreporttocongress.pdf. *See also* Robert B. Avery, Paul S. Calem, and Glenn B. Canner, *Credit Report Accuracy and Access to Credit*, Federal Reserve Bulletin (Summer 2004).

12 *Testimony of John A. Ford, Chief Privacy Officer for Equifax, Before the House Subcommittee on Financial Institutions and Consumer Credit* (June 4, 2003).

13 Robert B. Avery, Paul S. Calem, and Glenn B. Canner, *Credit Report and Accuracy to Credit*, Federal Reserve Board Bulletin (Summer 2004); Loretta Nott and Angle A. Welborn, *A Consumer's Access to a Free Report: A Legal and Economic Analysis*, Report to Congress by the Congressional Research Service 1–14 (Sept. 16, 2003).

14 Federal Trade Commission and Federal Reserve Board, Report to Congress on the Fair Credit Reporting Act Dispute Process (Aug. 2006), *available at* www.ftc.gov/os/comments/fcradispute/P044808fcradisputeprocessreporttocongress.pdf.

15 *See* § 2.6.2, *infra*.

In addition, some national firms specialize in particular consumer information, including medical records or payments, tenant history, check writing history, employment history, or insurance claims.

Consumer credit reporting can benefit both credit grantors and consumers. But the CRAs' extensive collection of information and the vast numbers of consumers on whom they report create serious concerns about the accuracy of information they keep, and about the adequacy of their measures designed to protect consumer privacy, including protection from identity theft.

A consumer report contains a substantial amount of information. To obtain a report, the CRA's customer typically uses a credit reporting terminal linked to the CRAs with which the customer has a subscription agreement, or connects through on-line access using specially developed software. Once appropriate passwords and consumer identifying information have been inputted, the CRA's search algorithm needs only seconds to return reports that match all, or even just some, of the identifying information. The report includes personal information such as name, age, Social Security number, home and business addresses, employment, previous addresses, marital status, and spouse's name. It contains financial information such as estimated income, value of car and home, bank accounts, credit accounts held, payment history and credit limits, and mortgages held. Public record information, such as tax liens, bankruptcies, or court judgments are also listed a credit report. A report will also indicate who has requested the individual's consumer report within the last two years.

A subset of consumer credit reports called "investigative reports" contains far more information than a standard consumer credit report. Besides the usual credit and financial information, investigative reports will include information related to a consumer's character, general reputation, personal characteristics, or mode of living. Investigative reports are used most often by insurance companies and prospective employers.

Credit scores are another important component of consumer reports. Creditors increasingly use these scores to determine whether to issue credit and the terms of that credit. Different types of credit scores are in use and most scores are based upon information contained in a consumer's credit file. Incorrect or omitted information in credit files may hurt such scores; however, there are also many uncertainties about whether these scores accurately reflect the risk associated with granting a particular consumer credit. In addition, many questions remain about how the credit scoring models are developed, whether these models have been properly and scientifically validated, and whether the validity holds up over time.

CRAs obtain their information for non-investigative reports from three sources: their subscribers; public records; and the information that consumers report on themselves (usually filtered through a subscriber). CRAs provide subscriber services to any number of kinds of creditors: banks; retailers; insurers; landlords; and others. These subscribers receive consumer reports from the CRA, and CRAs obtain a great deal of the information in their reports from their subscribers who regularly send the CRA information on the accounts of their customers so that the CRAs can constantly update the information. Frequently, a creditor will keep a record of all its customers in a computer file or tape, and periodically update or "dump" the information into the CRA's files. For investigative consumer reports, CRAs receive information from a fourth source: third-party interviews with a consumer's friends, neighbors, and colleagues.

Other information comes from public records—deaths, marriages, divorce notices, bankruptcies, court judgments, and dispositions of lawsuits. Often, CRAs will contract out the collection of public record information to other companies. Also, some federal, state, and local government agencies will sell information such as property tax rolls, motor vehicle registrations, workers' compensation filings, and police reports to CRA.

Consumers must keep in mind that CRAs' customers are *not* the consumers on whom they report. Rather, the real customers are the credit grantors who subscribe to the CRAs' services. This creates a precarious relationship between CRAs and consumers. The consumer's ability to access credit depends on the agencies' accuracy in documenting his or her credit history, as well as their prompt correction of mistakes once they are discovered. Yet, when consumers are confronted with a CRA that refuses to correct inaccurate information, the consumers cannot "vote with their feet" and change to another CRA.

This lack of power can cause large problems for consumers, because consumer reports are often inaccurate, and consumers have inordinate troubles in getting erroneous reports corrected. The Federal Reserve Board has reported that many consumer credit files contain incomplete or ambiguous information.[16] A report by the National Credit Reporting Association, a trade group of smaller CRAs, and the Consumer Federation of America found serious errors in a significant portion of consumer credit files.[17] An FTC report noted that the CRAs conduct investigations in over 20% of the instances where a consumer ordered his or her own credit report; presumably the investigations arose because of a dispute by the consumer.[18] A study by United

---

16 Robert Avery, Paul Calem, Glenn Canner, and Raphael Bostic, *An Overview of Consumer Data and Credit Reporting*, Federal Reserve Bulletin 70–71 (Feb. 2003).

17 Consumer Federation of America and National Credit Reporting Association, Credit Score Accuracy and Implications for Consumers (Dec. 17, 2002), *available at* www.consumerfed.org/121702CFA_NCRA_Credit_Score_Report_Final.pdf, *reprinted on the CD-Rom accompanying this manual.*

18 Federal Trade Commission and Federal Reserve Board, Report to Congress on the Fair Credit Reporting Act Dispute Process (Aug. 2006), *available* at www.ftc.gov/os/comments/fcradispute/P044808fcradisputeprocessreporttocongress.pdf.

States Public Interest Research Group found that nearly 80% of the consumer reports studied contained errors of some kind.[19] Alarmingly, 25% of the reports contained errors sufficiently serious to cause the denial of credit.[20] Among the errors were accounts mistakenly listed as delinquent or in for collection, loans listed twice, and inaccurate personal information including wrongly spelled names and incorrect addresses.[21]

With increased use of electronic information, several problems have arisen with CRAs. These include mismerged files, identity theft, and the failure of furnishers of information to properly investigate the accuracy of information they report to CRAs. Each of these are discussed in this manual. Other issues arise with respect to users of information.

1.3 About the FCRA

1.3.1 Overview

The Fair Credit Reporting Act (FCRA)[22] is a federal statute that first became effective April 25, 1971. It regulates the activities of consumer reporting agencies, the users of reports, and those who furnish information to consumer reporting agencies. The Act also provides remedies to consumers affected by such reports. A separate related statute, the federal Credit Repair Organization Act (CROA)[23] regulates credit repair organizations, businesses which for a fee, help improve a consumer's credit history. These Acts are part of the larger "package" of acts contained in the federal Consumer Credit Protection Act,[24] such as the Truth in Lending Act and the Fair Debt Collection Practices Act. Like other chapters of the federal Consumer Credit Protection Act, the Fair Credit Reporting Act is to be construed liberally.[25]

The FCRA's purpose is "to require that consumer reporting agencies adopt reasonable procedures for meeting the needs of commerce for consumer credit, personnel, insurance, and other information in a manner which is fair and equitable to the consumer, with regard to the confidentiality, accuracy, relevancy, and proper utilization of such information."[26] In general, the Act applies to situations in which a person collects information on a "consumer's credit worthiness, credit standing, credit capacity, character, general reputation, personal characteristics, or mode of living."[27] This information is used by a third party as a basis for denying or increasing the charge for "credit or insurance to be used primarily for personal, family, or household purposes."[28] The Act also applies if this information is used for purposes relating to employment opportunities, government benefits, or certain other business transactions.[29]

The FCRA attempts to protect consumers' privacy and reputations by placing various obligations on persons who use or disseminate credit information about consumers. Consumer reporting agencies must adopt reasonable procedures to ensure that the information they disseminate is accurate and up-to-date and that it is furnished only to users with certain permissible purposes.[30]

The Act imposes disclosure obligations for both reporting agencies and users. These are designed to ensure that consumers will know when a consumer report has been used as the basis of action adverse to their interest,[31] and that consumers will know about the information being disseminated about them.[32] Reporting agencies also must reinvestigate information that consumers dispute and inform users of the report of the dispute.[33] Those who furnish information to consumer reporting agencies must participate in an agency's reinvestigation.[34] Additionally, the Act makes it an offense for a user to obtain information on a consumer under false pretenses[35] and for an officer or an employee of a reporting agency to furnish such information to an unauthorized person.[36] The Act provides consumers with a civil remedy for most violations of the Act.[37]

---

19 National Association of State PIRGs, Mistakes DO Happen: A Look at Consumer Credit Reports 4 (June 2004).
20 *Id.*
21 *Id.* at 11–13.
22 15 U.S.C. §§ 1681–1681x.
23 15 U.S.C. §§ 1679–1679j
24 15 U.S.C. §§ 1601–1693r.
25 Jones v. Federated Fin. Reserve Corp., 144 F.3d 961, 964 (6th Cir. 1998) (the FCRA is to be construed liberally in favor of the consumer); Guimond v. Trans Union Credit Info. Co, 45 F.3d 1329 (9th Cir. 1995). *See also* Kates v. Crocker Nat'l Bank, 776 F.2d 1396, 1397 (9th Cir. 1985) (the FCRA is to be liberally construed, though read in such a way that the provisions give meaning to each other).
26 15 U.S.C. § 1681(b). *See also* S. Rep. No. 139, 91st Cong, 2d Sess. (1970); Hearings on H.R. 16340, *Subcommittee on Consumer Affairs of the House Committee on Banking and Currency*, 91st Cong., 2d Sess. (1970); Dea, FTC Informal Staff Opinion Letter (May 1, 1974), *reprinted on the CD-Rom accompanying this manual* (purpose of Act to "protect privacy of consumers from unrestricted dissemination of information about them by third parties in the business of compiling and selling reports," and to ensure accuracy of reported information).
27 15 U.S.C. § 1681a(d)(1).
28 15 U.S.C. § 1681a(d)(a)(A).
29 15 U.S.C. § 1681(b). *See also id.* §§ 1681b(a)(3), 1681d, 1681m.
30 15 U.S.C. §§ 1681e, 1681k, 1681l.
31 15 U.S.C. § 1681m.
32 15 U.S.C. §§ 1681d, 1681g, 1681h.
33 15 U.S.C. § 1681i.
34 15 U.S.C. § 1681s-2.
35 15 U.S.C. § 1681q.
36 15 U.S.C. § 1681r.
37 15 U.S.C. §§ 1681n, 1681o.

1.3.2 FCRA Litigation

Since many consumers are harmed by incomplete and inaccurate consumer reports, any remedies provided by the Act should be explored. For example, consumer reports may make it difficult for consumers to pull themselves out of poverty. A creditor may review reports and raise the interest rate on a loan if a negative item shows up on a borrower's report, furthering the consumer's debt load. Increasingly, landlords with available apartments rely on consumer reports before agreeing to rent to a new tenant. Prospective employers often use consumer reports to determine whether to hire a job applicant, even when filling jobs that do not involve the handling of money or other valuables. Consumers often need automobile insurance to get to decent jobs, but they are often denied insurance or forced to pay excessive rates for it because of unfavorable consumer reports. Given the importance of credit histories, and the high error rates which abound, it is not surprising that the amount of FCRA litigation is increasing.

The FCRA gives a consumer the right to learn what information is contained in a consumer report, including the right to a free report annually, and to dispute the accuracy of that information. If the consumer questions the accuracy of information in the file, the consumer reporting agency must take separate steps to correct the misinformation or, if it decides no correction is merited, must permit the consumer to add his or her own brief statement to the file. If these self-help remedies are not sufficient, an attorney may seek limited judicial remedies on behalf of a client.

Attorneys need to be alert to the power of a bad credit report when they litigate a debt on behalf of a consumer. A common problem confronting consumer attorneys is that although they may effectively argue valid defenses or counterclaims to a creditor's collection action, the creditor has already damaged the consumer's reputation by reporting the unpaid obligation to a consumer reporting agency. One solution is to specify in any settlement of the dispute that the agencies and creditors take steps to correct and protect the consumer's credit record. If a settlement does not protect a client's credit history, the consumer will probably continue to be plagued by the disputed debt. Settlement negotiations should always address what the creditor will report to a consumer reporting agency. Model settlement language is set out in § 12.6.4, *infra*.

Nonetheless, the FCRA is full of gaps and weaknesses. In some instances, the wrongs suffered by consumers are not addressed by the Act. In other instances, the Act imposes protections but does not provide consumers with a private remedy to seek redress when these protections are violated. Furthermore, the Act is so poorly drafted and difficult to understand that courts sometimes disagree over some fundamental questions. One of the chief objectives of this manual is to save consumer attorneys time by enabling them to quickly discover whether or not the Act will be useful. If the Act does apply, this manual will then assist the attorney in preparing the case.

1.3.3 Federal Agency Interpretations of the FCRA

1.3.3.1 FCRA Regulations

Congress has granted authority to the Federal Trade Commission (FTC), the Federal Reserve Board (FRB), the various banking regulators,[38] and, in some cases, the Securities and Exchange Commission (SEC) to issue regulations and interpretations for the FCRA. In addition to general rulemaking authority,[39] the agencies are specifically authorized to issue regulations pursuant to several provisions of the Fair and Accurate Credit Transactions Act of 2003 (FACTA) amendments to the FCRA.[40]

Prior to 1999, the FTC was prohibited from issuing regulations relating to the FCRA. In 1999, Congress lifted this restriction.[41] In addition to regulations, the rules of the FTC allow the agency to issue formal advisory opinions pursuant to request, and formal interpretations if an issue poses industry-wide concern.[42] However the FTC has not issued such a formal advisory opinion.

The FCRA did not require any regulations until the passage of the FACTA amendments. Thus, most, if not all, of the FCRA's regulations are promulgated pursuant to the FACTA amendments. As of mid-2006, only some of the regulations required by the FACTA amendments have been finalized by the FTC and other identified agencies. Appendix B, *infra*, includes copies of the final FACTA regulations issued so far.

FACTA's rulemaking scheme is extremely complex because there are several sets of regulations issued by different federal agencies. The FTC has promulgated regulations that apply to the CRAs and non-bank furnishers, reprinted in Appendix B.1, *infra*. The FRB has promulgated a limited number of regulations and model forms that generally apply to all furnishers or all non-bank furnishers, reprinted in Appendix B.2, *infra*. Finally, the banking regulators have promulgated regulations that govern the respective financial institutions that they supervise, reprinted in Appendix B.3, *infra*.

---

38 The banking regulators are the Office of the Comptroller of Currency (OCC) for national banks; the Office of Thrift Supervision (OTC) for federal thrifts; the Federal Deposit Insurance Corporation (FDIC) for certain state banks; the National Credit Union Administration (NCUA) for federal credit unions; and the Federal Reserve Board (FRB) for a set of other banks.
39 15 U.S.C. § 1681s(e).
40 Pub. L. No. 108-159 (2003).
41 Pub. L. No. 106-102, § 506(b) (Nov. 12, 1999) (striking 15 U.S.C. § 1681s(a)(4)). This amendment was part of the Gramm-Leach-Bliley Act of 1999.
42 *See* 16 C.F.R. §§ 1.1–1.4 (FTC Rules of Practice).

§ 1.3.3.1   Fair Credit Reporting

These regulations include:

- Regulations that create the centralized source through which consumers may request a free annual consumer report from a nationwide agency (FTC);[43]
- Regulations about how nationwide specialty consumer reporting agencies are to provide free annual credit reports (FTC);[44]
- Regulations imposing obligations on users for proper disposal of consumer report information and records (FTC, SEC, and federal banking regulators);[45]
- Regulations prohibiting nationwide consumer reporting agencies from circumventing their treatment under the FCRA (FTC);[46]
- Regulations that create exceptions to the prohibition against creditors obtaining or using medical information in connection with a determination of the consumer's eligibility for credit (federal banking regulators);[47]
- Regulations regarding the policies and procedures that a user of a consumer report that has an address discrepancy must employ (FTC and federal banking regulators);[48]
- Regulations defining what constitutes appropriate proof of identity for the purposes of 15 U.S.C. § 1681c-1 (identity theft prevention; fraud alerts; and active duty alerts), 15 U.S.C. § 1681c-2 (block of information resulting from identity theft), and 15 U.S.C. § 1681g(a)(1) (requiring a CRA to truncate the Social Security number of a consumer on a report issued to a consumer) (FTC);[49]
- Definitions of identity theft related terms, provisions regarding fraud alerts and active duty alerts, and identity theft report (FTC);[50]
- The red-flag guidelines that financial institutions are to follow to prevent and detect identity theft (FTC and federal banking regulators);[51]
- The model summary of rights to obtain and dispute information in consumer reports and to obtain credit scores (FTC);[52]
- The model summary of rights concerning identity theft (FTC);[53]
- Regulations with which creditors must comply regarding risk-based pricing notices (FTC and FRB);[54]
- Regulations identifying the circumstances under which a furnisher must reinvestigate information upon a consumer's direct dispute (FTC and federal banking regulators);[55]
- Guidelines for furnishers to follow regarding the accuracy and integrity of consumer information that they furnish to agencies (FTC and federal banking regulators);[56]
- The model disclosure for financial institutions to use to comply with the requirement that they disclose to a customer that the institution is furnishing negative information about that customer (FRB);[57]
- Regulations to implement the right of consumers to opt out of affiliate's use of information for marketing solicitations (FTC and federal banking regulators);[58]
- Designation of the effective dates for provisions within the FACTA amendments (FTC and FRB);[59]
- Creation of a severability rule (FTC);[60]
- Establishing fees for credit scores (FTC);[61] and
- The model disclosure to inform consumers of their right to opt out of prescreening lists (FTC).[62]

In addition to issuing regulations, the FTC and other agencies were required by the FACTA amendments to conduct several studies and issue reports on a broad range of

---

43   16 C.F.R. § 610.2; 15 U.S.C. § 1681j(a). *See* § 3.3.2, *infra*.

44   16 C.F.R. § 610.3; 15 U.S.C. § 1681j(a)(1)(C). *See* § 3.3.3, *infra*.

45   16 C.F.R. §§ 682.1–682.5 (FTC); 12 C.F.R. § 41.83 (OCC); 12 C.F.R. § 222.82 (FRB); 12 C.F.R. § 334.83 (FDIC); 12 C.F.R. § 571.83 (OTS); 12 C.F.R. § 717.83 (NCUA); 17 C.F.R. § 248.30 (SEC). 15 U.S.C. § 1681w(a).

46   16 C.F.R. Part 611; 15 U.S.C. § 1681x. *See* § 2.6.1.3, *infra*.

47   12 C.F.R. § 41.30 (OCC); 12 C.F.R. § 222.30 (FRB regulated banks); 12 C.F.R. § 334.30 (FDIC); 12 C.F.R. § 571.30 (OTS); 12 C.F.R. § 717.30 (NCUA). The FRB has also promulgated a set of regulations for non-bank creditors on this topic. *See* 12 C.F.R. § 232.3; 15 U.S.C. § 1681b(g)(5); § 5.4.1, *infra*.

48   15 U.S.C. § 1681c(h)(2). The FTC and banking regulators have issued a Notice of Proposed Rulemaking on this. 71 Fed. Reg. 40,786 (July 18, 2006).

49   16 C.F.R. § 614.1; Pub. L. No. 108-159, § 112(b) (2003). *See* § 9.2, *infra*.

50   16 C.F.R. §§ 603.1–603.3.

51   15 U.S.C. § 1681m(e). The FTC and banking regulators have issued a Notice of Proposed Rulemaking on this. 71 Fed. Reg. 40,786 (July 18, 2006). *See* § 9.2, *infra*.

52   16 C.F.R. §§ 698.1–698.3, and 16 C.F.R. Part 698 Appendix F; 15 U.S.C. § 1681g(c)(1). *See* § 8.2, *infra*.

53   16 C.F.R. §§ 698.1–698.3; 16 C.F.R. Part 698 Appendix E; 15 U.S.C. § 1681g(d). *See* § 8.2.3, *infra*.

54   15 U.S.C. § 1681m(h)(6). The agencies have not issued a proposal on this notice as of October 2006.

55   15 U.S.C. § 1681s-2(a)(8)(A). The FTC and banking regulators have only issued an Advanced Notice of Proposed Rulemaking on this. 71 Fed. Reg. 14,419 (Mar. 22, 2006). *See* § 8.2.8, *infra*.

56   15 U.S.C. § 1681s-2(e). The FTC and banking regulators have only issued an Advanced Notice of Proposed Rulemaking on this. 71 Fed. Reg. 14,419 (Mar. 22, 2006).

57   12 C.F.R. Part 222, Appendix B; 15 U.S.C. § 1681s-2(a)(7)(D). *See* § 8.2.10, *infra*.

58   15 U.S.C. § 1681s-3(a). The agencies have issued proposed rules, but have not finalized them as of mid-2006. 69 Fed. Reg. 33,324 (June 15, 2004); 69 Fed. Reg. 42,502 (July 15, 2004). *See* § 8.2.18, *infra*.

59   12 C.F.R. § 222.1; 16 C.F.R. § 602.1.

60   16 C.F.R. § 604.1.

61   15 U.S.C. § 1681g(f)(8). The FTC has issued a notice of proposed rulemaking on this. 69 Fed. Reg. 64,698 (Nov. 8, 2004).

62   16 C.F.R. Part 642, and 16 C.F.R. Part 698, Appendix A; 15 U.S.C. § 1681m(d). *See* § 8.2.2.2, *infra*.

credit reporting topics.[63] To the extent they have been completed, these studies are reproduced on the CD-Rom accompanying this manual.[64]

1.3.3.2 FTC Official Staff Commentary and Informal Opinion Letters

Prior to the 1996 Reform Act, the FTC issued an Official Staff Commentary (FTC Staff Commentary) interpreting many particulars of the FCRA. In addition, the FTC staff sometimes provided informal opinion letters upon request. The FTC Staff Commentary, as it is best known, is formally the *Statement of General Policy or Interpretation: Appendix—Commentary on the Fair Credit Reporting Act*.[65] While not binding, these FTC interpretations are an important resource that may affect court decision-making and analysis. The FTC Staff Commentary is reproduced at Appendix D, *infra*, while the FTC's informal staff opinion letters are included on the CD-Rom accompanying this manual, with an index at Appendix E, *infra*. In addition, annotations referring to these FTC resources may be found throughout the text of this manual.

It is unclear how much weight the courts will accord the FTC Staff Commentary in light of the rulemaking authority granted to the FTC by the 1999 and 2003 amendments. The FTC Staff Commentary is not analogous to the Federal Reserve Board's Regulation Z interpreting the Truth in Lending Act, because TILA specifically authorizes the Board to make rules and even staff interpretations. Judicial deference to the Regulation Z and its accompanying Official Staff Commentary is compelled by Supreme Court ruling.[66] By contrast, Congress in 1999 granted the FTC only limited rulemaking authority; not until the FACTA amendments did Congress expand that authority.[67] Furthermore, by its own terms, the FTC Staff Commentary is a "guideline intended to clarify how the Commission will construe the FCRA in light of Congressional intent" and will inform interested parties.[68] It was promulgated pursuant to administrative enforcement rules, making it "advisory in nature."[69] Consequently, courts need not, but still may, show deference to FTC Staff Commentary interpretations that predate the amendments.[70]

Nevertheless, although not requiring judicial deference,[71] a court may accord substantial weight to the FTC Staff Commentary.[72] The FTC Staff Commentary reflects the enforcement policy of the primary federal agency with responsibility for the FCRA;[73] it was promulgated only after publication in the *Federal Register* with an opportunity for public comment. However, the actual weight given the FTC Staff Commentary will depend upon the reasonableness, logic, and grounding in statutory language of a particular section, and its application to the circumstances of a specific case.

Prior to the FTC Staff Commentary, FTC staff issued hundreds of informal opinion letters. After the FTC Staff Commentary, the FTC issued only a trickle of letters. The volume of letters grew after passage of the Consumer Credit Reporting Reform Act of 1996 (1996 Reform Act) (amending the FCRA in many respects). The FTC last issued an FCRA-related informal staff opinion letter on June 28, 2001, and its website states that: "Except in unusual circumstances, the staff will no longer issue written interpretations of the FCRA."[74]

The informal staff opinion letters do not bind even the FTC, but do bear the imprimatur of an FTC employee.[75] The weight

---

63 These include studies on: (i) use of biometrics and other technologies to reduce identity theft; (ii) prescreened solicitations; (iii) the effects of a requirement that consumers who have experience an adverse action receive a copy of the same report as the user who took the adverse action; (iv) the comprehensibility of various forms and disclosures; (v) a study of the effects of credit scores on affordability and availability of financial products; (vi) furnishers' prompt investigation, completeness and correction or deletion of information reported to CRAs; (viii) a national strategy to promote financial literacy and financial education; and (ix) a study on the accuracy and completeness of credit reports. Pub. L. No. 108-159, §§ 157, 213, 214, 215, 313(h), 318, and 319 (2003).

64 *See, e.g.,* Federal Trade Commission and Federal Reserve Board, Report to Congress on the Fair Credit Reporting Act Dispute Process (Aug. 2006), *available at* www.ftc.gov/os/comments/fcradispute/P044808fcradisputeprocessreporttocongress.pdf; Federal Trade Commission, Report to Congress Under Sections 318 and 319 of the Fair and Accurate Credit Transactions Act of 2003 (Dec. 2004), *available at* www.ftc.gov/reports/facta/041209factarpt.pdf.

65 16 C.F.R. Part 600. The Commentary supersedes earlier statements of general policy and interpretations, compliance with the Fair Credit Reporting Act, and unofficial staff opinion letters issued prior to May 4, 1990. These superseded items are reproduced in the appendices because some of their analyses may still be compelling, and for historical purposes.

66 *See, e.g.,* Ford Motor Credit Co. v. Milhollin, 444 U.S. 555 (1980).

67 Pub. L. No. 106-102 (1999); Pub. L. No. 108-159 (2003).

68 16 C.F.R. §§ 600.1(b), 600.2; FTC Official Staff Commentary, Introduction-1, *reprinted at* Appx. D, *infra*.

69 16 C.F.R. §§ 1.71–1.73.

70 *See* Yonter v. Aetna Fin. Co., 777 F. Supp. 490 (E.D. La. 1991).

71 *See* Heintz v. Jenkins, 514 U.S. 291, 298 (1995) (noting that FTC's Official Staff Commentary on the Fair Debt Collection Practices Act did not bind courts).

72 *See, e.g., In re* Miller, 335 B.R. 335, 347 n.7 (Bankr. E.D. Pa. 2005) (court may "defer to the FTC's interpretations of the act on issues not expressly addresses by Congress"); Davis v. Equifax Info. Servs. L.L.C., 346 F. Supp. 2d 1164, 1172 (N.D. Ala. 2004) (relying on Commentary).

73 Yonter v. Aetna Fin. Co., 777 F. Supp. 490 (E.D. La. 1991).

74 www.ftc.gov/os/statutes/fcrajump.htm.

75 *See* Fischl v. GMAC, 708 F.2d 143, 149 n.4 (5th Cir. 1983) (letters provide "helpful guidance"). Informal FTC Staff Opinion Letters are also common under the Fair Debt Collection Practices Act. For the judicial weight accorded these analogous interpretations, see National Consumer Law Center, Fair Debt Collection § 6.12.2 (5th ed. 2004 and Supp.). *Cf.* Watts v. Key

accorded these letters should depend on their persuasiveness. The letters were written in response to written inquiries from consumer reporting agencies, users, and consumers.

1.4 FCRA Legislative History

1.4.1 Introduction

The FCRA has a curious legislative history. The impulse behind the FCRA was to protect consumers from abuses of the consumer reporting industry. Nevertheless, initial consumer support for the legislation turned to opposition, and it was the consumer reporting industry that embraced the Act with enthusiasm. Moreover, the most extensive and considered hearings and discussions occurred in the House of Representatives, but the final language was drafted almost entirely by the Senate with only little regard for House considerations. While the legislation sought to respond to public clamor for access to information, the final version was drafted in secrecy without explanation about some of the key provisions of the legislation. These ironies perhaps explain some of the difficulties inherent in the current law.

In the late 1960s, Congress was concerned with a broad range of consumer protection legislation. For example, Congress enacted the Truth in Lending Act, which revolutionized disclosure of credit terms and which set standards for private enforcement of consumer protection statutes. Privacy concerns were also paramount. Congressman Gallagher conducted a series of hearings which attracted wide public attention to the massive wealth of information compiled about individuals by both government and private agencies. The specter of huge data banks available electronically at the push of a button anywhere in the country loomed large. Many spoke to the urgent need to protect the rights and privacy of American citizens from "big brother." The notions of consumer protection legislation and privacy protection coalesced and gave rise to the FCRA.

The FCRA's legislative history is briefly discussed here for two reasons. First, the public history of the Act sheds considerable light on the general purposes and goals of the legislature. These congressional intentions can help guide judicial interpretation and application of the specific FCRA provisions. Second, the legislative history can help one understand the intent of specific FCRA provisions. Many provisions do not have any analogy in other consumer protection legislation. Some are difficult to understand on their face. Sometimes (but only sometimes) reviewing the debates of the time clarifies an issue. The material that follows sets out the legislative history in general. The broad outlines of various proposals are accompanied by various quotes and citations helping to explain the legislative authors' intent. More specific references to legislative history are sprinkled throughout the text in discussions of particular provisions.

1.4.2 Early Legislative History

The very first proposal in Congress for a Fair Credit Reporting Act arose as a proposed amendment to the original Truth in Lending Act. During the 1968 debate on the Truth in Lending Act in the House of Representatives, Congressman Zablocki offered an amendment which would have addressed the practices of consumer reporting agencies.[76] Although seldom recalled, Congressman Zablocki might thus be considered the father of the FCRA. The amendment was defeated, but it captured the attention of Senator Proxmire and Congresswoman Leonor Sullivan, the two legislators commonly credited with introducing credit reporting legislation.

Proxmire acted first, before the year was out. Addressing himself to the incidence of cases where a "consumer is unjustly denied credit because of faults or incomplete information in a credit report, or because he has been confused with another individual," the Senator announced his intention to alleviate these types of problems with legislation addressing the abuses of consumer credit reporting.[77] He announced that he would be introducing new legislation in the next session, and inserted a draft into the *Congressional Record*.[78] The specifics of this announcement and this draft proposal are important because this is the bill which, with amendments, later became the FCRA.

The title of the bill bespoke its purpose: A Bill To Protect Consumers Against Arbitrary Or Erroneous Credit Ratings, And The Unwarranted Publication Of Credit Information. As summarized by Proxmire, the bill was structured around three separate requirements. First, consumer reporting agencies were required to have procedures for guaranteeing the confidentiality of information they collected. Second, individuals were given the opportunity to correct adverse information in their credit records and to be notified when a derogatory item of public record is entered into their credit records. Third, consumer reporting agencies must have procedures for discarding irrelevant and outdated information from individuals' credit files. While these protections have been modified somewhat in the current law, they nevertheless continue to reflect the goals of the final legislation.

The necessity for legislation was clear to Proxmire, and soon the entire Congress. Proxmire explained the need for high standards in the credit reporting industry as follows:

> The increasing volume of complaints makes it clear that some regulations are vitally necessary to

---

Dodge Sales, Inc., 707 F.2d 847, 850–852 (5th Cir. 1983) (discussion of precedential value of official and unofficial staff interpretations of Federal Reserve Board).

76 H.R. 15627, 90th Cong., 2d Sess. (1968).
77 114 Cong. Rec. 24902 (Aug. 2, 1968).
78 *Id.* at 24904.

insure that higher standards are observed with respect to the information in the files of commercial credit bureaus. I cite what I consider to be the three most important criteria for judging the quality of these standards. They are first, confidentiality; second, accuracy; and third, currency of information.[79]

These three standards bear further elaboration. They are the three overriding themes of today's Fair Credit Reporting Act. Proxmire explained each in greater detail:[80]

Confidentiality:

> [Credit] information is furnished for a specific purpose, namely, in support of the application for credit. Without the consumer's knowledge or acquiescence this information should not be supplied to a noncreditor. It is the current practice for instance, of most consumer reporting agencies, with the notable exception of the Credit Data Corp, to grant free access to their files to various governmental investigatory agencies such as the FBI and the IRS. There have also been many stories telling of the ease with which an unauthorized person can get a look at an individual's file. Therefore, my bill requires that no one can engage in the business of credit reporting unless there are procedures in effect for guaranteeing the confidentiality of the information collected.

Accuracy:

> There are many varieties of inaccurate information, but I shall mention only two. One is the case of mistaken identity, where two individuals with the same names are confused, and the deserving individual is denied credit because of something done by the other person. . . . A second type of inaccuracy, or more precisely, incompleteness, has to do with so-called derogatory items from public records. Consumer reporting agencies seem very anxious to record the fact that a person has been sued for nonpayment, but they are in many cases not so diligent in noting the disposition of the case. For example, if a consumer refuses to pay because he cannot get satisfaction from a merchant with respect to a shoddy piece of merchandise, the merchant may sue him for nonpayment, and this fact is recorded by the consumer reporting agency. However, if the suit is subsequently decided in favor of the consumer, this would not be recorded and the consumer's credit rating would be unjustly jeopardized.

Currency of Information:

> The bill further provides that there be in effect procedures of information for evaluating and for keeping the information in an individual's credit file up to date. This requirement is related to the one I have just discussed: the requirement that the information be accurate. However, there is a further element here: that irrelevant and outdated information be discarded from the file.

These themes were made concrete in the draft bill presented by Proxmire. His bill proposed that consumer reports could be disseminated only to creditors, unless the consumer gave permission otherwise. It also required procedures for insuring confidentiality, for providing on consumer request an opportunity to correct information in consumer reporting agency files, for evaluating information about a consumer's creditworthiness, for keeping information current, and for notifying consumers whenever adverse public information has been obtained and permitting the consumer an opportunity to submit an explanatory statement.

1.4.3 Senate Bill 823

At the beginning of the new congressional session, Senator Proxmire and a bipartisan group of nine other senators, introduced Senate Bill 823, the bill which would eventually become law. For the first time, the legislation was called the Fair Credit Reporting Act. It was designed to "establish certain Federal safeguards over the activities of consumer reporting agencies in order to protect consumers against arbitrary, erroneous, and malicious credit information."[81]

Citing the vast size and scope of the credit reporting industry,[82] the Senator's introductory remarks noted the wide range of information included in consumer reports: financial status; bill paying records; items of public records including "arrests, suits, judgments, and the like"; dossiers on individuals; information on drinking; marital discords; adulterous behavior; general reputation; habits; and morals. "While the growth of this information network is somewhat alarming, what is even more alarming is the fact that the system has been built up with virtually no public regulation or supervision."[83]

The value of a credit reporting industry was recognized. Proxmire called consumer reporting agencies "absolutely essential."[84] Creditors need sound information about creditworthiness, quickly. The purpose of the bill was to "correct certain abuses which have occurred within the industry and

---

79 *Id.* at 24903.
80 *Id.*
81 115 Cong. Rec. 2410 (Jan. 31, 1969).
82 "Although a number of congressional committees have recently begun to investigate the activities of consumer reporting agencies, most Americans still do not realize the vast size and scope of today's credit reporting industry or the tremendous amount of information which these agencies maintain and distribute." 115 Cong. Rec. 2410 (Jan. 31, 1969).
83 *Id.*
84 *Id.* at 2411.

to ensure that the credit information system is responsive to the needs of consumers as well as creditors."[85]

The bill was designed to address three types of abuses: the problems of inaccuracies or inaccurate or misleading information; the problem of irrelevant information; and the problem of maintaining confidentiality.[86] Whether these abuses were adequately addressed by the legislation which emerged from Congress is subject to debate. Given the fact that the current FCRA addresses abuses of the reporting industry by establishing "reasonable procedures" and general rather than specific standards, it is especially helpful to note the original intentions of the Senate bill.

Inaccurate and misleading information was called the most serious problem in the credit reporting industry.[87] Inaccuracy is a general term which still bedevils the courts today. Proxmire listed five types of inaccuracies giving rise to abuses requiring a legislative response. The five are: the confusion of information about persons with similar or identical names,[88] biased or one-sided information,[89] malicious gossip and hearsay,[90] computer errors,[91] and incomplete information.[92]

---

[85] *Id.* Proxmire also put it this way: "Since the consumer pays the bill in the end, he has the right to have his interests represented and protected. The credit reporting system can only be justified if it serves the consumer as well as business." *Id.* at 2414.

[86] *Id.* at 2411.

[87] Perhaps the most serious problem in the credit reporting industry is the problem of inaccurate or misleading information. There have been no definitive studies made of just how accurate is the information in the files of consumer reporting agencies. Even if it is 99 percent accurate—and I doubt that it is that good—the 1 percent inaccuracy represents over a million people. While the credit industry might be satisfied with a 1 percent error, this is small comfort to the one million citizens whose reputations are unjustly maligned. Moreover, the composition of the 1 million persons is constantly shifting. Everyone is a potential victim of an inaccurate credit report. If not today, then perhaps tomorrow.

Id. at 2411.

[88] "Confusion with other persons: each year, millions of Americans get married, get divorced, change their name, their job or their residence. Millions of people have the same or similar name. Therefore, it is no wonder that credit bureaus frequently confuse one individual with another, sometimes with tragic results." *Id.*

[89] Biased information: A record of slow or nonpayment in a person's credit file does not necessarily mean he is a poor risk. Perhaps he had a legitimate dispute with a merchant and withheld payment until the merchant lived up to the terms of the contract. While merchants have a wide variety of collection weapons, about the only bargaining power consumers have is the threat to hold up payment. Unfortunately, the consumer's side of the story does not find its way as easily into the files of the credit bureau as does the merchant's version.

Id.

[90] Malicious gossip and hearsay: Perhaps the most serious misinformation in consumer reporting agency files is malicious gossip and hearsay. This type of information is most prevalent in the files of consumer reporting agencies which specialize in investigating people who apply for insurance or employment. The information is often obtained from neighbors or coworkers where the opportunity is ripe for anonymous character assassination. These kinds of investigations usually include detailed information on highly personal items. . . .

Id. This is the first reference in the legislative history to consumer reports compiled for insurance or employment purposes.

[91] "Computer errors: With the growing trend toward computerization, the incidence of computer errors is on the increase." *Id.* Also,

undoubtedly the computerization of personal information about millions of individuals gives this subject greater importance and urgency then it had in the days when the average businessman knew his customers personally and knew the good credit risks from the bad, and the insurance agent was an old acquaintance who knew the probably good actuarial risks from the probably bad ones. Today, such data is almost completely second-hand, third-hand or even more distant and impersonal, and it is almost impossible to find a human being to unravel a computer error once it is made. When the computer is half a continent away and connected to the store by electronics, the remoteness of the customer from the real arbiter of his creditworthiness becomes even pronounced.

Hearings Before Subcommittee on Consumer Affairs of House Committee on Banking and Currency on H.R. 16340, 91st Cong., 2d Sess. 1 (1970) (remarks of Congresswomen Leonor Sullivan).

[92] "Incomplete information: Because of the increased computerization and standardization of credit bureau files, all of the relevant information is not always reflected in a person's file." (For example, Proxmire notes, one may be classified as a "slow payer" despite the existence of extenuating circumstances which are not noted in a standardized computerized report.) *Id.* 115 Cong. Rec. 2410 (Jan. 31, 1969).

Another type of incomplete information is concerned with adverse items of public records. Most consumer reporting agencies assiduously cull adverse information on people from newspapers, court reports, and other public documents. These items include records of arrest, judgments, liens, bankruptcies, suits, and the like. However, most agencies are not anywhere nearly as diligent in following up on the case to record information favorable to the consumer. Action following arrest is often dropped because of evidence. Suits are dismissed or settled out of court. Judgments are reversed. However, these facts are seldom reported by the consumer reporting agencies with the result that their records are systematically biased against the consumers.

Irrelevant information is information which, while it may be "technically accurate, does not serve any useful or appropriate purpose."[93] Two types of irrelevant information were noted. First, some common irrelevant information concerns minor offenses committed years ago. A second type of irrelevant information goes beyond the immediate purpose for acquiring information and includes extraneous details and inappropriate personal information.[94]

Privacy and confidentiality were also major concerns of the time. The FCRA proponents addressed themselves to four aspects of confidentiality.[95] Many consumer reporting agencies supplied their reports to virtually anyone. Frequently, information was used by agencies inconsistently with the purposes indicated when the information was collected.[96] Internal security procedures were often inadequate.[97] And finally, information collected privately was often made available to governmental agencies.[98]

To address all these factors, Senate Bill 823 depended heavily upon rulemaking by the Federal Reserve Board. In the main, it set out objectives in general terms with the expectation that specifics would be promulgated by rule. The objectives were these: to ensure confidentiality; to provide a reasonable opportunity to correct information, upon request; to limit the collection, retention, or furnishing of information "bearing upon the credit rating of any individual to those items essential for the purposes for which the information is sought and to preclude the collection, retention, or furnishing of information which only marginally benefits the purposes for which the information is sought or which represents an undue invasion of the individual's right to privacy;" to keep information current and to destroy obsolete information; to notify an individual when adverse public record information is obtained by a reporting agency and to provide an opportunity to comment; and to ensure that information is provided only to persons with a legitimate business need and for the purposes disclosed in the collection of the information.[99]

In addition to these general objectives, Senate Bill 823 was more specific in three regards. First, it covered all reports making any representation as to creditworthiness or general reputation of an individual; it was not limited to credit, insurance, or employment purposes. Similarly, it covered all legitimate business uses in connection with consumer credit or other transactions with the individual on whom the information was furnished.[100] Second, whenever credit was denied in whole or in part because of a consumer report, notice of that fact together with the name and address of the reporting agency was to be given to the individual. Third, the bill provided for actual damages, and punitive damages of not less than $100 nor more than $1000, and attorney fees.

Public hearings,[101] secret negotiations,[102] a committee

Id. at 2412.
93 *Id.*
94 *Id.* at 2413.
95 "What is disturbing is the lack of any public standards to insure that the information is kept confidential and used only for its intended purpose. The growing accessibility of this information through computer- and data-transmission techniques makes the problem of confidentiality even more important." *Id.* at 2413.
96 When an individual seeks to buy an insurance policy, it might be argued that he has given his implied consent to be investigated. Likewise, when he applies for employment. But surely the doctrine of implied consent cannot be stretched to infer that the individual has agreed that information acquired in an insurance investigation or filled out on a credit application can be furnished to prospective employers. Considering the gossipy personal information included in . . . insurance investigations it is frightening to think such information could affect a person's entire career. It is bad enough to be turned down for insurance. It is much worse to lose a job on the basis of an erroneous piece of gossip in a credit file.

Id.
97 "Since credit bureaus are almost entirely responsive to the needs of business and have little responsibility to consumers, it is difficult to see major expenditures on security systems in the absence of public standards." *Id.*
98 One can certainly be sympathetic to the problems of the FBI and IRS in meeting their heavy responsibilities. But, nonetheless, their right to investigate is not absolute and is subject to various constitutional restraints. . . . Regardless of whether the individual has any legal control over the information on him in a consumer reporting agency's file, I certainly feel he has a moral claim to controlling its use. He should not be entirely dependent upon the policies of the particular consumer reporting agencies to protect his basic rights.

Id.

99 *See* S. 823, § 164, 91st Cong., 1st Sess. (15 Cong. Rec. 2415) (introduced Jan. 31, 1969).
100 S. 823 §§ 163, 164(f), 91st Cong., 1st Sess. (15 Cong. Rec. 2415) (introduced Jan. 31, 1969).
101 *Hearings on S. 823, Subcommittee on Financial Institutions of the Senate Banking and Currency Committee*, 91st Cong., 1st Sess. 2 (1969). In convening public hearings, Senator Proxmire set out a consumer bill of rights:

The Aim of the Fair Credit Reporting Act is to see that the credit reporting system serves the consumer as well as the industry. The consumer has a right to information which is accurate; he has a right to correct inaccurate or misleading information; he has a right to know when inaccurate information is entered into his file; he has a right to see that the information is kept confidential and is used for the purpose for which it is collected; and he has a right to be free from unwarranted invasions of his personal privacy. The Fair Credit Reporting Act seeks to secure these rights.

Also, "In a free society there is no place for protected character assassination masquerading under the guise of a credit report." *Id.*
102 Senator Bennett, the spokesperson for industry interests, characterized the negotiations as occurring between committee

§ 1.4.3   Fair Credit Reporting

compromise,[103] unanimous committee action,[104] and unanimous voice vote of the Senate[105] followed swiftly. All of this happened even before the main House bill was introduced. Moreover, the language of this Senate version is in most respects the language of the current law; it was largely unaffected by House deliberations. For this reason, a closer look at the changes which occurred in Senate Bill 832 is merited.

The most significant compromise in the Senate bill immunized consumer reporting agencies, informants, and users of consumer reports from substantial liability under state defamation laws in certain circumstances.[106] More than any other change, this concession won the industry's support for the bill[107] and the enmity of former consumer supporters.[108]

It did not start out this way. When the Senate public hearings were convened, Senator Proxmire intended to create new liability for consumer reporting agencies that violated the new federal Act and to retain liability under state laws for inaccurate or defamatory information.[109] Proxmire's original bill required reporting agencies to open their files to individuals about whom they collect information. The agencies objected strongly that this would leave them and their sources of information open to huge numbers of nuisance suits and dry up the flow of information necessary for the efficient operation of the credit market. Their then current policies usually were to permit consumer access to their files only if consumers waived their right to bring state law claims. Proxmire began to waiver and wonder aloud whether, in exchange for being required to open their files to consumers, credit agencies and others should be immunized from potential liability under state tort laws.[110] This is exactly the deal which was made.[111]

Another major change in the Senate legislation was the elimination of rulemaking. Rather than set forth objectives and require the Federal Reserve Board (or the Federal Trade Commission) to implement general goals through regulations, the Act was considerably more explicit in establishing its own standards and procedures.

The third major change was that consumer rights of access to files and for correcting information are set out more explicitly. In several instances, at the urging of the Nixon Administration, the rights are more beneficial for consumers than originally proposed by Senator Proxmire.[112] On the other hand, several consumer benefits which were anticipated to flow from rulemaking were not included in the legislation.[113] For example, agencies no longer had to notify a consumer when adverse information is included in any file; instead, a consumer who is turned down on the basis of a report, would have a right to find out what is in the credit file and have it corrected.[114]

A last major change involved the redrafting of the operative definition of consumer report.[115] For the first time, the definition incorporated information used for governmental benefits and business transactions involving consumers.[116] The intent and meaning of these changes is still debated today.[117]

---

members and industry representatives. "The committee members and representatives of both the reporting agencies and the industries which they serve have worked hard to reach agreement on responsible legislation which would protect the legitimate interests of both consumers and industry." 115 Cong. Rec. 33412 (1969).

103 "We have reached a compromise that I can enthusiastically support." 115 Cong. Rec. at 33413 (remarks of Sen. Proxmire).
104 *Id.* at 33408.
105 *Id.* at 33414.
106 See § 10.4, *infra* for exceptions to this immunity.
107 "It is an industry bill." *Hearings Before Subcommittee on Consumer Affairs of House Committee on Banking and Currency on H.R. 16340*, 91st Cong., 2d Sess. 108 (1970) (remarks of John L. Spafford, President, Associated Credit Bureaus Inc.). *See also* 115 Cong. Rec. 33412–33413 (1969) (remarks of Senator Bennett).
108 "If the choice is the Senate Bill or no bill, then I think it has to be no bill." *Hearings Before Subcommittee on Consumer Affairs of House Committee on Banking and Currency on H.R. 16340*, 91st Cong., 2d Sess. 84 (1970) (remarks of Anthony Roisman, Consumer Federation of America). "I have the feeling about S. 823 that it really is an act to protect and immunize the credit bureaus rather than an act to protect the individual who has been abused by credit information flow created by the bureaus." *Id.* at 190 (remarks of Prof. Arthur Miller, University of Michigan).
109 *Hearings on S. 823, Subcommittee on Financial Institutions of the Senate Banking and Currency Committee*, 91st Cong., 1st Sess. 24 (1969).

110 *Id.* For example, at page 104, Proxmire asks rhetorically:

> How about simply exempting the credit bureaus? After all, you have a situation here where you are recommending at least when this adverse information is entered, the consumer is notified he has an opportunity to come in and correct it. The credit bureau has complied with the law. What they have done is simply secure the information that the informant has given them, there has been an opportunity for correction made [sic]. Presumably if the consumer is right, the correction would be made. And under these circumstances, why should there be any basis for a suit?

111 115 Cong. Rec. 33411 (1969) ("That is the quid quo pro.") (remarks of Senator Proxmire).
112 *See Hearings on S. 823, Subcommittee on Financial Institutions of the Senate Banking and Currency Committee*, 91st Cong., 1st Sess. 11 (1969) (testimony of Virginia Knauer, Special Assistant to President Nixon) (e.g., consumers' right to learn contents of reports; right to submit explanatory statements; requirement that corrected version of reports be sent to earlier recipients).
113 *See generally Hearings Before Subcommittee on Consumer Affairs of House Committee on Banking and Currency on H.R. 16346*, 91st Cong., 2d Sess. (1970).
114 115 Cong. Rec. 33411 (1969) (remarks of Senator Proxmire).
115 *Compare* Senate Bill 823, 115 Cong. Rec. 2415 (1969) *with* today's statute.
116 15 U.S.C. § 1681a(d).
117 *See* § 2.3, *infra*.

1.4.4 Passage of the Fair Credit Reporting Act

On March 5, 1970, after Senate passage of Senate Bill 823, Congresswoman Leonor Sullivan introduced House of Representatives Bill 16340, the "Good Name Protection Act."[118] It was in general more pro-consumer than the Senate bill.[119] Extensive public hearings were held.

However, before the House was able to act on its own bill, the Senate bill become law. On May 25, 1970, the House of Representatives passed a Bank Records Foreign Transactions Act.[120] It contained no reference to consumer reporting. The Senate passed its own Financial Recordkeeping Bill on September 18th.[121] The Senate added Senate Bill 823 to the Senate Financial Recordkeeping Bill, and the matter went to a House-Senate Conference Committee. The Conference Committee kept the Fair Credit Reporting Act as part of this larger, more urgent bill.

Senate Bill 823 was accepted by the Conference Committee largely intact,[122] but with two quite significant changes. First, for the first time the bill required reporting agencies to follow reasonable procedures to ensure maximum possible accuracy in their reports. Second, the bill eliminated the floor and ceiling on punitive damages.[123]

The Senate voted to accept the Conference Report on September 9th, and the House on October 13th. Thus the FCRA become law without separate House action on its own bill and with few compromises between House and Senate interests.

1.4.5 FCRA Amendments Before the Consumer Credit Reporting Act of 1996

Although Senator Proxmire had his day with the House of Representatives, pressing his version of the FCRA on the House by parliamentary legerdemain, he came to have second thoughts. In 1973, Proxmire rose on the floor of the Senate and proposed a series of FCRA amendments reflecting earlier House and consumer concerns.[124] Acknowledging disappointment and shortcomings with the FCRA he drafted, he now proposed to correct deficiencies.

The seven proposals have proved to be an early recognition of areas where the Act has failed to achieve its original objectives. Proxmire proposed direct consumer access to all files;[125] the release of investigative reports only with the consumer's prior permission in writing; the provision of the consumer report by users who take adverse action (and if information were received from a third party (not an agency), the disclosure of the nature of the information); the override of FTC interpretations excluding government agencies such as the Civil Service Commission from FCRA coverage; FTC rulemaking power; minimum civil liability of $100 not to exceed $1000 for willful violations (because no punitive awards had been made by the courts to date); and, most significantly, the repeal of immunity from state tort actions granted reporting agencies and others. This bill never made it out of Committee. In 1975 and in 1979, Senator Proxmire again tried to amend and strengthen the Fair Credit Reporting Act.[126] Neither bill ever reached the public hearing stage.

Between its passage and the 1996 Reform Act, the FCRA was only infrequently amended, and then only in limited ways. As part of a reform of bankruptcy laws, the time period during which bankruptcy could be reported was shortened from fourteen to ten years.[127] Another amendment clarified that consumer reports may be provided in response to a federal grand jury subpoena.[128] The Ted Weiss Child-

---

118 116 Cong. Rec. 6200 (Mar. 5, 1970).

119 Some of the differences were that the House Bill provided for regulations and the Senate Bill did not; the House Bill provided for no immunity and the Senate Bill did; the House Bill permitted consumer access to the file itself without any waiver of state law tort rights while the Senate Bill required access only to information about the contents of the files and provided in return partial immunity from state tort laws; the House Bill required the grantor to disclose reasons for rejecting a consumer's application, but not the Senate Bill; under the House bill, but not the Senate bill, a grantor was required to disclose third party information; the House bill required a grantor to keep reports to reporting agencies current while the Senate Bill had no provisions in this regard; the House Bill required adverse information to be discarded after three years while the Senate had a seven year limitation; and the House Bill required notice to consumers when public record information is reported and required that it be updated within seven previous days, while the Senate Bill had no similar provisions.

120 H.R. 15073, 91st Cong. 2d Sess. (1970).

121 S. 3678, 91st Cong. 2d Sess. (1970).

122 Con. Rep. No. 1587, 91st Cong., 2d Sess. (1970), *reprinted in* 1970 U.S.C.C.A.N. 4394, 4414. Specific changes are noted throughout the text.

123 A consumer would no longer be entitled to a minimum of $100 and a maximum of $1000 of "punitive" damages. Instead, in order not to limit damages which a consumer might receive for injury to his reputation or harm to his access to credit, the limits on punitive damages were removed. *See Hearings on S. 823, Subcommittee on Financial Institutions of the Senate Banking and Currency Committee*, 91st Cong., 1st Sess. (1969) (testimony of Virginia Knauer).

124 S. 2360, 119 Cong. Rec. 27818–27819 (1973).

125 The proposal would have permitted consumers to inspect the files themselves and to get a copy of all information in the files. All information would have to be disclosed, including medical reports and sources for investigative reports. A consumer would be entitled to receive a copy of any consumer report through the mail and to obtain disclosures free by long distance telephone call whenever the consumer had been turned down.

126 S. 1840, 94th Cong., 1st Sess. (1975); S. 1928, 96th Cong. 1st Sess. (1979).

127 Pub. L. No. 95-598. *See also* § 5.2.3.7, *infra*.

128 Pub. L. No. 101-73.

hood Support Enforcement Act of 1992[129] required consumer reports to include information regarding failure to pay overdue child support. A number of bills enacted minor changes as to the responsibility of federal agencies to enforce the FCRA.[130] A 1994 amendment requires that negative information about a consumer's check cashing history in a reporting file be more fully disclosed to consumers upon request.[131] Two isolated 1996 amendments gave the FBI the right to obtain information from consumer reporting agencies for certain counterintelligence purposes[132] and gave state and local child support enforcement agencies the right to obtain information for purposes of setting child support payment levels.[133]

1.4.6 The Consumer Credit Reporting Reform Act of 1996

On September 30, 1996, culminating years of deliberation, Congress passed the Consumer Credit Reporting Reform Act of 1996 (the "1996 Reform Act"),[134] which revised nearly every section of the FCRA. Where appropriate, these revisions and their effects are discussed in this manual.

As discussed above, efforts at reform began in 1973, only a few years after the original enactment of the FCRA, although no sweeping changes were enacted. Starting in 1989, major efforts to reform the FCRA were made in Congress every year. In September 1996, Congress approved a modified version of Senate Bill 709, a bill proposed by Senator Bryan which was attached by the Senate Banking Committee to Senate Bill 650, the Economic Growth and Regulatory Paperwork Reduction Act of 1995, a draconian rollback of consumer laws. House Bill 561, similar to Senate Bill 709, was introduced in the House of Representatives by Congressmen Gonzalez and Kennedy, but no committee action was ever taken. In the end, the congressional consensus that had formed in 1994 and earlier allowed the Consumer Credit Reporting Reform Act of 1996 to be added without public debate as a small part of House Bill 3610, the so-called Continuing Budget Resolution[135] was adopted in the last hours of the fiscal year.[136]

The twin problems of consumer report inaccuracies and difficulties in fixing them were the primary motivation for reforming the FCRA. The Federal Trade Commission reported that errors in consumer credit reports were the number one item of complaint.[137] Forty-eight percent of the consumer reports studied by Consumers Union had errors, twenty percent had errors serious enough to cause credit to be denied.[138] Senators also cited the frustration of consumers who tried to correct inaccurate entries.[139] A 1991 study by US PIRG found that consumers who had filed complaints with the FTC had already complained to a consumer reporting agency for an average of twenty-three weeks, and sixty-three percent of the consumers had contacted the agency five times or more before contacting the FTC.[140]

Some attributed the accuracy problems to the increased use of computers to store and transfer consumer information, and the increased volume of that information.[141] Information that had once been kept on handwritten file cards was now stored on computer tapes that were updated daily, adding billions of entries each month.[142] Computers were also blamed for one of the most vexing issues of accuracy, the reinsertion of old, inaccurate information into a corrected consumer report. As explained in a statement before the House, the clerk in the office of the offending furnisher who processed the correction was not the same person who ran the data processing operation, so the inaccurate information was never removed from the magnetic tape before the furnisher resubmitted to the agency.[143]

Both the House and the Senate heard numerous horror stories from consumers regarding erroneous reports and the damage they caused.[144] Representative Sanders related in detail the continuing catastrophes caused by TRW (now

---

129 Pub. L. No. 102-537.
130 Pub. L. Nos. 98-443, 101-73, 102-242, 102-550.
131 See § 3.5.5, infra.
132 See § 7.2.10.4, infra.
133 See § 7.2.9, infra.
134 The Consumer Credit Reporting Reform Act of 1996, Pub. L. No. 104-208, 110 Stat. 3009 (Sept. 30, 1996).
135 Subtitle D, Chapter 1, of the Omnibus Consolidated Appropriations Act, Pub. L. No. 104-208, 110 Stat. 3009 (Sept. 30, 1996).
136 Id.
137 "Historically, credit bureaus have led the pack in terms of the number of the complaints that the agency receives." H. Rep. 45, 102d Cong., 1st Sess. 44 (statement of Ms. Noonan, Associate Director for Credit Practices, FTC). See also 142 Cong. Rec. S11869 (daily ed. Sept. 30, 1996) ("[e]rrors in credit reports have been the No. 1 item of complaint at the Federal Trade Commission and States attorneys general have experienced similar levels of complaint") (statement of Sen. Bryan, sponsor of S. 783); S. Rep. 925, 102d Cong., 1st Sess. 3 (1992) (statement of Hon. Del Papa, Attorney General, State of Nevada, stating that consumer complaints against consumer reporting agencies almost always concerned inaccuracies and the agencies' refusal to fix the problems).
138 H. Rep. 45, 102d Cong., 1st Sess. 12 (1991).
139 141 Cong. Rec. S5449 (daily ed. Apr. 6, 1995) (comments of Senators Bond and Bryan on S. 709).
140 Senate Committee on Banking, Housing and Urban Affairs, The Consumer Credit Reporting Reform Act of 1994, S. Rep. 209, 103d Cong., 1st Sess. 5 (1993) (to accompany S. 783).
141 141 Cong. Rec. E121 (daily ed. Jan. 18, 1995) (comments of Rep. Gonzalez in introducing H.R. 561).
142 140 Cong. Rec. S4973 (daily ed. May 2, 1994) (comments of Sen. Bryan regarding S. 783). See also H. Rep. 194, 102d Cong., 1st Sess. 11 (1991) ("[w]hen the [FCRA] was first drafted, no one envisioned the impact computer technology would have on the distribution of information").
143 H. Rep. 45, 102d Cong., 1st Sess. 63 (1991) (statement of Mr. Holstein, on behalf of Bank Card Holders of America).
144 See generally H. Rep. 45, 102d Cong., 1st Sess. (1991) (hearings on H.R. 194, H.R. 670, and H.R. 1751); S. Rep. 209, 103d Cong., 1st Sess. (1993) (hearings on S. 783).

Experian) when it listed every property taxpayer in Norwich, Vermont as delinquent, and subsequently failed to respond to efforts to clear up the mess.[145] The core problem, according to one industry expert, is that few market incentives exist to motivate the credit industry to voluntarily correct accuracy problems because consumers are not the agencies' paying customers.[146]

Most of the major changes to the FCRA by the 1996 Reform Act addressed, in some form, this issue of accuracy. Among the proposals finally enacted were those establishing obligations on furnishers,[147] a thirty-day deadline (with a conditional fifteen-day extension) on an agency's reinvestigation of information disputed by a consumer,[148] and protections against the reinsertion of previously deleted material.[149]

The thirty-day reinvestigation limit, described by one senator as the "single most important consumer protection provision" in the 1996 Reform Act,[150] did not raise much industry ire; one retailers' representative acknowledged it was "realistic."[151] However, a provision in Senate Bill 783 that would have required a consumer reporting agency to accept the consumer's version of disputed information, and to correct or delete it if the consumer provided confirming documentation from the source of the information, was kept out of the final bill.[152]

In contrast to the reinvestigation deadline, the provisions prescribing furnisher obligations and liability for failing those obligations caused great consternation. Creditor representatives argued vehemently against imposing any liability on furnishers, fearing a dramatic increase in litigation.[153] They contended that the proposed liability provisions would lead them to refuse to provide information to consumer reporting agencies, which would in turn hurt consumers seeking credit because their reports would not fully reflect their credit histories.[154]

The bill as passed compromised two main issues in favor of furnishers. First, while the 1996 Reform Act imposed obligations on furnishers, consumers were given the right to sue furnishers *only* after the furnisher has had an opportunity to reinvestigate and fix any mistakes after consumers have complained to the consumer reporting agency.[155] Consumers cannot privately enforce the provisions requiring furnishers to initially provide accurate information, to correct and update information, or to notify consumer reporting agencies of certain information about consumer accounts,[156] and even administrative enforcement of these provisions is greatly constricted.[157] The second compromised issue concerns the level of furnisher responsibility. Proposals that were rejected include: requiring furnishers to follow reasonable procedures to "assure the maximum possible accuracy" of any information furnished;[158] prohibiting them from furnishing information that the furnisher has "reasonable cause to believe is incomplete or inaccurate;"[159] prohibiting them from furnishing information if the consumer has notified the furnisher that the information is incomplete or inaccurate;[160] and requiring furnishers who furnish consumer information to consumer reporting agencies to notify consumers of that fact in writing before furnishing such information.[161] Even without these stricter provisions, however, the final version kept a privately enforceable obligation on furnishers to reinvestigate disputed information, and the Committee Report analyzing that version emphasized this responsibility:

> [T]he Committee does intend to impose an affirmative obligation on furnishers of information to establish, at a minimum, procedures through which an employee, who, in the ordinary course of business... determines that information furnished to a consumer reporting agency is not complete or accurate, can ensure that the results of this determination are communicated to the appropriate consumer reporting agencies.[162]

Furnishers' concerns about litigation were further assuaged with a provision requiring a party who in bad faith files an

---

145 H. Rep. 79, 102d Cong., 1st Sess. 5 (hearings on H. 3596).
146 H. Rep. 45, 102d Cong., 1st Sess. 60–61 (statement of Dr. Culnan, Georgetown University School of Business Administration).
147 See Ch. 6, *infra*.
148 See Ch. 4, *infra*.
149 See Ch. 4, *infra*.
150 141 Cong. Rec. S5449 (daily ed. Apr. 6, 1995) (statement of Sen. Bond).
151 H. Rep. 79, 102d Cong., 1st Sess. 70 (1991) (statement of Mr. Skinner, on behalf of the National Retail Federation).
152 S. 783, 103d Cong., 1st Sess. § 107 (1993).
153 *See, e.g.,* H. Rep 45, 102d Cong., 1st Sess. 84, 86; S. 486, 103d Cong., 1st. Sess 103 (1993).
154 *Id.*
155 15 U.S.C. § 1681s-2(e), *as amended by* Pub. L. No. 104-208, 110 Stat. 3009 (Sept. 30, 1996). See § 13.7, *infra*.
156 15 U.S.C. § 1681s-2, *as amended by* Pub. L. No. 104-208, 110 Stat. 3009 (Sept. 30, 1996).
157 *See* Chs. 3, 12, *infra*.
158 H.R. 3596, 102d Cong., 1st Sess. § 12 (1991); H.R. 1015, 103d Cong., 1st Sess. § 112 (1993) (as introduced).
159 *Id.* As passed, § 1681s-2(a)(1) only prohibits the furnishing of information that the furnisher "knows or consciously avoids knowing" is inaccurate. 15 U.S.C. § 1623s-2(a)(1), *as amended by* Pub. L. No. 104-208, 110 Stat. 3009 (Sept. 30, 1996).
160 S. 783, 103d Cong., 1st Sess. § 113 (1993).
161 *Id.* The provision would have applied only to furnishers who furnish information in the ordinary course of business and on a routine basis.
162 S. Rep. 486, 103d Cong., 1st Sess. 50 (1993). The Committee also stated that "[t]hese provisions are aimed at enhancing the quality and accuracy of the information provided to consumer reporting agencies and ensuring that furnishers of information respond in a reasonable and timely manner to consumer disputes about the accuracy and completeness of information in their credit files." *Id.* at 49.

unsuccessful pleading, motion, or other paper in a liability action to pay the opposing party's attorney fees.[163]

The issue of free consumer reports also drove much debate. The right to a free consumer report every year was seen as vital to the issue of maintaining accuracy by consumer advocates[164] and unacceptable by the consumer reporting industry, which feared not just the cost of the free reports but also the anticipated increase in workload to respond to consumers' concerns arising from their review of their reports.[165] House Bills 194 and 3596 would have allowed consumers one free report annually,[166] while Senate Bill 2776 would have allowed one free report biannually.[167] By contrast, Senate Bill 783 simply raised the cap on the cost of a report to three dollars,[168] then House Bill 1015 raised it to eight dollars.[169] The eight dollar cap was adopted in the final bill, with a provision that the FTC shall increase it each year in proportion to increases in the Consumer Price Index.[170] The ultimate result was a loss for consumers and for accuracy, as a consumer who did not fall within an exception may have had to pay twenty-four dollars (more in subsequent years) to get a report from each of the "Big Three" consumer reporting agencies[171] in order to check the information in his or her files. This remained the situation until the passage of the FACTA amendments in 2003, discussed *infra*.

Some proposed reform bills had sought a compromise, offering free reports to consumers whose files were found to have contained inaccurate information. House Bill 561 and one version of House Bill 1015 would have allowed one free report within twelve months after inaccurate or unverifiable information was deleted pursuant to a reinvestigation,[172] while another version would have required a consumer reporting agency to refund any charge for a report furnished to a consumer if that consumer then requested a reinvestigation that turned up inaccurate information.[173] A provision of Senate Bill 783 would have allowed a consumer to order one free report for a prior recipient designated by the consumer pursuant to section 1681i(d) following the deletion of inaccurate material;[174] as passed, the 1996 Reform Act allowed the consumer reporting agency to charge whatever the agency would otherwise charge the report's recipient, so long as the agency notifies the consumer ahead of time.[175] None of these free report provisions were enacted by the 1996 Reform Act despite their obvious incentive for accuracy—if the consumer's report was accurate, the agency would not be out the cost of the report.

The 1996 Reform Act did allow consumers free reports in limited circumstances. A consumer is not charged for a report requested within sixty days of receiving notice that a user of the report has taken an adverse action based on that report.[176] A consumer may also request a free report once a year if the consumer certifies that the consumer is unemployed and seeking employment, on welfare, or has reason to believe that the consumer's file contains inaccurate information due to fraud.[177]

Assorted other provisions relating to accuracy concerns were proposed but never enacted. House Bill 1015 and Senate Bill 783 would have required persons using a consumer report for employment purposes to provide the consumer a copy of the report *and* a reasonable opportunity to respond to any disputed information in the report before taking any adverse action.[178] House Bills 1751 and 630 would have required a consumer reporting agency to disclose to a consumer any piece of adverse information received by the agency within thirty days.[179] While such disclosures would have been very useful to consumers

---

163 15 U.S.C. § 1681n(c), *as amended by* Pub. L. No. 104-208, 110 Stat. 3009 (Sept. 30, 1996). See S. Rep. 209, 103d Cong., 1st Sess. 24 (1992) ("[t]he Committee intends this provision to apply to both plaintiffs and defendants"). *See also* § 11.6.1, *infra*.

164 *See, e.g.,* H. Rep. 45, 102d Cong., 1st Sess. 63 (1991); H. Rep. 79, 102d Cong., 1st Sess. 6–7 (1991) (statement of Hon. Morales, Attorney General, State of Texas); *id.* at 9 (statement of Hon. Amestoy, Attorney General, State of Vermont).

165 H. Rep. 45, 102d Cong., 1st Sess. 79 (1992).

166 H.R. 194, 102d Cong., 1st Sess. § 107 (1993); H.R. 3596, 102d Cong., 1st Sess. § 8 (1993). It is noteworthy that Dun & Broadstreet, a reporting agency providing information about businesses, sends a free report to each subject each year and asks for additions and corrections.

167 S. 2776, 102d Cong., 2d Sess. § 108 (1992).

168 S. 783, 103d Cong., 1st Sess. § 108 (1993). *See also* H.R. 561, 104th Cong., 1st Sess. § 11 (1995) ($3).

169 H.R. 1015, 103d Cong., 1st Sess. § 109 (1993).

170 15 U.S.C. § 1681j(a)(1), *as amended by* Pub. L. No. 104-208, 110 Stat. 3009 (Sept. 30, 1996). *See* § 3.3.9.2, *infra*.

171 Equifax, TransUnion, and Experian (formerly TRW).

172 H.R. 561, § 109, 104th Cong., 1st Sess. (1995); H.R. 1015, § 109, 103d Cong., 1st Sess. (1993).

173 H.R. 1015, 103d Cong., 1st Sess. § 109 (1993). The Committee Report on H.R. 1015 linked this provision to the reinsertion problem, stating that "[t]his report will benefit consumers faced with recurring errors in their consumer reports because it will provide them with an opportunity to ensure that errors, previously deleted from their consumer report, have not reappeared during the 12 month period following deletion. H. Rep. 486, 103d Cong., 2d Sess. 44 (1994).

174 S. 783, 103d Cong., 1st Sess. § 108 (1993).

175 15 U.S.C. § 1681j(a)(1)(B), *as amended by* Pub. L. No. 104-208, 110 Stat. 3009 (Sept. 30, 1996).

176 15 U.S.C. § 1681j(a)(2), *as amended by* Pub. L. No. 104-208, 110 Stat. 3009 (Sept. 30, 1996). A consumer is also allowed a free report within sixty days of notice from a debt collection agency affiliated with the consumer reporting agency that the consumer's credit rating may be or has been adversely affected. *Id. See* § 3.3.6, *infra*.

177 15 U.S.C. § 1681j(a)(3), *as amended by* Pub. L. No. 104-208, 110 Stat. 3009 (Sept. 30, 1996). *See* §§ 3.3.5, 3.3.7, *infra*.

178 H.R. 1015, 103d Cong., 1st Sess. § 103 (1993); S. 783, 103d Cong., 1st Sess. § 102 (1993) (Senate bill would have allowed an exception to the response period "if the person has a reasonable belief that the consumer has engaged in fraudulent or criminal activity").

179 H.R. 1751, 102d Cong., 1st Sess. § 2 (1991); H.R. 630, 103d Cong., 1st Sess. § 2 (1991).

seeking to maintain accurate files, it was likely seen as too burdensome on agencies, given the amount of data processed each day.

Though accuracy issues dominated, another set of issues yielding much difference of opinion revolved around privacy, including issues of prescreening lists, credit scores, use of reports by affiliates, and users' purposes for procuring reports.

In prescreening, a creditor asks a consumer reporting agency for a list of people who meet specified credit-granting criteria, though these people have not initiated a transaction with the creditor.[180] Under the 1996 Reform Act, such prescreening reports may be furnished only if the consumer authorizes the furnishing or if the transaction "consists of a firm offer of credit or insurance,"[181] and the agency complies with a provision allowing consumers to exclude themselves from prescreening lists.[182] Two early versions of the 1996 Reform Act would have prohibited prescreening entirely.[183] Retail representatives argued against the prohibition, claiming that consumers benefit from the abbreviated application process prescreening allows.[184] While "firm offer" prescreening prevailed, the definition of firm offer is pretty weak. In addition, while the 1996 Reform Act did provide consumers the right to opt out of prescreening through a toll-free telephone notification system, it limited the effect of the opt-out to two years unless the consumer submits a signed notice of election.[185] Earlier versions of the bill would not have limited the opt-out.[186] Earlier versions of the bill also would have prohibited[187] or limited[188] the use of consumer reports for direct marketing; these provisions were left out of the final bill.

House Bill 3596 would have required consumer reporting agencies that provide credit scores or ratings to explain the score and the credit scoring process;[189] the 1996 Reform Act expressly exempted consumer reporting agencies from having to disclose that information.[190]

Consumers lost another privacy battle when the 1996 Reform Act excluded from the scope of the FCRA information shared by entities related by common ownership or affiliated by corporate control.[191] Under prior law, when affiliates shared information, the information was deemed a consumer report and the sharer a consumer reporting agency, triggering FCRA requirements and consumer protections.[192] The 1996 Reform Act allowed affiliates to share information among themselves without FCRA protections, even to the extent of establishing in-house reporting agencies.[193] Only weak disclosure and a limited opt-out right are required.[194] This loophole was added in the process of passing House Bill 1015 and Senate Bill 783 and affects millions of consumers, as financial institutions continue to merge and branch into other activities, and as other retail conglomerates expand. One pro-consumer provision, imposing disclosure duties on persons who take adverse actions based on consumer information provided by an affiliate, did survive.[195]

Consumer advocates also sought to increase privacy by limiting the use of consumer reports for employment purposes. Early versions of the 1996 Reform Act would have allowed the furnishing of a report for employment purposes only where the consumer authorized the furnishing *and* the employment would require the employee to do one of the following: get a federal agency's security clearance; be covered by a fidelity bond; handle substantial amounts of cash or other valuables as part of normal duties; or engage in conduct with respect to which the employee has a fiduciary duty.[196] Though these provisions ultimately did not pass, the 1996 Reform Act does require users to obtain a consumer's written consent before procuring a report for employment purposes.[197]

---

180 See § 7.3.4, infra.

181 15 U.S.C. § 1681b(c), *as amended by* Pub. L. No. 104-208, 110 Stat. 3009 (Sept. 30, 1996). See § 7.3.4, infra.

182 15 U.S.C. § 1681b(e), *as amended by* Pub. L. No. 104-208, 110 Stat. 3009 (Sept. 30, 1996).

183 H.R. 421, 102d Cong., 1st Sess. § 3 (1991); H.R. 670, 102d Cong., 1st Sess. § 3 (1991).

184 H. Rep. 45, 102d Cong., 1st Sess. 86 (comments of representative for the National Retail Federation).

185 15 U.S.C. § 1681b(e), *as amended by* Pub. L. No. 104-208, 110 Stat. 3009 (Sept. 30, 1996). The FACTA amendments extended the time period to five years. See § 5.3.8.4.4, infra.

186 See, e.g., H.R. 1015, 103d Cong., 1st Sess. § 104 (1993); S. 783, 103d Cong., 1st Sess. § 103 (1993).

187 H. 561, 104th Cong., 1st Sess. § 104 (1995); H.R. 1015, 103d Cong., 1st Sess. § 104 (1993).

188 S. 709, 104th Cong., 1st Sess. § 104 (1992); S. 783, 103d Cong., 1st Sess. § 103 (1993).

189 Id. H.R. 1015 would have required, in the case of an adverse action based in whole or in part on a credit score or predictor, that the user provide to the consumer notice that the predictor was used and the principal factors used to determine that predictor, if required by the Equal Credit Opportunity Act. H.R. 1015, 103d Cong., 1st Sess. § 111 (1993) (as introduced).

190 15 U.S.C. § 1681g(a), *as amended by* Pub. L. No. 104-208, 110 Stat. 3009 (Sept. 30, 1996).

191 See § 2.4.3, infra.

192 15 U.S.C. § 1681a (1994).

193 See § 2.4.3, infra.

194 15 U.S.C. § 1681a(d)(2), *as amended by* Pub. L. No. 104-208, 110 Stat. 3009 (Sept. 30, 1996). See § 2.4.3, infra.

195 15 U.S.C. § 1681m(b)(2), *as amended by* Pub. L. No. 104-208, 110 Stat. 3009 (Sept. 30, 1996).

196 H.R. 561, 104th Cong., 1st Sess. § 103 (1995) (with exception for consumers to be employed in an executive or administrative position); H.R. 1015, 103d Cong., 2d Sess. § 103 (1993); H.R. 3596, 102d Cong., 1st Sess. § 3 (1991) (no such exception).

197 15 U.S.C. § 1681b(b)(2), *as amended by* Pub. L. No. 104-208, 110 Stat. 3009 (Sept. 30, 1996). See § 7.2.4.3.2, infra. The 1996 Reform Act also excludes from the definition of consumer report certain communications made by employment agencies, if the consumer gives permission and receives certain disclosures from the agency. 15 U.S.C. §§ 1681a(d)(2)(D), 1681a(o), *as amended by* Pub. L. No. 104-208, 110 Stat. 3009 (Sept. 30, 1996). See also § 2.4.4, infra.

Under prior versions of the 1996 Reform Act, consumers would have been entitled to know the reason users procured their reports. House Bills 1015 and 3596 would have required consumer reporting agencies to not only keep detailed records of the certified purpose for each report request, but to disclose the purpose to the consumer upon request.[198] House Bill 561 would also have required consumer reporting agencies to disclose the purpose, by category, for which each person procured a consumer report.[199]

Other proposed privacy provisions concerned obsolete information. House Bill 194 would have limited the report of chapter 13 bankruptcy cases to those within the last seven years, as opposed to ten.[200] That bill and House Bill 670 also proposed graduated periods for the reporting of overdue payments, such that payments that were not more than thirty days overdue would not be reported after three years; more than thirty days but not more than sixty, after four years; and more than sixty days but not more than ninety, after five years.[201] House Bills 561 and 1015 would have prohibited maintaining or furnishing any information as to a consumer's failure to make any payment during receipt of federal disaster aid or unemployment benefits, if the consumer so requested and if the consumer maintained the account current for a year following the request.[202] Senator Simon proposed an amendment to Senate Bill 783 that would have added a Privacy Protection Act to the bill, but that failed also.[203]

The last group of controversial issues concerned the force of the FCRA, in terms of its power to preempt state law and the FTC's power to enforce and strengthen it. Dispute over whether the FCRA should preempt all state laws governing consumer reporting prevented earlier passage.[204] The 1996 Reform Act preempted state laws which differ from certain FCRA language, but only until 2004 (this sunset was eliminated by the FACTA amendments), and grandfathered other state law provisions.[205] To balance this preemption, Senate Bill 783 would have allowed the FTC to promulgate regulations imposing more stringent requirements in the areas of reinvestigation time periods, adverse action disclosures, prescreening disclosures, and certain consumer notices.[206] This provision, and one that would have enhanced the FTC's enforcement authority and allowed it to impose civil penalties for initial violations[207] were not enacted.

1.4.7 1997 and 1999 Amendments

In 1997, Congress adopted a narrow exception to the rule that a person using a report of employment must make certain disclosures to the consumer before taking adverse action. For certain national security uses by the federal government, properly documented, the rule is superseded by other requirements.[208] In 1999, Congress amended the FCRA as part of the Gramm-Leach-Bliley Act to lift the prohibition against the FTC or other administrative enforcement agencies from prescribing trade regulation rules and other rules in relation to the FCRA.[209] Congress also removed the prohibition against the federal banking regula-

---

198 H.R. 1015, 103d Cong., 1st Sess. § 108 (1993) (as passed); H.R. 3596, 102d Cong., 1st Sess. § 7 (1991). H.R. 421, 102d Cong., 1st Sess. § 2 (1991), and H.R. 633, 102d Cong., 1st Sess. § 2 (1991) also would have required agencies to keep, with regard to every inquiry into a consumer's file, a record of the date of the inquiry, the identity of the inquirer and the nature of the inquiry.

199 H.R. 561, 104th Cong., 1st Sess. § 108 (1995). Under the 1996 Reform Act, a procurer of a consumer report must certify, through "a general or specific certification," the purpose for procuring the report; but the consumer reporting agency need not disclose the certified purpose to the consumer. 15 U.S.C. §§ 1681b(f), 1681g(a)(3), *as amended by* Pub. L. No. 104-208, 110 Stat. 3009 (Sept. 30, 1996). The classification of persons whose identification must be disclosed to the consumer upon request is, however, divided by purpose: if for employment purposes, the agency must disclose all within two years, for any other purpose, all within one year. 15 U.S.C. § 1681g(a)(3), *as amended by* Pub. L. No. 104-208, 110 Stat. 3009 (Sept. 30, 1996).

200 H.R. 194, 102d Cong., 1st Sess. § 103 (1991).

201 *Id.*; H.R. 670, 102d Cong., 1st Sess. § 4 (1991). Two other bills would have prohibited the reporting of certain payments late due to a bank holiday. H.R. 1197, 103d Cong., 1st Sess. § 1 (1993); H.R. 5859, 102d Cong., 1st Sess. § 1 (1991).

202 H.R. 561, 104th Cong., 1st Sess. § 106 (1995); H.R. 1015, 103d Cong., 1st Sess. § 6 (1993) (as passed).

203 140 Cong. Rec. S5195 (daily ed. May 4, 1994).

204 Preemption of state law was characterized as "essential" by a banking industry representative. H. Rep. 79, 102d Cong., 1st Sess. 40 (1991) (comments of Ms. Brinkley). *See also id.* at 64 (statement of Mr. Kurth, complaining that H. 3596 lacked a sufficiently strong preemption provision).

205 *See* § 10.4, *infra.* The preemption periods "should provide adequate time to demonstrate whether these Federal standards are sufficient." 140 Cong. Rec. S4973 (daily ed. May 2, 1994) (comments of Sen. Bryan on introducing S. 783).

206 S. 783, 103d Cong., 1st Sess. § 116 (1993). The Committee Report noted that:

> [W]hile the Committee has included preemption provisions in order to provide national uniformity . . . the Committee is concerned that consumers must be protected adequately and that the protections should continue to evolve as technology and the economy change. The Federal Trade Commission has suggested, for instance, that the 30-day reinvestigation period . . . may be unnecessarily long in the future as technology allows reinvestigations to be accomplished more quickly. The Committee has included this provision to enable the Commission to shorten the 30-day period if it becomes advisable.

S. Rep. 209, 103d Cong., 1st Sess. 28–29 (1993). *See also* S. 709, 104th Cong., 1st Sess. § 120 (1995); H.R. 561, 104th Cong., 1st Sess. § 120 (1995).

207 S. 783, 103d Cong., 1st Sess. § 113 (1993).

208 15 U.S.C. § 1681b(b)(4).

209 Pub. L. No. 106-102, § 506(b) (Nov. 12, 1999) (striking 15 U.S.C. § 1681s(a)(4)).

tors[210] conducting examinations of banks, savings associations or credit unions regarding FCRA compliance.[211] In addition, the amendments deleted a provision authorizing the Federal Reserve Board to issue interpretations of the FCRA in consultation with the FTC, and replaced it with a provision under which the federal banking regulators are authorized to jointly prescribe any regulations necessary to carry out the purposes of the FCRA with respect to designated banks and lending institutions.[212]

1.4.8 The USA PATRIOT Act

In 2001, Congress passed the USA PATRIOT Act which, among other changes, lightened the requirements for the FBI to gain access to consumer credit information.[213] Specifically, Congress amended section 1681u to reduce the administrative certification requirements for FBI access to credit information. This amendment was one of many contained in the USA PATRIOT Act intended to protect against international terrorism.

1.4.9 The Fair and Accurate Credit Transactions Act of 2003

1.4.9.1 Legislative History

In 2003, Congress made significant changes to the FCRA by passing the Fair and Accurate Credit Transactions Act (FACTA).[214] The impetus for the FACTA amendments was the industry's concern over the expiration of the FCRA's subject-matter-specific preemption of certain state laws.[215] These preemptions were due to sunset on January 1, 2004.[216] With the end of preemption looming, and the credit reporting and financial industry concerned about states enacting enhanced consumer protection laws, Congress sought to establish so-called "uniform" standards for the credit reporting industry, thus ensuring that existing preemptions continued.[217] In addition, Congress sought to address the problem of identity theft, viewed as reaching near epidemic proportions.[218] Other issues Congress focused on were accuracy, privacy, furnisher responsibilities, the protection of medical information, employee investigations, and financial literacy.[219]

Both the House and Senate held several hearings concerning the credit reporting industry and its practices. Many of the documents and testimony produced from these hearings, including Committee Reports, are available on the CD-Rom accompanying this manual, *infra*. The topics covered by hearings in the House included the following: fighting identity theft; the role of the FCRA in employee background checks; the collection of medical information; the role of the FCRA in the credit granting process; how the FCRA functions for consumers and the economy; and the importance of the national credit reporting system to consumers and the U.S. economy.[220] On the Senate side, the hearings related to a general overview of the credit reporting system,[221] identity theft,[222] affiliate sharing practices,[223] accuracy of credit report information,[224] consumer awareness and understanding of the credit granting process,[225] and measures to enhance the operation of the FCRA.[226]

Although several bills had been proposed on one or more FCRA issues since 1996, it was not until the House Committee on Financial Services drafted House Bill 2622 that Congress began the process of substantially amending the FCRA to address the preemption and identity theft issues that had become predominant. House Bill 2622 made it clear that the preemption provisions would become permanent. House Bill 2622 proponents professed that it would benefit consumers, asserting that it provided consumers with tools to fight identity theft and ensure accuracy. However it really only contained modest measures to protect consumers from identity theft, inaccuracies, and invasions of financial privacy.[227]

The Senate took a more balanced approach to the need for consumer protection and preemption. Its bill, Senate Bill 1753, the National Consumer Credit Reporting System Improvement Act of 2003, was the Senate's response to the House's House Bill 2622. This bill sought to address the needs of consumers while providing for the efficient opera-

---

210 The federal banking regulators are the Office of the Comptroller of the Currency, the Federal Reserve Board, the Federal Deposit Insurance Corporation, the Office of Thrift Supervision, and the National Credit Union Administration.
211 15 U.S.C. § 1681s(d), *as amended by* Pub. L. No. 106-102, § 506(a) (Nov. 12, 1999).
212 15 U.S.C. § 1681s(e), *as amended by* Pub. L. No. 106-102, § 506(a) (Nov. 12, 1999).
213 15 U.S.C. § 1681u, *as amended by* USA PATRIOT Act, Pub. L. No. 107-56, 115 Stat. 272 (2001). *See* § 5.2.12, *infra*.
214 Pub. L. No. 108-159 (2003).
215 15 U.S.C. § 1681t(d).
216 *Id.* (2002).
217 H.R. Rep. No. 108-263, at 23–25 (Sept. 4, 2003).
218 H.R. Rep. No. 108-263, at 25 (Sept. 4, 2003).
219 H.R. Rep. 108-263 (Sept. 4, 2003); S. Rep. 108-166 (Oct. 17, 2003).
220 *See* http://financialservices.house.gov/hearings.asp?formmode=All.
221 *Available at* http://banking.senate.gov/index.cfm?Fuseaction=Hearings.Detail&HearingID=26.
222 *Available at* http://banking.senate.gov/index.cfm?Fuseaction=Hearings.Detail&HearingID=43.
223 *Available at* http://banking.senate.gov/index.cfm?Fuseaction=Hearings.Testimony&TestimonyID=262&HearingID=46.
224 *Available at* http://banking.senate.gov/index.cfm?Fuseaction=Hearings.Detail&HearingID=49.
225 *Available at* http://banking.senate.gov/index.cfm?Fuseaction=Hearings.Detail&HearingID=55.
226 *Available at* http://banking.senate.gov/index.cfm?Fuseaction=Hearings.Detail&HearingID=56.
227 H.R. Rep. No. 108-263 (Sept. 4, 2003).

tion of the national credit markets.[228] The Senate Report for the Senate Banking Committee, which oversaw Senate Bill 1753, focused on several areas, including accuracy, risk-based pricing practices, identity theft, financial literacy, information use practices, and national standards for preemption.[229] The Committee was particularly concerned with the "tremendous significance" of consumer credit information,[230] especially in the form of credit scores:

> Increasingly, these scores determine whether a consumer can purchase a mortgage loan, a consumer loan, auto insurance, homeowners insurance, a rental unit and utilities, and at what price; and increasingly, these scores influence whether Americans can obtain and retain a job.[231]

The subsequent legislative history for the FACTA amendments is not extensive and neither the House nor the Senate engaged in much debate or substantive discussion. There are very few comments on the Senate floor concerning FACTA; only Senator Sarbanes provided meaningful comments.[232] On the House side, many members praised the Act's benefits, but offered little explanation of the Act's content.[233] The most extensive comments were made by Congressmen Oxley, who also provided supplemental comments several weeks after the FACTA amendments were passed.[234] On December 4, 2003, the President signed the FACTA amendments to the FCRA.

1.4.9.2 Key Provisions

The FCRA, as amended by FACTA, set up a web of communication among consumers, agencies, and furnishers that, if properly implemented and employed, could synchronize consumer reports and purge theft-related information from agencies' and furnishers' files. These communications include various notice requirements to consumers from consumer reporting agencies, furnishers, and debt collectors.[235]

The FACTA amendments contained several provisions intended to assist consumers with credit reporting problems. The Act provides for free annual credit reports from the "Big Three" nationwide consumer reporting agencies and newly defined nationwide specialty consumer reporting agencies (that is, tenant screening, insurance, and employment).[236] In addition to permanently extending existing preemption provisions in the FCRA, it added a long list of additional preemptions that significantly limited states' abilities to regulate much of the FCRA's subject matter and conduct requirements.[237] The full extent of the preemption and limitation of liability provisions is uncertain and will likely remain this way until courts interpret the various provisions added to the FCRA by FACTA.

To combat identity theft, the FACTA amendments allow consumers to place fraud alerts in their credit files[238] and to block information caused by identity theft or fraud.[239] Active military duty personnel can also add an alert to their files.[240]

The FACTA amendments provided the FTC and other federal regulatory agencies with significant rulemaking authority, something the FTC lacked for many years.[241] A list of these regulations is at § 1.3.3.1, *supra*. As of mid-2006, only some of the required regulations had been finalized by the FTC and the other federal agencies. Appendix B, *infra*, includes copies of the final FCRA regulations issued so far. In addition, the FACTA amendments required various studies or reports to be conduct by the FTC, other government agencies, and in some cases, the consumer reporting agencies. Such studies or reports cover a variety of consumer reporting issues, including the effectiveness of a FACTA provision requiring victims to receive identity theft transaction information from businesses that conducted business with an identity thief,[242] complaints received by the three nationwide consumer reporting agencies,[243] complaints to the FTC regarding accuracy and completeness of consumer reports,[244] reinvestigations of disputed information,[245] the efficacy of increasing the number of points of identifying information for matches before releasing consumer re-

---

228 S. Rep. No. 108-166, at 2 (Oct. 17, 2003).
229 S. Rep. No. 108-166 (Oct. 17, 2003).
230 S. Rep. No. 109-166 at 6–7 (Oct. 17, 2003).
231 *Id.* at 7.
232 Cong. Rec. S15806–15807 (Nov. 24, 2003).
233 Cong. Rec. H12198–H12224 (Nov. 21, 2003).
234 *Id. See* Cong. Rec. E2512–2519 (Dec. 9, 2003).
235 *See* § 8.2, *infra*.
236 15 U.S.C. § 1681j(a)(1)(C), *added by* Pub. L. No. 108-159, § 211(a)(2) (2003). The FTC is to issue regulations to establish a mechanism through which consumers can obtain reports from nationwide specialty consumer reporting agencies. *See* § 3.3.2, *infra*.
237 *See* § 10.7, *infra*.
238 15 U.S.C. §§ 1681c-1(a), (b), *added by* Pub. L. No. 108-159, § 112 (2003).
239 15 U.S.C. § 1681c-2, *added by* Pub. L. No. 108-159, § 152 (2003). *See* § 9.2, *infra*.
240 15 U.S.C. § 1681c-1(c), *added by* Pub. L. No. 108-159, § 112 (2003).
241 15 U.S.C. §§ 1681b(g)(5)(A), 1681c(h)(2)(A), 1681i(e)(4), 1681m(e), 1681m(h)(6), 1681s-2(a)(8)(A), 1681t(e)(1), 1681x, *added by* Pub. L. No. 108-159 (2003).
242 15 U.S.C. § 1681g(e)(13), *added by* Pub. L. No. 108-159, § 151(2003).
243 15 U.S.C. § 1681s(f)3), *added by* Pub. L. No. 108-159, § 153 (2003).
244 15 U.S.C. §§ 1681i(e)(1)(A), *added by* Pub. L. No. 108-159, § 313 (2003). *See also* Pub. L. No. 108-159, § 319 (2003).
245 Pub. L. No. 108-159, § 313(b) (2003). The FTC and Federal Reserve Board have issued this report. Federal Trade Commission and Federal Reserve Board, Report to Congress on the Fair Credit Reporting Act Dispute Process (Aug. 2006), *available* at www.ftc.gov/os/comments/fcradispute/P044808fcradisputeprocessreporttocongress.pdf.

ports,[246] the ability of consumers to avoid receiving written offers of credit or insurance in connection with transactions not initiated by the consumer,[247] and the effect of credit scores and credit-based insurance scores on the availability and affordability of financial products.[248]

Congress also created a new right for consumers to receive notices relating to risk-based pricing.[249] Whenever a creditor extends credit on terms "materially less favorable than the most favorable terms available to a substantial proportion of consumers," the creditor must provide to consumers a notice that explains that the terms are based on information in a consumer report and that the consumers can request a free copy of the report. This notice requirement will address a current flaw in the FCRA relating to failure by creditors to provide notice to consumers when they charge higher interest, fees, or other amounts based on an individual's consumer report. This flaw was specifically highlighted in testimony by FTC Chairman Timothy Muris.[250]

The FACTA amendments also modified the standard of accuracy for furnishers of information.[251] New duties for furnishers include requirements to prevent the "repollution" of consumer reports.[252] Furnishers must also have reasonable procedures in place to prevent them from refurnishing information that is the result of identity theft.[253]

Under FACTA, debt collectors are prohibited from selling or transferring for consideration, or placing for collection, a debt that they have been notified is the result of identity theft. Third-party debt collectors, once on notice that a debt may be the result of identity theft, must notify the creditor that the information may be the result of identity theft and, upon the request of the consumer, disclose to the consumer information about the transaction.[254]

The FACTA amendments also provide for the truncation of credit card numbers and Social Security numbers. Persons who accept credit cards or debit cards may print no more than the last five digits of the card or the expiration date on any receipt provided at the point of sale. This provision is only applicable to electronically printed receipts.[255] Consumers may also request that when providing a report to a particular consumer, consumer reporting agencies truncate the consumer's Social Security number to the last five numbers of the Social Security number.[256]

The prior version of the FCRA specifically provided that agencies were not required to disclose credit scores to consumers,[257] though it did not preempt states from requiring their disclosure. The FCRA now requires disclosure of credit scores and will standardize the fees for the disclosure, but it also preempts states from imposing new requirements.[258] Mortgage lenders must also disclose a credit score and certain other information.[259] Although state laws regarding these disclosures are preempted, several existing state laws are exempt from the preemption.[260]

The FACTA amendments also extend the opt-out period for prescreened offers from two years to five,[261] and give the FTC authority to issue regulations prescribing notices for this opt-out right.[262]

Another important area affected by the FACTA amendments is medical information and how furnishers and consumer reporting agencies handle such information. The FCRA was amended to provide for enhanced protection of medical information.[263]

Employee investigation communications was an important issue for Congress. Longstanding concerns over employee misconduct investigations and industry frustrations with FCRA notice requirements led Congress to restrict the rights of employees with respect to certain types of investigations. The FCRA now excludes certain communications related to employers' investigation of employees.[264] FACTA also amended the FCRA's statute of limitations to now provide that the two-year limitation period dates from the consumer's discovery of the violation, not the date of the violation itself.[265]

---

246 Pub. L. No. 108-159, § 318 (2003). The Federal Trade Commission has issued this report. Federal Trade Commission, Report to Congress under Sections 318 and 319 of the Fair and Accurate Credit Transactions Act of 2003 (Dec. 2004), available at www.ftc.gov/reports/facta/041209factarpt.pdf.
247 Pub. L. No. 108-159, § 213(e) (2003).
248 Pub. L. No. 108-159, § 215(a) (2003).
249 Pub. L. No. 108-159, § 311 (2003), amending 15 U.S.C. § 1681m(h). This provision became effective on December 1, 2004. 16 C.F.R. § 602.1(c)(3)(xiii), added by 69 Fed. Reg. 6,526 (Feb. 11, 2003).
250 Housing and Urban Affairs, Prepared Statement of the Federal Trade Commission on the Fair Credit Reporting Act Before the Senate Committee on Banking 11–12 (July 10, 2003) (statement of Timothy Muris, FTC Chairman).
251 15 U.S.C. § 1681s-2(a), as amended by Pub. L. No. 108-159, § 312(b). See § 6.4.2, infra.
252 Id.
253 Id. See § 6.4.3, infra.
254 15 U.S.C. § 1681m(g), as amended by Pub. L. No. 108-159, § 312(d). See § 6.3.3.8, infra.

255 15 U.S.C. § 1681c(g), added by Pub. L. No. 108-159, § 113 (2003).
256 15 U.S.C. § 1681g(a)(1), amended by Pub. L. No. 108-159, § 115 (2003).
257 15 U.S.C. § 1681g(a), as amended by Pub. L. No. 108-159, § 211 (2003).
258 15 U.S.C. § 1681g(a), as amended by Pub. L. No. 108-159, § 212 (2003).
259 15 U.S.C. § 1681g(a), as amended by Pub. L. No. 108-159, § 212 (2003).
260 15 U.S.C. § 1681m(b)(3), added by Pub. L. No. 108-159, § 212 (2003).
261 15 U.S.C. § 1681b(e), as amended by Pub. L. No. 108-159, § 213 (2003).
262 15 U.S.C. § 1681m(d)(2), as amended by Pub. L. No. 108-159, § 213 (2003).
263 See § 5.4.1, infra.
264 15 U.S.C. § 1681a(d)(2)(D), (x), amended by Pub. L. No. 108-159, § 611 (2003).
265 15 U.S.C. § 1681p, as amended by Pub. L. No. 108-159, § 156 (2003).

The FACTA amendments were signed into law on December 4, 2003, and certain provisions without a designated effective date went into effect on this date. However, the effective dates of most provisions were determined by the FTC and other federal agencies, which adopted regulations specifying effective dates for these provisions.[266] Still other FACTA provisions did or will not become effective until the FTC or other federal agencies enact regulations interpreting the provisions.

1.4.10 Legislation Since FACTA

In 2006, Congress modified the Fair Credit Reporting Act to respond to the perceived need for additional confidentiality in national security investigations.[267] The Act was amended to allow the FBI to prohibit a CRA from disclosing that the FBI sought information from the CRA.[268] Similarly, if "the head of a government agency authorized to conduct investigations of intelligence or counterintelligence activities or analysis related to international terrorism, or his designee" makes the same certification, the agency must also maintain the confidentiality of the request for consumer information.[269] In the USA PATRIOT Act Additional Reauthorizing Amendments Act of 2005,[270] Congress modified these provisions slightly to clarify that someone to whom a national security letter is issued need not disclose the name of an attorney from whom the letter recipient plans to seek legal advice about the letter.[271]

---

266 16 C.F.R. Part 602.
267 Pub. L. No. 109-177 § 116 (Mar. 9, 2006) (amending 15 U.S.C. §§ 1681u, 1681v).
268 *Id.*, *amending* 15 U.S.C. § 1681v.
269 *Id.*, *amending* 15 U.S.C. § 1681u.
270 Pub. L. No. 109-178 (Mar. 9, 2006).
271 *Id.* § 4, *amending* 15 U.S.C. §§ 1681u, 1681v.

Chapter 2 Scope: Consumer Reports and Consumer Reporting Agencies

2.1 Introduction

2.1.1 Definitions Analyzed in This Chapter

The FCRA regulates primarily "consumer reporting agencies" (CRAs) and "consumer reports." This chapter will address the scope of both of these terms, as well as how the FCRA governs transactions involving either of them. Furthermore, since FCRA rights generally apply only to consumers, this chapter will also analyze the Act's definition of "consumer."

Simply put, the Act defines a "CRA" as an entity that furnishes consumer reports and defines "consumer reports" as information communicated by a CRA. Clearly, these two terms are interdependent.

"Consumer reports" are defined and analyzed in § 2.3, *infra*. The FCRA's scope is broader than many consumer credit statutes, because it is not just concerned with consumer credit reports, but with information reported on individuals concerning their personal lives. The FCRA applies to information collected, used, or expected to be used to evaluate: an individual's eligibility for credit, insurance, and employment; the risk assessment and review of consumer accounts; certain government licenses or benefits and child support determinations; and other business transactions involving the consumer as a consumer.

That a report falls outside the FCRA's definition of a consumer report does not mean that CRAs cannot report this information and, conversely, it does not mean that consumers are without remedies when such non-consumer reports contain inaccurate information. If a report is a "consumer report," the FCRA regulates the transaction and the information can only be reported under certain conditions. If the report is not a "consumer report," there are no FCRA restrictions as to the report's use, but the CRA and the user may be subject to common law tort and other claims for improper use of the report.[1]

In addition to the fact that some reports will not fall into the definition of a "consumer report," there are a number of statutory and regulatory exclusions from the definition. These are discussed in § 2.4, *infra*.

The term "consumer reporting agency" is analyzed in § 2.5, *infra*. The FCRA also includes definitions and special requirements for several particular categories of CRAs, discussed in § 2.6, *infra*. The first is a CRA that "compiles and maintains files on consumers on a nationwide basis"—or a nationwide CRA, discussed in § 2.6.1, *infra*. The second is a "nationwide specialty consumer reporting agency," which maintains files on consumers on a nationwide basis, but restricted to one of five categories of records: medical records or payments; residential or tenant history; check-writing history; employment history; or insurance claims.[2] A third category is resellers; resellers are CRAs that buy consumer reports from other CRAs (such as one of the "Big Three") and then re-package the reports for banks and other third parties.[3]

The term "consumer reporting agency" refers not just to credit bureaus, but many other entities that meets the statutory definition. As described below in § 2.7, *infra*, this may include creditors, data brokers, collection agencies, check approval companies, attorneys, alternative credit bureaus, and others.

2.1.2 Concepts Analyzed in Other Chapters

In addition to "consumer reports" and "consumer reporting agencies," other key terms under the FCRA are "furnishers" and "users." These terms are largely discussed in other chapters. "Furnishers" are creditors and other third parties who provide information about consumers to the CRAs.[4] The FCRA prescribes standards for furnishing information and requires that furnishers be intimately involved when consumers ask a CRA to reinvestigate the accuracy of information in their files.[5]

"Users" are those who purchase consumer reports from CRAs, and even on occasion those who use information about consumers obtained from non-consumer reporting agencies. Under the FCRA, users may obtain consumer

---

1 See §§ 10.3, 10.5, 10.6, *infra*.
2 15 U.S.C. § 1681a(w). See § 2.6.2, *infra*.
3 See § 2.6.3, *infra*.
4 See § 6.2, *infra*.
5 See § 6.10, *infra*.

reports only for permissible purposes and must make certain disclosures to consumers related to their use of consumer information.[6]

This chapter examines the definition of a consumer report in general. The FCRA has special provisions dealing with investigative consumer reports, which are consumer reports that meet certain conditions. Chapter 13, *infra* on investigative consumer reports examines the special conditions that give rise to an investigative consumer report.

Although the Act is primarily concerned with the conveyance of personal information in consumer reports, the FCRA is concerned not just with the actual reports, but also with the CRA "files" from which they are culled. For example, the Act gives consumers the right know what is in their own files, which is discussed in Chapter 3, *infra*.[7]

2.2 FCRA Applies to "Consumers"

The FCRA applies to "consumers," which the Act defines as "an individual."[8] The definition only includes natural persons, not artificial entities such as partnerships, corporations, trusts, estates, cooperatives, associations, governments, government subdivisions, or agencies.[9] Even a nonprofit community organization is not a consumer.[10]

Unlike other statutes, the definition of "consumer" is not restricted to those involved in consumer transactions, i.e., transactions for personal, family, or household purposes. Instead, consumer is a broad term applying to any individual. It is the definition of "consumer report" that excludes from the Act many purely business or commercial transactions.[11]

2.3 Is a "Consumer Report" Involved?

2.3.1 Overview

2.3.1.1 General

The FCRA defines a "consumer report" as:[12]

> any written, oral, or other communication of any information by a consumer reporting agency bearing on a consumer's credit worthiness, credit standing, credit capacity, character, general reputation, personal characteristics, or mode of living which is used or expected to be used or collected in whole or in part for the purpose of serving as a factor in establishing the consumer's eligibility for—
>
> (A) credit or insurance to be used primarily for personal, family, or household purposes;
>
> (B) employment purposes; or
>
> (C) any other purpose authorized under section 1681b of this title."

The FCRA goes on to define a number of exclusions from "consumer report,"[13] which are discussed below.[14] Most FCRA provisions do not apply to a transaction unless the information about the consumer falls within the definition of a "consumer report."[15]

2.3.1.2 A Consumer Report Compared to a Consumer's File

A consumer report differs from the consumer's file at a consumer reporting agency (CRA).[16] The file is all information on that consumer recorded and retained by a CRA.[17] A consumer report is information from that file communi-

---

6 *See* Ch. 7, and §§ 2.3.5, 2.3.6, 8.2, 13.4, *infra*.
7 *See* §§ 3.3, 3.4, *infra*.
8 15 U.S.C. § 1681a(c); Leo Found., Inc. v. Dun & Bradstreet, Inc., [1974–1980 Decisions Transfer Binder] Consumer Cred. Guide (CCH) ¶ 98,798 (D. Conn. 1974).
9 *See* FTC Official Staff Commentary §§ 603(c), 603(d) item 3B, *reprinted at* Appx. D, *infra*.
10 *See* Carson, FTC Informal Staff Opinion Letter [1969–1973 Decisions Transfer Binder] Consumer Cred. Guide (CCH ¶ 99,532 (Mar. 20, 1971), *reprinted on the CD-Rom accompanying this manual*.
11 American Bankers Assoc. v. Lockyer, 2004 WL 1490432 (E.D. Cal. June 30, 2004), *rev'd, remanded*, 412 F.3d 1081 (9th Cir. 2005); Moore v. Equifax Info. Servs., L.L.C., 333 F. Supp. 2d 1360 (N.D. Ga. 2004) (FCRA does not apply to business or commercial transactions, citing Yeager v. TRW, Inc., 961 F. Supp. 161, 162 (E.D. Tex. 1997) ("FCRA does not apply to business transactions, even those involving consumers and their consumer credit information")). *Contra* Korotki v. Attorney Servs. Corp., 931 F. Supp. 1269, 1277 n.23 (D. Md. 1996) (where business debt involved individual, individual is a "consumer"), *aff'd*, 131 F.3d 135 (4th Cir. 1997) (table) (full opinion, 1997 WL 753322).

12 15 U.S.C. § 1681a(d)(1).
13 15 U.S.C. § 1681a(d)(2).
14 *See* § 2.4, *infra*.
15 The following four FCRA provisions apply to "information" as opposed to "consumer reports": § 1681(g)(a)(1) (CRA must disclose information to the consumer); § 1681m(b) (user of the information must disclose information to the consumer); § 1681q (persons obtaining information from a CRA under false pretenses subject to criminal liability), and § 1681r (officers or employees of CRAs who provide information to unauthorized persons subject to criminal liability). An "investigative consumer report" is a special type of consumer report for which additional duties are imposed upon the preparer and user. *See* Ch. 13, *infra*.
16 Nunnally, Jr. v. Equifax Info. Servs., 451 F.3d 768 (11th Cir. 2006); Campos v. ChoicePoint, Inc., __ F.R.D. __, 2006 WL 257891 (N.D. Ga. Mar. 27, 2006).
17 15 U.S.C. § 1681a(g).

cated to a third party; consumer reports involve "written, oral, or other communication of any information."[18] Moreover, a consumer report is derivative, or a subset, of the complete consumer file.[19]

A consumer report thus includes information provided over the telephone, through the mails, or by electronic means. However, information about the consumer that is collected and kept on file, but not communicated to a third party, is not a consumer report. The disclosure to the consumer of information in her file is also not considered to be a consumer report.[20] Instead, it is a consumer disclosure subject to the FCRA's dispute and reinvestigation procedures.[21] At least one court has also held that the transfer by sale of files from one CRA to another does not involve a consumer report.[22]

2.3.2 Information Must Be Communicated by a "Consumer Reporting Agency"

The definitions of a consumer report and a consumer reporting agency are mutually dependent and thus circular to some extent. A consumer report is a communication of certain information by a consumer reporting agency, and a consumer reporting agency is a person or business that collects certain information for the purpose of providing consumer reports.[23] Information communicated by anyone other than a reporting agency is not a consumer report. The definition of a consumer reporting agency is detailed in § 2.5, *infra*.

2.3.3 Report Must Bear On and Identify a Consumer

2.3.3.1 General

A consumer report is one "bearing on a *consumer's* credit worthiness" and other factors.[24] Consumer is defined in the FCRA as an individual.[25] A "consumer" must, at a minimum, be "an identifiable person"; therefore, a report on an anonymous computer username is not a consumer report.[26]

2.3.3.2 Coded Lists

A list "not consumer-specific" containing information such as telephone numbers and addresses, without names, used on fraudulent credit card applications is not a consumer report according to the FTC.[27] Similarly, the FTC Staff Commentary states that a report coded by Social Security or some other number, so that the consumer's identity is not disclosed, is not a consumer report.[28]

2.3.3.3 Reports on Businesses Are Not Consumer Reports

Because consumer is defined as an individual, a consumer report must bear on an individual's characteristics, not a business's or another artificial entity's characteristics.[29] Reports about corporations, associations, partnerships, or other entities are not consumer reports even if they contain information on individuals, because the report is not about a consumer.[30]

A report on a business entity is not a consumer report, even if the information is collected in connection with a transaction involving the consumer. Consumer reports on sole proprietorships as business entities (as opposed to on the owner's personal life) are also likely to be viewed as outside the scope of the term consumer report.[31]

---

18 15 U.S.C. § 1681a(d).
19 Nunnally, Jr. v. Equifax Info. Servs., 451 F.3d 768 (11th Cir. 2006).
20 *See* Cousin v. Trans Union Corp., 246 F.3d 359 (5th Cir. 2001).
21 Thomas v. Gulf Coast Credit Serv., Inc., 214 F. Supp. 2d 1228 (M.D. Ala. 2002). See § 3.3, *infra*.
22 State v. Credit Bureau of Nashua, Inc., 342 A.2d 640 (N.H. 1975).
23 15 U.S.C. § 1681a(f).
24 15 U.S.C. § 1681a(d)(1) (emphasis added).
25 15 U.S.C. § 1681a(c).
26 McCready v. Ebay, Inc., 453 F.3d 882, 889 (7th Cir. 2006) (finding that Ebay's Feedback Forum is not a consumer report).
27 Brinckerhoff, FTC Informal Staff Opinion Letter (June 3, 1987), *reprinted on the CD-Rom accompanying this manual*.
28 FTC Official Staff Commentary § 603(d) item 4B, *reprinted at* Appx. D, *infra*.
29 FTC Official Staff Commentary § 603(d) item 3A, *reprinted at* Appx. D, *infra*.
30 *Id.* item 3B. *See* Grimes, FTC Informal Staff Opinion Letter (July 14, 1987), *reprinted on the CD-Rom accompanying this manual*.
31 An interchange between the leading FCRA proponent, Senator Proxmire and the Committee voice for the industry, Senator Bennett went like this:

> *Bennett*: So if a man operates a business as a single proprietor, he is not protected by this legislation?
> *Proxmire*: The staff adviser, Mr. McLean, tells me if the report is on the individual proprietor, then he is covered. If the report is on the business he is not.

Hearings on S. 823, Subcommittee on Financial Institutions of the Senate Banking and Currency Committee, 91st Cong. 1st Sess. 16–17 (1969).

2.3.4 Information Must Bear On a Consumer's Creditworthiness, Credit Standing or Capacity, Character, Reputation, Personal Characteristics, or Mode of Living

2.3.4.1 General

The FCRA defines a consumer report as bearing on a consumer's "credit worthiness, credit standing, credit capacity, character, general reputation, personal characteristics, or mode of living. . . ."[32] Since a report need bear on only one of these seven factors,[33] a wide variety of information about a consumer satisfies this part of the definition of a consumer report.[34] Thus reports about renters' evictions, rental payment histories, or treatment of premises relate to character, general reputation, personal characteristics, and mode of living.[35] A list of consumers who have passed bad checks would also be covered, since the list reflects on the consumer's general reputation.[36] Likewise, a person's driving record contains information about the individual's personal characteristics, such as arrest information.[37] Even a report that the credit file is not being provided, or that the CRA has insufficient information on the consumer, conveys a message about creditworthiness and can be a consumer report.[38]

2.3.4.2 Identifying Information and Credit Header Information

2.3.4.2.1 General

Certain basic information about a consumer is not a consumer report if it does not bear on the seven FCRA characteristics. However, if the information falls within the Gramm-Leach-Bliley Act's definition of nonpublic personal information,[39] it may be protected from disclosure by that Act.[40]

A report limited solely to the consumer's name and address, with no connotations as to creditworthiness or other characteristics, does not constitute a consumer report because it does not bear on any of the seven factors.[41] Such reports are commonplace, and may be called "Address Update," or "Above the Line" reports, and may include additional information such as a Social Security number or other identifying information. Creditors, debt collectors, and others may use the information to keep track of or to locate consumers. With the growth of the Internet, many firms now provide "People Search" services that purport to try to match an address proffered by a consumer against a database collected from not just telephone books, but insurance, credit, and other sources.[42] These reports, that are merely attempting to validate an address, are not consumer reports.

As long as the information has no obvious bearing on the seven factors, the FTC Staff Commentary goes fairly far in indicating that certain basic information generally not associated with consumer reporting does not involve a consumer report. A telephone directory or a city directory containing only the consumer's name, address, telephone number, marital status, home ownership, and number of children is not a consumer report.[43] One court has held that even information about a consumer's credit card, dietary restrictions and

---

32. 15 U.S.C. § 1681a(d).
33. FTC Official Staff Commentary § 603(d) item 4A, *reprinted at* Appx. D, *infra*.
34. *See* Trans Union Corp. v. Fed. Trade Comm'n, 245 F.3d 809 (D.C. Cir. 2001).
35. *Id.*
36. Howard Enters., Inc., 93 F.T.C. 909 (1979). *See also* Lewis, Informal Staff Opinion Letter (June 11, 1998), *reprinted on the CD-Rom accompanying this manual*; Dea, FTC Informal Staff Opinion Letter (Oct. 29, 1974), *reprinted on the CD-Rom accompanying this manual*; Isaac, FTC Informal Staff Opinion Letter (Sept. 25, 1974), *reprinted on the CD-Rom accompanying this manual*; Grimes, FTC Informal Staff Opinion Letter (Jan. 9, 1974), *reprinted on the CD-Rom accompanying this manual* (bad check lists used for negative or positive information bears on creditworthiness, character and general reputation); Russell, FTC Informal Staff Opinion Letter (Dec. 3, 1973), *reprinted on the CD-Rom accompanying this manual*; Grimes, FTC Informal Staff Opinion Letter (Sept. 5, 1973), *reprinted on the CD-Rom accompanying this manual*.
37. FTC Official Staff Commentary § 603(d) item 4C, § 603(f) item 10, *reprinted at* Appx. D, *infra*; FTC Supplementary Information published with the commentary § II(1), 55 Fed. Reg. 18,804 (May 4, 1990), *reprinted at* Appx. D, *infra*. *See* § 2.5.7, *infra*.
38. Reynolds v. Hartford Fin. Servs. Group, Inc., 435 F.3d 1081 (9th Cir. 2006), *cert. granted on other grounds sub. Nom* GEICO Gen. Ins. Co. v. Edo, __ S. Ct. __, 2006 WL 2055539 (Sept. 26, 2006); Thompson v. Equifax Credit Inf. Servs., 2001 U.S. Dist. LEXIS 22666 (M.D. Ala. Nov. 14, 2001), *motion for reconsideration denied*, 2001 U.S. Dist. LEXIS 22640 (Dec. 14, 2001) (while "file unavailable online" and "contact bureau" may be neutral information, information used to deny credit, that consumer's "file under review," is a consumer report).
39. 15 U.S.C. § 6809(4)(A); 16 C.F.R. § 313.3(p).
40. *See* § 16.4.1, *infra*.
41. FTC Official Staff Commentary § 603(d) item 4F, *reprinted at* Appx. D, *infra*; Ali v. Vikar Mgmt. Ltd., 994 F. Supp. 492 (S.D.N.Y. 1998); Dotzler v. Perot, 914 F. Supp. 328 (E.D. Mo. 1996) (names, addresses and Social Security numbers do not bear on credit or general character), *aff'd without op.*, 124 F.3d 207 (8th Cir. 1997); Korotki v. Attorney Servs. Corp., 931 F. Supp. 1269 (D. Md. 1996) (permissible purpose to get address for service of process); Gomon v. TRW, Inc., 34 Cal. Rptr. 2d 256, 28 Cal. App. 4th 1161 (1994).
42. *See, e.g.*, www.ussearch.com.
43. FTC Official Staff Commentary § 603(d) item 5B, *reprinted at* Appx. D, *infra*. *See also* Brinckerhoff, FTC Informal Staff Opinion Letter (Sept. 22, 1987), *reprinted on the CD-Rom accompanying this manual*; Petruccelli, FTC Informal Staff Opinion Letter (Apr. 9, 1984), *reprinted on the CD-Rom accompanying this manual*; Muris, FTC Informal Staff Opinion Letter (Apr. 29, 1982), *reprinted on the CD-Rom accompanying this manual*. *But see* Brinckerhoff, FTC Informal Staff Opinion Letter (Dec. 21, 1983), *reprinted on the CD-Rom accompanying*

traveling partners is not information on the consumer's "personal characteristics" or "mode of living."[44]

Similarly, "credit header" information supplied by a CRA is generally not considered to be a consumer report. Credit header information customarily refers to a consumer's name, address, telephone number, Social Security number, mother's maiden name, and age. With the exception of age, this information has traditionally not been considered to constitute a consumer report because it has been thought not to bear on any of the seven factors.[45]

The FTC has distinguished age from other demographic information. Because age information bears on a consumer's credit capacity and is used in credit eligibility decisions, a report of age information does constitute a consumer report.[46] Accordingly, to retain its traditional exclusion from "consumer report," a credit header may not reference a consumer's age.

A list of credit header or other identifying information is, however, a series of consumer reports if it reflects on creditworthiness or other FCRA factors. For example, lists of creditworthy individuals or individuals with bad credit records are consumer reports.[47]

Reports on an individual containing solely public record information could be consumer reports if they reflect on one of the seven factors, such as records of arrest or the institution or disposition of criminal or civil proceedings.[48] The fact that information is taken from the public record is irrelevant; what matters is the nature of the information itself.[49] One case has held that a legal directory containing ratings of the legal abilities of lawyers does not constitute a consumer report.[50]

2.3.4.2.2 Gramm-Leach Bliley Act restrictions on disclosure of "credit header" information

Credit headers may not be consumer reports for purposes of the FCRA. However, the Gramm-Leach-Bliley Act (GLB), discussed in detail in Chapter 16, *infra* regulates how financial institutions may use consumers' "nonpublic personal information."[51] CRAs qualify as "financial institutions" under GLB,[52] and they are subject to its provisions.[53] Credit header information falls within the definition of nonpublic personal information,[54] and CRAs may only use the information in ways that comply with GLB.[55]

GLB has separate rules that apply (1) to those who report nonpublic personal information *to* CRAs, and (2) to the use of that information *by* CRAs. In general, GLB allows CRAs to obtain the information, but limits how they may distribute it.

GLB specifically exempts from its notice and opt-out requirements those disclosures "to a consumer reporting agency in accordance with the Fair Credit Reporting Act . . . [or] from a consumer report reported by a consumer reporting agency."[56] This exemption encompasses disclosures of credit header information even though they are not "consumer reports," and allows the traditional business of con-

---

this manual; Buffon, FTC Informal Staff Opinion Letter (June 16, 1983), *reprinted on the CD-Rom accompanying this manual* (report containing more than name and address by including property ownership is consumer report); Silbergeld, FTC Informal Staff Opinion Letter, [1969–1973 Decisions Transfer Binder] Consumer Cred. Guide (CCH) ¶ 99,525 (Apr. 1, 1971) (list would be a consumer report if indicated whether consumer rented or owned residence).

44 *In re* Northwest Airlines Privacy Litig., 2004 WL 1278459 (D. Minn. June 6, 2004).

45 Remsburg v. Docusearch, Inc., 2002 U.S. Dist. LEXIS 6231 (D.N.H. Apr. 4, 2002) (credit header information is not a consumer report); Ali v. Vikar Mgmt. Ltd., 994 F. Supp. 492 (S.D.N.Y. 1998); Dotzler v. Perot, 914 F. Supp. 328 (E.D. Mo. 1996) (names, addresses and Social Security numbers do not bear on credit or general character); FTC Official Staff Commentary § 603(d), item 4F, *reprinted at* Appx. D, *infra*.

46 *In re* Trans Union Corp., Dkt. No. 9255 (Mar. 1, 2000) (final order), *reprinted on the CD-Rom accompanying this manual*.

47 *Id.* item 4D; Supplementary Information published with the commentary, 55 Fed. Reg. 18,804 (May 4, 1990), *reprinted on the CD-Rom accompanying this manual*. *See also* Keller, FTC Informal Staff Opinion Letter (July 2, 1999) (a DTEC report that includes past employment information along with header information is a consumer report); Trans Union Corp. v. Fed. Trade Comm'n, 81 F.3d 228 (D.C. Cir. 1996) (remanding for factual determination as to whether information in specialized TransUnion lists would or could be used to determine credit eligibility).

48 FTC Official Staff Commentary § 603(d) item 4E, *reprinted at* Appx. D, *infra*. *But see* Ley v. Boron Oil Co., 419 F. Supp. 1240 (W.D. Pa. 1976) (list that indicated that individual had no suits and judgments against him and no criminal record was not a consumer report).

49 Sum, FTC Informal Staff Opinion Letter (Sept. 15, 1999), *reprinted on the CD-Rom accompanying this manual*.

50 Bergen v. Martindale-Hubbell, Inc., 176 Ga. App. 745, 337 S.E.2d 770 (1985).

51 15 U.S.C. § 6809.

52 Trans Union, L.L.C. v. Fed. Trade Comm'n, 295 F.3d 42, 48, 49 (D.C. Cir. 2002) (upholding FTC's construction of the term "financial institution").

53 The Gramm-Leach-Bliley Act has a savings clause that provides that it does not "modify, limit, or supersede the operation of the Fair Credit Reporting Act." 15 U.S.C. § 6806. The FTC has reasoned that since credit header information is not covered by the FCRA (because it falls outside the definition of "consumer report"), the GLB's regulation of such information does not affect the operation of the FCRA. 65 Fed. Reg. 33,668 (May 24, 2000).

54 15 U.S.C. § 6809(4); 16 C.F.R. § 313.3(n). The FTC's interpretation of "nonpublic personal information" as including credit header information has been upheld. Trans Union v. Fed. Trade Comm'n, 295 F.3d 42 (D.C. Cir. 2002). The Commission reasoned that such information is acquired through "[a] list, description, or other grouping of consumers (and publicly available information pertaining to them) that is derived using any personally identifiable financial information that is not publicly available." *Id.* at 51.

55 65 Fed. Reg. 33,668 (May 24, 2000); Trans Union v. Fed. Trade Comm'n, 295 F.3d 42, 50 (D.C. Cir. 2002).

56 15 U.S.C. § 6802(e)(6); 16 C.F.R. § 313.15(a)(5).

sumer reporting to continue by permitting financial institutions to disclose nonpublic personal information to CRAs.[57]

However, this exemption does *not* extend to the Act's limitations on the reuse and re-disclosure of consumer financial information.[58] Accordingly, "this exception does not allow consumer reporting agencies to re-disclose the nonpublic personal information it receives from financial institutions other than in the form of a consumer report. *Therefore, the exception does not operate to allow the disclosure of credit header information to individual reference services, direct marketers, or any other party that does not have a permissible purpose to obtain that information as part of a consumer report.*"[59]

This interpretation of the Gramm-Leach-Bliley Act has the potential to seriously impede some of the new products being offered by CRAs, such as those that trace people through nonpublic personal information. CRAs, who were once able to use credit header information with impunity, must now comport that use with GLB.

2.3.4.2.3 Prescreening lists

"Prescreening lists," which reflect the creditworthiness of those on the list, are a series of consumer reports.[60] Prescreening generally is a process by which a CRA, as a service, will compile lists of names of those fitting certain credit criteria supplied by the creditor. The creditor will then use the list to solicit consumers with a so-called firm offer of credit or other products and services. If compiled by CRAs, and if based on credit granting information and criteria, the FCRA applies and the use of such lists is restricted to the permissible purposes enumerated in the Act.[61] Prescreening lists are discussed in greater detail in Chapter 7.[62] Targeted marketing lists that are not prescreened based on creditworthiness or the other FCRA factors, such as those used to mail sweepstakes promotions, catalogues, and other junk mail, are generally not covered by the FCRA.

2.3.4.2.4 Inquiry Reports and trigger lists

The nationwide CRAs, as well as others, sell "inquiry activity reports" and "trigger lists." These reports provide information on requests that third parties have made for a consumer's report.

In one version of this service, the CRAs notify their subscribers when a third party inquires about a consumer whose report the subscriber had at one time requested. (This service may violate the permissible purposes section if the CRA has no reason to believe that the subscriber has a current permissible purpose for the information.)

In another version, lenders are notified when a competitor has requested a consumer's report. For example, a mortgage broker may purchase lists of consumers whose reports have been sought by a mortgage company so that the broker can make a competing offer. These trigger lists are a type of prescreened list, and may also violate the FCRA if the prescreening requirements are not followed.[63]

Inquiry activity reports and trigger lists bear on several of the enumerated factors in the definition of consumer report, such as an individual's "credit standing," "personal characteristics," and "mode of living."[64] These reports are consumer reports if they are collected or expected to be used for FCRA purposes, even if the ultimate use is not a listed purpose.[65]

2.3.5 Information Must Be Used, Expected to Be Used, or Collected for Certain Purposes

2.3.5.1 General

The FCRA provides that consumer reports involve information "used or expected to be used or collected in whole or in part for" various listed purposes.[66] (These listed purposes are discussed at § 2.3.6, *infra*.) That is, if a CRA expects a user to use a report for a listed purpose *or* if the CRA collected the information in the report for a listed purpose, the report is a consumer report even if the user applies the report to a different purpose.[67] The consumer need only show that a report meets one of these criteria: that the report was "used," "expected to be used," or "collected" for a listed purpose.[68] This interpretation of the

---

57 65 Fed. Reg. 33,668 (May 24, 2000); 16 C.F.R. § 313.15(a)(5).
58 15 U.S.C. § 6802(c) provides:

> Except as otherwise provided in this subchapter, a nonaffiliated third party that receives from a financial institution nonpublic personal information under this section shall not, directly or through an affiliate of such receiving third party, disclose such information to any other person that is a nonaffiliated third party of both the financial institution and such receiving third party, unless such disclosure would be lawful if made directly to such other person by the financial institution.

See also 16 C.F.R. § 313.11(a); § 16.4.1.5, *infra*.
59 65 Fed. Reg. 33,668 (May 24, 2000) (emphasis added).
60 See § 7.3.4, *infra*.
61 See § 7.3.4, *infra*.
62 See § 7.3.4, *infra*.

63 See § 7.3.8, *infra*.
64 Yang v. Gov't Employees Ins. Co., 146 F.3d 1320, 1324 (11th Cir. 1998).
65 *Id.*
66 15 U.S.C. § 1681a(d).
67 Permissible purposes are enumerated in the statute and are discussed at § 2.3.6, *infra* and Chapter 7, *infra*. Impermissible purposes are discussed at § 7.4, *infra*.
68 Yang v. Government Employees Ins. Co., 146 F.3d 1320 (11th Cir. 1998); Wilson v. Porter, Wright, Morris & Arthur, 921 F.

scope of the term consumer report not only tracks the statutory language, but is accepted by an overwhelming majority of courts[69] and by the Federal Trade Commission.[70]

For example, if the only purpose for which the information was used was to discredit the consumer in the community, the information was not used for a purpose listed in the Act's definition of a consumer report. Nevertheless, the consumer can show that the information is a consumer report if she can prove that the information was collected for use in connection with one of the listed purposes, or that its expected use was a use in connection with one or more of those purposes. That is, the CRA may have collected the information to help a user decide whether to employ the consumer (a listed purpose), or the CRA expected the user to utilize the report for that purpose. In either case, the court should find that the information was collected for a listed purpose or expected to be used for a listed purpose and, therefore, that it is a consumer report. Releasing or using the report for an impermissible purpose would therefore violate the Act.

To ignore the statute's plain language and limit consumer reports to ones where the user's actual use was one of those listed would have anomalous results. The listed purposes set forth in the definition of "consumer report" closely track (and, in fact, incorporate by reference) the list of permissible uses of consumer reports that appears in the next section of the statute, section 1681b. If a report only met the definition of "consumer report" if its actual use was permissible, then the FCRA requirement that consumer reports be released only to users with permissible purposes would be meaningless; if the information were used for an impermissible purpose, it would not be a consumer report, and the FCRA would not apply.[71]

2.3.5.2 Partial Use of a Prior Consumer Report Makes New Report a Consumer Report

If a new report contains just some of the information that was contained in a prior consumer report, the new report is also a consumer report, even if the new report was not used and not expected to be used for a listed purpose.[72] In addition, once information from the consumer's file is used as a "consumer report," then any subsequent use of the same information becomes a consumer report, even if that later report is not for a listed purpose.[73]

For example, information that is actually used for, and that the CRA expects to be used for, a purely commercial purpose (e.g., the decision of one company to merge with another) is still a consumer report if it is obtained from the consumer's file at a CRA. This is because the information was originally "collected" in whole or in part for consumer reporting purposes.[74]

This is a crucial aspect of the definition of a consumer report, because the consumer need not show that the actual report at issue was used or expected to be used for consumer reporting purposes. The consumer can instead show that a prior use of the file met the FCRA's standard for a consumer report.

Supp. 758 (S.D. Fla. 1995) (holds that a conclusory affidavit that the report is a consumer report does not satisfy this burden).

69 Comeaux v. Brown & Williamson Tobacco Co., 915 F.2d 1264 (9th Cir. 1990); St. Paul Guardian Ins. Co. v. Johnson, 884 F.2d 881 (5th Cir. 1989); Ippolito v. WNS, Inc., 864 F.2d 440 (7th Cir. 1988); Heath v. Credit Bureau of Sheridan, Inc., 618 F.2d 693 (10th Cir. 1980); Hansen v. Morgan, 582 F.2d 1214 (9th Cir. 1978); Hall v. Harleysville Ins. Co., 896 F. Supp. 478 (E.D. Pa. 1995); Allen v. Kirkland & Ellis, 1992 WL 206285 (N.D. Ill. Aug. 17, 1992); Zeller v. Samia, 758 F. Supp. 775 (D. Mass. 1991); Russell v. Shelter Fin. Servs., 604 F. Supp. 201 (W.D. Mo. 1984); Boothe v. TRW Credit Data, 523 F. Supp. 631 (S.D.N.Y. 1981), *modified*, 557 F. Supp. 66 (S.D.N.Y. 1982); Belshaw v. Credit Bureau, 392 F. Supp. 1356 (D. Ariz. 1975); Rasor v. Retail Credit Co., 87 Wash. 2d 516, 554 P.2d 1041 (1976). *See also* Kennedy v. Border City Sav. & Loan Assoc., 747 F.2d 367 (6th Cir. 1984); Mende v. Dun & Bradstreet, 670 F.2d 129 (9th Cir. 1982) (interpreting the California credit reporting statute, no consumer report where CRA required users to certify business purpose); Gardner v. Investigators, 413 F. Supp. 780 (M.D. Fla. 1976) (same); Doyle v. Chilton Corp., 289 Ark. 258, 711 S.W.2d 463 (1986), utilizing "intended use" as a threshold requirement to FCRA coverage; Note, *The Fair Credit Reporting Act: Are Business Credit Reports Regulated?*, 1971 Duke L. J. 1229 (1971). *But cf.* Houghton v. New Jersey Mfrs. Ins. Co., 795 F.2d 1144 (3d Cir. 1986), *rev'g* 615 F. Supp. 299 (E.D. Pa. 1985) (no consumer report where user clearly requested report not for permissible purpose, but CRA informed user that had checked credit sources); D'Angelo v. Wilmington Med. Ctr., 515 F. Supp. 1250 (D. Del. 1981); Henry v. Forbes, 433 F. Supp. 5 (D. Minn. 1976) (court failed to look beyond the actual use of the information).

70 FTC Official Staff Commentary § 603(d) items 5(A), 5(C), *reprinted at* Appx. D, *infra*; Tatelbaum, FTC Informal Staff Opinion Letter (July 26, 2000), *reprinted on the CD-Rom accompanying this manual*; Grimes, FTC Informal Staff Opinion Letter (Oct. 7, 1991), *reprinted on the CD-Rom accompanying this manual*; Noonan, FTC Informal Staff Opinion Letter (Aug. 22, 1990), *reprinted on the CD-Rom accompanying this manual*; Noonan, FTC Informal Staff Opinion Letter (Apr. 25, 1990), *reprinted on the CD-Rom accompanying this manual*. *See also* Howard Enters., Inc., 93 F.T.C. 909 (1979); FTC Informal Staff Opinion Letter [1969–1973 Decisions Transfer Binder], Consumer Cred. Guide (CCH) ¶ 99,424 (May 19, 1971).

71 *See* Ch. 7, *infra*.
72 FTC Official Staff Commentary § 603(d) item 5C, *reprinted at* Appx. D, *infra*. *See also* Grimes, FTC Informal Staff Opinion Letter (Mar. 4, 1992), *reprinted on the CD-Rom accompanying this manual*; FTC Informal Staff Opinion Letter [1969–1973 Decisions Transfer Binder] Consumer Cred. Guide (CCH) ¶ 99,424 (May 19, 1971).
73 FTC Official Staff Commentary § 603(d) item 5C, *reprinted at* Appx. D, *infra*.
74 *Id*.

2.3.5.3 Expected Use of Information

If a CRA provides a report with the expectation that the report will be used for one of the statute's listed purposes, the report is a consumer report under the Act; the ultimate use to which it is put is irrelevant.[75] It is enough if *one* of the anticipated uses is covered by the FCRA, even if it is not the *primary* expected use.[76]

While it is sufficient if the CRA anticipates a listed use, this is not even necessary. The statutory language "expected to be used" need not be limited to expectations by that particular CRA in that particular transaction. It should be enough if, in the usual course of events, one would expect that one of the uses of a report would be a listed one.[77]

CRAs cannot escape FCRA liability by proving that they knew the information would be used for an unlisted purpose, and arguing that the information is therefore not a consumer report. Such a reading would render meaningless the requirement that consumer reports be released only to users that the CRA has reason to believe have permissible purposes.[78] Furthermore, the FCRA requires CRAs to maintain reasonable procedures to ensure that they do not release reports for impermissible purposes.[79] Congress clearly intended CRAs to be liable under the Act when they know or reasonably should know that they are releasing reports to users with impermissible purposes.

It is illogical that the consumer should have to prove both that the CRA reasonably should have known that the report would be used impermissibly and that the CRA should have expected that the report would be used permissibly. The more logical interpretation is that a CRA's liability for violating the permissible purposes section depends on the CRA's expectations in the specific circumstances of the case, but that the definition of a consumer report depends on the expectations of a CRA in the usual course of events.

The structure of the phrase "used or expected to be used or collected"[80] indicates that the expected use should be given a meaning separate and distinct from the actual use of the information and the actual purpose for its collection. If the Act is narrowly interpreted to refer only to the actual expectations of the CRA in the specific fact situation before the court, "expected to be used" is likely to mean the same thing as "used" or "collected." For example, the purpose for which the information is "collected" clearly refers to the "state of mind" of the CRA. If the CRA collected the information pursuant to the request of a specific user, the purpose for which the CRA collected the information is the same as the purpose for which the CRA expected the information to be used. Thus a better interpretation is that the court should look at three separate factors in characterizing information as a consumer report:

- The actual use of the information (expectations of the user);
- The purpose for which the information was collected (expectations of that particular CRA); and
- The expected use of the information (expectations of any CRA in the usual course of events).

Thus, a consumer report exists where a CRA does not know the user's actual purpose, but there is no history of the CRA regularly releasing information to users for purposes outside the FCRA. In that situation, a presumption exists that the information is expected to be used for a listed purpose.[81] Prior consumer reporting activities of the person who requested the information are obviously important as well.[82] On the other hand, if the type of information requested about the individual is different from the type of information the CRA usually releases to other users, the CRA may be less likely to expect that the information would be used for purposes similar to the reasons other users request information.

The identity of the person who requests the information is also relevant. If the CRA has released information to the same person in the past and the information has always been used for a listed purpose, it is probably reasonable for the CRA to expect that it would be used for a permissible purpose in the present case. If, however, the user is generally known to be engaged in activities not listed in the Act, the CRA might reasonably expect that the information would be used for a purpose that is not covered by the definition of a consumer report.

The standard then is the CRA's reasonable expectation. The FTC Staff Commentary, for example, in discussing possible future use of information that might give rise to a consumer report, states that the standard is whether a CRA knows or should reasonably anticipate use as a consumer report.[83] Where one would not expect a use to be a covered one, the CRA can protect itself by requiring the user to

---

75 *See* Comeaux v. Brown & Williamson Tobacco Co., 915 F.2d 1264 (9th Cir. 1990); Pappas v. City of Calumet City, 9 F. Supp. 2d 943 (N.D. Ill. 1998); Zeller v. Samia, 758 F. Supp. 775 (D. Mass. 1991).

76 The definition of a consumer report includes information expected to be used "in whole *or in part*" for the listed purposes (emphasis added). 15 U.S.C. § 1681a(d).

77 *See* Ippolito v. WNS, Inc., 636 F. Supp. 471 (N.D. Ill. 1986), *aff'd in part, rev'd in part*, 864 F.2d 440 (7th Cir. 1988); Belshaw v. Credit Bureau, 392 F. Supp. 1356, 1359 (D. Ariz. 1975). *But see* Mende v. Dun & Bradstreet, 670 F.2d 129 (9th Cir. 1982); Henry v. Forbes, 433 F. Supp. 5 (D. Minn. 1976).

78 15 U.S.C. § 1681b.
79 15 U.S.C. § 1681e(a).
80 15 U.S.C. § 1681a(d).

81 Hansen v. Morgan, 582 F.2d 1214 (9th Cir. 1978).

82 Ippolito v. WNS, Inc., 864 F.2d 440 (7th Cir. 1988) (user generally requested business reports and CRA presumed report was for business purposes); Hansen v. Morgan, 582 F.2d 1214 (9th Cir. 1978).

83 FTC Official Staff Commentary § 603(d) item 5D, *reprinted at* Appx. D, *infra*.

certify that the report will not be used as a consumer report.[84] But such steps protect the CRA only where "it neither knows of, nor can reasonably anticipate such use."[85]

According to the FTC Staff Commentary, law enforcement bulletins with information on individuals being sought by law enforcement authorities for alleged crimes are not consumer reports because they are not collected for consumer purposes and it cannot be reasonably anticipated that they will be used for such purposes.[86] Likewise, the information in telephone directories and city directories is not collected for such purposes, and it cannot reasonably be anticipated that it will be used for such purposes.[87]

2.3.5.4 Purpose for Collecting Information

If information is originally collected for a purpose covered by the FCRA, a report containing that information is a consumer report even if the report is later used exclusively for business purposes or other transactions not covered by the FCRA.[88] The purpose for which the information is collected will be determined based on the reasonable expectations of the CRA at the time it collected the information.

For example, if an employer requests a report on a consumer and certifies that the information is required in connection with the consumer's employment application, and the CRA collects information pursuant to that request, the information is a consumer report.[89] When, at a later date, a bank requests information about the consumer to evaluate the consumer's request for a business loan, the information is still considered a consumer report and the requirements of the Act apply. This is true even had the bank been the first user to request that the information be collected, as long as the CRA collected the information with the expectation that it would be available both in connection with the business loan and for later purposes covered by the FCRA. The information would have been *collected* for a purpose covered by the Act.

The point is that a CRA may have many purposes when it collects information, but if one of the purposes involves a purpose covered by the FCRA, the information becomes a consumer report. Even if the CRA expects that only ten percent of the time the information will be put to purposes covered by the FCRA, this is enough for the information to be a consumer report, no matter the use to which it is actually put.[90]

One possible solution for the CRA is to collect from scratch information on the consumer for two different files, one for releasing consumer reports and one for business reports.[91] Nevertheless, the CRA must then be careful not to commingle the two files.

If information from the consumer file makes its way into the business file, then all future information from that file will be consumer reports as well.[92] Similarly, if information from the business file is ever put to a consumer purpose, any subsequent report from that file also becomes a consumer report.[93]

Setting up two databases creates another potential problem. If the CRA makes it easier or less expensive for a user

---

84 *Id.*
85 *Id. cf.* Harrington v. ChoicePoint, Inc., Slip. Op., No. CV 05-1294 MRP (C.D. Cal. Sept. 15, 2005), *available at* www.consumerlaw.org/unreported (rejecting argument that information was not a consumer report because defendant did not expect that information would be used for FCRA purposes; "Once the fraudsters indicated they intended to use the information for FCRA purposes, it does not matter that in another part of the agreement they promised not to do it. . . . Deciding otherwise would allow ChoicePoint to contract around FCRA liability.").
86 FTC Official Staff Commentary § 603(d) item 5A, *reprinted at* Appx. D, *infra. See also* Supplementary Information published with the Commentary, 55 Fed. Reg. 18,804–18,805 (May 4, 1990), *reprinted at* Appx. D, *infra*. Although the FTC stated its opinion in terms of "reasonable expectations," it appears that the result was also influenced by policy considerations that such lists are useful to law enforcement agencies. The public policy of preventing crime seems to have been balanced against the policies of the Act; the need to protect the public from alleged criminals was found to outweigh the need to ensure the accuracy of such lists and to protect the privacy rights of consumers.
87 *See* FTC Official Staff Commentary § 603(d) item 5B, *reprinted at* Appx. D, *infra*.
88 *See* Bakker v. McKinnon, 152 F.3d 1007 (8th Cir. 1998); Ippolito v. WNS, Inc., 864 F.2d 440 (7th Cir. 1988); Buchman, FTC Informal Staff Opinion Letter (Mar. 2, 1998), *reprinted on the CD-Rom accompanying this manual*; Grimes, FTC Informal Staff Opinion Letter (Aug. 3, 1984), *reprinted on the CD-Rom accompanying this manual*; FTC Informal Staff Opinion Letter [1969–1973 Decisions Transfer Binder] Consumer Cred. Guide (CCH) ¶ 99,424 (May 19, 1971); FTC, Compliance with the Fair Credit Reporting Act, at 46 (1977). *See also* St. Paul Guardian Ins. Co. v. Johnson, 884 F.2d 881 (5th Cir. 1989); Russell v. Shelter Fin. Servs., 604 F. Supp. 201 (W.D. Mo. 1984); Boothe v. TRW Credit Data, 523 F. Supp. 631 (S.D.N.Y. 1981), *modified*, 557 F. Supp. 66 (S.D.N.Y. 1982); Hall v. Harleysville Ins. Co., 896 F. Supp. 478 (E.D. Pa. 1995). *Cf.* Maloney v. City of Chicago, 678 F. Supp. 703 (N.D. Ill. 1987) (used to harass employee); Haynes, FTC Informal Staff Opinion Letter (Mar. 2, 1998), *reprinted on the CD-Rom accompanying this manual*.
89 The original version of S. 823, which eventually became the Fair Credit Reporting Act, added a major restriction to these permissible purposes. Use of consumer reports was restricted to those with a permissible purpose for the information as long as that purpose was also consistent with the purposes disclosed by the CRA at the time it collected the information. Thus, for example, information collected for credit purposes could not be used for employment purposes. *See* S. 823, 91st Cong., 1st Sess. § 164(f)(2) (1969) and discussion at 115 Cong. Rec. 2413, 2415 (1969).
90 Grimes, FTC Informal Staff Opinion Letter (Oct. 7, 1991), *reprinted on the CD-Rom accompanying this manual*.
91 *Id.*
92 Grimes, FTC Informal Staff Opinion Letter (Mar. 4, 1992), *reprinted on the CD-Rom accompanying this manual*.
93 *Id.*

§ 2.3.6   *Fair Credit Reporting*

to access the consumer database, it would create a built-in incentive for business users with no permissible purposes to improperly obtain reports from the consumer database instead of the business database.[94]

If a CRA collects information pursuant to a request by a user, the court will probably consider, in determining the CRA's purpose in collecting the information, the following factors: other consumer reporting activities of the CRA; the type of information requested; the stated purpose of the user who made the request; the identity of that user; and the CRA's prior dealings with that user. If the information was collected prior to any request for the information by a user, the court should not consider the identity and purpose of the eventual user of the report, but should instead focus its inquiry on the CRA's consumer reporting activities and the expected use of the type of information collected.

2.3.6 Purposes That Make Information a Consumer Report

2.3.6.1 General

To be a consumer report under section 1681a, information must be collected, used, or expected to be used at least in part for the purpose of serving as a factor in establishing the consumer's eligibility for: "(A) credit or insurance to be used primarily for personal, family or household purposes; (B) employment purposes; or (C) other purposes authorized under section 1681b" of the FCRA.[95]

Section 1681b, in turn, lists the permissible purposes for which consumer reports may be used. It reiterates (though in a somewhat different fashion) the permissible purposes for credit, employment, and insurance—uses already listed in the definition of consumer report. It also lists several other permissible purposes, which therefore become incorporated into the definition of consumer report:

- In response to a court order;
- At the consumer's written instruction;
- To review or collect credit accounts;
- To establish eligibility for government licenses or other benefits;
- To evaluate credit and prepayment risks of existing credit obligations;
- To respond to a legitimate business need for the information in connection with a transaction initiated by a consumer or account review; and
- For use by government officials in setting or modifying child support payment levels.

In the case of conflict between the specific purposes listed in section 1681a and the purposes incorporated by reference to section 1681b, courts have recognized section 1681a as the "primary" section defining "consumer report."[96] Thus, the broad language found in parts of section 1681b does not expand the definition of consumer report when it conflicts with the narrower language of section 1681a.[97] However, information is a consumer report—and therefore is covered by the FCRA—if it is collected or used for a purpose set forth in section 1681b, even if all of the specific requirements of section 1681b for the use of that report are not followed.[98]

Permissible purposes are generally discussed in Chapter 7, *infra*, but the interplay between each of those purposes and the definition of consumer report is discussed in the following sections (with the exception of the court order and consumer instructions purposes, which apparently have not been considered by either the FTC or the courts in connection with the definition of consumer report). The definition of consumer report was added to the FCRA during closed-door negotiations and drafting, so that little direct legislative history is available to resolve the ambiguities that have arisen.[99]

2.3.6.2 Reports on Individuals for Business, Not Consumer, Purposes Are Not Consumer Reports

As discussed above, a report on a business is not a consumer report.[100] Moreover, even a report on an individual is not a consumer report if it was collected, used and expected to be used to evaluate a business or for another commercial, nonpersonal purpose.[101]

The list of uses that make information a consumer report is prefaced by the requirement that the information be collected or used to establish "the consumer's eligibility" for those uses.[102] For example, information is a consumer report if it is used to determine a consumer's eligibility for credit, insurance, employment, government benefits, or a business transaction initiated by the consumer.[103] That is, a consumer report is involved if at least part of the information

---

94   *Id.*
95   15 U.S.C. § 1681a(d).
96   *See* Ippolito v. WNS, Inc., 864 F.2d 440 (7th Cir. 1988).
97   *See, e.g.,* Hoke v. Retail Credit Corp., 521 F.2d 1079 (4th Cir. 1975); Fernandez v. Retail Credit Corp., 349 F. Supp. 652 (E.D. La. 1972).
98   Hoke v. Retail Credit Corp., 521 F.2d 1079 (4th Cir. 1975). *See* § 2.3.5.3, *supra*.
99   *See* § 1.4.3, *supra*.
100   *See* § 2.3.3.3, *supra*.
101   FTC Official Staff Commentary § 603(d) item 3C, *reprinted at* Appx. D, *infra. See, e.g.,* Fernandez v. Retail Credit Corp., 349 F. Supp. 652 (E.D. La. 1972) (report secured for purpose of obtaining insurance on "key man," with company as beneficiary, not a consumer report).
102   15 U.S.C. § 1681a(d)(1).
103   15 U.S.C. §§ 1681a(d)(A), (C), 1681b(a)(3). It is not clear whether the reference to eligibility modifies each of the five permissible purposes; some of the purposes—such as court orders or child support enforcement—have nothing to do with

is collected, used, or expected to be used for personal reasons. If information is collected, used, *and* expected to be used solely to evaluate business credit, or other, purely commercial purposes, then a consumer report is not involved.[104]

The legislative history makes clear that the Act is not intended to regulate reporting for business purposes. The matter is stated formally in the Senate report accompanying the Senate bill (which was also enacted by the House): "The bill covers reports on consumers when used for obtaining credit, insurance or employment. However, the bill does not cover business credit or business insurance reports."[105] This emphasis on protecting individuals is also reflected in the final Senate report which refers to "individual" rights "whenever *an individual* is rejected . . . because of an adverse credit report" and to "prevent[ing] an undue invasion of *the individual's* right to privacy."[106]

Congresswoman Sullivan, the floor manager of the bill upon final House passage, commented:

> Insofar as reports of a business nature are concerned, this point was raised continually in our hearings in H.R. 16340 in the Subcommittee on Consumer Affairs, and I think we always made clear that we were not interested in extending this law to credit reports for business credit or business insurance. The conference bill spells this out, furthermore, in section 603(d), which defines a "consumer report" as a report, and so on, "which is used or expected to be used or collected in whole or in part for the purpose of serving as a factor in establishing the consumer's eligibility for (1) credit or insurance to be used primarily for personal, family, or household purposes" and so forth.[107]

She also stated:

> The purpose of the fair credit reporting bill is to protect consumers from inaccurate or arbitrary information in a consumer report, which is used as a factor in determining an individual's eligibility for credit, insurance or employment. It does not apply to reports utilized for business, commercial or professional purposes.[108]

This does not mean, notwithstanding dicta in some cases,[109] that reports collected on individuals for business purposes are never consumer reports. Information collected for business purposes, but used for consumer credit or other personal purposes, is a consumer report.[110] The statements in these cases are overly broad and in reality appear to be shorthand for the real reason for finding that a consumer report was not involved—the report was collected, used, *and* expected to be used solely concerning the individual acting in a business capacity.

Similarly, courts sometimes incorrectly state, often in *dicta*, that a report cannot be a consumer report if it is actually used for business purposes.[111] The proper test is whether the information was originally collected, used, or expected to be used for one or more of the purposes enumerated in the Act. If it was gathered for such purposes or ever used for such purposes, the information remains a consumer report even when later used for business purposes.[112]

---

eligibility. 15 U.S.C. § 1681b(a)(1), (4).

104 *E.g.*, McCready v. Ebay, Inc., 453 F.3d 882 (7th Cir. 2006); Mende v. Dun & Bradstreet, 670 F.2d 129 (9th Cir. 1982); Thomas v. Gulf Coast Credit Serv., Inc., 214 F. Supp. 2d 1228 (M.D. Ala. 2002); Cambridge Title Co. v. Transamerica Title Ins. Co., 817 F. Supp. 1263 (D. Md. 1992), *aff'd*, 989 F.2d 491 (4th Cir. 1993); Wrigley v. Dun & Bradstreet, 375 F. Supp. 969 (N.D. Ga. 1974) *aff'd*, 500 F.2d 1183 (5th Cir. 1974); Sizemore v. Bambi Leasing Corp., 360 F. Supp. 252 (N.D. Ga. 1973); Fernandez v. Retail Credit Corp., 349 F. Supp. 652 (E.D. La. 1972); FTC Official Staff Commentary § 603(d) item 6B, *reprinted at* Appx. D, *infra*. *See also* Grimes, FTC Informal Staff Opinion Letter (Aug. 22, 1990), *reprinted on the CD-Rom accompanying this manual*; Noonan, FTC Informal Staff Opinion Letter (Apr. 25, 1990), *reprinted on the CD-Rom accompanying this manual*; Brinckerhoff, FTC Informal Staff Opinion Letters (May 4, 1987) and (Sept. 3, 1986), *reprinted on the CD-Rom accompanying this manual*; Grimes, FTC Informal Staff Opinion Letter (May 12, 1987), *reprinted on the CD-Rom accompanying this manual*; Petruccelli, FTC Informal Staff Opinion Letter (Apr. 9, 1984), *reprinted on the CD-Rom accompanying this manual*; Conway, FTC Informal Staff Opinion Letter (Mar. 30, 1971), *reprinted on the CD-Rom accompanying this manual*. *See generally* G. Allan Van Fleet, Note, *Judicial Construction of the Fair Credit Reporting Act: Scope of Civil Liability*, 76 Colum. L. Rev. 458 (1976); Note *The Fair Credit Reporting Act: Are Business Credit Reports Regulated?*, 1971 Duke L.J. 1229.

105 S. Rep. No. 517, 91st Cong., 1st Sess. 1 (1969).

106 *Id.*

107 116 Cong. Rec. 36573 (Oct. 3, 1970).

108 *Id.*

109 *E.g.*, Boothe v. TRW Credit Data, 523 F. Supp. 631 (S.D.N.Y. 1981), *modified*, 557 F. Supp. 66 (S.D.N.Y. 1982); Fernandez v. Retail Credit Corp., 349 F. Supp. 652 (E.D. La. 1972) (never considered that original purpose report collected was a consumer purpose). *See also* Matthews v. Worthen Bank & Trust Co., 741 F.2d 217 (8th Cir. 1984); Mende v. Dun & Bradstreet, 670 F.2d 129 (9th Cir. 1982); Wrigley v. Dun & Bradstreet, 375 F. Supp. 969 (N.D. Ga. 1974).

110 *See* § 2.3.5.4, *supra*.

111 Matthews v. Worthen Bank & Trust Co., 741 F.2d 217 (8th Cir. 1984); Cook v. Equifax Info. Sys., Inc., 1992 WL 356119 (D. Md. Nov. 20, 1992); Allen v. Kirkland & Ellis, 1992 WL 206285 (N.D. Ill. Aug. 17, 1992); Ley v. Boron Oil Co., 419 F. Supp. 1240 (W.D. Pa. 1976); Sizemore v. Bambi Leasing Corp., 360 F. Supp. 252 (N.D. Ga. 1973).

112 *See* § 2.3.5.4, *supra*. *See also* Heath v. Credit Bureau of Sheridan, Inc., 618 F.2d 693 (10th Cir. 1980); Apodaca v. Discover Fin. Servs., 417 F. Supp. 2d 1220 (D.N.M. 2006) (notwithstanding testimony that plaintiff intended to use credit card for husband's business, factual issue remained as to whether report was a consumer report where plaintiff applied in her own name and application was denied based on her "*con*-

A contrary conclusion would make no sense, based on the Act's structure. If the use of a consumer report for an impermissible purpose made the report no longer a consumer report, then there would be no remedy for using the report for an impermissible purpose.[113] This would fly in the face of one of the primary purposes of the Act: to limit distribution of consumer reports to certain permissible purposes.

The FTC Staff Commentary, as it was originally proposed, contained language which would exclude reports with business purposes.[114] However, this was contradicted by other sections of the proposed commentary[115] and by earlier FTC staff opinion as well.[116] The final FTC Staff Commentary omitted the troubling language.[117]

2.3.6.3 Credit Purposes

2.3.6.3.1 General

The definition of "consumer report" incorporates two separate references to credit uses. First, the definition directly includes information collected or used for establishing the "consumer's eligibility for ... credit ... to be used primarily for personal, family, or household purposes."[118] Second, the definition incorporates section 1681b, which permits use of consumer reports "in connection with a credit transaction involving the consumer on whom the information is to be furnished and involving the extension of credit to, or review or collection of an account of, the consumer."[119]

"Credit" is defined in the FCRA[120] to have the same meaning as in the Equal Credit Opportunity Act (ECOA), which defines credit as "the right granted by a creditor to a debtor to defer payment of debt or to incur debts and defer is payment or to purchase property or services and defer payment therefore."[121]

There is no requirement in the ECOA that the credit be for personal, family, or household purposes.[122] Moreover, the "personal, family or household purposes" limitation of section 1681a does not appear in section 1681b.

It is unclear whether a consumer report may be released under section 1681b for purposes of business credit.[123] But this uncertainty affects only the use of consumer reports, not the threshold question of whether information is a consumer report in the first place. Since section 1681a is the primary section defining "consumer report," information that is collected, expected to be used, or actually used for credit purposes qualifies as a consumer report only if that credit is for "personal, family or household purposes." The FTC Staff Commentary specifically states that a report on a consumer for credit in connection with a business operated by the consumer is not a consumer report.[124] Though the FTC Staff Commentary overstates the issue somewhat—because the report would be a consumer report if it was originally collected or expected to be used for consumer purposes—it is clear that information on a consumer that is collected, expected to be used, *and* used for business credit purposes is not a consumer report.

The phrase "personal, family or household purposes" is not defined in either the ECOA or the FCRA. The FTC Staff Commentary has broadly interpreted the phrase to include, for example, credit relating to investment actions by consumers, as long as the consumer does not engage in such transactions as a business.[125] "Personal, family, or household purposes" is also identical to language found in the Truth in Lending Act (TILA), so TILA cases should be useful precedents for determining the scope of that phrase.[126]

The consumer report need not be the only basis for considering a consumer's eligibility for credit. As long as the report is one of the bases for deciding whether to grant credit, it would fall within the FCRA's definition of information used "in part" for that purpose. Characterizing the use of reports about consumers involved with fraud losses as a "checkpoint" rather than as a basis for denying credit does

---

sumer credit report" (original emphasis)); Russell v. Shelter Fin. Servs., 604 F. Supp. 201 (W.D. Mo. 1984); Boothe v. TRW Credit Data, 523 F. Supp. 631 (S.D.N.Y. 1981), *modified* 557 F. Supp. 66 (S.D.N.Y. 1982); FTC Official Staff Commentary § 603(d) item 5C, *reprinted at* Appx. D, *infra*; Supplementary Information published with the Commentary, 55 Fed. Reg. 18,806 (May 4, 1990), *reprinted at* Appx. D, *infra*. But see D'Angelo v. Wilmington Med. Ctr., 515 F. Supp. 1250 (D. Del. 1981).

113 *See also* Comeaux v. Brown & Williamson Tobacco Co., 915 F.2d 1264 (9th Cir. 1990); G. Allan Van Fleet, Note, *Judicial Construction of the Fair Credit Reporting Act: Scope of Civil Liability*, 76 Colum. L. Rev. 458 (1976).

114 Proposed FTC Official Staff Commentary § 604(3)(E) item 2, 53 Fed. Reg. 29,696, 29,706 (Aug. 8, 1988).

115 *Id.* § 603(d) item 5.

116 FTC, Compliance with the Fair Credit Reporting Act, at 21, 25, 46 (1977).

117 *See* Supplementary Information published with final FTC Official Staff Commentary, 55 Fed. Reg. 18,804–18,805 (May 4, 1990), *reprinted at* Appx. D, *infra*.

118 15 U.S.C. § 1681a(d)(1)(A).

119 15 U.S.C. § 1681b(a)(3)(A).

120 15 U.S.C. § 1681a(r)(5).

121 15 U.S.C. § 1691a(d); 12 C.F.R. § 202.2(j).

122 *See* National Consumer Law Center, Credit Discrimination, § 2.2.2.1.1 and 2.2.6.4 (4th ed. 2005 and Supp.).

123 *See* § 7.2.3.1.3, *infra*.

124 Lucchesi v. Experian Info. Solutions, Inc., 2003 WL 21542317 (S.D.N.Y. July 7, 2003); FTC Official Staff Commentary § 603(d) item 6B, *reprinted at* Appx. D, *infra*. See D'Angelo v. Wilmington Med. Ctr., 515 F. Supp. 1250 (D. Del. 1981).

125 Matise v. Trans Union Corp., 1998 WL 872511 (N.D. Tex. Nov. 30, 1998); FTC Official Staff Commentary § 615 item 7, *reprinted at* Appx. D, *infra*; Grimes, FTC Informal Staff Opinion Letter (Feb. 17, 1993).

126 National Consumer Law Center, Truth in Lending §§ 2.2.3, 2.2.4 (5th ed. 2003 and Supp.).

not remove it from the definition of consumer report.[127] Unless there are effective restrictions that prevent use of the report for FCRA-covered purposes, it would be a consumer report.[128]

The incorporation of section 1681b's broader credit provision means that information is considered a consumer report not only if it is collected or used to determine eligibility for credit, but also if it is used to review or collect any existing consumer credit account, as permitted under section 1681b.[129] According to the FTC Staff Commentary, the two sections of the statute (section 1681b and the definition of consumer reports in section 1681a) should be read together when possible.[130]

As a consequence, a straightforward reading of the statute indicates that the term consumer reports would include reports even if collected for or expected to be used solely for collection purposes, and not for purposes of extending credit. For example, if a skip tracing company sold lists of debtors' present whereabouts, this would seem to fall within the definition of a consumer report.

2.3.6.3.2 Check writing, check approval and similar lists

Reports or lists supplied to merchants, lenders, landlords, and banks on consumers' check writing history or other factors reflecting creditworthiness are generally considered to be a consumer reports. Two approaches have been taken in examining whether reports issued to banks by check guarantee companies are consumer reports under the FCRA. The first approach, taken by some courts, views such reports as consumer reports because they involve consumer credit.[131] A second approach, taken in the FTC Staff Commentary and by other courts, view them as consumer reports because they contain information used in connection with a business transaction initiated by the consumer.[132] The business transaction provision is discussed separately below.[133]

Both the courts and the FTC have agreed that a consumer report is implicated when a check guaranty agency or a check approval company, such as UniCheck, TeleCheck, SCAN, ChexSystems or RENTCHECK, provides lists of consumers with bad check cashing histories to merchants or landlords.[134] For example, the FTC Staff Commentary states the definition of consumer report includes information indicating that an individual has issued bad checks, provided by printed list or otherwise, to a business for use in determining whether to accept consumers' checks tendered in transactions primarily for personal, family, or household purposes.[135]

---

127 Grimes, FTC Informal Staff Opinion Letter (Mar. 3, 1993), *reprinted on the CD-Rom accompanying this manual.*
128 *Id.*
129 15 U.S.C. § 1681b(a)(3)(A).
130 FTC Official Staff Commentary §§ 603(d) item 6A, 604 item 1A, *reprinted at* Appx. D, *infra. See also* Houghton v. New Jersey Mfrs. Ins. Co., 795 F.2d 1144 (3d Cir. 1986); Greenway v. Information Dynamics, Ltd., 399 F. Supp. 1092 (D. Ariz. 1974), *aff'd per curiam*, 524 F.2d 1145 (9th Cir. 1975); Grimes, FTC Informal Staff Opinion Letter (Mar. 3, 1993), *reprinted on the CD-Rom accompanying this manual* (treating §§ 1681a(d)(A) and 1681b(a)(3)(A) as alternate tests). *But see* Ippolito v. WNS, Inc., 864 F.2d 440 (7th Cir. 1988).
131 Greenway v. Information Dynamics, Ltd., 524 F.2d 1145 (9th Cir. 1975) (checks are instruments of credit, and check cashing involves credit); Peasley v. TeleCheck of Kansas, 6 Kan. App. 2d 990, 637 P.2d 437 (1981). *Cf.* Bass v. Stolper, Koritzinsky, Brewster & Neider, S.C., 111 F.3d 1322 (7th Cir. 1997) (a consumer who issues a subsequently dishonored check has an obligation to pay that meets the definition of "debt" in the Fair Debt Collection Practices Act).
132 Estiverne v. Saks Fifth Avenue & JBS, 9 F.3d 1171 (5th Cir. 1993); FTC Official Staff Commentary § 603(d) item 6E, *reprinted at* Appx. D, *infra. See also* FTC Official Staff Commentary § 615 item 10, *reprinted at* Appx. D, *infra* (checks do not involve credit); Greenway v. Information Dynamics, Ltd., 399 F. Supp. 1092 (D. Ariz. 1974), *aff'd per curiam*, 524 F.2d 1145 (9th Cir. 1975); Peasley v. TeleCheck of Kansas, 6 Kan. App. 2d 990, 637 P.2d 437 (1981); Brinckerhoff, FTC Informal Staff Opinion Letter (July 16, 1998), *reprinted on the CD-Rom accompanying this manual;* Scholl, FTC Informal Staff Opinion Letter (Dec. 10, 1976), *reprinted on the CD-Rom accompanying this manual* (cites to Greenway); Grimes, FTC Informal Staff Opinion Letter (Sept. 5, 1973) (cashing of check is business transaction covered by § 604(3)(E) of Act); Howard Enters., Inc., 93 FTC 909 (1979).
133 *See* § 2.3.6.8, *infra.*
134 Estiverne v. Saks Fifth Avenue & JBS, 9 F.3d 1171 (5th Cir. 1993); Greenway v. Information Dynamics, Ltd., 524 F.2d 1145 (9th Cir. 1975); Oppenheimer v. Guzco Guarantee de Puerto Rico, Inc., 977 F. Supp. 549 (D. P.R. 1997); Alexander v. Moore & Associates, 553 F. Supp. 948 (D. Haw. 1982); Peasley v. TeleCheck of Kansas, 6 Kan. App. 2d 990, 637 P.2d 437 (1981); Howard Enters., Inc., 93 F.T.C. 909 (1979); Moore & Associates, 92 F.T.C. 440 (1978) (consent order) (settlement of FTC complaint against Uni-Check and RENTCHECK for FCRA violations); Interstate Check Sys., 88 F.T.C. 984 (1976) (consent order); Barnes t/a Nat'l Credit Exch., 85 F.T.C. 520 (1975) (consent order); Filmdex Chex Sys., 85 F.T.C. 889 (1975) (consent order); Checkmate Inquiry Serv., 86 F.T.C. 681 (1975) (consent order); FTC Official Staff Commentary § 603(d) item 6E, *reprinted at* Appx. D, *infra;* Scholl, FTC Informal Staff Opinion Letter (Dec. 10, 1976), *reprinted on the CD-Rom accompanying this manual* (cites to Greenway); Grimes, FTC Informal Staff Opinion Letter (Sept. 5, 1973) (cashing of check is business transaction covered by § 604(3)(E) of Act). *See also* Mangum v. Action Collection Serv., Inc., 2006 WL 2224067 (D. Idaho Aug. 2, 2006) (publication of a list of consumers from whom retailers should not accept checks may go beyond mere debt collection and constitute consumer reporting); Taylor v. Checkrite, Ltd., 627 F. Supp. 415 (S.D. Ohio 1986) (franchisor of a check collection company that issued procedural guidelines for its franchisees was found responsible for its franchisee's potential violations of the Act); FTC Official Staff Commentary § 604(3)(E) item 3, *reprinted at* Appx. D, *infra;* Grimes, FTC Informal Staff Opinion Letter (Jan. 22, 1991), *reprinted on the CD-Rom accompanying this manual;* Maine Bureau of Consumer Protection Advisory Ruling, Consumer Cred. Guide (CCH) ¶ 97,153 (May 29, 1981) (service organization providing checking account histories to financial institutions is a CRA).
135 FTC Official Staff Commentary § 603(d) item 6E, *reprinted at* Appx. D, *infra.*

A CRA that complies and maintains files on consumers' check writing histories on a nationwide basis is a "nationwide specialty consumer reporting agency," a subclass of CRA added to the FCRA by the Fair and Accurate Credit Transactions Act of 2003 (FACTA).[136] This provision bolsters the status of check approval lists or reports as "consumer reports."[137]

Check guaranty agencies sometimes argue that they are not CRAs because they do not provide information to merchants, but rather extend credit to consumers, and thus do not involve the transmission of information to third parties. If a consumer meets criteria established by a check guaranty agency, the agency guarantees payment of the check to merchants. When a check previously guaranteed by the agency is returned to the merchant as a "bad check," the agency pays the merchant the amount of the check, takes assignment of the check, and attempts to collect from the consumer. That is, the guarantee agencies claim that their recommendation to a merchant is merely a statement about whether they would extend credit, and is not a consumer report because such a use is specifically exempted from the definition of consumer report.[138]

This argument has been rejected by the courts. Guaranty companies provide merchants, landlords, and banks with informational services used by these businesses in their dealings with consumers without regard to any guarantee.[139] According to some courts, the primary purpose for obtaining the information is to determine whether the consumer has a good credit record, not the guarantee of a check.[140]

Banks use check writing databases in a different manner, to find out whether an applicant for a checking account owes a previous bank for charges related to a checking account. A bank may refuse to open an account if the company reports such charges. If the checking account is sought primarily for personal, family, or household purposes then the check approval company's report should be considered a consumer report.[141]

Another variation of a check approval company is TELE-TRACK, a subsidiary of First American Corporation, which is a company that specializes in providing information to rent-to-own stores and other sub-prime merchants and lenders. Unlike traditional CRAs, this company maintains a database containing only negative information. In addition to reporting on those who have written bad checks, it also reports on consumers who purportedly have not paid rent, used false Social Security numbers, have stolen merchandise or automobiles, or have not met terms under finance or service agreements with merchants.[142] These reports are also clearly consumer reports, as they bear on the consumer's creditworthiness and are used as a factor in granting or deny credit.

2.3.6.3.3 Reports on tenants

Tenant reports compiled by tenant screening companies are consumer reports under the Act. Less clear is whether this is so because leasing is a credit transaction, or because the reports fall under the separate business transaction provision.[143]

It is clear that tenant reports meet the general requirement that the information "bear" on the consumer's creditworthiness, credit standing, credit capacity, character, general reputation, personal characteristics, or mode of living.[144]

---

136 15 U.S.C. § 1681a(w).
137 See § 2.6.2, *infra*.
138 See 15 U.S.C. § 1681a(d)(2)(C), *as discussed at* § 2.4.6, *infra*.
139 Alexander v. Moore & Associates, 553 F. Supp. 948 (D. Haw. 1982); Nicholl v. NationsBank, 488 S.E.2d 751 (Ga. Ct. App. 1997); Peasley v. TeleCheck of Kansas, 6 Kan. App. 2d 990, 995–996, 637 P.2d 437 (1981). *See also* Moore & Associates, 92 F.T.C. 440 (1978) (consent order) (settlement of FTC complaint against Uni-Check and RENTCHECK for FCRA violations).
140 Alexander v. Moore & Associates, 553 F. Supp. 948 (D. Haw. 1982); Nicholl v. NationsBank, 488 S.E.2d 751 (Ga. Ct. App. 1997); Peasley v. TeleCheck of Kansas, 6 Kan. App. 2d 990, 995–996, 637 P.2d 437 (1981). *See also* Moore & Associates, 92 F.T.C. 440 (1978) (consent order) (settlement of FTC complaint against Uni-Check and RENTCHECK for FCRA violations).
141 FTC Official Staff Commentary § 604(3)(E) item 3, *reprinted at* Appx. D, *infra*.
142 *See* www.teletrack.com.
143 Ali v. Vikar Mgmt. Ltd., 994 F. Supp. 492 (S.D.N.Y. 1998) (while address information acquired by landlord on tenant did not constitute a consumer report, credit information did); Scott v. Real Estate Fin. Group, 956 F. Supp. 375 (E.D.N.Y. 1997), *aff'd*, Scott v. Real Estate Fin. Group, 183 F.3d 97 (2d Cir. 1999); Cotto v. Jenney, 721 F. Supp. 5 (D. Mass. 1989); Ferguson v. Park City Mobile Homes, 1989 WL 111916 (N.D. Ill. Sept. 18, 1989) (mobile home park used reports); Franco v. Kent Farm Vill., Clearinghouse No. 44,149 (D.R.I. Sept. 16, 1988) (public housing landlord used reports); Cisneros v. U.D. Registry, Consumer Cred. Guide ¶ 95,361 (Cal. Ct. App. Oct. 19, 1995); FTC Official Staff Commentary § 603(d) item 6F, *reprinted at* Appx. D, *infra*; Grimes, FTC Informal Staff Opinion Letter (Oct. 8, 1986), *reprinted on the CD-Rom accompanying this manual*; Brinckerhoff, FTC Informal Staff Opinion Letter (Nov. 10, 1983), *reprinted on the CD-Rom accompanying this manual*; Dea, FTC Informal Staff Opinion Letter (Mar. 31, 1975), *reprinted on the CD-Rom accompanying this manual*; Dea, FTC Informal Staff Opinion Letter (May 1, 1974), *reprinted on the CD-Rom accompanying this manual*.

Earlier California statutory provision restricting the truthful reporting of eviction cases was held unconstitutional. U.D. Registry, Inc. v. California, 34 Cal. App. 4th 107, 40 Cal. Rptr. 2d 228 (1995). California, has amended its statute expressly to include tenant reports and to prohibit reporting eviction cases unless the lessor is the prevailing party or the monthly rent exceeds $1,000. *See* Cal. Civil Code §§ 1785.13(a) and 1786.18(a)(4) (West).

Accord Washington v. CSC Credit Servs., 199 F.3d 263 (5th Cir. 2000). *See* § 12.7.3, *infra*. *See also* Conley v. TRW Credit Data, 381 F. Supp. 473 (N.D. Ill. 1974); Prospective Tenant Report v. Department of State, 629 So. 2d 894 (Fla. Dist. Ct. App. 1993); Mary A. Bernard, Note, *Fair Credit Reporting Act*, 71 Minn. L. Rev. 1319, 1365 (1987).
144 FTC Official Staff Commentary § 603(d) item 4G, *reprinted at* Appx. D, *infra*.

Rent payment history affects one's credit standing and worthiness, and the amount of rent affects credit capacity and worthiness. The fact that a consumer's residence is rented instead of owned is relevant to creditworthiness[145] and mode of living. Information about roommates and companions, hours, rent withholding, noisiness, complaints to housing authorities, recreational and work activities, attitudes, and other subjective information sometimes found in reports on rental habits all may reflect on the consumer's character, reputation, personal characteristics, or mode of living. When personal or subjective information is included in a tenant report, the report may be an "investigative" consumer report as well.[146]

Tenant reports are also used for a purpose listed in the FCRA, but which purpose is less certain. Courts have generally relied on the conclusion that the reports involve consumer credit,[147] while the FTC has relied only on the fact that the reports relate to information used in a business transaction for personal, family or household purposes.[148]

The distinction is not without consequence, because the landlord's duty to give a notice of adverse action,[149] and a landlord's ability to use consumer reports for collection efforts,[150] vary depending on whether a lease is seen as credit or merely a business transaction. The distinction is also relevant to the definition of some investigative reports.[151]

At one time tenant screening companies were largely localized, but the companies are increasingly consolidating, such that an eviction or similar problem that occurred in one state may still find its way onto a report issued to a landlord in another.[152] A CRA that complies and maintains files on consumers on a nationwide basis relating to their residential or tenant history is a "nationwide specialty consumer reporting agency," a subclass of agency added to the FCRA by the FACTA amendments in 2003.[153]

2.3.6.4 Employment Reports

2.3.6.4.1 General

Consumer reports include reports for "establishing the consumer's eligibility for... employment purposes."[154] The definition of a consumer report additionally incorporates the section 1681b permissible purposes, which also mentions "employment purposes."[155] Although the definition of consumer reports arguably is limited to establishing the consumer's "eligibility" for employment, and section 1681b just mentions employment purposes, the two provisions can be read together harmoniously in light of the fairly broad definition of "employment purposes" at section 1681a(h).

The term "employment purposes" includes evaluations of the consumer for "employment, promotion, reassignment or retention as an employee."[156] However, certain reports of employee misconduct or compliance investigations are excluded from the definition of consumer report.[157]

The FTC staff has expanded on the statutory definition of employment purposes to include employers who are even "considering the possibility" of actions such as termination,[158] promotion, and those who are determining whether an employee should have security clearance to certain areas of the place of eligibility for employment.[159] But not all reports used for such purposes will be consumer reports, because the reporting entity may not fall within the definition of a CRA if a transaction is directly between the consumer and an entity.[160] Permissible employment uses of

---

145 Silbergeld, FTC Informal Staff Opinion Letter (Apr. 1, 1971), *reprinted on the CD-Rom accompanying this manual.*
146 *See* § 13.3.3, *infra.*
147 Cotto v. Jenney, 721 F. Supp. 5 (D. Mass. 1989) (potential risk of allowing the applicant to occupy the apartment relates to creditworthiness); Ferguson v. Park City Mobile Homes, 1989 WL 111916 (N.D. Ill. Sept. 18, 1989) (lease to be paid in installments is a credit transaction); Franco v. Kent Farm Vill., Clearinghouse No. 44,149 (D.R.I. Sept. 16, 1988) ("whether the tenant is going to be able to pay rent"). *See also* Harris v. Capital Growth Investors, 52 Cal. 3d 1142, 805 P.2d 873, 278 Cal. Rptr. 614 (1991); Dea, FTC Informal Staff Opinion Letter (Mar. 31, 1975), *reprinted on the CD-Rom accompanying this manual*; Dea, FTC Informal Staff Opinion Letter (May 1, 1974), *reprinted on the CD-Rom accompanying this manual.*
148 FTC Official Staff Commentary §§ 603(d) item 6F, 604(3)(E) item 3, 615 item 10, *reprinted at* Appx. D, *infra*; Long, FTC Informal Staff Opinion Letter (July 6, 2000), *reprinted on the CD-Rom accompanying this manual* (a typical residential lease does not involve credit and an attorney therefore does not have a permissible purpose to use a consumer report to collect a debt not reduced to judgment); Grimes, FTC Informal Staff Opinion Letter (Oct. 8, 1986), *reprinted on the CD-Rom accompanying this manual*; Brinckerhoff, FTC Informal Staff Opinion Letter (Nov. 10, 1983), *reprinted on the CD-Rom accompanying this manual. See also* Mary A. Bernard, Note, *Fair Credit Reporting Act*, 71 Minn. L. Rev. 1319, 1365 (1987).
149 *See* § 8.2, *supra.*
150 *See* §§ 7.2.7, 7.2.8.3, 7.4.4, *infra.*
151 *See* § 13.3.3, *infra.*

152 White v. First Am. Registry, 230 F.R.D. 365 (S.D.N.Y. Aug. 12, 2005).
153 15 U.S.C. § 1681a(w).
154 15 U.S.C. § 1681a(d)(1)(B). See § 13.3.2, *infra* for a discussion of investigative reports that are prepared for employment purposes.
155 15 U.S.C. § 1681a(d)(1)(c), *incorporating* § 1681b(a)(3)(B).
156 15 U.S.C. § 1681a(h). *See also* S. Rep. No. 185, 104th Cong., 1st Sess. at 35 (Dec. 14, 1995).
157 *See* § 2.3.6.4.2, *infra.*
158 Grimes, FTC Informal Staff Opinion Letter (Oct. 23, 1985), *reprinted on the CD-Rom accompanying this manual.*
159 FTC Official Staff Commentary § 603(h) item 2. *See also* Brinckerhoff, FTC Informal Staff Opinion Letter (July 24, 1986), *reprinted on the CD-Rom accompanying this manual.*
160 Hodge v. Texaco, Inc., 975 F.2d 1093 (5th Cir. 1992) (even though one of testers conveyed information from a third party, not a CRA because it was a one-time rather than a regular activity); Martinets v. Corning Cable Sys., L.L.C., 237 F. Supp.

§ 2.3.6.4.2 Fair Credit Reporting

consumer reports, and the requirements imposed on employers, are discussed elsewhere in this manual.[161]

2.3.6.4.2 Employment agency and employee misconduct investigation report exceptions

Despite the generally broad understanding of "employment purposes," the FCRA contains two significant exclusions. First, the FCRA excludes from the definition of "consumer report" much information provided by employment agencies.[162] Employment agencies are unlikely to be considered CRAs despite the nature and purpose of information they provide employers.[163] Second, certain reports of employee misconduct or compliance investigations are excluded from the definition of consumer report.[164] Both of these exclusions are discussed later in this chapter.

2.3.6.5 Insurance Reports

2.3.6.5.1 Insurance underwriting purposes

The term consumer report includes a report to establish the consumer's eligibility for insurance to be used primarily for personal, family, or household purposes.[165] In addition, the definition of a consumer report incorporates by reference the permissible purposes listed in section 1681b including the use of consumer reports "in connection with the underwriting of insurance involving the consumer." Section 1681b does not, however, contain a requirement that the insurance be for personal, family, or household purposes.[166]

Almost all courts read these two provisions dealing with insurance purposes together to retain the requirement that the insurance be for personal, family, or household purposes.[167] Thus, consumer reports are information collected, used, or expected to be used to determine whether personal insurance should be offered to an individual.

Reports issued to help an insurer decide to offer commercial risk insurance on an individual or a business are not covered.[168] This reading comports with language in the Senate report accompanying the Senate bill, which was enacted by both Houses of Congress: "The bill does not cover business credit or business insurance reports."[169]

In *Fernandez v. Retail Credit Corp.*,[170] information was used in connection with an application for insurance on the life of the president of a corporation, with the corporation named as beneficiary. The court looked to the legislative history of the Act[171] and the FTC's interpretation of the Act[172] and found that Congress did not intend to include applications for insurance for business purposes. The court also stated that the purposes explicitly listed in the definition of a consumer report are primary and must control when there is a conflict with the purposes which are incorporated by the reference to section 1681b. Of course, a report remains a consumer report if the information is first collected for purposes of consumer credit, insurance, or employment, and then later used for commercial insurance.[173]

2.3.6.5.2 Insurance claims reports

Information collected, used *and* expected to be used solely for purposes of considering insurance claims is not a consumer report.[174] Both the definition of consumer report

---

2d 717 (N.D. Tex. 2002) (report of results from a breathalyzer test does not constitute a "consumer report" because the results are based on a "transaction or experience" between the employee and the clinic performing the screening).

161 See § 7.2.4, *infra*.
162 See § 2.4.4.2, *infra*.
163 *Id*.
164 See § 2.4.4.1, *infra*.
165 15 U.S.C. § 1681a(d)(1)(A).
166 15 U.S.C. § 1681a(d)(1)(C), *incorporating* § 1681b(a)(3)(C).
167 See Cochran v. Metropolitan Life Ins. Co., 472 F. Supp. 827 (N.D. Ga. 1979). See also Hovater v. Equifax, Inc., 823 F.2d 413 (11th Cir. 1987); Hoke v. Retail Credit Corp., 521 F.2d 1079 (4th Cir. 1975). But cf. Fernandez v. Retail Credit Corp., 349 F. Supp. 652 (E.D. La. 1972).
168 FTC Official Staff Commentary § 603(d) item 6B, *reprinted at* Appx. D, *infra*; Conway, FTC Staff Opinion Letter (Mar. 30, 1971), *reprinted on the CD-Rom accompanying this manual.* Cf. Ippolito v. WNS, Inc., 864 F.2d 440 (7th Cir. 1988) (definition of consumer reports in connection with business transaction is limited to credit and insurance for personal, family or household purposes; employment purposes; and licensing or governmental benefits). See also Cochran v. Metropolitan Life Ins. Co., 472 F. Supp. 827 (N.D. Ga. 1979) (stating in dicta that requirement of personal, family, or household purposes is preserved).
169 S. Rep. No. 517, 91st Cong., 1st Sess. 1 (1969). See also 116 Cong. Rec. 36573 (Oct. 3, 1970) (statement of Congresswoman Sullivan) ("we always made clear that we were not interested in extending this law to credit reports for business credit or business insurance").
170 349 F. Supp. 652 (E.D. La. 1972).
171 116 Cong. Rec. H 10,052 (Oct. 13, 1970); ("bill does not cover business credit or business insurance reports"). See also Conference Report on H.R. 15073, 116 Cong. Rec. 36572 (Oct. 13, 1970) ("the purpose of the fair credit reporting bill is to protect consumers from inaccurate or arbitrary information in a consumer report, which is used as a factor in determining an individual's eligibility for credit, insurance or employment. It does not apply to reports utilized for business, commercial or professional purposes").
172 FTC, Compliance with the Fair Credit Reporting Act, at 21 (1977). See also Conway, FTC Informal Staff Opinion Letter (Mar. 30, 1971), *reprinted on the CD-Rom accompanying this manual.*
173 See § 2.3.5, *supra*. *Fernandez* is criticized in G. Allan Van Fleet, Note, *Judicial Construction of the Fair Credit Reporting Act: Scope of Civil Liability*, 76 Colum. L. Rev. 458 (1976) because the court did not consider the possibility, indeed likelihood, that the information provided by the defendant was originally collected for consumer reporting purposes and thus was a consumer report at the time it was disseminated without regard to the business nature of the transaction. See also Rasor v. Retail Credit Co., 87 Wash. 2d 516, 554 P.2d 1041 (1976).
174 St. Paul Guardian Ins. Co. v. Johnson, 884 F.2d 881 (5th Cir.

in section 1681a,[175] and the specific permissible insurance uses of consumer reports listed in section 1681b,[176] are limited to eligibility and underwriting issues.

Insurance claims reports also do not become consumer reports under the separate provision, discussed below, governing the use of reports that fulfill "a legitimate business need for the information in connection with a business transaction that is initiated by the consumer."[177] Certainly they fulfill a legitimate business need of the insurance company evaluating an accident report or claim, and an insurance contract is an insurer's business transaction often involving a consumer. Nevertheless, courts and the FTC generally hold otherwise that insurance claims reports are not covered by the business transaction provision.[178]

Some courts hold that the specific insurance-related provisions govern and are not altered by the incorporation of section 1681b with its more general reference to legitimate business purposes.[179] Other courts draw on the legislative history of the Act, noting that three proposed amendments to include claims reports in the Act's coverage were never enacted.[180] The FTC staff also argues that the issuance of insurance benefits, which is what claims reports are usually used for, is not a "business transaction involving the consumer."[181]

Nevertheless, if a claims report includes information originally collected for consumer reporting purposes, or if it originally was used (or even later is used) for underwriting purposes, it then becomes a consumer report.[182] An insurance claims exchange, comprised of a group of insurance underwriters and adjusters who exchange information on consumers' prior claims in determining eligibility for insurance, issues consumer reports.[183] Moreover, if state law specifically regulates insurance claims reports, the CRA and user will have to comply with that state law.[184]

2.3.6.6 Governmental Licenses and Benefits

Consumer reports include information used for "other purposes authorized under section 1681b,"[185] and section 1681b permits CRAs to provide consumer reports when used in connection with a "determination of the consumer's eligibility for a license or other benefit granted by a governmental instrumentality required by law to consider an applicant's financial responsibility or status."[186]

The Fourth Circuit interprets this portion of the definition of a consumer report broadly to include reports used to determine the consumer's eligibility for a government license, even where the government agency is *not* required by law to consider an applicant's financial responsibility or

---

1989); Hovater v. Equifax, Inc., 823 F.2d 413 (11th Cir. 1987); Dickison v. Wal-Mart Stores, Inc., 2006 WL 1371653 (D. Or. May 16, 2006); Cochran v. Metropolitan Life Ins. Co., 472 F. Supp. 827 (N.D. Ga. 1979); Kemp v. County of Orange, 211 Cal. App. 3d 1422, 260 Cal. Rptr. 131 (1989).

175 15 U.S.C. § 1681a(d)(1).
176 15 U.S.C. § 1681b(a)(3)(C). *See* § 7.2.5, *infra*.
177 15 U.S.C. § 1681a(d)(1)(C), *incorporating* § 1681b(a)(3)(F). *See* § 2.3.6.8, *infra*.
178 Yang v. Gov't Employees Ins. Co., 146 F.3d 1320 (11th Cir. 1998) (noting that the outcome in *Hovater* was "undoubtedly correct" but limiting it to reports that were used, collected and expected to be used for insurance claims purposes); Hovater v. Equifax Servs., Inc., 823 F.2d 413 (11th Cir. 1987); Houghton v. New Jersey Mfrs. Ins. Co., 795 F.2d 1144 (3d Cir. 1986); Cochran v. Metropolitan Life Ins. Co., 472 F. Supp. 827 (N.D. Ga. 1979); Kemp v. County of Orange, 260 Cal. Rptr. 131 (App. 1989); Indiana Ins. Co. v. Plummer Power Mower & Tool Rental, Inc., 590 N.E.2d 1085 (Ind. Ct. App. 1992); Kiblen v. Pickle, 653 P.2d 1338, 1342 (Wash. Ct. App. 1982); Kane, FTC Informal Staff Opinion Letter (Aug. 9, 1993), *reprinted on the CD-Rom accompanying this manual*; FTC Official Staff Commentary §§ 603(d) item 6C, 604(3)(E) items 1 and 3, *reprinted at* Appx. D, *infra*; Supplementary Information published with the Commentary, 55 Fed. Reg. 18,804, 18,806 (May 4, 1990), *reprinted at* Appx. D, *infra*; FTC, Compliance with the Fair Credit Reporting Act, at 46 (1977). *See also* Soto v. Indus. Comm., 18 Ariz. App. 53, 500 P.2d 313 (1972). *But see* Beresh v. Retail Credit Co., 358 F. Supp. 260 (C.D. Cal. 1973).
179 Cochran v. Metropolitan Life Ins. Co., 472 F. Supp. 827 (N.D. Ga. 1979). *See also* Houghton v. New Jersey Mfrs. Ins. Co., 795 F.2d 1144 (3d Cir. 1986); Kemp v. County of Orange, 260 Cal. Rptr. 131 (App. 1989); Indiana Ins. Co. v. Plummer Power Mower & Tool Rental, Inc., 590 N.E.2d 1085 (Ind. Ct. App. 1992); Kiblen v. Pickle, 653 P.2d 1338, 1342 (Wash. Ct. App. 1982); FTC Official Staff Commentary §§ 603(d) item 6C, 604(3)(E) items 1 and 3, *reprinted at* Appx. D, *infra*; Supplementary Information published with the Commentary, 55 Fed. Reg. 18,804, 18806 (May 4, 1990), *reprinted at* Appx. D, *infra*.
180 Kiblen v. Pickle, 653 P.2d 1338, 1341 (Wash. Ct. App. 1982). *See also* Hovater v. Equifax Servs., Inc., 823 F.2d 413 (11th Cir. 1987); Houghton v. New Jersey Mfrs. Ins. Co., 795 F.2d 1144 (3d Cir. 1986); Cochran v. Metropolitan Life Ins. Co., 472 F. Supp. 827 (N.D. Ga. 1979).
181 Brinckerhoff, FTC Informal Staff Opinion Letter (July 29, 1985), *reprinted on the CD-Rom accompanying this manual*; FTC, Compliance with the Fair Credit Reporting Act, at 46 (1977); Feldman, FTC Informal Staff Opinion Letter (Apr. 15, 1971), *reprinted on the CD-Rom accompanying this manual*. *Cf.* Grimes, FTC Informal Staff Opinion Letter (Aug. 3, 1984), *reprinted on the CD-Rom accompanying this manual*.
182 Yang v. Government Employees Ins. Co., 146 F.3d 1320 (11th Cir. 1998) (limiting the effect of Hovater v. Equifax, Inc., 823 F.2d 413 (11th Cir. 1987)); St. Paul Guardian Inc. Co. v. Johnson, 884 F.2d 881 (5th Cir. 1989); Ippolito v. WNS, Inc., 864 F.2d 440 (7th Cir. 1988); d'Entremont, FTC Informal Staff Opinion Letter (Jan. 25, 1996), *reprinted on the CD-Rom accompanying this manual*; Brinckerhoff, FTC Informal Staff Opinion Letter (Mar. 4, 1994), *reprinted on the CD-Rom accompanying this manual. See* FTC Official Staff Commentary § 603(d) items 5C, 6C, § 603(f) item 5, *reprinted at* Appx. D, *infra*.
183 Grimes, FTC Informal Staff Opinion Letter (Apr. 30, 1986), *reprinted on the CD-Rom accompanying this manual. See also* FTC Official Staff Commentary § 603(f) item 5, *reprinted at* Appx. D, *infra*.
184 *See, e.g.*, Minn. Stat. § 72A.496.
185 15 U.S.C. § 1681a(d)(1)(c).
186 15 U.S.C. § 1681b(a)(3)(D).

§ 2.3.6.7   *Fair Credit Reporting*

status in determining whether to grant the license.[187] The specific requirements of section 1681b determine whether the use of the consumer report is permissible. But as to the threshold question of whether the information is a consumer report, the definition of a consumer report incorporates "only the general subject matter" of section 1681b and not "all the minutiae."[188] In other words, if information otherwise meets the definition of consumer report and is used for a general purpose set out in 1681b, it will be considered a consumer report even if its use does not comply with all of the requirements of section 1681b.

One court has found that a consumer report did not include information circulated among various adoption agencies used to determine the consumer's eligibility to adopt a child, despite the fact that courts were required by law to consider the financial responsibility of potential adoptive parents. The court viewed consumer reports as applying only to information collected and used for the purpose of affecting commercial decisions, and did not apply to information held by adoption agencies that were in effect social services agencies removed from the commercial world.[189]

An argument against this rationale is that the FCRA applies to government agencies when they act as employers, creditors, or insurers, and that there is no exception in those cases for the noncommercial nature of the government. Additionally, the governmental-license permissible purpose provision applies to benefits as well as licenses, and to decisions based on financial status as well as financial responsibility. Therefore, it should include the government agency determinations of eligibility for public assistance, Medicare, and other benefits based on financial need. Certainly, those are not commercial in nature. Whether adoption is such a "benefit" is a separate question.

2.3.6.7 Risk Assessment of Current Obligations

Another purpose incorporated into the definition of consumer report by the cross-reference to section 1681b is the use of reports by a person who "intends to use the information as a potential investor or servicer, or current insurer, in connection with a valuation of, or an assessment of the credit or prepayment risks associated with, an existing credit obligation."[190]

Consumer credit accounts are bought and sold in the marketplace by investors. Consumer home mortgages are often serviced by specialty companies who bill and collect monthly payments and manage related escrow accounts.[191] Insurers sometimes underwrite large blocks of such investments. Information on consumers is a consumer report if it is collected and used for the purpose of valuation or assessment of credit risk or prepayment risks before purchasing a consumer debt obligation or agreeing to service it.

Note that the risk assessment provision is separate from the credit provision that allows creditors to use consumer reports for the purpose of reviewing an existing credit account.[192] The risk assessment provision governs the use of consumer reports by third parties who generally do not have a direct transactional relationship with the consumer.

2.3.6.8 Legitimate Business Need for Information

One of the potentially broadest types of information incorporated into the definition of consumer report is information for which a person "otherwise has a legitimate business need" in one of two situations: "(i) in connection with a business transaction that is initiated by the consumer; or (ii) to review an account to determine whether the consumer continues to meet the terms of the account."[193]

The legitimate business need provision is discussed in detail in § 7.2.8, *infra*, concerning permissible uses of consumer reports. This subsection will merely highlight the role that the provision plays in the definition of consumer report.

The main thrust of this provision is to include within the definition of consumer report information provided on consumer transactions other than credit, employment, or insurance that otherwise are consistent with the FCRA's scope and purposes.[194] Examples from the FTC Staff Commentary of business transactions that are not necessarily considered credit, but are covered by the Act include consumers applying to rent an apartment, offering to pay for goods with a check, applying for a checking account or similar service, seeking to be included in a computer dating service, or those who have sought and received over-payments of government benefits that they are refusing to return.[195] Thus,

---

187 Hoke v. Retail Credit Corp., 521 F.2d 1079 (4th Cir. 1975). *Cf.* Grimes, FTC Informal Staff Opinion Letter (Mar. 7, 1986), *reprinted on the CD-Rom accompanying this manual* (board of law examiners has permissible purpose to obtain consumer reports where court rules require board to consider applicants' qualifications for admission, even though they do not specifically require consideration of financial responsibility).

188 Hoke v. Retail Credit Corp., 521 F.2d 1079, 1083 (4th Cir. 1975).

189 Porter v. Talbot Perkins Children's Servs., 355 F. Supp. 174 (S.D.N.Y. 1973).

190 15 U.S.C. § 1681b(a)(3)(E), *as amended by* Pub. L. No. 104-208

§ 2403, 110 Stat. 3009 (Sept. 30, 1996).

191 *See* National Consumer Law Center, Foreclosures Chs. 4A, 5, 6 (2005 and Supp.).

192 15 U.S.C. § 1681b(a)(3)(A). *See* § 2.3.6.2, *supra*, § 7.2.8.3, *infra*.

193 15 U.S.C. § 1681b(a)(3)(F). *See* 15 U.S.C. § 1681a(d).

194 Tatelbaum, FTC Informal Staff Opinion Letter (July 26, 2000), *reprinted on the CD-Rom accompanying this manual*; Williams v. AT&T Wireless Serv., Inc., 5 F. Supp. 2d 1142 (W.D. Wash. 1998) (finding that a business transaction involving a consumer must be similar to or associated with the other transactions listed in the Act).

195 FTC Official Staff Commentary § 604(3)(E) item 3, *reprinted at* Appx. D, *infra*.

reports collected or used for those purposes are consumer reports.[196] Residential leasing and check writing are sometimes also considered to be credit transactions, but the business need provision ensures that reports used in those transactions will fall under the FCRA regardless how they are characterized.[197] Other examples are discussed in Chapter 7, *infra*.[198]

Nonetheless, if information used in any business transaction involving a consumer is considered a consumer report, this provision has the potential to override the more limited terms of other provisions. For example, the credit provision is limited to personal, family, or household credit, and the insurance provision is limited to eligibility and underwriting. But neither of those limitations appear in the business need provision, which could arguably make any information provided to creditors or insurers a consumer report, even business reports that Congress clearly meant to exclude.

To avoid this result, courts have found that the specific credit, insurance, and employment provisions are "primary," and override the more general business need provision when the two are in conflict.[199] The FTC Staff Commentary takes the same position.[200]

Some courts have even stated that the business need provision should not be considered at all when determining whether information is a consumer report.[201] That is, the business need provision retains force to set out a permissible use of consumer reports, but it is not incorporated into the definition of consumer report.[202]

This approach is squarely rejected by the FTC Staff Commentary, and ignores the plan language of the statute.[203] It also reduces the courts' flexibility to deal with reports collected and used for tenants, check cashing, personal property leases, or other areas where credit or insurance may not be involved, but the purposes of the FCRA should apply.[204] There seems little reason for courts to read all these situations out of the FCRA's coverage of consumer reports.

It is noteworthy that the decisions that read the business need provision out of the definition of consumer report were all issued before 1996, when the provision was even broader and applied to any business transaction "involving" the consumer. In 1996, the provision was amended to apply only to business transactions "originated by" the consumer.[205]

Moreover, the superficially broad business need permissible purpose has been limited in ways that lessen the concern about incorporating it into the definition of consumer report. These limitations are discussed in Chapter 7, *infra*, and are only summarized here.

First, the business need provision has generally been interpreted to apply only to transactions or accounts that the consumer enters into for personal, family, or household purposes.[206] This is consistent with the legislative history that consumer reports do not include reports issued for business transactions,[207] and also with the interpretation of the credit and insurance provisions.[208] That is, a transaction is a "business" one from the point of view of the retailer or service provider but not from the perspective of the consumer.[209]

Second, the FTC has generally, though not completely consistently, interpreted the first subpart of the business need provision—"in connection with a business transaction that is initiated by the consumer"[210]—to permit use of consumer

---

196 FTC Official Staff Commentary § 603(d) items 6E, 6F, *reprinted at* Appx. D, *infra*. *See also* Estiverne v. Saks Fifth Avenue & JBS, 9 F.3d 1171 (5th Cir. 1993) (report used for check cashing is a consumer report).

197 *See* § 7.2.8, *infra*. The distinction does not matter for purposes of deciding whether the information is a consumer report, but it does matter when the report is used for collection purposes. *See* § 7.2.3.4, *infra*.

198 *See* § 7.2.8, *infra*. *See also* Williams v. AT&T Wireless Serv., Inc., 5 F. Supp. 2d 1142 (W.D. Wash. 1998) (whether the consumer could pay for cellular phone is similar to other permissible purposes even though no credit involved).

199 *See* Fernandez v. Retail Credit Corp., 349 F. Supp. 652 (E.D. La. 1972); Ippolito v. WNS, Inc., 864 F.2d 440 (7th Cir. 1988).

200 FTC Official Staff Commentary § 604(3)(E) item 1, *reprinted at* Appx. D, *infra*.

201 *See* Mone v. Dranow, 945 F.2d 306 (9th Cir. 1991); Ippolito v. WNS, Inc. 864 F.2d 440 (7th Cir. 1988); Houghton v. New Jersey Mfrs. Ins. Co., 795 F.2d 1144 (3d Cir. 1986); Arcidiacono v. American Express Co., 1993 WL 94327 (D.N.J. Mar. 29, 1993); Zeller v. Samia, 758 F. Supp. 775 (D. Mass. 1991); Ley v. Boron Oil Co., 419 F. Supp. 1240 (W.D. Pa. 1976); G. Allan Van Fleet, Note, *Judicial Construction of the Fair Credit Reporting Act: Scope of Civil Liability*, 76 Colum. L. Rev. 458 (1976). *Cf.* Greenway v. Information Dynamics, Ltd., 524 F.2d 1145 (9th Cir. 1975) (dissent, Wright J.).

202 *See* Ippolito v. WNS, Inc., 864 F.2d 440 (7th Cir. 1988) (noting that one way to read these two sections is to give § 1681a primacy when definitions are at issue, and § 1681b primacy when misuse is at issue).

203 FTC Official Staff Commentary § 603(d) items 6D, 6E, *reprinted at* Appx. D, *infra*; Houghton v. New Jersey Mfrs. Ins. Co., 795 F.2d 1144, 1150 (3d Cir. 1986) (Sloviter, J dissenting). This approach also provides no explanation why the same courts are willing to consider government licensing and benefits purposes, which are also found in section 1681b, in the definition of consumer report. *See* Ippolito v. WNS, Inc.; 864 F.2d 440, 451 (7th Cir. 1988).

204 For example, in Arcidiacono v. American Express Co., 1993 WL 94327 (D.N.J. Mar. 29, 1993), a company compiled and sold lists of consumers whose spending habits implied that they would be likely to respond to direct mail solicitations for merchandise. Since the court found that the use did not relate to credit, employment, insurance or benefits, the FCRA did not apply.

205 For a discussion of the effect of this change, see § 7.2.8.2.2.1, *infra*.

206 *See* § 7.2.8.2.2.1, *infra*.

207 *See* § 2.3.6.2, *supra*.

208 *See* §§ 2.3.6.3, 2.3.6.5, *supra*.

209 *See* Fernandez v. Retail Credit Corp., 349 F. Supp. 652 (E.D. La. 1972).

210 15 U.S.C. § 1681b(a)(3)(F)(i).

reports only for eligibility decisions.[211] This interpretation is consistent with most of the examples given in the FTC Staff Commentary.[212]

The second subpart allows use of reports after eligibility has been established, "to review an account to determine whether the consumer continues to meet the terms of the account."[213] But reports that are collected, expected to be used *and* actually used in connection with stages of a business transaction other than eligibility or account review would not be considered consumer reports. For example, litigation is not a permissible use of consumer reports under the business need provision, and reports collected and used solely for litigation (which do not otherwise meet the definition of consumer report) would not be consumer reports.[214] The scope of the business need provision is discussed further at § 7.2.8, *infra*.[215]

2.3.6.9 Government Determination of Child Support Payment Levels

Consumer reports include information used for "other purposes authorized under section 604 [15 U.S.C. § 1681b],"[216] and the final purpose in that section permits CRAs to release consumer reports to government officials to use for the purpose of establishing a person's capacity to make child support payments or to determine the level of child support awards.[217] Thus, financial information or other information bearing on creditworthiness, mode of living, or other FCRA factors is a consumer report if it is collected or provided to government officials for child support purposes. This permissible purpose does not extend to private individuals, and does not encompass reports to assist in establishing paternity.

2.4 Statutory Exemptions to Definition of Consumer Report

2.4.1 Overview

The FCRA statutorily excludes a number of reports from coverage under the FCRA, which otherwise would meet the definition of consumer report. These include first-hand experience information, information shared by affiliated companies, certain reports by employment agencies, and a credit card issuer's communication to a merchant of approval of a transaction. When determining FCRA coverage, these statutory exemptions must be considered.

2.4.2 Where Report Based on First-Hand Experience

The definition of a consumer report excludes information reported by a person or company whose own experience with the consumer is reflected in the information.[218] This information is sometimes termed "experience information."[219]

To be excluded as experience information, the information must relate *solely* to the person's or company's first-hand experience with the consumer.[220] For example, there is

---

211 *See* § 7.2.8.2.2.2, *infra*.
212 FTC Official Staff Commentary § 603(d) items 6D, 6E, § 604(3)(E) item 3, *reprinted at* Appx. D, *infra*. *See also* Williams v. AT&T Wireless Serv., Inc., 5 F. Supp. 2d 1142 (W.D. Wash. 1998) (whether the consumer could pay for cellular phone is similar to other permissible purposes even though no credit involved). The one example listed in the Commentary that does not fit the eligibility mold is consumers who have sought and received over-payments of government benefits that they are refusing to return.
213 15 U.S.C. § 1681b(a)(3)(F)(ii).
214 *See* § 7.4.4, *infra*.
215 15 U.S.C. § 1681a(d)(1)(C).
216 15 U.S.C. § 1681b(a)(4) and (5).
217 15 U.S.C. § 1681a(d)(2)(A)(i); DiGianni v. Stern's, 26 F.3d 346 (2d Cir. 1994); Hodge v. Texaco, Inc., 975 F.2d 1093 (5th Cir. 1992) (lab reports based on first-hand test not within FCRA); Garcia v. UnionBanCal Corp., 2006 WL 2619330 (N.D. Cal. Sept. 12, 2006) (bank's information on customer's accounts was first-hand experience information); Jonas v. International Airline Employees F.C.U., 2006 WL 1409721 (S.D.N.Y. May 19, 2006 S.D.N.Y); Lema v. Citibank (South Dakota), N.A., 935 F. Supp. 695 (D. Md. 1996); Podell v. Citicorp Diners Club, Inc., 859 F. Supp. 701 (S.D.N.Y. 1994); Oldroyd v. Associates Consumer Disc. Co., 863 F. Supp. 237 (E.D. Pa. 1994); Miranda-Rivera v. Bank One, 145 F.R.D. 614 (D. P.R. 1993); Chube v. Exxon Chem. Am., 760 F. Supp. 557 (M.D. La. 1991) (lab reports based on first-hand text not within FCRA); Nisenfeld v. American Express Co., 1989 WL 87017 (D. Md. July 28, 1989); Nuttleman v. Vossberg, 585 F. Supp. 133 (D. Neb. 1984); Rush v. Macy's New York, Inc., 596 F. Supp. 1540 (S.D. Fla. 1984), *aff'd*, 775 F.2d 1554 (11th Cir. 1985); Nikou v. INB Nat'l Bank, 638 N.E.2d 448 (Ind. Ct. App. 1994); Laracuente v. Laracuente, 252 N.J. Super. 384, 599 A.2d 968 (1991). *See* Moore v. Beneficial Nat'l Bank USA, 876 F. Supp. 1247 (M.D. Ala. 1995). *See also* Freeman v. Southern Nat'l Bank, 531 F. Supp. 94 (S.D. Tex. 1982); Grimes, FTC Informal Staff Opinion Letter (July 7, 1992), *reprinted on the CD-Rom accompanying this manual*; Fitzpatrick, FTC Informal Staff Opinion Letter (Mar. 8, 1985), *reprinted on the CD-Rom accompanying this manual*; Meyer, FTC Informal Staff Opinion Letter (June 21, 1983), *reprinted on the CD-Rom accompanying this manual. Cf.* Landrum v. Board of Commissioners, 758 F. Supp. 387 (E.D. La. 1991) (denying lab's action to dismiss FCRA claim).
218 American Bankers Ass'n v. Gould, 412 F.3d 1081 (9th Cir. 2005).
219 *See* FTC Official Staff Commentary § 603(d) item 7A(3), *reprinted at* Appx. D, *infra* (it may include opinion information such as "slow pay").
220 FTC Official Staff Commentary § 603(d) item 7A(2), *reprinted at* Appx. D, *infra*. *See* Nunnally v. Equifax Info. Servs., 451 F.3d 768 (11th Cir. 2006) (letters sent by CRA describing results of CRA's reinvestigations were not excluded as first-hand experience information because reinvestigations concerned consumers' experiences with third party creditors). *But see* § 2.4.3,

still a consumer report if a creditor or an insurance company reports the reasons for canceling credit or insurance, but such cancellation is based on information from an outside source.[221] Similarly, if a bank reports information gained from credit applications about experiences with others, that information is not the first-hand experience of the bank and it would be a consumer report when furnished to someone else.[222] If the report contains information in addition to first-hand experience, it is a consumer report.[223] Also, if first-hand experience information is then passed on to a third party, and the third party disseminates that information, a consumer report is involved.

The FTC Staff Commentary indicates that the first-hand experience exemption applies to reports that include opinions about the consumer (e.g., slow pay), but only if the facts underlying the opinions involve only transactions or experiences between the consumer and the reporting entity.[224] Thus a consumer report is involved where a creditor or employer reports to a third party its opinion of the consumer where that opinion is in part based on information the creditor or employer received from another source.

The purpose of the statutory exception is to allow persons doing business with the consumer (such as retail stores, hospitals, present and former employers, banks, mortgage servicing companies, credit unions, or universities[225]) to provide first-hand experience information to consumer reporting agencies (CRAs) without becoming CRAs themselves under the Act.[226] Unfortunately, this means that users (except for creditors and certain affiliated companies[227]) of experience information will not have to inform consumers that a denial or other adverse action was based on information reported directly from the company involved in the transaction with the consumer. It also means that there are no explicit standards as to permissible dissemination of such information.

Nevertheless, a party reporting its own experience with the consumer has a duty to provide full, accurate, and truthful information. It may be liable in deceit or negligent misrepresentation to someone who relies on the information provided.[228]

An interesting issue arises as to whether this exception for reporting one's own experience with a consumer applies to a creditor (or other party) who passes on information about an individual with whom the creditor *thinks* it has experience, but in fact does not. The Eleventh Circuit has applied the exception where another individual forged the consumer's application to a creditor, and the creditor reported the consumer's delinquency on the account. The consumer did not really have an account, but the creditor believed the consumer did.[229] This result can be criticized as failing to

---

infra regarding information sharing between affiliated companies.

221 Novak, FTC Informal Staff Opinion Letter (Sept. 9, 1998), *reprinted on the CD-Rom accompanying this manual*. However, one court has held that identifying information about the consumer, such as a Social Security number or address, is still considered first-hand experience information. Garcia v. Union-BanCal Corp., 2006 WL 2619330 (N.D. Cal. Sept. 12, 2006)

222 *See* Owner-Operator Indep. Driver Ass'n v. USIS Comm. Servs., Inc., 410 F. Supp. 2d 1005 (D. Colo. 2005) (completed "Termination Report" forms sent by employers to CRA not exempted from treatment as consumer reports, because forms were alleged to have contained information in addition to the first-hand experience of employers).

223 FTC Official Staff Commentary § 603(d) item 7A(3), *reprinted at* Appx. D, *infra*.

224 *Id.* item 7A(1).

225 *See* H.R. Rep. No. 1587, 91st Cong., 2d Sess. 28 (1970), *reprinted in* 1970 U.S.C.C.A.N. 4411, 4414 (protective bulletins issued by local trade associations excluded); Brinckerhoff, FTC Informal Staff Opinion Letter (Aug. 14, 1987), *reprinted on the CD-Rom accompanying this manual* (company that stores bad account information for credit card issuers who are customers of the company is not CRA); Brinckerhoff, FTC Informal Staff Opinion Letter (Jan. 28, 1987), *reprinted on the CD-Rom accompanying this manual* (insurer's disclosure to a CRA of its payment of a claim on a defaulted mortgage is not a consumer report); Grimes, FTC Informal Staff Opinion Letter (May 13, 1986), *reprinted on the CD-Rom accompanying this manual* (where stockbrokers are employed by a company and obtain information about the company's brokerage customers who are interested in obtaining residential mortgage loans from the company, neither company nor stockbrokers are subject to FCRA); Brinckerhoff, FTC Informal Staff Opinion Letter (June 11, 1985), *reprinted on the CD-Rom accompanying this manual* (a company servicing loans for the creditor may report its experiences with consumers, such as delinquencies, to others); Isaac, FTC Informal Staff Opinion Letter (Sept. 25, 1974), *reprinted on the CD-Rom accompanying this manual* (list of "bad check artists" wanted for criminal violations is not a consumer report); Grimes, FTC Informal Staff Opinion Letter (Sept. 5, 1973), *reprinted on the CD-Rom accompanying this manual* (check cashing lists are not excluded "protective bulletins" unless everyone on list has current warrant outstanding, company that furnishes such list is CRA); Feldman, FTC Informal Staff Opinion Letter (July 15, 1971), *reprinted on the CD-Rom accompanying this manual* ("protective bulletins" not covered by Act if purpose is to "warn potential victims of habits, practices and descriptions of alleged check forgers, swindlers and other criminals for whom arrest warrants are outstanding").

226 *See* §§ 2.4.3, 3.3.1.6, *infra*.

227 MSA Tubular Prods. Inc. v. First Bank & Trust Co., 869 F.2d 1422, 1424 (10th Cir. 1989); Ostlund Chem. Co. v. Norwest Bank, 417 N.W.2d 833, 836–837 (N.D. 1988). A creditor reporting inaccurate information may also be liable under a state law prohibiting reporting of inaccurate credit information, such as Conn. Gen. Stat. §§ 36a-645 to 36a-699e and Conn. Reg. State Agencies § 36-243c-6i. See Appendix H, *infra*, for a summary of state credit reporting laws.

228 Smith v. First Nat'l Bank of Atlanta, 837 F.2d 1575 (11th Cir. 1988). *See also* DiGianni v. Stern's, 26 F.3d 346 (2d Cir. 1994) (analogous fact patterns, but neither litigants nor court recognized issue); Lewis v. Ohio Prof'l Elec. Network L.L.C., 190 F. Supp. 2d 1049 (S.D. Ohio 2002); Miranda-Rivera v. Bank One, 145 F.R.D. 614 (D. P.R. 1993); Podell v. Citicorp Diners Club, Inc., 859 F. Supp. 701 (S.D.N.Y. 1994); Alvarez Melendez v. Citibank, 705 F. Supp. 67 (D. P.R. 1988).

229 15 U.S.C. § 1681a(d)(2)(A)(ii) and (iii). This exclusion was added by the 1996 Reform Act. Pub. L. No. 104-208 § 2402,

consider the statute's plain language limiting the exclusions to reports of information about one's experience with *the consumer*.

2.4.3 Information Shared by Affiliates

2.4.3.1 Types of Affiliate Sharing Excluded from Definition of Consumer Report

Information communicated between persons related by common ownership or affiliated by corporate control is excluded from the definition of a consumer report.[230] There are two types of information shared by affiliates that are excluded from coverage as consumer reports.

The first type is information based on first-hand experience of one of the affiliates.[231] This exception is like the first-hand experience exception, which generally permits anyone to report one's own experience with the consumer without being considered a consumer report.[232] However, in the context of affiliates, the effect is also to exempt from the definition of consumer report any communication of first-hand experience among affiliates even if the information is communicated through other related entities, and not directly by the affiliate that dealt with the consumer.[233]

The second exclusion is any other information shared by affiliates, provided that the sharing is disclosed to the consumer and the consumer is given the opportunity to direct that the information not be shared with related entities.[234] Thus, information gathered from third parties, even from CRAs, may be shared among affiliates. It must be clearly and conspicuously disclosed to the consumer that the information about the consumer may be communicated to a related entity. Additionally, the consumer must be given prior opportunity to opt out and direct that the information not be shared.[235] Finally, an affiliate must give notice if adverse action is taken based on the shared information.[236]

A common example of affiliate sharing occurs when a bank shares information about account holders and other customers with insurance or investment brokers and sellers affiliated with the bank. The bank may freely share customer lists and information relating to a customer's account. As first-hand information, no disclosure to the consumer is required. However, the bank could also share information about a consumer's personal finances and transactions with other creditors gleaned from the consumer's application for credit submitted to the bank, such as lists of a consumer's assets and liabilities with other entities. Because this information is not first-hand experience of the bank, the bank must give the consumer both prior notice that this kind of information may be shared with an affiliate and an opportunity to opt out of the sharing.[237]

This exclusion from the definition of consumer reports is potentially so broad that many purposes of the FCRA may be undermined. As financial institutions expand and merge, and nationwide conglomerates come to dominate credit and other markets, less and less information about consumers will be subject to the FCRA. Indeed, a likelihood exists that many banking establishments could establish their own in-house CRAs free from the consumer and privacy protections and other strictures of the FCRA.

Despite the breadth of this exclusion, the FCRA does impose some obligations on affiliates sharing information. Primarily, affiliates that share information must provide opportunities for consumers to opt out, discussed below. In addition, affiliates are required to send notices when taking an adverse action on the basis of information shared by affiliates.[238] They are also required to disclose, upon written request of the consumer, the nature of the information shared by the affiliates.[239]

2.4.3.2 Right to Opt Out from Affiliate Sharing

2.4.3.2.1 Two opt-out rights for affiliate sharing

There are two separate provisions in the FCRA that permit consumers to opt out of affiliate sharing. The first right applies only to information shared between affiliates that is gathered from third parties, i.e., is not first-hand experience information. The second right, added by the 2003 FACTA amendments, permits consumers to opt out of affiliate sharing for marketing purposes. This opt out right applies to both types of affiliate sharing information, i.e., it applies to affiliates sharing both first-hand experience and third party information.[240] This newer opt-out provision

---

[110] Stat. 3009 (Sept. 30, 1996). *See also* §§ 3.3.1.6, 3.3.6, 6.4.5, 8.2.7.5, 8.2.18, *infra*. Affiliates that share information are also excluded under the FCRA from the responsibilities of furnishers of information. *See* § 6.2.2.1, *infra*.

[230] 15 U.S.C. § 1681a(d)(2)(A)(ii).

[231] *See* § 2.4.2, *supra*.

[232] However, if the information is subsequently communicated by the affiliate who did not have the first-hand experience to an entity outside of the corporate family, it becomes a consumer report. Lewis v. Ohio Prof'l Elec. Network L.L.C., 190 F. Supp. 2d 1049 (S.D. Ohio 2002).

[233] 15 U.S.C. § 1681a(d)(2)(A)(iii).

[234] *See* § 2.4.3.2, Ch. 8, *infra*.

[235] *See* § 8.2.7.5, *infra*.

[236] Novak, FTC Informal Staff Opinion Letter (Sept. 9, 1998), *reprinted on the CD-Rom accompanying this manual*.

[237] *See* § 8.2.7.5, *infra*.

[238] *See* § 3.3.1.6, *infra*.

[239] 15 U.S.C. § 1681s-3.

[240] Both the FTC and the banking regulators have noted these opt out rights are separate. *See* Federal Trade Commission, Supplementary Information to Proposed Rule, 69 Fed. Reg. 33,324, 33,325 (June 15, 2004); Supplementary Information to Proposed Rule, 69 Fed. Reg. 42,502, 42,503 (July 15, 2004).

does not supersede or replace the older opt-out right, although there is some overlap between the two opt-out requirements.[241]

2.4.3.2.2 Opt-out right for affiliate sharing of third party information

Consumers must be notified of their right to opt out of affiliate sharing of third party information, along with the fact that the affiliate sharing will occur.[242] This disclosure is built into the definition of the affiliate-sharing exclusion for third party information; failure to provide this notice will disqualify the shared information from the exclusion and render it a consumer report.[243] The disclosure must be clear and conspicuous, and the opportunity to direct that the information not be communicated among affiliates must occur before the information is communicated.[244] Otherwise, however, the FCRA does not specify any procedures, forms, or language for this disclosure. This lack of specific statutory direction was a potential source of uncertainty.

In 2000, the FTC proposed interpretations of the terms and provisions of the affiliate opt-out exclusion;[245] these proposed interpretations were never finalized by the FTC. Under the proposed interpretations, "clear and conspicuous" would mean "reasonably understandable and ... designed to call attention to the nature and significance of the information."[246] The proposed interpretations provide examples of both "reasonably understandable" and "designed to call attention," and provide additional guidance as to what those terms might mean if the notice were to be posted on a company's website.[247] The proposed interpretations describe the content of a complying opt-out notice and further provide that a "reasonable opportunity to opt out" should extend for a period of at least thirty days.[248] Significantly, the proposed interpretations provided that, if a consumer opts out, the company must comply with the opt-out "as soon as reasonably practicable" after the company receives it.[249] Thereafter, the opt-out remains effective until revoked. The FTC provided a model notice.[250] The federal banking regulators issued similar proposed regulations on affiliate sharing.[251]

2.4.3.2.3 Opt-out right for affiliate sharing for marketing purposes

The opt-out right added by the FACTA amendments to the FCRA in 2003 specifically addresses affiliate sharing only with respect to marketing purposes. Consumers can prohibit an affiliate from using information for solicitation for marketing purposes when that information avoids being a consumer report, whether the information is first-hand experience information or third party information, due to the affiliate exceptions.[252] The right to opt out of such solicitations lasts for only five years, but can be renewed.[253] The user of the information must clearly and conspicuously disclose to consumers that affiliate information may be used for making solicitations and must provide the consumer with an opportunity to opt out and a simple method for doing so.[254]

However, a number of solicitations are exempted from this opt-out right, including: (i) solicitations by an entity that has a preexisting business relationship with the consumer; (ii) solicitations to facilitate communications to an individual to whom the entity provides employment benefit or similar services; and (iii) solicitations to perform services on behalf of an affiliate.[255]

The FTC, the banking agencies,[256] and the Securities and Exchange Commission have rulemaking authority with respect to this affiliate marketing opt-out right.[257] Pursuant to this authority, these agencies have issued proposed rules that in general prohibit a company from using certain information received from an affiliate to market products or services to a consumer, unless the consumer first has been given notice and an opportunity to opt out of receiving such solicitations.[258] As of October 2006, the agencies have not yet issued a final rule.

---

241 15 U.S.C. § 1681a(d)(2)(A)(iii).
242 See § 8.2.18.1, infra.
243 15 U.S.C. § 1681a(d)(2)(A)(iii).
244 65 Fed. Reg. 80,802 (Dec. 22, 2000). The proposal would add an Appendix B to 16 C.F.R. Part 600, entitled Commentary on the Amended Fair Credit Reporting Act (Affiliate Information Sharing). A copy of these proposed interpretations are reproduced on the CD-Rom accompanying this manual.
245 Id.
246 Id.
247 Id.
248 Id.
249 Id.
250 65 Fed. Reg. 80,809 (Dec. 22, 2000).
251 15 U.S.C. § 1681s-3.

252 15 U.S.C. § 1681s-3(a)(3).
253 15 U.S.C. § 1681s-3(a)(1). See § 8.2.18, infra.
254 15 U.S.C. § 1681s-3(a)(4). However, if using information on behalf of an affiliate, the person may not send solicitations on such affiliate's behalf if the consumer has opted out of marketing solicitations by that affiliate. 15 U.S.C. § 1681s-3(a)(4)(C).
255 The banking agencies are the Office of the Comptroller of the Currency, the Federal Reserve Board, the Federal Deposit Ins. Corp., the Office of Thrift Supervision, and the National Credit Union Administration.
256 This rulemaking authority was included in an uncodified section of FACTA. FACTA, Pub. L. No. 108-159, § 214(b) (2003).
257 See 69 Fed. Reg. 33,324 (June 15, 2004); 69 Fed. Reg. 42,502 (July 15, 2004). See § 8.2.18, infra.
258 15 U.S.C. § 1681t(b)(2). See § 10.7.6, infra. The only exception is that Vermont laws on affiliated sharing are specifically grandfathered and not preempted. Id.

2.4.3.2.4 Preemption of state regulation of affiliate sharing

The states are preempted from regulating the sharing of information between affiliates[259] or the use of information shared by affiliates for marketing purposes.[260] However, the Ninth Circuit has held that the FCRA preempts state laws on affiliate sharing only to the extent that they apply to information that falls within the FCRA's definition of "consumer report."[261] Preemption of state laws on affiliate sharing is more fully discussed at § 10.7.6, *infra*.

2.4.4 Certain Employment Reports

2.4.4.1 Employee Misconduct Investigation Reports

The FCRA was amended in 2003 by FACTA to exclude from the definition of consumer report certain communications made to an employer concerning investigations for employee misconduct or for compliance reasons from the definition of a "consumer report."[262] Under this exclusion, even if a particular report would otherwise be a consumer report, it will fall outside of the definition by virtue of being specifically excluded.[263] To be excluded, the communication must be made to an employer and must be in connection with an investigation of one of the following:[264]

- Suspected misconduct relating to employment;
- Compliance with federal, state, or local laws;
- Compliance with the rules of a self-regulatory organization; or
- Compliance with the preexisting written policies of the employer.

To limit the exclusion's scope, the FCRA further requires that the communication must *not* be for the purpose of investigating a consumer's creditworthiness, credit standing, or credit capacity (in other words, the communication must only bear on the employee's character, general reputation, personal characteristics, or mode of living). These limitations appear designed so that consumer credit reports from credit bureaus will not fall within the exclusion. However, one court has held that even a traditional credit report is not considered to be a consumer report as a result of this provision, if it is used in connection with an employee misconduct investigation.[265]

To fall within this exclusion, the report must only be provided to the employer (or the employer's agent), a governmental authority, or a self-regulatory organization with regulatory authority over the employer, and to no one else.[266] The FCRA defines a self-regulatory organization to be "any self-regulatory organization (as defined in section 3(a)(26) of the Securities Exchange Act of 1934),[267] any entity established under title I of the Sarbanes-Oxley Act of 2002,[268] any board of trade designated by the Commodity Futures Trading Commission, and any futures association registered with such Commission."[269]

The FCRA does maintain some regulation over employee misconduct investigation reports, notwithstanding that they are not "consumer reports." An employer who takes any adverse action based in whole or in part on the exempted communication must disclose to the consumer a summary of the communication, although the employer need not disclose any sources of information for use in preparing what would be, except for the exception, an investigative consumer report.[270]

2.4.4.2 Employment Agency Communications

2.4.4.2.1 Overview

Certain common communications made by employment agencies are excluded from the definition of consumer report.[271] Employment agencies are not exempted from the FCRA per se. The exclusion applies only if:

(1) The communication would otherwise be an investigative consumer report;
(2) The communication is made for certain purposes and used only for those purposes;
(3) The employment agency regularly performs employment procurement services; and

---

259 15 U.S.C. § 1681t(b)(1)(H). See § 10.7.6, *infra*.
260 American Bankers Ass'n v. Gould, 412 F.3d 1081, 1087 (9th Cir. 2005). On remand, the district court held that the California Act's affiliate sharing prohibition was entirely preempted. American Bankers Ass'n v. Lockyer, 2005 WL 2452798 (E.D. Cal. Oct. 5, 2005).
261 Pub. L. No. 108-159, § 611(b) (2003), *amending* 15 U.S.C. § 1681a(d)(2)(D) and adding § 1681a(x). See § 13.2.4.2, *infra*, for a discussion of the legislative history of this provision.
262 15 U.S.C. § 1681a(d)(2)(D).
263 15 U.S.C. § 1681a(x).
264 Millard v. Miller, 2005 WL 1899475, at *2 (W.D. Wis. Aug. 9, 2005) (workers' compensation investigation).
265 15 U.S.C. § 1681a(x)(1)(C). One court has held that an employer did not lose the protection of this provision by providing the report to the employer's worker's compensation carrier, reasoning that the carrier was an agent of the employer. Millard v. Miller, 2005 WL 1899475, at *3 (W.D. Wis. Aug. 9, 2005).
266 15 U.S.C. § 78c(a)(26).
267 15 U.S.C. §§ 7211–7218.
268 15 U.S.C. § 1681a(x)(3).
269 15 U.S.C. § 1681a(x)(2). See § 8.2.6.4.4.3 (notices) and 13.4 (investigative repots), *infra*.
270 15 U.S.C. § 1681a(d)(2)(D) and (o).
271 15 U.S.C. § 1681a(o). This exclusion was added by the 1996 Reform Act. Pub. L. No. 104-208 § 2402, 110 Stat. 3009 (Sept. 30, 1996). Prior to that time, these kind of employment reports would have been considered consumer reports.

(4) the consumer gives permission for the communication and receives certain disclosures from the CRA.[272]

In addition, even if all other factors are present, no exclusion applies if the employment agency makes inquiries that an employer would be prohibited from making by equal employment opportunity laws and regulations.[273] If this exclusion does not apply and an employment agency does qualify as a CRA, it may qualify as nationwide specialty CRA, if it compiles and maintains employment files on a nationwide basis.[274]

2.4.4.2.2 Investigative report

The first criterion for the employment agency exclusion is that the report would otherwise have qualified as an investigative report.[275] Investigative consumer reports are any consumer reports which contain information on the consumer's character or reputation or similar personal information, obtained through personal interviews with neighbors, friends, or associates.[276] Employment agencies, recruiting for an employer or seeking to place an individual in a job, commonly interview a potential employee's past and current employers or other associates. In order for a communication to be excluded from the definition of a consumer report, it must contain this kind of personal information obtained by personal interview.

2.4.4.2.3 Made for purposes of employment procurement

The second criterion for the employment agency exclusion is that the communication be made to a prospective employer either for the purpose of procuring an employee for the employer, or for the purpose of procuring an opportunity for a consumer to work for the employer.[277] In addition, the communication may not be used by any person for any other purpose.[278]

2.4.4.2.4 Regularly performs employment procurement services

The third criterion is that the person making the communication must be a person who regularly performs employment procurement services.[279] The effect of this criterion is to limit the exclusion to employment agencies, but the agency does not need to be incorporated or a partnership. Any person who regularly performs employment procurement services may qualify for the exclusion.

2.4.4.2.5 Consumer consent and required disclosures

The final criterion is that the consumer must consent to the employment agency communication and the agency must make certain disclosures to the consumer.[280] The consumer's consent may be oral or in writing.[281] If the consent is oral, then the employment agency must confirm it in writing within three business days.[282] The consumer must consent to the nature and scope of the communication, before information is collected for that purpose.[283] For example, consent is required before an employment agency may interview the consumer's colleagues or past employers. The consumer must also consent beforehand to the making of the communication to a prospective employer.[284]

The employment agency must also provide a written notice to the consumer disclosing that the consumer has a right to request the nature and substance of the information about the consumer in the employment agency's file.[285] No time period for providing this notice is specified, but as these disclosures are analogous to disclosures required for investigative consumer reports, the disclosure should normally be made prior to any communication of information resulting from personal interviews to the prospective employer.[286] If the consumer requests information about what is in the employment agency's files, then the employment agency must disclose the nature and substance of the information in its files within five business days.[287] The sources of the information do not have to be disclosed, as long as the information is communicated solely for procuring employment.[288]

2.4.5 Credit Card Issuer's Authorization to Extend Credit

The definition of a consumer report specifically excludes communication of the direct or indirect approval of a specific extension of credit by the issuer of a credit card or similar device.[289] Thus a card issuer's statement to a merchant that it will honor a consumer's credit card purchase is

---

272 15 U.S.C. § 1681a(o)(5)(B).
273 U.S.C. § 1681a(w). *See* § 2.6.1, *infra*.
274 15 U.S.C. § 1681a(o)(1).
275 15 U.S.C. § 1681a(e). *See* Ch. 13, *infra*.
276 15 U.S.C. § 1681a(o)(2).
277 15 U.S.C. § 1681a(o)(4).
278 15 U.S.C. § 1681a(o)(3).
279 15 U.S.C. § 1681a(o)(5)(A).
280 15 U.S.C. § 1681a(o)(5)(A)(i).
281 15 U.S.C. § 1681a(o)(5)(A)(iii).
282 15 U.S.C. § 1681a(o)(5)(A)(i).
283 15 U.S.C. § 1681a(o)(5)(A)(ii).
284 15 U.S.C. § 1681a(o)(5)(c)(ii).
285 *See* § 13.4, *infra*.
286 15 U.S.C. § 1681a(o)(5)(c)(i).
287 *Id.*
288 15 U.S.C. § 1681a(d)(2)(B).
289 *See* Wood v. Holiday Inns, Inc., 508 F.2d 167 (5th Cir. 1975) (no consumer report where viewed merchant as card issuer's agent, so no supply of information to third party).

not a consumer report. This exemption will likely be viewed also as applying to the issuer's *denial* or *disapproval* of a specific extension of credit.[290] However, if the issuer's denial is based on a consumer report or other information obtained from yet another party, the *card issuer* must comply with the obligations of users of consumer reports, including notice of the name of a CRA where such information was responsible in part for the denial.[291] That is, while the card issuer does not become a CRA in communicating with the merchant, it may be a user in receiving information from a third party in determining whether to approve the credit request.

Under the exclusion for credit card approvals, if a merchant refuses to extend its own credit directly to a consumer because an issuer has denied authorization of a credit card transaction between the merchant and the consumer, the merchant is *not* denying credit on the basis of a consumer report, and may not have to comply with the obligations of users of consumer reports. Nevertheless, the FCRA still requires creditors (in this case the merchant) to disclose information to the consumer where creditors use, at least in part, third party information that is not a consumer report in denying credit.[292] The Equal Credit Opportunity Act also requires the creditor (in this case the merchant) to disclose the reasons for the adverse credit action.[293]

2.4.6 Conveying Decision to Party Who Requested That Creditor Extend Credit to Consumer

The Act defines "consumer report" to exclude:

> any report in which a person who has been requested by a third party to make a specific extension of credit directly or indirectly to a consumer conveys his decision with respect to such request, if the third party advises the consumer of the name and address of the person to whom the request was made and such person makes the disclosures to the consumer required under section 1681m of the title.[294]

This exemption covers attempts by retailers to obtain credit for their individual customers from an outside source (such as a bank or a finance company), either by requesting that the financial institution extend credit directly to the consumer or purchase the retail sales agreement from the retailer.

There is no consumer report when the creditor communicates to the retailer its decision whether it will extend credit to the consumer.[295] For this exemption to apply, the retailer must inform the consumer of the potential creditor's name and address.[296] The creditor must also comply with the FCRA's requirements as to notice to consumers of adverse actions on their credit applications.[297]

A report falls under this exemption to the extent that it contains a simple indication whether credit was granted or denied and the basis for that action.[298] Inclusion of additional information may bring the report back under the definition of a consumer report. The exclusion is intended to permit sharing information relevant only to the making of a decision regarding a specific credit application. If the information is stored gratuitously or for the purpose of permitting the retailer to shop the information around to other creditors, as is common with automobile dealers, the communication may fall outside the intended scope of the exception.[299] Similarly, if the financial institution forwards to the retailer a consumer report it has obtained on the consumer, the financial institution may be a CRA.[300]

In addition, information provided to the retailer long after the applicant has been rejected would not seem to fall under this exemption. Nor should the exemption apply if the retailer first contacts the creditor concerning the consumer after the credit decision has been made.

The statutory exemption is designed primarily to protect the creditor from having to comply with the various obligations of CRAs because it has provided information to a retailer. The creditor loses that protection if the retailer does not provide the consumer with the name of the creditor to whom it has referred the consumer's application.[301] The FTC Staff Commentary suggests that creditors can protect themselves from retailers' failure to provide consumers with the name of the outside creditor by entering into a written agreement with the retailer requiring the retailer to make the required disclosures.[302] This probably overstates the matter, for the creditor's reliance on such an agreement may be attacked if it is unreasonable in the circumstances.

A related but different concept to this statutory exemption is that "joint users" of information in the same transaction

---

290 *See* Wood v. Holiday Inns, Inc., 508 F.2d 167 (5th Cir. 1975).
291 *See* § 8.2.7, *infra*.
292 *See* § 8.2.6.6, *infra*.
293 15 U.S.C. § 1681a(d)(2)(C).
294 FTC Official Staff Commentary § 603(d) item 7C(1), *reprinted at* Appx. D, *infra*.
295 15 U.S.C. § 1681a(d)(2)(C). *But see* Hageman v. Twin City Chrysler-Plymouth, 90 N.C. App. 594, 369 S.E.2d 99 (1988) (court fails to consider this requirement).
296 15 U.S.C. § 1681a(d)(2)(C). *See also* § 8.2.6, *infra*.
297 FTC Official Staff Commentary § 603(d) item 7C(2), *reprinted at* Appx. D, *infra*.
298 Brinckerhoff, FTC Staff Opinion Letter (Apr. 23, 1985), *reprinted on the CD-Rom accompanying this manual* (but a different result might occur if the bank and dealer are considered "joint users" of the consumer report). *See* § 2.5.5, *supra*.
299 Brinckerhoff, FTC Informal Staff Opinion Letter (Apr. 23, 1985), *reprinted on the CD-Rom accompanying this manual*.
300 15 U.S.C. § 1681a(d)(2)(C).
301 FTC Official Staff Commentary § 603(d) item 7C, *reprinted at* Appx. D, *infra*.
302 15 U.S.C. § 1681a(f).

may not become CRAs when they share third party information. The joint-user concept has been used to avoid two creditors' being considered CRAs or users when they share information. The joint-user exception does not have an explicit statutory basis, and is detailed in § 2.5.5, *infra*.

2.5 The Consumer Reporting Agency

2.5.1 General

Most FCRA provisions require both a consumer report and a consumer reporting agency (CRA). The two notions are interdependent because the definition of consumer report refers to consumer reporting agencies, and vice versa. Thus, for a transaction to be covered by the FCRA, usually there must be not only a consumer report, but also a consumer reporting agency.

The FCRA defines "consumer reporting agency" as

- Any person which, for monetary fees, dues, or on a cooperative nonprofit basis,
- Regularly engages in whole or in part in the practice of assembling or evaluating consumer credit information or other information on consumers,
- For the purpose of furnishing consumer reports to third parties, and
- Which uses any means or facility of interstate commerce for the purpose of preparing or furnishing consumer reports.[303]

Special issues are also raised concerning the coverage of joint users and government agencies.[304] The interstate commerce requirement has not generally been a contested issue.

2.5.2 "Any Person Which, For Monetary Fees, Dues, or on a Cooperative Nonprofit Basis"

A CRA must be a person, but person is broadly defined to include any individual, partnership, corporation, trust, estate, cooperative, association, government or governmental subdivision or agency, or other entity.[305] Nevertheless, issues as to government agencies acting as CRAs raise special concerns, as discussed in separate subsections below.[306]

A CRA assembles information for monetary fees, dues, or on a cooperative nonprofit basis.[307] For example, where a creditor, as part of its evaluation process, sends information from a consumer's application to a CRA to verify that information, and *provides* a fee to the CRA, the creditor is not acting as a CRA. Even though it is sending information collected from one party to another party, it has not done so for a fee or monetary dues or on a cooperative nonprofit basis.[308]

The House of Representatives considered a bill which would have defined CRAs more narrowly than the current statute and excluded loan cooperatives and other nonprofit cooperatives engaged in consumer reporting. Industry objected to this exclusion as a "loophole."[309]

According to one court, a social service CRA gathering information on a prospective adoptive parent's financial status is not a consumer reporting agency.[310] The court relied on the FTC interpretations of "consumer reporting agency" as dealing with "commercial purposes." The agencies characterized by the FTC are companies that "aid and support institutions making *economic* decisions...."[311] Probably a better justification in the social service case would be that no fee was exchanged between the adoption agencies for the information, and that no arrangement had been created to exchange information on a cooperative basis.

Certain activities of a corporation can involve the corporation as a CRA while other activities might not involve the same corporation as a CRA. For example, one division of a corporation could collect consumer reports, while another could collect business reports. As long as the business reports are not derived from a consumer report, but are independently collected solely for a business purpose, that division would not act as a CRA. However, the FTC's Circumvention Rule prohibits nationwide CRAs from reorganizing their operation to evade FCRA requirements.[312]

2.5.3 "Regularly Engages ... in the Practice of Assembling or Evaluating ... Information on Consumers"

2.5.3.1 Regularly Engages

The FTC Staff Commentary provides little guidance as to when a person "regularly engages" in consumer reporting activities. The FTC Staff Commentary only indicates that a creditor who only once furnishes information to a govern-

---

303 *See* §§ 2.5.5, 2.5.6, 2.5.7, *infra*.
304 15 U.S.C. § 1681a(b).
305 *See* §§ 2.5.6, 2.5.7, *infra*.
306 15 U.S.C. § 1681a(f).
307 FTC Official Staff Commentary § 603(f) item 12, *reprinted at* Appx. D, *infra*.
308 *See Hearings on H.R. 16340, Subcommittee on Consumer Affairs of the House Committee on Banking and Currency*, 91st Cong., 2d Sess. 132 (1970) (testimony of J. Spafford).
309 Porter v. Talbot Perkins Children's Servs., 355 F. Supp. 174 (S.D.N.Y. 1973).
310 *Id.* at 177.
311 *See* § 2.6.1.3, *infra*.
312 FTC Official Staff Commentary § 603(f) item 2, *reprinted at* Appx. D, *infra*.

ment agency is not a CRA, even if the creditor furnishes information beyond its own experience with the consumer.[313]

A few FCRA cases have addressed the issue of when a person "regularly engages" in consumer reporting activities. Courts have looked to case law under the Fair Debt Collection Practices Act (FDCPA), which defines a debt collector someone who "who regularly collects or attempt to collect" debts.[314] Relying on FDCPA case law, one court interpreted "regularly engages" as "at fixed and certain intervals, regular in point of time. In accordance with some consistent or periodical rule of practice." The term "regular" means "usual, customary, normal or general." It is the antonym of "casual" or "occasional."[315] Another court has suggested that an entity that provides only one or "isolated instances" of consumer reports does not engage "regularly" in consumer reporting activities.[316]

Another source of guidance may be the federal Truth in Lending Act (TILA), which requires that a business "regularly extends" credit in order to be covered by TILA;[317] the standard set by regulation is roughly whether one extended credit more than twenty-five times a year.[318] Prior to that regulation, the standard applied was whether the extension of credit was more than "an occasional, isolated, and incidental portion" of the business' activities.[319] Thus, the extension of credit in three-of-seven sales over a nineteen-month period was sufficient to characterize a business as a creditor subject to the Truth in Lending Act.[320] Given the similarity of the language in these Acts and their equally broad remedial purposes,[321] courts should interpret liberally this portion of the definition of a CRA.

2.5.3.2 Assemble or Evaluate

Another aspect of the definition of "consumer reporting agency" is that the activity involve the assembly or evaluation of the information reported to third parties. The terms "assemble" and "evaluate" are not defined in the FCRA and, except for a general tenor of casting a wide net, are unexplained in the legislative history. However, FTC staff opinion letters have occasionally addressed the issue,[322] and have noted that these terms cover a very broad range of activities.[323]

In general, the purely ministerial acts of obtaining and forwarding unaltered information to a third party would not make one a CRA. For example, an intermediary like a drug counselor merely forwarding or communicating laboratory reports is not thereby a CRA. Similarly, a firm which obtains doctor's statements and simply places them in an envelope and mails them to an insurer, without even keeping a copy, is not a CRA. One court has held that a debt collection attorney who merely furnishes information about a particular debt to a client, without assembling or evaluating information, is not a CRA.[324] On the other hand, if a person retains the information in its files or if it collects information from multiple sources and formats it in a report for a customer, the information is at least being assembled; the person is thereby a CRA; and the protections of the Act apply.[325]

Entities that market themselves as credit bureaus are unlikely to claim that they do not assemble or evaluate information.[326] But for entities that do not perceive themselves or market themselves as CRAs, the question whether they regularly assemble or evaluate information is critical.

If an entity meets the definition of CRA because it regularly assembles or evaluates information, it should still be considered a CRA even when it provides information that has not been assembled or evaluated to a third party. The FCRA does not require that the entity must meet the defi-

---

313 15 U.S.C. § 1692a(6). *See* National Consumer Law Center, Fair Debt Collection § 4.2.3 (5th ed. 2004 and Supp.).
314 Johnson v. Federal Express Corp., 147 F. Supp. 2d 1268 (M.D. Ala. 2001) (quoting Schroyer v. Frankel, 197 F.3d 1170, 1174 (6th Cir. 1999)). *See also* Lewis v. Ohio Prof'l Elec. Network L.L.C., 190 F. Supp. 2d 1049 (S.D. Ohio 2002) (accord).
315 Owner-Operator Indep. Driver Ass'n v. USIS Comm. Servs., Inc., 410 F. Supp. 2d 1005 (D. Colo. 2005).
316 15 U.S.C. § 1602(f).
317 12 C.F.R. 226.2(a)(17) at n.3. See National Consumer Law Center, Truth in Lending, § 2.3.3 (5th ed. 2003 and Supp.).
318 *See* Gerasta v. Hibernia Nat'l Bank, 411 F. Supp. 176, 185 (E.D. La. 1976), *rev'd on other grounds*, 575 F.2d 580 (5th Cir. 1978). *See generally* National Consumer Law Center, Truth in Lending § 2.3.3 (5th ed. 2003 and Supp.).
319 Eby v. Reb Realty, Inc., 495 F.2d 646, 649 (9th Cir. 1974).
320 *Compare* 15 U.S.C. § 1601 *with* 15 U.S.C. § 1681.
321 Lee, FTC Informal Staff Opinion Letter (June 26, 1998), *reprinted on the CD-Rom accompanying this manual*; Islinger, FTC Informal Staff Opinion Letters (June 9, 1998); LeBlanc, FTC Informal Staff Opinion Letters (June 9, 1998), *reprinted on the CD-Rom accompanying this manual. See also* Lewis v. Ohio Prof'l Elec. Network L.L.C., 190 F. Supp. 2d 1049 (S.D. Ohio 2002) (defining "assemble" and "evaluate").

322 Lee, FTC Informal Staff Opinion Letter (June 26, 1998), *reprinted on the CD-Rom accompanying this manual*; LeBlanc, FTC Informal Staff Opinion Letter (June 9, 1998), *reprinted on the CD-Rom accompanying this manual. See also* Morris v. Equifax Info. Servs., L.L.C., 457 F.3d 460 (5th Cir. 2006) (noting broad interpretation of "assemble" in FTC staff opinion letters).
323 Ditty v. Checkrite, Ltd., 973 F. Supp. 1320 (D. Utah 1997).
324 Lewis v. Ohio Prof'l Elec. Network L.L.C., 190 F. Supp. 2d 1049 (S.D. Ohio 2002) (defendants who assemble information about arrests from sheriffs in two states and furnish it for monetary compensation are subject to the FCRA).
325 *But see* Morris v. Equifax Info. Servs., L.L.C., 457 F.3d 460 (5th Cir. 2006) (Equifax claiming it was not a CRA in case at issue).
326 *But see* Garcia v. UnionBanCal Corp., 2006 WL 2619330 (N.D. Cal. Sept. 12, 2006) (even if bank sometimes functioned as a CRA, it was not liable as a CRA because it did not produce information at issue for purpose of providing it to a third party and thus was not acting as a CRA).

nition of CRA for each consumer report issued.³²⁷ Thus, if a CRA communicates "unassembled" and "unevaluated" information about a consumer, it should still be a CRA and the information is a consumer report. However, Equifax has argued before the Fifth Circuit that it was not acting as a CRA where it did not "own" a consumer's file, but merely stored it on its computers, and did not assemble or evaluate the file.³²⁸

2.5.4 Furnishing Consumer Reports to Third Party

The most important part of the definition of a consumer reporting agency is the requirement that the business be gathering information to furnish consumer reports to third parties. This part has two elements.

First, one must ascertain whether the information furnished qualifies as a "consumer report." The definition of "consumer report" in turn incorporates the definition of "consumer reporting agency," so there is some circularity to the analysis.³²⁹ Section 2.3, *supra*, discusses what constitutes a "consumer report" and § 2.4, *supra*, discusses statutory exceptions to the definition.

Second, the report must be to a third party.³³⁰ If a company uses its own employees to gather information, and those employees report the information to the company, the employees are not CRAs. The FTC Staff Commentary applies this notion generally to agents and employees sharing information with principals and employers.³³¹ An insurance company will not become a CRA merely by informing its agent of the cancellation of an insured's policy, since the agent is not considered a third person under the Act. However, the holder of a lien on the insured's car is considered a third party; if the insurer reports to the lienholder the reasons for cancellation that are based on information from an outside source, the insurer will become a CRA assuming it meets the other elements of the definition.³³² On the other hand, most transfers of information between a subsidiary and a parent corporation or among affiliates fall within a statutory exemption.³³³

Independent contractors hired by a company, when reporting information back to that company, may be CRAs, even when the same report by a company employee would not be covered. For example, if a company uses off-duty police officers or firefighters to gather information on a consumer's insurability, each police officer or firefighter is a CRA and must comply with the Act.³³⁴

A middleman who helps a retailer find a lender for a customer can also be a CRA. For example, a company that accepts inquiries from a car dealer seeking a lender for a customer, obtains a consumer report, and then furnishes the dealer with a list of potential lenders, is itself a CRA. The reports provided by this middleman are used and expected to be used to establish a consumer's eligibility for credit.³³⁵

Cooperative loan exchanges (offices that maintain information on applications for loans, names of finance companies, names of consumers, and amounts of credit requested or extended) are CRAs when they give this information to a finance company. This is true even if they do not give information about the consumer's payment record.³³⁶

2.5.5 Exception for Joint Lenders and Users

Although a person who furnishes a consumer report to a third party for that third party's use is generally considered a CRA, that is not the case when the person furnishing the report and the party receiving the report are joint lenders or joint users of the report, according to the FTC Staff Commentary.³³⁷ This is not a statutory exemption, but is based on the FTC's reading of the Act.

According to the FTC, entities that share consumer reports with others who are jointly involved in decisions for which there are permissible purposes to obtain the reports may be "joint users" rather than CRAs.³³⁸ For example, if a lender forwards consumer reports to government agencies administering loan guarantee programs or to other prospec-

---

327 Morris v. Equifax Info. Servs., L.L.C., 457 F.3d 460 (5th Cir. 2006).
328 See § 2.3, *supra* (discussion of what constitutes a consumer report).
329 15 U.S.C. § 1681a(f); Garcia v. UnionBanCal Corp., 2006 WL 2619330 (N.D. Cal. Sept. 12, 2006).
330 FTC Official Staff Commentary § 603(f) item 8, *reprinted at* Appx. D, *infra*.
331 Carson, FTC Informal Staff Opinion Letter (May 16, 1972), *reprinted on the CD-Rom accompanying this manual*.
332 See § 2.4.3, *supra*.
333 Carson, FTC Informal Staff Opinion Letter [1969–1973 Decisions Transfer Binder] Consumer Cred. Guide (CCH) ¶ 99,452 (June 9, 1971).

334 Grimes, FTC Informal Staff Opinion Letter (June 9, 1993), *reprinted on the CD-Rom accompanying this manual*.
335 FTC Official Staff Commentary § 603(f) item 9, *reprinted at* Appx. D, *infra* ("A loan exchange or any other exchange that regularly collects information bearing on decisions to grant consumers credit or insurance . . . or employment, is a 'CRA' "). See also FTC, Compliance with the Fair Credit Reporting Act, at 24 (1977). *Cf.* Grimes, FTC Informal Staff Opinion Letter (Apr. 30, 1986), *reprinted on the CD-Rom accompanying this manual* (insurance claims exchange is a CRA).
336 FTC Official Staff Commentary § 603(f) item 8, *reprinted at* Appx. D, *infra*.
337 *Id.*
338 *Id. See also* Brinckerhoff, FTC Informal Staff Opinion Letter (Apr. 23, 1985), *reprinted on the CD-Rom accompanying this manual*; Petruccelli, FTC Informal Staff Opinion Letter (Apr. 9, 1984), *reprinted on the CD-Rom accompanying this manual* (a broker may share a consumer report with the seller he is advising); FTC Informal Staff Opinion Letter, [1969–1973 Transfer Binder] Consumer Cred. Guide (CCH) ¶ 99,497 (May 6, 1971); Feldman, FTC Informal Staff Opinion Letter (May 5, 1971).

tive insurers or guarantors, the lender is not acting as a CRA.[339] This example would apply in the case of student loans and to FHA, Rural Housing Service (formerly FmHA), or VA insured home mortgages.

There is a statutory exemption for certain sharing of information between retailers and creditors,[340] but the joint-use exception has a different scope. The former exemption permits a financial institution to report its credit decision back to a retailer. The joint-use exclusion permits a lender to forward a consumer's information to a third party who must participate in the credit granting decision. For example, a retailer that is a retail installment seller who actually originates a loan may forward credit information to a financial institution in connection with a request that the financial institution purchase the retail installment contract.[341] The retailer would not become a CRA because the retailer is a joint lender with the financial institution.[342]

The joint-user exception also applies to other parties whose approval is needed before a lender grants credit,[343] and where the consumer asks one lender to forward information to a second creditor to help that second creditor evaluate the consumer's loan application with the second creditor.[344] The first scenario applies to government-sponsored enterprises (GSEs) Freddie Mac and Fannie Mae, who are considered joint users with lenders when they supply reports from their automated underwriting systems to these lenders.[345] Also, FTC staff have informally suggested that two potential lenders may share information if the consumer has filled out a loan application which identifies both potential lenders.[346]

The joint-use exception is not restricted to lenders. For example, a landlord sharing a consumer report with a state housing agency with authority to overrule the landlord's decision to deny housing to a tenant would be a joint user.[347]

FTC interpretations have suggested that the joint-use exception applies when a broker advising a seller shares a consumer report with the seller.[348] However, this kind of "joint use" has more commonly been dealt with by characterizing the advisor as an agent of the actual user.[349] If the advisor is more of an independent contractor, the exception may be necessary.

The joint-use exception applies to transactions where the two users are jointly involved in the decision. However, the exception should not apply where the information is shared for a subsequent transaction where the parties no longer share in the decision-making.[350]

2.5.6 Exception for Federal Government Agencies

Government agencies often collect and transmit information of the type that would qualify as a "consumer report," if collected and transmitted by a private business. The FTC has interpreted the FCRA to exempt the Office of Personnel Management and "similar federal agencies" from the scope of the definition of a CRA.[351] This ruling is based largely on the FTC's reading of the Act's legislative history, that indicates that the term "consumer reporting agency" was intended to include only "commercial enterprises engaged in mutually beneficial exchanges of information."[352]

The Ninth Circuit, in rejecting a consumer's FCRA suit requesting the FBI to amend records containing inaccurate information, has applied the FTC's exemption to all federal agencies, finding no legislative intent to cover such agencies

---

339 15 U.S.C. § 1681a(d), *as analyzed at* § 2.4.6, *supra*.
340 *See* FTC Informal Staff Opinion Letter, [1969–1973 Decisions Transfer Binder] Consumer Cred. Guide (CCH) ¶ 99,497 (May 6, 1971).
341 *Id.*
342 FTC Official Staff Commentary § 603(f) item 8, *reprinted at* Appx. D, *infra*; Isaac, FTC Informal Staff Opinion Letter (June 11, 1996), *reprinted on the CD-Rom accompanying this manual.* It does not apply to middlemen who use consumer reports to match a creditor's need to find a lender willing to make a loan to its customers. Grimes, FTC Informal Staff Opinion Letter (June 9, 1993), *reprinted on the CD-Rom accompanying this manual.*
343 FTC Official Staff Commentary § 603(f) item 8, *reprinted at* Appx. D, *infra*. *See also* Throne, FTC Informal Staff Opinion Letter (Nov. 20, 1998), *reprinted on the CD-Rom accompanying this manual*; Brinckerhoff, FTC Informal Staff Opinion Letter (May 1, 1987), *reprinted on the CD-Rom accompanying this manual.*
344 Weidman v. Federal Home Loan Mortgage Corp., 338 F. Supp. 2d 571 (Sept. 30, 2004). See § 14.5.3, *infra*, for a description of Freddie Mac's automated underwriting systems.
345 Isaac, FTC Informal Staff Opinion Letter (June 11, 1996), *reprinted on the CD-Rom accompanying this manual.*
346 *See* Brinckerhoff, FTC Informal Staff Opinion Letter (Dec. 30, 1988), *reprinted on the CD-Rom accompanying this manual.*
347 *See* Petruccelli, FTC Informal Staff Opinion Letter (Apr. 9, 1984), *reprinted on the CD-Rom accompanying this manual.*
348 *See* § 2.5.4, *supra*.
349 *See* Russell, FTC Informal Staff Opinion Letter (Sept. 27, 1973), *reprinted on the CD-Rom accompanying this manual.*
350 FTC Official Staff Commentary § 603(f) item 11, *reprinted at* Appx. D, *infra*. See also Supplementary Information published with the commentary, 55 Fed. Reg. 18,804, 18,805–18,806 (May 4, 1990), *reprinted at* Appx. D, *infra*.
351 *See* 116 Cong. Rec. 36,576 (1970) (remarks of Rep. Brown). *See also id.* at 35,941 (remarks of Sen. Proxmire); Conf. Rep. No. 1587, 91st Cong., 2d Sess. 1 (1970), *reprinted in* 1970 U.S.C.C.A.N. 4411, 4414. *But see* Remarks of Senator Proxmire, 119 Cong. Rec. 27818–19 (1973).
352 Ollestad v. Kelley, 573 F.2d 1109 (9th Cir. 1978). *See also* Ricci v. Key Bancshares of Maine, 768 F.2d 456 (1st Cir. 1985) (FBI agents not liable for contribution to bank that received information from the FBI); Fortney, FTC Informal Staff Opinion Letter (Jan. 30, 1986), *reprinted on the CD-Rom accompanying this manual* (Administrative Office of U.S. Courts not subject to FCRA when reporting information on bankruptcy filings to creditors and others). *Contra* Goldfarb, FTC Informal Staff Opinion Letter (July 9, 1980), *reprinted on the CD-Rom accompanying this manual* (FCRA applies to government agencies attempting to collect overpayments of government benefits and collection of guaranteed loans).

under the Act.[353] Note also that federal agencies do not usually issue reports to third parties, and when they do, it is rarely for a fee.

While the FCRA apparently will not provide protections for consumers when dealing with federal agencies as *reporting agencies*, federal agencies, as *users* of consumer reports, are subject to the Act's requirements for users. As a user, a federal agency may obtain information only for permissible purposes,[354] except that the FCRA specifically allows CRAs to release limited identifying information about a consumer to a governmental agency (name, address, former addresses, places of employment, or former place of employment).[355] Federal agencies may also act as *furnishers* of information, sometimes with limitations regarding the information they can furnish.[356] In addition, federal agencies have obligations under the Privacy Act.[357]

2.5.7 State and Local Government Agencies

A "consumer reporting agency" is defined in the FCRA as a "person,"[358] and the definition of a "person" includes a "government or governmental subdivision or agency."[359] Unlike federal agencies, the FTC has made clear that state and local government entities can be CRAs. For example, the FTC Staff Commentary states that state motor vehicle departments are CRAs if they regularly furnish (for a fee) motor vehicle reports containing information bearing on the consumer's personal characteristics, such as arrest information, to insurance companies for insurance underwriting purposes.[360]

Where a state motor vehicle department routinely sells reports on consumers' driving records to insurance companies, the department is a CRA in that respect. However, the FTC Staff Commentary finds that reports made by motor vehicle departments to other governmental authorities involved in licensing or law enforcement activities are not consumer reports because the consumer reports are between two governmental entities.[361]

Some states allow private entities electronic access to state unemployment insurance wage reporting records for the purpose of consumer credit verification. By doing so, these state agencies could become CRAs.[362]

FTC staff have suggested that state agencies which provide criminal record information to employers are not CRAs.[363] The rational for this suggestion is that the agencies have been designated by the state to provide such information and in fulfilling their public duties should not be covered by FCRA. No statutory language providing such an exemption is evident and no court has addressed this issue. On the other hand, similar federal agencies have been found exempt,[364] and a similar result involving state agencies is certainly possible.

As with federal agencies, state agencies may be users of consumer reports, and as such may obtain information only for permissible purposes,[365] except that the FCRA specifically allows CRAs to release limited identifying information about a consumer to a governmental agency (name, address, former addresses, places of employment, or former place of employment).[366] State agencies may also act as furnishers of information.

A consideration in bringing an action against a state for violation of the FCRA is that states and their respective agencies are protected by sovereign immunity. Under the Eleventh Amendment of the U.S. Constitution, states, as sovereigns, are immune from suit in federal court absent consent or a valid abrogation of that immunity by Congress.[367] This immunity extends to state agencies as

---

353 Edmond v. United States Postal Serv., 727 F. Supp. 7 (D.D.C. 1989) (question of fact whether postal inspector received copy of consumer report pursuant to court order or other lawful means), *rev'd in part on other grounds*, 949 F.2d 415 (D.C. Cir. 1991); § 7.2.1, *infra*.
354 15 U.S.C. § 1681f. See § 7.2.10.2, *infra*.
355 *See* § 5.5.3, *infra*.
356 5 U.S.C. §§ 552a(d), 552a(g)(1)(A). *See* § 16.2, *infra*.
357 15 U.S.C. § 1681a(f).
358 15 U.S.C. § 1681a(b).
359 FTC Official Staff Commentary § 603(f) item 10, *reprinted at* Appx. D, *infra*. *See also* Supplementary Information published with the Commentary, 55 Fed. Reg. 18,804–18,806 (May 4, 1990), *reprinted on the CD-Rom accompanying this manual*; FTC Informal Staff Opinion Letter [1969–1973 Decisions Transfer Binder] Consumer Cred. Guide (CCH) ¶ 99,487 (Apr. 28, 1971); Feldman, FTC Informal Staff Opinion Letter (Sept. 5, 1974), *reprinted on the CD-Rom accompanying this manual*.
360 FTC Official Staff Commentary § 603(d) item 4C, § 603(f) item 10, *reprinted at* Appx. D, *infra*; FTC Supplementary Information published with the Commentary § II(1), 55 Fed. Reg. 18,804 (May 4, 1990).

361 *See* 1996 Dep't of Labor, Office of Inspector General's Report. At one point, California had announced that its Employment Development Department would sell confidential wage data collected on 14 million people statewide to private information companies, car dealers and creditors wanting to check a consumer's income and who obtain the consumer's consent. *California Plans to Sell Confidential Wage Data*, Washington Post, June 4, 1999, at E02.
362 Pickett, FTC Informal Staff Opinion Letter (July 10, 1998), *reprinted on the CD-Rom accompanying this manual*; Copple, FTC Informal Staff Opinion Letter (June 10, 1998), *reprinted on the CD-Rom accompanying this manual*.
363 *See* § 2.5.6, *supra*.
364 Edmond v. United States Postal Serv., 727 F. Supp. 7 (D.D.C. 1989) (question of fact whether postal inspector got copy of consumer report pursuant to court order or other lawful means), *rev'd in part on other grounds*, 949 F.2d 415 (D.C. Cir. 1991); § 7.2.1, *infra*.
365 15 U.S.C. § 1681f. *See* § 7.2.10.2, *infra*.
366 *See* Kimel v. Florida Bd. of Regents, 528 U.S. 62 (2000); Sorrell v. Ill. Student Assistance Comm'n, 314 F. Supp. 2d 813 (C.D. Ill. 2004) (FCRA case); O'Diah v. New York City, 2002 WL 1941179 (S.D.N.Y. Aug. 21, 2002) (FCRA case).
367 Puerto Rico Aqueduct & Sewer Auth. v. Metcalf & Eddy, Inc., 506 U.S. 139 (1993).

well.³⁶⁸ Since Congress enacted the FCRA under the Commerce Clause, it was not empowered to abrogate a state's Eleventh Amendment immunity through the FCRA.³⁶⁹ As a result, neither a state nor its officers acting in their official capacities may be held liable for money damages in federal court. However, injunctive relief might be available against state officials when they are sued in their official capacity.³⁷⁰

2.6 The FCRA Distinguishes Special Types of Consumer Reporting Agencies

2.6.1 "Nationwide" Consumer Reporting Agencies

2.6.1.1 General

"Nationwide" consumer reporting agencies have a special status under the FCRA to which a few unique obligations attach. (The FCRA does not use the term "nationwide consumer reporting agency"; the phrase used throughout the Act is "consumer reporting agency that compiles and maintains files on consumers on a nationwide basis.") This subsection discusses the definition of a "nationwide" consumer reporting agency (CRA) and identifies their unique obligations.

The "nationwide" CRA is a actually a term of art, narrower than it sounds. A nationwide CRA not only must regularly assemble or evaluate and maintain information to provide consumer reports to third parties, but also must collect both public record information and credit account information on consumers residing nationwide.³⁷¹ Collecting or reporting just credit account information or just public record information is not enough; both are required to be considered a nationwide CRA.

This technical definition was intended to include, at the time of enactment, the "Big Three" credit bureaus: Equifax, Experian, and TransUnion.³⁷² However, the possibility that other nationwide CRAs might emerge was also contemplated.³⁷³

Regional CRAs are excluded. CRAs specializing in employment, landlord-tenant, check writing, medical, or other narrow fields are also excluded. However, these CRAs may be nationwide specialty CRAs if they compile such information on a nationwide basis.³⁷⁴

The definition of nationwide CRA appears to exclude so-called resellers who buy information from other CRAs (such as one of the "Big Three") and then re-package it for banks and other third parties without maintaining its own database of consumer credit information.³⁷⁵ However, the FCRA explicitly defines "resellers"³⁷⁶ and designates specific responsibilities for them.³⁷⁷

2.6.1.2 Responsibilities of Nationwide Consumer Reporting Agencies

The FCRA imposes a number of responsibilities on nationwide CRAs, some of which were added by the FACTA amendments to the FCRA in 2003. Nationwide CRAs must, *inter alia*:

- Provide free annual disclosures of consumer reports to consumers;³⁷⁸
- Maintain a toll-free telephone number during normal business hours with personnel accessible to consumers who have received their file disclosures.³⁷⁹ The Summary of Consumer Rights provided to consumers by CRAs and others must include that toll-free telephone number when appropriate;³⁸⁰
- Jointly maintain a notification system for consumers to opt out of being included in prescreening list mailings;³⁸¹
- Maintain an automated reinvestigation system so that the results of a furnisher's reinvestigation are reported to all the nationwide CRAs, as appropriate;³⁸²
- Insert fraud and active military duty alerts to consumer files³⁸³ and refer alerts to other such CRAs;³⁸⁴
- Review complaints of inaccuracy compiled by and transmitted by the FTC;³⁸⁵
- Coordinate consumer complaints of identity theft and

---

368 *See* Seminole Tribe of Florida v. Florida, 517 U.S. 44 (1996); Rovers v. Oregon Dep't of Justice, 2005 WL 2218457 (D. Or. Sept. 13, 2005); O'Diah v. New York City, 2002 WL 1941179 (S.D.N.Y. Aug. 21, 2002) ; Richmond v. TRW Info Servs. Div., 1997 WL 1037886 (S.D. Cal. July 22, 1997).
369 *Ex Parte* Young, 209 U.S. 123, 159–160; 28 S. Ct. 441, 52 L. Ed. 714 (1908). However, the ability of private parties to seek injunctive relief under the FCRA is questionable. *See* § 11.13, *infra*.
370 15 U.S.C. § 1681a(p).
371 *See* 140 Cong. Rec. 25,871 (1994) (remarks of Rep. Kennedy); Brinckerhoff, FTC Informal Staff Opinion Letter (June 29, 1999), *reprinted on the CD-Rom accompanying this manual*.
372 Brinckerhoff, FTC Informal Staff Opinion Letter (June 29, 1999), *reprinted on the CD-Rom accompanying this manual*.

373 *See* § 2.6.1.2, *infra*.
374 *See* § 2.6.3, *infra*.
375 15 U.S.C. § 1681a(u).
376 *See* § 2.6.3, *infra*.
377 15 U.S.C. § 1681j(a).
378 15 U.S.C. § 1681g(c)(1)(B). *See* § 8.2.6.2.3, *infra*.
379 15 U.S.C. § 1681g(c); § 8.2.6.2, *infra*.
380 15 U.S.C. § 1681b(e)(6); §§ 7.3.4, 8.2.9, *infra*.
381 15 U.S.C. § 1681i(a)(5)(D).
382 15 U.S.C. § 1681c-1(a)–(c).
383 15 U.S.C. §§ 1681c-1(e).
384 15 U.S.C. § 1681g(e)(3).
385 15 U.S.C. § 1681s(f)(1).

requesting fraud alerts or blocks;[386]
- Report annually to the FTC on consumer identity theft complaints and fraud alerts;[387]
- Abstain from corporate or technological means to try to circumvent the responsibilities of nationwide CRAs.[388]

In addition, a user that provides an adverse action notice to a consumer because it used information from a nationwide CRA must provide a toll-free number for that CRA.[389]

2.6.1.3 FTC Circumvention Rule

The FCRA, as amended by FACTA, requires the FTC to issue regulations preventing a CRA from circumventing or evading treatment as a nationwide CRA.[390] This provision specifically describes two types of conduct that Congress intended to prevent through the FTC Circumvention Rule:

- Corporate reorganization or restructuring, including a merger, acquisition, dissolution, divestiture, or asset sale of a CRA.[391]
- "Maintaining or merging public record and credit account information in a manner that is substantially equivalent to that described in § 1681a(p) of the FCRA."[392]

The FTC has issued a final circumvention rule.[393] The rule attempts to ensure a level playing field in the credit reporting industry so that newly formed CRAs are prohibited from circumventing or evading the responsibilities for nationwide CRAs in the initial organization and structuring of their entities.[394]

The FTC Circumvention Rule contains provisions that mirror the two types of circumvention conduct described in the statutory provision.[395] The FTC rule also contains a general prohibition against circumvention through any means.[396] The FTC concluded that Congress granted it broad authority to prevent all circumvention, by any means, including, but not limited to, the two types describe by Congress.[397]

In addition, the rule includes three examples of conduct that would violate the circumvention rule and one example that would not. The first example is of a nationwide CRA that restructures its operations so that public record information is assembled and maintained only by its corporate affiliate, so that the nationwide CRA ceases to comply with the requirements for nationwide CRAs because it no longer maintains public records.[398]

The second example is of a nationwide CRA that restructures its operations so that corporate affiliates separately assemble and maintain information in each state, so that the corporation ceases to comply with the requirements for nationwide agencies. This conduct would be a violation of the rule.[399]

This second example may actually be somewhat akin to the situation with respect to some of the "Big Three" nationwide CRAs. For example, Equifax contracts with a company called CSC Credit Services, which Equifax claims "owns" the consumer files for consumers in a certain geographic area.[400] Equifax has made the claim that it does not act as a CRA with respect to consumer files "owned" by CSC Credit Services, albeit not on the basis that Equifax does not operate in every state. Instead, Equifax argues that it merely stores the files on its computers, and does not assemble or evaluate the file.[401] It remains to be seen whether such an argument runs afoul of the FTC Circumvention Rule.

The third example provided by the FTC rule is of a new entrant into the marketplace for consumer reports that organizes itself into two entities. One entity assembles and maintains credit account information from furnishers. The second entity assembles and maintains public record information. Neither the corporation nor its affiliated entities comply with the requirements for nationwide agencies.[402] This conduct would also violate the rule.

The final example deals with a bona fide, arms-length transaction with an unaffiliated party. A nationwide CRA sells its public record information business to an unaffiliated company in a bona fide arms-length transaction. The nationwide CRA ceases to assemble and maintain public record information and ceases to offer reports containing public information. This conduct would not be a violation of the circumvention rule.[403]

One area the rule does not address is the use of outsourcing to circumvent coverage as a nationwide CRA. Advocates sought to have the rule explicitly apply to agents, independent contractors, partners, subsidiaries, and joint venturers, as well as anyone to whom the nationwide CRAs subcontract their work, but the rule does not mention these entities with respect to circumvention.

---

386 Id.
387 15 U.S.C. § 1681x. See 2.6.1.3, infra.
388 15 U.S.C. § 1681m(a)(2)(A); § 8.2.6.2, infra.
389 15 U.S.C. § 1681x.
390 15 U.S.C. § 1681x(1).
391 15 U.S.C. § 1681x(2).
392 16 C.F.R. Part 611.
393 69 Fed. Reg. 8,532, 8,533 (Feb. 24, 2004) (interim final rule).
394 16 C.F.R. § 611.2(a).
395 16 C.F.R. § 611.2(a).
396 69 Fed. Reg. 8,532, 8,533 (Feb. 24, 2004) (interim final rule).
397 16 C.F.R. § 611.2(b)(1).

398 16 C.F.R. § 611.2(b)(2).
399 Morris v. Equifax Info. Servs., L.L.C., 457 F.3d 460 (5th Cir. 2006).
400 Id.
401 16 C.F.R. § 611.2(b)(3).
402 16 C.F.R. § 611.2(b)(4).
403 16 C.F.R. § 611.3. A list of responsibilities of nationwide CRAs is included in § 2.6.1.2, supra.

§ 2.6.2   *Fair Credit Reporting*

A violation of the FTC Circumvention Rule could subject the violating CRA to liability pursuant to sections 1681n and 1681o of the FCRA. There appears to be no limitation on private enforcement of these requirements. The FTC Circumvention Rule provides a safe harbor that provides that any CRA which is otherwise in violation of the rule shall be deemed in compliance if the CRA complies with all of the responsibilities that the FCRA imposes on nationwide CRAs.[404]

2.6.2 Nationwide Specialty Consumer Reporting Agencies

2.6.2.1 General

The FACTA amendments to the FCRA in 2003 created a new category of CRA called a "nationwide specialty consumer reporting agency." These CRAs are defined as "consumer reporting agencies that compile and maintain files on a nationwide basis relating to consumers' medical records or payments, residential or tenant histories, check-writing histories, employment histories, or insurance claims."[405]

The significance of being a nationwide specialty CRA is that such CRAs, like general nationwide CRAs,[406] must provide a free consumer report.[407]

2.6.2.2 Types of Nationwide Specialty Consumer Reporting Agencies: Medical Information, Tenant Screening, and Check Writing Agencies

One type of nationwide specialty CRA would be a medical information CRA, set up primarily to assist in insurance underwriting by collecting medical information on consumers. The Medical Information Bureau (MIB) is the primary CRA collecting and selling personal health information.[408]

Tenant screening companies assist landlords in checking on prospective tenants. Even prior to the 2003 FACTA amendments, the FTC and the courts had agreed that tenant screening reports are consumer reports, and thus these companies are CRAs.[409] One of the largest of these nationwide tenant screening companies is First American Registry.[410] These services have been criticized as undermining the ability of tenants to enforce their rights under landlord-tenant law.[411]

Check approval companies guarantee consumers' checks for merchants and provide information to the merchant about a consumer's check writing history. Again, even prior to the FACTA amendments of 2003, the FTC and the courts agreed that check writing reports are consumer reports, and that these companies are CRAs.[412] Some nationwide check approval or check writing history databases are TeleCheck, SCAN, and ChexSystems.

2.6.3 Resellers of Consumer Reports

2.6.3.1 Overview

Resellers act as information brokers, buying large volumes of consumer reports at discount rates from other CRAs, and reselling the data to lower volume buyers. Banks and mortgage companies sometimes use resellers to procure reports from at least two of the "Big Three" nationwide CRAs, to combine the information into a single report, and to compute a credit score. These blended reports are commonplace and are generally called tri-merged reports.[413] Tenant screening companies also commonly supplement their own specialized information by providing a consumer report from one of the "Big Three."

2.6.3.2 FCRA Coverage of Resellers

The FCRA was amended by FACTA in 2003 to explicitly address resellers. The Act defines "reseller" as:[414]

> a consumer reporting agency that—
>
> (1) assembles and merges information contained in the database of another consumer reporting agency or multiple consumer reporting agencies concerning any consumer for purposes of furnishing such information to any third party, to the extent of such activities; and
>
> (2) does not maintain a database of the assembled or merged information from which new consumer reports are produced.

The FCRA's definition of "reseller" makes clear that these entities are CRAs.[415] This was true even prior to the

---

404   15 U.S.C. § 1681a(w).
405   15 U.S.C. § 1681a(p). *See* § 2.6.2, *supra*, § 3.4.2.1, *infra*.
406   15 U.S.C. § 1681j(a)(1)(C). *See* § 3.4.2.3, *infra*.
407   *See* § 3.5.1, *infra*.
408   *See* § 2.3.6.3.3, *supra*.
409   White v. First Am. Registry, 230 F.R.D. 365 (S.D.N.Y. Aug. 12, 2005).
410   Joe Lamport, Blacklisting Tenants, Gotham Gazette, Feb. 8, 2006, *available at* www.gothamgazette.com/article/housing/20060208/10/1753.
411   *See* § 2.3.6.3.2, *supra*.
412   *See* Standfacts Credit Servs., Inc. v. Experian Info. Solutions, Inc., 405 F. Supp. 2d 1141 (C.D. Cal. 2005).
413   15 U.S.C. § 1681a(u).
414   Poore v. Sterling Testing Sys., Inc., 410 F. Supp. 2d 557, 561 (E.D. Ky. 2006). *See also* Morris v. Equifax Info. Servs., L.L.C., 457 F.3d 460 (5th Cir. 2006).
415   Cohan, FTC Informal Staff Opinion Letter (Aug. 1, 2000), *reprinted on the CD-Rom accompanying this manual*; First Am. Real Estate Solutions, L.L.C., No. 952-3267 (F.T.C. 1998) (consent agreement); W.D.I.A. Corp (F.T.C. Dkt 9258 Mar. 3, 1994) (consent order); Inter-Fact, Inc. (F.T.C. Dkt C-3424 1993) (consent order); I.R.S.C., Inc. (F.T.C. Dkt C-3422 1993) (con-

FACTA amendments,[416] but the FACTA amendments clarify the status of a reseller as a CRA.[417]

Interestingly, some of the "Big Three" nationwide CRAs may actually be closer to resellers in some instances. For example, Equifax contracts with a company called CSC Credit Services, which it claims "owns" the consumer files for consumers in a certain geographic area.[418] However, these files are stored in Equifax's computer system[419] and thus Equifax does not meet the definition of "reseller," since it maintains a database of information from which new consumer reports are produced.[420]

As information brokers, resellers may also deal with non-consumer reports, and then need not comply with FCRA requirements concerning those reports. If a creditor itself purchases reports from multiple CRAs and merges them into a single document, the creditor is not considered a CRA or reseller unless it furnishes a report to a third party.[421]

2.6.3.3 Duties of Resellers

The FCRA exempts resellers from certain responsibilities and imposes modified responsibilities in other situations. With the exceptions of these exemptions and modifications, which are discussed below, resellers are subject to all of the general requirements imposed on CRAs by the FCRA.[422]

Any report by a reseller should be carefully evaluated to determine whether it comes within the definition of a consumer report under the FCRA or under some other protection provided by federal or state law. If the report is subject to FCRA protections, potential claims concerning accuracy, impermissible access, failure to reinvestigate, failure to provide appropriate notice may be available to consumers. On the other hand, if the report falls outside FCRA protections, there may be claims for invasion of privacy, unfair business practices, or other statutory and common law claims.[423]

Reselling often is associated with issues as to the accuracy of information reported. Resellers must establish procedures to ensure maximum possible accuracy of the consumer reports they sell.[424] However, the FCRA specifically provides that the general reinvestigation requirements applicable to ordinary CRAs do not apply to resellers.[425] Instead, resellers have specific reinvestigation responsibilities of their own.

A reseller that receives a notice from a consumer about an item in the reseller's report must investigate the item to determine whether or not it is incomplete or inaccurate as a result of some act or omission by the reseller.[426] If the reseller determines that the information was its responsibility, the reseller must correct or delete the information in the consumer's report within twenty days of receiving the original notice of dispute.[427] If, however, the item is the result of someone else's act or omission, the reseller need only convey the consumer's notice of the dispute to the CRA that originally provided the information.[428]

The FCRA extends the responsibility of CRAs to reinvestigate consumer information by requiring them to reinvestigate upon notice from a reseller that a consumer has disputed the item.[429] The CRA must then report the results of its reinvestigation back to the reseller, who must then reconvey the results back to the consumer.[430] This provision basically treats the reseller as a consumer for purposes of the CRA's reinvestigation responsibilities.

Special rules also apply to resellers that make it easier to trace information.[431] Anyone procuring a consumer report for purposes of reselling any part of the report must make prior disclosures to the CRA and must maintain reasonable procedures designed to ensure that information which it resells is used only for permissible purposes.[432]

A reseller may not procure a report from a CRA without disclosing to the CRA the identity of the end-user of information in the report,[433] and each permissible purpose for

---

sent order). The FTC enforcement actions are reprinted on the CD-Rom, see also Appx. K, *infra*.

416 Poore v. Sterling Testing Sys., Inc., 410 F. Supp. 2d 557, 561 (E.D. Ky. 2006). *But see* Lewis v. Ohio Prof'l Elec. Network L.L.C., 190 F. Supp. 2d 1049 (S.D. Ohio 2002) (defendant did not need to fit in the definition of a "CRA" in order to be considered a reseller subject to the FCRA; pre-FACTA decision).

417 Morris v. Equifax Info. Servs., L.L.C., 457 F.3d 460 (5th Cir. 2006).

418 *Id.*

419 In this instance, Equifax claimed it was a "procurer for resale" under § 1681e(e)(2). However, this provision is actually targeted at resellers but does not refer to the definition of reseller at § 1681a(u). The Court of Appeals in *Morris* declined to address this issue. Morris v. Equifax Info. Servs., L.L.C., 457 F.3d 460 (5th Cir. 2006).

420 Cast, FTC Informal Staff Opinion Letter (Oct. 27, 1997), *reprinted on the CD-Rom accompanying this manual*.

421 Poore v. Sterling Testing Sys., Inc., 410 F. Supp. 2d 557, 561 (E.D. Ky. 2006). *But see* Lewis v. Ohio Prof'l Elec. Network, L.L.C., 248 F. Supp. 2d 693 (S.D. Ohio 2003) (defendant was a reseller and not a CRA, thus not subject to duties of CRA under FCRA). The court in Poore v. Sterling Testing distinguished the *Lewis* case on the basis that *Lewis* was decided prior to the FACTA amendments that made clear resellers are CRAs.

422 *See* §§ 10.3–10.6, *infra*.

423 Poore v. Sterling Testing Sys., Inc., 410 F. Supp. 2d 557, 561 (E.D. Ky. 2006).

424 15 U.S.C. § 1681i(f)(1).

425 15 U.S.C. § 1681i(f)(2).

426 15 U.S.C. § 1681i(f)(2)(b)(i).

427 15 U.S.C. § 1681i(f)(2)(b)(ii).

428 15 U.S.C. § 1681i(a).

429 15 U.S.C. § 1681i(f).

430 15 U.S.C. § 1681e(e).

431 15 U.S.C. § 1681e(e)(1) and (2).

432 15 U.S.C. § 1681e(e)(1)(A). However, the end-user shall not be identified if it is a federal CRA using the report for certain national security reasons. 15 U.S.C. § 1681e(e)(3).

433 15 U.S.C. § 1681e(e)(1)(B).

which the information is furnished to the end-user.[434] This provision effectively prohibits a creditor or private investigator or other user from secretly obtaining a report by using a reseller as an intermediary.[435]

Additionally, the reseller must establish and comply with reasonable procedures designed to ensure that the information is resold only for permissible purposes. These procedures must include a requirement that each person to whom information is resold and who provides the report to another must identify each end-user, certify the purpose for which the information will be used, and certify that the information will be used for no other purpose.[436] Reasonable efforts to verify these certifications and the identity of each end-user must be made before reselling a report.[437] A creditor's notice of adverse action[438] will refer the consumer to the reseller.

Resellers operating on a national level, providing reports on consumers residing nationwide, may be subject to additional requirements. The FCRA's requirements for nationwide CRAs are listed in § 2.6.1.2, *supra*. On their face, most resellers of consumer reports meet the definition of a nationwide CRA.[439] They evaluate, assemble, and maintain credit information, including public record information, and use credit account information from persons who furnished such information. Nevertheless, relying upon legislative history, FTC staff has opined in the past that only the so-called "Big Three" CRAs, Equifax, Experian, and TransUnion are nationwide agencies under the FCRA.[440] However, these FTC staff opinions were written prior the 2003 FACTA amendments.

2.6.4 Trucker Database Services

The interstate trucking industry relies heavily on DAC Services, a subsidiary of USIS Commercial Services, to gather and disseminate truck driver employment histories and driving records to affiliated motor carriers.[441] Trucker database services such as DAC Services are clearly CRAs; however, employers who use these services may follow less stringent notice requirements for these reports than other users of employment reports.[442]

In addition to the trucker databases themselves, the employers who furnish information to these services might be considered CRAs in some instances. One court has found that motor carriers who provide completed "Termination Report" forms could be CRAs, because the reports included information pertaining not only to the first-hand experience of the carriers making the reports, but also to the interactions between drivers and shippers.[443] The court rejected the motor carriers' argument that they were not CRAs because they simply completed forms.[444] The court concluded that these reports were not isolated instances and that the motor carriers who supplied the report did so regularly and for a fee, thus bringing them within the FCRA's definition of a CRA.

2.7 Examples of Consumer Reporting Agencies

2.7.1 Credit Bureaus, Inspection Bureaus, and Consumer Reporting Agencies Collecting Public Record Data

Classic examples of consumer reporting agencies (CRAs) are the three major credit bureaus, Experian, TransUnion, and Equifax. In addition to the "Big Three," there are about 100 affiliate and independent local "credit bureaus" around the country.[445] The major purpose of these CRAs is to prepare consumer reports on consumers applying for credit.

Specialized CRAs were created to assist insurance companies and employers with investigative reports. These were sometimes called inspection bureaus, and are also CRAs.[446]

Yet another type of CRA specializes in public records information, and is typically used by law enforcement and government agencies to find assets, court records, and individuals.

2.7.2 Creditors As Consumer Reporting Agencies

Creditors frequently exchange credit information about consumers with other creditors, CRAs, retailers, brokers, and other parties. As such, creditors may be CRAs. Nevertheless, the FCRA contains numerous exceptions to limit the extent to which a creditor is treated as a CRA.

As discussed in an earlier section, a creditor is not a CRA where the creditor reports back to a retailer or dealer its credit decision, after the retailer requested that the creditor extend credit directly to the consumer or that it purchase the

---

434 Benner, FTC Informal Staff Opinion Letter (Apr. 30, 1999), *reprinted on the CD-Rom accompanying this manual.*
435 15 U.S.C. § 1681e(e)(2)(A).
436 15 U.S.C. § 1681e(e)(2)(B).
437 See § 8.2.6, *infra*.
438 15 U.S.C. § 1681a(p).
439 Cohan, FTC Informal Staff Opinion Letter (June 29, 1999), *reprinted on the CD-Rom accompanying this manual.*
440 See www.usis.com/commercialservices/transportation; Cassara v. DAC Servs., Inc., 276 F.3d 1210 (10th Cir. 2002).
441 See § 8.2.17.2.3, *infra*.
442 Owner-Operator Indep. Driver Ass'n v. USIS Comm. Servs., Inc., 410 F. Supp. 2d 1005 (D. Colo. 2005).

443 *Id.*
444 www.ncrainc.org.
445 *See Panacea or Placebo?, Actions for Negligent Non-Compliance Under the Fair Credit Reporting Act*, 47 S. Cal. L. Rev. 1070 (1974).
446 See § 2.4.6, *supra*.

retail sales agreement from the dealer.[447] However, this exception is only broad enough to allow the reporting back of the decision and the reasons. If the creditor gives the retailer more detailed reports on the consumers to whom it has denied credit so that the retailer can help get credit for the consumers elsewhere, the creditor may be a CRA.[448]

A loan company that, after rejecting a consumer's application for a residential mortgage loan, passes on the application and the files to other finance companies without the consumer's request in an attempt to obtain financing for the consumer, may well become a CRA.[449] However, if a creditor furnishes information to another party as part of their joint decision-making process about offering credit, the creditor is not a CRA because it is a "joint user" of credit information.[450]

Other exceptions include:

- A creditor that reports only information about its own experience with a consumer is not issuing a "consumer report," according to a specific exemption from the Act,[451] and so is not a CRA when it reports its own experience about a consumer to a CRA.
- An FCRA exemption permits sharing of information amongst a creditor and its affiliates.[452] However, if the creditor reports any information other than that obtained from its first-hand dealings with the consumer, and fails to provide the consumer with an opt-out right, it does become a CRA subject to the Act.

Several FTC informal staff opinion letters have dealt with other situations. For instance, a creditor does not become a CRA if, in evaluating a credit application, it transmits application information received from the consumer to a CRA, which in turn verifies the information and provides the creditor with a consumer report on the consumer.[453] Nor is a creditor a CRA if it rejects a credit applicant and then, at the applicant's request, forwards a consumer report it obtained on the applicant to another creditor.[454] If the creditor regularly conveys reports of rejected applicants without the applicants' specific request, it does become a CRA.[455]

A creditor that obtains consumer reports from CRAs, in connection with making credit decisions, is not a CRA itself when it releases copies of those reports to rejected credit applicants.[456] However, a retailer, whose customers finance purchases through a bank, becomes a CRA when (to avoid paying a fee to the bank) the retailer obtains information from the customers' references and furnishes it to the bank, which then decides whether to extend credit.[457]

2.7.3 Collection Agencies and Credit Bureau Collection Departments

Collection agencies and collection departments of credit bureaus are CRAs in certain circumstances. A collection agency becomes a CRA if it regularly furnishes information outside its own experience with the consumer to third parties for use in connection with consumer transactions.[458] For example, a collection agency that publishes a list of consumers from whom retailers should not accept checks is likely to be a CRA.[459] However, a collector is not a CRA if it only reports its own experiences with consumers.[460]

2.7.4 Data Brokers

Data brokers are companies that have developed highly sophisticated databases of consumer information, which may or may not be governed by the FCRA, the Gramm-Leach-Bliley Act or other laws and regulations intended to protect consumer data.[461] Data brokers typically provide information services to a variety of businesses and govern-

---

447 Brinckerhoff, FTC Staff Opinion Letter (Apr. 23, 1985), *reprinted on the CD-Rom accompanying this manual* (but a different result might occur if the bank and dealer are considered "joint users" of the consumer report. See § 2.5.5, *supra*.
448 Brinckerhoff, FTC Informal Staff Opinion Letter (Oct. 31, 1983), *reprinted on the CD-Rom accompanying this manual*.
449 See § 2.5.5, *supra* (discussion of "joint users").
450 15 U.S.C. § 1681a(d)(2)(A)(i); Daniels v. Carter One Bank, 39 Fed. Appx. 223, 2002 WL 1363525 (6th Cir. June 21, 2002). See § 2.4.2, *supra*.
451 15 U.S.C. § 1681a(d)(2)(A)(ii) and (iii). See § 2.4.3, *supra*.
452 FTC Official Staff Commentary § 603(f) item 12, *reprinted at* Appx. D, *infra*; Fortney, FTC Informal Staff Opinion Letter (May 2, 1986), *reprinted on the CD-Rom accompanying this manual*.
453 Brinckerhoff, FTC Informal Staff Opinion Letter (May 1, 1987), *reprinted on the CD-Rom accompanying this manual*.
454 *Id.*
455 15 U.S.C. § 1681e(c).
456 Grimes, FTC Informal Staff Opinion Letter (Aug. 6, 1986), *reprinted on the CD-Rom accompanying this manual*.
457 FTC Official Staff Commentary § 603(f) item 7, *reprinted at* Appx. D, *infra*. See National Consumer Law Center, Fair Debt Collection § 9.6 (5th 2004 and Supp.).
458 Mangum v. Action Collection Serv., Inc., 2006 WL 2224067 (D. Idaho Aug. 2, 2006).
459 Grimes, FTC Informal Staff Opinion Letter (July 7, 1992), *reprinted on the CD-Rom accompanying this manual* (not CRA when solely furnish information about own experience with consumer); Mitchell v. Surety Acceptance Corp., 838 F. Supp. 497 (D. Colo. 1993) (debt collector was not CRA where it only furnished information about debt it was collecting only to CRA); D'Angelo v. Wilmington Med. Ctr., 515 F. Supp. 1250 (D. Del. 1981) (collection CRA not CRA where it did not assemble or evaluate adverse information, and supplied it to CRA rather than directly to creditor).
460 See § 16.1, *infra*.
461 *Prepared Statement of the Federal Trade Commission Before the Subcommittee on Commerce, Trade, Consumer Protection Committee on Energy and Commerce, on Protecting Consumers' Data: Policy Issues Raised by ChoicePoint*, U.S. H.R. (Mar. 15, 2005), *available at* www.ftc.gov/os/2005/03/050315protectingconsumerdata.pdf.

ment entities, sometimes to detect fraudulent transactions or to assist in locating individuals.[462]

Data brokers obtain their information from different sources and use the information for a variety of purposes. The information is usually collected from three types of sources: public record information; publicly-available information; and non-public consumer information.[463] Public record information can include birth and death records, property records, tax lien records, voter registrations, licensing records, and court records (bankruptcy filings, criminal records, civil cases, and judgments). Publicly-available information may include phone directories, print publications, Internet sites, and other sources accessible to the general public. Non-public information is retrieved from identifying or contact information submitted to businesses by consumers to obtain products or services, transaction information about consumers with businesses (credit card numbers, products purchased, magazine subscriptions, travel records, types of accounts, claims filed, or fraudulent transactions).

Some data brokers include consumer report information in their databases, and thus would be considered "resellers" under the FCRA.[464] As resellers, they must comply with the various requirements imposed by the FCRA on that category.[465]

According to the FTC, one of many dilemmas presented by data brokers is that no one law governs all of the uses and disclosures of consumer information maintained in their files.[466] This leaves consumers with little or no protection from identity thieves who access this information.

Significant data security problems have arisen with data brokers such as ChoicePoint, which disclosed information on about 150,000 consumers to identity thieves posing as legitimate purchasers of such information.[467] In congressional hearings addressing the lack of oversight on data brokers, ChoicePoint implied that some of its products had not been subject to FCRA protections and limitations.[468] It is not clear why ChoicePoint had taken this position. Subsequently, the FTC brought an FCRA enforcement action against ChoicePoint over its release of information to identity thieves, alleging that the company did not have reasonable procedures to screen prospective subscribers to verify their identity and to make sure they had a permissible use for the information. ChoicePoint settled with the FTC, agreeing to pay $10 million in civil penalties and $5 million for consumer redress.[469]

ChoicePoint also has been the subject of a complaint to the FTC by the Electronic Privacy Information Center (EPIC), which argues that ChoicePoint's "AutoTrackXP" and Customer Identification Programs are subject to the FCRA.[470] While there is some dispute as to the source of information for these programs, the reports generated by these programs suggest that they originate from sources subject to the FCRA.[471] The FTC has not acted on EPIC's complaint.

2.7.5 Detective and Employment Agencies, Employers

An employment agency which gathers information about consumers and reports that information to prospective employers will often be a CRA under the FCRA. For example, an employment agency that prepares lists containing names of employees fired for cause is a CRA.[472] However, many communications by employment agencies that would otherwise be considered consumer reports are excluded from the definition of a consumer report.[473]

Private investigators and detective agencies that regularly obtain information about prospective employees or other information relating to a consumer report, and furnish that information to their clients, become CRAs.[474] The investigator's report is often likely to be an investigative consumer report.[475] However, reports compiled in connection with an

---

462 *Id.*
463 *See* § 2.6.3, *supra*.
464 *See* § 2.6.3.3, *supra*.
465 *Prepared Statement of the Federal Trade Commission Before the Subcommittee on Commerce, Trade, Consumer Protection Committee on Energy and Commerce, on Protecting Consumers' Data: Policy Issues Raised by ChoicePoint*, U.S. H.R. (Mar. 15, 2005), *available at* www.ftc.gov/os/2005/03/050315protectingconsumerdata.pdf.
466 U.S. v. ChoicePoint, Inc., CA 1 06-CV-0198 (N.D. Ga. Jan. 30, 2006) (complaint), *reprinted at* www.ftc.gov/os/caselist/choicepoint/0523069complaint.pdf, *reprinted on the CD-Rom accompanying this manual. See also* Appendix K, *infra*.
467 Written testimony of Derek Smith, Chairman and Chief Executive Officer, ChoicePoint Inc. Before the House Energy and Commerce Committee, Subcommittee on Commerce, Trade and Consumer Protection, on Protecting Consumers' Data: Policy Issues Raised by ChoicePoint, U.S. H.R. (Mar. 15, 2005), *available at* http://energycommerce.house.gov/108/Hearings/03152005hearing1455/Smith.pdf.
468 U.S. v. ChoicePoint, Inc., CA 1 06-CV-0198 (N.D. Ga. Jan. 30, 2006) (stipulated final judgment), *reprinted at* www.ftc.gov/os/caselist/choicepoint/choicepoint.htm, *reprinted on the CD-Rom accompanying this manual. See also* Appendix K, *infra*.
469 Letter to the Federal Trade Commission by Chris Jay Hoofnagle and Daniel Solove, Dec. 16, 2004, *available at* www.epic.org/privacy/choicepoint/fcraltr12.16.04.html.
470 *Id.*
471 Grimes, FTC Informal Staff Opinion Letter (Dec. 9, 1983), *reprinted on the CD-Rom accompanying this manual.*
472 15 U.S.C. § 1681a(d)(2)(D), (o). This exclusion is discussed in § 2.4.4.2, *supra*.
473 FTC Official Staff Commentary § 603(f) item 6, *reprinted at* Appx. D, *infra*; LeBlanc, FTC Informal Staff Opinion Letter (June 9, 1998), *reprinted on the CD-Rom accompanying this manual*. The California FCRA statute may exempt detective agencies. Cal. Civ. Code § 1785.4 (West) (*NB*: this section refers to a part of the Business and Professional Code which has since been renumbered several times, to unknown effect).
474 *See* § 13.3, *infra*.
475 15 U.S.C. § 1681a(x). *See* § 2.4.4.1, *supra*, Ch. 13, *infra*. This exclusion was added by the FACTA amendments in 2003. *Id.* Prior to that time, investigative reports concerning employee

investigation of employee misconduct or for compliance purposes are excluded from the definition of a consumer report under the employee misconduct investigation report exception.[476] Also, if the employer *itself* asks friends, neighbors, co-workers, and associates about an applicant, the employer is not a CRA because it is not a business gathering information for the purpose of furnishing a report to third parties.[477]

There are a number of other types of employment-related companies that might be considered CRAs. One such company is "The Work Number," an Internet-based employment verification database which maintains employee data on approximately 100 million American employees.[478] The Work Number verifies for users employee information concerning employment and income, to help those users evaluate applications for credit, employment, or a residential rental.[479] Reports issued by The Work Number appear to be consumer reports in that they are used for purposes of establishing a consumer's eligibility for credit, employment, and other FCRA-covered purposes.[480] However, there is no indication from The Work Number's website that it complies with FCRA provisions to provide consumer disclosures and follow FCRA dispute procedures.[481]

2.7.6 College Placement Offices

A college placement office may be a CRA if it collects and disburses information for a fee or on a cooperative nonprofit basis, and if the reports contain information not based on its own transactions or experiences with the consumer.[482]

2.7.7 Attorneys

Attorneys searching land records may be CRAs if they look for information that bears on creditworthiness, such as the existence of liens, judgments and other items affecting title, and render an opinion that is used by third parties, such as lenders and title insurance companies in determining whether to grant credit or insurance.[483] An attorney who regularly checks criminal records of a client's potential employees may be subject to FCRA.[484] Also, an attorney who requests a consumer report on potential buyers to help his or her client decide which home-purchase offer to accept, when the attorney knows the buyer is going to borrow money, is a CRA.[485] However, an attorney who merely furnishes information about a particular debt to its client, without assembling or evaluating information, is not a CRA.[486]

2.7.8 Accident Reporting Bureaus and Compilers of Insurance Claim Lists

Compiling a listing of policyholders who have received automobile claim payments in the past renders the compiler a CRA.[487] Accident bureaus that sell motor vehicle operating records to insurance companies may be CRAs,[488] but police or sheriff's departments which prepare accident reports are not.[489] State motor vehicle departments are CRAs when selling information to private parties, but not when cooperating with other government agencies.[490]

---

misconduct were considered consume reports. *See* Vail, FTC Informal Staff Opinion Letter (Apr. 5, 1999), *reprinted on the CD-Rom accompanying this manual. But see* Johnson v. Federal Express Corp., 147 F. Supp. 2d 1268 (M.D. Ala. 2001) (handwriting analysis as part of investigation of workplace violence is not a consumer report; use of outside CRA is within the exclusion for first-hand experience; declines to give deference to 1999 staff letters to Vail, Meisinger); Hartman v. Lisle Park Dist., 158 F. Supp. 2d 869 (N.D. Ill. 2001) (report issued to governing board by attorney it hired to investigate whistleblower and her allegations was not a consumer report because it did not bear on creditworthiness, etc., and it related solely to her dealings with the board for which attorney was acting as agent).

476 Pickett, FTC Informal Staff Opinion Letter (July 10, 1998), *reprinted on the CD-Rom accompanying this manual*; Kahn, FTC Informal Staff Opinion Letter [1969–1973 Decisions Transfer Binder] Consumer Cred. Guide (CCH) ¶ 99,447 (May 21, 1971).

477 *See* www.theworknumber.com/AboutUs.

478 *See* www.theworknumber.com/AboutUs/Verifiers/index.asp.

479 *See* § 2.3, *supra*.

480 *See* www.theworknumber.com.

481 Russell, FTC Informal Staff Opinion Letter (May 15, 1974), *reprinted on the CD-Rom accompanying this manual* (files containing recommendations from former employers of student not within "transaction or experience" exception).

482 Martin, FTC Informal Staff Opinion Letter (May 27, 1971), *reprinted on the CD-Rom accompanying this manual*.

483 Sum, FTC Informal Staff Opinion Letter (Sept. 15, 1999), *reprinted on the CD-Rom accompanying this manual*.

484 *See* Peeler, FTC Informal Staff Opinion Letter (July 24, 1978), *reprinted on the CD-Rom accompanying this manual. Cf.* Peeler, FTC Informal Staff Opinion Letter (Feb. 8, 1978), *reprinted on the CD-Rom accompanying this manual* (real estate brokers who obtain reports on potential home buyers).

485 Ditty v. Checkrite, Ltd., 973 F. Supp. 1320 (D. Utah 1997).

486 Brinckerhoff, FTC Informal Staff Opinion Letter (Nov. 23, 1983), *reprinted on the CD-Rom accompanying this manual*.

487 Opinion of Attorney General of Pennsylvania, [1974–1980 Decisions Transfer Binder] Consumer Cred. Guide (CCH) ¶ 98,549 (Aug. 7, 1975).

488 Opinion of Attorney General of Wisconsin, No. 98-74, [1974–1980 Decisions Transfer Binder] Consumer Cred. Guide (CCH) ¶ 98,736 (Sept. 17, 1974); Opinion of Attorney General of Arkansas, [1974–1980 Decisions Transfer Binder] Consumer Cred. Guide (CCH) ¶ 98,818 (Apr. 24, 1974).

489 FTC Official Staff Commentary § 603(d) item 4C, *reprinted at* Appx. D, *infra. See also* Opinion of Attorney General of New York, [1974–1980 Decisions Transfer Binder] Consumer Cred. Guide (CCH) ¶ 98,781 (July 17, 1974); Opinion of Attorney General of Texas, No. H-263, [1974–1980 Decisions Transfer Binder] Consumer Cred. Guide (CCH) ¶ 98,854 (Mar. 9, 1974). *See* § 2.5.7, *supra*.

490 *See* discussion at § 2.3.6.5.2, *supra*. However, if a user should later use the report for other purposes, it may then subject the CRA to the Act's provisions. *Cf.* FTC Official Staff Commen-

Insurance claim reports are generally not considered consumer reports when the reports are compiled and used by insurance companies (or adjusters) to adjust claims made by insureds.[491] However, if a business compiles claim payment histories and furnishes them to insurers for use in underwriting insurance policies, i.e., for use in deciding whether to insure applicants, the compilers would be CRAs.[492]

2.7.9 Telephone Companies

When a telephone company reports to others concerning its own experience with its own customers, a consumer report is *not* involved.[493] Nevertheless, local companies, long-distance companies, and other companies exchange information on customers. For example, some long-distance and 900-number companies bill through local telephone companies.

If a telephone company reports information on a customer not based on its own experience, but on the experience of another company, it is acting as a CRA. For example, if a consumer's old local telephone company reports to the consumer's new local telephone company the experience of a long-distance carrier with that consumer, the consumer's old local company is acting as a CRA within the scope of the FCRA. Similarly, if various telephone companies pool information in a centralized fashion, the central repository may be a CRA.[494]

2.7.10 Alternative Credit Bureaus

A number of "alternative" CRAs have been created, ostensibly to help consumers without a credit history. For example, Payment Reporting Builds Credit is a CRA that allows consumers to submit data about payment of rent, utilities, and other recurring bills, which can then be reported to creditors.[495]

The credit scoring company Fair Isaac has undertaken efforts to create credit scores using nontraditional credit information.[496] There are also subprime CRAs that provide credit assessment products using information from payday lenders, finance companies, subprime automobile lenders, landlord/tenant court records, and rent-to-own records.[497]

All of these entities are clearly CRAs. The concern over these alternative CRAs, especially based on subprime sources of credit, such as payday loans, is that such information will be used to market high-cost credit to these consumers.[498] Another concern is that these alternative sources of credit history will not be predictive of a consumer's credit risk, because these forms of credit are structured so differently (and so much more onerously) than traditional forms of credit.[499]

2.7.11 Retailer Database Services

There are a number of database services geared toward retailers, most of which focus on fraud prevention. Many of these database services have an on-line presence. In response to the growing e-commerce market, companies such as CyberSource have started collecting and analyzing data from Web merchants, and profiling consumers based on their purchase transactions for such characteristics as potential for fraud. Subscribers send the information of a potential customer to the service, which then returns a risk evaluation, which may just be a number between 0 and 99.[500] These companies appear to meet the definition of CRAs.[501]

Another example is a database that collects data on returned merchandise from retailers, and is used by retailers to decide whether to accept merchandise for return.[502] This company claims it does not share merchandise return history between retailers and bases its "return authorizations" (i.e., approvals as to whether a return should be accepted) only on the consumer's history with the retailer seeking the information.[503] It is unclear whether this company is a CRA, but its website does state it will provide disclosure of a consumer's history on the database to the consumer and does have a dispute process.

---

tary § 603(d) item 5D, *reprinted at* Appx. D, *infra*.
491 FTC Official Staff Commentary § 603(f) item 5, *reprinted at* Appx. D, *infra. See* § 2.3.6.5, *supra*.
492 *See* 15 U.S.C. § 1681(d), *as discussed at* § 2.4.2, *supra*.
493 The application of the Act to telephone companies is discussed in detail in *When the Phone Company Is Not the Phone Company: Credit Reporting in the Postdivestiture Era*, 24 Clearinghouse Rev. 98 (1990).
494 *See* www.prbc.com.
495 Isaac, FICO Expansion Score, *available at* www.fairisaac.com/Fairisaac/Solutions/FICO+Expansion+Score/Expansion+Score+Overview/FICO+Expansion+Score.htm.
496 Teletrack, Company Overview—Consumer Credit Information for Risk Mitigation, *available at* www.teletrack.com/company/overview.html.
497 Anna Afshar, *Use of Alternative Credit Data Offers Promise, Raises Issues*, New England Community Developments (Fed. Res. Bank of Boston 3d Quarter 2005).
498 Margot Saunders, National Consumer Law Center, *Testimony Regarding Helping Consumers Obtain the Credit They Deserve, Before the House Subcommittee on Financial Institutions and Consumer Credit*, May 12, 2005, at 6–7, *available at* www.consumerlaw.org.
499 *See* Bicknell, *Anti-Fraud That's Anti-Consumer*, Wired News, July 24, 2000.
500 *See* § 2.5, *supra*.
501 *See* www.returnexchange.com/faq/index/.asap.
502 *Id.*
503 *Id.*

Chapter 3   Obtaining and Examining a Report of the Consumer's File

3.1 Introduction

This chapter details how to examine a report of a consumer's file kept by a consumer reporting agency (CRA).[1] The chapter describes what information can be placed in the file,[2] the consumer's right to a free or low-cost report of the contents of that file,[3] and the mechanics of obtaining that report.[4] The chapter also examines what information from the file must be reported to the consumer,[5] the form of that disclosure,[6] and what use the consumer should make of that disclosure.[7]

A later chapter discusses notices and similar disclosures a consumer may receive from CRAs, creditors, insurers, employers, and others.[8] While these notices are helpful in motivating consumers to investigate their CRA files, consumers can also discover the contents of their files without waiting for a notice.

About 200 million Americans have files with CRAs, and the contents of these files are regularly reported to creditors, insurers, employers, landlords, merchants, and others. However, the major CRAs do not have files on everyone. Many American adults, especially immigrants, do not have consumer reporting files.

There are many reasons why a consumer or the consumer's attorney would want to examine the consumer's credit file. Consumers can review a report of the file contents to determine if there is inaccurate or incomplete information. Understanding the nature of negative information in the file also is an aid to improving the consumer's credit profile. Disclosure of the consumer's file is an essential first step to handling almost any problem relating to a consumer's credit file and consumer reports related to the file.

If a consumer or a consumer's attorney wants to know what information is actually being reported, there is no substitute for examining the consumer report. A consumer may fear that certain delinquencies appear in the consumer's file, when in fact that creditor is not a subscriber to the particular CRA and has not furnished the information to that CRA. Other times, older debts may just disappear from the system or a creditor may no longer report an account as delinquent. Conversely, since information can be reported for as long as seven years (more in certain cases),[9] consumers may not remember certain delinquencies, lawsuits, and blemishes on their credit record. Even worse, the credit record may contain inaccurate information about the consumer or even mistakenly report information about a completely different person. (Chapter 4, *infra*, explores consumer rights to correct such inaccuracies.)

One of the most important pieces of information for a creditor, employer, or insurer evaluating a consumer report is a credit score.[10] This is a number that is produced by an analysis of much of the information in the consumer's file. Different credit scores can be produced from the same file, depending on the formula used. The score is typically not provided to the consumer with the report, but the consumer can purchase disclosure of the score. Nevertheless, the score that a CRA provides a user may be different than the score it provides the consumer. As a consequence, while consumers certainly would like to know their credit score, purchasing the score may not prove as helpful as one would imagine.

There is a downside to a consumer requesting disclosure of the consumer's file through a consumer report. Under the FCRA, a consumer may be precluded from bringing a tort action in the nature of defamation, invasion of privacy, or negligence if such action is based on information disclosed pursuant to the consumer's request for disclosure.[11]

---

1 The information a consumer reporting agency (CRA) retains on a consumer is considered a "file" on the consumer. When the CRA provides certain contents of that file to a consumer or a user, the CRA provides a "report" to that person.
2 § 3.2, *infra*.
3 § 3.3, *infra*.
4 § 3.4, *infra*.
5 § 3.5, *infra*.
6 § 3.6, *infra*.
7 § 3.7, *infra*.
8 *See* Ch. 8, *infra*.

---

9 *See* § 5.2, *infra*.
10 Credit scores are examined in more detail at Ch. 14, *infra*.
11 15 U.S.C. § 1681h(e). *See* § 10.4, *infra*.

3.2 What Is Contained in a Consumer Reporting File

3.2.1 Investigative Reports Distinguished from Consumer Reports

Information in consumer reports is *not* obtained through personal interviews with friends, neighbors, business associates, or other third parties. If a consumer report contains any information obtained through an interview (whether in person or over the telephone), then the report is an investigative consumer report, a special type of consumer report to which additional procedures apply.[12] Users must give consumers special notices before seeking the investigative report and CRAs must engage in special procedures in supplying the investigative report.[13]

As a result, CRAs segregate investigative consumer report information from regular consumer report information. Investigative reports are chiefly sought by employers and insurers, particularly for high salary jobs or high face-value life insurance policies. The consumer will be notified before the report is sought, and the majority of consumers need not be concerned with this type of report.

3.2.2 Few Limits on Information That May Be Gathered and Filed on Consumers

The FCRA generally does not limit the kind of information that can be gathered in a consumer's file, except for the restrictions discussed in Chapter 5, *infra*, and the restrictions placed on the dissemination of information obtained by interview, discussed in § 3.2.1, *supra*. According to the FTC Staff Commentary, a consumer report may contain any information that is complete, accurate, and not obsolete on the consumer who is the subject of the report.[14] Federal and certain state laws do place specific restrictions on what can be reported or placed in the file in certain circumstances, as examined in Chapter 5, *infra*. Most significantly, obsolete information, usually information over seven years old cannot be reported.[15] Certain debts in dispute cannot be furnished to CRAs, and debts of active military personnel cannot be reported in certain circumstances.[16] The reporting and use of medical information is restricted.[17] State law may place certain additional restrictions as to what can be contained in a consumer's file, although such state laws may be preempted in certain cases.[18]

The term "file" in the FCRA is defined as information "on that consumer,"[19] so that it should contain information only on that consumer. CRAs must designate a separate file for each spouse, but, in an attempt to build up the credit histories of women without credit accounts in their own name, the Equal Credit Opportunity Act *requires* creditors to furnish information to both spouses' files reflecting the participation of both spouses in an account, if one spouse can use or is obligated on the other spouse's account.[20]

Apart from these restrictions, the general rule remains that any information can be placed in a file so long as it meets the FCRA's accuracy requirements. However, the fact that information *can* be placed in a consumer's file does not mean that it *will* be. CRAs tend to have a systematic approach to information, collecting only certain types and not others. The type of CRA that is collecting the data will have a profound effect on what is in the consumer's file with that CRA. Section 3.2.3, *infra*, examines what data is collected by the three major nationwide CRAs. Section 3.2.4, *infra*, looks at the information stored at a number of more specialized CRAs.

3.2.3 Information Found in Files with the "Big Three" Credit Bureaus

3.2.3.1 Introduction

The "Big Three" nationwide credit bureaus operating in the United States, Equifax, TransUnion and Experian (formerly TRW), keep files on about 200 million Americans.[21] More than one billion reports a year are issued in response to consumer applications for credit, employment, and insurance,[22] which works out to about six million per work day!

The information held in consumer files is updated constantly. The "Big Three" credit bureaus process massive amounts of information on a continual basis: each month, they enter about 4.5 billion pieces of information on consumers into their databases.[23]

3.2.3.2 Information Found in the File

Consumer files from the "Big Three" nationwide credit bureaus contain:

---

12 *See* Ch. 13, *infra*.
13 *See* §§ 13.4, 13.6, *infra*.
14 FTC Official Staff Commentary § 607 item 6, *reprinted at* Appx. D, *infra*.
15 *See* § 5.2, *infra*.
16 *See* §§ 5.3, 5.5.1, *infra*.
17 *See* § 5.4.1, *infra*.
18 *See* § 5.7, *infra*.
19 15 U.S.C. § 1681a(g).
20 *See* 12 C.F.R. § 202.10; § 5.6, *infra*; National Consumer Law Center, Credit Discrimination §§ 5.6, 9.4.2.1 (4th ed. 2005 and Supp.).
21 FTC Report to Congress Under Sections 318 and 319 of the Fair and Accurate Credit Transactions Act of 2003 8 (Dec. 2004), *available at* www.ftc.gov/reports/facta/041209factarpt.pdf.
22 *Id.*
23 *See* www.cdiaonline.org/about.cfm, About CDIA.

- Personal identifiers;
- Credit account information;
- Public record information;
- Credit scores;
- Inquiries from users; and
- Any consumer statements.[24]

Personal identification information includes the consumer's name (and aliases), current and previous addresses, and Social Security number. Files may also contain dates of birth, present and previous employment information, telephone numbers, and a spouse's name.

The credit account information details the consumer's payment history with certain creditors, including mortgage, auto, and installment loans, credit cards, and retail store cards. For each creditor, the file contains the creditor's name, the date the account was opened, and, if applicable, the date it was closed. Creditors who regularly furnish information to CRAs must also notify the CRA when the consumer voluntarily closed an account,[25] and the CRA must indicate the voluntary nature of the closure.[26]

Credit account information often indicates for each account the credit limit, balances, date of last payment, whether an account is in good standing or 30, 60, or 90 days overdue, whether it has been turned over to a collection agency or the collection office of a major creditor, and whether a repossession has occurred or an account has been charged off as uncollectible. Also indicated will be whether it is an individual or joint account, or whether a spouse is an authorized user.

The account information is limited to that furnished to the CRA. If a creditor is not a subscriber with that CRA, the consumer's account history with that creditor will not be included in the file. Typically, rent payments and most utility payments will not be supplied to the "Big Three" CRAs either, although there is beginning to be some movement toward supplying some utility data. Remittances that recent immigrants pay to family in other countries are also not supplied to the "Big Three" CRAs.

Public record information will be listed in a separate part of a report, obtained from public court files or other official sources. Public record information is always negative, such as tax liens, bankruptcies or court judgments (including default judgments), and foreclosures. Delinquent child support must be included if reported or verified by a state or local child support enforcement agency.[27]

A consumer report will show who has requested the report within the last two years for employment purposes and within the past year for other purposes, even simple credit inquiries. A single transaction, such as applying for a car loan, can result in multiple inquiries if an automobile dealer "shops" the loan among several potential financers.[28]

Other users of the consumer report listed in the file will not be responding to an application at all, but will use the report to send the consumer a pre-approved offer for a credit card or other credit. In addition, creditors with whom a consumer has an existing account may check the report as part of their review of the account, perhaps to increase the account's interest rate. Promotional inquiries appear in the nonpublic part of the consumer's file, and may be labeled PRM. Inquiries from existing creditors also appear here. Neither affects the credit score nor do they appear in consumer reports sent to users.

Reports sent to users (but not to consumers, unless specifically purchased) will also include a "credit score" or a rating of a consumer's so-called creditworthiness.[29] This score is based on information in the report, which is tabulated according to formulas that vary for different CRAs and even different creditors. Some files will not have sufficient data to produce a score, and these files will thus contain no credit score.

The report will also have any applicable alerts, such as that the consumer has requested that the file be blocked for promotional inquiries, that the file contain fraud alerts having to do with identity theft, or that the file contain active duty alerts relating to an individual's military status.[30] The consumer can also add a statement to the file in certain circumstances.[31]

3.2.3.3 Sources of Information in the File

The "Big Three" credit bureaus obtain their information from three sources. Most information comes from creditors and others who subscribe to the CRA and who provide current account information, generally on a monthly basis, electronically or by computer tape. The "Big Three" CRAs provide subscriber services to any number of creditors: banks; retailers; insurers; landlords; and others. These subscribers obtain consumer reports from the CRA, and the CRAs obtain a great deal of the information in their reports from their subscribers who regularly send the CRA information on the accounts of customers. Data is thus provided

---

24 *See* Robert B. Avery, Paul S. Calem, and Glenn B. Canner, *An Overview of Consumer Data and Credit Reporting*, Federal Reserve Board Bulletin (Feb. 2003), *available at* www.federalreserve.gov/pubs/bulletin/2003/0203/lead.pdf.

25 15 U.S.C. § 1681s-2(a)(4). The notification is to be included as part of the information regularly furnished for the period in which the account was closed.

26 15 U.S.C. § 1681c(e).

27 15 U.S.C. § 1681s-1.

28 This apparently can adversely affect a credit score. Some credit scoring models try to alleviate the effects of multiple inquiries related to a single transaction on a score by deleting them or clustering them. *See* § 14.5.2.1, *infra*.

29 Credit scores are analyzed at Ch. 14, *infra*.

30 *See* Ch. 9, *infra*.

31 *See* Ch. 4, *infra*.

by about 30,000 furnishers.[32] However, many other creditors do not supply information to the "Big Three" CRAs.

Court and other public records are another source of data: bankruptcies; court judgments; and dispositions of lawsuits. Often, CRAs will contract out the collection of public record information to other companies. Also, some federal, state and local government agencies will sell information to the "Big Three" CRAs. Finally, CRAs utilize information that consumers report on themselves, usually identification information when the consumer contacts the CRA.

3.2.4 Information Found in Files at More Specialized Reporting Agencies

Specialty CRAs obtain a narrow type of information on a consumer for special purposes, such as tenant screening services marketed to landlords for use in considering prospective tenants.[33] Information is culled from housing court and small claims court docket sheets, previous landlords, and sometimes other CRAs. The tenant screening file may list any back rent and rent payment history, sources of income (ranging from public assistance payments to return on investments), late payments, bounced checks, evictions, court proceedings and judgments.[34]

ChoicePoint maintains a number of different nationwide databases on consumers, including databases relating to automobile and homeowners insurance (Comprehensive Loss Underwriting Exchange or CLUE), employment (Workplace Solutions), and tenant history (Tenant History). The CLUE automobile insurance database retains a consumer's claims history with various insurance companies, assisting subscribers in their insurance underwriting and pricing. Its personal automobile reports have up to five years of claims information submitted by about 95% of all U.S. personal automobile insurers. The information includes data on the consumer's prior automobile insurance policies, and any claims submitted under those policies. The claims information includes the date of the loss, type of loss, whether the insured was at fault, the type of injury being compensated, the date and amount paid, and the type of vehicle insured, its vehicle identification number (VIN), and its disposition (repaired, stolen, totaled, etc.).[35]

CLUE apparently also includes information about automobile insurance claims by individuals residing at the same address as the consumer who is subject of the report.[36]

CLUE also retains information about additional drivers in the household, whether the consumer's home address is suspect or whether the area has high automobile insurance claims or crime, and six months history of insurance applications.[37] ChoicePoint also has a Motor Vehicle Records (MVR) database that contains driving records, with moving vehicle violations from all fifty states.

ChoicePoint has an analogous database for personal property insurance information, with more than 90% of personal property insurers submitting information to this database.[38] Data includes information on the consumer (name, date of birth, policy number), and claim information (date of loss, type of loss, and amounts paid). There are allegations that information is recorded even when the consumer just makes an inquiry about coverage, or reports a loss, but then decides not to file a claim.[39]

TeleCheck collects credit information on consumers from a variety of sources, including a history of prior checks returned for insufficient funds. Merchants and TeleCheck use this information to determine whether a merchant should accept a check and whether TeleCheck will guarantee the check. Equifax has developed the next generation of check approval software, an artificial intelligence system that uses information about the check writer, the current check, and recent check writing activity to predict whether a check will be honored. Check approval agencies are even used by some banks when consumers seek to open deposit accounts. A report by a bank to a check approval company that a consumer has had a bank account closed with a negative balance can prevent the consumer from opening an account at a new bank for several years.

The largest clearinghouse for medical record information is the Medical Information Bureau (MIB), that contains negative information acquired when insurers underwrite individual life, health, or disability insurance policies, including adverse health information and information about an individual's hazardous activities, such as hang-gliding or piloting airplanes.[40] Other agencies collect information on workers' compensation rolls, and then sell the data to employers who use these lists as blacklists, refusing to hire employees who have filed for workers' compensation in the past. Other agencies collect lists of individuals who have been involved in automobile lease fraud or financial services fraud. New types of databases are constantly emerging, and there are few limits to the types or amount of information that can be stored in these repositories.

---

32 FTC Report to Congress Under Sections 318 and 319 of the Fair and Accurate Credit Transactions Act of 2003 8 (Dec. 2004), available at www.ftc.gov/reports/facta/041209factarpt.pdf.
33 See §§ 2.6.2, supra, 13.3.3, infra. Some companies report the timeliness of rent payments directly to the "Big Three" CRAs.
34 Cotto v. Jenney, 721 F. Supp. 5 (D. Mass. 1989).
35 See www.choicepoint.com/business/pc_ins/us_5.html, Motor Vehicle Records.
36 See Evan Hendricks, Credit Scores & Credit Reports 244 (2d ed. 2005).
37 Id.
38 Id.
39 Id.
40 See www.mib.com.

3.3 Consumer's Right to Access the Consumer's File

3.3.1 Access from a User

3.3.1.1 Advantages

While a report can be obtained as a matter of right from a CRA, there are advantages in obtaining the report directly from a creditor or other entity that has recently used the consumer report. The user's report is the actual report that was the basis for the adverse action, not a report generated at a later date that may be significantly different than the report relied upon by the user. The user's report is thus the best evidence to explain why adverse action was taken against the consumer.

3.3.1.2 Can a CRA Prevent Users from Providing Reports to Consumers?

Where a user of a consumer report takes adverse action against the consumer based in whole or in part on a consumer report, the CRA cannot prohibit the user from disclosing that report to the consumer.[41] The user is not required to provide the report to the consumer, but the CRA cannot prevent the user from doing so, unless the user has taken no adverse action against the consumer. In addition, a CRA discouraging the user from providing this information should be viewed as hindering and delaying the consumer's ability to correct errors in the credit file. Nevertheless, many users, after taking adverse action, decline to reveal the contents of a consumer report to the consumer.

3.3.1.3 Mortgage Lenders Must Supply Credit Scores

The FCRA requires that mortgage lenders who use credit scores in connection with an application for residential real-estate-secured credit must provide, free of charge, the credit score and associated key factors that the lender used. The lender must provide either the score obtained from a CRA or a score developed and used by the lender.[42] Where a lender uses certain automated underwriting systems, such as those developed by Freddie Mac or Fannie Mae, the lender can satisfy this obligation by disclosing a credit score and associated key factors generated by a CRA, instead of reporting directly on the results of the automated underwriting system.[43] However, if the automated underwriting system generates a numerical score, the lender may disclose that numerical score and associated key factors.[44]

In addition to the disclosure of the actual credit score, the Act requires mortgage lenders to provide to the consumer a prescribed notice that includes the name, address, and telephone number of each CRA providing a credit score that was used.[45] The notice explains the nature of a credit score, its uses, and that the credit score is only as accurate as the credit information in the consumer's file.[46]

3.3.1.4 User Disclosure Where Report Will Lead to Adverse Employment Action

With certain minor exceptions,[47] whenever an employer decides to take an adverse action based in part upon a consumer report, the employer must provide the consumer with a copy of the report before the action is taken.[48] The employer cannot alter the report in any fashion before providing it to the consumer.[49]

However, the FCRA excludes certain reports for employee misconduct investigations from the scope of a "consumer report."[50] In those instances, the employer need only disclose a summary of the report if taking an adverse action.[51]

3.3.1.5 User Disclosure Where Information Obtained From a Person Other Than a Reporting Agency Leads to Credit Denial or an Increase in Credit Charges

Whenever consumer credit is denied, based at least in part on information obtained from a person other than a CRA, the creditor, when communicating the fact of the adverse credit action, must clearly and accurately disclose the consumer's right to obtain information about the reasons for the adverse credit action.[52] The consumer can send a written request for the reasons for the adverse action, if that request is received within sixty days of the consumer learning of the adverse action.[53]

The right only applies where the information obtained from a person other than a CRA bears on the person's credit

---

41 15 U.S.C. § 1681e(c).
42 15 U.S.C. § 1681g(g)(1)(A). *See also* § 14.4.1, *infra*.
43 15 U.S.C. § 1681g(g)(1)(B)(i). See §§ 14.2.2.4, 14.5.3., *infra*, for a discussion of automated underwriting systems.
44 15 U.S.C. § 1681g(g)(1)(B)(ii).
45 15 U.S.C. § 1681g(g)(1)(D).
46 15 U.S.C. § 1681g(g)(1)(D).
47 *See* 15 U.S.C. § 1581b(b)(3)(C) (employment subject to safety regulation by state transportation agency or over which Secretary of Transportation has oversight pursuant to 49 U.S.C. § 31502); 15 U.S.C. § 1681b(b)(4) (national security investigations).
48 15 U.S.C. § 1681b(b)(3)(A).
49 *See* § 8.2.6.2.5, *infra*.
50 *See* §§ 2.4.4, *supra*, 13.2.4.2, *infra*.
51 *See* § 13.4, *infra*
52 15 U.S.C. § 168 m(b)(1).
53 15 U.S.C. § 1681m(b)(1).

standing, character, reputation, personal characteristics, or mode of living.[54] This right does not apply where adverse action is taken as to employment, insurance, or activities other than credit. On the other hand, the right does apply even where the information leading to the credit denial is not related to past delinquencies or defaults, but relates to the consumer's character or life style. More on this right is found at § 8.2.7, *infra*.

3.3.1.6 User Disclosure of Adverse Information Obtained from an Affiliate

Information shared among affiliates related by common ownership or corporate control is generally not considered a consumer report, so that the consumer's rights under the FCRA to access a consumer report do not apply.[55] The Act though provides a limited right to learn about information shared by affiliates.

The right applies where an adverse action is taken against a consumer relating to credit, insurance, or employment, and that action is based on information furnished by a person related by common ownership or affiliated by common corporate control to the person taking the adverse action.[56] No disclosure need be made where the furnished information is based solely on transactions or experiences between the consumer and the furnisher, or upon a consumer report.[57] In other words, no disclosure need be made if Entity A tells affiliated Entity B about the consumer's credit experience solely with Entity A, or Entity A based its information on a consumer report it received on the consumer. In that latter case, presumably, Entity B should notify the consumer that adverse action was taken based upon a consumer report. The right to obtain the information from Entity B apparently only applies where Entity A furnishes information to Entity B that it received from a third party, not a CRA.

The user taking the adverse action must disclose "the nature of the information" to the consumer within thirty days of receipt of the request.[58] Compare this requirement with the FCRA's requirement that the CRA disclose "all information in the consumer's file at the time of the request."[59] This difference makes sense because a user only possesses the information supplied to it, and not all the information that the supplier maintains concerning the consumer.

The issue still remains whether "the nature" of the information refers to a complete description of the information, or just a summary of the type of information. At the time when this provision was drafted (as part of the Consumer Credit Reform Act of 1996[60]), CRA were required to disclose the "nature and substance" of all the information in a consumer's file.[61] That disclosure requirement applied to every item of information which the consumer reporting agency had in its possession at the time that the consumer requested disclosure, regardless of how the information is stored.[62] According to the Act's legislative history, this disclosure provision was intended "to permit the consumer to examine all the information in his file . . . while not giving the consumer the right to physically handle his file."[63] It would seem that the affiliated user's disclosure of the "nature" of the information must be similarly complete.

The policy behind the provision allowing access to information from non-reporting agencies leading to adverse credit actions would also suggest that "the nature of the information" must be a detailed description. The purpose of the disclosure is to enable a consumer to learn enough about the information to determine whether it is complete and accurate, and thus not an unfair basis for the action. Unless the information is sufficiently described, or itself revealed, the consumer will be unable to correct or supplement inaccurate or incomplete information. Note that the FCRA provides that no person can be held liable for a violation of the right to obtain this information if the person shows by a preponderance of evidence that reasonable procedures were maintained to ensure compliance.[64]

3.3.2 Right to a Free Annual Disclosure

Upon a consumer's request, nationwide CRAs (Equifax, Experian, and TransUnion) and nationwide specialty CRAs must provide the consumer with a free consumer report, once during any twelve-month period.[65] The report must be provided within fifteen days after the date on which the request is received.[66] The rules as to this free report are somewhat different for nationwide CRAs and nationwide specialty CRAs.

A "nationwide" CRA is one that regularly assembles or evaluates and maintains public record information and credit account information regarding consumers residing nationwide, for the purpose of furnishing reports to third parties concerning those consumers' creditworthiness, standing or capacity.[67] TransUnion, Equifax, and Experian are nationwide CRAs.

---

54 15 U.S.C. § 1681m(b)(1).
55 *See* § 2.4.3, *supra*.
56 15 U.S.C. § 1681m(b)(2). *See also* § 8.2.7, *infra*.
57 15 U.S.C. § 1681m(b)(2)(C)(ii).
58 15 U.S.C. § 1681m(b)(2)(A)(ii).
59 15 U.S.C. § 1681g(a)(1).

60 Pub. L. No. 104-208, 110 Stat. 3009 (Sept. 30, 1996).
61 Prior version of 15 U.S.C. § 1681g(a)(1) (Sept. 23, 1994).
62 15 U.S.C. § 1681a(g); FTC Official Staff Commentary §§ 603(g) item 2, 609 item 5, *reprinted at* Appx. D, *infra*. *See also* Trans Union Credit Co., 102 F.T.C. 1109 (1983) (consent order).
63 Conference Rep. No. 1587, 91st Cong., 2d Sess. *reprinted in* 1970 U.S.C.C.A.N. 4415.
64 15 U.S.C. § 1681m(c).
65 15 U.S.C. § 1681j(a)(1)(A).
66 15 U.S.C. § 1681j(a)(2).
67 15 U.S.C. § 1681a(p). *See also* 16 C.F.R. § 610.1(a)(9).

Nationwide CRAs must, upon the consumer's request and proper identification, provide an annual file disclosure to the consumer.[68] New nationwide CRAs in their first year of their operation do not have to provide a free annual report.[69] No matter from which of the three major nationwide CRAs the consumer seeks the free report, the consumer requests the report from one centralized source—whether via the Internet, a toll-free telephone number, or by mail.

FTC rules do not prohibit the centralized source from placing advertisements on its own website, or otherwise engage in marketing or advertising, but the rules do place restrictions on these efforts. The advertising or marketing cannot undermine the purpose of the centralized source to provide free consumer reports,[70] such as:

- Pop-up ads that make it difficult to fill in a request form on the website;[71]
- Representations that imply the consumer must purchase a product to receive or understand the report;[72]
- Representations that the report will not be free or will adversely affect the consumer's credit record;[73]
- Representations that an additional product sold by the centralized source is free when it is not; or
- The failure to prominently disclose that an initial free offer must be cancelled to avoid future charges.[74]

A "nationwide specialty agency" is one that compiles and maintains consumer files on a nationwide basis relating to medical records or payments, residential or tenant history, check writing history, employment history, or insurance claims.[75] Some of the more common of these specialty CRAs are described at §§ 2.6, 2.7, and 3.2.4, *supra*. Such CRAs must provide a toll-free telephone number and a streamlined process for consumers to request their reports.[76]

The process must provide clear and prominent instructions for requesting a report by any additional available request methods, but that do not undermine the ability of the consumer to request the report.[77] The toll-free telephone number must appear in all telephone directories where the CRA's other phone numbers appear,[78] and be prominently posted on the CRA's website.[79] If the consumer requests an annual file disclosure through a method other than the process established by the CRA, the CRA must either accept and process the request or instruct the consumer how to properly make the request.[80]

Both nationwide and specialty CRAs must have adequate capacity to meet a reasonably anticipated volume of consumer requests,[81] with adequate contingency plans for reasonably likely situations that might increase demand.[82] FTC regulations make certain provisions where request volume exceeds any reasonable anticipation.[83]

The CRA can only ask for the minimum of personal information necessary to be able to properly identify the consumer,[84] must provide clear and understandable instructions on how to obtain the requested report, and must provide directions as to the next step if the centralized source is having trouble identifying the consumer.[85] The FTC provides a sample standardized form which consumer can use to request a report.[86] The CRA can use the information provided by the consumer only to process the request, to process some other transaction requested by the consumer at the same time, to update the person's identifier with the CRA, or to comply with any FCRA requirements.[87]

3.3.3 "Free" Reports That Are Not Free

Section 3.3.2, *supra*, describes the consumer's right to an annual free report and the following subsections describe a number of other rights to obtain free or low-cost reports and credit scores. A number of companies market "free" consumer reports that are not free at all, but are only introductory teasers that convert to an expensive subscription service. For example, the FTC has settled charges that Experian Consumer Direct deceptively marketed free consumer reports by not adequately disclosing that consumers accepting the offer would automatically be signed up for a $79.95 monitoring service, if they did not affirmatively cancel within thirty days.[88] Visitors of the websites of the "Big Three" CRAs will have difficulty finding how to order a free report, because these websites promote a number of other offers that will result in substantial cost to the consumer.

---

68 16 C.F.R. § 610.2(d).
69 15 U.S.C. § 1681j(a)(4).
70 16 C.F.R. § 610.2(g)(1).
71 16 C.F.R. § 610.2(g)(2)(i).
72 16 C.F.R. § 610.2(g)(2)(ii).
73 16 C.F.R. § 610.2(g)(2)(iii).
74 16 C.F.R. § 610.2(g)(2)(iv).
75 15 U.S.C. § 1681a(w). *See also* 16 C.F.R. § 610.1(a)(10).
76 15 U.S.C. § 1681j(a)(C)(i).
77 16 C.F.R. §§ 610.3(a)(1)(i), 610.3(a)(2)(iii).
78 16 C.F.R. § 610.3(a)(1)(ii).
79 16 C.F.R. § 610.3(a)(1)(iii).
80 16 C.F.R. § 610.3(e).
81 16 C.F.R. §§ 610.2(b)(2)(i), 610.3(a)(2)(i).
82 16 C.F.R. §§ 610.2(c) 610.3(b).
83 16 C.F.R. §§ 610.2(e), 3(c).
84 16 C.F.R. §§ 610.2(b)(2)(ii), 610.3(a)(2)(ii). *See also* 15 U.S.C. § 1681h(a) (disclosures only made where there is proper identification).
85 16 C.F.R. §§ 610.2(b)(2), 610.3(a)(2)(iii)(C).
86 16 C.F.R. Part 698, Appendix D. A copy of this form is reproduced at Appx. C, *infra*.
87 16 C.F.R. §§ 610.2(f), 610.3(d).
88 FTC v. Consumerinfo.com, Inc., SACV05-801 AHS(MLGx) (C.D. Cal. Aug. 15, 2005) (stipulated final judgment and order for permanent injunction), *available on companion CD-Rom accompanying this manual*.

3.3.4 Right to Obtain a Credit Score

One of the key items in a consumer's file is a credit score, which is a single numerical representation of much of the information in the file.[89] When the consumer requests a consumer report, whether it is pursuant to a free annual report, in response to an adverse credit action, or any other type of request, the CRA is not required to include a credit score with that report.[90] Nevertheless, when the consumer makes a request for a report, the CRA must disclose that the consumer can pay a fee and obtain a credit score,[91] either by specifically requesting it at the same time as the consumer report, or by requesting it separately.

When the consumer makes such a request, the CRA must disclose either the current score or the most recent score that the CRA had calculated for a creditor,[92] the date the score was created,[93] the range of possible scores under the model used (that is the worst and best possible scores),[94] and the entity that provided the score.[95] The score must either (a) be generated using a scoring model that is widely distributed to users by the CRA or (b) assist the consumer in understanding the assessment by the credit scoring model of his or her credit behavior and predications about that behavior.[96]

The CRA must disclose the top four key factors (and no more) that adversely affected the credit score, listed in order of importance.[97] In addition, the CRA must also disclose if the number of inquiries on a consumer's file adversely affected the score, even if it was not one of the four top reasons.[98] The CRA is also required to provide a statement indicating that the information and credit scoring model may be different than the credit score used by a lender.[99]

The CRA can charge a fair and reasonable fee, as determined by the FTC.[100] As of October 2006, the FTC had not established such a fee. In its *Advanced Notice of Proposed Rulemaking*, the FTC appears to be considering setting the fee for obtaining a credit score at a price similar to the prices charged in the unregulated market, from about $4.00 to $8.00.[101]

CRAs are not required to develop or disclose the score if the CRA does not distribute scores that are used in connection with residential real property loans or does not develop scores that assist credit providers in understanding the general credit behavior of a consumer and predicting the future behavior of the consumer.[102] The FCRA requirements are not to be construed to require CRAs to maintain credit scores in their files.[103]

While the FCRA generally preempts state laws regarding disclosure of credit scores, California and Colorado state laws are grandfathered.[104] In addition, nothing prevents CRAs and others from voluntarily providing or selling a credit score to a consumer.[105]

3.3.5 Right to Free Reports Following a Fraud Alert or Other Fraud

A consumer who informs a CRA that there has been fraud relating to the consumer's identity or to his or her consumer reporting file has three separate rights to obtain a free consumer report. First, when a consumer asserts in good faith to a nationwide CRA[106] a suspicion that the consumer has been or is about to become a fraud victim, including identity theft, and provides appropriate proof of identity, the CRA must include a fraud alert in the consumer's file.[107] In that case, the CRA, upon the consumer's request, must provide a free copy of the consumer's report, within three business days of the request.[108] The CRA must also disclose this right to the consumer.[109] Presumably it must also disclose to the consumer the proper procedure to request the free report.

When the consumer informs one nationwide CRA of the fraud suspicion, that CRA must inform the other nationwide

---

89 Credit scores are examined at Ch. 14, *infra*. See § 8.2.4, *infra*, regarding disclosure of credit scores.
90 15 U.S.C. § 1681g(a)(1)(B).
91 15 U.S.C. § 1681g(a)(6). In addition, the Summary of Consumer Rights also must include a provision stating that the consumer has the right to obtain a credit score from a CRA and a description of how to obtain the score. 15 U.S.C. § 1681g(c)(1)(B)(iv).
92 15 U.S.C. § 1681g(f)(1)(A).
93 15 U.S.C. § 1681g(f)(1)(D).
94 15 U.S.C. § 1681g(f)(1)(B).
95 15 U.S.C. § 1681g(f)(1)(E).
96 15 U.S.C. § 1681g(f)(7)(A).
97 15 U.S.C. § 1681g(f)(1)(C), (f)(2)(B). For credit scores provided using Fair Isaac scoring models, the key factors are probably the "reason codes" provided by FICO. The most common of these codes involved a serious delinquency, a derogatory public record, or collection action. These three reasons accounted for 67% of all primary reasons provided. Consumer Federation of America and National Credit Reporting Ass'n, Credit Score Accuracy and Implications for Consumers 22–23 (Dec. 17, 2002), *available at* www.consumerfed.org/121702CFA_NCRA_Credit_Score_Report_Final.pdf.
98 15 U.S.C. § 1681g(f)(9).
99 15 U.S.C. § 1681g(f)(1).
100 15 U.S.C. § 1681g(f)(8).
101 69 Fed. Reg. 64,698 (Nov. 8, 2004).
102 15 U.S.C. § 1681g(f)(4).
103 15 U.S.C. § 1681g(f)(6).
104 15 U.S.C. § 1681t(b)(3), grandfathering Cal. Civ. Code § 1785.20.2 (West) and Colo. Rev. Stat. §§ 5-3-106(2) and 12-14.3-104.3. The Act refers to the latter Colorado statute as § 212-14.3, but this must be an error the reasonable conclusion is that Congress intended to refer to § 12-14.3-104.3 (credit scoring related to the extension of credit secured by a dwelling).
105 See 14.4, *infra*.
106 The definition of such a CRA is described in § 3.4.2.3, *infra*.
107 15 U.S.C. § 1681c-1(a)(1). See also § 9.2, *infra*.
108 15 U.S.C. §§ 1681c-1(a)(2)(B), 1681j(d).
109 15 U.S.C. §§ 1681c-1(a)(2)(A), 1681j(d).

CRAs of the suspicion,[110] which should trigger a fraud alert in the consumer's file at these other nationwide CRAs.[111] The fraud alerts in the consumer's file at the other nationwide CRAs should then provide the consumer with a free report from those CRAs as well, in addition to a disclosure from those CRAs of this right.[112]

A second right to a free report is triggered when a consumer submits to a nationwide CRA appropriate proof of identity and an identity theft report already submitted to a law enforcement agency.[113] In that case, the CRA must include an extended fraud alert in the consumer's file for up to seven years.[114] With an extended fraud alert, the CRA, upon the consumer's request, must provide two free copies of the consumer's report during the twelve-month period beginning on the date the fraud alert was included in the file.[115] The reports must be provided to the consumer within three business days of the request.[116] The CRA must also disclose these rights to the consumer when the identity theft report is forwarded to the CRA.[117] Presumably it must also disclose to the consumer the proper procedure to request the free report.

Suspicion of identity theft leads to a fraud alert; submission of an actual identity theft report leads to an "extended fraud alert." When the consumer submits such an identity theft report to one nationwide CRAs, that CRA must inform the other nationwide CRAs of the report,[118] which should trigger an extended fraud alert in the consumer's file at these other CRAs.[119] This, in turn, provides the consumer with two free reports from each of the nationwide CRAs.[120]

In addition to the right to free consumer reports from nationwide CRAs after a fraud alert or an extended fraud alert, a consumer who has reason to believe that the file at a CRA contains inaccurate information due to fraud is entitled to one free report in any twelve month period.[121] The consumer must provide the CRA with written certification of this belief.[122] There is no explicit requirement that the certification explain or detail the basis of the belief. The CRA must disclose all information the CRA is required to disclose upon any consumer request.[123]

Unlike fraud alert provisions that only apply to nationwide CRAs, this additional fraud provision applies to any CRA, such as one reporting on only information relating to medical records or payments, residential or tenant history, check writing history, employment history, or insurance claims. In addition, fraud alerts under the FCRA primarily relate to identity theft claims, but this latter provision applies to fraud generally. Thus, it should apply to many additional circumstances in which one's credit record may be inaccurate due to fraud, ranging from home improvement and telemarketing scams, lending abuses, and fraudulent sales, to the intentional furnishing of misleading information to the CRA.

3.3.6 Free Report Following Adverse Action or After Certain Communications from Affiliated Debt Collection Agencies

When a user takes an adverse action relating to credit, insurance, or employment, in part because of information in a consumer report, the user must provide to the consumer the name and address of the CRA that supplied the consumer report.[124] The consumer has sixty days to request a free consumer report from the CRA referenced in the notice.[125] This right is in addition to the right to a free annual report.

Even if the user's original denial is subsequently reversed, the consumer retains the sixty-day right to disclosure without charge.[126] The consumer is entitled to a free copy of the report even if the basis of the denial was that the consumer had supplied credit references that were too few in number or too new to appear in the credit file.[127] According to an informal FTC staff opinion, the right to free disclosure applies only to the CRA whose report was used in the denial.[128]

---

110 15 U.S.C. § 1681c-1(a)(1)(B).
111 15 U.S.C. § 1681c-1(e).
112 15 U.S.C. § 1681c-1(a)(2).
113 Identity theft report is defined at 16 C.F.R. § 603.3. *See also* § 9.2.2.3, *infra*.
114 15 U.S.C. § 1681c-1(b)(1).
115 15 U.S.C. §§ 1681c-1(b)(2)(B), 1681j(d).
116 15 U.S.C. §§ 1681c-1(b)(2)(B), 1681j(d).
117 15 U.S.C. §§ 1681c-1(b)(2)(A), 1681j(d).
118 15 U.S.C. § 1681c-1(b)(1)(C).
119 15 U.S.C. § 1681c-1(e).
120 15 U.S.C. § 1681c-1(b)(2).
121 15 U.S.C. § 1681j(c).
122 *Id.*
123 *See* § 3.5, *infra*.
124 *See* § 8.2.6, *supra*.
125 15 U.S.C. § 1681j(b). This applies to adverse actions based on medical information as well. The FTC and MIB have agreed to a policy requiring MIB members to inform applicants (1) that insurance has been denied, or made more expensive, because of information obtained from an investigation conducted as a result of MIB information; (2) the applicant's right to obtain a summary of the MIB report at no charge within 60 days; and (3) of a street address and telephone number at which the applicant can contact MIB. Medine, FTC Informal Staff Opinion Letter (May 31, 1995), *reprinted on the CD-Rom accompanying this manual*; Isaac, FTC Informal Staff Opinion Letter (July 5, 1995), *reprinted on the CD-Rom accompanying this manual*. The terms of the agreement provided for the applicant's right to obtain a summary of the MIB report at no charge within 30 days following adverse action. Since, the statute was amended to require free charges for reports obtained within 60 days of adverse action. *See* § 8.2.6, *infra*. Presumably, the statutory change applies to MIB.
126 FTC Official Staff Commentary § 612 item 1, *reprinted at* Appx. D, *infra*.
127 *Id.*
128 *See* Grimes, FTC Informal Staff Opinion Letter (Jan. 17, 1989), *reprinted on the CD-Rom accompanying this manual*.

When a debt collection agency affiliated with a CRA states that the consumer's credit rating may be or has been adversely affected, the consumer has sixty days to request a free consumer report, presumably from the CRA affiliated with the debt collector.[129] For example, TeleCheck Services is a CRA keeping track of dishonored checks. TeleCheck Recovery Systems collects on dishonored checks. If the collection effort mentions that nonpayment will affect the consumer's credit rating, the consumer can request a free report from TeleCheck Services. This right is in addition to the right to a free annual report.

3.3.7 Free Report for the Unemployed and for Public Assistance Recipients

Consumers who are unemployed and seeking employment,[130] and consumers receiving public assistance[131] are entitled to one free consumer report in any twelve month period. This right should be in addition to the right to a free annual report.

Consumers seeking a report to aid an employment search must provide the CRA with written certification that the consumer is unemployed *and* intends to apply for employment in the sixty-day period beginning on the date on which the certification is made. Because the consumer will not know which CRA will be used by a prospective employer, the best course of action is to request free disclosure of the contents of the consumer's file from each of the "Big Three" nationwide CRAs, and perhaps local ones as well.

Similarly, those receiving public assistance may make a request for free disclosure of the contents of the consumer's file to more than one CRA. The consumer must provide the CRA with written certification that the consumer is in fact a recipient of public assistance benefits. No requirement of public agency confirmation or certification exists.

Public welfare assistance, the term used in the Act, is not defined. Presumably it includes family welfare benefits to low-income children and households, Social Security benefits to older Americans, SSI benefits, state and federal food stamp programs, workers compensation benefits, fuel assistance benefits, Medicare and Medicaid coverage, and other state and federal and local benefit programs. The FCRA does not require the consumer to certify or reveal more than that the consumer is a "recipient of public welfare assistance."

3.3.8 State Law Right to Additional Free Reports

The FCRA provides for a free consumer report annually, and the Act indicates that states cannot change the frequency of this free consumer report.[132] Nevertheless, the Act specifies that certain states are grandfathered, allowing them to change the frequency of free reports. A Georgia statute that provides for two free consumer reports a year is one of those grandfathered.[133] The FCRA also allows Colorado, Maryland, Massachusetts, New Jersey, and Vermont to change the frequency of the free consumer report, and these states all allow residents to receive one free copy of their report each calendar year.[134] It would appear that this state-provided free copy should be in *addition* to the annual consumer report provided by federal law, otherwise there would be no purpose in providing special treatment for these statutes in the Act. Furthermore, the federal Act explicitly does not preempt a Colorado statute that provides a free consumer report when a Colorado resident's report has been subject to eight or more inquiries within a year or where a consumer report is received that would add negative information.[135]

3.3.9 Right to Obtain a Report for a Fee at Any Time from Any Type of Reporting Agency

3.3.9.1 General

In addition to the annual right to a free report from a nationwide CRA, and the special grounds for a free report from any type of CRA, the FCRA provides that every CRA of any type must, upon any consumer request, and upon proper identification,[136] clearly and accurately disclose to the consumer all information in the consumer's file at the time of the request.[137] Any consumer at any time has a statutory right to the disclosure of this information for a fee.[138] A CRA violates the FCRA by refusing to provide this information[139] or by providing only partial disclosure.[140]

---

129 15 U.S.C. § 1681j(b). Some CRAs have a collection agency component. Their collection letters may bear the CRA's name and make reference to the importance of good credit.
130 15 U.S.C. § 1681j(c)(1).
131 15 U.S.C. § 1681j(c)(2).
132 15 U.S.C. § 1681t(b)(4).
133 15 U.S.C. § 1681t(b)(4)(B) exempting Ga. Code § 10-1-393(29)(C) from the preemption provision.
134 15 U.S.C. § 1681t(b)(4). *See* Colo. Rev. Stat. § 12-14.3-104(2)(e); Md. Code Ann. Com. Law § 14-1209; Mass. Gen. Laws Ann. ch. 93, § 59; Vt. Stat. Ann. tit. 9, § 2480c.
135 Colo. Rev. Stat. § 12-14.3-104(2)(a).
136 *See* 15 U.S.C. § 1681h(a)(1).
137 15 U.S.C. § 1681g(a)(1).
138 *See* § 3.3.9.2, *infra*.
139 *See, e.g.*, Heath v. Credit Bureau of Sheridan, Inc., 618 F.2d 693 (10th Cir. 1980); Hauser v. Equifax, Inc., 602 F.2d 811 (8th Cir. 1979); Ackerley v. Credit Bureau of Sheridan, Inc., 385 F. Supp. 658 (D. Wyo. 1974). *Cf.* Wiggins v. Equifax Servs., Inc., 848 F. Supp. 213 (D.D.C. 1993).
140 *See, e.g.*, Collins v. Retail Credit Co., 410 F. Supp. 924 (E.D. Mich. 1976).

This is an important right when dealing with entities that may not consider themselves CRAs, but still fall within the FCRA definition.[141] For example, creditors, detective agencies, employment agencies, and others may have to provide consumers with the contents of their files on the consumer, if they meet the definition of a CRA.[142]

3.3.9.2 Legal Limits on the Price of a Report

The FCRA states that the charge for a consumer file disclosure shall be reasonable and not exceed $8.00, adjusted annually for inflation.[143] For 2006, the Federal Trade Commission has set that maximum charge as $10.[144] The charge is a maximum, and does not have to be imposed. If a charge will be imposed, it must be "indicated" to the consumer before the information is provided.[145]

State laws that set a lower maximum charge than found in the FCRA should not be preempted. While the Act preempts state laws that require free reports at a different *frequency* than the federal law, this preemption does not apply to state laws that require lower dollar *charges* for reports than specified in the FCRA. In addition, there is no conflict between the Act and such state laws because the FCRA does not require the imposition of a particular charge, but only specifies a maximum allowable charge. There is no conflict if states can require a lower maximum.[146]

A number of state statutes limit the amount the CRA may charge. California residents pay $8.00, but there is no charge if the report proves to be inaccurate.[147] Connecticut residents pay $5.00 for the first copy and $7.50 for each additional copy.[148] Maine residents pay $2.00.[149] Maryland residents pay $5.00 for copies beyond the first free copy.[150] Massachusetts law provides for a free report once per year from the nationwide CRA, $5.00 from local CRAs; and subsequent reports are $8.00.[151] Minnesota residents pay $3.00 for the first copy.[152] Vermont residents pay $7.50 for copies beyond the first free copy.[153]

3.3.9.3 Time Within Which Report Must Be Provided

Federal law requires that the first free annual report be provided within fifteen days, and reports following an identity theft notification must be made within three days.[154] The FCRA, though, does not specify a time period for other types of report requests. Nevertheless, undue delays are not permissible. For example, a CRA violated the Act by unreasonably forcing the consumer to make several visits to its office before it disclosed the nature and substance of some of the items in the consumer's file.[155] Some delays have been eliminated with the use of the Internet and the availability of consumer reports on-line. In addition, some state laws specify the time period the CRA has to respond.[156]

3.4 Mechanics of Obtaining a Consumer Report

3.4.1 Deciding from Which CRA to Seek a Report

In most cases, the consumer's file at one of the "Big Three" CRAs will be of most interest. These are the CRAs that provide most reports used by creditors, insurers, and even employers. Each of the "Big Three" CRAs have different systems to collect similar data. The actual information collected may be different in some cases, and the CRA may have a different algorithm to identify matches that are good enough to associate with the consumer. As a result, while the reports from each of the nationwide CRAs will often be similar, they also can contain different information.

Moreover, there may be even more variation in credit scores released to the consumer from the "Big Three" CRAs or from other sources. There are many potential credit scores. For example, at some lenders, the Classic FICO scoring model is being replaced by the NextGen model.[157] A score can be developed by a CRA to send to its users; certain users can request that the CRA produce a score tailored to that user's specifications, or third parties can produce a score using yet another different model.

Not only are the scoring systems different, but even when systems attempt to produce similar results on a similar scale, the same consumer can obtain significantly different scores from the different CRAs. An examination of over 500,000 consumer credit files found that 29% of consumers have

---

141 See § 2.5, *supra*.
142 See § 2.7, *supra*.
143 15 U.S.C. § 1681j(f).
144 Federal Trade Commission, Notice Regarding Charges for Certain Disclosures, 70 Fed. Reg. 94,816 (Dec. 30, 2005).
145 15 U.S.C. § 1681j.
146 Credit Data of Arizona, Inc. v. Arizona, 602 F.2d 195 (9th Cir. 1979).
147 Cal. Civ. Code § 1785 (West).
148 *See* Conn. Gen. Stat. §§ 36a-695 through 36a-704.
149 *See* Me. Rev. Stat. Ann. tit. 10, § 1316(z) (actual costs).
150 *See* Md. Code Ann. Com. Law § 14-1209.
151 Mass. Gen. Laws Ann. ch. 93, § 59.
152 *See* Minn. Stat. § 13C.01; Okla. Stat. tit 24, § 81–86. *See also* Opay v. Experian Info. Solutions, Inc., 681 N.W.2d 394 (Minn. Ct. App. 2004) (only if requested by regular mail).
153 *See* Vt. Stat. Ann. tit. 9, § 2480c (free once per year, subsequent reports no more than $7.50).

154 15 U.S.C. §§ 1681c-1(a)(2)(B), 1681j(a)(2).
155 Millstone v. O'Hanlon Reports, Inc., 383 F. Supp. 269 (E.D. Mo. 1974), *aff'd*, 528 F.2d 829 (8th Cir. 1976).
156 *See, e.g.*, R.I Gen. Laws § 6-13.1-20 (four working days).
157 Nathalie Mainland and Julia Wooding, *NextGen FICO Risk Score Conversion FAQ*, Fair Isaac 6 (Apr. 2002). *See also* Ch. 14, *infra*.

credit scores that differ by at least fifty points between CRAs, while 4% have scores that differ by at least 100 points.[158]

Where a consumer receives notice that a consumer report contributed to an adverse action, the notice will identify the CRA providing the report. The consumer may then want to obtain a report from that particular CRA, especially since the report will be free.[159] However, it is just as important to obtain reports from the other nationwide CRAs to make sure those files are accurate as well.

Consumers are entitled to one free report a year from each nationwide CRAs. One strategy is to go to the centralized source once a year, and order reports from all three CRAs at the same time. Another approach is to order them one by one throughout the year. The latter approach enables the consumer to do some rough monitoring for changes, although differences in the reports may just mean that the "Big Three" CRAs have not all used the same data sources. CRAs are also now aggressively marketing various products that allow continual monitoring of a report for a substantial fee.

Many specialty CRAs compile information about consumers on a nationwide basis relating to a specific subject, such as medical records, tenant history, check writing history, employment history, or insurance claims.[160] If a consumer is concerned with any of these issues, a free annual report should be obtained from them as well.

Finally, in addition to the "Big Three," there are smaller CRAs throughout the United States. These smaller CRAs tend to keep records only on consumers living within limited geographic areas. The majority are either affiliated with or fully owned by one of the "Big Three" nationwide CRAs, thus storing and distributing consumer reports through either Equifax, TransUnion, or Experian. However, some smaller CRAs gather their own information or are resellers.[161] Reports can be obtained from these CRAs, but there may be a minimal charge for these reports. This will certainly make sense where one of these CRAs is identified in a notice as being the source of a negative consumer report, and in addition the report will be free.

3.4.2 How to Request a Consumer Report

3.4.2.1 Free Annual Reports from the "Big Three" National Credit Bureaus

When seeking a free annual report from the nationwide CRAs, the consumer forwards the request to a centralized source,[162] which enables the consumer to obtain a consumer report from all nationwide CRAs.[163] The nationwide CRAs jointly design, fund, and operate the centralized source, and consumers can request a report from that source by any of the following three methods:

- On-line at www.annualcreditreport.com;
- By telephone, to 877-322-8228; or
- By letter to Annual Credit Report Request Service, P.O. Box 105281, Atlanta, GA 30374-5281.[164]

The consumer may be asked detailed information about existing credit accounts and employment, as a form of identification, in addition to the usual forms of identification.

3.4.2.2 Other Reports from the "Big Three" National Credit Bureaus

In addition to a free annual report, consumers have a number of other rights to obtain a consumer report from the "Big Three" nationwide CRAs. In general, there will be little difficulty in obtaining a paid report or purchasing one of the many other more expensive products that the nationwide CRAs are now selling. Going to their websites will provide easy access to all of these paid products. The consumer may have more difficulty obtaining information on how to request a free report other than an annual free report.

Nationwide CRAs must have toll-free numbers and personnel that are accessible to consumers within normal working hours, and these numbers must be disclosed in all CRA disclosures.[165] What follows is contact information that may work for the "Big Three" CRAs (note that these addresses are subject to change):

Equifax
www.equifax.com
800-685-1111
P.O. Box 740241
Atlanta, GA 30374-0241.
For inquiries concerning suspected fraud, call 800-525-6285.

Experian
www.experian.com
888-EXPERIAN (888-397-3742)
P.O. Box 2002
Allen, TX 75013

---

158 Consumer Federation of America and National Credit Reporting Ass'n, Credit Score Accuracy and Implications for Consumers 24 (Dec. 17, 2002), *available at* www.consumerfed.org/121702CFA_NCRA_Credit_Score_Report_Final.pdf.
159 *See* § 8.2.6, *infra*.
160 *See* §§ 2.6.2, 3.2.4, *supra*.
161 *See* § 2.6.3, *supra*.

162 15 U.S.C. § 1681j(a)(1)(B).
163 16 C.F.R. § 610.2(a).
164 16 C.F.R. § 610.2(b)(1). The exact website and mailing addresses and phone number are selected by the nationwide CRAs, and so could change in the future.
165 15 U.S.C. § 1681g(c)(2).

Fraud inquiries use the same phone number, but are sent to P.O. Box 9530.

TransUnion
www.transunion.com
800-888-4213
P.O. Box 1000
Chester, PA 19022
For inquiries concerning suspected fraud, 800-680-7289, Fraud Victim Assistance Division, P.O. Box 6790, Fullerton, CA 92634

It may be that free reports for reasons other than an annual report may be difficult to order from the website or even from the toll-free numbers, leaving a mail request as the best approach. Adverse action notices will also include information on contacting a CRA that was the source of the information leading to the action, and an appropriate phone number may be included there.

However a request is made, the consumer should retain as much documentation of the request as possible. Where a report is not forthcoming, it contains the wrong information, or the report is slow to arrive, the documentation may be useful in re-creating the CRA's failure to comply fully with FCRA requirements.

If a consumer wants to go to the CRA in person, the "Big Three" CRAs have about 150 offices around the country, and an additional 450 independent affiliates. There are also about 100 unaffiliated CRAs.[166] The best way to find the name and address of CRAs in a consumer's vicinity is to look in the telephone yellow pages or on the Internet.

The consumer requesting a free report not based upon the annual right should present some kind of documentation for this request. Usually a CRA will accept a copy of the notice of denial or the name of the creditor as verification of an adverse action. Other documentation may be required for the unemployed or those on public assistance.[167]

A consumer's inquiry should clearly be a request; a casual inquiry to a CRA's telephone receptionist asking generally what is going on is not a proper request for disclosure.[168] It is a safe procedure to specify that the request is for the complete file, including sources for the information in the file, information about persons who have procured a report on the consumer, and a record of inquiries. Nevertheless, if a consumer simply requests disclosure, without specifying which piece of information is sought, the CRA must disclose all three of these types of information.[169] The consumer will have to make a specific request for a credit score, and may have to pay for this information. The CRA will ask for extensive identification information, such as full name (e.g., middle initial, Junior), date of birth, Social Security number,

---

[166] See www.ncrainc.org.
[167] See § 3.3.7, supra.
[168] Clay v. Equifax, Inc., 762 F.2d 952 (11th Cir. 1985).
[169] Equifax Servs., Inc. v. Lamb, 621 S.W.2d 28 (Ky. Ct. App. 1981).

current and former addresses, current employer, daytime and nighttime telephone number, and the consumer's signature. Advocates report though that name, address, and Social Security number will generally suffice.

3.4.2.3 Obtaining Reports from Specialized CRAs, Local CRAs

Specialized nationwide CRAs must provide a toll-free number where the consumer can obtain a free annual report. Presumably the same number can be used to obtain reports on other bases. Here is the contact information for a number of the specialized CRAs (subject to change; readers are advised to verify these addresses before using):

C.L.U.E. Auto or Homeowners Reports
www.choicetrust.com
ChoicePoint Consumer Disclosure Center
P.O. Box 105295
Atlanta, GA 30348
866-312-8076

WorkPlace Solutions
www.choicetrust.com
ChoicePoint Consumer Disclosure Center
P.O. Box 105292
Atlanta, GA 30348
866-312-8075

Tenant History
www.choicetrust.com
Residential Data Consumer Disclosure Center
P.O. Box 850126
Richardson, TX 75085-0126
877-448-5732

Medical Information Bureau
www.mib.com
MIB Inc.
P.O. Box 105
Essex Station
Boston, MA 02112
866-692-6901

TeleCheck
www.telecheck.com
TeleCheck Services, Inc.
5251 Westheimer
Houston, TX 77056
800-TELECHECK

It is somewhat unclear whether local CRAs (those not meeting the definition of a nationwide or nationwide specialized CRA) must set up a toll-free number to accept calls where a consumer is entitled to a free report, or just a number where the consumer pays for the telephone charges. The Consumer Credit Reporting Reform Act of 1996 eliminated language specifically authorizing a requirement that consumers pay telephone toll charges in general.[170]

3.4.3 Requirement of Proper Consumer Identification

The FCRA mandates that CRAs require the consumer to supply "proper identification" as a condition of the consumer receiving a consumer report.[171] In addition to this legal mandate, CRAs have good reason to be careful to request proper identification from the consumer, because the CRA may be held liable for furnishing a report to a person who does not have a permissible purpose for obtaining it.[172]

The consumer must comply with a CRA's request for information which is reasonably required for verifying that the consumer is entitled to disclosure.[173] On the other hand, the CRA should not require more identifying information from consumers requesting their own reports than from subscribers requesting consumer reports.

When the consumer seeks a free annual report, the FCRA states that the CRA can ask for only the minimum of personal information necessary to be able to properly identify the consumer.[174] The FTC provides a sample standardized form which consumers can use to request a report,[175] that requires the consumer's full name, address, day and evening phone numbers, Social Security number, and date of birth. Despite this, some earlier informal FTC staff opinion letters state that consumers need not provide their Social Security number to receive FCRA disclosures if other sufficient identifying information is provided.[176]

While a CRA may request that the consumer fill out a standard form as part of the identification process, such forms are not required as a prerequisite for disclosure, and the form should not seek more than mere identification of the consumer.[177] In addition, in view of public policy established by state and federal law against discrimination on the basis of gender or marital status,[178] spousal information should normally be precluded as identifying information.

The need for proper identification may not be used as a pretext for collecting information which is not essential for that purpose. In an FTC action, a CRA agreed to stop collecting more information than it actually needed.[179] Examples of excessive information might include: five years of previous address history; five years of previous home and other telephone numbers; previous employment and past employment history; number of dependents; approximate annual worth; banking connections; real estate owned; court records pertaining to the consumer; names and addresses of references; and the nature of the consumer's business.[180]

When a consumer's identity cannot be established based upon the information supplied, the CRA may ask for additional information, such as copies of a driver's license, utility bill, bank statement, and the like. CRAs have been known to accept one clearly authenticated proof, such as a welfare check displaying a delivery address, or to accept authenticity letters from shelter directors, welfare officials, attorneys and other professionals.

3.4.4 Ability of a Consumer's Representative to Receive a Report

The FCRA states that a CRA may furnish a consumer report in accordance with written instructions of the consumer to whom it relates.[181] Thus even a spouse is not authorized to obtain a report on a partner, without the proper power of attorney from the partner.

The FTC Staff Commentary indicates that a CRA may disclose the contents of a consumer's file to a third party authorized by the consumer's written power of attorney to obtain the disclosure, if the third party presents adequate identification and fulfills other applicable conditions for

---

170 15 U.S.C. § 1681h, *as amended by* Pub. L. No. 104-208 § 2410, 110 Stat. 3009 (Sept. 30, 1996) *amending* § 1681(h)(b)(2). The FTC Official Staff Commentary § 610 item 5, *reprinted at* Appx. D, *infra*, stating that CRAs are not responsible for telephone toll charges, has not been reconsidered since enactment of the 1996 legislation. That FTC interpretation also states that where a consumer chooses to obtain disclosures by telephone, the CRA does not have to accept collect calls.
171 15 U.S.C. § 1681h(a)(i).
172 *See* § 7.6, *infra*.
173 *See* Sarver v. Experian Info. Solutions, Inc., 299 F. Supp. 2d 875 (N.D. Ill. 2004), *aff'd on other grounds*, 390 F.3d 969 (7th Cir. 2004) (reasonable to request Social Security number); Miller v. Credit Bureau, Inc., [1969–1973 Decisions Transfer Binder] Consumer Cred. Guide (CCH) ¶ 99,173 (D.C. Super. Ct. 1972).
174 16 C.F.R. §§ 610.2(b)(2)(ii), 610.3(a)(2)(ii).
175 16 C.F.R. Part 698, Appendix D. A copy of this form is reproduced at Appx. C, *infra*.
176 Meyer, FTC Informal Staff Opinion Letter (May 3, 1982), *reprinted on the CD-Rom accompanying this manual*; Goldfarb, FTC Informal Staff Opinion Letter (circa Sept. 1980), *reprinted on the CD-Rom accompanying this manual*. *Contra* Sarver v. Experian Info. Solutions, Inc., 299 F. Supp. 2d 875 (N.D. Ill. 2004), *aff'd on other grounds*, 390 F.3d 969 (7th Cir. 2004) (reasonable to request Social Security number).

177 Russell, FTC Informal Staff Opinion Letter (Sept. 18, 1973), *reprinted on the CD-Rom accompanying this manual*; Martin, FTC Informal Staff Opinion Letter (June 11, 1971), *reprinted on the CD-Rom accompanying this manual*. *See also* FTC Official Staff Commentary § 609 items 2 and 3, *reprinted at* Appx. D, *infra*, which would appear to allow a CRA to require use of a form, "if it does not use the form to inhibit disclosure." *Contra* Bragg, FTC Informal Staff Opinion Letter (May 15, 1972) ("[c]onsumer reporting agencies may not condition disclosure upon the completion of a form by the consumer, unless the in-person disclosure is to be made in the presence of a third party"), *reprinted on the CD-Rom accompanying this manual*.
178 National Consumer Law Center, Credit Discrimination §§ 3.3.4, 3.4.1, 5.5.2.2, 5.5.2.3 (4th ed. 2005 and Supp.).
179 *In re* Equifax, Inc., 96 F.T.C. 1045 (1980), *rev'd in part on other grounds*, 678 F.2d 1047 (11th Cir. 1982).
180 *E.g., In re* American Serv. Bureau, Inc., 92 F.T.C. 330, 336 (1978); *In re* Credit Bureau Assocs., 92 F.T.C. 837, 840 (1978).
181 15 U.S.C. § 1681b(a)(2).

disclosure.[182] However the CRA may also disclose the information directly to the consumer.[183]

This apparently means that the CRA can supply the information directly to the consumer *rather* than to the third party.[184] For example, if a "credit repair" company obtains the consumer's authorization to contact the CRA on the consumer's behalf, the CRA has the right to send the information directly to the consumer, and not to the credit repair company.[185] The practice of providing the report to the consumer rather than the third party apparently derived from a concern with bulk inquiries generated by credit repair organizations. The result should be different if an attorney representing a consumer makes a request with proof of the consumer's written authorization, since an attorney is traditionally allowed to act on behalf of a client in all capacities.[186]

3.4.5 Unreasonable Preconditions to Disclosure

A CRA cannot place unreasonable preconditions on the disclosure of the contents of the consumer's file. The FCRA states that the CRA "shall" provide the information,[187] and the CRA cannot thus refuse to provide information until the consumer meets preconditions created by the CRA. The CRA may not add conditions not set out in the FCRA as a prerequisite to the required disclosure.[188]

For example, a form which authorizes an investigation and authorizes any person to disclose information or records on the consumer as a prerequisite to disclosure is a questionable practice.[189] Similarly, a CRA may not utilize a standard form that includes a disclaimer of liability, even where the language of the disclaimer closely mirrors the language of the Act.[190] The CRA should not be able to require, as a precondition to receiving a report to which they have a legal right to receive, that consumers agree to arbitrate claims against the CRA. (On the other hand, CRAs may be able to require arbitration where the consumer purchases a product that the CRA does not have a legal obligation to provide.) Although a CRA has a legitimate interest in collecting information to ensure maximum possible accuracy, it should not be a prerequisite to the disclosure of a consumer report and should be solicited only *after* that mandatory disclosure is made.[191]

CRAs cannot take consumers "off-line" when the consumers bring suit, precluding the consumers from obtaining their consumer reports directly from the CRA. While initiation of litigation may raise issues regarding direct communications between the consumer's attorney and employees of the defendant CRA, the CRA continues to have a legal obligation to produce the file to the consumer pursuant to section 1681g. Failure to comply subjects the CRA to further claims and liability under the Act.[192]

The CRA also cannot impose unreasonable preconditions to an in-person disclosure. If the consumer specifies in-person disclosure at the CRA's place of business, the consumer must provide reasonable advance notice.[193] However, this notice requirement "should not be used as a means of making it difficult for the consumer to obtain information to which he is entitled."[194]

---

182 FTC Official Staff Commentary § 609 item 4, *reprinted at* Appx. D, *infra. See also* Grimes, FTC Informal Staff Opinion Letters (Oct. 8, 1986) and (Dec. 15, 1986), *reprinted on the CD-Rom accompanying this manual. Cf.* Pinner v. Schmidt, 617 F. Supp. 342 (E.D. La. 1985), *aff'd in part and rev'd in part on other grounds*, 805 F.2d 1258 (5th cir. 1986). Practitioners have reported, however, that some CRAs have refused to comply with an attorney's requests for a report, even when the request asks for the report to be sent directly to the consumer client.

183 FTC Official Staff Commentary § 609 item 4, *reprinted at* Appx. D, *infra*.

184 Supplementary information published with the FTC Official Staff Commentary, 55 Fed. Reg. 18,805 (May 4, 1990).

185 A-1 Credit & Assurance v. Trans Union Credit Info., 678 F. Supp. 1147 (E.D. Pa. 1988).

186 *E.g.*, Lunsford v. United States, 418 F. Supp. 1045, 1055–1056 (D.S.D. 1976) ("in my opinion, a signature as 'attorney for' . . . suffices to show capacity in which the claim is made"; non-FCRA case); Nathan v. United States Jewish Ctr., 20 Conn. Supp. 183 (Super. Ct. 1955) ("It is inconceivable to me that plaintiff's counsel would have written the letter . . . when he was authorized to do so"; non-FCRA case). *Cf.* Pinner v. Schmidt, 617 F. Supp. 342, 347 (E.D. La. 1985), *aff'd in part and rev'd in part*, 805 F.2d 1258, 1262 (5th Cir. 1986) (interpreting 15 U.S.C. § 1681i "Procedure in Case of Disputed Accuracy"). *But see* Cisneros v. U.D. Registry, 39 Cal. App. 4th 548 (1995) (request for disclosure must come from the consumer personally; a letter from the consumer's attorney is not sufficient).

187 15 U.S.C. §§ 1681g, 1681h.

188 *See* FTC Official Staff Commentary § 610 item 2, *reprinted at* Appx. D, *infra*.

189 Russell, FTC Informal Staff Opinion Letter (Sept. 18, 1973), *reprinted on the CD-Rom accompanying this manual. See also In re* Equifax, Inc., 96 F.T.C. 1045 (1980), *rev'd in part on other grounds*, 678 F.2d 1047 (11th Cir. 1982).

190 *In re* MIB, Inc. 101 F.T.C. 415 (1983) (consent order). *Contra* Peeler, FTC Informal Staff Opinion Letter (Mar. 23, 1977), *reprinted on the CD-Rom accompanying this manual*.

191 *In re* American Serv. Bureau, Inc., 92 F.T.C. 330, 336–337 (1978).

192 Spector v. Equifax Info. Servs., 338 F. Supp. 2d 378 (D. Conn. 2004) (cumbersome offline procedures that repeatedly resulted in failure to provide consumer with his credit file could warrant punitive damages).

193 15 U.S.C. § 1681h(b).

194 FTC, Compliance with the Fair Credit Reporting Act, at 31 (1977).

3.5 File Information That Must Be Disclosed

3.5.1 General

Virtually all information in the consumer's file at the time of the consumer's request must be provided to the consumer.[195] The Act explicitly requires CRA's to provide, upon request, *all* information in the consumer's file.[196] The intent is to ensure that the consumer will receive a copy of the consumer report, not a summary of information.[197] A file is defined as "all of the information on that consumer recorded and retained by a consumer reporting agency regardless of how the information is stored."[198] The consumer must be provided with information even if stored in other offices of the CRA.[199] Once a consumer has requested disclosure, the CRA should not change the file before disclosing it to the consumer.[200]

The Act specifies certain information that does not have to be disclosed to the consumer: the fact that the consumer report has been used for FBI counter-intelligence or to determine federal security clearance;[201] certain audit information;[202] and, upon the consumer's request, the last five digits of the consumer's Social Security number.[203] While the FCRA at one time had such an exception for medical information in the consumer's file, that is no longer the case.[204]

The consumer may request less than the complete file and, in such a circumstance, the CRA just discloses the requested information. This issue arose in correspondence between a CRA and the FTC about whether Social Security and consumer account numbers could be scrambled as a security measure. FTC staff opined that all information in the file must be disclosed, including unscrambled numbers, unless the consumer is given the option and does asks for less.[205]

The Act also requires that a Summary of Consumer Rights, drafted by the Federal Trade Commission, must be included with the disclosures.[206] This summary describes the consumer's rights to receive reports and credit scores, and to dispute information.[207] The CRA must also provide contact information for federal agencies enforcing the FCRA, a statement about rights under state law and state enforcement agencies, and a statement that a CRA is not required to remove accurate derogatory information.[208] Nationwide CRAs must also provide a toll-free telephone number at which personnel are accessible to consumers during normal business hours,[209] and contact information

3.5.2 Credit Scores

The FCRA provides certain disclosure rights as to a consumer's credit score.[210] However, the credit score the

---

195 15 U.S.C. § 1681g(a). *See also* Cohan, FTC Informal Staff Opinion Letter (Aug. 1, 2001), *reprinted on the CD-Rom accompanying this manual*.

196 15 U.S.C. § 1681g(a), *as amended by* Pub. L. No. 104-208, 110 Stat. 3009 (Sept. 30, 1996). Prior to the 1996 Amendments, CRAs were only required to disclose the "nature and substance" of all information in the consumer's file.

197 S. Rep. No. 185, 104th Cong., 1st Sess. at 41 (Dec. 14, 1995).

198 15 U.S.C. § 1681a(g); FTC Official Staff Commentary §§ 603(g) item 2, 609 item 5, *reprinted at* Appx. D, *infra*. *See also In re* Trans Union Credit Co., 102 F.T.C. 1109 (1983) (consent order).

199 FTC Official Staff Commentary § 609 item 5, *reprinted at* Appx. D, *infra*. *See also* FTC, Compliance with the Fair Credit Reporting Act, at 30 (1977). *But see In re* Equifax, Inc., 96 F.T.C. 1045 (1980), *rev'd in part on other grounds*, 678 F.2d 1047 (11th Cir. 1982) (disclosure did not have to be made in each suboffice as long as disclosure was available in each branch office).

200 An FTC staff attorney criticized the practice of changing the file before giving it to the consumer:

> However, we believe that a different case is presented in the situation where the credit bureau reinvestigates and deletes information *after* the consumer requests disclosure. Such deletion, in addition to preventing corrected information from being provided to a credit grantor, can also deprive the consumer of evidence of inaccurate information needed to make out a case against the credit bureau for violation of § 607(a) of the Act, 15 U.S.C. § 1681e(b). In that situation, we believe that the credit bureau violates Section 609 [§ 1681g], which requires disclosure of the nature and substance of all information in its files on the consumer *at the time of the request* (emphasis added). Liability for damages could be based either on § 617 (negligent non-compliance), or § 616 (willful non-compliance) if there has been a deliberate attempt by the bureau to deny consumer access to the information.

Federbush, FTC Informal Staff Opinion Letter (Mar. 10, 1983). *See also* Cong. Rec. H36,572, Oct. 13, 1970, 91st Cong. 2d Sess.; *In re* Equifax, 96 F.T.C. 844, 1068 (1980), *limited reversal on other grounds*, 678 F.2d 1047 (11th Cir. 1982).

201 *See* § 3.5.4.2, *infra*.

202 *See* § 3.5.8, *infra*.

203 15 U.S.C. § 1681g(a)(1)(A).

204 The exception was eliminated by Pub. L. No. 104-208, 110 Stat. 3009 (Sept. 30, 1996). *See also* Pub. L. No. 108-159, § 411(c) (2003), *amending* 15 U.S.C. § 1681a(i).

205 Darcy, FTC Informal Staff Opinion Letter (June 30, 2000), *reprinted on the CD-Rom accompanying this manual*.

206 15 U.S.C. § 1681g(c)(2)(A). The FTC model summary is reprinted at 16 C.F.R. Part 698, Appendix E, *reproduced at* Appx. C, *infra*. The FTC states that CRAs have flexibility as to the structure of the disclosure because it is a "model" form and a "substantially similar" summary will comply with the Commission's rule and statutory requirement. *Id.*

207 15 U.S.C. § 1681g(c)(1).

208 15 U.S.C. § 1681g(c)(2).

209 15 U.S.C. § 1681g(c)(2)(B).

210 15 U.S.C. § 1682g(f). *See* § 3.3.4, *supra*. Prior to changes to the FCRA added by Fair and Accurate Credit Transactions Act of

CRA provides to the consumer may not necessarily be the same score the CRA provides to creditors, since the Act allows the agency to provide either the current credit score or the score most recently calculated by the CRA for a credit-related purpose.[211] The Act generally preempts state statutes requiring disclosure of credit scores, but makes certain exceptions to that preemption.[212] Notably, California's statute requiring disclosure of credit scores[213] is not preempted.[214] A more general discussion of disclosure of credit scores is found at § 8.2.4, *infra*.

3.5.3 Disclosure of Sources of Reporting Information

The CRA must disclose to the consumer not only all information in the consumer's file at the time of the request, but also must clearly and accurately disclose the sources of that information.[215] This includes naming another CRA as a source if information in the file comes from that CRA.[216] The consumer need not specifically request that the CRA identify the sources.[217]

A CRA does not satisfy this requirement by saying it does not know the source of the information. In that event, it might be treated more properly as disputed information and deleted. The source of identifying information, such as an erroneous Social Security number and alias, must also be disclosed.[218]

The consumer's right does not extend to the sources of information in *investigative* consumer reports.[219] This FCRA exception was inserted in response to claims by the reporting industry that if the identities of the persons interviewed in investigations were not kept confidential, there would be a "drying up" of such sources of information.[220] Nevertheless, for the FCRA exception concerning sources of investigative consumer reports to apply, the information must have been "acquired solely for use in preparing an investigative consumer report and actually used for no other purpose."[221] This provision has two parts: for sources to be protected the information must be obtained solely for use in an investigative report and not for other types of consumer reports, and the report can only be subsequently used for the purposes originally specified.

Even when sources for investigative reports can generally be protected, the FCRA requires that such names shall be available to the consumer under appropriate discovery procedures if the consumer brings an FCRA action in court.[222] That is, if the consumer brings an FCRA action against the CRA, names of sources for an investigative report may be obtained through pre-trial discovery.

3.5.4 Identification of Users Receiving Reports

3.5.4.1 General

The CRA must disclose the names of all recipients of consumer reports about the consumer that were furnished within one year prior to the consumer's request for disclosure.[223] Additionally, the consumer must be told the names of any persons who received consumer reports on the consumer for employment purposes within two years before the request.[224] The CRA must also disclose the address and telephone number of the recipient, but only if specifically requested by the consumer.[225]

The CRA must maintain records of report recipients to comply with this provision of the Act.[226] Where the CRA has provided the report to a user at the request of another CRA, the CRA must disclose the ultimate recipient of the report, not just the name of the requesting CRA.[227] The list of recipients must also include any recipient of prescreened lists containing the consumer's name.[228]

Recipients of consumer reports, like the sources of information contained in the reports, must be identified pursuant to the consumer's general request for disclosure of the consumer's file, whether or not the consumer specifically requested that the recipients' names be disclosed.[229] The

---

2003 (FACTA), consumers were not entitled to learn their credit scores. Pub. L. No. 108-159, § 212 (2003). *See also* § 14.4, *infra*.

211 15 U.S.C. § 1681g(g)(1)(A).
212 15 U.S.C. § 1681t(b)(3).
213 *See* Cal. Civ. Code § 1785.11.15 (West).
214 15 U.S.C. § 1681t(b)(3)(A).
215 15 U.S.C. § 1681g(a)(2).
216 FTC Official Staff Commentary § 609 item 9, *reprinted at* Appx. D, *infra*.
217 *Id. See also* FTC, Compliance with the Fair Credit Reporting Act, at 30 (1977).
218 Guimond v. Trans Union Credit Info. Co., 45 F.3d 1329 (9th Cir. 1995).
219 15 U.S.C. § 1681g(a)(2). *See* § 13.4.2.3, *infra*.
220 The legislative history of this provision is discussed in Retail Credit Co. v. Dade County, 393 F. Supp. 577 (S.D. Fla. 1975).
221 15 U.S.C. § 1681g(a)(2).
222 *Id. See also* Retail Credit Co. v. United Family Life Ins. Co., 203 S.E.2d 760 (Ga. Ct. App. 1974).
223 15 U.S.C. § 1681g(a)(3).
224 *Id.* Employment purposes include decisions about "promotion, reassignment or retention" of the consumer, as well as hiring decisions. *Id.* § 1681a(h).
225 15 U.S.C. § 1681g(a)(3)(B)(ii).
226 FTC Official Staff Commentary § 609 item 10, *reprinted at* Appx. D, *infra*.
227 15 U.S.C. § 1681g(a)(3)(A). *See also* FTC Official Staff Commentary § 609 item 10, *reprinted at* Appx. D, *infra*; Benner, FTC Informal Staff Opinion Letter (Apr. 30, 1999), *reprinted on the CD-Rom accompanying this manual*; Jerison, FTC Informal Staff Opinion Letter (Aug. 3, 1988), *reprinted on the CD-Rom accompanying this manual*.
228 15 U.S.C. § 1681g(a)(5). *See also* FTC Official Staff Commentary § 609 item 11, *reprinted at* Appx. D, *infra*.
229 *See* § 3.5.1, *supra*. *See also* Guidelines for Financial Institutions in Complying with the Fair Credit Reporting Act (1971); FTC,

§ 3.5.4.2 Fair Credit Reporting

recipient must be identified by name or, if applicable, the full trade name under which the person does business.

3.5.4.2 Exception for FBI Counter-Intelligence and Government Security Clearance Usage

The FCRA grants the Federal Bureau of Investigation secret access, for certain purposes, to information kept by CRAs.[230] In these circumstances, CRAs may not reveal to the consumer, or any user, that the FBI obtained any information from the consumer reporting agency, or even sought to obtain any such information.[231] In addition, when the head of a federal agency or department provides a written finding[232] that a consumer report will be used for security clearance purposes, the CRA need not disclose, but also is not prohibited from disclosing that usage to the consumer.[233]

3.5.5 Identification of Checks upon Which Adverse Characterizations of the Consumer Are Based

The FCRA clarifies what information must be included in the report concerning consumer check-writing. The report must specify the dates, original payees, and amounts of any checks upon which is based any adverse characterization of the consumer, included in the file at the time of the disclosure.[234] For example, if a CRA has information about a bounced check in the consumer's file, disclosure of the contents of that file must include the date, payee, and amount of that bounced check.

3.5.6 Disclosure of Previously Reported Information

Consumer reports show the present status of a consumer's file, and do not disclose the information that may have been provided to a user in the past. An important issue is whether CRAs are in fact required to disclose the content of such prior reports, because it is the prior reports that form the basis of a user's adverse action.

The FTC Staff Commentary states that the term file "denotes all information on the consumer that is recorded and retained by a CRA that might be furnished, *or has been furnished*, in a consumer report on that consumer."[235] This language supports the argument that not only what currently is being reported, but also what has previously been reported must be disclosed to the consumer, as long as such information is retained by the CRA.

Nevertheless, Congress in 2003 required the FTC to study the effects of requiring consumers who have experienced adverse action based on a consumer report receive a copy of the same report that the creditor relied upon in taking the adverse action,[236] and the FTC concluded that the cost of providing the same report to consumers and users outweighs the benefits.[237] This report has been the subject of criticism.[238]

3.5.7 Disclosure of Other Persons in Consumer's File

The disclosure right is limited to information in the CRA's files "on the consumer."[239] The consumer has no right to information on other individuals. However, all information in the consumer's file must be disclosed, even if the information also relates to other individuals.[240] For example, practitioners report that CRAs sometimes provide their subscribers or users with reports that include more than one consumers' name. However the consumers who are the subject of such reports only receive information relevant to them, and not the other person also reported on. This practice is arguably a violation of the requirement to provide all information that "has been" furnished.[241] This is especially relevant in cases involving mismerged files or identity theft.[242]

3.5.8 Audit Trail and Other Ancillary Information

An audit trail is internal information that the CRA adds to the file as actions are taken on that file, so that an auditor can later review those actions, to verify that they were proper.[243]

Compliance with the Fair Credit Reporting Act, at 30 (1977).
230 See § 7.2.10, *infra*.
231 15 U.S.C. § 1681u(d).
232 Pursuant to 15 U.S.C. § 1681b(b)(4)(A).
233 15 U.S.C. § 1681g(a)(3)(c).
234 15 U.S.C. § 1681g(a)(4).
235 FTC Official Staff Commentary, § 603(g), item 2, *reprinted at* Appx. D, *infra* (emphasis added); Cohan, FTC Informal Staff Opinion Letter (Aug. 1, 2001), *reprinted on the CD-Rom accompanying this manual*.
236 FACTA, Pub. L. No. 108-159, § 318(A)(2)(C) (2003).
237 *See* FTC Report to Congress Under Sections 318 and 319 of the Fair and Accurate Credit Transactions Act of 2003 at 57 (Dec. 2004), available at www.ftc.gov/reports/facta/041209factarpt.pdf.
238 For example, critics claim it failed to address whether any measures could be taken to reduce any of these costs, and underestimated the benefits to consumers of seeing the report relied upon by the creditor.
239 15 U.S.C. § 1681g(a)(1).
240 FTC Official Staff Commentary § 609 item 8, *reprinted at* Appx. D, *infra*.
241 FTC Official Staff Commentary § 609 (g) item 2, *reprinted at* Appx. D, *infra*.
242 *See* §§ 7.2.4, 7.2.5, *infra*.
243 FTC Official Staff Commentary § 603(g) item 3, *reprinted at* Appx. D, *infra*.

The FTC staff deems that such information need not be disclosed because the information is not furnished in consumer reports or used as a basis in preparing them.[244] This, of course, will not prevent the consumer from seeking audit trail information through discovery if an action is filed in court.

The consumer's "file" also excludes other information which will not be included in a consumer report or used as a basis for preparing future reports.[245] Such other information includes billing records, customer relations information, and the like.[246] The FTC staff has also said that insurance claims reports which have not and will not appear in consumer reports do not have to be disclosed.[247]

3.6 The Form of the Disclosure

3.6.1 Electronic and Mail Disclosures

Unless otherwise authorized by the consumer, the report provided to the consumer must be in writing.[248] The consumer may authorize any other reasonable form of disclosure that is available from the CRA,[249] including electronic disclosure.[250] The FTC Staff Commentary allows mail disclosures with the consumer's actual or implied consent.[251] Disclosure by fax would seem to be another approach.

3.6.2 In-Person and Telephone Disclosures

The consumer can specify disclosure by telephone by making a written request for such disclosure,[252] although this will typically not be practical where the consumer requests disclosure of the complete file. The FTC Staff Commentary allows telephone disclosure without written request if the consumer is properly identified, but CRAs can still insist on a written request.[253]

The consumer can also receive the disclosures in person, upon the consumer's appearance at the CRA's place of business where disclosures are regularly provided, during normal business hours and upon reasonable notice.[254] If the consumer appears in person at the CRA and requests oral disclosure, the consumer has a right to such a disclosure.[255] CRAs cannot mislead consumers into believing that a written request with proper identification is a prerequisite to an in-person disclosure—the CRA must inform the consumer only that *telephone* disclosures will not be made until the consumer has complied with that prerequisite.[256]

In order to comply with the Act, the hours during which the CRA will provide disclosures must not be "unusual or restrictive."[257] If the consumer cannot come to the CRA's office during normal business hours, the CRA should specifically inform the consumer that disclosures may also be made available by other convenient means.[258]

Alternatively, the consumer and the CRA may arrange, by mutual agreement, to have disclosures made before or after normal business hours.[259] A CRA may make in-person disclosures to consumers who have made appointments ahead of other consumers, because the disclosures are only required to be made "on reasonable notice."[260]

The CRA may recommend that the consumer visit the office if it feels that in-person disclosure is a more effective way for the consumer to learn about the information in the consumer's file,[261] but the CRA may not imply that the

---

244 FTC Official Staff Commentary § 603(g) items 2, 3, *reprinted at* Appx. D, *infra. See also* Federbush, FTC Informal Staff Opinion Letter (Mar. 10, 1983), *reprinted on the CD-Rom accompanying this manual.*

245 FTC Official Staff Commentary § 609 item 7, *reprinted at* Appx. D, *infra. See also* Federbush, FTC Informal Staff Opinion Letter (Mar. 10, 1983), *reprinted on the CD-Rom accompanying this manual.*

246 FTC Official Staff Commentary § 609 item 7, *reprinted at* Appx. D, *infra. See also* Jerison, FTC Informal Staff Opinion Letter (Aug. 5, 1988), *reprinted on the CD-Rom accompanying this manual.*

247 FTC Official Staff Commentary § 609 item 7, *reprinted at* Appx. D, *infra. Contra In re* Equifax, Inc., 96 F.T.C. 1045 (1980), *rev'd in part on other grounds*, 678 F.2d 1047 (11th Cir. 1982).

248 15 U.S.C. § 1681h(a)(2).

249 15 U.S.C. § 1681h(b)(2)(D).

250 15 U.S.C. § 1681h(b)(2)(C).

251 FTC Official Staff Commentary § 610 item 3 ("with the consumer's actual or implied consent"); *Id.* § 609 item 5. *See also* Peeler, FTC Informal Staff Opinion Letter (Apr. 12, 1979), *reprinted on the CD-Rom accompanying this manual.*

252 15 U.S.C. § 1681h(b)(2)(B).

253 FTC Official Staff Commentary § 609 item 3, *reprinted at* Appx. D, *infra. See also* Peeler, FTC Informal Staff Opinion Letter (Apr. 12, 1979), *reprinted on the CD-Rom accompanying this manual.*

254 15 U.S.C. § 1681h(b)(2)(A). *Cf.* Cisneros v. U.D. Registry, 39 Cal. App. 4th 548 (1995) (tenant screening agency, which had closed its public office due to threats made against its personnel, could require a tenant wishing to review files in person to meet agency personnel in some public place like a restaurant).

255 *See* Feldman, FTC Informal Staff Opinion Letter (May 22, 1974), *reprinted on the CD-Rom accompanying this manual.*

256 *In re* Equifax, Inc., 96 F.T.C. 1045 (1980), *rev'd in part on other grounds*, 678 F.2d 1047 (11th Cir. 1982). *But see* Miller v. Credit Bureau, Inc., [1969–1973 Decisions Transfer Binder] Consumer Cred. Guide (CCH) ¶ 99,173 (D.C. Super. Ct. 1972) (written request could be required for in-person disclosures because the CRA's forms were designed to allow the CRA to verify the consumer's identity and to locate the proper files); FTC, Compliance with the Fair Credit Reporting Act, at 31 and App. 3 (1977) (suggesting written request forms as a method for obtaining proper identification of persons seeking in-person disclosure).

257 FTC, Compliance with the Fair Credit Reporting Act, at 31 (1977).

258 *Cf.* FTC, Compliance with the Fair Credit Reporting Act, at 31 (1977).

259 *See* FTC Official Staff Commentary § 610 item 1, *reprinted at* Appx. D, *infra.*

260 *Id.*

261 *In re* Equifax, Inc., 96 F.T.C. 1045 (1980), *rev'd in part on other grounds*, 678 F.2d 1047 (11th Cir. 1982).

information is not available by some other means by indicating that the consumer must come to a branch office.[262]

Consumers seeking in-person disclosures are also entitled to receive disclosures in the presence of one other person whom they have chosen to accompany them.[263] The CRA may require the consumer to furnish written permission for the CRA to discuss the consumer's file in front of the other person, and that other person must furnish the CRA with reasonable identification.[264] Unless the consumer refuses to comply with those requirements, the CRA may not refuse to make disclosure in the presence of another person.[265] The consumer may choose anyone as a companion for the disclosure.[266]

At the time that disclosure is made, the CRA's employee should have full knowledge of all relevant information in the CRA's files, so that the consumer is not forced to make repeated visits or telephone calls before obtaining a full disclosure and an adequate explanation of the items disclosed.[267] Similarly, the CRA may not interfere with the consumer's right to have the contents of the file clearly explained, by prohibiting its employees from referring to the actual file during the interview with the consumer.[268]

3.6.3 CRA Oral Assistance to Help Consumers Understand the Report

CRAs' employees must be trained to provide a full account of all information that the consumer is entitled to receive, and to explain all items that are disclosed.[269] The CRA's employees must be prepared to make thorough and efficient disclosures and to answer questions concerning the items disclosed. The procedures for disclosure, which employees are trained to follow, must not be inconsistent with the consumer's rights under the Act.

3.7 Examining the Consumer Report

3.7.1 The Consumer's Identity

The consumer report will have much information identifying the consumer: name; aliases; current address; previous addresses; telephone numbers; current and prior employer; Social Security number; and date of birth. It is tempting to skip over this information and go right to the substance of the report. However, one of the most important items on a consumer report is this identifying information. If the Social Security number or other information is inaccurate, this may result in data from another person being entered into the consumer's file. Make sure also that the Social Security number is accurate, and contains no transposed numbers or the like. If the consumer has a relative or someone else with a similar name and other similar identifying information, make sure there is no mix-up.

Of course, a creditor may be supplying the CRA with information on a consumer using less than optimal identification—such as misspelling a name or using a nickname—and in that case, the consumer file should include these aliases so as to properly match up the consumer's accounts and the consumer's file. But if there are real inaccuracies in the consumer's identification, this can cause all kinds of problems.

The consumer report may also identify the consumer by a file identification number assigned by the CRA. This number may be important because the CRA may ask that all inquiries, including dispute letters, include that file identification number.

3.7.2 Substance of the Report

3.7.2.1 A Report Is Just One Snapshot in Time

An important point in reviewing the consumer's report is to realize that it is a snapshot in time. It is not the same report that a potential creditor or other user saw in the past, if for no other reason than new information about the consumer is continually being furnished to CRAs. It is also not the current state of the consumer's accounts because there is a time lag. If a creditor makes a monthly dump of information to a CRA, and the consumer makes a payment two weeks later, that payment will not show up on the report until the creditor's next monthly dump. There can also be a time lag between when information is furnished to a CRA and when it gets reported to the consumer. The consumer report will indicate when an account was last updated with the CRA.

In other words, a report may show an account as past due, where the consumer has already made a payment to bring it up to date. Hopefully, a report issued the following month will reflect the payment. Similarly, new credit extended may not yet show up on the report either, and the account balance often will not be current. The only way to learn how the report reads over time is to obtain copies of the consumer's report periodically.

---

262 *Id.*
263 15 U.S.C. § 1681h(d).
264 *Id. See also* Bragg, FTC Informal Staff Opinion Letter (May 15, 1972), *reprinted on the CD-Rom accompanying this manual.*
265 *See* Collins v. Retail Credit Co., 410 F. Supp. 924 (E.D. Mich. 1976).
266 FTC Official Staff Commentary § 610 item 4, *reprinted at* Appx. D, *infra.*
267 *See* Millstone v. O'Hanlon Reports, Inc., 383 F. Supp. 269 (E.D. Mo. 1974), *aff'd*, 528 F.2d 829 (8th Cir. 1976).
268 *Id.*
269 15 U.S.C. § 1681h(c). *See also* FTC Official Staff Commentary § 609 item 5, *reprinted at* Appx. D, *infra.*

3.7.2.2 Differences in Reports Provided to the Consumer and to Users

What the consumer sees is not always the same as what a user sees. On the one hand, a user will often request a credit score, which will not be provided to the consumer unless the consumer specifically requests it and pays for it. Even then, the credit score the user sees may be a different one than that shown to the consumer. In addition, at least one of the "Big Three" CRAs sends out multiple reports on a consumer to some users, while only sending one report to the consumer. It states this happens about 1% of the time.[270] This occurs where the CRA is not sure whether information in its files belong to the consumer, so that it creates multiple files linked to that consumer, putting information it is unsure of in a second or even third file. Users are supplied reports on any file that may be a match, while the CRA provides consumers only one report that is the closest match.

In addition, practitioners report that CRAs will hide information in the report to the consumer by truncating or deleting account numbers, or deleting subscriber addresses, which hinders a consumer in directly disputing an account with a creditor. This sort of vandalism to the information associated with a consumer is in direct violation of the Act.[271]

On the other hand, sometimes the consumer sees more than the user. Promotional inquiries, review inquiries, and the CRA's activities in response to the consumer's request are shown on the report given to the consumer, but cloaked from creditors.[272] Obsolete negative information (generally information over seven years old) cannot be reported to users, while it can be included in the report provided to the consumer.[273] The fact that obsolete information has been reported to a consumer thus does not mean that the CRA has forwarded that information to a user. There is no simple way of determining whether that has in fact occurred. In a lawsuit, the consumer's attorney may be able to discover just what was reported to the creditor based on "frozen scans" or "name scans" kept by CRAs. However, no way exists to ensure that future creditors will get the same consumer report the consumer gets from the CRA.

3.7.2.3 Reading the Report

The actual format of the substance of the report will vary from CRA to CRA, and may even vary depending on whether the consumer receives the report on-line or in the mail. Samples of the reports from the "Big Three" CRAs are found at Appendix I, *infra*.

Perhaps the most important information to look at will be indications of any public records, because this can be some of the most damaging information for a consumer's credit standing. Verify each court judgment, bankruptcy, and the like. The CRA will only report negative information, so that if the public record section of the report has no data, this is the best possible result.

Much of the report will be taken up by a list of credit accounts (often called tradelines), with detailed information on each account. For example, the typical report from the "Big Three" CRAs will often contain at least the following information on each account supplied by a creditor:

- An abbreviated version of the creditor's name, some information about the creditor, the account number, and the type of the account;
- The relationship of the consumer to the account (sole owner, joint account, authorized user, etc.);
- Any collateral on the loan;
- The date the account was opened, the last update on the account, and other date information;
- The highest amount ever owed by the consumer on the account, the credit limit, and the current balance due;
- The loan terms, including number of payments, payment frequency, and dollar amount agreed upon; and
- The amount past due, any statement of dispute, the date and amount of the maximum delinquency on the account, and the number of times the consumer has been 30, 60, 90 days delinquent on the account.

It is important to examine each credit account not just for its current status, but also for information about past account payments. Delinquencies within the last seven years can continue to affect the credit score and the user's evaluation of the consumer's creditworthiness. Often CRAs keep accounts on file for ten years, even if such older information cannot be provided to report users because it exceeds the FCRA's standards for obsolete information. The fact that the consumer can see information on a report to the consumer does not mean it is being reported to others.

3.7.2.4 Errors to Look For

Billions of pieces of information get reported to CRAs, and the furnisher will often have incomplete or even inaccurate identification information for the consumer. The furnisher may not link the information to a Social Security number, may have a different address than what the CRA has on file, may use a different first name or even last name than what the CRA has. "Junior" may be left off, or any number of other identifying pieces of information may be inaccurate, transposed, or different than what the CRA has.

The CRA then must take this information and link it to an individual consumer. If it places the data in the wrong consumer's file, there is a mismatched or mixed file: Con-

---

270 FTC Report to Congress Under Sections 318 and 319 of the Fair and Accurate Credit Transactions Act of 2003 at 16 (Dec. 2004), *available at* www.ftc.gov/reports/facta/041209factarpt.pdf.
271 See § 3.5, *supra*.
272 See sample reports found at Appx. I, *infra*.
273 See § 5.2, *infra*.

sumer A has information in the file that belongs to Consumer B. If the CRA is not sure information is about Consumer B, it may decide not to include it in Consumer B's file, even though in fact it belongs to Consumer B. For example, a creditor may identify the consumer as K. Smith, and the CRA may not be sufficiently confident that this is Kevin Smith as to put the information in with others for Kevin Smith. The FTC found that about 4% of inquiries to the "Big Three" CRAs could call up such fragmented files, but that two CRAs never provide the fragmented file to consumers or users, and the third only provides the file when a user specifically requests it.[274] Thus information will be in a sort of limbo under K. Smith, not being available to users.

Examining a consumer report may help to identify mixed and fragmented files. Mixed or mis-matched accounts are the easiest to spot. The account will not be one belonging to the consumer. Note that CRAs will include accounts correctly where the consumer is only an authorized user.[275] Another reason why the consumer may not recognize an account is identity theft, that the thief has created an account using the consumer's identity.[276]

One way to check for fragmented files is to look for missing credit accounts that should be there in the report, but are not. Many creditors do not furnish data to CRAs, so there absence from the report is not remarkable. However, credit card issuers and similar large creditors invariably do furnish data to CRAs, and if such accounts are missing, it is very possible that the account has ended up in a fragmented file.

A list of accounts and their status may prove instructive to the consumer in two ways. First, certain delinquent accounts may not show up, and that will indicate that the creditor is not a subscriber with the CRA. This may be valuable information to a consumer concerned about which bills to pay first. Second, the consumer may not even remember certain older accounts that the creditor has written off and stopped collection efforts, but that remain in the consumer's file, adversely affecting the consumer's credit rating.

3.7.3 Information on Those Requesting Reports on the Consumer

The report to the consumer must list all persons who received a report on the consumer within the last year (two years if the report was for employment purposes).[277] The report the consumer sees will place these users into different categories, either in separate sections or providing different codes for each type of user.

One type of user is a company that receives prescreened information from the report in order to make a firm offer of credit and/or insurance to the consumer. This prescreening or promotional inquiry (which is often designated in the report as PRM) will not be shown to other users, and should not negatively affect the consumer's credit rating or record. Consumers can opt out of these promotional uses from the "Big Three" CRAs by calling 888-567-8688.[278]

A second type of user is a company that has an existing relationship with the consumer and is seeking the consumer report as part of a periodic review of the consumer's account. These account review inquiries (which are often designated in the report as AR) supposedly do not affect any other creditor's decision or the consumer's credit score. The report may also indicate a consumer's past requests for a copy of the consumer's own report. Finally, there will be listed those who use the consumer's report in conjunction with the consumer's application for credit, insurance, or employment.

There a number of reasons to scrutinize the list of users. First, look at each user to see if it has a permissible purpose for obtaining the report.[279] Specifically look at the users in the last category, those seeking the report for credit, insurance, or employment purposes. Do not worry about unfamiliar names if they are listed as part of the prescreening users, but do be concerned if they are listed as those obtaining the report in response to the consumer's application.

It will be particularly important to know who has received consumer reports on the consumer when the consumer's file contains incomplete or inaccurate information. If such information is deleted or updated, or the consumer files a statement of dispute, the consumer has the right to request that recipients of consumer reports be notified of such changes. The CRA must provide the requested notification to any recipient named by the consumer.[280]

Practitioners should also match up any notice of an adverse action, based on a report from a particular CRA, with the list of users found on that CRA's report. A user not being listed on that CRA's report may indicate that the user received a different person's report by mistake. Conversely, an inquiry indicating that the consumer applied for credit with a creditor that the consumer has never heard of may be an early warning sign of identity theft For instance, if a car dealer in Indiana pulled a Pennsylvania consumer's consumer report, that could be a "red flag" that someone is trying to finance a car in the consumer's name.

---

274 *Id.* at 58. FTC Report to Congress Under Sections 318 and 319 of the Fair and Accurate Credit Transactions Act of 2003 at 58 (Dec. 2004), *available at* www.ftc.gov/reports/facta/041209 factarpt.pdf.
275 *See* § 5.6.2, *infra.*
276 See Ch. 9, *infra*, on the FCRA's identity theft provisions.
277 *See* § 3.5.4, *supra.*
278 *See* § 7.3.4.4, *infra.*
279 *See* 15 U.S.C. §§ 1681b, 1681d. *See also* § 7.2, *infra.*
280 15 U.S.C. § 1681i(d).

Chapter 4 Accuracy in Consumer Reports

4.1 First Considerations

4.1.1 FCRA Places Two Separate Accuracy Obligations on Consumer Reporting Agencies

The FCRA does not impose liability on consumer reporting agencies (CRAs) simply for reporting inaccurate information. Instead, the Act requires that that CRAs utilize reasonable procedures to ensure maximum possible accuracy of the information in a report (as described in § 4.4, *infra*). The FCRA also requires that the CRA properly conduct a reinvestigation after the consumer disputes the accuracy of information (as described in §§ 4.5–4.7, *infra*), and provides the right for the consumer to file a statement of dispute after an unsuccessful dispute (as described in § 4.8, *infra*). Nevertheless, determining whether a report is in fact inaccurate is an important element in any litigation, especially involving reasonable procedures for maximum possible accuracy. Courts are unlikely to find procedures unreasonable if a report in fact is accurate. Section 4.2, *infra* examines standards for determining whether a report is in fact inaccurate.

It is also critical for practitioners to diagnose the form and cause of an inaccurate report before commencing litigation, or at least through discovery.[1] Did the error originate with the furnisher, or was the problem caused by the CRA after receiving the information? Section 4.3, *infra*, describes the types of inaccuracies that frequently occur, distinguishing between errors created by furnishers and those by CRAs.

Other chapters in this manual are also relevant. Chapters 10 and 11, *infra*, examine the claims and litigation against a CRA where its procedures are not reasonable to ensure accuracy or where it does not properly reinvestigate the consumer's dispute. Chapter 5, *infra*, discusses the types of information that are prohibited from being included in consumer reports, or require some sort of restriction; failure to follow these prohibitions or restrictions would also make the information inaccurate. Chapter 6, *infra*, considers the furnisher's obligations as to the accuracy of information it supplies to the CRA and as to reinvestigations of disputed information. Chapter 12, *infra*, reviews various techniques the consumer can utilize to try to correct inaccurate information and to respond to derogatory, but accurate items.

Because of the difficulties consumers face in correcting errors and keeping reports accurate, consumers will have to consider all possible options and aggressively pursue the most appropriate ones. Moreover, the same or different inaccuracies may be present in the files of various different CRAs. It is important for consumers to take a preemptory active role in monitoring the accuracy and completeness of their consumer reports, and not merely react after credit or employment is denied because of an inaccurate consumer report.

4.1.2 Congressional Intent to Combat Inaccurate Consumer Reports

The FCRA's legislative history shows a congressional intent that the Act protect consumers from the transmission of inaccurate information about them.[2] The FCRA was drafted to "prevent consumers from being unjustly damaged because of inaccurate or arbitrary information in a credit report."[3] One legislator has described the adverse effect of bad credit histories as: "A poor credit history is the 'Scarlet Letter' of 20th century America."[4]

Congress also explicitly recognized that the health of the consumer banking system is "dependent upon fair and accurate credit reporting" and that "[i]naccurate credit reports directly impair the efficiency of banking system."[5] An important theme underlying the statute is that the dissemination of accurate credit information is essential to maintain the vitality of the credit granting system for the benefit of creditors and consumers alike. Inaccurate derogatory infor-

---

1 See § 11.6, *infra*.

2 The following cases include discussion of the legislative history of the Act: Guimond v. Trans Union Credit Info. Co., 45 F.3d 1329, 1333 (9th Cir. 1995); Kates v. Croker National Bank, 776 F.2d 1396, 1397 (9th Cir. 1985). *See also* St. Paul Guardian Ins. v. Johnson, 884 F.2d 881, 883 (citing Pinner v. Schmidt, 805 F.2d 1258, 1261 (5th Cir. 1986)).

3 *See* Equifax, Inc. v. Fed. Trade Comm'n, 678 F.2d 1047, 1048 (11th Cir. 1982); Comeaux v. Experian Info. Solutions, 2004 WL 1354412 (E.D. Tex. June 8, 2004).

4 136 Cong. Rec. H5325-02 (daily ed. July 23, 1990) (statement of Rep. Annunzio), *cited in* Fed. Trade Comm'n v. Gill. 265 F.3d 944, 947 (9th Cir. 2001).

5 15 U.S.C. § 1681(a)(1).

§ 4.1.3   *Fair Credit Reporting*

mation will inappropriately keep businesses from selling and financing goods and services to consumers with otherwise acceptable credit. In considering the Consumer Credit Reporting Reform Act of 1996 (1996 Reform Act) amendments to the FCRA, Representative Kennedy explained, "[i]f these reports are not accurate, or if they are distributed without a legitimate purpose, then our whole society suffers. Consumers may be unfairly deprived of credit, employment, and their privacy. And businesses may lose out on the opportunity to gain new customers."[6]

Concern with inaccuracy in consumer reports was the primary theme throughout all the legislative debates leading up to the FCRA. Senator Proxmire, the father of the FCRA, called his first effort a "Bill to Protect Consumers Against Arbitrary or Erroneous Credit Ratings and The Unwarranted Publication of Credit Information."[7] The legislative purpose was to impose higher standards on CRAs with regard to the confidentiality, accuracy, and currency of information disseminated about consumers.[8]

Senator Proxmire expanded on the need for standards of accuracy when he introduced Senate Bill 823, the bill which, with changes, became the FCRA. Proclaiming that the Act would protect consumers against erroneous credit information,[9] he said the purpose of the bill was first to correct the abuse of "inaccurate or misleading" information.[10] He described the problem this way:

> Perhaps the most serious problem in the credit reporting industry is the problem of inaccurate or misleading information. There have been no definitive studies made of just how accurate is the information in the files of credit reporting agencies. But even if it is 99 percent accurate—and I doubt it is that good—the 1 percent inaccuracy represents over a million people. While the credit industry might be satisfied with a 1-percent error, this is small comfort to the 1 million citizens whose reputations are unjustly maligned. Moreover the composition of the 1 million is constantly shifting. Everyone is a potential victim of an inaccurate credit report. If not today, then perhaps tomorrow.[11]

Senator Proxmire then went on to discuss five types of inaccuracy: confusion with other persons; biased (one-sided) information; malicious gossip and hearsay; computer errors; and incomplete information.[12]

4.1.3 Prevalence of Inaccurate Consumer Reports

4.1.3.1 Studies and Reports Show Consumer Reports Prone to Errors

A number of surveys, studies and reports have shown that inaccuracies occur frequently in consumer reports. Inaccurate information is troublesome since it can adversely affect whether consumers are granted credit, and with the growth in risk-based pricing, how much they pay for it.[13]

One of the most well known studies on inaccuracies in consumer credit reports was a 1998 survey by U.S. Public Interest Research Group (U.S. PIRG) of 133 consumers who reviewed their own consumer reports.[14] This report found that 70% of these consumer reports contained an error and 29% contained an error serious enough (such as delinquencies or accounts that did not belong to the customer) to cause a denial of credit.[15] Six years later, another U.S. PIRG study of 154 consumers found that 79% of their consumer reports contained error, including 25% that contained serious errors which could cause a denial of credit and that 30% contained credit accounts listed as open that had been closed by the consumer.[16]

Consumers Union has undertaken similar studies of consumer credit report accuracy. A 1991 Consumers Union study found that almost half of the consumer reports studied contained at least one error, and many contained multiple errors. Twenty percent of these errors were serious enough to adversely affect an application for credit, housing, or employment.[17] In 2000, Consumers Union reviewed the consumer reports of twenty-five staffers and found that more than half of sixty-three reports contained inaccuracies.[18]

In 2002, the Consumer Federation of America (CFA) and the National Credit Reporting Association (NCRA) conducted a study that reviewed the files of more than 1700

---

6 140 Cong. Rec. H9809 (Sept. 27, 1994).
7 114 Cong. Rec. 24902 (1968).
8 [T]he increasing volume of complaints makes it clear that some regulations are vitally necessary to ensure that higher standards are observed with respect to the information in the files of commercial credit bureaus. I cite what I consider to be the three most important criteria for judging the quality of these standards. They are first, confidentiality; second, accuracy; and third, currency of information.

114 Cong. Rec. 24903 (1968).
9 115 Cong. Rec. 2410 (1970).
10 *Id.* at 2411.
11 *Id.*

12 *Id.*
13 *See* § 14.7.3, *infra*.
14 U.S. PIRG, Jon Golinger, Mistakes Do Happen: Credit Report Errors Mean Consumers Lose (Mar. 1998).
15 *Id.*
16 U.S. PIRG, Alison Cassidy, and Edmund Mierzwinski, Mistakes Do Happen: A Look at Errors in Consumer Credit Reports (June 2004).
17 Consumers Union, What Are They Saying About Me? The Results of a Review of 161 Credit Reports from the Three Major Credit Bureaus (Apr. 29, 1991).
18 Consumer Rep., Credit Reports: How Do Potential Lenders See You? (July 2000).

individuals.[19] The files were maintained by the three nationwide CRAs—Equifax, Experian, and TransUnion.[20] The report also included an in-depth analysis of fifty-one representative files for consistencies and inconsistencies. The report found common errors of omission (information not reported by all three nationwide CRAs) and commission (inconsistent information between the three nationwide CRAs). Errors included the failure to report negative and positive information. Negative information included delinquencies or charge-offs, whereas positive information included payments on accounts.

According to CFA/NCRA report, 78% of files were missing a revolving account in good standing, while one-third (33%) of files were missing a mortgage account that had never been late.[21] Serious errors of commission also appeared in a significant portion of files. The report found that files contained conflicting information on the same accounts regarding how often consumers had been late with payments.[22] The authors of the report acknowledged that a sample of fifty-one reports was too small to generalize for all files, however they concluded that "tens of millions of consumers are at risk of being penalized by inaccurate credit report information and incorrect credit scores."[23]

Government researchers have issued findings about inaccuracies in consumer credit reporting. A 2003 study by the Federal Reserve Board (FRB) found that information in credit reporting files is often incomplete and contains duplications and ambiguities.[24] The study looked at over 300,000 consumer files from one of the three nationwide CRAs. It found that the CRA's files often contained multiple entries involving public records, but these multiple entries frequently involved the same event or episode.[25] Similarly, many consumer files had multiple collection entries, but the entries often pertained to the same episode.[26] The FRB study also found that credit limits were typically not reported. The study noted problems with keeping consumer files up to date for those with negative credit histories. For consumer files with a major derogatory piece of information, almost three-fifths were not currently reported.[27] These accounts were likely to have been closed or transferred but were not reported as such.

An early study of 1500 reports from the three nationwide CRAs found that 43% contained errors. These errors included inaccurate or incomplete credit information, mismerged files, discrepancies among the three nationwide CRAs' reports on the same consumer, and erroneous public record information.[28] Moreover, this study reported that out of nine million consumers who *saw* their consumer reports in 1988 from the three nationwide CRAs, an astonishing one-third or three million had errors investigated and *corrected*.[29]

This last statistic points to another indicator that shows the prevalence of errors in consumer reports, i.e., the number of disputes filed after consumers see their consumer reports. More recent data shows a similarly high number of disputes over errors. The trade association for the CRAs, Consumer Data Industry Association, Inc. (CDIA, formerly the Associated Credit Bureaus, Inc.), reports that, out of the 57.4 million consumers who ordered their own consumer reports in 2003, 12.5 million (or 21.8%) filed a dispute that resulted in a reinvestigation.[30] A General Accounting Office (GAO) survey of 1578 found that about 18% of consumers had disputed information in their consumer reports at some point.[31]

---

19 Consumer Federation of America and National Credit Reporting Association, Credit Score Accuracy and Implications for Consumers (Dec. 17, 2002), *available at* www.consumerfed.org/121702CFA_NCRA_Credit_Score_Report_Final.pdf, *reprinted on the CD-Rom accompanying this manual.*

20 See § 14.8.1, *infra* for a discussion of the reports findings on credit scores; Consumer Federation of America and National Credit Reporting Association, Credit Score Accuracy and Implications for Consumers (Dec. 17, 2002), *available at* www.consumerfed.org/121702CFA_NCRA_Credit_Score_Report_Final.pdf, *reprinted on the CD-Rom accompanying this manual.*

21 Consumer Federation of America and National Credit Reporting Association, Credit Score Accuracy and Implications for Consumers (Dec. 17, 2002), at 29, *available at* www.consumerfed.org/121702CFA_NCRA_Credit_Score_Report_Final.pdf, *reprinted on the CD-Rom accompanying this manual.*

22 *Id.*

23 *Id.* at 37.

24 Robert Avery, Paul Calem, Glenn Canner, and Raphael Bostin, *An Overview of Consumer Data and Consumer Reporting*, Federal Reserve Bulletin 70 (Feb. 2003). This report also discussed the effects of credit reporting problems on access to credit, including simulating the effects of correcting each problem on the availability or price of credit as represented by the change in the individual's credit score. This is discussed further in § 14.8.1, *infra*.

25 Robert Avery, Paul Calem, Glenn Canner, and Raphael Bostin, *An Overview of Consumer Data and Consumer Reporting*, Federal Reserve Bulletin 70 (Feb. 2003).

26 *Id.*

27 *Id.* at 71.

28 Jan Lewis, *Credit Reporting: Paying for Others' Mistakes*, Trial 90 (Jan. 1992) (reporting on a 1988 study by Consolidated Information Services).

29 *Id.* Using the same data, the industry claimed a 99.5% accuracy rate. *Bad Credit, No Reason*, U.S. News & World Report, at 65 (Jan. 27, 1992) The industry compared the three million complaints to the four billion reports issued. The fair analysis compares the number of complaints with the number of consumers who actually saw their reports, an error rate of 33%.

30 Federal Trade Commission and Federal Reserve Board, Report to Congress on the Fair Credit Reporting Act Dispute Process (Aug. 2006), at 12, *available at* www.ftc.gov/os/comments/fcradispute/P044808fcradisputeprocessreporttocongress.pdf.

31 General Accounting Office, Report No. GAO-05-223, Credit Reporting Literacy: Consumers Understand the Basics But Could Benefit from Targeted Education Efforts (Mar. 2005).

This GAO report indicated a significant lack of knowledge about the credit reporting process, which does not bode well for the efficacy of self-help efforts to improve credit report accuracy. The study found that only about 60% of the consumers

The prevalence of inaccuracies in consumer credit reports is also indicated by the frequency of complaints to government regulators. FCRA-related complaints are one of the most frequent consumer complaints received by the Federal Trade Commission (FTC).[32] Complaints against the "Big Three" nationwide CRAs have increased, from 8000 in 2001 to 14,000 in 2002.[33] In the early 1990s, the FTC reported that approximately 20% of all complaints dealt with consumer reports,[34] even though most of these complaints occurred after the consumer had tried to resolve the complaint directly with the CRA—on average already having contacted the CRA about the particular problem more than *three* times.[35] Of these complainants, 61% had *already* been denied credit, jobs, housing, or insurance because of the errors in their reports. An additional 22% of complainants were likely to have similar adverse consequences because of inaccurate information in their reports.[36]

Some of the common themes in FTC complaints include:

- Failing to correct inaccuracies acknowledged by the furnisher or otherwise demonstrated by the consumer;
- Failing to forward critical information to the furnisher, resulting in an improper verification of the debt;
- Improper reinsertion of inaccurate information in the consumer's file, a particular concern for victims of identity theft; and
- Failing to address disputes within the statutorily-mandated deadline.[37]

Testimony by users of consumer credit reports have also shown a high rate of error. A mortgage reporting company's investigative supervisor testified by deposition that in her experience of reviewing reports from the major nationwide CRAs, she found error rates of between fifty and ninety percent. Persons with common last names experienced at least a ninety-percent error rate.[38]

While it is impossible to precisely measure the number of inaccurate consumer reports out of the billions of such reports made each year, these studies and other data all reach similar conclusions that a significant percentage of consumer reports contain inaccuracies and many of these errors are serious enough to affect the consumer's access to credit, housing, or employment. The GAO[39] and the FTC[40] have both noted the limitations of currently existing studies, and the need for more study concerning the accuracy of consumer reports. The GAO concluded that a meaningful independent review with the cooperation of industry would be necessary to assess the frequency of errors and the implications of errors for consumers.[41] The FTC will be undertaking its own study of consumer credit reporting accuracy, discussed in § 4.1.3.2, *infra*.

4.1.3.2 FACTA Requires FTC to Study the Accuracy of Consumer Reports

The Fair and Accurate Credit Transactions Act of 2003 (FACTA) amended the FCRA in part by directing the FTC to study and report to Congress on various issues related to the accuracy and completeness of consumer reports. The study is to occur over a period of eleven years, with a final report due to Congress in 2014. Five interim reports are to be completed, the first in 2004 and one every two years thereafter. These reports should include findings to date and recommendations for legislative or administrative action. The FTC is directed to study four specific proposals to improve the operation of the FCRA:

- Increasing the points of identifying information (e.g., name, Social Security number, address, etc.) used to match a consumer to a particular consumer credit file at a CRA.[42]
- Requiring that a consumer who has experienced an adverse action based on a consumer report receives a copy of the same report that the creditor relied on in taking the adverse action.[43]
- Requiring notification to consumers when negative information has been added to their reports.[44]
- Identifying any common financial transactions that are not generally reported to the CRAs, but that would provide useful information in determining creditwor-

---

surveyed had seen their consumer reports, and that many did not know more detailed information about the reports, such as how long items remained on their reports or the effect their credit history could have on insurance rates and potential employment. The GAO report also found that many consumers did not know specific information relating to their reports, such as names of the CRAs and the cost of ordering a report.

32 Remarks of J. Howard Beales, III, Before the Consumer Data Industry Association (Jan. 17, 2002), *available at* www.ftc.gov/speeches/other/bealesdia.htm.

33 Letter and enclosures from Joan E. Fina to Chris Hoofnagle in response to FOIA Request No. 2003-470 (June 23, 2003), *reprinted on the CD-Rom accompanying this manual*.

34 U.S. Public Interest Research Group, Credit Bureaus: Public Enemy #1 at the FTC (Oct. 1993). The total number of such complaints that the FTC received from 1990 through the first half of 1993 was 30,901.

35 *Id.*

36 *Id.*

37 *Id.*

38 R. Smith, *A Look Inside a Credit Bureau's Operation*, 22 Privacy Journal 5 (Apr. 1996).

39 General Accounting Office, Limited Information Exists on the Extent of Credit Report Errors and Their Implications for Consumers, GAO-03-1036T (July 31, 2003).

40 Federal Trade Commission, Report to Congress Under Sections 318 and 319 of the Fair and Accurate Credit Transactions Act of 2003, at 22–31 (Dec. 2004).

41 General Accounting Office, Limited Information Exists on the Extent of Credit Report Errors and Their Implications for Consumers, GAO-03-1036T (July 31, 2003).

42 Pub. L. No. 108-159, § 318(a)(2)(A) (2003).

43 Pub. L. No. 108-159, § 318(a)(2)(C) (2003).

44 Pub. L. No. 108-159, § 318(a)(2)(B) (2003).

thiness and any actions that might be taken to encourage greater reporting of such transactions.[45]

The FTC issued its first report to Congress in 2004.[46] The report addressed the four proposals discussed above, reviewing the background on each issue and the effect of implementing each proposal. The report concluded that there may be benefits to consumers from these proposals, but the costs to consumers and industry could be substantial. The FTC declined to offer any legislative or administrative action in furtherance of these four proposals based on in its analysis.[47]

This 2004 FTC report also addressed the accuracy and completeness of consumer reports, a subject that the FACTA amendments required the FTC to conduct a study on.[48] The FTC report reviewed the prior studies on accuracy, and noted the limitations of each study. In response to these limitations, the FTC has proposed a two-phase study. The first phase is a pilot study of approximately thirty-five consumers.[49] These consumers will receive assistance in obtaining and reviewing their consumer reports for errors. An independent contractor hired by the FTC will analyze the importance of the error, including helping the consumer resolve the error informally and through the dispute process to determine the effect on the consumer's credit score. Since statistical conclusions will not be drawn from the study due to the small size of the study group, the intent of the pilot study is to serve as a tool to design the second phase, a larger nationwide study.[50] This nationwide study will be based on a nationally representative sample, use a reliable method developed from the pilot to identify errors, and categorize errors based on their type and seriousness.[51]

4.2 What Is Accuracy?

4.2.1 Consumer Reporting Agency Must Do More Than Just Pass Along Information Provided by the Furnisher

Despite the importance of the term "accuracy" in interpreting the FCRA, the Act does not define the term. Dictionaries variously define "accuracy" to mean "freedom from mistake or error,"[52] "correct, exact and without any mistakes"[53] and "conformity to fact."[54] As one court has stated, accuracy "requires congruence between the legal status of a consumer's account and the status a CRA reports."[55]

Consumer reporting agencies (CRAs) commonly assert that information is "accurate" if the CRA accurately passes on the data provided by their furnishers. This argument has been almost universally rejected.[56] The concept of "accuracy" is an objective one.[57] A consumer report either is or is not accurate. If it is accurate when prepared a certain way, it will always be accurate when prepared that same way. As one court explained: "We begin, therefore, by presuming that Congress used the word 'accuracy' objectively throughout the FCRA. There is no basis for disturbing this presumption because a consistently objective interpretation of 'accuracy' does not render superfluous any part of the FCRA."[58] While credit information may be determined inaccurate by proof of how it was understood in a specific transaction[59], it may also be found inaccurate upon evidence of how it would be understood and interpreted in the industry.[60]

Merely parroting what a creditor reports may not fulfill the "maximum possible accuracy" obligation, once a CRA is notified of a dispute.[61] The accuracy of consumer reporting is not measured by consistency with a creditor's own internal records, but instead must be assessed by the true status of a debt. As described by a recent decision:

---

45 Pub. L. No. 108-159, § 318(a)(2)(D) and (E) (2003).
46 Federal Trade Commission, Report to Congress Under Sections 318 and 319 of the Fair and Accurate Credit Transactions Act of 2003, at 85–86 (Dec. 2004).
47 Id.
48 Pub. L. No. 108-159, § 319 (2003).
49 Federal Trade Commission, Report to Congress Under Sections 318 and 319 of the Fair and Accurate Credit Transactions Act of 2003, at 85–86 (Dec. 2004).
50 Id.
51 Id.
52 Merriam-Webster Online Dictionary (2006).
53 Cambridge Advanced Learner's Dictionary (2003).
54 The American Heritage® Dictionary of the English Language: Fourth Edition (2000).
55 Crane v. Trans Union, L.L.C., 282 F. Supp. 2d 311 (E.D. Pa. 2003).
56 Cushman v. Trans Union Corp., 115 F.3d 220, 224–225 (3d Cir. 1997); Henson v. CSC Credit Servs., 29 F.3d 280 (7th Cir. 1994); Cahlin v. General Motors Acceptance Corp., 936 F.2d 1151, 1158 (11th Cir. 1991); Sampson v. Equifax Info. Servs., L.L.C., 2005 WL 2095092 (S.D. Ga. Aug. 29, 2005); Diprinzio v. MBNA America Bank, N.A., 2005 WL 2039175 (E.D. Pa. Aug. 24, 2005); Crane v. Trans Union, L.L.C., 282 F. Supp. 2d 311 (E.D. Pa. 2003); Swoager v. Credit Bureau, 608 F. Supp. 972, 976 (D.C. Fla. 1985).
57 Cushman v. Trans Union Corp., 115 F.3d 220, 225 (3d Cir. 1995) (defining "accuracy" under the FCRA in an objective manner); Cahlin v. General Motors Acceptance Corp., 936 F.2d 1151, 1158 (11th Cir. 1991) ("[T]he standard of accuracy embodied in section 607(b) [§ 1681e(b)] is an objective measure."); Crane v. Trans Union, L.L.C., 282 F. Supp. 2d 311, 317 (E.D. Pa. 2003).
58 Crane v. Trans Union, L.L.C., 282 F. Supp. 2d 311, 317 n.7 (E.D. Pa. 2003).
59 Koropoulos v. Credit Bureau, Inc., 734 F.2d 37 (D.C. Cir. 1984).
60 Alexander v. Moore & Assocs., Inc., 553 F. Supp. 948 (D.C. Haw. 1982) (court considered "the potential that the information will create a misleading impression against the availability of more accurate information").
61 Crane v. Trans Union, L.L.C., 282 F. Supp. 2d 311 (E.D. Pa. 2003) and cases cited therein.

§ 4.2.2   *Fair Credit Reporting*

Defendant argues that the information it reported to the credit reporting agencies was "truthful" because it accurately reflected the status of plaintiff's account—i.e., "charged off." We find, however, that this reasoning erroneously conflates truth as it pertains to a customer's actions, and truth as it pertains to the content of a credit record.... Clearly, section 1681h(e) requires furnishers of credit information to accurately report what a consumer has done, not merely what a bank chooses to include in its records.... The defendant would have this Court believe that section 1681h(e) protects banks that furnish false facts about a customer, as long as the information matches what is stored in a customer database. Such logic defies common sense and the meaning of the Act.[62]

4.2.2 Accuracy Standard Applies to Report Actually Supplied to User, Not to Consumer Reporting Agency's Later Explanation of That Information

It is important to determine the specific information that was actually reported to a user and the accuracy of that information in the form it was reported to the user. The plain language, paper version of a consumer report usually produced in litigation, with easily-read narratives, is not the manner in which the "Big Three" nationwide CRAs typically supply a consumer report to users.

First, with the advent of credit scoring, that one number is sometimes the most critical, if not sole, criterion used by the creditor.[63] Second, the communication of a consumer's credit information to the actual user is almost always in coded format.[64] For example, the frequently used "MOP" payment status ratings, R-1 through R-9 are only summary values of ambiguous meaning. Each of these MOP summary codes could be descriptive of a dozen or more underlying Metro status codes. These undisclosed Metro 2 codes may be the very cause of the inaccuracy.[65] Thus, R-9, which means a revolving account chargeoff, could reflect a "paid chargeoff," an "unpaid chargeoff," a collection account, or even a "settlement for less than full balance." Each status will affect a consumer's credit score differently. What is at issue is not whether the CRA can describe the contents of the consumer's file in a manner where it is accurate, but whether the coded information in the Metro 2 Format actually supplied to the user accurately reflects the consumer's credit history.

4.2.3 Technically Accurate Reports Can Be Misleading and Inaccurate

The FCRA requires more than technical or literal accuracy;[66] it requires "maximum possible accuracy of the information concerning the individual about whom the report relates."[67] Courts agree that even "a technical truth ... can be as misleading as an outright untruth where it paints a misleading picture."[68] Thus, a consumer report is inaccurate if it is potentially misleading.[69] Whether information is accurate is usually a jury determination.[70] A report can be inaccurate, even if the report is technically true in some narrow sense, but the report is overly general, incomplete, out of date, or misleading.[71] In addition, information that is obsolete will also fail to meet as standard of "maximum

---

62 Diprinzio v. MBNA America Bank, N.A., 2005 WL 2039175 (E.D. Pa. Aug. 24, 2005) (citations omitted). The court also stated the following footnote: "In some accounts of lying there is no lie unless a false statement is made; in others a person may be lying even if the statement he makes is true, as long as he himself believes the statement is false and intends by making it to deceive." *Id.* at n.5. *See also* Saunders v. Equifax Info. Servs., L.L.C., 2006 WL 2850647 (E.D. Va. Oct. 3, 2006); Harry G. Frankfurt, On Bullshit 8 (2005).

63 *See* Ch. 14, *infra*.

64 *See* § 6.3, *infra*.

65 For such an example, see Schaffhausen v. Bank of America, N.A., 393 F. Supp. 2d 853 (D. Minn. 2005). See § 6.3, *infra*, for an explanation of the Metro 2 reporting format.

66 *See* 81 A.L.R. Fed. 207 (1987) (case annotation on accuracy plus practice hints).

67 15 U.S.C. § 1681e(b); Pinner v. Schmidt, 805 F.2d 1258, 1262–1263 (5th Cir. 1986); Koropoulos v. Credit Bureau, Inc., 734 F.2d 37, 40, 42 (D. C. Cir. 1984).

68 Dalton v. Capital Associated Indus., Inc., 257 F.3d 409, 415 (4th Cir. 2001); Sepulvado v. CSC Credit Servs., 158 F.3d 890, 895 (5th Cir. 1998) (consumer report is inaccurate if it is "misleading in such a way and to such an extent that it can be expected to adversely affect credit decisions"); Swoager v. Credit Bureau of Greater St. Petersburg, 608 F. Supp. 972, 977 (M.D. Fla. 1985) (entry misleadingly coded); Alexander v. Moore & Assocs., Inc., 553 F. Supp. 948, 952 (D. Haw. 1982).

69 Crabill v. Trans Union, L.L.C., 259 F.3d 662, 664 (7th Cir. 2001); Sepulvado v. CSC Credit Servs., 158 F.3d 890, 895 (5th Cir. 1998). *See also* Pinner v. Schmidt, 805 F.2d 1258, 1262 (5th Cir. 1986) (information was inaccurate because "any person could easily have" misconstrued the reporting).

70 Dalton v. Capital Associated Indus., Inc., 257 F.3d 409, 416 (4th Cir. 2001) ("If a jury concludes, as it reasonably could, that the report indicates that Dalton was guilty of a felony, inaccuracy would be established because it is undisputed that Dalton pleaded guilty to a misdemeanor.")

71 *See, e.g.*, Henson v. CSC Credit Servs., 29 F.3d 280 (7th Cir. 1994); Pinner v. Schmidt, 805 F.2d 1258 (5th Cir. 1986); Koropoulos v. Credit Bureau, Inc., 734 F.2d 37 (D.C. Cir. 1984); Thompson v. San Antonio Retail Merchants Ass'n, 682 F.2d 509 (5th Cir. 1982); Diprinzio v. MBNA America Bank, N.A., 2005 WL 2039175 (E.D. Pa. Aug. 24, 2005) ("In an effort to overcome plaintiff's contentions, defendant avers that 'incomplete information' is different from 'false information.' Such an argument, however, turns on a skewed interpretation of truthfulness."); Agosta v. Inovision, Inc., 2003 WL 22999213 (E.D. Pa. Dec. 16, 2003) (misleading or materially incomplete entry is inaccurate); Curtis v. Trans Union, L.L.C., 2002 WL 31748838 (N.D. Ill. Dec. 9, 2002); Alexander v. Moore & Assoc., 553 F. Supp. 948 (D. Haw. 1982) (technical accuracy is not the standard; a consumer report must be accurate to the

possible accuracy."[72] This view is also supported by the FTC in its FTC Official Staff Commentary (FTC Staff Commentary) and other interpretations.[73] The omission of a material fact, for example, constitutes misrepresentation under common law and deception under the Federal Trade Commission Act.[74]

Despite this majority view, industry litigants have asserted, and some courts have accepted a "technical accuracy" defense.[75] For example, a report might be technically accurate if it stated that a debt was turned over to a collection agency, but neglected to include that the debt was subsequently fully paid,[76] or if it reported a suit against an individual, but omitted that the individual was sued in his official capacity as deputy sheriff.[77]

The "technical accuracy" defense is primarily founded upon an unreported Sixth Circuit decision, *Dicken v. Trans Union Corp*.[78] In *Dicken*, the court dismissed a case in which the consumer did not dispute that the report was technically accurate because there was no evidence that the reported information was false.[79] While it may remain an open question in some circuits as to whether the "technical accuracy" standard is viable, the standard has been "universally criticized by commentators for taking an unjustifiably narrow view of 'maximum accuracy.'"[80]

Ironically, the phrase "technically accurate" was first used as an example of the abuses to be covered by the FCRA. Introducing the bill which was to become the FCRA, Senator Proxmire noted: "In addition to supplying inaccurate information, a second major abuse of credit reporting agencies is the dissemination of irrelevant information—that is, the information may be technically accurate but it may not serve any useful purposes."[81]

Indeed, a review the congressional history provides clear support that a "technically accurate" defense was never intended. Consider, for example, an exchange between Senator Bennett, the industry spokesman in debates, and Senator Proxmire:

> *Sen. Bennett*: It doesn't take any judgment in the end to discover whether or not something is accurate in terms of treatment.
>
> *Sen. Proxmire*: Well, here is a situation that has developed. One man's file had the charge in it that he had suffered a charge of assault. This was in the file. The information was not in the file that the charge had been dismissed because under the circumstances what had happened was that he had witnessed the mugging of an elderly person in the dark in the street and had gone to the elderly person's defense and in the course of doing this he had to assault the person who was mugging the elderly person. He was a hero. The person who had engaged in the mugging sued him for assault. Of course, it was dismissed.
>
> You can have a report which is accurate but not complete and not fair. I think this is one of the reasons why you have to go a little further than simple accuracy.

---

maximum possible extent); Bryant v. TRW, Inc., 487 F. Supp. 1234 (E.D. Mich. 1980), *aff'd*, 689 F.2d 72 (6th Cir. 1982); Miller v. Credit Bureau, Inc. of Washington, DC, [1969–1978 Decisions Transfer Binder] Consumer Cred. Guide (CCH) ¶ 99,173 (D.C. Super. Ct. 1972); Tracy v. Credit Bureau, Inc. of Georgia, 330 S.E.2d 921 (Ga. Ct. App. 1985); Note, *Fair Credit Reporting Act: Are Misleading Reports Reasonable?*, 55 N.Y.U.L. Rev. 111 (1980); Note, *Judicial Construction of the Fair Credit Reporting Act: Scope and Civil Liability*, 76 Colum. L. Rev. 458 (1976). *See also* Wilson v. Rental Research Serv., Inc., 165 F.3d 642 (8th Cir. 1999), *rehearing en banc without published opinion*, 206 F.3d 810 (8th Cir. 2000) (by vote of an equally divided court, the district court's order is affirmed) (case involved disclaimers placed in consumer reports); Neal v. CSC Credit Servs., Inc., 2004 WL 628214 (D. Neb. Mar. 30, 2004) (Wilson turns on warning that information might be inaccurate).

72 *See* § 5.2, *infra*.
73 FTC Official Staff Commentary §§ 607 items 3F(1), (2), (3), 611 items 5, 6, *reprinted at* Appx. D, *infra*; FTC, Compliance with the Fair Credit Reporting Act, at 28 (1977).
74 *See* 15 U.S.C. § 45; Restatement (Second) of Torts § 529; National Consumer Law Center, Unfair and Deceptive Acts and Practices § 4.2 (6th ed. 2004 and Supp.).
75 Dicken v. Trans Union Corp., 18 Fed. Appx. 315, 2001 WL 1006259 (6th Cir. Aug. 23, 2001); Sepulvado v. CSC Credit Servs., Inc., 158 F.3d 890 (5th Cir. 1998) (failure of CRA to include information that debt, shown to be recent, arose from a mortgage foreclosure several years old did not render report inaccurate); Spence v. TRW, Inc., 92 F.3d 380 (6th Cir. 1996); Heupel v. Trans Union, L.L.C., 193 F. Supp. 2d 1234 (N.D. Ala. 2002); Wright v. TRW Credit Data, 588 F. Supp. 112 (S.D. Fla. 1984); McPhee v. Chilton Corp., 468 F. Supp. 494 (D. Conn. 1978); Lowry v. Credit Bureau of Georgia, 444 F. Supp. 541 (N.D. Ga. 1978); Todd v. Associated Credit Bureau Servs., Inc., 451 F. Supp. 447 (E.D. Pa. 1977), *aff'd*, 578 F.2d 1376 (3d Cir. 1979); Roseman v. Retail Credit Co., 428 F. Supp. 643 (E.D. Pa. 1977); Middlebrooks v. Retail Credit Co., 416 F. Supp. 1013 (N.D. Ga. 1976); Austin v. Bankamerica Serv. Corp., 419 F. Supp. 730 (N.D. Ga. 1974). *Cf.* Cahlin v. General Motors Acceptance Corp., 936 F.2d 1151 (11th Cir. 1991) (not ruling on validity of technically accurate defense); Johnson v. Beneficial Fin. Corp., 466 N.Y.S.2d 553, 120 Misc. 2d 628 (Sup. Ct. 1983).
76 Todd v. Associated Credit Bureau Servs., Inc., 451 F. Supp. 447 (E.D. Pa. 1977), *aff'd*, 578 F.2d 1376 (3d Cir. 1979).
77 Austin v. Bankamerica Serv. Corp., 419 F. Supp. 730 (N.D. Ga. 1974).
78 18 Fed. Appx. 315, 2001 WL 1006259 (6th Cir. Aug. 23, 2001).
79 *Id.* at 318.
80 Koropoulos v. Credit Bureau, Inc., 734 F.2d 37, 41 n.7 (D.C. Cir. 1984). *See also* Dalton v. Capital Associated Indus. Inc., 257 F.3d 409, 415 (4th Cir. 2001); Crabill v. Trans Union, L.L.C., 259 F.3d 662, 665 (7th Cir. 2001); Sepulvado v. CSC Credit Servs., 158 F.3d 890, 895 (5th Cir. 1998); Wilson v. Rental Research Servs., Inc., 165 F.3d 642 (8th Cir. 1999), *vacated without opinion en banc*, 206 F.3d 810 (8th Cir. 2003) (equally divided en banc); Pinner v. Schmidt, 805 F.2d 1258, 1262 (5th Cir. 1987); Diprinzio v. MBNA America Bank, N.A., 2005 WL 2039175 (E.D. Pa. Aug. 24, 2005); Evantash v. G.E. Capital Mortgage Servs., Inc., 2003 WL 22844198 (E.D. Pa. Nov. 25, 2003); Spellman v. Experian Info. Solutions, Inc., 2002 WL 799876 (D. Nev. Jan. 10, 2002); Alexander v. Moore & Associates, Inc., 553 F. Supp. 948 (D. Haw. 1982).
81 115 Cong. Rec. 2412 (1969).

Sen. Bennett: I don't think a report that is that incomplete can be said to be accurate. But now we are talking about words.[82]

The cases permitting a "technically accurate" standard also make no sense when taken in conjunction with the FTC Staff Commentary position that CRAs must utilize procedures to ensure that information is complete and must correct incomplete information if disputed.[83] The same incompleteness, instead, should also lead to an inaccuracy finding triggering the consumer's ability to challenge the CRA procedures.[84]

Furthermore, the FTC staff, in its informal opinion letters, has repeatedly taken the view that, even where the accuracy of a report is not disputed, if the consumer provides additional information on an incomplete file, then the CRA must include the statement.[85] This is because a CRA must report significant additional information reflecting upon the accuracy or completeness of any item of information already in the file.[86] A CRA may not immunize itself from liability for inaccurate information by posting a warning that information in the report may not be accurate.[87]

Reports of delinquent accounts should note that the account has been paid if verified; a debt discharged in bankruptcy should be reported with an accurate account of its current status (e.g., voluntarily repaid); or a report of a bankruptcy which has been dismissed must report the dismissal.[88] If a consumer's obligation is based solely on that individual being a guarantor, this must also be disclosed in reporting the debt as delinquent.[89]

The same is the case with the FTC Staff Commentary's requirements on correcting files after consumers dispute incomplete information. It would make no sense to require CRAs to correct this information when disputed,[90] but then to find the same information to be "technically accurate" when considering whether the CRA's report was accurate.

Of course there are limits to the use of updated information in lieu of the original reported information. For example, where a debt marked uncollectible is later paid, a CRA is accurate in indicating the current balance owed as "0" and stating that the debt has been paid. The CRA can still indicate that at one point in time the debt was viewed by the creditor as uncollectible.[91]

4.2.4 Information Must Relate to the Consumer

Information that does not pertain to the consumer upon whom a report is furnished is not accurate under the FCRA.[92] A consumer report is one which "*bear[s] on a consumer's* credit worthiness, credit standing, credit capacity," and other individualized characteristics and which is to be used "as a factor in establishing *the consumer's eligibility*" for credit, employment, and other permissible purposes.[93] The CRA must follow procedures to "assure maximum possible accuracy of the information *concerning the individual about who the report relates.*"[94] A common thread throughout the FCRA is that a consumer report relates to the individual consumer.[95] One person's credit information does not bear on another consumer's creditworthiness or the other personal characteristics.[96]

---

82 Hearings on S. 823, Subcommittee on Financial Institutions on the Senate Banking and Currency Committee 91st Cong., 1st Sess. 34 (1969).
83 FTC Official Staff Commentary §§ 607 items 3F(1), (2), (3), 611 items 5, 6, *reprinted at* Appx. D, *infra*.
84 *But see* Grant v. TRW, Inc., 789 F. Supp. 690 (D. Md. 1992) (distinguishing § 1681i(a) which explicitly mentions "completeness" from § 1681e(b) which deals with accuracy).
85 Oliver, FTC Informal Staff Opinion Letter (June 10, 1983), *reprinted on the CD-Rom accompanying this manual*; Peeler, FTC Informal Staff Opinion Letter (July 25, 1978), *reprinted on the CD-Rom accompanying this manual* (reasons or circumstances of nonpayment go to completeness of report, therefore must include consumer's statement where requested); Peeler, FTC Informal Staff Opinion Letter (Aug. 23, 1976), *reprinted on the CD-Rom accompanying this manual*; Feldman, FTC Informal Staff Opinion Letter (Aug. 30, 1974), *reprinted on the CD-Rom accompanying this manual* (CRA's failure to include additional references provided by consumer would cause violation due to incompleteness of report); Feldman, FTC Informal Staff Opinion Letter (May 31, 1974), *reprinted on the CD-Rom accompanying this manual* (serious question exists whether CRA may continue to report incomplete information if consumer supplies additional information).
86 15 U.S.C. § 1681i(a); FTC Official Staff Commentary § 607 item 3F(2), *reprinted at* Appx. D, *infra*.
87 Wilson v. Rental Research Servs., Inc., 165 F.3d 642 (8th Cir. 1999), *rehearing en banc without published opinion*, 206 F.3d 810 (8th Cir. 2000) (by vote of an equally divided court, the district court's order is affirmed) (warning that information from public records that was based solely on name without further verification did not support summary judgment in favor of CRA).

88 FTC Official Staff Commentary § 607 items 3F(1) and (2), *reprinted at* Appx. D, *infra*. *See* § 5.6.2, *infra*.
89 FTC Official Staff Commentary § 607 item 3F(3).
90 FTC Official Staff Commentary § 611 items 5 and 6.
91 Cahlin v. General Motors Acceptance Corp., 936 F.2d 1151 (11th Cir. 1991).
92 Guimond v. Trans Union Credit Info. Co., 45 F.3d 1329, 1333 (9th Cir. 1995); Hansen v. Morgan, 582 F.2d 1214, 1220 (9th Cir. 1978). However, in certain circumstances, a furnisher may report information about a spouse's activities under the Equal Credit Opportunity Act. *See* § 5.6.1, *infra*.
93 15 U.S.C. § 1681a(d)(1).
94 15 U.S.C. § 1681e(b) (emphasis added).
95 *See also* 15 U.S.C. § 1681q ("information on a consumer"); 15 U.S.C. § 1681r ("concerning an individual").
96 Abbett v. Bank of America, 2006 WL 581193 (M.D. Ala. Mar. 8, 2006); Evantash v. G.E. Capital Mortgage Servs., Inc., 2003 WL 22844198 (E.D. Pa. Nov. 25, 2003); Spellman v. Experian Info. Solutions, Inc., 2002 WL 799876 (D. Nev. Jan. 10, 2002).

4.2.5 Consumer Reporting Agency May Not Report Unverifiable Information

While a CRA is entitled to presume that its furnisher is otherwise a reliable source, once it determines that a credit item cannot be "verified," it is no longer entitled to report it.[97] Typically, CRAs hold fast to the belief that they are entitled to report any information that cannot be conclusively determined to be inaccurate. This presumption is completely contrary to that demanded by the FCRA. A CRA may not report information which it concludes is unverified or indeterminable.[98] Similarly, a CRA must delete an item when it has attempted to determine whether the item is accurate and is unable to do so, whatever the reason.[99] CRAs are not entitled to report any information they wish. In light of the FCRA's remedial purpose and strict "maximum possible accuracy" standard, uncertainty or doubt should be resolved in the consumer's favor. Unverifiable information is tantamount to inaccurate information.

4.3 Types of Inaccurate Information

4.3.1 Introduction

There are a number of reasons why a consumer report may not be an accurate and complete representation of a consumer's actual credit history.[100] First, the data provided to the consumer reporting agency (CRA) by the furnisher or other source may itself be inaccurate or incomplete. Second, the CRA may fail to accurately assign reported information to the file of the consumer to whom it applies.[101] Third, the CRA may furnish to its subscriber a file which while otherwise correct does not regard the consumer upon whom the inquiry is made.[102] Each of these categories of inaccuracy are discussed below.

It is critical that practitioners diagnose the form and cause of a disputed inaccuracy before commencing litigation. Many inaccuracies may appear at first glance to be caused by inaccurate reporting by a furnisher, but discovery or other investigation will reveal that the error was caused by what the CRA did after it received the otherwise accurate data.

4.3.2 Inaccuracies Caused by Furnishers

4.3.2.1 Furnisher Provision of Inaccurate Data

Usually, information from creditors (also referred to as furnishers) on a consumer's account status is computerized, and the furnisher's computer files are periodically dumped into the CRA's computer. Any error in the furnisher's computer file automatically appears in the consumer's credit report. The furnisher often will have a relationship with one or more of the CRAs, and will make the computer tape available to each CRA. Thus it is likely that the same error will be sent to multiple CRAs.

Furnisher provision of inaccurate data is of two primary types. First, the furnisher might report the consumer's account with an incorrect payment history, current payment status, or balance. Alternately, a creditor may have attributed the account to a consumer who does not owe the debt. Most frequently, the furnisher is incorrectly attributing the "ownership" of the account to a spouse or other authorized user who is not contractually liable on the account.[103] Other times, the consumer may have been the victim of identity theft where a third party fraudulently opened an account for which the furnisher is now incorrectly attributing ownership.[104]

Many furnisher errors occur because the creditor has not complied with industry reporting standards, such as Metro 2. A series of cases over a six-year period challenged the practice of creditors that reported a single status—bankruptcy—for all obligors on an account even if only one debtor filed, contrary to Metro 2 standards.[105] An ongoing problem for the reporting of collection accounts is the date of status or delinquency. Many collectors "re-age" their accounts to report them as more recent than is accurate.[106]

One of the important points to realize is that correcting an error in a consumer's file at a CRA will not automatically correct the creditor's files. The problem of "re-insertion" is discussed at § 4.7, *infra*.

---

97 15 U.S.C. § 1681i(a). *See* § 4.6, *infra*.

98 *Cf.* FTC Official Staff Commentary § 607 item 3D ("Requirements are more stringent where the information furnished appears implausible or inconsistent, or where procedures for furnishing it seem likely to result in inaccuracies, or where the consumer reporting agency has had numerous problems regarding information from a particular source.").

99 15 U.S.C. § 1681i(a); Johnson v. MBNA America Bank, NA, 357 F.3d 426, 430 (4th Cir. 2004); Fed. Trade Comm'n v. Gill, 265 F.3d 944, 1035 (9th Cir. 2001) ("If an item is found to be inaccurate or unverifiable, the CRA must delete the information from the credit report."(emphasis added)). *See* § 4.6.2, *infra*.

100 Federal Trade Commission, Report to Congress Under Sections 318 and 319 of the Fair and Accurate Credit Transactions Act of 2003, at 12 (Dec. 2004).

101 The FTC describes process as "File Building." *Id.*

102 The FTC describes this process as "File Retrieval." *Id.*

103 Abbett v. Bank of America, 2006 WL 581193 (M.D. Ala. Mar. 8, 2006); Johnson v. MBNA America Bank, NA, 357 F.3d 426, 430 (4th Cir. 2004); Alabran v. Capital One Bank, 2005 WL 3338663 (E.D. Va. Dec. 8, 2005).

104 Cushman v. Trans Union Corp., 115 F.3d 220, 224–225 (3d Cir. 1997). *See* § 4.3.3.7, *infra*.

105 Clark v. Experian Info. Solutions, Inc., 2004 WL 256433 (D.S.C. Jan. 14, 2004); Evantash v. G.E. Capital Mortgage Servs., Inc., 2003 WL 22844198 (E.D. Pa. Nov. 25, 2003); Spellman v. Experian Info. Solutions, In, 2002 WL 799876 (D. Nev. Jan. 10, 2002). *But see* Dicken v. Trans Union Corp., 18 Fed. Appx. 215, 2001 WL 1006259 (6th Cir. Aug. 23, 2001). *See* § 4.4.6.9.3, *infra*.

106 *See* § 5.2.3.2.5, *infra*.

4.3.2.2 Failure of Many Creditors to Furnish Data to Consumer Reporting Agencies

A consumer's report is frequently incomplete, because it does not contain positive accounts that would otherwise render a more favorable and complete picture of a consumer's credit history. CRAs normally get most of their information from their subscribers, and do not receive information from creditors who do not subscribe to their services. A consumer's credit report from a given CRA, therefore, will likely contain only information on the accounts of creditors who subscribe to that CRA (plus public record information). The credit history may not include payment history to landlords, utilities, or others where the consumer's regular payments would reflect positively on the consumer's overall creditworthiness.

There are estimates that over one-in-ten non-incarcerated adults in the United States has no credit file at any CRA.[107] An additional group of such Americans—in excess of one in seven—has a "thin file" which does not contain sufficient reported credit data to generate a credit score.[108] Minorities and recent immigrants are disproportionately represented in these groups.[109] The CRAs rarely report the credit most often used by these groups—rent and utility payments. The 2003 FACTA amendments to the FCRA charged the FTC with the task of studying alternatives to this growing problem.[110] A number of "alternative" CRA have been established to address it as well.[111]

The credit files of consumers that are missing additional positive information are inaccurate because of their incompleteness. However, the remedy is not exactly clear. The FTC has indicated new items do not have to be added to the file.[112] The counter-argument would be that the file as a whole does not paint an accurate picture of the consumer, where missing information would help to correct the inaccuracy. A file showing a limited credit history would be inaccurate if the consumer had numerous other credit accounts not listed in the file.

Another argument regarding the CRAs' obligation to include new information not pertaining to existing items is that such information is important for purposes of credit scoring.[113] If missing information would alter the consumer's credit score, then this information must be added to the file to make an item in the file (the credit score) more accurate. This would be the case even if the information to be added involves completely new accounts.

Nevertheless, the FCRA does not explicitly require affirmative reporting by creditors; it merely governs the accuracy of the reporting for those that do. However, distinctions should be drawn between information needed to be added to items already in the file to make them accurate, and information that is not relevant to a particular item in the file, but that would make the whole file more complete. The former problem *is* governed by the FCRA and is discussed below.

4.3.2.3 Furnishers That Withhold Data

A different problem of incompleteness occurs when lenders intentionally withhold positive payment histories or reporting data from the CRAs for accounts they otherwise report. Mortgage lenders and credit card issuers often do so for strategic reasons. Their objective is to shield their customers from competing lenders who might otherwise solicit them.[114] This practice, which is especially common among subprime lenders, results in consumer reports that do not accurately reflect the positive payment histories for borrowers, especially high-interest borrowers in the subprime market.[115]

A number of attempts have been made to rectify this problem. At one time, Equifax and TransUnion attempted to establish policies intended to curtail the withholding of customer data.[116] Secondary lending giant Freddie Mac noted to its sellers and servicers that its Single-Family Seller/Servicer Guide requires monthly submission to all three nationwide CRAs of a *complete* file of mortgage information.[117] Similarly, the Federal Financial Institutions Examination Council (FFEIC)[118] notified institutions supervised by its members that they must take precautions to deal with the results of lenders' failure to report credit information to CRAs, noting in particular that certain large credit card issuers and some subprime lenders have stopped reporting consumer credit information in order to protect those accounts.[119] The FFEIC attributed this failure to "intense competition" among institutions, and advised financial institutions to put procedures in place to identify and com-

---

107 Federal Trade Commission, Report to Congress Under Sections 318 and 319 of the Fair and Accurate Credit Transactions Act of 2003, at 78 (Dec. 2004).
108 *Id.*
109 *Id.*
110 Pub. L. No. 108-159, §§ 318(a)(2)(D) and (E) (2003).
111 *See* § 2.7.10, *infra.*
112 Napier v. TRW/Credit Bureau Associates, Inc., 1997 Del. Super. LEXIS 546 (Del. Super. Ct. Sept. 15, 1997); FTC Official Staff Commentary § 611 item 3, *reprinted at* Appx. D, *infra.*
113 *See* Ch. 14, *infra.*
114 Federal Trade Commission, Report to Congress Under Sections 318 and 319 of the Fair and Accurate Credit Transactions Act of 2003, at 82 (Dec. 2004).
115 *Id.* at 12.
116 Fickenscher, *Credit Bureaus Move Against Lenders That Withhold Info*, American Banker (Dec. 30, 1999).
117 Freddie Mac, Industry Letter (Feb. 22, 2000).
118 The FFIEC is a formal interagency body that prescribes uniform standards for the examination of financial institutions by the Federal Reserve Board (FRB), the Federal Deposit Insurance Corporation (FDIC), the National Credit Union Administration (NCUA), the Office of the Comptroller of the Currency (OCC), and the Office of Thrift Supervision (OTS).
119 Fed. Fin. Insts. Examination Council, Advisory Letter (Jan. 18, 2000), *available at* www.ffiec.gov/press/pr011800a.htm.

pensate for missing data.[120] The Office of Comptroller of the Currency suggested that legislation may be required in order to ensure that such information is reported and consumers are protected from such incomplete reporting.[121]

Currently, several large credit card lenders, including Capital One, refuse to report the credit limit for their customer accounts.[122] One of the most heavily weighted parts of a credit score is "credit utilization" which measures the proportion of a consumer's available credit with the credit already being used.[123] When a credit card company does not report its customer's credit limit, the CRAs substitute the historical value for the highest amount of credit ever used on the account. This can negatively affect a consumer's credit score.[124] This inaccuracy is difficult to diagnose as the consumer will not receive a paper consumer report which lists the high credit value in the credit limit field. Instead, the CRAs' computers essentially publish two different reports—one that then enters the scoring algorithm and the one which is printed in narrative form and shown to the consumer.[125]

While the FCRA requires furnishers to report data that is both accurate and complete[126], one court has held that a creditor's refusal to report its credit limit field does not violate the FCRA.[127] While the suppression of good payment history might not violate the FCRA, it could possibly be attacked as an unfair or deceptive trade practice.

A Federal Reserve Board (FRB) study has also found that data maintained by CRAs is incomplete because many accounts contain incomplete or out-of-date information.[128] The FRB researchers found that creditors do not report or update information on consumers who make scheduled payments or on the accounts of those who have been seriously delinquent, particularly accounts with no change in status. Information also differs from CRA to CRA. CRAs also receive and post information at different times; furnishers may report to one or two nationwide CRAs, but not all three; and changes made to disputed information may be reflected in only in the CRA's file that received the dispute and not the others.[129] Such incomplete files may also negatively affect the credit score computed from such a file.[130]

Also troubling for consumers is the inclusion of information concerning preliminary actions that reflects negatively on the consumer without any follow up as to an eventual outcome that is more favorable to the consumer. For example, a CRA may record a collection lawsuit being filed, without indicating the eventual outcome (which may have been a dismissal), or might record that a debt was delinquent without indicating that it has now been paid. An insurance company may report that it has charged off a car loan on a car that has been totaled without reporting that the consumer continued to pay the note on time.

4.3.2.4 Furnisher Failure to Update Debts Discharged in Bankruptcy

One of the most prevalent consumer reporting problems over the last several years is the failure of the reporting system to provide consumers a "fresh start" after a bankruptcy discharge. Creditors frequently fail to report an updated status for discharged accounts or continue to report their pre-discharge status and balance. CRAs do not update tradelines and judgments they otherwise know have been discharged.[131]

The failure to update debts discharged in bankruptcy can have a significant effect on consumers. The effect of a bankruptcy on a consumer's credit score is of course initially devastating. However, it is a static event and, all other things equal, a consumer's credit score will continue to improve each day that passes post-discharge.[132] Failure to properly report the discharge of debts hampers that improvement. Another consequence of the failure to report that a debt has been discharged, as noted by one bankruptcy court, is that:

> [A] credit report entry that reflects a past due account is treated differently by prospective creditors in evaluating credit applications than an entry that reflects a debt that has been discharged in bankruptcy. The essential difference is that a discharged debt represents a historical fact, that the prospective borrower filed bankruptcy in the past and was relieved from the obligation. Nothing is now due. A past due debt represents a delinquent

---

120 *Id.*
121 Office of the Comptroller of the Currency, Press Release NR99-51 (June 6, 1999), *available at* www.occ.treas.gov/ftp/release/99-51.wpw.
122 Evan Hendricks, *Credit Scores & Credit Reports: How the System Really Works, What You Can Do*, Privacy Times, Ch. 22 (2d ed. 2005); Federal Trade Commission, Report to Congress Under Sections 318 and 319 of the Fair and Accurate Credit Transactions Act of 2003, at 12–13 (Dec. 2004).
123 Fair Isaac, Understanding Your FICO Score, at 9–15 (July 2005), *available at* www.myfico.com/Downloads/Files/myFICO_UYFS_Booklet.pdf.
124 *See* § 14.8.3.2, *infra*.
125 Bagby v. Experian Info. Solutions, 2004 WL 1244113 (N.D. Ill. June 7, 2004) (consumer failed to conduct discovery to obtain underlying reporting of data and instead relied only on the narrative reports which did not show the CRA's substitution of values).
126 15 U.S.C. § 1681s-2(a). *See* § 6.4, *infra*.
127 Baker v. Capital One Bank, 2006 WL 173668 (D. Ariz. Jan. 24, 2006) (*pro se*).
128 Robert B. Avery, Paul S. Calem, and Glenn B. Canner, *Credit Report Accuracy and Access to Credit*, Federal Reserve Bulletin, at 297–322 (Summer 2004), *available at* www.federalreserve.gov/pubs/bulletin/2004/summer04_credit.pdf.

129 *Id.*
130 *See* § 14.8.3.3, *infra*.
131 *See* § 4.4.6.9.3, *infra*.
132 *See* http://moneycentral.msn.com/content/Banking/bankruptcyguide/P108797.asp.

but legally enforceable obligation that must be resolved.[133]

Post-bankruptcy inaccuracies are caused by both furnishers and CRAs. Under the Metro 2 reporting format, a bankruptcy discharge is an account "condition" reported for each consumer who filed. A successful chapter 7 bankruptcy will result in the discharge of all unsecured debts, other than certain discrete debts such as:[134] (i) government-insured student loans and other statutorily nondischargeable debts;[135] (ii) debts that are subject to a signed reaffirmation agreement filed with the bankruptcy court;[136] and (iii) debts that have been subject to a successful objection or adversary action.[137] All of these exceptions to discharge of consumer debts are objectively determinable and identifiable.

A very significant number of creditors (also referred to as furnishers) never report a pre-bankruptcy petition tradeline or collection account as discharged or "included in bankruptcy." Often, when a creditor receives notice of a bankruptcy filing, it simply re-codes its internal account record to reflect the discharge and to avoid violating the bankruptcy stay. This may result in the account never again being reported to the CRAs. However, because the CRAs are accustomed to receiving only partial account information or histories, they continue to report the last known status and balance. For example, assume a lender reports a debt as 120 days late on December 31. On January 1, it receives notice of the bankruptcy and internally closes the account. Unless that creditor then re-reports with the new discharge status, the last reported information will be the pre-bankruptcy status of 120 days late.

Alternatively, some creditors may continue to report or report anew after the consumer's debts have been discharged. The reporting of a discharged debt as outstanding or owing is often accomplished by creditors to continue collection of an otherwise unenforceable debt.[138] One bankruptcy court, in concluding that such continued reporting may violate the bankruptcy stay, cautioned:

> We find that the latter most certainly must be done in an effort to effect collection of the account. See *In re* Spaulding, 116 B.R. 567, 570 (Bankr. S.D. Ohio 1990) (while it may be an increased burden for creditors to take extra steps to prevent violations of the automatic stay, creditors who fail to do so proceed at their own peril). Such a notation on a credit report is, in fact, just the type of creditor shenanigans intended to be prohibited by the automatic stay. H. R. Rep. No. 95-595, 95th Cong. 1st Sess. 342 (1977) reprinted in 1978 U.S. Cong. & Admin. News 5787, 6298 ("Paragraph (6) prevents creditors from attempting in any way to collect a pre-petition debt. Creditors in consumer cases occasionally telephone debtors to encourage payment in spite of bankruptcy. Inexperienced, frightened or ill-counseled debtors may succumb. . . .").[139]

4.3.2.5 Errors in Collection of Public Record Information

4.3.2.5.1 How public record information is collected

There are many different types of public record information that can appear in a consumer's file, e.g., bankruptcies, collection judgments, eviction proceedings, and tax liens. In contrast to how CRAs passively receive creditor data from their subscribers, they affirmatively seek out and obtain public record data from their own third party vendors. These vendors are also "furnishers" governed by the FCRA.[140]

Equifax has long relied on a company, National Data Retrieval, Inc. (NDR), to gather its public records data. NDR hires its own subcontract personnel to make weekly, bi-weekly, or monthly trips to the local courthouses to gather the judgment and tax lien dockets of various courthouses around the country. ChoicePoint, a former Equifax subsidiary has now purchased NDR and consolidated both the bankruptcy and judgment/liens docket contracts.

While each CRA at one point used different vendors (e.g., TransUnion uses Hogan Information Services Co., now a LexisNexis company), they sometimes use the same public records supplier. For example, Experian is now using ChoicePoint's data, as does Equifax. As a result, the same public records error in one CRA file will often appear in a competitor's file.

ChoicePoint's sale of public records data to Experian and Equifax creates an entirely new possibility of inaccuracy and FCRA governance. Unlike earlier public record vendors, ChoicePoint now sells its public records data out of its independent database. It is no longer simply a conduit to the courthouse, but is also an independent CRA. While it may remain governed by the FCRA's furnisher liability provisions, it is also governed by the FCRA provisions governing CRAs.

---

133 *In re* Helmes, 336 B.R. 105 (Bankr. E.D. Va. 2005).
134 National Consumer Law Center, Consumer Bankruptcy Law and Practice Ch. 14 (8th ed. 2006).
135 *See* 11 U.S.C. § 523.
136 11 U.S.C. § 524(c).
137 11 U.S.C. § 523(a)(2).
138 Carriere v. Proponent Federal Credit Union, 2004 WL 1638250 (W.D. La. July 12, 2004); *In re* Helmes, 336 B.R. 105 (Bankr. E.D. Va. 2005); *In re* Smith, 2005 WL 3447645 (Bankr. N.D. Iowa Dec. 12, 2005); *In re* Goodfellow, 298 B.R. 358 (Bankr. N.D. Iowa 2003); *In re* Singley, 233 B.R. 170 (Bankr. S.D. Ga. 1999); *In re* Sommersdorf, 139 B.R. 700 (Bankr. S.D. Ohio 1991).

139 *In re* Sommersdorf, 139 B.R. 700 (Bankr. S.D. Ohio 1991).
140 *See* Ch. 6, *supra*.

4.3.2.5.2 How errors occur in public record information

There are several ways that public record information in a consumer's file can end up with errors. Just like information from creditors, the source public record could itself contain an error. CRAs are not likely to discover and correct such errors on their own. In addition, errors are commonly made by CRAs (or the companies they hire) in copying information from public records. While more and more public records are computerized, the computer records may not be available to a CRA. Thus, an individual might have to visually inspect and interpret the record and copy down relevant information.

For example, in 1991, TRW (now Experian) contracted with an outside company to go through the public records in a town in Vermont to find those people delinquent on their property taxes. The researcher sent to do the job copied down the wrong roll, and, as a result, all property owners in the town were reported delinquent in paying their property taxes.[141] Ultimately, the CRA's tax lien data was found to be tainted in areas throughout Vermont, New Hampshire, Maine, and Rhode Island.[142]

It is not uncommon for a public records vendor to reverse the parties, or to reverse the outcome, of a judgment or lawsuit. For example, a plaintiff who obtains judgment against a debtor defendant may be mistakenly reported as the judgment debtor. Alternately, a defendant who succeeds in defending a lawsuit and obtains a dismissal may still find that the public record has been transcribed showing a judgment obtained. It is also not unusual for a corporate registered agent or a trustee named in a fiduciary capacity to find a public record judgment reported to their personal consumer reports. Even bankruptcy attorneys may find themselves listed as the bankrupt debtor.

Public records errors can also occur when the third party vendor itself makes an error in its judgment. In one instance, a CRA relied upon a subvendor to conduct criminal record checks. The subvendor, relying upon an informal but erroneous legal opinion from a court clerk, reported the plaintiff was convicted of a felony, which was inaccurate. The CRA's failure to have procedures in place to ensure the accuracy of the subvendor's sources of information was found to raise questions for the jury as to whether the CRA was negligent under the FCRA.[143] Similarly, it appears that some public record vendors have now been delegated the responsibility for merging and sorting data before it is delivered to the CRA. If the vendor itself mixes a data item and wrongfully attributes it to a consumer, it could be especially difficult to resolve.

A Federal Reserve Board study found that the degree to which lawsuits are reported is inconsistent. In some cases, there was more than one public record item associated with a single episode.[144] For example, there may be both a record of a lawsuit being filed and a judgment relating to the same debt. The report also found that there may be inconsistencies in reporting of public records across plaintiffs and geographic areas. For example, three states (Maryland, New York, and Pennsylvania) accounted for two thirds of all individuals with records of lawsuits in the files examined.[145] The report further found that some plaintiffs obtain separate judgments for individual unpaid items, while other plaintiffs in similar circumstances may have combined the bills.[146]

Creditors can also be the cause of errors in the public records when they fail to file a satisfaction of judgment or fail to inform the CRAs that the judgment has been satisfied. This problem is compounded by the CRAs' failure to update public information contained in consumer files.

4.3.3 Consumer Reporting Agency Errors in Matching Data to Consumer Files

4.3.3.1 Mixed or Merged Files

There are multiple causes of "ownership" inaccuracies in consumer files, i.e., inaccuracies in which a credit account or other item belonging to one person appears in the consumer report of another. One of the ways this can occur, as discussed in § 4.3.2, *supra*, is through inaccurate reporting by a furnisher. For example, a credit card company may incorrectly report a spouse as responsible for the debt signed for and agreed to only by her husband.[147] This error would be entirely and exclusively made by the furnisher.

However, furnisher error is not the only way that information belonging to one consumer can be placed in the consumer report of another. The first of two alternative explanations for another type of error—mixed or merged files—is caused by the way CRAs match data to files, and is discussed in § 4.3.4, *infra*. The second, discussed in § 4.3.3.3, *infra*, is caused by the way in which a CRA incorrectly retrieves otherwise correct files into a report.

---

141 Sharon Kindel, *Garbage In*, Financial World 60, 61 (Sept. 29, 1992).

142 In 1993, TRW agreed to pay monetary damages to all consumers who had credit denied or delayed as a result of the reporting errors. *See* Jeffrey Rothfeder, Privacy for Sale: How Computerization Has Made Everyone's Private Life an Open Secret (1992).

143 Dalton v. Capital Associated Industries, Inc., 257 F.3d 409 (4th Cir. 2001) (jury could properly conclude that it was unreasonable to rely on a clerk's informal opinion on the crucial question of whether a specific crime was a felony and the CRA should have procedures in place to instruct its subvendors on the appropriate sources for reliable information).

144 Robert Avery, Paul Calem, Glenn Canner, and Raphael Bostic, *An Overview of Consumer Data and Credit Reporting*, Federal Reserve Bulletin, at 68 (Feb. 2003).

145 *Id.*

146 *Id.*

147 Johnson v. MBNA America Bank, NA, 357 F.3d 426, 430 (4th Cir. 2004); Alabran v. Capital One Bank, 2005 WL 3338663 (E.D. Va. Dec. 8, 2005).

§ 4.3.3.2 *Fair Credit Reporting*

Mixed or mismerged files occur when credit information relating to one consumer is placed in the file of another, thus creating a false description of both consumers' credit histories. The FCRA clearly specifies that accuracy concerns the individual about whom the report relates.[148] Mismerging occurs most often when two or more customers have similar names, Social Security numbers, or other identifiers (for example, when information relating to John J. Jones is put in John G. Jones' file), but they also occur between total strangers without similarities of names or numbers.

4.3.3.2 How Consumer Reporting Agencies "Build" Their Files

To understand how a mixed file can occur, it is necessary to discover and obtain the procedures for matching and combining data into files at each CRAs. This information is closely guarded by CRA litigants, but has been produced in a sufficient number of cases that pleas of irreparable injury upon further production will not likely be justified. The basic system for matching data is the same for each CRA. Credit information is reported from multiple sources—furnishers, vendors, subscriber inquiries, and even consumers. Each is considered in turn.

Creditors (also referred to as furnishers) report information on their credit and collection trades. This is done by downloading from the creditor's computer to the CRA's computer, on a monthly basis, a list of the creditor's various accounts. Each is organized in the Metro 2 (or Metro) code format. Each account record will include identifying information such as name, Social Security number, address, and birth date. The CRAs organize these records into "files," which refer to all credit accounts and other information that the CRA believes to belong to the same person. Ideally, a CRA would maintain exactly one file for every credit-using consumer. Upon receipt of each account tradeline, the CRA uses an automated matching system which has been preprogrammed with defined rules. The CRA computer attempts to find in its database the existing credit file that most closely matches the identifying information in the reported account. The CRA matching criteria will assign different weights to each identifying segment. The Social Security number will be scored as the most relevant variable. Address and name follow in importance. An account with the same full Social Security number, consumer name, and address as an existing file would constitute a perfect match.

If there is not an existing file with an exact match to the account data, the CRA process will allow data that constitutes a partial match to be reported to a file. There may only be a file that matches some of the account identification segments. These could include a partial matching name, for example Amy Smith and Amy Saunders, or Jeff Franks and John Franks. Or the file and the account may only partially match with respect to address, such as 1200 Main Street and 4516 S. Main Street. Typically, the closeness of the match between account data and an existing file is scored or scaled and then placed in the credit file with the closest match. The closer the match to a file, the higher the correlation score. The FTC refers to this process as "file building."[149]

Mismerged files occur largely because the CRAs' computers do not use sufficiently rigorous score or scale thresholds to match consumer data precisely, even when such unique identifiers as Social Security numbers are present. For example, practitioners report that one nationwide CRA relies on a match of only five of the nine digits in a Social Security number, contending that this was reasonable, even when mismerges have been known to occur.

While the CRAs' justification for their over-inclusive reporting has been a claimed interest in completeness, the better explanation is the CRAs' over-emphasis of derogatory information is at the insistence of their creditor customers. As the FTC has acknowledged:

> When Congress passed the FCRA, it was responding in part to consumer concerns that the CRAs overemphasize completeness at the expense of accuracy. Many of the CRAs' customers are lenders, whose main concern in consulting a consumer report is assessing the likelihood that a borrower will default. For many lenders, the loss incurred when a borrower defaults is much larger than the profit earned when a borrower repays a loan. Because of this, lenders may prefer to see all potentially derogatory information about a potential borrower, even if it cannot all be matched to the borrower with certainty. This preference could give the CRAs an incentive to design algorithms that are tolerant of mixed files, which could harm consumers to whom derogatory information is mistakenly assigned.[150]

4.3.3.3 Studies on Mixed Files

Mismerged files are a frequent problem. One study found that 44% of consumer reporting complaints to the FTC

---

148 15 U.S.C. § 1681e(b). *See* § 4.2.4, *supra*. *See also* Wilson v. Rental Research Serv., Inc., 165 F.3d 642 (8th Cir. 1999), *rehearing en banc without published opinion*, 206 F.3d 810 (8th Cir. 2000) (by vote of an equally divided court, the district court's order is affirmed) (concerning efficacy of disclaimers placed in consumer reports).

149 Federal Trade Commission, Report to Congress Under Sections 318 and 319 of the Fair and Accurate Credit Transactions Act of 2003, at 9 (Dec. 2004). At an earlier stage, the CRA system for file building was not applied until an actual report was requested. Only then did the CRA cull, sort and match the accounts in its database to generate a matched report. However, none of the "Big Three" nationwide CRAs use this process anymore.

150 Federal Trade Commission, Report to Congress Under Sections 318 and 319 of the Fair and Accurate Credit Transactions Act of 2003, at 47 (Dec. 2004).

involved mismerged files. Of these complaints, 64% involved a total stranger's files mixed in with the consumer's, while 36% involved information belonging to relatives or former spouses.[151]

In another study, the Consumer Federation of America (CFA) and the National Credit Reporting Association (NCRA) found that one in ten files (155 out of 1545) contained at least one, but as many as three, additional consumer reports. The study also found it was very common for the additional reports to contain a mixture of credit information, some of which belonged to the subject of the report requested and some which did not.[152] Common reasons for the additional reports include:

— Confusion between generations with the same name (Jr., Sr., II, III, etc.);
— Mixed files with similar names, but different Social Security numbers;
— Mixed files with matching Social Security numbers, but different names;
— Mixed files that listed accounts recorded under the applicant's name, but with the Social Security number of the co-applicant;
— Name variations that appeared to contain transposed first and middle names;
— Files that appeared to track credit under the applicant's nickname;
— Spelling errors in the name;
— Transposing digits on the Social Security number.[153]

According to the CRA/NCRA report, CRAs all have their own rules for determining whether identifying information is sufficient to link information to a single individual. In addition to mixed files, the CRA rules sometimes results in "fragmentary files" that are multiple and incomplete consumer reports for the same individual.[154] These fragmentary files are created when there is neither an exact match nor a match of sufficient closeness to exceed the matching score threshold. When this occurs, the CRA's computer will generate a new file that contains that unmatched account and other data. When subsequent creditor data is furnished, this new "orphan" file will be compared to the data for its own closeness.

In a report to Congress, the FTC documented the inherent problems associated with credit reporting databases and the matching process. First, furnishers have their own unique systems for collecting and maintaining consumer information. Furnisher files, including form, content, updates, and inquiries can be inconsistent.[155] Second, consumer Social Security numbers have served as the unique identification number that is linked to consumer accounts, but such numbers are often missing from consumer information and errors are common in recording Social Security numbers.

Despite acknowledging the problem of mixed files, the FTC recommended against stricter rules on matching identifying information. The FTC concluded that stricter rules would result in fewer mixed files, but also result in an increase in cases where no matches were found or "no-hits."[156] The FTC noted that some no-hits reflect cases where identity theft may be prevented, but remarkably concluded that in most cases a no-hit does not provide a benefit to consumers.[157]

4.3.3.4 Mixed Public Records Information

Another source of reported data that undergoes a matching process is the public record vendor. Each public record contains some identifying criteria such as name, address, and sometimes Social Security number. The CRA matching process is applied to these items in much the same way as for furnished credit accounts.[158] Recently, it was discovered by a practitioner that this matching process may even occur first at the public records vendor. Public record mixed file problems can be as difficult to correct as any other type of mixed file.[159]

4.3.3.5 Mixed Files Resulting from Subscriber Inquiries

A significant source used by the CRAs to build and match data is the subscriber's inquiry. When a subscriber inputs identifying information into its credit reporting terminal to request a report, this information is then used by the CRA to

---

151 U.S. Public Interest Research Group, Credit Bureaus: Public Enemy #1 at the FTC (Oct. 1993). In this sample, U.S. PIRG analyzed 140 complaints to the FTC. See § 4.1.3.1, *infra*. Note that some of these errors could have been caused by the furnisher rather than in the file building. See § 4.3.2, *infra*.
152 Consumer Federation of America and National Credit Reporting Association, Credit Score Accuracy and Implications for Consumers, at 21 (Dec. 17, 2002), *available at* www.consumerfed.org/121702CFA_NCRA_Credit_Score_Report_Final.pdf, *reprinted on the CD-Rom accompanying this manual*.
153 *Id.*
154 *Id.* at 301.
155 Federal Trade Commission, Report to Congress Under Sections 318 and 319 of the Fair and Accurate Credit Transactions Act of 2003, at 37 (Dec. 2004).
156 *Id.* at 51.
157 *Id.*
158 A tension has arisen between public concern for privacy and against identity theft versus the access to identifying and personal information available in court records. CRA access to the later helps determine more precisely to whom a judgment or other public record should be attributed. National Center for State Courts, Susan J. Larson, *Court Record Access Policies: Under Pressure from State Security Breach Laws?*, Future Trends in State Courts (2006), *available at* www.ncsconline.org/WC/Publications/Trends/2006/PriPubRecordAccessTrends2006.pdf.
159 *See, e.g., Apodaca v. Discover Fin. Servs.*, 417 F. Supp. 2d 1220 (D.N.M. 2006).

§ 4.3.3.6   *Fair Credit Reporting*

do two things. Applying the same matching process and criteria as used to assign accounts to particular files, the inputted inquiry criteria is used to determine if there is an existing file with a sufficiently close matching score to permit the CRA to furnish a report. In addition, the inquiry criteria are used to determine into which file the inquiry history will be placed.

In one illustrative case detailed by a practitioner, inaccurate inquiry search criteria submitted by a collector caused a consumer's file to be mixed. In discovery, it was learned that the mixed file process occurred as follows: A collection company attempted a "skip trace" to obtain additional information about a third party with the same first and last name, as well as the same city of residence as the victim consumer.[160] It requested a consumer report using the third party's name and other criteria. There was no match found. However, because there was no existing file matching the debtor's identifiers, the CRA then created a new credit file containing nothing other than the inquiry. The CRA used the identifying information provided in the search to populate a set of identifying fields—the name and address in the file. The Social Security number was unknown.

Subsequently, the collector sued and obtained a default judgment against the correct debtor with the same first and last name and city of residence as the victim consumer. The public record of the judgment had no Social Security number, and contained a different street, but contained the same first and last name and city of residence as the innocent consumer. The full address of the debtor listed in the public record was not the victim's.

When the CRA received the details of the judgment from its public records vendor, its computer could not find an existing file (the third party was young) and the judgment did not contain a Social Security number. However, the address in the judgment correctly matched the inquiry-only fragment file and was thus updated to it.[161] Later, the collector sought to determine if a newly discovered Social Security number, which actually belonged to the innocent consumer, matched the address for the real debtor. It sought this information by requesting a consumer report using inquiry search criteria which itself incorrectly matched the innocent consumer's Social Security number with the debtor's address information.

When the CRA received this new search, it accepted the incorrect input criteria as actual reported data. Its computer applied the debtor's address to the innocent consumer's credit file. When that new address was added, the CRA computer then matched the existing fragment file of the debtor, which did not contain a Social Security number, to the innocent consumer's file. The files were merged. The judgments and inquiries were then placed in the consumer's file.

4.3.3.6 Consumer Source of Information Used for Matching

A final source that may influence mixed files is the consumer herself. While the CRAs' response to disputes over tradelines is often less than satisfactory,[162] the CRAs are more flexible when a consumer disputes a current or previous address reported in the file. If a consumer asks a CRA to add or remove an address, it will often do so. But unlike some identifying information in a file, such as apartment number, employer or age, the current and previous addresses are critical matching criteria. If an address is either removed from or added to a file, the change will often influence whether a subsequent reported account is matched to that file.

4.3.3.7 Mixed Files and Identity Theft

The problems that lead to mismerged files aggravate the effects of identity theft.[163] Most identity theft problems are actually caused by the CRAs' loose matching procedures. In fact, identity theft is a misnomer. The criminal actually steals from the creditor using only a partial set of a consumer's identifiers. For example, if an impostor has only adopted the victim's first name and Social Security number but not his or her last name or address, the algorithm used by CRAs to "merge" information often will nonetheless incorporate the impostor's information into the victim's file at the time the CRA compiles the report. It would make little practical sense for the criminal to open an account in the consumer's full name and have the credit cards sent to the victim's own home. Once the fraudulent debt is reported, often after default and nonpayment, and especially when collectors begin attempting skip trace searches, the account ends up merged into the victim's file even though many of the identifiers do not match. Accordingly, the "identity theft" is really only an initial genesis of the problem. It is instead better characterized as a hybrid of a mixed file problem.

In this era of heightened media attention to the problem of identity theft, many consumers incorrectly presume that the appearance of an item that is not theirs is the product of criminal activity, fraud, or identity theft. This is very often not the case. Instead, the CRA may simply have mismatched the accounts of two otherwise innocent consumers.

4.3.3.8 Fixing a Mixed File

Consumers face significant proof issues when trying to prove that a file does not belong to them. Trying to prove a negative such as "this is not my account" is a common

---

160 Chris Daniels v. Equifax, L.L.C., Civ. No. 3:05cv570 (E.D. Va. 2005).
161 *See* § 4.3.3.3, *supra*.
162 *See* § 4.5, *infra*.
163 *See* § 4.3.3.3, *supra*.

problem when files are mixed or mismerged. Consumers may have to submit affidavits or provide documentation such as birth certificates or driver's license numbers in order to prove that an account does not belong to them. The downside of disclosing such information is the potential for identity theft or other misuse of the information. The minimum consumers should do is dispute the accuracy of the incorrect information and assess what additional steps, including litigation, are necessary to clean up their credit files. It is also critical that consumers have the CRA correct and delete all identifying information such as previous addresses that could remain as an underlying cause of the mis-matching.

4.3.4 Consumer Reporting Agency Errors in Retrieving Consumer Files

Inaccuracies in a consumer report may also be caused by file retrieval—that is, when the CRA retrieves and sends a consumer's file in the consumer report it issues in response to an inquiry. For example, the CRA might send a single file that pertains to the wrong person; it might send multiple files in one report, one or more of which pertains to the wrong person; or it might send no report when the consumer in fact has a file in the CRA's system.[164] These problems arise not from the internal inaccuracy of individual accounts or in the files themselves, but rather because the CRA may permit credit inquiries without sufficiently detailed search criteria or because the CRA is over-inclusive and produces not just files that are exactly responsive to an inquiry, but also those that are merely close.

When a consumer requests a copy of his or her own consumer report or initiates a dispute, the CRA will usually require the consumer to provide complete identifying information including the full Social Security number, full name, and current address.[165] In contrast, subscribers are not required by the CRAs to submit a Social Security number as part of an inquiry.[166] In fact, as many as 10% of all inquiries do not include a valid Social Security number.[167] This use of limited identifying information from subscribers contributes to the mismerging of files.[168] It also means that consumers receive only consumer reports that exactly match their identifiers, whereas users have access to greater amounts of information, including credit information on consumers with similar identifiers.

The most common problem with file retrieval remains Equifax's willingness to furnish "probability files," also referred to as "possibility files."[169] When a subscriber requests a consumer report from Equifax, that CRA will sometimes furnish in the same response not only the credit file that most closely matches the inquiry, but also other files that are less exact. When Equifax does so, there is a reasonable chance that one of the files pertains to the wrong consumer. If one credit file is wrong, and the report's user does not discover the error, the consumer's application for credit might be adversely affected.[170] The CRA relies entirely on the user to sort out which file is actually responsive to the inquiry.[171]

The problem with the use of probability files is that they are often not interpreted by a user as an unrelated file, but instead as a multi-part consumer report. Equifax divides the files into two sections when it delivers its own reports. But when the files are resold by a tri-merge company,[172] they are combined in nearly every regard, with only a notation on tradeline such as "EQX-1" and "EQX-2" to identify from which of the separate files the account data was reported.[173] Fiserv/Chase Credit Research, a reseller of consumer reports, provided data to the FTC that independently confirms that Equifax furnishes multiple files in about 4% of the reports it sells to mortgage lenders.[174]

Equifax's defense of such practice is that it should be the user's responsibility to determine the relevance of each of the multiple files. While the consumer will claim that the multiple files were a statement by Equifax that they were relevant to that consumer's creditworthiness, the CRA will deny any such intended message. Equifax has claimed that it was not intending any particular statement as to the relevance of the secondary files to the primary consumer. This position places the CRA in an indefensible position. If true, then Equifax will have furnished the credit file of an unrelated consumer without a permissible purpose to do so.[175]

State laws may address file retrieval issues. For example, California law requires that when a retailer requests a

---

164 Federal Trade Commission, Report to Congress Under Sections 318 and 319 of the Fair and Accurate Credit Transactions Act of 2003, at 14 (Dec. 2004).
165 See § 4.5.2.2, infra. See also § 3.7.2.2, supra.
166 Federal Trade Commission, Report to Congress Under Sections 318 and 319 of the Fair and Accurate Credit Transactions Act of 2003, at 38 (Dec. 2004).
167 Id.
168 See § 4.3.3.3, supra.

169 Until recently, TransUnion also followed such procedures. As of December 2004, the FTC has reported that this is no longer so. Federal Trade Commission, Report to Congress Under Sections 318 and 319 of the Fair and Accurate Credit Transactions Act of 2003, at 16 (Dec. 2004). See also Rothery v. Trans Union, L.L.C., 2006 WL 1720498 (D. Or. Apr. 6, 2006).
170 Federal Trade Commission, Report to Congress Under Sections 318 and 319 of the Fair and Accurate Credit Transactions Act of 2003, at 16 (Dec. 2004).
171 Crabill v. Trans Union Corp., 259 F.3d 662 (7th Cir. 2000).
172 A tri-merge company is a type of "reseller" under the FCRA. See § 2.6.3, infra.
173 Rothery v. Trans Union, L.L.C., 2006 WL 1720498 (D. Or. Apr. 6, 2006).
174 Federal Trade Commission, Report to Congress Under Sections 318 and 319 of the Fair and Accurate Credit Transactions Act of 2003, at 16 n.50 (Dec. 2004).
175 15 U.S.C. § 1681b. See § 7.5, infra.

consumer report for a California applicant, the CRA may provide the consumer report only if the application matches the credit file on at least three points of identifying information.[176] An approach specifying a minimum number of matching elements is also analogous to one taken in the FTC's consent agreement with Equifax.[177]

The second most common "file retrieval" inaccuracy occurs when a CRA furnishes only a "short" or fragmentary, or "frag," file. These occur when the CRA business rules cannot match data to an existing file, and is the opposite problem of the mixed file.[178] The CRA may have created more than one file for the same individual. It then furnishes only one in response to an inquiry. While it might appear at first blush that the CRAs' attempts to prevent such fragmentary file reports could explain their use of multiple file reports, the better explanation is the failure of the CRA matching process to recognize and accept changes made to such files. Practitioners suggest that most frag file problems occur after a CRA has manually manipulated a credit file, such as in response to a consumer's dispute.

4.3.5 Identity Theft

Identity theft poses a unique combination of inaccuracy problems. It is caused by multiple failures of the credit industry to protect the privacy and accuracy of a consumer's credit file. The 2003 FACTA amendments to the FCRA added a number of protections intended to address identity theft, which are discussed in Chapter 9, *infra*.

Identity theft is a regular and predictable occurrence in the consumer reporting system. It occurs when an imposter uses information about a consumer to obtain credit in the consumer's name.[179] The thief may obtain and use the consumer's Social Security number, checking account number, credit card number, PIN, and other personal information, by a variety of means, and run up a string of debts before a consumer can react.

One contributing cause of identity theft is the willingness of CRAs to issue consumer reports, and of subscribers to readily extend credit, by automated means. As addressed in § 4.3.3.7, *supra*, however, most fraudulent credit applications are not submitted using all of the identifiers of the victim. Typically, an identity thief will use a variation of the consumer's name, changing the first or last name. Often this is done to make the listed account holder's name appear closer to the thief's. In addition, the identity thief will almost always use a different address, either in the original application or by requesting a change of address.[180]

When the identity thief's credit application is then processed and a credit inquiry is made using the hybrid identity—some segments of information from the fraudster and some from the victim—the CRA may then match the inquiry to the consumer's own credit file. When it does so, the CRA will add the thief's stated address and name variation to the victim's file, the latter as an "AKA." Thereafter, every time one of these incorrectly attributed identifiers is contained in a credit or public record item of data, that item will be matched to the victim's file. This is how the repercussions of a simple credit card theft can snowball and become so difficult for a consumer to resolve.

Thus, identity theft is actually a malevolent variation of a mixed or mismerged file inaccuracy. It is also, however, often the result of creditor error. Later after the debt is defaulted, the creditor may assign the debt to a collector. One of the first steps a debt collector will take is to obtain a current consumer report for the debtor listed in the account. When the CRA responds with a report containing the victim's actual address, the collector can "update" its internal account records and change the fraud account address to match the victim's real address. Thereafter, the account is reported to the CRA with the consumer's address, which would circumvent any intervening corrections or disputes by which the fraud address was deleted. An initial identity theft will therefore often cause inaccuracies at several levels of a consumer's credit profile.

4.3.6 Consumer Reporting Agency's Refusal to Provide Reports on Targeted Consumers

Incomplete or misleading reports are also furnished when a CRA responds to a prospective creditor's inquiry with the statement "FILE UNAVAILABLE ONLINE," "CONTACT BUREAU" or "FILE UNDER REVIEW."[181] Use of these terms leaves the creditor or user with questions about the creditworthiness of the consumer. CRAs should include available positive information, as well as other information that is in the consumer's credit file.

When a consumer applies for credit and the prospective creditor requests a consumer report from the CRA, if the CRA responds with any of the above responses, the statement that a credit file on the consumer cannot be located is often interpreted in the credit industry to mean that the credit file does not exist. This response is inaccurate and incom-

---

176 *See* Cal. Civ. Code § 1785.14(a)(1). The points of identifying information include, but are not limited to, name, address, Social Security number, and birth date.

177 *See* Equifax Credit Info. Servs., Inc, 120 F.T.C. 577 (1995).

178 *See* Robert B. Avery, Paul S. Calem, and Glenn B. Canner, *Credit Report Accuracy and Access to Credit*, Federal Reserve Bulletin, at 301 (Summer 2004), *available at* www.federalreserve.gov/pubs/bulletin/2004/summer04_credit.pdf. *See also* § 4.3.3.3, *supra*.

179 *See* § 9.2, *infra*, for a discussion of the FCRA's definition of identity theft.

180 The 2003 FACTA amendments to the FCRA imposed requirements of CRAs when faced with address discrepancies. *See* § 9.2.5.2, *infra*.

181 Thompson v. Equifax, 2001 U.S. Dist. LEXIS 22640 (M.D. Ala. Dec. 14, 2001).

plete and can likely give rise to a claim that the CRA has failed to "follow reasonable procedures to assure the maximum possible accuracy" of the information.[182]

Practitioners have reported that nationwide CRAs, particularly Equifax, block access to consumer credit reports when the consumer files suit against the CRA. This appears to be a growing practice by CRAs and may be a violation of the CRA's obligation to disclose all information in the consumer's file, upon request by the consumer.[183] If access is also blocked to subscribers or creditors seeking consumer reports, this practice violates the CRA's obligation to report accurately on the data in its possession.[184]

4.4 CRA Liability for Reporting Inaccurate Information

4.4.1 Introduction

The FCRA provides consumers with two primary inaccuracy claims against consumer reporting agencies (CRAs), one governing predispute accuracy and the other governing the dispute and reinvestigation process.[185] The first of these, 15 U.S.C. § 1681e(b), is the subject of this section and provides:

> (b) *Accuracy of report.* Whenever a consumer reporting agency prepares a consumer report it shall follow reasonable procedures to assure maximum possible accuracy of the information concerning the individual about whom the report relates.

A claim under section 1681e(b) will allege that the CRA published a consumer report to a third party without A reasonable procedures to assure maximum possible accuracy.

This requirement is independent of a consumer's right to dispute and obtain correction of inaccurate information. The right to dispute and correct inaccuracies is merely an alternative to a lawsuit over CRA procedures.[186] It is not a prerequisite to filing a lawsuit challenging CRA procedures.[187]

However, proof and prosecution of a "reasonable procedures" claim is difficult and should only be considered either in circumstances where the targeted inaccuracy would have been known and self-evident to the CRA or in conjunction with a reinvestigation claim.[188]

A CRA is not liable under the FCRA merely for reporting inaccurate information.[189] It is liable, whenever it prepares a consumer report, for failing to follow reasonable procedures to ensure maximum possible accuracy of the information about the consumer.[190] That is, the FCRA provides a cause of action for a CRA failing to enact and follow reasonable procedures, not for furnishing one particular inaccurate report.

The reasonable procedures must ensure "maximum possible accuracy."[191] The statute thus establishes a high standard for CRAs.[192] They must adopt procedures not just to catch many of the errors, but to ensure "maximum" possible accuracy. If the CRA's review of its procedures reveals, or the CRA should reasonably be aware of, steps it can take to improve the accuracy of its reports at a reasonable cost, it must take such steps.[193] In short, CRAs should be doing everything possible, within the limits of economic reality,[194] to ensure maximum accuracy.

Although much of the FCRA's legislative history is preoccupied with concerns for accurate reporting, the requirement for reasonable procedures to ensure maximum possible accuracy appeared first in the Conference Committee Report prepared just days before final enactment. The provision was agreed to by the Conference Committee upon the request of House members.[195]

---

182 15 U.S.C. § 1681e(b).
183 15 U.S.C. § 1681g; Spector v. Equifax Info. Servs., 338 F. Supp. 2d 378 (D. Conn. 2004). See § 3.4.5, *supra*.
184 15 U.S.C. § 1681b(e).
185 The second, 15 U.S.C. § 1681i is addressed at § 4.5, *infra*.
186 *See* the following FTC Informal Staff Opinion Letters [all found on the CD-Rom accompanying this manual], dealing with specific instances of disputed information: Grimes, FTC Informal Staff Opinion Letter (July 31, 1986), and Brinckerhoff, FTC Informal Staff Opinion Letter (Aug. 4, 1987) (both dealing with disclosures requested by "credit repair agencies"); Grimes, FTC Informal Staff Opinion Letter (July 23, 1986) and (Apr. 16, 1987); Brinckerhoff, FTC Informal Staff Opinion Letter (July 24, 1986) and (Jan. 29, 1987).
187 Thompson v. San Antonio Retail Merchants Ass'n, 682 F.2d 509 (5th Cir. 1982).
188 *Cf.* Spence v. TRW, Inc., 92 F.3d 380 (6th Cir. 1996) (since TRW was not aware of the inaccuracy, consumer's failure to use dispute procedure was fatal to consumer's "obsolete information" claim).
189 Guimond v. Trans Union Credit Info. Co., 45 F.3d 1329 (9th Cir. 1995); Bryant v. TRW, Inc., 689 F.2d 72 (6th Cir. 1982); Ladner v. Equifax Credit Info. Servs., Inc., 828 F. Supp. 427 (S.D. Miss. 1993); Jones v. Credit Bureau of Garden City, 703 F. Supp. 897 (D. Kan. 1988).
190 15 U.S.C. § 1681e(b).
191 15 U.S.C. § 1681e(b).
192 Andrews v. TRW, Inc., 225 F.3d 1063 (9th Cir. 2000) ("very high standard set by statute"), *rev'd on other grounds*, 534 U.S. 19 (2001).
193 FTC Official Staff Commentary § 607 item 3B, *reprinted at* Appx. D, *infra*.
194 *See* Henson v. CSC Credit Servs., 29 F.3d 280 (7th Cir. 1994).
195 "The House offered an amendment, which was agreed to by the conferees, to add the requirement that consumer reporting agencies must follow reasonable procedures to assure maximum possible accuracy of the information on an individual in all consumer credit reports." Conf. Rep. No. 1587, 91st Cong., 2d Sess. (1970) *reprinted in* 1970 U.S.C.C.A.N. 4394, 4411, 4415.

4.4.2 The Consumer Report Must Be Inaccurate

To challenge a CRA's procedures to ensure maximum possible accuracy, the procedures must not only be inadequate, but the report information must also be inaccurate.[196] In other words, if inadequate procedures produce a report on a consumer that is completely accurate, that consumer cannot bring a section 1681e(b) action.

The content of the report should be measured against the standard of "maximum possible accuracy."[197] The standard and requirements for proof of inaccuracy are discussed in § 4.2, *supra*. If the item is inaccurate, then the court can go on to determining if the CRA's procedures in preparing the report were reasonable.

4.4.3 The CRA Must Furnish a Consumer Report

Unlike an FCRA reinvestigation claim, which regulates the content of a consumer's "file,"[198] the accuracy requirements of section 1681e(b) govern the content of a "consumer report." As considered elsewhere in this manual, there is an important distinction between a "consumer report" and a consumer disclosure.[199] The latter is provided directly to the consumer by the CRA as a copy of the consumer's credit file pursuant to several notice provisions of the FCRA.[200] On the other hand, a consumer report is a report that is communicated to a third party, such as a prospective creditor or employer.[201] A consumer must do more than establish that there was an inaccuracy in her file, but also must establish that the inaccurate information was included in a consumer report.[202]

This is sometimes a challenge in litigation as the CRAs claim not to retain the reports they provide to users and may refuse to stipulate that the inaccurate information was within the consumer report furnished to a user as evidenced by an inquiry notation in the file. In litigation, the consumer should attempt to discover the copy of the inaccurate report from the third party user who received it.[203]

The FCRA requires that "whenever" a CRA "prepares a consumer report" it shall follow reasonable procedures.[204] Preparation of a report may be viewed as a continuing process of updating and maintaining files, and reasonable care is due at each step.[205]

Liability arises under section 1681e(b) when the CRA issues the inaccurate consumer report.[206] Each transmission of the same consumer report is a separate and distinct violation.[207]

4.4.4 Resellers Must Follow Reasonable Procedures

A reseller is a CRA that purchases a credit file or report from another CRA and then resells it to the end-user.[208] While a reseller has a different set of duties with respect to reinvestigations and other FCRA requirements, it is still subject to the FCRA's requirement that it use reasonable procedures to ensure maximum possible accuracy in its preparation of a report.[209] No FCRA provision contains any language that explicitly exempts a reseller from the obligation to ensure the accuracy of the information it resells.

While section 1681e contains a provision explicitly addressing a reseller's obligation to establish reasonable procedures to ensure that its report is sold for proper purposes, this provision does not state that these are the only obligations of a reseller under that section.[210] The FTC has explained that "[p]ersons who purchase consumer reports for resale (also known as 'resellers') are covered by the FCRA as consumer reporting agencies and have all the obligations of other CRAs, including the duty to reinvestigate information disputed by consumers."[211]

---

196 Spence v. TRW, Inc., 92 F.3d 380 (6th Cir. 1996). See § 4.3, *supra*, for a discussion of types of inaccuracy.
197 15 U.S.C. § 1681e(b). See §§ 4.2, 4.4.1, *supra*.
198 15 U.S.C. § 1681i. *But see* Casella v. Equifax Credit Info. Servs., 56 F.3d 469, 474 (2d Cir. 1995).
199 See § 2.3, *supra*.
200 See, e.g., 15 U.S.C. § 1681g; 1681i(a)(6). *See also* § 3.3, *supra*.
201 15 U.S.C. § 1681a(d).
202 The Ninth Circuit has ruled that damages must arise from the failure to follow reasonable procedures, but it is unnecessary for liability to flow from the transmission of the report to a third party. Guimond v. Trans Union Credit Info. Co., 45 F.3d 1329 (9th Cir. 1995). *But see* Casella v. Equifax Credit Info. Servs., 56 F.3d 469 (2d Cir. 1995).
203 See § 11.6.3, *infra*.
204 15 U.S.C. § 1681e(b).
205 Frost v. Experian, 1999 U.S. Dist. LEXIS 6783 (S.D.N.Y. May 6, 1999) (failure to update adverse item over 6 months old could lead to liability, even absent prior notice from the consumer that item was incorrect); Pinner v. Schmidt, 617 F. Supp. 342 (E.D. La. 1985), *rev'd on other grounds*, 805 F.2d 1258 (5th Cir. 1986); Lowry v. Credit Bureau of Georgia, 444 F. Supp. 541 (N.D. Ga. 1978).
206 Acton v. Bank One Corp., 293 F. Supp. 2d 1092, 1097 (D. Ariz. 2003); Lawrence v. Trans Union L.L.C., 296 F. Supp. 2d 582 (E.D. Pa. 2003).
207 *Id.*; Jaramillo v. Experian Info. Solutions. Inc., 155 F. Supp. 2d 356, 359–360 (E.D. Pa. 2001).
208 See § 2.6.3, *supra* and § 4.5.2.3, *infra*.
209 Poore v. Sterling Testing Sys., Inc, 410 F. Supp. 2d 557 (E.D. Ky. 2006).
210 Weidman v. Federal Home Loan Mortgage Corp., 338 F. Supp. 2d 571 (E.D. Pa. 2004).
211 *Prepared Statement of Federal Trade Commission on the Fair Credit Reporting Act Before the Senate Committee on Banking, Housing and Urban Affairs*, 2003 FTC LEXIS 101, 14–15 (July 10, 2003).

4.4.5 The Consumer Reporting Agency Must Follow Reasonable Procedures

4.4.5.1 Determining Reasonableness

4.4.5.1.1 No strict liability

The FCRA does not require error free reports. Liability does not flow automatically from the mere fact that the CRA reports inaccurate information but, instead, it must flow from its failure to follow reasonable procedures.[212] The statute does not impose strict liability for inaccurate entries in consumer reports.[213] A CRA will not be liable if it reported inaccurate information on an individual's consumer report provided it followed reasonable procedures to ensure maximum possible accuracy.[214]

4.4.5.1.2 Standard of reasonableness and the balancing test

Courts sometimes apply a "reasonable person" test in a section 1681e(b) case, although this test may vary greatly in application.[215] Using this standard of conduct, a trier of fact must judge the adequacy of a CRA's procedures by what a reasonably prudent person would do under the circumstances.[216] Thus, the CRA is held only to a standard of reasonable care.[217] As one court noted: "The standard of conduct by which the agency's action is to be judged is deeply rooted in the law of negligence: what a reasonably prudent person would do under the circumstances."[218]

Judging the reasonableness of a CRA's procedures involves weighing the potential harm from inaccuracy against the burden of safeguarding against such inaccuracy.[219] The most cited formulation of the reasonable procedures standard is a balancing test which weighs "the potential that the information will create a misleading impression against the availability of more accurate [or complete] information and the burden of providing such information."[220] This balancing test places the seriousness of the derogatory inaccuracy on a scale and compares it to a contrasting scale of the cost or burden of greater care. If the inaccuracy would cause significant harm to the consumer and could be prevented at little expense to the CRA, it would be unreasonable to fail to use such greater care. This is a variation of the *Henson* balancing test for reinvestigations discussed in § 4.5.3.2, *infra*.

This standard, now applied by most circuits, was first articulated in *Alexander v. Moore & Associates, Inc.*,[221] in which the court explained:

> Under this approach, the court, in determining whether a violation of § 1681e(b) has occurred, would weigh the potential that the information will create a misleading impression against the availability of more accurate information and the burden of providing such information. Clearly, the more misleading the information, and the more easily available the clarifying information, the greater is the burden upon the consumer reporting agency to provide this clarification. Conversely, if the misleading information is of relatively insignificant value, a consumer reporting agency should not be required to take on a burdensome task in order to discover or provide additional or clarifying data, and it should not be penalized under this section if the procedures used are otherwise reasonable.[222]

4.4.5.1.3 Establishing the availability and minimal burden of corrective measures

Although a plaintiff is not required to identify specific deficiencies in a CRA's practices or procedures,[223] she will be in a stronger position if she can articulate specific and

---

212 Bryant v. TRW, Inc., 689 F.2d 72 (6th Cir. 1982).
213 Spence v. TRW, Inc., 92 F.3d 380 (6th Cir. 1996); Enwonwu v. Trans Union, L.L.C., 364 F. Supp. 2d 1361 (N.D. Ga. 2005), *aff'd* 164 Fed. Appx. 914, 2006 WL 227585 (11th Cir. Jan. 31, 2006), *rehearing and rehearing en banc denied* 179 Fed. Appx. 686, 2006 WL 1173159 (11th Cir. Apr. 18, 2006) (table); Anderson v. Trans Union, L.L.C., 345 F. Supp. 2d 963 (W.D. Wis. 2004).
214 *Id.*; Jordan v. Equifax Info. Servs., L.L.C., 410 F. Supp. 2d 1349 (N.D. Ga. 2006).
215 Philbin v. Trans Union Corp., 101 F.3d 957, 963 (3d Cir. 1996); Pinner v. Schmidt, 805 F.2d 1258 (5th Cir. 1986); Bryant v. TRW, Inc., 689 F.2d 72 (6th Cir. 1982); Thompson v. San Antonio Retail Merchants Ass'n, 682 F.2d 509 (5th Cir. 1982); O'Brien v. Equifax Info. Servs., L.L.C., 382 F. Supp. 2d 733 (E.D. Pa. 2005); Houston v. TRW Info. Serv., 707 F. Supp. 689 (S.D.N.Y. 1989); Jones v. Credit Bureau of Garden City, 703 F. Supp. 897 (D. Kan. 1988).
216 Cousin v. Trans Union Corp., 246 F.3d 359 (5th Cir. 2001); Bryant v. TRW, Inc., 689 F.2d 72 (6th Cir. 1982); Thompson v. San Antonio Retail Merchants Ass'n, 682 F.2d 509 (5th Cir. 1982); Jordan v. Trans Union, L.L.C., 2006 WL 1663324 (N.D. Ga. June 12, 2006).
217 Spence v. TRW, Inc., 92 F.3d 380 (6th Cir. 1996).
218 Poore v. Sterling Testing Sys., Inc., 410 F. Supp. 2d 557 (E.D. Ky. 2006), *citing* Bryant v. TRW, Inc., 487 F. Supp. 1234, 1242 (E.D. Mich. 1980), *aff'd*, 689 F.2d 72 (6th Cir. 1982).
219 Philbin v. Trans Union Corp., 101 F.3d 957 (3d Cir. 1996); Stewart v. Credit Bureau, Inc., 734 F.2d 47 (D.C. Cir. 1984); Alexander v. Moore & Associates, Inc., 553 F. Supp. 948, 952 (D. Haw. 1982).
220 Wilson v. Rental Research Serv., Inc., 165 F.3d 642 (8th Cir. 1999), *rehearing en banc without published opinion*, 206 F.3d 810 (8th Cir. 2000) (by vote of an equally divided court, the district court's order is affirmed); Koropoulous v. Credit Bureau, Inc., 734 F.2d 37, 42 (7th Cir. 1984).
221 553 F. Supp. 948, 952 (D. Haw. 1982).
222 *Id.*
223 Nelski v. Trans Union, L.L.C., 86 Fed. Appx. 840, 2004 WL 78052 (6th Cir. Jan. 15, 2004); Morris v. Credit Bureau of Cincinnati, Inc., 563 F. Supp. 962 (D.C. Ohio 1983).

available procedures that the CRA has not followed. The objective should be to develop evidence that such procedures, implemented across the board at the CRA, would cost little or impose only a minimal additional burden. Simultaneously, practitioners will want to explain and develop the significance of and harm caused by the inaccuracy.

Two cases brought under section 1681e(b) provide a sharp contrast as to how the balancing test for reasonableness can be met. Both cases dealt with the same inaccuracy—the CRA had inaccurately reported that the consumer had an account that was included in bankruptcy. In both cases, the consumer argued that the CRA should have discovered contradictory information in the consumer report, the anomalous single bankruptcy account. In *Sarver v. Experian Information Solutions*,[224] the plaintiff went no further. As a result, the court was left with only Experian's claim that a cost effective automated procedure was unavailable.[225] In contrast, the plaintiff in *O'Brien v. Equifax Information Services, L.L.C.*[226] presented evidence of ways the CRA could address the inaccuracy:

> The O'Briens present evidence of an automated procedure that cross-references reports that a consumer has an account that is included in bankruptcy with the public records section of the consumer's credit file. (Hudziak Dep. at 21–23.) In generating a consumer credit report under this automated procedure, if the consumer supposedly has an account that is included in bankruptcy but there is no public record of the consumer ever filing bankruptcy, then the consumer's credit report would not indicate that the account was included in bankruptcy.[227]

The court in *O'Brien* thus held, "A trier of fact could also find that the potential harm from an inaccurate report that an account is included in bankruptcy outweighs the burden of automatically cross-referencing such reports with the public records section of a consumer's credit file."[228] The court also noted that the reasonableness of procedures and the burden of safeguards can change given newly available practices and procedures in the industry.[229]

Another means to establish the existence of reasonable alternative procedures to more accurately report is to compare the procedures at competing CRAs.[230]

Practitioners have cautioned that the "Big Three" nationwide CRAs regularly proffer declarations in litigation exaggerating the difficulties and expenses of more consumer-friendly procedures. For example, TransUnion successfully claimed that a system to reconcile an anomalous account indicating the consumer was deceased would have to be implemented manually at considerable expense.[231] Similarly, the Seventh Circuit held that despite evidence that a consumer's file contained facially inconsistent information concerning an account in bankruptcy, Experian's procedures for ensuring maximum possible accuracy were reasonable as a matter of law. The court relied upon Experian's expert to conclude that it would be unduly burdensome and unreasonable to require Experian to evaluate each computer record for anomalous information given the enormous volume of information processed.[232]

Unless practitioners have sought discovery of and challenged these positions in the litigation, they will be unprepared to refute the CRA's own application of the reasonableness balancing test. This is especially true in the Seventh Circuit and the Northern District of Illinois where courts have appeared to be uniquely tolerant of the CRAs' automation even as it leads to confirmed systematic errors.[233] In effect, these decisions have held that CRAs are not on notice of facially inconsistent information in their own files. Thus, it becomes even more important for practitioners to prove the CRAs' notice of defects in their procedures or of inaccurate information, through depositions or other appropriate evidence. Arguing that the CRAs knew or should have known of the inaccuracy based on the facially inaccurate information may not be enough, at least not in the Seventh Circuit.

4.4.5.1.4 Factors bearing on reasonableness

In addition to cost and the size of the CRA,[234] the reasonableness of procedures will depend upon the particular circumstances of the case. The FTC has construed the Act to require a CRA to do whatever is reasonable under the circumstances "to minimize the chances that consumers will be harmed by inaccurate reporting."[235]

When a CRA learns or should reasonably be aware of errors in its reports that may indicate systematic problems,

---

224 390 F.3d 969 (7th Cir. 2004).
225 390 F.3d at 972 ("In the absence of notice of prevalent unreliable information from a reporting lender, which would put Experian on notice that problems exist, we cannot find that such a requirement to investigate would be reasonable given the enormous volume of information Experian processes daily.").
226 382 F. Supp. 2d 733 (E.D. Pa. 2005).
227 *Id.*
228 *Id.*
229 *Id.*
230 Nelski v. Trans Union, L.L.C., 86 Fed. Appx. 840, 2004 WL 78052 (6th Cir. Jan. 15, 2004); Cousin v. Trans Union Corp.,

246 F.3d 359, 368 (5th Cir. 2001).
231 Anderson v. Trans Union, L.L.C., 345 F. Supp. 2d 963 (W.D. Wis. 2004).
232 Sarver v. Experian Info. Solutions, Inc., 390 F.3d 969 (7th Cir. 2004).
233 In addition to Sarver v. Experian Info. Solutions, 390 F.3d 969 (7th Cir. 2004).
234 FTC, Compliance with the Fair Credit Reporting Act, at 26 (1977).
235 *In re* Equifax, Inc., 96 F.T.C. 1045 (1980), *rev'd in part*, 678 F.2d 1047 (11th Cir. 1982).

it must review its procedures for ensuring accuracy.[236] This is the case whether the CRA discovers the problem from consumers, users, or its own internal reviews.[237] A consumer could establish the unreasonableness of CRA procedures through proof of prior notice of their defect, such as evidence that a CRA has been sued or notified of systemic problems on numerous occasions. Or the consumer could prove that the CRA procedures failed so often as to be unreasonable.[238]

Even when only one error is brought to its attention, the CRA should correct that consumer's file even if it does not warrant a change in overall procedures. That is, even if a CRA's procedures are otherwise generally reasonable, it must also have procedures to quickly and reliably correct unique errors that are brought to its attention. The CRA should correct any inaccuracies that come to its attention.[239] This latter point is important because many consumers find that multiple complaints to CRAs do not result in corrected files, and, even when a file is corrected, the same error crops up again shortly thereafter.

However, when a creditor reports one account under two or more different account numbers, it is not unreasonable for the CRA to report the multiple accounts absent notice of the inaccuracy.[240] "It would be unreasonable to hold that a credit reporting agency must anticipate every possible erroneous data entry that one of its customers might make."[241] A CRA is not held responsible for failing to foresee a complex programming error by the creditor.[242]

A consumer can meet her burden of showing unreasonable procedures by demonstrating that a CRA has no procedures in place to ensure that employees or vendors understand or cannot comprehend the status of a particular public record or account.[243] It may also be unreasonable to fail to use procedures sufficiently effective to prevent the reappearance of inaccurate information previously removed or suppressed.[244] This is in addition to any claim available after a CRA's reinvestigation.[245] In *Cousin v. Trans Union Corp.*,[246] the court found that it was incumbent on the CRA to permanently delete and cloak erroneous information it discovered. Cloaking of information for only twelve months, and allowing the erroneous information to return after the twelve months, was held to be unreasonable as a matter of law under the FCRA. As the Fifth Circuit explained in an earlier case, "[a]llowing inaccurate information back onto a credit report after deleting it because it is inaccurate is negligent."[247]

4.4.5.1.5 Consumer reporting agency must actually follow procedures that it establishes

Practitioners should consider not only whether the CRAs procedures are reasonably designed to prevent inaccuracies, but also "whether the agency actually followed its own procedures."[248] It is not enough that a CRA have procedures in place. The employees must follow those procedures in each and every report they prepare.[249] The CRA must not just have reasonable rules, but the employees must strictly follow those internal CRA rules.[250] The FTC staff indicates that "[o]ne of the most significant compliance procedures to assure accuracy will be the training of new personnel and the retraining of current employees from time to time. Even isolated instances of error should be followed up and procedures adjusted in order to correct the cause of the error."[251]

---

236 FTC Official Staff Commentary § 607 item 3B, *reprinted at* Appx. D, *infra*; Sheffer v. Experian Info. Solutions, Inc., 2003 WL 21710573 (E.D. Pa. July 24, 2003).
237 *Id.*
238 White v. Trans Union, L.L.C. (C.D. Cal. Oct. 13, 2006), *available at* www.consumerlaw.org/unreported (in 64% of surveyed reports an inaccuracy was discovered. "This allegation by itself is capable of demonstrating the type of repetitive and systematic errors in TransUnion's procedures that could render those procedures unreasonable.").
239 Cassara v. DAC Servs., Inc., 276 F.3d 1210, 1217 (10th Cir. 2002).
240 Nelski v. Trans Union, L.L.C., 86 Fed. Appx. 840, 2004 WL 78052 (6th Cir. Jan. 15, 2004); Jordan v. Equifax Info. Servs., L.L.C., 410 F. Supp. 2d 1349 (N.D. Ga. 2006); Jordan v. Trans Union, L.L.C., 2006 WL 1663324 (N.D. Ga. June 12, 2006).
241 Anderson v. Trans Union, L.L.C., 345 F. Supp. 2d 963 (W.D. Wis. 2004).
242 Schmitt v. Chase Manhattan Bank, N.A., 2005 WL 2030483 (D. Minn. Aug. 23, 2005).
243 Dalton v. Capital Associated Industries, Inc., 257 F.3d 409 (4th Cir. 2001). *See* § 4.3.2.5, *supra*.

244 Boris v. ChoicePoint Servs., Inc., 249 F. Supp. 2d 851 (W.D. Ky. 2003), *amended* 2003 WL 23009851 (W.D. Ky. Aug. 21, 2003).
245 15 U.S.C. § 1681i(a)(5)(C) ("A consumer reporting agency shall maintain reasonable procedures designed to prevent the reappearance in a consumer's file, and in consumer reports on the consumer, of information that is deleted pursuant to this paragraph (other than information that is reinserted in accordance with subparagraph (B)(i)).").
246 246 F.3d 359 (5th Cir. 2001).
247 Stevenson v. TRW, Inc., 987 F.2d 288, 296 (5th Cir. 1993). *See also* Morris v. Credit Bureau of Cincinnati, Inc., 563 F. Supp. 962, 967 (S.D. Ohio 1983).
248 Rothery v. Trans Union, L.L.C., 2006 WL 1720498 (D. Or. Apr. 6, 2006).
249 *See, e.g.*, Carroll v. Exxon Co., 434 F. Supp. 557 (E.D. La. 1977). *But see* Brinckerhoff and Grimes, FTC Informal Staff Opinion Letter (Mar. 8, 1988), *reprinted on the CD-Rom accompanying this manual* (a single typo does not violate the reasonable procedures standard; consideration of isolated incidence only without mention of standard procedures).
250 Carroll v. Exxon Co., 434 F. Supp. 557 (E.D. La. 1977).
251 FTC, Compliance with the Fair Credit Reporting Act, at 26 (1977). *See also In re* Equifax, Inc., 96 F.T.C. 1045 (1980), *rev'd in part*, 678 F.2d 1047 (11th Cir. 1982).

§ 4.4.5.2 Fair Credit Reporting

4.4.5.2 Proof Issues

4.4.5.2.1 Burden of proof

In the "overwhelming" majority[252] of cases, the reasonableness of the procedures will be a question for the jury.[253]

A plaintiff has the burden of proving that reasonable procedures were not followed in ensuring the maximum possible accuracy of the report.[254] The evidence that the consumer must show before shifting the burden of proof to the defendant has been described as "some evidence" from which it can be inferred that reasonable procedures were not utilized in the initial preparation of the report.[255]

There appears to be a variance amongst the circuits on the order and thresholds of proof for a claim under section 1681e(b) for failing to follow reasonable procedures. In *Cahlin v. General Motors Acceptance Corp.*, the Eleventh Circuit explained that a consumer satisfies her initial burden by presenting evidence tending to show that the CRA published a consumer report containing inaccurate data. Once this burden has been met, the CRA "can escape liability if it establishes that an inaccurate report was generated by following reasonable procedures, which will be a jury question in the overwhelming majority of cases."[256]

The Ninth Circuit expresses a similar opinion in *Guimond v. Trans Union Credit Information Co.*[257] The court held that "[i]n order to make out a prima facie violation under § 1681e(b), a consumer must present evidence tending to show that a credit reporting agency prepared a report con-

---

252 Guimond v. Trans Union Credit Info. Co., 45 F.3d 1329 (9th Cir. 1995) ("The issue of whether the agency failed to follow "reasonable procedures" will be a "jury question[] in the overwhelming majority of cases."); Dalton v. Capital Associated Indus., Inc., 257 F.3d 409, 416 (4th Cir. 2001).

253 Crabill v. Trans Union, 259 F.3d 662 (7th Cir. 2001) (determination of the "reasonableness" of the defendant's procedures is an application of a legal standard to given facts; must be treated as a factual question even when the underlying facts are undisputed and cannot be resolved on summary judgment unless reasonableness or unreasonableness of procedures is beyond question); Philbin v. Trans Union Corp., 101 F.3d 957 (3d Cir. 1996) (CRA can escape liability if it establishes that an inaccurate report was generated by following reasonable procedures, which will be a jury question in the overwhelming majority of cases); Bryant v. TRW, Inc., 487 F. Supp. 1234, 1242 (E.D. Mich. 1980), *aff'd*, 689 F.2d 72 (6th Cir. 1982) (if consumer report is determined to be inaccurate, "Congress has committed to a jury determination the question of whether the consumer reporting agency compiling the report followed reasonable procedures to assure maximum possible accuracy of the information contained in the report."). *See also* Cousin v. Trans Union Corp., 246 F.3d 359, 368–369 (5th Cir. 2001) (reasonableness of procedures was properly before jury where procedures are not justified by defendant); Dalton v. Capital Associated Indus., Inc., 257 F.3d 409, 418 (4th Cir. 2001) (jury question where defendant had no procedures in place to instruct subvendors on appropriate sources for reliable information); Andrews v. TRW, Inc., 225 F.3d 1063 (9th Cir. 2000), *rev'd and remanded*, 534 U.S. 19 (2001), *on remand, aff'd without op.*, 275 F.3d 893 (9th Cir. 2001) ("It would normally not be easy for a court as a matter of law to determine whether a given procedure was reasonable in reaching the very high standard set by the statute. . . ."), *modified, aff'd in part, rev'd in part*, 289 F.3d 600 (9th Cir. 2002); Guimond v. Trans Union Credit Info. Co., 45 F.3d 1329 (9th Cir. 1995) ("The issue of whether the agency failed to follow 'reasonable procedures' " will be a "jury question[] in the overwhelming majority of cases."); Cahlin v. Gen. Motors Acceptance Corp., 936 F.2d 1151, 1156 (11th Cir. 1991) (whether a CRA followed reasonable procedures when it generated an inaccurate consumer report is "a jury question in the overwhelming majority of cases."); Murphy v. Midland Credit Mgmt., Inc., __ F. Supp. 2d __, 2006 WL 2917355 (E.D. Mo. Oct. 11, 2006); Rothery v. Trans Union, L.L.C., 2006 WL 1720498 (D. Or. Apr. 6, 2006) (noting it is a "rare instance" where the CRA's procedures are clearly reasonable."); Poore v. Sterling Testing Sys., Inc., 410 F. Supp. 2d 557 (E.D. Ky. 2006) (determination of the "reasonableness" is treated a factual question even when the underlying facts are undisputed; summary judgment not appropriate for resolution of determination unless the reasonableness or of the procedures is beyond question.); Valvo v. Trans Union, L.L.C., 2005 WL 3618272 (D.R.I. Oct. 27, 2005); Swanson v. Central Bank & Trust Co., 2005 WL 1324887 (E.D. Ky. June 3, 2005) (whether defendants used reasonable procedures in initially reporting disputed accounts is a question for the jury); Sampson v. Equifax Info. Servs., 2005 WL 2095092 (S.D. Ga. Aug. 29, 2005); Schaffhausen v. Bank of America, N.A., 393 F. Supp. 2d 853 (D. Minn. 2005); Graham v. CSC Credit Servs., Inc., 306 F. Supp. 2d 873 (D. Minn. 2004); McKeown v. Sears Roebuck & Co., 335 F. Supp. 2d 917 (W.D. Wis. 2004); Boris v. ChoicePoint Servs., Inc., 249 F. Supp. 2d 851 (W.D. Ky. 2003), *amended* 2003 WL 23009851 (W.D. Ky. Aug. 21, 2003) (question of whether CRA followed "reasonable procedures" is typically a fact question reserved for the jury); Olwell v. Medical Inf. Bureau, 2003 WL 79035 (D. Minn. Jan. 7, 2003); Thomas v. Trans Union, L.L.C., 197 F. Supp. 2d 1233 (D. Or. 2002); Bruce v. First U.S.A. Bank, N.A., 103 F. Supp. 2d 1135, 1143 (E.D. Mo. 2000).

254 *See* Dalton v. Capital Associated Industries, Inc., 257 F.3d 409 (4th Cir. 2001) (nothing in the statute suggests that a plaintiff is relieved of the burden of showing that the CRA failed to follow reasonable procedures); Stewart v. Credit Bureau, Inc., 734 F.2d 47, 51 (D.C. Cir. 1984); Koropoulos v. Credit Bureau, 734 F.2d 37, 42 (D.C. Cir. 1984); Hussain v. Carteret Sav. Bank, 704 F. Supp. 567, 569 (D.N.J. 1989); Jones v. Credit Bureau of Garden City, 703 F. Supp. 897 (D. Kan. 1988).

255 Stewart v. Credit Bureau, Inc., 734 F.2d 47, 51 (D.C. Cir. 1984). *See also* Philbin v. Trans Union Corp., 101 F.3d 957 (3d Cir. 1996); Guimond v. Trans Union Credit Info. Co., 45 F.3d 1329 (9th Cir. 1995); Lendino v. Trans Union Credit Info. Co., 970 F.2d 1110 (2d Cir. 1992); Cahlin v. General Motors Acceptance Corp., 936 F.2d 1151 (11th Cir. 1991). *But see* Olwell v. Medical Info. Bureau, 2003 WL 79035 (D. Minn. Jan. 7, 2003) (plaintiff must offer specific facts that could allow a reasonable fact-finder to determine that defendant's procedures were not reasonable).

256 936 F.2d 1151, 1156 (11th Cir. 1991). *See also* Sampson v. Equifax Info. Servs., 2005 WL 2095092 (S.D. Ga. Aug. 29, 2005); Thomas v. Gulf Coast Credit Serv., Inc., 214 F. Supp. 2d 1228 (M.D. Ala. 2002); Parker v. Parker, 124 F. Supp. 2d 1216 (M.D. Ala. 2000); Natale v. TRW, Inc., 1999 U.S. Dist. LEXIS 3882 (N.D. Cal. Mar. 30, 1999).

257 45 F.3d 1329 (9th Cir. 1995).

taining inaccurate information."²⁵⁸ In the Ninth and Eleventh Circuits, "following reasonable procedures" is an affirmative defense that must be proven by the CRA.²⁵⁹

The Third Circuit carved out what it referred to as a "middle ground" in *Philbin v. Trans Union Corp.*²⁶⁰ Under this interpretation of section 1681e(b), the Third Circuit explained:

> A somewhat narrower, and more plausible, reading [of *Cahlin* and *Guimond*] is that a plaintiff may present his case to the jury on the issue of reasonable procedures merely by showing an inaccuracy in the consumer report and nothing more, but the burden does not shift to the defendant. Rather, a jury may, but need not, infer from the inaccuracy that the defendant failed to follow reasonable procedures.²⁶¹

Despite this holding, in the same decision, the Third Circuit in *Philbin* recognized that the CRA is "in a far better position to prove that reasonable procedures were followed than a plaintiff is to prove the opposite."²⁶²

At the opposite side of the spectrum from Ninth and Eleventh Circuits, the Fourth, Fifth, and D.C. Circuits have held that the consumer will always retain the burden of proving the unreasonableness of the CRA's procedures.²⁶³ A consumer plaintiff must minimally present some evidence from which a trier of fact could infer that the CRA failed to follow reasonable procedures in preparing the consumer report.²⁶⁴

The decisions from the Fourth, Fifth, and D.C. Circuits, however, hold out the possibility that a consumer may be able to prove the lack of reasonable procedures through circumstantial evidence of the egregiousness of the inaccuracy itself. In *Dalton v. Capital Associated Industries, Inc.*,²⁶⁵ the Fourth Circuit explained, "We express no view as to whether an inaccuracy can be so egregious that it creates a presumption that the agency's procedures were unreasonable." In *Stewart v. Credit Bureau, Inc.*,²⁶⁶ the D.C. Circuit accepted the viability of such non-direct evidence, stating, "[u]nder this standard a plaintiff need not introduce direct evidence of unreasonableness of procedures: In certain instances, inaccurate credit reports by themselves can fairly be read as evidencing unreasonable procedures, and we hold that in such instances plaintiff's failure to present direct evidence will not be fatal to his claim."

In *Stewart*, the D.C. Circuit suggested several examples of inaccuracies that would be sufficiently fundamental so as to provide adequate grounds for inferring that a CRA acted negligently. These included inconsistencies within a single report involving an inaccuracy as fundamental as a falsely reported bankruptcy, and inconsistencies between two files or reports involving less fundamental inaccuracies.²⁶⁷

This approach is also supported by several section 1681e(b) cases in which consumers prevailed despite their failure to present direct evidence on the reasonableness of the CRAs' reporting procedures. In *Bryant v. TRW, Inc.*,²⁶⁸ the court upheld a jury verdict against the CRA, which had reported inaccurate information supplied to it by several sources, concluding that such inconsistencies imposed a duty on the CRA to verify the information in those reports.²⁶⁹ In *Morris v. Credit Bureau, Inc.*,²⁷⁰ the CRA maintained two files on one consumer. The court found the existence of the two similar files to be a sufficient indication of unreasonable procedures to satisfy the consumer's burden of proving that the CRA did not follow reasonable procedures.²⁷¹ Inconsistencies or questionable transfers between two files may also imply negligence on the CRA's part.²⁷²

In the Seventh Circuit, however, it may be difficult to argue that a CRA knew or should have known of the inaccuracy based on the facially inaccurate information. The Seventh Circuit held in *Sarver v. Experian Info. Solutions, Inc.*²⁷³ that despite the fact that the consumer's file contained facially inconsistent information, Experian's procedures were reasonable as a matter of law. The court relied upon Experian's expert to conclude that it would be unduly burdensome and unreasonable to require Experian to evaluate each computer record for anomalous information given the enormous volume of information processed.²⁷⁴ Thus, it

---

258 *Id.* at 1333.
259 Sampson v. Equifax Info. Servs., 2005 WL 2095092 (S.D. Ga. Aug. 29, 2005).
260 101 F.3d 957 (3d Cir. 1996).
261 *Id.*
262 *Id. See also* Sampson v. Equifax Info. Servs., 2005 WL 2095092 (S.D. Ga. Aug. 29, 2005) (discussing this aspect of the *Philbin* opinion).
263 Dalton v. Capital Associated Industries, Inc., 257 F.3d 409 (4th Cir. 2001) (nothing in the statute suggests that a plaintiff is relieved of the burden of showing that the CRA failed to follow reasonable procedures); Sepulvado v. CSC Credit Servs., 158 F.3d 890, 895 (5th Cir. 1998); Stewart v. Credit Bureau, Inc., 734 F.2d 47, 51 (D.C. Cir. 1984); Koropoulos v. Credit Bureau, Inc., 734 F.2d 37, 42 (D.C. Cir. 1984); Gohman v. Equifax Info. Servs., L.L.C., 395 F. Supp. 2d 822 (D. Minn. 2005).
264 Stewart v. Credit Bureau, Inc., 734 F.2d 47, 51 (D.C. Cir. 1984).
265 257 F.3d 409 (4th Cir. 2001).
266 734 F.2d 47, 51 (D.C. Cir. 1984).
267 *Id.*
268 487 F. Supp. 1234 (E.D. Mich. 1980), *aff'd*, 689 F.2d 72 (6th Cir. 1982).
269 *Id.* at 1242. *See also* Jones v. Credit Bureau of Greater Garden City, 1989 WL 107747 (D. Kan. Aug. 28, 1989); Barron v. Trans Union Corp., 82 F. Supp. 2d 1288 (M.D. Ala. 2000).
270 563 F. Supp. 962 (S.D. Ohio 1983).
271 *Id.* at 968. *See also* Millstone v. O'Hanlon Reports, Inc., 383 F. Supp. 269, 275 (egregiousness of report's inaccuracy was evidence of "willful non-compliance" with § 1681e(b)), *aff'd*, 528 F.2d 829 (8th Cir. 1976).
272 *See* McKeown v. Sears Roebuck & Co., 335 F. Supp. 2d 917 (W.D. Wis. 2004) (only one furnisher reporting consumer's death); Jones v. Credit Bureau of Greater Garden City, 1989 LEXIS 11054 (D. Kan. Aug. 28, 1989).
273 390 F.3d 969 (7th Cir. 2004).
274 *Id.*

4.4.5.2.2 Sources of proof

If the plaintiff has the burden to show the unreasonableness of the CRA's procedures, there are a number of potential sources of evidence in addition to the consumer's file or report. Practitioners should seek to discover all prior consumer complaints and lawsuits against the defendant CRA alleging similar conduct or FCRA violations. Such evidence is directly relevant to the degree of unreasonableness.[275] It will constitute notice that the CRA cannot then refute. Practitioners confirm that each of the "Big Three" CRAs compile and have produced database lists of prior lawsuits on specific FCRA violations.

At one point or another, several of the nationwide CRAs were under court or FTC order to keep statistics on their own performance.[276] Practitioners might be able to obtain such internal reviews through discovery, and this may prove helpful to a case. For example, a court order required Experian (formerly TRW) to submit annual reports showing how changes in its algorithms reduce mixed files.[277] Experian was also required to report (1) the total number of reports issued to consumers; (2) the total number of consumer disputes; (3) the approximate number of disputed items; and (4) the total number of each type of dispute as reported on Experian's form 102.[278]

It may also prove helpful to request disclosure from the CRA of the contents of the consumer's file even after the CRA has corrected the file.[279] This post-correction disclosure must include the CRA's own audit trail as to its actions after it has reinvestigated the consumer's dispute, such as what information has been corrected and when.[280] The audit trail will thus provide evidence of inaccurate information that the consumer needs in an action against the CRA challenging the CRA's procedures to ensure accuracy.[281]

Another means to establish the existence of reasonable alternative procedures to more accurately report is to compare the procedures at competing CRAs.[282] In some cases, it may also be appropriate to identify and retain an expert witness with knowledge in the field.

4.4.5.3 Damages As an Element of a Reasonable Procedures Claim

Proof of actual damages is not a component of liability determination for a section 1681e(b) claim. While a consumer must ultimately prove that a negligent violation caused actual damages,[283] a willful violation may also entitle the consumer to recover statutory and punitive damages.[284] As one court noted, it needed to "first decide whether the preparing agency is liable before it determines whether the plaintiff has suffered recoverable damages."[285]

Despite this conclusion, a number of courts have imposed proof of "harm" as an element of a reasonable procedures claim. This requirement is derived from a formulation of the section 1681e(b) claim first suggested in *Whelan v. Trans Union Credit Reporting Agency*.[286] In *Whelan*, the court enunciated a four-step analysis:

> To succeed on a claim under this section, a plaintiff must establish that: (1) the consumer reporting agency was negligent in that it failed to follow reasonable procedures to assure the accuracy of its credit report; (2) the consumer reporting agency reported inaccurate information about the plaintiff; (3) the plaintiff was injured; and (4) the consumer reporting agency's negligence proximately caused the plaintiff's injury.[287]

This formulation is on its face unremarkable, because it requires proof of causation and harm for recovery upon a *negligent* FCRA violation. However, some courts have focused entirely on the "injury" or "harm" element and thus never reached a determination as to accuracy or the reasonableness of the CRA's conduct or procedures.[288] Without a

---

275 Dalton v. Capital Associated Industries, Inc., 257 F.3d 409, 418 (4th Cir. 2001) (court noted there was no evidence that other consumers had lodged complaints similar to plaintiff's against the defendant).
276 *See* Appx. K, *infra*.
277 See § 4.3.3, *supra*, for an explanation of mixed files.
278 Fed. Trade Comm'n v. TRW, Inc., 784 F. Supp. 361 (N.D. Tex. 1991); TRW, Inc. v. Morales, Civ. No. 3-91-1340-H (N.D. Tex. Dec. 10, 1991) (action involving a number of states' attorneys general), *reprinted on the CD-Rom accompanying this manual*.
279 *See* § 3.4, *supra*.
280 Federbush, FTC Informal Staff Opinion Letter (Mar. 10, 1983), *reprinted on the CD-Rom accompanying this manual*.
281 *Id.*
282 Nelski v. Trans Union, L.L.C., 86 Fed. Appx. 840, 2004 WL 78052 (6th Cir. Jan. 15, 2004); Cousin v. Trans Union Corp., 246 F.3d 359, 368 (5th Cir. 2001).
283 15 U.S.C. § 1681o.
284 15 U.S.C. § 1681n. *See also* §§ 11.11 and 11.12, *infra*.
285 Rothery v. Trans Union, L.L.C., 2006 WL 1720498 (D. Or. Apr. 6, 2006) *citing* Guimond v. Trans Union Credit Info. Co., 45 F.3d 1329, 1334 (9th Cir. 1995).
286 862 F. Supp. 824, 829 (E.D.N.Y. 1994).
287 *Id. See also* Cassara v. DAC Servs., Inc., 276 F.3d 1210, 1217 (10th Cir. 2002); Philbin v. Trans Union Corp., 101 F.3d 957, 963 (3d Cir. 1996); Gohman v. Equifax Info. Servs., L.L.C., 395 F. Supp. 2d 822 (D. Minn. 2005); Lawrence v. Trans Union, L.L.C., 296 F. Supp. 2d 582 (E.D. Pa. 2003).
288 Enwonwu v. Trans Union, L.L.C., 164 Fed. Appx. 914, 2006 WL 227585 (11th Cir. Jan. 31, 2006) (court held that plaintiff did not create a genuine issue of material fact that inaccurate information caused him harm, thus plaintiff failed to establish a prima facie case of a violation of § 1681e); Lamar v. Experian Info. Sys., 408 F. Supp. 2d 591 (N.D. Ill. 2006) (plaintiff's failure to raise a genuine issue of material fact as to any claimed damages that he assertedly sustained necessarily dooms his

determination as to the degree of inaccuracy or of the unreasonableness of a CRA's procedures, a court cannot consider the willfulness of the violation and the possibility of recovering statutory and punitive damages. This approach thus misconstrues the standard for a claim under section 1681e(b).

4.4.6 Reasonableness of Specific Consumer Reporting Agency Procedures

4.4.6.1 Management Policies Encouraging Unfavorable or Inaccurate Information

Reasonable procedures relating to accuracy include management practices that affect the manner in which information is collected and reported. The FTC prohibits CRA management policies that encourage or require investigators to prepare unfavorable consumer reports, such as investigator evaluations based on the percentage of adverse reports prepared.[289] However, the Eleventh Circuit reversed an FTC decision against Equifax, concluding that employee rankings based on the amount of adverse information produced was not actionable where the system did not pose a reasonable risk of inaccuracies—the FTC's massive and thorough investigation produced no evidence that the system caused inaccuracies.[290]

Inadequate procedures are also implicated where employees are encouraged to handle investigations in too cursory a fashion. For example, the court in *Millstone v. O'Hanlon Reports*[291] found inadequate procedures whereby investigators spent between ten minutes and half an hour in gathering information for automobile insurance reports, were paid on a commission basis of as little as $1.85 a report, and prepared an average of about 150 consumer reports in two weeks. The court held that this CRA's methods "were so slipshod and slovenly as to not even approach the realm of reasonable standards of care as imposed by the statute."[292]

Since the *Millstone* decision, industry methods have only gotten worse. Two of the three CRAs now outsource their dispute handling and much of their consumer contact work to third party vendors in foreign nations.[293]

---

entire claim, "for the Section 1681e(b) requirements are stated in the conjunctive.").

289 *See also* Collins v. Retail Credit Co., 410 F. Supp. 924 (E.D. Mich. 1976).
290 Equifax, Inc. v. Fed. Trade Comm'n, 678 F.2d 1047 (11th Cir. 1982).
291 383 F. Supp. 269 (E.D. Mo. 1974), *aff'd*, 528 F.2d 829 (8th Cir. 1976).
292 *Id.*
293 *See* § 4.5, *infra*. *See also* Cushman v. Trans Union Corp. 115 F.3d 220, 226 (3d Cir. 1997) (noting that CRA paid clerk $7.50 per hour to conduct ten reinvestigations per hour, or seventy-five cents per investigation).

4.4.6.2 Illogical Files and Internal Inconsistencies

CRAs must have procedures to compare recently obtained information with the information added to the file earlier to discover and correct inconsistent or contradictory information.[294] The FTC has required more stringent procedures where the information furnished appears implausible or inconsistent.[295] As a result of FTC enforcement action, Experian (formerly TRW) had formally agreed to use reasonable procedures to detect illogical information before it is furnished to users.[296]

There may be two pieces of reported information where it is impossible for both to be accurate, and the CRA may make no effort to unravel the inconsistency.[297] For example, a credit file may contain a consumer's age, previously reported by a creditor. If a newly reported account then reports a "date opened" which preceded the consumer's age of majority, a consumer can argue that the CRA could reasonably have cross-checked this inconsistency.[298]

One of the worst inconsistent file problems recurring in the case law is the reporting of a live consumer as deceased.[299] Usually the error mistakenly occurs internally in a creditor's records. When the creditor then furnishes the inaccurate account information to the CRA, the deceased condition is reported to the consumer's file. This results in the entire file essentially shutting down, as the file will no longer be able to generate a credit score. The relevant question that arises in these cases is whether the CRA was under a duty to recognize and reconcile the anomalous deceased account with the reporting of ongoing credit to the file from other creditors. The better reasoned cases have held the CRA responsible for such shockingly inconsistent reported data.[300] Such inconsistencies could lead a jury to infer that the CRA's failure to detect them was unreasonable.[301]

---

294 Bryant v. TRW, Inc., 487 F. Supp. 1234, 1237 (E.D. Mich. 1980), *aff'd*, 689 F.2d 72 (6th Cir. 1982).
295 FTC Official Staff Commentary § 607 item 3D, *reprinted at* Appx. D, *infra*.
296 Fed. Trade Comm'n v. TRW, 784 F. Supp. 361 (N.D. Tex. 1991).
297 *See* Wilson v. Rental Research Serv., Inc., 165 F.3d 642 (8th Cir. 1999), *rehearing en banc without published op.*, 206 F.3d 810 (8th Cir. 2000) (by vote of an equally divided court, the district court's order is affirmed).
298 Sheffer v. Experian Info. Solutions, Inc., 2003 WL 21710573 (E.D. Pa. July 24, 2003).
299 *Id.*; Gohman v. Equifax Info. Servs., L.L.C., 395 F. Supp. 2d 822 (D. Minn. 2005); Schmitt v. Chase Manhattan Bank, N.A., 2005 WL 2030483 (D. Minn. Aug. 23, 2005); Anderson v. Trans Union, L.L.C., 345 F. Supp. 2d 963 (W.D. Wis. 2004).
300 Gohman v. Equifax Info. Servs., L.L.C., 395 F. Supp. 2d 822 (D. Minn. 2005); McKeown v. Sears Roebuck & Co., 335 F. Supp. 2d 917, 930–931 (W.D. Wis. 2004) (summary judgment not warranted where erroneous deceased notation was inconsistent with other accounts); Sheffer v. Experian Info. Solutions, Inc., 2003 WL 21710573 (E.D. Pa. July 24, 2003).
301 Gohman v. Equifax Info. Servs., L.L.C., 395 F. Supp. 2d 822 (D. Minn. 2005) ('Plaintiff has also raised a disputed issue as to

§ 4.4.6.3   *Fair Credit Reporting*

However, some courts have held that tracking contradictory reporting by different credit furnishers was too heavy of a burden to place on a CRA.[302] In these cases, the CRAs have claimed, remarkably, that the reconciliation of accounts could not be performed electronically. It would therefore be too expensive to be reasonable.[303] These cases may be distinguished as they presented the unique circumstance in which the consumer had been reported dead because of an unusual coding glitch by the furnisher.[304] In addition, they evidence a failure of the consumer to have discovered and challenged the CRA assertions of burden and expense.

Another common inconsistent data inaccuracy occurs when one or more credit accounts are reported as "included in bankruptcy" even though the CRA file does not contain a reported public record bankruptcy case. These cases are discussed at § 4.4.6.9.2, *infra*.

4.4.6.3 Inaccurate Sources

CRAs rely for much of the information in their files on data provided by their subscribers, particularly by their creditor subscribers. Errors by those furnishing information on a consumer will lead to erroneous consumer reports,[305] unless the CRA takes appropriate preventative procedures.

CRAs cannot just report verbatim whatever is provided them by their sources; they must have procedures in place to ensure that the information from those sources is accurate.[306] The Sixth Circuit held that a CRA does not necessarily comply with section 1681e(b) by simply reporting in an accurate manner the information it receives from creditors.[307]

However, the prevalent view in the case law is that, generally, a CRA is permitted to rely on a furnisher, so long as it has no basis to question or doubt its reliability.[308] The Seventh Circuit in *Henson* ruled that CRAs are allowed to rely on information from the furnisher, absent prior information from the consumer that the information might be inaccurate.[309] Courts have found that the *Henson* reasoning, discussed *infra*,[310] excuses CRAs from independently verifying information provided by credit furnishers unless the CRA knew or had reason to know that the furnisher was unreliable or reporting inaccurate information.[311] While the reliability of a CRA's source is a question of fact,[312] a CRA is entitled to rely on its source when it had enjoyed a long term relationship with the credit furnisher with no report that it had provided unreliable information.[313]

If a CRA accurately transcribes, stores, and communicates information received from a source it reasonably believes to be reputable, and which is credible on its face, the CRA does not violate the FCRA provision of reasonable procedures just by reporting an item that turns out to be inaccurate.[314] The FTC Staff Commentary takes a similar position.[315]

Thus, the critical factor determining the reasonableness of a CRA's reliance on its credit furnisher is the degree of notice the CRA has as to unreliability. When a consumer makes a dispute, the CRA has been made aware of inaccurate information and it may not longer blindly parrot the furnisher.[316] If a CRA had reason to suspect the accuracy of a source of information, or if a consumer has already indicated a possible error, then the CRA has a responsibility to investigate more carefully.[317]

---

whether Equifax unreasonably failed to detect and inquire after a 'gross inconsistency' in her credit file. Plaintiff points to the fact that only her Wells Fargo account contained the deceased notation, while numerous other accounts were opened or remained active. Such inconsistencies could lead a jury to infer that Equifax's failure to detect them was unreasonable."); McKeown v. Sears Roebuck & Co., 335 F. Supp. 2d 917, 930–931 (W.D. Wis. 2004) (summary judgment not warranted where erroneous deceased notation was inconsistent with other accounts).

302 Schmitt v. Chase Manhattan Bank, N.A., 2005 WL 2030483 (D. Minn. Aug. 23, 2005).
303 Anderson v. Trans Union, L.L.C., 345 F. Supp. 2d 963 (W.D. Wis. 2004).
304 *Id.*
305 *See* § 4.3.2, *supra*.
306 Dalton v. Capital Associated Industries, Inc., 257 F.3d 409 (4th Cir. 2001); Poore v. Sterling Testing Sys., Inc, 410 F. Supp. 2d 557 (E.D. Ky. 2006); Soghomonian v. U.S., 278 F. Supp. 2d 1151 (E.D. Cal. 2003); Bryant v. TRW, Inc., 487 F. Supp. 1234, 1237 (E.D. Mich. 1980), *aff'd*, 689 F.2d 72 (6th Cir. 1982). A line of direct examination questions to establish that a CRA has not independently verified information supplied by a merchant is suggested in 4 Am. Jur. 2d *Proof of Fact* 261, 296.
307 Bryant v. TRW, Inc., 689 F.2d 72, 78 (6th Cir. 1982).
308 Henson v. CSC Credit Servs., 29 F.3d 280 (7th Cir. 1994); Morris v. Trans Union, L.L.C., 420 F. Supp. 733 (S.D. Tex. 2006). *See also* § 4.5.3.2, *infra*.
309 Henson v. CSC Credit Servs., 29 F.3d 280, 284 (7th Cir. 1994); Quinn v. Experian Solutions, 2004 WL 609357 (N.D. Ill. Mar. 24, 2004).
310 *See* § 4.5.3.2, *infra*.
311 Quinn v. Experian Solutions, 2004 WL 609357 (N.D. Ill. Mar. 24, 2004); Ruffin-Thompkins, 2003 U.S. Dist. LEXIS 23647, at *11–12 (quoting Zahran v. Trans Union Corp., 2003 U.S. Dist. LEXIS 5089, at *3 (N.D. Ill. Mar. 21, 2003) and Field v. Trans Union L.L.C., 2002 WL 849589, at *4 (N.D. Ill. May 3, 2002)), *aff'd* 422 F.3d 603 (7th Cir. 2005).
312 Campbell v. Chase Manhattan Bank, USA, N.A., 2005 WL 1514221 (D. N.J. June 27, 2005).
313 Morris v. Trans Union, L.L.C., 420 F. Supp. 733 (S.D. Tex. 2006).
314 Sarver v. Experian Info. Solutions, 390 F.3d 969 (7th Cir. 2004); Smith v. Auto Mashers, Inc., 85 F. Supp. 2d 638 (W.D. Va. 2000).
315 FTC Official Staff Commentary § 607 item 3A, *reprinted at* Appx. D, *infra*.
316 Graham v. CSC Credit Servs., Inc., 306 F. Supp. 2d 873 (D. Minn. 2004). *See* § 4.5.3.2, *infra*.
317 *See, e.g.*, Pinner v. Schmidt, 805 F.2d 1258 (5th Cir. 1986); Thomas v. GulfCoast Credit Serv., Inc., 214 F. Supp. 2d 1228 (M.D. Ala. 2002) (blind reliance on furnisher in the face of

For example, if a particular creditor (also referred to as furnisher) has furnished a significant amount of erroneous consumer account information, the CRA must require the furnisher to revise its procedures to correct whatever problems caused the errors or stop reporting information from that creditor.[318] If the CRA knew of a previous acrimonious personal relationship between the furnisher and the consumer, it could not rely on this source.[319] A CRA must also adopt reasonable procedures to eliminate errors that it knows about, or should reasonably be aware of, resulting from faulty procedures followed by furnishers.[320]

Also according to the FTC Staff Commentary, whether a CRA can rely on the accuracy of information from a source depends on the circumstances.[321] CRAs must take additional steps where the information appears implausible or inconsistent, where procedures for furnishing the information seem likely to result in inaccuracies, or where the CRA has had numerous problems regarding information from that source.[322] A necessary corollary of this analysis is that CRAs must keep track of the frequency of errors in information provided by each creditor or other party that furnishes information to the CRA.[323]

If the CRA knows about or should know about systematic errors from a furnisher, the FTC Staff Commentary requires the CRA to adopt reasonable procedures to eliminate these systematic errors resulting in new protocols to be followed.[324] For example, if a particular creditor frequently furnishes erroneous account information, the CRA must require the creditor to revise the creditor's procedures or the CRA must stop reporting information from that creditor.[325]

Because the CRAs use the same defense witnesses, and in most cases, even the same defense attorneys, their arguments supporting the reliability of data furnishers are usually generic and consistent from case to case. Accordingly, a wise practitioner can obtain CRA declarations and other filings from previous cases, many of which may be available on the PACER database.[326]

In addition, a CRA should take reasonable steps to tell the source of information what data should be supplied. CRAs, for example, must inform a source that if its customer disputes an account, the dispute should be noted in the information furnished to the CRA.[327] CRAs cannot take data compiled for one purpose and blindly report it as part of the consumer's file. The CRA has a duty to minimize the risk of incorrect interpretations of that data.

For example, a creditor may generate data for the creditor's own accounting or collection purposes, with no thought of its accuracy for credit reporting purposes. It might be irrelevant for the creditor's recordkeeping purposes when labeling a consumer's debt as "delinquent" whether the debt is three-days or three-months delinquent, or whether the consumer insists that no debt is owed. But a consumer report that contains only the information that the consumer is "delinquent" is likely to be misleading, and therefore inaccurate, when it is used by another subscriber for the purpose of evaluating the consumer's eligibility for credit, insurance, or employment.[328] Therefore, the Act requires that the CRA follow procedures for evaluating the information that it collects for use in consumer reports to determine whether it meets the standard of "maximum possible accuracy."[329]

4.4.6.4 Public Record Information

The gathering, interpreting and maintenance of public records pose unique accuracy problems for CRAs. Special problems exist where CRAs review, interpret, and then manually record judgments, tax liens, or bankruptcies. Errors can occur when the employee or vendor misunderstands

---

repeated consumer disputes is not reasonable); Swoager v. Credit Bureau, 608 F. Supp. 972 (M.D. Fla. 1976); FTC Official Staff Commentary § 607 items 3A and 3B, *reprinted at* Appx. D, *infra*.

318 *Id.*
319 Pinner v. Schmidt, 804 F.2d 1258, 1262 (5th Cir. 1987).
320 Cassara v. DAC Servs., Inc., 276 F.3d 1210 (10th Cir. 2002) (to ensure maximum possible accuracy, CRA collecting and reporting drivers' records and employment histories may be required to make sure the criteria defining categories of accidents reported by furnishers of information are made explicit and communicated to all who furnish information); Dalton v. Capital Associated Industries, Inc., 257 F.3d 409 (4th Cir. 2001); Poore v. Sterling Testing Sys., Inc., 410 F. Supp. 2d 557 (E.D. Ky. 2006).
321 FTC Official Staff Commentary § 607 item 3D, *reprinted at* Appx. D, *infra*.
322 *Id.*
323 *See* Bryant v. TRW, Inc., 487 F. Supp. 1234, 1237 (E.D. Mich. 1980), *aff'd*, 689 F.2d 72 (6th Cir. 1982). *Cf.* Houston v. TRW Info. Servs., Inc., 707 F. Supp. 689 (S.D.N.Y. 1989) (procedure held reasonable where TRW periodically verified the information provided to it by a clerical reporting service, which statistically had been highly accurate).
324 FTC Official Staff Commentary § 607 item 3B, *reprinted at* Appx. D, *infra*.
325 *Id.*

326 For example, the PACER file for Anderson v. Trans Union, L.L.C., 367 F. Supp. 2d 1225 (W.D. Wis. 2005), contains a complete description of reasons by a TransUnion employee justifying its reliance on its furnishers. The testimony of Experian employees is available in any number of cases in the Northern District of Illinois. *See, e.g.,* Sarver v. Experian Info. Solutions, 390 F.3d 969 (7th Cir. 2004).
327 Bryant v. TRW, Inc., 487 F. Supp. 1234, 1237 (E.D. Mich. 1980), *aff'd*, 689 F.2d 72 (6th Cir. 1982). *See also* 15 U.S.C. § 1681s-2(a)(3), discussed at Ch. 6, *supra* and added to the statute after the *Bryant* decision.
328 Bryant v. TRW, Inc., 487 F. Supp. 1234, 1237 (E.D. Mich. 1980), *aff'd*, 689 F.2d 72 (6th Cir. 1982).
329 *Id. See also* Miller v. Credit Bureau, Inc. of Washington, D.C., [1969–1973 Decisions Transfer Binder] Consumer Cred. Guide (CCH) ¶ 99,173 (D.C. Super. Ct. 1972).

§ 4.4.6.4 Fair Credit Reporting

or misinterprets the public record information, or makes errors in copying the information from the public record source.[330]

For example, a CRA may report that a tax lien was placed on a property by a tax assessor's office, but the report may not reflect a subsequent release of the lien because the assessor's office reported it incorrectly. Or the lien may be subject to interpretation not possible by the frontline vendor employee.[331] Some CRAs have asserted that the fact that the lien was placed is "technically accurate" and therefore may be reported, notwithstanding that the lien was subsequently released. This position highlights the inherent problem with using a "technically accurate" standard for accuracy.[332] In particular with respect to public records, the information is constantly changing based on correction of public record errors or change in a case's status. Often a governmental agency does not automatically report such changes to the CRA. Thus, a file's completeness may depend on how often the CRA reviews the public record information, and whether it even reviews changes in the information on record.

Furthermore, public record information requires special procedures because of the potential negative effect of errors on a consumer. For example, reports of a criminal record or an unpaid judgment may be enough for the consumer to be denied employment, insurance, credit, or other benefits.[333] In one case, even though the CRA used a "match logic" program and had a legal department review report of judgments, its procedure may be found unreasonable when the form used to report judgments had no space to indicate which defendant was subject to the judgment.[334]

While the CRA may not have to engage in extensive analysis to discover errors in public records, there are procedures CRAs should institute in dealing with public records. Consulting the public record is, as a matter of law, reasonable. A court docket is a "a presumptively reliable source."[335] Some cases have wrongly held or implied that CRAs may rely upon public records known or suspected of being false.[336] The better line of cases requires further investigation when reason exists to doubt the accuracy of a public record,[337] although the failure of a bankruptcy discharge to list a specific debt may have to be corrected by the debtor.[338]

The FCRA provides special procedures for dealing with public record information used for employment purposes, and these procedures are set out separately in § 4.4.7, *infra*. These special FCRA procedures are an indication of the importance of reasonable procedures when compiling public record information for other purposes as well. Also relevant are procedures to keep any information complete and up to date, and such procedures are discussed in § 4.4.6.8.4, *infra*.

Once a CRA undertakes to report public information, it is unreasonable to fail to update it. This would reduce the number of errors that occur when the CRAs rely upon stale public information.[339]

As this manual goes to press, substantial changes are occurring in the way in which the "Big Three" nationwide CRAs gather their public records data. In the past, each hired a third party vendor to gather the information directly from the courthouses across the country. As courts made their dockets available on-line, the vendors gathered some records, such as bankruptcy filings, by automated means. In each instance, however, the vendor was merely an information gatherer or conduit. They did not compile, match, or retain the data.

This is now changing. The primary public records vendors, Lexis-Nexis and ChoicePoint, are themselves national CRAs. The data that they sell to the "Big Three" bureaus is otherwise gathered, maintained, and retained in the vendor's own database. This raises a number of issues, most important among them the fact that the vendor is now also a CRA and thus governed by both the requirement that the CRA follow reasonable procedures to ensure accuracy under section 1681e(b) and the reinvestigation requirements of section 1681i.

The last five years have also seen the rise of numerous public records CRAs that do not compile credit data. Instead, they focus their business on criminal records checks,

---

330 *See* § 4.3.2.5, *supra*; Dalton v. Capital Associated Industries, Inc., 257 F.3d 409 (4th Cir. 2001); Apodaca v. Discover Fin. Servs., 417 F. Supp. 2d 1220 (D.N.M. 2006); Soghomonian v. United States, 278 F. Supp. 2d 1151 (E.D. Ca. 2003); Jones v. Credit Bureau of Garden City, Inc., 703 F. Supp. 899 (D. Kan. 1988).

331 Soghomonian v. United States, 278 F. Supp. 2d 1151 (E.D. Ca. 2003).

332 *See* § 4.2.3, *supra*.

333 Dalton v. Capital Associated Industries, Inc., 257 F.3d 409 (4th Cir. 2001); Poore v. Sterling Testing Sys., Inc., 410 F. Supp. 2d 557 (E.D. Ky. 2006); Apodaca v. Discover Fin. Servs., 417 F. Supp. 2d 1220 (D. N.M. 2006); Soghomonian v. United States, 278 F. Supp. 2d 1151 (E.D. Cal. 2003). *See* § 4.4.7, *infra*.

334 Matise v. Trans Union Corp., 1998 WL 872511 (N.D. Tex. Nov. 30, 1998).

335 Henson v. CSC Credit Servs., 29 F.3d 280, 285 (7th Cir. 1994).

336 Kettler v. CSC Credit Serv., Inc., 2003 WL 21975919 (D. Minn. Aug. 12, 2003) (consumer's dispute that she had never filed bankruptcy, without disclosing that her husband had mistakenly listed the accounts in his bankruptcy, was inadequate to obligate the CRA to look behind the public records); Williams v. Colonial Bank, 826 F. Supp. 415 (D.C. Ala. 1993); Grays v. Tans Union Credit Info. Co., 759 F. Supp. 390 (N.D. Ohio 1990).

337 Matise v. Trans Union Corp., 1998 WL 872511 (N.D. Tex. Nov. 30, 1998); Houston v. TRW Info. Servs., Inc., 707 F. Supp. 689 (S.D.N.Y. 1989); McPhee v. Chilton Corp., 468 F. Supp. 494 (D. Conn. 1978); Johnson v. Beneficial Fin. Corp., 466 N.Y.S.2d 553, 120 Misc. 2d 628 (1983).

338 Evans v. Credit Bureau, 904 F. Supp. 123 (W.D.N.Y. 1995).

339 *See* Frost v. Experian, 1999 U.S. Dist. LEXIS 6783 (S.D.N.Y. May 6, 1999) (reasonable jury could conclude that CRA's failure to verify accuracy of a judgment was unreasonable and in reckless disregard for the truth); FTC Official Staff Commentary § 607 item 3F(2) (if a reported bankruptcy has been dismissed, that fact should be reported).

mostly for employers. These CRAs are often unprepared for FCRA compliance. Experience has shown that these new CRAs often fail to correctly match public records, especially criminal records, to their proper owner. They also often fail to properly describe the history and status of such items.[340]

4.4.6.5 Mismerged Information and Wrong Consumer Identification

Mismerged information (where information on one consumer is incorrectly entered into another consumer's file) and CRAs issuing consumer reports to users on the wrong consumer are serious and frequent errors.[341] Such problems were one of the major reasons for the FCRA's enactment.[342]

CRAs must exercise reasonable care to verify that the individual about whom derogatory information is received is in fact the consumer into whose file they are inserting the information; CRAs must further exercise reasonable care that the individual whose report is furnished to the user is the same individual that is requested by the user.[343] This obvious point is confirmed by the FCRA's language that states that the CRA must follow reasonable procedures to ensure maximum possible accuracy of the information "concerning the individual about whom the report relates."[344] In addition, the requirement that consumer reports be released only for permissible purposes often requires a reasonable belief that the report is about the consumer on whom the information is to be provided.[345]

For example, CRAs cannot excuse mismatched information by telling consumers that "Brown" is a common last name and that such errors are bound to happen. The CRA must establish reasonable procedures to establish the maximum possible accuracy so that such errors will not happen, even if the individual's last name is Brown.[346]

These procedures logically should include a duty on the part of the CRA to obtain sufficient identifying information from both users and furnishers, and to make certain that such identifying information matches before the information provided by the furnisher is released to the user in a consumer report. This might require that CRAs compare individuals' middle names or initials, Social Security numbers, and other identifying data when matching a consumer's file with a request for a report or with new information being furnished to the CRA.[347]

Usually computers will be doing the matching and will search for the file that has the most points of identification matches with the individual whose report is requested or about whom information is being provided. Questions to ask in the case of a mismerged file are: what steps does a CRA take when the file that has the most matches also has several identification mismatches and what special procedures are followed. Generally these questions are appropriate for the jury.[348]

For example, the Fifth Circuit has found a CRA's procedures lacking where the CRA did not establish a minimum acceptable level of matching, but instead, furnished for user verification the file with the closest match.[349] Similarly, a special review may be required where the Social Security numbers do not match, since many experts view the Social Security number as the single most important identifying information in a consumer reporting file.[350]

---

340 *See, e.g.,* Dalton v. Capital Associated Industries, Inc., 257 F.3d 409 (4th Cir. 2001); Poore v. Sterling Testing Sys., Inc., 410 F. Supp. 2d 557 (E.D. Ky. 2006).

341 *See* § 4.3.3, *supra*.

342 When Senate Bill 823, the bill which eventually became the FCRA, was first introduced, its author explained the abuses in the credit reporting industry which required legislative action. The first abuse Senator Proxmire addressed was inaccurate reports, and the first example he gave involved the frequency with which consumer reporting agencies "confuse one individual with another." 115 Cong. Rec. 2411 (1968).

343 Andrews v. TRW, Inc., 225 F.3d 1063 (9th Cir. 2000), *rev'd on other grounds*, 534 U.S. 19 (2001); Philbin v. Trans Union Corp., 101 F.3d 957 (3d Cir. 1996); Bryant v. TRW, Inc., 689 F.2d 72 (6th Cir. 1982); Thompson v. San Antonio Retail Merchant Ass'n, 682 F.2d 509 (5th Cir. 1982); Rothery v. Trans Union, L.L.C., 2006 WL 1720498 (D. Or. Apr. 6, 2006); Valvo v. Trans Union, L.L.C., 2005 WL 3618272 (D.R.I. Oct. 27, 2005); Comeaux v. Experian Info. Solutions, 2004 WL 1354412 (E.D. Tex. June 8, 2004); Harris v. Equifax Credit Info. Servs., Inc., 2003 WL 23962280 (D. Or. Nov. 24, 2003); Jones v. Credit Bureau of Garden City, 1989 WL 107747 (D. Kan. Aug. 28, 1989); Jones v. Credit Bureau of Garden City, 703 F. Supp. 897 (D. Kan. 1988); Miller v. Credit Bureau, Inc., [1969–1973 Decisions Transfer Binder] Consumer Cred. Guide (CCH) ¶ 99,173 (D.C. Super. Ct. 1972). *Cf.* Lendino v. Trans Union Credit Info. Co., 970 F.2d 1110 (2d Cir. 1992); Tinsley v. TRW, Inc., 879 F. Supp. 550 (D. Md. 1995) (consumer's claim that information about his father was merged into his report was rejected because consumers failed to respond to CRA's request to particularize all information claimed to be in error); Lowry v. Credit Bureau, Inc. of Georgia, 444 F. Supp. 541 (N.D. Ga. 1978).

344 15 U.S.C. § 1681e(b).

345 15 U.S.C. § 1681b(a)(3); Andrews v. TRW, Inc., 225 F.3d 1063 (9th Cir. 2000), *rev'd on other grounds*, 534 U.S. 19 (2001).

346 Peeler, FTC Informal Staff Opinion Letter (Nov. 4, 1974), *reprinted on the CD-Rom accompanying this manual. See also* Jones v. Credit Bureau of Garden City, 1989 WL 107747 (D. Kan. Aug. 28, 1989).

347 *See* Jones v. Credit Bureau of Garden City, 1989 LEXIS 11054 (D. Kan. Aug. 28, 1989); Jones v. Credit Bureau of Garden City, 703 F. Supp. 897 (D. Kan. 1988). *See also* R. Smith, *A Look Inside a Credit Bureau's Operation*, 22 Privacy Journal 5 (Apr. 1996).

348 Andrews v. TRW, Inc., 225 F.3d 1063 (9th Cir. 2000) (reversing summary judgment for the CRA because trial court failed to leave the question of reasonableness to the jury), *rev'd on other grounds*, 534 U.S. 19 (2001).

349 Thompson v. San Antonio Retail Merchant Ass'n, 682 F.2d 509 (5th Cir. 1982). *Contra* Crabill v. Trans Union, L.L.C., 259 F.3d 662 (7th Cir. 2001) (when *pro se* consumer and his brother had a one-digit difference in their Social Security numbers and same first initial, court ruled that CRA procedures that released two files with similar but not identical data was reasonable).

350 Thompson v. San Antonio Retail Merchant Ass'n, 682 F.2d 509 (5th Cir. 1982).

It is unreasonable for a CRA to maintain two files under a single Social Security number, despite knowing that a Social Security number can belong to only one person.[351] The same should be true where other basic identifying characteristics do not match.[352] On the other hand, relying exclusively on Social Security numbers may be inadequate,[353] especially in light of the possibility of identity theft or the presence of other possibly inconsistent information. This is also a common problem for siblings as they often will share a similar Social Security number and have shared an address.[354] It is also a common problem for parents and their children when they share similar names.[355]

Because of the way that the CRAs merge and match credit files, the address is an important tool to understand and correct inaccuracy problems that arise from both mixed files and identity theft.[356] Accordingly, a jury could find that it is unreasonable for a CRA to fail to keep track of the source of the addresses that it reported on the consumer's report.[357] The 2003 FACTA amendments to the FCRA imposed requirements on CRAs when faced with address discrepancies, discussed at § 9.2.5.2, *infra*.

According to the FTC Staff Commentary, CRAs must review their procedures for ensuring accuracy when they discover that they have issued reports on a consumer other than the individual requested or have issued reports containing mismerged information.[358] The FTC views such errors as indicating systematic problems.[359] In other words, CRAs must have procedures in place so that such identification problems do not occur.

CRAs also have to take reasonable steps to ensure that mismerged information that is corrected does not reoccur at a later date.[360] The same weakness in a system that created one mismatch could create another.

Despite the well-known problems with mismerged files, the Seventh Circuit held in *Sarver v. Experian Information Solutions*,[361] that CRA procedures which resulted in another consumer's account being included in the plaintiff's file were reasonable as a matter of law, even though the resulting consumer report was facially inconsistent and the anomaly readily apparent. One potential rebuttal to the Seventh Circuit's decision is the fact that the nationwide CRAs have been on notice for several years that their files are mismerged, creating inaccuracies, and that the CRAs have done little to rectify the mistakes.[362] Both the FTC and state attorneys general entered into consent decrees with the three nationwide CRAs.[363] At trial, practitioners may seek to have these consent decrees admitted as evidence that mismerged files and failure to correct files is a systematic problem for which the CRA is on notice. If admitted, the consent decrees can be powerful evidence.

Even one instance of issuing a report on the wrong consumer would mean that the report is being issued without a permissible purpose.[364] This one violation should be an independent FCRA violation leading to a cause of action, whether or not the CRA has adopted reasonable procedures to prevent the misidentification from occurring.[365]

4.4.6.6 Identity Theft

The FACTA amendments to the FCRA mandated a number of procedures regarding identity theft. Most of these procedures must be invoked by notice from the consumer or identity theft victims. These procedures are discussed at length in Chapter 9, *infra*.

Given that in the nature of identity theft, the thief is posing as the consumer, accuracy procedures that are otherwise considered reasonable may not be sufficiently designed to catch fraudulent activities that are reported to a victim's account, at least before the victim or CRA learns of the fraud. Moreover, as identity theft has become increasingly more common, a CRA's failure to increase the sophistication of its procedures to respond to this problem is itself unreasonable.[366]

In fact, each of the "Big Three" nationwide CRAs advertises enhanced fraud detecting software that takes a consumer's name, address, telephone number, and Social Security number and other information and tries to verify them against a number of other data sources.[367] These products, developed to help businesses prevent losses suf-

---

351 Rothery v. Trans Union, L.L.C., 2006 WL 1720498 (D. Or. Apr. 6, 2006).
352 Jones v. Credit Bureau of Garden City, 1989 WL 107747 (D. Kan. Aug. 28, 1989).
353 Andrews v. TRW, Inc., 225 F.3d 1063 (9th Cir. 2000), *rev'd on other grounds*, 534 U.S. 19 (2001).
354 *See, e.g.,* Reed v. Experian Info. Solutions, Inc., 321 F. Supp. 2d 1109 (D. Minn. 2004).
355 Moore v. Equifax Info. Servs. L.L.C., 333 F. Supp. 2d 1360 (N.D. Ga. 2004).
356 Graham v. CSC Credit Servs., Inc., 306 F. Supp. 2d 873 (D. Minn. 2004).
357 *Id.*
358 FTC Official Staff Commentary § 607 item 3A, *reprinted at* Appx. D, *infra*.
359 *Id.*
360 Cousin v. Trans Union Corp., 246 F.3d 359 (5th Cir. 2001); Fed. Trade Comm'n v. TRW, 784 F. Supp. 361 (N.D. Tex. 1991).
361 390 F.3d 969 (7th Cir. 2004).
362 *See* § 4.3.3, *supra*.
363 *See* Appx. K, *infra*.
364 *See* § 7.4.6, *supra*.
365 *See* § 7.5.1, *supra*.
366 *See* FTC Commentary § 607, which states that "when a consumer reporting agency learns or should be reasonably aware of errors in its reports that may indicate systematic problems . . . it must review its procedures for assuring accuracy." *See also* Andrews v. TRW, Inc., 225 F.3d 1063 (9th Cir. 2000), *rev'd on other grounds*, 534 U.S. 19 (2001); Graham v. CSC Credit Servs., Inc., 306 F. Supp. 2d 873 (D. Minn. 2004) (CRA's failure to keep track of sources of addresses. which would have alerted CRA to identity theft, created issue of material fact).
367 For example, Equifax offers "FraudScan Plus," Experian offers "Fraud Shield," (advertised as recognizing, among other warning signs, a high chance that a Social Security number belongs

fered from application fraud, would do a great deal to help consumers prevent losses suffered from identity fraud. Where the CRA has the technology to conduct a "super-match" of consumer data or where software to prevent inconsistencies is available to the CRA, it can be argued it is unreasonable not to utilize these tools.[368]

CRAs have also developed identity theft products to sell directly to consumers, purportedly offering greater protection against fraud.[369] Rather than automatically program these safety measures into their credit reporting system, the CRAs have instead sought to profit from the burgeoning identity theft industry. It is arguable that the very existence of such products make CRAs' procedures unreasonable, and violates both the letter and spirit of the FCRA.

In addition to the remedies added by the FACTA amendments, once a victim has reported a theft to a CRA, there are several other steps that the CRA can take to prevent further damage to the victim's file: code the victim's reports to prevent automated application, batch or summary report processing; code the victim's report to prevent it from producing credit scores during the fraud period; and take the consumer reports off-line pursuant to VIP procedures, already in place, in order to prevent further access and allow screening of incoming false, fraud-related data.[370]

Even if a CRA maintains reasonable procedures to ensure accurate information, once an identity theft victim contests a false item on the report, the CRA must reinvestigate the disputed information. CRAs have been held liable in identity theft cases where they failed to conduct reasonable reinvestigations.[371] Even the mere presence of an inquiry on a consumer's report resulting from identity theft raises an issue of material fact as to whether the consumer's report was misleading.[372]

4.4.6.7 Transcription, Data Communication, and Interpretation

A CRA must establish reasonable procedures to ensure maximum possible accuracy where it is transcribing information into its file.[373] A common, therefore reasonable, procedure in data entry is to double check the information by having it entered twice, by separate data entry clerks, and then compare the two transcriptions.

When retrieving data from sources, it is important for the CRA to have procedures so that terminology used by the source is understood by the eventual user. For example, a source may describe a debt as delinquent, and then a CRA must be able to explain to users whether that is one day overdue or ninety days delinquent.[374]

According to the FTC Staff Commentary, CRAs that send data electronically should have reasonable procedures to ensure that the data is accurately converted into machine-readable format and not distorted by machine malfunction or transmission failure. CRAs must adopt reasonable security procedures to minimize theft or alteration of information, either by authorized or unauthorized users.[375]

4.4.6.8 Incomplete and Outdated Items in the File

4.4.6.8.1 General

A consumer's file at a CRA may be incomplete for several reasons: a creditor's failure to provide any information about a the consumer's account, a furnisher's failure to include complete information about existing items in a file, or the failure to update existing items in a file.[376] The consumer might lack any file at a CRA.[377] A CRA might also fail to include certain information even thought it has been furnished to the CRA.

The FTC Staff Commentary indicates that certain types of new information do not have to be added to the consumer's file, even when the information is furnished to the CRA. The CRA does not have to:

---

to another consumer), TransUnion offers "Fraud Detect."

368 Andrews v. TRW, Inc., 225 F.3d 1063 (9th Cir. 2000), *rev'd on other grounds*, 534 U.S. 19 (2001).

369 For example, Equifax offers "Credit Watch" (advertised to consumers as a means to monitor, manage, and protect their credit).

370 Equifax has advertised to its subscribers that its SAFESCAN program will flag files suspected of identity theft and compare every inquiry to a nationwide fraud system.

371 Cushman v. Trans Union Corp. 115 F.3d 220 (3d Cir. 1997); Stevenson v. TRW, Inc., 987 F.2d 288 (5th Cir. 1993); Graham v. CSC Credit Servs., Inc., 306 F. Supp. 2d 873 (D. Minn. 2004). *See also* Haque v. CompUSA, Inc., 2003 WL 117986 (D. Mass. Jan. 13, 2003); Thomas v. GulfCoast Credit Serv., Inc., 214 F. Supp. 2d 1228 (M.D. Ala. 2002); Field v. Trans Union, L.L.C., 2002 WL 849589 (N.D. Ill. May 3, 2002).

The court in Cushman v. Trans Union Corp. noted that the reinvestigation had been conducted by a clerk that the agency paid $7.50 per hour to conduct ten reinvestigations per hour: "[T]he jury could have concluded that seventy-five cents per investigation was too little to spend when weighed against Cushman's damages." 115 F.3d at 226.

372 Andrews v. Trans Union Corp., 7 F. Supp. 2d 1056, 1075 n.20 (C.D. Cal. 1998) (noting that "some creditors view the number and nature of inquiries present on a consumer report to be a relevant factor in evaluating credit applications"), *aff'd in part, rev'd in part on other grounds sub nom.* Andrews v. TRW, Inc., 225 F.3d 1063 (9th Cir. 2000), *rev'd on other grounds*, 534 U.S. 19 (2001) (statute of limitations issues).

373 *But cf.* Brinckerhoff and Grimes, FTC Informal Staff Opinion Letter (Mar. 8, 1988), *reprinted on the CD-Rom accompanying this manual* (a single "data entry error, standing alone" does not violate the "reasonable procedures" requirement).

374 Hauser v. Equifax Inc., 602 F.2d 811 (8th Cir. 1979); Morris v. Credit Bureau of Cincinnati, 563 F. Supp. 962 (S.D. Ohio 1983); Bryant v. TRW, Inc., 487 F. Supp. 1234, 1237 (E.D. Mich. 1980), *aff'd*, 689 F.2d 72 (6th Cir. 1982). *Cf.* Stewart v. Credit Bureau, Inc., 734 F.2d 47 (D.C. Cir. 1984).

375 FTC Official Staff Commentary § 607 item 3C, *reprinted at* Appx. D, *infra*.

376 *See* § 4.3.2, *supra*.

377 *See* § 4.3.2.2, *supra*.

- Open a new file on a consumer;
- Report new credit accounts not already listed in the consumer's file;
- Add explanations for why a debt was not paid; or
- Report the reasons that credit or some other benefit was denied when reporting on the existence of that denial.

The first two types of information are discussed in § 4.4.6.8.2, *infra*, while the latter two are discussed in § 4.4.6.8.3, *infra*. Both subsections discuss potential arguments to counter the FTC Staff Commentary position.

With respect items already in a file, CRAs must adopt reasonable procedures to ensure that information is complete, and not just a partial statement of the facts as then known, discussed in § 4.4.6.8.4, *infra*. A CRA's obligation to update an existing account is discussed in §§ 4.4.6.8.4 and 4.4.6.8.5, *infra*.

4.4.6.8.2 Missing accounts and other items not covered in a consumer's file

The FCRA does not require a CRA to include in reports to users all information it has about a consumer in its files. However, a CRA may not mislead its subscribers as to the completeness of its reports by deleting non-derogatory information and not disclosing its policy of making such deletions.[378]

The FTC Staff Commentary has interpreted both the consumer's right under the FCRA to dispute the accuracy of information in a CRA's files[379] and the CRA's obligation to try to maintain accurate files[380] in a manner that suggests that some new information does *not* have to be added to the files. The FTC Staff Commentary suggests that the right to dispute is limited to "items of information" in the consumer's file. If new information relevant to the accuracy of an item already in the file is provided by the consumer, it must be added to the file. However, if the new information pertains to a new account or new "items," the FTC Staff Commentary would not require such information be added to the files.[381]

This FTC interpretation is open to criticism. Although the right to dispute the completeness or accuracy of information is limited to "any item of information contained in [the consumer's] file,"[382] the general standards of accuracy imposed on CRAs relate to the "maximum possible accuracy of the information concerning the individual."[383] The obligations of accuracy are not limited to specific "items of information" but to "the information"—presumably the information in the report as a whole.

The FCRA is intended to ensure that CRAs exercise their obligations with "fairness" and "impartiality" and recognizes that the nation's banking system depends upon "fair and accurate" reporting.[384] These broad intentions would surely be undermined if a CRA could: choose to report the one existing adverse item of information and ignore numerous more telling items of favorable information; select older information of bad experiences and omit more recent patterns of responsibility; report a period of ill health and hospitalization but turn away information of later sustained perfect attendance on the job; or even list only good behavior at the expense of damaging information important to future users.[385]

Many circumstances may exist when the accuracy of a report as a whole, and an accurate understanding of the import of a specific item of information in particular, will be enhanced by the inclusion of additional items of information.[386] It is appropriate for a court to weigh the "reasonableness" of a CRA's procedures that exclude additional relevant information proffered by a consumer or any reliable source. Even if the FTC's position is a fair interpretation of the consumer's right to dispute items of information and the CRA's obligation to reinvestigate disputed information, the CRA may still have to include the consumer's submission to comply with its obligation to maintain reasonable procedures to ensure maximum possible accuracy of the information in its reports.[387]

The question of whether a CRA may reasonably be expected to create a new file upon request is different from the question of whether the accuracy of an existing file may be enhanced by additional information.[388] Nevertheless, if

---

378 FTC Official Staff Commentary § 607 item 7, *reprinted at* Appx. D, *infra*. *See also* Wharram v. Credit Servs. Inc., 2004 WL 1052970 (D. Minn. Mar. 12, 2004) (deleting entire tradeline, including positive history prior to dispute, did not ensure maximum possible accuracy).
379 *Id.* § 611 item 3.
380 *See id.* § 607 item 7 (CRAs are not required to include all existing information about a consumer in its reports); § 607 item 5. *Cf. id.* § 607 item 2.
381 *Id.* § 611 item 3.
382 15 U.S.C. § 1681i(a).
383 15 U.S.C. § 1681e(b).
384 15 U.S.C. § 1681(a).
385 FTC Official Staff Commentary § 607 item 7, *reprinted at* Appx. D, *infra*. This FTC Staff Commentary section, while suggesting that a consumer reporting agency does not have to issue complete reports, also states that the CRA may not mislead report users by deleting only nonderogatory information without disclosing its policy to the user. Query whether such a disclosure fulfills the CRA's obligations to maintain reasonable procedures to ensure maximum possible accuracy. *See also* Wharram v. Credit Servs. Inc., 2004 WL 1052970 (D. Minn. Mar. 12, 2004) (deleting entire tradeline, including positive history prior to dispute, did not ensure maximum possible accuracy).
386 *See* § 4.3.2.2, *supra* discussing problems created by the failure of some creditors to furnish information to CRAs.
387 *But see* FTC Official Staff Commentary § 607 item 7, *reprinted at* Appx. D, *infra*.
388 FTC Official Staff Commentary § 611 item 3, *reprinted at* Appx. D, *infra* (CRAs not required to create new files on consumers) (interpreting the section on Procedures in Case of Disputed Accuracy). *See also* Brinckerhoff, FTC Informal Staff Opinion Letter (July 30, 1985), *reprinted on the CD-Rom accompanying this manual*.

absence of a report about an individual will be construed unfavorably, it may be reasonable to require a new file be opened when verifiable information is submitted by a consumer. On the other hand, the Act does not establish any per se consumer right to be included in the files of a CRA.

4.4.6.8.3 Incomplete reporting of existing accounts

The prior subsection examines whether a CRA must have procedures to add new accounts to a file or create a new file. This subsection examines whether procedures must be in place to make sure that the information about an existing account is complete.

CRAs must adopt reasonable procedures to ensure that information when collected is complete, and not just a partial statement of the facts as then known.[389] Otherwise information that is technically accurate may be misleading because it is not complete or fails to convey the full picture. The CRA must balance whether the report's potential to mislead outweighs the availability of more accurate information and the burden of producing such information.[390] Of course, an incomplete report can still be accurate; the question is whether the incompleteness is misleading.[391]

Thus, CRAs must follow procedures to ensure that unfavorable information is not misleading *and* that the consumer report is complete in regard to information that might mitigate the adverse effect of such unfavorable information.[392] For example, reasonable procedures would add to a file's report of an unpaid hospital bill that the consumer disputed the bill.[393] Reasonable procedures would also result in a CRA noting that, while a debt is in litigation, it was the consumer who brought the action.[394] The CRA should follow reasonable procedures for gathering and reporting sufficient facts to ensure that the consumer report contains information that not only is technically true, but also presents an accurate picture of the consumer's status.[395]

Thus the Court of Appeals for the District of Columbia Circuit has questioned, without deciding, whether it would be per se unreasonable to code as a "9" all debts ranging from loans discharged in bankruptcy or paid off after collection referral to flagrant defaults where the debtor skipped town.[396] The theory would be that the "9" code would not present a complete or accurate picture of the consumer, even if technically accurate.

Reasonable procedures regarding inquiries would arguably require that CRAs adequately and completely identify the types of inquiries made regarding a consumer's report, rather than lump all inquiries into one category, making it impossible to determine which were for credit, account review, or prescreening. However, an FTC informal staff opinion letter does not require CRAs to adopt a uniform number or time period as a threshold for reporting inquiries about a consumer's report (a negative factor in some credit scoring calculations).[397]

In addition, the FTC Staff Commentary distinguishes additional information that must be included in a CRA's files for reasons of completeness and accuracy from extenuating circumstances as to why a debt is delinquent,[398] such as illness or loss of a job, which need not be reported, presumably because they do not enhance the accuracy of a report.[399] However, such a blanket rule preempts the statutory balanc-

---

389 Pinner v. Schmidt, 805 F.2d 1258 (5th Cir. 1986), *aff'g in part and rev'g in part*, 617 F. Supp. 342 (E.D. La. 1985); Koropoulos v. Credit Bureau, Inc., 734 F.2d 37, 45 (D.C. Cir. 1984); Alexander v. Moore & Associates, Inc., 553 F. Supp. 948 (D. Haw. 1982); Miller v. Credit Bureau, Inc., [1969–1973 Decisions Transfer Binder] Consumer Cred. Guide (CCH) ¶ 99,173 (D.C. Super. Ct. 1972). When Senate Bill 823, the bill which eventually became the FCRA, was first introduced, one of its principal targets was the reporting of incomplete information. 115 Cong. Rec. 2411–2412 (1969).

390 Koropoulos v. Credit Bureau, Inc., 734 F.2d 37, 45 (D.C. Cir. 1984); Alexander v. Moore & Associates, Inc., 553 F. Supp. 948 (D. Haw. 1982).

391 Sepulvado v. CSC Credit Servs., Inc., 158 F.3d 890 (5th Cir. 1998) (holding that describing a debt as "assigned" adequately indicated that the debt existed before the given date, particularly when the CRA's own research documented a much earlier date, seems unduly harsh. In any event, subsequent to the events in this case, the Act was amended to require furnishers to provide CRAs with the month and year a delinquency commenced. *See* § 5.2.3.3.3, *infra*).

392 Miller v. Credit Bureau, Inc., [1969–1973 Decisions Transfer Binder] Consumer Cred. Guide (CCH) ¶ 99,173 (D.C. Super. Ct. 1972).

393 *Id.*

394 Pinner v. Schmidt, 805 F.2d 1258 (5th Cir. 1986). *But see* Austin v. BankAmerica Serv. Corp., 419 F. Supp. 730 (N.D. Ga. 1974) (permissible for CRA to list consumer as defendant in lawsuit, failing to note that individual was sued in his official capacity as County Deputy Marshall. CRAs should not be forced to evaluate litigation).

395 *See* § 4.2.3, *supra*.

396 Koropoulos v. Credit Bureau, Inc., 734 F.2d 37, 45 (D.C. Cir. 1984). *But see* McClain v. Credit Bureau, [1980–1989 Decisions Transfer Binder] Consumer Cred. Guide (CCH) ¶ 96,703 (D.C. Cir. Mar. 14, 1983) (one digit code indicating a bad debt, debt placed for collection or skip creates no violation for failure to maintain procedures to ensure accuracy).

397 Brinckerhoff, FTC Informal Staff Opinion Letter (July 22, 1986), *reprinted on the CD-Rom accompanying this manual*; Grimes, FTC Informal Staff Opinion Letter (Feb. 27, 1986), *reprinted on the CD-Rom accompanying this manual*. *See* § 14.5.2.1, *infra*, regarding the effect of inquiries on a credit score.

398 *Cf.* FTC Official Staff Commentary § 611 item 4, *reprinted at* Appx. D, *infra*.

399 *See* FTC Official Staff Commentary § 611 items 4 and 5, *reprinted at* Appx. D, *infra*; Proposed FTC Official Staff Commentary, Supplementary Information, 53 Fed. Reg. 29,698 (Aug. 8, 1988). The Maine Bureau of Consumer Credit Protection interprets the Act more sensibly, ruling in effect that the consumer is disputing the significance of nonpayment in view of the circumstances and that a consumer report would be incomplete or inaccurate if it does not allow for exploration of nonpayments for potential creditors to evaluate. Maine Bureau of Consumer Credit Protection Fair Credit Reporting Act Ad-

ing test of reasonable procedures. If such additional information enhances the accuracy of a report *and* reasonable procedures could result in its inclusion, a CRA should include the information in its files and reports.

The FTC Staff Commentary also states that when reporting that a consumer was denied a benefit (such as credit), a CRA need not report the reasons for the denial.[400] This is also an over-generalization, in that reporting of the reasons for certain denials would certainly be appropriate. For example, a creditor could have denied a credit application because it was not accepting new applicants at that point in time, and the denial implies nothing as to the consumer's creditworthiness.

4.4.6.8.4 Reasonable methods to acquire updated information

CRAs must establish reasonable procedures to ensure that information is not outdated, even if the information is accurately reported as being current only as of a certain date, because the report produces a misleading picture of the consumer.[401] The user of a consumer report cannot be ensured of receiving the most accurate information reasonable under the circumstances if information is permitted to become misleading with the passage of time. This requirement is supported by the FCRA's language requiring accuracy, not when information is collected (which would imply that information which was accurate when collected would satisfy the statute), but when the report is "prepared,"[402] implying that the information must be accurate *each time* the information from the file is released to a user.

CRAs thus must employ reasonable procedures to keep their files current on past-due accounts.[403] For example, CRAs must require creditors to notify the CRA when past-due accounts have been paid or discharged in bankruptcy.[404] While it is not an FCRA violation if past-due accounts are out-of-date in a few instances, the CRA must maintain reasonable procedures to keep the file current.[405]

The circumstances in which a CRA must find additional or updated information to make a file more accurate is a balancing test. The CRA's interest in speed, lower expenses, and accessibility of information must be weighed against the consumer's interest in maximum possible accuracy and the likelihood of harm to the consumer.[406]

The Eleventh Circuit has seemingly recognized one exception to the rule that information be accurate as of the date the report is released to a user. In a questionable decision, the court suggests that procedural standards to ensure accuracy apply each time a report is prepared from materials in the files, except if a report is later copied and supplied to a user, with an express indication that it is a copy as well as the date and circumstances of the original report.[407]

4.4.6.8.5 Reporting of significant updated information that is furnished to a consumer reporting agency

If a CRA is informed of later developments relating to an item in the consumer's file, either by the furnisher or the consumer, the CRA must update the file.[408] A CRA must report significant, verified information it possesses about an item.[409] Even when the consumer does not formally dispute

---

visory Ruling 89-1, Consumer Cred. Guide (CCH) ¶ 95,760 (Oct. 31, 1989).
400 FTC Official Staff Commentary § 607 item 5, *reprinted at* Appx. D, *infra*.
401 Thompson v. San Antonio Retail Merchants Ass'n, 682 F.2d 509, 513 (5th Cir. 1982); Pinner v. Schmidt, 617 F. Supp. 342 (E.D. La. 1985), *aff'd in part and rev'd in part on other grounds*, 805 F.2d 1252 (5th Cir. 1986); Bryant v. TRW, Inc., 487 F. Supp. 1234 (E.D. Mich. 1980), *aff'd*, 689 F.2d 72 (6th Cir. 1982); Miller v. Credit Bureau, Inc. of Washington, D.C., [1969–1973 Decisions Transfer Binder] Consumer Cred. Guide (CCH) ¶ 99,173 (D.C. Super. Ct. 1972); FTC Official Staff Commentary § 607 item 3F(1), *reprinted at* Appx. D, *infra*; FTC, Compliance with the Fair Credit Reporting Act, at 20 (1977). *But see* Wright v. TRW Credit Data, 588 F. Supp. 112 (S.D. Fla. 1984); McPhee v. Chilton Corp., 468 F. Supp. 494 (D. Conn. 1978); Todd v. Associated Credit Bureau Servs., Inc., 451 F. Supp. 447 (E.D. Pa. 1977), *aff'd*, 578 F.2d 1376 (3d Cir. 1979); Austin v. Bankamerica Serv. Corp., 419 F. Supp. 730 (N.D. Ga. 1974).

Senator Proxmire, when he first introduced the bill which later became the FCRA, cited incomplete information as an example of inaccuracy:

> Most credit reporting agencies assiduously cull adverse information on people from newspapers, court records, and other public documents. These items include records of arrests, judgments, liens, bankruptcies, suits and the like. However, most agencies are not anywhere nearly as diligent in following up on the case to record information favorable to the consumer. Action following arrest is often dropped because of lack of evidence. Suits are dismissed or settled out of court. Judgments are reversed. However, these facts are seldom recorded by the credit reporting agencies with the result that their records are systematically biased against the consumer.

S. 823 introduced at 115 Cong. Rec. 2412 (1969).

402 15 U.S.C. § 1681e(b).
403 FTC Official Staff Commentary § 607 item 3F(1), *reprinted at* Appx. D, *infra*.
404 *Id. See* § 4.4.6.9.2, *infra*.
405 FTC Official Staff Commentary § 607 item 3F(1), *reprinted at* Appx. D, *infra*.
406 *See, e.g.*, Stewart v. Credit Bureau, Inc., 734 F.2d 47 (D.C. Cir. 1984); Koropoulos v. Credit Bureau, 734 F.2d 37 (D.C. Cir. 1984); Jones v. Credit Bureau of Garden City, Inc., 703 F. Supp. 897 (D. Kan. 1988); Alexander v. Moore & Associates, 553 F. Supp. 948 (D. Haw. 1982).
407 Clay v. Equifax, Inc., 762 F.2d 952 (11th Cir. 1985).
408 FTC Official Staff Commentary § 607 item 3F(1), *reprinted at* Appx. D, *infra*.
409 *Id.* item 3F(2). *But see* Sepulvado v. CSC Credit Servs., Inc., 158 F.3d 890 (5th Cir. 1998) (case implies that information which is not inaccurate or misleading does not have to be updated).

the accuracy of a report, if the consumer provides additional information on an incomplete file, then the CRA must include the statement.[410]

If a CRA has reported an account as delinquent, and obtains verified information that the account is paid, it must add that information to the file.[411] The same is true of information that a debt is discharged in bankruptcy or that a bankruptcy was involuntarily dismissed.[412] If a furnisher notifies a CRA that a consumer has voluntarily closed an account, the CRA must indicate that fact in any consumer report.[413] The CRA may not refuse to accept updated information because its contractual relationship with the furnisher is terminated.[414]

4.4.6.9 Bankruptcy Reporting

4.4.6.9.1 General

There are two contrasting and recurring inaccuracy problems with regards the reporting of bankruptcy in a consumer's credit report. The first problem is the CRAs' failure to report the discharge of an outstanding debt on an account when the consumer has completed a bankruptcy, discussed in § 4.4.6.9.2, *infra*.[415] The second is when a consumer has not filed bankruptcy, but the CRA reports otherwise, discussed in § 4.4.6.9.3, *infra*. In addition, the FTC Staff Commentary addresses other aspects of bankruptcy reporting, discussed in § 4.4.6.9.4, *infra*.

4.4.6.9.2 Reporting a debt discharged in bankruptcy

The FTC Staff Commentary requires that in reporting a debt discharged in bankruptcy, the balance should be reported as "0," although the report can indicate that the debt was not paid for a time and then was discharged in bankruptcy.[416] A debt discharged in bankruptcy may also be reported as charged off to profit or loss, if true, but only with the pre-discharge status.[417]

Despite this, account tradelines in consumer files often fail to indicate that the debts were discharged in bankruptcy.[418] The CRAs fail to reconcile obviously inconsistent information, i.e., a public record bankruptcy establishing that the consumer's debts are discharged versus prior reporting of a tradeline still showing the past-due status of the account. This inconsistency could be found to violate both relevant sections of the FCRA.[419] The FTC Staff Commentary cautions: "[A] consumer reporting agency may include delinquencies on debts discharged in bankruptcy in consumer reports, but must accurately note the status of the debt (e.g., discharged, voluntarily repaid)."[420]

A consumer report may include an account that was discharged in bankruptcy (as well as the bankruptcy itself), as long as it reports a zero balance due to reflect the fact that the consumer is no longer liable for the discharged debt.[421] A CRA must employ reasonable procedures to keep its file current on past due accounts (e.g., by requiring its creditors to notify the CRA when a previously past-due account has been paid or discharged in bankruptcy).[422]

Reliance on furnishers to correct inaccuracies in the status of accounts after bankruptcy will be unjustified. The FCRA has a single provision governing furnishers, 15 U.S.C. § 1681s-2. This section only governs a furnisher *when it reports*. It does not affirmatively require reporting to the CRAs. Thus, a creditor that simply ceases reporting after bankruptcy does not violate the FCRA. It is solely the fault of the CRA that the pre-bankruptcy reported status, never again updated, is retained in future consumer reports.

The second limitation on FCRA governance of furnishers is the fact that there is no private cause of action against furnishers for reporting inaccurate information or failing to maintain procedures for accuracy. The section of the FCRA that would require a furnisher to accurately report and update accounts discharged in bankruptcy, section 1681s-2(a), lacks any practical remedy.[423] Unlike the CRAs, a

---

410 Oliver, FTC Informal Staff Opinion Letter (June 10, 1983), *reprinted on the CD-Rom accompanying this manual*; Peeler, FTC Informal Staff Opinion Letter (July 25, 1978), *reprinted on the CD-Rom accompanying this manual* (reasons or circumstances of nonpayment go to completeness of report, therefore must include consumer's statement where requested); Peeler, FTC Informal Staff Opinion Letter (Aug. 23, 1976), *reprinted on the CD-Rom accompanying this manual*; Feldman, FTC Informal Staff Opinion Letter (Aug. 30, 1974), *reprinted on the CD-Rom accompanying this manual* (agency's failure to include additional references provided by consumer would cause violation due to incompleteness of report); Feldman, FTC Informal Staff Opinion Letter (May 31, 1974), *reprinted on the CD-Rom accompanying this manual* (serious question exists whether agency may continue to report incomplete information if consumer supplies additional information).
411 FTC Official Staff Commentary § 607 item 3F(2), *reprinted at* Appx. D, *infra*.
412 *Id.*
413 15 U.S.C. § 1681c(e). *See also* § 6.8, *infra*.
414 Harris, FTC Informal Staff Opinion Letter (Mar. 22, 1999), *reprinted on the CD-Rom accompanying this manual*.
415 *See* § 4.3.2.4, *infra*.

416 FTC Official Staff Commentary § 607 item 6, *reprinted at* Appx. D, *infra*. *See also* Learn v. Credit Bureau of Lancaster County, 664 F. Supp. 962 (E.D. Pa. 1987), *rev'd without op.*, 838 F.2d 461 (3d Cir. 1987); Brinckerhoff, FTC Informal Staff Opinion Letters (Mar. 19, 1987) and (Nov. 4, 1986), *reprinted on the CD-Rom accompanying this manual*.
417 McCorkell, FTC Informal Staff Opinion Letter (June 3, 1999), *reprinted on the CD-Rom accompanying this manual*.
418 *See* § 4.3.2.4, *supra*.
419 White v. Trans Union, L.L.C. (C.D. Cal. Oct. 13, 2006), *available at* www.consumerlaw.org/unreported.
420 FTC Official Staff Commentary § 607 item 3F(2), *reprinted at* Appx. D, *infra*.
421 *Id.* at § 607 item 3A(6).
422 *Id.* at § 607 item 3F(1).
423 15 U.S.C. § 1681s-2(c) (no private right of action for violations of 15 U.S.C. § 1681s-2(a)). *See also* § 6.1.2, *infra*.

furnisher can only be held accountable after the dispute process is completed.[424]

Note that reporting a debt after bankruptcy may not amount to a violation of the automatic stay as to the debtor,[425] but may be a violation of the stay as to a non-debtor cosigner in the debtor's chapter 13 proceedings.[426]

4.4.6.9.3 Included in bankruptcy

The second related bankruptcy inaccuracy problem is the CRA's incorrect reporting of a consumer as having been subject to a bankruptcy.[427] CRAs have a practice of including information on bankruptcy filings in the files of spouses, even when only one spouse filed for bankruptcy.[428] This practice also occurs even after the divorce. Notations in the report of the non-filing spouse or former spouse will state, "included in bankruptcy" or make some other reference about the bankruptcy, even though the consumer played no role in the bankruptcy action.[429]

This practice raises questions about the accuracy and relevancy of such reports. A CRA must have procedures to ensure that where an individual is acting solely as a guarantor of a debt, that any nonpayment of that debt listed in that individual's file must include a notation that the individual is only the guarantor and not the primary obligor.[430] The Metro 2 Format developed by the CRA industry gives specific instructions on the proper reporting of a bankruptcy for joint obligors.[431] As part of a class action settlement, the three nationwide CRAs committed to establishing procedures to prevent this error.[432]

Consumers who still are faced with erroneous bankruptcy notations should dispute the accuracy of them and request that such items be deleted or at least make the information truly accurate. If the CRAs fail to do either, they may be subject to claims under the FCRA.

4.4.6.9.4 Other bankruptcy issues

Any consumer report of a consumer's bankruptcy must identify the chapter under which the case arises, "if provided by the source of the information" about the bankruptcy.[433] Even before this language was added to the statute by amendment, the Conference Report, when the FCRA was first enacted, notes that the House conferees intended that the standards of accuracy shall impose a duty to distinguish between straight bankruptcies and wage earner plans.[434] Thus bankruptcies should commonly be reported as arising under chapter 7 or chapter 13.

If a bankruptcy filing is withdrawn by the consumer before final judgment, the CRA must, upon receipt of documentation certifying the withdrawal, include in any report that the filing was withdrawn.[435] Also, the bankruptcy court is not required to expunge its records for a debtor who, after discharge of debts, voluntarily paid his pre-petition creditors in full.[436]

The FCRA does not require a CRA to redesignate items as "bankruptcy vacated," rather than "bankruptcy dismissed," where a consumer withdraws a bankruptcy petition and pays off the debts.[437] On the other hand, a report

---

424 Nelson v. Chase Manhattan Mortgage Corp., 282 F.3d 1057, 1059 (9th Cir. 2002). *See also* § 6.10, *infra*.
425 Hickson v. Home Federal of Atlanta, 805 F. Supp. 1567 (N.D. Ga. 1992).
426 *In re* Singley, 233 B.R. 170 (Bankr. S.D. Ga. 1999) (even if creditor's report to a CRA concerning spouse/cosigner's credit contained truthful information that was a matter of public record, if made with intent to harass or coerce a debtor and/or co-debtor into paying a pre-petition debt, could violate the automatic stays for the debtor and or the non-debtor cosigner spouse); *In re* Sommersdorf, 139 B.R. 700 (Bankr. S.D. Ohio 1991).
427 Sarver v. Experian Info. Solutions, 390 F.3d 969 (7th Cir. 2004); Allen v. Experian Info. Solutions, Inc., 2006 WL 1388757 (S.D. Ill. May 12, 2006); O'Brien v. Equifax Info. Servs., L.L.C., 382 F. Supp. 2d 733 (E.D. Pa. 2005); Reed v. Experian Info. Solutions, Inc., 321 F. Supp. 2d 1109 (D. Minn. 2004).
428 *See, e.g.* Johnson v. MBNA America Bank, NA, 357 F.3d 426, 430 (4th Cir. 2004).
429 Spector v. Trans Union L.L.C., 301 F. Supp. 2d 231 (D. Conn. 2004) (question of fact for jury whether "included in bankruptcy" inaccurate); Spellman v. Experian, 2002 WL 799876 (D. Nev. Jan. 10, 2002) (failing to adequately and sufficiently identify that a mortgage was included in the bankruptcy of only one joint holder, and failing to adequately and sufficiently identify that only the liability of the joint holder was discharged by bankruptcy created a misleading report); Heupel v. Trans Union, L.L.C., 193 F. Supp. 2d 1234 (N.D. Ala. 2002) ("included in bankruptcy" technically accurate; entry in single tradeline reduced credit score). *Cf.* Trundle v. Homeside Lending, Inc., 162 F. Supp. 2d 396 (D. Md. 2001) (in a state defamation action it is not a false statement to say that mortgage loan was "included in bankruptcy" when co-obligor husband has filed for bankruptcy).
430 FTC Official Staff Commentary § 607 item 3F(3), *reprinted at* Appx. D, *infra*.
431 *See* § 6.3.3.12, *supra*.
432 Clark v. Experian Info. Solutions, 2004 WL 256433 (D.S.C. Jan. 14, 2004).
433 15 U.S.C. § 1681c(d).
434 Conf. Rep. No. 1587, 91st Cong., 2d Sess. (1970), *reprinted in* 1970 U.S.C.C.A.N. 4394, 4411, 4415; Isaac, FTC Informal Staff Opinion Letter (Nov. 5, 1998), *reprinted on the CD-Rom accompanying this manual*.
435 15 U.S.C. § 1681c(d).
436 *In re* Whitener, 57 B.R. 707 (Bankr. E.D. Va. 1986). Note, however, that the voluntary repayment of the debt should be included in any report of the discharge. FTC Official Staff Commentary § 607 item 2, *reprinted at* Appx. D, *infra*.
437 Brinckerhoff, FTC Informal Staff Opinion Letter (Oct. 29, 1985), *reprinted on the CD-Rom accompanying this manual*. [*Editor's Note*: This informal opinion may be challenged if it is shown vacated bankruptcies are less harmful to a consumer's credit history and reasonable procedures would permit the CRA to note the difference.]

should indicate when a bankruptcy petition was dismissed.[438]

4.4.7 Procedures for Reports of Adverse Public Record Information for Employment Purposes

4.4.7.1 General

The FCRA mandates specific procedures when the CRA furnishes "items of information on consumers which are matters of public record and are likely to have an adverse effect upon a consumer's ability to obtain employment."[439] This requirement applies only when the consumer report is furnished for employment purposes[440] *and* the public record information is adverse. The FCRA does not define adverse public record information, but the Act does mention certain types of information that, by implication, meet this standard: "items of public record relating to arrests, indictments, convictions, suits, tax liens, and outstanding judgments."[441]

The FCRA provides special consumer protections when this type of information is disclosed because such information is likely to have a significant effect on employment decisions. Consumers may be denied jobs or terminated from employment as a result of an arrest record, where the employer may not realize that the arrest never led to a conviction, that the arrest was due to a case of mistaken identity, that the arrest occurred when a personal foe filed a baseless criminal complaint and the charges were dropped as soon as the police conducted an initial inquiry, or where the arrest occurred when the individual was a juvenile.[442] An employer may also view negatively an unsatisfied court judgment against an individual, not knowing that the case involved only a default judgment that the consumer has since paid.

A CRA must comply with the special FCRA protections for public record information even if information is received from another CRA,[443] and even if the CRA does not actually include the public record information in the consumer report. For example, CRAs must comply with the public record requirement where a CRA sends a message to the user to "call" the CRA, where this is commonly understood to indicate that public record information exists.[444]

When public record information is likely to have an adverse effect on employment, the CRA must comply with at least one of the following two procedures, neither of which can be waived by the consumer.[445] The CRA must either notify the consumer of the release of the public record information or establish strict procedures to maintain complete and up-to-date public record information.[446]

4.4.7.2 Election to Notify Consumer of Release of Public Record Information

The option most CRAs choose is to notify the consumer, at the time that public record information is released, that the CRA is furnishing public record information to a user, together with the name and address of the person to whom such information is being released.[447] The FTC Staff Commentary indicates the notice can be by first class mail.[448]

4.4.7.3 Election to Establish Strict Procedures for Complete and Up-to-Date Public Record Information

The second option a CRA can elect is to maintain strict procedures to ensure that the public record information is both complete and up to date.[449] A recent court ruling has held that a reasonable juror could conclude that an item was not complete as to the record status of a conviction for driving under the influence where the report did not include the actual name, birth date, or Social Security number of the person who was convicted of the crime.[450]

For records relating to arrests, indictments, conviction, suits, tax liens, and outstanding judgments, "up to date" means "current public record status of the item at the time of the report is reported."[451] Relying upon database records

---

438 *Cf.* Anonymous, FTC Informal Staff Opinion Letter (Nov. 5, 1999), *reprinted on the CD-Rom accompanying this manual.*
439 15 U.S.C. § 1681k. A CRA must comply with this section even if the public record information is received from another CRA. *See* FTC Official Staff Commentary § 613 item 3, *reprinted at* Appx. D, *infra.*
440 Employment purposes include: "evaluating a consumer for employment, promotion, reassignment or retention as an employee." 15 U.S.C. § 1681a(h).
441 15 U.S.C. § 1681k(a)(2).
442 *See* Wiggins v. Equifax Servs., Inc., 848 F. Supp. 213 (D.D.C. 1993). State or federal laws, such as juvenile laws, might prohibit making arrest or conviction records public. Practitioners should check the laws of the jurisdiction to see if the CRA has complied. *See generally* Fite v. Retail Credit Co., 386 F. Supp. 1045 (D. Mont. 1975), *aff'd*, 537 F.2d 384 (9th Cir. 1976); Goodnough v. Alexander's, Inc., 82 Misc. 2d 662, 370 N.Y.S.2d 388 (Sup. Ct. 1975).

443 *See* FTC Official Staff Commentary § 613 item 3, *reprinted at* Appx. D, *infra.*
444 Brinckerhoff, FTC Informal Staff Opinion Letter (May 31, 1988), *reprinted on the CD-Rom accompanying this manual.*
445 FTC Official Staff Commentary § 613 item 5, *reprinted at* Appx. D, *infra.*
446 15 U.S.C. § 1681k(a).
447 15 U.S.C. § 1681k(a)(1).
448 FTC Official Staff Commentary § 613 item 4, *reprinted at* Appx. D, *infra.*
449 15 U.S.C. § 1681k(a)(2).
450 Poore v. Sterling Testing Sys., Inc., 410 F. Supp. 2d 557 (E.D. Ky. 2006).
451 15 U.S.C. § 1681k(a)(2).

updated every thirty days does not suffice.[452] The information must be checked almost simultaneously with the date of the report. The CRA must at least re-verify information that was collected prior to the current request for a consumer report for employment purposes to ensure that the status has not changed. It is not adequate to simply rely on a report obtained from another CRA.[453]

Unlike the provisions of the FCRA that deal with accuracy and obsolete information, which require "reasonable procedures,"[454] the section on public record information for employment purposes requires "strict procedures."[455] In contrast to "reasonable procedures," every CRA, no matter how small, must exercise the same high degree of care whenever it furnishes public record information for employment purposes.[456] The Act's requirement of strict procedures presupposes a finding that their cost is reasonably necessary, given the risk that the consumer will be seriously and unjustly harmed if this type of information is incomplete and out of date. In determining whether the CRA has complied with the requirement of strict procedures, the inquiry should be limited to the efficacy of its procedures in preventing the distribution to employers of adverse public record information that is incomplete or out of date.

The CRA logically must maintain procedures to ensure that it is aware when adverse public record information is being furnished for employment purposes and when the requirements of the Act must be met. Therefore, the CRA should maintain strict procedures for receiving certification of the user's purpose and for verifying that the certified purpose is true.[457] The CRA must also maintain strict procedures for evaluating public record information and determining whether that information is "likely to have an adverse effect upon a consumer's ability to obtain employment."[458]

In addition, the CRA must maintain procedures for training its employees. The CRA's employees should be instructed about the nature and amount of information required for the consumer report to be complete and up to date and about the methods by which such information can be obtained. Finally, the CRA arguably should maintain procedures designed to avoid any mistake and to catch any mistakes once made.[459] If the report is complete and up to date, no further inquiry into the reasonableness of the procedures is necessary.[460]

4.4.7.4 Exemption for National Security Investigations

The procedures required for the reporting of adverse public record information for employment purposes does not apply in the case where a United States agency or department seeks the report, if the head of that agency or department makes a written finding.[461] The finding must state that the report is relevant to a national security investigation, the investigation is within the jurisdiction of the agency or department, and there is reason to believe that one of six conditions will occur, if the exemption does not apply.[462] These six conditions include: (1) a person's safety will be endangered; (2) flight from prosecution will result; (3) evidence will be destroyed; (4) witnesses will be intimidated; (5) classified information will be compromised; or (6) the investigation will be jeopardized or delayed.[463] This exemption is peculiar in that national security may be endangered if the consumer is notified of the public record information, but this would not be the case if the CRA had just used the second option of strict procedures to ensure that the information was complete and up to date, something that would seem desirable in a national security investigation.

4.5 Consumer Reporting Agency Reinvestigation and Correction of Disputed Information

4.5.1 Introduction

A consumer reporting agency (CRA) on notice as to potentially inaccurate information in the consumer's file is in a very different position than a CRA without such no-

---

452 Allan, FTC Informal Staff Opinion Letter (May 5, 1999), *reprinted on the CD-Rom accompanying this manual.*
453 Poore v. Sterling Testing Sys., Inc., 410 F. Supp. 2d 557 (E.D. Ky. 2006).
454 15 U.S.C. § 1681e.
455 15 U.S.C. § 1681k(a)(2).
456 *See also* Poore v. Sterling Testing Sys., Inc., 410 F. Supp. 2d 557 (E.D. Ky. 2006) (heightened standards are required).
457 See § 7.5, *infra.*
458 15 U.S.C. § 1681k(a)(2). *See* Obabueki v. International Bus. Machs. Corp., 145 F. Supp. 2d 371 (S.D.N.Y. June 14, 2001) (despite listing several procedures, it remained a question of fact for the jury whether procedures were "strict"), *aff'd,* 319 F.3d 87 (2d Cir. 2003) (affirming judgment as a matter of law for CRA).

459 Mirabal v. General Motors Acceptance Corp., 537 F.2d 871 (7th Cir. 1976); Carroll v. Exxon Co., U.S.A., 434 F. Supp. 557 (E.D. La. 1977) (following *Mirabal*). *Mirabal* was a Truth in Lending case construing the provisions of 15 U.S.C. § 1640(c), that a creditor may not be held liable if it shows by a preponderance of the evidence that the violation was not intentional and resulted from a bona fide error notwithstanding the maintenance of procedures reasonably adapted to avoid such errors. *Carroll* applied the requirement of a "preventive mechanism" to the "reasonable procedures" defense in actions under FCRA § 1681m(c).
460 Obabueki v. International Bus. Machs. Corp., 145 F. Supp. 2d 371 (S.D.N.Y. June 14, 2001), *aff'd,* 319 F.3d 87 (2d Cir. 2003) (affirming judgment as a matter of law for CRA).
461 15 U.S.C. § 1681k(b).
462 *Id., referring to* 15 U.S.C. § 1681b(b)(4)(A).
463 15 U.S.C. § 1681b(b)(4)(A).

tice.[464] Most successful litigation against CRAs to challenge inaccuracy within a consumer's file comes after a consumer has made a dispute directly to the CRA. Upon receipt of a consumer dispute, the CRA must review and consider the information provided,[465] forward all relevant information to the creditor or other person who furnished the information,[466] and conduct its own "reasonable reinvestigation" to determine the accuracy or completeness of its reporting.[467] The CRA must correct information that is not verified.[468] In practice, this right can sometimes be difficult to exercise, and is the subject of vigorous litigation by CRAs.

The consumer's right to dispute information contained in a consumer report is an important safeguard necessary to ensure accuracy.[469] The legislative history rightly characterizes the dispute and correction process as "the heart of . . . efforts to ensure the ultimate accuracy of consumer report."[470]

Despite this, CRAs have little incentive to accommodate consumers because the CRAs' customers are their subscribers, rather than the consumers. Accordingly, CRAs are motivated to over-include items at the expense of accuracy. That is, a CRA will report items in its database that may, but may not, pertain to a consumer. The result will be that CRAs may report information that does not quite match the identifying information submitted with a request, i.e., information that is only a rough fit. This "over inclusion" of data may be justified absent notice to the CRA of its unreliability.[471] However, after a consumer dispute is made, a default to over-inclusion is improper.[472]

Consumers will frequently learn of their right to dispute inaccurate information from the Summary of Consumer Rights form drafted by the Federal Trade Commission.[473] CRAs must provide consumers with the Summary of Consumer Rights whenever consumers request a copy of their report. This form disclosure summarizes major rights consumers have under the FCRA, including the right to request a reinvestigation.

On the other hand, the FCRA does not explicitly require a CRA to inform the consumer of the right to dispute information in the consumer's file, and of the corresponding CRA duty to reinvestigate. Courts deciding cases involving an analogous provision[474] hold that the CRA has no affirmative duty to disclose to consumers their rights under the federal Act. Some state statutes, however, do impose this duty.[475]

This section discusses the CRA reinvestigation process. The consumer's request triggers the CRA reinvestigation.[476] While no special language is required to make the request, some care should be taken to appropriately identify which information is being disputed. A request which fails to provide sufficient information or is otherwise deemed to be frivolous will not lead to a reinvestigation.[477]

The CRA may avoid conducting a reinvestigation by simply deleting the disputed information.[478] Otherwise, an investigation to determine the accuracy of the disputed item is required.[479] Moreover, the CRA must involve the creditor or other party who furnished the disputed information in the reinvestigation process.[480] The whole reinvestigation will normally be over within thirty days.[481] If the result of the reinvestigation is inadequate, follow-up letters pointing out precisely what the CRA has done wrong help to set the stage for a strong legal claim for damages and help to create a claim that the failure to adequately reinvestigate was knowing or willful.[482]

Despite the acknowledged importance of the FCRA reinvestigation procedures, the current dispute process is not reliably effective. One study found that ninety-four percent of consumer complaints concerning consumer reporting involved uncorrected errors in reports, and the average consumer had already contacted the CRA over three times—

---

464 Henson v. CSC Credit Servs., 29 F.3d 280 (7th Cir. 1994).
465 15 U.S.C. § 1681i(a)(4).
466 15 U.S.C. § 1681i(a)(2).
467 15 U.S.C. § 1681i(a)(1)(A).
468 15 U.S.C. § 1681i(a)(5).
469 Equifax, Inc., 96 F.T.C. 1045, 1065 (1980), rev'd in part on other grounds, 678 F.2d 1047 (11th Cir. 1982). Note the comments of Senator Proxmire when the legislation was introduced in the Senate:

> It would be unrealistic to expect credit reporting agencies to be absolutely correct on every single case. But it seems to me that consumers affected by an adverse rating do have a right to present their side of the story and to have inaccurate information expunged from their file. Considering the growing importance of credit in our economy, the right to fair credit reporting is becoming more and more essential. We certainly would not tolerate a Government agency depriving a citizen of his livelihood or freedom on the basis of unsubstantiated gossip without an opportunity to present his case. And yet this is entirely possible on the part of a credit reporting agency.

115 Cong. Rec. 2412 (1969).
470 Committee Report accompanying S.650, S. Rep. No. 185, 104th Cong. 1st Sess., at 43 (Dec. 14, 1995).
471 Crabill v. Trans Union L.L.C., 259 F.3d 662 (7th Cir. 2001); Henson v. CSC Credit Servs., 29 F.3d 280 (7th Cir. 1994); Apodaca v. Discover Fin. Servs., 417 F. Supp. 2d 1220 (D.N.M. 2006).
472 Cushman v. Trans Union Corp., 115 F.3d 220 (3d Cir. 1997);

Henson v. CSC Credit Servs., 29 F.3d 280 (7th Cir. 1994); Apodaca v. Discover Fin. Servs., 417 F. Supp. 2d 1220 (D.N.M. 2006).
473 See § 8.2.2, infra.
474 15 U.S.C. § 1681i(b) (permitting consumer to file statement of dispute). See § 4.8.1, infra.
475 See, e.g., Mass. Gen. Laws Ann. ch. 93, § 56.
476 See § 4.5.2, infra.
477 See § 4.5.2.4, infra.
478 See § 4.5.2.1, infra.
479 See id.
480 See § 4.5.4, infra.
481 See § 4.5.5, infra.
482 See § 11.12.1.2, infra.

and waited without results for averages of between twenty-three to thirty-one weeks—before complaining to the FTC.[483]

4.5.2 The Consumer's Request for a Reinvestigation

4.5.2.1 When a Consumer Reporting Agency Must Reinvestigate

If a consumer conveys to the CRA a dispute over the completeness or accuracy of any item of information in the consumer's file,[484] the CRA must delete the disputed information[485] or conduct a reinvestigation.[486] The CRA cannot charge the consumer for the reinvestigation.[487] The obligation to reinvestigate is not contingent upon the consumer having been denied credit, employment, or other benefits, having requested a copy of the consumer report, or having asserted any other rights under the FCRA.[488] The CRA also cannot refuse a reinvestigation just because consumers say they will conduct their own investigation or just because consumers threaten to sue.[489]

A CRA may not impose unreasonable preconditions on the consumer before starting a reinvestigation. For example, the refusal to reinvestigate disputed information unless the consumer signs a form authorizing the CRA to obtain information from creditors, medical practitioners, employers, and the like, violates the FCRA.[490] The consumer's attorney should carefully examine any forms that the consumer is required to complete. Although the CRA has a legitimate interest in collecting information for its files, this cannot be a prerequisite to its obligation to reinvestigate disputed information.

A consumer's lack of precision as to the item being disputed is usually not a sufficient reason to refuse to reinvestigate.[491] But if the consumer does not provide a clear statement that the accuracy or completeness of specific information is "disputed" or "challenged," the consumer's statement may not be construed as an exercise of rights under the Act.

For example, the FTC Staff Commentary states that a consumer's mere explanation of the reason a debt was not paid does not constitute a dispute and does not require the CRA to reinvestigate.[492] Similarly, the FTC Staff Commentary takes the position that a consumer's request to add new lines of information about credit accounts not already included in the file is not a request to reinvestigate the existing account information.[493]

A CRA must reinvestigate if the consumer claims that a debt has subsequently been paid, or that an unpaid judgment has been satisfied.[494] If a file reflects a debt discharged in bankruptcy, the CRA must reinvestigate if the consumer alleges that the discharged debt has been reaffirmed or paid.[495] But a consumer's dispute that she had never filed bankruptcy, without disclosing that her husband had mis-

---

483 U.S. Public Interest Research Group, Credit Bureaus: Public Enemy #1 at the FTC (Oct. 1993).
484 See § 2.3.1.2, *supra* for a discussion of a consumer's "file."
485 See § 4.5.2.1, *infra*.
486 15 U.S.C. § 1681i(a); FTC Official Staff Commentary § 611 item 5, *reprinted at* Appx. D, *infra*. *See also* Dynes v. TRW Credit Data, 652 F.2d 35 (9th Cir. 1981); Collins v. Retail Credit Co., 410 F. Supp. 924 (E.D. Mich. 1976) (CRA refused to reinvestigate); Millstone v. O'Hanlon Reports, 383 F. Supp. 269 (E.D. Mo. 1974), *aff'd*, 528 F.2d 829 (8th Cir. 1976); Peeler, FTC Informal Staff Opinion Letter (Mar. 22, 1977), *reprinted on the CD-Rom accompanying this manual*; Peeler, FTC Informal Staff Opinion Letter (Aug. 23, 1976), *reprinted on the CD-Rom accompanying this manual* (CRA cannot make update of file contingent upon paid file disclosure under §§ 609 and 610); Peeler, FTC Informal Staff Opinion Letter (Mar. 8, 1976), *reprinted on the CD-Rom accompanying this manual*; Feldman, FTC Informal Staff Opinion Letter (Aug. 30, 1974), *reprinted on the CD-Rom accompanying this manual*; Dea, FTC Informal Staff Opinion Letter (July 19, 1974), *reprinted on the CD-Rom accompanying this manual*.
487 FTC Official Staff Commentary § 612 item 2, *reprinted at* Appx. D, *infra*.
488 Yolder v. Credit Bureau of Montgomery, L.L.C., 131 F. Supp. 2d 1275 (M.D. Ala. 2001) (insurer's oral dispute notice obligated CRA to supply verification request form). *See* FTC Official Staff Commentary § 611 item 9, *reprinted at* Appx. D, *infra*.
489 *In re* Equifax, Inc., 96 F.T.C. 1045 (1980), *rev'd in part on other grounds*, 678 F.2d 1047 (11th Cir. 1982).
490 Cisneros v. U.D. Registry, 39 Cal. App. 4th 548 (1995). *See also In re* Equifax, Inc., 96 F.T.C. 1045 (1980), *rev'd in part on other grounds*, 678 F.2d 1047 (11th Cir. 1982); Russell, FTC Informal Staff Opinion Letter (Sept. 18, 1973), *reprinted on the CD-Rom accompanying this manual*.
491 *In re* Equifax, Inc., 96 F.T.C. 1045 (1980), *rev'd in part on other grounds*, 678 F.2d 1047 (11th Cir. 1982).
492 FTC Official Staff Commentary § 611 item 4, *reprinted at* Appx. D, *infra*. *See* Yolder v. Credit Bureau of Montgomery, L.L.C., 131 F. Supp. 2d 1275 (M.D. Ala. 2001) (request for copy of report due to alleged fraud does not impose reinvestigation obligation). *See also* Brinckerhoff, FTC Informal Staff Opinion Letter (Jan. 29, 1987), *reprinted on the CD-Rom accompanying this manual*.
493 FTC Official Staff Commentary § 611 item 3, *reprinted at* Appx. D, *infra*. *See also* Brinckerhoff, FTC Informal Staff Opinion Letter (July 30, 1985), *reprinted on the CD-Rom accompanying this manual*. If a consumer provides additional information for an incomplete file, the CRA must include the additional relevant information to avoid potential liability, even if the specific accuracy of currently filed information is not challenged. Feldman, FTC Informal Staff Opinion Letter (Aug. 30, 1974), *reprinted on the CD-Rom accompanying this manual*. *See also* Feldman, FTC Informal Staff Opinion Letter (May 31, 1974), *reprinted on the CD-Rom accompanying this manual* (serious question exists whether CRA may continue to report incomplete if consumer supplies additional information).
494 FTC Official Staff Commentary § 611 item 5, *reprinted at* Appx. D, *infra*.
495 *Id.*

takenly listed the accounts in his bankruptcy, was inadequate to obligate the CRA to look behind the public records.[496]

A consumer's dispute will be most effective if it includes the following information about the consumer:

(1) Full name (including Jr., Sr., or the like);
(2) Current address and other addresses held within the previous two years;
(3) Date of birth;
(4) Telephone number;
(5) Social Security number;
(6) The name of the consumer's spouse, if married;
(7) Current employment information;
(8) A clear description of the item in the consumer report that the consumer is disputing, along with a copy of the consumer report on which the disputed item has been circled;
(9) An explanation of why the consumer is disputing the information (e.g., "This account does not belong to me"); and
(10) A request that the CRA delete or correct the information.

It is also important to include copies of any documentary evidence supporting the consumer's dispute, because this may shorten the investigation period and ensure that the particular errors are specifically examined.[497]

CRAs will often refuse to accept a consumer's dispute or conduct a reinvestigation unless the consumer's Social Security number is provided. The CRAs argue that such policy is justified because, without a Social Security number, the consumer has not provided "sufficient information" to investigate the dispute because the CRA cannot identify the proper consumer file.[498] However, there is no such requirement in the statute.[499] In fact, the CRAs regularly provide consumer reports to their subscribers without an identified Social Security number. The nationwide CRAs have also acknowledged their ability to identify and produce a consumer file without this identifier.[500] However, while a consumer's dispute without a Social Security number should not be rejected, a CRA that refuses to conduct a reinvestigation will be in a more defensible position if the consumer provides an incorrect identifier.[501]

4.5.2.2 The Consumer Must Make the Request to the Consumer Reporting Agency

In general, it is safest if the consumer directly sends the dispute and requests the reinvestigation from the CRA. The FTC Staff Commentary states that the CRA need not reinvestigate where a dispute is raised by a third party because the statute specifies that the file is disputed "by the consumer."[502] While an attorney representing a consumer should certainly be able to make the request for the consumer,[503] it is safest if the consumer actually signs the letter because of FTC staff opinion letters that hold that the attorney cannot make the request.[504]

Nationwide CRAs handle consumer disputes or requests for reinvestigation on attorney letterhead differently than disputes in the consumer's name. Each of the "Big Three" CRAs maintains a department to handle escalated or special disputes. Attorney letters are often handled in this fashion. Practitioners also report that each CRA handles what are deemed "VIP" disputes—disputes from a celebrity, industry employee, media source or politician—through a separate department. Sending an attorney letter has the advantage of better ensuring that a person will actually review and provide more personalized attention to the dispute. However, the disadvantage to such handling occurs when the dispute is then handled as if it possibly emanates from a credit repair organization. When it is coded by the CRA in such fashion, the details of the consumer's dispute are rarely conveyed to the information furnisher. Instead, the CRA may then request the furnisher to generally "verify all information."

The CRA is not required to respond to a dispute that is not conveyed directly to the CRA, but instead is conveyed to the source of the disputed information (such as the creditor) or to some other party.[505] That is, if the consumer wants the CRA to reinvestigate, the consumer must notify the CRA, and not solely the creditor or other related party.[506]

However, there are several exceptions to the requirement that the consumer directly notify the CRA of a dispute. First, a CRA that receives a consumer's complaint of identity theft

---

496 Kettler v. CSC Credit Serv., Inc., 2003 WL 21975919 (D. Minn. Aug. 12, 2003).
497 *See* FTC Official Staff Commentary § 611 item 10, *reprinted at* Appx. D, *infra*; § 4.5.2.5, *infra*.
498 15 U.S.C. § 1681i(a)(3)(A).
499 Menton v. Experian, 2003 WL 941388 (S.D.N.Y. Mar. 6, 2003).
500 *Id.*; Anderson v. Trans Union, 405 F. Supp. 2d 977 (W.D. Wis. 2005).
501 *Id.*

502 *Id.*
503 Milbauer v. TRW, Inc., 707 F. Supp. 92, 94 (E.D.N.Y. 1989); Pinner v. Schmidt, 617 F. Supp. 342 (E.D La. 1985) ("It is inconceivable to the Court that an attorney could not represent a consumer in this regard"), *aff'd in part and rev'd in part on other grounds*, 805 F.2d 1258 (5th Cir. 1986); Cisneros v. U.D. Registry, 39 Cal. App. 4th 548 (1995).
504 *See* Brinckerhoff, FTC Informal Staff Opinion Letters (Apr. 19, 1989) (Sept. 15, 1988) (two letters of same date), and (Aug. 4, 1987), *reprinted on the CD-Rom accompanying this manual. Cf.* Fitzpatrick, FTC Informal Staff Opinion Letter (Dec. 28, 1988), *reprinted on the CD-Rom accompanying this manual.*
505 FTC Official Staff Commentary § 611 item 7, *reprinted at* Appx. D, *infra*.
506 15 U.S.C. § 1681i(a)(1)(A).

is required to forward it to all other nationwide CRAs.[507] Second, when the FTC receives a consumer complaint that information in a credit file remains inaccurate or incomplete, it is obligated to forward the complaint to the respective CRA.[508] The CRAs are required to use reasonable procedures to review the consumer's complaint and file; the CRAs are also required to ensure that they have fully complied with the FCRA, including its accuracy and reinvestigation provisions.[509] Finally, the CRA might also receive notice of a consumer's dispute after an information furnisher makes a correction to its reporting, after receiving a dispute from another CRA.[510]

These indirect contacts may not expressly constitute a request for reinvestigation. However, even if a consumer has not properly triggered the FCRA's reinvestigation procedure, the CRA will still have been put on notice as to problems within the consumer's file. A CRA has a duty to correct errors that come to its attention,[511] even if someone other than the consumer brings it to their attention, or even if the consumer brings it to the attention of a third party who then passes the information on to the CRA.

4.5.2.3 Resellers and Affiliates

There are two categories of CRAs for which the FCRA reinvestigation requirements vary. The first category is a "reseller," which is a CRA that purchases, often combines and then resells a consumer's file from another CRA and does not itself maintain an independent database.[512] The most prominent resellers are CRAs that purchase and combine a consumer's credit reports from each of the "Big Three" CRAs into one "tri-merge report." These are most often used for mortgage credit.

The FTC has commented on the difficulties consumers may face when disputing information directly to the reseller and not the "Big Three" nationwide CRAs, noting that resellers have no relationship to the creditors and therefore may be ignored when attempting to reinvestigate a consumer's dispute.[513] Thus, the Fair and Accurate Credit Transactions Act of 2003 (FACTA) amendments to the FCRA specifically imposed a different set of reinvestigation duties on resellers.[514]

The underlying data in the reseller's report is obtained from another CRA. Accordingly, if there is an inaccuracy in this underlying data, the reseller may not have the means or furnisher relationship to conduct its own investigation. Thus, resellers are exempt from the general reinvestigation requirement by which a consumer disputes the underlying data in their file at the nationwide CRA.[515]

In some instances, the reseller itself may be responsible for the inaccuracy or error in the consumer's report. A reseller receives the underlying credit data from each nationwide CRA in code. Thereafter, it must translate and reformat the underlying data into a report format useful for its customer. In this process, it may create its own inaccuracy or, by omission of underlying information, incompleteness. When a consumer disputes inaccurate or incomplete information directly to a reseller, it must determine within five days whether it is responsible for the inaccuracy or incompleteness.[516] If the reseller determines that the information is incomplete or inaccurate as a result of the reseller's act or omission, the reseller must correct or delete the information within twenty days.[517]

If, however, the reseller does not find that the alleged inaccuracy resulted from the reseller's act or omission, the reseller must notify the CRA from whom the reseller obtained the information, and that CRA must then reinvestigate the information.[518] Once notified, the providing CRA must reinvestigate the alleged inaccuracy[519] and then report the results of its reinvestigation back to the reseller, who must then reconvey the results back to the consumer.[520] This provision substitutes the reseller as the consumer's proxy for purposes of the providing CRA's reinvestigation responsibilities. Although the reseller's reinvestigation duties are unique, such a CRA is not otherwise exempt from the FCRA's other accuracy provisions.[521]

The second category of CRAs that presents a unique circumstance are affiliates of the nationwide CRAs. While most consumer credit reports are prepared and furnished by the "Big Three" CRAs, in some parts of the country the data files of these CRAs are technically "owned" by an affiliate CRA. The original business model for the current "Big Three" CRAs involved the creation and maintenance of a

---

507 15 U.S.C. § 1681s(f)(1). *See* § 9.2.2, *infra*.
508 15 U.S.C. § 1681i(e)(1).
509 15 U.S.C. § 1681i(e)(3)(A).
510 15 U.S.C. § 1681s-2(b)(1)(D).
511 FTC Official Staff Commentary § 611 item 7, *reprinted at* Appx. D, *infra*. *See also* 15 U.S.C. § 1681e(b); § 4.4, *supra*.
512 The FCRA defines a reseller to be a CRA that meets the following criteria:

> (1) assembles and merges information contained in the database of another consumer reporting agency or multiple consumer reporting agencies concerning any consumer for purposes of furnishing such information to any third party, to the extent of such activities; and (2) does not maintain a database of the assembled or merged information from which new consumer reports are produced.

15 U.S.C. § 1681a(u). *See also* § 2.6.3, *supra*.

513 *See Testimony of Timothy J. Muris, Chairman, Federal Trade Commission, Before the Senate Banking Committee* (July 10, 2003).
514 Pub. L. No. 108-159, § 316 (2003).
515 15 U.S.C. § 1681i(f)(1).
516 15 U.S.C. § 1681i(f)(2).
517 15 U.S.C. § 1681i(f); 16 C.F.R. § 602.1(c)(3)(xviii).
518 15 U.S.C. § 1681i(f); 16 C.F.R. § 602.1(c)(3)(xviii).
519 15 U.S.C. § 1681i(a); 16 C.F.R. § 602.1(c)(3)(xvii).
520 15 U.S.C. § 1681i(f).
521 *See* § 2.6.3.7, *supra*.

national credit database and the wholesale leasing of that database to geographically defined affiliates. Over the last decade, the nationwide CRAs have steadily consolidated their businesses and have either purchased or severed their relationships with the regional affiliates. Now, if a creditor wishes to purchase a TransUnion consumer report regarding a Connecticut consumer, it will purchase that report directly from TransUnion instead of indirectly through a Connecticut affiliate company.

However, the nationwide CRAs have not severed all of their affiliate relationships. Equifax, more than any other, has retained some territorial affiliates. For example, while Equifax maintains the credit files on every consumer nationally, regardless of their domicile, it contractually does not "own" the credit files for consumers residing in some states, such as Texas, Indiana, Wisconsin or Tennessee. The credit files of consumers residing in the first three of these states are technically owned by Computer Sciences Corporation (CSC) and files for consumers residing in Tennessee are owned by ChoiceData. The credit reports for consumers in an affiliate state will look in every way like a report of the nationwide CRA, except for their branding.

Confusion can then arise when a consumer residing in an affiliate territory attempts to dispute information in their credit file. If the consumer directed their dispute or request for reinvestigation to Equifax, Equifax at one point refused to conduct the reinvestigation, and instead forwarded the dispute to its respective affiliate to do so. Neither the nationwide CRA nor its affiliate is a reseller because each "owns" and maintains a credit database.[522]

Accordingly, neither is exempt from the obligations to perform a reinvestigation. Even though the nationwide CRA may not technically "own" a credit file it maintains in its database for a particular state, it is still responsible to perform a reinvestigation of inaccurate information in that database if requested by a consumer.[523] However, if the consumer does not provide the dispute directly to the nationwide CRA and sends it only to the affiliate, only the affiliate is required to perform the reinvestigation.[524]

4.5.2.4 Frivolous or Irrelevant Disputes

The FCRA permits a CRA to refuse to delete or reinvestigate disputed information if the CRA "reasonably determines" a dispute is frivolous or irrelevant.[525] The FTC Staff Commentary states that CRAs must assume that a consumer's dispute is bona fide, unless there is evidence to the contrary.[526]

Such evidence may consist of receipt of letters disputing all information in the file without allegations concerning the specific items in the file.[527] Other evidence, according to the FTC Staff Commentary, would be a dispute made by a common format suggesting that a "credit repair" organization or similar entity is counseling consumers to dispute all items in their files, regardless of whether the information is known to be accurate.[528] If a request is from a credit repair organization, instead of the consumer, it is likely the CRA will refuse to reinvestigate because the request did not come from the consumer.[529] Currently, each CRA has established a specific process and dispute code for contacts it believes are sent by a "possible credit clinic." Often, disputes sent on attorney letterhead are handled as credit clinic disputes.

The Internet is filled with "*pro se*" advice and attorney websites which suggest that consumers make frequent and shallow disputes in the hope that the CRA will not timely process them, and thus have to delete the targeted account. Five years ago, this tactic may have had some success; however it is no longer viable. The CRAs have now completed the transition to full-automation, and all ordinary disputes are processed electronically through the e-Oscar system.[530] These "credit repair" type letters—e.g., a dispute which merely states, "This is not my account. Take it off my credit report"—have become virtually the entire focus of the CRA dispute processing system. Much, if not most, of the current reinvestigation process is designed to receive, code and turn around such generic disputes within minutes, if not seconds. The "credit repair" model was an attempt to overload the reinvestigation system, thereby forcing the deletion of the disputed information because of the FCRA's time requirements. However, CRAs can now process disputes almost as quickly as they can open the envelopes in which they arrive.

With respect to "relevancy," the FTC has ruled that a CRA may not properly conclude that a dispute is irrelevant, unless it can conclude that the disputed information is not adverse.[531] If the information may be used as a basis for denying credit, insurance, employment, or other benefits to the consumer, any dispute over the information is relevant.

---

522 15 U.S.C. § 1681a(u).
523 Morris v. Equifax Info. Servs., L.L.C., 457 F.3d 460 (5th Cir. 2006); Gohman v. Equifax Info. Servs., L.L.C., 395 F. Supp. 2d 822 (D. Minn. 2005).
524 Slice v. ChoiceData Consumer Servs., Inc., 2006 WL 686886 (E.D. Tenn. Mar. 16, 2006).
525 15 U.S.C. § 1681i(a)(3).
526 See FTC Official Staff Commentary § 611 item 11, *reprinted at* Appx. D, *infra*.
527 FTC Official Staff Commentary § 611 item 11, *reprinted at* Appx. D, *infra*.
528 *Id*. Regulation of credit repair organizations is discussed at Ch. 15, *infra*.
529 See § 4.5.2.4, *supra*.
530 The e-OSCAR system is the CRA industry's web-based, electronic dispute processing system. The CRA have apparently announced that they will require all furnishers to participate in the e-OSCAR system and will stop accepting paper-based disputes. Federal Trade Commission and Federal Reserve Board, Report to Congress on the Fair Credit Reporting Act Dispute Process (Aug. 2006), *available* at www.ftc.gov/os/comments/fcradispute/P044808fcradisputeprocessreporttocongress.pdf.
531 *In re* Equifax, Inc., 96 F.T.C. 1045 (1980), *rev'd in part on other grounds*, 678 F.2d 1047 (11th Cir. 1982). *See also* Gomon v. TRW, Inc., 34 Cal. Rptr. 2d 256, 28 Cal. App. 4th 1161 (1994).

Among the items in a consumer report file which may be disputed are reports of inquiries by creditors and other users. This information must be included in a CRA's disclosure of the file to the consumer, and may be included in the reports provided to users. Reports of numerous inquiries are commonly the basis for adverse action by creditors and will result in a lower credit score, since it appears that the consumer may be taking on too much credit.[532] Therefore, a CRA must reinvestigate a dispute which provides some basis to believe that an inquiry appearing in a report was not accurate, because, for example, it reflects an inquiry about another person.[533]

A CRA may not refuse to reinvestigate the consumer's dispute on the grounds that it is frivolous "unless it is clearly 'beyond credulity' or made in bad faith."[534] By statute, the consumer's failure to provide sufficient information to investigate the disputed information is sufficient reason for determining that a dispute is frivolous.[535] On the other hand, the presence of contradictory information in the consumer's file does not in and of itself constitute reasonable grounds for believing the dispute is frivolous or irrelevant.[536] That is, the CRA cannot decide that other information in the file will prove the consumer's dispute to be ill-grounded, and thus deny the reinvestigation. But if a consumer admits that public record information has been accurately retrieved, the CRA may be able to treat as frivolous the consumer's challenge that the CRA should never have entered the public record information.[537]

A consumer's repeated request for an investigation, after the CRA has already reinvestigated the same item, may be viewed as frivolous.[538] As a rule, the nationwide CRAs impose a window of six months before they will again process an identical dispute. However, CRA response is inconsistent, sometimes rejecting such disputes and other times processing them. The repeat request is not frivolous if the consumer provides additional evidence that the item is inaccurate or incomplete or alleges changed circumstances.[539] When a CRA adds new information to a file (even as a result of a reinvestigation), the consumer can again dispute the new information, and the CRA must then conduct another reinvestigation.[540]

If a reinvestigation request is deemed frivolous or irrelevant, the CRA must notify the consumer within five business days that such determination has been made, and give the reasons for the determination, and detail what additional information is required to initiate an investigation.[541] The description of the additional required information should be particularized enough to be helpful, but the statute permits a "standardized form describing the general nature of such information."[542] The notice must be made by mail, or, if the consumer authorizes, by any other means available to the CRA. State law in a few states also establishes deadlines for the CRA to inform the consumer of its decision not to reinvestigate.[543]

4.5.2.5 Practical Tips in Making a Dispute

Although not required by the statute,[544] it is safest if the consumer requests the reinvestigation in writing (keeping copies of all correspondence), or follows up a telephone request with a written confirmation. Telephone disputes do not create an adequate record in the event a consumer follows a failed dispute with litigation. In addition, the consumer will not be able to provide documentary support of the dispute by telephone. Furthermore, although the FCRA requires nationwide CRAs to maintain a toll-free number for consumers,[545] telephone access to the CRAs is not always consistent. Equifax, TransUnion and Experian paid a total of $2.5 million to settle charges by the FTC that

---

532 Philbin v. Trans Union Corp., 101 F.3d 957 (3d Cir. 1996); Palmiotto v. Bank of New York, 1989 WL 114156 (N.D.N.Y. 1989). See §§ 12.5.4 and 14.5.2, infra.
533 Grimes, FTC Informal Staff Opinion Letter (Aug. 1, 1994), reprinted on the CD-Rom accompanying this manual.
534 In re Equifax, Inc., 96 F.T.C. 1045 (1980), rev'd in part on other grounds, 678 F.2d 1047 (11th Cir. 1982).
535 15 U.S.C. § 1681i(a)(3)(A).
536 FTC Official Staff Commentary § 611 item 11, reprinted at Appx. D, infra. Prior to 1996, this was also provided by statute.
537 Williams v. Colonial Bank, 826 F. Supp. 415 (M.D. Ala. 1993).
538 FTC Official Staff Commentary § 611 item 11, reprinted at Appx. D, infra. See also Hauser v. Equifax, Inc., 602 F.2d 811 (8th Cir. 1979) (CRA not liable for failing to reinvestigate the disputed portion of the consumer report because CRA had "indirectly reinvestigated" the information when it prepared a subsequent, but undisclosed, report containing an accurate version of the disputed item. It would nonetheless appear that the CRA violated the Act by failing to delete the inaccurate information from the portion of the consumer's file that was disclosed to him).
539 McCelland v. Experian Info. Solutions, Inc., 2006 WL 2191973 (N.D. Ill. July 28, 2006); FTC Official Staff Commentary § 611 item 11, reprinted at Appx. D, infra.
540 Dynes v. TRW Credit Data, 652 F.2d 35 (9th Cir. 1981).
541 15 U.S.C. § 1681i(a)(3)(B) and (C).
542 15 U.S.C. § 1681i(a)(3)(C)(iii).
543 See, e.g. Cal. Civ. Code § 1785.16; Me. Rev. Stat. Ann. tit. 10, § 1317(2) (see also Me. Advisory Rulings of Bureau of Consumer Protection). See Appx. H, infra. See also Mass. Gen. Laws ch. 93, § 58; Wash. Rev. Code § 19.182.090. State laws on this point are preempted unless in effect on September 30, 1996. See § 10.7, infra.
544 Cf. Brady v. The Credit Recovery Co., 160 F.3d 64 (1st Cir. 1998) (federal Fair Debt Collection Practices Act, analogous to the FCRA, does not require consumer to notify debt collector in writing that the consumer disputes the debt to prevent collector from reporting to CRAs). An FTC report states that the CDIA reports 22% of consumer disputes to CRAs are submitted by telephone. Federal Trade Commission and Federal Reserve Board, Report to Congress on the Fair Credit Reporting Act Dispute Process (Aug. 2006), available at www.ftc.gov/os/comments/fcradispute/P044808fcradisputeprocessreporttocongress.pdf.
545 15 U.S.C. § 1681g(c)(1)(B).

they failed to meet the Act's requirement that the personnel be accessible to consumers during normal business hours.[546]

Internet disputes should also be avoided for some of the same reasons. When a consumer makes a dispute through a CRA website, the consumers are confined to a "check-box" dispute form, and cannot forward documentary support for their claim or conveniently copy the dispute to the information furnisher. It is especially ironic that CRA defenses are often premised on the lack of detail in a dispute when the Internet dispute process imposed by them prevents anything more.

When consumers request copies of their consumer reports from the "Big Three" major nationwide credit bureaus, Experian, TransUnion, and Equifax, they will receive a dispute form which the "Big Three" encourage consumers to use for making disputes. These forms attempt to pigeon hole the dispute into one of several general types, and do not facilitate a detailed consumer dispute. As with the Internet disputes, these forms provide only a list of "check box" dispute choices, and appear to discourage a more substantive dispute. Consumers using such forms for a dispute should supplement it with additional written details and documentary support.

As discussed below, a consumer's dispute may have to travel literally across the world and back before a response is rendered. There is thus at least a modest possibility that the dispute may be lost in the process and never reinvestigated. CRAs often deny receiving notices of disputes, so it is even advisable to send the request by certified mail, return receipt requested.[547] Even though the consumer retains a mailing presumption, this may still leave her with a marginal claim. If the CRA can claim that it never received the dispute, it will argue that it merely made a mistake, rather that be forced to defend a claim that its procedures themselves are inadequate.

In many cases, a request for reinvestigation is just the beginning of a protracted battle with the CRA that may ignore correspondence or fail to follow up as promised. Thus it is good practice for the consumer to establish a file of all correspondence sent to and received from the CRA, and to have proof that the CRA has received the consumer's correspondence.

Consumers should also directly notify the creditor or other furnisher of the disputed information at the same time, if not before.[548] Furnishers must participate in the CRA reinvestigation procedures and even conduct their own reinvestigation.[549] A information furnisher's investigation obligation arises when it receives the consumer's dispute indirectly through the CRA.[550] However, furnishers often claim that they did not receive adequate notice of the consumer's dispute from the CRA.

This problem is rooted in the fundamental nature of the credit industry's Automated Consumer Dispute Verification (ACDV) system. If the consumer does not make her dispute "indirectly" through the CRA, but instead sends it directly to the furnisher, she has no private right of action under the FCRA.[551] However, if the consumer sends a detailed, and well-documented, dispute directly to the CRA, she has little control over what information the CRA will actually forward to the furnisher. Under the "Big Three's" typical reinvestigation procedures, the consumer's dispute will be reduced to a one page, electronic ACDV message with the underlying dispute reduced to a generic two-digit dispute code (e.g. "01 not his/hers") and in some circumstances, a short, one-line paraphrase of some aspect of the dispute under the heading "FCRA Relevant Information" (e.g., "Consumer states belongs to husband only").[552] It will therefore be prudent to also directly notify furnishers of the dispute, to forestall the arguments that they did not receive adequate notice of the consumer's dispute from the ACDV.[553]

An additional, major problem in correcting consumer report errors occurs because the consumer's file at each CRA is independent of that at the other CRAs. Most consumer disputes and corrections made as a result are not reported between competing bureaus.[554] Therefore, even though a consumer has corrected a file at one CRA, if the incorrect information was furnished to other CRAs, the incorrect information will need to be corrected at these other CRAs as well. Unfortunately, a consumer may not realize this until an application for credit, employment, insurance, or housing is denied again.

To reduce the chance of an error remaining at other CRAs, at a minimum a consumer should try to correct inaccurate or incomplete items in their file at all of the "Big Three" nationwide CRAs—Experian, TransUnion and

---

546 The settlement agreements are reprinted on the CD-Rom accompanying this manual. The FTC charged that a substantial number of consumers encountered a busy signal or a message indicating the consumer must call back because all representatives were busy. The consent decrees contained specific injunctive provisions requiring the CRAs to maintain a blocked call rate of no greater than 10% and an average hold time of no greater than three minutes, thirty seconds.

547 Sampson v. Equifax Info. Servs., 2005 WL 2095092 (S.D. Ga. Aug. 29, 2005).

548 *See* Ch. 6, *infra*.

549 15 U.S.C. § 1681s-2b. *See* Ch. 6, *infra*.

550 *See* § 6.10, *infra*.

551 *See* § 6.5.2, *infra*; 15 U.S.C. § 1681s-2(c).

552 § 4.5.6, *infra*. A printout of an ACDV is reproduced at Appx. I.3, *infra*.

553 Westra v. Credit Control of Pinellas, 409 F.3d 825 (7th Cir. 2005); Malm v. Household Bank, N.A., 2004 U.S. Dist. LEXIS 12981 (D. Minn. July 7, 2004) (No. 03-4340).

554 *See also* 15 U.S.C. § 1681s-2(b)(1)(D) (if information furnisher's "investigation finds that the information is incomplete or inaccurate, report those results to all other consumer reporting agencies to which the person furnished the information and that compile and maintain files on consumers on a nationwide basis."). *But see* 15 U.S.C. § 1681s(f) (requiring CRAs to coordinate referral of consumer disputes of identity theft).

Equifax. A consumer who is aware of erroneous or incomplete information at one of the "Big Three" should request reports from the other two to help determine whether additional notices of dispute should be filed with them as well. Of course, even this will not correct items on the reports of CRAs which are not affiliated with the "Big Three" CRAs. Nor will it prevent different (or the same) inaccurate information being added back into the consumer's file after the initial correction.[555]

A more compelling need to contact more than one CRA can arise when the consumer is informed by a creditor (or other person) that adverse action was based on a consumer report received from a CRA which is not one of the "Big Three," such as a reseller.[556] While it is important to dispute the accuracy of information with the reseller who supplied it to the creditor, and while special rules require resellers to handle or forward the dispute,[557] a consumer should also consider going straight to the "Big Three."

For practitioners familiar with other federal consumer laws such as the Fair Debt Collection Practices Act or state UDAP statutes, there may be a temptation to view the dispute requirement merely as a technical threshold, used simply to trigger liability. This may tempt the advocate to send a pro forma dispute, without careful consideration. However, the FCRA is different because it does not provide for strict liability. Throughout the statute, the CRA's conduct is evaluated for its reasonableness. While sending a dispute is a condition precedent for liability, it is not, in and of itself, the only condition necessary to trigger liability. The dispute also has to fairly and adequately advise the CRA and the furnisher so that a "reasonable" person in their shoes could conduct a meaningful investigation.

Thus, the dispute notice should be clear, complete, and unambiguous. Vague dispute letters that fail to provide underlying details as to an identity theft or an ownership dispute may be inadequate to impose liability.[558] In addition to adequately identifying the consumer, the dispute notice should properly and fully identify the disputed information, and should explain why it is disputed. The CRAs will often take consumer disputes literally, and do nothing more than is expressly requested. If the consumer states, "I have never had a MBNA credit card, so delete MBNA account #1234," the CRA will only address that account. This is a problem when furnishers change account numbers after an initial dispute is made, leaving new and multiple tradelines reported in place of only a single account. The CRA then will ignore these additional tradelines, despite the fact they are clearly derived from the former, because these tradelines are not referenced in the dispute letter. Alternatively, the consumer may not know the actual account number that is used in her file at the CRA, since it could be different than the one provided in her bill or periodic statement.

To prevent these problems, a reinvestigation request should describe the full range of accounts the dispute covers. For example, a consumer could state, "I have never had a MBNA credit card. Any MBNA account in my credit file is not mine and should be deleted. This includes account number 1234, as well as any other account you may be reporting, as well as any account that may be reported by any debt collector who is reporting a debt originating from a MBNA account." For First USA accounts, which became Bank One and then Chase accounts, a consumer could state, "I am disputing the First USA account #2345. It may also be reported as a Bank One or a J.P. Morgan Chase account."

Having the consumer sign the dispute under oath will convert it into an affidavit, with several resulting benefits. This should provide greater credibility to the consumer's complaint, especially in contrast to the automated, unsworn response of a furnisher. This also advances a claim against the CRA that it failed to forward "all relevant information" to the information furnisher.[559] Furnishers may have policies which give greater weight to consumer affidavits and thereby more readily accept the consumer's version of the dispute and resolve it in their favor.

A consumer's request for reinvestigation should also include all documentary evidence and other information that supports the dispute. A consumer's word alone may not be sufficient.[560] While it is certainly not a threshold liability requirement, a consumer may choose to suggest what the CRA could do to best accomplish the reinvestigation.[561]

If the creditor has provided a letter or statement confirming its understanding that the reported information was inaccurate, the letter should be provided with the dispute to the CRA. In a dispute over ownership of an account, a consumer should request that the CRA obtain a copy of the underlying application or contract from the furnisher, and should provide several handwriting samples, such as copies of cancelled checks, a driver's license or backs of credit cards which include her signature.

CRAs may claim that it would be unreasonable to expect them to pay for a handwriting analysis.[562] To avoid this, the consumer could offer to pay this expense. Consumers can also provide the name and contact information of third-party witnesses who support their disputes. For example, if a consumer has been in direct contact with a furnisher repre-

---

555 See § 4.7, supra.
556 See §§ 2.6.3, 4.5.2.3, supra.
557 See id.
558 Perry v. Experian Info. Solutions, Inc., 2005 WL 2861078 (N.D. Ill. Oct. 28, 2005) ("Perry's terse dispute letters provided no detailed information regarding the alleged identity theft."); McCelland v. Experian Info. Solutions, Inc., 2006 WL 2191973 (N.D. Ill. July 28, 2006).
559 15 U.S.C. § 1681i(a)(2)(A).
560 Morris v. Trans Union, L.L.C., 420 F. Supp. 733 (S.D. Tex. 2006).
561 Perry v. Experian Info. Solutions, Inc., 2005 WL 2861078 (N.D. Ill. Oct. 28, 2005).
562 Bagby v. Experian Info. Solutions, Inc., 162 Fed. Appx. 600, 2006 WL 14580 (7th Cir. 2006) (unreported).

sentative who was helpful and agreed with her position, the dispute letter could provide the name and address of that person, and a request that the CRA manually send the dispute directly to that person, rather than through e-Oscar. If the dispute concerns a public record, a request for reinvestigation could include the name and telephone number of the court clerk. If there was prior litigation involved, the dispute letter could include the name and telephone number of the attorney who previously represented the creditor.

A dispute letter should also include any available information questioning the accuracy of the furnisher's information in other contexts, in order to rebut any claim that the furnisher's reporting could be considered presumptively accurate.[563] There are no limitations as to the nature of such additional information. It could include copies of relevant court opinions against the furnisher in the credit reporting contexts, or similar complaints by other consumers against that furnisher. A consumer could even include press clippings or excerpts from this manual that referenced a particular furnisher.

4.5.3 Nature of the Reinvestigation

4.5.3.1 Introduction

If a consumer disputes the accuracy of information in a consumer report, the CRA normally must conduct an investigation. The investigation is called a reinvestigation, presumably because the CRA initially added to its files the item of disputed information only after employing reasonable procedures to ensure maximum possible accuracy in the first place.[564] The CRA may avoid a reinvestigation by simply deleting the disputed information from its reports.[565]

An "investigation" is defined in the dictionary as a "detailed inquiry or systematic examination."[566] The plain meaning of "investigation" clearly requires some degree of careful inquiry.[567] When a reinvestigation is conducted, the CRA must investigate the underlying facts to determine whether the disputed information is accurate.[568] Perhaps most importantly, the reinvestigation must involve the person who furnished the disputed information to the CRA in the first place, and that person is required to conduct its own reinvestigation.[569] Some question exists about just what standards of reinvestigation apply.[570]

4.5.3.2 Heightened Standard and Balancing Test

Underlying the "reasonableness" of a CRA's compliance with its FCRA "accuracy" duties is a two step balancing test used expressly or implicitly by nearly every court to apply the statute. The balancing test was formulated by the Seventh Circuit in *Henson v. CSC Credit Services*:

> Whether the credit reporting agency has a duty to go beyond the original source will depend, in part, on whether the consumer has alerted the reporting agency to the possibility that the source may be unreliable or the reporting agency itself knows or should know that the source is unreliable. The credit reporting agency's duty will also depend on the cost of verifying the accuracy of the source versus the possible harm inaccurately reported information may cause the consumer.[571]

These two factors—the degree to which the CRA has been alerted as to the unreliability of the information furnisher and the cost of verifying the inaccuracy against its possible harm to the consumer—provide the framework for nearly all judicial analysis applying the CRA's accuracy obligation, and especially interpretations of the FCRA's reinvestigation provisions.[572] Both are integrated. The application of these factors was considered at § 7.2, *supra*, and will also be considered below.

A CRA may be entitled to initially rely on an information furnisher because of the inordinate costs in independently verifying a nearly infinite pool of data.[573] However, when a consumer makes a dispute to the CRA, the reasonableness of the CRA's conduct is measured against a heightened standard and the burden shifts to the CRA.[574]

---

563 *Id.*; Morris v. Trans Union, L.L.C., 420 F. Supp. 733 (S.D. Tex. 2006); Benson v. Trans Union, L.L.C., 387 F. Supp. 2d 834 (N.D. Ill. 2006).
564 *See* § 4.4.5, *infra*.
565 *See* § 4.5.2.1, *supra*.
566 Am. Heritage Dictionary 920 (4th ed. 2000). *See* Webster's Third New Int'l Dictionary 1189 (1981) (defining "investigation" as "a searching inquiry").
567 Johnson v. MBNA America Bank, N.A., 357 F.3d 426, 430 (4th Cir. 2004).
568 *See* § 4.5.3.3, *infra*.
569 *See* § 4.5.4, *infra*.
570 *See* § 4.5.3.3, *infra*.
571 29 F.3d 280 (7th Cir. 1994).
572 *See, e.g.*, Bagby v. Experian Info. Solutions, Inc., 162 Fed. Appx. 600, 2006 WL 14580 (7th Cir. 2006) (unreported); Cushman v. Trans Union Corp., 115 F.3d 220 (3d Cir. 1997); Henson v. CSC Credit Servs., 29 F.3d 280 (7th Cir. 1994); Apodaca v. Discover Fin. Servs., 417 F. Supp. 2d 1220 (D.N.M. 2006); Perry v. Experian Info. Solutions, Inc., 2005 WL 2861078 (N.D. Ill. Oct. 28, 2005); Sampson v. Equifax Info. Servs., 2005 WL 2095092 (S.D. Ga. Aug. 29, 2005); Campbell v. Chase Manhattan Bank, USA, N.A., 2005 WL 1514221 (D.N.J. June 27, 2005); Schmitt v. Chase Manhattan Bank, N.A., 2005 WL 2030483 (D. Minn. Aug. 23, 2005).
573 Henson v. CSC Credit Servs., 29 F.3d 280 (7th Cir. 1994).
574 Cushman v. Trans Union Corp., 115 F.3d 220 (3d Cir. 1997).

4.5.3.3 Nature of the Required Reinvestigation

A reinvestigation must be a good faith effort to determine the accuracy of the disputed item.[575] The CRA must reinvestigate, and cannot merely tell users that the consumer disputes the report.[576] A reinvestigation claim is properly raised when a consumer's credit file "contains a factual deficiency or error that could have been remedied by uncovering additional facts that provide a more accurate representation about a particular entry."[577]

Before the 2003 FACTA amendments to the FCRA, the Act did not specify a standard by which the CRA must reinvestigate. The FACTA amendments clarified that the reinvestigation must be "reasonable."[578] This addition was consistent with judicial interpretations of the pre-amendment provision.[579]

More is usually required than simply confirming that the disputed information was in fact reported as it was received from the original source.[580] The degree to which a CRA must investigate beyond reliance upon its original source will vary in direct correlation to the consumer's challenge of the reliability of that source. If a consumer creates a sufficient challenge to the reliability of its source, the CRA must conduct a full investigation of the underlying facts, to make sure not only that the information furnished by the original sources was accurately recorded, but that the information provided by those sources is accurate.[581]

New sources should be asked for their view of the disputed facts when appropriate. The consumer should specify other reliable sources for the CRA to contact, making clear why these sources will be useful, whenever these new sources will help resolve the dispute.[582] At a minimum, the CRA must check with both the original sources and other reliable sources of the disputed information.[583] The statute explicitly provides that the CRA shall provide the furnisher with all relevant information about the dispute,[584] and that the furnisher must conduct its own investigation.[585]

The extent of the investigation which is required will depend on the circumstances of the case.[586] If the consumer complains that the information in the file is incomplete, the CRA should investigate the entire matter and make a good faith effort to verify any additional information that the consumer has provided.[587] Where another party is fraudulently using the consumer's Social Security number, it is not enough for the CRA to publish a victim of fraud statement in the report, leaving the consumer to work out the fraud issues with the party furnishing the information. The CRA must also conduct an investigation and delete inaccurate information from the consumer's file.[588] An adequate reinvestigation should require the CRA to examine information received from the original source against information in its own files that would lead it to find the item inaccurate.

---

575 Curtis v. Trans Union, L.L.C., 2002 WL 31748838 (N.D. Ill. Dec. 9, 2002); FTC Official Staff Commentary § 611 item 2, *reprinted at* Appx. D, *infra*.

576 *In re* Equifax, Inc., 96 F.T.C. 1045 (1980), *rev'd in part on other grounds*, 678 F.2d 1047 (11th Cir. 1982).

577 Cahlin v. General Motors Acceptance Corp., 936 F.2d 1151 (11th Cir. 1991).

578 15 U.S.C. § 1681i(a), *amended by* Pub. L. No. 108-159, § 317 (2003); 16 C.F.R. § 602.1(c)(3)(xviii).

579 Cahlin v. Gen. Motors Acceptance Corp., 936 F.2d 1151, 1160 (11th Cir. 1991) (interpreting statute governing reinvestigations of consumer disputes by CRAs to require reasonable investigations); Pinner v. Schmidt, 805 F.2d 1258, 1262 (5th Cir. 1986) (same).

580 Cushman v. Trans Union Corp., 115 F.3d 220 (3d Cir. 1997) (in theft of identity case, CRA may not rely merely on creditor's information); Apodaca v. Discover Fin. Servs., 417 F. Supp. 2d 1220 (D.N.M. 2006); Sampson v. Equifax Info. Servs., 2005 WL 2095092 (S.D. Ga. Aug. 29, 2005); McKeown v. Sears Roebuck & Co., 335 F. Supp. 2d 917 (W.D. Wis. 2004); Evantash v. G.E. Capital Mortgage Serv., Inc., 2003 WL 22844198 (E.D. Pa. Nov. 25, 2003) (CRA may not merely parrot information provided to it but may have some duty to go beyond the source, depending on whether the consumer has alerted the CRA that the source may be unreliable and on the cost of verification compared with the harm to the consumer); Sheffer v. Experian Info. Solutions, Inc., 2003 WL 21710573 (E.D. Pa. July 24, 2003) (same); Soghomonian v. U.S., 278 F. Supp. 2d 1151 (E.D. Cal. 2003) (cannot defer to outside entity, especially when CRA does not consider information provided by consumer); Crane v. Trans Union, L.L.C., 282 F. Supp. 2d 311 (E.D. Pa. 2003) (accuracy "requires congruence between the legal status of a consumer's account and the status a CRA reports"); Olwell v. Medical Inf. Bureau, 2003 WL 79035 (D. Minn. Jan. 7, 2003) (failure to contact outside source could be unreasonable investigation); Curtis v. Trans Union, L.L.C., 2002 WL 31748838 (N.D. Ill. Dec. 9, 2002); Zala v. Trans Union, L.L.C., 2001 U.S. Dist. LEXIS 549 (N.D. Tex. Jan. 17, 2001); Frost v. Experian, 1998 WL 765178 (S.D.N.Y. Nov. 2, 1998) (required to go behind the court record if notified that it is inaccurate. *See* Guimond v. Trans Union, 45 F.3d 1329 (9th Cir. 1995); Lawrence v. Trans Union, 296 F. Supp. 2d 582,

589–590 (E.D. Pa. 2003); Connor v. Trans Union, 1999 WL 773504 (E.D. Pa. Sept. 29, 1999). *See also* FTC Official Staff Commentary § 611 item 2, *reprinted at* Appx. D, *infra*.

581 Bryant v. TRW, Inc., 487 F. Supp. 1234 (E.D. Mich. 1974), *aff'd*, 689 F.2d 72 (6th Cir. 1982).

582 *But see* Roseman v. Retail Credit Co., 428 F. Supp. 643 (E.D. Pa. 1977) (CRA not required to contact additional sources where consumer disputes reasons given by former employer for consumer's dismissal).

583 Zala v. Trans Union, L.L.C., 2001 U.S. Dist. LEXIS 549 (N.D. Tex. Jan. 17, 2001); FTC Official Staff Commentary § 611 item 2, *reprinted at* Appx. D, *infra*. *See also In re* MIB, Inc., 101 F.T.C. 415, 423 (1983) (consent order); FTC, Compliance with the Fair Credit Reporting Act, at 33 (1977).

584 *See* § 4.5.4.2, *infra*.

585 *See* § 4.5.4.1, *infra*.

586 Cushman v. Trans Union Corp., 115 F.3d 220 (3d Cir. 1997); Henson v. CSC Credit Servs., 29 F.3d 280 (7th Cir. 1994); Perry v. Experian Info. Solutions, Inc., 2005 WL 2861078 (N.D. Ill. Oct. 28, 2005).

587 FTC, Compliance with the Fair Credit Reporting Act, at 33 (1977).

588 Cushman v. Trans Union Corp., 115 F.3d 220 (3d Cir. 1997); Stevenson v. TRW, Inc., 987 F.2d 288 (5th Cir. 1993).

Over the last several years, the Seventh Circuit, as well as federal district courts in that Circuit, have considered a series of cases involving the CRAs' use of automated procedures to process the consumer's dispute, called Automated Consumer Dispute Verification forms (ACDVs).[589] In ruling generally in favor of the CRAs, these cases can be explained in large part because the courts were confronted with a unique set of facts in which the consumer had either not clearly articulated a comprehensible dispute[590] or had failed to establish notice to the CRA of the possible unreliability of its source.[591] This series of decisions—likely due in part to the lack of developed evidence challenging furnisher reliability—has been offered by CRA litigants as asserted support for the proposition that a CRA may rely entirely upon the verification and reporting of its creditor customers.

However, even these decisions all apply the same two-factor standard for a reasonable investigation: notice of reliability and cost-benefit analysis. Even the most CRA-friendly decision, *Lee v. Experian*, rejected the conclusion that the automated dispute verification system and its complete reliance on a furnisher are always appropriate:

> This does not of course negate the existence of a duty to conduct an independent investigation (L. Mem. 15; *Cushman*, 115 F.3d at 225). It rather means that given the absence of any indication of nonreliability here, Experian's CDV procedure was sufficiently interactive to satisfy Experian's section 1681i(a) obligation.[592]

No court has ever held that an independent investigation outside of the ACDV system is not required when the reliability of a furnisher's reporting has been effectively challenged. Put another way, no court has ever held that the ACDV system is proper as a matter of law.

Similarly, the CRAs have contended that the FCRA dispute mechanism for furnishers frees them of any independent responsibility. This position has been soundly rejected.[593] The obligations of CRAs and furnishers are independent.

It is nevertheless important that a consumer develop and raise sufficient challenges to the furnisher's reliability in order to satisfy the first *Henson* reasonability factor. Generally, the reliability of a furnisher is a question of fact.[594] The number of disputed accounts or an allegation of fraud may reasonably cause a CRA to doubt the reliability of its reported data.[595] A substantive dispute by the consumer may also provide its own basis for a CRA to doubt the reliability of its source, especially as a creditor will often have an obvious bias to verify the credit obligation.[596] But the consumer's word alone, disputing the debt at issue, has also been found insufficient.[597] A previous acrimonious relationship between the consumer and the furnisher may call source reliability into question.[598]

There are additional ways to challenge furnisher reliability. Determine if the furnisher has ever been sued or subject to administrative process connected with FCRA compliance. This information will be especially important if the CRA was also a party in that action. Establish through discovery that the furnisher's reinvestigation procedures are unreliable. This will contrast with the polished testimony of CRA witnesses attesting to the reliability of the underlying data reported by the furnisher. Practitioners should then argue that none of the CRA's testimony is relevant—it is not the underlying data that is challenged, but rather the furnisher's reinvestigation procedure when confronted with a dispute. It is also important to critically examine the claims and declarations of CRA witnesses who testify that a furnisher is reliable.

On the other hand, there are limits as to what is required of a reasonable reinvestigation. The cost of reinvestigating a particular "lead" can be a factor. Nevertheless, even then, the cost may be insignificant compared to the consumer's harm.[599]

A review of the furnishing creditor's ledger sheets may be sufficient. The FTC has stated that a CRA need not always

---

589 *See* § 4.5.6, *infra*. A printout of an ACDV is reproduced at Appx. I.3, *infra*.
590 Perry v. Experian Info. Solutions, Inc., 2005 WL 2861078 (N.D. Ill. Oct. 28, 2005) ("Perry's terse dispute letters provided no detailed information regarding the alleged identity theft."); McCelland v. Experian Info. Solutions, Inc., 2006 WL 2191973 (N.D. Ill. July 28, 2006) (vague dispute letters "not my account." Consumer could have cleared things up and assisted the CRA by telling it the judgment belonged to his son with the same name).
591 Bagby v. Experian Info. Solutions, Inc., 162 Fed. Appx. 600, 2006 WL 14580 (7th Cir. 2006) (unreported) (consumer offered no evidence "that Experian knew or should have known that the information provided in the CDVs was anything other than reliable."); Benson v. Trans Union, L.L.C., 387 F. Supp. 2d 834 (N.D. Ill. 2006) (deviation from standard procedures not required absent notice of prevalent unreliable information from a furnisher); Anderson v. Trans Union, L.L.C., et al., 367 F. Supp. 2d 1225 (W.D. Wis. 2005); Lee v. Experian Info. Solutions, 2003 WL 22287351 (N.D. Ill. Oct. 2, 2003).
592 Lee v. Experian Info. Solutions, 2003 WL 22287351 (N.D. Ill. Oct. 2, 2003).

593 Sampson v. Equifax Info. Servs., 2005 WL 2095092 (S.D. Ga. Aug. 29, 2005) (does not mean that the CRA has no "responsibility beyond serving as a conduit for consumers' complaints").
594 *Id.*; Campbell v. Chase Manhattan Bank, USA, N.A., 2005 WL 1514221 (D.N.J. June 27, 2005).
595 Stevenson v. TRW Inc., 987 F.2d 288 (5th Cir. 1993); Swoager v. Credit Bureau of Greater St. Petersburg, Fla., 608 F. Supp. 972 (D.C. Fla. 1985).
596 *Id.*
597 Morris v. Trans Union, L.L.C., 420 F. Supp. 733 (S.D. Tex. 2006).
598 Pinner v. Schmidt, 805 F.2d 1258, 1262 (5th Cir. 1986).
599 Cushman v. Trans Union Corp., 115 F.3d 220 (3d Cir. 1997).

§ 4.5.4 Fair Credit Reporting

review actual sales slips or similar documentation.[600] The FTC also has stated that an incentive system of paying the employee conducting the reinvestigation only if the reinvestigation confirmed the employee's initial investigation did not constitute an unreasonable procedure in violation of the Act.[601]

Nevertheless, it is not enough to determine whether the information was accurate or complete at the time it was furnished to the CRA. The CRA must "record the current status" of the information.[602] It must thus determine whether there is any change in the status of an ongoing matter, e.g., that a credit account has been closed, that a debt shown to be past due has been subsequently paid or discharged in bankruptcy, or that a debt discharged in bankruptcy has later been paid.[603]

The plain language of the FCRA requires CRAs to reinvestigate where the information in the file was accurate when furnished, but does not include subsequent developments in an account or does not include a lawsuit favorable to the consumer. The FCRA provides a right of reinvestigation where the consumer disputes the "completeness or accuracy" of any item in a file.[604] Obviously, the term "completeness" implies more than just accuracy, so that the consumer has a right to require reinvestigation if information relevant to an item is not included in the file. In addition, the FCRA requires the CRA to "record the current status" of the information.[605]

If the consumer provides written documents to the CRA that verify the incompleteness of a report, and the CRA refuses to enter that information, an FTC staff opinion letter suggests this denial would put the CRA in willful violation of the FCRA's reinvestigation requirement.[606] However, in order for a violation to occur due to an incomplete reinvestigation, the incompleteness must be of a fundamental nature.[607]

In investigating lawsuits and judgments, the CRA must inquire both of the original creditor, where relevant and possible, and also examine official records to determine if the judgment has been satisfied, the suit dismissed or other relevant action taken.[608] Even if a CRA was justified in relying on court docket summaries when originally compiling a report, once a notice of dispute has been received, the CRA can be expected to conduct a more thorough examination.[609]

4.5.4 Agency's Reinvestigation Must Involve the Person Who Furnished the Disputed Information to the Reporting Agency

4.5.4.1 General

The FCRA requires the creditor or other person who furnished the information disputed by the consumer to participate in the reinvestigation conducted by the CRA.[610] The only exceptions are if the CRA has determined the dispute to be frivolous[611] or has deleted the disputed information pursuant to an expedited dispute resolution process.[612] The furnisher who fails to properly participate in this reinvestigation may be liable to the consumer.[613]

When a furnisher confirms the substance of a consumer's dispute, the CRA will normally correct or delete the challenged information. However, if the furnisher reports back that the original information is accurate, the CRA nevertheless retains an independent responsibility to evaluate the accuracy of the disputed information.[614]

A CRA may not rely solely on the furnisher.[615] Reports from a creditor apparently biased against the consumer are not trustworthy.[616] In appropriate circumstances, the CRA

---

600 FTC Official Staff Commentary § 611 item 2, *reprinted at* Appx. D, *infra*. *See also* Brinckerhoff, FTC Informal Staff Opinion Letter (Jan. 31, 1985), *reprinted on the CD-Rom accompanying this manual*.
601 *In re* Equifax, Inc., 96 F.T.C. 1045 at 1063 (1980), *rev'd in part on other grounds*, 678 F.2d 1047 (11th Cir. 1982).
602 15 U.S.C. § 1681i(a).
603 FTC Official Staff Commentary § 611 item 6, *reprinted at* Appx. D, *infra*.
604 15 U.S.C. § 1681i(a).
605 *Id.*
606 Cook, FTC Informal Staff Opinion Letter (Apr. 22, 1977), *reprinted on the CD-Rom accompanying this manual* (written documents confirming that debts discharged in bankruptcy were subsequently reaffirmed and paid). *Cf.* Feldman, FTC Informal Staff Opinion Letter (Aug. 30, 1974), *reprinted on the CD-Rom accompanying this manual* (CRA may be liable for noncompliance if it fails to include in report credit history information volunteered by consumer). *See also* Zala v. Trans Union, L.L.C., 2001 U.S. Dist. LEXIS 549 (N.D. Tex. Jan. 17, 2001).
607 Koropoulos v. Credit Bureau, Inc., 734 F.2d 37, 45 (D.C. Cir. 1984); Stewart v. Credit Bureau, Inc., 734 F.2d 47, 55 (D.C. Cir. 1984).

608 Zala v. Trans Union, L.L.C., 2001 U.S. Dist. LEXIS 549 (N.D. Tex. Jan. 17, 2001); *In re* Credit Data Northwest, 86 F.T.C. 389, 396 (1975).
609 Cushman v. Trans Union Corp., 115 F.3d 220 (3d Cir. 1997); Henson v. CSC Credit Servs., 29 F.3d 280 (7th Cir. 1994); Curtis v. Trans Union, L.L.C., 2002 WL 31748838 (N.D. Ill. Dec. 9, 2002); Matise v. Trans Union Corp., 1998 U.S. Dist. LEXIS 19775 (N.D. Tex. Nov. 30, 1998).
610 15 U.S.C. §§ 1681i(a)(2), 1681s-2(b).
611 See § 4.5.2.4, *supra*.
612 See § 4.5.2.1, *supra*.
613 See § 10.2.4, *infra*.
614 Sampson v. Equifax Info. Servs., 2005 WL 2095092 (S.D. Ga. Aug. 29, 2005).
615 Cushman v. Trans Union Corp., 115 F.3d 220 (3d Cir. 1997); Stevenson v. TRW, Inc., 987 F.2d 288 (5th Cir. 1993); Cahlin v. GMAC, 936 F.2d 1151 (11th Cir. 1991); Bryant v. TRW, 689 F.2d 72 (6th Cir. 1982); Malhee v. Chilton Corp., 468 F. Supp. 494 (D.C. Conn. 1978). *But see* Podell v. Citicorp Diners Club, Inc., 112 F.3d 98 (2d Cir. 1997).
616 Swoager v. Credit Bureau of Greater St. Petersburg, 608 F. Supp. 972 (M.D. Fla. 1985).

must contact third parties for information,[617] and must consider all relevant information at its disposal. The Act also separately requires the CRA itself to review and consider all relevant information submitted by the consumer.[618] However, one court has refused to impose any objective or substantive meaning to this requirement.[619]

4.5.4.2 Consumer Reporting Agency Must Notify the Furnisher of the Disputed Information

Within five business days of receipt of a notice of dispute from a consumer, the CRA must provide a notice of the dispute to any person who furnished any item of information in dispute.[620] The notice must include "all relevant information regarding the dispute."[621] If the CRA receives additional, relevant information from the consumer during the dispute resolution period, that information too must be promptly provided to the furnisher.

Nationwide CRAs are now processing nearly all of their disputes electronically by using the Consumer Data Industry Association's (CDIA) Automated Consumer Dispute Verification (ACDV) Process, which transmits the information in question to the furnisher's electronic mailbox using standardized dispute codes. With an ACDV, the consumer's dispute—no matter how lengthy or thorough or well-documented—will be reduced to a one page, electronic ACDV message with the underlying dispute reduced to a generic two-digit dispute code (e.g., "01 not his/hers") and in some circumstances, a short, one-line paraphrase of some aspect of the dispute under the heading "FCRA Relevant Information (e.g. "Consumer states belongs to husband only").[622] Also, most disputes are processed through the e-Oscar system, which is an Internet-based dispute processing system developed by the consumer reporting industry.[623] According to the CDIA, more than 83% are processed through the e-OSCAR system.[624]

When a furnisher receives a notice of dispute, it is supposed to research the disputed information and transmit back a response. Under the FCRA, the CRA should be under a duty to ensure that the automated process incorporates "all relevant information" about the dispute in order to fulfill its obligations. If the CRA cannot fully describe all of the relevant information with the codes allowed by the automated process, it should find another way to adequately notify the furnisher of the dispute. Where the facts merit it, the original sources should not just be sent a form notice, but the CRA should communicate by telephone or in person.[625] This is almost never done.

Despite the duty to forward "all relevant information," an FTC report establishes that, when a consumer provides documents supporting a dispute, the standard practice of the "Big Three" CRAs is not to forward them to the furnisher.[626] In fact, the CDIA has even acknowledged that the e-OSCAR system is incapable of transmitting consumer-submitted documents to furnishers, and the possibility of being able to do so in the future is "questionable."[627] Furthermore, it appears that e-OSCAR may soon be the only way in which disputes will be communicated to furnishers. The "Big Three" nationwide CRAs have apparently announced that they will require all furnishers to participate in the e-OSCAR system and will stop accepting paper-based disputes.[628]

Thus, it is not likely that the CRA will forward copies of whatever it received from the consumer in the notice of dispute.[629] Without more detail than typically provided in a

---

617 Olwell v. Medical Info. Bureau, 2003 WL 79035 (D. Minn. Jan. 7, 2003) (reasonable jury could find that failure to contact outside sources was unreasonable investigation); Curtis v. Trans Union, L.L.C., 2002 WL 31748838 (N.D. Ill. Dec. 9, 2002); FTC Official Staff Commentary § 611 item 2, *reproduced at* Appx. D, *infra*.
618 15 U.S.C. § 1681i(a)(4).
619 Anderson v. Trans Union, L.L.C., 367 F. Supp. 2d 1225 (W.D. Wis. 2005).
620 15 U.S.C. § 1681i(a)(2). If the CRA fails to properly notify the furnisher or fails to revise the individual's consumer report to conform to the furnisher's reinvestigation, and the consumer sues the furnisher, the furnisher may cross-claim against the CRA. *See* Ch. 6, *infra*.
621 *Id.*
622 *See* § 4.5.6, *infra*. A printout of an ACDV is reproduced at Appx. I.3, *infra*.
623 Federal Trade Commission and Federal Reserve Board, Report to Congress on the Fair Credit Reporting Act Dispute Process (Aug. 2006), at 15, *available at* www.ftc.gov/os/comments/fcradispute/P044808fcradisputeprocessreporttocongress.pdf.
624 *Id.*
625 Stevenson v. TRW, Inc., 987 F.2d 288 (5th Cir. 1993).
626 Federal Trade Commission and Federal Reserve Board, Report to Congress on the Fair Credit Reporting Act Dispute Resolution Process (Aug. 2006), at 18, *available at* www.ftc.gov/os/comments/fcradispute/P044808fcradisputeprocessreporttocongress.pdf. The report states that "TransUnion stated that it typically does not supply copies of consumer-supplied documentation to furnishers" but may use the expedited dispute resolution procedure discussed in § 4.5.2.1, *supra* in some cases. It also states that Equifax "can" fax the consumer-submitted information to the furnisher "as appropriate," but does not indicate that this is Equifax's standard practice. The report does not describe Experian's practice. Nevertheless, practitioners confirm from CRA depositions that none of the "Big Three" nationwide CRAs forward dispute letters or any accompanying documents as part of their non-VIP reinvestigation process.
627 Federal Trade Commission and Federal Reserve Board, Report to Congress on the Fair Credit Reporting Act Dispute Resolution Process (Aug. 2006), at 18, *available at* www.ftc.gov/os/comments/fcradispute/P044808fcradisputeprocessreporttocongress.pdf.
628 *Id* at 16.
629 The FTC appears of two minds about this practice. While the FTC has stated that the failure to forward documents supplied the consumer does not mean that the CRAs fail to forward "all relevant information" to furnishers, it also has noted that this practice may lead to incorrect outcomes in certain situations. *Id.* at 33–34. Some furnishers, however, have agreed that the ACDV and e-OSCAR system are flawed, that the two-digit dispute codes are "vague and broad," and they the CRAs do not

"Big Three" CRA ACDV, and without prior notice of the dispute from the consumer,[630] the furnisher may be not be required to perform more than a cursory investigation.[631] Consequently, in drafting the notice of dispute for the CRA, the consumer or the consumer's attorney must specifically request that the information and any enclosed documents be forwarded to the furnisher and provide any readily available information that will help the furnisher to understand the dispute and locate relevant information.

4.5.5 Deadline for Reporting Agency to Respond

4.5.5.1 Generally Applicable Deadlines

The time period within which the CRA is to respond to the consumer's dispute depends upon the process through which the consumer obtained notice of the inaccurate information. The 2003 FACTA amendments to the FCRA added a new provision granting every consumer the right to a free annual consumer report from nationwide CRAs.[632] To receive the report from a nationwide CRA other than a nationwide specialty CRA,[633] the consumer must use a centralized source to make the request.[634] If a consumer requests a reinvestigation after receiving a free report under this provision, the CRA has forty-five days to complete the reinvestigation.[635]

Most other reinvestigations conducted by CRAs and initiated by a consumer's dispute must be completed within thirty days, with one fifteen-day extension allowed if the CRA receives information from the consumer during the thirty-day period that is relevant to the reinvestigation.[636] The thirty-day period begins on the date the CRA receives the consumer's notice of dispute.

One fifteen-day extension of the reinvestigation period is allowed in limited circumstances, but only if during the original thirty-day period additional information is received from the consumer relevant to the reinvestigation. The CRA may not extend the period to accommodate its procedures, or because it has not received a response from the furnisher of the information. No extension of time is permitted if the CRA has found, in the original thirty-day period, that the information is inaccurate, incomplete, or that it cannot be verified.

Some state laws set a maximum number of days that the CRA has to respond. The CRA will have to comply with the state standard if it is more restrictive and not preempted.[637] A few state statutes specify how quickly the CRA should begin contacting the sources of information,[638] and more state statutes specify the number of days allowed for the reinvestigation to be completed.[639]

At the end of the reinvestigation period, the disputed information must be deleted if it cannot be verified, or corrected or modified in light of the reinvestigation. If the reinvestigation is not completed in time, the disputed information must be deleted. If it is reinserted into the consumer's file later, perhaps after the CRA has obtained verification from the furnisher, the consumer must, at that time, be provided notice of the reinsertion.[640] Although the FCRA's reinvestigation provisions do not require the CRA to acknowledge in the file, while the reinvestigation is proceeding, that that the debt is disputed, nothing prevents it from doing so.

If the consumer does not receive a response from the CRA within thirty days, a follow-up letter should be sent—along with a copy of the original letter. The follow-up letter should request that the CRA either delete or correct the disputed item, since it did not initially respond within the required time, and state that the consumer will file a complaint with the FTC if this is not done.

Failure to comply with the statutory requirement of reinvestigation within the required time subjects the CRA to possible actual damages and attorney fees if the action is negligent.[641] If the failure is willful, the CRA can also be liable for punitive damages.[642]

---

always provide furnishers with sufficient information. *Id.* at 17
630 Alabran v. Capital One, 2005 WL 3338663 (E.D. Va. Dec. 8, 2005).
631 *See* Westra v. Credit Control of Pinellas, 409 F.3d 825 (7th Cir. 2005) (furnisher's investigation was reasonable given scant information it received from CRA in the form of a CDV; CDV only indicated dispute that account did not belong to consumer and did not provide any information about possible fraud or identity theft or include any of the documentation); Malm v. Household Bank, N.A., 2004 U.S. Dist. LEXIS 12981 (D. Minn. July 7, 2004) (No. 03-4340) (furnisher's investigation was reasonable given the cursory notice it received; furnisher verified that consumer's ; cryptic "Not his/hers" did not notify furnisher that additional inquiry was necessary.").
632 Pub. L. No. 108-159, § 211(a) (2003), *amending* 15 U.S.C. § 1681j(a). The CRAs that must provide free annual reports are those defined in 15 U.S.C. § 1681a(p). *See* § 3.3.2, *supra*.
633 These CRAs are defined in 15 U.S.C. § 1681a(w), *added by* Pub. L. No. 108-159, § 111 (2003).
634 *See* § 3.3.2, *supra*.
635 15 U.S.C. § 1681j(a)(3).
636 15 U.S.C. § 1681i(a)(1)(B).

637 State laws on this point are preempted unless in effect on September 30, 1996. 15 U.S.C. § 1681t(b)(1)(B). *See* § 10.7 and Appx. H, *infra*.
638 *See, e.g.*, Nev. Rev. Stat. § 598C.160 (5 days); Vt. Stat. Ann. tit. 9, § 2480d (5 days); Wash. Rev. Code § 19.182.090 (5 days).
639 *See, e.g.*, Ariz. Rev. Stat. Ann. § 44-1691 (30 days); Colo. Rev. Stat. § 12-14.3-106(1) (30 days); Me. Rev. Stat. Ann. tit. 10, § 1317(2) (21 days); Md. Code Ann. Com. Law § 14-1208 (30 days); Mass. Gen. Laws Ann. ch. 93, § 58 (30 days); Nev. Rev. Stat. § 598C.160 (30 days); N.H. Rev. Stat. Ann. § 359-B:11 (30 days); R.I. Gen. Laws § 6-13.1-23 (30 days); Vt. Stat. Ann. tit. 9, § 2480d (30 days); Wash. Rev. Code § 19.182.005 (same).
640 *See* § 4.7.4, *infra*.
641 *See* 15 U.S.C. § 1681n; Stevenson v. TRW, Inc., 987 F.2d 288 (5th Cir. 1993). *See also* § 10.2.2.2, *infra*.
642 *See* 15 U.S.C. § 1681o; § 11.12, *infra*. *But cf.* Stevenson v. TRW, Inc., 987 F.2d 288 (5th Cir. 1993) (no willfulness found).

4.5.5.2 Expedited Resolution of Disputes

In some instances, a CRA will want to delete information disputed by a consumer without initiating a reinvestigation. The CRA may resolve the dispute in expedited fashion by deleting the disputed information within three business days from receipt of the dispute.[643] For example, CRAs may choose to take this step when the consumer's dispute is accompanied by documentation from the original source confirming the consumer's version.[644] In fact, even prior to this statutory provision for expedited dispute resolution, Equifax and Experian (formerly TRW) agreed to accept the consumer's version of a dispute in this circumstance (unless Equifax/TRW in good faith doubted the documentation's authenticity).[645]

If the CRA follows the expedited dispute resolution procedure, it must give notice to the consumer, but is freed from other requirements of reinvestigation. The CRA must notify the consumer promptly, by telephone, that the disputed information has been deleted.[646] In addition, within five business days of the deletion, the CRA must provide the consumer with written confirmation of the deletion and a copy of the current, corrected report.[647] As part of either the telephone notification, or the written confirmation, the consumer must be informed of the right to have previous recipients of the report receive an updated, corrected report.[648]

If the consumer has been properly notified of the results of the expedited resolution of the dispute, the CRA does not have to notify the party who furnished the disputed information,[649] or provide other notices to the consumer of the results of a reinvestigation,[650] including a written description of the reinvestigation process.

In addition to these procedures, practitioners have reported that the nationwide CRAs have an expedited reinvestigation process which is used for "priority" credit applications, such as pending mortgages or student loans.

4.5.6 E-OSCAR and Other Aspects of the "Big Three's" Reinvestigation Procedures

4.5.6.1 E-OSCAR

The three major nationwide CRAs handle a large volume of consumer disputes and to handle those disputes use almost exclusively an electronic dispute processing system, known as e-OSCAR (Online Solution for Complete and Accurate Reporting). Understanding e-OSCAR is critical to understanding the CRAs dispute handling procedures.

E-OSCAR is web-based and permits furnishers to communicate with the CRA over the Internet. These communications utilize standard forms with codes, described elsewhere in this manual—Automated Consumer Dispute Verification forms (ACDVs)[651] and Automated Uniform Data Forms (AUDFs).[652] The CRA initiates a request for a reinvestigation with the furnisher by sending an ACDV through e-OSCAR.

The ACDV contains identifying information about the consumer in the CRA's file; one or two codes summarizing the consumer's dispute; and, if the CRA deems it necessary, a one-line free-form narrative field that supplements the dispute codes. This free-form field is sometimes referred to as the "FCRA Relevant Information field," but is rarely used. The CRAs' procedures manuals offer almost no instructions for their ACDV clerks as to what information should be placed in this one-line text field. As a result, many practitioners report that the field is often left blank.

ACDV clerks at the CRA select a specific dispute code from among twenty-six offered by the e-OSCAR system, such as "Not his/hers" and "Claims account closed." These codes are often contained in a dropdown "pick list" and the criteria for selecting the appropriate pick list value for a certain dispute is often more specifically detailed in the procedures manuals.

The CRAs encourage consumers to submit disputes using a limited set of dispute codes, either contained in a pre-created dispute form enclosed with every consumer disclosure, or, more recently, by having the consumer submit a dispute over the Internet using a list of on-line check-boxes to select the basis for the dispute. When such a dispute is submitted over the Internet, there may be no involvement of the CRA's personnel before the dispute is forwarded to the furnisher. The check-box selected by the consumer as most applicable to the dispute is matched to one of the pick-list ACDV dispute codes and automatically sent to the furnisher without any human intervention. Likewise, regardless of whether the dispute is submitted on-line, via mail, or via

---

643 15 U.S.C. § 1681i(a)(8).
644 CRAs are unlikely delete information and forego a reinvestigation in when the consumer does not provide documentation from the original source.
645 Fed. Trade Comm'n v. TRW, Inc., 784 F. Supp. 361 (N.D. Tex. 1991) (consent order), *reprinted on the CD-Rom accompanying this manual*; Equifax Agreement with Eighteen State Attorneys General Offices (June 22, 1992), *reprinted on the CD-Rom accompanying this manual*.
646 15 U.S.C. § 1681i(a)(8)(A).
647 15 U.S.C. § 1681i(a)(8)(C).
648 15 U.S.C. § 1681i(a)(8)(B). *See* § 4.6.2, *infra*.
649 *See* § 4.5.2.1, *infra*.
650 *See* § 4.6.1, *infra*.

651 *See* § 6.10, *infra*.
652 *See* § 6.5, *infra*.

telephone, the furnisher's response to the ACDV typically is automatically applied to the tradeline in question with minimal human intervention.[653]

It should be noted that certain attributes of a consumer's file may be updated upon dispute without the occurrence of an ACDV exchange. For example, addresses and employment information may be generally added, deleted, or modified based on receipt of a specific dispute by a consumer relating to the same. TransUnion additionally employs a policy of allowing certain public records and tradeline elements to be updated outside of the ACDV exchange process if the consumer provides what it internally categorizes as an adequate "proof document." A document such as a notice from a taxing authority releasing a tax lien, or a verifiable letter from a furnisher which includes a specific description of an authorized change to a tradeline and the name of an individual who will serve as the point of contact for questions regarding the authorization might be sufficient to process these categories of disputes.

4.5.6.2 The Processing of Consumer Disputes

Processing of consumer disputes is a fairly mechanical procedure. CRAs do not forward the actual dispute letters or any accompanying documents to the furnisher. The only contact is the one page electronic ACDV. Nor do CRA employees contact a live person as part of the dispute process and reinvestigation or exercise any personal discretion. The CRA dispute employee solely codes the dispute category and then forward the ACDV to the furnisher. The only changes that can be made to an account or public record are those dictated in the furnisher's response.

Of the three national CRAs, only Experian processes consumer disputes domestically. TransUnion receives disputes at its consumer relations facility near Philadelphia, scans the dispute into an electronic image and then transmits the image to Intelenet, its subcontractor located in Mumbai, India. Intelenet in Mumbai can connect directly to TransUnion's massive CRONUS database, retrieve a consumer's credit file and initiate the ACDV exchange. If a dispute falls into a certain category which requires "priority processing," such as when a consumer has a mortgage application pending, or the consumer falls with the VIP designation (e.g., a judge, attorney, or celebrity), Intelenet resends the electronic document back to the United States, where a TransUnion employee processes the dispute, albeit using the same CRA procedures manual that the Intelenet employees are contractually obligated to follow at the Mumbai facility. In either scenario, the furnisher's response to the ACDV is automatically reflected in the TransUnion database with no further interaction required and a letter confirming the results of the exchange is then mailed to the consumer.

Equifax maintains a similar dispute processing mechanism. The Equifax business rules require that the consumer's dispute is imaged by Intersource, based in Atlanta. A record of the dispute is logged into the consumer's file, and the dispute is then electronically transmitted to Jamaica, the Philippines, or Costa Rica. The foreign contractor accesses Equifax's database, retrieves the consumer's credit file and initiates the ACDV exchange as applicable. The results of the ACDV exchange are then auto-populated back into the tradelines and when all of the results have been received, the investigation responses are collectively sent to an Equifax employee to ensure that no data errors have occurred in the transmission and that the changes are applied to the proper consumer's file. This employee then prints a form letter to be sent to the consumer along with a copy of the changes that were made to the file.

CRAs have cost-efficiency motives to process disputes as rapidly and economically as possible. Practitioners report that depositions of CRA employees reveal that CRAs utilize evaluation and incentive programs to ensure that disputes are processed rapidly, meeting "quality" and "production" goals.

"Quality" is generally referred to as the precision with which the employee follows the investigation procedures set forth by the CRA in its manual—i.e., the Equifax Indicating Manual, the Experian Participant Guide or the TransUnion CRS Manual. Any deviation results in a lower score for that employee. "Production" is generally referred to as the raw number of disputes which are processed by the individual in a given day. CRAs may employ a weighted method for deriving this value by crediting the employee with a higher score for more complex disputes, such as those relating to identity theft or a mixed file, and a lower weight for more straightforward tasks, such as processing a request for a copy of a consumer disclosure. These two primary categories are sometimes supplemented by additional credits for perfect and punctual attendance and completion of required training. Employees are then evaluated on the basis of random audits performed by a executive-level group at each CRA responsible for sampling, processing, analyzing and incorporating the results into a monthly or quarterly employee evaluation upon which bonus and pay increase amounts are calculated.

CRA depositions conclusively confirm several additional major problems. None of the CRAs permit their employees to telephone or otherwise contact a live person as part of the dispute process and reinvestigation. Each of the "Big Three" CRAs also concedes that their employees are not permitted to exercise any personal discretion. The sole purpose of the CRA dispute employee is to code the dispute category and then forward the ACDV to the furnisher. The only changes that can be made to an account or public record are those dictated in the furnisher's response

---

653 The notable exception to this rule is disputes relating to mixed files. A specialist will generally review the furnisher's response to ensure that the identifying information provided by the furnisher closely matches more of the indicative information associated with the consumer's file.

4.5.6.3 Deposing the "Big Three" As to Reinvestigation Procedures

In litigation, the "Big Three" each tend to produce the same corporate witnesses from one case to another concerning that CRA's dispute and reinvestigation procedures. No matter the geographic location or issue involved in a case, the CRA will tend to utilize only one or two of a small number of individual employees, who specialize in being professional witnesses in these cases. It can be expected that these employee witnesses will be able to generally describe the CRA's procedures and will develop the CRA's position in the best possible light. Discovery of these individuals may not prove productive for a plaintiff's case. More meaningful discovery of a CRA's reinvestigation process would involve depositions of the frontline employees or agents who actually performed the reinvestigation at issue.

4.6 Corrections as a Result of Reinvestigations of Disputed Information

4.6.1 Notice to Consumer of Results of Reinvestigation

A consumer reporting agency (CRA) is required to notify the consumer of the results of its reinvestigation within five business days of the completion of the reinvestigation.[654] Notice must be by mail, unless the consumer authorizes the CRA to use some other means available to it.[655] Even though the CRA is permitted to provide the reinvestigation results by e-mail or other means with a consumer's permission, it is not obligated to do so.[656]

No matter how that initial notice is provided, the CRA must give the consumer, within the same five-day period, a written statement that the investigation is completed, together with a copy of any corrected report. The statute allows this information to be provided either as part of, or in addition to, the initial notice of the results of the reinvestigation,[657] so it should not be surprising if a single written notice is provided.

Presently, Equifax and Experian often provide only the portion of the consumer's credit file which was investigated and do not provide a full version of the consumer report. For example, if a consumer disputes a single tradeline, the CRA may provide only a single page showing that individual trade line. While this appears to be a violation of the FCRA's specific requirement that CRAs provide in writing "a consumer report that is based upon the consumer's file as that file is revised as a result of the reinvestigation,"[658] the Eleventh Circuit has held otherwise.[659] Furthermore, the CRA is not required to provide the consumer a copy of the ACDV or other specific documents sought.[660]

The written communication must also include a notice that the consumer may request a description of the procedure used to determine the accuracy and completeness of the disputed information, including the business name and address, and if reasonably available, the telephone number of any furnisher contacted during the reinvestigation.[661] This information may be particularly useful if a dispute remains, and if the consumer has had difficulty locating this creditor. If requested, this description must be provided within fifteen days.[662]

If a dispute remains after the reinvestigation is complete, the consumer may elect to have a statement of dispute included in the consumer's file.[663] The written communication must also include a notice of this right, as well as the right to have the CRA notify past users of a disputed report.[664] A consumer's right to insert a dispute statement is independent of all other rights under the FCRA, including its reinvestigation provisions.[665]

4.6.2 Correction or Deletion of Disputed Information

If the reinvestigation reveals that the disputed information is inaccurate or that it can no longer be verified, the CRA is required to delete the information, or modify it based on the results of the reinvestigation.[666] The CRA should act promptly.[667]

The CRA's file corrections will take different forms depending upon the nature of the inaccuracy. If the item was disputed as incomplete, the reinvestigation should correct the item so that the information is now complete.[668]

---

654 15 U.S.C. § 1681i(a)(6)(A).
655 15 U.S.C. § 1681i(a)(6)(A).
656 Baker v. Capital One Bank, 2006 WL 2523440 (D. Ariz. Aug. 29, 2006).
657 15 U.S.C. § 1681i(a)(b)(B).
658 15 U.S.C. § 1681i(a)(6)(B)(ii).
659 Nunnally v. Equifax Info. Servs., L.L.C., 451 F.3d 768 (11th Cir. 2006).
660 Morris v. Trans Union, L.L.C., 420 F. Supp. 733 (S.D. Tex. 2006).
661 15 U.S.C. § 1681a(6)(B)(iii).
662 15 U.S.C. § 1681i(a)(7).
663 15 U.S.C. § 1681i(b). See § 4.8, infra.
664 15 U.S.C. § 1681i(a)(b)(iv). See § 4.9, infra.
665 Cushman v. Trans Union Corp., 115 F.3d 220 (3d Cir. 1997).
666 15 U.S.C. § 1681i(a)(5). See also In re Trans Union Credit Info. Co., 102 F.T.C. 1109 (1983) (consent order) (CRA must record corrected information within a "reasonable" time); In re MIB, Inc., 101 F.T.C. 415, 423 (1983) (consent order) (unverifiable or inaccurate disputed item must be "promptly" deleted).
667 See Stevenson v. TRW, Inc., 987 F.2d 288 (5th Cir. 1993); § 4.5.5, supra.
668 In re MIB, Inc., 101 F.T.C. 415, 423 (1983) (consent order) (CRA must update incomplete item by "adding additional

If a correction is made to remove a tradeline from a consumer's credit file, for example after a dispute that the account does not belong to the consumer, the CRAs will only "soft-delete" the account, invoking a function that suppresses or cloaks the information while still leaving it in the database. The purpose for this function is to prevent a later re-reporting of the same account by the same furnisher. Such a function may not comply with the terms of the FCRA, which require the CRA to "delete" the information if the soft delete flag is not permanent and the suppressed information is later reinserted into consumer reports. TransUnion's cloaking procedures, which allowed for the information to be reinserted after one year, were found to be unreasonable under the FCRA.[669]

Other reporting inaccuracies caused by this suppression mechanism have been found to be potentially unreasonable.[670] The greatest limitation on the soft-delete solution is that the suppression tracks only a specific tradeline. For example, if a CRA conducts a reinvestigation and then soft deletes a credit card account, that same account can still return to the open file if any change is made to its Metro 2 code. If the account number is changed by the creditor—a common occurrence—the account will not be affected by the soft delete suppression flag.[671] Similarly, if an account is sold to a different creditor or collection company, the new subscriber number will circumvent the suppression.

If the consumer's dispute relates to a mixed file or identity theft, the CRA can make more substantial structural changes to the consumer's file. Often, the reason another person's tradelines or public records appear in a consumer's file is that the CRA's file includes an incorrect address for the consumer. To correct this problem, the first step with each of the "Big Three" CRAs should be to remove all incorrect addresses. Once an incorrect address is removed, new accounts associated with that address will not as easily merge. The most extreme solution is to have the CRA place a "Do Not Combine" file flag in the file. However, because some legitimate creditors may not report with the exact match identifiers, fewer legitimate accounts will be reported.

Among the items that the CRA should delete are inquiries resulting from fraud-related activities and reinvestigations.[672] Such "hard" inquiries can affect the consumer's credit score and influence creditors' decisions.[673]

The 2003 FACTA amendments to the FCRA added a provision that requires a CRA to notify the furnisher when the CRA corrects or deletes information as a result of the reinvestigation.[674] Such a notice should trigger a separate responsibility of the furnisher—to cease furnishing any information that the furnisher "knows or has reason to believe" is inaccurate[675]—since the correction/deletion notice from the CRA should serve as reason to believe that the information was inaccurate.

The CRA is not required to delete disputed information if it has been verified in the course of the reinvestigation. In addition, the CRA needs to verify or delete only disputed information. Thus, if information appears accurate, and is not disputed, the information can remain in the file even if not verified.[676]

4.6.3 Consumer Follow-Up Steps Where Corrections Made

Where the CRA corrects or deletes the disputed items, there are steps the consumer should take to follow up. First, obtain another copy of the information in the consumer's file to confirm that the corrections and deletions were made.[677] This is especially important if the CRA has provided only a partial file at the conclusion of the reinvestigation.

Second, decide if other CRAs have files on the consumer with the same error. This will be more likely where the source was a creditor's error rather than where information was mismerged. A creditor is required to notify all CRAs it has used of corrected information and the nationwide CRAs are required to maintain an automated reinvestigation system for this purpose;[678] nevertheless, a prudent consumer should never assume that other CRAs have picked up the correction. Even with public records information, the same error may appear with more than one CRA, since at least

---

information learned through the reinvestigation and necessary for a proper understanding of the disputed item"). *See also* FTC Official Staff Commentary § 611 item 6, *reprinted at* Appx. D, *infra*.

669 Cousin v. Trans Union Corp., 246 F.3d 359 (5th Cir. 2001).
670 Jordan v. Equifax Info. Servs., L.L.C., 410 F. Supp. 2d 1349 (N.D. Ga. 2006).
671 One court declined to hold that a CRA could be held liable for this phenomenon. Jordan v. Trans Union, L.L.C., 2006 WL 1663324 (N.D. Ga. June 12, 2006) (CRA could not know that the two student loan accounts were duplicative). However, another court has held that, where there was an unexplained "glitch" in the soft-delete function, it could not find the procedures reasonable as a matter of law. Jordan v. Equifax Info. Servs., L.L.C., 410 F. Supp. 2d 1349 (N.D. Ga. 2006).
672 Andrews v. Trans Union Corp., 7 F. Supp. 2d 1056, 1075 (C.D. Cal. 1998) (presence of inquiry, resulting from identity theft, that suggested that plaintiff had applied for credit raised issue of material fact as to whether listing of inquiry was misleading), *aff'd in part, rev'd in part on other grounds sub nom.* Andrews v. TRW Inc., 225 F.3d 1063 (9th Cir. 2000), *rev'd on other grounds*, 534 U.S. 19 (2001) (discovery rule not applicable to statute's general two-year statute of limitations).
673 *Id.* at 1056, n.20. *See also* § 14.5.2.1, *infra*. (credit scoring FICO factors).
674 Pub. L. 108-159, § 314(a) (2003), *amending* 15 U.S.C. § 1681i(a)(5)(A).
675 15 U.S.C. § 1681s-2(a)(1)(A). *See also* § 6.4.2, *supra*. Prior to the revision, the FCRA only prohibited furnishers from furnishing information to a CRA that the furnisher knew or "consciously avoided" knowing was inaccurate.
676 FTC Official Staff Commentary § 611 item 12, *reprinted at* Appx. D, *infra*.
677 *See* § 3.3, *supra*.
678 *See* Ch. 6, *infra*.

Equifax and Experian receive some public records from the same database and vendor. Accordingly, it remains important to review and make disputes of all three credit files.

Third, even if the CRA corrected the error, obtain a copy of the consumer's file again three or six months later to see if the offending information has been reinserted. This is particularly important where the information originated from a creditor and the consumer has not succeeded in dealing directly with the creditor to correct the information. A CRA may have acted to remove adverse information upon the complaint of the consumer or upon the failure of a creditor to confirm the information, yet nevertheless reinserted the information at a later time without question when the offending information was supplied by the creditor again.[679] Although a consumer is supposed to receive notice whenever deleted information is reinserted into the consumer's file,[680] this rarely occurs.

A fourth step a consumer should consider taking is to request that the CRA notify past users of the correction. This right is described below.[681] If the consumer does not specify which past users should receive notice, the CRA will not send notice to them.

4.7 Reinsertion of Information Previously Deleted from Consumer's File

4.7.1 The Problem of Reinsertion

One of the most pernicious reporting abuses suffered by consumers has been the repeated reintroduction of inaccurate information into one's consumer report after it has already been deleted once, twice, or even more times before. Consumer reporting agencies (CRAs) routinely recapture uncorrected information from monthly or periodic computer tapes or transmissions from creditors who have never corrected their own files. The result is that consumers have been frequently frustrated in their attempts to have inaccurate information permanently removed.[682]

Sometimes the problem arises at the CRA—not the creditor—level, where the a CRA has only suppressed or cloaked the information, called a "soft-delete," instead of performing a "hard-delete" that erases the information from the CRA's database.[683] Sometimes soft-deletes are on a timer and, when the programmed period expires, the soft-delete automatically terminates and the information reappears in the consumer's report. A further problem arises when a furnisher simply changes the account number on the consumer's account and then re-reports the disputed information under a new account number, thereby defeating the suppression of the item in the CRA's files. Another problem with reinserted information concerns the inability of some CRAs to prevent cloaked information from reappearing when an account is sold or sent to a collection agency which then reports it anew.

The problem was so pervasive that the Consumer Credit Reporting Reform Act of 1996 (1996 Reform Act) amended the FCRA to add specific provisions to prevent this abuse.[684] What constitutes a "reinsertion" for purposes of these provisions is discussed in § 8.2.12, *infra*. While these provisions, described below, improved matters, the problem of reinserted inaccurate information will not go away. It remains prudent for consumers to check back three to six months after information has been deleted to ensure that it has not erroneously found its way back into the CRA's files.[685]

The FCRA's provision governing the reinsertion of previously deleted information has three parts: (1) CRAs must adopt procedures to prevent the reappearance of material, except as specifically allowed;[686] (2) for previously deleted material to be reinserted the material must be certified by the furnisher;[687] and (3) if material is reinserted, the consumer must be promptly notified.[688] The 2003 FACTA amendments to the FCRA added another layer of protection against the refurnishing of inaccurate information. A furnisher who receives notice from a CRA that the consumer has disputed an item of information and who finds upon reinvestigation that the information is inaccurate, incomplete, or unverifiable, must modify, delete, or permanently block the information in its files for purposes of reporting to a CRA.[689]

---

679 In the early 1990s, Experian (formerly TRW) and Equifax agreed to implement procedures to prevent reinsertion. Fed. Trade Comm'n v. TRW, Inc., 784 F. Supp. 361 (N.D. Tex. 1991) (consent order), *reprinted on the CD-Rom accompanying this manual*; Equifax Agreement with Eighteen State Attorneys General Offices (June 22, 1992). *See also* Guimond v. Trans Union Credit Info. Co., 45 F.3d 1329 (9th Cir. 1995) (stating in dicta that since errors kept reappearing in file, it could not have been corrected).
680 *See* § 4.7.4, *infra*.
681 *See* § 4.9, *infra*.
682 15 U.S.C. § 1681i; S. Rep. No. 185, 104th Cong., 1st Sess. at 44 (Dec. 14, 1995).
683 Cousin v. Trans Union Corp., 246 F.3d 359 (5th Cir. 2001). *See* § 4.6.2, *supra*.
684 15 U.S.C. § 1681i(a)(5)(B), *as amended by* Pub. L. No. 104-208 § 2409. Cases prior to 1996 include: Stevenson v. TRW, Inc., 987 F.2d 288 (5th Cir. 1993); Morris v. Credit Bureau of Cincinnati, Inc., 563 F. Supp. 962 (S.D. Ohio 1983).
685 *See* § 4.6.2, *supra*.
686 15 U.S.C. § 1681i(a)(5)(C).
687 15 U.S.C. § 1681i(a)(5)(B)(i).
688 15 U.S.C. § 1681i(a)(5)(B)(ii).
689 15 U.S.C. § 1681s-2(b)(1)(E), *added by* Pub. L. No. 108-159, § 314(b) (2003); 16 C.F.R. § 602.1(c)(3)(xv). *See* § 6.10.5, *infra*.

4.7.2 Consumer Reporting Agency Must Maintain Procedures to Prevent Reinsertion

A CRA must maintain "reasonable procedures" designed to prevent the reappearance of information that has been deleted in a consumer's file and in a consumer report. At one level, it is hard to imagine what this adds to the standard that CRAs must maintain reasonable procedures to ensure maximum possible accuracy. It is, though, both a legislative imperative (which recognizes the particular importance of preventing abuses which have commonly occurred) and a prohibition intended to prevent the reinsertion of any material unless, and only if, certain specific steps are taken.

Despite the requirements to maintain procedures to prevent reinsertion, CRA procedures can sometimes exacerbate the problem. For example, a unique problem is caused by Equifax's continued use of "probability" files, consumer reports in which the CRA provides the credit file for more than one person.[690] The CRA creates such reports to ensure that it provides as much information as possible on a consumer. This type of reporting is deliberately over-inclusive.[691] The subscribing user will see the report with multiple consumer profiles listed. In fact, sometimes an individual consumer may have multiple files in a CRA database. In those cases, the consumer might receive a subscriber copy of the probability file report and begin a dispute, including providing her own identifying information. In response, Equifax will only review one file. The consumer report that Equifax subsequently provides the consumer will not show the disputed data. However, if a subscribing user requests the consumer report, the user will receive a new probability file, and it will appear as if the data has been reinserted even though in truth it was never previously investigated.

4.7.3 Furnisher Certification of Reinserted Information

Before information is reinserted into a consumer's file, the furnisher of the information must certify that the information is accurate and complete.[692] The form of certification is not specified and has not been considered by the courts. To be meaningful, the certification must reflect an individualized, separate determination by the furnisher that the particular information is both accurate and complete. If the requirement of certification is satisfied by a blanket statement accompanying, for example, every monthly submission of the current status of all of a creditor's consumer accounts, or by a contractual agreement that all information submitted at any time by the furnisher will be complete and accurate, the special protections intended for reinserted information will be undermined.

4.7.4 Notice of Reinsertion

Finally, before previously-deleted information is reinserted into a consumer's file, the CRA must notify the consumer.[693] Notice of the reinsertion must be prompt, within five business days, and must be in writing, or, if authorized by the consumer for this purpose, by any other means available to the CRA. Separately, or together, but also within the same five-day period, the CRA must provide a written statement that the disputed information has been reinserted.

In addition, the written notice must disclose the business name and address, and if reasonably available, the telephone number of any furnisher which contacted the CRA with regard to the reinsertion of the information.[694] This disclosure may be especially important if, as is likely, the consumer continues to dispute the accuracy of the information. In most instances, the consumer will find it necessary to dispute the accuracy with the furnisher as well as with the CRA.[695] The notice must also include a statement that the consumer has the right to add a statement to the consumer's file disputing the accuracy or completeness of the disputed information.[696] The notice of reinsertion is discussed further at § 8.2.13, *infra*.

4.8 Inclusion of Additional Information in Consumer's File

4.8.1 Consumer's Right to File Statement of Dispute

4.8.1.1 Overview

This section describes the obligation of a consumer reporting agency (CRA) with regard to the statement of dispute that a consumer files with it, following reinvestigation. The FCRA provides that if reinvestigation does not resolve the dispute, the consumer may file a brief statement setting forth the nature of the dispute.[697] If a consumer has

---

690 Experian and TransUnion no longer produce such reports.
691 See § 3.7.2.4, *supra*.
692 15 U.S.C. § 1681i(a)(5)(B)(i).
693 15 U.S.C. § 1681i(a)(5)(B)(ii).
694 15 U.S.C. § 1681i(a)(5)(B)(iii)(II).
695 *Id. See* Ch. 6, *infra*.
696 15 U.S.C. § 1681i(a)(5)(B)(iii)(III). *See* § 4.8, *infra*.
697 15 U.S.C. § 1681i(b). The notion of requiring CRAs to accept statements of dispute from consumers was first proposed by the administration of President Nixon. Letter to Sen. Sparkman from Special Assistant to the President Knauer (June 19, 1969), *reprinted at Hearings on S. 823, Subcommittee on Financial Institutions of the Senate Banking and Currency Committee 11 a–b*, 91st Cong., 1st Sess. (1969). The notion of the consumer's

filed a statement of dispute,[698] the CRA is required, in any subsequent consumer report concerning the consumer, to clearly note that the consumer disputes the information, and also to provide in the report either the consumer's statement or "a clear and accurate codification or summary" of that statement.[699] There can be no charge to the consumer for this.[700] A Government Account Office study found that 30% of consumers who are unsuccessful in their disputes with the CRAs subsequently submit a statement of dispute.[701]

This statement is not the same as a notice of dispute which triggers a reinvestigation; it must be filed separately and should clearly request that the statement be included in future consumer reports.[702] To maximize the effect of this statement, the consumer will have to file it with every CRA whose file contains the same inaccuracy. Courts have repeatedly rejected the argument that the reinvestigation procedures in 15 U.S.C. § 1681i provides the consumer's only remedy for an inaccurate report.[703]

Exercising this right to file a statement of dispute is rarely of great consequence. The statement, which appears at the bottom of the consumer report, is rarely seen by potential creditors. Moreover, the statements will not affect credit scores used by the vast majority of creditors.[704] Creditors will usually give more weight to the consumer report than to explanatory statements[705] or may ignore them altogether.

However, a consumer should exercise her right to add a dispute in order to improve her position if she later has to resort to litigation. Practitioners report that CRA litigants frequently raise a consumer's failure to insert a dispute statement as an indication that she has not acted to fully protect herself or otherwise cooperated with the CRA. While this argument is a red herring, a consumer could preempt it nonetheless by requesting the statement. Some courts may look less favorably at a consumer's subsequent lawsuit challenging an inaccurate report and the failure to correct it where the consumer does not even bother to enter a statement of dispute.[706]

The FCRA does not explicitly require the CRA to inform the consumer of the right to file a statement explaining the consumer's version of the dispute, and courts have held that the CRA has no affirmative duty to disclose this right.[707] If a CRA assists the consumer in writing a clear summary of the dispute, the statement may be limited to one hundred words for each disputed item of information.[708] If the CRA does not assist the consumer, there is no explicit limit on the length of the statement (although the statute describes it as a "brief" statement setting forth the nature of the dispute).[709] If a CRA even indirectly represents that the statement must be limited to 100 words (unless the CRA assists the consumer), the CRA has violated the FCRA.[710]

4.8.1.2 Consumer Reporting Agency Must Include Statement of Dispute in Subsequent Reports

If the consumer has filed a statement of dispute with the CRA, that statement must be noted in all subsequent reports containing the disputed information.[711] The CRA cannot tell the recipient of a subsequent report that the consumer's statement is on file, and will be provided when requested. The report must contain the actual statement or a summary of that statement.[712] When a user makes a telephonic request for information, the CRA must read the dispute statement or summary to the user *before* disclosing the disputed information in the consumer's file.[713]

Merely including the statement or summary in a consumer report does not satisfy the statute.[714] The report must also note that the information is disputed, although the report can use any appropriate terminology to convey this and may assign a negative rating to such items in a credit

---

right to correct adverse information on file was included in Senator Proxmire's original bill, S. 823, 115 Cong. Rec. 2415 (1969).

698 Guimond v. Trans Union Credit Info. Co., 45 F.3d 1329 (9th Cir. 1995); Mirocha v. TRW, Inc., 805 F. Supp. 663 (S.D. Ind. 1992).
699 15 U.S.C. § 1681i(c).
700 FTC Official Staff Commentary § 612 item 2, *reprinted at* Appx. D, *infra*.
701 Federal Trade Commission and Federal Reserve Board, Report to Congress on the Fair Credit Reporting Act Dispute Resolution Process (Aug. 2006), at 22, *available at* www.ftc.gov/os/comments/fcradispute/P044808fcradisputeprocessreporttocongress.pdf.
702 *See* Mirocha v. TRW, Inc., 805 F. Supp. 663 (S.D. Ind. 1992).
703 *See, e.g.*, Cushman v. Trans Union Corp., 115 F.3d 220 (3d Cir. 1997) and cases cited therein.
704 Federal Trade Commission and Federal Reserve Board, Report to Congress on the Fair Credit Reporting Act Dispute Resolution Process (Aug. 2006), at 22, *available at* www.ftc.gov/os/comments/fcradispute/P044808fcradisputeprocessreporttocongress.pdf.
705 *See* Sepulvado v. CSC Credit Servs., Inc., 158 F.3d 890 (5th Cir. 1998).

706 *See* Koropoulos v. Credit Bureau, Inc., 734 F.2d 37, 45 (D.C. Cir. 1984); Stewart v. Credit Bureau, Inc., 734 F.2d 47, 55 (D.C. Cir. 1984).
707 Roseman v. Retail Credit Co., 428 F. Supp. 643 (E.D. Pa. 1977); Middlebrooks v. Retail Credit Co., 416 F. Supp. 1013 (N.D. Ga. 1976).
708 15 U.S.C. § 1681i(b); FTC Official Staff Commentary § 611 item 13. *See also* Conway, FTC Informal Staff Opinion Letter (Aug. 27, 1973), *reprinted on the CD-Rom accompanying this manual*.
709 15 U.S.C. § 1681i(b).
710 *In re* MIB, Inc., 101 F.T.C. 415, 423 (1983) (consent order).
711 15 U.S.C. § 1681i(c).
712 FTC Official Staff Commentary § 611 item 14, § 612 item 2, *reprinted at* Appx. D, *infra*.
713 *In re* Trans Union Credit Info. Co., 102 F.T.C. 1109 (1983) (consent order).
714 Alexander v. Moore & Assocs., Inc., 553 F. Supp. 948, 954 (D. Haw. 1982). *See, e.g., In re* Credit Data Northwest, Inc., 86 F.T.C. 389, 397 (1975); *In re* Checkmate Inquiry Serv. Inc., 86 F.T.C. 681, 684 (1975) (consent order).

score.⁷¹⁵ It would also appear logical to note in the report that the credit score is also disputed if one of the score's components is disputed.

There are two limits on the requirement that the statement of dispute be included in the report. First, the statement of dispute (or a codification or summary) must be included only if a report contains "the information in question."⁷¹⁶ Second, the CRA is not required to note a consumer's dispute in subsequent consumer reports when the CRA has "reasonable grounds" to believe the statement itself is "frivolous or irrelevant."⁷¹⁷ Whether the CRA had reasonable grounds to believe the statement was frivolous or irrelevant is a question of fact for the jury.⁷¹⁸

4.8.2 Other Notations of Dispute; Fraud and Military Alerts

There is also a second kind of consumer dispute which must be noted by the CRA. If the consumer has disputed with a creditor/furnisher the accuracy of an item of information, either pursuant to the FCRA⁷¹⁹ or another consumer statute,⁷²⁰ the creditor/furnisher is required to note the consumer's dispute in its report to the CRA. The CRA in turn should, as a matter of accuracy, note the dispute in its own report. When a creditor/furnisher reports a tradeline account as "in dispute" pursuant to the FCRA or another consumer statute, practitioners note that the account is reported with a dispute condition that will cause the tradeline to be "unrated" and unscored in the CRA file. The creditor's obligation to note these disputes is discussed elsewhere.⁷²¹

The 2003 FACTA amendments to the FCRA also gave consumers a powerful new right to add what should be far more effective notices to a file: fraud alerts; extended fraud alerts; and active military duty alerts.⁷²² These alerts, unlike the statement of dispute discussed in § 4.8.1, *supra*, impose specific obligations on users of reports that contain such alerts.⁷²³ These alerts are discussed in § 9.2.2, *infra*.

4.8.3 Consumer Explanations for Adverse Information

The FTC Staff Commentary suggests that a CRA need not accept a consumer's statement as to extenuating circumstances for not paying a debt (e.g., illness, layoff), although the CRA can do so if it wishes, and may also charge a fee for inserting the information.⁷²⁴ The consumer only has a right to dispute the completeness or accuracy of an item, and such an explanation does not do either because "[m]ost creditors are aware that a variety of circumstances may render consumers unable to repay credit obligations."⁷²⁵ In other words, the FTC Staff Commentary discounts the possibility that the reason for a delinquency or default can ever make information about that default or delinquency more complete or more accurate.

The Maine Bureau of Consumer Protection, however, takes a more sensible approach, reasoning that, in effect, the consumer is disputing the significance of nonpayment in view of the circumstances; consequently, the consumer report would be incomplete or inaccurate if it does not allow consumers to explain nonpayment for potential creditors to evaluate.⁷²⁶ If additional information enhances the accuracy of the report, it should not be excluded.⁷²⁷

4.8.4 Consumer Offers of New Information

Earlier informal FTC staff interpretations would allow consumers to add, at no additional charge, new information to their file unrelated to any existing item in the file.⁷²⁸ Since CRAs often obtain credit account information only from creditors who subscribe to that particular CRA, a consumer's file often does not include relevant information, particularly a consumer's history in paying landlords or utilities.

---

715 *See* Grimes, FTC Informal Staff Opinion Letter (Apr. 16, 1987), *reprinted on the CD-Rom accompanying this manual* (while a CRA must clearly note the dispute, it may use any appropriate terminology and may nevertheless assign negative ratings to such items).
716 15 U.S.C. § 1681i(c).
717 *Id.*
718 Crane v. Trans Union, L.L.C., 282 F. Supp. 2d 311 (E.D. Pa. 2003).
719 15 U.S.C. § 1681s-2(a)(3). *See also* § 6.5.2, *infra*.
720 *E.g.*, Real Estate Settlement Procedures Act, 12 U.S.C. § 2605(e); Fair Credit Billing Act, 15 U.S.C. § 1666a. *See* § 5.3, *infra*.
721 *See* § 5.3, *infra*.
722 15 U.S.C. § 1681c-1, *added by* Pub. L. No. 108-159, § 112 (2003); 16 C.F.R. § 602.1(c)(3)(i).
723 *Id.*
724 Official Staff Commentary § 611 item 4, *reprinted at* Appx. D, *infra. See also* Boothe v. TRW Credit Data, 768 F. Supp. 434 (S.D.N.Y. 1991) (consumer report included bankruptcy which had been voluntarily dismissed. Since the information as to the bankruptcy was accurate, TRW had conclusively resolved the dispute and had no obligation to include a consumer's statement explaining why he went into bankruptcy).
725 Official Staff Commentary § 611 item 4, *reprinted at* Appx. D, *infra.*
726 Maine Bureau of Consumer Credit Protection Fair Credit Reporting Act Advisory Ruling 89-1, Consumer Cred. Guide (CCH) ¶ 95,760 (Oct. 31, 1989).
727 *See generally* § 4.8.4, *infra.*
728 Feldman, FTC Informal Staff Opinion Letter (Aug. 30, 1974), *reprinted on the CD-Rom accompanying this manual. See also* Peeler, FTC Informal Staff Opinion Letter (Mar. 20, 1977), *reprinted on the CD-Rom accompanying this manual*; Peeler, FTC Informal Staff Opinion Letter (Aug. 23, 1976), *reprinted on the CD-Rom accompanying this manual. But see* Brinckerhoff, FTC Informal Staff Opinion Letter (July 30, 1985), *reprinted on the CD-Rom accompanying this manual.*

The earlier FTC position was that information about such missing accounts should be included as a matter of right because credit can be denied based on incomplete credit history. Therefore, failure to include proffered additional information may place the CRA in violation of the provision requiring reasonable procedures to ensure the accuracy of credit information.

However, the FTC Staff Commentary signaled a change of course. It states that CRAs need not add new items of information to a file, create a file for a consumer for whom it has no file, or add new lines of information about new accounts not reflected in an existing file.[729] The consumer can only dispute the completeness or accuracy of particular items of information in the file. New information can be added as a matter of right, under this view, only if it increases the completeness or accuracy of an item already in the file.

While the FTC Staff Commentary finds that a CRA need not accept a statement of new information, the FTC Staff Commentary permits CRAs to charge a fee if they choose to add lines of information at the consumer's request.[730] In addition, the FTC Staff Commentary indicates that CRAs may charge fees for creating files on consumers at their request or for other services not required by the FCRA that are requested by consumers.[731]

4.9 Notification to Previous Users Who Received Disputed Information

4.9.1 Consumer Request for Notification

Following the deletion of information from the consumer's file pursuant to a reinvestigation or following the consumer's filing of a statement of dispute, the consumer reporting agency (CRA) must provide notice to past recipients of the consumer's report.[732] The notice indicates the items that were deleted, the consumer's statement, or a codification or summary of that statement.[733]

This notice requirement is triggered only by the consumer's request that the notice be sent, and only following the filing of a statement of dispute with the CRA. This notice requirement does not apply to notations of disputes added to the CRA's file because the consumer has disputed the accuracy of information with the creditor itself.[734] Although any report should note such a dispute, it does not give rise to the consumer's right to request that previous users be notified.

The notice to previous users may be sent only to past recipients of the report specifically designated by the consumer.[735] Moreover, the consumer may only specify users who have received the report within the prior six months (or two years if the user has received the report for employment purposes).[736]

A CRA cannot even indirectly report that an item has been deleted from the consumer's file to anyone other than those who were previously informed of the disputed item.[737] For example, where the CRA's records contain the notation "canceled" or "purged," these notations cannot appear in subsequent consumer reports.[738]

Certainly the CRA may not routinely send unsolicited corrected or updated reports even to past recipients of the disputed report unless so directed by the consumer. The FCRA restricts reports to users with permissible purposes,[739] and there is no guarantee that past users with permissible purposes still would have a permissible purpose to receive the report.

CRAs cannot assume that such users continue to have a permissible purpose and cannot rely on the users' blanket certification.[740] A state statute which requires a CRA to send changed reports to past recipients without the consumer's permission is preempted by the FCRA, because the CRA would have no "reason to believe that all past recipients would have a present permissible purpose to receive the information."[741]

4.9.2 Agency Disclosure to Consumer of Right to Request Notification

The CRA must disclose to the consumer the right to request that the CRA notify past users of a disputed report. When a reinvestigation of disputed information is concluded, the CRA must notify the consumer of the results and include a notice that the consumer also has the right to request that certain past users be notified of the results of the

---

729 FTC Official Staff Commentary § 611 item 3, *reprinted at* Appx. D, *infra*.
730 *Id.*
731 *Id.* § 612 item 3.
732 15 U.S.C. § 1681i(d). The notion that the CRA ought to be required to notify previous users of corrected information in a consumer's file came first from the administration of President Nixon. Letter to Sen. Sparkman from Special Assistant to the President Knauer (June 19, 1969), *reprinted at Hearings on S. 823, Subcommittee on Financial Institutions of the Senate Banking and Currency Committee 11a–b*, 91st Cong., 1st Sess. (1969).
733 15 U.S.C. § 1681i(d).
734 *See* Ch. 6, *infra*.
735 *Id. See also* Koros v. Credit Bureau, Inc., [1974–1980 Decisions Transfer Binder] Consumer Cred. Guide (CCH) ¶ 97,856 (N.D. Ga. 1977), *aff'd*, 577 F.2d 144 (5th Cir. 1977).
736 15 U.S.C. § 1681i(d).
737 *In re* MIB, Inc., 101 F.T.C. 415, 423 (1983) (consent order).
738 *Id.* at 417.
739 *See* Ch. 7, *infra*.
740 *In re* Equifax, Inc., 96 F.T.C. 844, 1000 (1980), *rev'd on other grounds*, 678 F.2d 1047 (11th Cir. 1982).
741 Peeler, FTC Informal Staff Opinion Letter (July 15, 1981), *reprinted on the CD-Rom accompanying this manual. See also* FTC Official Staff Commentary § 604(3)(A) item 1B, *reprinted at* Appx. D, *infra*.

reinvestigation (e.g., deletion of information).[742] The special rules for expedited dispute resolution have an essentially identical requirement.[743] This notice must be given in writing not later than five business days after completion of the reinvestigation, not contemporaneous with or prior to resolution of the reinvestigation or the dispute.[744]

There is no specific requirement that the notice be clear and conspicuous, as existed under prior law.[745] Nevertheless, to be effective the notice must be provided in a manner and form which usefully informs the consumer of the right to notify past users. The consumer's right to this notice is essential to the FCRA's remedial and protective scheme.[746]

4.9.3 Payment for Notification

There is no charge for the notice to past recipients following the deletion of information from the consumer's file or the consumer's filing of a statement of dispute,[747] but only if the consumer acts in a timely fashion.[748] The consumer must designate the past users to receive the notice within thirty days of being notified of the conclusion of the reinvestigation.[749]

After thirty days, a CRA may impose a reasonable charge for notification to past recipients.[750] The charge for the notification cannot exceed the charge that the CRA would impose on each designated recipient of a consumer report.[751] That is, the CRA must look at the rate it would charge each of the past recipients of a report for a similar report. If certain users receive volume discounts, the consumer must receive the same discount, thus requiring the CRA to compute charges for each particular user.

The Act does not require the CRA to disclose the fact that no charge may be imposed for notices to past recipients if the consumer so requests within thirty days. The Act does require disclosure of the charge that is permitted for sending notices to past recipients after the initial thirty days before any such notice is sent.[752]

---

742 15 U.S.C. § 1681i(a)(6)(B)(v); 15 U.S.C. § 1681i(d).
743 15 U.S.C. § 1681i(a)(8).
744 15 U.S.C. § 1681i(a)(6)(A), (B)(v).
745 *See, e.g.*, Stevenson v. TRW, Inc., 987 F.2d 288 (5th Cir. 1993).
746 Alexander v. Moore & Assocs. Inc., 553 F. Supp. 948, 954 (D. Haw. 1982); *In re* Credit Data Northwest, Inc., 86 F.T.C. 389, 396 (1975); *In re* Checkmate Inquiry Serv., Inc., 86 F.T.C. 681, 684 (1975) (consent order). *See also* Stevenson v. TRW, Inc., 987 F.2d 288 (5th Cir. 1993).
747 15 U.S.C. § 1681j(e).
748 15 U.S.C. § 1681j(f)(1)(B).
749 *Id.* The notice that the reinvestigation has been concluded is discussed at § 4.6.1, *supra*.
750 *Id.*
751 15 U.S.C. § 1681j(f)(1)(B)(i).
752 15 U.S.C. § 1681j(f)(1)(B)(ii).

Chapter 5   Restrictions on Information in Consumer Reports

5.1 Introduction

The Fair Credit Reporting Act (FCRA) prohibits certain information from being included in a consumer report and places restrictions on the inclusion of other information. The most significant restriction is the prohibition on reporting obsolete information, discussed in § 5.2, *infra*. The FCRA also places restrictions on the reporting of disputed information (§ 5.3, *infra*), medical information (§ 5.4.1, *infra*), and information from personal interviews (§ 5.4.2, *infra*).

Other federal consumer protection laws place limitations on the reporting of certain information in consumer reports, including the Fair Debt Collection Practices Act (§ 5.3.3, *infra*), the Fair Credit Billing Act (§ 5.3.4, *infra*), the Real Estate Settlement and Procedures Act (§ 5.3.5, *infra*), and the Servicemembers' Civil Relief Act (§ 5.5.1, *infra*). Finally, there are also state laws that place restrictions on the reporting of information (§ 5.7); however, some of these laws may be preempted under the FCRA.

5.2 Restrictions on the Obsolete Information

5.2.1 Overview

Reporting of obsolete *adverse* information is prohibited under the FCRA.[1] Congress did not want to burden consumers who demonstrated improved credit performances with old adverse information in current consumer reports.[2] As a result, most adverse information more than seven years old may not be reported.

The FCRA sets out five types of exceptions to this prohibition:

- The seven-year period is somewhat different for certain types of information;[3]
- A ten-year rule applies to bankruptcies;[4]
- A one-year rule applies to prescreening inquiries;[5]
- Criminal convictions never grow obsolete;[6] and
- Consumer reporting agencies (CRAs) can report even obsolete information in certain situations involving transactions exceeding a specific dollar amount.[7]

The FCRA prohibits inclusion of obsolete adverse information in a consumer report; it does not however prohibit inclusion of such information in the consumer's file.[8] Because there are situations where information can be reported even after the seven-year period, CRAs have valid reasons to retain old information in the consumer's file. The CRA must establish procedures so that obsolete adverse information is not reported in most situations.[9]

5.2.2 General Principles

5.2.2.1 No Restriction on Use of Favorable Information

The FCRA does not restrict reporting information that is not adverse (i.e., information favorable to the consumer).[10] Thus, CRAs can report favorable information beyond the seven-year period.[11] This may be helpful for a consumer with a sparse credit record, particularly where the consumer's credit activity has been limited in recent years. In addition, it is misleading for a CRA to purge its files of solely favorable information before the seven-year period and retain adverse information, unless it first advises its users that such purges are done periodically.[12]

The FCRA does not define "an adverse item of information," but one explanation from the FTC has been:

  information which may have, or may reasonably

---

1 15 U.S.C. § 1681c(a); FTC Official Staff Commentary § 605 item 1, *reprinted at* Appx. D, *infra*.
2 S. Rep. No. 517, 91st Cong., 1st Sess. 1 (1969).
3 *See* § 5.2.3, *infra*.
4 *See* § 5.2.3.7, *infra*.
5 *See* § 5.2.3.6, *infra*.
6 15 U.S.C. § 1681c.
7 *See* § 5.2.4, *infra*.
8 FTC Official Staff Commentary § 605 item 3, *reprinted at* Appx. D, *infra*.
9 *See* § 5.2.5.3, *infra*.
10 FTC Official Staff Commentary § 605 item 2, *reprinted at* Appx. D, *infra*.
11 *See* Conway, FTC Informal Staff Opinion Letter (Sept. 11, 1973), *reprinted on the CD-Rom accompanying this manual*.
12 Trans Union Credit Info. Co., 102 F.T.C. 1109 (1983) (consent order), *reprinted on the CD-Rom accompanying this manual*.

be expected to have, an unfavorable bearing on a consumer's eligibility or qualifications for credit, insurance, employment, or other benefit, including information which may result, or which may be reasonably expected to result, in a denial of or increased costs for such benefits.[13]

Certain information has been characterized as neutral by FTC staff, and, as neutral information, it may be reported indefinitely.[14] Education records of graduation and degrees and dates of past employment are not considered adverse information. Even if an inquiry reveals that the consumer has misrepresented information on his resume for example, the factual information—as opposed to the misrepresentation—is not adverse. The distinction between neutral and adverse information is a slippery one, and leaves many questions to be answered. When, for example, does the reporting of past grades or frequent job changes move from neutral to adverse?

The distinction between neutral and adverse information is also complicated by the practice of credit scoring. Information that may be neutral considered by itself can become adverse in the context of credit scoring.[15] For example, information regarding old credit card accounts in good standing might not be considered adverse by itself. However, a credit scoring model might deduct points for having too many credit card accounts, even if they were in good standing.

5.2.2.2 Deletion of Information Before It Is Obsolete

There is no requirement that CRAs must report information for the full seven years. CRAs can delete adverse or favorable information from reports whenever they wish before the seven-year period.[16] Indeed, the CRAs are not under any requirement to retain existing information about a consumer in their files.[17] However, CRAs should not purge favorable information sooner than adverse information.[18] Similarly, a CRA may not mislead its subscribers as to the completeness of its reports by deleting non-derogatory information and not disclosing its policy of making such deletions.[19]

In fact, as a practical matter, CRAs might not be able to verify five- or six-year-old debts. If a consumer challenges the accuracy of the information, and the CRA seeks verification from the creditor, enough time may have elapsed so that the creditor can no longer respond with information from its records. Other creditors may respond based upon computer records, but may not have the underlying documents to show liability of the consumer.[20]

In addition, it may be that information, although technically not yet obsolete, could be inaccurate. The CRA must still comply with the Act's accuracy requirements[21] for any information reported. Although the information's age may not yet make it obsolete, its very age may lead to its reporting being inaccurate.[22] For example, to be accurate the report may have to include more recent information that provides a more complete picture of the consumer's present status. Whether a report is accurate is detailed in Chapter 4, *supra*.

5.2.2.3 Consumer Reporting Agency Cannot Report Even Existence of Obsolete Information

It is improper to indicate the existence of obsolete adverse information, even if the information itself is not reported.[23] Even communication or reporting by implication is prohibited. This affords the consumer complete protection from the user's possible reliance on obsolete information.

For example, in *In re Equifax, Inc.*,[24] an FTC administrative law judge found that the CRA violated the Act by

---

13 *In re* Miller, 335 B.R. 335 (Bankr. E.D. Pa. 2005) (quoting Equifax, Inc. v. Federal Trade Comm'n, 678 F.2d 1047, 1050 (11th Cir. 1982), which in turn cited the FTC's Final Order to Cease and Desist issued Dec. 15, 1980).
14 Ovadell, FTC Informal Staff Opinion Letter (Dec. 10, 1998), *reprinted on the CD-Rom accompanying this manual*.
15 *See* § 14.5, *infra*. The FTC has acknowledged this issue in one of its reports to Congress, but has implied such information is still not considered adverse despite its negative effect on a credit score. FTC Report to Congress Under Sections 318 and 319 of the Fair and Accurate Credit Transactions Act of 2003, at 11 (Dec. 2004).
16 FTC Official Staff Commentary § 605 item 4, *reprinted at* Appx. D, *infra*. *See also* Grimes, FTC Informal Staff Opinion Letter (Aug. 28, 1986), *reprinted on the CD-Rom accompanying this manual* (creditor may delete favorable file information after five years or any other chosen time period).
17 FTC Official Staff Commentary § 607 item 7, *reprinted at* Appx. D, *infra*.
18 Trans Union Credit Info. Co., 102 F.T.C. 1109 (1983) (consent order), *reprinted on the CD-Rom accompanying this manual*.
19 FTC Official Staff Commentary § 607 item 7, *reprinted at* Appx. D, *infra*.
20 Some creditors have a policy of discarding documents regarding an account after a certain period of time. *See, e.g.*, Johnson v. MBNA Am. Bank, N.A., 357 F.3d 426 (4th Cir. 2004) (discussing MBNA's document retention policy to destroy original documents after five years).
21 *See* Ch. 4, *supra*.
22 *See* Ch. 4, *supra*. *But see* McPhee v. Chilton Corp., 468 F. Supp. 494 (D. Conn. 1978); Todd v. Associated Credit Bureau Servs., Inc., 451 F. Supp. 447 (E.D. Pa. 1977), *aff'd*, 578 F.2d 1376 (3d Cir. 1979) (CRA had not violated the Act by furnishing a report that the consumer owed a debt of $1200, although the debt had been fully paid more than a year prior to the report, because that information was not obsolete under the seven-year standard).
23 *See* FTC Official Staff Commentary § 605 item 6, *reprinted at* Appx. D, *infra*.
24 96 F.T.C. 854 (1977) (initial opinion), *aff'd*, 96 F.T.C. 1045 (1980) (final opinion), *rev'd in part on other grounds*, 678 F.2d 1047 (11th Cir. 1982). *Cf.* Brinckerhoff, FTC Informal Staff

inserting phrases in its reports such as, "[i]n compliance with the Fair Credit Reporting Act, no additional information can be reported from this former employer concerning employment experience prior to seven years ago." The quoted phrase was inserted into consumer reports only when Equifax believed it had *adverse* obsolete information. It was enough that use of that phrase indicated the presence of adverse information, even if users of the consumer report might not actually interpret the stock sentence as suggesting the presence of adverse information.

The FTC Official Staff Commentary (FTC Staff Commentary) gives another example. A CRA may not report that a creditor (whose debt is now obsolete) cannot locate the debtor.[25] Similarly, the CRA cannot include information that the consumer was denied a job with a certain employer because of a criminal record, if that criminal record is obsolete.

Note, however, that nothing in the FCRA prevents one from using obsolete information should it be wrongfully included in a consumer report. In other words, CRAs may be held accountable for inclusion of adverse obsolete information in a consumer report in violation of the FCRA, but users of such information face no liability when they rely on obsolete information included in the report.

5.2.3 Maximum Time Periods to Retain Adverse Information

5.2.3.1 Structure of the FCRA

The FCRA sets out various time periods for determining if information is obsolete. All applicable dates relate to the *occurrence* of events involving adverse information; the date the CRA *acquired* the adverse information is irrelevant.[26] Thus, a CRA generally can only report a defaulted loan for two years if it received information about the loan five years after the default.

The FCRA provides specific time frames for five specialized types of information—bankruptcies, suits and judgments, paid tax liens, accounts placed for collection or charged to profit or loss, and records relating to arrest—and then provides a general rule for "any other adverse item of information,"[27] excepting "records of convictions of crimes." No limit applies to criminal convictions.[28] In addition, other legislation sets out standards for reporting old student loan defaults.[29]

The standard automated data reporting format created by the consumer reporting industry, known as Metro 2,[30] refers to the date of commencement of the obsolescence period as the "date of last activity."[31] The Metro 2 manual contains several discussions of how to calculate this date.[32]

5.2.3.2 Any Other Adverse Item

As a general rule, any adverse item (other than criminal conviction records and the five types of information specifically listed in the statute) cannot antedate the report by more than seven years.[33] This rule applies to most information about delinquent loans other than those placed for collection or charged to profit and loss.[34]

If the account is not charged off or placed for collection, the existence of a delinquent account may be reported for seven years from the date of the last regularly scheduled payment before the account became delinquent.[35] The FTC Staff Commentary is ambiguous about whether the trigger for the seven-year period is the last regularly scheduled payment in the schedule of payments or the last payment scheduled before the account becomes delinquent. Since, however, the FCRA refers to reports of an "adverse item of information," the seven-year period should run from the last payment scheduled before the delinquency.[36]

There are three exceptions to this general rule. First, each of the five types of information specifically listed in the same part of the statute has its own rules. These are discussed in later sections of this manual. Second, criminal convictions do not fall within the rule and may effectively be reported without limit.[37] Third, transactions exceeding certain dollar amount thresholds are exempted and are also discussed below.[38]

Opinion Letter (May 31, 1988), *reprinted on the CD-Rom accompanying this manual*.

25 FTC Official Staff Commentary § 605 item 6, *reprinted at* Appx. D, *infra*.
26 FTC Official Staff Commentary § 605 item 7, *reprinted at* Appx. D, *infra*.
27 15 U.S.C. § 1681c(a)(5).
28 *Id*.
29 *See* § 5.2.3.6, *infra*
30 *See* §§ 6.3.2, 6.3.3, *infra*.
31 *See* § 6.3.3.7, *infra*.
32 *Id*.
33 *Id*.
34 FTC Official Staff Commentary § 605(a)(6) item 1, *reprinted at* Appx. D, *infra*. For what constitutes a "charge off," see § 5.2.3.3.2, *infra*.
35 FTC Official Staff Commentary § 605(a)(6) item 1, *reprinted at* Appx. D, *infra*. For what constitutes a "charge off," see § 5.2.3.3.2, *infra*. If the account is charged off or placed for collection, the account can be reported for seven years plus 180 days from the first delinquency. See § 5.2.3.3.1, *infra*.
36 15 U.S.C. § 1681c(a)(5). *See also* Brinckerhoff, FTC Informal Staff Opinion Letter (Aug. 10, 1988), *reprinted on the CD-Rom accompanying this manual*; Brinckerhoff, FTC Informal Staff Opinion Letter (Apr. 30, 1987), *reprinted on the CD-Rom accompanying this manual*; Brinckerhoff, FTC Informal Staff Opinion Letter (Nov. 6, 1985), *reprinted on the CD-Rom accompanying this manual*.
 For accounts charged off or placed for collection, it is clear that the trigger is the date of the first delinquency, since the act refers to the "commencement of the delinquency." 15 U.S.C. § 1781c(c)(1). *See also* § 5.2.3.3.1, *infra*.
37 *See* § 5.2.3.6, *infra*.
38 *See* § 5.2.4, *infra*.

§ 5.2.3.3   *Fair Credit Reporting*

Even when certain kinds of information must be excluded from consumer reports because the information is over seven years old, the creditor or employer may still obtain the information in direct communication with former creditors, employers, or other sources.

5.2.3.3 Accounts Placed for Collection or Charged Off

5.2.3.3.1 The 180-day rule

Accounts placed for collection and charged to profit and loss are subject to a slightly different seven-year rule.[39] The seven-year rule for these accounts is modified by tying the calculation to the preceding delinquency and allowing an extra half year.[40] If an account is placed for collection, charged to profit or loss, or subjected to similar action, more than 180 days after the preceding delinquency, the debt may still be included in consumer reports for only seven years and 180 days from the beginning of the delinquency, or about seven and one-half years. "Similar actions" would include voluntary and involuntary repossessions.[41] This 180-day rule was added by the 1996 Reform Act.[42]

---

39   15 U.S.C. § 1681c(c). *See* §§ 6.3.2, 6.3.3, *infra*, for a discussion of how debt collectors report collection accounts using the Metro 2 reporting system.

40   15 U.S.C. § 1681c(c)(1); Ch. 6, *infra*, discusses furnishing information about delinquent accounts.

41   Gillespie, FTC Informal Staff Opinion Letter (Mar. 10, 1998), *reprinted on the CD-Rom accompanying this manual*.

42   Pub. L. No. 104-208 § 2406, 110 Stat. 3009 (Sept. 30, 1996). The 180-day rule is effective for any item added to a consumer's reporting agency file after December 29, 1997. 15 U.S.C. § 1681c(c)(2); Waggoner v. Trans Union, L.L.C., 2003 WL 22220668 (N.D. Tex. July 17, 2003) (180-day rule did not apply to charge off added in 1995).

Prior to the 1996 Reform Act, the seven-year period for accounts placed for collection or charged off commenced at the time of placement or charge-off. The effect of this old rule was to extend the time many delinquent accounts could be included in a consumer report. Amason, FTC Informal Staff Opinion Letter (Feb. 15, 2000), *reprinted on the CD-Rom accompanying this manual*. The legislative history of the 1996 Reform Act notes:

> The Committee is concerned that this seven-year limitation is ineffective. In some cases, the collection action occurs months or even years after the commencement of the preceding delinquency. Under these circumstances, the consumer reporting agency may maintain the information for seven years beginning on the date that the collection action is first reported. Consequently, the consumer report may contain such information even if the delinquency commenced more than seven years before the date on which the report is provided to a user.
>
> [Under] the Committee bill . . . If a collection or similar action is reported, . . . , the seven-year reporting period will commence not later than 180 days

The FCRA is clear that the obsolescence period begins to run from 180 days after the *first* delinquency.[43] Thus, an account with repeated delinquencies, for example July 2003, August 2003, and continuing until the account closed in August, has a "commencement of delinquency" date of July 2003, the seven-year period would start 180 days later, or January 2004, and may be reported for seven years thereafter until January 2011.[44]

If an account is placed for collection before the expiration of the 180-day period, the seven-year period runs from the charge-off or placement for collection. The net effect of these rules is that the seven-year limitation may begin any time from the delinquency itself until 180 days thereafter, depending upon when the debt is placed for collection, charged off, or subjected to similar action.

The FTC Staff Commentary includes specific examples of when placement for collection or a charge-off is considered to have occurred; recall, however, that the FTC Staff Commentary predates the 1996 Reform Act and thus does not include the effect of the 180-day rule. An account is placed for collection (thus triggering a seven-year period) when dunning notices or other collection efforts begin, though not when the initial past-due notices are sent.[45] The collection efforts may be those either initiated by the creditor in-house or by an outside collection agency, whichever occurs first.[46] The FTC staff has issued several staff opinions prior to the 1996 Reform Act as well, stating that the seven-year period begins to run when an account is charged off or placed for collection, whichever occurs first.[47] The period is not

---

after the beginning of the delinquency rather than on the date of any subsequent action.

S. Rep. No. 185, 104th Cong., 1st Sess. at 40 (Dec. 14, 1995).

43   The Act explicitly refers to the "commencement of the delinquency" as the trigger. 15 U.S.C. § 1781c(c)(1). An FTC staff opinion letter states that "commencement" means when the first payment is missed. Johnson, FTC Informal Staff Opinion Letter (Aug. 31, 1998), *reprinted on the CD-Rom accompanying this manual*; Kosmerl, FTC Informal Staff Opinion Letter (June 4, 1999), *reprinted on the CD-Rom accompanying this manual*. *See also* Harvey, FTC Informal Staff Opinion Letter (Dec. 23, 1997), *reprinted on the CD-Rom accompanying this manual* (use of "paid-to-date" (the date of the last paid periodic installment) was not acceptable).

44   *See* Kosmerl, FTC Informal Staff Opinion Letter (June 4, 1999), *reprinted on the CD-Rom accompanying this manual*.

45   FTC Official Staff Commentary § 605(a)(4) item 1, *reprinted at* Appx. D, *infra. See also* Brinckerhoff, FTC Informal Staff Opinion Letter (Sept. 24, 1985), *reprinted on the CD-Rom accompanying this manual*.

46   FTC Official Staff Commentary § 605(a)(4) item 1, *reprinted at* Appx. D, *infra. See also* Brinckerhoff, FTC Informal Staff Opinion Letter (Sept. 24, 1985), *reprinted on the CD-Rom accompanying this manual*.

47   Brinckerhoff, FTC Informal Staff Opinion Letters (Nov. 6, 1985), (Sept. 24, 1985), (July 26, 1985), and (July 30, 1985), *reprinted on the CD-Rom accompanying this manual*; Childs, FTC Informal Staff Opinion Letter (Apr. 18, 1986), *reprinted on the CD-Rom accompanying this manual*; Grimes, FTC Informal

extended by later reporting of the delinquency by the creditor.[48]

5.2.3.3.2 Nature of charge-offs

A charge-off occurs when a creditor moves a debt from profit to loss on its balance sheet.[49] Creditors or debt collectors may still attempt to collect upon the underlying debt even after a charge-off has occurred. They may also attempt to collect upon the debt even after the account has become obsolete for consumer reporting purposes. Such collection efforts remain subject to the applicable statute of limitations defense, so long as the consumer has not made any payments, which might renew the statute.

5.2.3.3.3 Furnisher's duty to provide the date of delinquency, charge-off, collection, or other event

Unless informed by the creditor or person furnishing information about a delinquency, a CRA has no way of knowing when the delinquency commenced and hence when the information must be eliminated from reports as obsolete. The FCRA requires that any person who furnishes information about a delinquent account placed for collection or written off, must also inform the CRA when the preceding delinquency commenced.[50] The date of delinquency does not have to be provided until ninety days following the time the information is first furnished to the CRA. A CRA which does not receive the date of delinquency within ninety days risks reporting obsolete information.

Note that the furnisher of information about a delinquent account is only required to report the month and year of the delinquency, while the restriction on the CRA for reporting the information runs from 180 days after the date of delinquency. Thus, to avoid reporting the delinquency after it has become obsolete, the CRA may have to calculate the 180-day time period from the first day of the reported month. The FCRA has specific rules on how debt collectors should designate the date of delinquency to ensure that the date precedes the date the creditor placed the account for collection.[51]

This obligation to report the date of the delinquency is statutory, but, with one exception, the furnisher is not liable to the consumer for any failure to comply.[52] The CRA, on the other hand, must maintain reasonable procedures to avoid reporting obsolete information,[53] presumably including taking reasonable steps to ensure that it has in fact received this important date.

5.2.3.3.4 Effect of subsequent events

The FCRA's requirement that the period of obsolescence run from 180 days after the first delinquency is intended to establish a single date certain for calculation of the obsolescence period.[54] Thus, subsequent events, such as the sale of the charged off account by the creditor or payment by the consumer, do not alter the obsolescence period.[55]

Despite this, practitioners report frequent problems with the reporting of incorrect start dates for the obsolescence period. Some furnishers report charge-offs more than once by reversing the charge-off and then re-aging the charge-off once a delinquency occurs. A charge-off is only allowed to occur once. When a debt is reported as charged off it cannot be reported again and there cannot be "multiple dates" of delinquencies or charge-offs.[56]

Some furnishers, particularly debt collectors, will also report a new start date when the consumer even acknowledges a debt. While an acknowledgment or partial payment may re-start the statute of limitations anew in some states,[57] it does not restart the obsolescence period for FCRA pur-

---

Staff Opinion Letter (Sept. 24, 1985), *reprinted on the CD-Rom accompanying this manual*; Fortney, FTC Informal Staff Opinion Letter (Aug. 24, 1984), *reprinted on the CD-Rom accompanying this manual*; Fortney, FTC Informal Staff Opinion Letter (Nov. 23, 1983), *reprinted on the CD-Rom accompanying this manual*. Note that the FTC Official Staff Commentary is silent on this point, but Supplementary Information published with the FTC Staff Commentary suggests the seven-year period be separately calculated for charge-offs and for placement for collections. 55 Fed. Reg. 18,804, 18,807 (May 4, 1990).

48 *See, e.g.*, Brinckerhoff, FTC Informal Staff Opinion Letters (May 7, 1987), (Apr. 30, 1987), (Nov. 6, 1985), (Oct. 8, 1985), (Sept. 24, 1985), and (Sept. 17, 1985), *reprinted on the CD-Rom accompanying this manual*; Childs, FTC Informal Staff Opinion Letter (Apr. 18, 1986), *reprinted on the CD-Rom accompanying this manual*; Fitzpatrick, FTC Informal Staff Opinion Letter (Dec. 16, 1985), *reprinted on the CD-Rom accompanying this manual*; Grimes, FTC Informal Staff Opinion Letter (Sept. 24, 1985), *reprinted on the CD-Rom accompanying this manual*.

49 Certain creditors, such as depository financial institutions, are subject to rules as to when delinquent debts must be charged off. *See* Federal Fin. Insts. Examination Council, Uniform Retail Credit Classification and Account Management Policy, 64 Fed. Reg. 6,655 (Feb. 10, 1999).

50 15 U.S.C. § 1681s-2(a)(5)(A). *See* § 6.3.3.8, *infra*.

51 15 U.S.C. § 1681s-2(a)(5)(B). *See* § 5.2.3.3.6, *infra*.

52 The one exception is that a furnisher may be liable for reporting an inaccurate date of delinquency when responding to a reinvestigation instigated by the CRA. *See* § 6.10, *infra*.

53 *See* § 5.2.5, *infra*.

54 *See* Amason, FTC Informal Staff Opinion Letter (Feb. 15, 2000), *reprinted on the CD-Rom accompanying this manual*; Kosmerl, FTC Informal Staff Opinion Letter (June 4, 1999), *reprinted on the CD-Rom accompanying this manual*; Johnson, FTC Informal Staff Opinion Letter (Aug. 31, 1998), *reprinted on the CD-Rom accompanying this manual*.

55 *See* Amason, FTC Informal Staff Opinion Letter (Feb. 15, 2000), *reprinted on the CD-Rom accompanying this manual*.

56 *See* Kosmerl, FTC Informal Staff Opinion Letter (June 4, 1999), *reprinted on the CD-Rom accompanying this manual*.

57 *See e.g.*, Potterton v. Ryland Group, Inc., 424 A.2d 761 (Md. 1981) (partial payment or even acknowledgment of a debt can revive a debt or remove the limitation bar on the debt under Maryland law).

poses.[58] A later section in this manual discusses the problems of debt collectors who "re-age" obsolete debts.[59]

Even prior to the enactment of the 180-day rule, the FTC Staff Commentary had provided that the reporting period is not affected by subsequent events, such as assignment to another entity for further collection, or by a partial or full payment of an account.[60] According to the FTC Staff Commentary, a charge to profit or loss occurs on the date the creditor takes action to write off an account,[61] usually to bad debt. A subsequent repayment in part or in full does not extend the time period.[62] Otherwise, consumers who seek to repay outstanding obligations are punished, and those who do not are rewarded.[63] However, the FTC Staff Commentary states that if the account is brought completely up to date, and another default occurs subsequently, the seven-year reporting period will run from the date of the new default.[64] It is unclear whether this provision remains valid after the addition of the 180-day rule by the 1996 Reform Act.

It is also unclear whether the seven-year limitation period should begin anew if the consumer signs a repayment agreement. Such agreements, in effect, are one type of collection tool to ensure that the original debt is paid in full or in part. In this sense, it should be treated as a repayment which does not extend the obsolescence period. To do otherwise will punish those who agree to repay and reward those who do not. However, one pre-1996 Reform Act FTC staff opinion letter and the FTC Staff Commentary say that a repayment agreement may be considered a new transaction with a new seven-year limitation period.[65] It may be separately reported as long as the report does not imply that there was a default prior to the repayment agreement.[66]

5.2.3.3.5 Debt collectors and "re-aging"

Problems frequently arise when information about a debt is furnished to a CRA by a debt collector.[67] Debt collectors commonly report the date they received the account or assignment from the creditor as the initial date of delinquency, even though the creditor has almost certainly placed the debt for in-house collection or charged off the debt months earlier. Debt collectors also will sometimes report a new date of last activity if the consumer acknowledges the debt or even inquires about it.

CRAs, often unaware of the earlier dates of delinquency, use the dates furnished by the collector. The effect is to extend the seven-year period well beyond the statutory limits.

With many consumer debts being sold and even re-sold to debt collectors, some of these debts are not only obsolete, but even decades old.[68] The FTC has brought enforcement actions against two debt collectors, including one of the nation's largest debt collection firms, alleging they re-aged accounts by using later-than-actual delinquency dates.[69] One of these cases settled for 1.5 million dollars, one of the largest civil penalties ever obtained in an FCRA case.[70]

One solution for consumers faced with a "re-aged" debt is to dispute the debt. If during the reinvestigation the collector again reports the incorrect date as the date of delinquency, the collector can be liable for its violation of

---

58 *See* Amason, FTC Informal Staff Opinion Letter (Feb. 15, 2000), *reprinted on the CD-Rom accompanying this manual*. The Metro 2 manual clearly instructs furnishers to use the date of first delinquency for FCRA purposes in this situation. *See* § 6.3.3.7, *infra*.

59 § 5.2.3.3.5, *infra*.

60 FTC Official Staff Commentary § 605(a)(4) item 1, *reprinted at* Appx. D, *infra*. An FTC staff opinion had also stated that the use of a "paid-to-date" (the date of the last paid periodic installment) was not acceptable. Harvey, FTC Informal Staff Opinion Letter (Dec. 23, 1997), *reprinted on the CD-Rom accompanying this manual*.

61 FTC Official Staff Commentary § 605(a)(4) item 2, *reprinted at* Appx. D, *infra*. For example, use of a "paid-to-date" (the date of the last paid periodic installment) may not be used. Harvey, FTC Informal Staff Opinion Letter (Dec. 23, 1997), *reprinted on the CD-Rom accompanying this manual*.

62 FTC Official Staff Commentary § 605(a)(4) item 2.

63 Brinckerhoff, FTC Informal Staff Opinion Letters (July 26, 1985) and (July 30, 1985), *reprinted on the CD-Rom accompanying this manual*; Fitzpatrick, FTC Informal Staff Opinion Letter (Mar. 8, 1985), *reprinted on the CD-Rom accompanying this manual*; Peeler, FTC Informal Staff Opinion Letter (Aug. 8, 1979), *reprinted on the CD-Rom accompanying this manual*.

64 *See* FTC Official Staff Commentary § 605(a)(4) item 1, *reprinted at* Appx. D, *infra*. *But see* Brinckerhoff, FTC Informal Staff Opinion Letter (July 26, 1985), *reprinted on the CD-Rom accompanying this manual*; Peeler, FTC Informal Staff Opinion Letter (Aug. 8, 1979), *reprinted on the CD-Rom accompanying this manual*.

65 FTC Official Staff Commentary § 605(a)(4) item 1, *reprinted at* Appx. D, *infra*. *See also* Fortney, FTC Informal Staff Opinion Letter (Aug. 24, 1984), *reprinted on the CD-Rom accompanying this manual*.

66 Fortney, FTC Informal Staff Opinion Letter (Aug. 24, 1984), *reprinted on the CD-Rom accompanying this manual*. *See also* § 5.2.2.3, *supra*.

67 *See* § 6.3.3.8, *infra*, for a discussion of reporting requirements for debt collectors.

68 *See, e.g.*, Rosenberg v. Calvary Invs., L.L.C., 2005 WL 2490353 (D. Conn. Sept. 30, 2005) (claims brought under FCRA, FCDPA, and state UDAP against debt buyer that furnished information on debt possibly from 1976, or nearly three decades old). Re-aged debts have even driven some consumers into filing for bankruptcy. *See, e.g.*, In re Miller, 335 B.R. 335 (Bankr. E.D. Pa. 2005) (dismissing bankruptcy case and advising debtor to seek relief under the FCRA).

69 United States v. NCO Group, Inc., Civ. No. 922-3012. *See* www.ftc.gov/opa/2004/05/ncogroup.htm, *reprinted on the CD-Rom accompanying this manual*; U.S. v. Performance Capital Mgmt. (Bankr. C.D. Cal 2000) (complaint), *available at* www.ftc.gov/opa/2000/08/performance.htm, *reprinted on the CD-Rom accompanying this manual*.

70 United States v. NCO Group, Inc., Civ. No. 922-3012, *available at* www.ftc.gov/opa/2004/05/ncogroup.htm, *reprinted on the CD-Rom accompanying this manual*. *See* § 11.16.2.1, *infra*.

the Act.[71] The collector can be even liable for failing to conduct an adequate reinvestigation independent of whether it reported an obsolete debt.[72]

Re-aging may also be actionable under the Fair Debt Collection Practices Act. Under the FDCPA, a debt collector is prohibited from communicating to a CRA any information which is known or "should be known" to be false.[73] Reporting the wrong date of delinquency for a debt could be information the debt collector knows or should have known was false.

5.2.3.3.6 Debt collectors must use creditor's date of account delinquency

The FCRA provides specific rules regarding how debt collectors should designate the date to ensure that the date of delinquency precedes the date the creditor placed the account for collection.[74] These rules were added by Fair and Accurate Credit Transactions Act of 2003 (FACTA),[75] and it remains to be seen whether they will curb the reporting of obsolete information.

The FCRA provides that the debt collector must use the date of delinquency used by the original creditor, if the creditor reported a date to a CRA.[76] If the creditor did not report a date of delinquency to a CRA, the collector must establish and follow reasonable procedures to obtain the date of delinquency from the creditor or a reliable source.[77]

If no date can be determined by these procedures, then the furnisher must establish and follow reasonable procedures to ensure that the date reported precedes the date on which the account was placed for collection, charged to profit or loss, or subjected to any similar action.[78] A problem may exist here in that some collectors will claim a stale account was never placed for collection or charged to profit or loss until long after it actually went delinquent.

The requirements for debt collectors only exist under the section of the FCRA (15 U.S.C. § 1681s-2(a)) that is not subject to a private right of action under the FCRA.[79] However, the duty should be enforceable against debt collectors regulated by the Fair Debt Collection Practices Act.[80] States are preempted from regulating the subject matter covered.[81]

5.2.3.4 Suits and Judgments

Information concerning suits and judgments are obsolete after seven years from their "date of entry" or until the governing statute of limitations has expired, whichever is longer.[82] For suits, the "date of entry" is the date the suit was initiated and for judgments the "date of entry" is the date judgment was rendered.[83]

According to the FTC Staff Commentary, *paid* judgments cannot be reported more than seven years after the original judgment was entered because payment of the judgment eliminates any governing statute of limitations that might lengthen this period.[84] What remains then is the manner in which "the governing statute of limitations" extends the seven-year period for unpaid judgments and for the filing of suits. The FTC Staff Commentary states that a suit not resulting in a paid judgment can have its reporting extended until the statute of limitations has expired.[85] This is somewhat confusing in that the filing of the suit usually tolls the running of the limitations period.

---

71 *See* § 6.10, *infra*. Under the federal Fair Debt Collection Practices Act, a debt collector must notify the debtor of a 30-day validation period during which the consumer disputes the debt. *See* National Consumer Law Center, Fair Debt Collection § 5.7.2 (5th 2004 and Supp.). The debt collector may not engage in collection activity, including reporting the date to a CRA, between the time a written dispute from the consumer is received and the collector responds. LeFevre, FTC Informal Staff Letter (Dec. 23, 1997). *See* § 5.3.3, *infra*.

72 Rosenberg v. Calvary Invs., L.L.C., 2005 WL 2490353 (D. Conn. Sept. 30, 2005).

73 15 U.S.C. § 1692(e)(8). *See* National Consumer Law Center, Fair Debt Collection § 5.5.11 (5th 2004 and Supp.).

74 15 U.S.C. § 1681s-2(a)(5)(B).

75 Pub. L. No. 108-159, § 312 (2003).

76 15 U.S.C. § 1681s-2(a)(5)(B)(i).

77 15 U.S.C. § 1681s-2(a)(5)(B)(ii).

78 15 U.S.C. § 1681s-2(a)(5)(B)(iii).

79 *See* § 6.10, *infra*.

80 15 U.S.C. §§ 1692–1692o. *See generally* National Consumer Law Center, Fair Debt Collection Ch. 5 (5th 2004 and Supp.).

81 15 U.S.C. § 1681t(b)(1)(F).

82 15 U.S.C. § 1681c(a)(2). *See also* Beaver v. TRW Corp., 1988 WL 123636 (W.D.N.Y. Nov. 17, 1988) (a satisfied judgment less than seven years old may be reported); Mulkey v. Credit Bureau, Inc., [1980–1989 Decisions Transfer Binder] Consumer Cred. Guide (CCH) ¶ 96,739 (D.D.C. 1983), *aff'd*, 729 F.2d 863 (D.C. Cir. 1984).

83 FTC Official Staff Commentary § 605(a)(2) item 1, *reprinted at* Appx. D, *infra*. *See also* Fitzpatrick, FTC Informal Staff Opinion Letter (Mar. 8, 1985) (date judgment is entered), *reprinted on the CD-Rom accompanying this manual*; Grimes, FTC Informal Staff Opinion Letter (Dec. 9, 1983), *reprinted on the CD-Rom accompanying this manual*.

84 FTC Official Staff Commentary § 605(a)(2) item 2, *reprinted at* Appx. D, *infra*. *Cf*. Grays v. TransUnion Credit Info. Co., 759 F. Supp. 390 (N.D. Ohio 1990).

85 FTC Official Staff Commentary § 605(a)(2) item 2, *reprinted at* Appx. D, *infra*. *Cf*. Grays v. TransUnion Credit Info. Co., 759 F. Supp. 390 (N.D. Ohio 1990). One FTC staff letter has interpreted the term "statute of limitations" to apply not to the limitations period to bring an action, but rather to the state or federal limitations period to use court processes to compel payment of a judgment. Gold, FTC Informal Staff Opinion Letter (Jan. 26, 1977), *reprinted on the CD-Rom accompanying this manual*.

5.2.3.5 Tax Liens

Paid tax liens may not be reported more than seven years after the date of payment.[86] This allows the liens to be reported more than seven years from when the lien was first due.

On the face of the statute, unpaid tax liens and other liens, whether paid or unpaid, are within the catch-all seven-year limitations for any other adverse item of information.[87] The FTC Staff Commentary, nevertheless, takes the position that unpaid tax or other types of liens may be reported as long as they remain filed and effective.[88] There is no statutory basis for such an interpretation,[89] particularly for liens not dealing with taxes since the provision only applies to tax liens.

Tax liens can be one of the more difficult entries to remove from a consumer report because they are public records and CRAs are reluctant to delete information that is based on public records, even if the initial entry is wrong. A tax lien that is expunged may still be reported because CRAs may not pick up the new information about the lien being expunged. Consumers and advocates should take extra steps to dispute incorrect information on tax liens, and ensure that corrections become part of the public record.

5.2.3.6 Criminal Records

Criminal convictions may be reported indefinitely. The general seven-year rule explicitly excludes records of convictions of crimes, and thus no time limit exists.[90]

Such was not always the case. Until November 2, 1998, "records of arrest, indictment, or conviction of crime which, from date of disposition, release or parole, antedate the report by more than seven years" were obsolete and could not be reported. However, that language was deleted, and the exception to the seven-year limit for convictions was added in an add-on section to the Consumer Reporting Employment Clarification Act of 1998.[91] It is unclear whether a conviction which was more than seven years old, obsolete, and not reportable at the time, can now be "resurrected" as part of a consumer report and be reported henceforth without limit.

Records of arrest are treated like civil suits and judgments.[92] They may be reported for seven years or until the governing statute of limitations expires, whichever is longer. The date that the seven-year period runs would normally be the day of arrest. It is not clear what is meant by the statute of limitations in this connection. Although a warrant for arrest may be subject to a limitations period, the arrest itself is not the type of event that is generally subject to any period of limitations.

No special rule exists for other kinds of criminal records, including criminal complaints, warrants, indictments, parole and probation, and various possible criminal judgments or dispositions other than conviction. These events therefore fall within the general rule for any other adverse item of information,[93] and may be reported for only seven years.

For obsolescence purposes, the date of parole is determined from the beginning of parole and not from its completion.[94] A violation of parole, however, may be separately reported for seven years.[95] Confinement may be reported for seven years from the date of release or parole.[96] Acquittals and dismissed charges may be reported for seven years from the date of dismissal.[97] Warrants for arrest which remain outstanding can be reported beyond seven years, but only for seven years after execution or arrest.[98]

A person's criminal record, other than a conviction may be reported neither directly nor indirectly if it is obsolete under the text. For example, a CRA cannot include information that the consumer was denied a job with a certain employer because of a criminal complaint if that criminal record is obsolete.

5.2.3.7 Bankruptcy Reports Considered Obsolete After Ten Years

Bankruptcies more than ten years old cannot be included in a consumer report.[99] The ten-year rule applies to all bankruptcy filings under the United States Bankruptcy Code, whether they be under chapters 7, 11, 12, or 13.[100] Both direct and indirect references to a consumer's bank-

---

86 15 U.S.C. § 1681c(a)(3).
87 *See* § 5.2.3.2, *supra*.
88 FTC Official Staff Commentary § 605(a)(3) item 1, *reprinted at* Appx. D, *infra*.
89 *Compare* 15 U.S.C. § 1681c(a)(2) *with* 15 U.S.C. § 1681c(a)(3) and (a)(5). *See also* FTC Official Staff Commentary §§ 605(a)(3) item 1, 605(a)(6) item 2, *reprinted at* Appx. D, *infra*.
90 15 U.S.C. § 1681c(a)(5). *See* § 5.2.3.1, *supra*.
91 Pub. L. No. 905-347, 112 Stat. 3208 (Nov. 2, 1998). These amendments were retroactive to September 30, 1997. *Id.*
92 Fite v. Retail Credit Co., 386 F. Supp. 1045 (D. Mont. 1975), aff'd, 537 F.2d 384 (9th Cir. 1976) (a CRA may lawfully report the record of an arrest or indictment and judgment of acquittal). *See* § 5.2.3.4, *supra*.
93 Russell, FTC Informal Staff Opinion Letter (Jan. 21, 1974), *reprinted on the CD-Rom accompanying this manual*.
94 *See* FTC Official Staff Commentary § 605(a)(5) item 2, *reprinted at* Appx. D, *infra*.
95 Rosen, FTC Informal Staff Opinion Letter (June 4, 1999), *reprinted on the CD-Rom accompanying this manual*.
96 *Id.*
97 *Id.*
98 Holland, FTC Informal Staff Opinion Letter (Dec. 16, 1999), *reprinted on the CD-Rom accompanying this manual*.
99 15 U.S.C. § 1681c(a)(1). The time period was shortened in 1978 from fourteen years to ten years. *See* Pub. L. No. 95-598 (Nov. 6, 1978).
100 *See* FTC Official Staff Commentary § 605(a)(1) item 2, *reprinted at* Appx. D, *infra*. An early FTC informal opinion letter stated that chapter 13 wage-earner plans were not bankruptcies within the meaning of this provision and therefore could be reported for only seven years. Conway, FTC Informal Staff Opinion Letter (Nov. 15, 1973), *reprinted on the CD-Rom accompanying this manual*. The applicable FCRA provision

ruptcy should be deleted from reports after ten years. For example, the restriction on obsolete adverse information would be undermined by allowing a report containing information that the consumer was denied credit because the consumer declared bankruptcy more than ten years before.

The ten-year limitation on bankruptcy reporting begins from the date of entry of the order for relief or date of adjudication under the Bankruptcy Code.[101] In a voluntary bankruptcy case, the ten-year period begins with the *filing* by the consumer of the bankruptcy petition. That is because the filing of the petition itself is the entry of an "order for relief" according to the FTC.[102] The applicability of the ten-year rule to involuntary bankruptcies dismissed without an adjudication of bankruptcy is not clear.[103]

While the FCRA permits bankruptcy cases to be reported for up to ten years, this does not appear to extend the time that specific debts discharged in a bankruptcy case may be reported. For example, the FTC staff has suggested that a discharged debt or judgment may be reported for only seven years and should, during that time and as a matter of accuracy, be reported as discharged in bankruptcy.[104] The one court that held that discharged debts may be reported for ten years was reversed without an opinion.[105]

5.2.3.8 Prescreening Inquiries

Prescreening is the process whereby CRAs compile or edit mailing lists of consumers who meet particular credit or insurance related criteria, used by creditors or insurers to offer services or products to those consumers.[106] CRAs must keep a record for one year of all such "inquiries" that identified a consumer for such a list, and include that information in any file disclosure made to the consumer.[107] On the other hand, the CRA may not include such information in any consumer report furnished to others.[108]

5.2.3.9 Student Loans

The Higher Education Act sets out special rules as to when reports on defaulted, federally backed student loans become obsolete. There are two different sets of rules, depending on whether the student loan is a Federal Family Education Loan (FFEL) or a Perkins Loan. FFELs (including guaranteed student or Stafford Loans, SLS loans, and PLUS loans) are obligations owed to a lender, which are guaranteed by a guaranty agency and then reinsured by the United States. A Perkins or National Direct Student Loan is an obligation owed to a school as lender that may be assigned to the United States if the student does not repay the loan.[109]

Reports on FFEL defaults may be included in consumer reports for seven years from the latest of three dates. (All three of these dates occur months or even years after the student defaults on the loan.) The first date for triggering the seven-year period for FFELs is when the Secretary of Education or the guaranty agency pays a claim to the loan holder on the guaranty. This can take place months or even years after default, and, in effect, is the date the guaranty agency of the United States takes over the loan. The second date that initiates the running of the seven-year period is when the Secretary of Education, guaranty agency, lender, or any other loan holder first reported the account to the CRA. The third date occurs if a borrower re-enters repayment after defaulting on a loan and subsequently goes into default on the loan.[110]

In contrast, Perkins Loans are not subject to any limit on reporting.[111] A small consolation for borrowers, passed at the same time, requires Perkins institutions to report to CRAs when a borrower has made six consecutive monthly payments on a defaulted loan, and to disclose promptly any changes to information previously disclosed.[112]

---

was later amended by Pub. L. No. 95-598 (Nov. 6, 1978) to refer not to "bankruptcies," but to "cases under Title 11 or under the Bankruptcy Act." *See also* Ch. 4, *supra*.

101 15 U.S.C. § 1681c(a)(1). This refers to the actual entry of the order, not a judge's oral utterance during a hearing. Collier on Bankruptcy ¶ 102.07 (15th ed.).

102 FTC Official Staff Commentary § 605(a)(1) item 3, *reprinted at* Appx. D, *infra*. *See also* Matter of Tynan, 773 F.2d 177 (7th Cir. 1985); *In re* Martinson, 731 F.2d 543 (8th Cir. 1984); First Nat'l Sav. & Loan Ass'n v. Winkler, 29 B.R. 771 (N.D. Ill. 1983); Fortney, FTC Informal Staff Opinion Letter (Nov. 15, 1985), *reprinted on the CD-Rom accompanying this manual*. The fact that a petition is later dismissed upon the consumer's motion does not affect the reporting period, but may have to be noted. *See* Ch. 4, *supra*. Isaac, FTC Informal Staff Opinion Letter (Dec. 9, 1996), *reprinted on the CD-Rom accompanying this manual*.

103 An FTC staff opinion states that a dismissed involuntary bankruptcy can be reported from ten years from the order of dismissal. Anonymous, FTC Informal Staff Opinion Letter (Nov. 5, 1999), *reprinted on the CD-Rom accompanying this manual*.

104 Fitzpatrick, FTC Informal Staff Opinion Letter (Aug. 26, 1988), *reprinted on the CD-Rom accompanying this manual*; Grimes, FTC Informal Staff Opinion Letter (Apr. 11, 1986), *reprinted on the CD-Rom accompanying this manual*. *See also* FTC Official Staff Commentary § 605(a)(1) item 1, *reprinted at* Appx. D, *infra*.

105 Learn v. Credit Bureau of Lancaster County, 664 F. Supp. 962 (E.D. Pa. 1987), *rev'd and remanded without published opinion*, 838 F.2d 461 (3d Cir. 1989).

106 *See* § 7.3.4, *infra*.
107 15 U.S.C. § 1681g(a)(5).
108 15 U.S.C. § 1681b(c)(3).
109 For an updated description of the different types of student loan programs, see National Consumer Law Center, Student Loan Law (3d ed. 2006)
110 20 U.S.C. § 1080a.
111 20 U.S.C. § 1087cc(c)(3). This provision was amended in 1998. Pub. L. No. 105-224, § 3, 112 Stat. 1585 (1998). Prior to the 1998 amendments, the time limit was seven years from the date on which the Secretary accepted assignment or referral of the loan from the school or first reported the account to a CRA, whichever was later.
112 20 U.S.C. § 1087cc(c)(5); 34 C.F.R. § 674.45(b)(1).

5.2.4 Transactions Exceeding Monetary Thresholds

The FCRA provides three exemptions to the prohibition against reporting obsolete information, which involve transactions that exceed certain dollar amounts. In these three specific situations, CRAs may furnish consumer reports containing information that would normally be considered obsolete:[113]

- A "credit transaction involving, or which may reasonably be expected to involve, a principal amount of $150,000 or more;"[114]
- The "underwriting of life insurance involving, or which may reasonably be expected to involve, a principal amount of $150,000 or more;"[115] or
- The "employment of any individual at an annual salary which equals, or which may reasonably be expected to equal, $75,000 or more."[116]

These exemption amounts were updated by the 1996 Reform Amendments, but not since then.[117]

Because of these exemptions, CRAs have legitimate grounds for retaining otherwise obsolete information in their files,[118] as long as the CRA reports this information only when the user's need falls within one of the three itemized situations. Nevertheless, to reduce the danger of obsolete information making its way into a report not involving any of the three exemptions, CRAs must establish procedural safeguards. These procedures should ensure that obsolete information is only released after an internal decision is made that the release will not violate the statute.[119] Procedures for release of this information are detailed below.[120]

CRAs need not retain information longer than seven years in circumstances covered by these three exemptions; they are, however, permitted to do so. Often it will be difficult or impossible for a CRA to verify information more than seven years old, so that the CRA may not wish to retain the information. Moreover, retention of selected information that old may run afoul of the statute's accuracy requirements.[121]

5.2.5 Reasonable Procedures Concerning Obsolete Information

5.2.5.1 General

A CRA must "maintain reasonable procedures designed to avoid violations" of the requirements dealing with obsolete information.[122] FTC Staff Commentary also states that CRAs should establish procedures with their sources of adverse information that will avoid the risk of reporting obsolete information.[123]

Consequently, CRAs have two separate obligations, and must comply with both. CRAs cannot supply obsolete information in violation of the Act. In addition, CRAs must follow reasonable procedures designed to avoid violations of the Act's obsolete information requirements.

There is no merit to the argument that reasonable procedures can act as a defense to the reporting of obsolete information—reporting obsolete information remains an independent FCRA violation leading to private remedies.[124] Nevertheless, private remedies under the FCRA are available only if a CRA's action is negligent.[125]

Certainly, a CRA's failure to follow its own procedures is evidence of negligence. Similarly, adoption of improper procedures makes the report of obsolete information at least negligent. There will also be a question as to negligence when a CRA strictly follows it own reasonable procedures, but where obsolete information is still reported. (If procedures result in the reporting of obsolete information, this should lead to a questioning whether the procedures are, in fact, reasonable.[126])

---

113 15 U.S.C. § 1681c(b). This statutory provision is ambiguously drafted in that it allows the reporting of obsolete information in the case of a "consumer credit report" falling within three exceptions. "Consumer report" is the term generally used throughout the Act, and the term "consumer credit report" is not defined under the Act. One interpretation of the use of the term "consumer credit report" in § 1681c(b) is that the three exceptions only apply if a report concerns credit. The FTC staff instead treats § 1681c(b)'s use of the term "consumer credit report" as an oversight, and that Congress intended the exceptions to apply to any consumer report. Grimes, FTC Informal Staff Opinion Letter (Nov. 24, 1992), *reprinted on the CD-Rom accompanying this manual.*

114 15 U.S.C. § 1681c(b)(1).

115 15 U.S.C. § 1681c(b)(2).

116 15 U.S.C. § 1681c(b)(3). The dollar limitation was intended to apply to the initial or starting salaries in the employment involved. Conference Rep. No. 1587, 91st Cong., 2d Sess. (1970), *reprinted in* 1970 U.S.C.C.A.N. 4394, 4911, 4915. The limitation is not exceeded by temporary employment even at high wage levels if the employee does not reasonably expect to actually pay at least the $75,000 threshold amount. Isaac, FTC Informal Staff Opinion Letter (Mar. 13, 1996), *reprinted on the CD-Rom accompanying this manual.*

117 Pub. L. No. 104-208, 110 Stat. 3009 (Sept. 30, 1996).

118 *See* Herring v. Retail Credit Co., 224 S.E.2d 663 (S.C. 1976). *See also* Brinckerhoff, FTC Informal Staff Opinion Letter (July 30, 1985), *reprinted on the CD-Rom accompanying this manual.*

119 FTC Official Staff Commentary § 607 item 1B, *reprinted at* Appx. D, *infra. See also* 15 U.S.C. § 1681e(a).

120 *See* § 5.2.5, *infra.*

121 *See* § 5.2.2.1, *supra.*

122 15 U.S.C. § 1681e(a).

123 FTC Official Staff Commentary § 607 item 1A, *reprinted at* Appx. D, *infra.*

124 *See* § 10.2.2.3, *infra.*

125 *See* § 10.2.1, *infra.*

126 *See* Lendino v. Trans Union, 970 F.2d 110 (2d Cir. 1992) (issues of fact preclude summary judgment for CRA where CRA sent plaintiff three credit files, one of which contained obsolete

While reporting of obsolete information should generally involve negligence, it is probably the case that a CRA is not liable for punitive damages (i.e., its actions are not willful[127]) where it maintains reasonable procedures and followed those procedures, even if obsolete information was reported. On the other hand, the failure of a CRA to adopt any standards or the adoption of clearly inadequate procedures may be evidence of willfulness, leading to punitive damages. Intentional violation of a CRA's own procedures may also be evidence of willfulness.

5.2.5.2 What Are "Reasonable" Procedures?

The legal standard for what constitutes "reasonable procedures" has been formulated as a "reasonable person" test. The question for the trier of fact is whether the procedures used by the CRA were those which "a reasonably prudent person would [exercise] under the circumstances."[128]

The FTC has stated that the types of procedures required may vary. The cost, in time and money, of imposing specific procedural requirements on the CRA will be one likely factor that the court will consider in determining reasonableness in any given case.[129] General standards of when a procedure is "reasonable" are also discussed in another chapter dealing with inaccurate reports.[130]

5.2.5.3 Specific Procedural Requirements Regarding Obsolete Information

CRAs must maintain procedures for discovering and deleting obsolete information contained in their files. In collecting information, CRAs should maintain procedures to ensure that they may properly date information and then be able to determine when information becomes obsolete. For example, CRAs should maintain reasonable procedures to date when an account first became delinquent, and should be alerted by the failure of a creditor to provide such information.[131] In the absence of such information, the CRA should assign a conservative date, such as the date of the last regularly scheduled payment.[132]

5.2.5.4 Procedures Determining Whether an Exemption Applies

As described above, the FCRA restricts when obsolete information may be *reported*. CRAs can *retain* obsolete information in the consumer's file, and even report that information in limited, designated situations.[133] If the CRA releases obsolete information, it must first verify that the user's purpose falls within one of these designated situations. Consequently, the CRA must maintain procedures which "require that prospective users of the information identify themselves, certify the purposes for which the information is sought, and certify that the information will be used for no other purpose."[134]

The FTC has interpreted this section to require written certification by the user of the purpose for which the consumer report will be used,[135] or, at least, to require the CRA to keep a written record of the user's oral certification.[136] The FCRA explicitly requires the CRA to verify the prospective user's identity and stated purpose only if it is a user to which the CRA has not previously furnished a consumer report.[137] Nevertheless, even for a CRA's regular user, the CRA must have information on which to base a reasonable expectation that the use of the obsolete information will be limited to one of the designated exempt situations.

5.2.6 Preemption of State Obsolescence Laws

State laws that have obsolescence periods which differ from those in the FCRA are preempted unless they were in effect on September 30, 1996.[138] State laws that antedate this preemption are discussed in a later section.[139]

5.3 Restrictions for Disputed Information

5.3.1 General

A major purpose of the FCRA is to prevent the reporting of inaccurate information, which is primarily effected

---

information, and credit card issuer indicated that rejection was based on CRA's information, however a good credit rating in the report sent to the issuer would have provided no rational basis for the credit rejection); Batdorf v. Trans Union, 2002 WL 1034048 (N.D. Cal. May 15, 2002) (TransUnion criticized for reporting when furnisher did not provide a date from which the seven-year period can be calculated).

127 Under the Act willful violations may result in punitive damages. See §§ 10.2.1, 11.12.1, *infra*.
128 Thompson v. San Antonio Retail Merchants Ass'n, 682 F.2d 509, 513 (5th Cir. 1982). *See also* Bryant v. TRW, Inc., 689 F.2d 72 (6th Cir. 1982).
129 *Cf.* Austin v. Bankamerica Serv. Corp., 419 F. Supp. 730 (N.D. Ga. 1974).
130 *See* Ch. 4, *supra*.
131 *See* § 5.2.3.3, *supra*.

132 FTC Official Staff Commentary § 607 item 1A.
133 *See* § 5.2.5.1, *supra*.
134 15 U.S.C. § 1681e(a).
135 Carson, FTC Informal Staff Opinion Letter (Apr. 8, 1971).
136 FTC, Compliance with the Fair Credit Reporting Act, at 26 (1977).
137 15 U.S.C. § 1681e(a).
138 15 U.S.C. § 1681t(b)(1)(E).
139 *See* §§ 5.7, 10.7, *infra*.

§ 5.3.2 Fair Credit Reporting

through its accuracy requirements discussed in another chapter.[140] Part of the FCRA scheme to promote accuracy is the dispute and reinvestigation process.[141]

Furnishers are also subject to special rules when they furnish information which has been disputed by consumer. The FCRA is one source of these restrictions, but others also exist.

This section provides a summary of the restrictions on the reporting and furnishing of disputed information. Other chapters in this manual—and other manuals in this series—describe these requirements in greater detail.

5.3.2 FCRA Restrictions on Disputed Information

5.3.2.1 Restrictions on Consumer Reporting Agencies

The FCRA restricts the reporting of information that has been disputed as part of the reinvestigation process. At the end of the reinvestigation period, the consumer reporting agencies (CRAs) must delete disputed information if the information cannot be verified, or corrected or modified in light of the reinvestigation.[142] If reinvestigation does not resolve the dispute, the consumer may file a brief statement setting forth the nature of the dispute.[143]

5.3.2.2 Restrictions on the Furnishing of Disputed Information

Under the FCRA, if a consumer has disputed with the creditor or other furnisher the accuracy or completeness of information, the furnisher may not report that information to a CRA unless it also provides notice that the information is disputed.[144] In turn, the CRA must note the dispute in each consumer report which contains the disputed information.[145]

The obligations of the furnisher to note when information has been disputed by the consumer is discussed further in another chapter.[146] Private enforcement of this furnisher obligation, like so many others, is severely restricted.[147]

5.3.3 Fair Debt Collection Practices Act Restrictions

Reporting an outstanding debt to a CRA is a "powerful tool" to force payment.[148] A debt collector may not be able to report a debt at all under the Fair Debt Collection Practices Act (FDCPA).[149] Under the FDCPA, a debt collector is required to cease all collection efforts if a written dispute is received within the thirty-day validation period, until verification is provided.[150] (The validation period commences when the collector sends a required validation notice to the consumer at the beginning of the collection efforts.) An FTC staff opinion[151] states that reporting a charged-off debt to a CRA is collection activity and that the debt may not be reported at all during this period. Even if the collector ceases collection activity altogether during this period, it still may not report the debt. Further, if the debt collector has already reported the debt to a CRA (for example, in the period before a written dispute is received), the FDCPA requires the collector to report the debt as disputed in any subsequent report or communication.[152]

Separate from whether a dispute is timely or triggers the verification duties, a debt collector is prohibited from communicating to a CRA any debt which is known or "should be known" to be false. A debt collector is also prohibited from failing to report as disputed a debt which it knows to be disputed.[153] While the prohibition against furnishing *any* information is only applicable during the pendency of a verification request, the furnishing of information known to be false is prohibited at any time and is a violation of the FDCPA.

While the FCRA requires all furnishers, including debt collectors, to note when information it furnishes to a CRA has been disputed by the consumer, little consequence flows from a furnisher's failure to note the dispute, i.e., no private FCRA remedies are available to the consumer.[154] In contrast, the FDCPA provides for a private cause of action,

---

140 See Ch. 4, *supra*.
141 See § 6.10, *infra*.
142 See Ch. 4, *supra*.
143 See Ch. 4, *supra*.
144 15 U.S.C. § 1681s-2(a)(3).
145 15 U.S.C. § 1681c(f).
146 See § 6.6, *infra*.
147 See § 10.2.4, *infra*.

148 Sullivan v. Equifax, Inc., 2002 WL 799856 (E.D. Pa. Apr. 19, 2002), *aff'd sub nom*. Trans Union, L.L.C. v. Fed. Trade Comm'n, 295 F.3d 42 (D.C. Cir. 2002) and authorities cited therein.
149 15 U.S.C. §§ 1692–1692o; Individual Reference Servs. Group, Inc. v. Fed. Trade Comm'n, 145 F. Supp. 2d 6 (D.D.C. 2001) (upholding regulation against multiple challenges). *See* National Consumer Law Center, Fair Debt Collection (5th 2004 and Supp.).
150 15 U.S.C. § 1692g(b).
151 LeFevre, FTC Informal Staff Opinion Letter (Dec. 23, 1997).
152 15 U.S.C. § 1682e(8). *See* Brady v. Credit Recovery Co., 160 F.3d 64 (1st Cir. 1998); Sullivan v. Equifax, Inc., 2002 WL 799856 (E.D. Pa. Apr. 19, 2002). *See generally* National Consumer Law Center, Fair Debt Collection § 5.5.11 (5th 2004 and Supp.).
153 15 U.S.C. § 1692(e)(8). *See* National Consumer Law Center, Fair Debt Collection § 5.5.11 (5th 2004 and Supp.).
154 See § 10.2.4, *infra*.

including actual and statutory damages for the same failure by a debt collector.[155]

Thus, the private enforcement remedies of the FDCPA are an important supplement to the FCRA. As an industry with an unfortunate number of rogue members and a record of over-zealous behavior, debt collectors remain subject to stricter laws and a range of enforcement possibilities that do not exist for consumers directly in disputes with creditors themselves.

5.3.4 Limits on Furnishing Information on Disputed Credit Card and Open-End Accounts

The Fair Credit Billing Act (FCBA) regulates creditor activity when a consumer complains of a billing error.[156] FCBA applies to credit card bills and other open-end credit, such as home equity lines of credit.[157] A billing error is defined quite broadly to cover a wide variety of consumer complaints.[158]

To invoke FCBA, a consumer must send a written notification of a billing error to the creditor within sixty days of the periodic statement in which the error appeared.[159] After receiving this notice, the creditor may not directly or indirectly threaten to report to any person (such as a CRA) that the consumer has failed to pay an amount which is due.[160] The creditor is permitted to report that the consumer has disputed the amount. The creditor is prohibited from reporting the account as delinquent unless the consumer has still not paid the bill after the creditor has complied with all the requirements of FCBA, such as investigating the complaint, sending the consumer a written explanation of the creditor's determination, and allowing the consumer at least ten days to pay whatever the creditor claims is still owed.

FCBA contains additional restrictions if the consumer notifies the creditor, within the time limit for payment, that the consumer still disputes the matter after the creditor completes its investigation. Under these circumstances, the creditor can report to a CRA and others that the account is delinquent, but only if it also reports that the consumer disputes the delinquency and notifies the consumer in writing of the name and address of every person to whom it is reporting information about the disputed amount. Furthermore, the creditor must notify everyone to whom the delinquency has been reported of any subsequent resolution of the dispute.[161]

FCBA does not require the creditor to notify the CRA of the ultimate resolution of the dispute unless the creditor previously had informed the CRA that the account was delinquent. Therefore, if an account is reported only as being in dispute, the CRA and the user may never be told that, upon investigation, the creditor concluded that the consumer was correct and the disputed amount was never owed. Of course, under the FCRA, a creditor does have an obligation to correct and update information previously furnished to a CRA,[162] although creditor liability is severely restricted.[163] The consumer may, of course, request that the CRA reinvestigate the accuracy of its information.[164]

In addition to FCBA, the federal Truth in Lending Act's credit card protections allow credit cardholders to raise defenses against a card issuer based on the cardholder's claims against the merchant.[165] The cardholder must have first made a good faith attempt to resolve the dispute with the merchant, the amount involved must exceed $50, and the transaction must have occurred in the cardholder's state or within one hundred miles of the cardholder's residence.[166] The cardholder loses the right to raise defenses if payment for that charge has already been made to the card issuer.

Once the consumer has notified the card issuer that payment is being withheld because claims and defenses are being asserted, the amount is in dispute and may not be reported as a delinquent amount, at least until the dispute is settled or judgment rendered.[167] The creditor may report the amount as in dispute.[168] The card issuer can pursue normal collection routines on any undisputed and delinquent amount,[169] including filing suit, but cannot begin collection of the disputed amount until it has completed a reasonable investigation of the consumer's claim.[170] Often the card issuer will simply remove the debit from the consumer's account and charge back the amount to the merchant, although this is not required.

---

155 Brady v. Credit Recovery Co., 160 F.3d 64 (1st Cir. 1998). See National Consumer Law Center, Fair Debt Collection Ch. 6 (5th 2004 and Supp.).
156 15 U.S.C. § 1666.
157 Id. See generally National Consumer Law Center, Truth in Lending § 5.8 (5th ed. 2003 and Supp.).
158 See 12 C.F.R. § 226.13(a); National Consumer Law Center, Truth in Lending § 5.8.3 (5th ed. 2003 and Supp.).
159 15 U.S.C. § 1666(a); National Consumer Law Center, Truth in Lending § 5.8.4 (5th ed. 2003 and Supp.).
160 15 U.S.C. § 1666a; National Consumer Law Center, Truth in Lending § 5.8.7.3 (5th ed. 2003 and Supp.).

161 15 U.S.C. § 1666a(b); National Consumer Law Center, Truth in Lending § 5.8.7.3 (5th ed. 2003 and Supp.).
162 See § 6.5, infra.
163 See § 10.2.4, infra.
164 See § 6.10, infra.
165 15 U.S.C. § 1666i. See also National Consumer Law Center, Truth in Lending § 5.9.5 (5th ed. 2003 and Supp.).
166 The latter two requirements do not apply when the card issuer and merchant are closely connected. See Regulation Z, 12 C.F.R. § 226 n.26.
167 12 C.F.R. § 226.12(c)(2). This would also violate the consumer's rights under the Equal Credit Opportunity Act. 15 U.S.C. § 1691(e).
168 FRB Official Staff Commentary to Regulation Z § 226.12(c)(2)-1(i).
169 Id. § 226.12(c)(2)-1(ii).
170 Id. § 226.12(c)(2)-2.

5.3.5 Real Estate Settlement Procedures Act Restrictions

Federal law provides certain protections regarding billing errors and disputes that involve home mortgage payments, home improvement loans secured by a residence, home equity loans, and other first and junior loans secured by the consumer's dwelling. These disputes may include related sales transactions, credit origination practices, or the calculation of the amount due, and are not infrequent given the complications of escrow amounts, assignment of the loan to different servicers, and late payment charges.

The Real Estate Settlement Procedures Act (RESPA)[171] provides certain rights to consumers to dispute the amount owed with respect to all these different types of loans, and offers protection from adverse consumer reports during the dispute period. RESPA applies to federally related mortgage loans, which is a defined term that includes virtually all loans secured by a first or junior lien on residential real property (including individual condominium and cooperative units) designed for occupancy of one to four families.[172]

If a consumer disputes an amount being sought on a loan covered by RESPA, the consumer can send the servicer a qualified written request. A qualified written request is a request from the borrower written *not* on a payment coupon or other payment medium supplied by the servicer, identifying the borrower's name and account, explaining why the borrower believes the amount owed is in error or requesting in sufficient detail other information from the servicer.[173] Within sixty days, the servicer must make any necessary corrections to the account or provide the consumer with a statement why the servicer believes the account is correct. If the consumer merely sought information, the servicer must provide the information or explain why the information is unavailable.[174]

During the sixty-day period when a servicer is evaluating a borrower's qualified written request, a servicer may not provide any information to a CRA regarding an overdue payment that relates to the consumer's qualified written request.[175] The statute seems to prevent such communication with CRAs for sixty days, even if the servicer responds immediately.[176] This helps give the consumer time to evaluate the response and decide whether to pay.

A similar protection arises when the servicing of a RESPA-covered home loan is transferred from one servicer to another. During the sixty-day period following the transfer, the homeowner may send payment to the old servicer which the new servicer expects to receive. As long as the old servicer receives the payment on or before the due date, the new servicer may not impose a late fee and may not treat the payment as being late.[177] By implication, the servicer may not inform a CRA that the payment was late.

Noncompliance with these RESPA requirements subjects the servicer to an action for attorney fees, actual damages, and (if there is a pattern or practice of noncompliance) up to $1000 in statutory damages for each individual or up to $500,000 or one percent of the servicer's net worth in the case of a class action.[178]

5.4 Other FCRA Restrictions

5.4.1 Medical Information Restrictions

5.4.1.1 Medical Information Definition

The FCRA contains a number of restrictions pertaining to medical information, which are discussed below.[179] Medical information is defined as any data or information that relates to:[180]

- Past, present, or future physical, mental, or behavioral health or condition of an individual;
- Provision of health care to an individual; or

---

171 12 U.S.C. § 2601. *See* National Consumer Law Center, Foreclosures § 5.2.2 (2005).
172 12 U.S.C. § 2602(1)(A). The loan must involve a federally insured or regulated lender; the loan must be guaranteed by the FHA, FmHA, the VA, or other federal agency; the loan must be intended to be sold to FNMA, Freddie Mac, or GNMA; *or* the creditor must have more than $1 million a year in residential real estate loans. 12 U.S.C. § 2602(1)(B). The major area where RESPA may not apply involves a private individual who makes a small number of mortgage loans, even though a major institution acts as a broker for that and numerous other individuals who are acting as lenders.
173 12 U.S.C. § 2605(e)(1). National Consumer Law Center, Foreclosures § 5.2.2.2 (2005).
174 12 U.S.C. § 2605(e)(2). National Consumer Law Center, Foreclosures § 5.2.2.3 (2005).
175 12 U.S.C. § 2605(e)(3). National Consumer Law Center, Foreclosures § 5.2.2.3 (2005).
176 Note that other collection activity, including foreclosure, is not restricted during this sixty-day period.
177 12 U.S.C. § 2605(d). National Consumer Law Center, Foreclosures § 5.2.3 (2005).
178 12 U.S.C. § 2605(f).
179 Some states regulate medical information in consumer reports. *See* § 5.7.2, *infra*. Some states also prohibit furnishing information about medical debts in certain situations. *See, e.g.,* Mo. Rev. Stat. § 287-140(13) (prohibiting furnishing information of medical debt if provider receives worker's compensation notice concerning injury). However, these laws may be preempted by the FACTA amendments. *See* § 10.7.5.2, *infra*.
180 15 U.S.C. § 1681a(i)(1). The banking regulators have promulgated regulations defining "medical information" for the respective institutions they regulate. *See* 12 C.F.R. §§ 41.3(k) (OCC), 222.3(k) (FRB regulated banks), 334.3(k) (FDIC regulated banks), 571.3(k) (OTS), 717.3(k) (NCUA). The FRB has also promulgated a set of regulations for non-bank furnishers on this topic. *See* 12 C.F.R. § 232.1(c)(5).

- Payment for the provision of health care to an individual.

Such information can be oral or recorded, and may be in any form or medium.[181] The information must be created by or derived from either the consumer or a health care provider.[182]

The FCRA specifically provides that health care information does not include demographic information about a consumer, including age, gender, address of residence, or e-mail address.[183] It also does not include information that does not relate to the physical, mental, or behavioral health of a consumer, including the existence or value of any insurance policy.[184] Regulations issued by the banking regulators and Federal Reserve Board (for non-bank furnishers) create an additional exception, one which excludes information that does not identify a specific consumer from the definition of "medical information."[185]

The FCRA's definition of "medical information" was amended in 2003 by FACTA to remove the requirement that the information have been obtained with the consumer's consent.[186] In addition, many of the medical information provisions added by the FACTA amendments grant rule-making authority, not to the FTC, but the banking regulators for the respective institutions they regulate: Office of the Comptroller of Currency (OCC) for national banks; Office of Thrift Supervision (OTC) for federal thrifts; Federal Deposit Insurance Corporation (FDIC) for certain state banks; National Credit Union Administration (NCUA) for federal credit unions; and the Federal Reserve Board (FRB) for a set of other banks.

5.4.1.2 Consumer Reporting Agencies Required to Obtain Consent to Report Medical Information

The FCRA prohibits consumer reporting agencies (CRAs) from reporting medical information about consumers for employment purposes, or in connection with credit or insurance transactions without consumer consent.[187] If the use involves employment or credit related purposes, the consent must be in writing, must be specific, and must describe the use for which the CRA will furnish the information.[188] Furthermore, the medical information must to relevant for the employment or credit transaction at issue.[189]

A significant exception to this consent requirement is that a CRA may provide medical information if (a) the information pertains solely to financial transactions arising from medical services or products and (b) the CRA ensures that the information does not disclose the specific provider of medical services or the nature of services, but is coded pursuant to section 1681c(a)(6).[190]

The FCRA prohibits users from re-disclosing medical information that was permissibly obtained either through consent or because it was coded, unless re-disclosure is necessary for the purpose for which the information was initially obtained.[191] The banking regulators have issued similar regulations prohibiting the financial institutions they regulate from re-disclosing medical information obtained from a CRA or an affiliate.[192] Exceptions to re-disclosure can also be established by statute, regulation, or order.[193]

The requirements for consent are violated if the medical information is negligently reported. There is no "reasonable procedures" defense to the improper reporting of medical information without the required consumer consent. If medical information is released without such consent, it should create a prima facie case, or at least a rebuttable presumption, of negligence.

5.4.1.3 Restrictions on Reporting the Identifying Information of Medical Information Furnishers

The FCRA prohibits CRAs from including in consumer reports the name, address, and telephone number provided by furnishers of medical information.[194] An exception is provided if such information is restricted or reported using codes that do not identify, or provide information sufficient to infer, the specific provider or the nature of such services, products, or devices to a person other than the consumer.[195]

This restriction is intended to ensure that consumers who have medical transactions in their credit files are protected by requiring that the information be coded so that third parties cannot glean any health implications relating to the consumer.[196] It is not intended to prohibit the inclusion in a

---

181 15 U.S.C. § 1681a(i)(1).
182 *Id.*
183 15 U.S.C. § 1681a(i)(2). *See also* 12 C.F.R. §§ 41.3(k)(2) (OCC), 222.3(k)(2) (FRB regulated banks), 334.3(k)(2) (FDIC regulated banks), 571.3(k)(2) (OTS), 717.3(k)(2) (NCUA), 232.1(c)(5)(ii) (non-bank furnishers).
184 *Id.* This exclusion was added by the FACTA amendments in 2003. Pub. L. No. 108-159, § 411(c) (2003).
185 12 C.F.R. § 41.3(k)(2)(OCC); 12 C.F.R. §§ 222.3(k)(2)(iv) (FRB regulated banks), 334.3(k)(2)(iv) (FDIC regulated banks), 571.3(k)(2)(iv) (OTS), 717.3(k)(2)(iv) (NCUA), 232.1(c)(5)(ii)(D) (non-bank furnishers).
186 Pub. L. No. 108-159, § 411(c) (2003).
187 15 U.S.C. § 1681b(g).
188 15 U.S.C. § 1681b(g)(1)(B)(ii).
189 15 U.S.C. § 1681b(g)(1)(B)(i).
190 15 U.S.C. § 1681b(g)(1)(C). The coding requirements of 15 U.S.C. § 1681c(a)(6), are discussed in § 5.4.1.3, *infra*.
191 15 U.S.C. § 1681b(g)(4).
192 12 C.F.R. §§ 41.31 (OCC), 222.31 (FRB regulated banks), 334.31 (FDIC regulated banks), 571.31 (OTS), 717.31 (NCUA).
193 15 U.S.C. § 1681b(g)(4)
194 15 U.S.C. § 1681c(a)(6)(A).
195 *Id. See also* 15 U.S.C. § 1681(g)(1)(C).
196 H. Rep. No. 108-263, at 54 (2003).

consumer report of information relating to the consumer's place of employment.[197]

In order to ensure that the CRAs can properly implement this restriction, the FCRA requires furnishers whose primary business is providing medical services, products or devices to notify CRAs of such status.[198] Also, the exceptions contained in the FCRA that allow CRAs to include otherwise-to-be-excluded information in reports if the dollar value of the transaction meets or exceeds certain amounts[199] do not apply to the prohibition against identifying medical information furnishers and the coding requirements.[200]

There is an exception to the coding requirements that permits the CRAs to provide medical furnisher information in reports to insurance companies.[201] However, such reports must be used for a purpose relating to insurance other than property or casualty insurance.[202]

States are preempted from regulating the subject matter of this prohibition.[203]

5.4.1.4 Affiliate Sharing Exception Not Applicable to Medical Information

Under the FCRA, information shared between affiliates is excluded from the definition of a consumer report.[204] However, the affiliate sharing exclusion does not apply if the information is:[205]

- Medical information;
- An individualized list or description based on a consumer's payments for medical products or services; or
- An aggregate list of identified consumers based on payment for medical products or services.

To make matters even more complicated, this exception to the affiliate sharing exclusion has its own exceptions. Thus, the affiliate sharing exclusion *does* apply (and thus information is not considered a consumer report) if the medical information is disclosed in connection with the business of insurance or annuities.[206] The affiliate sharing exclusion also applies if the medical information is permitted to be disclosed without consent under the privacy rule for health information issued pursuant to the Health Insurance Portability and Accountability Act (HIPAA)[207] or is covered under certain exemptions[208] in the Gramm-Leach-Bliley Act (GLBA).[209]

The regulations issued by the banking regulators create an additional category permitting affiliate sharing for medical information. The regulations permit affiliate sharing for medical information that is used to determine eligibility for credit, consistent with the regulatory exceptions for creditor use of medical information.[210] Furthermore, the FCRA gives the FTC and banking regulators the authority to create additional affiliate sharing categories for medical information, either by regulation or administrative order,[211] consistent with other federal laws governing medical confidentiality.[212] Finally, if users receive medical information pursuant to the affiliate sharing exclusion, the FCRA prohibits users from re-disclosing such reports.[213]

5.4.1.5 Medical Information Creditor Restrictions

5.4.1.5.1 Creditors may not discriminate against applicants on the basis of medical information

The FCRA restricts creditors from obtaining or using medical information when they make a determination on the eligibility or continued eligibility of a consumer for credit.[214] This FCRA restriction is unusual in that it is not limited to information contained within a consumer file, but applies to *any* medical information about the consumer. It is essentially an anti-discrimination provision that prohibits creditors from using medical information adversely against applicants.

The FCRA provides the banking regulators, but not the FTC, with the authority to create exceptions to this restriction that are necessary and appropriate to protect the operational, transactional, risk, consumer, and other needs of the institutions they regulate.[215] Despite the fact that the FCRA

---

197 Id.
198 15 U.S.C. § 1681s-2(a)(9).
199 See § 5.2.4, *supra.*
200 15 U.S.C. § 1681c(b).
201 15 U.S.C. § 1681c(a)(6)(B).
202 Id.
203 15 U.S.C. § 1681t(b)(1)(E) and (F).
204 15 U.S.C. § 1681a(d)(2)(A)(ii) and (iii). See § 2.4.3, *supra.*
205 15 U.S.C. § 1681a(d)(3).
206 15 U.S.C. § 1681b(g)(3)(A). This includes the activities described in section 18B of the model Privacy of Consumer Financial and Health Information Regulation issued by the National Association of Insurance Commissioners as in effect January 1, 2003. Id.
207 Pub. L. No. 104-191 (1996). The HIPAA Privacy Rule is at 45 C.F.R. Parts 160 and 164. For a brief description of HIPAA protections, see National Consumer Law Center, Fair Debt Collection § 14.3.3 (5th ed. 2004 and Supp.).
208 The exemptions are enumerated in section 502(e) of the Gramm-Leach-Bliley Act, 15 U.S.C. § 6802(e), and are described in § 16.4.1.5, *infra.*
209 15 U.S.C. § 1681b(g)(3)(B). See 12 C.F.R. §§ 41.32(c)(4) (OCC), 222.32(c)(4) (FRB regulated banks), 334.32(c)(4) (FDIC regulated banks), 571.32(c)(4) (OTS), 717.32(c)(4) (NCUA).
210 See 12 C.F.R. §§ 41.32(c)(5) (OCC), 222.32(c)(5) (FRB regulated banks), 334.32(c)(5) (FDIC regulated banks), 571.32(c)(5) (OTS), 717.32(c)(5) (NCUA). The exceptions to the prohibition against creditor use of medical information are discussed in § 5.4.1.5.2, *infra.*
211 15 U.S.C. § 1681b(g)(3)(C).
212 15 U.S.C. § 1681b(g)(6).
213 15 U.S.C. § 1681b(g)(4).
214 15 U.S.C. § 1681b(g)(2).
215 15 U.S.C. § 1681b(g)(5).

granted rulemaking authority only to the banking regulators, and thus implicitly allows exceptions only for those financial institutions they regulate, the exceptions were extended to all creditors, in regulations promulgated by the Federal Reserve Board.[216]

5.4.1.5.2 Scope of prohibition

The prohibition against obtaining or using medical information applies in connection with a determination of a consumer's "eligibility, or continued eligibility," for credit.[217] This includes the qualification or fitness to receive credit, to continue to receive credit, and the terms on which credit is offered.[218] It does not include any determination concerning qualifications for employment, insurance (other than credit insurance), or other non-credit product or service.[219]

The prohibition also does not extend to maintaining or servicing a consumer's account, or to authorizing, processing or documenting a payment or transaction on behalf of a consumer, so long as these activities do not involve a determination of eligibility for credit.[220]

The prohibition is not limited to credit for personal, family, or household purposes, so long as the medical information relates to an individual and the individual is personally liable for the credit.[221] This is because FCRA defines "consumer" as an individual,[222] and uses the definition of "credit" and "creditor" from the Equal Credit Opportunity Act,[223] which is not limited to consumer credit.[224]

The FCRA excludes medical information that is coded in consumer reports pursuant to section 1681c(a)(6)[225] from the prohibition against obtaining or using medical information.[226] Also, a creditor does not violate the medical information use prohibition if it receives medical information without specifically requesting it, and does not use the information except pursuant to one of the exceptions established by regulation.[227]

5.4.1.5.3 Medical financial information exception

The major exception to the medical information use prohibition is for "medical financial information." This exception permits creditors to obtain and use medical information in connection with a determination of the consumer's eligibility for credit so long as three conditions are met:

- The information is the type routinely used in making credit eligibility determinations, such as information concerning debts, expenses, income, benefits, assets, collateral, or the purpose of the loan, including the use of proceeds.[228] Examples of this type of information includes the dollar amount of medical debts, the value of medical devices used to secure a loan, the amount and continued eligibility for disability income, and the identity of medical creditors.[229]
- The creditor uses the medical information in a manner and to an extent that is *no less favorable* than it would use comparable information that is not medical information in a credit transaction.[230]
- The creditor does not take the consumer's physical, mental, or behavioral health, condition or history, type of treatment, or prognosis into account in determining credit eligibility.[231]
- This exception essentially establishes a "no less favorable" standard for medical financial information. Thus, a creditor is permitted to deny credit to an applicant on

---

216 12 C.F.R. Part 232.
217 15 U.S.C. § 1681b(g)(2).
218 12 C.F.R. §§ 41.30(b)(2)(iii) (OCC), 222.30(b)(2)(iii) (FRB regulated banks), 334.30(b)(2)(iii) (FDIC regulated banks), 571.30(b)(2)(iii) (OTS), 717.30(b)(2)(iii) (NCUA), 232.1(c)(4) (non-bank furnishers).
219 12 C.F.R. §§ 41.30(b)(2)(iii)(A) (OCC), 222.30(b)(2)(iii)(A) (FRB regulated banks), 334.30(b)(2)(iii)(A) (FDIC regulated banks), 571.30(b)(2)(iii)(A) (OTS), 717.30(b)(2)(iii)(A) (NCUA), 232.1(c)(4)(i) (non-bank furnishers).
220 12 C.F.R. §§ 41.30(b)(2)(iii)(B) and (C) (OCC), 222.30(b)(2)(iii)(B) and (C) (FRB regulated banks), 334.30(b)(2)(iii)(B) and (C) (FDIC regulated banks), 571.30(b)(2)(iii)(B) and (C) (OTS), 717.30(b)(2)(iii)(B) and (C) (NCUA), 232.1(c)(4)(ii) and (iii) (non-bank furnishers).
221 The banking regulators had issued proposed rules that would have limited the prohibition to eligibility for credit for personal, family, or household purposes, but subsequently withdrew that limitation. 70 Fed. Reg. 33,958, 33,964 (June 10, 2005) (supplementary information to interim final rule).
222 15 U.S.C. § 1681a(c).
223 15 U.S.C. § 1681a(r)(5).
224 *See* National Consumer Law Center, Credit Discrimination § 2.2.2.1 (4th ed. 2005 and Supp.). The ECOA does contain some exemptions in its procedural requirements for business credit, but its anti-discrimination provisions apply fully. *Id.* § 2.2.6.4.

225 *See* § 5.4.1.3, *supra*.
226 15 U.S.C. § 1681b(g)(2).
227 12 C.F.R. §§ 41.30(c)(OCC), 222.30(c) (FRB regulated banks), 334.30(c) (FDIC regulated banks), 571.30(c) (OTS), 717.30(c) (NCUA), 232.2(a) and (b) (non-bank furnishers).
228 12 C.F.R. §§ 41.30(d)(1)(i) (OCC), 222.30(d)(1)(i) (FRB regulated banks), 334.30(d)(1)(i) (FDIC regulated banks), 571.30(d)(1) (OTS)(i), 717.30(d)(1)(i) (NCUA), 232.3(a)(1) (non-bank furnishers).
229 12 C.F.R. §§ 41.30(d)(2)(i) (OCC), 222.30(d)(2)(i) (FRB regulated banks), 334.30(d)(2)(i) (FDIC regulated banks), 571.30(d)(2)(i) (OTS), 717.30(d)(2)(i) (NCUA), 232.3(b)(1) (non-bank furnishers).
230 12 C.F.R. §§ 41.30(d)(1)(ii) (OCC), 222.30(d)(1)(ii) (FRB regulated banks), 334.30(d)(1)(ii) (FDIC regulated banks), 571.30(d)(1)(ii) (OTS), 717.30(d)(1)(ii) (NCUA), 232.3(a)(2) (non-bank furnishers).
231 12 C.F.R. §§ 41.30(d)(1)(iii) (OCC), 222.30(d)(1)(iii) (FRB regulated banks), 334.30(d)(1)(iii) (FDIC regulated banks), 571.30(d)(1)(iii) (OTS), 717.30(d)(1)(iii) (NCUA), 232.3(a)(3) (non-bank furnishers).

the basis of an overdue hospital debt, if the creditor would have made the same decision were the debt owed to a retailer.[232] However, if the creditor would have approved the loan had the debt been owed to a retailer, the creditor's use of medical information does not fall under this exception and the creditor will have violated the prohibition.[233]

In addition to prohibiting negative treatment on the basis of medical condition, the standard affords creditors the discretion to treat medically-related debt and expenses more leniently than other types of debt. Creditors will sometimes treat medical debt more leniently than non-medical debt because such debt often does not reflect a consumer's propensity to pay due to the circumstances under which it is incurred.[234] For instance, delinquent medical debt reported to a CRA is often the result of disputes between medical providers and insurers, where the consumer is "caught in the middle."[235]

5.4.1.5.4 Special purpose credit assistance and medical financing programs

The regulations permit use of medical information to determine a consumer's qualification for certain loan programs based on medical condition. First, the regulations create a category of special credit or credit-related assistance programs, similar to the special credit purpose programs established under the Equal Credit Opportunity Act.[236] Creditors may use medical information to determine eligibility for these special credit assistance programs so long as the programs are:[237]

- Designed to meet the special needs of consumers with medical conditions; and

- Established and administered pursuant to a written plan that (1) identifies the class of persons that the program is designed to benefit and (2) sets forth procedures and standards for granting credit or credit-related assistance.

An example of a special credit assistance program would be a loan program designed to assist disabled veterans. A creditor pursuant to such a program would be permitted to obtain medical information about the disability of the applicant to verify that the applicant qualifies for the program.[238]

Second, the regulations establish an exception for credit extended for the purpose of financing medical products or services. A creditor of medical financing may use medical information to verify the purpose of the loan and the use of proceeds.[239] For example, if a consumer applies for a loan to undertake a medical procedure, the creditor is permitted to verify that the procedure is actually going to be performed and the cost of the procedure.[240] Furthermore, if a medical loan program only finances certain procedures, it may deny an applicant on the basis that the applicant is undergoing a different procedure not eligible under the program.[241]

5.4.1.5.5 Other exceptions

The regulations create a number of other exceptions to the rule against obtaining or using medical information in determining credit eligibility. These exceptions include the following:

- To determine whether the use of a power of attorney or legal representative triggered by a medical condition or event is necessary and appropriate, or whether the consumer has the legal capacity to contract when a person seeks to exercise a power of attorney or act as legal representative based on medical condition or event;[242]

---

232 12 C.F.R. §§ 41.30(d)(2)(ii)(A) (OCC), 222.30(d)(2)(ii)(A) (FRB regulated banks), 334.30(d)(2)(ii)(A) (FDIC regulated banks), 571.30(d)(2)(ii)(A) (OTS), 717.30(d)(2)(ii)(A) (NCUA), 232.3(b)(2)(i) (non-bank furnishers).

233 12 C.F.R. §§ 41.30(d)(2)(iii)(A) (OCC), 222.30(d)(2)(iii)(A) (FRB regulated banks), 334.30(d)(2)(iii)(A) (FDIC regulated banks), 571.30(d)(2)(iii)(A) (OTS), 717.30(d)(2)(iii)(A) (NCUA), 232.3(b)(3)(i) (non-bank furnishers).

234 Eve Tahmincioglu, *Is Your Health Insurance Hurting Your Credit?*, New York Times, May 12, 2002.

235 Jennifer Steinhauer, *Will Doctors Make Your Credit Sick?*, New York Times, February 4, 2001; Consumer Federation of America and National Credit Reporting Association, Credit Score Accuracy and Implications for Consumers 31 (Dec. 17, 2002), *available at* www.consumerfed.org/121702CFA_NCRA_Credit_Score_Report_Final.pdf.

236 *See* National Consumer Law Center, Credit Discrimination § 3.9 (4th ed. 2005 and Supp.).

237 12 C.F.R. §§ 41.30(e)(1)(iii) (OCC), 222.30(e)(1)(iii) (FRB regulated banks), 334.30(e)(1)(iii) (FDIC regulated banks), 571.30(e)(1)(iii) (OTS), 717.30(e)(1)(iii) (NCUA), 232.4(a)(3) (non-bank furnishers).

238 12 C.F.R. §§ 41.30(e)(2) (OCC), 222.30(e)(2) (FRB regulated banks), 334.30(e)(2) (FDIC regulated banks), 571.30(e)(2) (OTS), 717.30(e)(2) (NCUA), 232.4(b) (non-bank furnishers).

239 12 C.F.R. §§ 41.30(e)(1)(v) (OCC), 222.30(e)(1)(v) (FRB regulated banks), 334.30(e)(1)(v) (FDIC regulated banks), 571.30(e)(1)(v) (OTS), 717.30(e)(1)(v) (NCUA), 232.4(a)(5) (non-bank furnishers).

240 12 C.F.R. §§ 41.30(e)(3)(i) and (ii) (OCC), 222.30(e)(3)(i) and (ii) (FRB regulated banks), 334.30(e)(3)(i) and (ii) (FDIC regulated banks), 571.30(e)(3)(i) and (ii) (OTS), 717.30(e)(3)(i) and (ii) (NCUA), 232.4(c)(1) and (2) (non-bank furnishers).

241 12 C.F.R. §§ 41.30(e)(3)(iii) (OCC), 222.30(e)(3)(iii) (FRB regulated banks), 334.30(e)(3)(iii) (FDIC regulated banks), 571.30(e)(3)(iii) (OTS), 717.30(e)(3)(iii) (NCUA), 232.4(c)(3) (non-bank furnishers).

242 12 C.F.R. §§ 41.30(e)(1)(i)(OCC), 222.30(e)(1)(i) (FRB regulated banks), 334.30(e)(1)(i) (FDIC regulated banks), 571.30(e)(1)(i) (OTS), 717.30(e)(1)(i) (NCUA), 232.4(a)(1) (non-bank furnishers).

- To comply with local, state, or federal laws;[243]
- For purposes of fraud prevention or detection;[244]
- To determine whether the consumer is eligible for a forbearance program that is triggered by a medical condition or event;[245]
- To make determinations regarding eligibility for, triggering of, or reactivation of a debt cancellation contract or credit insurance product, but only if a medical condition or event is a triggering event for the provision of benefits under that contract or product;[246] or
- If the consumer specifically requests that the creditor use medical information in determining the consumer's eligibility or continued eligibility for credit, to accommodate the consumer's particular circumstances, and such request is documented by the creditor.[247]

5.4.2 Information from Personal Interviews

Consumer reports cannot contain information from personal interviews with friends, neighbors, business associates, or other third parties, unless they comply with certain special restrictions. This is because a consumer report that contains any information obtained through an interview (whether in person or over the telephone) qualifies as an investigative consumer report under the FCRA, a special type of consumer report to which additional procedures apply.[248]

Investigatory reports are discussed in another chapter in this manual.[249] In short, users must give consumers special notices before seeking the report and CRAs must engage in special procedures in supplying the report.[250] As a result, CRAs segregate investigative consumer report material from regular consumer reports.

Investigative reports are chiefly sought by employers and insurers, particularly for high salary jobs or high face value life insurance policies. The consumer will be notified before the report is sought, and the majority of consumers need not be concerned with this type of report. Thus, the majority of consumers need not be concerned that their consumer reports will include information from personal interviews, hearsay, or gossip.

5.5 Other Federal Laws Restricting Information in Credit Records

5.5.1 Protection for Servicemembers

The Servicemembers Civil Relief Act (formerly the Soldiers' and Sailors' Civil Relief Act) provides some additional protection for military personnel. Under certain circumstances, military personnel have the right to defer civil and public debts, and to delay repossessions, foreclosures, lawsuits and other actions.[251] Adverse reports relating to creditworthiness resulting from a consumer's application to reduce financial obligations pursuant to the Servicemembers Civil Relief Act are strictly prohibited.[252]

5.5.2 Discrimination and Retaliation for Exercising Rights Is Prohibited

The Equal Credit Opportunity Act (ECOA) prohibits creditors from discriminating against consumers in credit transactions[253] including discrimination in the "furnishing of credit information." Consequently, the ECOA prohibits creditors from furnishing adverse credit information on a consumer when the real reason for furnishing the information is one of the prohibited bases. For example, a creditor may not be quicker to report defaults by black than white defaulters.

---

243 12 C.F.R. §§ 41.30(e)(1)(ii) (OCC), 222.30(e)(1)(ii) (FRB regulated banks), 334.30(e)(1)(ii) (FDIC regulated banks), 571.30(e)(1)(ii) (OTS), 717.30(e)(1)(ii) (NCUA), 232.4(a)(2) (non-bank furnishers).

244 12 C.F.R. §§ 41.30(e)(1)(iv) (OCC), 222.30(e)(1)(iv) (FRB regulated banks), 334.30(e)(1)(iv) (FDIC regulated banks), 571.30(e)(1)(iv) (OTS), 717.30(e)(1)(iv) (NCUA), 232.4(a)(4) (non-bank furnishers).

245 12 C.F.R. §§ 41.30(e)(1)(vii) (OCC), 222.30(e)(1)(vii) (FRB regulated banks), 334.30(e)(1)(vii) (FDIC regulated banks), 571.30(e)(1)(vii) (OTS), 717.30(e)(1)(vii) (NCUA), 232.4(a)(7) (non-bank furnishers).

246 12 C.F.R. §§ 41.30(e)(1)(viii) and (ix) (OCC), 222.30(e)(1)(viii) and (ix) (FRB regulated banks), 334.30(e)(1)(viii) and (ix) (FDIC regulated banks), 571.30(e)(1)(viii) and (ix) (OTS), 717.30(e)(1)(viii) and (ix) (NCUA), 232.4(a)(8) and (9) (non-bank furnishers).

247 12 C.F.R. §§ 41.30(e)(1)(vi) (OCC), 222.30(e)(1)(vi) (FRB regulated banks), 334.30(e)(1)(vi) (FDIC regulated banks), 571.30(e)(1)(vi) (OTS), 717.30(e)(1)(vi) (NCUA), 232.4(a)(vi) (non-bank furnishers).

The creditor use of boilerplate language that routinely requests medical information from the consumer does not qualify for this exception. 12 C.F.R. §§ 41.30(e)(4)(v) (OCC), 222.30(e)(4)(v) (FRB regulated banks), 334.30(e)(4)(v) (FDIC regulated banks), 571.30(e)(4)(v) (OTS), 717.30(e)(4)(v) (NCUA), 232.4(d)(5) (non-bank furnishers).

248 15 U.S.C. § 1681a(c).

249 *See* Ch. 13, *infra*.

250 *See* §§ 13.4, 13.6, *infra*.

251 50 U.S.C. App. §§ 501–591. *See* National Consumer Law Center, Fair Debt Collection § 9.12 (5th 2004 and Supp.).

252 50 U.S.C. App. § 518(3) (no adverse consumer reports if person in military service has applied for or received a stay, postponement, or suspension of a civil obligation). *See* Marin v. Armstrong, 1998 U.S. Dist. LEXIS 22792 (N.D. Tex. Sept. 1, 1998) (recognizing private cause of action for violations).

253 15 U.S.C. § 1691(a); 12 C.F.R. § 202.2(m). *See generally* National Consumer Law Center, Credit Discrimination (4th ed. 2005 and Supp.).

In addition, the ECOA prohibits discrimination based on an applicant's good faith exercise of rights under the federal Consumer Credit Protection Act (CCPA).[254] The CCPA[255] is the umbrella legislation that covers many of the important federal consumer protection statutes, including the Fair Credit Reporting Act.

Whenever consumers raise claims under any of these acts, the creditor may not furnish negative information to consumer reporting agencies (CRAs) when the consumer's claim is the basis for the creditor's decision to furnish the information. This is the case whether the information being furnished is about the consumer's CCPA claim or about some other aspect of the consumer's credit record.

5.5.3 Federal Agencies Are Restricted in Information They May Furnish

Federal agencies may report debts to CRAs, but only to a limited extent and only if certain procedures are established and followed.[256] The information which may be furnished is limited to name, address, Social Security number, and the amount of the claim. Perhaps more importantly, federal law specifies internal procedures which the government agency must follow, including providing prior notice to the consumer and keeping reported information up to date. Compliance with the Fair Credit Reporting Act is also required.

5.6 Information About Another

5.6.1 Spouse or Former Spouse

A consumer's file at a consumer reporting agency (CRA) should contain only information on that consumer. The term "file" in the FCRA is defined as information "on that consumer."[257] Thus a CRA must designate a separate file for each spouse. The information in the file can only relate to the consumer's conduct and credit history, and not to the spouse's.

Nevertheless, primarily in an attempt to assist women without credit accounts in their own name to build up their credit histories, the Equal Credit Opportunity Act *requires* creditors to furnish certain data to CRAs. If a consumer can use or is obligated on a spouse's account, the creditor must designate the account to reflect the participation of both spouses. Then, when the creditor furnishes the account information to CRAs, the information should be furnished in a way that enables the CRA to update the files for both spouses.[258]

On the other hand, if a spouse is not an authorized user or joint obligor on an account, account information should not be entered into that individual's file. For example, if a consumer has no connection with a spouse's credit account, the spouse's nonpayment of that account should not be included in the consumer's file. However, spousal reporting is complicated by state family expense or necessaries laws.[259] One court has held that liability for state law necessaries can be reported on both spouses' credit files, even if only one spouse has a contractual obligation.[260]

Divorce also complicates consumer reporting issues. A consumer who is going through a divorce should make sure that at least the minimum payment is made on joint accounts if possible. Late payments will appear on both parties' consumer reports and will impede future attempts to obtain credit. A divorce decree mandating that one spouse be responsible for the debt does not alter the contractual relationship with the creditor, who may continue to report the debt as to both obligated spouses.[261] The other party remains responsible unless the creditor agrees to release that party. It is a good idea to ask creditors to re-establish a joint account in just one party's name, so that that party alone is responsible for future charges.

5.6.2 Cosigners and Authorized Users

Cosigners are fully liable on a debt and thus reporting on an account on their consumer reports is permitted. A special problem for cosigners is that they may not know when a principal obligor is delinquent in repaying a debt. The FTC Staff Commentary requires that CRAs specify if an individual's delinquency is based on a debt that the individual only guarantees and is not the principal obligor.[262]

An authorized user, on the other hand, is different than a cosigner. An authorized user is someone listed in a cardholder's account as someone authorized by the cardholder to use the cardholder's credit card account. Depending on state law, an authorized user may not be liable to the creditor for charges on the card.[263]

---

254 *See* 15 U.S.C. § 1691(a)(3). *See also* National Consumer Law Center, Credit Discrimination § 3.4.4 (4th ed. 2002 and Supp.).
255 15 U.S.C. §§ 1601–1693.
256 31 U.S.C. § 3711(f). *See* National Consumer Law Center, Fair Debt Collection § 13.2.3 (5th 2004 and Supp.).
257 15 U.S.C. § 1681a(g).
258 *See* 12 C.F.R. § 202.10. *See also* §§ 12.2.5, 13.7.3, *infra*; National Consumer Law Center, Credit Discrimination §§ 5.5, 9.4.2.1 (4th ed. 2005 and Supp.).
259 *See* National Consumer Law Center, Fair Debt Collection § 14.6 (5th 2004 and Supp.) for a discussion of state necessaries laws.
260 Dunn v. Lehigh Valley Ctr. for Sight, P.C., 2003 WL 22299275 (E.D. Pa. Sept. 30, 2003).
261 Moline v. Experian Info. Solutions, Inc., 289 F. Supp. 2d 956 (N.D. Ill. 2003).
262 FTC Official Staff Commentary § 607(3)(F), item 3, *reprinted at* Appx. D, *infra*.
263 *See, e.g.,* Sears Roebuck & Co. v. Ragucci, 203 N.J. Super. 82, 495 A.2d 923 (Super. Ct. Law Div. 1985) (under N.J.'s retail installment sales act, authorized user is an agent for a disclosed

If the authorized user is not obligated to pay the debt, CRAs arguably should not report information about that credit account on the user's credit record. However, the provisions requiring spousal reporting in Regulation B, which implements the ECOA,[264] gives creditors the option to include information about an account on the consumer report of authorized users, even when the user is NOT a spouse.[265]

Although the creditor may report the debt in association with the name of the authorized user, the CRA remains responsible for how it tags that information and should not file it under the name of the authorized user in a way that will appear in a consumer report that the authorized user was responsible for the debt.

Another problem that occurs with joint obligors and even authorized users is that creditors will report bankruptcy information on an account for both consumers, even when only one obligor (the primary obligor in the case of authorized users) has filed for bankruptcy. Both the CRAs and furnishers have been challenged under the FCRA over this practice.[266]

5.6.3 State Law Restrictions Regarding Cosigners

Some state laws required creditors to notify the cosigner when they sends adverse information about an account,[267] or even to provide the cosigner notice before furnishing adverse information to a CRA, with the opportunity to make payment to forestall the negative credit rating.[268] However, the FCRA preempts state law requirements placed on those who furnish information to CRAs.[269]

5.7 State Law Restrictions

5.7.1 Restrictions on Child Support Debts

The FCRA requires a consumer reporting agency (CRA) to include overdue child support in any report issued for a permissible purpose if the overdue child support information is provided by a state or local child support enforcement agency.[270] If the information is provided by any other person or entity, its inclusion is mandated only if verified by a government agency—local, state, or federal.[271] The overdue support, like other information, can be reported only for seven years from the date it is overdue.[272]

Some state statutes require child support agencies to provide, at a CRA's request, information about child support debts. These statutes also require child support agencies to provide notice to the delinquent parent that the information is being furnished to a CRA, with the right to contest that information.[273] While these requirements appear to be preempted by the FCRA,[274] the preemption issues are complicated by the fact that the furnishers are themselves state agencies.

5.7.2 State Law Restrictions in General

State laws may restrict certain information from being included in consumer reports.[275] However, these state laws may preempted by the FCRA, unless they were adopted prior to September 30, 1996.[276]

State laws are preempted at least to the extent requirements and prohibitions are imposed relating to subject matter regulated under section 1681c.[277] Section 1681c governs obsolete information, restricts reporting of identifying information for medical information furnishers, and imposes a number of other requirements.[278]

Laws regarding whether information about things like race or religion, about polygraph tests, and other matters not addressed in section 1681c should not be preempted. For example, Maine and New York prohibit CRAs from listing a consumer as having been denied credit if the sole reason for the denial was insufficient information for granting credit.[279]

---

principle and is therefore not liable for the debts incurred on the card); First Nat'l Bank v. Fulk, 57 Ohio App. 3d 44, 566 N.E.2d 1270 (1989) (an authorized user of a credit card is not personally liable for the charges without an agreement to the contrary); Chevy Chase Sav. Bank v. Strong, 46 Va. Cir. 422 (1998). See generally National Consumer Law Center, Truth in Lending § 5.9.4.1.2 (5th ed. 2003 and Supp.).

264 See § 5.6.1, supra.
265 Official Staff Commentary to Regulation B, 12 C.F.R. § 202.10-2. See National Consumer Law Center, Credit Discrimination § 9.4.2.1 (4th ed. 2005 and Supp.).
266 See Ch. 4, supra.
267 See, e.g., Cal. Civ. Code § 1785.26 (West).
268 See, e.g., 815 Ill. Comp. Stat. § 505/25 (fifteen-day notice); Mich. Comp. Laws § 445.271 (thirty-day notice).
269 15 U.S.C. § 1681t(b)(1)(F). See § 10.7, infra.
270 15 U.S.C. § 1681s-1.
271 Id.
272 Id.
273 E.g., Colo. Rev. Stat. § 26-13-116; Conn. Gen. Stat. § 52-362c; Ga. Code Ann. § 19-11-25; Haw. Rev. Stat. § 576D-6(6); Kan. Stat. Ann. §§ 23-4, 23-145; Me. Rev. Stat. Ann. tit. 10, § 1329; Mich. Comp. Laws § 552.512; Mo. Rev. Stat. § 454.512; Mont. Code Ann. §§ 40-5-261, 40-5-262; N.J. Stat. Ann. § 2A:17-56.21 (West); Ohio Rev. Code Ann. § 2301.353 (West); 23 Pa. Cons. Stat. § 4303; R.I. Gen. Laws § 15-25-1; S.C. Code Ann. § 43-5-585 (Law Co-op.); Tenn. Code Ann. § 36-5-106; W. Va. Code § 48A-2-31; Wis. Stat. § 49.22(11).
274 15 U.S.C. § 1681t(b)(1)(F). See § 10.7, infra.
275 See Appx. H, infra.
276 See § 10.7, infra.
277 15 U.S.C. § 1681t(b)(1)(E). See § 10.7, supra.
278 15 U.S.C. § 1681c.
279 Me. Rev. Stat. Ann. tit. 10, § 1321(3) (report must state that credit was denied because of lack of sufficient information); Me. Advisory Rulings of Bureau of Consumer Protection; N.Y. Gen. Bus. Law § 380-j (McKinney).

Whether the FCRA preempts state laws that prohibit information for which section 1681c sets lesser restrictions is unclear. For example, whether reports of arrest records, which are addressed in section 1681c, can be forbidden altogether is one such category on information.

A list of state laws regarding the content of consumer reports that pre-date September 30, 1996 is included in another chapter.[280] Some of these restrictions are discussed below. California law prohibits CRAs from including medical information in their files.[281] Kentucky prohibits the reporting of criminal charges in a Kentucky court that did not result in conviction.[282] New York has a similar prohibition on reporting charges or arrests unless the case is pending or resulted in a conviction.[283] New York also provides that paid judgments can only be reported for five years; no information can appear in the record as to the consumer's race, religion, color, or national origin; no information can appear concerning polygraph tests; and there are limits as to reporting detentions for shoplifting.[284]

Sometimes state law imposes additional disclosure requirements when information is first gathered or reported. For example, California requires creditors to notify consumers and cosigners when first furnishing negative consumer reports to a CRA.[285] Minnesota requires that the consumer receive written disclosure prior to preparation of a report for employment purposes.[286]

State restrictions on the furnishing of information can come from surprising places. Consider, for example, a Massachusetts state bar ethical opinion regarding the collection of fees. In the opinion of the Massachusetts Bar Association's Ethics Committee, when a client fails to pay a lawyer for services rendered, the lawyer may not report the failure to consumer reporting services even if the lawyer initiates proceedings to collect the debt.[287] The indebtedness of the client is considered a confidential matter.

---

280 *See* § 10.7.5.3, *infra*.
281 Cal. Civ. Code § 1785.13(f) (West).
282 Ky. Rev. Stat. Ann. §§ 367.310, 367.990(16).
283 N.Y. Gen. Bus. Law § 380-j (McKinney).
284 *Id*.
285 Cal. Civ. Code § 1785.26 (West). However, this provision may be preempted under 15 U.S.C. § 1681t(b)(1)(F). *See* § 10.7.5.2, *infra*.
286 Minn. Stat. § 13C.02.
287 Mass. Bar Ass'n, Comm. on Prof'l Ethics, Op. 3 (2000).

Chapter 6 Activities and Duties of Furnishers of Information to Consumer Reporting Agencies

6.1 Introduction

6.1.1 Overview

Before 1996 furnishers of information[1] to consumer reporting agencies (CRAs) were essentially outside the scope of the Fair Credit Reporting Act (FCRA). Despite the central role that these entities played as the primary source of the data that the CRAs collected and disseminated, furnishers were effectively immune from federal oversight. Before 1996 furnishers were under no federal duty to provide CRAs with correct information, to respond to or investigate a consumer's dispute, or to cooperate with a CRA's reinvestigation of the completeness or accuracy of the information which the furnisher itself provided. This omission was significant and frustrating since the CRAs themselves were (and continue to be) bound to maintain the accuracy of their reports[2] and investigate a consumer's dispute that the information is incomplete or inaccurate.[3] The 1996 amendments partially eliminated furnishers' privileged status.[4]

The FCRA now imposes standards and obligations upon those who furnish information about consumers to CRAs. Many of these standards and duties were modified and in some instances expanded by the Fair and Accurate Credit Transactions Act of 2003 (FACTA).[5] This chapter discusses the standards and obligations applicable to furnishers, the industry standards and protocols for disseminating consumer credit information from furnishers to the CRAs, and issues surrounding furnishers' investigations of the accuracy of the information that they provide to CRAs.

The FCRA imposes several requirements on creditors or furnishers with respect to protecting consumers against identity theft. These requirements are discussed in detail in Chapter 9, *infra*.

Creditors, insurers, public agencies, and many others can and do furnish information about consumers to CRAs. Section 6.2, *infra*, explains who is a furnisher and when the FCRA applies.

Consumer information is usually transmitted to CRAs in electronic form, although manual submissions do occur. "Metro 2" is the ubiquitous industry-designed software or protocol used by creditors to regularly furnish information about their customers to CRAs, usually monthly or more frequently. The furnishing of information, including a description of Metro 2, is discussed in § 6.3, *infra*.

Understanding the standards for initially furnishing accurate information is important, but the crucial point for an attorney representing an aggrieved consumer is that the FCRA provides for no private enforcement and no statutory remedy for these initial reporting violations.[6] Nevertheless, the standards for the initial furnishing of information to CRAs should have an effect on creditor/furnisher behavior, and the failure to abide by the standards can be relevant if a private dispute against the furnisher later ends up in court. These standards include accuracy (§ 6.4, *infra*), a duty to correct and update (§ 6.5, *infra*), a requirement that consumer disputes be noted (§ 5.6, *infra*), and a requirement that the date of initial delinquency be provided (§ 6.7, *infra*). If an account has been voluntarily closed by the consumer, that information must be furnished as well (§ 6.8, *infra*). The duty of financial institutions to notify consumers when they submit negative information is discussed in § 6.9, *infra*.

The FCRA establishes a process for consumers to dispute information directly with the furnisher of that information and contains special rules with which furnishers must comply when a consumer sends them a report of identity theft.[7] However, Congress also eliminated any private right of action or private remedies for a breach of these direct investigation duties and identity theft rules.[8] The absence of private enforcement is discussed in § 6.1.2, *infra*. The substance of the duty to investigate disputes received di-

---

1 What constitutes a "furnisher" of information is discussed in § 6.2, *infra*.
2 15 U.S.C. § 1681e(b). *See* Ch. 4, *supra*.
3 15 U.S.C. § 1681i. *See* Ch. 4, *supra*.
4 Consumer Credit Reporting Reform Act of 1996, tit. II, subtit. D, ch. 1, of the Omnibus Consolidated Appropriations Act for Fiscal Year 1997, Pub. L. No. 104-208 (1996). *See* Nelson v. Chase Manhattan Mortgage Corp., 282 F.3d 1057, 1060 (9th Cir. 2002).
5 Fair and Accurate Credit Transactions Act of 2003, Pub. L. No. 108-159 (2003).

6 *See* § 6.10.2, *infra*.
7 15 U.S.C. § 1681s-2(a)(6) and (8).
8 *See* § 6.10.2, *infra*.

rectly from consumers is addressed in § 6.5.2, *infra*. Discussion of the special identity theft rules for furnishers is part of the comprehensive coverage of identity theft in Chapter 9, *infra*.

In some circumstances, state tort and statutory actions may be brought against the furnisher, but the FCRA's preemption provisions severely restrict the availability of those claims. This unsettled area of the law is discussed in §§ 6.12 and 10.4, *infra*.

Typically the only effective remedy available to the consumer will be the federal one under the FCRA discussed in § 6.10, *infra*. In order to trigger the formal FCRA dispute resolution process, the consumer must initiate a dispute with a CRA (or when applicable a reseller), as discussed in Chapter 4, *infra*.[9] The CRA must then formally notify the furnisher about the dispute (§ 6.10.3, *infra*). Once so notified by the CRA, the furnisher must conduct its own investigation (§ 6.10.4, *infra*) and then report the results of that investigation back to the CRA, usually in less than a month's time (§ 6.10.6, *infra*). Having received the furnisher's explanation, the CRA must then conduct its own reinvestigation of the consumer's dispute and ultimately correct the disputed information or delete the information which is inaccurate or which cannot be verified. A furnisher's violation of the duty to adequately investigate the disputed information or otherwise meet its obligations in this process subjects it to liability, as discussed in § 6.10.2, *infra*.

6.1.2 Congress Eliminated Private Enforcement of the Duties to Furnish Accurate and Complete Information or to Prevent and Investigate Identity Theft

Although private enforcement pervades the FCRA, the furnisher responsibilities other than those arising from their involvement in the formal dispute investigation process may not be enforced under the FCRA by private consumer litigation.[10] While the Act provides for civil liability for negligent or willful noncompliance with any provision of the FCRA,[11] the section on the responsibilities of furnishers states that these civil liability sections do not apply to any failure to comply with section 1681s-2(a).[12] Section 1681s-2(a) enumerates the essential furnisher duties for furnishing accurate and complete information to the CRAs[13] and for preventing identity theft and investigating direct consumer disputes.[14] In addition to these core responsibilities, section 1681s-2(a) also requires certain financial institutions that furnish negative information to CRAs to notify the affected consumer[15] and requires medical information furnishers to alert CRAs of their status to aid the CRAs in meeting their duty to protect that sensitive information.[16] Each of these requirements is thus immune from private enforcement under the FCRA.

---

9 A reseller's role in a formal furnisher liability case is essentially as a conduit with the consumer regarding those reseller consumer reports that it ultimately produces and that allegedly contain a third-party error. Where a consumer chooses to initiate a dispute with a reseller not alleging incompleteness or inaccuracy as a result of any act or omission of that reseller, the reseller's only function is to transfer the dispute to the applicable CRA. The CRA then treats the dispute as any other dispute received directly from the consumer. See § 6.13, *infra*.

10 15 U.S.C. § 1681s-2(c) and (d); Nelson v. Chase Manhattan Mortgage Corp., 282 F.3d 1057 (9th Cir. 2002); Washington v. CSC Credit Servs., Inc., 199 F.3d 263 (5th Cir. 2000); Ornelas v. Fidelity Nat'l Title Co. of Wash., Inc., 2005 WL 3359112 (W.D. Wash. Dec. 9, 2005); Sciria v. Huntington Bank, 2005 WL 3262954 (N.D. Ohio Dec. 1, 2005); Semper v. JBC Legal Group, 2005 WL 2172377 (W.D. Wash. Sept. 6, 2005); Pirouzian v. SLM Corp., 396 F. Supp. 2d 1124 (S.D. Cal. 2005); Dolan v. Fairbanks Capital Corp., 2005 WL 1971006 (E.D.N.Y. Aug. 16, 2005); Zager v. Deaton, 2005 WL 2008432 (W.D. Tenn. Aug. 16, 2005); Caltabiano v. BSB Bank & Trust Co., 387 F. Supp. 2d 135 (E.D.N.Y. 2005); King v. Equifax Info. Servs., 2005 WL 1667783 (S.D. Tex. July 15, 2005); Ruggiero v. Kavlich, 411 F. Supp. 2d 734 (N.D. Ohio 2005); Pitstick Farms, Inc. v. Sanders Sales and Serv., Inc., 2005 WL 1151684 (S.D. Ohio May 16, 2005); Kane v. Guaranty Residential Lending, Inc., 2005 WL 1153623 (E.D.N.Y. May 16, 2005); Gorman v. Wolpoff & Abramson, L.L.P., 370 F. Supp. 2d 1005 (N.D. Cal. 2005); Trikas v. Universal Card Servs. Corp., 351 F. Supp. 2d 37 (E.D.N.Y. 2005); Bach v. First Union Nat'l Bank, 149 Fed. Appx. 354 (6th Cir. Aug. 22, 2005) (unpublished); McKeown v. Sears Roebuck & Co., 335 F. Supp. 2d 917 (W.D. Wis. 2004); Gibbs v. SLM Corp., 336 F. Supp. 2d 1 (D. Mass. 2004); Elmore v. North Fork Bancorporation, Inc., 325 F. Supp. 2d 336 (S.D.N.Y. 2004); Evantash v. G.E. Capital Mortgage Serv., Inc., 2003 WL 22844198 (E.D. Pa. Nov. 25, 2003); Riley v. General Motors Acceptance Corp., 226 F. Supp. 2d 1316 (S.D. Ala. 2002); Vazquez-Garcia v. Trans Union de Puerto Rico, 222 F. Supp. 2d 150 (D. P.R. 2002); Hasvold v. First USA Bank, N.A., 194 F. Supp. 2d 1228 (D. Wyo. 2002); Redhead v. Winston & Winston, P.C., 2002 WL 31106934 (S.D.N.Y. Sept. 20, 2002); O'Diah v. New York City, 2002 WL 1941179 (S.D.N.Y. Aug. 21, 2002); Aklagi v. NationsCredit Fin. Servs. Corp., 196 F. Supp. 2d 1186 (D. Kan. 2002); Hasvold v. First USA Bank, N.A., 194 F. Supp. 2d 1228 (D. Wyo. 2002); Yelder v. Credit Bureau of Montgomery, L.L.C., 131 F. Supp. 2d 1275 (M.D. Ala. 2001); Fino v. Key Bank of New York, 2001 WL 849700 (W.D. Pa. July 27, 2001); Banks v. Stoneybrook Apartment, 2000 WL 1682979 (M.D.N.C. June 1, 2000), aff'd, 232 F.3d 888 (4th Cir. 2000) (table, text at 2000 WL 1578331); Ryan v. TransUnion Corp., 2000 WL 1100440 (N.D. Ill. Aug. 4, 2000); Johnson v. United States-Dep't of Defense, 2000 U.S. Dist. LEXIS 21087 (D. Minn. Aug. 4, 2000); Brown v. Maine Med. Ctr., 1999 WL 33117137 (D. Me. Mar. 18, 1999). *But see* Geeslin v. Nissan Motor Acceptance Corp., 1998 WL 433932 (N.D. Miss. June 3, 1998) (finding private cause of action without apparent awareness of the explicit contrary statutory limitation).

11 See Ch. 10, *infra*.

12 15 U.S.C. § 1681s-2(c).

13 15 U.S.C. § 1681s-2(a)(1)–(5). *See* §§ 6.3–6.8, *infra*.

14 15 U.S.C. § 1681s-2(a)(6) and (8).

15 15 U.S.C. § 1681s-2(a)(7). *See* § 6.9, *infra*.

16 15 U.S.C. § 1681s-2(a)(9). *See* 15 U.S.C. § 1681i(g).

Further exacerbating this void in effective enforcement is the provision that preempts most claims under state law relating to furnishing information to CRAs.[17] There remains some possibility of state tort liability for certain egregious misconduct, though a currently unresolved conflict between the furnisher preemption provision and the FCRA's general limitation on tort liability has only created additional confusion and uncertainty.[18]

In lieu of private actions, public enforcement may be undertaken by the Federal Trade Commission, by other federal agencies where appropriate, and by states.[19] The availability, scope, and limitations on public enforcement are addressed in Chapter 12, *infra*.

Quite apart from the normal furnishing of information to CRAs, sometimes a creditor who provides information to others is actually a CRA and not a furnisher.[20] In such a case, the creditor, like CRAs, will be liable for its negligent and willful violations of FCRA.

6.2 Creditors and Others Who Furnish Information to Consumer Reporting Agencies

6.2.1 Furnishers Provide Information to Consumer Reporting Agencies

Anyone who furnishes consumer information to a consumer reporting agency (CRA) is a "furnisher" of information under the FCRA. No special attribute is required and, in fact, the terms furnisher and furnishing are not defined.[21] The FCRA simply refers to "a person who furnishes information to a consumer reporting agency," or similar terms.[22] Merely reporting information to a CRA is sufficient to qualify as a furnisher. Furnishers include creditors, insurers, employers, landlords, banks, doctors, and lawyers as well as those who only occasionally report information to CRAs.[23] Even a neighbor or other person contacted by a CRA compiling an investigative report may be a furnisher under the Act.[24]

Public agencies may be furnishers as well, in which case special rules may apply. Federal agencies are authorized to disclose debtor information to CRAs, but restrictions apply to the nature of the information which may be furnished and when it may be furnished.[25] Federal law requires that defaults on student loans must be reported to CRAs as a means of encouraging debt repayment. A few restrictions apply. In addition, those with student loan debt should consider a range of remedies unique to the student loan situation.[26] Federal law also requires that if a spouse can use or is obligated on an open-end credit account, the creditor must furnish information in a manner that permits a CRA to use that information for each spouse.[27] Some states require that child support debts must be reported to CRAs, but the validity of these provisions and other state requirements in the face of federal preemption laws is in question.[28]

To be subject to the FCRA, the information which is furnished must be about a consumer and must be furnished to a CRA. A consumer is essentially any individual natural person.[29] A CRA may be a credit bureau, tenant screening business, check verification company, or a variety of other compilers of databases.[30]

A distinction is sometimes made between those who regularly furnish information to CRAs and those who provide information about consumers only occasionally or incidentally. The distinction does not arise often in practice because those who use and provide information to CRAs usually do so as a regular part of their business. Anyone who does furnish information regularly to a CRA must be given a notice by the CRA setting out the furnisher's obligations under the Act. The form of this notice is prescribed by the Federal Trade Commission and is reproduced in an appendix to this manual.[31] Most FCRA requirements apply equally to furnishers who regularly furnish information and to those who do so only occasionally. Two requirements apply only to furnishers who regularly furnish information: a furnisher must correct and update information[32] and must report when an account has been closed voluntarily.[33]

6.2.2 Limitations on Who Is a Furnisher

6.2.2.1 Special Rules for Affiliate Sharing

The rules of the FCRA, including those that apply to furnishers, generally do not apply to companies furnishing information to other entities affiliated by common owner-

---

17 15 U.S.C. § 1681t(b)(1)(F). See §§ 6.12, 10.5, *infra*.
18 15 U.S.C. § 1681t(b)(1)(F). See §§ 6.12, 10.5, *infra*.
19 15 U.S.C. § 1681s-2(d).
20 See § 2.7, *supra*.
21 Watson v. Trans Union Credit Bureau, 2005 WL 995687 (D. Me. Apr. 28, 2005); Carney v. Experian Info. Solutions, Inc., 57 F. Supp. 2d 496 (W.D. Tenn. 1999).
22 See, e.g., 15 U.S.C. § 1681s-2(a), (2), (4), (5).
23 Thomasson v. Bank One, 137 F. Supp. 2d 721 (E.D. La. 2001) (definition of furnisher provided by courts is "an entity which transmits information to a CRA concerning a particular debt owed by a consumer").
24 See Ch. 13, *infra*.
25 National Consumer Law Center, Fair Debt Collection § 10.2.3 (5th 2004 and Supp.).
26 See § 12.6.5, *infra*; National Consumer Law Center, Student Loan Law (3d ed. 2006).
27 See § 12.2.5, *infra*.
28 See § 10.7.3, *infra*.
29 See § 2.2, *supra*.
30 See § 2.6, *supra*.
31 See Appx. C, *infra*.
32 See § 6.5, *infra*.
33 See § 6.8, *infra*.

ship or corporate control, even if the receiving affiliate functions as an in-house credit reporting agency. Such affiliate sharing of information is generally outside the scope of the FCRA.[34] However, a consumer may opt out of the use by an affiliate of this exempt information when the information is used to market its products or services. Affiliates must also notify the consumer both of the possibility that an affiliate may use the consumer's information for marketing and of the consumer's right to opt out of such use.[35] Information that is excluded from the definition of consumer report because the information relates solely to the person's first-hand experience with the consumer or is a communication of information among persons related by common ownership or affiliated by corporate control is nonetheless subject to 15 U.S.C. § 1681s-3. This provision prohibits affiliates from using such excluded information for solicitation or marketing purposes unless the affiliate notifies the consumer that the consumer may opt-out of such use and provides the consumer with an opportunity to so opt out.[36] A consumer's election to opt out is effective for at least five years, beginning as soon as reasonably practicable.

Often a creditor may furnish information both to a CRA and to its own affiliates. Some limited opportunity exists for a consumer to direct that that information should not be shared among affiliates,[37] but the special rules regarding the obligations of furnishers will normally not apply to this kind of information sharing. However, the same information provided to a CRA will be subject to the FCRA rules governing the furnishing of information.

6.2.2.2 Direct Selling of Information Not Covered

Creditors have a booming business selling information about their customers. In addition to sharing information with their own affiliates, they will sell lists of customers meeting different criteria to other creditors, to direct marketers and mass mailing houses, and to other compilers of marketing databases. Sometimes, as on the Internet, these transactions occur instantaneously, and sometimes a creditor will compile information based on its past experiences with its own customer base. Although a creditor or other business may be furnishing information, it is not furnishing information to a CRA. Moreover, although the creditor is compiling a database about consumers to sell to others, as long as it is first-hand information based on its own experience with the customer, that creditor is not a CRA.[38] Other privacy regulations may apply,[39] but the FCRA rules on furnishers and on CRAs do not.

6.2.2.3 Certain State Laws Regarding Furnishers Are Preempted

The FCRA purports to preempt all state laws regarding the furnishing of information to CRAs, with two exceptions: California and Massachusetts.[40] Nevertheless, because of a facially conflicting preemption provision applicable to certain torts,[41] the courts have developed an assortment of inconsistent rules that have further muddled this area. See §§ 6.12 and 10.4, *infra*, for a detailed discussion of the preemption of state torts and statutory claims.

6.3 Furnishing Information to Consumer Reporting Agencies

6.3.1 Information Is Usually Furnished Electronically

In an effort to ensure uniformity and accuracy, the consumer reporting agencies (CRAs) typically accept information electronically from creditors and other furnishers of information. The trade association for the CRAs, Consumer Data Industry Association, Inc. (CDIA, formerly the Associated Credit Bureaus, Inc.), also encourages use of an electronic medium through Metro 2, the standard automated data reporting format created by CDIA.[42] While not required by law, the practical reality is that virtually all large furnishers of information, including credit card companies and mortgage bankers, provide information used by CRAs electronically. The CRAs report that up to 80% of their subscribers or furnishers have converted to the Metro 2 reporting system. However, consumer advocates have questioned whether the 80% figure is based on the data being reported and not the percentage of furnishers who submit the data.

Of course, information provided by consumers to CRAs is normally not communicated electronically. But once received, if it is to be used, the CRA will add it to its own electronic database. Even consumer disputes are regularly communicated electronically between the CRA and the furnisher, as discussed below.[43]

One consequence of this reliance upon electronic communication, even by furnishers of information, is that a correction of inaccurate information by a creditor is rarely effective if it is not reflected with precision in the same database used to report current information on a weekly or monthly basis to the CRAs. Any resolution of a dispute with

---

34 *See* § 2.4.3, *supra*.
35 15 U.S.C. § 1681s-3. Certain exemptions apply. *See* 15 U.S.C. § 1681s-3(a)(4).
36 15 U.S.C. § 1681s-3. *See also* §§ 2.4.3, *supra*, 8.2.2.2, *infra*.
37 *See* §§ 2.4.3, *supra*, 8.2.18, *infra*.
38 *See* § 2.4.2, *supra*.
39 *See* Ch. 16, *infra*.

40 15 U.S.C. § 1681t(b)(F).
41 15 U.S.C. § 1681h(e).
42 Consumer Data Indus. Ass'n, Inc., Credit Reporting Resources Guide (2004) (Metro 2 Manual).
43 *See* §§ 6.10.3, 6.10.6.4, *infra*.

a furnisher should ensure that the outcome is properly reported to the CRA and also properly updated and added to the correct database.[44]

Notwithstanding the industry's push for, and reliance on, electronic sharing of consumer credit information, a startling number of small companies furnish credit information by paper. This practice is especially prevalent among small collection agencies. Furthermore, due to the unsophisticated nature of the electronic medium or the people using it, essential information, such as whether the debt is disputed, is routinely not reported.

Creditors and others who use consumer reports are subscribers to one or more consumer reporting services. The subscriber or customer agreement normally requires the user to also furnish information about its own customers to the CRA. Many large and medium sized credit card companies and banks use another company to manage their customer data. While the creditor's employees may have a terminal and screen at the workplace, a data management company such as Electronic Data Systems, Inc. may maintain the data they are viewing using its own software. When it comes time to provide the information to CRAs (typically monthly), the data management company may be in charge of this process of direct communication with the CRAs, or in creating the medium to be provided to them. To determine the capabilities of this system or the records kept, it may be important to depose the data management company because of feigned or real lack of knowledge by the furnisher.

Information from courts, city halls, tax offices, and departments of motor vehicles is usually available and reported electronically as well, although sometimes CRAs will use contractors to collect the information by hand for conversion to electronic form.

The basics of database systems may be helpful when looking at the Metro 2 Format (also referred to as Metro 2). Metro 2 establishes the order and values of certain "fields" that are provided to it by furnishers of information. A "field" is a space allocated for a particular item of information.[45] Each field is given a name so it has an objective value. Fields may have "attributes" associated with them. A field can be "required," "optional" or "calculated."[46] A required field is one in which one must enter data, while an optional field is one that may be left blank. A calculated field's value is derived from a formula involving other fields. One does not enter data into a calculated field; instead the system automatically determines the correct value.[47] For instance, the last name of the person associated with an account may be a "required" field, whereas the middle name may be "optional." A "calculated field" may add two different entered numbers together or may use a formula to establish a number.

6.3.2 Metro 2: The Standard Automated Format for Furnishing Information to Consumer Reporting Agencies

Metro 2 is a reporting format used by furnishers to provide information about consumer accounts to CRAs. The Metro format software had been around since the 1970s. Metro 2 is the version created after the 1996 amendments to the FCRA. It was designed by the credit reporting industry, including the so-called "Big Three": Equifax, Experian, and TransUnion. The format and instructions are available for users from CDIA and from each of the major CRAs.[48] CDIA's website also contains valuable information about Metro 2, including instructions on how to access the Metro 2 Format and frequently asked questions and answers about Metro 2 reporting.[49] The format and instructions were initially published as the *Credit Reporting Resource Guide* in 2000, which is updated periodically. The book is also called *The Metro 2 Manual*. While Metro 2 is the current industry standard for furnishing consumer information to CRAs, some creditors may still be using an earlier version.

Not every CRA uses every field available in Metro 2. However, Metro 2 is considered a standard format for the consumer reporting industry and may safely be used by furnishers even though one CRA or another may ignore certain fields.

Creditors and other furnishers use the Metro 2 Format to report credit data and other personal information to the CRAs. The format may be used to furnish information to one or more of the major CRAs and is used by nearly all major creditors. An occasional large creditor may have unique adaptations, approved by the CRAs, but the Metro 2 Format is essentially ubiquitous.

As its name implies, the program provides a standard format, including standard codes, which can be used for virtually any consumer credit transaction. Creditors use Metro 2 to provide periodic reports to each CRA about all of its current accounts and those just closed out. Data may be transferred by electronic transmission, on data tapes, or by computer disks or cartridges. Normally the "computer dump" of credit data is made monthly, although it can be more or less frequent. Generally speaking, creditors convert or transfer their own data into the Metro 2 Format so that updated information on their entire active customer base is transferred to the CRAs at one time. The reliance on data furnished using Metro 2 is so complete that the latest Metro 2 "information dump" will often supersede a correction made earlier by a creditor if the creditor failed to also correct the data put into its Metro reports.

Reporting services are a highly computerized, sophisticated, technology-based industry. Information is stored, sorted, and transferred or printed electronically. Uniformity

---

44 See § 12.6.2, infra.
45 Webopedia at www.webopedia.com.
46 Id.
47 Id.

48 The website address is www.cdiaonline.org.
49 See www.cdiaonline.org/data.cfm.

is required if information is to be effectively manipulated by computer, so that the need to receive information electronically and in uniform format is critical. Any other information received by the CRAs must be converted into its standard formats. Metro 2 is designed to make the transfer of creditor information to the CRAs as seamless as possible.

Information may still be submitted manually to the CRAs, however. Some smaller entities, including small collection agencies, provide the data on paper that is then entered into a credit reporting database by the CRA with which it has an agreement. Some creditors and users are "limited manual reporters" who do not use Metro 2. However, it is also true that information from creditors and other users who are not equipped to use Metro 2 is sometimes discouraged or even excluded from the CRAs' databases. CRAs also sometimes arrange to collect information on a manual basis, especially public record information which is not available electronically. Information obtained manually is converted and added to each CRA's computer databases for eventual inclusion in consumer reports. Not surprisingly, the manual recording of information and its conversion to electronic data are error prone.

While Metro 2 is the overwhelmingly dominant way for information to be furnished to CRAs, Metro 2 users can and do submit information about consumers on an individualized basis in some circumstances. For example, when consumers have disputed the accuracy or completeness of information with a CRA, the CRA and the furnisher of that information will communicate about that specific transaction using a Consumer Dispute Verification (CDV). This communication, which is usually made electronically but can be made on paper, is discussed in a following section.[50]

A creditor may also use a Universal Data Form[51] to report new or updated information to a CRA or even to delete all information about a particular account. This one-page form can and often should be used to report the resolution of a dispute with a creditor over the status of a debt or to withdraw a report of a disputed debt as part of a settlement. The form can be used by any creditor or by anyone else who subscribes to the services of one of the major CRAs. Its uses are described further elsewhere in this manual.[52]

6.3.3 The Metro 2 Format Used by Creditors

6.3.3.1 Overview

The credit reporting industry distributes the *Metro 2 Format Manual* widely. Even so, when information about the Metro 2 Format is provided in discovery, many defendants routinely insist on confidentiality agreements or protective orders. The justification for these discovery restrictions is doubtful given that no competitive advantage is at stake and given the availability of much Metro 2 information on various websites. Nevertheless, should the nature of what and how information is furnished become a factor in litigation, a request for Metro 2 Format instructions and descriptions should be made of the defendant. What follows is an overview of how the format is organized to facilitate the furnishing of detailed information about an account to the CRAs.

The Metro 2 Format is divided into several "record layouts." Each layout is a separate chart or table used to collect a defined set of related information. For example, the so-called header record provides information identifying the furnisher, the CRA to which the information is being furnished, and information about the computer transmission itself. Another layout might be a segment used to communicate information about mortgages or employment. Each layout contains blanks to be filled in by the creditor or other furnisher, using uniform formats and codes, to describe in detail the transaction and current status of a customer's account. While the instructions look daunting, a creditor can organize its own computer records so that the Metro 2 information is provided automatically. That is why Metro 2 is called an automated format for reporting credit data.

The specific layouts, or parts, of the Metro 2 Format[53] include:

- The header record;
- The base segment—for basic information about an account and its status;
- The J1 segment—for information about an associated consumer at the same address;
- The J2 segment—for information about associated consumers at a different address;
- The K1 and K2 segments—for information about the original creditor when the account has been transferred, or about the sale of a portfolio of accounts;
- The K3 segment—for mortgage information;
- The K4 segment—for specialized payments like deferred and balloon payments;
- The L1 segment—for changing account and identification numbers;
- The N1 segment—for employment information; and
- Trailer records—used for processing purposes only.

6.3.3.2 Objective Standard

Metro 2 is useful for providing information to CRAs only to the extent that it creates a standard for the meaning given to each field provided under the Metro 2 Format. The

---

50 § 6.10, *infra*.
51 A sample Universal Data Form is reprinted at Appx. I, *infra*.
52 § 6.5, *infra*.

53 Consumer Data Indus. Ass'n, Inc., Credit Reporting Resources Guide (2004) (Metro 2 Manual).

usefulness of Metro 2 would be compromised if furnishers assigned different values to the information in the same field. For instance, if one mortgage company assigned a value to the "current balance" field (Base Segment, Field 21) to be the pay off balance and another used the field for the total amount of payments over the life of the entire loan, an identical loan could be reported by one creditor as $100,000 and by another as $290,000. The Metro 2 Format therefore makes the value of Base Segment, Field 21 the "payoff balance" (i.e., the principal balance plus the interest currently due) when a mortgage is being reported.

Maintaining the objective standard is also important because of the widespread use of credit scoring.[54] Credit scoring inputs the information in the various fields furnished to the consumer reporting agencies into a formula to derive a numerical score that reflects the relative strength and weakness of a consumer's credit data. Maintaining the objective value assigned to each item of information is essential since the formula cannot take into account different values assigned to the same field by different furnishers.

Because of the overriding need for the objective values, a furnisher reporting non-uniform information that may be accurate in lay terms or in accordance with its own database will compromise the system. For this reason, among others, the industry understanding of terms is one measure used to establish the accuracy of the report.[55]

6.3.3.3 Base Segment Contains Information About the Consumer and the Debt

The base segment is the most important part of the Metro report for anyone concerned with the accuracy of account and personal information furnished by a creditor to a CRA. This segment of the Metro 2 Format identifies the consumer, describes the transaction or account, and reports the consumer's payment history. A couple of fields (blanks to be filled in by the furnisher) capture information specifically required by the FCRA or the Fair Credit Billing Act (FCBA).

The fields used to identify the consumer include those for name (including generation codes for senior, junior, the III, etc.), address, whether one owns their home or rents, Social Security number, date of birth and telephone number. Because reports compiled by CRAs often improperly mix information about more than one consumer, sometimes based on address information, it is noteworthy that address information in Metro 2 can be modified by codes indicating whether it is known to be the address of the primary consumer, if it is not confirmed, or if it is a military or business address.

ECOA[56] codes are used to report the status of the consumer in relation to the transaction, for example, whether the consumer is jointly or individually liable.

The furnisher fills in enough fields about the transaction or account to describe it in some detail. In addition to the account number, information is requested about the date of the transaction, credit limits and loan amounts, and payment schedules and amounts. The portfolio type indicates whether the transaction is a mortgage, installment credit, a line of credit, or other kind of open account. More than sixty codes can be used to designate an account type. Some of the most common are: automobile, automobile lease, credit card, debit card, home equity, home equity line of credit, home improvement, household goods, installment sales contract, real estate, including conventional first mortgage real estate, junior liens, non-purchase money first liens, second mortgages, and secured home improvement. Some separate codes that might be routinely relevant to practitioners are: manufactured housing (formerly mobile homes), education loans, secured credit cards, child support, medical debts, debt consolidation, rental agreement, collection agencies, and utility companies. More esoteric codes abound, including attorney fees, debt counseling service, family support, and a range of codes for government and government-backed transactions. This level of detail can reasonably be included in consumer reports issued by the CRAs.

Of course the most critical part of the base segment is information about the account status and the consumer's payment history. This kind of information is familiar to anyone who has reviewed a typical consumer report. As might be expected, data is collected on payments received during the reporting period, a twenty-four month history of payments (or nonpayments), current balance, date of last payment, amount past due, charge-off amount, and date closed. The twenty-four month payment history profile includes codes for accounts placed for collection, foreclosure, repossession, and voluntary surrender.

In addition to such standard information as payment history, creditors summarize the current account status and can use special comment codes. The status codes themselves are rather ordinary, including such things as current account, account ninety-days past due, foreclosure, repossession, and other descriptions, often simply reflecting some of the credit history recorded in other fields. One code, though, causes the entire account to be deleted, although creditors are urged to use this code only to undo an error and not as a means of reporting "derogatory" accounts as paid.[57] A different delete code is used to delete accounts due to confirmed fraud.

---

54 See Ch. 14, infra.
55 See Cassara v. DAC Servs., Inc., 276 F.3d 1210 (10th Cir. 2002).
56 ECOA stands for Equal Credit Opportunity Act, 15 U.S.C. §§ 1691–1691f. To learn more about the ECOA's credit reporting requirements, see National Consumer Law Center, Credit Discrimination § 9.4 (4th ed. 2005 and Supp.).
57 ACA International, ACA Compliance Alert: Reporting Requirements for Metro-2 Format Users (Apr. 20, 2006) ("data furnishers should not delete paid in full collection accounts; rather

The status code can be further explained using special comment codes. The special comment codes can be particularly important to consumer attorneys concerned with how a dispute resolution may actually be reported to a CRA. Among the more useful codes that could be important in resolving disputes between creditor and consumer are those relating to special payment arrangements and legal actions. Dispute resolutions and settlements might, for example, be represented by codes for account paid in full for less than full balance, partial payment plan, payments through a credit counseling service, principal deferred with interest payment only, or even adjustment pending. The code indicating that the account was paid by the company that originally sold the merchandise could benefit the consumer. Other additional information represented by special comment codes includes: paid by insurance, paid by co-maker, payroll deduction, garnishment, and even natural disaster. The code for election of remedy is used when a car is repossessed and sold for less than the amount owed but the creditor is prohibited by operation of law from collecting the difference.[58] A catchall code simply indicating special handling suggests that a user might best contact the creditor directly to find out more.

Two special comment codes are especially pertinent in identity theft cases. The special handling designation alerts the CRA that identity theft or other special circumstances may be involved. Another code indicates that the first payment was never received, suggesting the possibility of fraud.

Other special comment codes delineate various ways an automobile lease can end and reasons an account has been closed (e.g., refinancing, lost credit card, closed by the creditor) or transferred to another (e.g., sold to another, student loan transferred to the government).

Compliance fields are used to ensure that various statutory requirements are met. One of the most important compliance fields requires the furnisher to indicate the date of the first delinquency that led to the reporting of a delinquent account. The FCRA generally prohibits CRAs from including debts more than seven years old from date of default (not charge-off) in consumer reports.[59] Without this information from the creditors, CRAs would likely continue to report debts after they become obsolete.

In order to avoid any unfair negative inference from a report that an account has been closed, both furnishers and CRAs must, when true, indicate that the closure was at the behest of the consumer.[60] Also, both the FCRA and the Fair Credit Billing Act require that consumer disputes over a debt must be noted.[61] A series of compliance condition codes used by the furnisher indicate that an account was closed at the request of the consumer, that consumer disputes are pending with the furnisher under the FCRA or with a creditor under the FCBA, or that, having been reinvestigated or resolved by the furnisher/creditor, the consumer still disputes the matter.

6.3.3.4 Associated Consumers Segment Has Information on Joint Debtors and Other Authorized Users of Credit

The Metro 2 base segment includes a fairly detailed identification of the main consumer, the consumer primarily responsible for the debt. The two J segments capture identifying information about additional consumers who are or may become obligated on the same debt. Frequently more than one consumer may be obligated on a single transaction or share some of its benefits. A spouse or child may be an authorized user of a credit card, two consumers may be jointly liable for a debt, or one may have guaranteed the debt of another and be liable if the primary consumer does not make timely payments. This relationship is captured by the ECOA codes included in both the base segment and the segments on associated consumers. The identity of the second (and additional) consumer is fleshed out in the J segments, using the same identifiers as used in the base segment for the primary consumer. The J1 segment is used only if the associated consumer is located at the same address as the primary consumer, and is shorter because it does not duplicate information already provided. The J2 segment is longer because it must include location information about the secondary consumer.

6.3.3.5 Transfers of Accounts Segment Tracks Holders of Debt

Consumer accounts are often transferred from one party to another. Delinquent debts are commonly transferred to debt collectors for collection. Also common is the sale of entire portfolios (groups) of debts from one creditor to another. These sales routinely occur with mortgages but occur with non-mortgage consumer credit transactions as well. Segments K1 and K2 identify these transfers. K1 is used by collection agencies to identify the original creditor and makes possible the use of the original creditor's name when the CRA reports the debt as delinquent. Absent the name of the creditor with whom the consumer did business, the consumer might have no idea what transaction is being reported. Similarly, student loan guaranty agencies and even the United States Department of Education must furnish the name of the original creditor in order to help keep track of

---

the account should be reported using the "62" account status code.").

58 See National Consumer Law Center, Repossessions (6th ed. 2005).
59 See § 5.2, supra.
60 See § 6.8, infra.
61 See § 6.6, infra. See also National Consumer Law Center, Truth in Lending, § 5.8 (5th ed. 2003 and Supp.) (discussion of the Fair Credit Billing Act).

which debt is which. This reporting should also help keep track of the first reported delinquency date for a transaction in order to avoid using obsolete information in consumer reports.[62]

6.3.3.6 Other Metro 2 Segments Serve Specialized Purposes

The remaining Metro 2 segments are short and specialized and used only as applicable. Segment K3, mortgage information, indicates when a secondary market agency has an interest in the mortgage and helps track so-called Mortgage Identification Numbers (MINs), which indicate that the mortgage is registered with the Mortgage Electronic Registration System (MERS) used to track mortgage ownership rights. Segment K4 reports information about balloon and deferred payments, more common in mortgages but applicable to other credit transactions as well. Segment L1 is used to change account numbers in the system, and the trailer records are used to help verify the completeness of each computer dump or monthly submission of information about a furnisher's current customer base. The employment segment (N1) is optional and identifies the primary consumer's occupation and the name and address of the employer. It does not have a field for income or pay.

6.3.3.7 Common Errors

FCRA Compliance Date/Date of Last Activity—Base Segment, Field 25. This field is extremely important as it sets the date for calculating the start of the obsolescence period under section 1681c of the FCRA.[63] This date is not literally the date of the last activity on the account. For example, an assignee of a bad debt may incorrectly state that this date is its recent purchase of the account, thus effectively (and illegally) extending the FCRA obsolescence period.[64] The *Credit Reporting Resource Guide* states repeatedly that the date of the first delinquency of the debt that is being collected sets this date. This is true regardless whether the debt was sold to subsequent entities. The date is also unaffected by subsequent repayment arrangements.[65] When a buyer of bad debt purchases an account, the original owner should zero out the "current balance" field and inform the purchaser of the debt the date the account first became delinquent.[66]

Incorrect "Date Opened"—Base Segment, Field 10. The Metro 2 Format requires the original creditor to report the date opened as the original date the account was opened. However, if a collection agency or purchaser begins reporting the debt, the opened date is the date the account was placed or assigned to the third party collection agency.[67] Thus, the account can appear as a newer account than it really is. The industry standard in this regard is confusing.

Bankruptcy Status Associated with Nonfiling Joint Obligor. The common error of reporting the bankruptcy of a joint obligor on the consumer report of the nonfiling consumer is wholly avoidable by following the requirements of Metro 2.[68] According the *Credit Reporting Resource Guide*, the status of such an account should be reflected as follows:

> For joint account holders where one borrower files bankruptcy, report one Base Segment for the account with the Consumer Information Indicator (CII) set to the appropriate bankruptcy code for the borrower who filed bankruptcy. The CII for the other consumer should be blank. The Account Status (field 17A) should reflect the status of the ongoing account for the consumer who did not file bankruptcy.[69]

Therefore, the account can reflect the status of the account (e.g., current, late, closed, etc.) for both obligors, but the bankruptcy status (e.g., petition for chapter 7 bankruptcy, discharged through chapter 7 bankruptcy, etc.) is segregated from the nonfiling joint account holder.[70]

Incorrect Status Codes—Base Segment, Field 17A. The Metro 2 Format allows the furnisher to provide the current status of the reported account based on a series of standardized codes. There are many codes that can be reported generally to reflect the account status. Many furnishers' data entry employees are not well trained in the variety of entries that can be made and therefore use an inapplicable code that incorrectly describes the consumer's precise circumstances. For instance, a vehicle may have been "account paid in full, was a repossession," "account paid in full, was a voluntary surrender," or "voluntary surrender," to name just a few.

---

62 See § 5.2, *supra*.
63 See § 5.2, *supra*.
64 See United States of Am. v. NCO Group, Inc., 2004 WL 1103323 (E.D. Pa. 2004) (consent decree requiring monitoring of FCRA complaints, particularly regarding delinquency date); U.S. v. Performance Capital Mgmt. (Bankr. C.D. Cal 2000) (complaint), *available at* www.ftc.gov/opa/2000/08/performance.htm.
65 Associated Credit Bureaus, Credit Reporting Resources Guide 10-4 (2000) (Metro Manual).
66 *Id.* at 6–7.
67 *Id.* at 4-8, 10-3.
68 This error is less common as a result of the settlement in Clark v. Experian Info. Solutions, 2004 WL 256433 (D.S.C. Jan. 14, 2004), in which the CRAs agreed to take steps to eliminate the practice, but still occurs. See § 6.3.3.4, *supra*.
69 Consumer Data Indus. Ass'n, Inc., Credit Reporting Resource Guide, *Frequently Asked Questions* 6-13 (2005) (Metro 2 Manual).
70 Nothing in the Equal Credit Opportunity Act or Regulation B § 202.10 requires a furnisher or CRA to report a spouse's bankruptcy on the nonfiling spouse's report, even if the latter is jointly liable. Following this Metro 2 protocol meets the directive of Regulation B § 202.10 to "reflect the participation of both spouses" without burdening the nonfiling spouse's report with the filing spouse's extraneous bankruptcy information. *See generally* National Consumer Law Center, Credit Discrimination § 9.4.2.1 (4th ed. 2005 and Supp.).

6.3.3.8 Metro 2 and Debt Collectors

Many debts are collected by someone other than the creditor. The debt may be assigned or sold to a debt collection agency or to an attorney. A factoring company is an old fashioned term, still used on occasion, for one who purchases debts with the intention of collecting amounts owed. In most instances these debt collectors will be covered by the Fair Debt Collection Practices Act and various state laws.[71] Under the FCRA, these collectors will usually be furnishers of information to CRAs. Once the debt is transferred to a collection agency, it is the collection agency and not the original creditor who will furnish updated information to the CRAs. Difficulties are not uncommon, first, because some debt collection agencies are notoriously sloppy in this regard and, second, because debt collectors are all too likely to report the date of first delinquency based on their acquisition of the debt and not, as required, the first delinquency experienced by the original creditor. This "error" is economically beneficial to the collector because it causes the debt to be reported well beyond the time it is obsolete.[72] The matter of reporting the date of first delinquency is discussed elsewhere in this chapter.[73]

Debt collectors, like other furnishers, are expected to fully fill in all appropriate segments and fields in the Metro 2 Format for identifying information to payment histories. Metro 2 materials provide additional instructions to collectors to ensure that accurate information is furnished and to avoid common errors. In litigation against a collector as a furnisher of information under the FCRA, the consumer's counsel may wish to discover what instructions have in fact been provided to the collector. Of course, one of the special concerns is the reporting of an accurate first date of delinquency, but some others bear noting.

The debt collector should report the name of the original creditor and the type of creditor involved. This information is furnished in the K1 segment. One purpose of this Metro 2 requirement is to identify the original creditor in the consumer report. Absent this information, a consumer may be unable to identify the source of the debt or to understand just what is being included in the consumer report. Often, the consumer will not recognize the name of the collector alone.

In identifying the account type, the collector should generally use one of only three codes: 48 for collection agency or attorney; 77 for returned checks; OC for debt purchaser. The guidelines for Metro 2 require the account status code for collectors to be one of three codes: 93 when the account is seriously past due or otherwise assigned for collection; 62 once it has been paid in full; or DA or DF to have the account deleted.

The collector should of course distinguish between the primary consumer and any secondary consumer, but normally would not furnish information on authorized users on a credit card account because such users are often not contractually liable. Presumably, if a collector did classify a consumer as an authorized user, the CRA would block that information from being included in that consumer's report.

The "Date Opened" field of the base segment is a common source of misunderstanding. Debts are frequently sold and transferred among collectors and other investors. The K and L segments of Metro 2 are important to a CRA as a means of keeping track of debts and avoiding inaccuracies and deceptions resulting from duplication. All creditors are expected to include in the base segment a Date Opened field, which is usually the date an account was opened. However, a debt collector is instructed to put into this field the date the debt was placed for collection, assigned, or purchased. When this date is included in consumer reports, it is frequently misunderstood.

6.3.3.9 Metro 2 and Student Loans

Most student loans are subject to extensive federal regulation, and borrowers have a variety of remedies available to them when they have been defrauded by a trade school or have experienced difficulty in making timely payments. These regulations are treated thoroughly elsewhere.[74] However, because of the unique treatment often required for student loans, some standardized ways of furnishing information to CRAs have been established.

No distinction is made in Metro 2 between different types of student loans; they are all reported as education loans. A student loan may be reported in good status when payments are being made and also when payments are deferred with a future payment obligation. Deferred payment loans are further distinguished between those where repayment has never (yet) been made and those where the account was previously being repaid. When payments are deferred, the start date for making payments should be included in the K-4 segment for specialized payments.

Student loans which are disbursed to students over a period of time are treated as a single account. The date opened is the date of the first disbursement, but the original loan amount, balance, and scheduled payment amounts would increase appropriately as disbursements are made. If the loans are truly multiple loans, then each one is treated as a separate account. If multiple loans are consolidated, it is considered a new loan initially in good standing. The consolidated loans should be recorded as paid or closed with zero balances, although a payment rating will reveal accounts which were not in good standing.

---

71 15 U.S.C. § 1692. *See generally* National Consumer Law Center, Fair Debt Collection (5th 2004 and Supp.).
72 *See* § 5.2, *supra*.
73 *See* § 6.7, *infra*.

---

74 *See generally* National Consumer Law Center, Student Loan Law (3d ed. 2006).

Status code 88 cases are those that have been referred to the Department of Education for payment of the insured balance on the loan. If the claim is denied, the lender or servicer must delete the account and furnish afresh information about the debt, using the original date opened, status, and other attributes. Of course, potential errors may result in the same student loan debt being reported twice.

Student loans can be forgiven for a variety of reasons. If the loan is forgiven due to a school closing, it is simply deleted. Similarly, in a false certification case, the loan report should also be deleted. Forgiveness for student disability may be reported one of two ways. If the loan never reached the repayment period, it too should be deleted. However, if repayments had begun, the loan should be designated as paid or closed, and the balance or amount due recorded as zero. Teacher forgiveness is treated in the same manner.

Student loans, like other debts, may be sold or transferred to others for collection. Generally speaking, the Metro 2 system relies upon the transferring creditor to delete the accounts from CRA files and the new creditor or servicing agent to begin furnishing information about the account. The new furnisher does not start with a new open date, payment history, or status or date of first delinquency but should retain prior information as furnished earlier on the account. A servicer, one who does not itself hold the note, must also continue to use the identification number of the holder. Mistakes when accounts are transferred can result in false or misleading information in consumer reports.

If a student loan is transferred to a student loan guaranty agency, the agency is supposed to record the loan as seriously past due. If the consumer is nonetheless making payments, the debt is still coded as seriously past due but the balance due should decline. A code also exists for accounts paid off by the government or insurer, or forgiven because the student has become totally and permanently disabled. If the guaranty agency itself transfers the account to a debt collection agency or the United States government, it should use a code (DA) to delete the account from the records reported to the CRAs. The collection agency or the government will then include the debt in its own Metro 2 submissions to the CRAs.

6.3.3.10 Metro 2 and Utility Bills

Utility company bills are unusual in that the amount due is generally not scheduled. Metro 2 guidelines unique to utilities call for standard codes for duration of payment terms (001) and scheduled monthly payment amounts (0) unless actual terms and schedule exist. Otherwise, payment history, identifying information, and other information are treated the same as for other creditors. Multiple accounts are treated separately. The purchase of merchandise such as an appliance is treated as installment credit. Account types can be utility company for the consumption of energy products, cellular for telecommunications, and installment sales contracts for merchandise sales.

6.3.3.11 Metro 2 and Dishonored Checks

Dishonored checks normally create a debt. Some CRAs specialize in dishonored checks or track check payment histories because they function as check guaranty companies.[75] A dishonored check, also called NSF (for Non-Sufficient Funds), usually creates a debt and is treated as a debt in Metro 2. The date opened is the date of the check; the loan amount is the amount of the check, excluding any fees or interest; the original creditor is the payee (the person to whom the check was made out); and the date of first delinquency is the date the check was returned for non-sufficient funds. If the return date is not known, Metro 2 allows substitution of the earlier date of the check itself.

NSF checks also affect Metro 2 reporting when the creditor has furnished information showing a payment, only to find out that the payment has to be reversed when the check is dishonored. Furnishers are expected to "correct" the information already provided via Metro 2 by adjusting future submissions to accurately reflect past history as if the bad check payment had never been made. Thus, the date of last payment, date of first delinquency, payment history profile, and actual payment amounts might all be adjusted for purposes of current and future Metro 2 computer dumps. As each periodic Metro 2 report contains past as well as current information, the new report should replace information reported earlier.

6.3.3.12 Metro 2 and Bankruptcy

Any report mentioning a bankruptcy can have a detrimental effect on the consumer. Thus it is important that the report accurately indicate what kind of bankruptcy is involved and the proper status of any bankruptcy proceeding.[76] The Metro 2 Format requires that a furnisher specify in some detail the nature of any reference to bankruptcy.

The Metro 2 base segment calls for a "consumer information indicator" or code designating specific bankruptcy information. The codes distinguish between chapter 7, 11, 12, and 13 bankruptcies on the one hand, and the filing of a petition, a discharge, dismissal, or withdrawal on the other. Reaffirmation of a debt and reaffirmation of a rescinded debt are also distinguished. Importantly, the "Q" code is used to remove a previously reported code. Bankruptcy status is reported only once—it does not have to be included in each monthly transmission of data by the furnisher—and will be deleted only upon a new or updated report by the furnisher.

---

75 See § 2.6.2.2, supra.
76 See Ch. 4, supra.

Metro 2 instructions require that debts discharged in bankruptcy be reported with a zero balance. However, furnishers often fail to properly report accounts discharged in bankruptcy.[77]

It is especially important to track separately the obligations and status of primary and associated consumers when one or the other has filed for bankruptcy. The bankruptcy of one should not be imputed to the other. CRAs should be able to make the appropriate distinctions because both the base segment and the associated consumer segments have a field for consumer information indicators. In the base segment, the consumer information indicator provides information about the primary consumer only; the furnisher should not report any bankruptcy information concerning an associated debtor here. The associated consumer segment of the Metro 2 Format has its own field for the bankruptcy codes appropriate to the secondary consumer(s). The record should therefore be clear which of two joint obligors has filed bankruptcy, and it should be entirely possible to separately track and report independently the accurate status of each consumer.

Although Metro 2 clearly distinguishes between the primary and secondary consumers, consumer reports on one consumer often include information about a bankruptcy filed by the other obligor.[78] Reportedly, this unfair reporting occurs even when the furnisher has properly categorized the bankruptcy information in the base segment or the associated consumer segment. No mention of the bankruptcy filed by one consumer should be included in a report on another because it is irrelevant to the creditworthiness of the other consumer. Of course, if the debt is delinquent, the delinquency may possibly be relevant to both consumers, but the fact that one has filed bankruptcy should not be imputed to the other.

6.4 Standards of Accuracy for Furnishers

6.4.1 Introduction

The FCRA establishes minimum standards of accuracy for creditors and other furnishers initially providing information about consumers to consumer reporting agencies (CRAs). These standards of accuracy are discussed in the following subsections. The standards are not unimportant but, given their status within the system for regulating the accuracy of consumer reports, their apparent import can be misleading. One way they are misleading is that they cannot be enforced by the consumer. Even if the creditor has ignored the standard altogether, no consumer may bring suit against the furnisher to enforce these provisions. Consumers are understandably incredulous when they learn that federal law requires accuracy when a creditor initially furnishes information to the CRA, but there is little one can do to enforce this requirement or remedy its breach.

The duties of accuracy described below may be enforced by the Federal Trade Commission, state attorneys general, and other public officials, but may not be enforced by private right of action.[79] The only privately enforceable FCRA standards covering the furnishers of information are those involving the reinvestigation which a creditor must perform after a consumer requests that a CRA reinvestigate.[80] In particularly egregious cases involving malice or willful intent to injure the consumer, some courts hold that a creditor may be liable for defamation or other torts,[81] but otherwise FCRA liability for furnishers derives from CRA reinvestigations and not from any independent standard of accuracy applicable to furnishers. As a result, a consumer attorney is likely to be primarily concerned with the reasonableness of the reinvestigation. These reinvestigation obligations are discussed elsewhere in this manual.[82]

Although there is no direct private enforcement, the standards of accuracy imposed on furnishers nevertheless set forth minimum criteria of acceptable creditor behavior. Thus, these standards may affect what is considered to be an accurate report in the context of litigation over the reinvestigation requirements that are privately enforceable.

6.4.2 General Duty to Report Accurately

Unlike the requirement placed on CRAs, the FCRA does not specify an affirmative standard of accuracy for those who furnish information to CRAs. CRAs must maintain reasonable procedures to ensure the maximum possible accuracy of the information they report.[83] The duty of furnishers to provide accurate information, on the other hand, is stated in the negative, as two prohibitions against reporting inaccurate information.

The first prohibition bars furnishing information that the furnisher "knows or has reasonable cause to believe is inaccurate."[84] The term "reasonable cause to believe" is defined as "having specific knowledge, other than solely

---

77 See Ch. 4, *supra*, for additional discussion on reports relating to bankruptcy.
78 This error is less common as a result of the settlement in *Clark v. Experian Info. Solutions*, 2004 WL 256433 (D.S.C. Jan. 14, 2004), in which the CRAs agreed to take steps to eliminate the practice, but still occurs.
79 15 U.S.C. § 1681s-2 (c) and (d); Riley v. General Motors Acceptance Corp., 226 F. Supp. 2d 1316 (S.D. Ala. 2002); Vazquez-Garcia v. Trans Union de Puerto Rico, 222 F. Supp. 2d 150 (D. P.R. 2002); Hasvold v. First USA Bank, N.A., 194 F. Supp. 2d 1228 (D. Wyo. 2002). See § 6.9, *infra*. See also § 10.2.4, *infra*.
80 See § 6.10, *infra*.
81 See § 10.5, *infra*.
82 See § 6.13, *infra*.
83 See Ch. 4, *supra*.
84 15 U.S.C. § 1681s-2(a)(1)(A).

allegations by the consumer, that would cause a reasonable person to have substantial doubts about the accuracy of the information."[85] This standard, however, is not applicable to furnishers who maintain a special address for notification of inaccuracies.[86]

Within this category of inaccurate information are those items that at least one CRA already has determined to be inaccurate, incomplete, or unverifiable. A CRA that concludes after reinvestigating a consumer's dispute that an item of information is "inaccurate or incomplete or cannot be verified" must "promptly" (1) delete or modify the information, as appropriate, and (2) notify the furnisher "that the information has been modified or deleted from the file of the consumer."[87] Such a notice should provide "reasonable cause to believe that the information is inaccurate" and meets the further requirement that its basis is more "than solely allegations by the consumer." A furnisher must then cease reporting the information, not simply because of the statutory mandate,[88] but also in the interest of maintaining consistently accurate information among the various CRAs and helping meet the separate directive that severely limits the reinsertion of deleted information.[89]

The second prohibition proscribes the furnishing of information where the consumer has notified the furnisher that the information is inaccurate and where the information is, in fact, inaccurate.[90]

The two accuracy standards must be read in conjunction with the subsection that immediately follows them establishing a duty to promptly correct and update furnished information determined to be incomplete or inaccurate.[91] This duty is applicable to furnishers who regularly and in the ordinary course of business furnish information to CRAs.[92] In general terms, furnishers are required to provide accurate, complete, and updated information.[93] Indeed, CRAs would be unable to provide accurate reports without generally accurate information from creditors and other furnishers. A reasonable level of accuracy is necessary to meet the goals of the FCRA, including the fair and accurate reporting of information useful to the banking system, as well as ensuring fairness to consumers.[94] This standard of accuracy, which includes completeness, is consistent with the general standards of accuracy applicable to other federal consumer protection statutes[95] and the common law.[96]

The FCRA also requires furnishers to assist in preventing the reporting of identity-theft-related debts. The Act requires furnishers to have reasonable procedures to prevent refurnishing identity theft information that a CRA has blocked.[97] Furnishers are also prohibited from refurnishing information that a consumer has identified to the furnisher at the address specified by such furnisher as resulting from identity theft.[98]

The Metro 2 standard operating procedure employed by most creditors for transmitting information to CRAs[99] has been painstakingly designed so that information vital to the preparation of accurate consumer reports is identified and defined in a manner to facilitate the routine provision of accurate and complete information. A furnisher is not free to ignore or selectively utilize the Metro 2 program in a manner which undermines the accuracy of the information provided.[100]

FTC staff have opined about what a furnisher may report. One creditor has been told that it may not submit information about delinquencies for which the consumer is not actually liable. The mortgage lender had been reporting payment histories of consumers who took title to mortgaged property (by will, for example) without formal obligation to make payments. The apparent reason for saying that the lender may not report delinquencies in the name of the new property owner is that, since the owner is not liable for the payments, the reports would be inaccurate.[101]

6.4.3 Accuracy and Integrity Regulations for Furnishers

The FCRA requires the federal agencies that enforce the Act to establish guidelines for furnishers regarding the "accuracy and integrity" of furnished information. The agencies must also issue regulations requiring furnishers to establish reasonable policies and procedures for implement-

---

85 15 U.S.C. § 1681s-2(a)(1)(D).
86 15 U.S.C. § 1681s-2(a)(1)(C). See § 6.4.4, infra.
87 15 U.S.C. § 1681i(a)(5)(A).
88 15 U.S.C. § 1681s-2(a)(1)(A).
89 15 U.S.C. § 1681i(a)(5)(B). See Ch. 4, supra.
90 15 U.S.C. § 1681s-2(a)(1)(B)(i) and (ii).
91 15 U.S.C. § 1681s-2(a)(2)(B).
92 Id.
93 Boynton, FTC Informal Staff Opinion Letter (Feb. 15, 2000), reprinted on the CD-Rom accompanying this manual. Cf. Jaffe, FTC Informal Staff Opinion Letter (July 17, 1998), reprinted on the CD-Rom accompanying this manual; Tabler, FTC Informal Staff Opinion Letter (Oct. 27, 1998), reprinted on the CD-Rom accompanying this manual.
94 15 U.S.C. § 1681(a).
95 Sterling Drugs, Inc. v. F.T.C., 741 F.2d 1146, 1154 (9th Cir. 1984) (omission of material information is deceptive even if the representation is not false); Simeon Mgmt. Corp. v. F.T.C., 579 F.2d 1136, 1146 (9th Cir. 1978) (same).
96 Restatement of Torts (Second) §§ 529 and 551 (omission of material fact constitutes misrepresentation just as an outright inaccuracy).
97 15 U.S.C. § 1681s-2(a)(6)(A). See also § 9.2, infra.
98 15 U.S.C. § 1681s-2(a)(6)(B). See also § 9.2, infra.
99 See § 6.3.2, supra.
100 See Cassara v. DAC Servs., Inc., 276 F.3d 1210 (10th Cir. 2002) (inaccuracy of report established by industry understanding of terms, even though report accurate by lay standards); § 6.3.3, supra.
101 Jaffe, FTC Informal Staff Opinion Letter (July 17, 1998), reprinted on the CD-Rom accompanying this manual. Cf. Tabler, FTC Informal Staff Opinion Letter (Oct. 27, 1998), reprinted on the CD-Rom accompanying this manual.

ing those guidelines.[102] It is unclear how the term "integrity" will be interpreted by the agencies and the extent to which it will be supplemental to the completeness duty for furnishers. By definition, integrity should include the soundness and completeness of information.[103] While Congress modified the standard for furnishers with respect to information they provide to CRAs, it did not provide for private enforcement of these new standards,[104] and states are preempted from regulating the subject matter of the provision.[105] As of mid-2006, no such regulations had been proposed by the federal agencies, and only the preliminary *Interagency Advance Notice of Proposed Rulemaking* had been published.[106]

6.4.4 Accuracy When Creditor Clearly and Conspicuously Maintains a Special Address for the Consumer to Give Notification of Inaccurate Information

Large national creditors and many others who furnish information to CRAs may maintain a special address which may be used to notify the creditor of inaccuracies. The address should be readily available to the consumer and may be used by the consumer in any effort to have the creditor correct information that may be provided to CRAs.

Many creditors will maintain addresses that a consumer may use to notify the creditor that specific information is inaccurate because it fosters good customer relations. In addition, creditors who maintain such an address for consumer use will thereby *not* be subject to the prohibition against furnishing information that is known (or should be known) to be inaccurate. A business that maintains this notification-of-error address avoids even that general accuracy requirement.[107]

That is, the general rule against reporting information known to be inaccurate does not apply to any furnisher of information who clearly and conspicuously specifies to a consumer an address for notices that specific information is inaccurate.[108] When this consumer-complaint address is maintained, the FCRA instead prohibits reporting information that has been specified by the consumer as inaccurate, in a notice sent to the address specified by the furnisher for consumer complaints, and that in fact is inaccurate. If the furnisher receives a notice of inaccuracy at that address, it no longer matters under the FCRA whether the furnisher "knows or has reason to know" that future reports are inaccurate.[109]

In a most fundamental way, this provision lowers the standard for the initial furnishing of information to CRAs, in that furnishers are not explicitly forbidden from providing information known to be false or that the furnisher has reasonable cause to believe is false.[110] However, for all but the casual supplier of information, this lowering of the standard is of little consequence. After all, anyone who regularly and in the ordinary course of business is furnishing information to CRAs is also required to promptly correct or update information determined not to be complete or accurate.[111] In addition, a furnisher who knows that information is inaccurate yet contemptuously still reports it to a CRA may well lose its immunity from state tort claims under the "willful intent to injure" standard.[112]

On the other hand, in one respect the rule is remarkably strict. If a consumer uses the complaint address to notify the creditor or furnisher that specific information is inaccurate, and the information is in fact inaccurate, the creditor is forbidden to furnish that information to a CRA at all. The imperative is unqualified by convenience, actual knowledge, or circumstance. All that matters is accuracy. Of course, much could depend upon the degree of understanding that the creditor can be expected to glean from the consumer's notice of inaccuracy. Nevertheless, the burden falls heavily upon the creditor to explain why any inaccuracy has been reported after notice from the consumer. Any prudent creditor must be required to reinvestigate the accuracy of the disputed information and to take into consideration any and all relevant information provided by the consumer or otherwise reasonably available to the creditor. In the end, if the creditor cannot confirm the accuracy of the contested information, it should not report the information at all.

Although many, if not most, furnishers will maintain this special address for consumer complaints in order to maintain good customer relations, the law introduces some incentive to obscure the address for FCRA purposes. Businesses which engage in predatory practices or which depend only upon initial sales and therefore care less about later customer relations have economic reasons to maintain an error notification address and hope that it is not widely used because complaints received at any other address do not trigger any accuracy standard. The general prohibition against knowing inaccuracy does not apply when a complaint address is maintained and, unless the notification is received at the specified address, even the lower standards

---

102 15 U.S.C. § 1681s-2(e). 16 C.F.R. § 602.1(c)(3)(xiv).

103 The Merriam-Webster definition of integrity includes "incorruptibility; and unimpaired condition, and the quality of being complete." *See* www.merriam-webster.com/cgi-bin/dictionary?book=Dictionary&va=integrity.

104 15 U.S.C. § 1681s-2(c)(2). However, consumers may bring an action against furnishers for behavior that independently violates 15 U.S.C. § 1681s-2(b). *Id.*

105 15 U.S.C. § 1681t(b)(1)(F). *See also* § 10.7, *infra*.

106 *See* 71 Fed. Reg. 14,419–14,425 (Mar. 22, 2006).

107 15 U.S.C. § 1681s-2(a)(1)(B).

108 *Id.*

109 *See* 15 U.S.C. § 1681s-2(a)(1)(A), (D), *as amended by* Pub. L. No. 108-159, § 312(b) (2003).

110 *Id.*

111 *See* § 6.5, *infra*.

112 15 U.S.C. § 1681h(e). *See* §§ 6.12, 10.4.6, *infra*.

arguably do not apply. Importantly, the Act requires that the address must be "clearly and conspicuously specified[d] *to the consumer*" (emphasis added).[113] The FTC brochure explains that clear and conspicuous means that it is reasonably easy to read and understand and cannot be buried in a mailing.[114]

If a creditor/furnisher provides an address to lodge complaints, consumers should use that address whenever directly disputing a debt (as well as when sending the creditor/furnisher a courtesy copy of a formal dispute submitted to a CRA). The consumer should be as specific as possible in explaining and documenting the dispute. According to reports from practitioners and consumers, creditors sometimes deny that a dispute was ever received. For this reason, the general admonition that consumers should always use return receipt mail is particularly appropriate when sending any correspondence to a creditor (and when writing to a CRA as well).

6.4.5 Duty of Accuracy When Creditor Furnishes Information to an Affiliate

The differing duties of a creditor to furnish accurate information to a CRA, discussed in the preceding sections, do not apply to companies furnishing information to other entities affiliated by common ownership or corporate control even if the receiving affiliate functions as an in-house CRA. Such affiliate sharing of information is generally outside the scope of the FCRA.[115]

Often, a consumer disputing a debt will not know whether the creditor is furnishing information to a CRA, to an affiliated company, or to both. A consumer will likely only know that inaccurate information is being furnished if it has been revealed by an actual consumer report. Normally, though, a consumer will be moved to dispute a debt because the creditor is demanding sums the consumer believes are not owed.

6.5 Furnishers Have Duty to Correct and Update Furnished Information

6.5.1 Creditors Must Promptly Correct and Update Information

If a creditor or other furnisher determines that information it has provided to a consumer reporting agency (CRA) is inaccurate or incomplete, the creditor must promptly inform the CRA of the determination and provide corrected information.[116] This correction procedure will occur most frequently in response to a dispute by the consumer. If, after considering a consumer dispute, the creditor determines that the consumer was correct, or finds in any way that it has furnished inaccurate information, the creditor must correct itself. However, the creditor may also learn of its mistakes through a variety of other ways, from internal audits to complaints from third parties. No matter how the creditor makes its determination of error, steps to correct the information must be promptly taken.

The creditor must not only inform the CRA that it has determined that information previously provided was inaccurate or incomplete and provide updated information, it must also ensure that it does not thereafter furnish the uncorrected information. Frequently, even when creditors have corrected information once, the inaccurate information reappears in future reports. One reason this occurs is that the computer tapes or other internal records of the creditor are not adequately corrected. The next time the creditor "dumps" its records into the CRA's computerized system, the inaccurate information is furnished again and supersedes whatever corrected information has made it into the CRA's consumer records. Creditors are required to prevent the reappearance of this inaccurate information.

Consumer attorneys report instances in which CRAs fail to update files with information provided by creditors who are no longer customers of that CRA. To circumvent this unlawful obstacle, the consumer can notify the CRA directly that the item is in dispute. Under the law, a CRA must drop the information from its reports unless the creditor verifies it; as the information has already been determined to be inaccurate, the creditor should not verify it and the CRA should thereafter delete it.[117] The creditor, of course, should be taking steps to make sure that the information is not unwittingly verified. A reminder from the consumer's attorney of the furnisher's obligations may help.

Most creditors who furnish information to CRAs do so on a regular and ongoing basis. A creditor who does not "regularly and in the ordinary course of business" furnish information on at least one consumer is not subject to the FCRA duty to correct. Actually, the duty is not just to correct inaccurate information but to update information that has been previously reported. A consumer or attorney coping with inaccurate consumer reports will be most concerned with the duty to correct. However, the continuing duty to update information—as payments are made, for example—is fundamentally important to ensure that consumer reports remain accurate even in the absence of disputes.

---

113 15 U.S.C. § 1681s-2(a)(1)(C).
114 Fed. Trade Comm'n, Credit Reports: What Information Providers Need to Know (Mar. 1999), *available at* www.ftc.gov/bcp/conline/pubs/buspubs/infopro.pdf.
115 See § 2.4.3, *supra*.

116 15 U.S.C. § 1681s-2(a)(2). See Ch. 4, *supra*.
117 15 U.S.C. § 1681i. See Ch. 4, *supra*.

6.5.2 Disputing Inaccurate Information with the Creditor

A furnisher of information is liable under the FCRA only after the consumer notifies a CRA (or a reseller when appropriate) of the dispute, the dispute is conveyed to the furnisher by the CRA, and the furnisher does not conduct a reasonable investigation.[118] The furnisher's mere knowledge of the dispute without a formal dispute to the CRA does not impose FCRA liability.[119] Consumers and practitioners must be vigilant to initiate the formal dispute process with the CRAs or reseller in order to preserve any remedy under the FCRA. Nevertheless, a dispute with the creditor may be efficacious so long as one formally renews the dispute with the CRA in the event that the informal effort with the creditor does not fully resolve the reporting error.

Prior to the FACTA amendments, the FCRA had no provision at all by which a consumer could formally or informally dispute an inaccurate item of information and request a reinvestigation directly with the furnisher; rather, the consumer had to dispute the item with the CRA, which was then required to notify the furnisher.[120] Prior to the FACTA amendments, the FCRA required the furnisher to reinvestigate the item only upon receiving the CRA's notice; a notice from the consumer was irrelevant and ineffective.[121] Now a consumer may trigger a furnisher's responsibility to reinvestigate by disputing the item directly with the furnisher when the circumstances of the dispute meet the conditions of to-be-prescribed provisions.[122] This new provision specifically provides, however, that such a reinvestigation responsibility will not be initiated by a notice from or prepared by a credit repair organization,[123] and furnishers need not respond to "frivolous" or "irrelevant" disputes.[124] However, if the furnisher considers the dispute frivolous, the furnisher must notify the consumer within five business days of this determination, of the reason it considers the dispute frivolous, and what information the consumer must provide to convert the dispute into one that will trigger a reinvestigation.[125]

The furnisher must investigate the dispute and report the results back to the consumer in the same time frame allowed CRAs for reinvestigation.[126] If the furnisher finds that the information is inaccurate, the furnisher must correct the information with each CRA to which it furnished the information.[127] As with formal investigation responsibilities that arise upon notice from a CRA, states are preempted from regulating the subject matter of this provision.[128] However, unlike those responsibilities under the formal investigation process, under this provision consumers may not privately enforce violations of this direct furnisher's dispute of right.[129]

A problem may occur when information has previously been disputed but not properly investigated. The consumer will still need the relief, but the furnisher can consider a second investigation request frivolous and refuse to perform any new investigation. This provision only exists under section 1681s-2(a), so the consumer should continue to dispute the debt through the CRA.[130]

Although the process has no private enforcement mechanism, dealing with the source of information furnished to the CRA may be advisable for several reasons. Contacting the creditor or other furnishing source certainly makes sense when the error originates from that source. Even when the CRA has inaccurately transcribed information or mismerged files, the CRA is also likely to respond readily to corrections coming from the information's source. When information is incomplete and the original source supplies the CRA with additional information, it is also likely that the CRA will include this information in the consumer's file.

In addition, the source of inaccurate information is likely to have reported the same information to a number of different CRAs. The correction of information at one CRA may have no effect on the same error at other CRAs. The source of the incorrect information, on the other hand, can report the correction to all CRAs originally furnished with the inaccurate information.

Also, the source of inaccurate information is likely to continue furnishing the same inaccurate information to CRAs until the problem is fixed at the source. Even if the CRA has deleted or corrected the information once, the possibility exists that the information will be added to the consumer's file again.

---

118 See § 6.10, *infra*.
119 See § 6.10.3, *infra*.
120 15 U.S.C. § 1681i(a)(2).
121 15 U.S.C. § 1681s-2(b). See § 6.10.3, *infra*.
122 15 U.S.C. § 1681s-2(a)(8). The effective date for the new regulations is December 1, 2003; yet, as of mid-2006, no regulations had been proposed.
123 15 U.S.C. § 1681s-2(a)(8)(G). Even notices from or prepared by organizations that are not defined as credit repair organizations under the Credit Repair Organizations Act (16 U.S.C. § 1679a) because of their non-profit status will not trigger a reinvestigation. *Id.*
124 Such a determination may arise by reason of the consumer's failure to provide sufficient information to allow the furnisher to investigate the disputed information, 15 U.S.C. § 1681s-2(a)(8)(F)(i)(I), or when the submitted dispute reiterates a dispute made by the consumer to either the furnisher or a CRA and which the furnisher has already reinvestigated, 15 U.S.C. § 1681s-2(a)(8)(F)(i)(II).

125 15 U.S.C. § 1681t(a)(8)(F).
126 15 U.S.C. § 1681t(a)(8)(E).
127 *Id.*
128 15 U.S.C. § 1681t(b)(1)(F).
129 Peasley v. Verizon Wireless, 364 F. Supp. 2d 1198 (S.D. Cal. 2005). There may be a possibility that state UDAP laws could be a source by which to attach a remedy to violations of this duty, but such an effort would need to address the preemption issue. See § 10.7, *infra*.
130 See § 6.10, *infra*.

Another reason to contact the creditor is that the CRA may respond faster to a creditor correction furnished to the CRA than it would to a consumer request to reinvestigate information in the consumer's file. The creditor's monthly computer transmission of information may automatically correct the consumer's file at the CRA, and it is quite unlikely that a CRA would refuse a subscriber's request to correct information previously furnished. Experian and Equifax have also agreed that they will accept a consumer's version of a dispute if it is accompanied by documentation from the CRA's source confirming the consumer's version (unless Experian or Equifax in good faith doubts the authenticity of the documentation).[131]

A dispute over accuracy between a consumer and a creditor or furnisher may also be relevant to formal reinvestigation processes with the CRA which could lead to furnisher liability. The fact that a consumer has contacted the creditor and complained about the inaccurate information or contested the creditor's claims and the inaccurate information still appears in a consumer report will buttress the claim that the creditor failed to reasonably correct the inaccuracy during the formal reinvestigation initiated with the CRA.

Of course, a creditor saying that it will correct information does not mean it will. Similarly, the creditor may make the correction but not follow through and pass this correction on to all relevant CRAs. The CRAs themselves may not enter the information properly in the consumer's file. While 16% of complaints reviewed in one study involved the creditor continuing to furnish inaccurate information, another 11% of complaints involved cases where the reporting creditor had fixed an error but the CRA had not.[132]

The clear implication is that consumers may have to deal both with the source furnishing the information and the CRA to correct inaccuracies. Even if information appears corrected, it is important to follow up several months later to make sure the information has stayed corrected.

Again, it must be emphasized that the FCRA provides consumers with no private remedy for any violation of a furnisher's initial reporting obligations or for any violation of the statutory dispute process that permits consumers to initiate direct disputes with a furnisher; instead, the FCRA allows consumers to sue a furnisher only for failing to meet its duties within the formal dispute process initiated directly with the CRA or reseller.[133] Therefore, the most important litigation advice is to proceed immediately to this formal dispute procedure.

6.5.3 Sometimes Adverse Information May Not Be Furnished During a Dispute

While the FCRA does not prohibit the furnishing of information that has been disputed by the consumer but not yet resolved, other parts of the federal Consumer Protection Act do. Restrictions on information that may be furnished to a CRA are discussed more fully in another chapter.[134]

In brief:

- Under the Fair Debt Collection Practices Act, a debt collector is prohibited from furnishing disputed information without noting that dispute.[135]
- The Fair Credit Billing Act limits the furnishing of disputed information on credit card and other open-end accounts.[136]
- The Real Estate Settlement Procedures Act protects consumers from adverse consumer reports during periods of disputes involving mortgages and home equity loans.[137]
- The Equal Credit Opportunity Act restricts creditors when furnishing credit information from discriminating against a consumer on any prohibited basis.[138]

6.5.4 Universal Data Form May Be Used to Make Corrections

A creditor may correct information which it has previously provided to a CRA in at least two ways. A creditor can simply correct its own internal records and supply this corrected information to the CRA as part of its regular submission of information on its customer base. Most creditors do provide routine, updated information on all of their customers to the CRAs on a periodic basis, frequently using the Metro 2 reporting system.[139] The newly supplied information will normally replace the older incorrect information, and only the most recent information will be included in future consumer reports.

An alternative way to correct information is to use the Universal Data Form.[140] The Universal Data Form was designed in 1990 by the CRA trade association, Associated Credit Bureaus (now the Consumer Data Industry Association), and may be used to update information with any of the major nationwide CRAs. The single page form may be filled out manually, or an automated version may be used to

---

131 *See* Fed. Trade Comm'n v. TRW, Inc., 784 F. Supp. 361 (N.D. Tex. 1991) (consent order), *reprinted on the CD-Rom accompanying this manual*; Equifax Agreement with Eighteen State Attorneys General Offices (June 22, 1992), *reprinted on the CD-Rom accompanying this manual. See also* summary in Appx. K, *infra*.
132 U.S. Pub. Interest Research Group, Credit Bureaus: Public Enemy #1 at the FTC (Oct. 1993).
133 *See* § 6.10, *infra*.
134 *See* Ch. 5, *supra*.
135 National Consumer Law Center, Fair Debt Collection § 5.5.11 (5th 2004 and Supp.).
136 *See* National Consumer Law Center, Truth in Lending, § 5.8.7.3 (5th ed. 2003 and Supp.).
137 *See* National Consumer Law Center, Foreclosures, § 5.2.2.3 (2005 and Supp.).
138 *See* § 6.11, *infra*.
139 *See* § 6.3.2, *supra*.
140 A sample Universal Data Form is reprinted in Appx. I, *infra*.

transmit the information via computer connections. Attorneys coping with inaccurate reports or settling litigation[141] will normally want the creditor to use the Universal Data Form, both to ensure that the correction is properly made and to document the change.

While the Universal Data Form is commonly used by creditors to correct and update information about a particular customer, it is generally not sufficient on its own. A correction made using the form will be superseded by the later (re)submission of the original inaccurate information. A creditor must also update its own internal records to ensure that the data it regularly submits electronically to the CRAs is correct. If the computer tapes or other format used to update information contains the earlier inaccurate information, that erroneous information will be incorporated into the CRA's files and used in future reports. Significantly, if this common occurrence leads to litigation, the creditor will also have violated one of the terms of the form itself: the form contains a clause stating, in bold, "When you sign this form, you certify that your computer and/or manual records have been adjusted to reflect any changes made."

The FCRA requires creditors to correct erroneous information promptly. Using the Universal Data Form is generally more prompt than waiting for the next routine transmission of customer base information to the CRA. It also provides easy documentation that the change was submitted. It is appropriate to use when a creditor finds it necessary to change information as a result of customer contact or of discovery through internal processes that updating is required. For example, upon consumer complaint, a creditor might discover that it has misapplied a payment it actually did receive or that an account has been opened fraudulently as a result of identity theft. The form may also be important to quickly communicate information that is urgent, for example, when a consumer pays off a mortgage or an account in full in order to qualify for a new mortgage or credit account.

The Universal Data Form can be used to submit changes in balances, payment history, current status and, importantly, to delete account information. The form is based on the Metro 2 Format. Basically, the same codes used for Metro 2 are used on the Universal Data Form. In addition, it has a simple check-off box to have the entire "tradeline" or account deleted. Any settlement agreement in which a creditor must change or delete an account should include a requirement that the creditor use the Universal Data Form to correct or change the incorrect information on the account.[142]

6.6 Furnisher Must Note Disputes

If a consumer disputes the accuracy or completeness of any information which has been furnished to a consumer reporting agency (CRA), the furnisher may not in the future report this information to a CRA unless it notes that it has been disputed.[143] Even if the creditor determines that the disputed information was neither inaccurate nor incomplete, or is unable to make any determination about the dispute raised by the consumer, the creditor must note that the information is disputed whenever it furnishes the information to a CRA in the future. As a result, if information furnished to one CRA is disputed and then furnished to another CRA, the report to the second CRA must note that the information has been disputed by the consumer.

There is a more important application of this provision, however. While one might doubt whether this rule would have any effect on information previously furnished to the original CRA, it will often be quite important. Many creditors—and, perhaps, most nationwide creditors—automatically report each month, by computer hook-up with a CRA, the current status of all outstanding consumer accounts. Once a consumer has disputed a debt, all future reports to the same CRA must note that the account has been disputed. Thus, many disputes will be noted in the files of a CRA even though the originally furnished information indicated no dispute at all.

This rule applies to all parties who furnish information to a CRA. The rule is not restricted to those who regularly furnish information to CRAs or to those who do so in the ordinary course of business. The rule is also not dependent upon whether the consumer uses an error-notification address, which many creditors will maintain to escape the general rule for reporting accurate information.[144] This is one more reason for a consumer to dispute information with the furnisher at the same time, if not before it disputes information with the CRA.

The Metro 2 Format[145] has a section in the base segment that is used for noting disputes required by the FCRA and the Fair Credit Billing Act.[146] Creditors and debt collectors can use the Metro 2 compliance condition code for account information disputed by consumer. Credit card creditors can use the codes to indicate Account In Dispute Under Fair Credit Billing Act and for FCBA Dispute Resolved—Consumer Disagrees.

---

141 See § 12.6.4, *infra*.
142 See § 12.6.4, *infra*.
143 15 U.S.C. § 1681s-2(a)(3). As this provision of the FCRA does not require that the consumer notify the furnisher of the dispute in writing, a consumer's oral notice should be sufficient. *Cf.* Brady v. The Credit Recovery Co., 160 F.3d 64 (1st Cir. 1998) (FDCPA does not require a consumer to notify a debt collector in writing that the consumer disputes the debt to prevent collector from reporting the debt to CRAs).
144 See § 6.4, *supra*.
145 See § 6.3, *supra*.
146 See § 6.3.4, *supra*.

6.7 Furnisher Must Furnish Dates of Delinquency

Accounts placed for collection or charged to profit and loss may not be included in consumer reports after seven years.[147] The information is then considered obsolete.[148] The seven-year period begins when the account is placed for collection or charged to profit and loss. Unless informed by the creditor or by the person furnishing information about a delinquency, a consumer reporting agency (CRA) has no way of knowing when the delinquency commenced and, hence, when the information must be eliminated from reports as obsolete. Any person who provides information about a delinquent account placed for collection or written off must also inform the CRA when the delinquency commenced.[149]

The date of the delinquency does not have to be provided by the furnisher until ninety days after the information is first provided to the CRA. However, a CRA which does not receive the date of delinquency within ninety days risks reporting obsolete information. Perhaps for this reason the Metro 2 Format appears to require that the date of first delinquency be reported without delay. For example, in the base segment, the date of first delinquency must be reported regardless of the status codes. Most status codes are for varying degrees of delinquency; if the code for a current account is used, the date of first delinquency is to be given as zero.

Problems frequently arise when information about a debt is furnished to a CRA by a debt collector. Debt collectors commonly report the date they received the account or assignment from the creditor as the initial date of delinquency, even though the creditor has almost certainly placed the debt for in-house collection or charged off the debt much earlier. This noncompliance occurs despite the fact that the FCRA specifies that the date of delinquency for an account placed for collection must be a date that immediately preceded the placement.[150] It also occurs even though the Metro 2 Format requires debt collectors to use the date of delinquency from the original creditor and instructs debt collectors who do not know the date of first delinquency with the original creditor to use the earlier date for when the account was opened by the creditor.[151] When CRAs are unaware of the earlier, proper date of delinquency, the date furnished by the collector may well be used. The effect is to extend the seven-year period well beyond the statutory limits.

A debt collector that reports such erroneous information to a CRA typically violates the FDCPA, which, unlike the FCRA, provides a private remedy for this misconduct.[152] In addition, the consumer should still dispute the information under the FCRA. If, during the reinvestigation, the collector again reports the date of its first activity as the date of delinquency, the collector can be liable for its violation of the FCRA.[153]

6.8 Furnishers Must Provide Notice of Closed Account

An indication in a consumer report that an account has been closed may be interpreted negatively even if a consumer has voluntarily asked that the account be closed. Concerned that such reports may be read as suggesting that an account was closed because the consumer did not meet the account's terms, Congress required that creditors who regularly and in the ordinary course of business furnish information to the consumer reporting agency (CRA) must also notify the CRA when an account has been voluntarily closed by the consumer.[154] A CRA which receives such a notice must indicate the voluntary nature of the closure in any report which includes information about the closed account.[155]

Under the Metro 2 Format,[156] the reason for a closed account can be coded in several ways. Only "XA" for "account closed at consumer's request" has no apparent or likely negative connotation to a future user. Other codes, like those for "account closed at consumer's request and in dispute under FCRA," or "account closed at consumer's request and dispute investigation completed, consumer disagrees," clearly provide information allowing a skeptical user to surmise that this consumer may be troublesome regardless of the bona fides of the matter.

6.9 "Financial Institution" As Defined by Gramm-Leach-Bliley Must Notify Customers of Negative Information Furnished to Reporting Agencies

The FCRA requires that a "financial institution" must notify a customer that it is furnishing negative information about that customer.[157] The notice must be given within

---

147 See § 5.2, *supra*.
148 Obsolete information is discussed in detail at § 5.2, *supra*.
149 15 U.S.C. § 1681s-2(a)(5).
150 15 U.S.C. § 1681s-2(a)(5).
151 See § 6.3.3.8, *supra*.
152 See 15 U.S.C. § 1692e(8); National Consumer Law Center, Fair Debt Collection § 5.5.10 (5th 2004 and Supp.).
153 See § 10.2.4.2, *infra*. See also § 6.3.4.2, *supra*.
154 15 U.S.C. § 1681s-2(a)(4). The notification is to be included as part of the information regularly furnished for the period in which the account was closed.
155 15 U.S.C. § 1681c(e).
156 See § 6.3.2, *supra*.
157 15 U.S.C. § 1681s-2(a)(7).

thirty days of reporting negative information.[158] This requirement applies to financial institutions as defined by cross reference to the Gramm-Leach-Bliley definition of a financial institution.[159] This furnisher notification requirement is further limited by the FCRA to only those financial institutions that (1) extend credit and regularly and in the course of business furnish information to a nationwide consumer reporting agency (CRA), and (2) furnish negative information to such a CRA regarding credit extended to a customer.[160] Such a financial institution needs only to provide the customer with one notice, and does not need to provide further notice when additional negative information is later reported about that account.[161]

The Federal Reserve Board has issued two model notices that a financial institution may use. One model notice is applicable when the institution provides notice in advance of providing negative information to a CRA. This notice appears to serve as a sort of "boilerplate" without providing actual notice when negative information is furnished. The other model notice is applicable when an institution provides the notice after furnishing negative information to a CRA.[162] The notice must be clear and conspicuous.[163] Use of a model form, while not required, constitutes compliance with this statutory provision.[164] The notice may not be included with disclosures under section 127 of the Truth in Lending Act.[165] As with all furnisher obligations (other than those arising during participation in the formal reinvestigation process), this provision is not enforceable by private consumer actions.[166]

The fact that Congress chose to impose this notification obligation only on the limited category of defined financial institutions and that it omitted any similar notification duty on furnishers as a whole presumably demonstrates that other furnishers who report negative information do not need to provide the consumer with notification. Further discussion of this notification obligation is found in § 6.8, *infra*.

6.10 Formal Consumer Reporting Agency Dispute Process Subjects the Furnisher to Obligations That Are Enforceable by the Consumer

6.10.1 Overview

Furnishers are subject to a single category of duties and standards that may be enforced by consumers—the people with the greatest incentive and ability to police their own consumer reports. These privately enforceable duties are limited to the formal process where consumers may dispute the accuracy and completeness of information by initiating a reinvestigation under section 1681i with the consumer reporting agency (CRA) (and where applicable via a reseller),[167] not with the person who furnished the information to the CRA. A consumer who fails to initiate the dispute with the CRA or reseller under section 1681i and instead deals directly with the furnisher cannot invoke any FCRA remedies whatsoever; private consumer enforcement is only available for a breach of the section 1681s-2(b) furnisher obligations triggered by a formal section 1681 dispute with a CRA or reseller.[168]

Absent such a formal dispute lodged with a CRA or reseller, furnishers are simply not liable to the consumer for a breach of any of their other FCRA duties, such as to initially to report accurate information,[169] to correct and update furnished information,[170] and to comply with the other FCRA requirements for furnishing information. The economic incentive that the private enforcement of the Act provides is missing with regard to the furnishing of accurate information to CRAs. Perhaps as a consequence, compliance with these standards is abysmally low. All too commonly, creditors and others maintain inadequate procedures to ensure accuracy and fail to take complaints from consumers either seriously or seriously enough.

Moreover, the system for handling consumer disputes is also inadequate given the enormity of the task. Testimony in cases suggests that CRAs receive tens of thousands of consumer disputes each week (one CRA reportedly receives between 35,000 and 50,000 per week). Approximately 80% of such complaints are written.[171] Some CRAs have procedures that require quotas for the number of consumer disputes CRA employees must process. One former CRA

---

158 15 U.S.C. § 1681s-2(a)(7)(B)(i).
159 15 U.S.C. § 1681s-2(a)(7)(G)(ii), incorporating § 5089 of Pub. L. No. 106-102, the Gramm-Leach-Bliley definition codified in 15 U.S.C. § 6809. See § 16.4.1.2, *infra*. N.B. The FCRA contains a general definition of "financial institution" in § 1681a(t) that, by operation of § 1681s-2(a)(7)(G)(ii), does not apply to § 1681s-2(a)(7) and instead applies to its usage in § 1681u(a) and (d).
160 15 U.S.C. § 1681s-2(a)(7)(A)(i).
161 15 U.S.C. § 1681s-2(a)(7)(A)(ii).
162 69 Fed. Reg. 33,281–33,285 (June 15, 2005), *codified at* 12 C.F.R. Part 222. See Appx. C, *infra*.
163 15 U.S.C. § 1681s-2(a)(7)(C)(ii).
164 15 U.S.C. § 1681s-2(a)(7)(D)(iii).
165 15 U.S.C. § 1681s-2(a)(7)(B)(ii).
166 15 U.S.C. § 1681s-2(c)(1). See § 6.10, *infra*.

167 *See* Ch. 4, *supra*. Where applicable, a dispute may be initiated with a reseller, as discussed in § 6.13, *infra*.
168 *See* § 6.10.2, *infra*.
169 *See* § 6.4, *supra*.
170 *See* § 6.5, *supra*.
171 *See* Deposition of Eileen Little, Evantash v. G.E. Capital Mortgage, Civ. Action No. 02-CV-1188 (E.D. Pa. Jan. 25, 2003), *reprinted on the CD-Rom accompanying this manual*.

employee testified that employees were required to process one dispute every four minutes in order to meet quotas.[172]

Each CRA has a different process for handling disputed information, but all three collaborated through CDIA to create an automated on-line reinvestigation processing system: "E-OSCAR,"[173] touted by the consumer reporting industry as a state-of-the-art solution for processing Automated Consumer Dispute Verifications (ACDVs) and Automated Universal Data Forms (AUDFs). However, use of this automated system has resulted in a perfunctory data verification procedure, not a reinvestigation process. Written disputes from consumers, often containing a detailed letter and supporting documentation, are translated into a two digit code that a CRA employee believes best describes the dispute. Only the code is sent to the furnisher for verification. A more thorough reinvestigation in which documents are reviewed and the substance of the consumer's dispute is investigated appears to be the exception, if not a rarity, rather than the rule.

The process typically is as follows: the CRA first receives a formal dispute from the consumer or reseller.[174] The CRA generally must forward the complaint to the furnisher. The furnisher must conduct an investigation and report the results back to the CRA. Then the CRA must investigate the disputed information. The CRAs then send generic and uninformative letters stating that an investigation has been made, without including any details as to whom they have contacted and what information was obtained or relied upon for a final determination. This missing information is important, however, because it reflects the fact that the CRA received the dispute, that the dispute was in fact forwarded to the furnisher, and that a substantive determination was made with respect to the accuracy or completeness of the disputed information.

A failure of the CRA to forward the dispute to the furnisher relieves the furnisher of its obligation to investigate.[175] However, the furnisher that establishes this defense necessarily establishes the consumer's alternative claim that the CRA breached its statutory duty to notify the furnisher.[176] These litigation alternatives illustrate that whether the CRA or the furnisher (or both) is ultimately responsible for the failure to properly investigate the consumer's dispute is virtually impossible to know prior to formal discovery. Accordingly, the consumer is well advised to join claims against both the furnisher and the CRA when suing either for breaching its reinvestigation duties.[177]

After receiving the CRA's notice of the consumer's dispute, a furnisher can be liable to the consumer for its failures to participate in the reinvestigation process as required by the statute. Furnisher liability under these provisions of the FCRA is a frequent subject of litigation. Therefore, initiating a reinvestigation of inaccurate information with the CRA or reseller can be far more efficacious than relying upon an unenforceable complaint to the creditor/furnisher to clear up its mistakes.

This is not to say one should not dispute matters directly with creditors/furnishers. Indeed, resolution can be swift. Moreover, should a creditor fail to correct a dispute sent directly by the consumer to it and also fail to conduct an adequate investigation following a formal dispute lodged with the CRA, its knowledge of the dispute and culpability in eventual litigation will be all the more apparent.[178]

A formal reinvestigation involves both the CRA and the person who furnished the information to the CRA. The obligations of the CRAs are discussed in an earlier chapter.[179] The subsections which follow discuss the obligations and the bases for liability of the furnisher once it has been notified by the CRA of the dispute.

Because the FCRA is not a strict liability statute, merely showing that the furnisher did not comply with one of its formal investigation duties will not establish liability. Establishing liability by proving negligent noncompliance with these provisions is discussed in Chapter 10, *infra*; proving willful noncompliance is discussed in Chapter 11, *infra*.

6.10.2 Furnishers Are Liable to Consumers in Private Suits for Breach of the Formal Investigation Responsibilities

The investigation procedures that a CRA undertakes when a consumer disputes the accuracy or completeness of

---

172 Deposition of Regina Sorenson, Fleischer v. Trans Union, Civ. Action No. 02-71301 (E.D. Mich. Jan 9, 2002), *reprinted on the CD-Rom accompanying this manual.*

173 Online Solution for Complete and Accurate Reporting. *See* www.cdiaonline.org/eoscar/eoscarintro.cfm.

174 A reseller's role in a formal furnisher liability case is essentially as a conduit with the consumer regarding those reseller consumer reports that it ultimately produces and that allegedly contain a third-party error. Where a consumer chooses to initiate a dispute with a reseller not alleging incompleteness or inaccuracy as a result of any act or omission of that reseller, the reseller's only function is to transfer the dispute to the applicable CRA. The CRA then treats the dispute as any other dispute received directly from the consumer. *See* § 6.13, *infra*.

175 *See* § 6.10.4, *infra*.

176 15 U.S.C. § 1681i(a)(2). *See* Ch. 4, *supra*.

177 *See* Jaramillo v. Experian Inf. Solution, Inc., 155 F. Supp. 2d 356 (E.D. Pa. 2001), *vacated in part on other grounds*, 2001 U.S. Dist. LEXIS 10221 (E.D. Pa. June 20, 2001) (vacated as to § 1681t(b) preemption holding) (the consumer complaining of an insufficient reinvestigation cannot be expected to know at the pleading stage whether the CRA properly notified the furnisher of the dispute). *Cf.* Whitesides v. Equifax Credit Info. Servs., Inc., 125 F. Supp. 2d 307, 812 n.5 (W.D. La. 2000) (commenting that neither party had yet established whether the CRA conveyed the consumer's dispute to the furnisher).

178 *Cf.* Bruce v. First U.S A. Bank, 103 F. Supp. 2d 1135 (E.D. Mo. 2000).

179 *See* Ch. 4, *supra*.

§ 6.10.2 Fair Credit Reporting

information must involve the person who furnished the disputed information to the CRA.[180] Any furnisher who fails to comply with its duties pursuant to section 1681s-2(b) in this investigation process is liable to the consumer in a private cause of action for its negligent or willful noncompliance.[181]

Section 1681s-2(b)(1) clearly conditions its five enumerated furnisher investigation duties on the furnisher's receipt from the CRA of notice of the consumer's dispute.[182] Therefore, the furnisher is required to act, and accordingly is liable, only if the investigation process is triggered by a consumer dispute lodged directly with a CRA.[183] Some courts hold that even the failure to allege in the complaint the CRA's transmittal of the section 1681i consumer dispute to the furnisher constitutes a failure to state a claim for relief under Federal Rule of Civil Procedure 12(b)(6).[184] Others reject that pleading omission as at most a technical deficiency.[185] But all courts enforce the condition precedent that the consumer initiated a direct section 1681i dispute with a

---

180 See § 6.10.3, infra.
181 Nelson v. Chase Manhattan Mortgage Corp., 282 F.3d 1057 (9th Cir. 2002); Bach v. First Union Nat'l Bank, 149 Fed. Appx. 354 (6th Cir. Aug 22, 2005) (unpublished); King v. Equifax Info. Servs., 2005 WL 1667783 (S.D. Tex. July 15, 2005); Howard v. Blue Ridge Bank, 371 F. Supp. 2d 1139 (N.D. Cal. 2005); Nelski v. Risk Mgmt. Alternatives, Inc., 2005 WL 1038788 (E.D. Mich. Apr. 21, 2005) (negligent or willful noncompliance with § 1681s-2(b)is an element of the claim); Johnson v. CGR Servs., Inc., 2005 WL 991770 (N.D. Ill. Apr. 7, 2005) (damages are an essential element of a negligence claim); Caltabiano v. BSB Bank & Trust Co., 387 F. Supp. 2d 135 (E.D.N.Y. 2005) (damages are an essential element of a negligence claim); Schaffhausen v. Bank of America, N.A., 393 F. Supp. 2d 853 (D. Minn. 2005) (damages are an essential element of a negligence claim); Hurocy v. Direct Merchants Credit Card Bank, N.A., 371 F. Supp. 2d 1058 (E.D. Mo. 2005); Akalwadi v. Risk Mgmt. Alternatives, Inc., 336 F. Supp. 2d 492 (D. Md. 2004); McKeown v. Sears Roebuck & Co., 335 F. Supp. 2d 917 (W.D. Wis. 2004) (deletion instead of reinvestigation does not comply); Carriere v. Proponent Fed. Credit Union, 2004 WL 1638250 (W.D. La. July 12, 2004); Gibbs v. SLM Corp., 336 F. Supp. 2d 1 (D. Mass. 2004); Gonzalez v. Ocwen Fin. Servs., Inc., 2003 WL 23939563 (N.D. Cal. Dec. 2, 2003) (plaintiff can file claim under § 1681s-2(b), but failed to allege furnisher received notice of the dispute from a CRA); Olwell v. Medical Info. Bureau, 2003 WL 79035 (D. Minn. Jan. 7, 2003); Redhead v. Winston & Winston, P.C., 2002 WL 31106934 (S.D.N.Y. Sept. 20, 2002); Yutesler v. Sears Roebuck & Co., 263 F. Supp. 2d 1209 (D. Minn. 2003); Mendoza v. Experian Info. Solutions, Inc., 2003 WL 2005832 (S.D. Tex. Mar. 25, 2003); Sheffer v. Experian Info. Solutions, Inc., 249 F. Supp. 2d 560 (E.D. Pa. 2003); Betts v. Equifax Credit Info. Servs., Inc., 245 F. Supp. 2d 1130 (W.D. Wash. 2003); Whisenant v. First Nat'l Bank & Trust Co., 258 F. Supp. 2d 1312 (N.D. Okla. 2003); Carlson v. Trans Union, L.L.C., 259 F. Supp. 2d 517 (N.D. Tex. 2003); Stafford v. Cross Country Bank, 262 F. Supp. 2d 776 (W.D. Ky. 2003); Vasquez-Garcia v. Trans Union de Puerto Rico, 222 F. Supp. 2d 150 (D. P.R. 2002); Hawthorne v. Citicorp Data Sys., 216 F. Supp. 2d 45, 47–48 (E.D.N.Y. 2002), vacated on other grounds, 219 F.R.D. 47 (E.D.N.Y. 2003); Yelder v. Credit Bureau of Montgomery, 131 F. Supp. 2d 1275 (M.D. Ala. 2001); Jaramillo v. Experian Info. Solutions, Inc., 155 F. Supp. 2d 356 (E.D. Pa. 2001), vacated in part on other grounds, 2001 U.S. Dist. LEXIS 10221 (June 20, 2001); Fino v. Key Bank of New York, 2001 WL 849700 (W.D. Pa. July 27, 2001); Scott v. AmEx/Centurion, 2001 WL 1645362 (N.D. Tex. Dec. 18, 2001); Thomasson v. Bank One, Louisiana, N.A., 137 F. Supp. 2d 721 (E.D. La. 2001); DiMezza V. First USA Bank, Inc., 103 F. Supp. 2d 1296 (D.N.M. 2000); McMillan v. Experian Info. Servs., Inc., 119 F. Supp. 2d 84 (D. Conn. 2000); Dornhecker v. Ameritech Corp., 99 F. Supp. 2d 918 (N.D. Ill. 2000); Banks v. Stoneybrook Apartment, 2000 WL 1682979 (M.D.N.C. June 1, 2000), aff'd, 232 F.3d 888 (4th Cir. 2000) (table, text at 2000 WL 1578331); Bruce v. First U.S.A. Nat'l Ass'n, 103 F. Supp. 2d 1135 (E.D. Mo. 2000); Campbell v. Baldwin, 90 F. Supp. 2d 754 (E.D. Tex. 2000); Johnson v. United States-Dep't of Defense, 2000 U.S. Dist. LEXIS 21087 (D. Minn. Oct. 17, 2000); Mandly v. Bank One Dayton, 2000 U.S. Dist. LEXIS 16269 (D. Ariz. Sept. 18, 2000); Olexy v. Interstate Assurance Co., 113 F. Supp. 2d 1045 (S.D. Miss. 2000); Ryan v. Trans Union Corp., 2000 WL 1100440 (N.D. Ill. Aug. 4, 2000); Thompson v. The Elec. Transaction Corp., 2000 U.S. Dist. LEXIS 5275 (N.D. Miss. Mar. 28, 2000); Whitesides v. Equifax Credit Info. Servs., Inc., 125 F. Supp. 2d 807 (W.D. La. 2000); Brown v. Maine Med. Ctr., 1999 WL 33117137 (D. Me. Mar. 18, 1999); Geeslin v. Nissan Motor Acceptance Corp., 1998 WL 433932 (N.D. Miss. June 3, 1998), aff'd, 228 F.3d 408 (5th Cir. 2000); Brinckerhoff, FTC Informal Staff Opinion Letter (June 24, 1999) (Watkins) (§ 1681s-2[b] affords a private right of action). See also Young v. Equifax Credit Info. Servs., Inc., 294 F.3d 631 (5th Cir. 2002) (dicta). But see Carney v. Experian Info. Solutions, Inc., 57 F. Supp. 2d 496 (W.D. Tenn. 1999) (finding no private right of action on basis of reliance on overtly inapplicable section of the FCRA).
182 15 U.S.C. § 1681s-2(b)(1)("After receiving notice pursuant to section 1681i(a)(2) of this title of a dispute with regard to the completeness or accuracy of any information provided by a person to a consumer reporting agency, the person shall. . . .").
183 See § 10.2.4, infra.
184 Roybal v. Equifax, 405 F. Supp. 2d 1177 (E.D. Cal. 2005); Peasley v. Verizon Wireless (VAW), 364 F. Supp. 2d 1198 (S.D. Cal. 2005); Banks v. Stoneybrook Apartment, 2000 WL 1682979 (M.D.N.C. June 1, 2000), aff'd, 232 F.3d 888 (4th Cir. 2000) (table, text at 2000 WL 1578331); Moline v. Trans Union, 2003 WL 21878728 (N.D. Ill. Aug. 7, 2003); DiMezza v. First USA Bank, Inc., 103 F. Supp. 2d 1296 (D.N.M. 2000); Thompson v. The Elec. Transaction Corp., 2000 U.S. Dist. LEXIS 5275 (N.D. Miss. Mar. 28, 2000); Dolan v. Fairbanks Capital Corp., 2005 WL 1971006 (E.D.N.Y. Aug. 16, 2005); Ruggiero v. Kavlich, 411 F. Supp. 2d 734 (N.D. Ohio 2005). Accord Rovers v. Providian Nat'l Bank, 2006 WL 305915 (D. Or. Feb 7, 2006) (granting furnisher's Rule 12(c) motion for judgment on the pleadings for absence of any allegation that the furnisher received notice of the dispute from a CRA).
185 Young v. Equifax Credit Inf. Serv., Inc., 294 F.3d 631 (5th Cir. 2002); Thompson v. Homecomings Fin., 2005 WL 3534234 (N.D. Tex. Dec. 19, 2005); Ornelas v. Fidelity Nat'l Title Co. of Wash., Inc., 2005 WL 3359112 (W.D. Wash. Dec. 9, 2005); King v. Equifax Info. Servs., 2005 WL 1667783 (S.D. Tex. July 15, 2005); Watson v. Trans Union Credit Bureau, 2005 WL 995687 (D. Me. Apr. 28, 2005); Cook v. Experian Inf. Solutions, Inc., 2002 WL 31718624 (N.D. Ill. Nov. 27, 2002); Jaramillo v. Experian Info. Solutions, Inc., 155 F. Supp. 2d 356 (E.D. Pa. 2001), vacated in part on other grounds, 2001 U.S. Dist. LEXIS 10221 (E.D. Pa. June 20, 2001).

CRA or reseller and that the CRA met its obligation to convey notice of the dispute to the furnisher as an element of establishing furnisher liability under section 1681s-2(b).[186]

The FCRA civil liability rules make no exception for furnishers who violate their obligations as part of the investigation procedures pursuant to section 1681s-2(b).[187] Thus, any furnisher who negligently fails to comply with any of these investigation requirements is liable to the consumer for actual damages, the costs of litigation, and attorney fees.[188] If the violation is willful, the furnisher is liable for actual damages or minimum statutory damages between $100 and $1000, for punitive damages, as well as for costs and attorney fees.[189] To maintain a claim under section 1681s-2(b), the consumer must either establish a willful violation or suffer damages in connection with a negligent violation.[190] A merely negligent failure to complete the investigation resulting in no actual damages entitles the furnisher to judgment as a matter of law.[191] These private remedies are discussed in Chapter 10, *infra*.

Congress carefully distinguished between section 1681s-2(a), requiring furnishers initially to report accurate and complete information but omitting any private enforcement mechanism, and section 1681s-2(b), permitting private enforcement of any breach by furnishers of their subsequent duty to help investigate consumer disputes. In effect, Congress decided that furnishers are entitled to the proverbial "one free bite," as confirmed by the Ninth Circuit in the seminal case recognizing the right of consumers to enforce a furnisher's breach of its investigation duties:

> It can be inferred from the structure of the statute that Congress did not want furnishers of credit information exposed to suit by any and every consumer dissatisfied with the credit information furnished. Hence, Congress limited the enforcement of the duties imposed by § 1681s-2(a) to governmental bodies. But Congress did provide a filtering mechanism in § 1681s-2(b) by making the disputatious consumer notify a credit reporting agency and setting up the credit reporting agency to receive notice of the investigation by the furnisher. See 15 U.S.C. § 1681i(a)(3) (allowing the credit reporting agency to terminate reinvestigation of disputed item if the credit reporting agency "reasonably determines that the dispute by the consumer is frivolous or irrelevant"). With this filter in place and opportunity for the furnisher to save itself from liability by taking the steps required by § 1681s-2(b), Congress put no limit on private enforcement under §§ 1681n and o.[192]

This congressionally imposed "filtering mechanism" requiring a consumer dispute helps ensure that only the most meritorious claims are actually litigated. The hallmark of a successful FCRA case is that the defendant is on notice of the error or inaccuracy.[193] Every furnisher (and CRA) necessarily will be on notice of the erroneous report once informed of the consumer's dispute. The only exceptions will occur when the consumer does not explain the dispute adequately (a condition easily remedied before filing suit) or the CRA breaches its obligation under section 1681i(a)(2)(A) (and thereby establishes another claim against the CRA) to advise the furnisher of "all relevant information regarding the dispute that the agency has received from the consumer."[194]

---

186 Young v. Equifax Credit Inf. Serv., Inc., 294 F.3d 631 (5th Cir. 2002); Nelson v. Chase Manhattan Mortgage Corp., 282 F.3d 1057 (9th Cir. 2002); Stiff v. Wilshire Credit Corp., 2006 WL 141610 (D. Ariz. Jan. 17, 2006); Thompson v. Homecomings Fin., 2005 WL 3534234 (N.D. Tex. Dec. 19, 2005); Sciria v. Huntington Bank, 2005 WL 3262954 (N.D. Ohio Dec. 1, 2005); Westbrooks v. Fifth Third Bank, 2005 WL 3240614 (M.D. Tenn. Nov. 30, 2005); Semper v. JBC Legal Group, 2005 WL 2172377 (W.D. Wash. Sept. 6, 2005); Pirouzian v. SLM Corp., 396 F. Supp. 2d 1124 (S.D. Cal. 2005); Steele v. Chase Manhattan Mortg. Corp., 2005 WL 2077271 (E.D. Pa. Aug. 26, 2005); Zager v. Deaton, 2005 WL 2008432 (W.D. Tenn. Aug. 16, 2005); Pitstick Farms, Inc. v. Sanders Sales and Serv., Inc., 2005 WL 1151684 (S.D. Ohio May 16, 2005); Kane v. Guaranty Residential Lending, Inc., 2005 WL 1153623 (E.D.N.Y. May 16, 2005); Watson v. Trans Union Credit Bureau, 2005 WL 995687 (D. Me. Apr. 28, 2005); Robinson v. American Honda Fin. Corp., 2005 WL 1009568 (W.D. Tenn. Mar. 31, 2005); Aklagi v. NationsCredit Fin. Servs. Corp., 196 F. Supp. 2d 1186 (D. Kan. 2002); Yelder v. Credit Bureau of Montgomery, 131 F. Supp. 2d 1275 (M.D. Ala. 2001); Scott v. Amex/Centurion S&T, 2001 WL 1645362 (N.D. Tex. Dec. 18, 2001).
187 See § 6.10.2, *supra*.
188 15 U.S.C. § 1681o.
189 15 U.S.C. § 1681n.
190 Johnson v. CGR Servs., Inc., 2005 WL 991770 (N.D. Ill. Apr. 7, 2005) (damages are an essential element of a negligence claim); Caltabiano v. BSB Bank & Trust Co., 387 F. Supp. 2d 135 (E.D.N.Y. 2005) (damages are an essential element of a negligence claim); Schaffhausen v. Bank of America, N.A., 393 F. Supp. 2d 853 (D. Minn. 2005) (damages are an essential element of a negligence claim); Rosenberg v. Cavalry Invs., L.L.C., 2005 WL 2490353 (D. Conn. Sept. 30, 2005) (even in the absence of actual damages, plaintiff was entitled to prove willful violation for which relief is available without a showing of damages).
191 Trikas v. Universal Card Servs. Corp., 351 F. Supp. 2d 37 (E.D.N.Y. 2005).
192 Nelson v. Chase Manhattan Mortgage Corp., 282 F.3d 1057, 1060 (9th Cir. 2002).
193 *See e.g.* Cushman v. Trans Union Corp., 115 F.3d 220 (3d Cir. 1997); Dalton v. Capital Associated Industries, Inc., 257 F.3d 409, 418 (4th Cir. 2001); Crabill v. Trans Union, 259 F.3d 662 (7th Cir. 2001) (contrasting the instant mismerged case finding no violation for the initial merged reporting by the CRA with its higher duty if it were "alerted to a potential error"); Schaffhausen v. Bank of America, N.A., 393 F. Supp. 2d 853 (D. Minn. 2005) (proof that the furnisher continued misreporting after acknowledging errors is evidence of unreasonable investigation procedures and willfulness).
194 *See* Ch. 4, *supra*.

Another component of meritorious claims is informed case selection. The strongest case is one where reasonable minds cannot differ because the disputed information is objectively incorrect or incomplete. In that event, if the furnisher still rejects the dispute or the CRA continues to report the information, each necessarily will be shown to have breached its duties to conduct a reasonable investigation since it will have disregarded incontrovertible facts. The circumstances meeting this standard are as varied as the data appearing on consumer reports. Examples include situations in which the creditor misapplied payments for which the consumer has receipts or the consumer is the continuing victim of theft of identity (TOI) because the furnisher persists in reporting the identity thief's fraud as the consumer's own. The common thread is that no one taking the time to review these types of disputes and their supporting documentation can doubt their merit.

6.10.3 Consumer Reporting Agency Investigation Must Involve the Furnisher

After a consumer has initiated a reinvestigation of inaccurate or incomplete information by submitting a dispute to a CRA (or as appropriate with a reseller),[195] the CRA must notify the person who furnished any item of disputed information.[196] The CRA must provide this notice of dispute within five days after receipt of the dispute and must include "all relevant information" provided by the consumer. If the CRA receives additional information from the consumer before the furnisher completes its own investigation, that information also must be forwarded to the furnisher.

In practice, the dispute is communicated using a Consumer Dispute Verification form, known colloquially as a CDV or a "611 notice." An automated version of the form, communicated entirely electronically, is known as an ACDV. According to one nationwide CRA, 52% of its data furnishers participate in the Automated Consumer Dispute Verification (ACDV) system.[197] Although the statute does not specify any particular form, it does require notification "in a manner" established by the CRA with the furnisher.[198]

The CDV, like the Metro 2 Format used to furnish information to the CRAs in the first instance, was designed by an industry task force under the auspices of the Associated Credit Bureaus (now the Consumer Data Industry Association).[199] Like Metro 2, a CDV is heavily dependent upon standardized dispute codes used to communicate the nature of the dispute. Receipt of the CDV triggers the time period for the furnisher to conduct its own investigation and to report results back to the CRA.[200]

The industry has been put on notice of the problems with the use of CDVs because they are communicated without supporting documentation and without explaining the consumer's actual dispute.[201] The requirement that "all relevant information" received from the consumer must be forwarded to the furnisher is thus ignored as a matter of course. A typical consumer's painstaking description of a specific dispute, fashioned to make detection and correction easy, may at best be relegated to a generalized code. In addition, the dispute codes are not uniformly applied among the major CRAs, so the same information disputed in the same manner by a consumer may be categorized differently by different CRAs.

The CRA's failure to provide the furnisher with "all relevant information" often may naturally prevent the furnisher from fulfilling its obligation to investigate and accordingly may spare the furnisher from liability.[202] If a CRA does not convey the actual dispute, the furnisher cannot be expected to intuit the claim in order to investigate it.

Nevertheless, the failure of the CRA to fully apprise the furnisher of the nature of the dispute or provide it with "all relevant information" does not automatically excuse a furnisher who fails to act when that furnisher knows or reasonably can ascertain the pertinent facts. A furnisher may have a complete understanding of the dispute and of the consumer's supporting evidence from, for example, the consumer's earlier communications with it and/or receipt of a courtesy copy from the consumer of the dispute letter sent to the CRA. Ultimately, the standard for FCRA compliance is reasonableness;[203] and therefore a furnisher who has "additional information at its disposal to at least clarify . . . insufficient notification" from the CRA and who fails or refuses to refer to and act on that clarifying information will

---

195 See § 6.13, infra.
196 15 U.S.C. § 1681i(a)(2). See Young v. Equifax Credit Info. Servs., Inc., 294 F.3d 631 (5th Cir. 2002). See also Ch. 4, supra.
197 Statement of Harry Gambill, Chief Executive Officer, Trans-Union, Before the Subcommittee on Financial Institutions and Consumer Credit (June 4, 2003).
198 15 U.S.C. § 1681i(a)(2)(A).
199 See § 6.3.2, supra.
200 See § 6.7, supra.
201 Westra v. Credit Control of Pinellas, 409 F.3d 825 (7th Cir. 2005) (CRA's CDV provided "scant information" that prevented the furnisher from conducting a thorough investigation); Ruffin-Thompkins v. Experian Info. Solutions, Inc., 422 F.3d 603, 610–611 (7th Cir. 2005) (contradicting and overruling the unexamined dicta in Lee v. Experian Info. Solutions, 2003 WL 22287351, *6 (N.D. Ill. Oct. 2, 2003), purporting to approve the CDV system "as an adequate method both for assuring accuracy and for reinvestigation"). See Apodoca v. Discover Fin. Servs., 417 F. Supp. 2d 1220 (D.N.M. 2006) (explaining and rejecting the Lee dicta).
202 Robinson v. Equifax Info. Servs., 2005 WL 1712479 (S.D. Ala. July 22, 2005); Westra v. Trans Union, 2004 WL 1794482 (N.D. Ill. Aug. 5, 2004); Malm v. Household Bank (SB), 2004 WL 1559370 (D. Minn. July 7, 2004) (consumer's dispute cursory: not his/hers).
203 15 U.S.C. § 1681o ("[a]ny person who is negligent in failing to comply with any requirement imposed under this subchapter with respect to any consumer is liable. . . ."). See § 10.2.2, infra.

still be liable if its conduct is unreasonable, so long as it is otherwise notified by the CRA of the consumer's dispute.[204]

6.10.4 Furnisher's Duty upon Notification of Dispute by the Reporting Agency to Conduct a Reasonable Investigation

One role of the furnisher in conducting its own investigation of disputed information is to help the CRAs meet their duty to ensure that consumer reports are accurate and complete. For this reason, the FCRA specifically requires that the furnisher not only investigate the disputed information[205] but report the results of its investigation back to the CRA.[206] The FCRA requires CRAs to maintain reasonable procedures to ensure maximum possible accuracy of consumer reports.[207] The furnisher's investigation of disputed information cannot serve either the general purposes of the FCRA or the specific purposes of the reinvestigation process unless the furnisher provides complete and accurate information to the extent it is reasonably available.[208]

After receiving notice from a CRA that information provided by the furnisher has been disputed, the furnisher must review the information provided by the CRA and conduct its own investigation of the accuracy and completeness of the disputed information.[209] While the FCRA does not contain specific standards or procedures for the furnisher's investigation, the courts consistently have adopted the "reasonable investigation" standard,[210] the same standard as applicable to CRAs under section 1681i.[211] A "reasonable investigation" is also the standard required of creditors responding to a formal dispute under the Fair Credit Billing Act.[212]

The furnisher's reasonable investigation must be a good faith effort to ascertain the truth. Therefore, a reasonable investigation must answer the substance of the consumer's dispute and may not simply be a *pro forma* record review that simply begs the question. The CDV permits a furnisher to simply check a box indicating that the disputed information has been verified. Checking the box without conducting the underlying investigation of the claim is also inadequate.

The exact nature of the investigation will depend on a number of factors, including how the dispute is framed and what information is available to the furnisher. One specific obligation is that the furnisher must consider the information communicated in or with the notice of dispute from the CRA.[213] In addition, the furnisher must also consider other information available to it, including earlier complaints or other communications received from the consumer before reinvestigation was even begun.[214] Where appropriate and practical, a reasonable investigation may require a furnisher to go beyond its own records and obtain information from a third party.[215] In addition to demonstrating what the furnisher did or did not do, relevant evidence of whether an investigation is reasonable may include the amount of time allocated or permitted by the furnisher for its employees to perform the investigation.[216] The reasonableness of the investigation is a question of fact for jury determination.[217]

---

204 Alabran v. Capital One Bank, 2005 WL 3338663, *7 (E.D. Va. Dec. 8, 2005); Semper v. JBC Legal Group, 2005 WL 2172377 (W.D. Wash. Sept. 6, 2005). *But see* Rollins v. Peoples Gas Light and Coke Co., 379 F. Supp. 2d 964 (N.D. Ill. July 27, 2005) ("only proper notice, including all relevant information received from the consumer, triggers the furnisher's obligation to conduct an investigation under § 1681s-2(b).").

205 15 U.S.C. § 1681s-2(b)(1)(A).

206 15 U.S.C. § 1681s-2(b)(1)(C). See § 6.10.6, *infra*. See also Johnson v. MBNA Am. Bank, NA, 357 F.3d 426, 432 n.4 (4th Cir. 2003).

207 See Ch. 4, *supra*.

208 A furnisher who properly conducts a reasonable investigation that sustains the consumer's dispute but who fails to accurately convey the results to the CRA accordingly will be liable for violating these investigation duties. Evantash v. G.E. Capital Mortgage Serv., Inc., 2003 WL 22844198 (E.D. Pa. Nov. 25, 2003).

209 15 U.S.C. § 1681s-2(b); Cohan, Informal Staff Opinion Letter (Aug. 1, 2000), *reprinted on the CD-Rom accompanying this manual*.

210 Johnson v. MBNA Am. Bank, NA, 357 F.3d 426 (4th Cir. 2004); Hurocy v. Direct Merchants Credit Card Bank, N.A., 371 F. Supp. 2d 1058 (E.D. Mo. 2005); Schaffhausen v. Bank of Am., N.A., 393 F. Supp. 2d 853 (D. Minn. 2005); DiPrinzio v. MBNA America Bank, N.A., 2005 WL 2039175 (E.D. Pa. Aug. 24, 2005); Farren v. RJM Acquisition Funding, 2005 WL 1799413 (E.D. Pa. July 26, 2005); Hinton v. USA Funds, 2005 WL 730963 (N.D. Ill. Mar. 30, 2005); Danielson v. Experian Info. Solutions Inc., 2004 WL 1729871 (D. Minn. July 30, 2004); Ayers v. Equifax Inf. Servs., 2003 WL 23142201 (E.D. Va. Dec. 16, 2003); Buxton v. Equifax Info. Servs., 2003 WL 22844245 (N.D. Ill. Dec. 1, 2003) (when furnisher timely changed its records in response to the dispute, investigation was reasonable as a matter of law); Zotta v. Nationscredit Fin. Servs., 297 F. Supp. 2d 1196 (E.D. Mo. 2003); Evantash v. G.E. Capital Mortgage Serv., Inc., 2003 WL 22844198 (E.D. Pa. Nov. 25, 2003); Wade v. Equifax, 2003 WL 22089694 (N.D. Ill. Sept. 8, 2003) (when furnisher confirmed to CRA that last name on the account it was reporting was not the plaintiff's, investigation was adequate); Betts v. Equifax Credit Info. Servs., Inc., 245 F. Supp. 2d 1130 (W.D. Wash. 2003); Bruce v. First U.S.A. Bank, 103 F. Supp. 2d 1135 (E.D. Mo. 2000).

211 15 U.S.C. § 1681i(a)(1)(A). See Ch. 4, *supra*.

212 Federal Reserve Board, Regulation Z, 12 C.F.R. § 226.13(f). See National Consumer Law Center, Truth in Lending § 5.8 (5th ed. 2003 and Supp.). *Cf.* Erickson v. Johnson, 2006 WL 453201 (D. Minn. Feb. 22, 2006) (contrasting this higher FCRA standard of "investigation" versus the Fair Debt Collection Practices Act requirement of a mere "verification").

213 15 U.S.C. § 1681s-2(b)(1)(B).

214 Alabran v. Capital One Bank, 2005 WL 3338663, *7 (E.D. Va. Dec. 8, 2005); Semper v. JBC Legal Group, 2005 WL 2172377 (W.D. Wash. Sept. 6, 2005); Bruce v. First U.S.A. Bank, 103 F. Supp. 2d 1135 (E.D. Mo. 2000).

215 Bruce v. First U.S.A. Bank, 103 F. Supp. 2d 1135 (E.D. Mo. 2000).

216 DiPrinzio v. MBNA America Bank, N.A., 2005 WL 2039175 (E.D. Pa. Aug. 24, 2005).

217 Farren v. RJM Acquisition Funding, 2005 WL 1799413 (E.D.

Significant cases illustrate the furnisher's duty and the consumer's burden of proof. The Fourth Circuit, in the seminal decision on furnisher liability, confirmed that the investigation must be a substantive examination of the merits of the consumer's dispute: "We therefore hold that § 1681s-2(b)(1) requires creditors [furnishers], after receiving notice of a consumer dispute from a credit reporting agency, to conduct a reasonable investigation of their records to determine whether the disputed information can be verified."[218] The court stated that a reasonable investigation "requires some degree of careful inquiry" as opposed to a merely "superficial" inquiry.[219] As a result, the court sustained the jury's finding of furnisher liability where, when faced with the claim that the consumer was not obligated on the credit card account as reported but simply an authorized user, the furnisher (1) only reviewed the computer summary that contained the disputed information that showed that the consumer was an obligor and that the consumer was challenging and (2) failed to consult the underlying documents necessary to refute or verify the validity of her dispute.[220] Therefore, just as the CRA's "reasonable investigation" may not simply "parrot" the furnisher's position,[221] the furnisher's "reasonable investigation" must contain a "qualitative component" and thus may not merely beg the question by confirming simply that the disputed information itself is being faithfully conveyed to the CRA.[222]

Similarly, the Federal Trade Commission (FTC), in its first enforcement action under section 1681s-2,[223] imposed the requirement that a furnisher must refer to original account records and even consult third parties when necessary to actually investigate the merits of a dispute. Thus, according to the FTC, a furnisher cannot merely rely on the disputed information itself but must verify the debt with the original account records in its or the original creditor's possession. If no original records exist, the FTC required that the information must be deleted. This FTC enforcement position, formally adopted by the Commission and entered through a consent decree, is precedential.[224]

Because the furnisher must actually conduct an investigation and because the accuracy of the information is so important to both credit grantors and consumers, the furnisher may not instruct deletion instead of conducting a reasonable investigation.[225] Similarly, a consumer may maintain a claim to redress the furnisher's failure to conduct a reasonable investigation irrespective of whether the information is in fact inaccurate or incomplete.[226]

6.10.5 Furnishers Must Permanently Delete, Modify, or Block Inaccurate, Incomplete, or Unverifiable Information

When its investigation determines that disputed information is "inaccurate or incomplete or cannot be verified," the furnisher must, "as appropriate," modify, delete, and/or "permanently block the reporting of that item of information" to prevent its re-reporting.[227] Because this duty is codified as part of section 1681s-2(b), it is subject to private enforcement under the same terms that recognize the consumer's private right of action to enforce the formal investigation duties.[228]

One reference point for determining whether the information is accurate and complete is the standard recited in section 1681s-2(a) for initially furnishing accurate and complete information and continuing to update it. For example, the omission of specific information that must be included in a furnisher's initial and updated reports, such as noting

---

Pa. July 26, 2005); Hinton v. USA Funds, 2005 WL 730963 (N.D. Ill. Mar. 30, 2005); Akalwadi v. Risk Mgmt. Alternatives, Inc., 336 F. Supp. 2d 492 (D. Md. 2004); McKeown v. Sears Roebuck & Co., 335 F. Supp. 2d 917 (W.D. Wis. 2004); Osuna v. Equifax Credit Info. Servs., 2004 WL 1874985 (N.D. Ill. Feb. 4, 2004); Betts v. Equifax Credit Info. Servs., Inc., 245 F. Supp. 2d 1130 (W.D. Wash. 2003); Bruce v. First U.S.A. Bank, 103 F. Supp. 2d 1135 (E.D. Mo. 2000). *Cf.* Johnson v. MBNA Am. Bank, NA, 357 F.3d 426 (4th Cir. 2004).

218 Johnson v. MBNA Am. Bank, NA, 357 F.3d 426, 431 (4th Cir. 2003). *See also* Malm v. Household Bank (SB), 2004 WL 1559370 (D. Minn. July 7, 2004); Agosta v. Inovision, Inc., 2003 WL 22999213, at *5 (E.D. Pa. Dec. 16, 2003); Buxton v. Equifax Credit Info. Servs., Inc., 2003 WL 22844245 (N.D. Ill. Dec. 1, 2003); Wade v. Equifax, 2003 WL 22089694 (N.D. Ill. Sept. 8, 2003); Betts v. Equifax Credit Info. Servs., Inc., 245 F. Supp. 2d 1130 (W.D. Wash. 2003); Olwell v. Med. Info. Bureau, 2003 WL 79035 (D. Minn. Jan. 7, 2003); Kronstedt v. Equifax, 2001 WL 34124783 (W.D. Wis. Dec. 14, 2001); Bruce v. First U.S.A. Bank, 103 F. Supp. 2d 1135 (E.D. Mo. 2000).

219 Johnson v. MBNA Am. Bank, NA, 357 F.3d 426, 430 (4th Cir. 2003). *Accord* Schaffhausen v. Bank of America, N.A., 393 F. Supp. 2d 853 (D. Minn. 2005).

220 Johnson v. MBNA Am. Bank, NA, 357 F.3d 426, 430 (4th Cir. 2003). *Accord* Schaffhausen v. Bank of America, N.A., 393 F. Supp. 2d 853 (D. Minn. 2005).

221 Cushman v. Trans Union Corp., 115 F.3d 220 (3d Cir. 1997). *See* Ch. 4, *supra*.

222 Johnson v. MBNA Am. Bank, NA, 357 F.3d 426, 430 (4th Cir. 2003).

223 U.S. v. Performance Capital Mgmt. (Bankr. C.D. Cal. Aug. 24, 2000) (consent decree), *available at* www.ftc.gov/os/2000/08/performconsent.htm, complaint *available at* www.ftc.gov/os/2000/08/performcomp.htm, and FTC News Release *available at* www.ftc.gov/opa/2000/08/performance.htm and 2000 WL 1204636 (F.T.C. Aug. 24, 2000).

224 National Consumer Law Center, Unfair and Deceptive Acts and Practices § 3.4.5.3 (6th ed. 2004).

225 McKeown v. Sears Roebuck & Co., 335 F. Supp. 2d 917 (W.D. Wis. 2004).

226 Rosenberg v. Cavalry Invs., 2005 WL 2490353 (D. Conn. Sept. 30, 2005).

227 15 U.S.C. § 1681s-2(b)(1)(E).

228 *See* § 6.10.2, *supra*.

disputed debts, voluntary closures of accounts, and the dates of delinquency,[229] constitutes per se incompleteness; conversely, the absence in section 1681s-2(a) and in any other authority or relevant industry standard of any requirement to include specific items of information may be considered in determining whether that omission is actionable.[230]

6.10.6 Furnisher Must Report Investigation Results

6.10.6.1 Furnisher Must Report the Results of Its Investigation to the Reporting Agency That Provided Notice of the Dispute

The furnisher must report the results of its investigation to the CRA that notified it of the dispute and triggered the furnisher's duties.[231] It is not sufficient for a furnisher to merely conduct a reasonable investigation; it must also convey the results back to the CRA. Failing to convey the investigation results to the CRA or reporting false, confusing, or inconsistent information to the CRA is a separate basis for liability.[232]

6.10.6.2 Corrected Information Must Be Reported to Other Agencies As Well

Information about a consumer is routinely included in the files of multiple CRAs. Resolving an error in the files of one CRA may be ineffective unless the files of other CRAs are corrected as well. To help ensure that corrected information is appropriately disseminated, a furnisher whose investigation finds that the disputed information was inaccurate or incomplete must report the result to all CRAs which operate on a nationwide basis and to which the information had been furnished.[233]

Noncompliance with this requirement will subject the furnisher to civil liability, as is true for any violation of its reinvestigation duties pursuant to section 1681s-2(b).[234] This report of investigation results must be made by the same deadline as the report to the CRA which initiated the reinvestigation in the first place.

In addition, each nationwide CRA must create and maintain an automated reinvestigation system.[235] Furnishers must be able to use the system to report to the other CRAs the results of a reinvestigation that finds incomplete or inaccurate information. In practice, a report to this clearinghouse should be a report to the major nationwide CRAs.

The furnisher is not required to report its findings to the consumer. Only the CRA[236] or reseller[237] with whom the dispute is lodged must inform the consumer of the results of the reinvestigation.[238]

6.10.6.3 Time for Investigation and Reporting Results Is Limited

The furnisher must complete its investigation and report the results before expiration of the time allowed to the CRA to complete its reinvestigation.[239] Normally, reinvestigations conducted by CRAs must be completed within thirty days, with one extension allowed when the CRA receives additional information from the consumer in the interim.[240] The thirty-day period begins on the date that the CRA receives the consumer's notice of dispute.[241] If, however, the consumer discovered the basis for the dispute through a free annual report provided pursuant to section 1681j(a), the CRA has forty-five days in which to complete the investigation.[242] The timing for the CRA to complete their reinvestigation is further discussed in § 8.1.2.2, *infra*.

A furnisher's failure to complete its investigation within the statutory deadline is an actionable violation.[243]

6.10.6.4 Report of Investigation Results May Be Electronic

The nationwide CRAs maintain an automated clearinghouse, as required by law, for furnishers to use to report the

---

229 See §§ 6.4–6.7, *supra*.
230 Baker v. Capital One Bank, 2006 WL 173668 (D. Ariz. Jan. 24, 2006) (holding that the consumer's § 1681s-2(b) dispute that the credit card company failed to furnish the account's credit limit was properly rejected since no authority, specifically including § 1681s-2(a), required the furnisher to report that information) (*N.B.* Apparently unbeknownst to the court in Baker, and in any event not considered by it, reporting the credit limit on credit card tradelines is the prevailing Metro 2 industry standard and therefore should have provided the basis for reaching the opposite result. See §§ 6.3.3, 6.4, *supra*. See generally Ch. 4, *supra*). *Cf.* DiPrinzio v. MBNA America Bank, N.A., 2005 WL 2039175 (E.D. Pa. Aug. 24, 2005) (incomplete report that failed to note that the debt was disputed constituted false information for purposes of state law).
231 15 U.S.C. § 1681s-2(b)(1)(C). *See* Johnson v. MBNA Am. Bank, NA, 357 F.3d 426, 432 n.4 (4th Cir. 2003).
232 Evantash v. G.E. Capital Mortgage Serv., Inc., 2003 WL 22844198 (E.D. Pa. Nov. 25, 2003).
233 15 U.S.C. § 1681s-2(b)(1)(D).

234 See § 6.10.2, *supra*.
235 15 U.S.C. § 1681i(a)(5)(D).
236 15 U.S.C. § 1681i(a)(6).
237 15 U.S.C. § 1681i(f)(3).
238 See § 8.2.12, *infra*.
239 15 U.S.C. § 1681s-2(b)(2); Trikas v. Universal Card Servs., Corp., 2005 WL 17867 (E.D.N.Y. Jan. 3, 2005) (furnisher failed to comply with its reinvestigation duty by not completing the reinvestigation in thirty days).
240 15 U.S.C. § 1681i(a)(1).
241 15 U.S.C. § 1681i(a)(1)(A).
242 15 U.S.C. § 1681j(a)(3).
243 Trikas v. Universal Card Servs. Corp., 351 F. Supp. 2d 37 (E.D.N.Y. 2005).

results of investigations that find inaccurate or incomplete information.[244] Furnishers are not legally required to use this automated clearinghouse but are strongly urged to do so by the major CRAs. Consequently most results are reported electronically, using the clearinghouse, and in response to the automated version of the Consumer Dispute Verification form (ACDV).

The obligations of CRAs and the right of a consumer to file a "Statement of Dispute" are discussed at Chapter 4, *supra*.

6.10.7 Private Enforcement Is Subject to the FCRA's Hybrid Two-Year Statute of Limitations

The FCRA's statute of limitations expires two years after the date of discovery by the plaintiff of the violation, but in no event more than five years after the date of the violation.[245] The furnisher's duties under section 1681s-2(b) commence at the earliest only when it receives a request for investigation from a CRA,[246] and an actionable violation can only occur when it breaches one of those duties, not when it reported the underlying inaccurate information or otherwise took action for which there is no private remedy.[247]

If the furnisher does not respond at all to the request for reinvestigation, the furnisher's liability arises thirty days after receipt of the request for reinvestigation, which is the deadline for completing the reinvestigation.[248] If the furnisher responds within the thirty-day period, but the response is inadequate, liability might arise on the date of the violative response or at the conclusion of the thirty-day period, the last opportunity that the furnisher had to comply. Caution commands that a practitioner calculate the limitations period in the event of an inadequate response from no later than the earliest date that the furnisher acted.[249] Filing within two years of lodging the dispute with the CRA or reseller removes all risk.[250]

6.11 Furnisher Liability for Discrimination, Including Retaliating Against a Consumer for Exercising Federal Statutory Rights

The Equal Credit Opportunity Act (ECOA) and Federal Reserve Board Regulation B prohibit creditors from discriminating against consumers in credit transactions based on several familiar and two less familiar prohibited bases. As is found in some other anti-discrimination statutes, the ECOA prohibits credit discrimination on the basis of race, color, religion, national origin, sex, marital status, or age; in addition, a creditor may not discriminate because the consumer's income derives from any public assistance program or because the consumer in good faith exercised any rights under the federal Consumer Credit Protection Act (CCPA).[251] These protections create significant overlap with the FCRA.

The ECOA specifies that the prohibition against discrimination in a credit transaction applies to "every aspect" of the consumer's dealings with a creditor, including discrimination in the "furnishing of credit information."[252] Thus, for example, the ECOA prohibits creditors from furnishing adverse credit information on a consumer when the real reason for furnishing the information is one of the prohibited bases. Consequently, creditor may not be quicker to report defaults by minorities than white defaulters. Because the prohibition applies to "every aspect" of the parties' dealings, a creditor may not discriminate in reporting information even after it has closed an account.

---

244 *See* 15 U.S.C. § 1681i(a)(5)(D).

245 15 U.S.C. § 1681p.

246 Zotta v. Nationscredit Fin. Servs., 297 F. Supp. 2d 1196 (E.D. Mo. 2003).

247 Deaton v. Chevy Chase Bank, 157 Fed. Appx. 23 (9th Cir. Nov 28, 2005) (unpublished) (acknowledging the principle, and observing that the action was timely because the consumer filed within two years of lodging the dispute with the CRA); Dornhecker v. Ameritech Corp., 99 F. Supp. 2d 918, 927, 928 (N.D. Ill. 2000) (plaintiff had two years after furnisher's failure to comply with reinvestigation request to sue, even though furnisher's initial report of the inaccurate information occurred earlier); Zotta v. Nationscredit Fin. Servs., 297 F. Supp. 2d 1196 (E.D. Mo. 2003). *Cf.* Young v. Equifax Credit Info. Servs., Inc., 294 F.3d 631 (5th Cir. 2000) (republication of credit information resulting in a new denial of credit is a distinct harm that gives rise to new cause of action; furnisher's reinvestigation duties exist only after it receives reinvestigation request from CRA); Jaramillo v. Experian Info. Solutions, Inc., 155 F. Supp. 2d 356 (E.D. Pa. 2001) (furnisher's republication of old inaccurate information, apparently in response to reinvestigation request, within two-year period satisfies statute of limitations), *vacated in part on other grounds*, 2001 U.S. Dist. LEXIS 10221 (E.D. Pa. June 20, 2001). *But cf.* Ryan v. Trans Union Corp., 2000 WL 1100440 (N.D. Ill. Aug. 4, 2000) (no FCRA claim where plaintiff did not allege that furnisher failed to comply with reinvestigation duties after 1996 amendments; court erroneously suggests in dictum that a request for reinvestigation cannot create a cause of action where the inaccurate information is old).

248 *See* Lawrence v. Trans Union, L.L.C., 296 F. Supp. 2d 582 (E.D. Pa. 2003) (two-year limitation for failure to reinvestigate begins thirty days after CRA receives the dispute); Acton v. Bank One Corp., 293 F. Supp. 2d 1092 (D. Ariz. 2003) (same); § 6.10.6.3, *supra*.

249 *See* § 11.5, *infra*, for further discussion of the statute of limitations.

250 Deaton v. Chevy Chase Bank, 157 Fed. Appx. 23, 2005 WL 3150258 (9th Cir. Nov. 28, 2005) (unpublished).

251 15 U.S.C. § 1691(a). *See generally* National Consumer Law Center, Credit Discrimination Ch. 3 (4th ed. 2005 and Supp.).

252 *See* 12 C.F.R. § 202.2(m).

Another important and potentially the most useful ECOA application to credit reporting is the fact that the consumer in good faith exercised any rights under the federal Consumer Credit Protection Act (CCPA) is an additional prohibited basis for discrimination.[253] The CCPA[254] is the umbrella legislation that covers many of the important federal consumer protection statutes:

- Truth in Lending Act (including the right to raise merchant defenses against a card issuer);
- Fair Credit Billing Act;
- Consumer Leasing Act;
- Federal Credit Repair Organizations Act;
- Federal Garnishment Act;
- Fair Credit Reporting Act;
- Fair Debt Collection Practices Act;
- Electronic Funds Transfer Act; and
- Equal Credit Opportunity Act.

Whenever consumers raise claims under any of these acts, the creditor should not furnish negative information to consumer reporting agencies (CRAs) if the consumer's claim is the basis for the creditor's decision to furnish the information. This is the case whether the information being furnished is about the consumer's CCPA claim or about some other aspect of the consumer's credit record. These rules supplement the related duties that limit the furnishing of disputed information on credit card and other open-end accounts under the Fair Credit Billing Act and that protect consumers from adverse consumer reports during periods of disputes involving mortgages and home equity loans under the Real Estate Settlement Procedures Act.[255]

6.12 Furnisher Liability for Related Torts

Because of the limitation on private enforcement other than in the context of a dispute and reinvestigation initiated through a consumer reporting agency (CRA), the consumer must often turn to legal theories outside the FCRA to establish liability of a creditor or other party furnishing inaccurate information to a CRA. The most readily available alternative is a tort claim, such as defamation.

The FCRA expressly restricts a consumer's right to bring a proceeding in the nature of defamation, invasion of privacy, or negligence with respect to the reporting of information against any person who furnishes information to a CRA.[256] There are two important caveats about this qualified immunity of furnishers. First, if the furnisher provides false information with malice or a willful intent to injure the consumer, the FCRA provides no immunity for such an act.[257] The consumer can then bring a tort action against the creditor or other party furnishing the information and, in such circumstances, should also seek punitive damages where available.

Second, the limited immunity only applies when the information at issue was disclosed to the consumer pursuant to one of the various FCRA disclosure requirements to consumers—disclosure of the contents of the consumer's file or disclosure after a consumer report leads to a denial of credit, insurance or employment.[258] If the consumer obtained the information directly from the furnisher, the immunity should not apply. Similarly, the immunity should not apply if the consumer obtained the information from a user who did not notify the consumer of a denial of employment, insurance or credit based on the report.[259]

Another issue is whether the FCRA's limited qualified immunity applies to tort claims other than the three explicitly mentioned. The FCRA immunity provision applies to actions in the "nature" of the three torts, so the immunity will likely extend to other tort claims that essentially are the same but bear names other than defamation, invasion of privacy or negligence. Nevertheless, the immunity may not apply to actions for intentional infliction of emotional distress, misrepresentation, injurious falsehood, intentional interference with prospective contractual relations, or breach of fiduciary duty.[260]

Concurrently with adopting in 1996 the furnisher liability provisions of section 1681s-2(b), Congress also expanded the preemption provisions to further insulate furnishers from most state law obligations.[261] While this preemption of state law on furnisher duties appears plenary, it must be read in conjunction with section 1681h(e), which, as mentioned above, expressly retains the right of a consumer to sue a furnisher in tort for providing "false information furnished with malice or willful intent to injure." If section 1681t(b)(1)(F) were a blanket preemption of state claims against a furnisher, then the savings provision of section 1681h(e) for furnisher torts committed with malice or willful intent to injure would be impermissibly rendered a nullity. Therefore, in order to give effect to this savings provision, the general preemption of section 1681t(b)(1)(F) must still recognize at least the right of a consumer to file suit under the limited, specific conditions of section

---

253 See 15 U.S.C. § 1691(a)(3).
254 15 U.S.C. §§ 1601–1693.
255 See § 6.5.3, supra.
256 15 U.S.C. § 1681h(e). This provision is discussed in more detail at § 10.4, infra.
257 15 U.S.C. § 1681h(e). See also § 10.4.6, infra.
258 15 U.S.C. § 1681h(e).
259 See § 10.4.3, infra (discussing in detail such exclusions from the limited immunity).
260 See § 10.4.4, infra.
261 15 U.S.C. § 1681t(b)(1)(F) (preempting any state law "requirement or prohibition . . . relating to the responsibilities of persons who furnish information to consumer reporting agencies," except specific portions of Massachusetts and California statutes). See § 10.7, infra.

1681h(e).[262] This conflict between the furnisher preemption provision and the FCRA's general limitation on tort liability remains essentially unresolved and has created confusion and uncertainty. A detailed discussion of these and other preemption issues affecting furnishers is analyzed in a later chapter.[263]

6.13 Reinvestigation Requirements Applicable to Resellers

Resellers occupy a mixture of roles in the dispute resolution process that is part user, part furnisher, and part consumer reporting agency (CRA). In general, resellers are exempt from reinvestigation requirements.[264] However, if a reseller receives a notice from a consumer of a dispute concerning the completeness or accuracy of any item in a consumer report produced by the reseller, the reseller must, within five business days of receipt of the notice, determine whether the item of information is complete or inaccurate as a result of an act or omission of the reseller. If the reseller determines that the item of information is incomplete or inaccurate as a result of an act or omission on its part, it must correct the information in the consumer report or delete it no later than twenty days after receipt of the notice.

If the reseller determines that the information is not incomplete or inaccurate as a result of its act or omission, it is required to convey the notice of the dispute, together with all relevant information provided by the consumer, to each CRA that provided the reseller with the information in dispute, using the notification mechanism specified by the CRA for such notices.[265] Receipt by the CRA of such a consumer dispute from a reseller then triggers all of the CRA's reinvestigation obligations as when the consumer lodges a dispute directly with the CRA, including notifying and involving the furnisher.[266] CRAs that complete reinvestigations based on notice from resellers must notify the consumer through the reseller of the results of the investigation.[267]

6.14 Furnishers Subject to Identity Theft Duties and Responsibilities

The FCRA imposes several requirements on creditors or furnishers with respect to protecting consumers against identity theft. As all other furnisher obligations except those created by the formal dispute process initiated with a consumer reporting agency (and where applicable a reseller), the FCRA's private enforcement provisions are not available to remedy a breach of these duties.[268] These requirements are discussed in detail in Chapter 9, *infra*.

---

262 Jaramillo v. Experian Info. Solution, Inc., 155 F. Supp. 2d 356 (E.D. Pa. 2001), *vacated in relevant part*, 2001 U.S. Dist. LEXIS 10221 (June 20, 2001) (vacating on reconsideration its earlier ruling that section 1681t(b)(F) preempted a claim against a furnisher for defamation with malice after being alerted by the consumer's counsel that its ruling impermissibly eliminated the efficacy of the savings provision of section 1681h(e)).
263 *See* § 10.7, *infra*.
264 15 U.S.C. § 1681i(f)(1); 16 C.F.R. § 602.1(c)(3)(xviii).

265 15 U.S.C. § 1681i(f)(1), (2).
266 15 U.S.C. § 1681i(a)(1)(A).
267 15 U.S.C. § 1681i(f)(3).
268 *See* § 6.10.2, *supra*.

Chapter 7 Permissible Releases and Uses of Consumer Reports

7.1 General

7.1.1 Background

One of the primary reasons for enactment of the Fair Credit Reporting Act (FCRA) was protection of confidential information and individual privacy.[1] When Senator Proxmire first introduced S. 823, the bill which ultimately became the Fair Credit Reporting Act, he stressed the importance of assuring confidentiality:

> The fact that credit reporting agencies maintain files on millions of Americans, including their employment, income, bill paying record, marital status, habits, character and morals is not in and of itself so disturbing. What is disturbing is that this practice will continue, and will have to continue, if we continue to have an insurance system and a consumer credit system of the kind we have. What is disturbing is the lack of any public standards to ensure that the information is kept confidential and used only for its intended purpose. The growing accessibility of this information through computer- and data-transmission techniques makes the problem of confidentiality even more important.[2]

The four aspects of confidentiality addressed more specifically by Senator Proxmire were: (1) policies as to whom information may be released; (2) use of information inconsistent with the purposes for which the information was collected; (3) maintenance of adequate internal security procedures; and (4) the availability of information to government agencies. From these initial concerns, the FCRA emerged with specific restrictions on the release of consumer reports.

When the FCRA was amended by the Fair and Accurate Credit Transactions Act of 2003 (FACTA), privacy and the protection of consumer financial information from identity theft were two of the major objectives behind many of the amendments.[3] Most of these amendments are addressed in other chapters in this manual, however some of the amendments affect the release of information to users of consumer reports.

7.1.2 Reports May Be Released Only for Permissible Purposes

Because of Congress' concern with a consumer's privacy, consumer reports can only be disseminated for certain designated purposes. The statute enumerates specific purposes authorizing release of a consumer report.[4] These specific purposes are each analyzed in §§ 7.2 and 7.3, infra. The only permissible purposes are listed in the statute; consumer reports can be released for those purposes "and no other."[5] Section 7.2, infra, lists some but not all common impermissible purposes. Whether a use is permissible can be a question of law for the court [6]

In general, a consumer reporting agency (CRA) may release a report whenever the CRA "has reason to believe" that the user intends to use the information for a permissible purpose.[7] This "reason to believe" language only prefaces some of the listed permissible purposes, but the other permissible purposes generally relate to the status of the requester—i.e., child support agencies or one who has a court order or the consumer's consent—and not to the requester's ultimate purpose for seeking the report.[8]

---

1 See 15 U.S.C. § 1681(a)(4), (b).
2 115 Cong. Rec. 2413 (1969). See also 114 Cong. Rec. 24,903 (1968) (remarks of Sen. Proxmire).
3 Fair and Accurate Credit Transactions Act of 2003, Pub. L. No. 108-159 (2003). See Ch. 9, infra, for a discussion of the FACTA amendments' identity theft provisions.
4 In the case of release to government agencies of identifying information which falls short of being a consumer report, the FCRA places limits on what identifying information may be disseminated. See § 7.2.10.2, infra.
5 15 U.S.C. § 1681b(a); Cole v. U.S. Capital, 389 F.3d 719 (7th Cir. 2004); Trans Union L.L.C. v. F.T.C., 295 F.3d 42, 49 n.4 (D.C. Cir. 2002).
6 Stonehart v. Rosenthal, 2001 U.S. Dist. LEXIS 11566 (S.D.N.Y. Aug. 13, 2001) (whether permissible purpose exists is a legal issue which may be resolved on summary judgment); Edge v. Professional Claims Bureau, Inc., 64 F. Supp. 2d 115 (E.D.N.Y. 1999); aff'd without op., 234 F.3d 1261 (2d Cir. 2000).
7 15 U.S.C. § 1681b(a)(3). Cf. Shah v. Collecto, 2005 WL 2216242 (D. Md. Sept. 12, 2005) (collection agency had reason to believe that consumer owed a debt on an account that the merchant actually referred in error).
8 See 15 U.S.C. § 1681b(a)(1), (2), (4), (5).

A CRA must maintain reasonable procedures to avoid releases for impermissible purposes, and may not furnish a report if the CRA has reason to believe the use will be impermissible, even if the user has stated a facially valid purpose.[9] The procedures that a CRA must maintain are discussed in § 7.5, *infra*.

If a user wants to obtain information about a consumer for a purpose not listed in the FCRA, the user must obtain the consumer's written authorization[10] or must obtain the information from a source other than a consumer report.[11]

A CRA is not required to provide a report to a user and may refuse such a request.[12] However, it is required to disclose the contents of a consumer's file to the consumer upon request.[13]

A CRA may release a report only if the user has a permissible purpose at the time the report is requested.[14] The CRA may not provide an unsolicited report even to a prior recipient, because the recipient may no longer have a permissible purpose for obtaining a report.[15] An example of this kind of practice occurred when one of the largest investigative CRAs furnished follow-up reports on consumers to insurance companies that previously requested reports but, at the time of the follow-up reports, were not considering any application from the consumer. This was found to be in violation of the Act.[16]

7.1.3 Can a Consumer Deny Permission for a Release of a Consumer Report?

If a user has a permissible purpose, however, the consumer cannot stop the CRA from furnishing the report. A consumer's written objection to the release has no effect,[17] unless the intended use is impermissible.

A consumer can condition an offer or willingness to enter a transaction so that a permissible purpose to obtain and use a consumer report never arises. When a consumer states that he will not enter a transaction if it means that a consumer report will be obtained, then a permissible purpose for using a report may not exist.

In an example from the Second Circuit,[18] a prospective tenant tells a landlord he wants to rent an apartment unless it means that the landlord will use a consumer report. The consumer has effectively conditioned the offer to rent upon the landlord's willingness to forgo a credit check. If the landlord insists upon a credit check, agreement is not possible and the landlord has no legitimate need for a consumer report.

On the other hand, if the CRA is unaware of the consumer's instructions, it might not be liable for releasing a report in a situation in which the creditor would normally have a permissible purpose.[19]

This ability of the consumer to structure a transaction so that a consumer report is not used is not absolute. Sometimes a user has a permissible purpose to obtain a report without regard to the wishes of the consumer, as for example when reports are used for child support enforcement purposes or for valuations of current accounts. On the other hand, consumers considering a new credit transaction, applying for insurance or a license, or initiating other business transactions can condition their interest on an assurance that a consumer report will not be used. The user then must choose between striking a deal with no credit checks and no deal at all.

---

9 *See* 15 U.S.C. § 1681e(a); Levine v. World Fin. Network Nat'l Bank, 473 F.3d 1118 (11th Cir. 2006). *Cf.* Harrington v. ChoicePoint, Inc., Slip. Op., No. CV 05-1294 MRP (C.D. Cal. Sept. 15, 2005), *available at* www.consumerlaw.org/unreported (rejecting argument that information was not a consumer report because defendant did not expect that information would be used for FCRA purposes; "Once the fraudsters indicated they intended to use the information for FCRA purposes, it does not matter that in another part of the agreement they promised not to do it. . . . Deciding otherwise would allow ChoicePoint to contract around FCRA liability.").

10 *See* § 7.2.2, *infra*.

11 The permissible purposes allowed under the Act also form part of the definition of "consumer report," see 15 U.S.C. § 1681a(d)(1), but the fact that a report's use is impermissible does not make the report no longer a consumer report. *See* § 7.1.8, *infra*.

12 FTC Official Staff Commentary § 604(2) item 2, *reprinted at* Appx. D, *infra*; Oliver, FTC Informal Staff Opinion Letter (Mar. 23, 1982), *reprinted on the CD-Rom accompanying this manual*. *See also* Venable v. Equifax, 1993 U.S. Dist. LEXIS 7684 (E.D. Pa. June 8, 1993) (may refuse to issue report except as retaliation against consumer). A CRA refusal to issue a report to a user because of a consumer's exercise of FCRA rights should be a violation of the Equal Credit Opportunity Act, 15 U.S.C. § 1691(a)(3) *as discussed in* National Consumer Law Center, Credit Discrimination §§ 3.4.4, 6.2.2.7 (3d ed. 2002 and Supp.).

13 *See* § 3.3, *supra*.

14 *See* § 7.7, *infra*.

15 FTC Official Staff Commentary § 604(3)(A) item 1B, *reprinted at* Appx. D, *infra*. *Cf.* Levine v. World Fin. Network Nat'l Bank, 473 F.3d 1118 (11th Cir. 2006) (former creditor could not obtain reports on accounts closed and paid in full for purpose of marketing new credit).

16 *In re* Equifax, Inc., 96 F.T.C. 1045 (1980), *rev'd in part on other grounds*, 678 F.2d 1047 (11th Cir. 1982).

17 Frederick v. Marquette National Bank, 911 F.2d 1 (7th Cir. 1990); Scott v. Real Estate Fin. Group, 956 F. Supp. 375 (E.D.N.Y. 1997), *aff'd in part, and rev'd in part*, 183 F.3d 97 (2d Cir. 1999) (consumer's instruction not to access consumer report irrelevant if permissible purpose); A-1 Credit & Assurance v. Trans Union Credit Info., 678 F. Supp. 1147 (E.D. Pa. 1988); Grimes, FTC Informal Staff Opinion Letter (July 20, 1992), *reprinted on the CD-Rom accompanying this manual*; Grimes, FTC Informal Staff Opinion Letter (July 31, 1986), *reprinted on the CD-Rom accompanying this manual*.

18 Scott v. Real Estate Fin. Group, 183 F.3d 97 (2d Cir. 1999). *See also* Uhlig v. Berge Ford, Inc., 257 F. Supp. 2d 1228 (D. Ariz. 2003).

19 *See* Short v. Allstate Credit Bureau, 270 F. Supp. 2d 1173 (M.D. Ala. 2005) (farm loan agency ignored wife's instructions not to obtain her consumer report).

7.1.4 Reports May Be Used Only for Permissible Purposes

Although the FCRA is structured as a list of permissible circumstances under which CRAs may release reports, the Act also governs the *users* of consumer reports. The purposes listed in the FCRA govern both users' ability to obtain consumer reports and also their use of those reports once they have been released.[20]

"User" is not a defined term under the FCRA. Anyone receiving a consumer report and applying it to a consumer is a user and must comply with the Act,[21] whether the user obtains or uses the report directly or indirectly.[22] One who merely reports information[23] is not a user,[24] nor is a merchant who does not obtain the report or participate in a financing decision.[25]

As long as the user obtained a report for one permissible purpose, it can use the report for other permissible purposes.[26] However, the Act may be violated if the report is initially obtained for a permissible purpose but is later used for an impermissible purpose.[27] A user with a permissible purpose cannot pass the report on to a third party with an impermissible purpose.[28] Conversely, a user with an impermissible purpose cannot evade liability by giving the report to a third party with a permissible purpose.[29]

"Resellers" are companies that purchase reports from CRAs and pass these on to users.[30] The same rules (and additional ones as well[31]) apply to resellers as CRAs: they must have a permissible purpose for obtaining and for releasing a report.[32]

7.1.5 Users Must Be Informed of FCRA Requirements

CRAs are required to give to each user to whom a consumer report is provided a statement of the user's responsibilities under the Act.[33] The content of the notice is prescribed by the Federal Trade Commission (FTC), and is reprinted at Appendix C, *infra*.

This notice ensures that users are in an easy position to know what is required of them as users of consumer reports. The notice outlines in simple form: (1) the requirement that a user must have a permissible purpose to request a report,

---

20 15 U.S.C. § 1681b(f) ("A person shall not *use or obtain* a consumer report for any purpose unless [in accordance with the Act]") (emphasis added). *See* Lukens v. Dunphy Nissan, Inc., 2004 WL 1661220 (E.D. Pa. July 26, 2004) ("Although it would be nonsensical to interpret the FCRA to allow the improper use of consumer reports as long as such reports were originally obtained for permissible purposes, this Court does not reach the issue."); Chester v. Purvis, 260 F. Supp. 2d 711, 718 (S.D. Ind. 2003) (concluding that reading the FCRA as a whole requires user liability); Castro v. Union Nissan, Inc., 2002 WL 1466810 (N.D. Ill. July 8, 2002) (car dealership could be liable under FCRA for obtaining spouse's consumer report without a permissible purpose); § 7.7, *infra*. *But see* Kodrick v. Ferguson, 54 F. Supp. 2d 788 (N.D. Ill. 1999) (holding that the FCRA is aimed primarily at CRAs and refusing to extend liability to users without a more definite statement by Congress).

21 Zeller v. Samia, 758 F. Supp. 775 (D. Mass. 1991); Rylewicz v. Beaton Servs., Ltd., 698 F. Supp. 1391, 1400 (N.D. Ill. 1988), *aff'd*, 888 F.2d 1175 (7th Cir. 1989) (user includes persons who acquire report for another); Boothe v. TRW Credit Data, 557 F. Supp. 66, 71 (S.D.N.Y. 1982). *See also* Yohay v. City of Alexandria Employees Credit Union, 827 F.2d 967, 973 (4th Cir. 1987).

22 Padin v. Oyster Point Dodge, 397 F. Supp. 2d 712 (E.D. Va. 2005) (automobile dealer that was listed as "Creditor-Seller" on sales contract and that forwarded consumer's information, though not report itself, to various lenders was user and had to disclose adverse action by lender denying credit); Adams v. Phillips, 2002 WL 31886737 (E.D. La. Dec. 19, 2002) (impostor is user where fraudulent conduct was sole cause of issuance of consumer report to retailers); Klapper v. Shapiro, 586 N.Y.S.2d 846 (Sup. Ct. 1992) (attorney who submitted consumer report as evidence is a user). *But see* Dennis v. Turner, 1999 U.S. Dist. LEXIS 3322 (S.D. Ala. Mar. 2, 1999) (FCRA does not provide a right of action against a third party FBI agent who obtained consumer information from the user and had no contact with the consumer reporting agency).

23 One who reports information to a CRA for its use in compiling consumer reports is a furnisher of information, not a user. The obligations of furnishers are set out at Ch. 6, *supra*.

24 Lema v. Citibank (South Dakota), N.A., 935 F. Supp. 695 (D. Md. 1996).

25 *See* Castro v. Union Nissan, Inc., 2002 WL 1466810 (N.D. Ill. July 8, 2002) (automobile dealer that did not access consumer report is not user and is not liable for actions of financing agencies).

26 Minter v. AAA Cook County Consol., Inc., 2004 WL 1630781 (N.D. Ill. July 19, 2004); Marzluff v. Verizon Wireless, 785 N.E.2d 805 (Ohio Ct. App. 2003). *Cf.* Scott v. Real Estate Fin. Group, 183 F.3d 97 (2d Cir. 1999) ("a report requester does not violate [the false pretenses section] by giving a false reason for its request if it has an independent legitimate basis for requesting the report"). *But see* Daley v. Haddonfield Lumber Inc., 943 F. Supp. 464 (D.N.J. 1996) ("[The FCRA] allows release of consumer reports only to specific parties and under specific circumstances. . . . [T]he credit reporting agency . . . did not release the information generally to any potential user who may indeed maintain a permissible purpose for obtaining the report.").

27 15 U.S.C. § 1681b(f); Lukens v. Dunphy Nissan, Inc., 2004 WL 1661220 (E.D. Pa. July 26, 2004); Henry v. Forbes, 433 F. Supp. 5 (D. Minn. 1976) (owner of railroad company that previously obtained reports for permissible purposes obtained report for political purposes). *See also* § 7.7.1, *infra*. *But see* Stonehart v. Rosenthal, 2001 U.S. Dist. LEXIS 11566 (S.D.N.Y. Aug. 13, 2001) (showing of permissible purpose is a complete defense).

28 *See, e.g.*, Hansen v. Morgan, 582 F.2d 1214 (9th Cir. 1978) (president of jewelry store that was member of local CRA obtained report for use by politician's allies in congressional investigation of politician's adversary).

29 Daley v. Haddonfield Lumber, Inc., 943 F. Supp. 464 (D.N.J. 1996).

30 For a discussion of resellers, see § 2.6.3, *supra*.

31 *Id.*

32 *See* § 7.1.7, *infra*.

33 15 U.S.C. § 1681e(d)

listing the specific permissible purposes; (2) the requirement that a user certify the permissible purpose it is using; and (3) the requirement that users notify consumers when adverse action is taken. This notice also contains sections that set forth the special obligations of: (1) users of reports for employment purposes; (2) users of investigative reports; (3) users of reports containing medical information; (4) users of prescreened lists; and (4) resellers of consumer reports.

Another significance of this required notice is that when a question of liability arises under the FCRA, no user may reasonably claim that it did not know what the law required.

7.1.6 Agents of the User

An agent of a party with a permissible purpose may obtain a consumer report on behalf of the principal where the agent is involved in the decision that gives rise to the permissible purpose.[34] (The access to consumer reports by third parties who are involved in transactions but are not agents of other parties is discussed in § 7.4.6, *infra*.)

Such involvement may include the agent's making the decision or taking action for the principal, or helping to evaluate the information.[35] By implication, an agent without such an involvement does not have a permissible purpose.[36]

However, where an agent does have such an involvement, not only does the agent have a permissible purpose to receive the report, but the agent can share the report with the principal without becoming a CRA.[37]

FTC Official Staff Commentary (FTC Staff Commentary) gives several examples of agents who have a permissible purpose in obtaining a report for their principal. A real estate agent may obtain a report on behalf of a seller to evaluate a prospective purchaser.[38] A private detective agency may obtain a report for a client if the client has a permissible purpose.[39] A rental agency or apartment manager that receives reports to assist owners of residential property in screening consumers as tenants has a permissible purpose, if it uses the reports to apply the landlord's criteria to approve or disapprove applicants.[40] Similarly, an attorney has the same permissible purpose as the attorney's client when acting for that client.[41]

Nevertheless, a CRA may choose to refuse to release a consumer report to the agent, and insist on providing the report directly to a user. CRAs may elect to insist on providing a report to the principal directly to avoid the need to ascertain particulars of the relationship between the representative and the user. In fact, a CRA is not even required to provide a report to a user, and may refuse a request, or establish any conditions it wishes on provision of the report.[42]

7.1.7 Release by One Reporting Agency to Another

The FTC Staff Commentary allows a CRA to release a consumer report to another CRA in order for the second CRA to furnish the report to a requesting subscriber. In this circumstance, one CRA is acting on behalf of another.[43] In other words, the CRA receiving a request from a user is responsible for determining the permissible purpose, and the CRA providing the report to another CRA need only determine if the requesting CRA's purpose is to provide the report to a user with a permissible purpose. At least one court has made an exception even to this obligation when one CRA sells its files in bulk to another CRA.[44] However, the second CRA, often a "reseller,"[45] is responsible for complying with all the requirements imposed by the FCRA on CRAs.[46]

---

34 Trans Union Corp. v. Fed. Trade Comm'n, 81 F.3d 228, 233 (D.C. Cir. 1996) (finding that communication to merchant's mailing service was equivalent to communication with merchant itself); Breese v. Triadvantage Credit Serv., 393 F. Supp. 2d 819, 821, n.3 (D. Minn. 2005) (grandson who obtained report for his grandfather); FTC Official Staff Commentary § 604(3)(E) item 6A, *reprinted at* Appx. D, *infra*. *See also* Petruccelli, FTC Informal Staff Opinion Letter (Apr. 9, 1984), *reprinted on the CD-Rom accompanying this manual*; Garman, FTC Informal Staff Opinion Letter (June 17, 1985), *reprinted on the CD-Rom accompanying this manual*. *Cf.* FTC Official Staff Commentary § 603(f) item 8.
35 Weidman v. Federal Home Loan Mortgage Corp., 338 F. Supp. 2d 571 (E.D. Pa. 2004) (Freddie Mac); FTC Official Staff Commentary § 604(3)(E) item 6A, *reprinted at* Appx. D, *infra*.
36 Scott v. Real Estate Fin. Group, 956 F. Supp. 375 (E.D.N.Y. 1997); Daley v. Haddonfield Lumber, Inc., 943 F. Supp. 464 (D.N.J. 1996).
37 *Cf.* FTC Official Staff Commentary § 603(f) item 8, *reprinted at* Appx. D, *infra*.
38 FTC Official Staff Commentary § 604(3)(E) item 6B, *reprinted at* Appx. D, *infra*.
39 *Id.* item 6C. Davis v. Asset Servs., 46 F. Supp. 2d 503 (M.D. La. 1998); Korotki v. Attorney Servs. Corp., 931 F. Supp. 1269 (D. Md. 1996) (agent had "reason to believe" there was permissible purpose); Cambridge Title Co. v. Transamerica Title Ins. Co., 817 F. Supp. 1263, 1278 (D. Md. 1992), *aff'd*, 989 F.2d 491 (4th Cir. 1993); Zeller v. Samia, 758 F. Supp. 775, 781–782 (D. Mass. 1991) (reason to believe).
40 FTC Official Staff Commentary § 604(3)(E) item 6D, *reprinted at* Appx. D, *infra*.
41 *Id.*
42 *Id.* § 604(2) item 2.
43 FTC Official Staff Commentary § 604 General item 1.
44 State v. Credit Bureau of Nashua, Inc., 115 N.H. 455, 342 A.2d 640 (1975).
45 *See* § 2.6.3, *supra*.
46 *See, e.g.*, First Am. Real Estate Solutions, L.L.C., No. 952-3267 (F.T.C. 1998) (consent agreement).

7.1.8 Is Information a Consumer Report If Released for Impermissible Purposes?

The permissible purposes allowed under the FCRA also form part of the definition of "consumer report," because information becomes a "consumer report" if it is used or expected to be used in the manner described by the Act.[47] CRAs have on occasion defended unlawful releases of consumer reports by arguing that information released for impermissible purposes is not a "consumer report" and the FCRA therefore does not apply. What is considered a consumer report is discussed at § 2.3, *supra*.

The FTC and the courts generally reject this argument. The mere fact that the report was used for an impermissible purpose is not enough to exclude the transaction from the Act's coverage.[48] If a report at any point in time qualifies as a consumer report, then the report is protected by the FCRA. Similarly, if the information was originally collected for a permissible purpose or the CRA expected it to be used for a permissible purpose, the Act applies to the information, regardless of its actual use.[49] The limits on releases and uses of consumer reports would be meaningless if violation of those limits were itself a defense to the Act.[50] The issue of whether the information is a consumer report is separate from the issue of the CRA's compliance with the permissible purposes section of the Act.

7.1.9 Discovering an Impermissible Use

It is not always easy to discover if a consumer report has been used for an impermissible purpose. Under the FCRA, a user must provide a notice disclosing the use of a consumer report when denying credit, insurance, or employment.[51] However, those receiving reports for impermissible purposes are unlikely to provide these notices.

In any instance where a client has been subjected to adverse action in a business or government benefits situation, or other areas listed below as impermissible purposes,[52] the attorney should inquire whether a consumer report may have been used. In any litigation, this should be added as an item in a discovery request.

Probably the best approach is to request a copy of the individual's consumer report from Experian, Equifax, and TransUnion.[53] Most, but not all consumer reports are from these three sources. The consumer's report will list "inquiries," i.e., the names and addresses of all persons who have previously received the consumer report.[54] It can sometimes be difficult for consumers to determine whether the inquiries are permissible or not because creditors use many different names, some of which may not be familiar to the consumer.

The consumer should consider the nature of any contact which the consumer has had with each named recipient. If any of the named users are not familiar to the consumer, or the consumer's contact with a particular user does not seem to constitute a legitimate business reason for obtaining a consumer report, the consumer may have a cause of action against the user and/or the CRA. Nevertheless, when a consumer is added to a prescreening list (e.g., for solicitation for a credit card or another offer), the user requesting the list will be added to the consumer's file as a user.[55] It is thus important to differentiate between users of prescreening lists and those who do not have a permissible purpose to receive a report on the consumer.

7.2 Permissible Uses

7.2.1 In Response to a Court Order

A report may be furnished "[i]n response to the order of a court having jurisdiction to issue such an order, or a subpoena issued in connection with proceedings before a Federal grand jury."[56] A consumer report furnished pursu-

---

47 *See* 15 U.S.C. § 1681a(d)(1).
48 *See, e.g.*, Ippolito v. WNS, Inc., 864 F.2d 440 (7th Cir. 1988); Heath v. Credit Bureau of Sheridan, Inc., 618 F.2d 693 (10th Cir. 1980); Boothe v. TRW Credit Data, 523 F. Supp. 631 (S.D.N.Y. 1981), *modified*, 557 F. Supp. 66 (S.D.N.Y. 1982). *See also* Grimes, FTC Informal Staff Opinion Letter (Aug. 22, 1990), *reprinted on the CD-Rom accompanying this manual*; FTC Informal Staff Opinion Letter [1969–1973 Decisions Transfer Binder] Consumer Cred. Guide (CCH) ¶ 99,424 (May 19, 1971).
49 15 U.S.C. § 1681a(d). *See generally* § 2.3.5, *supra*.
50 Belshaw v. Credit Bureau, 392 F. Supp. 1356 (D. Ariz. 1975). *But see* Henry v. Forbes, 433 F. Supp. 5 (D. Minn. 1976) (actual use is dispositive).
51 *See* § 8.2.6, *infra*.
52 *See* § 7.4, *infra*.
53 *See* §§ 3.3, 3.4, *supra*, for a discussion of how to obtain a consumer report.
54 15 U.S.C. § 1681g(a)(3) *See also* § 3.7, *supra*.
55 Prescreening is treated in more detail at § 7.3.4, *infra*.
56 15 U.S.C. § 1681b(a)(1). *See* Hahn v. Star Bank, 190 F.3d 708 (6th Cir. 1999) (leaves unresolved issue of whether a subpoena actually issued by court order); Etefia v. Credit Technologies, Inc., 628 N.W.2d 577 (Mich. Ct. App. 2001) (a subpoena issued by an attorney was an order of the court for purposes of § 1681b(a)(1) of the FCRA). *See also* Schoka v. General Motors Acceptance Corp., 1 F.3d 1247 (9th Cir. 1993) (subpoena issued by court creates a permissible purpose); FTC Official Staff Commentary § 604(i), item 1, *reprinted at* Appx. D, *infra* (a subpoena is not an order of the court unless signed by a judge); Morris, FTC Informal Staff Opinion Letter (July 26, 1979), *reprinted on the CD-Rom accompanying this manual* (state and local child support enforcement agencies may receive report if used to collect child support enforcement payments subject to existing court order). *Cf.* White, FTC Informal Staff Opinion Letter (Feb. 18, 1977), *reprinted on the CD-Rom accompanying this manual* (county attorney does not have permissible purpose

ant to a court order may still be permissible, even if the purpose may be otherwise prohibited under the Act.

This permissible purpose is interpreted very strictly, so that even law enforcement requests for information—with the exception of Internal Revenue Service (IRS) summons—are not permitted under this provision unless they are pursuant to a court order. (However, there are several other provisions in the FCRA that authorize releases to specific government agencies.[57]) Even if the request is pursuant to an administrative summons or subpoena, it is not considered a court order unless it is signed by a judge.[58] Thus, even a government agency conducting a criminal investigation would need to obtain a court order before it sought information from consumer reporting agencies, unless the request satisfied one of the Act's other permissible purposes. (For example, the FCRA allows release to a government agency of basic identifying information.[59] In addition, a government agency may have a permissible use when attempting to collect on a judgment,[60] even if it does not have authority to seek a report prior to that court order.)[61]

An IRS summons is an exception to the requirement that an order be signed by a judge before it constitutes an order of the court. Congress has amended the Tax Code to require consumer reporting agencies (CRAs) to open their files upon receipt of a summons and a specific IRS certificate that the subject of the files has not moved in a timely fashion to quash the summons.[62]

Disputes have arisen relating to attorney-issued subpoenas and whether or not they are "court orders" under the Act. Some CRAs have taken the position that attorney-issued subpoenas are not court orders under the FCRA unless they are signed by a judge and thus they do not have to release consumer reports. Rule 45 of the Federal Rules of Civil Procedure was amended to specifically provide for issuance of subpoenas by attorneys as officers of the court. Defiance of a subpoena, even if issued by an attorney, "is nevertheless an act in defiance of a court order" thereby exposing the recipient to contempt sanctions.[63] Attorneys who are merely seeking the consumer reports of their clients may also obtain appropriate authorizations from the clients and submit the request and authorization to the CRA.[64]

The language allowing release of information pursuant to a subpoena issued in connection with proceedings before a *federal* grand jury was added in 1988.[65] Case law prior to that date had typically found that a grand jury subpoena was not a court order,[66] often viewing the grand jury as more a tool of the prosecutor than of the court. Consequently, even after the 1989 amendment, a *state* grand jury subpoena provides a permissible purpose to release a consumer report only if the subpoena is signed by a judge or magistrate.

A court order must be by the court having jurisdiction to issue such an order. Thus the FTC, in a formal advisory opinion, has found that the United States District Court judges of South Carolina could not issue a general order for use in all cases in that court, making consumer reports on potential jurors available to attorneys for *voir dire* purposes. Such a general order was not an "order of court having jurisdiction" to issue such an order under the FCRA.[67]

---

if used to investigate welfare fraud; needs court order); Scholl, FTC Informal Staff Opinion Letter (Dec. 10, 1976), *reprinted on the CD-Rom accompanying this manual* (law enforcement not permissible purpose). *Contra* Etefia v. Credit Technologies, Inc., 245 Mich. App. 466, 628 N.W.2d 577 (2001) (subpoena issued by attorney is a court order; relying on dictum in *Hahn*).

57 *See* § 7.2.10, *infra*.
58 *See* United States v. Puntorieri, 379 F. Supp. 332 (E.D.N.Y. 1974) (administrative summons from I.R.S. not sufficient permissible purpose for CRA to release information. A 1976 statutory change to the tax code now allows the I.R.S. to obtain reports pursuant to a summons in certain situations); FTC Official Staff Commentary § 604(1) item 1, *reprinted at* Appx. D, *infra*; Brinckerhoff, FTC Informal Staff Opinion Letter (Apr. 23, 1986), *reprinted on the CD-Rom accompanying this manual* (a subpoena is not a court order unless signed by a judge); Peeler, FTC Informal Staff Opinion Letter (Feb. 26, 1979), *reprinted on the CD-Rom accompanying this manual*; FTC Informal Staff Opinion Letter [1969–1973 Decisions Transfer Binder] Consumer Cred. Guide (CCH) ¶ 99,422 (May 18, 1971). *Cf.* Morris, FTC Informal Staff Opinion Letter (July 26, 1979), *reprinted on the CD-Rom accompanying this manual* (order must be issued by court, not by administrative tribunal of limited jurisdiction).
59 *See* § 7.2.10.2, *infra*.
60 *See* § 7.2.3.4, *infra*.
61 *See also* § 7.2.10.4, *infra* (FBI access to consumer reports for counterintelligence purposes).
62 26 U.S.C. § 7609. *See also* FTC Official Staff Commentary § 604(1) item 2, *reprinted at* Appx. D, *infra*.

63 Fed. R. Civ. P. 45(a)(3), Notes of Advisory Committee on December 1991 Amendment of Rule, Subdivision (a). *See also* Etefia v. Credit Technologies, Inc., 628 N.W.2d 577 (Mich. Ct. App. 2001). *See* § 11.6.3.6, *infra*.
64 *See* 15 U.S.C. § 1681b(a)(2); § 11.6.3.6, *infra*.
65 15 U.S.C. § 1681b(a)(1).
66 United States v. TRW (*In re* Gren), 633 F.2d 825 (9th Cir. 1980); *In re* Grand Jury Subpoena to Credit Bureau, 594 F. Supp. 229 (M.D. Pa. 1984); *In re* Special October 1981 Grand Jury, [1980–1989 Decisions Transfer Binder] Consumer Cred. Guide (CCH) (N.D. Ill. 1984); *In re* Application to Quash Grand Jury Subpoena, 526 F. Supp. 1253 (D. Md. 1981); *In re* Grand Jury Subpoena Duces Tecum Concerning Credit Bureau, Inc., 498 F. Supp. 1174 (N.D. Ga. 1980); *In re* Vaughn, 496 F. Supp. 1080 (N.D. Ga. 1980); *In re* Credit Info. Corp., 457 F. Supp. 969 (S.D.N.Y. 1978); *In re* TRW Credit Data, 415 N.Y.S.2d 1976 (Nassau County Ct. 1979); FTC Official Staff Commentary § 604(1) item 1, *reprinted at* Appx. D, *infra*; Supplementary Information published with commentary, 55 Fed. Reg. 18,804, 18,806–18,807 (May 4, 1990); Brinckerhoff, FTC Informal Staff Opinion Letter (Nov. 4, 1983), *reprinted on the CD-Rom accompanying this manual* (grand jury subpoena duces tecum is not a court order unless signed by a judge). *But see* United States v. Retail Credit Men's Ass'n, 501 F. Supp. 21 (M.D. Fla. 1980); *In re* Grand Jury Proceedings, 503 F. Supp. 9 (D.N.J. 1980); *In re* TRW, Inc., 460 F. Supp. 1007 (E.D. Mich. 1978).
67 Federal Trade Commission Advisory Opinion, [1969–1973 De-

7.2.2 Consumer's Written Instructions

A consumer report may be furnished when the consumer gives the CRA written instructions or permission to provide a report to the user,[68] whether or not the report would otherwise be for a permissible purpose.[69] On the other hand, the CRA may refuse to furnish the report, despite these instructions, because the statute is permissive.[70] (The CRA must disclose to the consumer the contents of the consumer's file on request,[71] but the CRA need not furnish reports to users at the consumer's instructions.[72])

An informal FTC staff opinion interprets the term "written instruction" as requiring less than a power of attorney; a dated written authorization that designates who is to send and who is to receive the consumer report is sufficient.[73] Under the federal E-Sign Act, an electronic authorization may suffice.[74]

With incidents of identity theft increasing, CRAs should take extra care to be certain that the consumer providing the written permission is indeed actually the consumer who is the subject of the report. With the proliferation of consumer credit information and instant access to consumer credit files by computer, the potential for impermissible access to consumer reports and invasion of consumer privacy increases.

User abuse of the written instruction provision (such as not explaining to the consumer that the user does not otherwise have a right to obtain the report) may violate the FCRA provision prohibiting anyone from willfully obtaining information from a CRA under false pretenses.[75] Similarly, a consumer's acknowledgment in an application that an employer may seek consumer reports on the consumer is not a written permission from the consumer for the employer to obtain reports for impermissible purposes.[76]

There have been instances of CRAs have taking advantage of this written instruction permissible use provision for marketing purposes. For example, TransUnion partnered with an Internet marketing firm to offer cash to consumers for their written permission for access to their credit data.[77]

A consumer's written permission allowing a user to receive a report does not waive the user's and the CRA's obligations under the FCRA. For example, the consumer should still be entitled to notice when the report leads to a denial of the consumer's application, or if an investigative consumer report is involved, notice of the types of sources from which the information will be collected, as well as the name and address of the CRA.[78] The user should explain to the consumer that the Act prevents it from receiving the report for its intended use unless the consumer specifically authorizes it.

7.2.3 Permissible Use in Connection with Credit

7.2.3.1 General

7.2.3.1.1 Overview

Users have a permissible use for a consumer report "in connection with a credit transaction involving the consumer on whom the information is to be furnished and involving the extension of credit to, or review or collection of an

---

cisions Transfer Binder] Consumer Cred. Guide (CCH) ¶ 99,134 (Sept. 29, 1972).
68 15 U.S.C. § 1681b(a)(2).
69 Hammons v. Enterprise Leasing Co.—Southwest, 993 F. Supp. 1388 (W.D. Okla. 1998). *See also* FTC Official Staff Commentary § 604(2) item 1, *reprinted at* Appx. D, *infra*; Brinckerhoff, FTC Informal Staff Opinion Letter (Feb. 5, 1985), *reprinted on the CD-Rom accompanying this manual*; Petruccelli, FTC Informal Staff Opinion Letter (Apr. 9, 1984), *reprinted on the CD-Rom accompanying this manual*.
70 Frederick v. Marquette National Bank, 911 F.2d 1 (7th Cir. 1990); A-1 Credit & Assurance v. Trans Union Credit Info., 678 F. Supp. 1147 (E.D. Pa. 1988); FTC Official Staff Commentary § 604(2) item 2, *reprinted at* Appx. D, *infra*; FTC Official Staff Commentary § 604-general, item 2, *reprinted at* Appx. D, *infra*; Grimes, FTC Informal Staff Opinion Letter (July 20, 1992), *reprinted on the CD-Rom accompanying this manual*; Grimes, FTC Informal Staff Opinion Letter (July 31, 1986), *reprinted on the CD-Rom accompanying this manual*; Oliver, FTC Informal Staff Opinion Letter (Mar. 23, 1982), *reprinted on the CD-Rom accompanying this manual* (CRA may refuse so long as not in restraint of trade or acting illegally).
71 *See* § 3.3, *supra*.
72 FTC Official Staff Commentary § 604(2) item 2, *reprinted at* Appx. D, *infra*.
73 *See also* Malbrough v. State Farm Fire & Cas. Co., 1997 U.S. Dist. LEXIS 4122 (E.D. La. Mar. 30, 1997) (rejecting argument that "authorization" is not "instruction"); Oliver, FTC Informal Staff Opinion Letter (Mar. 23, 1982), *reprinted on the CD-Rom accompanying this manual*. *See also* Brinckerhoff, FTC Informal Staff Opinion Letter (Nov. 14, 1994), *reprinted on the CD-Rom accompanying this manual*.
74 Electronic Signatures in Global and National Commerce Act (E-Sign Act), 15 U.S.C. §§ 7001–7031. Such an electronic authorization must be in a form capable of being retained and reproduced for later reference. *See also* Zalenski, FTC Informal Staff Opinion Letter (May 24, 2001), *reprinted on the CD-Rom accompanying this manual*.

75 15 U.S.C. § 1681q. *See also* § 7.7, *infra*. *But see* Hammons v. Enterprise Leasing Co.—Southwest, 993 F. Supp. 1388 (W.D. Okla. 1998) (automobile ease's provision authorizing lessor to verify personal and credit information provided by the consumer allowed the lessor to obtain consumer report, no false pretenses).
76 Grimes, FTC Informal Staff Opinion Letter (July 20, 1992), *reprinted on the CD-Rom accompanying this manual*. *Cf.* Sibley, FTC Informal Staff Opinion Letter (June 8, 1999), *reprinted on the CD-Rom accompanying this manual* ("I understand that where appropriate, CRA reports may be obtained" is not adequate authorization language).
77 Kristen Brenner, Consumers Can Trade Credit Data for Cash, *available at* Dmnews.com, Aug. 16, 2000.
78 *See* Carson, FTC Informal Staff Opinion Letter (June 3, 1971), *reprinted on the CD-Rom accompanying this manual*.

account of, the consumer."[79] This provision governs three separate situations: decisions to extend credit; account review of current credit customers; and collection.

7.2.3.1.2 Definition of "credit transaction"

"Credit" is defined in the FCRA[80] to have the same meaning as in section 1691a of the Equal Credit Opportunity Act (ECOA). Under the ECOA, credit is defined as "the right granted by a creditor to a debtor to defer payment of debt or to incur debts and defer its payment or to purchase property or services and defer payment therefor."[81]

The term "credit" is used in the FCRA both to define what information is entitled to protection as a "consumer report," and also to describe situations when a consumer's information may be released or used. Ironically, therefore, a broad definition of "credit" simultaneously extends the Act's protection to more types of consumer information while weakening the privacy protection that the information receives by allowing its release. For example, a check has been considered an instrument of credit, which subjects check guarantee and check approval agencies to the requirements of the Act, but also allows merchants to check the consumer's check writing history before accepting a check and to obtain a consumer report in order to collect a bounced check.[82]

Even if a transaction is not considered credit, a user may be able to access and use a consumer report if needed for a business transaction, as discussed in § 7.2.8, *infra*. The characterization typically matters only in the collection context, because a user may access a consumer report to collect on a credit account but not to collect on a business debt, unless that debt is reduced to judgment.[83] For example, it is unclear whether a residential lease is a credit or a business transaction. Under either view, the report of a tenant screening agency is a consumer report and a landlord has a permissible purpose to review the report in deciding whether to accept a rental application.[84] However, if a residential lease is credit, the landlord could access a consumer report in order to collect on back rent, but not if the lease is merely a business transaction, unless the debt is reduced to judgment.[85]

7.2.3.1.3 Must credit be for personal, family, or household purposes?

It is unclear whether consumer reports may be released in connection with a credit transaction that is not for personal, family, or household purposes. The FTC Official Staff Commentary (FTC Staff Commentary) states that the credit transaction provision must be read together with the Act's definition of "consumer report" so that the permissible credit transaction purposes must involve credit "primarily for personal, family, or household purposes."[86]

On the other hand, since the Fair and Accurate Credit Transactions Act of 2003 (FACTA) amendments, "credit" has been defined under the FCRA to have the same meaning as under the Equal Credit Opportunity Act (ECOA), which does not have any requirement that the credit be for "consumer" purposes.[87] Moreover, unlike the definition of a consumer report, the permissible purposes section does not explicitly require that the credit be "primarily for personal, family, or household purposes."

Also, an informal FTC staff opinion letter concurred with the position of federal banking agencies that a creditor has a permissible purpose to obtain a consumer report on a consumer in connection with a business credit transaction if the consumer is or will be personally liable on the loan, such as in the case of a guarantor, cosigner, or, in most instances, an individual proprietor.[88] Another FTC opinion letter also suggests that consumer reports may be used to collect business debts.[89]

Even if the credit transaction is limited to "personal, family, and household purposes," the FTC defines that phrase broadly. Thus personal credit includes credit for securities transactions,[90] and even credit related to real

---

79 15 U.S.C. § 1681b(a)(3)(A).
80 15 U.S.C. § 1681a(r)(5).
81 15 U.S.C. § 1691a(d); 12 C.F.R. § 202.2(j).
82 *See* § 2.3.6.3.2, *supra*.
83 *Compare* 15 U.S.C. § 1681b(a)(3)(A) (permitting use for "collection" in connection with credit transactions) *with id.* § 1681b(a)(F) (omitting any collection purpose in connection with business transactions); §§ 7.2.8.2.2.2, 7.2.8.3, *infra*.
84 *See* § 2.3.6.3.3, *supra*.
85 *See* § 7.2.3.4, *infra*.

86 FTC Official Staff Commentary § 604 item 1A, *reprinted at* Appx. D, *infra*. *See also* Goldfarb, FTC Informal Staff Opinion Letter (July 9, 1980), *reprinted on the CD-Rom accompanying this manual* (permissible purpose exists for government agency to obtain report in collection of guaranteed loan); Feldman, FTC Informal Staff Opinion Letter (Apr. 15, 1971), *reprinted on the CD-Rom accompanying this manual*; Cook v. Equifax Info. Sys., Inc., 1992 WL 356119 (D. Md. Nov. 20, 1992); Allen v. Kirkland & Ellis, 1992 U.S. Dist. LEXIS 12383 (N.D. Ill. Aug. 14, 1992); Sizemore v. Bambi Leasing Corp., 360 F. Supp. 252 (N.D. Ga. 1973).
87 15 U.S.C. § 1691a(d); 12 C.F.R. § 202.2(j). *See* National Consumer Law Center, Credit Discrimination § 2.2.2.1.1, 2.2.6.4 (4th ed. 2005 and Supp.).
88 *See* Letter from Joel Winston to Julie L. Williams, J. Virgil Mattingly, William F. Kroener, III, and Carolyn Buck (June 22, 2001). A copy of this letter is available from the FTC's Internet website at www.ftc.gov/os/statutes/fcra/tatelbaum2.htm.
89 Grimes, FTC Informal Staff Opinion Letter (Feb. 17, 1993), *reprinted on the CD-Rom accompanying this manual. But cf.* FTC Official Staff Commentary § 604 item 1A, *reprinted at* Appx. D, *infra*.
90 *See* FTC Official Staff Commentary § 615 item 7, *reprinted at* Appx. D, *infra*.

estate investments,[91] as long as the consumer is not engaged in such transactions as a business.[92]

7.2.3.2 Extension of Credit

A user may request a consumer report when the consumer is seeking an extension of credit, including credit used to finance a purchase. However, the consumer must actually express a desire to obtain credit. A seller or creditor does not have a permissible purpose to obtain a consumer report if the consumer is merely comparison shopping, by asking about price and financing, or has offered to make a purchase without requesting financing.[93] For example, automobile dealers sometimes request driver's licenses and use them to obtain consumer reports when a consumer is merely taking a test drive, which is a clear violation of the Act. Similarly, if an automobile dealer wishes to see an individual's consumer report before answering questions about the availability of financing, the dealer must request the consumer's formal authorization.[94]

The "extension of credit" provision does not permit obtaining a consumer report simply to see if a consumer is a potential customer. However, a separate provision, discussed in § 7.3.4, *infra*, allows creditors to engage in prescreening of potential customers under certain circumstances.

Even if the consumer has requested financing, merchants such as car dealers often shop for financing from third parties, usually without the consumer's knowledge. Consumers purchasing automobiles are often unaware that the dealer is shopping their retail installment contract around for financing. This practice can result in many inquiries that pull down a credit score.[95] Nevertheless, the potential third party lenders contacted by the car dealer have a permissible purpose to access the consumer's report even if the consumer is unaware that they are doing so.[96]

A user has a permissible purpose to obtain a consumer report on the person it thinks is applying for credit, even if it is mistaken that the consumer wants credit.[97] On the other hand, if the credit application was taken for the purpose of identity theft and not for the purpose of extending credit, there would be no permissible purpose.[98]

7.2.3.3 Account Review

A creditor may obtain a consumer report in connection with a credit transaction and involving "review ... of an account."[99] Thus, a creditor may obtain a report on a current customer to determine whether the consumer continues to meet the terms of the account, or for the purpose of deciding to retain or modify current accounts.[100] These purposes normally apply to open-end credit transactions only; a close-end creditor would not ordinarily have a permissible reason to review a consumer report because the terms are predetermined and generally may not be changed unilaterally.[101]

Once an account is closed and paid in full, the creditor does not have a permissible purpose to review the account, for example for the purpose of identifying new marketing

---

91 Grimes, FTC Informal Staff Opinion Letter (Feb. 17, 1993), *reprinted on the CD-Rom accompanying this manual*.

92 *See* FTC Official Staff Commentary § 615 item 7, *reprinted at* Appx. D, *infra*; Grimes, FTC Informal Staff Opinion Letter (Feb. 17, 1993), *reprinted on the CD-Rom accompanying this manual*.

93 Shibley, FTC Informal Staff Opinion Letter (June 8, 1999), *reprinted on the CD-Rom accompanying this manual* (dentist has no permissible purpose for obtaining a consumer report when a patient comes in for a free office visit); Coffey, FTC Informal Staff Opinion Letter (Feb. 11, 1998), *reprinted on the CD-Rom accompanying this manual*; Fisher v. Quality Hyundai, Inc., 2002 U.S. Dist. LEXIS 407 (N.D. Ill. Jan. 11, 2002) (allegation that consumer told dealer she did not want credit because she had loan from credit union withstands motions to dismiss on impermissible access/false pretenses claim); Scott v. Real Estate Fin. Group, 956 F. Supp. 375 (E.D.N.Y. 1997) (discussion between the parties had progressed to the point prospective tenants had made an offer), *aff'd in part, rev'd in part*, Scott v. Real Estate Fin. Group, 183 F.3d 97 (2d Cir. 1999) (offer was conditioned by insistence that a consumer report not be used).

94 Coffey, FTC Informal Staff Opinion Letter (Feb. 11, 1998), *reprinted on the CD-Rom accompanying this manual*; Medine, FTC Informal Staff Opinion Letter (Feb. 11, 1998), *reprinted on the CD-Rom accompanying this manual. See* § 7.2.2, *supra. See also* La. Rev. Stat. Ann. § 9:3571.2 (West) (limiting circumstances under which a motor vehicle dealer may request, obtain or review an individual's consumer report).

95 *See* Andrews v. Trans Union Corp., 7 F. Supp. 2d 1056, 1075 (C.D. Cal. 1998) (presence of inquiry, resulting from identity theft, that suggested that plaintiff had applied for credit raised issue of material fact as to whether listing of inquiry was misleading), *aff'd in part, rev'd in part on other grounds sub nom.* Andrews v. TRW Inc., 225 F.3d 1063 (9th Cir. 2000), *rev'd on other grounds*, 534 U.S. 19 (2001). *See* § 12.2.2.3, *infra*. Some credit scoring models try to adjust for the effect of multiple inquiries related to a single transaction by omitting or clustering them. *Id.*

96 *See* Sterigiopoulos v. First Midwest Bancorp., Inc., 472 F.3d 1043 (7th Cir. 2005) (third party lender need only be engaged in a credit transaction in which the consumer is participating; the consumer need not be aware of which lenders might pull their reports). *See also* Castro v. Union Nissan, Inc., 2002 WL 1466810 (N.D. Ill. July 8, 2002) (earlier decision in same case finding that automobile dealer was not a "user" and was not liable for potential FCRA violations by third party lenders).

97 Kennedy v. Victoria's Secret Stores Inc., 2004 WL 2186613 (E.D. La. Sept. 29, 2004) (consumer alleged that employee surreptitiously opened account without consumer's permission).

98 Lukens v. Dunphy Nissan, Inc., 2004 WL 1661220 (E.D. Pa. July 26, 2004).

99 15 U.S.C. § 1681b(a)(3)(A).

100 *See* Benner, FTC Informal Staff Opinion Letter (Apr. 30, 1999), *reprinted on the CD-Rom accompanying this manual*; Gowen, FTC Informal Staff Opinion Letter (Apr. 29, 1999), *reprinted on the CD-Rom accompanying this manual*.

101 Gowen, FTC Informal Staff Opinion Letter (Apr. 29, 1999), *reprinted on the CD-Rom accompanying this manual*.

opportunities.[102] The use of consumer reports for prescreening offers of credit is discussed in § 7.3.4, infra.

If a credit account has an unpaid balance, the creditor may permissibly review the account for collection purposes (but not if it is a noncredit account).[103] An unretained debt collector cannot invoke the account review provision to obtain consumer reports for the purpose of seeking the business of the creditors.[104]

Account reviews are increasingly relied upon as grounds to access consumer reports. The practice of accessing consumer reports for account reviews takes various forms. Some creditors purportedly conduct account reviews on consumers who have previously discharged their debts in bankruptcy. Others access consumer reports even though the statute of limitations period to report the debt has run, asserting that even though the creditor's legal remedies may be barred, the debt is not extinguished. It is unclear whether access to consumer reports in permissible in these situations.

7.2.3.4 Collection of Credit Accounts and Judgment Debts

A consumer report may be used in "in connection with a credit transaction involving the consumer . . . and involving . . . collection of an account of [] the consumer."[105]

The word "credit" is important in this context.[106] Consumer reports may be used to further collection efforts only if the account was a credit account, or if another type of account or debt has been reduced to judgment. The FCRA does not permit access to consumer reports to assist in collecting noncredit business transactions unless those transactions have been reduced to a judgment debt.[107]

The FTC has interpreted the collection provision to allow use of consumer reports for "skip tracing," in which the creditor hires a person to locate a debtor to facilitate the collection of a consumer account.[108] Collection agencies thus have a permissible purpose for receiving consumer reports, and CRAs are permitted to furnish a consumer report to an attorney for use in a lawsuit involving a credit account.[109] A collection agency has a permissible purpose to obtain a consumer report if the agency has reason to believe that the consumer owes the debt, even if it turns out that the account was turned over to the collection agency by the merchant in error.[110] A collection agency does not have a permissible

---

102 Levine v. World Fin. Network Nat'l Bank, 473 F.3d 1118 (11th Cir. 2006) (consumer stated viable claim that former creditor unlawfully reviewed consumer's closed account for purpose of trolling for new business); Fed. Trade Comm'n v. Citigroup Inc., 239 F. Supp. 2d 1302 (N.D. Ga. 2001) (denying motion to dismiss allegations that Associates used or obtained consumer reports for impermissible purposes of soliciting additional loan products or to solicit the consumer for a credit transaction that the consumer did not initiate); Gowen, FTC Informal Staff Opinion Letter (Apr. 29, 1999), reprinted on the CD-Rom accompanying this manual; Benner, FTC Informal Staff Opinion Letter (Apr. 30, 1999), reprinted on the CD-Rom accompanying this manual. But cf. Trikas v. Universal Card Servs., Corp., 351 F. Supp. 2d 37 (E.D.N.Y. 2005) (bank's inquiries on account erroneously left open were not made with an impermissible purpose); Geer v. Medallion Homes Ltd. P'ship, 2005 WL 2708992 (E.D. Mich. Oct 20, 2005) (creditor could obtain second consumer report after credit application was denied and file was closed because consumers indicated that they had been working to clean up their credit and creditor was attempting to see what corrections had been made).
103 See § 7.2.3.4, infra.
104 Benner, FTC Informal Staff Opinion Letter (Apr. 30, 1999), reprinted on the CD-Rom accompanying this manual.
105 15 U.S.C. § 1681b(a)(3)(A) as renumbered by Pub. L. No. 104-208, 110 Stat. 3009 (Sept. 30, 1996). See, e.g., Grenier v. Equifax Credit Info. Servs., Inc., 892 F. Supp. 57 (D. Conn. 1995). See also Brinckerhoff, FTC Informal Staff Opinion Letter (July 7, 1995), reprinted on the CD-Rom accompanying this manual; Brinckerhoff, FTC Informal Staff Opinion Letter (Nov. 14, 1994), reprinted on the CD-Rom accompanying this manual (concerning consumer credit counseling agencies which provide information about all of a consumer's debts to a creditor); Meyer, FTC Informal Staff Opinion Letter (Oct. 21, 1982),

reprinted on the CD-Rom accompanying this manual (CRA may furnish consumer report on consumer whose name was forged on application for credit, to enable creditor to locate the person extended credit, so long as consumer merely denies responsibility for the account, without more).
106 For a discussion of the types of transactions that qualify as "credit," see § 7.2.3.1, supra.
107 See Smith v. Bob Smith Chevrolet, Inc., 275 F. Supp. 2d 808 (W.D. Ky. 2003) (though car dealer could access consumer report in assessing consumer's eligibility for financing, it had no permissible purpose to obtain another report later, after the dealer had been paid, in order to assess how much additional money it could collect with respect to a dispute that arose about the contract price).
108 FTC Official Staff Commentary § 604(3)(A) item 1A, reprinted at Appx. D, infra. See also Phillips v. Grendahl, 312 F.3d 357 (8th Cir. 2002); Washington v. South Shore Bank, 2004 WL 2038425 (N.D. Ill. Aug. 27, 2004) (permissible purpose to locate debtor, determine whether account fraudulently opened, and whether debtor could pay); Stonehart v. Rosenthal, 2001 U.S. Dist. LEXIS 11566 (S.D.N.Y. Aug. 13, 2001) (the CRA that obtains the report need not be the one to which an unpaid account has been referred; permissible to outsource skip-tracing); Korotki v. Attorney Servs. Corp., 931 F. Supp. 1269 (D. Md. 1996); Carson, FTC Informal Staff Opinion Letter (Apr. 29, 1971), reprinted on the CD-Rom accompanying this manual.
109 Perretta v. Capital Acquisitions & Mgmt. Co., 2003 WL 21383757 (N.D. Cal. May 5, 2003); Edge v. Professional Claims Bureau, Inc., 64 F. Supp. 2d 115 (E.D.N.Y. 1999) (permissible purpose, even though determined later not to be an attempt to collect the debt); Allen v. Kirkland & Ellis, 1992 LEXIS 12383 (N.D. Ill. Aug. 14, 1992); FTC Official Staff Commentary § 604(3)(A) item 1A, reprinted at Appx. D, infra (attorney use in deciding whether to sue). See also Brinckerhoff, FTC Informal Staff Opinion Letter (Nov. 22, 1991), reprinted on the CD-Rom accompanying this manual. Cf. FTC Informal Staff Opinion Letter [1969–1973 Decisions Transfer Binder] Consumer Cred. Guide (CCH) ¶ 99,444 (May 18, 1971). But see the discussion of impermissible uses of consumer reports in litigation at § 7.4.4, infra.
110 See Shah v. Collecto, Inc., 2005 WL 2216242 (D. Md. Sept. 12, 2005).

purpose to review accounts that it has not been retained to collect in an effort to identify potential creditor customers.[111]

The FTC Staff Commentary states that a party attempting to collect on a returned check has a permissible purpose to obtain a report concerning the maker of the check,[112] although the FTC has been inconsistent about whether check writing involves credit.[113]

Whether a residential lease is a credit transaction, allowing use of consumer reports to collect past-due rent, is not uniformly resolved. The FTC takes the view that residential leases do not involve credit, and therefore an attorney cannot legitimately seek a consumer report to collect past-due rent unless she is enforcing a judgment.[114] This approach is consistent with interpretations of the term "credit" under the ECOA,[115] which is now incorporated into the FCRA. On the other hand, before the FCRA was linked to the ECOA, courts usually held that a lease is a credit transaction, allowing access to consumer reports for collection purposes.[116]

The FTC Staff Commentary indicates that, even if there originally was no credit relationship between a consumer and another, the relationship becomes a creditor/debtor relationship when judgment is secured against the consumer. Thereafter, the judgment creditor may obtain a consumer report on the judgment debtor in an effort to locate the consumer or the consumer's assets.[117] Thus, a federal agency seeking to collect a money judgment has a permissible purpose to receive a consumer report on the individual who owes the judgment, since a "credit" relationship exists, although it could not receive such a report prior to the judgment.[118]

The IRS has a permissible collection purpose to obtain a consumer report where it has either obtained a judgment or filed a tax lien against a taxpayer, or has entered into a formal repayment agreement with a taxpayer.[119] Of course, the IRS has even broader authority under the permissible purpose involving court orders, discussed above, which in the case of the IRS extends to summons.[120]

It is unclear whether a creditor seeking to collect a judgment may obtain the consumer report of a spouse when the debt is community property. One court has held that the creditor may obtain the spouse's report, even if state law creates only a rebuttable presumption that the debt is community property.[121] However, the FTC has issued an opinion letter stating that there is no clear and concrete credit relationship between a creditor and the spouse of the judgment debtor, and that no credit-based permissible purpose exists to obtain a report on spouses, joint owners of property, or others absent a judgment or lien against that person.[122]

The child support collection unit of a district attorney's office may obtain a consumer report in an effort to collect amounts due[123] (as well as under a separate provision related to child support enforcement, discussed below[124]). Consumer reports may also be furnished on parents to child support enforcement agencies where quasi-judicial administrative orders have been entered which establish liability for the payments.[125] Several states use administrative process, rather than judicial process, to establish the obligation. Once the obligation is established, whether by court decree or administrative order, the child support agency becomes a

---

111 *See* Levine v. World Fin. Network Nat'l Bank, 473 F.3d 1118 (11th Cir. 2006).
112 FTC Official Staff Commentary § 604(3)(A) item 9, *reprinted at* Appx. D, *infra. See also* Grimes, FTC Informal Staff Opinion Letter (Feb. 10, 1987), *reprinted on the CD-Rom accompanying this manual.*
113 *See* § 2.3.6.3.2, *supra.*
114 *See* Long, FTC Informal Staff Opinion Letter (July 6, 2000), *reprinted on the CD-Rom accompanying this manual.*
115 *See* Laramore v. Richie Realty Mgmt. Co., 397 F.3d 544 (7th Cir. 2005); National Consumer Law Center, Credit Discrimination, § 2.2.2.2.4 (4th ed. 2005 and Supp.).
116 *See* § 2.3.6.3.3, *supra.*
117 FTC Official Staff Commentary § 604(3)(A) item 2, *reprinted at* Appx. D, *infra. See* Sather v. Weintraut, 2003 WL 21692111 (D. Minn. July 10, 2003) (attorney may not obtain report of someone who is not personally liable for the judgment, such as owner or officer of corporation against whom judgment was entered); Morgovsky v. Creditors' Collection Serv., 1995 LEXIS 7055 (N.D. Cal. May 16, 1995); Baker v. Bronx-Westchester Investigations, Inc., 850 F. Supp. 260 (S.D.N.Y. 1994). *See also* Grimes, FTC Informal Staff Opinion Letter (Aug. 14, 1985), *reprinted on the CD-Rom accompanying this manual*; Garman, FTC Informal Staff Opinion Letter (June 17, 1985), *reprinted on the CD-Rom accompanying this manual* (but pre-judgment writ of attachment does not give rise to a creditor/debtor relationship).
118 Noonan, FTC Informal Staff Opinion Letter (Dec. 18, 1986), *reprinted on the CD-Rom accompanying this manual.*

119 Brinckerhoff, FTC Informal Staff Opinion Letter (May 28, 1986), *reprinted on the CD-Rom accompanying this manual.*
120 *See* § 7.2.1, *supra.*
121 *See* Simoneaux v. Brown, 403 F. Supp. 2d 526 (M.D. La. 2005) (employer could access wife's credit information to collect on husband's embezzlement restitution order because it could rely on presumption under Louisiana law that debt was a community obligation). *See also* Thibodeaux v. Rupers, 196 F. Supp. 2d 585 (S.D. Ohio 2001) (indicating in dicta that creditor of wife could obtain consumer report of husband who was unaware of loans; under Ohio law, the husband could have been held liable for the loans because they were used for marital purposes).
122 Baucher, FTC Informal Staff Opinion Letter (Aug. 5, 1998), *reprinted on the CD-Rom accompanying this manual.*
123 Hasbun v. County of Los Angeles, 323 F.3d 801 (9th Cir. 2003) (no need to comply with certification requirements when collecting overdue support); FTC Official Staff Commentary § 604(3)(A) item 3, *reprinted at* Appx. D, *infra. See also* Isaac, FTC Informal Staff Opinion Letter (Oct. 30, 1986), *reprinted on the CD-Rom accompanying this manual.*
  A separate permissible purpose exists allowing certain child support enforcement agencies limited access to consumer reports. *See* § 7.2.9, *infra.*
124 *See* § 7.2.9, *infra.*
125 Fortney, FTC Informal Staff Opinion Letter (Dec. 2, 1983), *reprinted on the CD-Rom accompanying this manual. See also* § 7.2.9, *infra*; Isaac, FTC Informal Staff Opinion Letter (Oct. 30, 1986), *reprinted on the CD-Rom accompanying this manual.*

judgment creditor having a permissible purpose to obtain a consumer report,[126] as does the parent/creditor.[127]

The ability of government agencies to obtain consumer reports in the child support context before an order of support has been made is discussed in § 7.2.9, *infra*.

7.2.4 Permissible Use in Connection with Employment

7.2.4.1 Overview

CRAs may release a report "for employment purposes,"[128] but only if the employer certifies that it has advised the employee that it will be requesting a report, that the employee has consented in writing to the release, and that the employer will make certain disclosures if adverse action is taken based in any part on the report.[129] The CRA is required to enclose with the consumer report a copy of the FTC Statement of Consumer Rights for the employer to use.

Employment purposes are broadly defined, but certain employee misconduct and compliance investigations are excluded from the definition of a consumer report and are provided more limited protection.[130]

7.2.4.2 Employment Purposes

"Employment purposes"[131] is defined to mean "evaluating a consumer for employment, promotion, reassignment or retention as an employee."[132] The FTC staff has expanded on this definition to include employers who are even "considering the possibility" of actions such as termination,[133] who are investigating a current employee concerning disappearance of money from the employment premises (because the employee's retention is at issue),[134] trucking firms who are hiring drivers as independent contractors,[135] and those who are determining whether a government contractor's employee should have security clearance.[136] However, investigative reports regarding some of these purposes are now exempted from coverage as a consumer report by the FCRA because they would constitute employee misconduct investigations.[137]

Employment purposes do not include inquiries into why an employee quit.[138] If former employee is no longer employed, the employer will be making no decision concerning the former employee's retention, hire, or promotion. Jury duty, on the other hand, is a civic duty, rather than employment, and therefore counsel has no permissible purpose to obtain reports on potential jurors.[139]

The FTC has taken the position that investigation of workers' compensation claims is not an "employment purpose," and does not constitute a permissible purpose to obtain a consumer report.[140] Note, however, that one court has held that a workers' compensation investigation is "related to employment" under the newer, separate provision exempting employee misconduct investigations from the definition of consumer reports.[141]

An employer may not obtain a consumer report on someone other than the subject of its decision-making.[142] For example, there is no permissible purpose for a user to obtain consumer reports on an employment applicant's relatives, even where the applicant is being considered for a security-sensitive position and the report is obtained to evaluate the applicant's trustworthiness for the position.[143]

---

126 Woolford, FTC Informal Staff Opinion Letter (Aug. 6, 1999), *reprinted on the CD-Rom accompanying this manual*; Fortney, FTC Informal Staff Opinion Letter (Dec. 2, 1983), *reprinted on the CD-Rom accompanying this manual*.

127 Baker v. Bronx-Westchester Investigations, Inc., 850 F. Supp. 260 (S.D.N.Y. 1994).

128 15 U.S.C. § 1681b(a)(3)(B).

129 See § 8.2.17, *infra*.

130 15 U.S.C. §§ 1681a(d)(2)(D), 1681a(x). *See* § 7.2.4.5 and Ch. 13, *infra*.

131 15 U.S.C. § 1681b(a)(3)(B).

132 15 U.S.C. § 1681a(h); Wiggins v. Philip Morris, Inc., 853 F. Supp. 470 (D.D.C. 1994).

133 Grimes, FTC Informal Staff Opinion Letter (Oct. 23, 1985), *reprinted on the CD-Rom accompanying this manual*.

134 Official Staff Commentary § 604(3)(B) item 1, *reprinted at* Appx. D, *infra* (use of report in connection with theft investigation if retention of employee is at stake). *See* Kelchner v. Sycamore Manor Health Ctr., 135 Fed. Appx. 499 (3d Cir. 2005) (employer could obtain report to investigate possible theft, fraud or other dishonesty by employee). [*Editor's Note*: presumably such use is permissible only if employment of consumer likely to be affected.]

135 Allison, FTC Informal Staff Opinion Letter (Feb. 23, 1998), *reprinted on the CD-Rom accompanying this manual*.

136 FTC Official Staff Commentary § 603(h) item 2. Other examples of a broad definition of "employment" for this purpose include: Solomon, FTC Informal Staff Opinion Letter (Oct. 7, 1998), *reprinted on the CD-Rom accompanying this manual*. *See also* Brinckerhoff, FTC Informal Staff Opinion Letter (July 24, 1986), *reprinted on the CD-Rom accompanying this manual*. Special rules apply to trucking firms. *See* § 8.2.17.2.3, *infra*.

137 See § 7.2.4.5 and Ch. 13, *infra*.

138 Russell v. Shelter Fin. Servs., 604 F. Supp. 201 (W.D. Mo. 1984).

139 *Cf.* FTC Official Staff Commentary § 604(3)(B) item 3, *reprinted at* Appx. D, *infra*.

140 Greathouse, FTC Informal Staff Opinion Letter (Oct. 20, 1998), *reprinted on the CD-Rom accompanying this manual*.

141 Millard v. Miller, 2005 WL 1899475, at *2 (W.D. Wis. Aug. 9, 2005). *See* § 7.2.4.5, *infra*.

142 FTC Official Staff Commentary § 604(3)(B) item 2, *reprinted at* Appx. D, *infra*; Zamora v. Valley Fed. Sav. & Loan Ass'n, 811 F.2d 1368 (10th Cir. 1987); Andrews v. TRW, Inc., 225 F.3d 1063 (9th Cir. 2000) (it is for the jury to decide whether it was reasonable to disclose information about someone else), *rev'd and remanded on other grounds*, 534 U.S. 19 (2001); Conway, FTC Informal Staff Opinion Letter [1969–1973 Decisions Transfer Binder] Consumer Cred. Guide (CCH) ¶ 99,520 (Apr. 19, 1971).

143 Zamora v. Valley Fed. Sav. & Loan Ass'n, 811 F.2d 1368 (10th Cir. 1987).

The Fourth Circuit found that a state licensing board has an employment purpose in receiving a consumer report in order to evaluate an applicant for a professional license,[144] even if there is no employer-employee relationship between the board and applicant. Because of this employment purpose, the Fourth Circuit found the report falls within the definition of a consumer report. Since the Act's definition of "employment purposes"[145] applies equally to consumer reports and permissible uses of reports,[146] this case is precedent for the proposition that a CRA can furnish a report to a licensing board that intends to use it in connection with an evaluation of the consumer's right to practice a trade or profession.[147]

Once an employment relationship has ended, and re-employment is not contemplated, the former employer no longer has an "employment purpose" for a consumer report on the former employee. Thus, a former employer has been found liable for improperly obtaining a consumer report on an employee who had quit unexpectedly the previous day.[148] There was no employment purpose for obtaining the report, even if the employer suspected embezzlement, because there was no present employment relationship. However, the former employer is not restricted from *providing* information on the former employee to a CRA.[149]

Again, note that the separate provision exempting employee misconduct investigations from the definition of consumer reports might apply in post-termination settings.[150]

7.2.4.3 Employer Must Provide Prior Certification

7.2.4.3.1 General

A CRA may not release a consumer report for employment purposes unless the employer certifies that the employer has already made required disclosures to the employee and that the employer will, if adverse action is taken, make future disclosures as well.[151] The CRA is required only to have received the employer's certification. It is not required to obtain further documentation of compliance.[152]

Exceptions exist for security-clearance-related employment decisions by agencies of the United States, and for the trucking industry.[153] In addition, the FCRA provides for exceptions for certain communications relating to employee misconduct investigations, which are not considered consumer reports.[154]

7.2.4.3.2 Employer must obtain employee's consent

The FCRA requires the employer to obtain the employee's authorization in order to procure a consumer report.[155] The employer must certify that it has clearly and conspicuously disclosed to the consumer that a consumer report may be obtained for employment purposes, and that the consumer has authorized in writing the procurement of the report.[156]

An employer can require prospective employees to authorize consumer reports as part of the application process. One court has also held that an employer can require current employees to provide a blanket advance authorization for release of reports for investigating possible future theft, fraud, or dishonesty, and that an employee who refuses to give authorization may be terminated.[157] The court reasoned that the Act permits an employer to obtain authorization "at any time before the report is procured."[158]

Note that, because of the FACTA amendments, advance authorization is no longer required when a report is obtained for the purpose of investigating an employee's suspected misconduct as long as the FCRA guidelines are followed. It is unclear if this exception applies to traditional consumer reports obtained for investigative purposes, or only to reports created as part of an employee misconduct investigation.[159]

The pre-consent disclosure requirement is discussed in greater detail in § 8.2.17, *infra*.

7.2.4.3.3 Employer must make disclosures in case of adverse action

The employer must certify to the CRA that, prior to taking adverse action based in full or in part on the consumer

---

144 Hoke v. Retail Credit Corp., 521 F.2d 1079 (4th Cir. 1975) (Texas Board of Medical Examiners has permissible purpose in evaluating application for license to practice medicine).
145 15 U.S.C. § 1681a(h).
146 Compare 15 U.S.C. § 1681a(d)(1) with 15 U.S.C. § 1681b(a)(3)(B).
147 See also Grimes, FTC Informal Staff Opinion Letter (Mar. 7, 1986), *reprinted on the CD-Rom accompanying this manual* (state board of bar examiners may obtain consumer reports on applicants for a license to practice law).
148 Russell v. Shelter Fin. Servs., 604 F. Supp. 201 (W.D. Mo. 1984).
149 Grimes, FTC Informal Staff Opinion Letter (Oct. 4, 1985), *reprinted on the CD-Rom accompanying this manual*.
150 Millard v. Miller, 2005 WL 1899475, at *2 (W.D. Wis. Aug. 9, 2005) (workers compensation investigation). See § 7.2.4.5, *infra*.
151 15 U.S.C. § 1681b(b). See §§ 7.2.4.3.2, 7.2.4.3.3, *infra*.
152 See Kilgo, FTC Informal Staff Opinion Letter (July 28, 1998), *reprinted on the CD-Rom accompanying this manual*.
153 See § 8.2.17.2.3, *infra*.
154 See §§ 7.2.4.5, 13.5.1, *infra*.
155 15 U.S.C. § 1681b(b)(2)(A)(ii).
156 15 U.S.C. § 1681b(b)(1)(A).
157 Kelchner v. Sycamore Manor Health Ctr., 305 F. Supp. 2d 429 (M.D. Pa. 2004) (employee who refuses to give authorization may be terminated), *aff'd*, 135 Fed. Appx. 499 (3d Cir. 2005).
158 *Kelchner*, 305 F. Supp. 2d at 433 (quoting 15 U.S.C. § 1681b(b)(2)(A)(i)).
159 See § 7.2.4.5, *infra*.

report, the employer will give the consumer a copy of the consumer report along with a Summary of Consumer Rights as prescribed by the FTC. This disclosure requirement is discussed in greater detail in § 8.2.6.2.5, *infra*.

7.2.4.4 Agency Must Enclose Summary of Consumer Rights

To release a consumer report for employment purposes, the CRA must also provide a Summary of Consumer Rights.[160] In fact, the report may be released "only if" the CRA provides or has provided the summary.[161] The employer in turn is required to provide an employee or potential employee with a copy of the report and the summary in the event the employer takes adverse action on the basis of the consumer report.[162] However, if the report pertains to an employee misconduct investigation that falls outside coverage as a consumer report, the employee is only entitled to a summary of the report if adverse action is taken. They are not entitled to the Summary of Consumer Rights.[163]

One would expect that a CRA would attach to each report the Summary of Consumer Rights or, in the event an employer obtains the report through a computer connection, would cause the summary to print out along with the report. However, FTC staff has suggested that a CRA may provide sufficient copies to the employer so that a copy may be attached to each report at the time it is given to the consumer. The CRA remains responsible for compliance, and must ensure that the employer "will comply as appropriate."[164]

7.2.4.5 Employee Misconduct Investigations Not Considered Consumer Reports

The FCRA excludes from the definition of consumer reports communications related to employer investigations by third parties of employees for certain conduct.[165] To fall within this exclusion the communication must be made to an employer by a third party and must be in connection with an investigation of one of the following:

- Suspected misconduct relating to employment;
- Compliance with federal, state or local laws;
- Compliance with the rules of a self-regulatory organization; or
- Compliance with any preexisting written policies of the employer.

Furthermore, the communication must not be made for the purpose of investigating a consumer's creditworthiness, credit standing, or credit capacity. In other words, the communication must only bear on the employee's character, general reputation, personal characteristics, or mode of living. These limitations appear designed to exclude traditional consumer reports from CRAs. However, one court has held that even a traditional consumer report is not considered to be a consumer report as a result of this provision if it is used in connection with an employee misconduct investigation.[166]

The communication must not be provided to anyone other than the employer or the employer's agent, a governmental authority, or a self-regulatory organization with regulatory authority over the employer.[167]

Employees who are the subject of these types of investigations and communications have the right to notification only if adverse action is taken based on the communication resulting from the investigation. The notice thus comes after the adverse action. They also have a right to a summary of the nature and substance of the communications.

The employee misconduct investigation exclusion was added by the 2003 FACTA amendments, and prior to that time, such employees would have been entitled to a copy of the actual report, not simply a summary of the nature and substance of the report.[168] This exclusion and the legislative history behind it are discussed more fully in § 2.4.4.1, *supra*.

7.2.5 Permissible Use in Connection with Insurance

Another permissible purpose for furnishing consumer reports to users is "in connection with the underwriting of insurance involving the consumer."[169] Underwriting activities include deciding whether to issue or cancel a policy and determination of coverage, terms, rates, and similar items.[170] One court has ruled that an actual application for insurance is not necessary as long as the insurer intends to use the report for underwriting.[171] In the event there is any adverse action, such as charging a higher rate based on information contained in a report, insurance companies are required to

---

160 FACTA amended the FCRA to require the FTC to revise the model Summary of Consumer Rights. 15 U.S.C. § 1681g, *added by* Pub. L. No. 108-159, § 211 (2003). *See* § 8.2.2, *infra*. A copy of the FTC's revised Summary of Consumer Rights can be found in Appx. C.2, *infra*.
161 15 U.S.C. § 1681b(b).
162 15 U.S.C. § 1681b(b)(3). *See* § 8.2.6.2.5, *infra*.
163 15 U.S.C. § 1681a(x)(2). *See* §§ 7.2.4.5, 13.4, *infra*.
164 Haynes, FTC Informal Staff Opinion Letter (Dec. 23, 1997), *reprinted on the CD-Rom accompanying this manual*.
165 15 U.S.C. §§ 1681a(d)(2)(D), 1681a(x).
166 Millard v. Miller, 2005 WL 1899475, at *2 (W.D. Wis. Aug. 9, 2005) (workers' compensation investigation).
167 15 U.S.C. § 1681a(x).
168 *See* § 7.2.4.4, *supra*.
169 15 U.S.C. § 1681b(a)(3)(C).
170 *See* FTC Official Staff Commentary § 604(3)(C) item 1, *reprinted at* Appx. D, *infra*.
171 Scharpf v. AIG Mktg., Inc., 242 F. Supp. 2d 455 (W.D. Ky. 2003) (the adverse action notice provision thus also applies despite absence of an actual application).

provide notice to the consumer.[172] This adverse action must be provided despite the absence of an application for insurance.[173]

Underwriting does not include marketing activities.[174] However, a separate provision, discussed in § 7.3.4, *infra*, permits CRAs to provide prescreened lists of consumers meeting certain criteria to insurers who intend to make an offer to those on the list.

Underwriting also does not include investigating an insurance claim after the insurance has been written. Therefore consumer reports obtained for insurance-claims purposes involve an impermissible purpose.[175]

The FTC Staff Commentary has interpreted permissible insurance purposes in the same manner as permissible credit purposes and, therefore, consumer reports may be furnished for insurance use only when the insurance is for personal, non-business purposes.[176] The FTC's position has the merit of ensuring that the privacy rights of consumers are protected. If an insurer considering underwriting business insurance is unable to obtain sufficient information from a business report, the consumer has the option of authorizing the insurer to obtain the consumer's consumer report.[177]

Several states also have passed laws governing the issuance and use of consumer reports and credit scores for insurance purposes.[178] Many states also require notice to consumers if a consumer report is to be used for underwriting purposes. For example, Maine requires users of consumer reports to disclose at the time of application for insurance the fact that it will use credit information. If the insurer takes adverse action, it must explain the reasons to the consumer, and provide notice pursuant to state law and the FCRA.[179] Many state laws also prohibit insurers from requesting credit information, including credit scores, based on protected status including race, ethnicity, color, religion, marital status, age, gender, and other categories.[180]

7.2.6 Permissible Use in Connection with Government Licenses or Other Benefits

Another permissible use of a consumer report is "in connection with a determination of the consumer's eligibility for a license or other benefit granted by a governmental instrumentality required by law to consider an applicant's financial responsibility or status."[181] This provision allows public assistance agencies, for example, to obtain consumer reports for use in evaluating the consumer's eligibility for benefits.

The FCRA does not require that the user of the report be the governmental instrumentality itself. Any party charged by law (including regulations having the force of law) with responsibility for assessing the consumer's eligibility for the benefit has a permissible purpose.[182] For example, a district attorney's office, or a social services bureau, required by law to determine an individual's eligibility for public assistance benefits has a permissible purpose.[183] A township required to consider a consumer's financial status in connection with assistance has a permissible purpose. A professional board that must consider an applicant's admission to practice (e.g., law, medicine) has a permissible purpose.[184] A state may use reports as part of its determination to grant or withdraw an insurance agent's license.[185] Even a private landlord has a permissible purpose to obtain reports on those applying for a tenancy where the landlord is authorized to screen the applications to determine tenants' eligibility for governmental rental payment subsidies.[186]

On the other hand, parties without responsibility for determining a consumer's eligibility for a governmental benefit do not have a permissible purpose to obtain a consumer report.[187] For example, a party competing for an FCC radio station construction permit would not have a permissible purpose to obtain a consumer report on a competing bidder.[188]

The FTC Staff Commentary would not limit governmental use of consumer reports to the time at which eligibility for benefits is first considered. Although the FCRA appears to contemplate use of reports on applicants only, the FTC Staff Commentary would permit use of reports after an

---

172 See § 8.2.6, *infra*.
173 Scharpf v. AIG Mktg., Inc., 242 F. Supp. 2d 455 (W.D. Ky. 2003).
174 Buchman, FTC Informal Staff Opinion Letter (Mar. 2, 1998), *reprinted on the CD-Rom accompanying this manual*.
175 See § 7.4.7, *infra*.
176 FTC Official Staff Commentary § 604 item 1B, *reprinted at* Appx. D, *infra*. See also Feldman, FTC Informal Staff Opinion Letter (Apr. 15, 1971), *reprinted on the CD-Rom accompanying this manual*; FTC, Compliance with the Fair Credit Reporting Act, at 46 (1977).
177 15 U.S.C. § 1681b(a)(2).
178 See Appx. H, *infra*. See also § 14.10, *infra*.
179 Me. Rev. Stat. Ann. tit. 24A, § 2169-B. See Appx. H, *infra*.
180 See Appx. H, *infra*.

181 15 U.S.C. § 1681b(a)(3)(D).
182 FTC Official Staff Commentary § 604(3)(D) item 1, *reprinted at* Appx. D, *infra*.
183 *Id.*
184 *Id.*
185 Greathouse, FTC Informal Staff Opinion Letter (Oct. 20, 1998), *reprinted on the CD-Rom accompanying this manual*.
186 See Franco v. Kent Farm Vill., Clearinghouse No. 44,149 (D.R.I. Sept. 16, 1988) (bench opinion) (Civil Action No. 88-0115 T).
187 FTC Official Staff Commentary § 604(3)(D) item 2, *reprinted at* Appx. D, *infra*.
188 *Id.*

application for benefits is granted whenever the government on its own initiative is reviewing a recipient's qualifications or continuing eligibility for the benefits.[189]

If the governmental body has reason to believe a particular consumer's eligibility is in doubt, or wishes to conduct random checks to confirm eligibility, it has a permissible purpose.[190]

The permissible purpose involving government benefits only applies where an entity is "required by law to consider an applicant's financial responsibility or status."[191] The issue is not whether the consumer's financial responsibility or status is relevant to the governmental decision, but whether a statute or regulation requires financial responsibility or status to be considered in the granting of the benefit or license. The user will have to point to a specific provision in the enabling statute or regulations requiring the user to consider this.

7.2.7 Risk Assessment of Existing Credit Obligations

Consumer reports may be provided to "a potential investor or servicer, or current insurer, in connection with a valuation of, or an assessment of the credit or prepayment risks associated with, an existing credit obligation."[192]

Creditors often sell installment contracts, home mortgages, and other credit obligations. The potential investor, or purchaser, may use information in a consumer report in connection with a valuation or assessment of the credit or prepayment risks associated with the consumer debt.

The risk assessment provision only applies to those considering involvement with "an *existing* credit obligation."[193] Thus, this provision does not justify release of a consumer report in connection with a potential or as yet unconsummated credit obligation, though other provisions may apply.[194]

Similarly, banks and others who extend or own home mortgages often arrange for servicing agencies to "service" the transactions, that is to bill, collect, and otherwise monitor and enforce the transactions on their behalf. These servicers will also want to evaluate the existing mortgage or credit obligation, and may use consumer reports for that purpose.

---

189 *Id*. item 3.
190 *Id*.
191 15 U.S.C. § 1681b(a)(3)(D).
192 15 U.S.C. § 1681b(a)(3)(E). *See also* § 2.3.6.7, *supra*.
193 15 U.S.C. § 1681b(a)(3)(E) (emphasis added).
194 *See* Stergiopoulos v. First Midwest Bancorp., Inc., 472 F.3d 1043 (7th Cir. 2005) (lender considering financing automobile purchase could not rely on risk assessment provision, 15 U.S.C. § 1681b(a)(3)(E), to justify request for consumer report, but was entitled to request report under credit transaction provision, 15 U.S.C. § 1681b(a)(3)(A)).

Insurers often underwrite large bundles of credit obligations, and will wish to use consumer reports to assess changing risks involved.

Insurance companies will sometimes seek an individual's consumer report after that consumer files a claim. Although they may argue that they are entitled to the report under the risk assessment provision, it is far more likely that they are accessing the consumer's credit file for purposes of settling the claim, which is not a permissible purpose and should accordingly cause liability under the FCRA.[195]

7.2.8 Legitimate Business Need

7.2.8.1 Overview

In addition to the specific purposes described above (in connection with credit transactions, employment, insurance, government benefits and licenses, and risk assessment), the FCRA also lists a more general permissible purpose. The Act authorizes releases of consumer reports to a user who "otherwise has a legitimate business need for the information" in one of two situations: "in connection with a business transaction initiated by the consumer,"[196] or "to review an account to determine whether the consumer continues to meet the terms of the account."[197]

7.2.8.2 Business Transaction Initiated by the Consumer

7.2.8.2.1 General

The first legitimate business need for consumer reports is "in connection with a business transaction initiated by the consumer."[198] Three separate questions arise in determining whether a report may be used under this provision. First, what types of business transactions qualify? Second, was the transaction initiated by the consumer? And third, is the business need legitimate?

7.2.8.2.2 Business transaction

7.2.8.2.2.1 Business transaction for personal, family, or household purposes

A "business transaction" is "an arm's length transaction between the consumer and the person requesting the report

---

195 *See* §§ 7.4.7, 10.2.4.1, *infra*.
196 15 U.S.C. § 1681b(a)(3)(F)(i).
197 15 U.S.C. § 1681b(a)(3)(F)(ii).
198 15 U.S.C. § 1681b(a)(3)(F)(i).

or his agent."[199] It must involve an action by the consumer from which the consumer reasonably expects to benefit.[200] The FTC Staff Commentary takes the view that the business transaction must be "with a consumer primarily for personal, family or household purposes."[201] Courts have generally agreed.[202] The "business" aspect of the transaction relates to the user's purpose, not the consumer's. Obtaining a consumer report for a business transaction that involves purely commercial purposes on both ends is not a permissible use.[203]

Of course, if a report is compiled and used purely for business purposes, it may not qualify as a consumer report, in which case the FCRA does not restrict its use.[204] For example, reports on businesses or commercial enterprises are not consumer reports because they are not about individuals.

Examples of permissible consumer-related business transactions, according to the FTC Staff Commentary, include consumers applying to rent an apartment, offering to pay for goods with a check, applying for a checking account or similar service, seeking to be included in a computer dating service, or who have sought and received overpayments of government benefits that they are refusing to return.[205] If a consumer is seeking legal assistance from an attorney for personal, family, or household purposes, the attorney may have a permissible business transaction purpose to obtain the consumer's report.[206] An FTC staff letter adds as a permissible purpose a consumer's application for a land contract (even if the contract is not treated as an application for credit).[207] One FTC staff letter indicates that investments such as limited partnerships are considered transactions for personal, family, or household purposes if the consumers are not engaged for their livelihood in the investment business.[208]

Litigation does not usually constitute a consumer relationship or business transaction,[209] nor do property or custody disputes between suspicious, divorcing, or ex-spouses.[210] Even if the user has an otherwise legitimate need for information about a consumer, the need does not constitute permissible grounds for releasing a consumer report unless there is a consumer relationship.[211]

Prior to the Consumer Credit Reporting Reform Act of 1996 (1996 Reform Act), a minority of courts took a broader view of business transactions, allowing consumer reports to be used even for transactions that were not for personal,

---

199 Carson, FTC Informal Staff Opinion Letter (Apr. 29, 1971), *reprinted on the CD-Rom accompanying this manual*.

200 Brinkerhoff, FTC Informal Staff Opinion Letter (Nov. 26, 1984), *reprinted on the CD-Rom accompanying this manual*. See also FTC Official Staff Commentary § 604(3)(E) item 3, *reprinted at* Appx. D, *infra*; Mone v. Dranow, 945 F.2d 306 (9th Cir. 1991) (desire to see if potential defendant could satisfy a judgment is not a business transaction); Geer v. Medallion Homes Ltd. P'ship, 2005 WL 2708992 (E.D. Mich. Oct. 20, 2005) (obtaining second consumer report after file was closed but consumers indicated that they had been working to clean up their credit benefited consumers to assist them with their credit application).

201 *See* FTC Official Staff Commentary § 604(3)(E) item 2, *reprinted at* Appx. D, *infra*; Noonan, FTC Informal Staff Opinion Letter (Aug. 22, 1990), *reprinted on the CD-Rom accompanying this manual*. But see Tatelbaum 2, FTC Informal Staff Opinion Letter (June 22, 2001), *reprinted on the CD-Rom accompanying this manual* (permitting a lender to obtain a consumer report when the consumer will be personally liable in connection with a commercial credit application).

202 Bakker v. McKinnon, 152 F.3d 1007 (8th Cir. 1998); Mone v. Dranow, 945 F.2d 306 (9th Cir. 1991) (desire to see if potential defendant could satisfy a judgment is not a business transaction); Daley v. Haddonfield Lumber, Inc., 943 F. Supp. 464 (D.N.J. 1996); Zeller v. Samia, 758 F. Supp. 775 (D. Mass. 1991); Russell v. Shelter Fin. Servs., 604 F. Supp. 201 (W.D. Mo. 1984); Henry v. Forbes, 433 F. Supp. 5 (D. Minn. 1976); Ley v. Boron Oil Co., 419 F. Supp. 1240 (W.D. Pa. 1976).

203 Tatelbaum, FTC Informal Staff Opinion Letter (July 26, 2000), *reprinted on the CD-Rom accompanying this manual*.

204 *See* § 2.3.6.2, *supra*.

205 Kvalheim v. Checkfree Corp., 2000 U.S. Dist. LEXIS 1959 (S.D. Ala. Feb. 17, 2000) (home computer banking service); FTC Official Staff Commentary § 604(3)(E) item 3, *reprinted at* Appx. D, *infra*. Courts have not always accepted these FTC classifications, sometimes ruling that a permissible use in connection with credit exists. *See* § 2.3.6.3, 2.3.6.4, *supra* and § 8.2.6.4.3.2, *infra*. *See also* Estiverne v. Saks Fifth Avenue & JBS, 9 F.3d 1171 (5th Cir. 1993) (check cashing); Long, FTC Staff Opinion Letter (July 6, 2000), *reprinted on the CD-Rom accompanying this manual*; Brinckerhoff, FTC Informal Staff Opinion Letter (Feb. 5, 1985), *reprinted on the CD-Rom accompanying this manual* (provisional checking accounts and similar financial services); Goldfarb, FTC Informal Staff Opinion Letter (July 9, 1980), *reprinted on the CD-Rom accompanying this manual* (government agency has a permissible purpose when seeking to collect over-payments of government benefits, where the consumer has resisted initial voluntary repayment. If the consumer has made a voluntary repayment, then there is no legitimate business need, and no permissible purpose, to obtain the report).

206 Carson, FTC Informal Staff Opinion Letter (Apr. 29, 1971), *reprinted on the CD-Rom accompanying this manual*.

207 Petruccelli, FTC Informal Staff Opinion Letter (Apr. 9, 1984), *reprinted on the CD-Rom accompanying this manual*.

208 Grimes, FTC Informal Staff Opinion Letter (Feb. 17, 1993), *reprinted on the CD-Rom accompanying this manual*.

209 *See* § 5.3.4, *infra*. *Cf*. Spence v. TRW, Inc., 92 F.3d 380 (6th Cir. 1996) (user could obtain consumer report for use in defending suit claiming user had falsely reported a debt). But *cf*. Duncan v. Handmaker, 149 F.3d 424 (6th Cir. 1998) (attorney defending mortgage company in negligence suit by consumers had no permissible purpose in accessing consumers' report; business transaction underlying suit did not extend to the litigation itself). A settlement agreement might, however, justify access to a consumer report for the purposes of confirming that information has not been provided to the CRA contrary to the terms of the settlement, or at least so holds a loosely reasoned judicial opinion. Wilting v. Progressive County Mut. Ins. Co., 227 F.3d 474 (5th Cir. 2000).

210 Cole v. American Family Mut. Ins. Co., 2006 WL 158688 (D. Kan. Jan. 18, 2006) (citing cases); Thibodeaux v. Rupers, 196 F. Supp. 2d 585 (S.D. Ohio 2001).

211 Boothe v. TRW Credit Data, 523 F. Supp. 631 (S.D.N.Y. 1981), *modified*, 557 F. Supp. 66 (S.D.N.Y. 1982).

family, or household purposes.[212] At that time, the transaction needed only to be one "involving the consumer." The 1996 Reform Act amendments, requiring that the transaction be "initiated by the consumer," strengthens the view of other courts that the transaction must be initiated for consumer purposes. That is, the transaction must be initiated by a consumer *in his or her capacity as a consumer*: i.e., for personal, family, or household purposes.[213]

Allowing the business transaction provision to apply to any type of non-consumer transaction would be inconsistent with the interpretation of the insurance and credit provisions. The predominant view of those provisions is that only consumer insurance and credit, not business or commercial credit or insurance, qualified as a permissible purpose.[214] Similarly, consumer reports may not be used for evaluating any type of insurance claim.[215]

If insurance or credit is involved, the business transaction provision does not apply; the purpose must be one permitted under the specific insurance or credit provision, respectively.[216] The limitations in those provisions would be meaningless if the general business transaction provision could be used to justify any credit or insurance use, even one unrelated to consumer purposes. Rather, the catch-all business transaction provision "is designed to provide a permissible purpose to a business that is considering a *consumer* application for a purpose *other than* credit, employment, or insurance," which are set forth elsewhere in the Act.[217]

7.2.8.2.2.2 Business transaction must relate to eligibility

The FTC has interpreted the business transaction provision to apply only at the point of initiation—that is, for the purpose of determining the consumer's *eligibility* for the business transaction at hand.[218] The existence of a separate business transaction provision that provides a permissible purpose for account reviews,[219] which applies *after* an account has been established, bolsters the view that the first provision applies only to initial eligibility decisions.[220]

For example, when an automobile dealer mistakenly wrote up a transaction more favorably to the consumer, the dealer did not have a permissible purpose to obtain the report once the sale was consummated, even though the dealer thought the consumer should reimburse the dealer for an excessive discount.[221] Similarly, a landlord cannot rely on the consumer-initiated business transaction provision to justify obtaining a report for use in collecting disputed rent after a tenant has vacated the apartment.[222]

On the other hand, one FTC staff letter stated that the business transaction purpose applied to a user who was attempting to collect on defaulted promissory notes.[223] Similarly, a court has found that a grandfather could obtain his granddaughter's report to investigate possible identity theft by her after he cosigned her car loan.[224] Neither the staff letter nor the court decision discussed the possible limitation of the business transaction provision to eligibility situations.

7.2.8.2.3 Initiated by the consumer

The business transaction must be "initiated by the consumer." Prior to the 1996 Reform Act amendments, the business transaction needed only to "involve" the consumer.[225] The language now makes clear that the consumer must at least evidence interest in a transaction and perhaps

---

212 *E.g.*, Ippolito v. WNS, Inc., 864 F.2d 440 (7th Cir. 1988); Korotki v. Attorney Servs. Corp., 931 F. Supp. 1269 (D. Md. 1996) (permissible to obtain individual's consumer report in course of collecting a business debt), *aff'd without published op.* 131 F.3d 135 (4th Cir. 1997); Advanced Conservation Sys., Inc. v. Long Island Lighting Co., 934 F. Supp. 53 (E.D.N.Y. 1996) (permissible to access report of sole shareholders of business contractor).
213 Tatelbaum, FTC Informal Staff Opinion Letter (July 26, 2000), *reprinted on the CD-Rom accompanying this manual* (noting that an application for commercial purposes is not a "*consumer* application") (original emphasis).
214 *See* §§ 7.2.5, 7.2.7, *supra*.
215 *See* § 7.4.7, *infra*.
216 FTC, Compliance with the Fair Credit Reporting Act, at 46–47 (1977). *See also* FTC Official Staff Commentary § 604(3)(E) item 1, *reprinted at* Appx. D, *infra*. Similarly, in the context of defining a "consumer report," the courts have found that the explicit provisions dealing with credit and insurance uses are "primary" and, therefore, the use of information in connection with credit and insurance transactions not specified in the definition cannot be included under the business transaction provision.
217 Tatelbaum, FTC Informal Staff Opinion Letter (July 26, 2000), *reprinted on the CD-Rom accompanying this manual* (original emphasis).

218 Buchman, FTC Informal Staff Opinion Letter (Mar. 2, 1998), *reprinted on the CD-Rom accompanying this manual*; Long, FTC Informal Staff Opinion Letter (July 6, 2000), *reprinted on the CD-Rom accompanying this manual. Accord* Smith v. Bob Smith Chevrolet, Inc., 275 F. Supp. 2d 808 (W.D. Ky. 2003).
219 15 U.S.C. § 1681b(a)(3)(F)(ii). *See* § 7.2.8.3, *infra*.
220 Furthermore, 15 U.S.C. § 1681a(d) defines a consumer report as containing information "for the purpose of serving as a factor in establishing the consumer's eligibility for" credit, insurance, and other permitted purposes. Unless otherwise expanded by the list of permissible purposes (15 U.S.C. § 1681b(a)), the argument goes, reports may be requested only for eligibility determinations. *See* Buchman, FTC Informal Staff Opinion Letter (Mar. 2, 1998), *reprinted on the CD-Rom accompanying this manual*.
221 Smith v. Bob Smith Chevrolet, Inc., 275 F. Supp. 2d 808 (W.D. Ky. 2003).
222 Long, FTC Informal Staff Opinion Letter (July 6, 2000), *reprinted on the CD-Rom accompanying this manual*.
223 Grimes, FTC Informal Staff Opinion Letter (Feb. 17, 1993), *reprinted on the CD-Rom accompanying this manual*.
224 *See* Breese v. Triadvantage Credit Servs., Inc., 393 F. Supp. 2d 819 (D. Minn. 2005).
225 15 U.S.C. § 1681(a)(3)(F), *as amended by* Pub. L. No. 104-208 § 2403, 110 Stat. 3009 (Sept. 30, 1996).

take an explicit first step to initiate the transaction in order for the business to have a legitimate permissible use of a consumer report.

Thus, the business transaction provision does not permit consumer reports to be used for marketing purposes. The older language, it was sometimes argued, allowed access to consumer reports for target marketing purposes.[226] The current requirement that the consumer initiate the transaction clarifies that solicitations are not a permissible business transaction purpose. A separate provision, governing "credit or insurance transactions that are *not* initiated by the consumer" (used for prescreening firm offers of credit or insurance) is the only provision that permits limited use of consumer reports for the purposes of marketing.[227]

The question that most commonly arises is determining *when* has a transaction been initiated, or put another way, at what point does a user have a permissible purpose for requesting a consumer report. Consumers' mere inquiries about prices and product availability, comparison shopping, or asking if financing is available do not constitute the initiation of a transaction.[228] FTC staff has opined that even when a consumer asks to take a test drive, the car dealer does not have a permissible purpose for obtaining a consumer report.[229] Once a consumer has made an offer that requires credit, however, the transaction has been initiated.[230]

7.2.8.2.4 Legitimate business need

Even if the consumer has initiated a business transaction, the user must still have "a legitimate business need" for the report. As FTC staff has pointed out, a car dealer has no legitimate need for a consumer report in order to negotiate a cash sale.[231] In order to obtain a report in connection with a cash sale, the dealer would need the consumer's authorization.[232] Similarly, a landlord has no permissible business purpose to access a consumer report on a tenant who is entitled to lease renewal without regard to her creditworthiness.[233] On the other hand, a court has found that a grandfather had a legitimate business need to review his granddaughter's consumer report, after he cosigned a car loan for her, to determine if she had stolen his identity and was the cause of his low credit score.[234]

7.2.8.3 Business Need to Review a Consumer's Account

Even if the consumer has not initiated a new transaction, businesses and others who hold consumer accounts have a permissible purpose to obtain a consumer report if they have a legitimate business need "to review an account to determine whether the consumer continues to meet the terms of the account."[235] The user does not have to be a creditor and can be anyone with consumer accounts.[236] (In fact, a creditor has a permissible purpose to obtain a consumer report to review a credit account under the permissible use relating to credit.[237]) The principal effect of this separate provision is to extend the right to use consumer reports to a review of deposit and other non-credit accounts.[238]

The purpose of the review must be to determine whether the consumer "continues to meet the terms of the account."[239] Reviews frequently occur when creditors seek to determine whether an account should be retained or closed out, or whether to modify current terms for the account. For example, if the consumer is experiencing other credit problems, a creditor may seek additional security or reduce or eliminate a line of credit. Conversely, if the consumer has an improved credit history or increased income, a creditor may offer to increase available credit. Insurers may review their customers' consumer reports for similar reasons. Banks managing checking accounts, investment firms, and landlords may have reason to obtain consumer reports under this provision.

As with transactions initiated by the consumer, consumer reports may be used under the account review provision only if there is a "legitimate business need."[240] One may not obtain reports on consumers who are not their customers or when the transaction has been terminated. For example, a

---

226 See § 7.3.4, *infra*.
227 15 U.S.C. § 1681b(c). See § 7.4.8, *infra*.
228 See Coffey, FTC Informal Staff Opinion Letter (Feb. 11, 1998), *reprinted on the CD-Rom accompanying this manual*; Foster, FTC Informal Staff Opinion Letter (Sept. 2, 1998), *reprinted on the CD-Rom accompanying this manual*. Contra Anderson v. Ray Brandt Nissan, Inc., 1991 U.S. Dist. LEXIS 14550 (E.D. La. Oct. 8, 1991) (predates 1996 FCRA amendments).
229 Coffey, FTC Informal Staff Opinion Letter (Feb. 11, 1998), *reprinted on the CD-Rom accompanying this manual*.
230 See Uhlig v. Berge Ford, Inc., 257 F. Supp. 2d 1228 (D. Ariz. 2003). Note, however, that an offer may be conditioned with the understanding that a consumer report will not be used. *See id.*; Scott v. Real Estate Fin. Group, 183 F.3d 97 (2d Cir. 1999).
231 Shibley, FTC Informal Staff Opinion Letter (June 8, 1999), *reprinted on the CD-Rom accompanying this manual* (no right to obtain consumer report on a patient on a free office visit); Coffey, FTC Informal Staff Opinion Letter (Feb. 11, 1998), *reprinted on the CD-Rom accompanying this manual*.
232 See § 7.2.2, *supra*.

233 Ali v. Vikar Mgmt. Ltd., 994 F. Supp. 492 (S.D.N.Y. 1998).
234 Breese v. Triadvantage Credit Servs., Inc., 393 F. Supp. 2d 819 (D. Minn. 2005). While the grandfather's legitimate need might be obvious, it is not clear that the transaction was one that qualified under this provision, since it did not involve eligibility and actually concerned identity theft separate and apart from the completed loan transaction. See § 7.2.8.2.1, *supra*.
235 15 U.S.C. § 1681b(a)(3)(F)(ii).
236 See § 2.3.6.11, *supra*.
237 See § 5.2.4, *supra*.
238 Stonehart v. Rosenthal, 2001 U.S. Dist. LEXIS 11566 (S.D.N.Y. Aug. 13, 2001) (the underlying unpaid account need not be a credit account in order for user to have permissible purpose); Gowen, FTC Informal Staff Opinion Letter (Apr. 29, 1999), *reprinted on the CD-Rom accompanying this manual*.
239 15 U.S.C. § 1681b(a)(3)(F)(ii).
240 See § 7.2.8.2.4, *supra*.

§ 7.2.9 *Fair Credit Reporting*

debt collector may not review accounts for the purpose of identifying defaults and to solicit the creditors for business.[241] Nor may an automobile dealer obtain a consumer report after the transaction has been finalized, just because it wrote up the terms more favorably than it meant to and is looking for an excuse to change it.[242]

When Congress added the subsection permitting consumer reports to be used for reviewing accounts, the legislative history made clear that this permissible purpose does not permit access to consumer report information for the purpose of offering unrelated products or services.[243] The provision also does not provide authority for using a consumer report in litigation if authority to do so does not otherwise exist.[244]

7.2.9 Use by Officials to Determine Child Support Payment Levels

Two separate provisions permit government agencies to obtain consumer reports for use in connection with determining ability to pay and the appropriate level of child support awards. The first allows releases to child support enforcement agencies, which may be state or local.[245] The second applies to the single state agency that administers the federal child support enforcement state plan.[246]

Under the first provision, the head of a state or local child support enforcement agency, or an official authorized by the head, may obtain a consumer report by certifying:

- The report is needed to determine the capacity to make, or the level of, child support payments;
- Paternity has been established or acknowledged by the consumer;
- The consumer has been provided at least ten-days' notice that the report will be requested, by certified or registered mail to the consumer's last known address; and
- The report will be kept confidential, and will not be used in connection with any other purpose, including other civil, administrative, or criminal proceedings.[247]

Thus, reports may be released under this provision only for the purposes of determining the parent's ability to pay support and at what level. However, if a child support order has been entered, the child support enforcement agency may also obtain consumer reports for collection purposes under the general provision permitting release of reports for purposes of collecting a credit account, discussed above.[248] If the agency operates under that provision, it need not provide the certification or notice required under the child support enforcement provision.[249]

In addition to the child support enforcement agency, an agency administering a state plan under Title IV-D of the Social Security Act[250] may obtain a consumer report to set an initial child support award or to later modify it.[251] Generally speaking, in order for states to receive certain federal monies related to the provision of public benefits, states must have a child support enforcement plan. Most, if not all, states have such plans. The FCRA allows releases of consumer reports to the administering agency and does not require the certification under the separate provision described above, though the report may only be used for setting or modifying the award level. Prior to the amendment permitting this public agency use of consumer reports, a child support agency seeking to establish the duty to pay child support did not have a permissible purpose for obtaining a consumer report.[252]

7.2.10 Other Permissible Uses by Government Agencies

7.2.10.1 Introduction

Although the permissible purposes section of the FCRA states that consumer reports may be released under the listed circumstances "and no other,"[253] the FCRA actually contains a smattering of provisions elsewhere in the Act that authorize various releases to and uses by government agencies.

7.2.10.2 Identifying Information Furnished to the Government

Even if a government agency does not have a permissible purpose described by the Act, a CRA may furnish certain

---

241 Long, FTC Informal Staff Opinion Letter (July 6, 2000), *reprinted on the CD-Rom accompanying this manual*; Benner, FTC Informal Staff Opinion Letter (Apr. 30, 1999), *reprinted on the CD-Rom accompanying this manual*; Levine v. World Fin. Network Nat'l Bank, 473 F.3d 1118 (11th Cir. 2006).

242 Smith v. Bob Smith Chevrolet, Inc., 275 F. Supp. 2d 808 (W.D. Ky. 2003).

243 S. Rep. No. 185, 104th Cong., 1st Sess. at 35 (Dec. 14, 1995); Fed. Trade Comm'n v. Citigroup Inc., 239 F. Supp. 2d 1302 (N.D. Ga. 2001) (denying motion to dismiss allegations that Associates used or obtained consumer reports for impermissible purposes of soliciting additional loan products or to solicit the consumer for a credit transaction that the consumer did not initiate).

244 Long, FTC Staff Opinion Letter (July 6, 2000), *reprinted on the CD-Rom accompanying this manual*.

245 15 U.S.C. § 1681b(a)(4). *See also* § 2.3.6.9, *supra*.

246 15 U.S.C. § 1681b(a)(5).

247 15 U.S.C. § 1681b(a)(4).

248 *See* § 7.2.3.4, *supra*. *See also* § 7.4.2, *infra*.

249 Hasbun v. County of Los Angeles, 323 F.3d 801 (9th Cir. 2003).

250 42 U.S.C. § 654.

251 15 U.S.C. § 1681b(a)(5).

252 FTC Official Staff Commentary § 604(3)(A) item 3, *reprinted at* Appx. D, *infra*.

253 15 U.S.C. § 1681b(a).

"identifying information" short of a full consumer report to governmental agencies.[254] This information is the consumer's name, address, former addresses, places of employment, or former places of employment.[255] A government agency without an otherwise permissible purpose cannot obtain information beyond that specified above.[256]

The term governmental agency includes federal, state, county, and municipal agencies, and grand juries, but not non-governmental entities.[257] A private investigator, for example, cannot receive identifying information under this provision.[258]

A question exists whether identifying information may be furnished to a government agency, when disclosure of the identifying information would also imply negative information. For example, the FTC staff construes as consumer reports the identifying information contained in lists which include only individuals who are in financial difficulty, since the list would also reflect on the individuals' character, reputation, and personal characteristics.[259] Where any list is being furnished that contains only the names and addresses of individuals who fall into a certain category, for example from a CRA which reports only on those who have previously been fired for cause, then practitioners should argue that this list of identifying information may be furnished to the government only if it can certify that it has a permissible purpose for the list beyond the release of identifying information.

7.2.10.3 Investigation of FCRA Violations

The FCRA provides the FTC with investigational powers concerning FCRA violations, including the power to require the production of documents.[260] This gives the FTC the power to subpoena consumer reports in connection with any investigation under the Fair Credit Reporting Act.[261] Other federal agencies with enforcement authority under the FCRA should have the same power,[262] as should state officials with authority under state "little FCRA" statutes.[263]

7.2.10.4 Permissible Use by FBI for Counterintelligence Purposes

The FCRA grants the FBI access to three different types of consumer information from CRAs if the FBI[264] certifies that the information is "sought for the conduct of an authorized investigation to protect against international terrorism or clandestine intelligence activities, provided that such an investigation of an United States person is not conducted solely upon the basis of activities protected by the first amendment to the Constitution of the United States."[265] The 2001 USA PATRIOT Act removed the earlier requirement that the information be "necessary" to the investigation.[266]

Note that a separate provision, discussed in § 7.2.10.5, *infra*, gives additional authority to federal governmental agencies generally, including the FBI, for investigations related to international terrorism.

Under the FBI-specific provision, the FBI may first obtain the names and addresses of all financial institutions at which a consumer maintains or has maintained an account.[267]

Second, the FBI may obtain identifying information on the consumer, limited to name, address, former addresses, places of employment, or former places of employment.[268]

Third, the FBI may obtain a full consumer report by an *ex parte*, *in camera*, application to a court. The court order itself may not disclose that it is issued for purposes of a counterintelligence investigation.

Information obtained by the FBI pursuant to these purposes may not be disseminated further except to other federal agencies as a necessary part of the investigation or except to the military as appropriate and necessary for the conduct of a joint investigation.

---

254 15 U.S.C. § 1681f; FTC Official Staff Commentary § 608 item 1, *reprinted at* Appx. D, *infra*. Special rules sometimes apply to requests for information from the FBI made for counterintelligence purposes. *See* § 7.2.10.4, *infra*.

255 FTC Official Staff Commentary § 608 item 1, *reprinted at* Appx. D, *infra*.

256 Soghomonian v. U.S., 278 F. Supp. 2d 1151 (E.D. Cal. 2003) (rejecting argument that "may" is permissive; instead, it is limiting); FTC Official Staff Commentary § 608 item 1, *reprinted at* Appx. D, *infra*. *See* Pub. L. No. 90-321, § 502 (May 29, 1968), 82 Stat. 146, 147, reported as a note following 15 U.S.C. § 1601 (the Consumer Credit Protection Act), which provides in pertinent part: "(1) The word 'may' is used to indicate that an action either is authorized or is permitted. (2) The word 'shall' is used to indicate that an action is both authorized and required. (3) The phrase 'may not' is used to indicate that an action is both unauthorized and forbidden. (4) Rules of law are stated in the indicative mood."

257 *Id.*

258 Grimes, FTC Informal Staff Opinion Letter (Sept. 11, 1975), *reprinted on the CD-Rom accompanying this manual*.

259 White, FTC Informal Staff Opinion Letter (Nov. 24, 1976), *reprinted on the CD-Rom accompanying this manual. See also* Petruccelli, FTC Informal Staff Opinion Letter (Apr. 9, 1984), *reprinted on the CD-Rom accompanying this manual*; Muris, FTC Informal Staff Opinion Letter (Apr. 29, 1982), *reprinted on the CD-Rom accompanying this manual*.

260 15 U.S.C. § 1681s(a).

261 Fed. Trade Comm'n v. Manager, Retail Credit Co., Miami Branch Office, 515 F.2d 988 (D.C. Cir. 1975). *See also* Fed. Trade Comm'n v. TRW Inc., 628 F.2d 207 (D.C. Cir. 1980); FTC Official Staff Commentary § 622 item 4, *reprinted at* Appx. D, *infra*.

262 *See* FTC Official Staff Commentary § 622 item 4, *reprinted at* Appx. D, *infra*.

263 *Id.* See Appx. H, *infra*, for a summary of state credit reporting laws.

264 The certification must be made by the director or the director's designee "in a position not lower than Deputy Assistant Director at Bureau headquarters or a Special Agent in Charge of a Bureau field office."

265 15 U.S.C. § 1681u(a), (b), (c).

266 USA PATRIOT Act, Pub. L. No. 107-56, 115 Stat. 272 (2001).

267 15 U.S.C. § 1681u(a).

268 15 U.S.C. § 1681u(b).

§ 7.2.10.5   Fair Credit Reporting

If a federal agency violates this section, the consumer may claim statutory damages of one hundred dollars in addition to actual and punitive damages and attorney fees.[269] Injunctive relief is also available.[270]

If the FBI certifies that confidentiality is necessary, then the fact that the FBI has accessed CRA files may not be reported to anyone except those persons necessary to comply with the request or an attorney to obtain legal advice about the request.[271] The CRA also may not include in any consumer report information that would indicate that the FBI has sought information on a consumer report.

7.2.10.5 Disclosures to Governmental Agencies for Counterterrorism Purposes

The FCRA requires CRAs to provide consumer reports and any other information in a consumer's file to a federal government agency authorized to conduct investigations, intelligence or counterintelligence, or analysis related to international terrorism.[272] The federal agency must present the CRA with a certification that the information "is necessary" for the agency's activities.[273]

This provision is in addition to the separate provision authorizing FBI access to consumer information, discussed in § 7.2.10.4, *supra*. That provision does not require certification that the information is "necessary," though it does require court approval, *ex parte*, if the FBI seeks a full consumer report. The general counterterrorism provision does not require court approval. The FBI may operate under either provision.[274]

The CRA may not disclose the fact that a government agency has sought information under this section.[275]

Unlike the FBI provision, the counterterrorism provision does not contain a section providing damages or attorney fees for violations.

A CRA that discloses information to a government agency under this provision in good faith reliance on the agency's certification may not be held liable for the disclosure.[276]

7.3 Permissible Uses of Consumer Lists

7.3.1 General

Users often seek from consumer reporting agencies (CRAs) lists of consumers with certain relevant characteristics, or lists which specify the varying characteristics of individuals on the list. Many, but not all, of these lists are considered to be a series of consumer reports on each consumer on the list. If the list is considered to be series of consumer reports, the user must have a permissible purpose for every consumer on the list.

The permissible purposes discussed above[277] are the only ones permitting access to a full consumer report. However, lists of consumers containing limited information—little more than names and addresses, prescreened based on credit criteria supplied by the requester—may be released for one additional purpose: making a "firm offer of credit or insurance."[278]

As discussed below, a firm offer is often not very firm, and this provision has created a major exception to the general rule that consumer lists may not be used for marketing purposes. Prescreening is a common source of junk mail. It is at the heart of all the literally billions of pre-approved credit card solicitations that inundate many households.[279]

7.3.2 When a List Is a Consumer Report Requiring a Permissible Purpose

7.3.2.1 General

A list of consumers is considered to be a series of consumer reports on each individual named on the list if the list meets the general definition of "consumer report": that is, the list bears on "a consumer's credit worthiness, credit standing, credit capacity, character, general reputation, personal characteristics, or mode of living" and is collected, used, or expected to be used for the purpose of establishing the consumer's eligibility for credit, insurance, employment, or another permissible purpose set forth in the FCRA.[280]

Lists of consumers that meet the definition of consumer reports are prohibited, unless at the time the list is furnished to the user, the user has a permissible purpose to obtain the information about *every* consumer on the list.[281] Except in the prescreening context, discussed in § 7.3.4, *infra*, this generally requires the user to be involved in a transaction with each consumer.

---

269   15 U.S.C. § 1681u(i).
270   15 U.S.C. § 1681u(m).
271   15 U.S.C. § 1681u(d).
272   15 U.S.C. § 1681v.
273   15 U.S.C. § 1681v(a).
274   15 U.S.C. § 1681v(d).
275   15 U.S.C. § 1681v(c).
276   15 U.S.C. § 1681v(e).

277   See § 7.2, *supra*.
278   15 U.S.C. § 1681b(c)(1)(B)(i). *See also* 1681a(l).
279   Neal Walters, *The Fair Credit Reporting Act: Issues and Policies*, AARP Public Policy Institute Issue Brief No. 58, at 2 (Jan. 2003) (in 2000, 3.5 billion prescreened offers sent to consumers based on lists created by CRAs).
280   15 U.S.C. § 1681a(d); FTC Official Staff Commentary § 603(d) item 4B, *reprinted at* Appx. D, *infra* (credit guides); FTC Official Staff Commentary § 604(3)(A) items 6 (prescreening lists) and 8 (uncoded credit guides), *reprinted at* Appx. D, *infra*.
281   FTC Official Staff Commentary § 604(3)(A) item 8, *reprinted at* Appx. D, *infra*.

7.3.2.2 Credit Guides

Thus, "credit guides" (frequently used before enactment of the FCRA), containing the names and credit ratings of large numbers of consumers, are consumer lists. Credit granters would collect these lists in the expectation that at some time in the future they might have a transaction with some of the consumers on the list.

The FTC, in a formal interpretation, found such lists illegal.[282] Thus creditors have no permissible use for lists of consumers who have passed uncollectible checks[283] or who have delinquent accounts with any creditor.[284] There is no permissible use for bulletins designed to protect potential creditors from consumers with bad credit histories,[285] or even for lists of creditworthy individuals.[286]

A discussed below,[287] however, coded credit guides may be provided as long as a consumer's identity is not decoded until the creditor has a permissible purpose concerning that consumer.

7.3.2.3 Coded Lists

Lists are not considered to be a series of consumer reports if they are coded so that the consumer's identity is not disclosed and is not decoded until the user has a permissible purpose involving that consumer.[288] For example, the list is not a series of consumer reports, according to the FTC, if the list does not include the consumers' names, but only identification based on the consumers' Social Security numbers, driver's license numbers, or bank account numbers.[289] Demonstrating how far this non-statutory exception has been stretched, in one coding scheme the list contained the first letter of the consumer's middle name, the surname, numbers of the street address, state, the last four digits of the consumer's driver's license and Social Security number, followed by the last five digits of his or her checking account number.[290]

The list becomes a series of consumer reports when the list is decoded.[291] At that time, the user must have a permissible purpose for each report (i.e., on each individual) that is decoded. For example, a CRA might provide a user with a list of individual coded bad check writers. The CRA also provides the user with additional information to "break" the code. This is permissible as long as the user does not break the code on an individual until that individual seeks to write a check with that creditor.[292]

7.3.2.4 Target Marketing Lists

CRAs compile and sell many kinds of mailing lists to retailers to use to solicit business from consumers. These so-called target marketing lists compete with thousands of other mailing lists of consumers sold by every imaginable kind of business.

Target marketing lists, like any other type of list, constitute consumer reports if they bear on creditworthiness[293] and are compiled from information collected, used, or expected to be used for the purpose of determining credit eligibility or other FCRA purposes. Target marketing lists are not restricted by the FCRA if they do not meet the FCRA's definition of consumer report.

The issue is trickier if the information was collected by a CRA, which presumably collects most of its information for consumer reporting purposes, even if not all of the information bears on creditworthiness. The FTC has distinguished between (1) the use of generic identification information to generate mailing lists, and (2) lists compiled from credit information (and presumably employment or insurance information) used as a factor in determining a consumer's eligibility for credit. Lists compiled from generic data,

---

282 *See also* FTC Official Staff Commentary § 603(d) item 4B, *reprinted at* Appx. D, *infra*; FTC Official Staff Commentary § 604(3)(A) item 8, *reprinted at* Appx. D, *infra*; Silbergeld, FTC Informal Staff Opinion Letter (Apr. 1, 1975), *reprinted on the CD-Rom accompanying this manual*; FTC Informal Staff Opinion Letter [1969–1973 Decisions Transfer Binder] Consumer Cred. Guide (CCH) ¶¶ 99,484 (Apr. 15, 1971), 99,531 (Mar. 26, 1971).

283 FTC Official Staff Commentary § 603(d) item 6E, *reprinted at* Appx. D, *infra*; Greenway v. Information Dynamics, Ltd., 399 F. Supp. 1092 (D. Ariz. 1974), *aff'd per curiam*, 524 F.2d 1145 (9th Cir. 1975); Howard Enterprises, Inc., 93 F.T.C. 909 (1979). *See also* Moore & Assocs., Inc., 92 F.T.C. 440 (Aug. 18, 1978) (consent order).

284 FTC Informal Staff Opinion Letter [1969–1973 Decisions Transfer Binder] Consumer Cred. Guide (CCH) ¶ 99,531 (Mar. 26, 1971).

285 Silbergeld, FTC Informal Staff Opinion Letter (Apr. 1, 1971), *reprinted on the CD-Rom accompanying this manual. Cf.* Martin, FTC Informal Staff Opinion Letter (May 26, 1971), *reprinted on the CD-Rom accompanying this manual* (lists of liens and mortgages prohibited).

286 FTC Official Staff Commentary § 603(d) item 4D, *reprinted at* Appx. D, *infra*. *See also* Carson, FTC Informal Staff Opinion Letter (Apr. 15, 1971) [1969–1973 Decisions Transfer Binder] Consumer Cred. Guide (CCH) ¶ 99,484.

287 *See* § 7.3.2.3, *infra*.

288 FTC Official Staff Commentary § 603(d) item 4B, *reprinted at* Appx. D, *infra*. *See also id.* § 604(3)(A) item 8.

289 FTC Official Staff Commentary § 603(d) item 4B, *reprinted at* Appx. D, *infra*.

290 *See* FTC Informal Staff Opinion Letter, [1980–1989 Decisions Transfer Binder] Consumer Cred. Guide (CCH) ¶ 96,733 (Dec. 10, 1982).

291 FTC Official Staff Commentary § 603(d) item 4B, *reprinted at* Appx. D, *infra*.

292 *See* FTC Informal Staff Opinion Letter, [1980–1989 Decisions Transfer Binder] Consumer Cred. Guide (CCH) ¶ 96,733 (Dec. 10, 1982).

293 A marketing list would presumably also qualify as a consumer list if it bears on character, general reputation, personal characteristics, or mode of living and is compiled for FCRA purposes. *See* 15 U.S.C. § 1681a(d)(1).

§ 7.3.3 *Fair Credit Reporting*

which does not bear on creditworthiness, are not consumer reports; lists compiled from information bearing on creditworthiness are.

Thus, in a settlement with TRW (now Experian) in the early 1990s, the FTC permitted TRW to freely use names, telephone numbers, mother's maiden names, addresses, zip codes, years of birth, ages, generational definitions, Social Security numbers, and "substantially similar" identifiers to compile lists of consumers for marketing purposes.[294] The FTC considers target marketing lists based on such generic data to be outside the scope of FCRA, and FCRA restrictions do not apply.[295]

TransUnion went much further. It compiled lists from information collected and used by retailers in determining creditworthiness. That is, the lists reflected specific credit-based factors such as number of car loans, open credit card accounts and credit limits, presence of second mortgages, and/or credit scores.[296] These lists were heavily marketed to send catalogues, sweepstakes promotions, product offers, and invitations to apply for services (goods and services that are not offers of credit or insurance under the prescreening exception).

The FTC found that the TransUnion lists were consumer reports and prohibited TransUnion from selling them because target marking is not a permissible purpose.[297] The District of Columbia Court of Appeals upheld the decision, finding substantial evidence that the TransUnion lists were consumer reports because they were based on information—including the consumer's credit limits, open dates of loans, number of tradelines,[298] type of tradeline and existence of a tradeline—that is used in credit scoring and credit making decisions.[299]

7.3.3 No FCRA Restriction Where List Not Collected or Used for FCRA Purpose

Lists which are not used or collected for evaluating consumers for credit, insurance, employment, or other permissible purposes, and which do not bear on creditworthiness or other FCRA factors, are not consumer reports and are not subject to the Act.[300] Examples may include telephone directories, lists of individuals with checking accounts, lists used only for law enforcement purposes, lists used for target marketing that do not bear on creditworthiness (i.e., mailing lists), and trade directories, such as lists of insurance agents.[301] However, the issue is a factual one which must be resolved based on the expected and actual uses of the lists.

The FTC Staff Commentary declares that protective bulletins listing alleged criminals who are wanted by law enforcement agencies are not consumer reports if they include only limited information about the named individuals, such as physical descriptions or photographs and the alleged criminal violations.[302] Therefore, such bulletins are not subject to the requirements of the Act.[303]

There also appears to have been a Congressional intent not to include protective bulletins issued by local hotel and motel associations circulated only to members and dealing solely with transactions between the individuals and association members.[304]

The publisher of a directory rating the legal abilities of listed lawyers was found not to be dealing in information concerning the individuals' credit, general reputation, personal characteristics or mode of living, and so was found not to be distributing "consumer reports" subject to the Act.[305]

Although the FCRA may not prohibit a CRA from reporting lists that do not involve consumer reports, if the information on the list falls within the Gramm-Leach-Bliley

---

294 Fed. Trade Comm'n v. TRW, Inc., (Dec. 10, 1991) (Agreed Order Amending Consent Decree), *reprinted on the CD-Rom accompanying this manual.*

295 *See* § 2.3.4, *supra.* The D.C. Court of Appeals has noted a potential inconsistency between the FTC's position on the TRW lists and the TransUnion lists, since factors such as age and use of a post office box, permitted on the TRW lists, also bear on creditworthiness, personal characteristics, or mode of living, 15 U.S.C. § 1681a(d)(1), and serve as a factor bearing on eligibility for credit. Trans Union Corp. v. Fed. Trade Comm'n, 245 F.3d 809, 816–817 (D.C. Cir. 2001). The court refused, however, to resolve the inconsistency.

296 *In re* Trans Union Corp., No. 9255 (F.T.C. 1998), *reprinted on the CD-Rom accompanying this manual.*

297 *In re* Trans Union Corp., No. 9255 (F.T.C. Feb. 10, 2000) (final order). *See also In re* Trans Union Corp., No. 9255 (F.T.C. 1998), *reprinted on the CD-Rom accompanying this manual.* In Trans Union Corp. v. Fed. Trade Comm'n, 81 F.3d 228 (D.C. Cir. 1996), the appeals court agreed with the FTC that such target marketing lists do not serve a legitimate business purpose under the FCRA, but remanded the case to the FTC for a factual determination of whether Trans Union's reports actually do convey information used by credit grantors in eligibility determinations.

298 A tradeline contains information about the status and history of a consumer's account with a company. A tradeline typically includes the name of the company, account type, opening date of account, credit limit, account status, balance owed, and payment history.

299 Trans Union Corp. v. Fed. Trade Comm'n, 245 F.3d 809, 815 (D.C. Cir. 2001). The court also rejected TransUnion's arguments that the Commission's ruling violated the First and Fifth Amendments of the U.S. Constitution. *Id.* at 817–818.

300 *See* § 2.3.4, *supra.*

301 FTC Official Staff Commentary § 603(d) item 5B, *reprinted at* Appx. D, *infra. See also* Grimes, FTC Informal Staff Opinion Letter (Jan. 22, 1991), *reprinted on the CD-Rom accompanying this manual.*

302 *See* § 2.3.4, *supra* for a more detailed discussion.

303 FTC Official Staff Commentary § 603(d) item 5A, *reprinted at* Appx. D, *infra.*

304 Conf. Rep. No. 1587, 91st Cong., 2d Sess. (1970), *reprinted in* 1970 U.S.C.C.A.N. 4394, 4411, 4415.

305 Bergen v. Martindale-Hubbell, Inc., 337 S.E.2d 770 (Ga. Ct. App. 1985).

Act's definition of nonpublic personal information,[306] it may be protected from disclosure by that Act.[307]

7.3.4 Lists for Prescreening "Firm Offers" of Credit or Insurance

7.3.4.1 General

The FCRA permits CRAs to furnish lists containing limited consumer information, short of a full consumer report, for purposes of making a "firm offer of credit or insurance."[308] The title of this section of the FCRA refers to "credit or insurance transaction that are not initiated by the consumer,"[309] but in the popular vernacular, it is simply called prescreening. Although the formal title would suggest something more, the terms in the title are defined elsewhere to exclude the possibility that this section allows reports relating to a review of existing accounts or to the collection of an account.[310]

The Act allows prescreening for credit and insurance purposes only,[311] requires that a "firm offer" be made,[312] requires that the CRAs maintain a comprehensive system permitting consumers to elect to be excluded from pre-screened lists,[313] and imposes notice requirements on both the CRAs and users of prescreening lists.[314]

A CRA may supply only limited information for pre-screening purposes. The user can receive little more than the name and the address of the consumer.[315] An identifier may be provided, but it must not be unique to the consumer, such as a Social Security number, and is to be used solely for the purpose of verifying the identity of the consumer. Other information about the consumer may be provided, but it must not identify the relationship or the experience of the consumer with a particular creditor, insurer, or other entity.

The user may obtain a full consumer report, under the separate credit or insurance provisions, only after a particular consumer has responded to an offer.

State laws relating to the creation and use of prescreened reports are preempted.[316]

7.3.4.2 Prescreened Lists Are a Type of Consumer Report

Prescreening is the process whereby CRAs compile or edit lists of consumers who meet specific criteria, and then provide the lists to the user or third party (such as a mailing service), who uses the lists to solicit consumers with a firm offer for the users' products or services, usually by mail.[317]

The lists are often compiled by using a search algorithm on the CRA's database to identify consumers who meet the special criteria approved by the user. The process may also include demographic or other analysis of the consumers on the list (e.g., use of census tract data reflecting real estate values) by the CRA or by a third party employed for that purpose (either by the CRA or its client) before the list sent to the client.[318]

In prescreening, the user may provide the list to the CRA, who then edits out those who the CRA's own files indicate have a credit problem, or the CRA may generate its own lists from its own files, using criteria agreed to specified by the user. The process may also include demographic or other analysis of the consumers on the list.[319] The CRA might provide multiple lists, each with different levels of credit-worthiness or insurability criteria, with the user planning on making different offers to those on the different lists.[320]

The prescreened list is a series of consumer reports because the list conveys information on each individual's creditworthiness or insurability.[321] The permissible purpose is in connection with a credit or insurance transaction involving the consumer.[322] Nevertheless, the list is not coded because the user wishes to mail an offer to individuals on the list. As a result, the user will have to show that its permissible purpose of extending credit or underwriting insurance applies to each individual on the list. Otherwise the user will be receiving consumer reports on some individuals with no permissible purpose.

---

306 Pub. L. No. 106-102, § 509(4); 16 C.F.R. § 313.3(p). See § 16.4.1.4, *infra*.
307 See § 2.3.4.2.2, *supra*.
308 15 U.S.C. § 1681b(c)(1)(B)(i). See 15 U.S.C. § 1681a(l) (defining "firm offer of credit or insurance").
309 The phrase "credit or insurance transaction that is not initiated by the consumer" is used throughout the legislation to "describe prescreening transactions." S. Rep. No. 104-186, 104th Cong., 1st Sess. at 33 (1995).
310 15 U.S.C. § 1681a(m). Another section in this chapter discuss permissible purposes for reviewing or collecting accounts. See § 7.2.3.4, *supra*.
311 15 U.S.C. § 1681b(c), (e).
312 15 U.S.C. § 1681b(c)(1)(B)(i). See § 7.3.4.3, *infra*.
313 15 U.S.C. § 1681b(e). See § 7.3.4.4, *infra*.
314 15 U.S.C. §§ 1681b(e). See §§ 7.3.4.4, 8.2.9, *infra*.
315 15 U.S.C. § 1681b(c)(2).

316 15 U.S.C. § 1681t(b)(1)(A); Kennedy v. Chase Manhattan Bank, 369 F.3d 833 (5th Cir. 2004). See § 10.7, *infra*.
317 Cole v. U.S. Capital, Inc., 389 F.3d 719 (7th Cir. 2004); Gamble v. Citifinancial, 2002 WL 31643028 (D. Conn. 2002); FTC Official Staff Commentary § 604(3)(A) item 6, *reprinted at* Appx. D, *infra*.
318 *Id.*
319 FTC Official Staff Commentary § 604(3)(A) item 6, *reprinted at* Appx. D, *infra*.
320 *Id.*
321 *Id. See also In re* Trans Union Corp., Dkt. No. 9255 (F.T.C. Mar. 1, 2000) (final order) (tradeline information in target marketing lists qualified as consumer report because contained information lenders would use in evaluating credit eligibility, including the fact that a consumer had a credit relationship with a creditor, and the consumer's age).
322 FTC Official Staff Commentary § 604(3)(A) item 6, *reprinted at* Appx. D, *infra*.

7.3.4.3 A "Firm Offer" Is Required

A CRA may provide a prescreened list of consumers only if the user makes a so-called "firm offer" of credit or insurance to each consumer on the list, or if the consumer authorizes a CRA to include the consumer's name and address on prescreening lists. A firm offer is necessary in the logic of the statute because the report can be used only in connection with a consumer transaction. Having a firm offer apparently is close enough.

A "firm offer" does not have to be very firm. Earlier standards of the FTC Staff Commentary[323] have been loosened by the Consumer Credit Reporting Reform Act of 1996 (1996 Reform Act) amendments.[324] As one court noted, "the Act permits a creditor to make a 'conditional' firm offer of credit. . . . [A] a 'firm offer' really means a 'firm offer if you meet certain criteria.'"[325] The general rule is that the offer is considered "firm" if it will be honored as long as, based on the information in the consumer report, the consumer meets the criteria specified for the prescreening list.[326] However, the FCRA's definition of firm offer is qualified by three contingencies.[327]

First, the user may require the consumer to submit an application demonstrating that the consumer meets the user's specific criteria "bearing on credit worthiness or insurability."[328] These criteria must be established before selection of the consumer for the offer and be for the purpose of determining whether to extend credit or insurance pursuant to the offer.[329] It appears that the user may specify one set of criteria for generating the prescreened lists of consumers to receive the offer, and a different set of criteria for evaluating the consumer's application, as long as both criteria are established before the consumers are selected.[330]

Second, the user may retain the right to verify that the consumer meets the criteria used to select the prescreening list.[331] Verification may be based on: information in a consumer report, presumably a full consumer report, not the truncated prescreened report; information in the consumer's application for credit or insurance; or on other information bearing on creditworthiness or insurability.[332]

The third condition that a user may place on the "firm offer" is that the consumer must provide sufficient collateral for the offered credit or insurance.[333] The collateral requirement must be established before selecting the consumer for the offer and be disclosed to the consumer in the offer.[334]

These conditions, especially those allowing required application and verification, pose the threat of blurring the distinction between solicitations with firm offers and those without.

In addition, courts have generally concluded that "sham" offers—those that provide no meaningful benefit to consumers in exchange for giving up statutorily protected privacy rights in consumer reports—are not "firm offers."[335] An offer of credit without value, which is not expected to be accepted, is the equivalent of an advertisement or solicitation, which is not a purpose for which consumer reports may be used.

The Seventh Circuit has found that an offer of a minimum of $300 in credit to buy a car at interest rates anywhere from 2.9% to 24.9% had no real value to the consumer and was not a firm offer.[336] The court rejected the argument that an offer of credit can be of any amount, however nominal, concluding that such a definition would eviscerate the statutory purpose behind the FCRA to protect consumer data and privacy. Rather, the "*entire* offer and the effect of *all* material conditions" must be considered, and if "the 'offer' was a guise for solicitation rather than a legitimate credit product, the communication cannot be considered a firm offer of credit."[337]

Other courts have found that similar flyers mailed to consumers also might not have value or be firm offers, especially if the offers fail to specify material terms such as credit amounts, interest rates, or repayment periods.[338]

On the other hand, a third Seventh Circuit panel found 2-1, over a strong dissent, that a credit card offer had value even though the card was admittedly not an attractive deal for "the great majority" of consumers.[339] The defendant offered a credit card with a $250 credit limit and with $184

---

323 FTC Official Staff Commentary § 604(3)(A) item 6, *reprinted at* Appx. D, *infra*; Grimes, FTC Informal Staff Opinion Letter (July 8, 1993), *reprinted on the CD-Rom accompanying this manual*; Grimes, FTC Informal Staff Opinion Letter (Aug. 1, 1990), *reprinted on the CD-Rom accompanying this manual*.
324 FCRA § 603(*l*), 15 U.S.C. § 1681a(*l*), *as amended by* Pub. L. No. 104-208 § 2402, 110 Stat. 3009 (Sept. 30, 1996).
325 Kennedy v. Chase Manhattan Bank, 369 F.3d 833 (5th Cir. 2004).
326 15 U.S.C. § 1681a(l).
327 15 U.S.C. § 1681a(l).
328 15 U.S.C. § 1681a(l)1.
329 15 U.S.C. § 1681a(l)(1)(A), (B).
330 Kennedy v. Chase Manhattan Bank USA, N.A., 369 F.3d 833 (5th Cir. 2004).
331 15 U.S.C. § 1681a(l)(2).
332 *Id.*
333 15 U.S.C. § 1681a(l)(3).
334 *Id.*
335 Cole v. U.S. Capital, Inc., 389 F.3d 719 (7th Cir. 2004); Hyde v. RDA, Inc., 389 F. Supp. 2d 658 (D. Md. 2005). *But see* Putkowski v. Irwin Home Equity Corp., 423 F. Supp. 2d 1053 (N.D. Cal. 2006). An amicus brief in support of the plaintiff in Cole is available at www.ftc.gov/ogc/briefs/cole.pdf and is reproduced on the accompanying CD-Rom.
336 Cole v. U.S. Capital, Inc., 389 F.3d 719 (7th Cir. 2004).
337 *Id.* at 728.
338 *See* Murray v. E*Trade Fin. Corp., 2006 WL 2054381 (N.D. Ill. July 19, 2006) (offer that specified rate of 1.99% for first three months but did not disclose subsequent rate was not firm offer); Hyde v. RDA, Inc., 389 F. Supp. 2d 658 (D. Md. 2005) (flyer from car dealer); Murray v. Flexpoint Funding Corp., 2005 WL 1463500 (N.D. Ill. June 17, 2005) (mortgage flyer); Murray v. Sunrise Chevrolet, 2005 WL 2284245 (N.D. Ill. Sept. 15, 2005) (flyer from car dealer).
339 Perry v. First National Bank, 459 F.3d 816 (7th Cir. 2006).

in fees for opening the account. The court noted that the offer did specify the material terms and might have value to a consumer who charged and paid off $250 in purchases each month and was trying to build up or reestablish credit. The dissent argued that anyone who could pay off the balance each month did not need credit, and that the offer was "an unconscionably one-side financial deal that defies a reasonable concept of sufficient value."[340]

Another court found that a similar offer, "while plainly a lousy deal," nonetheless had some value and was not a solicitation—even though the mailer included an unrelated solicitation to purchase membership in a club.[341] This approach appears to sanction access to consumer reports for purposes of prescreening offers that are neither firm nor credit, as long as the solicitation includes some kind of offer of credit, no mater how "lousy."

Whether or not an offer has value is determined by looking at the offer itself and its value to the "*normal consumer,*" not by the way in which individual consumers react.[342] Thus, courts have found class actions appropriate to challenge purported firm offers of credit,[343] and have found that discovery about the financial circumstances of the proposed class representatives is irrelevant to the issue of whether an offer has value.[344]

Note that a firm offer of credit may not be accompanied by a credit card; if it is, the issuer has violated the Truth in Lending Act's prohibition against unsolicited credit cards.[345]

One court has held that an offer does not lose its status as a firm offer of credit if it fails to include required disclosures about a consumer's right to be removed from marketing lists.[346]

7.3.4.4 Consumers Can Elect to Be Excluded from Prescreening Lists

Recognizing the intrusive nature of direct marketing campaigns, the FCRA gives consumers the right to remove their names from prescreening lists; requires CRAs to maintain a joint notification system for removing names from prescreening lists; and requires that both CRAs and users of prescreened lists notify consumers of their right to be removed and the procedures for doing so.[347]

Consumers may instruct a CRA to remove the consumer's name from prescreening lists either by calling or by submitting a signed notice of election form issued by the CRA.[348] If the consumer calls, the opt-out is effective for only five years.[349] A consumer who submits a proper, signed form should henceforth be excluded from prescreening permanently.[350] However, the consumer may notify the CRA at any time that the election is no longer effective. Indications are that consumers overwhelmingly choose to opt out permanently.[351]

The right to opt out of prescreening lists should not be confused with the right of consumers to opt out of the use of their information by affiliates for marketing purposes.[352] This right applies to information that falls outside of the FCRA's definition of consumer report—and would therefore be available for marketing purposes—pursuant to either the first-hand knowledge exception or the affiliate exception.[353]

The FCRA requires that each CRA that compiles prescreening lists create and maintain a notification system. The nationwide CRAs must operate a joint notification system, so that an opt-out notice to one is effectively an opt-out notice to all.[354] Similarly, notice to one CRA is effective for all affiliates of that same CRA.[355]

Each notification system must have a toll-free number consumers may call to opt out, and must advertise at least annually to inform consumers that prescreening occurs and that they may opt out by calling toll-free 888-567-8688 (888-5-OPT-OUT).[356]

If the consumer calls or writes to the notification system, and provides appropriate identification, the consumer should

---

340 *Id.* (Evans, dissenting).
341 Bonner v. Cortrust Bank, N.A., 2006 WL 1980183 (N.D. Ind. July 12, 2006).
342 Murray v. GMAC Mortgage Corp., 434 F.3d 948 (7th Cir. 2006) (vacating denial of class certification); White v. E-Loan, Inc., 2006 WL 2411420 (N.D. Cal. Aug. 18, 2006).
343 *Id.*
344 Hernandez v. Citifinancial Servs., Inc., 2006 WL 1749649 (N.D. Ill. June 21, 2006).
345 Munoz v. Seventh Avenue, Inc., 2004 WL 1593906 (N.D. Ill. July 15, 2004).
346 Murray v. Household Bank (SB), N.A., 386 F. Supp. 2d 993 (N.D. Ill. 2005). See § 8.2.9, *infra.*

347 15 U.S.C. § 1681b(e).

> The Committee is aware that some consumers may find that direct marketing and prescreening entail an undesirable invasion of their privacy. Therefore, while this section facilitates prescreening ... it creates an "opt-out" procedure through which a consumer may elect to have his or her name excluded from any list provided by the consumer reporting agency....

S. Rep. No. 185, 104th Cong., 1st Sess. at 38 (Dec. 14, 1995).
348 15 U.S.C. § 1681b(e)(2).
349 15 U.S.C. §§ 1681b(e)(3)(A), 1681b(e)(4)(B)(1). This period was extended from two years by FACTA, Pub. L. No. 108-159 § 213(c) (2003), effective Dec. 1, 2004. 16 C.F.R. § 602.1(c)(3)(x).
350 15 U.S.C. § 1681b(e)(4)(C).
351 *In re* Trans Union Corp., No. 9255 (F.T.C. 1998), *reprinted on the CD-Rom accompanying this manual.*
352 15 U.S.C. § 1681s-3. This opt-out right was added by FACTA in 2003. Pub. L. No. 108-159 § 213(c) (2003).
353 *See also* §§ 2.4.2, 2.4.3, *supra.*
354 15 U.S.C. § 1681b(e)(6). See § 2.6.1, *supra*, for a discussion of "nationwide reporting agency."
355 15 U.S.C. § 1681b(e)(4)(D).
356 15 U.S.C. § 1681b(e)(5).

be told that he or she will be excluded from all prescreening lists compiled by the CRA for a five-year period, unless the consumer completes and submits a signed written form issued by the notification system requesting permanent exclusion. If the consumer requests the notice of election form, the notification system must provide it within five business days.

The FCRA requires that consumers be notified in two different ways of their right to be excluded from prescreening lists. First, if the consumer receives a solicitation (i.e., a "firm offer" of credit or insurance) based on a prescreened list, the solicitation must disclose the fact that it was based on information in a consumer report; the conditions on the offer; and the procedure for removing one's name from prescreening lists.[357] The specific disclosure requirements are discussed in § 8.2.9, *supra*.

Second, CRAs are required to advertise in a publication of general circulation at least annually notifying consumers of their right to be excluded from prescreening lists.[358] Either way, the consumer will be provided with an address and a toll-free number to use to make such an election.

7.4 Potentially Impermissible Purposes

7.4.1 General

The FCRA does not itemize impermissible purposes. Those impermissible purposes discussed in the following sections constitute only a partial list of some of the more common wrongful uses which arise. The rule is that a user must have a permissible purpose for obtaining a report; all other uses are impermissible. A user can be liable for either using or obtaining a consumer report impermissibly.[359]

7.4.2 Use in Divorce, Child Support, or Paternity Proceedings

A consumer report cannot be used by suspicious, divorcing, or ex-spouses in property or child custody disputes.[360] However it can be used under the collection provision in order to collect alimony after a payment schedule is set by a court.[361] A child support order, whether judicial or administrative, creates a debtor-creditor relationship with the consumer.[362]

It is impermissible for an individual to obtain a consumer report to check to see if her ex-spouse was improperly using credit cards that were formerly jointly used.[363]

As discussed above, certain public officials also have a permissible purpose to use consumer reports for use in connection with child support.[364]

7.4.3 Use in Tax Collection Proceedings

Although one of the original concerns giving rise to the FCRA was the free availability of confidential information to the IRS,[365] Consumer reporting agencies (CRAs) have been required since 1976 to provide consumer reports in response to a summons issued by the IRS (but not other tax collection agencies).[366] The IRS must first provide a designated IRS certificate that the consumer has not filed a timely motion to quash the summons. The FTC considers these IRS summons to fall within the permissible purpose for court orders.[367]

Apart from this one exception for the IRS, a tax collection agency has no general permissible purpose to obtain a consumer report to collect delinquent tax accounts. Until the tax amount is reduced to some kind of judgment, there is no debtor-creditor relationship.[368]

However, a tax collection agency does have a permissible purpose after it has acquired a tax lien having the same effect as a judgment or after it has obtained a judgment.[369] Similarly, if the taxpayer entered into an agreement with the tax

---

357 15 U.S.C. § 1681m(d); 16 C.F.R. § 642.3. See § 8.2.9, *infra*.
358 15 U.S.C. § 1681b(e)(5)(A)(ii).
359 15 U.S.C. § 1681b(f); Chester v. Purvis, 260 F. Supp. 2d 711 (S.D. Ind. 2003).
360 *See* Cole v. American Family Mut. Ins. Co., 2006 WL 158688 (D. Kan. Jan. 18, 2006) (husband could not obtain wife's report for use in divorce proceeding to determine what she had done with joint marital assets) (citing cases in other contexts); Thibodeaux v. Rupers, 196 F. Supp. 2d 585 (S.D. Ohio 2001).
361 *See* Chiappetta v. Tellefson, 1985 WL 1951 (N.D. Ill. July 9, 1985). *See also* § 7.4.4, *infra*.
362 *See* § 5.2.4.2, *supra*; FTC Official Staff Commentary § 604(3)(A) item 3, *reprinted at* Appx. D, *infra*; Morris, FTC Informal Staff Opinion Letter (July 26, 1979), *reprinted on the CD-Rom accompanying this manual* (a child support order establishes the agency as a creditor); Isaac, FTC Informal Staff Opinion Letter (Oct. 30, 1986), *reprinted on the CD-Rom accompanying this manual* (same). The FTC Staff Commentary replaced prior inconsistent staff opinions.
363 Yohay v. City of Alexandria Employees Credit Union, Inc., 827 F.2d 967 (4th Cir. 1987).
364 *See* § 7.2.9, *supra*.
365 "One can certainly be sympathetic to the problems of the FBI and IRS in meeting their heavy responsibilities. But, nonetheless, their right to investigate is not absolute. . . . Regardless of whether the individual has any legal control over the information on him in a credit reporting agency's file, I certainly feel he has a moral claim to controlling its use. He should not be entirely dependent upon the policies of the particular CRAs to protect his basic rights." 115 Cong. Rec. 2413 (1969) (comments of Sen. Proxmire introducing the Fair Credit Reporting Act bill on the floor of the Senate).
366 26 U.S.C. § 7609. *See also* FTC Official Staff Commentary § 604(1) item 2, *reprinted at* Appx. D, *infra*. *See* § 2.4.1, *supra*.
367 FTC Official Staff Commentary § 604(1) item 2, *reprinted at* Appx. D, *infra*.
368 FTC Official Staff Commentary § 604(3)(A) item 4, *reprinted at* Appx. D, *infra*. *See also* Peeler, FTC Informal Staff Opinion Letter (Nov. 1, 1983), *reprinted on the CD-Rom accompanying this manual*.
369 FTC Official Staff Commentary § 604(3)(A) item 4, *reprinted at* Appx. D, *infra*.

collection agency to pay taxes according to a timetable, that agreement would create a debtor-creditor relationship.[370]

7.4.4 Use in Civil or Criminal Litigation

Generally, a party involved or potentially involved in litigation does not have a permissible purpose to receive a consumer report, unless the subject matter of the litigation itself provides the permissible purpose (such as a suit on a credit account, actions to collect on a judgment, or a business transaction between the two parties).[371] For example, there is no permissible purpose to obtain a consumer report in tort litigation[372] or a divorce proceeding.[373] There is no court order to provide the report, the other party has not provided written instructions, there is not yet a debtor-creditor relationship, and there is no employment, insurance, government benefit, or business transaction related purpose. Litigation between two parties is not considered itself a business transaction[374]—although, of course, a business transaction between the two parties could lead to litigation.

If litigation is brought to collect on a consumer credit account, a consumer report may be used, just as it could be without litigation.[375] However, the report may not be used if the suit does not involve collection of the debt. For example, if a debtor sues the creditor for violation of a federal or state consumer statute, the creditor would not have a permissible purpose for obtaining a consumer report on the plaintiff, unless the creditor is also trying to collect on the underlying debt.[376] An FTC staff opinion indicates that a suit against a former tenant does not involve credit and a consumer report may not be used for this purpose, though some courts would disagree.[377]

Thus, potential plaintiffs may not use consumer reports to determine whether potential defendants are worth suing, such as to evaluate a defendant or potential defendant's ability to pay a judgment, the existence of outstanding judgments or previous lawsuits involving the consumer, the consumer's employment record, or the consumer's personal background (divorce or separation, mode of living, or creditworthiness).[378] It is inappropriate to use a consumer report to impugn a litigant's credibility.[379] Likewise, it is impermissible to obtain a defendant's consumer report with the intent of forcing a party to settle litigation.[380] A tenant may not obtain a landlord's report to determine whether the landlord can pay a proposed settlement.[381]

If there is no permissible purpose relating to the litigation, a consumer report cannot be obtained for the purpose of locating a defendant for service of process or otherwise to locate a person in connection with litigation.[382] Consumer reports cannot be used to discredit a witness at trial, to locate

---

370 *Id. See also* Brinckerhoff, FTC Informal Staff Opinion Letter (May 28, 1986), *reprinted on the CD-Rom accompanying this manual.*

371 FTC Official Staff Commentary § 604(3)(E) item 4, *reprinted at* Appx. D, *infra*; Korotki v. Attorney Servs. Corp., 931 F. Supp. 1269 (D. Md. 1996) (permissible to obtain consumer's consumer report to obtain address for service of notice of mechanic's lien arising out of business transaction), *aff'd*, 131 F.3d 135 (4th Cir. 1997). *See also* § 7.2.3.4, *supra*.

372 *Id. See also* Jerison, FTC Informal Staff Opinion Letter (Dec. 12, 1988), *reprinted on the CD-Rom accompanying this manual.*

373 Cole v. American Family Mut. Ins. Co., 2006 WL 158688 (D. Kan. Jan. 18, 2006); Rodgers v. McCullough, 296 F. Supp. 2d 895 (W.D. Tenn. 2003); Chiappetta v. Tellefson, 1985 WL 1951 (N.D. Ill. July 9, 1985).

374 *See* Bakker v. McKinnon, 152 F.3d 1007 (8th Cir. 1998); Duncan v. Handmaker, 149 F.3d 424 (6th Cir. 1998); Comeaux v. Brown & Williamson Tobacco Co., 915 F.2d 1264 (9th Cir. 1990); Cole v. American Family Mut. Ins. Co., 2006 WL 158688 (D. Kan. Jan. 18, 2006); Auriemma v. City of Chicago, 1990 WL 36774 (N.D. Ill. Mar. 2, 1990); Maloney v. City of Chicago, 678 F. Supp. 703 (N.D. Ill. 1987); FTC Official Staff Commentary § 604(3)(E) item 4, *reprinted at* Appx. D, *infra*. *Contra* Minter v. AAA Cook County Consol., Inc., 2004 WL 1630781 (N.D. Ill. July 19, 2004) (dictum).

375 *See* § 7.2.3.4, *supra*.

376 *See* Chester v. Purvis, 2003 WL 22454885 (S.D. Ind. Oct. 22, 2003); Peeler, FTC Informal Staff Opinion Letter (Aug. 27, 1977), *reprinted on the CD-Rom accompanying this manual.*

377 Long, FTC Staff Opinion Letter (July 6, 2000), *reprinted on the CD-Rom accompanying this manual. But see* §§ 2.3.6.3.3, 7.2.3.1.2, *supra*.

378 FTC Official Staff Commentary § 604(3)(E) item 4, *reprinted at* Appx. D, *infra*; Bakker v. McKinnon, 152 F.3d 1007 (8th Cir. 1998); Mone v. Dranow, 945 F.2d 306 (9th Cir. 1991); Chester v. Purvis, 2003 WL 22454885 (S.D. Ind. Oct. 22, 2003). *See also* Jerison, FTC Informal Staff Opinion Letter (Dec. 12, 1988), *reprinted on the CD-Rom accompanying this manual*; FTC Informal Staff Opinion Letter [1969–1973 Decisions Transfer Binder] Consumer Cred. Guide (CCH) ¶ 99,444 (May 27, 1971).

379 Klapper v. Shapiro, 586 N.Y.S.2d 846 (1992) (attorney's use of opposing counsel's consumer report was improper under § 1681b and New York's parallel statute; there was no rational basis or relevance in submitting to a court a consumer report on an attorney representing a party).

380 Bakker v. McKinnon, 152 F.3d 1007 (8th Cir. 1998); Chester v. Purvis, 260 F. Supp. 2d 711 (S.D. Ind. 2003).

381 Popik v. American Int'l Mtg. Co., 936 F. Supp. 173 (S.D.N.Y. 1996).

382 FTC Informal Staff Opinion Letter [1969–1973 Decisions Transfer Binder] Consumer Cred. Guide (CCH) ¶ 99,444 (May 27, 1971). *See also* Mullen v. Al Castrucci Ford, Inc., 537 N.E.2d 1307 (Ohio Ct. Com. Pl. 1986) (improperly used consumer report to locate former car salesman for litigation).

See also FTC Official Staff Commentary § 604(3)(E) item 4, *reprinted at* Appx. D, *infra*. *Contra* Spence v. TRW, Inc., 92 F.3d 380 (6th Cir. 1996) (dicta; allowed creditor to obtain report to defend suit claiming creditor made false consumer report). *Cf.* Duncan v. Handmaker, 149 F.3d 424 (6th Cir. 1998) (tort action brought against mortgagee); Myshrall v. Keybank National Assoc., 2001 Me. Super. LEXIS 29 (Mar. 5, 2001) (permissible purpose to access consumer report when loan still outstanding despite fact that bank's purpose was to verify allegation in litigation. The court followed *Spence* on the theory that the creditor would have no other way of confirming the allegation—ignoring the fact that discovery procedures/court orders were other avenues.).

a witness or to evaluate a prospective juror,[383] even if the litigation involves collection of a credit account or a business transaction between the parties. The witness or juror does not have a debtor-creditor or business transaction relationship with the user. Nor may consumer reports be obtained to settle pending litigation, or be used in connection with depositions or enforcement of prejudgment writs of attachment.[384]

Consequently, whenever a party is involved in litigation, it may be prudent to determine through discovery (or by requesting the consumer's report from the major nationwide CRAs) whether the other side has received a consumer report on the consumer. If so, there may be an FCRA violation giving rise to a cause of action against the CRA and/or the opposing party and attorney.

An attorney for a collection agency has no immunity from suit under the FCRA simply because he obtained and used a consumer report in the course of his duties as a lawyer in the context of litigation.[385]

While the opposing attorney may not be able to obtain a report on a consumer, an attorney may have a permissible purpose to obtain a consumer report on a prospective client. If a consumer is seeking legal assistance from an attorney for personal, family, or household purposes, the relationship is covered by the permissible purpose of a business transaction involving the consumer.[386]

In addition, the FCRA only applies to consumer reports, so that if a litigant obtains a report that is *not* a consumer report, then the FCRA restrictions do not apply. For example, if information is collected, used, and expected to be used solely for litigation purposes not covered by the FCRA, the FCRA does not restrict the use by an attorney of such information.[387] Litigants are also not restricted in their use of business reports. Similarly, a non-consumer report is not rendered a consumer report if it is used in litigation for purposes other than those specified in the FCRA.[388]

7.4.5 Use by Investigators

Detectives and other investigators are covered by the same rules relating to permissible purposes as are their clients for whom they are seeking information. Thus, consumer reports could be released to a detective for skip tracing purposes while investigating a consumer for employment, insurance, credit, or debt collection purposes, or in relationship to a business transaction, but not for other purposes.[389] An investigator may obtain a report on a judgment debtor on behalf of an attorney trying to collect a judgment debt, but not for an attorney pursuing a personal injury claim.[390]

Consumer reports cannot be used for the purposes of locating a person suspected of committing a crime.[391] A permissible purpose does not exist to release a consumer report to a district attorney's office to "investigate welfare fraud" or to investigate or prosecute criminal or civil cases.[392] Nevertheless, *government* agencies can obtain specified limited identifying information and any user can obtain a consumer report pursuant to a court order.[393]

Private investigators are restricted from obtaining consumer reports for impermissible purposes even if the investigator only seeks basic identifying information and the consumer's home or work address; the FCRA's exception

---

383 FTC Official Staff Commentary § 604(3)(E) item 4, *reprinted at* Appx. D, *infra. See also* Federal Trade Commission Advisory Opinion, [1969–1973 Decisions Transfer Binder] Consumer Cred. Guide (CCH) ¶ 99,134 (Sept. 29, 1972); Garman, FTC Informal Staff Opinion Letter (June 17, 1985), *reprinted on the CD-Rom accompanying this manual*; Brinckerhoff, FTC Informal Staff Opinion Letter (Oct. 31, 1983), *reprinted on the CD-Rom accompanying this manual*; Peeler, FTC Informal Staff Opinion Letter (July 24, 1978), *reprinted on the CD-Rom accompanying this manual* (CRA may not enter into general contract with attorney); Russell, FTC Informal Staff Opinion Letter (Sept. 26, 1973), *reprinted on the CD-Rom accompanying this manual*; FTC Informal Staff Opinion Letter [1969–1973 Decisions Transfer Binder] Consumer Cred. Guide (CCH) ¶ 99,444 (May 27, 1971).

384 Jerison, FTC Informal Staff Opinion Letter (Dec. 12, 1988), *reprinted on the CD-Rom accompanying this manual* (may obtain report once settlement of tort claim is reached in principle to decide whether to accept payments in installments); Garman, FTC Informal Staff Opinion Letter (June 17, 1985), *reprinted on the CD-Rom accompanying this manual*; Peeler, FTC Informal Staff Opinion Letter (Aug. 27, 1977), *reprinted on the CD-Rom accompanying this manual*.

385 Chester v. Purvis, 260 F. Supp. 2d 711 (S.D. Ind. 2003).

386 Carson, FTC Informal Staff Opinion Letter (Apr. 29, 1971), *reprinted on the CD-Rom accompanying this manual*.

387 *Id.*

388 *See* Ippolito v. WNS, Inc., 864 F.2d 440 (7th Cir. 1988).

389 Phillips v. Grendahl, 312 F.3d 357 (8th Cir. 2002) (investigation of boyfriend not permissible purpose); FTC Official Staff Commentary § 604(3)(E) item 6C, *reprinted at* Appx. D, *infra*; Kane, FTC Informal Staff Opinion Letter (Aug. 9, 1993), *reprinted on the CD-Rom accompanying this manual* (investigation has no permissible purpose for skip tracing report related to insurance accident claims); Muris, FTC Informal Staff Opinion Letter (Apr. 29, 1982), *reprinted on the CD-Rom accompanying this manual*; Grimes, FTC Informal Staff Opinion Letter (Sept. 11, 1975), *reprinted on the CD-Rom accompanying this manual*; Carson, FTC Informal Staff Opinion Letter (Apr. 29, 1971), *reprinted on the CD-Rom accompanying this manual* (investigator has no permissible purpose for report other than tracing persons for collection of account). *Cf.* Liu v. DeFelice, 6 F. Supp. 2d 106 (D. Mass. 1998).

390 Grimes, FTC Informal Staff Opinion Letter (Aug. 14, 1985), *reprinted on the CD-Rom accompanying this manual*.

391 FTC Official Staff Commentary § 604(3)(E) item 4, *reprinted at* Appx. D, *infra*.

392 Peeler, FTC Informal Staff Opinion Letter (Feb. 26, 1979), *reprinted on the CD-Rom accompanying this manual*; White, FTC Informal Staff Opinion Letter (Feb. 18, 1977), *reprinted on the CD-Rom accompanying this manual. Cf.* d'Entremont, FTC Informal Staff Opinion Letter (Jan. 25, 1996), *reprinted on the CD-Rom accompanying this manual*.

393 *See* §§ 7.2.1, 7.2.10.2, *supra*.

for basic identifying information applies only to requests by government agencies.[394] On the other hand, if simple identifying information does not qualify as a consumer report, the FCRA's restrictions do not apply.[395]

The investigator will need a permissible purpose at the time it is seeking a report, even if the investigator had a permissible purpose at some time in the past. For example, there may no longer be a permissible purpose for an investigator to obtain a consumer report after the investigator's client has agreed to underwrite an insurance policy for the consumer.[396]

7.4.6 Use of Reports on the Consumer's Spouse, Relatives, or Other Third Parties

7.4.6.1 General Rule

The FCRA generally permits release of a consumer report in connection with uses *involving that consumer*.[397] Consequently, with the exceptions discussed below, there is no permissible purpose to obtain a consumer report on one individual to assist the user in making a determination on a different individual.

Of course, in certain circumstances, information from a third party's report may become relevant to and part of the consumer's report.[398] Some courts have gone so far as to say that one spouse's consumer report could at times constitute the other spouse's consumer report, though such a broad approach seems inconsistent with the limitations in the Act.[399]

7.4.6.2 Exceptions for Credit Transactions

For *credit* transactions, a creditor may seek information on a spouse when:

- The spouse will be an authorized user of the account;[400]
- The spouse will be liable for the account (i.e., contractually or through community property law);[401] or
- The applicant is relying on the spouse's income as a basis for repayment of the credit requested.[402]

The last rule allows creditors to obtain reports of *former* spouses as well, if the consumer is relying on alimony, child support, or separate maintenance payments to repay the account.[403]

With respect to the second rule, a spouse may be liable for the account if a state law doctrine of necessaries applies to the transaction (whereby the spouse would be liable for goods or services from which the spouse benefited);[404] if the applicant resides in a community property state or the property upon which the applicant is relying is in a community property state; or if the applicant is acting as the nonapplicant spouse's agent in requesting the credit.[405] Even

---

394 Grimes, FTC Informal Staff Opinion Letter (Sept. 11, 1975), *reprinted on the CD-Rom accompanying this manual.*

395 Muris, FTC Informal Staff Opinion Letter (Apr. 29, 1982), *reprinted on the CD-Rom accompanying this manual.*

396 Equifax, Inc., 96 F.T.C. 1045 (1980), *rev'd in part on other grounds*, 678 F.2d 1047 (11th Cir. 1982).

397 15 U.S.C. § 1681b(3); Koropoulos v. Credit Bureau, Inc., 734 F.2d 37 (D.C. Cir. 1984). The employment purposes provision does not explicitly limit the permissible purpose of a consumer report to employment of the subject of the consumer report, but the legislative intent is clear. Andrews v. TRW, Inc., 225 F.3d 1063 (9th Cir. 2000) (it is for the jury to decide whether it was reasonable to disclose information about someone else), *rev'd and remanded on other grounds*, 534 U.S. 19 (2001). *See* Zamora v. Valley Fed. Sav. & Loan Ass'n, 811 F.2d 1368 (10th Cir. 1987); Conway, FTC Informal Staff Opinion Letter [1969–1973 Decisions Transfer Binder] Consumer Cred. Guide (CCH) ¶ 99,520 (Apr. 19, 1971).

398 *See* § 7.4.6.4, *infra.*

399 *See* § 7.4.6.4, *infra.*

400 FTC Official Staff Commentary § 604(3)(A) item 5A, *reprinted at* Appx. D, *infra. See also* Equal Credit Opportunity Act, Regulation B, 12 C.F.R. § 202.5(c)(2).

401 FTC Official Staff Commentary § 604(3)(A) item 5A, *reprinted at* Appx. D, *infra. See also* Equal Credit Opportunity Act, Regulation B, 12 C.F.R. § 202.5(c)(2); Moore v. Credit Info. Corp., 673 F.2d 208 (8th Cir. 1982) (defamation action arising from the reporting of a bad debt which the spouse agreed to assume as part of a dissolution decree); Peeler, FTC Informal Staff Opinion Letter (May 27, 1982), *reprinted on the CD-Rom accompanying this manual.*

402 FTC Official Staff Commentary § 604(3)(A) item 5A, *reprinted at* Appx. D, *infra. See also* Equal Credit Opportunity Act, Regulation B, 12 C.F.R. § 202.5(c)(2).

403 Equal Credit Opportunity Act, Regulation B, 12 C.F.R. § 202.5(c)(2).

404 *See* National Consumer Law Center, Fair Debt Collection § 14.6 (5th ed. 2004 and Supp.) for a discussion of the doctrine of necessaries.

405 FTC Official Staff Commentary § 604(3)(A) item 5A, *reprinted at* Appx. D, *infra*; Equal Credit Opportunity Act, Regulation B, 12 C.F.R. § 202.5(c)(2); Oliver, FTC Informal Staff Opinion Letter (June 10, 1983), *reprinted on the CD-Rom accompanying this manual* (state law determines if husband liable for wife's debt and report on him can be obtained); Peeler, FTC Informal Staff Opinion Letter (Mar. 20, 1977), *reprinted on the CD-Rom accompanying this manual* (if personally liable for judgment, CRA may report information even if name not on contract); Feldman, FTC Informal Staff Opinion Letter (Mar. 29, 1976), *reprinted on the CD-Rom accompanying this manual* (used business transaction rationale); Peeler, FTC Informal Staff Opinion Letter (Apr. 1976), *reprinted on the CD-Rom accompanying this manual* (if relying on community property to show ability to repay); Feldman, FTC Informal Staff Opinion Letter (Aug. 5, 1974), *reprinted on the CD-Rom accompanying this manual* (CRA may obtain report on surviving spouse or divorced spouse if it can legally obtain judgment against them for debt); Simoneaux v. Brown, 403 F. Supp. 2d 526 (M.D. La. 2005) (creditor of criminal restitution order could obtain consumer report of wife of embezzler since Louisiana is an community property state and wife failed to rebut presumption that the funds were not used for the benefit of the community); Olson v. Six Rivers Nat'l Bank, 111 Cal. App. 4th 1, 3 Cal. Rptr. 3d

§ 7.4.6.3   Fair Credit Reporting

if a divorce decree assigns responsibility for a debt to one spouse, the other spouse may still be potentially liable for it if the first spouse defaults.[406]

If none of the narrow grounds for requesting a spouse's report apply, then the creditor cannot obtain a consumer report on the spouse in connection with a credit transaction.[407] Regulation B to the Equal Credit Opportunity Act codifies the rules set forth above, and prohibits a creditor from requesting any information concerning a credit applicant's spouse or former spouse except in those circumstances.[408] The FTC Staff Commentary in turn states that there is never a permissible purpose for making a consumer report on a nonapplicant spouse if Regulation B prohibits the creditor from requesting the information.[409]

Similarly, the FTC Staff Commentary specifies that if, at the time of a credit application, the applicant makes it clear that he or she is relying solely on separate property, not acting as the agent for the spouse, and that no necessaries will be involved, then no permissible purpose exists for the creditor to seek the spouse's report.[410] The FTC Staff Commentary also states that at the time of default or collection, it should be clear whether the spouse is liable for the debt under state law, and there would be no permissible purpose to obtain a report on that spouse at that time if the spouse has no such liability.[411]

The FTC Staff Commentary states that there is no permissible purpose to obtain a consumer report on a nonapplicant former spouse, a legally separated spouse, or one who has otherwise indicated an intent to legally disassociate with the marriage.[412] This rule presumably does not apply if the consumer is relying on alimony or child support from the former spouse in a credit application.[413]

Even if the user does not have a permissible reason for requesting a spouse's report, a CRA may still have "reason to believe" that a permissible purpose exists if the CRA is not made aware of instructions or other circumstances that negate what would normally be a permissible purpose. For example, a CRA was not liable for releasing a report for use in considering the husband's farm loan application, when the CRA did not know that the wife had instructed the creditor not to obtain her report.[414]

7.4.6.3 Other Types of Transactions

The exceptions set forth above, permitting release of a spouse's report for use in connection with some credit transactions, do not apply when a report is sought for use in connection with insurance, employment, a government license or benefit, or a business transaction with the consumer alone. Thus, there is generally no permissible purpose to release or use the report of the consumer's spouse or another third party for use in noncredit transactions not involving that party.[415]

For example, there is no permissible purpose for a potential employer to obtain consumer reports on anyone other than the applicant him or herself.[416] Reports on relatives are

---

301 (Cal. Ct. App. 2003) (community property state; applying parallel state law).

406 Petruccelli, FTC Informal Staff Opinion Letter (Feb. 13, 1984), *reprinted on the CD-Rom accompanying this manual* (if divorce decree assigns payment of account to husband only, but state law makes wife liable upon default, may report payment history on both husband and wife's files with comment on wife's that husband is responsible for payment).

407 FTC Official Staff Commentary § 604(3)(A) item 5B, *reprinted at* Appx. D, *infra*.

408 12 C.F.R. 202.5(c). *See* National Consumer Law Center, Credit Discrimination § 5.5.2.4 (4th ed. 2005 and Supp.).

Under the Equal Credit Opportunity Act, information from a married person's files may be designated as relating to a consumer's joint or individual experience. 12 C.F.R. § 202.10. *See* National Consumer Law Center, Credit Discrimination § 9.4 (4th ed. 2005 and Supp.). CRAs must maintain reasonable procedures to ensure that "undesignated information," as it is called, is not improperly included in a report on a spouse. *See* FTC Official Staff Commentary § 607 item 3E, *reprinted at* Appx. D, *infra*.

409 FTC Official Staff Commentary § 604(3)(A) item 5B, *reprinted at* Appx. D, *infra*.

410 FTC Official Staff Commentary § 604(3)(A) item 5B, *reprinted at* Appx. D, *infra*. *See also* FTC, Compliance with the Fair Credit Reporting Act, at 20.3 (1977).

411 FTC Official Staff Commentary § 604(3)(A) item 5B, *reprinted at* Appx. D, *infra*; Peeler, FTC Informal Staff Opinion Letter (May 27, 1982), *reprinted on the CD-Rom accompanying this manual*. *But see* Simoneaux v. Brown, 403 F. Supp. 2d 526 (M.D. La. 2005) (creditor was entitled to obtain spouse's report in order to collect on restitution order because spouse failed to rebut presumption of community obligation under Louisiana law and creditor acted in good faith in relying on that presumption).

412 FTC Official Staff Commentary § 604(3)(A) item 5B, *reprinted at* Appx. D, *infra*. *See also* Oliver, FTC Informal Staff Opinion Letter (June 10, 1983), *reprinted on the CD-Rom accompanying this manual*.

This does not preclude reporting a prior joint account of former spouses for which the spouse that is the subject of the report is still contractually liable. FTC Official Staff Commentary § 604(3)(A) item 5B, *reprinted at* Appx. D, *infra*. *See also* Peeler, FTC Informal Staff Opinion Letter (Mar. 8, 1976), *reprinted on the CD-Rom accompanying this manual*.

413 Equal Credit Opportunity Act, Regulation B, 12 C.F.R. § 202.5(c)(2)(iv); FTC Official Staff Commentary § 604(3)(A) item 5A, *reprinted at* Appx. D, *infra*.

414 Short v. Allstate Credit Bureau, 370 F. Supp. 2d 1173 (M.D. Ala. 2005). *Cf.* Simoneaux v. Brown, 403 F. Supp. 2d 526 (M.D. La. 2005) (even if husband's debt was a separate obligation, creditor acted reasonably in relying on presumption of community obligation under Louisiana law).

415 *See* § 7.4.6.1, *supra*.

416 Zamora v. Valley Fed. Sav. & Loan Ass'n, 811 F.2d 1368 (10th Cir. 1987); FTC Official Staff Commentary § 604(3)(B) item 2, *reprinted at* Appx. D, *infra*; Conway, FTC Informal Staff Opinion Letter [1969–1973 Decisions Transfer Binder] Consumer Cred. Guide (CCH) ¶ 99,520 (Apr. 19, 1971). One court has ruled, with little discussion, that the U.S. Postal Service did not violate the FCRA by obtaining an employee's spouse's report for employment and investigative purposes. Jones v.

impermissible even where the applicant is being considered for a security-sensitive position and the report is obtained to evaluate the applicant's trustworthiness for the position.[417] Similarly, a health care insurer does not have a permissible purpose under either the insurance or business transaction provision to obtain report on applicant's spouse.[418]

7.4.6.4 Joint Information

A former spouse has a permissible purpose to obtain a joint consumer report of herself and her former husband when the information contained in the report related to her own creditworthiness, credit standing, and credit capacity and their ability to discharge their parental duties under state law.[419]

A consumer report can also include information about a joint account where the credit applicant was liable on that account, even if the creditor could not otherwise obtain a report on the applicant's spouse.[420] However, where a bankruptcy or negative credit information accrues against one spouse before marriage, no permissible purpose exists for the user to obtain that information if the other spouse was not involved and files a separate application for credit.[421]

The FTC Staff Commentary states that information appearing solely in the report of a consumer's spouse or former spouse may be reported in response to a request for a report on the consumer, when the consumer applies for separate credit, only if the information relates to accounts for which the consumer was either a user or was contractually liable, or the user has a permissible purpose for a report on the spouse.[422]

Some courts have stated a more general rule that information about a consumer's spouse or the spouse's report may be released as long as it has a bearing on the consumer's creditworthiness, because such information would constitute a consumer report on the consumer him or herself.[423] But such a broad rule is inconsistent with the narrow rules governing when a spouse's report can be requested.[424] This approach also does not justify the release of a spouse's entire consumer report, which may contain information that does not bear on the creditworthiness of the consumer.

7.4.7 Use in Connection with Insurance Claims

Most courts and FTC opinions have held that insurance claims reports are not consumer reports when information is used, expected to be used, and collected solely for that purpose.[425] Consequently, the use of such reports to evaluate insurance claims (as opposed to insurance underwriting) is not covered by the Act, and the FCRA does not restrict their release.

Nevertheless, there is still the question whether information that *is* a consumer report can be released to a user whose purpose involves investigation of an insurance claim. Many reports that could be used for such purposes clearly fall within the definition of consumer reports, such as a typical report from a CRA. Moreover an insurance claim report also is a consumer report if it is compiled in whole or in part from information in a consumer report.

The FTC Staff Commentary finds no permissible purpose to use consumer reports for insurance claims purposes.[426] The FCRA's language clearly supports this interpretation. Permissible insurance purposes include only those uses "connected with the underwriting of insurance."[427] Determinations of eligibility for insurance coverage are included, but determinations of eligibility for insurance benefits are not.

Runyon, 32 F. Supp. 2d 873 (N.D. W. Va. 1998), *aff'd without op.*, 173 F.3d 850 (4th Cir. 1999). However, the plaintiff was in pro per and the court did not discuss why or whether those purposes extended to release of a spouse's report.

417 Zamora v. Valley Fed. Sav. & Loan Ass'n, 811 F.2d 1368 (10th Cir. 1987).

418 Brinckerhoff, FTC Informal Staff Opinion Letter (Dec. 21, 1983), *reprinted on the CD-Rom accompanying this manual*.

419 Spencer v. Spencer, 52 Fed. Appx. 874 (9th Cir. 2002) (local court rules may limit citation to this case). *See* 9th Cir. R. 36-3.

420 *See* Moore v. Credit Info. Corp., 673 F.2d 208 (8th Cir. 1982) (defamation claim arising from the reporting of bad debts which the spouse agreed to assume under the term of a dissolution decree). *See generally* § 7.7.1 regarding the ability to include information about a spouse's credit history in a consumer report.

421 Feldman, FTC Informal Staff Opinion Letter (Dec. 24, 1974), *reprinted on the CD-Rom accompanying this manual*.

422 FTC Official Staff Commentary § 607 item 3E, *reprinted at* Appx. D, *infra*.

423 *See* Short v. Allstate Credit Bureau, 370 F. Supp. 2d 1173 (M.D. Ala. 2005). The *Short* decision relied on Koropoulos v. Credit Bureau, 734 F.2d 37 (D.C. Cir. 1984) and Smith v. GSH Residential Real Estate Corp., 935 F.2d 1287 (4th Cir. 1991) (unpublished opinion). The *Koropoulos* discussion was dicta, however, and the Fourth Circuit in *Smith* was merely describing the district court's reasoning, while ultimately affirming on much narrower grounds consistent with the FTC Staff Commentary. Moreover, both *Koropoulos* and *Smith* noted that the plain language of the credit transaction provision—which only authorizes reports on the consumer involved in the transaction—seems to prohibit releases of spousal reports.

424 *See* §§ 7.4.6.1–7.4.6.3.

425 *See* § 2.3.6.5.2, *supra*.

426 FTC Official Staff Commentary § 604(3)(C) item 2, *reprinted at* Appx. D, *infra*. *See also* Kane, FTC Informal Staff Opinion Letter (Aug. 9, 1993), *reprinted on the CD-Rom accompanying this manual* (skip tracing reports on drivers involved in accidents with insureds); Grimes, FTC Informal Staff Opinion Letter (Aug. 3, 1984), *reprinted on the CD-Rom accompanying this manual*; Feldman, FTC Informal Staff Opinion Letter (Apr. 15, 1971), *reprinted on the CD-Rom accompanying this manual*; Brinckerhoff, FTC Informal Staff Opinion Letter (July 29, 1985), *reprinted on the CD-Rom accompanying this manual*. *See also* Greathouse, FTC Informal Staff Opinion Letter (Oct. 20, 1998), *reprinted on the CD-Rom accompanying this manual*. *Cf.* Kiblen v. Pickle, 653 P.2d 1338, 1341 (Wash. Ct. App. 1982).

427 15 U.S.C. § 1681b(a)(2)(c). *See* § 7.2.5, *infra*.

§ 7.4.8   *Fair Credit Reporting*

While it is clear that the insurance permissible purpose does not apply to insurance claims activity, but only to underwriting, there is a question whether the permissible purpose involving business transactions applies. Nevertheless, courts usually find that the explicit provision dealing with insurance is "primary" and, therefore, the use of information in connection with insurance claims transactions not specified in the insurance provision cannot be included under the business transaction provision.[428]

Practitioners also report that insurance companies utilize waivers containing vague but broad language in connection with processing insurance claims. Such waivers are then used as grounds to access consumer reports and gather information on the consumers. This practice undermines the FCRA's protections against accessing consumer reports for impermissible purposes.

7.4.8 Marketing

The only marketing-related permissible purpose under the Act is prescreening firm offers of credit or insurance, under the limitations of the prescreening provision.[429] Otherwise, marketing is not a permissible purpose under the Act.[430] "It is clear that Congress did not intend to allow access to consumer credit information 'for catalogs and sales pitches.' "[431] Thus, neither full consumer reports nor consumer lists that qualify as consumer reports, unless they meet the prescreening requirements, can be used for marketing research. Marketing research must be based on other information not qualifying as consumer reports.

Thus, once a credit account is closed and paid in full, the creditor does not have a permissible purpose to review the account for the purpose of identifying new marketing opportunities.[432]

Similarly, the insurance provision does not permit use of consumer reports for marketing activities separate and apart from underwriting decisions.[433]

The business transaction provision also cannot justify marketing uses of consumer reports. The business transaction either must be initiated by the consumer,[434] or must involve legitimate account review unrelated to marketing.[435]

7.4.9 Other Impermissible Uses

There is no exclusive list of impermissible uses. Instead, there are only limited *permissible* uses, and *any* other uses are impermissible. Many of the impermissible uses have been described above, but certainly not all possible improper uses are listed here.

For example, it is impermissible for an individual to obtain a consumer report to check to see if her ex-spouse was improperly using credit cards that were formerly jointly used.[436] It would also be impermissible to obtain a consumer report as part of a vendetta against that individual,[437] or even just to satisfy the requester's curiosity.[438] A reporter has no permissible purpose to receive a consumer report for use in preparing a media story.[439] A tenant may not obtain a landlord's report to determine whether the landlord can pay a proposed settlement.[440]

---

428 Cochran v. Metropolitan Life Ins. Co., 472 F. Supp. 827 (N.D. Ga. 1979); FTC Official Staff Commentary § 604(3)(C) item 2, *reprinted at* Appx. D, *infra*; Grimes, FTC Informal Staff Opinion Letter (Aug. 3, 1984), *reprinted on the CD-Rom accompanying this manual*; Feldman, FTC Informal Staff Opinion Letter (Apr. 15, 1971), *reprinted on the CD-Rom accompanying this manual*. *See also* § 5.2.4.3, *supra*. *But see* Houghton v. New Jersey Mfrs. Ins. Co., 615 F. Supp. 299 (E.D. Pa. 1985), *rev'd*, 795 F.2d 1144 (3d Cir. 1986); Beresh v. Retail Credit Co., 358 F. Supp. 260 (C.D. Cal. 1973).

429 15 U.S.C. § 1681b(c). *See* § 7.3.4, *infra*.

430 *See* Carson, FTC Informal Staff Opinion Letter (Apr. 29, 1971), *reprinted on the CD-Rom accompanying this manual*; FTC, Compliance with the Fair Credit Reporting Act, at 23 (1977); Trans Union Corp. v. Fed. Trade Comm'n, 81 F.3d 228 (D.C. Cir. 1996).

431 Cole v. U.S. Capital, Inc., 389 F.3d 719, 727 (7th Cir. 2004) (quoting Trans Union Corp. v. Fed. Trade Comm'n, 267 F.3d 1138, 1143 (D.C. Cir. 2001)). *See Trans Union*, 267 F.3d at 1143 ("the FCRA's express purpose is to facilitate credit, not target marketing").

432 Levine v. World Fin. Network Nat'l Bank, 473 F.3d 1118 (11th Cir. 2006) (consumer stated claim that former creditor unlawfully reviewed consumer's closed account for purpose of trolling for new business); Fed. Trade Comm'n v. Citigroup Inc., 239 F. Supp. 2d 1302 (N.D. Ga. 2001) (denying motion to dismiss allegations that Associates used or obtained consumer reports for impermissible purposes of soliciting additional loan products or to solicit the consumer for a credit transaction that the consumer did not initiate); Gowen, FTC Informal Staff Opinion Letter (Apr. 29, 1999), *reprinted on the CD-Rom accompanying this manual*; Benner, FTC Informal Staff Opinion Letter (Apr. 30, 1999), *reprinted on the CD-Rom accompanying this manual*. *But cf*. Trikas v. Universal Card Servs., Corp., 351 F. Supp. 2d 37 (E.D.N.Y. 2005) (bank's inquiries on account erroneously left open were not made with an impermissible purpose).

433 Buchman, FTC Informal Staff Opinion Letter (Mar. 2, 1998), *reprinted on the CD-Rom accompanying this manual*.

434 *See* § 7.2.8.2.3, *supra*.

435 S. Rep. No. 185, 104th Cong., 1st Sess. at 35 (Dec. 14, 1995); Fed. Trade Comm'n v. Citigroup Inc., 239 F. Supp. 2d 1302 (N.D. Ga. 2001) (denying motion to dismiss allegations that Associates used or obtained consumer reports for impermissible purposes of soliciting additional loan products or to solicit the consumer for a credit transaction that the consumer did not initiate). *See* § 7.2.8.3, *supra*.

436 Yohay v. City of Alexandria Employees Credit Union, Inc., 827 F.2d 967 (4th Cir. 1987).

437 This was alluded to as the impermissible purpose in Yohay v. City of Alexandria Employees Credit Union, Inc., 827 F.2d 967 (4th Cir. 1987).

438 FTC Official Staff Commentary § 604(3)(E) item 5, *reprinted at* Appx. D, *infra*.

439 *Id. See* W.D.I.A. Corp. v. McGraw-Hill, Inc. 34 F. Supp. 2d 612 (S.D. Ohio 1998).

440 Popik v. American Int'l Mtg. Co., 936 F. Supp. 173 (S.D.N.Y. 1996).

A business' interest in a consumer report, no matter how legitimate and proper in a commercial sense, is not a permissible ground for releasing a consumer report unless there is a consumer relationship between the requester and the consumer, or the consumer was seeking credit, insurance, employment, or some public benefit from the business concern, or other particular purpose specified in the Act.[441] For example, a company's investigation to determine whether the subject of a consumer report was selling contraband liquor is an impermissible reason for a CRA to release a consumer report.[442] Likewise, a rent stabilized landlord may not access a tenant's consumer report to check the tenant's principal residence where the law requires renewal of the lease without regard to creditworthiness.[443]

7.5 Agency Procedures Insuring That Only Users with Permissible Purposes Obtain Reports

7.5.1 General

Consumer reporting agencies (CRAs) have two separate obligations concerning when they can release consumer reports to users, and they should be liable under the FCRA for failing to comply with *either* provision. First, CRAs cannot release consumer reports for impermissible purposes, and both negligent and willful violations of this requirement are actionable under the Act.[444] In addition, the Act requires CRAs to "maintain reasonable procedures . . . to limit the furnishing of consumer reports to the purposes listed."[445] Failure to comply with this provision should be actionable under the FCRA as well. That is, CRAs are liable if they *either* negligently or willfully release reports for impermissible purposes *or* if they negligently or willfully do not maintain reasonable procedures.[446]

If a CRA employee releases information for an impermissible purpose, even if the CRA is not vicariously liable for the employee's actions, the CRA would still be liable if its procedures were faulty, permitting the employee to violate the FCRA.[447] Another example would relate to punitive damages, where a CRA may not have intentionally released information improperly, but where it intentionally failed to maintain proper procedures. Punitive damages should then be available.[448] However, if no information about the consumer has been released for an impermissible purpose, or even if faulty procedures resulted only in a permissible use of a consumer report, courts may decline to find any violation of the Act.[449]

The FCRA requires that the procedures for limiting the use of reports be reasonable. In addition, the Act requires that procedures be established so that, *prior* to releasing a consumer report:

- Prospective users identify themselves;
- Prospective users certify the purpose for which the information is sought;
- Prospective users certify that the information will be used for no other purpose; and
- The CRA makes a reasonable effort to verify the identity of new prospective users and the uses certified by those prospective users.[450]

In addition, no CRA may release a report to anyone if it has reasonable grounds for believing that the consumer report will not be used for a permissible purpose.[451]

The Act places affirmative requirements on CRAs to determine the user's purpose. The requirements are not satisfied by a system that places the burden on its users to notify the CRA when a use is impermissible, and until then the CRA continues to supply reports to those users.[452]

---

441 Russell v. Shelter Fin. Servs., 604 F. Supp. 201 (W.D. Mo. 1984); Boothe v. TRW Credit Data, 523 F. Supp. 631 (S.D.N.Y. 1981), *modified*, 557 F. Supp. 66 (S.D.N.Y. 1982). *See also* Henry v. Forbes, 433 F. Supp. 5 (D. Minn. 1976); Ley v. Boron Oil Co., 419 F. Supp. 1240 (W.D. Pa. 1976); § 7.2.8, *supra*.
442 Boothe v. TRW Credit Data, 994 F. Supp. 492 (S.D.N.Y. 1998).
443 Ali v. Vikar Mgmt. Ltd., 97 Civ. 1501 (D.C.) (S.D.N.Y. Feb. 19, 1988).
444 15 U.S.C. §§ 1681b, 1681n, 1681o.
445 15 U.S.C. § 1681e(a).
446 *See* § 10.2.2.4, *infra*. *Cf.* Kennedy v. Border City Sav. & Loan Ass'n, 747 F.2d 367 (6th Cir. 1984); Batdorf v. Equifax, 949 F. Supp. 777 (D. Haw. 1996) (describing TRW's extensive procedures), *aff'd without op.*, 176 F.3d 481 (9th Cir. 1999); New Palm Gardens, Inc. v. Bentley, [1980–1989 Decisions Transfer Binder] Consumer Cred. Guide (CCH) ¶ 96,648 (D. Mass. 1983); Peeler, FTC Informal Staff Opinion Letter (Aug. 27, 1977), *reprinted on the CD-Rom accompanying this manual*. *But see* Dobson v. Holloway, 828 F. Supp. 975 (M.D. Ga. 1993) (better justification of ruling would have been that CRA not negligent in refusing report for impermissible purpose, rather than reasonable procedures provide a defense); Dotzler v. Perot, 876 F. Supp. 207 (E.D. Mo. 1995).
447 *See* § 7.6, *infra*.
448 *See* § 11.12, *infra*, for a discussion when punitive damages are available.
449 *See* § 10.2.2.4, *infra*.
450 15 U.S.C. § 1681e.
451 15 U.S.C. § 1681e(a); Levine v. World Fin. Network Nat'l Bank, 473 F.3d 1118 (11th Cir. 2006). *Cf.* Harrington v. ChoicePoint, Inc., Slip. Op., No. CV 05-1294 MRP (C.D. Cal. Sept. 15, 2005), *available at* www.consumerlaw.org/unreported (rejecting argument that information was not a consumer report because defendant did not expect that information would be used for FCRA purposes; "Once the fraudsters indicated they intended to use the information for FCRA purposes, it does not matter that in another part of the agreement they promised not to do it. . . . Deciding otherwise would allow ChoicePoint to contract around FCRA liability.").
452 Grimes, FTC Informal Staff Opinion Letter (Oct. 15, 1974), *reprinted on the CD-Rom accompanying this manual*.

7.5.2 User Identification and Certifications

7.5.2.1 Nature of Certification

The CRA must require prospective users to identify themselves, certify the purpose for which they intend to use the information, and certify that the information will not be used for other purposes.[453] The CRA must obtain a specific, *written* certification that the recipient will obtain reports for certain specific purposes and for no others.[454] If the report is obtained by a reseller to release to someone else, the reseller must identify the end-user.[455]

The FCRA also prohibits a user from obtaining or using a report unless the report was obtained for an authorized purpose that was certified in accordance with section 1681e, which requires the user to certify that the information will be used for no other purpose.[456] The user's certification should expressly state that the user is prohibited from sharing the report or providing it to anyone else, except the subject of the report or a joint user having the same purpose.[457] FTC consent orders also indicate that the certification should state that the user understands that any report obtained under false pretenses will subject the user to a maximum $5000 fine and/or one-year imprisonment.[458] If a user refuses to provide the certification, the CRA should refuse to provide reports to that user.[459]

If an investigative consumer report has been requested, the user must certify to the CRA that it has already made the required disclosures to the subject of the report, and further that upon written request the user will make a complete and accurate disclosure of the nature and scope of the investigation requested.[460]

Where reports are to be used for employment purposes, and sometimes when they are requested by a child support enforcement agency, the user must also certify additional information specified by the statute. These requirements are discussed elsewhere.[461]

7.5.2.2 Blanket Certifications

A CRA can obtain a blanket certification from a user (such as a creditor) that typically has a permissible purpose for receiving a consumer report, stating that it will use all reports it receives only for specified permissible purposes and for no others. Then certification need not be provided for each individual report released, as long as there is no reason to believe the user may be violating its certification.[462] In such instances of suspected violation, the CRA should require a specific certification and retain at least a single copy of the statement in its records.[463]

When doubt arises as to the continuing accuracy of the user's blanket certification, the CRA must take additional steps to ensure compliance and to limit access to information for permissible purposes only. The most obvious precaution is to require separate, advance certification for each request. Additional steps may include use of random checks, new computer passwords, and the like.

In addition, if a user (e.g., an attorney or detective agency) is likely to have both permissible and impermissible purposes for ordering consumer reports, the CRA can *never* rely on a blanket certification. Instead, the CRA must require the user to provide a separate certification each time it requests a consumer report.[464]

---

453 15 U.S.C. § 1681e(a). *See also* FTC Official Staff Commentary § 607 item 2B, *reprinted at* Appx. D, *infra*.

454 FTC Official Staff Commentary § 607 item 2B, *reprinted at* Appx. D, *infra*. *See also* Morris, FTC Informal Staff Opinion Letter (July 26, 1979), *reprinted on the CD-Rom accompanying this manual*; Grimes, FTC Informal Staff Opinion Letter (May 22, 1975), *reprinted on the CD-Rom accompanying this manual*; Grimes, FTC Informal Staff Opinion Letter (Oct. 15, 1974), *reprinted on the CD-Rom accompanying this manual*; Conway, FTC Informal Staff Opinion Letter (May 6, 1971), *reprinted on the CD-Rom accompanying this manual*; Carson, FTC Informal Staff Opinion Letter (Apr. 8, 1971), *reprinted on the CD-Rom accompanying this manual*. *But see* Meyer, FTC Informal Staff Opinion Letter (Mar. 22, 1983), *reprinted on the CD-Rom accompanying this manual* (oral certification permissible).

455 *See* § 2.6.3, *supra*.

456 15 U.S.C. § 1681b(f).

457 FTC Official Staff Commentary § 607 item 2B, *reprinted at* Appx. D, *infra*.

458 Southern Maryland Credit Bureau, Inc., 101 F.T.C. 19, 23 (1983) (consent order); Trans Union Credit Info. Co., 102 F.T.C. 1109 (1983) (consent order).

459 FTC Official Staff Commentary § 607 item 2B, *reprinted at* Appx. D, *infra*.

460 *See* § 13.4.1, *infra*.

461 For employment purposes, see § 7.2.4.3, *supra*; by child support enforcement agencies, see § 7.2.9, *supra*.

462 Greenhouse v. TRW, Inc., 1998 U.S. Dist. LEXIS 1973 (E.D. La. Feb. 12, 1998); Davis v. Asset Servs., 46 F. Supp. 2d 503 (M.D. La. 1998); FTC Official Staff Commentary § 607 items 2B, 2C, *reprinted at* Appx. D, *infra*. *See also* Klapper v. Chapiro, 154 Misc. 2d 459, 586 N.Y.S.2d 846 (Sup. Ct. 1992); Peeler, FTC Informal Staff Opinion Letter (Aug. 27, 1977), *reprinted on the CD-Rom accompanying this manual* (minimum standard requires CRA to have written agreement with customers' that reports are not used for impermissible purpose); Dea, FTC Informal Staff Opinion Letter (Apr. 2, 1975), *reprinted on the CD-Rom accompanying this manual*; Dea, FTC Informal Staff Opinion Letter (Nov. 28, 1974), *reprinted on the CD-Rom accompanying this manual*; FTC Informal Staff Opinion, [1969–1973 Decisions Transfer Binder] Consumer Cred. Guide (CCH) ¶ 99,493 (May 16, 1971). *Cf.* Breese v. Triadvantage Credit Servs., Inc., 393 F. Supp. 2d 819 (D. Minn. 2005) (defendant, whose employee obtained consumer report for use by his grandfather, could rely on its general certification and did not need to specifically certify grandfather's purpose, which was permissible).

463 Hiemstra v. Crocker National Bank, 195 Cal. App. 3d 1629, 241 Cal. Rptr. 564 (1987).

464 Allen v. Kirkland & Ellis, Clearinghouse No. 49,963 (N.D. Ill. Mar. 14, 1994) (law firm cannot use blanket certification); FTC Official Staff Commentary § 607 item 2C, *reprinted at* Appx. D,

In determining whether users have both permissible and impermissible purposes, the FTC has suggested that a CRA should utilize its area's yellow pages to compile a list of all detectives, private investigators, and attorneys in the area.[465]

Some car dealers have also been reported to pull customer reports before any actual application for credit has been made in order to increase negotiating power. Louisiana has even specifically addressed this abuse by statute, prohibiting dealers from requesting, obtaining, or reviewing an individual's consumer report in connection with: (1) a test drive; (2) a request for information about pricing or financing; or (3) for negotiating with the consumer, unless the dealer received an application from the consumer to lease or finance or has written authorization from the consumer to obtain or review the consumer report.[466] Even without such a statute, if abuse by car dealers is sufficiently widespread that a CRA may not reasonably rely on a dealer's blanket certification, the CRA should require additional separate certifications from the dealer to ensure that the dealer has a permissible purpose, such as an application for financing or for a lease, to obtain the report.

7.5.2.3 Follow-Up and Continuing Reports

It is not enough for a user to certify that its initial use of a report will be for a permissible purpose, if there is a risk that follow-up reports will no longer be for a permissible purpose. The CRA will have to obtain a separate certification for each follow-up report on the consumer.[467]

Similarly, if a CRA provides activity reports on customers with open-end accounts (that is periodic reports to the creditor on its open-end customers), the CRA must make certain that the creditor notifies the CRA when an account is closed and paid in full. Once the account is closed, the creditor no longer has a permissible purpose to receive the report.[468]

7.5.3 Agency Verification Procedures

It is not enough that the CRA obtain a certification from the user. The CRA must have a system to verify that it is dealing with a legitimate business having a legitimate permissible purpose for the report being requested.[469] A CRA has a duty to investigate a facially valid request when there are reasonable indications that the request is for impermissible purposes.[470] What constitutes adequate verification will vary with the circumstances.[471]

If the CRA is not familiar with a user, appropriate procedures might require an on-site visit to the user's place of business or a check of the user's bank or other references.[472] If the CRA already has a blanket certification from a user, the CRA should still ensure that the company requesting a report is in fact the company that has issued the blanket certification. The CRA could accomplish this by assigning its subscribers or members an identification number which they must supply each time a consumer report is requested.[473]

When doubt arises concerning a particular user's compliance with its contractual certification, the CRA must take steps to ensure compliance, such as requiring a separate, advance certification for each report it releases to that user or auditing that user to verify that it is obtaining reports only for a permissible purpose.[474] Of course, if a user repeatedly requests reports for impermissible purposes, the CRA should stop supplying reports to such user.[475]

---

infra; Southern Maryland Credit Bureau, Inc., 101 F.T.C. 19, 23 (1983) (consent order); Trans Union Credit Info. Co., 102 F.T.C. 1109 (1983) (consent order). *See also* Grimes, FTC Informal Staff Opinion Letter (Dec. 9, 1983), *reprinted on the CD-Rom accompanying this manual* (detective agency or private investigator); Meyer, FTC Informal Staff Opinion Letter (Mar. 22, 1983), *reprinted on the CD-Rom accompanying this manual* (child support agency); Peeler, FTC Informal Staff Opinion Letter (Feb. 26, 1979), *reprinted on the CD-Rom accompanying this manual*; Morris, FTC Informal Staff Opinion Letter (July 26, 1979), *reprinted on the CD-Rom accompanying this manual*; Peeler, FTC Informal Staff Opinion Letter (July 24, 1978), *reprinted on the CD-Rom accompanying this manual* (attorney). *Accord* Peeler, FTC Informal Staff Opinion Letter (Nov. 1, 1983), *reprinted on the CD-Rom accompanying this manual* (detective agency has mixed use, unclear whether Franchise Tax Board falls into mixed use category mandating individual certification).

465 Southern Maryland Credit Bureau, Inc., 101 F.T.C. 19, 23 (1983) (consent order). *See also* Allen v. Kirkland & Ellis, Clearinghouse No. 49,963 (N.D. Ill. Mar. 14, 1994) (law firm cannot use blanket certification).

466 La. Rev. Stat. Ann. § 9:3571.2 (West).

467 Equifax, Inc., 96 F.T.C. 1045 (1980), *rev'd in part on other grounds*, 678 F.2d 1047 (11th Cir. 1982). *See also* Southern Maryland Credit Bureau, Inc., 101 F.T.C. 19, 23 (1983) (consent order).

468 FTC Official Staff Commentary § 607 item 2G, *reprinted at* Appx. D, *infra*; Levine v. World Fin. Network Nat'l Bank, 473 F.3d 1118 (11th Cir. 2006). *See also* Ch. 4, *supra*.

469 FTC Official Staff Commentary § 607 item 2G, item 2A, *reprinted at* Appx. D, *infra*.

470 Levine v. World Fin. Network Nat'l Bank, 473 F.3d 1118 (11th Cir. 2006).

471 *Id*. One large CRA, TRW (now Experian), has asserted it conducts both precautionary and investigative activities on the uses to which its clients put the reports. Klapper v. Shapiro, 154 Misc. 2d 459, 586 N.Y.S.2d 846 (Sup. Ct. 1992).

472 FTC Official Staff Commentary § 607 item 2A, *reprinted at* Appx. D, *infra*.

473 *But see* National Account Sys., Inc., 89 F.T.C. 282 (1977), *modified sub nom.* Diners Club, Inc., 94 F.T.C. 297 (1979) (consent order) (subsidiary of Diners Club obtained reports under false pretenses by using code numbers of other, legitimate businesses).

474 FTC Official Staff Commentary § 607 item 2D, *reprinted at* Appx. D, *infra*.

475 *Id.*; *see* Commonwealth v. Source One, 763 N.E.2d 42 (Mass. 2002) (Equifax terminated user's account after receiving and investigating consumer complaint and concluding that defen-

7.5.4 Electronic Communication of Reports

Electronic communication of consumer reports to users is common. The FTC Staff Commentary permits users to access the files of CRAs through in-house computer terminals.[476] CRAs may provide consumer reports in this manner provided that they take the necessary steps to ensure that the users have a permissible purpose.[477] The CRA must also be able to know and retain a record of what users have obtained access to consumer reports on which consumers, so that the CRA can comply with other FCRA provisions that necessitate that CRAs know who has used which consumer reports.[478]

In addition, if a CRA has doubts about whether a user that is obtaining reports via computer hook-up has a permissible purpose for each report it obtains, the CRA must take special steps to prevent abuse. For example, different procedures may be necessary where a user routinely has permissible and impermissible uses or reports.

Before the Internet age, a court held that when a user normally has primarily permissible purposes to request a report, direct teletype hookups may be utilized between the user and the CRA upon the user's advance certification that all requests would be in connection with legitimate purposes.[479] But an FTC staff letter refuses to authorize direct, automatic relay of information between a CRA and private investigators, reasoning that since these agencies have substantial impermissible, as well as permissible purposes for the report, the individual certification necessary for the reports could not be obtained.[480] The same principles undoubtedly apply to Internet access.

On the other hand, another early FTC staff letter expressly allows the use of direct computer linkups between a CRA and a child support agency where an adequate certification process for the reports was implemented. The process approved was one in which: (1) the support agency initially would file with the CRA a letter certifying that all inquiries made would be in compliance with the Act; (2) after each actual inquiry, the child support agency would send a form certifying a permissible purpose exists, along with the judgment number from an adjudicated child support obligation; (3) a monthly audit would be made by the CRA to ensure that certification was made for each inquiry and that a permissible purpose was found in each certified purpose; and (4) if an impermissible purpose or no certification is found in the audit, the CRA will promptly terminate the service.[481]

If a CRA suspects that a third party is breaking into the user's computer to improperly access consumer reports, the CRA should take appropriate action, such as creating passwords or codes to restrict access to reports or to make random checks as to the actual user.[482] Similarly, if a user or its employees are inadvertently, or with intent, obtaining reports for an impermissible purpose, the CRA should require an individual written certification for each report request or randomly monitor the user's purposes in requesting reports.[483]

7.5.5 Retention of Request Records

It is important for the CRA to keep an accurate record of persons who receive consumer reports. A consumer report may be used on many occasions before the consumer learns that it exists. Once the consumer is informed that the CRA has released a report about the consumer, the consumer has a right to disclosure of the names of all persons who have received the report (often called "inquiries").[484] If the consumer discovers that the consumer report contains inaccurate or inadequate information, the consumer will want to ensure that all past users of the report are notified of corrections or additions to the consumer report. Additionally, the consumer will be able to discover users that may have used the report for impermissible purposes or under false pretenses.[485]

7.6 Liability of Reporting Agency Employees for Impermissible Uses

The FCRA imposes criminal liability on "[a]ny officer or employee of a CRA who knowingly and willfully provides

---

dants were using consumer reports for impermissible purposes).
476 FTC Official Staff Commentary § 607 item 2D, *reprinted at* Appx. D, *infra*.
477 *Id*.
478 *Id. See* § 7.5.5, *infra*.
479 Boothe v. TRW Credit Data, 557 F. Supp. 66, 71 (S.D.N.Y. 1982) (advance certification by user with primary proper purpose protects CRA without knowledge of improper use of report, even though program could be written to require individual certification for each report). Advance certification does not protect the user who then obtains a consumer report for illegitimate reasons. Russell v. Shelter Fin. Servs., 604 F. Supp. 201 (W.D. Mo. 1984).
480 Muris, FTC Informal Staff Opinion Letter (Apr. 29, 1982), *reprinted on the CD-Rom accompanying this manual* (should method be found to individually certify the purpose for each report, then teletype hookups may be allowed).

481 Meyer, FTC Informal Staff Opinion Letter (Mar. 22, 1983), *reprinted on the CD-Rom accompanying this manual*.
482 FTC Official Staff Commentary § 607 item 2E, *reprinted at* Appx. D, *infra*. Even this may not be enough, though. *See* Diners Club, *sub. nom.* National Account Sys., Inc., 89 F.T.C. 282 (1977), *modified sub nom.* Diners Club, Inc., 94 F.T.C. 297 (1979) (consent order) (debt collection agency broke into computer using other users' secret codes and improperly obtained consumer reports).
483 FTC Official Staff Commentary § 607 item 2E, *reprinted at* Appx. D, *infra. See* National Consumer Law Center, Consumer Law Pleadings No. 3 § 5.1 (Cumulative CD-Rom and Index Guide).
484 15 U.S.C. § 1681g(a)(3). *See* § 3.5.4, *supra*.
485 Such users would then be liable under 15 U.S.C. § 1681q.

information... from the agency's files to a person not authorized to receive that information."[486] The FTC has not issued an interpretation of this FCRA provision, and no criminal suits have been brought under it. Like the criminal false pretenses section, though, it is likely that a consumer reporting agency (CRA) employee's violation of this provision is also actionable through the civil provision for willful violations.[487]

This provision is useful where a CRA employee is acting beyond the scope of employment, so that issues would be raised whether the CRA is liable for the employee's release of information for an impermissible use. Where a user with an impermissible purpose obtains a consumer report from CRA personnel without the CRA's knowledge, the consumer may be able to obtain a judgment against the individual CRA personnel, even if there may not be a cause of action against the CRA.

In such a situation, however, the consumer's attorney should investigate the consumer CRA's procedures and personnel training. The consumer's attorney can argue that the employee would not have been able to release the consumer report to an unauthorized user were it not for the CRA's failure to "maintain reasonable procedures... to limit the furnishing of consumer reports to the purposes listed."[488] The CRA should be required to maintain procedures limiting its employees' access to consumers' files to those situations where the employees are acting as agents of the CRA. If an employee of the CRA has violated the criminal provision of the Act[489] and the CRA cannot be held liable for violating the Act's substantive permissible purposes requirement,[490] the CRA nevertheless may be liable for failing to comply with the Act's procedural requirement.[491]

7.7 User Liability for Impermissible Purposes

7.7.1 General

Notwithstanding the consumer reporting agency's (CRA) reasonable efforts to verify the user's identification and purpose for requesting information, some users will obtain consumer reports through misrepresentation. In light of the difficulty which the CRA may have in discovering fictitious creditors, it may be that the consumer will have more success suing the user than the CRA.

The Act imposes liability on "any person" who fails to comply with any "requirement" of the Act with respect to consumers, with separate provisions for willful and negligent violations.[492] Users are clearly covered by these liability provisions. Since 1997,[493] the Act has specifically imposed requirements on users, as well as on CRAs.[494] The Act also directly imposes criminal liability on users who obtain information under false pretenses,[495] a provision that has been held to create a "requirement," the violation of which is civilly enforceable as well.[496]

Thus, users may be liable for failing to certify their purpose for obtaining a consumer report, for obtaining or using a report without a permissible purpose, or for obtaining any information from a CRA under false pretenses.[497] On the other hand, an individual who inadvertently received a report that she did not request or use might not be liable.[498] The specific remedies available for violations of the Act are discussed in Chapters 10 and 11, *infra*.

---

486 15 U.S.C. § 1681r.
487 See § 7.7, *infra*.
488 15 U.S.C. § 1681e(a).
489 15 U.S.C. § 1681r.
490 15 U.S.C. § 1681b.
491 15 U.S.C. § 1681e(a).
492 15 U.S.C. §§ 1681n, 1681o. *See* § 10.2.1, *infra*.
493 15 U.S.C. § 1681b(f), *added by* Pub. L. No. 104-208, 110 Stat. 3009 (1996). Thus pre-1997 cases holding that users cannot be liable for negligently obtaining reports for impermissible purposes should no longer be applicable. *See, e.g.,* Ippolito v. WNS, Inc., 864 F.2d 440 (7th Cir. 1988); Frederick v. Marquette National Bank, 911 F.2d 1 (7th Cir. 1990).
494 15 U.S.C. § 1681b(f) ("A person shall not *use or obtain* a consumer report for any purpose unless [in accordance with the Act]") (emphasis added). *See* Lukens v. Dunphy Nissan, Inc., 2004 WL 1661220 (E.D. Pa. July 26, 2004) ("Although it would be nonsensical to interpret the FCRA to allow the improper use of consumer reports as long as such reports were originally obtained for permissible purposes, this Court does not reach the issue."); Chester v. Purvis, 260 F. Supp. 2d 711, 718 (S.D. Ind. 2003) (concluding that reading the FCRA as a whole requires user liability); Castro v. Union Nissan, Inc., 2002 WL 1466810 (N.D. Ill. July 8, 2002) (car dealership could be liable under FCRA for obtaining spouse's consumer report without a permissible purpose). *But see* Kodrick v. Ferguson, 54 F. Supp. 2d 788 (N.D. Ill. 1999) (holding that the FCRA is aimed primarily at CRAs and refusing to extend liability to users without a more definite statement by Congress).
495 15 U.S.C. § 1681q.
496 *See* § 7.7.4, *supra*, § 10.2.5, *infra*.
497 15 U.S.C. §§ 1681b(f), 1681q; Ausherman v. Bank of Am. Corp., 352 F.3d 896 (4th Cir. 2003); Padin v. Oyster Point Dodge, 397 F. Supp. 2d 712, 720 n.13 (E.D. Va. 2005); Hinton v. Trans Union L.L.C., 2004 WL 1114744 (N.D. Ill. May 4, 2004) (lender and furnisher of information that accessed individual's consumer report after loan was paid in full can be liable for obtaining individual's consumer report without permissible purpose); Quigley v. Pennsylvania Higher Educ. Assistance Agency 2000 U.S. Dist. LEXIS 19847 (N.D. Cal. Nov. 8, 2000) (private right of action against creditor who reviewed debtor's consumer report without permission and under false pretenses); Commonwealth v. Source One, 763 N.E.2d 42 (Mass. 2002) (users obtained consumer reports using false pretenses and for impermissible purposes when they had no reasons for use of the reports by third parties); Cohen v. Sheehy Ford, 27 Va. Cir. 161 (1992) (employer and employee can be liable under FCRA for violations of § 1681b). Separate provisions apply to CRAs which violate the provisions granting the FBI secret access to information in consumer reporting files, including statutory damages.
498 Phillips v. Grendahl, 312 F.3d 357 (8th Cir. 2002).

7.7.2 Uncertified Uses of a Consumer Report

A person cannot use or obtain a consumer report for any purpose unless the purpose is a permissible one that has been certified to the CRA.[499] This rule, which applies to users, references the separate provision requiring CRAs to maintain procedures requiring users to certify that the information will be used for the permissible purpose specified and no other purpose.[500]

The conjunction of these two provisions appears to establish that a use is impermissible if it is not the one certified to the CRA. Note, however, that some courts have held that a user who obtained a report for one permissible purpose may use it without liability for another permissible purpose.[501] Moreover, courts are divided on whether a user who certifies a false purpose for the report may be held liable for obtaining it under false pretenses if the ultimate use of the report is permissible.[502]

A user who negligently or willfully violates the certification requirements is liable under the general liability provisions of the FCRA.[503] By adding subsection 1681b(f) in 1997,[504] Congress clarified that a plaintiff need not meet the willfulness standard of FCRA's criminal false pretenses provision to demonstrate liability for violating the Act's certification requirements.[505]

7.7.3 Willful Noncompliance of User

The Act imposes higher penalties for willful violations. The consumer is entitled to statutory and punitive damages, in addition to actual damages and attorney fees, which are also available for negligent violations.[506]

For willful violations of the FCRA, the Act generally provides for actual damages "or damages of not less than $100 and not more than $1,000."[507] However, in the specific case of liability of a *natural person* for obtaining a consumer report under false pretenses or knowingly without a permissible purpose, the consumer is entitled to a minimum of $1000 or actual damages, whichever is higher.[508] In the case of a corporation or other entity, it appears that the general FCRA liability provision could also be used to obtain statutory damages for false pretenses, but potentially in a lower amount.[509]

Willfulness is generally discussed in § 11.12, *infra*, but some specific examples involving users are provided below.

Familiarity with the FCRA or general knowledge that reports can be obtained under limited circumstances is sufficient to support an inference of knowingly obtaining a consumer report in conscious disregard of the target's legal rights.[510] Repeatedly obtaining a consumer's report after notices that the consumer had no account with user is sufficient to defeat a motion to dismiss a claim that the user willfully obtained the consumer's report without a permissible purpose.[511]

Intentionally misleading a CRA about the use to which the report will be put is a knowing violation.[512] The false pretense may be as simple as signing a certification not to put information to an impermissible purpose, and then

---

499 15 U.S.C. § 1681b(f) (effective Sept. 30, 1997). See § 7.5.2, *supra*.
500 15 U.S.C. § 1681e(a). See also § 10.2.2.4, *infra*.
501 Minter v. AAA Cook County Consol., Inc., 2004 WL 1630781 (N.D. Ill. July 19, 2004); Marzluff v. Verizon Wireless, 785 N.E.2d 805 (Ohio Ct. App. 2003).
502 Compare Daley v. Haddonfield Lumber Inc., 943 F. Supp. 464 (D. N.J. 1996) ("[The FCRA] allows release of credit reports only to specific parties and under specific circumstances. . . . [T]he credit reporting agency . . . did not release the information generally to any potential user who may indeed maintain a permissible purpose for obtaining the report.") with Scott v. Real Estate Fin. Group, 183 F.3d 97 (2d Cir. 1999) ("a report requester does not violate [the false pretenses section] by giving a false reason for its request if it has an independent legitimate basis for requesting the report").
503 See § 10.2.5.1, *infra*.
504 Pub. L. No. 104-208, 110 Stat. 3009 (1996).
505 Ausherman v. Bank of Am. Corp., 352 F.3d 896 (4th Cir. 2003) (recognizing § 1681b(f) is now primary source of civil liability rather than § 1681q); Sather v. Weintraut, 2003 WL 21692111 (D. Minn. July 10, 2003) (same). See § 7.7.3, *infra*.
506 15 U.S.C. § 1681n. Cf. id. § 1681o.
507 15 U.S.C. § 1681n(a)(1)(A).
508 15 U.S.C. § 1681n(a)(1)(B).
509 See Schroeder v. Capitol Indemnity Corp., 2006 WL 2009053 (E.D. Wis. July 17, 2006). But see Phillips v. Grendahl, 312 F.3d 357 (8th Cir. 2002) (noting that 15 U.S.C. § 1681n(a)(1)(B) provides for statutory damages only against natural persons, but failing to discuss § 1681n(a)(A)); Lamar v. Experian Info. Sys., 408 F. Supp. 2d 591 (N.D. Ill. 2006) (same).
510 Phillips v. Grendahl, 312 F.3d 357 (8th Cir. 2002); Sather v. Weintraut, 2003 WL 21692111 (D. Minn. July 10, 2003).
511 Sather v. Weintraut, 2003 WL 21692111 (D. Minn. July 10, 2003); Veno v. AT&T Corp., 297 F. Supp. 2d 379 (D. Mass. 2003).
512 Duncan v. Handmaker, 149 F.3d 424 (6th Cir. 1998) (dicta); Yohay v. City of Alexandria Employees Credit Union, Inc., 827 F.2d 967 (4th Cir. 1987) (attorney used her connection with a credit union, that had a computer link with a CRA, to obtain credit information on her ex-husband; action subjected both herself and the credit union to civil and criminal liability); Pappas v. City of Calumet City, 9 F. Supp. 2d 943 (N.D. Ill. 1998) (police certified employment purposes but actual use was to investigate owner of towing business; no business transaction between city and towing company); Popik v. American Int'l Mtg. Co., 936 F. Supp. 173 (S.D.N.Y. 1996) (intent to deceive factual question); Daley v. Haddonfield Lumber, Inc., 943 F. Supp. 464 (D.N.J. 1996) (individual liable for false pretenses where he represented that he was acting as employee of lumber company, when in fact he wanted report for condominium association of which he was board of directors member; permissible purpose of the condominium association was irrelevant); Rylewicz v. Beaton Servs., Ltd., 698 F. Supp. 1391 (N.D. Ill. 1988) (defendants obtained report during litigation to harass and intimidate), *aff'd*, 886 F.2d 1175 (7th Cir. 1989). See Comeaux v. Brown & Williamson Tobacco Co., 915 F.2d 1264 (9th Cir. 1990).

putting the information to an impermissible purpose, even where the user disclosed the intended purpose.[513]

If a user had previously obtained reports for permissible purposes from the CRA, but did not disclose the user's present (impermissible) purpose, this could arguably still involve false pretenses because the CRA could assume that the user would be using the current report for a permissible purpose.[514] Providing a blanket certification is no defense if one report is obtained for an impermissible purpose.[515]

The false pretenses section applies to "any person" obtaining information under false pretenses, whether the person obtained the report directly from the CRA or indirectly.[516]

A person who obtains information under false pretenses or knowingly without a permissible purpose is also liable to the CRA. The Act provides the CRA a separate remedy and minimum damages of $1000.[517] Apart from this provision, most courts have found that the FCRA does not allow defendants to cross claim for contribution or indemnity.[518]

7.7.4 User's Liability for Criminal False Pretenses

The Act now clearly imposes civil liability for willfully obtaining consumer information under false pretenses.[519] However, prior to the 1997 effective date of 15 U.S.C. § 1681b(f), which explicitly imposed the Act's requirements on users, civil liability for users was less clear. Courts reached users by looking to the Act's criminal provision, section 1681q, which applies to "[a]ny person who knowingly and willfully obtains information on a consumer from a CRA under false pretenses."[520] The civil provision, section 1681n, imposes liability for violation of "any requirement" of the Act. Courts held that section 1681q imposes a "requirement" on users not to obtain information on false pretenses (i.e., without a permissible purpose)—a requirement that, if violated, is actionable through section 1681n.

With the addition of section 1681b(f), the direct use of section 1681q in civil cases is "anachronistic," since section 1681n suffices.[521] But the requirements of section 1681q are still incorporated into section 1681n and can provide the basis for civil liability.

In particular, courts have noted that the criminal provision forbids use of false pretenses to obtain any "information on a consumer from a consumer reporting agency," not limited to information that qualifies as a "consumer report" under the Act.[522] The criminal section prohibits using false pre-

---

513 *See* Maloney v. City of Chicago, 678 F. Supp. 703 (N.D. Ill. 1987).

514 *But see* Henry v. Forbes, 433 F. Supp. 5 (D. Minn. 1976).

515 Russell v. Shelter Fin. Servs., 604 F. Supp. 201 (W.D. Mo. 1984).

516 *See* Yohay v. City of Alexandria Employees Credit Union, Inc., 827 F.2d 967 (4th Cir. 1987) (attorney used her connection with a credit union, that had a computer link with a CRA, to obtain credit information on her ex-husband; action subjected both herself and the credit union to civil and criminal liability); Daley v. Haddonfield Lumber, Inc., 943 F. Supp. 464 (D.N.J. 1996); Allen v. Miller, 1993 LEXIS 4879 (D. Or. Apr. 12, 1993) (federal employee).

517 15 U.S.C. § 1681n(b).

518 *See* § 11.8, *infra*.

519 15 U.S.C. §§ 1681n.

520 15 U.S.C. § 1681q. *See* Bakker v. McKinnon, 152 F.3d 1007 (8th Cir. 1998); Duncan v. Handmaker, 149 F.3d 424 (6th Cir. 1998); Northrop v. Hoffman of Simsbury, Inc., 134 F.3d 41 (2d Cir. 1997); Comeaux v. Brown & Williamson Tobacco Co., 915 F.2d 1264 (9th Cir. 1990) (noncompliance with § 1681q forms the basis for civil liability under § 1681n); Zamora v. Valley Fed. Sav. & Loan Ass'n, 811 F.2d 1368 (10th Cir. 1987); Yohay v. City of Alexandria Employees Credit Union, Inc., 827 F.2d 967 (4th Cir. 1987); Kennedy v. Border City Sav. & Loan Ass'n, 747 F.2d 367 (6th Cir. 1984) (§ 617, not § 616, gives rise to the private cause of action); Hansen v. Morgan, 582 F.2d 1214 (9th Cir. 1978); Popik v. American Int'l Mtg. Co., 936 F. Supp. 173 (S.D.N.Y. 1996); Daley v. Haddonfield Lumber, Inc., 943 F. Supp. 464 (D.N.J. 1996); Milgram v. Advanced Cellular Sys., Inc., 1990 U.S. Dist. LEXIS 4675 (E.D. Pa. Apr. 18, 1990); Auriemma v. City of Chicago, 1990 U.S. Dist. LEXIS 2335 (N.D. Ill. Mar. 2, 1990); Maloney v. City of Chicago, 678 F. Supp. 703 (N.D. Ill. 1987); Chiappetta v. Tellefson, 1985 WL 1951 (N.D. Ill. July 9, 1985); New Palm Gardens, Inc. v. Bentley, 1983 U.S. Dist. LEXIS 14710 (D. Mass. Aug. 11, 1983); Boothe v. TRW Credit Data, 557 F. Supp. 66, 70–71 (S.D.N.Y. 1982) (the "user" found liable was firm which impermissibly acquired report destined for another business); Klapper v. Shapiro, 154 Misc. 2d 459, 586 N.Y.S.2d 846 (Sup Ct. 1992) (attorney's use to impugn plaintiff's credibility is impermissible purpose; attorney deemed to have employed false pretenses); Mullen v. Al Castrucci Ford, Inc., 42 Ohio Misc. 2d 35, 537 N.E.2d 1307 (Ct. Com. Pl. 1986); Peeler, FTC Informal Staff Opinion Letter (Aug. 27, 1977), *reprinted on the CD-Rom accompanying this manual* (§ 616 creates consumer private cause of action for knowingly and willfully obtaining information on consumer under false pretenses). *See also* Scott v. Real Estate Fin. Group, 183 F.3d 97 (2d Cir. 1999) (false pretenses not actionable when user had a permissible, though undisclosed, purpose) (dicta); Matthews v. Worthen Bank & Trust Co., 741 F.2d 217 (8th Cir. 1984); Baker v. Bronx-Westchester Investigations, Inc., 850 F. Supp. 260 (S.D.N.Y. 1994) (false pretenses not actionable when user had a permissible, though undisclosed, purpose); Russell v. Shelter Fin. Servs., 604 F. Supp. 201 (W.D. Mo. 1984); Rice v. Montgomery Ward & Co., 450 F. Supp. 668 (M.D.N.C. 1978); Henry v. Forbes, 433 F. Supp. 5 (D. Minn. 1976). *Cf.* Allen v. Kirkland & Ellis, 1992 U.S. Dist. LEXIS 12383 (N.D. Ill. Aug. 14, 1992) (false pretenses not actionable when user had a permissible but undisclosed purpose). Dicta to the contrary, without benefit of briefing, in Frederick v. Marquette National Bank, 911 F.2d 1 (7th Cir. 1990) is simply wrong.

521 Phillips v. Grendahl, 312 F.3d 357 (8th Cir. 2002).

522 *See* Northrop v. Hoffman of Simsbury, Inc., 134 F.3d 41 (2d Cir. 1997) ("user" includes a party that in the ordinary course of business obtains consumer reports, as well as the ultimate recipient of the report); Ippolito v. WNS, Inc., 864 F.2d 440 n.8 (7th Cir. 1988); Kennedy v. Border City Sav. & Loan Ass'n, 747 F.2d 367, 369 (6th Cir. 1984); Berman v. Parco, 986 F. Supp. 195 (S.D.N.Y. 1997); Ali v. Vikar Mgmt. Ltd., 994 F. Supp. 492 (S.D.N.Y. 1998) (above the line information); New Palm Gardens, Inc. v. Bentley, 1983 U.S. Dist. LEXIS 14710 (D. Mass. Aug. 11, 1983) (civil and criminal liability may result if any information obtained from CRA under false pretenses); Rice v.

tense even to obtain an address or a Social Security number or other identifying information, which alone is not a consumer report.[523] Thus, it may still be useful in some cases to look to section 1681q as a substantive requirement for users. For example, a CRA could collect and expect to use information solely for business reports and even though the information is not a consumer report, a person would be liable under the criminal false pretenses provision if the person obtained the business report under false pretenses.

But if there is no intent to obtain a report improperly, then the user obviously did not "knowingly and willfully" obtain the report under false pretenses.[524]

7.7.5 Vicarious Liability of User for Acts of Employees

Employers may be held vicariously liable for employees who obtain reports for impermissible purposes, even while the employee may be separately liable.[525] The Act does not address employer liability per se, but courts have generally found that common law theories of vicarious liability are consistent with and even necessary to fulfill the FCRA's privacy and consumer protection purposes.[526]

An employer may be held liable for acts of an employee in three ways. First, if the employer expressly or implicitly authorizes or ratifies the conduct of the employee, that conduct is imputed to the employer.[527] Second, if the employee (as agent) acts for the benefit of the employer and within the scope of employment, the employer is liable under the doctrine of *respondeat superior*.[528]

Third, under the doctrine of apparent authority, an employer is liable for the acts of its employee when the employer puts the employee in a position which communicates to third parties that the employee possesses the authority to request the consumer report. Whenever a creditor, for example, has expressly allowed an employee to access consumer reports on its behalf, that person will invariably have apparent authority in the eyes of the CRA to request and receive a consumer report. If the employee abuses that authority by obtaining a report for impermissible purposes, the creditor can be liable.[529] This doctrine makes sense because, after all, the employer is in the best position to protect consumers with internal safeguards.[530]

In addition, apart from vicarious liability, an employer can be directly liable if it is negligent in its selection or supervision of its employees, or has policies permitting or encouraging violations of the Act.[531]

Montgomery Ward & Co., 450 F. Supp. 668 (M.D.N.C. 1978). *Cf.* 15 U.S.C. § 1681n(a)(1)(B) (setting forth damages for "obtaining a *consumer report* under false pretenses or knowingly without a permissible purpose) (emphasis added).

523 Ali v. Vikar Mgmt. Ltd., 994 F. Supp. 492 (S.D.N.Y. 1998).

524 *See* Duncan v. Handmaker, 149 F.3d 424 (6th Cir. 1998); Davis v. Asset Servs., 46 F. Supp. 2d 503 (M.D. La. 1998); Graziano v. TRW, Inc., 877 F. Supp. 53 (D. Mass. 1995); Allen v. Calvo, 832 F. Supp. 301 (D. Or. 1993); Allen v. Miller, 1993 U.S. Dist. LEXIS 4879 (D. Or. Apr. 12, 1993).

525 *See* Myers v. Bennett Law Offices, 238 F.3d 1068 (9th Cir. 2001), *on remand*, 238 F. Supp. 2d 1196 (D. Nev. 2002); Jones v. Federated Fin. Reserve Corp., 144 F.3d 961 (6th Cir. 1998). The Act defines "person" broadly to include "any individual, partnership, corporation, trust, estate, cooperative, association, government or governmental subdivision or agency, or other entity." 15 U.S.C. § 1681a(b).

526 *See* Myers v. Bennett Law Offices, 238 F.3d 1068 (9th Cir. 2001), *on remand*, 238 F. Supp. 2d 1196 (D. Nev. 2002); Jones v. Federated Fin. Reserve Corp., 144 F.3d 961 (6th Cir. 1998). *But see* Kodrick v. Ferguson, 54 F. Supp. 2d 788 (N.D. Ill. 1999) (Congress did not provide for vicariously liability under FCRA); Smith v. Sears, Roebuck & Co., 276 F. Supp. 2d 603 (S.D. Miss. 2003) (rejecting respondeat superior, apparent authority, and aided-in-the-agency analyses of other courts); Graves v. Tubb, 281 F. Supp. 2d 886 (N.D. Miss. 2003) (same; nothing in the FCRA makes employer liable for employees who knowingly obtain reports for impermissible purposes).

527 *See, e.g.,* Myers v. Bennett Law Offices, 238 F.3d 1068 (9th Cir. 2001), *on remand*, 238 F. Supp. 2d 1196 (D. Nev. 2002); Jones v. Federal Fin. Reserve Corp., 144 F.3d 961 (6th Cir. 1998).

528 *See, e.g.,* Jones v. Federal Fin. Reserve Corp., 144 F.3d 961 (6th Cir. 1998). *But see* Smith v. Sears, Roebuck & Co., 276 F. Supp. 2d 603 (S.D. Miss. 2003) (rejecting respondeat superior liability).

529 Myers v. Bennett Law Offices, 238 F.3d 1068 (9th Cir. 2001), *on remand*, 238 F. Supp. 2d 1196 (D. Nev. 2002); Jones v. Federal Fin. Reserve Corp., 144 F.3d 961 (6th Cir. 1998); Yohay v. City of Alexandria Employees Credit Union, Inc., 827 F.2d 967 (4th Cir. 1987); Cole v. American Family Mut. Ins. Co., 333 F. Supp. 2d 1038 (D. Kan. 2004) (discussing, without deciding, whether apparent authority or aided-in-the-agency-relation is the proper agency theory for vicarious liability); Del Amora v. Metro Ford Sales and Serv., Inc. 206 F. Supp. 2d 947 (N.D. Ill. 2002) (violation accomplished by virtue of employment position and access to CRA computer); Del Amora v. Metro Ford Sales and Serv., Inc. 206 F. Supp. 2d 947 (N.D. Ill. 2002); Adams v. Berger Chevrolet, Inc., 2001 U.S. Dist. LEXIS 6174 (W.D. Mich. May 7, 2001) (car dealer vicariously liable for salesman's intentional acts of identity theft, despite no contemporaneous knowledge or approval of the acts, because salesman had apparent authority and under respondeat superior doctrine); Cohen v. Sheehy Ford, 27 Va. Cir. 161 (1992) (employer who cloaked employees with actual or apparent authority to obtain credit information could be vicariously liable, and possibly directly liable, for the wrongful accessing of plaintiff's credit information by an employee, regardless of whether that employee acted outside the scope of his authority). *But see* Smith v. Sears, Roebuck & Co., 276 F. Supp. 2d 603 (S.D. Miss. 2003) (rejecting respondeat superior, apparent authority, and aided-in-the-agency analyses of other courts); Kodrick v. Ferguson, 54 F. Supp. 2d 788 (N.D. Ill. 1999) (Congress did not provide for vicarious liability).

530 Jones v. Federal Fin. Reserve Corp., 144 F.3d 961 (6th Cir. 1998); Yohay v. City of Alexandria Employees Credit Union, Inc., 827 F.2d 967 (4th Cir. 1987); Myers v. Bennett Law Offices, 238 F. Supp. 2d 1196 (D. Nev. 2002).

531 Yohay v. City of Alexandria Employees Credit Union, Inc., 827 F.2d 967, 973–974 (4th Cir. 1987) (credit union was liable for employee's violation of the FCRA where anyone using the credit union's computers had access to consumer reports, and the credit union posted no guidelines for obtaining them). *Cf.* Myers v. Bennett Law Offices, 238 F. Supp. 2d 1196 (D. Nev. 2002) (finding employer not negligent where there was no evidence the employer failed to properly supervise the employee).

Chapter 8 Notices Concerning Consumer Reports

8.1 Introduction and Structure of Chapter

Information about consumers flows freely from creditors and public record vendors to consumer reporting agencies (CRAs). In turn, often unsuspected by consumers, this information can be recirculated back to creditors, employers, and others. This flow of information may improve the ability of users to predict the outcome of some anticipated transaction or relationship with a consumer if the information flowing through the system is accurate and timely. When that information is inaccurate, the flow of information unfairly deprives people of opportunities for credit, employment, or other improvements to their lives.

For many consumers, the first notice of some inaccuracy may be an adverse action notice from a creditor or potential employer. While these kinds of notices are commonplace, they are by no means the only notices required under the Fair Credit Reporting Act (FCRA). The FCRA provides for a number of notices designed to ensure that the information in the credit reporting system is accurate, private, and fairly used. The FCRA was amended by the Fair and Accurate Credit Transactions Act of 2003 (FACTA),[1] which provided for a variety of additional notices triggered by a wide range of circumstances, including identity theft (Chapter 9, *infra*), risk-based pricing, *infra*), negative information furnished by financial institutions to CRAs (Chapter 6, *infra*), key factors in credit scores (Chapter 14, *infra*), fraud alerts (§ 9.2.2, *infra*), blocks for identity theft information (§ 9.2.4, *infra*).

Some of these notices provide simple summaries of rights and duties under the Act, while others can be highly specific in nature and inform recipients and others of claims of non-compliance with the Act. These notices fall into two broad categories.

Status Notices: These notices are given in response to some predetermined triggering event and advise the recipient of a current or changed status. These notices may be accompanied by a summary or restatement of the recipient's legal rights and duties. In some instances, notification that a status has changed (such as a consumer's decision to opt out of receiving prescreened notices) will require that the recipient of the notice (such as the CRA) to take some action.

Dispute Notices: These notices advise a party that some dispute has arisen over the content of information or its use, and some corrective action is required by the recipient.

This chapter reviews each of the notices required to be given to consumers by the FCRA. The chapter is broken down into four parts based on who is receiving the notice. Thus, all notices sent to the consumer—irrespective of who has sent the notice or what the notice describes—are discussed in § 8.2, *infra*. Notices to CRAs are discussed in § 8.3, *infra*. Notices to furnishers are discussed in § 8.4, *infra*. Finally, notices to users are discussed in § 8.5, *infra*. Where appropriate, these sections are cross-referenced to other sections of the manual which may treat the subject matter in greater detail.

In reviewing the provisions regarding the new notices, practitioners should be aware that the increased number of notices does not necessarily correspond to new rights for the consumer. In many instances, notices inform the consumer of some change in status or action without providing concrete remedies or direct access to information. For example, the notices regarding risk-based pricing may notify consumers that their credit histories have affected the price received for goods or services, but does not necessarily indicate how or to what extent the price was affected. And while an adverse action notice may, in some circumstances, notify the consumer that improper information was used to render an adverse credit decision, there is no corresponding right to have only accurate information appear in a consumer report or to require that only accurate information be used.[2] More important, a number of the notice requirements are not actionable. Practitioners must make sure to understand the precise requirements of each notice and whether that an FCRA violation related to that notice—or failure to provide that notices—is actionable.

8.2 Notices to Consumers

8.2.1 Overview

The FCRA requires a number of notices to be provided to consumers in various circumstances. Perhaps the most im-

---

[1] Fair and Accurate Credit Transactions Act of 2003, Pub. L. No. 108-159, 117 Stat 1952 (Dec. 4, 2003).

[2] *See* 12 C.F.R. Part 202.6(b).

portant role of these notices is that receipt of a notice can trigger a consumer's inquiry into just what personal information is being reported and what a consumer can do to correct misinformation. The chain of events which leads consumers to seek legal counsel about an FCRA matter often begins with an FCRA-required notice to the consumer. These notices can, in turn, trigger a number of statutorily mandated responses, a variety of additional notices, and possible corrective action.

There is no single notice that is given to every consumer about whom information is stored by a consumer reporting agency (CRA) or released to a user. Each notice has a particular purpose and is required only in particular circumstances.

The FCRA, as amended by FACTA and interpreted by the FTC, provides opportunities for consumer relief where a CRA, furnisher, or user fails to comply with certain FCRA notice requirements or fails to take the corrective action required by the notice. The consumer may be able to obtain actual damages and attorney fees and, in certain situations, statutory damages and punitive damages.[3] Nevertheless, consumer litigants bringing such claims must take great care to explain the intent and purposes of the FCRA, particularly the FACTA amendments, especially in regards to why a private right of action remains for adverse action notices,[4] and regarding the relationship between adverse action notices and the new risk-based pricing notice.[5] Additionally, for some of these notice requirements, the user's maintenance of proper procedures may act as a defense.[6]

8.2.2 Notice of Summary of Consumers Rights Under the FCRA: "The Summary of Consumer Rights Notice"

8.2.2.1 Content of Notice

One of the most significant disclosure requirements under the FCRA is that a consumer reporting agency (CRA) must provide consumers with a "Summary of Consumer Rights."[7] For practical purposes, this notice will serve as the consumer's guide to:

- Understanding the credit reporting process;
- The consumer's right to receive the file; and
- The means by which the consumer can correct inaccuracies in the file.

In 2003, FACTA amended the FCRA by revising the Summary of Consumer Rights and requiring the Federal Trade Commission (FTC) to promulgate a model form conforming to the requirements of the Act.[8] The FTC has issued a model form,[9] which is reproduced at Appendix C.2, *infra*.

Prior to the FACTA amendments in 2003, CRAs had discretion in the formulation of these notices so long as the notice contained the all required information and substantially met the requirements. The FACTA amendments, however, eliminated that discretion and instead require that CRAs use the model form promulgated by the FTC.[10] The FACTA amendments require this model Summary of Consumer Rights to be included with each written disclosure to a consumer provided by CRAs.[11]

The Summary of Consumer Rights must include a description of—

- The right of consumers to obtain a copy of their report from each CRA;
- The frequency and circumstances under which a consumer is entitled to receive a consumer report without charge from a nationwide CRA;
- The right of a consumer to dispute information in that consumer's file;
- The right of a consumer to obtain a credit score from a CRA, and a description of how to obtain a credit score;
- The method by which a consumer can contact, and obtain a consumer report from, a nationwide CRA without charge, as provided for by FTC regulations; and
- The method by which a consumer can contact, and obtain a consumer report from, a nationwide specialty CRA, as provided for by FTC regulations.[12]

The FCRA also requires the FTC to actively publicize the availability of this form, conspicuously post its availability on the FTC website, and promptly make the summary available to consumers upon request.[13]

Along with this model form, CRAs must provide additional information about enforcement of the act when providing consumers with copies of their credit files.[14] If a CRA operates as a nationwide CRA,[15] that CRA must also disclose a toll-free telephone number, which must be staffed by personnel who are accessible to consumers during normal working hours.[16]

---

3 See Ch. 11, *infra*.
4 See § 10.2.5.2, *infra*.
5 See §§ 8.2.6, 8.2.8, *infra*.
6 See § 10.2.5.2, *infra*.
7 15 U.S.C. § 1681g(c).
8 15 U.S.C. § 1681g(c), *as amended by* Pub. L. No. 108-159, § 211(c), 117 Stat 1952 (Dec. 4, 2003).
9 16 C.F.R. § 698, Appendix F.
10 15 U.S.C. § 1681g(c)(2)(A).
11 *Id.*
12 15 U.S.C. § 1681g(c).
13 15 U.S.C. § 1681g(c)(1)(C).
14 15 U.S.C. § 1681g(c)(2).
15 15 U.S.C. § 1681a(p). For a complete discussion of the definition of nationwide CRAs, see § 2.6.1, *supra*.
16 15 U.S.C. § 1681g(c)(2)(B).

The Summary of Consumer Rights must also include the following:

- A list of all federal agencies responsible for enforcing the FCRA, and the address and phone number of each such agency;
- A statement that the consumer may have additional rights under state law, and that the consumer may wish to contact a state or local consumer protection agency or a state attorney general or the equivalent thereof to learn of those rights; and
- A statement that the CRA is not required to remove accurate derogatory information from the file of a consumer, unless the information is outdated under section 1681c[17] or cannot be verified.[18]

8.2.2.2 Time and Manner of Notice

A CRA must provide the FCRA Summary of Consumer Rights notice every time it makes a disclosure to a consumer under section 1681g. These qualifying disclosures include a disclosure of the CRA's file relating to the consumer[19] or a disclosure of a credit score relating to the consumer.[20]

8.2.2.3 Enforcement of Notice Rights

The failure of a CRA to deliver the prescribed notice is subject to the usual private remedies of the FCRA including claims for actual damages, punitive damages, costs and attorney fees.[21] This contrasts with the absence of a right to sue for failure to provide a number of other notices under the FCRA.[22]

8.2.3 Summary of Consumer Rights for Identity Theft Victims: "The Summary of Consumer Identity Theft Rights Notice"

8.2.3.1 Content of Notice

The FCRA requires consumer reporting agencies (CRAs) to provide a notice of rights to consumers who are believed to be victims of fraud or identity theft involving credit, an electronic fund transfer, or an account or transaction at or with a financial institution or other creditor.[23]

The FCRA directs the FTC, federal banking agencies, and the National Credit Union Administration to prepare a model notice of those rights.[24] The regulatory agencies have issued a model form,[25] which is included in Appendix C.3, *infra*. This form requires disclosure of:

- The right to place initial and extended fraud alerts in the consumer's file.[26]
- The right to free copies of their credit file with the CRAs.[27]
- The victim's right to obtain documents relating to the transactions involving the fraudster's use of the consumer's personal identification information.[28]
- The right to obtain information from a debt collector regarding the debt.[29]
- The right to request that suspected identity theft credit information be blocked from publication by a CRA[30] or a furnisher of credit data.[31]

8.2.3.2 Time and Manner of Notice

The duty of a CRA to provide the ID Theft Rights Notice is triggered any time that a consumer contacts the CRA and either expresses a belief that she is a victim of fraud or identity theft involving credit, an electronic fund transfer, or an account or transaction involving a financial institution or creditor.[32] The notice for identity theft victims is in addition to any other disclosures which the CRA is required to provide. The statute provides that the notice must be given using the written form prescribed by the FTC.[33]

8.2.3.3 Enforcement of Notice Rights

The failure of a CRA to deliver the prescribed notice is subject to the usual private remedies of the FCRA. This contrasts with the absence of a right to sue for failure to provide a number of other notices under the FCRA.[34]

---

17 *See* § 5.2, *supra*.
18 15 U.S.C. § 1681g(c)(2)(A).
19 15 U.S.C. § 168g(a). *See* § 3.3, *supra*.
20 15 U.S.C. § 1681g(f). *See* § 14.4, *infra*.
21 15 U.S.C. §§ 1681n and 1681o.
22 Whether the is a private cause of action for a particular notice requirement is discussed at the end of each subsection of this chapter.
23 15 U.S.C. § 1681g(d).
24 *Id.*
25 The FTC published this form at 16 C.F.R. 698, Appendix E.
26 *See* § 9.2.2, *infra*.
27 15 U.S.C. §§ 1681g(a) and 1681j(c)(3). *See* § 3.3, *supra*.
28 15 U.S.C. § 1681g(e). Note that this subsection of § 1681g is not actionable by consumers under either of the private remedy sections of the FCRA, 15 U.S.C. §§ 1681n or 1681o.
29 15 U.S.C. § 1681g(e). *See* § 9.2.3.2, *infra*.
30 15 U.S.C. § 1681c-2. *See* § 9.2.4, *infra*.
31 15 U.S.C. § 1681s-2a(6).
32 15 U.S.C. § 1681g(d)(2).
33 *Id.*
34 Whether the is a private cause of action for a particular notice requirement is discussed at the end of each subsection of this chapter.

8.2.4 Notices of Preparation of Credit Score and Scoring Model: "The Credit Score Notice"[35]

8.2.4.1 Nature and Content of Notice

Under the FCRA, consumers may request and obtain disclosure of their credit score. Even though these scores are part of the consumer's file, which the consumer can review once a year free of charge,[36] credit scores need not be disclosed in the absence of a specific request from the consumer[37] and payment of a fee.[38] If the consumer does request disclosure of a credit score from a consumer reporting agency (CRA) the disclosure of the score must be accompanied by a notice to the consumer describing the scoring factors and events surrounding any recent scoring.[39] In particular, the notice must include:

- The current credit score of the consumer or the most recent credit score of the consumer calculated by the CRA;[40]
- The range of possible credit scores under the model used;[41]
- All of the top four key factors that adversely affected the credit score of the consumer in the model used;[42]
- The date on which the credit score was created;[43] and
- The name of the person or entity that provided the credit score or credit file upon which the credit score was created.[44]

This notice may greatly assist the consumer in understanding which items on the consumer report are causing the greatest harm to her ability to obtain credit. Likewise, a disclosure of the factors affecting the score which is given close to the time of a credit denial may greatly assist an practitioner in building a damage case.[45]

In addition to the credit score notice, when consumers request their credit files, but not their credit scores, the FCRA also requires the CRAs to disclose the fact that consumers have a right to obtain their credit scores.[46]

8.2.4.2 Time and Manner of Notice

CRAs must disclose a credit score and provide the credit score notice "within the same timeframes and manner" as they would provide a disclosure of the consumer's file under section 1681g(a).[47] Given that there is no timeframe actually specified for disclosures under section 1681g(a), one interpretation would be that credit scores and the credit scoring notice must be provided at the same time as disclosures of the consumer's credit file when the consumer request both. However, note that section 1681g(a) specifically does not require disclosure of the credit score if the consumer's requests only her file.[48] Another interpretation would be that the CRA must disclose credit scores and provide the credit score notice with the same expediency and using the same methods as disclosures of the consumer's file.

8.2.4.3 Enforcement of Right

The failure of a CRA to deliver the notice of the most recent score and description of the scoring process is subject to the usual private remedies of the FCRA, including actual damages, punitive damages, costs, and attorney fees.[49]

8.2.5 Notices of Use of Credit Score and Scoring Model Relating to Mortgage Transactions: "The Mortgage Scoring Notice"

8.2.5.1 Content of Notice

8.2.5.1.1 Overview

In those instances when a credit score is used in conjunction with the extension of credit secured by residential real estate, the user must provide the credit score free of charge, as well as information regarding the factors used in making up the credit score and additional disclosures relating to the scoring process.[50]

The Mortgage Scoring Notice requires disclosure of two separate segments of information, each of which will be discussed below. The gist of the notice is that consumers who are engaged in mortgage transactions will be provided with information about the credit score that was used, how the score was derived, and how that score may have affected the credit application process. Thus, the first segment of

---

35 This section deals only with notices to the consumer which accompany a credit score disclosure. See § 14.3, infra for a discussion of the disclosure of the score and its contents.
36 See § 3.3, supra.
37 15 U.S.C. § 1681g(a)(1)(B). See § 14.4, infra.
38 15 U.S.C. § 1681g(c)(1)(B)(iv); 15 U.S.C. § 1681g(f)(8). See § 14.4, infra.
39 15 U.S.C. § 1681g(f).
40 15 U.S.C. § 1681g(f)(1)(A).
41 15 U.S.C. § 1681g(f)(1)(B).
42 15 U.S.C. § 1681g(f)(1)(C).
43 15 U.S.C. § 1681g(f)(1)(D).
44 15 U.S.C. § 1681g(f)(1)(E).
45 See § 11.10, infra.
46 15 U.S.C. § 1681g(a)(6). The Summary of Consumer Rights also includes a statement that the consumer has the right to obtain a credit score from a CRA and a description of how to obtain the score. See § 14.4, infra.
47 15 U.S.C. § 1681g(f)(3).
48 15 U.S.C. § 1681g(a)(1)(B).
49 15 U.S.C. §§ 1681n and 1681o.
50 15 U.S.C. § 1681g(g)(1)(A).

information is specific to the consumer, the consumer's credit score, and the transaction at hand. The second segment of information is a form notice explaining the general manner in which credit score information may have affected the consumer in the mortgage transaction at hand.

The FCRA, however, recognizes that lenders utilize a variety of different scoring mechanisms, some of which involve analysis of other factors which fall outside conventional data maintained within consumer credit files.[51] Likewise, the Act recognizes that scores and other statistical predictors may come not only from consumer reporting agencies (CRAs), but also from non-consumer reporting sources that may be internal or external to the user's business.[52] Accordingly, the Mortgage Scoring Notice provisions focus primarily on providing consumers information about those processes and sources that are most closely related to the consumer reporting and scoring processes of CRAs, rather than those of any proprietary systems actually used in the transaction at hand.[53]

8.2.5.1.2 Credit score information from consumer reporting agencies

The first segment of information that a mortgage user must disclose is credit scoring information. The FCRA's specific requirement is that the mortgage user give the consumer the information identified in section 1681g(f) that it obtained from a CRA or that it developed itself.[54] That subsection describes disclosures that CRAs must make when responding to requests from consumers for copies of their credit scores. Thus, in the context of the Mortgage Scoring Notice, the user of a credit score in a mortgage transaction must provide the consumer with the information it received from the CRA corresponding to section 1681g(f). This information would include:

- The actual score used;[55]
- The range of possible scores under the model;[56]
- The four primary factors adversely affecting the score;[57]
- The date of the score;[58] and
- The entity that provided the score.[59]

This information is only required to the extent that it was used and either provided to the user by a CRA or developed by the user itself.[60] To the extent that section 1681g(f) requires disclosure of any information not provided to the mortgage user or developed by the mortgage user, this information need not be disclosed in the Mortgage Scoring Notice.[61]

The FCRA exempts certain automated underwriting systems from the requirement that mortgages users provide the actual credit score they used.[62] This exemption (which, in section 1681g, immediately follows those relating to the notice requirements) recognizes that credit scores can be generated by CRAs or created by other entities using raw data provided by the CRAs.

When the user develops and uses its own scoring system in conjunction with an automated underwriting process, that user clearly could not provide the consumer with the credit score given by the CRA; no such score was in fact generated or used. Thus, in order to comply with the mandates of the Mortgage Scoring Notice, the user would normally be required to provide the score developed by the user itself.[63] However, when a user employs an automated underwriting system, the FCRA provides those users with the choice of either disclosing the score actually developed and employed by the user, or obtaining and disclosing a score and the associated risk factors from a CRA, even though the CRA score was not actually used.[64]

It is apparent from the use of the permissive language "may" that the user has the option of disclosing the actual score used. The actual score used, while accurate, may be of more limited value to the consumer since it is particular to the user of the report and its affiliates. At the same time, murky draftsmanship casts doubt on whether users need ever disclose an internally generated score without also providing a score generated by a CRA. Specifically, the FCRA[65] permits users who obtain a score from sources other than a CRA provide a CRA score and associated key factors.[66] Examining these requirements in totality, it appears that the Act permits disclosure of internal scores and factors, but favors the disclosure of CRA scores and factors by allowing the disclosure of scores and factors from a CRA even if they were not used in the actual transaction.

Thus, the intention of the statute appears to be to use the opportunity of a mortgage transaction to provide the consumer with educational information about the credit scoring process and an impetus to request a copy of his or her credit file from a CRA. Put another way, the FCRA favors a process where the consumer is guided to obtain information from the most universally accepted sources, namely the CRAs.

---

51 15 U.S.C. § 1681g(g)(1)(F)(I).
52 15 U.S.C. § 16812g(g)(1)(C).
53 *Id.*
54 15 U.S.C. § 1681g(g). The specific requirements of § 1681g(f) are discussed § 8.2.4.1, *supra*.
55 15 U.S.C. § 1681g(f)(1)(A).
56 15 U.S.C. § 1681g(f)(1)(B).
57 15 U.S.C. § 1681g(f)(1)(C).
58 15 U.S.C. § 1681g(f)(1)(D).
59 15 U.S.C. § 1681g(f)(1)(E).

60 15 U.S.C. § 1681g(f)(1)(A)(I).
61 15 U.S.C. § 1681g(f)(1)(A)(ii).
62 15 U.S.C. § 1681g(g)(1)(B).
63 15 U.S.C. §§ 1681g(f)(1)(A) and 1681g(g)(1)(A)(I).
64 15 U.S.C. § 1631g(g)(1)(B)(i).
65 15 U.S.C. § 1631g(g)(1)(B)(ii).
66 15 U.S.C. § 1681g(g)(1)(C).

Additionally, the user's obligations are limited expressly, and the user has no obligation to:

- Provide an explanation of the information relating to the preparation of the score;[67]
- Disclose any information other than a credit score or key factors;[68]
- Disclose any credit score or related information obtained by the user after a loan has closed;[69]
- Provide more than one disclosure per loan transaction;[70] or
- Provide the disclosure required by section 1681g(g) when another person has made the disclosure to the consumer for that loan transaction.[71]

8.2.5.1.3 Home loan notice

Credit applicants whose mortgage application relates to a home loan are entitled to a specific notice describing how credit scores are used and their role in the mortgage process, along with information on where the consumer may learn more about the scores relating to their application. The language of the notice is prescribed by the Act.[72]

8.2.5.2 Time and Manner of Notice

The FCRA requires that the user provide notices under section 1681g(g) as soon as is reasonably practicable.[73] As such, this notice should be provided at the time the mortgage user receives and makes use of the score.

8.2.5.3 Enforcement of Right

In general, the failure of a mortgage user to deliver the notices relating to the preparation and use of the score is subject to the usual private remedies of the FCRA, including actual damages, punitive damages, costs and attorney fees.[74] However, a significant safe harbor is provided to mortgage users. Users are not liable for the substance of the information disclosed to a consumer, if the information was provided to the user by a CRA.[75] Thus, to the extent that the user provides information that it received from a CRA, the user is liable only for its transmittal, but not for the content of that information or any omissions in it.[76]

---

67 15 U.S.C. § 1681g(g)(1)(E)(i). *See also* 15 U.S.C. § 1681(f).
68 15 U.S.C. § 1681g(g)(1)(E)(ii).
69 15 U.S.C. § 1681g(g)(1)(E)(iii).
70 15 U.S.C. § 1681g(g)(1)(E)(iv).
71 15 U.S.C. § 1681g(g)(1)(E)(v).
72 15 U.S.C. § 1681g(g)(1)(D).
73 15 U.S.C. § 1681g(g)(1).
74 15 U.S.C. §§ 1681n and 1681o.
75 15 U.S.C. § 1681g(g)(1)(F)(ii).
76 15 U.S.C. § 1681g(g)(1)(F)(i).

8.2.6 Adverse Action Based upon Consumer Report: "The Adverse Action Notice"

8.2.6.1 Nature and Importance of Adverse Action Notice

Users of consumer reports who take adverse action against consumers must provide notice of that adverse action.[77] For consumers with a bad credit history, this notice, given at the moment when the consumer is expecting to receive an approval, constitutes a "teachable moment" which may drive the consumer to improve her credit. If the information is inaccurate or misleading, the consumer may try to reverse the adverse action by correcting or explaining the third party information.[78] If this is too late, the notices provide a clear warning that steps must be taken before the consumer applies with another creditor, landlord, insurer, or employer. A sensible follow-up to this notice would be to request that the consumer reporting agency (CRA) disclose the exact contents of the file, and to request from a creditor (if the creditor has not already provided) the exact reason for the denial of credit.

Second, the notices of adverse action provide the consumer with the name, address, and telephone number of the CRA providing the report. This is useful information because there are hundreds of CRAs. Most information comes from the "Big Three" nationwide CRAs—Experian (formerly TRW), Equifax, and TransUnion (or their affiliates)—and most consumers have files with the "Big Three" nationwide CRAs. Nevertheless, notice that a particular CRA has a file on the consumer and that it was that particular CRA that reported negative information helps consumers narrow down their initial requests for the contents of their files. This information becomes essential when one of the smaller, regional CRAs made the report, not one of the "Big Three" nationwide CRAs.

Third, the notices of adverse action generally provide the consumer with the right to obtain at no charge the contents of the file from the CRA making the negative report. If the consumer makes the request within sixty days, then the CRA has no right to seek any payment for disclosure of the report. Consumers can request disclosure by any reasonable means available from the CRA, including electronic transmission. The nationwide CRAs maintain toll-free telephone numbers which can be used to obtain disclosure.

The following portions of this chapter will detail:

- The content of the adverse action notice;
- The definition of adverse action under the existing case law;

---

77 15 U.S.C. § 1681m.
78 *See* 12 C.F.R. § 202.6(b)(6)(ii).

- The circumstances requiring adverse actions notification to the consumer because they relate to credit, employment, insurance, and government benefits and licenses;
- A discussion of whether notification is required for other types of adverse actions, including those related to transactions initiated by consumers; and
- Changes to the FCRA's adverse action notice requirement by the FACTA amendments, including changes to the private right of enforcement.

In reviewing each of the following subsections, practitioners should be aware that following the enactment of FACTA, this area has been subject to conflicting interpretations. As of the date of publication of this manual, whether violations of the adverse action notice provisions are privately enforceable remains an open question, and there is no firm consensus among the U.S. Circuit Courts or the U.S. District Courts. Before undertaking a case, practitioners should research the most recent decisions in their jurisdiction.

8.2.6.2 Content of Notice

8.2.6.2.1 General

The adverse action notice must include the following:

- A statement of the adverse action taken;[79]
- The name, address, and phone number of the CRA which supplied the report.[80]
- A statement that the CRA did not make the decision and cannot supply the reasons for the adverse action.[81]
- A notice that upon a request by the consumer made within sixty days, the consumer may obtain a free copy of his or her consumer report;[82] and
- Disclosure of the consumer's right to dispute with the CRA the accuracy or completeness of the report.[83]

While the notice need not indicate what about the file led to the denial, the Equal Credit Opportunity Act requires a creditor to specify the reasons for the denial.[84]

8.2.6.2.2 Content of notice: identification of action and actor

An adverse action notice must at minimum reasonably identify that an adverse action was taken and provide sufficient information to allow the consumer to determine, clearly and unequivocally, the nature of that adverse action.[85] Additionally, the notice must provide the identity of the person who has taken the adverse action.[86] There is no requirement similar to that in the ECOA that the user provide a statement of the reasons for the adverse action or identify the items which caused the adverse action.[87]

8.2.6.2.3 Content of notice: identity of the consumer reporting agency

The FCRA requires a user who takes an adverse action to inform the consumer of the name and address of the CRA that issued the report to the user.[88] The user must provide the telephone number of the CRA, and in the case of one of the "Big Three" CRAs or any other CRA which compiles information on a nationwide basis, a toll-free number.[89]

When disclosing a CRA's address, the user must disclose the complete street address of the CRA, and not merely the post office box number, so that the consumer may ascertain the exact location of the CRA involved.[90] However, one court has held that disclosing only the name of the CRA that issued the report, where the consumer was subsequently able to determine the address of the CRA was "substantial compliance" and sufficient under the Act.[91] Of course, nothing in the FCRA prevents a user from providing more information about the report, and a CRA may not prohibit the user from providing a copy of the report to the consumer

---

79 15 U.S.C. § 1681m(a)(1).
80 15 U.S.C. § 1681m(a)(2)(A).
81 15 U.S.C. § 1681m(a)(2)(B). If the CRA did in fact make the adverse decision, applying, for example, criteria provided by an employer or a creditor, this statement would be misleading and should be omitted from the disclosure statement. Allan, FTC Informal Staff Opinion Letter (Feb. 14, 2000), *reprinted on the CD-Rom accompanying this manual*.
82 15 U.S.C. § 1681m(a)(3)(A) and (B). *See* § 3.3, *supra*.
83 *See* Ch. 4, *supra*.
84 *See* § 8.2.6.6, *infra*.

85 Reynolds v. Hartford Fin. Servs. Group, Inc., 435 F.3d 1081, 1094 (9th Cir. 2006), *cert. granted, sub nom.* GEICO Gen. Ins. Co. v. Edo, __ S. Ct. __, 2006 WL 2055539 (Sept. 26, 2006), *citing* Fischl v. General Motors Acceptance Corp., 708 F.2d 143, 150 (5th Cir. 1983).
86 *Id.*
87 *See* National Consumer Law Center, Credit Discrimination § 10.5.4.2 (4th ed. 2005 and Supp.). *Cf.* 15 U.S.C. § 1691; 12 C.F.R. § 202.9.
88 FTC Official Staff Commentary § 615 item 13, *reprinted at* Appx. D, *infra*.
89 15 U.S.C. § 1681m(a). With regard to which CRAs are nationwide, see § 2.6, *supra*; Brinckerhoff, FTC Informal Staff Opinion Letter (June 29, 1999), *reprinted on the CD-Rom accompanying this manual* (mortgage reporting services and resellers are not so-called nationwide CRAs for this purpose).
90 FTC Official Staff Commentary § 615 item 12, *reprinted at* Appx. D, *infra*. *See also* Bragg, FTC Informal Staff Opinion Letter (Dec. 3, 1971), *reprinted on the CD-Rom accompanying this manual*.
91 Kiblen v. Pickle, 653 P.2d 1338, 1342 (Wash. Ct. App. 1982) (insurance company disclosed only name of detective agency who prepared report).

when adverse action has been taken.[92] It will often be helpful to ask the user what aspect of the report led to the adverse action.[93]

Even if a local CRA makes a report based on information entirely obtained from a foreign CRA (e.g., a nationwide chain), the user must disclose the name of the local CRA, as the last CRA in the reporting chain. Then, when the consumer seeks disclosure of the contents of the local CRA's file, the consumer can discover if the local CRA made any mistakes in the transmission of information, or added any additional information.[94]

Two courts have wrongly said the user need not also notify the consumer of the name of the intermediary CRA, but only the name of the CRA actually making the report.[95] Even when the intermediary CRA is not identified in the notice, the consumer should eventually be able to obtain the names of intermediary CRAs because the consumer has the right to receive from the CRA making the report not only the nature of the report, but also the sources of the report.[96] Usually, though, the user will identify the intermediary CRA, known as a reseller, and the reseller will identify the CRA from which it obtained the information.[97] If the user has obtained the same adverse information from more than one CRA, the user must identify each CRA.[98]

8.2.6.2.4 Content of notice: other mandatory information

In addition to the items set forth above, the notice must include other mandatory information concerning the consumer's rights under the Act. In specific, the notice must include:

- A statement that the CRA did not make the decision and cannot supply the reasons for the adverse action;[99]
- A notice that upon a request by the consumer made within sixty days, the consumer may obtain a free copy of his or her consumer report;[100]
- Disclosure of the consumer's right to dispute with the CRA the accuracy or completeness of the report.[101]

8.2.6.2.5 Content of notice: copy of report for adverse action relating to employment

When an employer takes adverse action based upon a consumer report, that employer must also provide a copy of the actual consumer report.[102] An employer who has provided that report to the consumer may note in the notice of adverse action that the consumer has already received a copy of the report and a Summary of Consumer Rights, and that the name, address, and phone number of the CRA may be contained in those materials.[103]

8.2.6.3 Manner of Giving Notice

8.2.6.3.1 Who must provide notice

The complexities of corporate structures have added a corresponding layer of complexity to the requirements of adverse action notices. Often, corporations that extend credit or issue insurance must consult with affiliates or obtain underwriting approval from third parties before approving a consumer's application. In these situations, multiple parties may access or use a given individual's consumer' report even though only one of those entities has the legal authority to provide the services, and another may actually render the decision.

Users of consumer reports have used this complexity as a defense to the requirement of issuing adverse action notices, in some instances claiming that they did not take action or use the report. A consensus now holds that all parties involved in rendering decisions which rely on the report must issue the notice.[104] Such relationships include affiliated companies using reports, as well as parent companies and their subsidiaries.[105] Thus, privity is not a condition prece-

---

92 15 U.S.C. § 1681e(c). See § 3.3.1.2, supra.
93 See § 8.2.6.6, infra.
94 Peeler, FTC Informal Staff Opinion Letter (Jan. 4, 1978), reprinted on the CD-Rom accompanying this manual.
95 See Morrisey v. TRW Credit Data, 434 F. Supp. 1107 (E.D.N.Y. 1977) (need only inform the consumer of the CRA from which the report ultimately came, not other CRAs used as intermediaries); Green v. Stores Mut. Protective Ass'n, [1974–1980 Decisions Transfer Binder] Consumer Cred. Guide (CCH) 98,527 (S.D.N.Y. 1975) (user does not need to volunteer this information); Conference Rep. No. 1587, 91st Cong., 2d Sess. (1970), reprinted in 1970 U.S.C.C.A.N. 4394, 4411, 4416 (addition of provision requiring user to convey this information upon denial of credit, insurance, or employment). See § 2.6.3, supra.
96 See § 3.2.3.3, supra.
97 See § 2.6.3, supra.
98 Cast, FTC Informal Staff Opinion Letter (Oct. 27, 1997), reprinted on the CD-Rom accompanying this manual.
99 15 U.S.C. § 1681m(a)(2)(B). If the CRA did in fact make the adverse decision, applying, for example, criteria provided by an employer or a creditor, this statement would be misleading and should be omitted from the disclosure statement. Allan, FTC Informal Staff Opinion Letter (Feb. 14, 2000), reprinted on the CD-Rom accompanying this manual.
100 15 U.S.C. § 1681m(a)(3)(A), (B). See § 3.3.6, supra.
101 See § 6.10, supra, § 12.6.2.1, infra.
102 See § 8.2.6.4.4.3, infra.
103 See § 8.2.6.4.4.3, infra.
104 Reynolds v. Hartford Fin. Servs. Group, Inc., 435 F.3d 1081 (9th Cir. 2006), cert. granted, sub nom. GEICO Gen. Ins. Co. v. Edo, __ S. Ct. __, 2006 WL 2055539 (Sept. 26, 2006); Thomas v. Cendant Mortgage, 2004 WL 2600772 (E.D. Pa. Nov. 15, 2004).
105 Whitfield v. Radian Guar., Inc., 395 F. Supp. 2d 234 (E.D. Pa. 2005) (granting summary judgment for defendant on grounds that action was not adverse to consumer); Broessel v. Triad Guar. Ins. Corp., 2005 WL 2260498 (W.D. Ky. Sept. 15, 2005).

dent to liability for failure to send the notice.[106] Nonetheless, to the extent that the individual's consumer' report affects costs to third parties which are not necessarily passed on to the consumer, the notice may not be required.[107] Likewise, joint users of a consumer report who anticipate extending credit in a car transaction must provide the notice.[108]

8.2.6.3.2 Oral, electronic, or written

The FCRA contains three separate provisions concerning the manner of giving notice: subsections 1681m(a)(1), (2), and (3). Each of these provisions specifies that the notice may be made orally, electronically, or in writing. Based on this repetitive structure, it appears that Congress intended to allow each of the separate components to be disclosed independently, but did not restrict the manner of delivery. For all purposes, however, the complexity of the notice requirements and need for records would ordinarily dictate that the notice be in writing. Creditors taking adverse action are likely to use a single form combined with an ECOA adverse action notice.[109]

Furthermore, the FTC Staff Commentary recommends the notice be in writing so that users have evidence in writing that they have taken reasonable steps to comply.[110] Moreover, if a user provides written notice, but that notice is not adequate, the CRA may not be able to correct the defect orally.[111]

The Electronic Signatures in Global and National Commerce Act (E-Sign)[112] provides that disclosures *required* to be made in writing to consumers may be made electronically if several conditions are met. These conditions include: informing the consumer about rights under the Act; providing a statement of the hardware and software necessary for access and retention of the electronic record; and having the consumer either consent electronically or confirm consent electronically.[113] However, as the FCRA does not require that the adverse action notice and accompanying disclosures be made in writing, and already provides that they may be made electronically without any additional procedures, E-Sign's safeguards likely do not apply to an FCRA-compelled notice or disclosure.

8.2.6.4 When Notice Required

8.2.6.4.1 General requirements

For purposes of notice under the FCRA, "adverse action" serves as both the triggering event as well as the subject of the notice. Thus, when a user of a consumer report takes adverse action, that user is required to notify the consumer of the action taken. The FCRA does not state how quickly the user must provide this information, but the FTC and case law have illuminated this provision as requiring simultaneous notification.[114]

For purposes of case law and litigation, more important than the time for delivery is whether the notice is required to be delivered at all. When a user of a consumer report uses the information in the report to take an adverse action, that user must notify the consumer.[115] Notice is not required only where the information is obtained: directly from the consumer's application; from a third party which is not a CRA; or from the user's own past experience in direct transactions with the consumer.[116] It is irrelevant that the report itself is not seriously adverse to the consumer, as long as it led to adverse action.[117] For example, the Fifth Circuit required notice where credit was denied because a generally excellent report was not considered sufficient in the lender's eyes.[118]

If a user did not rely on information in a consumer report, but instead based its actions on information obtained else-

---

106 Treadway v. Gateway Chevrolet Oldsmobile Inc., 362 F.3d 971, 974 (7th Cir. 2004); Whitfield v. Radian Guar., Inc., 395 F. Supp. 2d 234 (E.D. Pa. 2005); Crane v. American Home Mortgage, Corp., 2004 WL 1529165 (E.D. Pa. July 7, 2004).

107 Whitfield v. Radian Guar., Inc., 395 F. Supp. 2d 234 (E.D. Pa. 2005). *Cf.* Broessel v. Triad Guar. Ins. Corp., 2005 WL 2260498 (W.D. Ky. Sept. 15, 2005).

108 Padin v. Oyster Point Dodge, 397 F. Supp. 2d 712 (E.D. Va. 2005).

109 12 C.F.R. § 202 Appendix C Form C-1 through C-9, *reprinted in* Appx. C.9, *infra*.

110 FTC Official Staff Commentary § 615 item 3, *reprinted at* Appx. D, *infra. See also* FTC, Compliance with the Fair Credit Reporting Act, at 38–39 (1977).

111 *See* Fischl v. GMAC, 708 F.2d 143, 150 (5th Cir. 1983).

112 15 U.S.C. §§ 7001–7031.

113 15 U.S.C. § 7001(c)(1)(A)–(D).

114 *See In re* Farmers Ins. Co., FCRA Litig., 2006 WL 1042450, n.11 (W.D. Okla. Apr. 13, 2006); Ashby v. Farmers Ins. Co. of Oregon, 2004 WL 2297468 (D. Or. Oct. 7, 2004) (citing Carroll v. Exxon Co.); Thomas v. Cendant Mortgage, 2004 WL 2600772 (E.D. Fa. Nov. 15, 2004); Drury v. TNT Holland Motor Exp., Inc., 885 F. Supp. 161 (W.D. Mich. 1994); Carroll v. Exxon Co., USA, 434 F. Supp. 557 (E.D. La. 1977); Conf. Rep. No. 1587, 91st Cong., 2d Sess., *reprinted in* 1970 U.S.C-.C.A.N. 4416 ('immediately upon denial"). *See also* H.R. 15073, 91st Cong., 2d Sess., 116 Cong. Rec. 36571 (1970) ("assuring immediate notification").

115 15 U.S.C. § 1681m(a).

116 FTC Official Staff Commentary § 615 item 4, *reprinted at* Appx. D, *infra*.

117 Costa v. Mauro Chevrolet, Inc., 390 F. Supp. 2d 720, 730–731 (N.D. Ill. 2005). *See* FTC Official Staff Commentary § 615 item 11, *reprinted at* Appx. D, *infra* (e.g., "the user must give the notice if the denial is based wholly or partly on the absence of a file or on the fact that the file contained insufficient references"). *See also* Fischl v. GMAC, 708 F.2d 143, 149 (5th Cir. 1983); Hospital & Health Servs. Credit Union, 104 F.T.C. 589 (1984) (consent order); FTC Informal Staff Opinion Letter, [1969–1973 Decisions Transfer Binder] Consumer Cred. Guide (CCH) & 98,989 (July 5, 1973); Wan, FTC Informal Staff Opinion Letter (July 5, 1973), *reprinted on the CD-Rom accompanying this manual*; FTC, Compliance with the Fair Credit Reporting Act, at 38–39 (1977).

118 Fischl v. GMAC, 708 F.2d 143, 149–150 (5th Cir. 1983).

where, the user need not provide the adverse action notice even if the user received a consumer report that contained some of the same information as that obtained elsewhere.[119] Instead, a different user notice to the consumer may be required if the user obtains information from a source other than a CRA that resulted in an adverse credit determination.[120]

At the same time, there need not even be a file on the consumer in order to trigger the required notice. If a user took an adverse action because a CRA had no file on a consumer (e.g., the consumer had no credit history), or the file had insufficient references, then the user must still make the disclosure.[121] It is irrelevant that the report itself contains no adverse information on the consumer, as long as it led to adverse action.[122]

A report does not need to be the only grounds for a user's adverse determination, or even the major grounds. It need only be one of the grounds for the determination.[123] If, however, the report contains information the user has obtained from other sources and that information is the basis for the adverse action, the user is not required to notify the consumer.[124]

8.2.6.4.2 Overview and summary of what is an "adverse action"?

Adverse action occurs when any of the following actions are taken by a user.[125] In connection with credit,[126] adverse action has the same meaning as it does in the Equal Credit Opportunity Act, and, includes:

- Refusal to grant credit in substantially the amount or terms as requested;
- Termination of an account or an unfavorable change in its terms;
- Refusal to increase a line of credit.

In connection with employment,[127] an adverse action occurs whenever:

- Employment is denied;
- Any employment decision adversely affects a current or prospective employee.

In connection with the underwriting of new or existing insurance,[128] adverse action means:

- Denial or cancellation of coverage;
- Increase in any charge;
- Any reduction or adverse or unfavorable change in coverage or amounts of insurance.

In connection with government benefits and licenses,[129] notice of adverse action is required upon:

- Denial or cancellation;
- An increase in any charge;
- Any other unfavorable or adverse change in terms.

In addition, there is a sweeping catchall.[130] Adverse action also includes any action adverse to the interests of the consumer in connection with any application or transaction initiated by the consumer, or in connection with any review of an account to determine whether the consumer continues to meet the requirements of the account. Even if an action does not clearly fall within one of the other kinds of adverse action, it may be covered by this catchall.

---

119 Wood v. Holiday Inns, Inc., 508 F.2d 167 (5th Cir. 1975). However, if the notice asserts that a report served as a basis for the adverse action but the user contradicts the notice, advocates should carefully evaluate the actual use of the consumer report and whether a permissible purpose existed for any access or use of the report.
120 See § 8.2.7, *infra*.
121 Reynolds v. Hartford Fin. Servs. Group, Inc., 435 F.3d 1081 (9th Cir. 2006), *cert. granted, sub nom.* GEICO Gen. Ins. Co. v. Edo, __ S. Ct. __, 2006 WL 2055539 (Sept. 26, 2006); FTC Official Staff Commentary § 615 item 11, *reprinted at* Appx. D, *infra*. *See also* Anderson v. Capital One Bank, 224 F.R.D. 444 (W.D. Wis. 2004) (allowing individual action to proceed when user based decision on inaccurate report that consumer was deceased); Goldfarb, FTC Informal Staff Opinion Letter (Dec. 6, 1977), *reprinted on the CD-Rom accompanying this manual* ("no file" response deals with consumer's creditworthiness, so notice must be given). *Cf.* Peeler, FTC Informal Staff Opinion Letter (Mar. 8, 1976), *reprinted on the CD-Rom accompanying this manual* (unclear whether CRA must add information to correct "no file" report); Feldman, FTC Informal Staff Opinion Letter (Aug. 30, 1974), *reprinted on the CD-Rom accompanying this manual* (unclear whether CRA must open new file on consumer denied credit due to "no file").
122 *See* FTC Official Staff Commentary § 615 item 11, *reprinted at* Appx. D, *infra*. *See also* Fischl v. GMAC, 708 F.2d 143, 149 (5th Cir. 1983); Hospital & Health Servs. Credit Union, 104 F.T.C. 589 (1984) (consent order); FTC Informal Staff Opinion Letter, [1969–1973 Decisions Transfer Binder] Consumer Cred. Guide (CCH) 98,989 (July 5, 1973); Wan, FTC Informal Staff Opinion Letter (July 5, 1973), *reprinted on the CD-Rom accompanying this manual*.
123 15 U.S.C. § 1681m(a); Woodell v. United Way of Dutchess County, 357 F. Supp. 2d 761 (S.D.N.Y. 2005); FTC Official Staff Commentary § 615 item 14, *reprinted at* Appx. D, *infra*.
124 Wood v. Holiday Inns, Inc., 508 F.2d 167 (5th Cir. 1975).

125 15 U.S.C. § 1681a(k). Adverse action was not separately defined in the Act prior to the Reform Act of 1996. Instead, 15 U.S.C. § 1681m specifically stated the circumstances when such a notice was required under §§ 1681m(a) and 1681m(b). The 1996 Reform Act was intended to expand the circumstances under which adverse action notices under § 1681m(a) were required. Pub. L. No. 104-208 § 2402, 110 Stat. 3009 (Sept. 30, 1996).
126 15 U.S.C. § 1681a(k)(1)(A). *See* § 8.2.6.4.3.2, *infra*.
127 15 U.S.C. § 1681a(k)(B)(ii). *See* §§ 8.2.6.2.5, 8.2.6.4.4, *infra*.
128 15 U.S.C. § 1681a(k)(B)(i). *See* § 8.2.6.4.5, *infra*.
129 15 U.S.C. § 1681a(k)(B)(iii). *See* § 8.2.6.4.6, *infra*.
130 15 U.S.C. § 1681a(k)(B)(iv). *See* § 8.2.6.4.7, *infra*.

8.2.6.4.3 When notice required: following adverse action on credit

8.2.6.4.3.1 General requirement

A user must notify the consumer whenever adverse action, based at least in part on a consumer report, is taken in connection with a credit transaction.[131] The FCRA gives the term "adverse action" the same meaning as it has under the Equal Credit Opportunity Act (ECOA).[132] Under the ECOA, adverse action has been defined to include: (1) any refusal to grant credit in substantially the amount or on substantially the terms requested in an application; (2) a termination of an account or an unfavorable change in the terms of an account; and (3) a refusal to increase the amount of credit upon application. Interpretations of the ECOA on what constitutes adverse action directly apply. Readers should consider the relevant discussions in NCLC's *Credit Discrimination*.[133]

In addition to adverse actions described in the ECOA, notification by the user is required by the FCRA upon any action adverse to the interests of the consumer in connection with any transaction initiated by the consumer or application made by the consumer, so long as the adverse action is based in whole or in part on any information in the consumer's report.[134] This is the so-called catchall category of adverse action under the FCRA.[135]

Adverse action does not occur where application is withdrawn by a credit grantor based solely on the refusal of the consumer to provide verifications necessary to complete the credit application process.[136] If a yo-yo car sale is subject to a condition subsequent that the dealer obtain financing, denial based on inability to obtain financing (rather than on information in the consumer report) does not require an adverse action notice under section 1681m(a) (even though a notice would be required under the ECOA and 15 U.S.C. § 161m(b)).[137]

Adverse action, requiring user notification, includes both consumer and business credit. The statutory language limiting coverage to credit for personal, family, or household purposes was eliminated in 1996[138] and now echoes the ECOA's coverage to include business as well as consumer credit.

8.2.6.4.3.2 Definition of "credit"

The term "credit" is defined in the FCRA[139] to have the same meaning as in section 1691a of the ECOA. Under the ECOA, credit is defined as "the right granted by a creditor to a debtor to defer payment of debt or to incur debts and defer its payment or to purchase property or services and defer payment therefor,"[140] The definition of "credit" under the ECOA is broader than under the Truth in Lending Act (TILA) and thus it should not be limited to transactions covered by TILA.[141] It should apply to any type of credit, including a straight loan, a credit sale, or any right to put off payment.[142] Thus, notification should be required if a seller refuses to sell an item to the consumer on credit because of information in a consumer report.[143] The same may be the case if a home seller, based on information in a consumer

---

131 15 U.S.C. § 1681m(a).
132 15 U.S.C. § 1681a(k), *citing* 15 U.S.C. § 1691(d)(6); Baynes v. Alltel, 322 F. Supp. 2d 1307 (M.D. Ala. 2004); Thomas v. Cendant Mortgage, 2004 WL 2600772 (E.D. Pa. Nov. 15, 2004) ("adverse action" has same meaning as under ECOA); Crane v. American Home Mortgage, Corp., 2004 WL 1529165 (E.D. Pa. July 7, 2004).
133 National Consumer Law Center, Credit Discrimination (4th ed. 2005 and Supp.).
134 Treadway v. Gateway Chevrolet Oldsmobile, Inc., 362 F.3d 971 (7th Cir. 2004) (obligations under § 1681m are not limited to persons granting final approval of credit.); Thomas v. Cendant Mortgage, 2004 WL 2600772 (E.D. Pa. Nov. 15, 2004) ("adverse action" has same meaning as under ECOA); Crane v. American Home Mortgage, Corp., 2004 WL 1529165 (E.D. Pa. July 7, 2004); Cannon v. Metro Ford, Inc., 242 F. Supp. 2d 1322 (S.D. Fla. 2002) (repossession could be adverse action if based on consumer report); Castro v. Union Nissan, Inc., 2002 WL 1466810 (N.D. Ill. July 8, 2002) (same). See § 8.2.6.4.7, *infra*.

FTC staff have opined that the failure to grant a good credit discount based on a consumer report is an adverse action. This is true whether or not the consumer applied for the discount or was even aware of the possibility of lower charges. This implies that a decision not to extend some benefits to an applicant or to an existing customer, based on a consumer report, even if no new charges or rate increases are levied, is adverse action triggering notification requirement. Ball, FTC Informal Staff Opinion Letter (Mar. 1, 2000), *reprinted on the CD-Rom accompanying this manual*.
135 Barnes v. Ditech.Com, 2005 WL 913090 (E.D. Pa. Apr. 19, 2005); Baynes v. Alltel, 322 F. Supp. 2d 1307 (M.D. Ala. 2004). See § 8.2.6.4.7, *infra*.

136 Kirk v. Kelley Buick of Atlanta, Inc., 336 F. Supp. 2d 1327 (N.D. Ga. 2004). *But see* Treadway v. Gateway Chevrolet Oldsmobile, Inc., 362 F.3d 971 (7th Cir. 2004) (obligations under § 1681m are not limited to persons granting final approval of credit.); Padin v. Oyster Point Dodge, 397 F. Supp. 2d 712 (E.D. Va. 2005) (dealer must notify consumer of denial of credit by finance company).
137 Brand v. Rohr-Ville Motors, Inc., 2003 WL 21078022 (N.D. Ill. May 9, 2003).
138 15 U.S.C. § 1681m(a), *as amended by* Pub. L. No. 104-208 § 2411, 110 Stat. 3009 (Sept. 30, 1996).
139 15 U.S.C. § 1681a(r)(5).
140 15 U.S.C. § 1691a(d); 12 C.F.R. § 202.2(j).
141 *See* National Consumer Law Center, Credit Discrimination § 2.2.2.1.1 (4th ed. 2005 and Supp.).
142 Such extensions of credit include typical car finance transactions where credit is denied by a proposed assignee. Padin v. Oyster Point Dodge, 397 F. Supp. 2d 712 (E.D. Va. 2005).
143 Payne v. Ken Dipeholz Ford Lincoln Mercury, Inc., 2004 WL 40631 (N.D. Ill. Jan 5, 2004) (requiring cosigner is adverse action); Brand v. Rohr-Ville Motors, Inc., 2003 WL 21078022 (N.D. Ill. May 9, 2003) (question of fact whether adverse action was based on consumer report instead of on third party's refusal to buy the loan); Peeler, FTC Informal Staff Opinion Letter (Feb. 8, 1978), *reprinted on the CD-Rom accompanying this manual*.

report, rejects a consumer's attempt to condition a home purchase on the consumer finding suitable financing.[144]

8.2.6.4.3.3 "Denial" of credit defined

Because of the number of terms involved in a credit transaction, questions arise as to when credit as requested has been denied. Clearly, notice is required where credit is denied outright, where less credit is provided than requested, where an increase in the amount of credit is denied, or where the charge for the credit is increased.[145] In this sense, a denial of credit can also occur when a creditor reviews a current account and unfavorably changes its terms.[146]

If any condition is imposed, without which credit will not be extended, *and* it is imposed because of information in the consumer report, there is a "denial" which requires a notice. This would include cases where a larger down payment, a shorter maturity, a cosigner, a guarantor, or additional collateral is required as a condition of extending credit. If a consumer applies, for example, for a credit card limit of $1500, and only $1000 is approved because of information in a consumer report, a "denial" has occurred.[147] Similarly, suppose a bank notifies a consumer that, based on a consumer report, it would approve a loan only if the consumer makes a larger down payment. The larger down payment could result in a *lower* charge for the credit, but notice is still required. Similarly, a notice will be required where a bank, based on a consumer report, requires the consumer to obtain a cosigner or put up collateral, even if the bank then lowers the interest rate because of the lower risk of the loan as restructured. Any refusal to grant credit on the terms originally requested by the consumer should be a denial of credit which requires notice of adverse action. Such denials would include the refusal of a car dealer to sell a vehicle on credit.[148]

When credit is denied because the creditor does not ordinarily offer the kind of credit plan requested by the consumer, there is no adverse action.[149] Some courts have ruled that there is no denial if the consumer accepts a counteroffer made by the creditor,[150] but such a conclusion is not necessarily controlling and arguments can be made that acceptance of counteroffer terms adverse to the consumer still violate the FCRA if notice is not given.[151] Furthermore, there is clearly a denial where a consumer applied for credit on particular terms, was offered credit with a higher interest rate based on a credit score derived from information in a consumer report, and refused to accept those terms or use the credit offered.[152] Additionally, it has been held that a user takes "adverse action" when it requires the consumer to obtain a cosigner for the credit obligation.[153]

---

144 Peeler, FTC Informal Staff Opinion Letter (Feb. 8, 1978), *reprinted on the CD-Rom accompanying this manual.*

145 Thomas v. Cendant Mortgage, 2004 WL 2600772 (E.D. Pa. Nov. 15, 2004) (telephone denial of mortgage application constitutes adverse action where credit application was used to prequalify eligibility for mortgage program); Crane v. American Home Mortgage, Corp., 2004 WL 1529165 (E.D. Pa. July 7, 2004). *See also* Hospital & Health Servs. Credit Union, 104 F.T.C. 589 (1984) (consent order); *In re* Alden's, Inc., 92 F.T.C. 901 (1978) (consent order); Reynolds, FTC Informal Staff Opinion Letter (May 14, 1979), *reprinted on the CD-Rom accompanying this manual. But see* Kirk v. Kelley Buick of Atlanta, Inc., 336 F. Supp. 2d 1327 (N.D. Ga. 2004) (consumer's failure to provide requested verification necessary to complete credit application does not constitute adverse action on part of user); Weidman v. Fed. Home Loan Mortgage Corp., 338 F. Supp. 2d 571 (E.D. Pa. 2004) (creating an exemption without statutory support that precludes a non-creditor from acting adversely to the interests of a consumer in a credit transaction); FTC Official Staff Commentary § 615 item 9, *reprinted at* Appx. D, *infra.*

146 *See* § 8.2.6.4.3.9, *infra.*

147 Guidelines for Financial Institutions in Complying with Fair Credit Reporting Act (1971). *See also* FTC Official Staff Commentary § 615 item 9, *reprinted at* Appx. D, *infra.*

148 *See, e.g.,* Padin v. Oyster Point Dodge, 397 F. Supp. 2d 712 (E.D. Va. 2005).

149 Reg. B, 12 C.F.R. § 202.2(c)(2)(iv).

150 Lopez v. Platinum Home Mortg. Corp., 2006 WL 2269154 (W.D. Mich. Aug. 8, 2006); Baynes v. Alltel, 322 F. Supp. 2d 1307 (M.D. Ala. 2004) (rejecting argument that consumer must affirmatively allege rejection of counteroffer); Thomas v. Cendant Mortgage, 2004 WL 2600772 (E.D. Pa. Nov. 15, 2004) (where creditor denies credit but consumer accepts counteroffer, there is no "adverse action" under § 1681a(k)(1)(A), but extension of the counter offer may constitute "adverse action" for purposes of catch-all definition under § 1681a(k)(10(B)(iv)); Harper v. Lindsay Chevrolet Oldsmobile, L.L.C., 212 F. Supp. 2d 582 (E.D. Va. 2002); Mayberry v. Ememessay Inc., 201 F. Supp. 2d 687 (W.D. Va. 2002); Austin v. J.C. Penney Co., 162 F. Supp. 2d 495 (E.D. Va. 2001) (without deciding the conflicting authority as to whether a check is a credit instrument, court determines that initial refusal to accept check due to consumer report, and acceptance of the check 45 minutes later, is not adverse action within the meaning of FCRA. Court deems notice burden on merchants too great); National Consumer Law Center, Credit Discrimination § 10.4 (4th ed. 2005 and Supp.).

151 *See* § 8.2.6.4.3.5, *infra.*

152 Latour, FTC Informal Staff Opinion Letter (June 28, 2001), *reprinted on the CD-Rom accompanying this manual.* There is no denial where a dealer merely submitted consumer report to potential lenders and made it clear that without lender approval there was no sale. Treadway v. Gateway Chevrolet Oldsmobile, Inc., 362 F.3d 971 (7th Cir. 2004); Barnes v. Ditech.Com, 2005 WL 913090 (E.D. Pa. Apr. 19, 2005) (FCRA does not require "final action" on credit application); Thomas v. Cendant Mortgage, 2004 WL 2600772 (E.D. Pa. Nov. 15, 2004); Crane v. American Home Mortgage, Corp., 2004 WL 1529165 (E.D. Pa. July 7, 2004); Najieb v. Chrysler-Plymouth, 2002 WL 31906466 (N.D. Ill. Dec. 31, 2002). *Cf.* Kirk v. Kelley Buick of Atlanta, Inc., 336 F. Supp. 2d 1327 (N.D. Ga. 2004) (no adverse action where consumer fails to provide verification necessary to complete credit application and creditor withdraws application); Rausch v. Hartford Fin. Servs. Group, Inc., 2003 WL 22722061 (D. Or. July 31, 2003) (no increase in rate or "adverse action" occurs in context of insurance transaction where insurance issuer uses consumer report in determining initial rate offering).

153 Rodriquez v. Lynch Ford, Inc., 2004 WL 2958772 (N.D. Ill. Nov. 18, 2004).

8.2.6.4.3.4 Special situation: risk-based pricing

The FACTA amendments in 2003 added a notice to risk-based pricing. Whenever a creditor extends credit on terms "materially less favorable than the most favorable terms available to a substantial proportion of consumers," the creditor must provide to consumers a notice that explains that the terms are based on information in a consumer report and that the consumers can request a free copy of the report.[154] This notice is discussed in § 8.2.8, infra.

Prior to the FACTA amendments to the FCRA, advocates argued—based on the plain language of the catchall definition of adverse action and its supporting FTC Staff Commentary—that risk-based pricing constituted adverse action. Despite the addition of the new notice requirement, the issue of whether instances of risk-based pricing[155] fall within the definition of adverse action will be crucial, since the notices required under these separate provisions are entirely different. While a creditor who issues an adverse action notice need not issue a risk-based pricing notice, the FTC and Federal Reserve Board (FRB) have been granted rule making authority over the latter notice,[156] including the power to determine who would not benefit from a risk-based pricing notice, thereby limiting the class of persons entitled to that notice.

As a result, consumers who have been subject to forms of risk-based pricing may be entitled to an adverse action notice if the FTC and FRB choose to exempt those consumers from receipt of the risk-based pricing notice. However, because enforcement of rights for all notices required under section 1681m are currently in flux, it appears that for the time being, the FTC and FRB's regulations on this will likely be the last word for the immediate future. Practitioners who wish to litigate in this area should familiarize themselves with the history of this provision and its prior staff interpretations.

Prior to the FACTA amendments to the FCRA in 2003, the FTC Staff Commentary, which had not changed following the Consumer Credit Reporting Reform Act of 1996 (1996 Reform Act),[157] and an FTC informal staff opinion letter[158] reflected the fact that risk-based pricing constituted adverse action under 15 U.S.C. § 1681m.[159] Consistent with this position, the FTC's Notice to Users of Consumer Reports required that users provide adverse action notices when "unfavorably changing credit or contract terms or conditions" and when "offering credit on less favorable terms than requested."[160] Thus, although creditors are not required to issue written adverse action notices under the ECOA when the consumer accepts a counteroffer of credit which provided less favorable terms,[161] that same creditor is required to provide an adverse action notice under the FCRA. Courts deciding cases under the pre-FACTA amendment provisions of section 1681m consistently agreed with this analysis that properly applied the catchall provision.[162]

After the FACTA amendments, the FTC revised its Notice to Users of Consumer Reports.[163] In the process, the FTC added the following statement to its previously unambiguous stance regarding the necessity that creditors provide the section 1681m notice when issuing counteroffers, irrespective of whether such offers are accepted: "No adverse action occurs in a credit transaction where the creditor makes a counteroffer that is accepted by the consumer."[164] The FTC additionally deleted the references to "unfavorably changing credit or contract terms or conditions" and "offering credit on less favorable terms than requested" as adverse actions.

The consequence of this policy reversal, despite no change in the statutory definitions, is to provide users of consumer reports with a possible defense of good faith reliance on the information in the FTC-promulgated notice. Erroneously, the FTC's revised notice instructs users that the section 1681m notice is no longer required where the consumer accepts a counteroffer on less favorable terms than those initially sought by the consumer.

Based on the pre-FACTA amendment cases, the FTC's own prior construction of the Act, and the fact that the adverse action definition was not amended in FACTA, it appears that this position exceeds the authority Congress granted to the FTC. In so doing, the FTC has improperly instructed creditors to withhold adverse action notices when they should appropriately be issued under the FCRA's catch-all provision. Due to the current confusion regarding the availability of a private right of action under section 1681m, case law developments in this area may not resolve this question absent a challenge to the FTC under the Administrative Procedures Act or by further revisions by the FTC to its notice.

---

154 15 U.S.C. § 1681m(h)(6).
155 See, e.g., Crane v. American Home Mortgage, Corp., 2004 WL 1529165 (E.D. Pa. July 7, 2004).
156 15 U.S.C. § 1681m(h)(6).
157 FTC Official Staff Commentary § 615(9), reprinted at Appx. D, infra.
158 Brinkerhoff, FTC Informal Staff Opinion Letter (May 31, 1996), reprinted on the CD-Rom accompanying this manual.
159 See § 8.2.6.4.3.5, infra.
160 Notice to Users of Consumer Reports: Obligations of Users Under the FCRA, as adopted by the FTC pursuant to the 1996 Reform Act, (I)(c), cited in Baynes v. Alltel, 322 F. Supp. 2d 1307, 1314 (M.D. Ala. 2004). See § 8.5.2, infra.
161 See 12 C.F.R. § 202.9; National Consumer Law Center, Credit Discrimination § 10.4 (4th ed. 2005 and Supp.).
162 See § 8.2.6.4.3.1, supra.
163 See § 8.5.2, infra.
164 Notice to Users of Consumer Reports: Obligations of Users Under the FCRA, 16 C.F.R. 698 Appx. H, reprinted at Appx. C.6, infra.

8.2.6.4.3.5 Special situation: accepted counteroffers

An issue closely related to risk-based pricing is whether acceptance of a counteroffer in a credit transaction initiated by the consumer will trigger the FCRA adverse action notice requirement. This issue is closely related to the issue of adverse action notices based on risk-based pricing and often are one and the same.[165]

For example, automobile dealers and other retailers currently offer "zero percent financing" and other teaser rates, but many consumers do not qualify for such offers because of information in their consumer reports. These consumers still enter into the transactions at the higher rate, yet they do not receive adverse action notices and are thus unaware that they are paying higher costs because of their consumer report or credit score. Does the FCRA require an adverse action notice under these circumstances? The answer to this question hinges on the interpretation of section 1681a(k)(1)(A) (which incorporates the ECOA definition) and section 1681a(k)(1)(B)(iv) (which includes any action "adverse to the consumer.").

The ECOA defines adverse action as a denial or revocation of credit, a change in the terms of an existing credit arrangement, or a refusal to grant credit in substantially the same amount or on substantially the terms requested. The term does not include a refusal to extend additional credit under an existing credit arrangement where the applicant is delinquent or otherwise in default, or where such additional credit would exceed a previously established credit limit.[166]

In addition, Regulation B specifically states that adverse action is a "refusal to grant credit in substantially the terms requested in an application *unless the creditor makes a counteroffer (to grant the credit in a different amount or on other terms) and the applicant uses or expressly accepts the credit offered.*"[167] For purposes of determining whether an action constitutes an adverse action under the FCRA, all FRB findings, decisions, commentaries, and orders under the ECOA apply.[168]

These definitions must be compared to section 1681a(k)(1)(B)(iv), which defines adverse action as "an action taken or determination that is (I) made in connection with an application that was made by, or a transaction that was initiated by, any consumer . . . and (II) *adverse to the interests of the consumer.*"[169] This definition must be read as a supplement to section 1681a(k)(1)(A) because of the use of the word "and." Moreover, section 1681a(k)(1)(B)(iv) and other subsections clearly go beyond the more limited ECOA definitions.

The FTC has issued contradictory staff opinion letters relating to this issue. The first FTC staff opinion letter supports the argument that a counteroffer with adverse terms is the type of action for which the FCRA notice was created.[170] The example used in the opinion letter is an applicant for a car loan who had to pay more to finance an automobile purchase than she would have been charged if her credit record had been better. According to this opinion, the increase in charge triggers the notice required under section 1681m of the FCRA.[171] A subsequent FTC staff opinion letter does not address the analysis and conclusion contained in the first letter and instead simply follows the definition of adverse action contained in Regulation B.[172]

A court in Virginia has held that a change in interest rate from 23% to 25% in an automobile financing deal did not constitute adverse action as required by section 1681m.[173] The court relied upon the ECOA's Regulation B definition of adverse action as a basis for its decision. The decision did not include any analysis relating to the broader definition of adverse action contained in section 1681a(k)(1)(B)(iv). A Michigan court, however, has concluded that acceptance of a counteroffer of credit exempts a creditor from the requirement of sending an adverse action notice under the FCRA.[174] But as of this date, there is no clear consensus at either the circuit or district court level and the issue remains unresolved.

8.2.6.4.3.6 Special situation: price quotes

Where the credit score or other information contained within the consumer report adversely affects the interest rate found in an initial quote offered to a consumer, the increase in rate constitutes adverse action.[175] Such is the case even where the consumer withdraws the application based upon the quote, rather than awaiting a firm commitment offer of credit at the higher rate.

8.2.6.4.3.7 Special situation: cosigners

Often in consumer credit transactions, more than one consumer signs a credit application. For example, a co-

---

165 See § 8.2.6.4.3.4, *supra*.
166 15 U.S.C. § 1691d(6).
167 12 C.F.R. § 202.2(c)(I).
168 15 U.S.C. § 1681a(k)(2).
169 15 U.S.C. § 1681a(k)(1)(B)(iv)(I) and (II).

170 Brinkerhoff, FTC Informal Staff Opinion Letter (May 31, 1996), *reprinted on the CD-Rom accompanying this manual*.
171 *Id.*
172 Keller, FTC Staff Opinion Letter (July 14, 2000), *reprinted on the CD-Rom accompanying this manual*; Berger, FTC Staff Opinion Letter (June 28, 2003), *reprinted on the CD-Rom accompanying this manual*.
173 Harper v. Lindsay Chevrolet Oldsmobile, L.L.C., 212 F. Supp. 2d 582 (E.D. Va. 2002).
174 Lopez v. Platinum Home Mortg. Corp., 2006 WL 2269154 (W.D. Mich. Aug. 8, 2006).
175 Reynolds v. Hartford Fin. Servs. Group, Inc., 435 F.3d 1081 (9th Cir. 2006), *cert. granted, sub nom.* GEICO Gen. Ins. Co. v. Edo, __ S. Ct. __, 2006 WL 2055539 (Sept. 26, 2006); Barnes v. Ditech.Com, 2005 WL 913090 (E.D. Pa. Apr. 19, 2005) (FCRA does not require "final action" on credit application). *See also* Thomas v. Cendant Mortgage, 2004 WL 2600772 (E.D. Pa. Nov. 15, 2004) (consumer need not provide completed credit application in order to trigger requirements of § 1681m(a)).

maker, guarantor, or surety may sign. The FCRA requires notice of adverse action in connection with transactions initiated by *any* consumer.[176] In its guidelines, the federal financial regulatory CRAs declare the disclosures, which must be made to the consumer who originally and primarily applied for credit, must also be made to the co-maker, guarantor, or surety to whom the information relates.[177] Additionally, it has been held that a user takes "adverse action" where it requires the consumer to obtain a cosigner for the credit obligation.[178]

8.2.6.4.3.8 Special situation: prescreening offers

Creditors often offer credit to those on a mailing list compiled or edited by a CRA. That is, only individuals meeting certain credit criteria are included on the list, and others are deleted from the list because of information from a CRA.[179] Nevertheless, the FTC Staff Commentary indicates that users of these "prescreened" lists need not notify those deleted from the list that a consumer report has led to denial of credit.[180] The FTC Staff Commentary's rationale is that the consumers deleted from the list have not requested credit and, therefore, credit has not been denied to those individuals.

8.2.6.4.3.9 Special situation: account reviews

From time to time, many users who have an ongoing relationship with consumers will review their accounts with a consumer to determine whether the consumer continues to meet the requirements of the account. Users may rely upon consumer reports to make these determinations. Under the Act, if any action is taken adverse to the interest of the consumers, user notification is required.[181] No notification is required where a creditor, for example, obtains consumer reports on a customer in connection with a review of its credit or other portfolio, and as a result of the review, the consumer's account is not changed, or is changed in a way that is not less favorable to the interest of that consumer, even if the accounts of other consumers are changed in a more favorable manner.[182]

It has become commonplace for major providers of open-end credit, especially credit card issuers, to periodically review existing accounts and to adjust interest rates upwards based on a credit score or consumer report. This so-called "universal default" increase may be triggered by delinquencies on other credit cards or accounts, new secured credit, errors, or other factors.[183] A notice of adverse action is required at the time of an increase by both the FCRA and the Equal Credit Opportunity Act.[184]

8.2.6.4.3.10 Other situations constituting credit

Whether or not check cashing, leasing, and sale of property constitute credit for purposes of the FCRA remains an open question. But, under the inclusive catchall definition of adverse action,[185] it is clear that each of these situations would require a notice if any action was taken contrary to the interest of the consumer based on the use of a consumer report. These situations are considered in another section.[186]

8.2.6.4.4 Time for notice: following adverse action on employment

8.2.6.4.4.1 Overview

Employers are required to provide adverse action notices whenever adverse employment decisions were based, at least in part, on consumer reports. Additional disclosures prior to the adverse action are required as well. These disclosures for adverse action are in addition to and separate from the notice and employee authorization required when an employer first seeks to use a consumer report for employment purposes. That notice and authorization are provided before the employer accesses the consumer report.[187]

The FACTA amendments of 2003 significantly reduced the circumstances in which adverse action notices are pro-

---

176 15 U.S.C. § 1681a(k)(1)(B)(iv).
177 Guidelines for Financial Institutions in Complying with the Fair Credit Reporting Act Question 9 (May 24, 1971); Spritz, FTC Informal Staff Opinion Letter (Nov. 5, 1998), *reprinted on the CD-Rom accompanying this manual. But see* Stinneford, FTC Informal Staff Opinion Letter (July 14, 2000), *reprinted on the CD-Rom accompanying this manual* (notice not required for guarantors).
178 Rodriquez v. Lynch Ford, Inc., 2004 WL 2958772 (N.D. Ill. Nov. 18, 2004).
179 *See* § 7.3.4, *supra*.
180 *See* FTC Official Staff Commentary § 615 item 5, *reprinted at* Appx. D, *infra. See also* Gowen, FTC Informal Staff Opinion Letter (Apr. 29, 1999), *reprinted on the CD-Rom accompanying this manual*; Grimes, FTC Informal Staff Opinion Letter (Jan. 22, 1988), *reprinted on the CD-Rom accompanying this manual*.
181 15 U.S.C. §§ 1681m(a) and 1681a(k)(1)(B)(iv)(I).

182 S. Rep. No. 185, 104th Cong., 1st Sess. at 32 (Dec. 14, 1995). *See* Ball, FTC Informal Staff Opinion Letter (Mar. 1, 2000), *reprinted on the CD-Rom accompanying this manual*.
183 National Consumer Law Center, The Cost of Credit: Regulation, Preemption, and Industry Abuses 11.7.2.3.1 (3d ed. 2005 and Supp.).
184 Letter, Director, Compliance Policy, Office of Thrift Supervision, U.S. Department of the Treasury, Sept. 30, 1997, Clearinghouse No. 52,160.
185 15 U.S.C. § 1681a(k)(1)(B)(iv)(II).
186 *See* § 2.3.6, *supra*.
187 15 U.S.C. § 1681b(b)(2). The disclosures that must be made for an adverse action based on a consumer report are discussed at § 8.2.6.2, *supra*.

vided to existing employees. As a result, notice requirements prior to FACTA are applicable in most cases to prospective employees who are new applicants and those employees who are subject to transfers or promotions.

8.2.6.4.4.2 Employee misconduct investigations

The FCRA, as amended by FACTA, excluded certain communications made to an employer concerning investigations for employee misconduct or for compliance reasons from the definition of a "consumer report."[188] To fall within the exclusion, the communication must be made to an employer and must be in connection with an investigation of one of the following:

- Suspected misconduct relating to employment;
- Compliance with federal, state, or local laws;
- Compliance with the rules of a self-regulatory organization; or
- Compliance with the preexisting written policies of the employer.[189]

In addition, this exemption applies only if the communication was not for the purpose of investigating an employee's creditworthiness, credit standing, or credit capacity, and the communication must only have been made to the employer, the employer's agent, a governmental agency, or a self-regulatory organization.[190]

For those investigations that meet the exemption, the employee will not be entitled to the standard adverse action notice of section 1681m or the Summary of Consumer Rights. However, these employees will have the right to a summary of the exempted report.[191] In contrast to other employment-related investigations, the employer need not provide any notice beforehand.[192] The effect of this amendment is to remove FCRA protections for misconduct investigations concerning current employees, leaving only post-facto disclosure of the summary of the exempted report.

8.2.6.4.4.3 Notice requirements for employment adverse actions

Under the FCRA, employers are still required to provide adverse action notices (or other notices required by the FCRA)[193] to (1) consumers who are being investigated for a new position or a new job by a third party hired by the employer for that purpose, or (2) any consumers, whether they are existing employees or not, whom the employer decides to evaluate via a consumer report in the employment context. Employers are required to disclose their reliance on a consumer report—or a third-party investigative report—any time they deny initial employment, promotion, or job transfer to an employee.[194]

Except for employee misconduct investigations, an employer intending to take adverse action based, at least in part, on a consumer report must provide to the consumer/employee beforehand a copy of the report itself and an FTC Summary of Consumer Rights.[195] The copy of the report may not be altered, even to exclude the names of confidential sources.[196] This prior disclosure is unique to employment decisions.[197]

The amount of time which must elapse between this pre-adverse action disclosure and the adverse action itself is not specified. The reason for prior disclosure of the report is clearly to provide the consumer with an opportunity to clear up any misstatements in the consumer report, and to address any misunderstandings the report may have engendered in the mind of the employer. The fact that the Summary of Consumer Rights must also be provided to the consumer suggests that the period should be long enough for the consumer to exercise rights to correct errors in the report. However, an FTC staff attorney has suggested informally that five days between the pre-adverse action disclosures and the adverse action appears reasonable, even though the facts of a particular circumstance may require a different time period.[198]

---

188 Pub. L. No. 108-159, § 611(b), 117 Stat 1952 (Dec. 4, 2003), *amending* 15 U.S.C. § 1681a(d)(2)(D). *See* § 2.3.6.4.2, *supra*, Ch. 13, *infra*.
189 Pub. L. No. 108-159, § 611(b), 117 Stat 1952 (Dec. 4, 2003), *amending* 15 U.S.C. § 1681a(d)(2)(D). *See* § 2.3.6.4.2, *supra*, Ch. 13, *infra*.
190 15 U.S.C. § 1681a(x)(D)(i)–(iii).
191 15 U.S.C. § 1681a(x)(2). *See* § 2.3.6.4.2, *supra*, § 13.4, *infra*.
192 *See* 15 U.S.C. § 1681b(b)(3).
193 *See* § 13.4.1.3, *infra*.
194 *See* 15 U.S.C. § 1681a(h). *See also* Silbergeld, FTC Informal Staff Opinion Letter (Apr. 15, 1971), *reprinted on the CD-Rom accompanying this manual. See also* FTC, Compliance with the Fair Credit Reporting Act, at 41. *Cf.* Maloney, FTC Staff Opinion Letter (Sept. 4, 1984), *reprinted on the CD-Rom accompanying this manual*.
195 15 U.S.C. § 1681b(b)(3); Obabueki v. Int'l Bus. Machs. Corp., 145 F. Supp. 2d 371 (S.D.N.Y. 2001). The Summary of Consumer Rights is described at § 4.6, *supra*.
196 Hahn, FTC Informal Staff Opinion Letter (July 8, 1998), *reprinted on the CD-Rom accompanying this manual*; Leathers, FTC Informal Staff Opinion Letter (Sept. 9, 1998), *reprinted on the CD-Rom accompanying this manual* (suggesting further that if the consumer report is delivered to the employer orally, the "copy" of the report may be given to the consumer orally as well).
197 Special rules exist for government agencies using consumer reports for employment purposes where the use is part of a national security investigation. Nevertheless, upon the conclusion of the investigation, notice of adverse action and a copy of the report (redacted if necessary) must be given to the consumer. *See* 15 U.S.C. § 1681b(b)(4).
198 Weisberg, FTC Informal Staff Opinion Letter (June 27, 1997), *reprinted on the CD-Rom accompanying this manual. See also* Haynes, FTC Informal Staff Opinion Letter (Dec. 18, 1997), *reprinted on the CD-Rom accompanying this manual* ("Employers may wish to consult with their counsel so that they

The pre-adverse action disclosures overlap with the notice of adverse action in that the notice of adverse action informs the consumer of the right to obtain a copy of the consumer report while the pre-adverse action disclosures will have already provided the consumer with a copy of the report itself. To minimize any possible confusion or duplication of effort, an employer may note in the notice of adverse action that a copy of the report and the Summary of Consumer Rights has already been provided.[199]

One group of employers is subject to different rules. By the terms of the so-called "trucker's amendment," when a consumer is applying for a job regulated by the Secretary of Transportation, or subject to certain state safety regulations, pre-adverse action disclosure may not be required.[200] If the application has been made by mail or electronically, and not in person, the employer may notify the applicant of adverse action without first providing a copy of the consumer report or the Summary of Consumer Rights. If the consumer does request a copy of the report, the employer must provide it.

A second group of employers which may be exempted from the adverse notice rules is federal agencies and departments who use a consumer report for employment purposes, if the report is relevant to a national security investigation.[201] Precise steps must be taken by the federal agency head for this exemption to apply.

Note that information communicated by an employment agency to a prospective employer may be excluded from the definition of a consumer report. Consequently, an employer who declines to hire a consumer recommended by an employment agency, even if the decision is based on information gleaned by the agency from a consumer report, may not be required to make any disclosure of adverse action. The scope of this exception is discussed in an earlier section.[202] When an employment agency is involved, consumer attorneys should consider whether this exception applies.

Even if an employer or employment agency has no duty in certain situations to disclose use of a consumer report to the consumer, the FCRA requires a *CRA* to notify the consumer whenever it provides a consumer report to a user with an employment purpose and the report contains public record information that is likely to have an adverse effect on the consumer's ability to obtain employment.[203] The notice also must contain the name and address of the report user.

The CRA can avoid this disclosure requirement by maintaining strict procedures to ensure that the public record information is complete and up to date.[204]

8.2.6.4.5 Time for notice: following adverse action on insurance

Whenever insurance is denied or the charge for the insurance is increased either wholly or partly because of information contained in a consumer report, the insurer must notify the consumer.[205] Notification is also required for any other adverse or unfavorable change in the terms or amount of insurance.[206] In other words, notice is required when an insurer decides to issue a substandard policy as opposed to one of its preferred (and lower-priced) policies because of the applicant's consumer report from a CRA. The notification requirement also applies to all users of the report who participate in the underwriting decision, irrespective of whether the user itself will underwrite the policy.[207] Even if the consumer has not applied for the insurance, notice to the consumer is required if insurance is denied based on the report about the consumer.[208] For example, if a mortgage insurer or credit insurer refuses, on the basis of a consumer report, to issue insurance which protects the lender from the consumer's default, a notice of adverse action must be given

---

develop procedures that are appropriate, keeping in mind the clear purpose . . . to allow consumers to discuss reports with employers or otherwise respond before adverse action is taken.").

199 Weisberg, FTC Informal Staff Opinion Letter (June 27, 1997), *reprinted on the CD-Rom accompanying this manual*; Haynes, FTC Informal Staff Opinion Letter (Dec. 18, 1997), *reprinted on the CD-Rom accompanying this manual*.

200 15 U.S.C. § 1681b(b)(3)(B).

201 15 U.S.C. § 1681b(b)(4).

202 *See* § 2.4.4.2, *supra*.

203 *See* § 8.2.20, *infra*.

204 *Id*.

205 15 U.S.C. § 1681m(a); Reynolds v. Hartford Fin. Servs. Group, Inc., 435 F.3d 1081 (9th Cir. 2006), *cert. granted, sub nom.* GEICO Gen. Ins. Co. v. Edo, __ S. Ct. __, 2006 WL 2055539 (Sept. 26, 2006); Karwo v. Citimortgage, Inc., 2005 WL 670640 (N.D. Ill. Mar. 21, 2005) ("increase" in rates subsumes those instances where the price initially quoted to consumer is greater than those generally made available); Karwo v. Citimortgage, Inc., 2004 WL 2033445 (N.D. Ill. Sept. 2, 2004).

206 *See* Isaac, FTC Informal Staff Opinion Letter (Oct. 13, 1995), *reprinted on the CD-Rom accompanying this manual* ("Insurers, unlike creditors under the Equal Credit Opportunity Act, are not required to disclose to consumers the specific reasons for denying insurance. However, we would encourage insurers to disclose this information, especially if the denial was based on information obtained from a CRA, as this would better enable consumers to readily identify and correct any inaccurate information being reported about them."). Prior to 1996 Reform Act, notification was only required where insurance was denied for personal, family, or household purposes or the charge for the insurance was increased either wholly or partly because of information contained in a consumer report.

207 Reynolds v. Hartford Fin. Servs. Group, Inc., 435 F.3d 1081 (9th Cir. 2006), *cert. granted, sub nom.* GEICO Gen. Ins. Co. v. Edo, __ S. Ct. __, 2006 WL 2055539 (Sept. 26, 2006); Karwo v. Citimortgage, Inc.. 2004 WL 2033445 (N.D. Ill. Sept. 2, 2004) (requirements may apply to those significantly involved in underwriting process but not actually issuing insurance policy); FTC Official Staff Commentary § 615 item 6, *reprinted at* Appx. D, *infra*.

208 Reynolds v. Hartford Fin. Servs. Group, Inc., 435 F.3d 1081 (9th Cir. 2006), *cert. granted, sub nom.* GEICO Gen. Ins. Co. v. Edo, __ S. Ct. __, 2006 WL 2055539 (Sept. 26, 2006).

to the consumer.[209] Similarly, a decision not to offer a discount based on a consumer report, even if the consumer did not ask for the discount, may require the adverse action notice.[210]

An Alabama district court certified a class action against an insurer who allegedly raised premiums by fifty percent or more in reliance on information contained in consumer reports and allegedly failed to send adverse action notice pursuant to section 1681m.[211] The insurer used Insurance Bureau Codes (ICBs) as one factor in setting the amounts of homeowners' renewal premiums. ICBs are generated by Fair Issac, Inc.[212] and are based on information contained in consumer reports.[213]

Although not yet commonplace, insurers may use pre-screening mailing lists to market their products. By analogy to credit purposes, deletion of a consumer from a pre-screened list used for insurance purposes is not an adverse action giving rise to any consumer notice requirement.[214]

One practice reportedly used by insurance companies is accessing consumer reports of non-applicants for insurance and making determinations on whether to grant insurance or charge higher premiums for the insurance based on the non-applicant's credit history. This practice raises issues regarding adverse action notices and who is entitled to an adverse action notice when insurance is denied or is granted but only at a higher rate because of the consumer report of the non-applicant. Should the applicant, the non-applicant, or both receive an adverse action notice? No court has ruled on this issue, but advocates have filed actions complaining of this practice.

8.2.6.4.6 Time for notice: following adverse action on government benefits

Government agencies may use consumer reports when they are required by law to consider an individual applicant's financial responsibility or status in order to determine the individual's eligibility for a license or other benefit.[215] Whenever such an agency denies, conceals, increases a charge, or otherwise imposes an adverse or unfavorable change in the terms of a license or government benefit, based in whole or in part on a consumer report, the agency must notify the consumer.[216]

Required notification may arise in a number of common situations ranging from granting and denial of professional licenses to use of consumer reports in connection with public housing and public assistance benefits.

8.2.6.4.7 Other situations

8.2.6.4.7.1 Transactions initiated by the consumer

The notice required when adverse action is based on a consumer report is not limited to credit, employment, and insurance purposes. Notice is triggered by adverse action relating to any transaction initiated by the consumer.[217] Indeed, this broad standard encompasses most credit, employment, and insurance purposes, and extends much further. Notice is also required following adverse action based on a review of a consumer's account, even if the review was not initiated by the consumer.[218]

Many potential transactions do not relate to credit, employment, insurance, or governmental licenses and benefits. Nevertheless, the user of a consumer report may be required to notify the consumer of adverse action under the most sweeping of all adverse notice provisions. The FCRA provides that notification must be made whenever any action adverse to the interests of the consumer is taken in connection with an application made by the consumer or in connection with any transaction initiated by the consumer, based in whole or in part on information contained in the consumer's report.[219]

Transactions which may give rise to notification clearly include: requirements that consumer pay a deposit; landlord denial of apartment rentals, or even a landlord's decision to increase the required deposit; denial of check writing privileges by merchants or by financial institutions; sales of property; investment opportunities; business transactions; and a wide array of other potential arrangements which a consumer may seek. The breadth of this provision removed a number of previously contentious issues over the Act's

---

209 Hall, FTC Informal Staff Opinion Letter (Oct. 26, 1998), reprinted on the CD-Rom accompanying this manual; Schieber, FTC Informal Staff Opinion Letter (Mar. 3, 1998), reprinted on the CD-Rom accompanying this manual.
210 See § 8.2.6.4.3.1, supra.
211 Braxton v. Farmers Ins. Group, 209 F.R.D. 654 (N.D. Ala. 2002).
212 See Ch. 14, infra, for a discussion of credit scores.
213 Braxton v. Farmers Ins. Group, 209 F.R.D. 654 (N.D. Ala. 2002). See § 11.2.2, infra.
214 See § 8.2.6.4.3.8, supra.
215 See § 2.3.6.6, supra.
216 15 U.S.C. §§ 1681m(a) and 1681a(k). Prior to the 1996 Reform Act, notice of adverse action was not required.
217 15 U.S.C. § 1681a(k)(1)(B)(iv)(I).
218 See § 8.2.6.4.3.9, supra.
219 15 U.S.C. §§ 1681m(a) and 1681a(k)(1)(B)(iv); Barnes v. Ditech.Com, 2005 WL 913090 (E.D. Pa. Apr. 19, 2005) (increased price quote for credit constitutes "adverse action" under "catch all" definition in § 1681a(k)(B)(iv)); Karwo v. Citimortgage, Inc., 2005 WL 670640 (N.D. Ill. Mar. 21, 2005) (increase charges for mortgage insurance may constitute adverse action under the "catch all" definition of "adverse action" found in 15 U.S.C. § 1681a(k)(B)(iv) as well as the more specific insurance provisions of 15 U.S.C. § 1681a(k)(B)(i)); Baynes v. Alltel, 322 F. Supp. 2d 1307 (M.D. Ala. 2004) (determination of charges for wireless telephone service may constitute "adverse action" under § 1681a(k)(B)(iv). See also Everson, FTC Informal Staff Opinion Letter (July 28, 1998), reprinted on the CD-Rom accompanying this manual.

scope and coverage. The provision recognizes that user notice is fundamentally important in assuring the accuracy of consumer reports.[220]

8.2.6.4.7.2 Check writing or approval services

Merchants often rely on check-approval services that furnish reports on individuals who want to pay by check, and the question arises whether notice must be provided to consumers where check-writing privileges are denied because of a consumer report. These reports are generally treated as consumer reports,[221] so the issue will be whether denial of check-writing privileges is an adverse action.

In the typical situation, a consumer presents a check to a merchant as payment for purchase of an item. The merchant then calls a check-approval service before accepting the check. If the check-approval service provides a negative report on the consumer (often meaning it has records of a check previously bounced by the consumer), the merchant will decline the check. The consumer may or may not have alternative means for making payment.

The Ninth Circuit, in finding check-approval reports to be consumer reports, stated that checks are essentially instruments of credit and not cash.[222] In addition, the definition of adverse action was expanded after the Ninth Circuit's decision to include any action adverse to the interests of consumers made in connection with an application made by the consumer or a transaction initiated by the consumer.[223] The proffer by the consumer of a personal check can be considered either an application to make payment by check, or an essential element of a purchase transaction initiated by the consumer. Either way, the merchant, as user, would have to notify the consumer of the adverse action based on a consumer report.

8.2.6.4.7.3 Leases

The issue of whether the denial of a lease is an adverse action should be clear.[224] Adverse action includes any action adverse to the interests of the consumer made in connection with any application made by the consumer or any transaction initiated by the consumer. If a consumer has asked to lease any property, and the lessor has turned the consumer down on the basis of a consumer report, the lessor must give notice of the adverse action.[225] However, it is less clear that the ECOA notice is required when a consumer is denied a lease because of a consumer report.[226]

8.2.6.4.7.4 Sale of property

Adverse action includes any action adverse to the interests of the consumer made in connection with any application made by the consumer or any transaction initiated by the consumer.[227] If a consumer applies to purchase property or initiated a purchase transaction, and the seller turns the consumer down based in whole or in part on a consumer report, the seller must give notice with the adverse action.

---

220 This was the position taken by a series of FTC letters, (although not the FTC Staff Commentary) even under the FCRA prior to the 1996 Reform Act. Brinckerhoff, FTC Informal Staff Opinion Letter (Nov. 10, 1983), *reprinted on the CD-Rom accompanying this manual* (the user "should" make disclosure); Peeler, FTC Informal Staff Opinion Letter (Dec. 11, 1978), *reprinted on the CD-Rom accompanying this manual*; Grimes, FTC Informal Staff Opinion Letter (Jan. 9, 1974), *reprinted on the CD-Rom accompanying this manual* (citing the unfairness standard of § 5 of the Federal Trade Commission Act). *See also* Crane v. American Home Mortgage, Corp., 2004 WL 1529165 (E.D. Pa. July 7, 2004); Razilov v. Nationwide Mut. Ins. Co., 242 F. Supp. 2d 977, 989 (D. Or. 2003); Scholl, FTC Informal Staff Opinion Letter (Dec. 10, 1976), *reprinted on the CD-Rom accompanying this manual* (citing the FTC Act).

221 *See* § 2.3.6.3.2, *supra*.

222 Greenway v. Information Dynamics, Ltd., 524 F.2d 1145 (9th Cir. 1975). *See also* Peasley v. TeleCheck of Kansas, 6 Kan. App. 2d 990, 637 P.2d 437 (1981) (that check involves credit one of two alternative grounds for finding existence of a consumer report); Maine Bureau of Consumer Protection Advisory Ruling, Consumer Cred. Guide (CCH) ¶ 97,153 (May 29, 1981) (service organization providing checking account histories to financial institutions is a CRA).

223 15 U.S.C. § 1681a(k)(1)(B)(iv). Prior to the 1996 Reform Act, the FTC Staff Commentary took the position that the denial of check writing privileges did not require notice because no credit was involved. FTC Official Staff Commentary § 615 item 10, *reprinted at* Appx. D, *infra*.

224 15 U.S.C. § 1681a(k)(1)(B)(iv); Riddle, FTC Informal Staff Opinion Letter (Mar. 17, 1999), *reprinted on the CD-Rom accompanying this manual*. Earlier court precedent held that the denial of a residential leases involved credit and was therefore adverse action. Ferguson v. Park City Mobile Home, 1989 WL 111916 (N.D. Ill. Sept. 18, 1989) ("the Court concludes that the lease of a mobile home lot is a credit transaction within the meaning of the FCRA"); Franco v. Kent Farm Vill., Clearinghouse No. 44,149, Civil Action No. 88-0115-T (D.R.I. Sept. 16, 1989) (bench opinion) (subsidized housing project). *See also* Cotto v. Jenney, 721 F. Supp. 5 (D. Mass. 1989). *Cf.* Smith v. Better Bus. Bureau, 858 F.2d 774 (D.C. Cir. 1988) (unpublished) (disclosure of CRA's name and address to the prospective tenant satisfied landlord's disclosure obligations).

225 Notice may also be due any cosigner or guarantor on the application. *See* § 8.2.6.4.3.7, *supra*; Spritz, FTC Informal Staff Opinion Letter (Nov. 5, 1998), *reprinted on the CD-Rom accompanying this manual*.

226 *See* Laramore v. Richie Realty Mgmt. Co., 397 F.3d 544 (7th Cir. 2005); National Consumer Law Center, Credit Discrimination § 2.2.2.2.4 (4th ed. 2005 and Supp.).

227 15 U.S.C. § 1681a(k)(1)(B)(iv). Prior to the 1996 Reform Act, adverse action in connection with the sale of property arguably required notice to the consumer only if credit was involved. Grimes, FTC Informal Staff Opinion Letter (Feb. 10, 1994), *reprinted on the CD-Rom accompanying this manual*, credit was not involved when the VA administration sold houses after the 1996 Reform Act, and therefor adverse action notices were not required, opinion is no longer valid.

8.2.6.5 Enforcement of Right

The FACTA amendments to the FCRA in 2003 cast serious doubt upon the ability of consumers to privately enforce the adverse action notice requirements of the FCRA. As part of those amendments, Congress added the following language to 15 U.S.C. § 1681m:

> (8) Enforcement
>
> (A) No civil actions
>
> Sections 1681n and 1681o of this title shall not apply to any failure by any person to comply with this section.
>
> (B) Administrative enforcement This section shall be enforced exclusively under section 1681s of this title by the Federal agencies and officials identified in that section.

Based upon this language, the Seventh Circuit and several district courts have issued decisions concluding that section 1681m is not privately enforceable.[228]

These decisions fail to correctly decide two arguments against the elimination of the private right of action. First, an uncodified provision of the FACTA amendments makes clear that none of the amendments to the Act were intended to abrogate private rights of action in relation to any claims that existed before those amendments. Section 312(f) of the FACTA amendments reads:

> Nothing in this section, the amendments made by this section [amending 15 U.S.C.A. §§ 1681s and 1681s-2 and enacting this note], or any other provision of this Act [the Fair and Accurate Credit Transactions Act of 2003, which enacted 15 U.S.C.A. §§ 1681c-1, 1681c-2, 1681s-3, 1681w, and 1681x and chapter 77 of Title 20, 20 U.S.C.A. §§ 9701 to 9708, amended 15 U.S.C.A. §§ 1681a to 1681c, 1681g, 1681i, 1681j, 1681m, 1681o, 1681p, 1681s, 1681s-2, and 1681t to 1681v, and 31 U.S.C.A. § 5318, enacted provisions set out as notes under this section and 15 U.S.C.A. §§ 1681, 1681a to 1681c, 1681c-1, 1681i, 1681j, 1681m, 1681n, 1681s-2, and 1681s-3, and amended provisions set out as a note under 15 U.S.C.A. § 1601; for complete classification, see Tables] shall be construed to affect any liability under section 616 or 617 of the Fair Credit Reporting Act (15 U.S.C. 1681n, 1681o) [this section and 15 U.S.C.A. § 1681o] that existed on the day before the date of enactment of this Act [Dec. 4, 2003]. (Bracketed material in original).[229]

This provision of the Public Law stands as binding authority through the Statutes at Large.[230] Accordingly, consumers should retain the right to sue on those provisions which were actionable prior to the FACTA amendments. One district court has concluded that this rule of construction dispositively establishes that the provisions of section 1681m which were actionable prior to the FACTA amendments remain actionable after the FACTA amendments.[231]

Second, the provisions of the FACTA amendments which were added to section 1681m were enacted as their own independent "section" of the Public Law, even though they were ultimately codified as "subsections" to section 1681m. Thus, an ambiguity arises between whether the term "section"—as used in the amendments—was intended to refer only to the amendments themselves, or was it intended to refer to the "section" of the FCRA into which those amendments would ultimately be codified. The courts that have considered this argument have failed to apprehend the import of the drafting history through which this language was added, and have erroneously concluded that Congress must have used the word "section" consistently throughout 15 U.S.C. § 1681m without ever analyzing whether those provisions should be considered to have been drafted at the same time.

In any event, practitioners should not expect that these rights are *a priori* enforceable by private litigants and should be prepared to meet these arguments as they are raised by the courts and opposing parties. Briefings on both issues are included on the CD-Rom accompanying this manual.

8.2.6.6 Comparison to ECOA Notice

The federal Equal Credit Opportunity Act (ECOA)[232] requires creditors to provide borrowers and potential borrowers with notice of any adverse action taken by the creditor.[233] For purposes of ECOA, creditors include "any person who regularly extends, renews, or continues credit; any person who regularly arranges for the extension, renewal or continuation of credit; or any assignee of an original creditor who participates in the decision to extend, renew, or continue credit."[234] The Federal Reserve Board

---

228 Perry v. First Nat'l Bank, 459 F.3d 816 (7th Cir. 2006) (collecting cases); Putkowski v. Irwin Home Equity Corp., 423 F. Supp. 2d 1053, 1060–1062 (N.D. Cal. 2006); Villagran v. Freeway Ford, Ltd., 2006 WL 964731 (S.D. Tex. Jan. 19, 2006).

229 Pub. L. No. 108-159, Title III, § 312(f), 117 Stat 1993 (Dec. 4, 2003), reported as a note following 15 U.S.C. § 1681n (rule of construction).

230 *See* United States Nat'l Bank v. Independent Ins. Agents of Am., Inc., 508 U.S. 439, 448, 113 S. Ct. 2173, 124 L. Ed. 2d 402 (1993) (stating that an uncodified provision shall have the force of law).

231 Barnette v. Brook Road, Inc., 429 F. Supp. 2d 741 (E.D. Va. 2006).

232 15 U.S.C. § 1691.

233 *See* 12 C.F.R. § 202.9(a). *See also* National Consumer Law Center, Credit Discrimination § 10.5 (4th ed. 2005 and Supp.).

234 15 U.S.C. § 1691a(e). *See* FRB Official Staff Commentary on Regulation B § 202.2(1)-1 (Official Staff Commentary) (creditor also includes an assignee or potential purchaser of the obligation who influences the credit decision by indicating whether or not

(FRB) has provided model forms,[235] discussed below, which may be used by a creditor when adverse action is taken based on information from a CRA, a third party other than a CRA, or from an affiliate. The ECOA notice requirement does not apply to adverse employment or insurance actions.

An important distinction between the ECOA and FCRA notice requirements is that the ECOA notice must be given within thirty days of a credit application.[236] The FCRA notice should be sent at the same time as the denial, but there is no requirement that the denial meet any time deadlines. The FCRA,[237] like the ECOA, requires notice for any adverse credit action.

Another distinction between the ECOA and FCRA notice requirements is that an FCRA notice of adverse action may be required even when an ECOA notice is not. Under the ECOA, where a creditor responds to a credit application, based on a consumer report, with a counteroffer with terms less advantageous to the consumer (such as a higher rate), and the consumer accepts the counteroffer, the rejection of the initial application based on the initial terms of an offer is not considered an adverse action.[238] However, under the FCRA, the rejection of the initial application, or even the failure to offer a discount, is an adverse action if it is based on a consumer report.[239] In such circumstance, a notice of adverse action would be required under the FCRA, but not the ECOA.

The ECOA notice provides a statement of the action taken, the creditor's name and address, the name and address of the federal agency with enforcement authority over the transaction, and the specific reasons for the action taken or a statement of the applicant's right to a statement of those reasons.[240] The statement of reasons for the action taken must be specific—it is inadequate to say that a consumer had insufficient credit references where the consumer had finance company references and the creditor meant that the consumer had insufficient *bank* references.[241]

It is also inadequate to state that credit was denied based on a consumer report—the creditor must state what in the report led to the adverse action. For example, a creditor cannot state that a consumer report led to an adverse action, but must instead indicate that the action was based on a delinquent debt.[242]

Listing only one of several reasons is not sufficient. The creditor must list the principal reasons, although the Federal Reserve Board (FRB) has suggested that more than four reasons is not likely to be helpful to the applicant.[243] The stated reason for the denial must be the real one,[244] but it need not be a good reason, as long as the reason does not involve illegal discrimination.[245]

The FRB has provided creditors with model forms that combine both the FCRA notice and the ECOA notice separately on the same disclosure.[246] However, the required notices under the FCRA and ECOA serve different purposes and have separate requirements.[247] These forms generally provide a check-off list of reasons for the denial of credit or other adverse action. As a result, a statement of reasons will seldom go beyond those provided as examples in the FRB model forms. A sample of the reasons which may be checked off are: your income is below our minimum; your income could not be verified; your credit score was inadequate because of insufficient bank references, or type of occupation, or insufficient credit experiences; bankruptcy; length of employment; temporary residence; garnishment; and many others.

While the FRB forms are illustrative and not mandatory, proper use of the FRB forms will satisfy the ECOA notice requirement.[248] Compliance with just the FCRA notice requirements will ordinarily not comply with the ECOA requirement.[249]

The ECOA notice will often be helpful for consumers in allowing them to better understand their FCRA denial notice. The FCRA notice will only indicate that a consumer report was involved in the denial. The ECOA notice will state the particular reason for the denial, allowing the consumer to determine what in the report (or what that was missing from the report) led to the denial.[250]

The ECOA also requires one additional notice to consumers that may prove helpful. Creditors must provide applicants with notice of their right to receive a copy of any appraisal report if a dwelling is to secure the loan being sought.[251] This can provide another piece in the puzzle as to why a mortgage or home equity loan is denied.

Finally, Regulation B provides that a creditor that uses a computerized system need not keep a written copy of the

---

it will purchase the obligation if the transaction is consummated).

235 *See* Appx. C.9, *infra*.
236 12 C.F.R. § 202.9(a)(1)(I).
237 15 U.S.C. § 1681m(a).
238 Regulation B, 12 C.F.R. § 202.9; National Consumer Law Center, Credit Discrimination § 10.5 (4th ed. 2005 and Supp.).
239 *See* § 8.2.6.4.3, *supra*.
240 12 C.F.R. § 202.9(a)(2).
241 12 C.F.R. § 202 Appendix C.
242 FRB Official Staff Commentary on Regulation B § 202.9(b)(2)-9.
243 FRB Official Staff Commentary on Regulation B § 202.9(b)(2)-1.
244 *See* National Consumer Law Center, Credit Discrimination § 10.5.4.2.2 (4th ed. 2005 and Supp.).
245 *Id.* § 7.5.9.3.
246 12 C.F.R. § 202 Appx. C Form C-1 through C-9. *See* Appx. C.9, *infra*. Also reprinted in National Consumer Law Center, Credit Discrimination Apxx. B (3d ed. 2002 and Supp.).
247 FRB Official Staff Commentary on Reg. B § 202.9(b)(2)-9.
248 12 C.F.R. § 202, Appendix C.
249 FTC Official Staff Commentary § 615 item 1, *reprinted at* Appx. D, *infra*.
250 *See* Fischl v. General Motors Acceptance Corp., 708 F.2d 143 (5th Cir. 1983) (notification will enable the consumer to request disclosure from the CRA of the nature and scope of information in file).
251 15 U.S.C. § 1691(e).

adverse action if it can regenerate all pertinent information in a timely manner for examination or other purposes.[252] It has been reported that this provision has been misused by some creditors to assert that they do not have to produce copies of ECOA adverse action notices because they are not required to maintain copies of such notices. This position appears to ignore the requirement that the creditor be able to regenerate such notices.

8.2.7 Notice of Adverse Use of Information Other Than Consumer Report

8.2.7.1 Nature and Content of Notice

The FCRA places notice requirements on creditors when they take adverse action based on information obtained from a person *other than* a consumer reporting agency (CRA).[253] This notice requirement does not apply to denials of insurance or employment, but only to denials of credit for personal, family, or household purposes where the information bears upon the consumer's creditworthiness, credit standing, credit capacity, character, general reputation, personal characteristics, or mode of living.[254]

When a creditor communicates its adverse credit action to the consumer, if the creditor used third party information other than from a CRA, the creditor must clearly and accurately disclose the consumer's right to request the reasons for the adverse action.[255] There appears to be no requirement that this notice be in writing,[256] as long as the communication of the adverse action was not in writing.[257]

There is no requirement that the notice contain the identity of the source from which the information was obtained.[258]

At the time of the notice of adverse action, the consumer must be informed that a right exists to make a written request, within sixty days, of the reasons for the adverse action. But if the creditor sets forth its reasons in the original notice of adverse action, the creditor need not notify the consumer of his or her right to request the reasons for the action.[259]

8.2.7.2 Residential Lease As Credit

Whether a landlord's rejection of a rental applicant, based on information obtained from prior landlords, is a denial of credit that is subject to this notice requirement has been called into question. A string of court cases had held that a denial of a residential lease involves credit,[260] implicitly rejecting the FTC stance that no credit is involved.[261] A more recent informal FTC staff opinion letter has reiterated that a landlord-tenant relationship does not involve credit and that a landlord who rejects an applicant based on information obtained from prior landlords does not have to give notice of adverse action.[262] Furthermore, the FTC's approach is consistent with interpretations of the term "credit" under the ECOA,[263] which is now incorporated into the FCRA.[264]

All of the above arguments would apply with equal force to situations involving a denial of a lease based upon a consumer report; however, the expansive catchall category of adverse action when a consumer report is involved covers leases whether or not they constitute credit.[265]

252　FRB Official Staff Commentary on Reg. B § 212(b).
253　15 U.S.C. § 1681m(b); Thomas v. Cendant Mortgage, 2004 WL 260072 (E.D. Pa. Nov. 15, 2004) (notice under § 1681m(b) must be provided when adverse action is predicated upon information pertaining to the consumer's creditworthiness, credit standing, credit capacity, character, general reputation, person characteristics, or mode of living and is provided by a person other than a CRA. *See also* FTC Official Staff Commentary § 615 item 15, *reprinted at* Appx. D, *infra*; Brinckerhoff, FTC Informal Staff Opinion Letter (Dec. 28, 1984), *reprinted on the CD-Rom accompanying this manual.*
254　15 U.S.C. § 1681m(b).
255　15 U.S.C. § 1681m(b).
256　*See* Guidelines for Financial Institutions in Complying with the Fair Credit Reporting Act (1971). *See also* form adopted in Hospital & Health Servs. Credit Union, 104 F.T.C. 589 (1984) (consent order).
257　*See* § 8.2.6.6, *supra* for a discussion of Equal Credit Opportunity Act requirements as to notice of adverse action.
258　Barnes v. Ditech.Com, 2005 WL 913090 (E.D. Pa. Apr. 19, 2005); Thomas v. Cendant Mortgage, 2004 WL 2600772 (E.D. Pa. Nov. 15, 2004).
259　FTC Official Staff Commentary § 615 item 16, *reprinted at* Appx. D, *infra*. *See also* Brinckerhoff, FTC Informal Staff Opinion Letter (Feb. 16, 1989), *reprinted on the CD-Rom accompanying this manual.*
260　See cases cited at § 8.2.6.4.7.3, *supra*.
261　Official Staff Commentary § 603(d) item 4h and 6f, § 604(3)(E) item 3, § 615 item 10 (Feb. 11, 1992).
262　Riddle, FTC Informal Staff Opinion Letter (Mar. 17, 1999), *reprinted on the CD-Rom accompanying this manual.* The matter was complicated further by the effect of the 1996 Reform Act amendments to the FCRA. All of the earlier cases referred to in the text generally held that because credit is involved, landlords who turn down applicants on the basis of consumer reports must give notice of adverse action. The 1996 Reform Act amendments extended the adverse notice requirements to all adverse actions based on consumer reports, regardless of whether credit was involved. 15 U.S.C. § 1681a(k)(1)(B)(iv), *as amended by* Pub. L. No. 104-208 § 2402, 100 Stat. 3009 (Sept. 30, 1996). The amendments did not extend the requirement of notice of adverse use of information other than consumer reports to apply where credit is not involved. The March 1999 staff letter argues that this omission affirms the earlier FTC opinion that leases are not credit, ignoring that, given the gist of all earlier cases, the matter might already have been resolved to the contrary by the courts.
263　*See* Laramore v. Richie Realty Mgmt. Co., 397 F.3d 544 (7th Cir. 2005); National Consumer Law Center, Credit Discrimination § 2.2.2.2.4 (4th ed. 2005 and Supp.).
264　15 U.S.C. § 1681a(r)(5).
265　*See* § 2.3.6.3.3, *supra*.

8.2.7.3 Time and Manner of Notice

The nature of this notice is twofold. The user must give an initial notice of the adverse action along with notice of the consumer's other rights. This notice of rights must include disclosure of the consumer's right to request the reasons for the adverse action. This notice is not required, however, where the creditor obtained the information from a CRA, its own files, or directly from the consumer.[266]

A second, or follow-up notice, is required when the consumer tenders a written request for the reason underlying the adverse action. Within a "reasonable time" after receiving that request, the user must disclose the "nature of the information" upon which the adverse action was based.[267] The FTC advises that the consumer must be told "the information itself plus sufficient identifying information concerning the source to permit him to verify the accuracy of the information."[268] However, the user need not disclose the source of the information by name.[269] Nevertheless, "it may be impossible to identify the nature of certain information without also revealing the source."

The FTC Staff Commentary ties the disclosure standards to those for the Equal Credit Opportunity Act.[270] A statement of the main reasons for adverse action based on third party information which complies with the ECOA is sufficient for the FCRA disclosures as well.[271] Under the ECOA, the statement of reasons must contain "specific reasons for the adverse action taken."[272] A creditor may use a model form which only lists reasons such as "your income is below our minimum requirement" or "your application lacks a sufficient number of credit references."[273] These descriptions may be inadequate to permit the consumer to verify the accuracy of the information where the source of the information is not known (if a consumer report had been the source, instead of a third party, the consumer could have eventually discovered the name of the CRA and the name of that CRA's sources).[274]

8.2.7.4 Application to Particular Transactions

8.2.7.4.1 Example: car financing transactions

The required disclosures should apply when a financial institution is a purchaser of dealer paper and the institution refuses to accept certain paper from the dealer based on information from an outside source. For example, if, after a car dealer calls a bank to ask whether it will purchase a customer's contract, the bank refuses to extend credit on the basis of information from an outside source, then both the dealer and the bank may have to make disclosures to the consumer.[275]

8.2.7.4.2 Example: verification of loan information

These disclosures would also apply to businesses engaged in obtaining bank loans for consumers. In this case, the bank, the loan broker who obtains the fees and credit information from the consumer and decides whether or not to forward the application to the bank, and the loan verifier who verifies the consumer's information with that listed in a consumer report, all must make disclosures if credit is denied.[276]

8.2.7.4.3 Example: accommodation parties

Where credit is denied based on adverse information obtained from an outside source that relates to the bad credit history of an accommodation party (e.g., cosigner or guarantor), the FTC and the federal finance regulatory agencies require that notice be given to the accommodation party, rather than to the primary credit applicant.[277] This notification allows the accommodation party to determine whether the information is accurate and to correct inaccurate information.

8.2.7.4.4 Example: investigation of information in a consumer report

The notice provisions should apply when the creditor obtains information on its own as a result of obtaining

---

266 *Id.*; Matthiesen v. Banc One Mortg. Corp., 173 F.3d 1242 (10th Cir. 1999) (notice not required for information obtained from the consumer); Barnes v. Ditech.Com, 2005 WL 913090 (E.D. Pa. Apr. 19, 2005) (no notice need be given when a creditor acts on information which is derived from the consumer but analyzed by third party). Thomas v. Cendant Mortgage, 2004 WL 2600772 (E.D. Pa. Nov. 15, 2004) (notice requirement is not triggered where third party merely provides analytical tools for determining suitability of consumer loan for resale on secondary market but makes no actual review of the consumer's credit information).
267 15 U.S.C. § 1681m(b).
268 FTC, Compliance with the Fair Credit Reporting Act, at 39–40.
269 FTC Official Staff Commentary § 615 item 16, *reprinted at* Appx. D, *infra*.
270 *See* § 8.2.6.6, *supra*.
271 FTC Official Staff Commentary § 615 item 16.
272 15 U.S.C. § 1691(d); Regulation B, 12 C.F.R. § 202.9 and Appendix C. These requirements are discussed more extensively in National Consumer Law Center, Credit Discrimination § 10.5.4.2 (4th ed. 2005 and Supp.).
273 Reg. B, 12 C.F.R. Part 202 Appendix C. These forms are reprinted in Appx. C.9, *infra*.
274 *See* § 3.2.3.3, *supra*.
275 *See* § 2.7.3, *supra* (financial institution as purchaser of dealer paper).
276 Carson, FTC Informal Staff Opinion Letter (May 21, 1971), *reprinted on the CD-Rom accompanying this manual*.
277 Guidelines for Financial Institutions in Complying with the Fair Credit Reporting Act (1971); Noonan, FTC Informal Staff Opinion Letter (Jan. 11, 1980), *reprinted on the CD-Rom accompanying this manual*.

information from a CRA. For example, if a creditor learns from a consumer report that the consumer was considered for credit by another lender, calls that lender, and learns directly of the lender's bad experience, which becomes the basis of the creditor's denial of a credit application, the creditor must give the third party notice.[278] If there has been a misunderstanding between the consumer and the prior lender, the consumer will thereby gain the opportunity to pursue the matter directly with the prior lender.

8.2.7.5 Special Rules for Information Shared by Affiliates

8.2.7.5.1 Overview

Information which is shared among companies who are affiliated by common ownership or corporate control is excluded from the definition of consumer report and from the protections that normally attach to the use of consumer reports.[279] Even so, notice of adverse action is required when it is based on information obtained from the user's affiliate.

A consumer is unlikely to know whether information upon which an adverse decision is made originates from a consumer report or upon in-house affiliate reports. The first hint will come when the user makes an adverse decision based on affiliate-supplied information and provides the disclosure which must accompany the adverse action. The user must notify the consumer of the action, and tell the consumer that it—the user—will disclose to the consumer the nature of the affiliate-supplied information upon which the action is based within thirty days of the consumer's request.[280] There is no requirement that this disclosure be made in writing.

The adverse actions which trigger the requirement for an affiliate to notify the consumer are less inclusive than when consumer reports are used. Included are: credit transactions (but only for adverse actions taken in connection with a transaction initiated by the consumer); employment uses; and uses in connection with insurance underwriting.[281] Excluded are: other transactions initiated by consumers; account reviews; and governmental licenses and benefits.

Adverse actions by affiliates are also covered only if the information that is used is obtained from an affiliate and also bears on the creditworthiness, credit standing, credit capacity, character, general reputation, personal characteristics, or mode of living of the consumer.[282] This restriction uses language similar to the definition of a consumer report.[283] Adverse action for this purpose, however, does not include information in a consumer report, nor information solely as to the experiences between the consumer and the affiliate.[284]

8.2.7.5.2 Enforcement of right

The affiliate sharing adverse action notices are required by section 1681m of the FCRA. The FACTA amendments to the FCRA have cast doubt on the ability of consumers to seek private enforcement of these provisions under section 1681m or its adverse action notice requirements.[285] As such, the viability of any claims for violation of these notice requirements is unresolved. Practitioners seeking to enforce such claims should review the extended discussion of enforceability in § 8.2.6.5, *supra*.

8.2.8 Increased Price Based Upon Use of Consumer Report: "The Risk-Based Pricing Notice"

8.2.8.1 General

One problem Congress sought to address with the passage of the FACTA amendments in 2003 is the frequent occurrence of creditors reviewing individuals' consumer' reports and making risk-based adjustments to the terms offered to consumers.[286] A common example occurs when creditors offering credit but at an increased price to consumers based on information in the individuals' consumer' reports. The consumers may accept the proposed terms but be unaware that information in their consumer reports caused their credit to be more expensive. In such situations, consumers were not being provided with adverse action notices.[287]

Industry argued that no adverse action notice requirements were triggered, relying on Regulation B, which

---

278 *See* FTC Official Staff Commentary § 615 item 15, *reprinted at* Appx. D, *infra*.
279 *See* § 2.4.3, *supra*.
280 15 U.S.C. § 1681m(b)(2)(A). The consumer must request such information within 60 days of this notice. *Id.*
281 15 U.S.C. § 1681m(b)(2)(B).
282 15 U.S.C. § 1681m(b)(2)(C)(i)(II).
283 *See* § 2.3.4, *supra*.
284 15 U.S.C. § 1681m(b)(2)(C)(ii).
285 Perry v. First Nat'l Bank, 459 F.3d 816 (7th Cir. 2006); Putkowski v. Irwin Home Equity Corp., 423 F. Supp. 2d 1053 (N.D. Cal. 2006); Villagran v. Freeway Ford, Ltd., 2006 WL 964731 (S.D. Tex. Jan. 19, 2006). *But see* Barnette v. Brook Road, Inc., 2006 WL 1195913 (E.D. Va. May 3, 2006).
286 Sen. Rep. No. 312, at 20 (Oct. 17, 2003).
287 This flaw was specifically highlighted in testimony by the FTC. Housing and Urban Affairs, Prepared Statement of the Federal Trade Commission on the Fair Credit Reporting Act Before the Senate Banking Committee on Banking 11–12 (July 10, 2003). The initial proposal to address this flaw was in Senate Bill 1753, which proposed that regulatory agencies promulgate rules requiring notice to consumers when they have accepted, by way of a counteroffer, terms that are materially less favorable than those generally available because of the individuals' consumer reports. This proposal was modified by the Joint Conference Committee of the House and Senate so that the notice requirement would not be limited only to counteroffers.

implements the ECOA and excludes from the definition of adverse action a counteroffer that is accepted by the consumer. Consumer advocates had argued that the FCRA's catchall definition of adverse action still required notice to the consumer.[288] A more detailed discussion of the interplay between the ECOA and FCRA adverse action requirements can be found at § 8.2.6.6, *supra*.

In response to this issue, the FACTA amendments to the FCRA require users to provide a notice informing consumers about risk-based pricing.[289] This notice may have a tremendous effect throughout the credit industry. It makes clear that risk-based pricing notices must be provided even if the consumer is given credit and accepts it. Thus, it clearly requires FCRA notices even when ECOA notices are not required.

The FACTA amendments granted rulemaking authority to the Federal Trade Commission (FTC) and the Federal Reserve Board (FRB) to issue regulations specifying how this risk-based pricing notice requirement is to be implemented.[290] As of late 2006, proposed regulations had not yet been issued. Because of the broad scope of regulatory authority granted to those agencies, the effectiveness of this notice will be determined by the regulations that are adopted. Note that the risk-based pricing requirement has gone into effect even without the promulgation of regulations by the FTC and FRB.[291]

8.2.8.2 Nature and Content of Notice

The risk-based pricing notice must inform "the consumer that the terms offered to the consumer are set based on information from a consumer report."[292] It must also identify the consumer reporting agency (CRA) that furnished the report[293] and inform the consumer of her right to obtain a copy of a consumer report from that CRA without charge.[294] It must also include contact information specified by that CRA for obtaining consumer reports.[295]

The risk-based pricing notice is not a substitute for an adverse action notice;[296] however, when an adverse action notice is given, the risk-based pricing notice need not be given.[297] The risk-based pricing notice is not required when the consumer applies for specific material terms and is granted those terms, unless those terms were initially specified by the grantor after the transaction was initiated by the consumer and after the grantor obtained a consumer report.[298] Unfortunately, this exemption excludes a broad class of people who are targeted with specific solicitations from prescreened lists generated for specific risk factors. In this way, the creditor could induce the consumer to apply for specific terms that have increased the cost of the credit based on the pre-selection criteria. Because the consumer would be applying for specific material terms, the risk-based pricing notice would not be required despite the fact that information in the individual's consumer' report caused some material terms to be materially less favorable.

In addition to the statutory exemptions, the rulemaking authority granted to the FRB and the FTC permits these agencies to exempt "classes of persons or transactions regarding which the agencies determine that notice would not significantly benefit consumers."[299] Consequently, the final regulations will determine eligibility for receipt of the notice.

8.2.8.3 Time and Manner of Notice

The risk-based pricing notice is required when "any person uses a consumer report in connection with an application for, or a grant, extension, or other provision of, credit on material terms that are materially less favorable than the most favorable terms available to a substantial proportion of consumers from or through that person."[300] The FTC and the FRB are to jointly promulgate regulations that will further define what credit terms are "material," and when credit terms are "materially less favorable."[301]

The risk-based pricing notice may be given at the time of application or communication of the approval,[302] but the specific time requirement will be decided by the FRB and the FTC. The regulations to be issued by those agencies will determine the timing of the risk-based pricing notice, including "the circumstances under which the notice must be provided after the terms offered to the consumer were set based on information from a consumer report.[303]

This notice may be given orally, in writing, or electronically, but the specific manner of disclosure will be determined by the regulations issued by the FTC and the FRB.[304]

---

288 15 U.S.C. § 1681a(k)(1)(B)(iv). See § 8.2.6.4.3.5, *supra*.
289 15 U.S.C. § 1681m(h), *added by* Pub. L. No. 108-159, § 311, 117 Stat 1952 (Dec. 4, 2003).
290 15 U.S.C. § 1681m(h)(6).
291 12 C.F.R. § 222.1(c)(3))(xiii); 16 C.F.R. § 602.1(c)(3)(xiii) (effective date for FACTA amendments to 15 U.S.C. § 1681m(h) is December 1, 2004).
292 15 U.S.C. § 1681m(h)(5)(A).
293 15 U.S.C. § 1681m(h)(5)(B).
294 15 U.S.C. § 1681m(h)(5)(C).
295 15 U.S.C. § 1681m(h)(5)(D).
296 15 U.S.C. § 1681m(h)(4).
297 15 U.S.C. § 1681m(h)(3)(B). The risk-based pricing notice is in addition to other notices that are required under the FCRA except the adverse action notice.
298 15 U.S.C. § 1681m(h)(3)(A).
299 15 U.S.C. § 1681m(h)(6)(B)(3).
300 15 U.S.C. § 1681m(h)(1).
301 15 U.S.C. § 1681m(h)(6).
302 15 U.S.C. § 1681m(h)(2).
303 15 U.S.C. § 1681m(h)(6)(b)(v).
304 15 U.S.C. § 1681m(h)(1).

8.2.8.4 Enforcement of Notice Rights

A major drawback to the new risk-based pricing notice requirement is that no private right of action exists.[305] It can only be enforced through federal agencies and officials under section 1681s of the FCRA.[306] Furthermore, states are preempted from regulating the subject matter of the provision.[307]

8.2.9 Notice When Information Is Used for Prescreening Purposes: "The Prescreening Use Notice"

8.2.9.1 Content and Nature of Notice

Prescreening is the process whereby consumer reporting agencies (CRAs) compile or edit lists of consumers who meet specific criteria, often specified by the user, and then provide the lists to users who solicit consumers with firm offers for credit and for insurance purposes.[308] The user of these prescreened lists must include with each written solicitation to the consumer a clear and conspicuous statement containing each of the following items of information:

- Information from the individual's consumer report has been used;[309]
- The consumer received the solicitation because the consumer met the criteria for the credit or insurance solicitation;[310]
- The offered credit or insurance may not be extended: if it turns out the consumer does not meet the criteria for the solicitation, if the consumer does not meet any applicable criteria bearing on creditworthiness or insurability, or if the consumer does not furnish any required collateral (this part of the notice is required only if it is applicable);[311]
- The consumer can prohibit the use of information in his or her consumer reporting files from being used in future solicitations (i.e., the "opt out right").[312] The statement must include the toll-free telephone number and address of the notification system which the consumer must notify to opt out of future such solicitations.[313]

The FTC has issued regulations prescribing the form of this notice,[314] and has issued a model form.[315]

The notice serves two purposes. First, it provides the consumer with information about the immediate transaction. The consumer is given to believe that he or she preliminarily qualifies for the offered transaction, but is warned that if he or she responds, further evaluation may determine that the consumer does not qualify after all. This is a partial description of how prescreening is allowed to work.

The second purpose of the notice has broader applicability. It informs consumers that their consumer reports have been used. This should alert the consumer to the fact that personal information has been collected and is being used, and that consumer may wish take steps to ensure the accuracy of that information. (The specific CRA may or may not be identified, however.) The notice also informs the consumer of the right to opt out of future solicitations, and provides the telephone number and address for the consumer to use for that purpose. This notification system is described more fully in § 7.3.4.4, *supra*, but a consumer's request is valid for five years.

8.2.9.2 Time and Manner of Notice

Users of prescreened lists must include in their solicitations certain disclosures which inform the consumer that consumer reports have been used, and that consumers may take steps to prevent future use.[316] The disclosures must be "clear and conspicuous,"[317] which has been ordinarily a question for the court to determine.[318]

In determining whether a disclosure is "clear and conspicuous," courts have draw upon the body of case law developed under the Uniform Commercial Code and the Truth in Lending Act for guidance construing those terms.[319] Whether or not a disclosure complies can be determined by evidence within the four corners of the document.[320] Firm offers do not meet the standard of a clear conspicuous notice if the terms and conditions are subject to

---

305 15 U.S.C. § 1681m(h)(8)(A).
306 15 U.S.C. § 1681m(h)(8)(B).
307 15 U.S.C. § 1681t(b)(1)(I).
308 *See* § 7.3.4, *supra*.
309 15 U.S.C. § 1681m(d)(1)(A).
310 15 U.S.C. § 1681m(d)(1)(B).
311 15 U.S.C. § 1681m(d)(1)(C).
312 15 U.S.C. § 1681m(d)(1)(D).
313 15 U.S.C. § 1681m(d)(1)(E).

314 16 C.F.R. Part 642.
315 16 C.F.R. Part 698 Appendix A. A copy of this model notice is included in Appx. C.7, *infra*.
316 15 U.S.C. § 1681m(d). *See In re* Unicor Funding, Inc., F.T.C. File No. 982 3251 (Oct. 14, 1999) (consent decree providing for $100,000 civil penalty by marketer of federally insured home improvement loans who was alleged to have violated the FCRA by using consumer reports to prescreen without providing required notices).
317 15 U.S.C. § 1681m(d)(1).
318 Cole v. U.S. Capital, 389 F.3d 719 (7th Cir. 2004); Sampson v. W. Sierra Acceptance Corp., 2003 WL 21785612 (N.D. Ill. Aug. 1, 2003); Tucker v. Olympia Dodge of Countryside, Inc., 2003 WL 21230604 (N.D. Ill. May 28, 2003).
319 Cole v. U.S. Capital, 389 F.3d 719 (7th Cir. 2004); Hyde v. RDA, Inc., 389 F. Supp. 2d 658, 667 (D. Md. 2005).
320 Murray v. GMAC Mortg. Corp., 434 F.3d 948 (7th Cir. 2006).

change at any time.[321] Likewise, these offers are not firm if they do not provide anything of value sufficient to justify the invasion of privacy.[322] To determine whether the offer of credit comports with the statutory definition, a court must consider the entire offer and the effect of all the material conditions that comprise the credit product in question to determine whether the "offer" contains a legitimate extension of credit.[323]

In 2005, the FTC issued a regulation on prescreening notices requiring that the notices be both "clear and conspicuous," as well as "simple and easy to understand."[324] The regulation contains specific guidance as to what constitutes "simple and easy to understand, such as:[325]

- Plain language designed to be understood by ordinary consumers;
- Use of clear and concise sentences, paragraphs, and sections;
- Use of short explanatory sentences;
- Use of definite, concrete, everyday words;
- Use of active voice;
- Avoidance of multiple negatives;
- Avoidance of legal and technical business terminology;
- Avoidance of explanations that are imprecise and reasonably subject to different interpretations; and
- Use of language that is not misleading.

The FTC's regulation requires that all prescreened offers of credit contain: (1) a short but more conspicuous notice informing consumers of their right to opt out and listing the toll-free number to call and (2) a longer but relatively less conspicuous notice on the back of the offer providing additional information about prescreening.[326] The FTC has issued a model notice in both English and Spanish.[327] The rule also specifies that the short portion of the notice should appear on the document that the offeror intends to be seen first by the consumer, such as the cover letter.[328] The rule also establishes other baseline requirements for the format and type size of the notices.[329]

8.2.9.3 Enforcement of Right

The prescreening use notices are required by section 1681m of the FCRA. Revisions to the FCRA by the FACTA amendments have been interpreted as removing any private rights of action to enforce the provisions of section 1681m or its prescreening notice requirements.[330] As such, the viability of any claims for violation of these notice requirements are in flux. Practitioners seeking to enforce such claims should review the extended discussion of enforceability in § 8.2.6.5, *supra*.

8.2.10 Notice When Negative Information Provided by Financial Institutions: "The Negative Information Reporting Notice"

The FCRA as amended by FACTA in 2003 requires a one-time consumer notice when a financial institution furnishes negative information about that customer.[331] However, a financial institution may take advantage of a safe-harbor provision if it maintained reasonable compliance policies and procedures or reasonably believed that it was prohibited from contacting the consumer.[332] Once notified about an account, it appears that there is no other requirement entitling the consumer to receive further notices when additional negative information is reported about that account.[333] The notice must be given within thirty days of reporting negative information.[334]

The Federal Reserve Board promulgated a regulation that implements the negative information reporting requirement, providing model notices and safe harbor provisions.[335] Under this regulation, the financial institution may provide the notice even if it has not submitted any negative information.[336] This is an unusual means of providing notice since it would not be accurate. The negative information reporting notice may not be included with the initial disclosures for open-end credit[337] required by the Truth in Lending Act.[338]

---

321 Kudlicki v. Farragut Fin. Corp., 2006 WL 927281 (N.D. Ill. Jan. 20, 2006).
322 Hyde v. RDA, Inc., 389 F. Supp. 2d 658, 666 (D. Md. 2005).
323 Cole v. U.S. Capital, 389 F.3d 719 (7th Cir. 2004); Hyde v. RDA, Inc., 389 F. Supp. 2d 658 (D. Md. 2005) (finding sufficient allegations to sustain complaint where offer to lend $300 for purchase of vehicle did not meet the statutory requirements where no vehicles were available at that price).
324 16 C.F.R. § 642.3(a) and (b).
325 16 C.F.R. §§ 642.2(a).
326 16 C.F.R. § 642.3.
327 16 C.F.R. Part 698 Appendix A. A copy of this model notice is included in Appx. C.7, *infra*.
328 16 C.F.R. § 642.3(a)(2)(ii).
329 16 C.F.R. § 642.3.
330 Perry v. First Nat'l Bank, 459 F.3d 816 (7th Cir. 2006); Putkowski v. Irwin Home Equity Corp., 423 F. Supp. 2d 1053 (N.D. Cal. 2006); Villagran v. Freeway Ford, Ltd., 2006 WL 964731 (S.D. Tex. Jan. 19, 2006). *But see* Barnette v. Brook Road, Inc., 2006 WL 1195913 (E.D. Va. May 3, 2006).
331 15 U.S.C. § 1681s-2(a)(7), *added by* Pub. L. No. 108-159, § 217, 117 Stat 1952 (Dec. 4, 2003).
332 15 U.S.C. § 1681s-2(a)(7)(F).
333 15 U.S.C. § 1681s-2(a)(7)(A)(ii).
334 15 U.S.C. § 1681s-2(a)(7)(B)(i).
335 12 C.F.R. § 222. (2)(ii); 12 C.F.R. Part 222 Appendix B. The model notices are reprinted in Appx. C.8, *infra*.
336 12 C.F.R. Part 222 Appendix B, para. b.
337 15 U.S.C. § 1637(a). *See* National Consumer Law Center, Truth in Lending § 5.5 (5th ed. 2003 and Supp.).
338 15 U.S.C. § 1681s-2(a)(7)(D)(i).

This provision is not to be enforceable by private right of actions.[339]

8.2.11 Notice Required Before Federal Agency May Disclose Debtor Information: "The Governmental Agency Reporting Notice"

8.2.11.1 Introduction

The Debt Collection Improvement Act amended the Federal Claims Collection Act to authorize federal agencies to disclose debtor information to consumer reporting agencies (CRAs).[340] However, prior to such a disclosure, the federal agency must notify the consumer in writing that the claim is overdue and that the agency intends to notify a CRA of the debt no sooner than sixty days from the date of the notice, and must describe the specific information the federal agency intends to disclose to the CRA.[341] The federal agency must also disclose to the CRA that it has given the prescribed notice to the consumer.[342]

Furthermore, the federal agency cannot contact a CRA at all if a repayment plan has been agreed upon or administrative review requested.[343] A federal agency planning to release information to a CRA must establish procedures for ensuring that the information held remains accurate and up to date and for ensuring that the CRA is complying with the FCRA and other applicable statutes concerning consumer credit information.[344]

8.2.11.2 Content of Notice

The federal agency's notice to the consumer must state:

- That payment of the claim is overdue;[345]
- That after sixty days, information will be disclosed to a CRA;[346]
- The nature of the information to be disclosed;[347] and
- A statement of the consumer's rights to a complete explanation of the claim, to dispute information, and to administrative repeal or review of the claim.[348]

8.2.11.3 Time and Manner of Notice

The Governmental Agency Reporting Notice must be given at least sixty days before the federal agency provides the data to a CRA, and the notice must be in writing.[349]

8.2.12 Notice of Results of Consumer Reporting Agency Reinvestigation: "The Reinvestigation Results Notice"

8.2.12.1 General

Following the completion of a reinvestigation of disputed information in the consumer's credit file, the consumer reporting agency (CRA) must notify the consumer upon completion of that reinvestigation.[350] This notice informs the consumer not only of the results of the investigation, but also the consumer's further rights. As such, the notice provides the consumer with the opportunity to lodge a further dispute and take limited steps to address a CRA's refusal to remove disputed information.

8.2.12.2 Nature and Content of Notice

The CRA must send a written notice informing the consumer of the results on the reinvestigation.[351] In addition, it must include in its notice (or a separate notice sent within five days of concluding the reinvestigation) information about the reinvestigation process, including:

- A statement that the reinvestigation is completed;[352]
- A copy of the consumer's file as revised following the reinvestigation;[353]
- A notice that the consumer may request a description of the procedure used to determine the accuracy and completeness of the information, including the business name and address of any furnisher of information contacted in connection with such information and the telephone number of such furnisher, if reasonably available;[354]
- A notice that the consumer has the right to add a statement to the consumer's file disputing the accuracy or completeness of the information;[355] and
- A notice that the consumer has the right to request that the CRA provide updated copies of the individual's

---

339 15 U.S.C. § 1681s-2(c)(1).
340 31 U.S.C. § 3711(e). Information that may be released is limited to the name, address, and Social Security number of the obligor, the amount of the claim, and the CRA involved. 31 U.S.C. § 3711(e)(1)(F).
341 31 U.S.C. § 3711(e)(1)(C).
342 31 U.S.C. § 3711(e)(1).
343 31 U.S.C. § 3711(e)(1).
344 31 U.S.C. § 3711(e)(1)(E).
345 31 U.S.C. § 3711(e)(1)(C)(i).
346 31 U.S.C. § 3711(e)(1)(C)(ii).
347 31 U.S.C. § 3711(e)(1)(C)(iii).
348 31 U.S.C. § 3711(e)(1)(C)(iv).

349 31 U.S.C. § 3711(e)(1)(C).
350 15 U.S.C. § 1681i(a)(6).
351 15 U.S.C. § 1681i(a)(6)(A).
352 15 U.S.C. § 1681i(a)(6)(B)(i).
353 15 U.S.C. § 1681i(a)(6)(B)(ii).
354 15 U.S.C. § 1681i(a)(6)(B)(iii).
355 15 U.S.C. § 1681i(a)(6)(B)(iv).

consumer' report to identified persons who have received the report within the preceding six months or two years if the report was used for employment purposes.[356]

8.2.12.3 Time and Manner of Notice

The CRA must notify the consumer of the results of the reinvestigation within five days of completing the reinvestigation.[357] The notice must be in writing and sent by mail unless the consumer has authorized the CRA to notify the consumer by a different method.[358] At least one court has held that the CRA need not disclose a complete copy of the consumer's credit file following the reinvestigation, but may instead provide a copy of those portions of the report that were reinvestigated.[359]

8.2.12.4 Enforcement

The failure of a CRA to deliver the prescribed notice is subject to the usual private remedies of the FCRA under 15 U.S.C. §§ 1681n and 1681o. Unlike a number of the other notice provisions under the FCRA, the failure to provide the notice of result can readily and foreseeably cause actual damages to the consumer. Consumers are regularly advised to check their consumer reports and correct their files before applying for credit or concluding a credit transaction. Because the notice provision is applicable only in those circumstances where the consumer has sought to dispute credit information, it is entirely likely that the consumer has lodged the dispute in the midst of a credit application process or in anticipation of an application.

In those instances, consumers often await the results of the reinvestigation before concluding any deal to ensure that they will not be denied and receive the lowest rate available. As such, the failure of a CRA to advise the consumer of the results may cause a delay in the credit process or even the outright loss of the credit opportunity. Practitioners are well advised to investigate any potential claims from the issuance of a defective or incomplete notice, or the complete failure to issue the notice.

At the same time, practitioners should be aware that courts have been hesitant to permit these claims to go forward to the jury absent actual damages.[360] Additionally, at least one court has held that the results of reinvestigation need not include a complete copy of the consumer's credit file, and that the CRA need only disclose the results of the consumer's specific dispute.[361]

8.2.13 Notice That Deleted Information Has Been Reinserted Into a Consumer Report File: "The Reinsertion Notice"

8.2.13.1 General

One of the most frustrating and pernicious reporting abuses has been the reappearance in a consumer's file of inaccurate or incomplete information which was previously deleted. Several provisions of the FCRA are meant to guard against this practice.[362] One of the most important of those safeguards is the requirement that consumer reporting agencies (CRAs) must notify the consumer whenever once-deleted information is reinserted into the files.[363] The notice is important because it is a sign of potential difficulty and a possible indication that the consumer should consider initiating a fresh dispute with the CRA, contacting the furnisher who furnished the information to the CRA, filing a consumer statement for inclusion in the report, or taking other steps.[364]

8.2.13.2 Nature and Content of Notice

Upon reinsertion of previously deleted material, the CRA must provide the consumer with a basic notice of the reinsertion.[365] In addition to that basic notice, the CRA must provide a more detailed notice including:

- A statement that the information has been reinserted;
- The business name, address, and phone number (if reasonably available) of any furnisher of information that was contacted by the CRA or that contacted the CRA in connection with the reinsertion of the information;
- A notice that the consumer's has the right to add a statement to his or her file disputing the accuracy or completeness of the disputed information.

This notice, in effect, serves to inform the consumer that the results of a former reinvestigation have been redetermined

---

356 15 U.S.C. § 1681i(a)(6)(B)(v).
357 15 U.S.C. § 1861i(a)(6)(A).
358 15 U.S.C. § 1861i(a)(6)(A).
359 Nunnally v. Equifax Info. Servs., L.L.C., 451 F.3d 768 (11th Cir. 2006).
360 See Kuehling v. Trans Union, L.L.C., 137 Fed. Appx. 904 (7th Cir. 2006) (in the absence of actual damages arising from the failure to send notice of reinvestigation results, plaintiff's case was properly dismissed).
361 Nunnally v. Equifax Info. Servs., L.L.C., 451 F.3d 768 (11th Cir. 2006).
362 See Ch. 4, supra.
363 15 U.S.C. § 1681i(a)(5)(B).
364 See Chs. 4 and 6, supra.
365 15 U.S.C. § 1681i(a)(5)(B)(ii). See Jackson v. Equifax Info. Servs., L.L.C., 157 Fed. Appx. 144 (11th Cir. 2006); Boris v. ChoicePoint Servs., Inc., 249 F. Supp. 2d 851 (W.D. Ky. 2003) (finding sufficient evidence to support jury verdict that ChoicePoint wrongfully reinserted deleted information without notice to the consumer).

by the CRA. As such, practitioners who find such a notice in the consumer's materials should view any credit denials or other damage following the reinsertion as an element of damages which might be ascribed to the CRA's duty to properly reinvestigate or prepare consumer reports.

8.2.13.3 Time and Manner of Notice

The basic notice may be given in writing or by any other means authorized by the consumer.[366] The detailed notice, however, must in writing.[367] The FCRA authorizes CRAs to send these two notices at the same time,[368] and as a practical matter it is likely that these notices will be combined and sent in writing to the consumers.

The notice of reinsertion is required only if the reinserted information was deleted as a result of an earlier notice of dispute provided to the CRA by the consumer, which will be a common circumstance.[369] Once the information is reinserted, the CRA must provide these notices (the basic notice and detailed notice) within five business days.[370]

This notice of reinsertion is unrelated to the actual or imminent use of a consumer report. Rather, the issuance of this notice is triggered when a CRA determines that it is prepared to change its prior decision to remove information from the consumer's credit file. This notice is especially important because CRA's commonly reinsert deleted information, even where is it inaccurate and should be known by the CRA to be inaccurate. The notice can serve as an alarm to the consumer to check the reinserted information and, if necessary, to take steps to challenge the reinsertion, to have it corrected, or to be prepared to explain it in the best light.

8.2.13.4 Enforcement of Notice Rights

The failure of a CRA to deliver notice of reinsertion of previously deleted material is subject to the usual private remedies of the FCRA under sections 1681n and 1681o.[371]

8.2.13.5 Bringing Reinsertion Cases

8.2.13.5.1 What constitutes reinsertion

While the reinsertion of previously deleted account data is one of the most common and frustrating problems faced by consumers, little treatment has been given to this problem in the case law. To the extent that courts have dealt with this issue head on, they have taken a far narrower view of the requirements of the FCRA relating to reinsertion than would be necessary to properly address consumer problems.

Typically, the courts that have reviewed these cases have been unwilling to find a "reinsertion" unless there is a complete identity of account data between the account that has been reinserted and the account that was removed.[372] Thus, courts have treated accounts with separate account numbers as different accounts and not subject the requirements of section 1681i(a)(5)(B). The rulings in these cases do not appear to deal with the vast amount of data which is available for use by CRAs to identify reinserted accounts as relating to the same underlying debt.

Thus, practitioners who are preparing to file cases involving claims relating to reinsertion should be aware that courts will not treat violations of section 1681i(a)(5)(b) as "self evident" or negligence per se. Rather, practitioners must acquaint themselves with the content of the data that is required by the CRA[373] as well information available in the various consumer reports, consumer disclosures, and disputes. After discovery of these items, practitioners must be prepared to explain how a reasonable person would have used the available data in order to identify the account information as relating to the same debt.

8.2.13.5.2 Strategies for litigating reinsertion cases

While many consumers may easily recognize items which have been reinserted into the consumer report, the courts have yet to allow juries to determine whether such reinsertions were reasonable. Therefore, before commencing litigation, a practitioner should prepare the case by developing a discovery and litigation plan aimed at determining what information was available to the CRA and what steps were taken to utilize this information.

Practitioners should not rely solely on the reappearance of the item to carry the day. Rather, practitioners must be aware that the CRAs have more data about the accounts available than has been provided in either the consumer disclosures or the consumer reports issued to third parties. The CRAs will often defend these cases by claiming that some portion of the account data, no matter how insignificant, has changed, causing the system to not identify two accounts as relating to the same debt.

With this legal and factual landscape in mind, practitioners should focus their attention on four factors in discovery in order to establish a question of fact relating to a violation of the reinsertion provisions.

---

366 15 U.S.C. § 1681i(a)(5)(B)(ii).
367 15 U.S.C. § 1681i(a)(5)(B)(iii).
368 15 U.S.C. § 1681i(a)(5)(B)(iii).
369 15 U.S.C. § 1681i(a)(5)(B)(i).
370 15 U.S.C. § 1681i(a)(5)(B)(ii) and (iii).
371 Advocates should refer to § 11.10–11.12, *infra*, for information relating to the litigation of these matters and proving damages.
372 Jordan v. Trans Union L.L.C., 2006 WL 1663324 (N.D. Ga. June 12, 2006) (change of account number by furnisher of fraud account vitiates duty of CRA to notify the consumer of reinsertion); Anderson v. Trans Union L.L.C., 367 F. Supp. 2d 1225 (W.D. Wis. 2005) (questioning whether account is reinserted for purposes of the FCRA when new account information is included).
373 See § 6.3.3, *supra* (description of Metro 2 Format).

1. What are the known risks leading to reinsertion of information relating to a deleted debt?
2. What information or processes are available to ameliorate those risks?
3. What has the CRA actually done to ameliorate those risks?
4. What are the relative costs to the consumer and the CRA of taking corrective action against known risks?

If discovery is performed on each of these four factors, the court will be in a far better position to understand how it is that the consumer reporting processes might have been inadequate to protect the consumer, and find a question of fact for the jury.

Litigation experience establishes three principal scenarios leading to the reinsertion of account information. Practitioners should be aware of each and be prepared to address the specific cause of the reinsertion and explain how the information in hand would have led a reasonable person to identify two separate pieces of information as relating to the same underlying debt:

1. *Account number change*: Often, when creditors identify some problem or situation with a specific account, that creditor will flag the account with a new account number. Thus, it is not uncommon to see creditors flag accounts that are disputed as fraudulent with a prefix or a suffix while leaving the remaining account numbers and all other account information intact. Similarly, large creditors may often internally transfer accounts between different servicers. Again, account numbers may change *in toto* or simply receive a new prefix or suffix to denote the change in servicer. Practitioners should discover these procedures for changes in account numbers from the furnisher. In turn the practitioner should attempt to discover the CRA's familiarity with such policies, prior litigation involving the same situation, and possible remedial changes made when confronted with the policy.
2. *Subscriber number change*: Many large creditors have multiple subscriber numbers associated with their reports to CRAs. In many instances, accounts may retain the same account data but be reported under a different subscriber number associated with the creditor. Practitioners should focus discovery efforts on the matching algorithms used to determine the identity of two accounts and procedures used in cases where creditors have been assigned multiple subscriber numbers.
3. *Transfer of debt:* While similar to the problem of altered subscriber numbers, debts that are transferred pose specific problems and opportunities. Accounts which are transferred will often carry much of the same account information as before they were transferred. Additionally, accounts that are transferred should be identified in the Metro 2 data as being transferred.[374] Specifically, the K1 and K2 segments of that data are used to identify transferred portfolios and the L1 segment is used to identify prior account number information. Practitioners should focus their attention on the data that was present and the efforts made to ensure that all the necessary data was received and validated before the information was allowed into the consumer's credit file.

8.2.14 Notice of Frivolous Dispute

8.2.14.1 Nature and Content of Notice

A consumer reporting agency (CRA) need not conduct a reinvestigation of every dispute tendered by a consumer. The FCRA provides that a CRA may terminate a reinvestigation of disputed information if it reasonably determines that the consumer's request is frivolous or irrelevant.[375] Under this standard, the CRA may not simply reject a notice out of hand. Rather, its determination must be reasonable under the circumstances. If the CRA makes that determination, it must notify the consumer and provide two pieces of information. First, the CRA must inform the consumer of the reason for the determination.[376] Second, the CRA must identify any information which is required to conduct a reinvestigation of the disputed item.[377]

Ostensibly, if a CRA provides this notice to the consumer, it should contain sufficient information to assist the consumer in understanding why the reinvestigation request was rejected and the steps necessary to have the information reinvestigated. In effect the notice should serve as a roadmap to resubmitting the request.

8.2.14.2 Time and Manner of Notice

A CRA must notify consumers of its determination within five days of finding the request to be frivolous or irrelevant. The notice must be in writing and sent by mail, unless the consumer has authorized another means of communication.[378]

8.2.14.3 Enforcement of Notice Rights

The determination that a request is frivolous or irrelevant is not without limitation. Rather, that determination must be reasonable.[379] To the extent that the determination is not reasonable or is not followed by an appropriate notice, the

---
374 See § 6.3.3, *supra*, (description of Metro 2 reporting format).
375 15 U.S.C. § 1681i(a)(3)(A).
376 15 U.S.C. § 1681i(a)(3)(C)(i).
377 15 U.S.C. § 1681i(a)(3)(C)(ii).
378 15 U.S.C. § 1681i(a)(3)(B).
379 15 U.S.C. § 1681i(a)(3)(A).

failure of the CRA to comply with these requirements is subject to the usual civil remedies including actual damages, statutory damages, punitive damages, costs, and attorney fees.[380]

8.2.15 Notice in Cases of Fraud Alert That Consumer May Request a Free Copy of the File

8.2.15.1 Nature and Content of Notice

When consumer reporting agencies (CRAs) place an initial fraud alert in a consumer file, the CRA must disclose that the consumer may request a free copy of his or her file.[381] When CRAs place an extended fraud alert in a consumer file, the CRA must disclose that the consumer may request two free copies of his or her file during the twelve-month period beginning on the date on which the fraud alert was included in the file.[382]

8.2.15.2 Time and Manner of Notice

The notice of the consumer's right to free disclosures is required any time a CRA posts a fraud alert to the consumer's credit file.[383]

8.2.15.3 Enforcement of Notice Rights

The failure of a CRA to provide notice of the consumer's right to free disclosures is subject to the usual private remedies of the FCRA under sections 1681n and 1681o.[384]

8.2.16 Notice to Consumer If Agency Refuses to Block Alleged Identity Theft Information

Under the FACTA amendments to the FCRA in 2003, consumers have the right to seek a block of the reporting of information resulting from identity theft.[385] If a consumer reporting agency (CRA) declines to block identity theft information or rescinds a block, the effected consumer must be notified promptly.[386] This notification must be made in the same manner that consumers are notified when information is reinserted into their file upon certification of accuracy.[387] Thus, consumers must be notified regarding the reinsertion of information within five days of the CRA's reinsertion of information.[388] This five-day period should be the same limitation for purposes of notification when a block is declined or rescinded.

Resellers that maintain consumer files must also promptly provide notice to consumers of their decision to block the file relating to identity theft information.[389] Such notice must contain the name, address, and telephone number of each CRA from which the consumer information was obtained for resale.[390]

8.2.17 Notice from an Employer That It May Obtain a Consumer Report: "The Employment Use Notice"

8.2.17.1 Nature and Content of Notice

Prior to using a consumer report in connection with employment, a consumer must be given notice that a consumer report may be used for such purposes.[391] This notice is in addition to and separate from the notice an employer must give when taking an adverse action on the basis of a consumer report. If adverse action is taken, the employer must make the disclosures again prior to the adverse action.[392] These notices are intended to provide the consumer whose employment may be affected by a consumer report the time and means to ensure that adverse action will not be taken based on inaccurate information.

8.2.17.2 Time and Manner of Notice

8.2.17.2.1 General

The notice may be provided any time before the employer accesses and uses the report, and may even be part of the sign-up process for a new employee.[393] In addition to the notice, the employee must also have given the employer a written authorization if the employer is to obtain a consumer report.[394] The authorization may itself be a condition of employment.[395] Absent such an employee authorization, no

---

380 15 U.S.C. §§ 1681n and 1681o.
381 15 U.S.C. § 1681c-1(a)(2)(A). *See* § 3.3.5, *supra*, § 9.2.2, *infra*.
382 15 U.S.C. § 1681c-1(b)(2)(A). *See* § 3.3.5, *supra*, § 9.2.2, *infra*.
383 15 U.S.C. § 1681c-1(a)(2) and (b)(2).
384 Advocates should refer to §§ 11.10–11.12, *infra*, for information relating to the litigation of these matters and proving damages.
385 15 U.S.C. § 1681c-2(a). *See* § 9.2.4, *infra*.
386 15 U.S.C. § 1681c-2(c)(2).
387 *Id. See* 15 U.S.C. § 1681i(a)(5)(B); § 8.2.13, *supra*.
388 15 U.S.C. § 1681i(a)(5)(B)(ii) and (iii).
389 15 U.S.C. § 1681c-2(d)(3).
390 *Id.*
391 15 U.S.C. § 1681b(b)(2).
392 15 U.S.C. § 1681b(b)(3). The disclosures that must be made for an adverse action based on a consumer report are discussed at § 8.2.6, *supra*.
393 Meisinger, FTC Informal Staff Opinion Letter (Aug. 31, 1999), *reprinted on the CD-Rom accompanying this manual*.
394 15 U.S.C. § 1681b(b)(3).
395 Kelchner v. Sycamore Manor Health Ctr., 135 Fed. Appx. 499 (3d Cir. 2005).

report should be released or used for employment purposes, including investigative reports.[396] A consumer's authorization that an employer may seek a consumer report is not written permission to obtain a report for otherwise impermissible purposes.[397] The authorization need not be contemporaneous with the notice so long as both requirements are met prior to the access and use of the report.[398]

In practice, the two requirements may be met in a single disclosure form. The separate document disclosing that a consumer report may be obtained for employment purposes can also include the employee's' authorization[399] and may additionally include the required disclosure that an investigative consumer report may be requested;[400] however, it may not include any other information.[401] If an application for employment or the employment contract itself contains the authorization, then the disclosure form must be provided separately, then or later.[402] The form must be separate, and must be clear and conspicuous, but no particular size or print or language is specified.[403] If a blanket authorization is used, covering future reports that may arise during the course of employment, that fact should be clearly stated.[404]

8.2.17.2.2 Exception: investigation of employee misconduct

Communications are not consumer reports if they are made to employers in connection with the investigation of suspected employment-related misconduct or the employee's compliance with federal, state, or local laws and regulations, the rules of a self-regulatory organization, or any preexisting written policies of the employer.[405] This exemption applies only if the communication was not for the purpose of investigating an employee's creditworthiness, credit standing, or credit capacity, and the communication must only have been made to the employer, the employer's agent, a governmental agency, or a self-regulatory organization.[406] Thus, in most cases, only new applicants and employees being subject to transfer or promotion will receive notice prior to any adverse action being taken.[407] Investigations of existing employees for alleged misconduct fall within the exception and do not require prior notice.

However, if an employer asks a consumer reporting agency (CRA) to check references or to do a background check for a job applicant or a candidate for transfer or promotion, the report will almost certainly be an investigative consumer report.[408] These types of investigations remain subject to the usual notice requirements. The additional requirement that a user of an investigative report disclose to the applicant or candidate that such a report may be required is discussed in a later section.[409]

8.2.17.2.3 Exception: truckers

One group of employers is treated differently. Under the so-called "trucker's amendment," an employer regulated by the Secretary of Transportation or subject to certain state safety regulations may be permitted to make the required disclosure orally and obtain the consumer's authorization orally.[410] This exception, commonplace enough in the trucking industry, only arises if all interaction between the consumer and the employer with regards to the application has been in person.

8.2.17.3 Enforcement of Right

The failure of an employer to provide notice and obtain authorization prior to obtaining a consumer report subjects the employer to the usual private remedies of the FCRA including actual damages, punitive damages, costs and attorney fees.[411]

---

396 *Cf.* Haynes, FTC Informal Staff Opinion Letter (Dec. 18, 1997), *reprinted on the CD-Rom accompanying this manual*. Investigative reports are discussed at Ch. 13, *infra*.

397 Grimes, FTC Informal Staff Opinion Letter (July 20, 1992), *reprinted on the CD-Rom accompanying this manual*.

398 Kelchner v. Sycamore Manor Health Ctr., 135 Fed. Appx. 499 (3d Cir. 2005).

399 15 U.S.C. § 1681b(b)(2)(A)(ii); Willner, FTC Informal Staff Opinion Letter (Mar. 25, 1999), *reprinted on the CD-Rom accompanying this manual*. Steer, FTC Informal Staff Opinion Letter (Oct. 21, 1997), *reprinted on the CD-Rom accompanying this manual*.

400 Willner, FTC Informal Staff Opinion Letter (Mar. 25, 1999), *reprinted on the CD-Rom accompanying this manual*. The disclosure that an investigative consumer report may be requested is discussed at § 13.2, *infra*.

401 Willner, FTC Informal Staff Opinion Letter (Mar. 25, 1999), *reprinted on the CD-Rom accompanying this manual*. But see Coffey, FTC Informal Staff Opinion Letter (Feb. 11, 1998), *reprinted on the CD-Rom accompanying this manual*.

402 Coffey, FTC Informal Staff Opinion Letter (Feb. 11, 1998), *reprinted on the CD-Rom accompanying this manual*; Haynes, FTC Informal Staff Opinion Letter (Dec. 18, 1997), *reprinted on the CD-Rom accompanying this manual*.

403 Coffey, FTC Informal Staff Opinion Letter (Feb. 11, 1998), *reprinted on the CD-Rom accompanying this manual*.

404 James, FTC Informal Staff Opinion Letter (Aug. 5, 1998), *reprinted on the CD-Rom accompanying this manual*.

405 15 U.S.C. § 1681a(d)(2)(D). *See* §§ 2.3.6.4.2, 2.4.4, *supra*, Ch. 13, *infra*.

406 15 U.S.C. § 1681a(x)(D)(i)-(iii), *added by* Pub. L. No. 108-159, § 611, 117 Stat 1952 (Dec. 4, 2003).

407 *See* §§ 8.2.6.2.5, 3.2.6.4.4.2, *supra*.

408 15 U.S.C. § 1681a(e). *See* Ch. 13, *infra*.

409 *See* § 8.2.2.1, *supra*, § 13.4.1, *infra*.

410 15 U.S.C. § 1681b(b)(2)(B) and (C).

411 15 U.S.C. §§ 1681n and 1681o.

8.2.18 Notice When Credit Information May Be Used by Affiliates: "The Affiliate Sharing Notice"

8.2.18.1 Content and Nature of Notice

Consumer information which is shared among companies or other entities related by common ownership or affiliated by corporate control may be excluded from the definition of consumer report.[412] The FCRA regulates this internal sharing (known as "affiliate" sharing) by requiring users to notify consumers of the intended use and providing them with opportunities to opt out of that sharing.[413] There are two types of information affiliate sharing that are excluded from coverage as consumer reports. The first type is affiliate sharing of first-hand experience, which does not require any notice to consumers.[414] The second type of affiliate sharing involves information provided by third parties and requires the consumer be given a notice and the opportunity to opt out.[415] If the consumer is given the proper notice and opportunity to opt out, the provisions of section 1681a(d)(2)(A)(iii) operate to exclude the shared information from the definition of a "consumer report" and therefore avoid the restrictions for consumer reports under the FCRA. If, however, the user fails to provide the notice and opportunity to exclude, the shared information retains its overall character as a "consumer report" and the protections of the FCRA for consumer reports apply in full force. There are two natural consequences of a failure to provide notice and an opt-out. First, the company that shares the information becomes a consumer reporting agency (CRA) and may not provide the report without a permissible purpose. Second, the affiliate must have a permissible purpose under section 1681b if it wishes to access or use the information. The absence of a permissible purpose would render both entities in violation of the FCRA.

In addition to the opt-out right provided in the definition of the affiliate sharing exclusion in section 1681a(d)(2)(A)(iii), the FACTA amendments of 2003 added a second, separate opt-out right for use of affiliate sharing in marketing, in section 1681s-3.[416] Sections 1681s-3 and 1681a(d)(2)(A)(iii) —though not identical in scope—operate in tandem to establish this regulatory framework. Section 1681a(d)(2)(A)(iii) only requires notice and opt-out to the consumer when information from third parties outside of the affiliated companies is involved. On the other hand, section 1681s-3(a) covers all affiliate sharing,[417] but specifically restricts use of affiliate information for marketing and solicitations; as such the FCRA requires specific notice that the information may be used for these purposes before the information can be shared.

Thus, it is conceivable that a company may provide a generalized notice of sharing and opt-out under section 1681a(d)(2)(A), and still not be able to share the information for marketing purposes. Conversely, the more specific notice of section 1681s-3 would suffice to allow intercorporate first-hand experience communications to be used for marketing purposes, but would not suffice to exclude information from outside of the company from being a consumer report when shared between affiliates. Practitioners should read these two sections together for a compete understanding of the subject.

8.2.18.2 Time and Manner of Notice

8.2.18.2.1 General

8.2.18.2.1.1 Affiliate sharing marketing notice

For purposes of section 1681s-3, in relation to marketing material, the notice to the consumer must clearly and conspicuously disclose that the information may be communicated among affiliates.[418] Presumably, a clear notice, to be effective, must adequately identify "the information" which is to be communicated. A written notice is not required, but any other method of disclosure is subject to attack as less than conspicuous.

The election to opt out is effective for a period of five years.[419] At the conclusion of the five years, an affiliate that wishes to use the information for sharing must again notify the consumer of the right to opt out before that affiliate may use the information for marketing.[420]

The FTC, the banking agencies,[421] and the Securities and Exchange Commission have rulemaking authority with respect to the affiliate sharing marketing opt out right.[422] Pursuant to this authority, these agencies have issued a proposed rule that in general prohibits a company from using certain information received from an affiliate to market products or services to a consumer, unless the consumer first has been given notice and an opportunity to opt out of

---

412 15 U.S.C. § 1681a(d)(2)(A). See § 2.4.3, *supra*.
413 15 U.S.C. § 1681a(d)(2)(A)(ii) and 15 U.S.C. § 1681s-3.
414 15 U.S.C. § 1681a(d)(2)(A)(ii). See § 2.4.3, *supra*, for further discussion.
415 15 U.S.C. § 1681a(d)(2)(A)(iii). See § 2.4.3, *supra*, for further discussion.
416 15 U.S.C. § 1681s-3.
417 15 U.S.C. § 1681s-3(a)(1) (referring to both affiliate sharing exclusions under § 1681a(d)(2)(A)).
418 15 U.S.C. § 1681s-3(a)(1)(A).
419 15 U.S.C. § 1681s-3(a)(3)(A).
420 15 U.S.C. § 1681s-3(a)(3)(B).
421 The banking agencies are the Office of the Comptroller of the Currency, the Federal Reserve Board, the Federal Deposit Insurance Corporation, the Office of Thrift Supervision, and the National Credit Union Administration.
422 This rulemaking authority was included in an uncodified section of the FACTA amendments. FACTA, Pub. L. No. 108-159, § 214(b), 117 Stat 1952 (Dec. 4, 2003).

receiving such solicitations.[423] As of mid-2006, the agencies have not yet issued a final rule.

8.2.18.2.1.2 Affiliate sharing exclusion notice

The provisions of section 1681a(d)(2)(A)(iii) do not prescribe the manner in which the notice and opt-out right must be communicated and exercised, but they do require the notice must be clear and conspicuous. However, the opt-out election does not have an expiration date, and thus the consumer's choice to opt out appears to be permanent, while the choice to opt of affiliate marking solicitations expires and must be renewed every five years.

In 2000, the FTC had proposed interpretations of the terms and provisions of the affiliate opt-out exclusion;[424] these proposed interpretations were never finalized. The proposed interpretations described the content of a complying opt-out notice, and further provide that a "reasonable opportunity to opt out" should be a period of at least thirty days.[425] The notice must be clear and conspicuous, meaning "reasonably understandable and . . . designed to call attention to the nature and significance of the information."

The "reasonable means of opting out" must be convenient and can be met by designating check-off boxes in a prominent position, including a reply form with an address to which the form should be mailed, providing a toll-free number to call, or providing electronic means to opt out *if* the consumer agrees to the electronic delivery of information.[426] The proposed interpretations provided that if a consumer does opt out, the company must comply with the opt-out "as soon as reasonably practicable" after the company receives it.[427] To facilitate this process, the FTC proposed a model notice.[428]

8.2.18.2.2 Relation to the Gramm-Leach-Bliley Act

The FCRA only requires that the consumer be given a one-time notice of the right to opt out of affiliate information sharing. However, the Gramm-Leach-Bliley Act,[429] a federal statute concerning the privacy of consumer financial information, requires an annual notice to the customers of financial institutions of their privacy policies and of a consumer's right to opt out from the sharing of personal information with non-affiliate third parties.

The Gramm-Leach-Bliley Act does not, by its own terms, alter a consumer's rights under the FCRA.[430] However, because it does require an annual disclosure of a company's financial privacy practices, and because the FCRA affiliate information sharing opt-out is a required element of a privacy policy, the FCRA opt-out right must be disclosed in the annual Gramm-Leach-Bliley notice whenever appropriate.[431]

8.2.18.3 Enforcement of Right

The failure to comply with the affiliate sharing provisions of the FCRA is subject to the usual private remedies of the FCRA including actual damages, punitive damages, costs and attorney fees.[432] To the extent that these requirements overlap with those of the Gramm-Leach-Bliley Act, which has no private right of action,[433] these requirements should be remediable under the FCRA. In specific, if affiliates share information which would be a consumer report without providing the appropriate notice and opportunity to opt out, both companies are subject to liability for impermissible use of a consumer report. Second, if an affiliate uses shared information to market or solicit the consumer without having provided the proper notice and opportunity to opt out, that affiliate would be subject to liability under section 1681s-3(a).

States are, however, preempted from regulating the subject matter of this provision.[434]

8.2.19 Notice That Government Official Plans to Obtain a Consumer Report for Child Support Purposes: "The Child Support Use Notice"

8.2.19.1 Content and Nature of Notice

Consumers are entitled to notice from certain state officials requesting a consumer report for child support purposes. Under the FCRA, two separate provisions permit state and local government officials to obtain consumer reports to help determine an individual's capacity to make child support payments.[435] The first provision applies to child support enforcement in general agencies, which may

---

423 69 Fed. Reg. 33,324–33,341 (June 15, 2004); 69 Fed. Reg. 42,502 (July 15, 2004).
424 65 Fed. Reg. 80,802 (Dec. 22, 2000). The proposal would add an Appendix B to 16 C.F.R. Part 600, entitled Commentary on the Amended Fair Credit Reporting Act (Affiliate Information Sharing). Other agencies had issued similar proposals: Office of the Comptroller of the Treasury, 12 C.F.R. Part 41; Fed. Reserve Sys., 12 C.F.R. Part 222; Fed. Deposit Ins. Corp., 12 C.F.R. Part 334; Dep't of the Treasury, 12 C.F.R. Part 571.
425 65 Fed. Reg. 80,808 (Dec. 22, 2000).
426 *Id.*
427 *Id.* at 80,809.
428 65 Fed. Reg. 80,809 (Dec. 22, 2000).
429 15 U.S.C. §§ 6802–6809. *See* § 16.4.1, *infra*.

430 15 U.S.C. § 6806.
431 *See* 16 C.F.R. Part 313, and discussion at 65 Fed. Reg. 33,646, 33,663 (May 24, 2000).
432 15 U.S.C. §§ 1681n and 1681o.
433 *See* §§ 16.4.1.10–16.4.1.11, *infra*.
434 15 U.S.C. § 1681t(b)(1)(H).
435 *See* § 7.4.2, *supra*.

be state or local.[436] The second provision[437] applies to the single state agency that administers the federal child support enforcement state plan under Title IV-D of the Social Security Act.[438] State officials are required to provide notice only under the first provision.[439]

Usually, notice to the consumer will not be necessary because the requesting agency is administering a state plan under Title IV-D. However, if the request comes from any other official, the official must certify to the CRA that a prior notice to the consumer has been provided in order to establish a permissible purpose for the request. If the notice is not provided, the official does not have a permissible purpose and the liability attaches for violation of section 1681b.

8.2.19.2 Time and Manner of Notice

The notice must be sent by certified or registered mail to the last known address of the consumer, at least ten days in advance of the request. Proof of receipt is not necessary.[440]

8.2.19.3 Enforcement of Right

The failure to comply with the requirements of prior notice for child support uses by state agencies other than a Title IV-D agency renders the access or use of such a reporting impermissible. As such, that access or use would be subject to the usual private remedies of the FCRA including actual damages, punitive damages, costs and attorney' fees.[441]

8.2.20 Public Record Information for Employment Purposes

8.2.20.1 Content and Nature of Notice

When a consumer reporting agency (CRA) supplies public record information to a user for employment purposes, and that information is likely to have an adverse effect on employment, the CRA must comply with at least one of the following two procedures.[442] The first (and most common) option requires the CRA to provide notice to the consumer that the CRA is supplying the public record information to a user. The CRA must include the name and address of the user to whom such information is being supplied in the notice.[443] The FTC Staff Commentary indicates the notice can be by first class mail.[444]

The other option is to maintain strict procedures to ensure that the public record information is complete and up to date.[445] For arrests, indictments, convictions, suits, tax liens, and outstanding judgments, "up to date" means that the CRA reports the *current* public record status of the item, "current" meaning at the time of the report.[446]

These options may not be waived by the consumer.[447]

The FCRA provides these special consumer protections when this type of information is disclosed because such information is likely to have a significant effect on employment decisions. Consumers may be denied jobs or terminated from employment as a result of an arrest record if the employer does not realize all the circumstances. For example, the arrest may not have led to a conviction; it may have been due to a case of mistaken identity; it may have occurred when a personal foe filed a baseless criminal complaint, and charges were dropped as soon as the police conducted an initial inquiry; or it may have occurred when the individual was a juvenile.[448] An employer may also view negatively an unsatisfied court judgment against an individual, not knowing that the case involved only a default judgment which the consumer has since paid.

A CRA must comply with the special FCRA protections for public record information even if the information is received from another CRA,[449] and even if the CRA does not actually include the public record information in the consumer report. For example, CRAs must comply with the public record requirement where a CRA sends a message to the user to "call" the CRA, where this is commonly understood to indicate that public record information exists.[450]

---

436 15 U.S.C. § 1681b(a)(4).
437 15 U.S.C. § 1681b(a)(5).
438 42 U.S.C. § 654.
439 15 U.S.C. § 1681b(a)(4)(C).
440 Baughn, FTC Informal Staff Opinion Letter (Apr. 30, 1999), *reprinted on the CD-Rom accompanying this manual.*
441 15 U.S.C. §§ 1681n and 1681o.
442 15 U.S.C. § 1681k(a).
443 15 U.S.C. § 1681k(1).
444 FTC Official Staff Commentary § 613 item 4, *reprinted at* Appx. D, *infra.*
445 15 U.S.C. § 1681k(2).
446 *Id.*; Brinckerhoff, FTC Informal Staff Opinion Letter (Dec. 16, 1999), *reprinted on the CD-Rom accompanying this manual.*
447 FTC Official Staff Commentary § 613 item 5, *reprinted at* Appx. D, *infra*; Feldman v. Comprehensive Info. Servs., Inc., 2003 WL 22413484 (Conn. Super. Ct. Oct. 6, 2003) (procedures are alternative). *See* Ch. 4, *supra.*
448 *See* Wiggins v. Equifax Servs., Inc., 848 F. Supp. 213 (D.D.C. 1993). State or federal laws, such as juvenile laws, might prohibit making arrest or conviction records public. The consumer's attorney should check the laws of the jurisdiction to see if the CRA has complied. *See generally* Fite v. Retail Credit Co., 386 F. Supp. 1045 (D. Mont. 1975), *aff'd*, 537 F.2d 384 (9th Cir. 1976); Goodnough v. Alexander's, Inc., 82 Misc. 2d 662, 370 N.Y.S.2d 388 (Sup. Ct. 1975).
449 *See* FTC Official Staff Commentary § 613 item 3, *reprinted at* Appx. D, *infra.*
450 Brinckerhoff, FTC Informal Staff Opinion Letter (May 31, 1988), *reprinted on the CD-Rom accompanying this manual.*

8.2.20.2 Time and Manner of Notice

8.2.20.2.1 General

The CRA must follow specific requirements whenever the CRA furnishes "items of information on consumers which are matters of public record and are likely to have an adverse effect upon a consumer's ability to obtain employment."[451] The FTC indicates that this section applies not only when the information is likely to have an adverse effect on an individual's obtaining employment, but also when the information will adversely affect the consumer's ability to retain employment or obtain promotion.[452]

This section applies only when the consumer report is furnished for employment purposes *and* the public record information is adverse. Examples of public record information are arrests, indictments, convictions, suits, tax liens, and outstanding judgments.[453] This notice is separate and in addition to the notice and employee authorization required of the employer when the employer first seeks to use a consumer report for employment purposes.[454] It is also separate and in addition to the notice that the employer must give to the consumer whenever an adverse employment action is based on a consumer report.[455] These other two notices are provided by the employer, not the CRA, and applied whether or not public record information is included in the consumer report.

8.2.20.2.2 Exception for government agencies

Despite the persuasive reasons to the contrary, the protections do not apply when a federal government agency uses a consumer report for employment purposes related to a national security investigation.[456] For this exception to apply, the head of the agency must make certain findings.[457]

8.2.20.3 Enforcement of Right

The failure of a CRA to either take the required steps insuring accuracy of public record information or else to provide notice that a report has been provided is subject to the usual private remedies of the FCRA including actual damages, punitive damages, costs, and attorney fees.[458]

8.2.21 Notice of Preparation of Investigative Consumer Reports: "The Investigative Report Notice"

When a user requests an investigative consumer report (subjective information based on personal interviews), special notice requirements are placed on the *user*. The content, timing and enforcement of these notices are discussed in detail in § 13.4.1, *infra*.

8.2.22 Notice of Right to Opt Out of Prescreening

8.2.22.1 Content of Notice

Each consumer reporting agency (CRA) that sells prescreened lists must maintain a system through which consumers may elect to opt out of prescreening.[459] The system must include the maintenance of a toll-free number through which consumers may notify the CRA of their election.[460] Additionally, the CRAs must annually publish notice that this system is maintained.[461]

If a consumer calls and elects to be removed from the prescreened lists over the telephone, that election stands as effective for five years.[462] However, after the consumer has made the election using the toll-free number, the CRA must also send a written notice of the election along with a form to complete that election.[463] If the consumer completes the form, the election remains valid until the consumer revokes the request, thereby opting out indefinitely.[464]

This notice of the right to opt out of prescreening, sent only after the consumer contacts the CRAs' toll-free number, is separate and in addition to the notice sent by users of prescreened lists, discussed at § 8.2.9, *supra*.

8.2.22.2 Time and Manner of Notice

The CRAs must annually publish notice of the existence of the toll-free system that consumers may use to opt out of prescreening. Within five days of receipt of a notice over the toll-free telephone system from the consumer, the CRA must send notice to opt out and a form for the consumer to fill out if the consumer wishes to be permanently excluded from prescreening lists and the five-year limitation on that right. The notification must also notify the consumer that the

---

451 15 U.S.C. § 1681k.
452 FTC, Compliance with the Fair Credit Reporting Act, at 35 (1977). *See also* 15 U.S.C. § 1681a(h) which defines "employment purposes" as including Aevaluating a consumer for employment, promotion, reassignment or retention as an employee.
453 15 U.S.C. § 1681k(2).
454 *See* § 7.2.4.1, *supra*.
455 *See* § 8.2.6.4.4.3, *supra*.
456 15 U.S.C. § 1681k(b).
457 *Id.* referring to the findings required by 15 U.S.C. § 1681b(b)(4)(A).
458 15 U.S.C. §§ 1681n and 1681o.

459 15 U.S.C. § 1681b(e)(5)(A)(i). *See* §§ 7.3.4.4, *supra*.
460 15 U.S.C. § 1681b(e)(5)(A)(i).
461 15 U.S.C. § 1681b(e)(5)(A)(ii).
462 15 U.S.C. § 1681b(e)(3)(A).
463 15 U.S.C. § 1681b(e)(3)(B).
464 15 U.S.C. § 1681b(e)(3)(A).

8.2.22.3 Enforcement of Right

The failure of a CRA to provide notices of the consumer's right to opt out of prescreening remain enforceable under section 1681b. Violations are subject to the usual private remedies of the FCRA including actual damages, statutory damages, punitive damages, costs, and attorney fees.[466]

8.2.23 Special State Law Requirements

Sometimes state law imposes additional disclosure requirements when information is first gathered or reported.[467] For example, Minnesota requires that the consumer receive written disclosure prior to preparation of a report for employment purposes.[468] California requires creditors to notify consumers and cosigners when first furnishing negative consumer reports to a consumer reporting agency (CRA).[469] Before practitioners rely on any state law requirements, the effect of federal preemption must be considered.[470]

8.2.24 Other Notices

Consumers are entitled to a number of other notices, most of which relate to possibly fraudulent use of credit. In specific, consumers are entitled to notice when a furnisher receives notice of a change of address from the consumer,[471] when fraud blocks are removed from the consumer's credit file,[472] and when accounts that have been inactive for two or more years are reactivated.[473] These notices are discussed elsewhere in this manual.

8.3 Notices to Consumer Reporting Agencies

A number of consumer rights under the FCRA are triggered by a consumer or other person's notice directly to the consumer reporting agencies (CRAs). Most significantly, a consumer's challenge to inaccuracies in his or her credit file at a CRA is made by way of a notice of dispute.[474] Likewise, consumer must sent certain notices to in order to be excluded from prescreened solicitations and lists,[475] and to place fraud alerts on their files[476] that limit the ability of creditors to open new accounts. Each of these notices is discussed elsewhere in this manual.

Similarly, corrections made by furnishers to a consumer's credit file are sometimes made by way of notice. The FCRA prescribes two situations in which notice of changes must be delivered to CRAs by the furnisher of account information. First, the furnisher must give notice when an account is closed by the consumer.[477] Second, when the consumer has directly notified a furnisher that account information is disputed, the furnisher must notify the CRAs.[478] Each of these notices triggers obligations by the CRAs.[479] In addition, these notices should be analyzed under the provisions applicable to CRAs to maintain maximum possible accuracy[480] for possible violations.

8.4 Notices to Furnishers of Credit Information

8.4.1 Notices of Furnisher's Duties Under the Act

Consumer reporting agencies (CRAs) must provide a notice to each furnisher describing their responsibilities under the FCRA.[481] The form of the notice is prescribed by the FTC under its rulemaking authority[482] and a model form has been promulgated.[483]

This notice establishes that the furnisher was informed of its legal responsibilities. It will likely appear in every contract between CRAs and their furnishers. A troubling aspect of the notice is that it informs furnishers that they are not subject to the general prohibition against providing information they know or have reasonable cause to believe is inaccurate, if the furnisher clearly and conspicuously specifies an address to which consumers may write to provide notice the information is inaccurate.[484]

---

465 Id.
466 15 U.S.C. §§ 1681n, 1681o.
467 See Appx. H, infra.
468 Minn. Stat. § 13C.02.
469 Cal. Civ. Code § 1785.26.
470 15 U.S.C. § 1681t. See § 10.7, infra.
471 15 U.S.C. § 1681m(e)(1). See § 9.2.6, infra.
472 15 U.S.C. § 1681c-2(2). See § 9.2.4.1, infra.
473 15 U.S.C. § 1681m(e)(2). See § 9.2.6, infra.
474 15 U.S.C. § 1681i. See Ch. 4, § 6.10, supra.
475 15 U.S.C. § 1681b(e). See § 7.3.4.4, supra.
476 15 U.S.C. § 1681c-1(h); 15 U.S.C. § 1681a(q); 15 U.S.C. § 1681c-2(a).
477 15 U.S.C. § 1681s-2(a)(4) See § 6.8, supra.
478 15 U.S.C. § 1681s-2(a)(3) See § 6.6, supra.
479 15 U.S.C. § 1681c(e) and (f).
480 15 U.S.C. § 1681e(b). See Ch. 4, supra.
481 15 U.S.C. § 1681e(d).
482 15 U.S.C. § 1681e(d)(2).
483 16 C.F.R. Part 698 Appendix G, reprinted at Appx. C.5, infra, restating 15 U.S.C. § 1681s-2(1)(C).
484 Id. While this is a restatement of 15 U.S.C. § 1681s-2(a)(1)(C), it fails to note potential other liability for a furnisher that furnishes information that it knows or has reasonable cause to believe is inaccurate. See § 6.4.2, supra.

8.4.2 Other Notices

A number of other notices may be provided to furnishers of credit information. These notices usually relate to the reports that the furnisher has made in reference to a particular account. Specifically, notices may be given when fraud-related information is blocked,[485] when account information has been modified or deleted by a CRAs,[486] or when a consumer disputes credit information directly with the furnisher.[487] These notices and the procedures under them are discussed more fully elsewhere in this manual.

8.5 Notices to Users of Consumer Reports

8.5.1 Overview

Users of consumer reports are the end users of the information maintained within the credit reporting system. Because the use of this information will often determine whether a consumer will have access to goods, services, or employment opportunities, the FCRA has put in place mechanisms to ensure that the information is properly used. And in those instances when the information is suspicious or subject to dispute, the Act puts in place a series of notice requirements to ensure that information is used appropriately.

Thus, where a consumer has disputed an item which has not been removed, the FCRA provides that a notice be given to users of that information.[488] Where identifying information does not match that information on file with a consumer reporting agency (CRA), the CRA must notify the user, thereby alerting the user of the potentially fraudulent use the consumer's credit history.[489]

This section will discuss the most relevant of these notices to users of consumer reports and briefly identify other notices which are required by the FCRA. Civil remedies will be discussed only where relevant to the consumer.

8.5.2 Notices of User's Duties Under the Act

CRAs must provide a notice to each user of consumer reports describing their responsibilities under the FCRA.[490] The form of the notice is prescribed by the FTC under its rulemaking authority[491] and a model form has been promulgated.[492]

This notice establishes that the user was informed of its legal responsibilities. It will likely appear in every contract between CRAs and their subscribers who use consumer reports.

8.5.3 Notices of Address Discrepancy

8.5.3.1 Nature and Content of Notice

One of the most well documented causes of identity theft has been the failure of creditors and CRAs to note and take action when a new account is opened using an undocumented address. Consumer advocates had contended that both the creditors and the CRAs were in a position to immediately catch fraudulent uses of credit by noting these address discrepancies, which were apparent from the reports being requested.

The FACTA amendments to the FCRA in 2003 recognized this problem. FACTA mandated procedures by the CRAs and users to make use of this already-available information and catch address discrepancies before they result in identity theft.[493] Under these provisions, CRAs must monitor the addresses relating to the consumers whose reports have been requested. If there is any discrepancy between the address listed in the request for a consumer report and the address in the consumer's file with that CRA, the CRA must notify the user of the address discrepancy.[494] In this fashion, the CRA places the user on notice that the application in question may be fraudulent in nature. Furthermore, the CRA is on notice any time a new (and potentially fraudulent) address comes into the system. Ultimately, this provision places the burden of preventing identity theft squarely on shoulders of the users and CRAs who are in the best position to prevent the fraud.

The FCRA directs the federal banking agencies and the FTC to jointly develop regulations providing guidance as to reasonable policies and procedures to be employed by users who receive this notice from CRAs.[495] Those regulations must, at a minimum describe

- Procedures the user should use to form a reasonable belief that the user knows the identity of the person to whom the consumer report pertains; and
- Where the user establishes a continuing relationship with the consumer and will be furnishing information

---

485 15 U.S.C. § 1681c-3(b). *See* § 9.2.4.1, *infra*.
486 15 U.S.C. § 1681i(a)(5)(3). *See* Ch. 4, *supra*.
487 15 U.S.C. § 1681s-2(a)(8). *See* § 6.10, *supra*.
488 *See* Ch. 4, *supra*.
489 *See* § 9.2.5.2, *infra*.
490 15 U.S.C. § 1681e(d).

491 15 U.S.C. § 1681e(d)(2).
492 16 C.F.R. Part 698 Appendix G, *reprinted at* Appx C.6, *infra*, *restating* 15 U.S.C. § 1681s-2(1)(C).
493 15 U.S.C. § 1681c(h).
494 15 U.S.C. § 1681c(h)(1).
495 15 U.S.C. § 1681c(h)(2)(A).

on that consumer to the CRA that identified the address discrepancy, the procedures by which the user should furnish the address to the CRA to reconcile the discrepancy.[496]

As of late 2006, only proposed regulations had been promulgated under this provision.[497] Once promulgated, these provisions will hopefully ensure that both users and CRAs make due note of address discrepancies which might lead to identity theft and fraudulent uses of consumer reports. Likewise, these provisions will create a documentary trail of those notices.

In those instances where an identity theft does result, this documentary trail may then be used to establish a number of claims which are typical in identity theft situations. More particularly, when the address discrepancy notice is provided and the user fails to implement reasonable policies and procedures, any subsequent use of a consumer report may be prima facie in violation of this section or the provisions of section 1681b(a).[498] Likewise, where a CRA has notified a user of an address discrepancy, that CRA has itself generated notice of the possible identity theft. Consequently, that CRA would be required to implement reasonable procedures to ensure that the item was bona fide before reporting the address or accepting any reports relating to any new account from that user.[499]

8.5.3.2 Time and Manner of Notice

The provisions of the FCRA do not specify a time for the notice. Nonetheless, if the notice is to serve the function anticipated by Congress, the notice should be provided along with the requested report so as to allow the user of the report to take preventive action and avoid fraudulent use of the consumer report.

8.5.3.3 Enforcement of Notice Rights

The violation of these address discrepancy notice provisions by a either a CRA or user are privately enforceable, as violations of section 1681c are not excluded from the FCRA's private right of action. Violations are subject to the usual private remedies of the FCRA including actual damages, statutory damages, punitive damages, costs, and attorney fees.[500] The failure of either the CRAs to provide the required notice and the failure of a user to heed that notice could foreseeably lead to identity theft and harm to the consumer's credit file. As such, the failure of either party to comply with these requirements could lead to damages.

8.5.4 Notices of Deletion or Dispute

8.5.4.1 Nature and Content of Notice

It often happens that, after a reinvestigation, a CRA refuses to delete or modify the disputed credit information. In those instances, the consumer has a remedy which can be used to inform potential creditors, employers, and insurers that this information may not be reliable. Under the reinvestigation procedures of the FCRA, consumers are entitled to request that a disputed be noted in conjunction with a disputed account.[501] Following the addition of a disputed notation to the consumer's file, the consumer may request that the CRA provide notice of that dispute to all users who have received the file within the preceding six months, or to those who have received the file within the preceding two years for employment purposes.[502]

8.5.4.2 Time and Manner of Notice

The FCRA does not direct either the time or manner of the notice. However, the nature of the request and the anticipated response would dictate that the notice be given within a reasonable time and in a fashion that is reasonable under the circumstances.

8.5.4.3 Enforcement of Notice Rights

The violation of these dispute notice provisions by a CRA or user is enforceable, as violations of section 1681i are not excluded from the FCRA's private right of action. Violations are subject to the usual private remedies of the FCRA including actual damages, statutory damages, punitive damages, costs, and attorney fees.[503]

Advocates should note that creditors are required under the ECOA to consider any information from the consumer questioning the reliability of a consumer report that was relied on to deny credit.[504] As such, this provision can provide documentary support in such a request, and should be used in conjunction with a request to a user/creditor to reconsider the credit application in light of the dispute.

---

496 15 U.S.C. § 1681c(h)(2)(B).
497 71 Fed. Reg. 40,786 (July 18, 2006).
498 See § 9.2.5.2, infra.
499 15 U.S.C. § 1681e(b). See Ch. 4, supra.
500 15 U.S.C. §§ 1681n and 1681o.

501 15 U.S.C. § 1681i(b).
502 15 U.S.C. § 1681i(d).
503 15 U.S.C. §§ 1681n and 1681o.
504 Regulation B, 12 C.F.R. § 202.6(b)(6)(ii).

Chapter 9   Identity Theft

9.1 General

Inaccurate information in a credit history can present serious, if not devastating, problems for a consumer; unauthorized access to a consumer report represents a significant breach a consumer's financial privacy. The worst manifestation of these offenses may be when information is taken by a culprit with malicious intentions for the data. Identity theft has become an alarmingly frequent invasion of privacy: in 2005, 255,565 complaints of identity theft were filed with the FTC's Identity Theft Clearinghouse.[1] Identity theft occurs when an imposter obtains information about a consumer then uses that information to pose as the consumer to fraudulently obtain credit, goods, or services in the consumer's name. Once the impostor has established himself or herself as the consumer, the impostor may leave unpaid credit cards, cleaned-out checking accounts, foreclosed mortgages, default judgments, bankruptcy declarations, and, at worst, arrest warrants all firmly stuck to the consumer's financial identity.

Identity theft causes substantial costs to consumers and businesses, whether in terms of money or time. A comprehensive study released by the Council for Better Business Bureaus spanning 2003–2006 found that 8.9 million people were victims of identity theft in the last year surveyed, and that the one-year cost of identity theft had risen to $56.6 billion.[2] The study also reported that while many identity theft victims incurred no out-of-pocket expenses, a significant percentage did. Furthermore, the time to resolve identity theft cases increased from 33 hours in 2003 to 40 hours—an entire work week—in 2006.

The FTC provides an array of resources in educating consumers about identity theft and providing informational tools for victims to combat it. The FTC maintains a website through which consumers can file a complaint,[3] staffs a hotline (877-ID-THEFT (877-438-4338)) through which consumers can speak to consumer counselors and get information about identity theft, and provides an identity theft affidavit form that a victim can fill out, execute, and provide to consumer reporting agencies (CRAs) and financial institutions that have issued credit or provided goods or services to a thief in the consumer's name.[4]

This chapter discusses the legal protections for identity theft victims provided by the FCRA, other federal statutes, and in state law. It contains some practical advice for victims; additional practical advice for coping with identity theft can be found in Chapter 12, *infra*, which discusses nonlitigation remedies.

9.2 The FCRA's Identity Theft Prevention and Credit History Restoration Provisions

9.2.1 Overview

The effect of identity theft on consumers was one of the motivating factors that led to the passage of Fair and Accurate Transactions Act of 2003 (FACTA). FACTA amended the FCRA to provide identity theft victims with tools to halt a thief's use of the victim's identity and to repair the damage done by a thief to the victim's credit record.[5] Prior to the FACTA amendments, consumers had to seek relief through the FCRA's preexisting mechanisms for addressing ordinary inaccuracies in a report[6] or through state identity theft laws.[7]

The FACTA amendments added to the FCRA significant provisions designed to prevent identity theft, limit the consequences of identity theft to victims' credit records, and help victims clear their credit records of identity-theft related information. The FCRA defines "identity theft" as "a

---

1 Identity Theft Data Clearinghouse: Identity Theft Victim Complaints Trends by State (Jan. 1–Dec. 31, 2005), *available at* www.consumer.gov/idtheft/pdf/clearinghouse_2005.pdf.
2 Council of Better Business Bureaus and Javelin Strategy & Research, 2006 Identity Fraud Survey Report, *available at* www.bbbonline.org/idtheft/safetyQuiz.asp.
3 www.consumer.gov/idtheft.
4 www.consumer.gov/idtheft/affidavit. A copy of the affidavit form can be found at Appx. C.4, *infra*. The FTC also maintains on its site a list of companies that accept the affidavit.
5 Pub. L. No. 108-159 (2003).
6 *See* Ch. 7, *supra*.
7 *See* § 9.4, Appx. B.3, *infra*. Although Congress enacted the Identity Theft and Assumption Deterrence Act to formally criminalize identity theft, the Act does not provide consumers with the ability to enforce it. *See* § 9.3, *infra*.

fraud committed or attempted using the identifying information of another person" and gives the FTC authority to further define the term.[8]

The FCRA, as amended, sets up a web of communication among consumers, consumer reporting agencies (CRAs), and furnishers that—if properly implemented and employed—could allow them, once they learn that a consumer's identity has been stolen, to synchronize consumer reports and purge theft-related information from CRAs' and furnishers' files.

As described in more detail below, a consumer who is the victim of identity theft can require a nationwide CRA to put a fraud alert in the victim's file;[9] the CRA must then notify the other nationwide CRAs of the alert, who then must also place the alert in their files. The CRA also has to provide the victim with a summary of identity theft victim's rights under the Act.[10]

The victim can also identify fraudulent information in the victim's report; the CRA must block that fraudulent information and notify the furnisher of the block.[11] Once notified, the furnisher must both reinvestigate the information and take steps to prevent it from being refurnished to any CRA.

In addition, furnishers must have reasonable procedures to respond to notices of information blocked due to identity theft[12] and, if furnished with an identity theft report, the furnisher must stop furnishing that information.[13] Furnishers are prohibited from transferring a debt that a CRA has blocked as resulting from identity theft.[14] Also, if a debt collector learns that any information relating to a debt sought to be collected may either be fraudulent or may be the result of identity theft, the debt collector must notify the creditor and, upon the consumer's request, provide the consumer with the same information about the debt that the consumer would have been entitled to had the consumer actually incurred the debt.[15]

The FCRA includes a potentially powerful tool that allows an identity theft victim to obtain information from any business that transacted with the thief in the victim's name. This information may allow a victim to more quickly find and stop the thief.[16] Fraud victims also have a right to a free consumer report, over and above the free annual report that all consumers are now entitled to.[17] These reports should help fraud victims track and block false debts accrued in their names. Furthermore, each nationwide CRA must prepare and submit to the FTC an annual report summarizing consumer complaints received on identity theft or fraud alerts, which should lead to a nationwide picture of the effect of identity theft on the accuracy and integrity of consumers' credit files.[18]

The FCRA goes beyond the surface problem of identity theft by addressing its underlying cause: the failure of businesses to properly verify, protect, and dispose of consumer financial information. The FACTA amendments require regulations that establish "red flag guidelines" for the use of institutions to identify identity fraud risks to account holders or customers.[19] Furnishers must comply with accuracy and integrity guidelines that will be established by the FTC and banking regulators.[20] Those entities that collect consumers' information must protect it by disposing of it in a manner required by regulation.[21]

However, consumers may not realize the full value of the FACTA amendments' anti-fraud provisions. While at first glance these provisions appear to give identity theft victims significant rights, what the amendments gave with one hand, they took away with another. The FACTA amendments added provisions to the FCRA preempting certain state laws

---

8 15 U.S.C. § 1681a(q)(3). The FTC has further defined "identity theft" to mean "a fraud committed or attempted using the identifying information of another person without authority." 16 C.F.R. § 603.2(a). The FTC defines

> "identifying information" to mean "any name or number that may be used, alone or in conjunction with any other information, to identify a specific person, including any—
> (1) Name, Social Security number, date of birth, official State or government issued driver's license or identification number, alien registration number, government passport number, employer or taxpayer identification number;
> (2) Unique biometric data, such as fingerprint, voice print, retina or iris image, or other unique physical representation;
> (3) Unique electronic identification number, address, or routing code; or
> (4) Telecommunication identifying information or access device (as defined in 18 U.S.C. 1029(e)).

16 C.F.R. § 603.2(b).

9 15 U.S.C. § 1681c-1; 16 C.F.R. § 602.1(c)(3)(xi). A nationwide CRA is one that "that regularly engages in the practice of assembling or evaluating, and maintaining, for the purpose of furnishing consumer reports to third parties bearing on a consumer's credit worthiness, credit standing, or credit capacity . . . [p]ublic record information [and] [c]redit account information from persons who furnish that information regularly and in the ordinary course of business" about consumers "residing nationwide." 15 U.S.C. § 1681a(p).

10 15 U.S.C. § 1681g(d); 16 C.F.R. § 698, Appendix E. *See also* § 8.2.3, *supra*.

11 15 U.S.C. § 1681c-2(a).

12 15 U.S.C. § 1681s-2(a)(6); 16 C.F.R. § 602.1(c)(3)(vii).

13 *Id.*

14 15 U.S.C. § 1681m(f); 16 C.F.R. § 602.1(c)(3)(vii).

15 15 U.S.C. § 1681m(g); 16 C.F.R. § 602.1(c)(3)(viii).

16 15 U.S.C. § 1681c(e).

17 15 U.S.C. § 1681j(d).

18 15 U.S.C. § 1681i(e).

19 15 U.S.C. § 1681m(e). The FTC and banking regulators have issued a Notice of Proposed Rulemaking on this. 71 Fed. Reg. 40,786 (July 18, 2006). *See* § 9.2.6, *infra*.

20 15 U.S.C. § 1681s-2(e). The FTC and banking regulators have only issued an Advanced Notice of Proposed Rulemaking on this. 71 Fed. Reg. 14,419 (Mar. 22, 2006). *See* § 9.2.4.2, *infra*.

21 15 U.S.C. § 1681w.

that address identity theft.[22] Furthermore, the FCRA specifically prohibits consumers from enforcing many of the rights added by FACTA, stating that the liability provisions of the Act[23] do not apply to most of the obligations of furnishers or to any violations of the accuracy and integrity regulations or red flag guidelines.[24] In addition, identity theft victims may not enforce the obligation of businesses to provide them with the thief's transaction information.[25] Consumers must rely on the FTC and state agencies to enforce these provisions.

9.2.2 Fraud Alerts and Active Military Duty Alerts

9.2.2.1 General

9.2.2.1.1 Overview

As amended by FACTA, the FCRA provides for three varieties of alerts that consumers may add to their files with nationwide CRAs. These alerts differ in their initiation requirements, time periods, and demands imposed on users. However, all three alerts require the CRA receiving the alert to refer it to the other nationwide CRAs; in theory, this process allows consumers to issue the alert to all the CRAs with "one call."

The form of these alerts and their effects on users should make them significantly more effective than the dispute process set forth in the preexisting provision of the FCRA for all types of inaccuracies.[26] Furthermore, the provisions that set forth the three types of alerts do not limit liability, thus consumers can enforce their rights against CRAs and users pursuant to the willful and negligent noncompliance provisions of the FCRA.[27] States, however, are preempted from imposing any "requirement or prohibition" with respect to the "conduct required" by the fraud alerts provision.[28]

9.2.2.1.2 Appropriate proof of identity

A prerequisite to obtaining any of the three alerts discussed below is that the consumer must provide the CRA with "appropriate proof of identity."[29] The FTC has issued a regulation requiring CRAs to develop and implement "reasonable requirements" to verify identity.[30] In developing these requirements, the CRAs must:[31]

- Ensure that the information is sufficient to enable the CRA to match consumers with their files; and
- Adjust the information to be commensurate with an identifiable risk of harm arising from misidentifying the consumer.

One example the FTC provides as being appropriate would have the CRA demanding from the consumer the following: (1) his or her first name, middle initial, last name, and any suffix; (2) current and, if applicable, recent full addresses; (3) the full nine digits of the consumer's Social Security number; and (4) the consumer's date of birth.[32] The CRA can demand additional information from the consumer, such as copies of government-issued identification documents, utility bills, and possibly answers to "questions to which only the consumer might be expected to know the answer."[33]

9.2.2.2 Initial Fraud Alerts

With respect to the first type of alert, the FCRA allows consumers who believe that they are or might be victimized by identity theft fraud or any other sort of fraud to require all nationwide CRAs to add a fraud alert to their files simply by calling one such CRA.[34] Note that consumers may seek an initial fraud alert merely upon a "good faith suspicion" that they are about to be victimized by identity theft or other fraud;[35] consumers do not need to know definitively that they actually have been or will be victimized by identity theft. The consumer must provide appropriate proof of identity in order to obtain an initial fraud alert.[36]

The initial fraud alert is called a "one-call" alert because the CRA must refer the alert to other nationwide CRAs and all the nationwide CRAs must not only include the alert in the consumer's file, but provide the alert each time they generate that consumer's credit score.[37]

To implement the alert, the CRAs must present to any user a "clear and conspicuous" view of the alert,[38] which must notify users of the consumer's report that the consumer

---

22 15 U.S.C. § 1681t. See § 10.7, infra.
23 15 U.S.C. §§ 1681n, 1681o. See § 10.2, infra.
24 15 U.S.C. § 1681s-2(c).
25 15 U.S.C. § 1681g(e)(6).
26 15 U.S.C. § 1681i(b). See Ch. 4, supra.
27 15 U.S.C. §§ 1681n, 1681o. See, e.g., Collins v. Experian Credit Reporting Serv., 2005 WL 2042071 (D. Conn. Aug. 24, 2005) (denying motion to dismiss claims under §§ 1681c-1 and 1681c-2).
28 15 U.S.C. § 1681t(b)(5)(B). See § 10.7, supra.
29 15 U.S.C. § 1681c-1(a), (b), (c).
30 15 U.S.C. § 614.1. This regulation also applies when the consumer is seeking to block information resulting from identity theft, 15 U.S.C. § 1681c-2, and when the consumer is seeking a disclosure of his or her file pursuant to 15 U.S.C. § 1681g(a)(1).
31 15 U.S.C. § 614.1(a).
32 16 C.F.R. § 614.1(b)(1).
33 16 C.F.R. § 614(b)(2).
34 15 U.S.C. § 1681c-1(a)(1).
35 Id.
36 Id. See § 9.2.2.1, supra.
37 15 U.S.C. § 1681c-1(a)(1).
38 15 U.S.C. § 1681a(q)(2)(B).

may be a victim of fraud—including, but not limited to, identity theft.[39] In addition to placing the alert, the CRA must provide the consumer with the Summary of Consumer Rights under the identity theft provisions of the Act,[40] must notify the consumer of the consumer's right to a free consumer report, and must provide a requested report within three business days of the consumer's request.[41]

A fraud alert stays active for only ninety days.[42] However, a consumer may request the CRA to lift the alert earlier and a CRA is permitted to provide the alert for a longer period.[43] For a sustained alert of longer duration, the consumer may obtain an extended fraud alert, described in § 9.2.2.3, *infra*. However, only consumers who file an identity theft report may seek an extended fraud alert.[44] Accordingly, the initial fraud alert is appropriate for consumers who are unsure whether they have actually been defrauded or who believe they may be the victim of a fraud other than identity theft.

9.2.2.3 Extended Fraud Alerts

9.2.2.3.1 Overview

An identity theft victim can seek a second type of alert, an extended fraud alert. The extended fraud alert lasts seven years.[45] In order to obtain this alert, the consumer must: (1) file a qualifying "identity theft report" with a law enforcement agency; and (2) provide the CRA with "appropriate proof of identity."[46]

9.2.2.3.2 Identity theft report

The FTC has issued regulations that define the term "identity theft report."[47] This definition imposes some significant burdens on consumers. Thus, any consumer seeking to invoke the extended fraud alert, as well as the blocking provisions of the FCRA,[48] should check to make sure that any police report meets the regulation's requirements.

To qualify as an "identity theft report" under the FCRA, the report must: (1) allege identity theft with as much specificity as the consumer can provide; (2) be a copy of an official, valid report filed by the consumer with a law enforcement agency; and (3) its filing must expose the person to criminal penalties relating to the filing of false information if the information in the report is false.[49]

Furthermore, even if a report meets these requirements, a furnisher or CRA may require the report to include "additional information" to determine the validity of the "alleged identity theft" so long as the furnisher or CRA makes the request within fifteen days of receiving the report.[50] The furnisher or CRA can make a second request for information within another fifteen days of its first request for information.[51] The furnisher or CRA must makes its decision regarding acceptance of the identity theft report within fifteen days after its initial request for information or within five days of receiving requested information, if the CRA or furnisher receives the requested information between the 11th and 15th day of the second fifteen-day period.[52]

The regulation thus allows the CRA or furnisher to demand more information and more specificity than a law enforcement agency would require to make a criminal report. Not even the FTC's own Identity Theft Affidavit will necessarily suffice to meet the regulation's definition. The regulation provides examples of the degree of specificity that a furnisher or CRA can require.[53]

9.2.2.3.3 Effects of the extended fraud alert

By submitting the identity theft report and providing satisfactory proof of identification to a nationwide CRA, the consumer may add to his or her credit file an extended fraud alert that can last for seven years.[54] As with the initial fraud alert, the CRA must refer the alert to the other nationwide CRAs, all of whom must provide a "clear and conspicuous view" of the alert each time they generate the consumer's credit score.[55]

The extended fraud alert provides additional protection to identity theft victims by requiring the CRAs to exclude the consumer, for five years, from any lists generated to sell to users for transactions not initiated by the consumer (prescreening lists),[56] a provision that should curtail access by new thieves to the consumer's identity.[57] This feature, along with the extended term of the alert—which lasts as long as the seven-year period of obsolescence for most negatives items in a credit file[58]—are what distinguish the extended fraud alert from the initial alert. The CRAs must also notify

---

39 "Identity theft" is "a fraud committed using the identifying information of another person." 15 U.S.C. § 1681a(q)(4).
40 15 U.S.C. § 1681g(d). See also § 8.2.3, *supra*.
41 15 U.S.C. § 1681j(d).
42 15 U.S.C. § 1681c-1(1)(A).
43 *Id*.
44 See § 9.2.2.3, *infra*.
45 15 U.S.C. § 1681c-1(b)(1).
46 *Id*. See §§ 9.2.2.1.2, *supra*, and 9.2.2.3.2, *infra*.
47 16 C.F.R. § 603.3.
48 15 U.S.C. § 1681c-2(a). See § 9.2.4, *infra*.
49 16 C.F.R. § 603.3(a)(1)–(2).
50 16 C.F.R. § 603.3(a)(3)(i).
51 16 C.F.R. § 603.3(a)(3)(ii).
52 16 C.F.R. § 603.3(a)(3)(ii)–(iii).
53 16 C.F.R. § 603.3(b).
54 15 U.S.C. § 1681c-1(b).
55 15 U.S.C. § 1681c-1(b)(1)(A); 15 U.S.C. § 1681a(q)(2)(B) (requiring alert to be "clear and conspicuous").
56 For a discussion of prescreening lists, see § 7.3.4, *supra*.
57 15 U.S.C. § 1681c-1(b)(1)(B). Note that this exclusion is separate from the consumer's right to opt out of prescreening lists for five years pursuant to 15 U.S.C. § 1681b(e). See § 7.3.4, *supra*.
58 15 U.S.C. § 1681c(a)(5). See also § 5.2, *supra*.

the consumer of the consumer's right to two free consumer reports over the subsequent twelve months.[59] As with the fraud alert, a CRA must provide the consumer's file to the consumer within three business days of the consumer's request.[60]

9.2.2.4 Active Military Duty Alerts

Consumers on active military duty can inform users of their status by adding an alert to their files.[61] The FCRA defines an "active duty military consumer" to mean "a consumer in military service who . . . is on active duty or a reservist called to active duty . . . and who is assigned to service away from the usual duty station of the consumer."[62]

Once a military consumer requests the active duty alert, it will become part of the consumer report for twelve months.[63] Similar to an extended fraud alert, an active military duty alert gives the consumer relief from prescreening lists, though for only two years as opposed to five.[64] As with the other two types of alerts, the consumer must provide "appropriate proof" of identity to obtain an active duty alert.[65]

The active duty alert should also be used by creditors to comply with the Servicemembers' Civil Relief Act[66] when engaged in collection activity. It can help to prevent identity thieves from victimizing military personnel who are stationed away from old addresses. However, unlike the fraud alert and extended alert, an active duty alert does not entitle a consumer to a free consumer report.

9.2.2.5 Effects of Alerts

All three varieties of alerts must notify users that the consumer does not authorize new credit, an additional card on an existing account, or any increase in the credit limit of any existing account.[67] However, an extension of credit under an existing open-end credit account, (e.g., a credit card) is excepted from this limitation.[68] In addition, a CRA must provide a consumer with an FTC-prescribed summary of rights when that consumer contacts the CRA and expresses a belief that the consumer is a victim of fraud or identity theft involving credit, an electronic funds transfer, or an account or transfer at or with another financial institution or other creditor.[69] The nationwide CRAs must refer consumer complaints of identity theft to one another, and the notified CRAs must include the alert in their files as well.[70]

The alerts also impose new responsibilities on users to verify the identity of credit applicants, provisions that should interrupt a thief's abuse of a consumer's identity. A user of a report containing an initial fraud alert or active military duty alert may not proceed with a credit transaction unless the user "utilizes reasonable policies and procedures to form a reasonable belief that the user knows the identity of the person making the request."[71] If the alert is an extended fraud alert, the prohibition extends to users of credit scores as well.[72]

Consumers may provide a telephone number in the alert; in the case of an extended fraud alert the user *must* use the number to verify the requester's identity.[73] However, if the alert is an initial fraud alert or an active duty alert, the user can "take reasonable steps" to verify the consumer's identity instead of calling the consumer.[74]

9.2.3 Identity Theft Victim's Access to Information About the Theft

9.2.3.1 Access to Thief's Transaction Information

The FCRA requires businesses that have dealt with an identity thief to provide information about the transactions to the thief's victim and to law enforcement agencies, a requirement that may help a consumer to document fraud transactions and find the thief.[75] Finding the thief is necessary to prosecute and convict the thief; some states' identity theft laws allow a judge to order a thief to compensate a victim and to order record rehabilitation, but only upon actual conviction.[76]

The provision allows identity theft victims access to the thief's application for credit and any business records—information that could reveal the source of the theft.[77] The consumer must request the information in writing, mailing

---

59 15 U.S.C. § 1681c-1(b)(2).
60 *Id.*
61 § 15 U.S.C. § 1681c-1(c).
62 15 U.S.C. § 1681a(q)(1) (citing 10 U.S.C. §§ 101(d)(1) and (a)(13)).
63 15 U.S.C. § 1681c-1(c)(1); 16 C.F.R. § 610.1.
64 15 U.S.C. § 1681c-1(c)(2).
65 15 U.S.C. § 1681c-1(c). *See* § 9.2.2.1.2, *supra*.
66 50 U.S.C. App. §§ 501–591. *See* § 5.5.1, *supra*.
67 15 U.S.C. §§ 1681c-1(h)(1)(A) (initial fraud and active military duty alerts), 1681c-1(h)(2)(A) (extended fraud alerts).
68 *Id.*
69 15 U.S.C. § 1681g(d). Note that "credit," "creditor," and "electronic funds transfer" are all defined terms. 15 U.S.C. § 1681a(r).
70 15 U.S.C. § 1681s(f); 16 C.F.R. § 602.1(c)(3)(vi).
71 15 U.S.C. § 1681c-1(h)(1)(B)(i).
72 15 U.S.C. § 1681c-1(h)(2)(b).
73 15 U.S.C. § 1681c-1(h)(2)(B). The consumer may provide another "reasonable contact method." 15 U.S.C. § 1681c-1(h)(2)(A)(ii).
74 15 U.S.C. § 1681c-1(h)1)(B)(ii). *See also* 16 C.F.R. § 614.1 (describing appropriate identity proof).
75 15 U.S.C. § 1681g(e).
76 *See, e.g.*, Md. Code Ann. Crim. Law § 8-301. *See also* Appx. H, *infra*.
77 15 U.S.C. § 1681g(e)(1).

the request to the address specified by the business entity, and including any relevant information about the transaction requested by the business.[78]

There are several other requirements for the victim to access the theft information. First, the victim must provide proof of positive identification, consisting, at the business's election, of one of the following: (1) a government-issued identification card; (2) personally identifying information of the same type as the thief provided to the business; or (3) personally identifying information of the type that the business usually requests from new applicants.[79] Ironically, an identity theft victim may have to provide more identifying information to see the records of the thief's transactions than the thief had to provide to create those transactions.

Second, the victim must provide proof of the identity theft claim. In order to prove the claim, the business can require the consumer to provide both a copy of a police report evidencing the claim,[80] and either a properly completed FTC Identity Theft Affidavit or another affidavit acceptable to the business.[81] Upon receiving this information, the business should provide the victim with copies of the application and business transaction records within thirty days.[82] The information should be provided whether the business maintains the records, or a third person maintains the records on the business's behalf.[83]

Nonetheless, a business can thwart a victim's access to such records. Even if a victim complies with all the prerequisites to obtain the transaction information, a business may still decline to provide the information if the business determines "in the exercise of good faith" that any of the following exceptions exists:

- The business does not have a "high degree of confidence in knowing the true identity of the individual" requesting the information, notwithstanding the victim's satisfaction of the identity verification requirements;
- The request is based on a misrepresentation of fact; or
- The information requested is "Internet navigational data or similar information."[84]

One concern is that businesses may use this last exception to shield a thief's on-line applications and transactions from the victim without providing an adequate substitute for the information.

Consumers have no ability to privately enforce this right to obtain information about identity theft transactions.[85] Furthermore, states are preempted from regulating not just the conduct required by the new provision but the subject matter itself.[86] Thus, the effectiveness of this provision may depend solely upon the willingness of businesses to comply with it.

9.2.3.2 Debt Collectors Must Provide Information to Victims and Notify Creditors

The FCRA imposes notification responsibilities on debt collectors that should help victims identify the original entities that provided credit to a thief in the victim's name. Once a consumer notifies a debt collector that a debt may be fraudulent or may have resulted from identity theft, the debt collector must notify the creditor of that allegation and must provide the consumer with all information about the debt to which the consumer would be entitled if the consumer were in fact the liable party.[87] Debt collectors are defined the same as in the Fair Debt Collection Practices Act (FDCPA).[88]

This provision appears to simply require that the collector treat the victim as the actual consumer in complying with dispute rights that the consumer would have under various laws,[89] including the FDCPA.[90] For example, the FDCPA's notice provisions require a debt collector to provide a written notice containing the amount of the debt, the name of the creditor to whom the debt is owed, a statement that unless the consumer disputes the validity of the debt within thirty days the debt collector will assume the debt to be valid, and a statement that, if the consumer disputes the debt in writing within that period, the collector will provide verification of the debt and the name and address of the original creditor.[91]

It is unclear whether consumers can enforce this right to obtain from a debt collector the identity of the original creditor. FACTA's revisions have been interpreted as removing any private rights of action for violations of this consumer right. Practitioners seeking to enforce claims should review the extended discussion of enforceability in § 10.2, *infra*.

---

78 15 U.S.C. § 1681g(e)(3).
79 15 U.S.C. § 1681g(e)(2)(A). The FCRA does not clarify the distinction between the proof of identification required from the consumer in this section and the "proper identification" required for fraud alerts and consumer report disclosures under § 1681g(a)(1). 16 C.F.R. § 614.1. *See* § 3.4, *supra*.
80 15 U.S.C. § 1681g(e)(2)(B)(i). A document meeting the Act's definition of "identity theft report" should qualify. 15 U.S.C. § 1681a(q)(4); 16 C.F.R. § 603.3. *See* § 9.2.2.3.2, *supra*.
81 15 U.S.C. § 1681g(e)(2)(B)(ii). Note that Congress could have designated the Commission's affidavit as acceptable, which would have furthered the goal of standardizing identity theft prevention.
82 15 U.S.C. § 1681g(e)(1).
83 *Id.*
84 15 U.S.C. § 1681g(e)(5).

85 15 U.S.C. § 1681g(e)(6).
86 15 U.S.C. § 1681t(b)(1)(G).
87 15 U.S.C. § 1681m(g).
88 *Id. See* 15 U.S.C. § 1692a(6); National Consumer Law Center, Fair Debt Collection § 4.2 (5th 2004 and Supp.).
89 *See* § 5.3, *supra*.
90 15 U.S.C. § 1681m(g)(2).
91 15 U.S.C. § 1692g. *See* National Consumer Law Center, Fair Debt Collection § 5.7 (5th 2004 and Supp.).

9.2.4 Blocking of Fraudulent Information

9.2.4.1 Agency Responsibilities

Under the FCRA, victims of identity theft can require nationwide CRAs[92] to block theft-related debts from their files.[93] To activate a block, a consumer must provide the CRA with the following:[94]

- Proof of the consumer's identity;[95]
- Copy of an identity theft report;[96]
- The consumer's identification of the fraudulent information; and
- The consumer's statement that the information does not relate to any transaction by the consumer.

Once the CRA has received this information, the CRA must block the identified items from the consumer's file within four business days.[97] The CRA must also notify the furnisher of the blocked information about the block, that the information may have resulted from identity theft, and an identity theft report has been filed.[98] Blocking the information should help the consumer's file with that CRA; the consumer can request the same block from the other nationwide CRAs. Furthermore, the FCRA requires a nationwide CRA that receives a consumer's complaint of identity theft, including a block, to notify the other nationwide CRAs of the complaint.[99]

A CRA can decline or rescind a block if the CRA "reasonably determines" that one of the following circumstances exists: (a) the consumer erroneously requested the information; (b) the consumer made a material misrepresentation of fact relevant to the block request; or (c) the consumer acquired goods, services, or money as a result of the blocked transaction.[100] Apparently, this right to decline or rescind a block seeks to prevent consumers from abusing the blocking provision by requesting that genuine debts be blocked.

If the CRA decides to decline or rescind a block, the CRA must notify the consumer of both this decision and the specific reason for the decision within five business days, in the same manner and timeframe that a CRA must notify a consumer that it is reinserting formerly deleted information.[101] Thus, when a CRA has improperly determined that it should decline or rescind a block, the consumer will learn of the decision and can then reassert the fraud claim.

Resellers[102] also have blocking responsibilities, but only if the reseller has a file that contains the information sought to be blocked.[103] If the consumer notifies a reseller that a report contains identity-theft information, the reseller must block the report from subsequent use by the reseller.[104] Upon blocking the file, the reseller must notify the consumer of the block and provide the name, address, and telephone number of the CRA from which the reseller acquired the consumer's file.[105] Although a reseller need not notify the original furnisher of the information, identifying the CRA from which the reseller obtained the fraudulent information allows the consumer to enforce the right to block the information with that CRA, who will then be required to notify the original furnisher.

Check services companies are exempted from the blocking requirements, although if the consumer sends them the information ordinarily required for a block, such companies are required to cease furnishing the fraudulent information to a nationwide CRA.[106]

The states are preempted from regulating the conduct required of CRAs and resellers under the FCRA's blocking provisions.[107] However, there is no prohibition against consumers using the FCRA's liability provisions to enforce the blocking requirements.[108]

9.2.4.2 Furnisher Responsibilities

Requesting a block also pulls the furnisher of the fraudulent information into the credit restoration process. When a block is properly requested, the CRA must notify the furnisher that the blocked information may be the result of identity theft, that the consumer has filed an identity theft report, and that the consumer has requested that the CRA block the information that the furnisher furnished, along with the effective date of the block.[109] Once notified, furnishers must implement procedures to prevent them from re-furnishing such information (to anyone, apparently, not just the notifying CRA).[110] Similar to the provision that

---

92 See § 2.6.1, supra.
93 15 U.S.C. § 1681c-2(a); 16 C.F.R. § 602.1(c)(3)(v).
94 15 U.S.C. § 1681c-2(a).
95 See § 9.2.2.1.2, supra.
96 See § 9.2.2.3.2, supra.
97 15 U.S.C. § 1681c-2(a).
98 15 U.S.C. § 1681c-2(b).
99 15 U.S.C. § 1681s(f). Here, too, states are preempted from regulating the required conduct. 15 U.S.C. § 1681t(b)(5)(G). An argument exists that, since the new provisions only directly impose requirements on the identified agencies and not on furnishers, actions against the furnishers are not preempted.
100 15 U.S.C. § 1681c-2(c)(1).
101 15 U.S.C. § 1681c-2(c)(2) (citing 15 U.S.C. § 1681i(a)(5)). See § 8.2.13, supra.
102 The term "reseller" is defined in 15 U.S.C. § 1681a(u).
103 15 U.S.C. § 1681c-2(d)(1) (no blocking responsibilities if reseller does not have file with information to be blocked).
104 15 U.S.C. § 1681c-2(d)(2).
105 15 U.S.C. § 1681c-2(d)(3).
106 15 U.S.C. § 1681c-2(e).
107 15 U.S.C. § 1681t(b)(5)(C).
108 15 U.S.C. §§ 1681n, 1681o. See, e.g., Collins v. Experian Credit Reporting Serv., 2005 WL 2042071 (D. Conn. Aug. 24, 2005) (denying motion to dismiss claims under §§ 1681c-1 and 1681c-2).
109 § 15 U.S.C. § 1681c-2(b)(1)–(4).
110 15 U.S.C. § 1681s-2(a)(6).

requires furnishers to cease furnishing information that a consumer has disputed,[111] this provision should help the CRA maintain the purged version of the victim's file. The consumer can also trigger that responsibility by submitting an identity theft report to the furnisher directly at the address specified for such reports.[112]

Once the consumer submits the report and states that the information resulted from identity theft, the furnisher must cease furnishing the fraudulent information unless the furnisher subsequently "knows" that the information is correct.[113] This appears to be a very high standard.

However, consumers have no right to enforce these provisions against furnishers,[114] and states are preempted from regulating the subject matter of the provisions.[115] Accordingly, they may provoke little change in furnishers' behavior. But notice of a block should also trigger a separate responsibility, that a furnisher not furnish information it "knows or has reason to believe" is inaccurate.[116] States are not preempted from regulating this conduct.

A CRA's notice to a furnisher that it has blocked information has another effect. Once a furnisher has been notified that a CRA has blocked a consumer's information as having resulted from identity theft, the furnisher may not sell or transfer the debt or place it for collection.[117] The notice triggering this protection must come from the CRA and must be pursuant to the FCRA's blocking provisions.[118] Thus, a consumer who informs a creditor or debt collector that a debt is the result of identity theft, such as pursuant to section 1681m(g)[119] or section 1692g of the FDCPA,[120] will not trigger this particular prohibition. Accordingly, identity theft victims should be advised to notify both the CRAs and the furnishers of the theft in order to put into play the full range of rights under the FCRA and other laws.

This prohibition against sale or transfer of identity theft debts should help victims by pinning the debt to one furnisher, so that the victim does not have to chase down a moving target. However, states are preempted from regulating this conduct.[121] Furthermore, the prohibition does not extend to the following:[122]

- The repurchase of a debt because the assignee requires such repurchase due to identity theft;
- The transfer of a debt as a result of a merger, acquisition, purchase and assumption transaction, or transfer of substantially all of the assets of an entity; or
- The securitization of a debt or the pledging of a portfolio of debt as collateral in connection with a borrowing.

This last exception creates some concern, since many types of debts are regularly securitized on the secondary market and may fall into this exception.

The ability of consumers to enforce this prohibition on transferring debts is unclear, because of FACTA's revisions to the FCRA section containing this prohibition. Those revisions have been interpreted as removing a private right of action for any violation of the prohibitions of the FCRA section. Practitioners seeking to enforce claims should review the extended discussion of enforceability in § 10.2, *infra*.

9.2.5 Preventing Theft of Consumer's Identification Information

9.2.5.1 Card Number and Social Security Number Truncation

The FCRA includes several provisions added by the FACTA amendments that seek to protect sensitive consumer information, thus decreasing the chance of identity theft. Merchants that accept credit cards or debit cards[123] must truncate credit and debit card numbers on electronically printed receipts.[124] The Act preempts states from regulating the printing of account numbers on card receipts.[125]

Consumers requesting a copy of their consumer reports can direct the CRA to withhold the first five digits of the consumer's Social Security number on the report.[126] How

---

111 *See* Ch. 4, *supra*.
112 15 U.S.C. § 1681s-2(a)(6)(B).
113 *Id.*; 16 C.F.R. § 602.1(c)(3)(vii). The furnisher can also commence re-furnishing of the information if the consumer informs the furnisher that the information is correct. 15 U.S.C. § 1681s-2(a)(6)(B).
114 15 U.S.C. § 1681s-2(c).
115 15 U.S.C. § 1681t(b)(5)(H).
116 15 U.S.C. § 1681s-2(a)(1)(A).
117 15 U.S.C. § 1681m(f).
118 15 U.S.C. § 1681m(f)(1) citing 15 U.S.C. § 1681c-2.
119 *See* § 9.2.2, *supra*.
120 15 U.S.C. § 1692g(b). *See* National Consumer Law Center, Fair Debt Collection § 5.7 (5th 2004 and Supp.).
121 15 U.S.C. § 1681t(b)(5)(f).
122 15 U.S.C. § 1681m(f)(3).

123 These terms are defined in 15 U.S.C. § 1681a(r)(2) and (3).
124 15 U.S.C. § 1681c(g). The truncation provision will become effective on December 4, 2006, for receipt-printing machines in use before January 1, 2005, and became effective December 4, 2004, with respect to machines first put into use on or after January 1, 2005. 15 U.S.C. § 1681c(g)(3)(A), (B).
125 15 U.S.C. § 1681t(b)(1)(E). Some states have enacted provisions requiring similar, and possibly identical, conduct, but, arguably, even if they were subject to the preemption, they would remain in effect until the Act's provision becomes effective, under the reasoning that the Act does not "require" the truncation conduct until that time. *See, e.g.*, Ariz. Rev. Stat. § 44-1367; Cal. Civ. Code § 1747.9; 815 Ill. Comp. Stat. 616/50 (violation is a deceptive trade practice); Me. Rev. Stat. § 1149. Note that the FCRA's provision may not fully substitute for such state statutes because to state a claim under the FCRA a consumer must show negligence or willfulness, whereas a state may impose liability under a lesser standard. *See* 15 U.S.C. §§ 1681n, 1681o.
126 15 U.S.C. § 1681g(a)(1).

9.2.5.2 Address Discrepancies

A CRA that receives a request for a consumer's report that includes an address for the consumer that substantially differs from the addresses in the file of the CRA must notify the requester of the discrepancy if the CRA provides a consumer report in response to the request.[127] In addition, the FCRA requires the FTC and banking regulators to issue regulations that provide guidance to users regarding the reasonable policies and procedures that they should employ when they receive an address discrepancy notice.[128]

The FTC and banking regulators have issued proposed regulations for this requirement.[129] These regulations would require a user to "develop and implement reasonable policies and procedures" to verify the consumer's address after receiving such an address discrepancy notice,[130] and to furnish to the CRA an address that the user has "reasonably confirmed is accurate."[131] To confirm a consumer's address, a user could verify the address with the consumer; review its own records of the address provided to request the report; verify the address through third parties; or use "other reasonable means."[132]

The Act preempts states from regulating the conduct required by this FCRA section on address discrepancies.[133]

9.2.5.3 Disposal of Consumer Information

Regulations promulgated by the FTC, the Securities and Exchange Commission, and the banking regulators[134] require users to properly dispose of the consumer information they acquire through consumer reports.[135] These regulations should help prevent the illicit disclosure and use of consumer financial information. Note that the FCRA provides that the regulations cannot be inconsistent with the requirements of the Gramm-Leach-Bliley Act (GLB).[136]

The FTC has issued a set of regulations, while the banking regulator's regulations refer to the Interagency Guidelines Establishing Information Security Standards.[137] For purposes of the FTC regulations, "consumer information" means "any record about an individual, whether in paper, electronic, or other form, that is a consumer report or is derived from a consumer report."[138] Consumer information also means a compilation of such records, but does not include information that does not identify individuals, such as aggregate or blind data.[139] "To dispose" means "(1) [t]he discarding or abandonment of consumer information, or (2) [t]he sale, donation, or transfer of any medium, including computer equipment, upon which consumer information is stored."[140]

To comply with the regulation, anyone "who maintains or otherwise possesses consumer information for a business purpose" must take "reasonable measures to protect against unauthorized access to or use of the information in connection with its disposal."[141] The FTC has provided examples of satisfactory disposal, which generally consist of destroying the record, in the case of paper records, or destroying or erasing the records, in the case of electronic media, so that, regardless of medium, "the information cannot practicably be read or reconstructed."[142] The information possessor may contract with another to do the destruction, so long as the possessor exercises due diligence in doing so.[143] Those subject to the Gramm-Leach-Bliley Act's safeguard rule[144] can satisfy their obligations under the FTC's disposal regulations by complying with the GLB safeguard rule.[145]

9.2.6 Creditor Implementation of Red Flag Guidelines

The FCRA as amended by FACTA calls for the FTC and the banking regulators issue "red flag" guidelines for use by financial institutions[146] and creditors[147] regarding identity theft.[148] In addition, the FTC and banking regulators must issue regulations that will require each financial institution

---

127 15 U.S.C. § 1681c(h).
128 15 U.S.C. § 1681c(h).
129 71 Fed. Reg. 40,786 (July 18, 2006).
130 71 Fed. Reg. at 40,795–40,796.
131 Id.
132 Id.
133 15 U.S.C. § 1681t(b)(1)(E).
134 The banking regulators are the Office of the Comptroller of Currency (OCC) for national banks; the Office of Thrift Supervision (OTC) for federal thrifts; the Federal Deposit Insurance Corporation (FDIC) for certain state banks; the National Credit Union Administration (NCUA) for federal credit unions; and the Federal Reserve Board (FRB) for a set of other banks.
135 15 U.S.C. § 1681w. The FTC's regulations are codified at 16 C.F.R. §§ 682.1–682.5; the SEC at 17 C.F.R. § 248.30; the OCC at 12 C.F.R. § 41.83; the FRB at 12 C.F.R. § 222.82; the FDIC at 12 C.F.R. § 334.83; the OTS at 12 C.F.R. § 571.83; NCUA at 12 C.F.R. § 717.83.
136 15 U.S.C. § 1681w(a)(2)(B).
137 12 C.F.R. § 41.83 (OCC); 12 C.F.R. § 222.82 (FRB); 12 C.F.R. § 334.83 (FDIC); 12 C.F.R. § 571.83 (OTS); 12 C.F.R. § 717.83 (NCUA).
138 16 C.F.R. § 682.1.
139 Id.
140 16 C.F.R. § 682.1.
141 16 C.F.R. § 682.3(a).
142 16 C.F.R. § 682.2(b)(1)–(2), (4).
143 16 C.F.R. § 682.2(b)(3).
144 16 C.F.R. Part 314.
145 16 C.F.R. § 682.2(b)(5).
146 Defined in 15 U.S.C. § 1681a(t).
147 Defined in 15 U.S.C. § 1681a(r).
148 15 U.S.C. § 1681m(e)(1)(A).

and creditor to establish reasonable policies and procedures to implement these red flag guidelines.[149]

The FCRA also specifically requires the FTC and banking regulators to issue guidelines for credit and debit card issuers[150] to prevent "account-takeover" identity theft by imposing special verification procedures on issuers that receive a request for an additional or a replacement card on an existing account within thirty days of receiving a change of address notice.[151] Before issuing the card the issuer must do one of the following:

- Notify the cardholder of the request at the former address;
- Notify the cardholder of the request by such other agreed means; or
- Validate the change of address using other means in accordance with the red flag procedures established pursuant to regulation.[152]

In response to these provisions, the FTC and banking agencies issued proposed red flag guidelines and regulations;[153] as of October 2006, final regulations had not been issued. The proposed rulemaking also contained provisions implementing the FCRA's address discrepancy provisions.[154]

The regulations create a flexible approach intended to evolve as risks of identity theft change. They require financial institutions and creditors to implement a written "Identity Theft Prevention Program."[155] The program must include "policies and procedures to identify Red Flags" and to prevent and mitigate identity theft in connection with accounts.[156] Creditors and financial institutions are permitted to use the same procedures to identify customers as in their Customer Identification Programs established pursuant to the USA PATRIOT Act.[157] The proposed regulations would require institutions and creditors to train staff to implement the program, to oversee service providers that perform activities subject to the program, and to have the program approved by the entity's board of directors or a committee thereof.[158]

The regulations define "red flag" as a "a pattern, practice, or specific activity that indicates the possible risk of identity theft."[159] The program must meet a floor level, incorporating not only red flags identified by the regulations, but also any from any incidents of identity theft experienced or methods of identity theft that reflect changes in risks.[160]

The regulations set forth a number of pre-defined red flags. Of these, there are three red flags that can arise from information received from a CRA:

- A fraud or active duty alert is included with a consumer report;
- An address discrepancy notice from a CRA; and
- A consumer report indicating a pattern of activity that is inconsistent with the history and usual pattern of activity of an applicant or customer, such as:
  a. A recent and significant increase in the volume of inquiries;
  b. An unusual number of recently established credit relationships;
  c. A material change in the use of credit, especially with respect to recently established credit relationships;
  d. An account was closed for cause or identified for abuse of account privileges by a financial institution or creditor.[161]

The proposed regulations also address the requirements of the FCRA on card issuers who receive address changes followed shortly by a request for an additional or replacement card.[162]

The FCRA does not permit private actions to enforce the red flag guidelines.[163] States are preempted from regulating the conduct required by the FCRA's red flag provisions.[164]

9.3 Identity Theft and Assumption Deterrence Act

Under the federal Identity Theft and Assumption Deterrence Act,[165] one who transfers or uses another's identification with the intent to commit, or to aid or abet a violation of federal law or a felony under state law commits a federal crime. "Means of identification" is defined broadly to include "any name or number that may be used, alone or in conjunction with any other information, to identify a specific individual." "Means of identification" specifically includes not just traditional forms of identification, such as name, Social Security number, and date of birth, but also "unique biometric data," "unique electronic identification number," and "telecommunication identifying information or access device."[166] This Act requires the Federal Trade Commission to set up a centralized complaint department to

---

149 15 U.S.C. § 1681m(e)(1)(B).
150 Defined in 15 U.S.C. § 1681a(r)(1).
151 15 U.S.C. § 1681m(e)(1)(B).
152 15 U.S.C. § 1681m (e)(1)(C).
153 71 Fed. Reg. 40,786 (July 18, 2006).
154 15 U.S.C. § 1681c(h). See § 9.2.5.2, supra.
155 71 Fed. Reg. 40,786, 40,788 (July 18, 2006).
156 71 Fed. Reg. 40,786, 40,789 (July 18, 2006).
157 71 Fed. Reg. 40,786, 40,792 (July 18, 2006). The Customer Identification Program regulations are at 31 C.F.R. Part 103.
158 71 Fed. Reg. 40,786, 40,793 (July 18, 2006).
159 71 Fed. Reg. 40,786, 40,790 (July 18, 2006).

160 71 Fed. Reg. 40,786, 40,791 (July 18, 2006).
161 71 Fed. Reg. 40,786, 40,810–40,811 (July 18, 2006).
162 71 Fed. Reg. 40,786, 40,794 (July 18, 2006).
163 15 U.S.C. § 1681s-2(c).
164 15 U.S.C. § 1681t(b)(5)(F).
165 18 U.S.C. § 1028, 28 U.S.C. § 994.
166 18 U.S.C. § 1028(d)(3).

receive reports from identity theft victims, provide informational materials to the victims, and refer the complaints to "appropriate entities."[167]

A primary motivation for the Act was law enforcement's failure to recognize that the consumer whose identity is stolen is a victim. Since the consumer is not legally obligated to pay the charges rung up by the impostor, police considered the credit issuers and merchants, and not the consumer, the "true" victim of the crime, even though it was the consumer's information that was misused and the consumer's credit record that suffered damage.[168] Though existing federal legislation prohibited the fraudulent use of identification, bank cards, and Social Security numbers,[169] as a practical matter federal investigators would only investigate multistate fraud rings and cases worth over $200,000.[170]

Though the Act advances the fight against identity theft, there is much that it does not do. It does not regulate consumer reporting agencies (CRAs) and their treatment of identity theft; a victim must rely on the FCRA identity theft provisions to try to clean up a credit record.[171] The Act does not require creditors to exercise care in extending credit by properly verifying the identity of the credit applicant, even though such care would forestall a great deal of identity theft. The Act does not require a judge to order restitution to a victim but leaves it to the judge's discretion; a prior version of the bill, which would have mandated restitution and defined it to include the costs incurred in clearing the credit history, was not adopted.[172] Consumers may not base a private claim on a defendant's violation of the Act.[173]

9.4 State Identity Theft Statutes

Nearly every state has explicitly criminalized identity theft, enacting a special statute to combat this particular violation that does not fit neatly into classic common law categories of offenses.[174] These statutes are summarized at Appendix H, *infra*. A typical statute prohibits a person from obtaining identification information of another person and using it to obtain credit, property, or services without that person's authorization. Most such statutes impose only criminal penalties, and only a tiny fraction of thefts get prosecuted because states have insufficient resources to pursue them.[175] However, Alabama,[176] Delaware,[177] Kentucky,[178] Massachusetts,[179] Minnesota,[180] Mississippi,[181] Nevada,[182] New Hampshire,[183] New Mexico,[184] Tennessee,[185] and Virginia[186] provide for mandatory restitution, while some other states allow the court to order restitution in its discretion.[187] Some states specifically provide victims

---

167 Pub. L. No. 105-318, § 5, 112 Stat. 3007 (codified as note to 18 U.S.C. § 1028).
168 *See, e.g., "Identity Theft": Hearings Before the Subcomm. on Technology, Terrorism and Government Information of the Senate Comm. of the Judiciary*, 105th Cong., 1st Sess. 9 (1998) (prepared statement of the Federal Trade Commission); Michael Higgins, *Identity Thieves*, ABA Journal 43 (Oct. 1998).
169 18 U.S.C. § 1028; 42 U.S.C. § 408.
170 Michael Higgins, *Identity Thieves*, ABA Journal 43 (Oct. 1998).
171 See § 9.2, *supra*.
172 S. 512, 105th Cong., 1st Sess. (1997). *See also* 143 Cong. Rec. S2741 (daily ed. Mar. 21, 1997) (statement of Sen. Kyl).
173 Garay v. U.S. Bancorp, 303 F. Supp. 2d 299, 302–303 (E.D.N.Y. 2004) (dismissing claim that credit card issuer aided and abetted identity theft by issuing card in plaintiff's name to imposter).
174 Ala. Code §§ 13A-192 to 200; Alaska Stat. §§ 11.46.565 and 11.46.570; Ariz. Rev. Stat. § 13-2008; Ark. Code Ann. § 5-37-227; Cal. Penal Code §§ 530.5 to 530.7; Cal. Civ. Code §§ 1798.92 to 1798.97, 1785.11.1 and 11.2, 1785.16, 1785.16.1 and 1785.16.2 and 1785.20.3; Colo. Rev. Stat. Ann. §§ 18-5-901 to 18-5-905; Conn. Gen. Stat. §§ 53a-129a, 52-571h; Del. Code Ann. tit. 11, § 854; D.C. Stat. §§ 22-3227.01 to 22-3227.08; Fla. Stat. Ann. § 817.568; Ga. Code Ann. §§ 16-9-121 to 16-9-127; Haw. Rev. Stat. Ann. §§ 708-839.6 to 708-839.8; Idaho Code §§ 18-3126, 18-3123, 28-51-101 and 28-51-102 (identity theft); 720 Ill. Comp. Stat. § 5/16G-1 to 5/16G-25; Ind. Code § 35-43-5-1 and 35-43-5-3.5; Iowa Code §§ 714.16B, 715A.8 and 715A.9; Kan. Stat. Ann. § 21-4018; Ky. Rev. Stat. Ann. §§ 411.201, 514.160 and 514.170, 532.034; La. Rev. Stat. Ann. § 14:67.16; Md. Code Ann. art. 27, § 231; Md. Govt. Code § 6-202; Mass. Gen. Laws ch. 266, § 37E; Mich. Comp. Laws § 750.285; Minn. Stat. § 609.527; Miss. Code Ann. § 97-19-85; Mo. Rev. Stat. § 570.223; Mont. Code Ann. § 45-6-332; Neb. Rev. Stat. § 28-608; Nev. Rev. Stat. §§ 41.1345, 205.463 and 205.465; N.H. Rev. Stat. Ann. §§ 638:25 to 638:27; N.J. Stat. Ann. § 2C:21-17; N.M. Stat. Ann. § 30-16-24.1; N.Y. Pen. Law §§ 190.77-190.83; N.C. Gen. Stat. § 14-113.20 to 14-113.23; N.D. Cent. Code § 12.1-23-11; Ohio Rev. Code Ann. § 2913.49; Okla. Stat. tit. 21, § 1533.1; Or. Rev. Stat. § 165.800; 18 Pa. Cons. Stat. §§ 4120, 4142, 9720.1; R.I. Gen. Laws § 11-49.1-1 to 11-49.1-5; S.C. Code Ann. §§ 16-13-500 to 16-13-530; S.D. Codified Laws §§ 22-30A-3.1 to 22-30A-3.3; Tenn. Code Ann. §§ 39-14-150, 39-16-303, 47-18-2101 to 47-18-2106; Tex. Penal Code Ann. § 32.51; Utah Code Ann. §§ 76-6-1101 to 76-6-1104; Vt. Stat. Ann. § 2030; Va. Code Ann. § 18.2-186.3; Wash. Rev. Code §§ 9.35.001 to 9.35.902; W. Va. Code § 61-3-54; Wis. Stat. §§ 943.201, 895.80; Wyo. Stat. §§ 1-1-128, 6-3-901.
175 In an analysis of prosecutions in ten states, the U.S. Government Accounting Office cited shortages of both funds and trained personnel to explain the few prosecutions of identity thefts. U.S. General Accounting Office, Rep. No. GAO-02-766, Identity Theft: Greater Awareness and Use of Existing Data Are Needed 17 (June 2002).
176 Ala. Code § 13A-8-195.
177 Del. Code Ann. tit. 11, § 854(e).
178 Ky. Rev. Stat. Ann. § 532.034 (including costs incurred to correct credit history).
179 Mass. Gen. Laws ch. 266, § 37E(c) (including costs incurred to correct credit history).
180 Minn. Stat. § 609.527(4) (up to $1000).
181 Miss. Code Ann. § 97-19-85(1).
182 Nev. Rev. Stat. § 205.463 (including costs incurred to correct credit history).
183 N.H. Rev. Stat. Ann. § 638:26(III).
184 N.M. Stat. Ann. § 30-16-24.1(F).
185 Tenn. Code Ann § 47-18-2105(f).
186 Va. Code § 18.2-186.3(E) (may include costs incurred to correct credit history, as judge deems appropriate).
187 *E.g.*, D.C. Stat. § 22-3227.04; Fla. Stat. Ann. § 817.568(6)(a);

with a private cause of action against the thief, an element missing from the federal Identity Theft and Assumption Deterrence Act.[188] Other states specifically designate a violation of the identity theft statute as an unfair practice for purposes of the state's unfair and deceptive practices act.[189]

While a right of restitution and a private cause of action against the thief satisfy a sense of justice, in all likelihood the thief will be as judgment proof as a stone, and a victim will be able to realize little real reimbursement from that source. The thief, however, would be unable to carry out the theft without the unintended cooperation of retailers, banks, and others who extend credit to the thief in the consumer's name without verifying the identity of the applicant. California recognizes that those who extend credit to thieves contribute to the victim's loss and therefore should also have liability when they overlook indications that someone other than the consumer is acting in the consumer's name.

Accordingly, California's statute imposes two obligations on those who use consumer reports. First, any person who uses a consumer report in connection with a credit transaction, and who discovers that the address on the consumer report does not match the address of the consumer requesting or being offered credit, must take reasonable steps to verify the accuracy of the consumer's address, and must confirm with the consumer that the credit transaction is not the result of identity theft.[190] Second, if a person using a consumer report receives a "clearly identifiable notification" that the report's information has been blocked as a result of identity theft, that person may not extend credit without taking reasonable steps to verify the consumer's identity and to confirm that the credit transaction is not the result of identity theft.[191] Those who fail these obligations may be liable to the consumer for losses incurred, and for punitive damages of up to $30,000.[192] This statute appears to have been a precursor to some of the FACTA amendments' identity theft provisions, and indeed is perhaps more effective by providing substantial economic disincentives for violating its provisions.

Some states address the problem of identity theft by requiring consumer reporting agencies (CRAs) to cooperate with the victim by blocking information in the consumer's report related to the thief's transactions, and providing the consumer with a cause of action for the CRA's failure to do so.[193] About two dozen states have enacted "security freeze" laws that allow consumers to deny access by users to their consumer reports, thus preventing the thieves from obtaining extensions of credit based on these reports.[194] Washington requires those who may have done business with a thief to provide the victim with all relevant information related to the transaction.[195]

An ideal statute would incorporate the above elements from state laws and the FACTA amendments, and would add a cause of action against those who negligently allow the thief to take out credit or acquire goods or services in the consumer's name, and a right of restitution from the thief as well. Note, however, that many protections of state identity theft statutes may be preempted by the preemption provisions added by the FACTA amendments, which generally bar states from regulating any "conduct required by" the new identity theft provisions.[196]

La. Rev. Stat. Ann. § 14:67.16(E); Md. Crim. Law Code Ann. § 8-301 (including costs incurred to correct credit history); Mo. Rev. Stat. § 570.223(3); Mont. Code Ann. 45-6-332(4) (including costs incurred to correct credit history); 42 Pa. Cons. Stat. § 9720.1(A) (including costs incurred to correct credit history); S.C. Code Ann. § 16-13-510; Tex. Penal Code §§ 32.51(d), 6-3-901(d).

188 Ala. Code § 13A-8-199; Cal. Civ. Code § 1798.93; Conn. Gen. Stat. § 52-571h; Iowa Code § 714.16B (treble damages); Ky. Rev. Stat. Ann. § 411.210 (compensatory and punitive damages); Nev. Rev. Stat. § 41.1345; Tenn. Code Ann. § 47-18-2104; Wash. Rev. Code § 9.35.010; Wis. Stat. § 895.80(1) (treble damages); Wyo. Stat. Ann. § 1-1-128.

189 Ark. Code Ann. § 5-37-227(d)(1); Iowa Code § 715A.8(4); Tenn. Code Ann. § 47-18-2106; Wash. Rev. Code § 9.35.800.

190 Cal. Civ. Code § 1785.20.3(a).

191 Cal. Civ. Code § 1785.20.3(b).

192 Cal. Civ. Code § 1785.20.3(c).

193 See, e.g., Ala. Code § 13A-8-200 (CRA must use "reasonable procedures" to block any information described in a court order issued upon conviction under the identity theft statute); Cal. Civ. Code Ann. § 1785.16(k) (requiring CRAs to "promptly and permanently" block information that a consumer alleges to be present due to identity theft, substantiated by a police report; information may only be unblocked if furnisher meets the statute's criteria for showing that item was legitimate); Conn. Gen. Stat. § 36a-699f; Idaho Code § 28-51-102 (if consumer submits a certified copy of a police report establishing probable cause of a violation, the CRA must block the information that the consumer identifies as being a result of the theft unless the consumer benefited from the blocked transaction, made a misrepresentation to the CRA, or agrees that the information will not be blocked; CRA must notify furnisher of blocked information); Mont. Code § 31-3-115; Wash. Rev. Code § 19.182.160. See also Cal. Civ. Code Ann. § 1785.11.2 (allowing consumers to put a security freeze on the consumer's report so that the CRA is prohibited from releasing the report without the consumer's express authorization; exceptions provided).

194 See, e.g., Cal. Civ. Code § 1785.11.2; Del. Code Ann. tit. 6, § 2203; Fla. Stat. § 501.005; 815 Ill. Comp. Stats. Ann. 505/2MM; La. Rev. Stat. § 9:3571.1; Md. Rev. Stat. art. 10, § 1313-C; Nev. Rev. Stat. § 598C.300; N.H. Rev. Stat. §§ 359-B:22-23; N.J. Stat. Ann. § 56:11-46; N.Y. Gen. Bus. Law § 380-t; N.C. Gen. Stat. § 75-63; S.D. Codified Laws §§ 54-15-1 to -15; Utah Code § 3-45-2004 (effective Sept. 1, 2008); Vt. Stat. Ann. tit. 9, § 2840h; Wash. Rev. Code § 19.182.170.

195 Wash. Rev. Code § 9.35.040 (violation is deemed to also be a UDAP violation).

196 See 15 U.S.C. § 1681t(b)(5). With respect to the right to obtain identity theft transaction information, provided in 15 U.S.C. § 1681g(e), the FACTA amendments preempt not just the conduct required by the provision but the entire subject matter. 15 U.S.C. § 1681t(b)(1)(g). See § 10.7, infra.

9.5 Filing Suit Under the FCRA and Other Laws to Rectify Identity Theft

A hard fact of life is that many consumers find consumer reporting agencies (CRAs) and creditors less than helpful when dealing with identity theft, and legal action or the threat of legal action is often needed. Identity theft is one of the leading reasons consumers with bad consumer reports turn to attorneys for assistance. There are many claims that should be considered in an identity theft case.

First, a number of the FACTA amendments' identity theft provisions are privately enforceable and should be considered, including:

- The right to an initial fraud alert, extended fraud alert or active military alert;[197]
- The requirement that CRAs block information resulting from identity theft;[198]
- The requirement for merchants to truncate credit and debit card numbers on electronically printed receipts;[199]
- The requirement for CRAs to notify users of any address discrepancies between the user's request and the CRA's files, and the user's responsibilities in response;[200]
- The requirement that users properly dispose of the consumer information they acquire through consumer reports.[201]

Second, practitioners should not ignore the possibility of claims under those FCRA provisions that pre-date the FACTA amendments. Some of these claims have been use quite effectively in identity theft cases, and include:

- FCRA claims based on any violations by the CRA of its duties when dealing with disputed debts, such as failing to initiate a reinvestigation, failing to delete a debt after reinvestigation has shown it to be fraudulent, reinsertion of previously deleted items, failing to include the consumer's dispute statement in the report if the disputed entry is not deleted, and failure to use reasonable procedures to ensure maximum possible accuracy.[202]
- FCRA claims that a furnisher failed to conduct a proper reinvestigation of the alleged debt as requested by the CRA after the consumer sent the CRA a dispute letter.[203]

Finally, there are also potential claims under other federal and state laws. These include:

- Claims under the Equal Credit Opportunity Act if a creditor turns down the victim's credit application because of delinquencies that the creditor knows were incurred by the thief rather than the consumer;[204]
- Common law claims against the creditor;[205]
- Claims under a state identity theft statute, if one exists that creates a private cause of action;[206]
- A claim for restitution if the offender is criminally prosecuted;[207]
- A claim against a government agency that may have violated privacy laws by providing information to a thief.[208]

A creditor who posts a thief's delinquencies to the victim's credit record may be liable for failing to use due care in opening the account. By extending credit or providing goods or services to the thief without properly verifying the thief's identity, the creditor facilitates the conduct that leads to catastrophic consequences to the victim's credit record. This extension necessarily occurs well before the responsibilities imposed on furnishers by section 1681s-2 arise, and therefore an action based on it will not be preempted by section 1681t.[209]

Several courts have held that credit card issuers have a duty to ensure that card applicants are who they say they are.[210] However, cases based on a common law duty or theory are not easy, and many more identity theft victims have lost than won when suing creditors who enabled the theft.[211] Counsel should carefully identify the precise duty

---

197 See § 9.2.2, supra.
198 See § 9.2.4, supra.
199 See § 9.2.5.1, supra.
200 See § 9.2.5.2, supra.
201 See § 9.2.5.3, supra.
202 See Ch. 4, supra.
203 See Ch. 6, supra

204 Cf. § 8.2.6.6, supra.
205 See § 10.5, infra.
206 State identity theft statutes are summarized in Appx. H, infra, and discussed at § 9.4, supra.
207 In a few states, the criminal court can also order the victim's credit record cleared. See Appx. H, infra (summaries of state identity theft statutes).
208 See, e.g., Smith v. Illinois Sec. of State, 2003 WL 1908020 (N.D. Ill. Apr. 21 2003) (denying defendant's motion to dismiss plaintiff's claim that defendant had violated the federal Driver's Privacy Protection Act by providing an identity thief with a false Illinois driver's license that bore the plaintiff's name, date of birth, and Social Security number).
209 Stafford v. Cross Country Bank, 262 F. Supp. 2d 776 (W.D. Ky. 2003). See also § 10.7, infra.
210 Patrick v. Union State Bank, 681 So. 2d 1364 (Ala. 1996); Lechmere Tire & Sales Co. v. Burwick, 277 N.E.2d 503, 507 (Mass. 1972) (credit card issuer has duty to use due care to ensure that the person using the card is its proper holder or authorized user); Bradshaw v. Mich. Nat'l Bank, 197 N.W.2d 531, 531 (Mich. Ct. App. 1972) (affirming denial of motion for summary judgment).
211 See Garay v. U.S. Bancorp, 303 F. Supp. 2d 299, 302, 303 (E.D.N.Y. 2004) (rejecting all of identity theft victim's claims against creditor who issued a credit card in victim's name to identity thief, including claims that creditor aided and abetted

the creditor owes to the victim, and use appropriate evidence to establish the breach of that duty. Victims generally cannot rely on the mere fact that the identity theft occurred to establish that the creditor breached a duty, and may instead need to put on expert testimony to substantiate the creditor's negligence.

It has been held that an identity theft victim may not rely on the doctrine of *res ipsa loquitur* to establish that a credit card provider had failed to abide by a standard of care when it issued a card to a thief in the victim's name.[212] The court reasoned that the fraud could have occurred even had the provider strictly followed the verification procedures the plaintiff asserted would have been reasonable, therefore the doctrine did not apply.[213] The court further found that the plaintiff failed to show that the creditor had not acted in accordance with commercially reasonable practices. The creditor had the practice of verifying credit card applications by comparing the name, address and Social Security number on the application with information contained in consumer reports.[214] Where, as in the plaintiff's case, the applicant's address differed from the address given by the applicant, the creditor would call the telephone number listed by the applicant to verify the application information.[215] Though it could perhaps be easily foreseen that an identity thief would in fact list his or her own telephone number and thereby be given the opportunity to explain away the discrepancy to the creditor, the court ruled against the victim because she failed to offer expert testimony about whether more thorough verification procedures would have been commercially reasonable.[216]

That case followed the reasoning of an earlier identity theft case in which the plaintiff sued two credit card companies that had issued cards in his name to his ex-girlfriend, even though the applications were filled with wrong information.[217] That court, too, ruled against the use of *res ipsa loquitur*, and held that without expert testimony, the plaintiff simply could not show that the merchants had acted outside the duty of care.[218]

However, by offering convincing expert testimony a plaintiff may well succeed on a claim that a bank or creditor failed to act reasonably in ensuring that the person who opened an account was in fact the person they purported to be. For example, the Alabama Supreme Court overturned a summary judgment in favor of a bank on an identity theft victim's claim that the bank had breached its duty of care to her by allowing an impostor to open an account in her name and write $1500 worth of bad checks on it.[219] The plaintiff offered the affidavit of a bank security expert who testified that the bank clerk, who opened the account without requiring picture identification, without verifying the offered Social Security number, and without inquiring why the impostor's signature did not match that on the plaintiff's temporary—and pictureless—driver's license, did not comport with industry fraud-prevention standards.[220] As the incidence of identity theft increases, the degree of diligence and standard of care considered reasonable to counteract fraud may well rise.

---

the identity theft); Huggins v. Citibank, N.A., 585 S.E.2d 275 (S.C. 2003) (state does not recognize tort of negligent enablement of imposter fraud); Polzer v. TRW, Inc., 682 N.Y.S.2d 194 (App. Div. 1998) (affirming summary judgment in favor of creditor in case in which identity theft victims had alleged negligence, intentional and negligent infliction of emotional distress, and UDAP claims, ruling that credit issuers owed no special duty to victims). In Stevens v. First Interstate Bank, 167 Or. App. 280, 999 P.2d 551, 554 (2000) the court held that a bank could not be liable for either breach of duty of confidentiality or infliction of emotional distress to customers whose financial information had been misappropriated by a rogue employee to obtain credit. Curiously, the plaintiffs did not allege a respondeat superior claim against the bank for its employee's fraud. *See also* Rivera-Lebron v. Cellular One, 13 F. Supp. 2d 235 (D. P.R. 1998) (plaintiff, who alleged cellular telephone company negligently issued a telephone to an impostor under plaintiff's name, had no cause of action under FCRA, other claims dismissed for lack of jurisdiction).

212 Yelder v. Credit Bureau of Montgomery, L.L.C., 131 F. Supp. 2d 1275, 1285 (M.D. Ala. 2001).
213 *Id.* at 1285.
214 *Id.* at 1285–1286.
215 *Id.*
216 *Id.* at 1286.
217 Beard v. Goodyear Tire & Rubber Co., 587 A.2d 195 (D.C. 1991).
218 *Id.* at 199–200. The plaintiff had not shown that any of the merchants had his consumer report, which would have illuminated the discrepancies in the applications, and since the discrepancies were not obvious on the face of the applications, the court ruled that the plaintiff failed to adequately counter the affidavits offered by the defendants that their verification practices met industry standard. *Id.*
219 Patrick v. Union State Bank, 681 So. 2d 1364 (Ala. 1996).
220 *Id.* at 1367.

Chapter 10   Available Claims for Consumer Reporting Disputes

10.1 Introduction

This chapter focuses on consumer claims relating to consumer reporting injury. Prior chapters examine in detail the Fair Credit Reporting Act (FCRA) obligations of consumer reporting agencies (CRAs), users and furnishers. This chapter looks to the elements of a consumer's claim for a violation of those obligations, and also looks to related claims under other federal statutes, common law tort theories, and under state statutes. Section 10.4, *infra*, analyzes the limited immunity that CRAs, furnishers and users have from various tort claims, while § 10.7, *infra* examines when the FCRA preempts claims under state statutes.

Section 10.2, *infra*, focuses on FCRA claims based on negligence. Enhanced remedies are also available under the FCRA for willful violations, and these are examined in Chapter 11, *infra* in the context of punitive damages. Chapter 11, *infra* also considers other aspects of the FCRA remedies and litigation, including selecting the appropriate plaintiffs,[1] defendants,[2] fact patterns,[3] and courts (i.e., federal or state court),[4] the FCRA statute of limitations, tips on both informal and formal case discovery,[5] jury trials,[6] damages, punitive damages, attorney fees, and other remedy issues. Sample pleadings and discovery are found at Appendix J, *infra*, and additional FCRA pleadings are found on the CD-Rom accompanying this manual.

Special care should be taken before raising a tort claim, as discussed in § 10.5, *infra*. Case law is sparse concerning consumer reporting tort claims, particularly as they relate to the FCRA's qualified immunity. The case easily may be sidetracked on motions to dismiss the tort claim because of this qualified immunity.

Generally, a state credit reporting act statutory claim will raise fewer preliminary issues as long as specific FCRA preemptions do not apply. But, as examined at § 10.7, *infra*, the FCRA preempts a number of state laws, and the range of this preemption is still quite unclear. Moreover, the state claim may not make sense if it exactly mirrors the federal statute, unless the consumer wants to stay in state court, or unless there is some other specific reason to bring the state law claim. If the consumer wants to stay in state court, another approach is to bring a state deceptive acts challenge based on the fact that it is a deceptive practice to violate the federal FCRA.[7] Less common will be federal claims not based on the FCRA. Nevertheless, § 10.3, *infra*, reviews potential federal claims in lieu of or in addition to a federal FCRA claim.

10.2 FCRA Claims

10.2.1 General

FCRA claims can be raised in a private action for either willful or negligent non-compliance with the Act,[8] and the two may be pleaded in the alternative.[9] This section focuses on the elements of FCRA claims based on negligent non-compliance. The elements of a claim for willful non-compliance (and punitive damages) are discussed in the next chapter.

Although there is a private right of action for violation of most FCRA requirements, there are a number of provisions that explicitly state that their violation does not lead to a private right of action.[10] But for other FCRA provisions, any "person" who fails to comply regarding a consumer is liable to that consumer.[11] Any "person" includes not only consumer reporting agencies (CRAs), including re-sellers, but also those using information from CRAs, and also those furnishing information to CRAs, including creditors.

To recover damages for an FCRA violation, the consumer must show that the defendant's noncompliance was negli-

---

1 See § 11.2.1, *infra*.
2 See § 11.2.3, *infra*.
3 See § 11.3, *infra*.
4 See § 11.4, *infra*.
5 See § 11.6, *infra*.
6 See § 11.7, *infra*.

7 State v. TRW, Clearinghouse No. 49,967 (D. Vt. 1991).
8 15 U.S.C. §§ 1681n, 1681o.
9 Stevenson v. Employers Mut. Ass'n, 960 F. Supp. 141 (N.D. Ill. 1997).
10 See, e.g., § 10.2.4, *infra*.
11 15 U.S.C. §§ 1681, 1681n, 1681o, as amended by Pub. L. No. 104-208 § 2412, 110 Stat. 3009 (Sept. 30, 1996, generally effective Sept. 30, 1997).

gent.[12] Congress explicitly rejected a gross negligence standard.[13] The *Restatement (Second) of Torts* defines negligence as "conduct which falls below the standard established by law for the protection of others against unreasonable risk of harm."[14] This would indicate that any violation of the FCRA is negligent, because it is a standard established by law.

Nevertheless, some courts view the FCRA's phrase "negligent failure" as a reflection that Congress intended not to impose a duty of strict liability whereby a person would be automatically liable for any innocent, unintentional "slip-up not attributable to lack of due care."[15] As a result, it will be prudent for the consumer to show that the violation was more than an isolated, innocent, unintentional error.

Whether a defendant is negligent may depend on applicable standards in the consumer reporting industry. Even so, the industry standards as to normal practices may themselves fall below a reasonable standard of care.[16] If the industry practice is not facially inadequate, plaintiffs may need an expert witness as to the standard of care.[17]

10.2.2 FCRA Claims Against Reporting Agencies

10.2.2.1 Claims Relating to Inaccurate Reports

10.2.2.1.1 General

The FCRA does not require that all consumer reports be accurate,[18] but instead requires that CRAs follow reasonable procedures to ensure maximum possible accuracy of information in a consumer report.[19] To prove negligent noncompliance with this requirement, the consumer must show by a preponderance of evidence that:

- The defendant failed to follow procedures to ensure maximum possible accuracy;[20]
- The consumer report in fact contained an inaccurate entry;[21]
- The consumer suffered injury; and
- The injury was caused, in part, by the inaccuracy.[22]

The consumer can recover even if the consumer did not first provide notice of the inaccuracy to the CRA.[23] The FCRA does not define accuracy.[24]

10.2.2.1.2 Reasonable procedures

The consumer must first show that the CRA was negligent in failing to "follow reasonable procedures to assure the maximum possible accuracy" of the reported information.[25] Whether procedures are adequate and reasonable under the FCRA is for a jury to decide.[26]

Where procedures that should be in place are not in place, the consumer litigant will have little difficulty establishing a violation. For example, a CRA is negligent where it has no procedure to verify the fact that the individual about whom

---

12 15 U.S.C. § 1681*o*.
13 Note, *Judicial Construction of the Fair Credit Reporting Act: Scope and Civil Liability*, 76 Colo. L. Rev. 458, 503 (1976). Gross negligence may be said to occur when the cost of taking precautions, which have not been taken, is substantially less than the benefits of the precautions. Simple negligence may be said to occur when the cost of taking precautions, which have not been taken, is less than their benefits.
14 Restatement (Second) of Torts § 282 (1965).
15 Thomas v. Trans Union, L.L.C., 197 F. Supp. 2d 1233 (D. Or. 2002) (FCRA is not a strict liability law). *See also* Dalton v. Capital Associated Ind., Inc., 257 F.3d 409, 417 (4th Cir. 2001); Guimond v. Trans Union Credit Inf. Co., 45 F.3d 1329, 1333 (9th Cir. 1995); Olwell v. Medical Info. Bureau, 2003 WL 79035 (D. Minn. Jan. 7, 2003); Curtis v. Trans Union, L.L.C., 2002 WL 31748838 (N.D. Ill. Dec. 9, 2002); Rasor v. Retail Credit Co., 87 Wash. 2d 516, 554 P.2d 1041, 1048 (1976), *rehearing denied* (Dec. 2, 1976); Note, *Panacea or Placebo? Actions for Negligent Noncompliance Under the Fair Credit Reporting Act*, 47 S. Cal. L. Rev. 1070, 1110 (1974).
16 Beard v. Goodyear Tire & Rubber Co., 587 A.2d 195 (D.C. Ct. App. 1991) (a merchant's evidence of conformity to industry practice is not conclusive and cannot set the standard of conduct; the case involved standards for approval of credit card applications and detection of fraudulent applications, not FCRA).
17 *Id.*
18 One approach to seeking strict liability for any inaccurate report is for the consumer to bring a breach of contract action against the CRA, based on the consumer being a third party beneficiary of the user's contract with the CRA. Such an action was dismissed in Lazar v. Trans Union, L.L.C., 195 F.R.D. 665, 674 (C.D. Cal. 2000).
19 15 U.S.C. § 1681e(b).
20 *See* Ch. 4, *supra*.
21 *See id.*
22 Philbin v. Trans Union Corp., 101 F.3d 957 (3d Cir. 1996); Zala v. Trans Union, L.L.C., 2001 U.S. Dist. LEXIS 549 (N.D. Tex. Jan. 17, 2001); Lang v. Trans Union Corp., 1999 U.S. Dist. LEXIS 18584 (W.D. Pa. July 16, 1999). *See also* Crabill v. Trans Union, L.L.C., 259 F.3d 662, 664–665 (7th Cir. 2001) (granting summary judgment to defendant CRA on grounds that plaintiff failed to show that the credit denial he had suffered was due to the inaccurate information in the report).
23 O'Connor v. Trans Union Corp., 1999 U.S. Dist. LEXIS 14917 (E.D. Pa. Sept. 28, 1999); Lang v. Trans Union Corp., 1999 U.S. Dist. LEXIS 18584 (W.D. Pa. July 16, 1999).
24 *See* Ch. 4, *supra*.
25 15 U.S.C. §§ 1681e(b), 1681*o*. *See* Ch. 4, *supra*. As discussed below, causes of action relating to inaccurate reports may arise from negligent acts other than the failure to follow reasonable procedures to ensure maximum accuracy. For example, there is no "reasonable procedures" defense where CRAs fail to re-verify adverse information in subsequent investigative reports. *See* § 10.2.2.2, *infra*.
26 Crabill v. Trans Union, L.L.C., 259 F.3d 662 (7th Cir. 2001); Dalton v. Capital Associated Industries, Inc., 257 F.3d 409 (4th Cir. 2001); McCauley v. Trans Union, L.L.C., 2003 WL 22845741 (S.D.N.Y. Nov. 26, 2003); Acton v. Bank One Corp., 293 F. Supp. 2d 1092 (D. Ariz. 2003).

it receives unfavorable information is the same person about whom it is preparing a report.[27] Where the CRA itself has a procedure requiring verification of unfavorable information by at least one other source, failure to verify is negligent misconduct.[28] Whether procedures are reasonable may be judged by what a reasonably prudent person would do under the circumstances.[29]

Although most FCRA provisions require an entity to "maintain" reasonable procedures, the FCRA section regarding "maximum possible accuracy" requires the CRA to "follow" such reasonable procedures.[30] "Follow" implies a double requirement, that the CRA have reasonable procedures in place, and that the CRA actually follow those procedures. The CRA should be liable if it maintains reasonable procedures, but its employees do not follow them.[31]

The FCRA requirement also states that the procedures should "assure" maximum possible accuracy. The *Webster's Dictionary* definition of "assure" is, among others, "to make safe," "to insure," "to make certain."[32] Procedures do not make accuracy certain if they are followed sometimes and not others. CRAs must institute additional procedures to ensure that the basic procedures are consistently followed.

Special procedures should be instituted to ensure that deleted inaccurate information is not reinserted into the consumer's file. Such reinsertion will face greater scrutiny than the original inaccuracy, because it is reasonable for a CRA to follow procedures that make especially certain that such incorrect information does not reappear.

Nevertheless, the FCRA standard is that a CRA must be found to be *negligent* in failing to follow procedures. One instance of a trusted employee's failure to follow procedures because of an unavoidable accident, which is unique in that employee's ten years of preparing reports, is unlikely to be viewed as negligence on the part of the CRA. The consumer must show that the lapse was not an isolated instance, in other words, that the inaccuracy could happen again.

Consumers will often want to establish that a CRA violated the reasonable procedures standard when the CRA furnishes a report that mixes in, or mismerges, information about another consumer. However, the Seventh Circuit has found that such mismerging may be justified, reasoning that it is more important to over-include information that may, but may not, refer to the subject consumer, than to omit an item that was intended to be tagged to that consumer but, because of data miscollection, was not.[33] The court appeared to misread the language of the statute to require only that the CRA have reasonable procedures to "avoid inaccuracy," where in fact the CRA must have procedures to "assure maximum possible accuracy."[34]

Information as to a defendant's procedures and whether the CRA followed them is, of course, exclusively within the defendant's knowledge and control. The consumer, however, must show at least an inaccuracy in order to shift the burden to the defendant, who will then have to show what procedures it followed.[35] A minority of courts require a plaintiff to show more than a mere inaccuracy at this stage of the proceedings.[36] For those courts, indirect evidence can allow a fact-finder to infer absence of reasonable procedures, such as inconsistencies between two reports.[37]

10.2.2.1.3 The report must in fact be inaccurate

While the FCRA standard is that CRA's must follow reasonable procedures to ensure accuracy, courts usually require consumers to prove not only that a CRA failed to follow such procedures, but that the report was in fact

---

27 Dalton v. Capital Associated Industries, Inc., 257 F.3d 409 (4th Cir. 2001) (a CRA's failure to have procedures to investigate the accuracy of subvendors on appropriate sources for reliable information could cause a reasonable jury to conclude that the CRA was negligent); Miller v. Credit Bureau, [1969–1973 Decisions Transfer Binder] Consumer Cred. Guide (CCH) ¶ 99,173 (D.C. Super. Ct. 1973).

28 Millstone v. O'Hanlon Reports, Inc., 383 F. Supp. 269 (E.D. Mo. 1974).

29 See Ch. 4, *supra*.

30 15 U.S.C. § 1681e(b).

31 King v. Credit Bureau, Inc. of Georgia, [Decisions Transfer Binder] Consumer Cred. Guide (CCH) ¶ 98,635 (D.D.C. 1975).

32 Webster's Seventh New Collegiate Dictionary 54 (1969).

33 Crabill v. Trans Union, L.L.C., 259 F.3d 662–663 (7th Cir. 2001). The court agreed with Trans Union that it would be useful for creditors to have all the information and use their own judgment about whether the information referred to two different people. *Id.* at 663. However, the court also found that once the CRA was notified that it was mismerging the information, it might not be reasonable for the CRA to continue to supply information about both consumers in response to an inquiry about just one and, in such a case, summary judgment would not be appropriate. *Id.* at 664. According to one CRA's website, reasons for the over-inclusion of information include creditors failing to give all the identifying information when submitting a report on an account, consumers giving incorrect information or using different names on different accounts, and typographical errors made by those setting up the account. *See* www.experian.com/corporate/max/max0901097.htm.

34 15 U.S.C. § 1681e(b); 259 F.3d 662–663 (7th Cir. 2001). *See also* Ch. 4, *supra*.

35 Philbin v. Trans Union Corp., 101 F.3d 957 (3d Cir. 1996) (analogizing to the tort theory of *res ipsa loquitur*); Lendino v. Trans Union Credit Info. Co., 970 F.2d 1110, 1111–1112 (2d Cir. 1992); Thomas v. Gulf Coast Credit Serv., Inc., 214 F. Supp. 2d 1228 (M.D. Ala. 2002); O'Connor v. Trans Union Corp., 1999 U.S. Dist. LEXIS 14917 (E.D. Pa. Sept. 28, 1999).

36 Crabill v. Trans Union L.L.C., 259 F.3d 662 (7th Cir. 2001); Stewart v. Credit Bureau, Inc., 734 F.2d 47 (D.C. Cir. 1984).

37 Philbin v. Trans Union Corp., 101 F.3d 957 (3d Cir. 1996). It is important for the consumer to request the "audit trail" in discovery to see what the creditor actually received. Often, the CRA will send a consumer a report different from what the creditor received. This is because the CRA asks the consumer for a great deal more identifying information than it asks the creditor to provide, so that what it sends the consumer will be more precisely tailored than what the creditor received.

inaccurate.[38] This extra hurdle is not found in the statute, and stems from a judicial aversion to hearing complaints where the report was in fact accurate. Nonetheless, since showing a report is inaccurate is not part of the statutory provision, the consumer need not show that the inaccuracy in the particular report arose from negligence, only that there was an inaccuracy, and that the CRA was negligent in failing to follow reasonable procedures to prevent that or other inaccuracies.

10.2.2.1.4 Injury and causation

Courts also require that the inaccuracy injure the consumer, although courts differ on whether the consumer must prove a denial of credit in order to satisfy the element.[39] All courts agree that emotional distress is one of the components of damages.[40]

Causation, the link between the inaccuracy and the injury, may be based on inference.[41] It is enough that a reasonable fact-finder could infer that the inaccurate entry was a "substantial factor" in the denial.[42] But where the CRA shows that the inaccurate entry was not the basis for a credit denial, for instance by affidavit of the creditor, the consumer's proof requirements become that much greater.[43]

10.2.2.1.5 Relation of claim to one based on the failure to reinvestigate

Where difficulties arise in showing that the CRA was negligent in failing to follow reasonable procedures to ensure maximum accuracy, a better approach may be to show that the CRA was negligent in failing to correct the report after the inaccuracy was brought to the CRA's attention. The FCRA specifies in detail requirements on handling consumer disputes of inaccurate or incomplete information.[44] As described in § 10.2.2.2, *infra*, negligent noncompliance with these procedures violates the Act irrespective of CRA procedures to prevent the inaccuracy from first occurring. Of course, this FCRA claim is applicable only if the consumer disputed the report with the CRA, the CRA did not properly respond, and this improper response (as opposed to the initial inaccuracy) damaged the consumer.

In addition, even where the claim is based upon the failure to follow reasonable procedures in the initial receipt of the information, it is helpful to also point out the CRA's failure to properly reinvestigate. Damage awards are likely to be greatest where the consumer has made repeated vain attempts to correct a report.

10.2.2.2 Claims for Failure to Properly Handle Consumer Disputes, Reinvestigations

The FCRA establishes procedures in case of disputed accuracy of a report.[45] The dispute resolution process has several statutorily required steps, including reinvestigation, correction, or deletion of inaccurate or unverifiable information, notification of the results of reinvestigation, and notification when information has been reinserted into a consumer's file. Unless the consumer is notified that the CRA has deemed the dispute frivolous, the investigation at the very least must involve the creditor or other person who furnished the information to the CRA in the first place.[46]

Negligent or willful failure to follow those procedures is actionable.[47] Even if inaccurate information in a report was not initially actionable because the CRA had followed reasonable procedures, the CRA's failure to properly handle a consumer's dispute concerning that information provides a separate cause of action for the consumer. Of course, in that case the consumer can only obtain damages flowing from the CRA's subsequent failure to correct the information, and not from the CRA's initial publication of the inaccurate information. Moreover, the consumer must have properly disputed the information to trigger operation of these procedures.[48]

---

38 *See* Ch. 4, *supra*.
39 *Compare* Cassella v. Equifax Credit Info. Servs., 56 F.3d 469 (2d Cir. 1995) *with* Guimond v. Trans Union Credit Info. Co., 45 F.3d 1329 (9th Cir. 1995). *See also* § 11.10.2, *infra*.
40 *See* § 11.10.2.3, *infra*.
41 Philbin v. Trans Union Corp., 101 F.3d 957, 968 (3d Cir. 1996); Sampson v. Equifax Info. Servs., L.L.C., 2005 WL 2095092, at *4 (S.D. Ga. Aug. 29, 2005). *But see* Valvo v. Trans Union L.L.C., 2005 WL 3618272, at *5 (D.R.I. Oct. 27, 2005) (granting summary judgment to the CRA where the plaintiff did not establish the reasons for the credit denials or link the denials to the reports issued by the CRA).
42 Philbin v. Trans Union Corp., 101 F.3d 957 (3d Cir. 1996) (and cases cited therein); Soghomonian v. U.S., 278 F. Supp. 2d 1151 (E.D. Cal. 2003); Frost v. Experian, 1999 U.S. Dist. LEXIS 6783 (S.D.N.Y. May 6, 1999); O'Connor v. Trans Union Corp., 1999 U.S. Dist. LEXIS 14917 (E.D. Pa. Sept. 28, 1999); Lang v. Trans Union Corp., 1999 U.S. Dist. LEXIS 18584 (W.D. Pa. July 16, 1999) (granting summary judgment to the defendant where the inaccurate item was just one of several derogatory entries and therefore was not a substantial factor in credit denials).
43 *E.g.*, Cahlin v. General Motors Acceptance Corp., 936 F.2d 1151 (11th Cir. 1991); Heupel v. Trans Union, L.L.C., 193 F. Supp. 2d 1234 (N.D. Ala. 2002); Zala v. Trans Union, L.L.C., 2001 U.S. Dist. LEXIS 549 (N.D. Tex. Jan. 17, 2001). Unfortunately, this result may encourage collusion between the CRA and its creditor-subscriber.

44 *See* Ch. 4, *supra*.
45 15 U.S.C. § 1681i. *See* Ch. 4, *supra*.
46 *See* Ch. 4, *supra*.
47 15 U.S.C. §§ 1681n, 1681o. Note however that one court held that a CRA is not liable for inadequate reinvestigation if the disputed information was in fact accurate. Batdorf v. Equifax, 949 F. Supp. 777 (D. Haw. 1996).
48 *See* Ruffin-Thompkins v. Experian Info. Solutions, Inc., 422 F.3d 603, 608–609 (7th Cir. 2005) (affirming summary judgment for the CRA where the plaintiff failed to establish damages suffered during the CRA's period of liability, which did not start

To establish a right of relief under the reinvestigation section, the consumer must demonstrate the following elements:

- The consumer disputed the completeness or accuracy of an item of information contained in the consumer's file and notified the CRA directly of that dispute;
- The CRA either
  - reinvestigated but failed to record in the file the current status of the dispute or
  - did not reinvestigate and failed to properly delete the item from the file;
- The noncompliance was negligent;
- The consumer suffered injury; and
- The consumer's injury was caused by the CRA's failure to properly reinvestigate.[49]

These dispute and reinvestigation procedures present bright-line obligations for CRAs. The maintenance of reasonable procedures is not a defense to a failure to fulfill these obligations. Nor should it be difficult to show that failure to fulfill these specific obligations was negligent in most cases.[50] Nevertheless, issues will arise as to negligence. For example, is a CRA negligent if it believes (incorrectly) that it has reasonable grounds for treating a dispute as frivolous? Has the degree of diligence in the reinvestigation inquiry been sufficient? How much reliance may the CRA continue to place on the party who furnished the disputed information? While the total failure to follow prescribed reinvestigation procedures is almost certainly negligent, or willful, the actual practice can raise serious, triable questions of reasonableness.[51]

10.2.2.3 Claims Relating to Obsolete Reports

CRAs can violate the FCRA by issuing obsolete reports in two different ways. First, the CRA is liable under section 1681c if it is negligent in making any consumer report that contains any obsolete information.[52] Second, the CRA is liable under section 1681e(a) if it is negligent in maintaining reasonable procedures designed to avoid reporting of obsolete information.[53]

Thus, consumers can bring actions based on reporting of obsolete information whether or not a CRA's procedures are reasonable, as long as the CRA is negligent in reporting the information. If the consumer cannot prove negligence in reporting the obsolete information, the consumer instead can show negligence in failing to maintain reasonable procedures.

This distinction is largely academic, because in most cases, the two claims should involve the same proof. Nonetheless, occasionally a consumer can show that a CRA negligently provided an obsolete report, but will not want to become enmeshed in a CRA's general procedures for preventing the reporting of obsolete information. There may also be situations where a consumer cannot show that the reporting of obsolete information on that person was willful, so cannot meet the punitive damages standard through that avenue, but can show that the CRA intentionally failed to maintain proper procedures in general, and that failure should trigger punitive damages.[54]

There is also no merit to CRA claims, when reporting obsolete information, that reasonable procedures are a defense. The defense instead is that the CRA was not negligent. The FCRA, when it wants a CRA's reasonable procedures to serve as a defense, explicitly so provides.[55] In the case of obsolete information, maintaining reasonable procedures is a defense to an attack on the CRA's procedures relating to obsolete information, not on a claim based on the CRA's negligent reporting of obsolete information.

10.2.2.4 Claims Relating to Consumer Reporting Agencies Furnishing Reports for Impermissible Purposes

FCRA liability concerning the providing of reports for impermissible purposes is very similar to liability concerning providing obsolete reports.[56] The Act establishes CRA liability under two different provisions. First, the CRA is liable if it is negligent in providing any consumer report in any circumstance other than the circumstances explicitly

---

until she notified the CRA of her dispute); Caltabiano v. BSB Bank & Trust Co., 387 F. Supp. 2d 135, 140 (E.D.N.Y. 2005) (granting summary judgment to CRAs where the plaintiff's asserted damages were incurred prior to his notifying the CRAs of his dispute).

49 Zala v. Trans Union, L.L.C., 2001 U.S. Dist. LEXIS 549 (N.D. Tex. Jan. 17, 2001). *See also* Bagby v. Experian Info. Solutions, Inc., 162 Fed. Appx. 600, 604 (7th Cir. 2006) (dismissing the plaintiff's claim where she could not show she suffered a denial of credit or other pecuniary damages based on the CRA's failure to properly reinvestigate her disputes).

50 Cousin v. Trans Union Corp., 246 F.3d 359 (5th Cir. 2001) (allowing inaccurate information back into a consumer report after deleting it because of its inaccuracy is negligent); Pinner v. Schmidt, 805 F.2d 1258 (5th Cir. 1986) (CRA negligent for not reverifying disputed consumer debt beyond contacting manager of creditor); Silver v. Credit Bureau of Greater Kansas City, Inc., 816 S.W.2d 23 (Mo. Ct. App. 1991) (directed verdict where CRA failed to add consumer's statement of dispute to file).

51 McKeown v. Sears Roebuck & Co., 335 F. Supp. 2d 917 (W.D. Wis. 2004). *See* Ch. 4, *supra*.

52 15 U.S.C. §§ 1681c, 1681o. *See* § 5.2, *supra*.
53 15 U.S.C. §§ 1681e(a), 1681o. *See* § 5.2.5, *supra*.
54 See § 5.2.5.1, *supra*, for further discussion of this issue.
55 *See, e.g.*, 15 U.S.C. § 1681m(c).
56 *See* § 10.2.2.3, *supra*.

permitted in the statute.⁵⁷ Second, the CRA is liable if it is negligent in maintaining reasonable procedures designed to avoid such reporting.⁵⁸

In other words, just as with obsolete information, a consumer can sue when a CRA provides a report for impermissible purposes, whether or not the CRA's procedures are reasonable, as long as the CRA was negligent in providing the information. Some courts suggest that if the CRA has reason to believe the requestor has a permissible purpose to use the report, the CRA is not negligent, even if the user ends up putting the report to an improper use.⁵⁹ In such circumstances, if the consumer cannot prove the CRA's negligence in the provision of the specific information, the consumer instead can try to show that the CRA was negligent in its efforts to maintain reasonable procedures.

The Act clarifies what those reasonable procedures are. To meet the standard for permissible purposes, the CRA must maintain procedures to require that prospective users identify themselves, certify the purpose for which the information is sought, and promise that the information will be used for no other purpose.⁶⁰ A CRA's failure to maintain all specified procedures should clearly suffice to show negligent noncompliance with the requirements for permissible purposes, even if the consumer cannot prove negligence in providing the report to a particular user. Intentional failure to comply with the specified procedures may also support a punitive damages claim, even if the CRA did not intend to provide the report for an impermissible purpose.

Nevertheless, the consumer should still prove that the CRA in fact provided the report for an impermissible purpose, even if the consumer proves that it was negligent in its procedures. As with the accuracy standards,⁶¹ courts may not be impressed with cases where faulty procedures nonetheless produced correct results.⁶²

A history of reports given to users without permissible purposes can be a key factor in proving that a CRA has not maintained reasonable procedures. What is reasonable depends in part on patterns and practices of abuse by particular users or groups of users. When a CRA has reason to doubt a user's compliance, it must take additional steps to ensure compliance or to deny the user access to reports altogether.⁶³ For example, when Vermont found that Equifax was failing to reasonably ensure that users obtained prior consumer consent to access consumer reports, as required by Vermont law, Equifax agreed to require audits of user practices and to terminate users who failed to promise to follow new prophylactic procedures imposed by Equifax.⁶⁴ Evidence of prior abuse by a particular user, or widespread abuse in a particular industry such as car dealers, is relevant to the reasonableness of CRA procedures to avoid the provision and use of consumer reports for impermissible purposes.

On the other hand, even if a CRA maintains all the procedures specified in the statute, the consumer still has a valid claim if the CRA was negligent in providing a particular report on the consumer for an impermissible use. "Reasonable procedures" is not a defense to a consumer's action for negligent provision of a report—the CRA can only defend itself on the ground that it was not negligent. The FCRA, when it wants reasonable procedures to act as a defense, explicitly so provides.⁶⁵ In the case of reports provided without permissible purposes, maintaining reasonable procedures is a defense to an attack on the CRA's procedures relating to permissible purposes, not on a claim based on the CRA's negligent reporting of information without a permissible purpose.

10.2.2.5 Claims Relating to Medical Information Reported Without Consumer Consent

The FCRA has strict rules about a CRA releasing medical information to a user without the consumer's consent, as

---

57 *See* 15 U.S.C. §§ 1681, 1681b(a). The Consumer Credit Reporting Reform Act of 1996 added two permissible purposes to the FCRA's original seven: A CRA may furnish a consumer report to a person who the CRA has reason to believe (1) intends to use the information, as a potential investor or servicer, or current insurer, in connection with a valuation of, or an assessment of the credit or prepayment risks associated with, an existing credit obligation, or (2) has a legitimate business need for the information to review an account to determine whether the consumer continues to meet the terms of the account. Pub. L. No. 104-208, § 2403, 110 Stat. 3009 (Sept. 30, 1996). *See also* § 10.2.2.3, *supra*.

58 15 U.S.C. §§ 1681e(a), 1681o. *See* Ch. 7, *supra*.

59 Andrews v. TRW Inc., 225 F.3d 1063 (9th Cir. 2000), *cert. granted*, 532 U.S. 902 (2001), *rev'd and remanded*, 534 U.S. 19 (2001), *on remand, aff'd without op.*, 275 F.3d 893 (9th Cir. 2001), *modified, aff'd in part, rev'd in part*, 289 F.3d 600 (9th Cir. 2002); Spence v. TRW, 92 F.2d 380, 382 (6th Cir. 1996) (dicta); Greenhouse v. TRW, Inc., 1998 U.S. Dist. LEXIS 1973 (E.D. La. Feb. 12, 1998); King v. MTA Bridges & Tunnels, 933 F. Supp. 220 (E.D.N.Y. 1996); Dobson v. Holloway, 828 F. Supp. 975, 977 (M.D. Ga. 1993); Zeller v. Samia, 758 F. Supp. 775 (D. Mass. 1991); Klapper v. Shapiro, 586 N.Y.S.2d 846 (N.Y. Sup. Ct. 1992).

60 15 U.S.C. § 1681e(a). *See* Levine v. World Fin. Network Nat'l Bank, 437 F.3d 1118, 1125 (11th Cir. 2006) (holding that the plaintiff stated claims for both negligent and willful violations of section 1681e(a) where the CRA provided a report to a creditor after the plaintiff had closed his account); § 7.5, *supra*.

61 *See* Ch. 4, *supra*.

62 Washington v. CSC Credit Servs., 199 F.3d 263 (5th Cir. 2000) (holding that employer's disclosure is required before the question of reasonable procedures can be reached); Middlebrooks v. Retail Credit Co., 416 F. Supp. 1013 (N.D. Ga. 1976). *See also* Wright v. TRW Credit Data, 588 F. Supp. 112 (S.D. Fla. 1984); Todd v. Associated Credit Bureau Servs., Inc., 451 F. Supp. 447 (E.D. Pa. 1977); Peller v. Retail Credit Co., 359 F. Supp. 1235 (N.D. Ga. 1973), *aff'd*, 505 F.2d 733 (5th Cir. 1974).

63 *Cf.* FTC Official Staff Commentary § 607 item 2, *reprinted at* Appx. D, *infra*.

64 The Vermont consent decree with Equifax is reprinted on the companion CD-Rom.

65 *See, e.g.*, 15 U.S.C. § 1681m(c). *See also* Note, *The Consumer Guide to Litigatory Remedies Under the Fair Credit Reporting Act*, 8 Val. L. Rev. 377, 385 (1974).

detailed at § 5.4.1, *supra*, and a consumer has a cause of action against a CRA that negligently fails to follow those rules. There is no "reasonable procedures" defense to the improper furnishing of medical information without the required consumer consent. If medical information is released without proper consent, it should create a prima facie case, or at least a rebuttable presumption, of negligence.

10.2.2.6 Claims Relating to Investigative Reports

A CRA may not prepare or furnish an investigative report unless it has received a proper certification from the person requesting the report.[66] The CRA also has additional obligations to reverify negative information in an investigative report, and it may not prepare a report for employment purposes if the making of investigative inquiries by an employer would violate any federal or state equal employment opportunity law.

A CRA's negligent failure to comply with these requirements is actionable. The FCRA provides no "reasonable procedures" defense for the CRA. For example, a CRA will normally be liable to the consumer when a report is provided without the proper certifications required from an employer.[67] The only defense for the failure to obtain certification is that the CRA's conduct was not negligent.

10.2.2.7 Claims Relating to Adverse Public Record Information for Employment Purposes

A CRA must either notify the consumer that adverse public record information is being reported for employment purposes or must maintain strict procedures to ensure that the information is complete and up to date.[68] The CRA can defend against an allegation that it failed to send a notice by alleging that the CRA had instituted strict procedures, and vice versa. The consumer will have to allege that the CRA complied with neither option, and was negligent in that failure. "Strict procedures" appears to be a more stringent requirement than reasonable procedures, so it should be easier to show that a CRA's failure in procedures was negligent.

10.2.2.8 Claims for Failure to Disclose the Content of a Consumer's File

The FCRA requires that CRAs disclose the contents of the consumer's file to the consumer under specified conditions, and in specified ways.[69] Negligent failure to comply with these requirements is actionable. The Act does not mention reasonable procedures as either a substantive requirement or as a defense. Accordingly, the only possible defense to failure to act as required is that the CRA's conduct was not negligent.

10.2.3 Claims Against Resellers

A growing industry of information brokers, "superbureaus," and others buy information from CRAs for resale to various end-users, including detective agencies, attorneys, and mortgage lenders. Most typically, these agencies merely purchase information from the three major nationwide CRAs and recompile it for an end-user, often providing a credit rating or score.

These resellers are CRAs, and are subject to all of the restrictions and mandates that the FCRA places on CRAs.[70] Resellers must also meet additional requirements, which focus on their role as a conduit of consumer reporting information, requiring a reseller to establish and comply with reasonable procedures to ensure that reports or information within reports are resold only for permissible purposes.[71]

Failure by a reseller to establish reasonable procedures to ensure that reports are resold only for permissible purposes and to previously identified end-users suffices to show negligent noncompliance with the requirements. Even if the reseller has established reasonable procedures, the consumer may still have a valid claim against a reseller who has resold consumer reporting information for an impermissible purpose or to an end-user who was not properly identified to the original CRA. In addition, the reseller, like any CRA, is liable for negligently furnishing a consumer report to a user without a permissible purpose; there is no separate requirement for reasonable procedures.[72] A reseller may also be liable for negligently failing to maintain or comply with its own procedures. Resellers now have an explicit, though limited, obligation to reinvestigate a dispute.[73]

---

66 15 U.S.C. § 1681d.
67 Obabueki v. Int'l Bus. Machs. Corp., 2001 U.S. Dist. LEXIS 4092 (S.D.N.Y. Mar. 30, 2001) (the CRA, not the employer, was held liable), *aff'd*, 319 F.3d 87 (2d Cir. 2003).
68 15 U.S.C. § 1681k. *See* Ch. 4, § 8.2.6.4.4, *supra*.
69 15 U.S.C. §§ 1681g, 1681h. *See* §§ 3.3, 3.4, *supra*.
70 While resellers fit the definition of a CRA, at least one court has ruled that the 1996 amendment applicable to resellers, 15 U.S.C. § 1681e(e), is the only provision with which they must comply. Lewis v. Ohio Prof'l Elec. Network L.L.C., 248 F. Supp. 2d 693 (S.D. Ohio 2003). However, now that the FACTA amendments at 15 U.S.C. § 1681a(u) specifically designates resellers as CRAs, courts should impose liability on resellers for failing to abide by general CRA responsibilities. *See* Poore v. Sterling Testing Sys., Inc., 410 F. Supp. 2d 557, 567 (E.D. Ky. 2006) (noting new definition and disapproving of *Lewis*).
71 *See* § 7.1.4, *supra*.
72 *See* § 10.2.2.4, *supra*.
73 15 U.S.C. § 1681i(f).

10.2.4 FCRA Claims Against Creditors and Others Furnishing Information to Consumer Reporting Agencies

10.2.4.1 Private FCRA Right of Action Not Available for Many Furnisher Violations

Creditors, and others who furnish information to CRAs are subject to a number of FCRA requirements placed on such furnishers,[74] but the FCRA explicitly states that there is no private right of action for many of these requirements.[75] There is no private right of action, for example, related to the obligation of furnishers:

- To refrain from furnishing information about a consumer to a CRA if the furnisher knows or has reason to believe that the information is inaccurate;[76]
- Not to furnish information if the furnisher has been notified by a consumer that the information is inaccurate and is in fact inaccurate;[77]
- To reinvestigate the accuracy of information upon consumer's notice that the information is inaccurate;[78]
- To correct and update information;[79]
- To notify a CRA that a consumer has disputed the furnished information;[80]
- To notify a CRA that a consumer has voluntarily closed an account;[81]
- To comply with date delinquency provisions when furnishing account delinquency information;[82]
- To put in place reasonable procedures for responding to a CRA's notice that the CRA has blocked furnished information on the grounds that it was the result of fraud or identity theft;[83]
- Who are financial institutions to notify customers that the institution has furnished negative information about the customer to a nationwide CRA;[84] and
- To notify a CRA of the furnisher's status as one furnishing medical information.[85]

In short, furnishers are not liable under the FCRA for inaccuracies in the initial information they furnish, and are not even liable for their misconduct where the consumer contacts the furnisher to dispute information or seeks a reinvestigation from the furnisher.

Creditor and other furnisher liability is further diminished by two additional FCRA provisions. One provides that no state law may impose any responsibility or prohibition with respect to the subject matter of section 1681s-2, relating to the obligations of persons who furnish information to CRAs.[86] The other relates to a qualified immunity that parties have from certain tort claims. The extent to which these two provisions do or do not protect creditors is examined at §§ 10.4 and 10.7, *infra*.

Nevertheless, as discussed in the next subsection, there is an FCRA private right of action to sue creditors and other furnishers who fail to properly participate in any CRA reinvestigation concerning the accuracy or completeness of information they supplied to the CRA, including steps to correct erroneous information. This private right of action is only triggered where a CRA asks the furnisher to reinvestigate, and not where a consumer disputes the information directly with the furnisher.[87] If a creditor has provided a CRA with inaccurate information, the consumer should initiate a reinvestigation with the CRA, not just the creditor. Then, if the creditor persists in furnishing the inaccurate information, the consumer can sue the creditor for failing to appropriately reinvestigate and correct the disputed information.

10.2.4.2 Claims Relating to Furnisher's Reinvestigation in Response to a Consumer Reporting Agency Request

Creditors and others who furnish information to CRAs must participate in reinvestigations conducted by the CRAs

---

74 See Ch. 6, *supra*.
75 15 U.S.C. § 1681s-2(c).
76 15 U.S.C. § 1681s-2(a)(1)(A), *amended by* Pub. L. No. 108-159, § 312(b) (2003). See also § 6.4.2, *supra*.
77 15 U.S.C. § 1681s-2(a)(1)(B), *amended by* Pub. L. No. 108-159, § 312(b) (2003).
78 15 U.S.C. § 1681s-2(a)(8), *added by* Pub. L. No. 108-159, § 312(c) (2003). This provision became effective on December 1, 2004. 16 C.F.R. § 602.1(c)(3)(xiv), *added by* 69 Fed. Reg. 6,526–6,531 (Feb. 5, 2004). The obligations will not arise until the identified agencies prescribe regulations that identify circumstances under which a furnisher will be required to reinvestigate a dispute made directly by a consumer. 15 U.S.C. § 1681s-2(a)(8)(C). See also § 6.5, *supra*.
79 15 U.S.C. § 1681s-2(a)(2).
80 15 U.S.C. § 1681s-2(a)(3).
81 15 U.S.C. § 1681s-2(a)(4).
82 15 U.S.C. § 1681s-2(a)(5), *amended by* Pub. L. No. 108-159, § 312(d) (2003). See also § 6.7, *supra*.
83 15 U.S.C. § 1681s-2(a)(6), *added by* Pub. L. No. 108-159, § 154 (2003). This provision became effective on December 1, 2004. 16 C.F.R. § 602.1(c)(3)(vii), *added by* 69 Fed. Reg. 6,526–6,531 (Feb. 5, 2004). See also § 9.2, *supra*.
84 15 U.S.C. § 1681s-2(a)(7), *added by* Pub. L. No. 108-159, § 217 (2003). This provision became effective on December 1, 2004. 16 C.F.R. § 602.1(c)(3)(xii), *added by* 69 Fed. Reg. 6,526–6,531 (Feb. 5, 2004).
85 15 U.S.C. § 1681s-2(a)(9), *added by* Pub. L. No. 108-159, § 412(a) (2003). This provision does not become effective until March 4, 2005. *Id.* See also § 8.3, *supra*.
86 15 U.S.C. § 1681t(b)(1)(F). The statute specifically grandfathers laws of Massachusetts and California regarding duties of furnishers. Cal. Civ. Code § 17.85.25(a) (West) (as in effect on Sept. 30, 1996); Mass. Gen. Laws. ch. 93, § 54A(a) (as in effect on Sept. 30, 1996). See also §§ 10.7, *infra*.
87 15 U.S.C. § 1681s-2(a)(8), *as amended by* Pub. L. No. 108-159, § 312 (2003). This provision became effective on December 1, 2004. 16 C.F.R. § 602.1(c)(3)(xiv), *added by* 69 Fed. Reg. 6,526–6,531 (Feb. 5, 2004).

when consumers dispute the accuracy or completeness of information with the CRA.[88] Specifically, once a furnisher has received notice of a consumer's dispute from a CRA, the furnisher must:

- Conduct an investigation of the dispute;
- Review all relevant information provided by the CRA;
- Report the results of the investigation to the CRA;
- If the information is incomplete or inaccurate, report those results to the other nationwide CRAs to which the furnisher has furnished the information; and
- In the case of inaccurate, incomplete, or unverifiable information, promptly modify, delete, or permanently block the reporting of the information.[89]

Consumers may bring claims for damages against furnishers who fail to comply with these reinvestigation requirements.[90]

Litigation under this section is likely to be substantial until creditors begin to take seriously their obligation to conduct reasonable reinvestigations. Several courts have confirmed that the statute allows consumers to bring a private action for civil damages against furnishers who fail to comply with their reinvestigation obligations.[91] Only one decision, which grows increasingly isolated with each new opinion upholding private actions, has misconstrued the provision as only allowing CRAs—and not consumers—to bring civil actions.[92] Nevertheless, counsel should not assume that the plain language of the Act will automatically prevail, and should carefully explain the importance of private enforcement in the statutory scheme.

To sustain a claim against a furnisher, consumers should allege that they notified the CRA of a dispute,[93] with "all relevant information."[94] Some courts have, perhaps wrongly, held that the consumer must also allege that notice of the dispute was in fact received by the furnisher from the CRA. Thus it would be prudent for the consumer's claim to include this allegation.[95]

Once the furnisher receives notice of the dispute from the CRA, the furnisher must then conduct a timely investigation of the disputed information and review all relevant information provided by the CRA. The furnisher must then report the results of the investigation to the CRA and, if the investigation reveals that the original information is incomplete or inaccurate, the information furnisher must report the results to all other CRAs to which it supplied such information.[96]

Negligence will be apparent where the furnisher makes no attempt to reinvestigate,[97] or fails to report the results to the CRA requesting the reinvestigation and, when required, to other CRAs as well. Moreover, as part of its reinvestigation, the furnishers must review all relevant information provided by the CRA. Failure to telephone or send a facsimile to the CRA, in addition to attempting correction by electronic Automated Consumer Dispute Verification (ACDV), when the consumer continues to dispute an item, may show negligence.[98]

Although the FCRA does not designate specific requirements for the furnisher's reinvestigation, clearly the reinvestigation must be conducted in good faith and not be simply pro forma. A reasonable investigation would require a furnisher to consider and evaluate the specific dispute framed by the consumer, along with other facts and concerns evidenced in the materials provided by the CRA to the furnisher. If differences exist, the furnisher should weigh the differences and make a determination of accuracy.

The furnisher must consider information reasonably available to it. For example, if in addition to a final ledger, the furnisher has other information from or about the consumer which relates to the dispute, the furnisher should consider that information in addition to, say, its final ledger. The purpose of the reinvestigation is not simply to confirm that the CRA has recorded accurately the information initially furnished by the creditor, but also to determine in good faith the accuracy of the information itself in light of all available information.

The reasonableness of a reinvestigation will depend on the circumstances, including the nature of the dispute and available documentation.[99] The allegation that a report is inaccurate, without explanation, will require a different investigation than a consumer complaint that specifies which payment is missing or that the creditor agreed to

---

88 15 U.S.C. § 1681s-2(b). *See also* Ch. 6, *supra*.
89 15 U.S.C. § 1681s-2(b)(1)(A)–(E).
90 *See* Ch. 6, *supra*.
91 *Id.*
92 Carney v. Experian Info. Solutions, Inc., 57 F. Supp. 2d 496 (W.D. Tenn. 1999). Reasoning that a furnisher's duties under this section "appear" to exist solely for the benefit of the CRAs, misreading a case from before this section of the FCRA was enacted, and ignoring the plain language of the Act, the court wrote that an individual cannot state a claim under this section. Even so, all this is arguably dicta because, as noted by the court, the plaintiff failed to allege that the furnisher received any notice from a CRA triggering the requirement to reinvestigate.
93 *See* Ch. 4, *supra*.
94 Varnado v. Trans Union, L.L.C., 2004 WL 1093488 (N.D. Ill. Apr. 29, 2004).
95 Densmore v. Gen. Motors Acceptance Corp., 2003 WL 22220177 (N.D. Ill. Sept. 25, 2003) (court was not aware that the CRAs merely parrot the requirements of the FCRA when describing the procedures used to investigate rather than provide information sufficient to allow a factual allegation of notice to the furnisher); Moline v. Trans Union, L.L.C., 2003 WL 21878728 (N.D. Ill. Aug. 7, 2003).
96 15 U.S.C. § 1681s-2(b)(1) and (2). *See* Ch. 6, *supra*.
97 McKeown v. Sears Roebuck & Co., 335 F. Supp. 2d 917 (W.D. Wis. 2004) (it is improper to delete rather than reinvestigate, since the FCRA protects the credit industry as well as consumers).
98 Evantash v. G.E. Capital Mortg. Serv., Inc., 2003 WL 22844198 (E.D. Pa. Nov. 25, 2003).
99 *See* Ch. 6, *supra*.

§ 10.2.5   *Fair Credit Reporting*

waive a late payment on a specific date.[100] The more specific the dispute, the more likely the creditor will correct it.

Whether a reinvestigation was adequate will be a question for the trier of facts. As with other claims under the FCRA, the best cases include evidence of damages such as a denial of credit, and monetary and emotional harm that resulted from the failure to comply with the FCRA's reinvestigation requirements.[101]

10.2.5 FCRA Claims Against Users of Consumer Reports

10.2.5.1 Claims Against Those Obtaining Reports Without a Permissible Purpose or Under False Pretenses

The FCRA has a number of remedy provisions relating to users who obtain reports without a permissible purpose or under false pretenses. 15 U.S.C. § 1681q provides only criminal penalties against any person who knowingly and willfully obtains information on a consumer from a CRA under false pretenses. At one time, this provisions was important because courts found a private civil action implicit in violation of this criminal standard where other avenues for such relief were not available.[102] This included liability based on the knowing and willful misconduct of a user's employees.[103]

Litigants today can rely on a more direct provision of civil liability. The FCRA prohibits any person from using or obtaining a consumer report unless the report is obtained for a permissible purpose and such purpose is certified by the user in accordance with the Act.[104] Certification includes a promise that the information will be used for no other purpose.[105] A cause of action arises against a person who negligently uses or obtains a consumer report for an impermissible purpose or without the proper certification.[106] A "user" includes the person who actually requests or obtains the report, the person who is the ultimate destination of the report, and one who fraudulently causes a report to be issued (such as an impostor who applies for credit using someone else's personal identifiers).[107]

In order to succeed on a claim of obtaining a report without a permissible purpose against a user or other recipient, the consumer must show: (1) the report was a consumer report;[108] (2) the user obtained the report for use other than a properly certified use;[109] and (3) the consumer suffered

---

100   Malm v. Household Bank (SB), 2004 WL 1559370 (D. Minn. July 7, 2004); Quinn v. Experian Solutions, 2004 WL 609357 (N.D. Ill. Mar. 24, 2004) (customer's statement that the account was "not mine" was too terse to require a full reinvestigation by the furnisher, although "not mine" is one of the check boxes provided by the CRAs on the dispute form they ask consumers to fill out).
101   Bach v. First Union Nat'l Bank, 149 Fed. Appx. 354, 361 (6th Cir. 2005) (affirming award of compensatory damages based on violation of section 1681s-2(b); rejecting furnisher's argument that the plaintiff's testimony as to damages was insufficient to impose liability); Trikas v. Universal Card Servs., Corp., 351 F. Supp. 2d 37 (E.D.N.Y. 2005) (failure to present sufficient evidence of damages resulted in summary judgment).
102   *See* § 7.7, *supra*.
103   Jones v. Federated Fin. Reserve Corp., 144 F.3d 961 (6th Cir. 1998); Northrop v. Hoffman of Simsbury, Inc., 134 F.3d 41, 49 (2d Cir. 1997); Yohay v. City of Alexandria Employees Credit Union, 827 F.2d 967 (4th Cir. 1987); Myers v. Bennett Law Offices, 238 F. Supp. 2d 1196 (D. Nev. 2002); Del Amora v. Metro Ford Sales and Serv., Inc. 206 F. Supp. 2d 947 (N.D. Ill. 2002) (employer liable for rogue employee because of employee's access to computer); *But see* Kodrick v. Ferguson, 54 F. Supp. 2d 788 (N.D. Ill. 1999) (employer not liable for acts of rogue employee).
104   15 U.S.C. § 1681b(f). *See* § 7.7, *supra*.
105   15 U.S.C. § 1681e(a).
106   15 U.S.C. § 1681*o*.
107   Adams v. Phillips, 2002 WL 31886737 (E.D. La. Dec. 19, 2002). If the employer expressly or implicitly authorizes the conduct of the employee, that conduct may be imputed to the employer. An employer may also be liable under the doctrine of respondeat superior. Under the doctrine of apparent authority, an employer is liable for the acts of its employee when the employer gives the employee apparent authority by putting the employee in a position that communicates to third parties that the employee has the authority to request the consumer's report. *See* Jones v. Federated Fin. Reserve Corp., 144 F.3d 961, 965 (6th Cir. 1998) (a principal may be held liable for FCRA violations of its agent under the doctrine of apparent authority); Northrop v. Hoffman of Simsbury, Inc., 134 F.3d 41, 49 (2d Cir. 1997) (automobile dealership could be liable for the actions of its employees in impermissibly acquiring plaintiff's consumer report). *See also* Jaycox v. GC Servs. Ltd. P'ship-Delaware, 2006 WL 2061348, at *1–2 (E.D. Mo. July 26, 2006) (denying the defendant's motion to dismiss claim that was based on apparent authority of the defendant over its employee); § 7.7.5, *supra*.

   In addition, the employees themselves can be liable for their knowing and willful conduct, since the provision applies to "any person," and not just to users. Mone v. Dranow, 945 F.2d 306 (9th Cir. 1991) (chief executive officer acting on behalf of corporation is personally liable for the tort-like act of obtaining consumer report for impermissible purpose); Yohay v. City of Alexandria Employees Credit Union, 827 F.2d 967 (4th Cir. 1987). *But see* Austin v. BankAmerica Serv. Corp., 419 F. Supp. 730 (N.D. Ga. 1974) (mere employers of a user acting within their scope of employment were not themselves users and not subject to the Act; however, as the court found no violation of the Act, the finding regarding user employees may be dicta). Consequently, it was generally better to bring actions involving false pretenses against both the user and its employees involved in the illegal retrieval of the information. Razilov v. Nationwide Mut. Ins. Co., 242 F. Supp. 2d 977 (D. Or. 2003); Ashby v. Farmers Group, Inc., 261 F. Supp. 2d 1213 (D. Or. 2003); Spano v. Safeco Ins. Co., 215 F.R.D. 601 (D. Or. 2003). *But see* Kodrick v. Ferguson, 54 F. Supp. 2d 788 (N.D. Ill. 1999) (employer not liable for acts of rogue employee).
108   Korotki v. Attorney Servs. Corp., 931 F. Supp. 1269 (D. Md. 1996), *aff'd*, 131 F.3d 135 (4th Cir. 1997). *See* § 2.3, *supra*.
109   Edge v. Professional Claims Bureau, Inc., 64 F. Supp. 2d 115 (E.D.N.Y. 1999) (any permissible purpose is a complete defense

damages substantially attributable to the unauthorized access.[110] However, a consumer does not need to show that the user had reason to believe the purpose was impermissible, only that the defendant used a report for an impermissible purpose or even a permissible purpose other than the purpose certified by the user.

Like all FCRA provisions that provide for a private damage action for a negligent violation, a willful violation under section 1681n(1)(A) leads to additional actual damages or at least $100 to $1000 in minimum damages, punitive damages and attorney fees. Where a natural person willfully obtains a consumer report under false pretenses or knowingly without a permissible purpose, such a natural person's minimum liability under section 1681n(1)(B) is the greater of actual damages or $1000 plus punitive damages and attorney fees.

10.2.5.2 Claims Against Users for Failure to Provide Required Notices

The FCRA requires users of consumer reports to provide certain notices to consumers.[111] Among the notices a user must provide are notices of adverse actions based on consumer reports, notices to the consumer prior to employers requesting certain information, and notices relating to medical records, certain information used by affiliates, and government officials' use of information for child support purposes.

Negligent or willful failure to provide such notices is actionable.[112] A user has a defense to such an action "if he shows by a preponderance of the evidence" that at the time of the violation or alleged violation "he maintained reasonable procedures to assure compliance" with the provisions requiring such notice.[113]

In other words, the consumer must show the user was negligent in not complying with the notice requirements. The user would then have to show that, even though negligent, it maintained reasonable procedures to "assure" compliance. In practice, the two steps may become blurred, because an important way to show negligence is to demonstrate that the user did not institute proper procedures. But while the consumer has the burden of showing negligence, the user has the burden of showing that the user instituted reasonable procedures.[114]

However, actions against users for failure to provide required notices now face a new challenge. The Fair and Accurate Credit Transactions Act of 2003 (FACTA) amended the FCRA adding a subsection to the user liability section, 15 U.S.C. § 1681m(h), that requires users to notify consumers when a consumer's report leads the user to offer the consumer credit on materially less favorable terms than the best available to others.[115] The FACTA amendments provided that this new requirement would not be subject to the private cause of action provisions of sections 1681n and 1681o, but rather would be enforced only by public authorities.[116] However, instead of limiting the claims exception to just the new subsection, Congress stated that the liability provisions "shall not apply to any failure by any person to comply with this section."[117]

Many courts have read this language as exempting all obligations under section 1681m, not just the new ones under subsection 1681m(h), from any liability under the Act.[118] However, in the most thorough analysis of the subsection and Congress' intent, the court in *Barnette v. Brook Road, Inc.* held that the use of the word "section"

---

to false pretenses); Korotki v. Attorney Servs. Corp., 931 F. Supp. 1269 (D. Md. 1996), aff'd, 131 F.3d 135 (4th Cir. 1997). See McNamara v. Guazzoni, 1999 U.S. Dist. LEXIS 7373 (S.D.N.Y. May 20, 1999) (where plaintiffs offered no consumer report or other evidence to rebut defendant's denial that a consumer report was obtained, cause of action dismissed); § 2.3.6, *supra*.

110 Korotki v. Attorney Servs. Corp., 931 F. Supp. 1269 (D. Md. 1996), aff'd, 131 F.3d 135 (4th Cir. 1997). See Ch. 11, *infra*.

111 15 U.S.C. §§ 1681d, 1681m. See Ch. 8, *supra*.

112 While a user's failure to provide required notice is actionable, it may not provide a defense to an employer's termination of an employee. Salazar v. Golden State Warriors, 2000 U.S. Dist. LEXIS 2366 (N.D. Cal. Feb. 29, 2000).

113 15 U.S.C. §§ 1681d(c), 1681m(c). See § 7.5, *supra*.

114 *See* Matthews v. Government Employees Ins. Co., 23 F. Supp. 2d 1160 (S.D. Cal. 1998) (reasonable procedure defense was rejected where failure to give notice to non-hired employment applicants was not an isolated instance).

115 15 U.S.C. § 1681m(h)(1).

116 15 U.S.C. § 1681m(h)(8).

117 *Id.*

118 Bonner v. CorTrust Bank, N.A., 2006 WL 1980183, at *3–4 (N.D. Ind. July 12, 2006); Miller v. CoreStar Fin. Group of Pa., Inc., 2006 WL 1876584, *2–3 (E.D. Pa. June 29, 2006); Bruce v. Wells Fargo Bank, N.A., 2006 WL 1195210, at *2 (N.D. Ind. May 2, 2006); Crowder v. PMI Mortg. Ins. Co., 2006 WL 1528608, at *4 (M.D. Ala. May 26, 2006) (rejecting argument that section 1681m(h)(8) should not be applied retroactively); Bonner v. Home123 Corp., 2006 WL 1518974, at *4 (N.D. Ind. May 25, 2006); Bruce v. Grieger's Motor Sales, Inc., 422 F. Supp. 2d 994, 998 (N.D. Ind. 2006); Putkowski v. Irwin Home Equity Corp., 2006 WL 741387, at *8 (N.D. Cal. Mar. 23, 2006); Bonner v. H&R Block Mortg. Corp., 2006 WL 760258, at *3 (N.D. Ind. Mar. 23, 2006); Phillips v. New Century Fin. 2006 WL 517653, at *2–4 (C.D. Cal., Mar. 1, 2006); Harris v. Fletcher Chrysler Prods., Inc., 2006 WL 279030, at *2 (S.D. Ind. Feb. 2, 2006); White v. E-Loan, Inc., 409 F. Supp. 2d 1183, 1184–1187; Killingsworth v. Household Bank (SB), N.A., 2006 WL 250704, at *3 (N.D. Ill. Jan. 31, 2006); Stavroff v. Gurley Leep Dodge, Inc., 2006 WL 196381, at *2–5 (N.D. Ind. Jan. 20, 2006); Villagran v. Freeway Ford, Ltd., 2006 WL 964731 (S.D. Tex. Jan. 19, 2006); Murray v. Cross Country Bank, 399 F. Supp. 2d 843, 844 (N.D. Ill. 2005); Murray v. Household Bank, 386 F. Supp. 2d 993, 997–999 (N.D. Ill. 2005); Hernandez v. Citifinancial Servs., Inc., 2005 WL 3430858, at *6 (N.D. Ill. Dec. 9, 2005); McCane v. America's Credit Jewelers, Inc., 2005 WL 3299371, at *3 (N.D. Ill. Dec. 1, 2005); Phillips v. New Century Fin. Corp., No. SA CV 05-0692, Order at 5 (C.D. Cal. Nov. 9, 2005); Pietras v. Curfin Oldsmobile, Inc., 2005 WL 2897386, at *4 (N.D. Ill. Nov. 1, 2005).

rather than "subsection" was a scrivener's error.[119] The court relied heavily on FACTA § 312(f) which provides that "[n]othing in this section, the amendments made by this section, or any other provision of this Act shall be construed to affect any liability under section 616 or 617 of the Fair Credit Reporting Act (15 U.S.C. 1681n, 1681o) that existed on the day before the date of enactment of this Act."[120] The court reasoned that had Congress intended the nonliability provision to apply to the whole of section 1681m, the logical location for it would be in a new subsection 1681m(i), rather than within 1681m(h)(8).[121] In addition, reading the provision to apply to all of section 1681m would render another FACTA provision, codified at subsection 1681s-2(c)(3), superfluous.[122] Finally, the court pointed out that had Congress intended to eliminate the ability of consumers to enforce a key right of the FCRA, some legislator would have noted it.[123] In any event, the FACTA provision should not apply retroactively to bar claims based on events that took place before the provision's effective date.[124]

10.2.5.3 Claims Against Users for Failing to Comply with Requirements for Investigative Reports

The FCRA prohibits any person from procuring an investigative consumer report without disclosure to the consumer,[125] and a certification to the CRA that it has made this disclosure.[126] Negligent failure to comply with these disclosure and certification requirements is actionable. A user may defend such an action "if he shows by a preponderance of the evidence that at the time of the violation he maintained reasonable procedures to assure compliance" with the requirements.[127] The consumer must therefore show that the user was negligent in not complying with the disclosure and certification requirements and that the user did not maintain reasonable procedures to ensure compliance.

10.2.5.4 Claims Relating to Prescreening Lists

Creditors and insurers may use prescreened lists of potential customers to market their products,[128] but each written prescreened solicitation to the consumer must include a set of disclosures which lets the consumer know that a consumer report has been used, that the consumer can opt out of future prescreened mailings, and applicable criteria relating to the terms of the so-called firm offer which must be extended.[129] The negligent violation of these disclosure requirements, or the misuse of consumer reports used for the prescreening subjects the user to liability under the Act. One court granted summary judgment in the plaintiff's favor on a claim of a willful violation of the firm offer provision where the offer specifically stated that "[a]ll loans subject to approval" and "[r]ates and terms subject to change at any time."[130]

10.3 Other Federal Statutory Claims

A consumer may have recourse under other federal laws against a creditor or debt collector who improperly furnishes information to a consumer reporting agency (CRA). Under the Fair Credit Billing Act, after a creditor has received a notice of a billing error, pending resolution of the claim the creditor may not make or threaten to make an adverse report about the consumer's credit standing or report that an amount or account is delinquent, because the consumer failed to pay the disputed amount or related finance or other charges.[131] Even after the creditor completes its investigation and resolution of the error, if the consumer still disputes the charge, the creditor must not report to a CRA that the account is delinquent unless it also reports that the account is in dispute.[132]

Under the Real Estate Settlement Procedures Act, the consumer can make a qualified written request questioning the amount due on a home mortgage. Then for the next sixty days, the creditor cannot adversely report to a CRA any payment relating to the request.[133]

The Fair Debt Collection Practices Act prohibits a debt collector from communicating or threatening to communicate to any person credit information which is known or which should be known to be false, including the failure to communicate that a disputed debt is disputed.[134] Under the

---

119 429 F. Supp. 2d 741 (E.D. Va. 2006).
120 Pub. L. No. 108-159, § 312(f), 117 Stat. 1952, 1993 (codified as amended at 15 U.S.C. § 1681n, Historical and Statutory Notes (2003)).
121 Id.
122 Id.
123 Id.
124 See, e.g., Hogan v. PMI Mortg. Ins. Co., 2006 WL 1310461, at *8 (N.D. Cal. May 12, 2006) (reasoning that provision did not bar the plaintiff's claim because the amendment eliminated "an entire category of plaintiffs").
125 See Ch. 13, infra. The FCRA as originally enacted, effective until September 30, 1997, contained an exception to this requirement for reports to be used for employment for which the consumer has not applied. 15 U.S.C. § 1681d(a)(2).
126 15 U.S.C. § 1681d.
127 15 U.S.C. § 1681d(c).

128 See § 7.3.4, supra.
129 §§ 7.3.4, 8.2.9, supra.
130 Kudlicki v. Farragut Fin. Corp., 2006 WL 927281, at *2 (N.D. Ill. Jan. 20, 2006).
131 12 C.F.R. § 226.13(d)(2).
132 15 U.S.C. § 1666l(b). See also National Consumer Law Center, Truth in Lending § 5.8 (5th ed. 2003 and Supp.).
133 24 C.F.R. § 3500.21(e)(4).
134 15 U.S.C. § 1692(e). See National Consumer Law Center, Fair Debt Collection Ch. 5 (5th 2004 and Supp.).

Equal Credit Opportunity Act, creditors may not discriminate in furnishing credit information.[135]

A federal computer fraud statute may have applicability to a person obtaining consumer reports without a permissible purpose by use of a computer. The statute prohibits unauthorized computer access to consumer reporting files, and provides for compensatory damages and injunctive relief.[136] A private action is only available where the person is responsible for the loss of at least $5000 during any one-year period, and even then the consumer can only recover economic damages.[137] There is a two-year statute of limitations, and no attorney fee-shifting provision. To succeed, the plaintiff must show that the defendant acted intentionally.[138]

It has been unsuccessfully argued that abuses associated with consumer reporting constitute violations of federal civil rights laws. Section 1983 civil rights claims[139] usually fail for lack of complicity of state or federal authorities (state action).[140] Section 1985 claims[141] have failed for lack of a colorable equal protection claim and for failure to do more than merely allege conspiracy.[142] In addition, one court has ruled that violations of the FCRA may never form the basis for a section 1985 claim as a matter of law.[143]

If a creditor continues to report a debt discharged in bankruptcy, it may be found to have violated the automatic stay imposed by the Bankruptcy Code, leading to a charge of contempt.[144] While a few consumers have alleged RICO claims in addition to FCRA violations,[145] there are no reported cases where a RICO claim has succeeded. It may also be difficult to allege a requisite predicate act under RICO.[146] Accordingly, counsel should be aware of the need to draft such a claim carefully and in accordance with local requirements to avoid a Federal Rule of Civil Procedure Rule 11 motion.[147]

10.4 The FCRA's Qualified Immunity for Tort Claims

10.4.1 Background

Prior to the FCRA's enactment, the traditional remedy for a consumer harmed by false consumer reports or investigative reports was to bring an action for libel. In addition, at the time the FCRA was enacted, the common law was changing and actions for invasion of privacy and negligence were beginning to threaten the consumer reporting industry. As a quid pro quo for the FCRA requiring certain disclosures to consumers and providing remedies to consumers, the FCRA limits the tort liability of consumer reporting agencies (CRAs), users, and suppliers if the consumer acquired knowledge of the information through an FCRA-required disclosure.[148]

Congress intended this limited immunity to balance the FCRA's requirements that consumer reports and related information be disclosed to consumers.[149] Throughout congressional considerations, a tension existed between the desire to require CRAs to disclose fully to consumers the contents of their files, and the fear that these required disclosures would lead to a barrage of lawsuits against CRAs and their informants, which would dry up needed sources of information.[150]

The bill's primary sponsor, Senator Proxmire, originally intended to create new liability for failure to abide by new federal standards of conduct (now reflected in the civil liability provisions of the Act[151]), but also to fully preserve state law remedies for inaccurate information reported by

---

135 Reg. B, 12 C.F.R. §§ 202.2(m), 202.2(z), 202.4. *See* National Consumer Law Center, Credit Discrimination § 3.4, Ch. 9 (4th ed. 2004 and Supp.).
136 18 U.S.C. § 1030(a)(2) and (g).
137 18 U.S.C. § 1030(a)(5)(B)(i).
138 18 U.S.C. § 1030(a)(2); Letscher v. Swiss Bank Corp., 1997 LEXIS 7909 (S.D.N.Y. June 5, 1997).
139 42 U.S.C. § 1983.
140 Wright v. TRW Credit Data, 588 F. Supp. 112 (S.D. Fla. 1984). *See also* Houghton v. New Jersey Mfrs. Co., 795 F.2d 1144 (3d Cir. 1986), *rev'g* 615 F. Supp. 299 (E.D. Pa. 1985).
141 42 U.S.C. § 1985.
142 Wright v. TRW Credit Data, 588 F. Supp. 112 (S.D. Fla. 1984).
143 Wiggins v. Philip Morris, Inc., 853 F. Supp. 470 (D.D.C. 1994); Wiggins v. Hitchins, 853 F. Supp. 505 (D.D.C. 1994).
144 11 U.S.C. § 362. *See In re* Sommersdorf, 239 B.R. 700 (S.D. Ohio 1992) (creditor's refusal to remove write-off notation on non-debtor comaker's consumer report violated automatic stay); *In re* Singley, 233 B.R. 170 (Bankr. S.D. Ga. 1999) (even if creditor's report to a CRA concerning spouse/cosignor's credit contained truthful information that was a matter of public record, if made with intent to harass or coerce a debtor and/or co-debtor into paying a pre-petition debt, could violate the automatic stays for the debtor and or the non-debtor cosignor spouse).
145 *See, e.g.*, Hovater v. Equifax, Inc., 823 F.2d 413 (11th Cir. 1987) (affirming summary judgment for defendant on RICO claims, and reversing judgment for plaintiff on RICO claims); Management Info. Techs. v. Alyeska Pipeline Co., 151 F.R.D. 478 (D.D.C. 1993) (does not address substance of claims).
146 *See, e.g.*, Wiggins v. Equifax Servs., 848 F. Supp. 213 (D.D.C. 1993).
147 *Cf.* Malbrough v. Kilpatrick & Stockton, 1999 U.S. Dist. LEXIS 13066 (E.D. La. Aug. 23, 1999) (denying defendant's motion for sanctions where plaintiff's counsel dismissed "frivolous" RICO claim).
148 15 U.S.C. § 1681h(e).
149 McAnly v. Middleton & Rentlinger, P.S.C., 77 F. Supp. 2d 810 (W.D. Ky. 1999). *See* Remarks of Sen. Proxmire, 115 Cong. Rec. 33411 (1969) ("That is the quid pro quo...."). *See also* Alvarez Melendez v. Citibank, 705 F. Supp. 67 (D. P.R. 1988); Freeman v. Southern National Bank, 531 F. Supp. 94 (S.D. Tex. 1982); Retail Credit Co. v. Dade County, 393 F. Supp. 577, 584 (S.D. Fla. 1975); Peller v. Retail Credit Co., 359 F. Supp. 1235 (N.D. Ga. 1973), *aff'd per curiam*, 505 F.2d 733 (5th Cir. 1974).
150 *See* Hearings on S. 823, Subcommittee on Financial Institutions of the Senate Banking and Currency Committee, 91st Cong., 1st Sess. 71 (1969).
151 15 U.S.C. §§ 1681n, 1681o.

CRAs.[152] That is, the failure to maintain reasonable procedures, for example, would give rise to FCRA claims, while specific inaccuracies would still be subject to defamation and other state claims.

However, as the hearings proceeded, he began to propose that, in exchange for requiring that consumers be given access to CRA files, CRAs would be given a limited, qualified immunity from state law libel claims based on information disclosed as required by the Act.[153] The immunity is limited to information learned from required disclosures because of the nature of the legislative compromise.[154] This bargain, hammered out behind closed doors with the consumer reporting industry over vehement opposition from the consumer side, secured industry support for the bill which then became law.

The provision for qualified immunity is distinct from FCRA provisions added in 1996 and 2003 establishing preemption of certain state statutes. However, the courts are having difficulty in reconciling the qualified immunity provision with these new state law preemption provisions, as described at § 10.7, *infra*.

The FCRA prohibits any action:

> in the nature of defamation, invasion of privacy, or negligence with respect to the reporting of information against any CRA, any user of information, or any person who furnishes information to a CRA, based on information disclosed pursuant to [the sections concerning disclosures to consumers, conditions of disclosure to consumers, and disclosure requirements for users of consumer reports] of this title or based on information disclosed by a user of a consumer report to or for a consumer against whom the user has taken adverse action, based in whole or in part on the report, except as to false information furnished with malice or willful intent to injure such consumer.[155]

This section establishes a limited qualified immunity for the CRA, user, and furnisher from liability under three tort theories, unless the conduct involves malice or willful intent.[156] The immunity applies only if the consumer's case is based on specified information that a CRA or user was required to provide the consumer under the FCRA. Qualified immunity has been held to extend to claims involving business credit.[157]

10.4.2 Immunity Only Applies to the "Reporting" of Information

The limited immunity arises only when the consumer's claim is "with respect to the reporting of information."[158] Accordingly, when the claim is based on other behavior, the immunity should not arise. So, for example, the immunity should not be available for claims based on the new responsibilities of debt collectors who are notified that information related to the debt may be fraudulent or the result of identity theft.[159] Though the FCRA now requires such collectors to disclose to the consumer all information to which the consumer would be entitled if the consumer were actually the debtor, since an action based on such disclosures would not be with respect to the reporting of information, the qualified immunity provision should not be an obstacle. Similarly, certain creditors will now have to issue risk-based pricing notices when they offer credit on "material terms that are materially less favorable" than those offered to other consumers.[160] But actions based on those disclosures should not be subject to qualified immunity if they are not based on the reporting of information.

---

152 Hearings on S. 823, Subcommittee on Financial Institution of the Senate Banking and Currency Committee, 91st Cong., 1st Sess. 24 (1969).

153 *Id.* at 104.

154 *See* Watson v. Credit Bureau, Inc., 660 F. Supp. 48 (S.D. Miss. 1986); Freeman v. Southern National Bank, 531 F. Supp. 94 (S.D. Tex. 1982); Mitchell v. First Nat'l Bank of Dozier, 505 F. Supp. 176 (M.D. Ala. 1981). *Cf.* Pinner v. Schmidt, 617 F. Supp. 342 (E.D. La. 1985), *aff'd in part and rev'd in part*, 805 F.2d 1258 (5th Cir. 1986).

155 15 U.S.C. § 1681h(e). The 1996 amendment added to this section, near its end, this language: "of this title or based on information disclosed by a user of a consumer report to or for a consumer against whom the user has taken adverse action, based in whole or in part on the report."

156 Rhodes v. Ford Motor Credit Co., 951 F.2d 905 (8th Cir. 1991) (summary judgment granted to creditor which negligently furnished false information; apology and correction indicates lack of willful intent/malice); Schaffhausen v. Bank of America, N.A., 393 F. Supp. 2d 853, 859–860 (D. Minn. 2005) (granting the defendant's motion for summary judgment because the facts failed to show malice or intent to injure); Watson v. Trans Union Credit Bureau, 2005 WL 995687, at *8–9 (D. Me. Apr. 28, 2005) (recommendation by magistrate that the court grant the defendant's motion to dismiss because the plaintiff had failed to allege malice or willfulness); Feldman v. Comprehensive Info. Servs., Inc., 2003 WL 22413484, at *2 (Conn. Super. Ct. Oct. 6, 2003) (qualified immunity provision barred plaintiff's claim for reckless common law libel when plaintiff failed to show evidence of reckless disregard for the truth); Larobina v. First Union National Bank, 2001 Conn. Super. LEXIS 3549 (Dec. 13, 2001) (*pro se* allegations that defendant furnished inaccurate information to CRAs complaint preempted by FCRA immunity; no allegation that defendant's reporting false information was intentional, even though plaintiff alleged it was wanton, willful and with malicious regard); Gibson v. Decatur Fed. S&L Ass'n, 508 S.E.2d 788 (Ga. Ct. App. 1998); Laracuente v. Laracuente, 252 N.J. Super. 384, 599 A.2d 968 (1991).

This section does not create any federal cause of action. Alvarez Melendez v. Citibank, 705 F. Supp. 67 (D. P.R. 1988); Mitchell v. First National Bank of Dozier, 505 F. Supp. 176 (M.D. Ala. 1981).

157 Frost v. Experian, 1999 U.S. Dist. LEXIS 6783 (S.D.N.Y. May 6, 1999). *Contra* Frost v. Experian, 1998 WL 765178 (S.D.N.Y. Nov. 2, 1998).

158 15 U.S.C. § 1681h(e).

159 15 U.S.C. § 1681m(e), *added by* Pub. L. No. 108-159, § 155 (2003). *See also* § 9.2.3.2, *supra*.

160 15 U.S.C. § 1681m(h) *added by* Pub. L. No. 108-159, § 311 (2003).

10.4.3 Immunity Applies Only to Information Discovered Exclusively Through FCRA-Required Disclosure

The qualified immunity arises only for claims based on information disclosed to consumers[161] pursuant to sections 1681g, 1681h, and 1681m, three FCRA sections requiring specified disclosures to consumers.[162] Consequently, the limited immunity applies when the consumer discovers reporting inaccuracies based on review of the consumer's file, as disclosed to the consumer by the CRA. The limited immunity does not apply when the consumer has discovered the reporting inaccuracies elsewhere.

Sections 1681g and 1681h require CRAs to disclose to consumers the information in their files about the consumer.[163] Less clear is the operation of immunity based on the third FCRA disclosure section, section 1681m, which requires various disclosures by users, including disclosure to consumers of the fact that an adverse action has been taken on the basis of information contained in a consumer report and disclosure that credit was denied on the basis of other third-party information, including information provided by an affiliate.[164] This notice will not specify the reason for, or what in the report led to, the adverse action or denial of credit. The notice of adverse action will, however, notify the consumer of his or her right to obtain a free copy of the consumer report from the CRA, and the notice of credit denial based on third party information will inform the consumer of the right to disclosure of the "nature of the information" which led to the adverse action. When credit is involved, the FCRA notice usually follows a notice required under the Equal Credit Opportunity Act (ECOA), and it is the ECOA notice that is more likely to provide the exact reason why the consumer report led to the denial.[165]

A tort claim would not normally be based on the reporting of information disclosed pursuant to the user's FCRA notice that an adverse action was taken based on information in a consumer report or information from a third party, because the notice alone will not reveal what information was reported to the user. This leaves open the question as to the immunity's application where the consumer's claim is not based on the user's FCRA notice, but on the user's ECOA notice. Alternatively, what if the consumer's suspicion is triggered by the FCRA notice, but the consumer discovers the actual tortious conduct from conversations with the furnishing creditor or the user? What if the FCRA notice is not the trigger, but the ECOA notice is? None of these issues have been addressed by the case law. Presumably, common law rights will not be unduly restricted absent a clear mandate from Congress, and courts will therefore allow tort claims based on knowledge gained by the consumer which does not come directly and specifically from FCRA-mandated disclosures. In any event, as discussed immediately below, the legislative history indicates that a tort is actionable if information is gleaned both from other sources and from FCRA-required disclosures.

The immunity clearly does not extend to information disclosed or obtained by means other than through one of the designated mandatory disclosures.[166] In fact, consistent with the very limited nature of the qualified immunity, no

---

161 McKeown v. Sears Roebuck & Co., 335 F. Supp. 2d 917 (W.D. Wis. 2004). The FTC Commentary treats, for purposes of the immunity, disclosure to a consumer's representative the same as information disclosed to the consumer directly. FTC Official Staff Commentary § 610 item 6, *reprinted at* Appx. D, *infra*.

162 15 U.S.C. §§ 1681g, 1681h, 1681m.

163 15 U.S.C. §§ 1681g, 1681h.

164 15 U.S.C. § 1681m. The FACTA amendments added to § 1681m a provision that will eventually require financial institutions or creditors to establish policies to implement the forthcoming red flag guidelines that certain federal agencies will issue to prevent identity theft. 15 U.S.C. § 1681m(e), *added by* Pub. L. No. 108-159, § 114 (2003). *See also* § 9.2.4, *supra*. However, since this new provision does not require any disclosures, it should not be subject to the qualified immunity provision.

165 *See* § 8.2.6.6, *supra*.

166 FTC Official Staff Commentary § 610 item 6, *reprinted at* Appx. D, *infra*. The Senate Committee Report similarly found no immunity where information is "acquired by a consumer through other means." S. Rep. No. 517, 91st Cong., 1st Sess. 6 (1969) (report on S. 823 § 610). Poore v. Sterling Testing Sys., Inc., 410 F. Supp. 2d 557, 573–574 (E.D. Ky. 2006) (no immunity where claim was based on information the defendant reported to a potential employer); Roybal v. Equifax, 2006 WL 902276, at *4 (E.D. Cal. Apr. 4, 2006) (provision did not protect CRA where tort claims were based on the CRA's failure to properly maintain information); Abbett v. Bank of Am., 2006 WL 581193, at *7 (M.D. Ala. Mar. 8, 2006) (immunity did not arise where tort claims were based on bank's management of an account, its attempts to collect the debt, and disclosing information to its hired collection agencies); Jordan v. Trans Union L.L.C., 377 F. Supp. 2d 1307, 1309 (N.D. Ga. 2005) (provision did not protect furnisher where tort claim based on act other than a required disclosure); Pinckney v. SLM Fin. Corp., 2005 WL 4065029, at *5 (N.D. Ga. Apr. 27, 2005) (no immunity where claim based on conduct other than that required by one of the three designated provisions); Webb v. Bob Smith Chevrolet, Inc., 2005 WL 2065237, at *5 (W.D. Ky. Aug. 24, 2005) (no immunity where information was not disclosed pursuant to one of the three designated provisions); Carriere v. Proponent Fed. Credit Union, 2004 WL 1638250, at *6 (W.D. La. July 12, 2004) (recommendation of magistrate against dismissal of tort claims brought against furnisher where the allegedly inaccurate information was not disclosed pursuant to one of the provisions eligible for qualified immunity); Kronstedt v. Equifax, 2001 WL 34124783, at *20 (W.D. Wis. July 14, 2001) (qualified immunity provision does not protect defendant, which had attributed debts incurred by an identity thief to the plaintiff); Williams v. Experian Info. Solutions, Inc., 2002 WL 31133235, at *1 (E.D. Tex. Aug. 6, 2002) (denying furnisher's motion to dismiss plaintiff's negligence claims); Whiteside v. Equifax Credit Info. Servs., Inc., 125 F. Supp. 2d 807 (W.D. La. 2000) (no immunity based on information provided to potential creditor). *Cf.* McAnly v. Middleton & Rentlinger, P.S.C., 77 F. Supp. 2d 810 (W.D. Ky. 1999).

immunity arises even when information is gleaned from required disclosures, as long as the information is also acquired elsewhere.[167] That is, a consumer who has learned of inaccurate information in a consumer report as a result of disclosures required by the Act may nevertheless bring tort actions without qualification if the consumer also learns of the information some other way. Some courts, however, apply qualified immunity where the consumer learned of the information from a third party, and later received the information from the CRA.[168]

Some common sources of harmful reports other than those required to make the designated FCRA-required disclosures include the following:

- *The furnisher of information.* The furnisher may be a creditor, bank, employer, debt collector or other person who furnishes information to a CRA or to another creditor, bank, employer, or other user. The furnisher may provide the information to the consumer as part of a threat to obtain collection or just as part of its relationship with a customer. Discovery of this information from the furnisher can clearly lead to tort liability for the supplier, and in certain cases for the CRA as well.

- *A user of information from a non-reporting CRA.* Such a user is required to make disclosures to consumers only when credit is denied or the charge for credit is increased based on the information provided.[169] If the user has used the information for employment, insurance, or other non-credit purposes, and the consumer learns of the report from the user, then the qualified immunity does not arise.

- *A user of information that does not take an adverse action.* The user is required to make disclosures to consumers only when it takes an adverse action based on information in a consumer report or denies or increases the cost of credit based on third party information. If the user has used the information for some other purpose, the qualified immunity would not arise with respect to information obtained from the user. For example, if the user has not taken an adverse action but has disclosed information about the file, that information is not subject to the immunity. Banks and mortgage companies commonly provide a copy of the consumer report to the consumer, as a courtesy and to encourage accuracy, regardless of whether they extend a mortgage.

- *A CRA not responding to the consumer's request for disclosure.* A CRA is required to disclose information in its files to consumers upon request,[170] and such information triggers the qualified immunity. However, for a fee, some CRAs provide the service of sending consumers a copy of their report periodically. This is not a disclosure required by the FCRA, but rather an ordinary business transaction. Similarly, creditors or others sometimes arrange, as a promotional offer, for the consumer to obtain a copy of a consumer report by purchasing an item or service. Such a disclosure is unlikely to involve an FCRA-required disclosure of the file. In these instances, the information would be furnished voluntarily and not pursuant to a requirement imposed by the FCRA. Therefore, the qualified immunity would not apply.

- *Other third parties.* A consumer may learn of reported information from third parties, i.e., persons or organizations who are not strictly suppliers, users, or CRAs under the Act. This could be anyone who has obtained the information on their own, properly or improperly, as long as they did not receive the information as a user or CRA. One not unlikely possibility suggested by a commentator[171] is that the consumer may learn the contents of a consumer report from an organization, such as a consumer debt counseling agency, which obtained the information pursuant to the consumer's written instructions.

10.4.4 Immunity Applies Only to Enumerated Tort Claims

The qualified immunity applies only to actions and proceedings in the "nature of" defamation, invasion of privacy, and negligence. Few cases discuss whether other torts are also in the "nature of" defamation, invasion of privacy, or negligence.[172] Assuming other torts are independent claims and not in the "nature of" these three torts, then the FCRA immunity does not restrict other such common law actions. Examples might include intentional infliction of emotional

---

167 Congresswoman Leonor Sullivan, House sponsor of the Fair Credit Reporting Act, put it this way:

> The bill bars defamation and the invasion of privacy suits against an agency, but only if the individual bases his suit on information disclosed under the act. If the individual uses information obtained through independent sources, whether he has also obtained disclosures under the act or not, he may of course bring any action allowed by common law or statute. It is not intended that the bill grant any immunity to an agency from such suits by individuals whenever the agency has furnished information under this act.

116 Cong. Rec. 36573 (1970).

168 Thornton v. Equifax, Inc., 619 F.2d 700, 703 (8th Cir. 1980); Graham v. CSC Credit Servs., Inc., 306 F. Supp. 2d 873 (D. Minn. 2004).

169 15 U.S.C. § 1681m(b).

170 15 U.S.C. §§ 1681g and 1681h.

171 Note, *The Consumer Guide to Litigatory Remedies Under the Fair Credit Reporting Act*, 8 Val. L. Rev. 375, 395 n.93 (1974).

172 McAnly v. Middleton & Rentlinger, P.S.C., 77 F. Supp. 2d 810 (W.D. Ky. 1999) (tort of intrusion upon seclusion is in the nature of invasion of privacy).

distress,[173] misrepresentation,[174] intentional interference with prospective contractual relations,[175] or injurious falsehood.[176] Other examples might include tortious interference with prospective advantage, tortious interference with contract, prima facie tort, and injurious falsehood.[177] Additional examples of tort actions courts have found not subject to the limited immunity include tortious interference with employment,[178] and conspiracy to violate the FCRA or to commit unlawful acts.[179]

The immunity clearly does not apply to claims not based in tort at all. Examples include state credit reporting statutes,[180] state deceptive practices statutes,[181] state and federal debt collection statutes,[182] and contract claims.[183] Whether these state statutes are preempted is examined at § 10.7, infra.

10.4.5 A Furnisher of Information to a Non-Reporting Agency Is Not Immunized

Not only does the FCRA limit liability of persons who furnish information to CRAs,[184] it also protects furnishers through the qualified immunity provision, which expressly applies to "any person who furnishes information to a consumer reporting agency."[185] By these very terms, the immunity does not apply when the person furnishes information to someone other than a CRA. For example, the provision does not protect a creditor reporting its own experience with its customer to another creditor. Nor does the immunity apply when a furnisher furnishes information to a prospective employer.[186] The creditor has a duty to

---

173 Rivera v. Countrywide Fin. Corp., 2006 WL 1586555, at *2–3 (S.D. Miss. June 8, 2006) (refusing to dismiss claim). Such an action requires, inter alia, outrageous conduct and conspicuous disregard of consequences. E.g., Pulver v. Avco Fin. Servs., 182 Cal. App. 3d 622, 227 Cal. Rptr. 491, 499 (1986).

174 A misrepresentation, to be actionable, must be aimed at the plaintiff, not at a third party such as a CRA. E.g., Pulver v. Avco Fin. Servs., 182 Cal. App. 3d 622, 227 Cal. Rptr. 491, 500 (1986).

175 The tort requires a prospective contractual relationship, purpose to harm the plaintiff, absence of privilege, and actual damages. Zions First National Bank, N.A. v. Limited Health Club, 704 F.2d 120, 123 (3d Cir. 1983); Maberry v. Said, 911 F. Supp. 1393 (D. Kan. 1995); Restatement (Second) Torts § 766B (1979). One court has held in a case involving a negative consumer report that a valid or reasonable expectancy of credit can satisfy the requirement of a prospective contractual relationship; although a pending credit application is not necessary, the plaintiff must have a reasonable chance of obtaining credit, a jury question. Bell v. May Dep't Stores Co., 6 S.W.3d 871 (Mo. 1999) (en banc), overruling in part Haas v. Town & Country Mortg. Co., 886 S.W.2d 225 (Mo. Ct. App. 1994). See also Bruce v. First U.S.A. Bank, 103 F. Supp. 2d 1135, 1142–1143 (E.D. Mo. 2000) (reciting elements, denying furnisher's motion for summary judgment).

176 The tort requires intent (or likelihood) to harm the pecuniary interests of another, and knowledge or reckless disregard of falsity. It is usually applied to disparagement of property or intangible things. Restatement (Second) Torts §§ 623A-652 (1979). E.g., reporting a lien or attachment on property could be disparagement of title, to which truth would be a defense. Another tort, malicious prosecution, could not be established under New York Law by an allegation that a lawsuit caused a diminished credit rating. A diminished credit rating does not make the required showing of "some interference with person or property." Diamond v. Strassberg, 751 F. Supp. 1152 (S.D.N.Y. 1990).

177 Yeager v. TRW Inc., 984 F. Supp. 517 (E.D. Tex. 1997); Maberry v. Said, 911 F. Supp. 1393 (D. Kan. 1995) (applying Missouri law) (creditor had submitted negative consumer report after notification that consumer had legitimate reasons to withhold payments).

178 Wiggins v. Philip Morris, Inc., 853 F. Supp. 470 (D.D.C. 1994); Wiggins v. District Cablevision, Inc., 853 F. Supp. 484 (D.D.C. 1994).

179 Wiggins v. Philip Morris, Inc., 853 F. Supp. 470 (D.D.C. 1994); Wiggins v. District Cablevision, Inc., 853 F. Supp. 484 (D.D.C. 1994); Wiggins v. Hitchins, 853 F. Supp. 505 (D.D.C. 1994) (no conspiracy as to employees of plaintiff's employer).

180 See § 10.6.1, infra. See also Apodaca v. Discover Fin. Servs., 417 F. Supp. 2d 1220 (2006), 1235 (D.N.M. 2006) (§ 1681h(e) did not apply to claim brought under state credit reporting act).

181 See § 10.6.2, infra.

182 But see Greenwood Trust Co. v. Conley, 938 P.2d 1141 (Colo. 1997) (allegation that creditor wrongly reported a debt to a CRA without disclosing that it was disputed was an unconscionable practice under a state debt collection statute was in the nature of defamation, and thereby "preempted" by the FCRA's qualified immunity. The statute list several factors for determining unconscionability; plaintiff relied upon only one factor—injury to reputation or economic status. The court indicated that had plaintiff also relied upon any other factor, the state claim would not have been preempted. At p.149. Although the court held that the FCRA qualified immunity applied, it remanded the case for further proceedings because a genuine dispute existed over whether the defendant acted with malice.).

183 Larobina v. First Union Nat'l Bank, 2004 WL 1664230 (Conn. Super. Ct. June 28, 2004) (breach of contract not preempted); Hoglan v. First Sec. Bank, 120 Idaho 682, 819 P.2d 100 (1991) (plaintiff alleged that the bank wrongly listed and reported an account as charged off). But see McAnly v. Middleton & Rentlinger, P.S.C., 77 F. Supp. 2d 810 (W.D. Ky. 1999) (consumer is not a third party beneficiary of contract between CRA and user of report).

184 See § 10.2.4, supra.

185 15 U.S.C. § 1681h(e). See also Bloom v. I.C. Sys., Inc., 753 F. Supp. 314 (D. Or. 1990) (defamation claim preempted absent allegation of malice or willful intent even though debt collector continued to report a disputed debt after notified by creditor no debt was ever owed), aff'd, 972 F.2d 1067 (9th Cir. 1992); Pan Am. Bank of Miami v. Osgood, 383 So. 2d 1095 (Fla. Dist. Ct. App. 1980), review denied, 392 So. 2d 1377 (Fla. 1980) (bank liable for negligent reporting of information to CRA; failed to timely plead FCRA immunity defense); Parker v. Laurance Eustis Mortg. Corp., 615 So. 2d 1102 (La. Ct. App. 1993); Dominick v. Sears, Roebuck & Co., 741 S.W.2d 290 (Mo. Ct. App. 1987) (vacating jury verdict for consumer on libel claim against creditor that reported information for the wrong "Janet Dominick" in its records).

186 Poore v. Sterling Testing Sys., Inc., 410 F. Supp. 2d 557, 573–574 (E.D. Ky. 2006).

provide full, accurate, and truthful information, and may be subject to a tort claim by the consumer or other creditor if it does not.[187]

In addition, as with the tort immunity for CRAs and users, this is a limited immunity. It applies only where a claim in the nature of defamation, invasion of privacy, or negligence is based on information disclosed pursuant to the three specified FCRA disclosure provisions, and not obtained by the plaintiff from independent sources. Moreover, the immunity applies only if the furnisher acted without malice or willfulness.

10.4.6 No Immunity Where Malice or Willful Intent

The FCRA's qualified immunity raises the level of proof required by a consumer to prevail in state defamation, privacy, and negligence actions. The qualified immunity does not preclude these tort claims, but requires that the consumer prove that the defendant acted with malice or willful intent to injure, and that the reported information was false.[188] The FCRA imposes higher standards than normally required under most if not all tort claims. For example, since negligence is inconsistent with willfulness, courts have dismissed claims of negligence and negligent infliction of emotional distress.[189]

The FCRA does not define malice. Two Circuits, the Fifth and the Eighth, have referred to the Supreme Court's definition of malice in the First Amendment case of *New York Times v. Sullivan*,[190] where the Court defined actual malice as acting with knowledge that the information is false or with reckless disregard of whether or not it is false.[191] In contrast, state common law standards of malice as applied to CRAs, at least prior to the federal law, were quite varied and in some instances tended towards more lenient standards akin to negligence.[192] The Act similarly fails to define "willful," but courts have borrowed from cases interpreting the liability section 1681n to interpret the term as requiring a showing that the CRA "knowingly and intentionally committed an act in conscious disregard for the rights of others."[193]

---

187 *See* MSA Tubular Prods., Inc. v. First Bank & Trust Co., 869 F.2d 1422, 1424 (10th Cir. 1989); Ostlund Chem. Co. v. Norwest Bank, 417 N.W.2d 833, 836–837 (N.D. 1988).

188 Lawrence v. Trans Union L.L.C., 296 F. Supp. 2d 582, 591 (E.D. Pa. 2003) (holding, without extensive analysis, that the plaintiff had sufficiently showed willful intent to survive summary judgment); Borner v. Zale Lipshy Univ. Hosp., 2002 WL 449576 (N.D. Tex. Mar. 20, 2002) (false report quickly corrected shows lack of malice); Whiteside v. Equifax Credit Info. Servs., Inc., 125 F. Supp. 2d 807 (W.D. La. 2000) (question of fact whether willful when repeatedly notified of error); Olson v. Atlantic Mortg. & Ins. Corp., 24 F. Supp. 2d 976 (D. Mich. 1998); Frost v. Experian, 1998 WL 765178 (S.D.N.Y. Nov. 2, 1998) (failure to reinvestigate can show willfulness); Blanche v. First Nationwide Mortg. Corp., 74 S.W.3d 444 (Tex. App. 2002) (whether defendant acted with malice or willful intent when it knowingly reported plaintiffs as delinquent even though it knew of a federal court ruling that plaintiff's were not liable was a factual issue precluding summary judgment).

189 Carlson v. Trans Union, L.L.C., 259 F. Supp. 2d 517 (N.D. Tex. 2003); Socorro v. IMI Data Search, Inc., 2003 WL 1964269 (N.D. Ill. Apr. 28, 2003); Carlson v. Trans Union, L.L.C., 261 F. Supp. 2d 663 (N.D. Tex. 2003).

190 376 U.S. 254, 279 (1964). Cases applying this standard include: Bruce v. First U.S.A. Bank, 103 F. Supp. 2d 1135, 1142–1143 (E.D. Mo. 2000) (granting furnisher's motion for summary judgment on defamation claim) and Yeager v. TRW Inc., 984 F. Supp. 517 (E.D. Tex. 1997) (citing further examples).

191 Rhodes v. Ford Motor Credit Co., 951 F.2d 905, 907 (8th Cir. 1991) (declining to rule on whether the New York Times standard was the law of the Eighth Circuit, but affirming summary judgment for the defendant on the issue of malice); Thornton v. Equifax, Inc., 619 F.2d 700 (8th Cir. 1980) (reversing judgment for the plaintiff because the trial judge had instructed the jury that defamation liability could be found if the acts were wanton or oppressive); Cousin v. Trans Union Corp., 246 F.3d 359 (5th Cir. 2001) (relying on Mississippi state law). Many district courts have borrowed the New York Times standard. *See, e.g.*, Beuster v. Equifax Info. Servs., 2006 WL 1669790, at *4 (D. Md. June 15, 2006) (denying defendant's motion to dismiss); Thurman v. Case Credit Corp., 2005 WL 3074149, at *6 (E.D. Mo. Nov. 16, 2005) (granting defendant's motion for summary judgment); DiPrinzio v. MBNA America Bank, N.A., 2005 WL 2039175, at *5 (E.D. Pa. Aug. 24, 2005) (denying defendant's motion for summary judgment); Gohman v. Equifax Info. Servs., L.L.C., 395 F. Supp. 2d 822, 829 (D. Minn. July 21, 2005) (granting defendant's motion for summary judgment); Jordan v. Trans Union L.L.C., 377 F. Supp. 2d 1307, 1309 (N.D. Ga. 2005) (denying motion); Johnson v. Citimortgage, Inc., 351 F. Supp. 2d 1368, 1376 (N.D. Ga. 2004) (denying defendant's motion to dismiss); Anderson v. Trans Union, L.L.C., 345 F. Supp. 2d 963, 973–974 (D. Wis. 2004) (granting summary judgment to CRA); Graham v. CSC Credit Servs., Inc., 306 F. Supp. 2d 873, 882 (D. Minn. 2004) (denying defendant's motion for summary judgment); Cisneros v. Trans Union, L.L.C., 293 F. Supp. 2d 1167, 1177 (D. Haw. 2003) (denying defendant's motion to dismiss); Gordon v. Greenpoint Credit, 266 F. Supp. 2d 1007, 1013 (S.D. Iowa 2003) (denying defendant's motion to dismiss); Yutesler v. Sears Roebuck & Co., 263 F. Supp. 2d 1209, 1212 (D. Minn. 2003) (denying defendant's motion to dismiss). *But see* McCloud v. Homeside Lending, 309 F. Supp. 2d 1335 (N.D. Ala. 2004) (citing state statutory definition of malice). Cases in which malice was established include: Credit Bureau v. LaVoie, 627 S.W.2d 49 (Ky. Ct. App. 1982); Sateren v. Montgomery Ward & Co., 362 S.E.2d 324 (Va. 1987). *See also* Wiggins v. Equifax Servs., Inc., 848 F. Supp. 213 (D.D.C. 1993); McDowell v. Credit Bureau, No. 51192 (Mo. Ct. App. June 23, 1987), *aff'd*, 747 S.W.2d 630 (Mo. 1988) (qualified privilege). *But see* Rhodes v. Ford Motor Credit Co., 951 F.2d 905, 907 (8th Cir. 1991) (declining to rule on whether the New York Times standard was the law of the Eighth Circuit, but affirming summary judgment for the defendant on the issue of malice); Pinner v. Schmidt, 805 F.2d 1258 (5th Cir. 1986); Boydston v. Chrysler Credit Co., 511 N.E.2d 318 (Ind. Ct. App. 1987).

192 *See* § 10.5, *infra*.

193 Whelan v. Trans Union Credit Reporting Agency, 862 F. Supp. 824, 833 (E.D.N.Y. 1994) (quoting Stevenson v. TRW Inc., 987 F.2d 288, 293 (5th Cir. 1993).

In any case, whenever counsel makes a claim against a party that is eligible for section 1681h(e)'s qualified immunity, counsel should plead malice or willful intent to injure. In general, such pleading should allow the claim to survive a motion to dismiss.[194] Malice need not be plead with particularity, but can be averred generally.[195] Once discovery commences, counsel should prepare to defend a summary judgment motion with evidence that could meet the stringent *New York Times* standard.[196] For example, evidence that a furnisher verified false information as part of a reinvestigation of a dispute, after receiving strong evidence that the item was false, could suffice to survive a furnisher's motion for summary judgment.[197] Evidence of a consumer's direct disputes with a furnisher can also support the claim that the furnisher has lost the qualified immunity.[198] As for CRAs, one court ruled that evidence that the CRA had deliberately adopted a system that allowed an inaccurate report justified denying the CRA's motion for summary judgment on the issue of qualified immunity.[199]

So long as the plaintiff either pleads malice or the trier of fact finds it, a court need not expressly refer to the FCRA's qualified immunity provision. In *Hoglan v. First Security Bank of Idaho*,[200] the jury found for plaintiff on counts of libel, breach of contract, and negligence. The jury instructions made no mention of the FCRA or of a qualified immunity, but did instruct the jury that defendant must have acted with malice, that is "something that was said, made, or done with knowledge that was false or with reckless disregard of whether it was false or not." On appeal, the Idaho Supreme Court ruled that because the qualified immunity was effectively contained in the jury instructions, there was no error in not applying the FCRA.

The FCRA's qualified immunity provision requires that the tort claims not only establish malice or willful intent to injure, but also that the reported information was false.[201] This imposes no new requirement for defamation claims where falsehood is an element of the tort and truth is a complete defense. But this does add a new element to negligence claims and may limit the effect of privacy torts.

Falsehood is not normally an element of a negligence claim, only injury which is negligently caused. Injury can result from the imprudent release of accurate or inaccurate information. However, if the doctrine of qualified immunity is invoked, the consumer will need to base all negligence claims on false information.[202]

Invasion of privacy torts normally are based on the infringement of one's right to privacy without regard to truthfulness.[203] In this sense, this tort complements the law of defamation: for one truthfulness is not relevant and for the other a falsehood is required. By imposing a requirement that the information is necessarily false, the likelihood of successfully claiming an invasion of privacy is diminished.

10.5 Common Law Tort Claims Where Immunity Does Not Apply

10.5.1 Advantages of a Tort Claim

Common law tort claims are still widely used to challenge inaccurate reports on commercial businesses (often called "mercantile reports" in the case law). But the FCRA has largely replaced tort claims as a cause of action for consumer reporting issues. One reason for this is that the FCRA, like the tort claims, provides a cause of action for actual and punitive damages. But, unlike tort claims, the FCRA also provides for the consumer's attorney fees. Moreover, where a consumer's attorney does not want to plead a federal cause of action (to prevent removal of the case to federal court), a state credit reporting statute is often a superior choice to a tort claim.

Nevertheless, tort claims may be useful to an injured consumer. The FCRA provides a cause of action only if a specific FCRA provision is violated. The Act requires a showing of negligence, and often requires the plaintiff to show that reasonable procedures were not followed. Furthermore, although any "person" may be liable for violating specific provisions of the FCRA, the available remedies, particularly those against furnishers of information, are

---

194 *See, e.g.*, Jordan v. Trans Union L.L.C., 377 F. Supp. 2d 1307, 1309 (N.D. Ga. 2005).

195 Fed. R. Civ. P. 9(b); Jordan v. Trans Union L.L.C., 377 F. Supp. 2d 1307, 1309 (N.D. Ga. 2005).

196 For example, in Gohman v. Equifax Info. Servs., L.L.C., 395 F. Supp. 2d 822, 828–829 (D. Minn. 2005), the court, in granting summary judgment to the defendant on the plaintiff's state law claims of defamation and interference with credit expectancy, pointed to the plaintiff's own deposition testimony that the defendant had not acted with malice.

197 *See, e.g.*, McMillan v. Experian, 170 F. Supp. 2d 278, 287 (D. Conn. 2001) (reasonable jury could conclude that a furnisher whose investigation consisted of nothing more than comparing plaintiff's name and Social Security number with the account holder's—whose address, telephone, date of birth, employment and work telephone were different—acted with reckless disregard for the truth or falsity of the information for the purpose of a defamation claim). *See also* McCloud v. Homeside Lending, 309 F. Supp. 2d 1335 (N.D. Ala. 2004) (allegations that holder of mortgage acted willfully sufficiently alleged malice as defined by state statute, denying motion to dismiss defamation and invasion of privacy claims).

198 *See* DiPrinzio v. MBNA America Bank, N.A., 2005 WL 2039175, at *4 (E.D. Pa. Aug. 24, 2005) (denying the defendant's motion for summary judgment).

199 Graham v. CSC Credit Servs., Inc., 306 F. Supp. 2d 873, 882 (D. Minn. 2004).

200 120 Idaho 682, 819 P.2d 100 (1991) (on appeal the libel verdict was held to have been barred by the state statute of limitation; the verdicts for breach of contract and negligence, and a $20,000 award, were affirmed.).

201 15 U.S.C. § 1681h(e).

202 Nikou v. INB Nat'l Bank, 638 N.E.2d 448 (Ind. Ct. App. 1994).

203 *See* § 10.5.3, *infra*.

limited.²⁰⁴ Thus the FCRA does not private a private remedy for creditors furnishing inaccurate information.

Also the FCRA does not provide a cause of action against consumer reporting agencies (CRAs) for the reporting of inaccurate information, as long as the procedures followed were reasonable, and the error is corrected when brought to the CRA's attention. Where the FCRA does not provide an avenue to challenge inaccurate reports, tort claims may provide a better avenue. In addition, a tort claim may have a longer statute of limitations and certainly has a broader scope.

10.5.2 Elements of a Defamation Claim

The traditional non-statutory remedy for inaccurate consumer reports is libel. Libel is the written form of defamation, and slander is the oral form. Both libel and slander require prejudice to the consumer's reputation or livelihood, resulting from a communication to a third party, such as a creditor.²⁰⁵ Statements commonly contained in consumer reports are often libelous if false.²⁰⁶ Malice is often presumed,²⁰⁷ but must be pleaded if the claim is subject to a qualified immunity defense.²⁰⁸ Each transmission of the same information is a separate and distinct tort.²⁰⁹ On the other hand, defamation actions generally must be pleaded with a higher degree of specificity than most claims.²¹⁰

Actual (general or special), punitive, and nominal damages are recoverable in libel actions.²¹¹

The issue of proof is usually not the libelous nature of the report or information, but whether the CRA or the supplier of information is protected by a conditional privilege. The common law tort doctrine of conditional privilege allows the CRA or the supplier a defense in actions of defamation, a defense that strongly resembles the FCRA's qualified immunity provision.²¹² Under the doctrine of conditional privilege, a CRA may not be held liable for defamation unless malice and falsehood are proved by the complainant. Once the defense is raised, the consumer must show actual malice.²¹³

---

204 See §§ 10.2.4, 10.4, supra, § 10.7, infra.

205 See Restatement (Second) of Torts § 558.

206 Trundle v. Homeside Lending, Inc., 162 F. Supp. 2d 396 (D. Md. 2001) (granting summary judgment for creditor against plaintiff, who had not submitted opposing evidence, on state law defamation and invasion of privacy claims arising from report on mortgage debt as "included in bankruptcy" because it was literally true and thus not defamatory even though only spouse filed bankruptcy); Spencer v. Hendersen-Webb, Inc., 81 F. Supp. 2d 582 (D. Md. 1999) (report of debt barred by the 3-year statute of limitations is a false report). See Note, *The Consumer Guide to Litigatory Remedies Under the Fair Credit Reporting Act*, 8 Val. L. Rev. 375, 387 (1974).

207 Matthews v. Deland State Bank, 334 So. 2d 164 (Fla. Ct. App. 1976) (bank's knowledge that the amount it reported as due was wrong, coupled with repeated refusal to correct it, is libel per se pursuant to which malice is presumed). *But see* Denney v. Northwestern Credit Ass'n, 55 Wash. 331, 104 P. 769, 770 (Wash. 1909) (when words contained in report were innocent when considered in their natural sense without special knowledge, malice not implied).

208 Thornton v. Equifax, 619 F.2d 700 (8th Cir. 1980); Mitchell v. Surety Acceptance Corp., 838 F. Supp. 497 (D.C. Colo. 1993). *See also* § 10.4.6, supra.

209 Young v. Equifax Credit Info. Serv., Inc., 294 F.3d 631, 636 (5th Cir. 2002); Hyde v. Hibernia Nat'l Bank in Jefferson Parish, 861 F.2d 446 (5th Cir. 1988); Matise v. Trans Union Corp., 1998 WL 872511 (N.D. Tex. Nov. 30, 1998) (but rejecting defamation claim under doctrine of self-publication); Musto v. Bell South Telecomms. Corp., 748 So. 2d 296 (Fla. Ct. App. 1999); Swafford v. Memphis Individual Practice Ass'n, 1998 WL 281935, at *6 (Tenn. Ct. App. June 2, 1998).

210 Wiggins v. District Cablevision, Inc., 853 F. Supp. 484, 494 (D.D.C. 1994) (citing 5 Wright and Miller, Federal Practice and Procedure § 1309 (1990)). *See also* Wiggins v. Philip Morris, Inc., 853 F. Supp. 470 (D.D.C. 1994); Wiggins v. Hitchins, 853 F. Supp. 505 (D.D.C. 1994).

211 W. Page Keeton, Prosser & Keeton on Torts § 116A (5th ed. 1984). At common law actual damages were available without any proof of damage to reputation—special damages—where the libel was classified as "libel per se" because it pertained to one of: a crime; a loathsome disease; a business, trade profession or office; or unchastity. However, Gertz v. Robert Welch, Inc., 418 U.S. 323 (1974) ruled that such damages were unconstitutional as against the mass media and those who used them without proof the libel was made with knowledge of its falsity or reckless disregard thereof. *Id.* §§ 112, 116A. Defamation as to personal creditworthiness would not be libel per se and accordingly, a plaintiff suing for false credit reporting will likely have to make some showing of damage to his or her reputation. Fisher v. Quality Hyundai, Inc., 2002 U.S. Dist. LEXIS 407 (N.D. Ill. Jan. 11, 2002) (statements concerning consumer's credit reputation are not defamation per se). A defamation plaintiff may be able to recover punitive damages even without demonstrating actual malice where the subject is not a matter of public concern; the Constitution does not require it, though state law may. *Id.* at 116A. *See* Dun & Bradstreet v. Greenmoss Builders, 472 U.S. 749 (1985) (where matter does not involve matter of public concern, plaintiff need not prove actual malice to obtain punitive damages). Since personal consumer reports are not matters of public concern, state law should define the requirements for their recovery. Sunward Corp. v. Dun & Bradstreet, Inc., 811 F.2d 511 (10th Cir. 1987) (Colorado law). The consumer's reputation is presumed to have been good until the defendant establishes the contrary. Rasor v. Retail Credit Co., 554 P.2d 1041 (Wash. 1976).

212 See Ullman, *Liability of Credit Bureau After the Fair Credit Reporting Act: The Need for Future Reform*, 17 Vill. L. Rev. 44, 44–45 (1971). *See also* Moore v. Credit Info. Co., 673 F.2d 208, 210 (8th Cir. 1982) (consumer reports issued in good faith to one with legitimate interest are qualifiedly privileged); Hood v. Dun & Bradstreet, Inc., 486 F.2d 25, 32 (5th Cir. 1973); Hargrow v. Long, 760 F. Supp. 1 (D.D.C. 1989) (qualified privilege protected consumer's former employer, who told CRA that consumer was "ineligible for hire" and "wholly incompetent"); Sondak v. Dun & Bradstreet, Inc., 39 Misc. 2d 13, 239 N.Y.S.2d 697 (Sup. Ct. 1963) (qualified privilege protected CRA who made a "reasonable effort" to obtain facts from defamation claim); Lomas Bank USA v. Flatow, 880 S.W.2d 52 (Tex. App. 1994). *See generally* 30 A.L.R.2d 776.

213 In point of fact, malice may be established by conduct which evidences ill will, indifference or reckless disregard for the

The doctrine is premised on the policy that the free flow of credit information is more important than individual claims of personal injury, and on the fear that, absent some protection from defamation liability, CRAs would not provide valuable information. However, the FCRA arguably undermines the underlying policy determination that commercial interests should predominate over individual interests and may justify the elimination of the doctrine.[214] Moreover, the privilege is not universal,[215] it is in decline, and its absence has not dampened CRA activities.[216]

10.5.3 Elements of Invasion of Privacy Claim

Invasion of privacy comprises four torts: appropriation of name or likeness, intrusion upon seclusion, publicity given to private life, and publicity placing one in a false light.[217]

The last three of these have the most potential to apply to a consumer report situation, and are discussed in more detail in Chapter 16, *infra*.

At the time of the FCRA's enactment, no reported cases had held a CRA liable for invasion of privacy,[218] and none have since.[219] Nevertheless, public and academic concerns with privacy rights were in the air[220] and continue. This concern probably explains why the tort of invasion of privacy was included among those claims which, if the FCRA's qualified immunity arises, must also include proof of malice or willful intent to injure.

The FCRA goes one step further, however, by specifying that if the qualified immunity arises, a claim for invasion of privacy must also establish that the personal information is in fact false. This additional requirement eviscerates traditional notions of invasion of privacy which remedy the collection or dissemination of personal information without regard to its truthfulness. Thus it is likely that the development and application of the tort of invasion of privacy to consumer reporting activities will occur only when no qualified immunity protects the opposing party.

10.5.4 Elements of Negligence Claim

The development and application of negligence law to consumer reporting activities was advancing when the FCRA was enacted. A few courts had expressly held CRAs liable for negligence,[221] and another implied the possibility of a claim for negligent misstatements injuring a consumer.[222] Moreover, the proof required to establish malice to overcome a CRA's conditional privilege defense was beginning to approach traditional negligence standards.

The FCRA itself adopted a negligence standard for liability.[223] Actions for common law negligence must overcome the FCRA's qualified immunity. A negligence verdict for charging off and reporting a credit card debt was upheld in *Hoglan v. First Security Bank*.[224] The jury instructions had

---

rights of others, lack of good faith, and actual knowledge of falsehood. *See, e.g.*, Luster v. Retail Credit Co., 575 F.2d 609 (8th Cir. 1978) (applying Arkansas law) (conditional privilege not available when false information reported with reckless disregard; however no punitive damages allowed without proof of actual ill will or malice); Dun & Bradstreet, Inc. v. Robinson, 345 S.W.2d 34 (Ark. 1961) (reckless disregard of the rights or feelings of others sufficient to overcome the conditional privilege); Dun & Bradstreet, Inc. v. O'Neill, 456 S.W.2d 896 (Tex. 1970) (failure to investigate the truth or falsity of a statement before it is published is insufficient to show the actual malice needed to overcome the conditional privilege). *See generally* 40 A.L.R.3d 1049. Even so, CRAs acting in good faith are widely protected by the doctrine of conditional privilege. Note, *Credit Investigations and the Right to Privacy: Quest for a Remedy*, 57 Geo. L.J. 509, 516 (1969).

214 Vinson v. Ford Motor Credit Co., 259 So. 2d 768 (Fla. Dist. Ct. App. 1972) abolished the conditional privilege, saying:

> Times change and principles of law change with them. "A man's credit in this day and age is one of his most valuable assets and without it, a substantial portion of the American people would be without . . . necessities of life." The impersonal and concerned attitude displayed by business machines as to the impact of their actions upon an individual consumer . . . was the catalyst for our National Congress to pass the Fair Credit Reporting Act, which provides protection for consumers from irresponsible credit reporting agencies.

Id. at 771 (footnotes omitted). See discussion at Note, The Consumer Guide to Litigatory Remedies Under the Fair Credit Reporting Act, 8 Val. L. Rev. 375, 399 (1974).

215 Vinson v. Ford Motor Credit Co., 259 So. 2d 768 (Fla. Dist. Ct. App. 1972); Johnson v. Bradstreet Co., 77 Ga. 172 (1886); Pac. Packing Co. v. Bradstreet Co., 25 Idaho 696, 139 P. 1007 (1914).

216 Ullman, *Liability of Credit Bureau After the Fair Credit Reporting Act: The Need for Future Reform*, 17 Vill. L. Rev. 44, 50 (1971).

217 *See* Restatement (Second) Torts §§ 652B–652E (1979).

218 *E.g.*, Shorter v. Retail Credit Co., 251 F. Supp. 329 (D.S.C. 1966).

219 See Chapter 16, *supra*, for a discussion of privacy laws and concerns.

220 For example, one of the findings and purposes of the Act itself recognizes a need to respect the privacy of consumers. 15 U.S.C. § 1681(a)(4).

221 *E.g.*, Roemer v. Retail Credit Co., 3 Cal. App. 2d 368, 83 Cal. Rptr. 540 (1970); Bartels v. Retail Credit Co., 185 Neb. 304, 175 N.W.2d 292 (1970).

222 H.E. Crawford Co. v. Dun & Bradstreet, Inc., 241 F.2d 387 (4th Cir. 1957). *See also* Watson v. Credit Bureau, Inc., 660 F. Supp. 48 (S.D. Miss. 1986) (case brought against CRA under common law negligence rather than FCRA; court applied FCRA "reasonableness" standard to find that report of "voluntary repossession" was accurate, even though consumer had returned automobile after initiating litigation claiming automobile was defective).

223 15 U.S.C. § 1681o.

224 120 Idaho 682, 819 P.2d 100 (1991) (opinion contains excerpts

stated that "negligence involves the furnishing of false information with malice . . . or willful intent to injure," thus overcoming any bar which the FCRA qualified immunity may have raised. In addition, a court may apply the common law doctrine of conditional privilege to negligence claims, in which case a consumer would have the burden of proving malice even in a negligence claim not affected by the FCRA's immunity.[225]

10.6 State Statutory Claims

10.6.1 State Credit Reporting Statutes

Most states have laws relating to consumer reporting agencies (CRAs).[226] Often, these laws mirror the federal statute. However in many instances the state laws will provide important additional protections for consumers, or contain different statutes of limitation, remedies, or scope. Consequently, it is generally best to bring an action under both the federal and state statutes. In fact, where a consumer does not want an action removed to federal court, raising only the state law claim may be preferable to bringing an FCRA action. A state-by-state summary of these laws is found at Appendix H, *infra*, but consumer attorneys should rely on a careful reading of their own statutes. An important limitation to the use of state credit reporting statutes is the question whether the FCRA preempts their applicability. This subject is explored in depth at § 10.7, *infra*.

10.6.2 State Deceptive Practices Statutes

Every state has a deceptive practices statute that, with few exceptions, provides important consumer remedies for marketplace misconduct.[227] Remedies, depending on the state, might include attorney fees, actual damages, treble damages, punitive damages, and/or statutory damages for deceptive conduct. In addition, many of these statutes also prohibit unfair or unconscionable conduct, and not just deceptive conduct. The statutes are generally patterned after the Federal Trade Commission Act's (FTC Act) prohibition of unfair and deceptive acts and practices, and violations of the FTC Act will usually violate these statutes.[228] Moreover, allegations of unfair or illegal practices have the advantage of entitling consumers to introduce evidence not only of practices applied to them individually, but also of practices involving members of the public generally or to individuals not a party to the suit.[229]

Consumer litigants may want to argue that violations of the FCRA or state credit reporting statutes[230] are per se state UDAP violations.[231] The FCRA explicitly provides that an FCRA violation shall constitute an unfair or deceptive act or practice under the FTC Act.[232] Thus, consumers may be able to bring suit under their state's deceptive practices act for violation of the FCRA and also for other related unfair and deceptive practices that do not explicitly violate the FCRA.

A UDAP challenge may be appropriate even where the deceptive or unfair practices do not expressly violate the FCRA. For example, in *In re Equifax*,[233] the FTC found certain CRA practices not covered by the FCRA to still be unfair and deceptive. The FTC ruled that it was deceptive for CRA interviewers to misrepresent that they worked for an insurance agency, or conversely to claim that they were preparing a consumer report when they were observing the consumer's health for purposes of an insurance claim.[234] Nor may CRAs retain and use medical records and related information for uses other than those specifically authorized by the consumer.[235] The FTC also ruled in *In re Equifax* that the FCRA does not preempt other FTC action against CRAs.

The FCRA's qualified tort immunity should not apply to deceptive practices claims because they are statutory causes of action not "in the nature of defamation, invasion of privacy, or negligence."[236] Whether the specific subject matter preemptions in the FCRA preempt a state claim of unfair and deceptive acts and practices will depend upon the

---

225 Lomas Bank USA v. Flatow, 880 S.W.2d 52 (Tex. App. 1994) (consumers must establish malice in a negligence claim against a creditor alleged to have supplied false information to a CRA). See § 10.5.4, *supra*.
226 *See* Appx. H, *infra*.
227 *See* National Consumer Law Center, Unfair and Deceptive Acts and Practices Appx. A (6th ed. 2004). *See also* Ch. 6, *supra*.
228 *See* Commonwealth v. Source One Associates, Inc., 763 N.E.2d 42 (Mass. 2002) (conduct clashed with the norms established by the FTC, the FCRA, the state equivalent of FCRA and other state law).
229 *See* Cisneros v. U.D. Registry, 39 Cal. App. 4th 548, 46 Cal. Rptr. 2d 233 (1995).
230 *See, e.g.*, Ga. Code Ann. § 10-1-393(b)(29). *See* Appx. H, *infra*.
231 Cisneros v. U.D. Registry, 39 Cal. App. 4th 548, 46 Cal. Rptr. 2d 233 (1995) (violation of state and federal fair credit reporting statutes is a violation of California's UDAP statute).
232 15 U.S.C. § 1681s; Beattie v. Nations Credit Fin. Servs. Corp., 69 Fed. Appx. 585 (4th Cir. 2003) (unpublished) (not immoral, unethical, or oppressive to falsely report that mortgage is in foreclosure); Fisher v. Quality Hyundai, Inc., 2002 U.S. Dist. LEXIS 407 (N.D. Ill. Jan. 11, 2002) (consumer stated a claim for unfair or deceptive practices when dealer misrepresented to finance company that consumer was applying for credit and finance company relied on the representation).
233 96 F.T.C. 884 (1980), *rev'd in part on other grounds*, 678 F.2d 1047 (11th Cir. 1982).
234 96 F.T.C. 884 (1980).
235 *Id.*
236 Agosta v. Inovision, Inc., 2003 WL 22999213 (E.D. Pa. Dec. 16, 2003) (UDAP claim for intentional failure to reinvestigate is preempted); Jaramillo v. Experian Inf. Solutions, Inc., 155 F. Supp. 2d 356 (E.D. Pa. 2001), *vacated in part*, 2001 U.S. Dist. LEXIS 10221 (June 20, 2001) (vacated as to § 1681t(b) preemption holding). *But see* Polzer v. TRW, Inc., 682 N.Y.S.2d 194 (N.Y. App. Div. 1998).

nature of the activity and the breadth of the preemptions analyzed at § 10.7, *infra*.

10.6.3 State Identity Theft Laws

Many states have enacted criminal and civil laws that target identity theft.[237] As discussed below, however, the FCRA specifically preempts states from imposing any requirement or prohibition with respect to the "conduct required" by many of the new provisions of the FCRA aimed at preventing and remediating identity theft. Nonetheless, other aspects of state identity theft statutes should not be preempted.

10.7 FCRA's Preemption of State Law Claims

10.7.1 No "Field" Preemption

By its express language, the general preemption rule under the FCRA provides, subject to a number of important exceptions, that the Act does not preempt state law claims:

> Except as provided in subsections (b) and (c), this title does not annul, alter, affect, or exempt any person subject to the provisions of this title from complying with the laws of any State with respect to the collection, distribution, or use of any information on consumers or for the prevention or mitigation of identity theft, except to the extent that those laws are inconsistent with any provision of this title, and then only to the extent of the inconsistency.[238]

According to this savings clause, the FCRA does not generally preempt state credit reporting or other laws, unless there is a specific inconsistency between the FCRA and the state law,[239] or unless certain explicit FCRA exceptions apply. Courts have consistently found that this savings clause shows that Congress did not intend to comprehensively preempt states from the field of credit reporting

regulation.[240] Furthermore, in 2003, Congress added to the savings clause state laws "for the prevention or mitigation of identity theft." This evinces a strong presumption in favor of the rights of states to protect their citizens from identity theft, and implies a continuing congressional approval of the savings clause in general.

10.7.2 When Is State Law Inconsistent with the FCRA?

The FCRA does preempt state law "to the extent that those laws are inconsistent with any provision of this title, and then only to the extent of the inconsistency."[241] State law is inconsistent, for preemption purposes, only where the actor would violate the FCRA by complying with the state statute.[242] For example, a state fair credit reporting act that provided attorney fees to a prevailing consumer reporting agency (CRA) was held not to be preempted by the FCRA because a consumer could avoid the risk of becoming responsible for such fees by electing to sue under the FCRA without invoking state law.[243]

A state law is not inconsistent with the FCRA merely because it gives consumers more protection than does the federal act.[244] The Eighth Circuit has ruled that the FCRA did not preempt a state statutory provision requiring insurance companies doing business in the state to notify applicants and policyholders of the company's intent to obtain their personal information, and to state its purpose in col-

---

237 *See* § 9.4, *supra*, Appx. H, *infra*.
238 15 U.S.C. § 1681t(a). *See also* Davenport v. Farmers Ins. Group, 378 F.3d 839, 842 (8th Cir. 2004) (in ruling that the FCRA did not preempt a state statutory provision requiring insurance companies doing business in the state to notify applicants and policyholders if the company intends to obtain their personal information, "FCRA makes clear that it is not intended to occupy the entire regulatory field with regard to consumer reports").
239 Credit Data of Arizona, Inc. v. Arizona, 602 F.2d 195 (9th Cir. 1979); Sherron v. Private Issue By Discover, 977 F. Supp. 804 (N.D. Miss. 1997); Hughes v. Fidelity Bank, 709 F. Supp. 639, 641 (E.D. Pa. 1989); Equifax Servs., Inc. v. Cohen, 420 A.2d 189, 211 (Me. 1980).
240 Credit Data of Ariz., Inc. v. State of Ariz., 602 F.2d 195, 197 (9th Cir. 1979) (provision demonstrates Congress did not intend to preempt the field of claims); Sehl v. Safari Motor Coaches, Inc., 2001 WL 940846, at *5 (N.D. Cal. Aug. 13, 2001) (FCRA preemption not complete, therefore removal of plaintiff's libel action was improper); Watkins v. Trans Union, L.L.C., 118 F. Supp. 2d 1217, 1222 (N.D. Ala. 2000) (holding that court did not have removal jurisdiction).
241 15 U.S.C. § 1681t(a).
242 FTC Official Staff Commentary § 622 item 1, *reprinted at* Appx. D, *infra*. *See also* Goldfarb, FTC Informal Staff Opinion Letter (Sept. 20, 1978), *reprinted on the CD-Rom accompanying this manual*; Supplementary Information published with the FTC Official Staff Commentary, 55 Fed. Reg. 18,804, 18,808 (May 4, 1990). *But see* Retail Credit Co. v. Dade County, 393 F. Supp. 577, 580–581 (S.D. Fla. 1975) (look to see if state law consistent with all the express purposes of the FCRA); Equifax Servs., Inc. v. Cohen, 420 A.2d 189, 211 (Me. 1980).
243 Cisneros v. U.D. Registry, Consumer Cred. Guide, 46 Cal. Rptr. 2d 233, 252–253 (Cal. Ct. App. Oct. 19, 1995).
244 Petruccelli, FTC Informal Staff Opinion Letter (July 15, 1981), *reprinted on the CD-Rom accompanying this manual*; Goldfarb, FTC Informal Staff Opinion Letter (Sept. 20, 1978), *reprinted on the CD-Rom accompanying this manual*. *See also* Comment, *Preemption of State Credit Reporting Legislation: Toward Validation of State Authority*, 24 UCLA L. Rev. 83, 99–103 (1979); Validity and Construction of State Fair Credit Reporting Act, 12 A.L.R.4th 294 (1984). The principal report in the Act's legislative history stated that "no state law would be preempted unless compliance would involve a violation of Federal law." S. Rep. No. 517, 91st Cong., 1st Sess. 8 (Nov. 5, 1969).

lecting such information.[245] The court reasoned that since the FCRA neither specifically required insurance companies to notify consumers before obtaining their personal information, nor affirmatively permitted companies to procure such information without notice, the state statute was not inconsistent with the FCRA.[246]

Similarly, the Ninth Circuit upheld an Arizona statute that required disclosure of the consumer's file to the consumer at no charge, even though the federal statute authorized assessment of a reasonable charge.[247] The state law was not inconsistent with the federal law; it merely provided additional protection to the consumer, for whose benefit the FCRA was intended.[248] Similarly, before the FCRA itself was strengthened by amendment, the FTC Staff Commentary found no inconsistency in more protective state law provisions that required employers to notify consumers before ordering a consumer report or that require CRAs to provide the contents of a consumer's file to the consumer in writing.[249]

The FTC Staff Commentary also gives examples of inconsistent state laws that the FCRA preempts. A state law authorizing grand juries to compel CRAs to provide them with consumer reports would conflict with the FCRA's requirement that the reports only be provided for purposes explicitly permitted in the FCRA.[250] Similarly, the FCRA requires CRAs to notify past users if a file has been corrected or a statement of dispute filed, if the consumer so requests. Otherwise the CRA has no permissible purpose to send the information to the past user. Accordingly, a state statute requiring CRAs to notify past users without the consumer's consent would require CRAs to violate the FCRA by disseminating consumer information without a permissible purpose in violation of the FCRA.[251]

A state law may be inconsistent with the Act even when it offers more protection to the consumer than the federal act does, if it frustrates some other objective of the Act.[252] Thus, to determine whether state law frustrates any particular provision of the federal act the specific requirements must be compared not only in terms of their particular content vis-à-vis each other but also in relation to whether the content of the state law would thwart the "full purposes and objectives" of Congress.[253]

Two cases applied the general FCRA preemption standard to state statutes and came to opposite conclusions. At the time of the decisions, the FCRA did not require a CRA to disclose to the consumer medical information in its files.[254] One of several purposes of this provision was to prevent the disclosure of raw medical information to a consumer without the counsel of a physician.[255] In light of this congressional intent, a Florida federal court held that a local ordinance requiring disclosure that made no exception for the disclosure of medical information was preempted by the FCRA.[256] On the other hand, Maine's highest court held that a similar state law withstood preemption since the state law authorized disclosure of medical information only to a licensed physician, providing an opportunity for the counsel that the FCRA envisioned.[257]

The same two cases also came to opposite conclusions in applying the general FCRA preemption standard to state statutes that did not have qualified immunity provisions to protect CRAs from tort actions. The federal court ruled that the failure of county ordinances to provide similar qualified immunity was inconsistent with the federal act and therefore the Act preempted the ordinances.[258] However, the Maine court's more considered opinion upheld the even more stringent requirements of a state law that also failed to provide any immunity.[259] The Maine Supreme Judicial Court found that the omission of immunity was a mere "incidental aspect" of the state statute that did not prevent

---

245 Davenport v. Farmers Ins. Group, 378 F.3d 839, 842 (8th Cir. 2004).
246 Id.
247 Credit Data of Arizona, Inc. v. Arizona, 602 F.2d 195, 198 (9th Cir. 1979). Note that this case predates FACTA's amendment to the FCRA that allows consumers one free consumer report per year. Pub. L. No. 108-159, §§ 211, 212 (2003), *amending* 15 U.S.C. § 1681j(a)(1). *See also* § 3.3.8, *supra*. If state law imposes liability for acts authorized by the FCRA, the state law may be inconsistent and therefore preempted. Korotki v. Attorney Servs. Corp., 931 F. Supp. 1269, 1280 (D. Md. 1996) (dicta), *aff'd*, 131 F.3d 135 (4th Cir. 1997).
248 Credit Data of Arizona, Inc. v. Arizona, 602 F.2d 195, 198 (9th Cir. 1979).
249 FTC Official Staff Commentary § 622 item 2, *reprinted at* Appx. D, *infra*. The FCRA did not then require the disclosure be in writing. The statute was amended and strengthened with respect to employer investigations by the Omnibus Consolidated Appropriations Act of 1996, Pub. L. No. 104-208, 110 Stat. 3009 (Sept. 30, 1996), then weakened somewhat by FACTA, Pub. L. No. 108-159, § 111 (2003), *adding* 15 U.S.C. § 1681a(d)(2)(D)(x). *See also* Equifax Servs., Inc. v. Cohen, 420 A.2d 189, 211–215 (Me. 1980) (upholding various state credit reporting provisions).
250 FTC Official Staff Commentary § 622 item 3, *reprinted at* Appx. D, *infra*.
251 Id.
252 *See* Equifax Servs., Inc. v. Cohen, 420 A.2d 189, 211 (Me. 1980) (reasoning that the question of inconsistency requires not only a comparison between the specific requirements of the state and federal acts, but also a comparison of the state provision with the " 'full purposes and objectives' " of Congress).
253 Id.
254 Today, the consumer is entitled to this information, see § 3.5.1, *supra*.
255 H.R. Rep. No. 975, 91st Cong., 2d Sess. 28 (1970), *reprinted in* 1970 U.S.C.C.A.N. 4394, 4414.
256 Retail Credit Co. v. Dade County, 393 F. Supp. 577, 582 (S.D. Fla. 1975).
257 Equifax Servs., Inc. v. Cohen, 420 A.2d 189, 211, 212–213 (Me. 1980).
258 Retail Credit Co. v. Dade County, 393 F. Supp. 577, 584 (S.D. Fla. 1975).
259 Equifax Servs., Inc. v. Cohen, 420 A.2d 189, 214, 215 (Me. 1980).

the state statute from fulfilling the FCRA's dominant purpose by assuring "the full disclosure to consumers of all information ... to allow consumers ... to participate in the process of reviewing, refining, and correcting for accuracy the body of information" compiled about them.[260]

10.7.3 Overview Concerning Explicit FCRA Preemption Language

10.7.3.1 A Roadmap

The general FCRA rule is that state law is not preempted unless it is inconsistent with the FCRA or unless it is explicitly preempted by section 1681t(b).[261] Section 1681t(b) states that "[n]o requirement or prohibition may be imposed under the laws of any State" with respect to five different areas:[262]

- The "subject matter regulated by" eleven specific FCRA provisions;[263]
- The exchange of information among affiliates;[264]
- Designated disclosures required by section 1681g;[265]
- The frequency with which consumers can obtain free consumer reports;[266] and
- The "conduct required by" twelve specific FCRA provisions.[267]

Sections 10.7.4–10.7.9, *infra*, analyze these five different FCRA preemptions of state law found in section 1681t(b). While a state law must be scrutinized as it relates to each of these five preemption provisions, in general the following types of state laws should be reviewed closely:

- State laws placing requirements on furnishers as to the accuracy of information they provide, their obligations to correct inaccurate information, their response to consumer disputes and requests to reinvestigate the accuracy of that information, and their obligation to notify CRAs when an account is closed voluntarily, to specify the date of any delinquency, and to respond to notice of an identity theft.[268]
- State laws placing obligations on furnishers when they are notified of identity theft;[269]
- State laws placing obligations on financial institutions to notify customers when they furnish negative information to CRAs and furnishers of medical information to notify CRAs of their medical status;[270]
- State laws dealing with the exchange of information among affiliates;[271]
- State laws related to CRA prescreening of consumer reports, responding to consumer disputes of information in their files, and their reporting of information to users;[272]
- State laws requiring CRAs to make disclosures to consumers,[273] and specifying the frequency with which CRAs must provide free consumer reports;[274]
- State laws relating to obligation of users of consumer reports and other third party information when the user takes adverse actions, makes a firm offer of credit or insurance, uses information for marketing purposes, or provides notices of risk-based loan pricing;[275]
- State laws relating to the obligations of users when they are notified of identity theft, and also the obligations of users to comply with "red flag" guidelines and also to properly dispose consumer information;[276]
- State laws placing obligations on businesses that accept credit or debit cards not to print out more than the last five digits of the card number,[277] or to provide certain information to identity theft victims when they receive reports of identify theft related to that business;[278]
- State laws relating to the obligations of debt collectors when they are notified that information related to a debt may be fraudulent or the result of identity theft.

This explicit preemption of certain state laws should not be confused with the FCRA's creation in a separate section of a limited immunity provided to CRAs, users, and furnishers against tort claims for defamation, invasion of privacy, or negligence.[279] While courts sometimes interpret section 1681t(b) in ways to harmonize it with this limited immunity, the two sections are distinct. This section interprets only section 1681t(b).

---

260 *Id.*
261 15 U.S.C. § 1681t(a). In addition, § 1681t(c) states that the term "firm offer of credit or insurance" or any equivalent term used in a state law shall have the same meaning at that term has under the FCRA. *See* 15 U.S.C. § 1681a(l). *See also* Cole v. U.S. Capital, 389 F.3d 719, 726 (7th Cir. 2004) (rejecting plaintiff's argument that a proposal insufficient to qualify as an offer under state law could not justify release of her consumer report under the FCRA's prescreened offer provision).
262 These specific preemptions of state law do not affect any settlement agreement or consent judgment between any state attorney general and any CRA in effect on Sept. 30, 1996. 15 U.S.C. § 1681t(d).
263 15 U.S.C. § 1681t(b)(1). *See* §§ 10.7.4, 10.7.5, *infra*.
264 15 U.S.C. § 1681t(b)(2). *See* § 10.7.6, *infra*.
265 15 U.S.C. § 1681t(b)(3). *See* § 10.7.7, *infra*.
266 15 U.S.C. § 1681t(b)(4). *See* § 10.7.8, *infra*.
267 15 U.S.C. § 1681t(b)(5). *See* § 10.7.9, *infra*.
268 *See* § 10.7.5.2, *infra*.
269 § 10.7.9.4, *infra*.
270 § 10.7.5.2, *infra*.
271 *See* § 10.7.6, *infra*.
272 § 10.7.5.3, *infra*.
273 § 10.7.7, *infra*.
274 § 10.7.8, *infra*.
275 *See* § 10.7.5.4, *infra*.
276 § 10.7.9.3, *infra*.
277 § 10.7.9.6, *infra*.
278 *See* §§ 10.7.5.5, 10.7.7, *infra*.
279 15 U.S.C. § 1681h(e), *discussed at* § 10.4, *supra*.

10.7.3.2 General Principles of Interpretation

When Congress employs express preemption in a federal act, the scope of the clause depends on its language, along with that of any savings clause in the act.[280] When examining an express preemption clause, a court must focus on the plain wording of the clause, because that wording is "the best evidence of Congress' pre-emptive intent."[281] When the state statute pertains to "a field which the States have traditionally occupied," the federal Act will preempt the state's laws only when "that was the clear and manifest purpose of Congress."[282] Consumer protection is just such a field that the states have traditionally occupied.[283]

10.7.3.3 Applicability of Pre-FACTA Case Law to Current FCRA Preemption Provisions

The FCRA's explicit preemption provisions were due to expire on January 1, 2004,[284] but the Fair and Accurate Credit Transactions Act of 2003 (FACTA) removed this sunset clause, thus retaining the earlier preemption language. The FACTA amendments to the FCRA also added new language whereby additional FCRA provisions preempted state law. Case law prior to the FACTA amendments will still be good precedent for the preemption language that has been retained unchanged, but only partially relevant to the new preemption language.

Most of the older cases interpreting the preexisting FCRA preemption language examine section 1681t(b)(1): "No requirement or prohibition may be imposed under the laws of any State" with respect to "any subject matter regulated under" enumerated FCRA provisions. FACTA did not amend this language, only adding several FCRA provisions to which the language applies. Thus case law interpreting section 1681t(b)(1) continues to be directly relevant to section 1681t(b)(1) cases,[285] and is analyzed at § 10.7.4, *infra*.

The FACTA amendments added a new subsection 1681t(b)(5) that states that no requirement or prohibition may be imposed under the laws of any state with respect to "the conduct required by" other enumerated FCRA provisions. Limiting state law with respect to "the conduct required by" a section is less restrictive than limiting state law with respect to "subject matter regulated under" a section. Consequently, existing case law interpreting section 1681t(b)(1) will only be partially relevant to issues arising under new section 1681t(b)(5).

The preemption language found in sections 1681t(b)(2) and 1681t(c) are unchanged, that found in section 1681t(b)(3) has been expanded, and a new section 1681t(b)(4) has been added. For this preemption language, the case law interpreting section 1681t(b)(1) is only partially relevant.

10.7.4 Interpretations of "With Respect to the Subject Matter Regulated"

10.7.4.1 Overview of Case Law Interpreting § 1681t(b)(1)

While the majority of the preemption analysis in this area has centered around requirements relating to furnishers, the analysis applies to other types of requirements as well. Courts have differed significantly over the meaning of the phrase that "no requirement or prohibition may be imposed under" state law "with respect to the subject matter regulated under" the specified FCRA provisions. A small minority of courts preempt virtually all state statutory and common law tort claims in any way relating to the subject of credit reporting. The majority of courts limit the preemptive effect of the provision in three different ways. First, the preemption language is interpreted as only applying to statutory, and not to tort or other common law claims. Second, preemption of state claims is limited in time to only those state claims based on conduct occurring after FCRA liability is triggered. Third, only state claims are preempted whose elements closely resemble those of the substantive FCRA provision.

---

280 Sprietsma v. Mercury Marine, a Div. of Brunswick Corp., 537 U.S. 51, 63 (2002); Cipollone v. Liggett Group, Inc. 505 U.S. 504 (1992) (where Congress preempted state law "requirements or prohibitions" based on smoking and health advertising, even some common law remedies were preempted, but claims with respect to express warranties, fraud, misrepresentation, and conspiracy were not preempted because they were predicated on a general standard not to deceive which is not a duty based on "smoking or health").
281 CSX Transp., Inc. v. Easterwood, 507 U.S. 658, 664 (1993).
282 Rice v. Santa Fe Elevator Corp., 331 U.S. 218, 230 (1947). *See also* Medtronic, Inc. v. Lohr, 518 U.S. 470, 485 (1996) (plurality opinion) (federal Medical Device Amendments provisions did not preempt state products liability claims).
283 General Motors Corp. v. Abrams, 897 F.2d 34, 41 (2d Cir. 1990) ("[b]ecause consumer protection law is a field traditionally regulated by the states, compelling evidence of an intention to preempt is required in this area").
284 15 U.S.C. § 1681t(d) (2000).
285 One court held that a state statute requiring a creditor to notify its customer that it was furnishing negative information about the customer was not preempted by the pre-FACTA preemption provision. Banga v. World Sav. and Loan Ass'n, 2006 WL 1467967, at *4–5 (Cal. Ct. App. May 30, 2006) (citing Cal. Civ. Code § 1785.26). The court reasoned that the creditor could comply with both its obligations under the state statute and under the FCRA without conflict. *Id.* at *4. However, the court noted, without elaboration, that the FACTA amendments added a provision similar to the state notification statute after the events giving rise to the case; if the state provision is construed as regulating the same "subject matter" as the new provision, it would now be preempted.

10.7.4.2 Minority Cases Find Statutory and Common Law Claims Generally Preempted

In a decision that has subsequently been vacated by the judge who issued it, a Pennsylvania district court held that section 1681t(b)(1) preempted all actions against furnishers.[286] This interpretation carries two flaws. It ignores the language which limits the sorts of state laws preempted to those that relate to the "subject matter regulated under" certain provisions. It also effectively renders superfluous furnishers' qualified immunity from tort claims found in another FCRA provision.[287] If section 1681t(b)(1) preempts all state causes of action against furnishers, there would be no need to offer furnishers in that other section the qualified immunity from the listed tort actions.[288] Since this decision has been vacated, it should not be cited as precedent. Nonetheless a number of courts have followed it.[289]

10.7.4.3 Only Statutory, Not Common Law Claims Are Preempted

The FCRA's express preemption provision applies not to all state law claims, but only to the "requirement or prohibition of any State." That language, when read in conjunction with the FCRA provision limiting furnishers' qualified immunity from tort claims only where the furnisher acted without malice or willful intent,[290] strongly suggests that Congress did not intend to preempt state common law claims, as opposed to state statutory or regulatory claims, brought for behavior that may also violate the FCRA.[291] If section 1681t(b) preempts all state causes of action against furnishers, there would be no need to offer furnishers qualified immunity from the listed tort actions.[292] Congress ignored its opportunity with the FACTA amendments to clarify the relationship of section 1681t(b) with FCRA's qualified immunity provision for furnishers; that omission in the face of existing preemption decisions further indicates that it did not intend section 1681t(b) to apply to tort

---

286 Jaramillo v. Experian Info. Solutions, Inc., 155 F. Supp. 2d 356, 362 (E.D. Pa. 2001), *vacated in relevant part*, Jaramillo v. Experian Info. Solutions, Inc., 2001 WL 1762626 (E.D. Pa. June 20, 2001).
287 15 U.S.C. § 1681h(e).
288 *See* § 10.4, *supra*.
289 *See* Cope v. MBNA Am. Bank N.A., 2006 U.S. Dist. LEXIS 10937, at *24 (D. Or. Mar. 8, 2006) (holding that provision preempted a defamation claim); Abbett v. Bank of Am., 2006 WL 581193, at *5 (M.D. Ala. Mar. 8, 2006) (holding that provision preempted state defamation, invasion of privacy, negligence, and conspiracy claims); Schade v. MBNA Am. Bank, N.A., 2006 WL 212147, at *7 (W.D.N.C. Jan. 26, 2006) (holding that provision preempted state UDAP claim); Campbell v. Chase Manhattan Bank, USA, N.A., 2005 U.S. Dist. LEXIS 16402, 51–53 (D.N.J. June 27, 2005) (holding that provision preempted intentional infliction of emotional distress, negligent infliction of emotional distress, and misrepresentation and injurious falsehood claims); Hutchinson v. Del. Sav. Bank F.S.B., 410 F. Supp. 2d 374, 384–385 (D.N.J. 2006) (holding that provision preempted state negligence, intentional tort, breach of contract, and state UDAP claims); Roybal v. Equifax, 405 F. Supp. 2d 1177, 1181–1182 (E.D. Cal. 2005) (holding that section 1681t(b)(1)(F) preempted all state claims, both statutory and common law, against furnishers); Pirouzian v. SLM Corp., 396 F. Supp. 2d 1124, 1130 (S.D. Cal. 2005) (holding that provision preempted a state debt collection statute); Howard v. Blue Ridge Bank, 371 F. Supp. 2d 1139, 1143–1144 (N.D. Cal. 2005) (holding that provision preempted a state unfair competition claim); Shah v. Collecto, Inc., 2005 WL 2216242, at *14 (D. Md. Sept. 12, 2005) (holding that provision preempted state tort claims against a debt collector, which the court reasoned was subject to the provisions of 15 U.S.C. § 1681s-2(b)); Henry v. Fleet Boston, 2003 WL 22401247, at *2 (D.N.H. Oct. 20, 2003) (granting summary judgment to furnisher on plaintiffs' defamation and negligent infliction of emotional distress claims without deciding which of the two provisions controlled); Purcell v. Universal Bank, N.A. 2003 WL 1962376, at *4 (E.D. Pa. Apr. 28, 2003) (relying on *Jaramillo*, *Riley*, and *Vasquez-Garcia* to hold that section 1681t(b)(1)(F) preempts any state law claims based on reports to CRAs); Agosta v. Inovision, Inc., 2003 WL 22999213, at *8 (E.D. Pa. Dec. 16, 2003) (dismissing plaintiff's claims for defamation, negligence, and invasion of privacy); Riley v. Gen Motors Acceptance Corp., 226 F. Supp. 2d 1316 (S.D. Ala. 2002) (section 1681t preempts all state causes of action against furnishers, both statutory and common law, where the state law claim is based on the same conduct that gives rise to the FCRA claim); Davis v. Maryland Bank, 2002 WL 32713429, at *12, 14 (N.D. Cal. June 19, 2002) (stating in dicta that section 1681t(b)(1)(F) preempted all claims against furnishers, whether based on 1681s-2(a) or 1681s-2(b)); Hasvold v. First U.S. Bank, N.A., 194 F. Supp. 2d 1228, 1239 (D. Wyo. 2002) (citing *Jaramillo* with approval, holding that § 1681t barred plaintiff, an identity theft victim, from suing a furnisher for defamation and invasion of privacy). *See also* Jarrett v. Bank of Am., 2006 WL 709322, at *3 (D. Kan. Mar. 20, 2006) (stating that preemption provision "appear[ed] to preempt" an invasion of privacy action against a furnisher).
290 15 U.S.C. § 1681h(e).
291 *See also* Sprietsma v. Mercury Marine, 537 U.S. 51, 63 (2002) (in construing section 10 of the Federal Boat Safety Act, 46 U.S.C. § 4306, holding that the term "law or regulation" in an express preemption clause referred only to positive state enactments, and not to state common law tort claims).
292 TRW Inc. v. Andrews, 534 U.S. 19, 31 (2001) ("'[i]t is 'a cardinal principle of statutory construction' that 'a statute ought, upon the whole, to be so construed that, if it can be prevented, no clause, sentence, or word shall be superfluous, void, or insignificant' ") (quoting Duncan v. Walker, 533 U.S. 167, 174 (2001)). Other courts have also agreed that Congress's failure to remove furnishers from section 1681h(e) when it added section 1681t indicated that it did not intend for the new section to preempt all claims against them. Johnson v. Citimortgage, Inc., 351 F. Supp. 2d 1368, 1374 (N.D. Ga. 2004); Mattice v. Equifax, 2003 WL 21391679, at *2 (D. Minn. June 13, 2003) (rejecting furnisher's argument that § 1681t completely subsumed § 1681h(e)); Stafford v. Cross Country Bank, 262 F. Supp. 2d 776 (W.D. Ky. 2003) (provisions must be read together); Vazquez-Garcia v. Trans Union de Puerto Rico, 222 F. Supp. 2d 150 (D. P.R. 2002) (rejecting argument that § 1681t completely bars state actions against furnishers on grounds that such a reading would in fact nullify part of § 1681h(e)). *See also* Woltersdorf v. Pentagon Fed. Credit Union, 320 F. Supp. 2d 1222 (N.D. Ala. 2004).

claims.293 As a result, the more thoughtful courts have limited the subject matter preemption to statutory claims, and not tort claims.294

For example, a Texas district court interpreted the provision as preempting only state statutes, not common law actions, on the grounds that the two specific state laws exempted from the preemption provision were both credit reporting statutes that specifically referenced furnishers.295 Similarly, a Minnesota district court rejected a furnisher's argument that the immunity and preemption provisions together barred any action based on any matter regulated by the FCRA provisions relating to furnishers.296 The court reasoned that such a reading would render the general immunity provision superfluous as to furnishers.297 Yet another interpretation uses the statutory construction rule that specific provisions prevail over general, and therefore the specific language of the qualified immunity provision preserved claims that would otherwise be considered preempted by the more general language of section 1681t(b).298

10.7.4.4 Preemption Only Where State Statute Closely Resembles FCRA Provision

A number of cases have limited section 1681t(b)(1) preemption only to where the state statute closely relates to the subject matter regulated by one of the enumerated provision listed in section 1681t(b)(1). For example, in the identity theft case of *Carlson v. Trans Union, L.L.C.*,299 the court framed its analysis around the elements of the particular claims, and held that a consumer's defamation claim withstood preemption.300 The court reasoned that the proof required for each claim determined the scope of each claim's subject matter, notwithstanding that the same underlying acts gave rise to all the claims.301 A claim under section 1681s-2 would require the plaintiff to show that the defendant violated a duty to thoroughly investigate the plaintiff's claim that his credit record was inaccurate. In contrast, a defamation claim would require proof of publication of a defamatory statement that concerned the plaintiff, made with negligence.302 Dissimilar proof, dissimilar claims.

A claim may also be dissimilar if it imposes a general duty on the public at large, as opposed to a duty imposed only on those playing a designated role in a consumer reporting transaction. A federal court ruled that section 1681t(b)(1) does not preempt state common law tort claims such as negligence, defamation, or invasion of privacy against furnishers, because those torts did not in and of themselves impose any special duty on furnishers that did

---

293 *See* Stafford v. Cross Country Bank, 262 F. Supp. 2d 776, 786 (W.D. Ky. 2003) (provisions must be read together).

294 Beuster v. Equifax Info. Servs., 2006 WL 1669790, at *5–6 (D. Md. June 15, 2006); Islam v. Option One Mortg. Corp., 2006 WL 1216617, *7–8 (D. Mass. May 5, 2006) (dicta); Johnson v. MBNA Am. Bank Nat'l Ass'n, 2006 WL 618077, at *7 (M.D.N.C. Mar. 9, 2006); Alabran v. Capital One Bank, 2005 WL 3338663, at *5 (E.D. Va. Dec. 8, 2005); DiPrinzio v. MBNA America Bank, N.A., 2005 WL 2039175, at *7 (E.D. Pa. Aug. 24, 2005); Barnhill v. Bank of Am., N.A., 378 F. Supp. 2d 696, 704 (D.S.C. 2005); Jordan v. Trans Union L.L.C., 377 F. Supp. 2d 1307, 1309 (D. Ga. 2005); Gorman v. Wolpoff & Abramson, L.L.P., 370 F. Supp. 2d 1005, 1009–1011 (D. Cal. 2005); Watson v. Trans Union Credit Bureau, 2005 U.S. Dist. LEXIS 7376, at *26 (D. Me. Apr. 28, 2005) (magistrate's recommendation); McCloud v. Homeside Lending, 309 F. Supp. 2d 1335, 1341 (N.D. Ala. 2004); Woltersdorf v. Pentagon Fed. Credit Union, 320 F. Supp. 2d 1222 (N.D. Ala. 2004); Jeffrey v. Trans Union, 273 F. Supp. 2d 725, 728 (E.D. Va. 2003); Gordon v. Greenpoint Credit, 266 F. Supp. 2d 1007 (S.D. Iowa 2003); Sheffer v. Experian Info. Solutions, Inc., 249 F. Supp. 2d 560 (E.D. Pa. 2003); Carlson v. Trans Union L.L.C., 259 F. Supp. 2d 517 (N.D. Tex. 2003) (relying in part on the fact that the furnisher action preemption section specifically exempted two state statutes from the preemption. Given that none of the new subject-matter-preemption provisions have any similar exemptions, the court's reasoning may not apply to the interpretation of the new provisions); Yutesler v. Sears Roebuck & Co., 263 F. Supp. 2d 1209 (D. Minn. 2003); Nelski v. Ameritech, 2004 WL 1460001 (Mich. Ct. App. June 29, 2004).

295 Carlson v. Trans Union, L.L.C., 259 F. Supp. 2d 517 (N.D. Tex. 2003). *See also* Manno v. Am. Gen. Fin. Co., 2006 WL 1967338, at *7 (E.D. Pa. July 12, 2006) (section 1681t(b)(1)(F) preempted the plaintiff's state UDAP claim); Johnson v. Citimortgage, Inc., 351 F. Supp. 2d 1368, 1376 (N.D. Ga. 2004) (holding that section 1681t(b)(1)(F) applied to state statutory claims and section 1681h(e) applied to state common law claims); Jeffery v. Trans Union, L.L.C., 273 F. Supp. 2d 725, 728 (E.D. Va. 2003) (denying defendant's motion for judgment on the pleadings on plaintiff's defamation claim on the grounds that section 1681t(b)(1)(F) preempted only state statutory claims; Sheffer v. Experian Info. Solutions, Inc., 249 F. Supp. 2d 560 (E.D. Pa. 2003) (refusing to dismiss plaintiff's defamation claim on grounds that neither section 1681h(e) or section 1681t(b)(1) apply when false information is furnished with malice or willful intent to injure, an interpretation that grafts the qualification of section 1681h(e)'s immunity onto section 1681t, but without thorough analysis); Nelski v. Ameritech, 2004 WL 1460001, at *6 (Mich. Ct. App. June 29, 2004) (relying on *Carney* and *Carlson* to hold that section 1681t(1)(F) preempted only state statutory claims, not state common law claims, and that accordingly the provision did not bar identity theft victim's defamation claim against furnisher).

296 Yutesler v. Sears Roebuck & Co., 263 F. Supp. 2d 1209, 1211–1212 (D. Minn. 2003) (holding that plaintiff's common law claim for defamation of credit that asserted gross negligence survived both the general immunity and supplemental preemption provisions).

297 *Id.* at 1212.

298 McCloud v. Homeside Lending, 309 F. Supp. 2d 1335, 1341 (N.D. Ala. 2004) (holding that since section 1681h(e) took precedence over section 1681t(b)(1)(F) because it was more specific); Gordon v. Greenpoint Credit, 266 F. Supp. 2d 1007 (S.D. Iowa 2003) (holding that negligence and defamation claims against furnisher were not preempted).

299 259 F. Supp. 2d 517 (N.D. Tex. 2003).

300 The suit alleged that the defendant, a telephone company had furnished false reports. *Id.* at *1.

301 *Id.* at *3.

302 *Id.* The court did not employ the elevated standard of section 1681h(e).

not apply to the public at large.³⁰³ The court further stated that the section would not preempt any claims based on the furnisher's improper opening of an account for the thief, because those would be actions not covered by the FCRA, that is, not "subject matter regulated by" section 1681s-2.³⁰⁴

The degree of similarity necessary to pull the claim into the preemption provision varies from decision to decision. While *Carlson* compared the proof necessary to establish the elements of the tort claim and the section 1681s-2 violation, to rule that the plaintiff's defamation claim was not preempted, another identity theft case, *Stafford v. Cross Country Bank*,³⁰⁵ focused on the role of the defendant at the time the actionable conduct occurred, and ruled that the plaintiff's defamation claim was preempted. The court reasoned that section 1681t(b)(1) preempted only those tort claims that implicated conduct falling within section 1681s-2, which the court interpreted to be the conduct involved in the reporting of credit information after receiving notice of a dispute.³⁰⁶ In contrast, those claims that involved the bank's actions that were "independent of its function as a furnisher of credit information" were not preempted.³⁰⁷

Applying this distinction, the court struck the defamation, slander and UDAP claims, along with certain aspects of an invasion of privacy claim, but allowed other aspects of the invasion of privacy claim along with a harassment claim to proceed.³⁰⁸ Similarly, the victim's claim that the bank acted unconscionably in verifying the identity of its applicants was not preempted for it did not go to the bank's furnishing function.³⁰⁹ Under this analysis, the issue is whether the creditor is wearing its furnisher's hat when it commits the injuring acts (state claim preempted), as opposed to its creditor's or banker's hat (state claim preserved).

10.7.4.5 Preemption Applies Only to Claims Based on Conduct Occurring *After* FCRA Liability Is Triggered

Courts following a "before and after" approach focus on when the conduct that gave rise to the plaintiff's claim against the furnisher occurred, on the theory that section 1681s-2 regulates furnisher conduct only after a specific event has occurred:

- The furnisher has reported information with actual knowledge of errors (triggering section 1681s-2(a)(1)(A));
- The furnisher has received notice from a consumer that specific information is inaccurate (triggering section 1681s-2(a)(1)(B)); or
- A CRA has notified the furnisher that a reported item is in dispute (triggering section 1681s-2(b)).

Under this analysis, each provision's obligations set the circumference of that provision's "subject matter;" the preemption provision bars state claims based on the furnisher's behavior after the furnisher's responsibilities under section 1681s-2 have arisen.

So, for example, in *Aklagi v. Nationscredit Financial*,³¹⁰ a federal court held that a defamation claim was preempted to the extent that it was based on a furnisher's furnishing of inaccurate information to a CRA after the furnisher received notice that the consumer disputed the information. This suit was brought by an identity theft victim after the defendant made a mortgage loan to a person posing as the plaintiff, a loan that subsequently defaulted and led to the furnisher's damaging the plaintiff's credit record. The court reasoned

---

303 Dornhecker v. Ameritech Corp. 99 F. Supp. 2d 918, 931 (N.D. Ill. 2000). *See also* Brown v. Bank One Corp., 2002 WL 31654950, at *2–3 (N.D. Ill. Nov. 22, 2002) (relying on *Dornecker* to hold that since bank's alleged misconduct in issuing false loans in plaintiffs' names was not regulated by the FCRA, section 1681t(b)(1)(F) did not preempt their state consumer fraud act claim).

304 *Id. See also* Carney v. Experian Info. Solutions, Inc., 57 F. Supp. 2d 496 (W.D. Tenn. 1999) (section 1681t preempted state UDAP claim based on furnisher's failure to provide accurate information after being notified by a consumer of a dispute).

305 262 F. Supp. 2d 776, 787 (W.D. Ky. May 8, 2003).

306 *Id.* at 787.

307 *Id. See also* Massey v. MBNA Am. Bank, N.A., 2005 WL 3099011, at *2 (W.D. Ky. Nov. 17, 2005) (following *Stafford* to hold that the plaintiff's "state law claim of loss of economic and business opportunities relates directly to MBNA's reporting of credit information and is thus, preempted").

308 *Id.*

309 *Id.*

310 196 F. Supp. 2d 1186, 1195 (D. Kan. 2002). One potential problem to applying this line of cases to define the effect of subject matter preemption of FCRA to claims under sections 1681g(e) or 1681m(e) is that unlike section 1681s-2, the section that this line interpreted and which defines a group of obligations of furnishers for which a consumer can bring a private cause of action distinct from a group for which a consumer may not, the FACTA amendments specifically provides that no private cause of action exists under section 1681g(e) or 1681m(e). 15 U.S.C. §§ 1681t(3)(6), 1681s(c)(3). Furthermore, section 1681h(e)'s qualified immunity provision, which by its terms could apply to state claims brought against a furnisher for conduct violating the provisions of section 1681s-2, does not appear to be relevant to the sort of suit that could be brought to enforce rights of the sort given by section 1681g(e). Accordingly, neither the temporal split nor the preemption/qualified immunity conflict that led to the result in *Aklagi* are necessarily present in a case brought to enforce such rights, and arguably the logic of *Aklagi* may not work to preserve any state claims. However, given that these cases preempt only those claims arising after the prerequisites of section 1681s-2(b), notice of a dispute from a CRA, have arisen, *Aklagi* could be adapted to interpret "subject matter" preemption as preempting only those claims where the FCRA's provision prerequisites have been met and have imposed an affirmative duty on the actor.

that the subject matter of the suit was regulated by section 1681s-2(a)(1)(B), and therefore section 1681t(b)(1) preempted the state law claims.[311] The court distinguished, in its analysis, the portion of the plaintiff's claim that was based on information furnished by the furnisher after it made the loan but *before* it received notice of the consumer's dispute, ruling that such a time period is not regulated under section 1681s-2, given that no evidence indicated that the furnisher had known or consciously avoided knowing that the information was inaccurate, which would have been conduct within the strictures of the Act.[312] Accordingly, the subject matter preemption provision did not bar the plaintiff's prenotice action.[313]

Similarly, another federal court interpreted section 1681t(b)(1) as barring all state actions against a furnisher that are based on conduct occurring after the furnisher received the notice from a CRA that triggers the furnisher's obligations under section 1681s-2.[314] Several courts have also followed this construction.[315]

311　196 F. Supp. 2d at 1195.
312　*Id.*
313　*Id.* However, her victory was brief. The court then ruled that the general qualified immunity provision found in section 1681h(e) did bar the action, because the plaintiff had failed to show the malice or willful intent necessary to remove the action from immunity. *Id.* at 1196. A similar result occurred in Reed v. Experian Info. Solutions, Inc., 321 F. Supp. 2d 1109, 1116–1117, 1117 n.4 (D. Minn. 2004).
314　Vazquez-Garcia v. Trans Union de Puerto Rico, 222 F. Supp. 2d 150, 162 (D. P.R. 2002) (construing section 1681s-2 obligations as arising once the CRA, rather than the furnisher, receives notice of the consumer's dispute).
315　Holland v. GMAC Mortg. Corp., 2006 WL 1133224, at *12 (D. Kan. Apr. 26, 2006) (holding that notice from the consumer, as opposed to notice from a CRA, suffices); Larobina v. First Union Nat'l Bank, 2006 WL 437396, at *5–6 (Conn. Super. Ct. Feb. 1, 2006) (denying the defendant's motion for summary judgment on the grounds that the time of notice of "specific information" being in error was a factual dispute); Ryder v. Wash. Mut. Bank, FA, 371 F. Supp. 2d 152, 155 (D. Conn. 2005) (dismissing state UDAP and defamation claims where the plaintiff had notified the furnisher of his dispute); Kane v. Guaranty Residential Lending, Inc., 2005 U.S. Dist. LEXIS 17052, at *29 (E.D.N.Y. May 9, 2005) (holding that notice need not be from a CRA to trigger preemptive protection); Millett v. Ford Motor Credit Co., 2005 U.S. Dist. LEXIS 8806, at *7–9 (D. Kan. Apr. 20, 2005); Cox v. Beneficial Kansas, Inc. 2005 WL 627974, *3 (D. Kan. Mar. 9, 2005); Malm v. Household Bank (SB), N.A., 2004 WL 1559370 (D. Minn. July 7, 2004) (dismissing claim based on inaccurate information that furnisher furnished after plaintiff had notified the furnisher that he was not liable for the debt); Woltersdorf v. Pentagon Fed. Credit Union, 2004 WL 504659 (N.D. Ala. Mar. 12, 2004) (preserving possibility of claims arising based on disclosures unrelated to defendant's furnishing of information; defamation, libel, and slander claims arising before information was furnished; and claims that defendant recklessly failed to adopt training policies and to train and supervise its employees); Mattice v. Equifax, 2003 WL 21391679 (D. Minn. June 13, 2003) (adopting *Aklagi*'s reasoning in refusing to dismiss claim against furnisher); Bank One, N.A. v. Colley, 294 F. Supp. 2d 864, 869 (M.D. La.

10.7.5 Section 1681t(b)(1) Preemption Language Applies to Eleven FCRA Provisions

10.7.5.1 Introduction

The FCRA lists eleven provisions the subject matter of which is to be free from any state "requirement or prohibition:"

- Section 1681s-2 concerning furnishers;
- Sections 1681b(c), 1681b(e), 1681(c), and 1681i concerning CRAs;
- Sections 1681m(a), (b), (d), and (h), and 1681s-3 all concerning users; and
- Section 1681g(e) relating to business' obligations for identity theft victims.

Eight of these pre-dated the FACTA amendments, and three were added by the FACTA amendments.

10.7.5.2 Provisions Regarding Furnishers

15 U.S.C. § 1681s-2 imposes the following specific types of obligations on furnishers that are subject to subject matter preemption through section 1681t(b)(1):

- Not to report information the furnisher "knows or has reasonable cause to believe" is inaccurate;[316]
- Not to furnish inaccurate information if the consumer has notified the furnisher that the information is inaccurate, the consumer gave that notice at the address specified by the furnisher for such notices, and the information is in fact inaccurate;[317]
- Where a furnisher determines that it has provided inaccurate or incomplete information to a CRA to promptly inform the CRA of the determination and to

---

2003) (subject matter preemption provision barred plaintiffs' negligence and defamation claims that arose from conduct occurring after the furnisher was notified of an inaccuracy in their report); Mendoza v. Experian Info. Solutions, Inc., 2003 WL 2005832 (S.D. Tex. Mar. 25, 2003) (whether cause of action survived depended upon whether CRAs fulfilled their responsibilities to notify furnisher of dispute; if they did, state claims were preempted, if they did not, claims could survive because cause of action would not relate to subject matter regulated under § 1681s-2(b)); Aklagi v. Nationscredit Fin., 196 F. Supp. 2d 1186, 1195 (D. Kan. 2002); Vazquez-Garcia v. Trans Union de Puerto Rico, 222 F. Supp. 2d 150 (D. P.R. 2002); Larobina v. First Union Nat'l Bank, 2004 WL 1664230 (Conn. Super. Ct. June 28, 2004) (relying on *Colley* to deny plaintiff's motion to strike furnisher's section 1681t(b)(1)(F) defense to plaintiff's negligence and negligent infliction of emotional distress claims).
316　15 U.S.C. § 1681s-2(a)(1)(A). *See* § 3.4.2, *supra*.
317　15 U.S.C. § 1681s-2(a)(1)(B). *See* § 6.4.2, *supra*.

provide corrected information;³¹⁸
- Once a consumer has disputed an item's accuracy, to notify the CRA of the dispute upon refurnishing it;³¹⁹
- If a creditor who regularly and in the ordinary course of business furnishes information to a CRA, to notify the CRA when a consumer voluntarily closes the account;³²⁰
- If a person who furnishes information to a CRA regarding a delinquent account placed for collection or charged to profit or loss, to inform the CRA of the date of the delinquency;³²¹
- If a furnisher that has received notice of a consumer's dispute from a consumer must reinvestigate the disputed information, to review all relevant information provided by the CRA, and to take action to correct any inaccuracy;³²²
- Requirements that furnishers have in place reasonable procedures to respond to a CRA's notice of a block of identity theft information, and, when they receive an identity theft report from the consumer, to stop furnishing the fraudulent information;³²³
- A requirement that a financial institution notify a customer that it is furnishing negative information about that consumer to a CRA;³²⁴
- A provision that allows a consumer to dispute an inaccurate report directly with a furnisher. Until regulations are issued, the furnisher need not reinvestigate upon receipt of this notice;³²⁵
- A requirement that furnishers whose primary business is providing medical services, products, or devices to notify the CRA of such status.³²⁶

The FCRA explicitly lists two state statutes, one in Massachusetts and one in California, regarding furnisher liability, that are *not* preempted as those statutes were in effect on September 30, 1996.³²⁷ However, while the substantive California statute is not preempted, courts have held that the California law providing a private right of action to enforce that prohibition is preempted.³²⁸ Other preexisting state laws, being not explicitly referenced in the FCRA, do not receive this immunity from preemption.³²⁹

10.7.5.3 Provisions Regarding Consumer Reporting Agencies

The subject matter preemption provision in section 1681t(b)(1) covers claims against CRAs relating to:

- The prescreening of consumer reports;³³⁰
- A consumer's election to be removed from prescreened lists;³³¹
- The time by which a CRA must take any action in any procedure related to disputed information in a consumer's file;³³² and
- Information contained in consumer reports.³³³

State credit reporting laws in effect on September 30, 1996 are protected from preemption with respect to the subject matter of the last two listed items.³³⁴ To the extent a tort claim is a state "law," arguably any such tort existing on the

---

318 15 U.S.C. § 1681s-2(a)(2). See § 6.5, *supra*.
319 15 U.S.C. § 1681s-2(a)(3). See § 6.6, *supra*.
320 15 U.S.C. § 1681s-2(a)(4). See § 6.8, *supra*.
321 15 U.S.C. § 1681s-2(a)(5). See § 6.7, *supra*.
322 15 U.S.C. § 1681s-2(b).
323 15 U.S.C. § 1681s-2(6). See § 9.2, *supra*. See also § 10.7.9.4, *infra*, arguing that this provision should be particularly narrowed to harmonize with another FCRA preemption provision.
324 15 U.S.C. § 1681s-2(a)(7). See § 6.9, *supra*.
325 15 U.S.C. § 1681s-2(a)(8). See § 6.5.2, *supra*.
326 15 U.S.C. § 1681s-2(a)(9).
327 15 U.S.C. § 1681t(b)(1)(F). See 15 U.S.C. § 1681s-2. The Massachusetts law is referred to as § 54A of Chapter 93 of Massachusetts Annotated Laws. The California law is referred to as § 1785.25(a) of the California Civil Code. *See also* Appx. H, *infra*.
328 Gorman v. Wolpoff & Abramson, L.L.P., 370 F. Supp. 2d 1005, 1011 (D. Cal. 2005); Lin v. Universal Card Servs. Corp., 238 F. Supp. 2d 1147, 1151–1153 (N.D. Cal. 2002); Quigley v. Pennsylvania Higher Educ. Assistance Agency, 2000 WL 1721069, at *3 (N.D. Cal. Nov 8, 2000) (dismissing section 1785.25(g) action); Potter v. Illinois Student Assistance Comm'n, 2004 WL 1203156, at *7 (Cal. Ct. App. June 2, 2004) (although FCRA preserved Cal. Civ. Code § 1785.25(a) from preemption, the private action provision to enforce that section, § 1785.25(g), was not preserved and accordingly plaintiff could not bring private claim based on state provision).
329 These statutes are found in: Colorado (to extent furnishers required to use Social Security numbers), Illinois (a creditor may not furnish adverse information relating to a cosignor without first notifying the cosignor), Iowa (prohibiting the reporting of a mortgagor's delinquency if the mortgagor agrees to alternative non-judicial voluntary foreclosure procedures), Michigan (requiring that a creditor may not furnish adverse information relating to a cosignor without first notifying the cosignor) and Utah (notification to consumer that negative information has been reported). An Arizona law regulating the calculation of days of delinquency was effective after Sept. 30, 1996, so is not excluded from the preemption provision. *See also* Ch. 6, *supra*, and Appx. H, *infra*.
In addition, several state laws regarding the furnishing by public agencies of child support debt information are preempted, including: Connecticut, Georgia, Hawaii, Kansas, Michigan, Missouri, Montana, New Jersey, Ohio, Pennsylvania, Rhode Island, South Carolina, Tennessee, West Virginia and Wisconsin. See Appx. H, *infra*.
330 15 U.S.C. § 1681b(c). *See also* Kennedy v. Chase Manhattan Bank, 369 F.3d 833 (5th Cir. 2004) (dismissing claim that bank's failure to honor "firm offer" did not violate the FCRA); § 7.3.4, *supra*.
331 15 U.S.C. § 1681(b)(e). *See also* § 7.3.4, *supra*.
332 15 U.S.C. § 1681i. *See also* Ch. 4, *supra*.
333 15 U.S.C. § 1681c.
334 15 U.S.C. § 1681t(b)(1)(B), (E). With respect to section 1681i, such existing state laws include Arizona (no 15-day extension); Maine (21-day period for reinvestigation; immediate notification that dispute deemed frivolous); Maryland (no 15-day extension; time period for notice of results); Massachusetts (no

§ 10.7.5.4 *Fair Credit Reporting*

designated date continues to be available as a remedy for CRA behavior violating one of these two FCRA provisions.

10.7.5.4 Provisions Regarding Users

The subject matter preemption provision extends to five different user provisions. These are the duties of users:

- Taking adverse action based on a consumer report;[335]
- Taking adverse action based on other third party information;[336]
- In connection with any credit or insurance transaction that is not initiated by the consumer and that consists of a firm offer of credit or insurance;[337]
- Relating to the exchange and use of information to make a solicitation for marketing purposes;[338] and
- Providing notices of risk-based loan pricing.[339]

Note that the risk-based loan pricing provision, by its terms, extends not to risk-based pricing itself, but only to notices concerning risk-based pricing, and specifically the timing and content of such notices. Accordingly, the subject matter of the provision is restricted to required notices, not

required behavior of other sorts. The greater the difference between the proof required for the state law claim and for the FCRA claim, the less similar the claims and the more likely the state law claim will survive.[340]

10.7.5.5 Provision Regarding Businesses and Identity Theft

Business entities must provide a thief's information to an identify theft victim.[341] Even though there is no private right of action to enforce this provision,[342] it preempts state law that have the same subject matter. Nonetheless, this provision should not preempt actions alleging that the business entity was negligent at common law in providing an identity thief with the credit, goods, or services in the victim's name, either because such claims fall outside the "subject matter" of the provision, which pertains to information access, not credit granting, or because they are common law torts, viable under the "common law torts permitted" construction.

However, claims brought under comparable state statutes are far more likely to fall victim to the preemption provision.[343] In such a case, practitioners may want to fall back on the *Aklagi* line of "up until obligations arise" construction, that allows state law claims if they are based on conduct arising before a consumer can bring an action under the FCRA provision.[344] Since a business entity has no obligation to provide the thief's information to the consumer until the victim makes a written request to the business entity, and, if requested, provides certain additional information,[345] under this construction, the preemption provision would not bar any state claim based on the business entity's conduct before that time.

10.7.6 Affiliate Exchange Preemption— § 1681t(b)(2)

Section 1681t(b)(2) preempts state requirements and prohibitions "with respect to the exchange of information among persons affiliated by common ownership or common corporate control,"[346] with the exception of a Vermont

---

15-day extension); Nevada (no 15-day extension); New Hampshire (no 15-day extension); Rhode Island (no 15-day extension); Texas (relating to time periods for reinvestigation); Vermont (no 15-day extension); Washington (relating to time periods for reinvestigation). *See* Appx. H, *infra*.

With respect to section 1681c, among states that had preexisting laws regulating the content of consumer reports are California (relating to obsolete information), Kentucky (relating to criminal charges), Maine (relating to denials for insufficient credit history; reverification of adverse information in investigative reports), Maryland (relating to reverification of adverse information in investigative reports), Massachusetts (relating to reverification of adverse information in investigative reports), Montana (relating to reverification of investigative reports), Nevada (relating to reporting of medical information), New Hampshire (relating to reverification of investigative reports); New Mexico (relating to merging of specialized personal information with credit information) and New York (relating to denials due to insufficient information; race, religion, or ethnic origin; polygraph information; detention by retail establishments; paid judgments). A Colorado law prohibiting the reporting of inquiries, a California law prohibiting reporting of liens against property of public officials struck by court order, and an Arizona law regulating the calculation of days of delinquency were effective after Sept. 30, 1996. *See* Appx. H, *infra*. To the extent these laws are construed as regulating the subject matter regulated by section 1681c, they may be subject to preemption pursuant to section 1681t(b)(1)(E).

335 15 U.S.C. § 1681m(a). *E.g.*, Washington; possibly Arkansas (only if adverse action relating to additional credit found to apply to credit denials not covered by federal act); possibly Oklahoma (to the extent a rating book, for example, is based on consumer report(s)). *See also* § 8.2.6, *supra* and Appx. H, *infra*.
336 15 U.S.C. § 1681m(b).
337 15 U.S.C. § 1681m(d).
338 15 U.S.C. § 1681s-3. *See also* § 2.4.3, *supra*.
339 15 U.S.C. § 1681m(h). *See also* § 8.2.8, *supra*.

340 *See* Carlson, 359 F. Supp. 2d 517 (N.D. Tex. 2003).
341 *See* 15 U.S.C. § 1681g(e); § 9.2.3, *infra*.
342 15 U.S.C. § 1681g(e)(6).
343 *See, e.g.*, Cal. Fin. Code § 22470 (West) (right of victim to receive copies of forms or other information from finance lender); La. Rev. Stat. Ann. § 9:3568(B) (creditors to make information available).
344 *See* § 10.7.4.5, *supra*.
345 15 U.S.C. § 1681g(e)(1), (3). *See also* 16 C.F.R. § 614.1 (describing "appropriate proof of identity").
346 15 U.S.C. § 1681t(b)(2). One reported decision, later vacated when the appeal was dismissed, held that this provision preempted three California county ordinances that barred financial institutions operating in the relevant jurisdictions from disclos-

statute, as it existed in 1996, that requires a consumer's consent to obtain a consumer report, unless the report is obtained pursuant to a court order.[347] An important question is whether this preemption only applies to state laws regulating the exchange of consumer reports between affiliates, or more broadly to the exchange of any information between affiliates. The Ninth Circuit, in interpreting a provision of the new California Information Privacy Act,[348] held that the FCRA preempted the California act only to the extent that it applies to information that falls within the FCRA's definition of "consumer report."[349]

10.7.7 Disclosure Preemption— § 1681t(b)(3)

Section 1681t(b)(3) preempts state requirements or prohibitions with respect to disclosures required by section 1681g(c), (d), (e), and (g) and by section 1681g(f) relating to credit score disclosures for credit granting purposes.[350] Section 1681t(b)(3)'s preemption provision explicitly preserves California's[351] and Colorado's[352] existing disclosure statutes, as in effect on December 4, 2003. It also specifically preserves state insurance laws that require disclosure of credit-based insurance scores.[353]

Sections 1681g(c) and (d) require disclosure of summaries of consumer rights under the FCRA. As such, the FCRA preemption provision would not apply to a state requirement that requires disclosure of different rights, such as rights under state law,[354] but would apply to a state claim based on a CRA's failure to comply with its FCRA disclosure obligations.[355]

The provision also limits state laws relating to the disclosure of credit scores, and as such does not preempt state law regulating the use of credit scores or other aspects of credit scores.[356] Of course, the limitation on state regulation of credit scores does not affect a claim based on a federal statute, such as the Federal Fair Housing Act,[357] the Truth in Lending Act,[358] and the Equal Credit Opportunity Act.[359] However, state statutes that require CRAs to disclose credit scores[360] or to provide information about a score,[361] may well be preempted.

15 U.S.C. § 1681g(e), allowing identity theft victims certain information from business entities that participated in the theft, is a new provision that is preempted three ways— under both sections 1681t(b)(1) and (3), and also under section 1681g(e)(7) that states that a business entity cannot be liable under federal or state law for a good faith disclosure made pursuant to section 1681g(e).

To the extent that section 1681g(e) does not require an entity to make any disclosures whatsoever until the consumer has met all of the subsection's prerequisites, a state

---

ing or sharing confidential consumer information to affiliates or non-affiliated third parties unless the institution notified the consumer in writing and acquired the consumer's consent. Bank of Am., N.A. v. City of Daly City, Cal., 279 F. Supp. 2d 1118, 1124 (N.D. Cal. 2003), *judgment vacated, appeal dismissed* (May 14, 2004). *See also* Cline v. Hawke, 51 Fed. Appx. 392, 397 (4th Cir. 2002) (upholding preemption letter from Office of Comptroller of the Currency that found that portions of West Virginia's Insurance Sales Consumer Protection Act were preempted by section 1681t(b)(2)); 15 U.S.C. § 1681a(d); § 2.4.3, *supra*.

347 9 Vt. Stat. Ann. § 2480e.
348 2003 Cal. Leg. c. 241, *codified at* Cal. Fin. Code §§ 4050–4059.
349 American Bankers Ass'n v. Gould, 412 F.3d 1081, 1087 (9th Cir. 2005). On remand, the district court held that the California Act's affiliate sharing prohibition was entirely preempted. American Bankers Ass'n v. Lockyer, 2005 WL 2452798, at *3 (E.D. Cal. Oct. 5, 2005).
350 Prior to the FACTA amendments, the FCRA preempted state laws that imposed a requirement or prohibition on the form or content of disclosures required by old section 1681g(c).
351 Cal. Civ. Code §§ 1785.10 (inspection of files by consumer; advice to consumer; coded files; availability of information; disclosure of recipients of consumer reports and inquiries; reselling report or information; exemptions), 1785.16 (disputes as to completeness or accuracy of information in file; reinvestigation and recording of current status; notice of results; deletion and reinsertion of information; statement of dispute; CRA procedures; block of information appearing as a result of Penal Code § 530.5; unblocking information), 1785.20.2 (adverse action based on consumer report information; notice and disclosure to consumer; denial of credit or insurance or increase in charge because of information from one other than CRA; liability), 1785.15 (supplying files and information; right to information), 1785.15.1 (credit scores supplied upon request by consumer; key factors), and 1785.15.2 (credit scoring model), apparently regardless of the date) (West).
352 Colo. Rev. Stat. §§ 5-3-106(2) (requiring creditors making loans secured by a dwelling, to disclose the consumer's credit score and related information upon a consumer's request), and 12-14.3-104.3 (detailing the information that must be provided with a credit score).
353 15 U.S.C. § 1681t(b)(3)(C). *See, e.g.*, Ark. Code Ann. §§ 23-67-401 to 23-67-415; Colo. Rev. Stat. § 10-4-110.7; Fla. Stat. § 626.9741; La. Rev. Stat. Ann. § 1484; Md. Code Ann., Ins. § 27-605 (West); Minn. Stat. § 58.13(36); Mo. Rev. Stat. § 375.918; N.C. Gen. Stat. § 58-36-90; Tenn. Code Ann. §§ 56-5-401 to 56-5-407; Tex. Ins. Code Ann. § 21.49-2U (Vernon); Utah Code Ann. § 31A-22-320; Va. Code Ann. §§ 38-2-2126, 38-2-2234.
354 *See, e.g.*, Cal. Civ. Code § 1785.15(8) (West); Wash. Rev. Code § 19.182.080(7)(a).
355 *See, e.g.*, Conn. Gen. Stat. §§ 36a-696, 36a-699a; Me. Rev. Stat. Ann. tit. 10, § 1313-A; N.J. Stat. Ann. § 56:11-31(b)(2) (West).
356 D.C. Code § 16-1152.06 (unfair steering or improper use of credit scores); Minn. Stat. § 58.13 (prohibiting mortgage originators and servicers from arranging a loan of a lower investment grade if the consumer's credit score indicates that the consumer might qualify for a higher grade loan).
357 42 U.S.C. §§ 3601–3619. *See also* National Consumer Law Center, Credit Discrimination Ch. 4 (4th ed. 2004 and Supp.).
358 15 U.S.C. §§ 1601–1615.
359 15 U.S.C. § 1691. *See also* National Consumer Law Center, Credit Discrimination Ch. 4 (4th ed. 2004 and Supp.).
360 *See, e.g.*, Vt. Stat. Ann. tit. 9, § 2480b; Wash. Rev. Code § 19.182.080.
361 *See, e.g.*, Wash. Rev. Code § 19.182.080(5) (requiring CRA that provides credit score to a consumer to explain it).

claim based on a failure to disclose any particular information before the consumer has met those prerequisites should not be preempted, because until then no "disclosures [are] required to be made." Furthermore, the FCRA saving clause's specific reservation of state laws "for the prevention or mitigation of identity theft"[362] indicates that Congress intended a very narrow construction of this preemption provision. Accordingly, actions under state laws, such as those of California[363] and Louisiana,[364] that require businesses that have done business with a thief to make the transaction information available to an identity theft victim may not be preempted to the extent that the business incurs a duty to act under the state statute before it incurs a duty to act under section 1681g(e).

10.7.8 Preemption Related to Frequency of Free Consumer Report Disclosures—§ 1681t(b)(4)

Section 1681t(b)(4) prohibits a state from imposing any state requirement or prohibition "with respect to the frequency of any disclosure under section 1681j(a)," that requires nationwide CRAs to provide consumers, upon request, with a free consumer report once during any twelve month period. Section 1681t(b)(4) expressly exempts from this preemption specific Colorado, Georgia, Maine, Maryland, Massachusetts, New Jersey, and Vermont statutes, as in effect on December 4, 2003.[365] Other than these seven states, any state statute requiring CRAs to offer free consumer reports more often than once per year is likely preempted.

Thus, state identity theft statutes that require CRAs to provide free consumer reports more often than once a year will have to contend with this preemption provision.[366] There is an argument, though, that this preemption does not apply to state identity theft statutes because of the FCRA saving clause's specific reservation of state laws "for the prevention or mitigation of identity theft."[367] In addition, section 1681t(b)(4) applies only to the frequency of disclosure, not to the content of the disclosure, although state law regulating the content of this disclosure must deal with other FCRA preemption provisions, most specifically section 1681t(b)(5).

10.7.9 Preemption Related to "Conduct Required by" Twelve FCRA Provisions—§ 1681t(b)(5)

10.7.9.1 Narrow Construction

Section 1681t(b)(5) preempts state laws that impose a requirement or prohibition "with respect to the conduct required by twelve FCRA subsections. Both the term "conduct required by" and the term "the specific provisions of" argue in favor of the narrowest possible preemption construction, since such plain language is "the best evidence of Congress' pre-emptive intent."[368] State statutes should survive to the extent that they require conduct additional to that mandated by the FCRA, and would only be preempted where they regulate conduct identical to or a subset of the conduct required by the FCRA provision.

Except for the new right to a free annual consumer report,[369] all of the provisions listed under section 1681t(b)(5) relate to identity theft. The FCRA savings clause's specific reservation of state laws "for the prevention or mitigation of identity theft,"[370] further argues for a strict construction of this preemption provisions.

10.7.9.2 Reporting Agency Provisions That Preempt State Law

Section 1681t(b)(5) preempts conduct required by a number of FCRA provisions dealing with CRA obligations, and that thus preempt state laws that regulate the same conduct. One provision is section 1681c-1, relating to identity theft prevention, fraud alerts, and active duty alerts. In general, the provision requires more of nationwide CRAs than other CRAs, imposing few duties on resellers and non-nationwide CRAs. Accordingly, state statutes that may be preempted as they apply to nationwide CRAs may not be preempted as to other CRAs. For example, a state statute that requires CRAs other than nationwide CRAs to provide specified fraud alerts or to act with a particular level of care may well still be a viable option.[371]

Even nationwide CRAs are not subject to rules of conduct under section 1681c-1 until certain prerequisites have occurred, so that a state claim based on conduct arising before those prerequisites have occurred should survive. Until that time, no conduct has been "required" of the CRA, and the provision does not apply to conduct before that trigger.[372]

---

362 15 U.S.C. § 1681t(a).
363 Cal. Fin. Code §§ 4002, 22470 (West).
364 La. Rev. Stat. Ann. § 3568(B).
365 15 U.S.C. § 1681t(b)(4)(A)–(G).
366 *See, e.g.*, Cal. Civ. Code § 1785.15.3 (West) (requiring CRAs to provide identity theft victims with 12 free reports per year).
367 15 U.S.C. § 1681t(a).

368 CSX Transp., Inc. v. Easterwood, 507 U.S. 658, 664 (1993).
369 15 U.S.C. § 1681j(a).
370 15 U.S.C. § 1681t(a).
371 *See, e.g.*, La. Rev. Stat. Ann. § 9:3571.1(H) (effective July 1, 2005) (imposing fraud alert responsibilities on all CRAs meeting statute's definition, not just nationwide CRAs).
372 *See, e.g.*, Cal. Civ. Code §§ 1785.11.1–1785.11.6 (West) (security alerts and freezes in consumer reports); La. Rev. Stat. Ann.

Another provision referred to in section 1681t(b)(5) is section 1681c-2, requiring CRAs in certain situations to block information resulting in identity theft. A number of states also require CRAs to block identity theft information,[373] and such statutes may not be preempted if they require CRAs to block information before the FCRA so requires or in different situations than required by the FCRA.

Section 1681t(b)(5) also preempts state laws from regulating conduct required by section 1681g(a)(1)(A). That section mandates that CRAs, upon the consumer's request, delete the first five digits of a consumer's Social Security number in a report provided to that consumer. What if a state law prohibited disclosure of the Social Security number? The FCRA requires disclosure to the consumer of all the information in the consumer's file (including, presumably, a Social Security number) section 1681g(a)(1)(A) is a limited exception to that provision. Thus, a more restrictive state law would put the CRA in the position of being unable to comply with both the state and federal provisions.[374]

Section 1681t(b)(5) also lists section 1681j(a) concerning free annual disclosures of a consumer's report. This preemption provision seems intended to preempt only those state laws that provide for a different process by which to get a free consumer report.[375] Section 1681t(b)(4) preempts state laws that specify the frequency of such a free disclosure.

Finally, section 1681t(b)(5) lists section 1681s(f), requiring coordination between nationwide CRAs concerning identity theft reports. Since the provision applies only to nationwide CRAs, it should not preempt state laws placing requirements on other CRAs. Nor should this provision preempt state laws regulating other aspects of identity theft.

10.7.9.3 User Provisions That Preempt State Law

Section 1681t(b)(5) refers to a number of provisions that require conduct of users of information from CRAs, and that thus preempt state laws that regulate the same conduct. One provision is section 1681c-1, relating to identity theft prevention, fraud alerts, and active duty alerts, requiring specific conduct of users when they are alerted to potential identity theft. Thus, state statutes that impose specific requirements on credit card issuers who learn that an applicant's file has been contaminated by identity theft are at the highest risk of preemption.[376] However, users only become obligated when using a file that has an FCRA-defined alert; any other notice of financial information fraud has no effect. Accordingly, state regulation relating to a user's conduct before receiving such an FCRA-defined report should survive, because at that point in time the FCRA does not require any conduct from the user.

Furthermore, to the extent that a state statute imposes any additional obligations on users, such as more stringent identity verification procedures,[377] a claim possibly could overcome preemption on the theory that such conduct exceeded that imposed by the FCRA, and that complying with the state obligations would not in any way prevent the user from complying with its FCRA-imposed responsibilities.[378] So, for example, this preemption provision should not bar a claim against a credit card issuer who did not comply with the provisions of Georgia's UDAP statute requiring issuers to verify the identity of an applicant when the application's address differs from that on the issuer's solicitation or in the issuer's file for that consumer.[379] For similar reasons, a state common law claim alleging liability for such conduct should survive preemption as well.[380]

The user's obligation to verify identity arises only when the user is extending certain types of credit. A state statute should not be preempted where it requires verification of identity before entering into another sort of transaction, for example, a lease or a rental agreement for goods.[381]

Another provision referred to by section 1681t(b)(5) is section 1681m(e), requiring federal agencies to issue guidelines and regulations for creditors to help curtail identity theft and to establish reasonable policies and procedures for implementing the red flag guidelines. Since the agencies have not yet created any red flag guidelines, this provision presently requires no conduct from financial institutions or

---

§ 9:3571.1(H) (effective July 1, 2005); Vt. Stat. Ann. tit. 9, §§ 2480h (security freeze by CRA; time in effect), 2480i (CRA duties if security freeze in place).

373 *See, e.g.,* Cal. Civ. Code § 1785.16(k) (West); Colo. Rev. Stat. § 12-14.3-106.5; Conn. Gen. Stat. § 36a-699f; Idaho Code Ann. § 28-51-102; Va. Code Ann. § 18.2-186.3:1.

374 *See* English v. General Elec. Co., 496 U.S. 72, 79 (1990); Shaw v. Delta Air Lines, Inc., 463 U.S. 85, 95–98 (1983).

375 *See* § 3.3.8, *supra*.

376 *See, e.g.,* Ga. Code Ann. § 10-1-393(29.1); 815 Ill. Comp. Stat. § 505/2MM; Vt. Stat. Ann. tit. 9, § 2480l.

377 *See, e.g.,* La. Rev. Stat. Ann. § 3568(C)(2) (requiring user to use a consumer-supplied telephone number to verify identity).

378 *See* English v. General Elec. Co., 496 U.S. 72, 79 (1990); Shaw v. Delta Air Lines, Inc., 463 U.S. 85, 95–98 (1983).

379 Ga. Code Ann. § 10-1-393(29.1). *See also* Cal. Civ. Code §§ 1799.1b, 1747.06 (West) (requiring credit card issuer to verify a change of address); Colo. Rev. Stat. § 5-3.7-101 (requiring one who issues a firm offer of credit to verify a change of address); 815 Ill. Comp. Stat. § 505/2MM (imposing verification procedures on users who learn that the consumer has filed an identity theft report); Mont. Code Ann. § 30-14-1721 (requiring credit card issuer to verify change of consumer's address); Vt. Stat Ann. tit. 9, § 2480l (same). However, this provision could be challenged pursuant to section 1681t(b)(5)(F), discussed further on in this section.

380 Such claims suffer from other frailties, however. *See* § 10.5, *supra*.

381 *See, e.g.,* La. Rev. Stat. Ann. § 3568(C)(1) (imposing an obligation to verify an applicant's identity upon receipt of a security alert before entering into a wide variety of transactions, including "non-credit related service[s]").

creditors, and accordingly should at this point have no preemptive effect.

Even after the guidelines are issued, the provision should not preempt any state law applying to a non-creditor who would not be subject to the guidelines. Furthermore, a state statute should not be preempted to the extent that it requires conduct different in type from that in the forthcoming regulations. So, for example, claims against financial institutions for violating California's Financial Information Privacy Act should survive so long as the conduct that the specific California provision requires differs from that required by the forthcoming regulations.[382] Similarly, state statutes requiring those who keep confidential personal information to notify consumers of any security breach should survive as well.[383] However, once the red flag regulations for card issuers are promulgated, state statutes that require card issuers to take specific steps to verify a cardholder's identity may be challenged as preempted.[384]

Another provision referred to by 1681t(b)(5) is section 1681w, requiring federal agencies to issue regulations requiring any person that possesses consumer information derived from consumer reports for a business purpose to properly dispose of any such information. These regulations have been issued,[385] and accordingly the provision likely extends to the conduct required by those regulations.

A state statute regulating a person's treatment of information is not preempted unless it relates to the disposal of that information. Thus, a state statute requiring a keeper of consumer information derived from consumer reports to protect the information from unlawful use should escape preemption. Furthermore, a state statute that requires such a person to notify consumers of a security breach should likewise be exempt.[386] However, an action based on a person's carelessness in disposing of consumer information that otherwise meets the requirements of the federal regulation would likely be preempted.[387]

---

382 *See* Cal. Fin. Code §§ 4050–4059 (West).
383 *See, e.g.*, Cal. Fin. Code § 1798.25 (West).
384 *See, e.g.*, Ga. Code Ann. § 10-1-393(29.2) (state UDAP provision requiring card issuers who receive an application in response to the issuer's solicitation to verify the identity of an applicant when the application's address differs from that on the issuer's solicitation or in the issuer's file for that consumer).
385 69 Fed. Reg. 68,690 (Nov. 24, 2004) (FTC); 69 Fed. Reg. 69,209 (Nov. 29, 2004) (National Credit Union Administration); 69 Fed. Reg. 70,322 (Dec. 14, 2004) (SEC); 69 Fed. Reg. 77,610 (Dec. 28, 2004) (Department of the Treasury, Office of Thrift Supervision; Federal Reserve System; FDIC; Department of the Treasury, Comptroller of the Currency).
386 *See, e.g.*, Cal. Fin. Code § 1798.25 (West).
387 *See, e.g.*, Colo. Rev. Stat. § 6-1-713 (disposal of personal identifying documents—policy).

10.7.9.4 Furnisher Provisions That Preempt State Law

Section 1681t(b)(5) refers to a number of provisions that require conduct of furnishers, and that thus preempt state laws that regulate the same conduct. One provision is section 1681m(f). Where identity theft leads to an FCRA block on the reporting of information about a debt, and the CRA so notifies the furnisher, the furnisher cannot sell or collect on that debt.

A state statute should still apply where no block has been placed on a debt. Thus, there is no preemption where a state statute prohibits a creditor from selling a debt that the creditor has learned pursuant to the state information-blocking provision was the result of identity theft, at least if the creditor has yet to receive an FCRA-compliant notice.[388] In addition, if a CRA has failed to abide by its obligations to notify the creditor, the creditor remains vulnerable to state law claims based on the sale or placement for collection of that debt, because such notice is a prerequisite to the furnisher's conduct under the provision. Furthermore, since an FCRA notice only goes to furnishers, claims against parties other than furnishers based on similar conduct should not be preempted, because the conduct required under section 1681m(f) is required only of furnishers.[389]

A similar provision listed in section 1681t(b)(5) is section 1681s-2(a)(6), prohibiting furnishers from reporting information on identity theft victims and requiring them to have reasonable procedures to respond to notices of identity theft. This preemption is redundant with that provided by section 1681t(b)(1) for any law relating to the subject matter regulated under section 1681s-2 regards to furnishers. One argument for harmonizing these two provisions is to use the rule of statutory construction that the specific should prevail over the general,[390] and that accordingly actions based on the subject matter of this particular provision, section 1681s-2(a)(6), are preempted only to the extent that they are based on conduct required by the provision. Otherwise, the less specific of the two provisions will preempt a broader class of laws than does section 1681t(b)(5). Because there are no private FCRA remedies under section 1681s-2(a),[391] the extent of this preemption of state law is particularly significant.

Since one part of the provision only requires the furnisher to adopt reasonable procedures upon receiving notice, a state law may not be preempted to the extent the law

---

388 *See, e.g.*, Cal. Civ. Code § 1785.16.2(a) (West).
389 *See, e.g.*, Cal. Civ. Code § 1788.18 (West) (debtor as an alleged victim of identity theft; sworn statement; inferences and presumptions; duties after collection terminated) (requiring a debt collector to cease collection activities if the debt is the result of identity theft and if specified prerequisites have been met).
390 *See, e.g.*, Morales v. Trans World Airlines, Inc., 504 U.S. 374, 384–385 (1992).
391 15 U.S.C. § 1681s-2(c)(1).

requires the furnisher to cease refurnishing identity theft information, whether or not it receives notice from the CRA. The other part of section 1681s-2(a)(6) requires furnishers to cease furnishing information if the consumer submits a report at an address specified by the furnisher, stating that the furnisher's information resulted from identity theft. Accordingly, any state law action based on conduct that arose before this notice should escape preemption, because, until that point, the provision requires no conduct of the furnisher.

10.7.9.5 Debt Collector Provisions That Preempt State Law

Section 1681t(b)(5) refers to one provision that requires conduct of debt collectors, and that thus preempts state laws that regulate the same conduct. Section 1681m(g) requires certain conduct from a debt collector collecting on a debt owed a third party, after the collector has been notified that information related to the debt may be fraudulent the result of identity theft. Once so notified, the debt collector must pass this information on to the party owed the debt. The debt collector must also give the identity theft victim the same information as it would be required to do, for example, under the Fair Debt Collection Practices Act, if the consumer were in fact the person initiating the debt. State law actions based on traditional debt collection statutes should be free from preemption, to the extent that they address conduct different from the specific conduct required of debt collectors under this subsection.[392]

10.7.9.6 Preemption by Provision Relating to Those Accepting Credit or Debit Cards

Section 1681t(b)(5) refers to section 1681c(g), that requires conduct of those accepting credit or debit cards, and that thus preempts state laws that regulate the same conduct. The provision requires the business to print out no more than the last five digits of the account number. A number of states have already enacted similar legislation,[393] with remedies ranging from deceptive trade practices act actions to criminal penalties. Because the FCRA provision does not become effective until December 4, 2006 for electronic printing devices that were in use before January 1, 2005,[394] similar state statutes were not be preempted until that date.[395]

A number of states prohibit printing more than four digits of the account number,[396] where the FCRA allows up to five.[397] Such state laws may not be preempted because a merchant could easily comply with both provisions simply by truncating the account number at four digits.[398]

---

392 *Cf.* Cal. Civ. Code § 1788.18 (West) (debtor as an alleged victim of identity theft; sworn statement; inferences and presumptions; duties after collection terminated).

393 *See, e.g.*, Ariz. Rev. Stat. Ann. § 44-1367 (no more than last five digits); Ark. Code Ann. § 4-107-303 (no more than last five digits); Cal. Civ. Code § 1747.09 (West) (no more than last five digits); Colo. Rev. Stat. § 6-1-711 (no more than last five digits); Conn. Gen. Stat. § 42-133hh (no more than last five digits); 815 Ill. Comp. Stat. § 505/2MM (last four digits only); Kan. Stat. Ann. § 50-669b (no more than last five digits); Md. Code Ann., Com. Law § 14-1318 (no more than eight digits); Mich. Comp. Laws § 445.903(ii) (no more than last four digits); Nev. Rev. Stat. § 597.945 (no more than last five digits); N.J. Stat. Ann. § 56:11-42 (West) (no more than last five digits); N.D. Cent. Code § 51-07-27 (no more than last five digits); Ohio Rev. Code Ann. § 1349.18 (West) (no more than last five digits); Okla. Stat. tit. 15, § 752A (no more than last five digits); Tex. Bus. & Comm. Code Ann. § 35.58 (Vernon) (no more than last four digits; prohibiting class actions based on the provision); Wash. Rev. Code §§ 19.200.010, 63.14.123 (no more than last five digits); Wis. Stat. § 134.74 (no more than last five digits).

394 15 U.S.C. § 1681c(g)(3). The provision became effective on December 4, 2004 for machines put in use on or after January 1, 2005. *Id.*

395 *See also* Effective Dates for the Fair and Accurate Credit Transactions Act of 2003, 69 Fed. Reg. 6,528 (Feb. 11, 2004) (stating that "the Agencies believe that a requirement that applies under an existing State law will remain in effect until the applicable specific provision of the FCRA, as amended by the FACT Act, becomes effective").

396 *See, e.g.*, 815 Ill. Comp. Stat. 505/2MM (last four digits only); Mich. Comp. Laws § 445.903(ii) (no more than last four digits); Tex. Bus. & Comm. Code Ann. § 35.58 (Vernon) (no more than last four digits; prohibiting class actions based on the provision).

397 15 U.S.C. § 1681c(g)(1).

398 *See* English v. General Elec. Co., 496 U.S. 72, 79 (1990); Shaw v. Delta Air Lines, Inc., 463 U.S. 85, 95–98 (1983).

Chapter 11   Private Remedies and Public Enforcement

11.1 Introduction

Once the theory of the case and the nature of the claims have been decided upon,[1] the practicalities of litigation must be considered. This chapter covers everything from selection of parties and court to private remedies following a successful court challenge to credit reporting practices. It is worth noting, however, that consumers also have non-litigation approaches to dealing with credit reporting problems—approaches provided by the Fair Credit Reporting Act (FCRA) (e.g., disputing an inaccurate report, or discovering the contents of the consumer's file), avenues provided by other laws (e.g., Real Estate Settlement Procedures Act and Fair Credit Billing Act dispute rights), or by no particular law (e.g., explaining a bad credit rating to a potential creditor). These non-litigation consumer options are described throughout this manual. This chapter focuses specifically on litigation and its remedies, with a brief discussion of public enforcement as well.

An FCRA case should be undertaken from the beginning with an eye to establishing damages and obtaining an award of attorney fees. The scope of damages under the Act is broad, and may include actual, statutory, and punitive damages. The damages suffered by an individual consumer from an inaccurate consumer report or from other FCRA violations may not always be apparent. Building a case for damages begins with an attorney's initial contact with the consumer. Similarly, a successful claim for attorney fees will depend upon accurate timekeeping records from the very first contact with the client.

Maximizing damage awards and recovering the full amount of attorney fees to which one is entitled serves several purposes. In addition to fully recompensing injury and the expense of litigation, adequate awards to plaintiffs create incentives for defendants to police themselves and avoid further FCRA violations. The large volume of bad reporting and unresolved consumer complaints is evidence of the need for greater enforcement of the FCRA. Since little public enforcement occurs, private enforcement is the primary method of assuring compliance and policing the industry.[2] Substantial damage awards should bring about greater compliance and serve users and consumers well. Likewise, full and adequate attorney fee awards will promote private attorney involvement in FCRA cases.

11.2 Selecting the Parties

11.2.1 Plaintiffs

The FCRA provides that any person who fails to comply with any FCRA requirement with respect to any consumer is liable to that consumer.[3] A consumer is broadly defined as any individual.[4] Consequently, any individual can bring an FCRA action where an FCRA requirement has been violated "with respect to" that individual.

Thus a consumer may have standing to sue even where the report at issue is on the consumer's spouse, not on the consumer, and contains no information about the consumer, provided that the information in the file adversely affects the consumer.[5] A wife, for example, may sue where information in the husband's report impaired the wife's ability to obtain financing on jointly owned property.[6] On the other hand, a merely derivative claim, where the information does not refer or relate to the plaintiff at all, will likely be dismissed.[7] Because the FCRA is remedial in nature, the estate of a decedent may sue.[8]

Nor is there any requirement that the plaintiff have "clean hands" or that the action be in the public interest. For

---

1 See Ch. 10, supra.
2 The Consumer Credit Reporting Reform Act of 1996 increased the powers of public officials and agencies to enforce the FCRA. See Ch. 11.16, infra. For the foreseeable future, however, private enforcement will remain the primary method of assuring compliance and policing the industry.
3 15 U.S.C. §§ 1681n, 1681o.
4 See § 2.2, supra.
5 Koropoulos v. Credit Bureau, Inc., 734 F.2d 37 (D.C. Cir. 1984); Haque v. CompUSA, Inc., 2003 WL 117986 (D. Mass. Jan. 13, 2003); Soghomonian v. U.S., 278 F. Supp. 2d 1151 (E.D. Cal. 2003); Oppenheimer v. Guzco Guarantee de Puerto Rico, Inc., 977 F. Supp. 549 (D. P.R. 1997); Middlebrooks v. Retail Credit Co., 416 F. Supp. 1013 (N.D. Ga. 1976). Cf. Conley v. TRW Credit Data, 381 F. Supp. 473 (N.D. Ill. 1974).
6 Williams v. Equifax Credit Info. Servs., 892 F. Supp. 951 (E.D. Mich. 1995).
7 Barron v. Trans Union Corp., 82 F. Supp. 2d 1288 (M.D. Ala. 2000) (one spouse applying for credit for himself alone); Wiggins v. Equifax Servs., Inc., 848 F. Supp. 213 (D.D.C. 1993).
8 Saturno v. Dovenmuehle Funding, Inc., 2001 Conn. Super. LEXIS 564 (Conn. Super. Ct. Feb. 21, 2001).

§ 11.2.2   *Fair Credit Reporting*

example, a consumer can bring an FCRA claim against a user even if the consumer had submitted a fraudulent insurance claim to the user.[9]

11.2.2 Class Actions

Class actions provide a potentially effective tool for ameliorating many abuses in the consumer reporting industry. Federal Trade Commission investigations and actions, studies, and private suits have demonstrated the existence of widespread *systematic* illegal practices.[10] In addition, it may be easier, or at least more cost-effective, to show that a consumer reporting agency's (CRA) procedures are not reasonable in a class action than in an individual action. A number of publications can assist the consumer's attorney in bringing a class action under the FCRA.[11]

Whether class actions may be brought for declaratory or injunctive relief under the FCRA is problematic.[12] In addition, putative class actions for monetary relief which would have the potential for catastrophic damages are sometimes but not always denied certification as not being the superior method for resolving the controversy.[13]

Apart from these concerns, since the FCRA is silent on class actions, such actions are generally allowed in federal courts as provided in Rule 23 of the Federal Rules of Civil Procedure,[14] and in state courts as state procedure or law allows.

For example, a class was certified in an FCRA action against the "Big Three" nationwide CRAs based on their practice of indicating that plaintiffs were involved in bankruptcy proceedings when the named plaintiffs had not, themselves, filed for bankruptcy but were merely joint account holders with, or cosigners for, persons who later filed for bankruptcy.[15] After initially denying class certification over concerns of adequacy of representation, and the fact that the plaintiffs originally sought only statutory damages and class members would be barred from pursuing actual damages claims, the court reconsidered its decision. The court noted that the complaint was amended to include both willful and negligent claims against the CRAs and that class certification could not be defeated by mere hypothetical conflicts of interest, as opposed to demonstrating that the alleged potential conflicts were real possibilities. Based on the plaintiffs' showing that only a very small number of alternative claims had been filed in the past, the court concluded that the plaintiffs adequately represented the proposed class. The court further held that the proposed class had the following facts in common: (1) they were individuals who had not filed for bankruptcy; (2) their consumer reports had a tradeline with the word "bankruptcy" on it; and (3) the tradeline did not reference that the account was jointly held. Thus there were common legal issues including: whether the information in the tradeline was misleading; whether the CRAs had a particular practice or policy of writing consumer reports in this manner; and, if so, whether this was reasonable. Notwithstanding the fact that individual actual damages inquiries would be required for class members that chose to pursue such damages, the

---

9 St. Paul Guardian Ins. Co. v. Johnson, 884 F.2d 881 (5th Cir. 1989). *See also* Klapper v. Shapiro, 154 Misc. 2d 459, 586 N.Y.S.2d 846 (Sup. Ct. 1992) (user held to have obtained consumer report under false pretenses for impermissible purpose in response to plaintiff's similar tactics; plaintiff's dirty tricks "cannot validate the improper use of the credit report or shield defendant from liability").

10 *See* Appx. K, *infra*.

11 *See* Note, *Panacea or Placebo? Actions for Negligent Noncompliance Under the Federal Fair Credit Reporting Act*, 47 S. Cal. L. Rev. 1070, 1114–1122 (1974); National Consumer Law Center, Consumer Class Actions (6th ed. 2006); Newberg & Conte, Newberg on Class Actions (4th ed.).

12 *See* § 11.13, *infra*. *See also* Washington v. CSC Credit Servs., 199 F.3d 263 (5th Cir. 2000) (class status for declaratory relief under Rule 23(b)(2) denied when damages were the predominant form of relief sought by the plaintiffs).

13 *In re* Trans Union Corp. Privacy Litig., 211 F.R.D. 328, 351 (N.D. Ill. 2002) ("Although certification should not be denied solely because of the possible financial impact it would have on a defendant, consideration of the financial impact is proper when based on the disproportionality of a damage award that has little relation to the harm actually suffered by the class, and on the due process concerns attended upon such an impact."). *See also In re* Trans Union Corp. Privacy Litig., 2005 WL 2007157, at *4 (N.D. Ill. Aug. 17, 2005) (citing the same concerns and denying certification of a nationwide punitive damage class). *But see* Murray v. GMAC Mortgage Corp., 434 F.3d 948, 953–954 (7th Cir. 2006).

14 *See, e.g.*, Murray v. GMAC Mortgage Corp., 434 F.3d 948 (7th Cir. 2006) (noting that statutory damages require willful conduct and setting forth that class seeking statutory damages should be certified); White v. Imperial Adjustment Corp., 75 Fed. Appx. 972 (5th Cir. 2003) (unpublished); Bruce v. Keybank Nat'l Ass'n, 2006 WL 2334846 (N.D. Ind. Aug. 7, 2006); Kudlicki v. Farragut Fin. Corp., 2006 WL 927281, at *2 (N.D. Ill. Jan. 20, 2006) (finding defendant willfully failed to comply with FCRA on a classwide basis); Perry v. FleetBoston Fin. Corp., 229 F.R.D. 105 (E.D. Pa. 2005) (settlement class); *In re* Trans Union Corp. Privacy Litig., 2005 WL 2007157, *4 (N.D. Ill. Aug. 17, 2005) (certifying class consisting of Illinois consumers whose telephone numbers or other personal information was improperly sold in connection with a firm offer of credit or insurance); Washington v. CSC Credit Servs., Inc., 178 F.R.D. 95 (E.D. La. 1998) (granting motion to certify class in suit claiming CRAs failed to use reasonable procedures to ensure that user insurance companies were obtaining appropriate authorizations from consumers), *motion for reconsideration denied*, 180 F.R.D. 309 (E.D. La. 1998) (holding that even if class certification inappropriate under Fed. R. Civ. Pro. 23(b)2), it was appropriate under Rule 23(b)(3)), *rev'd in part, remanded in part*, 199 F.3d 263 (5th Cir. 2000); Greenway v. Information Dynamics, Ltd., 399 F. Supp. 1092 (D. Ariz. 1974), *aff'd on other grounds*, 524 F.2d 1145 (9th Cir. 1975). *But see* Kekich v. Traveler's Indemnity, 64 F.R.D. 660 (W.D. Pa. 1974).

15 Clark v. Experian Info. Solutions, Inc. 2002 WL 2005709 (D.S.C. June 26, 2002) (order on plaintiffs' motion for class certification).

court concluded that common questions predominated over individual questions and certified the class.[16]

Another court certified a class of homeowners who did not receive adverse action notices when their insurance premiums were raised by fifty percent or more based on information in their consumer report.[17] The insured class representative alleged that the insurer negligently and/or willfully failed to comply with the FCRA's adverse action notice requirements.[18] Class certification was sought pursuant to Federal Rule of Civil Procedure 23(b)(3).[19] The insurance company claimed that the insured representative did not have standing because he actually received notice and suspected that his consumer report had been accessed, and also because he had no actual damage since he bought replacement coverage at a cheaper premium. However the court found that the insurer misunderstood the insured's claim, which was not that the notice was not sent, but that it had been sent too late to comply with the FCRA. The court concluded that the insured would be entitled to an award of damages if the insurance company's notice failed to comply with the Act's requirements and the failure was negligent or willful, and thus he had standing.

The court also found that the class met the numerosity requirement. The court relied on discovery from the insurance company that revealed the company "took adverse action against 5,000 or more" of its customers in Alabama based in whole or in part on consumer reports. Commonality was found because all class members were mailed letters similar to the letter received by the class representative, thus presenting a question of law common to all class members. The court also found that the insured met the typicality requirement, even though the insurance company argued that the named insured's claims were not typical because he received notice, suspected his credit had been accessed and changed carriers at a premium savings.[20] No conflicts of interest were found by the court to make the insured an inadequate class representative, and the court concluded that since common questions of law and fact predominated, the class would be conditionally certified.[21]

Unlike the Truth in Lending Act,[22] the Equal Credit Opportunity Act,[23] and certain other federal credit statutes, the FCRA does *not* contain restrictions on the total amount of a class action award for statutory damages. As a result, there is no limit to the size of such an award that can be made in a class action under the FCRA, and there is, of course, no firm limit to the size of a class action award for actual or punitive damages.[24]

11.2.3 Defendants

Any "person" who fails to comply with any requirement with respect to a consumer may be liable under the FCRA.[25] CRAs, users of consumer reports and those who furnish information to CRAs are liable for violations.[26] "Consumer reporting agency" is a defined term,[27] but "user" and "furnisher of information" are not. Nevertheless, the FCRA sets out several requirements for those who use consumer reports as well as for those who furnish information to CRAs. While there should generally be little question whether an entity is covered as a user or furnisher of information, issues sometimes arise. In *Reynolds v. Hartford Financial Services Group, Inc.*,[28] for example, the Ninth Circuit recently held that several affiliated insurers could be held liable as users for failing to provide adverse action notices even though only one of them issued a policy to the insured. Whether an employer of a user may *also* be a user, subject to suit, will depend upon whether the employee-user is acting within the scope of employment.[29]

In suing a CRA, consider any corporation in the chain of corporate ownership and all the CRAs in the chain of distribution. For example, a consumer may sue both the national repository of credit information, and the local, or regional entity which provided the consumer report based on information gleaned from the national repository.[30] Also

---

16 *Id.*
17 Braxton v. Farmer's Ins. Group, 209 F.R.D. 654 (N.D. Ala. 2002), *aff'd*, 91 Fed. Appx. 656 (11th Cir. 2003) (table).
18 15 U.S.C. § 1681m(a).
19 Common questions predominate and a class action is the superior method to resolve the controversy. *See* National Consumer Law Center, Consumer Class Actions (6th ed. 2006).
20 *Id.* at 659.
21 *Id.*
22 15 U.S.C. § 1640(a)(2)(B).
23 15 U.S.C. § 1691e.
24 *But see In re* Trans Union Corp. Privacy Litig., 211 F.R.D. 328, 351 (N.D. Ill. 2002).
25 15 U.S.C. §§ 1681n, 1681o. Prior to the 1996 Reform Act only users and CRAs were liable under the Act. Pub. L. No. 104-208, 110 Stat. 3009 (Sept. 30, 1996).
26 The question of contribution between the defendants for violations of the FCRA is a question of federal law, and one court has ruled that, because the Act does not provide for such contribution, a CRA could not claim contribution against the subscriber who requested the consumer report. Kay v. First Cont'l Trading Co., 966 F. Supp. 753, 754–755 (N.D. Ill. 1997).
27 *See* § 2.5, *supra*.
28 435 F.3d 1081 (9th Cir. 2006), *cert. granted, sub nom.* GEICO Gen. Ins. v. Edo, __ S. Ct. __, 2006 WL 2055539 (Sept. 26, 2006).
29 Graves v. Tubb, 281 F. Supp. 2d 886 (N.D. Miss. 2003) ("no record evidence showing that Delta was aware of [employee's] impermissible conduct much less that Delta expressly or implicitly authorized Tubb to use their facilities to obtain reports for impermissible [personal] purposes"); Kodrick v. Ferguson, 54 F. Supp. 2d 788 (N.D. Ill. 1999) (no alter ego or user liability for rogue employee "where the employee of the subscriber obtained the report under false pretenses and for personal use without the express or implied approval of her supervisors"). *Compare* Austin v. BankAmerica Serv. Corp., 419 F. Supp. 730 (N.D. Ga. 1974) *with* Wiggins v. Hitchins, 853 F. Supp. 505 (D.D.C. 1994).
30 Verdin v. Equifax Servs., Inc., 1992 WL 111223 (E.D. La. May

consider not only the corporate entities involved in violating the Act, but also individuals who actually participated in the violation, for instance by obtaining a report for impermissible purposes.[31] Remember, however, that the Act permits information to be shared freely among affiliates outside the strictures of the law, largely without regard for FCRA privacy protections and requirements for accuracy.[32]

Where a creditor is found to have furnished inaccurate information to one CRA, it probably has furnished the same inaccurate information to other CRAs as well. Information obsolete at one CRA will be obsolete in another CRA as well. Where an individual has no permissible purpose to obtain reports from one CRA, it will have no permissible purpose to obtain the report from another CRA. There is thus a strong potential that where one CRA has violated the FCRA, another has too in the same way. It thus may make sense to bring different, but similar actions against various CRAs.

An additional reason to sue more than one CRA is that losing a case against a CRA may bar a separate case raising the same issue against a different CRA, but the reverse is not true. A (*pro se*) consumer who litigated the reasonableness of one CRA's procedures has been held to be collaterally estopped from re-litigating the reasonableness of the same procedures against a different CRA.[33]

In considering which defendants to include in the action, attention should also be paid to whether there is a colorable claim of personal jurisdiction over the particular defendant. This subject is discussed at Section 11.4.3, *infra*.

11.3 Case Selection

There is no magic formula for winning an FCRA case. The odds of prevailing are high if the facts strongly point to a clear injustice: where common sense indicates that there has been a violation and the result emerges without any apparent weighing or balancing test. Examples include where a file is on the wrong consumer because the consumer reporting agency (CRA) ignored the proper Social Security number, or where a CRA is specifically apprised of an error and asked to correct it, but continues to furnish incorrect reports or reinserts the same erroneous information after deleting it.

A case is more attractive if the consumer suffered direct injury from the violation, such as being turned down for credit. Nevertheless, compelling evidence of mental anguish, embarrassment, humiliation, and/or loss of reputation will enhance damages from what may be difficult-to-quantify economic losses.

It also helps a case to emphasize CRA delays, runarounds, and obfuscations. Detail the amount of time the consumer spent trying to straighten out the record. Often CRAs can take up to six months to handle a complaint, and this may not appear reasonable to judges or juries.

As in any area of litigation, filing a frivolous case can subject the consumer and her attorney to monetary sanctions for violation of Rule 11 of the Federal Rules of Civil Procedure or 28 U.S.C. § 1927, which requires an attorney who "multiplies the proceedings in any case unreasonably and vexatiously" to pay "fees reasonably incurred because of such conduct." Further, in FCRA litigation, 18 U.S.C. § 1681n(c) entitles a prevailing defendant to reasonable attorney fees from a plaintiff who proceeded under the FCRA "in bad faith or for the purposes of harassment."[34] For this reason, it is also prudent to resolve questionable claims by settlement and mutual release in order to prevent a subsequent motion for fees by defense counsel.

11.4 Selecting the Court

11.4.1 FCRA Claims May Be Brought in Federal or State Court

The FCRA provides that actions may be brought in federal courts without regard to the amount in controversy, or in any other court of competent jurisdiction.[35] Bringing an action in state court does not alter substantive rights.[36] If state court is the preferred forum, one advantage of including an FCRA claim is that it authorizes an award of punitive damages under certain circumstances, while state claims may not. However, if an FCRA claim is included in the state court action, the defendant has the option of removing the case to federal court.

8, 1992) (liability under FCRA does not depend on ownership of data). See also Stern v. Credit Bureau of Milwaukee, 105 Wis. 2d 647, 315 N.W.2d 511 (Ct. App. 1981) (court refused to consider certain claims against the defendant, a local CRA which supplied the consumer report, because there was no evidence of an agency relationship with the nationwide company which compiled the erroneous report).

31 Mone v. Dranow, 945 F.2d 306 (9th Cir. 1991) (chief executive officer acting on behalf of corporation is personally liable for the tort-like act of obtaining consumer report for impermissible purpose); Yohay v. City of Alexandria Employees Credit Union Inc., 827 F.2d 967 (4th Cir. 1987).

32 See § 2.4.3, *supra*.

33 Houston v. Trans Union Credit Info. Co., 1990 U.S. Dist. LEXIS 12833 (S.D.N.Y. Sept. 28, 1990) (non-mutual defensive collateral estoppel applied).

34 See Mayle v. Equifax Info. Sys., L.L.C., Civ. No. 03C8746 (N.D. Ill. Mar. 18, 2005) (monetary sanctions ordered for frivolous claim on disputed debt involving funds deposited into plaintiff's account), *subsequent proceedings are reported at* 2006 WL 398076 (2006).

35 15 U.S.C. § 1681p.

36 Ackerley v. Credit Bureau of Sheridan, Inc., 385 F. Supp. 658 (D. Wyo. 1974); Emerson v. J.F. Shea Co., 76 Cal. App. 3d 579, 143 Cal. Rptr. 170 (1978).

11.4.2 Bringing Related State Law Claims in Federal Court

It often makes sense to join various related common law tort or state statutory claims to an FCRA claim in federal court.[37] Like most other federal statutes, the FCRA contains no provision on joining state law claims, so the advocate must turn to the federal statute on supplemental jurisdiction.[38] The test is whether the claim for which jurisdiction is sought as "part of the same case or controversy [as the FCRA claim] under Article III of the United States Constitution."[39] If this test is met, the district court nevertheless has discretion to decline to exercise supplemental jurisdiction over the state law claim if:

> (1) The claim raises a novel or complex issue of State law;
> (2) The claim substantially predominates over the claim or claims over which the district court has original jurisdiction;
> (3) The district court has dismissed all claims over which it has original jurisdiction; or
> (4) In exceptional circumstances, there are other compelling reasons for declining jurisdiction.[40]

This statutory test is somewhat more conducive to a court accepting supplemental jurisdiction than that on pendent jurisdiction which prevailed prior to the statute's enactment in 1990,[41] so caution should be exercised in relying on prior case law.[42]

Defendant furnishers may file a state law counterclaim against the consumer to collect the underlying debt. If the case is in state court, there is no bar to this effort. In federal court, however, such a counterclaim raises a jurisdictional issue; it must either meet the statutory supplemental jurisdiction requirements discussed at the beginning of this subsection[43] or fulfill the demands of diversity jurisdiction, including the requisite $75,000 amount in controversy.[44]

Most federal courts use the "same transaction or occurrence" test to determine whether the claim meets the supplemental jurisdiction statute's requirement that it be "part of the same case or controversy." Even if a counterclaim meets this requirement, a court has discretion as to whether to exercise its supplemental jurisdiction, as discussed above. In an analogous context, federal courts have generally declined to exercise supplemental jurisdiction over a debt collector's counterclaim in Fair Debt Collection Practices Act (FDCPA) cases.[45] This is because establishing the underlying debt requires evidence of the existence, performance, validity, and breach of a contract, none of which are necessary to prove a violation of the FDCPA. Courts have also expressed concern that allowing such counterclaims would discourage consumers from bringing suit, which would frustrate the broad public policy of the Act, not to mention impede the workflow of the federal courts.[46] These decisions likewise support the argument that a federal court should not exercise jurisdiction over a furnisher's collection counterclaim in an FCRA suit. A claim against a furnisher for its failure to comply with its FCRA-imposed obligation to reinvestigate a disputed debt,[47] for example, requires evidence of facts separate in time, place, and substance from those related to the original debt. Furthermore, allowing such counterclaims would be at odds with the FCRA's consumer protection purposes.

11.4.3 Personal Jurisdiction

Personal jurisdiction must exist to proceed against a defendant. Whether personal jurisdiction exists will generally be a matter of state law even for cases brought in federal court. If suit is brought in state court, state jurisdictional rules will, of course, apply. If brought in federal court, the Federal Rules of Civil Procedure limit federal courts to service over non-resident defendants only as authorized by the forum state's law.[48] When personal jurisdiction is raised as an issue, courts will determine whether the forum state's long-arm statute provides a basis for jurisdiction. If a basis for jurisdiction exists, it is possible a second question will arise, that is whether the defendant has had sufficient minimum contacts with the forum state to satisfy questions of the

---

37 See § 10.2, supra.
38 28 U.S.C. § 1367.
39 28 U.S.C. § 1367(a).
40 Id. § 1367(c).
41 Judicial Improvements Act of 1990, Pub. L. No. 101-650 § 310(c) (eff. Dec. 1, 1990).
42 See United Mine Workers v. Gibbs, 383 U.S. 713 (1966); 16 Moore's Federal Practice § 106.05[4] (3d ed. 2005). Older FCRA cases raising this issue include Belshaw v. Credit Bureau of Prescott, 392 F. Supp. 1356 (D. Ariz. 1975) (certain state claims not related to FCRA claim); Austin v. Bankamerica Serv. Corp. 419 F. Supp. 730 (N.D. Ga. 1974) (state claims dismissed where FCRA claims dismissed).
43 Further, claims that "arise out of the transaction or occurrence that is the subject matter of the opposing party's claim" are compulsory counterclaims under Federal Rule of Civil Procedure 13(a), and are entitled to supplemental jurisdiction. See 3 Moore's Federal Practice § 13.10[3] (3d ed. 2005). Those that do not meet this test are permissive counterclaims, as to which there must be an independent basis for jurisdiction. See 3 Moore's Federal Practice § 13.30 (3d ed. 2005).
44 28 U.S.C. § 1332.
45 See National Consumer Law Center, Fair Debt Collection § 7.4 (5th 2004 and Supp.).
46 Id.
47 15 U.S.C. § 1681s-2(b). See § 6.10, 10.2.4, supra. There is no civil liability for a furnisher's failure to comply with 15 U.S.C. § 1681s-2(a), which pertains to the furnisher's obligations to provide accurate information; however liability may be imposed for failure to comply with § 1681s-2(b), which pertains to the furnisher's obligations upon notice of dispute. 15 U.S.C. § 1681s-2(d).
48 Fed. R. Civ. Pro. 4(e).

Fourteenth Amendment Due Process rights.[49] As a practical matter, most cases will be decided on the basis of state law, not constitutional law.

In suits against consumer reporting agencies (CRAs), the question of personal jurisdiction will rarely arise. Most CRAs, and certainly the nationwide CRAs, will be doing business in every state. However, when the defendant is out of state *and* a user of a consumer report or a furnisher of information to a CRA, or has obtained a report improperly, questions of personal jurisdiction can sometimes arise. In such cases, the law of the state in which the court is located must be considered. Often, state law permits personal jurisdiction to the maximum extent allowed by due process, i.e., provided there are minimum contacts.

The Supreme Court has held that "where a defendant who purposefully has directed his activities at forum residents seeks to defeat jurisdiction, he must present a compelling case that the presence of some other considerations would render jurisdiction unreasonable."[50] It has also held that personal jurisdiction is available in defamation cases where the victim is harmed even if "publication" originates elsewhere.[51]

Personal jurisdiction has thus frequently been found proper in the state where the subject of the consumer report resides.[52] For example, personal jurisdiction was found where the defendant knew that the disputed consumer report had adverse effects in the plaintiff's forum, and voluntarily generated contacts in the forum to collect the disputed debt.[53] Similarly, personal jurisdiction was held proper even if defendant intended to target a debtor in another state, but was informed of the harm to plaintiff's credit record in the state for which jurisdiction is sought.[54] Likewise, a complaint sufficiently alleged jurisdiction by asserting that the defendant, an investigative services company, "cause[d] tortious injury by an act or omission in this commonwealth" when it obtained her consumer report without a permissible purpose because the defendant knew that the effects of his actions were going to be felt within Massachusetts.[55] Although the defendant's place of business was in New York and he made the inquiry from a computer in New York to a CRA located in New York, the court ruled that it was reasonable to conclude that the defendant knew his actions would have specific effect in Massachusetts because he had inputted the plaintiff's Massachusetts address in order to obtain the report. Furthermore, the knowledge fulfilled the Constitution's requirement that the defendant "reasonably anticipate being hailed into court"[56] in Massachusetts.

However, where the tortious conduct is not expressly aimed at the forum state, jurisdiction may be lacking.[57] Even where some conduct is aimed at the forum state, it may be insufficient to establish personal jurisdiction. Thus a New York investigator who obtained a consumer report on a Maryland resident, and hired a Maryland company to conduct a criminal check, has been held not subject to personal

---

49 This inquiry involves "traditional notions of fair play and substantial justice" including the burden on the defendant, the interests of the forum State, and the plaintiff's interest in obtaining relief. *See, e.g.*, International Shoe Co. v. Washington, 326 U.S. 310, 66 S. Ct. 154, 90 L. Ed. 95 (1945); Asahi Metal Indus. Co. v. Superior Court of California, Solano County, 480 U.S. 102, 113, 107 S. Ct. 1026, 1033, 94 L. Ed. 2d 92 (1987); Obabueki v. IBM, 2001 U.S. Dist. LEXIS 11810 (S.D.N.Y. Aug. 14, 2001) (finding personal jurisdiction because of Internet application form), *aff'd on other grounds*, 319 F.3d 87 (2d Cir. 2003). *See also* Myers v. Bennett Law Offices, 238 F.3d 1068 (9th Cir. 2001).

50 Burger King Corp. v. Rudzewicz, 471 U.S. 462, 477, 105 S. Ct. 84, 85 L. Ed. 2d 528 (1985).

51 Calder v. Jones, 465 U.S. 783, 104 S. Ct. 1482, 79 L. Ed. 2d 804 (1984). *See also* Brown v. Flowers Industries, Inc., 688 F.2d 328 (5th Cir. 1982); Bils v. Nixon, Hargrave, Devans & Doyle, 880 P.2d 743 (Ariz. Ct. App. 1994); Shaw v. North Am. Title Co., 876 P.2d 1291 (Haw. 1994).

52 Scott v. Real Estate Fin. Group, 183 F.3d 97 (2d Cir. 1999) (personal jurisdiction obtained under Massachusetts law over an out of state investigator who accessed plaintiff's consumer report; although defendant had no contact with the state, defendant knew his actions would have a specific effect in the state); Hahn v. Star Bank, 190 F.3d 708 (6th Cir. 1999) (jurisdiction existed over out of state bank which refused to correct inaccurate information; defendant knew actions would be felt specifically in Puerto Rico); Cole v. American Family Mut. Ins. Co., 333 F. Supp. 2d 1038 (D. Kan. 2004) (impermissible access aimed at Kansas resident); Bertolet v. Bray, 277 F. Supp. 2d 835 (S.D. Ohio 2003) (consumer is injured in state of residence by impermissible access to individual's consumer report); Bickford v. Onslow Mem'l Hosp. Found., Inc., 855 A.2d 1150 (Me. 2004) ("[i]f a creditor actively refuses to correct the false consumer report of a Maine resident, Maine has a legitimate interest in protecting the resident, whether or not the creditor is located outside of Maine's boundaries").

53 Miranda Rivera v. Bank One, 145 F.R.D. 614 (D. P.R. 1993) (tortious act within the forum); Bils v. Nixon, Hargrove, Devans & Doyle, 880 P.2d 743 (Ariz. Ct. App. 1994).

54 Harris v. Equifax Credit Info. Sys., 2002 WL 32770554 (D. Or. May 31, 2002).

55 Liu v. DeFelice, 6 F. Supp. 2d 106 (D. Mass. 1998) (citing Mass. Gen. Laws ch. 223A, § 3(c)).

56 World-Wide Volkswagen Corp. v. Woodson, 444 U.S. 286, 297, 100 S. Ct. 559, 62 L. Ed. 2d 490 (1980).

57 Lockard v. Equifax, Inc., 163 F.3d 1259 (11th Cir. 1998) (Georgia did not have jurisdiction over collection agency which sent tape containing allegedly false information about the plaintiff to Equifax, a Credit Reporting Agency, in Atlanta; mailing did not amount to committing a tortious act under state long-arm statute); Screen v. Equifax Info. Sys., L.L.C., 303 F. Supp. 2d 685 (D. Md. 2004) (out-of-state creditor's response to verification requests was not affirmative conduct aimed at forum); Cisneros v. Trans Union, L.L.C., 293 F. Supp. 2d 1156 (D. Haw. 2003) (no personal jurisdiction in state of temporary residence; furnisher did not know of the location, purposefully avail itself of that forum, or aim its conduct there); Harris v. Trans Union, L.L.C., 197 F. Supp. 2d 200 (E.D. Pa. 2002) (furnisher's failure to mark CDV forms confirming plaintiff's address in forum state and its failure to attempt to collect erroneous debt lead court to conclude that furnisher did not expressly aim its tortious conduct activity in the forum state).

jurisdiction in Maryland. The actions causing injury in Maryland were taken outside Maryland.[58]

Personal jurisdiction over employees of a CRA may also be more difficult to obtain. A state's long-arm statute may not reach individuals whose only connection with the local jurisdiction is activity within the scope of their employment with the CRA.[59]

11.4.4 Selecting the Appropriate Court

Because an FCRA claim may be brought in either state or federal court, the consumer's attorney should carefully analyze the features of the case to determine which forum will be most beneficial. Relevant factors in deciding between federal and state court include:

- Whether the local courts lack prior experience and familiarity with FCRA cases;
- Whether a federal court will find supplemental jurisdiction for state law claims;
- Whether a jury trial will be requested and where juries are more likely to be favorably inclined toward plaintiffs;
- Whether opposing counsel is familiar with and comfortable in federal court;
- The relative merits of federal versus state court discovery rules;
- The relative ease of service of process;
- How quickly cases are processed in the different court systems;
- Where personal jurisdiction can be obtained.[60]
- The likelihood of removal if the case is brought in state court, thereby giving defendants the opportunity to forum-shop.

In some jurisdictions, the client can get a quicker determination from a more sympathetic judge with adequate discovery in a state court; in others, the opposite is true. Often, there is no clearly preferable forum when the relevant factors are considered.

Once a court has been selected, and the case goes to judgment, the consumer will not have a second chance to forum-shop because of collateral estoppel.[61]

---

58 Stover v. O'Connell Assocs., Inc., 84 F.3d 132 (4th Cir. 1996) (constitutional questions). *See also* Texas Guaranteed Student Loan Corp. v. Ward, 696 So. 2d 930 (Fla. Dist. Ct. App. 1997) (under Florida law, calls and letters to a Florida resident insufficient for long arm jurisdiction).
59 Wiggins v. Equifax Servs., Inc., 853 F. Supp. 500 (D.D.C. 1994). *But see* Dotzler v. Perot, 899 F. Supp. 416 (E.D. Mo. 1995); Way v. Barr, 1995 U.S. Dist. LEXIS 6342 (D. Md. May 9, 1995).
60 § 11.4.3, *supra*.
61 *See, e.g.*, Spence v. TRW, Inc., 92 F.3d 380 (6th Cir. 1996).

11.4.5 Removal

FCRA claims may be brought in state or federal court. If the consumer prefers state court, it has to be anticipated that the defendants may prefer federal court.

The FCRA is silent as to whether an FCRA claim can be removed from state to federal court pursuant to the general federal removal statute.[62] In general, an action brought in a state court can be removed to federal court when a federal district court also has original jurisdiction unless Congress has expressly prohibited removal. There are not many such prohibitions, and when Congress has decided that justifications exist to prohibit removal, it has made the prohibition clear by unambiguous language in the statute.[63] While the majority of courts hold that the general removal statute applies to FCRA claims brought in state court,[64] a few have found that Congress did not intend to require individual consumers to go to a potentially distant federal court in cases where claim sizes are relatively small and not worth the time, expense, and inconvenience of litigation in that forum.[65]

The best way to avoid removal is to bring an action in state court utilizing only state causes of action. Including federal claims and planning to dismiss them if the case is removed to federal court is usually a successful strategy, but carries some risk.[66] Most courts hold that the FCRA does

---

62 28 U.S.C. § 1441(a).
63 *See, e.g.*, 28 U.S.C. § 1445(a) (FELA cases "may not be removed"), § 1445(b) (suit against a common carrier for shipping damages "may not be removed to any district court of the United States unless the matter in controversy exceeds $3,000"), § 1445(c) (workers' compensation cases "may not be removed"); Securities Act of 1933, 15 U.S.C. § 77v ("no case . . . brought in any State court of competent jurisdiction shall be removed").
64 Lockard v. Equifax, Inc., 163 F.3d 1259 (11th Cir. 1998) ("We hold that the sole purpose of the language at issue here is to allow state courts concurrent jurisdiction for actions brought under the FCRA, and that the provision of concurrent jurisdiction does not prohibit removal."); Salei v. Boardwalk Regency Corp., 913 F. Supp. 993 (E.D. Mich. 1996) (remanding state claims); McGilvray v. Hallmark Fin. Group, Inc., 891 F. Supp. 265 (E.D. Va. 1995); Rhea v. Amrescc, Inc., 871 F. Supp. 283 (N.D. Tex. 1994); Duff v. C.S.C. Credit Servs., Inc., 1993 U.S. Dist. LEXIS 8520 (W.D. Mo. May 27, 1993); Broom v. TRW Credit Data, 732 F. Supp. 66 (E.D. Mich. 1990); Pinner v. Schmidt, 617 F. Supp. 342 (E.D. La. 1985), *aff'd in part and rev'd in part on other grounds*, 805 F.2d 1258 (5th Cir. 1986); Sicinski v. Reliance Funding Corp., 461 F. Supp. 649 (S.D.N.Y. 1978); Haun v. Retail Credit Co., 420 F. Supp. 859 (W.D. Pa. 1976).
65 Harper v. TRW, Inc., 831 F. Supp. 294, 299 (E.D. Mich. 1995) (holding in a privacy action that "[t]here is nothing in the legislative history or the FCRA itself to establish that Congress intended that state law causes of action such as Plaintiff's should be removable"); Ruth v. Westinghouse Credit Co., 373 F. Supp. 468 (W.D. Okla. 1974).
66 A plaintiff's right to amend the complaint to dismiss the FCRA claim upon removal is subject to Fed. R. Civ. P. 41. Further, amendment will not automatically succeed in defeating jurisdiction as it is determined at the time of removal. If the state and

not *completely preempt*⁶⁷ state law claims against a CRA, such as for defamation, and therefore may not be used as a basis for removal of a state court action to federal court.⁶⁸ Indeed, a state deceptive practices statute case cannot be removed to federal court even if the sole allegation is that the FCRA has been violated, and that the FCRA violation is a deceptive trade practice.⁶⁹ Nor does the fact that the FCRA may grant immunity to the defendant on some or all of plaintiff's state-law tort claims provide any basis for defendant to remove a state-law based case.⁷⁰

Even this approach to retaining the state court forum, however, is not ironclad protection; care must be taken in drafting the complaint not to assert a claim available only under the FCRA.⁷¹ Also, another maneuver to attempt to avoid removal—first serving an unsophisticated defendant who is the least likely to attempt removal, so that removal will be untimely because the limitation period for removal technically begins when any defendant is served—may fail if the court sees through this attempt at forum manipulation.⁷² Also, if a consumer brings a suit in state court under the state fair credit reporting statute, and another in federal court under the FCRA, the state court action may be stayed.⁷³

11.5 Statute of Limitations

11.5.1 FCRA Limitations Period

In 2003, FACTA amended the FCRA's statute of limitations to provide that the two-year limitations period dates from the consumer's discovery of the violation, not the date of the violation itself.⁷⁴ This effectively overrules *TRW v. Andrews*,⁷⁵ which had held that the discovery rule did not apply to the FCRA's limitations period. However, the consumer must bring the action within five years of the date of the violation, regardless of the discovery date.⁷⁶ The effective date for this change to the statute of limitation was March 31, 2004.⁷⁷

11.5.2 Limitations Period for Other Legal Claims

The limitations period for a common law tort claim will vary by state and may differ for different types of torts, but will often be one or two years. In some states, the tort limitations period will begin when the liability first arose,

---

federal claims form part of the same case or controversy, the federal court would still have supplemental jurisdiction of the state claims. Many courts nevertheless exercise their discretion to decline such jurisdiction when the federal claims are dismissed, and permit remand on plaintiff's motion. *See* 16 Moore's Federal Practice § 107.14[3][b](3d ed. 2005).

67 The FCRA preempts state law defamation claims "except as to false information furnished with malice or willful intent to injure such consumer," 15 U.S.C. 1681h(e); 15 U.S.C. 1681t(b). While this type of preemption precludes the pursuit of such claims in state or federal court, see, e.g., Johnson v. MBNA Am. Bank, N.A., 2006 WL 618077, *5–6 (M.D.N.C. Mar. 9, 2006) and Gorman v. Wolpoff & Abramson, 370 F. Supp. 2d 1005, 1009–1010 (N.D. Cal. 2005), it is different than the complete preemption discussed in the cases in the next footnote. *See generally* § 10.7.5, *supra*.

68 Sehl v. Safari Motor Coaches, Inc., 2001 WL 940846, *7 (N.D. Cal. Aug. 13, 2001) (removal of state claims based on federal preemption does not apply to FCRA since FCRA is not a "complete preemption" statute); Watkins v. Trans Union, L.L.C., 118 F. Supp. 2d 1217 (N.D. Ala. 2000) (no complete preemption for removal purposes—defamation); Swecker v. Trans Union Corp., 31 F. Supp. 2d 536, 539 (E.D. Va. 1998) ("The complete preemption exception to the well-pleaded complaint rule only applies where the federal preemption provision preempts all possible causes of action in a certain area, not just where it preempts some causes of action or even the specific cause of action at issue"). *See* Griffin v. Hooper-Holmes Bureau, Inc., 413 F. Supp. 107 (M.D. Fla. 1976). *See also* Shaner v. Fleet Bank, 132 F. Supp. 2d 953 (M.D. Ala. 2001) (remanded where only state claims for negligent or wanton reporting to CRA, libel, slander, false light invasion of privacy were asserted; "merely because a plaintiff could have stated a federal claim instead of, or in addition to, a state law claim will not sustain removal jurisdiction"); Rule v. Ford Receivables, 36 F. Supp. 2d 335, 339 (S.D. Va. 1999) (sole potential federal question is defendants' potential FCRA preemption defense, but "[s]uch a defense, which may be asserted, successfully or unsuccessfully, in the state court, does not provide a basis for removal"); Sherron v. Private Issue By Discover, 977 F. Supp. 804 (N.D. Miss. 1997) (cannot remove based on FCRA defenses to state claims).

69 State v. TRW, Clearinghouse No. 49,967 (D. Vt. 1991).

70 Wells v. Shelter Gen. Ins. Co., 217 F. Supp. 2d 744 (S.D. Miss. 2002); Sehl v. Safari Motor Coaches, Inc., 2001 WL 940846 (N.D. Cal. Aug. 13, 2001) (FCRA's preemption of libel claim not sufficient to support removal because of the statutory exceptions to preemption); Watkins v. Trans Union, L.L.C., 118 F. Supp. 2d 1217 (N.D. Ala. 2000). *See* Shaner v. Fleet Bank, 132 F. Supp. 2d 953 (M.D. Ala. 2001); Rule v. Ford Receivables, Inc., 36 F. Supp. 2d 335 (W.D. W. Va. 1999) (granting motion to remand; defendant may not remove a civil action on the basis of a defense of federal preemption); Swecker v. Trans Union Corp., 31 F. Supp. 2d 536 (E.D. Va. 1998) (granting motion to remand); Harper v. TRW, Inc., 881 F. Supp. 294 (E.D. Mich. 1995).

71 Taylor v. Wells Fargo Home Mortgage, Inc., 2004 WL 856673 (E.D. La. Apr. 20, 2004) (even though plaintiff had not pleaded a claim under the FCRA, defendant could remove where punitive damages remedy sought was available only under FCRA, citing Medina v. Ramsey Steel Co., 238 F.3d 674, 680 (5th Cir. 2001). *But see* Hughes v. Fidelity Bank, 709 F. Supp. 639 (E.D. Pa. 1989) (defendant removed, asserting "artfully pleaded" cause of action was actually under FCRA. Court remanded, allowing plaintiff to forego FCRA claims).

72 White v. White, 32 F. Supp. 2d 890 (W.D. 1998) (magistrate judge) (motion to remand granted despite technical untimeliness).

73 Houston v. Trans Union Credit Info., 546 N.Y.S.2d 600 (App. Div. 1989).

74 15 U.S.C. § 1681p.

75 TRW Inc. v. Andrews, 534 U.S. 19, 122 S. Ct. 441, 151 L. Ed. 2d 339 (2001).

76 15 U.S.C. § 1681p.

77 *Id.*

not when the consumer discovered or should have discovered the violation. Consequently, in many situations, a tort limitations period will be less than the two years for an FCRA claim which now begins only upon discovery. For the common law tort of credit slander, however, each publication of the consumer report is a new violation for statute of limitations purposes.[78]

State credit reporting statutes often have the identical limitations period as the federal statute, but in some states the statute may differ. In addition, where a limitation period is not found in the statute, a state's general statutory limitations period may apply instead. Consequently, the limitation period may be shorter or longer than that provided by the FCRA, perhaps depending on whether state law begins the period from when the consumer discovered or should have discovered the violation.

The same can be said for state deceptive practices statutes. These may be as short as one or two years but may be three, four, or even more years. In addition, limitations periods usually begin to run from when the consumer discovered or should have discovered the deception.[79]

11.6 Discovery and Litigation Strategies

11.6.1 General

Development and implementation of a comprehensive discovery plan is essential for success in litigating FCRA cases. Consumer attorneys should establish a plan that will provide access to necessary documents and electronic information such as consumer reports, consumer reporting agency (CRA) manuals, policies and procedures, and, at the same time, lay the foundation for admitting such documents and other information into evidence. Practitioners should also be cognizant of common defense strategies that impede these efforts, including challenges to attorney-issued subpoenas, use of confidentiality agreements, and other measures that are aimed at limiting both access to, and the admissibility of, information that is maintained by CRAs, furnishers, and users of consumer credit information. This section provides some practical discovery and other litigation suggestions on these important issues.

11.6.2 Informal Discovery

It is possible to gather much useful information very easily in an informal manner. As an initial step, consumers or their attorneys should normally request disclosure of the contents of the consumer's file, which the "Big Three" nationwide CRAs must supply for free on an annual basis,[80] as well as the consumer's credit score (available for a fee). Consumers or their attorneys should request creditors to provide the exact reasons for credit denial if not already provided,[81] and request follow-up information where notice of an investigative report is provided.[82]

In addition to the free annual reports from the "Big Three," the consumer is entitled to receive from an employer a copy of any consumer report if the employer intends to take an adverse action based on the report.[83] Furthermore, following an adverse action based on information in a consumer report, the consumer is entitled to a free copy of the report from the CRA, and following a denial or increase in the charge for credit based on information from a third party, the consumer is entitled to disclosure from the user of the nature of the information.[84] The consumer has a statutory right to all of this information.

Alternatively, a consumer can request a report from a consolidation service, also known as a "reseller," that combines information from all three CRAs into one combined report, sometimes called a "trimerger," and identifies which CRA reported each item of information. Obtaining reports from all three CRAs can be helpful because evidence that another CRA handled the information at issue differently and better can show that the defendant CRA has been unreasonable.[85] In addition, the consumer has a right to the names of persons who have received reports on the consumer.[86]

The consumer's lawyer can also learn a great deal simply by telephoning the CRA and/or user and making inquiries. Practitioners should consider having clients execute a power of attorney to aid in acquisition of the information. CRAs sometimes demand a power of attorney signed by the consumer before releasing reports or other information to the attorney, even though a release signed by the consumer should be sufficient.

It may be wise to inquire about the CRA's business relationships with other CRAs. Sometimes a local CRA may contract with a national CRA to broaden its information base. In such cases, the consumer report provided by the local CRA may have been compiled by the national CRA. If such a relationship is discovered, one should consider the merits of adding the national CRA as a party to the suit.[87]

---

78 *See, e.g.*, Musto v. Bell South Telecomms. Corp., 748 So. 2d 296 (Fla. Dist. Ct. App. 1999).
79 *See* National Consumer Law Center, Unfair and Deceptive Acts and Practices § 7.3.2 (6th ed. 2004 and Supp.).
80 *See* § 3.3.2, *supra*.
81 *See* § 8.2.6.6, *supra*.
82 *See* § 13.4.2, *supra*.
83 *See* § 8.2.6.2.5, *supra*.
84 *See* § 8.2.6.4.3, *supra*.
85 Cousin v. Trans Union Corp., 246 F.3d 359 (5th Cir. 2001).
86 *See* § 3.5.4, *supra*.
87 *See, e.g.*, Stern v. Credit Bureau of Milwaukee, 105 Wis. 2d 647, 315 N.W.2d 511 (Ct. App. 1981) (court refused to consider certain claims against the defendant, a local CRA which supplied the consumer report, because there was no evidence of an agency relationship with the nationwide company which compiled the erroneous report).

Consumer advocates may consider the use of "testers" to establish that CRAs are in violation of the Act, but caution is in order. For instance, a friendly creditor could tell the CRA it was processing a loan application and thus obtain a report on a consumer, with the actual purpose being to obtain a sample of the CRA's consumer report format for the consumer's attorney. This might reveal that different information is being furnished to users than appears on the report made available to the consumer.[88] However, anyone considering the use of such testers should be advised that the Department of Justice has informally indicated that, unless the "tester" had a permissible purpose for obtaining the report, it would potentially be violating the Act's criminal sanctions against obtaining reports by false pretenses.[89]

11.6.3 Formal Discovery

11.6.3.1 General

Through motions to produce documents and electronic files, interrogatories, depositions, and subpoenas, the consumer's attorney can discover much information that is useful to prove a claim. This includes information specific to the consumer's individual situation, such as credit scores or communications with users, as well as information regarding CRA practices and policies generally. Both types of discovery are discussed below.

Sample discovery requests provided by attorneys based on their own experience are available in Appendix J, *infra*, on the CD-Rom accompanying this manual, and in NCLC's *Consumer Law Pleadings*.[90]

In some cases, the consumer must show that the CRA or user did not follow or maintain reasonable procedures. It is then appropriate to probe the company's system-wide operation in order to determine its procedures. The consumer's attorney should examine the training program provided for employees, as well as the manner in which employees' preparation of reports is supervised by superiors. Request all documents that affect the CRA's preparation and treatment of data pertaining to the consumer, including its policy and procedure manuals. In some cases office manuals, internal memoranda, and other material have demonstrated a lack of reasonable procedures or company policies to provide accurate reports.[91] For example, the CRA may not have a reasonable procedure to ensure that the John Jones about whom it has received information is definitely the same John Jones about whom it is preparing a report.[92] Indeed, practitioners have reported that sometimes the only written office procedures produced by local CRAs is a document written by the CRAs' trade association, Consumer Data Industry Association (formerly the Associated Credit Bureaus, Inc.), titled *How to Comply with the Fair Credit Reporting Act*. This extended discussion of the FCRA falls far short of establishing or explaining a CRA's reasonable procedure for reporting activities. Also, discovery has sometimes revealed that employees conducting investigations have been required to produce such high quotas of reports every week that accuracy was impossible.[93]

Practitioners should inquire into the CRA's handling of consumer disputes, including disputes from consumer attorneys and how all disputes are logged, both manually and by computer. Specific inquiries should be made into how the CRA maintains all dispute logs, how the CRA maintains letters from consumers and the consumers' attorneys, as well as how the CRA handles the consumer dispute verification forms (CDVs).[94] The actual handling of such information should also be compared to the CRA's manuals governing the processing of this information to determine if employees of the CRA are following the protocols and policies outlined in the manual, which are the presumptively reasonable procedures established by the CRA.

It may be helpful to ascertain how users receive information from the CRA. If it is provided over the phone, what procedures are used to ensure errors are not made in transmitting the information in this fashion?[95] If the matter concerns mixed files or erroneous information, the header information will show what identifying factors were given to the CRA, and the audit trail will show what information appeared in a consumer report at various times.

Practitioners should also request copies of CRA manuals for reinvestigation of consumer disputes, including all forms and other documents relating to the CRA's compliance with the FCRA. This is especially important with respect to the CRA's policies and protocols for investigating disputes from consumers. A CRA may insist on a protective order governing the confidentiality of such materials.[96] In some cases, the CRA may claim that it did not conduct the reinvestigation, but instead outsourced this responsibility to its trade association,

---

88 See Ch. 3, *supra* (how consumers may obtain copies of their reports).
89 This opinion was expressed by S. Kurn, attorney in the Department of Justice's Office of Consumer Litigation, in a letter of Feb. 22, 1988 (Clearinghouse No. 45,505). *See also* W.D.I.A. Corp. v. McGraw-Hill, Inc., 34 F. Supp. 2d 612 (S.D. Ohio 1998).
90 National Consumer Law Center, Consumer Law Pleadings (Cumulative CD-Rom and Index Guide).
91 *See, e.g.*, Jones v. Credit Bureau of Huntington, Inc., 399 S.E.2d 694 (W. Va. 1990) (granting discovery of portions of TRW's Consumer Relations Policy and Procedure Manual over relevancy objections); Equifax, Inc., 96 F.T.C. 1045 (1980), *rev'd in part*, 678 F.2d 1047 (11th Cir. 1982).
92 *See, e.g.*, Miller v. Credit Bureau of Washington, D.C., [1969–1973 Decisions Transfer Binder] Consumer Cred. Guide (CCH) ¶ 99,173 (D.C. Super. Ct. 1973).
93 *See, e.g.*, Cushman v. Trans Union Corp., 115 F.3d 220, 224–225 (3d Cir. 1997); Millstone v. O'Hanlon Reports, 383 F. Supp. 269 (E.D. Mo. 1974), *aff'd*, 528 F.2d 829 (8th Cir. 1976).
94 See Ch. 4, *supra*.
95 Privacy Protection Study Commission, Personal Privacy in an Information Society at 73, 163 (1977).
96 *See* § 11.6.3.4, *infra*.

Consumer Data Information Association (formerly Associated Credit Bureaus). Thus, the manuals may not produce a complete picture of the reinvestigation process and practitioners may have to subpoena documents from CDIA regarding its reinvestigation policies and practices.

Some CRAs claim they are unable to produce archived reports, but litigators recount that, despite such claims, CRAs often have copies of their database system that were downloaded for backup purposes, and that these reports are archived at least monthly, notwithstanding CRA claims that they are done no more than quarterly. Archived reports are also sometimes available as "snapshots" or "frozen data sheets."[97] These archival systems are reportedly accessible to CRA employees. Practitioners report that they have received, over the objection of CRA attorneys, reports generated by these archival systems. Practitioners also report that the CRAs sometimes attempt to charge for these reports, purportedly because they are expensive to produce, but others have been able to obtain this information without charge. Cost-shifting should be considered *only* when discovery imposes an "undue burden or expense" on the responding party.[98] It may also be helpful to request reports from the past to determine what information may have been in the CRA's database at various times in order to establish the contents of a report conveyed to a user.

A wide variety of other useful documents and electronic information can be sought from users, furnishers, and CRAs. For example, a "terminal audit trail" is a record of the exact keystrokes inputted by a user to retrieve a report. From this audit trail, consumer attorneys can access what has transpired on the consumer's account and within a particular tradeline during a defined period of time. This would be useful to determine when information was added or deleted from a consumer's file. Copies of subscriber contracts may contain the terms under which the subscriber is allowed to access the CRA's reports. An inquiry invoice may establish that a user requested and paid for a particular report. This is especially important in cases where insurance companies and others who have blanket agreements to access consumer reports may be obtaining reports for unauthorized purposes.

From a user, consider requesting not only all documents related to the consumer's account, but specifically any information, including credit scores, obtained from any CRA that pertained to the consumer's credit account or application. If the case concerns a failure to reinvestigate a dispute, request copies of any electronic Automated Consumer Dispute Verification (ACDV)[99] process items. Practitioners should be aware of the CRA's use of the Metro 2 Format and how information is furnished to the CRA.[100] Advocates may also have to seek information from third parties with whom a CRA has contracted to conduct the re-investigation of disputed information. The outsourcing of investigations appears to be an increasing practice by some CRAs. Since prior similar complaints and prior knowledge are relevant to willfulness, they should be discoverable and admissible in any action seeking statutory or punitive damages.

Consumers are entitled to all information in their file, not just their consumer reports.[101] They are also entitled to their credit scores for a fee.[102] Creditors rely more and more on credit scores, so scores should be requested as a part of formal discovery, especially since consumers may not receive the same scores as those provided to users.[103] Moreover, if a score was a possible factor in a denial or more especially in the cost of credit offered the consumer, one should request the score as originally calculated and a recomputed score based on corrected information. A significant difference may correlate to the price or type of credit made available to the consumer, and help prove actual damages.

Upon commencing litigation, practitioners should send a letter to opposing counsel requesting preservation of categories of current and ongoing data that ultimately will be requested in discovery. Case law recognizes a party's duty to preserve unique, relevant evidence that might be useful to an adversary. Failure to do so may be deemed spoliation. "While a litigant is under no duty to keep or retain every document in its possession . . . it is under a duty to preserve what it knows, or reasonably should know, is relevant in the action, is reasonably calculated to lead to the discovery of admissible evidence, is reasonably likely to be requested during discovery and/or is the subject of a pending discovery request."[104] This duty extends, for example, to backup tapes.[105]

---

97 *See* Young v. Equifax, Inc., 294 F.3d 631 (5th Cir. 2002); TransUnion also maintains monthly snapshots. Experian has more traditional "files" for each consumer.
98 The Supreme Court has instructed that "the presumption is that the responding party must bear the expense of complying with discovery requests. . . ." *Oppenheimer Fund*, 437 U.S. 340, 358, 98 S. Ct. 2380, 57 L. Ed. 2d 253 (1978). *See* Fed. R. Civ. P. 26(c).
99 *See* Ch. 4, *supra*.
100 *See* § 6.3.2, *supra*.
101 15 U.S.C. § 1681g(a)(1). *See* § 3.5, *supra*.
102 15 U.S.C. § 1681g(a)(f). *See* § 14.4, *supra*.
103 *See* § 14.4.3, *supra*.
104 Marrocco v. General Motors, 966 F.2d 220, 224–225 (7th Cir. 1997); Kemper Mortg., Inc. v. Russell, 2006 WL 2319858 (S.D. Ohio Apr. 18, 2006); Mosaid Technologies, Inc. v. Samsung Elecs. Co., 348 F. Supp. 2d 332, (D.N.J. 2004) (awarding sanction of adverse inference jury instruction for spoliation of e-mail evidence); *In re* Prudential Ins. Co. of Am. Sales Practices Litig., 169 F.R.D. 598, 615 (D.N.J. 1997); Nat'l Assoc. of Radiation Survivors v. Turnage, 115 F.R.D. 543, 557–558 (N.D. Cal. 1987); William T. Thompson Co. v. General Nutrition Corp., 593 F. Supp. 1443, 1445 (C.D. Cal. 1984). "Whether a responding party is required to preserve unsearched sources of potentially responsive information that it believes are not reasonably accessible depends on the circumstances of each case. It is often useful for the parties to discuss this issue early in discovery." Report of the Advisory Committee on Rule 26(b)(2), *available at* www.uscourts.gov/rules/EDiscovery_w_Notes.pdf.
105 Zubulake v. UBS Warburg, 220 F.R.D. 212, 218 (S.D.N.Y. 2003) (Zubulake IV).

Do not lose confidence in your case just because company documents do not prove your claims. For example, in one case, TransUnion's records indicated that an obsolete debt had *not* been reported to a user. However, a TransUnion representative told the plaintiff it had been reported, and there was no other apparent reason for denying the plaintiff credit. Based on these facts, the Second Circuit ruled that the lower court had erred in granting summary judgment to TransUnion and that the question must go to the trier of facts—the inferences to be drawn from these indirect proofs raised material issues of fact as to credibility.[106]

11.6.3.2 Electronic Discovery

At this writing, the Federal Rules of Civil Procedure governing electronic discovery are about to be amended, effective December 1, 2006, absent Congressional disapproval.[107] The commentary by the Rules' Advisory Committee tempers somewhat the obligation to preserve electronic evidence, acknowledging "the balance between the competing needs to preserve relevant evidence and to continue routine operations critical to ongoing activities. Complete or broad cessation of a party's routine computer operations could paralyze the party's activities."[108] For this reason, Rule 37(f) creates a "safe harbor" that protects a party from sanctions for failing to provide electronically stored information lost because of the routine operation of the party's computer system.

Codification of the ground rules governing accessibility of electronic discovery is one of the most significant provisions of the proposed amendments to the Federal Rules of Civil Procedure. As a starting point and potential source of valuable information in evaluating claims of inaccessibility, Rule 26(a)(1) has been amended to expressly require that initial disclosures about individuals with discoverable information and documents include disclosures about electronically stored information. This obligation should result in defendants disclosing which specific electronic databases they maintain and utilize that are relevant to the plaintiff's claims. Proposed Rule 26(b)(2)(B) then creates a shifting burden on what need not be produced as "inaccessible" because of "undue burden or cost." The requesting party may need discovery to test the responding party's assertion that identified sources of information are not reasonably accessible because of undue burden or cost. "Such discovery might take the form of requiring the responding party to conduct a sampling of information contained on the sources identified as not reasonably accessible; allowing some form of inspection of such sources; or taking depositions of witnesses knowledgeable about the responding party's information systems."[109] As noted above, cost-shifting to the requesting party should be considered *only* when electronic discovery imposes an "undue burden or expense" on the responding party.[110]

11.6.3.3 Company Information About Defendants

CRAs and other defendants will of course be unwilling to produce information on net worth. For punitive damage claims, however, it is appropriate to use discovery to ascertain the defendant's financial status.[111] To establish a claim for punitive damages, the complaint must allege that the defendant acted willfully, in violation of section 1681n.[112] General information about the CRAs and the structure of the industry may also be helpful. For example, if the CRA that prepared the report about the client is Equifax, it is useful to know that it has been the subject of many lawsuits and Federal Trade Commission actions, and is the current name of what used to be called Retail Credit Co.

If the consumer files a claim against an officer or employer of a CRA, user, or furnisher, information concerning that person's economic interests and benefits relating to the CRA should be discoverable along with similar information about the CRA itself. Practitioners have reported incidents where tax returns showed that all of the CRA profits were paid out to the owner, and the CRA paid no taxes. Reluctance to have such information placed before the jury and made public has contributed to a willingness to settle litigation.

11.6.3.4 Confidentiality Agreements and Protective Orders

CRAs often request that discovery be disclosed under the cloak of a protective order, claiming that the information requested is confidential, proprietary, or includes a trade

---

106 Lendino v. Trans Union Credit Info. Co., 970 F.2d 1110 (2d Cir. 1992).
107 The Judicial Conference and the Supreme Court have approved them. *See* Report to the Standing Committee on Rules of Practice and Procedure, Judicial Conference of the United States by the Advisory Committee on the Federal Rules of Civil Procedure (Sept. 2005).
108 Advisory Committee, *citing* the Manual for Complex Litigation (4th) § 11.422A. *See, e.g.*, Sedona Conference Working Group Series, The Sedona Principles: Best Practices, Recommendations & Principles for Addressing Electronic Document Discovery cmt. 6.h (2003) ("Absent specific circumstances, preservation obligations should not extend to disaster recovery backup tapes. . . .").

109 Report of the Advisory Committee on Rule 26(b)(2), *available at* www.uscourts.gov/rules/EDiscovery_w_Notes.pdf.
110 The Supreme Court has instructed that "the presumption is that the responding party must bear the expense of complying with discovery requests. . . ." *Oppenheimer Fund*, 437 U.S. 340, 358, 98 S. Ct. 2380, 57 L. Ed. 2d 253 (1978). *See* Fed. R. Civ. P. 26(c).
111 Thornton v. Equifax, 467 F. Supp. 1008 (E.D. Tenn. 1979), *rev'd*, 619 F.2d 700 (8th Cir. 1980); Collins v. Retail Credit Co., 410 F. Supp. 924 (E.D. Mich. 1976). *See also* Sutherland v. TRW, Inc., 1995 WL 275578 (N.D. Ill. May 8, 1995).
112 *See* § 11.12, *infra*.

secret. Federal Rule of Civil Procedure 26(c) allows a judge "for good cause shown" to issue a protective order, but the burden is on the party seeking the order, who must make a particular and specific demonstration that failure to issue the order will cause a clearly defined, serious injury.[113] Consumer attorneys should closely examine the factual record the CRA purportedly relies upon to assert the existence of trade secrets and good cause for the issuance of the protective order. The public has an interest in court proceedings at all stages, and protective orders should not be granted carte blanche, without review.[114] Consumer attorneys should be wary of such orders since confidentiality agreements hinder litigation and keep the wrongdoing by credit reporting industry hidden from public scrutiny.

In addition, any limitation is a restraint on First Amendment speech and any such order must advance "an important and substantial government interest unrelated to the suppression of speech" and must be "no greater than is necessary or essential to the protection of the particular governmental interest involved."[115]

A CRA may seek such an order to preclude the plaintiff's attorney from consulting with or sharing information with other attorneys who have handled FCRA cases. In the meantime, of course, the CRA remains free to consult with other CRAs and their attorneys to mount its defense, and the plaintiff's attorney should assert that the inequity that would result from a protective order argues against it. One commentator has suggested that in an appropriate case, a protective order can be crafted that prohibits disclosure of trade secrets to competitors while still allowing the sharing of documents among plaintiffs with similar cases.[116] Indeed, since the real motive for secrecy often is to shield practices and procedures which, if known, would lead to other lawsuits by other wronged individuals, one court has suggested that persons who are not party to the lawsuit should be able to challenge the secreting of particular documents.[117]

Sometimes, the CRA's attorney and the consumer's attorney may be able to negotiate a confidentiality agreement concerning the materials to be revealed, although often a CRA will begin with an absurdly broad claim of confidentiality that has to be whittled down. With respect to such an agreement, the consumer's attorney should seek an express provision permitting the documents to be shared with anyone designated as a "consultant" or an expert. Be wary of any request by the CRA to redact any information on a credit or administrative report before turning it over. Deletion of internal codes may make the report impossible to decipher, even by one familiar with the codes.

Some CRAs have insisted on protective orders to protect the privacy of third-party consumers who may have been linked with the consumer litigant in a consumer report. This strategy by CRAs should not be permitted to hinder the litigant's right to obtain information necessary to pursue his or her FCRA and related claims.

11.6.3.5 Consumer Reports and Evidentiary Issues

Though it may be the centerpiece of any FCRA litigation, actually getting a consumer report into evidence can be difficult. At a minimum and as a first step, the defendants should be willing to stipulate to its authenticity. An objection to admissibility is frequently made, however, on the ground that it is hearsay.[118] For example, CRAs sometimes assert that tradelines within consumer reports are out-of-court statements of third party non-defendants and thus non-admissible hearsay.

Preliminary consideration should be given to whether the report is being admitted for its truthfulness or accuracy, or whether instead it is simply evidence that a report was generated or pulled by a user. If the latter, then the report is not hearsay, and it is unnecessary to consider whether it is admissible under some exception to the hearsay rule.[119]

In the course of a deposition, practitioners may wish to lay appropriate evidentiary foundations for authentication of documents and to establish that documents like consumer reports are "business records" for purposes of overcoming a hearsay objection. Authentication can also be accomplished through requests for admissions.

The business records exception allows hearsay to be admitted unless the source of information or the method or circumstances of preparation indicate lack of trustworthiness.[120] This presumption of trustworthiness for business records is especially applicable to consumer reports because Congress has set up an elaborate statutory framework to

---

113 Fed. R. Civ. P. 26(c). *See* Phillips v. General Motors, 289 F.3d 1117 (9th Cir. 2002), *as amended*, 307 F.3d 1206 (9th Cir. 2002); Citizens First National Bank of Princeton v. Cincinnati, 178 F.3d 943 (7th Cir. 1999); 23 Am. Jur. 2d *Depositions & Discovery* § 89 (1983). The affidavit of an expert in the field, who can testify as to the necessity or lack of necessity for protecting the information, will bolster a motion opposing a protective order. A sample confidentiality order proposed by consumer counsel and keeping the burden of proof on the CRA is reproduced at Appx. J.7, *infra*.

114 Zahran v. Trans Union Corp., 2002 WL 31010822 (N.D. Ill. Sept. 9, 2002) (TransUnion's dispute manuals and subscriber agreements are not confidential). *See* Citizens First National Bank of Princeton v. Cincinnati Ins. Co., 178 F.3d 943 (7th Cir. 1999).

115 Seattle Times Co. v. Rhinehart, 467 U.S. 20 (1984).

116 Richard A. Rosen, *Confidentiality Agreements Become Increasingly Elusive; Several States Have Limited the Availability of Protective Orders, and Judges Are Now More Skeptical About Issuing Such Orders*, National L. J., at B7, col. 1 (July 20, 1998).

117 Citizens First National Bank of Princeton v. Cincinnati Ins. Co., 178 F.3d 943 (7th Cir. 1999).

118 Davis v. Equifax Info. Servs. L.L.C., 346 F. Supp. 2d 1164 (N.D. Ala. 2004) (n.13 remarks that plaintiff's testimony about reports given to third party was inadmissible hearsay).

119 Fed. R. Evid. 801(c).

120 Fed. R. Evid. 803(6). *See, e.g.*, Semper v. JBC Legal Group, 2005 WL 2172377, n.11 (W.D. Wash. Sept. 6, 2005).

ensure that consumer reports are accurate and complete.[121] Thus there is a compelling argument that consumer reports are reliable and admissible under the business records exception to the hearsay rule. However, this argument of course should not be made if plaintiff's claim is that the report contains harmful inaccuracies.

Other theories for getting the report admitted into evidence over a hearsay objection include the following:

- In a case against a furnisher, if the furnisher supplied data on which the consumer report is based, or otherwise ratified or participated in publishing the report, the report is not hearsay and may be admissible against the furnisher;[122]
- The report is not hearsay if it is the opposing party's own statement or a statement of which the party or an authorized person or agent of the party has manifested an adoption or belief in its truth;[123]
- The report is admissible to show the state of mind of the credit grantor in making a credit granting decision;[124]
- The report is admissible as a statement of the plaintiff's character or reputation;[125]
- The report is evidence of a material fact that is more probative than other evidence that can be procured through reasonable efforts, and admission of the report will best serve the interests of justice.[126]

11.6.3.6 Subpoenas

The FCRA provides that any CRA may furnish a consumer report in response to the order of a court having jurisdiction to issue such an order, or a subpoena issued in connection with proceedings before a federal grand jury.[127] Practitioners report that discovery disputes have arisen relating to attorney-issued subpoenas and whether or not they are "court orders" under the Act. Some CRAs take the incorrect position that attorney-issued subpoenas are not court orders under the FCRA unless they are signed by a judge. Rule 45 of the Federal Rules of Civil Procedure was amended in 1991 to specifically provide for issuance of a subpoena by attorneys as officers of the court and states that defiance of a subpoena, even if issued by an attorney, "is nevertheless an act in defiance of a court order" thereby exposing the recipient to contempt sanctions.[128] When the deposition is to be taken in another district, the subpoena should be issued in the name of the court in that district.[129] In some cases if all that is needed is the consumer report of the client, a subpoena is unnecessary. Simply obtain an appropriate authorization from the client and submit the request and authorization to the CRA.[130]

11.6.3.7 Insurance Coverage for FCRA Liability

Reportedly, the "Big Three" nationwide CRAs are self-insured. For local CRAs, information about liability insurance coverage often aids settlement discussions. Consumer Data Information Association (formerly Associated Credit Bureaus, Inc.) and others market professional liability insurance to CRAs covering consumer reporting activities, check verification and recovery activities, and even debt collection activities. Such policies also frequently include as named insureds the officers, directors, stockholders, trustees, partners, and employees of the insured credit agency. At times, such insurance has satisfied the claims of consumers suing under the Fair Credit Reporting Act. Usually, the policy excludes intentional acts, so a defendant's liability for willful violation of the FCRA or defamation might not be covered.

The existence and contents of such insurance agreements are expressly discoverable in federal courts.[131] Also, some states provide by statute for direct actions by claimants against insurers. In other states, such an insurance agreement may be subject to attachment in aid of execution. Upon determining that the defendant is insured, plaintiff's counsel should consider bringing the insurer directly into the negotiations, as the insurer may be more cooperative than the defendant itself, particularly where hostility has developed between the plaintiff and the defendant. Doing so may also avert any claim by the insurer that coverage is waived due to the insured's noncooperation. Noncooperation should not be an issue where the insurer provides the lawyers for the insured's defense. Otherwise, send copies of demand letters, the complaint and motions to the insurer to avoid this issue.

11.6.4 Record Retention

The Fair Credit Reporting Act has no specific record retention requirement and imposes no obligation that a CRA, furnisher, or user keep information for any length of time. CRAs also tend not to retain important documents. For example, practitioners report that the "Big Three" nationwide CRAs do not retain consumer dispute verification forms or records of the automated dispute verification

---

121 15 U.S.C. § 1681.
122 Philip Van Heusen, Inc. v. Korn, 204 Kan. 172, 460 P.2d 549, 552 (1969).
123 Fed. R. Evid. 801(d)(1), (2).
124 Fed. R. Evid. 803(3).
125 Fed. R. Evid. 803(21). See 15 U.S.C. § 1681(a)(2).
126 Fed. R. Evid. 807.
127 15 U.S.C. § 1681b(a)(1).
128 Fed. R. Civ. P. 45 (a)(3), Notes of Advisory Committee on December 1991 Amendment of Rule, Subdivision (a).
129 Potomac Elec. Power Co. v. Electric Motor Supply Inc., 190 F.R.D. 372, 380 (D. Md. 1999). See Fed. R. Civ. P. 45, referencing geographical limits imposed upon service of subpoenas.
130 See 15 U.S.C. § 1681b(a)(2).
131 Fed. R. Civ. P. 26(a)(1)(D); Aetna Cas. & Surety Co. v. Sunshine Corp., 74 F.3d 685 (6th Cir. 1996) (insurer's obligation to defend). However, evidence of insurance liability is not generally admissible against the insured. Fed. R. Evid. 411.

forms. Information about a consumer could be used by the CRA without even being filed or kept for later usage, disclosure, or discovery.[132] While the Equal Credit Opportunity Act requires creditors to maintain records for twenty-five months following notice to a consumer of adverse action,[133] this requirement does not reach CRAs and others. Even so, the absence of a record retention requirement does not usually present a problem. Records and information are plentiful because information used by CRAs has a useful life of several years until it becomes obsolete, CRAs, users, and furnishers remain potentially liable for violation under an up-to-five-year statute of limitations, and businesses need to track and organize billions of bits of information, to bill users, and manage sources of information electronically. Usually, the greater challenge is to locate and obtain the precise information relevant to particular circumstances.

Although there is no record retention requirement, the FACTA amendments of 2003 required federal agencies and the CRAs to adopt consistent and comparable rules regarding the proper *disposal* of consumer report information and records in order to reduce the risk of consumer fraud, including identity theft.[134]

11.7 Right to Jury Trial; Jury Instructions

The FCRA is silent on whether the consumer has a right to a jury trial. Juries have been permitted in cases involving FCRA claims *and* related state claims where punitive damages were sought.[135] Jury trials also have been permitted where the complaint was based solely on FCRA claims.[136] Section 11.15, *infra*, provides a list of jury awards in FCRA cases.[137]

Although no decision directly addresses whether parties have a Seventh Amendment right to a jury trial in FCRA actions, cases involving the Fair Debt Collection Practices Act[138] and the Truth in Lending Act[139] make a strong argument that under the Supreme Court's reasoning in *Curtis v. Loether*,[140] the Seventh Amendment affords the right to a jury trial in an FCRA action, whether for actual, statutory, or punitive damages. Under *Curtis*, if the claim involves rights and remedies of the type traditionally enforced in an action at law, the Seventh Amendment requires the right to a jury trial.[141] Actions under the FCRA, it can be argued, are actions to enforce legal rights that closely resemble the tort actions of defamation, invasion of privacy, and negligence. Events giving rise to an FCRA action will often also state a claim under one or more of these torts, hence the Act's grant of qualified immunity from them.[142] Furthermore, the actual, statutory, and punitive damages[143] available to consumers under the FCRA have all been found to provide a basis for a jury trial in cases involving other consumer protection statutes and are considered to be among the sorts of relief traditionally offered in courts of law.[144]

The appendices and the CD-Rom accompanying this manual include sample testimony and closing statements to a jury. In fashioning instructions to the jury, the judge has considerable leeway.[145] Sample jury instructions are included at Appendix J.8, *infra*.

11.8 Defenses, Counterclaims, and Third Party Claims

Defendants typically raise boilerplate defenses to FCRA claims.[146] Unlike other titles of the Consumer Credit Pro-

---

132 *See* Lee, FTC Informal Staff Opinion Letter (June 26, 1998), *reprinted on the CD-Rom accompanying this manual*.

133 *See* § 8.2.6.6, *supra*; and especially National Consumer Law Center, Credit Discrimination § 10.12 (4th ed. 2005 and Supp.).

134 15 U.S.C. § 1681w(a)(1). *See* § 9.2.5.3, *supra*.

135 *See, e.g.,* Bach v. First Union National Bank, 149 Fed. Appx. 354, 361 (6th Cir. 2005); Johnson v. MBNA Am. Bank, N.A., 357 F.3d 426 (4th Cir. 2004); Pinner v. Schmidt, 617 F. Supp. 342 (E.D. La. 1985), *aff'd in part, rev'd in part*, 805 F.2d 1258 (5th Cir. 1986); Thornton v. Equifax, 467 F. Supp. 1008 (E.D. Ark. 1979), *rev'd on other grounds*, 619 F.2d 700 (8th Cir. 1980); Collins v. Retail Credit Co., 410 F. Supp. 924 (E.D. Mich. 1976).

136 *E.g.,* Colletti v. Credit Bureau Servs., 644 F.2d 1148 (5th Cir. 1981); Evers v. Equifax, 650 F.2d 793 (5th Cir. 1981); Russell v. Shelter Fin. Servs., 604 F. Supp. 201 (W.D. Mo. 1984); Bryant v. TRW, Inc., 487 F. Supp. 1234 (E.D. Mich. 1980), *aff'd*, 689 F.2d 72 (6th Cir. 1982).

137 *See* § 11.15, *infra*.

138 15 U.S.C. §§ 1692–1692o. *See* National Consumer Law Center, Fair Debt Collection (5th 2004 and Supp.).

139 15 U.S.C. §§ 1601–1615. *See* National Consumer Law Center, Truth in Lending (5th ed. 2003 and Supp.).

140 415 U.S. 189 (1972). *See also* Feltner v. Columbia Pictures Television, 523 U.S. 340, 118 S. Ct. 1279, 140 L. Ed. 2d 438 (1998) (Seventh Amendment provides a right to a jury trial in an action for statutory damages under the Copyright Act).

141 *Id.* at 195–196 (action under Title VIII of the Civil Rights Act of 1968 is an action to enforce legal rights, sounding basically in tort, and that the relief sought, actual and punitive damages, is the traditional form of relief offered in courts of law).

142 15 U.S.C. § 1681h(e). *See* Ch. 10, *supra*. *See also* Thompson v. Homecomings Fin. Network, 2005 WL 3534234 (N.D. Tex. Dec. 19, 2005) (since a claim for negligence is inconsistent with a claim of malice or willfulness, the exception to qualified immunity does not apply to such a claim).

143 15 U.S.C. §§ 1681n and 1681o(a)(2).

144 *See* National Consumer Law Center, Fair Debt Collection § 6.2.4 (5th 2004 and Supp.) and cases cited therein; National Consumer Law Center, Truth in Lending § 8.10 (5th ed. 2003 and Supp.) and cases cited therein; § 11.12.3, *infra*. In federal court, all damage issues, including punitive damages, are to be decided by the jury. Feltner v. Columbia Pictures Television, Inc., 523 U.S. 340, 118 S. Ct. 1279, 140 L. Ed. 2d 438 (1998); Kobs v. Arrow Serv. Bureau, Inc., 134 F.3d 893 (7th Cir. 1998); McGuire v. Russell Miller, Inc., 1 F.3d 1306 (2d Cir. 1993); Kampa v. White Consol. Inc., 115 F.3d 585, 586 (8th Cir. 1997).

145 Colletti v. Credit Bureau Servs., 644 F.2d 1148 (5th Cir. 1981).

146 County Vanlines, Inc. v. Experian Inf. Solutions, Inc., 205 F.R.D. 148 (S.D.N.Y. 2002) (denial as premature of motion to strike affirmative defenses of failure to state a claim, truth,

tection Act, there are no statutory defenses, such as bona fide error. Reasonableness of a consumer reporting agency's (CRA) procedures is an affirmative defense as to which the defendant has the burden of proof,[147] as is reasonableness of a user's procedures.[148]

Equitable defenses, such as unclean hands, do not provide an excuse for failure to comply with statutory obligations and a claim for damages, and are improperly asserted.[149] Mitigation of damages is also ordinarily an improper defense to a statutory violation.[150] The First Amendment has been rejected as a defense.[151]

The consumer is under no duty to exhaust other FCRA remedies or rights before filing suit.[152] For example, there is no obligation to dispute the information in the CRA's files before bringing suit for a violation of the Act against the CRA.[153] While the FCRA explicitly provides for the consumer's right to dispute information, and provides remedies where the CRA does not agree with the consumer, such as the consumer's right to have the consumer's own statement included in the file,[154] these consumer rights need not be exhausted as prerequisites to an FCRA suit for actual damages.

There is no litigation privilege or immunity which can be raised as a defense to a claim based on improperly using a consumer report during litigation.[155]

A defendant may not implead a third party for the purpose of obtaining indemnification.[156] A plaintiff will often sue both the CRA that prepared a report and the user that requested it. Those defendants may seek to file cross-claims for contribution or indemnity. One court rejected the claim of a CRA, which had prepared a report that wrongfully attributed a criminal charge to a consumer, against the user (the consumer's employee), stating that a CRA should not be able to slough off liability for failing to comply with its extensive obligations under the Act onto a user, on whom Congress put far less substantial requirements.[157] The defendant could not assert contribution under a state joint tortfeasor act, because contribution and indemnity for violation of a federal statute is a matter of federal law.[158] Without an express or implied congressional enactment for contribution or a private contractual provision,[159] the CRA

---

third-party causation, independent intervening cause, failure to mitigate damages, plaintiff's negligence, fault, unclean hands, statute of limitation, release, state law qualified privilege, but striking affirmative defense reserving the "right" to add affirmative defenses).

147 Guimond v. Trans Union Credit Info. Co., 45 F.3d 1329 (9th Cir. 1995); Cahlin v. General Motors Acceptance Corp., 936 F.2d 1151, 1156 (11th Cir. 1991); Sampson v. Equifax Info. Servs., L.L.C., 2005 WL 2095092, at *5 (S.D. Ga. Aug. 29, 2005); Thomas v. Trans Union L.L.C., 197 F. Supp. 2d 1233 (D. Or. 2002) (reasonable procedures defense permitted as to alleged reinvestigation violations, and as to failure to provide proper statutory notice after reinvestigation). See Ch. 4, supra.

148 See § 10.2.5.2, supra.

149 See, e.g., Obabueki v. Int'l Bus. Machs. Corp., 137 F. Supp. 2d 320 (S.D.N.Y. 2001), aff'd, 319 F.3d 87 (2d Cir. 2003) (words "unclean hands" insufficient; defense stricken); Kiblen v. Pickle, 653 P.2d 1338 (Wash. Ct. App. 1982).

150 Silver Sage Partners, Ltd. v. City of Desert Hot Springs, 251 F.3d 814 (9th Cir. 2001) (Fair Housing Act) (citing Curtis v. Loether, 415 U.S. 189, 195 (1974)).

151 Schoendorf v. U.D. Registry, 97 Cal App. 4th 227, 118 Cal. Rptr. 2d 313 (2002) (neither First Amendment nor litigation privilege protects tenant registry from FCRA liability).

152 Cushman v. Trans Union Corp., 115 F.3d 220 (3d Cir. 1997) (rejecting suggestion that no cause of action lies pursuant to § 1681i(a) on the ground that § 1681i(b) and (c) provide the exclusive remedy when a consumer disputes information that has been placed on her consumer report); Thompson v. San Antonio Retail Merchants Ass'n, 682 F.2d 509 (5th Cir. 1982) (consumer need not pursue remedies under § 1681i before suing under § 1681e). But see Hyde v. Hibernia Nat'l Bank, 861 F.2d 446 (5th Cir. 1988) (failure to mitigate damages does not preclude damage claim, but may bear upon jury's calculation of damages). See also Graham v. CSC Credit Servs., Inc., 306 F. Supp. 2d 873, 880 (D. Minn. 2004) (finding that CRA failed to show that consumer could have mitigated his damages by refinancing his mortgage at a lower rate once the CRA corrected his report).

153 Cushman v. Trans Union Corp., 115 F.3d 220 (3d Cir. 1997). However, the consumer DOES need to file a dispute with the CRAs in order to bring a claim against a furnisher. See § 6.10, supra.

154 See Ch. 4, supra.

155 Chester v. Purvis, 260 F. Supp. 2d 711 (S.D. Ind. 2003) (defendant attorney did not have absolute immunity from suit under the FCRA simply because he obtained and used the consumer report in the course of his duties as a lawyer in the context of previous FDCPA litigation).

156 Kudlicki v. MDMA, Inc., 2006 WL 1308617 (N.D. Ill. May 10, 2006) (citing cases); Fields v. Experian Info. Solutions, Inc., 2003 WL 1960010 (N.D. Miss. Apr. 16, 2003) (denying motion to add impostor); McMillan v. Equifax Credit Inf. Servs., Inc., 153 F. Supp. 2d 129 (D. Conn. 2001) (FCRA does not provide a right of indemnification; furnisher's motion to implead plaintiff's son denied; son's acts did not cause inadequate investigation); Kay v. First Cont'l Trading, Inc., 966 F. Supp. 753 (N.D. Ill. 1997) (CRA may not seek indemnity against user). See Doherty v. Wireless Broad. Sys. of Sacramento, Inc., 151 F.3d 1129, 1131 (9th Cir. 1998) ("A defendant held liable under a federal statute has a right to indemnification or contribution from another only if such right arises: (1) through the affirmative creation of a right of action by Congress, either expressly or implicitly, or (2) under the federal common law."). But see Yohay v. City of Alexandria Employees Credit Union, Inc., 827 F.2d 967 (4th Cir. 1987) (applying state law); Scott v. Real Estate Fin. Group, 956 F. Supp. 375 (E.D.N.Y. 1997), rev'd on other grounds, 183 F.3d 97 (2d Cir. 1999).

157 Kay v. First Cont'l Trading, Inc., 966 F. Supp. 753 (N.D. Ill. 1997).

158 Id. at 754.

159 The court ruled that the indemnity provision in the contract between the agency and the user had been drawn too narrowly to cover the circumstances here, and further suggested that, even had the indemnity provision purported to cover the agency's own wrongdoing, enforcing the provision "would be to exculpate [the agency] entirely from any liability based on its own misconduct, at the expense of its customer who relied on the reporting." Id. at 756 n.5. That in turn could result in the user having to pay the CRA more than it might have to pay the

had no grounds upon which to claim contribution or indemnity. In short, a primary wrongdoer under the FCRA may not "lay off its own liability" onto another defendant.[160] Although not addressing the issue of settlement, the case would strongly militate against a CRA being able to benefit from a plaintiff's settlement with a user or furnisher.

In a case of identity theft, a defendant may seek to file a third party complaint against the thief. Many times a plaintiff prefers to keep the thief out of the action, perhaps because the thief is a family member. The plaintiff should be able to keep the thief out because the FCRA does not provide causes of action to users or furnishers for indemnification or contribution, and only provides a cause of action to CRAs against users or furnishers, not against other third parties.[161] Nor is the third party an indispensable or necessary party to an FCRA suit.[162] Whether a third party claim is viable with respect to a state law claim may depend on applicable state law.[163] Hence, where the plaintiff prefers not to include the thief in the action, advocates should exercise caution in including state causes of action in identity theft consumer reporting suits if duplicative of an FCRA claim.

11.9 Enforceability of Arbitration Agreements

Although consumers are usually completely unaware of them, arbitration clauses are now found in most consumer contracts, including agreements for credit cards, loans, and utilities. These may affect a consumer's FCRA claim against the other party to a consumer contract, for example a furnisher of credit information. The enforceability of such provisions, ways to avoid arbitration, and the effects of arbitration on consumers are all discussed in detail in NCLC's *Consumer Arbitration Agreements*.[164]

Consumer reporting agencies (CRAs) have also included such clauses in agreements with consumers who seek disclosure of their own consumer reports, at least those who order their reports online through the centralized source and directly through the CRA's website. The legality of including arbitration clauses as a prerequisite for consumers to obtain their own consumer reports, an unconditional right granted under the FCRA, is very questionable.

In *Frerichs v. Credential Services International*,[165] an arbitration agreement in an FCRA case was held enforceable by the credit card issuer, First USA. However the court declined to mandate arbitration of FCRA claims against the two CRAs, CSI and Experian, who were also named as defendants. The court found that CSI and Experian were not "the employees, agents or assigns" of First USA, as required for coverage by the terms of the arbitration agreement in the credit card agreement. The court also rejected First USA's argument that arbitration of the claims against the CRAs should be required, finding that the FCRA claims against the three defendants were not so intertwined with the facts surrounding the underlying contract containing the arbitration agreement as to mandate arbitration.[166]

In a case against a wireless service provider for FCRA violations, a New York district court upheld the arbitration provisions in a cellular service agreement.[167] The arbitration provision stated: "INSTEAD OF SUING IN COURT, YOU'RE AGREEING TO ARBITRATE DISPUTES ARISING OUT OF OR RELATED TO THIS OR PRIOR AGREEMENTS."[168] The court found that the FCRA claims arose out of and were related to the agreement and thus were presumptively arbitrable. The court also rejected plaintiff's arguments that the service provider had waived its right to arbitrate by placing the account for collection and that compelling arbitration would be improper because it would force the plaintiff to waive her rights under the FCRA.[169] Inasmuch as new decisions on the enforceability of arbitration agreements generally and also the validity of specific restrictions in such clauses appear frequently, when such issues arise, advocates would be well advised to consult the latest edition of NCLC's *Consumer Arbitration Agreements*.[170]

---

plaintiff itself, which the court found would be "an impermissible consequence." *Id.*

160 *Id.* at 756. The court distinguished Yohay v. City of Alexandria Employees Credit Union, Inc., 827 F.2d 967 (4th Cir. 1987), which upheld the indemnification claim of a user against the employee who actually requested the report, because in that case the employee had sought the report for her own independent purposes, not as part of her employment, with "the indemnitor being the 'active' or 'primary' wrongdoer and the indemnitee being the 'passive' or 'secondary' wrongdoer." 966 F. Supp. at 756.

161 McSherry v. Capital One F.S.B., 236 F.R.D. 516 (W.D. Wash. 2006). *See, e.g.*, 15 U.S.C. § 1681s-2(b), (c) (allowing CRA to sue furnisher that does not comply with statute's reinvestigation obligations).

162 Pinckney v. SLM Fin. Corp., 236 F.R.D. 587 (N.D. Ga. 2005).

163 *Cf.* McSherry v. Capital One F.S.B., 236 F.R.D. 516 (W.D. Wash. 2006).

164 National Consumer Law Center, Consumer Arbitration Agreements (4th ed. 2004 and Supp.).

165 Frerichs v. Credential Servs. Int'l, 1999 U.S. Dist. LEXIS 22811 (N.D. Ill. Sept. 30, 1999). *See* Walton v. Experian, 2003 WL 22110788 (N.D. Ill. Sept. 9, 2003) (also enforcing an arbitration clause in a credit card); Niederriter v. CSC Credit Servs., Inc., 2005 WL 2647951 (E.D. Mo. Oct. 17, 2005) (enforcing arbitration).

166 Frerichs v. Credential Servs. Int'l, 1999 U.S. Dist. LEXIS 22811, at *29 (N.D. Ill. Sept. 30, 1999). *See also* Greene v. Chase Manhattan Auto. Fin. Corp., 2003 WL 22872102 (E.D. La. Dec. 3, 2003).

167 DeGraziano v. Verizon Communications, Inc., 325 F. Supp. 2d 238 (E.D.N.Y. 2004).

168 *Id.* at 243.

169 *Id.* at 244–245, *citing* Green Tree Fin. Corp. v. Randolph, 531 U.S. at 90, 121 S. Ct. 513, 148 L. Ed. 2d 373 (2000).

170 National Consumer Law Center, Consumer Arbitration Agreements (4th ed. 2004 and Supp.).

11.10 Damages

11.10.1 Damages Generally

For most FCRA requirements, any person who negligently fails to comply with the requirement is liable to the consumer for actual damages sustained as a result of the failure and court costs, together with reasonable attorney fees.[171] For willful violations, a consumer is entitled to actual damages *or* statutory damages ranging from $100 to $1000 and such punitive damages as the court may allow.[172] Each failure to comply with the FCRA is a separate violation, the consumer is potentially entitled to multiple awards of statutory damages for multiple violations.[173] With the possible exception of claims against users,[174] the FACTA amendments of 2003 did not amend the relevant FCRA provisions that provide for relief when there are negligent or willful FCRA violations.[175]

A separate provision makes a natural person who obtains a consumer report under false pretenses or knowingly without a permissible purpose liable to the consumer for actual damages or $1000, whichever is greater.[176] Liability also includes punitive damages for willful violations as appropriate, costs, and attorney fees.[177]

During legislative debates over statutory damages, consumer reporting agencies (CRAs) and furnishers of information expressed concern that the availability of statutory damages would encourage unwarranted litigation. To balance this concern with the rights of consumers, Congress provided that either the defendant or the plaintiff can recover reasonable attorney fees if a court finds that an unsuccessful pleading, motion, or other paper was filed in an FCRA action in bad faith or for purposes of harassment.[178]

Any person who violates the FCRA may be liable for damages, including CRAs, users of consumer reports, and those who furnish information to CRAs. Liability is not limited just to CRAs and users, as was the case before the Consumer Credit Reporting Reform Act of 1996 (1996 Reform Act) amendments to the FCRA which extended potential liability to "any person."[179] The primary effect of the change was to create FCRA liability for creditors and others who furnish information to CRAs.[180]

However, other provisions added to the FCRA at the same time limit enforcement of some of the furnisher obligations to government officials and state attorneys general, and not by the consumer's private right of action.[181] Essentially, those obligations requiring that information furnished to CRAs be accurate may not be privately enforced under the FCRA, and actual, statutory, and punitive damages are not available. On the other hand, and importantly, furnishers are liable for damages and fees for failing to participate as required in reinvestigations of accuracy and completeness conducted by the CRAs themselves.[182]

The FACTA amendments to the FCRA added several new obligations and standards for CRAs and users and furnishers of credit information. The FACTA amendments also provided consumers with additional rights, especially with respect to identity theft and restoration of credit information. Unfortunately, the FACTA amendments limited the ability of consumers to privately enforce some of these new rights.[183]

State credit reporting statutes generally offer remedies similar to those provided by the FCRA. Several of these statutes also offer additional remedies. For example, some state credit reporting statutes provide consumers with minimum damages of several hundred dollars whenever even a negligent violation is proven.[184] State deceptive practices statutes in many states also provide minimum statutory or treble damages.[185] Common law tort claims generally provide for actual and punitive damages (where state law punitive damages standards are met), but no attorney fees.

Mitigation of damages is ordinarily an improper defense to a statutory violation.[186]

---

171 15 U.S.C. § 1681o(a).
172 15 U.S.C. § 1681n(a). Prior to the 1996 amendments, this civil liability section applied only to violations by CRAs and users, and did not include statutory damages.
173 White v. Imperial Adjustment Corp., 2002 WL 1809084 (E.D. La. Aug. 6, 2002), *aff'd on other grounds, remanded*, 75 Fed. Appx. 972 (5th Cir. 2003) (unpublished).
174 *See* § 10.2.5, *supra*.
175 *Compare* Perry v. First Nat'l Bank, 459 F.3d 816 (7th Cir. 2006) *with* Barnette v. Brook Road, Inc., 429 F. Supp. 2d 741 (E.D. Va. 2006).
176 15 U.S.C. § 1681n(b).
177 15 U.S.C. § 1681n(a)(2).
178 15 U.S.C. §§ 1681n(c); S. Rep. No. 185, 104th Cong., 1st Sess. 49 (Dec. 14, 1995). *See also* § 11.14.1, *infra*.
179 15 U.S.C. §§ 1681n(a) and 1681o(a), *as amended by* Pub. L. No. 104-208 § 2412, 110 Stat. 3009 (Sept. 30, 1996). *See* Hawthorne v. Citicorp Data Sys., 216 F. Supp. 2d 45 (E.D.N.Y. 2002), *vacated on other grounds*, 219 F.R.D. 47 (E.D.N.Y. 2003) ("expansive" language "clearly expands" scope of FCRA liability).
180 *See* Ch. 6, *supra*.
181 15 U.S.C. § 1681s-2(d), *as added by* Pub. L. No. 104-208 § 2413, 110 Stat. 3009 (Sept. 30, 1996). *See* Ch. 6, *supra* and § 11.16, *infra*.
182 *See* Ch. 6, § 10.2.4, *supra*. Some courts, however, hold that 15 U.S.C. § 1681t(b)(1)(F) preempts all state claims, both statutory and common law, against furnishers. *See, e.g.*, Roybal v. Equifax, 405 F. Supp. 2d 1177, 1181–1182 (E.D. Cal. 2005) and cases discussed in § 10.7, *supra*. Others hold that this provision preempts only state statutory claims. *See, e.g.*, Pinckney v. SLM Fin. Corp., 433 F. Supp. 2d 1316, 1320–1321 (N.D. Ga. 2005).
183 *See* § 10.2, *supra*.
184 *See* § 11.11, *infra*.
185 *Id.*
186 Silver Sage Partners, Ltd. v. City of Desert Hot Springs, 251 F.3d 814 (9th Cir. 2001) (Fair Housing Act) (citing Curtis v. Loether, 415 U.S. 189, 195 (1974)).

11.10.2 Actual Damages

11.10.2.1 General

For a consumer to recover for a defendant's negligent failure to comply with the FCRA, the consumer will have to prove actual damages[187] which were a result of the defendant's failure to comply with an FCRA requirement.[188] As will be described below, these damages can be intangible in nature (such as pain and suffering or humiliation), and need not be pecuniary in nature.[189]

Actual damages are also available for willful violations of the Act.[190] However, proof of actual damages where the FCRA violation is willful, while always helpful, may not be required for two reasons. First, punitive damages are generally available even without proof of actual damages.[191] Second, modest statutory damages are available as an alternative to actual damages.[192]

The term actual damages is nowhere defined or explained in the FCRA or the FCRA's legislative history.[193] The succeeding subsections analyze what type of pecuniary and non-pecuniary loss may be recovered as FCRA actual damages. It is important to keep in mind that proof of FCRA actual damages is very different from proving defamation damages at common law, where injury is often presumed once publication is proven.

11.10.2.2 Damages for Pecuniary Loss

Pecuniary loss proximately caused by FCRA violations is one type of actual damages that may be recompensed by a damage award. For example, an inaccurate consumer report may cause credit to be denied, a job opportunity to be lost, or an insurance policy to be refused. These denials may result in financial loss to the consumer which, if proved, entitles the consumer to an actual damage award.

Actual damages should include pecuniary business losses, but some confusion exists. A report on a business, or even on an individual in a business capacity, is not a consumer report[194] and would not give rise to damages under the FCRA.[195] However, a consumer report used for business

---

187 Guimond v. Credit Bureau Inc., 1992 WL 33144 (4th Cir. Feb. 25, 1992) (no inaccurate information; no damages; challenge only to disclosure procedures); Cahlin v. General Motors Acceptance Corp., 936 F.2d 1151 (11th Cir. 1991); Spector v. Experian Info. Servs., Inc., 321 F. Supp. 2d 348, 357 (D. Conn. 2004) (granting summary judgment to furnisher); Minter v. AAA Cook Cty. Consolidation, Inc., 2004 WL 1630781 (N.D. Ill. July 19, 2004) (dismissing claim where plaintiff failed to support claim for actual damages); McMillan v. Experian, 170 F. Supp. 2d 278 (D. Conn. 2001) (possibility of lost opportunities or subprime offers from prescreening is too speculative for damages); Sternaman v. Experian Inf. Solutions, Inc., 2001 U.S. Dist. LEXIS 19561 (D. Minn. Nov. 19, 2001) (judgment for Experian where plaintiff offered only hearsay about the credit denial; the denial notice did not state that information was obtained from a CRA; and for furnisher; no damages where plaintiff's credit denial was before Cross Country verified the disputed information); Greenhouse v. TRW, Inc., 1997 WL 191491 (E.D. La. Apr. 17, 1997) (citing Hyde v. Hibernia Nat'l Bank, 861 F.2d 446, 448 (5th Cir. 1988)); Guimond v. Trans Union Credit Info. Co., 1993 WL 102756 (N.D. Cal. Mar. 22, 1993); Neptune v. Trans Union Corp., 1993 WL 505601 (E.D. Pa. Dec. 8, 1993); Eisenberg v. Progress Fed. Sav., 1992 WL 333894 (E.D. Pa. Nov. 5, 1992); Cook v. Equifax Info. Sys., Inc., 1992 WL 356119 (D. Md. Nov. 20, 1992) (damages can include out-of-pocket expenses for attorney fees, expenditure of time and money to get credit at higher rate); Mulkey v. Credit Bureau Inc., Consumer Cred. Guide (CCH) ¶ 96,739 (D.D.C. 1983), aff'd, 729 F.2d 863 (D.C. Cir. 1984). Nominal damages have been held to be unavailable. See Lambert v. Credit Bureau, Inc., Consumer Cred. Guide (CCH) ¶ 96,300 (4th Cir. 1985). But see Russell v. Shelter Fin. Servs., 604 F. Supp. 201 (W.D. Mo. 1984) (with no proof of actual damages, the court awarded nominal and punitive damages for willful violation). On the other hand, an action for willful noncompliance may succeed without proof of actual damages. See § 11.12.1.3, infra.

188 Cousin v. Trans Union Corp., 246 F.3d 359 (5th Cir. 2001) (reversing verdict due to insufficient evidence of actual damages); Crabill v. Trans Union, 259 F.3d 662 (7th Cir. 2001) (no actual damages because insufficient evidence of causation); Philbin v. Trans Union Crop., 101 F.3d 957 (3d Cir. 1996) (consumer must produce evidence from which trier of fact can infer inaccuracy was a substantial factor in the denial of credit); Casella v. Equifax Credit Info. Servs., 56 F.3d 469 (2d Cir. 1995) (consumer did not show any person had access to false derogatory information); Guimond v. Trans Union Credit Info. Co., 45 F.3d 1329 (9th Cir. 1995) (consumer must show damages flow from failure to follow reasonable procedures, and need not show damages arise from transmission of the report to third parties); Cahlin v. General Motors Acceptance Corp., 936 F.2d 1151 (11th Cir. 1991) (consumer did not prove any credit denied based on mistaken report); Pettus v. TRW Consumer Credit Serv., 879 F. Supp. 695 (W.D. Tex. 1994) (consumer did not prove employment or credit denied based on mistaken report); Mirocha v. TRW, Inc., 805 F. Supp. 663 (S.D. Ind. 1992) (while unemployment could have been a sufficient reason for denial, it was not the stated reason; summary judgment could not be granted because defendants did not foreclose possibility that credit was denied because of the adverse consumer report); Houston v. TRW Info. Servs., Inc., 1989 WL 59850 (S.D.N.Y. May 2, 1989) (consumer may not be able to prove actual damages if other items on the consumer report could have led to the credit denials); Mulkey v. Credit Bureau Inc., Consumer Cred. Guide (CCH) ¶ 96,739 (D.D.C. 1983), aff'd, 729 F.2d 863 (D.C. Cir. 1984) (information reported was less prejudicial than if it had been completely accurate and therefore no injury or actual damages resulted).

189 See § 11.10.2.3, infra.
190 15 U.S.C. § 1681n(a)(1).
191 See § 11.12.1.3, infra.
192 See § 11.11, infra.
193 Note, *Panacea or Placebo? Actions for Negligent Noncompliance Under the Fair Credit Reporting Act*, 47 S. Cal. L. Rev. 1070, 1111 (1974).
194 See § 2.3.6.2, supra.
195 See, e.g., Thomas v. Gulf Coast Credit Serv., Inc., 214 F. Supp. 2d 1228 (M.D. Ala. 2002) (denial of credit for investment purposes is not covered by the FCRA); Jones v. Credit Bureau of Huntington, Inc., 399 S.E.2d 694 (W. Va. 1990) (evidence showed reduction in plaintiff's business). Contra Natale v. TRW, Inc., 1999 WL 179678 (N.D. Cal. Mar. 30, 1999); Hussain v.

purposes is still a consumer report[196] and if the consumer suffers damages from its misuse, the damages should be recoverable. The plain language of the damages provisions allows a consumer to recover "any actual damages sustained by the consumer as a result of the failure."[197] Congress did not choose to limit the damages to non-business losses. Accordingly, there is no reason why the consumer should not recover damages if the report is otherwise a consumer report and is misused in a way that causes injury to the consumer with respect to a business transaction. Questions concerning the business/non-business distinction arise when determining whether the Act applies, but should not bar damages actually incurred by a consumer due to violations of the statute.

The consumer must show a causal relation between the violation of the statute and the loss of credit or other harm.[198] The plaintiff need not show that the erroneous negative information is the only cause of the loss, but only that it was a substantial factor.[199] Nonetheless, proof of pecuniary loss is sometimes difficult. Assume, for example, that a bank has denied a consumer's mortgage application on a new home, and, as a result, the purchase and sale agreement is canceled and the opportunity to buy the home is lost. At trial, the issue may become whether the denial was based on a particular error in the consumer report, or whether there were other items in the report or in the review of the consumer's mortgage application which could explain the loan denial.[200] Another question may be whether credit was available to this consumer elsewhere, and if so at what cost.[201] Causation may be difficult in the case of a consumer whose legitimate credit record is less than enviable, but borderline consumers can least afford to have a CRA corrupt their reports, and are much more likely to suffer negative results than a consumer whose otherwise pristine record has only one or two false negatives on it. However, if the consumer's true record is so bad that proving pecuniary damages seems doubtful, and other forms of actual damages are also unavailable, consider bringing an action for declaratory judgment, an injunction,[202] and attorney fees instead. If the violation can be characterized as willful, an action for statutory and punitive damages can succeed without proof of actual damages.[203]

The growing reliance upon credit scores may sometimes aid the proof of actual damages.[204] Creditors, especially

---

Carteret Sav. Bank, F.A., 704 F. Supp. 567 (D.N.J. 1989).
196 See §§ 2.3.5, 2.3.5.4, supra.
197 15 U.S.C. § 1681n(a)(1)(A).
198 Crabill v. Trans Union, 259 F.3d 662 (7th Cir. 2001); Philbin v. Trans Union Corp., 101 F.3d 957, 963 (3d Cir. 1996); Casella v. Equifax Credit Info. Serv., 56 F.3d 469, 473 (2d Cir. 1995); Cahlin v. General Motors Acceptance Corp., 936 F.2d 1151, 1160, 1161 (11th Cir. 1991); Sampson v. Equifax Info. Servs., L.L.C., 2005 WL 2095092, at *4 (S.D. Ga. Aug. 29, 2005) (affidavit that plaintiff was denied credit; Lawrence v. Trans Union, L.L.C., 296 F. Supp. 2d 582 (E.D. Pa. 2003) (loss of credit opportunity); Heupel v. Trans Union, L.L.C., 193 F. Supp. 2d 1234 (N.D. Ala. 2002). See also Reed v. Experian Info. Solutions, Inc., 321 F. Supp. 2d 1109, 1114–1115 (D. Minn. 2004) (granting summary judgment to CRA where evidence did not show that erroneous notation on plaintiff's consumer report was a substantial factor in the denial of credit); Comeaux v. Experian Info. Solutions, 2004 WL 1354412, at *7–9 (E.D. Tex. June 8, 2004) (plaintiff created genuine issue of material fact on issue of whether inaccurate reporting by CRA caused her application for a mortgage and for credit cards to be denied).
199 Philbin v. Trans Union Corp., 101 F.3d 957 (3d Cir. 1996); Richardson v. Fleet Bank, 190 F. Supp. 2d 81 (D. Mass. 2001); Sampson v. Equifax Info. Servs., L.L.C., 2005 WL 2095092, at *4 (S.D. Ga. Aug. 29, 2005). But see Elliott v. TRW, Inc., 889 F. Supp. 960 (N.D. Tex. 1995) (causation not shown where potential lender's letter listed not only the contested portion of the consumer report but also a second reason for denying credit; no discussion of "substantial factor" rule).
200 See Cousin v. Trans Union Corp., 246 F.3d 359 (5th Cir. 2001) (no actual damages flowed from GMAC's denial of credit that was based on its own information and report from different CRA, even though automobile dealer that was arranging credit had this defendant's report); Philbin v. Trans Union Corp., 101 F.3d 957 (3d Cir. 1996) (plaintiff only need produce evidence from which trier of fact can infer that the consumer report entry is a "substantial factor" in the denial of credit); Obabueki v. ChoicePoint, 236 F. Supp. 2d 278 (S.D.N.Y. 2002), aff'd, 319 F.3d 87 (2d Cir. 2003) (plaintiff failed to establish that consumer report was proximate cause of loss where employer initially received inaccurate report, but withdrew job offer only after receiving corrected information); Riley v. Equifax Credit Info. Servs., 194 F. Supp. 2d 1239 (S.D. Ala. 2002) (must show that denial of credit was based not just on the consumer report but on the particular inaccuracy in the report); Huepel v. Trans Union, 193 F. Supp. 2d 1234 (N.D. Ala. 2002) (no actual damages were denial of credit based on accurate portion of consumer report, even though other portions were inaccurate); Richardson v. Fleet Bank, 190 F. Supp. 2d 81 (D. Mass. 2001) (plaintiff must show that inaccurate entry was substantial factor that brought about the denial of credit); Zala v. Trans Union, L.L.C., 2001 U.S. Dist. LEXIS 549 (N.D. Tex. Jan. 17, 2001) (several other account delinquencies shown as basis for denial of credit); Elliott v. TRW, Inc., 889 F. Supp. 960 (N.D. Tex. 1995) (causation not shown where potential lender's letter listed not only the contested portion of the consumer report but also a second reason for denying credit); Evans v. Credit Bureau, 904 F. Supp. 123 (W.D.N.Y. 1995) (bankruptcy, not inaccuracy, was basis of credit denial). See also Thomas v. Gulf Coast Credit Servs., 214 F. Supp. 2d 1228 (M.D. Ala. 2002) (no actual damages where inaccuracies in this defendant's consumer report would not have prevented loan approval; bank denied credit because it also had other consumer reports); Kabakjian v. United States, 92 F. Supp. 2d 435, 445 (E.D. Pa. 2000) (granting summary judgment to defendant in suit for damages under IRS Code when evidence showed credit denied in part because of a history of delinquency, and unclear whether disputed item had any influence), aff'd on other grounds, 267 F.3d 208 (3d Cir. 2001).
201 "Pre-approved" credit offers from subprime lenders or for greater-than-market rates may demonstrate these sorts of damages.
202 See § 11.13, infra. However, courts are split over whether declaratory and injunctive relief are available under the Act.
203 See §§ 11.11, 11.12, infra.
204 Heupel v. Trans Union, L.L.C., 193 F. Supp. 2d 1234 (N.D. Ala.

mortgage financers, often use credit scores to determine not only whether to accept or reject an application, but to determine what to charge the consumer. Consumers with worse scores may be classified as higher risk borrowers and may either be denied credit completely or required to pay higher interest rates, greater points or additional fees. For discovery, a consumer's attorney should request that the credit score be recalculated based on corrected information, and compare the results with the lender's pricing criteria. If the consumer would have been eligible for a less expensive loan, the difference may be actual damages. Similarly, expenses incurred due to improperly impaired credit are recoverable consequential damages.[205]

Where the plaintiff claims that the CRA failed to conduct a proper reinvestigation of a dispute, damage must be tied to reports released after the demand for reinvestigation.[206] Where the violation is a failure to send an adverse action letter, the Fifth Circuit suggests that actual damages exist only if the consumer shows that the credit denial was based on erroneous information in the consumer report, so that the consumer could have corrected the problem if the adverse action letter had been sent.[207]

There is no requirement that the consumer actually be denied credit; however it is unclear whether damages are available to a consumer who was prevented from applying for credit by knowledge that a report would contain false derogatory information.[208] The consumer must be prepared to build the damage case with care.[209] In some cases, it may make sense for the consumer to follow through with credit applications notwithstanding the incorrect information in the consumer report. If the consumer gets the desired credit, then the consumer will have mitigated his or her losses. The downside is that the consumer's application may be denied because of the inaccurate report, which will create a new negative entry on the credit record, but then at least the consumer will know the precise scope of the problem and it will be easier to quantify the necessary redress.

The Third Circuit has held that introduction of denial letters from creditors may be sufficient to prove that credit was denied because of the erroneous consumer report.[210] Indeed, the court held that this may be the case even when the denial letter does not specify the aspect of the consumer's credit history that led to the denial, as long as the jury can infer, by a process of elimination, that the erroneous information in the consumer report was the cause. It is much preferable, however, to present testimony from the individuals who made the decision to turn down the plaintiff's application, particularly since some courts have subjected FCRA damage claims to a high standard of proof of causation. The consumer's testimony about credit denials is unlikely to be sufficient, as the consumer normally will not have personal knowledge of the reasons a potential lender refused to extend credit.[211]

Another kind of pecuniary loss which may be easier to prove as actual damages is out-of-pocket losses. Such losses

---

2002) (credit score reduced because of notation in one trade line of a chapter 13 bankruptcy). See Ch. 14, *infra*, for a discussion of credit scores.

205 *See, e.g.*, City Nat'l Bank of Charleston v. Wells, 84 S.E.2d 374 (W. Va. 1989).
206 Kettler v. CSC Credit Serv., Inc., 2003 WL 21975919 (D. Minn. Aug. 12, 2003); Thomas v. Gulf Coast Credit Servs., 214 F. Supp. 2d 1228 (M.D. Ala. 2002). *See also* Casella v. Equifax Credit Info. Servs., 56 F.3d 469 (2d Cir. 1995) (expenses are only actual damages if incurred after CRA committed the FCRA violation).
207 Sapia v. Regency Motors, 276 F.3d 747 (5th Cir. 2002).
208 Guimond v. Trans Union Credit Info. Co., 45 F.3d 1329 (9th Cir. 1995) (damages available even absent a denial of credit); Casella v. Equifax Credit Info. Servs., 56 F.3d 469 (2d Cir. 1995) (no damages where consumer never applied for or was denied credit, absent evidence that some creditor was interested in lending to him); Soghomonian v. U.S., 278 F. Supp. 2d 1151 (E.D. Cal. 2003); Gill v. Kostroff, 2000 U.S. Dist. LEXIS 1161 (M.D. Fla. Feb. 8, 2000) (consumer satisfied *Casella* standards by showing credit denial); Cushman v. Trans Union Corp., 920 F. Supp. 80 (E.D. Pa. 1996) (consumer may recover for emotional distress even when no credit denial). *See also* Tinsley v. TRW, Inc., 879 F. Supp. 550 (D. Md. 1995), *aff'd per curiam*, 64 F.3d 659 (4th Cir. Aug. 15, 1995) (unpublished).

Casella v. Equifax Credit Info. Servs., 56 F.3d 469 (2d Cir. 1995), which involved a claim against a CRA, may be distinguished from cases against furnishers by the court's focus on the plaintiff's failure to show that the damages he claimed to have suffered were caused by the CRA's retention of the false information, and not the furnisher's furnishing of it, a causation issue that actually argues in favor of finding a furnisher liable. 56 F.3d

at 474–475. With respect to damages, the court did not hold that a plaintiff must have been denied credit to prove damages, just that, without evidence that someone actually learned of the false information in the consumer's file with the CRA, the consumer could not show compensable damages. *Id.* at 475. *See also* Northrop v. Hoffman of Simsbury, Inc., 2000 WL 436612 (D. Conn. Mar. 15, 2000) (no actual damages where plaintiff withdrew loan application after lender inquired about unauthorized credit check that appeared on report; court suggests that result might be different if lender had required an explanation before processing loan application), *aff'd in relevant part, vacated in part on other grounds*, 2001 WL 682301, 12 Fed. Appx. 44 (2d Cir. June 14, 2001) (unpublished). *But see* Sternaman v. Experian Inf. Solutions, Inc., 2001 U.S. Dist. LEXIS 19561 (D. Minn. Nov. 19, 2001) (judgment for Experian where plaintiff offered only hearsay about the credit denial; the denial notice did not state that information was obtained from a CRA; and for furnisher; no damages where plaintiff's credit denial was before Cross Country verified the disputed information).

209 *See* Elliott v. TRW, Inc., 889 F. Supp. 960 (N.D. Tex. 1995).
210 Philbin v. Trans Union Corp., 101 F.3d 957, 963 (3d Cir. 1996). *Accord* Richardson v. Fleet Bank, 190 F. Supp. 2d 81 (D. Mass. 2001); McMillan v. Experian, 170 F. Supp. 2d 278 (D. Conn. 2001) (denial after accessing report sufficient for trier of fact to infer causation).
211 Riley v. Equifax Credit Info. Servs., 194 F. Supp. 2d 1239 (S.D. Ala. 2002); McMillan v. Experian, 170 F. Supp. 2d 278 (D. Conn. 2001) (consumer's affidavit about insurer's reasons for denying insurance is inadmissible, but mere proof that insurer accessed the report and then issued denial would allow jury to infer that consumer report was cause of denial).

include expenses related to seeking to have an improper report corrected, such as costs associated with long-distance telephone calls, multiple visits to CRA or creditor offices, and the like.[212] In a case of identity theft that involves numerous erroneous entries, out-of-pocket expenses for mailings, telephone calls, mileage, and the like can be substantial. Consumers should be encouraged to keep documentation of expenses related to improper consumer reports, and attorneys should seek other evidence to substantiate such expenses as soon as a client broaches a possible FCRA claim. Losses on personal investments, but not business investments, have been held to constitute damages under the FCRA.[213] Itemizing the damages can be helpful in settlement negotiations to demonstrate that the loss of creditworthiness affected the client's life in many different ways, resulting in different kinds of expenses.

11.10.2.3 Intangible Damages

11.10.2.3.1 Are intangible damages available?

In many cases, the most significant damage sustained by a consumer is the emotional distress and vexation of dealing with the repercussions of an inaccurate consumer report and the often frustrating ordeal of trying to set the record straight. A consumer may also have had the privacy of his or her financial affairs invaded.[214] Such an invasion of privacy is little different from that by a criminal who breaks into a cabinet and steals a person's bills, paystubs, receipts, and other financial documentation. Although the statute is silent about whether such emotional damages are actual damages which may be recompensed under the Act, case law is clear: the term "actual damages" is to be broadly construed to include such non-pecuniary damages. Accordingly, the terms "pecuniary losses" and "non-pecuniary losses" are more appropriate than "actual damages" and "no actual damages."

The common law of actual damages traditionally had limited recovery for torts not involving physical impact to pecuniary injury, although there was significant variation among states on this.[215] In 1974, the Supreme Court ruled in *Gertz v. Robert Welch, Inc.*,[216] a defamation case raising First Amendment issues, that actual injury was not limited to out-of-pocket loss. The Court noted that the more common types of harm inflicted by defamatory falsehoods include loss of reputation and standing in the community, personal humiliation, and mental anguish and suffering.[217]

Four years later, in a procedural due process case brought under 42 U.S.C. § 1983, the Court stated that "[d]istress is a personal injury familiar to the law," and that "[w]e use the term 'distress' to include mental suffering or emotional anguish."[218] The Court thus defined actual injury to include a variety of psychological harms, as well as pecuniary loss and physical injury.

FCRA cases reach a similar result, that actual damages for intangible injury are recoverable under the FCRA. No matter the limits that a state would place on recovery through a tort claim for such injury, the FCRA provides an independent basis for this recovery.[219] It is not necessary to show monetary loss or an actual denial of a credit opportunity.[220] However, for any type of emotional distress damages, particular care should be taken in developing causation.[221]

There is a dispute regarding whether intangible damages are available under the FCRA for a CRA's failure to follow reasonable procedures when the inaccurate information has not been included in a damaging report transmitted to a third party. One argument in favor of permitting damages without publication is that the mere knowledge that a CRA's file likely contains false derogatory information may cause distress and anguish and even deter a consumer from applying for credit. The Ninth Circuit holds that liability is not tied to

---

212 *See* Casella v. Equifax Credit Info. Servs., 56 F.3d 469 (2d Cir. 1995) (fees paid by consumer for lawyer to notify a CRA of inaccurate information not actual damages where CRA's FCRA violation occurred only after it received the notification).
213 Matise v. Trans Union Corp., 1998 WL 872511 (N.D. Tex. Nov. 30, 1998).
214 Cases which have analogized FCRA violations to invasion of privacy include: Myers v. Bennett Law Offices, 238 F.3d 1068 (9th Cir. 2001); Bakker v. McKinnon, 152 F.3d 1007 (8th Cir. 1998); Yang v. Gov't Employees Ins. Co., 146 F.3d 1320 (11th Cir. 1998); Zamora v. Valley Fed. Sav. & Loan Ass'n, 811 F.2d 1368 (10th Cir. 1987); Hansen v. Morgan, 582 F.2d 1214 (9th Cir. 1978).
215 *See* Rasor v. Retail Credit Co., 87 Wash. 2d 516, 554 P.2d 1041, 1048–1049 (1976).
216 418 U.S. 323, 94 S. Ct. 2997, 41 L. Ed. 2d 789 (1974).
217 *Id.* at 350.
218 Carey v. Piphus, 435 U.S. 247, 263, n.20, 98 S. Ct. 1042, 55 L. Ed. 2d 252 (1978).
219 Millstone v. O'Hanlon Reports, Inc., 383 F. Supp. 269 (E.D. Mo. 1974), aff'd, 528 F.2d 829 (8th Cir. 1976); Rasor v. Retail Credit Co., 87 Wash. 2d 516, 554 P.2d 1041 (1976). Accord Smith v. Law Offices of Mitchell N. Kay, 124 B.R. 182 (D. Del. 1991) (dicta). *See also* Bryant v. TRW, Inc., 487 F. Supp. 1234 (E.D. Mich. 1980), aff'd, 689 F.2d 72 (6th Cir. 1982).
220 Levine v. World Fin. Network Nat'l Bank, 437 F.3d 1118, 1124 (11th Cir. 2006); Cousin v. Trans Union Corp., 246 F.3d 359 (5th Cir. 2001) (emotional distress damages may be awarded even if there are no out-of-pocket losses); Bakker v. McKinnon, 152 F.3d 1007, 1013(8th Cir. 1998); Casella v. Equifax Credit Info. Servs., 56 F.3d 469, 474 (2d Cir. 1995) (emotional distress damages can be awarded even in absence of out-of-pocket losses); Thomas v. Gulf Coast Credit Servs., 214 F. Supp. 2d 1228 (M.D. Ala. 2002); Field v. Trans Union, 2002 WL 849589 (N.D. Ill. May 3, 2002); Richardson v. Fleet Bank, 190 F. Supp. 2d 81 (D. Mass. 2001).
221 *See* Thomas v. Gulf Coast Credit Servs., 2002 WL 1813463 (M.D. Ala. July 22, 2002) (distress caused by collection call not compensable without evidence that inaccuracies in consumer report led to the call); Field v. Trans Union, 2002 WL 849589 (N.D. Ill. May 3, 2002) (no damages where distress not caused by CRA's failure to investigate or adopt reasonable procedures).

the transmission of a report to a third party.[222] On the other hand, the Second Circuit holds that a creditor or some third party must have learned of the report from the CRA.[223]

Examples of awards for actual damages in FCRA cases without proof of pecuniary loss include damages for:

- Loss of sleep, nervousness, frustration, and mental anguish over the consumer report;[224]
- Injury to reputation, family, work, and sense of well-being;[225] and
- Humiliation, embarrassment, and mental distress.[226]

Future damages can be included in the verdict where the loss caused by the FCRA violation is of a continuing nature.[227]

The FCRA is one title of the federal Consumer Credit Protection Act, and cases under other titles should be helpful precedent as well concerning recovery of non-pecuniary damages. In particular, reference should be made to cases under the Equal Credit Opportunity Act[228] and the Fair Debt Collection Practices Act.[229] Courts have awarded large amounts for intangible injuries under these statutes.

11.10.2.3.2 Proving intangible damages

The general rule in cases outside the FCRA is that non-pecuniary damages must be based on competent evidence, but do not require evidence of the actual monetary value of the mental injury or suffering.[230] Courts in FCRA cases have similarly held that, while damages must be more than speculative, the dollar amount of intangible damages need not be proved.[231]

Consumer litigants will be well served to produce as much evidence as possible that a claimed injury occurred, and the

---

222 Guimond v. Trans Union Credit Info. Co., 45 F.3d 1329 (9th Cir. 1995). *See also* Matise v. Trans Union Corp., 1998 WL 872511 (N.D. Tex. Nov. 30, 1998); Cushman v. Trans Union Corp., 920 F. Supp. 80 (E.D. Pa. 1996) (consumer may recover for emotional distress even if no credit denied).

223 Casella v. Equifax Credit Info. Servs., 56 F.3d 469 (2d Cir. 1995), *applied in* Renninger v. ChexSystems, Inc., 1998 WL 295497 (N.D. Ill. May 21, 1998). The Fifth Circuit has declined to rule whether publication and denial of credit is required to award damages for an inaccurate report. Instead, the court, over a dissent, imposed unreasonably high standards of proof of intangible damages to void a jury award. Cousin v. Trans Union Corp., 246 F.3d 359 (5th Cir. 2001). *See also* Field v. Trans Union, L.L.C., 2002 WL 849589 (N.D. Ill. May 3, 2002); Thomas v. Gulf Coast Credit Servs., 214 F. Supp. 2d 1228 (M.D. Ala. 2002) (worry about effect of inaccurate consumer report not compensable where CRA had not actually released report to any lender); McMillan v. Experian, 170 F. Supp. 2d 278 (D. Conn. 2001) (for negligent violation plaintiff must prove actual damages, which may include denial of insurance together with a demonstration that he obtained coverage at a higher cost or was unable to get insurance and suffered an uninsured loss (economic damages). Actual damages may also include emotional distress from the denial or nondisclosure of the erroneous information to inquirers). *See also* Field v. Trans Union, 2002 WL 849589 (N.D. Ill. May 3, 2002) (emotional distress due to knowledge of inaccuracies in report not compensable where actual disclosure of inaccuracies did not cause distress).

224 Acton v. Bank One Corp., 293 F. Supp. 2d 1092 (D. Ariz. 2003); Millstone v. O'Hanlon Reports, Inc., 383 F. Supp. 269 (E.D. Mo. 1974), *aff'd*, 528 F.2d 829 (8th Cir. 1976) ($2500); Rasor v. Retail Credit Co., 87 Wash. 2d 516, 554 P.2d 1041 (1976). *See also* Thomas v. Gulf Coast Credit Servs., 214 F. Supp. 2d 1228 (M.D. Ala. 2002) (plaintiff may recover for emotional distress but must show objective physical manifestations; changes in complexion and demeanor are sufficient); Bryant v. TRW, Inc., 487 F. Supp. 1234 (E.D. Mich. 1980), *aff'd*, 689 F.2d 72 (6th Cir. 1982). *Cf.* Pinner v. Schmidt, 805 F.2d 1258 (5th Cir. 1986) (consumer given choice of reduction of damages to $25,000 or new trial, where no out-of-pocket damages were shown).

225 Morris v. Credit Bureau of Cincinnati, 563 F. Supp. 962 (S.D. Ohio 1983) ($10,000). In Rasor v. Retail Credit Co., 87 Wash. 2d 516, 554 P.2d 1041 (1976), in which damages were awarded for injury to reputation, the lower court issued a jury instruction that the reputation of the consumer is presumed good at the time of the violation, unless evidence to the contrary is established. *See also* Dalton v. Capital Assoc. Indus., 257 F.3d 409 (4th Cir. 2001) (damages for loss of reputation are available under FCRA); White v. Imperial Adjustment Corp., 2002 WL 1809084 (E.D. La. Aug. 6, 2002), *aff'd on other grounds*, 75 Fed. Appx. 972 (5th Cir. 2003) (unpublished) (noting that damages for injury to reputation and creditworthiness are available even without proof of pecuniary damages).

226 Fischl v. GMAC, 708 F.2d 143 (5th Cir. 1983); Thompson v. San Antonio Retail Merchants Ass'n, 682 F.2d 509 (5th Cir. 1982) ($8000); Sheffer v. Experian Info. Solutions, Inc., 2003 WL 21710573 (E.D. Pa. July 24, 2003); Lawrence v. Trans Union, L.L.C., 296 F. Supp. 2d 582 (E.D. Pa. 2003); Zala v. Trans Union, L.L.C., 2001 U.S. Dist. LEXIS 549 (N.D. Tex. Jan. 17, 2001); Bruce v. First U.S.A. Bank, 103 F. Supp. 2d 1135 (E.D. Mo. 2000); Matise v. Trans Union Corp., 1998 WL 872511 (N.D. Tex. Nov. 30, 1998); Pinner v. Schmidt, 617 F. Supp. 342 (E.D. La. 1985), *aff'd in part, rev'd in part*, 805 F.2d 1258 (5th Cir. 1986) (court upheld $100,000 jury award with no out-of-pocket loss shown); Swoager v. Credit Bureau, 608 F. Supp. 972 (M.D. Fla. 1985); Bryant v. TRW, Inc., 487 F. Supp. 1234 (E.D. Mich. 1980), *aff'd*, 689 F.2d 72 (6th Cir. 1982) ($8000); Collins v. Retail Credit Co., 410 F. Supp. 924 (E.D. Mich. 1976) ($21,750); Jones v. Credit Bureau of Huntington, Inc., 399 S.E.2d 694 (W. Va. 1990). *See also* Dalton v. Capital Assoc. Indus., 257 F.3d 409 (4th Cir. 2001) (damages for emotional distress are available under FCRA); White v. Imperial Adjustment Corp., 2002 WL 1809084 (E.D. La. Aug. 6, 2002), *aff'd on other grounds*, 75 Fed. Appx. 972 (5th Cir. 2003) (unpublished) (noting that damages for humiliation and mental distress are available even without proof of pecuniary damages). *Cf.* Field v. Trans Union, 2002 WL 849589 (N.D. Ill. May 3, 2002) (emotional distress due to knowledge of inaccuracies in report not compensable where actual disclosure of inaccuracies did not cause distress).

227 Collins v. Retail Credit Co., 410 F. Supp. 924 (E.D. Mich. 1976).

228 National Consumer Law Center, Credit Discrimination § 11.7.2.3 (4th ed. 2005 and Supp.).

229 National Consumer Law Center, Fair Debt Collection § 6.3 (5th ed. 2004 and Supp.).

230 Carey v. Piphus, 435 U.S. 247, 264, 98 S. Ct. 1042, 55 L. Ed. 2d 252 (1978); Gertz v. Robert Welch, Inc., 418 U.S. 323, 351, 94 S. Ct. 2997, 41 L. Ed. 2d 789 (1974); Shuman v. Standard Oil Co., 453 F. Supp. 1150, 1154 (N.D. Cal 1978).

231 Ackerley v. Credit Bureau, 385 F. Supp. 658, 661 (D. Wyo.

extent and duration of the injury.[232] Evidence of the injured party's conduct and observations of others may be necessary.[233] While no court has required medical evidence, it can be persuasive, as can supporting testimony from friends, family, co-workers, and others who observed the plaintiff's behavior.[234] The plaintiff's testimony alone may not suffice to recover for emotional distress damages if it is not sufficiently specific and concrete, and it may even need to be supported by corroborating evidence. Summary judgment has been granted against a plaintiff who does not present sufficient independent evidence of emotional distress.[235] But once injury is proven, the amount of damages is a jury question.[236]

It is often not evident to a lawyer when a client has suffered emotional distress. Many consumers will not volunteer the emotional content of their experience. They may be unaware of its legal relevance, may have suppressed past unpleasantness, or simply may be naturally reticent. It is important to probe the full extent of a client's emotional distress early, while it is still fresh in his or her mind. Emotional distress might better be referred to as non-economic damage or non-pecuniary harm to allay the perception that someone pleading emotional distress is a complainer or of precarious mental health. Frustration, aggravation, and humiliation are all valid examples of compensable non-economic damage, and a jury may be more willing to identify with such emotions than with the idea of "emotional distress."[237] Practitioners report that juries are often particularly sensitive to the outrage and offense of an unwarranted invasion of privacy. Stressing the pain of not being able to obtain credit to fulfill a specific hope or dream, such as to pay for a wedding or to buy a house, can have a strong effect on a jury, and can help them to understand the role credit can play both in ordinary life and for extraordinary occasions.

Relying on a client's narrative accounting may not suffice; repeated questioning during the interview about how the

---

1974); Rasor v. Retail Credit Co., 87 Wash. 2d 516, 530, 554 P.2d 1041, 1050 (1976).

232 *See, e.g.*, Bach v. First Union National Bank, 149 Fed. Appx. 354, 361 (6th Cir. 2005) (unpublished) (injured person's testimony alone may suffice to establish damages for emotional distress provided that she reasonably and sufficiently explains the circumstances surrounding the injury and does not rely on mere conclusory statements) (upholding jury award of $400,000 in compensatory damages); McKeown v. Sears Roebuck & Co., 335 F. Supp. 2d 917, 933 (W.D. Wis. 2004) (consumer need not show that forms of emotional distress other than embarrassment were caused by publication of erroneous report to third party); Rasor v. Retail Credit Co., 87 Wash. 2d 516, 530, 554 P.2d 1041, 1050 (1976). *See also* Minter v. AAA Cook Cty. Consolidation, Inc., 2004 WL 1630781, at *6 (N.D. Ill. July 19, 2004) (plaintiff must sufficiently support claim for emotional distress damages); Quinn v. Experian Solutions, 2004 WL 609357, at *5 (N.D. Ill. Mar. 24, 2004) (plaintiff must explain the circumstances of the emotional distress); Graham v. CSC Credit Servs., Inc., 306 F. Supp. 2d 873, 880 (D. Minn. 2004) (consumer's testimony about his frustration, anxiety, and humiliation created an issue of fact regarding his damages for emotional distress); Riley v. Equifax Credit Info. Servs., 194 F. Supp. 2d 1239 (S.D. Ala. 2002) (consumer's imprecise and conclusory statements re emotional distress are insufficient). The burden on the consumer is especially difficult in the Fifth Circuit. Cousin v. Trans Union Corp., 246 F.3d 359 (5th Cir. 2001) (consumer's testimony about emotional distress insufficient).

233 Cousin v. Trans Union Corp., 246 F.3d 359 (5th Cir. 2001), *citing* Carey v. Piphus, 435 U.S. 247, 98 S. Ct. 1042, 1052 n.20, 55 L. Ed. 2d 252 (1978). *See also* Wantz v. Experian Info. Solutions, 386 F.3d 829, 834 (7th Cir. 2004) (plaintiff may not support emotional distress damages with no more than the plaintiff's own "conclusory statements").

234 *See, e.g.*, McKeown v. Sears Roebuck & Co., 335 F. Supp. 2d 917, 932 (W.D. Wis. 2004) (refusing to grant CRA's motion for summary judgment on emotional distress claim where plaintiff submitted an affidavit from his wife chronicling his distress). *But see* Wecht v. PG Publishing Co., 725 A.2d 788 (Pa. Super. Ct. 1999) (plaintiff who claimed false light invasion of privacy must prove emotional distress damages through expert testimony).

235 Bagby v. Experian Info. Solutions, Inc., 162 Fed. Appx. 600 (7th Cir. 2006) (unpublished) (consumer did not seek medical or psychological treatment for emotional distress, and consumer failed to explain her emotional injury in detail); Ruffin-Thompkins v. Experian Info. Solutions, Inc., 422 F.3d 603 (7th Cir. 2005) (consumer provided only conclusory statements about her emotional distress, and failed to explain her emotional injury in detail); Wantz v. Experian Info. Solutions, 386 F.3d 829, 834 (7th Cir. 2004) (plaintiff may not support emotional distress damages with no more than the plaintiff's own "conclusory statements"); Nagle v. Experian Info. Solutions, Inc., 297 F.3d 1305 (11th Cir. 2002); Cousin v. Trans Union Corp., 246 F.3d 359 (5th Cir. 2001) (consumer's testimony about emotional distress insufficient); Riley v. Gen. Motors Acceptance Corp., 226 F. Supp. 2d 1316 (S.D. Ala. 2002); Thomas v. GulfCoast Credit Serv., Inc., 214 F. Supp. 2d 1228 (M.D. Ala. 2002); Myers v. Bennett Law Offices, 238 F. Supp. 2d 1196 (D. Nev. 2002); Field v. Trans Union, L.L.C., 2002 WL 849589 (N.D. Ill. May 3, 2002). *See* Sampson v. Equifax Info. Servs., L.L.C., 2005 WL 2095092, at *5 (S.D. Ga. Aug. 29, 2005) (denying defendant's motion for summary judgment, but noting that plaintiff "must produce some form of independent, corroborating evidence of her humiliation and embarrassment at trial."). *But see* Bach v. First Union National Bank, 149 Fed. Appx. 354, 361 (6th Cir. 2005) (unpublished) (injured person's testimony alone may suffice to establish damages for emotional distress provided that she reasonably and sufficiently explains the circumstances surrounding the injury and does not rely on mere conclusory statements) (upholding jury award of $400,000 in compensatory damages); Graham v. CSC Credit Servs., Inc., 306 F. Supp. 2d 873, 880 (D. Minn. 2004) (consumer's testimony about his frustration, anxiety, and humiliation created an issue of fact regarding his damages for emotional distress).

236 *See* Evers v. Equifax, 650 F.2d 793 (5th Cir. 1981) (limits on a jury award of actual damages); Comeaux v. Experian Info. Solutions, 2004 WL 1354412, at *10 (E.D. Tex. June 8, 2004) (recommending that CRA's motion for summary judgment should be denied).

237 *See, e.g.*, Morris v. Credit Bureau of Cincinnati, 563 F. Supp. 962 (S.D. Ohio 1983) (awarding $10,000 for, among other damages, plaintiff's nervousness, irritation and loss of sleep caused by FCRA violation).

client felt at each step may elicit helpful information. If the consumer felt emotional distress, it is appropriate to ask further about whether the client cried, took medicine, complained to others, discussed the problem with friends, family or doctor, lost sleep, became irritable, and the like. Early documentation and gathering of substantiating evidence will help preserve the evidence of actual damages for trial. Also, examine the law of the jurisdiction to determine whether expert testimony may be required to obtain emotional distress damages.[238]

11.10.2.4 Nominal Damages

An open question is whether an FCRA plaintiff can recover nominal damages as an alternative to actual damages. Nominal damages mean a trivial sum, usually one dollar, awarded to recognize the defendant's violation of the plaintiff's rights.[239] The issue is significant not only because such damages give the plaintiff a sense of vindication, but also because the FCRA's attorney fees provision provides that fees and costs are recoverable "in the case of any successful action."[240] An Eleventh Circuit decision, while holding that an FCRA plaintiff who had not recovered any damages could not claim fees, suggested that an action that resulted in mere nominal damages would be "successful," and thereby qualify for fees.[241] The FCRA's attorney fees provisions are discussed in more detail in § 11.14, *infra*. Nominal damages might also be recoverable under certain state credit reporting statutes or UDAP statutes.[242]

There are two theories justifying nominal damages. Under the first, nominal damages are recoverable when the defendant has violated plaintiff's rights, but that violation did not cause any actual damages.[243] Under the other, nominal damages are awarded to a plaintiff who proved both a violation and some sort of injury, but the damages suffered were either difficult to quantify in dollar terms, or were inadequately substantiated at trial.[244]

In general, to recover nominal damages under the first theory, that is, in the absence of any actual damages, the claim involved must be one which is complete without proof of such damages. Common examples include breach of contract,[245] claims filed under civil rights statutes,[246] and certain intentional torts, such as assault,[247] false imprisonment,[248] trespass,[249] and conversion.[250] False light and invasion of privacy cases have also yielded nominal damages without proof of injury.[251] For claims based on statutes, whether nominal damages are available may depend upon whether the statute is constructed to impose liability upon proof of a violation, without regard to injury, or whether the plaintiff must demonstrate some injury to make a successful claim.[252]

---

238 *See, e.g.*, Wecht v. PG Publishing Co., 1999 Pa. Super. 28, 725 A.2d 788 (1999) (plaintiff who claimed false light invasion of privacy must prove emotional distress damages through expert testimony).

239 *See, e.g.*, Wilson v. Eberle, 18 F.R.D. 7, 9 (D. Alaska 1955). *See also* Tatum v. Morton, 386 F. Supp. 1308 (D.D.C. 1974) (nominal damages are presumed to follow from the violation of any legal right, even if no actual damages are involved), *aff'd in part, rev'd in part on other grounds*, 562 F.2d 1279 (D.C. Cir. 1977).

240 15 U.S.C. §§ 1681n(a)(3) (willful noncompliance), 1681o(a)(2) (negligent noncompliance).

241 Nagle v. Experian Info. Solutions, Inc., 297 F.3d 1305, 1307 (11th Cir. 2002).

242 *See, e.g.*, Cisneros v. U.D. Registry, Inc., 46 Cal. Rptr. 2d 233, 255 (Cal. Ct. App. 1995) (upholding award of $350 as justifiable nominal damages under state credit reporting act).

243 *See, e.g.*, *In re* Wiggins, 273 B.R. 839, 881 (Bankr. D. Idaho 2001) (plaintiff who failed to prove amount of damages suffered from defendant's fraud entitled to nominal award of $100); D'Addario v. Viera, 510 A.2d 1382, 1382 (Conn. App. Ct. 1986) (plaintiff who proved defendant had converted roofing materials but who failed to itemize his losses or introduce any evidence beyond oral testimony as to their amount entitled to only nominal damages); Western Union Tel. Co. v. Guard, 139 S.W.2d 722, 728 (Ky. Ct. App. 1940); 22 Am. Jur. 3d *Damages* § 5.

244 22 Am. Jur. 3d *Damages* § 5

245 *See, e.g.*, Hutchison v. Tompkins, 259 So. 2d 129 (Fla. 1972); Damiano v. National Grange Mut. Liab. Co., 56 N.E.2d 18 (Mass. 1944); Manhattan Sav. Inst. v. Gottfried Baking Co., 36 N.E.2d 637 (N.Y. 1941) Lee Cycle Cent., Inc. v. Wilson Cycle Ctr., Inc., 545 S.E.2d 745, 750, 751 (N.C. Ct. App. 2001) (nominal damages allowed where contract breached but no substantial loss or injury), *aff'd per curiam*, 556 S.E.2d 293 (N.C. 2001); DeCastro v Wellston City Sch. Dist. Bd. of Educ., 761 N.E.2d 612, 615 (Ohio 2002) (nominal damages appropriate for plaintiff who proves breach of contract but fails to prove actual damages).

246 *See, e.g.*, Carey v. Piphus, 435 U.S. 247, 266, 97 S. Ct. 1642, 52 L. Ed. 2d 355 (1978) (right to procedural due process is absolute, and therefore nominal damages are awardable even without proof of actual injury); Schneider v. County of San Diego, 285 F.3d 784, 794 (9th Cir. 2002) (holding trial court erred in failing to award $2 in nominal damages on procedural due process claim); Craig v. Carson, 449 F. Supp. 385, 396 (M.D. Fla. 1978) (owner of car wrongfully impounded entitled to nominal damages even though she failed to prove any actual damages).

247 Simpkins v. Ryder Freight Sys., Inc., 855 S.W.2d 416, 421 (Mo. Ct. App. 1993) (damages imputed to vindicate the violation of plaintiff's rights).

248 Wilson v. Eberle, 18 F.R.D. 7, 9 (D. Alaska 1955). *See also* Zok v. State, 903 P.2d 574, 573 (Alaska 1995) (false arrest).

249 Indiana State Highway Comm. v. Pappas, 349 N.E.2d 808, 812 (Ind. Ct. App. 1976).

250 Save Charleston Found. v. Murray, 333 S.E.2d 60, 65 (S.C. Ct. App. 1985) (nominal damages available in action for conversion of promissory note, even when no actual loss has occurred).

251 *See, e.g.*, Wecht v. PG Pub Co., 725 A.2d 788, 792 (Pa. Super. Ct. 1999) (nominal damages recoverable for false light even without proof of pecuniary loss or physical harm); Barr v. Southern Bell Tel. & Tel. Co., 185 S.E.2d 714, 717 (N.C. Ct. App. 1972); LeCrone v. Ohio Bell Tel. Co., 201 N.E.2d 533, 536 (Ohio Ct. App. 1963) (intrusion upon seclusion action primarily protects mental rather than economic or pecuniary interests, therefore nominal damages awardable without proof of actual damages).

252 *See, e.g.*, Griffin v. Steeltek, Inc., 261 F.3d 1026, 1028, 1029 (10th Cir. 2001) (Americans with Disabilities Act requires plaintiff to

If actual damages are an element of the prima facie case, nominal damages may not be awardable without proof that the plaintiff suffered some injury. So, for example, a court may deny nominal damages in a common law fraud action if the plaintiff fails to prove the fact of injury on the grounds that the plaintiff has not satisfied all the elements of the claim, and therefore has not established a right to any judgment.[253] For the same reason, several cases have held that nominal damages are unavailable in negligence actions without proof of actual damages.[254] Under these cases, a right to compensatory damages is a prerequisite to nominal damages. Not all courts agree, however. Nominal damages have been held to be available in a fraud action, without proof of actual damages.[255] Two North Carolina decisions, both involving malpractice,[256] and one Kentucky decision, against a negligent telegram carrier,[257] have ruled that nominal damages were available even though the plaintiff failed to meet the element of actual damages.

Some authority exists for awarding nominal damages to a plaintiff who has proven an FCRA violation but has not proven actual damages. For example, in *Russell v. Shelter Financial Services*,[258] a district court awarded one dollar in nominal damages to a plaintiff who had successfully shown that the defendant had obtained his report without a permissible purpose, even though he had not shown any actual injury from the violation. The court then directed the jury to determine punitive damages.[259] Similarly, the Sixth Circuit affirmed a lower court's award of one dollar in nominal damages and $500 in punitive damages even though the lower court had found that the plaintiffs had not suffered any actual damages.[260]

Other decisions have held that without proving actual damages, an FCRA plaintiff cannot recover even a nominal award. One court has ruled that nominal damages are not available under a section 1681o action, reasoning that damages are a required element of an FCRA negligent noncompliance action just as they are of a common law negligence action.[261] Decisions in the Fifth Circuit have adopted similar logic.[262] Nonetheless, in jurisdictions that have allowed nominal damages without proof of actual damages in negligence cases, courts should be receptive to an argument that a plaintiff who has established an FCRA violation should recover a nominal sum without proving actual damages.

Even in jurisdictions that deny nominal damages where no actual damages have been shown, nominal damages should still be awardable to FCRA plaintiffs who prove the existence, but not the extent, of actual damages, or whose damages are difficult to quantify in monetary terms, like intangible injuries of humiliation, embarrassment, or mental distress. These sorts of intangible injuries have been grounds for nominal damages in other actions.[263] The damages flowing from an FCRA violation may be difficult to assess when no immediate and direct consequence, such as the loss of a loan, occurs. Nonetheless, when a CRA issues wrong credit information about a consumer, some injury can be presumed. The nature of the injury is similar to that suffered by someone whose bank wrongfully dishonors a

---

prove injury from intentional discrimination to recover any damages); Abrams v. Communications Workers of America, AFL-CIO, 23 F. Supp. 2d 47, 52 (D.D.C. 1998) (rights of workers to notice under National Labor Relations Act was absolute, and nominal damages awardable without any pecuniary injury), *vacated on other grounds by* 221 F.3d 195 (D.C. Cir. 2000).

253 *See, e.g.*, Olson v. Fraase, 421 N.W.2d 820, 827 (N.D. 1988).
254 *See, e.g.*, Vivian Arnold Realty Co. v. McCormick, 506 P.2d 1074, 1079 (Ariz. Ct. App. 1973) (no nominal damages in negligence action without proof of actual injury); William v. Wiggins, 285 So. 2d 163, 165 (Miss. 1973); Beavers v. Christensen, 176 Neb. 162, 125 N.W.2d 551, 554 (1963); Bird v. Rozier, 948 P.2d 888, 892 (Wyo. 1997) (no nominal damages for negligence actions without proof of actual damages); W. Page Keeton, Prosser & Keeton on Torts, § 30 at 165 (5th ed. 1984).
255 Clearview Concrete Prods. Corp. v. S. Charles Gherardi, Inc., 453 N.Y.S.2d 750, 756 (N.Y. App. Div. 1982).
256 Nick v. Baker, 481 S.E.2d 412, 414 (N.C. Ct. App. 1997); Title Ins. Co. of Minn. v. Smith, Debnam, Hibbert & Pahl, 459 S.E.2d 801, 804 (N.C. Ct. App. 1995), *aff'd in part, dismissed in part*, 467 S.E.2d 241 (1996).
257 Western Union Tel. Co. v. Guard, 139 S.W.2d 722, 728 (Ky. Ct. App. 1940).
258 604 F. Supp. 201 (W.D. Mo. 1984) (granting plaintiff's motion for directed verdict).
259 *Id.* at 203.
260 Lodise v. Lodise, 9 F.3d 108 (table), 1993 WL 441787, at *2 (6th Cir. Oct. 29, 1993). *See also* Wright v. TRW, Inc., 872 F.2d 420 (table), 1989 WL 27516, at *4 (4th Cir. Mar. 20, 1989) (nominal damages may be awarded for technical violation of FCRA, but plaintiff not entitled to them where jury found no willful violation of FCRA and plaintiff had not pleaded negligent violation); Gray v. Experian Info. Solutions, Inc., 2001 U.S. Dist. LEXIS 5466, at *32 (D. Ariz. Mar. 22, 2001) (though plaintiffs did not show actual damages from apparent FCRA violation, they might be able to recover nominal damages, denying, in part, defendant's motion for summary judgment).
261 *In re* Trans Union Corp. Privacy Litig., 211 F.R.D. 328 (N.D. Ill. 2002) (striking prayer for nominal damages). The court dismissed the plaintiffs' claim for nominal damages under § 1681n, the willful noncompliance provision, on the grounds that the statutory damages provided for by that section rendered nominal damages unnecessary. *Id.* at 16.
262 Cousin v. Trans Union Corp., 246 F.3d 359, 371 n.19 (5th Cir. 2001) (plaintiff who failed to produce adequate actual damages evidence of his emotional distress could not recover nominal damages); Larson v. Groos Bank, N.A., 204 B.R. 500, 502 (Bankr. W.D. Tex. 1996) (nominal damages cannot be recovered under the FCRA unless plaintiff has shown actual loss). *See also* Hyde v. Hibernia Nat'l Bank, 861 F.2d 446, 448 (5th Cir. 1988).
263 *See* Parton v. GRE North, Inc., 802 F. Supp. 241, 255 (W.D. Mo. 1991) (nominal damages are appropriate to recognize a violation of rights when a monetary value cannot be attached, awarding nominal damages in Title VII action), *aff'd*, 971 F.2d 150 (8th Cir. 1992); Minger v. Reinhard Distrib. Co., 943 P.2d 400, 403 (Wash. Ct. App. 1997) (nominal damages awarded in civil rights action to compensate for hurt feelings, embarrassment, and humiliation, injuries proof cannot entirely show). See also § 11.10.2.3, *supra*, for a discussion of intangible damages.

check; in awarding nominal damages in such a case, one court justified the damages as follows:

> In the modern world the financial credit of a man, particularly of one engaged in commercial pursuits, is a much prized and valuable asset. Although laboriously built it is easily destroyed.... Hence when a check of a depositor is refused at the counter of his bank, that portion of the commercial world, greater or less, that comes within the sphere of his transactions, promptly imputes the blame to him rather than to the bank.[264]

Similarly, a report user will likely attribute negative credit information to the consumer, not to a CRA's or furnisher's error. It is fair to characterize an incorrect attribution as an injury, and by allowing nominal damages a fact finder who could not assess the dollar value of that injury would still be able to impose a judgment against the wrongdoer. Likewise, a CRA's refusal to disclose records to which a consumer is entitled inflicts some injury, for a consumer without that information has less power and knowledge than he or she would have with it.[265] The wrongful disclosure of a consumer's report causes an injury like that from other invasions of privacy,[266] an injury that is mental, not economic, but nonetheless real.

11.11 Statutory Damages

Statutory damage awards are available for willful violations of the FCRA, but not for negligent violations.[267] Any person who willfully fails to comply with the FCRA with respect to any consumer is liable to the consumer for either (a) actual damages sustained or (b) damages ranging from $100 to $1000.[268] Consumers should normally request in their pleadings actual damages or statutory damages, whichever is greater.[269] As discussed in § 11.12, *infra*, punitive damages may also be available for willful violations of the FCRA. In addition, a natural person who obtains a consumer report under false pretenses or knowingly without a permissible purpose is liable to the consumer for the greater of actual damages or $1000.[270]

Statutory damages for willful violations are available when actual damages are difficult to prove or nonexistent;[271] however, at least one court has stated that common sense indicates that evidence of actual damages is "at least potentially quite meaningful" in determining statutory damages.[272] Statutory damages are well suited to class treatment.[273]

Unlike the Fair Debt Collection Practices Act, which expressly provides factors for the court to consider when setting statutory damages,[274] the FCRA does not specify any criteria for determining the amount of statutory damages, other than a floor and a ceiling. Presumably the amount is left to the discretion of the court.[275]

A defendant may argue that because Congress failed to explicitly provide that a plaintiff is entitled to the *higher* of actual or statutory damages, the defendant should only be liable for the *lower* amount. However, if the $1000 ceiling on statutory damages was also intended to cap actual damages, then a consumer who proves that a defendant willfully violated the FCRA could receive a lower actual damage award than if the consumer had merely proven negligence, for the negligence provision provides for actual damages with no limit.[276] It is unlikely Congress intended to provide less compensation to a plaintiff who has been subjected to willful misconduct than one who has been the victim of negligence. Furthermore, the section of the 1996 Reform Act that amends 15 U.S.C. 1681n to provide for statutory damages is entitled *Minimum* Civil Liability for Willful Non-Compliance, indicating that statutory damages are

---

264 American Fletcher Nat'l Bank & Trust Co. v. Flick, 252 N.E.2d 839, 846 (Ind. Ct. App. 1969) (quoting Weiner v. North Penn. Bank, Inc., 65 Pa. Super. 290 (1916)).
265 *Cf.* Abrams v. Communications Workers of America, AFL-CIO, 23 F. Supp. 2d 47, 52 (D.D.C. 1998) (nominal damages appropriate where union failed to give workers notices required by the National Labor Relations Act), *vacated on other grounds*, 221 F.3d 195 (D.C. Cir. 2000).
266 *See, e.g.*, LeCrone v. Ohio Bell Tel. Co., 201 N.E.2d 533, 536 (Ohio Ct. App. 1963) (intrusion upon seclusion action primarily protects mental rather than economic or pecuniary interests, therefore nominal damages are an appropriate remedy).
267 A narrow exception provides for statutory damages for violations of the provision granting the FBI secret access to information for counterintelligence purposes. See § 7.2.10.4, *supra*. Willfulness is discussed at § 11.12.1, *infra*.
268 15 U.S.C. § 1681n(a).
269 15 U.S.C. § 1681n(a)(1)(A) does not specify that the court must award the greater of actual or statutory damages. *Cf.* 15 U.S.C. § 1681n(a)(1)(B). Until 1996, actual damages but not statutory damages were available. Statutory damages were added in order to provide minimum damages, not to limit actual damages.
270 15 U.S.C. § 1681n(b).
271 Murray v. Finance America, 2006 WL 862832 (N.D. Ill. Apr. 4, 2006).
272 Andrade v. Chase Home Fin., 2005 WL 3436400, *6 (N.D. Ill. Dec. 12, 2005) (motion to transfer venue).
273 Murry v. GMAC Mort. Corp., 434 F.3d 948 (7th Cir. 2006). *See also* Kudlicki v. Farragut Fin. Corp., 2006 WL 927281, at *2 (N.D. Ill. Jan. 20, 2006) (summary judgment granted to plaintiff on claim that defendant obtained consumer report for impermissible purpose; only statutory damages sought; class action complaint.
274 15 U.S.C. § 1692k(b)(1). These factors are the frequency and persistence of noncompliance by the debt collector, the nature of noncompliance, and the intent of the noncompliance. *Id. See* National Consumer Law Center, Fair Debt Collection § 6.4.3 (5th ed. 2004 and Supp.).
275 *Cf.* 15 U.S.C. § 1681n(a)(1)(B).
276 15 U.S.C. § 1681o. While a plaintiff who proves willful noncompliance becomes eligible for punitive damages, those damages, unlike actual damages, are discretionary: "as the court may allow." 15 U.S.C. § 1681n(a)(2).

§ 11.12   *Fair Credit Reporting*

meant to compensate consumers who are unable to prove a higher amount of actual damages.[277]

Analysis of cases awarding statutory damages under the Fair Debt Collection Practices Act reveals that certain factors have been considered relevant by courts in determining damages, and these factors may guide consumers arguing for statutory damages under the FCRA.[278] The factors include: the defendant's sophistication; the clarity of the requirements the defendant violated; the defendant's persistent denial of its illegal act; the defendant's failure to bring its practices into compliance despite ample time to do so; prior violations and liability of the defendant for the same illegal act; multiple violations; multiple accounts or transactions that were the subject of the same violation; the importance of deterrence; the consumer's injury; the egregiousness of the violation; and the existence of the defendant's liability insurance.

Like other titles in the Consumer Credit Protection Act,[279] enforcement of the FCRA is largely dependent upon private litigation, or so-called private attorney general enforcement. The addition of statutory damages promotes the private enforcement of the law, in this case of a law which suffered greatly from lack of compliance and enforcement. However, Congress was aware of industry fears that statutory damages would result in unwarranted suits. Consequently, a provision was included providing that when an unsuccessful pleading is filed in bad faith, the prevailing party may recover reasonable attorney fees.[280]

In at least a few states, the state credit reporting statute provides minimum statutory damages, in some instances even when willfulness is not proved.[281] At least one state credit reporting statute also provides treble damages for willful violations.[282]

Additional remedies may be available if a violation of the FCRA is found to be a violation of a state deceptive practices statute.[283] This is because many deceptive practices statutes provide for either minimum statutory damages or treble damages for prevailing consumers.[284] Usually statutory damages are available even for negligent violations, but treble damages will require willfulness.[285]

11.12 Punitive Damages

11.12.1 *Prerequisites for Punitive Damages*

11.12.1.1 Relation to Common Law Standards

The FCRA specifies that if the failure by a person to comply with the FCRA is willful, then the person is liable for such punitive damages as the court will allow.[286] Punitive damages are also expressly allowed for the willful violation of obtaining a consumer report under false pretenses or knowingly without a permissible purpose.[287] The function of FCRA punitive damages is deterrence.[288] The appropriateness of punitive damages also depends on whether the wrongdoer's conduct was egregious and whether it is necessary to "punish" that person.[289]

Punitive damages under a tort claim will follow state law standards as to punitive damages, but punitive damages under the FCRA will be pursuant to the federal standard enunciated in the statute itself. The standard of "willfulness" will generally be somewhat different from a particular state's common law standard for punitive damages, which might be reckless and wanton disregard of societal interests, proof of malice or evil motive, or one of any number of different formulae.[290]

11.12.1.2 Proving Willfulness

As described above,[291] punitive damage recoveries under the FCRA require only a defendant's willful violation of an FCRA requirement. If adequately pleaded, willfulness is

---

277 Omnibus Consolidated Appropriations Act, subtit. D, ch. 1, § 2412(b), Pub. L. No. 104-208, 110 Stat. 3009 (Sept. 30, 1996).
278 *See* National Consumer Law Center, Fair Debt Collection § 6.4.3.2 (5th 2004 and Supp.).
279 *See* § 1.3.1, *supra*.
280 S. Rep. No. 185, 104th Cong., 1st Sess. 49 (Dec. 14, 1995).
281 Cal. Civ. Code § 1785.31; Me. Rev. Stat. Ann. tit. 10, § 1323; Vt. Stat. Ann. tit. 9, § 2480f(b); Wash. Rev. Code § 19.182.150.
282 Me. Rev. Stat. Ann. tit. 10, § 1322.
283 *See* § 10.6.2, *supra*. The Washington credit reporting statute explicitly provides that a violation of the credit reporting act is an unfair or deceptive act in trade or commerce and an unfair method of competition under the state deceptive practices statute. Wash. Rev. Code § 19.182.150.
284 National Consumer Law Center, Unfair and Deceptive Acts and Practices § 8.4, Appx. A (6th ed. 2004).
285 *Id*.

286 15 U.S.C. § 1681n(a)(2).
287 *Id*.
288 Northrop v. Hoffman, 12 Fed. Appx. 44, 2001 WL 682301 (2d Cir. June 14, 2001) (unpublished).
289 *Id. See* W.D.I.A. Corp. v. McGraw-Hill, Inc., 34 F. Supp. 2d 612 (S.D. Ohio 1998) (CRA's request for punitive damages against publication rejected; "testers" serve an important role in policing FCRA compliance).
290 Northrop v. Hoffman, 12 Fed. Appx. 44, 2001 WL 682301 (2d Cir. June 14, 2001) (unpublished);Philbin v. Trans Union Corp., 101 F.3d 952 (3d Cir. 1996); Fischl v. GMAC, 708 F.2d 143 (5th Cir. 1983); Thornton v. Equifax, Inc., 619 F.2d 700 (8th Cir. 1980); Bruce v. First U.S.A. Bank, 103 F. Supp. 2d 1135 (E.D. Mo. 2000); Oppenheimer v. Guzco Guarantee de Puerto Rico, Inc., 977 F. Supp. 549 (D. P.R. 1997) (willfulness or malice could be shown by failure to note or investigate the dispute so that erroneous information is again provided); Jones v. Credit Bureau of Greater Garden City, 1989 WL 107747 (D. Kan. Aug. 28, 1989); Pinner v. Schmidt, 617 F. Supp. 342 (E.D. La. 1985), *aff'd in part and rev'd in part*, 805 F.2d 1258 (5th Cir. 1986); Boothe v. TRW Credit Data, 557 F. Supp. 66, 72 (S.D.N.Y. 1982); Tans Union Corp. v. Crisp, 896 S.W.2d 446 (Ark. Ct. App. 1995).
291 *See* § 11.12.1.1, *supra*.

usually an issue of fact for the jury.[292] The plaintiff need only produce sufficient evidence to establish the failure to comply with a requirement by circumstantial evidence or otherwise, and that this failure was willful.[293]

In determining willfulness, some courts may be influenced by the number of violations proven. Violation of one or two requirements that do not seem very important to the court may be characterized as negligence. However, violation of a number of requirements or repeated failure to comply with one requirement may be seen as willful, and the resulting frustration of the consumer's ability to obtain information or gain relief will more likely be regarded as willful.

Under the most widely adopted definition of willfulness, the plaintiff must show that the defendant "knowingly and intentionally committed an act in conscious disregard for the rights of others," but need not show "malice or evil motive."[294] "Willful misrepresentations or concealments" have been held sufficient in the Third and Fifth Circuits.[295] The Eighth Circuit requires "knowing and intentional commission of an act the defendant knows to violate the law." A defendant's general familiarity with the FCRA's requirements can support an inference of willfulness.[296]

Some courts, considering the particular circumstances before them, have applied this standard to require near-blind indifference to the consumer's rights. Under these harsh decisions, where the defendant attempted to respond to the consumer's complaint, however ineptly, the consumer reporting agency (CRA) was found to have been merely negligent. For example, in *Philbin v. Trans Union Corp.*,[297] a CRA's reinsertion of an item of bad information, previously deleted after the plaintiff complained, was found not willful even though the defendant had failed to re-correct the item after the plaintiff notified the CRA of the error's reappearance.[298] This decision preceded the amendment of the Act to add specific anti-reinsertion provisions, violation of which should be stronger evidence of willfulness.[299]

Similarly, in *Stevenson v. TRW, Inc.*,[300] a Fifth Circuit panel reversed an award of punitive damages where the CRA had taken months to complete its reinvestigation and to delete inaccurate items: "TRW moved slowly in completing its investigation and was negligent in its compliance with the prompt deletion requirement. The record does not reveal, however, any intention to thwart consciously Stevenson's right to have inaccurate information removed promptly from his report."[301] The court noted that TRW had

---

292 Rodgers v. McCullough, 296 F. Supp. 2d 895 (W.D. Tenn. 2003); Thibodeaux v. Rupers, 196 F. Supp. 2d 585 (S.D. Ohio 2001); Whitesides v. Equifax Credit Info. Servs., Inc., 125 F. Supp. 2d 807 (W.D. La. 2000). *See also* Dalton v. Capital Assoc. Indus., 257 F.3d 409 (4th Cir. 2001) (summary judgment is seldom appropriate on question of willfulness, but here evidence of willfulness was wholly lacking).

293 *See, e.g.,* Beechum v. Isgett, 2001 U.S. Dist. LEXIS 18688 (E.D.N.C. Sept. 24, 2001) (female employee of finance company liability for willful violation as a matter of law where she obtained consumer report on male not transacting business with the company. Conscious disregard shown where employee had no permissible purpose and acquired and stored the consumer report without plaintiff's consent, for personal purposes such as peace of mind, and without authority from employer); Cushman v. Trans Union Corp., 920 F. Supp. 80 (E.D. Pa. 1996) (in theft of identity case, jury could conclude that CRA acted willfully by failing to adequately reinvestigate). *See also* Evers v. Equifax, 650 F.2d 793 (5th Cir. 1981); Oppenheimer v. Guzco Guarantee de Puerto Rico, Inc., 977 F. Supp. 549 (D. P.R. 1997) (willfulness or malice could be shown by failure to note or investigate the dispute so that erroneous information is again provided); Wiggins v. District Cablevision, Inc., 853 F. Supp. 484 (D.D.C. 1994); Swoager v. Credit Bureau, 608 F. Supp. 972 (M.D. Fla. 1985); Boothe v. TRW Credit Data, 557 F. Supp. 66, 72 (S.D.N.Y. 1982); Marrinan v. Compliance Data Ctr., Inc., [1974–1980 Decisions Transfer Binder] Consumer Cred. Guide (CCH) ¶ 97,482 (S.D.N.Y. 1980). *But see* Rhodes v. Ford Motor Credit Co., 951 F.2d 905 (8th Cir. 1991) (false adverse report kept reappearing even though FMCC had issued correction; consumer failed to establish willfulness).

294 Sapia v. Regency Motors, 276 F.3d 747 (5th Cir. 2002) (must show conscious disregard or willful and deliberate actions; mere violation of law is not enough); Northrop v. Hoffman, 12 Fed. Appx. 44, 2001 WL 682301 (2d Cir. June 14, 2001) (unpublished) (no need to show malice or evil motive; conscious disregard is enough); Dalton v. Capital Assoc. Indus., 257 F.3d 409 (4th Cir. 2001); Bakker v. McKinnon, 152 F.3d 1007 (8th Cir. 1998); Pinner v. Schmidt, 805 F.2d 1258, 1263 (5th Cir. 1986); Riley v. Equifax Credit Info. Servs., 194 F. Supp. 2d 1239 (S.D. Ala. 2002); Thomas v. GulfCoast Credit Serv., Inc., 214 F. Supp. 2d 1228 (M.D. Ala. 2002); Richardson v. Fleet Bank, 190 F. Supp. 2d 81 (D. Mass. 2001) (no issue of willfulness where consumer did not allege that Equifax adopted its reinvestigation policies with knowledge or reckless disregard as to whether the policies contravened rights under the FCRA); Whitesides v. Equifax Credit Info. Servs., 125 F. Supp. 2d 807 (W.D. La. 2000) (no need to produce "smoking gun"); Bruce v. First U.S.A. Bank, 103 F. Supp. 2d 1135 (E.D. Mo. 2000); Davis v. Asset Servs., 46 F. Supp. 2d 503 (M.D. La. 1998); Feldman v. Comprehensive Info. Servs., Inc., 2003 WL 22413484 (Conn. Super. Ct. Oct. 6, 2003). *See also* Philbin v. Trans Union Corp., 101 F.3d 957, 960 (3d Cir. 1996); Casella v. Equifax Credit Info. Servs., 56 F.3d 469, 486 (2d Cir. 1995); Berman v. Parco, 986 F. Supp. 195, 199 (S.D.N.Y. 1997). *Cf.* Cousin v. Trans Union Corp., 246 F.3d 359 (5th Cir. 2001) (articulating this standard but finding no willfulness despite CRA's repeated reinsertion of erroneous information; note strong dissent on this issue); Huepel v. Trans Union, 193 F. Supp. 2d 1234 (N.D. Ala. 2002) (applying *Cousin* standard and finding insufficient evidence of willfulness).

295 Cousin v. Trans Union Corp., 246 F.3d 359 (5th Cir. 2001); Cushman v. Trans Union Corp., 115 F.3d 220, 227 (3d Cir. 1997); Stevenson v. TRW, Inc. 987 F.2d 288, 293–294 (5th Cir. 1993).

296 Phillips v. Grendahl, 312 F.3d 357 (8th Cir. 2002).

297 101 F.3d 957 (3d Cir. 1996).

298 *Id.* at 970. *Accord* Cousin v. Trans Union Corp., 246 F.3d 359 (5th Cir. 2001) (note strong dissent on this issue); Richardson v. Fleet Bank, 190 F. Supp. 2d 81 (D. Mass. 2001).

299 15 U.S.C. § 1681i(a)(5)(B), *as amended by* Pub. L. No. 104-208, 110 Stat. 3009 (Sept. 30, 1996). *See also* Ch. 4, *supra.*

300 Stevenson v. TRW, Inc. 987 F.2d 288, 293–294 (5th Cir. 1993).

301 *Id.* at 294.

given the plaintiff his report on request, had investigated (however slowly) the disputed accounts, and had attempted to resolve his complaints.[302] *Stevenson* was decided before the 1996 Reform Act's amendments, which imposed a thirty-day deadline (with conditional extension) on reinvestigations.[303] Under the revised statute, the sort of gross delay involved in that case might present a case of willfulness.

The repeated failure by a CRA to respond adequately to a consumer's disputes and reasonable inquiries adds to the likelihood that a court or jury will make a finding of willfulness.[304] Similarly, a user which repeatedly obtains an individual's consumer report despite efforts by a consumer to stop such actions may also be liable for willful noncompliance.[305] For this reason, consumers should keep good records of their contacts with CRAs, users, and furnishers. Lawyers who are assisting clients prior to any lawsuit may want to draft correspondence to the recalcitrant CRA or user so that any failure to respond adequately is readily apparent and not easily explained away.

In many cases that find willfulness, the courts lump the relevant facts together to reach a conclusion that a willful violation was proven, without clearly analyzing what crucial features of the fact pattern made it a willful rather than a negligent violation.[306] Willfulness may be found where there are multiple violations of FCRA requirements, where the defendant adopted a policy that violates the FCRA, when the CRA knew that the report was inaccurate,[307] where there has been a single violation of an important requirement (particularly where acrimony is present), where the defendant has poor procedures to ensure compliance with the FCRA, or where a CRA has resisted a consumer's repeated efforts to fix a problem. Evidence of complaints by other consumers can help establish the defendant's willfulness.[308]

A good example is *Millstone v. O'Hanlon Reports, Inc.*,[309] in which the court upheld an award of punitive damages where the CRA's investigator spent thirty minutes preparing the report, which was "rife with innuendo, misstatement and slander" and was garnered only from one biased informant, and where the CRA's reinvestigation found that every allegation in the report was untrue. The investigator did not even follow the company's own policy of verifying the informant's story. In addition, when the consumer tried to discover the nature and substance of the information in the file, the CRA delayed and misled the consumer. Full disclosure was not made until the lawsuit was in progress. The court found this a willful failure to

---

302 *Id. See also* Pinner v. Schmidt, 805 F.2d 1258 (5th Cir. 1986) (1987) (reversing punitive damage award because CRA had promptly furnished the report upon request and had not attempted to conceal anything, though CRA had verified disputed account only with one biased source, had failed to note the consumer's dispute in the file, and had marked the file with a misleading comment that indicated the creditor had filed suit on the account); Berman v. Parco, 986 F. Supp. 195 (S.D.N.Y. 1997); Swoager v. Credit Bureau of Greater St. Petersburg, Fla., 608 F. Supp. 972 (M.D. Fla. 1985) (though unreasonable for CRA to merely rely on creditor's information once CRA became aware of dispute between creditor and consumer, CRA was not willful); Morris v. Credit Bureau of Cincinnati, Inc., 563 F. Supp. 962 (S.D. Ohio 1983) (though CRA was negligent in allowing deleted information to reappear, not willful where CRA had exhibited no ill will toward that plaintiff and had acted to fix the problem).

303 15 U.S.C. § 1681i(a)(1), *as amended by* Pub. L. No. 104-208, 110 Stat. 3009 (Sept. 30, 1996).

304 Sheffer v. Experian Info. Solutions, Inc., 2003 WL 21710573 (E.D. Pa. July 24, 2003) (systemic errors, not merely human error, and not promptly cured); Soghomonian v. U.S., 278 F. Supp. 2d 1151 (E.D. Cal. 2003) (failure to pick up the phone to find out the status of tax liens until after suit was filed can show willfulness); Whitesides v. Equifax Credit Info. Servs., Inc., 125 F. Supp. 2d 807 (W.D. La. 2000) (question of fact whether furnisher was willful when repeatedly notified of error yet continued to report that fraudulent account was plaintiff's). *See also* McKeown v. Sears Roebuck & Co., 335 F. Supp. 2d 917, 941–942 (W.D. Wis. 2004) (a plaintiff may be entitled to punitive damages from furnisher if furnisher did not conduct any investigation of dispute or conducted an investigation that it knew to be inadequate).

305 Veno v. AT&T Credit Corp., 297 F. Supp. 2d 379 (D. Mass. 2003).

306 *See, e.g.,* Thompson v. Equifax Credit Inf. Servs., 2001 U.S. Dist. LEXIS 22666 (M.D. Ala. Nov. 14, 2001), *motion for reconsideration denied*, 2001 U.S. Dist. LEXIS 22640 (Dec. 14, 2001) (in order to establish reckless disregard, plaintiff must establish that defendant entertained doubt about the truth of the report, such as being put on notice repeatedly about inaccuracy). *See also* Evers v. Equifax, 650 F.2d 793 (5th Cir. 1981); Zala v. Trans Union, L.L.C., 2001 U.S. Dist. LEXIS 549 (N.D. Tex. Jan. 17, 2001) (policy of refusal to deal with credit repair organization could show malice; for CRA to send out consumer reports with proof in hand of the errors shows reckless disregard); Bruce v. First U.S.A. Bank, 103 F. Supp. 2d 1135 (E.D. Mo. 2000); Russell v. Shelter Fin. Servs., 604 F. Supp. 201 (W.D. Mo. 1984). *Contra* Richardson v. Fleet Bank, 190 F. Supp. 2d 81 (D. Mass. 2001) (insufficient evidence of willful noncompliance by mere failure to correct the report after receiving several notices of the error).

307 Thomas v. GulfCoast Credit Serv., Inc., 214 F. Supp. 2d 1228 (M.D. Ala. 2002).

308 Dalton v. Capital Assoc. Indus., 257 F.3d 409 (4th Cir. 2001) (plaintiff "has not shown, for example, that it was aware that its subvendors relied upon informal legal opinions from court clerks. There is no evidence that other consumers have lodged complaints similar to [plaintiff's]. . . .").

309 383 F. Supp. 269 (E.D. Mo. 1974), *aff'd*, 528 F.2d 829 (8th Cir. 1976). *See* Stevenson v. Employer's Mut. Ass'n, 960 F. Supp. 141 (N.D. Ill. 1987) (allegations that the defendant confused the plaintiff with a convicted felon despite obvious inconsistencies, continued to wrongly assert that the two birthdays matched even after a reinvestigation, and continued to maintain that the plaintiff had committed two of the other man's felonies even after reinvestigation revealed he was not the man who committed the first felony, sufficed to state a claim of willful noncompliance); Collins v. Retail Credit Co., 410 F. Supp. 924 (E.D. Mich. 1976) (upholding a jury's award of punitive damages where CRA violated multiple provisions of the FCRA, including failing to reveal whole report to the plaintiff, refusing to allow the plaintiff to bring a friend with her to review the report, and failing to reinvestigate disputed items).

follow reasonable procedures to maintain maximum possible accuracy.

Willfulness sometimes can be based on a company's general policy that directly violates the FCRA.[310] For example, in one case, willfulness was found where a user admitted that it would supply required disclosures only when the consumer requested them, while the FCRA required the disclosures to be made automatically without the consumer first having to request them.[311] Likewise, if the CRA "adopted its reinvestigation policy either knowing that policy to be in contravention of the rights possessed by consumers pursuant to the FCRA or in reckless disregard of whether the policy contravened those rights, [the consumer] may be awarded punitive damages."[312] A CRA's design of a system that fails to allow the CRA to comply with the FCRA's requirements may also show willfulness.[313]

Once a CRA is on notice of a problem, whether because of consumer complaints or otherwise, willfulness may be shown if it fails to address the problem.[314]

Willfulness can also be shown by a single instance of a CRA's flat out refusal to comply with an FCRA requirement. Thus a court has found willfulness where a CRA refused to reinvestigate an item upon the consumer's request.[315] The amount of acrimony displayed by the CRA or user may prove willfulness.[316]

Evidence of poor compliance procedures may also lead to a finding of willfulness. Thus, evidence that a defendant knew that its employee was not properly trained, and that it made a voluntary and conscious decision not to spend time or money on training or double checking its employee's work, supported an award of punitive damages.[317]

---

310 Evantash v. G.E. Capital Mortgage Serv., Inc., 2003 WL 22844198 (E.D. Pa. Nov. 25, 2003) (policy not to provide consumer's dispute documentation to furnisher; policy to report whatever information creditors provide); Sheffer v. Experian Info. Solutions, Inc., 2003 WL 21710573 (E.D. Pa. July 24, 2003) (same); Lawrence v. Trans Union, L.L.C., 296 F. Supp. 2d 582 (E.D. Pa. 2003) (same); Soghomonian v. U.S., 278 F. Supp. 2d 1151 (E.D. Cal. 2003), *vacated by agreement of the parties pursuant to settlement*, 2005 WL 1972594 (E.D. Cal. June 20, 2005).

311 Carroll v. Exxon Co., U.S.A., 434 F. Supp. 557 (N.D. La. 1977) (disclosure of name of CRA on basis of whose information credit is refused). *See* Cushman v. Trans Union Corp., 115 F.3d 220 (3d Cir. 1997) (in identity theft case, where CRA reinserted previously deleted information after verifying only that the cardholder's name, address and Social Security number matched those in its files, court held that if plaintiff could prove that the defendant adopted its reinvestigation policy either knowing it to be in contravention of consumer rights under the FCRA or in reckless disregard of whether it contravened those rights, she could be awarded punitive damages).

312 Cushman v. Trans Union Corp., 115 F.3d 220 (3d Cir. 1997). *See also* Reynolds v. Hartford Fin. Servs. Group, Inc., 435 F.3d 1081 (9th Cir. 2006), *cert. granted, sub nom.* GEICO Gen. Ins. v. Edo, ___ S. Ct. ___, 2006 WL 2055539 (Sept. 26, 2006) (reckless disregard is a basis for punitive damages under the FCRA); Graham v. CSC Credit Servs., Inc., 306 F. Supp. 2d 873 (D. Minn. 2004) (inability to track source of disputed address may warrant punitive damages); McKeown v. Sears Roebuck & Co., 335 F. Supp. 2d 917 (W.D. Wis. 2004) (same); McMillan v. Experian, 170 F. Supp. 2d 278 (D. Conn. 2001) (reasonable jury could conclude that a furnisher whose investigation consisted of nothing more than comparing plaintiff's name and Social Security number with the account holder's—whose address, telephone, date of birth, employment and work telephone were different—acted with reckless disregard for the truth or falsity of the information for the purpose of a defamation claim).

313 *See* Graham v. CSC Credit Servs., Inc., 306 F. Supp. 2d 873, 881 (D. Minn. 2004) (CRA's decision to design a system that failed to record the source of the address information it included in its consumer reports presented question of material fact on punitive damages claim); McKeown v. Sears Roebuck & Co., 335 F. Supp. 2d 917, 940–941 (W.D. Wis. 2004) (plaintiff raised issue of material fact on punitive damages claim where CRA designed system that failed to record the source of addresses and aliases).

314 Dalton v. Capital Assoc. Indus., 257 F.3d 409 (4th Cir. 2001) (prior similar consumer complaints, or knowledge of its subvendor's faulty procedures, could show CRA's willfulness, but not shown here); Comeaux v. Experian Info. Solutions, 2004 WL 1354412, at *10 (E.D. Tex. June 8, 2004) (in mixed file case, recommending that CRA's motion for summary judgment on plaintiff's claim for punitive damages should be denied, where plaintiff provided evidence that CRA had consciously and intentionally disregarded discrepancies and inaccuracies in the plaintiff's file, falsely informed the plaintiff that her Social Security number was not on file or attainable, and placed a fraud alert in her file without ascertaining whether the plaintiff was in fact a victim of fraud).

315 Collins v. Retail Credit Co., 410 F. Supp. 924 (E.D. Mich. 1976). *See also* Bryant v. TRW, Inc., 487 F. Supp. 1234 (E.D. Mich. 1980), *aff'd*, 689 F.2d 72 (6th Cir. 1982) (sufficient to send issue of willfulness to the jury).

316 Mirocha v. TRW, Inc., 805 F. Supp. 663 (S.D. Ind. 1992) (intent may be deduced from circumstances, including acrimonious dealings between the parties); Trans Union Corp. v. Crisp, 896 S.W.2d 446 (Ark. Ct. App. 1995) (failure to help consumer seeking information about inaccurate reports).

317 Adams v. Berger Chevrolet, Inc., 2001 U.S. Dist. LEXIS 16015 (W.D. Mich. Sept. 27, 2001) (proper considerations for punitive damage claims include the personnel file of the wrongdoing employee to show the dealer was on notice that employee was a convicted felon. It is 'important for the jury to understand now the corporate structure hired, supervised and facilitated [employee] to have a full appreciation of the degree to which the corporation acted reprehensibly." Likewise, evidence as to misappropriation of others' credit information is "highly relevant to the issue of punitive damages in that it relates directly to the extent of the wrongful conduct and to whether the Defendant had engaged in a pattern of wrongful conduct." Testimony that consumer reports and applications were stored in unsecured locations, including a cardboard box, is important to allow the jury to fully assess the blameworthiness of the whole of Defendant's relevant corporate conduct); Jones v. Credit Bureau of Huntington, Inc., 184 W. Va. 112, 399 S.E.2d 694 (1990). *See also* Dalton v. Capital Assoc. Indus., 257 F.3d 409 (4th Cir. 2001) (evidence that CRA knew of its subvendor's faulty procedures could show willfulness, but not shown here); Nitti v. Credit Bureau of Rochester, Inc., 84 Misc. 2d 277, 375 N.Y.S.2d 817 (Sup. Ct. 1975) (evidence that the defendant CRA authenticated only 2% of the more than 50,000 reports prepared each month, and that the defendant's system did not include independent verification of outstanding judgments or liens,

Willfulness also includes reckless disregard of whether a policy or practice violates FCRA rights.[318] Where headquarters drafted a manual advising staff about the notice to be given rejected employment applicants, but a senior official did not read the manual, a jury could find reckless disregard:

> Congress did not intend to enable mass-users of credit reports to evade meaningful liability [punitive damages] for repeated violations of their "grave responsibilities" under the FCRA by sticking their heads in the sand and pleading ignorance of the law.[319]

Finally, a CRA's callous disregard of a consumer's repeated attempts to fix an error can be found to be a willful violation of the FCRA.[320] One court, affirming a jury's award of punitive damages, described the defendant's behavior with exasperation likely familiar to suffering consumers:

> Time and time again the plaintiff came to the defendant's office and went over the same credit information with the defendant's employees, pointing out the errors, all to no purpose. . . . Like a character in Kafka, he was totally powerless to move or penetrate the implacable presence brooding, like some Stone Moloch, within the Castle.[321]

On the other hand, a continuing failure to correct a report is not always proof of willfulness where there is a reasonable basis for the CRA's continuing errors.[322] Similarly, mixing the files of two James Jones may involve only a negligent and not willful violation.[323]

11.12.1.3 No Need to Prove Actual Damages

Although proof of actual damages is essential for any recovery for negligent noncompliance,[324] it is not required for an award of statutory[325] or punitive damages in an instance of willful noncompliance with the Act.[326] The Supreme Court has endorsed this view, stating that punitive damages can be awarded when there is a willful violation, even if no actual damages have accrued.[327]

---

supported jury's award of punitive damages).

318 *See, e.g.,* Reynolds v. Hartford Fin. Servs. Group, Inc., 435 F.3d 1081 (9th Cir. 2006), *cert. granted, sub nom.* GEICO Gen. Ins. v. Edo, __ S. Ct. __, 2006 WL 2055539 (Sept. 26, 2006); Cushman v. Trans Union Corp., 115 F.3d 220 (3d Cir. 1997). *Contra* Phillips v. Grendahl, 312 F.3d 357, 370 (8th Cir. 2002); Duncan v. Handmaker, 149 F.3d 424, 429 (6th Cir. 1998).

319 Matthews v. Gov't Employees Ins. Co., 23 F. Supp. 2d 1160, 1164 (S.D. Cal. 1998). *See also* Richardson v. Fleet Bank, 190 F. Supp. 2d 81 (D. Mass. 2001) (reckless disregard would show willfulness, but not shown here).

320 White v. Imperial Adjustment Corp., 2002 WL 1809084 (E.D. La. Aug. 6, 2002) (willfulness may be shown by course of conduct that exhibits conscious disregard or deliberate and purposeful actions against plaintiff's rights); Thompson v. Equifax Credit Inf. Servs., 2001 U.S. Dist. LEXIS 22666 (M.D. Ala. Nov. 14, 2001), *motion for reconsideration denied*, 2001 U.S. Dist. LEXIS 22640 (Dec. 14, 2001) (issue of material fact as to willfulness in failing to accurately report despite being notified of falsity "more than a couple of times"; and in failing to include consumer's explanation of dispute); Whitesides v. Equifax Credit Info. Servs., 125 F. Supp. 2d 807 (W.D. La. 2000) (punitive damages may be available where consumer repeatedly informed CRA of errors yet it continued to report them). *See, e.g.,* Stevenson v. Employer's Mut. Ass'n, 960 F. Supp. 141 (N.D. Ill. 1987) (CRA's refusal to correct mix-up between plaintiff and convicted felon, even after faced with indisputable evidence, could be considered willful). *But cf.* Cousin v. Trans Union Corp., 246 F.3d 359 (5th Cir. 2001) (no willfulness despite CRA's repeated reinsertion of erroneous information; note strong dissent on this issue); Thomas v. Gulf Coast Credit Servs., 214 F. Supp. 2d 1228 (M.D. Ala. 2002) (insufficient evidence of conscious disregard); Field v. Trans Union, 2002 WL 849589 (N.D. Ill. May 3, 2002) (need for repeated requests to remove inaccurate information insufficient where no evidence of substantial delay by CRA); Parker v. Parker, 124 F. Supp. 2d 1216 (M.D. Ala. 2000) (no willfulness shown where all information disputed by plaintiff was deleted and did not reappear, even though a new inaccuracy appeared).

321 Nitti v. Credit Bureau of Rochester, Inc., 84 Misc. 2d 277, 375 N.Y.S.2d 817, 822 (Sup. Ct. 1975). *Accord* White v. Imperial Adjustment Corp., 2002 WL 1809084 (E.D. La. Aug. 6, 2002) (named plaintiff had sizeable statutory and punitive damages claims since her consumer report had been accessed no less than six times by insurance company).

322 Casella v. Equifax Credit Info. Servs., 56 F.3d 469, 486 (2d Cir. 1995); Stevenson v. TRW, Inc., 987 F.2d 288 (5th Cir. 1993); Pinner v. Schmidt, 805 F.2d 1258 (5th Cir. 1986), *aff'g in part and rev'g in part*, 617 F. Supp. 342 (E.D. La. 1985). *Cf.* Hoglan v. First Sec. Bank, 120 Idaho 682, 819 P.2d 100 (1991) (applying state standards to state tort law claims, the court overturned a punitive damage award because there was insufficient proof of any extreme deviation from reasonable conduct).

323 Jones v. Credit Bureau of Garden City, 703 F. Supp. 897 (D. Kan. 1988).

324 *See* § 11.10.2.1, *supra.*

325 *See* § 11.11, *supra.*

326 Northrop v. Hoffman, 12 Fed. Appx. 44, 2001 WL 682301 (2d Cir. June 14, 2001) (unpublished); Bakker v. McKinnon, 152 F.3d 1007 (8th Cir. 1998) (dicta); Casella v. Equifax Credit Info. Servs., 56 F.3d 469, 486 (2d Cir. 1995); Lodise v. Lodise, 9 F.3d 108 (6th Cir. 1993) ($1 nominal damages but $500 punitive damages); Yohay v. City of Alexandria Employees Credit Union, Inc., 827 F.2d 967 (4th Cir. 1987); Riley v. Equifax Credit Info. Servs., 194 F. Supp. 2d 1239 (S.D. Ala. 2002); Beechum v. Isgett, 2001 U.S. Dist. LEXIS 18688 (E.D.N.C. Sept. 24, 2001) (award of punitive damages may be made in an appropriate case even if no actual damages); Washington v. CSC Credit Serv., Inc., 178 F.R.D. 95 (E.D. La. 1998), *rev'd on other grounds*, 199 F.3d 263 (5th Cir. 2000); Matise v. Trans Union Corp., 1998 WL 872511 (N.D. Tex. Nov. 30, 1998); Russell v. Shelter Fin. Servs., 604 F. Supp. 201 (W.D. Mo. 1984) (no actual damages but awarded $1.00 nominal damages and left the amount of punitive damages to be settled by a jury); Boothe v. TRW Credit Data, 557 F. Supp. 66, 71 (S.D.N.Y. 1982) ($15,000 punitive damages granted where no actual damages alleged or proven); Ackerley v. Credit Bureau, 385 F. Supp. 658 (D. Wyo. 1974).

327 TRW, Inc. v. Andrews, 534 U.S. 19, 122 S. Ct. 441, 451, 151 L.

Case law as to whether actual damages are a prerequisite for punitive damages under a common law tort claim should not determine this issue for the FCRA, particularly since the general federal rule is not to require proof of actual damages. Moreover, the Act itself[328] does not make actual damages a prerequisite; the Act lists the defendant's liability for various potential monetary awards—actual or statutory damages, punitive damages, costs, and attorney fees. Actual damages is simply one of the several types of awards that might be granted.[329]

Some violations of the FCRA are in essence a form of invasion of privacy. As one court recognized, "[t]he mere issuance of the reports themselves under improper procedures constitutes an invasion of privacy if not under the common law, then at least as contemplated by the FCRA. In an era where information is instantly transmissible and easily shared, and where consumer reports can determine a person's access to a wide range of goods and services, having one's own credit history released into electronic circulation without reasonable procedures in place to ensure permissible use is cause for sufficient anxiety and invasion of privacy to constitute an injury-in-fact in and of itself."[330] The best example perhaps is the section prohibiting obtaining information under false pretenses.[331] Punitive damages for violations of this provision do not require that the victims suffer economic harm.[332]

11.12.2 Determining the Amount of Punitive Damages

11.12.2.1 No Fixed Upper Limit on Size of Award

The position that there is no fixed cap on punitive damages under the FCRA is supported by the legislative history, the text of the statute, and a comparison with other similar statutes. The original legislative proposals for a Fair Credit Reporting Act provided for actual damages, punitive damages of not less than $100 nor more than $1000, and attorney fees for any willful violation of the Act.[333] The limits on punitive damages were eliminated in response to arguments that, where a person's reputation or character may be maligned, punitive damages serve an extremely valuable prophylactic purpose.[334] Moreover, since 1996, damages of from $100 to $1000 have been available as statutory damages for willful violations, in lieu of actual damages,[335] but no similar limit was placed on the award of punitive damages.

The Equal Credit Opportunity Act,[336] for example, places caps on punitive damages in individual and in class actions. In contrast, the FCRA leaves punitive damages to the discretion of the courts. There is no firm limit to the size of punitive damages in either an individual or a class action.

Due process may, however, place a cap on the size of a particular award in an FCRA case, as in any other type of case. In *State Farm Mut. Auto. Ins. Co. v. Campbell*,[337] for example, an award of $145 million in punitive damages on a $1 million compensatory judgment was held to have violated due process. Each case is fact dependent, and ratios of punitive to compensatory damages in excess of the 145:1 ratio at issue in *State Farm* have been permitted in cases decided subsequent to it.[338]

11.12.2.2 Determining the Size of the Award

The cases do not establish clear standards for determining the appropriate amount of punitive damages.[339] Among the factors which might be considered in assessing punitive damages are: (1) the remedial purpose of the FCRA; (2) the consumer harm intended to be addressed by the Act; (3) the way the CRA conducted its business, including whether the CRA acted with malice; and (4) the CRA's income and net worth.[340] Punitive damages do not have to be directly proportional to actual damages, but, as noted in the preced-

---

Ed. 2d 339 (2001) (analyzing time when statute of limitations began to run).
328 15 U.S.C. § 1681n.
329 Ackerley v. Credit Bureau, 385 F. Supp. 658 (D. Wyo. 1974); Nitti v. Credit Bureau of Rochester, Inc., 84 Misc. 2d 277, 375 N.Y.S.2d 817 (Sup. Ct. 1975).
330 Matise v. Trans Union Corp., 1998 WL 872511 (N.D. Tex. Nov. 30, 1998).
331 See §§ 7.7, 10.2.5.1, supra.
332 United States v. Valenzeno, 123 F.3d 365 (6th Cir. 1997) (dissent).
333 See S. 823, 115 Cong. Rec. 2415 (1969).
334 See, e.g., Hearings on S. 823, Subcommittee on Financial Institutions of the Senate Banking and Currency Committee, 91st Cong., 1st Sess. 14 (1969) (testimony of Virginia Knauer, Special Assistant to the President).
335 See § 11.11, supra.
336 15 U.S.C. § 1691e(b). See National Consumer Law Center, Credit Discrimination § 11.7.4.3 (4th ed. 2005 and Supp.).
337 538 U.S. 408, 123 S. Ct. 1513, 155 L. Ed. 2d 585 (2003).
338 See, e.g., Kemp v. American Tel. & Tel. Co., 393 F.3d 1354 (11th. Cir. 2004) (reducing $1,000,000 in punitive damages to $250,000, but actual damages were just $115.05; thus ratio in excess of 2000:1 allowed).
339 See, e.g., Bach v. First Union National Bank, 149 Fed. Appx. 354, 361 (6th Cir. 2005) (unpublished) (reversing as excessive jury award to seventy-seven year old widow of $2,628,600 in punitive damages for willful violation of FCRA); Yohay v. City of Alexandria Employees Credit Union, 827 F.2d 967 (4th Cir. 1987) (punitive damages could be based on willful violation of "false pretenses" provision); Zamora v. Valley Fed. Sav. & Loan Ass'n, 811 F.2d 1368 (10th Cir. 1987) (award of $61,500 not excessive for willful violation, although jury verdict did not separately list actual and punitive damages).
340 See, e.g., Thornton v. Equifax, 467 F. Supp. 1008 (E.D. Ark. 1979), rev'd on other grounds, 619 F.2d 700 (8th Cir. 1980); Collins v. Retail Credit Co., 410 F. Supp. 924 (E.D. Mich. 1976); Jones v. Credit Bureau of Huntington, Inc., 399 S.E.2d 694 (W. Va. 1990) (citing Nitti v. Credit Bureau of Rochester, Inc., 89 Misc. 2d 277, 375 N.Y.S.2d 817, 821 (Sup. Ct. 1975)).

ing subsection of this manual, due process may be violated by excessive disproportionality.

Other factors a court may review in determining whether the jury's award is excessive include: (1) the degree of reprehensibility of the defendant's conduct, such as whether it was part of a larger pattern of misconduct; (2) the relationship between the punitive damages and the harm suffered; and (3) the existence of sanctions, such as criminal penalties for similar misconduct.[341]

In a case decided prior to *State Farm Mut. Auto. Ins. Co. v. Campbell*,[342] a jury award of $250,000 in punitive damages against a CRA was upheld.[343] The court rejected the defendant's argument that there was a huge discrepancy between the punitive damage award and the much smaller actual damage award.[344] "[T]he exemplary damage statute is addressed to restraining the malefactor. Thus the Plaintiff is only an accidental beneficiary of the jury's decision as to the amount necessary to impose an adequate restraint on the malefactor."[345] In that case, the trial court upheld the plaintiff's submission of evidence of the defendant's worth: profit-and-loss statements extracted from brochures published by the defendant that showed that $300,000 amounted to the company's profits for two hours of operation.

Another federal court (while later reversed on substantive grounds) upheld a $100,000 jury award of punitive damages because a lesser amount would not affect the CRA's future conduct.[346] In another case, the jury awarded the consumer $300,000 in punitive damages. The federal judge noted that the record established willful and reckless wrongdoing and found the jury's decision was not the result of "passion and prejudice." However, the court held the award to be excessive and reduced it to $50,000.[347] The standard announced by that court is vague: the amount of punitive damages must be "reasonable" in light of "the deterrent purpose to be achieved, as well as the corporate defendant's reckless indifference to the plaintiff's rights."[348]

Serious deficiencies in the defendant's initial procedures to ensure accuracy may also warrant punitive damages. Thus, in one case, even though an erroneous report was corrected a week later, the court upheld a jury verdict of $42,500 in punitive damages based on multiple factors substantiating the willfulness and dereliction of the CRA: the CRA's decision not to spend time or money training the employee who prepared the erroneous report or double-checking her work; the employee's failure to read the entire source document; the high evaluation of the employee by a supervisor who never checked her work; and the possibility that users will not see corrections.[349]

11.12.3 Punitive Damages: Decided by Judge or Jury?

Although the FCRA does not address whether consumers have a right to a jury trial, numerous FCRA cases have gone to juries and punitive damages have been awarded for willful violations of the Act.[350] Similarly, courts deciding non-FCRA cases have held that the issue of punitive damage awards historically has been a matter for determination by a jury.[351]

Defendants may contend that the judge must determine the size of punitive damages because the FCRA states that the CRA or user is liable for "such amount of punitive damages as the court may allow."[352] Courts have rejected this reasoning, finding that the phrase "as the court may allow" means only that the court had a duty to review excessive verdicts and to eliminate any elements of emotion and prejudice reflected in the verdict.[353] However, when a court determines that no reasonable jury could find the

---

341 Adams v. Phillips, 2002 WL 31886737 (E.D. La. Dec. 19, 2002).
342 538 U.S. 408, 123 S. Ct. 1513, 155 L. Ed. 2d 585 (2003). See § 11.12.2.1, *supra*.
343 Thornton v. Equifax, 467 F. Supp. 1008 (E.D. Ark. 1979), *rev'd on other grounds*, 619 F.2d 700 (8th Cir. 1980). The court of appeals reversed because of faulty jury instructions and did not discuss the size of the monetary award.
344 *Id.*
345 *Id.* at 1012.
346 Pinner v. Schmidt, 617 F. Supp. 342 (E.D. La. 1985), *aff'd in part, rev'd in part*, 805 F.2d 1258 (5th Cir. 1986).
347 Collins v. Retail Credit Co., 410 F. Supp. 924 (E.D. Mich. 1976). *See also* Northrop v. Hoffman of Simsbury, Inc., 2000 WL 436612 (D. Conn. Mar. 15, 2000) (reducing jury's punitive damages awards from $300,000 to $75,000 against one defendant and $50,000 against another where consumer report was wrongfully disclosed to only one person and there were no actual damages), *aff'd in part, rev'd in part*, 12 Fed. Appx. 44, 2001 WL 682301 (2d Cir. June 14, 2001) (unpublished) (affirming trial court's exercise of discretion in reducing punitive damage award, but remanding for trial court to offer plaintiff the option of a new trial).
348 Collins v. Retail Credit Co., 410 F. Supp. 924 (E.D. Mich. 1976).
349 Jones v. Credit Bureau of Huntington, Inc., 399 S.E.2d 694 (W. Va. 1990).
350 *See* §§ 11.7, *supra*, 11.15, *infra*.
351 *See, e.g.,* Hartford Fire Ins. Co. v. First Nat'l Bank of Atmore, 198 F. Supp. 2d 1308 (S.D. Ala. 2002) (insured had right to jury trial as to amount of punitive damages on its claim against insurer for bad faith); Todd v. Roadway Express Inc., 178 F. Supp. 2d 1244 (M.D. Ala. 2001) (it is the function of the jury to determine the amount of punitive damages once it has determined that an award of punitive damages is proper and the role of the court, whether trial or appellate, to determine whether the jury has set an amount which is constitutionally excessive). *See* § 11.7, *supra*. In federal court, all damage issues, including punitive damages, are to be decided by the jury. Feltner v. Columbia Pictures Television, Inc., 523 U.S. 340, 348, 118 S. Ct. 1279, 140 L. Ed. 2d 438 (1998); Kobs v. Arrow Serv. Bureau, Inc., 134 F.3d 893 (7th Cir. 1998); Kampa v. White Consol. Inc., 115 F.3d 585, 586 (8th Cir. 1997); McGuire v. Russell Miller, Inc., 1 F.3d 1306 (2d Cir. 1993).
352 15 U.S.C. § 1681n(a)(2).
353 Northrup v. Hoffman, 2001 WL 682301 (2d Cir. June 14, 2001); Barron v. Trans Union Corp., 82 F. Supp. 2d 1288 (M.D. Ala.

defendant's actions to be willful, it may enter summary judgment for defendant on the claims for punitive damages.[354]

Under the Federal Rules of Civil Procedure, any party may make a timely demand for a jury trial of any issue triable of right by a jury by timely serving upon the other parties a demand in writing. Failure so to do so constitutes a waiver of the right.[355]

11.13 Injunctive and Declaratory Relief

With one exception that does not aid consumers, the FCRA does not explicitly provide for injunctive relief in a private action.[356] Enforcement agencies, such as the FTC, can seek such relief,[357] and the FCRA explicitly acknowledges the FTC's right to seek an injunction in its administrative enforcement provision.[358] This explicit grant of authority to the FTC, when contrasted with the absence of such an explicit grant to consumers, has lead some courts to hold that consumers may not obtain injunctive or declaratory relief under the FCRA. Others, however, have held that their inherent equitable powers may permit them to enjoin conduct that violates the FCRA.

District courts have inherent power to issue equitable relief, and while Congress may limit that power with respect to a particular statute, the Supreme Court has made clear that such limits are *not* assumed. *Califano v. Yamasaki*[359] provides that "[a]bsent the clearest command to the contrary from Congress, federal courts retain their equitable power to issue injunctions in suits over which they have jurisdiction."[360] Accordingly, courts presumptively can enjoin conduct that violates a statute, and the presumption cannot be overturned without convincing evidence that Congress intended to deprive the court of its traditional equity powers when adjudicating rights and liabilities under a particular statute.

Under *Yamasaki*, a district court can enjoin a consumer reporting agency (CRA) from violating the FCRA unless some text within the statute or legislative history demonstrates a "clear command" from Congress to disable that power. Decisions on the issue have been uneven. In one of the few opinions favorable to consumers on this subject, a California federal district court applied the *Yamasaki* standard and held that "[t]he FCRA contains no 'clear command' that injunctive relief is unavailable; consequently, it is available."[361] Beyond finding no such command, the court further reasoned that equity powers were justified to further the FCRA's goals of protecting consumers from the transmission of inaccurate information and of establishing credit reporting practices that use accurate information.[362] The court then issued an injunction requiring TransUnion to remove an inaccurate credit item from the plaintiff's file—precisely the sort of order that fulfills the FCRA's goals in a way that a pure damages award might not.

Although the availability of injunctive relief was not specifically made an issue in the case, it is noteworthy that the Ninth Circuit affirmed an FCRA case awarding injunctive relief, adopting the careful reasoning of the district court judge.[363] A subsequent Seventh Circuit opinion also suggests that FCRA plaintiffs can seek injunctive relief.[364]

On the other hand, numerous district court decisions have held that courts do not have the power to issue an injunction in FCRA cases because doing so could undermine the FTC's discretion to seek equitable relief.[365] Some of these cases, however, lack precedential value because they neither cite to *Yamasaki* nor apply its stringent test for divesting a court of its equitable powers.[366] These cases did not start their

---

2000) (issue of fact for jury); Russell v. Shelter Fin. Serv., 604 F. Supp. 201 (W.D. Mo. 1984); Collins v. Retail Credit Co., 410 F. Supp. 924 (D. Mich. 1976) (court found congressional history inconclusive on this point).

354 Castro v. Union Nissan, 2002 WL 1466810 (N.D. Ill. July 8, 2002); Gill v. Kostroff, 2000 U.S. Dist. LEXIS 1161 (M.D. Fla. Feb. 8, 2000); Natale v. TRW, Inc., 1999 WL 179678 (N.D. Cal. Mar. 30, 1999); O'Connor v. Trans Union Corp., 1999 U.S. Dist. LEXIS 14917 (E.D. Pa. Sept. 28, 1999).

355 Fed. R. Civ. P. 38; Fed. R. Civ. P. 39.

356 The FCRA authorizes injunctive relief for the purpose of enforcing the section on FBI access to information for counterintelligence reasons. 15 U.S.C. § 1681u(m). See § 7.2.10.4, *supra*. The FCRA's liability provisions, §§ 1681n (willful noncompliance) and 1681o (negligent noncompliance) refer to liability for "any actual damages sustained by the consumer," along with fees and costs; the willful noncompliance subsection also provides for statutory damages of $100 to $1000 and punitive damages. See §§ 11.10–11.12, *supra*.

357 See §§ 11.16.1–11.16.2, *infra*.

358 15 U.S.C. § 1681s.

359 442 U.S. 682, 99 S. Ct. 2545, 61 L. Ed. 2d 176 (1979).

360 *Id.* at 705.

361 Andrews v. Trans Union Corp., 7 F. Supp. 2d 1056, 1084 (C.D. Cal. 1998), *rev'd on other grounds sub nom.* Andrews v. TRW, Inc., 225 F.3d 1063 (9th Cir. 2000), *rev'd*, 534 U.S. 19, 122 S. Ct. 441, 151 L. Ed. 2d 339 (2001) (statute of limitations issues) (criticized, Yeagley v. Wells Fargo & Co., 2006 WL 193257 (N.D. Cal. Jan. 23, 2006) and Howard v. Blue Ridge Bank, 371 F. Supp. 2d 1139 (N.D. Cal. 2005)).

362 *Id.*

363 Greenway v. Info. Dynamics, Ltd., 399 F. Supp. 1092 (D. Ariz. 1974), *aff'd per curiam*, 524 F.2d 1145 (9th Cir. 1975). *See also* Wenger v. Trans Union Corp., 1995 U.S. Dist. LEXIS 22214 (C.D. Cal. Nov. 14, 1995).

364 Crabill v. Trans Union, L.L.C., 259 F.3d 662, 664 (7th Cir. 2001).

365 *See, e.g.*, Yeagley v. Wells Fargo & Co., 2006 WL 193257 (N.D. Cal. Jan. 23, 2006); Owner-Operator Indep. Driver Ass'n v. USIS Comm. Servs., Inc., 410 F. Supp. 2d 1005 (D. Colo. 2005); Howard v. Blue Ridge Bank, 371 F. Supp. 2d 1139 (N.D. Cal. 2005); Thompson v. Homecomings Fin. Network, 2005 WL 3534234 (N.D. Tex. Dec. 19, 2005); *In re* Trans Union Corp. Privacy Litig., 211 F.R.D. 328 (N.D. Ill. 2002); Bumgardner v. Lite Cellular, Inc., 996 F. Supp. 525 (E.D. Va. 1998) (refusing to enjoin consumer report user).

366 Bittick v. Experian Info. Solutions, Inc., 419 F. Supp. 2d 917 (N.

analysis from the point that courts retain their inherent authority to issue an injunction until convincingly proved otherwise.

Some of these decisions, along with one Fifth Circuit court of appeals decision,[367] mention *Yamasaki* but fail to appropriately apply its rule by giving the weight to the presumption of equity powers that *Yamasaki* prescribes. These decisions reasoned that by expressly providing for the FTC to seek injunctive relief, Congress adequately conveyed its intent to deprive courts of such a remedy in cases of individual litigants.[368] However, other cases that have applied *Yamasaki* to other statutes have not found that Congress' express acknowledgment of an enforcement agency's right to seek an injunction equaled a "clear command" to curtail the court's powers to do equity for other parties. For example, the Eleventh Circuit and Third Circuits have ruled that a statute's express provision of equitable remedies for the Secretary of Agriculture did not deprive a private litigant of those same remedies.[369] To meet *Yamasaki*'s test, said the court, it must be shown that "the statute or its legislative history clearly states that Congress intended to preclude such relief to private parties;"[370] silence does not suffice. Other courts have similarly ruled that courts retain the authority to enjoin notwithstanding that a statute omits mention of the remedy, but not all these cases involve statutory schemes granting enforcement powers to a federal agency.[371]

There is no reason to believe that the FTC would be thwarted in its attempts to force CRAs to comply with the FCRA if courts retained their inherent powers to issue injunctions in appropriate private actions. Rather, the goal of the FCRA to "assure maximum possible accuracy" of consumer reports[372] would be furthered by allowing courts to order CRAs to delete inaccurate information from their files and to cease issuing inaccurate reports. Injunctive relief is particularly important since many FCRA violations cause injuries to privacy or reputation that a damage award cannot undo. Judicial efficiency would also be served; if injunctive relief is unavailable, a consumer may be forced to file repeated actual damage actions. Furthermore, injunctions would provide relief to consumers who had not yet actually suffered an injury from a denial of credit or other actual damages by reason of an inaccurate report, but who still had wrong credit information associated with their names. Injunctive relief would enable these consumers to prevent actual damage from occurring, rather than having to suffer damage and only then seek relief.

Aside from the FCRA, state credit reporting statutes[373] and state deceptive practices statutes[374] sometimes explicitly authorize injunctive relief. The courts are divided as to whether the FCRA preempts such state statutes and common law bases for injunctive relief.[375]

Consumers who may not have suffered damages that would be recoverable under the FCRA should also consider a declaratory judgment action under the Declaratory Judgment Act (DJA).[376] Few such actions have been filed under

---

D. Tex. 2006); Jones v. Sonic Auto., Inc., 391 F. Supp. 2d 1064 (M.D. Ala. 2005); White v. First Am. Registry, Inc., 378 F. Supp. 2d 419 (S.D.N.Y. 2005); Lin v. Universal Card Servs. Corp., 238 F. Supp. 2d 1147, 1152 (N.D. Cal. 2002); Ditty v. Checkrite Ltd., Inc., 973 F. Supp. 1320 (D. Utah 1999); Mangio v. Equifax, Inc., 887 F. Supp. 283 (S.D. Fla. 1995); Kekich v. Travelers Indemnity Co., 64 F.R.D. 660 (W.D. Pa. 1974).

367 Washington v. CSC Credit Servs., 199 F.3d 263 (5th Cir.).

368 *Id.* at 268; *In re* Trans Union Corp. Privacy Litig., 211 F.R.D. 328, 339, 340 (N.D. Ill. 2002); Bumgardner v. Lite Cellular, Inc., 996 F. Supp. 525, 527 (E.D. Va. 1998).

369 Frio Ice, S.A. v. Sunfruit, Inc., 918 F.2d 154, 157 (11th Cir. 1990) (Perishable Agriculture Commodities Act); Tanimura & Antle, Inc. v. Packed Fresh Produce, Inc., 222 F.3d 132, 138 (3d Cir. 2000) (also under Perishable Agriculture Commodities Act).

370 Tanimura & Antle, Inc. v. Packed Fresh Produce, Inc., 222 F.3d 132, 138 (3d Cir. 2000) (also under Perishable Agriculture Commodities Act); Frio Ice, S.A. v. Sunfruit, Inc., 918 F.2d 154, 157 (11th Cir. 1990) (Perishable Agriculture Commodities Act).

371 *See, e.g.,* U.S. v. Princeton Gamma-Tech, Inc., 31 F.3d 138, 147, 148 (3d Cir. 1994) (injunctive relief available under CERCLA); Alabama-Tombigbee Rivers Coalition v. Department of Interior, 26 F.3d 1103, 1107 (11th Cir. 1994) (injunctive relief available under Federal Advisory Committee Act); Sierra Club, Lone Star Chapter v. F.D.I.C., 992 F.2d 545, 549 (5th Cir. 1993) (FDIC could be enjoined in its corporate capacity, rejecting argument that statutory limit on injunctions that applied to FDIC acting in its receiver capacity carried over); T & E Industries, Inc. v. Safety Light Corp., 680 F. Supp. 696, 705 (D.N.J. 1988) (CERCLA). *But see* Wheeling-Pittsburgh Steel Corp. v. Mitsui & Co., 221 F.3d 924, 928 (6th Cir. 2000) (injunctive relief not available under anti-dumping statute; could conflict with presidential power over foreign affairs); Religious Tech. Ctr. v. Wollersheim, 796 F.2d 1076, 1082 (9th Cir. 1986) (no injunctive relief under civil RICO; notes that Congress rejected versions of the act that would have expressly allowed it); Utah State Dep't of Health v. Ng, 649 F. Supp. 1102 (D. Utah 1986) (no injunctive relief under CERCLA; little analysis).

372 15 U.S.C. § 1681e.

373 *See* Appx. H, *infra*. *See, e.g.,* Cal. Civ. Code § 1785.31 (West).

374 National Consumer Law Center, Unfair and Deceptive Acts and Practices, Appx. A (6th ed. 2004 and Supp.). *See, e.g.,* Mass. Gen. Laws ch. 93A, § 4.

375 *Compare* Albert v. Trans Union Corp., 346 F.3d 734, 739–740 (7th Cir. 2003) (in dicta, noting that even though district court denied injunctive relief under FCRA, essentially same relief is available under state law) *and* White v. First Am. Registry, Inc., 378 F. Supp. 2d 419, 424–425 (S.D.N.Y. 2005) (also finding injunctive and declaratory relief unavailable under FCRA, but overruling motion to dismiss claim against CRA for injunctive relief under New York statute) *with* Jarrett v. Bank of America, 421 F. Supp. 2d 1350 (D. Kan. 2006) (an injunction would "essentially subject[] the credit reporting agency defendants to strict liability for inaccuracies that appear on plaintiff's future credit reports"); Bittick v. Experian Info. Solutions, Inc., 419 F. Supp. 2d 917 (N. D. Tex. 2006); Lin v. Universal Card Servs. Corp., 238 F. Supp. 2d 1147, 1152(N.D. Cal. 2002).

376 28 U.S.C. §§ 2201, 2202. The Act provides: "In a case of actual controversy within its jurisdiction . . . any court of the United States, upon the filing of an appropriate pleading, may declare the rights and other legal relations of any interested party

the FCRA, and the decisions are split. One court held that it had jurisdiction to hear a suit for relief under the DJA in a case alleging that the defendant had violated the FCRA by obtaining the plaintiffs' consumer reports in connection with the investigation of their insurance claims.[377] However, other courts have held that an FCRA plaintiff should not be able to use the DJA to supplement a claim for damages.[378] Such an action would not serve the purposes of the DJA, which one court characterized as "to avoid accrual of avoidable damages to one not certain of his rights and to afford him early adjudication without waiting until his adversary should see fit to begin suit, after damage has accrued."[379] Here, the court viewed the damages remedy as more complete than a declaratory judgment, and given that damages were available it chose not to exercise jurisdiction under the DJA. Nonetheless, a court with a less restrictive view of the appropriate role of the DJA may permit a plaintiff to use it to establish that particular conduct violates the FCRA, regardless of damages. And while a court may be unwilling to grant injunctive relief due to concerns about interfering with the FTC's discretionary enforcement powers, no such concern should apply to issuing a declaratory judgment.

11.14 Attorney Fees and Costs

11.14.1 When Are Fees and Costs Awarded?

The FCRA provides that a prevailing consumer is entitled to recover from the defendant the costs of the action as well as reasonable attorney fees as determined by the court.[380] When applying for fees, the consumer's attorney must be mindful of the fourteen-day time limitation found in Federal Rule of Civil Procedure 54(d)(2)(B), the Rule's format requirements, and any applicable local rules.[381]

Although an FCRA case has yet to rule squarely on the point, it is clear that an award of attorney fees to a successful plaintiff is mandatory.[382] The statute provides that a consumer reporting agency (CRA) or user "is" liable for reasonable fees. The Truth in Lending Act[383] uses identical language and the United States Supreme Court has cited that language as an example of mandatory fees.[384] Other courts have also found the Truth in Lending Act to require an award of attorney fees in a successful action.[385] The same is the case with the federal Fair Debt Collection Practices Act, which has identical attorney fee language as the FCRA.[386]

As with any fee shifting statute, issues will arise as to what is a "successful action" and to what extent an attorney's time on the case is related to it. Two circuit courts have held that a consumer has not brought a "successful" action and is not entitled to any fee award where there was proof of liability but no award of money damages (or possibly some other relief such as an injunction).[387] Also, fees may not be available for attorneys litigating *pro se*.[388]

There is little FCRA case law evaluating whether particular aspects of the attorney's work is related to the success and therefore compensable. In one case, an award was allowed for litigation to recover previously-awarded fees under the FCRA.[389] Decisions under other fee shifting statutes should be instructive on this general subject. For example, and most closely related, there is more extensive case law under other titles of the Consumer Credit Protec-

---

seeking such declaration, whether or not further relief is or could be sought. Any such declaration shall have the force and effect of a final judgment or decree and shall be reviewable as such." 28 U.S.C. § 2201(a).

377 Malbrough v. State Farm Fire & Cas. Co., 1996 WL 517702 (E.D. La. Sept. 11, 1996).

378 Anderson v. Capital One Bank, 224 F.R.D. 444, 449 (W.D. Wis. 2004); *In re* Trans Union Corp. Privacy Litig., 211 F.R.D. 328, 340 (N.D. Ill. 2002) (wrongful sale of target marketing lists).

379 *In re* Trans Union Corp. Privacy Litig., 211 F.R.D. 328, 340 (N.D. Ill. 2002).

380 15 U.S.C. §§ 1681n(a)(3), 1681o(a)(2); Sheffer v. Experian Info. Solutions, 290 F. Supp. 2d 538 (E.D. Pa. 2003).

381 *See* Bruce v. Cascade Collections, Inc., 110 P.2d 587 (Or. Ct. App. 2005) (discussing requirements of state rules of procedure with respect to attorney fees to be awarded under the FCRA).

382 Lodise v. Lodise, 9 F.3d 108 (6th Cir. 1993) comes very close to finding fees to be mandatory.

383 15 U.S.C. § 1640.

384 Christiansburg Garment Co. v. EEOC, 434 U.S. 412, 415, n.5, 98 S. Ct. 694, 54 L. Ed. 2d 648 (1978); Alyeska Pipeline Serv. Co. v. Wilderness Soc'y, 421 U.S. 240, 261, n.34, 95 S. Ct. 1612, 44 L. Ed. 2d 141 (1975) ("statutes which are mandatory in terms of awarding attorney's fees include . . . the Truth in Lending Act, 15 U.S.C § 1640(a). . . ."). *See also* Pub. L. No. 90-321, § 503(4) ("Rules of law [in the Consumer Credit Protection Act] are stated in the indicative mood"). This uncodified provision of the Consumer Credit Protection Act is printed as a note following 15 U.S.C. § 1601 in West's U.S. Code Annotated.

385 DeJesus v. Banco Popular de Puerto Rico, 918 F.2d 232 (1st Cir. 1990) and other cases cited at National Consumer Law Center, Truth in Lending § 8.9.2.1 (5th ed. 2003 and Supp.).

386 *See, e.g.,* Tolentino v. Friedman, 46 F.3d 645, 651 (7th Cir. 1995). *See generally* National Consumer Law Center, Fair Debt Collection § 6.8.1 (5th 2004 and Supp.).

387 Nagle v. Experian Info. Solutions, Inc., 297 F.3d 1305 (11th Cir. 2002) (jury found negligent violation, but no damages of any kind); Crabill v. Trans Union, 259 F.3d 662 (7th Cir. 2001). *Accord* Bumgardner v. Lite Cellular, Inc., 996 F. Supp. 525 (E.D. Va. 1998) (jury verdict finding liability but awarding no damages is not successful action, so plaintiff cannot recover fees). FDCPA cases to the contrary include Zagorski v. Midwest Billing Servs., Inc., 128 F.3d 1164 (7th Cir. 1997); Pipiles v. Credit Bureau of Lockport, 886 F.2d 22 (2d Cir. 1989); Emanuel v. American Credit Exch., 870 F.2d 805 (2d Cir. 1989).

388 Menton v. Experian Corp., 2003 WL 21692820 (S.D.N.Y. July 21, 2003); Hawthorne v. Citicorp Data Sys., 216 F. Supp. 2d 45 (E.D.N.Y. 2002), *vacated on other grounds*, 219 F.R.D. 47 (E.D.N.Y. 2003).

389 Mares v. Credit Bureau, 801 F.2d 1197 (10th Cir. 1986).

tion Act interpreting identical statutory language as to when attorney time is related to a successful action. The two most analogous titles are the federal Truth in Lending and Fair Debt Collection Practices Acts. Decisions under these titles are detailed in other NCLC manuals.[390]

The FCRA as originally enacted provided no attorney fees for a prevailing FCRA *defendant*. The law was amended by the 1996 Reform Act to provide that, upon a finding by a court that an unsuccessful pleading, motion, or other paper was filed in bad faith or for purposes of harassment, the prevailing party may recover attorney fees reasonable in relation to the work expended in responding to the pleading, motion, or other paper.[391] This provision applies to plaintiffs and defendants alike.[392] The section allows recovery of attorney fees only against the party, not against the party's attorney.[393] Under some state statutes, a prevailing CRA may be entitled to attorney fees.[394] Similarly, as in any other federal court case, the court has discretion to award costs to a prevailing defendant.[395]

11.14.2 Calculating the Size of the Attorney Fee Award

11.14.2.1 FCRA Awards Will Be Based on Standards Enunciated in Other Federal Fee-Shifting Statutes

The United States Supreme Court has stated that the standards used for the Civil Rights Attorney's Fees Awards Act are generally applicable in all cases in which Congress has authorized an award of attorney fees for a prevailing party.[396] Therefore, a single body of law has developed under all the federal fee-shifting statutes as to how to calculate a reasonable attorney fee award. Attorney fee awards in FCRA cases thus will be calculated using the same standards as civil rights, Truth in Lending, antitrust, RICO, and other federal fee-shifting statutes.[397] The standards for all such cases, established by the Supreme Court as further developed by the particular circuit at any given point in time, will control.[398]

FCRA cases have followed the Supreme Court's guidance that because fee-shifting statutes are meant to encourage private attorney general enforcement of their provisions, the fee award need not be proportional to the damage award.[399] That a CRA or user chooses to litigate a relatively small matter aggressively, and this results in a fee many times the actual damages awarded, is no justification to lower the attorney fee award. Defendants must bear the consequences of their own conduct.[400] As the United States Supreme Court has said about a government defendant,

---

390 National Consumer Law Center, Truth in Lending § 8.9.2 (5th ed. 2003 and Supp.); National Consumer Law Center, Fair Debt Collection § 6.8 (5th 2004 and Supp.).

391 15 U.S.C. §§ 1681n(c), 1681o(b), *as amended by* Pub. L. No. 104-208 § 2412 (Sept. 30, 1996). *See* River Oaks Homeowners Prot. Comm. v. Edington & Assocs., 32 Fed. Appx. 929 (9th Cir. 2002) (unpublished) (vacating fee award that court entered against plaintiff after dismissing complaint, since plaintiff should have been given leave to amend complaint, and defendant presented no evidence of bad faith); Battley v. City Fin. Corp., 2002 WL 1379204 (M.D. La. June 18, 2002) (defendant's failure to respond to pre-litigation inquiry shows plaintiff acted in good faith); Edge v. Professional Claims Bureau, Inc., 64 F. Supp. 2d 115 (E.D.N.Y. 1999) (declining to award fees merely because defendant prevailed), *aff'd without op.*, 234 F.3d 1261 (2d Cir. 2000).

392 S. Rep. No. 185, 104th Cong., 1st Sess. 49 (Dec. 14, 1995); Morgovsky v. Creditor Collection Serv., 166 F.3d 343 (9th Cir. 1998) (unpublished) (award of attorney fees against *pro se* plaintiffs who brought and pursued FCRA litigation in bad faith, including a prior unreported appeal (19 F.3d 28 (1994))).

393 Ryan v. Trans Union Corp., 2001 U.S. Dist. LEXIS 1239 (N.D. Ill. Feb. 8, 2001).

394 *E.g.*, Cal. Civ. Code § 1785.31 (West). *See* Guimond v. Trans Union Credit Info. Co., 45 F.3d 1329 (9th Cir. 1995) (notes chilling effect upon consumers).

395 Waggoner v. Trans Union, L.L.C., 2003 WL 22838718 (N.D. Tex. Nov. 24, 2003) (awarding $6000 in costs to Trans Union; citing 28 U.S.C. § 1920). As discussed above, the FCRA itself provides for an award of costs to a prevailing plaintiff.

396 *See* Hensley v. Eckerhart, 461 U.S. 424, 103 S. Ct. 1933, 76 L. Ed. 2d 40 (1983). *See also* DeJesus v. Banco Popular de Puerto Rico, 918 F.2d 232 (1st Cir. 1990).

397 City of Burlington v. Dague, 505 U.S. 557, 562, 112 S. Ct. 2638, 120 L. Ed. 2d 449 (1992) ("[O]ur case law construing what is a 'reasonable' fee applies uniformly to all" fee shifting statutes.).

398 Sheffer v. Experian Info. Solutions, Inc., 290 F. Supp. 2d 538 (E.D. Pa. 2003); Jones v. Credit Bureau of Greater Garden City, 1989 WL 134945 (D. Kan. Oct. 24, 1989) (FCRA case, followed standards announced in Pennsylvania v. Delaware Valley Citizens Council, 478 U.S. 546, 566–567 (1986)). The standards in Johnson v. Georgia Highway Express, 488 F.2d 714 (5th Cir. 1974) were applied to an FCRA award in Thompson v. San Antonio Retail Merchants Ass'n, 682 F.2d 509 (5th Cir. 1982). The Sixth Circuit standards set out in Northcross v. Board of Educ., 611 F.2d 624 (6th Cir. 1969) were applied to an FCRA case in Bryant v. TRW, Inc., 689 F.2d 72 (6th Cir. 1982). Houghton v. New Jersey Mfgrs. Ins. Co., 615 F. Supp. 299 (E.D. Pa. 1985), *rev'd on other grounds*, 795 F.2d 1144 (3d Cir. 1986) applied Lindy Bros. Builders, Inc. v. American Radiator & Standard Sanitary Corp., 487 F.2d 161 (3d Cir. 1973), *refined*, 540 F.2d 102 (3d Cir. 1976) (en banc).

399 Yohay v. Alexandria Employees' Credit Union, 827 F.2d 967 (4th Cir. 1987) (proportionality would discourage vigorous enforcement of the Act); Northrup v. Hoffman of Simsbury, Inc., 2000 WL 436612 (D. Conn. Mar. 15, 2000), *aff'd in relevant part, vacated in part on other grounds*, 12 Fed. Appx. 44, 2001 WL 682301 (2d Cir. June 14, 2001) (unpublished); Hall v. Harleysville Ins. Co., 943 F. Supp. 536 (E.D. Pa. 1996) ($88,000 fee award on $115,000 application); Jones v. Credit Bureau of Greater Garden City, 1989 WL 134945 (D. Kan. Oct. 24, 1989) (citing City of Riverside v. Rivera, 477 U.S. 561, 575–579, 106 S. Ct. 2686, 91 L. Ed. 2d 466 (1986)). *See also* Bryant v. TRW, Inc., 689 F.2d 72 (6th Cir. 1982) (FCRA case rejecting notion that fees are contingent on size of award and upholding fee awarded greater than the amount of damages).

400 *E.g.*, Fleet Inv. Co. v. Rogers, 620 F.2d 792 (10th Cir. 1980); Postow v. Oriental Bldg. Ass'n, 455 F. Supp. 781 (D.D.C. 1978).

... petitioners could have avoided liability for the bulk of the attorney's fees for which they now find themselves liable by making a reasonable settlement offer in a timely manner.... "The government cannot litigate tenaciously and then be heard to complain about the time necessarily spent by the plaintiff in response."[401]

11.14.2.2 Current Federal Fee-Shifting Standards

This section is not a comprehensive guide to the latest precedent as to how to compute attorney fee awards pursuant to a federal fee-shifting statute. Two other NCLC manuals offer more detail, and are especially relevant because they interpret virtually identical attorney fee language in two more frequently utilized sister titles in the federal Consumer Credit Protection Act—the Truth in Lending and Fair Debt Collection Practices Acts.[402]

Generally, courts adopt a lodestar approach, where the time reasonably expended is multiplied by the average rate for an attorney of that experience and skill in that locality. The hourly rate is not reduced because the attorney is a legal services or other attorney who handles the case for no charge.[403]

Attorney fees are central to the FCRA's enforcement, which chiefly relies on consumers to act as private attorneys general. As a court has said concerning another federal consumer statute, "The value of an attorney's services is not only measured by the amount of the recovery to the plaintiff, but also the non-monetary benefit accruing to others, in this case the public at large from this successful vindication of a national policy...."[404]

The lodestar figure is presumed reasonable unless one of the parties carries the burden of showing unusual circumstances that justify adjusting it up or down.[405] Courts have considerable discretion in this regard.[406]

Counsel in one FCRA case, following settlement of class action, were held entitled to 1.5 lodestar multiplier as encouragement for this type of litigation.[407] In another FCRA case, after taking into account the difficulty of the case, skill in trial work, and the results obtained, the court specifically noted that its award did not cover time expected to be necessary to respond to post-trial motions.[408] In another FCRA case, the consumer's rejection of a mid-trial settlement offer more favorable than the eventual court judgment did not impede an award of fees.[409]

11.14.3 Maximizing the Chances of an Adequate Fee Award

A plaintiff's attorney can take several steps to maximize an attorney fee recovery in an FCRA case. The first step is to keep excellent time records which not only record all time spent on an FCRA case by each attorney and paralegal involved, but also indicate why the time was necessary for the case. This will help avoid a reduction in the lodestar amount where the court or defendant views the amount spent as possibly excessive.[410]

Special timekeeping requirements should be instituted where a tort or other non-fee shifting claim is added to the plaintiff's case. Then the time spent on that claim must be separately recorded from the time spent on the FCRA claim. Where work is necessary to the development of both claims, this should also be noted on the time sheet.

It is important to justify the hourly rate for each attorney and paralegal with reference to rates charged in the community by similarly experienced advocates.[411] This will

---

401 City of Riverside v. Rivera, 477 U.S. 561, 580 n.11, 106 S. Ct. 2686, 91 L. Ed. 2d 466 (1986) (citations omitted).
402 National Consumer Law Center, Truth in Lending § 8.9.4 (5th ed. 2003 and Supp.); National Consumer Law Center, Fair Debt Collection § 6.8 (5th 2004 and Supp.).
403 Blanchard v. Bergeron, 489 U.S. 87, 109 S. Ct. 939, 103 L. Ed. 2d 67 (1989); Blum v. Stenson, 465 U.S. 886, 895, 104 S. Ct. 1541, 79 L. Ed. 2d 891 (1983).
404 Fleet Inv. Co. v. Rogers, 620 F.2d 792 (10th Cir. 1980) (odometer law).
405 City of Burlington v. Dague, 505 U.S. 557, 112 S. Ct. 2638, 120 L. Ed. 2d 449 (1992). See, e.g., Fischel v. Equitable Life Assur. Soc'y of U.S. 307 F.3d 997, 1007 (9th Cir. 2002) (listing factors); Mealer v. Serv. Vending Co., 22 Fed. Appx. 700 (8th Cir. 2002) (unpublished) (trial court had discretion to reduce lodestar amount by 42% in light of limited success, lack of difficulty or novelty, and amount of awards in similar cases); Perry v. FleetBoston Fin. Corp., 229 F.R.D. 105 (E.D. Pa. 2005) (settlement class) (1.5 times lodestar awarded in FCRA case with settlement class); Ciccarone v. B.J. Marchese, Inc., 2004 WL 2966932, at *9 (E.D. Pa. Dec. 22, 2004) (when using lodestar method to calculate fee award, court should cross-check amount by calculating it as a percentage recovery of the approximate valuation of the total relief provided, awarding total of more than $1.2 million in fees). See also Stoner v. CBA Info. Servs., 352 F. Supp. 2d 549, 553 (E.D. Pa. 2005) (granting motion for award of attorney fees and expenses in amount of 33% of settlement fund of $772,000).
406 Sheffer v. Experian Info. Solutions, Inc., 290 F. Supp. 2d 538 (E.D. Pa. 2003).
407 Perry v. FleetBoston Fin. Corp., 229 F.R.D. 105 (E.D. Pa. 2005).
408 Pinner v. Schmidt, 617 F. Supp. 342 (E.D. La. 1985), aff'd in part, rev'd in part, 805 F.2d 1258 (5th Cir. 1986).
409 Lawhorn v. Trans Union Credit Info. Corp., 519 F. Supp. 455 (E.D. Mo. 1981).
410 Sheffer v. Experian Info. Solutions, Inc. 290 F. Supp. 2d 538 (E.D. Pa. 2003). See Collins v. Retail Credit Co., 410 F. Supp. 924 (E.D. Mich. 1976) (awarding $21,000 in attorney fees after attorney submitted affidavits with detailed lists of how he and his associate spent their time). See also Peck, Taxation of Costs in the United States District Court, 37 F.R.D. 481 (1965). But cf. Mares v. Credit Bureau, 801 F.2d 1197 (10th Cir. 1986) (allowing the consumer's attorney to recover fees for litigation to recover previously-awarded fees, but affirming the lower court's reduction of recoverable hours for that attorney and totally disallowing fees for a second "expert counsel" who assisted the consumer's attorney).
411 Sheffer v. Experian Info. Solutions, Inc. 290 F. Supp. 2d 538 (E.D. Pa. 2003) (court determines reasonable hourly rate by

require careful presentation of the plaintiff attorney's experience and skill and proof of the hourly rate in the community for that level of experience and skill. Expert testimony or affidavits by attorneys who have knowledge and experience regarding community rates for the type of legal work are generally necessary.

Another useful step where the attorney fee request is contested is to engage in discovery as to the *defendant* attorney's hourly rate and the time the defendant's attorney expended in the case.[412] This will not only point out the reasonableness of the plaintiff's request, but also may speed settlement of the attorney fee award. Some courts allow discovery as to defense counsel's hours and fees when defendant is challenging the reasonableness of plaintiff's hours and fees.[413]

11.14.4 Preserving Fee Entitlement When Case Is Settled

Attorneys should take care about the manner in which a settlement is consummated and commemorated in light of the United States Supreme Court's decision in *Buckhannon Board and Care Home v. West Virginia Dept. of Health and Human Resources*.[414] Although the case deals with the fee-shifting provisions of the fair housing laws and the Americans with Disabilities Act, the Supreme Court made clear that it was announcing a general rule that applied to most if not all federal fee-shifting statutes.[415]

Buckhannon was a suit for injunctive and declaratory relief. The Court rejected the "catalyst" theory, under which courts had held that a plaintiff is a prevailing party entitled to attorney fees even if a favorable order was never entered, as long as the suit achieved the desired result by bringing about a "voluntary" change in the defendant's behavior. This decision greatly diminished the incentive of plaintiffs' attorneys to bring certain kinds of suits for injunctive relief, where the defendant might simply cease the challenged behavior, thus mooting the case and blocking the award of attorney fees. In rejecting the catalyst theory, however, the Court reaffirmed its view that both "enforceable judgments on the merits and court-ordered consent decrees" can establish that a party has prevailed and is entitled to a fee award.[416] On the other hand, the Court, in *dicta*,[417] also suggested that a "private settlement" is insufficient to trigger the consumer's right to attorney fees because the consumer is not a prevailing party. The decision states that a "court-ordered consent decree" is sufficient, contrasted in a footnote to "private settlements," which "do not entail the judicial approval and oversight involved in consent decrees."[418]

What is a "court-ordered consent decree" and what is a "private settlement"? The key distinction is likely to be that a consumer will be considered to have prevailed and be entitled to fees when a final order is entered in the case which permits the court to retain jurisdiction for enforcement purposes. An order need not include an admission of liability by the defendant to qualify as a consent decree.[419] One court held that an order that recited steps that the defendant agreed to take, thereby subjecting the parties' agreement to judicial oversight and enforcement, qualified as a court-ordered consent decree.[420] Another decision holds that a signed order that referred to and ordered compliance with a separate settlement agreement was a consent decree for *Buckhannon* purposes even though it was not titled "Consent Decree." The order retained jurisdiction to enforce the agreement, and "the appropriateness of an award of fees surely ought not turn on whether the court does or does not retype the provisions of a settlement agreement as part of an order compelling compliance."[421] On the other hand, a mere stipulation, even if filed with the court and even if it includes the defendant's agreement to all of the relief the plaintiff sought, may not be sufficient.[422] A stipulation of dismissal is also unlikely to qualify,[423] even if it

---

assessing the prevailing party's attorneys' experience and skill compared to the market rates in the relevant community for lawyers of reasonably comparable skill, experience, and reputation).

412 Real v. Continental Group, 116 F.R.D. 211 (N.D. Cal. 1986); Mitroff v. Xomox Corp., 731 F. Supp. 25 (S.D. Ohio 1985). *But see* Chambless v. Masters, Mates & Pilots Pension Plan, 885 F.2d 1053, 1059 (2d Cir. 1989).

413 *See, e.g.*, Henson v. Columbus Bank & Trust Co., 770 F.2d 1566, 1575 (11th Cir. 1985); Chicago Prof'l Sports v. National Basketball Assoc., 1996 U.S. Dist. LEXIS 1525, 1526, (N.D. Ill. Feb. 13, 1996) (defendant's fees may provide the best available comparable standard to measure the reasonableness of plaintiffs' expenditures in litigating the issues of the case). Decisions going both ways on this issue are collected in Cohen v. Brown Univ., 1999 WL 695235, at *2 (D.R.I. May 19, 1999).

414 532 U.S. 598, 121 S. Ct. 1835, 149 L. Ed. 2d 855 (2001).

415 *Id.*, 532 U.S. at 603, n.4.

416 *Id.*, 532 U.S. at 604.

417 *See* Barrios v. Cal. Interscholastic Fed'n, 277 F.3d 1128, 1134, n.5 (9th Cir. 2002) (characterizing *Buckhannon*'s discussion of private settlements as *dicta*).

418 *Buckhannon*, 532 U.S. at 604, n.7.

419 *Buckhannon*, 532 U.S. at 604.

420 Johnny's Icehouse, Inc. v. Amateur Hockey Ass'n, 2001 WL 893840, 2001 U.S. Dist. LEXIS 11671 (N.D. Ill. Aug. 7, 2001). *But cf.* Smyth v. Rivero, 282 F.3d 268 (4th Cir. 2002) (entry dismissing case as moot because of defendant's change in policy was not a "consent decree" even though it referred to the parties' agreement on one issue).

421 Nat'l Coalition for Students with Disabilities v. Bush, 173 F. Supp. 2d 1272 (N.D. Fla. 2001). *Cf.* Smyth v. Rivero, 282 F.3d 268 (4th Cir. 2002) (either incorporation of the agreement into the order or a separate provision retaining jurisdiction over it would have sufficed, but mere acknowledgment and approval of agreement is insufficient).

422 Dorfsman v. Law Sch. Admission Council, 2001 WL 1754762 (E.D. Pa. Nov. 28, 2001).

423 Oil, Chem. and Atomic Workers Int'l Union v. Dep't of Energy, 288 F.3d 452 (D.C. Cir. 2002); Perez-Arellano v. Smith, 279 F.3d 791 (9th Cir. 2002); Dorfsman v. Law Sch. Admission Council, 2001 WL 1754762 (E.D. Pa. Nov. 28, 2001) (stipula-

recites the steps that the defendant has taken that have resolved the dispute.[424]

After *Buckhannon*, the following ways of settling an FCRA case are likely to preserve entitlement to fees:

- Negotiation of payment of fees in an acceptable amount as part of the settlement on the merits.
- An agreed judgment for money, as long as it is clear that fees have not been waived.
- An agreed order that specifies the steps the defendant will take (e.g., correction of a consumer report), as long as the court retains jurisdiction to enforce it.[425] It is clearer that the plaintiff is the prevailing party if the order the court signs actually recites the steps the defendant will take, rather than referring to a separate document, although the latter format is probably also sufficient.[426]
- An agreed order of any sort that includes a finding or stipulation that the plaintiff is the prevailing party. Even a stipulation between the parties, not signed by the court, that the plaintiff is the prevailing party is probably sufficient. While *Buckhannon* does not explicitly endorse this method of preserving the right to attorney fees, the Court never indicated that winning an enforceable judgment or a court-ordered consent decree is a jurisdictional requirement that cannot be satisfied by a stipulation. Merely reserving the issue of attorney fees for the court, without stipulating that the plaintiff is the prevailing party, is probably insufficient, however.[427]

Settlement methods that are less likely to preserve the right to fees are:

- A stipulation that is filed with the court but is signed only by the parties and does not state that the plaintiff is the prevailing party.
- A dismissal entry, even if the case is dismissed pursuant to an agreement signed by the parties under which the defendant agrees to the relief the plaintiff sought.[428]

11.14.5 Rule 68 and Attorney Fee Awards

Rule 68 of the Federal Rules of Civil Procedure allows a defendant to serve upon the plaintiff an offer of judgment for a sum of money "with costs then accrued." The plaintiff has ten days to accept the offer. If the plaintiff does not accept it, and then recovers judgment for less than the offer, the plaintiff must pay the costs incurred after the making of the offer.

Rule 68 offers are common in litigation under some consumer laws such as the Fair Debt Collection Practices Act, but less so in FCRA litigation.[429] One reason may be that a Rule 68 offer, if accepted, is a judgment on the record against the defendant, which CRAs tend to want to avoid.

In the event that a Rule 68 offer is made in an FCRA case, an important question is whether a plaintiff who rejects the offer and then recovers a judgment for a smaller amount, loses the right to claim attorney fees accrued after the date of the offer. The clear answer is no, because Rule 68 only

---

tion followed by dismissal); Former Employees of Motorola Ceramic Prods. v. U.S., 176 F. Supp. 2d 1370 (U.S. Ct. Int'l Trade 2001) (plaintiffs not prevailing parties when government moved to remand case to administrative agency, which then rewarded the relief sought, and parties then stipulated to dismissal). *See also* John T. v. Delaware County Intermediate Unit, 318 F.3d 545 (3d Cir. 2003) (preliminary injunction insufficient); Brickwood Contractors, Inc. v. U.S., 288 F.3d 1371 (Fed. Cir. 2002) (plaintiff was not prevailing party where court dismissed case as moot, even though it had commented favorably on merits at TRO hearing); J.C. v. Reg'l Sch. Dist. 10, 278 F.3d 119 (2d Cir. 2002) (order dismissing hearing as moot after school board adopted individualized educational plan granting all relief sought was insufficient for fee award); Sileikis v. Perryman, 2001 WL 965503, 2001 U.S. Dist. LEXIS 12737 (N.D. Ill. Aug. 20, 2001) (suit which sought order requiring I.N.S. to adjudicate two applications was dismissed when I.N.S. did so); Thayer v. Principi, 15 Vet. App. 204 (2001).

424 Oil, Chem. and Atomic Workers Int'l Union v. Dep't of Energy, 288 F.3d 452 (D.C. Cir. 2002).

425 *Buckhannon*, 532 U.S. at 604, n.7. *See* Kokkonen v. Guardian Life Ins. Co., 511 U.S. 375, 114 S. Ct. 1673, 128 L. Ed. 2d 391 (1994) (stating that district court can enforce settlement agreement if it is embodied in dismissal order or if order states that court retains jurisdiction to enforce it). *See also* Truesdell v. Phila. Hous. Auth., 290 F.3d 159 (3d Cir. 2002) (order entered upon parties' agreement, which contained mandatory language, was entitled "Order," and was signed by the judge rather than the parties' attorneys, was a proper vehicle for making plaintiff the prevailing party); American Disability Ass'n v. Chmielarz, 289 F.3d 1315 (11th Cir. 2002) (dismissal order that approved, adopted, and ratified settlement, and retained jurisdiction to enforce it, met *Kokkonen* standards, so fees could be awarded); Smyth v. Rivero, 282 F.3d 268 (4th Cir. 2002) (consent decree on which fees can be based is one that is enforceable as a judicial decree by the court that entered it, but this order does not meet that standard).

426 *See* Smyth v. Rivero, 282 F.3d 268 (4th Cir. 2002) (either incorporation of the agreement into the order or a separate provision retaining jurisdiction over it will suffice).

427 Dorfsman v. Law Sch. Admission Council, 2001 WL 1754762 (E.D. Pa. Nov. 28, 2001). *See also* Oil, Chem. and Atomic Workers Int'l Union v. Dep't of Energy, 288 F.3d 452 (D.C. Cir. 2002) (plaintiff not prevailing party under stipulation of dismissal that was "without prejudice to the right of plaintiff to obtain . . . an award of attorney's fees," although court does not address the argument that this language was sufficient in and of itself).

428 Oil, Chem. and Atomic Workers Int'l Union v. Department of Energy, 288 F.3d 452 (D.C. Cir. 2002) (dismissal entry that recited the steps defendant had taken was insufficient); Smyth v. Rivero, 282 F.3d 268 (4th Cir. 2002) (dismissal order that merely acknowledges, refers to, or approves settlement agreement is insufficient).

429 *See* National Consumer Law Center, Fair Debt Collection § 2.4.13 (5th 2004 and Supp.).

shifts liability for costs, and fees are not treated as part of costs under the FCRA.[430]

The second important question is how attorney fees are treated if the plaintiff accepts a Rule 68 offer in an FCRA case. This question can be particularly tricky if the defendant makes an offer but does not specify whether it is intended to cover both the award to the plaintiff and attorney fees. A number of decisions under other similar statutes hold that an offer of judgment is to be construed against the drafter, and if it is ambiguous about whether a lump sum is intended to cover attorney fees it will be construed not to, thereby allowing the court to award fees.[431] Some cases adopt a contrary view, though, construing a lump-sum Rule 68 offer that is silent about fees to cover both the award to the plaintiff and attorney fees even if the offer does not make this clear.[432]

Rule 68 case law is highly complex and varied, and before accepting or rejecting a Rule 68 offer the attorney should check the controlling decisions in the jurisdiction. Immediately requesting clarification of an unclear offer is also a good idea; not only may the defendant's response clear up the ambiguity, but any evasiveness on the part of the defendant will be an additional factor that may persuade the court to construe the offer against the defendant.[433]

If an offer of judgment under Rule 68 represents everything the plaintiff could possibly recover, the case may be dismissed. "Everything" is read literally, so that in a *pro se* FCRA case, the court held that an offer of judgment covering all actual damages was insufficient to justify dismissal because of the remote possibility of punitive damages at the time of the offer.[434]

11.14.6 Interest on Judgments

Pursuant to federal statute, interest accrues from the date of judgment on any money judgment obtained in a federal district court.[435]

11.15 Quick Reference to Published Awards

Listed alphabetically, some published damage awards include:

- *Adams v. Phillips*, 2002 WL 31886737 (E.D. La. Dec. 19, 2002): $225,000 actual damages and $275,000 punitive damages against impostor.
- *Anderson v. Conwood Co.*, 34 F. Supp. 2d 650 (W.D. Tenn. 1999): $35,000 punitive damage award vacated; $2,000,000 compensatory award reduced to $50,000 in absence of testimony other than worry, stress, anxiety.
- *Bach v. First Union Nat'l Bank*, 149 Fed. Appx. 354 (6th Cir. 2005) (unpublished): Jury award of $400,000 in compensatory damages to 77-year-old widow upheld; punitive damages of $2,628,600 reversed and remanded as unconstitutionally excessive.
- *Bakker v. McKinnon*, 152 F.3d 1007 (8th Cir. 1998) $500 actual damages; $5000 punitive damages.
- *Barnett Bank v. Hazel*, 555 S.E.2d 195 (Ga. Ct. App. 2001): Judgment of $75,000 against bank for providing false information to CRAs with malice or willful intent to injure.
- *Boothe v. TRW Credit Data*, 557 F. Supp. 66 (S.D.N.Y. 1982): $15,000 punitive damages against entity which had gotten consumer report under false pretenses, plus attorney fees.
- *Boris v. ChoicePoint Servs., Inc.*, 249 F. Supp. 2d 851 (W.D. Ky. 2003): Jury award of $197,000 actual damages remitted to $100,000; $250,000 punitive damages not excessive.
- *Bryant v. TRW Inc.*, 689 F.2d 72 (6th Cir. 1982): Jury awarded "relatively modest verdict" of $8000 for embarrassment and humiliation; attorney fees $13,705.
- *Collins v. Retail Credit Co.*, 410 F. Supp. 924 (E.D. Mich. 1976): $21,750 loss of reputation, embarrass-

---

430 15 U.S.C. §§ 1681n(a)(3), 1681o(a)(2) (defendant is liable for "the costs of the action together with reasonable attorney's fees"). See Marek v. Chesny, 473 U.S. 1, 105 S. Ct. 3012, 87 L. Ed. 2d 1 (1985) (note that the frequently-cited appendix to J. Brennan's dissent lists the FCRA as one of the statutes that treats attorney fees as separate from costs). See also Fegley v. Higgins, 19 F.3d 1126 (6th Cir. 1994) (Fair Labor Standards Act); Knight v. Snap-On Tools Corp., 3 F.3d 1398, 1403 (10th Cir. 1993) (state UDAP statute).

431 Hennessy v. Daniels Law Office, 270 F.3d 551 (8th Cir. 2001) (defendant is liable for fees in FDCPA case after plaintiff accepted ambiguous offer of judgment that was silent about fees); Webb v. James, 147 F.3d 617 (7th Cir. 1998) (plaintiff became prevailing party by accepting defendant's deliberately vague Rule 68 offer that was silent about whether it included fees, so was entitled to petition for fees); Nusom v. Comh Woodburn, Inc., 122 F.3d 830 (9th Cir. 1997) (fees may be awarded on TILA and state RICO claims after plaintiff's acceptance of undifferentiated lump sum offer that did not clearly and unambiguously exclude fees).

432 Oates v. Oates, 866 F.2d 203 (6th Cir. 1989) (wiretapping provisions of Crime Control Act); Keffer v. Cigna Corp., 1990 U.S. Dist. LEXIS 8532, at *9, *10 (E.D. Pa. July 9, 1990) (ERISA).

433 Solomon v. Onyx Acceptance Corp., 222 F.R.D. 418, 423 (C.D. Cal. 2004) (where case ultimately settles, to determine whether cost-shifting provision of Rule 68 applies court must determine reasonable fees and costs as of the date of the offer, subtract that figure from the amount of the offer, and compare it to the settlement amount). See Webb v. James, 147 F.3d 617 (7th Cir. 1998) (defendant's deliberately vague offer was insufficient to preclude fee award).

434 McCauley v. Trans Union, L.L.C., 2003 WL 22845741 (S.D.N.Y. Nov. 26, 2003).

435 28 U.S.C. § 1961(a). See also W.D.I.A. Corp. v. McGraw-Hill, Inc., 34 F. Supp. 2d 612 (S.D. Ohio 1998) (awarding post-judgment interest on FCRA claim).

ment, humiliation, in recognition of the "many subtle and indirect adverse effects upon her personal, social and economic life." $300,000 punitive reduced to $50,000 by the court; $21,000 attorney fees.
- *Hall v. Harleysville Ins. Co.*, 943 F. Supp. 536 (E.D. Pa. 1996): No damages, attorney fees and costs $87,821.48.
- *Hoglan v. First Security Bank*, 120 Idaho 682, 819 P.2d 100 (1991): The court upheld a jury verdict of $20,000 for breach of contract and negligence, and overturned a $200,000 award of punitive damages.
- *Jones v. Credit Bureau of Greater Garden City*, 1989 WL 134945 (D. Kan. Oct. 24, 1989): $500 for expenses, lost wages, mental anguish, and embarrassment; $10,620 attorney fees.
- *Jones v. Credit Bureau of Huntington, Inc.*, 399 S.E.2d 694 (W. Va. 1990): Jury award of $4000 compensatory, $42,500 punitive, upheld. Report was corrected one week after publication.
- *Milgram v. Advanced Cellular Systems, Inc.*, 1990 WL 116322 (E.D. Pa. Aug. 8, 1990): Jury award of $20,000; $20,224 attorney fees.
- *Millstone v. O'Hanlon Reports, Inc.*, 383 F. Supp. 269 (E.D. Mo. 1974): $2500 compensatory, $10,000 punitive, $12,500 attorney fees.
- *Morris v. Credit Bureau*, 563 F. Supp. 962 (S.D. Ohio 1983): $10,000 for stress, anxiety, humiliation, injury to his reputation, his work, his family, his sense of well-being.
- *Nitti v. Credit Bureau of Rochester, Inc.*, 84 Misc. 2d 277, 375 N.Y.S.2d 817 (Sup. Ct. 1975): $10,000 punitive; $8000 attorney fees.
- *Northrop v. Hoffman*, 12 Fed. Appx. 44, 2001 WL 682301 (2d Cir. June 14, 2001): Punitive damages totaling $125,000 against two defendants, plus attorney fees and costs of $54,962, where defendants obtained consumer report under false pretenses.
- *Pinner v. Schmidt*, 617 F. Supp. 342 (E.D. La. 1985): Jury awarded $100,000 actual and $100,000 punitive. On appeal, conditional remittitur reduced actual damages to $25,000 and reversed the award of punitive damages for negligent violations. 805 F.2d 1258 (5th Cir. 1991).
- *Sheffer v. Experian Info. Solutions, Inc.*, 290 F. Supp. 2d 538 (E.D. Pa. 2003): $1000 actual damages, $25,000 fees, $7500 costs.
- *Stevenson v. TRW*, 987 F.2d 288 (5th Cir. 1993): The trial court awarded $30,000 in mental anguish and embarrassment damages, $100,000 in punitive damages, plus $20,700 in attorney fees. The Fifth Circuit overturned only the punitive damages award because the violations were not willful.
- *Thompson v. San Antonio Retail Merchants Ass'n*, 682 F.2d 509 (5th Cir. 1982): $10,000 actual damages for humiliation and mental distress even when no out-of-pocket expenses for three credit denials resulting from CRA error. Also $4485 attorney fees at $90 per hour.
- *Thornton v. Equifax Inc.*, 467 F. Supp. 1008 (E.D. Ark. 1979): $5000 compensatory and $250,000 punitive in light of defendant's annual gross income of $300,000,000.
- *Trans Union Corp. v. Crisp*, 896 S.W.2d 446 (Ark. Ct. App. 1995): Jury awarded $15,000 in compensatory damages and $25,000 in punitive damages in a case involving reports which did not show that debts had been satisfied and unhelpfulness when consumer tried to raise matter with company.
- *Yohay v. Alexandria Employees Credit Union Inc.*, 827 F.2d 967 (4th Cir. 1987): no actual damages; $10,000 punitive damages.

11.16 Public Enforcement

11.16.1 Administrative Enforcement Agencies

A plethora of federal agencies are invested with enforcement powers by the FCRA. The Federal Trade Commission (FTC) is the FCRA's primary administrative enforcer. The FTC has administrative enforcement power over all consumer reporting agencies (CRAs) and other persons subject to the Act, except to the extent enforcement authority has been reserved for the federal banking regulators and other specialized federal agencies.[436] The federal financial regulators have FCRA enforcement authority over the institutions they regulate—the Office of the Comptroller of the Currency (national banks), the Office of Thrift Supervision (federal savings banks or thrifts), the Federal Deposit Insurance Corporation (state-chartered banks), the Federal Reserve Board (FRB member banks other than national banks), and the National Credit Union Administration (credit unions).[437] The other specialized agencies include the Secretary of Transportation (carriers subject to the jurisdiction of the Surface Transportation Board and for air carriers), and the Secretary of Agriculture (for those subject to the Packers and Stockyards Act).[438]

A violation of the FCRA is a violation of the various statutes providing general enforcement powers to each of the federal agencies with FCRA administrative enforcement jurisdiction.[439] In general, the agencies may utilize their normal statutory enforcement authority to enforce the FCRA.[440]

---

[436] 15 U.S.C. § 1681s(a). *See generally* Feldman, *The Fair Credit Reporting Act—from the Regulators Vantage Point*, 14 Santa Clara Lawyer 459 (1974).
[437] 15 U.S.C. § 1681s(b)(1)–(3).
[438] 15 U.S.C. § 1681s(b)(4)–(6).
[439] 15 U.S.C. § 1681s(d).
[440] 15 U.S.C. § 1681s(d). Prior to 1999, the Act provided that any agency with FCRA administrative enforcement authority was prohibited from examining a bank, savings association, or credit

11.16.2 Federal Trade Commission Enforcement

11.16.2.1 General FTC Enforcement Powers

Most administrative enforcement of the FCRA will come from the FTC. FTC administrative enforcement jurisdiction includes credit bureaus, the "Big Three" nationwide CRAs as well as other CRAs, retailers, finance companies, mortgage companies, other non-bank creditors, most employers, lawyers and private investigators, check guaranty companies, tenant screening companies and landlords. Jurisdiction extends to every entity subject to the FCRA and not explicitly excepted by the statute as regulated by another federal agency.[441]

The FTC can use the powers it has under the FTC Act to secure compliance, irrespective of whether the defendant is engaged in "commerce" or meets any other jurisdictional tests in the FTC Act.[442] The FTC's authority encompasses the United States, the District of Columbia, the Commonwealth of Puerto Rico, and all the United States territories, but does not extend to activities outside those areas.[443] This breadth of jurisdiction has made the FTC the principal enforcement agency to which the other agencies defer on matters of FCRA enforcement policy.

The FCRA explicitly states that any violation of any FCRA requirement or prohibition is an unfair or deceptive act or practice in violation of section 5(a) of the FTC Act and subject to enforcement under that Act.[444] The FTC is authorized to require the filing of reports, the production of documents,[445] and the appearance of witnesses as if it were enforcing the FTC Act.[446] The FTC can also use all its normal enforcement powers—administrative cease-and-desist orders, consent decrees, and federal court restitution, injunction, and civil penalty orders.

The FCRA also allows the FTC to commence a civil action to recover a civil penalty of not more than $2500 per violation in the event of a knowing violation of the FCRA which constitutes a pattern or practice of violations.[447] Such action must be brought in a federal district court. In determining the amount of the civil penalty, the court "shall take into account the degree of culpability, any history of prior such conduct, ability to pay, effect on ability to continue to do business, and such other matters as justice may require."[448]

With the exception of reinvestigation duties, private enforcement under the FCRA against creditors and others for furnishing information to CRAs is generally not permitted.[449] Consumers have tried to force the FTC to use its powers to assist their personal grievances against CRAs, seeking a mandamus order from a court to compel the FTC to seize certain records in the CRA's possession. Courts hold that the FTC's power to order production of documents is discretionary and the FTC can exercise that power only in the public interest, not in the personal interest of a single consumer.[450]

However, when the FTC does act and enters into a consent decree with the offending party, those consent decrees have some precedential value that can aid consumers who seek to bring their own case. Strictly speaking, an FTC consent order or settlement does not adjudicate disputed issues of fact and does not decide a disputed issue of law. Nonetheless, an FTC complaint establishes that certain practices are impermissible under the statute, even while it only alleges that such practices occur.[451] Although an FTC consent decree that provides that it is not an admission of wrong-doing may not be used as evidence of wrong-doing, it is evidence that a defendant has been put on notice that certain alleged activity is illegal and improper. A decree proscribing future conduct is evidence of what a party to the consent decree believed to be reasonable behavior in compliance with the law.[452]

Although violations of the FCRA are one of the most common complaints received by the FTC,[453] FTC enforce-

---

union for FCRA compliance except in response to a complaint (or if the agency otherwise had knowledge) of an FCRA violation. Congress struck this restriction in the Gramm-Leach-Bliley Act of 1999. Pub. L. No. 106-102, § 510, 113 Stat. 1338 (1999).

441 15 U.S.C. § 1681s(a)(1).
442 *Id.*
443 FTC Official Staff Commentary § 621 item 2, *reprinted at* Appx. D, *infra*.
444 15 U.S.C. § 1681s(a)(1). *See, e.g.*, Equifax, Inc., 96 FTC 1045 (1980), *rev'd in part on other grounds*, 678 F.2d 1047 (11th Cir. 1982), in which the Commission considered several allegations of violations of the Fair Credit Reporting Act and several alleged violations of section 5 of the Federal Trade Commission Act. The FTC Act charges included the misrepresentation of the identity of CRA employees, the use of deception to induce participation in interviews, and the acquisition of medical information without proper authorization.
445 15 U.S.C. § 1681s(a)(1). This power was affirmed in Fed. Trade Comm'n v. Manager, Retail Credit Co., 515 F.2d 988 (D.C. Cir. 1975). *See also* Fed. Trade Comm'n v. TRW, 628 F.2d 207 (9th Cir. 1980).
446 15 U.S.C. § 1681s(a)(1).

447 15 U.S.C. § 1681s(a)(2)(A).
448 15 U.S.C. § 1681s(a)(2)(B).
449 *See* Ch. 6, § 10.2.4.1, *supra*.
450 Rush v. Macy's New York, Inc., 596 F. Supp. 1540 (S.D. Fla. 1984), *aff'd*, 775 F.2d 1554 (11th Cir. 1985); Pendleton v. TransUnion Sys. Corp., 430 F. Supp. 95 (E.D. Pa. 1977); Sauke v. Fed. Trade Comm'n, 333 F. Supp. 1197 (N.D. Ga. 1971).
451 *See* Fed. Trade Comm'n v. Mandel Bros., Inc., 359 U.S. 385, 391 (1959) (an FTC construction is "entitled to great weight . . . even though it was applied in cases settled by consent rather than in litigation").
452 *See* National Consumer Law Center, Unfair and Deceptive Acts and Practices § 3.4.5.3 (6th ed. 2004 and Supp.).
453 U.S. Public Interest Research Group, Credit Bureaus: Public Enemy #1 at the FTC (Oct. 1993). The total number of com-

ment resources are limited. The FTC is more likely to take action over an FCRA violation when evidence suggests a pattern of serious violations. Even though administrative action is unlikely in response to a single complaint by an individual, it is still important for individual complaints to be sent to the FTC because a pattern of complaints may cause the FTC staff to consider enforcement action. Complaints may be sent to the Division of Credit Practices, Federal Trade Commission, Washington, D.C. 20580, or to a regional FTC office.

Summaries of enforcement orders the FTC has obtained against CRAs, resellers of consumer reports, and others are included in Appendix K, *infra*; full versions of the enforcement orders are included in the CD-Rom accompanying this manual.[454] Some more recent examples of the FTC's FCRA enforcement efforts include the following:

In 2002, the FTC filed a complaint against D.C. Credit Services, a debt collection agency, and its owner for allegedly furnishing information to a CRA that the defendants knew or consciously avoided knowing was inaccurate; for failing to notify promptly a CRA that previously-furnished information was incomplete or inaccurate, even after making such a determination; for furnishing adverse information to CRAs without disclosing that the consumer previously had disputed the information; and for falsely reporting the date of delinquency of a debt. The FTC ultimately settled with D.C. Credit Services and its owner, requiring them to pay $300,000 in civil penalties, to notify CRAs, to delete all adverse information previously provided for the past seven years by the defendants and only allowing the defendants to re-report information after a determination that it is accurate and reportable.[455]

In 2002, the FTC brought an enforcement action against a user of consumer reports for failing to provide adverse action notices.[456] According to the FTC,[457] the user was a lender who offered "prequalify" or "preapprove" the consumer for a loan over the Internet based in part on the individual's consumer report. Consumers whom the lender denied preapproval on-line were informed of the denial, but did not receive the required adverse action notice under the FCRA.[458] The FTC subsequently settled with the lender, requiring the lender to notify consumers for taking adverse action based in whole or in part on information in a consumer report.[459]

In 2004, the FTC charged a debt collection agency with reporting accounts with incorrect delinquency dates and causing negative information to remain in consumer files longer than the seven-year period permitted under the FTC. The debt collection agency entered into a consent agreement with the FTC, agreeing to a $1.5 million civil penalty.[460] The decree permanently barred the defendant from reporting inaccurate delinquency dates to CRAs and required it to establish a monitoring program on complaints it receives.[461]

In 2005, the FTC settled a case against Consumerinfo.com, Inc., d.b.a. Experian Consumer Direct, which it alleged deceptively marketed "free credit reports" by not adequately disclosing that consumers who requested the "free" reports would automatically be signed up for a consumer report monitoring service and charged.[462]

In 2005, data broker ChoicePoint acknowledged that the personal financial records of more than 163,000 consumers in its database had been compromised. The FTC filed an action alleging that ChoicePoint did not have reasonable procedures to screen prospective users to verify their identity and to make sure they had a permissible use for the information.[463] Some subscribers had commercial mail drops as addresses or in other ways indicated a high likelihood that they were not real businesses or did not have a permissible purpose. ChoicePoint agreed to a stipulated final judgment requiring the company to pay $10 million in civil penalties and $5 million for consumer redress, barring the company from furnishing consumer reports to people who do not have a permissible purpose, and requiring the company to maintain reasonable procedures to ensure that consumer reports are provided only to those with a permissible purpose, including the verification of the user's identity.[464]

---

plaints that the FTC received from 1990 through the first half of 1993 was 30,901.

454 Most of these enforcement orders pre-date the Fair and Accurate Transactions Act (FACTA) of 2003 and many even pre-date the Consumer Credit Reporting Reform Act of 1996. Therefore, they may not reflect the current state of the law.

455 United States v. DC Credit Servs., Inc., Civil Action No. 02-5115 (W.D. Cal. June 27, 2002), *reprinted on the CD-Rom accompanying this manual*.

456 *See In re* Quicken Loans, Inc., Docket No. 9304, (Dec. 30, 2002) (consent decree), *reprinted on the CD-Rom accompanying this manual*.

457 *Id.*

458 *Id.*

459 The FTC did permit the defendant some exceptions in order to obtain additional information offline, if certain precautions and conditions were met. *See In re* Quicken Loans, Inc., Docket No. 9304 (Dec. 30, 2002) (consent decree), *reprinted on the CD-Rom accompanying this manual*.

460 United States v. NCO Group, Inc., Civ. No. 922-3012. *See* www.ftc.gov/opa/2004/05/ncogroup.htm (a copy of the consent decree is reproduced on the CD-Rom accompanying this manual).

461 *Id.*

462 Federal Trade Commission v. Consumerinfo.com, CV SACV05-801 AHS (Aug. 15, 2005) (stipulated final judgment), *available at* www.ftc.gov/os/caselist/0223263/050816stipfnl0223263.pdf. This case was technically brought under Section 5 of the FTC Act, 15 U.S.C. § 45, but is described because it was brought against a CRA.

463 U.S. v. ChoicePoint, Inc., CA 1 06-CV-0198 (N.D. Ga. Jan. 30, 2006) (complaint), *reprinted at* www.ftc.gov/os/caselist/choicepoint/0523069complaint.pdf (available on the CD-Rom accompanying this manual; *see also* Appx. K, *infra*).

464 U.S. v. ChoicePoint, Inc., CA 1 06-CV-0198 (N.D. Ga. Jan. 30, 2006) (stipulated final judgment), *reprinted at* www.ftc.gov/os/caselist/choicepoint/choicepoint.htm (available on the CD-Rom accompanying this manual; *see also* Appx. K, *infra*).

In 2006, the FTC filed a complaint against CRA Far West Credit, Inc., in which it alleged Far West did not follow reasonable procedures to ensure the accuracy of the information in the consumer reports it sold to mortgage companies.[465] In particular, it alleged that when the information Far West purchased from the nationwide CRAs was insufficient, Far West accepted documentation from the consumer or other interested party on behalf of the consumer, such as the mortgage broker or originator, purporting to show sources of credit and credit status with businesses that do not report to the nationwide CRAs, and merged it into the other information it had purchased.[466] Since Far West did not adequately review or verify this information, many of the reports it generated were inaccurate, leading to origination of FHA loans that subsequently defaulted.[467] Far West entered into a consent decree with the FTC, agreeing to implement reasonable procedures to ensure the maximum possible accuracy of information in consumer reports that it prepares, and to pay $120,000 in civil penalties.[468]

The FTC has also stepped up enforcement and other activities concerning adverse action notices. The FTC charged Sprint and AT&T with using individuals' consumer reports to deny telephone service and to place restrictions on consumers' service, without providing complete adverse action notices required under the FCRA and ECOA.[469] Sprint sometimes failed to provide any notice at all. Under consent decrees reached with the FTC, Sprint agreed to a civil penalty of over one million dollars and AT&T agreed to pay $365,000. The decrees barred both companies from failing to comply with the FCRA's and ECOA's adverse action notice requirement. The decrees also included record-keeping and monitoring requirements.[470]

In addition to bringing cases for violations of the FCRA, the FTC filed several amicus briefs in support of consumer FCRA claims. In three cases before the Ninth Circuit, the FTC argued that insurance companies take "adverse action" when they charge a consumer a higher price based on information in the consumer's report.[471] In another case, the FTC asserted in an amicus brief that it was improper for a district court to dismiss an impermissible access claim without evaluating the substance of an offer of credit to determine whether the offer might be a sham that precluded the creditor from obtaining the individual's consumer report.[472] The Seventh Circuit agreed with the FTC and reversed the lower court's dismissal of the consumer's claims.[473] In another case, the FTC asserted that an insurance provider that increases consumers' private mortgage insurance premium based on their consumer reports has an obligation to provide notice of "adverse action" even if the mortgagee is the policy's beneficiary.[474]

The FTC also created a new complaint referral program, required by the FACTA amendments, in which the FTC will refer to the CRAs complaints the FTC receives from consumers who maintain that their disputes about accuracy or completeness have not been resolved to their satisfaction. The FTC will not make any determination about the merits of the complaints. The CRAs will review the complaints to make sure they have complied with the applicable provisions of the FCRA, and periodically provide reports to the FTC on the disposition of a sample of the complaints. The program does not limit the FTC's ability to pursue law enforcement under the FCRA.[475]

Consumers and advocates often complain about the lack of responsiveness by the FTC to complaints, but the complaints also serve to document problematic trends with CRAs, furnishers, and users of consumer reports. It is also more likely that a high volume of complaints on a particular topic will generate closer scrutiny by the FTC and other agencies.

11.16.2.2 FTC Enforcement Powers Against Information Furnishers Are Limited

There is a significant limitation on the FTC's authority to seek civil penalties for violations of the FCRA against information furnishers. The FCRA imposes several duties on furnishers when they furnish information to CRAs.[476] One of the most critical duties is a limited duty not to report inaccurate information, which is not privately enforce-

---

465 States v. Far West Credit, Inc., Civ. No. 2:06-CV-00041 (D. Utah Jan. 12, 2006) (complaint), *available at* www.ftc.gov/os/caselist/0423185/060112farwestcreditcmplt.pdf.
466 *Id.*
467 *Id.*
468 States v. Far West Credit, Inc., Civ. No. 2:06-CV-00041 (D. Utah Jan. 12, 2006) (consent decree), *available at* www.ftc.gov/os/caselist/0423185/060113farwestcreditconsentdecree.pdf.
469 United States v. AT&T Corp., Civ. No. 022-3159 (N.D.N.J. Sept. 9, 2004); United States v. Sprint Corp., Civ. No. 022-3160 (N.D. Fla.). *See* www.ftc.gov/opa/2004/09/sprintatt.htm.
470 United States v. AT&T Corp., Civ. No. 022-3159 (N.D.N.J. Sept. 9, 2004); United States v. Sprint Corp., Civ. No. 022-3160 (N.D. Fla.). *See* www.ftc.gov/opa/2004/09/sprintatt.htm.
471 *See* Spano v. Safeco Ins. Co., Civ. No. 04-3514 (9th Cir. 2004) (amicus brief); Rausch v. Hartford Fin. Servs. Group, Inc., Civ. No. 03-35695 (9th Cir. 2004) (amicus brief); Willes v. State Farm Cas. Co., Civ. No. 03-35848 (9th Cir.) (amicus brief) (copies of the amicus briefs are reproduced on the CD-Rom accompanying this manual). These were the cases decided by the Ninth Circuit's decision in Reynolds v. Hartford Fin. Servs. Group, Inc., 435 F.3d 1081 (9th Cir. 2006), *cert. granted, sub nom.* GEICO Gen. Ins. v. Edo, __ S. Ct. __, 2006 WL 2055539 (Sept. 26, 2006). *See* § 6.4.2.5, *supra*.
472 Cole v. U.S. Capital, Inc., Civ. No. 03-3331 (7th Cir. 2004) (amicus brief) (a copy of the amicus brief is reproduced on the CD-Rom accompanying this manual). *See* § 8.2.6.4, *supra*.
473 Cole v. U.S. Capital, Inc., 389 F.3d 719, 727–728 (7th Cir. 2004). *See* § 8.2.6, *supra*.
474 *See* Whitfield v. Radian Guar., Inc., Civ. No. 05-5017 (3d Cir. 2005) (amicus brief), *available at* www.ftc.gov/os/2006/03/BriefAmicusCuriaeoftheFTCinWhitfieldv.Radian.pdf.
475 15 U.S.C. § 1681s(f). *See* www.ftc.gov/opa/2004/04/cra.htm.
476 *See* Ch. 5, *supra*.

able.[477] It is also this duty for which the FTC's authority to impose civil penalties is sharply curtailed.

The FTC may not impose a civil penalty on a person for violating the duty not to furnish inaccurate information to CRAs, *unless*: (1) the person has been previously enjoined from committing the violation, or ordered not to commit the violation, in an action or proceeding brought by or on behalf of the FTC; and (2) the person has violated the injunction or order.[478]

This limitation on the FTC's civil penalty authority applies only to furnishers' general duty to provide accurate information to CRAs under 15 U.S.C. § 1681s-2(a)(1). It does not apply with regard to furnishers' other FCRA obligations, including their duties to:

- Correct and update inaccurate information;
- Provide notice that the accuracy of information has been disputed by a consumer;
- Provide notice of voluntarily closed accounts;
- Provide the date of a delinquency on an account commenced;
- Have reasonable procedures for responding to a notice from a CRA that that CRA has blocked furnished information on the grounds that it was the result of fraud or identity theft;
- Reinvestigate the accuracy of information upon consumer's notice that the information is inaccurate;
- For medical information furnishers, to notify CRAs of their status as a furnisher of medical information;
- For financial institution furnishers, to notify customers when they furnish negative information about the customer to a nationwide CRA.

11.16.2.3 FTC and Federal Banking Agencies Rulemaking, FTC Staff Commentary and Opinion Letters

As described more fully in Chapter 1, *supra* Congress has granted authority to the FTC, the FRB, and the various banking regulators to issue regulations and interpretations for the FCRA. In addition to general rulemaking authority,[479] the FCRA requires these agencies to issue regulations for several of its provisions, especially those added by the FACTA amendments in 2003.[480] The FTC is also authorized to issue formal advisory opinions pursuant to request and formal interpretations of the Act if the issue's scope is industry wide.[481]

Prior to 1999, the FTC was prohibited from issuing regulations under the FCRA.[482] Instead, the FTC issued an Official Staff Commentary (FTC Staff Commentary) interpreting many particulars of the Act. The FTC staff also sometimes provides informal opinion letters upon request. The FTC last issued an FCRA-related informal staff opinion letter on June 28, 2001, and its website states that: "Except in unusual circumstances, the staff will no longer issue written interpretations of the FCRA."[483]

The Official Staff Commentary is reproduced in Appendix D, *infra*, the informal staff opinion letters can be found on the CD-Rom accompanying this manual, and an index of the informal FTC staff opinion letters is included in Appendix E, *infra*. Annotations referring to these FTC resources may be found throughout the text of this manual, and an analysis of the precedential value of these FTC resources is found at § 1.3.3.2, *supra*.

11.16.3 Criminal Enforcement

In 1996, Congress provided for criminal enforcement of two of the FCRA's provisions. Any person who knowingly and willfully obtains information on a consumer from a CRA under false pretenses shall be subject to certain criminal penalties.[484] In addition, any officer or employee of a CRA who knowingly and willfully provides information concerning an individual from the CRA's files to a person not authorized to receive that information shall also be subject to criminal sanctions.[485] The penalty for either violation is a fine pursuant to title 18 of the United States Code, or imprisonment for not more than two years, or both.[486]

In addition, federal computer fraud law provides an additional source of criminal penalties for credit reporting violations. It is a crime to intentionally access a computer without authority, or in excess of authority, and obtain information from a consumer report.[487] Employees of CRAs, users, and employers of users, as well as others, may

---

477 15 U.S.C. § 1681s-2(a)(1). See § 10.2.4.1, *supra*.
478 15 U.S.C. § 1681s(a)(3). These limitations on the FTC's ability to seek civil penalties in connection with section 1681-s2(a)(1) violations parallel the restrictions on states' ability to recover damages on behalf of residents in connection with section 623(a)(1); § 11.16.4.2, *infra*.
479 15 U.S.C. § 1681s(e).
480 See §§ 1.3.3, 1.4.9.2, *supra*, Appx. B, *infra*.
481 See 16 C.F.R. §§ 1.1–1.4 (FTC Rules of Practice).
482 Pub. L. No. 106-102, 113 Stat. 1338 (Nov. 12, 1999) (striking 15 U.S.C. § 1681s(a)(4)).
483 www.ftc.gov/os/statutes/fcrajump.htm.
484 15 U.S.C. § 1681q.
485 15 U.S.C. § 1681r.
486 15 U.S.C. §§ 1681q, 1681r.
487 18 U.S.C. § 1030(a)(2). Section 1030 Fraud and Related Activity In Connection with Computers reads in pertinent part as follows:

   (a) Whoever—
   . . .
   (2) intentionally accesses a computer without authorization or exceeds authorized access, and thereby obtains information contained in a financial record of a financial institution, or of a card issuer as defined in section 1602(n) of title 15, or contained in a file of a consumer reporting agency on a consumer, as such terms are defined in the Fair Credit Reporting Act (15 U.S.C. 1681 et seq.).

be subject to this provision if they access information from a consumer report under false pretenses, for impermissible purposes, or without proper authority. Creditors that obtain consumer reports via direct computer hook-up to CRAs may now be subject to this part of the criminal code. No cases have been reported under this part of the computer fraud law relating to the FCRA.

In its 2001 annual report, the FTC identified approximately 200 firms using false pretenses to obtain consumer's financial information for the purpose of selling it to third parties, a practice known as "pretexting."[488]

11.16.4 State Enforcement

11.16.4.1 General State Enforcement Powers

State attorneys general are frequently the first governmental authorities to whom consumers turn when they experience consumer reporting problems. Congress recognized this fact[489] when it provided state officials with FCRA enforcement authority.[490]

If the chief law enforcement officer of a state, or an official or agency designated by a state, has reason to believe that any person has violated or is violating the FCRA, the official may bring an action to enjoin the violation in an appropriate United States district court or in any other court of competent jurisdiction.[491]

In addition, the state official may bring an action on behalf of the residents of the state to recover:

- Damages for which any person who has willfully or negligently violated the FCRA is liable to the state's residents under section 1681n or 1681o; or
- In the case of a violation of section 1681s-2(a) (the subsection relating to the furnishing of information by creditors and others to CRAs), damages for which the person would be liable to the state's residents as a result of the violation but for the prohibition against private actions over section 1681s-2(a) violations;[492] or
- Statutory damages of not more than $1000 for each willful or negligent violation.[493]

In the case of any successful action, the state official shall be awarded costs and reasonable attorney fees.[494]

11.16.4.2 State Enforcement Powers Against Information Furnishers Are Extremely Limited

As mentioned earlier,[495] private citizens may not sue furnishers of information for damages resulting from a failure to provide accurate or complete information to CRAs as required by the Act.[496] Instead, public officials or federal or state agencies are permitted to enforce these requirements.[497] (Similar restrictions do not apply to the enforcement of the Act, requiring those who furnish information to CRAs to participate in reinvestigations conducted by the CRAs.[498])

State officials have severe limitations in seeking civil penalties for violations of the FCRA against information furnishers. Similar to the FTC,[499] state officials may not bring an action on behalf of residents to recover damages resulting from the furnishing of inaccurate information unless: (1) the information furnisher has been enjoined from committing the violation in an action brought by the state and (2) the information furnisher has violated the injunction.[500] In addition, the state may not recover any damages incurred before the date of the violation of the injunction.[501]

However, the FACTA amendments in 2003 expanded this limitation to apply, unlike the FTC, to state actions over all of the other duties the FCRA imposes on furnishers, with the exception of the duty to reinvestigate after notice from a CRA.[502] State officials, like injured consumers, may enforce the requirement that furnishers conduct such reinvestigations when they receive notice from a CRA that a consumer has disputed the accuracy or completeness of information.[503] Note that the restrictions on state officials enforcing the FCRA is in addition to the preemption provisions of the FCRA precluding states from imposing requirements on furnishers.[504]

11.16.4.3 State Notification of Federal Regulators

Prior to bringing any action, a state official must serve prior written notice of such action upon the FTC or the

---

See also U.S. v. Petersen, 98 F.3d 502, 504 (9th Cir. 1996); U.S. v. Morris, 928 F.2d 504, 507 (2d Cir. 1991).
488 Available at www.ftc.gov/reports/index.htm.
489 S. Rep. No. 185, 104th Cong., 1st Sess. at 53 (Dec. 14, 1995).
490 15 U.S.C. § 1681s(c).
491 15 U.S.C. § 1681s(c)(1)(A). *See* Commonwealth v. Source One Assocs., Inc., 436 Mass. 118 (2002).
492 But see § 11.16.4.2, *infra*, for limitations on states' ability to recover damages for violations by furnishers under the FCRA.
493 15 U.S.C. § 1681s(c)(1)(B).

494 15 U.S.C. § 1681s(c)(1)(C).
495 *See* § 10.2.4.1, *supra*.
496 15 U.S.C. § 1681s-2(a).
497 15 U.S.C. § 1681s-2(d).
498 15 U.S.C. § 1681s-2(b).
499 *See* § 11.16.2.2, *supra*.
500 15 U.S.C. § 1681s(c)(5)(A).
501 15 U.S.C. § 1681s(c)(5)(B).
502 15 U.S.C. § 1681s(c)(5)(A), *as amended by* Pub. L. No. 108-159, § 312(e) (2003).
503 *See* § 6.10, *supra*.
504 15 U.S.C. § 1681t(b)(1)(F); Ameritech Mich. v. Michigan Pub. Servs. Comm'n, 658 N.W.2d 849 (Mich. Ct. App. 2003).

appropriate federal regulator and provide a copy of the complaint. If, however, prior written notice is not feasible, the state must serve the required notice immediately upon instituting the action. The FTC or appropriate federal regulator then has the right to intervene in the action, and upon so intervening, to be heard on all matters arising therein, to remove the action to the appropriate United States district court, and to file petitions for appeal.[505]

11.16.4.4 State Investigatory Powers

Nothing in the FCRA's provision on state enforcement shall prevent the chief law enforcement officer of a state from exercising the powers to conduct investigations or to administer oaths or affirmations or to compel the attendance of witnesses or the production of documentary and other evidence in connection with any FCRA enforcement action brought by the state.[506]

11.16.4.5 Limitation on State Action While Federal Action Is Pending

If the FTC or other appropriate federal regulator has instituted a civil or administrative action in connection with a violation of the FCRA, no state may, during the pendency of the action, bring an action under the FCRA against any defendant named in the federal government's complaint in connection with any FCRA violation that is alleged in that complaint.[507]

---

505 15 U.S.C. § 1681s(c)(2).
506 15 U.S.C. § 1681s(c)(3).
507 15 U.S.C. § 1681s(c)(4).

Chapter 12   Consumer Self-Help: Advising Consumers Concerning Their Credit History and Rating

12.1 Introduction

While this manual focuses on the Fair Credit Reporting Act (FCRA) requirements and litigation, clients often need advice about their credit record, but the matter does not merit litigation. This chapter details information consumers need about their credit record that will allow them to make rational decisions about their economic lives.

While consumers justifiably are concerned about their credit record, sometimes this concern is misplaced and leads to improper choices. Thus § 12.2, *infra*, examines impermissible uses of consumer reports, even where some consumers take actions to avoid such uses. Section 12.3, *infra*, explains why collectors' threats to ruin a consumer's credit record are largely hollow. Section 12.4, *infra*, details situations where withholding payment to dispute a debt will not injure a consumer's credit record.

Nevertheless, in many situations a consumer's credit record will affect access to and the cost of credit and insurance, and have other major implications. Section 12.6, *infra*, summarizes techniques the consumer can use to improve a credit history. Just as important, § 12.5, *infra*, lists tactics to improve a credit record that are not recommended, that can just get the consumer in more trouble.

Often, no matter the consumer's efforts, a credit record will be blemished or insufficient. In that case, § 12.7, *infra*, discusses the effect of such a record on important consumer transactions, such as car and mortgage loan applications, insurance, utilities, and apartment applications. Advice is provided as to how to avoid or reduce the negative consequences of such a record for each of the types of transaction. Finally, § 12.8, *infra*, examines special consumer reporting issues related to immigrants.

These and related topics are also discussed in the *NCLC Guide to Surviving Debt*,[1] which presents advice on such topics as what debts to pay first, establishing a budget, the pros and cons of credit counseling, credit cards, refinancing loans, raising money to repay debts, responding to debt collectors and collection lawsuits, mortgage workouts, student loans, and bankruptcy.

12.2 Impermissible Uses of Consumer Reports

12.2.1 Introduction

Consumers are justifiably concerned with the real life consequences of a blemished or insufficient credit history. But sometimes this concern is not justified. Consumers should understand that certain uses of a consumer report are not allowed. The general rule is that a party has access to an individual's consumer report only for purposes related to credit, insurance, employment, public benefits and licenses, child support enforcement, counter-intelligence, and "business transactions" initiated by the consumer.[2] Where the user's purpose does not fall within one of these categories, the user may not see the report. Unauthorized access to a consumer report may result in liability for both the user and the consumer reporting agency (CRA).[3] Some areas of frequent, but unfounded, consumer concern about the use of credit records are listed below.

12.2.2 User's Curiosity; General Publication in the Community

An individual cannot obtain a consumer report solely for curiosity, gossip, or to determine an individual's general reputation.[4] These are not permissible purposes to obtain the report under the FCRA. Not only is a person prohibited from seeking a report for an impermissible purpose, but when someone obtains a report for a legitimate purpose (e.g., to evaluate a credit application), that person cannot then use the report for an impermissible purpose, such as to spread gossip about the applicant's credit record. Such an impermissible use violates both the FCRA and the person's certification to the CRA as to how that person will use the information.[5] Similarly it is illegal for a relative or potential in-law to ask a friend who has access to consumer reports to obtain a report on an individual.

---

1 NCLC Guide to Surviving Debt (2006).

2 *See* § 7.2, *supra*.
3 *See* §§ 7.5, 7.6, 7.7, *supra*.
4 *See* § 7.4.9, *supra*.
5 *See* § 7.5.2, *supra*.

12.2.3 Publication of Bad Debt Lists

Consumer reporting agencies (CRAs) cannot publish bad debt lists, because every reader of the lists will not have a permissible purpose to obtain information on every individual on the list. The CRA can use a coded list, that allows individuals on the list to be decoded only when the user has a permissible purpose to obtain information on that individual.[6] But CRAs cannot publish bad debt lists of consumers where the consumers are identifiable to the public.

Sometimes debt collection agencies who are not covered by this FCRA prohibition threaten to publish similar lists, but the federal Fair Debt Collection Practices Act prohibits third party debt collectors from publishing such lists.[7] A collection agency may not publish, for the general public or for a group of creditors, a list of debtors simply to further its own collection activities.[8] A collector may not report a debtor's delinquency to creditors subscribing to its mailing service, since not every creditor has a legitimate business need for the information.[9] There may be certain exceptions to this general rule, such as when the collection agency furnishes coded lists of bad check writers;[10] uses newspaper advertisements offering rewards for the return of specified leased cars, at least as long as they do not identify the lessee by name;[11] and provides lists of judgment debtors to an investigator for locating the debtors.[12]

12.2.4 Divorce and Custody Proceedings, Tort Suits, Criminal Actions, Immigration Matters, and Other Litigation

There is generally no permissible purpose for a spouse or other individual to obtain an individual's consumer report for the purposes of litigating a divorce or a child custody proceeding, or as an aid in computing a child support award.[13] Creditors may have a permissible purpose in discovering the existence or outcome of such litigation, and a spouse may be able to obtain a consumer report to assist in collecting payment pursuant to an order or agreement establishing a creditor-debtor relationship related to those matters. But there is no permissible purpose for obtaining the report in order to build a case for litigation.

Similarly, litigants other than creditors enforcing debt obligations have no permissible purpose to obtain consumer reports to assist them in the conduct of lawsuits. The report can only be ordered after a judgment is issued against the consumer, and the plaintiff becomes a judgment creditor.[14] The same is true in criminal investigations and prosecutions involving the consumer. In that context, not even a government agency can obtain the consumer report, except pursuant to a court order or for certain national security investigations.[15] A consumer report cannot be used for purposes related to an immigration proceeding, an application for citizenship, or voter registration.

12.2.5 Using a Consumer's Credit History to Evaluate Other Family Members and Associates

Consumers may fear that their poor credit record will reflect badly on their associates or family members. There is a blanket rule that the consumer's report cannot be used when a spouse or other associate applies for insurance, employment, or for other non-credit matters.[16] Where the spouse or other associate applies for credit, the consumer's credit history can only be used where that person is relying on the consumer's income or assets in the credit application, or where the consumer will be liable on the account.[17] (This exception allows the creditor to look at a spouse's consumer report if: the applicant lives in a community property state; the property on which the applicant relies as a basis for repayment is located in such a state; or the applicant is acting as the spouse's agent.[18])

---

6 See § 7.3.2.3, supra.
7 15 U.S.C. § 1692d(3). See generally National Consumer Law Center, Fair Debt Collection § 5.5.5 (5th 2004 and Supp.).
8 See National Consumer Law Center, Fair Debt Collection § 5.5.5.1 (5th 2004 and Supp.).
9 FTC Official Staff Commentary on the Fair Debt Collection Practices Act, § 806(4), 3; Clement, FTC Informal Staff Letter (Nov. 12, 1985) (bad check writer lists prohibited); Cathcart, FTC Informal Staff Letter (Aug. 24, 1981) (distribution by collection agency to retailers of lists of people who allegedly wrote checks subsequently dishonored violates FDCPA since retailers are not CRAs and do not have a legitimate business need for the name of everyone on the list); Woosley, FTC Informal Staff Letter (May 30, 1978); Dean, FTC Informal Staff Letter (May 30, 1978). All these materials are available at National Consumer Law Center, Fair Debt Collection Appx. B, C (5th 2004 and Supp.).
10 See Campbell v. Thompson, 1990 WL 71348 (N.D. Ala. May 23, 1990). See also § 12.7.7, infra.
11 Farmer, FTC Informal Staff Letter (Sept. 26, 1989).
12 FTC Official Staff Commentary on the Fair Debt Collection Practices Act, § 806(4)-5, reproduced in National Consumer Law Center, Fair Debt Collection Appx. C (5th 2004 and Supp.).

13 See § 7.4.2, supra.
14 See § 7.4.4, supra.
15 See §§ 7.2.1, 7.4.4, 7.4.5, supra. See also § 7.2.3, supra.
16 See § 7.4.6, supra.
17 FTC Official Staff Commentary § 604(3)(A) item 5A, reprinted at Appx. D, infra. See also § 7.4.6, supra.
18 Id.

In addition, the Equal Credit Opportunity Act (ECOA) not only prohibits access to the spouse's consumer report, but even prohibits a creditor from making any inquiry about an applicant's spouse or former spouse.[19] For example, if a wife is not relying on the husband's income or assets, the husband will not be obligated on the credit account, and the wife does not live in a community property state, the husband's credit record should in no way interfere with the wife obtaining credit. According to the FTC Official Staff Commentary (FTC Staff Commentary), a permissible purpose for making a consumer report on a non-applicant spouse can never exist under the FCRA where the ECOA prohibits the creditor from requesting the information[20] or where a non-applicant is a former spouse, a legally separated spouse, or has otherwise indicated an intent to legally disassociate with the marriage.[21] But a consumer report of a present or former spouse is accessible where a credit applicant is relying on alimony, child support, or separate maintenance payments from that spouse for repayment of the credit.[22]

Nevertheless, while the spouse's consumer report may be off limits, the spouse's credit actions may find their way on to the other spouse's consumer report. The ECOA requires that a creditor that furnishes credit information to a consumer reporting agency (CRA) must designate any account to reflect the participation of both spouses, if both spouses are permitted to use or are contractually liable on the account.[23] Then that information is entered into both spouses' files at the CRA. These procedures are designed to ensure that each spouse may build a credit history on the basis of accounts which they both use or for which both are contractually liable, even if only one spouse is listed as the primary obligor.

12.3 Consumers Should Not Fear a Collector's Threats to Report a Debt to a Consumer Reporting Agency

A common creditor and collection agency threat is that, if a consumer does not pay a debt, the consumer's credit record will be ruined. Such threats are "a powerful tool designed, in part, to wrench compliance with payment terms."[24] Consumers in financial trouble should not fear these threats.

Most creditors subscribe to one or more consumer reporting agencies (CRAs), allowing the creditor not only to receive reports, but also obligating the creditor to supply information to the CRA. Typically, information is reported in a standardized fashion each month by computer on all of the creditor's accounts. The consumer's file at a CRA is constantly updated with the current payment status, the amount owed, how many days a debt is delinquent, and what collection actions have been taken. This happens automatically. Creditors do not withhold adverse information, giving consumers another chance to pay. Each month, the exact status of the debt is updated.

When a creditor or collector is threatening to report a debt to a CRA, creditors who subscribe to the CRA have already reported the debt's status. Despite the threat, there will be nothing else for the creditor to report. The threat is meaningless because it has already been carried out. If a creditor does not subscribe to CRA, it is highly unlikely that the creditor will respond to a consumer's nonpayment by attempting to furnish that fact to a CRA with whom it is not associated, and the CRA will not accept the information from a non-subscriber.

It is also unlikely that an independent collection agency hired by a creditor will report information to a CRA just because the consumer does not respond to the debt collector's collection attempts. Although some large collection agencies subscribe to CRAs, some do not want to go to the expense of collecting and sending the information. If a collection agency does furnish information to a CRA, the damage will have already been done, as discussed below. Paying that collector first is unlikely to prevent future damage.

Implicit in a threat to ruin a consumer's credit record is the suggestion that the consumer's credit record will best be served by paying that creditor's debt ahead of other creditors. This is very important to collectors. Collectors realize that when consumers are seriously delinquent, it is almost always because consumers do not have enough money to pay all their debts. Consumers must decide which debts to pay first. The collector's job is to get the consumer to pay its creditor's debt first. The threat thus is that nonpayment of a particular creditor's debt will be especially damaging to a consumer's credit record.

In reality, almost all the consumer's creditors are regularly reporting on their accounts to CRAs. The fact that a particular collector threatens to report a debt to a CRA bears no relationship to whether that debt's delinquency is more or less likely to be furnished to a CRA than other debts. In fact, debts being collected by an independent collection agency often are less likely to be furnished to a CRA. Large creditors that do their own collecting usually will subscribe to a CRA and regularly furnish month-to-month reports on

---

19 Reg. B, 12 C.F.R. § 202.5(c)(1).
20 *Id.*
21 FTC Official Staff Commentary § 604(3)(A) item 5B, *reprinted at* Appx. D, *infra*.
22 *Id.* § 202.5(c)(2)(v). FTC, Compliance with the Fair Credit Reporting Act, at 20 (1977).
23 ECOA Reg. B, 12 C.F.R. § 202.10(a)(1). *See* National Consumer Law Center, Credit Discrimination § 9.4 (4th ed. 2005 and Supp.).
24 Rivera v. Bank One, 145 F.R.D. 614 (D. P.R. 1993). *Accord*

Matter of Sommersdorf, 139 B.R. 700, 701 (Bankr. S.D. Ohio 1991).

all their accounts. On the other hand, hospitals, doctors, and others who are likely to hire an independent collection agency are less likely to subscribe to a CRA, and thus are less likely to furnish information to a CRA. The independent collection agency itself is also unlikely to supply information to the CRA.

Moreover, the debt will already have been reported as delinquent. Stopping payment on another debt to pay the collector will only mean that the individual's consumer report will show two delinquencies instead of one. And if this second debt is a home mortgage, car payment, or the like, this new delinquency will not only be a much greater weight hanging over the family, but it may put the consumer's home or car (and thus ability to get to work) at risk. Paying an account that is already in default is not likely to improve a credit record because the account still stays on the report as a negative account.

Some collectors will promise to remove the account from the consumer report as an incentive to pay. These promises are not likely to be kept. First, the collector can remove only its own information, not the creditor's. Second, unless the consumer gets the promise to remove in writing before payment, the collector can easily deny having made the promise. Sample language for a written agreement to remove bad credit information is provided in Appendix J.9 and discussed at § 12.6.4.6, *infra*.

12.4 Does Withholding Payment As Part of a Dispute Ruin a Consumer's Credit Record?

12.4.1 Introduction

One of the most effective self-help strategies for a consumer who is disputing a debt is to withhold payment, whether it is a dispute as to the nature of product or service delivered, defects in the product, overcharges, or any other aspect of a transaction. Withholding payment is far more practical than paying in full and then seeking a refund from the company. When the consumer withholds payment, companies are unlikely to sue for a small amount in dispute, and will thus be encouraged to settle. On the other hand, if the consumer pays, the consumer will be the one who will find it impractical to bring a lawsuit seeking to recover a relatively small amount in dispute.

A major impediment to withholding payment is that those from whom money is withheld will often threaten to or in fact will supply negative information to a consumer reporting agency (CRA) about the consumer's nonpayment of the obligation. This concern over a consumer's credit record is a major reason why more consumers do not withhold payment when they have valid disputes as to an obligation. This section reviews legal restrictions on a company reporting negative information about a disputed debt when the consumer is withholding payment.

In addition, consumers should not assume that every company they deal with sends information to a CRA. Disputing certain debts with a merchant who does not subscribe to a CRA will have no effect on an individual's consumer report. For example, doctors, hospitals, lawyers, smaller landlords, and other small merchants are unlikely to have a relationship with a CRA.

If the dispute has resulted in litigation, another way to protect an individual's consumer report is for the consumer's attorney to seek the creditor's agreement not to furnish adverse information while the suit is pending. If the creditor refuses, application can be made to the court.

12.4.2 Disputes Relating to Credit Card Charges

Federal law provides consumers with two different rights to dispute credit card charges, and provides protections against the card issuer furnishing CRAs adverse information during that dispute. In many disputes, the consumer can utilize either of these protections or both. The first is provided by the Fair Credit Billing Act, discussed in more detail in another NCLC manual.[25] If the consumer notifies the creditor of a billing error within sixty days after it first appears on a periodic statement, the consumer can withhold payment relating to the dispute, and adverse reports or threats of adverse reports are prohibited until the creditor completes its investigatory obligations under the Fair Credit Billing Act.[26] If the consumer still disputes the item, the creditor can report that the account is delinquent only if it also reports that the consumer disputes the delinquency.[27]

A second consumer right provided by Truth in Lending applies where the consumer has a complaint with the merchant relating to a credit card charge, and an attempt to resolve the matter with the merchant fails. The consumer can then withhold payment on the credit card, and adverse reports are prohibited until the card issuer investigates and resolves the dispute.[28] The card issuer cannot report or threaten to report the amount as delinquent, but can report the amount as in dispute and can report other charges that are delinquent. If the consumer has acted in good faith, the

---

25 National Consumer Law Center, Truth in Lending § 5.8 (5th ed. 2003 and Supp.). *See also* § 5.3.4, *supra*.
26 15 U.S.C. § 1666; 12 C.F.R. § 226.13(b).
27 12 C.F.R. § 226.13(g)(4).
28 15 U.S.C. § 1666i. This right only applies if the cardholder has first made a good faith attempt to resolve the dispute with the merchant, and, except when the card issuer and the merchant are closely connected, the amount involved exceeds $50 and the transaction occurred in the consumer's state or within 100 miles of the consumer's residence. In addition, the right only applies if the consumer has not yet paid the disputed charge. *See also* National Consumer Law Center, Truth in Lending § 5.9.5 (5th ed. 2003 and Supp.).

card issuer cannot close or restrict the account. Even after the investigation, if the card issuer decides the consumer owes the amount, and the consumer continues to dispute the amount, the card issuer can only report the amount as delinquent if it also reports the amount is in dispute.[29] This right is also examined in more detail in another NCLC manual.[30]

12.4.3 Telephone and Other Utility Charges

A consumer may wish to dispute many different types of utility charges—local telephone, long-distance telephone, cell phone, water, gas, electric, and cable, to mention the most common. Different utilities will involve different protections while the dispute is pending. Many such utilities will not even furnish information to CRAs. Those regulated by a state public utility commission (typically local phone, gas, and electric) will also be subject to regulations that limit their ability to take adverse actions while a dispute is pending.[31]

The Fair Credit Billing Act and Truth in Lending rights, described in the prior section, to dispute bills without an adverse effect on a consumer report, do not apply to regulated utilities. But they apply to unregulated utilities whose payment procedures meet the definition of a credit card. For example, long-distance calling cards are not regulated and the cards would meet the TILA definition of a credit card.[32] TILA defines a credit card as "any card, plate, coupon book, or other single credit device that may be used from time to time to obtain credit."[33] Although no court or agency has ruled on the question, there is an argument that a cell phone used to make a call or receive a service for which payment is deferred qualifies as a "device" used to obtain credit. FCBA and TILA rights would then apply to these cell phone charges. In addition, FCBA rights should apply whenever a unregulated utility's payment plan meets the definition of open-end credit.

12.4.4 Home Mortgages and Home Equity Lines of Credit

A consumer can dispute the amount owed on various types of mortgage loans without an immediate adverse effect on the consumer's credit record, by first sending a "qualified written request." This right applies to disputes regarding a home mortgage loan, a home improvement loan secured by the residence, a home equity loan, or another first or junior loan secured by the consumer's dwelling. No adverse reports are allowed during the sixty-day period that the Real Estate Settlement Procedures Act (RESPA) gives the servicer to evaluate the dispute.[34] This right is examined in more detail in another NCLC manual.[35]

HUD states that the RESPA right to dispute or request information on a mortgage loan does not apply to home equity lines of credit, but this is contrary to the statute and may not be enforceable.[36] In any event, as discussed above, the FCBA rights regarding open-end credit apply and provide different and probably stronger consumer protections. These protections apply to open-end credit plans—a home equity line of credit meets this definition.

12.4.5 Student Loans and Other Government Debts

Before a guaranty agency can report a student loan delinquency to a CRA, the consumer must have an opportunity to inspect and copy the records concerning the debt, and obtain an administrative review of the enforceability of the debt and whether the student loan is past due.[37] The rule is similar for other types of debts owed to the United States. Before any information can be furnished to a CRA, the consumer must first receive notice of the intent to report the information,[38] and the consumer can request a review of the obligation, including an opportunity for reconsideration of the initial determination that the consumer owes the debt.[39]

12.4.6 Debt Being Collected by a Debt Collector

The Fair Debt Collection Practices Act requires third party collectors to provide consumers with a "validation notice" offering them the right to request that the collector verify the debt within the first thirty days after the consumer receives the notice. If a written request to verify is sent to the collector, the collector can take no collection action until it provides the requested verification. This has generally been interpreted as preventing the collector or creditor from

---

29 12 C.F.R. § 226.13(g).
30 National Consumer Law Center, Truth in Lending § 5.9 (5th ed. 2003 and Supp.).
31 See National Consumer Law Center, Access to Utility Service (3d ed. 2004 and Supp.).
32 FCBA applies to a creditor, and 15 U.S.C. § 1602(f) states that, for purposes of the FCBA, the term "creditor" applies to any card issuer, and that the FCBA applies to card issuers even if otherwise limited to creditors offering open-end credit plans. See also 12 C.F.R. § 226.2(15).
33 15 U.S.C. § 1602(k).

34 12 U.S.C. § 2605(e). These rights apply only to "federally related mortgage loans" as defined in 12 U.S.C. § 2602(1)(A).
35 National Consumer Law Center, Foreclosures § 5.2.2 (2005 and Supp.). See also § 5.3.5, supra.
36 National Consumer Law Center, Foreclosures (2005 and Supp.).
37 34 C.F.R. § 682.410(b)(5)(ii)(B), (C).
38 31 U.S.C. § 3711(e)(1).
39 31 U.S.C. § 3711(e)(2).

§ 12.4.7 FCRA Protections Where Consumer Disputes a Debt

For any type of credit, when a consumer disputes a debt, the creditor, in furnishing information on that debt to a CRA, must include notice that the information is disputed by the consumer.[41] In turn, the CRA must note the consumer's dispute in any report that includes the information.[42] The creditor also risks tort liability if it furnishes inaccurate information.[43] These rights are explored in more detail elsewhere in this manual.[44]

§ 12.4.8 ECOA Protections When Raising Federal Statutory Rights

The Equal Credit Opportunity Act prohibits creditors from furnishing adverse credit information on consumers because of the consumer's good faith exercise of rights under the federal Consumer Credit Protection Act.[45] The federal Consumer Credit Protection Act is an umbrella name for many of the federal consumer protection statutes, including the Truth in Lending, the Fair Credit Billing Act, the Consumer Leasing Act, the Fair Credit Reporting Act, the Fair Debt Collection Practices Act, the Garnishment Act, the Credit Repair Organizations Act, the Electronic Funds Transfer Act, and the Equal Credit Opportunity Act.

12.5 The Wrong Way to Improve a Credit Record

12.5.1 Credit Repair

Credit repair organizations (sometimes referred to as credit clinics, or credit service companies) offer an expensive service that may not do anything to improve a credit record. Typically the consumer's own efforts will be more effective than that of the credit repair organizations, because consumer reporting agencies (CRAs) ignore dispute letters coming from such organizations or even coming from consumers using forms provided by such organizations. What such organizations provide may in fact make matters worse or lead the consumer to violate the law. These organizations are so suspect that Congress enacted the Credit Repair Organizations Act to attempt to prevent many of the abuses. That Act and credit repair in general is discussed in more detail at Chapter 15, *infra*.

12.5.2 Debt Elimination, Debt Settlement, and Debt Adjustment

Debt termination or debt elimination companies claim to be able to eliminate debts, for a charge, usually through use of specially prepared documents with names such as "Declaration of Voidance," "Bond for Discharge of Debt," and "Redemption Certificate." These documents will be based on outlandish theories, such as challenging the authority of the Federal Reserve Board or the legitimacy of the U.S. currency. Other times, phony arbitration proceedings will claim to cancel the indebtedness. Whatever the scam, the consumer will just lose money, obtain no relief, and will probably further blemish a credit record, if these schemes lead the consumer to skip additional loan obligations.

Debt settlement companies can be even more costly to the consumer, and be even more damaging to a credit record. They encourage consumers not to pay their debts, but to put money away in a separate account. At some point, the agency will negotiate with the creditor, trying to make a lump-sum settlement for less than is owed, paid out of the money put away in a separate account. The settlement company though will be taking large fees out of the money set aside, and another fee if the debt is settled. The fees are so high that this strategy rarely works, and the consumer would have been better off settling the debt on his or her own. In the meantime, by encouraging the consumer not to make payments to the creditor, the consumer's credit record will be worsened.

Credit counseling is more of a mixed bag. Some agencies charge high fees for little service. Even many supposed non-profit agencies are losing this status because the companies were using the fiction of a non-profit status to hide their real profit motive. Legitimate agencies can offer advice, and they can facilitate payment to creditors. A debt management plan will be disclosed on a consumer report, but a debt management plan with a credit counselor is unlikely to have a significant positive or negative effect on a consumer's credit record. The *NCLC Guide to Surviving Debt*[46] discusses credit counseling in greater depth.

12.5.3 Making Payments on Old Defaults

It may be counter-productive to make payments on old defaults, in an attempt to make a credit record look better.

---

40 LeFevre, FTC Informal Staff Opinion Letter (Dec. 4, 1997), *interpreting* 15 U.S.C. § 1692g(b). *See also* National Consumer Law Center, Fair Debt Collection § 5.7 (5th ed. 2004 and Supp.) and § 5.3.3, *supra*.
41 15 U.S.C. § 1681s-2(a)(3). *See* § 6.5.2, *supra*.
42 15 U.S.C. § 1681c(f).
43 *See* Ch. 10, *supra*.
44 § 6.5.2, *supra*.
45 12 C.F.R. § 202.2(m), (z); 15 U.S.C. § 1691(a)(3). *See* National Consumer Law Center, Credit Discrimination § 3.4.4 (4th ed. 2005 and Supp.).

46 NCLC Guide to Surviving Debt Ch. 4 (2006).

After seven years, such defaults will be removed from the report in any event.[47] Making payments on older debt also is unlikely to improve a credit score, and may make the old debt look more recent, particularly if the debt is not paid in full.[48] Even more significantly, such payments will reduce the consumer's cash flow, and may prevent payment on current debts that are not yet delinquent. Placing those other debts into a delinquent status is certain to do more damage than making a payment on an older debt will help.

12.5.4 Taking on New Debt

Consumers may be tempted to bulk up a credit record by seeking to establish new credit accounts, and pay those accounts in a timely fashion. There are several problems with this approach. First, not all creditors furnish information to CRAs. Although almost every credit card issuer and car lender will, many merchants appealing to those with a marginal credit history will not furnish data to CRAs. For example, even if a "buy here, pay here" car dealer advertises that no credit is necessary and that a purchase through them will improve a credit record, the dealer may in fact not furnish its payment experience to CRAs.

In addition, it may take a number of credit inquiries before the consumer is accepted for credit, and the frequency of those inquiries will damage a consumer's credit rating. Even more significantly, relative debt burden to income is an important factor in qualifying for credit, so that adding new debt may be counterproductive. In the rush to establish a credit history, consumers may overextend themselves. If delinquencies and defaults result, the consumer has made a blemished credit record worse, or exchanged an insufficient credit history for a bad credit history. Even if the consumer is able to stay current on the payments, it is best to keep balances low so that creditors perceive the consumer as having the capacity to undertake more credit.

The worst effect of a consumer trying too hard to obtain additional credit is where the consumer falls victim to predatory lenders or brokers targeting those with marginal credit records. These scam operators charge exorbitant rates and assess hidden charges. Rather than clean up a credit record, such creditors may rob the consumer of income, more severely blemish the credit record when the consumer cannot pay the inflated payments, and seize the consumer's home or other key assets.

12.5.5 File Segregation Is Not Recommended

One strategy that is not recommended to clean up a blemished consumer report is the so-called "file segregation" technique. Various for-profit "credit repair clinics"[49] and even some consumer self-help manuals suggest this approach. A consumer tries to confuse the CRAs about his or her identity, so that the CRA will create a new, "clean" file that does not contain the negative credit information. The file segregation technique takes advantage of CRAs' failure to identify consumers with precision, even when such universal identifiers as Social Security numbers are present. Basically, a consumer changes as much identifying information as possible—name, and even Social Security number[50]—so that a CRA will not be able to find the file when a potential creditor asks for it. If a CRA cannot find a consumer on whom a report is demanded, it will create a new file for the consumer.

The consumer then tries to put as much of his or her good credit history as possible into the new file (by changing the address/name/Social Security number on accounts that are current, for example) while leaving out delinquent accounts. When this is done, the consumer can apply for credit (probably as fast as possible, since conceivably the bad information the consumer is trying to outrun is not far behind).

While those who advocate file segregation insist that it is entirely legal as long as the consumer has no intent to defraud creditors, there is, of course, a very real possibility that the intent to defraud is the consumer's motivation. In addition, as CRAs improve the sophistication of their computer identification systems (for example, to prevent mismerged files and wrongly identified consumers), this technique should work less and less. Instead, the very attempt may reflect poorly on the consumer both in dealings with the CRA and potential creditors.

12.6 Ways to Improve a Credit Record

12.6.1 First Considerations

Some perspective is necessary before consumers attempt to improve their credit records. A consumer's credit history is only one factor that a lender will consider in deciding whether to extend credit to the consumer. Another factor will be the consumer's ability to present a pattern of stability in employment and income and a reasonable debt burden in relation to income.[51] For example, continuous employment for the last two years may be a better indicator of a consumer's ability to repay a loan than a debt that was once delinquent for several months four years ago. Similarly, mortgage lenders, landlords, and certain other creditors may

---

47 *See* § 5.2, *supra*.
48 *See* Ch. 14, *infra*.
49 *See* Ch. 15, *infra*.
50 It has been suggested that individuals can get a new Social Security number if they demonstrate a need for it, such as a founded fear of fraud.
51 *See, e.g.*, Federal Home Loan Mortgage Corporation, Single-Family Seller/Service Guide §§ 37.13, 37.15, 37.16 (2000).

be more likely to extend credit to an individual who has a reasonable debt level, even if one or two accounts were recently delinquent, than to someone with excessive debt, even if that individual has not yet defaulted on any of the loans. The further in the past a default gets, the less weight a creditor is likely to give it, so the mere passage of time can improve a consumer report as long as the consumer is not running up new defaults, making several credit applications, or becoming overloaded with debt.

Creditors know that virtually all delinquencies are based on a consumer's inability to pay, and not a consumer's intent to avoid legitimate obligations. Unless a credit record shows a pattern of intentional avoidance of valid obligations, the creditor will be more concerned with whether the consumer will have the present and future ability to repay the loan.

Consumers should focus their energies on achieving this stability of income and employment, and keeping their debt burden under control. This is usually a higher priority than worrying how to clear up an old blemish on a credit record. Stable income and a low debt burden may be the best way to clean up a credit record. Moreover, consumers can actually make matters worse if they go about cleaning up their record in the wrong way. Section 12.5, *infra*, examines such tactics that can get consumers into trouble.

In any effective attempt to improve a consumer's credit record, the first step is to read the consumer report. Many consumers should seek out someone to help them review the report, because it is not always easy to read and understand. Once the report is understood, its contents may surprise the consumer—delinquent debts they were worried about may not even show up on the report, while others will be listed that the consumer may not have been aware of or even have been responsible for. Reading the report will also uncover errors and may make apparent items that have the most serious adverse consequences.

There are different schools of thought as to whether the consumer should obtain an annual free report from the "Big Three" nationwide consumer reporting agencies (CRAs) immediately, or stagger the receipt of these free reports over a period of many months.[52] There will be significant similarities between the three reports, and staggering allows three free requests over the year. But, as set out in § 3.3, *supra*, there are other grounds to obtain additional free consumer reports, and other reports can be obtained at a minimal charge.

In many cases, a report from a specialized CRA is the cause of a consumer's problems in obtaining a residential tenancy, insurance, a bank account, or certain other transactions. In these cases, the consumer should obtain a report from the specialized CRA providing the negative report. As with the reports from the nationwide CRAs, the consumer usually has a right to obtain such a report free of charge.[53]

Another initial point to make is that often credit decisions will be based on a credit score, rather than a copy of the complete report. It may be more difficult for the consumer to see the actual score relied upon by the creditor, and it will be even more difficult to understand how that score was derived.[54] Probably the best approach is to make the individual's consumer report look as clean as possible, and the credit score will probably follow.

12.6.2 Correcting Inaccurate Information

12.6.2.1 Disputing the Information

A consumer report often contains a number of inaccurate or incomplete items that will adversely affect the consumer's credit standing. For example, negative information about a consumer with a similar name may be mixed in with the consumer's report, or consumer payments will not be reflected in the report, indicating a delinquency that does not exist. Consumers should dispute all such items, even when an item is technically accurate, but does not tell the whole picture.[55] For example, a report may indicate a cosigner was months delinquent on a debt not paid by the principal obligor, where the cosigner paid in full immediately upon learning of the delinquency. Similarly, an account may look like it is maxed out, but the creditor has failed to furnish the CRA with the higher credit limit.

Even if the consumer has notified the creditor about an inaccuracy, it is imperative that the consumer also dispute the item directly with the CRA. This triggers potential liability for both the creditor (often called the furnisher) and the CRA if they do not respond properly. On the other hand, if the consumer only disputes the item with the creditor, the creditor and CRA's liability is extremely circumscribed, and neither CRA will have much incentive to correct inaccurate information.

Check the CRA's materials or its website for the current address to send disputes. If that fails, the FTC's website, www.ftc.gov, usually indicates the correct postal addresses to dispute an item with a CRA. Although the dispute need not be in writing, it is prudent to put everything in writing and keep copies, and to send the dispute return receipt requested. Using a CRA's website to submit disputes is not recommended because it reduces the chances that human eyes will ever see the dispute. The consumer may need to dispute information with all three of the nationwide CRAs if inaccurate information is found in the files for all three.

Do not use a form provided by a credit repair organization. CRAs receive large numbers of disputes on those forms and may treat them as frivolous, and thus ignore them.

---

52 *See* § 3.3.2, *supra*.
53 *See id.*
54 *See* Ch. 14, *infra*.
55 15 U.S.C. § 1681i(a)(1). For an extensive discussion of the legal requirements of the FCRA dispute process, see Chs. 4, 6, *supra*.

Instead, use the CRA's own form or a simple letter drafted by the consumer or the consumer's attorney. Be specific and precise as to the dispute. Do not dispute everything in the file, but specify certain items with clear reasons why the items themselves are inaccurate or incomplete.

Many attorneys prefer to have consumers write and send dispute letters on their own, using guidelines supplied by the attorney (and possibly reviewed and edited by the attorney). This is less expensive for the client, and it prevents the attorney from being dragged into the case as a fact witness if the mailing or receipt of the letter becomes an issue. On the other hand, some CRAs may treat dispute letters from attorneys with more care.[56]

12.6.2.2 Steps the Consumer Reporting Agency and Creditor Must Take in Response to the Consumer's Dispute

When a CRA receives the consumer's dispute, it first determines if the dispute is frivolous or irrelevant.[57] If the CRA terminates a reinvestigation because it deems the dispute frivolous, it must notify the consumer and give reasons for its determination.[58] Alternatively, the CRA may simply delete the disputed information, without contacting the furnisher. This is called an expedited dispute resolution, and must occur within three days, with notice to the consumer.[59] This is relatively rare—CRAs generally will not delete an item simply because a consumer disputes it.

More typically, within five days after receiving the consumer's dispute, the CRA provides the consumer's notice of dispute to the party who furnished the information to the CRA (typically a creditor, often referred to as a furnisher).[60] The furnisher is then required to conduct its own investigation,[61] including review of all information about the dispute forwarded by the CRA.[62] If the furnisher cannot verify the original item, or does not respond to the request for verification, the consumer's view must prevail.[63] Future reports must not contain the deleted information,[64] and it is important for consumers to verify this by periodically reviewing their consumer report.[65] The consumer can also require the CRA to notify past report users of the correction or deletion.[66]

12.6.2.3 Contacting the Creditor

Disputing a debt with the creditor should never be a substitute for disputing the item with the CRA, but the consumer can consider contacting the creditor in addition to contacting the CRA. The creditor (often referred to as the furnisher) may agree to clear up the problem. If not, the consumer's notice to the creditor will make the consumer's case stronger if the matter goes to litigation.

Whenever disputing a debt with the furnisher, consumers should use the address the creditor provides for that purpose, if there is one on the bill. The dispute letter must identify the specific information that is disputed, explain the basis for the dispute, and include any supporting documentation required by the furnisher.[67] Submit the dispute in writing, using return receipt mail, so that the furnisher does not deny receipt of the dispute.[68]

When a consumer has used the address provided by the creditor to specify that information is inaccurate, the creditor is prohibited from furnishing information that "is, in fact, inaccurate."[69] While the Fair and Accurate Credit Transactions Act of 2003 (FACTA) amendments to the FCRA imposed a duty of investigation upon the creditor, a creditor's failure under this section is not privately enforceable.[70] However, any prudent creditor can be expected to reinvestigate the accuracy of the disputed information, and to take into consideration any and all relevant information provided by the consumer and otherwise reasonably available to the creditor.

If the creditor does not have an address for consumer complaints, the consumer should still write and dispute the debt and the inaccurate reporting of the debt with just as much specificity. Although no duty arises to furnish only information that is in fact accurate, the creditor nevertheless remains obligated not to furnish information it knows or consciously avoids knowing is inaccurate.[71] Thus, when the creditor next furnishes information about the debt (and most creditors do so at least monthly), it will be obligated to reasonably evaluate the information provided by the consumer.

12.6.3 Dealing with Public Record Information

Some of the most damaging information in a consumer report does not come from creditors, but from CRAs retrieving public record information, such as judgments against the consumer, foreclosures, tax takings, liens, and

---

56 For a comparison of the advantages and disadvantages of these two approaches, see L. Bennett, *Attorneys Should Draft Dispute Letters for Their Clients in FCRA Cases* and R. Sola, *Why Attorneys Should Not Write Dispute Letters*, both found at The Consumer Advocate, vol. 12, no. 1, at 3 (Jan.–Mar. 2006).
57 15 U.S.C. § 1681i(a)(3).
58 *Id.*
59 15 U.S.C. § 1681i(a)(8).
60 15 U.S.C. § 1681i(a)(2).
61 15 U.S.C. § 1681s-2(b)(1).
62 15 U.S.C. § 1681s-2(b)(1)(A), (B).
63 15 U.S.C. § 1681i(a)(5)(A).
64 15 U.S.C. § 1681i(a)(5)(B).
65 Ch. 4, *supra*.
66 15 U.S.C. § 1681i(d).

67 15 U.S.C. § 1681s-2(c)(8)(D).
68 However, since the FCRA does not provide that the consumer must notify the furnisher of the dispute in writing, a consumer's oral notice should be sufficient.
69 15 U.S.C. § 1681s-2(c)(8)(D).
70 15 U.S.C. § 1681s-2(a)(8). See § 6.10, *supra*.
71 15 U.S.C. § 1681s-2(a)(1)(A).

the like. This information can have a strong negative effect and should be cleared up where possible.

The best approach is to improve the public record information at its source, and then make sure that the CRA deletes the outdated information in its files. For example, any information in error should be corrected. Alternatively, where a creditor that has taken a default judgment against the consumer, improving a public record might involve reaching an agreement to vacate the judgment and dismiss the case in return for lump-sum payment. Other ways of cleaning up public record information include getting a lawsuit or an arrest warrant dismissed or expunged, and arranging for liens to be removed. Once the public record is improved, the consumer can dispute the CRA's version, and the CRA will have to correct its file to reflect the updated status of the record.[72]

12.6.4 Dealing with Negative Information When Settling Non-FCRA Litigation

12.6.4.1 Importance of Resolving Credit Reporting Issues

There is no better time to clear up a consumer's credit record than when settling a lawsuit with a creditor that has furnished negative information on the consumer.[73] Failure of a settlement to protect a client's credit record will probably mean that the consumer will be plagued by a bad credit record for at least seven years. As a matter of routine, practitioners should demand that all settlements related to credit accounts include a provision dealing directly with what the creditor should and should not report to a CRA. Depending on the circumstances, practitioners may want to consider adding such provisions in any repayment agreement (which should be in writing) with a creditor.[74]

If a dispute involves the consumer defending a collection action, the creditor will already have reported its unfavorable experience with the consumer to at least one and probably more CRAs. Even if the consumer later pays the amount being sought in full, the existence of the default, the collection action, and the extended period of nonpayment may remain on consumer reports for seven years.

The solution is to make sure that any settlement or repayment agreement on the debt deals with consumer reporting issues. The settlement should contain a clear and unequivocal requirement that, as part of the resolution of differences, the creditor will undertake to remove unfavorable information from the individual's consumer reporting file.[75] Model language which may be adapted and included in settlement agreements is at Appendix J.9, *infra*.

It is important to note that CRAs are not required to withdraw information upon the request of the creditor who supplied the information initially.[76] However, the CRA is held to a standard of accuracy which, if violated, may render the CRA liable for civil damages. Thus, in practice, if the source of information in a credit file requests that the information be withdrawn, thereby suggesting that the information is not entirely accurate or reliable, the CRA is likely to comply. Moreover, even if the CRA does not comply, the consumer can dispute the item. The CRA will have to obtain re-verification of the item from the creditor. If the terms of the settlement preclude the creditor from verifying the information, the CRA, unable to obtain verification, will have to delete the information.[77] Also, regardless of a CRA's decision not to remove unfavorable information, the creditor will often have already reported the debt as disputed, as required, and the CRA must note the dispute in its reports.[78]

When settling a foreclosure case, a deed in lieu of foreclosure may have some advantage over a foreclosure judgment. In a judicial foreclosure state, a foreclosure judgment will appear in court records, which the CRAs are sure to pick up. A deed in lieu of foreclosure will appear on an individual's consumer report only if the lender reports it. Of course, the creditor will already have reported any default, and the filing of any foreclosure action will also appear in public records.

12.6.4.2 Negotiating Settlement Covering Credit Reporting

Practitioners may find the creditor (sometimes referred to as the furnisher) reluctant to agree to cease furnishing unfavorable credit information to the CRAs. The creditor may harbor resentment of "irresponsible" consumer behavior, and wish to avoid any "generous" concessions. More importantly, the creditor may feel a moral obligation to report its experiences so that the integrity of the consumer reporting system upon which all creditors rely is not undermined.

On the other hand, the information reported by the creditor may not reflect an accurate summary of the whole credit experience, and may conflict in important aspects with the consumer's version. This is almost always the case where the consumer disputes whether he or she owed the full amount the creditor reported as delinquent. Moreover, the

---

72 See Ch. 4, *supra*.
73 See, *e.g.*, Cahlin v. General Motors Acceptance Corp., 936 F.2d 1151 (11th Cir. 1991) (GMAC removed adverse report as part of settlement efforts).
74 See § 12.6.7.3, *infra*.
75 A creditor may be able to access a consumer report to make sure information has in fact been deleted as promised. Wilting v. Progressive County Mut. Ins. Co., 227 F.3d 474 (5th Cir. 2000).
76 See Watson v. Credit Bureau, Inc., 660 F. Supp. 48 (S.D. Miss. 1986).
77 See Ch. 4, *supra*.
78 See § 12.6.2, *supra*.

paramount responsibility of a credit manager to maximize the amount collected from its consumer debtors should generally outweigh the intangible concern for keeping a blemish on the individual's consumer report. It should cost the creditor essentially nothing to revise or withdraw an earlier report.

Settlement negotiations should always include a discussion of consumer reports, even if it is unlikely that the final agreement will provide a more accurate report. At best, the creditor may be amenable to the consumer's concerns. At worst, the consumer may be able to obtain the names of any CRA used by the creditor. Then, after settlement, the consumer or counsel may write the CRAs directly to correct or dispute any inaccurate or incomplete information remaining on file.[79]

Once counsel has established the precedent that settlement agreements with a creditor must address consumer reporting, it will become easier to obtain similar agreements in the future. When inclusion of reporting issues in a settlement becomes routine in the community, consumers regularly will be protected from some of the potentially devastating effects of bad consumer reports.

12.6.4.3 Selecting the Correct Settlement Language

Practitioners can consider two alternative types of settlement provisions, which are included in Appendix J.9, *infra*. The first type requires the creditor (often referred to as the furnisher) to contact the CRA and request that the entire report of the disputed debt be withdrawn. This withdrawal is sometimes referred to as a "hard delete." The consumer report will then be altogether silent about the debt and will not even provide a basis for another creditor, interested in the creditworthiness of the consumer, to inquire further. This is often the simplest solution for the consumer and the safest.[80] One drawback is that sometimes if the debt is deleted, the consumer's credit record will be too sparse.

Some advocates report that a "soft delete" such as "cloaking" or "suppression" is inadequate and seems to lead to later re-reporting of the information. These advocates favor a "hard delete." Others report that re-insertion of the deleted information is actually easier after a "hard delete."[81] The key for the consumer is that the agreement must include an iron-clad prohibition against re-reporting the debt or transferring or selling it, and the consumer must monitor his or her consumer report to make sure the information does not reappear. The agreement should address the possibility that the CRA will not delete the report despite the creditor's request. In that event, the consumer should plan to dispute the debt, and the creditor should agree that it will not verify the debt if it receives a reinvestigation request from a CRA.

The second alternative permits reporting of the debt, but requires the creditor to take steps to avoid having unfavorable information about the debt included in any consumer report. The consumer may benefit from this approach, especially if the consumer report contains only information which suggests a good consumer experience with the creditor. It may benefit the creditor because it permits the reporting of the debt and any information which is uncontested or undisputed. The report could also thus accurately reflect a debt, a dispute, and a successful resolution of the dispute.

For the second alternative to be successful, the settlement provisions must carefully delineate what information cannot be furnished to a CRA because it might be construed unfavorably to the client. The model language found at Appendix J.9, *infra*, suggests some possibilities. Even so, there is always the risk that even the limited information reported, though accurate in a narrow sense, will permit another creditor using the report to fill in the gaps incorrectly or to draw its own negative inferences. For example, if there was a dispute, a creditor might suppose there was a default as well.

There is another risk inherent in the second alternative, which should be addressed in the settlement agreement. The mere reporting of the existence of a debt may lead a future report user to call the creditor listed in the consumer report. A credit manager receiving such a call will naturally be inclined to give only the creditor's version of the facts, tinged perhaps with latent anger. As a result, the settlement must deal explicitly with oral inquiries made to the creditor directly. However, this will be a difficult provision to police.

Creditors may balk at promising to correct credit information before they can verify that the consumer will live up to the consumer's side of the settlement. To meet this concern, the consumer can agree that unfavorable information will be withdrawn or withheld only so long as the consumer complies with the settlement agreement. If the consumer breaches any part of the settlement agreement, for example by missing a payment, then the creditor may make a full report to the CRA without the limitations otherwise inherent in the agreement. Nevertheless, because of the possibilities that a consumer will miss a payment, the settlement might only allow the creditor to report this delinquency in the rescheduled payment plan.

---

79 See Ch. 4, *supra*.

80 Some practitioners have encountered creditors who assert that they are unable to withdraw the entire report. On the contrary, however, the deletion can be accomplished through the Consumer Data Industry Association's Universal Data Form, or through the its Metro 2 Format. Information regarding these mechanisms can be obtained from CDIA's website: www.cdiaonline.org. *See also* § 6.3, *supra* (discussion of Metro 2 and Universal Data Form); Appx. I, *infra* (copy of Universal Data Form). The settlement agreement can provide that the creditor will give the consumer's attorney a copy of the form that the creditor submits to the agency.

81 See Ch. 4, *supra*.

Creditors who routinely report their experiences to CRAs by computer tape or transmission will generally simply correct their tapes.[82] Other creditors may notify the CRA by letter. The consumer's attorney may wish to retain a hand in the drafting of the letter the creditor will submit to the CRA.[83] In an appropriate case, the consumer's attorney may want to specify the CRA-specific codes that will be used in the creditor's report on the debt's status to the CRA.[84] It is important, especially under the second alternative, that the tone of the letter reflect the true nature of the settlement and not seem to mask some mismanagement of the credit by the consumer. This can be resolved by providing that the notice to the CRA shall be in a letter using language agreed to at the time of settlement by both parties. Upon posting, a copy of the letter should be sent to the consumer.

A common problem is the "recapture" of information from the monthly or periodic computer tapes or transmissions from creditors who fail to adjust their internal records to reflect the corrections made to the tradeline. The result is that the inaccurate information will then resurface in the consumer's report. The FCRA contains a provision to prevent this abuse.[85] However, the settlement agreement itself should provide for the creditor to correct its internal records, including those already stored, with the specific intent to prevent accidental re-reporting of the transactions involved. If the settlement is with a CRA, the agreement can provide for a periodic review of the consumer's file to ensure that the offending information has not been reinserted. Although the FCRA provides that the CRA is supposed to notify the consumer when once-deleted information is reinserted,[86] the settlement agreement should provide for additional verification.

The settlement agreement should also provide that the creditor will not assign the debt. A collection agency or assignee creditor can cause the disputed information to reappear in the individual's consumer report, and they may claim that the settlement agreement does not bind them.

Finally, in light of the frequency of reinsertion problems, the consumer should consider requiring the settlement agreement to include a provision for attorney fees in the event of a breach. For example, the agreement could provide that the creditor or CRA "shall be liable to [consumer] for damages, reasonable attorney fees and costs, and any reasonable expert witness fees incurred as a result of any breach of this Agreement or any needed enforcement of the this Agreement." The agreement could also include acceptance of the reasonableness of the consumer's attorney's hourly rate. A liquidated damages provision is another possibility.

12.6.4.4 Obtaining Court Approval

Practice varies by jurisdiction and by status of a case as to whether courts must approve a settlement agreement. Nevertheless, it may be in the consumer's interest, where possible, to obtain a court approval of any settlement involving correction of a consumer report. A CRA is not required to take any action requested by a creditor, but only has an obligation to ensure maximum possible accuracy. Having the request for correction appear in a document approved by a court may prove more persuasive to a CRA.

12.6.4.5 Court Orders Should Cover Consumer Reporting Issues

Practitioners must consider a consumer's credit record not only while drafting settlement agreements, but also when the dispute will be resolved through a court order. If the consumer has prevailed or partially prevailed in an action, the consumer should seek a court order that the creditor take action to clear up the consumer's credit record relating to the dispute. Otherwise, even if the debt is no longer listed as currently due, an indication that the debt was once considered delinquent and once subject to a collection action may remain on the consumer's record, unless corrective action is taken.

Even if a consumer loses a case, the consumer should consider seeking a court order that will minimize the effect of the dispute on the consumer's credit record. For example, consider the situation where a consumer disputed a debt in good faith, and thus did not pay the debt for several years pending resolution of the case. The consumer might seek a court order that the creditor should attempt to correct any reference to the two year delinquency in the consumer's reporting file, if the consumer pays the judgment promptly.

---

82 Some consumer attorneys have found that CRAs will refuse to delete derogatory information that is "technically accurate" when the creditor submits it manually. In such a case, having the creditor submit the updated information via automated tape may accomplish the change. Failing that, the consumer may dispute the information directly with the CRA. The CRA must drop the information from the report unless the creditor verifies it. 15 U.S.C. § 1681i. See Ch. 4, supra. The agreement can require that the creditor not verify it, and the creditor should take steps to make sure that the information is not unwittingly verified. A reminder of the new obligations imposed on furnishers may help. 15 U.S.C. § 1681s-2. See Ch. 6, supra.

83 In drafting a letter for the creditor to submit to a CRA, it may be prudent to identify the consumer by present and any recent address, Social Security number, and name(s). Many creditors use a "Universal Data Form" to correct consumer credit records. The form allows the option of deleting or updating account information, and can be included in the letter if appropriate. The Consumer Data Industry Association (formerly Associated Credit Bureaus, Inc.), a trade association of CRAs, makes such a form available to its members and includes it in a universal electronic reporting program, called Metro 2, which also may be used to submit changes to all the major CRAs.

84 See sample consumer reports in Appx. I, infra.

85 See Ch. 4, supra.

86 15 U.S.C. § 1681i(a)(5)(B). See also Ch. 4, supra.

12.6.4.6 Cleaning Up the Consumer's File Where Dispute Settlement Does Not Deal with Consumer Reporting

Even where there is no obligation in a settlement for a creditor to clear up a consumer's credit record, it is just as important to ensure that the dispute was properly reported in the consumer's credit history. The first step, several months after the dispute is resolved, is to obtain from the relevant CRAs disclosure of the contents of the consumer's file. If the fact of the dispute is not reported, the consumer should notify the CRA and the creditor of the dispute.[87] If the debt represents a judgment in a former lawsuit that has been satisfied, counsel should file in that lawsuit a motion to set aside and vacate the judgment and stipulate the dismissal of the suit; once entered, copies of the court's order setting aside the judgment can be sent to the CRAs.

12.6.4.7 Monitoring the Consumer's File After Resolution of a Dispute

It is important to check that the creditor and CRA follow through with their obligations in a settlement. Where the file does not accurately and completely reflect the resolution of the dispute, the consumer can also dispute with the CRA the inaccurate or incomplete information. If the consumer disputes a debt and the CRA deletes it, the FCRA requires the CRA to notify the consumer if it reinserts it.[88] At the same time, the consumer should notify the creditor that, under the settlement agreement, it should not verify the inaccurate information when requested by the CRA. Because the CRA cannot obtain verification, it will have to delete the information from the file. Sometimes, at this point, it makes sense for the consumer's attorney to contact the CRA directly to explain the situation.

Where the creditor has properly corrected the consumer's file, the consumer may also want to request that the CRA forward that correction to certain users who had received an uncorrected report.[89] Consumers have a right under the FCRA to require that a correction be sent to past users, but only if the change in the file is made pursuant to the consumer's dispute to the CRA. A CRA may still agree to send corrections to past users, even if the change is based on the creditor's correction, not the consumer's.

12.6.5 Cleaning Up Student Loan Defaults

Issues relating to government-backed student loans can become quite complex, varying by loan program and other factors. This section summarizes issues examined in more detail in another NCLC publication.[90] A consumer can remove a student loan default from both the current account information and the historical portion of the report by obtaining a closed school, false certification, or unpaid refund discharge on the student loan.[91] These three types of discharges apply mainly to borrowers that attended fraudulent trade schools. Borrowers that qualify for any of these three discharges are no longer obligated to repay, are no longer regarded in default, and are no longer regarded as ever having been in default.[92]

The closed school discharge applies to most government-backed student loans where the student attended a school that closed while the student was still enrolled or within ninety days of when the student withdrew.[93] Borrowers qualify for a false certification discharge for most government-backed student loans if their eligibility to borrow was falsely certified by the school.[94] This includes:

- The school falsifies a non-high school graduate's ability to benefit from the program;[95]
- The school enrolls a student unable to meet minimum state employment requirements for the job for which the student is being trained;[96] or
- The school forges or alters the student loan note or check endorsements.[97]

The third type of discharge also applies to most government-backed loans, where a school failed to make an owed refund to the student.[98]

When a discharge is granted, that fact is reported to all CRAs who had been furnished with the original default "so as to delete all adverse credit history assigned to the loan."[99] The CRA should be told not only that the loan is no longer in default, but that the reporting of the loan as ever being in default was in error. Borrowers can follow up a discharge by

---

87 See § 12.6.2, supra.
88 15 U.S.C. § 1681i(a)(B)(ii).
89 See Ch. 4, supra.
90 National Consumer Law Center, Student Loan Law (2d. ed. 2002 and Supp.)
91 For unpaid refund discharges, it is possible that only a portion of the loan may be paid off. The consumer report therefore may still show that the borrower is delinquent on a portion of the loan.
92 Note that the unpaid refund discharge will cancel the loan only up to the amount of refund owed but not paid. In some cases, borrowers may still be left with balances on their loans.
93 34 C.F.R. §§ 682.402(d)(1)(i) (FFEL), 685.214 (Direct Loans), 674.33(g) (Perkins). The rules on the six main discharges are substantially the same for the different programs. See generally National Consumer Law Center, Student Loan Law Ch. 6 (3d ed. 2006).
94 20 U.S.C. § 1087(c)(1). This discharge does not apply to Perkins Loans, but Perkins borrowers should be able to raise the school's misconduct as a defense to loan repayment.
95 See National Consumer Law Center, Student Loan Law § 6.3.2 (3d. ed. 2006).
96 See id. § 6.3.3.
97 See id. § 6.3.4
98 34 C.F.R. §§ 682.402(l) (FFEL), 685.215 (Direct Loans).
99 34 C.F.R. §§ 682.402(d)(2)(iv), 682.402(e)(2)(iv).

obtaining a copy of their consumer report and determining if the current and historical information on the loan has been corrected. If has not been corrected, that information should be disputed with both the CRA and the furnisher (the U.S. Department of Education or a state guaranty agency). The furnisher in turn should refuse to verify to the CRA that a default ever existed.

If a borrower was defrauded, but is not entitled to a discharge, another option is to raise the borrower's claims against the school as a defense to repayment of the loan.[100] In settling such a case, it will be important that the borrower's credit record be cleaned up as part of any settlement.[101] Some states also have tuition recovery funds to help pay defaulted loans of victims of trade school fraud.[102]

Federal law provides additional rights to remove the default status of a student loan, beyond just repaying the loan in full. The student can rehabilitate the loan by making twelve reasonable and affordable monthly payments; when the loan is then resold to another lender, it will no longer be in default even though a significant part of the loan is still unpaid.[103] Another option is a consolidation loan; whereby the consumer refinances the old loan or loans into a new loan, with a repayment schedule that takes into account the consumer's income.[104] As long as the consumer is current on the consolidation loan, the consumer is no longer in default. Consolidation results in a notation on a borrower's consumer report that the defaulted loan was paid in full. In contrast, rehabilitation may remove the default notation completely.[105]

Another popular option to repay defaulted student loans will not erase the default—entering into a reasonable and affordable payment plan. Six payments under such a plan will renew eligibility for new student loans, but will not erase the student's current default status on the consumer's report.

12.6.6 Identity Theft

12.6.6.1 Cleaning Up After Identity Theft

Identity theft is examined in detail in Chapter 9, *supra*; this subsection summarizes the consumer rights detailed in that chapter. Identity theft leads to serious problems for a consumer's credit record, because the thief will have taken out, but made no payments on new loans that the consumer does not discover until months or even years later and are marked as delinquent or defaulted on the consumer's credit record.

Consumers have FCRA rights to respond to these identity theft problems. A consumer can request that a CRA block the reporting of any fraudulent information in the consumer's file. The consumer must provide the CRA with proof of the consumer's identity, a copy of an identity theft report filed with a government agency, a description of what information in the report is fraudulent, and a statement that the thief, not the consumer was involved in the transaction.[106]

The CRA must then block that information within four business days and notify the creditor who furnished the information of the block. That creditor (often referred to as the furnisher) must then reinvestigate and take steps to prevent the information from being furnished to a CRA again. Once a CRA has notified a creditor of the identify theft, the creditor cannot sell or transfer the debt or send it out for collection.[107]

The consumer can also provide a copy of an identity theft report directly to a creditor from whom the thief obtained credit, and the creditor must then cease furnishing that information to CRAs, until it subsequently "knows" that the information in fact is correct.[108] The consumer should contact the security or fraud department of each creditor involved in the theft, and follow up with a written notice, with a return receipt requested, to the address for billing inquiries. The consumer should also ask also for written confirmation when a creditor agrees that charges do not belong to the consumer.

To aid in the creation of an identity theft report, a consumer can seek information from any business that transacted with the thief in the victim's name. The consumer can gain access to the thief's application for credit and any business transaction records relating to the transaction. The consumer should make a written request to the business and must prove the consumer's identification and the validity of the identity theft claim, by providing information as requested by the business.[109]

Throughout the process of correcting the credit record, the victim should keep records of all expenses, including paper, postage, long-distance charges, copying charges, travel expenses, and fees for consultations with attorneys. It may be possible to recover these amounts as restitution if the thief is criminally prosecuted. In addition, some of these amounts may be actual damages if the victim has to sue a CRA or creditor for failing to correct the credit record.[110]

---

100 National Consumer Law Center, Student Loan Law Ch. 9 (3d. ed. 2006).
101 *See* § 12.6.4, *supra*.
102 National Consumer Law Center, Student Loan Law § 9.8 (3d ed. 2006).
103 34 C.F.R. § 682.405(b)(2).
104 *See* National Consumer Law Center, Student Loan Law § 8.2 (3d. ed. 2006).
105 *See generally* National Consumer Law Center, Student Loan Law § 8.4 (3d ed. 2006) (rehabilitation). There is some confusion whether rehabilitating a loan will also clean up the historical section of the student's credit rating. *See id.* § 8.4.

106 15 U.S.C. § 1681c-2.
107 *Id.*
108 15 U.S.C. § 1681s-2(a)(6).
109 15 U.S.C. § 1681g(e).
110 *See* § 11.10, *supra*.

The victim should keep a record of all telephone calls and should follow up telephone conversations with confirming letters sent by certified mail, return receipt requested.

12.6.6.2 Heading Off New Identity Theft Problems

The consumer should not stop at cleaning up the problems the identity thief caused on the consumer's current credit record. It is very likely that additional credit will be taken out in the consumer's name or fraudulent checks cashed. It is important to continue to monitor the individual's consumer report to make sure that the fraudulent items are not reinserted and that new fraudulent accounts are not added. The consumer should obtain a copy of his or her report every several months from each of the "Big Three" CRAs.

To protect against new fraudulent accounts being opened, the consumer can call a toll-free number for any of the "Big Three" nationwide CRAs,[111] to request that a fraud alert be placed in the consumer's file. The CRA called must contact the other two nationwide CRAs, and then, whenever new credit is sought in the consumer's name, a creditor contacting one of these CRAs is told to take extra steps to verify the consumer's identity. This initial alert stays on the consumer's file for ninety days. The consumer can also file an identity theft report and seek an extended alert for seven years.[112]

To find out if the identity thief has been passing bad checks in a consumer's name, contact SCAN.[113] To notify retailers not to accept checks drawn on a fraudulent account in the consumer's name, contact companies such as Tele-Check,[114] Certegy,[115] CheckRite,[116] National Processing Co. (NPC),[117] CrossCheck,[118] and ChexSystems.[119]

In one form of identity theft, a thief files a change of address form with the consumer's local post office to divert bank statements, credit card statements, credit applications and the like. If a consumer suspects this has happened, both the local Postal Inspector and the United States Postal Inspector should be contacted to obtain the forwarding address, and to arrange to have all mail forwarded in the consumer's name re-forwarded back to the consumer's own address.

If a consumer's Social Security number has been misused, the consumer should immediately notify the Social Security Administration.[120] If a driver's license has been stolen or its number appropriated, the consumer should call the state department or registry of motor vehicles and follow their fraud investigation process. If a civil judgment has been entered in the consumer's name for actions taken by an impostor, the consumer should contact an attorney.

12.6.7 Removing Recent Delinquencies

12.6.7.1 Introduction

Part of an individual's consumer report will list current accounts, indicating how many days each account is delinquent.[121] The creditor will update this information electronically, often on a monthly basis. As a result, this portion of the report will continuously be replaced by more current information. Old delinquencies will disappear if the consumer catches up on payments, the amount owing will change, and the summary status of the account (e.g., "I9") will change as payments are made.

Elsewhere on the report, the CRA will include historical information on defaults, delinquencies, and the like. For example, a report might list the current status of each account, then provide a summary payment history, and then the number of times any of the consumer's accounts were 30, 60, or 90 days past due, the date of the most recent delinquency, and the date of the most severe delinquency.[122]

Because the current status of the listed accounts may be of greater relevance to potential creditors than the summary of payment history, one approach to cleaning up a credit record is to clear up the current status of delinquent accounts. Usually, though, consumers do not pay on their account because they do not have sufficient income to make the payment or there are more pressing accounts to pay. This subsection looks at ways of clearing up a delinquency involving taking out new loans, refinancing, shifting payment choices, and negotiating new payment schedules.

12.6.7.2 New Loans, Refinancing, and Shifting Payment Priorities

In general, trying to clear up a delinquency by taking out new loans, refinancing existing loans, or shifting payments from other obligations all have serious pitfalls. One approach that may work is to move credit card balances to cards with lower rates. Transferring balances so that no card has a balance above 50% of the available line of credit may also improve a credit score. However, the consumer should be careful of teaser rates. Many credit cards offer what looks to be a lower rate, but the rate goes up after an initial period,

---

111 For Equifax, 800-525-6285; for Experian, 888-397-3742; for TransUnion, 800-680-7289.
112 15 U.S.C. § 1681c-1. See § 9.2.2, supra.
113 800-262-7771.
114 800-710-9898 or 800-927-0188.
115 800-437-5120.
116 800-766-2748.
117 800-526-5380.
118 707-586-0551.
119 800-428-9623.

120 800-269-0271.
121 See § 3.2.3, supra.
122 See id.

or the creditor reserves the right to raise the rate if the consumer is late on a payment or the consumer's credit score declines. In addition, many cards impose a "balance transfer fee" that will add to the consumer's debt burden. Also watch out that the new credit card does not transfer over extremely old credit card balances, that are so old they may not be legally enforceable and whose default will not show up on a consumer report. The consumer should also be aware that having a large number of credit cards by itself can reduce a credit score.

The worst thing that can happen is if the consumer turns to a predatory lender for new loans or to refinance existing debt. As a general rule, avoid any lender that comes to the consumer's home or otherwise seeks out the consumer. Many scam operators charge exorbitant rates and assess hidden charges. Rather than clean up a credit record, such creditors may rob the consumer of income, more severely blemish the credit record when the consumer cannot pay the inflated payments, and seize the consumer's home or other key assets.

Similarly, it does not make sense to make another obligation delinquent just to take the first loan out of its delinquency status. This will actually make a credit record look worse. Another key question is whether nonpayment of the other obligation is going to have greater adverse consequences for the consumer. For example, one should not stop making payments on a car loan to bring a credit card debt up to date. The car could be repossessed, while nonpayment of the credit card would just add interest charges.

12.6.7.3 Negotiating Repayment Schedules

Where an account is about to become delinquent or has recently become delinquent, the consumer can attempt to negotiate with the creditor to establish a more affordable payment schedule, with the understanding that the creditor not report the account as delinquent if the consumer keeps to the new repayment schedule. (This approach is less desirable for accounts that have been in default status for a period of years, as explained in § 12.5.3, *supra*.) Ideally, the creditor will accept partial payment on the amount due, paid out over a series of months, rather than receive nothing.

It is critical though that consumers only agree to modified payment schedules that they can meet, while still being able to keep current on their other loan and financial obligations. A creditor may be less likely to agree to a second repayment agreement if the consumer fails to make payments as originally negotiated.

Any negotiated repayment agreement should require the creditor to supply updated account information to all relevant CRAs, indicating the account is now current. Only when the consumer misses a payment pursuant to the repayment agreement should the creditor report the account as delinquent. Sometimes, it may be simplest for the creditor to mark the old account paid in full, and set up a new account with the consumer under a new number, and report that new account status to the CRA.

The negotiation with the creditor can occur either before or after the account becomes delinquent. From the point of view of the individual's consumer report, negotiation before an account is delinquent is preferable. Not only will the report show no delinquency in the account's current status, but there will be no history in the file of a default or delinquency relating to the account. Nevertheless, creditors are often not willing to negotiate repayment terms until a consumer is delinquent.

In any negotiation, consumers should not be affected by threats to turn accounts over for collection (collectors cannot do anything to a consumer that the creditor could not). Similarly, the threat to furnish negative credit information to a CRA should not be effective because the creditor has already done so, and the issue in the negotiation is what type of payment will the creditor accept in return for cleaning up the credit record.[123]

Be aware whether one is negotiating with the original creditor or a debt buyer (those purchasing credit accounts for pennies on the dollar from the original creditor). Debt buyers are not interested in payment schedules, but only want a lump-sum payment. Because they have paid so little for a debt, they often will accept only 10% or 15% on the dollar. But it is essential to obtain a written release, or the debt could be sold again to another debt buyer, who will initiate collection efforts.

In negotiating with a creditor, an attorney's presence is helpful. Where this is not possible, the consumer should enlist the aid of a sophisticated friend or associate to provide moral support and to make sure the consumer is not talked into a bad deal by the creditor. Other helpful approaches include having a maximum repayment figure written down in advance, or contacting a nonprofit consumer credit counselor, whose job is to negotiate repayment agreements with creditors.

Consumers should definitely avoid debt elimination and debt settlement companies. As discussed at 12.5.1, *supra*, these companies do not offer any real relief, and in fact will make matters worse for a consumer. Consumers should also be very leery of for-profit credit counselors, who often charge high fees for limited assistance. Even nonprofit consumer credit counselors may receive funding from creditors, creating a conflict of interest that prevents them from recommending bankruptcy or pointing out legal defenses the consumer may have. And some nonprofit counselors are affiliates of for-profit companies, or are nonprofit only in name, simply funneling money to the principals as salary rather than as profits. A fuller discussion of credit counseling issues may be found in NCLC's UDAP manual.[124]

---

123 See § 12.3, *supra*.
124 National Consumer Law Center, Unfair and Deceptive Acts and Practices § 5.1.2.3 (6th ed. 2004 and Supp.).

A negotiation with a creditor can also attempt to clean up the historical information in the report about past delinquencies. There are two ways of enlisting the creditor's assistance to clean up older blemishes. The creditor can contact the CRA and correct the erroneous or incomplete credit history. For example, the creditor could agree to contact the CRA and indicate that there was good reason for the consumer's late payment and the payment had not in fact been delinquent. The other approach is for the creditor to agree not to verify its original information if asked by the CRA. Then, when the consumer disputes the item, the information will not be verified on reinvestigation, and it will have to be deleted.

Creditors will have differing views on these two options. Some creditors will refuse to alter earlier information, insisting that it was correct. Consumers in a negotiation will thus have to show these creditors why the information they originally furnished to the CRA was not fully accurate or complete. Of course, a creditor's main interest is recovering as much money from a delinquent account as possible. But some creditors will also be concerned with the integrity of the consumer reporting process, as they see it.

There is some evidence that doctors, hospitals, and some retailers are more likely to enter into an agreement to remove adverse historical information, and may accept installment for less than the full amount owed. Consumers may need to be persistent in order to arrive at an agreement, and will probably need to talk with supervisors.

However, many creditors may be unwilling to enter into this kind of agreement, either because of hostility towards the consumer, or perhaps out a natural reluctance to change the information they furnished to the CRAs. A consumer should be sure that any agreement with the creditor to contact the CRA and request that the historical information be withdrawn is clear and in writing. Otherwise, creditors may not, in fact, follow through in requesting that the information be withdrawn. Sample language to include in a written agreement is set forth at Appendix J.9, *infra*.[125]

12.6.8 Discharging Obligations in Bankruptcy

Some creditors, such as many home mortgage lenders, will not extend credit to anyone who has filed bankruptcy recently. And the bankruptcy will be listed in the individual's consumer reports for ten years. Often, though, filing bankruptcy will actually improve a consumer's credit record.[126] A bankruptcy discharge gets a consumer off to a fresh start and should reduce a consumer's debt burden and enhance stable employment and income. Stability of income and lowered debt burden may be more important to a potential creditor than the fact that certain older debts were discharged in bankruptcy.[127] The bankruptcy also will instantly reduce the overall amount of debt outstanding. Some lenders will not extend mortgage loans to consumers with outstanding defaults, but will do so to consumers who have discharged debts in bankruptcy, at least those whose bankruptcy discharge is a few years old.[128]

By eliminating older obligations, the bankruptcy will allow the consumer to make more timely payments on credit obligations incurred post-petition. A recent history of post-bankruptcy timely payments may be more attractive to a creditor, even with the bankruptcy notation, than a list of numerous delinquent bills with no current history of on-time payments.

What is less obvious is the salutary effect of the bankruptcy in stabilizing a consumer's employment picture. Wage garnishments, continuous collection calls, car repossessions, telephone disconnections, and other consequences of an unaffordable debt burden are not conducive to finding and holding steady employment. All of these distractions are significantly reduced after a bankruptcy filing.

To ensure the benefits of a bankruptcy on a consumer's current debt picture, the consumer should send the CRAs a copy of the time-stamped bankruptcy petition, the schedules of debts, and the discharge. Listing the "Big Three" nationwide CRAs on the address matrix when filing the bankruptcy petition ensures that they get notice of the bankruptcy and the discharge. If debts appear on the debtor's consumer report that should have been discharged through the bankruptcy, but were inadvertently omitted from the schedules, the debtor should consider reopening the bankruptcy to list the omitted debts.[129]

One caveat to the benefits of bankruptcy is that there have been significant problems with the failure of creditors (often referred to as furnishers) to accurately report debts discharged in bankruptcy. Debts discharged in bankruptcy should be reported with a zero balance. Yet often furnishers will continue to inaccurately report a debt as seriously past due with a significant balance, information which is much more negative than correctly reporting that the debt has been discharged in bankruptcy.[130]

Well-intentioned consumers may inadvertently undo the clearing effects of the bankruptcy by continuing to make payments on the debt, perhaps in order to retain possession of the collateral of a secured loan. An FTC staff member has indicated that, when a consumer continues or resumes payments on an obligation discharged in bankruptcy, a creditor may report delinquencies subsequent to the bankruptcy, so

---

125 *See also* § 12.6.4, *supra*.
126 *See* Teresa Sullivan, Elizabeth Warren, Jay Lawrence Westbrook, As We Forgive Our Debtors: Bankruptcy and Consumer Credit in America (1989) (bankrupt persons can and do return eventually to normal credit ratings).
127 *See* § 12.6.1, *supra*.
128 *See* § 12.7.2, *infra*.
129 *See* National Consumer Law Center, Consumer Bankruptcy Law and Practice § 14.4.3.3 (8th ed. 2006).
130 *See* Ch. 4, *supra*.

long as the information is accurate, complete, updated, and otherwise in compliance with the FCRA.[131]

Of course, the listing of a bankruptcy may prove a stigma for certain creditors. But others look at the fact that the consumer cannot receive a second chapter 7 (straight) bankruptcy discharge for another seven years, and that fewer debts are now competing for the consumer's stream of income.

Bankruptcies stay on a consumer's credit record for ten years from the bankruptcy filing, while the underlying debts are usually only reported for seven years from the delinquency.[132] Thus, if a consumer's delinquencies are mostly five or six years old, bankruptcy may not be the best option to deal with the credit record issues. The debts will have to be deleted from consumer reports within another year or two, while the bankruptcy will stay on the record for ten years.

12.6.9 Providing Additional Information to the Creditor

There are a number of reasons why a consumer report may not be an accurate reflection of a consumer's bill-paying history. Some creditors, such as utilities (e.g., telephone, gas, electric, cable television, water and sewer), landlords, and small merchants may not report a consumer's payment record to any CRA. There can also be good explanations for delinquencies and other adverse information. Much more productive than trying to submit such additional information to a CRA is to supply it directly to a creditor evaluating the consumer's creditworthiness. For example, where a credit history is lacking, the consumer might supply statements from landlords, utilities, and others as to the consumer's creditworthiness.

The Equal Credit Opportunity Act (ECOA) requires a prospective creditor to consider information provided by the consumer, and not to rely exclusively on consumer reports. Whenever a creditor considers credit history in evaluating an applicant's creditworthiness, a creditor shall consider, on the applicant's request, any information the applicant may present that tends to indicate that the credit history being considered does not accurately reflect the applicant's creditworthiness.[133]

The ECOA also requires that a creditor must consider, on the applicant's request, the credit history, when available, of any account reported in the name of the applicant's spouse or former spouse which the applicant can demonstrate accurately reflects the applicant's own creditworthiness.[134] The burden is placed on the applicant to present such information on these other accounts, without any affirmative duty on the creditor to request the information. The applicant carries the further burden of demonstrating that these other accounts "accurately reflect" the applicant's own creditworthiness.[135] One method of doing so is to produce checks written on a joint account as payments on accounts listed in the spouse's name. Another is to produce employment records or deposit slips indicating that the applicant actually provided funds which paid accounts in the spouse's name.

How carefully a creditor will consider such an explanation will depend on the creditor. For home mortgage loans, creditors generally will carefully consider consumer explanations. For example, the Federal National Mortgage Association (Fannie Mae) requires that lenders determine the cause and significance of derogatory credit information.[136] On the other hand, for credit cards and other small credit applications, the potential lender may be less interested in investigating the reasons behind a credit blemish, and will instead be processing thousands of applications almost mechanically.

Any explanation provided a creditor should be a compelling one (e.g., illness, death in the family, plant closing leading to layoffs) and one that is well documented and succinctly stated. A rambling and unpersuasive explanation may raise more questions than it settles.

Some credit blemishes on an individual's consumer report are not caused by the consumer, but by the consumer's spouse or by other third parties by their nonpayment of jointly used or obligated accounts. For example, in an attempt to build up credit histories for women without credit accounts in their own names, ECOA requires creditors to furnish account information to CRAs in such a way that the CRA can include the information in both spouses' files, as long as both spouses use or are obligated on the account.[137] Because this protection may backfire when the other party causes an account to be delinquent, the ECOA provides consumers with the right to explain to potential creditors that adverse information in their consumer report does not accurately reflect the applicant's creditworthiness, that the blemish was due to the other spouse's culpability, and not the consumer's.[138] Similarly, indicate to the creditor that the consumer is merely an authorized user on a delinquent

---

131 Foster, FTC Informal Staff Opinion Letter (Feb. 15, 2000), *reprinted on the CD-Rom accompanying this manual.*
132 *See* § 5.2, *supra.*
133 ECOA Reg. B, 12 C.F.R. § 202.6(b)(6)(ii).
134 ECOA Reg. B, 12 C.F.R. § 202.6(b)(6)(iii).
135 *Id.*
136 Federal National Mortgage Association Selling Guide Part X, § 803.02 (2001).
137 *See* § 12.2.5, *supra.*
138 Reg. B, 12 C.F.R. § 202.6(b)(6)(ii). For instance, an applicant could show that she was unemployed at a time when a joint account went into default and had no way to ensure that her then-spouse, who was employed, would make payments. *See* FTC Informal Staff Opinion, Clearinghouse No. 37,088 (Apr. 5, 1983) (where unmarried cohabitants share use of an account and the accountholder's negative credit history is imputed to another cohabitant, the cohabitant may make countervailing information available, and the creditor must consider it).

account, and not responsible for payment. The creditor has no affirmative duty to request this information; the burden is placed on the applicant to explain why the applicant should not be denied credit. The creditor has an obligation to consider expiating information presented by an applicant, but it is not required to ignore the bad history altogether.

Another approach is to request a creditor to obtain a report from one of the new, alternative CRAs that are created to help consumers with non-traditional payment histories.[139] For example, Payment Reporting Builds Credit is a CRA that allows consumers to submit data about payment of rent, utilities, and other recurring bills, which can then be reported to creditors.[140]

12.7 Coping with a Substandard Credit Record

12.7.1 Automobile Loans and Leases

A substandard credit record is more likely to have a significant effect on the cost of a car loan or lease, rather than prevent the consumer from obtaining a motor vehicle loan. Many standard market automobile lenders will distinguish between "A," "B," "C," and "D" risks, based primarily on the consumer's credit score. The lower the credit score, the higher the interest rate the lender will require from the dealer. This rate is called the "buy rate." Those who do not meet the "D" criteria of a standard car lender will often still qualify for credit in the substandard market, where the lender will again offer the dealer a buy rate. "Buy here, pay here" dealers and certain other high-cost automobile lenders charging even more than substandard lenders have entered the market to capture consumers who believe, rightly or wrongly, they cannot obtain even substandard financing.

However, there is a second way in which a substandard credit record affects the cost of a car loan or lease. Dealers mark up the "buy rate" so that the effective interest rate the consumer pays is higher than the consumer's risk requires. This mark-up is not based on the consumer's creditworthiness, but is based on the dealer's perception as to how much extra profit it can make off a particular consumer, how vulnerable the consumer is to overcharges. Experts believe that, in today's market, dealers on average mark up a higher risk customer over the buy rate than a lower risk customer. This mark-up takes the form of a higher differential between the buy rate and the actual rate charged the consumer, higher prices for service contracts, rust proofing, and other add-ons, and a higher price for the vehicle itself. The most extreme case is a "buy here, pay here" dealer selling low-cost vehicles at very high prices, with very expensive add-ons, and with very high stated interest rates.

---

139 See § 2.7.10, supra.
140 See www.prbc.com.

The consumer, without even changing the consumer's credit standing, can take a number of steps to reduce the costs of financing a vehicle. The consumer can find a cosigner, or can put the vehicle in the name of a relative, thus relying on that other person's superior creditworthiness. The obvious risks to the cosigner or other purchaser should be explained carefully, but these risks will often be acceptable to help family members. For example, where a husband and wife wish to purchase a car, it may make sense to determine which is the more creditworthy and then have that individual purchase the car and obtain the car loan. The lender should not be able to run a credit history on the other spouse whose income and assets are not being relied upon to take out the loan.

Another tactic is to purchase a less expensive car and put up a higher cash down payment, reducing the loan's riskiness. Carefully evaluate what it really happening when the consumer trades in an older vehicle that still has a large balance on its car loan. Dealers will often hide this "negative equity" in the new paperwork, but the negative equity will increase the amount financed being secured by the new car purchase, making that loan far more risky for the lender. True disclosure of the effect of the trade-in may lead the consumer to decide it is wiser to stay in the old vehicle until its loan is paid down more.

The most important step a consumer can take to lower the cost of car financing is to shop around and negotiate a better deal, so the consumer's interest rate is close to the buy rate, so that expensive add-ons are not purchased, and so that the car itself is competitively priced. This is particularly important before going to a dealer who specializes in consumers who perceive they have bad credit or no credit. Contacting more traditional lenders first may pleasantly surprise the consumer that one of those standard lenders is willing to make them a car loan.

Effective negotiation requires the consumer not to rush to drive home with a car. Do not take possession before financing is unalterably approved. The "yo-yo" sale is a common dealer tactic, putting in the fine print that the sale is contingent on the dealer obtaining financing. Days or even weeks later, with the consumer's trade-in gone and friends and neighbors having been shown the consumer's new car, the dealer calls back and says financing has not been approved. The consumer must either return the vehicle or pay a higher down payment and/or interest rate. Instead, no matter the dealer pressure, do not drive the car home, and do not commit to the purchase, but instead wait for the financing to be approved and compare this rate with others available at other lenders.

Consumers often mistakenly believe that a lease will be a more attractive option than a credit sale if they have a substandard credit record, and that they can put down less money up-front in a lease. The opposite is usually the case. The complexities of a lease transaction provide the dealer for more opportunities for extra charges, including using a higher price for the vehicle than in a credit sale. Moreover, there is a very real risk that the consumer will default or otherwise have to terminate the lease early, and virtually all automobile leases today charge excessive and very large penalties at such lease early termination, as much as $5000 or $10,000.

12.7.2 Home Mortgage Applications

Most home mortgage applications will be evaluated using one of several standardized underwriting programs. Key to these programs will be the consumer's credit score and the contents of the consumer's credit report. Often the lender will obtain information from the "Big Three" nationwide consumer reporting agencies (CRAs) and will review several different credit scores for the consumer. But mortgage lenders will also base their decision on other information as well—the size of the mortgage, the value of the home, the applicant's income, the size of the down payment, and the like. For example, the Federal Home Loan Mortgage Corporation (Freddie Mac) lists on its website the relative importance of various factors. Credit history and credit risk are listed as high, but so is the size of the down payment, the type of property (e.g., one-family or condominium), and whether the property is owner-occupied or an investment.[141]

The exact standards will typically be determined not by the entity originating the loan, but by the party that will eventually purchase or insure the mortgage. Many mortgages today will be purchased by the Federal National Mortgage Association (FNMA) or Freddie Mac, and other mortgages are insured by Federal Housing Administration (FHA), Veterans Administration (VA), Rural Housing Service (RHS) (formerly Farmers Home Administration or FmHA) and private mortgage insurers. These insurers and secondary market purchasers will establish the underwriting guidelines. Some banks and other lenders do not sell their mortgages on the secondary market, and will devise their own underwriting guidelines, which may be more flexible than guidelines published by FNMA, Freddie Mac or other underwriters with national standards.

In addition, underwriting guidelines in the conventional market can also vary depending on the interest rate being offered. Those who score lower on the underwriting guidelines may be offered mortgages at higher interest rates. A lender may classify mortgage loans as A, A minus, B, C, and D, and then offer an A loan at 6.5%, an A minus at 7%, and a C or D at 10%. Although the difference between an A and a D loan may add substantially to a mortgage payment, this may still be significantly less than rates charged by high-rate mortgage lenders and by most other types of non-mortgage lenders.

Consumers should definitely avoid extraordinarily high-rate lenders that prey on minorities, inner city residents, the elderly, and others who may believe that they are unable to obtain standard mortgages. These lenders may charge rates as high as 15% to 25% and also charge excessive points, broker fees, and other inflated charges. These payments may be so high as to almost guarantee foreclosure, which may be exactly what these lenders want. A good rule of thumb is to avoid any mortgage lender that actively solicits the consumer door-to-door or over the telephone. Consumers will always be better off finding financing elsewhere. A much better option is to explore special community reinvestment programs and other mortgage programs charging low interest rates, but specially designed for those traditionally excluded from the low-risk mortgage market.

Mortgage applicants should obtain a copy of their consumer report from several of the major nationwide CRAs well before applying for the mortgage loan. As described below, it is not too early to begin planning a mortgage application over a year in advance, because the mortgage lender will be looking in particular for late payments within a year of the application. Moreover, consumers filing bankruptcy, losing a court judgment on a debt, or experiencing a home foreclosure may even decide to wait several years before applying for a mortgage. Before the application is made, the consumer should do whatever is possible to improve a credit record, bringing all debts current, reducing high balances, paying off any liens and outstanding judgments, and the like.

There are no hard and fast rules about what types of credit problems will lead to denial of a mortgage application, because there are so many different underwriting guidelines, depending on whether a mortgage will be purchased by FNMA, Freddie Mac, or some other secondary market player, and whether the mortgage will be insured by FHA, VA, FHS, or a private mortgage insurer. Underwriting criteria for an "A" mortgage will necessarily be tougher than for a "D" mortgage or one from a substandard lender. Federal agencies disposing of an inventory of foreclosed housing may be more lenient, and exceptions may be made for special community reinvestment programs and other mortgage programs specially designed for those traditionally excluded from the low-risk mortgage market.

Nevertheless, certain generalizations will not be too far off the mark for most conventional mortgages. Certain items will usually be fatal to a mortgage loan application. This would include within the last few years a foreclosure on a prior mortgage, a bankruptcy discharge, or a court judgment on a debt against the consumer.

Lenders will look at the bankruptcy discharge date, which occurs significantly after the date of filing—around six months after a chapter 7 filing and from three to five years after a chapter 13 filing. Lenders will also look at, but give less weight to, older foreclosures, bankruptcy discharges, and judgments going back seven years. The consumer can attempt to explain away the foreclosure, bankruptcy, or judgment, but the reason must be compelling and unlikely to

---

141 www.freddiemac.com/corporate/au-works/factors.html.

recur, such as a serious illness, death of a wage earner, layoff due to a plant closing, and the like.[142]

Another key factor is a consumer's track record in making payments on a prior mortgage. All payments within a year of the application should be on time. Outstanding judgments, garnishments, and liens should all be paid in full before the application, and certainly before the closing. Some mortgage lenders make the consumer pay, from closing funds escrowed for that purpose, all outstanding delinquent debt appearing in the individual's consumer report, even if the debt is legitimately disputed.

For more minor credit issues, such as delinquencies on credit cards and installment loans, underwriting guidelines generally give more weight to delinquencies occurring within the last year or two before the application. The consumer should avoid having any credit cards or other revolving credit payments being sixty or more days late and should minimize having payments that are even just thirty days late in the year or two prior to applying for the loan.

Lenders will also use the consumer report to spot errors in the consumer's application. For example, they may note on the report the identities of other creditors who have received the consumer's report, because this may help them uncover undisclosed debts, which indicate that the consumer is less able to afford a mortgage than was indicated in the application.

Whenever a problem area in a consumer report cannot be cleared up before a mortgage application, the applicant should provide the mortgage lender with explanations, additional relevant material, and other evidence of creditworthiness (e.g., history in making rent and utility payments). Most home mortgage lenders, for example, use complex and non-mechanical procedures to evaluate loan applications; these procedures often leave considerable room for subjectivity and discretion. Another option are businesses that assist consumers in correcting errors in their credit files and getting their files "re-scored."[143]

A consumer may have to shop around to find a lender who will overlook certain blemishes. It is the best course to be honest with the lender and see if it will make the loan despite certain marks on the credit record. If one lender does not work, move on to the next one. Mortgage brokers also offer to help find a willing lender, but often arrange mortgages with higher rates and fees, sometimes of scandalous size. Obtaining pre-approval from a mortgage lender may be a helpful option. A cosigner can help as well, but the attendant risks must be carefully explained to the cosigner.

12.7.3 Residential Lease Applications

There is a growing utilization of consumer reports by landlords in evaluating residential rental applications. Landlords can obtain not only a traditional credit score or consumer report, but also a report from a specialized tenant screening company that will look at the applicant's residential rental history. Some landlords use both, some only one or the other, and some neither. It is hard to predict what a particular landlord will do, and there may even be variations geographically. But, in general, the more sophisticated the person handling the application, the more likely that some form or report will be used. Thus, larger landlords are more likely to use such reports. Real estate agents acting for a landlord are likely to run a report for the landlord as well. So are management companies hired to handle applications for a landlord.

Less likely to run a consumer report is an owner renting half of a two family home or some one who rents a small number of residences a year. Reports are mixed as to whether landlords in subsidized housing are more or less likely to use a consumer report. Clearly, landlords will be more selective in a tight rental market than where there is a high vacancy rate. One piece of advice is to keep trying different landlords, if a consumer report is preventing access to an apartment. Another is to put the tenancy in the name of a roommate who may have a better credit record.

It is also a good idea to look at consumer reports from one or more of the nationwide CRAs and also one or more tenant screening CRAs that landlords in the area utilize.[144] Because the consumer will invariably be in personal contact with the landlord or the landlord's agent, this provides a good opportunity to explain any blemishes or inaccuracies.

12.7.4 Utility Service

Generally speaking, even a seriously blemished credit record will not prevent a consumer from obtaining basic utility service. Because a utility has a monopoly in a service area, usually it has a common law duty to serve all members of the public within its service area.[145] The general rule is that utilities cannot deny service because of collateral matters.[146] On the other hand, the utility can deny service if there are any outstanding obligations to that utility. For example, past-due gas bills usually have no effect on an applicant obtaining electric service, but may prevent the applicant from obtaining new gas service.

The typical reason not to qualify for a utility service is an applicant's outstanding bill with the same utility from a prior address. Even then, the old delinquency will not prevent

---

142 Federal Home Loan Mortgage Corporation, Single-Family Seller/Servicer Guide, at 37.7 (2000) (circumstances beyond the borrower's control that are not ongoing and are unlikely to recur). *See also* Federal National Mortgage Association, Selling Guide Part X, § 803.02 (2001).
143 See § 14.6.3, *infra*.
144 See Ch. 3, *supra*.
145 National Consumer Law Center, Access to Utility Service § 3.1 (3d ed. 2004 and Supp.).
146 *Id.* § 3.2.

service, but payment of the old bill will be a precondition of new service. Issues sometimes arise as to whether one utility can deny service for nonpayment of service with a sister utility company owned by the same holding company. More frequently, issues arise about whether an individual can be denied service if a spouse or roommate failed to pay for service.[147]

Utilities are beginning to use credit scores and credit history. For example, Equifax has developed an Energy Risk Assessment Model (ERSM) to develop credit scores for use by utilities. At present, regulated utilities' chief use of these scores is to determine the size of a security deposit. (Some utilities have unsuccessfully sought to set different pricing levels for customers dependent on their credit score.) Even then, the size of these deposits will typically be determined by state public utility commission policy, and will not be dependent on the individual's credit record. However, if the public utility commission allows a range of deposit amounts, or allows the utility company discretion about whether to require a deposit, the utility company may decide to obtain a consumer report to make this decision.

If the deposit is unaffordable, explore cosigners or other forms of security. A bankruptcy filing also entitles the consumer to utility service—new service, reconnection of disconnected service, or continuation of service despite a shut-off notice.[148] Within twenty days, the consumer has to provide the utility with adequate security to ensure payment of future bills; the utility can take no action against the consumer for nonpayment of pre-bankruptcy service.[149] Adequate security is usually a security deposit in an amount the bankruptcy trustee deems reasonable.

On the other hand, a cell phone service or cable Internet provider may not have a common law duty to serve, and a credit check may be used to determine whether to grant service. Where a consumer's credit record prevents access to service, prepaid service is an option, such as prepaid phone cards or cell phone service. Putting the service in the name of another consumer is another option.

12.7.5 Insurance

Insurers can use a consumer report to decide whether to insure an individual, whether to place the individual with one of their preferred, standard, or substandard companies (thus affecting their rates), and whether to non-renew or even cancel an insured. Some companies may even raise premiums for lower credit scores. Insurers use both standard consumer reports from the "Big Three" CRAs and also more specialized reports indicating claim history and medical information. Nevertheless, insurers' use of consumer reports may be limited by state insurance department regulations or guidelines. State law as to allowable grounds for non-renewal and cancellation may also limit the use of credit scores in this regard.[150]

An insurer has no permissible purpose under the FCRA to obtain a consumer report to evaluate a consumer's claim for benefits, once coverage has been granted.[151] However, sometimes insurers will seek to evade this rule by using separate files on consumers that are created solely for purposes of evaluating insurance claims and do not otherwise meet the definition of a consumer report.[152] Files maintained and used exclusively for claims purposes are not consumer reports: the FCRA does not apply, including its restrictions on use for permissible purposes only.

This means that files used for insurance claims purposes and for underwriting purposes must be strictly segregated. Using an insurance claim file for insurance underwriting purposes will make future reports from that file consumer reports, meaning they cannot be used for insurance claims purposes. Nor can the insurer use information from the underwriting file for claims purposes, because this is an impermissible use of a consumer report.

12.7.6 Access to a Credit Card

Use of credit scores and other credit history is pervasive in the credit card industry. Not only will credit history affect a consumer's access to a credit card, but, as the credit score changes over time, it can change the consumer's credit limit, credit card fees, and even interest rate. Under a provision called universal default, the card issuer grants itself authority to dramatically increase the interest rate and certain fees if the consumer is delinquent in any other loan with another creditor or even if the consumer's credit score drops.[153]

The average American household is flooded with offers from credit card issuers. When a direct mail solicitation offers a credit card to a consumer, the CRA has sold a list to the creditor that the CRA has vetted for one or two characteristics. Nevertheless, credit card issuers can deny credit even when they solicit the consumer. The card issuer runs the full consumer report only after the consumer sends in the application.[154]

If a card cannot be obtained from a major national card issuer, another approach is to seek one from a local bank or credit union. Another way to get access to a credit card, if a credit record prevents other access, is to become an authorized user of another individual's card. This of course

---

147 *See* National Consumer Law Center, Access to Utility Service § 6.2.4 (3d ed. 2004 and Supp.).
148 11 U.S.C. § 366. *See also* National Consumer Law Center, Consumer Bankruptcy Law and Practice § 9.8 (8th ed. 2006).
149 *Id.*
150 *See* § 14.10, *infra*.
151 *See* § 7.2.5, *supra*.
152 *See* § 2.3.6.5, *supra*.
153 For a discussion of universal default, see National Consumer Law Center, The Cost of Credit: Regulation, Preemption, and Industry Abuses 11.7.2.3.1 (3d ed. 2005 and Supp.).
154 *See* § 7.3.4, *supra*.

presents risks for the principal cardholder, who should be carefully advised of the possible problems.

A more doubtful option is a secured credit card, where the consumer keeps a cash balance with the card issuer, and the consumer in effect draws down on this amount with the credit card. For example, the consumer keeps $500 in an account with the card issuer, and the consumer obtains a credit card with a $500 limit. This does not provide a consumer with new credit, but only provides a convenient way to pay for everyday purchases, and provides identification and security where necessary.

Secured credit cards have high interest rates and high annual fees. Some cards have large fees ($40 to $65) just to apply for the card, with no guaranty that the consumer will be accepted. Consumers should shop around not only for an issuer that has low fees and interest rates, but for one who will also be willing to increase the credit limit or decrease the cash deposit over time, if the consumer is responsible in making payments.

An alternative to a secured credit card that may prove less expensive is a debit card from the consumer's bank. It offers many of the conveniences of a credit card (ordering merchandise over the phone or Internet, reserving hotel rooms, and the like), but its cost may be less than a secured credit card.

12.7.7 Banking and Check Cashing

Consumers may be surprised to learn that banks may obtain a specialized consumer report before they accept an applicant for a deposit account. Even though no credit may be involved, the bank is concerned with overdrafts and fraud, and these specialized reports will indicate if any such events occurred in a consumer's past.

Similarly, when a consumer attempts to make a purchase by check, the merchant may compare the check with a list of consumers who have written bad checks, developed by a CRA. Typically the list will only be a numerical order listing of driver's license numbers or lists of bad check writers alphabetically by various codes. Other merchants may use specially designed software that purports to predict whether a check will be honored based on the consumer's credit information, the current check, and recent check writing activity.[155]

It is illegal for merchants to post bad checks in their place of business, and even bad check lists must be coded, making it more difficult for a consumer on the list to be recognized except by a merchant when the consumer seeks to cash a check. On the other hand, some coding schemes are not too sophisticated, and it would not be difficult, especially in a small town, for someone to speculate from the information provided about who was bouncing bad checks. For example, the FTC has given approval to a coded list involving the first three letters in the consumer's last name, their first initial and their street or post office box number and drivers' license number.[156] Thus the "code" of "DAV K 352" might mean Keith Davis of 352 First Street.

If inaccurate information has led to a bank denying a deposit account, a merchant refusing to accept a check, or even just to the consumer's inclusion on a bad check list, the consumer can seek to correct this in the same way as any other consumer report. Such lists also can only report bad check experiences going back seven years.

12.7.8 Student Loans and Grants

A consumer's credit record with a CRA is irrelevant to obtaining most types of subsidized, federally guaranteed student loans. (PLUS loans, taken out by parents of students are one exception, as are certain unsubsidized loans.) On the other hand, an existing default in another guaranteed student loan does affect a student's eligibility for new loans and grants.

Even then, there are several ways, short of paying off the defaulted student loan, to regain eligibility for new loans and grants. The student can make six monthly payments, in an amount determined by the loan holder, but one that is reasonable and affordable to the consumer considering the consumer's total financial circumstances.[157] Other options available to student loan debtors include loan consolidation, discharge, and rehabilitation, discussed in § 12.6.5, *supra*. Those discharging student loans in bankruptcy also remain eligible for new loans and grants, even when they do not reaffirm the discharged loans.[158]

12.7.9 Eligibility for Public Assistance

In a twist from most uses of a consumer report, government agencies may look at a consumer's credit history to determine if the individual has too much income or assets, not too little. The government agency will be looking for unreported income or assets or payments beyond the applicant's reported income.

Government agencies have a permissible purpose to obtain a consumer report in connection with a determination of the consumer's eligibility for needs-based public assistance.[159] So does any party charged by law with responsibility for assessing the consumer's eligibility for the ben-

---

155 *See* § 2.6.2.2, *supra*.

156 Fleming, FTC Informal Staff Letter (Apr. 1, 1982). *See also* FTC Official Staff Commentary on FDCPA § 806(4), 53 Fed. Reg. 50,097 (Dec. 13, 1998).
157 *See* 34 C.F.R. §§ 682.200, (satisfactory repayment arrangement), 682.401(b)(4); National Consumer Law Center, Student Loan Law § 8.3 (3d ed. 2006).
158 11 U.S.C. § 525(c).
159 15 U.S.C. § 681b(a)(3)(D). *See* § 7.2.6, *supra*.

efit.[160] For example, a district attorney, a social services agency, or township required by law to determine an individual's eligibility for public assistance benefits has a permissible purpose to obtain a consumer report on an individual.[161] Even a private landlord has a permissible purpose to obtain reports on those applying for a tenancy where the landlord is authorized to screen the applications to determine tenants' eligibility for governmental rental payment subsidies.[162] Similarly, a utility authorized to determine eligibility for a low-income home energy assistance program may have a permissible purpose to obtain consumer reports. However, the permissible purpose only applies to parties responsible for determining a consumer's eligibility for a governmental benefit.[163]

The FTC Staff Commentary does not limit governmental use of consumer reports to the time at which eligibility for benefits is first considered. Although the FCRA appears to contemplate the use of reports on applicants only, the FTC Staff Commentary would permit the use of reports after an application for benefits is granted whenever the government on its own initiative is reviewing a recipient's continuing eligibility for the benefits.[164]

12.8 Consumer Reporting Issues for Immigrants

Immigrants have unique consumer reporting issues, relating both to their lack of a credit history and insufficient documentation as to their identities, especially for undocumented immigrants. Insufficient identification prevents immigrants from opening up deposit accounts and accessing other banking services, including loans.

One step that undocumented immigrants can take is to obtain an Individual Taxpayer Identification Number (ITIN).[165] An ITIN is issued by the Internal Revenue Service for tax purposes for those who cannot obtain a Social Security number. It consists of a nine-digit number, beginning with the number "9." At one least one consumer reporting agency (CRA), Experian, has implied that it does use ITINs to create credit files.[166]

The IRS has established a number of requirements to obtain an ITIN. Applicants must use a Form W-7, Individual Taxpayer Identification Number Application. ITIN applicants must show that they cannot obtain a Social Security number and must provide proof that the ITIN will be used for tax administration purposes.[167] For applicants seeking an ITIN in order to file a tax return, the return must be filed along with the W-7.

The Mexican government has offered a form of identification for immigrants from Mexico, called a *matriculas consulares*. Many banks, cities, counties, and local law enforcement agencies are accepting the *matriculas* for identification purposes. Under the Treasury Department's Customer Identification Program regulations promulgated pursuant to the USA PATRIOT Act, banks are permitted to accept *matriculas* for customer identification purposes.[168]

Immigrants can also rely on family members or friends who are legal residents or citizens to open joint accounts, using the joint account holder's Social Security number. There are risks associated with this practice, and immigrant consumers should be advised to choose a joint account holder they can trust.

Finally, some banks have offered secured credit cards to undocumented consumers to establish credit. The consumer must retain a cash balance in a deposit account with the card issuer to offset the line of credit accompanying the card. Use of secured cards comes with significant costs, including high application, processing, and annual fees, plus interest rates that often are higher than those associated with unsecured credit cards.

---

160 FTC Official Staff Commentary § 604(3)(D) item 1, *reprinted at* Appx. D, *infra*.
161 *Id*.
162 *See* Franco v. Kent Farm Vill., Clearinghouse No. 44,149, Civil Action No. 88-0115 T (D.R.I. Sept. 16, 1988) (bench opinion).
163 FTC Official Staff Commentary § 604(3)(D) item 2, *reprinted at* Appx. D, *infra*.
164 *Id*. item 3.
165 *See* National Consumer Law Center, Guide to Consumer Rights For Immigrants (2002). *See also* www.irs.gov/individuals/article/0,,id=96287,00.html.
166 *See* www.experian.com/ask_max/max111605b.html.
167 *See* Internal Revenue Service, Instructions for Form W-7, Application for IRS Individual Taxpayer Identification Number (Jan. 2006).
168 31 C.F.R. § 103.121(b)(2).

Chapter 13 Investigative Consumer Reports

13.1 Introduction

13.1.1 What Is an Investigative Consumer Report?

A typical consumer report lists specific objective information concerning a consumer's credit history, criminal record, employment, address, or related subjects. The information is obtained from creditor, public, or other written records. However, sometimes a user, usually an insurance company or prospective employer, requests an investigative consumer report. This contains more detailed, personal, and subjective information than a regular consumer report, and may include material concerning an individual's lifestyle, such as details about an individual's marital or sex life, drinking habits, friends, and behavior.[1]

An investigator will question neighbors, co-workers, and others concerning their opinion and knowledge of the consumer. Such an investigation obviously has worrisome potential for bias, abuse and error, with serious adverse consequences for the consumer. A report based on such an investigation, in addition to leading to denial of insurance or employment, could damage a person's reputation in the community. The investigation itself can be a form of intimidation and harassment.

Because of these concerns, the FCRA provides certain specific consumer protections for "investigative consumer reports." If an investigation falls within the FCRA's definition of an investigative consumer report, users requesting the report and consumer reporting agencies (CRAs) compiling the report will have certain specified obligations over and beyond those present for other types of consumer reports. However, the FCRA, as amended by the Fair and Accurate Credit Transactions Act of 2003 (FACTA), excludes certain reports of employee misconduct from the definition of "consumer report," and thereby from the definition of "investigative consumer report." Nonetheless, employers must make certain disclosures to benefit from the exclusion; these are discussed elsewhere in this manual.[2]

Most CRAs specializing in investigative reports are smaller companies that have developed a niche making employment, insurance, or landlord/tenant related investigative reports. These smaller CRAs and detective agencies that prepare investigative consumer reports commonly refer to them as "background checks."

13.1.2 Overview of Additional Obligations Required for an Investigative Consumer Report

Investigative consumer reports are subject to additional requirements, beyond those applicable to an ordinary consumer report. Specifically, those who procure an investigative consumer report must disclose to the consumer the fact that such a report may be prepared, and upon request, must also completely disclose the nature and scope of the investigation requested.[3]

If an investigative consumer report includes certain types of negative public record information, the CRA must verify the information within thirty days prior to issuing the report.[4] If the report contains adverse information obtained through an interview with anyone who is not the best possible source of the information, the CRA may not prepare or furnish the report unless it has followed reasonable procedures to confirm the adverse information with an additional source that has direct and independent knowledge of the information.[5] Finally, the Act restricts the CRA's reuse of any adverse information in an investigative consumer report; the information cannot be included in a subsequent consumer report (investigative or otherwise) unless the CRA has verified the information in the process of making the subsequent report, or the information was received within three months prior to the furnishing of the subsequent report.[6] Each of these special provisions is discussed below.

---

1 See Note, Judicial Construction of the Fair Credit Reporting Act: Scope and Civil Liability, 76 Colum. L. Rev. 458 (1976); Privacy Protection Study Commission, Personal Privacy in an Information Society, at 73 (1977).

2 See § 7.2.4, supra.
3 15 U.S.C. §§ 1681d(a), (b).
4 15 U.S.C. § 1681d(3).
5 15 U.S.C. § 1681d(4).
6 15 U.S.C. § 1681l.

13.2 FCRA Definition

13.2.1 General

The Act's definition of "investigative consumer report" provides as follows:

> The term "investigative consumer report" means a consumer report or portion thereof in which information on a consumer's character, general reputation, personal characteristics, or mode of living is obtained through personal interviews with neighbors, friends, or associates of the consumer reported on or with others with whom he is acquainted or who may have knowledge concerning any such items of information. However, such information shall not include specific factual information on a consumer's credit record obtained directly from a creditor of the consumer or from a consumer reporting agency (CRA) when such information was obtained directly from a creditor of the consumer or from the consumer.[7]

Accordingly, a report must fall within this definition of an "investigative consumer report" in order to invoke the FCRA's special protections for such reports.[8] Note that an investigative consumer report is a "consumer report" at least a portion of which contains investigative information.[9] Consequently, the investigatory report must first meet the definition of a "consumer report" in order to be an investigative consumer report.[10]

Under the FCRA, a consumer report must have a specific kind of content; it must contain information bearing on one of seven listed aspects of a consumer: creditworthiness, credit standing, credit capacity, character, general reputation, personal characteristics, or mode of living.[11] In addition, the use or expected use of the information must be in whole or in part for the purpose of serving as a factor in establishing the consumer's eligibility for credit or insurance to be used primarily for personal, family or household purposes; for employment purposes; or for some other purpose permitted by the Act.[12]

Furthermore, to be consumer report the report's information must have been communicated by a "consumer reporting agency."[13] A "consumer reporting agency" is defined as one who furnishes consumer reports to third parties.[14] Thus, consumer reports, and correspondingly, investigative consumer reports, do not involve entities performing their own investigation to determine if the consumer should be granted credit, insurance, employment, or other benefits. Instead, there must be an entity requesting the report and a separate entity conducting the interviews that form the basis of the report.

Apart from meeting the definition of a consumer report, the FCRA's definition of an investigative consumer report requires that the report have three particular elements that relate to the substance of the information in the report, the manner in which it is acquired, and the source from which it is required. As to substance, the report must contain information on any of four aspects of a consumer: character, general reputation, personal characteristics, or mode of living. Thus, a report that is deemed a consumer report because it bears on one of the other three aspects of a consumer set forth in the Act's definition of "consumer report," creditworthiness, credit standing, and credit capacity, will not meet the substance element.

The manner in which the CRA acquires the report's information is the primary factor that distinguishes an investigative consumer report from an ordinary consumer report. The information must be "obtained through personal interviews,"[15] with one of the designated sources. In contrast, a typical consumer report includes information transmitted to the CRA by a consumer's creditors by tape or similar computer transmission, without any interpersonal communication.

Finally, the definition has a source element: the personal interview must be with "neighbors, friends, or associates of the consumer . . . or with others with whom he is acquainted or who may have knowledge" concerning the substantive information. The definition thus is sufficiently broad to include anyone who is in a position to convey information about the consumer. Each of these elements is discussed more thoroughly below.

13.2.2 Report Must Concern Character, General Reputation, Personal Characteristics, or Mode of Living

The first element deals with the report's subject matter, which must concern character, general reputation, personal characteristics, or mode of living. In contrast, a consumer report can arise from information regarding any of these four qualities, or regarding a consumer's creditworthiness, credit standing, or credit capacity.[16] This distinction suggests that the special provisions for investigative consumer

---

7 15 U.S.C. § 1681a(e).
8 *Id.*
9 *Id. See also* Ippolito v. WNS, Inc., 864 F.2d 440, 448 (7th Cir. 1988); FTC Official Staff Commentary § 603(e) item 1, *reprinted at* Appx. D, *infra*.
10 15 U.S.C. § 1681a(d). See § 2.3, *supra*, for a thorough discussion of the FCRA's definition of "consumer report."
11 15 U.S.C. § 1681a(d).
12 *Id. See also* § 2.3, *supra*.
13 *Id.*
14 15 U.S.C. § 1681a(f). See § 2.5, *supra* for a thorough discussion of the FCRA's definition of "consumer reporting agency."
15 15 U.S.C. § 1681a(d).
16 15 U.S.C. § 1681a(d)(1).

reports are not thought necessary when only credit-related information is acquired from third party interviews, as opposed to other personal information.

Another subject matter distinction between consumer reports and investigative consumer reports pertains to the role the information plays in the report. A "consumer report" is defined as including information *bearing on* the consumer's character and general reputation,[17] while the FCRA defines an "investigative consumer report" as including information *on* those matters.[18] This difference in language would appear to require that an investigative report must directly concern these subjects. Under this interpretation, objective information, such as the fact that a consumer is employed by a certain company, is not an investigative report, whereas information about the consumer's work habits would fall within the substance element of the definition of an investigative report.

13.2.3 Information Must Be Obtained from Third Party Personal Interviews

The second principle element of the definition of an investigative report involves the manner in which the report's information was procured. Some portion of the substantive information in the report must have been obtained by a "personal interview" with neighbors, friends, associates or others.[19] "Personal interview" is not restricted to in-person inquiries, but also includes inquiries made by telephone, or other method of transmission.[20] It does not matter who conducts the interview, whether it be an employee of the CRA or anyone else.[21] However, some communication with a third party is necessary; information obtained by an investigator observing a consumer's home will not turn a consumer report into an investigative report because no interview occurred.[22]

The definition provides that the interview must be with neighbors, friends, associates, "or with others with whom [the consumer] is acquainted or who may have knowledge concerning any such items of information."[23] Consequently, the interview may be with *any* source who is a third party,[24] including members of the consumer's family.[25] However, an interview directly with the consumer would not qualify, since the consumer is not a third party.[26]

13.2.4 Reports Excluded from the Definition

13.2.4.1 General

The Act specifically excludes from the definition of investigative consumer report a report that consists *solely* of specific factual information on a consumer's credit record obtained directly from a creditor or a CRA (where the CRA obtained the information from a creditor or the consumer).[27] A report with both non-investigative and investigative information is still an investigative consumer report, since the statutory definition of an investigative consumer report is a consumer report "or portion thereof" that contains investigative information.[28]

In addition, any report excluded from the definition of "consumer report" will be excluded from the definition of "investigative consumer report." Thus, reports based on the reporter's first-hand experience with the consumer,[29] certain communications among affiliates,[30] and reports by employment agencies that meet the requirements of the employment agency exception[31] will all shield a report from the extra requirements applied to investigative consumer reports.

---

17 15 U.S.C. § 1681a(d).
18 15 U.S.C. § 1681a(e).
19 15 U.S.C. § 1681a(e). *See also* Hinckle, FTC Informal Staff Opinion Letter (July 9, 1998) (mere confirmation of facts stated on a job application is not an interview, but questioning which goes beyond fact-checking, such as asking if one was terminated for cause, would constitute an interview), *reprinted on the CD-Rom accompanying this manual*.
20 FTC Official Staff Commentary § 603(e) item 4, *reproduced at* Appx. D, *infra*; Peeler, FTC Informal Staff Opinion Letter (May 5, 1976), *reprinted on the CD-Rom accompanying this manual*.
21 FTC Official Staff Commentary § 603(e) item 5, *reprinted at* Appx. D, *infra*.
22 FTC Official Staff Commentary § 603(e) item 7, *reprinted at* Appx. D, *infra*.
23 15 U.S.C. § 1681a(e).
24 FTC Official Staff Commentary § 603(e) item 3, *reprinted at* Appx. D, *infra*.
25 An early FTC informal opinion, [1969–1973 Decisions Transfer Binder] Consumer Cred. Guide (CCH) ¶ 99,425 (May 20, 1971), to the contrary has clearly been reversed. *See* FTC Official Staff Commentary § 603(e) item 3, *reprinted at* Appx. C, *infra*; Dea, FTC Informal Staff Opinion Letter (Sept. 24, 1975), *reprinted on the CD-Rom accompanying this manual*.
26 FTC Official Staff Commentary § 603(e) item 3, *reprinted at* Appx. D, *infra*.
27 15 U.S.C. § 1681a(e).
28 FTC Official Staff Commentary § 603(e) item 6, *reprinted at* Appx. D, *infra*.
29 15 U.S.C. § 1681a(d)(2)(A)(i). *See* § 2.4.2, *supra*. This exception applies only to transactions or experiences between the consumer and the person making the report. Accordingly, a CRA may not take advantage of the first-hand experience exception to keep a report that contains information from the first-hand experiences of a third party, such as an employer, with the consumer from being considered a consumer report because the transactions referred to in the communications are not between the job applicant and the CRA. Kane, FTC Informal Staff Opinion Letter (July 9, 1998), *reprinted on the CD-Rom accompanying this manual*.
30 15 U.S.C. § 1681a(d)(2)(A)(ii), (iii). *See* § 2.4.3, *supra*.
31 15 U.S.C. § 1681a(d)(2)(D).

13.2.4.2 Employee Misconduct Investigation Reports

The FCRA was amended in 2003 by FACTA to meet a rising demand by employers to exempt certain reports about employees from the requirements for investigative consumer reports. Employers had complained that the FCRA unfairly undercut meaningful investigations of employee misconduct by requiring the employer to provide FCRA notices ahead of time, notices that effectively alerted the employee to the employer's suspicions.[32]

Under this exclusion, even if a particular investigation would otherwise be an investigative consumer report, it will fall outside of the definition by virtue of being specifically exempted from the definition of "consumer report."[33] To fall within the exclusion the communication must be made to an employer and must be in connection with an investigation of one of the following:

- Suspected misconduct relating to employment;
- Compliance with federal, state, or local laws;
- Compliance with the rules of a self-regulatory organization; or
- Compliance with the preexisting written policies of the employer.[34]

A concern is that the last of the qualifying reasons is subject to the employer's control; conceivably an employer could draft very broad written policies in order to expand the breadth of this exception. One court has construed the first qualifying reason broadly, finding that an employer's investigation of an ex-employee's allegedly false misrepresentation with respect to a worker's compensation claim was one "relating to employment," notwithstanding that the claimant no longer worked for the employer.[35]

To limit the exclusion's scope, the FCRA further requires that the communication must *not* be for the purpose of investigating a consumer's creditworthiness, credit standing, or credit capacity (in other words, the communication must only bear on the employee's character, general reputation, personal characteristics, or mode of living) and must not be provided to anyone other than the employer (or the employer's agent), a governmental authority, or a self-regulatory organization with regulatory authority over the employer.[36] The FCRA defines a self-regulatory organization to be "any self-regulatory organization (as defined in section 3(a)(26) of the Securities Exchange Act of 1934),[37] any entity established under title I of the Sarbanes-Oxley Act of 2002,[38] any board of trade designated by the Commodity Futures Trading Commission, and any futures association registered with such Commission."[39]

Despite taking employee misconduct investigation reports outside the scope of a consumer report, the Act still requires employers to disclose certain information to an employee in connection with such a report. If the employer takes adverse action based on an employee misconduct report, it must disclose to the employee a summary of the nature and substance of the report (but need not disclose sources of information).[40]

13.3 Types of Investigative Reports

13.3.1 Reports for Insurance Purposes

Insurance purposes are the most common basis for an investigative consumer report. According to the FCRA, a permissible purpose for a consumer report (and correspondingly, an investigative consumer report) is the "underwriting" of insurance involving the consumer,[41] meaning the decision whether or not to issue a policy to the consumer, the amount and terms of coverage, the duration of the policy, the rates or fees charged, or the renewal or cancellation of a

---

32 *See* 149 Cong. Rec. H8123 (daily ed. Sept. 10, 2003). Rep. Jackson explained the problem as follows:

> [I]t deals with or undermines or did undermine the ability of employers to use experienced, outside organizations or individuals to investigate allegations of drug use or sales, violence, sexual harassment, other types of harassment, employment discrimination, job safety and health violations, as well as criminal activity, including theft, fraud, embezzlement, sabotage or arson, patient or elder abuse, child abuse and other types of misconduct related to employment. This was not the intention of the Fair Credit Reporting Act, but by its interpretation this is what occurred.

> *Id.* Among the Act's requirements that were perceived as impeding such investigations were the following: (1) Notice to the consumer (in this case, the employee) of the investigation; (2) The employee's consent prior to the investigation; (3) A description of the nature and scope of the proposed investigation, if the employee requested it; (4) A release of a full, un-redacted investigative report to the employee; and (5) Notice to the employee of his or her rights under FCRA prior to taking any adverse employment action. 15 U.S.C. § 1681 b(b). *See* § 7.2.4.5, *supra*.

33 15 U.S.C. § 1681a(d)(2)(D).
34 15 U.S.C. § 1681a(x).
35 Millard v. Miller, 2005 WL 1899475, at *2 (W.D. Wis. Aug. 9, 2005).
36 15 U.S.C. § 1681a(x)(1)(C). One court has held that an employer did not lose the protection of this provision by providing the report to the employer's worker's compensation carrier, reasoning that the carrier was an agent of the employer. Millard v. Miller, 2005 WL 1899475, at *3 (W.D. Wis. Aug. 9, 2005).
37 15 U.S.C. § 78c(a)(26).
38 15 U.S.C. §§ 7211–7218.
39 15 U.S.C. § 1681a(x)(3).
40 15 U.S.C. § 1681a (x)(2).
41 15 U.S.C. § 1681b(a)(3)(c).

policy.[42] However, the evaluation an insurance claim is not a permissible purpose for a consumer report because it does not relate to underwriting.[43]

Entities that prepare consumer reports for insurers are often called inspection bureaus. Inspection bureaus often limit their efforts to public record searches.[44] Through public record searches, these inspection bureaus can obtain information about a consumer's personal life and reputation without conducting personal interviews, thus avoiding the Act's requirements concerning investigative consumer reports.[45] While reports that reference public record information do fall under the FCRA as consumer reports, claim reports that expand beyond public record information to involve interviews with neighbors and colleagues will be investigative consumer reports.

13.3.2 Reports for Employment Purposes

Another common example of an investigative consumer report is a report prepared for employment purposes. Employers may want more in-depth information about an employee or a prospective employee than is available in a typical consumer report, and will request that personal interviews be conducted with former associates or employers. Investigative reports for employment purposes relate not only to hiring, but also to promotions, demotions, transfers, discharges, and related employment decisions.[46]

Contrast this sort of report, which falls with the FCRA's definition of a consumer report, with the employee misconduct investigation report noted in the previous subsection. As discussed above, the FCRA excludes certain employee misconduct investigation reports from the definition of consumer report and accordingly from the definition of investigative consumer report.[47] Should information from a particular employee investigation not meet the criteria of an exempt employer report, the employer will have to comply with the requirements discussed below, assuming the report meets the additional criteria of an investigative consumer report. Even where an employee misconduct investigation report meets the criteria for an exempt report, employees have a right to a summary of the nature and substance of the report upon which the employer's adverse action is based.[48]

The simple procedure of checking out someone's references would qualify as an interview for purposes of that element of an investigative consumer report.[49] Although pure fact-checking of an employee's period of employment, job titles, and salaries would not give rise to an investigative consumer report, any information regarding the individual's job performance, or whether he or she had ever been disciplined or terminated for cause would constitute an interview, and thereby yield an investigative consumer report.[50]

Interviews conducted by the employer or the employer's staff do not involve investigative consumer reports[51]—a third party must perform the interviews for the FCRA's investigative consumer report protections to apply,[52] such as when an employer hires a detective agency[53] or consumer reporting agency (CRA) to conduct the interviews.[54]

Pursuant to a specific exception in the Act, interviews and investigations conducted by employment agencies are usually not investigative consumer reports.[55] If the employment agency is communicating to a prospective employer, with the consent of the consumer, either for the purpose of procuring a work opportunity for the consumer or for the purpose of procuring an employee for the employer, then the communication is not a consumer report at all. This major exclusion from the definition of consumer report is discussed in more detail elsewhere in this manual.[56] If, however, the employment agency does not fulfill each criterion required to be excluded from coverage, then the agency's investigation will likely be an investigative report.

Specific requirements and protections apply to consumer reports requested for employment purposes, whether or not the report is an investigative one. The requirements, summarized here for convenience, are in addition to the special requirements for all investigative reports discussed in the remainder of this chapter.[57]

---

42 FTC Official Staff Commentary § 604(3)(C) item 1, *reprinted at* Appx. D, *infra*.
43 *Id.* item 2. *See* § 7.2.5, *supra*.
44 Privacy Protection Study Commission, Personal Privacy in an Information Society 324–325 (1977), *available at* http://aspe.hhs.gov/datacncl/1977privacy/c5.htm.
45 *See* 15 U.S.C. § 1681a(e). *See also* 15 U.S.C. § 1681l.
46 Under the FCRA as originally enacted, an employer was not required to notify a current employee that it had requested an investigative consumer report if the investigative consumer report was to be used for a promotion or other employment purpose for which the consumer had not specifically applied. *See* 15 U.S.C. §§ 1681a(h), 1681d(a)(2) (1982). Amendments in 1996 eliminated this exception to the notice requirements. 15 U.S.C. § 1681d(a), Pub. L. No. 104-208 § 2414, 110 Stat. 3009 (Sept. 30, 1996).
47 *See* § 7.2.4.5, *supra*, § 13.4.1.4, *infra*.
48 15 U.S.C. § 1681a(x)(2).
49 Willner, FTC Informal Staff Opinion Letter (Mar. 25, 1999), *reprinted on the CD-Rom accompanying this manual*.
50 Kane, FTC Informal Staff Opinion Letter (July 9, 1998), *reprinted on the CD-Rom accompanying this manual*.
51 Kahn, FTC Informal Staff Opinion Letter [1969–1973 Decisions Transfer Binder] Consumer Cred. Guide (CCH) ¶ 99,447 (May 21, 1971).
52 *See* § 13.2.1, *supra*.
53 *See* § 2.7.5, *supra*.
54 FTC Official Staff Commentary § 603(f) item 4, *reprinted at* Appx. D, *infra*. *See also* Grimes, FTC Informal Staff Opinion Letter (Dec. 9, 1983) (agency that prepares lists containing names of employees fired for cause a CRA), *reprinted on the CD-Rom accompanying this manual*; Martin, FTC Informal Staff Opinion Letter (May 26, 1971), *reprinted on the CD-Rom accompanying this manual*; FTC, Compliance with the Fair Credit Reporting Act, at 24.
55 15 U.S.C. § 1681a(o).
56 *See* § 2.4.4, *supra*.
57 15 U.S.C. § 1681b(b)(2). *See also* § 7.2.4, *supra*.

Employers are required to obtain written permission from the consumer before requesting any consumer report, investigative or otherwise. Such permission may be obtained at any time, however, so that an employee's general authorization may remain valid for the duration of employment.[58] The employer must certify to the CRA both that (1) it has notified the consumer that a consumer report may be obtained and (2) the consumer has authorized in writing the procurement of the report. The employer must also certify to the CRA that information in the consumer report will not be used in violation of any federal or state equal employment opportunity law. CRAs are prohibited from furnishing consumer reports for employment purposes without receiving such certifications from the employer. Furthermore, the CRA must provide, when it furnishes the consumer report, a summary of the consumer's rights under the FCRA for the employer's use.[59] If an employer intends to take an adverse action based on information in a consumer report, the employer must provide to the consumer a copy of the report and a description of the consumer's rights under the FCRA.[60]

In the context of investigative reports, the last requirement that a copy of the report sometimes must be given to the consumer takes on added significance. As a general rule, confidential sources for investigative reports do not have to be disclosed.[61] However, if sources are included in a report to an employer, the whole report—sources and all—must be provided to the employee prior to adverse action.[62]

13.3.3 Reports for Landlords

A third common basis for an investigative report is to evaluate a prospective tenant on behalf of a landlord. Such reports are significant not only for their frequency, but also because of the high likelihood that landlords will not comply with the FCRA's requirements concerning such reports.

Investigative reports for landlords may involve personal interviews of a tenant's former landlords, employers, or other references. The investigative report may also involve one of a growing number of tenant screening companies that in effect blacklist certain tenants because of their past practices.[63] Such tenant screening companies not only cull information from court dockets (not likely to entail an investigative consumer report), but also often from former landlords (likely to entail such a report).

It is generally recognized that tenant screening and other reports on tenants are consumer reports.[64] A landlord's report that meets the definition of a consumer report must also meet the substance, manner and source elements of an investigative consumer report to invoke the Act's special protections. There is not much likelihood that questions to a former landlord concerning verification of the existence and dates of a former tenancy and payment records will involve an investigative report. However, any subjective information that pertains to any of the four aspects of the consumer (character, general reputation, personal characteristics, or mode of living) will cause the report to meet the substance element of an investigative consumer report regardless of whether other, business record type, information is also reflected in the report. Thus, nearly any information about a tenant's behavior or even comments such as that the tenant "was very irresponsible in making rent payments" can turn a consumer report into an investigative report.

As with any investigative consumer report, the subjective information about the tenant must have been acquired by a third party through a personal interview. Where a landlord interviews former landlords or other references itself, there will be no investigative consumer report. But where a landlord hires a firm to manage the building, including investigating prospective tenants, it might be argued that the management company is acting as a CRA.[65] Similarly, where a real estate agent is paid a fee for finding tenants, and the landlord asks the real estate agent to conduct personal interviews of former landlords, the real estate agent should be considered a CRA and an investigative consumer report should be involved.

One court has held that where a tenant screening company simply gathers subjective information by asking its subscribing landlords to fill out a questionnaire, the inquiry is not a "personal" interview because it is not conducted "in person."[66] Such an unwarranted loophole, if it is recognized elsewhere, will permit many tenant screening companies to escape the strictures of an investigative consumer report. In any case, inquiries made over the telephone would meet the personal interview element,[67] although whether inquiries made via e-mail would is an open question.

Including subjective information about a tenant obtained through a personal interview will convert the report into an investigative consumer report if it was obtained from any

---

58 Kelchner v. Sycamore Manor Health Ctr., 135 Fed. Appx. 499, 2005 WL 503774, at *2 (3d Cir. Mar. 3, 2005) (holding that a blanket, one-time authorization form meets the Act's requirements).
59 15 U.S.C. § 1681b(b)(1)(B). *See* § 8.2.2, *supra*.
60 *See* § 8.2.6, *supra*.
61 *See* § 13.4.2.3, *infra*.
62 *See* Hahn, FTC Informal Staff Opinion Letter (July 8, 1998), *reprinted on the CD-Rom accompanying this manual*; Kane, FTC Informal Staff Opinion Letter (July 9, 1998), *reprinted on the CD-Rom accompanying this manual*.
63 *See* § 2.6.2.2, *supra*.

64 *See* § 2.6.2.2, *supra*.
65 *But see* Dea, FTC Informal Staff Opinion Letter (Mar. 31, 1975), *reprinted on the CD-Rom accompanying this manual*.
66 Cisneros v. U.D. Registry, 46 Cal. Rptr. 2d 233, 247 (Cal. Ct. App. 1995) (interpreting parallel provision in California's credit reporting act statute).
67 FTC Official Staff Commentary § 603(e) item 4, *reproduced at* Appx. D, *infra*; Peeler, FTC Informal Staff Opinion Letter (May 5, 1976), *reprinted on the CD-Rom accompanying this manual*.

third party source. It might be argued that tenant reports based on information from former landlords are not investigative consumer reports because the FCRA exempts from the definition of investigative consumer report "specific factual information" on a consumer's "credit record" *obtained from the consumer's creditor*. However, a landlord should not be considered a creditor, and therefore this exception should not apply to tenant reports.[68] Even if a former landlord is treated as a creditor, reports dealing with subjective information about a tenant can *not* be said to involve "specific factual information," and certainly will not involve specific factual information about the consumer's "credit record."[69] Accordingly, if any information on the tenant's character, general reputation, personal characteristics or mode of living appears in the report, it will be an investigative consumer report notwithstanding that the report also contains certain credit record information that would be exempted from the definition if it was in its own, separate report.

In addition to the FCRA, tenants should also look to state credit reporting legislation for protections concerning tenant investigative reports. The California Fair Credit Reporting Act, for example, expressly applies to investigative tenant reports.[70] However, a related provision which prohibited the reporting of eviction cases unless the landlord was the prevailing party or the monthly rent exceeded $1000, was held to be unconstitutional.[71]

13.3.4 Other Types of Investigative Reports

Although most investigative consumer reports involve queries by employers, insurers, or landlords, an investigative report can be produced for any purpose that a consumer report is issued. An investigative report is just a consumer report that includes subjective information from third party interviewees.[72]

Accordingly, investigative reports can be used to evaluate a consumer for credit purposes, to review or collect an existing credit account, to determine the consumer's eligibility for a license or other benefit granted by a governmental unit required to consider an applicant's financial status, or, in the case of a potential investor or servicer or a current insurer, to evaluate or assess the credit or prepayment risks associated with an existing credit obligation.[73] The Act also permits investigative reports where a user has a "legitimate business need for the information—(i) in connection with a business transaction that is initiated by the consumer; or (ii) to review an account to determine whether the consumer continues to meet the terms of the account,"[74] as described in § 7.2.8, *supra*. Just as with an ordinary consumer report, an investigative consumer report must be issued for one of the FCRA's listed permissible purposes; if for any other purpose, the investigative consumer report will violate the Act regardless of whether the special requirements pertaining to investigative consumer reports were met.

13.4 Disclosure to Consumer of Investigative Report's Existence

13.4.1 Notice That User Has Requested an Investigative Report

13.4.1.1 General

Any "person" requesting an investigative report must provide notice to the consumer that an investigative consumer report may be made;[75] the FCRA defines person as including individuals, corporations, trusts, governments, governmental subdivisions or agencies, or any other entity.[76] In addition, the user must certify to the consumer reporting agency (CRA) that it has provided this notice to the consumer and will upon proper request disclose the nature and scope of the investigation.[77] In the employment context, the employer must also have written permission from the employee.[78]

13.4.1.2 When Notice Must Be Sent

The user's notice of the investigative report must be mailed to the consumer not later than three days after the user's first request to the CRA that a report be prepared on the consumer.[79] Unfortunately, this notice may arguably be made at any time prior to the request for an investigation, and therefore not necessarily alert the consumer that an investigation is imminent.[80] An employer, who must also

---

68 As discussed in § 2.6.2.2, *supra*. FTC Official Staff Commentary §§ 604(3)(E) item 3 and 615 item 10, *reprinted at* Appx. D, *infra*, do not view landlords as creditors, but a number of courts find leases to involve credit.
69 *Cf.* Grimes, FTC Informal Staff Opinion Letter (Dec. 9, 1983), *reprinted on the CD-Rom accompanying this manual*.
70 *See* Cal. Civ. Code § 1785.11.
71 U.D. Registry, Inc. v. California, 34 Cal. App. 4th 107, 40 Cal. Rptr. 2d 228 (1995).
72 15 U.S.C. § 1681a(e).
73 *See* § 7.2, *supra*.
74 15 U.S.C. § 1681b(3)(F).
75 15 U.S.C. § 1681a(b).
76 15 U.S.C. § 1681d(a)(1).
77 *See* § 13.4.1.5, *infra*.
78 *See* § 13.5.1, *infra*.
79 15 U.S.C. § 1681d(a)(1).
80 *See* Haynes, FTC Informal Staff Opinion Letter (Dec. 18, 1997), *reprinted on the CD-Rom accompanying this manual*; Kelchner v. Sycamore Manor Health Ctr., 135 Fed. Appx. 499, 2005 WL 503774 at *2 (3d Cir. Mar. 3, 2005) (holding that a blanket, one-time authorization form meets the Act's requirements). Maine has its own fair credit reporting statute that requires notice three days prior to the start of the investigation. This provides the consumer with a more timely notice. *See* Me. Rev.

have a signed authorization from an employee, could avoid alerting a particular subject by giving notice and obtaining authorization from all current employees at one time.[81]

Since the notice is given by the user before an investigation is completed or sometimes even before it is initiated, it can easily be abused. For example, a debt collector could inform debtors that an investigation into their private lives will be initiated because of nonpayment of a debt, without any real intent to pursue that investigation. Though the use of such a false threat in an attempt to collect a debt is illegal for other reasons, it may still satisfy the FCRA's notice requirement.[82]

In contrast to some other disclosure notices required by the Act,[83] the notice regarding an investigative consumer report is to be given by the person who requests an investigation, not the CRA.[84] The CRA has no obligation to inform consumers that information will be gathered or that reports will be furnished about them.[85] The CRA is not free from responsibilities, however; it must have the user's certification of compliance prior to preparing a report.[86]

Additional requirements apply if the user requesting an investigative consumer report is an employer. Whether or not a requested consumer report is an investigative report, employers must have disclosed in a separate document that a report may be obtained for employment purposes. This requirement is discussed in an earlier section.[87]

13.4.1.3 Content of Notice

The notice should inform the consumer that a request for an investigative consumer report may be made and should describe the information that the report will seek, including, as applicable, information on the consumer's character, general reputation, personal characteristics, and mode of living.[88] In addition, the disclosure must also state that an investigative consumer report involves personal interviews with sources such as friends, neighbors, and associates.[89] This is the information that will alert a consumer to the fact that something beyond an ordinary consumer report is being sought. If, however, the investigation will actually have a much narrower scope, such as involving only former employers of the consumer, the disclosure may be so modified, thus sparing the consumer unnecessary anxiety.[90] Of course, if the scope of the investigation is subsequently broadened, the consumer must then be informed by a correspondingly broader disclosure. The notice may include any additional accurate information about the report, such as the types of interviews that will be conducted.[91]

While this initial notice will often be fairly cursory, the consumer has the right to receive more detailed information about the investigative report.[92] The notice must include a statement informing the consumer of this right to request additional disclosures concerning the nature and scope of the investigation.[93] In some limited circumstances, when the person requesting the report is able to do so, the notice that an investigative report may be requested can be combined with the more detailed disclosure of the nature and scope of the investigation itself.[94] State law may create additional disclosure requirements.[95]

13.4.1.4 Form of Notice

The notice must be in writing[96] and must be mailed or otherwise delivered to the consumer.[97] The information in the notice must be clearly and accurately disclosed.[98] The FTC staff has drafted and published a form that it deems adequate.[99]

The user may include the notice in an application for insurance, employment, or credit, so long as it is clear and

---

Stat. Ann. tit. 10, § 1314(1). *See also* Mass. Gen. Laws Ann. ch. 93, § 53 (requiring prior notice and consumer's written permission).

81 Meisinger, FTC Informal Staff Opinion Letter (Aug. 31, 1999), *reprinted on the CD-Rom accompanying this manual.*

82 *See* National Consumer Law Center, Fair Debt Collection § 5.1.1 (5th 2004 and Supp.); National Consumer Law Center, Unfair and Deceptive Acts and Practices § 5.1.1 (6th ed. 2004 and Supp.).

83 *See, e.g.,* 15 U.S.C. § 1681g.

84 FTC Official Staff Commentary § 606 item 2, *reprinted at* Appx. D, *infra.*

85 *Id.*

86 *See* § 7.5, *supra.*

87 *See* § 8.2.17, *supra.*

88 15 U.S.C. § 1681d(a)(1). *See* Wilmore, FTC Informal Staff Opinion Letter (Jan. 18, 1994), *reprinted on the CD-Rom accompanying this manual.*

89 FTC Official Staff Commentary § 606 item 6, *reprinted at Appx. C, infra. See also* Petruccelli, FTC Informal Staff Opinion Letter (Nov. 14, 1983), *reprinted on the CD-Rom accompanying this manual*; FTC, Compliance with the Fair Credit Reporting Act, at 40–41 (1977); National Indemnity Co., 92 F.T.C. 426, 428 (1978) (consent order).

90 Dea, FTC Informal Staff Opinion Letter (Dec. 30, 1974), *reprinted on the CD-Rom accompanying this manual.*

91 FTC Official Staff Commentary § 606 item 6, *reprinted at* Appx. D, *infra.*

92 *See* § 13.4.2, *infra.*

93 15 U.S.C. § 1681d(a)(1); FTC Official Staff Commentary § 606 item 6, *reprinted at* Appx. D, *infra.*

94 Willner, FTC Informal Staff Opinion Letter (Mar. 25, 1999), *reprinted on the CD-Rom accompanying this manual.*

95 *See, e.g.,* N.Y. Gen. Bus. Law §§ 380-a, 380-c (disclosure of name of CRA and rights to obtain copy of report).

96 15 U.S.C. § 1681d(a)(1); FTC Official Staff Commentary § 606 item 5, *reprinted at* Appx. D, *infra. See also* Bragg, FTC Informal Staff Opinion Letter (Sept. 16, 1971), *reprinted on the CD-Rom accompanying this manual.*

97 FTC Official Staff Commentary § 606 item 5, *reprinted at* Appx. D, *infra.*

98 FTC Official Staff Commentary § 606 item 5, *reprinted at* Appx. D, *infra.*

99 *See* Feldman, FTC Informal Staff Opinion Letter (Mar. 12, 1971), *reprinted on the CD-Rom accompanying this manual. See also* White, FTC Informal Staff Opinion Letter (Dec. 22, 1975), *reprinted on the CD-Rom accompanying this manual.*

conspicuous and not obscured by other language.[100] However, according to FTC staff, the Act requires employers to provide the notice separate from the employment application itself.[101] If another type of user opts to include the notice in the application, the user must provide the consumer with an extra copy so that the consumer will have a copy after sending the original application back to the user.[102]

13.4.1.5 Certification to Consumer Reporting Agency of Notice to Consumer

The user procuring an investigative consumer report must specifically notify the consumer that a report may be made and that the consumer has the right to request that the nature and scope of the investigation be completely and accurately disclosed. The user must also certify to the CRA that the user has done so.[103] The FCRA prohibits a CRA from preparing or furnishing an investigative consumer report without receiving this certification from the user of the report.[104] Responsibility for compliance with the certification requirements therefore falls both on the user and the CRA: the user may not procure the investigative report without making the required certification to the CRA, and the CRA may not prepare the investigative report without receiving such certification from the user.

13.4.1.6 Relationship to Notice of Adverse Action Based on Consumer Report

The requisite notice of the possibility that a user may procure an investigative consumer report alerts a consumer that an investigation may occur. In addition, since an investigative consumer report is also a consumer report,[105] a user of an investigative consumer report must notify the consumer when it takes adverse action based at least in part on information in the report, and must supply the name, address and telephone number of the CRA making the report.[106] The user must also notify the consumer of the right to obtain a free copy of the report within sixty days.

Consequently, consumers who may be the subject of an investigative consumer report will receive at least one and often two notices. One that must be given no later than three days after the user's request for the report (often no more than a notice that an investigative report may be requested at some time in the future) and, if the user subsequently takes an adverse action, one at a later date notifying the consumer of the adverse action. The first disclosure reveals somewhat more about the nature of the report, and the second disclosure provides the address and telephone number of the CRA making the report as well as information regarding the consumer's rights to obtain a free copy of the report from the CRA and to dispute the report. (This second disclosure could be conveyed in a separate notice.) The first notice of the investigative report must be in writing. The notice(s) following an adverse action may be oral, written or electronic.[107]

Both notices must also explain how the consumer can obtain more information about the report, although the information to be obtained, and the source from which to obtain it, will be somewhat different. When an investigatory report may be requested, the consumer is informed of the right to obtain additional information about the nature and scope of the requested report from the *user*.[108] When adverse action is taken, the consumer is informed of the right to obtain a copy of the report from the *CRA*.[109]

13.4.2 Consumer's Right to Additional Disclosures

13.4.2.1 General

The FCRA gives consumers who may be the subject of an investigative consumer report a second right of disclosure in addition to the initial notice that an investigative consumer report about the consumer may be made.[110] Within a reasonable amount of time from the receipt of the initial notice, the consumer can seek from the person requesting the report a complete and accurate disclosure of the nature and scope of the investigation requested.[111] Note that this second disclosure is still provided by the person requesting the investigation, and not from the individual who in fact conducts the investigation. Thus, the requester/user is disclosing what the requester is asking the investigator to investigate, not what in fact is investigated. According to FTC staff,[112] the user requesting the investigation may preempt the consumer by disclosing the nature and scope of the investigation even before the consumer asks for such

---

100 FTC Official Staff Commentary § 606 item 5, *reprinted at* Appx. D, *infra*.
101 See § 8.2.17, *supra*.
102 *See* Bragg, FTC Informal Staff Opinion Letter (Sept. 16, 1971), *reprinted on the CD-Rom accompanying this manual*; Bragg, FTC Informal Staff Opinion Letter (Aug. 27, 1971), *reprinted on the CD-Rom accompanying this manual*; Carson, FTC Informal Staff Opinion Letter (June 3, 1971), *reprinted on the CD-Rom accompanying this manual*; Feldman, FTC Informal Staff Opinion Letter (Mar. 12, 1971) (specifies what form of disclosure needed in separate notice and in application), *reprinted on the CD-Rom accompanying this manual*.
103 15 U.S.C. § 1681d(a)(2).
104 *See* § 7.5, *supra*.
105 *See* § 13.2.1, *supra*.
106 *See* § 8.2.6, *supra*.
107 *See* § 8.2.6, *supra*.
108 *See* § 13.4.2, *infra*.
109 *See* § 13.4.3, *infra*.
110 *See* § 13.4.1, *supra*.
111 15 U.S.C. § 1681d(b). No guidelines are provided on what constitutes a "reasonable amount of time" under this section.
112 Willner, FTC Informal Staff Opinion Letter (Mar. 25, 1999), *reprinted on the CD-Rom accompanying this manual*.

information, and even as part of the user's disclosure that an investigative report may be requested. Of course, this combination of disclosures is only possible when the person who might request an investigation already knows with requisite detail the nature and scope of the investigation itself.

The notice that an investigation may be requested does not necessarily mean that an investigation has been or even will be requested. The notice may be included with an application for employment or insurance, without an investigation ever being conducted; the user may include the notice merely to keep open the option of someday procuring an investigative consumer report. A consumer who prudently requests disclosure of the nature and scope of the investigation must be provided complete and accurate information about the investigation within five days of the time the user requests an investigation, even if the request occurs much later. In effect the consumer may only trigger a standing obligation on the part of the user to disclose the additional information about an investigation if and when it occurs. At least one court has decided that it is not an FCRA violation to fail to respond to a request for additional disclosures where the investigation was never initiated.[113] The consumer may be left in an uncomfortable limbo, wondering whether an intrusive investigation into his or her personal habits may be forthcoming. However, the possibility of such an investigation should terminate with the permissible purpose that presumably would underlie an investigative report.

13.4.2.2 User Must Disclose Questions Asked, Not Answers Given

The FCRA requires that upon the consumer's request, the person procuring the report must completely and accurately disclose "the nature and scope of the investigation requested."[114] According to an FTC staff opinion, the requester's disclosure must include a complete and accurate description of the types of questions asked, the number and types of persons interviewed, and the name and address of the investigating agency.[115] The user need not provide the consumer with a copy of the actual report,[116] unless state law requires it[117] or unless the user is an employer who intends to take an adverse action based on a consumer report procured for employment purposes.[118] As discussed earlier, the CRA must provide a free copy of the report if the consumer requests it following an adverse action.[119]

Except in the case of an employer who intends to take an adverse action based on a consumer report,[120] nothing in the Act requires *users*, as opposed to CRAs, to provide consumers with copies of reports. Of course, nothing in the FCRA prohibits a user from giving a copy of the report to its consumer subject if it decides to do so.[121] The practice whereby CRAs enter into agreements with users specifying that users cannot disclose contents of reports to consumer subjects[122] is not legal where adverse action occurs, because the Act provides that CRAs may not prohibit users from disclosing the contents of the consumer report when adverse action has been taken.[123] A user's disclosure of a report to the consumer subject does not turn the user into a CRA because the user is not disclosing the information to a third party.[124] Users must certify to CRAs that they will not share information in a report with others, but this prohibition does not apply to the sharing of the information with the consumer.[125] If a user directly provides the consumer with the report, any inaccuracies in the report can be corrected much more quickly, which would contribute to the CRA's ability to ensure maximum possible accuracy.[126]

13.4.2.3 Disclosure of Names of Sources Interviewed Not Required

The FTC Staff Commentary states that users need not disclose the names of sources of information, that is, the names of individuals interviewed. This is derived from the FCRA's provision that protects CRAs (though not users) from the obligation to provide names of individuals interviewed for investigative consumer reports.[127] This FCRA exception was inserted in response to claims by the reporting industry that if the identities of the persons interviewed in investigations were not kept confidential, such sources of

---

113 Kates v. Crocker Nat'l Bank, 776 F.2d 1396 (9th Cir. 1985).
114 15 U.S.C. § 1681d(b).
115 FTC Official Staff Commentary § 606 item 7, *reprinted at* Appx. D, *infra*. *See also* Feldman, FTC Informal Staff Opinion Letter (Aug. 21, 1974), *reprinted on the CD-Rom accompanying this manual*.
116 FTC Official Staff Commentary § 606 item 7, *reprinted at* Appx. D, *infra*. *See also* Feldman, FTC Informal Staff Opinion Letter (Aug. 21, 1974), *reprinted on the CD-Rom accompanying this manual*.
117 *See, e.g.*, Mass. Gen. Laws Ann. ch. 93, § 53.
118 *See* § 13.3.2, *supra*.
119 *See* § 3.3.6, *supra*.
120 As discussed in § 13.3.2, *supra*, the employer who intends to take an adverse action based on information in a consumer report must provide the consumer with a copy of the report and a description of the consumer's rights under the FCRA.
121 FTC Official Staff Commentary § 604-General item 3, *reprinted at* Appx. D, *infra*. *See also* FTC Official Staff Commentary § 606 item 7, *reprinted at* Appx. D, *infra*; Brinckerhoff, FTC Informal Staff Opinion Letter (June 3, 1989). *See also* Feldman, FTC Informal Staff Opinion Letter (Aug. 21, 1974), *reprinted on the CD-Rom accompanying this manual*.
122 *See, e.g.*, A-1 Credit & Assurance v. Trans Union Credit Info., 678 F. Supp. 1147, 1148 (E.D. Pa. 1988).
123 15 U.S.C. § 1681e(c).
124 FTC Official Staff Commentary § 603(f) item 3, *reprinted at* Appx. D, *infra*.
125 *Id*.
126 *See* § 13.4.3, *infra*.
127 15 U.S.C. § 1681g(a)(2).

information would "dry up."[128] An exception will exist, however, where the user is an employer who intends to take an adverse action based on the report and the report does not fall under the employee misconduct investigation report exception. In that case, since that user must provide the consumer with a copy of the report itself, the consumer will thereby learn the names of any sources in the report.

For the FCRA exception concerning sources of investigative consumer reports to apply, the information must have been "acquired solely for use in preparing an investigative consumer report and actually used for no other purpose."[129] This provision has two parts: for sources to be protected the information must be obtained solely for use in an investigative report and not for other types of consumer reports, and the report can only be subsequently used for the purposes originally specified.

Even if sources for investigative reports are generally protected, a consumer who brings an FCRA action in court may use appropriate discovery procedures to obtain those names.[130] That is, the protection does not create a litigation privilege.

13.4.2.4 Form of Disclosure

The user must disclose to the consumer the nature and scope of the requested investigation in writing, and must mail or otherwise deliver it to the consumer within five days of receipt of the consumer's request for the disclosure or of the date the investigation was requested, whichever is later.[131] The FTC Staff Commentary suggests that the user can properly disclose the nature (but not the scope) of the requested investigation by providing the consumer with a blank copy of the standardized form used to transmit the report from the CRA to the user.[132] Obviously not any form will suffice, because the standardized form could contain virtually no information at all about the nature of the investigation. Nevertheless, the FTC Staff Commentary example is instructive. It indicates that the user must disclose to the consumer very specifically and accurately the type of issues being investigated, but need not disclose what actually has been discovered about the consumer.

13.4.3 Consumer Reporting Agency Must Disclose Consumer Report

As with any ordinary consumer report, a consumer has a right to additional information about an investigative consumer report not just from the user but also from the CRA directly. In fact, the information received from the CRA may be more useful than that received from the user. Upon the request of a consumer, a CRA must disclose all information in the consumer's file at the time of the request.[133] The CRA must also provide the names, addresses, and telephone numbers of any recipients of a report on the consumer within the last year (two years for reports with employment purposes).[134] In addition, the CRA must provide a free copy of the report to the consumer upon the consumer's request following an adverse action based in part on a consumer report.[135] As noted above,[136] the CRA need not disclose the names of individuals interviewed for an investigative consumer report if the information was "acquired solely for use in preparing an investigative consumer report and actually used for no other purpose."[137]

Obviously, to be able to request information in the consumer's file from the CRA, the consumer will need to know the name and address of the CRA. The FCRA's investigative consumer report provision requires the user to disclose this information upon the consumer's request.[138] In addition, since an investigative consumer report is also a consumer report, the Act's requirement that the user must disclose this information on its own whenever it takes adverse action against the consumer based at least in part on a consumer report also applies to an investigative consumer report.[139] A user who takes an adverse action must also provide the CRA's telephone number, including a toll-free telephone number for any CRA that operates nationwide.[140]

It would be unusual for a consumer to discover (from friends or associates) that someone is conducting an investigation concerning him or her and not to have received a notice from the individual requesting the investigative report. This might take place only when the user has violated the FCRA by failing to notify the consumer of its request for an investigative report.[141] In such a situation, it will be difficult for the consumer to discover who has ordered the investigation. Investigators usually do not reveal to those they interview why or for whom they are conducting the investigation. Nevertheless, if friends can identify the name of the investigator, the consumer is entitled to seek from the

---

128 The legislative history of this provision is discussed in Retail Credit Co. v. Dade County, 393 F. Supp. 577 (S.D. Fla. 1975).
129 15 U.S.C. § 1681g(a)(2).
130 Id. See also Retail Credit Co. v. United Family Life Ins. Co., 203 S.E.2d 760 (Ga. Ct. App. 1974).
131 15 U.S.C. § 1681d.
132 FTC Official Staff Commentary § 606 item 7, reprinted at Appx. D, infra.
133 See § 3.5, supra.
134 See § 3.5.4, supra.
135 See § 3.3.6, supra.
136 See § 13.4.2.3, supra.
137 15 U.S.C. § 1681g(a)(2). However, the names of the sources are available to a plaintiff who brings an action under the FCRA in accordance with appropriate discovery procedures. Id.
138 FTC Official Staff Commentary § 606 item 7, reprinted at Appx. D, infra. See also FTC Official Staff Commentary § 606 item 7, reprinted at Appx. D, infra; Feldman, FTC Informal Staff Opinion Letter (Aug. 21, 1974). See also Feldman, FTC Informal Staff Opinion Letter (Aug. 21, 1974), reprinted on the CD-Rom accompanying this manual.
139 15 U.S.C. § 1681m.
140 15 U.S.C. § 1681m(a).
141 See § 13.4.1.2, supra.

investigator not only the information the investigator obtained about the consumer, but also the recipients of any consumer report produced on the consumer.[142]

13.4.4 Users' Reasonable Procedures Defense

As described above, there are four different disclosures concerning investigative reports, one whereby *CRAs* must disclose information in their files to consumers[143] and three disclosure requirements placed on *users*—disclosure that an investigatory consumer report may be requested, provision of additional information about an investigative consumer report upon the consumer's request, and notification that a consumer report is at least in part the basis for an adverse determination against the consumer.[144] Users cannot be held liable for a violation of any of their three disclosure requirements relating to investigative reports if the user can show "by a preponderance of the evidence that at the time of the violation he maintained reasonable procedures to assure compliance" with these requirements.[145]

The FCRA does not specify the types of procedures that must be shown to avoid liability under this section. Ordinarily, the reasonableness of procedures is a question of fact.[146] However, interpretations of other FCRA "reasonable procedures" provisions, discussed elsewhere in this manual, give some indication of what the user must establish.[147]

13.4.5 Waiver of Consumer Rights

Employers, insurers, or others requesting investigative reports may attempt to avoid the FCRA notice requirements by seeking a waiver from the consumer. For example, an employer might require all job applicants to sign a form that contains an express waiver of their right to request disclosure of the nature and scope of any investigative report. The employer might even seek a broader waiver of all disclosure rights the consumer might have concerning any consumer report.

The FTC staff, when requested to provide an opinion of such a waiver, found the waiver to be ineffective, and concluded that the very inclusion of the waiver would be an unfair and deceptive act or practice. The FTC staff stated:

It is the view of the staff of this Division that the inclusion of such a waiver would be unfair to the consumer and of doubtful validity as well. It is a generally accepted principle that a right afforded by Federal law may not be waived unless the statute creating the right expressly allows for such waiver. In this case, unlike the Truth in Lending Act, the statute does not provide for such a waiver. Accordingly, we would view such a waiver as invalid, and would, in all probability, recommend to the Commission in the appropriate case that it proceed administratively against users of consumer reports, subject to our enforcement jurisdiction, who employed a waiver of the type described in your letter in their applications.[148]

The FTC has also determined that a CRA cannot condition disclosure upon the execution by the consumer of a waiver of claims, even where the waiver closely conforms to the language contained in the Act.[149] Waivers are strictly construed against the drafter; preprinted waivers with potential employees of unequal bargaining power demand careful judicial scrutiny when they are "so broad as to afford protection for all conduct no matter how egregious."[150]

13.5 Consumer Utilization of Investigative Report Notices

13.5.1 Consumer's Permission Necessary for Employee Investigation Report, Except for Employee Misconduct Investigation Reports

An employer may not procure a consumer report (investigative or otherwise) for employment purposes without the written permission of the employee.[151] Thus, a consumer may prevent some investigations for employment purposes

---

142 15 U.S.C. § 1681g.
143 *See* § 13.4.3, *supra*.
144 *See* § 13.4.2, *supra*.
145 15 U.S.C. § 1681d(c).
146 Feldman v. Comprehensive Info. Servs., Inc., 2003 WL 22413484 (Conn. Super. Ct. Oct. 6, 2003) (unknown to the employer, the CRA did not physically inspect the criminal records but the employer required neither a physical inspection in the written contract nor an affidavit that such an inspection had been done).
147 *See* Chs. 4, 6, § 7.5, *supra*.

148 FTC Official Staff Commentary § 606 item 7, *reprinted at* Appx. D, *infra;* Carson, FTC Informal Staff Opinion Letter (June 3, 1971). *See also* Feldman, FTC Informal Staff Opinion Letter (Aug. 21, 1974), *reprinted on the CD-Rom accompanying this manual*.
149 MIB, Inc., 101 FTC 415, 423 (1983) (consent order). Contra FTC Official Staff Commentary § 606 item 7, *reprinted at* Appx. D, *infra;* Peeler, FTC Informal Staff Opinion Letter (Mar. 23, 1977). *See also* Feldman, FTC Informal Staff Opinion Letter (Aug. 21, 1974), *reprinted on the CD-Rom accompanying this manual*.
150 Feldman v. Comprehensive Info. Servs., Inc., 2003 WL 22413484 (Conn. Super. Ct. Oct. 6, 2003).
151 *See* §§ 7.2.4, 13.3.2, *supra*. Nothing in the Act authorizes or prohibits employer to terminate or refuse to hire someone who refuses to give an employer permission to obtain a consumer report. *See* FTC Official Staff Commentary § 606 item 7, *reprinted at* Appx. D, *infra;* Fischel, FTC Informal Staff Opinion Letter (Oct. 1, 1999). *See also* Feldman, FTC Informal Staff

by withholding permission. A major exception to this rule is the FCRA's exclusion of employee misconduct investigation reports from the definition of consumer report and accordingly from the definition of investigative consumer report.[152] This exemption allows an employer to avoid the special requirements applicable to other types of consumer reports used for employment purposes, although the employer must comply with new exemption's disclosure requirements.[153]

In the event an employer has kept an old open-ended permission form on file, the consumer presumably may withdraw the grant of permission to prevent an investigation. No case has addressed whether the consumer may restrict the scope of the investigation by placing limitations on the permission itself.

Other than in the employment context, however, a consumer who receives notice that an investigative consumer report may be requested has only limited options. As long as an investigative consumer report is for a permissible purpose,[154] the consumer cannot stop the investigation.[155] A consumer reporting agency (CRA) or a user need not obtain the consumer's permission before initiating an investigation,[156] unless a state law requires such permission.[157]

On the other hand, if a report described as for a permissible purpose is really for an impermissible purpose, the consumer may seek relief under the FCRA.[158] The consumer's signing of a statement in an application providing such permission probably does not suffice to give the report a permissible purpose.[159] This is the case even though the FCRA lists as a permissible purpose a report "in accordance with the written instructions of the consumer."[160] According to one FTC informal staff opinion letter, a consumer's acknowledgment that an employer may seek subsequent consumer reports for employment purposes does not rise to be a "written instruction[]."[161]

13.5.2 Steps the Consumer Can Take upon Notice of Request for an Investigative Report

The first step in responding to a notice that an investigatory report may be requested is to ask the user for additional information about the requested investigation. The consumer should seek this information promptly, because the Act requires the user to provide additional information only if the consumer requests it within a reasonable period after receiving the first notice of the user's request for an investigatory report. If the consumer's request for that disclosure is timely, the user must provide a complete and accurate disclosure of the nature and scope of the investigation, including the name of the investigating agency.[162] Disclosure must occur not later than five days from the request by the consumer, or from the date the investigation is requested by the user. If the investigation is initiated well after the consumer's request, the consumer may not receive a quick response, and may not even receive a response at all if the user never initiates the investigation.[163]

If the consumer wants to stop the investigation for privacy reasons, the consumer can try to do so by notifying the user that the consumer wants to withdraw the application for credit, insurance, employment, or whatever other action that triggered the user's request for the report. Once the application is withdrawn, the user probably has no reason to go to the expense of procuring the investigative report. Nevertheless, the consumer does not have a legal right to compel the user to stop the investigation.[164]

The consumer can also try to limit the investigation by requesting former employers, friends, and neighbors not to cooperate with the investigation. The consumer will not be given a list of the individuals to be contacted,[165] so the consumer will have to guess who will be interviewed.

In most cases, the consumer will want the investigation to proceed, but to keep inaccurate or biased information out of the report. The best approach, as with any ordinary consumer report, is to make use of the FCRA's reinvestigation provisions that apply to all consumer reports. The consumer should first obtain the substance of the report from the investigating agency,[166] and then dispute the accuracy or completeness of information in the file, which will trigger the CRA's obligation to reinvestigate the disputed information.[167]

Reinvestigation of personal interviews will usually require the CRA to re-contact those individuals initially in-

---

Opinion Letter (Aug. 21, 1974), *reprinted on the CD-Rom accompanying this manual.*

152 *See* §§ 7.2.4.5, 13.4.1.4, *supra.*
153 15 U.S.C. § 1681a(x)(2).
154 *See* § 7.2, *supra.*
155 *But see* Mass. Gen. Laws Ann. ch. 93, § 53 (requiring consumer's prior written authorization of any investigative consumer report); N.J. Stat. Ann. § 56:11-33 (the disclosure must include the precise nature of the investigation requested and the consumer's right to have a copy of the report on request).
156 *See* FTC Official Staff Commentary § 606 item 7, *reprinted at* Appx. D, *infra;* Grimes FTC Informal Staff Opinion Letter (July 20, 1992). *See also* Feldman, FTC Informal Staff Opinion Letter (Aug. 21, 1974), *reprinted on the CD-Rom accompanying this manual.*
157 *See, e.g.,* N.Y. Gen. Bus. Law. § 380-c (permission required).
158 *See* §§ 7.6, 7.7, *supra.*
159 *See* Grimes FTC Informal Staff Opinion Letter (July 20, 1992), *reprinted on the CD-Rom accompanying this manual.*
160 15 U.S.C. § 1681b(2).
161 *See* Grimes FTC Informal Staff Opinion Letter (July 20, 1992), *reprinted on the CD-Rom accompanying this manual.*

162 15 U.S.C. § 1681d(b). *See also* FTC Official Staff Commentary § 606 item 7, *reprinted at* Appx. D, *infra;* § 13.4.2, *supra.*
163 *See* § 13.4.2.1, *supra.*
164 *See* § 13.5.1, *supra.*
165 *See* § 13.4.2.3, *supra.*
166 *See* § 13.4.3, *supra.*
167 *See* Ch. 4, *supra.*

terviewed who provided the disputed information. These individuals must be told that their original statement is disputed, and the nature of the consumer's objection should be fully disclosed before they are asked to verify the information that they originally furnished.[168] An earlier FTC guide indicated that sources who furnish information used in an investigative report also should be informed that the consumer may discover their names in any resulting litigation.[169]

If the CRA cannot verify the information, the information must be deleted from the file.[170] If the information remains in the file, the consumer can still provide a brief statement to be inserted in his or her file setting forth the nature of the dispute.[171] Unfortunately, this reinvestigation and statement of dispute may take place after the user has received and acted upon the initial investigatory report. The damage may not be able to be undone.[172]

The consumer can request that the CRA provide updated information to the user, such as that the information cannot be verified or that the consumer disputes the information.[173] Obviously the consumer can also send directly to the user any information that the consumer wishes. The consumer need not wait to do this until the CRA has reinvestigated a disputed item. In fact, it may even make sense for the consumer to send certain information to the user *before* the investigative agency completes its report; by the time the report is completed and its contents disclosed to the consumer, the user may already have acted on the report.

13.6 Consumer Reporting Agency Procedures for Investigative Reports

13.6.1 Procedures Required for Any Consumer Report

Consumer reporting agencies (CRAs) have an obligation to ensure that information in consumer reports is accurate[174]

and not obsolete.[175] These requirements apply to investigative reports as they do to any other consumer reports.[176]

Accordingly, in preparing an investigative consumer report, a CRA must follow reasonable procedures to ensure maximum possible accuracy of the information concerning the consumer.[177] Procedures for seeking subjective information from personal interviews[178] will differ from procedures for seeking objective information from creditors or public records. In any case, however, the procedures should be reasonably designed to ensure maximum possible accuracy.

The standards for obsolete information also apply to investigative consumer reports. In general information cannot be more than seven years old.[179] Nevertheless, the Act provides for three situations where obsolete information may be included in any report, and these three situations frequently apply to investigative consumer reports. Obsolete information can be included in a report where the report is used in connection with (i) a credit transaction whose principal amount is $150,000 or more, (ii) a life insurance transaction whose principal amount is $150,000 or more, or (iii) the employment of an individual at an annual salary of $75,000 or more.[180]

13.6.2 Special Procedures for Investigative Consumer Reports

13.6.2.1 General

Because of the sensitive nature of many investigative consumer reports, CRAs must follow special procedures to ensure their accuracy. Information based on personal interviews, certain adverse information from public records, as well as information which an agency seeks to re-use in a subsequent investigative report must all be verified in accordance with the FCRA.

13.6.2.2 Information from Personal Interviews

To guard against the inclusion of unsubstantiated information in investigative consumer reports, a CRA that interviews a consumer's neighbor, friend, or other associate must follow "reasonable procedures" to confirm any interview information that is adverse to the consumer with an additional source having independent and direct knowledge of the information.[181] The CRA may escape this confirmation

---

168 *See* FTC Official Staff Commentary § 611 item 2, *reprinted at* Appx. D, *infra*. *See also* FTC, Compliance with the Fair Credit Reporting Act, at 33 (1977).
169 *See* FTC, Compliance with the Fair Credit Reporting Act, at 33 (1977).
170 15 U.S.C. § 1681i(a). *See* Ch. 4, *supra*.
171 15 U.S.C. § 1681i(b). *See* Ch. 4, *supra*.
172 *See, e.g.*, Poore v. Sterling Testing Sys., Inc., 410 F. Supp. 2d 557, 561 (E.D. Ky. 2006) (employer filled the position with another applicant before the plaintiff was able to show that an arrest that the investigating agency had attributed to him in a pre-employment report was not in fact his).
173 15 U.S.C. § 1681i(d).
174 *See* Ch. 4, *supra*.

175 *See* § 5.2, *supra*.
176 *See, e.g.*, 15 U.S.C. § 1681g(a)(2).
177 15 U.S.C. § 1681e(b).
178 *See* § 13.6.2.1, *infra*.
179 *See* § 5.2, *supra*.
180 *See* § 5.2.4, *supra*.
181 15 U.S.C. § 1681d(d)(4).

requirement, however, if the person interviewed is the "best possible source of the information."[182]

13.6.2.3 Adverse Information Based on Public Records

Certain adverse information that is a matter of public record must be verified before the release of the investigative report. A CRA may not furnish an investigative consumer report that includes public record information relating to an arrest, indictment, conviction, civil judicial action, tax lien, or outstanding judgment, unless the CRA has verified the accuracy of the information within thirty days prior to releasing the information.[183] Certain additional standards apply to public record information contained in consumer reports used for employment purposes, as discussed elsewhere.[184]

13.6.2.4 Verification of Information for Re-Use in Subsequent Investigative Report

If a CRA prepares an investigative consumer report that contains adverse information, the CRA may not include that information in a subsequent consumer report unless the information "has been verified in the process of making such subsequent consumer report."[185] The required verification does not refer to the initial process to obtain the information, but to a verification made at the time of a subsequent report of the same information.

For example, consider where a CRA conducts an initial set of interviews at the request of one user and provides a report to that user. If another user also wants an investigative report on the same individual, the CRA cannot merely copy the old report. The CRA must, at that later point in time, verify the information in the report. However, one court has held that verification may not be required when a user requests a copy of an old report if no new report is prepared and the copy supplied clearly states that it is dated and does not provide fresh information.[186] When a new report is prepared, that may be the first time that the information is verified, since adverse information in the original report need not be confirmed with another source if the person interviewed was the best possible source of the information.[187]

One exception exists to the FCRA verification requirement for re-use of an investigative consumer report.[188] Investigative information that "was received within the three-month period preceding the date the subsequent report is furnished" is exempted.[189] This exemption indicates that one of the purposes of the requirement is to ensure that the information in investigative reports is complete and up-to-date.

In order to verify information that has been on file for more than three months, the CRA will, in effect, have to reinvestigate the consumer. The CRA must delete any information that cannot be verified at the time the later report is prepared.[190] The CRA may not simply add more recent information to the investigative report. Accordingly, the verification requirement prevents the continued distribution of subjective evaluations of the consumer's conduct that were included in the original report but which sources can no longer confirm.

An investigative report can contain information from a previous report as long as that information has been reverified.[191] But even if reverified, the CRA may discover new information that puts the older information in a different light. While the CRA can keep the older information in its files as long as it has been recently reverified, the CRA may have to add the newer information as well to ensure maximum accuracy.[192]

The Act's legislative history indicates that the drafters felt that the "highly personal nature of these investigative reports requires reverification of specific details."[193] Although this explanation is somewhat ambiguous, the reverification requirement may have been intended to protect the consumer's privacy by prohibiting the distribution of personal information that is not currently a matter of common knowledge among the consumer's friends, neighbors, or associates. Unfortunately, to reverify information the CRA must renew inquiries about the consumer's personal life, an additional intrusion into the consumer's privacy. The cost of

---

182 15 U.S.C. § 1681d(d)(4)(B).
183 15 U.S.C. § 1681d(d)(3).
184 15 U.S.C. § 1681k. See § 8.2.20, supra. When an investigative consumer report contains such adverse public record information, the more strict requirements of section 1681k take precedence over those of section 1681d. Poore v. Sterling Testing Sys., Inc., 410 F. Supp. 2d 557, 571 (E.D. Ky. 2006).
185 15 U.S.C. § 1681l.
186 Clay v. Equifax, Inc., 762 F.2d 952 (11th Cir. 1985).
187 15 U.S.C. § 1581d(d)(4). See § 13.6.2.2, supra.

---

188 A second possible exception exists. Section 1681l, requiring reverification, does not apply to "information which is a matter of public record." However, § 1681d(d) effectively requires reverification of public record information relating to arrest, indictment, conviction, civil judicial action, tax lien, or outstanding judgment. Other forms of adverse public record information are apparently not subject to unique reverification requirements.
189 15 U.S.C. § 1681l.
190 15 U.S.C. § 1681l.
191 The term "reverified" is used for the § 1681l process although it is possible that the information was not confirmed at the time of the original report. See 15 U.S.C. § 1681d(d)(4). See also § 13.6.2.2, supra.
192 See 15 U.S.C. § 1681e(b).
193 Hearings on H.R. 16340 Before the Subcommittee on Consumer Affairs of the House Committee on Banking and Currency, 91st Cong., 2d Sess. 13 (1970) (section-by-section summary and analysis of H.R. 16340).

reverification may, however, discourage the CRA from preparing, and users from requesting, unnecessary investigative reports.[194]

13.7 State Laws on Investigative Reports

Several states also have laws regulating investigative reports,[195] often filling the void left by the FCRA and providing consumers with enhanced protections against the unfair and improper use of investigative reports for employment and insurance purposes. Most of these statutes use the same definition of an investigative report found in the FCRA, but California's statute does not require a personal interview, part of the FCRA's definition.[196] State laws on consumer investigative reports usually govern insurance and employment investigative reports and typically require certain disclosures and notices when such reports are requested.

For example, in California, if an investigative report is requested for insurance purposes, a written disclosure must be provided to the consumer at the time the consumer signs the application, medical form, or binder. If there is no signed application, medical form, or binder, the disclosure must be made in writing and mailed or otherwise delivered within three days after the report was first requested.[197]

The disclosure warns the consumer that an investigative report regarding the consumer's character, general reputation, personal characteristics, and mode of living may be made. The disclosure must include the name and address of the investigative consumer reporting agency conducting the investigation and the nature and scope of the investigation requested.

For investigative reports for an employment purpose, California law requires employers to show the consumer the report and identify who asked for the report and how to contact them.[198] The California statute has an employee misconduct investigation report exception similar to that found in the FCRA. Notice is not required if the reports are made because of a "suspicion of wrongdoing by the subject of the investigation."[199]

---

194 The user must not only bear the costs of reverification that the CRA passes on, but also the expense of providing notice to the consumer when an investigative consumer report is requested.

195 *See, e.g.,* Ariz. Rev. Stat. Ann. § 20-2107; Cal. Civ. Code § 1786.16 (West); Conn. Gen. Stat. § 38a-982; Ga. Code Ann. § 33-39-8; 215 Ill. Comp. Stat. 5/1008.73; Kan. Stat. Ann. § 50-705; Me. Rev. Stat. Ann. tit. 10, § 1312-1319; Me. Rev. Stat. Ann. tit. 24, § 2209; Mass. Gen. Laws ch. 93, § 53; Minn. Stat. § 72A.496; Mont. Code Ann. § 31-3-113; N.H. Rev. Stat. Ann. §§ 359-B:6, 359-B:14; N.J. Stat. Ann. §§ 17:23A-7, 56:11-33 (West); N.Y. Gen. Bus. Law § 380-c (McKinney); N.C. Gen. Stat. § 58-39-40; Ohio Rev. Code Ann. § 3904.07 (West); Or. Rev. Stat. § 746.635; Va. Code Ann. § 38.2-607; Wash. Rev. Code § 19.182.050.

196 Cal. Civ. Code § 1786.2 (West).

197 Cal. Civ. Code § 1781.16(a)(1) (West).

198 *Id.*

199 Cal. Civ. Code § 1781.16(a)(2) (West).

Chapter 14 Credit Scoring

14.1 Introduction

A credit score is a number compiled from a consumer's file at a consumer reporting agency (CRA), sometimes in conjunction with information obtained from a credit application or other sources. Credit scores are used as a factor, sometimes the sole factor, in determining whether to grant credit to a consumer. The credit score may be the single most influential, critical piece of information associated with a consumer's file at a CRA. Despite their importance, the FCRA specifically exempted credit scores from disclosure until the passage of the Fair and Accurate Credit Transactions Act of 2003 (FACTA) amendments to the FCRA.[1]

This chapter gives an overview of credit scores. It discusses what credit scores are,[2] the variations on credit scoring,[3] and how credit scores are generated.[4] The discussion of these issues in this chapter is admittedly sparse, because how credit scores are generated is a secret closely guarded by industry.[5] Any attempt to break into this "black box" or challenge credit scoring will need to address the fact that there is little law that directly regulates this very important information about a consumer's credit history.

This chapter provides some practical advice on how to improve a credit score.[6] It also discusses some of the policy issues, controversies, and practical problems with credit scoring.[7] One particular controversy involves the use of credit scores for a seemingly unrelated purpose, insurance underwriting and rate setting.[8] Another controversy arises when credit scoring disproportionately harms minorities and other groups, an issue discussed more fully in another manual in this series.[9]

---

1 See § 14.4.1, infra.
2 See § 14.2.1, infra.
3 See § 14.2.2, infra.
4 See § 14.5.2, infra.
5 See § 14.5.1, infra.
6 See § 14.6, infra.
7 See §§ 14.7, 14.8, infra.
8 See § 14.10, infra.
9 See National Consumer Law Center, Credit Discrimination § 6.4 (4th ed. 2005 and Supp.).

14.2 What Is Credit Scoring?

14.2.1 The Basics

A credit scoring system is one that numerically weighs or "scores" some or all of the factors considered in the underwriting process. Factors are developed based on data about past borrowers from their files at consumer reporting agencies (CRAs) and sometimes from other sources. Examples of factors used in a credit scoring system include payment history of past obligations, amounts owed, length of credit history, and types of credit already held. The number of points received often determines whether the consumer is offered credit, how much credit is granted, and at what price.

Credit scores are used to predict the probability that consumers with a certain score will engage in a particular behavior, e.g., delinquency, default, or bankruptcy. Credit scores cannot predict if any particular person will actually engage in the behavior. In fact, oftentimes the probability is that a particular low-scoring person will not engage in the behavior. For example, a score of 620 is generally used as a cut-off between prime and subprime credit.[10] It is estimated that about 11% of borrowers with a credit score of under 620 will become delinquent.[11] Thus, if a score of 620 is used as a cut-off in determining whether to grant a loan, the vast majority of applicants who are denied would probably have not been delinquent.[12]

---

10 Freddie Mac advises lenders that a credit score below 620 indicates high risk, between 620 and 660 indicates an uncertain credit profile, and above 660 means the applicant is likely to have an acceptable credit reputation. Freddie Mac, Automated Underwriting: Making Mortgage Lending Simpler and Fairer for America's Families 25 (Sept. 1996), available at www.freddiemac.com/corporate/reports/moseley/mosehome.htm.
11 Freddie Mac, Automated Underwriting: Making Mortgage Lending Simpler and Fairer for America's Families 14 (Sept. 1996), available at www.freddiemac.com/corporate/reports/moseley/mosehome.htm.
12 In addition, while credit scores may be good at predicting the risk of an event, they are not good at measuring the magnitude of that risk. For example, while credit scores can predict the risk of delinquency, they cannot predict the dollar amount lost as a result of the delinquency. John R. Davies, *Watch Out When Using Credit Scores to Drive a Forecast!*, Signals (Strategic Analytics Spring 2003).

§ 14.2.2   *Fair Credit Reporting*

Exactly what is meant by a "credit score" can vary depending on the score's creator and the specific industry involved. There are a number of types of credit scores, a fact which itself can create confusion for consumers. The following are descriptions of different variations of credit scoring models.

14.2.2 The Variations

14.2.2.1 Credit Risk Scores

A credit risk score is a number calculated based on information obtained from a consumer's credit file at a CRA. This number purports to predict the risk that the consumer will default on credit in the future, based on the historic performance of credit extended to people with similar characteristics. The number is calculated from an algorithm or mathematical model. This is the most well-known type of credit score.

The leading creator of models is Fair Isaac & Co. ("Fair Isaac"), also known as FICO. Even though FICO develops other types of credit scores, a credit risk score is sometimes referred to as a "FICO score." Fair Isaac has developed credit scoring models for each of the "Big Three" CRAs: FICO Risk Score at TransUnion, Experian/Fair Isaac at Experian, and BEACON at Equifax.[13]

FICO scores generally fall within a range from a low of 300 to a high of 850. A borrower with a score of 660 or greater is generally considered to be less of a risk for the lender,[14] although some lenders are now differentiating by credit score within their prime categories, offering their best rates to consumers with scores over 720.[15] A score of 620 or lower is considered a poor risk.[16]

Fair Isaac has also developed a newer scoring model called "NextGen." NextGen scores range from 150 to 950.[17] In addition, the "Big Three" CRAs have developed their own scoring model, called the "Vantage Score," which ranges from 501 to 990.[18] The CRAs claim that the Vantage Score is expected to reduce the variance in an individual consumer's credit scores, discussed in § 14.4.3, *infra*, by about 30%.[19]

Because a credit score is generated based on information in a consumer's credit file, it will change as the information in the consumer's credit file is constantly updated. According to Fair Isaac, however, most credit scores do not change more than 20 points in a three month period.[20]

14.2.2.2 Custom Versus Generic Scores

Historically, most credit scoring systems were custom models built for a particular lender or user. These models were developed using data in the lender's own customer files. The factors in the model and the weights assigned to each factor were derived from the characteristics of the lender's customer base, and the lender's experience with each customer.[21]

Many lenders and users now use "generic" or "off the shelf" scoring models, which are developed for generalized use. These systems are built from data derived from across the files of multiple lenders or users. Credit risk scores are an example of generic credit scores.

14.2.2.3 Specialty Scores

Some credit scoring models are designed for specific purposes or for specific industries. For example, the CRAs offer specialty "Auto Industry Option" scores for automobile finance.[22] Some score models, such as the FICO Bankruptcy Risk Score (from Fair Isaac and TransUnion), are designed to predict the risk of a specific event, such as bankruptcy. Other models, such as those used for pre-screened credit card offers, are used to predict not only risk

---

13   Fair Isaac, Understanding Your FICO Score 8 (July 2005), *available at* www.myfico.com/Downloads/Files/myFICO_UYFS_Booklet.pdf.

14   Freddie Mac, Automated Underwriting: Making Mortgage Lending Simpler and Fairer for America's Families 25 (Sept. 1996), *available at* www.freddiemac.com/corporate/reports/moseley/mosehome.htm.

15   For example, the Fair Isaac website lists sample mortgage rates, with the best rates requiring a credit score of 720 or higher. www.myfico.com. *See also* Evan Hendricks, *Credit Scores & Credit Reports: How the System Really Works, What You Can Do*, Privacy Times 7 (2d ed. 2005). One advertisement for automobile financing required a FICO score of 775 for the best rate. Robert C. Mitchell, Letter to FTC Chairman Timothy Muris and Federal Reserve Board Chair Alan Greenspan 1 (Oct. 11, 2002).

16   Freddie Mac, Automated Underwriting: Making Mortgage Lending Simpler and Fairer for America's Families 25 (Sept. 1996), *available at* www.freddiemac.com/corporate/reports/moseley/mosehome.htm.

17   Nathalie Mainland and Julia Wooding, Fair Isaac, NextGen FICO Risk Score Conversion FAQ, at 2 (Apr. 2002).

18   VantageScore Solutions, L.L.C., VantageScore: The Tri-Bureau Model (2006), www.vantagescore.com/docs/VantageScore_Product_Fact_Sheet_wwwvantagscorecom.pdf.

19   Eileen Alt Powell, *Major Credit Agencies Adopt Uniform Score*, Associated Press, Mar. 14, 2006 (quoting David Rubinger, spokesperson for Equifax).

20   Fair Isaac, Understanding Your FICO Score 3 (July 2005), *available at* www.myfico.com/Downloads/Files/myFICO_UYFS_Booklet.pdf.

21   *See* Federal Trade Commission, Public Forum on The Consumer and Credit Scoring, Matter No. P994810, at 37 (July 22, 1999) (statement of Peter McCorkell, General Counsel, Fair Isaac), *available at* www.ftc.gov/bcp/creditscoring.

22   Fair Isaac, *For Auto Lenders, Sharper Risk Assessment Now More Critical Than Ever*, Viewpoints (June 2002), *available at* www.fairisaac.com/NR/rdonlyres/BF7B99B8-F546-4000-9812-880C814D6422/0/NextGen_AutoLenders_AR.pdf.

but also whether a consumer is a good prospect for accepting a credit offer.[23] There are also models that screen for the risk of credit application fraud.[24]

Experian has developed custom scores specifically focused on the subprime market.[25] Fair Isaac states that its latest generation of credit scoring models, NextGen, had especially strong predictive value in the subprime market.[26]

14.2.2.4 Credit Application Scores

Credit application scores combine credit history information with information derived from an application for a particular type of credit. This information may include employment history, income, loan collateral, debt-to-income ratio and cash reserves. Credit application scores are often used for automobile loan and mortgage applications.

Credit application scores are also used in the form of "automated underwriting systems." These systems are computerized decision-making programs that determine whether or not an applicant should receive a loan. The best-known automated underwriting systems are the ones developed by Freddie Mac and Fannie Mae for purposes of deciding whether they will consider purchasing a loan on the secondary market.[27]

14.2.3 Definition of Credit Score

14.2.3.1 FCRA Definition

The Fair Credit Reporting Act defines a credit score as:

> a numerical value or a categorization derived from a statistical tool or modeling system used by a person who makes or arranges a loan to predict the likelihood or certain credit behaviors, including default (and the numerical value or the categorization derived from such analysis may be referred to as a "risk predictor" or "risk score").[28]

The FCRA specifically excludes from the definition of "credit score" any score or rating from a mortgage automated underwriting system and any other elements of the underwriting process.[29]

14.2.3.2 Regulation B Definition

In addition to the FCRA definition, there is a definition of a credit score in Regulation B,[30] the implementing regulation for the Equal Credit Opportunity Act.[31] This definition is different than the FCRA definition. Regulation B specifically defines an "empirically derived, demonstrably and statistically sound, credit scoring system," which is a system that compares, by assignment of points or by other methods, certain key attributes of the applicant or of the transaction to sample groups or to the population of creditworthy and non-creditworthy applicants of a creditor who have applied within a "reasonably preceding" period of time.[32] The total score, taken alone or in conjunction with other information about the applicant, is used to determine whether credit should be granted or denied.[33]

Regulation B requires that a credit scoring system satisfy four criteria:[34]

- The data used to develop the system must constitute either the entire applicant file or an appropriate sample of it;[35]
- The system must have the purpose of predicting applicants' creditworthiness with respect to "legitimate business interests" of the creditor using it;[36]
- The system must be "developed and validated using accepted statistical principles and methodology";[37] and
- The system should be periodically reviewed and revalidated as to its predictive ability and adjusted accordingly.[38]

Regulation B itself makes limited use of this definition of a credit scoring system, referring to it only with respect to when creditors may consider information about age and

---

23 Fair Isaac, Fair Isaac Qualify Marketing Score (Sept. 2004), *available at* www.fairisaac.com/NR/rdonlyres/5D51DEF5-3726-486A-A9B1-8A6E78DF7BA4/0/Qualify_Score_Product_Sheet__new_format.pdf
24 Fair Isaac, Application Fraud Scores, *available at* www.fairisaac.com/Fairisaac/Solutions/Product+Index/Credit+Bureau+Fraud+Risk+Scores.
25 Experian, Advanced Select for Non-Prime (June 2001), *available at* www.experian.com/products/pdf/advanced_select_nonprime.pdf.
26 W.A. Lee, *Experian and Fair Isaac Tweak Subprime Scoring*, American Banker, Dec. 28, 2001.
27 Freddie Mac's automated underwriting system is known as "Loan Prospector." Fannie Mae's system is called "Desktop Underwriter." Freddie Mac's system is described at § 14.5.3, *infra*.
28 15 U.S.C. § 1681g(f)(2)(A)(ii).
29 15 U.S.C. § 1681g(f)(2)(A)(ii). See §§ 14.2.2.4, *supra*, and 14.5.3, *infra*, for a discussion of automated underwriting systems.
30 Reg. B, 12 C.F.R. Part 202.
31 15 U.S.C. §§ 1691–1691f.
32 Reg. B, 12 C.F.R. § 202.2(p)(1). *See also* Official Staff Commentary to Regulation B § 202.2(p)-1.
33 Reg. B, 12 C.F.R. § 202.2(p)(1). *See also* Official Staff Commentary to Regulation B § 202.2(p)-1.
34 Reg. B, 12 C.F.R. § 202.2(p)(1). *See also* Official Staff Commentary to Regulation B § 202.2(p)-1.
35 Reg. B, 12 C.F.R. § 202.2(p)(1)(i).
36 *Id.* § 202.2(p)(1)(ii).
37 *Id.* § 202.2(p)(1)(iii).
38 *Id.* § 202.2(p)(1)(iv). No definition of "periodically" is given in the regulation. *See also* Official Staff Commentary to Regulation B § 202.2(p)-2, which gives some guidance on revalidation procedures.

public assistance status.[39] However, the practical importance of this definition is much greater, because some of the banking regulators have required the banks they regulate to meet Regulation B's requirements for credit scoring models.[40]

14.3 Widespread Use of Credit Scores

The use of credit scores in determining whether to extend consumer credit, and the terms of that credit, has grown dramatically in the past decade, particularly in the home mortgage business. Over 90% of mortgage lenders and credit-card issuers use credit scores in making lending decisions.[41]

Credit scores are also increasingly being used for purposes well beyond initial evaluation of whether to grant loans. For example, scoring systems are used to prescreen and preselect consumers for direct marketing, to determine interest rates and credit limits, to collect on mortgage loans, and for sale of loans to Wall Street and secondary market purchasers.[42] Some credit card issuers periodically review cardholders' credit scores to decide whether to re-issue the card and for how long, whether to send special promotions,[43] and in a particularly controversial application called "universal default," whether to charge consumers a penalty interest rate.[44] Payday lenders use specialty scores to determine whether to grant a payday loan.[45] Scoring is also used to increase recovery rates from debt collection and to detect credit card fraud.[46]

The use of credit scores for non-credit related purposes has grown dramatically. Credit scores are being used to determine eligibility and rates for automobile and homeowner's insurance.[47] Businesses use them for employment purposes.[48] Utilities use credit scores to determine whether consumers must pay a deposit for utility service.[49] Under the FCRA's standard of permissible use of consumer reports for "a legitimate business need for the information in connection with a business transaction initiated by the consumer," there may be few limits on the use of credit scores for non-credit related consumer transactions.[50]

In the mortgage lending arena, one reason for the growth in the use of credit scores is that Freddie Mac and Fannie Mae, who together dominate the secondary market for home mortgages, recommend that mortgage lenders use automated underwriting systems based upon credit scores in deciding whether to grant a mortgage request. Another reason is that automated underwriting allows lenders to make decisions on loans more quickly, cutting down the

---

39 *See* Official Staff Commentary to Regulation B § 202.2(p)-1 that describes the difference only as relating to how age is used as a predictive factor.

40 For example, the Office of the Comptroller of Currency has required the national banks that it regulates to ensure that the bank's scoring models meet the validation requirements of Regulation B's definition of credit scoring. Office of the Comptroller of the Currency, *Credit Scoring Models*, OCC Bull. 97-24 (May 20, 1997). The National Credit Union Administration has similarly required that the credit scoring systems used by the credit unions that NCUA regulates meet the criteria of Regulation B's definition of credit scoring. National Credit Union Administration, NCUA Letter to Credit Unions No. 174 (Aug. 1995). *See also* Fed. Fin. Insts. Examination Council, *Interagency Fair Lending Examination Procedures Guide*, Appendix—Credit Scoring Analysis, Clearinghouse No. 53,526 (1999), *available at* www.ffiec.gov/PDF/fairlend.pdf (interagency examination procedures for reviewing a financial institution's credit scoring models).

41 Federal Trade Commission, Report to Congress Under Sections 318 and 319 of the Fair and Accurate Credit Transactions Act of 2003, at 79 (Dec. 2004); Andrea Coombes, *CBS Marketwatch: Spread of Credit Scoring: Consumer Boon or Bane* (television broadcast Nov. 11, 2004), *available at* www.marketwatch.com (noting that credit scores are used by the top 20 automobile lenders, the top 25 credit card issuers, and 40 out of 50 of the largest banks).

42 *See* Federal Trade Commission, Public Forum on the Consumer and Credit Scoring, Matter No. P994810, at 40 (July 22, 1999) (statement of Peter McCorkell, General Counsel, Fair Isaac), *available at* www.ftc.gov/bcp/creditscoring; Edward Kulkosky, *Credit Scoring Appeal Transcends Underwriting*, American Banker, May 15, 1996, at 8.

43 Federal Trade Commission, Public Forum on The Consumer and Credit Scoring, Matter No. P994810, at 39 (July 22, 1999) (statement of Peter McCorkell, General Counsel, Fair Isaac), *available at* www.ftc.gov/bcp/creditscoring; Kenneth Harney, *A Clearer View of Credit Scores*, Washington Post, Feb. 21, 2004, at F1 (National Credit Reporting Association stating that mortgage servicers regularly order credit scores on homeowners, often on a quarterly basis).

44 *See* National Consumer Law Center, The Cost of Credit: Regulation, Preemption, and Industry Abuses § 11.7.2.3.1 (3d ed. 2005 and Supp.).

45 For example, Teletrack offers an automated decision-making application for payday lenders. *See* Teletrack, Payday Advance, *available at* www.teletrack.com/industries/payday.html. The use of specialty scores for payday lending is ironic, given that one of the selling points for these often abusive loans is the ability to obtain them despite a negative credit history.

46 Fair Isaac, *Custom Scoring for Collections and Recovery* (Jan. 2006), *available at* www.fairisaac.com/NR/rdonlyres/EA7E1827-AD3C-4E1B-9910-2C43106BE1BB/0/CustomScoringProductSheet.pdf. Fair Isaac, Fraud Predictor with Merchant Profiles (Sept. 2004), *available at* www.fairisaac.com/NR/rdonlyres/EECD2BD3-1482-4358-B9C2-73B7DC32AB72/0/FraudPredMerchProf_PS.pdf. Debt collectors use credit scores to determine which borrowers to contact, how soon the borrower should be contacted in the month, what method of collection to use (phone versus letters) and how frequently to contact the borrower. Elizabeth Mays, *The Role of Credit Scores in Consumer Lending Today*, RMA Journal, Oct. 1, 2003 (reprinting Chapter One of Elizabeth Mays, Credit Scoring for Risk Managers: The Handbook for Lenders (2004)).

47 *See* § 14.11, *infra*.

48 Christopher Conkey, *How to Boost Your Credit Score*, Wall Street Journal, Nov. 19, 2005, at B1 (citing Society of Human Resource Management finding that 19% of employers always conduct credit checks on job applicants).

49 *See* § 14.10, *infra*. *See also* National Consumer Law Center, Access to Utility Service, § 3.7.4 (3d ed. 2004 and Supp.).

50 15 U.S.C. § 1681(b)(a)(3)(F). *See generally* § 7.2.8, *supra*.

time necessary to review an application from several hours to a matter of minutes.[51] This allows a lender to make a decision within days instead of weeks.

Despite the widespread and ever-increasing use of credit scores, many consumers do not understand their nature or what they measure. According to one survey, almost half of consumers do not know that credit scores are intended to measure credit risk.[52]

14.4 Disclosure to Consumers of Credit Score

14.4.1 FCRA Disclosure Requirements

The FCRA requires the consumer reporting agencies (CRAs) to disclose credit scores to consumers upon their request.[53] The CRAs may charge a fee for the credit score, to be determined by the Federal Trade Commission.[54] As of mid-2006, the FTC had yet to set a fee.

In particular, the FCRA requires the CRAs to disclose the following:

- The current credit score of the consumer or most recent credit score that was previously calculated by the CRA related to the extension of credit.[55] The score must either (a) be generated using a scoring model that is widely distributed to users by the CRA in connection with residential real property loans or (b) assist the consumer in understanding the assessment by the credit scoring model of his or her credit behavior and predications about that behavior.[56]
- A statement indicating that the information and credit scoring model may be different than the credit score used by a lender.[57]
- The range of possible credit scores used by the scoring system, e.g., 400 to 900, that generated the disclosed credit score.[58]

- The key factors that adversely affected the credit score of the consumer,[59] listed in order of impact.[60] The CRA cannot provide more than 4 key factors,[61] unless one of the factors is the number of "enquiries," in which case that factor must be included notwithstanding the 4 factor limit.[62]
- The date on which the credit score was created.[63]
- The name of the provider of the credit score or the credit file used to generate the score.[64]

When consumers request their credit files, but not their credit scores, the FCRA also requires the CRAs to disclose the fact that consumers have a right to obtain their credit scores.[65]

A CRA is required to disclose a credit score if the CRA distributes scores that are used in connection with residential real property loans or develops scores that assist credit providers in understanding the general credit behavior of a consumer and predicting the future behavior of the consumer.[66] Thus, the three major nationwide CRAs are required to disclose credit scores, but some smaller CRAs that do not distribute scores may not be. The FCRA provides that the requirement to disclose credit scores is not to be construed as requiring CRAs to maintain credit scores in their files.[67]

In addition, the FCRA requires mortgage lenders who use credit scores in connection with an application for residential real-estate secured credit to provide, free of charge, the credit score and accompanying information that is either obtained from a CRA or was developed and used by the lender.[68] If the lender uses an automated underwriting system that does not provide a numerical score, the disclosure of the credit risk score and associated key factors is sufficient.[69] However, if the automated underwriting system generates a numerical score, the lender may disclose that

---

51 Freddie Mac, Automated Underwriting: Making Mortgage Lending Simpler and Fairer for America's Families, Ch. 2 (Sept. 1996), *available at* www.freddiemac.com/corporate/reports/moseley/mosehome.htm.
52 Press Release, Consumer Federation of America and Fair Isaac & Co., Many Americans Misunderstand Credit Scores According to New National Survey (Mar. 15, 2005).
53 15 U.S.C. § 1681g(f)(1).
54 15 U.S.C. § 1681g(f)(8). In its Advanced Notice of Proposed Rulemaking, the Federal Trade Commission appears to be considering setting the fee for obtaining a credit score at a price similar to the prices charged in the unregulated market, which the FTC cited as $4 to $8. 69 Fed. Reg. 64,698 (Nov. 8, 2004).
55 15 U.S.C. § 1681g(f)(1)(A).
56 15 U.S.C. § 1681g(f)(7)(A).
57 15 U.S.C. § 1681g(f)(1).
58 15 U.S.C. § 1681g(f)(1)(B).
59 15 U.S.C. § 1681g(f)(1)(C). For credit scores provided using Fair Isaac scoring models, the key factors are probably the "reason codes" provided by FICO. See § 8.2.5, *supra*, for a discussion of reason codes.
60 15 U.S.C. § 1681g(f)(2)(B).
61 15 U.S.C. § 1681g(f)(1)(C).
62 15 U.S.C. § 1581g(f)(9).
63 15 U.S.C. § 1581g(f)(1)(D).
64 15 U.S.C. § 1681g(f)(1)(E).
65 15 U.S.C. § 1681g(a)(6). In addition, the Summary of Consumer Rights also must include a provision stating that the consumer has the right to obtain a credit score from a CRA and a description of how to obtain the score. 15 U.S.C. § 1681g(c)(1)(B)(iv).
66 15 U.S.C. § 1681g(f)(4).
67 15 U.S.C. § 1681g(f)(6).
68 15 U.S.C. § 1681g(g)(1)(A) (requiring disclosure of the same information identified in FCRA, § 609(f), that is, the information described in the bullet list in this section).
69 15 U.S.C. § 1681g(g)(1)(B)(i). See §§ 14.2.2.4, *supra*, and 14.5.3, *infra*, for a discussion of automated underwriting systems.

§ 14.4.2 Fair Credit Reporting

numerical score or a credit risk score and associated key factors.[70] Mortgage lenders must also give a prescribed notice to the consumers.[71]

Finally, state laws regarding disclosure of credit scores are preempted, except for existing state laws in California and Colorado.[72] The FCRA's preemption of state credit scoring disclosure laws is discussed in full at § 10.7.7, *supra*.

14.4.2 How to Obtain a Credit Score

Consumers who wish to obtain their credit scores have the following options:

- They can go to the Fair Isaac website, which offers a number of different FICO score products to consumers. Consumers can purchase a copy of their FICO score based upon either their Equifax, Experian or TransUnion file.[73] Consumers can also get credit reports from all three CRAs from the myfico.com website, with their FICO score based on each report. They can even purchase celebrity-promoted FICO "kits" which purport to assist consumers in improving their score.[74]
- TransUnion sells a stand-alone credit score if the consumer obtains a credit report from TransUnion, either paid or free. However, it is difficult to find the information to order the stand-alone credit score, as TransUnion's website heavily promotes other, more costly services.
- Experian offers a product called "Experian PLUS Score" which it offers along with a credit report. The only score that Experian appears to offer as a stand-alone product is the VantageScore, discussed at § 14.4.3, *infra*, and even then it is hard to find the appropriate information for ordering on the Experian website.
- Equifax's website offers a FICO score and credit report but does not appear to offer the credit score as a stand-alone product.
- Consumers who obtained their free annual consumer reports from www.annualcreditreport.com have the option of purchasing a credit score as part of that process.

In addition to providing the credit scores, the CRAs and Fair Isaac now offer an array of higher priced services, such as "credit monitoring" and personalized analyses of how to improve credit scores. These services may constitute "credit repair organizations" under federal and state law.[75] Fair Isaac and the CRAs have also been accused of misleading advertising for these services, promising personalized assistance in improving credit scores but delivering computer-generated generic advice of limited value.[76]

14.4.3 Variations in Credit Score by Consumer Reporting Agencies

There will likely be significant variations in the credit scores provided by the three CRAs. An examination of over 500,000 consumer credit files found that 29% of consumers have credit scores that differ by at least 50 points between CRAs, while 4% have scores that differ by at least 100 points.[77] The median spread between the high score and low score for these consumer credit files was 35 points.[78]

One reason for this variation is that the information in a consumer's file is different for each CRA. Another reason is that the credit score products sold by TransUnion and Experian may not utilize their respective FICO scoring systems.

Even a consumer's FICO score could vary, depending on whether it is generated by a classic FICO scoring model or by the NextGen model.[79] To add more confusion, the CRAs are offering their own scoring product, called VantageScore, which is not produced by a Fair Isaac scoring model. The CRAs are touting VantageScore as an improved product, claiming it is expected to reduce the variance in a consumer's credit scores by about 30%.[80]

Finally, it is unclear just how much resemblance these credit scores bear to the ones actually provided to lenders. The TransUnion and Experian credit scores are not produced from FICO scoring models, and even the FICO score from Equifax may not be the one provided to a lender.[81] All of

---

70 15 U.S.C. § 1681g(g)(1)(B)(ii).
71 15 U.S.C. § 1681g(g)(1)(D).
72 15 U.S.C. § 1681t(b)(3).
73 It appears that www.myfico.com only accepts major credit or debit cards as a form of payment, which may present a practical barrier to consumers with low FICO scores who do not qualify for a credit or debit card. In addition, www.myfico.com only offers credit scores on-line, so consumers without Internet access will have difficulty obtaining their FICO scores. Fair Isaac, myFICO Questions, www.myfico.com, click Support Center, Answer ID 148.
74 Selling credit scores has become a profitable business for Fair Isaac, which claims to have sold 10 million scores to consumers in four and a half years and earned $32 million in one year from consumer sales. Damon Darlin, *Credit: For Those of You Keeping Score at Home*, New York Times, Aug. 27, 2005, at C1.
75 Slack v. Fair Isaac Corp., 390 F. Supp. 2d 906 (N.D. Cal. 2005). See Ch. 15, *infra*.
76 Slack v. Fair Isaac Corp., 390 F. Supp. 2d 906 (N.D. Cal. 2005).
77 Consumer Federation of America and National Credit Reporting Association, Credit Score Accuracy and Implications for Consumers 24 (Dec. 17, 2002), *available at* www.consumerfed.org/pdfs/121702CFA_NCRA_Credit_Score_Report_Final.pdf.
78 *Id.*
79 Nathalie Mainland and Julia Wooding, Fair Isaac, NextGen FICO Risk Score Conversion FAQ, at 6 (Apr. 2002).
80 Eileen Alt Powell, *Major Credit Agencies Adopt Uniform Score*, Associated Press, Mar. 14, 2006 (quoting David Rubinger, spokesperson for Equifax).
81 Evan Hendricks, *Credit Scores & Credit Reports: How the System Really Works, What You Can Do*, Privacy Times 37 (2d ed. 2005). *See also* Neal Walters and Sharon Hermanson, Credit

these scores are generally higher than the FICO score used by lenders.[82] One expert has noted that consumers cannot rely on a score bought at a website, even it is from FICO's website.[83]

If CRAs are not providing the actual scores that they provide to lenders, the FCRA is unlikely to force them to. The FCRA permits a CRA to disclose, when a consumer requests a credit score, either a score derived from a model widely distributed to users *or* a score that assists the consumer in understanding the model's assessment and prediction about her credit behavior.[84] The latter description may permit CRAs to disclose credit scores that are not used by lenders at all. Furthermore, the FCRA requires the CRAs to provide, when disclosing a credit score, a statement indicating that the credit scoring model may be different than the credit score used by a lender,[85] which implies that the CRAs are not required provide scores actually used by lenders.

14.5 How a Credit Score Is Calculated

14.5.1 The Black Box

One reason for the controversy over credit scores is that the method by which they are calculated has been kept secret from consumers, advocates, and regulators. The process by which a credit score is calculated has been likened to a "black box."

Fair Isaac has disclosed a generalized list of the factors it uses in generating credit scores and the general level of importance of each factor.[86] Freddie Mac has provided similar information.[87] However, critical information is still lacking from the industry's new disclosures. For example, while Fair Isaac has disclosed the five major categories of factors it uses in its scoring models, not all of the factors within those categories are known. It is estimated that the models actually contain about twenty factors.[88] Furthermore, neither FICO nor Freddie Mac has identified the algorithms or mathematical models used to calculate the credit scores.

Another part of the mystery is how the scoring models are developed. In general, Fair Isaac develops its models from a random sample of files that are analyzed for attributes that correlate with creditworthiness. It is unknown how Fair Isaac selects factors and attributes, why attributes are given particular weightings, how they correlate with creditworthiness, and how this translates into the scoring model.

Also, Fair Isaac has stated that there are many correlations between different factors that one could consider in a credit decision. For example, the factor of age correlates with home ownership. That factor in turn correlates with the factor of length of time at address.[89] Thus, FICO models may only use one of these factors, because having more would not add predictive value. One major question is whether any of the factors used by FICO models correlate with race, gender, or any of the bases prohibited for use in credit decisions by the Equal Credit Opportunity Act.[90]

14.5.2 How Fair Isaac Scores Are Developed

14.5.2.1 Fair Isaac's Scoring Factors

Fair Isaac has identified the following categories of factors used to derive FICO scores, including a generalized weighting of these factors given in parentheses.[91]

- Payment History (35%)

    This category includes information about late payments, defaults, collections, repossessions, bankruptcies and judgments. This is the most important factor in a credit score. Fair Isaac claims that about 60 to 65% of credit files show no late payments at all,[92] and a Fair Isaac representative has stated that 85% of consumers do not have a serious problem in this category.[93]

    Fair Isaac claims that late payments do not necessarily result in a bad score. The age of delinquencies and other adverse events is important, with newer events costing applicants more points. There is an indication that delinquent accounts that have shown no activity in

---

Scores and Mortgage Lending, AARP Public Policy Institute 3 (Aug. 2001).

82 Evan Hendricks, *Credit Scores & Credit Reports: How the System Really Works, What You Can Do,* Privacy Times 37 (2d ed. 2005).

83 *Id.*

84 15 U.S.C. § 1681g(f)(7)(A). See § 14.4.1, *supra*.

85 15 U.S.C. § 1681g(f)(1).

86 Fair Isaac, Understanding Your FICO Score 9–15 (July 2005), available at www.myfico.com/Downloads/Files/myFICO_UYFS_Booklet.pdf.

87 *See* Freddie Mac, Factors Used in Loan Prospector, *available at* www.freddiemac.com/homeownership/au-works/factors.html.

88 John R. Engen, *Blind Faith*, Banking Strategies (Nov./Dec. 2000), *available at* www.bai.org/bankingstrategies/2000-nov-dec/articles/blindfaith/index.html.

89 Federal Trade Commission, Public Forum on The Consumer and Credit Scoring, Matter No. P994810, at 28–29 (July 22, 1999) (statement of Peter McCorkell, General Counsel, Fair Isaac), *available at* www.ftc.gov/bcp/creditscoring.

90 *See* National Consumer Law Center, Credit Discrimination § 6.4 (4th ed. 2005 and Supp.).

91 Fair Isaac, Understanding Your FICO Score 9–15 (July 2005), *available at* www.myfico.com/Downloads/Files/myFICO_UYFS_Booklet.pdf.

92 *Id.* at 10.

93 Federal Trade Commission, Public Forum on The Consumer and Credit Scoring, Matter No. P994810, at 43 (July 22, 1999) (statement of Peter McCorkell, General Counsel, Fair Isaac), *available at* www.ftc.gov/bcp/creditscoring.

a year may have a limited effect on a credit score.[94] Non-delinquent accounts and accounts with minor delinquencies also appear to be subject to a similar one-year "stale account" rule.[95]

Some advocates have expressed concern that the payment history factor hurts low- and moderate-income consumers more, because they have fewer credit accounts, so one late payment could have a disproportionate effect.[96] On the other hand, high-scoring consumers may also experience severe adverse effects from a single late payment, because it may lower a high FICO score by about 100 points.[97] The larger the late or missed payment, the greater the adverse effect on a FICO score.[98]

Another issue appears to be small dollar amount delinquencies that are sent to collections or appear in public records, such as parking tickets, video rental fees, and library fines, which depress a consumer's credit score. Fair Isaac's latest version of NextGen supposedly reduces the effect of these items by ignoring any collections or public record items under $100.[99]

- Amounts Owed (30%)

This category includes information on the amount owed by a consumer on each account as well as the total credit limit permitted for that account. Consumers are considered ideal if they have only utilized about 10–20% of their available credit limit. In contrast, consumers will be penalized for using over 50% of available credit.[100]

Revolving credit, that is, credit cards, appears to be given more weight in the "amount owed" category than installment loans.[101] If consumers do not utilize their credit cards at all, they may score lower.[102] Interestingly, scoring models appear to treat a home equity line of credit differently depending on the amount withdrawn. A sizable withdrawal is treated as an installment loan, while a small withdrawal is treated as revolving credit.[103]

- Length of Credit History (15%)

This category includes information on the age of a consumer's accounts, including the age of the oldest account and an average age of all accounts. Generally, consumers with longer credit histories are seen as less risky. This category also considers the time that has elapsed since the last use of an account. Note that this category considers old accounts that have been closed.[104] According to Fair Isaac, the average consumer's oldest account is 14 years old.[105]

- New Credit (10%)

This category includes information about new accounts as well as inquiries by lenders for the consumer's credit file. Evidence of opening several accounts in a short period of time is taken as an indicator of risk. Excessive inquiries will lower a credit score. According to Fair Isaac, its scoring models only consider inquiries by creditors within the past twelve months, and do not consider self-inquiries, account reviews, or prescreening inquiries.[106] In the past, there were criticisms that scoring models penalized consumers for rate shopping, because each lender the consumer contacted would make an inquiry that would lower the consumer's score. Fair Isaac developed a process to address this issue by counting inquiries for home and automobile loans with a certain time period, such as 14 or 30 days, as a single inquiry.[107] According to Fair Isaac, the average consumer has only about one inquiry within the past year.[108]

---

94 Robert B. Avery, Paul S. Calem, and Glenn B. Canner, *Credit Report Accuracy and Access to Credit*, Federal Reserve Bulletin 310 (Summer 2004).
95 *Id.*
96 One study has noted that an item of derogatory information has a greater effect on "thin" files. Consumer Federation of America and National Credit Reporting Association, Credit Score Accuracy and Implications for Consumers 27 (Dec. 17, 2002), *available at* www.consumerfed.org/pdfs/121702CFA_NCRA_Credit_Score_Report_Final.pdf.
97 Sharon Epperson, *One Missed Bill Saps Your Credit*, USA Weekend, May 15, 2005 (consumers with one late payment have credit scores 160 points lower than those without missed payment). Use of the FICO Score Simulator supports this theory. Supposedly, Fair Isaac's NextGen scoring systems is less drastic with this situation, giving higher scores to consumers who have just one or a few late payments. On the other hand, NextGen gives lower scores to consumers with more serious adverse events, such as collections, charge-offs, and bankruptcies. Nathalie Mainland and Julia Wooding, Fair Isaac, NextGen FICO Risk Score Conversion FAQ, at 5 (Apr. 2002).
98 Cybele Weisser, *Getting Behind the Numbers*, Money Magazine, Nov. 1, 2003, at 157.
99 Fair Isaac, NextGen FICO Score Version 2.0 (May 2003).
100 Evan Hendricks, *Credit Scores & Credit Reports: How the System Really Works, What You Can Do*, Privacy Times 7 (2d ed. 2005).

101 Cybele Weisser, *Getting Behind the Numbers*, Money Magazine, Nov. 1, 2003, at 157.
102 Fair Isaac, Understanding Your FICO Score 11 (July 2005), *available at* www.myfico.com/Downloads/Files/myFICO_UYFS_Booklet.pdf.
103 Cybele Weisser, *Getting Behind the Numbers*, Money Magazine, Nov. 1, 2003, at 157.
104 Federal Trade Commission, Public Forum on The Consumer and Credit Scoring, Matter No. P994810, at 43 (July 22, 1999) (statement of Peter McCorkell, General Counsel, Fair Isaac), *available at* www.ftc.gov/bcp/creditscoring. The issue of having old, closed accounts considered in a credit score is discussed at § 14.8.3.7, *infra*.
105 Fair Isaac, Average Credit Statistics, *available at* www.myfico.com/CreditEducation/AverageStats.aspx?fire=5.
106 Fair Isaac, Understanding Your FICO Score 13 (July 2005), *available at* www.myfico.com/Downloads/Files/myFICO_UYFS_Booklet.pdf.
107 Fair Isaac, Understanding Your FICO Score 15 (July 2005), *available at* www.myfico.com/Downloads/Files/myFICO_UYFS_Booklet.pdf.
108 Fair Isaac, Average Credit Statistics, *available at* www.myfico.com/CreditEducation/AverageStats.aspx?fire=5.

- Types of Credit in Use (10%)

    This category considers the mix of credit accounts that a consumer has. A good mix includes some credit cards, a mortgage loan, an installment loan and retail store cards. Given that a good mix includes a mortgage loan, it appears FICO's scoring models favor homeowners over renters.[109] Indeed, one consumer reporting agency (CRA) has stated that not having a mortgage "means that your credit score is not as high as it could be."[110] Also, Fair Isaac states that having no credit card accounts will lower a FICO score.[111]

Fair Isaac's credit scoring models generally will not score an applicant whose credit file does not have at least one account or other tradeline with updated activity in the past six months.[112] Thus, consumers who have not previously used much credit may be shut out from getting more. Fair Isaac's latest version of NextGen supposedly has more liberal criteria for generating a credit score, permitting consumer files with one tradeline to be scored if there is any activity within the past twelve months.[113]

14.5.2.2 FICO Scorecards

The guts of Fair Isaac scoring models are called "scorecards."[114] These are preset tables, with the factors listed on the left-hand side (e.g., number of recent inquiries) and attributes for each factor on the top row (e.g., 0, 1, 2). Each attribute is assigned a point value, which can be positive or negative, and the point values fill the cells in the scorecard. Points are developed based on a sample of previous borrowers whose creditworthiness (i.e., whether their loans were good or bad) is already known. A consumer's score is derived by seeing how many points he or she gets for each attribute, and adding up the points.

Fair Isaac has developed different scorecards tailored to different groups of consumers, e.g., consumers with serious delinquencies, or those with only a single tradeline.[115] To generate an overall credit score, the consumer's credit history may be sequentially processed through multiple scorecards.[116]

14.5.3 Factors in Freddie Mac's Automated Underwriting System

Freddie Mac's website lists the categories of factors used in its automated underwriting system, Loan Prospector.[117] Freddie Mac has not provided the weighting given each category, but has described the relative importance of each (in parentheses):

- Collateral (High)

    Collateral factors include amount of down payment or equity, type of property (e.g., one-family, condo), and use of property (owner-occupied versus investment).
- Credit history and credit risk score (High)
- Capacity (Low)

    Capacity factors include debt-to-income ratios, salaried versus self-employed borrower, number of borrowers, and cash reserves.
- Loan characteristics (Medium)

    Loan characteristics include what type of loan product (e.g., fixed 30-year loan versus 1-year adjustable rate with 30-year term) and the purpose of the loan (purchase money or refinance)).

14.5.4 Ideas on How to Peek into the Black Box

Even with these revelations by the credit score industry, much of the "black box" nature of credit scoring systems

---

109 At least two studies have noted that homeowners have higher credit scores than renters, although this is probably due to a number of factors, including that homeowners might start off with the good score and income necessary to obtain a mortgage. Raphael W. Bostic, Paul S. Calem, and Susan M. Wachter, Joint Center for Housing Studies of Harvard University, Hitting the Wall: Credit As an Impediment to Homeownership (Feb. 2004); David K. Musto and Nicholas Souleles, *A Portfolio View of Consumer Credit* (Federal Reserve Bank of Philadelphia—Research Department, Working Paper No. 05-25 Sept. 2005).
110 Experian, Credit Score Basics FAQs, *available at* www.experian.com/consumer/credit_score_faqs.html. *See also* Cybele Weisser, *Getting Behind the Numbers*, Money Magazine, Nov. 1, 2003, at 157 (noting that lenders prefer that a credit history include a mix of credit, such as student loans, a mortgage and credit cards; however, also quoting Fair Isaac's spokesperson claiming that a "clean track record" on two credit cards is just as good as having several installment loans and a mortgage).
111 Fair Isaac, Understanding Your FICO Score 14 (July 2005), *available at* www.myfico.com/Downloads/Files/myFICO_UYFS_Booklet.pdf.
112 *Id.* at 7.
113 Fair Isaac, NextGen FICO Score Version 2.0 (May 2003).
114 Federal Trade Commission, Public Forum on the Consumer and Credit Scoring, Matter No. P994810, at 17–18 (July 22, 1999) (statement of Peter McCorkell, General Counsel, Fair Isaac), *available at* www.ftc.gov/bcp/creditscoring. A sample FICO scorecard was presented at this FTC hearing on credit scoring as part of Mr. McCorkell's Powerpoint presentation, and can be viewed at www.ftc.gov/bcp/creditscoring. The FTC administrative decision of *In re* Trans Union Corp. also offers some insight into both how models are structured and what data they select out of the consumer's file, even though the decision has been redacted of some of the most sensitive information in the case. No. D-9255, at 29 (F.T.C. July 31, 1998) (Initial Decision).
115 *Id.* at 60, 61
116 Federal Trade Commission, Public Forum on the Consumer and Credit Scoring, Matter No. P994810, at 47 (July 22, 1999) (statement of Peter McCorkell, General Counsel, Fair Isaac), *available at* www.ftc.gov/bcp/creditscoring.
117 Freddie Mac, Factors Used In Loan Prospector, *available at* www.freddiemac.com/corporate/au-works/factors.html.

§ 14.6 Fair Credit Reporting

still persists. Those seeking detailed information about how credit scores are calculated in general or for a specific person will be told initially that the actual process is a trade secret. However, if this information is sought during the discovery process in litigation, the "trade secret" obstacle may not be insurmountable.[118] While Rule 26(c) of the Federal Rules of Civil Procedure allows a business to seek a protective order barring or restricting discovery of trade secret information, if the information sought is relevant and necessary to the initial presentation of the plaintiff's claim, it must be produced.[119]

Some potential arguments to gain access to inner workings of credit scoring model information are:

- In an FCRA action over failure to remove inaccurate information, discovery of credit scoring models may be necessary to show exactly how the inaccurate information lowered a credit score and the damaging consequences of the lower score.
- As discussed in § 14.8.3, *infra*, there is certain information that by itself does not seem adverse, but can lower a credit score (e.g., reporting an account several times). Information about how the credit score model works may be necessary to prove that the information is actually adverse.
- As discussed in § 14.8.2, *infra*, credit scores may conflict with a consumer's right under the FCRA to include a written protest concerning a disputed amount. Information about how credit scoring models work may be necessary to determine whether there is actually such a conflict.
- Detailed information about credit scoring systems may also be relevant and necessary in litigating other types of consumer credit claims, such as discrimination claims under the Equal Credit Opportunity Act.[120] For example, in a disparate impact action, plaintiffs would need to establish that a scoring model includes factors which are neutral but have a disparate impact on minorities. They would also have to rebut the inevitable argument that the factors in the scoring model are required because of business necessity. In order to rebut the argument, the plaintiffs might try to show that there is a less discriminatory alternative. A disparate treatment claim might be based on the argument that scoring models contain forbidden factors such as race or that correlate strongly with race.

14.6 How Consumers Can Improve Their Credit Scores

14.6.1 Industry's Advice

Since they are based on consumer credit files that are constantly changing, credit scores will also change over time. Consumers can take steps to improve their credit score, although it may take time for some of their actions to be reflected in a new score. Fair Isaac gives the following advice on improving a credit score:[121]

- Pay bills on time;
- Keep balances low on credit cards and other revolving bank products;
- Do not open a lot of new accounts too rapidly;
- Conduct rate shopping for a given automobile or mortgage loan within a short period of time;
- Do not close unused credit card accounts, as this may lower a credit score;
- Make sure all joint accounts are listed. Married consumers, especially women, should also make sure if they are authorized users on their spouse's accounts, the account histories are reflected in their credit files (if the account has a good history).[122]

14.6.2 Additional Advice

There are other steps consumers can take themselves to attempt to improve their credit scores, or at least avoid the negative effect of a low score. For example, a consumer could:

- Dispute inaccurate information. Not only may this help remove adverse information, but the fact that the consumer report is in dispute means the consumer may be able to convince a lender to ignore the credit score.[123]

---

118 See § 11.6.3.4, *supra*.
119 See, e.g., Federal Open Market Comm. v. Merrill, 443 U.S. 340 (1979); Carter Products, Inc. v. Eversharp, Inc., 360 F.2d 868 (7th Cir. 1966); United States v. Aluminum Co. of Am., 193 F. Supp. 249 (N.D.N.Y. 1960). See also 4 J. Moore, *Federal Practice* § 26.105[8][a], 26.60 (3d ed. 1997) (discussion of trade secrets discovery); § 11.6.3.4, *supra*.
120 See National Consumer Law Center, Credit Discrimination § 6.4 (4th ed. 2005 and Supp.). The ECOA states nothing in the statute shall be construed to prohibit discovery of a creditor's credit granting standards under appropriate discovery procedures 15 U.S.C. § 1691e(j).
121 Fair Isaac, Understanding Your Credit Score 9–15 (July 2005), *available at* www.myfico.com/Downloads/Files/myFICO_UYFS_Booklet.pdf.
122 Regulation B, 12 C.F.R. § 202.10(a)(1) requires that creditors provide this information to CRAs. See Ch. 4, *supra*, and National Consumer Law Center, Credit Discrimination § 9.4.2.1 (4th ed. 2005 and Supp.). The flip side of this requirement is that a married consumer's credit score will suffer if the spouse's authorized user account includes adverse events.
123 Some lenders will ignore credit scores if there is a dispute. Federal Trade Commission, Public Forum on the Consumer and Credit Scoring, Matter No. P994810, at 94–95 (July 22, 1999) (statement of Carroll Justice, Executive Vice President, FT Mortgage Companies), *available at* www.ftc.gov/bcp/creditscoring.

Credit Scoring § 14.7.2

- Contact the issuer for an already existing credit card account and ask for the credit limit to be raised. This will not generate an inquiry since the issuer will only conduct an account review which does not affect a credit score. The percentage of available credit will be increased and may raise the consumer's score since it is not picked up as "new" credit.[124]
- Have information on duplicate or old, closed accounts removed from the consumer report. Sometimes an account with negative information gets reported twice, especially if there is a collection agency involved. A consumer may also want to have extraneous accounts removed if a consumer's score is being lowered because of too many credit card or revolving accounts. Be careful to ensure that this does not lower the "age of credit history" factor.
- Do not pay off old collection accounts without reaching an agreement with the creditor or collection agency that addresses the consumer credit reporting issues. Otherwise, payment may "re-age" the account, showing it as current collection activity.[125] In fact, Fair Isaac in its advice on improving a credit score states that paying off a collection account does not remove it from the consumer report, implying that it also does not help raise a credit score to pay it off.[126]
- Find out on what day a credit card issuer furnishes information to the consumer reporting agencies (CRAs). Pay the balance off before that day to create a zero ratio of credit used to credit limit, which will increase the "available credit" factor.
- Seek permission to be added as an authorized user to someone else's mature credit-card account with no delinquencies. The account will probably appear on the consumer's file[127] and increase her score.

14.6.3 Re-Scoring

There are a number of organizations that offer services to raise a consumer's credit score, most particularly during the mortgage lending process. These businesses assist consumers in correcting errors in their credit files and getting their files "re-scored." Many of these firms work by referral from mortgage lenders and brokers.[128]

14.7 Policy Concerns with Credit Scoring Systems

14.7.1 Lack of Transparency

One of the original congressional purposes in passing the FCRA was to make consumer credit reporting data accessible, understandable and correctable. In other words, the FCRA was intended to make the credit reporting process "transparent" for consumers, who could now learn what was in their credit files and how to correct mistakes.

Credit scoring, on the other hand, lacks transparency. Credit scoring does not allow consumers to obtain information about how their credit scores were calculated or why their credit scores are low or high. For many years, consumers did not even have access to their credit scores. Consumers still cannot be certain they have obtained the same scores as creditors. As a result, consumers are returned to a pre-FCRA state, in which they are left in the dark about information critical to determine whether they will be able to obtain credit and obtain it at a fair price.[129] Thus, credit scoring undermines the fundamental purpose of the FCRA.

14.7.2 Lack of Flexibility

A fundamental discomfort with credit scoring systems is the idea that a person's entire "credit persona" is reduced to a number. The rigidity of a credit scoring system and its mechanistic application leave no room for the exercise of human insight and discretion in evaluating applicants. Someone who may be a very questionable risk in some respects might qualify under a rigid credit scoring system, while someone else who is in every respect dependable and

---

Fannie Mae and Freddie Mac advise lenders to ignore a credit score if a consumer report is inaccurate. *See* § 14.8.1, *infra*. Also, during the pendency of a dispute, the credit scoring system supposedly will not take the disputed information into account in calculating the credit score. Anne Kadet, *How to Boost Credit Score*, Wall Street Journal, May 4, 2003, at 2.

124 Anne Kadet, *FICO Frenzy*, SmartMoney, May 1, 2002, at 104.
125 Kathy Kristof, *Knowing the Score on Credit Can Help*, Los Angeles Times, May 25, 2003, at C3. If the consumer does want to pay off an old collection account, she should first condition that payment on the creditor agreeing to either to remove or modify the negative information, or not to verify the information if the consumer disputes it. Any such agreement must be in writing. *See* § 12.6.7.3, *supra*.
126 Fair Isaac, Understanding Your Credit Score 9 (July 2005), *available at* www.myfico.com/Downloads/Files/myFICO_UYFS_Booklet.pdf.
127 Official Staff Commentary to Regulation B § 202.10-2 (creditor may designate all authorized user accounts to reflect the participation of both parties, whether or not married). This tactic should be used with great caution, and only with account holders that the consumer trusts, because if the account holder does subsequently become delinquent or default, this adverse information will end up on the consumer's credit report. In general, this section of the Commentary of Regulation B is not without controversy. *See* National Consumer Law Center, Credit Discrimination § 9.4.2.1 (4th ed. 2005 and Supp.).
128 Evan Hendricks, *Credit Scores & Credit Reports: How the System Really Works, What You Can Do*, Privacy Times Ch. 3 (2d ed. 2005).
129 One state regulator has described this effect as the "re-mystification" of the credit reporting system. Fed. Reserve Bank of Boston, *Perspectives on Credit Scoring and Fair Lending: Part 4*, Communities & Banking 18 (Spring 2002) (interview with William N. Lund, Maine Office of Consumer Credit Regulation).

conscientious may not qualify because of a temporary financial setback, such as a medical emergency or short-term unemployment, that could not be justified numerically. There is some evidence that low-income and minority households are more prone to these setbacks or "application idiosyncrasies."[130]

Reliance on credit scoring does not permit the flexibility to consider mitigating factors that would turn an otherwise unacceptable risk into a successful loan. Human judgment is by no means infallible, but contains insight that is not quantifiable.

On the other hand, some humans exercise their judgment in a discriminatory way so that certain applicants benefit from the human element while other similarly situated applicants do not. Often, people are not even aware of the discriminatory element of their judgment. Credit scoring proponents have consistently argued that removing the human discretion from credit evaluation also removes potential for discrimination.

The inflexibility of credit scores may have particularly negative consequences for low-income consumers.[131] Both Freddie Mac and Fannie Mae have issued guidelines for lenders on what they consider to be an acceptable FICO score.[132] While Freddie Mac and Fannie Mae state that they instruct lenders not to exclude borrowers solely on the basis of their credit scores, but to work with them,[133] lenders may be tempted to err on the side of denying loans or to steer lower-scoring applicants to subprime loan products. As a result, more low-income borrowers and those who do not have a conventional credit background may be unnecessarily forced into the fringe or subprime market where interest rates are considerably higher and many lenders charge excessive points and fees.

14.7.3 Credit Scores, Risk-based Pricing, and Subprime Loans

The current trend is to use credit scores to determine, not only whether a consumer will be approved for credit, but at what price the credit will be provided. Essentially, the higher the credit score, the lower the price for credit. The website for Fair Isaac even provides interest rates quotes for home mortgages based upon a consumer's credit score. However, there are questions as to the justifiability of risk-based pricing, i.e., whether the additional price charged by some lenders for so-called "risky" loans legitimately compensates them for additional risk, or represent pure additional profit.[134] Furthermore, credit scores may not accurately predict risk with respect to high-priced, subprime mortgage loans. The risk of default for these loans, which is what credit scoring best predicts, does not equal the risk of loss, because of the presence of substantial equity in the home.

There has also been a concern raised that credit scores do not predict risk very well with respect to home mortgages. Credit scoring models are best at predicting early default within the first few months of a loan, while most mortgage defaults and foreclosures take place several years into the loan.[135] Credit scoring models can only predict early default because they do not incorporate many of the factors that cause defaults, such as job loss, divorce and medical problems.

The FCRA requires creditors to give consumers a notice relating to risk-based pricing.[136] The notice became effective on March 31, 2004.[137] Federal Trade Commission and Federal Reserve Board will be issuing regulations that prescribe the form and content of the notice.[138]

---

130   Stanley D. Longhofer, Federal Reserve Bank of Boston, *Mortgage Scoring and the Myth of Overrides*, Perspectives on Credit Scoring and Fair Mortgage Lending, Part 5: Communities & Bank 19 (Fall 2002).

131   Low-income consumers do have lower credit scores as a group. Thirty-three percent of households living in neighborhoods with low family incomes have low credit scores, whereas only 17% of households in high-income neighborhoods have low credit scores. Brent W. Ambrose, Thomas G. Thibodeau, and Kenneth Temkin, U.S. Department of Housing and Urban Development, An Analysis of the Effects of the GSE Affordable Goals on Low- and Moderate-Income Families 13 (May 2002).

132   Freddie Mac advises lenders that applicants with FICO scores below 620 indicates high risk, between 620 and 660 indicates an uncertain credit profile, and above 660 means they are likely to have acceptable credit reputations. *See* Freddie Mac, Automated Underwriting: Making Mortgage Lending Simpler and Fairer for America's Families 25 (Sept. 1996), *available at* www.freddiemac.com/corporate/reports/moseley/mosehome.htm.

133   Henry Cassidy and Robert Englestad, Credit Scoring and the Secondary Market: Perceptions, Policies, Practices, Community Investments 5 (Summer 1998); Federal Trade Commission, Public Forum on the Consumer and Credit Scoring, Matter No. P994810, at 66–69 (July 22, 1999) (statement of Pamela Johnson, Vice President of Single Family Mortgage Business, Fannie Mae) (stating that Desktop Underwriter will approve loans with scores under 620 and that if the system does not approve the loan, the lender should try to work with the applicant), *available at* www.ftc.gov/bcp/creditscoring.

134   For a critique of risk-based pricing, see National Consumer Law Center, The Cost of Credit: Regulation, Preemption, and Industry Abuses § 11.3 (3d ed. 2005 and Supp.).

135   Federal Reserve Board Mortgage Credit Partnership Credit Scoring Committee, Statement of Calvin Bradford, *Perspectives on Credit Scoring and Fair Mortgage Lending*, First Installment 7 (Spring 2000). *Cf.* Bonnie Sinnock, *Changing Definitions Pose Challenge in Valuing Jumbo, Alt-A Loan Pools*, National Mortgage News, May 12, 2003, at 20 (noting that FICO scores are better at sizing up short-duration credit risks than long ones and scores are generally less important in the long term.).

136   15 U.S.C. § 1681m(h)(1); 16 C.F.R. § 602.1(c)(3)(xiii). This notice is discussed in depth at § 8.2.8, *supra*.

137   12 C.F.R. § 222.1(c)(1)(i) and 16 C.F.R. § 602.1(c)(1)(i).

138   15 U.S.C. § 1681m(h)(6). *See* § 8.2.8, *supra*.

14.8 Concerns About the Accuracy of Credit Scores

14.8.1 Garbage In, Garbage Out: The Effect of Consumer Reporting Inaccuracies on Credit Scores

No matter how valid a model may be, it is no better than the data it is given. If a consumer's credit history contains inaccuracies, his or her credit score will be inaccurate. In other words, credit scoring models are developed to assume perfection in credit reporting, which is a fundamentally flawed assumption. Credit history files at the major consumer reporting agencies (CRAs) are notorious for their lack of accuracy.[139] With credit scoring, consumers are penalized twice for inaccuracies.

One study has estimated that at least one in five borrowers is likely being penalized because of an inaccurate credit score due to credit reporting problems, but that one in five at risk borrowers is benefiting from scores that are inflated because of incomplete credit information.[140] The study authors posited an interesting theory as to why credit scores are predictive despite substantial inaccuracies—that given the large number of borrowers most lenders have, lenders suffer little harm from inaccuracies so long as there is statistical equilibrium between the number of positive versus negative mistakes, that is, the mistakes cancel each other out.[141]

A study by the Federal Reserve Board of over 300,000 credit history files analyzed the effect of inaccurate and missing information on credit scores.[142] The study found that the effect of these problems was modest in most cases (causing a decrease of less than 10 points in credit score), but was more substantial when the errors involved collection tradelines. Individuals with low credit scores or thin files also experienced greater adverse effects from errors or omissions. The FRB study found that none of the problems affected a great proportion of the population, with the exception of missing credit limits.[143] However, consumers living in minority and lower-income neighborhoods experienced errors or omissions in credit data more frequently.[144]

Inaccuracies in credit scoring may be one area in which challenges under the FCRA are possible, since the CRAs are required to have procedures to "assure maximum possible accuracy of the information concerning the individual about whom the report relates."[145] Credit scores are certainly "information concerning" a consumer. If scores are inaccurate on a systemic basis, then the CRAs may be in violation of the requirement for maximum possible accuracy.

Some lenders will make exceptions to credit scoring in the case of an inaccurate credit file.[146] Fannie Mae has stated that it instructs lenders to disregard a credit score if the credit file information is wrong or inaccurate.[147] Freddie Mac states that it permits lenders to disregard a credit score in the same situation.[148]

14.8.2 Credit Scores Do Not Allow the FCRA's Dispute Mechanisms to Work As Intended

Credit scoring sometimes may conflict with the FCRA's fundamental consumer protections to correct inaccurate information. First, the speed of lending decisions based on credit scoring does not allow time for a consumer to dispute inaccurate information if it is discovered during the credit application process.

Second, if a CRA or creditor refuses to delete negative information from a consumer's file after a dispute, the FCRA allows consumers to include a written statement.[149]ABi Yet it is unclear whether the consumer's credit score will reflect a written statement.[150]

---

139 See Ch. 7, supra.
140 Consumer Federation of America and National Credit Reporting Association, Credit Score Accuracy and Implications for Consumers 23–24 (Dec. 17, 2002), available at www.consumerfed.org/pdfs/121702CFA_NCRA_Credit_Score_Report_Final.pdf.
141 Consumer Federation of America and National Credit Reporting Association, Credit Score Accuracy and Implications for Consumers 24 (Dec. 17, 2002), available at www.consumerfed.org/pdfs/121702CFA_NCRA_Credit_Score_Report_Final.pdf. See also Bruce Kellison and Patrick Brockett, Check the Score; Credit Scoring and Insurance Losses: Is There a Connection?, Tex. Bus. Rev. 1 (Jan. 1, 2003) (noting that random and occasional errors will not significantly weaken the statistical correlation between credit scores and insurance loss history).
142 Robert B. Avery, Paul S. Calem, and Glenn B. Canner, Credit Report Accuracy and Access to Credit, Federal Reserve Bulletin 321 (Summer 2004).
143 See § 14.8.4, infra.
144 Robert B. Avery, Paul S. Calem, and Glenn B. Canner, Credit Report Accuracy and Access to Credit, Federal Reserve Bulletin 319 (Summer 2004).
145 15 U.S.C. § 1681e(b). See Ch. 4, supra.
146 Federal Trade Commission, Public Forum on the Consumer and Credit Scoring, Matter No. P994810, at 94–95 (July 22, 1999) (statement of Carroll Justice, Executive Vice President, FT Mortgage Companies), available at www.ftc.gov/bcp/creditscoring.
147 Henry Cassidy and Robert Englestad, Credit Scoring and the Secondary Market: Perceptions, Policies, Practices, Community Investments 5 (Summer 1998); Federal Trade Commission, Public Forum on the Consumer and Credit Scoring, Matter No. P994810, at 169, 170 (July 22, 1999) (statement of Pamela Johnson, Vice President of Single Family Mortgage Business, Fannie Mae), available at www.ftc.gov/bcp/creditscoring.
148 Henry Cassidy and Robert Englestad, Credit Scoring and the Secondary Market: Perceptions, Policies, Practices, Community Investments 5 (Summer 1998).
149 See Ch. 4, supra.
150 Helen Huntley, Making Your Credit Score Soar, St. Petersburg Times, Jan. 26, 2003, at 1H (noting that the consumer's submission of a written statement will not change a credit score).

During the pendency of a dispute over inaccurate derogatory information, the credit scoring system supposedly will not take that information into account in calculating the credit score.[151] However, this may be only true if it is the creditor who reports that the information is disputed.

Furthermore, disputed information can affect a consumer's credit score in ways other than being treated as a delinquency, default, or collection item. For example, if a consumer disputes a single charge on a credit card bill, the amount in dispute will not be considered delinquent but will be included in the balance for that credit card. If the amount in dispute is significant, that can result in a lower credit score because it appears that the consumer's ratio of amount owed to available credit is too high.

If credit scores are at odds with the FCRA's protections regarding inaccurate information, this aspect of credit scoring may be vulnerable to legal challenge under the FCRA. Credit scores may conflict with the dispute resolution protections of other consumer protection statutes as well, such as the Fair Credit Billing Act, which is the statute that governs consumer disputes involving credit card transactions.[152]

There may also be a cause of action under the Equal Credit Opportunity Act. The ECOA prohibits discrimination against a consumer for invoking any of her rights under the Consumer Credit Protection Act, which includes the FCRA.[153] The theory would be that credit scores, if they do not allow the FCRA's dispute mechanisms to work or if they ignore written protests, automatically penalize applicants who invoke their FCRA rights in violation of the ECOA.

14.8.3 The Effect of Inaccurate, Non-derogatory Information

14.8.3.1 General

Because of the way credit scoring models weigh data from a credit file, certain information that is not negative in the abstract will have an adverse effect on a credit score. This information may or may not be accurate. It may be considered "technically accurate," which some courts, but not others, have held complies with the FCRA.[154] However if information artificially lowers a credit score, one could argue that it can never be considered accurate because of its significant effect on a credit score.[155]

14.8.3.2 Missing Limits

A very common problem affecting credit scores is the failure of certain credit card issuers to report the credit limits on their cardholder's accounts. Instead, the CRAs will often substitute the highest balance on that account as the credit limit for that tradeline. Since one of the factors in a scoring model is the ratio of credit used to credit available, these accounts will depress a credit score by making it seem that a consumer is "maxed out" on the account.[156]

The failure to report credit limits appears to be a common problem. An initial study by Federal Reserve Board researchers indicates about 70% of consumers have at least one revolving account in their credit files that does not contain information about the credit limit.[157] A later study by the FRB found that the percentage of consumers whose credit files had missing credit limit information had declined to 46%, due to efforts to encourage reporting of credit limits.[158] Still, nearly half of all consumers and 14% of all credit card accounts remain affected by the practice. Furthermore, the study found that over 60% of these consumers would have experienced an increase in their credit scores if the credit card issuer had not withheld the credit limit information.[159]

The failure to report credit card limits appears in some cases to be intentional and calculated to affect consumers. One issuer of credit cards has admitted that it deliberately failed to report credit limits of its customers as a way to artificially depress credit scores, citing "competitive advan-

---

151 Anne Kadet, *How to Boost Credit Score*, Wall Street Journal, May 4, 2003, at 2.

152 15 U.S.C. § 1666. *See generally* National Consumer Law Center, Truth in Lending § 5.8 (5th ed. 2003 and Supp.). FCBA prohibits the creditor from reporting disputed amounts as delinquent, but does allow creditors to report them as disputed. The question is how does a credit scoring system treat these disputed amounts? If the system does lower a credit score for disputed amounts, the consumer may not have a cause of action under FCBA because the creditor reported the dispute correctly. However, the consumer may have a cause of action under the FCRA.

153 15 U.S.C. § 1691(a)(3). *See* National Consumer Law Center, Credit Discrimination § 3.4.4 (4th ed. 2005 and Supp.).

154 *See* Ch. 4, *supra*.

155 *But see* Baker v. Capital One Bank, 2006 WL 173668 (D. Ariz. Jan. 24, 2006) (failure to report credit limits does not violate FCRA even though it lowers a credit score); Heupel v. Trans Union, 193 F. Supp. 2d 1234 (N.D. Ala. 2002) (holding that "included in bankruptcy" designation did not violate FCRA because it was "technically accurate" even though it had lowered the plaintiff's credit score enough to cause a rejection by a credit card issuer.).

156 Evan Hendricks, *Credit Scores & Credit Reports: How the System Really Works, What You Can Do,* Privacy Times Ch. 22 (2d ed. 2005).

157 Robert Avery, Paul Calem, Glenn Canner, and Raphael Bostic, Federal Reserve Bulletin, An Overview of Consumer Data and Credit Reporting, Feb. 2003, at 71. *See also* Federal Financial Institutions Examination Council, Advisory Letter (Jan. 18, 2000) (stating that "certain large credit card issuers are no longer reporting customer credit lines of high credit balances or both."), *available at* www.ffiec.gov/press/pr011800a.htm.

158 Robert B. Avery, Paul S. Calem, and Glenn B. Canner, Federal Reserve Bulletin, Credit Report Accuracy and Access to Credit 306 (Summer 2004).

159 *Id.* at 316.

tage."[160] For other creditors, such as charge card companies like American Express, their products are designed not to have credit limits.

One court has held that a consumer could not use the FCRA's re-investigation mechanism to require a furnisher to report credit limit information, because such information is not required for the account information to be complete, despite the effect on the consumer's credit score.[161] It remains to be seen whether the failure of the CRAs to require furnishers to report credit limits violates the FCRA's requirement to use reasonable procedures to ensure maximum possible accuracy.[162]

14.8.3.3 Unreported Information

Another problem occurs when creditors fail to furnish information, particularly positive information, to the CRAs.[163] The lack of positive information may artificially depress a consumer's credit score. The Office of the Comptroller of Currency has expressed concerns that certain lenders deliberately fail to report positive information to CRAs.[164] There are allegations that some subprime lenders engage in this omission for the purpose of keeping their borrower's credit scores artificially low, so that the borrowers do not have better credit alternatives.[165] Since a disproportionate number of subprime borrowers are in nonwhite neighborhoods,[166] this practice would have a disparate impact on minority groups.

However, the practice of withholding credit information is not limited to subprime lenders. For a period of time, student loan giant Sallie Mae stopped reporting about its student loan customers to TransUnion and Experian.[167] Sallie Mae took this action to prevent other lenders from soliciting its customers (and thus to preserve its advantage in cross-marketing to this lucrative young market). Sallie Mae's actions artificially depressed the credit scores of its customers; in one case, a borrower's score dropped 40 points after his Sallie Mae loans were removed from his Experian and TransUnion files.[168] Sallie Mae's actions were especially problematic because the method by which many young consumers establish their credit histories is through repayment of student loans.

Another common occurrence is that information will be missing from files at one CRA, but be present in another CRA's files, because of mistakes or the fact that creditors do not report to all three major CRAs. One study found, from a limited sample of 51 consumer files, that 78% of these consumers had a revolving account in good standing missing from their files at one of the three major CRAs.[169] One third of these files were missing a mortgage account that had never been late.[170] An earlier study examining over 1700 files from the three major CRAs revealed that 44% of these files had missing information in them.[171]

14.8.3.4 Student Loan Deferments

Another example that may affect a great number of consumers is student loan deferments. For certain student loans, a deferment will result in a loan balance that exceeds the original loan amount. Apparently, credit scoring models consider this to be negative, and will lower a consumer's credit score because of student loan deferments.

---

160 Eric Dash, *Up Against the Plastic Wall*, New York Times, May 21, 2005; Kenneth Harney, *Credit Card Limits Often Unreported*, Washington Post, Dec. 25, 2004; Michele Heller, *FCRA Hearing to Shine Spotlight on Credit Reports*, American Banker, June 12, 2003, at 10.
161 Baker v. Capital One Bank, 2006 WL 173668 (D. Ariz. Jan. 24, 2006).
162 *See* Ch. 4, *supra*.
163 *See* Ch. 4, *supra*.
164 Federal Trade Commission, Public Forum on the Consumer and Credit Scoring, Matter No. P994810, at 205 (July 22, 1999) (statement of Russ Bailey, Fair Lending Team Leader, Community and Consumer Policy Division, Office of the Comptroller of Currency), *available at* www.ftc.gov/bcp/creditscoring; Press Release, Office of the Comptroller of the Currency, Comptroller Urges Industry to End Abusive Practices and Elevate Customer Service Standards (June 7, 1999) (No. 99-51), *available at* www.occ.treas.gov/ftp/release/99-51.txt.
165 Kenneth Harney, *Improve Credit Rating By Paying On Time? Don't Count On It*, Washington Post, Jan. 29, 2000, at G1.
166 *See* National Consumer Law Center, Credit Discrimination § 8.2.2 (4th ed. 2005 and Supp.).
167 W.A. Lee, *Credit Data or Customer List? Sallie's Stance Drawing Heat*, American Banker, Oct. 7, 2003. Salle Mae has apparently ceased its withholding of borrower information. Robert B. Avery, Paul S. Calem, and Glenn B. Canner, *Credit Report Accuracy and Access to Credit*, Federal Reserve Bulletin 310 (Summer 2004).
168 *Id.*
169 Consumer Federation of America and National Credit Reporting Association, Credit Score Accuracy and Implications for Consumers 30 (Dec. 17, 2002), *available at* www.consumerfed.org/pdfs/121702CFA_NCRA_Credit_Score_Report_Final.pdf. While the sample size for this finding was limited, the study's authors noted that many of the findings are consistent with those reported in research by the Federal Reserve Board. Travis B. Plunkett, *Testimony Before the House Committee on Financial Services*, Subcommittee on Financial Institutions and Consumer Credit 5, n.8 (June 12, 2003).
170 Consumer Federation of America and National Credit Reporting Association, Credit Score Accuracy and Implications for Consumers 30 (Dec. 17, 2002), *available at* www.consumerfed.org/pdfs/121702CFA_NCRA_Credit_Score_Report_Final.pdf.
171 Consumer Federation of America and National Credit Reporting Association, Credit Score Accuracy and Implications for Consumers 7 (Dec. 17, 2002) (describing 1994 study conducted by the National Association of Independent Credit Reporting Agencies), *available at* www.consumerfed.org/pdfs/121702CFA_NCRA_Credit_Score_Report_Final.pdf.

14.8.3.5 Duplicate Accounts

Sometimes a credit account will show up multiple times in a credit file.[172] If it is an account in collection, it may be reported by both the collection agency and the creditor, creating a false double negative effect on the creditor score.[173] The failure of the CRAs to have procedures to prevent duplicate tradelines may violate the FCRA's requirement to use reasonable procedures to ensure maximum possible accuracy.[174]

Even if the account is not in default, reporting it twice could lower the credit score. The account might be a new account and thus the consumer appears to have too much "new" credit. It might be a credit card account, and the consumer may be in a situation where the scoring model deducts points for having too many revolving accounts.

14.8.3.6 Wrong Account Type

Misreporting the type of account may lower a credit score.[175] For example, consider if a mortgage account is reported as a revolving account. Suddenly, the consumer seems very over-extended.

14.8.3.7 Too Many Accounts

Even simply reporting old, closed credit card accounts with no balance may hurt a credit score, if the consumer is considered to have too many of these accounts.[176] Yet the FCRA arguably permits reporting these accounts indefinitely, because it is not technically negative information and thus not subject to the seven-year limit.[177]

14.8.4 Lack of Validation and Re-Validation

Credit scoring models must be initially validated when they are developed. This means the model must be tested against databases of loan files where the results of the loans (good or bad) are known. The models must also be re-validated periodically. Without re-validation, a credit scoring model can lose its accuracy. The Federal Reserve Board (FRB) has warned that validity can deteriorate over time, and must be rechecked periodically.[178] The Office of the Comptroller of the Currency (OCC) has reported that some banks have been unable to track the validity of the credit scoring model over time.[179] The definition of credit scoring system under Regulation B includes a requirement that the system be "validated using accepted statistical principles and methodology,"[180] and periodically re-validated as to its predictive ability and adjusted accordingly.[181]

Re-validation is particular important when economic situations changed. Many credit scoring models were developed in booming economic times of the 1990s and there are questions about how predictive they were during the economic recession.[182] For example, one study showed that credit scores are not as predictive for home mortgage defaults as the volatility of the local economy. High scoring homeowners in volatile areas in the Northeast (defined as areas hard hit by local economic problems and declining property values) were 60% more likely to lose their homes than low scoring homeowners in the stable Midwest.[183] Federal Reserve Board researchers have noted that economic conditions, such as unemployment rates by locality, housing prices, and income levels significantly affect predictions of consumer behavior.[184]

Credit scoring models may have underestimated the effect of the economic slowdowns on credit card borrowers.[185]

---

172 According to one study, an examination of over 1700 consumer files from the three major nationwide CRAs revealed that 29% of tradelines, 15% of inquiries, and 26% of public record entries were duplicates. Consumer Federation of America and National Credit Reporting Association, Credit Score Accuracy and Implications for Consumers 7 (Dec. 17, 2002) (describing 1994 study conducted by the National Association of Independent Credit Reporting Agencies), *available at* www.consumerfed.org/pdfs/121702CFA_NCRA_Credit_Score_Report_Final.pdf.

173 *Id.* at 34 (in 5.9% of all files examined, a collection action was reported more than once on a single credit report, artificially lowering the credit score). *See also* Robert Avery, Paul Calem, Glenn Canner, and Raphael Bostic, *An Overview of Consumer Data and Credit Reporting*, Federal Reserve Bulletin, Feb. 2003, at 71 (40% of collection agency trades have multiple record items, many of which appeared to refer to the same episode).

174 Kohut v. Trans Union, L.L.C., 2004 WL 1882239 (N.D. Ill. Aug. 11. 2004) (denying motion to dismiss in action challenging duplicate tradelines under § 1681e). *See* Ch. 4, *supra*.

175 Consumer Federation of America and National Credit Reporting Association, Credit Score Accuracy and Implications for Consumers 34 (Dec. 17, 2002) (21.6% of all files contained errors regarding what type of account was involved in a tradeline), *available at* www.consumerfed.org/pdfs/121702CFA_NCRA_Credit_Score_Report_Final.pdf.

176 One of the reasons that may be given for a lower credit score is "too many revolving" accounts.

177 *See* § 5.2.2.1, *supra*.

178 *See Credit Risk, Credit Scoring, and the Performance of Home Mortgages*, Federal Reserve Bulletin, July 1996, at 621, 628. *See also* Press Release, Office of the Comptroller of the Currency, OCC Alerts Banks to Potential Benefits and Risks of Credit Scoring Models (May 20, 1997) (No. 97-46), *available at* www.occ.treas.gov.

179 Office of the Comptroller of the Currency, *Credit Scoring Models*, OCC Bull., May 20, 1997, at 97-24.

180 Reg. B, 12 C.F.R. § 202.2(p)(1)(iii).

181 *Id.* at § 202.2(p)(1)(iv). No definition of "periodically" is given in the regulation.

182 John R. Engen, *The Recession Question*, Banking Strategies (Nov./Dec. 2000), *available at* www.bai.org/bankingstrategies/2000-nov-dec/articles/blindfaith/sidearticle.html (quoting Jeffrey Brown, Director of Risk Analysis for the OCC).

183 Kenneth Harney, *Study Produces Surprises on Credit Risks*, Washington Post, Nov. 10, 2001, at H1.

184 Federal Reserve Bank of Philadelphia—Payments Card Center, Highlights from the Conference on Credit Modeling and Decisioning (Fall 2002).

185 Isabelle Lindenmayer, *Report Scores FICO-Based Lending, Teasers*, American Banker, Sept. 8, 2005 (researcher warning

Many credit card issuers rely solely on the credit score in approving an account, and do not consider the borrower's income or other debt. Thus, these lenders may grant credit to borrowers who are already overextended.[186]

14.8.5 Lender Misuse of Credit Scoring Models

Even if a credit scoring model is perfect and the data is 100% accurate, the model may produce wrong results if it is not properly used by lenders. There are a number of problems stemming from lender misuse of credit scoring models.

Some lenders or their employees may use a credit scoring model for a purpose for which it was not intended. The OCC has reported finding problems of the application of models to products or customers or neighborhoods for which they were not designed, and that bank staff were often poorly trained in the use of models.[187] Some lenders encounter problems when they use a generic or "off-the-shelf" scoring model, when they should be using a custom model.

Problems can arise when lenders do not understand the scoring model they are using. Like consumers, lenders may also view credit scoring as a black box. This is problematic because it means the lenders will not understand the basis on which they approve or deny loans. The OCC requires that bank management thoroughly understand the scoring models that they use.[188] Furthermore, the OCC requires that lenders carefully evaluate their scoring models, which is not possible if they do not understand the models.[189] Finally, credit discrimination laws prohibit lenders from discriminating against protected groups.[190] It is the lender, not the scoring model developer, that bears ultimate responsibility if a scoring model has an unlawful discriminatory effect on protected groups. Lenders need to understand their scoring models so that they do not violate credit discrimination laws.[191]

14.9 Do Credit Scores Discriminate?

14.9.1 Credit Scoring's Disparate Impact

As long as there have been credit scores, there have been concerns that scoring systems contain biases that disproportionately impact minorities and other groups protected by credit discrimination laws.[192] Several studies have found that minorities as a group have lower credit scores than whites.[193] A full analysis of this issue and implications under fair lending laws is included in another manual in this series.[194]

One concern is that scoring models often fail to adequately weigh rent, utility, and other nonstandard payment histories that are more typical in lower-income populations. Thus, the models may unwittingly overestimate the real risk of nonpayment for these groups.

To address these concerns, there have been several initiatives to establish "alternative" credit profiles for popu-

---

that lenders' reliance on inflated credit scores was resulting in consumers to take on unsustainable debt). As early as 1997, the Office of Comptroller of Currency had warned banks to closely monitor the performance of their credit scoring models throughout economic cycles, advising them to retest models developed in prosperous times. Office of the Comptroller of the Currency, *Credit Scoring Models*, OCC Bull., May 20, 1997, at 97-24.

186 *In re* Mercer, 246 F.3d 391 (5th Cir. 2001) (credit card issuer sent debtor a pre-approved card with a $3000 limit based on a FICO score of 735, even though the debtor earned less than $25,000 annually and had recently acquired four other credit cards); *In re* Akins, 235 B.R. 866 (Bankr. W.D. Tex. 1999) (debtor obtained approval to use a convenience check up to her full $4000 credit limit based on acceptable FICO score even though she had two other credit cards totaling approximately $30,000 in debt, or 150% of her gross income); *In re* Ellingsworth, 212 B.R. 326 (Bankr. W.D. Mo. 1997) (debtor sent a pre-approved credit card with credit limit of $4000 based on her FICO score of 759 even though she had 16 other credit cards).

187 Office of the Comptroller of the Currency, *Credit Scoring Models* OCC Bull., May 20, 1997, at 97-24.
188 *Id.*
189 *Id.*
190 *See generally* National Consumer Law Center, Credit Discrimination (4th ed. 2005 and Supp.).

191 Press Release, Office of the Comptroller of the Currency, OCC Alerts Banks to Potential Benefits and Risks of Credit Scoring Models (May 20, 1997) (No. 97-46), *available at* www.occ.treas.gov.

192 *See* National Consumer Law Center, Credit Discrimination § 6.4 (4th ed. 2005 and Supp.). The Federal Reserve Board has published a five part series on this topic. Fed. Reserve Bank of Boston, Perspectives on Credit Scoring and Fair Lending in Communities & Banking (2000–2002).

193 Matt Fellowes, Brookings Institution, Credit Scores, Reports, and Getting Ahead in America (May 2006) (finding that counties with relatively high proportions of racial and ethnic minorities are more likely to have lower average credit scores; although study author cautions that this finding is not evidence of bias); Raphael W. Bostic, Paul S. Calem, and Susan M. Wachter, Joint Center for Housing Studies of Harvard University, Hitting the Wall: Credit as an Impediment to Homeownership (Feb. 2004) (finding that the median credit score for whites increased significantly during the 1990s, from 727 to 738, while the median credit score for African Americans dropped from 693 to 676); Robert E. Avery, Paul S. Calem, and Glenn B. Canner, *Credit Report Accuracy and Access to Credit*, Federal Reserve Bulletin (Summer 2004) (fewer than 40% of consumers who lived in high minority neighborhoods had credit scores over 701, while nearly 70% of consumers who lived in mostly white neighborhoods had scores over 701). *See also* Freddie Mac, Automated Underwriting: Making Mortgage Lending Simpler and Fairer for America's Families (Sept. 1996) (noting African-Americans are three times as likely to have FICO scores below 620 as whites), *available at* www.freddiemac.com/corporate/reports/moseley/mosehome.htm.

Studies of insurance credit scores have resulted in similar findings, see National Consumer Law Center, Credit Discrimination § 6.4.5.2 (4th ed. 2005 and Supp.).

194 *See* National Consumer Law Center, Credit Discrimination § 6.4 (4th ed. 2005 and Supp.).

lations without a credit history. PRBC is a consumer reporting agency (CRA) that compiles credit histories using rent, utility, insurance, and other monthly payments.[195] Fair Isaac has undertaken efforts to create credit scores using nontraditional credit information.[196] There are also subprime CRAs that provide credit assessment products using information from payday lenders, finance companies, subprime automobile lenders, landlord/tenant court records, and rent-to-own records.[197]

The development of credit scoring models based on subprime sources of credit, such as payday loans, has created concerns that such scores will be used to market high-cost credit to these consumers.[198] Another concern is that these alternative scores will not be predictive of a consumer's credit risk, because these forms of credit are structured so differently (and so much more onerously) than traditional forms of credit.[199] One CRA has stated that the presence of a finance company tradeline negatively affects a credit score because they often carry high interest rates, which hampers the consumer's ability to repay.[200] If a finance company loan is considered negative because of high interest rates, the use of even more expensive credit sources (such as payday loans and subprime mortgages) to develop scoring models would logically create a database of "bad scorers."

14.9.2 The Growing Credit Scoring Gap

In addition to disparate impact on racial minorities, research indicates that low-income consumers, renters, and other groups have lower credit scores as a group.[201] More troubling, the gap between "good" and "bad" scorers appears to be growing, reflecting an increasing divide between the credit haves and have-nots.

First, there is a question as to how much of the population has poor or marginal credit scores. According to Fair Isaac, the median score is 723,[202] and about 73% of FICO scores are over 650.[203] Research from the Brookings Institution, however, has found that the average credit score is around 650 (which is considered a marginal credit score) and only 55% of consumers have scores between 600 and 800.[204] Furthermore, the Brookings Institution found that counties in the South had the highest concentration of low scorers, with an average of 635.[205]

Most important, the Brookings Institution found that counties with lower average credit scores saw a decline in those scores by 17% on average over a five-year period, while counties with higher average scores saw them improve slightly.[206] This trend suggests that credit scores are "path dependent," i.e., low scoring consumers tend to see their scores decline while high scorers see them improve. The Brookings report expressed concern that this trend pointed to a "potentially ruinous fiscal cycle" for consumers with low credit scores.[207]

A study by the Joint Center for Housing Studies at Harvard University revealed similar results. This study was based on a simulation of credit scores using 200,000 credit files matched with data from the triennial Survey of Consumer Finances.[208] The study's researchers found that, for the period of 1989 to 2001, the median credit score had increased slightly for the general population. However, this increase masked a tremendous divergence in credit scores during that same period of time. The study's researchers

---

195 PRBC stands for "Payment Reporting Builds Credit." See PRBC, PRBC Overview, available at http://prbc.com/pub/PRBC_Consumer_Overview.pdf.
196 Fair Isaac, FICO Expansion Score, available at www.fairisaac.com/Fairisaac/Solutions/FICO+Expansion+Score/Expansion+Score+Overview/FICO+Expansion+Score.htm.
197 Teletrack, Company Overview—Consumer Credit Information for Risk Mitigation, available at www.teletrack.com/company/overview.html.
198 Kathy Kristof, New Credit Score System Has Mixed Reviews, Los Angeles Times, Aug. 12, 2004.
199 Testimony of Margot Saunders, National Consumer Law Center, Helping Consumers Obtain the Credit They Deserve: Hearing Before the House Subcommittee on Financial Institutions and Consumer Credit 6–7 (May 12, 2005), available at www.consumerlaw.org.
200 Experian, Credit Score Basics FAQs, available at www.experian.com/consumer/credit_score_faqs.html#17.
201 One study found that 33% of households living in neighborhoods with low family incomes have low credit scores, whereas only 17% of households in high-income neighborhoods have low credit scores. Brent W. Ambrose, Thomas G. Thibodeau & Kenneth Temkin, U.S. Dep't of Hous. and Urban Dev., An Analysis of the Effects of the GSE Affordable Goals on Low- and Moderate-Income Families 13 (May 2002). At least one study of insurance credit scores also indicated that scores were significantly worse for residents of low-income zip codes. See,

e.g., Brent Kabler, Mo. Dep't of Ins., Insurance-Based Credit Scores: Impact on Minority and Low Income Populations in Missouri (Jan. 2004).
202 Fair Isaac, Credit Education, available at www.myfico.com/CreditEducation/?fire=1.
203 Fair Isaac, Understanding Your FICO Score 7 (July 2005), available at www.myfico.com/Downloads/Files/myFICO_UYFS_Booklet.pdf.
204 Matt Fellowes, Brookings Institution, Credit Scores, Reports, and Getting Ahead in America 10 (May 2006).
205 Id. at 6. A study from the Federal Reserve Bank of Philadelphia also has found that measures of credit risk are higher in the South. David K. Musto and Nicholas Souleles, A Portfolio View of Consumer Credit 21 (Federal Reserve Bank of Philadelphia—Research Department, Working Paper No. 05-25 Sept. 2005). This study noted the relationship between credit scores and other economic indicators. Higher credit scores are found in states with lower unemployment rates, lower divorce rates and most significantly, higher rates of health insurance coverage.
206 David K. Musto and Nicholas Souleles, A Portfolio View of Consumer Credit 8 (Federal Reserve Bank of Philadelphia—Research Department, Working Paper No. 05-25 Sept. 2005).
207 Id.
208 Raphael W. Bostic, Paul S. Calem, and Susan M. Wachter, Joint Center for Housing Studies of Harvard University, Hitting the Wall: Credit as an Impediment to Homeownership (Feb. 2004).

observed that the median credit score for the top quintile of income increased significantly during the 1990s, from 729 to 754, while the median credit score for the bottom quintile dropped from 703 to 688.[209] Moreover, the percentage of consumers who scored under 660, and thus have marginal or worse credit, increased from 19% to 25% of the overall population.[210]

14.10 Credit Scores and Insurance

A particularly controversial issue is the use of credit scores by automobile and homeowner's insurers to determine whether to insure a consumer and at what price. The credit scores used by insurers, or "insurance scores," are specially developed for insurance purposes and not the same as credit scores for credit-granting purposes, but they nonetheless are based solely on credit history. Consumers can obtain one version of their insurance scores from Choice-Point.[211]

The practice of using insurance scores has become widespread, with an early survey showing that 92% of automobile insurers surveyed use them.[212] As a result, a consumer with a poor credit history may be charged 40 to 75% more in premiums for automobile insurance.[213]

This practice has been criticized as being fundamentally unfair as well as being particularly burdensome to low-income consumers least able to afford high insurance rates. In addition, the use of insurance scores probably disproportionately burdens racial minorities, given that they have lower credit scores as a group.[214] Insurance companies defend their actions by noting the high correlation between credit scores and loss experience.[215]

A number of states have passed legislation regulating the practice.[216] Many of these statutes are based on model legislation written by the National Conference of Insurance Legislators and supported by the insurance industry.[217] While the FCRA generally preempts state laws governing credit score disclosure, it specifically exempts from preemption any state law regulating insurance scores.[218]

A number of class actions have been filed challenging the practice under anti-discrimination and state insurance laws.[219] Other lawsuits allege violation of the FCRA's notice requirements.[220] Insurance regulators in both Texas and California have taken enforcement actions against insurance companies over this practice.[221]

---

209 *Id.* at 18.
210 *Id.*
211 *See* ChoicePoint's consumer website at www.choicetrust.com.
212 Brian Grow and Pallavi Gogoi, *Insurance: A New Way to Squeeze the Weak?*, Business Week, Jan. 28, 2002, at 92 (citing study by Conning & Co.).
213 Pamela Yip, *One Number, Many Uses*, Dallas Morning News, Apr. 8, 2002, at 1D.
214 *See* National Consumer Law Center, Credit Discrimination § 6.4 (4th ed. 2005 and Supp.).
215 Michael J. Miller and Richard A. Smith, EPIC Actuaries, The Relationship of Credit-Based Insurance Scores to Private Passenger Automobile Insurance Loss Propensity (June 2003) (study commissioned by the insurance industry finding that individuals with the lowest insurance scores incurred 33% higher losses than average, while the highest scorers incurred 19% lower losses).
216 *See, e.g.*, Ark. Code Ann. §§ 23-67-401 to -415; Colo. Rev. Stat. Ann. § 10-4-110.7; Fla. Rev. Stat. Ann. § 626.9741; Haw. Rev. Stat. §§ 431:10C-207 and 431:10C-409; 2002 Idaho Sess. Laws 264; La. Rev. Stat. § 1484; Md. Ins. Code Ann. § 27-605; Minn. Stat. Ann. § 58.13(36); Mo. Rev. Stat. Ann. § 375.918; N.C. Gen. Stat. Ann. § 58-36-90; Tenn. Code Ann. §§ 56-5-401 to -407; Tex. Ins. Code Ann. § 21.49-2U; Utah Code Ann. § 31A-22-320; Va. Code Ann. §§ 38-2-2126, 38-2-2234. A summary of some of the state insurance laws governing use of credit information is included in Appx. H, *infra*.
217 National Conference of Insurance Legislators, Model Act Regarding Use of Credit Information in Personal Insurance (Nov. 22, 2002). *See* National Ass'n of Mut. Ins. Cos., NAMIC's State Laws and Legislative Trends State Laws Governing Insurance Scoring Practices, undated, *available at* www.namic.org/reports/credithistory/credithistory.asp.
218 15 U.S.C. § 1681t(b)(3)(C). The FCRA's preemption of state credit scoring disclosure laws is discussed in full at § 10.7.7, *supra*.
219 DeHoyos v. Allstate Corp, 345 F.3d 290 (5th Cir. 2003) (holding that a challenge to credit scoring under the Fair Housing Act and federal Civil Rights Acts was not preempted by the McCarran-Ferguson Act); Melder v. Allstate Corp., 404 F.3d 328 (class action alleging that insurer's use of credit scoring violated state insurance law's prohibition on unfair discrimination; Fifth Circuit upheld denial of motion to remand to state court); Owens v. Nationwide Mut. Ins. Co., 2005 WL 1837959 (N.D. Tex. Aug. 2, 2005) (granting summary judgment to insurance company on claims alleging that use of credit scores for homeowners insurance violates section 3604 of the FHA and the federal Civil Rights Acts); Nat'l Fair Housing Alliance v. Prudential Ins. Co., 208 F. Supp. 2d 46 (D.D.C. 2002) (class action alleging that the use of credit scores to determine eligibility for homeowners insurance has a disparate impact on minorities in violation of the Fair Housing Act); Wells v. Shelter Gen. Ins. Co., 217 F. Supp. 2d 744 (S.D. Miss. 2002) (class action challenging use of credit scores under Mississippi insurance law).
220 Reynolds v. Hartford Fin. Servs. Group, 435 F.3d 1081 (9th Cir. 2006) (insurer is required to provide an adverse action notice under the Fair Credit Reporting Act if the insurer would have charged the consumer a lower rate for insurance had the consumer's insurance credit score been more favorable), *abrogating* Ashby v. Farmers Group, Inc., 261 F. Supp. 2d 1213 (D. Or. 2003) (dismissal of FCRA claim against insurance management services company that used credit scores in rate setting).
221 R.J. Lehman, *Allstate Settles California Insurance-Scoring Dispute for $3 Million*, Bestwire, Mar. 5, 2004 (Allstate allegedly violated California law prohibiting use of credit information in underwriting or rate setting for automobile insurance; settlement prohibits use of credit scores and imposes a $3 million fine); Press Release, Texas Department of Insurance, State of Texas, Farmers Insurance Reach Agreement (Nov. 30, 2003) (resulting in a $100 million settlement, including $30 million in refunds for improper use of credit scores. Settlement does not prohibit use of credit scoring in insurance, and requires only disclosures acceptable to the Attorney General). The Texas settlement was reversed by the Texas Court of Appeals, on the basis that the Attorney General could not bring a class action without having a class representative, and that he did not have *parens patriae* authority to bring an

A number of state insurance commissions have conducted studies on the relationship between insurance scores and certain demographic characteristics, including race, gender, age, and income. These studies are discussed in another manual in this series.[222]

14.11 Credit Scores and Utility Service

Another controversial use of credit scores involves the determination of whether a consumer will receive utility service and have to pay a deposit for such services. The use of credit scores by utility companies has been challenged as undermining their common law duty to serve the public and violating the prohibition against consideration of a "collateral" matter in determining whether to provide service.[223]

As with insurance scores, there are specialty scores that have been developed for use by utility companies. For example, Equifax has established an Energy Risk Assessment Model (ERAM) to create risk assessment scores specifically for electric and natural gas utility providers.[224] Fair Isaac offers a specialty credit score for telecommunication providers.[225] Experian developed a telecommunications, energy, and cable (TEC) risk model.[226]

A more extensive discussion of the use of utility scores is included in another manual in this series.[227]

---

action on behalf of insurance consumers. Lubin v. Farmers Group, Inc., 157 S.W.3d 113 (Tex. App. 2005).

222 National Consumer Law Center, Credit Discrimination § 6.4.6.2 (4th ed. 2005 and Supp.).

223 National Consumer Law Center, Access to Utility Service § 3.7.4.4 (3d ed. 2004 and Supp.).

224 Petition of Columbia Gas of Pennsylvania, Inc. & PPL Electric Utilities Corporation for Limited Waiver of 52 Pa. Code § 56.32(2), Penn. P.S.C. Dockets P-00001807 and P-00001808, March 8, 2001 (relating to residential deposits).

225 Fair Isaac, Scoring—Predictive Modeling—Telecom Scores, *available at* www.fairisaac.com/Fairisaac/Solutions/Product+Index/Telecom+Models.

226 *See* www.experian.com/products/tec_risk_model.html.

227 National Consumer Law Center, Access to Utility Service § 3.7.4 (3d ed. 2004 and Supp.).

Chapter 15 Credit Repair Legislation

15.1 General

15.1.1 Nature of Credit Repair Organizations

Financially-troubled consumers are likely to be attracted to credit repair organizations. Credit repair organizations solicit consumers who believe they have bad consumer reports, often using advertising promising to eliminate bad credit histories. Many, perhaps most, credit repair organizations are fraudulent, either promising help that they cannot deliver or using illegal methods to disguise a consumer's negative credit history.[1] Consumers with troubled finances are generally better off using the procedures and tactics discussed in the preceding chapters of this manual than using (and paying for) the services of a credit repair organization.

These organizations commonly call themselves "credit repair" or "credit service" agencies, "credit clinics," or similar titles. They often promise consumers that for a fee,[2] negative items will be eliminated from a credit history. Sometimes, they encourage consumers to establish a new credit identity by using an Employer Identification Number instead of their Social Security number, a seemingly fraudulent and possibly criminal solution to a bad situation. Others assist consumers in disputing items in their credit histories. Some flood the consumer reporting agencies (CRAs) with dispute letters in hopes that the CRAs will be unable to respond in a timely manner and will delete negative information at least temporarily.

Other credit repair organizations do not promise to make the actual improvements to the consumer report, but sell credit repair books, CD-Roms, or other materials, often accompanied by a promise to provide personal credit repair advice to the consumer. There have been reports of creditors selling these services, or even requiring consumers to buy them, as a condition of an extension of credit.

Frequently, these organizations do nothing consumers cannot do for themselves free of charge. Indeed, consumers may be better positioned to deal with their credit histories by themselves. The FCRA allows CRAs and creditors to disregard disputes of items on consumer reports that are generated by credit repair organizations.[3] As a result, even a consumer bent upon filing groundless disputes will have far greater success by drafting individualized letters to CRAs and will save paying the repair organization's fee.

Anyone litigating against a credit repair organization should anticipate having to untangle a web of related corporations.[4] Credit repair organizations may seek to present themselves as exempt non-profit organizations or as agents for such organizations.[5]

A portion of the blame for the ready market for credit repair organizations lies with the consumer reporting industry. The frequency and regularity with which inaccurate information is maintained and reported is appalling,[6] and consumers are rightfully outraged when they suffer the consequences of the incompetence of the consumer reporting system. In despair because of delays, failure to make corrections, and the repeated reintroduction of past errors, consumers understandably look for someone to help. But the barrage of additional, often illegitimate dispute letters that credit repair organizations send to CRAs on behalf of consumers can get the consumer into greater difficulty and often compounds a CRA's problem of sorting accurate from inaccurate information.

15.1.2 Overview of Credit Repair Laws

To address common abuses, the federal Credit Repair Organization Act (CROA) was adopted in 1996.[7] CROA's broad definitions and prohibitions make it applicable not just to traditional credit repair organizations, but also to a wide

---

1 For a discussion of credit repair organizations, see Nehf, *Legislative Framework for Reducing Fraud in the Credit Repair Industry*, 70 N C.L. Rev. 781 (1992).
2 In addition to fees, consumers may be directed to use 900-number telephone numbers where charges accrue by the minute. The use of such numbers may be governed by 47 U.S.C. § 228, 15 U.S.C. § 5711, 47 C.F.R. Part 64, and 16 C.F.R. Part 308.
3 15 U.S.C. § 1681i(a)(3) (CRAs), 1861s-2(a)(8)(F) (creditors); FTC Official Staff Commentary § 611 item 11, *reprinted at* Appx. C, *infra*. See Ch. 4, *supra*.
4 *See, e.g.*, Asmar v. Benchmark Literacy Group, Inc., 2005 WL 2562965 (E.D. Mich. Oct. 11, 2005).
5 *See id.*; § 15.2.2.3.2, *infra*.
6 *See* § 1.2, *supra*.
7 15 U.S.C. § 1679, passed by Congress as part of the Omnibus Consolidated Appropriations Act of 1996, Pub. L. No. 104-208, § 2451, 110 Stat. 3009 (Sept. 30, 1996). *See* § 15.2, *infra*.

§ 15.1.3   *Fair Credit Reporting*

range of other entities.[8] It offers a private cause of action with powerful remedies. In mid-2006, Congress was considering amendments that would significantly weaken the Act, but it was not yet clear whether they would be adopted.

Many states also have their own statutes specifically regulating practices of credit repair businesses.[9] These state statutes are worth separate consideration because they do not necessarily mirror the federal law. For example, while the federal act generally applies only to those who assist consumers in improving credit records, state law may also apply to entities that help consumers obtain financing.

State and federal telemarketing laws are also important in the credit repair context. The Federal Trade Commission's telemarketing rule imposes specific restrictions on credit repair organizations that market their services by telephone.[10] A second federal statute, the Telephone Consumer Protection Act, does not have any specific provisions regarding credit repair services, but restricts calling times, unsolicited faxes, calls to consumers who have registered on the nationwide do-not-call list, and other abusive methods of contacting consumers.[11] In addition, state telemarketing laws restrict deceptive practices in general and some also have specific provisions regulating credit repair services.[12] These sources of law are discussed in the following sections.

15.1.3 The Surprising Reach of Credit Repair Laws

A signal characteristic of state and federal credit repair laws is their surprising reach. The federal statute includes a broad definition of "credit repair organization" that may apply to credit counseling agencies, debt collectors, retail sellers, and other entities that are not traditional credit repair organizations.[13] Moreover, many of the federal statute's prohibitions apply to any person, not just credit repair organizations.[14]

State credit repair laws are often even broader than the federal statute, applying not just to credit repair organizations but also to entities that obtain extensions of credit for consumers. These laws have been applied to credit card finders, loan brokers, and foreclosure rescue scam operators, and appear to be applicable to many other types of fringe lenders as well.[15]

---

8   *See* §§ 15.2.2, 15.2.7, *infra*.
9   *See* § 15.3, *infra*. *See also* Appx. H, *infra*.
10 *See* § 15.4.1, *infra*.
11 *See* § 15.4.2, *infra*.
12 *See* § 15.4.3, *infra*.
13 *See* § 15.2.2.2.1, *infra*.
14 *See* §§ 15.2.7, 15.2.2.1, *infra*.
15 *See* § 15.3.2, *infra*.

15.2 Federal Credit Repair Organizations Act

15.2.1 Introduction

To address the abuses associated with credit repair organizations, Congress passed the Credit Repair Organizations Act (CROA)[16] in 1996, imposing stringent limitations on activities of credit repair organizations. CROA, Title IV of the Federal Consumer Credit Protection Act, was passed by Congress as part of the 1996 Omnibus Appropriations Act, and became effective April 1, 1997.[17] There is minimal legislative history, mostly relating to prior versions of the bill.[18]

The legislation passed with little opposition, and with the support of the consumer reporting industry. In fact, the initiative for the legislation, at the federal and at the state level, did not come from consumers. Consumer reporting companies felt the burden of large numbers of inquiries, complaints, and petitions from repair groups who sometimes mass-produced such correspondence to consumer reporting agencies (CRAs). Swamped by what they perceived as harassing and irresponsible requests, CRAs sometimes refused to respond at all, and pushed legislation designed to curtail not just the abuses but the viability of credit repair organizations. Consumer advocates did not object.

Congress formally found that "[c]onsumers have a vital interest in establishing and maintaining their creditworthiness and credit standing in order to obtain and use credit"[19] and that certain advertising and business practices of some credit repair organizations "have worked a financial hardship upon consumers, particularly those of limited economic means and who are inexperienced in credit matters."[20] The purpose of CROA is to provide consumers "with the information necessary to make an informed decision regarding the purchase of [credit repair] services" and "to protect the public from unfair or deceptive advertising and business practices by credit repair organizations."[21]

---

16 15 U.S.C. §§ 1679–1679j. Pub. L. No. 104-208, 110 Stat. 3009 (Sept. 30, 1996), *reprinted at* Appx. F, *infra*.
17 Section 413 of the Act states that contracts entered into by a credit repair organization prior to that date are exempt. *See* 15 U.S.C. § 1679 and accompanying note. *See also* Shulman v. CRS Fin. Servs., Inc., 2003 WL 22400211 (N.D. Ill. Oct. 21, 2003) (refusing to apply CROA to contract entered into before effective date); Appx. F, *infra*.
18 H.R. Rep. 486, 103d Cong., 2d Sess. (Apr. 28, 1994) (relating to H.R. 1015); H.R. Rep. 692, 102d Cong. (July 23, 1992) (relating to H.R. 3596); S. Rep. 209, 103d Cong., 2d Sess. (Dec. 9, 1993) (relating to S. 783).
19 15 U.S.C. § 1679(a)(1).
20 15 U.S.C. § 1679(a)(2). This language is cited in *In re* National Credit Mgmt. Group, L.L.C., 21 F. Supp. 2d 424 (D.N.J. 1998) and in Parker v. 1-800 Bar None, 2002 WL 215530 (N.D. Ill. Feb. 12, 2002).
21 15 U.S.C. § 1679(b).

Some of CROA's prohibitions apply only to "credit repair organizations," while others apply to any person. CROA defines "credit repair organization" broadly as any person who, in return for money or other valuable consideration, provides services to improve a consumer's credit record. Only non-profit organizations and a few others are excepted.[22] A credit repair organization must make key disclosures prior to entering into a contract with a consumer.[23] The contract itself must contain certain stringent terms, including a three-day right to cancel.[24] Credit repair organizations must not accept payment before services are fully performed.[25] The Act also prohibits any person—not just any credit repair organization—from engaging in certain deceptive acts.[26] Violations may lead to civil liability, including actual and punitive damages and reasonable attorney fees.[27]

CROA is entitled to a liberal construction in favor of consumers.[28] Credit repair laws do not impinge on First Amendment rights.[29] CROA rights are non-waivable, and any waiver is void.[30]

15.2.2 Scope

15.2.2.1 Some CROA Restrictions Apply to "Credit Repair Organizations" While Others Apply to Any Person

A number of CROA's provisions—disclosures, the three-day right to cancel, requirements for contracts, and the prohibition on advance payment—apply only to "credit repair organizations" as defined by the statute. This definition is discussed in the following subsections.

The scope of the Act goes well beyond "credit repair organizations," however. Many of the most important prohibitions of the Act apply not just to credit repair organizations but to any "person." Thus, individuals and organizations that do not meet the definition of "credit repair organization" can still be subject to liability if they violate or assist in a violation of these prohibitions.[31] The prohibitions that apply to any person are analyzed in § 15.2.7, *infra*.

---

22 *See* § 15.2.2.3, *infra*.
23 *See* § 15.2.4, *infra*.
24 *See* § 15.2.5, *infra*.
25 *See* § 15.2.6, *infra*.
26 *See* § 15.2.7, *infra*.
27 *See* § 15.2.8, *infra*.
28 Helms v. ConsumerInfo.com, Inc., 436 F. Supp. 2d 1220, 1229 (N.D. Ala. 2005); Parker v. 1-800 Bar None, 2002 WL 215530 (N.D. Ill. Feb. 12, 2002). *See also* Zimmerman v. Cambridge Credit Counseling Corp., 409 F.3d 473 (1st Cir. 2005) (CROA is a remedial statute and exceptions should be read narrowly).
29 *In re* National Credit Mgmt. Group, L.L.C., 21 F. Supp. 2d 424 (D.N.J. 1998).
30 15 U.S.C. § 1679f. *See* Polacsek v. Debticated Consumer Counseling, Inc., 413 F. Supp. 2d 539, 549 n.5 (D. Md. 2005).
31 Helms v. ConsumerInfo.com, Inc., 436 F. Supp. 2d 1220, 1229 (N.D. Ala. 2005) (noting that the prohibitions of § 1679b(a)

15.2.2.2 Definition of "Credit Repair Organization"

15.2.2.2.1 Broad Definition Covers Wide Array of Entities

The Credit Repair Organizations Act contains an exceptionally broad definition of the credit repair organizations that are subject to its requirements.[32] A credit repair organization means any person who performs or offers to perform any service, "in return for the payment of money or other valuable consideration," for the express or implied purpose of—

(i) improving any consumer's credit record, credit history, or credit rating; or
(ii) providing advice and assistance to any consumer with regard to any activity or service described in clause (i).[33]

The definition only applies if the organization uses an instrumentality of interstate commerce, such as mail or telephone, in these activities.[34]

Many courts have held that the definition is broad enough to cover entities beyond traditional credit repair organizations, as long as they perform or offer to perform credit repair services for a fee or other valuable consideration. Thus, courts have held that the definition may apply to a credit counseling agency that promised to improve participants' credit ratings,[35] debt collectors that offer improvement of the debtor's credit rating in return for payment on the debt,[36] and a company that generated subprime financing leads for car dealers by advertising that it could restore

---

apply to any person); Rodriguez v. Lynch Ford, Inc., 2004 WL 2958772 (N.D. Ill. Nov. 18, 2004); Lacey v. William Chrysler Plymouth Inc., 2004 U.S. Dist. LEXIS 2479 (N.D. Ill. Feb. 20, 2004); Parker v. 1-800 Bar None, 2002 WL 215530 (N.D. Ill. Feb. 12, 2002); Bigalke v. Creditrust Corp., 162 F. Supp. 2d 996, 999 (N.D. Ill. 2001); Vance v. Nat'l Benefit Ass'n, 1999 WL 731764 (N.D. Ill Aug. 30, 1999). *See also* § 15.2.7, *infra*.
32 15 U.S.C. § 1679a(3).
33 15 U.S.C. § 1679a(3)(A).
34 15 U.S.C. § 1679a(3)(A). *See* Baker v. Family Credit Counseling Corp., 2006 WL 2089153, at *7 (E.D. Pa. July 28, 2006) (use of e-mail, fax, and mail sufficient); Polacsek v. Debticated Consumer Counseling, Inc., 413 F. Supp. 2d 539, 548 (D. Md. 2005) (use of telephone, Internet, and mail sufficient).
35 Baker v. Family Credit Counseling Corp., 2006 WL 2089153 (E.D. Pa. July 28, 2006); Polacsek v. Debticated Consumer Counseling, Inc., 413 F. Supp. 2d 539 (D. Md. 2005). *But cf.* Plattner v. Edge Solutions, Inc., 422 F Supp. 2d 969 (N.D. Ill. 2006) (CROA does not apply to debt settlement organization where it stated that its program would probably worsen participants' credit ratings, but it would help them restore their credit ratings after they completed the program).
36 *See* § 15.2.2.6, *infra*.

consumers' credit.[37] Courts have also suggested that retail sellers may be credit repair organizations under certain conditions.[38] The definition includes individuals engaging in credit repair activities.[39]

Whether the organization actually performs the services it promises is irrelevant to the question whether it meets the definition of "credit repair organization."[40] Placing a disclaimer in the contract that the organization makes no claims to improve or remove any credit reference on the consumer report is ineffective if the organization has promised credit repair.[41] A successor corporation may be liable for a credit repair organization's violation if the new corporation is merely a continuation of the original one.[42]

There is no requirement that one be engaged in a business, or have multiple customers. A single instance of providing credit repair services can constitute the acts of a credit repair organization if undertaken for a fee. Simply because an organization offers some other service, such as a debt management plan to reduce a consumer's credit rates and payments, does not mean that it cannot meet the definition of "credit repair organization."[43] The definition is not confined to fraudulent agencies, but includes non-fraudulent organizations as well.[44]

15.2.2.2.2 "In return for the payment of money or other valuable consideration"

To be a credit repair organization, the organization must offer or provide its services "in return for the payment of money or other valuable consideration."[45] To meet this requirement, some courts require that the consumer pay additional consideration for the credit repair services, separate from any fee for other goods or services.[46] The fee need not be paid by the consumer, however; payment by some other party is sufficient to meet this coverage requirement.[47] The fee requirement is met if the credit repair organization offers its services for a fee or the consumer pays a fee, even if the fee is held by a payment intermediary instead of going directly to the credit repair organization.[48]

Characterizing the fee as a voluntary contribution does not avoid CROA's reach when the contribution is in fact a fee for the service provided.[49] Likewise, characterizing the credit repair services as free, but linking them to other services that require payment, is unlikely to avoid the definition as long as the credit repair services are provided "in return for" the payment.[50] Such a ploy is also likely to run afoul of state UDAP statutes, which generally prohibit deceptive use of the word "free," and will constitute a violation of the CROA prohibition at 15 U.S.C. § 1679b(a)(3) of deceptive statements regarding the credit repair organization's services.

---

37 Parker v. 1-800 Bar None, 2002 WL 215530 (N.D. Ill. Feb. 12, 2002).
38 Wojcik v. Courtesy Auto Sales, Inc., 2002 WL 31663298, at *8 (D. Neb. Nov. 25, 2002) ("A car dealership could obviously fit into the credit repair organization category" but not shown here where plaintiffs were not lured in by any credit repair advertising).
39 Baker v. Family Credit Counseling Corp., 2006 WL 2089153, at *9–10 (E.D. Pa. July 28, 2006); Polacsek v. Debticated Consumer Counseling, Inc., 413 F. Supp. 2d 539, 547 n.4 (D. Md. 2005) (individual's control of credit repair organization and participation in or acquiescence in CROA violations sufficient for liability); Limpert v. Cambridge Credit Counseling Corp., 328 F. Supp. 2d 360 (E.D.N.Y. 2004) (individuals may be credit repair organizations). But see Asmar v. Benchmark Literacy Group, Inc., 2005 WL 2562965 (E.D. Mich. Oct. 11, 2005) (corporate officers not credit repair organizations where they did not personally perform credit repair activities but only made decisions, formulated policies, and directed the companies).
40 Asmar v. Benchmark Literacy Group, Inc., 2005 WL 2562965 (E.D. Mich. Oct. 11, 2005) (for-profit entity that sells credit repair services is credit repair organization even if the actual services are performed by a non-profit affiliate and even if it shares the fee with that affiliate); Browning v. Yahoo!, Inc., 2004 WL 2496183 (N.D. Cal. Nov. 4, 2004) (denial of motion to dismiss) (company that represented that it could provide credit services can be credit repair organization even though another entity actually provided the services); Parker v. 1-800 Bar None, 2002 WL 215530 (N.D. Ill. Feb. 12, 2002) (company that provided no credit repair services itself, but just referred the consumer to another organization, is covered). See also 15 U.S.C. § 1679d(b)(1), (2)(B)(i) (requiring contract with credit repair organization to disclose payments to be made to others and timeline for services to be performed by others).
41 Polacsek v. Debticated Consumer Counseling, Inc., 413 F. Supp. 2d 539, 549 n.5 (D. Md. 2005).
42 Asmar v. Benchmark Literacy Group, Inc., 2005 WL 2562965 (E.D. Mich. Oct. 11, 2005).
43 Baker v. Family Credit Counseling Corp., 2006 WL 2089153, at *7 (E.D. Pa. July 28, 2006).
44 Helms v. ConsumerInfo.com, Inc., 436 F. Supp. 2d 1220, 1233–1234 (N.D. Ala. 2005). But cf. Baker v. Family Credit Counseling Corp., 2006 WL 2089153, at *7 (E.D. Pa. July 28, 2006) (implying that organization is credit repair organization only if it makes false representations).
45 15 U.S.C. § 1679a(3)(A).
46 Rodriguez v. Lynch Ford, Inc., 2004 WL 2958772 (N.D. Ill. Nov. 18, 2004); Wojcik v. Courtesy Auto Sales, Inc., 2002 WL 31663298 (D. Neb. Nov. 25, 2002) (must be additional fee for credit repair service); Sannes v. Jeff Wyler Chevrolet, Inc., 1999 WL 33313134, 1999 U.S. Dist. LEXIS 21748 (S.D. Ohio Mar. 31, 1999). See also Banks v. Capital Credit Alliance, Inc., 2005 WL 1563220 (N.D. Ill. June 28, 2005) (denial of motion to dismiss) (requirement of additional consideration may be met where defendants withdrew $200 fee from plaintiff's bank account in connection with offer of credit card that would allegedly improve plaintiff's credit rating). But see Bigalke v. Creditrust Corp., 162 F. Supp. 2d 996, 999 (N.D. Ill. 2001) (debt collector's demand for payment of debt sufficient). See generally § 15.3.4.2, infra (discussion of similar issue under state credit repair laws).
47 Parker v. 1-800 Bar None, 2002 WL 215530 (N.D. Ill. Feb. 12, 2002).
48 Asmar v. Benchmark Literacy Group, Inc., 2005 WL 2562965 (E.D. Mich. Oct. 11, 2005).
49 Polacsek v. Debticated Consumer Counseling, Inc., 413 F. Supp. 2d 539, 548–549 (D. Md. 2005).
50 15 U.S.C. § 1679a(3)(A).

On the other hand, if no money or other valuable consideration is paid or requested, the entity is not a credit repair organization. Thus, social workers or union shop stewards who help individuals without charge will not be credit repair organizations, even if they are acting within the scope of their employment.

15.2.2.2.3 Types of advertisements and services that meet the definition

An entity is a credit repair organization even if its services are offered for the implied rather than the express purpose of credit repair.[51] Promising that accepting an offered credit card will improve the consumer's credit rating,[52] or that debt consolidation plans will "help repair bad credit negatives on your credit report"[53] may be sufficient to establish coverage. Using terms such as "establish," "rebuild," "raise," and "improve" to describe the effect of the organization's services on a consumer's credit rating is sufficient, even if some of these representations refer to free products or services.[54]

A credit counseling agency that stated that its services would "improve credit" and "keep your credit protected and clean" was offering credit repair services, as was its for-profit affiliate that communicated with creditors and received, deposited, and disbursed consumers' payments.[55] Advertising "personalized tips and analysis" on how consumers can improve their credit scores and information on factors that positively and negatively affect credit standing is sufficient.[56] But one court held that an organization that offered to negotiate and settle consumers' debts was not a credit repair organization where its overall purpose was not to improve consumers' credit scores and in fact its materials warned consumers that their credit scores might worsen.[57]

Simply advertising or claiming to provide credit repair services is sufficient for coverage.[58] In determining whether an entity is a credit repair organization, the issue is the nature of the entity's business, not whether the particular consumer was deceived. Accordingly, the court need not limit itself to the advertisements the particular plaintiff saw, but may look to the entire nature of the entity's business and the representations it makes.[59] An organization that merely advises or assists a consumer in credit repair is a credit repair organization even if all actual credit repair steps are undertaken by the consumer.[60]

15.2.2.2.4 Other Definitions

Other definitions in the Act may be important from time to time in determining whether the Act applies to a given circumstance. For the most part, these definitions track those in other titles of the Consumer Credit Protection Act. A consumer is defined as an individual.[61] Credit is the right granted by a creditor to defer payment of a debt.[62] The definition of "creditor" is discussed in § 15.2.2.3.3, *infra*.

The Act defines "consumer credit transaction" as one in which credit is offered or extended for personal, family or household purposes,[63] but, oddly, never uses this term after having defined it. As a result, nothing in the Act prevents it from applying to organizations that offer to repair an individual's business credit rating.

15.2.2.3 Exceptions to Definition of "Credit Repair Organization"

15.2.2.3.1 Introduction

The sweeping definition of "credit repair organization" has three exceptions. It does not include: non-profit organizations that are exempt from taxation under section 501(c)(3) of the Internal Revenue Code; creditors who are restructuring consumers' debts; and depository institutions,

---

51 15 U.S.C. § 1679a(3)(A) ("for the express or implied purpose"). *See* Helms v. ConsumerInfo.com, Inc., 436 F. Supp. 2d 1220, 1232 (N.D. Ala. 2005).
52 Banks v. Capital Credit Alliance, Inc., 2005 WL 1563220 (N.D. Ill. June 28, 2005).
53 Baker v. Family Credit Counseling Corp., 2006 WL 2089153, at *7 (E.D. Pa. July 28, 2006).
54 Helms v. ConsumerInfo.com, Inc., 436 F. Supp. 2d 1220, 1232 (N.D. Ala. 2005).
55 Polacsek v. Debticated Consumer Counseling, Inc., 413 F. Supp. 2d 539, 548 (D. Md. 2005).
56 Browning v. Yahoo!, Inc., 2004 WL 2496183 (N.D. Cal. Nov. 4, 2004) (denial of motion to dismiss). *See also* Helms v. ConsumerInfo.com, Inc., 436 F. Supp. 2d 1220, 1232 (N.D. Ala. 2005) (offering "tips" to help customers improve credit ratings falls squarely within definition).
57 Plattner v. Edge Solutions, Inc., 422 F. Supp. 2d 969 (N.D. Ill. 2006).
58 Asmar v. Benchmark Literacy Group, Inc., 2005 WL 2562965 (E.D. Mich. Oct. 11, 2005); Parker v. 1-800 Bar None, 2002 WL 215530 (N.D. Ill. Feb. 12, 2002); Sannes v. Jeff Wyler Chevrolet, Inc., 1999 WL 33313134, 1999 U.S. Dist. LEXIS 21748

(S.D. Ohio Mar. 31, 1999); *In re* National Credit Mgmt. Group, L.L.C., 21 F. Supp. 2d 424, 457 (D.N.J. 1998) (promising personal credit analysis and information to help consumers establish or re-establish their credit is sufficient). *See also* Limpert v. Cambridge Credit Counseling Corp., 328 F. Supp. 2d 360 (E.D.N.Y. 2004) (representing the ability to perform credit repair services may be sufficient for coverage); Browning v. Yahoo!, Inc., 2004 WL 2496183 (N.D. Cal. Nov. 4, 2004) (denial of motion to dismiss) (company that represented that it could provide credit services can be credit repair organization even though another entity actually provided the services).
59 Helms v. ConsumerInfo.com, Inc., 436 F. Supp. 2d 1220, 1231 n.13 (N.D. Ala. 2005).
60 15 U.S.C. § 1679a(3)(A)(ii).
61 15 U.S.C. § 1679a(1).
62 15 U.S.C. § 1679a(4) (cross-referencing 15 U.S.C. § 1602(e), which defines credit as "the right granted by a creditor to a debtor to defer payment of debt or to incur debt and defer its payment).
63 15 U.S.C. § 1679a(2).

credit unions, and their subsidiaries or affiliates.[64] Since the Act is remedial, these exceptions should be narrowly construed.[65]

An entity that falls within one of these exceptions is not exempt from all requirements of the Act. Rather, it is only exempt from those requirements—the disclosures, right to cancel, contract format requirements, restrictions on contract terms, and prohibition of advance payment[66]—that apply exclusively to "credit repair organizations." The Act's other prohibitions apply to any person or organization regardless of whether it is a "credit repair organization."[67]

15.2.2.3.2 Non-Profit Organizations

The first exception is for non-profit organizations that are exempt from taxation under section 501(c)(3).[68] As a result, the provisions of the Act that apply only to credit repair organizations do not apply to non-profit legal services programs or to non-profit credit counseling organizations, notably those which intend to educate and help consumers manage their debt. To be exempt, the organization must not only have an IRS determination that it qualifies under section 501(c)(3), but must in fact be operating as a non-profit organization.[69]

A for-profit entity that sells credit repair services is a credit repair organization even if the actual services are performed by a non-profit affiliate and even if it shares the fee with that affiliate.[70] Likewise, where an ostensibly non-profit entity offers credit repair services, but the actual work is performed by a related for-profit company, both may be credit repair organizations.[71]

Some credit repair organizations have abused this exception by incorporating as non-profits while funneling substantial profits to officers and related for-profit organizations. In 2004, the Internal Revenue Service began cracking down on spurious non-profits, issuing a series of letters denying applications for tax-exempt status by credit counseling organizations.[72] IRS concluded that the applicants were seeking tax-exempt status in order to perform credit repair services while evading regulation, and that they were operating as the intake arms of for-profit providers. In 2006, Congress enacted special additional requirements for credit counseling organizations seeking tax-exempt status.[73] These and other issues regarding credit counseling are discussed in detail in another NCLC manual.[74]

If a credit repair organization claims to be a non-profit but appears to be operating as a for-profit entity, it may be worthwhile to review its annual tax return forms (Form 990). IRS regulations require section 501(c)(3) organizations to post their tax return forms on the Internet, or provide copies of their three most recent annual returns within thirty days of a written request at no charge other than a reasonable fee to cover photocopying and mailing.[75]

15.2.2.3.3 Creditors who are restructuring a consumer's debt

CROA's definition of "credit repair organization" also excludes any creditor to the extent it is restructuring a consumer's debt to it.[76] This exception excludes some creditors who, in the process of collecting their own debts, promise consumers that payment or restructuring will improve their credit rating. The exception is narrower than it appears, however.

The exception applies only to entities that meet the Truth in Lending Act's definition of "creditor":

> a person who both (1) regularly extends, whether in connection with loans, sales of property or services, or otherwise, consumer credit which is payable by agreement in more than four installments or for which the payment of a finance charge is or may be required, and (2) is the person to whom the debt arising from the consumer credit transaction is initially payable on the face of the evidence of indebtedness or, if there is no such evidence of indebtedness, by agreement.[77]

The most significant part of this definition is that an entity is a "creditor" only if the obligation is initially payable to it. As a result, a company that purchases or is assigned a debt from the entity to which it was originally owed will not fall into this exception even if it is involved in attempting to restructure the debt. Thus, if such a company represents to the consumer that it will improve the consumer's credit

---

64 15 U.S.C. § 1679a(3)(B).
65 Zimmerman v. Cambridge Credit Counseling Corp., 409 F.3d 473 (1st Cir. 2005).
66 15 U.S.C. §§ 1679b(b), 1679c, 1679d, 1679e.
67 See § 15.2.7, infra.
68 15 U.S.C. § 1679a(3)(B)(i). But see Fed. Trade Comm'n v. Gill, 265 F.3d 944 (9th Cir. 2001) (defendants' conversion of credit repair business to a purportedly non-profit corporation was a means of evading preliminary injunction and justifies harsher permanent injunction).
69 Zimmerman v. Cambridge Credit Counseling Corp., 409 F.3d 473 (1st Cir. 2005); Baker v. Family Credit Counseling Corp., 2006 WL 2089153, at *8 (E.D. Pa. July 28, 2006) (allowing CROA claims to proceed against § 501(c)(3) organizations that allegedly funneled money to related for-profit corporations); Polacsek v. Debticated Consumer Counseling, Inc., 413 F. Supp. 2d 539, 550 (D. Md. 2005).
70 Asmar v. Benchmark Literacy Group, Inc., 2005 WL 2562965 (E.D. Mich. Oct. 11, 2005).
71 Polacsek v. Debticated Consumer Counseling, Inc., 413 F. Supp. 2d 539 (D. Md. 2005).
72 Internal Revenue Service letter, Clearinghouse No. 55607 (Oct. 21, 2004); Internal Revenue Service letter, Clearinghouse No. 55608 (Oct. 19, 2004).
73 Pub. Law No. 109-280, § 1220, 120 Stat. 780 (Aug. 17, 2006).
74 National Consumer Law Center, Unfair and Deceptive Acts and Practices § 5.1.2.3 (6th ed. 2004 and Supp.).
75 26 C.F.R. §§ 301.6104(d)-1, 301.6104(d)-2.
76 15 U.S.C. § 1679a(3)(B)(ii).
77 15 U.S.C. § 1602(f).

rating if the consumer pays the debt, it may be a credit repair organization as defined by the Act.⁷⁸

Even an originating creditor may find that it is a credit repair organization if it falls outside the Truth in Lending definition of "creditor" because it does not extend credit "regularly" or because the debt is not payable in more than four installments or subject to a finance charge. Further, a creditor that does not offer to restructure the debt cannot take advantage of this exception.

Even if a creditor does not fall within this exception, there still may be issues about whether it meets the general definition of "credit repair organization." In particular, the consumer will have to show that the creditor is offering its credit repair services in return for a fee or other valuable consideration.⁷⁹

The applicability of CROA to creditors who promise improvement of a consumer's credit rating while collecting their own debts is particularly significant since the Fair Debt Collection Practices Act does not generally cover creditors. While creditors who use deceptive tactics in collecting their own debts can be sued under UDAP statutes or special debt collection laws in most states, a CROA claim has a number of advantages. It offers attorney fees to successful consumers, damages in the amount of all payments made regardless of any actual injury, punitive damages, probably federal jurisdiction, and explicit provisions for class actions.

In addition to the exception for creditors that are restructuring their debts, depository institutions, credit unions, and their subsidiaries and affiliates are completely excluded from the definition of "credit repair organization."⁸⁰ This exception is discussed in the next subsection.

15.2.2.3.4 Depository institutions and credit unions

The final exception from the definition of "credit repair organization" is for depository institutions, credit unions, and their subsidiaries or affiliates.⁸¹ There is no exception for other financial institutions, lenders, and creditors, however, or for brokers, so they may be credit repair organizations if they offer or sell credit repair services along with the extension of credit.⁸² Further, even a depository institution, credit union, or subsidiary or affiliate may be liable under the Act if it violates one of the substantive prohibitions that is applicable to any "person."⁸³

---

78 *See* Bigalke v. Creditrust Corp., 162 F. Supp. 2d 996 (N.D. Ill. 2001). *See generally* § 15.2.2.6, *infra*.
79 *See* § 15.2.2.2.2, *supra*.
80 15 U.S.C. § 1679a(3)(B)(iii). *See* § 15.2.2.3.4, *infra*.
81 15 U.S.C. § 1679a(3)(B)(iii).
82 *But cf.* § 15.2.2.4, *infra* (discussion of coverage of ancillary services).
83 *See* Vance v. Nat'l Benefit Ass'n, 1999 WL 731764 (N.D. Ill. Aug. 30, 1999) (bank may be liable for violation of § 1679b(a) even though it is exempt from definition of "credit repair organization"); § 15.2.2.7, *infra*.

15.2.2.4 Credit Repair Services That Are Ancillary to Another Activity

Some courts have held that credit repair services that are ancillary to another activity do not make an organization a credit repair organization as defined by the Act. In a case involving an automobile dealer, one of the reasons the court found the Act not to apply was that the credit repair services were merely ancillary to the dealer's main business.⁸⁴ Another decision held that a debt collector was not a credit repair organization even though its letters referred to the possibility that payment would improve the debtor's credit rating, because the Act was aimed at companies in the business of credit repair, not debt collectors.⁸⁵ In a third decision, the court held that an organization that offered to negotiate and settle consumers' debts was not a credit repair organization because its "overall purpose" was not improving the consumers' credit scores.⁸⁶ The credit repair services the organization offered were merely intended to repair the damage to consumers' credit scores caused by participating in the debt settlement program.

The flaw in these cases is the lack of any statutory language that might support such an exception. If an entity is offering or providing services, for a fee, for the express or implied purpose of improving a consumer's credit rating, it meets the statutory definition of "credit repair organization" regardless of whether those activities are ancillary to its primary business activities. CROA's language does suggest, however, that offering or providing services that have merely an ancillary *effect* on a consumer's credit rating may not make an entity a credit repair organization, because the services would not be offered for the express or implied purpose of improving the consumer's credit rating.⁸⁷ Thus, an attorney who files bankruptcy or litigates a case for a client would not be a credit repair organization even though those services might have the ancillary effect of improving the consumer's credit rating. Likewise, the services of financial advisors or college financial aid counselors might have an effect on their clients' credit ratings, but if they did

---

84 *See* Sannes v. Jeff Wyler Chevrolet, Inc., 1999 WL 33313134, 1999 U.S. Dist. LEXIS 21748 (S.D. Ohio Mar. 31, 1999) (credit repair services advertised by automobile dealer were ancillary to its main business so did not make it a credit repair organization).
85 White v. Fin. Credit Corp., 2001 WL 1665386 (N.D. Ill. Dec. 27, 2001).
86 Plattner v. Edge Solutions, Inc., 422 F Supp. 2d 969 (N.D. Ill. 2006). *See also* Polacsek v. Debticated Consumer Counseling, Inc., 413 F. Supp. 2d 539, 546 (D. Md. 2005) (arguably an organization is exempt if its credit repair activities are ancillary and de minimis).
87 15 U.S.C. § 1679a(3)(A). *See* Plattner v. Edge Solutions, Inc., 422 F Supp. 2d 969, 975 (N.D. Ill. 2006) (advice to consumers about developing creditworthy behavior and paying their debts does not make organization a credit repair organization even though an improved credit rating may be a collateral consequence; assistance in rehabilitating credit after completion of company's debt settlement service is also ancillary).

not advertise or offer services for that purpose they would not be credit repair organizations.

15.2.2.5 Attorneys

It is clear that the Act applies to lawyers who offer or provide credit repair activities as defined by the Act. An earlier version of the bill exempted attorneys,[88] but this exemption did not get into the final bill. The FTC's suit against an attorney who allowed a credit repair operative to work out of his office was upheld by the Ninth Circuit.[89]

Despite the Act's broad definitions, lawyers who are performing legitimate services such as litigating FCRA violations or advising or representing clients in bankruptcy matters should not fall within the definition of "credit repair organization."[90] CROA defines as credit repair organizations those who perform or offer to perform services for the purpose of "improving" a person's credit record.[91] By contrast, the purpose of FCRA litigation is to recover the relief—primarily damages—authorized by the FCRA.

The fact that CROA was adopted as part of the same statute that expanded the FCRA's private cause of action is further evidence that Congress did not intend FCRA litigation to be restricted by CROA. The expanded FCRA private cause of action, which includes a fee-shifting provision, is clearly intended to encourage "private attorney general" enforcement of the FCRA, which would be inconsistent with treating attorneys who handle FCRA cases as credit repair organizations. Even pre-litigation steps such as dispute letters should not bring attorneys within the definition of "credit repair organization," but should be considered part of the FCRA litigation.

Another distinction is that, by preparing dispute letters as a preliminary step before FCRA litigation, attorneys are seeking correction of the consumer's credit record rather than improvement. Correction is different from improvement because correction is only possible when the consumer report is inaccurate, while improvement (at least in the form practiced by credit repair organizations that Congress had in mind when adopting CROA) involves obscuring or deleting negative credit history regardless of its accuracy.

Likewise, the purpose of bankruptcy litigation is to discharge debts. Whether the bankruptcy results in an improvement, a deterioration, or no change in the debtor's credit rating depends on the circumstances and is entirely tangential to the purpose of the representation.

In order to make it crystal clear that they are not credit repair organizations, some attorneys who handle FCRA matters draft initial dispute letters, or help their clients to do so, without charge. Since the definition of "credit repair organization" only applies to persons who perform credit repair services for a fee, attorneys who prepare dispute letters free of charge are not credit repair organizations. Many practitioners report that an FCRA practice can still be financially viable if this service is provided free of charge, as it generates good will and winnows out the cases that can be resolved without litigation.

For attorneys who charge a fee for drafting a dispute letter, the retainer should be drafted so that it does not promise to improve any consumer's credit rating, but simply agrees to prepare a dispute letter. The attorney should, of course, avoid making any oral representations that are inconsistent with the retainer. As a precaution, some attorneys who charge fees for dispute letters comply with the requirements of CROA that are applicable to credit repair organizations: disclosures; contract format and terms; a right to cancel; and a prohibition of advance payment of fees. The prohibition on advance payment of fees means that the client should be billed for services only after they are performed, without any up-front retainer.

15.2.2.6 Debt Collectors

Several courts have held that debt collectors may be credit repair organizations if they promise improvement of the debtor's credit record in return for payment of the debt. In *Bigalke v. Creditrust Corp.*,[92] a company that had purchased a delinquent debt sent the debtor a letter falsely representing that if the debtor settled the debt, the company would "completely remove the entire outstanding balance from your credit report." The court held that this letter constituted the use of an instrumentality of interstate commerce to offer to provide the debtor a service which purported to improve the consumer's credit record. As for the requirement that the service be offered "in return for the payment of money or other valuable consideration,"[93] the court considered this criterion satisfied by the demand for payment of the debt. The court noted that the original creditor might fall within the exception for workouts,[94] but this exception was not available to an entity that had purchased the debt.

---

88 H.R. Rep. 486, 103d Cong., 2d Sess., tit. II, § 201 (adding Tit. IV § 403(3)(B)(ii) to the Consumer Credit Protection Act).

89 Fed. Trade Comm'n v. Gill, 265 F.3d 944 (9th Cir. 2001) (applying CROA to attorney who allowed credit repair operative to work out of his office). *See also* Iosello v. Lexington Law Firm, 2003 WL 21920237 (N.D. Ill. Aug. 7, 2003) (attorneys who act in the manner of a credit repair organization are covered); State of Tennessee v. Lexington Law Firms, 1997-1 Trade Cases (CCH) 71,820, 1997 WL 367409, 1997 U.S. Dist. LEXIS 7403 (M.D. Tenn. May 14, 1997) (defendant law firm, seeking to establish an exemption from the FTC Telemarketing Rule, claimed to be governed by the Credit Repair Organizations Act).

90 *See* Consumer Justice Ctr. v. Trans Union L.L.C., 2004 WL 885781 (Minn. Ct. App. Apr. 27, 2004) (unpublished) (reversing summary judgment that consumer law firm was credit repair organization).

91 15 U.S.C. § 1679a(3)(A).

92 162 F. Supp. 2d 996 (N.D. Ill. 2001).

93 15 U.S.C. § 1679a(3)(A).

94 15 U.S.C. § 1679a(3)(B)(ii). *See* § 15.2.2.3.3, *supra*.

Debt collectors who have not purchased a debt should also be considered credit repair organizations as defined by the Act when offering improvement of the debtor's credit rating in return for a payment on the debt.[95] Debt collectors may try to take advantage of the exception for creditors who arrange workouts by arguing that the debt collector is merely acting as an agent of the original creditor to try to restructure the debt. In responding to such a claim, the consumer's attorney should seek discovery of the agreement between the creditor and the debt collector to see if the debt collector really is given the authority of an agent to restructure the debt on behalf of the creditor. Most debt collectors merely seek repayment, rather than restructuring the debt. The attorney should also check whether the current holder of the debt is itself an assignee of the original creditor.

CROA offers distinct advantages over the Fair Debt Collection Practices Act as a basis for suit against debt collectors. It allows punitive damages without a cap in either an individual action or a class action. It also allows minimum damages in the amount of all payments made to the defendant, without regard to actual damages.[96] Significantly, an entity that is excluded from the FDCPA because it acquired the debt before it went into default can still meet the CROA definition of "credit repair organization." For creditors collecting their own debts, however, an additional question is whether it falls into the exception, discussed in § 15.2.2.3.3, *supra*, for creditors who are restructuring a consumer's debt.

15.2.2.7 Sellers Who Advertise Credit Repair

Another potential application of the Act is to sellers who advertise credit repair as part of the sales pitch for their product. For example, one car dealer advertised: "Have you wrecked your credit? . . . Reestablish your credit through one of the largest banks in Ohio!"[97] Such ads are surprisingly common among low-end automobile dealers.

These dealers meet the requirement of using an instrumentality of interstate commerce if they advertise in a regionally-distributed newspaper[98] or in the telephone book. The question is whether they can be said to charge or accept money in return for the credit repair service. One court found no coverage where a dealer did not charge a separate fee for arranging for financing, but charged the same purchase price for cash and credit customers.[99] Courts have tended to take this same position when interpreting similar language in state credit repair statutes.[100]

If it is necessary to show that a separate charge was imposed for arranging the credit, discovery may show that the creditor kicked back a portion of the interest rate to the dealer. Since this "yield spread premium" diverts a portion of the consumer's payment back to the dealer, it should be considered a payment by the consumer for the credit improvement service, thus establishing coverage. Even if the court declines to trace the payment back to the consumer, the transaction should still be covered. The Credit Repair Organizations Act merely requires that the services be provided in return for payment, not that the payment come from the consumer.[101]

Dealers may also argue that the Act should not apply because their credit repair services are merely ancillary to their main business of selling cars.[102] This argument should carry little weight where the dealer is advertising credit repair services, thus affirmatively entering the marketplace that Congress sought to regulate. One court, though, found that advertising credit repair services was not enough where the advertisements were placed only in the automotive section of a newspaper's classified ads, not in the credit repair section.[103] This decision should be entitled to little weight as it reads an exemption into the statute beyond those that Congress created. But some dealers actually advertise

---

95 *See* Nielsen v. United Creditors Alliance Corp., 1999 WL 674740, 1999 U.S. Dist. LEXIS 13267 (N.D. Ill. Aug. 18, 1999) (denying motion to dismiss claim that debt collector was covered by CROA). *But see* Oslan v. Collection Bureau, 206 F.R.D. 109 (E.D. Pa. 2001) (debt collector is covered only if receives or solicits payment beyond repayment of debt); White v. Fin. Credit Corp., 2001 WL 1665386 (N.D. Ill. Dec. 27, 2001) (debt collector's reference to improving consumer report did not make it a credit repair organization).
96 15 U.S.C. § 1679g.
97 Sannes v. Jeff Wyler Chevrolet, Inc., 1999 WL 33313134, 1999 U.S. Dist. LEXIS 21748 (S.D. Ohio Mar. 31, 1999). *See also* Rodriguez v. Lynch Ford, Inc., 2004 WL 2958772 (N.D. Ill. Nov. 18, 2004). *But cf.* Wojcik v. Courtesy Auto Sales, Inc., 2002 WL 31663298 (D. Neb. Nov. 25, 2002) (automobile dealer not credit repair organization where plaintiffs were not lured in by any credit repair advertising).

98 Sannes v. Jeff Wyler Chevrolet, Inc., 1999 WL 33313134, 1999 U.S. Dist. LEXIS 21748 (S.D. Ohio Mar. 31, 1999).
99 Sannes v. Jeff Wyler Chevrolet, Inc., 1999 WL 33313134, 1999 U.S. Dist. LEXIS 21748 (S.D. Ohio Mar. 31, 1999). *Accord* Rodriguez v. Lynch Ford, Inc., 2004 WL 2958772 (N.D. Ill. Nov. 18, 2004). *See also* Wojcik v. Courtesy Auto Sales, Inc., 2002 WL 31663298 (D. Neb. Nov. 25, 2002) (must be additional fee for credit repair service).
100 *See* § 15.3.4.2, *infra*.
101 Parker v. 1-800 Bar None, 2002 WL 215530 (N.D. Ill. Feb. 12, 2002).
102 *See* Sannes v. Jeff Wyler Chevrolet, Inc., 1999 WL 33313134, 1999 U.S. Dist. LEXIS 21748 (S.D. Ohio Mar. 31, 1999) (credit repair services advertised by automobile dealer were ancillary to its main business so did not make it a credit repair organization). *See also* White v. Fin. Credit Corp., 2001 WL 1665386 (N.D. Ill. Dec. 27, 2001) (CROA is aimed at companies in the businesses of credit repair, not debt collectors even if they refer to the possibility that payment will improve credit rating). *But cf.* Wojcik v. Courtesy Auto Sales, Inc., 2002 WL 31663298, at *8 (D. Neb. Nov. 25, 2002) (noting that a dealership "could obviously fit into the credit repair organization category" but finding this dealership not covered for other reasons). *See generally* § 15.2.2.4, *supra*.
103 Sannes v. Jeff Wyler Chevrolet, Inc., 1999 WL 33313134, 1999 U.S. Dist. LEXIS 21748 (S.D. Ohio Mar. 31, 1999).

under "credit repair" so could be covered even under this decision's rationale. Further, the proposition that selling automobiles is the main business of a car dealership should also not be accepted at face value. Many dealers make a surprising percentage of their profit through financing cars, which offers the possibility of many add-ons and kickbacks.

15.2.3 Credit Repair Organizations Must Make Specific Disclosures

A credit repair organization must provide a form disclosure to the consumer prior to executing any agreement with the consumer.[104] The agreement or contract itself must disclose the credit repair organization's name and address, the payment terms, the services to be provided, and the consumer's three-day right to cancel. The form disclosure is described here; the requirements for the contract are discussed in the next subsection.

The statute sets out specific language which must be provided to the consumer before the consumer signs any contract.[105] The disclosure must be written and on a separate sheet of paper.[106] No requirement about type face is stated, but a reasonable disclosure surely should not be in fine print or otherwise obscured by its presentation to the consumer. The credit repair organization must retain a copy of the disclosure statement signed by the consumer.[107]

The gist of the disclosure, titled "Consumer Credit File Rights Under State and Federal Law," informs the consumer of rights under the Fair Credit Reporting Act to obtain a copy of a consumer report, to dispute its accuracy, and to file a brief statement if the dispute is not resolved satisfactorily. It warns that no right exists to have accurate, current, verifiable information removed from one's consumer report. And it discloses the consumer's right to sue a credit repair organization for deceptive practices, and to cancel the contract within three business days. The statute sets forth the exact language of the required statement, in quotation marks, thereby indicating that it is not enough to disclose the general tenor of this information; the credit repair organization must use the specific language of the statute.[108] The disclosure statement has not been updated to reflect the 2003 amendments to the Fair Credit Reporting Act, such as the requirement that consumer reporting agencies provide free consumer reports to consumers.

---

104 15 U.S.C. § 1679c(a). *See In re* Zuniga, 332 B.R. 760, 788 (Bankr. S.D. Tex. 2005) (finding violation).
105 15 U.S.C. § 1679c(a).
106 15 U.S.C. § 1679c(b).
107 15 U.S.C. § 1679c(c).
108 *See also In re* National Credit Mgmt. Group, L.L.C., 21 F. Supp. 2d 424, 458 (D.N.J. 1998) (finding violation where cancellation notice did not include language required by CROA).

> 5 U.S.C. § 1679c. Disclosures
> (a) Disclosure Required.—Any credit repair organization shall provide any consumer with the following written statement before any contract or agreement between the consumer and the credit repair organization is executed:
>
> Consumer Credit File Rights Under State and Federal Law
>
> You have a right to dispute inaccurate information in your credit report by contacting the CRA directly. However, neither you nor any "credit repair" company or credit repair organization has the right to have accurate, current, and verifiable information removed from your credit report. The CRA must remove accurate, negative information from your report only if it is over seven years old. Bankruptcy information can be reported for ten years.
>
> You have a right to obtain a copy of your credit report from a CRA. You may be charged a reasonable fee. There is no fee, however, if you have been turned down for credit, employment, insurance, or a rental dwelling because of information in your credit report within the preceding 60 days. The CRA must provide someone to help you interpret the information in your credit file. You are entitled to receive a free copy of your credit report if you are unemployed and intend to apply for employment in the next 60 days, if you are a recipient of public welfare assistance, or if you have reason to believe that there is inaccurate information in your credit report due to fraud.
>
> You have a right to sue a credit repair organization that violates the Credit Repair Organization Act. This law prohibits deceptive practices by credit repair organizations.
>
> You have the right to cancel your contract with any credit repair organization for any reason within 3 business days from the date you signed it.
>
> Credit bureaus are required to follow reasonable procedures to ensure that the information they report is accurate. However, mistakes may occur.
>
> You may, on your own, notify a credit bureau in writing that you dispute the accuracy of information in your credit file. The credit bureau must then reinvestigate and modify or remove inaccurate or incomplete information. The credit bureau may not charge any fee for this service. Any pertinent information and copies of all documents you have concerning an error should be given to the credit bureau.
>
> If the credit bureau's reinvestigation does not resolve the dispute to your satisfaction, you may send a brief statement to the credit bureau, to be kept in your file, explaining why you think the record is inaccurate. The credit bureau must include a summary of your statement about disputed information with any report it issues about you.
>
> The Federal Trade Commission regulates credit bureaus and credit repair organizations. For more information contact:
>
> The Public Reference Branch
> Federal Trade Commission
> Washington, D.C. 20580.

15.2.4 Requirements for Credit Repair Contracts

A credit repair organization may not provide services without a signed written and dated contract,[109] or before the expiration of a three-day right to cancel.[110] Similar language in a state credit repair law has been interpreted as requiring not only the initial contract, but also all modifications of that contract, to be in writing and signed.[111] The consumer must be given a copy of the completed contract, the disclosure form, and any other document the consumer is required to sign, at the time of signature.[112]

In addition to the name and principal business address of the credit repair organization, the contract must include a statement of the consumer's three-day right to cancel the contract, which is discussed in § 15.2.5, *infra*. It must also set forth the terms and conditions of payment, including the total amount of all payments to be made to the credit repair organization or any other person.[113] A "full and detailed" description of services to be provided by the organization must be set forth. This description must include all guarantees of performance, and the date or estimate of how long these services will take, whether performed by the credit repair organization or by any other person.[114]

As described in § 15.2.6, *infra*, a credit repair organization may not receive payment for services until those services are fully performed. The schedule of services which must be set forth in the contract should be read in this light. The organization will have reason to describe services in a manner which will enable early payment from the consumer. Counsel for the consumer should consider whether the services described in the contract are illusory or are real and concrete and have in fact been "fully performed."[115]

15.2.5 Three-Day Right to Cancel

A consumer has the right to cancel any contract with a credit repair organization within three business days, ending at midnight of the third day after the date the agreement is executed.[116] The contract must include a conspicuous, bold face disclosure of this three-day right to cancel "in immediate proximity" to the consumer's signature.[117] In addition, each contract must be accompanied by a notice of cancellation form, in duplicate, explaining the right.[118] The form must use the exact language specified in the Act.[119] Although the required notice of the right of cancellation indicates that to cancel the contract the consumer should mail or deliver a signed and dated notice to the organization,[120] the statute itself does not require any particular manner of cancellation. The consumer is required only to notify the credit repair organization of the intention to cancel.[121] Cancellation may occur even if no notice of the right to cancel has been provided,[122] and may presumably be provided in any reasonable form, even orally. Written notice, of course, is the wiser course.

In fact, the consumer has no obligation to a credit repair organization without a contract which meets the requirements of the Act, and without receipt of the required "Notice of Cancellation." This result occurs for two reasons. First, a credit repair organization may not provide services without a written contract setting forth all of the terms described above, including the notice of right to cancel.[123] Second, the Act provides that a contract for service which does not meet the Act's requirements shall be treated as void and unenforceable.[124] Since a contract not meeting the requirements of the Act is void and unenforceable, the unqualified right to cancel is effectively extended until three days after the credit repair organization complies with the Act.

15.2.6 Prohibition of Advance Payment to Credit Repair Organization

No credit repair organization may charge or receive payment for services before the services are "fully performed."[125] This restriction strikes at the heart of the tactics used by credit repair organizations and threatens to eliminate the financial imbalance that has made the organizations

---

109 *See* Helms v. ConsumerInfo.com, Inc., 436 F. Supp. 2d 1220, 1234 (N.D. Ala. 2005) (finding violation).
110 15 U.S.C. § 1679d(a). *See* U.S. v. Cornerstone Wealth Corp., 2006 WL 522124 (N.D. Tex. Mar. 3, 2006) (credit repair organization may begin providing services only after written contract has been signed and three days have passed); *In re* Zuniga, 332 B.R. 760, 788 (Bankr. S.D. Tex. 2005) (finding violation where credit repair organization entered into contract with consumer by telephone).
111 Mitchell v. Am. Fair Credit Ass'n, 122 Cal. Rptr. 2d 193 (Cal. Ct. App. 2002).
112 15 U.S.C. § 1679e(c).
113 15 U.S.C. § 1679d(b)(1).
114 15 U.S.C. § 1679d(b)(2).
115 *See* § 15.2.6, *infra*.
116 15 U.S.C. § 1679e(a). *See* Helms v. ConsumerInfo.com, Inc., 436 F. Supp. 2d 1220, 1234 (N.D. Ala. 2005) (finding violation); *In re* Zuniga, 332 B.R. 760, 788 (Bankr. S.D. Tex. 2005) (finding violation where notice of right to cancel stated that the three days ran from date of entering into contract rather than date of signing).
117 15 U.S.C. § 1679d(b).
118 15 U.S.C. § 1679e(b).
119 *In re* National Credit Mgmt. Group, L.L.C., 21 F. Supp. 2d 424, 458 (D.N.J. 1998).
120 15 U.S.C. § 1679e(b).
121 15 U.S.C. § 1579e(a).
122 15 U.S.C. § 1579c(a).
123 15 U.S.C. § 1679d(a).
124 15 U.S.C. § 1679f(a). *See* § 15.2.8.1, *infra*.
125 15 U.S.C. § 1679b(b). *See In re* Zuniga, 332 B.R. 760, 788 (Bankr. S.D. Tex. 2005) (finding violation).

profitable. Many agencies are not well financed, and will not want to expend resources prior to payment. Moreover, any delay in the time for payments increases the risk of consumer dissatisfaction or change of heart and therefore nonpayment. Violation of this prohibition is widespread.

Accepting a down payment after giving the consumer an initial free consultation violates this prohibition,[126] as does charging a fee in advance for a "credit analysis."[127] Charging for a year of credit monitoring before the consumer has actually received the complete service is a violation.[128]

This payment provision has the potential of driving or keeping some credit repair organizations out of business. To minimize the risk, agencies may engage in possibly unfair or deceptive pricing techniques. Counsel for consumers should be alert to disproportionately high prices for early advice-giving or to services defined in small increments only distantly related to the ultimate goal of an improved credit record. In one case, a credit repair organization characterized its fees as payment for only the initial tasks of setting up a file, reviewing the consumer report, and preparing verification requests to CRAs. It also promised up to two years of requests for re-verification, but characterized this work as a guarantee that was provided free of charge. The court had no trouble concluding that the fee was not only for the initial services but also for the two years of reverifications, so was impermissibly charged in advance.[129] The court further held that the parol evidence rule did not bar evidence about the credit repair organization's oral descriptions of its services. Other credit repair organizations may advertise their credit repair services as free, but link them to other services for which an advance fee is required. This ploy is unlikely to be successful since the statutory language prohibits acceptance not only of money but also of any "other valuable consideration" before the services are performed.[130]

15.2.7 Prohibitions of Deceptive Practices, Applicable to Any Person

15.2.7.1 Overview

Section 1679b(a) of the Act prohibits four deceptive practices in very general terms.[131] Taken as a group, the prohibitions forbid untrue or misleading statements to consumers about the organization's services, to consumer reporting agencies about the credit standing of a consumer, and to actual or potential creditors of the consumer. In addition, they forbid actions intended to alter a consumer's identification for the purpose of concealing information. These prohibitions are discussed in the following subsections.

These prohibitions apply not just to credit repair organizations, but to "any person."[132] "Person" is clearly a broader term than "credit repair organization," and courts should give effect to the apparent intent of Congress when it chose this broader term to define the scope of these prohibitions.[133] Since these prohibitions are not confined to entities that meet the definition of "credit repair organization," the consumer need not show that the defendant promised credit repair services or provided them in return for money or other valuable consideration.[134]

15.2.7.2 Misstatements to Consumer Reporting Agencies or Creditors

No person may make any statement to a CRA or an actual or potential creditor which is untrue or misleading with respect to the consumer's creditworthiness, credit standing or credit capacity.[135] Counseling or advising the consumer to make such a misstatement is also prohibited. An organization is liable for any statement which it, its officer, its employee, its agent, or other person should, upon the exercise of reasonable care, know is untrue or misleading.[136] This prohibition, like the others in section 1679b(a), applies to any "person," not just to entities that meet the statutory definition of a "credit repair organization."[137]

---

126 Fed. Trade Comm'n v. Gill, 265 F.3d 944 (9th Cir. 2001).
127 *In re* National Credit Mgmt. Group, L.L.C., 21 F. Supp. 2d 424, 458 (D.N.J. 1998) (granting preliminary injunction based on violations of CROA, FTC Act, FTC telemarketing rule, and New Jersey UDAP statute).
128 Helms v. ConsumerInfo.com, Inc., 436 F. Supp. 2d 1220, 1234 (N.D. Ala. 2005).
129 U.S. v. Cornerstone Wealth Corp., 2006 WL 522124 (N.D. Tex. Mar. 3, 2006).
130 15 U.S.C. § 1679b(b).
131 15 U.S.C. § 1679b(a).
132 15 U.S.C. § 1679b(a). *See* Helms v. ConsumerInfo.com, Inc., 436 F. Supp. 2d 1220, 1229 (N.D. Ala. 2005) (noting that the prohibitions of § 1679b(a) apply to any person); Costa v. Mauro Chevrolet, Inc., 390 F. Supp. 2d 720, 727–728 (N.D. Ill. 2005); Rodriguez v. Lynch Ford, Inc., 2004 WL 2958772 (N.D. Ill. Nov. 18, 2004); Bigalke v. Creditrust Corp., 162 F. Supp. 2d 996 (N.D. Ill. 2001); Vance v. Nat'l Benefit Ass'n, 1999 WL 731764 (N.D. Ill. Aug. 30, 1999).
133 Costa v. Mauro Chevrolet, Inc., 390 F. Supp. 2d 720, 727 (N.D. Ill. 2005).
134 Rodriguez v. Lynch Ford, Inc., 2004 WL 2958772 (N.D. Ill. Nov. 18, 2004); Lacey v. William Chrysler Plymouth Inc., 2004 U.S. Dist. LEXIS 2479 (N.D. Ill. Feb. 20, 2004) (prohibition against counseling a consumer to make false statements regarding creditworthiness applies to car dealer even though it is not a credit repair organization).
135 15 U.S.C. § 1679b(a)(1). *See* Fed. Trade Comm'n v. IRC Servs. (N.D. Ill. Aug. 11, 2003) (consent order against credit repair organization that made untrue and misleading statements to CRAs), *available at* www.ftc.gov/opa/2003/08/nationwide.htm.
136 15 U.S.C. § 1679b(a)(1).
137 Rodriguez v. Lynch Ford, Inc., 2004 WL 2958772 (N.D. Ill. Nov. 18, 2004); Lacey v. William Chrysler Plymouth Inc., 2004 U.S. Dist. LEXIS 2479 (N.D. Ill. Feb. 20, 2004) (prohibition against counseling a consumer to make false statements regard-

This prohibition should apply to a loan broker or retailer who falsifies a consumer's credit application and submits it to a potential creditor. The consumer may be able to show actual damages if the falsified credit application was the means by which the defendant bound the consumer to an unaffordable, disadvantageous transaction. Even without actual damages, the consumer is entitled to punitive damages.[138] A claim along these lines will raise difficult issues if the consumer was complicit in the falsification, so the attorney should investigate the facts carefully.

15.2.7.3 Concealment of the Consumer's Identity

No person may make any statement to a CRA or an actual or potential creditor which is intended to alter the consumer's identification for the purpose of concealing adverse information which is accurate and not obsolete.[139] Advising the consumer to take these steps is also prohibited. Like the other prohibitions in section 1679b(a), this prohibition applies to any "person," not just entities that meet the definition of "credit repair organization."

This prohibition applies to a car dealer who sets up a sale with a "straw purchaser" to conceal the real buyer's identity from the entity financing the sale.[140] Such a claim will raise difficult issues, however, if the consumer was complicit in the falsification, so the attorney should investigate the facts carefully.

15.2.7.4 Misrepresentations Regarding the Services of a Credit Repair Organization

No person may make "any untrue or misleading representation" about the services of a credit repair organization.[141] The statute prohibits such statements in broad terms. A false representation would violate this prohibition whether it was made to the consumer, to the public generally, or even to creditors and CRAs. A statement is misleading if it would deceive the least sophisticated consumer.[142]

An untrue or misleading representation about a credit repair organization's services is a violation whether or not it is made for the purpose of inducing consumers to buy the services.[143] Indeed, the statute does not require that the deception involve the organization's *credit repair* services, but prohibits deception about any aspect of the organization's services. Even if there are no explicit misrepresentations, the Act is violated if the overall net impression of the defendant's statements is misleading.[144]

A credit repair organization violates this prohibition by claiming that it can legally and permanently get negative information removed from consumer reports even if the information is accurate, complete, and not obsolete.[145] Promising to improve a person's credit rating, but then merely referring her to another organization, which instructed her to take steps that could actually damage her credit rating, would be a violation.[146] A debt collector may violate this prohibition by claiming that payment of the debt will remove the adverse entry from the consumer's credit rating, if the claim is untrue.[147] Promising customized advice but then providing only a general assessment generated by a computer may be a violation.[148]

15.2.7.5 Fraud and Deception

The final prohibition of section 1679b(a) is that no person may "engage, directly or indirectly, in any act, practice, or course of business" that constitutes the commission of, or an attempt to commit, fraud or deception in connection with the offer or sale of the services of a credit repair organization.[149] One court, inexplicably ignoring the reference to deception, held that the reference to fraud meant that the consumer must show reliance and damages.[150] The same court held that, for a claim based on an attempt to commit fraud rather than completed fraud, the consumer need not show reliance but must show specific intent to defraud.[151]

This provision appears to apply to advertising and solicitations, as well as generally to communications with potential clients. An organization violated this prohibition when it advertised credit repair but then referred the consumer to

---

ing creditworthiness applies to car dealer even though it is not a credit repair organization).

138 15 U.S.C. § 1679g(a)(2). *See* § 15.2.8.5.3, *infra*.
139 15 U.S.C. § 1679b(a)(2).
140 Costa v. Mauro Chevrolet, Inc., 390 F. Supp. 2d 720, 728 (N.D. Ill. 2005) (denial of motion to dismiss); Rodriguez v. Lynch Ford, Inc., 2004 WL 2958772 (N.D. Ill. Nov. 18, 2004).
141 15 U.S.C. § 1679b(a)(3).
142 Helms v. ConsumerInfo.com, Inc., 436 F. Supp. 2d 1220, 1236 (N.D. Ala. 2005) (fact question whether defendant's references to its expertise were deceptive).
143 Fed. Trade Comm'n v. Gill, 265 F.3d 944 (9th Cir. 2001).
144 *Id.* at 956; Slack v. Fair Isaac Corp., 390 F. Supp. 2d 906 (N.D. Cal. 2005).
145 Fed. Trade Comm'n v. Gill, 265 F.3d 944, 956 (9th Cir. 2001); Slack v. Fair Isaac Corp., 390 F. Supp. 2d 906, 912–913 (N.D. Cal. 2005).
146 Parker v. 1-800 Bar None, 2002 WL 215530 (N.D. Ill. Feb. 12, 2002).
147 Nielsen v. United Creditors Alliance Corp., 1999 WL 674740, 1999 U.S. Dist. LEXIS 13267 (N.D. Ill. Aug. 18, 1999) (denying motion to dismiss). *See also* Bigalke v. Creditrust Corp., 162 F. Supp. 2d 996 (N.D. Ill. 2001) (denial of motion to dismiss) (debt collector that sent similar letter was covered by CROA), *later op. at* 2001 WL 1098047, 2001 U.S. Dist. LEXIS 14591 (N.D. Ill. Sept. 11, 2001) (certifying class). *But see* White v. Fin. Credit Corp., 2001 WL 1665386 (N.D. Ill. Dec. 27, 2001) (consumer's evidence did not establish that debt collector's representation that payment would improve credit history was misleading).
148 Slack v. Fair Isaac Corp., 390 F. Supp. 2d 906 (N.D. Cal. 2005).
149 15 U.S.C. § 1679b(a)(4).
150 Helms v. ConsumerInfo.com, Inc., 436 F. Supp. 2d 1220, 1237 (N.D. Ala. 2005).
151 *Id.* at 1237.

another organization that instructed her to write a post-dated check that she did not have the funds to cover, with the expectation that at a later point the check would be refinanced.[152] This advice would more likely harm than help her credit rating. Promising customized advice but then providing only a general assessment generated by a computer may be a violation.[153]

The "directly or indirectly" language extends liability to individuals and entities that not only do not meet the definition of "credit repair organization" but also have not had direct contact with the consumer or direct involvement with the sale of the credit repair services. Thus, a bank that agreed that a credit repair organization could sponsor people for the bank's credit card was subject to suit under the Act.[154] Likewise, assignees of the credit repair organization's contract can be liable, as can the individual owners of the credit repair company.[155] Companies who help credit repair telemarketers process credit card payments or submit "telechecks" for payment out of the consumer's bank account may also be liable.[156] Whether a particular defendant actually received the consumer's payments, or just assisted someone else who did, is immaterial.[157]

15.2.8 Private Remedies

15.2.8.1 Noncomplying Contract Is Void

In addition to the right to cancel, described in § 15.2.5, *supra*, any contract not in compliance with the Act is treated as void. It may not be enforced by any court or other person.[158] If the contract fails to include the right to cancel and notice thereof, or fails to include any of the terms and conditions required by the Act, or if the contract requires any act or statement which is prohibited, the contract is effectively void. On the other hand, if the contract is otherwise in compliance, even if the acts or statements of the organization in the performance of the contract violate one of the Act's prohibitions, the remedy is damages and not that the contract is void.

A void contract may not be enforced against the consumer. Whether the contract is void ab initio and the consumer entitled to the return of any payments made is moot because in any event the consumer is entitled to at least those payments under the civil liability provisions discussed below.

A consumer may not waive the provision which effectively voids the contract, nor for that matter any other protection provided by the Act.[159] Any attempt to obtain a waiver is itself a violation of the Act.[160]

15.2.8.2 Who May Sue

Any person may sue a credit repair organization, as long as the credit repair organization has violated a requirement relating to the person suing.[161] Thus, not only consumers but also creditors, CRAs, and others may sue. For example, if the provision proscribing misleading statements to a creditor or a CRA is violated, the creditor or the CRA could sue for damages. CRAs, which bear the brunt of many credit repair abuses, have a special incentive and the resources to enforce the Act.

Significantly, there is no requirement that the party suing have suffered actual injury. A credit repair organization that violates the Act is strictly liable for damages in the amount of all money paid. The formula for the damage award—any actual damage *or* the amount paid by the person to the credit repair organization—makes it clear that restitution of the amount paid is available in the absence of actual damages. The Ninth Circuit, in a suit brought by the FTC, cited this provision in affirming an award in the amount of all sums paid by consumers to the credit repair organization even though no actual damages were proven.[162] Likewise, a district court held that consumers who had received a misleading letter from a credit repair organization could recover without showing actual damages or that they were actually misled.[163] The ease of establishing liability for damages makes class actions particularly attractive under this statute. Some injury may be required in order to meet constitutional standing requirements, however.[164]

---

152 Parker v. 1-800 Bar None, 2002 WL 215530 (N.D. Ill. Feb. 12, 2002).
153 Slack v. Fair Isaac Corp., 390 F. Supp. 2d 906 (N.D. Cal. 2005).
154 Parker v. 1-800 Bar None, 2002 WL 215530 (N.D. Ill. Feb. 12, 2002) (even if defendant were not a credit repair organization, prohibition would apply to it); Vance v. National Benefit Ass'n, 1999 WL 731764, 1999 U.S. Dist. LEXIS 13846 (N.D. Ill. Aug. 26, 1999) (prohibition applied to bank).
155 Vance v. National Benefit Ass'n, 1999 WL 731764, 1999 U.S. Dist. LEXIS 13846 (N.D. Ill. Aug. 26, 1999).
156 *See* National Consumer Law Center, Unfair and Deceptive Acts and Practices §§ 5.9.4.8.3, 5.9.6 (6th ed. 2004 and Supp.) (description of entities that process payments for telemarketers).
157 Fed. Trade Comm'n v. Gill, 265 F.3d 944 (9th Cir. 2001).
158 15 U.S.C. § 1679f(c).
159 15 U.S.C. § 1679f. *See* Alexander v. U.S. Credit Mgmt., Inc., 384 F. Supp. 2d 1003 (N.D. Tex. 2005) (right to punitive damages is not waivable); Polacsek v. Debticated Consumer Counseling, Inc., 413 F. Supp. 2d 539, 549 n.5 (D. Md. 2005) (credit repair organization's attempt to disavow its offer to improve consumers' credit scores is an ineffective waiver under CROA).
160 15 U.S.C. § 1679f(b).
161 15 U.S.C. § 1679g(a) (violation must be "with respect to" the plaintiff).
162 Fed. Trade Comm'n v. Gill, 265 F.3d 944 (9th Cir. 2001).
163 Bigalke v. Creditrust Corp., 2001 U.S. Dist. LEXIS 14591 (N.D. Ill. Sept. 11, 2001).
164 Asmar v. Benchmark Literacy Group, Inc., 2005 WL 2562965 (E.D. Mich. Oct. 11, 2005) (standing established where consumer paid fee to credit repair organization, even though it was refunded as soon as consumer filed suit).

15.2.8.3 Liability Not Limited to Credit Repair Organizations

Liability under the Act is not confined to credit repair organizations, but applies to "any person" who fails to comply with the Act.[165] Thus, other entities that are directly or indirectly involved in deception or other violations of the Act—such as assignees of a credit repair organization's contracts, the owner or employees of the credit repair organization, creditors who agree to accept referrals from the credit repair organization, or persons who assist in concealment of a credit applicant's identification or in misrepresentation of an applicant's creditworthiness—may be liable.[166] The Ninth Circuit affirmed a $1.3 million restitution award against an attorney who allowed a credit repair operator to work out of his offices and under his supervision.[167] Although the plaintiff in that case was the FTC and the court applied a different analysis of the question of the attorney's liability, the decision demonstrates the scope of the Act.

15.2.8.4 Does an Arbitration Clause Apply to CROA Claims?

Credit repair organizations may include clauses in their consumer contracts that require any dispute to be resolved by binding arbitration, thus attempting to keep consumer litigation out of the courts. Another NCLC manual, *Consumer Arbitration Agreements*,[168] examines whether such arbitration clauses are enforceable. This subsection reviews several issues as to the enforceability of such clauses of special relevance to a consumer's CROA claims.

CROA states that any contract for services which does not comply with the Act is void, and this might lead to an argument that the arbitration clause is void as well.[169] But the U.S. Supreme Court, in *Buckeye Check Cashing, Inc. v. Cardegna*, established a bright-line test as to whether a court or an arbitrator decides if an arbitration agreement is enforceable.[170] The arbitration clause is treated as a separate agreement. A court decides a challenge directed to that separate agreement—such as that it is unconscionable or misrepresented. An arbitrator decides challenges to the rest of the contract. Thus a claim that a credit repair contract is void for violating CROA goes to the contract as a whole, and not specifically to the arbitration clause. Therefore an arbitrator, not the court, decides if CROA has been violated, making the contract void.

If the consumer instead takes advantage of the CROA right to cancel the contract by sending timely notice to the repair organization, however, the result should be different. If the defendant does not dispute the effectiveness of the cancellation (i.e., does not dispute that it received a timely cancellation notice), then the contract and with it the arbitration clause are cancelled.[171] Any subsequent litigation can proceed in court.

Of special significance for CROA cases, a recent federal decision in *Alexander v. U.S. Credit Management, Inc.* holds that a mandatory arbitration requirement conflicts with congressional intent in enacting CROA.[172] CROA has an unusually specific anti-waiver clause: "Any waiver by any consumer of any protection provided by or any right of the consumer under this subchapter shall be treated as void; and may not be enforced by any Federal or State court of any other person."[173] CROA also states: "Any attempt by any person to obtain a waiver from any consumer of any protection provided by or any right of the consumer under this subchapter shall be treated as a violation of this subchapter."[174] *Alexander* thus holds that it is the arbitration clause that is void as an impermissible waiver, not the whole contract. Since this challenge goes to the arbitration clause and not to the contract as a whole, *Alexander* is consistent with the U.S. Supreme Court ruling in *Cardegna* that a court and not an arbitrator determines the challenge to the arbitration clause specifically.

Alexander looks to CROA's explicit language requiring disclosure to the consumer of the "right to sue a credit repair organization that violates the Credit Repair Organization Act."[175] It finds the right to sue in court (not some other proceeding) specifically protected by the Act. An arbitration clause would waive this right, and is thus unenforceable.[176]

---

165 15 U.S.C. § 1679g(a).
166 Baker v. Family Credit Counseling Corp., 2006 WL 2089153, at *9–10 (E.D. Pa. July 28, 2006); Polacsek v. Debticated Consumer Counseling, Inc., 413 F. Supp. 2d 539, 547 n.4 (D. Md. 2005) (individual's control of credit repair organization and participation in or acquiescence in CROA violations sufficient for liability); Vance v. National Benefit Ass'n, 1999 WL 731764, 1999 U.S. Dist. LEXIS 13846 (N.D. Ill. Aug. 26, 1999). *But see* Asmar v. Benchmark Literacy Group, Inc., 2005 WL 2562965 (E.D. Mich. Oct. 11, 2005) (corporate officers not liable under CROA and not credit repair organizations where they did not personally perform credit repair activities but only made decisions, formulated policies, and directed the companies).
167 Fed. Trade Comm'n v. Gill, 265 F.3d 944 (9th Cir. 2001).
168 (4th ed. 2004 and Supp.).
169 *See* Cortese v. Edge Solutions, Inc., 2005 WL 1804472 (E.D.N.Y. July 28, 2005).
170 Buckeye Check Cashing, Inc v. Cardegna, 126 S. Ct. 1204, 163 L. Ed. 2d 1038 (2006).
171 *See* Chapman v. Mortgage One Corp., 2005 WL 656222 (E.D. Mo. Mar. 8, 2005). *See also* Large v. Conseco Fin. Servicing Corp., 292 F.3d 49, 55 (1st Cir. 2002) (distinguishing cases where cancellation not in dispute from those where there is a dispute).
172 Alexander v. U.S. Credit Mgmt., Inc., 384 F. Supp. 2d 1003 (N.D. Tex. 2005).
173 15 U.S.C. § 1679f(a).
174 15 U.S.C. § 1679f(b).
175 15 U.S.C. § 1679c(a).
176 Alexander v. U.S. Credit Mgmt., Inc., 384 F. Supp. 2d 1003 (N.D. Tex. 2005).

Alexander distinguishes CROA from other statutes both in the explicit nature of the right to sue and the detailed anti-waiver provision, and also by examining CROA's legislative history in detail.[177]

Moreover, the anti-waiver provision is particularly applicable where the arbitration clause either explicitly or by reference to the rules of an arbitration service provider limits the consumer's right to punitive damages, attorney fees, or a class claim, all of which are rights explicitly granted by CROA. Although some courts will only strike an arbitration clause where it limits the consumer's substantive rights, *Alexander* states that it is not necessary to determine if punitive damages, attorney fees, or class claims are substantive CROA rights, because the anti-waiver language applies to *any* waiver.[178]

Another unique challenge to an arbitration clause may be available under certain state credit services organization acts that require all contracts to be in writing and signed by the consumer. A California appellate court has held that the state credit repair law, which so requires, applies not just to the initial contract but also to any later modification.[179] As a result, an arbitration clause added to existing customers' contracts was ineffective except as to those consumers who had signed it.

Of course, other grounds to challenge an arbitration clause also apply to CROA cases as well. For example, since consumers seek the services of a credit repair organization only when they are in dire financial straits, an arbitration clause that imposes high up-front costs on the consumer is particularly vulnerable to an unconscionability challenge.[180] A detailed analysis of unconscionability and other challenges to arbitration clauses is found at NCLC's *Consumer Arbitration Agreements*.[181]

15.2.8.5 Damages

15.2.8.5.1 Statutory formula for damages

Any person who violates the Act is liable for damages in the sum of:

- The greater of actual damages or the amount paid to the credit repair organization;
- Such additional punitive damages as the court may allow; and
- Costs and reasonable attorney fees.[182]

The Act contains no authorization for the award of attorney fees to a prevailing defendant, allowing fees only for "any successful action to enforce any liability" thereunder.[183]

15.2.8.5.2 Actual damages

Any loss that results from the violation of the Act can be awarded as actual damages. Where a consumer was lured by a credit repair organization into buying a car, but backed out of the deal after discovering the falsity of the company's representations, money she spent in repairs before canceling the contract would be actual damages.[184] The amount paid to the credit repair organization may be awarded as damages even if the consumer does not prove any injury beyond paying that amount.[185]

15.2.8.5.3 Punitive damages

Punitive damages are available whether or not the consumer proves actual damages or has paid any money to the organization.[186] The Act authorizes punitive damages not just in individual suits but also in class actions.[187] The right to punitive damages, like other rights under the Act, is non-waivable.[188]

In awarding punitive damages, the Act directs courts to use as factors the frequency, persistence, and nature of the noncompliance, the extent to which the violation was intentional, and, in a class action, the number of consumers adversely affected.[189] Several other consumer protection statutes[190] list similar factors, and decisions interpreting those statutes may be persuasive. The Act allows the court to consider "other relevant factors" as well,[191] and one court has allowed discovery of a defendant's net worth as relevant to punitive damages.[192]

---

177 *Id.*
178 Alexander v. U.S. Credit Mgmt., Inc., 384 F. Supp. 2d 1003 (N.D. Tex. 2005).
179 Mitchell v. Am. Fair Credit Ass'n, 122 Cal. Rptr. 2d 193 (Cal. Ct. App. 2002) .
180 *See* Plattner v. Edge Solutions Inc., 2003 WL 22859532 (N.D. Ill. Dec. 2, 2003) (finding arbitration clause in credit repair contract unconscionable).
181 (4th ed. 2004 and Supp.).
182 15 U.S.C. § 1679g(a).
183 15 U.S.C. § 1679g(a)(3).
184 Parker v. 1-800 Bar None, 2002 WL 215530 (N.D. Ill. Feb. 12, 2002).
185 *See* § 15.2.8.5.1, *supra*.
186 Parker v. 1-800 Bar None, 2002 WL 215530 (N.D. Ill. Feb. 12, 2002).
187 *See* § 15.2.8.6, *infra*.
188 15 U.S.C. § 1679f. *See* Alexander v. U.S. Credit Mgmt., Inc., 384 F. Supp. 2d 1003 (N.D. Tex. 2005).
189 15 U.S.C. § 1679g(b).
190 *See* 15 U.S.C. § 1692k(b) (Fair Debt Collection Practices Act), discussed in National Consumer Law Center, Fair Debt Collection § 6.4.3 (5th ed. 2004 and Supp.); 15 U.S.C. § 1640(a) (Truth in Lending Act), *discussed in* National Consumer Law Center, Truth in Lending § 8.8.3.2 (5th ed. 2003 and Supp.); 15 U.S.C. § 1691e(b) (Equal Credit Opportunity Act), *discussed in* National Consumer Law Center, Credit Discrimination § 11.7.4.3 (4th ed. 2005 and Supp.).
191 15 U.S.C. § 1679g(b).
192 Iosello v. Lawrence, 2004 WL 1194741 (N.D. Ill. May 26, 2004).

15.2.8.6 Class Actions

The Act specifically contemplates class actions. It sets forth a special rule for determining the amount of punitive damages in a class action: the aggregate amount the court allows for each named plaintiff, plus the aggregate amount it allows for each other class member without regard to any minimum individual recovery.[193] Class actions must meet the usual requirements of Rule 23 of the Federal Rules of Civil Procedure.[194]

15.2.8.7 Jurisdiction

Unlike the other titles of the Consumer Credit Protection Act which provide for enforcement through private rights of action,[195] the Credit Repair Organization Act does not contain a specific grant of jurisdiction in the federal district courts. To date, courts have not viewed this issue with concern, but have exercised federal question jurisdiction[196] over CROA claims.[197] Diversity jurisdiction is also possible if the amount in controversy exceeds $75,000.[198]

Credit repair organizations often operate across state lines, raising questions whether the consumer's home state has jurisdiction over an out-of-state entity. An interactive website that allows out-of-state consumers to enroll in a credit repair program may be sufficient for courts in the consumer's home state to exercise long-arm jurisdiction over the credit repair organization.[199]

15.2.8.8 Pleading

Allegations of violations of the Credit Repair Organization Act involving fraudulent, deceptive, or misleading statements may have to be pleaded with particularity pursuant to Federal Rule of Civil Procedure 9(b) and similar state rules.[200] Courts have split on the analogous question of whether allegations of violations of state deceptive practices statutes must meet Rule 9(b) standards, with the better-reasoned decisions finding that deception is a less-demanding standard than fraud so need not meet the same pleading requirements.[201]

Courts have applied Rule 9(b) to allegations under section 1679b(a)(3), which prohibits certain untrue or misleading representations,[202] and section 1679b(a)(4), which prohibits fraud and deception in connection with the offer or sale of a credit repair organization's services.[203] Even if these decisions are correct, Rule 9(b) should not be applicable to the other CROA prohibitions, which do not include fraud or deception as an element.

15.2.8.9 Statute of Limitations

The statute of limitations for an action under the Credit Repair Organizations Act is five years from the occurrence

---

193 15 U.S.C. § 1679g(2)(B)(ii). *See also* 15 U.S.C. § 1679g(b)(4) (specifically referring to class actions in listing the factors for determining the amount of punitive damages).
194 Iosello v. Lawrence, 2004 WL 1194741 (N.D. Ill. May 26, 2004) (denying class certification because of insufficient evidence of numerosity and failure to narrow class to those who entered into same contract or viewed same website). *See also* Helms v. ConsumerInfo.com, Inc., 236 F.R.D. 561 (N.D. Ala. 2005) denying class certification because classwide statutory damages would be overwhelming, even though all requirements of Rule 23 were met).
195 Title I, Truth in Lending Act, 15 U.S.C. §§ 1601–1667e; Title IV; Fair Credit Reporting Act, 15 U.S.C. §§ 1681–1681t; Title VII, Equal Credit Opportunity Act, 15 U.S.C. §§ 1691–1691f; Title VIII, Fair Debt Collection Practices Act, 15 U.S.C. §§ 1692–1692o; and Title IX, Electronic Fund Transfer Act, 15 U.S.C. §§ 1693–1693r.
196 28 U.S.C. § 1331.
197 *See, e.g.,* Lacey v. William Chrysler Plymouth, 2004 WL 415972 (N.D. Ill. Feb. 23, 2004) (stating that court has jurisdiction over CROA claim under 28 U.S.C. § 1331); Sannes v. Jeff Wyler Chevrolet, Inc., 1999 WL 33313134, at *4 (S.D. Ohio Mar. 31, 1999) (asserting that court had jurisdiction over CROA claim under 28 U.S.C. § 1331). *Cf.* Arnold v. Goldstar Fin. Sys., Inc., 2002 WL 1941546, at *6 (N.D. Ill. Aug. 22, 2002) (finding federal jurisdiction because defendant did not fall into exemption for non-profits at time of alleged violations). *See generally* Grable & Sons Metal Prods., Inc. v. Darue Eng'g & Mfg., 125 S. Ct. 2363, 162 L. Ed. 2d 257 (2005) (allowing federal question jurisdiction over state claim that raised substantial disputed federal issue); McCready v. White, 417 F.3d 700, 702 (7th Cir. 2005) (assertion of claim under a federal statute is sufficient for federal question jurisdiction).
198 28 U.S.C. § 1332.
199 Asmar v. Benchmark Literacy Group, Inc., 2005 WL 2562965 (E.D. Mich. Oct. 11, 2005); Arnold v. Goldstar Fin. Sys., Inc., 2002 WL 1941546, at *6 (N.D. Ill. Aug. 22, 2002) (maintenance of interactive website and entering into 5-year service contract with forum state resident sufficient for jurisdiction; active telephone solicitation in forum state also sufficient where defendant knowingly enters into long-term contracts with forum state residents). *See generally* National Consumer Law Center, The Cost of Credit: Regulation, Preemption, and Industry Abuses § 10.2.2 (3d ed. 2005 and Supp.).
200 Banks v. Capital Credit Alliance, 2005 WL 1563220 (N.D. Ill. June 28, 2005); Slack v. Fair Isaac Corp., 390 F. Supp. 2d 906 (N.D. Cal. 2005); Parker v. 1-800 Bar None, 2002 WL 215530 (N.D. Ill. Feb. 12, 2002) (applying Rule 9(b) without discussion of whether it should apply; pleading found sufficiently detailed). *See also* Costa v. Mauro Chevrolet, Inc., 390 F. Supp. 2d 720 (N.D. Ill. 2005) (applying Rule 9(b) to complaint and finding it sufficient).
201 *See* National Consumer Law Center, Unfair and Deceptive Acts and Practices § 7.7.6 (6th ed. 2004 and Supp.).
202 Slack v. Fair Isaac Corp., 390 F. Supp. 2d 906 (N.D. Cal. 2005); Browning v. Yahoo!, Inc., 2004 WL 2496183 (N.D. Cal. Nov. 4, 2004). *See also* Costa v. Mauro Chevrolet, Inc., 390 F. Supp. 2d 720 (N.D. Ill. 2005) (applying Rule 9(b) to complaint and finding it sufficient).
203 Banks v. Capital Credit Alliance, Inc., 2005 WL 1563220 (N.D. Ill. June 28, 2005); Slack v. Fair Isaac Corp., 390 F. Supp. 2d 906 (N.D. Cal. 2005); Browning v. Yahoo!, Inc., 2004 WL 2496183 (N.D. Cal. Nov. 4, 2004).

of the violation.[204] Where the violation relates to the organization's material and willful failure to disclose, the five years begins to run when the consumer discovers the misrepresentation.[205]

15.2.8.10 Jury Trial

As is the case with regard to other titles of the Consumer Credit Protection Act, CROA is silent as to the right to trial by jury. Consistent with the Seventh Amendment and the case law under these related statutes, a jury should be available.[206]

15.2.9 Relation to State Laws

The Credit Repair Organizations Act does not preempt state credit repair statutes, except to the extent to which the two are inconsistent, and then only to the extent of such inconsistency.[207] This standard is essentially identical to the general preemption provision under the Fair Credit Reporting Act[208] and preemption provisions of the Truth in Lending Act,[209] the Equal Credit Opportunity Act,[210] and the Fair Debt Collection Practices Act,[211] so decisions under those statutes should be persuasive. Additional remedies for the same deceptive acts are not inconsistent with CROA, so the advocate can use remedies under state UDAP statutes and other consumer laws in addition to CROA remedies.[212]

15.2.10 Federal and State Enforcement of the Federal Act

The Federal Trade Commission enforces the Credit Repair Organizations Act under the Federal Trade Commission Act (FTC Act), whether or not the organization comes under the jurisdictional tests for the FTC Act.[213] Over a period of years, the Federal Trade Commission has charged many such organizations and their principals with misleading consumers by falsely and deceptively claiming the ability to improve credit records and by not honoring refund guarantees, not only under CROA and the FTC Telemarketing Sales Rule but also under its general authority to proceed against unfair and deceptive practices in or affecting commerce.[214] In one case against a lawyer, the FTC obtained equitable disgorgement of $1.3 million for numerous violations.[215]

State enforcement officials can also bring actions under the Credit Repair Organizations Act to enjoin violations, to act on behalf of state residents to recover damages that the residents could have recovered in private actions.[216] If successful, the state may recover the state's costs and attorney fees.[217]

15.3 State Credit Repair Laws

15.3.1 Introduction

Most states have passed their own statutes to deal with abuses by credit repair organizations.[218] These statutes, often termed the state Credit Services Organization Act, typically follow the federal Credit Repair Organizations Act closely in some respects, but differ in significant ways, often imposing additional requirements such as registration and bonding. Many are broader than the federal statute, covering not only credit repair organizations but also loan brokers and sometimes other entities as well. These statutes have a broad remedial purpose[219] and should be construed accordingly.

In some states, violation of the state credit repair law carries criminal penalties. In Ohio, operating an unlicensed credit services organization is a predicate offense under the state RICO statute.[220]

---

204 15 U.S.C. § 1679i.
205 *Id.*
206 *See* Sibley v. Fulton DeKalb Collection Serv., 677 F.2d 830 (11th Cir. 1982) (Fair Debt Collection Practices Act); Barber v. Kimbrell's Inc., 577 F.2d 216 (4th Cir. 1978) (Truth in Lending Act).
207 15 U.S.C. § 1679j. *See* § 15.3.8, *infra* (effect on state credit repair laws).
208 15 U.S.C. § 1681t(a). *See* § 10.7.1, *supra*.
209 15 U.S.C. § 1610(a)(1). *See* National Consumer Law Center, Truth in Lending § 2.6.3 (5th ed. 2003 and Supp.).
210 15 U.S.C. § 1691d(f). *See* National Consumer Law Center, Credit Discrimination § 11.6.1.3 (4th ed. 2005 and Supp.).
211 15 U.S.C. § 1692n. *See* National Consumer Law Center, Fair Debt Collection § 6.13.1 (5th ed. 2004 and Supp.).
212 *In re* National Credit Mgmt. Group, L.L.C., 21 F. Supp. 2d 424 (D.N.J. 1998).
213 15 U.S.C. § 1679h(a), (b).
214 *See, e.g.*, Fed. Trade Comm'n v. Gill, 265 F.3d 944 (9th Cir. 2001) (suit under Credit Repair Organizations Act); *In re* National Credit Mgmt. Group, L.L.C., 21 F. Supp. 2d 424 (D.N.J. 1998); *In re* Anderson, 107 F.T.C. 437 (1986); *In re* Everts, 107 F.T.C. 450 (1986); *In re* Hakim, 107 F.T.C. 459 (1986); *In re* Herndon, 107 F.T.C. 468 (1986); *In re* Hull, 107 F.T.C. 477 (1986); *In re* Tannous, 107 F.T.C. 488 (1986). A multitude of unreported court orders and consent orders obtained by the FTC against credit repair organizations may be found on the FTC's website, www.ftc.gov.
215 Fed. Trade Comm'n v. Gill, 265 F.3d 944 (9th Cir. 2001). The case describes a litany of activities fully justifying the need for CROA.
216 15 U.S.C. § 1679h(c)(1). *See, e.g.*, *In re* National Credit Mgmt. Group, L.L.C., 21 F. Supp. 2d 424 (D.N.J. 1998) (CROA suit brought jointly by FTC and state attorney general).
217 15 U.S.C. § 1679h(c)(1)(c).
218 *See* Appx. H, *infra*. *See also* Mitchell v. Am. Fair Credit Ass'n, 122 Cal. Rptr. 2d 193 (Cal. Ct. App. 2002) (reciting purposes of Cal. credit repair law).
219 Mitchell v. Am. Fair Credit Ass'n, 99 Cal. App. 4th 1345, 122 Cal. Rptr. 2d 193 (2002) (statute explicitly requires liberal construction).
220 Ohio Rev. Code § 2923.31(I). *See* State v. Schlosser, 79 Ohio St. 3d 329, 681 N.E.2d 911 (Ohio 1997) (affirming conviction of

Another issue relating to state credit repair laws is that high-rate lenders may exploit these laws as a way of evading state usury caps. For example, the Fifth Circuit dealt with a company that registered under the state credit repair law and then charged $1500 to arrange a $2000 loan from a separate entity. The $2000 loan ostensibly bore interest that complied with the state usury statute, and the court held that the credit repair organization's fee did not count as additional interest.[221] These issues are discussed in another NCLC manual.[222]

15.3.2 Coverage

The most far-reaching difference between state and federal credit repair organization laws is coverage. All or nearly all of the state statutes duplicate the federal law's coverage of organizations that offer to improve an individual's credit rating. Accordingly, they generally cover the same variety of organizations as the federal statute.[223] But most of the state statutes also cover organizations that assist or offer to assist consumers in obtaining extensions of credit. As a result, loan brokers and credit card finders are covered by the substantive requirements of these state laws, including registration, bonding, and the right to cancel. Sellers who arrange credit may also be covered.

Entities potentially covered by the "obtaining credit" branch of state credit repair laws include:

- Credit card "finders" that claim to be able to procure credit cards for consumers.[224]
- Loan brokers and mortgage brokers.[225] Most state credit repair statutes exclude licensed real estate brokers and securities brokers, but few exclude loan brokers. The West Virginia Supreme Court, interpreting language that is found in many other states' statutes, has held that a loan broker meets the definition of "credit services organization."[226]

- Tax preparers who offer, for a fee, to arrange refund anticipation loans for their clients. While tax preparers may not disclose any special fee for arranging a refund anticipation loan, most receive a substantial fee in the form of a kickback of part of the borrower's payment to the lender.
- "Home finders" that promise to help people buy homes. These operations often appear in cities and are usually fraudulent.
- Foreclosure rescue scam operators who approach homeowners who are in foreclosure and offer to secure financing to enable them to save their homes.[227]
- Scholarship location services that purport, for a fee, to locate college scholarship money for students.

State laws typically limit this branch of the definition of "credit services organization" to those arranging consumer credit rather than business credit. They accomplish this by defining "extension of credit" so that it is limited to credit for personal, family, or household use.[228]

Many of the organizations that fall into this branch of the definition make no attempt to comply with the state statute. Indeed, registration, bonding, restrictions on advance payment, and a right to cancel would so impede these organizations' ability to take advantage of people that fraudulent operators will rarely comply with these requirements.

The typical state credit repair law only applies to organizations that provide their services "in return for the payment of money or other valuable consideration." The meaning of this language has been litigated in the context of whether retailers are covered and is discussed in § 15.3.4.2, *infra*.

State credit repair laws can be applied to in-state organizations even if they direct their activities solely toward non-residents.[229] In addition, others involved in the credit

---

credit card finder under state RICO statute based on predicate offense of operating unlicensed credit services organization).

221 Lovick v. Ritemoney Ltd., 378 F.3d 433 (5th Cir. 2004).
222 National Consumer Law Center, The Cost of Credit: Regulation, Preemption, and Industry Abuses § 7.5.5.7 (2005 Supp. and Supp.).
223 See § 15.2.2.2.1. *supra*.
224 See State v. Schlosser, 79 Ohio St. 3d 329, 681 N.E.2d 911 (Ohio 1997) (affirming conviction of credit card finder under state RICO statute based on predicate offense of operating unlicensed credit services organization); State v. New Beginning Credit Ass'n, 2006 WL 1472284 (Tenn. Ct. App. May 25, 2006) (unpublished) (statute covers company that offered to help people reestablish their credit with an unsecured credit card).
225 See, e.g., State v. Berks Fin., 2004 WL 3736495 (Ohio Com. Pleas Aug. 4, 2005) (unpublished) (state credit repair law applies to advance fee loan scam).
226 Arnold v. United Companies Lending Corp., 511 S.E.2d 854 (W. Va. 1998). *See also* Lovick v. Ritemoney Ltd., 378 F.3d 433 (5th

Cir. 2004) (state credit services law covers loan broker and authorizes it to charge fees); *In re* Bell, 309 B.R. 139 (Bankr. E.D. Pa. 2004) (mortgage loan broker meets Pennsylvania definition of "credit services organization"); Lewis v. Delta Funding Corp. (*In re* Lewis), 290 B.R. 541 (Bankr. E.D. Pa. 2003) (mortgage loan broker met Pennsylvania definition of "credit services organization"); Barker v. Altegra Corp. (*In re* Barker), 251 B.R. 250 (Bankr. E.D. Pa. 2000) (finding that loan broker was covered under Pennsylvania credit repair statute, but basing decision on language that does not appear in most states' statutes). *But cf.* Brown v. Mortgagestar, Inc., 194 F. Supp. 2d 473 (S.D. W. Va. 2002) (company that had a lending license was exempt even though it was operating as a broker rather than as a lender).
227 Moore v. Cycon Enters., Inc., 2006 WL 2375477, at *14 (W.D. Mich. Aug. 16, 2006) (applying state credit repair law to foreclose rescue scam operator).
228 *See* Del. Fin. Mgmt. Corp. v. Steen, 1998 WL 961772, 1998 Del. Super. LEXIS 516 (Oct. 13, 1998) (broker that arranged commercial loan not covered; court does not state rationale other than referring to statutory definitions), *aff'd on other grounds*, 734 A.2d 640 (Del. 1999).
229 State *ex rel.* Woods v. Sgrillo, 176 Ariz. 148, 859 P.2d 771 (Ariz. Ct. App. 1993) (affirming civil penalties of $2,038,000).

repair organization's activities may be liable. Many state statutes explicitly apply their prohibitions not only to the organization itself, but also to its agents and representatives, including independent contractors. One decision finds that a lender who prepared the broker agreement for the mortgage broker, and then funded the loan, violated the state credit repair law even though only the broker met the statutory definition of "credit services organization."[230] But another decision from the same district holds that others who participate in the scheme with a credit repair organization but do not themselves meet the statutory definition are not subject to the statute.[231] And the West Virginia Supreme Court has held that a lender did not have a legal duty to ensure that an independent broker complied with the state credit repair law.[232]

15.3.3 Exemptions

Another important difference between state and federal credit repair laws is that the state laws tend to have more exceptions than the federal statute. For example, state laws typically exempt attorneys, while the federal law does not. This means that a parallel state cause of action will not be available against some of the entities covered by the federal law.

State statutes vary in the parties they exempt, but most exempt non-profit organizations;[233] licensed real estate brokers and attorneys when acting within the scope of their licenses; broker-dealers registered with the SEC or CFTC; consumer reporting agencies (CRAs); credit unions; banks eligible for FDIC or FSLIC insurance; banks and other entities authorized to extend credit under federal or state law;[234] and lenders approved by HUD for participation in federal mortgage insurance. A smaller number exempt debt collectors, debt adjusters, mortgage brokers, accountants, holders of other licenses, or other entities. Many statutes provide that the burden of proving an exemption is upon the party claiming it.

A Pennsylvania trial court concluded that licensed real estate brokers were operating within the scope of their licenses and were therefore exempt from the state credit repair law when they held credit workshops.[235] The workshops were limited to the realtors' clients; the only business of the workshops was to help these clients get mortgages; and the realtors' employees supervised the workshop employees and paid the expenses of the workshops. A federal court held that an exemption for licensed lenders applied to a loan broker that had a lending license, even when it was operating as a broker rather than as a lender.[236]

15.3.4 Do State Credit Repair Laws Apply to Retailers Who Arrange Credit for Customers?

15.3.4.1 Introduction

A highly significant question is whether car dealers or home improvement contractors who arrange credit for their customers are covered by state credit services acts that apply not only to entities that offer credit repair services but also to entities that offer to arrange credit for consumers. One reason this question is important is that car dealers and other sellers do not consider themselves covered by such statutes and never comply with the detailed requirements regarding cooling-off periods, not accepting payment until the service is completed, disclosures, registration with the state, and the like.[237] Where the seller is in fact covered by the state credit repair statute, but fails to comply, consumer remedies are quite powerful and may include voiding the transaction, punitive damages, and attorney fees.[238]

Whether sellers who arrange credit are covered by a state credit services act depends on careful analysis of the exact language of the statute. Two issues are particularly important: whether the statute requires that the consumer pay money specifically for the credit services and whether the dealer falls within an exemption for entities authorized by state or federal law to extend credit.

15.3.4.2 Requirement of Payment of Fee for the Credit Services

Unlike most state credit repair statutes, the coverage provisions of Ohio's credit repair statute formerly required that the consumer pay money without specifically saying that the money had to be *for* the credit services. A series of cases held that car dealerships that arranged credit for their customers were regulated by the Ohio Credit Services Or-

---

230 Lewis v. Delta Funding Corp. (*In re* Lewis), 290 B.R. 541 (Bankr. E.D. Pa. 2003). *But cf.* Strang v. Wells Fargo Bank, 2005 WL 1655886 (E.D. Pa. July 13, 2005) (lender had no derivative liability under state credit repair law for acts of closing agent and loan broker who were not shown to be covered by that law).

231 Allen v. Advanta Fin. Corp., 2002 U.S. Dist. LEXIS 11650 (E.D. Pa. Jan. 3, 2002).

232 Herrod v. First Republic Mortg. Corp., 625 S.E.2d 373 (W. Va. 2005).

233 *See In re* Zuniga, 332 B.R. 760, 786 (Bankr. S.D. Tex. 2005) (rejecting company's claim to be exempt where evidence showed that it did not have non-profit status).

234 *See* McMaster v. CIT Group/Consumer Fin., Inc., 2006 WL 1314379, at *9 (E.D. Pa. May 11, 2006) (licensed lender is exempt).

235 King v. Rubin, 35 Phila. 571, 1998 Phila. Cty. Rptr. LEXIS 73 (Pa. C.P. July 1, 1998).

236 Brown v. Mortgagestar, Inc., 194 F. Supp. 2d 473 (S.D. W. Va. 2002).

237 *See* § 15.3.5, *infra*.

238 *See* § 15.3.6, *infra*.

ganization Act as long as the dealer accepted any money from the consumer, even if no part of the payment was designated in any way for arranging the credit.[239] The first appellate decision on the question, however, read into the definition of "buyer" a requirement that the consumer show either payment of a fee specifically for the service of arranging credit or that the cost of this service was included in the price of the vehicle.[240] This decision, while requiring that there be a specific charge for the service of arranging credit, still recognizes that dealers can and will be covered by the state credit repair law if a specific charge is shown. In any event, while these cases were being decided, the statute was amended to insert a requirement that the consumer's payment be *for* the credit services[241] and to explicitly exclude car dealers when acting within the scope of their licenses.[242]

The Illinois credit services organization statute is more typical in that it only applies if the credit repair services are provided in return for the payment of money or other valuable consideration. Applying this definition, an intermediate appellate court held that a retail seller—specifically, a home improvement contractor—who arranged financing for consumers must comply with the Illinois Credit Services Organizations Act.[243] The court held that the seller's provision of credit services was "in return for" the payment of money because it was part of the seller's agreement with the buyer so was supported by the same consideration that supported the rest of the contract. However, the Illinois Supreme Court reversed this decision, holding that there had to be a specific payment for the credit services; a payment for other goods or services is insufficient.[244]

In courts that require the consumer to show that the retailer accepted money specifically for the purpose of arranging credit, the consumer will have to examine the transaction carefully to see if there is a charge earmarked for the dealer's assistance in obtaining credit. Since dealers invariably make money from a credit transaction through yield spread premiums or other kickbacks, this should not be difficult to show.[245] The dealership may also have made a special payment from the proceeds of the sale to the "F & I" employee who arranged the credit.

Another possibility is that the dealership may have charged the consumer a document preparation fee.[246] The

---

239 Snook v. Ford Motor Co., 2000 Ohio Misc. LEXIS 7 (C.P. Jan. 6, 2000) (summary judgment that Ohio Credit Services Organization Act applied and that dealer had violated the Act), *rev'd, remanded*, 142 Ohio App. 3d 212, 755 N.E.2d 380 (2001) (remanding for finding whether plaintiffs meet definition of "buyer," which requires transfer of money or other consideration specifically for credit services); Hester v. Alan Besco Cars-Trucks, Inc., 1999 Ohio Misc. LEXIS 62 (C.P. Aug. 9, 1999) (summary judgment that Ohio Credit Services Organization Act applied and that dealer had violated the Act); Bailey v. Ford Motor Co., 1999 Ohio Misc. LEXIS 61 (C.P. Aug. 10, 1999) (summary judgment that Ohio Credit Services Organization Act applied to dealer who had arranged a lease, that dealer had violated the Act, and that violation was per se UDAP violation); Sannes v. Jeff Wyler Chevrolet, Inc., 1999 Ohio Misc. LEXIS 63 (C.P. Mar. 15, 1999), *upheld on reconsideration*, 107 Ohio Misc. 2d 11, 736 N.E.2d 116 (C.P. 1999) (the state's automobile dealer association and retail merchant association filed amicus briefs in opposition to the initial decision); Hall v. Jack Walker Pontiac, Toyota, Inc., 1999 Ohio Misc. LEXIS 65 (C.P. Mar. 1, 1999) (magistrate's decision), *adopted by* 1999 Ohio Misc. LEXIS 64 (C.P. Sept. 24, 1999), *aff'd on other grounds*, 758 N.E.2d 1151 (Ohio Ct. App. 2000) (affirming denial of class certification). *But see* Blinkoff v. Ricart Ford, Inc., 2000 Ohio Misc. LEXIS 8 (C.P. Jan. 18, 2000) (consumer's payment of money must be for the credit services, not merely to lease the vehicle). *But cf.* Clark v. D.O.W. Fin. Co., 2000 WL 973092, 2000 Del. Super. LEXIS 238 (May 26, 2000) (automotive finance company itself is not a credit services organization as it does not obtain extensions of credit by others for consideration).

240 Snook v. Ford Motor Co., 142 Ohio App. 3d 212, 755 N.E.2d 380 (Ohio Ct. App. 2001) (2-1 decision; dissent would have affirmed, based on buyer's affidavit that she paid dealer for an inseparable "bundle" consisting of the vehicle plus the assistance in obtaining credit). *Accord* Blinkoff v. Ricart Ford, Inc., 2000 Ohio Misc. LEXIS 8 (C.P. Jan. 18, 2000).

241 Ohio Rev. Code § 4712.01, *as amended by* Am. Sub. H.B. 283, effective 90 days from June 30, 1999.

242 Ohio Rev. Code § 4712.01(C)(2)(k).

243 Midstate Siding & Window Co. v. Rogers, 309 Ill. App. 3d 610, 243 Ill. Dec. 87, 722 N.E.2d 1156 (1999), *review granted*, 204 Ill. 2d 314 (2003). *See also* Harris v. River View Ford, Inc., 2001 WL 1155279, 2001 U.S. Dist. LEXIS 15714 (N.D. Ill. Sept. 27, 2001) (finding *Midstate Siding* persuasive and provisionally following it while awaiting ruling from Illinois Supreme Court); Brugger v. Elmhurst Kia, 2001 WL 845472, 2001 U.S. Dist. LEXIS 10298 (N.D. Ill. July 18, 2001) (same); Jafri v. Lynch Ford, 2000 U.S. Dist. LEXIS 20736 (N.D. Ill. Aug. 25, 2000) (same). *Cf* Alvizo v. Metro Ford Sales & Serv., Inc., 2002 WL 10470 (N.D. Ill. Jan. 3, 2002) (provisionally following *Midstate Siding* while awaiting ruling from Illinois Supreme Court); Crowe v. Joliet Dodge, 2001 WL 811655, 2001 U.S. Dist. LEXIS 10066 (N.D. Ill. July 17, 2001) (same); Harris v. Castle Motor Sales, Inc., 2001 WL 477241, 2001 U.S. Dist. LEXIS 5797 (N.D. Ill. May 4, 2001) (same); Strohmaier v. Yemm Chevrolet, 211 F. Supp. 2d 1036 (N.D. Ill. 2001) (same). *But see* Fogle v. William Chevrolet/Geo, Inc., 2000 WL 1129983, 2000 U.S. Dist. LEXIS 11556 (N.D. Ill. Aug. 8, 2000) (holding, based on court's perception of legislative intent and public policy, that credit repair organization statute does not apply to car dealers).

244 Midstate Siding & Window Co. v. Rogers, 204 Ill. 2d 314, 789 N.E.2d 1248, 273 Ill. Dec. 816 (2003). *Accord* Thele v. Sunrise Chevrolet, Inc., 2004 WL 1194751 (N.D. Ill. May 28, 2004) (car dealer was not credit services organization where it did not charge fee for forwarding credit application to potential lenders). *See also* Oslan v. Collection Bureau, 206 F.R.D. 109 (E.D. Pa. 2001) (debt collector is covered by federal CROA only if receives or solicits payment beyond repayment of debt).

245 *But see* Cannon v. William Chevrolet/Geo, Inc., 341 Ill. App. 3d 674, 794 N.E.2d 843, 276 Ill. Dec. 593 (2003) (finding car dealership not to be a credit repair organization even though it required consumer to pay a 4.5% higher interest rate than bank required).

246 *But see* Cannon v. William Chevrolet/Geo, Inc., 341 Ill. App. 3d 674, 794 N.E.2d 843, 276 Ill. Dec. 593 (2003) (finding car dealership not to be a credit repair organization even though it

consumer can probably show through discovery that the primary purpose of such a fee was to compensate the retailer for preparing the credit contract, the credit application, and other credit documents. If no special charge for arranging the credit can be identified, some decisions suggest that the consumer may still be able to establish coverage by showing that the charge was buried in the cost of the product.[247]

15.3.4.3 Do Retailers Fall Within a Specific Statutory Exemption?

In some states dealers and other sellers may claim that they fall within an exemption for entities that are authorized to extend credit under state or federal laws. Some dealers may hold a license under the state Retail Installment Sales Act or Motor Vehicle Installment Sales Act. Such a license allows the dealer to enter into retail installment contracts, which most sellers then assign to a financing entity.

On the other hand, such an exemption will not help a seller, such as a home improvement contractor, who merely arranges a direct loan between the consumer and a third-party lender. There may be no difference in the consumer's eyes between a direct loan and an installment contract that is assigned to a financing entity, but in the first case the obligation is originally payable to the seller, while, in the case of a loan, the debt is owed to the lender from the outset. With a direct loan, the seller itself is not extending credit, but merely arranging for a loan from a third party, so will not be covered by its retail installment sales license. The fact that it acts as the lender's agent for the purposes of obtaining the consumer's signature on the loan papers does not mean that it shares in the lender's exemption.[248] Any other conclusion would nullify the application of state credit repair statutes to entities that obtain or offer to obtain extensions of credit for the consumer.

Retailers may also push special exemptions through their state legislatures. An immediate response to the Ohio cases discussed in § 15.3.4.2, *supra*, was that the Ohio legislature amended the Credit Services Organization Act to explicitly exclude car dealers when acting within the scope of their licenses.[249] The amendment has not been applied retroactively, however.[250] Moreover, there is some doubt that the legislation comported with the Ohio Constitution, because it was attached to an unrelated bill.

15.3.4.4 Legislative Intent

Retailers typically argue that the legislature could not have intended that they be included under the state credit repair law. The legislature's specific list of entities that are exempt is, however, strong evidence that others are not exempt.[251] In addition, there are strong reasons why a legislature would want a state credit repair law to cover dealers who arrange credit. These sellers often make most of their profit through arranging credit, not selling goods or services. They are in an excellent position to slip terms into financing contracts that are profitable to them but highly disadvantageous to the consumer. Prohibiting deception, requiring registration, and affording a right to cancel would directly address these abuses.

15.3.5 *Substantive Prohibitions*

Typical requirements of state credit repair statutes include:

- Registration and bonding,[252] requirements that go beyond the federal statute.
- Disclosures to the buyer about rights available under the FCRA. In contrast to the federal statute, state statutes usually describe the disclosures that must be made rather than specifying the exact language that must be used.
- Written contracts with specified provisions, including a description of the services to be provided.[253] A California appellate court has held that the state credit repair law, which requires that contracts be in writing and signed by the consumer, applies not just to the initial

---

required consumer to pay documentary fee of $46.88).

247 *See* Snook v. Ford Motor Co., 142 Ohio App. 3d 212, 755 N.E.2d 380 (Apr. 6, 2001) (state CRO statute will apply if cost of the credit services is included in the cost of the vehicle).

248 Hester v. Alan Besco Cars-Trucks, Inc., 1999 Ohio Misc. LEXIS 62 (C.P. Aug. 9, 1999).

249 Amended Substitute House Bill 283, *adding* Ohio Rev. Code § 4712.01(C)(2)(k) (June 30, 1999).

250 *See* Snook v. Ford Motor Co., 2000 Ohio Misc. LEXIS 7 (C.P. Jan. 6, 2000), *rev'd, remanded on other grounds*, 142 Ohio App. 3d 212, 755 N.E.2d 380 (2001); Hall v. Jack Walker Pontiac, Toyota, Inc., 1999 Ohio Misc. LEXIS 65 (C.P. Mar. 1, 1999) (magistrate's decision), *adopted by* 1999 Ohio Misc. LEXIS 64 (C.P. Sept. 24, 1999), *aff'd on other grounds*, 758 N.E.2d 1151 (Ohio Ct. App. 2000) (affirming denial of class certification).

251 Hester v. Alan Besco Cars-Trucks, Inc., 1999 Ohio Misc. LEXIS 62 (C.P. Aug. 9, 1999).

252 *See* Illinois v. National Credit Mgmt. Group, 1996 WL 351196, 1996 U.S. Dist. LEXIS 8722 (N.D. Ill. June 20, 1996) (denying motion to dismiss claim that credit repair organization violated state credit repair law by violating bonding requirements); *In re* Zuniga, 332 B.R. 760, 786–787 (Bankr. S.D. Tex. 2005) (credit repair organization violated statute by failing to register).

253 *See* Illinois v. National Credit Mgmt. Group, 1996 WL 351196, 1996 U.S. Dist. LEXIS 8722 (N.D. Ill. June 20, 1996) (denying motion to dismiss claim that credit repair organization violated state credit repair law by failing to comply with requirements for form of contracts); *In re* Zuniga, 332 B.R. 760, 787 (Bankr. S.D. Tex. 2005) (violation shown where credit repair organization merely sent a welcome letter that did not describe its services and was sent only after services began). *Cf.* Herrod v. First Republic Mortg. Corp., 625 S.E.2d 373 (W. Va. 2005) (lender not liable for broker's failure to give copy of contract to borrowers).

contract but also to any later modifications of it.[254] As a result, an arbitration clause added to existing customers' contracts was ineffective except as to those consumers who signed it.
- A prohibition against charging the consumer for a referral to a retail seller who will or may extend credit to the consumer on the same terms as those available to the general public.
- A three- or five-day right to cancel.
- A prohibition against certain misrepresentations and deceptive acts.[255]

Some state credit repair laws identify certain charges as illegal. The West Virginia Supreme Court has ruled, however, that yield spread premiums do not violate its statute's prohibition.[256] A number of state statutes explicitly prohibit waivers of the statutory protections.

The right to cancel under state credit repair laws is particularly important in transactions involving real estate. For example, "home savers" who approach homeowners facing foreclosure and offer to arrange credit to save the home may be covered by a state credit repair law. Then the contract with the home saver—which sometimes includes conveyance of the home or a lien on the home to the home saver—is subject to cancellation. A particular advantage of this approach is that the right to rescind under the Truth in Lending Act expires after three years,[257] while there is no such limit for cancellation under the typical state credit repair statute.

Some state credit repair statutes, like the federal statute, prohibit organizations from accepting payment from the buyer before performing services.[258] Many allow advance payment once the organization has posted a bond, however.

15.3.6 Private Causes of Action

Almost all state credit repair statutes provide a private right of action to consumers. Some do so both by making a violation actionable under the state UDAP statute[259] and by creating a special cause of action. For many claims under state credit repair statutes, intent is not an element.[260]

The special causes of action offered by state credit repair laws are often broader than those authorized by the state UDAP statute. Usually the statutes that create special causes of action authorize punitive damages and attorney fees. Many, like the federal statute,[261] set as minimum damages the total amount paid by the consumer.[262] A few set a dollar amount, such as $1000, as minimum damages. The minimum damage awards involve few or no individual fact questions so are well-suited for class action treatment.

A few state statutes, like the federal law, do not require the consumer to have suffered actual damages, but most afford a cause of action only to an "injured person." Presumably any payment to a credit repair organization will constitute injury.

A number of state laws, like the federal Act, make non-complying contracts void and unenforceable.[263] A declaration that all contracts are void, with an ancillary order for restitution, could conceivably be won in a Rule 23(b)(2) class action, which is easier to certify than a 23(b)(3) action.

Pleading a parallel claim under state law in a suit alleging violations of the federal statute offers a number of advantages. UDAP claims in particular often allow multiple damages, a remedy that the federal law does not include. Even if the state credit repair law does not explicitly state that a violation is a UDAP violation, in many states any violation of a consumer protection law is a per se UDAP violation.[264] In addition, the credit repair organization is likely to have made many misstatements that will be actionable under a state UDAP statute. Cases filed in states with a bonding requirement should combine claims under the state and federal acts in order to maximize the availability of the bond to satisfy any judgment ultimately received.

---

254 Mitchell v. Am. Fair Credit Ass'n, 122 Cal. Rptr. 2d 193 (Cal. Ct. App. 2002).

255 Slack v. Fair Isaac Corp., 390 F. Supp. 2d 906 (N.D. Cal. 2005) (allegation that defendant promised customized advice but provided only a general assessment generated by a computer states claim).

256 Herrod v. First Republic Mortg. Corp., 625 S.E.2d 373 (W. Va. 2005).

257 See National Consumer Law Center, Truth in Lending § 6.3.3 (5th ed. 2003 and Supp.).

258 See In re Zuniga, 332 B.R. 760, 787 (Bankr. S.D. Tex. 2005) (violation shown where credit repair organization that had not posted bond charged fee before rendering any service); State v. New Beginning Credit Ass'n, 2006 WL 1472284 (Tenn. Ct. App. May 25, 2006) (unpublished) (credit repair organization must forego any compensation from consumer prior to completion of every service; characterizing fee as down payment, deposit, or layaway plan does not evade prohibition).

259 See Illinois v. National Credit Mgmt. Group, 1996 WL 351196, 1996 U.S. Dist. LEXIS 8722 (N.D. Ill. June 20, 1996) (denying motion to dismiss claim that credit repair organization violated state credit repair law by violating bonding requirements); Barker v. Altegra Corp. (*In re* Barker), 251 B.R. 250 (Bankr. E.D. Pa. 2000) (any violation of state credit repair law is UDAP violation).

260 Westfield Group v. Campisi, 2006 WL 328415, at *19 (W.D. Pa. Feb. 10, 2006).

261 15 U.S.C. § 1679g(a)(1)(B).

262 See In re Bell, 309 B.R. 139 (Bankr. E.D. Pa. 2004) (awarding as damages the amount consumer paid to mortgage loan broker, including yield spread premium), *reconsideration granted in part* 314 B.R. 54, 60 (Bankr. E.D. Pa. 2004) (violation of credit repair law is UDAP violation, but consumer suffers no actual damages where loan is rescinded, so is not entitled to have any amount trebled under UDAP statute); Barker v. Altegra Corp. (*In re* Barker), 251 B.R. 250 (Bankr. E.D. Pa. 2000) (amount paid must be awarded regardless of amount of actual damages).

263 See § 15.2.8.1, *supra*.

264 See National Consumer Law Center, Unfair and Deceptive Acts and Practices § 3.2.7 (6th ed. 2004 and Supp.).

15.3.7 State Remedies

The typical state credit repair statute permits state enforcement as well as a private cause of action. Restitution of fees paid by consumers is an appropriate remedy.[265]

15.3.8 Federal Preemption

The federal Credit Repair Organizations Act provides that it does not annul, alter, affect, or exempt any person subject to its provisions from complying with state laws except to the extent that the state law is inconsistent with the federal law, and then only to the extent of the inconsistency.[266] Since this language is identical to the general preemption language in the Fair Credit Reporting Act, it should be interpreted similarly.[267] Interpretations of the similar language in the Truth in Lending Act,[268] the Equal Credit Opportunity Act,[269] and the Fair Debt Collection Practices Act,[270] should also be persuasive.

State law should be considered preempted where compliance with the state statute would result in a violation of the federal law,[271] but state laws that provide more protections to consumers should not be preempted.[272] This interpretation of the preemption provision is confirmed by the legislative history of CROA. A House Report on a predecessor bill, referring to language identical to that ultimately adopted, states: "Any weaker state law would be inconsistent with this Title. A state law is not inconsistent if it provides greater consumer protection than this Title."[273]

Applying these standards, state registration and bonding requirements would not be preempted, since an organization can comply with them without running afoul of CROA in any way. State laws that require contract terms or disclosures would be preempted only if those terms or disclosures conflicted with those required by the federal law.[274]

States that provide a longer cancellation period than federal law should also avoid preemption. A credit repair organization does not violate the federal statute by providing a five-day right to cancel in addition to the three-day cancellation right mandated by the federal law. The credit repair organization must, however, take care not to disclose the two cancellation rights so that they obscure or undercut each other.[275] In states that require a five-day right to cancel, a credit repair organization that merely complies with the federal law will be subject to suit under the state law.

On the other hand, state laws that allow credit repair organizations to accept payment before the services are fully performed as long as they have posted a bond will be preempted. An organization that accepted advance payment under this state law provision would be in violation of the federal law.

A final preemption issue involves the disclosures that state credit repair laws require. Many of these laws specify disclosures about the consumer's rights that were accurate when the state law was passed but were rendered inaccurate by the 1996 amendments to the Fair Credit Reporting Act. The state law provisions requiring disclosure of outdated information are probably preempted by the federal Credit Repair Organization Act if the organization is subject to that Act, as it would probably be considered a violation of CROA to make disclosures that contradict the disclosures it requires.[276] Even for organizations not covered by CROA, however, state credit repair laws are probably preempted by the Fair Credit Reporting Act[277] to the extent that they require disclosure about consumer reporting rights that is no longer accurate.

Of course, to the extent that state laws cover entities that the federal law does not cover, there are no preemption concerns other than the outdated disclosure requirements. These entities must comply with the state law.

15.4 Federal Telemarketing Statutes and Regulations

15.4.1 Federal Telemarketing and Consumer Fraud and Abuse Prevention Act

Congress enacted the Telemarketing and Consumer Fraud and Abuse Prevention Act of 1994 (FTC Telemarketing Rule) in response to concerns over an estimated $40 billion lost annually by consumers to telemarketing fraud.[278] The Act directs the FTC to "prescribe rules prohibiting decep-

---

265 State v. New Beginning Credit Ass'n, 2006 WL 1472284 (Tenn. Ct. App. May 25, 2006) (unpublished) (reversing trial court's refusal to order restitution).
266 15 U.S.C. § 1679j.
267 See § 10.7.1, supra.
268 15 U.S.C. § 1610(a)(1). See National Consumer Law Center, Truth in Lending § 2.6.3 (5th ed. 2003 and Supp.).
269 15 U.S.C. § 1691d(f). See National Consumer Law Center, Credit Discrimination § 11.6.1.3 (4th ed. 2005).
270 15 U.S.C. § 1692n. See National Consumer Law Center, Fair Debt Collection § 6.13.1 (5th ed. 2004 and Supp.).
271 See FTC Official Staff Commentary on FCRA § 622 item 1, reprinted in Appx. D, infra.
272 See id. item 2 (example of statute that is not preempted).
273 H.R. Rep. 486, 103d Cong., 2d Sess. (relating to H.R. 1015). Accord H.R. Rep. 692, 102d Cong. (July 23, 1992) (relating to H.R. 3596). See generally § 1.4.6, supra (legislative history of the bill that included CROA).
274 15 U.S.C. § 1679d.

275 Cf. Williams v. Empire Funding Corp., 109 F. Supp. 2d 352 (E.D. Pa. 2000) (seller violated Truth in Lending Act by disclosing one-day state right to cancel that made 3-day TIL rescission period unclear).
276 15 U.S.C. § 1679c.
277 15 U.S.C. § 1681t. See § 10.7.1, supra.
278 Pub. L. No. 103-297, 108 Stat. 1545 (1994), codified at 15 U.S.C. §§ 6101–6108.

tive telemarketing acts or practices and other abusive telemarketing acts or practices" and to enforce those rules.[279] The Act further allows states to bring civil actions for violations of those rules.[280] It provides consumers a private right of action for telemarketing fraud, but only if the amount in controversy exceeds $50,000.[281]

In 1995, the FTC adopted its Telemarketing Rule[282] pursuant to this Act.[283] The FTC Telemarketing Rule was extensively amended effective March 31, 2003,[284] but the amendments did not have a significant effect on the restrictions that apply to credit repair organizations.

The FTC Telemarketing Rule explicitly applies to credit repair services that are marketed through at least one interstate telephone call without a face-to-face meeting.[285] It specifically covers cases where the consumer makes the first call to the credit repair organization in response to an advertisement or direct mail solicitation, including those transmitted by fax, e-mail, or similar methods.[286] It does not, however, cover 900-number calls to credit repair clinics, because these are regulated by different statutes and rules.[287] The FTC Telemarketing Rule does not cover charitable organizations but covers for-profit organizations that solicit contributions or sell goods or services on behalf of non-profit organizations.[288]

One area in which the FTC Telemarketing Rule provides greater consumer protection than the Credit Repair Organizations Act is payment for services. The Credit Repair Organizations Act prohibits credit repair organizations from charging or receiving payment for their services until the service is fully performed.[289] The FTC's Telemarketing Rule, on the other hand, requires the credit repair organization to wait even longer. It prohibits a credit repair clinic from requesting or receiving any payment for its services until the seller has provided the consumer with a consumer report, issued at least six months after the credit repair services were provided, that demonstrates that the promised results have been achieved.[290] Since fraudulent credit repair clinics have difficulty achieving an improvement in the consumer's credit record that lasts six months, the FTC Telemarketing Rule comes close to outlawing their activities to the extent that they fall within its coverage.

The FTC Telemarketing Rule also applies special restrictions to telemarketers who offer to arrange loans or other extensions of credit for consumers. These telemarketers are prohibited from requesting or receiving payment of any fee or consideration in advance of obtaining the loan or extension of credit.[291] This prohibition only applies, however, if the telemarketer represents that there is a high likelihood of success in obtaining credit. Credit repair clinics are likely to violate this prohibition since they often offer not only to improve the consumer's credit but also to help obtain credit cards or loans.

The FTC Telemarketing Rule also imposes general proscriptions against facilitating or engaging in deceptive telemarketing.[292] It requires disclosures of the total costs of the goods or services sold, their quantity, all material restrictions, limitations, or conditions, and information about the seller's refund policy.[293] Credit repair organizations are likely to run afoul of these prohibitions as well.

The 2003 amendments to the FTC Telemarketing Rule establish a nationwide do-not-call list.[294] Consumers who have received telephone solicitations from credit repair organizations should consider adding their names to the do-not-call list.[295]

Unfortunately, neither the Act nor the FTC Telemarketing Rule is likely to provide a consumer with a private cause of action against a credit repair organization. The Act does create a private cause of action for violations of the FTC Telemarketing Rule, but only where each plaintiff's damages exceed $50,000. Usually damages will be far less. Consumers may instead invoke the FTC Telemarketing Rule as a per se violation of state UDAP statutes.[296] A UDAP violation will entitle the consumer to actual or statutory damages, sometimes double or triple damages, plus attorney fees and costs.[297]

---

279 15 U.S.C. §§ 6102(a)(1), 6105.
280 15 U.S.C. § 6103.
281 15 U.S.C. § 6104.
282 16 C.F.R. Part 310. The rule was published at 60 Fed. Reg. 43,842 (Aug. 23, 1995) (effective Dec. 31, 1995).
283 15 U.S.C. §§ 6101–6108. *See* National Consumer Law Center, Unfair and Deceptive Acts and Practices § 5.9.4 and Appxs. D.1.1, D.2.1 (6th ed. 2004 and Supp.).
284 68 Fed. Reg. 4,530 (Jan. 29, 2003).
285 16 C.F.R. §§ 310.2(cc) (definition of "telemarketing"), 310.6(b)(3) (former §§ 310.2(u), 310.6(c)).
286 16 C.F.R. § 310.6(b)(5), (6), *as amended by* 68 Fed. Reg. 4,530 (Jan. 29, 2003). The former version of these sections of the rule, 16 C.F.R. § 310.6(e), (f), did not specifically mention fax and e-mail transmission.
287 16 C.F.R. § 310.6(b)(1) (formerly § 310.6(a)). *See* 47 U.S.C. § 228, 15 U.S.C. § 5711, 47 C.F.R. Part 64, and 16 C.F.R. Part 308, for the statutes, FCC rules, and FTC rules relating to 900-number abuses.
288 *See* 68 Fed. Reg. 4,530, 4,589–4,590 (Jan. 29, 2003).
289 15 U.S.C. § 1679b(b).
290 16 C.F.R. § 310.4(a)(2). *See* Illinois v. National Credit Mgmt. Group, 1996 WL 351196, 1996 U.S. Dist. LEXIS 8722 (N.D. Ill. June 20, 1996) (refusing to dismiss state's suit for violation of FTC telemarketing rule's prohibition against accepting payment prior to time specified in the rule).
291 16 C.F.R. § 310.4(a)(4).
292 16 C.F.R. § 310.3.
293 16 C.F.R. § 310.3(a)(1).
294 16 C.F.R. § 310.4(b)(iii)(B).
295 Consumers may add their names to the do-not-call list by calling 888-382-1222 (TTY 866-290-4236) or on-line at www.ftc.gov/donotcall.
296 *See* National Consumer Law Center, Unfair and Deceptive Acts and Practices §§ 3.2.7.3.6, 3.4.5 (6th ed. 2004 and Supp.).
297 *See* National Consumer Law Center, Unfair and Deceptive Acts and Practices Ch. 8 (6th ed. 2004 and Supp.).

15.4.2 Federal Telephone Consumer Protection Act

The federal Telephone Consumer Protection Act of 1991 (TCPA)[298] provides certain protections against telemarketing calls. It covers both interstate and intrastate calls.[299] It has no restrictions specifically aimed at credit repair clinics, but has general restrictions that fraudulent credit repair clinics may violate. It is discussed in detail in another NCLC manual.[300]

FCC regulations under this statute prohibit telephone solicitations before 8:00 a.m. or after 9:00 p.m., local time (determined by the called party's location).[301] The statute and regulations also prohibit:

- The use of a telephone fax machine, a computer, or any other device to send an unsolicited advertisement to a telephone fax machine (with an exception if the sender has an established business relationship with the recipient);[302]
- Placing calls by means of an automatic dialing system or using an artificial or prerecorded voice to emergency telephone lines, to patient or guest rooms at nursing homes, hospitals, and similar health facilities, or to pagers, cellular phones, or other services in which the called party is charged for the call (with exceptions for emergency calls or with the prior express consent of the called party);[303]
- Placing a call that uses an artificial or prerecorded voice to a residence, unless the caller is a tax-exempt non-profit organization, the call is for emergency purposes, the caller has an established business relationship with the called party, the call is for non-commercial purposes, or the call is for commercial purposes but does not include any unsolicited advertisements;[304]
- Calling consumers who have registered with the national do-not-call list.[305]

These restrictions are constitutional as content-neutral restrictions on the time, place and manner of protected speech[306] and do not violate the Equal Protection Clause.[307]

The Telephone Consumer Protection Act explicitly grants consumers the right to bring suit for violations in state court "if otherwise permitted by the laws or rules of court" of the state.[308] The consumer may seek an injunction and may also seek the greater of actual monetary loss or up to $500 for each violation.[309] The consumer need not prove actual damages in order to recover the statutory damages.[310] The statute's provision for a minimum penalty of $500 regardless of the actual amount of monetary damages incurred does not violate the Constitution's Due Process Clause.[311] The court may treble the damages if it finds that the defendant's violation was willful or knowing.[312] There is no provision for an attorney fee award, but the consumer may be able to assert a parallel claim under the state UDAP statute and win fees under that statute. Consumers also have the alternative of filing complaints with the FCC.[313]

15.4.3 State Telemarketing Statutes

Almost all states have their own telemarketing laws that afford a private cause of action to consumers.[314] Most of these statutes do not place special restrictions on credit repair clinics, but in many cases a credit repair clinic that has conducted a sale over the telephone will have violated one of the more general prohibitions of the state telemarketing statute. For example, many require specific disclosures and a written contract or confirmation of the transaction.

---

298 47 U.S.C. § 227. This statute and the regulations under it are reproduced in National Consumer Law Center, Unfair and Deceptive Acts and Practices Appx. D (6th ed. 2004 and Supp.).
299 47 U.S.C. § 152(b). *See* Hooters of Augusta, Inc. v. Nicholson, 245 Ga. App. 363, 537 S.E.2d 468 (2000).
300 National Consumer Law Center, Unfair and Deceptive Acts and Practices § 5.9.3 (6th ed. 2004 and Supp.).
301 47 C.F.R. § 64.1200(c)(1).
302 47 U.S.C. § 227(b)(1)(C); 47 C.F.R. § 64.1200(a)(3).
303 47 U.S.C. § 227(b)(1)(A); 47 C.F.R. § 64.1200(a)(1).
304 47 U.S.C. § 227(b)(1)(B); 47 C.F.R. § 64.1200(a)(2).
305 47 C.F.R. § 64.1200(c).
306 Moser v. Fed. Communications Comm'n, 46 F.3d 970 (9th Cir. 1995); Texas v. American Blast Fax, Inc., 121 F. Supp. 2d 1085 (W.D. Tex. 2000); Kenro, Inc. v. Fax Daily, Inc., 962 F. Supp. 1162 (S.D. Ind. 1997). *See also* Destination Ventures, Ltd. v. Fed. Communications Comm'n, 46 F.3d 54 (9th Cir. 1995) (restriction on unsolicited fax transmissions directly advances substantial governmental interest in manner that is no more extensive than necessary), *aff'd,* 46 F.3d 54 (9th Cir. 1995); State *ex rel.* Humphrey v. Casino Mktg. Group, Inc., 491 N.W.2d 882 (Minn. 1992) (Minnesota's statutory restriction on automatic dialing announcement devices upheld).
307 Texas v. American Blast Fax, Inc., 121 F. Supp. 2d 1085 (W.D. Tex. 2000).
308 47 U.S.C. § 227(b)(3), (c)(5). Most courts have held that federal courts do not have jurisdiction over consumer suits to enforce the statute. *See, e.g.,* Murphey v. Lanier, 204 F.3d 911 (9th Cir. 2000). This and other jurisdictional questions under this statute are discussed at National Consumer Law Center, Unfair and Deceptive Acts and Practices § 5.9.3.9.2 (6th ed. 2004 and Supp.).
309 47 U.S.C. § 227(b)(3), (c)(5).
310 Kaplan v. Democrat & Chronicle, 698 N.Y.S.2d 799 (N.Y. Ct. App. Div. 1999) (statutory damages are punitive, not compensatory, in nature).
311 Kenro, Inc. v. Fax Daily, Inc., 962 F. Supp. 1162 (S.D. Ind. 1997).
312 47 U.S.C. § 227(b)(3).
313 Complaints can be filed through the FCC's website, www.fcc.gov/ccb/enforce/index-complaints.html.
314 State telemarketing laws are discussed and summarized in National Consumer Law Center, Unfair and Deceptive Acts and Practices § 5.9.5.3 and Appx. E (6th ed. 2004 and Supp.).

Chapter 16 Privacy Protection

16.1 Overview

The Fair Credit Reporting Act (FCRA) protects a narrow segment of financial privacy by regulating consumer reporting agencies (CRAs) that collect credit information about consumers, those who provide information to the CRAs, and those who seek information from CRAs. However, many consumer financial transactions do not fall within the FCRA and other sources of privacy law must be examined for how they can protect personal financial data from those who seek to acquire and exploit it. Discussed below are some federal statutes, state statutes, common law tort claims and identity theft laws that may serve to shield consumers' economic conduct.

As the world goes digital, consumers' records, both financial and otherwise, are increasingly vulnerable to exposure. Transactions that were once fleeting, recorded only on paper and filed in some cabinet or perhaps reduced to microfiche, are now but mouse-clicks away from duplication and dissemination.

Unregulated databases, escalating numbers of mergers, and the proliferation of information brokers—private investigators who specialize in obtaining computerized records—all threaten privacy. As noted in Congress, "databases of personal identifiable information are increasingly prime targets of hackers, identity thieves, rogue employees, and other criminals, including organized and sophisticated criminal operations."[1]

The Internet raises particular privacy concerns, as information sent over the World Wide Web may pass through dozens of different computer systems, each of which can snatch and hold the information in its coffers. In addition, website owners can track consumers' on-line behavior and gather information about their preferences, often without their knowledge. Web bugs, tiny graphics that are put into web pages and e-mails, can monitor who views the information. Clickstream data can tell website owners which pages of the site were viewed and for how long. "Cookies" dropped onto a computer may not identify the user by name but do identify the particular computer, which allows an interested party to assemble a great deal of information about that computer's user.[2]

Financial information is especially sensitive, able to reveal not just a consumer's standard of living and debt load, but also personal preferences and lifestyle details ranging from books bought to prescriptions purchased. In *California Bankers Association v. Shultz*,[3] Justice Powell pointed out that "[f]inancial transactions can reveal much about a person's activities, associations, and beliefs." Justice Douglas elaborated further:

> A checking account ... may well record a citizen's activities, opinion, and beliefs as fully as transcripts of his telephone conversations. ... In a sense a person is defined by the checks he writes. By examining them the agents get to know his doctors, lawyers, creditors, political allies, social connections, religious affiliation, educational interests, the papers and magazines he reads, and so on ad infinitum.[4]

The same can be said of credit card charges, debit purchases, and on-line transactions. A quarter-century later, the details of these revealing consumer activities are easily collected, compiled, analyzed, and accessed, and thus have created a lucrative market for their trade. Data aggregation companies such as ChoicePoint maintain billions of consumer transaction records,[5] which they analyze, compile, and sell to their customers for target marketing and other purposes.[6] In 2005, ChoicePoint was duped into disclosing hundreds of thousands of their consumer reports to persons who posed as legitimate users of such reports, further revealing the vulnerability of consumers to the careless use of their personal information.[7]

---

1 Personal Data Privacy and Security Act of 2005, S. 1332, 109th Cong. (June 29, 2005).

2 *See* www.epic.org/privacy/internet/cookies.

3 416 U.S. 21 (1974).

4 *Id.* at 85, 90 (Douglas, J., dissenting).

5 Duane D. Stanford, *All Our Lives Are on File, for Sale*, Atl. J. Const., Mar. 20, 2004. The company adds 40,000 new public records each day from courthouses and government agencies nationwide. *Id.*

6 www.choicepoint.com.

7 The FTC brought an enforcement action against ChoicePoint over this incident, alleging that CRA did not have reasonable procedures to screen prospective subscribers to verify their identity and to make sure they had a permissible use for the information. ChoicePoint settled with the FTC, agreeing to pay

Marketers are intensely interested in consumers' web searches, and can acquire that data from those search engines that register their users.[8] Businesses—and increasingly since 9/11, the federal government—want to learn as much about consumers as possible.[9] Recently even political groups have started to seek and aggregate information about consumer choices to "microtarget" them for particular campaign materials.[10] Even the mundane task of grocery shopping is considered sufficiently informative that supermarkets use "loyalty cards" to track every item purchased by every card-holder, and they are free to sell that information to anyone who might be interested. There is a near insatiable hunger to learn how consumers get and spend their money.

Notwithstanding the sensitivity embedded in a person's financial choices, they are, for the most part, fair game for trade. While federal law protects against disclosure of video rental preferences,[11] cable viewing preferences,[12] medical records,[13] and student records,[14] it does not yet prevent financial or other institutions from selling their customers' Social Security numbers, account balances, maturity dates, securities holdings, or other information to private entities.[15]

Though the FCRA limits some disclosures by private parties of consumer financial information, it does not give consumers the right to prohibit a CRA from disclosing accurate, non-obsolete information to those deemed to have a permissible purpose.[16] The FACTA amendments to the FCRA in 2003 set the table for more thorough protection of financial information—at least of information acquired from CRAs—by requiring those who have information from consumer reports to properly dispose of it pursuant to authorized regulations.[17]

The Gramm-Leach-Bliley Act gives consumers a limited right to "opt out" of certain disclosures by financial institutions to non-affiliated third parties.[18] However, its abundant exceptions arguably all but destroy the protection it purports to provide.

American privacy law is poorly suited to protecting privacy, especially of computerized consumer information. Aside from the FCRA, privacy laws largely fall into three categories: laws protecting personal privacy from invasions by governments, federal or local; the common law tort of invasion of privacy; and statutes and case law that prohibit private parties from gaining[19] or disclosing[20] specific types of information. Relevant provisions of the Gramm-Leach-Bliley Act[21] will be described in this last category;[22] they impose certain notice requirements on financial institutions

---

$10 million in civil penalties and $5 million for consumer redress. U.S. v. ChoicePoint, Inc., CA 1 06-CV-0198 (N.D. Ga. Jan. 30, 2006) (stipulated final judgment), *reprinted at* www.ftc.gov/os/caselist/choicepoint/choicepoint.htm (available on the CD-Rom accompanying this manual).

8 *See* Tom Zeller, Jr., *You Life as an Open Book; Privacy versus Viewing the Internet User as a Commodity*, N.Y. Times (Aug. 12, 2006).

9 *See Your Privacy for Sale*, Consumer Rep. (Oct. 2006).

10 *See* Chris Cilliza and Jim VandeHei, *In Ohio, a Battle of Databases*, Wash. Post A01 (Sept. 26, 2006) (discussing Republicans' use of information about Ohio voters).

11 Video Privacy Protection Act of 1988, 18 U.S.C. § 2710.

12 Cable Communications Policy Act of 1984, 47 U.S.C. § 551(c). Note that the USA PATRIOT Act expanded the list of disclosures permitted by the Cable Communications Policy Act by adding certain disclosures made to specified government authorities. Pub. L. No. 107-56, § 211 (Oct. 26, 2001), *amending* 47 U.S.C. § 551(c).

13 Most health insurers and providers must comply with the Privacy Rule promulgated pursuant to the Health Insurance Portability and Accountability Act (HIPAA). 45 C.F.R. §§ 160.101–160.312, 164.102–164.534. The HIPAA Privacy Rule generally prohibits covered entities from using or disclosing protected health information except as specifically allowed. Among the permitted disclosures are those to CRAs for purposes of payment, so long as the disclosure is limited to the following information: name and address, date of birth, Social Security number, payment history, account number, and name and address of the health care provider. 45 C.F.R. §§ 164.501, 164.506(c)(1). For a discussion of the HIPAA Privacy Rule, see National Consumer Law Center, Fair Debt Collection, § 14.3.3 (5th ed. 2004 and Supp.). See § 5.4.1, *supra*, for discussion of the FCRA's restrictions on medical information.

14 Family Educational Rights & Privacy Act of 1974, 20 U.S.C. § 1232g.

15 Federal law prohibits firms and persons who regularly prepare income tax returns for others from disclosing personal tax information or using it for other purposes, with a few excep-

tions. 26 U.S.C. § 7216. The Privacy Act of 1974, 5 U.S.C. § 552a, requires all government agencies, whether federal, state, or local, that request Social Security numbers to provide a disclosure statement that explains whether the consumer is required to provide the number, how it will be used, and under what statutory authority the agency is requesting the number. The Act provides that a consumer cannot be denied a benefit for refusing to provide the number unless the number is required by federal law (or the disclosure is to an agency that had been using Social Security numbers prior to enactment of the Privacy Act). Although usually a consumer is not compelled to disclose her Social Security number to a private business, no federal law prohibits them from asking for it or from refusing to do business with a consumer who refuses to provide it.

16 The Act additionally imposes some restrictions on users of consumer reports and imposes obligations on those that furnish information to CRAs to provide accurate information. *See* Chs. 4, 5, and 7, *supra*.

17 15 U.S.C. § 1681w, *added by* Pub. L. No. 108-159, § 216 (2003). The FTC's regulations are codified at 16 C.F.R. §§ 682.1–682.5; the Securities and Exchange Commission's, at 17 C.F.R. § 248.30; the Comptroller of the Currency's, at 12 C.F.R. § 41.83; the Board of Governors, Federal Reserve System, at 12 C.F.R. § 222.82; the FDIC's, at 12 C.F.R. § 334.83; the Office of Thrift Supervision's, at 12 C.F.R. § 571.83; the National Credit Union Administration's at 12 C.F.R. § 717.83.

18 *See* § 16.4.1, *infra*.

19 For example, through wiretapping. *See, e.g.*, 18 U.S.C. § 2510; Cal. Penal Code §§ 631 to 637; Conn. Gen. Stat. Ann. § 53a-187; Haw. Rev. Stat. § 711-1111.

20 For example, the disclosure of customers' videotape rentals. *See, e.g.*, Cal. Civ. Code § 1799.3; Conn. Gen. Stat. Ann. § 53-450; Iowa Code Ann. § 727.11.

21 15 U.S.C. §§ 6801–6810.

22 *See* § 16.4.1, *infra*.

who disclose financial data and a limited right for consumers to opt out of some kinds of disclosures.

16.2 Privacy from Governmental Intrusion

Many constitutions and statutes create a right of privacy against intrusion by a government and its agencies. For example, the United States Constitution prohibits governments from conducting unreasonable searches and seizures[23] and from enacting laws that violate the Fourteenth Amendment's guarantee of privacy.[24] Government agencies cannot freely disclose the information they have gathered on individuals. For example, with a few exceptions, the Internal Revenue Service is forbidden from disclosing tax return information.[25] Other government agencies are prohibited by the Privacy Act of 1974 from disclosing personal information, again with some exceptions.[26] Some states similarly limit disclosures by their governmental agencies,[27] and the federal Driver Privacy Protection Act restricts state motor vehicle departments from disclosing personal information in their records.[28]

Other laws, in turn, prevent private entities from disclosing information to the government; for example, the federal Right to Financial Privacy Act[29] restricts disclosures that financial institutions may give to a government. However, it does not prohibit them from giving that same information to telemarketers, insurance companies, or other private entities. Similarly, many states prohibit financial institutions from disclosing their customer records to government authorities without the customer's consent unless required by a subpoena or search warrant.[30] These sorts of provisions, while necessary to protect personal privacy from governmental intrusion, do not protect personal privacy from commercial intrusion.

However, the ability of the federal government to obtain information, including financial information, about an individual from third parties expanded significantly with the USA PATRIOT Act.[31] Among other provisions that diminish privacy, the USA PATRIOT Act allows the FBI to seek a judicial order that requires a third party to produce all tangible things that party holds with respect to a specified person.[32] The FBI is entitled to the order upon merely asserting that the items are sought for an authorized investigation to protect against international terrorism or clandestine intelligence activities, so long as the agency alleges an association with a foreign power as specified by the Act.[33] Furthermore, the Act prohibits the third party from disclosing that the FBI has sought or obtained the records and immunizes it from liability for its disclosures.[34]

16.3 Tort of Invasion of Privacy

Protection of individuals from invasions and disclosures by non-governmental entities developed at common law with the tort of invasion of privacy. This tort actually comprises four different torts: appropriation; false light in the public eye; unreasonable intrusion; and public disclosure of private facts.[35] Nearly every state recognizes at least one form of the tort, some through statute rather than by common law.[36]

Appropriation consists of the use, for the defendant's benefit, of the plaintiff's name or likeness.[37] False light in the public eye allows an action for publicity that is highly offensive to the ordinary person, even if the publicity is not defamatory.[38] The First Amendment strictly limits awards

---

23 U.S. Const. amend. IV.
24 Katz v. U.S., 389 U.S. 347 (1967). *See, e.g.*, Griswold v. Connecticut, 381 U.S. 479 (1965).
25 26 U.S.C. § 6103.
26 5 U.S.C. §§ 552, 552a(b). Prior to enactment of the Debt Collection Improvement Act, 31 U.S.C. § 3711(e), federal agencies were required to comply with the Privacy Act of 1974 in furnishing information to CRAs. The Debt Collection Improvement Act amended the Privacy Act by specifically excluding reports to CRAs from Privacy Act requirements. Pub. L. No. 97-365, § 2 (1982) (amending 5 U.S.C. § 552a(b)). National Consumer Law Center, Fair Debt Collection, § 13.2.3 (5th ed. 2004 and Supp.).
27 *See, e.g.*, Cal. Civ. Code § 1798; Colo. Rev. Stat. §§ 24-72-204(3)(a), 24-90-119; Ky. Rev. Stat. Ann. § 61.878; Minn. Stat. § 13.04; Ohio Rev. Code § 1347.07.
28 18 U.S.C. §§ 2721–2725. The Supreme Court has upheld the constitutionality of the Act, resolving a split in the circuits. Reno v. Condon, 528 U.S. 141 (2000).
29 12 U.S.C. § 3401.
30 *See, e.g.*, Cal. Gov. Code § 7470; Mont. Code Ann. § 32-8-503; N.H. Rev. Stat. Ann. § 359-C:4; Or. Rev. Stat. § 192.565.
31 Pub. L. No. 107-56, 115 Stat. 272 (2001); USA PATRIOT Improvement and Reauthorization Act of 2005, Pub. L. No. 109-177 (2006).
32 Pub. L. No. 109-177 § 106 (2005). This provision modifies and extends section 215 of the original USA PATRIOT Act, a section that was due to expire in 2005.
33 *Id.*
34 *Id.* The revised Act designates certain exceptions to the non-disclosure rule. *Id.*
35 *See generally* W.P. Keeton, Prosser & Keeton on the Law of Torts 849–869 (5th ed. 1984); Restatement (Second) of Torts §§ 625A–625L A nineteenth-century law review article considerably advanced the concept of legal protection of privacy in American tort law. Samuel D. Warren & Louis D. Brandeis, *The Right to Privacy*, 4 Harvard L. Rev. 193 (1890). The authors, who deplored the "overstepping" of the press and the "numerous mechanical devices" that were breaching privacy cited the "general right of the individual to be let alone" as the basis of the tort.
36 *See, e.g.*, N.Y. Civ. Rights Law § 50.
37 W.P. Keeton, Prosser & Keeton on the Law of Torts 851 (5th ed. 1984); Restatement (Second) of Torts § 625C. *See also* Sloan v. S.C. Dep't of Pub. Safety, 586 S.E.2d 108, 110 (S.C. 2003) (because state law authorized sale of images on drivers' licenses, no liability for misappropriation).
38 Restatement (Second) of Torts § 625E; Blakey v. Victory Equip. Sales, Inc., 576 S.E.2d 288, 292 (Ga. Ct. App. 2002) (no false

under this tort when the information concerns public figures or matters of public interest,[39] and its overlap with the tort of defamation has led some states to decline to recognize it.[40] Unreasonable intrusion allows a cause of action for the intentional interference with a person or that person's private affairs.[41] The tort of public disclosure of private facts prohibits the disclosure of private facts to the public when that disclosure would be highly offensive and objectionable to a reasonable person.[42] Here, too, the First Amendment limits awards when the facts disclosed are contained in a public record.[43]

Even if one of these torts may be appropriate for a particular consumer, remember that the FCRA provides qualified immunity for privacy actions based on information disclosed pursuant to specific provisions of the FCRA, immunity that extends to consumer reporting agencies (CRAs) and those who use their information and furnish information to them.[44] If the immunity applies, the plaintiff must show that the information was both false and furnished with malice or willful intent to injure the consumer.[45]

Of these four varieties of common law invasion of privacy, public disclosure of private facts has the most potential to constrict the flow of personal financial information. However, it is not particularly well suited to keeping financial information private. The tort, where recognized, requires proof of the following elements: publicity was given to matters concerning the plaintiff's private life; publication of those matters would be highly offensive to a reasonable person of ordinary sensibilities; and the matter publicized was not of legitimate public concern.[46] It is the first element, publicity, that keeps the tort from effectively protecting routine disclosures. The matter must be communicated to not just one or a small group of persons, but to the public at large such that it becomes a matter of public knowledge.[47] Few disclosures of personal financial information are going to have that large an audience.[48] Nonetheless, even an

---

light claim where defendant disclosed information only to CRA, not to "public"). *See also* Miller v. Javitch, Block & Rathbone, L.L.P., 397 F. Supp. 2d 991, 1006 (N.D. Ind. 2005) (dismissing false light claim based on the defendants' filing of a lawsuit to collect disputed debt from plaintiff on the grounds that consumer report that listed debt detracted from the element of knowledge or reckless disregard of falsity); Regions Bank v. Plott, 897 So. 2d 239 (Ala. 2004) (in action brought by account holders whose checks were stolen, holding that stamping of "refer to maker" on check was not an assertion that could support false light claim and that return of two forged checks to presenting banks stamped "insufficient funds" did not meet "giving publicity" element of false light claim).

39 *See, e.g.*, Time, Inc. v. Hill, 385 U.S. 374 (1967) (no recovery for false light for publication of fictionalized version of plaintiffs' hostage experience, portrayed as re-enactment, without showing actual malice, applying New York Times Co. v. Sullivan, 376 U.S. 254 (1964)). *See also* Cantrell v. Forest City Publishing Co., 419 U.S. 245 (1974) (false light recovery upheld where newspaper published false feature story about the plaintiffs and jury instructed on actual malice).

40 *See, e.g.*, Lake v. Wal-Mart Stores, Inc., 582 N.W.2d 231 (Minn. 1998) (recognizing appropriation, seclusion, and publication of private facts, but declining to recognize false light); Sullivan v. Pulitzer Broad. Co., 709 S.W.2d 475 (Mo. 1986); Renwick v. News & Observer Publishing Co., 312 S.E.2d 405 (N.C. 1984); Cain v. Hearst Corp., 878 S.W.2d 577 (Tex. 1994).

41 W.P. Keeton, Prosser & Keeton on the Law of Torts 854 (5th ed. 1984); Restatement (Second) of Torts § 625B.

42 W.P. Keeton, Prosser & Keeton on the Law of Torts 856–857 (5th ed. 1984); Restatement (Second) of Torts § 625D.

43 *See, e.g.*, Cox Broad. Corp. v. Cohn, 420 U.S. 469 (1975) (states may not impose sanctions for the publication of truthful information contained in official records open to public inspection).

44 *See* § 10.4, *supra*.

45 *Id.*

46 *See, e.g.*, Phillips v. Grendahl, 312 F.3d 357, 371–372 (8th Cir. 2002); Johnson v. Sawyer, 980 F.2d 1490 (5th Cir. 1993) (applying Texas law), *rev'd*, 47 F.3d 716 (5th Cir. 1995) (en banc), *vacated and remanded after remand*, 120 F.3d 716 (5th Cir. 1997); Robins v. Conseco Fin. Loan Co., 656 N.W.2d 241 (Minn. Ct. App. 2003).

47 Phillips v. Grendahl, 312 F.3d 357, 371 (8th Cir. 2002). *See also* Richard S. Murphy, *Property Rights in Personal Information: An Economic Defense of Privacy*, 84 Georgetown L.J. 2381, 2392 (1996) (pointing out that the more publicity the information gets, the more likely it will be considered newsworthy and thus protected by the First Amendment).

48 *See, e.g.*, Phillips v. Grendahl, 312 F.3d 357, 372 (8th Cir. 2002) (disclosure of consumer report to just one person failed publicity element); Olwell v. Med. Info. Bureau, 2003 WL 79035 (D. Minn. Jan. 7, 2003) (granting summary judgment to defendant on publication of private facts claim that alleged the defendant improperly disclosed the results of plaintiff's drug test to three insurance company); Peacock v. Retail Credit Co., 302 F. Supp. 418, 423–424 (N.D. Ga. 1969) (disclosure of consumer report, regardless of its falsity, to CRA's customers did not meet publicity element), *aff'd*, 429 F.2d 31 (5th Cir. 1970); Blakey v. Victory Equip. Sales, Inc., 576 S.E.2d 288, 292 (Ga. Ct. App. 2002) (publication of information to single CRA failed to meet publicity element of public disclosure of private facts claim); Peterson v. Idaho First Nat'l Bank, 367 P.2d 284 (Idaho 1961) (bank whose employee had written to plaintiff's boss regarding his financial situation not liable for invasion of privacy because dissemination was not public); Rush v. Maine Sav. Bank, 387 A.2d 1127 (Me. 1978) (bank that disclosed customer's loan information to IRS not liable for invasion of privacy because disclosure not public); Robins v. Conseco Fin. Loan Co., 656 N.W.2d 241 (Minn. Ct. App. 2003) (plaintiff failed to establish publicity element of public disclosure of private facts claim based on lender's disclosure of plaintiff's poor credit history to a co-worker, from whom plaintiff sought to purchase a mobile home); Bodah v. Lakeville Motor Express, Inc., 663 N.W.2d 550 (Minn. 2003) (employer's disclosure of 204 employee names and Social Security numbers to sixteen trucking terminals in six states did not meet publicity element of public disclosure of private facts claim; specifically evaluating the publicity element); Rycroft v. Gaddy, 281 S.C. 119, 314 S.E.2d 39 (S.C. Ct. App. 1984) (bank's delivery of customer's checks to litigant pursuant to a subpoena not invasion of privacy because disclosure not public); Blanche v. First Nationwide Mortg. Corp., 74 S.W.3d 444, 454–455 (Tex. App. 2002) (creditor's reporting of allegedly false information about mortgagee to CRA did not meet publicity element; furthermore, if information was false it could not meet private fact element); Olson v. Red Cedar Clinic, 681 N.W.2d 306, 309 (Wis. Ct. App. 2004) (dis-

audience as small as one can be significant, for example, an employer who has acquired information about an employee's bank account and purchasing habits. The "highly offensive" element may also be difficult to meet when the disclosure is of mundane personal information; one court held that a bank's disclosure of a depositor's unlisted telephone number to another customer was not sufficiently objectionable to give rise to liability under this tort.[49] However, a Wisconsin case upheld an invasion of privacy verdict based on a single disclosure to a single person, stating that the jury may consider the type and character of the person to whom the defendant disclosed the information in determining whether the plaintiff satisfied the publicity element of the tort.[50] Furthermore, if the persons to whom the defendant discloses the private matter have a special relationship with the plaintiff, disclosure to just a couple of people may satisfy the element.[51] However, the "special relationship" exception to the publicity element may not apply when the person to whom the information is disclosed has an appropriate interest in the information.[52]

The tort of intrusion can also apply to the disclosure of financial information.[53] The tort, also sometimes called "intrusion into seclusion," or "unreasonable intrusion," creates liability for the intentional intrusion upon another person's solitude, seclusion, or private affairs in a manner that would be highly offensive to a reasonable person.[54] Generally the intrusion need not be physical, it can lead to liability for the unauthorized prying into a bank account,[55]

---

closure of counseling records to one person did not meet "public disclosure" element of state invasion of privacy statute).

49 Taylor v. NationsBank N.A., 128 Md. App. 414, 738 A.2d 893, 897 (1999), *rev'd on other grounds*, 776 A.2d 645 (2001). In this case, the bank disclosed to a customer that his paycheck had been accidentally deposited into the account of the plaintiff, a co-worker of the defendant, and gave the plaintiff's name and unlisted telephone number to the customer in the course of seeking to clear up the mix up. The co-worker had an account number on his pay advice; by making these other disclosures the bank revealed to the co-worker that the account number belonged to the plaintiff. Though disclosure of an account number might be far more objectionable than mere disclosure of a name and telephone number, the appellate court chose to characterize the account number as already being in the co-worker's possession—and therefore not disclosed by the bank to the co-worker—notwithstanding that without the bank's disclosures the co-worker would have had nothing more than a number with no name. *Id.* On review, the Maryland Supreme Court—though not addressing the invasion of privacy issue—noted this analytical error. 776 A.2d at 654 (ruling that the disclosure could have violated the bank's duty of confidentiality, reversing summary judgment for the defendant). *See also* Busse v. Motorola, Inc., 813 N.E.2d 1013, 1017–1018 (Ill. App. Ct. 2004) (cellular telephone company's provision of customers' names, addresses, and Social Security numbers to research company did not create liability under tort of public disclosure of private facts because such information did not comprise "private facts").

50 Pachowitz v. Ledoux, 666 N.W.2d 88 (Wis. Ct. App. 2003). A Wisconsin court of appeals later distinguished *Paschowitz* in *Olson v. Red Cedar Clinic*, 273 Wis. 2d 728, 733, 681 N.W.2d 306, 308 (2004), ruling that a clinic's disclosure of the records of a student's mother to the student's school psychologist did not meet the publicity element of the tort, given that the psychologist was prohibited from further disclosure.

51 Chisholm v. Foothill Capital Corp., 3 F. Supp. 2d 925, 941 (N.D. Ill. 1998) (disclosure of plaintiff's affair with a married man to two of her potential business clients could satisfy publicity element; however, plaintiff failed to show that the information was private and that its disclosure would be highly offensive to a reasonable person, therefore action dismissed). *See also* Hill v. MCI WorldCom Communications, Inc., 141 F. Supp. 2d 1205, 1212–1213 (S.D. Iowa 2001) (telecommunications carrier's disclosure to customer's ex-husband of customer's billing information and names of parties she'd called stated claim because of special relationship between customer and ex-husband); Munoz v. Chicago Sch. Reform Bd. of Trs., 2000 WL 152138, at *10 (N.D. Ill. Feb. 4, 2000) (teacher who alleged that her personnel file was disclosed to students' parents met publicity element because she had a special relationship with those parents); Pinkston-Adams v. Nike, Inc., 1999 WL 543202, at *4 (N.D. Ill. July 22, 1999) (communication of personal information to plaintiff's employees could meet publicity element); Miller v. Motorola, Inc., 560 N.E.2d 900, 903 (Ill. App. Ct. 1990) (plaintiff could meet publicity element of tort based on employer's disclosure of her surgery to her co-workers because of her special relationship with them).

52 Doe v. TCF Bank Illinois, F.S.B., 707 N.E.2d 220, 222 (Ill. App. Ct. 1999) (loan officer's disclosure of plaintiff's credit card debt to plaintiff's spouse did not meet publicity element; "special relationship" exception did not apply because spouse had "natural and proper" interest in the information).

53 *See, e.g.*, Rodgers v. McCullough, 296 F. Supp. 2d 895, 904 (W.D. Tenn. 2003) (in case alleging tort where the opposing attorney in a custody dispute used the plaintiff's consumer report without a permissible purpose, acknowledging that Tennessee recognized the tort but ruling that a fact issue existed as to whether the use would have been highly offensive to a reasonable person). Not every state recognizes the tort of intrusion, though most do. *See, e.g.*, Hougum v. Valley Mem'l Homes, 1998 N.D. 24, 574 N.W.2d 812 (N.D. 1998) (declining to decide whether tort of invasion of seclusion exists in North Dakota).

54 Phillips v. Grendahl, 312 F.3d 357, 372 (8th Cir. 2002); Olwell v. Med. Info. Bureau, 2003 WL 79035 (D. Minn. Jan. 7, 2003); Joseph v. J.J. Mac Intyre Cos., L.L.C., 238 F. Supp. 2d 1158, 1169 (N.D. Cal. 2002); Barler v. Erie Ins. Exch., 344 Md. 515, 687 A.2d 1375, 1380, 1381 (1997); Irvine v. Akron Beacon Journal, 770 N.E.2d 1105 (Ohio Ct. App. 2002) (affirming jury's award of $100,000 in punitive damages for defendant's repeated computer-dialed sales calls to plaintiff's home). *See also* Lovgren v. Citizens First Nat'l Bank, 126 Ill. 2d 411, 534 N.E.2d 987, 989 (1989) (declining to decide whether tort recognized in Illinois); Lake v. Wal-Mart Stores, Inc., 582 N.W.2d 231, 233 (Minn. 1998); Remsburg v. Docusearch, Inc., 816 A.2d 1001 (N.H. 2003); Household Credit Servs., Inc. v. Driscol, 989 S.W.2d 72, 84 (Tex. App. 1998); Restatement (Second) of Torts § 652B.

55 *See, e.g.*, Zimmermann v. Wilson, 81 F.2d 847 (3d Cir. 1936), *rev'd on other grounds*, 105 F.2d 583 (3d Cir. 1939); Lowe v. Surpas Res. Corp., 253 F. Supp. 2d 1209 (D. Kan. 2003) (for jury to decide whether debt collector's actions intruded upon borrower's seclusion); Pulla v. Amoco Oil Co., 882 F. Supp. 836 (S.D. Iowa 1994) (affirming verdict that defendant had intruded upon the seclusion of plaintiff, who was defendant's employee, by accessing his credit card records to check his activities on

or access to a consumer report.[56] The plaintiff must prove not just an intrusion, but an intrusion that would be offensive or objectionable to a reasonable person.[57] While Social Security numbers are private, courts differ as to whether transmission of Social Security numbers can constitute an intrusion upon seclusion.[58]

The tort can serve to protect bank account records from intrusion. For example, in *McGuire v. Shubert*,[59] a Pennsylvania court held that a bank employee's unwarranted access of the plaintiffs' account gave rise to an intentional intrusion on the seclusion of private concerns, specifically finding that the intrusion "was substantial and highly offensive to a reasonable person."[60] However, the tort only addresses the intrusion into the plaintiffs affairs, not the exposure of the information acquired,[61] so while it may offer a cause of action against one who *invades* a person's financial matters, it does not impose liability on one who *discloses* information acquired without such intrusion.[62]

Although the tort may have limited utility for consumers seeking to protect their financial data, identity theft victims who are wrongfully held to account for charges run up by the thief may be able to use it against creditors who overreach into the victim's solitude. For example, a credit card issuer who issued a card in the name of the applicant's brother was found liable for intrusion into seclusion for its tactics used to collect the debt from the brother.[63] A federal court used a similar theory to uphold a claim against a creditor who had repeatedly contacted the plaintiffs seeking collection on an automobile loan taken out by a third party, and who had even sought to repossess the plaintiffs' car, notwithstanding that they had informed the creditor and its collection agency that the debtor did not live with them and in fact was wholly unknown to them.[64]

---

days he had called in sick; rejecting defense that defendant had a legitimate objective in reviewing the records), *aff'd in part, rev'd in part on other grounds*, 72 F.3d 648 (8th Cir. 1995); Remsburg v. Docusearch, Inc., 816 A.2d 1001, 1008–1009 (N.H. 2001) (people have a reasonable expectation that someone to whom they disclose their Social Security numbers will keep the numbers private, and therefore the wrongful disclosure of the number may be considered sufficiently offensive to support an action based on intrusion upon seclusion; however, people do not have a similar expectation of privacy as to their work addresses, and therefore no intrusion upon seclusion action can be based on the release of that information); McGuire v. Shubert, 722 A.2d 1087 (Pa. Super. Ct. 1998). *But see* Phillips v. Grendahl, 312 F.3d 357, 372 (8th Cir. 2002) (future mother-in-law's improper purpose to obtain consumer report on plaintiff did not render acquisition "highly offensive" for purposes of intrusion upon seclusion invasion of privacy tort); *In re* Trans Union Corp. Privacy Litig., 211 F.R.D. 328, 343–342 (N.D. Ill. 2002) (CRA's disclosure of plaintiffs' consumer reports to target marketing firms did not meet highly offensive element of intrusion upon seclusion invasion of privacy claim); Fabio v. Credit Bureau of Hutchison, Inc., 210 F.R.D. 688 (D. Minn. 2002) (debt collector's use of curse words in telephone demands for payment did not render intrusion highly offensive); Cummings v. Walsh Constr. Co., 561 F. Supp. 72 (S.D. Ga. 1983) (under Georgia law, tort requires physical invasion akin to trespass).

56 Smith v. Bob Smith Chevrolet, Inc., 275 F. Supp. 2d 808, 822 (W.D. Ky. 2003) (denying defendant's motion for summary judgment).

57 W.P. Keeton, Prosser & Keeton on the Law of Torts 855 (5th ed. 1984).

58 Phillips v. Grendahl, 312 F.3d 357 (8th Cir. 2002) (no); Bodah v. Lakeville Motor Express, Inc., 649 N.W.2d 859, 863 (Minn. Ct. App. 2002) (recognizing privacy of social security numbers), *rev'd on other grounds*, 663 N.W.2d 550 (Minn. 2003); Remsburg v. Docusearch, 816 A.2d 1001 (N.H. 2003) (yes). *Cf.* Meyerson v. Prime Realty Servs., L.L.C., 7 Misc. 3d 911, 796 N.Y.S.2d 848 (N.Y. Sup. Ct. 2005) (discussing privacy of Social Security numbers in denying landlord's motion to dismiss a state UDAP claim brought by a tenant who alleged that the landlord had misrepresented that she was required by law to provide the Social Security numbers of other occupants of her apartment).

59 722 A.2d 1087 (Pa. Super. Ct. 1998).

60 *Id.* at 1092.

61 *See, e.g., In re* Trans Union Corp. Privacy Litig., 326 F. Supp. 2d 893, 901–902 (N.D. Ill. 2004) (CRA's disclosure of consumers' information did not create intrusion action; furthermore, agency's access of information in its own files was not unlawful intrusion on consumers' affairs); Dwyer v. American Exp. Co., 652 N.E.2d 1351, 1354 (Ill. App. Ct. 1995) (credit card companies did not intrude without authorization on cardholders' privacy by compiling the information voluntarily given to it and then renting its compilation); Blanche v. First Nationwide Mortg. Corp., 74 S.W.3d 444 (Tex. App. 2002) (where information disclosed by bank came from its own records, and no evidence showed that bank had intruded into the plaintiff's private affairs, bank entitled to summary judgment on intrusion of privacy claim).

62 *See, e.g.*, Fisher v. Quality Hyundai, Inc., 2002 U.S. Dist. LEXIS 407, at *16, 17 (N.D. Ill. Jan. 8, 2002) (plaintiff, a car buyer for whom the dealer fraudulently arranged financing against her will for a car for which she'd already arranged independent financing, properly alleged intrusion into seclusion with allegations that dealer had harassed her on the telephone; however, allegations that dealer had contacted her credit union, her employer, and her family members did not support the claim); Blanche v. First Nationwide Mortg. Corp., 2002 Tex. Ct. App. LEXIS 1892, at *19 (Mar. 14, 2002) (where information disclosed by bank came from its own records, and no evidence showed that bank had intruded into the plaintiff's private affairs, bank entitled to summary judgment on intrusion of privacy claim). *See* Remsburg v. Docusearch, Inc., 816 A.2d 1001 (N.H. 2003). *See also* Remsburg v. Docusearch, Inc., 2002 U.S. Dist. LEXIS 7952 (D.N.H. Apr. 26, 2002) (certifying to New Hampshire Supreme Court questions of whether a private investigator or information broker commits the tort by deceitfully obtaining a person's work address by means of a pretextual telephone call, or by obtaining a person's Social Security number from a credit header through a CRA).

63 Montgomery Ward v. Larragoite, 81 N.M. 383, 467 P.2d 399, 401 (N.M. 1970).

64 Bauer v. Ford Motor Credit Co., 149 F. Supp. 2d 1106, 1110 (D. Minn. 2001) (such persistence in the face of "highly reliable confirmations" of the inaccuracy of the creditor's records could, said the court, be considered by a reasonable person as "highly offensive conduct," to the point of invasion of privacy, reversing summary judgment for defendants). *See also* Lowe v. Surpas Res. Corp., 253 F. Supp. 2d 1209 (D. Kan. 2003) (debt collector's repeated calls to identity theft victim could be basis of intrusion upon seclusion claim); National Consumer Law Cen-

Privacy Protection § 16.4.1.1

The tort of appropriation at first glance appears to be apropos to identity theft. After all, the essence of identity theft is the thief's appropriation the victim's name or likeness for the thief's own benefit.[65] Traditionally, the elements of the tort have been: (1) an appropriation of the plaintiff's name or likeness for the value associated with it, and not in an incidental manner or for a newsworthy purpose; (2) a publication with which the plaintiff can be identified; and (3) an advantage or benefit to the defendant.[66] The traditional use of the tort has been read to intend to protect the value of an individual's celebrity or image, such as when an advertiser pastes a picture of a star athlete onto an advertisement to market a product or service without actually obtaining the athlete's endorsement. Arguably, an identity thief seizes a plaintiff' name (and Social Security number) to take advantage of the credit reputation associated with it. The thief then uses that information in a way in which the plaintiff is identified. In fact it is in a way where only the plaintiff is identified. The thief does this for the thief's benefit—to obtain goods and services without the burden of paying for them. Nonetheless, as yet appropriation has not been recognized as a viable claim in ordinary identity theft cases.[67] Likewise, courts have rejected appropriation claims brought against financial institutions that sell their customers' financial information, on the grounds that each individual's name has no intrinsic value, but rather the value arises only from the institution's aggregation and organization of groups of names.[68]

These traditional torts are useful (although sometimes unwieldy) instruments with which to shield financial information from disclosure. While they do offer an opportunity for punitive damages, they are ineffective in the age of networked databases and the Internet to instill apprehension in those who collect and disseminate financial data. Once confidentiality is breached it is too late for perfect redress—what is said cannot be unsaid, and once information is digitized, copied, and transferred to other systems, it is an unbottled genie.

16.4 Statutory Protection of Financial Information

16.4.1 The Gramm-Leach-Bliley Act

16.4.1.1 Overview

Title V of the Gramm-Leach-Bliley Act (GLB)[69] addresses financial institutions' use of consumers' "nonpublic personal information."[70] That term is defined to mean any personally identifiable financial information that is: provided by the consumer to the financial institution;[71] results from any transaction with the consumer or service performed for the consumer; or is otherwise obtained by the financial institution, but which is not "publicly available information."[72] At its heart, GLB is a notification statute, one that requires certain notices to be given to "consumers"[73] and "customers."[74]

The Federal Trade Commission (FTC), the federal banking agencies, and Securities and Exchange Commission have both rulemaking and enforcement authority under GLB.[75] These agencies have all issued regulations under the GLB Act, all of which are substantially the same.[76] Most

---

ter, Fair Debt Collection § 10.3.2 (5th 2004 and Supp.). *But see* Mlynek v. Household Fin. Corp, 2000 U.S. Dist. LEXIS 13783, at *8, 9 (N.D. Ill. Sept. 11, 2000) (no cause of action against creditor who made one call to person creditor mistakenly believed to have cosigned a loan where creditor ceased calling after being notified of the mistake).

65 Restatement (Second) of Torts § 652C ("[o]ne who appropriates to his own use or benefit the name or likeness of another is subject to liability to the other for invasion of his privacy").

66 Matthews v. Wozencraft, 15 F.3d 432, 437 (5th Cir. 1994).

67 *Cf.* Remsburg v. Docusearch, Inc., 816 A.2d 1001 (N.H. 2001) (investigator who sells personal information cannot be liable for appropriation because the benefit to the investigator does not derive from the social or commercial standing of the persona whose information is sold, but from the client's willingness to pay for the information).

68 *In re* Trans Union Corp., Privacy Litig., 326 F. Supp. 2d 893, 903 (N.D. Ill. 2004); Dwyer v. American Exp. Co., 652 N.E.2d 1351, 1356 (Ill. App. Ct. 1995).

69 15 U.S.C. §§ 6801–6809. *See* Appx. G.1, *infra*. The Act is also known as the Financial Services Modernization Act of 1999. The FTC has issued its final rules regarding Title V of the Act. 16 C.F.R. Part 313. *See* Appx. G, *infra*, for relevant sections discussed in this section. A complete version of GLB is available on the CD-Rom accompanying this manual.

70 15 U.S.C. § 6809(4).

71 The Gramm-Leach-Bliley Act defines "financial institution" to include any institution the business of which is engaging in financial activities as described in section 4(k) of the Bank Holding Company Act of 1956. 15 U.S.C. § 6809(3). *See* § 16.4.1.2, *infra*.

72 15 U.S.C. § 6809(4). The statute provides for "publicly available information" to be further defined by regulations. *See* § 16.4.1.4, *infra*.

73 Consumer "means an individual who obtains or has obtained a financial product or service from you that is to be used primarily for personal, family, or household purposes, or that individual's legal representative." 16 C.F.R. § 313.3(e). *See* § 16.4.1.3, *infra*.

74 A customer is a consumer who has a customer relationship with the financial institution, meaning "a continuing relationship between a consumer and you under which you provide one or more financial products or services to the consumer that are to be used primarily for personal, family, or household purposes," codifying 16 C.F.R. § 313.3(h). *See* § 16.4.1.3, *infra*.

75 15 U.S.C. §§ 6804 and 6805. The banking agencies are the Office of the Comptroller of the Currency, the Federal Reserve Board, the Federal Deposit Insurance Corporation, the Office of Thrift Supervision, and the National Credit Union Administration. *See* § 15.4.1.10, *infra*.

76 The Comptroller of the Currency's regulations are codified at 12 C.F.R. § 40; the Federal Reserve Board's at 12 C.F.R. § 216; the FDIC's at 12 C.F.R. § 332; the Office of Thrift Supervision's at 12 C.F.R. § 573; the NCUA's at 12 C.F.R. § 716; and the SEC's at 12 C.F.R. § 248.

critical for the discussion below are the regulations that are collectively known as the "FTC Privacy Rule."[77] The remaining discussion of GLB's regulations will cite to the FTC's version of the Privacy Rule.

16.4.1.2 "Financial Institutions"—Entities That Must Comply with Gramm-Leach-Bliley

GLB applies to "financial institutions." Whether an entity is a "financial institution" is determined by whether it engages in "financial activities" as that term is defined by the Bank Company Holding Act of 1956.[78] That Act describes five different categories of financial activities that cover lending, insuring, financial advising, issuing or selling asset pool instruments, and underwriting securities.[79] Under the FTC Privacy Rule not every institution that engages in financial activities will be a financial institution covered by GLB; the institution must be "significantly engaged" in those financial activities to be subject to GLB.[80]

The FTC has provided examples of covered financial institutions, such as a retailer that issues its own credit card to consumers, an automobile dealership that leases cars for at least ninety-day terms, a check cashing business, and an accountant or tax preparation service.[81] Consumer reporting agencies (CRAs) fall within the FTC's definition.[82] Credit counseling organizations do as well.[83] However, attorneys who provide legal services in areas such as real estate settlement, tax-planning, and tax preparation do not.[84] The size of the institution does not control, even a diminutive business can be a subject financial institution if it significantly engages in financial activities.

16.4.1.3 "Customers" and "Consumers"—Those Protected by Gramm-Leach-Bliley

GLB protects both "customers" and "consumers." All customers are consumers, but not all consumers are customers. Customers and consumers are equally protected by the opt-out and nondisclosure provisions of GLB and the FTC Privacy Rule.[85] The difference is only relevant to whether the institution must provide an initial privacy notice and annual privacy notices to the individual, and turns on the individual's particular relationship with the financial institution.

A consumer is anyone who "obtains, from a financial institution, financial products or services which are to be used primarily for personal, family, or household purposes."[86] Although GLB does not define "financial products or services," the FTC Privacy Rule does so by referring back to the source of the definition of "financial activities;" they include any product or service that could be offered by an entity engaging in a financial activity.[87]

A customer is a consumer with whom the financial institution has established a "customer relationship,"[88] which is described as being a "continuing relationship" through which the financial institution provides financial products or services that the consumer will use primarily for personal, household or family purposes.[89] The FTC Privacy Rule sets forth a variety of examples of such relationships, including loans, insurance product sales, personal property leases, and the like.[90] The FTC Privacy Rule also describes incidents that do not yield such a relationship, including the isolated provision of a financial service, such as through an ATM from which the consumer gets cash from another institution.[91]

---

77 16 C.F.R. § 313.
78 15 U.S.C. § 6809(3); 12 U.S.C. § 1843(k). See also Lacerte Software Corp. v. Prof'l Tax Servs., L.L.C., 2004 WL 180321 at *1–2 (N.D. Tex. Jan. 6, 2004) (finding software company not a financial institution, denying defendant's motion to dismiss based on argument that plaintiff included defendant's personal credit card number and signature in exhibit to complaint); N.Y. State Bar Ass'n v. F.T.C., 276 F. Supp. 2d 110, 146 (D.D.C. 2003) (holding that Gramm-Leach-Bliley's privacy provisions did not apply to attorneys and suggesting that, even if it were, the FTC should consider whether attorneys are entitled to a *de minimis* exemption under the Act).
79 12 U.S.C. § 1843(k)(4) further incorporates by reference 12 C.F.R. §§ 225.28 and 225.86. These three sources together encompass a wide scope of financially-related activities, including lenders, loan brokers and servicers, collection agencies, financial advisors, tax preparers, real estate settlement services, property appraisers, and others. Notwithstanding this definition of "financial activities," GLB specifically exempts activities covered by the Commodity Futures Trading Commission under the Commodity Exchange Act. 15 U.S.C. § 6809(3)(B). GLB also specifically exempts from the definition of "financial institution" the Federal Agricultural Mortgage Corporation and entities chartered under the Farm Credit Act of 1971. *Id.* § 6809(3)(C).
80 16 C.F.R. § 313.3(k)(4).
81 16 C.F.R. § 313.3(k)(1), (2).
82 Trans Union, L.L.C. v. Fed. Trade Comm'n, 295 F.3d 42, 48, 49 (D.C. Cir. 2002) (upholding FTC's construction of the term "financial institution").
83 F.T.C. v. AmeriDebt, Inc., 343 F. Supp. 2d 451, 461–462 (D. Md. 2004) (construing 12 U.S.C. § 1843(k)(4)(C) and 12 C.F.R. § 225.28(b)(6)(v) to hold that credit counseling activities were "well within the reach of the FTC Act").
84 N.Y. State Bar Ass'n v. F.T.C., 430 F.3d 457, 472 (2005) (holding that the Federal Trade Commission's interpretation of Gramm-Leach-Bliley as applying to such attorneys was "not reasonable").
85 15 U.S.C. § 6802(b)–(d); 16 C.F.R. §§ 313.10–313.12.
86 15 U.S.C. § 6809(9).
87 16 C.F.R. § 313.3(d).
88 16 C.F.R. § 313.3(h).
89 16 C.F.R. § 313.3(i).
90 *Id.*
91 *Id.*

16.4.1.4 "Nonpublic Personal Information"—the Information Covered by Gramm-Leach-Bliley

GLB does not prevent financial institutions from revealing any information that they get from consumers; the only information restricted by the Act is "nonpublic personal information." Nonpublic personal information is deemed to be personally identifiable financial information that is not publicly available.[92] The Act does not defined "personally identifiable financial information"; nonetheless the FTC's authority to define the term, and to define the term broadly, has been upheld.[93] Under the FTC Privacy Rule, the source, not the substance, of the information matters. Information is deemed to be personally identifiable financial information if it meets any of the following criteria: (1) the information was provided by the consumer to obtain a financial product or service; (2) the information was about a consumer resulting from any transaction involving a financial product or service between the institution and the consumer; or (3) the information was otherwise obtained about a consumer in connection with a financial product or service.[94] In short, if the information is about a consumer and pertains to an institution's financial product or service, it is considered personally identifiable financial information without reference to the content of the data itself.

In addition, the FTC Privacy Rule tags as nonpublic personal information any "list, description, or other grouping of consumers"—including any publicly available information pertaining to them—"that is *derived* using any personally identifiable financial information that is not publicly available."[95] Thus, the FTC intends to protect derivative information such as a list of consumers' names and addresses that was derived using information such as account numbers or other information not publicly available, *even if* the information on the list itself is publicly available

and therefore would not be protected if derived from another source, or in a manner that did not use any personally identifiable financial information.[96] GLB does not control publicly available information, so long as the institution did not derive it from personally identifiable financial information that was not publicly available.[97]

Although "publicly available" information might seem to be a broad term that could encompass any data acquired from any non-restricted source, or which the consumer has not taken specific steps to protect, the FTC Privacy Rule narrows the scope of the term. The FTC Privacy Rule provides that it includes *only* such information that the institution has a reasonable basis to believe is lawfully made available to the general public from government records, widely disseminated media, and disclosures made to the general public to meet a legal requirement.[98] Accordingly, information acquired from government records, telephone books, newspapers, and similar media is publicly available.[99] However, it would appear that information that has been disclosed to third parties, but not in publication form or pursuant to a legal requirement, does not falls outside the FTC Privacy Rule's definition of "publicly available information." Furthermore, a financial institution cannot merely claim a reasonable belief that information is public without justification, the regulations require it to take steps to ascertain that the information is public.[100]

16.4.1.5 Exempt Disclosures

16.4.1.5.1 Overview

At first glance the scope of information GLB protects from disclosure appears to be expansive—including all nonpublic personal information about a consumer. However, a raft of exceptions removes significant categories out of the protected class of information.

16.4.1.5.2 Disclosures to affiliates

Though not expressly labeled as an exception, a key feature of GLB is that disclosures to an institution's own

---

92 15 U.S.C. § 6809(4)(A). *See also* Landry v. Union Planters Corp., 2003 WL 21355462 at *6–7 (E.D. La. June 6, 2003) (Gramm-Leach-Bliley Act's privacy provisions do not apply to redacted or aggregated financial data; such data is not "nonpublic information"; party's discovery of customer information would not violate Gramm-Leach-Bliley Act so long as all nonpublic personal information was redacted from the materials); Union Planters Bank, N.A. v. Gavel, 2003 WL 1193671 (E.D. La. Mar. 12, 2003) (granting bank a permanent injunction against party who had been issued a subpoena for the disclosure of information that related to plaintiff bank's customers, on grounds that the Gramm-Leach-Bliley Act prohibited the defendant from revealing that information without the customers' consent; it is unclear whether the defendant sought to employ the Act's exception for subpoenas, found at 16 C.F.R. § 313.15), *rev'd and remanded on other grounds sub nom.*, Union Planters Bank, N.A. v. Salih, 369 F.3d 457 (5th Cir. 2004).

93 Trans Union, L.L.C. v. Fed. Trade Comm'n, 295 F.3d 42, 50 (D.C. Cir. 2002).

94 16 C.F.R. § 313.3(o).

95 16 C.F.R. § 313.3(n)(i), (ii) (emphasis added).

96 16 C.F.R. § 313.3(n)(3).

97 16 C.F.R. § 313.3(n)(2).

98 16 C.F.R. § 313.3(p)(1) (defining "publicly available information" as information from "(i) Federal, State, or local government records; (ii) Widely distributed media; or (iii) Disclosures to the general public that are required to be made by Federal, State, or local law.").

99 16 C.F.R. § 313.3(p)(3).

100 The financial institution must "have taken steps to determine: (i) That the information is of the type that is available to the general public; and (ii) Whether an individual can direct that the information not be made available to the general public and, if so, that [the] consumer has not done so." 16 C.F.R. § 313.3(p)(2).

affiliate are completely unrestricted by the Act and the FTC Privacy Rule.[101] An affiliate is "any company that controls, is controlled by, or is under common control with another company."[102] Thus private consumer information may flow freely throughout a company's extended family, and every acquisition by a financial institution expands the scope of consumer information the entity can share with and acquire from its parent, sibling, and subsidiary companies.

16.4.1.5.3 Categories of exempted disclosures

In addition to affiliate disclosures, the FTC Privacy Rule describes three sets of exempt disclosures. The first two sets of disclosures are exempt not just from the privacy notices but also from the consumer's opt-out rights. That is, a financial institution need not disclose that it will make these disclosures, even to nonaffiliated third parties (beyond a statement that the institution will "make disclosures to nonaffiliated third parties as permitted by law"),[103] and furthermore a consumer has no power to stop—to opt out of—these exempt disclosures.

The first set of exempt disclosures are those needed in connection with processing or servicing the consumer's transaction.[104] The second set consists of a laundry list of exempt disclosures, unshielding information that is disclosed:[105]

- At the consumer's direction or consent;
- To protect the confidentiality or security of the institution's records;
- To protect against fraud or other liability;
- For required institutional risk control;
- To resolve consumer disputes or inquiries;
- To persons holding a legal or beneficial interest relating to the consumer;
- To persons acting in a fiduciary or representative capacity to the consumer;[106]
- To insurance rate advisory organizations, or guaranty funds or agencies;
- To agencies rating the institution;
- To persons assessing the institution's compliance with industry standards;
- To the institution's attorneys, accountants, and auditors;
- To law enforcement agencies (to the extent permitted under other provisions of law);
- To self-regulatory organizations;
- For an investigation on a matter related to public safety;
- In connection with a proposed or actual sale, merger, transfer, or exchange of all or a portion of a business or operating unit (so long as the disclosure concerns solely consumers of such business or unit);
- To comply with federal, state, or local laws or rules;
- To comply with a properly authorized civil, criminal or regulatory investigation, subpoena, or summons;[107]
- To respond to judicial process or government regulatory authorities that have jurisdiction over the institution;[108]

---

101 15 U.S.C. § 6802. The Act and the FTC Privacy Rule only require that the institution's privacy notice must disclose its policy with respect to the disclosure of nonpublic personal information to affiliates. 15 U.S.C. § 6802(a)(1); 16 C.F.R. § 313.6.
102 16 C.F.R. § 313.3(a).
103 16 C.F.R. § 313.6(b).
104 15 U.S.C. § 6802(e)(1); 16 C.F.R. § 313.14(a). The full text of this exemption provides:

> Exceptions for processing transactions at consumer's request. The requirements for initial notice in § 313.4(a)(2), for the opt out in §§ 313.7 and 313.10, and for service providers and joint marketing in § 313.13 do not apply if you disclose nonpublic personal information as necessary to effect, administer, or enforce a transaction that a consumer requests or authorizes, or in connection with:
> (1) Servicing or processing a financial product or service that a consumer requests or authorizes;
> (2) Maintaining or servicing the consumer's account with you, or with another entity as part of a private label credit card program or other extension of credit on behalf of such entity; or
> (3) A proposed or actual securitization, secondary market sale (including sales of servicing rights), or similar transaction related to a transaction of the consumer.

105 16 C.F.R. § 313.15.
106 *See* ArborPlace, L.P. v. Encore Opportunity Fund, L.L.C., 2002 WL 205681 (Del. Ch. Ct. Jan. 29, 2002) (Gramm-Leach-Bliley regulations did not require limited liability company to shield its membership lists from limited partner, information was exempt from notice and opt-out requirements by 17 C.F.R. § 248.15, the SEC's equivalent to the FTC's regulation at 16 C.F.R. § 313.15).
107 *See* Cash Today of Texas, Inc. v. Greenberg, 2002 WL 31414138 (D. Del. Oct. 23, 2002) (ruling against bank that objected to a subpoena for the production of documents relating to transactions between bank and plaintiff on the grounds that the Gramm-Leach-Bliley Act prohibited such disclosure; court applied subpoena exception in Act, found at 16 C.F.R. § 313.15).
108 Marks v. Global Mortgage Group, Inc., 218 F.R.D. 492, 496 (S.D. W. Va. 2003) (judicial process exception permitted defendant to disclose its customers' nonpublic personal information in response to plaintiffs' discovery request); *Ex parte* Nat'l Western Life Ins. Co., 899 So. 2d 218 (Ala. 2004) (reading section 6802(e)(8)'s exemption for judicial process to cover a party's request for discovery of documents, but counseling that courts should also issue a comprehensive protective order to guard the privacy of consumers whose information might be disclosed by such discovery); *Ex parte* Mut. Sav. Life Ins. Co., 899 So. 2d 986 (Ala. 2004) (same); *In re* Lexington Ins. Co., 2004 WL 210576, at *4 (Tex. App. Feb. 2, 2004) (upholding order to insurance company to produce documents that were to be redacted of private, personal, and nonpublic information of insureds); Martino v. Barnett, 595 S.E.2d 65 (W. Va. 2004) (Gramm-Leach-Bliley Act allows use of judicial process to obtain information relevant to a judicial proceeding; nonetheless, trial courts should balance the interests at stake to limit discovery to necessary information only).

- To a consumer reporting agency in accordance with the FCRA; or
- From a consumer report reported by a consumer reporting agency.

With respect to the last two items, note that the list exempts not just those FCRA disclosures made to a consumer reporting agency (CRA) in accordance with the FCRA, but those from a consumer report reported by a CRA, regardless of whether the report was obtained or issued in accordance with the FCRA.[109] Thus, anything the institution learns from a consumer report acquired from a CRA is completely unprotected by GLB, only the FCRA can restrict those disclosures.

A third set of information is exempt from the opt-out, but not the notice, provisions of GLB. This category comprises information disclosed to a nonaffiliated third party that provides services to the institution, including the marketing of services of either the institution itself or offered in connection with a joint agreement with some other financial institution.[110] To take advantage of the servicing exemption, however, the financial institution must have complied with the initial privacy notice requirements, and further must have agreed with the nonaffiliated third party that the party will not disclose or use the information except to carry out the purposes for which the institution disclosed the information to the party.[111] However, the nonaffiliated third party may make use of any of the exempt disclosures described above.[112]

Amassed together, these exemptions pull a significant amount of information out of GLB's protections, large enough to take an extensive bite out of consumer privacy. An institution that intends to maximize its use of consumer financial information can quite likely find shelter under the guise of one exceptions or another. By including not just so many exemptions, but also so many exemptions with blurry boundaries that are open to broad interpretation, the Act significantly cuts into the core of protection it purports to offer.

16.4.1.5.4 Gramm-Leach-Bliley's limits on redisclosure and reuse of the information

While GLB exempts from its notice requirement and opt-out right provisions disclosures for servicing and processing the consumer's transaction and disclosures falling within GLB's laundry list of exemptions, the Act restricts what the receiver of an exempt disclosure may do with the information once it has been disclosed. The receiver of an exempt disclosure may redisclose the information only to affiliates of the financial institution from which it received the information and its own affiliates (who in turn take the information subject to the same limitations that apply to the initial receiver).[113] In other words, the exception that exempts the particular disclosure attaches to the disclosure and follows it as it travels from institution to institution, shaping the scope of the use and further disclosure of the information. However, the receiver may itself take advantage of the exempt disclosure provisions, so long as it is acting in the ordinary course of business to carry out the activity covered by the particular exemption.[114]

16.4.1.6 Gramm-Leach-Bliley's Privacy Notices Requirement

Fundamentally, GLB is a notice statute, not a privacy protection statute. The Act describes two sets of notices: privacy notices and opt-out notices. Opt-out notices are discussed in § 16.4.1.7.2, *infra*. In addition, there are two kinds of privacy notices: the initial notice and the annual notice.

A privacy notice is a "clear and conspicuous notice that accurately reflects [the institution's] privacy policies."[115] The time the institution must give the notice depends on whether the consumer has customer status.[116] Customers must be given the notice no later than the time the customer relationship starts,[117] except in two cases: when someone other than the customer establishes the customer relationship,[118] or when providing the notice would substantially delay the customer's transaction and the customer agrees to receive notice at a later time.[119] In those cases, the institution can delay giving the notice for a reasonable time.[120]

Consumers who are not customers, that is, do not have a continuing relationship with the institution,[121] are entitled to an initial privacy notice as well, if the institution wants to disclose nonpublic personal information to a nonaffiliated third party, and the disclosure is not exempted by the statute. The institution must give the notice before making the disclosure.[122] An institution that does not make any nonexempt disclosures to any nonaffiliated third parties need not give non-customer consumers any sort of notice.[123]

In addition to initial privacy notices, customers—but not consumers—are entitled to an annual privacy notice regard-

---

109 15 U.S.C. § 6802(6); 16 C.F.R. § 313.15(a)(5).
110 15 U.S.C. § 6802(a)(2); 16 C.F.R. § 313.13(a).
111 15 U.S.C. § 6802(a)(2); 16 C.F.R. § 313.13(a).
112 16 C.F.R. § 313.13(a)(ii).
113 15 U.S.C. § 6802(c); 16 C.F.R. § 313.11(a).
114 16 C.F.R. § 313.11(a)(1)(iii).
115 16 C.F.R. § 313.4. See also 15 U.S.C. § 6804(a).
116 See 16.4.1.3, *supra*.
117 15 U.S.C. § 6803(a); 16 C.F.R. § 313.4(a).
118 16 C.F.R. § 313.4(e)(i).
119 16 C.F.R. § 313.4(e)(ii). Existing customers who have already received a privacy notice do not need a new notice when obtaining a new financial product or service if the previous notice was accurate with respect to what's now being offered. 16 C.F.R. § 313.3(d).
120 16 C.F.R. § 313.4(e).
121 15 U.S.C. § 6809(9), (10); 16 C.F.R. § 313.3(h).
122 16 C.F.R. §§ 313.4(b), 313.13, 313.14.
123 15 U.S.C. § 6803(a); 16 C.F.R. § 313.4(b).

ing the institution's privacy policies and practices.[124] The customer's right to any annual notice ends once the customer relationship ends.[125]

The required contents of the privacy notices revolve around the concept of "categories;" the notices, whether initial, annual, or revised, must include the following:

(1) The categories of nonpublic personal information that the institution collects;

(2) The categories of nonpublic personal information that the institution discloses;

(3) The categories of affiliates and nonaffiliated third parties to whom the institution discloses nonpublic information, other than those to whom the institution makes exempt disclosures;

(4) The categories of nonpublic personal information about the institution's former customers that the institution discloses;

(5) The categories of affiliates and nonaffiliated third parties to whom the institution discloses nonpublic personal information about former customers, except those to whom the institution makes exempt disclosures;

(6) If the institution discloses nonpublic personal information to a nonaffiliated third party pursuant to the Act's special provision for disclosures to service providers,[126] the categories of information that the institution discloses and the categories of the servicer providing third parties with whom the institution has contracted.[127]

In addition to these categorical items, the privacy notices must further set forth the consumer's right to opt out of those disclosures for which the Act gives such a right. The notice must further set out any disclosures the institution makes pursuant to the FCRA's provision regarding sharing of information among affiliates,[128] the institution's policies and practices with respect to protecting the confidentiality and security of nonpublic personal information,[129] and if the institution makes exempt disclosures, a statement that it will make disclosures to nonaffiliated third parties as permitted by law.[130]

---

124 15 U.S.C. § 6803(a); 16 C.F.R. § 313.5.
125 16 C.F.R. § 313.3(b).
126 See § 16.4.1.5, supra.
127 15 U.S.C. § 6803(b); 16 C.F.R. § 313.6(a).
128 16 C.F.R. § 313.6(a)(7); 15 U.S.C. § 1681a(d)(2)(A)(iii). This provision of the FCRA provides that information shared among an institution's affiliates is outside the definition of a "consumer report"—and thereby largely outside the scope of FCRA regulation—so long as the institution has first disclosed to the consumer that it may share that information and gives the consumer the opportunity to opt out of such sharing. See also § 8.2.18, supra.
129 16 C.F.R. § 313.6(a)(8).
130 16 C.F.R. § 313.6(b).

Note that the FTC Privacy Rule allows the institution to describe the categories in broad and loose terms. The FTC Privacy Rule lists as an example of how an institution might describe categories of nonpublic personal information that it collects as "(i) information from the consumer; (ii) information about the consumer's transactions with the institution or its affiliates; (iii) information about the consumer's transactions with nonaffiliated third parties; and (iv) information from a consumer reporting agency."[131] The institution need not give specific examples of the information it intends to disclose, and accordingly consumers may be left unclear as to what specific information has been put at risk.

16.4.1.7 Opting Out

16.4.1.7.1 General

The opt-out right is the core privacy protection of GLB, but it applies only to nonexempt disclosures of nonpublic personal information to a nonaffiliated third party. A financial institution may not make a nonexempt disclosure of nonpublic personal information about a consumer to a nonaffiliated third party unless:

(1) It has provided the consumer with an initial privacy notice;

(2) It has provided the consumer with an opt-out notice;

(3) It has given the consumer a reasonable opportunity to opt out; and

(4) The consumer has not opted out.[132]

16.4.1.7.2 The opt-out notice

If an institution wants to disclose, or to reserve the right to disclose, nonpublic personal information about a consumer to a nonaffiliated third party, the institution must furnish the consumer with an opt-out notice that meets the Act's requirements, the foremost of which is that it provide "a clear and conspicuous notice . . . that accurately explains the right to opt out."[133] The notice must state that the institution might make such disclosures and that the consumer has the right to opt out of the disclosures, and must provide a reasonable means for the consumer to exercise the opt-out right.[134]

The FTC Privacy Rule provides many examples of the various elements of an adequate opt-out notice, and some examples of inadequate notices.[135] The FTC Privacy Rule requires the institution to do *something* to facilitate the opting-out. Requiring the consumer to write a letter to

---

131 16 C.F.R. § 313.6(c)(1).
132 15 U.S.C. § 6802(b)(1); 16 C.F.R. § 313.10(a)(1).
133 16 C.F.R. § 313.7.
134 16 C.F.R. § 313.7.
135 16 C.F.R. § 313.7(a)(2).

exercise the opt-out right is unreasonable and does not comply with the statute.[136] Reasonable opt-out means include: designating a check-off box in a prominent position on the opt-out notice form; including a reply form that includes the address to which the form should be mailed; providing an electronic means to opt out; or providing a toll-free number that the consumer may call.[137] The institution need not supply postage for a mail-in response, however. The FTC Privacy Rule details how opt-out notices can be supplied to and acted upon by consumers who have a joint relationship with the institution.[138]

The FTC Privacy Rule requires the opt-out notice to be "clear and conspicuous,"[139] meaning that the notice must be both "reasonably understandable" and "designed to call attention to the nature and significance of the information in the notice."[140] The FTC Privacy Rule considers a notice to be "reasonably understandable" if it:[141]

(A) Presents the information in clear, concise sentences, paragraphs, and sections;
(B) Uses short explanatory sentences or bullet lists whenever possible;
(C) Uses definite, concrete, everyday words and active voice whenever possible;
(D) Avoids multiple negatives;
(E) Avoids legal and highly technical business terminology whenever possible; and
(F) Avoids explanations that are imprecise and readily subject to different interpretations.

The FTC Privacy Rule considers a notice to be "designed to call attention to the nature and significance of the information" if the notice:[142]

(A) Uses a plain-language heading to call attention to the notice;
(B) Uses a typeface and type size that is easy to read;
(C) Provides wide margins and ample line spacing;
(D) Uses boldface or italics for key words; and
(E) Uses distinctive type size, style, and graphic devices, such as shading or sidebars, when combined with other information when the notice is in a form that combines the notice with other information.

Despite the FTC Privacy Rule's guidelines, evidence suggests that many of the notices sent to consumers in the initial years after the Act's passage lacked the clarity and simplicity many consumers need to fully understand their right to opt out of disclosures and the method by which they can do so.[143] One study found that typical opt-out notices fail to adequately advise consumers of their protection rights.[144] The analysis of sixty financial privacy notices found that they were written at an average of a third- to fourth-year college reading level, and were graded as ranging from difficult to very difficult on the Flesch Reading Ease measure.[145] The analysis also showed that the notices often failed to be clear; examples showed that many institutions incorporated the legal terminology of the Act and its regulations instead of translating the provisions into concrete terms, e.g., "financial transactions," rather than "checks and credit card charges."

In fact, the FTC's own suggested clauses do not use the sort of down-to-earth terms that would catch the eye of many consumers.[146] Though nominally requiring the notice to be "clear and conspicuous," the FTC failed to pin the requirement to an objective standard, such as a certain score on the Flesch Reading Ease scale, that would have ensured that a large pool of consumers would be able to understand the notices and thereby be able to act on them.[147] Such a requirement is not unprecedented, as several states have required that certain consumer documents, most commonly insurance policies, meet a particular Flesch score, usually 40 to 50.[148]

In a report to the FTC, Privacy Rights Clearinghouse, a nonprofit consumer organization, reported an opt-out rate of less than five percent.[149] Based on its own survey of consumers, though, Privacy Rights Clearinghouse attributed this low rate not to a lack of interest in maintaining privacy, but to the complication of notices and the burden of the opt out election process;[150] about 65% of consumers had a low understanding of GLB and the notices they received.

---

136 16 C.F.R. § 313.6(a)(2)(B).
137 Id.
138 16 C.F.R. § 313.7(d).
139 16 C.F.R. § 313.7(a)(1).
140 16 C.F.R. § 313.3(b)(1).
141 16 C.F.R. § 313.3(b)(2).
142 Id.
143 Mark Hochhauser, *Lost in the Fine Print: Readability of Financial Privacy Act Notices*, available at www.privacyrights.org/ar/GLB-reading htm.
144 Id.
145 Id.
146 16 C.F.R. Part 313, App. A.
147 The Flesch Reading Ease score is based on a 100 point scale; the higher the score, the easier the document is to read. The formula for the Flesch Reading Ease score is: $206.835 - (1.015 \times ASL) - (84.6 \times ASW)$, where: ASL = average sentence length (the number of words divided by the number of sentences), and ASW = average number of syllables per word (the number of syllables divided by the number of words).
148 See, e.g., Ala. Code § 23-80-206 (insurance policies, 40); Conn. Gen. Stat. § 38a-297 (insurance policies, 45); Del. Code Ann. tit. 18, § 2741 (automobile insurance policies, 40); Me. Rev. Stat. Ann. tit. 24-A, § 2441 (insurance policies, 50); Minn. Stat. § 17.944 (agricultural contracts, score considered relevant to contract's readability); Va. Code Ann. § 31.1-330.2 (managed care program information documents, 40).
149 Privacy Rights Clearinghouse, *2001: The GLB Odyssey—We're Not There Yet, How Consumers Responded to Financial Privacy Notices & Recommendations for Improving Them* (Dec. 4, 2001), available at www.privacyrights.org/ar/fp-glb-ftc.htm.
150 Id.

Consumers reportedly have complained about the time, cost, and confusion in trying to exercise the opt-out right, and reported that many financial institutions handled their inquiries ineptly, which suggests that GLB is not fully understood by the regulated financial institutions themselves. Based on these comments, the Privacy Rights Clearinghouse recommended that institutions write notices at an eighth grade level, place the opt-out right disclosure at the top of the notice, minimize marketing messages in the materials, and send the notices separately from other information.[151]

16.4.1.7.3 Exercise of the opt-out right

The FTC Privacy Rule requires the institution to comply with a consumer's opt-out direction "as soon as reasonably practicable after [the institution] receives it,"[152] and the opt-out continues until the consumer revokes it in writing or electronically.[153] Until revoked, the consumer may exercise the opt-out right at any time.[154]

16.4.1.8 Limits on Sharing Account Number Information for Marketing Purposes

The only category of information that GLB protects from disclosure outright, without any action on the consumer's part, is the highly potent information of account numbers and similar forms of access codes. Financial institutions are prohibited from disclosing these numbers or codes to any nonaffiliated third party for marketing use *other than to a consumer reporting agency*, even if the financial institution has given the consumer a conforming opt-out notice.[155]

However, the FTC Privacy Rule carves two exceptions into even this narrow protection.[156] First, an institution may disclose such numbers or codes to an agent or service provider providing marketing services to the institution, as long as the agent or service provider is not authorized to directly initiate charges to the account.[157] Second, an institution may disclose account numbers to a participant in a private-label credit card program or an affinity or similar program where the participants in the program are identified to the customer when the customer enters into the program.[158]

As for the exception for CRAs, the FTC construes it as limited to such disclosures that the FCRA permits only "in connection with [a] credit or insurance transaction that is not initiated by the consumer" if it consists of a "firm offer"[159]—known as the "prescreening" exception. The District of Columbia Circuit Court of Appeals has upheld this construction, rejecting a CRA's contention that the GLB provision exempted CRAs from *all* restrictions on marketing of account numbers.[160]

16.4.1.9 Impact on Fair Credit Reporting Act

GLB specifically provides that it does not "modify, limit, or supersede the operation of the Fair Credit Reporting Act."[161] The FTC has proposed interpretations of the FCRA that recognize that financial institutions will design information-sharing policies that will simultaneously comply with GLB and the FCRA.[162] As discussed above,[163] GLB specifically exempts disclosures made to a CRA in accordance with the FCRA, and from a consumer report issued by a CRA. However, the savings clause does *not* prevent the FTC from restricting a CRA from making any disclosure that is not expressly permitted by the FCRA.[164]

16.4.1.10 Implementation and Enforcement of Gramm-Leach Bliley

A variety of federal and even state agencies have jurisdiction over the financial institutions covered by GLB. The respective banking regulators[165] and Securities and Exchange Commission have rulemaking authority over the institutions they regulate.[166] In addition, these agencies have enforcement authority to bring actions against financial

---

151 *Id.*
152 16 C.F.R. § 313.7(e).
153 16 C.F.R. § 313.7(h).
154 16 C.F.R. § 313.7(g).
155 15 U.S.C. § 6802(d).
156 16 C.F.R. § 313.12. Though these exceptions were not in the original proposed rule, after receiving comments the FTC loosened its proposed rule to allow such disclosures. 65 Fed. Reg. 33,686 (codified at 16 C.F.R. § 313.12).
157 16 C.F.R. § 313.12(b)(1).
158 16 C.F.R. § 313.12(b)(2).
159 15 U.S.C. § 1681b(c)(1)(B). See § 7.3.4, *supra*.
160 Trans Union, L.L.C. v. Fed. Trade Comm'n, 295 F.3d 42, 52 (D.C. Cir. 2002). The court reasoned that Congress could not have intended for account numbers to have even less protection than other nonpublic personal financial information. *Id.*
161 15 U.S.C. § 6806.
162 65 Fed. Reg. 80,802 (Dec. 22, 2000). These proposed interpretations, intended to become part of Appendix B to 16 C.F.R. Part 600, target the affiliate sharing exception to the Fair Credit Reporting Act, § 603(d)(2)(A)(iii), and the consumer's right to opt out of such sharing. Other federal agencies have also furnished proposed FCRA regulations on affiliate sharing, to be codified as follows: Office of the Comptroller of the Treasury, 12 C.F.R. Part 41; Federal Reserve System, 12 C.F.R. Part 222; Federal Deposit Insurance Corp., 12 C.F.R. Part 334; Department of the Treasury, 12 C.F.R. Part 571. These interpretations are discussed at § 2.4.3, *supra*.
163 *See* § 16.4.1.5, *supra*.
164 Trans Union, L.L.C. v. Fed. Trade Comm'n, 295 F.3d 42, 49 (D.C. Cir. 2002).
165 These agencies are the Office of the Comptroller of the Currency for national banks, the Office of Thrift Supervision for federal savings banks, the Federal Deposit Insurance Corporation for state chartered banks, the Federal Reserve System for its member banks, the National Credit Union Administration for credit unions.
166 15 U.S.C. § 6804.

institutions for violations of the GLB Act, as do state insurance regulators for insurers.[167]

The FTC has catch-all authority over those financial institutions and persons that are not subject to the jurisdiction of any of the others; the FTC describes these remaining institutions as including mortgage lenders, "payday" lenders, finance companies, mortgage brokers, non-bank lenders, account servicers, check cashers, wire transferors, travel agencies operated in connection with financial services, collection agencies, credit counselors and other financial advisors, tax preparation firms, non-federally insured credit unions, and investment advisors that are not required to register with the Securities and Exchange Commission.[168]

The government agencies have all issued regulations pursuant to GLB, which are substantially similar.[169] The FTC's authority to issue the regulations survived a challenge brought by TransUnion, one of the three major CRAs.[170] The most critical regulations which have been the subject of the discussion above are the ones collectively known as the FTC Privacy Rule.[171] GLB also requires agencies subject to the Act to establish standards "relating to administrative, technical, and physical safeguards" to ensure security and confidentiality of customer information, protect against any anticipated threats or hazards to those records, and protect against unauthorized access to those records.[172] The FTC has issued its Safeguard Rules, which require financial institutions within the FTC's jurisdiction to develop and maintain an information security program that contains certain designated elements.[173]

The FTC also issued regulations under the GLB Act to close the FCRA's "credit header" information loophole, which was a significant step for consumers' privacy. Thus, under the regulations governing reuse of information, a CRA may not redisclose nonpersonal public information—even name, address, and telephone number—that it acquires from a nonaffiliated financial institution, except in the form of a consumer report provided for a permissible purpose under the provisions of the FCRA.[174]

16.4.1.11 No Private Right of Action under Gramm-Leach-Bliley

A fundamental flaw of the GLB Act is that it fails to provide consumers with a private cause of action. This renders the Act of little practical value to those who seek to limit, or even monitor, the use of their private data.[175] The failure to provide a private cause of action puts extra demands on such government agencies, who will have to balance the demand of pursuing violations of GLB against all the other competing demands for limited resources.

On the other hand, however, GLB does not preempt more protective state laws,[176] allowing states themselves to address this significant privacy protection problem. Since, a violation of GLB may give rise to a claim under a state's UDAP statute,[177] consumers may be able to enforce GLB's provisions through this device.

In part due to the lack of a private cause of action, not many cases have tested the contours of Gramm-Leach-Bliley. Most uses of GLB have been to defend against a litigation opponent's discovery request for customer information.[178] The statute has also been invoked as a defense in

---

167 15 U.S.C. § 6805.
168 16 C.F.R. § 313.1(b). See also Federal Trade Commission, Frequently Asked Questions for Privacy Regulation, Dec. 2001, available at www.ftc.gov/privacy/glbact/glb-faq.htm.
169 The OCC's regulations are codified at 12 C.F.R. § 40; the FRB's at 12 C.F.R. § 216; the FDIC's at 12 C.F.R. § 332; the OTS at 12 C.F.R. § 573; the NCUA's at 12 C.F.R. § 716; and the SEC's at 12 C.F.R. § 248.
170 Trans Union, L.L.C. v. Fed. Trade Comm'n, 295 F.3d 42 (D.C. Cir. 2002). The decision not only ruled that the FTC had authority to issue the regulations at issue, but also that they did not violate TransUnion's right to free speech, expressly affirming that the government has a substantial interest in protecting the privacy of consumers' credit information. *Id.* at 22–24 (citing Trans Union Corp. v. Fed. Trade Comm'n, 245 F.3d 809 (D.C. Cir. 2001)).
171 16 C.F.R. § 313.
172 15 U.S.C. § 6801.
173 16 C.F.R. Part 314. The institution must designate an employee to coordinate the program, identify reasonably foreseeable risks to customer information, design and implement information safeguards to control those risks, oversee service providers by requiring them by contract to implement and maintain their own safeguards, and evaluate and adjust the program. 16 C.F.R. § 314.4(a)–(e). The FTC has brought two actions to enforce the Safeguard Rules. *In re* Sunbelt Lending Servs., (Docket No. C-4129) (Jan. 3, 2005) (consent order), available at www.ftc.gov/os/caselist/0423153/050107do0423153.pdf; *In re* Nationwide Mortgage Group, Inc., (Docket No. 9319) (Mar. 4, 2005) (consent order), available at www.ftc.gov/os/adjpro/d9319/050304agreeconorder.pdf. See also Federal Trade Commission, Protecting Consumer's Data: Policy Issues Raised by ChoicePoint, Statement Before the Subcommittee on Commerce, Trade, and Consumer Protection (Mar. 15, 2005), available at www.ftc.gov/os/2005/03/050315protectingconsumerdata.pdf.
174 65 Fed. Reg. at 33,668, 33,685 (codifying 16 C.F.R. § 313.11). Trans Union L.L.C. v. Fed. Trade Comm'n, 295 F.3d 42 (D.C. Cir. 2002) (upholding regulation against multiple challenges).
175 See Farley v. Williams, 2005 WL 3579060, at *3 (W.D.N.Y. Dec. 30, 2005). Briggs v. Emporia State Bank and Trust Co., 2005 WL 2035038, at *2–3 (D. Kan. Aug. 23, 2005); Borinski v. Williamson, 2004 WL 433746 at *3 (N.D. Tex. Mar. 1, 2004) (no private cause of action under Gramm-Leach-Bliley); Lacerte Software Corp. v. Prof'l Tax Servs., L.L.C., 2004 WL 180321, at *2 (N.D. Tex. Jan. 6, 2004) (same); Menton v. Experian Corp., 2003 WL 21692820, at *3 (S.D.N.Y. July 21, 2003) (same).
176 15 U.S.C. § 6807. See § 16.4.2.4, *infra*.
177 See § 10.6.2, *supra*. See also National Consumer Law Center, Unfair and Deceptive Acts and Practices (6th ed. 2004 and Supp.).
178 See, e.g., *In re* Boston Herald, Inc., 321 F.3d 174, 190 (1st Cir. 2003) (citing Gramm-Leach-Bliley in support of its ruling that newspaper could not have access to sealed financial documents submitted by a criminal defendant who sought government funding for his legal bills; stating that "[p]ersonal financial

suits alleging violations of the Fair Debt Collection Practices Act,[179] but even if a financial institution has properly notified a consumer that it may disclose the consumer's information to third parties, the disclosure may nonetheless violate another consumer protection act, including the Fair Debt Collection Practices Act.[180] In other words, a defendant cannot avoid a claim that its disclosure of a consumer's financial information violated the consumer's privacy rights by asserting that it properly warned the consumer pursuant to Gramm-Leach-Bliley that it intended to disclose that information.[181]

16.4.1.12 Limited Preemption of State Law

The Gramm-Leach-Bliley Act expressly preserves the right of states to protect the privacy of consumers' financial information. The Act provides that it supersedes state laws only to the extent that such laws are inconsistent with the Act,[182] and specifically grants states permission to enact greater protections.[183]

16.4.1.13 Weaknesses of Gramm-Leach-Bliley

While any privacy protection is welcome, GLB blocks only a very few of the many channels through which financial institutions distribute consumers' financial information. This becomes apparent if the focus shifts from what GLB prohibits to what it permits. A financial institution can always disclose any consumer financial information to any of its affiliates. If a financial institution provides the prescribed privacy policy and opt-out notice, and a consumer does not opt out, the financial institution becomes free to market to any third party any of the information it has about a consumer and that consumer's account (apart from the actual account numbers and access codes). Such information can include credit limits, when and where a consumer used a debit card or charged a purchase, and which ATMs a consumer frequents.

Furthermore, even if a consumer opts out, financial institutions may still disclose consumer information to nonaffiliated third parties that perform services or functions on behalf of the financial institution and may disclose information pursuant to any one of a myriad of listed exceptions, without even notifying the consumer that it will do so.[184] Finally, even further inroads into prohibited disclosures are possible, as the Act authorizes the rulemaking agencies to include even more exceptions "as are deemed consistent" with the Act.[185]

To be effective, this legislation should have prohibited financial institutions from disclosing nonpublic personal information unless the consumer specifically authorized it by "opting in" to such use of the consumer's information. The selection of opt-out over opt-in means that the consumer bears the burden not just of understanding and heeding the opt-out notice, but also of complying with the necessary procedures to actually opt out. There is no universal opt-out, a consumer has to follow each different financial institution's own individual opt-out requirements in order to make the most of what little protection the Act provides. If the consumer does not opt out, her financial information becomes fair fodder for the marketing industry, at least to the extent state laws do not curb such information trafficking, and the average consumer may never be aware of who reaches for their information and where they take it.

The legislation's failure to put any limits on information that an institution may share with an affiliate greatly weakens the purported protection. As financial institutions continue to align and merge with not just other financial institutions, but financial services entities of all sorts—the main point of the Gramm-Leach-Bliley Act in fact being to remove barriers between insurance and banking and secu-

---

information, such as one's income or bank account balance, is universally presumed to be private, not public, for disclosure purposes"); Landry v. Union Planters Corp., 2003 WL 21355462 (E.D. La. June 6, 2003) (party's discovery of customer information would not violate Gramm-Leach-Bliley Act so long as all nonpublic personal information was redacted from the materials); Union Planters Bank, N.A. v. Gavel, 2003 WL 1193671 (E.D. La. Mar. 12, 2003) (granting bank a permanent injunction against party who had been issued a subpoena for the disclosure of information that related to plaintiff bank's customers, on grounds that the Gramm-Leach-Bliley Act prohibited the defendant from revealing that information without the customers' consent), *rev'd and remanded*, Union Planters Bank, N.A. v. Salih 369 F.3d 457 (5th Cir. 2004); *Ex parte* Nat'l Western Life Ins. Co., 2004 WL 2260308, at *7 (Ala. Oct. 8, 2004) (reading section 6802(e)(8)'s exemption for judicial process to cover a party's request for discovery of life insurance policies and other documents containing nonpublic personal information from petitioner, an insurance company, in suit alleging petitioner negligently issued a policy); ArborPlace, L.P. v. Encore Opportunity Fund, L.L.C., 2002 WL 205681 (Del. Ch. Ct. Jan. 29, 2002) (Gramm-Leach-Bliley regulations did not require limited liability company to shield its membership lists from limited partner, information was exempt from notice and opt-out requirements by 17 C.F.R. § 248.15, the SEC's equivalent to the FTC's regulation at 16 C.F.R. § 313.15); *In re* Lexington Ins. Co., 2004 WL 210576, at *4 (Tex. App. Feb. 2, 2004) (upholding order to insurance company to produce documents that were to be redacted of private, personal, and nonpublic information of insureds).

179 15 U.S.C. §§ 1692–1692o. *See also* National Consumer Law Center, Fair Debt Collection (5th ed. 2004 and Supp.).
180 Blair v. Sherman Acquisition, 2004 WL 2870080, at *4 (N.D. Ill. Dec. 13, 2004) (denying defendants' motion to dismiss in part).
181 *Id.*
182 15 U.S.C. § 6807(a).
183 15 U.S.C. § 6807(b). *See also* American Council of Life Insurers v. Vermont Dep't of Banking, Ins., Sec., & Healthcare Admin., 2004 WL 578737 (Vt. Feb. 12, 2004) (upholding

administrative regulation requiring "opt-in" rule for various financial institutions).
184 16 C.F.R. § 313.15.
185 15 U.S.C. § 6804(b).

rities and banking[186]—personal financial information will become available to larger and larger pools of companies.

Finally, a very significant weakness in the GLB Act is its failure to provide injured consumers with an effective remedy to seek redress.[187] Even if a financial institution violates GLB's limited protections, a consumer is powerless to take action and must rely on overburdened federal agencies to address violations.

16.4.2 Other State and Federal Protections

16.4.2.1 Protections Related to Computers and the Internet

The federal Computer Fraud and Abuse Act criminalizes various forms of unauthorized use of federal government and financial institution computers.[188] Although the Act prohibits the unauthorized, intentional access of a computer to obtain the records of a financial institution, a card issuer, or a CRA, the Act's limited private right of action provision provides relief for a violation only in unusual circumstances.[189] Furthermore, a federal district court has held that the Act did not bar the use of cookies or other data mining activities.[190]

Other statutes enacted in the era of computer crime may prohibit the unauthorized access of databases more effectively than the tort of intrusion, though, again, usually without providing a private cause of action.[191] These statutes, however, are not directed towards those who, with authorized access, disseminate data to someone not entitled to it. Accordingly, these statutes do not protect against one of the most common breaches of privacy, personal information given to an information broker who has used a false "pretext" or impersonation designed to overcome the privacy barriers kept by a particular data-keeping entity such as a bank.[192] Since the broker does not access the computer, but

---

186 146 Cong. Rec. S4616 (May 4, 1999).
187 *See* § 16.4.1.11, *supra*.
188 18 U.S.C. § 1030.
189 18 U.S.C. § 1030(c). A person whose records were wrongfully accessed could assert a cause of action under 18 U.S.C. § 1030(a)(5)(A), but would have to additionally meet one of the factors listed in § 1030(a)(5)(B)(i)–(v). As a practical matter, the victim would have to prove a loss of at least $5000. 18 U.S.C. § 1030(a)(5)(B)(1). *Cf.* Doe v. Dartmouth-Hitchcock Med. Ctr., 2001 U.S. Dist. LEXIS 10704 (D.N.H. July 19, 2001) (no vicarious liability for violations of Computer Fraud & Abuse Act).
190 *In re* DoubleClick Inc. Privacy Litig., 154 F. Supp. 2d 497, 519 (S.D.N.Y. 2001).
191 Most states also criminalize computer hacking. *See, e.g.*, Ala. Code § 13A-8-101 (unauthorized disclosure of computer data is a crime); Alaska Stat. § 11.81.900(b)(48) (criminal code defines "property" to include "tangible personal property including data or information stored in a computer program, system or network"); Ariz. Rev. Stat. § 13-2316; Ark. Code Ann. § 5-41-104 (computer trespassing a misdemeanor); Cal. Penal Code § 484j (malicious access; publishing a PIN, password, access code, debt card number, or bank account number, is a crime); Colo. Rev. Stat. § 18-5.5-102 (accessing a computer system without authorization, to defraud, for theft or to interrupt); Conn. Gen. Stat. § 53a-251 (unauthorized access); Del. Code tit. 11, §§ 931–939 (intentionally accessing a computer system for an improper purpose); Fla. Stat. Ann. § 815.04 (West) (prohibits willful disclosure of computer information); Ga. Code Ann. § 16-9-93 (accessing or attempting to access a computer system owned by the state or by any business); Haw. Rev. Stat. § 708-891 (computer fraud includes accessing a system to get credit information); Idaho Code § 18-2202 (Michie) (wrongfully accessing computer system); 720 Ill. Comp. Stat. 5/16D-3 (illegal to access a system, or use or benefit from it, without consent); Ind. Code § 35-43-2-3 (accessing a computer system without consent; Iowa Code § 716.6B (crime to access a system to obtain information without authority); Kan. Stat. Ann. § 21-3755 (disclosing or copying); Ky. Rev. Stat. Ann. § 434.845 (Michie) (accessing computer information or misusing computer information) La. Rev. Stat. §§ 14:73.1 to 14:73.5; Me. Rev. Stat. Ann. tit. 17-A, § 432 (West); Md. Ann. Code art. 27, § 146, *as amended by* 2000 Md. Laws 7, § 1 (access without authorization); Mass. Gen. Laws Ann. ch. 266, § 30(2) ("property" as defined in the larceny statute includes "electronically processed or stored data, either tangible or intangible, and data while in transit"); Mich. Comp. Laws § 752.795 (illegal to access or disrupt a computer system without authorization); Miss. Code Ann. § 97-45-5 (disclosure or misuse of codes or passwords; Mont. Code Ann. §§ 45-6-310, 45-6-311 (prohibits unauthorized use of computer); Neb. Rev. Stat. § 28-1346 (unauthorized access of confidential information); Nev. Rev. Stat. § 205.4765 (unauthorized use of a computer to get personal information on another); N.H. Rev. Stat. Ann. § 638:17 (unauthorized access); N.J. Stat. Ann. § 2C:20-25; N.M. Stat. Ann. § 30-45-4 (Michie) (misuse of a computer); N.Y. Penal Law para. 156 (intrusion into a computer system with confidential medical or personal information, unauthorized duplication of data); N.C. Gen Stat. § 14-454 (wrongful access); N.D. Cent. Code § 12.1-06.1-08 (unauthorized access with intent to defraud, deceive, or control property or services); Ohio Rev. Code. Ann. §§ 2901.01, 2913.01 (definition of stolen property includes computer media); Okla. Stat. tit. 21, §§ 1951–1958 (authorizes civil action) (computer hacking); Or. Rev. Stat. § 164.377 (unauthorized access); Pa. Stat. Ann. tit. 18, § 3933 (access with criminal intent and tampering); R.I. Gen. Laws § 11-52-1 (unauthorized access); S.C. Code § 16-16-10 (computer hacking); S.D. Codified Laws § 43-43B-1 (computer hacking, use or disclosure of passwords, accessing or disclosing computerized information); Tenn. Code Ann. § 39-14-602; Tex. Penal Code Ann. § 33.02 (Vernon) (use or gain access without consent); Utah Code Ann. § 76-6-703 (wrongful access); Va. Code Ann. § 18.2-152.4 (Michie) (invasion of privacy to peruse medical, employment, salary, credit or other financial or personal data stored in a computer); Vt. Stat. Ann. § 4104; Wash. Rev. Code Ann. § 9A.48.100 (physical damage includes damage to computers, computer information and computer services); W. Va. Code §§ 61-3C-4 through 61-3C-12 (unauthorized access); Wis. Stat. § 943.70 (access or copy data); Wyo. Stat. Ann. §§ 6-3-501 to 6-3-504.
192 Federal prosecutors have charged one information broker with violating federal racketeering laws—though not privacy laws. Douglas Frantz, *Law Confronts Seller of Private Data*, N.Y. Times, July 1, 1999.

merely manipulates an institution's employee into doing it, the hacking laws will not apply.

Other computer-relevant legislation indirectly addresses consumer privacy. The federal Electronic Communications Privacy Act of 1986 outlaws the interception of certain wire, oral, and electronic communications, and provides a cause of action to those whose privacy has been breached in that manner.[193] However, that act does not restrict surreptitious Internet data collection. The Children's Online Privacy Protection Act (COPPA) restricts website operators and on-line services from collecting identifying information from children, but does not provide private parties with enforcement power.[194] The Telecommunications Act of 1996 contains a customer privacy provision that imposes on telecommunications carriers a duty to protect the confidentiality of customers' proprietary information, prohibits them from using information acquired from another carrier for marketing efforts, and requires customer approval to disclose customer proprietary network information.[195]

16.4.2.2 The Financial Information Privacy Act

The Financial Information Privacy Act criminalizes obtaining customer information from a financial institution by pretext or through the use of an illegitimate document.[196] The statute covers both communications with a financial institution's agents and employees and with a customer of the institution, and further prohibits the solicitation of someone to obtain such information—attempting to reach those who hire the information brokers.[197] The statute exempts information that is otherwise available from a public record, and does not apply to private investigators seeking to enforce child support judgments.[198] Significantly, state laws are not preempted.[199] While the statute provides for a fine and for imprisonment of up to five years, it does not provide for a private cause of action.[200]

---

193 18 U.S.C. §§ 2510–2522. However, if the subject of the intercepted communication involves a matter of public interest, the First Amendment may prohibit a private action based on its disclosure. Bartnicki v. Vopper, 532 U.S. 514 (2001).
194 13 U.S.C. §§ 1301–1308.
195 47 U.S.C. § 222. See also 47 C.F.R. § 2005 (corresponding privacy regulation issued by the FCC). The FCC's regulation was struck down by the Tenth Circuit on First Amendment grounds, the court holding that the FCC had failed to show that the dissemination of the information would inflict "specific or significant harm on individuals," rejecting the government's assertion that a broad privacy interest justified the restriction on the carriers' commercial speech. U.S. West, Inc. v. FCC, 182 F.3d 1224 (10th Cir. 1999).
196 15 U.S.C. §§ 6821–6827.
197 15 U.S.C. § 6821.
198 15 U.S.C. § 6821(f), (g).
199 15 U.S.C. § 6824.
200 15 U.S.C. § 6823. The statute further imposes an enhanced penalty for those who violate or attempt to violate the section while violating another U.S. law or as part of a pattern of illegal

16.4.2.3 The Federal Trade Commission Act

The Federal Trade Commission Act[201] prohibits unfair methods of competition and unfair or deceptive acts and practices. The FTC has used the FTC Act to pursue information brokers who obtain private financial information by "pretexting," that is, by misleading the institution into believing that the broker is someone entitled to the information.[202] Though there is no private right of action under the FTC Act,[203] state unfair and deceptive acts and practices statutes may draw upon the FTC Act to find that a practice violates a state statute by the fact that it violates the FTC standard.[204]

16.4.2.4 State Statutes

State laws that specifically prohibit the disclosure of financial data to non-governmental third parties might be more effective than the traditional torts. For example, New York law prohibits credit card registration services from selling or disclosing the names, addresses, and account numbers of cardholders for use in direct-mail marketing without the cardholder's prior written approval;[205] however, the statute does not specifically provide for a private cause of action.[206] Many other states prohibit financial institutions from disclosing certain kinds of customer information to a non-governmental party in the absence of a statutory exception.[207]

---

activity involving greater than $100,000 in a 12 month period. § 523(b).
201 15 U.S.C. § 45. See generally National Consumer Law Center, Unfair and Deceptive Acts and Practices (6th ed. 2004 and Supp.).
202 Fed. Trade Comm'n v. Rapp, 2000 U.S. Dist. LEXIS 20627 (D. Colo. June 22, 2000) (settlement agreement, enjoining defendant from obtaining the private financial information of consumers through misleading statements and from disclosing any financial information so obtained).
203 See National Consumer Law Center, Unfair and Deceptive Acts and Practices § 9.1 (6th ed. 2004 and Supp.).
204 See id. § 3.4.5.
205 N.Y. Gen. Bus. Law § 521-c.
206 Id. § 521-f.
207 See, e.g., Ala. Code § 5-5A-43 (comment states that customer records should be disclosed only upon legal process); Alaska Stat. §§ 06.01.028 (bank records), 21.36.162 (requiring issuance of regulations protecting consumer financial and health information in insurance transactions); Ariz. Rev. Stat. § 20-2104 (requiring that specified notices must comply either with Gramm-Leach-Bliley Act or with state's specifications); Ark. Code Ann. § 23-61-113 (prohibiting disclosures that violate the Gramm-Leach-Bliley Act); Cal. Fin. Code §§ 4050–4060 (California's Financial Information Privacy Act, providing at section 4051, that the California legislature intended to provide greater privacy protections than those of the Gramm-Leach-Bliley Act); Cal. Ins. Code § 1861.16(c)(2) (restricting sharing of information between insurers); Colo. Rev. Stat. §§ 11-37.5-205 (prohibiting disclosure by a foreign capital depository of customer

financial records to private individuals) 11-37.5-214 (civil liability of $10,000 plus actual damages plus costs and attorney fees); Conn. Gen. Stat. § 36a-42; Del. Stat. Ann § 535 (prohibiting disclosures of nonpublic personal information that violate the Gramm-Leach-Bliley Act); Fla. Stat. § 655.059 (financial institution's books and records are confidential); Haw. Rev. Stat. § 412:2-603 (misdemeanor for institution to disclose any information derived from a financial institution's records except in the regular course of business); Idaho Stat. Ann. § 41-1334 (prohibiting disclosures of nonpublic personal information that violate the Gramm-Leach-Bliley Act); 205 Ill. Comp. Stat. § 5/48.1, *as amended by* 1999 Ill. Laws 330 § 95 (now includes any financial statements or other financial information provided by the customer to the bank) (disclosure of customer information is prohibited without authorization, subpoena, or regulatory agency request, or credit exchange; exempts exchanges with banks and other financial institutions); Iowa Code § 527.10 (prohibiting satellite terminals or data processing centers from permitting any person to obtain information concerning the account of any person with a financial institution, unless essential to complete or prevent the completion of a transaction then being engaged in through the use of that facility); Kan. Stat. Ann. § 40-2404 (providing that disclosures of nonpublic personal information that violate the Gramm-Leach-Bliley Act also violate the state's UDAP statute); La. Rev. Stat. Ann. §§ 6:333, 9:3571 (West) (a financial institution or credit card company may release personal credit or financial information only under subpoena with advance notice to customer, except for exchanges among credit grantors and other businesses and for non-tax law enforcement investigations); Me. Rev. Stat. Ann. tit. 9-A, §§ 3-314, 9-310 (requiring creditors to comply with the Gramm-Leach-Bliley Act and Privacy of Consumer Information regulations), 9-A, § 11-122 (requiring merchants who enter into consumer rental-purchase agreements to comply with the Gramm-Leach-Bliley Act and Privacy of Consumer Information regulations), tit. 9-B, § 162 (West) (bank records confidential except for matching of government records, for supervisory audit, with consent of customer, or by legal process), tit. 9-B, § 241 (requiring financial institutions and credit unions to comply with the Gramm-Leach Bliley Act), tit. 30-A, § 3963-A (requiring pawnbrokers to comply with the Gramm-Leach-Bliley Act and Privacy of Consumer Information regulations), tit. 32, § 6146 (requiring check cashing and foreign currency exchange businesses to comply with the Gramm-Leach-Bliley Act and Privacy of Consumer Information regulations), tit. 32, § 6162 (requiring cash-dispensing machine operators to comply with the Gramm-Leach-Bliley Act and Privacy of Consumer Information regulations), tit. 32, § 10313 (providing that broker-dealer's violation of the privacy provisions of the Gramm-Leach-Bliley Act is a ground for action against dealer's license), tit. 32, § 11018 (requiring collection agencies and repossession companies to comply with the Gramm-Leach-Bliley Act and Privacy of Consumer Information regulations), tit. 33, § 528 (requiring settlement agents to comply with the Gramm-Leach-Bliley Act and Privacy of Consumer Information regulations); Md. Code Ann., Fin. Inst. § 1-302 (fiduciary institution may not disclose records unless customer has authorized or pursuant to a subpoena); Minn. Stat. § 47.69 (with respect to electronic financial terminals); Miss. Code Ann. § 81-5-55 (forbids disclosure of depositor's name or amount of deposit to any unapproved party); Mo. Rev. Stat. §§ 326.105 (prohibiting disclosures by a financial institution that violate Gramm-Leach-Bliley), 362.422 (prohibiting disclosures that violate the Gramm-Leach-Bliley Act), 375.918 (limiting disclosures by credit scoring entities of nonpublic personal information); Neb. Rev. Stat. §§ 44-901 to -925 (Privacy of Insurance Consumer Information Act, modeled after GLB); N.H. Rev. Stat. Ann. § 406-C:9 (prohibiting disclosures that do not comply with Gramm-Leach-Bliley Act); N.C. Stat. Ann. §§ 58-39-130 to 58-39-165 (establishing insurance customer information safeguards); N.D. Cent. Code §§ 6.08.1-03 (financial institution may not disclose customer's records without consent unless meets an exemption), 6-08.1-08 (liable for greater of $1000 or actual damages), 26.1-02-27 (prohibiting insurance companies, nonprofit health service corporations, and health maintenance organizations from making disclosures that would violate the Gramm-Leach-Bliley Act); Okla. Stat. Ann. tit. 36, § 307.2 (prohibiting disclosures that violate the Gramm-Leach-Bliley Act); Tenn. Code Ann. § 45-10-104 (forbids disclosure of any financial records unless authorized by customer or pursuant to a lawful subpoena); Vt. Stat. Ann. tit. 8, §§ 10201–10205, (prohibiting financial institutions from disclosing customer information, though with exceptions); W. Va. Code Ann. § 33-6F-1 (prohibiting disclosures that violate the Gramm-Leach-Bliley Act); Vt. Admin. Code 21 010 016 and Reg. B-2001-01; Wis. Stat. § 214.37 (restricting access to books and records of savings banks). *See also* McCarty v. McCarty, 2003 WL 721681 (Conn. Super. Ct. Jan. 22, 2003) (though bank failed to fully comply with state statute's requirements regarding a bank's duties upon receiving a subpoena for customer records, sanctions were not appropriate because evidence did not show that bank willfully subverted the plaintiff's rights); Milohnich v. First Nat'l Bank of Miami Springs, 224 So. 2d 759 (Fla. 1969) (banks to keep information secret except to comply with government orders or to exchange credit data); Peterson v. Idaho First Nat'l Bank, 83 Idaho 578, 367 P.2d 284 (1961) (bank owes customer duty of confidentiality); Burford v. First Nat'l Bank in Mansfield, 557 So. 2d 1147 (La. Ct. App. 1990) (state privacy statute imposed on bank a duty to maintain the confidentiality of plaintiff's financial statement); Taylor v. NationsBank N.A., 365 Md. 166, 776 A.2d 645, 656 (2001) (construing anti-disclosure statute strictly, statute did not prohibit disclosure about financial records, as opposed to the records themselves); Brex v. Smith, 146 A. 34 (Ch. N.J. 1924) (unauthorized prying into a bank account is a tortious invasion of privacy); Sparks v. Union Trust Co., 256 N.C. 478, 124 S.E.2d 365 (1962) (implies that bank depositors have a right of confidentiality); Walker v. White, 89 S.W.3d 573 (Tenn. Ct. App. 2002) (customers had no cause of action against bank under Tennessee Financial Records Privacy Act because Act did not apply to subpoena issued by a federal agency). Many states have separate statutes that restrict disclosures of customer financial information to governmental agencies. *See, e.g.*, N.H. Rev. Stat. Ann. § 359-C:5.

208 Cal. Fin. Code §§ 4050–4060.
209 *Id.* § 4053(a).
210 *Id.* § 4053(b). Certain designated types of affiliates are exempt from the opt-out requirement. *Id.* § 4053(c).

California has enacted a comprehensive statute, the Financial Information Privacy Act,[208] which, among other protections, prohibits financial institutions from disclosing consumer information to others unless the consumer "opts-in" to the disclosure,[209] and allows consumers to "opt-out" of disclosures between affiliated institutions.[210] An entity that negligently violates the Act may suffer a civil penalty in the amount of up to $2500 per violation (for disclosure of one individual's information), or of up to $500,000 (for disclosure of more than one individual's information).[211] These penalties double if the violation results in the theft of a consumer's identity.[212] However, only the California's Attorney General and other designated officials may pursue penalties under the Act.[213]

A few states specifically protect the privacy of electronic fund transfers.[214] A state's UDAP statute may provide a remedy if private information is demanded of a consumer with the misrepresentation that the information is required by law.[215] A number of states have recently enacted statutes specifically targeted to identity theft, these are discussed in § 9.4, *supra*. Finally, some state constitutions contain privacy provisions that may be a source of policy, if not actual precedent, to support a privacy claim.[216]

16.5 Common Law Protection of Financial Information

In addition to statutes, common law may impose on banks an implied contractual duty to keep financial information concerning a depositor confidential.[217] Explained one court, "[i]nviolate secrecy is one of the inherent and fundamental precepts of the relationship of the bank and its customers or depositors."[218] Accordingly, if the state recognizes a duty of confidentiality in its case law, the bank may be liable for all damages proximately caused by the bank's wrongful disclosure of information.[219] However, this theory of liability under common law may not protect a customer when a rogue employee of the bank misuses the information, as opposed to disclosing it to a third party.[220]

---

211 Cal. Fin. Code § 4057(a). The unlawful use or obtaining of personal financial information can also incur a civil penalty of up to $2500; *id.* § 4057(b).

212 *Id.* § 4057(d).

213 *Id.* § 4057(e).

214 *See, e.g.*, Mass. Gen. Laws ch. 167B, § 16 (electronic fund transfer services providers may not disclose customer information without customer's authorization, except to a party to the transaction, government regulators, a CRA, the representative of a collection agency, or pursuant to legal process); Mich. Comp. Laws § 488.12; Mont. Code Ann. § 32-6-105; N.J. Rev. Stat. § 17:16k-3.

215 Meyerson v. Prime Realty Servs., L.L.C., 7 Misc. 3d 911, 796 N.Y.S.2d 848 (N.Y. Sup. Ct. 2005) (denying landlord's motion to dismiss a state UDAP claim brought by a tenant who alleged that the landlord had misrepresented that she was required by law to provide the Social Security numbers of other occupants of her apartment).

216 Alaska Const. art. I, § 22; Ariz. Const. art. II, § 8; Cal. Const. art. I, § 1; Mont. Const. art. II, § 10; Wash. Const. art. I, § 7. Some other state constitutions have privacy provisions that mirror the Fourth Amendment to the U.S. Constitution, targeted toward people's right to privacy from governmental, as opposed to general, intrusion. *See, e.g.*, Fla. Const. art. I, § 23; Ill. Const. art. I, § 6; La. Const. art. I, § 5; N.Y. Const. art. I, § 12; S.C. Const. art. I, § 10.

217 *See, e.g.*, Jordan v. Shattuck Nat'l Bank, 868 F.2d 383 (10th Cir. 1989) (plaintiff stated a cause of action against his bank for its wrongful disclosure of confidential loan application information); Barnett Bank v. Hooper, 498 So. 2d 923 (Fla. 1986); Peterson v. Idaho First Nat'l Bank, 83 Idaho 578, 367 P.2d 284 (1961); Indiana Nat'l Bank v. Chapman, 482 N.E.2d 474 (Ind. Ct. App. 1985); Suburban Trust Co. v. Waller, 44 Md. App. 335, 408 A.2d 758 (1979) (unless required by law, bank may not make any disclosures concerning a depositor's account without the express or implied consent of the depositor); Taylor v. NationsBank, N.A., 365 Md. 166, 776 A.2d 645, 654 (2001) (bank's disclosure of plaintiff's name and unlisted telephone number to another customer, in context of which customer learned plaintiff's account number, could be breach of duty); Richfield Bank & Trust Co. v. Sjogren, 309 Minn. 362, 244 N.W.2d 648 (1976); Pigg v. Robertson, 549 S.W.2d 597 (Mo. Ct. App. 1977) (bank's duty of confidentiality may extend to third party authorized by bank to advise customers); Djowharzadeh v. City Nat'l Bank & Trust Co., 646 P.2d 616 (Okla. Ct. App. 1982) (bank liable for loan officer's disclosure of applicant's financial information even if officer acted outside scope of employment); McGuire v. Shubert, 722 A.2d 1087 (Pa. Super. Ct. 1998). *See also* O'Halloran v. First Union Nat'l Bank of Fla., 205 F. Supp. 2d 1296, 1301 (M.D. Fla. 2002), *vacated and remanded on other grounds*, 350 F.3d 1197 (11th Cir. 2003) (bank owed duty of confidentiality to depositor and therefore could not be liable for failing to disclose to plaintiffs, who alleged that they were defrauded by depositor's Ponzi scheme, the depositor's transactions; granting defendant's motion to dismiss); Ryan v. Hunton & Williams, 2000 U.S. Dist. LEXIS 13750, at *16, 17 (E.D.N.Y. Sept. 20, 2000) (bank could not be liable to investors for failing to advise them of suspicious activities in depositor's account because bank owed duty of confidentiality to depositor); Milohnich v. First Nat'l Bank, 224 So. 2d 759 (Fla. Ct. App. 1969); Roth v. First Nat'l State Bank of N.J., 404 A.2d 1182 (N.J. Super. Ct. App. Div. 1979) (bank was not liable for teller's disclosure to accomplice that bank customer's custom of withdrawing large amounts of cash at particular times, on the agency grounds that teller's behavior was outside the scope of her employment); Roth v. First Nat'l State Bank, 169 N.J. Super. 280, 404 A.2d 1182 (1979) (while bank owes duty of confidentiality to depositor, bank not liable for teller's disclosure where teller acted outside the scope of her employment); R.A. Peck, Inc. v. Liberty Fed. Sav. Bank, 108 N.M. 84, 766 P.2d 928 (N.M. Ct. App. 1988); Heritage Surveyors & Eng'rs, Inc. v. Nat'l Penn Bank, 801 A.2d 1248, 1252–1253 (Pa. Super. 2002) (bank owed duty of confidentiality to depositor, and thus had no duty to disclose to another customer, who was depositor's creditor, information about depositor's account).

218 Peterson v. Idaho First Nat'l Bank, 83 Idaho 578, 367 P.2d 284, 290 (1961) (finding no invasion of privacy tort, because no public dissemination, but upheld breach of implied contract of confidentiality).

219 Suburban Trust Co. v. Waller, 44 Md. App. 335, 408 A.2d 758, 764 (1979) (bank that notified law enforcement authorities after becoming suspicious of the bank notes plaintiff deposited liable to depositor for the wrongful arrest he subsequently suffered).

220 Roth v. First Nat'l State Bank of N.J., 404 A.2d 1182 (N.J. Super. Ct. App. Div. 1979) (bank was not liable for teller's disclosure to accomplice that bank customer's custom of withdrawing large amounts of cash at particular times, on the agency grounds that teller's behavior was outside the scope of her employment); Stevens v. First Interstate Bank, 167 Or. App. 280, 999 P.2d 551, 554 (2000) (employee of bank misappropriated plaintiffs' financial information to obtain credit).

Some courts have ruled that the duty of confidentiality does not exist between a borrower and a bank, as opposed to a depositor.[221] On that basis, one court ruled that a customer who was both a borrower and depositor of the defendant bank had no cause of action for the disclosure by an employee of the bank to the customer's family that she was "in trouble" and would soon lose everything.[222] However, at least one court has suggested that borrowers may be entitled to expect their lender to keep confidential the information they have given to the lender in the course of the relationship.[223]

Representations made by the bank in its contract with the customer or in its published privacy policy or other promotional materials should be a basis for a cause of action when the bank discloses information in violation of those representations.[224] However, a New York court dismissed a class action brought by credit card holders and mortgagors against a bank based on its release of their information to marketers, on the grounds that the customers had failed to fulfill the damage element required by either a UDAP claim or a breach of contract claim.[225] In the court's view, the only consequences to the bank's customers were that they were "offered products and services which they were free to decline. This does not qualify as actual harm."[226] The case illustrates the trivial value many courts put on personal privacy.[227]

A bank customer whose financial information is mishandled might also argue that the bank breached its fiduciary duty, which is a duty distinct from the duty of confidentiality. Though courts generally find that banks do not owe a fiduciary duty to borrowers, particular circumstances surrounding a borrower's relationship with its lender may give rise to a fiduciary duty not to disclose the borrower's financial information.[228] While sounding in contract, at least one court has held that a bank's breach of its fiduciary duty not to disclose confidential information gives rise to a tort that supports a claim for exemplary damages.[229]

The drawback of these statutes and case law decisions is that they are narrow—they apply to banks, but likely not to merchants, credit card companies, website owners, or others who collect consumers' financial information. Furthermore, statutes and decisions vary greatly from state to state, but computer networks cross state boundaries at the speed of light, leading to vexing choice of law issues.

16.6 Interests Impeding Legislative Protection of Financial Information

Expanding privacy law to cover more consumer protections has and will continue to meet with resistance: there is simply too much money to be had in the disclosure of personal identifying information. A trade organization of direct marketers predicted that marketers would spend $1.61 billion in 2005, generating $1.85 trillion in sales.[230] U.S. Bank received $4 million for its customers' account information.[231] Indeed, scholars from the law and economics

---

221 Hopewell Enters. v. Trustmark Nat'l Bank, 680 So. 2d 812, 817 (Miss. 1996); Boccardo v. Citibank, N.A., 579 N.Y.S.2d 836 (N.Y. Sup. Ct. 1991) (bank did not owe customer with line of credit a duty of confidentiality notwithstanding that customer had not yet drawn on line of credit); Graney Dev. Corp. v. Taksen, 92 Misc. 2d 764, 400 N.Y.S.2d 717, aff'd, 66 A.D.2d 1008, 411 N.Y.S.2d 756 (1978). See also Sharma v. Skaarup Ship Mgmt. Corp., 699 F. Supp. 440, 448 (S.D.N.Y. 1988) (bank's duty of confidentiality runs to depositors, not debtors), aff'd, 916 F.2d 820 (2d Cir. 1990). Cf. Parham v. Congress Talcott Corp., 219 A.D.2d 522, 631 N.Y.S.2d 671, 672 (1995) (no duty of confidentiality arises between bank and guarantor of loan).
222 Schoneweis v. Dando, 231 Neb. 180, 435 N.W.2d 666, 672, 673 (1989).
223 Jordan v. Shattuck Nat'l Bank, 868 F.2d 383 (10th Cir. 1989) (reversing lower court's directed verdict in favor of the bank); Rubenstein v. South Denver Nat'l Bank, 762 P.2d 755, 756, 757 (Colo. Ct. App. 1988) (reversing summary judgment for bank against plaintiff who was both a borrower and a depositor).
224 See, e.g., Taylor v. NationsBank N.A., 365 Md. 166, 776 A.2d 645, 651–652 (2001) (bank who disclosed customer's name and telephone number in context which also revealed his account number could be liable pursuant to account agreement).
225 Smith v. Chase Manhattan Bank, USA, 741 N.Y.S.2d 100 (N.Y. App. Div. 2002). The court also rejected an unjust enrichment claim by framing the alleged enrichment as the payments made by the customers for products and services marketed to them, finding that since the purchasers received the benefit of the products and services, no unjust enrichment arose. Id. at 102–103. However, the court framed the enrichment as arising from the profits the bank earned as commissions on the purchases made as a result of the marketing. The framing overlooks that the bank received the commission as a result not just of the sale of products to the customers who wished to purchase from marketers, but also from the disclosure of the financial information of all the members of the class, including the (probably majority) group who did not buy anything from the marketers to whom their confidential information was disclosed, and who thus received absolutely no benefit from the disclosure.
226 Id. at 102.
227 See § 11.10, supra.
228 Dolton v. Capitol Federal Sav. & Loan Ass'n, 642 P.2d 21, 23, 24 (Colo. Ct. App. 1981) (reversing summary judgment for lender in case where plaintiff asserted that lender usurped plaintiff's real estate opportunity after plaintiff approached lender for financing of the intended purchase). See also Commercial Cotton Co. v. United Cal. Bank, 163 Cal. App. 3d 511, 516 (1985) (upholding verdict against bank in case claiming that it breached its covenant of good faith and fair dealing with a depositor, describing a bank's relationship with its depositor as "at least quasi-fiduciary").
229 Rubenstein v. South Denver Nat'l Bank, 762 P.2d 755 (Colo. Ct. App. 1988).
230 Direct Marketing Association, *Direct Marketing is Not What You Think: Annual Report 2005* at 1 (2005), available at www.the-dma.org/aboutdma/annualreport.pdf.
231 *Hatch Sues U.S. Bank for Selling Out Customers to Telemarketers*, Minn. Att'y Gen. Press Release, July 9, 1999. U.S. Bancorp settled this suit, without admitting any wrongdoing, by

school of jurisprudence argue that protecting consumer data would inhibit the flow of accurate information and decrease efficiency,[232] that more information, not less, is needed, and that restrictions on information restrain decision-making, increase transaction costs, and encourage fraud.[233] However, it is not inconceivable that the knowledge that every purchase, every check, every ATM withdrawal can be made available to telemarketers, insurance companies and even identity thieves may ultimately discourage consumers from freely participating in the marketplace. Such fears may particularly inhibit Internet transactions. In a report to Congress, the FTC cited a survey that showed that consumers who did not use the Internet named concerns for the security of their personal information as the main reason for their reluctance.[234]

With passage of the Gramm-Leach-Bliley Act[235] and its restrictions, however weak, on disclosure of financial information by financial institutions, Congress has recognized some intrinsic value in protecting financial information from disclosure. However, given that it requires consumers to "opt out" of disclosure, and continues to allow financial institutions to share information with affiliates and with those who fall within one of the Act's numerous exceptions, the Act will likely do little to slow the traffic in this valuable data.

The Fair and Accurate Credit Transaction Act of 2003 (FACTA) did little to change this trend. Consumer information furnishers arguably received a good deal more than they lost in the FACTA amendments to the FCRA. In return for reasonably mild requirements on CRAs to issue fraud alerts and block information and to comply with eventual accuracy and integrity guidelines,[236] they won freedom from any new state laws regulating furnishers through the revocation of the sunset provision that would have allowed states to regulate furnishers as of January 1, 2004.[237] They were also freed from most state identity theft laws that applied to their conduct.[238] Accordingly, they were able to significantly narrow their responsibilities to comply with state laws, past and future, protecting consumers from identity theft. Furthermore, the FCRA, as amended, shields most of the duties demanded from furnishers from private enforcement and from meaningful state enforcement In short, the FCRA's new privacy protections may be mere paper privileges.

---

agreeing to stop sharing customer account information with third parties for marketing nonfinancial products and services, and by contributing over $3,000,000 to various charities. Hatch v. U.S. Bank N.A., No. 99-872 (D.C. Minn. June 14, 1999) (settled). *See also* Gail Appleson, *States Probe Banks for Selling Customer Data*, Reuters Sept. 27, 1999.

232 *See, e.g.*, R. Posner, Overcoming Law 539–551 (1995).
233 Richard S. Murphy, *Property Rights in Personal Information: An Economic Defense of Privacy*, 84 Georgetown L.J. 2381, 2382 (1996).
234 FTC, *Privacy Online: A Report to Congress* at 3 (June, 1998) (citing *Business Week/Harris Poll, Online Security*, Business Week, Mar. 16, 1998, at 102).
235 *See* § 16.4.1, *supra*.

236 *See* § 9.2, *supra*.
237 15 U.S.C. § 1681t(d) (2002).
238 15 U.S.C. § 1681t(b).

Appendix A Fair Credit Reporting Act

A.1 Cross-Reference Table of 15 U.S.C. Section Numbers with Fair Credit Reporting Act Section Numbers

When referring to the Fair Credit Reporting Act, this manual cites the section numbers as contained in Title 15 of the United States Code. However, many cases and articles refer to the Act's uncodified section numbers instead. To assist the attorney when reading material using the FCRA's uncodified section numbers, the following table is provided. Also, there are parenthetical references to the FCRA's sections in each of U.S.C. sections reprinted in this appendix.

Note that the FCRA's sections were renumbered as a result of the Fair and Accurate Credit Transactions Act (FACTA) of 2003.

U.S.C. Section	FCRA § Pre-FACTA	FCRA § Post-FACTA	FCRA Heading
§ 1681.	602	602	Congressional findings and statement of purpose
§ 1681a.	603	603	Definitions; rules of construction
§ 1681b.	604	604	Permissible purposes of consumer reports
§ 1681c.	605	605	Requirements relating to information contained in consumer reports
§ 1681c-1.	—	605A	Identity theft prevention; fraud alerts and active duty alerts
§ 1681c-2.	—	605B	Block of information resulting from identity theft
§ 1681d.	606	606	Disclosure of investigative consumer reports
§ 1681e.	607	607	Compliance procedures
§ 1681f.	608	608	Disclosures to governmental agencies
§ 1681g.	609	609	Disclosures to consumers
§ 1681h.	610	610	Conditions and form of disclosure to consumers
§ 1681i.	611	611	Procedure in case of disputed accuracy
§ 1681j.	612	612	Charges for certain disclosures
§ 1681k.	613	613	Public record information for employment purposes
§ 1681*l*.	614	614	Restrictions on investigative consumer reports
§ 1681m.	615	615	Requirements on users of consumer reports
§ 1681n.	616	616	Civil liability for willful noncompliance
§ 1681*o*.	617	617	Civil liability for negligent noncompliance
§ 1681p.	618	618	Jurisdiction of courts; limitation of actions
§ 1681q.	619	619	Obtaining information under false pretenses
§ 1681r.	620	620	Unauthorized disclosures by officers or employees
§ 1681s.	621	621	Administrative enforcement
§ 1681s-1.	622	622	Information on overdue child support obligations
§ 1681s-2.	623	623	Responsibilities of furnishers of information to consumer reporting agencies
§ 1681s-3.	—	624	Affiliate sharing
§ 1681t.	624	625	Relation to State laws
§ 1681u.	625	626	Disclosures to FBI for counterintelligence purposes
§ 1681v.	626	627	Disclosures to governmental agencies for counterterrorism purposes
§ 1681w.	—	628	Disposal of records
§ 1681x.	—	629	Corporate and technological circumvention prohibited

A.2 The Fair Credit Reporting Act

The Fair Credit Reporting Act as amended through Pub. L. No. 109-178, 4(c)(2), 120 Stat. 280 (Mar. 9, 2006) is set forth below. Bracketed material indicating amendments can be found following each section. For more detail about these amendments to the Act and their effective dates, see the CD-Rom accompanying this volume.

The FCRA has undergone two major revisions in its history. In 2003, Congress made significant changes to the FCRA by passing the Fair and Accurate Credit Transactions Act (FACTA), Pub. L. No. 108-159, 117 Stat. 1970 (Dec. 4, 2003). The effective date for the FACTA amendments is Dec. 4, 2003, unless otherwise noted. The CD-Rom accompanying this volume contains both the text of FACTA and a redline version of the FCRA reflecting the 2003 FACTA amendments as well those contained in Pub. L. No. 108-177, tit. III, § 361(j), 117 Stat. 2625 (Dec. 13, 2003) and Pub. L. No. 108-458, tit. VI, § 6203(1), 118 Stat. 3747 (Dec. 17, 2004). The effective dates for the FACTA amendments are noted on the CD-Rom as well.

The Fair Credit Reporting Act was also extensively amended by the Consumer Credit Reporting Reform Act of 1996, part of the Omnibus Consolidated Appropriations Act of 1996, Pub. L. No. 104-208, 110 Stat. 3009 (Sept. 30, 1996). The CD-Rom accompanying this volume contains a version of the Fair Credit Reporting Act prior to the 1996 amendments, as well as a copy of the 1996 amendments and a version of the Act after the 1996 amendments, but prior to FACTA.

§ 1681. Congressional findings and statement of purpose [FCRA § 602]

(a) Accuracy and fairness of credit reporting

The Congress makes the following findings:

(1) The banking system is dependent upon fair and accurate credit reporting. Inaccurate credit reports directly impair the efficiency of the banking system, and unfair credit reporting methods undermine the public confidence which is essential to the continued functioning of the banking system.

(2) An elaborate mechanism has been developed for investigating and evaluating the creditworthiness, credit standing, credit capacity, character, and general reputation of consumers.

(3) Consumer reporting agencies have assumed a vital role in assembling and evaluating consumer credit and other information on consumers.

(4) There is a need to insure that consumer reporting agencies exercise their grave responsibilities with fairness, impartiality, and a respect for the consumer's right to privacy.

(b) Reasonable procedures

It is the purpose of this subchapter to require that consumer reporting agencies adopt reasonable procedures for meeting the needs of commerce for consumer credit, personnel, insurance, and other information in a manner which is fair and equitable to the consumer, with regard to the confidentiality, accuracy, relevancy, and proper utilization of such information in accordance with the requirements of this subchapter.

[Pub. L. No. 90-321, tit. VI, § 602, *as added* Pub. L. No. 91-508, tit. VI, § 601, 84 Stat. 1128 (Oct. 26, 1970)]

§ 1681a. Definitions; rules of construction [FCRA § 603]

(a) Definitions and rules of construction set forth in this section are applicable for the purposes of this subchapter.

(b) The term "person" means any individual, partnership, corporation, trust, estate, cooperative, association, government or governmental subdivision or agency, or other entity.

(c) The term "consumer" means an individual.

(d) Consumer report.—

(1) In general.—The term "consumer report" means any written, oral, or other communication of any information by a consumer reporting agency bearing on a consumer's credit worthiness, credit standing, credit capacity, character, general reputation, personal characteristics, or mode of living which is used or expected to be used or collected in whole or in part for the purpose of serving as a factor in establishing the consumer's eligibility for—

(A) credit or insurance to be used primarily for personal, family, or household purposes;

(B) employment purposes; or

(C) any other purpose authorized under section 1681b of this title.

(2) Exclusions.—Except as provided in paragraph (3), the term "consumer report" does not include—

(A) subject to section 1681s-3, any—[1]

(i) report containing information solely as to transactions or experiences between the consumer and the person making the report;

(ii) communication of that information among persons related by common ownership or affiliated by corporate control; or

(iii) communication of other information among persons related by common ownership or affiliated by corporate control, if it is clearly and conspicuously disclosed to the consumer that the information may be communicated among such persons and the consumer is given the opportunity, before the time that the information is initially communicated, to direct that such information not be communicated among such persons;

(B) any authorization or approval of a specific extension of credit directly or indirectly by the issuer of a credit card or similar device;

(C) any report in which a person who has been requested by a third party to make a specific extension of credit directly or indirectly to a consumer conveys his or her decision with respect to such request, if the third party advises the consumer of the name and address of the person to whom the request was made, and such person makes the disclosures to the consumer required under section 1681m of this title; or

---

1 *Editor's Note*: The effective date for the FACTA amendments (Pub. L. No. 108-159 (Dec. 4, 2003)) to 15 U.S.C. § 1681a(d)(2)(A) is Dec. 31, 2003. *See* 12 C.F.R. § 222.1(c)(1)(i) and 16 C.F.R. § 602.1(c)(1)(i).

(D) a communication described in subsection (*o*) or (x) of this section.[2]

(3) Restriction on sharing of medical information.—Except for information or any communication of information disclosed as provided in section 1681b(g)(3), the exclusions in paragraph (2) shall not apply with respect to information disclosed to any person related by common ownership or affiliated by corporate control, if the information is—

  (A) medical information;

  (B) an individualized list or description based on the payment transactions of the consumer for medical products or services; or

  (C) an aggregate list of identified consumers based on payment transactions for medical products or services.

(e) The term "investigative consumer report" means a consumer report or portion thereof in which information on a consumer's character, general reputation, personal characteristics, or mode of living is obtained through personal interviews with neighbors, friends, or associates of the consumer reported on or with others with whom he is acquainted or who may have knowledge concerning any such items of information. However, such information shall not include specific factual information on a consumer's credit record obtained directly from a creditor of the consumer or from a consumer reporting agency when such information was obtained directly from a creditor of the consumer or from the consumer.

(f) The term "consumer reporting agency" means any person which, for monetary fees, dues, or on a cooperative nonprofit basis, regularly engages in whole or in part in the practice of assembling or evaluating consumer credit information or other information on consumers for the purpose of furnishing consumer reports to third parties, and which uses any means or facility of interstate commerce for the purpose of preparing or furnishing consumer reports.

(g) The term "file," when used in connection with information on any consumer, means all of the information on that consumer recorded and retained by a consumer reporting agency regardless of how the information is stored.

(h) The term "employment purposes" when used in connection with a consumer report means a report used for the purpose of evaluating a consumer for employment, promotion, reassignment or retention as an employee.

(i) Medical information.—The term 'medical information'—

  (1) means information or data, whether oral or recorded, in any form or medium, created by or derived from a health care provider or the consumer, that relates to—

    (A) the past, present, or future physical, mental, or behavioral health or condition of an individual;

    (B) the provision of health care to an individual; or

    (C) the payment for the provision of health care to an individual.

  (2) does not include the age or gender of a consumer, demographic information about the consumer, including a consumer's residence address or e-mail address, or any other information about a consumer that does not relate to the physical, mental, or behavioral health or condition of a consumer, including the existence or value of any insurance policy.

(j) Definitions relating to child support obligations

  (1) Overdue support

  The term "overdue support" has the meaning given to such term in section 666(e) of Title 42.

  (2) State or local child support enforcement agency

  The term "State or local child support enforcement agency" means a State or local agency which administers a State or local program for establishing and enforcing child support obligations.

(k) Adverse action.—

  (1) Actions included.—The term "adverse action"—

    (A) has the same meaning as in section 1691(d)(6) of this title; and

    (B) means—

      (i) a denial or cancellation of, an increase in any charge for, or a reduction or other adverse or unfavorable change in the terms of coverage or amount of, any insurance, existing or applied for, in connection with the underwriting of insurance;

      (ii) a denial of employment or any other decision for employment purposes that adversely affects any current or prospective employee;

      (iii) a denial or cancellation of, an increase in any charge for, or any other adverse or unfavorable change in the terms of, any license or benefit described in section 1681b(a)(3)(D) of this title; and

      (iv) an action taken or determination that is—

        (I) made in connection with an application that was made by, or a transaction that was initiated by, any consumer, or in connection with a review of an account under section 1681b(a)(3)(F)(ii) of this title; and

        (II) adverse to the interests of the consumer.

  (2) Applicable findings, decisions, commentary, and orders.—For purposes of any determination of whether an action is an adverse action under paragraph (1)(A), all appropriate final findings, decisions, commentary, and orders issued under section 1691(d)(6) of this title by the Board of Governors of the Federal Reserve System or any court shall apply.

(*l*) Firm offer of credit or insurance.—The term "firm offer of credit or insurance" means any offer of credit or insurance to a consumer that will be honored if the consumer is determined, based on information in a consumer report on the consumer, to meet the specific criteria used to select the consumer for the offer, except that the offer may be further conditioned on one or more of the following:

  (1) The consumer being determined, based on information in the consumer's application for the credit or insurance, to meet specific criteria bearing on credit worthiness or insurability, as applicable, that are established—

    (A) before selection of the consumer for the offer; and

    (B) for the purpose of determining whether to extend credit or insurance pursuant to the offer.

  (2) Verification—

    (A) that the consumer continues to meet the specific criteria used to select the consumer for the offer, by using information

---

2 *Editor's Note*: The effective date for the FACTA amendments (Pub. L. No. 108-159 (Dec. 4, 2003)) to 15 U.S.C. § 1681a(d)(2)(D) is Mar. 31, 2004. *See* 12 C.F.R. § 222.1(c)(1)(i) and 16 C.F.R. § 602.1(c)(1)(i).

in a consumer report on the consumer, information in the consumer's application for the credit or insurance, or other information bearing on the credit worthiness or insurability of the consumer; or

(B) of the information in the consumer's application for the credit or insurance, to determine that the consumer meets the specific criteria bearing on credit worthiness or insurability.

(3) The consumer furnishing any collateral that is a requirement for the extension of the credit or insurance that was—

(A) established before selection of the consumer for the offer of credit or insurance; and

(B) disclosed to the consumer in the offer of credit or insurance.

(m) Credit or insurance transaction that is not initiated by the consumer.—The term "credit or insurance transaction that is not initiated by the consumer" does not include the use of a consumer report by a person with which the consumer has an account or insurance policy, for purposes of—

(1) reviewing the account or insurance policy; or

(2) collecting the account.

(n) State.—The term "State" means any State, the Commonwealth of Puerto Rico, the District of Columbia, and any territory or possession of the United States.

(o) Excluded communications.—A communication is described in this subsection if it is a communication—

(1) that, but for subsection (d)(2)(D) of this section, would be an investigative consumer report;

(2) that is made to a prospective employer for the purpose of—

(A) procuring an employee for the employer; or

(B) procuring an opportunity for a natural person to work for the employer;

(3) that is made by a person who regularly performs such procurement;

(4) that is not used by any person for any purpose other than a purpose described in subparagraph (A) or (B) of paragraph (2); and

(5) with respect to which—

(A) the consumer who is the subject of the communication—

(i) consents orally or in writing to the nature and scope of the communication, before the collection of any information for the purpose of making the communication;

(ii) consents orally or in writing to the making of the communication to a prospective employer, before the making of the communication; and

(iii) in the case of consent under clause (i) or (ii) given orally, is provided written confirmation of that consent by the person making the communication, not later than 3 business days after the receipt of the consent by that person;

(B) the person who makes the communication does not, for the purpose of making the communication, make any inquiry that if made by a prospective employer of the consumer who is the subject of the communication would violate any applicable Federal or State equal employment opportunity law or regulation; and

(C) the person who makes the communication—

(i) discloses in writing to the consumer who is the subject of the communication, not later than 5 business days after receiving any request from the consumer for such disclosure, the nature and substance of all information in the consumer's file at the time of the request, except that the sources of any information that is acquired solely for use in making the communication and is actually used for no other purpose, need not be disclosed other than under appropriate discovery procedures in any court of competent jurisdiction in which an action is brought; and

(ii) notifies the consumer who is the subject of the communication, in writing, of the consumer's right to request the information described in clause (i).

(p) Consumer reporting agency that compiles and maintains files on consumers on a nationwide basis.—The term "consumer reporting agency that compiles and maintains files on consumers on a nationwide basis" means a consumer reporting agency that regularly engages in the practice of assembling or evaluating, and maintaining, for the purpose of furnishing consumer reports to third parties bearing on a consumer's credit worthiness, credit standing, or credit capacity, each of the following regarding consumers residing nationwide:

(1) Public record information.

(2) Credit account information from persons who furnish that information regularly and in the ordinary course of business.

(q) Definitions relating to fraud alerts.—[3]

(1) Active duty military consumer.—The term 'active duty military consumer' means a consumer in military service who—

(A) is on active duty (as defined in section 101(d)(1) of title 10, United States Code) or is a reservist performing duty under a call or order to active duty under a provision of law referred to in section 101(a)(13) of title 10, United States Code; and

(B) is assigned to service away from the usual duty station of the consumer.

(2) Fraud alert; active duty alert.—The terms 'fraud alert' and 'active duty alert' mean a statement in the file of a consumer that—

(A) notifies all prospective users of a consumer report relating to the consumer that the consumer may be a victim of fraud, including identity theft, or is an active duty military consumer, as applicable; and

(B) is presented in a manner that facilitates a clear and conspicuous view of the statement described in subparagraph (A) by any person requesting such consumer report.

(3) Identity theft.—The term 'identity theft' means a fraud committed using the identifying information of another person, subject to such further definition as the Commission may prescribe, by regulation.

(4) Identity theft report.—The term 'identity theft report' has the meaning given that term by rule of the Commission, and means, at a minimum, a report—

(A) that alleges an identity theft;

(B) that is a copy of an official, valid report filed by a consumer with an appropriate Federal, State, or local law enforcement agency, including the United States Postal In-

---

3 *Editor's Note*: The effective date for the FACTA amendments (Pub. L. No. 108-159 (Dec. 4, 2003)) to 15 U.S.C. § 1681a(q) is Mar. 31, 2004. *See* 12 C.F.R. § 222.1(c)(1)(i) and 16 C.F.R. § 602.1(c)(1)(i).

spection Service, or such other government agency deemed appropriate by the Commission; and

(C) the filing of which subjects the person filing the report to criminal penalties relating to the filing of false information if, in fact, the information in the report is false.

(5) **New credit plan.**—The term 'new credit plan' means a new account under an open end credit plan (as defined in section 103(i) of the Truth in Lending Act) or a new credit transaction not under an open end credit plan.

(r) **Credit and debit related terms.**—[4]

(1) **Card issuer.**—The term 'card issuer' means—

(A) a credit card issuer, in the case of a credit card; and

(B) a debit card issuer, in the case of a debit card.

(2) **Credit card.**—The term 'credit card' has the same meaning as in section 103 of the Truth in Lending Act.

(3) **Debit card.**—The term 'debit card' means any card issued by a financial institution to a consumer for use in initiating an electronic fund transfer from the account of the consumer at such financial institution, for the purpose of transferring money between accounts or obtaining money, property, labor, or services.

(4) **Account and electronic fund transfer.**—The terms 'account' and 'electronic fund transfer' have the same meanings as in section 903 of the Electronic Fund Transfer Act.

(5) **Credit and creditor.**—The terms 'credit' and 'creditor' have the same meanings as in section 702 of the Equal Credit Opportunity Act.

(s) **Federal banking agency.**—[5] The term 'Federal banking agency' has the same meaning as in section 3 of the Federal Deposit Insurance Act.

(t) **Financial institution.**—[6] The term 'financial institution' means a State or National bank, a State or Federal savings and loan association, a mutual savings bank, a State or Federal credit union, or any other person that, directly or indirectly, holds a transaction account (as defined in section 19(b) of the Federal Reserve Act) belonging to a consumer.

(u) **Reseller.**—[7] The term 'reseller' means a consumer reporting agency that—

(1) assembles and merges information contained in the database of another consumer reporting agency or multiple consumer reporting agencies concerning any consumer for purposes of furnishing such information to any third party, to the extent of such activities; and

(2) does not maintain a database of the assembled or merged information from which new consumer reports are produced.

(v) **Commission.**—[8] The term 'Commission' means the Federal Trade Commission.

(w) **Nationwide specialty consumer reporting agency.**—[9] The term 'nationwide specialty consumer reporting agency' means a consumer reporting agency that compiles and maintains files on consumers on a nationwide basis relating to—

(1) medical records or payments;

(2) residential or tenant history;

(3) check writing history;

(4) employment history; or

(5) insurance claims.

(x) **Exclusion of certain communications for employee investigations.**—[10]

(1) **Communications described in this subsection.**—A communication is described in this subsection if—

(A) but for subsection (d)(2)(D), the communication would be a consumer report;

(B) the communication is made to an employer in connection with an investigation of—

(i) suspected misconduct relating to employment; or

(ii) compliance with Federal, State, or local laws and regulations, the rules of a self-regulatory organization, or any preexisting written policies of the employer;

(C) the communication is not made for the purpose of investigating a consumer's credit worthiness, credit standing, or credit capacity; and

(D) the communication is not provided to any person except—

(i) to the employer or an agent of the employer;

(ii) to any Federal or State officer, agency, or department, or any officer, agency, or department of a unit of general local government;

(iii) to any self-regulatory organization with regulatory authority over the activities of the employer or employee;

(iv) as otherwise required by law; or

(v) pursuant to section 1681f.

(2) **Subsequent disclosure.**—After taking any adverse action based in whole or in part on a communication described in paragraph (1), the employer shall disclose to the consumer a summary containing the nature and substance of the communication upon which the adverse action is based, except that the sources of information acquired solely for use in preparing what would be but for subsection (d)(2)(D) an investigative consumer report need not be disclosed.

---

4 *Editor's Note*: The effective date for the FACTA amendments (Pub. L. No. 108-159 (Dec. 4, 2003)) to 15 U.S.C. § 1681a(r) is Mar. 31, 2004. See 12 C.F.R. § 222.1(c)(1)(i) and 16 C.F.R. § 602.1(c)(1)(i).

5 *Editor's Note*: The effective date for the FACTA amendments (Pub. L. No. 108-159 (Dec. 4, 2003)) to 15 U.S.C. § 1681a(s) is Mar. 31, 2004. See 12 C.F.R. § 222.1(c)(1)(i) and 16 C.F.R. § 602.1(c)(1)(i).

6 *Editor's Note*: The effective date for the FACTA amendments (Pub. L. No. 108-159 (Dec. 4, 2003)) to 15 U.S.C. § 1681a(t) is Mar. 31, 2004. See 12 C.F.R. § 222.1(c)(1)(i) and 16 C.F.R. § 602.1(c)(1)(i).

7 *Editor's Note*: The effective date for the FACTA amendments (Pub. L. No. 108-159 (Dec. 4, 2003)) to 15 U.S.C. § 1681a(u) is Mar. 31, 2004. See 12 C.F.R. § 222.1(c)(1)(i) and 16 C.F.R. § 602.1(c)(1)(i).

8 *Editor's Note*: The effective date for the FACTA amendments (Pub. L. No. 108-159 (Dec. 4, 2003)) to 15 U.S.C. § 1681a(v) is Mar. 31, 2004. See 12 C.F.R. § 222.1(c)(1)(i) and 16 C.F.R. § 602.1(c)(1)(i).

9 *Editor's Note*: The effective date for the FACTA amendments (Pub. L. No. 108-159 (Dec. 4, 2003)) to 15 U.S.C. § 1681a(w) is Mar. 31, 2004. See 12 C.F.R. § 222.1(c)(1)(i) and 16 C.F.R. § 602.1(c)(1)(i).

10 *Editor's Note*: The effective date for the FACTA amendments (Pub. L. No. 108-159 (Dec. 4, 2003)) to 15 U.S.C. § 1681a(x) is Mar. 31, 2004. See 12 C.F.R. § 222.1(c)(1)(i) and 16 C.F.R. § 602.1(c)(1)(i).

(3) **Self-regulatory organization defined.**—For purposes of this subsection, the term 'self-regulatory organization' includes any self-regulatory organization (as defined in section 3(a)(26) of the Securities Exchange Act of 1934), any entity established under title I of the Sarbanes-Oxley Act of 2002, any board of trade designated by the Commodity Futures Trading Commission, and any futures association registered with such Commission.

[Pub. L. No. 90-321, tit. VI, § 603, *as added* Pub. L. No. 91-508, tit. VI, § 601, 84 Stat. 1128 (Oct. 26, 1970), *and amended* Pub. L. No. 102-537, § 2(b), 106 Stat. 3531 (Oct. 27, 1992); Pub. L. No. 104-208, div. A, tit. II, § 2402(a)–(g), 110 Stat. 3009–428 (Sept. 30, 1996); Pub. L. 105-347, § 6(1)–(3), 112 Stat. 3211 (Nov. 2, 1998); Pub. L. No. 108-159, tit. I, § 111, tit. II, § 214(c)(1), tit. IV, § 411(b), (c), tit. VI, § 611, 117 Stat. 1954, 1983, 2001, 2010 (Dec. 4, 2003)]

§ 1681b. Permissible purposes of consumer reports [FCRA § 604]

(a) In general.—Subject to subsection (c) of this section, any consumer reporting agency may furnish a consumer report under the following circumstances and no other:

(1) In response to the order of a court having jurisdiction to issue such an order, or a subpoena issued in connection with proceedings before a Federal grand jury.[11]

(2) In accordance with the written instructions of the consumer to whom it relates.

(3) To a person which it has reason to believe—

(A) intends to use the information in connection with a credit transaction involving the consumer on whom the information is to be furnished and involving the extension of credit to, or review or collection of an account of, the consumer; or

(B) intends to use the information for employment purposes; or

(C) intends to use the information in connection with the underwriting of insurance involving the consumer; or

(D) intends to use the information in connection with a determination of the consumer's eligibility for a license or other benefit granted by a governmental instrumentality required by law to consider an applicant's financial responsibility or status; or

(E) intends to use the information, as a potential investor or servicer, or current insurer, in connection with a valuation of, or an assessment of the credit or prepayment risks associated with, an existing credit obligation; or

(F) otherwise has a legitimate business need for the information—

(i) in connection with a business transaction that is initiated by the consumer; or

(ii) to review an account to determine whether the consumer continues to meet the terms of the account.

---

11 *Editor's Note*: The effective date for the FACTA amendments (Pub. L. No. 108-159 (Dec. 4, 2003)) to 15 U.S.C. § 1681b(a)(1)–(5) is Mar. 31, 2004. *See* 12 C.F.R. § 222.1(c)(1)(i) and 16 C.F.R. § 602.1(c)(1)(i). The § 811 of the FACTA amendments were technical in nature (moving § 1681b(a)(1)–(5) two ems to the right).

(4) In response to a request by the head of a State or local child support enforcement agency (or a State or local government official authorized by the head of such an agency), if the person making the request certifies to the consumer reporting agency that—

(A) the consumer report is needed for the purpose of establishing an individual's capacity to make child support payments or determining the appropriate level of such payments;

(B) the paternity of the consumer for the child to which the obligation relates has been established or acknowledged by the consumer in accordance with State laws under which the obligation arises (if required by those laws);

(C) the person has provided at least 10 days' prior notice to the consumer whose report is requested, by certified or registered mail to the last known address of the consumer, that the report will be requested; and

(D) the consumer report will be kept confidential, will be used solely for a purpose described in subparagraph (A), and will not be used in connection with any other civil, administrative, or criminal proceeding, or for any other purpose.

(5) To an agency administering a State plan under section 654 of Title 42 for use to set an initial or modified child support award.

(b) Conditions for furnishing and using consumer reports for employment purposes.—

(1) **Certification from user.**—A consumer reporting agency may furnish a consumer report for employment purposes only if—

(A) the person who obtains such report from the agency certifies to the agency that—

(i) the person has complied with paragraph (2) with respect to the consumer report, and the person will comply with paragraph (3) with respect to the consumer report if paragraph (3) becomes applicable; and

(ii) information from the consumer report will not be used in violation of any applicable Federal or State equal employment opportunity law or regulation; and

(B) the consumer reporting agency provides with the report, or has previously provided, of the consumer's rights under this subchapter, as prescribed by the Federal Trade Commission under section 1681g(c)(3) of this title.

(2) **Disclosure to consumer.**—

(A) **In general.**—Except as provided in subparagraph (B), a person may not procure a consumer report, or cause a consumer report to be procured, for employment purposes with respect to any consumer, unless—

(i) a clear and conspicuous disclosure has been made in writing to the consumer at any time before the report is procured or caused to be procured, in a document that consists solely of the disclosure, that a consumer report may be obtained for employment purposes; and

(ii) the consumer has authorized in writing (which authorization may be made on the document referred to in clause (i)) the procurement of the report by that person.

(B) **Application by mail, telephone, computer, or other similar means.**—If a consumer described in subparagraph (C) applies for employment by mail, telephone, computer, or other similar means, at any time before a consumer report is procured or caused to be procured in connection with that application—

(i) the person who procures the consumer report on the consumer for employment purposes shall provide to the consumer, by oral, written, or electronic means, notice that a consumer report may be obtained for employment purposes, and a summary of the consumer's rights under section 1681m(a)(3); and

(ii) the consumer shall have consented, orally, in writing, or electronically to the procurement of the report by that person.

(C) Scope.—Subparagraph (B) shall apply to a person procuring a consumer report on a consumer in connection with the consumer's application for employment only if—

(i) the consumer is applying for a position over which the Secretary of Transportation has the power to establish qualifications and maximum hours of service pursuant to the provisions of section 31502 of title 49, or a position subject to safety regulation by a State transportation agency; and

(ii) as of the time at which the person procures the report or causes the report to be procured the only interaction between the consumer and the person in connection with that employment application has been by mail, telephone, computer, or other similar means.

(3) Conditions on use for adverse actions.—

(A) In general.—Except as provided in subparagraph (B), in using a consumer report for employment purposes, before taking any adverse action based in whole or in part on the report, the person intending to take such adverse action shall provide to the consumer to whom the report relates—

(i) a copy of the report; and

(ii) a description in writing of the rights of the consumer under this title, as prescribed by the Federal Trade Commission under section 1681g(c)(3) of this title.[12]

(B) Application by mail, telephone, computer, or other similar means.—

(i) If a consumer described in subparagraph (C) applies for employment by mail, telephone, computer, or other similar means, and if a person who has procured a consumer report on the consumer for employment purposes takes adverse action on the employment application based in whole or in part on the report, then the person must provide to the consumer to whom the report relates, in lieu of the notices required under subparagraph (A) of this section and under section 1681m(a) of this title, within 3 business days of taking such action, an oral, written or electronic notification—

(I) that adverse action has been taken based in whole or in part on a consumer report received from a consumer reporting agency;

(II) of the name, address and telephone number of the consumer reporting agency that furnished the consumer report (including a toll-free telephone number established by the agency if the agency compiles and maintains files on consumers on a nationwide basis);

(III) that the consumer reporting agency did not make the decision to take the adverse action and is unable to provide to the consumer the specific reasons why the adverse action was taken; and

(IV) that the consumer may, upon providing proper identification, request a free copy of a report and may dispute with the consumer reporting agency the accuracy or completeness of any information in a report.

(ii) If, under clause (B)(i)(IV), the consumer requests a copy of a consumer report from the person who procured the report, then, within 3 business days of receiving the consumer's request, together with proper identification, the person must send or provide to the consumer a copy of a report and a copy of the consumer's rights as prescribed by the Federal Trade Commission under section 1681g(c)(3) of this title.

(C) Scope.—Subparagraph (B) shall apply to a person procuring a consumer report on a consumer in connection with the consumer's application for employment only if—

(i) the consumer is applying for a position over which the Secretary of Transportation has the power to establish qualifications and maximum hours of service pursuant to the provisions of section 31502 of title 49, or a position subject to safety regulation by a State transportation agency; and

(ii) as of the time at which the person procures the report or causes the report to be procured the only interaction between the consumer and the person in connection with that employment application has been by mail, telephone, computer, or other similar means.

(4) Exception for national security investigations.—

(A) In general.—In the case of an agency or department of the United States Government which seeks to obtain and use a consumer report for employment purposes, paragraph (3) shall not apply to any adverse action by such agency or department which is based in part on such consumer report, if the head of such agency or department makes a written finding that—

(i) the consumer report is relevant to a national security investigation of such agency or department;

(ii) the investigation is within the jurisdiction of such agency or department;

(iii) there is reason to believe that compliance with paragraph (3) will—

(I) endanger the life or physical safety of any person;

(II) result in flight from prosecution;

(III) result in the destruction of, or tampering with, evidence relevant to the investigation;

(IV) result in the intimidation of a potential witness relevant to the investigation;

(V) result in the compromise of classified information; or

(VI) otherwise seriously jeopardize or unduly delay the investigation or another official proceeding.

(B) Notification of consumer upon conclusion of investigation.—Upon the conclusion of a national security investigation described in subparagraph (A), or upon the determination that the exception under subparagraph (A) is no longer required for the reasons set forth in such subparagraph, the official exercising the authority in such subparagraph shall

---

12 *Editor's Note*: The references in §§ 1681b(b)(3)(A) and 1681b(b)(3)(B) should be to § 1681g(c)(1), not (c)(3) that no longer exists as the result of congress' re-organization of § 1681g in 2003 (FACTA).

provide to the consumer who is the subject of the consumer report with regard to which such finding was made—

(i) a copy of such consumer report with any classified information redacted as necessary;

(ii) notice of any adverse action which is based, in part, on the consumer report; and

(iii) the identification with reasonable specificity of the nature of the investigation for which the consumer report was sought.

(C) **Delegation by head of agency or department.**—For purposes of subparagraphs (A) and (B), the head of any agency or department of the United States Government may delegate his or her authorities under this paragraph to an official of such agency or department who has personnel security responsibilities and is a member of the Senior Executive Service or equivalent civilian or military rank.

(D)[13] **Definitions.**—For purposes of this paragraph, the following definitions shall apply:

(i) **Classified information.**—The term "classified information" means information that is protected from unauthorized disclosure under Executive Order No. 12958 or successor orders.

(ii) **National security investigation.**—The term "national security investigation" means any official inquiry by an agency or department of the United States Government to determine the eligibility of a consumer to receive access or continued access to classified information or to determine whether classified information has been lost or compromised.

(F) **Redesignated (D)**[14]

(c) **Furnishing reports in connection with credit or insurance transactions that are not initiated by the consumer.**—

(1) **In general.**—A consumer reporting agency may furnish a consumer report relating to any consumer pursuant to subparagraph (A) or (C) of subsection (a)(3) of this section in connection with any credit or insurance transaction that is not initiated by the consumer only if—

(A) the consumer authorizes the agency to provide such report to such person; or

(B)(i) the transaction consists of a firm offer of credit or insurance;

(ii) the consumer reporting agency has complied with subsection (e) of this section; and

(iii) there is not in effect an election by the consumer, made in accordance with subsection (e), to have the consumer's name and address excluded from lists of names provided by the agency pursuant to this paragraph.

(2) **Limits on information received under paragraph (1)(B).** —A person may receive pursuant to paragraph (1)(B) only—

(A) the name and address of a consumer;

(B) an identifier that is not unique to the consumer and that is used by the person solely for the purpose of verifying the identity of the consumer; and

(C) other information pertaining to a consumer that does not identify the relationship or experience of the consumer with respect to a particular creditor or other entity.

(3) **Information regarding inquiries.**—Except as provided in section 1681g(a)(5) of this title, a consumer reporting agency shall not furnish to any person a record of inquiries in connection with a credit or insurance transaction that is not initiated by a consumer.

(d) **Reserved**

(e) **Election of consumer to be excluded from lists.**—

(1) **In general.**—A consumer may elect to have the consumer's name and address excluded from any list provided by a consumer reporting agency under subsection (c)(1)(B) of this section in connection with a credit or insurance transaction that is not initiated by the consumer, by notifying the agency in accordance with paragraph (2) that the consumer does not consent to any use of a consumer report relating to the consumer in connection with any credit or insurance transaction that is not initiated by the consumer.

(2) **Manner of notification.**—A consumer shall notify a consumer reporting agency under paragraph (1)—

(A) through the notification system maintained by the agency under paragraph (5); or

(B) by submitting to the agency a signed notice of election form issued by the agency for purposes of this subparagraph.

(3) **Response of agency after notification through system.**— Upon receipt of notification of the election of a consumer under paragraph (1) through the notification system maintained by the agency under paragraph (5), a consumer reporting agency shall—

(A) inform the consumer that the election is effective only for the 5-year period following the election if the consumer does not submit to the agency a signed notice of election form issued by the agency for purposes of paragraph (2)(B); and[15]

(B) provide to the consumer a notice of election form, if requested by the consumer, not later than 5 business days after receipt of the notification of the election through the system established under paragraph (5), in the case of a request made at the time the consumer provides notification through the system.

(4) **Effectiveness of election.**—An election of a consumer under paragraph (1)—

(A) shall be effective with respect to a consumer reporting agency beginning 5 business days after the date on which the consumer notifies the agency in accordance with paragraph (2);

(B) shall be effective with respect to a consumer reporting agency—

(i) subject to subparagraph (C), during the 5-year period beginning 5 business days after the date on which the consumer notifies the agency of the election, in the case of an election for which a consumer notifies the agency only in accordance with paragraph (2)(A); or[16]

---

13 *Editor's Note*: Amended by Pub. L. No. 108-177, tit. III, § 361(j), 117 Stat. 2625 (Dec. 13, 2003).

14 *Editor's Note*: Amended by Pub. L. No. 108-177, tit. III, § 361(j), 117 Stat. 2625 (Dec. 13, 2003).

15 *Editor's Note*: The effective date for the FACTA amendments (Pub. L. No. 108-159 (Dec. 4, 2003)) to 15 U.S.C. § 1681b(e)(3)(A) is Dec. 1, 2004. *See* 12 C.F.R. § 222.1(c)(1)(i) and 16 C.F.R. § 602.1(c)(1)(i).

16 *Editor's Note*: The effective date for the FACTA amendments

(ii) until the consumer notifies the agency under subparagraph (C), in the case of an election for which a consumer notifies the agency in accordance with paragraph (2)(B);

(C) shall not be effective after the date on which the consumer notifies the agency, through the notification system established by the agency under paragraph (5), that the election is no longer effective; and

(D) shall be effective with respect to each affiliate of the agency.

(5) **Notification system.—**

(A) **In general.—**Each consumer reporting agency that, under subsection (c)(1)(B) of this section, furnishes a consumer report in connection with a credit or insurance transaction that is not initiated by a consumer, shall—

(i) establish and maintain a notification system, including a toll-free telephone number, which permits any consumer whose consumer report is maintained by the agency to notify the agency, with appropriate identification, of the consumer's election to have the consumer's name and address excluded from any such list of names and addresses provided by the agency for such a transaction; and

(ii) publish by not later than 365 days after September 30, 1996, and not less than annually thereafter, in a publication of general circulation in the area served by the agency—

(I) a notification that information in consumer files maintained by the agency may be used in connection with such transactions; and

(II) the address and toll-free telephone number for consumers to use to notify the agency of the consumer's election under clause(i).

(B) **Establishment and maintenance as compliance.—**Establishment and maintenance of a notification system (including a toll-free telephone number) and publication by a consumer reporting agency on the agency's own behalf and on behalf of any of its affiliates in accordance with this paragraph is deemed to be compliance with this paragraph by each of those affiliates.

(6) **Notification system by agencies that operate nationwide.—**Each consumer reporting agency that compiles and maintains files on consumers on a nationwide basis shall establish and maintain a notification system for purposes of paragraph (5) jointly with other such consumer reporting agencies.

(f) **Certain use or obtaining of information prohibited.—**A person shall not use or obtain a consumer report for any purpose unless—

(1) the consumer report is obtained for a purpose for which the consumer report is authorized to be furnished under this section; and

(2) the purpose is certified in accordance with section 1681e of this title by a prospective user of the report through a general or specific certification.

(g) **Protection of medical information.—**

(1) **Limitation on consumer reporting agencies.—**A consumer reporting agency shall not furnish for employment purposes, or in connection with a credit or insurance transaction, a consumer report that contains medical information (other than medical contact information treated in the manner required under section 1681c(a)(6)) about a consumer, unless—

(A) if furnished in connection with an insurance transaction, the consumer affirmatively consents to the furnishing of the report;

(B) if furnished for employment purposes or in connection with a credit transaction—

(i) the information to be furnished is relevant to process or effect the employment or credit transaction; and

(ii) the consumer provides specific written consent for the furnishing of the report that describes in clear and conspicuous language the use for which the information will be furnished; or

(C) the information to be furnished pertains solely to transactions, accounts, or balances relating to debts arising from the receipt of medical services, products, or devises, where such information, other than account status or amounts, is restricted or reported using codes that do not identify, or do not provide information sufficient to infer, the specific provider or the nature of such services, products, or devices, as provided in section 1681c(a)(6).

(2) **Limitation on creditors.—**Except as permitted pursuant to paragraph (3)(C) or regulations prescribed under paragraph (5)(A), a creditor shall not obtain or use medical information (other than medical information treated in the manner required under section 1681c(a)(6)) pertaining to a consumer in connection with any determination of the consumer's eligibility, or continued eligibility, for credit.

(3) **Actions authorized by federal law, insurance activities and regulatory determinations.—**Section 1681a(d)(3) shall not be construed so as to treat information or any communication of information as a consumer report if the information or communication is disclosed—

(A) in connection with the business of insurance or annuities, including the activities described in section 18B of the model Privacy of Consumer Financial and Health Information Regulation issued by the National Association of Insurance Commissioners (as in effect on January 1, 2003);

(B) for any purpose permitted without authorization under the Standards for Individually Identifiable Health Information promulgated by the Department of Health and Human Services pursuant to the Health Insurance Portability and Accountability Act of 1996, or referred to under section 1179 of such Act, or described in section 502(e) of Public Law 106-102; or

(C) as otherwise determined to be necessary and appropriate, by regulation or order and subject to paragraph (6), by the Commission, any Federal banking agency or the National Credit Union Administration (with respect to any financial institution subject to the jurisdiction of such agency or Administration under paragraph (1), (2), or (3) of section 1681s(b), or the applicable State insurance authority (with respect to any person engaged in providing insurance or annuities).

(4) **Limitation on redisclosure of medical information.—**Any person that receives medical information pursuant to paragraph (1) or (3) shall not disclose such information to any other person, except as necessary to carry out the purpose for which

---

(Pub. L. No. 108-159 (Dec. 4, 2003)) to 15 U.S.C. § 1681b(e)(4)(B)(i) is Dec. 1, 2004. *See* 12 C.F.R. § 222.1(c)(1)(i) and 16 C.F.R. § 602.1(c)(1)(i).

the information was initially disclosed, or as otherwise permitted by statute, regulation, or order.

  (5) **Regulations and effective date for paragraph (2).**—
    (A) **Regulations required.**—Each Federal banking agency and the National Credit Union Administration shall, subject to paragraph (6) and after notice and opportunity for comment, prescribe regulations that permit transactions under paragraph (2) that are determined to be necessary and appropriate to protect legitimate operational, transactional, risk, consumer, and other needs (and which shall include permitting actions necessary for administrative verification purposes), consistent with the intent of paragraph (2) to restrict the use of medical information for inappropriate purposes.
    (B) **Final regulations required.**—The Federal banking agencies and the National Credit Union Administration shall issue the regulations required under subparagraph (A) in final form before the end of the 6-month period beginning on the date of enactment of the Fair and Accurate Credit Transactions Act of 2003.
  (6) **Coordination with other laws.**—No provision of this subsection shall be construed as altering, affecting, or superseding the applicability of any other provision of Federal law relating to medical confidentiality.

[Pub. L. No. 90-321, tit. VI, § 604, *as added* Pub. L. No. 91-508, tit. VI, § 601, 84 Stat. 1129 (Oct. 26, 1970), *and amended* Pub. L. No. 101-73, tit. IX, § 964(c), 103 Stat. 506 (Aug. 9, 1989); Pub. L. No. 104-193, tit. III, § 352, 110 Stat. 2240 (Aug. 22, 1996); Pub. L. No. 104-208, div. A, tit. II, §§ 2403, 2404(a), (b), 2405, 110 Stat. 3009–430, 3009–433, 3009–434 (Sept. 30, 1996); Pub. L. No. 105-107, tit. III, § 311(a), 111 Stat. 2255 (Nov. 20, 1997); Pub. L. No. 105-347, §§ 2, 3, 6(4), 112 Stat. 3208, 3210, 3211 (Nov. 2, 1998); Pub. L. No. 107-306, tit. VIII, § 811(b)(8)(A), 116 Stat. 2426 (Nov. 27, 2002); Pub. L. No. 108-159, tit. II, § 213(c), tit. IV, § 411(a), (f), tit. VIII, § 811(b), 117 Stat. 1979, 1999, 2003, 2011 (Dec. 4, 2003); Pub. L. No. 108-177, tit. III, § 361(j), 117 Stat. 2625 (Dec. 13, 2003)]

§ 1681c. Requirements relating to information contained in consumer reports [FCRA § 605]

(a) Information excluded from consumer reports—Prohibited items

Except as authorized under subsection (b) of this section, no consumer reporting agency may make any consumer report containing any of the following items of information:

  (1) Cases[17] under Title 11 or under the Bankruptcy Act that, from the date of entry of the order for relief or the date of adjudication, as the case may be, antedate the report by more than 10 years.
  (2) Civil suits, civil judgments, and records of arrest that, from date of entry, antedate the report by more than seven years or until the governing statute of limitations has expired, whichever is the longer period.
  (3) Paid tax liens which, from date of payment, antedate the report by more than seven years.
  (4) Accounts placed for collection or charged to profit and loss which antedate the report by more than seven years.[18]
  (5) Any other adverse item of information, other than records of convictions of crimes, which antedates the report by more than seven years.[19]
  (6) The name, address, and telephone number of any medical information furnisher that has notified the agency of its status, unless—
    (A) such name, address, and telephone number are restricted or reported using codes that do not identify, or provide information sufficient to infer, the specific provider or the nature of such services, products, or devices to a person other than the consumer; or
    (B) the report is being provided to an insurance company for a purpose relating to engaging in the business of insurance other than property and casualty insurance.

(b) Exempted cases

The provisions of paragraphs (1) through (5) of subsection (a) of this section are not applicable in the case of any consumer credit report to be used in connection with—

  (1) a credit transaction involving, or which may reasonably be expected to involve, a principal amount of $150,000 or more;
  (2) the underwriting of life insurance involving, or which may reasonably be expected to involve, a face amount of $150,000 or more; or
  (3) the employment of any individual at an annual salary which equals, or which may reasonably be expected to equal $75,000, or more.

(c) Running of reporting period

  (1) **In general.**—The 7-year period referred to in paragraphs (4) and (6)[20] of subsection (a) of this section shall begin, with respect to any delinquent account that is placed for collection (internally or by referral to a third party, whichever is earlier), charged to profit and loss, or subjected to any similar action, upon the expiration of the 180-day period beginning on the date of the commencement of the delinquency which immediately preceded the collection activity, charge to profit and loss, or similar action.

---

17 *Editor's Note*: The effective date for the FACTA amendments (Pub. L. No. 108-159 (Dec. 4, 2003)) to 15 U.S.C. § 1681c(a) is Mar. 31, 2004. *See* 12 C.F.R. § 222.1(c)(1)(i) and 16 C.F.R. § 602.1(c)(1)(i). The § 811 of the FACTA amendments were technical in nature (capitalizing "Cases").

18 *Editor's Note*: The reporting periods have been lengthened for certain adverse information pertaining to U.S. Government insured or guaranteed student loans, or pertaining to national direct student loans. See sections 430A(f) and 463(c)(3) of the Higher Education Act of 1965, 20 U.S.C. § 1080a(f) and 20 U.S.C. § 1087cc(c)(3), respectively.

19 *Editor's Note*: The reporting periods have been lengthened for certain adverse information pertaining to U.S. Government insured or guaranteed student loans, or pertaining to national direct student loans. See sections 430A(f) and 463(c)(3) of the Higher Education Act of 1965, 20 U.S.C. § 1080a(f) and 20 U.S.C. § 1087cc(c)(3), respectively.

20 This provision, added in September 1996, should read "paragraphs (4) and (5)...." Prior § 1681c(a)(6) was amended and re-designated as § 1681c(a)(5) in November 1998. The current § 1681c(a)(6), added in December 2003 and now containing no reference to any 7-year period, is obviously inapplicable.

Fair Credit Reporting Act

(2) Effective date.—Paragraph (1) shall apply only to items of information added to the file of a consumer on or after the date that is 455 days after Sept. 30, 1996.

(d) Information required to be Disclosed

(1) **Title 11 information.**—[21] Any consumer reporting agency that furnishes a consumer report that contains information regarding any case involving the consumer that arises under Title 11, shall include in the report an identification of the chapter of such Title 11 under which such case arises if provided by the source of the information. If any case arising or filed under Title 11, is withdrawn by the consumer before a final judgment, the consumer reporting agency shall include in the report that such case or filing was withdrawn upon receipt of documentation certifying such withdrawal.

(2) **Key factor in credit score information.**—[22] Any consumer reporting agency that furnishes a consumer report that contains any credit score or any other risk score or predictor on any consumer shall include in the report a clear and conspicuous statement that a key factor (as defined in section 1681g(f)(2)(B)) that adversely affected such score or predictor was the number of enquiries, if such a predictor was in fact a key factor that adversely affected such score. This paragraph shall not apply to a check services company, acting as such, which issues authorizations for the purpose of approving or processing negotiable instruments, electronic fund transfers, or similar methods of payments, but only to the extent that such company is engaged in such activities.

(e) Indication of closure of account by consumer

If a consumer reporting agency is notified pursuant to section 1681s-2(a)(4) of this title that a credit account of a consumer was voluntarily closed by the consumer, the agency shall indicate that fact in any consumer report that includes information related to the account.

(f) Indication of dispute by consumer

If a consumer reporting agency is notified pursuant to section 1681s-2(a)(3) of this title that information regarding a consumer who was furnished to the agency is disputed by the consumer, the agency shall indicate that fact in each consumer report that includes the disputed information.

(g) Truncation of credit card and debit card numbers.—

(1) **In general.**—Except as otherwise provided in this subsection, no person that accepts credit cards or debit cards for the transaction of business shall print more than the last 5 digits of the card number or the expiration date upon any receipt provided to the cardholder at the point of the sale or transaction.

(2) **Limitation.**—This subsection shall apply only to receipts that are electronically printed, and shall not apply to transactions in which the sole means of recording a credit card or debit card account number is by handwriting or by an imprint or copy of the card.

(3) **Effective date.**—This subsection shall become effective—

(A) 3 years after the date of enactment of this subsection, with respect to any cash register or other machine or device that electronically prints receipts for credit card or debit card transactions that is in use before January 1, 2005; and

(B) 1 year after the date of enactment of this subsection, with respect to any cash register or other machine or device that electronically prints receipts for credit card or debit card transactions that is first put into use on or after January 1, 2005.

(h) Notice of discrepancy in address.—[23]

(1) **In general.**—If a person has requested a consumer report relating to a consumer from a consumer reporting agency described in section 1681a(p), the request includes an address for the consumer that substantially differs from the addresses in the file of the consumer, and the agency provides a consumer report in response to the request, the consumer reporting agency shall notify the requester of the existence of the discrepancy.

(2) **Regulations.**—

(A) **Regulations required.**—The Federal banking agencies, the National Credit Union Administration, and the Commission shall jointly, with respect to the entities that are subject to their respective enforcement authority under section 1681s, prescribe regulations providing guidance regarding reasonable policies and procedures that a user of a consumer report should employ when such user has received a notice of discrepancy under paragraph (1).

(B) **Policies and procedures to be included.**—The regulations prescribed under subparagraph (A) shall describe reasonable policies and procedures for use by a user of a consumer report—

(i) to form a reasonable belief that the user knows the identity of the person to whom the consumer report pertains; and

(ii) if the user establishes a continuing relationship with the consumer, and the user regularly and in the ordinary course of business furnishes information to the consumer reporting agency from which the notice of discrepancy pertaining to the consumer was obtained, to reconcile the address of the consumer with the consumer reporting agency by furnishing such address to such consumer reporting agency as part of information regularly furnished by the user for the period in which the relationship is established.

[Pub. L. No. 90-321, tit. VI, § 605, *as added* Pub. L. No. 91-508, tit. VI, § 601, 84 Stat. 1129 (Oct. 26, 1970), *and amended* Pub. L. No. 95-598, tit. III, § 312(b), 92 Stat. 2676 (Nov. 6, 1978); Pub. L. No. 104-208, div. A, tit. II, §§ 2406(a)–(e), 110 Stat. 3009–434, 3009–435 (Sept. 30, 1996); Pub. L. No. 105-347, § 5, 112 Stat. 3211 (Nov. 2, 1998); Pub. L. No. 108-159, tit. II, §§ 113, 212(d), tit. III, § 315, tit. IV, § 412(a), (c), tit. VIII, § 811(c)(1), (2)(A), 117 Stat. 1959, 1977, 1996, 2002, 2011 (Dec. 4, 2003)]

---

21 *Editor's Note*: The effective date for the FACTA amendments (Pub. L. No. 108-159 (Dec. 4, 2003)) to 15 U.S.C. § 1681c(d)(1) is Dec. 1, 2004. *See* 12 C.F.R. § 222.1(c)(1)(i) and 16 C.F.R. § 602.1(c)(1)(i).

22 *Editor's Note*: The effective date for the FACTA amendments (Pub. L. No. 108-159 (Dec. 4, 2003)) to 15 U.S.C. § 1681c(d)(2) is Dec. 1, 2004. *See* 12 C.F.R. § 222.1(c)(1)(i) and 16 C.F.R. § 602.1(c)(1)(i).

23 *Editor's Note*: The effective date for the FACTA amendments (Pub. L. No. 108-159 (Dec. 4, 2003)) to 15 U.S.C. § 1681c(h) is Dec. 1, 2004. *See* 12 C.F.R. § 222.1(c)(1)(i) and 16 C.F.R. § 602.1(c)(1)(i).

§ 1681c-1. Identity theft prevention; fraud alerts and active duty alerts [FCRA § 605A][24]

(a) One-call fraud alerts.—

(1) Initial alerts.—Upon the direct request of a consumer, or an individual acting on behalf of or as a personal representative of a consumer, who asserts in good faith a suspicion that the consumer has been or is about to become a victim of fraud or related crime, including identity theft, a consumer reporting agency described in section 1681a(p) that maintains a file on the consumer and has received appropriate proof of the identity of the requester shall—

(A) include a fraud alert in the file of that consumer, and also provide that alert along with any credit score generated in using that file, for a period of not less than 90 days, beginning on the date of such request, unless the consumer or such representative requests that such fraud alert be removed before the end of such period, and the agency has received appropriate proof of the identity of the requester for such purpose; and

(B) refer the information regarding the fraud alert under this paragraph to each of the other consumer reporting agencies described in section 1681a(p), in accordance with procedures developed under section 1681s(f).

(2) Access to free reports.—In any case in which a consumer reporting agency includes a fraud alert in the file of a consumer pursuant to this subsection, the consumer reporting agency shall—

(A) disclose to the consumer that the consumer may request a free copy of the file of the consumer pursuant to section 1681j(d); and

(B) provide to the consumer all disclosures required to be made under section 1681g, without charge to the consumer, not later than 3 business days after any request described in subparagraph (A).

(b) Extended alerts.—

(1) In general.—Upon the direct request of a consumer, or an individual acting on behalf of or as a personal representative of a consumer, who submits an identity theft report to a consumer reporting agency described in section 1681a(p) that maintains a file on the consumer, if the agency has received appropriate proof of the identity of the requester, the agency shall—

(A) include a fraud alert in the file of that consumer, and also provide that alert along with any credit score generated in using that file, during the 7-year period beginning on the date of such request, unless the consumer or such representative requests that such fraud alert be removed before the end of such period and the agency has received appropriate proof of the identity of the requester for such purpose;

(B) during the 5-year period beginning on the date of such request, exclude the consumer from any list of consumers prepared by the consumer reporting agency and provided to any third party to offer credit or insurance to the consumer as part of a transaction that was not initiated by the consumer,

unless the consumer or such representative requests that such exclusion be rescinded before the end of such period; and

(C) refer the information regarding the extended fraud alert under this paragraph to each of the other consumer reporting agencies described in section 1681a(p), in accordance with procedures developed under section 1681s(f).

(2) Access to free reports.—In any case in which a consumer reporting agency includes a fraud alert in the file of a consumer pursuant to this subsection, the consumer reporting agency shall—

(A) disclose to the consumer that the consumer may request 2 free copies of the file of the consumer pursuant to section 1681j(d) during the 12-month period beginning on the date on which the fraud alert was included in the file; and

(B) provide to the consumer all disclosures required to be made under section 1681g, without charge to the consumer, not later than 3 business days after any request described in subparagraph (A).

(c) Active duty alerts.—Upon the direct request of an active duty military consumer, or an individual acting on behalf of or as a personal representative of an active duty military consumer, a consumer reporting agency described in section 1681a(p) that maintains a file on the active duty military consumer and has received appropriate proof of the identity of the requester shall—

(1) include an active duty alert in the file of that active duty military consumer, and also provide that alert along with any credit score generated in using that file, during a period of not less than 12 months, or such longer period as the Commission shall determine, by regulation, beginning on the date of the request, unless the active duty military consumer or such representative requests that such fraud alert be removed before the end of such period, and the agency has received appropriate proof of the identity of the requester for such purpose;

(2) during the 2-year period beginning on the date of such request, exclude the active duty military consumer from any list of consumers prepared by the consumer reporting agency and provided to any third party to offer credit or insurance to the consumer as part of a transaction that was not initiated by the consumer, unless the consumer requests that such exclusion be rescinded before the end of such period; and

(3) refer the information regarding the active duty alert to each of the other consumer reporting agencies described in section 1681a(p), in accordance with procedures developed under section 1681s(f).

(d) Procedures.—Each consumer reporting agency described in section 1681a(p) shall establish policies and procedures to comply with this section, including procedures that inform consumers of the availability of initial, extended, and active duty alerts and procedures that allow consumers and active duty military consumers to request initial, extended, or active duty alerts (as applicable) in a simple and easy manner, including by telephone.

(e) Referrals of alerts.—Each consumer reporting agency described in section 1681a(p) that receives a referral of a fraud alert or active duty alert from another consumer reporting agency pursuant to this section shall, as though the agency received the request from the consumer directly, follow the procedures required under—

---

[24] *Editor's Note*: The effective date for the FACTA enactment (Pub. L. No. 108-159 (Dec. 4, 2003)) of 15 U.S.C. § 1681c-1 is Dec. 1, 2004. *See* 12 C.F.R. § 222.1(c)(1)(i) and 16 C.F.R. § 602.1(c)(1)(i).

(1) paragraphs (1)(A) and (2) of subsection (a), in the case of a referral under subsection (a)(1)(B);
(2) paragraphs (1)(A), (1)(B), and (2) of subsection (b), in the case of a referral under subsection (b)(1)(C); and
(3) paragraphs (1) and (2) of subsection (c), in the case of a referral under subsection (c)(3).

(f) Duty of reseller to reconvey alert.—A reseller shall include in its report any fraud alert or active duty alert placed in the file of a consumer pursuant to this section by another consumer reporting agency.

(g) Duty of other consumer reporting agencies to provide contact information.—If a consumer contacts any consumer reporting agency that is not described in section 1681a(p) to communicate a suspicion that the consumer has been or is about to become a victim of fraud or related crime, including identity theft, the agency shall provide information to the consumer on how to contact the Commission and the consumer reporting agencies described in section 1681a(p) to obtain more detailed information and request alerts under this section.

(h) Limitations on use of information for credit extensions.—
  (1) Requirements for initial and active duty alerts.—
    (A) Notification.—Each initial fraud alert and active duty alert under this section shall include information that notifies all prospective users of a consumer report on the consumer to which the alert relates that the consumer does not authorize the establishment of any new credit plan or extension of credit, other than under an open-end credit plan (as defined in section 103(i)), in the name of the consumer, or issuance of an additional card on an existing credit account requested by a consumer, or any increase in credit limit on an existing credit account requested by a consumer, except in accordance with subparagraph (B).
    (B) Limitation on users.—
      (i) In general.—No prospective user of a consumer report that includes an initial fraud alert or an active duty alert in accordance with this section may establish a new credit plan or extension of credit, other than under an open-end credit plan (as defined in section 103(i)), in the name of the consumer, or issue an additional card on an existing credit account requested by a consumer, or grant any increase in credit limit on an existing credit account requested by a consumer, unless the user utilizes reasonable policies and procedures to form a reasonable belief that the user knows the identity of the person making the request.
      (ii) Verification.—If a consumer requesting the alert has specified a telephone number to be used for identity verification purposes, before authorizing any new credit plan or extension described in clause (i) in the name of such consumer, a user of such consumer report shall contact the consumer using that telephone number or take reasonable steps to verify the consumer's identity and confirm that the application for a new credit plan is not the result of identity theft.
  (2) Requirements for extended alerts.—
    (A) Notification.—Each extended alert under this section shall include information that provides all prospective users of a consumer report relating to a consumer with—
      (i) notification that the consumer does not authorize the establishment of any new credit plan or extension of credit described in clause (i), other than under an open-end credit plan (as defined in section 103(i)), in the name of the consumer, or issuance of an additional card on an existing credit account requested by a consumer, or any increase in credit limit on an existing credit account requested by a consumer, except in accordance with subparagraph (B); and
      (ii) a telephone number or other reasonable contact method designated by the consumer.
    (B) Limitation on users.—No prospective user of a consumer report or of a credit score generated using the information in the file of a consumer that includes an extended fraud alert in accordance with this section may establish a new credit plan or extension of credit, other than under an open-end credit plan (as defined in section 103(i)), in the name of the consumer, or issue an additional card on an existing credit account requested by a consumer, or any increase in credit limit on an existing credit account requested by a consumer, unless the user contacts the consumer in person or using the contact method described in subparagraph (A)(ii) to confirm that the application for a new credit plan or increase in credit limit, or request for an additional card is not the result of identity theft.

[Pub. L. No. 90-321, tit. VI, § 605A, *as added* Pub. L. No. 108-159, tit. I, § 112(a), 117 Stat. 1955 (Dec. 4, 2003)]

§ 1681c-2. Block of information resulting from identity theft [FCRA § 605B][25]

(a) Block.—Except as otherwise provided in this section, a consumer reporting agency shall block the reporting of any information in the file of a consumer that the consumer identifies as information that resulted from an alleged identity theft, not later than 4 business days after the date of receipt by such agency of—
  (1) appropriate proof of the identity of the consumer;
  (2) a copy of an identity theft report;
  (3) the identification of such information by the consumer; and
  (4) a statement by the consumer that the information is not information relating to any transaction by the consumer.

(b) Notification.—A consumer reporting agency shall promptly notify the furnisher of information identified by the consumer under subsection (a)—
  (1) that the information may be a result of identity theft;
  (2) that an identity theft report has been filed;
  (3) that a block has been requested under this section; and
  (4) of the effective dates of the block.

(c) Authority to decline or rescind.—
  (1) In general.—A consumer reporting agency may decline to block, or may rescind any block, of information relating to a consumer under this section, if the consumer reporting agency reasonably determines that—

---

25 *Editor's Note*: The effective date for the FACTA enactment (Pub. L. No. 108-159 (Dec. 4, 2003)) of 15 U.S.C. § 1681c-2 is Dec. 1, 2004. *See* 12 C.F.R. § 222.1(c)(1)(i) and 16 C.F.R. § 602.1(c)(1)(i).

(A) the information was blocked in error or a block was requested by the consumer in error;

(B) the information was blocked, or a block was requested by the consumer, on the basis of a material misrepresentation of fact by the consumer relevant to the request to block; or

(C) the consumer obtained possession of goods, services, or money as a result of the blocked transaction or transactions.

(2) **Notification to consumer.**—If a block of information is declined or rescinded under this subsection, the affected consumer shall be notified promptly, in the same manner as consumers are notified of the reinsertion of information under section 1681i(a)(5)(B).

(3) **Significance of block.**—For purposes of this subsection, if a consumer reporting agency rescinds a block, the presence of information in the file of a consumer prior to the blocking of such information is not evidence of whether the consumer knew or should have known that the consumer obtained possession of any goods, services, or money as a result of the block.

(d) **Exception for resellers.**—

(1) **No reseller file.**—This section shall not apply to a consumer reporting agency, if the consumer reporting agency—

(A) is a reseller;

(B) is not, at the time of the request of the consumer under subsection (a), otherwise furnishing or reselling a consumer report concerning the information identified by the consumer; and

(C) informs the consumer, by any means, that the consumer may report the identity theft to the Commission to obtain consumer information regarding identity theft.

(2) **Reseller with file.**—The sole obligation of the consumer reporting agency under this section, with regard to any request of a consumer under this section, shall be to block the consumer report maintained by the consumer reporting agency from any subsequent use, if—

(A) the consumer, in accordance with the provisions of subsection (a), identifies, to a consumer reporting agency, information in the file of the consumer that resulted from identity theft; and

(B) the consumer reporting agency is a reseller of the identified information.

(3) **Notice.**—In carrying out its obligation under paragraph (2), the reseller shall promptly provide a notice to the consumer of the decision to block the file. Such notice shall contain the name, address, and telephone number of each consumer reporting agency from which the consumer information was obtained for resale.

(e) **Exception for verification companies.**—The provisions of this section do not apply to a check services company, acting as such, which issues authorizations for the purpose of approving or processing negotiable instruments, electronic fund transfers, or similar methods of payments, except that, beginning 4 business days after receipt of information described in paragraphs (1) through (3) of subsection (a), a check services company shall not report to a national consumer reporting agency described in section 1681a(p), any information identified in the subject identity theft report as resulting from identity theft.

(f) **Access to blocked information by law enforcement agencies.**—No provision of this section shall be construed as requiring a consumer reporting agency to prevent a Federal, State, or local law enforcement agency from accessing blocked information in a consumer file to which the agency could otherwise obtain access under this title.

[Pub. L. No. 90-321, tit. VI, § 605B, *as added* Pub. L. No. 108-159, tit. I, § 152(a), 117 Stat. 1964 (Dec. 4, 2003)]

§ 1681d. Disclosure of investigative consumer reports [FCRA § 606]

(a) **Disclosure of fact of preparation**

A person may not procure or cause to be prepared an investigative consumer report on any consumer unless—

(1) it is clearly and accurately disclosed to the consumer that an investigative consumer report including information as to his character, general reputation, personal characteristics, and mode of living, whichever are applicable, may be made, and such disclosure (A) is made in a writing mailed, or otherwise delivered, to the consumer, not later than three days after the date on which the report was first requested, and (B) includes a statement informing the consumer of his right to request the additional disclosures provided for under subsection (b) of this section and the written summary of the rights of the consumer prepared pursuant to section 1681g(c) of this title; and

(2) the person certifies or has certified to the consumer reporting agency that—

(A) the person has made the disclosures to the consumer required by paragraph (1); and

(B) the person will comply with subsection (b) of this section.

(b) **Disclosure on request of nature and scope of investigation**

Any person who procures or causes to be prepared an investigative consumer report on any consumer shall, upon written request made by the consumer within a reasonable period of time after the receipt by him of the disclosure required by subsection (a)(1) of this section, shall make a complete and accurate disclosure of the nature and scope of the investigation requested. This disclosure shall be made in a writing mailed, or otherwise delivered, to the consumer not later than five days after the date on which the request for such disclosure was received from the consumer or such report was first requested, whichever is the later.

(c) **Limitation on liability upon showing of reasonable procedures for compliance with provisions**

No person may be held liable for any violation of subsection (a) or (b) of this section if he shows by a preponderance of the evidence that at the time of the violation he maintained reasonable procedures to assure compliance with subsection (a) or (b) of this section.

(d) **Prohibitions**

(1) **Certification.**—A consumer reporting agency shall not prepare or furnish investigative consumer report unless the agency has received a certification under subsection (a)(2) from the person who requested the report.

(2) **Inquiries.**—A consumer reporting agency shall not make an inquiry for the purpose of preparing an investigative consumer report on a consumer for employment purposes if the making of the inquiry by an employer or prospective employer of the

consumer would violate any applicable Federal or State equal employment opportunity law or regulation.

(3) Certain public record information.—Except as otherwise provided in section 1681k of this title, a consumer reporting agency shall not furnish an investigative consumer report that includes information that is a matter of public record and that relates to an arrest, indictment, conviction, civil judicial action, tax lien, or outstanding judgment, unless the agency has verified the accuracy of the information during the 30-day period ending on the date on which the report is furnished.

(4) Certain adverse information.—A consumer reporting agency shall not prepare or furnish an investigative consumer report on a consumer that contains information that is adverse to the interest of the consumer and that is obtained through a personal interview with a neighbor, friend, or associate of the consumer or with another person with whom the consumer is acquainted or who has knowledge of such item of information, unless—

(A) the agency has followed reasonable procedures to obtain confirmation of the information, from an additional source that has independent and direct knowledge of the information; or

(B) the person interviewed is the best possible source of the information.

[Pub. L. No. 90-321, tit. VI, § 606, *as added* Pub. L. No. 91-508, tit. VI, § 601, 84 Stat. 1130 (Oct. 26, 1970); *amended* Pub. L. No. 104-208, div. A, tit. II, §§ 2408(d)(2), 2414(1)–(3), 110 Stat. 3009-438, 3009-449 (Sept. 30, 1996)]

§ 1681e. Compliance procedures [FCRA § 607]

(a) Identity and purposes of credit users

Every consumer reporting agency shall maintain reasonable procedures designed to avoid violations of section 1681c of this title and to limit the furnishing of consumer reports to the purposes listed under section 1681b of this title. These procedures shall require that prospective users of the information identify themselves, certify the purposes for which the information is sought, and certify that the information will be used for no other purpose. Every consumer reporting agency shall make a reasonable effort to verify the identity of a new prospective user and the uses certified by such prospective user prior to furnishing such user a consumer report. No consumer reporting agency may furnish a consumer report to any person if it has reasonable grounds for believing that the consumer report will not be used for a purpose listed in section 1681b of this title.

(b) Accuracy of report

Whenever a consumer reporting agency prepares a consumer report it shall follow reasonable procedures to assure maximum possible accuracy of the information concerning the individual about whom the report relates.

(c) Disclosure of consumer reports by users allowed

A consumer reporting agency may not prohibit a user of a consumer report furnished by the agency on a consumer from disclosing the contents of the report to the consumer, if adverse action against the consumer has been taken by the user based in whole or in part on the report.

(d) Notice to users and furnishers of information

(1) Notice requirement.—A consumer reporting agency shall provide to any person—

(A) who regularly and in the ordinary course of business furnishes information to the agency with respect to any consumer; or

(B) to whom a consumer report is provided by the agency; a notice of such person's responsibilities under this subchapter.

(2) Content of notice.—The Federal Trade Commission shall prescribe the content of notices under paragraph (1), and a consumer reporting agency shall be in compliance with this subsection if it provides a notice under paragraph (1) that is substantially similar to the Federal Trade Commission prescription under this paragraph.

(e) Procurement of consumer report for resale

(1) Disclosure.—A person may not procure a consumer report for purposes of reselling the report (or any information in the report) unless the person discloses to the consumer reporting agency that originally furnishes the report—

(A) the identity of the end-user of the report (or information); and

(B) each permissible purpose under section 1681b of this title for which the report is furnished to the end-user of the report (or information).

(2) Responsibilities of procurers for resale.—A person who procures a consumer report for purposes of reselling the report (or any information in the report) shall—

(A) establish and comply with reasonable procedures designed to ensure that the report (or information) is resold by the person only for a purpose for which the report may be furnished under section 1681b of this title, including by requiring that each person to which the report (or information) is resold and that resells or provides the report (or information) to any other person—

(i) identifies each end user of the resold report (or information);

(ii) certifies each purpose for which the report (or information) will be used; and

(iii) certifies that the report (or information) will be used for no other purpose; and

(B) before reselling the report, make reasonable efforts to verify the identifications and certifications made under subparagraph (A).

(3) Resale of consumer report to a federal agency or department.—Notwithstanding paragraph (1) or (2), a person who procures a consumer report for purposes of reselling the report (or any information in the report) shall not disclose the identity of the end-user of the report under paragraph (1) or (2) if—

(A) the end user is an agency or department of the United States Government which procures the report from the person for purposes of determining the eligibility of the consumer concerned to receive access or continued access to classified information (as defined in section 604(b)(4)(E)(i)); and

(B) the agency or department certifies in writing to the person reselling the report that nondisclosure is necessary to protect classified information or the safety of persons employed by or contracting with, or undergoing investigation for work or contracting with the agency or department.

[Pub. L. No. 90-321, tit. VI, § 607, *as added* Pub. L. No. 91-508, tit. VI, § 601, 84 Stat. 1130 (Oct. 26, 1970); *amended* Pub. L. No. 104-208, div. A, tit. II, § 2407, 110 Stat. 3009–435 (Sept. 30, 1996); Pub. L. No. 105-107, tit. III, § 311(b), 111 Stat. 2256 (Nov. 20, 1997)]

§ 1681f. Disclosures to governmental agencies [FCRA § 608]

Notwithstanding the provisions of section 1681b of this title, a consumer reporting agency may furnish identifying information respecting any consumer, limited to his name, address, former addresses, places of employment, or former places of employment, to a governmental agency.

[Pub. L. No. 90-321, tit. VI, § 608, *as added* Pub. L. No. 91-508, tit. VI, § 601, 84 Stat. 1131 (Oct. 26, 1970)]

§ 1681g. Disclosures to consumers [FCRA § 609]

(a) Information on file; sources; report recipients

Every consumer reporting agency shall, upon request, and subject to section 1681h(a)(1) of this title, clearly and accurately disclose to the consumer:

(1) All information in the consumer's file at the time of the request, except that—[26]

(A) if the consumer to whom the file relates requests that the first 5 digits of the social security number (or similar identification number) of the consumer not be included in the disclosure and the consumer reporting agency has received appropriate proof of the identity of the requester, the consumer reporting agency shall so truncate such number in such disclosure; and

(B) nothing in this paragraph shall be construed to require a consumer reporting agency to disclose to a consumer any information concerning credit scores or any other risk scores or predictors relating to the consumer.

(2) The sources of the information; except that the sources of information acquired solely for use in preparing an investigative consumer report and actually used for no other purpose need not be disclosed: *Provided*, That in the event an action is brought under this subchapter, such sources shall be available to the plaintiff under appropriate discovery procedures in the court in which the action is brought.[27]

(3)(A) Identification of each person (including each end-user identified under section 1681e(e)(1)) that procured a consumer report—

(i) for employment purposes, during the 2-year period preceding the date on which the request is made; or
(ii) for any other purpose, during the 1-year period preceding the date on which the request is made.

(B) An identification of a person under subparagraph (A) shall include—

(i) the name of the person or, if applicable, the trade name (written in full) under which such person conducts business; and
(ii) upon request of the consumer, the address and telephone number of the person.

(C) Subparagraph (A) does not apply if—[28]

(i) the end user is an agency or department of the United States Government that procures the report from the person for purposes of determining the eligibility of the consumer to whom the report relates to receive access or continued access to classified information (as defined in section 1681b(b)(4)(E)(i) of this title); and
(ii) the head of the agency or department makes a written finding as prescribed under section 1681b(b)(4)(A) of this title.

(4) The dates, original payees, and amounts of any checks upon which is based any adverse characterization of the consumer, included in the file at the time of the disclosure.

(5) A record of all inquiries received by the agency during the 1-year period preceding the request that identified the consumer in connection with a credit or insurance transaction that was not initiated by the consumer.

(6) If the consumer requests the credit file and not the credit score, a statement that the consumer may request and obtain a credit score.[29]

(b) Exempt information

The requirements of subsection (a) of this section respecting the disclosure of sources of information and the recipients of consumer reports do not apply to information received or consumer reports furnished prior to the effective date of this subchapter except to the extent that the matter involved is contained in the files of the consumer reporting agency on that date.

(c) Summary of rights to obtain and dispute information in consumer reports and to obtain credit scores.—[30]

(1) Commission summary of rights required.—

(A) In general.—The Commission shall prepare a model summary of the rights of consumers under this title.

(B) Content of summary.—The summary of rights prepared under subparagraph (A) shall include a description of—

(i) the right of a consumer to obtain a copy of a consumer report under subsection (a) from each consumer reporting agency;
(ii) the frequency and circumstances under which a con-

---

26 *Editor's Note*: The effective date for the FACTA amendments (Pub. L. No. 108-159 (Dec. 4, 2003)) to 15 U.S.C. § 1681g(a)(1) is Dec. 1, 2004. *See* 12 C.F.R. § 222.1(c)(1)(i) and 16 C.F.R. § 602.1(c)(1)(i).

27 *Editor's Note*: The effective date for the FACTA amendments (Pub. L. No. 108-159 (Dec. 4, 2003)) to 15 U.S.C. § 1681g(a)(2) is Mar. 31, 2004. *See* 12 C.F.R. § 222.1(c)(1)(i) and 16 C.F.R. § 602.1(c)(1)(i). The § 811 of the FACTA amendments were technical in nature (moving § 1681g(a)(2) two ems to the right).

28 *Editor's Note*: The effective date for the FACTA amendments (Pub. L. No. 108-159 (Dec. 4, 2003)) to 15 U.S.C. § 1681g(a)(3)(C) is Mar. 31, 2004. *See* 12 C.F.R. § 222.1(c)(1)(i) and 16 C.F.R. § 602.1(c)(1)(i). The § 811 of the FACTA amendments were technical in nature (moving § 1681g(a)(3)(C) two ems to the right).

29 *Editor's Note*: The effective date for the FACTA amendments (Pub. L. No. 108-159 (Dec. 4, 2003)) to 15 U.S.C. § 1681g(a)(6) is Dec. 1, 2004. *See* 12 C.F.R. § 222.1(c)(1)(i) and 16 C.F.R. § 602.1(c)(1)(i).

30 *Editor's Note*: The effective date for the FACTA amendments (Pub. L. No. 108-159 (Dec. 4, 2003)) to 15 U.S.C. § 1681g(c) is Dec. 1, 2004. *See* 12 C.F.R. § 222.1(c)(1)(i) and 16 C.F.R. § 602.1(c)(1)(i).

sumer is entitled to receive a consumer report without charge under section 1681j;

(iii) the right of a consumer to dispute information in the file of the consumer under section 1681i;

(iv) the right of a consumer to obtain a credit score from a consumer reporting agency, and a description of how to obtain a credit score;

(v) the method by which a consumer can contact, and obtain a consumer report from, a consumer reporting agency without charge, as provided in the regulations of the Commission prescribed under section 211(c) of the Fair and Accurate Credit Transactions Act of 2003; and

(vi) the method by which a consumer can contact, and obtain a consumer report from, a consumer reporting agency described in section 1681a(w), as provided in the regulations of the Commission prescribed under section 1681j(a)(1)(C).

(C) **Availability of summary of rights.**—The Commission shall—

(i) actively publicize the availability of the summary of rights prepared under this paragraph;

(ii) conspicuously post on its Internet website the availability of such summary of rights; and

(iii) promptly make such summary of rights available to consumers, on request.

(2) **Summary of rights required to be included with agency disclosures.**—A consumer reporting agency shall provide to a consumer, with each written disclosure by the agency to the consumer under this section—

(A) the summary of rights prepared by the Commission under paragraph (1);

(B) in the case of a consumer reporting agency described in section 1681a(p), a toll-free telephone number established by the agency, at which personnel are accessible to consumers during normal business hours;

(C) a list of all Federal agencies responsible for enforcing any provision of this title, and the address and any appropriate phone number of each such agency, in a form that will assist the consumer in selecting the appropriate agency;

(D) a statement that the consumer may have additional rights under State law, and that the consumer may wish to contact a State or local consumer protection agency or a State attorney general (or the equivalent thereof) to learn of those rights; and

(E) a statement that a consumer reporting agency is not required to remove accurate derogatory information from the file of a consumer, unless the information is outdated under section 1681c or cannot be verified.

(d) **Summary of rights of identity theft victims.**—[31]

(1) **In general.**—The Commission, in consultation with the Federal banking agencies and the National Credit Union Administration, shall prepare a model summary of the rights of consumers under this title with respect to the procedures for remedying the effects of fraud or identity theft involving credit, an electronic fund transfer, or an account or transaction at or with a financial institution or other creditor.

(2) **Summary of rights and contact information.**—Beginning 60 days after the date on which the model summary of rights is prescribed in final form by the Commission pursuant to paragraph (1), if any consumer contacts a consumer reporting agency and expresses a belief that the consumer is a victim of fraud or identity theft involving credit, an electronic fund transfer, or an account or transaction at or with a financial institution or other creditor, the consumer reporting agency shall, in addition to any other action that the agency may take, provide the consumer with a summary of rights that contains all of the information required by the Commission under paragraph (1), and information on how to contact the Commission to obtain more detailed information.

(e) **Information available to victims.**—[32]

(1) **In general.**—For the purpose of documenting fraudulent transactions resulting from identity theft, not later than 30 days after the date of receipt of a request from a victim in accordance with paragraph (3), and subject to verification of the identity of the victim and the claim of identity theft in accordance with paragraph (2), a business entity that has provided credit to, provided for consideration products, goods, or services to, accepted payment from, or otherwise entered into a commercial transaction for consideration with, a person who has allegedly made unauthorized use of the means of identification of the victim, shall provide a copy of application and business transaction records in the control of the business entity, whether maintained by the business entity or by another person on behalf of the business entity, evidencing any transaction alleged to be a result of identity theft to—

(A) the victim;

(B) any Federal, State, or local government law enforcement agency or officer specified by the victim in such a request; or

(C) any law enforcement agency investigating the identity theft and authorized by the victim to take receipt of records provided under this subsection.

(2) **Verification of identity and claim.**—Before a business entity provides any information under paragraph (1), unless the business entity, at its discretion, otherwise has a high degree of confidence that it knows the identity of the victim making a request under paragraph (1), the victim shall provide to the business entity—

(A) as proof of positive identification of the victim, at the election of the business entity—

(i) the presentation of a government-issued identification card;

(ii) personally identifying information of the same type as was provided to the business entity by the unauthorized person; or

(iii) personally identifying information that the business entity typically requests from new applicants or for new transactions, at the time of the victim's request for information, including any documentation described in clauses (i) and (ii); and

---

31 *Editor's Note*: The effective date for the FACTA amendments (Pub. L. No. 108-159 (Dec. 4, 2003)) to 15 U.S.C. § 1681g(d) is Dec. 1, 2004. *See* 12 C.F.R. § 222.1(c)(1)(i) and 16 C.F.R. § 602.1(c)(1)(i).

32 *Editor's Note*: The effective date for the FACTA amendments (Pub. L. No. 108-159 (Dec. 4, 2003)) to 15 U.S.C. § 1681g(e) is Dec. 1, 2004. *See* 12 C.F.R. § 222.1(c)(1)(i) and 16 C.F.R. § 602.1(c)(1)(i).

(B) as proof of a claim of identity theft, at the election of the business entity—
  (i) a copy of a police report evidencing the claim of the victim of identity theft; and
  (ii) a properly completed—
    (I) copy of a standardized affidavit of identity theft developed and made available by the Commission; or
    (II) an affidavit of fact that is acceptable to the business entity for that purpose.

(3) **Procedures.**—The request of a victim under paragraph (1) shall—
  (A) be in writing;
  (B) be mailed to an address specified by the business entity, if any; and
  (C) if asked by the business entity, include relevant information about any transaction alleged to be a result of identity theft to facilitate compliance with this section including—
    (i) if known by the victim (or if readily obtainable by the victim), the date of the application or transaction; and
    (ii) if known by the victim (or if readily obtainable by the victim), any other identifying information such as an account or transaction number.

(4) **No charge to victim.**—Information required to be provided under paragraph (1) shall be so provided without charge.

(5) **Authority to decline to provide information.**—A business entity may decline to provide information under paragraph (1) if, in the exercise of good faith, the business entity determines that—
  (A) this subsection does not require disclosure of the information;
  (B) after reviewing the information provided pursuant to paragraph (2), the business entity does not have a high degree of confidence in knowing the true identity of the individual requesting the information;
  (C) the request for the information is based on a misrepresentation of fact by the individual requesting the information relevant to the request for information; or
  (D) the information requested is Internet navigational data or similar information about a person's visit to a website or online service.

(6) **Limitation on liability.**—Except as provided in section 1681s, sections 1681n and 1681o do not apply to any violation of this subsection.

(7) **Limitation on civil liability.**—No business entity may be held civilly liable under any provision of Federal, State, or other law for disclosure, made in good faith pursuant to this subsection.

(8) **No new recordkeeping obligation.**—Nothing in this subsection creates an obligation on the part of a business entity to obtain, retain, or maintain information or records that are not otherwise required to be obtained, retained, or maintained in the ordinary course of its business or under other applicable law.

(9) **Rule of construction.**—
  (A) **In general.**—No provision of subtitle A of title V of Public Law 106-102, prohibiting the disclosure of financial information by a business entity to third parties shall be used to deny disclosure of information to the victim under this subsection.
  (B) **Limitation.**—Except as provided in subparagraph (A), nothing in this subsection permits a business entity to disclose information, including information to law enforcement under subparagraphs (B) and (C) of paragraph (1), that the business entity is otherwise prohibited from disclosing under any other applicable provision of Federal or State law.

(10) **Affirmative defense.**—In any civil action brought to enforce this subsection, it is an affirmative defense (which the defendant must establish by a preponderance of the evidence) for a business entity to file an affidavit or answer stating that—
  (A) the business entity has made a reasonably diligent search of its available business records; and
  (B) the records requested under this subsection do not exist or are not reasonably available.

(11) **Definition of victim.**—For purposes of this subsection, the term 'victim' means a consumer whose means of identification or financial information has been used or transferred (or has been alleged to have been used or transferred) without the authority of that consumer, with the intent to commit, or to aid or abet, an identity theft or a similar crime.

(12) **Effective date.**—This subsection shall become effective 180 days after the date of enactment of this subsection.

(13) **Effectiveness study.**—Not later than 18 months after the date of enactment of this subsection, the Comptroller General of the United States shall submit a report to Congress assessing the effectiveness of this provision.

(f) **Disclosure of credit scores.**—[33]
(1) **In general.**—Upon the request of a consumer for a credit score, a consumer reporting agency shall supply to the consumer a statement indicating that the information and credit scoring model may be different than the credit score that may be used by the lender, and a notice which shall include—
  (A) the current credit score of the consumer or the most recent credit score of the consumer that was previously calculated by the credit reporting agency for a purpose related to the extension of credit;
  (B) the range of possible credit scores under the model used;
  (C) all of the key factors that adversely affected the credit score of the consumer in the model used, the total number of which shall not exceed 4, subject to paragraph (9);
  (D) the date on which the credit score was created; and
  (E) the name of the person or entity that provided the credit score or credit file upon which the credit score was created.

(2) **Definitions.**—For purposes of this subsection, the following definitions shall apply:
  (A) **Credit score.**—The term 'credit score'—
    (i) means a numerical value or a categorization derived from a statistical tool or modeling system used by a person who makes or arranges a loan to predict the likelihood of certain credit behaviors, including default (and the numerical value or the categorization derived from such analysis may also be referred to as a 'risk predictor' or 'risk score'); and
    (ii) does not include—
      (I) any mortgage score or rating of an automated underwriting system that considers one or more factors in addition to credit information, including the loan to

---

[33] *Editor's Note*: The effective date for the FACTA amendments (Pub. L. No. 108-159 (Dec. 4, 2003)) to 15 U.S.C. § 1681g(f) is Dec. 1, 2004. *See* 12 C.F.R. § 222.1(c)(1)(i) and 16 C.F.R. § 602.1(c)(1)(i).

value ratio, the amount of down payment, or the financial assets of a consumer; or

(II) any other elements of the underwriting process or underwriting decision.

(B) Key factors.—The term 'key factors' means all relevant elements or reasons adversely affecting the credit score for the particular individual, listed in the order of their importance based on their effect on the credit score.

(3) Timeframe and manner of disclosure.—The information required by this subsection shall be provided in the same timeframe and manner as the information described in subsection (a).

(4) Applicability to certain uses.—This subsection shall not be construed so as to compel a consumer reporting agency to develop or disclose a score if the agency does not—

(A) distribute scores that are used in connection with residential real property loans; or

(B) develop scores that assist credit providers in understanding the general credit behavior of a consumer and predicting the future credit behavior of the consumer.

(5) Applicability to credit scores developed by another person.—

(A) In general.—This subsection shall not be construed to require a consumer reporting agency that distributes credit scores developed by another person or entity to provide a further explanation of them, or to process a dispute arising pursuant to section 1681i, except that the consumer reporting agency shall provide the consumer with the name and address and website for contacting the person or entity who developed the score or developed the methodology of the score.

(B) Exception.—This paragraph shall not apply to a consumer reporting agency that develops or modifies scores that are developed by another person or entity.

(6) Maintenance of credit scores not required.—This subsection shall not be construed to require a consumer reporting agency to maintain credit scores in its files.

(7) Compliance in certain cases.—In complying with this subsection, a consumer reporting agency shall—

(A) supply the consumer with a credit score that is derived from a credit scoring model that is widely distributed to users by that consumer reporting agency in connection with residential real property loans or with a credit score that assists the consumer in understanding the credit scoring assessment of the credit behavior of the consumer and predictions about the future credit behavior of the consumer; and

(B) a statement indicating that the information and credit scoring model may be different than that used by the lender.

(8) Fair and reasonable fee.—A consumer reporting agency may charge a fair and reasonable fee, as determined by the Commission, for providing the information required under this subsection.

(9) Use of enquiries as a key factor.—If a key factor that adversely affects the credit score of a consumer consists of the number of enquiries made with respect to a consumer report, that factor shall be included in the disclosure pursuant to paragraph (1)(C) without regard to the numerical limitation in such paragraph.

(g) Disclosure of credit scores by certain mortgage lenders.—[34]

(1) In general.—Any person who makes or arranges loans and who uses a consumer credit score, as defined in subsection (f), in connection with an application initiated or sought by a consumer for a closed end loan or the establishment of an open end loan for a consumer purpose that is secured by 1 to 4 units of residential real property (hereafter in this subsection referred to as the 'lender') shall provide the following to the consumer as soon as reasonably practicable:

(A) Information required under subsection (f).—

(i) In general.—A copy of the information identified in subsection (f) that was obtained from a consumer reporting agency or was developed and used by the user of the information.

(ii) Notice under subparagraph (d).—In addition to the information provided to it by a third party that provided the credit score or scores, a lender is only required to provide the notice contained in subparagraph (D).

(B) Disclosures in case of automated underwriting system.—

(i) In general.—If a person that is subject to this subsection uses an automated underwriting system to underwrite a loan, that person may satisfy the obligation to provide a credit score by disclosing a credit score and associated key factors supplied by a consumer reporting agency.

(ii) Numerical credit score.—However, if a numerical credit score is generated by an automated underwriting system used by an enterprise, and that score is disclosed to the person, the score shall be disclosed to the consumer consistent with subparagraph (C).

(iii) Enterprise defined.—For purposes of this subparagraph, the term 'enterprise' has the same meaning as in paragraph (6) of section 1303 of the Federal Housing Enterprises Financial Safety and Soundness Act of 1992.

(C) Disclosures of credit scores not obtained from a consumer reporting agency.—A person that is subject to the provisions of this subsection and that uses a credit score, other than a credit score provided by a consumer reporting agency, may satisfy the obligation to provide a credit score by disclosing a credit score and associated key factors supplied by a consumer reporting agency.

(D) Notice to home loan applicants.—A copy of the following notice, which shall include the name, address, and telephone number of each consumer reporting agency providing a credit score that was used:

Notice to the Home Loan Applicant

In connection with your application for a home loan, the lender must disclose to you the score that a consumer reporting agency distributed to users and the lender used in connection with your home loan, and the key factors affecting your credit scores.

The credit score is a computer generated summary calculated at the time of the request and based on information that a consumer reporting

---

[34] *Editor's Note*: The effective date for the FACTA amendments (Pub. L. No. 108-159 (Dec. 4, 2003)) to 15 U.S.C. § 1681g(g) is Dec. 1, 2004. *See* 12 C.F.R. § 222.1(c)(1)(i) and 16 C.F.R. § 602.1(c)(1)(i).

agency or lender has on file. The scores are based on data about your credit history and payment patterns. Credit scores are important because they are used to assist the lender in determining whether you will obtain a loan. They may also be used to determine what interest rate you may be offered on the mortgage. Credit scores can change over time, depending on your conduct, how your credit history and payment patterns change, and how credit scoring technologies change.

Because the score is based on information in your credit history, it is very important that you review the credit-related information that is being furnished to make sure it is accurate. Credit records may vary from one company to another.

If you have questions about your credit score or the credit information that is furnished to you, contact the consumer reporting agency at the address and telephone number provided with this notice, or contact the lender, if the lender developed or generated the credit score. The consumer reporting agency plays no part in the decision to take any action on the loan application and is unable to provide you with specific reasons for the decision on a loan application.

If you have questions concerning the terms of the loan, contact the lender.

(E) **Actions not required under this subsection.**—This subsection shall not require any person to—
(i) explain the information provided pursuant to subsection (f);
(ii) disclose any information other than a credit score or key factors, as defined in subsection (f);
(iii) disclose any credit score or related information obtained by the user after a loan has closed;
(iv) provide more than 1 disclosure per loan transaction; or
(v) provide the disclosure required by this subsection when another person has made the disclosure to the consumer for that loan transaction.

(F) **No obligation for content.**—
(i) **In general.**—The obligation of any person pursuant to this subsection shall be limited solely to providing a copy of the information that was received from the consumer reporting agency.
(ii) **Limit on liability.**—No person has liability under this subsection for the content of that information or for the omission of any information within the report provided by the consumer reporting agency.

(G) **Person defined as excluding enterprise.**—As used in this subsection, the term 'person' does not include an enterprise (as defined in paragraph (6) of section 1303 of the Federal Housing Enterprises Financial Safety and Soundness Act of 1992).

(2) **Prohibition on disclosure clauses null and void.**—
(A) **In general.**—Any provision in a contract that prohibits the disclosure of a credit score by a person who makes or arranges loans or a consumer reporting agency is void.
(B) **No liability for disclosure under this subsection.**—A lender shall not have liability under any contractual provision for disclosure of a credit score pursuant to this subsection.

[Pub. L. No. 90-321, tit. VI, § 609, *as added* Pub. L. No. 91-508, tit. VI, § 601, 84 Stat. 1131 (Oct. 26, 1970), *and amended* Pub. L. No. 103-325, tit. III, § 339, 108 Stat. 2237 (Sept. 23, 1994); Pub. L. No. 104-208, div. A, tit. II, § 2408(a)–(d)(1), (e)(5)(A), 110 Stat. 3009–436, 3009–437, 3009–439 (Sept. 30, 1996); Pub. L. No. 105-347, § 4(a), 112 Stat. 3210 (Nov. 2, 1998); Pub. L. No. 108-159, tit. I, §§ 115, 151(a)(1), tit. II, §§ 211(c), 212(a)–(c), tit. VIII, § 811(d), 117 Stat. 1961, 1970, 1973–1975, 2011 (Dec. 4, 2003)]

§ 1681h. Conditions and form of disclosure to consumers [FCRA § 610]

(a) In general
(1) **Proper identification.**—A consumer reporting agency shall require, as a condition of making the disclosures required under section 1681g of this title, that the consumer furnish proper identification.
(2) **Disclosure in writing.**—Except as provided in subsection (b) of this section, the disclosures required to be made under section 1681g of this title shall be provided under that section in writing.

(b) Other forms of disclosure
(1) **In general.**—If authorized by a consumer, a consumer reporting agency may make the disclosures required under 1681g of this title—
(A) other than in writing; and
(B) in such form as may be—
(i) specified by the consumer in accordance with paragraph (2); and
(ii) available from the agency.
(2) **Form.**—A consumer may specify pursuant to paragraph (1) that disclosures under section 1681g of this title shall be made—
(A) in person, upon the appearance of the consumer at the place of business of the consumer reporting agency where disclosures are regularly provided, during normal business hours, and on reasonable notice;
(B) by telephone, if the consumer has made a written request for disclosure by telephone;
(C) by electronic means, if available from the agency; or
(D) by any other reasonable means that is available from the agency.

(c) Trained personnel

Any consumer reporting agency shall provide trained personnel to explain to the consumer any information furnished to him pursuant to section 1681g of this title.

(d) Persons accompanying consumer

The consumer shall be permitted to be accompanied by one other person of his choosing, who shall furnish reasonable identification. A consumer reporting agency may require the consumer to furnish a written statement granting permission to the consumer reporting agency to discuss the consumer's file in such person's presence.

(e) Limitation of liability

Except as provided in sections 1681n and 1681*o* of this title, no consumer may bring any action or proceeding in the nature of defamation, invasion of privacy, or negligence with respect to the reporting of information against any consumer reporting agency, any user of information, or any person who furnishes information to a consumer reporting agency, based on information disclosed pursuant to section 1681g, 1681h, or 1681m of this title, or based on information disclosed by a user of a consumer report to or for a consumer against whom the user has taken adverse action, based in whole or in part on the report except as to false information furnished with malice or willful intent to injure such consumer.

[Pub. L. No. 90-321, tit. VI, § 610, *as added* Pub. L. No. 91-508, tit. VI, § 601, 84 Stat. 1131 (Oct. 26, 1970), *and amended* Pub. L. No. 104-208, div. A, tit. II, § 2408(e)(1), (e)(4), (e)(5)(B), 110 Stat. 3009–438, 3009–439 (Sept. 30, 1996)]

§ 1681i. Procedure in case of disputed accuracy [FCRA § 611]

(a) Reinvestigations of disputed information

(1) Reinvestigation required.—

(A) In general.—[35] Subject to subsection (f), if the completeness or accuracy of any item of information contained in a consumer's file at a consumer reporting agency is disputed by the consumer and the consumer notifies the agency directly, or indirectly through a reseller, of such dispute, the agency shall, free of charge, conduct a reasonable reinvestigation to determine whether the disputed information is inaccurate and record the current status of the disputed information, or delete the item from the file in accordance with paragraph (5), before the end of the 30-day period beginning on the date on which the agency receives the notice of the dispute from the consumer or reseller.

(B) Extension of period to reinvestigate.—Except as provided in subparagraph (C), the 30-day period described in subparagraph (A) may be extended for not more than 15 additional days if the consumer reporting agency receives information from the consumer during that 30-day period that is relevant to the reinvestigation.

(C) Limitations on extension of period to reinvestigate.—Subparagraph (B) shall not apply to any reinvestigation in which, during the 30-day period described in subparagraph (A), the information that is the subject of the reinvestigation is found to be inaccurate or incomplete or the consumer reporting agency determines that the information cannot be verified.

(2) Prompt notice of dispute to furnisher of information.—

(A) In general.—[36] Before the expiration of the 5-business-day period beginning on the date on which a consumer reporting agency receives notice of a dispute from any consumer or a reseller in accordance with paragraph (1), the agency shall provide notification of the dispute to any person who provided any item of information in dispute, at the address and in the manner established with the person. The notice shall include all relevant information regarding the dispute that the agency has received from the consumer or reseller.

(B) Provision of other information.—[37] The consumer reporting agency shall promptly provide to the person who provided the information in dispute all relevant information regarding the dispute that is received by the agency from the consumer or the reseller after the period referred to in subparagraph (A) and before the end of the period referred to in paragraph (1)(A).

(3) Determination that dispute is frivolous or irrelevant.—

(A) In general.—Notwithstanding paragraph (1), a consumer reporting agency may terminate a reinvestigation of information disputed by a consumer under that paragraph if the agency reasonably determines that the dispute by the consumer is frivolous or irrelevant, including by reason of a failure by a consumer to provide sufficient information to investigate the disputed information.

(B) Notice of determination.—Upon making any determination in accordance with subparagraph (A) that a dispute is frivolous or irrelevant, a consumer reporting agency shall notify the consumer of such determination not later than 5 business days after making such determination, by mail or, if authorized by the consumer for that purpose, by any other means available to the agency.

(C) Contents of notice.—A notice under subparagraph (B) shall include—

(i) the reasons for the determination under subparagraph (A); and

(ii) identification of any information required to investigate the disputed information, which may consist of a standardized form describing the general nature of such information.

(4) Consideration of consumer information.—In conducting any reinvestigation under paragraph (1) with respect to disputed information in the file of any consumer, the consumer reporting agency shall review and consider all relevant information submitted by the consumer in the period described in paragraph (1)(A) with respect to such disputed information.

(5) Treatment of inaccurate or unverifiable information.—

(A) In general.—[38] If, after any reinvestigation under paragraph (1) of any information disputed by a consumer, an item of the information is found to be inaccurate or incomplete or cannot be verified, the consumer reporting agency shall—

(i) promptly delete that item of information from the file of the consumer, or modify that item of information, as appropriate, based on the results of the reinvestigation; and

(ii) promptly notify the furnisher of that information that the information has been modified or deleted from the file of the consumer.

---

35 *Editor's Note*: The effective date for the FACTA amendments (Pub. L. No. 108-159 (Dec. 4, 2003)) to 15 U.S.C. § 1681i(a)(1)(A) is Dec. 1, 2004. *See* 12 C.F.R. § 222.1(c)(1)(i) and 16 C.F.R. § 602.1(c)(1)(i).

36 *Editor's Note*: The effective date for the FACTA amendments (Pub. L. No. 108-159 (Dec. 4, 2003)) to 15 U.S.C. § 1681i(a)(2)(A) is Dec. 1, 2004. *See* 12 C.F.R. § 222.1(c)(1)(i) and 16 C.F.R. § 602.1(c)(1)(i).

37 *Editor's Note*: The effective date for the FACTA amendments (Pub. L. No. 108-159 (Dec. 4, 2003)) to 15 U.S.C. § 1681i(a)(2)(B) is Dec. 1, 2004. *See* 12 C.F.R. § 222.1(c)(1)(i) and 16 C.F.R. § 602.1(c)(1)(i).

38 *Editor's Note*: The effective date for the FACTA amendments (Pub. L. No. 108-159 (Dec. 4, 2003)) to 15 U.S.C. § 1681i(a)(5)(A) is Dec. 1, 2004. *See* 12 C.F.R. § 222.1(c)(1)(i) and 16 C.F.R. § 602.1(c)(1)(i).

(B) Requirements relating to reinsertion of previously deleted material.—

(i) Certification of accuracy of information.—If any information is deleted from a consumer's file pursuant to subparagraph (A), the information may not be reinserted in the file by the consumer reporting agency unless the person who furnishes the information certifies that the information is complete and accurate.

(ii) Notice to consumer.—If any information that has been deleted from a consumer's file pursuant to subparagraph (A) is reinserted in the file, the consumer reporting agency shall notify the consumer of the reinsertion in writing not later than 5 business days after the reinsertion or, if authorized by the consumer for that purpose, by any other means available to the agency.

(iii) Additional information.—As part of, or in addition to, the notice under clause (ii), a consumer reporting agency shall provide to a consumer in writing not later than 5 business days after the date of the reinsertion—

(I) a statement that the disputed information has been reinserted;

(II) the business name and address of any furnisher of information contacted and the telephone number of such furnisher, if reasonably available, or of any furnisher of information that contacted the consumer reporting agency, in connection with the reinsertion of such information; and

(III) a notice that the consumer has the right to add a statement to the consumer's file disputing the accuracy or completeness of the disputed information.

(C) Procedures to prevent reappearance.—A consumer reporting agency shall maintain reasonable procedures designed to prevent the reappearance in a consumer's file, and in consumer reports on the consumer, of information that is deleted pursuant to this paragraph (other than information that is reinserted in accordance with subparagraph (B)(i)).

(D) Automated reinvestigation system.—Any consumer reporting agency that compiles and maintains files on consumers on a nationwide basis shall implement an automated system through which furnishers of information to that consumer reporting agency may report the results of a reinvestigation that finds incomplete or inaccurate information in a consumer's file to other such consumer reporting agencies.

(6) Notice of results of reinvestigation.—

(A) In general.—A consumer reporting agency shall provide written notice to a consumer of the results of a reinvestigation under this subsection not later than 5 business days after the completion of the reinvestigation, by mail or, if authorized by the consumer for that purpose, by other means available to the agency.

(B) Contents.—As part of, or in addition to, the notice under subparagraph (A), a consumer reporting agency shall provide to a consumer in writing before the expiration of the 5-day period referred to in subparagraph (A)—

(i) a statement that the reinvestigation is completed;

(ii) a consumer report that is based upon the consumer's file as that file is revised as a result of the reinvestigation;

(iii) a notice that, if requested by the consumer, a description of the procedure used to determine the accuracy and completeness of the information shall be provided to the consumer by the agency, including the business name and address of any furnisher of information contacted in connection with such information and the telephone number of such furnisher, if reasonably available;

(iv) a notice that the consumer has the right to add a statement to the consumer's file disputing the accuracy or completeness of the information; and

(v) a notice that the consumer has the right to request under subsection (d) that the consumer reporting agency furnish notifications under that subsection.

(7) Description of reinvestigation procedure.—A consumer reporting agency shall provide to a consumer a description referred to in paragraph (6)(B)(iii) by not later than 15 days after receiving a request from the consumer for that description.

(8) Expedited dispute resolution.—If a dispute regarding an item of information in a consumer's file at a consumer reporting agency is resolved in accordance with paragraph (5)(A) by the deletion of the disputed information by not later than 3 business days after the date on which the agency receives notice of the dispute from the consumer in accordance with paragraph (1)(A), then the agency shall not be required to comply with paragraphs (2), (6), and (7) with respect to that dispute if the agency—

(A) provides prompt notice of the deletion to the consumer by telephone;

(B) includes in that notice, or in a written notice that accompanies a confirmation and consumer report provided in accordance with subparagraph (C), a statement of the consumer's right to request under subsection (d) of this section that the agency furnish notifications under that subsection; and

(C) provides written confirmation of the deletion and a copy of a consumer report on the consumer that is based on the consumer's file after the deletion, not later than 5 business days after making the deletion.

(b) Statement of dispute

If the reinvestigation does not resolve the dispute, the consumer may file a brief statement setting forth the nature of the dispute. The consumer reporting agency may limit such statements to not more than one hundred words if it provides the consumer with assistance in writing a clear summary of the dispute.

(c) Notification of consumer dispute in subsequent consumer reports

Whenever a statement of a dispute is filed, unless there is reasonable grounds to believe that it is frivolous or irrelevant, the consumer reporting agency shall, in any subsequent consumer report containing the information in question, clearly note that it is disputed by the consumer and provide either the consumer's statement or a clear and accurate codification or summary thereof.

(d) Notification of deletion of disputed information

Following any deletion of information which is found to be inaccurate or whose accuracy can no longer be verified or any notation as to disputed information, the consumer reporting agency shall, at the request of the consumer, furnish notification that the item has been deleted or the statement, codification or summary pursuant to subsection (b) or (c) of this section to any person specifically designated by the consumer who has within two years prior thereto received a consumer report for employment purposes, or within six months prior thereto received a consumer report for any other purpose, which contained the deleted or disputed information.

(e) Treatment of complaints and report to Congress.—[39]
  (1) In general.—The Commission shall—
    (A) compile all complaints that it receives that a file of a consumer that is maintained by a consumer reporting agency described in section 1681a(p) contains incomplete or inaccurate information, with respect to which, the consumer appears to have disputed the completeness or accuracy with the consumer reporting agency or otherwise utilized the procedures provided by subsection (a); and
    (B) transmit each such complaint to each consumer reporting agency involved.
  (2) Exclusion.—Complaints received or obtained by the Commission pursuant to its investigative authority under the Federal Trade Commission Act shall not be subject to paragraph (1).
  (3) Agency responsibilities.—Each consumer reporting agency described in section 1681a(p) that receives a complaint transmitted by the Commission pursuant to paragraph (1) shall—
    (A) review each such complaint to determine whether all legal obligations imposed on the consumer reporting agency under this title (including any obligation imposed by an applicable court or administrative order) have been met with respect to the subject matter of the complaint;
    (B) provide reports on a regular basis to the Commission regarding the determinations of and actions taken by the consumer reporting agency, if any, in connection with its review of such complaints; and
    (C) maintain, for a reasonable time period, records regarding the disposition of each such complaint that is sufficient to demonstrate compliance with this subsection.
  (4) Rulemaking authority.—The Commission may prescribe regulations, as appropriate to implement this subsection.
  (5) Annual report.—The Commission shall submit to the Committee on Banking, Housing, and Urban Affairs of the Senate and the Committee on Financial Services of the House of Representatives an annual report regarding information gathered by the Commission under this subsection.

(f) Reinvestigation requirement applicable to resellers.—[40]
  (1) Exemption from general reinvestigation requirement.—Except as provided in paragraph (2), a reseller shall be exempt from the requirements of this section.
  (2) Action required upon receiving notice of a dispute.—If a reseller receives a notice from a consumer of a dispute concerning the completeness or accuracy of any item of information contained in a consumer report on such consumer produced by the reseller, the reseller shall, within 5 business days of receiving the notice, and free of charge—
    (A) determine whether the item of information is incomplete or inaccurate as a result of an act or omission of the reseller; and
    (B) if—
      (i) the reseller determines that the item of information is incomplete or inaccurate as a result of an act or omission of the reseller, not later than 20 days after receiving the notice, correct the information in the consumer report or delete it; or
      (ii) if the reseller determines that the item of information is not incomplete or inaccurate as a result of an act or omission of the reseller, convey the notice of the dispute, together with all relevant information provided by the consumer, to each consumer reporting agency that provided the reseller with the information that is the subject of the dispute, using an address or a notification mechanism specified by the consumer reporting agency for such notices.
  (3) Responsibility of consumer reporting agency to notify consumer through reseller.—Upon the completion of a reinvestigation under this section of a dispute concerning the completeness or accuracy of any information in the file of a consumer by a consumer reporting agency that received notice of the dispute from a reseller under paragraph (2)—
    (A) the notice by the consumer reporting agency under paragraph (6), (7), or (8) of subsection (a) shall be provided to the reseller in lieu of the consumer; and
    (B) the reseller shall immediately reconvey such notice to the consumer, including any notice of a deletion by telephone in the manner required under paragraph (8)(A).
  (4) Reseller reinvestigations.—No provision of this subsection shall be construed as prohibiting a reseller from conducting a reinvestigation of a consumer dispute directly.

[Pub. L. No. 90-321, tit. VI, § 611, *as added* Pub. L. No. 91-508, tit. VI, § 601, 84 Stat. 1132 (Oct. 26, 1970), *and amended* Pub. L. No. 104-208, div. A, tit. II, § 2409(a), (b), 110 Stat. 3009–439, 3009–442 (Sept. 30, 1996); Pub. L. No. 105-347, § 6(5), 112 Stat. 3211 (Nov. 2, 1998); Pub. L. No. 108-159, tit. III, §§ 313(a), 314(a), 316, 317, 117 Stat. 1994, 1995, 1996, 1998 (Dec. 4, 2003)]

§ 1681j. Charges for certain disclosures [FCRA § 612]

(a) Free annual disclosure.—
  (1) Nationwide consumer reporting agencies.—
    (A) In general.—All consumer reporting agencies described in subsections (p) and (w) of section 1681a shall make all disclosures pursuant to section 1681g once during any 12-month period upon request of the consumer and without charge to the consumer.
    (B) Centralized source.—Subparagraph (A) shall apply with respect to a consumer reporting agency described in section 1681a(p) only if the request from the consumer is made using the centralized source established for such purpose in accordance with section 211(c) of the Fair and Accurate Credit Transactions Act of 2003.
    (C) Nationwide specialty consumer reporting agency.—
      (i) In general.—The Commission shall prescribe regulations applicable to each consumer reporting agency described in section 1681a(w) to require the establishment of a streamlined process for consumers to request consumer reports under subparagraph (A), which shall include, at a

---

[39] *Editor's Note*: The effective date for the FACTA amendments (Pub. L. No. 108-159 (Dec. 4, 2003)) to 15 U.S.C. § 1681i(e) is Mar. 31, 2004. *See* 12 C.F.R. § 222.1(c)(1)(i) and 16 C.F.R. § 602.1(c)(1)(i).

[40] *Editor's Note*: The effective date for the FACTA amendments (Pub. L. No. 108-159 (Dec. 4, 2003)) to 15 U.S.C. § 1681i(f) is Dec. 1, 2004. *See* 12 C.F.R. § 222.1(c)(1)(i) and 16 C.F.R. § 602.1(c)(1)(i).

minimum, the establishment by each such agency of a toll-free telephone number for such requests.

(ii) **Considerations.**—In prescribing regulations under clause (i), the Commission shall consider—

(I) the significant demands that may be placed on consumer reporting agencies in providing such consumer reports;

(II) appropriate means to ensure that consumer reporting agencies can satisfactorily meet those demands, including the efficacy of a system of staggering the availability to consumers of such consumer reports; and

(III) the ease by which consumers should be able to contact consumer reporting agencies with respect to access to such consumer reports.

(iii) **Date of issuance.**—The Commission shall issue the regulations required by this subparagraph in final form not later than 6 months after the date of enactment of the Fair and Accurate Credit Transactions Act of 2003.

(iv) **Consideration of ability to comply.**—The regulations of the Commission under this subparagraph shall establish an effective date by which each nationwide specialty consumer reporting agency (as defined in section 1681a(w)) shall be required to comply with subsection (a), which effective date—

(I) shall be established after consideration of the ability of each nationwide specialty consumer reporting agency to comply with subsection (a); and

(II) shall be not later than 6 months after the date on which such regulations are issued in final form (or such additional period not to exceed 3 months, as the Commission determines appropriate).

(2) **Timing.**—A consumer reporting agency shall provide a consumer report under paragraph (1) not later than 15 days after the date on which the request is received under paragraph (1).

(3) **Reinvestigations.**—Notwithstanding the time periods specified in section 1681i(a)(1), a reinvestigation under that section by a consumer reporting agency upon a request of a consumer that is made after receiving a consumer report under this subsection shall be completed not later than 45 days after the date on which the request is received.

(4) **Exception for first 12 months of operation.**—This subsection shall not apply to a consumer reporting agency that has not been furnishing consumer reports to third parties on a continuing basis during the 12-month period preceding a request under paragraph (1), with respect to consumers residing nationwide.

(b) Free disclosure after adverse notice to consumer

Each consumer reporting agency that maintains a file on a consumer shall make all disclosures pursuant to section 1681g of this title without charge to the consumer if, not later than 60 days after receipt by such consumer of a notification pursuant to section 1681m of this title, or of a notification from a debt collection agency affiliated with that consumer reporting agency stating that the consumer's credit rating may be or has been adversely affected, the consumer makes a request under section 1681g of this title.

(c) Free disclosure under certain other circumstances

Upon the request of the consumer, a consumer reporting agency shall make all disclosures pursuant to section 1681g of this title once during any 12-month period without charge to that consumer if the consumer certifies in writing that the consumer—

(1) is unemployed and intends to apply for employment in the 60-day period beginning on the date on which the certification is made;

(2) is a recipient of public welfare assistance; or

(3) has reason to believe that the file on the consumer at the agency contains inaccurate information due to fraud.

(d) Free disclosures in connection with fraud alerts.—Upon the request of a consumer, a consumer reporting agency described in section 1681a(p) shall make all disclosures pursuant to section 1681g without charge to the consumer, as provided in subsections (a)(2) and (b)(2) of section 1681c-1, as applicable.

(e) Other charges prohibited

A consumer reporting agency shall not impose any charge on a consumer for providing any notification required by this subchapter or making any disclosure required by this subchapter, except as authorized by subsection (f) of this section.

(f) Reasonable charges allowed for certain disclosures.

(1) **In general.**—In the case of a request from a consumer other than a request that is covered by any of subsections (a) through (d), a consumer reporting agency may impose a reasonable charge on a consumer—

(A) for making a disclosure to the consumer pursuant to section 1681g of this title, which charge—

(i) shall not exceed $8;[41] and

(ii) shall be indicated to the consumer before making the disclosure; and

(B) for furnishing, pursuant to section 1681i(d) of this title, following a reinvestigation under section 1681i(a) of this title, a statement, codification, or summary to a person designated by the consumer under that section after the 30-day period beginning on the date of notification of the consumer under paragraph (6) or (8) of section 1681i(a) of this title with respect to the reinvestigation, which charge—

(i) shall not exceed the charge that the agency would impose on each designated recipient for a consumer report; and

(ii) shall be indicated to the consumer before furnishing such information.

(2) **Modification of amount.**—The Federal Trade Commission shall increase the amount referred to in paragraph (1)(A)(i) on January 1 of each year, based proportionally on changes in the Consumer Price Index, with fractional changes rounded to the nearest fifty cents.

[Pub. L. No. 90-321, tit. VI, § 612, *as added* Pub. L. No. 91-508, tit. VI, § 601, 84 Stat. 1132 (Oct. 26, 1970), *and amended* Pub. L. No. 104-208, div. A, tit. II, § 2410, 110 Stat. 3009–442 (Sept. 30, 1996); Pub. L. No. 108-159, tit. II, § 211(a), 117 Stat. 1968 (Dec. 4, 2003)]

---

41 Pursuant to § 1681j(d)(2), the Federal Trade Commission increased the maximum allowable charge to $9.50, effective January 1, 2005. *See* 69 Fed. Reg. 76767 (Dec. 22, 2004).

§ 1681k. Public record information for employment purposes [FCRA § 613]

(a) In General.—

A consumer reporting agency which furnishes a consumer report for employment purposes and which for that purpose compiles and reports items of information on consumers which are matters of public record and are likely to have an adverse effect upon a consumer's ability to obtain employment shall—

(1) at the time such public record information is reported to the user of such consumer report, notify the consumer of the fact that public record information is being reported by the consumer reporting agency, together with the name and address of the person to whom such information is being reported; or

(2) maintain strict procedures designed to insure that whenever public record information which is likely to have an adverse effect on a consumer's ability to obtain employment is reported it is complete and up to date. For purposes of this paragraph, items of public record relating to arrests, indictments, convictions, suits, tax liens, and outstanding judgments shall be considered up to date if the current public record status of the item at the time of the report is reported.

(b) Exemption for National Security Investigations.—Subsection (a) does not apply in the case of an agency or department of the United States Government that seeks to obtain and use a consumer report for employment purposes, if the head of the agency or department makes a written finding as prescribed under section 1681b(b)(4)(A) of this title.

[Pub. L. No. 90-321, tit. VI, § 613, *as added* Pub. L. No. 91-508, tit. VI, § 601, 84 Stat. 1133 (Oct. 26, 1970), *and amended* Pub. L. No. 105-347, § 4(b), 112 Stat. 3210 (Nov. 2, 1998)]

§ 1681*l*. Restrictions on investigative consumer reports [FCRA § 614]

Whenever a consumer reporting agency prepares an investigative consumer report, no adverse information in the consumer report (other than information which is a matter of public record) may be included in a subsequent consumer report unless such adverse information has been verified in the process of making such subsequent consumer report, or the adverse information was received within the three-month period preceding the date the subsequent report is furnished.

[Pub. L. No. 90-321, tit. VI, § 614, *as added* Pub. L. No. 91-508, tit. VI, § 601, 84 Stat. 1133 (Oct. 26, 1970)]

§ 1681m. Requirements on users of consumer reports [FCRA § 615]

(a) Duties of users taking adverse actions on the basis of information contained in consumer reports

If any person takes any adverse action with respect to any consumer that is based in whole or in part on any information contained in a consumer report, the person shall—

(1) provide oral, written, or electronic notice of the adverse action to the consumer;

(2) provide to the consumer orally, in writing, or electronically—

(A) the name, address, and telephone number of the consumer reporting agency (including a toll-free telephone number established by the agency if the agency compiles and maintains files on consumers on a nationwide basis) that furnished the report to the person; and

(B) a statement that the consumer reporting agency did not make the decision to take the adverse action and is unable to provide the consumer the specific reasons why the adverse action was taken; and

(3) provide to the consumer an oral, written, or electronic notice of the consumer's right—

(A) to obtain, under section 1681j of this title, a free copy of a consumer report on the consumer from the consumer reporting agency referred to in paragraph (2), which notice shall include an indication of the 60-day period under that section for obtaining such a copy; and

(B) to dispute, under section 1681i of this title, with a consumer reporting agency the accuracy or completeness of any information in a consumer report furnished by the agency.

(b) Adverse action based on information obtained from third parties other than consumer reporting agencies.

(1) In general.—Whenever credit for personal, family, or household purposes involving a consumer is denied or the charge for such credit is increased either wholly or partly because of information obtained from a person other than a consumer reporting agency bearing upon the consumer's credit worthiness, credit standing, credit capacity, character, general reputation, personal characteristics, or mode of living, the user of such information shall, within a reasonable period of time, upon the consumer's written request for the reasons for such adverse action received within sixty days after learning of such adverse action, disclose the nature of the information to the consumer. The user of such information shall clearly and accurately disclose to the consumer his right to make such written request at the time such adverse action is communicated to the consumer.

(2) Duties of person taking certain actions based on information provided by affiliate.—

(A) Duties, generally.—If a person takes an action described in subparagraph (B) with respect to a consumer, based in whole or in part on information described in subparagraph (C), the person shall—

(i) notify the consumer of the action, including a statement that the consumer may obtain the information in accordance with clause (ii); and

(ii) upon a written request from the consumer received within 60 days after transmittal of the notice required by clause (i), disclose to the consumer the nature of the information upon which the action is based by not later than 30 days after receipt of the request.

(B) Action described.—An action referred to in subparagraph (A) is an adverse action described in section 1681a(k)(1)(A) of this title, taken in connection with a transaction initiated by the consumer, or any adverse action described in clause (i) or (ii) of section 1681a(k)(1)(B) of this title.

(C) Information described.—Information referred to in subparagraph (A)—
  (i) except as provided in clause (ii), is information that—
    (I) is furnished to the person taking the action by a person related by common ownership or affiliated by common corporate control to the person taking the action; and
    (II) bears on the credit worthiness, credit standing, credit capacity, character, general reputation, personal characteristics, or mode of living of the consumer; and
  (ii) does not include—
    (I) information solely as to transactions or experiences between the consumer and the person furnishing the information; or
    (II) information in a consumer report.

(c) Reasonable procedures to assure compliance

No person shall be held liable for any violation of this section if he shows by a preponderance of the evidence that at the time of the alleged violation he maintained reasonable procedures to assure compliance with the provisions of this section.

(d) Duties of users making written credit or insurance solicitations on the basis of information contained in consumer files
  (1) In general.—Any person who uses a consumer report on any consumer in connection with any credit or insurance transaction that is not initiated by the consumer, that is provided to that person under section 1681b(c)(1)(B) of this title, shall provide with each written solicitation made to the consumer regarding the transaction a clear and conspicuous statement that—
    (A) information contained in the consumer's consumer report was used in connection with the transaction;
    (B) the consumer received the offer of credit or insurance because the consumer satisfied the criteria for credit worthiness or insurability under which the consumer was selected for the offer;
    (C) if applicable, the credit or insurance may not be extended if, after the consumer responds to the offer, the consumer does not meet the criteria used to select the consumer for the offer or any applicable criteria bearing on credit worthiness or insurability or does not furnish any required collateral;
    (D) the consumer has a right to prohibit information contained in the consumer's file with any consumer reporting agency from being used in connection with any credit or insurance transaction that is not initiated by the consumer; and
    (E) the consumer may exercise the right referred to in subparagraph (D) by notifying a notification system established under section 1681b(e) of this title.
  (2) Disclosure of address and telephone number; format.—A statement under paragraph (1) shall—
    (A) include the address and toll-free telephone number of the appropriate notification system established under section 1681b(e); and
    (B) be presented in such format and in such type size and manner as to be simple and easy to understand, as established by the Commission, by rule, in consultation with the Federal banking agencies and the National Credit Union Administration.

  (3) Maintaining criteria on file.—A person who makes an offer of credit or insurance to a consumer under a credit or insurance transaction described in paragraph (1) shall maintain on file the criteria used to select the consumer to receive the offer, all criteria bearing on credit worthiness or insurability, as applicable, that are the basis for determining whether or not to extend credit or insurance pursuant to the offer, and any requirement for the furnishing of collateral as a condition of the extension of credit or insurance, until the expiration of the 3-year period beginning on the date on which the offer is made to the consumer.
  (4) Authority of federal agencies regarding unfair or deceptive acts or practices not affected.—This section is not intended to affect the authority of any Federal or State agency to enforce a prohibition against unfair or deceptive acts or practices, including the making of false or misleading statements in connection with a credit or insurance transaction that is not initiated by the consumer.

(e) Red Flag Guidelines and Regulations Required.—[42]
  (1) Guidelines.—The Federal banking agencies, the National Credit Union Administration, and the Commission shall jointly, with respect to the entities that are subject to their respective enforcement authority under section 1681s—
    (A) establish and maintain guidelines for use by each financial institution and each creditor regarding identity theft with respect to account holders at, or customers of, such entities, and update such guidelines as often as necessary;
    (B) prescribe regulations requiring each financial institution and each creditor to establish reasonable policies and procedures for implementing the guidelines established pursuant to subparagraph (A), to identify possible risks to account holders or customers or to the safety and soundness of the institution or customers; and
    (C) prescribe regulations applicable to card issuers to ensure that, if a card issuer receives notification of a change of address for an existing account, and within a short period of time (during at least the first 30 days after such notification is received) receives a request for an additional or replacement card for the same account, the card issuer may not issue the additional or replacement card, unless the card issuer, in accordance with reasonable policies and procedures—
      (i) notifies the cardholder of the request at the former address of the cardholder and provides to the cardholder a means of promptly reporting incorrect address changes;
      (ii) notifies the cardholder of the request by such other means of communication as the cardholder and the card issuer previously agreed to; or
      (iii) uses other means of assessing the validity of the change of address, in accordance with reasonable policies and procedures established by the card issuer in accordance with the regulations prescribed under subparagraph (B).
  (2) Criteria.—
    (A) In general.—In developing the guidelines required by paragraph (1)(A), the agencies described in paragraph (1)

---

[42] *Editor's Note*: The effective date for the FACTA amendments (Pub. L. No. 108-159 (Dec. 4, 2003)) to 15 U.S.C. § 1681m(e) is Dec. 1, 2004. *See* 12 C.F.R. § 222.1(c)(1)(i) and 16 C.F.R. § 602.1(c)(1)(i).

shall identify patterns, practices, and specific forms of activity that indicate the possible existence of identity theft.

(B) Inactive accounts.—In developing the guidelines required by paragraph (1)(A), the agencies described in paragraph (1) shall consider including reasonable guidelines providing that when a transaction occurs with respect to a credit or deposit account that has been inactive for more than 2 years, the creditor or financial institution shall follow reasonable policies and procedures that provide for notice to be given to a consumer in a manner reasonably designed to reduce the likelihood of identity theft with respect to such account.

(3) Consistency with verification requirements.—Guidelines established pursuant to paragraph (1) shall not be inconsistent with the policies and procedures required under section 5318(l) of title 31, United States Code.

(f) Prohibition on Sale or Transfer of Debt Caused by Identity Theft.—[43]

(1) In general.—No person shall sell, transfer for consideration, or place for collection a debt that such person has been notified under section 1681c-2 has resulted from identity theft.

(2) Applicability.—The prohibitions of this subsection shall apply to all persons collecting a debt described in paragraph (1) after the date of a notification under paragraph (1).

(3) Rule of construction.—Nothing in this subsection shall be construed to prohibit—

(A) the repurchase of a debt in any case in which the assignee of the debt requires such repurchase because the debt has resulted from identity theft;

(B) the securitization of a debt or the pledging of a portfolio of debt as collateral in connection with a borrowing; or

(C) the transfer of debt as a result of a merger, acquisition, purchase and assumption transaction, or transfer of substantially all of the assets of an entity.

(g) Debt Collector Communications Concerning Identity Theft.—[44] If a person acting as a debt collector (as that term is defined in title VIII) on behalf of a third party that is a creditor or other user of a consumer report is notified that any information relating to a debt that the person is attempting to collect may be fraudulent or may be the result of identity theft, that person shall—

(1) notify the third party that the information may be fraudulent or may be the result of identity theft; and

(2) upon request of the consumer to whom the debt purportedly relates, provide to the consumer all information to which the consumer would otherwise be entitled if the consumer were not a victim of identity theft, but wished to dispute the debt under provisions of law applicable to that person.

(h)[45] **Duties of users in certain credit transactions.**—

(1) In general.—Subject to rules prescribed as provided in paragraph (6), if any person uses a consumer report in connection with an application for, or a grant, extension, or other provision of, credit on material terms that are materially less favorable than the most favorable terms available to a substantial proportion of consumers from or through that person, based in whole or in part on a consumer report, the person shall provide an oral, written, or electronic notice to the consumer in the form and manner required by regulations prescribed in accordance with this subsection.

(2) Timing.—The notice required under paragraph (1) may be provided at the time of an application for, or a grant, extension, or other provision of, credit or the time of communication of an approval of an application for, or grant, extension, or other provision of, credit, except as provided in the regulations prescribed under paragraph (6).

(3) Exceptions.—No notice shall be required from a person under this subsection if—

(A) the consumer applied for specific material terms and was granted those terms, unless those terms were initially specified by the person after the transaction was initiated by the consumer and after the person obtained a consumer report; or

(B) the person has provided or will provide a notice to the consumer under subsection (a) in connection with the transaction.

(4) Other notice not sufficient.—A person that is required to provide a notice under subsection (a) cannot meet that requirement by providing a notice under this subsection.

(5) Content and delivery of notice.—A notice under this subsection shall, at a minimum—

(A) include a statement informing the consumer that the terms offered to the consumer are set based on information from a consumer report;

(B) identify the consumer reporting agency furnishing the report;

(C) include a statement informing the consumer that the consumer may obtain a copy of a consumer report from that consumer reporting agency without charge; and

(D) include the contact information specified by that consumer reporting agency for obtaining such consumer reports (including a toll-free telephone number established by the agency in the case of a consumer reporting agency described in section 1681a(p)).

(6) Rulemaking.—

(A) **Rules required.**—The Commission and the Board shall jointly prescribe rules.

(B) **Content.**—Rules required by subparagraph (A) shall address, but are not limited to—

(i) the form, content, time, and manner of delivery of any notice under this subsection;

(ii) clarification of the meaning of terms used in this subsection, including what credit terms are material, and when credit terms are materially less favorable;

(iii) exceptions to the notice requirement under this sub-

---

43 *Editor's Note*: The effective date for the FACTA amendments (Pub. L. No. 108-159 (Dec. 4, 2003)) to 15 U.S.C. § 1681m(f) is Dec. 1, 2004. *See* 12 C.F.R. § 222.1(c)(1)(i) and 16 C.F.R. § 602.1(c)(1)(i).

44 *Editor's Note*: The effective date for the FACTA amendments (Pub. L. No. 108-159 (Dec. 4, 2003)) to 15 U.S.C. § 1681m(g) is Dec. 1, 2004. *See* 12 C.F.R. § 222.1(c)(1)(i) and 16 C.F.R. § 602.1(c)(1)(i).

45 *Editor's Note*: The effective date for the FACTA amendments (Pub. L. No. 108-159 (Dec. 4, 2003)) to 15 U.S.C. § 1681m(h) is Dec. 1, 2004. *See* 12 C.F.R. § 222.1(c)(1)(i) and 16 C.F.R. § 602.1(c)(1)(i).

section for classes of persons or transactions regarding which the agencies determine that notice would not significantly benefit consumers;

(iv) a model notice that may be used to comply with this subsection; and

(v) the timing of the notice required under paragraph (1), including the circumstances under which the notice must be provided after the terms offered to the consumer were set based on information from a consumer report.

(7) **Compliance.**—A person shall not be liable for failure to perform the duties required by this section if, at the time of the failure, the person maintained reasonable policies and procedures to comply with this section.

(8) **Enforcement.**—

(A) **No civil actions.**—Sections 1681n and 1681o shall not apply to any failure by any person to comply with this section.

(B) **Administrative enforcement.**—This section shall be enforced exclusively under section 1681s by the Federal agencies and officials identified in that section.

[Pub. L. No. 90-321, tit. VI, § 615, *as added* Pub. L. No. 91-508, tit. VI, § 601, 84 Stat. 1133 (Oct. 26, 1970), *and amended* Pub. L. No. 104-208, div. A, tit. II, § 2411(a), (b), (d), (e), 110 Stat. 3009–443, 3009–444, 3009–445 (Sept. 30, 1996); Pub. L. No. 108-159, tit. I, §§ 114, 154(b), 155, tit. II, § 213(a), tit. III, § 311(a), tit. VIII, § 811(h), 117 Stat. 1960, 1967, 1978, 1988, 2012 (Dec. 4, 2003)]

§ 1681n. Civil liability for willful noncompliance [FCRA § 616]

(a) In general

Any person who willfully fails to comply with any requirement imposed under this subchapter with respect to any consumer is liable to that consumer in an amount equal to the sum of—

(1)(A) any actual damages sustained by the consumer as a result of the failure or damages of not less than $100 and not more than $1,000; or

(B) in the case of liability of a natural person for obtaining a consumer report under false pretenses or knowingly without a permissible purpose, actual damages sustained by the consumer as a result of the failure or $1,000, whichever is greater;

(2) such amount of punitive damages as the court may allow; and

(3) in the case of any successful action to enforce any liability under this section, the costs of the action together with reasonable attorney's fees as determined by the court.

(b) Civil liability for knowing noncompliance

Any person who obtains a consumer report from a consumer reporting agency under false pretenses or knowingly without a permissible purpose shall be liable to the consumer reporting agency for actual damages sustained by the consumer reporting agency or $1,000, whichever is greater.

(c) Attorney's fees

Upon a finding by the court that an unsuccessful pleading, motion, or other paper filed in connection with an action under this section was filed in bad faith or for purposes of harassment, the court shall award to the prevailing party attorney's fees reasonable in relation to the work expended in responding to the pleading, motion, or other paper.

[Pub. L. No. 90-321, tit. VI, § 616, *as added* Pub. L. No. 91-508, tit. VI, § 601, 84 Stat. 1134 (Oct. 26, 1970), *and amended* Pub. L. No. 104-208, div. A, tit. II, § 2412(a)–(c), (e)(1), 110 Stat. 3009–446 (Sept. 30, 1996)]

§ 1681o. Civil liability for negligent noncompliance [FCRA § 617]

(a) In general

Any person who is negligent in failing to comply with any requirement imposed under this subchapter with respect to any consumer is liable to that consumer in an amount equal to the sum of—

(1) any actual damages sustained by the consumer as a result of the failure; and[46]

(2) in the case of any successful action to enforce any liability under this section, the costs of the action together with reasonable attorney's fees as determined by the court.

(b) Attorney's fees

On a finding by the court that an unsuccessful pleading, motion, or other paper filed in connection with an action under this section was filed in bad faith or for purposes of harassment, the court shall award to the prevailing party attorney's fees reasonable in relation to the work expended in responding to the pleading, motion, or other paper.

[Pub. L. No. 90-321, tit. VI, § 617, *as added* Pub. L. No. 91-508, tit. VI, § 601, 84 Stat. 1134 (Oct. 26, 1970), *and amended* Pub. L. No. 104-208, div. A, tit. II, § 2412(d), (e)(2), 110 Stat. 3009–446 (Sept. 30, 1996); Pub. L. No. 108-159, tit. VIII, § 811(e), 117 Stat. 2012 (Dec. 4, 2003)]

§ 1681p. Jurisdiction of courts; limitation of actions [FCRA § 618]

An action to enforce any liability created under this title may be brought in any appropriate United States district court, without regard to the amount in controversy, or in any other court of competent jurisdiction, not later than the earlier of—[47]

(1) 2 years after the date of discovery by the plaintiff of the violation that is the basis for such liability; or

(2) 5 years after the date on which the violation that is the basis for such liability occurs.

---

46 *Editor's Note*: The effective date for the FACTA amendments (Pub. L. No. 108-159 (Dec. 4, 2003)) to 15 U.S.C. § 1681o(a)(1) is Mar. 31, 2004. *See* 12 C.F.R. § 222.1(c)(1)(i) and 16 C.F.R. § 602.1(c)(1)(i).

47 *Editor's Note*: The effective date for the FACTA amendments (Pub. L. No. 108-159 (Dec. 4, 2003)) to 15 U.S.C. § 1681p is Mar. 31, 2004. *See* 12 C.F.R. § 222.1(c)(1)(i) and 16 C.F.R. § 602.1(c)(1)(i).

[Pub. L. No. 90-321, tit. VI, § 618, *as added* Pub. L. No. 91-508, tit. VI, § 601, 84 Stat. 1134 (Oct. 26, 1970), *and amended* Pub. L. No. 108-159, tit. I, § 156, 117 Stat. 1968 (Dec. 4, 2003)]

§ 1681q. Obtaining information under false pretenses [FCRA § 619]

Any person who knowingly and willfully obtains information on a consumer from a consumer reporting agency under false pretenses shall be fined under Title 18, imprisoned for not more than 2 years, or both.

[Pub. L. No. 90-321, tit. VI, § 619, *as added* Pub. L. No. 91-508, tit. VI, § 601, 84 Stat. 1134 (Oct. 26, 1970), *and amended* Pub. L. No. 104-208, div. A, tit. II, § 2415(a), 110 Stat. 3009–450 (Sept. 30, 1996)]

§ 1681r. Unauthorized disclosures by officers or employees [FCRA § 620]

Any officer or employee of a consumer reporting agency who knowingly and willfully provides information concerning an individual from the agency's files to a person not authorized to receive that information shall be fined under Title 18, imprisoned for not more than 2 years, or both.

[Pub. L. No. 90-321, tit. VI, § 620, *as added* Pub. L. No. 91-508, tit. VI, § 601, 84 Stat. 1134 (Oct. 26, 1970), *and amended* Pub. L. No. 104-208, div. A, tit. II, § 2415(b), 110 Stat. 3009–450 (Sept. 30, 1996)]

§ 1681s. Administrative enforcement [FCRA § 621]

(a) Federal Trade Commission; powers

(1) Enforcement by Federal Trade Commission. Compliance with the requirements imposed under this subchapter shall be enforced under the Federal Trade Commission Act [15 U.S.C. 41 et seq.] by the Federal Trade Commission with respect to consumer reporting agencies and all other persons subject thereto, except to the extent that enforcement of the requirements imposed under this subchapter is specifically committed to some other government agency under subsection (b) hereof. For the purpose of the exercise by the Federal Trade Commission of its functions and powers under the Federal Trade Commission Act, a violation of any requirement or prohibition imposed under this subchapter shall constitute an unfair or deceptive act or practice in commerce in violation of section 5(a) of the Federal Trade Commission Act [15 U.S.C. 45(a)] and shall be subject to enforcement by the Federal Trade Commission under section 5(b) thereof [15 U.S.C. 45(b)] with respect to any consumer reporting agency or person subject to enforcement by the Federal Trade Commission pursuant to this subsection, irrespective of whether that person is engaged in commerce or meets any other jurisdictional tests in the Federal Trade Commission Act. The Federal Trade Commission shall have such procedural, investigative, and enforcement powers, including the power to issue procedural rules in enforcing compliance with the requirements imposed under this subchapter and to require the filing of reports, the production of documents, and the appearance of witnesses as though the applicable terms and conditions of the Federal Trade Commission Act were part of this subchapter. Any person violating any of the provisions of this subchapter shall be subject to the penalties and entitled to the privileges and immunities provided in the Federal Trade Commission Act as though the applicable terms and provisions thereof were part of this subchapter.

(2)(A) In the event of a knowing violation, which constitutes a pattern or practice of violations of this subchapter, the Commission may commence a civil action to recover a civil penalty in a district court of the United States against any person that violates this subchapter. In such action, such person shall be liable for a civil penalty of not more than $2,500 per violation.

(B) In determining the amount of a civil penalty under subparagraph (A), the court shall take into account the degree of culpability, any history of prior such conduct, ability to pay, effect on ability to continue to do business, and such other matters as justice may require.

(3) Notwithstanding paragraph (2), a court may not impose any civil penalty on a person for a violation of section 1681s-2(a)(1) of this title unless the person has been enjoined from committing the violation, or ordered not to commit the violation, in an action or proceeding brought by or on behalf of the Federal Trade Commission, and has violated the injunction or order, and the court may not impose any civil penalty for any violation occurring before the date of the violation of the injunction or order.

(4) Neither the Commission nor any other agency referred to in subsection (b) may prescribe trade regulation rules or other regulations with respect to this subchapter.

(b) Enforcement by other agencies

Compliance with the requirements imposed under this subchapter with respect to consumer reporting agencies, persons who use consumer reports from such agencies, persons who furnish information to such agencies, and users of information that are subject to subsection (d) of section 1681m of this title shall be enforced under—

(1) section 8 of the Federal Deposit Insurance Act [12 U.S.C. § 1818], in the case of—

(A) national banks, and Federal branches and Federal agencies of foreign banks, by the Office of the Comptroller of the Currency;

(B) member banks of the Federal Reserve System (other than national banks), branches and agencies of foreign banks (other than Federal branches, Federal agencies, and insured State branches of foreign banks), commercial lending companies owned or controlled by foreign banks, and organizations operating under section 25 or 25A of the Federal Reserve Act [12 U.S.C. §§ 601 et seq., 611 et seq.], by the Board of Governors of the Federal Reserve System; and[48]

(C) banks insured by the Federal Deposit Insurance Corporation (other than members of the Federal Reserve System)

---

[48] *Editor's Note*: The effective date for the FACTA amendments (Pub. L. No. 108-159 Dec. 4, 2003)) to 15 U.S.C. § 1681s(b)(1)(B) is Mar. 31, 2004. *See* 12 C.F.R. § 222.1(c)(1)(i) and 16 C.F.R. § 602.1(c)(1)(i).

and insured State branches of foreign banks, by the Board of Directors of the Federal Deposit Insurance Corporation;

(2) Section 8 of the Federal Deposit Insurance Act [12 U.S.C. § 1818], by the Director of the Office of Thrift Supervision, in the case of a savings association the deposits of which are insured by the Federal Deposit Insurance Corporation.

(3) the Federal Credit Union Act [12 U.S.C. 1751 et seq.], by the Administrator of the National Credit Union Administration with respect to any Federal credit union;

(4) subtitle IV of Title 49, by the Secretary of Transportation, with respect to all carriers subject to the jurisdiction of the Surface Transportation Board;

(5) part A of subtitle VII of title 49, by the Secretary of Transportation with respect to any air carrier or foreign air carrier subject to that part; and

(6) the Packers and Stockyards Act, 1921 [7 U.S.C. 181 et seq.] (except as provided in section 406 of that Act [7 U.S.C. 226, 227]), by the Secretary of Agriculture with respect to any activities subject to that Act.

The terms used in paragraph (1) that are not defined in this subchapter or otherwise defined in section 3(s) of the Federal Deposit Insurance Act (12 U.S.C. 1813(s)) shall have the meaning given to them in section 1(b) of the International Banking Act of 1978 (12 U.S.C. 3101).

(c) State action for violations

   (1) Authority of States.—In addition to such other remedies as are provided under State law, if the chief law enforcement officer of a State, or an official or agency designated by a State, has reason to believe that any person has violated or is violating this subchapter, the State—

   (A) may bring an action to enjoin such violation in any appropriate United States district court or in any other court of competent jurisdiction;

   (B) subject to paragraph (5), may bring an action on behalf of the residents of the State to recover—

   (i) damages for which the person is liable to such residents under sections 1681n and 1681o of this title as a result of the violation;

   (ii) in the case of a violation described in any of paragraphs (1) through (3) of section 1681s-2(c) of this title, damages for which the person would, but for section 1681s-2(c) of this title, be liable to such residents as a result of the violation; or[49]

   (iii) damages of not more than $1,000 for each willful or negligent violation; and

   (C) in the case of any successful action under subparagraph (A) or (B), shall be awarded the costs of the action and reasonable attorney fees as determined by the court.

   (2) Rights of Federal regulators.—The State shall serve prior written notice of any action under paragraph (1) upon the Federal Trade Commission or the appropriate Federal regulator determined under subsection (b) of this section and provide the Commission or appropriate Federal regulator with a copy of its complaint, except in any case in which such prior notice is not feasible, in which case the State shall serve such notice immediately upon instituting such action. The Federal Trade Commission or appropriate Federal regulator shall have the right—

   (A) to intervene in the action;

   (B) upon so intervening, to be heard on all matters arising therein;

   (C) to remove the action to the appropriate United States district court; and

   (D) to file petitions for appeal.

   (3) Investigatory powers.—For purposes of bringing any action under this subsection, nothing in this subsection shall prevent the chief law enforcement officer, or an official or agency designated by a State, from exercising the powers conferred on the chief law enforcement officer or such official by the laws of such State to conduct investigations or to administer oaths or affirmations or to compel the attendance of witnesses or the production of documentary and other evidence.

   (4) Limitation on State action while Federal action pending.—If the Federal Trade Commission or the appropriate Federal regulator has instituted a civil action or an administrative action under section 1818 of Title 12 for a violation of this subchapter, no State may, during the pendency of such action, bring an action under this section against any defendant named in the complaint of the Commission or the appropriate Federal regulator for any violation of this subchapter that is alleged in that complaint.

   (5) Limitations on state actions for certain violations.—[50]

   (A) Violation of injunction required.—A State may not bring an action against a person under paragraph (1)(B) for a violation described in any of paragraphs (1) through (3) of section 1681s-2(c) of this title, unless—

   (i) the person has been enjoined from committing the violation, in an action brought by the State under paragraph (1)(A); and

   (ii) the person has violated the injunction.

   (B) Limitation on damages recoverable.—In an action against a person under paragraph (1)(B) for a violation described in any of paragraphs (1) through (3) of section 1681s-2(c) of this title, a State may not recover any damages incurred before the date of the violation of an injunction on which the action is based.

(d) Enforcement under other authority

For the purpose of the exercise by any agency referred to in subsection (b) of this section of its powers under any Act referred to in that subsection, a violation of any requirement imposed under this subchapter shall be deemed to be a violation of a requirement imposed under that Act. In addition to its powers under any provision of law specifically referred to in subsection (b) of this section, each of the agencies referred to in that subsection may exercise, for the purpose of enforcing compliance with any requirement imposed under this subchapter any other authority conferred on it by law.

(e) Regulatory Authority.—

   (1) The Federal banking agencies referred to in paragraphs (1)

---

[49] *Editor's Note*: The effective date for the FACTA amendments (Pub. L. No. 108-159 (Dec. 4, 2003)) to 15 U.S.C. § 1681s(c)(1)(B)(ii) is Mar. 31, 2004. *See* 12 C.F.R. § 222.1(c)(1)(i) and 16 C.F.R. § 602.1(c)(1)(i).

[50] *Editor's Note*: The effective date for the FACTA amendments (Pub. L. No. 108-159 (Dec. 4, 2003)) to 15 U.S.C. § 1681s(c)(5) is Mar. 31, 2004. *See* 12 C.F.R. § 222.1(c)(1)(i) and 16 C.F.R. § 602.1(c)(1)(i).

and (2) of subsection (b) shall jointly prescribe such regulations as necessary to carry out the purposes of this Act with respect to any persons identified under paragraphs (1) and (2) of subsection (b), and the Board of Governors of the Federal Reserve System shall have authority to prescribe regulations consistent with such joint regulations with respect to bank holding companies and affiliates (other than depository institutions and consumer reporting agencies) of such holding companies.

(2) The Board of the National Credit Union Administration shall prescribe such regulations as necessary to carry out the purposes of this Act with respect to any persons identified under paragraph (3) of subsection (b).

(f) Coordination of Consumer Complaint Investigations.—[51]
(1) **In general.**—Each consumer reporting agency described in section 1681a(p) shall develop and maintain procedures for the referral to each other such agency of any consumer complaint received by the agency alleging identity theft, or requesting a fraud alert under section 1681c-1 or a block under section 1681c-2.

(2) **Model form and procedure for reporting identity theft.**—The Commission, in consultation with the Federal banking agencies and the National Credit Union Administration, shall develop a model form and model procedures to be used by consumers who are victims of identity theft for contacting and informing creditors and consumer reporting agencies of the fraud.

(3) **Annual summary reports.**—Each consumer reporting agency described in section 1681a(p) shall submit an annual summary report to the Commission on consumer complaints received by the agency on identity theft or fraud alerts.

(g) FTC regulation of coding of trade names.—If the Commission determines that a person described in paragraph (9) of section 1681s-2(a) has not met the requirements of such paragraph, the Commission shall take action to ensure the person's compliance with such paragraph, which may include issuing model guidance or prescribing reasonable policies and procedures, as necessary to ensure that such person complies with such paragraph.

[Pub. L. No. 90-321, tit. VI, § 621, *as added* Pub. L. No. 91-508, tit. VI, § 601, 84 Stat. 1134 (Oct. 26, 1970), *and amended* Pub. L. No. 98-443, § 9(n), 98 Stat. 1708 (Oct. 4, 1984); Pub. L. No. 101-73, tit. VII, § 744(l), 103 Stat. 439 (Aug. 9, 1989); Pub. L. No. 102-242, tit. II, § 212(c), 105 Stat. 2300 (Dec. 19, 1991); Pub. L. No. 102-550, tit. XVI, § 1604(a)(6), 106 Stat. 4082 (Oct. 28, 1992); Pub. L. No. 104-88, tit. III, § 314, 109 Stat. 948 (Dec. 29, 1995); Pub. L. No. 104-208, div. A, tit. II, §§ 2416–2418, 110 Stat. 3009–450, 3009–452 (Sept. 30, 1996); Pub. L. No. 105-347, § 6(6), 112 Stat. 3211 (Nov. 2, 1998); Pub. L. No. 106-102, tit. V, § 506(a), (b), 113 Stat. 1441, 1442 (Nov. 12, 1999); Pub. L. No. 108-159, tit. I, § 153, tit. III, § 312(e)(2), tit. IV, § 411(e), tit. VIII, § 811(f), 117 Stat. 1966, 1993, 2003, 2012 (Dec. 4, 2003)]

§ 1681s-1. Information on overdue child support obligations [FCRA § 622]

Notwithstanding any other provision of this subchapter, a consumer reporting agency shall include in any consumer report furnished by the agency in accordance with section 1681b of this title, any information on the failure of the consumer to pay overdue support which—
(1) is provided—
(A) to the consumer reporting agency by a State or local child support enforcement agency; or
(B) to the consumer reporting agency and verified by any local, State, or Federal government agency; and
(2) antedates the report by 7 years or less.

[Pub. L. No. 90-321, tit. VI, § 622, *as added* Pub. L. No. 102-537, § 2(a), 106 Stat. 3531 (Oct. 27, 1992)]

§ 1681s-2. Responsibilities of furnishers of information to consumer reporting agencies [FCRA § 623]

(a) Duty of furnishers of information to provide accurate information.—
(1) Prohibition
(A) Reporting information with actual knowledge of errors
A person shall not furnish any information relating to a consumer to any consumer reporting agency if the person knows or has reasonable cause to believe that the information is inaccurate.[52]
(B) Reporting information after notice and confirmation of errors
A person shall not furnish information relating to a consumer to any consumer reporting agency if—
(i) the person has been notified by the consumer, at the address specified by the person for such notices, that specific information is inaccurate; and
(ii) the information is, in fact, inaccurate.
(C) No address requirement
A person who clearly and conspicuously specifies to the consumer an address for notices referred to in subparagraph (B) shall not be subject to subparagraph (A); however, nothing in subparagraph (B) shall require a person to specify such an address.
(D) Definition.—For purposes of subparagraph (A), the term 'reasonable cause to believe that the information is inaccurate' means having specific knowledge, other than solely allegations by the consumer, that would cause a reasonable person to have substantial doubts about the accuracy of the information.[53]

---

51 *Editor's Note*: The effective date for the FACTA amendments (Pub. L. No. 108-159 (Dec. 4, 2003)) to 15 U.S.C. § 1681s(f) is Dec. 1, 2004. *See* 12 C.F.R. § 222.1(c)(1)(i) and 16 C.F.R. § 602.1(c)(1)(i).

52 *Editor's Note*: The effective date for the FACTA amendments (Pub. L. No. 108-159 (Dec. 4, 2003)) to 15 U.S.C. § 1681s-2(a)(1)(A) is Dec. 1, 2004. *See* 12 C.F.R. § 222.1(c)(1)(i) and 16 C.F.R. § 602.1(c)(1)(i).

53 *Editor's Note*: The effective date for the FACTA amendments (Pub. L. No. 108-159 (Dec. 4, 2003)) to 15 U.S.C. § 1681s-2(a)(1)(D) is Dec. 1, 2004. *See* 12 C.F.R. § 222.1(c)(1)(i) and 16 C.F.R. § 602.1(c)(1)(i).

(2) Duty to correct and update information
A person who—
(A) regularly and in the ordinary course of business furnishes information to one or more consumer reporting agencies about the person's transactions or experiences with any consumer; and
(B) has furnished to a consumer reporting agency information that the person determines is not complete or accurate,

shall promptly notify the consumer reporting agency of that determination and provide to the agency any corrections to that information, or any additional information, that is necessary to make the information provided by the person to the agency complete and accurate, and shall not thereafter furnish to the agency any of the information that remains not complete or accurate.

(3) Duty to provide notice of dispute
If the completeness or accuracy of any information furnished by any person to any consumer reporting agency is disputed to such person by a consumer, the person may not furnish the information to any consumer reporting agency without notice that such information is disputed by the consumer.

(4) Duty to provide notice of closed accounts
A person who regularly and in the ordinary course of business furnishes information to a consumer reporting agency regarding a consumer who has a credit account with that person shall notify the agency of the voluntary closure of the account by the consumer, in information regularly furnished for the period in which the account is closed.

(5) Duty to provide notice of delinquency of accounts
(A) **In general.**—[54] A person who furnishes information to a consumer reporting agency regarding a delinquent account being placed for collection, charged to profit or loss, or subjected to any similar action shall, not later than 90 days after furnishing the information, notify the agency of the date of delinquency on the account, which shall be the month and year of the commencement of the delinquency on the account that immediately preceded the action.

(B) **Rule of construction.**—[55] For purposes of this paragraph only, and provided that the consumer does not dispute the information, a person that furnishes information on a delinquent account that is placed for collection, charged for profit or loss, or subjected to any similar action, complies with this paragraph, if—
(i) the person reports the same date of delinquency as that provided by the creditor to which the account was owed at the time at which the commencement of the delinquency occurred, if the creditor previously reported that date of delinquency to a consumer reporting agency;
(ii) the creditor did not previously report the date of delinquency to a consumer reporting agency, and the person establishes and follows reasonable procedures to obtain the date of delinquency from the creditor or another reliable source and reports that date to a consumer reporting agency as the date of delinquency; or
(iii) the creditor did not previously report the date of delinquency to a consumer reporting agency and the date of delinquency cannot be reasonably obtained as provided in clause (ii), the person establishes and follows reasonable procedures to ensure the date reported as the date of delinquency precedes the date on which the account is placed for collection, charged to profit or loss, or subjected to any similar action, and reports such date to the credit reporting agency.

(6) Duties of furnishers upon notice of identity theft-related information.—[56]
(A) **Reasonable procedures.**—A person that furnishes information to any consumer reporting agency shall have in place reasonable procedures to respond to any notification that it receives from a consumer reporting agency under section 1681c-2 relating to information resulting from identity theft, to prevent that person from refurnishing such blocked information.

(B) **Information alleged to result from identity theft.**—If a consumer submits an identity theft report to a person who furnishes information to a consumer reporting agency at the address specified by that person for receiving such reports stating that information maintained by such person that purports to relate to the consumer resulted from identity theft, the person may not furnish such information that purports to relate to the consumer to any consumer reporting agency, unless the person subsequently knows or is informed by the consumer that the information is correct.

(7) Negative information.—[57]
(A) **Notice to consumer required.**—
(i) **In general.**—If any financial institution that extends credit and regularly and in the ordinary course of business furnishes information to a consumer reporting agency described in section 1681a(p) furnishes negative information to such an agency regarding credit extended to a customer, the financial institution shall provide a notice of such furnishing of negative information, in writing, to the customer.

(ii) **Notice effective for subsequent submissions.**—After providing such notice, the financial institution may submit additional negative information to a consumer reporting agency described in section 1681a(p) with respect to the same transaction, extension of credit, account, or customer without providing additional notice to the customer.

(B) **Time of notice.**—
(i) **In general.**—The notice required under subparagraph (A) shall be provided to the customer prior to, or no later than 30 days after, furnishing the negative information to a consumer reporting agency described in section 1681a(p).

---

54 *Editor's Note*: The effective date for the FACTA amendments (Pub. L. No. 108-159 (Dec. 4, 2003)) to 15 U.S.C. § 1681s-2(a)(5)(A) is Mar. 31, 2004. *See* 12 C.F.R. § 222.1(c)(1)(i) and 16 C.F.R. § 602.1(c)(1)(i).

55 *Editor's Note*: The effective date for the FACTA amendments (Pub. L. No. 108-159 (Dec. 4, 2003)) to 15 U.S.C. § 1681s-2(a)(5)(B) is Mar. 31, 2004. *See* 12 C.F.R. § 222.1(c)(1)(i) and 16 C.F.R. § 602.1(c)(1)(i).

56 *Editor's Note*: The effective date for the FACTA amendments (Pub. L. No. 108-159 (Dec. 4, 2003)) to 15 U.S.C. § 1681s-2(a)(6) is Dec. 1, 2004. *See* 12 C.F.R. § 222.1(c)(1)(i) and 16 C.F.R. § 602.1(c)(1)(i).

57 *Editor's Note*: The effective date for the FACTA amendments (Pub. L. No. 108-159 (Dec. 4, 2003)) to 15 U.S.C. § 1681s-2(a)(7) is Dec. 1, 2004. *See* 12 C.F.R. § 222.1(c)(1)(i) and 16 C.F.R. § 602.1(c)(1)(i).

(ii) Coordination with new account disclosures.—If the notice is provided to the customer prior to furnishing the negative information to a consumer reporting agency, the notice may not be included in the initial disclosures provided under section 127(a) of the Truth in Lending Act.

(C) Coordination with other disclosures.—The notice required under subparagraph (A)—

(i) may be included on or with any notice of default, any billing statement, or any other materials provided to the customer; and

(ii) must be clear and conspicuous.

(D) Model disclosure.—

(i) Duty of board to prepare.—The Board shall prescribe a brief model disclosure a financial institution may use to comply with subparagraph (A), which shall not exceed 30 words.

(ii) Use of model not required.—No provision of this paragraph shall be construed as requiring a financial institution to use any such model form prescribed by the Board.

(iii) Compliance using model.—A financial institution shall be deemed to be in compliance with subparagraph (A) if the financial institution uses any such model form prescribed by the Board, or the financial institution uses any such model form and rearranges its format.

(E) Use of notice without submitting negative information.—No provision of this paragraph shall be construed as requiring a financial institution that has provided a customer with a notice described in subparagraph (A) to furnish negative information about the customer to a consumer reporting agency.

(F) Safe harbor.—A financial institution shall not be liable for failure to perform the duties required by this paragraph if, at the time of the failure, the financial institution maintained reasonable policies and procedures to comply with this paragraph or the financial institution reasonably believed that the institution is prohibited, by law, from contacting the consumer.

(G) Definitions.—For purposes of this paragraph, the following definitions shall apply:

(i) Negative information.—The term 'negative information' means information concerning a customer's delinquencies, late payments, insolvency, or any form of default.

(ii) Customer; financial institution.—The terms 'customer' and 'financial institution' have the same meanings as in section 509 Public Law 106-102.

(8) Ability of consumer to dispute information directly with furnisher.—[58]

(A) In general.—The Federal banking agencies, the National Credit Union Administration, and the Commission shall jointly prescribe regulations that shall identify the circumstances under which a furnisher shall be required to reinvestigate a dispute concerning the accuracy of information contained in a consumer report on the consumer, based on a direct request of a consumer.

---

58 *Editor's Note*: The effective date for the FACTA amendments (Pub. L. No. 108-159 (Dec. 4, 2003)) to 15 U.S.C. § 1681s-2(a)(8) is Dec. 1, 2004. *See* 12 C.F.R. § 222.1(c)(1)(i) and 16 C.F.R. § 602.1(c)(1)(i).

(B) Considerations.—In prescribing regulations under subparagraph (A), the agencies shall weigh—

(i) the benefits to consumers with the costs on furnishers and the credit reporting system;

(ii) the impact on the overall accuracy and integrity of consumer reports of any such requirements;

(iii) whether direct contact by the consumer with the furnisher would likely result in the most expeditious resolution of any such dispute; and

(iv) the potential impact on the credit reporting process if credit repair organizations, as defined in section 403(3), including entities that would be a credit repair organization, but for section 403(3)(B)(i), are able to circumvent the prohibition in subparagraph (G).

(C) Applicability.—Subparagraphs (D) through (G) shall apply in any circumstance identified under the regulations promulgated under subparagraph (A).

(D) Submitting a notice of dispute.—A consumer who seeks to dispute the accuracy of information shall provide a dispute notice directly to such person at the address specified by the person for such notices that—

(i) identifies the specific information that is being disputed;

(ii) explains the basis for the dispute; and

(iii) includes all supporting documentation required by the furnisher to substantiate the basis of the dispute.

(E) Duty of person after receiving notice of dispute.—After receiving a notice of dispute from a consumer pursuant to subparagraph (D), the person that provided the information in dispute to a consumer reporting agency shall—

(i) conduct an investigation with respect to the disputed information;

(ii) review all relevant information provided by the consumer with the notice;

(iii) complete such person's investigation of the dispute and report the results of the investigation to the consumer before the expiration of the period under section 1681i(a)(1) within which a consumer reporting agency would be required to complete its action if the consumer had elected to dispute the information under that section; and

(iv) if the investigation finds that the information reported was inaccurate, promptly notify each consumer reporting agency to which the person furnished the inaccurate information of that determination and provide to the agency any correction to that information that is necessary to make the information provided by the person accurate.

(F) Frivolous or irrelevant dispute.—

(i) In general.—This paragraph shall not apply if the person receiving a notice of a dispute from a consumer reasonably determines that the dispute is frivolous or irrelevant, including—

(I) by reason of the failure of a consumer to provide sufficient information to investigate the disputed information; or

(II) the submission by a consumer of a dispute that is substantially the same as a dispute previously submitted by or for the consumer, either directly to the person or through a consumer reporting agency under subsection (b), with respect to which the person has already performed the person's duties under this paragraph or subsection (b), as applicable.

(ii) **Notice of determination.**—Upon making any determination under clause (i) that a dispute is frivolous or irrelevant, the person shall notify the consumer of such determination not later than 5 business days after making such determination, by mail or, if authorized by the consumer for that purpose, by any other means available to the person.

(iii) **Contents of notice.**—A notice under clause (ii) shall include—

(I) the reasons for the determination under clause (i); and

(II) identification of any information required to investigate the disputed information, which may consist of a standardized form describing the general nature of such information.

(G) **Exclusion of credit repair organizations.**—This paragraph shall not apply if the notice of the dispute is submitted by, is prepared on behalf of the consumer by, or is submitted on a form supplied to the consumer by, a credit repair organization, as defined in section 403(3), or an entity that would be a credit repair organization, but for section 403(3)(B)(i).

(9) **Duty to provide notice of status as medical information furnisher.**—A person whose primary business is providing medical services, products, or devices, or the person's agent or assignee, who furnishes information to a consumer reporting agency on a consumer shall be considered a medical information furnisher for purposes of this title, and shall notify the agency of such status.

(b) **Duties of furnishers of information upon notice of dispute**

(1) **In general**

After receiving notice pursuant to section 1681i(a)(2) of this title of a dispute with regard to the completeness or accuracy of any information provided by a person to a consumer reporting agency, the person shall—

(A) conduct an investigation with respect to the disputed information;

(B) review all relevant information provided by the consumer reporting agency pursuant to section 1681i(a)(2) of this title;

(C) report the results of the investigation to the consumer reporting agency;[59]

(D) if the investigation finds that the information is incomplete or inaccurate, report those results to all other consumer reporting agencies to which the person furnished the information and that compile and maintain files on consumers on a nationwide basis; and[60]

(E) if an item of information disputed by a consumer is found to be inaccurate or incomplete or cannot be verified after any reinvestigation under paragraph (1), for purposes of reporting to a consumer reporting agency only, as appropriate, based on the results of the reinvestigation promptly—[61]

(i) modify that item of information;

(ii) delete that item of information; or

(iii) permanently block the reporting of that item of information.

(2) **Deadline**

A person shall complete all investigations, reviews, and reports required under paragraph (1) regarding information provided by the person to a consumer reporting agency, before the expiration of the period under section 1681i(a)(1) of this title within which the consumer reporting agency is required to complete actions required by that section regarding that information.

(c) **Limitation on liability.**—[62] Except as provided in section 1681s(c)(1)(B), sections 1681n and 1681o do not apply to any violation of—

(1) subsection (a) of this section, including any regulations issued thereunder;

(2) subsection (e) of this section, except that nothing in this paragraph shall limit, expand, or otherwise affect liability under section 1681n or 1681o, as applicable, for violations of subsection (b) of this section; or

(3) subsection (e) of section 1681m.

(d) **Limitation on enforcement.**—[63] The provisions of law described in paragraphs (1) through (3) of subsection (c) (other than with respect to the exception described in paragraph (2) of subsection (c)) shall be enforced exclusively as provided under section 1681s by the Federal agencies and officials and the State officials identified in section 1681s.

(e) **Accuracy guidelines and regulations required.**—[64]

(1) **Guidelines.**—The Federal banking agencies, the National Credit Union Administration, and the Commission shall, with respect to the entities that are subject to their respective enforcement authority under section 1681s, and in coordination as described in paragraph (2)—

(A) establish and maintain guidelines for use by each person that furnishes information to a consumer reporting agency regarding the accuracy and integrity of the information relating to consumers that such entities furnish to consumer reporting agencies, and update such guidelines as often as necessary; and

(B) prescribe regulations requiring each person that furnishes information to a consumer reporting agency to establish

---

59 *Editor's Note*: The effective date for the FACTA amendments (Pub. L. No. 108-159 (Dec. 4, 2003)) to 15 U.S.C. § 1681s-2(b)(1)(C) is Dec. 1, 2004. *See* 12 C.F.R. § 222.1(c)(1)(i) and 16 C.F.R. § 602.1(c)(1)(i).

60 *Editor's Note*: The effective date for the FACTA amendments (Pub. L. No. 108-159 (Dec. 4, 2003)) to 15 U.S.C. § 1681s-2(b)(1)(D) is Dec. 1, 2004. *See* 12 C.F.R. § 222.1(c)(1)(i) and 16 C.F.R. § 602.1(c)(1)(i).

61 *Editor's Note*: The effective date for the FACTA amendments (Pub. L. No. 108-159 (Dec. 4, 2003)) to 15 U.S.C. § 1681s-2(b)(1)(E) is Dec. 1, 2004. *See* 12 C.F.R. § 222.1(c)(1)(i) and 16 C.F.R. § 602.1(c)(1)(i).

62 *Editor's Note*: The effective date for the FACTA amendments (Pub. L. No. 108-159 (Dec. 4, 2003)) to 15 U.S.C. § 1681s-2(c) is Mar. 31, 2004. *See* 12 C.F.R. § 222.1(c)(1)(i) and 16 C.F.R. § 602.1(c)(1)(i).

63 *Editor's Note*: The effective date for the FACTA amendments (Pub. L. No. 108-159 (Dec. 4, 2003)) to 15 U.S.C. § 1681s-2(d) is Mar. 31, 2004. *See* 12 C.F.R. § 222.1(c)(1)(i) and 16 C.F.R. § 602.1(c)(1)(i).

64 *Editor's Note*: The effective date for the FACTA amendments (Pub. L. No. 108-159 (Dec. 4, 2003)) to 15 U.S.C. § 1681s-2(e) is Dec. 1, 2004. *See* 12 C.F.R. § 222.1(c)(1)(i) and 16 C.F.R. § 602.1(c)(1)(i).

reasonable policies and procedures for implementing the guidelines established pursuant to subparagraph (A).

(2) **Coordination.**—Each agency required to prescribe regulations under paragraph (1) shall consult and coordinate with each other such agency so that, to the extent possible, the regulations prescribed by each such entity are consistent and comparable with the regulations prescribed by each other such agency.

(3) **Criteria.**—In developing the guidelines required by paragraph (1)(A), the agencies described in paragraph (1) shall—

(A) identify patterns, practices, and specific forms of activity that can compromise the accuracy and integrity of information furnished to consumer reporting agencies;

(B) review the methods (including technological means) used to furnish information relating to consumers to consumer reporting agencies;

(C) determine whether persons that furnish information to consumer reporting agencies maintain and enforce policies to assure the accuracy and integrity of information furnished to consumer reporting agencies; and

(D) examine the policies and processes that persons that furnish information to consumer reporting agencies employ to conduct reinvestigations and correct inaccurate information relating to consumers that has been furnished to consumer reporting agencies.

[Pub. L. No. 90-321, tit. VI, § 623, *as added* Pub. L. No. 104-208, div. A, tit. II, § 2413(a)(2), 110 Stat. 3009–447 (Sept. 30, 1996), *and amended* Pub. L. No. 108-159, tit. I, § 154(a), tit. II, § 217(a), tit. III, §§ 312(a)–(e)(1), 314(b), tit. IV, § 412(a), (f), 117 Stat. 1966, 1986, 1989 to 1993, 1995, 2002, 2003 (Dec. 4, 2003)]

§ 1681s-3. Affiliate sharing [FCRA § 624]

(a) **Special rule for solicitation for purposes of marketing.**—

(1) **Notice.**—Any person that receives from another person related to it by common ownership or affiliated by corporate control a communication of information that would be a consumer report, but for clauses (i), (ii), and (iii) of section 1681a(d)(2)(A), may not use the information to make a solicitation for marketing purposes to a consumer about its products or services, unless—

(A) it is clearly and conspicuously disclosed to the consumer that the information may be communicated among such persons for purposes of making such solicitations to the consumer; and

(B) the consumer is provided an opportunity and a simple method to prohibit the making of such solicitations to the consumer by such person.

(2) **Consumer choice.**—

(A) **In general.**—The notice required under paragraph (1) shall allow the consumer the opportunity to prohibit all solicitations referred to in such paragraph, and may allow the consumer to choose from different options when electing to prohibit the sending of such solicitations, including options regarding the types of entities and information covered, and which methods of delivering solicitations the consumer elects to prohibit.

(B) **Format.**—Notwithstanding subparagraph (A), the notice required under paragraph (1) shall be clear, conspicuous, and concise, and any method provided under paragraph (1)(B) shall be simple. The regulations prescribed to implement this section shall provide specific guidance regarding how to comply with such standards.

(3) **Duration.**—

(A) **In general.**—The election of a consumer pursuant to paragraph (1)(B) to prohibit the making of solicitations shall be effective for at least 5 years, beginning on the date on which the person receives the election of the consumer, unless the consumer requests that such election be revoked.

(B) **Notice upon expiration of effective period.**—At such time as the election of a consumer pursuant to paragraph (1)(B) is no longer effective, a person may not use information that the person receives in the manner described in paragraph (1) to make any solicitation for marketing purposes to the consumer, unless the consumer receives a notice and an opportunity, using a simple method, to extend the opt-out for another period of at least 5 years, pursuant to the procedures described in paragraph (1).

(4) **Scope.**—This section shall not apply to a person—

(A) using information to make a solicitation for marketing purposes to a consumer with whom the person has a pre-existing business relationship;

(B) using information to facilitate communications to an individual for whose benefit the person provides employee benefit or other services pursuant to a contract with an employer related to and arising out of the current employment relationship or status of the individual as a participant or beneficiary of an employee benefit plan;

(C) using information to perform services on behalf of another person related by common ownership or affiliated by corporate control, except that this subparagraph shall not be construed as permitting a person to send solicitations on behalf of another person, if such other person would not be permitted to send the solicitation on its own behalf as a result of the election of the consumer to prohibit solicitations under paragraph (1)(B);

(D) using information in response to a communication initiated by the consumer;

(E) using information in response to solicitations authorized or requested by the consumer; or

(F) if compliance with this section by that person would prevent compliance by that person with any provision of State insurance laws pertaining to unfair discrimination in any State in which the person is lawfully doing business.

(5) **No retroactivity.**—This subsection shall not prohibit the use of information to send a solicitation to a consumer if such information was received prior to the date on which persons are required to comply with regulations implementing this subsection.

(b) **Notice for other purposes permissible.**—A notice or other disclosure under this section may be coordinated and consolidated with any other notice required to be issued under any other provision of law by a person that is subject to this section, and a notice or other disclosure that is equivalent to the notice required by subsection (a), and that is provided by a person described in subsection (a) to a consumer together with disclosures required by any other provision of law, shall satisfy the requirements of subsection (a).

(c) User requirements.—Requirements with respect to the use by a person of information received from another person related to it by common ownership or affiliated by corporate control, such as the requirements of this section, constitute requirements with respect to the exchange of information among persons affiliated by common ownership or common corporate control, within the meaning of section 1681t(b)(2).

(d) Definitions.—For purposes of this section, the following definitions shall apply:

   (1) Pre-existing business relationship.—The term 'pre-existing business relationship' means a relationship between a person, or a person's licensed agent, and a consumer, based on—

     (A) a financial contract between a person and a consumer which is in force;

     (B) the purchase, rental, or lease by the consumer of that person's goods or services, or a financial transaction (including holding an active account or a policy in force or having another continuing relationship) between the consumer and that person during the 18-month period immediately preceding the date on which the consumer is sent a solicitation covered by this section;

     (C) an inquiry or application by the consumer regarding a product or service offered by that person, during the 3-month period immediately preceding the date on which the consumer is sent a solicitation covered by this section; or

     (D) any other pre-existing customer relationship defined in the regulations implementing this section.

   (2) Solicitation.—The term 'solicitation' means the marketing of a product or service initiated by a person to a particular consumer that is based on an exchange of information described in subsection (a), and is intended to encourage the consumer to purchase such product or service, but does not include communications that are directed at the general public or determined not to be a solicitation by the regulations prescribed under this section.

[Pub. L. No. 90-321, tit. VI, § 624, *as added* Pub. L. No. 108-159, tit. II, § 214(a)(2), 117 Stat. 1980 (Dec. 4, 2003)]

§ 1681t. Relation to State laws [FCRA § 625]

(a) In general

Except as provided in subsections (b) and (c) of this section, this subchapter does not annul, alter, affect, or exempt any person subject to the provisions of this subchapter from complying with the laws of any State with respect to the collection, distribution, or use of any information on consumers, or for the prevention or mitigation of identity theft, except to the extent that those laws are inconsistent with any provision of this subchapter, and then only to the extent of the inconsistency.[65]

(b) General exceptions

No requirement or prohibition may be imposed under the laws of any State—

(1) with respect to any subject matter regulated under—

   (A) subsection (c) or (e) of section 1681b of this title, relating to the prescreening of consumer reports;

   (B) section 1681i of this title, relating to the time by which a consumer reporting agency must take any action, including the provision of notification to a consumer or other person, in any procedure related to the disputed accuracy of information in a consumer's file, except that this subparagraph shall not apply to any State law in effect on September 30, 1996;

   (C) subsections (a) and (b) of section 1681m of this title, relating to the duties of a person who takes any adverse action with respect to a consumer;

   (D) section 1681m(d) of this title, relating to the duties of persons who use a consumer report of a consumer in connection with any credit or insurance transaction that is not initiated by the consumer and that consists of a firm offer of credit or insurance;

   (E) section 1681c of this title, relating to information contained in consumer reports, except that this subparagraph shall not apply to any State law in effect on September 30, 1996;[66]

   (F) section 1681s-2 of this title, relating to the responsibilities of persons who furnish information to consumer reporting agencies, except that this paragraph shall not apply—

     (i) with respect to section 54A(a) of chapter 93 of the Massachusetts Annotated Laws (as in effect on September 30, 1996); or

     (ii) with respect to section 1785.25(a) of the California Civil Code (as in effect on September 30, 1996);

   (G) section 1681g(e), relating to information available to victims under section 1681g (e);[67]

   (H) section 1681s-3, relating to the exchange and use of information to make a solicitation for marketing purposes; or[68]

   (I) section 1681m(h), relating to the duties of users of consumer reports to provide notice with respect to terms in certain credit transactions;[69]

(2) with respect to the exchange of information among persons affiliated by common ownership or common corporate control, except that this paragraph shall not apply with respect to subsection (a) or (c)(1) of section 2480e of title 9, Vermont Statutes Annotated (as in effect on September 30, 1996);[70]

---

65 *Editor's Note*: The effective date for the FACTA amendments (Pub. L. No. 108-159 (Dec. 4, 2003)) to 15 U.S.C. § 1681t(a) is Dec. 31, 2003. *See* 12 C.F.R. § 222.1(c)(1)(i) and 16 C.F.R. § 602.1(c)(1)(i).

66 *Editor's Note*: The effective date for the FACTA amendments (Pub. L. No. 108-159 (Dec. 4, 2003)) to 15 U.S.C. § 1681t(b)(1)(E) is Dec. 31, 2003. *See* 12 C.F.R. § 222.1(c)(1)(i) and 16 C.F.R. § 602.1(c)(1)(i).

67 *Editor's Note*: The effective date for the FACTA amendments (Pub. L. No. 108-159 (Dec. 4, 2003)) to 15 U.S.C. § 1681t(1)(G) is Dec. 31, 2003. *See* 12 C.F.R. § 222.1(c)(1)(i) and 16 C.F.R. § 602.1(c)(1)(i).

68 *Editor's Note*: The effective date for the FACTA amendments (Pub. L. No. 108-159 (Dec. 4, 2003)) to 15 U.S.C. § 1681t(b)(1)(H) is Dec. 31, 2003. *See* 12 C.F.R. § 222.1(c)(1)(i) and 16 C.F.R. § 602.1(c)(1)(i).

69 *Editor's Note*: The effective date for the FACTA amendments (Pub. L. No. 108-159 (Dec. 4, 2003)) to 15 U.S.C. § 1681t(b)(1)(I) is Dec. 31, 2003. *See* 12 C.F.R. § 222.1(c)(1)(i) and 16 C.F.R. § 602.1(c)(1)(i).

70 *Editor's Note*: The effective date for the FACTA amendments (Pub. L. No. 108-159 (Dec. 4, 2003)) to 15 U.S.C. § 1681t(b)(2)

(3) with respect to the disclosures required to be made under subsection (c), (d), (e), or (g) of section 1681g, or subsection (f) of section 1681g relating to the disclosure of credit scores for credit granting purposes, except that this paragraph—

(A) shall not apply with respect to sections 1785.10, 1785.16, and 1785.20.2 of the California Civil Code (as in effect on the date of enactment of the Fair and Accurate Credit Transactions Act of 2003) and section 1785.15 through section 1785.15.2 of such Code (as in effect on such date);

(B) shall not apply with respect to sections 5-3-106(2) and 212-14.3-104.3 of the Colorado Revised Statutes (as in effect on the date of enactment of the Fair and Accurate Credit Transactions Act of 2003); and

(C) shall not be construed as limiting, annulling, affecting, or superseding any provision of the laws of any State regulating the use in an insurance activity, or regulating disclosures concerning such use, of a credit-based insurance score of a consumer by any person engaged in the business of insurance;

(4) with respect to the frequency of any disclosure under section 1681j(a), except that this paragraph shall not apply—[71]

(A) with respect to section 12-14.3-105(1)(d) of the Colorado Revised Statutes (as in effect on the date of enactment of the Fair and Accurate Credit Transactions Act of 2003);

(B) with respect to section 10-1-393(29)(C) of the Georgia Code (as in effect on the date of enactment of the Fair and Accurate Credit Transactions Act of 2003);

(C) with respect to section 1316.2 of title 10 of the Maine Revised Statutes (as in effect on the date of enactment of the Fair and Accurate Credit Transactions Act of 2003);

(D) with respect to sections 14-1209(a)(1) and 14-1209(b)(1)(i) of the Commercial Law Article of the Code of Maryland (as in effect on the date of enactment of the Fair and Accurate Credit Transactions Act of 2003);

(E) with respect to section 59(d) and section 59(e) of chapter 93 of the General Laws of Massachusetts (as in effect on the date of enactment of the Fair and Accurate Credit Transactions Act of 2003);

(F) with respect to section 56:11-37.10(a)(1) of the New Jersey Revised Statutes (as in effect on the date of enactment of the Fair and Accurate Credit Transactions Act of 2003); or

(G) with respect to section 2480c(a)(1) of title 9 of the Vermont Statutes Annotated (as in effect on the date of enactment of the Fair and Accurate Credit Transactions Act of 2003); or

(5) with respect to the conduct required by the specific provisions of—[72]

(A) section 1681c(g);

(B) section 1681c-1;

(C) section 1681c-2;

(D) section 1681g(a)( )(A);

(E) section 1681j(a);

(F) subsections (e), (f), and (g) of section 1681m;

(G) section 1681s(f);

(H) section 1681s-2(a)(6); or

(I) section 1681w

(c) Definition of firm offer of credit or insurance

Notwithstanding any definition of the term "firm offer of credit or insurance" (or any equivalent term) under the laws of any State, the definition of that term contained in section 1681a(l) of this title shall be construed to apply in the enforcement and interpretation of the laws of any State governing consumer reports.

(d) Limitations[73]

Subsections (b) and (c) do not affect any settlement, agreement, or consent judgment between any State Attorney General and any consumer reporting agency in effect on September 30, 1996.

[Pub. L. No. 90-321, tit. VI, § 625, *formerly § 622, as added* Pub. L. No. 91-508, tit. VI, § 601, 84 Stat. 1136 (Oct. 26, 1970), *and renumbered § 623*, Pub. L. No. 102-537, § 2(a), 106 Stat. 3531 (Oct. 27, 1992); *renumbered § 624 and amended* Pub. L. No. 104-208, div. A, tit. II, §§ 2413(a)(1), 2419, 110 Stat. 3009–447, 3009–452 (Sept. 30, 1996); *renumbered § 625 and amended* Pub. L. No. 108-159, tit. I, § 151(a)(2), tit. II, §§ 212(e), 214(a)(1), (c)(2), tit. III, § 311(b), tit. VII, § 711, 117 Stat. 1964, 1977, 1980, 1983, 1989, 2011 (Dec. 4, 2003)]

§ 1681u. Disclosures to FBI for counterintelligence purposes [FCRA § 626]

(a) Identity of financial institutions

Notwithstanding section 1681b of this title or any other provision of this subchapter, a consumer reporting agency shall furnish to the Federal Bureau of Investigation the names and addresses of all financial institutions (as that term is defined in section 3401 of Title 12) at which a consumer maintains or has maintained an account, to the extent that information is in the files of the agency, when presented with a written request for that information, signed by the Director of the Federal Bureau of Investigation, or the Director's designee in a position not lower than Deputy Assistant Director at Bureau headquarters or a Special Agent in Charge of a Bureau field office designated by the Director, which certifies compliance with this section. The Director or the Director's designee may make such a certification only if the Director or the Director's designee has determined in writing, that such information is sought for the conduct of an authorized investigation to protect against international terrorism or clandestine intelligence activities, provided that such an investigation of a United States person is not conducted solely upon the basis of activities protected by the first amendment to the Constitution of the United States.

---

is Dec. 31, 2003. *See* 12 C.F.R. § 222.1(c)(1)(i) and 16 C.F.R. § 602.1(c)(1)(i).

71 *Editor's Note*: The effective date for the FACTA amendments (Pub. L. No. 108-159 (Dec. 4, 2003)) to 15 U.S.C. § 1681t(b)(4) is Dec. 31, 2003. *See* 12 C.F.R. § 222.1(c)(1)(i) and 16 C.F.R. § 602.1(c)(1)(i).

72 *Editor's Note*: The effective date for the FACTA amendments (Pub. L. No. 108-159 (Dec. 4, 2003)) to 15 U.S.C. § 1681t(b)(5) is Dec. 31, 2003. *See* 12 C.F.R. § 222.1(c)(1)(i) and 16 C.F.R. § 602.1(c)(1)(i).

73 *Editor's Note*: The effective date for the FACTA amendments (Pub. L. No. 108-159 (Dec. 4, 2003)) to 15 U.S.C. § 1681t(d) is Dec. 31, 2003. *See* 12 C.F.R. § 222.1(c)(1)(i) and 16 C.F.R. § 602.1(c)(1)(i).

(b) Identifying information

Notwithstanding the provisions of section 1681b of this title or any other provision of this subchapter, a consumer reporting agency shall furnish identifying information respecting a consumer, limited to name, address, former addresses, places of employment, or former places of employment, to the Federal Bureau of Investigation when presented with a written request, signed by the Director or the Director's designee in a position not lower than Deputy Assistant Director at Bureau headquarters or a Special Agent in Charge of a Bureau field office designated by the Director, which certifies compliance with this subsection. The Director or the Director's designee may make such a certification only if the Director or the Director's designee has determined in writing that such information is sought for the conduct of an authorized investigation to protect against international terrorism or clandestine intelligence activities, provided that such an investigation of a United States person is not conducted solely upon the basis of activities protected by the first amendment to the Constitution of the United States.

(c) Court order for disclosure of consumer reports

Notwithstanding section 1681b of this title or any other provision of this subchapter, if requested in writing by the Director of the Federal Bureau of Investigation, or a designee of the Director in a position not lower than Deputy Assistant Director at Bureau headquarters or a Special Agent in Charge in a Bureau field office designated by the Director, a court may issue an order ex parte directing a consumer reporting agency to furnish a consumer report to the Federal Bureau of Investigation, upon a showing in camera that the consumer report is sought for the conduct of an authorized investigation to protect against international terrorism or clandestine intelligence activities, provided that such an investigation of a United States person is not conducted solely upon the basis of activities protected by the first amendment to the Constitution of the United States.

The terms of an order issued under this subsection shall not disclose that the order is issued for purposes of a counterintelligence investigation.

(d) Confidentiality

(1) If the Director of the Federal Bureau of Investigation, or his designee in a position not lower than Deputy Assistant Director at Bureau headquarters or a Special Agent in Charge in a Bureau field office designated by the Director, certifies that otherwise there may result a danger to the national security of the United States, interference with a criminal, counterterrorism, or counterintelligence investigation, interference with diplomatic relations, or danger to the life or physical safety of any person, no consumer reporting agency or officer, employee, or agent of a consumer reporting agency shall disclose to any person (other than those to whom such disclosure is necessary to comply with the request or an attorney to obtain legal advice or legal assistance with respect to the request) that the Federal Bureau of Investigation has sought or obtained the identity of financial institutions or a consumer report respecting any consumer under subsection (a), (b), or (c), and no consumer reporting agency or officer, employee, or agent of a consumer reporting agency shall include in any consumer report any information that would indicate that the Federal Bureau of Investigation has sought or obtained such information on a consumer report.

(2) The request shall notify the person or entity to whom the request is directed of the nondisclosure requirement under paragraph (1).

(3) Any recipient disclosing to those persons necessary to comply with the request or to an attorney to obtain legal advice or legal assistance with respect to the request shall inform such persons of any applicable nondisclosure requirement. Any person who receives a disclosure under this subsection shall be subject to the same prohibitions on disclosure under paragraph (1).

(4) At the request of the Director of the Federal Bureau of Investigation or the designee of the Director, any person making or intending to make a disclosure under this section shall identify to the Director or such designee the person to whom such disclosure will be made or to whom such disclosure was made prior to the request, except that nothing in this section shall require a person to inform the Director or such designee of the identity of an attorney to whom disclosure was made or will be made to obtain legal advice or legal assistance with respect to the request for the identity of financial institutions or a consumer report respecting any consumer under this section.

[Pub. L. No. 109-177, tit. I, 116(b), 120 Stat. 214 (Mar. 9, 2006); Pub. L. No. 109-178, 4(c)(1), 120 Stat. 280 (Mar. 9, 2006)]

(e) Payment of fees

The Federal Bureau of Investigation shall, subject to the availability of appropriations, pay to the consumer reporting agency assembling or providing report or information in accordance with procedures established under this section a fee for reimbursement for such costs as are reasonably necessary and which have been directly incurred in searching, reproducing, or transporting books, papers, records, or other data required or requested to be produced under this section.

(f) Limit on dissemination

The Federal Bureau of Investigation may not disseminate information obtained pursuant to this section outside of the Federal Bureau of Investigation, except to other Federal agencies as may be necessary for the approval or conduct of a foreign counterintelligence investigation, or, where the information concerns a person subject to the Uniform Code of Military Justice, to appropriate investigative authorities within the military department concerned as may be necessary for the conduct of a joint foreign counterintelligence investigation.

(g) Rules of construction

Nothing in this section shall be construed to prohibit information from being furnished by the Federal Bureau of Investigation pursuant to a subpoena or court order, in connection with a judicial or administrative proceeding to enforce the provisions of this subchapter. Nothing in this section shall be construed to authorize or permit the withholding of information from the Congress.

(h) Reports to Congress

On a semiannual basis, the Attorney General shall fully inform the Permanent Select Committee on Intelligence and the Committee on Banking, Finance and Urban Affairs of the House of Representatives, and the Select Committee on Intelligence and the Committee on Banking, Housing, and Urban Affairs of the Senate concerning all requests made pursuant to subsections (a), (b), and (c) of this section.

(i) Damages

Any agency or department of the United States obtaining or disclosing any consumer reports, records, or information contained therein in violation of this section is liable to the consumer to whom such consumer reports, records, or information relate in an amount equal to the sum of—

(1) $100, without regard to the volume of consumer reports, records, or information involved;

(2) any actual damages sustained by the consumer as a result of the disclosure;

(3) if the violation is found to have been willful or intentional, such punitive damages as a court may allow; and

(4) in the case of any successful action to enforce liability under this subsection, the costs of the action, together with reasonable attorney fees, as determined by the court.

(j) Disciplinary actions for violations

If a court determines that any agency or department of the United States has violated any provision of this section and the court finds that the circumstances surrounding the violation raise questions of whether or not an officer or employee of the agency or department acted willfully or intentionally with respect to the violation, the agency or department shall promptly initiate a proceeding to determine whether or not disciplinary action is warranted against the officer or employee who was responsible for the violation.

(k) Good-faith exception

Notwithstanding any other provision of this subchapter, any consumer reporting agency or agent or employee thereof making disclosure of consumer reports or identifying information pursuant to this subsection in good-faith reliance upon a certification of the Federal Bureau of Investigation pursuant to provisions of this section shall not be liable to any person for such disclosure under this subchapter, the constitution of any State, or any law or regulation of any State or any political subdivision of any State.

(*l*) Limitation of remedies

Notwithstanding any other provision of this subchapter, the remedies and sanctions set forth in this section shall be the only judicial remedies and sanctions for violation of this section.

(m) Injunctive relief

In addition to any other remedy contained in this section, injunctive relief shall be available to require compliance with the procedures of this section. In the event of any successful action under this subsection, costs together with reasonable attorney fees, as determined by the court, may be recovered.

[Pub. L. No. 90-321, tit. VI, § 625, *formerly § 624, as added* Pub. L. No. 104-93, tit. VI, § 601(a), 109 Stat. 974 (Jan. 6, 1996); *renumbered § 625 and amended* Pub. L. No. 107-56, tit. III, § 358(g)(1)(A), tit. V, § 505(c), 115 Stat. 327, 366 (Oct. 26, 2001); Pub. L. No. 107-306, tit. VIII, § 811(b)(8)(B), 116 Stat. 2426 (Nov. 27, 2002); *renumbered § 626,* Pub. L. No. 108-159, tit. II, § 214(a)(1), 117 Stat. 1980 (Dec. 4, 2003); Pub. L. No. 109-177, tit. I, § 116(b), 120 Stat. 214 (Mar. 9, 2006); Pub. L. No. 109-178, § 4(c)(1), 120 Stat. 280 (Mar. 9, 2006)]

§ 1681v. Disclosures to governmental agencies for counterterrorism purposes [FCRA § 627]

(a) Disclosure

Notwithstanding section 1681b or any other provision of this title, a consumer reporting agency shall furnish a consumer report of a consumer and all other information in a consumer's file to a government agency authorized to conduct investigations of, or intelligence or counterintelligence activities or analysis related to, international terrorism when presented with a written certification by such government agency that such information is necessary for the agency's conduct or such investigation, activity or analysis.

(b) Form of Certification

The certification described in subsection (a) shall be signed by a supervisory official designated by the head of a Federal agency or an officer of a Federal agency whose appointment to office is required to be made by the President, by and with the advice and consent of the Senate.

(c) Confidentiality

(1) If the head of a government agency authorized to conduct investigations of intelligence or counterintelligence activities or analysis related to international terrorism, or his designee, certifies that otherwise there may result a danger to the national security of the United States, interference with a criminal, counterterrorism, or counterintelligence investigation, interference with diplomatic relations, or danger to the life or physical safety of any person, no consumer reporting agency or officer, employee, or agent of such consumer reporting agency, shall disclose to any person (other than those to whom such disclosure is necessary to comply with the request or an attorney to obtain legal advice or legal assistance with respect to the request), or specify in any consumer report, that a government agency has sought or obtained access to information under subsection (a).

(2) The request shall notify the person or entity to whom the request is directed of the nondisclosure requirement under paragraph (1).

(3) Any recipient disclosing to those persons necessary to comply with the request or to any attorney to obtain legal advice or legal assistance with respect to the request shall inform such persons of any applicable nondisclosure requirement. Any person who receives a disclosure under this subsection shall be subject to the same prohibitions on disclosure under paragraph (1).

(4) At the request of the authorized government agency, any person making or intending to make a disclosure under this section shall identify to the requesting official of the authorized government agency the person to whom such disclosure will be made or to whom such disclosure was made prior to the request, except that nothing in this section shall require a person to inform the requesting official of the identity of an attorney to whom disclosure was made or will be made to obtain legal advice or legal assistance with respect to the request for information under subsection (a).

[Pub. L. No. 109-177, tit. I, 116(c), 120 Stat. 214 (Mar. 9, 2006); Pub. L. No. 109-178, 4(c)(2), 120 Stat. 280 (Mar. 9, 2006)]

(d) Rule of Construction[74]

Nothing in section 1681u shall be construed to limit the authority of the Director of the Federal Bureau of Investigation under this section.

(e) Safe Harbor

Notwithstanding any other provision of this title, any consumer reporting agency or agent or employee thereof making disclosure of consumer reports or other information pursuant to this section in good-faith reliance upon a certification of a government[75] agency pursuant to the provisions of this section shall not be liable to any person for such disclosure under this subchapter, the constitution of any State, or any law or regulation of any State or any political subdivision of any State.

(f) Reports to Congress

(1) On a semi-annual basis, the Attorney General shall fully inform the Committee on the Judiciary, the Committee on Financial Services, and the Permanent Select Committee on Intelligence of the House of Representatives and the Committee on the Judiciary, the Committee on Banking, Housing, and Urban Affairs, and the Select Committee on Intelligence of the Senate concerning all requests made pursuant to subsection (a).

(2) In the case of the semiannual reports required to be submitted under paragraph (1) to the Permanent Select Committee on Intelligence of the House of Representatives and the Select Committee on Intelligence of the Senate, the submittal dates for such reports shall be as provided in section 507 of the National Security Act of 1947 (50 U.S.C. 415b).

[Pub. L. No. 90-321, tit. VI, § 627, *formerly § 626, as added* Pub. L. No. 107-56, tit. III, § 358(g)(1)(B), 115 Stat. 327 (Oct. 26, 2001); *renumbered § 627 and amended* Pub. L. No. 108-159, tit. II, § 214(a)(1), (c)(3), 117 Stat. 1980, 1983 (Dec. 4, 2003); Pub. L. No. 108-458, tit. VI, § 6203(l), 118 Stat. 3747 (Dec. 17, 2004); Pub. L. No. 109-177, tit. I, §§ 116(c), 118(b), 120 Stat. 214, 217 (Mar. 9, 2006); Pub. L. No. 109-178, § 4(c)(2), 120 Stat. 280 (Mar. 9, 2006)]

§ 1681w. Disposal of records [FCRA § 628]

(a) Regulations.—

(1) **In general.**—Not later than 1 year after the date of enactment of this section, the Federal banking agencies, the National Credit Union Administration, and the Commission with respect to the entities that are subject to their respective enforcement authority under section 1681s, and the Securities and Exchange Commission, and in coordination as described in paragraph (2), shall issue final regulations requiring any person that maintains or otherwise possesses consumer information, or any compilation of consumer information, derived from consumer reports for a business purpose to properly dispose of any such information or compilation.

(2) **Coordination.**—Each agency required to prescribe regulations under paragraph (1) shall—

(A) consult and coordinate with each other such agency so that, to the extent possible, the regulations prescribed by each such agency are consistent and comparable with the regulations by each such other agency; and

(B) ensure that such regulations are consistent with the requirements and regulations issued pursuant to Public Law 106-102 and other provisions of Federal law.

(3) Exemption authority.—In issuing regulations under this section, the Federal banking agencies, the National Credit Union Administration, the Commission, and the Securities and Exchange Commission may exempt any person or class of persons from application of those regulations, as such agency deems appropriate to carry out the purpose of this section.

(b) Rule of construction.—Nothing in this section shall be construed—

(1) to require a person to maintain or destroy any record pertaining to a consumer that is not imposed under other law; or

(2) to alter or affect any requirement imposed under any other provision of law to maintain or destroy such a record.

[Pub. L. No. 90-321, tit. VI, § 628, *as added* Pub.L. 108-159, tit. II, § 216(a), 117 Stat. 1985 (Dec. 4, 2003)]

§ 1681x. Corporate and technological circumvention prohibited [FCRA § 629]

The Commission shall prescribe regulations, to become effective not later than 90 days after the date of enactment of this section, to prevent a consumer reporting agency from circumventing or evading treatment as a consumer reporting agency described in section 1681a(p) for purposes of this title, including—

(1) by means of a corporate reorganization or restructuring, including a merger, acquisition, dissolution, divestiture, or asset sale of a consumer reporting agency; or

(2) by maintaining or merging public record and credit account information in a manner that is substantially equivalent to that described in paragraphs (1) and (2) of section 1681a(p), in the manner described in section 1681a(p).

[Pub. L. No. 90-321, tit. VI, § 629, *as added* Pub.L. 108-159, tit. II, § 211(b), 117 Stat. 1970 (Dec. 4, 2003)]

---

74 *Editor's Note*: The effective date for the FACTA amendments (Pub. L. No. 108-159 (Dec. 4, 2003)) to 15 U.S.C. § 1681v(d) is Dec. 31, 2003. *See* 12 C.F.R. § 222.1(c)(1)(i) and 16 C.F.R. § 602.1(c)(1)(i).

75 *Editor's Note*: Amended by Pub. L. No. 108-458, tit. VI, § 6203(*l*), 118 Stat. 3747 (Dec. 17, 2004).

Appendix B FCRA Regulations, Interpretations, and Guidelines

The FCRA did not grant rulemaking authority to the Federal Trade Commission until 1999, and did not mandate any regulations until the passage of the Fair and Accurate Credit Transactions Act (FACTA) of 2003. Thus, the majority of FCRA regulations are promulgated pursuant to FACTA.

FACTA amended the FCRA to require rulemaking in variety of areas. This rulemaking scheme is complex because there are several sets of regulations issued by different federal agencies. The Federal Trade Commission has promulgated regulations that apply to credit reporting agencies and non-bank furnishers, which are set forth in Appendix B.1. The Federal Reserve Board has promulgated a limited number of regulations and model forms that generally apply to all furnishers or all non-bank furnishers, which are set forth in Appendix B.2. Finally, the banking regulators (Office of Comptroller of Currency, Office of Thrift Supervision, Federal Deposit Insurance Corporation, National Credit Union Administration and Federal Reserve Board in its role as a banking regulator) have promulgated FCRA regulations that govern the respective financial institutions that they supervise, which are set forth in Appendix B.3.

In addition to regulations, the FTC and banking regulators have jointly promulgated Interagency Guidelines Establishing Information Security Standards. These Interagency Guidelines were originally issued pursuant to the Gramm-Leach-Bliley Act, but were amended in 2004 to address standards with respect to disposal of consumer report information as mandated by FACTA. The Interagency Guidelines can be found at Appx. G.3, *infra*.

At the time of this printing, only some of regulations required by FACTA have been finalized by the FTC and the banking regulators.

B.1 Federal Trade Commission Regulations

TITLE 16—COMMERCIAL PRACTICES

CHAPTER I—FEDERAL TRADE COMMISSION

* * *

SUBCHAPTER F—FAIR CREDIT REPORTING ACT

* * *

PART 600—STATEMENTS OF GENERAL POLICY OR INTERPRETATIONS

600.1 Authority and purpose.
600.2 Legal effect.

Editor's note: Appendix to Part 600 is reprinted at Appx. C, *infra*.

PART 601—[RESERVED]

PART 602—FAIR AND ACCURATE CREDIT TRANSACTIONS ACT OF 2003

602.1 Effective dates.

PART 603—DEFINITIONS

603.1 Terms defined in the Fair Credit Reporting Act.
603.2 Identity theft.
603.3 Identity theft report.

535

PART 604—FAIR CREDIT REPORTING ACT RULES

604.1 Severability.

PART 610—FREE ANNUAL FILE DISCLOSURES

610.1 Definitions and rule of construction.
610.2 Centralized source for requesting annual file disclosures from nationwide consumer reporting agencies.
610.3 Streamlined process for requesting annual file disclosures from nationwide specialty consumer reporting agencies.

PART 611—PROHIBITION AGAINST CIRCUMVENTING TREATMENT AS A NATIONWIDE CONSUMER REPORTING AGENCY

611.1 Rule of construction.
611.2 General prohibition.
611.3 Limitation on applicability.

PART 613—DURATION OF ACTIVE DUTY ALERTS

613.1 Duration of active duty alerts.

PART 614—APPROPRIATE PROOF OF IDENTITY

614.1 Appropriate proof of identity.

PART 642—PRESCREEN OPT-OUT NOTICE

642.1 Purpose and scope.
642.2 Definitions.
642.3 Prescreen opt-out notice.
642.4 Effective date.

PART 682—DISPOSAL OF CONSUMER REPORT INFORMATION AND RECORDS

682.1 Definitions.
682.2 Purpose and scope.
682.3 Proper disposal of consumer information.
682.4 Relation to other laws.
682.5 Effective date.

PART 698—MODEL FORMS AND DISCLOSURES

698.1 Authority and purpose.
698.2 Legal effect.
698.3 Definitions.
Appendix A to Part 698 Model Prescreen Opt-Out Notices
Appendix B to Part 698 [Reserved]
Appendix C to Part 698 [Reserved]
Appendix D to Part 698 Standardized form for requesting annual file disclosures.
Appendix E to Part 698 Summary of Consumer Identity Theft Rights
Appendix F to Part 698 General Summary of Consumer Rights
Appendix G to Part 698 Notice of Furnisher Responsibilities
Appendix H to Part 698 Notice of User Responsibilities

* * *

TITLE 16—COMMERCIAL PRACTICES

CHAPTER I—FEDERAL TRADE COMMISSION

SUBCHAPTER F—FAIR CREDIT REPORTING ACT

* * *

PART 600—STATEMENTS OF GENERAL POLICY OR INTERPRETATIONS

16 C.F.R. § 600.1 Authority and purpose.

(a) *Authority*. This part is issued by the Commission pursuant to the provisions of the Fair Credit Reporting Act. Pub.L. 91-508, approved October 26, 1970. 84 Stat. 1127–36 (15 U.S.C. 1681 *et seq.*).

(b) *Purpose*. The purpose of this part is to clarify and consolidate statements of general policy or interpretations in a commentary in the Appendix to this part. The Commentary will serve as guidance to consumer reporting agencies, their customers, and consumer representatives. The Fair Credit Reporting Act requires that the manner in which consumer reporting agencies provide information be fair and equitable to the consumer with regard to the confidentiality, accuracy, and proper use of such information. The Commentary will enable interested parties to resolve their questions more easily, present a more comprehensive treatment of interpretations and facilitate compliance with the Fair Credit Reporting Act in accordance with Congressional intent.

16 C.F.R. § 600.2 Legal effect.

(a) The interpretations in the Commentary are not trade regulation rules or regulations, and, as provided in § 1.73 of the Commission's rules, they do not have the force or effect of statutory provisions.

(b) The regulations of the Commission relating to the administration of the Fair Credit Reporting Act are found in subpart H of 16 CFR part 1 (§§ 1.71–1.73).

[*Editor's note*: Appendix to Part 600 is reprinted at Appx. D, *infra*.]

PART 601—[RESERVED]

[69 Fed. Reg. 69784 (Nov. 30, 2004)]

PART 602—FAIR AND ACCURATE CREDIT TRANSACTIONS ACT OF 2003

16 C.F.R. § 602.1 Effective dates.

(a) [Reserved]

(b) [Reserved]

(c) The applicable provisions of the Fair and Accurate Credit Transactions Act of 2003 (FACT Act), Pub.L. 108-159, 117 Stat. 1952, shall be effective in accordance with the following schedule:

(1) *Provisions effective December 31, 2003.*

(i) Sections 151(a)(2), 212(e), 214(c), 311(b), and 711, concerning the relation to state laws; and

(ii) Each of the provisions of the FACT Act that authorizes an agency to issue a regulation or to take other action to implement the applicable provision of the FACT Act or the applicable provision of the Fair Credit Reporting Act, as amended by the FACT Act, but only with respect to that agency's authority to propose and adopt the implementing regulation or to take such other action.

(2) *Provisions effective March 31, 2004.*

(i) Section 111, concerning the definitions;

(ii) Section 156, concerning the statute of limitations

(iii) Sections 312(d), (e), and (f), concerning the furnisher liability exception, liability and enforcement, and rule of construction, respectively;

(iv) Section 313(a), concerning action regarding complaints;

(v) Section 611, concerning communications for certain employee investigations; and

(vi) Section 811, concerning clerical amendments.

(3) *Provisions effective December 1, 2004.*

(i) Section 112, concerning fraud alerts and active duty alerts;

(ii) Section 114, concerning procedures for the identification of possible instances of identity theft;

(iii) Section 115, concerning truncation of the social security number in a consumer report;

(iv) Section 151(a)(1), concerning the summary of rights of identity theft victims;

(v) Section 152, concerning blocking of information resulting from identity theft;

(vi) Section 153, concerning the coordination of identity theft complaint investigations;

(vii) Section 154, concerning the prevention of repollution of consumer reports;

(viii) Section 155, concerning notice by debt collectors with respect to fraudulent information;

(ix) Section 211(c), concerning a summary of rights of consumers;

(x) Section 212(a)–(d), concerning the disclosure of credit scores;

(xi) Section 213(c), concerning duration of elections;

(xii) Section 217(a), concerning the duty to provide notice to a consumer;

(xiii) Section 311(a), concerning the risk-based pricing notice;

(xiv) Section 312(a)–(c), concerning procedures to enhance the accuracy and integrity of information furnished to consumer reporting agencies;

(xv) Section 314, concerning improved disclosure of the results of reinvestigation;

(xvi) Section 315, concerning reconciling addresses;

(xvii) Section 316, concerning notice of dispute through reseller; and

(xviii) Section 317, concerning the duty to conduct a reasonable reinvestigation.

[69 Fed. Reg. 6526 (Feb. 11, 2004) (Effective Date: Mar. 12, 2004) (reprinted on CD-Rom accompanying this volume); 69 Fed. Reg. 29061 (May 20, 2004) (Effective Date: June 21, 2004)]

PART 603—DEFINITIONS

16 C.F.R. § 603.1 Terms defined in the Fair Credit Reporting Act.[1]

Any term used in any part in this subchapter, if defined in the Fair Credit Reporting Act (FCRA) and not otherwise defined in that rule, has the same meaning provided by the FCRA.

[69 Fed. Reg. 8531 (Feb. 24, 2004) (Effective Date: Mar. 3, 2004) (reprinted on CD-Rom accompanying this volume); 69 Fed. Reg. 29061 (May 20, 2004) (Effective Date: June 21, 2004) (reprinted on CD-Rom accompanying this volume); 69 Fed. Reg. 63922 (Nov. 3, 2004) (Effective Date: Dec. 1, 2004)]

16 C.F.R. § 603.2 Identity theft.

(a) The term "identity theft" means a fraud committed or attempted using the identifying information of another person without authority.

(b) The term "identifying information" means any name or number that may be used, alone or in conjunction with any other information, to identify a specific person, including any—

(1) Name, social security number, date of birth, official State or government issued driver's license or identification number, alien registration number, government passport number, employer or taxpayer identification number;

(2) Unique biometric data, such as fingerprint, voice print, retina or iris image, or other unique physical representation;

(3) Unique electronic identification number, address, or routing code; or

(4) Telecommunication identifying information or access device (as defined in 18 U.S.C. 1029(e)).

[69 Fed. Reg. 8531 (Feb. 24, 2004) (Effective Date: Mar. 3, 2004) (reprinted on CD-Rom accompanying this volume); 69 Fed. Reg. 63922 (Nov. 3, 2004) (Effective Date: Dec. 1, 2004)]

16 C.F.R. § 603.3 Identity theft report.

(a) The term "identity theft report" means a report—

(1) That alleges identity theft with as much specificity as the consumer can provide;

(2) That is a copy of an official, valid report filed by the consumer with a Federal, State, or local law enforcement agency, including the United States Postal Inspection Service, the filing of which subjects the person filing the report to criminal penalties relating to the filing of false information, if, in fact, the information in the report is false; and

(3) That may include additional information or documentation that an information furnisher or consumer reporting agency reasonably requests for the purpose of determining the validity of the alleged identity theft, provided that the information furnisher or consumer reporting agency:

(i) Makes such request not later than fifteen days after the date of receipt of the copy of the report form identified in paragraph (a)(2) of this section or the request by the consumer for the particular service, whichever shall be the later;

(ii) Makes any supplemental requests for information or documentation and final determination on the acceptance of the identity theft report within another fifteen days after its initial request for information or documentation; and

(iii) Shall have five days to make a final determination on the acceptance of the identity theft report, in the event that the consumer reporting agency or information furnisher receives any such additional information or documentation on the eleventh day or later within the fifteen day period set forth in paragraph (a)(3)(ii) of this section.

(b) Examples of the specificity referenced in paragraph (a)(1) of this section are provided for illustrative purposes only, as follows:

(1) Specific dates relating to the identity theft such as when the loss or theft of personal information occurred or when the fraud(s) using the personal information occurred, and how the consumer discovered or otherwise learned of the theft.

(2) Identification information or any other information about the perpetrator, if known.

(3) Name(s) of information furnisher(s), account numbers, or other relevant account information related to the identity theft.

(4) Any other information known to the consumer about the identity theft.

(c) Examples of when it would or would not be reasonable to request additional information or documentation referenced in paragraph (a)(3) of this section are provided for illustrative purposes only, as follows:

(1) A law enforcement report containing detailed information about the identity theft and the signature, badge number or other identification information of the individual law enforcement official taking the report should be sufficient on its face to support a victim's request. In this case, without an identifiable concern, such as an indication that the report was fraudulent, it would not be reasonable for an information furnisher or consumer reporting agency to request additional information or documentation.

(2) A consumer might provide a law enforcement report similar to the report in paragraph (c)(1) of this section but certain important information such as the consumer's date of birth or Social Security number may be missing because the consumer chose not to provide it. The information furnisher or consumer reporting agency could accept this report, but it would be reasonable to require that the consumer provide the missing information.

(3) A consumer might provide a law enforcement report generated by an automated system with a simple allegation that an identity theft occurred to support a request for a tradeline block or cessation of information furnishing. In such a case, it would be reasonable for an information furnisher or consumer reporting agency to ask that the consumer fill out and have notarized the Commission's ID Theft Affidavit or a similar form and provide some form of identification documentation.

(4) A consumer might provide a law enforcement report generated by an automated system with a simple allegation that an identity theft occurred to support a request for an extended fraud alert. In this case, it would not be reasonable for a consumer reporting agency to require additional documentation or information, such as a notarized affidavit.

[69 Fed. Reg. 8531 (Feb. 24, 2004) (Effective Date: Mar. 3, 2004) (reprinted on CD-Rom accompanying this volume); 69 Fed. Reg. 63922 (Nov. 3, 2004) (Effective Date: Dec. 1, 2004)]

PART 604—FAIR CREDIT REPORTING ACT RULES

16 C.F.R. § 604.1 Severability.

All parts and subparts of this subchapter are separate and severable from one another. If any part or subpart is stayed or determined to be invalid, the Commission intends that the remaining parts and subparts shall continue in effect.

[69 Fed. Reg. 29061 (May 20, 2004) (Effective Date: June 21, 2004)]

PART 610—FREE ANNUAL FILE DISCLOSURES

16 C.F.R. § 610.1 Definitions and rule of construction.

(a) The definitions and rule of construction set forth in this section apply throughout this part.

(b) *Definitions.*

(1) *Annual file disclosure* means a file disclosure that is provided to a consumer, upon consumer request and without charge, once in any 12-month period, in compliance with section 612(a) of the Fair Credit Reporting Act, 15 U.S.C. 1681j(a).

(2) *Associated consumer reporting agency* means a consumer reporting agency that owns or maintains consumer files housed within systems operated by one or more nationwide consumer reporting agencies.

(3) *Consumer* means an individual.

(4) *Consumer report* has the meaning provided in section 603(d) of the Fair Credit Reporting Act, 15 U.S.C. 1681a(d).

(5) *Consumer reporting agency* has the meaning provided in section 603(f) of the Fair Credit Reporting Act, 15 U.S.C. 1681a(f).

(6) *Extraordinary request volume*, except as provided in sections 610.2(i) and 610.3(g) of this part, occurs when the number of consumers requesting or attempting to request file disclosures during any 24-hour period is more than 175% of the rolling 90-day daily average of consumers requesting or attempting to request file disclosures. For example, if over the previous 90 days an average of 100 consumers per day requested or attempted to request file

disclosures, then extraordinary request volume would be any volume greater than 175% of 100, i.e., 176 or more requests in a single 24-hour period.

(7) *File disclosure* means a disclosure by a consumer reporting agency pursuant to section 609 of the Fair Credit Reporting Act, 15 U.S.C. 1681g.

(8) *High request volume*, except as provided in sections 610.2(i) and 610.3(g) of this part, occurs when the number of consumers requesting or attempting to request file disclosures during any 24-hour period is more than 125% of the rolling 90-day daily average of consumers requesting or attempting to request file disclosures. For example, if over the previous 90 days an average of 100 consumers per day requested or attempted to request file disclosures, then high request volume would be any volume greater than 125% of 100, i.e., 126 or more requests in a single 24-hour period.

(9) *Nationwide consumer reporting agency* means a consumer reporting agency that compiles and maintains files on consumers on a nationwide basis as defined in section 603(p) of the Fair Credit Reporting Act, 15 U.S.C. 1681a(p).

(10) *Nationwide specialty consumer reporting agency* has the meaning provided in section 603(w) of the Fair Credit Reporting Act, 15 U.S.C. 1681a(w).

(11) *Request method* means the method by which a consumer chooses to communicate a request for an annual file disclosure.

(c) *Rule of construction*. The examples in this part are illustrative and not exclusive. Compliance with an example, to the extent applicable, constitutes compliance with this part.

[69 Fed. Reg. 35467 (June 24, 2004) (Effective Date: Dec. 1, 2004)]

16 C.F.R. § 610.2 Centralized source for requesting annual file disclosures from nationwide consumer reporting agencies.

(a) *Purpose*. The purpose of the centralized source is to enable consumers to make a single request to obtain annual file disclosures from all nationwide consumer reporting agencies, as required under section 612(a) of the Fair Credit Reporting Act, 15 U.S.C. 1681j(a).

(b) *Establishment and operation*. All nationwide consumer reporting agencies shall jointly design, fund, implement, maintain, and operate a centralized source for the purpose described in paragraph (a) of this section. The centralized source required by this part shall:

(1) Enable consumers to request annual file disclosures by any of the following request methods, at the consumer's option:

(i) A single, dedicated Internet website;

(ii) A single, dedicated toll-free telephone number; and

(iii) Mail directed to a single address;

(2) Be designed, funded, implemented, maintained, and operated in a manner that:

(i) Has adequate capacity to accept requests from the reasonably anticipated volume of consumers contacting the centralized source through each request method, as determined in accordance with paragraph (c) of this section;

(ii) Collects only as much personally identifiable information as is reasonably necessary to properly identify the consumer as required under the Fair Credit Reporting Act, section 610(a)(1), 15 U.S.C. 1681h(a)(1), and other applicable laws and regulations, and to process the transaction(s) requested by the consumer;

(iii) Provides information through the centralized source website and telephone number regarding how to make a request by all request methods required under section 610.2(b)(1) of this part; and

(iv) Provides clear and easily understandable information and instructions to consumers, including, but not necessarily limited to:

(A) Providing information on the progress of the consumer's request while the consumer is engaged in the process of requesting a file disclosure;

(B) For a website request method, providing access to a "help" or "frequently asked questions" screen, which includes specific information that consumers might reasonably need to request file disclosures, the answers to questions that consumers might reasonably ask, and instructions whereby a consumer may file a complaint with the centralized source and with the Federal Trade Commission;

(C) In the event that a consumer requesting a file disclosure through the centralized source cannot be properly identified in accordance with the Fair Credit Reporting Act, section 610(a)(1), 15 U.S.C. 1681h(a)(1), and other applicable laws and regulations, providing a statement that the consumer's identity cannot be verified; and directions on how to complete the request, including what additional information or documentation will be required to complete the request, and how to submit such information; and

(D) A statement indicating that the consumer has reached the website or telephone number operated by the national credit reporting agencies for ordering free annual credit reports, as required by federal law; and

(3) Make available to consumers a standardized form established jointly by the nationwide consumer reporting agencies, which consumers may use to make a request for an annual file disclosure, either by mail or on the Internet website required under section 610.2(b)(1) of this part, from the centralized source required by this part. The form provided at 16 CFR Part 698, Appendix D, may be used to comply with this section.

(c) *Requirement to anticipate*. The nationwide consumer reporting agencies shall implement reasonable procedures to anticipate, and to respond to, the volume of consumers who will contact the centralized source through each request method, to request, or attempt to request, a file disclosure, including developing and implementing contingency plans to address circumstances that are reasonably likely to occur and that may materially and adversely impact the operation of the nationwide consumer reporting agency, a centralized source request method, or the centralized source.

(1) The contingency plans required by this section shall include reasonable measures to minimize the impact of such circumstances on the operation of the centralized source and on consumers contacting, or attempting to contact, the centralized source.

(i) Such reasonable measures to minimize impact shall include, but are not necessarily limited to:

(A) To the extent reasonably practicable under the circumstances, providing information to consumers on how to use another available request method;

(B) To the extent reasonably practicable under the circumstances, communicating, to a consumer who attempts but is unable to make a request, the fact that a condition exists that has precluded the centralized source from accepting all requests, and the period of time after which the centralized source is reasonably anticipated to be able to accept the consumer's request for an annual file disclosure; and

(C) Taking all reasonable steps to restore the centralized source to normal operating status as quickly as reasonably practicable under the circumstances.

(ii) Reasonable measures to minimize impact may also include, as appropriate, collecting request information but declining to accept the request for processing until a reasonable later time, provided that the consumer is clearly and prominently informed, to the extent reasonably practicable under the circumstances, of when the request will be accepted for processing.

(2) A nationwide consumer reporting agency shall not be deemed in violation of section 610.2(b)(2)(i) of this part if a centralized source request method is unavailable to accept requests for a reasonable period of time for purposes of conducting maintenance on the request method, provided that the other required request methods remain available during such time.

(d) *Disclosures required.* If a nationwide consumer reporting agency has the ability to provide a consumer report to a third party relating to a consumer, regardless of whether the consumer report is owned by that nationwide consumer reporting agency or by an associated consumer reporting agency, that nationwide consumer reporting agency shall, upon proper identification in compliance with section 610(a)(1) of the Fair Credit Reporting Act, 15 U.S.C. 1681h(a)(1), provide an annual file disclosure to such consumer if the consumer makes a request through the centralized source.

(e) *High Request volume and extraordinary request volume.*

(1) *High request volume.* Provided that a nationwide consumer reporting agency has implemented reasonable procedures developed in accordance with paragraph (c) of this section, entitled "requirement to anticipate," the nationwide consumer reporting agency shall not be deemed in violation of paragraph (b)(2)(i) of this section for any period of time in which a centralized source request method, the centralized source, or the nationwide consumer reporting agency experiences high request volume, if the nationwide consumer reporting agency:

(i) Collects all consumer request information and delays accepting the request for processing until a reasonable later time; and

(ii) Clearly and prominently informs the consumer of when the request will be accepted for processing.

(2) *Extraordinary request volume.* Provided that the nationwide consumer reporting agency has implemented reasonable procedures developed in compliance with paragraph (c) of this section, entitled "requirement to anticipate," the nationwide consumer reporting agency shall not be deemed in violation of paragraph (b)(2)(i) of this section for any period of time during which a particular centralized source request method, the centralized source, or the nationwide consumer reporting agency experiences extraordinary request volume.

(f) *Information use and disclosure.* Any personally identifiable information collected from consumers as a result of a request for annual file disclosure, or other disclosure required by the Fair Credit Reporting Act, made through the centralized source, may be used or disclosed by the centralized source or a nationwide consumer reporting agency only:

(1) To provide the annual file disclosure or other disclosure required under the FCRA requested by the consumer;

(2) To process a transaction requested by the consumer at the same time as a request for annual file disclosure or other disclosure;

(3) To comply with applicable legal requirements, including those imposed by the Fair Credit Reporting Act and this part; and

(4) To update personally identifiable information already maintained by the nationwide consumer reporting agency for the purpose of providing consumer reports, provided that the nationwide consumer reporting agency uses and discloses the updated personally identifiable information subject to the same restrictions that would apply, under any applicable provision of law or regulation, to the information updated or replaced.

(g) *Communications provided by centralized source.*

(1) Any communications or instructions, including any advertising or marketing, provided through the centralized source shall not interfere with, detract from, contradict, or otherwise undermine the purpose of the centralized source stated in paragraph (a) of this section.

(2) Examples of interfering, detracting, inconsistent, and/or undermining communications include:

(i) A website that contains pop-up advertisements or other offers or promotions that hinder the consumer's ability to complete an online request for an annual file disclosure;

(ii) Centralized source materials that represent, expressly or by implication, that a consumer must purchase a paid product in order to receive or to understand the annual file disclosure;

(iii) Centralized source materials that represent, expressly or by implication, that annual file disclosures are not free, or that obtaining an annual file disclosure will have a negative impact on the consumer's credit standing; and

(iv) Centralized source materials that falsely represent, expressly or by implication, that a product or service offered ancillary to receipt of a file disclosure, such as a credit score or credit monitoring service, is free, or fail to clearly and prominently disclose that consumers must cancel a service, advertised as free for an initial period of time, to avoid being charged, if such is the case.

(h) *Effective date.* Sections 610.1 and 610.2 shall become effective on December 1, 2004.

(i) *Transition.*

(1) *Regional rollout.* The centralized source required by this part shall be made available to consumers in a cumulative manner, as follows:

(i) For consumers residing in Alaska, Arizona, California, Colorado, Hawaii, Idaho, Montana, New Mexico, Nevada, Oregon, Utah, Washington, and Wyoming, the centralized source shall become available on or before December 1, 2004;

(ii) For consumers residing in Illinois, Indiana, Iowa, Kansas, Michigan, Minnesota, Missouri, Nebraska, North Dakota, Ohio, South Dakota, and Wisconsin, the centralized source shall become available on or before March 1, 2005;

(iii) For consumers residing in Alabama, Arkansas, Florida, Georgia, Kentucky, Louisiana, Mississippi, Oklahoma, South Carolina, Tennessee, and Texas, the centralized source shall become available on or before June 1, 2005; and

(iv) For all other consumers, including consumers residing in Connecticut, Delaware, District of Columbia, Maine, Maryland, Massachusetts, New Hampshire, New Jersey, New York, North Carolina, Pennsylvania, Rhode Island, Vermont, Virginia, West Virginia, and all United States territories and possessions, the centralized source shall become available on or before September 1, 2005.

(2) *High request volume during transition.*

(i) *During the period of December 1, 2004 through December 7, 2004*, high request volume shall mean the following:

(A) For an individual request method: High request volume occurs when the number of consumers contacting or attempting to contact the centralized source through the request method in any 24-hour period is more than 115% of the daily total number of consumers that were reasonably anticipated to contact the centralized source, in compliance with paragraph (c) of this section, through that request method.

(B) For the centralized source as a whole: High request volume occurs when the number of consumers contacting or attempting to contact the centralized source in any 24-hour period is more than 115% of the daily total number of consumers that were reasonably anticipated to contact the centralized source, in compliance with paragraph (c) of this section, through any request method.

(C) For a nationwide consumer reporting agency: High request volume occurs when the number of consumers contacting or attempting to contact the nationwide consumer reporting agency to request file disclosures in any 24-hour period is more than 115% of the daily total number of consumers that were reasonably anticipated to contact that nationwide consumer reporting agency to request file disclosures, in compliance with paragraph (c) of this section.

(ii) *During the period of December 8, 2004 through August 31, 2005*, high request volume shall mean the following:

(A) For an individual request method: High request volume occurs when the number of consumers contacting or attempting to contact the centralized source through the request method in any 24-hour period is more than 115 % of the rolling 7-day daily average number of consumers who contacted or attempted to contact the centralized source to request file disclosures through that request method.

(B) For the centralized source as a whole: High request volume occurs when the number of consumers contacting or attempting to contact the centralized source in any 24-hour period is more than 115% of the rolling 7-day daily average number of consumers who contacted or attempted to contact the centralized source to request file disclosures through any request method.

(C) For a nationwide consumer reporting agency: High request volume occurs when the number of consumers contacting or attempting to contact the nationwide consumer reporting agency to request file disclosures in any 24-hour period is more than 115% of the rolling 7-day daily average of consumers who requested any type of file disclosure from that nationwide consumer reporting agency.

(3) *Extraordinary request volume during transition.*

(i) *During the period of December 1, 2004 through December 7, 2004*, extraordinary request volume shall mean the following:

(A) For an individual request method: Extraordinary request volume occurs when the number of consumers contacting or attempting to contact the centralized source through the request method in any 24-hour period is more than 175% of the daily total number of consumers that were reasonably anticipated to contact the centralized source, in compliance with paragraph (c) of this section, through that request method.

(B) For the centralized source as a whole: Extraordinary request volume occurs when the number of consumers contacting or attempting to contact the centralized source in any 24-hour period is more than 175% of the daily total number of consumers that were reasonably anticipated to contact the centralized source, in compliance with paragraph (c) of this section, through any request method.

(C) For a nationwide consumer reporting agency: Extraordinary request volume occurs when the number of consumers contacting or attempting to contact the nationwide consumer reporting agency to request file disclosures in any 24-hour period is more than 175% of the daily total number of consumers that were reasonably anticipated to contact that nationwide consumer reporting agency to request their file disclosures, in compliance with paragraph (c) of this section.

(ii) *During the period of December 8, 2004 through August 31, 2005*, extraordinary request volume shall mean the following:

(A) For an individual request method: Extraordinary request volume occurs when the number of consumers contacting or attempting to contact the centralized source through the request method in a 24-hour period is more than 175% of the rolling 7-day daily average number of consumers who contacted or attempted to contact the centralized source to request file disclosures through that request method.

(B) For the centralized source as a whole: Extraordinary request volume occurs when the number of consumers contacting or attempting to contact the centralized source in a 24-hour period is more than 175% of the rolling 7-day daily average number of consumers who contacted or attempted to contact the centralized source to request file disclosures through any request method.

(C) For a nationwide consumer reporting agency: Extraordinary request volume occurs when the number of consumers contacting or attempting to contact the nationwide consumer reporting agency to request file disclosures in a 24-hour period is more than 175% of the rolling 7-day daily average of consumers who requested any type of file disclosure from that nationwide consumer reporting agency.

[69 Fed. Reg. 35467 (June 24, 2004) (Effective Date: Dec. 1, 2004)]

16 C.F.R. § 610.3 Streamlined process for requesting annual file disclosures from nationwide specialty consumer reporting agencies.

(a) *Streamlined process requirements*. Any nationwide specialty consumer reporting agency shall have a streamlined process for accepting and processing consumer requests for annual file disclosures. The streamlined process required by this part shall:

(1) Enable consumers to request annual file disclosures by a toll-free telephone number that:

(i) Provides clear and prominent instructions for requesting disclosures by any additional available request methods, that do not interfere with, detract from, contradict, or otherwise undermine the ability of consumers to obtain annual file disclosures through the streamlined process required by this part;

(ii) Is published, in conjunction with all other published numbers for the nationwide specialty consumer reporting agency, in any telephone directory in which any telephone number for the nationwide specialty consumer reporting agency is published; and

(iii) Is clearly and prominently posted on any website owned or maintained by the nationwide specialty consumer reporting agency that is related to consumer reporting, along with instructions for requesting disclosures by any additional available request methods; and

(2) Be designed, funded, implemented, maintained, and operated in a manner that:

(i) Has adequate capacity to accept requests from the reasonably anticipated volume of consumers contacting the nationwide specialty consumer reporting agency through the streamlined process, as determined in compliance with paragraph (b) of this section;

(ii) Collects only as much personal information as is reasonably necessary to properly identify the consumer as required under the Fair Credit Reporting Act, section 610(a)(1), 15 U.S.C. 1681h(a)(1), and other applicable laws and regulations; and

(iii) Provides clear and easily understandable information and instructions to consumers, including but not necessarily limited to:

(A) Providing information on the status of the consumer's request while the consumer is in the process of making a request;

(B) For a website request method, providing access to a "help" or "frequently asked questions" screen, which includes more specific information that consumers might reasonably need to order their file disclosure, the answers to questions that consumers might reasonably ask, and instructions whereby a consumer may file a complaint with the nationwide specialty consumer reporting agency and with the Federal Trade Commission; and

(C) In the event that a consumer requesting a file disclosure cannot be properly identified in accordance with the Fair Credit Reporting Act, section 610(a)(1), 15 U.S.C. 1681h(a)(1), and other applicable laws and regulations, providing a statement that the consumer's identity cannot be verified; and directions on how to complete the request, including what additional information or documentation will be required to complete the request, and how to submit such information.

(b) *Requirement to anticipate.* A nationwide specialty consumer reporting agency shall implement reasonable procedures to anticipate, and respond to, the volume of consumers who will contact the nationwide specialty consumer reporting agency through the streamlined process to request, or attempt to request, file disclosures, including developing and implementing contingency plans to address circumstances that are reasonably likely to occur and that may materially and adversely impact the operation of the nationwide specialty consumer reporting agency, a request method, or the streamlined process.

(1) The contingency plans required by this section shall include reasonable measures to minimize the impact of such circumstances on the operation of the streamlined process and on consumers contacting, or attempting to contact, the nationwide specialty consumer reporting agency through the streamlined process.

(i) Such reasonable measures to minimize impact shall include, but are not necessarily limited to:

(A) To the extent reasonably practicable under the circumstances, providing information to consumers on how to use another available request method;

(B) To the extent reasonably practicable under the circumstances, communicating, to a consumer who attempts but is unable to make a request, the fact that a condition exists that has precluded the nationwide specialty consumer reporting agency from accepting all requests, and the period of time after which the agency is reasonably anticipated to be able to accept the consumer's request for an annual file disclosure; and

(C) Taking all reasonable steps to restore the streamlined process to normal operating status as quickly as reasonably practicable under the circumstances.

(ii) Measures to minimize impact may also include, as appropriate, collecting request information but declining to accept the request for processing until a reasonable later time, provided that the consumer is clearly and prominently informed, to the extent reasonably practicable under the circumstances, of when the request will be accepted for processing.

(2) A nationwide specialty consumer reporting agency shall not be deemed in violation of section 610.3(a)(2)(i) if the toll-free telephone number required by this part is unavailable to accept requests for a reasonable period of time for purposes of conducting maintenance on the request method, provided that the nationwide specialty consumer reporting agency makes other request methods available to consumers during such time.

(c) *High request volume and extraordinary request volume.*

(1) *High request volume.* Provided that the nationwide specialty consumer reporting agency has implemented reasonable procedures developed in accordance with paragraph (b) of this section, entitled "requirement to anticipate," a nationwide specialty consumer reporting agency shall not be deemed in violation of paragraph (a)(2)(i) of this section for any period of time during which a streamlined process request method or the nationwide specialty consumer reporting agency experiences high request volume, if the nationwide specialty consumer reporting agency:

(i) Collects all consumer request information and delays accepting the request for processing until a reasonable later time; and

(ii) Clearly and prominently informs the consumer of when the request will be accepted for processing.

(2) *Extraordinary request volume.* Provided that the nationwide specialty consumer reporting agency has implemented reasonable procedures developed in accordance with paragraph (b) of this section, entitled "requirement to anticipate," a nationwide specialty consumer reporting agency shall not be deemed in violation of paragraph (a)(2)(i) of this section for any period of time during which a streamlined process request method or the nationwide specialty consumer reporting agency experiences extraordinary request volume.

(d) *Information use and disclosure.* Any personally identifiable information collected from consumers as a result of a request for annual file disclosure, or other disclosure required by the Fair Credit Reporting Act, made through the streamlined process, may be used or disclosed by the nationwide specialty consumer reporting agency only:

(1) To provide the annual file disclosure or other disclosure required under the FCRA requested by the consumer;

(2) To process a transaction requested by the consumer at the same time as a request for annual file disclosure or other disclosure;

(3) To comply with applicable legal requirements, including those imposed by the Fair Credit Reporting Act and this part; and

(4) To update personally identifiable information already maintained by the nationwide specialty consumer reporting agency for the purpose of providing consumer reports, provided that the nationwide specialty consumer reporting agency uses and discloses the updated personally identifiable information subject to the same restrictions that would apply, under any applicable provision of law or regulation, to the information updated or replaced.

(e) *Requirement to accept or redirect requests.* If a consumer requests an annual file disclosure through a method other than the streamlined process established by the nationwide specialty consumer reporting agency in compliance with this part, a nationwide specialty consumer reporting agency shall:

(1) Accept the consumer's request; or

(2) Instruct the consumer how to make the request using the streamlined process required by this part.

(f) *Effective date.* This section shall become effective on December 1, 2004.

(g) *High request volume and extraordinary request volume during initial transition.*

(1) During the period of December 1, 2004 through February 28, 2005, high request volume shall mean the following:

(i) For an individual request method: High request volume occurs when the number of consumers contacting or attempting to contact the nationwide specialty consumer reporting agency through a streamlined process request method in any 24-hour period is more than 115% of the daily total number of consumers who were reasonably anticipated to contact that request method, in compliance with paragraph (b) of this section.

(ii) For a nationwide specialty consumer reporting agency: High request volume occurs when the number of consumers contacting or attempting to contact the nationwide specialty consumer reporting agency to request file disclosures in any 24-hour period is more than 115% of the number of consumers who were reasonably anticipated to contact the nationwide specialty consumer reporting agency to request their file disclosures, in compliance with paragraph (b) of this section.

(2) *Extraordinary request volume.* During the period of December 1, 2004 through February 28, 2005, extraordinary request volume shall mean the following:

(i) For an individual request method: Extraordinary request volume occurs when the number of consumers contacting or attempting to contact the nationwide specialty consumer reporting agency through a streamlined process request method in any 24-hour period is more than 175% of the daily total number of consumers who were reasonably predicted to contact that request method, in compliance with paragraph (b) of this section.

(ii) For a nationwide specialty consumer reporting agency: Extraordinary request volume occurs when the number of consumers contacting or attempting to contact the nationwide specialty consumer reporting agency to request file disclosures in any 24-hour period is more than 175% of the number of consumers who were reasonably anticipated to contact the nationwide specialty consumer reporting agency to request their file disclosures, in compliance with paragraph (b) of this section.

[69 Fed. Reg. 35467 (June 24, 2004) (Effective Date: Dec. 1, 2004)]

PART 611—PROHIBITION AGAINST CIRCUMVENTING TREATMENT AS A NATIONWIDE CONSUMER REPORTING AGENCY

16 C.F.R. § 611.1 Rule of construction.

The examples in this part are illustrative and not exclusive. Compliance with an example, to the extent applicable, constitutes compliance with this part.

[69 Fed. Reg. 29061 (May 20, 2004) (Effective Date: June 21, 2004)]

16 C.F.R. § 611.2 General prohibition.

(a) A consumer reporting agency shall not circumvent or evade treatment as a "consumer reporting agency that compiles and maintains files on consumers on a nationwide basis' as defined under section 603(p) of the Fair Credit Reporting Act, 15 U.S.C. 1681a(p), by any means, including, but not limited to:

(1) Corporate organization, reorganization, structure, or restructuring, including merger, acquisition, dissolution, divestiture, or asset sale of a consumer reporting agency; or

(2) Maintaining or merging public record and credit account information in a manner that is substantially equivalent to that described in paragraphs (1) and (2) of section 603(p) of the Fair Credit Reporting Act, 15 U.S.C. 1681a(p).

(b) *Examples*:

(1) *Circumvention through reorganization by data type.* XYZ Inc. is a consumer reporting agency that compiles and maintains files on consumers on a nationwide basis. It restructures its operations so that public record information is assembled and maintained only by its corporate affiliate, ABC Inc. XYZ continues operating as a consumer reporting agency but ceases to comply with the FCRA obligations of a consumer reporting agency that compiles and maintains files on consumers on a nationwide basis, asserting that it no longer meets the definition found in FCRA section 603 (p), because it no longer maintains public record information. XYZ's conduct is a circumvention or evasion of treatment as a consumer reporting agency that compiles and maintains files on consumers on a nationwide basis, and thus violates this section.

(2) *Circumvention through reorganization by regional operations.* PDQ Inc. is a consumer reporting agency that compiles and maintains files on consumers on a nationwide basis. It restructures its operations so that corporate affiliates separately assemble and maintain all information on consumers residing in each state. PDQ continues to operate as a consumer reporting agency but ceases to comply with the FCRA obligations of a consumer reporting agency that compiles and maintains files on consumers on a nationwide basis, asserting that it no longer meets the definition found in FCRA section 603(p), because it no longer operates on a nationwide basis. PDQ's conduct is a circumvention or evasion of treatment as a consumer reporting agency that compiles and maintains files on consumers on a nationwide basis, and thus violates this section.

(3) *Circumvention by a newly formed entity.* Smith Co. is a new entrant in the marketplace for consumer reports that bear on a consumer's credit worthiness, standing and capacity. Smith Co. organizes itself into two affiliated companies: Smith Credit Co. and Smith Public Records Co. Smith Credit Co. assembles and maintains credit account information from persons who furnish that information regularly and in the ordinary course of business on consumers residing nationwide. Smith Public Records Co. assembles and maintains public record information on consumers nationwide. Neither Smith Co. nor its affiliated organizations comply with FCRA obligations of consumer reporting agencies that compile and maintain files on consumers on a nationwide basis. Smith Co.'s conduct is a circumvention or evasion of

treatment as a consumer reporting agency that compiles and maintains files on consumers on a nationwide basis, and thus violates this section.

(4) Bona fide, arms-length transaction with unaffiliated party. Foster Ltd. is a consumer reporting agency that compiles and maintains files on consumers on a nationwide basis. Foster Ltd. sells its public record information business to an unaffiliated company in a bona fide, arms-length transaction. Foster Ltd. ceases to assemble, evaluate and maintain public record information on consumers residing nationwide, and ceases to offer reports containing public record information. Foster Ltd.'s conduct is not a circumvention or evasion of treatment as a consumer reporting agency that compiles and maintains files on consumers on a nationwide basis. Foster Ltd.'s conduct does not violate this part.

[69 Fed. Reg. 29061 (May 20, 2004) (Effective Date: June 21, 2004)]

16 C.F.R. § 611.3 Limitation on applicability.

Any person who is otherwise in violation of § 611.2 shall be deemed to be in compliance with this part if such person is in compliance with all obligations imposed upon consumer reporting agencies that compile and maintain files on consumers on a nationwide basis under the Fair Credit Reporting Act, 15 U.S.C. 1681 et seq.

[69 Fed. Reg. 29061 (May 20, 2004) (Effective Date: June 21, 2004)]

PART 613—DURATION OF ACTIVE DUTY ALERTS

16 C.F.R. § 613.1 Duration of active duty alerts.

The duration of an active duty alert shall be twelve months.

[69 Fed. Reg. 63922 (Nov. 3, 2004) (Effective Date: Dec. 1, 2004)]

PART 614—APPROPRIATE PROOF OF IDENTITY

16 C.F.R. § 614.1 Appropriate proof of identity.

(a) Consumer reporting agencies shall develop and implement reasonable requirements for what information consumers shall provide to constitute proof of identity for purposes of sections 605A, 605B, and 609(a)(1) of the Fair Credit Reporting Act. In developing these requirements, the consumer reporting agencies must:

(1) Ensure that the information is sufficient to enable the consumer reporting agency to match consumers with their files; and

(2) Adjust the information to be commensurate with an identifiable risk of harm arising from misidentifying the consumer.

(b) Examples of information that might constitute reasonable information requirements for proof of identity are provided for illustrative purposes only, as follows:

(1) Consumer file match: The identification information of the consumer including his or her full name (first, middle initial, last, suffix), any other or previously used names, current and/or recent full address (street number and name, apt. no., city, state, and zip code), full 9 digits of Social Security number, and/or date of birth.

(2) Additional proof of identity: copies of government issued identification documents, utility bills, and/or other methods of authentication of a person's identity which may include, but would not be limited to, answering questions to which only the consumer might be expected to know the answer.

[69 Fed. Reg. 63922 (Nov. 3, 2004) (Effective Date: Dec. 1, 2004)]

PART 642—PRESCREEN OPT-OUT NOTICE

16 C.F.R. § 642.1 Purpose and scope.

(a) *Purpose.* This part implements section 213(a) of the Fair and Accurate Credit Transactions Act of 2003, which requires the Federal Trade Commission to establish the format, type size, and manner of the notices to consumers, required by section 615(d) of the Fair Credit Reporting Act ("FCRA"), regarding the right to prohibit ("opt out" of) the use of information in a consumer report to send them solicitations of credit or insurance.

(b) *Scope.* This part applies to any person who uses a consumer report on any consumer in connection with any credit or insurance transaction that is not initiated by the consumer, and that is provided to that person under section 604(c)(1)(B) of the FCRA (15 U.S.C. 1681b(c)(1)(B)).

[70 Fed. Reg. 5021 (Jan. 31, 2005) (Effective Date: Aug. 1, 2005)]

16 C.F.R. § 642.2 Definitions.

As used in this part:

(a) *Simple and easy to understand* means:

(1) A layered format as described in § 642.3 of this part;

(2) Plain language designed to be understood by ordinary consumers; and

(3) Use of clear and concise sentences, paragraphs, and sections.

(i) *Examples.* For purposes of this part, examples of factors to be considered in determining whether a statement is in plain language and uses clear and concise sentences, paragraphs, and sections include:

(A) Use of short explanatory sentences;

(B) Use of definite, concrete, everyday words;

(C) Use of active voice;

(D) Avoidance of multiple negatives;

(E) Avoidance of legal and technical business terminology;

(F) Avoidance of explanations that are imprecise and reasonably subject to different interpretations; and

(G) Use of language that is not misleading.

(ii) [Reserved]

(b) *Principal promotional document* means the document designed to be seen first by the consumer, such as the cover letter.

[70 Fed. Reg. 5021 (Jan. 31, 2005) (Effective Date: Aug. 1, 2005)]

16 C.F.R. § 642.3 Prescreen opt-out notice.

Any person who uses a consumer report on any consumer in connection with any credit or insurance transaction that is not initiated by the consumer, and that is provided to that person under section 604(c)(1)(B) of the FCRA (15 U.S.C. 1681b(c)(1)(B)), shall, with each written solicitation made to the consumer about the transaction, provide the consumer with the following statement, consisting of a short portion and a long portion, which shall be in the same language as the offer of credit or insurance:

(a) *Short notice*. The short notice shall be a clear and conspicuous, and simple and easy to understand statement as follows:

(1) *Content*. The short notice shall state that the consumer has the right to opt out of receiving prescreened solicitations, and shall provide the toll-free number the consumer can call to exercise that right. The short notice also shall direct the consumer to the existence and location of the long notice, and shall state the heading for the long notice. The short notice shall not contain any other information.

(2) *Form*. The short notice shall be:

(i) In a type size that is larger than the type size of the principal text on the same page, but in no event smaller than 12-point type, or if provided by electronic means, then reasonable steps shall be taken to ensure that the type size is larger than the type size of the principal text on the same page;

(ii) On the front side of the first page of the principal promotional document in the solicitation, or, if provided electronically, on the same page and in close proximity to the principal marketing message;

(iii) Located on the page and in a format so that the statement is distinct from other text, such as inside a border; and

(iv) In a type style that is distinct from the principal type style used on the same page, such as bolded, italicized, underlined, and/or in a color that contrasts with the color of the principal text on the page, if the solicitation is in more than one color.

(b) *Long notice*. The long notice shall be a clear and conspicuous, and simple and easy to understand statement as follows:

(1) *Content*. The long notice shall state the information required by section 615(d) of the Fair Credit Reporting Act (15 U.S.C. 1681m(d)). The long notice shall not include any other information that interferes with, detracts from, contradicts, or otherwise undermines the purpose of the notice.

(2) *Form*. The long notice shall:

(i) Appear in the solicitation;

(ii) Be in a type size that is no smaller than the type size of the principal text on the same page, and, for solicitations provided other than by electronic means, the type size shall in no event be smaller than 8-point type;

(iii) Begin with a heading in capital letters and underlined, and identifying the long notice as the "PRESCREEN & OPT-OUT NOTICE";

(iv) Be in a type style that is distinct from the principal type style used on the same page, such as bolded, italicized, underlined, and/or in a color that contrasts with the color of the principal text on the page, if the solicitation is in more than one color; and

(v) Be set apart from other text on the page, such as by including a blank line above and below the statement, and by indenting both the left and right margins from other text on the page.

[70 Fed. Reg. 5021 (Jan. 31, 2005) (Effective Date: Aug. 1, 2005)]

16 C.F.R. § 642.4 Effective date.

This part is effective on August 1, 2005.

[70 Fed. Reg. 5021 (Jan. 31, 2005) (Effective Date: Aug. 1, 2005)]

PART 682—DISPOSAL OF CONSUMER REPORT INFORMATION AND RECORDS

16 C.F.R. § 682.1 Definitions.

(a) *In general*. Except as modified by this part or unless the context otherwise requires, the terms used in this part have the same meaning as set forth in the Fair Credit Reporting Act, 15 U.S.C. 1681 *et seq*.

(b) "*Consumer information*" means any record about an individual, whether in paper, electronic, or other form, that is a consumer report or is derived from a consumer report. Consumer information also means a compilation of such records. Consumer information does not include information that does not identify individuals, such as aggregate information or blind data.

(c) "*Dispose*," "*disposing*," or "*disposal*" means:

(1) The discarding or abandonment of consumer information, or

(2) The sale, donation, or transfer of any medium, including computer equipment, upon which consumer information is stored.

[69 Fed. Reg. 68689 (Nov. 24, 2004) (Effective Date: June 1, 2005)]

16 C.F.R. § 682.2 Purpose and scope.

(a) *Purpose*. This part ("rule") implements section 216 of the Fair and Accurate Credit Transactions Act of 2003, which is designed to reduce the risk of consumer fraud and related harms, including identity theft, created by improper disposal of consumer information.

(b) *Scope*. This rule applies to any person over which the Federal Trade Commission has jurisdiction, that, for a business purpose, maintains or otherwise possesses consumer information.

[69 Fed. Reg. 68689 (Nov. 24, 2004) (Effective Date: June 1, 2005)]

16 C.F.R. § 682.3 Proper disposal of consumer information.

(a) *Standard*. Any person who maintains or otherwise possesses consumer information for a business purpose must properly dispose of such information by taking reasonable measures to protect against unauthorized access to or use of the information in connection with its disposal.

(b) *Examples*. Reasonable measures to protect against unauthorized access to or use of consumer information in connection with its disposal include the following examples. These examples are illustrative only and are not exclusive or exhaustive methods for complying with the rule in this part.

(1) Implementing and monitoring compliance with policies and procedures that require the burning, pulverizing, or shredding of papers containing consumer information so that the information cannot practicably be read or reconstructed.

(2) Implementing and monitoring compliance with policies and procedures that require the destruction or erasure of electronic media containing consumer information so that the information cannot practically be read or reconstructed.

(3) After due diligence, entering into and monitoring compliance with a contract with another party engaged in the business of record destruction to dispose of material, specifically identified as consumer information, in a manner consistent with this rule. In this context, due diligence could include reviewing an independent audit of the disposal company's operations and/or its compliance with this rule, obtaining information about the disposal company from several references or other reliable sources, requiring that the disposal company be certified by a recognized trade association or similar third party, reviewing and evaluating the disposal company's information security policies or procedures, or taking other appropriate measures to determine the competency and integrity of the potential disposal company.

(4) For persons or entities who maintain or otherwise possess consumer information through their provision of services directly to a person subject to this part, implementing and monitoring compliance with policies and procedures that protect against unauthorized or unintentional disposal of consumer information, and disposing of such information in accordance with examples (b)(1) and (2) of this section.

(5) For persons subject to the Gramm-Leach-Bliley Act, 15 U.S.C. 6081 *et seq.*, and the Federal Trade Commission's Standards for Safeguarding Customer Information, 16 CFR part 314 ("Safeguards Rule"), incorporating the proper disposal of consumer information as required by this rule into the information security program required by the Safeguards Rule.

[69 Fed. Reg. 68689 (Nov. 24, 2004) (Effective Date: June 1, 2005)]

16 C.F.R. § 682.4 Relation to other laws.

Nothing in the rule in this part shall be construed:

(a) To require a person to maintain or destroy any record pertaining to a consumer that is not imposed under other law; or

(b) To alter or affect any requirement imposed under any other provision of law to maintain or destroy such a record.

[69 Fed. Reg. 68689 (Nov. 24, 2004) (Effective Date: June 1, 2005)]

16 C.F.R. § 682.5 Effective date.

The rule in this part is effective on June 1, 2005.

[69 Fed. Reg. 68689 (Nov. 24, 2004) (Effective Date: June 1, 2005)]

PART 698—MODEL FORMS AND DISCLOSURES

16 C.F.R. § 698.1 Authority and purpose.

(a) *Authority.* This part is issued by the Commission pursuant to the provisions of the Fair Credit Reporting Act (15 U.S.C. 1681 *et seq.*), as amended by the Consumer Credit Reporting Reform Act of 1996 (Title II, Subtitle D, Chapter 1, of the Omnibus Consolidated Appropriations Act for Fiscal Year 1997), Public Law 104-208, 110 Stat. 3009-426 (Sept. 30, 1996), and the Fair and Accurate Credit Transactions Act of 2003, Public Law 108-159, 117 Stat. 1952 (Dec. 4, 2003).

(b) *Purpose.* The purpose of this part is to comply with sections 607(d), 609(c), 609(d), 612(a), and 615(d) of the Fair Credit Reporting Act, as amended by the Fair and Accurate Credit Transactions Act of 2003, and Section 211 of the Fair and Accurate Credit Transactions Act of 2003.

[69 Fed. Reg. 35467 (June 24, 2004) (Effective Date: Dec. 1, 2004) (reprinted on CD-Rom accompanying this volume); 69 Fed. Reg. 69775 (Nov. 30, 2004) (Effective Date: Jan. 31, 2005) (reprinted on CD-Rom accompanying this volume); 70 Fed. Reg. 5021 (Jan. 31, 2005) (Effective Date: Aug. 1, 2005)]

16 C.F.R. § 698.2 Legal effect.

These model forms and disclosures prescribed by the FTC do not constitute a trade regulation rule. The issuance of the model forms and disclosures set forth below carries out the directive in the statute that the FTC prescribe these forms and disclosures. Use or distribution of these model forms and disclosures will constitute compliance with any section or subsection of the FCRA requiring that such forms and disclosures be used by or supplied to any person.

[69 Fed. Reg. 35467 (June 24, 2004) (Effective Date: Dec. 1, 2004) (reprinted on CD-Rom accompanying this volume); 69 Fed. Reg. 69775 (Nov. 30, 2004) (Effective Date: Jan. 31, 2005)]

16 C.F.R. § 698.3 Definitions.

As used in this part, unless otherwise provided:

(a) *Substantially similar* means that all information in the Commission's prescribed model is included in the document that is distributed, and that the document distributed is formatted in a way consistent with the format prescribed by the Commission. The document that is distributed shall not include anything that interferes with, detracts from, or otherwise undermines the information contained in the Commission's prescribed model.

[69 Fed. Reg. 69775 (Nov. 30, 2004) (Effective Date: Jan. 31, 2005)]

Appendix A to Part 698—Model Prescreen Opt-Out Notices

In order to comply with part 642 of this title, the following model notices may be used:

(a) English language model notice.
(1) Short notice.
[*Editor's note*: This notice is reprinted in Appx. C, *infra.*]
(2) Long notice.
[*Editor's note*: This notice is reprinted in Appx. C, *infra.*]
(b) Spanish language model notice.
(1) Short notice.
[*Editor's note*: This notice is reprinted in Appx. C, *infra.*]
(2) Long notice.

[*Editor's note*: This notice is reprinted in Appx. C, *infra*.]

[70 Fed. Reg. 5021 (Jan. 31, 2005) (Effective Date: Aug. 1, 2005)]

Appendix B to Part 698—[Reserved]

[69 Fed. Reg. 35496 (June 24, 2004); 69 Fed. Reg. 35500 (June 24, 2004); 69 Fed. Reg. 69784 (Nov. 30, 2004)]

Appendix C to Part 698—[Reserved]

[69 Fed. Reg. 35496 (June 24, 2004); 69 Fed. Reg. 35500 (June 24, 2004); 69 Fed. Reg. 69784 (Nov. 30, 2004)]

Appendix D to Part 698—Standardized form for requesting annual file disclosures.

[*Editor's note*: This notice is reprinted in Appx. C, *infra*.]

[69 Fed. Reg. 35496 (June 24, 2004); 69 Fed. Reg. 35500 (June 24, 2004); 69 Fed. Reg. 69784 (Nov. 30, 2004)]

Appendix E to Part 698—Summary of Consumer Identity Theft Rights

The prescribed form for this summary is a disclosure that is substantially similar to the Commission's model summary with all information clearly and prominently displayed. A summary should accurately reflect changes to those items that may change over time (such as telephone numbers) to remain in compliance. Translations of this summary will be in compliance with the Commission's prescribed model, provided that the translation is accurate and that it is provided in a language used by the recipient consumer.

[*Editor's note*: This notice is reprinted in Appx. C, *infra*.]

[69 Fed. Reg. 69775 (Nov. 30, 2004) (Effective Date: Jan. 31, 2005)]

Appendix F to Part 698—General Summary of Consumer Rights

The prescribed form for this summary is a disclosure that is substantially similar to the Commission's model summary with all information clearly and prominently displayed. The list of federal regulators that is included in the Commission's prescribed summary may be provided separately so long as this is done in a clear and conspicuous way. A summary should accurately reflect changes to those items that may change over time (e.g., dollar amounts, or telephone numbers and addresses of federal agencies) to remain in compliance. Translations of this summary will be in compliance with the Commission's prescribed model, provided that the translation is accurate and that it is provided in a language used by the recipient consumer.

[*Editor's note*: This notice is reprinted in Appx. C, *infra*.]

[69 Fed. Reg. 69775 (Nov. 30, 2004) (Effective Date: Jan. 31, 2005)]

Appendix G to Part 698—Notice of Furnisher Responsibilities

The prescribed form for this disclosure is a separate document that is substantially similar to the Commission's model notice with all information clearly and prominently displayed. Consumer reporting agencies may limit the disclosure to only those items that they know are relevant to the furnisher that will receive the notice.

[*Editor's note*: This notice is reprinted in Appx. C, *infra*.]

[69 Fed. Reg. 69775 (Nov. 30, 2004) (Effective Date: Jan. 31, 2005)]

Appendix H to Part 698—Notice of User Responsibilities

The prescribed form for this disclosure is a separate document that is substantially similar to the Commission's notice with all information clearly and prominently displayed. Consumer reporting agencies may limit the disclosure to only those items that they know are relevant to the user that will receive the notice.

[*Editor's note*: This notice is reprinted in Appx. C, *infra*.]

[69 Fed. Reg. 69775 (Nov. 30, 2004) (Effective Date: Jan. 31, 2005)]

B.2 Federal Reserve System Regulations

TITLE 12—BANKS AND BANKING

* * *

CHAPTER II—FEDERAL RESERVE SYSTEM

SUBCHAPTER A—BOARD OF GOVERNORS OF THE FEDERAL RESERVE SYSTEM

PART 222—FAIR CREDIT REPORTING (REGULATION V)

SUBPART A—GENERAL PROVISIONS

222.1 Purpose, scope, and effective dates.

* * *

PART 232—OBTAINING AND USING MEDICAL INFORMATION IN CONNECTION WITH CREDIT (REGULATION FF)

232.1 Scope, General Prohibition and Definitions
232.2 Rule of construction for obtaining and using unsolicited medical information.
232.3 Financial information exception for obtaining and using medical information.
232.4 Specific exceptions for obtaining and using medical information.

TITLE 12—BANKS AND BANKING

* * *

CHAPTER II—FEDERAL RESERVE SYSTEM

SUBCHAPTER A—BOARD OF GOVERNORS OF THE FEDERAL RESERVE SYSTEM

PART 222—FAIR CREDIT REPORTING (REGULATION V)

SUBPART A—GENERAL PROVISIONS

12 C.F.R. § 222.1 Purpose, scope, and effective dates.

* * *

(b) *Scope.*

* * *

(2) *Institutions covered.*

* * *

(ii) For purposes of Appendix B to this part, financial institutions as defined in section 509 of the Gramm-Leach-Bliley Act (12 U.S.C. 6809), may use the model notices in Appendix B to this part to comply with the notice requirement in section 623(a)(7) of the Fair Credit Reporting Act (15 U.S.C. 1681s-2(a)(7)).

* * *

[69 Fed. Reg. 6526 (Feb. 11, 2004) (Effective Date: Mar. 12, 2004); 69 Fed. Reg. 33281 (June 15, 2004) (Effective Date: July 16, 2004); 69 Fed. Reg. 77618 (Dec. 28, 2004) (Effective Date: July 1, 2005)]

* * *

PART 232—OBTAINING AND USING MEDICAL INFORMATION IN CONNECTION WITH CREDIT (REGULATION FF)

12 C.F.R. § 232.1 Scope, General Prohibition and Definitions

(a) *Scope.* This part applies to creditors, as defined in paragraph (c)(3) of this section, except for creditors that are subject to §§ 41.30, 222.30, 334.30, 571.30, or 717.30.

(b) *In general.* A creditor may not obtain or use medical information pertaining to a consumer in connection with any determination of the consumer's eligibility, or continued eligibility, for credit, except as provided in this section.

(c) *Definitions.* (1) *Consumer* means an individual.

(2) *Credit* has the same meaning as in section 702 of the Equal Credit Opportunity Act, 15 U.S.C. 1691a.

(3) *Creditor* has the same meaning as in section 702 of the Equal Credit Opportunity Act, 15 U.S.C. 1691a.

(4) *Eligibility, or continued eligibility, for credit* means the consumer's qualification or fitness to receive, or continue to receive, credit, including the terms on which credit is offered. The term does not include:

(i) Any determination of the consumer's qualification or fitness for employment, insurance (other than a credit insurance product), or other non-credit products or services;

(ii) Authorizing, processing, or documenting a payment or transaction on behalf of the consumer in a manner that does not involve a determination of the consumer's eligibility, or continued eligibility, for credit; or

(iii) Maintaining or servicing the consumer's account in a manner that does not involve a determination of the consumer's eligibility, or continued eligibility, for credit.

(5) *Medical information* means:

(i) Information or data, whether oral or recorded, in any form or medium, created by or derived from a health care provider or the consumer, that relates to—

(A) The past, present, or future physical, mental, or behavioral health or condition of an individual;

(B) The provision of health care to an individual; or

(C) The payment for the provision of health care to an individual.

(ii) The term does not include:

(A) The age or gender of a consumer;

(B) Demographic information about the consumer, including a consumer's residence address or e-mail address;

(C) Any other information about a consumer that does not relate to the physical, mental, or behavioral health or condition of a consumer, including the existence or value of any insurance policy; or

(D) Information that does not identify a specific consumer.

(6) *Person* means any individual, partnership, corporation, trust, estate cooperative, association, government or governmental subdivision or agency, or other entity.

[70 Fed. Reg. 33957 (June 10, 2005) (Effective Date: Apr. 1, 2006, *as amended* 70 Fed. Reg. 70663 (Nov. 22, 2005)); 70 Fed. Reg. 70663 (Nov. 22, 2005) (Effective Date: Apr. 1, 2006; 70 Fed. Reg. 75931 (Dec. 22, 2005) (Effective Date: Dec. 22, 2005) (technical amendments to 70 Fed. Reg. 70663 (Nov. 22, 2005) (Effective Date: Apr. 1, 2006))]

12 C.F.R. § 232.2 Rule of construction for obtaining and using unsolicited medical information.

(a) *In general.* A creditor does not obtain medical information in violation of the prohibition if it receives medical information pertaining to a consumer in connection with any determination of the consumer's eligibility, or continued eligibility, for credit without specifically requesting medical information.

(b) *Use of unsolicited medical information.* A creditor that receives unsolicited medical information in the manner described in paragraph (a) of this section may use that information in connection with any determination of the consumer's eligibility, or continued eligibility, for credit to the extent the creditor can rely on at least one of the exceptions in § 232.3 or § 232.4.

(c) *Examples.* A creditor does not obtain medical information in violation of the prohibition if, for example:

(1) In response to a general question regarding a consumer's debts or expenses, the creditor receives information that the consumer owes a debt to a hospital.

(2) In a conversation with the creditor's loan officer, the consumer informs the creditor that the consumer has a particular medical condition.

(3) In connection with a consumer's application for an extension of credit, the creditor requests a consumer report from a consumer reporting agency and receives medical information in the consumer report furnished by the agency even though the creditor did not specifically request medical information from the consumer reporting agency.

[70 Fed. Reg. 33957 (June 10, 2005) (Effective Date: Apr. 1, 2006, *as amended* 70 Fed. Reg. 70663 (Nov. 22, 2005)); 70 Fed. Reg. 70663 (Nov. 22, 2005) (Effective Date: Apr. 1, 2006);70 Fed. Reg. 75931 (Dec. 22, 2005) (Effective Date: Dec. 22, 2005) (technical amendments to 70 Fed. Reg. 70663 (Nov. 22, 2005) (Effective Date: Apr. 1, 2006))]

12 C.F.R. § 232.3 Financial information exception for obtaining and using medical information.

(a) *In general.* A creditor may obtain and use medical information pertaining to a consumer in connection with any determination of the consumer's eligibility, or continued eligibility, for credit so long as:

(1) The information is the type of information routinely used in making credit eligibility determinations, such as information relating to debts, expenses, income, benefits, assets, collateral, or the purpose of the loan, including the use of proceeds;

(2) The creditor uses the medical information in a manner and to an extent that is no less favorable than it would use comparable information that is not medical information in a credit transaction; and

(3) The creditor does not take the consumer's physical, mental, or behavioral health, condition or history, type of treatment, or prognosis into account as part of any such determination.

(b) *Examples.* (1) Examples of the types of information routinely used in making credit eligibility determinations. Paragraph (a)(1) of this section permits a creditor, for example, to obtain and use information about:

(i) The dollar amount, repayment terms, repayment history, and similar information regarding medical debts to calculate, measure, or verify the repayment ability of the consumer, the use of proceeds, or the terms for granting credit;

(ii) The value, condition, and lien status of a medical device that may serve as collateral to secure a loan;

(iii) The dollar amount and continued eligibility for disability income, workers' compensation income, or other benefits related to health or a medical condition that is relied on as a source of repayment; or

(iv) The identity of creditors to whom outstanding medical debts are owed in connection with an application for credit, including but not limited to, a transaction involving the consolidation of medical debts.

(2) Examples of uses of medical information consistent with the exception.

(i) A consumer includes on an application for credit information about two $20,000 debts. One debt is to a hospital; the other debt is to a retailer. The creditor contacts the hospital and the retailer to verify the amount and payment status of the debts. The creditor learns that both debts are more than 90 days past due. Any two debts of this size that are more than 90 days past due would disqualify the consumer under the creditor's established underwriting criteria. The creditor denies the application on the basis that the consumer has a poor repayment history on outstanding debts. The creditor has used medical information in a manner and to an extent no less favorable than it would use comparable non-medical information.

(ii) A consumer indicates on an application for a $200,000 mortgage loan that she receives $15,000 in long-term disability income each year from her former employer and has no other income. Annual income of $15,000, regardless of source, would not be sufficient to support the requested amount of credit. The creditor denies the application on the basis that the projected debt-to-income ratio of the consumer does not meet the creditor's underwriting criteria. The creditor has used medical information in a manner and to an extent that is no less favorable than it would use comparable non-medical information.

(iii) A consumer includes on an application for a $10,000 home equity loan that he has a $50,000 debt to a medical facility that specializes in treating a potentially terminal disease. The creditor contacts the medical facility to verify the debt and obtain the repayment history and current status of the loan. The creditor learns that the debt is current. The applicant meets the income and other requirements of the creditor's underwriting guidelines. The creditor grants the application. The creditor has used medical information in accordance with the exception.

(3) *Examples of uses of medical information inconsistent with the exception.* (i) A consumer applies for $25,000 of credit and includes on the application information about a $50,000 debt to a hospital. The creditor contacts the hospital to verify the amount and payment status of the debt, and learns that the debt is current and that the consumer has no delinquencies in her repayment history. If the existing debt were instead owed to a retail department store, the creditor would approve the application and extend credit based on the amount and repayment history of the outstanding debt. The creditor, however, denies the application because the consumer is indebted to a hospital. The creditor has used medical information, here the identity of the medical creditor, in a manner and to an extent that is less favorable than it would use comparable non-medical information.

(ii) A consumer meets with a loan officer of a creditor to apply for a mortgage loan. While filling out the loan application, the consumer informs the loan officer orally that she has a potentially terminal disease. The consumer meets the creditor's established requirements for the requested mortgage loan. The loan officer recommends to the credit committee that the consumer be denied credit because the consumer has that disease. The credit committee follows the loan officer's recommendation and denies the application because the consumer has a potentially terminal disease. The creditor has used medical information in a manner inconsistent with the exception by taking into account the consumer's physical, mental, or behavioral health, condition, or history, type of treatment, or prognosis as part of a determination of eligibility or continued eligibility for credit.

(iii) A consumer who has an apparent medical condition, such as a consumer who uses a wheelchair or an oxygen tank, meets with a loan officer to apply for a home equity loan. The consumer meets the creditor's established requirements for the requested home equity loan and the creditor typically does not require consumers to obtain a debt cancellation contract, debt suspension agreement, or credit insurance product in connection with such loans. However, based on the consumer's apparent medical condition, the loan officer recommends to the credit committee that credit be extended to the consumer only if the consumer obtains a debt cancellation contract, debt suspension agreement, or credit insurance product from a nonaffiliated third party. The credit committee agrees with the loan officer's recommendation. The loan officer informs the consumer that the consumer must obtain a debt cancellation contract, debt suspension agreement, or credit insurance product from a nonaffiliated third party to qualify for the loan. The consumer obtains one of these products and the creditor approves the loan. The creditor has used medical information in a manner inconsistent with the exception by taking into account the consumer's physical, mental, or behavioral health, condition, or history, type of treatment, or prognosis in setting conditions on the consumer's eligibility for credit.

[70 Fed. Reg. 33957 (June 10, 2005) (Effective Date: Apr. 1, 2006, *as amended* 70 Fed. Reg. 70663 (Nov. 22, 2005));70 Fed. Reg. 70663 (Nov. 22, 2005) (Effective Date: Apr. 1, 2006); 70 Fed. Reg. 75931 (Dec. 22, 2005) (Effective Date: Dec. 22, 2005) (technical amendments to 70 Fed. Reg. 70663 (Nov. 22, 2005) (Effective Date: Apr. 1, 2006))]

12 C.F.R. § 232.4 Specific exceptions for obtaining and using medical information.

(a) *In general.* A creditor may obtain and use medical information pertaining to a consumer in connection with any determination of the consumer's eligibility, or continued eligibility, for credit:

(1) To determine whether the use of a power of attorney or legal representative that is triggered by a medical condition or event is necessary and appropriate or whether the consumer has the legal capacity to contract when a person seeks to exercise a power of attorney or act as legal representative for a consumer based on an asserted medical condition or event;

(2) To comply with applicable requirements of local, state, or Federal laws;

(3) To determine, at the consumer's request, whether the consumer qualifies for a legally permissible special credit program or credit-related assistance program that is—

(i) Designed to meet the special needs of consumers with medical conditions; and

(ii) Established and administered pursuant to a written plan that—

(A) Identifies the class of persons that the program is designed to benefit; and

(B) Sets forth the procedures and standards for extending credit or providing other credit-related assistance under the program;

(4) To the extent necessary for purposes of fraud prevention or detection;

(5) In the case of credit for the purpose of financing medical products or services, to determine and verify the medical purpose of a loan and the use of proceeds;

(6) Consistent with safe and sound practices, if the consumer or the consumer's legal representative specifically requests that the creditor use medical information in determining the consumer's eligibility, or continued eligibility, for credit, to accommodate the consumer's particular circumstances, and such request is documented by the creditor;

(7) Consistent with safe and sound practices, to determine whether the provisions of a forbearance practice or program that is triggered by a medical condition or event apply to a consumer;

(8) To determine the consumer's eligibility for, the triggering of, or the reactivation of a debt cancellation contract or debt suspension agreement if a medical condition or event is a triggering event for the provision of benefits under the contract or agreement; or

(9) To determine the consumer's eligibility for, the triggering of, or the reactivation of a credit insurance product if a medical condition or event is a triggering event for the provision of benefits under the product.

(b) *Example of determining eligibility for a special credit program or credit assistance program.* A not-for-profit organization establishes a credit assistance program pursuant to a written plan that is designed to assist disabled veterans in purchasing homes by subsidizing the down payment for the home purchase mortgage loans of qualifying veterans. The organization works through mortgage lenders and requires mortgage lenders to obtain medical information about the disability of any consumer that seeks to qualify for the program, use that information to verify the consumer's eligibility for the program, and forward that information to the organization. A consumer who is a veteran applies to a creditor for a home purchase mortgage loan. The creditor informs the consumer about the credit assistance program for disabled veterans and the consumer seeks to qualify for the program. Assuming that the program complies with all applicable law, including applicable fair lending laws, the creditor may obtain and use medical information about the medical condition and disability, if any, of the consumer to determine whether the consumer qualifies for the credit assistance program.

(c) *Examples of verifying the medical purpose of the loan or the use of proceeds.* (1) If a consumer applies for $10,000 of credit for the purpose of financing vision correction surgery, the creditor may verify with the surgeon that the procedure will be performed. If the surgeon reports that surgery will not be performed on the consumer, the creditor may use that medical information to deny the consumer's application for credit, because the loan would not be used for the stated purpose.

(2) If a consumer applies for $10,000 of credit for the purpose of financing cosmetic surgery, the creditor may confirm the cost of the procedure with the surgeon. If the surgeon reports that the cost of the procedure is $5,000, the creditor may use that medical information to offer the consumer only $5,000 of credit.

(3) A creditor has an established medical loan program for financing particular elective surgical procedures. The creditor receives a loan application from a consumer requesting $10,000 of credit under the established loan program for an elective surgical procedure. The consumer indicates on the application that the purpose of the loan is to finance an elective surgical procedure not eligible for funding under the guidelines of the established loan program. The creditor may deny the consumer's application because the purpose of the loan is not for a particular procedure funded by the established loan program.

(d) *Examples of obtaining and using medical information at the request of the consumer.* (1) If a consumer applies for a loan and specifically requests that the creditor consider the consumer's medical disability at the relevant time as an explanation for adverse payment history information in his credit report, the creditor may consider such medical information in evaluating the consumer's willingness and ability to repay the requested loan to accommodate the consumer's particular circumstances, consistent with safe and sound practices. The creditor may also decline to consider such medical information to accommodate the consumer, but may evaluate the consumer's application in accordance with its otherwise applicable underwriting criteria. The creditor may not deny the consumer's application or otherwise treat the consumer less favorably because the consumer specifically requested a medical accommodation, if the creditor would have extended the credit or treated the consumer more favorably under the creditor's otherwise applicable underwriting criteria.

(2) If a consumer applies for a loan by telephone and explains that his income has been and will continue to be interrupted on account of a medical condition and that he expects to repay the loan liquidating assets, the creditor may, but is not required to, evaluate the application using the sale of assets as the primary source of repayment, consistent with safe and sound practices, provided that the creditor documents the consumer's request by recording the oral conversation or making a notation of the request in the consumer's file.

(3) If a consumer applies for a loan and the application form provides a space where the consumer may provide any other information or special circumstances, whether medical or non-medical, that the consumer would like the creditor to consider in evaluating the consumer's application, the creditor may use medical information provided by the consumer in that space on that application to accommodate the consumer's application for credit, consistent with safe and sound practices, or may disregard that information.

(4) If a consumer specifically requests that the creditor use medical information in determining the consumer's eligibility, or continued eligibility, for credit and provides the creditor with medical information for that purpose, and the creditor determines that it needs additional information regarding the consumer's circumstances, the creditor may request, obtain, and use additional medical information about the consumer as necessary to verify the information provided by the consumer or to determine whether to make an accommodation for the consumer. The consumer may decline to provide additional information, withdraw the request for an accommodation, and have the application considered under the creditor's otherwise applicable underwriting criteria.

(5) If a consumer completes and signs a credit application that is not for medical purpose credit and the application contains boilerplate language that routinely requests medical information from the consumer or that indicates that by applying for credit the consumer authorizes or consents to the creditor obtaining and using medical information in connection with a determination of the consumer's eligibility, or continued eligibility, for credit, the consumer has not specifically requested that the creditor obtain and use medical information to accommodate the consumer's particular circumstances.

(e) *Example of a forbearance practice or program.* After an appropriate safety and soundness review, a creditor institutes a program that allows consumers who are or will be hospitalized to defer payments as needed for up to three months, without penalty, if the credit account has been open for more than one year and has not previously been in default, and the consumer provides confirming documentation at an appropriate time. A consumer is hospitalized and does not pay her bill for a particular month. This consumer has had a credit account with the creditor for more than one year and has not previously been in default. The creditor attempts to contact the consumer and speaks with the consumer's adult child, who is not the consumer's legal representative. The adult child informs the creditor that the consumer is hospitalized and is unable to pay the bill at that time. The creditor defers payments for up to three months, without penalty, for the hospitalized consumer and sends the consumer a letter confirming this practice and the date on which the next payment will be due. The creditor has obtained and used medical information to determine whether the provisions of a medically-triggered forbearance practice or program apply to a consumer.

[70 Fed. Reg. 33957 (June 10, 2005) (Effective Date: Apr. 1, 2006, *as amended* 70 Fed. Reg. 70663 (Nov. 22, 2005)); 70 Fed. Reg. 70663 (Nov. 22, 2005) (Effective Date: Apr. 1, 2006); 70 Fed. Reg. 75931 (Dec. 22, 2005) (Effective Date: Dec. 22, 2005) (technical amendments to 70 Fed. Reg. 70663 (Nov. 22, 2005) (Effective Date: Apr. 1, 2006))]

* * *

B.3 Banking Agency Regulations

B.3.1 *Office of the Comptroller of the Currency Regulations*

TITLE 12—BANKS AND BANKING

CHAPTER I—COMPTROLLER OF THE CURRENCY, DEPARTMENT OF THE TREASURY

* * *

PART 41—FAIR CREDIT REPORTING

SUBPART A—GENERAL PROVISIONS

41.2	Examples.
41.3	Definitions.

SUBPARTS B–C—[Reserved]

SUBPART D—MEDICAL INFORMATION

41.30	Obtaining or using medical information in connection with a determination of eligibility for credit.
41.31	Limits on redisclosure of information.
41.32	Sharing medical information with affiliates.

SUBPARTS E TO H—[RESERVED]

SUBPART I—DUTIES OF USERS OF CONSUMER REPORTS REGARDING IDENTITY THEFT

41.80–41.82 [Reserved]
41.83 Disposal of consumer information.

TITLE 12—BANKS AND BANKING

CHAPTER I—COMPTROLLER OF THE CURRENCY, DEPARTMENT OF THE TREASURY

* * *

PART 41—FAIR CREDIT REPORTING

SUBPART A—GENERAL PROVISIONS

12 C.F.R. § 41.2 Examples.

The examples in this part are not exclusive. Compliance with an example, to the extent applicable, constitutes compliance with this part. Examples in a paragraph illustrate only the issue described in the paragraph and do not illustrate any other issue that may arise in this part.

[69 Fed. Reg. 77610 (Dec. 28, 2004) (Effective Date: July 1, 2005); 70 Fed. Reg. 33957 (June 10, 2005) (Effective Date: Apr. 1, 2006, *as amended* 70 Fed. Reg. 70663 (Nov. 22, 2005)); 70 Fed. Reg. 70663 (Nov. 22, 2005) (Effective Date: Apr. 1, 2006); 70 Fed. Reg. 75931 (Dec. 22, 2005) (Effective Date: Dec. 22, 2005) (technical amendments to 70 Fed. Reg. 70663 (Nov. 22, 2005) (Effective Date: Apr. 1, 2006))]

12 C.F.R. § 41.3 Definitions.

As used in this part, unless the context requires otherwise:

(a) *Act* means the Fair Credit Reporting Act (15 U.S.C. 1681 *et seq.*).

(b) *Affiliate* means any company that is related by common ownership or common corporate control with another company.

(c) [Reserved]

(d) *Company* means any corporation, limited liability company, business trust, general or limited partnership, association, or similar organization.

(e) *Consumer* means an individual.

(f)–(h) [Reserved]

(i) *Common ownership or common corporate control* means a relationship between two companies under which:

(1) One company has, with respect to the other company:

(i) Ownership, control, or power to vote 25 percent or more of the outstanding shares of any class of voting security of a company, directly or indirectly, or acting through one or more other persons;

(ii) Control in any manner over the election of a majority of the directors, trustees, or general partners (or individuals exercising similar functions) of a company; or

(iii) The power to exercise, directly or indirectly, a controlling influence over the management or policies of a company, as the OCC determines; or

(2) Any other person has, with respect to both companies, a relationship described in paragraphs (i)(1)(i)–(i)(1)(iii) of this section.

(j) [Reserved]

(k) *Medical information* means:

(1) Information or data, whether oral or recorded, in any form or medium, created by or derived from a health care provider or the consumer, that relates to:

(i) The past, present, or future physical, mental, or behavioral health or condition of an individual;

(ii) The provision of health care to an individual; or

(iii) The payment for the provision of health care to an individual.

(2) The term does not include:

(i) The age or gender of a consumer;

(ii) Demographic information about the consumer, including a consumer's residence address or e-mail address;

(iii) Any other information about a consumer that does not relate to the physical, mental, or behavioral health or condition of a consumer, including the existence or value of any insurance policy; or

(iv) Information that does not identify a specific consumer.

(l) *Person* means any individual, partnership, corporation, trust, estate cooperative, association, government or governmental subdivision or agency, or other entity.

[69 Fed. Reg. 77610 (Dec. 28, 2004) (Effective Date: July 1, 2005); 70 Fed. Reg. 33957 (June 10, 2005) (Effective Date: Apr. 1, 2006, *as amended* 70 Fed. Reg. 70663 (Nov. 22, 2005)); 70 Fed. Reg. 70663 (Nov. 22, 2005); 70 Fed. Reg. 75931 (Dec. 22, 2005) (Effective Date: Dec. 22, 2005) (technical amendments to 70 Fed. Reg. 70663 (Nov. 22, 2005) (Effective Date: Apr. 1, 2006))]

SUBPARTS B–C—[RESERVED]

[69 Fed. Reg. 77610 (Dec. 28, 2004) (Effective Date: July 1, 2005)]

SUBPART D—MEDICAL INFORMATION

12 C.F.R. § 41.30 Obtaining or using medical information in connection with a determination of eligibility for credit.

(a) *Scope.* This section applies to:

(1) Any person that participates as a creditor in a transaction and that is a national bank, a Federal branch or agency of a foreign bank, and their respective subsidiaries; or

(2) Any other person that participates as a creditor in a transaction involving a person described in paragraph (a)(1) of this section.

(b) *General prohibition on obtaining or using medical information.*—(1) *In general.* A creditor may not obtain or use medical information pertaining to a consumer in connection with any determination of the consumer's eligibility, or continued eligibility, for credit, except as provided in this section.

(2) *Definitions.*—(i) *Credit* has the same meaning as in section 702 of the Equal Credit Opportunity Act, 15 U.S.C. 1691a.

(ii) Creditor has the same meaning as in section 702 of the Equal Credit Opportunity Act, 15 U.S.C. 1691a.

(iii) *Eligibility, or continued eligibility, for credit* means the consumer's qualification or fitness to receive, or continue to receive, credit, including the terms on which credit is offered. The term does not include:

(A) Any determination of the consumer's qualification or fitness for employment, insurance (other than a credit insurance product), or other non-credit products or services;

(B) Authorizing, processing, or documenting a payment or transaction on behalf of the consumer in a manner that does not involve a determination of the consumer's eligibility, or continued eligibility, for credit; or

(C) Maintaining or servicing the consumer's account in a manner that does not involve a determination of the consumer's eligibility, or continued eligibility, for credit.

(c) *Rule of construction for obtaining and using unsolicited medical information.*—(1) *In general.* A creditor does not obtain medical information in violation of the prohibition if it receives medical information pertaining to a consumer in connection with any determination of the consumer's eligibility, or continued eligibility, for credit without specifically requesting medical information.

(2) *Use of unsolicited medical information.* A creditor that receives unsolicited medical information in the manner described in paragraph (c)(1) of this section may use that information in connection with any determination of the consumer's eligibility, or continued eligibility, for credit to the extent the creditor can rely on at least one of the exceptions in § 41.30(d) or (e).

(3) *Examples.* A creditor does not obtain medical information in violation of the prohibition if, for example:

(i) In response to a general question regarding a consumer's debts or expenses, the creditor receives information that the consumer owes a debt to a hospital.

(ii) In a conversation with the creditor's loan officer, the consumer informs the creditor that the consumer has a particular medical condition.

(iii) In connection with a consumer's application for an extension of credit, the creditor requests a consumer report from a consumer reporting agency and receives medical information in the consumer report furnished by the agency even though the creditor did not specifically request medical information from the consumer reporting agency.

(d) *Financial information exception for obtaining and using medical information.*—(1) *In general.* A creditor may obtain and use medical information pertaining to a consumer in connection with any determination of the consumer's eligibility, or continued eligibility, for credit so long as:

(i) The information is the type of information routinely used in making credit eligibility determinations, such as information relating to debts, expenses, income, benefits, assets, collateral, or the purpose of the loan, including the use of proceeds;

(ii) The creditor uses the medical information in a manner and to an extent that is no less favorable than it would use comparable information that is not medical information in a credit transaction; and

(iii) The creditor does not take the consumer's physical, mental, or behavioral health, condition or history, type of treatment, or prognosis into account as part of any such determination.

(2) *Examples.*—(i) *Examples of the types of information routinely used in making credit eligibility determinations.* Paragraph (d)(1)(i) of this section permits a creditor, for example, to obtain and use information about:

(A) The dollar amount, repayment terms, repayment history, and similar information regarding medical debts to calculate, measure, or verify the repayment ability of the consumer, the use of proceeds, or the terms for granting credit;

(B) The value, condition, and lien status of a medical device that may serve as collateral to secure a loan;

(C) The dollar amount and continued eligibility for disability income, workers' compensation income, or other benefits related to health or a medical condition that is relied on as a source of repayment; or

(D) The identity of creditors to whom outstanding medical debts are owed in connection with an application for credit, including but not limited to, a transaction involving the consolidation of medical debts.

(ii) *Examples of uses of medical information consistent with the exception.*—(A) A consumer includes on an application for credit information about two $20,000 debts. One debt is to a hospital; the other debt is to a retailer. The creditor contacts the hospital and the retailer to verify the amount and payment status of the debts. The creditor learns that both debts are more than 90 days past due. Any two debts of this size that are more than 90 days past due would disqualify the consumer under the creditor's established underwriting criteria. The creditor denies the application on the basis that the consumer has a poor repayment history on outstanding debts. The creditor has used medical information in a manner and to an extent no less favorable than it would use comparable non-medical information.

(B) A consumer indicates on an application for a $200,000 mortgage loan that she receives $15,000 in long-term disability income each year from her former employer and has no other income. Annual income of $15,000, regardless of source, would not be sufficient to support the requested amount of credit. The creditor denies the application on the basis that the projected debt-to-income ratio of the consumer does not meet the creditor's underwriting criteria. The creditor has used medical information in a manner and to an extent that is no less favorable than it would use comparable non-medical information.

(C) A consumer includes on an application for a $10,000 home equity loan that he has a $50,000 debt to a medical facility that specializes in treating a potentially terminal disease. The creditor contacts the medical facility to verify the debt and obtain the repayment history and current status of the loan. The creditor learns that the debt is current. The applicant meets the income and other requirements of the creditor's underwriting guidelines. The creditor grants the application. The creditor has used medical information in accordance with the exception.

(iii) *Examples of uses of medical information inconsistent with the exception.*—(A) A consumer applies for $25,000 of credit and includes on the application information about a $50,000 debt to a hospital. The creditor contacts the hospital to verify the amount and payment status of the debt, and learns that the debt is current and that the consumer has no delinquencies in her repayment history. If the existing debt were instead owed to a retail department store, the creditor would approve the application and extend credit based on the amount and repayment history of the outstanding debt. The creditor, however, denies the application because the consumer is indebted to a hospital. The creditor has used medical information, here the identity of the medical creditor, in a manner and to an extent that is less favorable than it would use comparable non-medical information.

(B) A consumer meets with a loan officer of a creditor to apply for a mortgage loan. While filling out the loan application, the consumer informs the loan officer orally that she has a potentially terminal disease. The consumer meets the creditor's established requirements for the requested mortgage loan. The loan officer recommends to the credit committee that the consumer be denied credit because the consumer has that disease. The credit committee follows the loan officer's recommendation and denies the application because the consumer has a potentially terminal disease. The creditor has used medical information in a manner inconsistent with the exception by taking into account the consumer's physical, mental, or behavioral health, condition, or history, type of treatment, or prognosis as part of a determination of eligibility or continued eligibility for credit.

(C) A consumer who has an apparent medical condition, such as a consumer who uses a wheelchair or an oxygen tank, meets with a loan officer to apply for a home equity loan. The consumer meets the creditor's established requirements for the requested home equity loan and the creditor typically does not require consumers to obtain a debt cancellation contract, debt suspension agreement, or credit insurance product in connection with such loans. However, based on the consumer's apparent medical condition, the loan officer recommends to the credit committee that credit be extended to the consumer only if the consumer obtains a debt cancellation contract, debt suspension agreement, or credit insurance product from a nonaffiliated third party. The credit committee agrees with the loan officer's recommendation. The loan officer informs the consumer that the consumer must obtain a debt cancellation contract, debt suspension agreement, or credit insurance product from a nonaffiliated third party to qualify for the loan. The consumer obtains one of these products and the creditor approves the loan. The creditor has used medical information in a manner inconsistent with the exception by taking into account the consumer's physical, mental, or behavioral health, condition, or history, type of treatment, or prognosis in setting conditions on the consumer's eligibility for credit.

(e) *Specific exceptions for obtaining and using medical information.*—(1) *In general.* A creditor may obtain and use medical information pertaining to a consumer in connection with any determination of the consumer's eligibility, or continued eligibility, for credit:

(i) To determine whether the use of a power of attorney or legal representative that is triggered by a medical condition or event is necessary and appropriate or whether the consumer has the legal capacity to contract when a person seeks to exercise a power of attorney or act as legal representative for a consumer based on an asserted medical condition or event;

(ii) To comply with applicable requirements of local, state, or Federal laws;

(iii) To determine, at the consumer's request, whether the consumer qualifies for a legally permissible special credit program or credit-related assistance program that is:

(A) Designed to meet the special needs of consumers with medical conditions; and

(B) Established and administered pursuant to a written plan that:

(1) Identifies the class of persons that the program is designed to benefit; and

(2) Sets forth the procedures and standards for extending credit or providing other credit-related assistance under the program;

(iv) To the extent necessary for purposes of fraud prevention or detection;

(v) In the case of credit for the purpose of financing medical products or services, to determine and verify the medical purpose of a loan and the use of proceeds;

(vi) Consistent with safe and sound practices, if the consumer or the consumer's legal representative specifically requests that the creditor use medical information in determining the consumer's eligibility, or continued eligibility, for credit, to accommodate the consumer's particular circumstances, and such request is documented by the creditor;

(vii) Consistent with safe and sound practices, to determine whether the provisions of a forbearance practice or program that is triggered by a medical condition or event apply to a consumer;

(viii) To determine the consumer's eligibility for, the triggering of, or the reactivation of a debt cancellation contract or debt suspension agreement if a medical condition or event is a triggering event for the provision of benefits under the contract or agreement; or

(ix) To determine the consumer's eligibility for, the triggering of, or the reactivation of a credit insurance product if a medical condition or event is a triggering event for the provision of benefits under the product.

(2) *Example of determining eligibility for a special credit program or credit assistance program.* A not-for-profit organization establishes a credit assistance program pursuant to a written plan that is designed to assist disabled veterans in purchasing homes by subsidizing the down payment for the home purchase mortgage loans of qualifying veterans. The organization works through mortgage lenders and requires mortgage lenders to obtain medical information about the disability of any consumer that seeks to qualify for the program, use that information to verify the consumer's eligibility for the program, and forward that information to the organization. A consumer who is a veteran applies to a creditor for a home purchase mortgage loan. The creditor informs the consumer about the credit assistance program for disabled veterans and the consumer seeks to qualify for the program. Assuming that the program complies with all applicable law, including applicable fair lending laws, the creditor may obtain and use medical information about the medical condition and disability, if any, of the consumer to determine whether the consumer qualifies for the credit assistance program.

(3) *Examples of verifying the medical purpose of the loan or the use of proceeds.*—(i) If a consumer applies for $10,000 of credit for the purpose of financing vision correction surgery, the creditor may verify with the surgeon that the procedure will be performed. If the surgeon reports that surgery will not be performed on the consumer, the creditor may use that medical information to deny the consumer's application for credit, because the loan would not be used for the stated purpose.

(ii) If a consumer applies for $10,000 of credit for the purpose of financing cosmetic surgery, the creditor may confirm the cost of the procedure with the surgeon. If the surgeon reports that the cost of the procedure is $5,000, the creditor may use that medical information to offer the consumer only $5,000 of credit.

(iii) A creditor has an established medical loan program for financing particular elective surgical procedures. The creditor receives a loan application from a consumer requesting $10,000 of credit under the established loan program for an elective surgical procedure. The consumer indicates on the application that the purpose of the loan is to finance an elective surgical procedure not eligible for funding under the guidelines of the established loan program. The creditor may deny the consumer's application because the purpose of the loan is not for a particular procedure funded by the established loan program.

(4) *Examples of obtaining and using medical information at the request of the consumer.*—(i) If a consumer applies for a loan and specifically requests that the creditor consider the consumer's medical disability at the relevant time as an explanation for adverse payment history information in his credit report, the creditor may consider such medical information in evaluating the consumer's willingness and ability to repay the requested loan to accommodate the consumer's particular circumstances, consistent with safe and sound practices. The creditor may also decline to consider such medical information to accommodate the consumer, but may evaluate the consumer's application in accordance with its otherwise applicable underwriting criteria. The creditor may not deny the consumer's application or otherwise treat the consumer less favorably because the consumer specifically requested a medical accommodation, if the creditor would have extended the credit or treated the consumer more favorably under the creditor's otherwise applicable underwriting criteria.

(ii) If a consumer applies for a loan by telephone and explains that his income has been and will continue to be interrupted on account of a medical condition and that he expects to repay the loan by liquidating assets, the creditor may, but is not required to, evaluate the application using the sale of assets as the primary source of repayment, consistent with safe and sound practices, provided that the creditor documents the consumer's request by recording the oral conversation or making a notation of the request in the consumer's file.

(iii) If a consumer applies for a loan and the application form provides a space where the consumer may provide any other information or special circumstances, whether medical or nonmedical, that the consumer would like the creditor to consider in evaluating the consumer's application, the creditor may use medical information provided by the consumer in that space on that application to accommodate the consumer's application for credit, consistent with safe and sound practices, or may disregard that information.

(iv) If a consumer specifically requests that the creditor use medical information in determining the consumer's eligibility, or continued eligibility, for credit and provides the creditor with medical information for that purpose, and the creditor determines that it needs additional information regarding the consumer's circumstances, the creditor may request, obtain, and use additional medical information about the consumer as necessary to verify the information provided by the consumer or to determine whether to make an accommodation for the consumer. The consumer may decline to provide additional information, withdraw the request for an accommodation, and have the application considered under the creditor's otherwise applicable underwriting criteria.

(v) If a consumer completes and signs a credit application that is not for medical purpose credit and the application contains boilerplate language that routinely requests medical information from the consumer or that indicates that by applying for credit the consumer authorizes or consents to the creditor obtaining and using medical information in connection with a determination of the consumer's eligibility, or continued eligibility, for credit, the consumer has not specifically requested that the creditor obtain and use medical information to accommodate the consumer's particular circumstances.

(5) *Example of a forbearance practice or program.* After an appropriate safety and soundness review, a creditor institutes a program that allows consumers who are or will be hospitalized to defer payments as needed for up to three months, without penalty, if the credit account has been open for more than one year and has not previously been in default, and the consumer provides confirming documentation at an appropriate time. A consumer is hospitalized and does not pay her bill for a particular month. This consumer has had a credit account with the creditor for more than one year and has not previously been in default. The creditor attempts to contact the consumer and speaks with the consumer's adult child, who is not the consumer's legal representative. The adult child informs the creditor that the consumer is hospitalized and is unable to pay the bill at that time. The creditor defers payments for up to three months, without penalty, for the hospitalized consumer and sends the consumer a letter confirming this practice and the date on which the next payment will be due. The creditor has obtained and used medical information to determine whether the provisions of a medically-triggered forbearance practice or program apply to a consumer.

[70 Fed. Reg. 33957 (June 10, 2005) (Effective Date: Apr. 1, 2006, *as amended* 70 Fed. Reg. 70663 (Nov. 22, 2005)); 70 Fed. Reg. 70663 (Nov. 22, 2005) (Effective Date: Apr. 1, 2006); 70 Fed. Reg. 75931 (Dec. 22, 2005) (Effective Date: Dec. 22, 2005) (technical amendments to 70 Fed. Reg. 70663 (Nov. 22, 2005) (Effective Date: Apr. 1, 2006))]

12 C.F.R. § 41.31 Limits on redisclosure of information.

(a) *Scope.* This section applies to national banks, Federal branches and agencies of foreign banks, and their respective operating subsidiaries.

(b) *Limits on redisclosure.* If a person described in paragraph (a) of this section receives medical information about a consumer from a consumer reporting agency or its affiliate, the person must not disclose that information to any other person, except as necessary to carry out the purpose for which the information was initially disclosed, or as otherwise permitted by statute, regulation, or order.

[70 Fed. Reg. 33957 (June 10, 2005) (Effective Date: Apr. 1, 2006, *as amended* 70 Fed. Reg. 70663 (Nov. 22, 2005)); 70 Fed. Reg. 70663 (Nov. 22, 2005) (Effective Date: Apr. 1, 2006); 70 Fed. Reg. 75931 (Dec. 22, 2005) (Effective Date: Dec. 22, 2005) (technical amendments to 70 Fed. Reg. 70663 (Nov. 22, 2005) (Effective Date: Apr. 1, 2006))]

12 C.F.R. § 41.32 Sharing medical information with affiliates.

(a) *Scope.* This section applies to national banks, Federal branches and agencies of foreign banks, and their respective operating subsidiaries.

(b) *In general.* The exclusions from the term "consumer report" in section 603(d)(2) of the Act that allow the sharing of information with affiliates do not apply if a person described in paragraph (a) of this section communicates to an affiliate:

(1) Medical information;

(2) An individualized list or description based on the payment transactions of the consumer for medical products or services; or

(3) An aggregate list of identified consumers based on payment transactions for medical products or services.

(c) *Exceptions.* A person described in paragraph (a) may rely on the exclusions from the term "consumer report" in section 603(d)(2) of the Act to communicate the information in paragraph (b) to an affiliate:

(1) In connection with the business of insurance or annuities (including the activities described in section 18B of the model Privacy of Consumer Financial and Health Information Regulation issued by the National Association of Insurance Commissioners, as in effect on January 1, 2003);

(2) For any purpose permitted without authorization under the regulations promulgated by the Department of Health and Human Services pursuant to the Health Insurance Portability and Accountability Act of 1996 (HIPAA);

(3) For any purpose referred to in section 1179 of HIPAA;

(4) For any purpose described in section 502(e) of the Gramm-Leach-Bliley Act;

(5) In connection with a determination of the consumer's eligibility, or continued eligibility, for credit consistent with § 41.30; or

(6) As otherwise permitted by order of the OCC.

[70 Fed. Reg. 33957 (June 10, 2005) (Effective Date: Apr. 1, 2006, *as amended* 70 Fed. Reg. 70663 (Nov. 22, 2005)); 70 Fed. Reg. 70663 (Nov. 22, 2005) (Effective Date: Apr. 1, 2006); 70 Fed. Reg. 75931 (Dec. 22, 2005) (Effective Date: Dec. 22, 2005) (technical amendments to 70 Fed. Reg. 70663 (Nov. 22, 2005) (Effective Date: Apr. 1, 2006))]

SUBPARTS E–H—[RESERVED]

SUBPART I—DUTIES OF USERS OF CONSUMER REPORTS REGARDING IDENTITY THEFT

12 C.F.R. §§ 41.80–41.82 [Reserved]

[69 Fed. Reg. 77610 (Dec. 28, 2004) (Effective Date: July 1, 2005)]

12 C.F.R. § 41.83 Disposal of consumer information.

(a) *Definitions as used in this section.*—(1) *Bank* means national banks, Federal branches and agencies of foreign banks, and their respective operating subsidiaries.

(b) *In general.* Each bank must properly dispose of any consumer information that it maintains or otherwise possesses in accordance with the Interagency Guidelines Establishing Information Security Standards, as set forth in appendix B to 12 CFR part 30, to the extent that the bank is covered by the scope of the Guidelines.

(c) *Rule of construction.* Nothing in this section shall be construed to:

(1) Require a bank to maintain or destroy any record pertaining to a consumer that is not imposed under any other law; or

(2) Alter or affect any requirement imposed under any other provision of law to maintain or destroy such a record.

[69 Fed. Reg. 77610 (Dec. 28, 2004) (Effective Date: July 1, 2005)]

B.3.2 Federal Reserve System Regulations

TITLE 12—BANKS AND BANKING

* * *

CHAPTER II—FEDERAL RESERVE SYSTEM

SUBCHAPTER A—BOARD OF GOVERNORS OF THE FEDERAL RESERVE SYSTEM

PART 222—FAIR CREDIT REPORTING (REGULATION V)

SUBPART A—GENERAL PROVISIONS

222.1 Purpose, scope, and effective dates.
222.2 Examples.
222.3 Definitions.

SUBPARTS B, C—[RESERVED]

SUBPART D—MEDICAL INFORMATION

222.30 Obtaining or using medical information in connection with a determination of eligibility for credit.
222.31 Limits on redisclosure of information.
222.32 Sharing medical information with affiliates.

SUBPARTS E–H—[RESERVED]

SUBPART I—DUTIES OF USERS OF CONSUMER REPORTS REGARDING IDENTITY THEFT

222.80–222.82 [Reserved]
222.83 Disposal of consumer information.

TITLE 12—BANKS AND BANKING

* * *

CHAPTER II—FEDERAL RESERVE SYSTEM

SUBCHAPTER A—BOARD OF GOVERNORS OF THE FEDERAL RESERVE SYSTEM

* * *

PART 222—FAIR CREDIT REPORTING (REGULATION V)

SUBPART A—GENERAL PROVISIONS

12 C.F.R. § 222.1 Purpose, scope, and effective dates.

(a) [Reserved]

(b) *Scope.* (1) [Reserved]

(2) *Institutions covered.* (i) Except as otherwise provided in this part, the regulations in this part apply to banks that are members of the Federal Reserve System (other than national banks), branches and Agencies of foreign banks (other than Federal branches, Federal Agencies, and insured State branches of foreign banks), commercial lending companies owned or controlled by foreign banks, organizations operating under section 25 or 25A of the Federal Reserve Act (12 U.S.C. 601 *et seq.*, and 611 *et seq.*), and bank holding companies and affiliates of such holding companies (other than depository institutions and consumer reporting agencies).

(ii) For purposes of Appendix B to this part, financial institutions as defined in section 509 of the Gramm-Leach-Bliley Act (12 U.S.C. 6809), may use the model notices in Appendix B to this part to comply with the notice requirement in section 623(a)(7) of the Fair Credit Reporting Act (15 U.S.C. 1681s-2(a)(7)).

(c) *Effective dates.* The applicable provisions of the Fair and Accurate Credit Transactions Act of 2003 (FACT Act), Pub.L. 108-159, 117 Stat. 1952, shall be effective in accordance with the following schedule:

(1) *Provisions effective December 31, 2003.*

(i) Sections 151(a)(2), 212(e), 214(c), 311(b), and 711, concerning the relation to state laws; and

(ii) Each of the provisions of the FACT Act that authorizes an agency to issue a regulation or to take other action to implement the applicable provision of the FACT Act or the applicable provision of the Fair Credit Reporting Act, as amended by the FACT Act, but only with respect to that agency's authority to propose and adopt the implementing regulation or to take such other action.

(2) *Provisions effective March 31, 2004.*

(i) Section 111, concerning the definitions;

(ii) Section 156, concerning the statute of limitations;

(iii) Sections 312(d), (e), and (f), concerning the furnisher liability exception, liability and enforcement, and rule of construction, respectively;

(iv) Section 313(a), concerning action regarding complaints;

(v) Section 611, concerning communications for certain employee investigations; and

(vi) Section 811, concerning clerical amendments.

(3) *Provisions effective December 1, 2004.*

(i) Section 112, concerning fraud alerts and active duty alerts;

(ii) Section 114, concerning procedures for the identification of possible instances of identity theft;

(iii) Section 115, concerning truncation of the social security number in a consumer report;

(iv) Section 151(a)(1), concerning the summary of rights of identity theft victims;

(v) Section 152, concerning blocking of information resulting from identity theft;

(vi) Section 153, concerning the coordination of identity theft complaint investigations;

(vii) Section 154, concerning the prevention of repollution of consumer reports;

(viii) Section 155, concerning notice by debt collectors with respect to fraudulent information;

(ix) Section 211(c), concerning a summary of rights of consumers;

(x) Section 212(a)–(d), concerning the disclosure of credit scores;

(xi) Section 213(c), concerning enhanced disclosure of the means available to opt out of prescreened lists;

(xii) Section 217(a), concerning the duty to provide notice to a consumer;

(xiii) Section 311(a), concerning the risk-based pricing notice;

(xiv) Section 312(a)–(c), concerning procedures to enhance the accuracy and integrity of information furnished to consumer reporting agencies;

(xv) Section 314, concerning improved disclosure of the results of reinvestigation;

(xvi) Section 315, concerning reconciling addresses;

(xvii) Section 316, concerning notice of dispute through reseller; and

(xviii) Section 317, concerning the duty to conduct a reasonable reinvestigation.

[69 Fed. Reg. 6526 (Feb. 11, 2004) (Effective Date: Mar. 12, 2004); 69 Fed. Reg. 33281 (June 15, 2004) (Effective Date: July 16, 2004); 69 Fed. Reg. 77618 (Dec. 28, 2004) (Effective Date: July 1, 2005)]

12 C.F.R. § 222.2 Examples.

The examples in this part are not exclusive. Compliance with an example, to the extent applicable, constitutes compliance with this part. Examples in a paragraph illustrate only the issue described in the paragraph and do not illustrate any other issue that may arise in this part.

[70 Fed. Reg. 33957 (June 10, 2005) (Effective Date: Apr. 1, 2006, *as amended* 70 Fed. Reg. 70663 (Nov. 22, 2005)); 70 Fed. Reg. 70663 (Nov. 22, 2005) (Effective Date: Apr. 1, 2006); 70 Fed. Reg. 75931 (Dec. 22, 2005) (Effective Date: Dec. 22, 2005) (technical amendments to 70 Fed. Reg. 70663 (Nov. 22, 2005) (Effective Date: Apr. 1, 2006))]

12 C.F.R. § 222.3 Definitions.

As used in this part, unless the context requires otherwise:

(a) *Act* means the Fair Credit Reporting Act (15 U.S.C. 1681 *et seq.*).

(b) *Affiliate* means any company that is related by common ownership or common corporate control with another company.

(c) [Reserved]

(d) *Company* means any corporation, limited liability company, business trust, general or limited partnership, association, or similar organization.

(e) *Consumer* means an individual.

(f)–(h) [Reserved]

(i) *Common ownership or common corporate control* means a relationship between two companies under which:

(1) One company has, with respect to the other company:

(i) Ownership, control, or power to vote 25 percent or more of the outstanding shares of any class of voting security of a company, directly or indirectly, or acting through one or more other persons;

(ii) Control in any manner over the election of a majority of the directors, trustees, or general partners (or individuals exercising similar functions) of a company; or

(iii) The power to exercise, directly or indirectly, a controlling influence over the management or policies of a company, as the Board determines; or

(2) Any other person has, with respect to both companies, a relationship described in paragraphs (i)(1)(i) through (i)(1)(iii) of this section.

(j) [Reserved]

(k) *Medical information* means:

(1) Information or data, whether oral or recorded, in any form or medium, created by or derived from a health care provider or the consumer, that relates to:

(i) The past, present, or future physical, mental, or behavioral health or condition of an individual;

(ii) The provision of health care to an individual; or

(iii) The payment for the provision of health care to an individual.

(2) The term does not include:

(i) The age or gender of a consumer;

(ii) Demographic information about the consumer, including a consumer's residence address or e-mail address;

(iii) Any other information about a consumer that does not relate to the physical, mental, or behavioral health or condition of a consumer, including the existence or value of any insurance policy; or

(iv) Information that does not identify a specific consumer.

(l) *Person* means any individual, partnership, corporation, trust, estate cooperative, association, government or governmental subdivision or agency, or other entity.

[70 Fed. Reg. 33957 (June 10, 2005) (Effective Date: Apr. 1, 2006, *as amended* 70 Fed. Reg. 70663 (Nov. 22, 2005)); 70 Fed. Reg. 70663 (Nov. 22, 2005) (Effective Date: Apr. 1, 2006); 70 Fed. Reg. 75931 (Dec. 22, 2005) (Effective Date: Dec. 22, 2005) (technical amendments to 70 Fed. Reg. 70663 (Nov. 22, 2005) (Effective Date: Apr. 1, 2006))]

SUBPARTS B, C—[RESERVED]

[69 Fed. Reg. 77610 (Dec. 28, 2004) (Effective Date: July 1, 2005)]

SUBPART D—MEDICAL INFORMATION

12 C.F.R. § 222.30 Obtaining or using medical information in connection with a determination of eligibility for credit.

(a) *Scope.* This section applies to

(1) Any of the following that participates as a creditor in a transaction—

(i) A bank that is a member of the Federal Reserve System (other than national banks) and its subsidiaries;

(ii) A branch or Agency of a foreign bank (other than Federal branches, Federal Agencies, and insured State branches of foreign banks) and its subsidiaries;

(iii) A commercial lending company owned or controlled by foreign banks;

(iv) An organization operating under section 25 or 25A of the Federal Reserve Act (12 U.S.C. 601 *et seq.*, and 611 *et seq.*);

(v) A bank holding company and an affiliate of such holding company (other than depository institutions and consumer reporting agencies); or

(2) Any other person that participates as a creditor in a transaction involving a person described in paragraph (a)(1) of this section.

(b) *General prohibition on obtaining or using medical information.* (1) *In general.* A creditor may not obtain or use medical information pertaining to a consumer in connection with any determination of the consumer's eligibility, or continued eligibility, for credit, except as provided in this section.

(2) *Definitions.* (i) *Credit* has the same meaning as in section 702 of the Equal Credit Opportunity Act, 15 U.S.C. 1691a.

(ii) *Creditor* has the same meaning as in section 702 of the Equal Credit Opportunity Act, 15 U.S.C. 1691a.

(iii) *Eligibility, or continued eligibility, for credit* means the consumer's qualification or fitness to receive, or continue to receive, credit, including the terms on which credit is offered. The term does not include:

(A) Any determination of the consumer's qualification or fitness for employment, insurance (other than a credit insurance product), or other non-credit products or services;

(B) Authorizing, processing, or documenting a payment or transaction on behalf of the consumer in a manner that does not involve a determination of the consumer's eligibility, or continued eligibility, for credit; or

(C) Maintaining or servicing the consumer's account in a manner that does not involve a determination of the consumer's eligibility, or continued eligibility, for credit.

(c) *Rule of construction for obtaining and using unsolicited medical information.* (1) *In general.* A creditor does not obtain medical information in violation of the prohibition if it receives medical information pertaining to a consumer in connection with any determination of the consumer's eligibility, or continued eligibility, for credit without specifically requesting medical information.

(2) *Use of unsolicited medical information.* A creditor that receives unsolicited medical information in the manner described in paragraph (c)(1) of this section may use that information in connection with any determination of the consumer's eligibility, or continued eligibility, for credit to the extent the creditor can rely on at least one of the exceptions in § 222.30(d) or (e).

(3) *Examples.* A creditor does not obtain medical information in violation of the prohibition if, for example:

(i) In response to a general question regarding a consumer's debts or expenses, the creditor receives information that the consumer owes a debt to a hospital.

(ii) In a conversation with the creditor's loan officer, the consumer informs the creditor that the consumer has a particular medical condition.

(iii) In connection with a consumer's application for an extension of credit, the creditor requests a consumer report from a consumer reporting agency and receives medical information in the consumer report furnished by the agency even though the creditor did not specifically request medical information from the consumer reporting agency.

(d) *Financial information exception for obtaining and using medical information.* (1) *In general.* A creditor may obtain and use medical information pertaining to a consumer in connection with any determination of the consumer's eligibility, or continued eligibility, for credit so long as:

(i) The information is the type of information routinely used in making credit eligibility determinations, such as information relating to debts, expenses, income, benefits, assets, collateral, or the purpose of the loan, including the use of proceeds;

(ii) The creditor uses the medical information in a manner and to an extent that is no less favorable than it would use comparable information that is not medical information in a credit transaction; and

(iii) The creditor does not take the consumer's physical, mental, or behavioral health, condition or history, type of treatment, or prognosis into account as part of any such determination.

(2) *Examples.* (i) *Examples of the types of information routinely used in making credit eligibility determinations.* Paragraph (d)(1)(i) of this section permits a creditor, for example, to obtain and use information about:

(A) The dollar amount, repayment terms, repayment history, and similar information regarding medical debts to calculate, measure, or verify the repayment ability of the consumer, the use of proceeds, or the terms for granting credit;

(B) The value, condition, and lien status of a medical device that may serve as collateral to secure a loan;

(C) The dollar amount and continued eligibility for disability income, workers' compensation income, or other benefits related to health or a medical condition that is relied on as a source of repayment; or

(D) The identity of creditors to whom outstanding medical debts are owed in connection with an application for credit, including but not limited to, a transaction involving the consolidation of medical debts.

(ii) *Examples of uses of medical information consistent with the exception.* (A) A consumer includes on an application for credit information about two $20,000 debts. One debt is to a hospital; the other debt is to a retailer. The creditor contacts the hospital and the retailer to verify the amount and payment status of the debts. The creditor learns that both debts are more than 90 days past due. Any two debts of this size that are more than 90 days past due would disqualify the consumer under the creditor's established underwriting criteria. The creditor denies the application on the basis that the consumer has a poor repayment history on outstanding debts. The creditor has used medical information in a manner and to an extent no less favorable than it would use comparable non-medical information.

(B) A consumer indicates on an application for a $200,000 mortgage loan that she receives $15,000 in long-term disability income each year from her former employer and has no other income. Annual income of $15,000, regardless of source, would not be sufficient to support the requested amount of credit. The creditor denies the application on the basis that the projected debt-to-income ratio of the consumer does not meet the creditor's underwriting criteria. The creditor has used medical information in a manner and to an extent that is no less favorable than it would use comparable non-medical information.

(C) A consumer includes on an application for a $10,000 home equity loan that he has a $50,000 debt to a medical facility that specializes in treating a potentially terminal disease. The creditor contacts the medical facility to verify the debt and obtain the repayment history and current status of the loan. The creditor learns that the debt is current. The applicant meets the income and other requirements of the creditor's underwriting guidelines. The creditor grants the application. The creditor has used medical information in accordance with the exception.

(iii) *Examples of uses of medical information inconsistent with the exception.* (A) A consumer applies for $25,000 of credit and includes on the application information about a $50,000 debt to a hospital. The creditor contacts the hospital to verify the amount and payment status of the debt, and learns that the debt is current and that the consumer has no delinquencies in her repayment history. If the existing debt were instead owed to a retail department store, the creditor would approve the application and extend credit based on the amount and repayment history of the outstanding debt. The creditor, however, denies the application because the consumer is indebted to a hospital. The creditor has used medical information, here the identity of the medical creditor, in a manner and to an extent that is less favorable than it would use comparable non-medical information.

(B) A consumer meets with a loan officer of a creditor to apply for a mortgage loan. While filling out the loan application, the consumer informs the loan officer orally that she has a potentially terminal disease. The consumer meets the creditor's established requirements for the requested mortgage loan. The loan officer recommends to the credit committee that the consumer be denied credit because the consumer has that disease. The credit committee follows the loan officer's recommendation and denies the application because the consumer has a potentially terminal disease. The creditor has used medical information in a manner inconsistent with the exception by taking into account the consumer's physical, mental, or behavioral health, condition, or history, type of treatment, or prognosis as part of a determination of eligibility or continued eligibility for credit.

(C) A consumer who has an apparent medical condition, such as a consumer who uses a wheelchair or an oxygen tank, meets with a loan officer to apply for a home equity loan. The consumer meets the creditor's established requirements for the requested home equity loan and the creditor typically does not require consumers to obtain a debt cancellation contract, debt suspension agreement, or credit insurance product in connection with such loans. However, based on the consumer's apparent medical condition, the loan officer recommends to the credit committee that credit be extended to the consumer only if the consumer obtains a debt cancellation contract, debt suspension agreement, or credit insurance product from a nonaffiliated third party. The credit committee agrees with the loan officer's recommendation. The loan officer informs the consumer that the consumer must obtain a debt cancellation contract, debt suspension agreement, or credit insurance product from a nonaffiliated third party to qualify for the loan. The consumer obtains one of these products and the creditor approves the loan. The creditor has used medical information in a manner inconsistent with the exception by taking into account the consumer's physical, mental, or behavioral health, condition, or history, type of treatment, or prognosis in setting conditions on the consumer's eligibility for credit.

(e) *Specific exceptions for obtaining and using medical information.* (1) *In general.* A creditor may obtain and use medical information pertaining to a consumer in connection with any determination of the consumer's eligibility, or continued eligibility, for credit—

(i) To determine whether the use of a power of attorney or legal representative that is triggered by a medical condition or event is necessary and appropriate or whether the consumer has the legal capacity to contract when a person seeks to exercise a power of attorney or act as legal representative for a consumer based on an asserted medical condition or event;

(ii) To comply with applicable requirements of local, state, or Federal laws;

(iii) To determine, at the consumer's request, whether the consumer qualifies for a legally permissible special credit program or credit-related assistance program that is—

(A) Designed to meet the special needs of consumers with medical conditions; and

(B) Established and administered pursuant to a written plan that—

(1) Identifies the class of persons that the program is designed to benefit; and

(2) Sets forth the procedures and standards for extending credit or providing other credit-related assistance under the program;

(iv) To the extent necessary for purposes of fraud prevention or detection;

(v) In the case of credit for the purpose of financing medical products or services, to determine and verify the medical purpose of a loan and the use of proceeds;

(vi) Consistent with safe and sound practices, if the consumer or the consumer's legal representative specifically requests that the creditor use medical information in determining the consumer's eligibility, or continued eligibility, for credit, to accommodate the consumer's particular circumstances, and such request is documented by the creditor;

(vii) Consistent with safe and sound practices, to determine whether the provisions of a forbearance practice or program that is triggered by a medical condition or event apply to a consumer;

(viii) To determine the consumer's eligibility for, the triggering of, or the reactivation of a debt cancellation contract or debt suspension agreement if a medical condition or event is a triggering event for the provision of benefits under the contract or agreement; or

(ix) To determine the consumer's eligibility for, the triggering of, or the reactivation of a credit insurance product if a medical condition or event is a triggering event for the provision of benefits under the product.

(2) *Example of determining eligibility for a special credit program or credit assistance program.* A not-for-profit organization establishes a credit assistance program pursuant to a written plan that is designed to assist disabled veterans in purchasing homes by subsidizing the down payment for the home purchase mortgage loans of qualifying veterans. The organization works through mortgage lenders and requires mortgage lenders to obtain medical information about the disability of any consumer that seeks to qualify for the program, use that information to verify the consumer's eligibility for the program, and forward that information to the organization. A consumer who is a veteran applies to a creditor for a home purchase mortgage loan. The creditor informs the consumer about the credit assistance program for disabled veterans and the consumer seeks to qualify for the program. Assuming that the program complies with all applicable law, including applicable fair lending laws, the creditor may obtain and use medical information about the medical condition and disability, if any, of the consumer to determine whether the consumer qualifies for the credit assistance program.

(3) *Examples of verifying the medical purpose of the loan or the use of proceeds.* (i) If a consumer applies for $10,000 of credit for the purpose of financing vision correction surgery, the creditor may verify with the surgeon that the procedure will be performed. If the surgeon reports that surgery will not be performed on the consumer, the creditor may use that medical information to deny the consumer's application for credit, because the loan would not be used for the stated purpose.

(ii) If a consumer applies for $10,000 of credit for the purpose of financing cosmetic surgery, the creditor may confirm the cost of the procedure with the surgeon. If the surgeon reports that the cost of the procedure is $5,000, the creditor may use that medical information to offer the consumer only $5,000 of credit.

(iii) A creditor has an established medical loan program for financing particular elective surgical procedures. The creditor receives a loan application from a consumer requesting $10,000 of credit under the established loan program for an elective surgical procedure. The consumer indicates on the application that the purpose of the loan is to finance an elective surgical procedure not eligible for funding under the guidelines of the established loan program. The creditor may deny the consumer's application because the purpose of the loan is not for a particular procedure funded by the established loan program.

(4) *Examples of obtaining and using medical information at the request of the consumer.* (i) If a consumer applies for a loan and specifically requests that the creditor consider the consumer's medical disability at the relevant time as an explanation for adverse payment history information in his credit report, the creditor may consider such medical information in evaluating the consumer's willingness and ability to repay the requested loan to accommodate the consumer's particular circumstances, consistent with safe and sound practices. The creditor may also decline to consider such medical information to accommodate the consumer, but may evaluate the consumer's application in accordance with its otherwise applicable underwriting criteria. The creditor may not deny the consumer's application or otherwise treat the consumer less favorably because the consumer specifically requested a medical

accommodation, if the creditor would have extended the credit or treated the consumer more favorably under the creditor's otherwise applicable underwriting criteria.

(ii) If a consumer applies for a loan by telephone and explains that his income has been and will continue to be interrupted on account of a medical condition and that he expects to repay the loan by liquidating assets, the creditor may, but is not required to, evaluate the application using the sale of assets as the primary source of repayment, consistent with safe and sound practices, provided that the creditor documents the consumer's request by recording the oral conversation or making a notation of the request in the consumer's file.

(iii) If a consumer applies for a loan and the application form provides a space where the consumer may provide any other information or special circumstances, whether medical or non-medical, that the consumer would like the creditor to consider in evaluating the consumer's application, the creditor may use medical information provided by the consumer in that space on that application to accommodate the consumer's application for credit, consistent with safe and sound practices, or may disregard that information.

(iv) If a consumer specifically requests that the creditor use medical information in determining the consumer's eligibility, or continued eligibility, for credit and provides the creditor with medical information for that purpose, and the creditor determines that it needs additional information regarding the consumer's circumstances, the creditor may request, obtain, and use additional medical information about the consumer as necessary to verify the information provided by the consumer or to determine whether to make an accommodation for the consumer. The consumer may decline to provide additional information, withdraw the request for an accommodation, and have the application considered under the creditor's otherwise applicable underwriting criteria.

(v) If a consumer completes and signs a credit application that is not for medical purpose credit and the application contains boilerplate language that routinely requests medical information from the consumer or that indicates that by applying for credit the consumer authorizes or consents to the creditor obtaining and using medical information in connection with a determination of the consumer's eligibility, or continued eligibility, for credit, the consumer has not specifically requested that the creditor obtain and use medical information to accommodate the consumer's particular circumstances.

(5) *Example of a forbearance practice or program.* After an appropriate safety and soundness review, a creditor institutes a program that allows consumers who are or will be hospitalized to defer payments as needed for up to three months, without penalty, if the credit account has been open for more than one year and has not previously been in default, and the consumer provides confirming documentation at an appropriate time. A consumer is hospitalized and does not pay her bill for a particular month. This consumer has had a credit account with the creditor for more than one year and has not previously been in default. The creditor attempts to contact the consumer and speaks with the consumer's adult child, who is not the consumer's legal representative. The adult child informs the creditor that the consumer is hospitalized and is unable to pay the bill at that time. The creditor defers payments for up to three months, without penalty, for the hospitalized consumer and sends the consumer a letter confirming this practice and the date on which the next payment will be due. The creditor has obtained and used medical information to determine whether the provisions of a medically-triggered forbearance practice or program apply to a consumer.

[70 Fed. Reg. 33957 (June 10, 2005) (Effective Date: Apr. 1, 2006, *as amended* 70 Fed. Reg. 70663 (Nov. 22, 2005)); 70 Fed. Reg. 70663 (Nov. 22, 2005); 70 Fed. Reg. 75931 (Dec. 22, 2005) (Effective Date: Dec. 22, 2005) (technical amendments to 70 Fed. Reg. 70663 (Nov. 22, 2005) (Effective Date: Apr. 1, 2006))]

12 C.F.R. § 222.31 Limits on redisclosure of information.

(a) *Scope.* This section applies to banks that are members of the Federal Reserve System (other than national banks) and their respective operating subsidiaries, branches and agencies of foreign banks (other than Federal branches, Federal Agencies, and insured State branches of foreign banks), commercial lending companies owned or controlled by foreign banks, organizations operating under section 25 or 25A of the Federal Reserve Act (12 U.S.C. 601 *et seq.*, and 611 *et seq.*), and bank holding companies and affiliates of such holding companies (other than depository institutions and consumer reporting agencies).

(b) *Limits on redisclosure.* If a person described in paragraph (a) of this section receives medical information about a consumer from a consumer reporting agency or its affiliate, the person must not disclose that information to any other person, except as necessary to carry out the purpose for which the information was initially disclosed, or as otherwise permitted by statute, regulation, or order.

[70 Fed. Reg. 33957 (June 10, 2005) (Effective Date: Apr. 1, 2006, *as amended* 70 Fed. Reg. 70663 (Nov. 22, 2005)); 70 Fed. Reg. 70663 (Nov. 22, 2005) (Effective Date: Apr. 1, 2006); 70 Fed. Reg. 75931 (Dec. 22, 2005) (Effective Date: Dec. 22, 2005) (technical amendments to 70 Fed. Reg. 70663 (Nov. 22, 2005) (Effective Date: Apr. 1, 2006))]

12 C.F.R. § 222.32 Sharing medical information with affiliates.

(a) *Scope.* This section applies to banks that are members of the Federal Reserve System (other than national banks) and their respective operating subsidiaries, branches and agencies of foreign banks (other than Federal branches, Federal Agencies, and insured State branches of foreign banks), commercial lending companies owned or controlled by foreign banks, organizations operating under section 25 or 25A of the Federal Reserve Act (12 U.S.C. 601 *et seq.*, and 611 *et seq.*).

(b) *In general.* The exclusions from the term "consumer report" in section 603(d)(2) of the Act that allow the sharing of information with affiliates do not apply to a person described in paragraph (a) of this section if that person communicates to an affiliate:

(1) Medical information;

(2) An individualized list or description based on the payment transactions of the consumer for medical products or services; or

(3) An aggregate list of identified consumers based on payment transactions for medical products or services.

(c) *Exceptions.* A person described in paragraph (a) of this section may rely on the exclusions from the term "consumer report" in section 603(d)(2) of the Act to communicate the information in paragraph (b) of this section to an affiliate:

(1) In connection with the business of insurance or annuities (including the activities described in section 18B of the model Privacy of Consumer Financial and Health Information Regulation issued by the National Association of Insurance Commissioners, as in effect on January 1, 2003);

(2) For any purpose permitted without authorization under the regulations promulgated by the Department of Health and Human Services pursuant to the Health Insurance Portability and Accountability Act of 1996 (HIPAA);

(3) For any purpose referred to in section 1179 of HIPAA;

(4) For any purpose described in section 502(e) of the Gramm-Leach-Bliley Act;

(5) In connection with a determination of the consumer's eligibility, or continued eligibility, for credit consistent with § 222.30 of this part; or

(6) As otherwise permitted by order of the Board.

[70 Fed. Reg. 33957 (June 10, 2005) (Effective Date: Apr. 1, 2006, *as amended* 70 Fed. Reg. 70663 (Nov. 22, 2005)); 70 Fed. Reg. 70663 (Nov. 22, 2005) (Effective Date: Apr. 1, 2006); 70 Fed. Reg. 75931 (Dec. 22, 2005) (Effective Date: Dec. 22, 2005) (technical amendments to 70 Fed. Reg. 70663 (Nov. 22, 2005) (Effective Date: Apr. 1, 2006))]

SUBPARTS E–H—[RESERVED]

SUBPART I—DUTIES OF USERS OF CONSUMER REPORTS REGARDING IDENTITY THEFT

12 C.F.R. §§ 222.80–222.82 [Reserved]

[69 Fed. Reg. 77610 (Dec. 28, 2004) (Effective Date: July 1, 2005)]

12 C.F.R. § 222.83 Disposal of consumer information.

(a) *Definitions as used in this section.* (1) *You* means member banks of the Federal Reserve System (other than national banks) and their respective operating subsidiaries, branches and agencies of foreign banks (other than Federal branches, Federal agencies and insured State branches of foreign banks), commercial lending companies owned or controlled by foreign banks, and organizations operating under section 25 or 25A of the Federal Reserve Act (12 U.S.C. 601 *et seq.*, 611 *et seq.*).

(b) *In general.* You must properly dispose of any consumer information that you maintain or otherwise possess in accordance with the Interagency Guidelines Establishing Information Security Standards, as required under sections 208.3(d) (Regulation H), 211.5(l) and 211.24(i) (Regulation K) of this chapter, to the extent that you are covered by the scope of the Guidelines.

(c) *Rule of construction.* Nothing in this section shall be construed to:

(1) Require you to maintain or destroy any record pertaining to a consumer that is not imposed under any other law; or

(2) Alter or affect any requirement imposed under any other provision of law to maintain or destroy such a record.

[69 Fed. Reg. 77610 (Dec. 28, 2004) (Effective Date: July 1, 2005)]

* * *

B.3.3 Federal Deposit Insurance Corporation Regulations

TITLE 12—BANKS AND BANKING

* * *

CHAPTER III—FEDERAL DEPOSIT INSURANCE CORPORATION

* * *

SUBCHAPTER B—REGULATIONS AND STATEMENTS OF GENERAL POLICY

* * *

PART 334—FAIR CREDIT REPORTING

SUBPART A—GENERAL PROVISIONS

334.1 [Reserved]
334.2 Examples.
334.3 Definitions.

SUBPARTS B, C—[RESERVED]

SUBPART D—MEDICAL INFORMATION

334.30 Obtaining or using medical information in connection with a determination of eligibility for credit.
334.31 Limits on redisclosure of information.
334.32 Sharing medical information with affiliates.

SUBPARTS E TO H—[RESERVED]

SUBPART I—DUTIES OF USERS OF CONSUMER REPORTS REGARDING IDENTITY THEFT

334.80–334.82 [Reserved]
334.83 Disposal of consumer information.

TITLE 12—BANKS AND BANKING

* * *

CHAPTER III—FEDERAL DEPOSIT INSURANCE CORPORATION

* * *

SUBCHAPTER B—REGULATIONS AND STATEMENTS OF GENERAL POLICY

* * *

PART 334—FAIR CREDIT REPORTING

SUBPART A—GENERAL PROVISIONS

12 C.F.R. § 334.1 [Reserved]

[70 Fed. Reg. 33957 (June 10, 2005) (Effective Date: Apr. 1, 2006, as amended 70 Fed. Reg. 70663 (Nov. 22, 2005))]

12 C.F.R. § 334.2 Examples.

The examples in this part are not exclusive. Compliance with an example, to the extent applicable, constitutes compliance with this part. Examples in a paragraph illustrate only the issue described in the paragraph and do not illustrate any other issue that may arise in this part.

[70 Fed. Reg. 33957 (June 10, 2005) (Effective Date: Apr. 1, 2006, as amended 70 Fed. Reg. 70663 (Nov. 22, 2005)); 70 Fed. Reg. 70663 (Nov. 22, 2005) (Effective Date: Apr. 1, 2006); 70 Fed. Reg. 75931 (Dec. 22, 2005) (Effective Date: Dec. 22, 2005) (technical amendments to 70 Fed. Reg. 70663 (Nov. 22, 2005) (Effective Date: Apr. 1, 2006))]

12 C.F.R. § 334.3 Definitions.

As used in this part, unless the context requires otherwise:

(a) *Act* means the Fair Credit Reporting Act (15 U.S.C. 1681 et seq.).

(b) *Affiliate* means any company that is related by common ownership or common corporate control with another company.

(c) [Reserved]

(d) *Company* means any corporation, limited liability company, business trust, general or limited partnership, association, or similar organization.

(e) *Consumer* means an individual.

(f)–(h) [Reserved]

(i) *Common ownership or common corporate control* means a relationship between two companies under which:

(1) One company has, with respect to the other company:

(i) Ownership, control, or power to vote 25 percent or more of the outstanding shares of any class of voting security of a company, directly or indirectly, or acting through one or more other persons;

(ii) Control in any manner over the election of a majority of the directors, trustees, or general partners (or individuals exercising similar functions) of a company; or

(iii) The power to exercise, directly or indirectly, a controlling influence over the management or policies of a company, as the FDIC determines; or

(2) Any other person has, with respect to both companies, a relationship described in paragraphs (i)(1)(i) through (i)(1)(iii) of this section.

(j) [Reserved]

(k) *Medical information* means:

(1) Information or data, whether oral or recorded, in any form or medium, created by or derived from a health care provider or the consumer, that relates to:

(i) The past, present, or future physical, mental, or behavioral health or condition of an individual;

(ii) The provision of health care to an individual; or

(iii) The payment for the provision of health care to an individual.

(2) The term does not include:

(i) The age or gender of a consumer;

(ii) Demographic information about the consumer, including a consumer's residence address or e-mail address;

(iii) Any other information about a consumer that does not relate to the physical, mental, or behavioral health or condition of a consumer, including the existence or value of any insurance policy; or

(iv) Information that does not identify a specific consumer.

(l) *Person* means any individual, partnership, corporation, trust, estate cooperative, association, government or governmental subdivision or agency, or other entity.

[70 Fed. Reg. 33957 (June 10, 2005) (Effective Date: Apr. 1, 2006, as amended 70 Fed. Reg. 70663 (Nov. 22, 2005)); 70 Fed. Reg. 70663 (Nov. 22, 2005) (Effective Date: Apr. 1, 2006); 70 Fed. Reg. 75931 (Dec. 22, 2005) (Effective Date: Dec. 22, 2005) (technical amendments to 70 Fed. Reg. 70663 (Nov. 22, 2005) (Effective Date: Apr. 1, 2006))]

SUBPARTS B, C—[RESERVED]

SUBPART D—MEDICAL INFORMATION

12 C.F.R. § 334.30 Obtaining or using medical information in connection with a determination of eligibility for credit.

(a) *Scope.* This section applies to:

(1) Any of the following that participates as a creditor in a transaction:

(i) A State bank insured by the FDIC (other than members of the Federal Reserve System);

(ii) An insured State branch of a foreign bank; or

(2) Any other person that participates as a creditor in a transaction involving a person described in paragraph (a)(1) of this section.

(b) *General prohibition on obtaining or using medical information.*—(1) *In general.* A creditor may not obtain or use medical information pertaining to a consumer in connection with any determination of the consumer's eligibility, or continued eligibility, for credit, except as provided in this section.

(2) *Definitions.* (i) *Credit* has the same meaning as in section 702 of the Equal Credit Opportunity Act, 15 U.S.C. 1691a.

(ii) *Creditor* has the same meaning as in section 702 of the Equal Credit Opportunity Act, 15 U.S.C. 1691a.

(iii) *Eligibility, or continued eligibility, for credit* means the consumer's qualification or fitness to receive, or continue to receive, credit, including the terms on which credit is offered. The term does not include:

(A) Any determination of the consumer's qualification or fitness for employment, insurance (other than a credit insurance product), or other non-credit products or services;

(B) Authorizing, processing, or documenting a payment or transaction on behalf of the consumer in a manner that does not involve a determination of the consumer's eligibility, or continued eligibility, for credit; or

(C) Maintaining or servicing the consumer's account in a manner that does not involve a determination of the consumer's eligibility, or continued eligibility, for credit.

(c) *Rule of construction for obtaining and using unsolicited medical information.* (1) *In general.* A creditor does not obtain medical information in violation of the prohibition if it receives medical information pertaining to a consumer in connection with any determination of the consumer's eligibility, or continued eligibility, for credit without specifically requesting medical information.

(2) *Use of unsolicited medical information.* A creditor that receives unsolicited medical information in the manner described in paragraph (c)(1) of this section may use that information in connection with any determination of the consumer's eligibility, or continued eligibility, for credit to the extent the creditor can rely on at least one of the exceptions in § 334.30(d) or (e).

(3) *Examples.* A creditor does not obtain medical information in violation of the prohibition if, for example:

(i) In response to a general question regarding a consumer's debts or expenses, the creditor receives information that the consumer owes a debt to a hospital.

(ii) In a conversation with the creditor's loan officer, the consumer informs the creditor that the consumer has a particular medical condition.

(iii) In connection with a consumer's application for an extension of credit, the creditor requests a consumer report from a consumer reporting agency and receives medical information in the consumer report furnished by the agency even though the creditor did not specifically request medical information from the consumer reporting agency.

(d) *Financial information exception for obtaining and using medical information.*

(1) *In general.* A creditor may obtain and use medical information pertaining to a consumer in connection with any determination of the consumer's eligibility, or continued eligibility, for credit so long as:

(i) The information is the type of information routinely used in making credit eligibility determinations, such as information relating to debts, expenses, income, benefits, assets, collateral, or the purpose of the loan, including the use of proceeds;

(ii) The creditor uses the medical information in a manner and to an extent that is no less favorable than it would use comparable information that is not medical information in a credit transaction; and

(iii) The creditor does not take the consumer's physical, mental, or behavioral health, condition or history, type of treatment, or prognosis into account as part of any such determination.

(2) *Examples.* (i) *Examples of the types of information routinely used in making credit eligibility determinations.* Paragraph (d)(1)(i) of this section permits a creditor, for example, to obtain and use information about:

(A) The dollar amount, repayment terms, repayment history, and similar information regarding medical debts to calculate, measure, or verify the repayment ability of the consumer, the use of proceeds, or the terms for granting credit;

(B) The value, condition, and lien status of a medical device that may serve as collateral to secure a loan;

(C) The dollar amount and continued eligibility for disability income, workers' compensation income, or other benefits related to health or a medical condition that is relied on as a source of repayment; or

(D) The identity of creditors to whom outstanding medical debts are owed in connection with an application for credit, including but not limited to, a transaction involving the consolidation of medical debts.

(ii) *Examples of uses of medical information consistent with the exception.* (A) A consumer includes on an application for credit information about two $20,000 debts. One debt is to a hospital; the other debt is to a retailer. The creditor contacts the hospital and the retailer to verify the amount and payment status of the debts. The creditor learns that both debts are more than 90 days past due. Any two debts of this size that are more than 90 days past due would disqualify the consumer under the creditor's established underwriting criteria. The creditor denies the application on the basis that the consumer has a poor repayment history on outstanding debts. The creditor has used medical information in a manner and to an extent no less favorable than it would use comparable non-medical information.

(B) A consumer indicates on an application for a $200,000 mortgage loan that she receives $15,000 in long-term disability income each year from her former employer and has no other income. Annual income of $15,000, regardless of source, would not be sufficient to support the requested amount of credit. The creditor denies the application on the basis that the projected debt-to-income ratio of the consumer does not meet the creditor's underwriting criteria. The creditor has used medical information in a manner and to an extent that is no less favorable than it would use comparable non-medical information.

(C) A consumer includes on an application for a $10,000 home equity loan that he has a $50,000 debt to a medical facility that specializes in treating a potentially terminal disease. The creditor contacts the medical facility to verify the debt and obtain the repayment history and current status of the loan. The creditor learns that the debt is current. The applicant meets the income and other requirements of the creditor's underwriting guidelines. The creditor grants the application. The creditor has used medical information in accordance with the exception.

(iii) *Examples of uses of medical information inconsistent with the exception.* (A) A consumer applies for $25,000 of credit and includes on the application information about a $50,000 debt to a hospital. The creditor contacts the hospital to verify the amount and payment status of the debt, and learns that the debt is current and that the consumer has no delinquencies in her repayment history. If the existing debt were instead owed to a retail department store, the creditor would approve the application and extend credit based on the amount and repayment history of the outstanding debt. The creditor, however, denies the application because the consumer is indebted to a hospital. The creditor has used medical information, here the identity of the medical creditor, in a manner and to an extent that is less favorable than it would use comparable non-medical information.

(B) A consumer meets with a loan officer of a creditor to apply for a mortgage loan. While filling out the loan application, the consumer informs the loan officer orally that she has a potentially terminal disease. The consumer meets the creditor's established requirements for the requested mortgage loan. The loan officer recommends to the credit committee that the consumer be denied credit because the consumer has that disease. The credit committee follows the loan officer's recommendation and denies the application because the consumer has a potentially terminal disease. The creditor has used medical information in a manner inconsistent with the exception by taking into account the consumer's physical, mental, or behavioral health, condition, or history, type of treatment, or prognosis as part of a determination of eligibility or continued eligibility for credit.

(C) A consumer who has an apparent medical condition, such as a consumer who uses a wheelchair or an oxygen tank, meets with a loan officer to apply for a home equity loan. The consumer meets the creditor's established requirements for the requested home equity loan and the creditor typically does not require consumers to obtain a debt cancellation contract, debt suspension agreement, or credit insurance product in connection with such loans. However, based on the consumer's apparent medical condition, the loan officer recommends to the credit committee that credit be extended to the consumer only if the consumer obtains a debt cancellation contract, debt suspension agreement, or credit insurance product from a nonaffiliated third party. The credit committee agrees with the loan officer's recommendation. The loan officer informs the consumer that the consumer must obtain a debt cancellation contract, debt suspension agreement, or credit insurance product from a nonaffiliated third party to qualify for the loan. The consumer obtains one of these products and the creditor approves the loan. The creditor has used medical information in a manner inconsistent with the exception by taking into account the consumer's physical, mental, or behavioral health, condition, or history, type of treatment, or prognosis in setting conditions on the consumer's eligibility for credit.

(e) *Specific exceptions for obtaining and using medical information.* (1) *In general.* A creditor may obtain and use medical information pertaining to a consumer in connection with any determination of the consumer's eligibility, or continued eligibility, for credit:

(i) To determine whether the use of a power of attorney or legal representative that is triggered by a medical condition or event is necessary and appropriate or whether the consumer has the legal capacity to contract when a person seeks to exercise a power of attorney or act as legal representative for a consumer based on an asserted medical condition or event;

(ii) To comply with applicable requirements of local, state, or Federal laws;

(iii) To determine, at the consumer's request, whether the consumer qualifies for a legally permissible special credit program or credit-related assistance program that is:

(A) Designed to meet the special needs of consumers with medical conditions; and

(B) Established and administered pursuant to a written plan that:

(1) Identifies the class of persons that the program is designed to benefit; and

(2) Sets forth the procedures and standards for extending credit or providing other credit-related assistance under the program;

(iv) To the extent necessary for purposes of fraud prevention or detection;

(v) In the case of credit for the purpose of financing medical products or services, to determine and verify the medical purpose of a loan and the use of proceeds;

(vi) Consistent with safe and sound practices, if the consumer or the consumer's legal representative specifically requests that the creditor use medical information in determining the consumer's eligibility, or continued eligibility, for credit, to accommodate the consumer's particular circumstances, and such request is documented by the creditor;

(vii) Consistent with safe and sound practices, to determine whether the provisions of a forbearance practice or program that is triggered by a medical condition or event apply to a consumer;

(viii) To determine the consumer's eligibility for, the triggering of, or the reactivation of a debt cancellation contract or debt suspension agreement if a medical condition or event is a triggering event for the provision of benefits under the contract or agreement; or

(ix) To determine the consumer's eligibility for, the triggering of, or the reactivation of a credit insurance product if a medical condition or event is a triggering event for the provision of benefits under the product.

(2) *Example of determining eligibility for a special credit program or credit assistance program.* A not-for-profit organization establishes a credit assistance program pursuant to a written plan that is designed to assist disabled veterans in purchasing homes by subsidizing the down payment for the home purchase mortgage loans of qualifying veterans. The organization works through mortgage lenders and requires mortgage lenders to obtain medical information about the disability of any consumer that seeks to qualify for the program, use that information to verify the consumer's eligibility for the program, and forward that information to the organization. A consumer who is a veteran applies to a creditor for a home purchase mortgage loan. The creditor informs the consumer about the credit assistance program for disabled veterans and the consumer seeks to qualify for the program. Assuming that the program complies with all applicable law, including applicable fair lending laws, the creditor may obtain and use medical information about the medical condition and disability, if any, of the consumer to determine whether the consumer qualifies for the credit assistance program.

(3) *Examples of verifying the medical purpose of the loan or the use of proceeds.* (i) If a consumer applies for $10,000 of credit for the purpose of financing vision correction surgery, the creditor may verify with the surgeon that the procedure will be performed. If the surgeon reports that surgery will not be performed on the consumer, the creditor may use that medical information to deny the consumer's application for credit, because the loan would not be used for the stated purpose.

(ii) If a consumer applies for $10,000 of credit for the purpose of financing cosmetic surgery, the creditor may confirm the cost of the procedure with the surgeon. If the surgeon reports that the cost of the procedure is $5,000, the creditor may use that medical information to offer the consumer only $5,000 of credit.

(iii) A creditor has an established medical loan program for financing particular elective surgical procedures. The creditor receives a loan application from a consumer requesting $10,000 of credit under the established loan program for an elective surgical procedure. The consumer indicates on the application that the purpose of the loan is to finance an elective surgical procedure not eligible for funding under the guidelines of the established loan program. The creditor may deny the consumer's application because the purpose of the loan is not for a particular procedure funded by the established loan program.

(4) *Examples of obtaining and using medical information at the request of the consumer.* (i) If a consumer applies for a loan and specifically requests that the creditor consider the consumer's medical disability at the relevant time as an explanation for adverse payment history information in his credit report, the creditor may consider such medical information in evaluating the consumer's willingness and ability to repay the requested loan to accommodate the consumer's particular circumstances, consistent with safe and sound practices. The creditor may also decline to consider such medical information to accommodate the consumer, but may evaluate the consumer's application in accordance with its otherwise applicable underwriting criteria. The creditor may not deny the consumer's application or otherwise treat the consumer less favorably because the consumer specifically requested a medical accommodation, if the creditor would have extended the credit or treated the consumer more favorably under the creditor's otherwise applicable underwriting criteria.

(ii) If a consumer applies for a loan by telephone and explains that his income has been and will continue to be interrupted on account of a medical condition and that he expects to repay the loan by liquidating assets, the creditor may, but is not required to, evaluate the application using the sale of assets as the primary source of repayment, consistent with safe and sound practices, provided that the creditor documents the consumer's request by recording the oral conversation or making a notation of the request in the consumer's file.

(iii) If a consumer applies for a loan and the application form provides a space where the consumer may provide any other information or special circumstances, whether medical or nonmedical, that the consumer would like the creditor to consider in evaluating the consumer's application, the creditor may use medical information provided by the consumer in that space on that application to accommodate the consumer's application for credit, consistent with safe and sound practices, or may disregard that information.

(iv) If a consumer specifically requests that the creditor use medical information in determining the consumer's eligibility, or continued eligibility, for credit and provides the creditor with medical information for that purpose, and the creditor determines that it needs additional information regarding the consumer's circumstances, the creditor may request, obtain, and use additional medical information about the consumer as necessary to verify the information provided by the consumer or to determine whether to make an accommodation for the consumer. The consumer may decline to provide additional information, withdraw the request for an accommodation, and have the application considered under the creditor's otherwise applicable underwriting criteria.

(v) If a consumer completes and signs a credit application that is not for medical purpose credit and the application contains boilerplate language that routinely requests medical information from the consumer or that indicates that by applying for credit the consumer authorizes or consents to the creditor obtaining and using medical information in connection with a determination of the consumer's eligibility, or continued eligibility, for credit, the consumer has not specifically requested that the creditor obtain and use medical information to accommodate the consumer's particular circumstances.

(5) *Example of a forbearance practice or program.* After an appropriate safety and soundness review, a creditor institutes a program that allows consumers who are or will be hospitalized to defer payments as needed for up to three months, without penalty, if the credit account has been open for more than one year and has not previously been in default, and the consumer provides confirming documentation at an appropriate time. A consumer is hospitalized and does not pay her bill for a particular month. This consumer has had a credit account with the creditor for more than one year and has not previously been in default. The creditor attempts to contact the consumer and speaks with the consumer's adult child, who is not the consumer's legal representative. The adult child informs the creditor that the consumer is hospitalized and is unable to pay the bill at that time. The creditor defers payments for up to three months, without penalty, for the hospitalized consumer and sends the consumer a letter confirming this practice and the date on which the next payment will be due. The creditor has obtained and used medical information to determine whether the provisions of a medically-triggered forbearance practice or program apply to a consumer.

[70 Fed. Reg. 33957 (June 10, 2005) (Effective Date: Apr. 1, 2006, *as amended* 70 Fed. Reg. 70663 (Nov. 22, 2005)); 70 Fed. Reg. 70663 (Nov. 22, 2005) (Effective Date: Apr. 1, 2006); 70 Fed. Reg. 75931 (Dec. 22, 2005) (Effective Date: Dec. 22, 2005) (technical amendments to 70 Fed. Reg. 70663 (Nov. 22, 2005) (Effective Date: Apr. 1, 2006))]

12 C.F.R. § 334.31 Limits on redisclosure of information.

(a) *Scope.* This section applies to State banks insured by the FDIC (other than members of the Federal Reserve System) and insured State branches of foreign banks.

(b) *Limits on redisclosure.* If a person described in paragraph (a) of this section receives medical information about a consumer from a consumer reporting agency or its affiliate, the person must not disclose that information to any other person, except as necessary to carry out the purpose for which the information was initially disclosed, or as otherwise permitted by statute, regulation, or order.

[70 Fed. Reg. 33957 (June 10, 2005) (Effective Date: Apr. 1, 2006, *as amended* 70 Fed. Reg. 70663 (Nov. 22, 2005)); 70 Fed. Reg. 70663 (Nov. 22, 2005) (Effective Date: Apr. 1, 2006); 70 Fed. Reg. 75931 (Dec. 22, 2005) (Effective Date: Dec. 22, 2005) (technical amendments to 70 Fed. Reg. 70663 (Nov. 22, 2005) (Effective Date: Apr. 1, 2006))]

12 C.F.R. § 334.32 Sharing medical information with affiliates.

(a) *Scope.* This section applies to State banks insured by the FDIC (other than members of the Federal Reserve System) and insured State branches of foreign banks.

(b) *In general.* The exclusions from the term "consumer report" in section 603(d)(2) of the Act that allow the sharing of information with affiliates do not apply if a person described in paragraph (a) of this section communicates to an affiliate—

(1) Medical information;

(2) An individualized list or description based on the payment transactions of the consumer for medical products or services; or

(3) An aggregate list of identified consumers based on payment transactions for medical products or services.

(c) *Exceptions.* A person described in paragraph (a) of this section may rely on the exclusions from the term "consumer report" in section 603(d)(2) of the Act to communicate the information in paragraph (b) of this section to an affiliate—

(1) In connection with the business of insurance or annuities (including the activities described in section 18B of the model Privacy of Consumer Financial and Health Information Regulation issued by the National Association of Insurance Commissioners, as in effect on January 1, 2003);

(2) For any purpose permitted without authorization under the regulations promulgated by the Department of Health and Human Services pursuant to the Health Insurance Portability and Accountability Act of 1996 (HIPAA);

(3) For any purpose referred to in section 1179 of HIPAA;

(4) For any purpose described in section 502(e) of the Gramm-Leach-Bliley Act;

(5) In connection with a determination of the consumer's eligibility, or continued eligibility, for credit consistent with § 334.30; or

(6) As otherwise permitted by order of the FDIC.

[70 Fed. Reg. 33957 (June 10, 2005) (Effective Date: Apr. 1, 2006, *as amended* 70 Fed. Reg. 70663 (Nov. 22, 2005)); 70 Fed. Reg. 70663 (Nov. 22, 2005) (Effective Date: Apr. 1, 2006); 70 Fed. Reg. 75931 (Dec. 22, 2005) (Effective Date: Dec. 22, 2005) (technical amendments to 70 Fed. Reg. 70663 (Nov. 22, 2005) (Effective Date: Apr. 1, 2006))]

SUBPARTS E TO H—[RESERVED]

SUBPART I—DUTIES OF USERS OF CONSUMER REPORTS REGARDING IDENTITY THEFT

12 C.F.R. §§ 334.80–334.82 [Reserved]

[69 Fed. Reg. 77610 (Dec. 28, 2004) (Effective Date: July 1, 2005)]

12 C.F.R. § 334.83 Disposal of consumer information.

(a) *In general.* You must properly dispose of any consumer information that you maintain or otherwise possess in accordance with the Interagency Guidelines Establishing Information Security Standards, as set forth in appendix B to part 364 of this chapter, prescribed pursuant to section 216 of the Fair and Accurate Credit Transactions Act of 2003 (15 U.S.C. 1681w) and section 501(b) of the Gramm-Leach-Bliley Act (15 U.S.C. 6801(b)), to the extent the Guidelines are applicable to you.

(b) *Rule of construction.* Nothing in this section shall be construed to:

(1) Require you to maintain or destroy any record pertaining to a consumer that is not imposed under any other law; or

(2) Alter or affect any requirement imposed under any other provision of law to maintain or destroy such a record.

[69 Fed. Reg. 77610 (Dec. 28, 2004) (Effective Date: July 1, 2005)]

B.3.4 Office of Thrift Supervision Regulations

TITLE 12—BANKS AND BANKING

* * *

CHAPTER V—OFFICE OF THRIFT SUPERVISION, DEPARTMENT OF THE TREASURY

* * *

PART 571—FAIR CREDIT REPORTING

SUBPART A—GENERAL PROVISIONS

571.1 Purpose and scope.
571.2 Examples.
571.3 Definitions.

SUBPARTS B, C—[RESERVED]

SUBPART D—MEDICAL INFORMATION

571.30 Obtaining or using medical information in connection with a determination of eligibility for credit.
571.31 Limits on redisclosure of information.
571.32 Sharing medical information with affiliates.

SUBPARTS E TO H—[RESERVED]

SUBPART I—DUTIES OF USERS OF CONSUMER REPORTS REGARDING IDENTITY THEFT

571.80–571.82 [Reserved]
571.83 Disposal of consumer information.

Appx. B.3.4 § 571.1   *Fair Credit Reporting*

TITLE 12—BANKS AND BANKING

* * *

CHAPTER V—OFFICE OF THRIFT SUPERVISION, DEPARTMENT OF THE TREASURY

* * *

PART 571—FAIR CREDIT REPORTING

SUBPART A—GENERAL PROVISIONS

12 C.F.R. § 571.1 Purpose and scope.

(a) *Purpose.* The purpose of this part is to establish standards regarding consumer report information. In addition, the purpose of this part is to specify the extent to which you may obtain, use, or share certain information. This part also contains a number of measures you must take to combat consumer fraud and related crimes, including identity theft.

(b) *Scope.*

(1)–(3) [Reserved]

(4) The scope of Subpart D of this part is stated in §§ 571.30(a), 571.31(a), and 571.32(a) of this part.

(5)–(8) [Reserved]

(9) Subpart I of this part applies to savings associations whose deposits are insured by the Federal Deposit Insurance Corporation (and federal savings association operating subsidiaries in accordance with § 559.3(h)(1) of this chapter).

[69 Fed. Reg. 77610 (Dec. 28, 2004) (Effective Date: July 1, 2005); 70 Fed. Reg. 33957 (June 10, 2005) (Effective Date: Apr. 1, 2006, *as amended* 70 Fed. Reg. 70663 (Nov. 22, 2005)); 70 Fed. Reg. 70663 (Nov. 22, 2005) (Effective Date: Apr. 1, 2006); 70 Fed. Reg. 75931 (Dec. 22, 2005) (Effective Date: Dec. 22, 2005) (technical amendments to 70 Fed. Reg. 70663 (Nov. 22, 2005) (Effective Date: Apr. 1, 2006))]

12 C.F.R. § 571.2 Examples.

The examples in this part are not exclusive. Compliance with an example, to the extent applicable, constitutes compliance with this part. Examples in a paragraph illustrate only the issue described in the paragraph and do not illustrate any other issue that may arise in this part.

[69 Fed. Reg. 77610 (Dec. 28, 2004) (Effective Date: July 1, 2005); 70 Fed. Reg. 33957 (June 10, 2005) (Effective Date: Apr. 1, 2006, *as amended* 70 Fed. Reg. 70663 (Nov. 22, 2005)); 70 Fed. Reg. 70663 (Nov. 22, 2005) (Effective Date: Apr. 1, 2006); 70 Fed. Reg. 75931 (Dec. 22, 2005) (Effective Date: Dec. 22, 2005) (technical amendments to 70 Fed. Reg. 70663 (Nov. 22, 2005) (Effective Date: Apr. 1, 2006))]

12 C.F.R. § 571.3 Definitions.

As used in this part, unless the context requires otherwise:

(a) *Act* means the Fair Credit Reporting Act (15 U.S.C. 1681 *et seq.*).

(b) *Affiliate* means any company that is related by common ownership or common corporate control with another company.

(c) [Reserved]

(d) *Company* means any corporation, limited liability company, business trust, general or limited partnership, association, or similar organization.

(e) *Consumer* means an individual.

(f)–(h) [Reserved]

(i) *Common ownership or common corporate control* means a relationship between two companies under which:

(1) One company has, with respect to the other company:

(i) Ownership, control, or power to vote 25 percent or more of the outstanding shares of any class of voting security of a company, directly or indirectly, or acting through one or more other persons;

(ii) Control in any manner over the election of a majority of the directors, trustees, or general partners (or individuals exercising similar functions) of a company; or

(iii) The power to exercise, directly or indirectly, a controlling influence over the management or policies of a company, as the OTS determines; or

(2) Any other person has, with respect to both companies, a relationship described in paragraphs (i)(1)(i)–(i)(1)(iii) of this section.

(j) [Reserved]

(k) *Medical information* means:

(1) Information or data, whether oral or recorded, in any form or medium, created by or derived from a health care provider or the consumer, that relates to—

(i) The past, present, or future physical, mental, or behavioral health or condition of an individual;

(ii) The provision of health care to an individual; or

(iii) The payment for the provision of health care to an individual.

(2) The term does not include:

(i) The age or gender of a consumer;

(ii) Demographic information about the consumer, including a consumer's residence address or e-mail address;

(iii) Any other information about a consumer that does not relate to the physical, mental, or behavioral health or condition of a consumer, including the existence or value of any insurance policy; or

(iv) Information that does not identify a specific consumer.

(l) *Person* means any individual, partnership, corporation, trust, estate cooperative, association, government or governmental subdivision or agency, or other entity.

(m), (n) [Reserved]

(o) *You* means savings associations whose deposits are insured by the Federal Deposit Insurance Corporation and federal savings association operating subsidiaries.

[69 Fed. Reg. 77610 (Dec. 28, 2004) (Effective Date: July 1, 2005); 70 Fed. Reg. 33957 (June 10, 2005) (Effective Date: Apr. 1, 2006, *as amended* 70 Fed. Reg. 70663 (Nov. 22, 2005)); 70 Fed. Reg. 70663 (Nov. 22, 2005) (Effective Date: Apr. 1, 2006); 70 Fed. Reg. 75931 (Dec. 22, 2005) (Effective Date: Dec. 22, 2005) (technical amendments to 70 Fed. Reg. 70663 (Nov. 22, 2005) (Effective Date: Apr. 1, 2006))]

SUBPARTS B, C—[RESERVED]

SUBPART D—MEDICAL INFORMATION

12 C.F.R. § 571.30 Obtaining or using medical information in connection with a determination of eligibility for credit.

(a) *Scope.* This section applies to:

(1) Any of the following that participates as a creditor in a transaction—

(i) A savings association;

(ii) A subsidiary owned in whole or in part by a savings association;

(iii) A savings and loan holding company;

(iv) A subsidiary of a savings and loan holding company other than a bank or subsidiary of a bank; or

(v) A service corporation owned in whole or in part by a savings association; or

(2) Any other person that participates as a creditor in a transaction involving a person described in paragraph (a)(1) of this section.

(b) *General prohibition on obtaining or using medical information.*—(1) *In general.* A creditor may not obtain or use medical information pertaining to a consumer in connection with any determination of the consumer's eligibility, or continued eligibility, for credit, except as provided in this section.

(2) *Definitions.* (i) *Credit* has the same meaning as in section 702 of the Equal Credit Opportunity Act, 15 U.S.C. 1691a.

(ii) *Creditor* has the same meaning as in section 702 of the Equal Credit Opportunity Act, 15 U.S.C. 1691a.

(iii) *Eligibility, or continued eligibility, for credit* means the consumer's qualification or fitness to receive, or continue to receive, credit, including the terms on which credit is offered. The term does not include:

(A) Any determination of the consumer's qualification or fitness for employment, insurance (other than a credit insurance product), or other non-credit products or services;

(B) Authorizing, processing, or documenting a payment or transaction on behalf of the consumer in a manner that does not involve a determination of the consumer's eligibility, or continued eligibility, for credit; or

(C) Maintaining or servicing the consumer's account in a manner that does not involve a determination of the consumer's eligibility, or continued eligibility, for credit.

(c) *Rule of construction for obtaining and using unsolicited medical information.*—(1) *In general.* A creditor does not obtain medical information in violation of the prohibition if it receives medical information pertaining to a consumer in connection with any determination of the consumer's eligibility, or continued eligibility, for credit without specifically requesting medical information.

(2) *Use of unsolicited medical information.* A creditor that receives unsolicited medical information in the manner described in paragraph (c)(1) of this section may use that information in connection with any determination of the consumer's eligibility, or continued eligibility, for credit to the extent the creditor can rely on at least one of the exceptions in § 571.30(d) or (e).

(3) *Examples.* A creditor does not obtain medical information in violation of the prohibition if, for example:

(i) In response to a general question regarding a consumer's debts or expenses, the creditor receives information that the consumer owes a debt to a hospital;

(ii) In a conversation with the creditor's loan officer, the consumer informs the creditor that the consumer has a particular medical condition; or

(iii) In connection with a consumer's application for an extension of credit, the creditor requests a consumer report from a consumer reporting agency and receives medical information in the consumer report furnished by the agency even though the creditor did not specifically request medical information from the consumer reporting agency.

(d) *Financial information exception for obtaining and using medical information.*—(1) *In general.* A creditor may obtain and use medical information pertaining to a consumer in connection with any determination of the consumer's eligibility, or continued eligibility, for credit so long as:

(i) The information is the type of information routinely used in making credit eligibility determinations, such as information relating to debts, expenses, income, benefits, assets, collateral, or the purpose of the loan, including the use of proceeds;

(ii) The creditor uses the medical information in a manner and to an extent that is no less favorable than it would use comparable information that is not medical information in a credit transaction; and

(iii) The creditor does not take the consumer's physical, mental, or behavioral health, condition or history, type of treatment, or prognosis into account as part of any such determination.

(2) *Examples.* (i) *Examples of the types of information routinely used in making credit eligibility determinations.* Paragraph (d)(1)(i) of this section permits a creditor, for example, to obtain and use information about:

(A) The dollar amount, repayment terms, repayment history, and similar information regarding medical debts to calculate, measure, or verify the repayment ability of the consumer, the use of proceeds, or the terms for granting credit;

(B) The value, condition, and lien status of a medical device that may serve as collateral to secure a loan;

(C) The dollar amount and continued eligibility for disability income, workers' compensation income, or other benefits related to health or a medical condition that is relied on as a source of repayment; or

(D) The identity of creditors to whom outstanding medical debts are owed in connection with an application for credit, including but not limited to, a transaction involving the consolidation of medical debts.

(ii) *Examples of uses of medical information consistent with the exception.* (A) A consumer includes on an application for credit information about two $20,000 debts. One debt is to a hospital; the other debt is to a retailer. The creditor contacts the hospital and the retailer to verify the amount and payment status of the debts. The creditor learns that both debts are more than 90 days past due. Any two debts of this size that are more than 90 days past due would disqualify the consumer under the creditor's established underwriting criteria. The creditor denies the application on the basis that the consumer has a poor repayment history on outstanding debts. The creditor has used medical information in a manner and to an extent no less favorable than it would use comparable non-medical information.

(B) A consumer indicates on an application for a $200,000 mortgage loan that she receives $15,000 in long-term disability income each year from her former employer and has no other income. Annual income of $15,000, regardless of source, would not be sufficient to support the requested amount of credit. The creditor denies the application on the basis that the projected debt-to-income ratio of the consumer does not meet the creditor's underwriting criteria. The creditor has used medical information in a manner and to an extent that is no less favorable than it would use comparable non-medical information.

(C) A consumer includes on an application for a $10,000 home equity loan that he has a $50,000 debt to a medical facility that specializes in treating a potentially terminal disease. The creditor contacts the medical facility to verify the debt and obtain the repayment history and current status of the loan. The creditor learns that the debt is current. The applicant meets the income and other requirements of the creditor's underwriting guidelines. The creditor grants the application. The creditor has used medical information in accordance with the exception.

(iii) *Examples of uses of medical information inconsistent with the exception.* (A) A consumer applies for $25,000 of credit and includes on the application information about a $50,000 debt to a hospital. The creditor contacts the hospital to verify the amount and payment status of the debt, and learns that the debt is current and that the consumer has no delinquencies in her repayment history. If the existing debt were instead owed to a retail department store, the creditor would approve the application and extend credit based on the amount and repayment history of the outstanding debt. The creditor, however, denies the application because the consumer is indebted to a hospital. The creditor has used medical information, here the identity of the medical creditor, in a manner and to an extent that is less favorable than it would use comparable non-medical information.

(B) A consumer meets with a loan officer of a creditor to apply for a mortgage loan. While filling out the loan application, the consumer informs the loan officer orally that she has a potentially terminal disease. The consumer meets the creditor's established requirements for the requested mortgage loan. The loan officer recommends to the credit committee that the consumer be denied credit because the consumer has that disease. The credit committee follows the loan officer's recommendation and denies the application because the consumer has a potentially terminal disease. The creditor has used medical information in a manner inconsistent with the exception by taking into account the consumer's physical, mental, or behavioral health, condition, or history, type of treatment, or prognosis as part of a determination of eligibility or continued eligibility for credit.

(C) A consumer who has an apparent medical condition, such as a consumer who uses a wheelchair or an oxygen tank, meets with a loan officer to apply for a home equity loan. The consumer meets the creditor's established requirements for the requested home equity loan and the creditor typically does not require consumers to obtain a debt cancellation contract, debt suspension agreement, or credit insurance product in connection with such loans. However, based on the consumer's apparent medical condition, the loan officer recommends to the credit committee that credit be extended to the consumer only if the consumer obtains a debt cancellation contract, debt suspension agreement, or credit insurance product from a nonaffiliated third party. The credit committee agrees with the loan officer's recommendation. The loan officer informs the consumer that the consumer must obtain a debt cancellation contract, debt suspension agreement, or credit insurance product from a nonaffiliated third party to qualify for the loan. The consumer obtains one of these products and the creditor approves the loan. The creditor has used medical information in a manner inconsistent with the exception by taking into account the consumer's physical, mental, or behavioral health, condition, or history, type of treatment, or prognosis in setting conditions on the consumer's eligibility for credit.

(e) *Specific exceptions for obtaining and using medical information.*—(1) *In general.* A creditor may obtain and use medical information pertaining to a consumer in connection with any determination of the consumer's eligibility, or continued eligibility, for credit—

(i) To determine whether the use of a power of attorney or legal representative that is triggered by a medical condition or event is necessary and appropriate or whether the consumer has the legal capacity to contract when a person seeks to exercise a power of attorney or act as legal representative for a consumer based on an asserted medical condition or event;

(ii) To comply with applicable requirements of local, state, or federal laws;

(iii) To determine, at the consumer's request, whether the consumer qualifies for a legally permissible special credit program or credit-related assistance program that is—

(A) Designed to meet the special needs of consumers with medical conditions; and

(B) Established and administered pursuant to a written plan that—

(1) Identifies the class of persons that the program is designed to benefit; and

(2) Sets forth the procedures and standards for extending credit or providing other credit-related assistance under the program;

(iv) To the extent necessary for purposes of fraud prevention or detection;

(v) In the case of credit for the purpose of financing medical products or services, to determine and verify the medical purpose of a loan and the use of proceeds;

(vi) Consistent with safe and sound practices, if the consumer or the consumer's legal representative specifically requests that the creditor use medical information in determining the consumer's eligibility, or continued eligibility, for credit, to accommodate the consumer's particular circumstances, and such request is documented by the creditor;

(vii) Consistent with safe and sound practices, to determine whether the provisions of a forbearance practice or program that is triggered by a medical condition or event apply to a consumer;

(viii) To determine the consumer's eligibility for, the triggering of, or the reactivation of a debt cancellation contract or debt suspension agreement if a medical condition or event is a triggering event for the provision of benefits under the contract or agreement; or

(ix) To determine the consumer's eligibility for, the triggering of, or the reactivation of a credit insurance product if a medical condition or event is a triggering event for the provision of benefits under the product.

(2) *Example of determining eligibility for a special credit program or credit assistance program.* A not-for-profit organization establishes a credit assistance program pursuant to a written plan that is designed to assist disabled veterans in purchasing homes by subsidizing the down payment for the home purchase

mortgage loans of qualifying veterans. The organization works through mortgage lenders and requires mortgage lenders to obtain medical information about the disability of any consumer that seeks to qualify for the program, use that information to verify the consumer's eligibility for the program, and forward that information to the organization. A consumer who is a veteran applies to a creditor for a home purchase mortgage loan. The creditor informs the consumer about the credit assistance program for disabled veterans and the consumer seeks to qualify for the program. Assuming that the program complies with all applicable law, including applicable fair lending laws, the creditor may obtain and use medical information about the medical condition and disability, if any, of the consumer to determine whether the consumer qualifies for the credit assistance program.

(3) *Examples of verifying the medical purpose of the loan or the use of proceeds.* (i) If a consumer applies for $10,000 of credit for the purpose of financing vision correction surgery, the creditor may verify with the surgeon that the procedure will be performed. If the surgeon reports that surgery will not be performed on the consumer, the creditor may use that medical information to deny the consumer's application for credit, because the loan would not be used for the stated purpose.

(ii) If a consumer applies for $10,000 of credit for the purpose of financing cosmetic surgery, the creditor may confirm the cost of the procedure with the surgeon. If the surgeon reports that the cost of the procedure is $5,000, the creditor may use that medical information to offer the consumer only $5,000 of credit.

(iii) A creditor has an established medical loan program for financing particular elective surgical procedures. The creditor receives a loan application from a consumer requesting $10,000 of credit under the established loan program for an elective surgical procedure. The consumer indicates on the application that the purpose of the loan is to finance an elective surgical procedure not eligible for funding under the guidelines of the established loan program. The creditor may deny the consumer's application because the purpose of the loan is not for a particular procedure funded by the established loan program.

(4) *Examples of obtaining and using medical information at the request of the consumer.* (i) If a consumer applies for a loan and specifically requests that the creditor consider the consumer's medical disability at the relevant time as an explanation for adverse payment history information in his credit report, the creditor may consider such medical information in evaluating the consumer's willingness and ability to repay the requested loan to accommodate the consumer's particular circumstances, consistent with safe and sound practices. The creditor may also decline to consider such medical information to accommodate the consumer, but may evaluate the consumer's application in accordance with its otherwise applicable underwriting criteria. The creditor may not deny the consumer's application or otherwise treat the consumer less favorably because the consumer specifically requested a medical accommodation, if the creditor would have extended the credit or treated the consumer more favorably under the creditor's otherwise applicable underwriting criteria.

(ii) If a consumer applies for a loan by telephone and explains that his income has been and will continue to be interrupted on account of a medical condition and that he expects to repay the loan by liquidating assets, the creditor may, but is not required to, evaluate the application using the sale of assets as the primary source of repayment, consistent with safe and sound practices,

provided that the creditor documents the consumer's request by recording the oral conversation or making a notation of the request in the consumer's file.

(iii) If a consumer applies for a loan and the application form provides a space where the consumer may provide any other information or special circumstances, whether medical or nonmedical, that the consumer would like the creditor to consider in evaluating the consumer's application, the creditor may use medical information provided by the consumer in that space on that application to accommodate the consumer's application for credit, consistent with safe and sound practices, or may disregard that information.

(iv) If a consumer specifically requests that the creditor use medical information in determining the consumer's eligibility, or continued eligibility, for credit and provides the creditor with medical information for that purpose, and the creditor determines that it needs additional information regarding the consumer's circumstances, the creditor may request, obtain, and use additional medical information about the consumer as necessary to verify the information provided by the consumer or to determine whether to make an accommodation for the consumer. The consumer may decline to provide additional information, withdraw the request for an accommodation, and have the application considered under the creditor's otherwise applicable underwriting criteria.

(v) If a consumer completes and signs a credit application that is not for medical purpose credit and the application contains boilerplate language that routinely requests medical information from the consumer or that indicates that by applying for credit the consumer authorizes or consents to the creditor obtaining and using medical information in connection with a determination of the consumer's eligibility, or continued eligibility, for credit, the consumer has not specifically requested that the creditor obtain and use medical information to accommodate the consumer's particular circumstances.

(5) *Example of a forbearance practice or program.* After an appropriate safety and soundness review, a creditor institutes a program that allows consumers who are or will be hospitalized to defer payments as needed for up to three months, without penalty, if the credit account has been open for more than one year and has not previously been in default, and the consumer provides confirming documentation at an appropriate time. A consumer is hospitalized and does not pay her bill for a particular month. This consumer has had a credit account with the creditor for more than one year and has not previously been in default. The creditor attempts to contact the consumer and speaks with the consumer's spouse, who is not the consumer's legal representative. The spouse informs the creditor that the consumer is hospitalized and is unable to pay the bill at that time. The creditor defers payments for up to three months, without penalty, for the hospitalized consumer and sends the consumer a letter confirming this practice and the date on which the next payment will be due. The creditor has obtained and used medical information to determine whether the provisions of a medically-triggered forbearance practice or program apply to a consumer.

[70 Fed. Reg. 33957 (June 10, 2005) (Effective Date: Apr. 1, 2006, *as amended* 70 Fed. Reg. 70663 (Nov. 22, 2005)); 70 Fed. Reg. 70663 (Nov. 22, 2005) (Effective Date: Apr. 1, 2006); 70 Fed. Reg. 75931 (Dec. 22, 2005) (Effective Date: Dec. 22, 2005) (technical amendments to 70 Fed. Reg. 70663 (Nov. 22, 2005) (Effective Date: Apr. 1, 2006))]

12 C.F.R. § 571.31 Limits on redisclosure of information.

(a) *Scope.* This section applies to savings associations and federal savings association operating subsidiaries.

(b) *Limits on redisclosure.* If a person described in paragraph (a) of this section receives medical information about a consumer from a consumer reporting agency or its affiliate, the person must not disclose that information to any other person, except as necessary to carry out the purpose for which the information was initially disclosed, or as otherwise permitted by statute, regulation, or order.

[70 Fed. Reg. 33957 (June 10, 2005) (Effective Date: Apr. 1, 2006, *as amended* 70 Fed. Reg. 70663 (Nov. 22, 2005)); 70 Fed. Reg. 70663 (Nov. 22, 2005) (Effective Date: Apr. 1, 2006); 70 Fed. Reg. 75931 (Dec. 22, 2005) (Effective Date: Dec. 22, 2005) (technical amendments to 70 Fed. Reg. 70663 (Nov. 22, 2005) (Effective Date: Apr. 1, 2006))]

12 C.F.R. § 571.32 Sharing medical information with affiliates.

(a) *Scope.* This section applies to savings associations and federal savings association operating subsidiaries.

(b) *In general.* The exclusions from the term "consumer report" in section 603(d)(2) of the Act that allow the sharing of information with affiliates do not apply if a person described in paragraph (a) of this section communicates to an affiliate:

(1) Medical information;

(2) An individualized list or description based on the payment transactions of the consumer for medical products or services; or

(3) An aggregate list of identified consumers based on payment transactions for medical products or services.

(c) *Exceptions.* A person described in paragraph (a) of this section may rely on the exclusions from the term "consumer report" in section 603(d)(2) of the Act to communicate the information in paragraph (b) of this section to an affiliate:

(1) In connection with the business of insurance or annuities (including the activities described in section 18B of the model Privacy of Consumer Financial and Health Information Regulation issued by the National Association of Insurance Commissioners, as in effect on January 1, 2003);

(2) For any purpose permitted without authorization under the regulations promulgated by the Department of Health and Human Services pursuant to the Health Insurance Portability and Accountability Act of 1996 (HIPAA);

(3) For any purpose referred to in section 1179 of HIPAA;

(4) For any purpose described in section 502(e) of the Gramm-Leach-Bliley Act;

(5) In connection with a determination of the consumer's eligibility, or continued eligibility, for credit consistent with § 571.30; or

(6) As otherwise permitted by order of the OTS.

[70 Fed. Reg. 33957 (June 10, 2005) (Effective Date: Apr. 1, 2006, *as amended* 70 Fed. Reg. 70663 (Nov. 22, 2005)); 70 Fed. Reg. 70663 (Nov. 22, 2005) (Effective Date: Apr. 1, 2006); 70 Fed. Reg. 75931 (Dec. 22, 2005) (Effective Date: Dec. 22, 2005) (technical amendments to 70 Fed. Reg. 70663 (Nov. 22, 2005) (Effective Date: Apr. 1, 2006))]

SUBPARTS E TO H—[RESERVED]

SUBPART I—DUTIES OF USERS OF CONSUMER REPORTS REGARDING IDENTITY THEFT

12 C.F.R. §§ 571.80–571.82 [Reserved]

[69 Fed. Reg. 77610 (Dec. 28, 2004) (Effective Date: July 1, 2005)]

12 C.F.R. § 571.83 Disposal of consumer information.

(a) *In general.* You must properly dispose of any consumer information that you maintain or otherwise possess in accordance with the Interagency Guidelines Establishing Information Security Standards, as set forth in appendix B to part 570, to the extent that you are covered by the scope of the Guidelines.

(b) *Rule of construction.* Nothing in this section shall be construed to:

(1) Require you to maintain or destroy any record pertaining to a consumer that is not imposed under any other law; or

(2) Alter or affect any requirement imposed under any other provision of law to maintain or destroy such a record.

[69 Fed. Reg. 77610 (Dec. 28, 2004) (Effective Date: July 1, 2005)]

B.3.5 National Credit Union Administration Regulations

TITLE 12—BANKS AND BANKING

* * *

CHAPTER VII—NATIONAL CREDIT UNION ADMINISTRATION

SUBCHAPTER A—REGULATIONS AFFECTING CREDIT UNIONS

* * *

PART 717—FAIR CREDIT REPORTING

SUBPART A—GENERAL PROVISIONS

717.1 Purpose.
717.2 Examples.
717.3 Definitions.

SUBPARTS B, C—[RESERVED]

SUBPART D—MEDICAL INFORMATION

717.30 Obtaining or using medical information in connection with a determination of eligibility for credit.
717.31 Limits on redisclosure of information
717.32 Sharing medical information with affiliates.

SUBPARTS E–H—[RESERVED]

SUBPART I—DUTIES OF USERS OF CONSUMER REPORTS REGARDING IDENTITY THEFT

717.80–717.82 [Reserved]
717.83 Disposal of consumer information.

TITLE 12—BANKS AND BANKING

* * *

CHAPTER VII—NATIONAL CREDIT UNION ADMINISTRATION

SUBCHAPTER A—REGULATIONS AFFECTING CREDIT UNIONS

* * *

PART 717—FAIR CREDIT REPORTING

SUBPART A—GENERAL PROVISIONS

12 C.F.R. § 717.1 Purpose.

(a) *Purpose.* The purpose of this part is to establish standards for Federal credit unions regarding consumer report information. In addition, the purpose of this part is to specify the extent to which Federal credit unions may obtain, use or share certain information. This part also contains a number of measures Federal credit unions must take to combat consumer fraud and related crimes, including identity theft.

(b) [Reserved]

[69 Fed. Reg. 69269 (Nov. 29, 2004) (Effective Date: Dec. 29, 2004); 70 Fed. Reg. 33957 (June 10, 2005) (Effective Date: Apr. 1, 2006, *as amended* 70 Fed. Reg. 70663 (Nov. 22, 2005)); 70 Fed. Reg. 70663 (Nov. 22, 2005) (Effective Date: Apr. 1, 2006); 70 Fed. Reg. 75931 (Dec. 22, 2005) (Effective Date: Dec. 22, 2005) (technical amendments to 70 Fed. Reg. 70663 (Nov. 22, 2005) (Effective Date: Apr. 1, 2006))]

12 C.F.R. § 717.2 Examples.

The examples in this part are not exclusive. Compliance with an example, to the extent applicable, constitutes compliance with this part. Examples in a paragraph illustrate only the issue described in the paragraph and do not illustrate any other issue that may arise in this part.

[69 Fed. Reg. 69269 (Nov. 29, 2004) (Effective Date: Dec. 29, 2004); 70 Fed. Reg. 33957 (June 10, 2005) (Effective Date: Apr. 1, 2006, *as amended* 70 Fed. Reg. 70663 (Nov. 22, 2005)); 70 Fed. Reg. 70663 (Nov. 22, 2005) (Effective Date: Apr. 1, 2006); 70 Fed. Reg. 75931 (Dec. 22, 2005) (Effective Date: Dec. 22, 2005) (technical amendments to 70 Fed. Reg. 70663 (Nov. 22, 2005) (Effective Date: Apr. 1, 2006))]

12 C.F.R. § 717.3 Definitions.

As used in this part, unless the context requires otherwise:

(a) *Act* means the Fair Credit Reporting Act (15 U.S.C. 1681 *et seq.*).

(b) *Affiliate* means any company that is related by common ownership or common corporate control with another company. For example, an affiliate of a Federal credit union is a credit union service corporation (CUSO), as provided in 12 CFR part 712, that is controlled by the Federal credit union.

(c) [Reserved]

(d) *Company* means any corporation, limited liability company, business trust, general or limited partnership, association, or similar organization.

(e) *Consumer* means an individual.

(f)–(h) [Reserved]

(i) *Common ownership or common corporate control* means a relationship between two companies under which:

(1) One company has, with respect to the other company:

(i) Ownership, control, or power to vote 25 percent or more of the outstanding shares of any class of voting security of a company, directly or indirectly, or acting through one or more other persons;

(ii) Control in any manner over the election of a majority of the directors, trustees, or general partners (or individuals exercising similar functions) of a company; or

(iii) The power to exercise, directly or indirectly, a controlling influence over the management or policies of a company, as the NCUA determines; or

(iv) *Example.* NCUA will presume a credit union has a controlling influence over the management or policies of a CUSO, if the CUSO is 67% owned by credit unions.

(2) Any other person has, with respect to both companies, a relationship described in paragraphs (i)(1)(i) through (i)(1)(iii) of this section.

(j) [Reserved]

(k) *Medical information* means:

(1) Information or data, whether oral or recorded, in any form or medium, created by or derived from a health care provider or the consumer, that relates to:

(i) The past, present, or future physical, mental, or behavioral health or condition of an individual;

(ii) The provision of health care to an individual; or

(iii) The payment for the provision of health care to an individual.

(2) The term does not include:

(i) The age or gender of a consumer;

(ii) Demographic information about the consumer, including a consumer's residence address or e-mail address;

(iii) Any other information about a consumer that does not relate to the physical, mental, or behavioral health or condition of a consumer, including the existence or value of any insurance policy; or

(iv) Information that does not identify a specific consumer.

(l) *Person* means any individual, partnership, corporation, trust, estate cooperative, association, government or governmental subdivision or agency, or other entity.

[69 Fed. Reg. 69269 (Nov. 29, 2004) (Effective Date: Dec. 29, 2004); 70 Fed. Reg. 33957 (June 10, 2005) (Effective Date: Apr. 1, 2006, *as amended* 70 Fed. Reg. 70663 (Nov. 22, 2005)); 70 Fed. Reg. 70663 (Nov. 22, 2005) (Effective Date: Apr. 1, 2006); 70 Fed. Reg. 75931 (Dec. 22, 2005) (Effective Date: Dec. 22, 2005) (technical amendments to 70 Fed. Reg. 70663 (Nov. 22, 2005) (Effective Date: Apr. 1, 2006))]

SUBPARTS B, C—[RESERVED]

SUBPART D—MEDICAL INFORMATION

12 C.F.R. § 717.30 Obtaining or using medical information in connection with a determination of eligibility for credit.

(a) *Scope.* This section applies to:

(1) A Federal credit union that participates as a creditor in a transaction; or

(2) Any other person that participates as a creditor in a transaction involving a person described in paragraph (a)(1) of this section.

(b) *General prohibition on obtaining or using medical information.*—(1) *In general.* A creditor may not obtain or use medical information pertaining to a consumer in connection with any determination of the consumer's eligibility, or continued eligibility, for credit, except as provided in this section.

(2) *Definitions.* (i) Credit has the same meaning as in section 702 of the Equal Credit Opportunity Act, 15 U.S.C. 1691a.

(ii) *Creditor* has the same meaning as in section 702 of the Equal Credit Opportunity Act, 15 U.S.C. 1691a.

(iii) *Eligibility, or continued eligibility, for credit* means the consumer's qualification or fitness to receive, or continue to receive, credit, including the terms on which credit is offered. The term does not include:

(A) Any determination of the consumer's qualification or fitness for employment, insurance (other than a credit insurance product), or other non-credit products or services;

(B) Authorizing, processing, or documenting a payment or transaction on behalf of the consumer in a manner that does not involve a determination of the consumer's eligibility, or continued eligibility, for credit; or

(C) Maintaining or servicing the consumer's account in a manner that does not involve a determination of the consumer's eligibility, or continued eligibility, for credit.

(c) *Rule of construction for obtaining and using unsolicited medical information.*—(1) *In general.* A creditor does not obtain medical information in violation of the prohibition if it receives medical information pertaining to a consumer in connection with any determination of the consumer's eligibility, or continued eligibility, for credit without specifically requesting medical information.

(2) *Use of unsolicited medical information.* A creditor that receives unsolicited medical information in the manner described in paragraph (c)(1) of this section may use that information in connection with any determination of the consumer's eligibility, or continued eligibility, for credit to the extent the creditor can rely on at least one of the exceptions in § 717.30(d) or (e).

(3) *Examples.* A creditor does not obtain medical information in violation of the prohibition if, for example:

(i) In response to a general question regarding a consumer's debts or expenses, the creditor receives information that the consumer owes a debt to a hospital.

(ii) In a conversation with the creditor's loan officer, the consumer informs the creditor that the consumer has a particular medical condition.

(iii) In connection with a consumer's application for an extension of credit, the creditor requests a consumer report from a consumer reporting agency and receives medical information in the consumer report furnished by the agency even though the creditor did not specifically request medical information from the consumer reporting agency.

(d) *Financial information exception for obtaining and using medical information.*—(1) *In general.* A creditor may obtain and use medical information pertaining to a consumer in connection with any determination of the consumer's eligibility, or continued eligibility, for credit so long as:

(i) The information is the type of information routinely used in making credit eligibility determinations, such as information relating to debts, expenses, income, benefits, assets, collateral, or the purpose of the loan, including the use of proceeds;

(ii) The creditor uses the medical information in a manner and to an extent that is no less favorable than it would use comparable information that is not medical information in a credit transaction; and

(iii) The creditor does not take the consumer's physical, mental, or behavioral health, condition or history, type of treatment, or prognosis into account as part of any such determination.

(2) *Examples.* (i) *Examples of the types of information routinely used in making credit eligibility determinations.* Paragraph (d)(1)(i) of this section permits a creditor, for example, to obtain and use information about:

(A) The dollar amount, repayment terms, repayment history, and similar information regarding medical debts to calculate, measure, or verify the repayment ability of the consumer, the use of proceeds, or the terms for granting credit;

(B) The value, condition, and lien status of a medical device that may serve as collateral to secure a loan;

(C) The dollar amount and continued eligibility for disability income, workers' compensation income, or other benefits related to health or a medical condition that is relied on as a source of repayment; or

(D) The identity of creditors to whom outstanding medical debts are owed in connection with an application for credit, including but not limited to, a transaction involving the consolidation of medical debts.

(ii) *Examples of uses of medical information consistent with the exception.* (A) A consumer includes on an application for credit information about two $20,000 debts. One debt is to a hospital; the other debt is to a retailer. The creditor contacts the hospital and the retailer to verify the amount and payment status of the debts. The creditor learns that both debts are more than 90 days past due. Any two debts of this size that are more than 90 days past due would disqualify the consumer under the creditor's established underwriting criteria. The creditor denies the application on the basis that the consumer has a poor repayment history on outstanding debts. The creditor has used medical information in a manner and to an extent no less favorable than it would use comparable non-medical information.

(B) A consumer indicates on an application for a $200,000 mortgage loan that she receives $15,000 in long-term disability income each year from her former employer and has no other income. Annual income of $15,000, regardless of source, would not be sufficient to support the requested amount of credit. The creditor denies the application on the basis that the projected debt-to-income ratio of the consumer does not meet the creditor's underwriting criteria. The creditor has used medical information in a manner and to an extent that is no less favorable than it would use comparable non-medical information.

(C) A consumer includes on an application for a $10,000 home equity loan that he has a $50,000 debt to a medical facility that specializes in treating a potentially terminal disease. The creditor contacts the medical facility to verify the debt and obtain the repayment history and current status of the loan. The creditor learns that the debt is current. The applicant meets the income and other requirements of the creditor's underwriting guidelines. The creditor grants the application. The creditor has used medical information in accordance with the exception.

(iii) *Examples of uses of medical information inconsistent with the exception.* (A) A consumer applies for $25,000 of credit and includes on the application information about a $50,000 debt to a hospital. The creditor contacts the hospital to verify the amount and payment status of the debt, and learns that the debt is current and that the consumer has no delinquencies in her repayment history. If the existing debt were instead owed to a retail department store, the creditor would approve the application and extend credit based on the amount and repayment history of the outstanding debt. The creditor, however, denies the application because the consumer is indebted to a hospital. The creditor has used medical information, here the identity of the medical creditor, in a manner and to an extent that is less favorable than it would use comparable non-medical information.

(B) A consumer meets with a loan officer of a creditor to apply for a mortgage loan. While filling out the loan application, the consumer informs the loan officer orally that she has a potentially terminal disease. The consumer meets the creditor's established requirements for the requested mortgage loan. The loan officer recommends to the credit committee that the consumer be denied credit because the consumer has that disease. The credit committee follows the loan officer's recommendation and denies the application because the consumer has a potentially terminal disease. The creditor has used medical information in a manner inconsistent with the exception by taking into account the consumer's physical, mental, or behavioral health, condition, or history, type of treatment, or prognosis as part of a determination of eligibility or continued eligibility for credit.

(C) A consumer who has an apparent medical condition, such as a consumer who uses a wheelchair or an oxygen tank, meets with a loan officer to apply for a home equity loan. The consumer meets the creditor's established requirements for the requested home equity loan and the creditor typically does not require consumers to obtain a debt cancellation contract, debt suspension agreement, or credit insurance product in connection with such loans. However, based on the consumer's apparent medical condition, the loan officer recommends to the credit committee that credit be extended to the consumer only if the consumer obtains a debt cancellation contract, debt suspension agreement, or credit insurance product from a nonaffiliated third party. The credit committee agrees with the loan officer's recommendation. The loan officer informs the consumer that the consumer must obtain a debt cancellation contract, debt suspension agreement, or credit insurance product from a nonaffiliated third party to qualify for the loan. The consumer obtains one of these products and the creditor approves the loan. The creditor has used medical information in a manner inconsistent with the exception by taking into account the consumer's physical, mental, or behavioral health, condition, or history, type of treatment, or prognosis in setting conditions on the consumer's eligibility for credit.

(e) *Specific exceptions for obtaining and using medical information.*—(1) *In general.* A creditor may obtain and use medical information pertaining to a consumer in connection with any determination of the consumer's eligibility, or continued eligibility, for credit:

(i) To determine whether the use of a power of attorney or legal representative that is triggered by a medical condition or event is necessary and appropriate or whether the consumer has the legal capacity to contract when a person seeks to exercise a power of attorney or act as legal representative for a consumer based on an asserted medical condition or event;

(ii) To comply with applicable requirements of local, state, or Federal laws;

(iii) To determine, at the consumer's request, whether the consumer qualifies for a legally permissible special credit program or credit-related assistance program that is:

(A) Designed to meet the special needs of consumers with medical conditions; and

(B) Established and administered pursuant to a written plan that:

(1) Identifies the class of persons that the program is designed to benefit; and

(2) Sets forth the procedures and standards for extending credit or providing other credit-related assistance under the program;

(iv) To the extent necessary for purposes of fraud prevention or detection;

(v) In the case of credit for the purpose of financing medical products or services, to determine and verify the medical purpose of a loan and the use of proceeds;

(vi) Consistent with safe and sound practices, if the consumer or the consumer's legal representative specifically requests that the creditor use medical information in determining the consumer's eligibility, or continued eligibility, for credit, to accommodate the consumer's particular circumstances, and such request is documented by the creditor;

(vii) Consistent with safe and sound practices, to determine whether the provisions of a forbearance practice or program that is triggered by a medical condition or event apply to a consumer;

(viii) To determine the consumer's eligibility for, the triggering of, or the reactivation of a debt cancellation contract or debt suspension agreement if a medical condition or event is a triggering event for the provision of benefits under the contract or agreement; or

(ix) To determine the consumer's eligibility for, the triggering of, or the reactivation of a credit insurance product if a medical condition or event is a triggering event for the provision of benefits under the product.

(2) *Example of determining eligibility for a special credit program or credit assistance program.* A not-for-profit organization establishes a credit assistance program pursuant to a written plan that is designed to assist disabled veterans in purchasing homes by subsidizing the down payment for the home purchase mortgage loans of qualifying veterans. The organization works through mortgage lenders and requires mortgage lenders to obtain medical information about the disability of any consumer that seeks to qualify for the program, use that information to verify the consumer's eligibility for the program, and forward that information to the organization. A consumer who is a veteran applies to a creditor for a home purchase mortgage loan. The creditor informs the consumer about the credit assistance program for disabled veterans and the consumer seeks to qualify for the program. Assuming that the program complies with all applicable law, including applicable fair lending laws, the creditor may obtain and use medical information about the medical condition and disability, if any, of the consumer to determine whether the consumer qualifies for the credit assistance program.

(3) *Examples of verifying the medical purpose of the loan or the use of proceeds.* (i) If a consumer applies for $10,000 of credit for the purpose of financing vision correction surgery, the creditor may verify with the surgeon that the procedure will be performed. If the surgeon reports that surgery will not be performed on the consumer, the creditor may use that medical information to deny the consumer's application for credit, because the loan would not be used for the stated purpose.

(ii) If a consumer applies for $10,000 of credit for the purpose of financing cosmetic surgery, the creditor may confirm the cost of the procedure with the surgeon. If the surgeon reports that the cost of the procedure is $5,000, the creditor may use that medical information to offer the consumer only $5,000 of credit.

(iii) A creditor has an established medical loan program for financing particular elective surgical procedures. The creditor receives a loan application from a consumer requesting $10,000 of credit under the established loan program for an elective surgical procedure. The consumer indicates on the application that the purpose of the loan is to finance an elective surgical procedure not eligible for funding under the guidelines of the established loan program. The creditor may deny the consumer's application because the purpose of the loan is not for a particular procedure funded by the established loan program.

(4) *Examples of obtaining and using medical information at the request of the consumer.* (i) If a consumer applies for a loan and specifically requests that the creditor consider the consumer's medical disability at the relevant time as an explanation for adverse payment history information in his credit report, the creditor may consider such medical information in evaluating the consumer's willingness and ability to repay the requested loan to accommodate the consumer's particular circumstances, consistent with safe and sound practices. The creditor may also decline to consider such medical information to accommodate the consumer, but may evaluate the consumer's application in accordance with its otherwise applicable underwriting criteria. The creditor may not deny the consumer's application or otherwise treat the consumer less favorably because the consumer specifically requested a medical accommodation, if the creditor would have extended the credit or treated the consumer more favorably under the creditor's otherwise applicable underwriting criteria.

(ii) If a consumer applies for a loan by telephone and explains that his income has been and will continue to be interrupted on account of a medical condition and that he expects to repay the loan by liquidating assets, the creditor may, but is not required to, evaluate the application using the sale of assets as the primary source of repayment, consistent with safe and sound practices, provided that the creditor documents the consumer's request by recording the oral conversation or making a notation of the request in the consumer's file.

(iii) If a consumer applies for a loan and the application form provides a space where the consumer may provide any other information or special circumstances, whether medical or non-medical, that the consumer would like the creditor to consider in evaluating the consumer's application, the creditor may use medical information provided by the consumer in that space on that application to accommodate the consumer's application for credit, consistent with safe and sound practices, or may disregard that information.

(iv) If a consumer specifically requests that the creditor use medical information in determining the consumer's eligibility, or continued eligibility, for credit and provides the creditor with medical information for that purpose, and the creditor determines that it needs additional information regarding the consumer's circumstances, the creditor may request, obtain, and use additional medical information about the consumer as necessary to verify the information provided by the consumer or to determine whether to make an accommodation for the consumer. The consumer may decline to provide additional information, withdraw the request for an accommodation, and have the application considered under the creditor's otherwise applicable underwriting criteria.

(v) If a consumer completes and signs a credit application that is not for medical purpose credit and the application contains boilerplate language that routinely requests medical information from the consumer or that indicates that by applying for credit the consumer authorizes or consents to the creditor obtaining and using medical information in connection with a determination of the consumer's eligibility, or continued eligibility, for credit, the consumer has not specifically requested that the creditor obtain and use medical information to accommodate the consumer's particular circumstances.

(5) *Example of a forbearance practice or program.* After an appropriate safety and soundness review, a creditor institutes a program that allows consumers who are or will be hospitalized to defer payments as needed for up to three months, without penalty, if the credit account has been open for more than one year and has not previously been in default, and the consumer provides confirming documentation at an appropriate time. A consumer is hospitalized and does not pay her bill for a particular month. This consumer has had a credit account with the creditor for more than one year and has not previously been in default. The creditor attempts to contact the consumer and speaks with the consumer's adult child, who is not the consumer's legal representative. The adult child informs the creditor that the consumer is hospitalized and is unable to pay the bill at that time. The creditor defers payments for up to three months, without penalty, for the hospitalized consumer and sends the consumer a letter confirming this practice and the date on which the next payment will be due. The

creditor has obtained and used medical information to determine whether the provisions of a medically-triggered forbearance practice or program apply to a consumer.

[70 Fed. Reg. 33957 (June 10, 2005) (Effective Date: Apr. 1, 2006, *as amended* 70 Fed. Reg. 70663 (Nov. 22, 2005)); 70 Fed. Reg. 70663 (Nov. 22, 2005) (Effective Date: Apr. 1, 2006); 70 Fed. Reg. 75931 (Dec. 22, 2005) (Effective Date: Dec. 22, 2005) (technical amendments to 70 Fed. Reg. 70663 (Nov. 22, 2005) (Effective Date: Apr. 1, 2006))]

12 C.F.R. § 717.31 Limits on redisclosure of information

(a) *Scope.* This section applies to Federal credit unions.

(b) *Limits on redisclosure.* If a Federal credit union receives medical information about a consumer from a consumer reporting agency or its affiliate, the person must not disclose that information to any other person, except as necessary to carry out the purpose for which the information was initially disclosed, or as otherwise permitted by statute, regulation, or order.

[70 Fed. Reg. 33957 (June 10, 2005) (Effective Date: Apr. 1, 2006, *as amended* 70 Fed. Reg. 70663 (Nov. 22, 2005)); 70 Fed. Reg. 70663 (Nov. 22, 2005) (Effective Date: Apr. 1, 2006); 70 Fed. Reg. 75931 (Dec. 22, 2005) (Effective Date: Dec. 22, 2005) (technical amendments to 70 Fed. Reg. 70663 (Nov. 22, 2005) (Effective Date: Apr. 1, 2006))]

12 C.F.R. § 717.32 Sharing medical information with affiliates.

(a) *Scope.* This section applies to Federal credit unions.

(b) *In general.* The exclusions from the term "consumer report" in section 603(d)(2) of the Act that allow the sharing of information with affiliates do not apply if a Federal credit union communicates to an affiliate:

(1) Medical information;

(2) An individualized list or description based on the payment transactions of the consumer for medical products or services; or

(3) An aggregate list of identified consumers based on payment transactions for medical products or services.

(c) *Exceptions.* A Federal credit union may rely on the exclusions from the term "consumer report" in section 603(d)(2) of the Act to communicate the information in paragraph (b) to an affiliate:

(1) In connection with the business of insurance or annuities (including the activities described in section 18B of the model Privacy of Consumer Financial and Health Information Regulation issued by the National Association of Insurance Commissioners, as in effect on January 1, 2003);

(2) For any purpose permitted without authorization under the regulations promulgated by the Department of Health and Human Services pursuant to the Health Insurance Portability and Accountability Act of 1996 (HIPAA);

(3) For any purpose referred to in section 1179 of HIPAA;

(4) For any purpose described in section 502(e) of the Gramm-Leach-Bliley Act;

(5) In connection with a determination of the consumer's eligibility, or continued eligibility, for credit consistent with § 717.30; or

(6) As otherwise permitted by order of the NCUA.

[70 Fed. Reg. 33957 (June 10, 2005) (Effective Date: Apr. 1, 2006, *as amended* 70 Fed. Reg. 70663 (Nov. 22, 2005)); 70 Fed. Reg. 75931 (Dec. 22, 2005) (Effective Date: Dec. 22, 2005) (technical amendments to 70 Fed. Reg. 70663 (Nov. 22, 2005) (Effective Date: Apr. 1, 2006))]

SUBPARTS E–H—[RESERVED]

SUBPART I—DUTIES OF USERS OF CONSUMER REPORTS REGARDING IDENTITY THEFT

12 C.F.R. §§ 717.80–717.82 [Reserved]

[69 Fed. Reg. 69269 (Nov. 29, 2004) (Effective Date: Dec. 29, 2004)]

12 C.F.R. § 717.83 Disposal of consumer information.

(a) *In general.* You must properly dispose of any consumer information that you maintain or otherwise possess in a manner consistent with the Guidelines for Safeguarding Member Information, in appendix A to part 748 of this chapter.

(b) *Examples.* Appropriate measures to properly dispose of consumer information include the following examples. These examples are illustrative only and are not exclusive or exhaustive methods for complying with this section.

(1) Burning, pulverizing, or shredding papers containing consumer information so that the information cannot practicably be read or reconstructed.

(2) Destroying or erasing electronic media containing consumer information so that the information cannot practicably be read or reconstructed.

(c) *Rule of construction.* This section does not:

(1) Require you to maintain or destroy any record pertaining to a consumer that is not imposed under any other law; or

(2) Alter or affect any requirement imposed under any other provision of law to maintain or destroy such a record.

(d) *Definitions.* As used in this section:

(1) *Consumer information* means any record about an individual, whether in paper, electronic, or other form, that is a consumer report or is derived from a consumer report and that is maintained or otherwise possessed by or on behalf of the credit union for a business purpose. Consumer information also means a compilation of such records. The term does not include any record that does not identify an individual.

(i) *Consumer information* includes:

(A) A consumer report that you obtain;

(B) Information from a consumer report that you obtain from your affiliate after the consumer has been given a notice and has elected not to opt out of that sharing;

(C) Information from a consumer report that you obtain about an individual who applies for but does not receive a loan, including any loan sought by an individual for a business purpose;

(D) Information from a consumer report that you obtain about an individual who guarantees a loan (including a loan to a business entity); or

(E) Information from a consumer report that you obtain about an employee or prospective employee.

(ii) *Consumer information* does not include:

(A) Aggregate information, such as the mean credit score, derived from a group of consumer reports; or

(B) Blind data, such as payment history on accounts that are not personally identifiable, you use for developing credit scoring models or for other purposes.

(2) *Consumer report* has the same meaning as set forth in the Fair Credit Reporting Act, 15 U.S.C. 1681a(d). The meaning of consumer report is broad and subject to various definitions, conditions and exceptions in the Fair Credit Reporting Act. It includes written or oral communications from a consumer reporting agency to a third party of information used or collected for use in establishing eligibility for credit or insurance used primarily for personal, family or household purposes, and eligibility for employment purposes. Examples include credit reports, bad check lists, and tenant screening reports.

[69 Fed. Reg. 69269 (Nov. 29, 2004) (Effective Date: Dec. 29, 2004)]

B.3.6 Security and Exchange Commission Regulations

TITLE 17—COMMODITY AND SECURITIES EXCHANGES

* * *

CHAPTER II—SECURITIES AND EXCHANGE COMMISSION

* * *

PART 248—REGULATION S-P: PRIVACY OF CONSUMER FINANCIAL INFORMATION

* * *

SUBPART D—RELATION TO OTHER LAWS; EFFECTIVE DATE

* * *

248.30 Procedures to safeguard customer records and information; disposal of consumer report information.

TITLE 17—COMMODITY AND SECURITIES EXCHANGES

* * *

CHAPTER II—SECURITIES AND EXCHANGE COMMISSION

* * *

PART 248—REGULATION S-P: PRIVACY OF CONSUMER FINANCIAL INFORMATION

* * *

SUBPART D—RELATION TO OTHER LAWS; EFFECTIVE DATE

* * *

17 C.F.R. § 248.30 Procedures to safeguard customer records and information; disposal of consumer report information.

(a) Every broker, dealer, and investment company, and every investment adviser registered with the Commission must adopt written policies and procedures that address administrative, technical, and physical safeguards for the protection of customer records and information. These written policies and procedures must be reasonably designed to:

(1) Insure the security and confidentiality of customer records and information;

(2) Protect against any anticipated threats or hazards to the security or integrity of customer records and information; and

(3) Protect against unauthorized access to or use of customer records or information that could result in substantial harm or inconvenience to any customer.

(b) *Disposal of consumer report information and records*—(1) *Definitions* (i) *Consumer report* has the same meaning as in section 603(d) of the Fair Credit Reporting Act (15 U.S.C. 1681a(d)).

(ii) *Consumer report information* means any record about an individual, whether in paper, electronic or other form, that is a consumer report or is derived from a consumer report. Consumer report information also means a compilation of such records. Consumer report information does not include information that does not identify individuals, such as aggregate information or blind data.

(iii) *Disposal* means:

(A) The discarding or abandonment of consumer report information; or

(B) The sale, donation, or transfer of any medium, including computer equipment, on which consumer report information is stored.

(iv) *Notice-registered broker-dealers* means a broker or dealer registered by notice with the Commission under section 15(b)(11) of the Securities Exchange Act of 1934 (15 U.S.C. 78o(b)(11)).

(v) *Transfer agent* has the same meaning as in section 3(a)(25) of the Securities Exchange Act of 1934 (15 U.S.C. 78c(a)(25)).

(2) *Proper disposal requirements*—(i) *Standard.* Every broker and dealer other than notice-registered broker-dealers, every investment company, and every investment adviser and transfer agent registered with the Commission, that maintains or otherwise possesses consumer report information for a business purpose must properly dispose of the information by taking reasonable measures to protect against unauthorized access to or use of the information in connection with its disposal.

(ii) *Relation to other laws.* Nothing in this section shall be construed:

(A) To require any broker, dealer, or investment company, or any investment adviser or transfer agent registered with the Commission to maintain or destroy any record pertaining to an individual that is not imposed under other law; or

(B) To alter or affect any requirement imposed under any other provision of law to maintain or destroy any of those records.

* * *

[69 Fed. Reg. 71321 (Dec. 8, 2004) (Effective Date: Jan. 11, 2005; Paragraph (b) Compliance Date: July 1, 2006)]

Appendix C FTC and FRB Model Forms

The Fair Credit Reporting Act requires the Federal Trade Commission and Federal Reserve Board to develop a number of model forms for credit reporting agencies and furnishers to use. A table of these forms is set forth below. The authority, purpose, and legal effect of these model forms are set forth in 16 C.F.R. §§ 642.1–.3 and §§ 698.1–.3 (reprinted at Appx. B.1, *supra*) and 12 C.F.R. § 222.1(b)(2)(ii) (reprinted at Appx. B.2, *supra*)

This appendix also contains five sample notification forms issued by the Federal Reserve Board, concerning notice to consumers of adverse action on a credit application. These forms are used when creditors comply simultaneously with the requirements of both the Equal Credit Opportunity Act and the Fair Credit Reporting Act.

C.1 Standardized Form for Requesting Annual File Disclosures (Requesting a Free Credit Report)
C.2 General Summary of Consumer Rights
C.3 Summary of Consumer Identity Theft Rights
C.4 FTC Identity Theft Affidavit
C.5 Notice of Furnisher Responsibilities
C.6 Notice to Users of Consumer Reports
C.7 Model Prescreen Opt-Out Notices
C.8 Model Notices of Furnishing Negative Information
C.9 ECOA Adverse Action Forms (Regulation B, 12 C.F.R. Part 202, Appendix C)

C.1 Standardized Form for Requesting Annual File Disclosures (Requesting a Free Credit Report)

FACTA requires the FTC to adopt a standardized form for consumers to request a free annual file disclosure (credit report) from each nationwide consumer reporting agency.[1] In 2004, the FTC adopted the following sample form to be utilized by consumers seeking a free credit report.[2]

---

1 Pub. L. No. 108-159, § 211(d) (Dec. 4, 2003). *See* § 3.3.2 *supra*.
2 69 Fed. Reg. 35468 (June 24, 2004).

REQUEST FOR FREE CREDIT REPORT

> *Note to Consumers:* **You have the right to obtain a free copy of your credit report once every 12 months (also known as an "annual file disclosure"), from each of the nationwide consumer reporting agencies. Your report may contain information on where you work and live, the credit accounts that have been opened in your name, if you've paid your bills on time, and whether you have been sued, arrested, or have filed for bankruptcy. Businesses use this information in making decisions about whether to offer you credit, insurance, or employment, and on what terms.**

Use this form to request your credit report from any, or all, of the nationwide consumer reporting agencies.

The following information is required to process your request:

Your Full Name: _____

Your Street Address: _____

Your City, State & Zip Code: _____

Your Telephone Numbers (with area code): Day: _____
　　　　　　　　　　　　　　　　　　　　　Evening: _____

Your Social Security number: _____ Your Date of Birth_____

Place a check next to each credit report you want.

　　_____ I want a credit report from each of the nationwide consumer reporting agencies

OR

　　_____ I want a credit report from:
　　　　　_____ [name of nationwide consumer reporting agency]
　　　　　_____ [name of nationwide consumer reporting agency]
　　　　　_____ [name of nationwide consumer reporting agency]

Please check how you would like to receive your report. (Note: because of the need to accurately identify you before we send you your credit report, we may not be able to offer every delivery method to every consumer. We will try to honor your preference.)

_____ [available delivery method]
_____ [available delivery method]
_____ [available delivery method]

_____ Check here if, for security purposes, you want your copy of your credit report to include only the last four digits of your Social Security number (SSN), rather than your entire SSN.

For more information on obtaining your free credit report, visit [insert appropriate website address], call [insert appropriate telephone number], or write to [insert appropriate address].

Mail this form to:
[insert appropriate address]

Your report(s) will be sent within 15 days after we receive your request.

By direction of the Commission.

Donald S. Clark,
Secretary.
[FR Doc. 04–14388 Filed 6–23–04; 8:45 am]
BILLING CODE 6750-01-C

C.2 General Summary of Consumer Rights

Section 1681g(c) of the FCRA requires the FTC to issue a general summary of consumer rights.[3] The Summary of Consumer Rights is perhaps the single most common explanation of the FCRA most consumers will ever receive. Consumer reporting agencies must provide a copy of the Summary of Consumer Rights whenever a consumer requests disclosure of a consumer's file.

---

3 See § 8.2.2, *supra*.

Para informacion en espanol, visite www.ftc.gov/credit o escribe a la FTC Consumer Response Center, Room 130-A 600 Pennsylvania Ave. N.W., Washington, D.C. 20580.

A Summary of Your Rights Under the Fair Credit Reporting Act

The federal Fair Credit Reporting Act (FCRA) promotes the accuracy, fairness, and privacy of information in the files of consumer reporting agencies. There are many types of consumer reporting agencies, including credit bureaus and specialty agencies (such as agencies that sell information about check writing histories, medical records, and rental history records). Here is a summary of your major rights under the FCRA. **For more information, including information about additional rights, go to www.ftc.gov/credit or write to: Consumer Response Center, Room 130-A, Federal Trade Commission, 600 Pennsylvania Ave. N.W., Washington, D.C. 20580.**

- **You must be told if information in your file has been used against you.** Anyone who uses a credit report or another type of consumer report to deny your application for credit, insurance, or employment – or to take another adverse action against you – must tell you, and must give you the name, address, and phone number of the agency that provided the information.

- **You have the right to know what is in your file.** You may request and obtain all the information about you in the files of a consumer reporting agency (your "file disclosure"). You will be required to provide proper identification, which may include your Social Security number. In many cases, the disclosure will be free. You are entitled to a free file disclosure if:
  - a person has taken adverse action against you because of information in your credit report;
  - you are the victim of identify theft and place a fraud alert in your file;
  - your file contains inaccurate information as a result of fraud;
  - you are on public assistance;
  - you are unemployed but expect to apply for employment within 60 days.

  In addition, by September 2005 all consumers will be entitled to one free disclosure every 12 months upon request from each nationwide credit bureau and from nationwide specialty consumer reporting agencies. See www.ftc.gov/credit for additional information.

- **You have the right to ask for a credit score.** Credit scores are numerical summaries of your credit-worthiness based on information from credit bureaus. You may request a credit score from consumer reporting agencies that create scores or distribute scores used in residential real property loans, but you will have to pay for it. In some mortgage transactions, you will receive credit score information for free from the mortgage lender.

- **You have the right to dispute incomplete or inaccurate information.** If you identify information in your file that is incomplete or inaccurate, and report it to the consumer reporting agency, the agency must investigate unless your dispute is frivolous. See www.ftc.gov/credit for an explanation of dispute procedures.

- **Consumer reporting agencies must correct or delete inaccurate, incomplete, or unverifiable information.** Inaccurate, incomplete or unverifiable information must be removed or corrected, usually within 30 days. However, a consumer reporting agency may continue to report information it has verified as accurate.

- **Consumer reporting agencies may not report outdated negative information.** In most cases, a consumer reporting agency may not report negative information that is more than seven years old, or bankruptcies that are more than 10 years old.

- **Access to your file is limited.** A consumer reporting agency may provide information about you only to people with a valid need -- usually to consider an application with a creditor, insurer, employer, landlord, or other business. The FCRA specifies those with a valid need for access.

- **You must give your consent for reports to be provided to employers.** A consumer reporting agency may not give out information about you to your employer, or a potential employer, without your written consent given to the employer. Written consent generally is not required in the trucking industry. For more information, go to www.ftc.gov/credit.

- **You may limit "prescreened" offers of credit and insurance you get based on information in your credit report.** Unsolicited "prescreened" offers for credit and insurance must include a toll-free phone number you can call if you choose to remove your name and address from the lists these offers are based on. You may opt-out with the nationwide credit bureaus at 1-800-XXX-XXXX.

- **You may seek damages from violators.** If a consumer reporting agency, or, in some cases, a user of consumer reports or a furnisher of information to a consumer reporting agency violates the FCRA, you may be able to sue in state or federal court.

- **Identity theft victims and active duty military personnel have additional rights.** For more information, visit www.ftc.gov/credit.

States may enforce the FCRA, and many states have their own consumer reporting laws. In some cases, you may have more rights under state law. For more information, contact your state or local consumer protection agency or your state Attorney General. Federal enforcers are:

TYPE OF BUSINESS:	CONTACT:
Consumer reporting agencies, creditors and others not listed below	Federal Trade Commission: Consumer Response Center - FCRA Washington, DC 20580 1-877-382-4357
National banks, federal branches/agencies of foreign banks (word "National" or initials "N.A." appear in or after bank's name)	Office of the Comptroller of the Currency Compliance Management, Mail Stop 6-6 Washington, DC 20219 800-613-6743
Federal Reserve System member banks (except national banks, and federal branches/agencies of foreign banks)	Federal Reserve Board Division of Consumer & Community Affairs Washington, DC 20551 202-452-3693
Savings associations and federally chartered savings banks (word "Federal" or initials "F.S.B." appear in federal institution's name)	Office of Thrift Supervision Consumer Complaints Washington, DC 20552 800-842-6929
Federal credit unions (words "Federal Credit Union" appear in institution's name)	National Credit Union Administration 1775 Duke Street Alexandria, VA 22314 703-519-4600
State-chartered banks that are not members of the Federal Reserve System	Federal Deposit Insurance Corporation Consumer Response Center, 2345 Grand Avenue, Suite 100 Kansas City, Missouri 64108-2638 1-877-275-3342
Air, surface, or rail common carriers regulated by former Civil Aeronautics Board or Interstate Commerce Commission	Department of Transportation , Office of Financial Management Washington, DC 20590 202-366-1306
Activities subject to the Packers and Stockyards Act, 1921	Department of Agriculture Office of Deputy Administrator - GIPSA Washington, DC 20250 202-720-7051

C.3 Summary of Consumer Identity Theft Rights

Section 1681g(d) of the FCRA requires the FTC, in consultation with the federal banking agencies and the National Credit Union Administration, to prepare a model summary of the rights of consumers "with respect to the procedures for remedying the effects of fraud or identity theft." Consumer reporting agencies must distribute this form to any consumer who "contacts a consumer reporting agency and expresses a belief that the consumer is a victim of fraud or identity theft."

Para informacion en espanol, visite www.consumer.gov/idtheft o escribe a la FTC, Consumer Response Center, Room 130-B, 600 Pennsylvania Avenue, N.W. Washington, D.C., 20580.

Remedying the Effects of Identity Theft

You are receiving this information because you have notified a consumer reporting agency that you believe that you are a victim of identity theft. Identity theft occurs when someone uses your name, Social Security number, date of birth, or other identifying information, without authority, to commit fraud. For example, someone may have committed identity theft by using your personal information to open a credit card account or get a loan in your name. For more information, visit www.consumer.gov/idtheft or write to: FTC, Consumer Response Center, Room 130-B, 600 Pennsylvania Avenue, N.W. Washington, D.C., 20580.

The Fair Credit Reporting Act (FCRA) gives you specific rights when you are, or believe that you are, the victim of identity theft. Here is a brief summary of the rights designed to help you recover from identity theft.

1. **You have the right to ask that nationwide consumer reporting agencies place "fraud alerts" in your file** to let potential creditors and others know that you may be a victim of identity theft. A fraud alert can make it more difficult for someone to get credit in your name because it tells creditors to follow certain procedures to protect you. It also may delay your ability to obtain credit. You may place a fraud alert in your file by calling just one of the three nationwide consumer reporting agencies. As soon as that agency processes your fraud alert, it will notify the other two, which then also must place fraud alerts in your file.

    - Equifax: 1-800-XXX-XXXX; www.equifax.com
    - Experian: 1-800-XXX-XXXX; www.experian.com
    - TransUnion: 1-800-XXX-XXXX; www.transunion.com

    An <u>initial fraud alert</u> stays in your file for at least 90 days. An <u>extended alert</u> stays in your file for seven years. To place either of these alerts, a consumer reporting agency will require you to provide appropriate proof of your identity, which may include your Social Security number. If you ask for an extended alert, you will have to provide an *identity theft report*. An *identity theft report* includes a copy of a report you have filed with a federal, state, or local law enforcement agency, and additional information a consumer reporting agency may require you to submit. For more detailed information about the *identity theft report*, visit www.consumer.gov/idtheft.

2. **You have the right to free copies of the information in your file (your "file disclosure").** An <u>initial fraud alert</u> entitles you to a copy of all the information in your file at each of the three nationwide agencies, and an <u>extended alert</u> entitles you to two free file disclosures in a 12-month period following the placing of the alert. These additional disclosures may help you detect signs of fraud, for example, whether fraudulent accounts have been opened in your name or whether someone has reported a change in your address. Once a year, you also have the right to a free copy of the information in your file

at any consumer reporting agency, if you believe it has inaccurate information due to fraud, such as identity theft. You also have the ability to obtain additional free file disclosures under other provisions of the FCRA. See www.ftc.gov/credit.

3. **You have the right to obtain documents relating to fraudulent transactions made or accounts opened using your personal information.** A creditor or other business must give you copies of applications and other business records relating to transactions and accounts that resulted from the theft of your identity, if you ask for them in writing. A business may ask you for proof of your identity, a police report, and an affidavit before giving you the documents. It also may specify an address for you to send your request. Under certain circumstances, a business can refuse to provide you with these documents. See www.consumer.gov/idtheft.

4. **You have the right to obtain information from a debt collector.** If you ask, a debt collector must provide you with certain information about the debt you believe was incurred in your name by an identity thief – like the name of the creditor and the amount of the debt.

5. **If you believe information in your file results from identity theft, you have the right to ask that a consumer reporting agency block that information from your file.** An identity thief may run up bills in your name and not pay them. Information about the unpaid bills may appear on your consumer report. Should you decide to ask a consumer reporting agency to block the reporting of this information, you must identify the information to block, and provide the consumer reporting agency with proof of your identity and a copy of your *identity theft report*. The consumer reporting agency can refuse or cancel your request for a block if, for example, you don't provide the necessary documentation, or where the block results from an error or a material misrepresentation of fact made by you. If the agency declines or rescinds the block, it must notify you. Once a debt resulting from identity theft has been blocked, a person or business with notice of the block may not sell, transfer, or place the debt for collection.

6. **You also may prevent businesses from reporting information about you to consumer reporting agencies if you believe the information is a result of identity theft.** To do so, you must send your request to the address specified by the business that reports the information to the consumer reporting agency. The business will expect you to identify what information you do not want reported and to provide an *identity theft report*.

To learn more about identity theft and how to deal with its consequences, visit www.consumer.gov/idtheft, or write to the FTC. You may have additional rights under state law. For more information, contact your local consumer protection agency or your state attorney general.

In addition to the new rights and procedures to help consumers deal with the effects of identity theft, the FCRA has many other important consumer protections. They are described in more detail at www.ftc.gov/credit.

C.4 FTC Identity Theft Affidavit

The FTC developed an ID Theft Affidavit to assist victims who dispute fraudulent debts and accounts opened by an identity thief. The FTC's ID Theft Affidavit is intended to simplify this process. Instead of completing different forms, consumers can use the ID Theft Affidavit to alert companies where a new account was opened in the identity theft victim's name. The company can then investigate the fraud and decide the outcome of the consumer's claim.

Instructions for Completing the ID Theft Affidavit

To make certain that you do not become responsible for the debts incurred by the identity thief, you must provide proof that you didn't create the debt to each of the companies where accounts where opened or used in your name.

A working group composed of credit grantors, consumer advocates and the Federal Trade Commission (FTC) developed this ID Theft Affidavit to help you report information to many companies using just one standard form. Use of this affidavit is optional for companies. While many companies accept this affidavit, others require that you submit more or different forms. Before you send the affidavit, contact each company to find out if they accept it.

You can use this affidavit where a **new account** was opened in your name. The information will enable the companies to investigate the fraud and decide the outcome of your claim. (If someone made unauthorized charges to an **existing account**, call the company to find out what to do.)

This affidavit has two parts:

- **ID Theft Affidavit** is where you report general information about yourself and the theft.

- **Fraudulent Account Statement** is where you describe the fraudulent account(s) opened in your name. Use a separate Fraudulent Account Statement for each company you need to write to.

When you send the affidavit to the companies, attach copies (**NOT** originals) of any supporting documents (for example, drivers license, police report) you have. Before submitting your affidavit, review the disputed account(s) with family members or friends who may have information about the account(s) or access to them.

Complete this affidavit as soon as possible. Many creditors ask that you send it within two weeks of receiving it. Delaying could slow the investigation.

Be as accurate and complete as possible. You *may* choose not to provide some of the information requested. However, incorrect or incomplete information will slow the process of investigating your claim and absolving the debt. Please print clearly.

When you have finished completing the affidavit, mail a copy to each creditor, bank or company that provided the thief with the unauthorized credit, goods or services you describe. Attach to each affidavit a copy of the Fraudulent Account Statement with information only on accounts opened at the institution receiving the packet, as well as any other supporting documentation you are able to provide.

Send the appropriate documents to each company by certified mail, return receipt requested, so you can prove that it was received. The companies will review your claim and send you a written response telling you the outcome of their investigation. **Keep a copy of everything you submit for your records**.

If you cannot complete the affidavit, a legal guardian or someone with power of attorney may complete it for you. Except as noted, the information you provide will be used only by the company to process your affidavit, investigate the events you report and help stop further fraud. If this affidavit is requested in a lawsuit, the company might have to provide it to the requesting party.

Completing this affidavit does not guarantee that the identity thief will be prosecuted or that the debt will be cleared.

DO NOT SEND AFFIDAVIT TO THE FTC OR ANY OTHER GOVERNMENT AGENCY

If you haven't already done so, report the fraud to the following organizations:

1. Each of the three **national consumer reporting agencies**. Ask each agency to place a "fraud alert" on your credit report, and send you a copy of your credit file. When you have completed your affidavit packet, you may want to send them a copy to help them investigate the disputed accounts.

- **Equifax Credit Information Services, Inc.**
(800) 525-6285/ TDD 1-800-255-0056 and ask the operator to call the Auto Disclosure Line at 1-800-685-1111 to obtain a copy of your report.
P.O. Box 740241, Atlanta, GA 30374-0241
www.equifax.com

- **Experian information Solutions, Inc.**
(888) 397-3742/ TDD (800) 972-0322
P.O. Box 9530, Allen, TX 75013
www.experian.com

- **TransUnion**
(800) 680-7289/ TDD (877) 553-7803
Fraud Victim Assistance Division
P.O. Box 6790, Fullerton, CA 92634-6790
www.transunion.com

2. The **fraud department at each creditor, bank, or utility/service** that provided the identity thief with unauthorized credit, goods or services. This would be a good time to find out if the company accepts this affidavit, and whether they require notarization or a copy of the police report.

3. Your local **police department**. Ask the officer to take a report and give you a copy of the report. Sending a copy of your police report to financial institutions can speed up the process of absolving you of wrongful debts or removing inaccurate information from your credit reports. If you can't get a copy, at least get the number of the report.

4. The FTC, which maintains the Identity Theft Data Clearinghouse – the federal government's centralized identity theft complaint database – and provides information to identity theft victims. You can visit **www.consumer.gov/idtheft** or call toll-free **1-877-ID-THEFT (1-877-438-4338)**.

The FTC collects complaints from identity theft victims and shares their information with law enforcement nationwide. This information also may be shared with other government agencies, consumer reporting agencies, and companies where the fraud was perpetrated to help resolve identity theft related problems.

DO NOT SEND AFFIDAVIT TO THE FTC OR ANY OTHER GOVERNMENT AGENCY

FTC and FRB Model Forms   **Appx. C.4**

Name _____ Phone number _____ Page 1

ID Theft Affidavit

Victim Information

(1) My full legal name is _____
                  (First)   (Middle)   (Last)   (Jr., Sr., III)

(2) (If different from above) When the events described in this affidavit took place, I was known as

_____
  (First)   (Middle)   (Last)   (Jr., Sr., III)

(3) My date of birth is _____
               (day/month/year)

(4) My Social Security number is _____

(5) My driver's license or identification card state and number are _____

(6) My current address is _____

    City _____ State _____ Zip Code _____

(7) I have lived at this address since _____
                             (month/year)

(8) (If different from above) When the events described in this affidavit took place, my address was

_____

    City _____ State _____ Zip Code _____

(9) I lived at the address in Item 8 from _____ until _____
                                     (month/year) (month/year)

(10) My daytime telephone number is (____)_____

     My evening telephone number is (____)_____

DO NOT SEND AFFIDAVIT TO THE FTC OR ANY OTHER GOVERNMENT AGENCY

593

Name _____ Phone number _____ Page 2

How the Fraud Occurred

Check all that apply for items 11 - 17:

(11) ❑ I did not authorize anyone to use my name or personal information to seek the money, credit, loans, goods or services described in this report.

(12) ❑ I did not receive any benefit, money, goods or services as a result of the events described in this report.

(13) ❑ My identification documents (for example, credit cards; birth certificate; driver's license; Social Security card; etc.) were ❑ stolen ❑ lost on or about _____.
(day/month/year)

(14) ❑ To the best of my knowledge and belief, the following person(s) used my information (for example, my name, address, date of birth, existing account numbers, Social Security number, mother's maiden name, etc.) or identification documents to get money, credit, loans, goods or services without my knowledge or authorization:

_____ _____
Name (if known)   Name (if known)

_____ _____
Address (if known)   Address (if known)

_____ _____
Phone number(s) (if known)   Phone number(s) (if known)

_____ _____
Additional information (if known) Additional information (if known)

(15) ❑ I do NOT know who used my information or identification documents to get money, credit, loans, goods or services without my knowledge or authorization.

(16) ❑ Additional comments: (For example, description of the fraud, which documents or information were used or how the identity thief gained access to your information.)

_____
_____
_____
_____

(Attach additional pages as necessary.)

DO NOT SEND AFFIDAVIT TO THE FTC OR ANY OTHER GOVERNMENT AGENCY

FTC and FRB Model Forms   Appx. C.4

Name _____ Phone number _____ Page 3

Victim's Law Enforcement Actions

(17) (check one) I ❏ am ❏ am not willing to assist in the prosecution of the person(s) who committed this fraud.

(18) (check one) I ❏ am ❏ am not authorizing the release of this information to law enforcement for the purpose of assisting them in the investigation and prosecution of the person(s) who committed this fraud.

(19) (check all that apply) I ❏ have ❏ have not reported the events described in this affidavit to the police or other law enforcement agency. The police ❏ did ❏ did not write a report. *In the event you have contacted the police or other law enforcement agency, please complete the following:*

_____ _____
(Agency #1) (Officer/Agency personnel taking report)

_____ _____
(Date of report) (Report number, if any)

_____ _____
(Phone number) (email address, if any)

_____ _____
(Agency #2) (Officer/Agency personnel taking report)

_____ _____
(Date of report) (Report number, if any)

_____ _____
(Phone number) (email address, if any)

Documentation Checklist

Please indicate the supporting documentation you are able to provide to the companies you plan to notify. Attach copies (NOT originals) to the affidavit before sending it to the companies.

(20) ❏ A copy of a valid government-issued photo-identification card (for example, your driver's license, state-issued ID card or your passport). If you are under 16 and don't have a photo-ID, you may submit a copy of your birth certificate or a copy of your official school records showing your enrollment and place of residence.

(21) ❏ Proof of residency during the time the disputed bill occurred, the loan was made or the other event took place (for example, a rental/lease agreement in your name, a copy of a utility bill or a copy of an insurance bill).

DO NOT SEND AFFIDAVIT TO THE FTC OR ANY OTHER GOVERNMENT AGENCY

Appx. C.4   *Fair Credit Reporting*

Name _____ Phone number _____ Page 4

(22) ❏   A copy of the report you filed with the police or sheriff's department. If you are unable to obtain a report or report number from the police, please indicate that in Item 19. Some companies only need the report number, not a copy of the report. You may want to check with each company.

Signature

I declare under penalty of perjury that the information I have provided in this affidavit is true and correct to the best of my knowledge.

_____   _____
(signature)   (date signed)

Knowingly submitting false information on this form could subject you to criminal prosecution for perjury.

_____
(Notary)

[Check with each company. Creditors sometimes require notarization. If they do not, please have one witness (non-relative) sign below that you completed and signed this affidavit.]

Witness:

_____   _____
(signature)   (printed name)

_____   _____
(date)   (telephone number)

DO NOT SEND AFFIDAVIT TO THE FTC OR ANY OTHER GOVERNMENT AGENCY

FTC and FRB Model Forms   **Appx. C.4**

Name _____ Phone number _____ Page 5

Fraudulent Account Statement

> **Completing this Statement**
> - Make as many copies of this page as you need. **Complete a separate page for each company you're notifying and only send it to that company.** Include a copy of your signed affidavit.
> - List only the account(s) you're disputing with the company receiving this form. **See the example below.**
> - If a collection agency sent you a statement, letter or notice about the fraudulent account, attach a copy of that document (**NOT** the original).

I declare (check all that apply):

☐ As a result of the event(s) described in the ID Theft Affidavit, the following account(s) was/were opened at your company in my name without my knowledge, permission or authorization using my personal information or identifying documents:

Creditor Name/Address *(the company that opened the account or provided the goods or services)*	Account Number	Type of unauthorized credit/goods/services provided by creditor *(if known)*	Date issued or opened *(if known)*	Amount/Value provided *(the amount charged or the cost of the goods/services)*
Example Example National Bank 22 Main Street Columbus, Ohio 22722	01234567-89	auto loan	01/05/2002	$25,500.00

☐ During the time of the accounts described above, I had the following account open with your company:

Billing name _____

Billing address _____

Account number _____

DO NOT SEND AFFIDAVIT TO THE FTC OR ANY OTHER GOVERNMENT AGENCY

C.5 Notice of Furnisher Responsibilities

Section 1681e(d)(1) of the FCRA requires that consumer reporting agencies distribute to each person that regularly furnishes information to the agency or that receives information from the agency a notice of the person's responsibilities under the FCRA. The FCRA requires the FTC to "prescribe" the content of model notices that can be used to comply with section 1681e(d)(1). The FTC issued a notice explaining the duties of persons furnishing information to consumer reporting agencies in 1997, which the FTC amended in 2004 in response to new furnisher duties added by FACTA.[4]

---

[4] 69 Fed. Reg. 69776 (Nov. 30, 2004).

All furnishers subject to the Federal Trade Commission's jurisdiction must comply with all applicable regulations, including regulations promulgated after this notice was prescribed in 2004. Information about applicable regulations currently in effect can be found at the Commission's Web site, www.ftc.gov/credit. Furnishers who are not subject to the Commission's jurisdiction should consult with their regulators to find any relevant regulations.

NOTICE TO FURNISHERS OF INFORMATION: OBLIGATIONS OF FURNISHERS UNDER THE FCRA

The federal Fair Credit Reporting Act (FCRA), 15 U.S.C. 1681-1681y, imposes responsibilities on all persons who furnish information to consumer reporting agencies (CRAs). These responsibilities are found in Section 623 of the FCRA, 15 U.S.C. 1681s-2. State law may impose additional requirements on furnishers. All furnishers of information to CRAs should become familiar with the applicable laws and may want to consult with their counsel to ensure that they are in compliance. The text of the FCRA is set forth in full at the Website of the Federal Trade Commission (FTC): www.ftc.gov/credit. A list of the sections of the FCRA cross-referenced to the U.S. Code is at the end of this document.

Section 623 imposes the following duties upon furnishers:

Accuracy Guidelines

The banking and credit union regulators and the FTC will promulgate guidelines and regulations dealing with the accuracy of information provided to CRAs by furnishers. The regulations and guidelines issued by the FTC will be available at www.ftc.gov/credit when they are issued. Section 623(e).

General Prohibition on Reporting Inaccurate Information

The FCRA prohibits information furnishers from providing information to a CRA that they know or have reasonable cause to believe is inaccurate. However, the furnisher is not subject to this general prohibition if it clearly and conspicuously specifies an address to which consumers may write to notify the furnisher that certain information is inaccurate. Sections 623(a)(1)(A) and (a)(1)(C).

Duty to Correct and Update Information

If at any time a person who regularly and in the ordinary course of business furnishes information to one or more CRAs determines that the information provided is not complete or accurate, the furnisher must promptly provide complete and accurate information to the CRA. In addition, the furnisher must notify all CRAs that received the information of any corrections, and must thereafter report only the complete and accurate information. Section 623(a)(2).

Duties After Notice of Dispute from Consumer

If a consumer notifies a furnisher, at an address specified for the furnisher for such notices, that specific information is inaccurate, and the information is, in fact, inaccurate, the furnisher must thereafter report the correct information to CRAs. Section 623(a)(1)(B).

If a consumer notifies a furnisher that the consumer disputes the completeness or accuracy of any information reported by the furnisher, the furnisher may not subsequently report that information to a CRA without providing notice of the dispute. Section 623(a)(3).

The federal banking and credit union regulators and the FTC will issue regulations that will identify when an information furnisher must investigate a dispute made directly to the furnisher by a consumer. Once these regulations are issued, furnishers must comply with them and complete an investigation within 30 days (or 45 days, if the consumer later provides relevant additional information) unless the dispute is frivolous or irrelevant or comes from a "credit repair organization." The FTC regulations will be available at www.ftc.gov/credit. Section 623(a)(8).

Duties After Notice of Dispute from Consumer Reporting Agency

If a CRA notifies a furnisher that a consumer disputes the completeness or accuracy of information provided by the furnisher, the furnisher has a duty to follow certain procedures. The furnisher must:

- Conduct an investigation and review all relevant information provided by the CRA, including information given to the CRA by the consumer. Sections 623(b)(1)(A) and (b)(1)(B).

- Report the results to the CRA that referred the dispute, and, if the investigation establishes that the information was, in fact, incomplete or inaccurate, report the results to all CRAs to which the furnisher provided the information that compile and maintain files on a nationwide basis. Section 623(b)(1)(C) and (b)(1)(D).

- Complete the above steps within 30 days from the date the CRA receives the dispute (or 45 days, if the consumer later provides relevant additional information to the CRA). Section 623(b)(2).

- Promptly modify or delete the information, or block its reporting. Section 623(b)(1)(E).

Duty to Report Voluntary Closing of Credit Accounts

If a consumer voluntarily closes a credit account, any person who regularly and in the ordinary course of business furnishes information to one or more CRAs must report this fact when it provides information to CRAs for the time period in which the account was closed. Section 623(a)(4).

Duty to Report Dates of Delinquencies

If a furnisher reports information concerning a delinquent account placed for collection, charged to profit or loss, or subject to any similar action, the furnisher must, within 90 days after reporting the information, provide the CRA with the month and the year of the commencement of the delinquency that immediately preceded the action, so that the agency will know how long to keep the information in the consumer's file. Section 623(a)(5).

Any person, such as a debt collector, that has acquired or is responsible for collecting delinquent accounts and that reports information to CRAs may comply with the requirements of Section 623(a)(5) (until there is a consumer dispute) by reporting the same delinquency date previously reported by the creditor. If the creditor did not report this date, they may comply with the FCRA by establishing reasonable procedures to obtain and report delinquency dates, or, if a delinquency date cannot be reasonably obtained, by following reasonable procedures to ensure that the date reported precedes the date when the account was placed for collection, charged to profit or loss, or subjected to any similar action. Section 623(a)(5).

Duties of Financial Institutions When Reporting Negative Information

Financial institutions that furnish information to "nationwide" consumer reporting agencies, as defined in Section 603(p), must notify consumers in writing if they may furnish or have furnished negative information to a CRA. Section 623(a)(7). The Federal Reserve Board has prescribed model disclosures, 12 CFR Part 222, App. B.

Duties When Furnishing Medical Information

A furnisher whose primary business is providing medical services, products, or devices (and such furnisher's agents or assignees) is a medical information furnisher for the purposes of the FCRA and must notify all CRAs to which it reports of this fact. Section 623(a)(9). This notice will enable CRAs to comply with their duties under Section 604(g) when reporting medical information.

Duties When ID Theft Occurs

All furnishers must have in place reasonable procedures to respond to notifications from CRAs that information furnished is the result of identity theft, and to prevent refurnishing the information in the future. A furnisher may not furnish information that a consumer has identified as resulting from identity theft unless the furnisher subsequently knows or is informed by the consumer that the information is correct. Section 623(a)(6). If a furnisher learns that it has furnished inaccurate information due to identity theft, it must notify each consumer reporting agency of the correct information and must thereafter report only complete and accurate information. Section 623(a)(2). When any furnisher of information is notified pursuant to the procedures set forth in Section 605B that a debt has resulted from identity theft, the furnisher may not sell, transfer, or place for collection the debt except in certain limited circumstances. Section 615(f).

The FTC's Web site, www.ftc.gov/credit, has more information about the FCRA, including publications for businesses and the full text of the FCRA.

Citations for FCRA sections in the U.S. Code, 15 U.S.C. § 1681 et seq.:

Section 602	15 U.S.C. 1681	Section 615	15 U.S.C. 1681m
Section 603	15 U.S.C. 1681a	Section 616	15 U.S.C. 1681n
Section 604	15 U.S.C. 1681b	Section 617	15 U.S.C. 1681o
Section 605	15 U.S.C. 1681c	Section 618	15 U.S.C. 1681p
Section 605A	15 U.S.C. 1681cA	Section 619	15 U.S.C. 1681q
Section 605B	15 U.S.C. 1681cB	Section 620	15 U.S.C. 1681r
Section 606	15 U.S.C. 1681d	Section 621	15 U.S.C. 1681s
Section 607	15 U.S.C. 1681e	Section 622	15 U.S.C. 1681s-1
Section 608	15 U.S.C. 1681f	Section 623	15 U.S.C. 1681s-2
Section 609	15 U.S.C. 1681g	Section 624	15 U.S.C. 1681t
Section 610	15 U.S.C. 1681h	Section 625	15 U.S.C. 1681u
Section 611	15 U.S.C. 1681i	Section 626	15 U.S.C. 1681v
Section 612	15 U.S.C. 1681j	Section 627	15 U.S.C. 1681w
Section 613	15 U.S.C. 1681k	Section 628	15 U.S.C. 1681x
Section 614	15 U.S.C. 1681*l*	Section 629	15 U.S.C. 1681y

C.6 Notice to Users of Consumer Reports

Many consumers learn of errors in a consumer report only when a creditor or other user informs the consumer that adverse action has been based on a report. Users must also certify to the agency that the user has a permissible purpose for obtaining a consumer report. Some users, including employers, users of investigative consumer reports, users of reports containing medical information, users of prescreened lists, and resellers of credit reports have additional obligations. In 1997, the FTC issued a notice explaining the duties of persons using information obtained from consumer reporting agencies ("user notice"), which the FTC amended in 2004 in response to new duties added by FACTA for users, especially resellers.[5]

---

5   69 Fed. Reg. 69776 (Nov. 30, 2004).

> All users subject to the Federal Trade Commission's jurisdiction must comply with all applicable regulations, including regulations promulgated after this notice was prescribed in 2004. Information about applicable regulations currently in effect can be found at the Commission's Web site, www.ftc.gov/credit. Persons not subject to the Commission's jurisdiction should consult with their regulators to find any relevant regulations.

NOTICE TO USERS OF CONSUMER REPORTS: OBLIGATIONS OF USERS UNDER THE FCRA

The Fair Credit Reporting Act (FCRA), 15 U.S.C. 1681-1681y, requires that this notice be provided to inform users of consumer reports of their legal obligations. State law may impose additional requirements. The text of the FCRA is set forth in full at the Federal Trade Commission's Website at www.ftc.gov/credit. At the end of this document is a list of United States Code citations for the FCRA. Other information about user duties is also available at the Commission's Web site. **Users must consult the relevant provisions of the FCRA for details about their obligations under the FCRA.**

The first section of this summary sets forth the responsibilities imposed by the FCRA on all users of consumer reports. The subsequent sections discuss the duties of users of reports that contain specific types of information, or that are used for certain purposes, and the legal consequences of violations. If you are a furnisher of information to a consumer reporting agency (CRA), you have additional obligations and will receive a separate notice from the CRA describing your duties as a furnisher.

I. OBLIGATIONS OF ALL USERS OF CONSUMER REPORTS

A. Users Must Have a Permissible Purpose

Congress has limited the use of consumer reports to protect consumers' privacy. All users must have a permissible purpose under the FCRA to obtain a consumer report. Section 604 contains a list of the permissible purposes under the law. These are:

- As ordered by a court or a federal grand jury subpoena. Section 604(a)(1)

- As instructed by the consumer in writing. Section 604(a)(2)

- For the extension of credit as a result of an application from a consumer, or the review or collection of a consumer's account. Section 604(a)(3)(A)

- For employment purposes, including hiring and promotion decisions, where the consumer has given written permission. Sections 604(a)(3)(B) and 604(b)

- For the underwriting of insurance as a result of an application from a consumer. Section 604(a)(3)(C)

- When there is a legitimate business need, in connection with a business transaction that is <u>initiated</u> by the consumer. Section 604(a)(3)(F)(i)

- To review a consumer's account to determine whether the consumer continues to meet the terms of the account. Section 604(a)(3)(F)(ii)

- To determine a consumer's eligibility for a license or other benefit granted by a governmental instrumentality required by law to consider an applicant's financial responsibility or status. Section 604(a)(3)(D)

- For use by a potential investor or servicer, or current insurer, in a valuation or assessment of the credit or prepayment risks associated with an existing credit obligation. Section 604(a)(3)(E)

- For use by state and local officials in connection with the determination of child support payments, or modifications and enforcement thereof. Sections 604(a)(4) and 604(a)(5)

In addition, creditors and insurers may obtain certain consumer report information for the purpose of making "prescreened" unsolicited offers of credit or insurance. Section 604(c). The particular obligations of users of "prescreened" information are described in Section VII below.

B. Users Must Provide Certifications

Section 604(f) prohibits any person from obtaining a consumer report from a consumer reporting agency (CRA) unless the person has certified to the CRA the permissible purpose(s) for which the report is being obtained and certifies that the report will not be used for any other purpose.

C. Users Must Notify Consumers When Adverse Actions Are Taken

The term "adverse action" is defined very broadly by Section 603. "Adverse actions" include all business, credit, and employment actions affecting consumers that can be considered to have a negative impact as defined by Section 603(k) of the FCRA – such as denying or canceling credit or insurance, or denying employment or promotion. No adverse action occurs in a credit transaction where the creditor makes a counteroffer that is accepted by the consumer.

1. Adverse Actions Based on Information Obtained From a CRA

If a user takes any type of adverse action as defined by the FCRA that is based at least in part on information contained in a consumer report, Section 615(a) requires the user to notify the consumer. The notification may be done in writing, orally, or by electronic means. It must include the following:

- The name, address, and telephone number of the CRA (including a toll-free telephone number, if it is a nationwide CRA) that provided the report.

- A statement that the CRA did not make the adverse decision and is not able to explain why the decision was made.

- A statement setting forth the consumer's right to obtain a free disclosure of the consumer's file from the CRA if the consumer makes a request within 60 days.

- A statement setting forth the consumer's right to dispute directly with the CRA the accuracy or completeness of any information provided by the CRA.

2. Adverse Actions Based on Information Obtained From Third Parties Who Are Not Consumer Reporting Agencies

If a person denies (or increases the charge for) credit for personal, family, or household purposes based either wholly or partly upon information from a person other than a CRA, and the information is the type of consumer information covered by the FCRA, Section 615(b)(1) requires that the user clearly and accurately disclose to the consumer his or her right to be told the nature of the information that was relied upon if the consumer makes a written request within 60 days of notification. The user must provide the disclosure within a reasonable period of time following the consumer's written request.

3. Adverse Actions Based on Information Obtained From Affiliates

If a person takes an adverse action involving insurance, employment, or a credit transaction initiated by the consumer, based on information of the type covered by the FCRA, and this information was obtained from an entity affiliated with the user of the information by common ownership or control, Section 615(b)(2) requires the user to notify the consumer of the adverse action. The notice must inform the consumer that he or she may obtain a disclosure of the nature of the information relied upon by making a written request within 60 days of receiving the adverse action notice. If the consumer makes such a request, the user must disclose the nature of the information not later than 30 days after receiving the request. If consumer report information is shared among affiliates and then used for an adverse action, the user must make an adverse action disclosure as set forth in I.C.1 above.

D. Users Have Obligations When Fraud and Active Duty Military Alerts are in Files

When a consumer has placed a fraud alert, including one relating to identity theft, or an active duty military alert with a nationwide consumer reporting agency as defined in Section 603(p) and resellers, Section 605A(h) imposes limitations on users of reports obtained from the consumer reporting agency in certain circumstances, including the establishment of a new credit plan and the issuance of additional credit cards. For initial fraud alerts and active duty alerts, the user must have reasonable policies and procedures in place to form a belief that the user knows the identity of the applicant or contact the consumer at a telephone number specified by the consumer; in the case of extended fraud alerts, the user must contact the consumer in accordance with the contact information provided in the consumer's alert.

E. Users Have Obligations When Notified of an Address Discrepancy

Section 605(h) requires nationwide CRAs, as defined in Section 603(p), to notify users that request reports when the address for a consumer provided by the user in requesting the report is substantially different from the addresses in the consumer's file. When this occurs, users must comply with regulations specifying the procedures to be followed, which will be issued by the Federal Trade Commission and the banking and credit union regulators. The Federal Trade Commission's regulations will be available at www.ftc.gov/credit.

F. Users Have Obligations When Disposing of Records

Section 628 requires that all users of consumer report information have in place procedures to properly dispose of records containing this information. The Federal Trade Commission, the Securities and Exchange Commission, and the banking and credit union regulators have issued regulations covering disposal. The Federal Trade Commission's regulations may be found at www.ftc.gov/credit.

II. CREDITORS MUST MAKE ADDITIONAL DISCLOSURES

If a person uses a consumer report in connection with an application for, or a grant, extension, or provision of, credit to a consumer on material terms that are materially less favorable than the most favorable terms available to a substantial proportion of consumers from or through that person, based in whole or in part on a consumer report, the person must provide a risk-based pricing notice to the consumer in accordance with regulations to be jointly prescribed by the Federal Trade Commission and the Federal Reserve Board.

Section 609(g) requires a disclosure by all persons that make or arrange loans secured by residential real property (one to four units) and that use credit scores. These persons must provide credit scores and other information about credit scores to applicants, including the disclosure set forth in Section 609(g)(1)(D) ("Notice to the Home Loan Applicant").

III. OBLIGATIONS OF USERS WHEN CONSUMER REPORTS ARE OBTAINED FOR EMPLOYMENT PURPOSES

A. Employment Other Than in the Trucking Industry

If information from a CRA is used for employment purposes, the user has specific duties, which are set forth in Section 604(b) of the FCRA. The user must:

- Make a clear and conspicuous written disclosure to the consumer before the report is obtained, in a document that consists solely of the disclosure, that a consumer report may be obtained.

- Obtain from the consumer prior written authorization. Authorization to access reports during the term of employment may be obtained at the time of employment.

- Certify to the CRA that the above steps have been followed, that the information being obtained will not be used in violation of any federal or state equal opportunity law or regulation, and that, if any adverse action is to be taken based on the consumer report, a copy of the report and a summary of the consumer's rights will be provided to the consumer.

- **Before** taking an adverse action, the user must provide a copy of the report to the consumer as well as the summary of consumer's rights. (The user should receive this summary from the CRA.) A Section 615(a) adverse action notice should be sent after the adverse action is taken.

An adverse action notice also is required in employment situations if credit information (other than transactions and experience data) obtained from an affiliate is used to deny employment. Section 615(b)(2)

The procedures for investigative consumer reports and employee misconduct investigations are set forth below.

B. Employment in the Trucking Industry

Special rules apply for truck drivers where the only interaction between the consumer and the potential employer is by mail, telephone, or computer. In this case, the consumer may provide consent orally or electronically, and an adverse action may be made orally, in writing, or electronically. The consumer may obtain a copy of any report relied upon by the trucking company by contacting the company.

IV. OBLIGATIONS WHEN INVESTIGATIVE CONSUMER REPORTS ARE USED

Investigative consumer reports are a special type of consumer report in which information about a consumer's character, general reputation, personal characteristics, and mode of living is obtained through personal interviews by an entity or person that is a consumer reporting agency. Consumers who are the subjects of such reports are given special rights under the FCRA. If a user intends to obtain an investigative consumer report, Section 606 requires the following:

- The user must disclose to the consumer that an investigative consumer report may be obtained. This must be done in a written disclosure that is mailed, or otherwise delivered, to the consumer at some time before or not later than three days after the date on which the report was first requested. The disclosure must include a statement informing the consumer of his or her right to request additional disclosures of the nature and scope of the investigation as described below, and the summary of consumer rights required by Section 609 of the FCRA. (The summary of consumer rights will be provided by the CRA that conducts the investigation.)

- The user must certify to the CRA that the disclosures set forth above have been made and that the user will make the disclosure described below.

- Upon the written request of a consumer made within a reasonable period of time after the disclosures required above, the user must make a complete disclosure of the nature and scope of the investigation. This must be made in a written statement that is mailed, or otherwise delivered, to the consumer no later than five days after the date on which the request was received from the consumer or the report was first requested, whichever is later in time.

V. SPECIAL PROCEDURES FOR EMPLOYEE INVESTIGATIONS

Section 603(x) provides special procedures for investigations of suspected misconduct by an employee or for compliance with Federal, state or local laws and regulations or the rules of a self-regulatory organization, and compliance with written policies of the employer. These investigations are not treated as consumer reports so long as the employer or its agent complies with the procedures set forth in Section 603(x), and a summary describing the nature and scope of the inquiry is made to the employee if an adverse action is taken based on the investigation.

VI. OBLIGATIONS OF USERS OF MEDICAL INFORMATION

Section 604(g) limits the use of medical information obtained from consumer reporting agencies (other than payment information that appears in a coded form that does not identify the medical provider). If the information is to be used for an insurance transaction, the consumer must give consent to the user of the report or the information must be coded. If the report is to be used for employment purposes – or in connection with a credit transaction (except as provided in regulations issued by the banking and credit union regulators) – the consumer must provide specific written consent and the medical information must be relevant. Any user who receives medical information shall not disclose the information to any other person (except where necessary to carry out the purpose for which the information was disclosed, or as permitted by statute, regulation, or order).

VII. OBLIGATIONS OF USERS OF "PRESCREENED" LISTS

The FCRA permits creditors and insurers to obtain limited consumer report information for use in connection with unsolicited offers of credit or insurance under certain circumstances. Sections 603(l), 604(c), 604(e), and 615(d). This practice is known as "prescreening" and typically involves obtaining from a CRA a list of consumers who meet certain preestablished criteria. If any person intends to use prescreened lists, that person must (1) before the offer is made, establish the criteria that will be relied upon to make the offer and to grant credit or insurance, and (2) maintain such criteria on file for a three-year period beginning on the date on which the offer is made to each consumer. In addition, any user must provide with each written solicitation a clear and conspicuous statement that:

- Information contained in a consumer's CRA file was used in connection with the transaction.

- The consumer received the offer because he or she satisfied the criteria for credit worthiness or insurability used to screen for the offer.

- Credit or insurance may not be extended if, after the consumer responds, it is determined that the consumer does not meet the criteria used for screening or any applicable criteria bearing on credit worthiness or insurability, or the consumer does not furnish required collateral.

- The consumer may prohibit the use of information in his or her file in connection with future prescreened offers of credit or insurance by contacting the notification system established by the CRA that provided the report. The statement must include the address and toll-free telephone number of the appropriate notification system.

In addition, once the Federal Trade Commission by rule has established the format, type size, and manner of the disclosure required by Section 615(d), users must be in compliance with the rule. The FTC's regulations will be at www.ftc.gov/credit.

VIII. OBLIGATIONS OF RESELLERS

A. Disclosure and Certification Requirements

Section 607(e) requires any person who obtains a consumer report for resale to take the following steps:

- Disclose the identity of the end-user to the source CRA.

- Identify to the source CRA each permissible purpose for which the report will be furnished to the end-user.

- Establish and follow reasonable procedures to ensure that reports are resold only for permissible purposes, including procedures to obtain:
  (1) the identity of all end-users;
  (2) certifications from all users of each purpose for which reports will be used; and
  (3) certifications that reports will not be used for any purpose other than the purpose(s) specified to the reseller. Resellers must make reasonable efforts to verify this information before selling the report.

B. Reinvestigations by Resellers

Under Section 611(f), if a consumer disputes the accuracy or completeness of information in a report prepared by a reseller, the reseller must determine whether this is a result of an action or omission on its part and, if so, correct or delete the information. If not, the reseller must send the dispute to the source CRA for reinvestigation. When any CRA notifies the reseller of the results of an investigation, the reseller must immediately convey the information to the consumer.

C. Fraud Alerts and Resellers

Section 605A(f) requires resellers who receive fraud alerts or active duty alerts from another consumer reporting agency to include these in their reports.

IX. LIABILITY FOR VIOLATIONS OF THE FCRA

Failure to comply with the FCRA can result in state government or federal government enforcement actions, as well as private lawsuits. Sections 616, 617, and 621. In addition, any person who knowingly and willfully obtains a consumer report under false pretenses may face criminal prosecution. Section 619.

The FTC's Web site, www.ftc.gov/credit, has more information about the FCRA including publications for businesses and the full text of the FCRA.

Citations for FCRA sections in the U.S. Code, 15 U.S.C. § 1681 et seq.:

Section 602	15 U.S.C. 1681
Section 603	15 U.S.C. 1681a
Section 604	15 U.S.C. 1681b
Section 605	15 U.S.C. 1681c
Section 605A	15 U.S.C. 1681cA
Section 605B	15 U.S.C. 1681cB
Section 606	15 U.S.C. 1681d
Section 607	15 U.S.C. 1681e
Section 608	15 U.S.C. 1681f
Section 609	15 U.S.C. 1681g
Section 610	15 U.S.C. 1681h
Section 611	15 U.S.C. 1681i
Section 612	15 U.S.C. 1681j
Section 613	15 U.S.C. 1681k
Section 614	15 U.S.C. 1681*l*
Section 615	15 U.S.C. 1681m
Section 616	15 U.S.C. 1681n
Section 617	15 U.S.C. 1681o
Section 618	15 U.S.C. 1681p
Section 619	15 U.S.C. 1681q
Section 620	15 U.S.C. 1681r
Section 621	15 U.S.C. 1681s
Section 622	15 U.S.C. 1681s-1
Section 623	15 U.S.C. 1681s-2
Section 624	15 U.S.C. 1681t
Section 625	15 U.S.C. 1681u
Section 626	15 U.S.C. 1681v
Section 627	15 U.S.C. 1681w
Section 628	15 U.S.C. 1681x
Section 629	15 U.S.C. 1681y

FTC and FRB Model Forms

C.7 Model Prescreen Opt-Out Notices

The FCRA directs the FTC, in consultation with the federal banking agencies and the National Credit Union Administration, to adopt a rule to improve the required notice to consumers regarding the right to opt out of prescreened solicitations for credit or insurance.[6] The FTC issued such a rule, 16 C.F.R. § 642.3 (reprinted at Appendix B.1, *supra*), and that rule requires that consumers be provided with a statement in specific language, consisting of a short portion and a long portion, which shall be in the same language as the offer of credit or insurance. To assist in compliance, the FTC rules provide four model notices: a short and long notice in English, and a short and long notice in Spanish.

---

6   15 U.S.C. § 1681m(d). *See* § 8.2.9, *supra*.

(a) *English language model notice.* (1) *Short notice.*

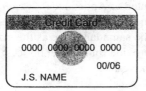

Here's a Line About Credit

J.S. Name
12345 Friendly Street
City, ST 12345

Dear Ms. Name,

Back in the last century, we saw how technology was changing the way people do things. So we set out to create a the last century, we saw how technology was changing the way people do things. Back in the last century, we saw how technology was changing the way people do things. So we set out to create a the last century, we saw how technology was changing the way people do things.

Back in the last century, we saw how technology was changing the way people do things. So we set out to create a smart kind of credit card. Back in the last century, we saw how technology was changing the way. Back in the last century, we saw how technology was changing the way people do things. So we set out to create a the last century, we saw how technology was changing the way people do things.

Back in the last century, we saw how technology was changing the way people do things. So we set out to create a smart kind of credit card. Back in the last century, we saw how technology was changing the way peop. So we set out to create a smart kind of credit card. Back in the last century, we saw how technology was changing the way people do things. So we set out to create a smart kind of credit a smart kind of credit card.

So we set out to create a smart kind of credit card. Back in the last century, we saw how technology was changing the way people. Back in the last century, we saw how technology was changing the way people do things. So we set out to create a smart kind of credit card.

We saw how technology was changing the way people do things. So we set out to create a smart kind of credit card. Back in the last century, we saw how technology.

Sincerely,

John W. Doe
President, Credit Card Company

PFOR 00 MON
FIXED ABC

■

BALANCE TR
FOR 00 MONTHS

■

NO MONTHS FEE

■

INTERNET SECURITY
SECURITY

■

ONLINE FRAUD PRO
GUARANTEE

■

YOUR BALANCE
PAY YOUR BILL

■

FEE-FREE REWARDS
PROGRAM

You can choose to stop receiving "prescreened" offers of [credit or insurance] from this and other companies by calling toll-free [toll-free number]. See <u>PRESCREEN & OPT-OUT NOTICE</u> on other side [or other location] for more information about prescreened offers.

FTC and FRB Model Forms **Appx. C.7**

Federal Register / Vol. 70, No. 19 / Monday, January 31, 2005 / Rules and Regulations **5035**

(2) *Long notice.*

Back in the last century, we saw how technology was changing the way people do things. So we set out to create a smart kind of credit card. Back in the last century, we saw how technology was changing the way. Back in the last century, we saw how technology was changing the way people do things. So we set out to create a the last century, we saw how technology was changing the way people do things.

HEADER

Percent Rate for	Other ABCs	Variable info material	Grace or repases Are placed here	Computing the balast	Annual Fee	Usual Place Finance Charge
Back in the last century, we saw how technology was changing the way people do things. So we set out to create a smart kind of credit card.	Back in the last century, we saw how technology was changing the way people do things. So we set out to create a smart kind of credit card. Back in the last century, we saw how technology was changing the way.	Back in the last century, we saw how technology was changing the way people do things. So we set out to create a smart kind of credit card.	Back in the last century, we saw how technology was changing.	Back in the last century, we saw how technology was changing the way people do things. So we set out to create a smart kind of credit card.	Back long ago.	Back in the last century, we saw how technology.

Back in the last century, we saw how technology was changing the way people do things. So we set out to create a smart kind of credit card. Back in the last century, we saw how technology was changing the way. Back in the last century, we saw how technology was changing the way people do things. So we set out to create a smart kind of credit card. Back in the last century, we saw how technology was changing the way people do things. So we set out to create a smart kind of credit card. Back in the last century, we saw how technology was changing the way.

Back in the last century, we saw how technology was changing the way people do things. So we set out to create a smart kind of credit card. Back in the last century, we saw how technology was changing the way. Back in the last century, we saw how technology was changing the way people do things. So we set out to create a smart kind of credit card. Back in the last century, we saw how technology was changing the way. Back in the last century, we saw how technology was changing the way people do things. So we set out to create a smart kind of credit card. Back in the last century, we saw how technology was changing the way. Back in the last century, we saw how technology was changing the way people do things. So we set out to create a smart kind of credit card. Back in the last century, we saw how technology was changing the way.

Back in the last century, we saw how technology was changing the way. Back in the last century, we saw how technology was changing the way people do things. So we set out to create a smart kind of credit card. Back in the last century, we saw how technology was changing the way.

Back in the last century, we saw how technology was changing the way. Back in the last century, we saw how technology was changing the way people do things. So we set out to create a smart kind of credit card. Back in the last century, we saw how technology was changing the way.

TERMS AND CONDITIONS

Back in the last century, we saw how technology was changing the way people do things. So we set out to create a smart kind of credit card. Back in the last century, we saw how technology was changing the way. Back in the last century, we saw how technology was changing the way people do things. So we set out to create a smart kind of credit card. Back in the last century, we saw how technology was changing the way. Back in the last century, we saw how technology was changing the way people do things. So we set out to create a smart kind of credit card. Back in the last century, we saw how technology was changing the way. Back in the last century, we saw how technology was changing the way people do things. So we set out to create a smart kind of credit card. Back in the last century, we saw how technology was changing the way people do things. So we set out to create a smart kind of credit card. Back in the last century, we saw how technology was changing the way. Back in the last century, we saw how technology was changing the way people do things. So we set out to create a smart kind of credit card. Back in the last century, we saw how technology was changing the way. Back in the last century, we saw how technology was changing the way people do things. So we set out to create a smart kind of credit card. Back in the last century, we saw how technology was changing the way. Back in the last century, we saw how technology was changing the way people do things. So we set out to create a smart kind of credit card. Back in the last century, we saw how technology was changing the way. Back in the last century, we saw how technology was changing the way people do things. So we set out to create a smart kind of credit card. Back in the last century, we saw how technology was changing the way. Back in the last century, we saw how technology was changing the way people do things. So we set out to create a smart kind of credit card. Back in the last century, we saw how technology was changing the way. Back in the last century, we saw y, we saw how technology was changing the way. Back in the last century, we saw how technology was changing the way people do things.

Act Notice: the a smart kind of credit card. Back in the last century, we saw how technology was changing the way people do things. So we set out to create a smart kind of credit card. Back in the last century, we saw how technology was changing the way. Back in the last century, we saw.

PRESCREEN & OPT-OUT NOTICE: This "prescreened" offer of [credit or insurance] is based on information in your credit report indicating that you meet certain criteria. This offer is not guaranteed if you do not meet our criteria [including providing acceptable property as collateral]. If you do not want to receive prescreened offers of [credit or insurance] from this and other companies, call the consumer reporting agencies [or name of consumer reporting agency] toll-free, [toll-free number]; or write: [consumer reporting agency name and mailing address].

Notice to Some Residents: te a smart kind of credit card. Back in the last century, we saw how technology was changing the way. Back in the last century, we saw how technology was changing the way people do things. So we set out to create a smart kind of credit card. Back in the last century, we saw how technology was changing the way. Back in the last century. So we set out to create a smart kind of credit card. Back in the last century, we saw how technology was changing the way.

(b) *Spanish language model notice.*
(1) *Short notice.*

Aquí están líneas crédito

J.S. Nombre
1234 Calle Amistosa
Ciudad, ST 12345

Estimada Señora Nombre:

En el siglo pasado vimos como la tecnología estaba cambiando la manera en que la gente hace las cosas. Así que creamos una tarjeta de crédito inteligente, vimos como la tecnología estaba cambiando la manera en que la gente hace las cosas. En el siglo pasado vimos como la tecnología estaba cambiando la manera en que la gente hace las cosas. Así que creamos una tarjeta de crédito inteligente. Vimos como la tecnología estaba cambiando la manera en que la gente hace las cosas.

Así que creamos una tarjeta de crédito inteligente. Vimos como la tecnología estaba cambiando la manera en que la gente hace las cosas. En el siglo pasado vimos como la tecnología estaba cambiando la manera en que la gente hace las cosas. Así que creamos una tarjeta de crédito inteligente, vimos como la tecnología estaba cambiando la manera en que la gente hace las cosas.

Vimos como la tecnología estaba cambiando la manera en que la gente hace las cosas. En el siglo pasado vimos como la tecnología estaba cambiando la manera en que la gente hace las cosas. Así que creamos una tarjeta de crédito inteligente, vimos como la tecnología estaba cambiando la manera en que la gente hace las cosas. En el siglo pasado vimos como la tecnología estaba cambiando la manera en que la gente hace las cosas.

Así que creamos una tarjeta de crédito inteligente. Vimos como la tecnología estaba cambiando la manera en que la gente hace las cosas. En el siglo pasado vimos como la tecnología estaba cambiando la manera en que la gente hace las cosas. Así que creamos una tarjeta de crédito inteligente. Vimos como la tecnología estaba cambiando la manera en que la gente hace las cosas.

Sinceramente,

John W. Doe
Presidente, Compañía

PFOR 00 MON FIJO ABC

TRANSFERENCIA DE BALANCE POR MESES

SIN CUOTA MENSUAL

PAGO ELECTRÓNICO SEGURO

PROTECCIÓN CONTRA FRAUDE EN LÍNEA GARANTIZADO

SU BALANCE PAGA SU CUENTA

PROGRAMA DE RECOMPENSAS SIN CUENTA

Usted puede elegir no recibir más "ofertas de [crédito o seguro] pre-investigadas" de esta y otras compañías llamando sin cargos al [número sin cargo]. Ver la <u>NOTIFICACIÓN DE PRE-INVESTIGACIÓN Y EXCLUSIÓN VOLUNTARIA</u> al otro lado de esta página [o en otro lugar] para más información sobre ofertas pre-investigadas.

(2) *Long notice.*

En el siglo pasado vimos como la tecnología estaba cambiando la manera en que la gente hace las cosas. Así que creamos una tarjeta de crédito inteligente, vimos como la tecnología estaba cambiando la manera en que la gente hace las cosas. En el siglo pasado vimos como la tecnología estaba cambiando la manera en que la gente hace las cosas. Así que creamos una tarjeta de crédito inteligente.

AQUÍ ESTÁN

Protección Contra Fraude	Programa de Recompensas	Su Balance Paga	Sin Cuota Mensual	Protección Contra Fraude	Recompensas Sin Cuenta	Sin Cuota Mensual
En el siglo pasado vimos como la tecnología estaba cambiando la manera en que la gente hace las cosas.	Vimos como la tecnología estaba cambiando la manera en que la gente hace las cosas. Vimos como la tecnología estaba cambiando la manera en que la gente hace las cosas.	En el siglo pasado vimos como la tecnología estaba cambiando la manera en que la gente hace las cosas. En el siglo pasado vimos como la gente hace las cosas. Así que cremos.	Así que creamos una tarjeta de crédito inteligente.	En el siglo pasado vimos como la tecnología estaba cambiando la manera en que la gente hace las cosas.	Así que cremos.	Vimos como la tecnología estaba cambiando la manera en que la gente hace las cosas.

En el siglo pasado vimos como la tecnología estaba cambiando la manera en que la gente hace las cosas. Así que creamos una tarjeta de crédito inteligente, vimos como la tecnología estaba cambiando la manera en que la gente hace las cosas. En el siglo pasado vimos como la tecnología estaba cambiando la manera en que la gente hace las cosas. Así que creamos una tarjeta de crédito inteligente. Vimos como la tecnología estaba cambiando la manera en que la gente hace las cosas. Así que creamos una tarjeta de crédito inteligente. Vimos como la tecnología estaba cambiando la manera en que la gente hace las cosas.

Así que creamos una tarjeta de crédito inteligente, vimos como la tecnología estaba cambiando la manera en que la gente hace las cosas. En el siglo pasado vimos como la tecnología estaba cambiando la manera en que la gente hace las cosas. Así que creamos una tarjeta de crédito inteligente. Vimos como la tecnología estaba cambiando la manera en que la gente hace las cosas. Así que creamos una tarjeta de crédito inteligente. Vimos como la tecnología estaba cambiando la manera en que la gente hace las cosas. En el siglo pasado vimos como la tecnología estaba cambiando la manera en que la gente hace las cosas. Así que creamos una tarjeta de crédito inteligente, vimos como la tecnología estaba cambiando la manera en que la gente hace las cosas.

Vimos como la tecnología estaba cambiando la manera en que la gente hace las cosas. En el siglo pasado vimos como la tecnología estaba cambiando la manera en que la gente hace las cosas. Así que creamos una tarjeta de crédito inteligente, vimos como la tecnología estaba cambiando la manera en que la gente hace las cosas. En el siglo pasado vimos como la tecnología estaba cambiando la manera en que la gente hace las cosas. Así que creamos una tarjeta de crédito inteligente. Vimos como la tecnología estaba cambiando la manera en que la gente hace las cosas. En el siglo pasado vimos como la tecnología estaba cambiando la manera en que la gente hace las cosas. En el siglo pasado vimos como la tecnología estaba cambiando la manera en que la gente hace las cosas.

TERMINOS Y CONDICIONA

En el siglo pasado vimos como la tecnología estaba cambiando la manera en que la gente hace las cosas. Así que creamos una tarjeta de crédito inteligente, vimos como la tecnología estaba cambiando la manera en que la gente hace las cosas. En el siglo pasado vimos como la tecnología estaba cambiando la manera en que la gente hace las cosas. Así que creamos una tarjeta de crédito inteligente. Vimos como la tecnología estaba cambiando la manera en que la gente hace las cosas.

Así que creamos una tarjeta de crédito inteligente. Vimos como la tecnología estaba cambiando la manera en que la gente hace las cosas. En el siglo pasado vimos como la tecnología estaba cambiando la manera en que la gente hace las cosas. Así que creamos una tarjeta de crédito inteligente, vimos como la tecnología estaba cambiando la manera en que la gente hace las cosas.

Vimos como la tecnología estaba cambiando la manera en que la gente hace las cosas. En el siglo pasado vimos como la tecnología estaba cambiando la manera en que la gente hace las cosas. Así que creamos una tarjeta de crédito inteligente, vimos como la tecnología estaba cambiando la manera en que la gente hace las cosas. En el siglo pasado vimos como la tecnología estaba cambiando la manera en que la gente hace las cosas.

Así que creamos una tarjeta de crédito inteligente. Vimos como la tecnología estaba cambiando la manera en que la gente hace las cosas. En el siglo pasado vimos como la tecnología estaba cambiando la manera en que la gente hace las cosas. Así que creamos una tarjeta de crédito inteligente. Vimos como la tecnología estaba cambiando la manera en que la gente hace las cosas.

En el siglo pasado vimos como la tecnología estaba cambiando la manera en que la gente hace las cosas. Así que creamos una tarjeta de crédito inteligente, vimos como la tecnología estaba cambiando la manera en que la gente hace las cosas. En el siglo pasado vimos como la tecnología estaba cambiando la manera en que la gente hace las cosas. Así que creamos una tarjeta de crédito inteligente. Vimos como la tecnología estaba cambiando la manera en que la gente hace las cosas. Así que creamos una tarjeta de crédito inteligente. Vimos como la tecnología estaba cambiando la manera en que la gente hace las cosas. En el siglo pasado vimos como la tecnología estaba cambiando la manera en que la gente hace las cosas. Así que creamos una tarjeta de crédito inteligente. Vimos como la tecnología estaba cambiando la manera en que la gente hace las cosas. Vimos como la tecnología estaba cambiando la manera en que la gente hace las cosas. Vimos como la tecnología estaba cambiando la manera en que la gente hace las cosas. Vimos como la tecnología estaba cambiando la manera en que la gente hace las cosas.

<u>NOTIFICACIÓN DE PRE-INVESTIGACIÓN Y EXCLUSIÓN VOLUNTARIA</u>: Esta oferta de [crédito o seguro] está basada en información contenida en su informe de crédito que indica que usted cumple con ciertos criterios [incluyendo la condición de tener propiedades aceptables como colateral]. Si usted no cumple con nuestros criterios, esta oferta no está garantizada. Si usted no desea recibir ofertas de [crédito o seguro] pre-investigadas de ésta y otras compañías, llame a las agencias de información del consumidor [o nombre de la agencia de información del consumidor] sin cargos, [número sin cargo]; o escriba a: [nombre de la agencia de información del consumidor y dirección de correo].

En el siglo pasado vimos como: la tecnología estaba cambiando la manera en que la gente hace las cosas. Así que creamos una tarjeta de crédito inteligente. Vimos como la tecnología estaba cambiando la manera en que la gente hace las cosas. Vimos como la tecnología estaba cambiando la manera en que la gente hace las cosas. Vimos como la tecnología estaba cambiando la manera en que la gente hace las cosas. Vimos como la tecnología estaba cambiando la manera en que la gente hace las cosas.

C.8 Model Notices of Furnishing Negative Information

The FCRA requires a financial institution to provide a one-time consumer notice when it furnishes negative information about customers and requires the Federal Reserve Board to develop a model disclosure.[7] The Federal Reserve Board promulgated Regulation V, 12 C.F.R. § 222, which contains the requirements of the negative information notice and model disclosures. A financial institution may provide the notice without actually submitting the negative information.

12 C.F.R. Appendix B to Part 222—Model Notices of Furnishing Negative Information

a. Although use of the model notices is not required, a financial institution that is subject to section 623(a)(7) of the FCRA shall be deemed to be in compliance with the notice requirement in section 623(a)(7) of the FCRA if the institution properly uses the model notices in this appendix (as applicable).

b. A financial institution may use Model Notice B-1 if the institution provides the notice prior to furnishing negative information to a nationwide consumer reporting agency.

c. A financial institution may use Model Notice B-2 if the institution provides the notice after furnishing negative information to a nationwide consumer reporting agency.

d. Financial institutions may make certain changes to the language or format of the model notices without losing the safe harbor from liability provided by the model notices. The changes to the model notices may not be so extensive as to affect the substance, clarity, or meaningful sequence of the language in the model notices. Financial institutions making such extensive revisions will lose the safe harbor from liability that this appendix provides. Acceptable changes include, for example,

1. Rearranging the order of the references to "late payment(s)," or "missed payment(s)"
2. Pluralizing the terms "credit bureau," "credit report," and "account"
3. Specifying the particular type of account on which information may be furnished, such as "credit card account"
4. Rearranging in Model Notice B-1 the phrases "information about your account" and "to credit bureaus" such that it would read "We may report to credit bureaus information about your account."

Model Notice B-1

We may report information about your account to credit bureaus. Late payments, missed payments, or other defaults on your account may be reflected in your credit report.

Model Notice B-2

We have told a credit bureau about a late payment, missed payment or other default on your account. This information may be reflected in your credit report.

[69 Fed. Reg. 33281 (June 15, 2004) (Effective Date: July 16, 2004)]

---

7   15 U.S.C. § 1681s-2(a)(7). See § 8.2.10, supra.

C.9 ECOA Adverse Action Forms (Regulation B, 12 C.F.R. Part 202, Appendix C)

This section contains five sample notification forms. These forms are intended for use in fulfilling notification requirements of both the Fair Credit Reporting Act and the Equal Credit Opportunity Act (ECOA), 15 U.S.C. 1691–1691f.

Form C-1 contains the FCRA disclosure as required by sections 1681m(a) and (b) of that Act. Forms C-2 through C-5 contain only the section 1681m(a) disclosure (that a creditor obtained information from a consumer reporting agency that played a part in the credit decision). A creditor must provide the 1681m(a) disclosure when adverse action is taken against a consumer based on information from a consumer reporting agency. A creditor must provide the section 1681m(b) disclosure when adverse action is taken based on information from an outside source other than a consumer reporting agency. In addition, a creditor must provide the section 1681m(b) disclosure if the creditor obtained information from an affiliate other than information in a consumer report or other than information concerning the affiliate's own transactions or experiences with the consumer. Creditors may comply with the disclosure requirements for adverse action based on information in a consumer report obtained from an affiliate by providing either the section 1681m(a) or 1681m(b) disclosure.

With respect to the ECOA, Forms C-1 through C-4 are intended for use in notifying an applicant that adverse action has been taken on an application or account under section 202.9(a)(1) and (2)(i) of the Federal Reserve Board's Regulation B, 12 C.F.R. Part 202. Form C-5 is a notice disclosing the right to request specific reasons for adverse action under section 202.9(a)(1) and (2)(ii).

The sample forms are illustrative and may not be appropriate for all creditors. They were designed to include some of the factors that creditors most commonly consider. If a creditor chooses to use the checklist of reasons provided in one of the sample forms in this appendix and if reasons commonly used by the creditor are not provided on the form, the creditor should modify the checklist by substituting or adding other reasons. For example, if "inadequate down payment" or "no deposit relationship with us" are common reasons for taking adverse action on an application, the creditor ought to add or substitute such reasons for those presently contained on the sample forms.

If the reasons listed on the forms are not the factors actually used, a creditor will not satisfy the notice requirement by simply checking the closest identifiable factor listed. For example, some creditors consider only references from banks or other depository institutions and disregard finance company references altogether; their statement of reasons should disclose "insufficient bank references," not "insufficient credit references." Similarly, a creditor that considers bank references and other credit references as distinct factors should treat the two factors separately and disclose them as appropriate. The creditor should either add such other factors to the form or check "other" and include the appropriate explanation. The creditor need not, however, describe how or why a factor adversely affected the application. For example, the notice may say "length of residence" rather than "too short a period of residence."

A creditor may design its own notification forms or use all or a portion of the forms contained in this appendix.

Form C-1—Sample Notice of Action Taken and Statement of Reasons

Statement of Credit Denial, Termination, or Change

Date _____

Applicant's Name: _____

Applicant's Address: _____

Description of Account, Transaction, or Requested Credit:

_____

Description of Action Taken:

_____

_____

Part I— PRINCIPAL REASON(S) FOR CREDIT DENIAL, TERMINATION, OR OTHER ACTION TAKEN CONCERNING CREDIT.

This section must be completed in all instances.

_____ Credit application incomplete

_____ Insufficient number of credit references provided

_____ Unacceptable type of credit references provided

_____ Unable to verify credit references

_____ Temporary or irregular employment

_____ Unable to verify employment

_____ Length of employment

_____ Income insufficient for amount of credit requested

_____ Excessive obligations in relation to income

_____ Unable to verify income

_____ Length of residence

_____ Temporary residence

_____ Unable to verify residence

_____ No credit file

_____ Limited credit experience

_____ Poor credit performance with us

_____ Delinquent past or present credit obligations with others

_____ Garnishment, attachment, foreclosure, repossession, collection action, or judgment

_____ Bankruptcy

_____ Value or type of collateral not sufficient

_____ Other, specify: _____

Part II— DISCLOSURE OF USE OF INFORMATION OBTAINED FROM AN OUTSIDE SOURCE.

This section should be completed if the credit decision was based in whole or in part on information that has been obtained from an outside source.

_____ Our credit decision was based in whole or in part on information obtained in a report from the consumer reporting agency listed below. You have a right under the Fair Credit Reporting Act to know the information contained in your credit file at the consumer reporting agency. The reporting agency played no part in our decision and is unable to supply specific reasons why we have denied credit to you. You also have a right to a free copy of your report from the reporting agency, if you request it no later than 60 days after you receive this notice. In addition, if you find that any information contained in the report you receive is inaccurate or incomplete, you have the right to dispute the matter with the reporting agency.

Name: _____

_____

Address: _____

_____

[Toll-free] Telephone number: _____

_____ Our credit decision was based in whole or in part on information obtained from an affiliate or from an outside source other than a consumer reporting agency. Under the Fair Credit Reporting Act, you have the right to make a written request, no later than 60 days after you receive this notice, for disclosure of the nature of this information.

If you have any questions regarding this notice, you should contact:

Creditor's name: _____

Creditor's address: _____

Creditor's telephone number: _____

NOTICE

The federal Equal Credit Opportunity Act prohibits creditors from discriminating against credit applicants on the basis of race, color, religion, national origin, sex, marital status, age (provided the applicant has the capacity to enter into a binding contract); because all or part of the applicant's income derives from any public assistance program; or because the applicant has in good faith exercised any right under the Consumer Credit Protection Act. The federal agency that administers compliance with this law concerning this creditor is (name and address as specified by the appropriate agency listed in appendix A).

Form C-2—Sample Notice of Action Taken and Statement of Reasons

Date _____

Dear Applicant:

Thank you for your recent application. Your request for [a loan/a credit card/an increase in your credit limit] was carefully considered, and we regret that we are unable to approve your application at this time, for the following reason(s):

Your Income:

_____ is below our minimum requirement.

_____ is insufficient to sustain payments on the amount of credit requested.

_____ could not be verified.

Your Employment:

_____ is not of sufficient length to qualify.

_____ could not be verified.

Your Credit History:

_____ of making payments on time was not satisfactory.

_____ could not be verified.

Your Application:

_____ lacks a sufficient number of credit references.

_____ lacks acceptable types of credit references.

_____ reveals that current obligations are excessive in relation to income.

Other: _____

The consumer reporting agency contacted that provided information that influenced our decision in whole or in part was [name, address and [toll-free] telephone number of the reporting agency]. The reporting agency is unable to supply specific reasons why we have denied credit to you. You do, however, have a right under the Fair Credit Reporting Act to know the information contained in your credit file. You also have a right to a free copy of your report from the reporting agency, if you request it no later than 60 days after you receive this notice.

In addition, if you find that any information contained in the report you receive is inaccurate or incomplete, you have the right to dispute the matter with the reporting agency. Any questions regarding such information should be directed to [consumer reporting agency].

If you have any questions regarding this letter you should contact us at [creditor's name, address and telephone number].

NOTICE: The federal Equal Credit Opportunity Act prohibits creditors from discriminating against credit applicants on the basis of race, color, religion, national origin, sex, marital status, age (provided the applicant has the capacity to enter into a binding contract); because all or part of the applicant's income derives from any public assistance program; or because the applicant has in good faith exercised any right under the Consumer Credit Protection Act. The federal agency that administers compliance with this law concerning this creditor is (name and address as specified by the appropriate agency listed in Appendix A).

Form C-3—Sample Notice of Action Taken and Statement of Reasons (Credit Scoring)

Date_____

Dear Applicant:

Thank you for your recent application for _____. We regret that we are unable to approve your request.

Your application was processed by a credit scoring system that assigns a numerical value to the various items of information we consider in evaluating an application. These numerical values are based upon the results of analyses of repayment histories of large numbers of customers.

The information you provided in your application did not score a sufficient number of points for approval of the application. The reasons why you did not score well compared to other applicants were:

- Insufficient bank references
- Type of occupation
- Insufficient credit experience

In evaluating your application the consumer reporting agency listed below provided us with information that in whole or in part influenced our decision. The reporting agency played no part in our decision other than providing us with credit information about you. Under the Fair Credit Reporting Act, you have a right to know the information provided to us. It can be obtained by contacting: [name, address, and [toll-free] telephone number of the consumer reporting agency]. You also have a right to a free copy of your report from the reporting agency, if you request it no later than 60 days after you receive this notice. In addition, if you find that any information contained in the report you receive is inaccurate or incomplete, you have the right to dispute the matter with the reporting agency.

If you have any questions regarding this letter, you should contact us at:

Creditor's Name: _____

Address: _____

_____

Telephone: _____

Sincerely,

NOTICE: The federal Equal Credit Opportunity Act prohibits creditors from discriminating against credit applicants on the basis of race, color, religion, national origin, sex, marital status, age (with certain limited exceptions); because all or part of the applicant's income derives from any public assistance program; or because the applicant has in good faith exercised any right under the Consumer Credit Protection Act. The federal agency that administers compliance with this law concerning this creditor is (name and address as specified by the appropriate agency listed in Appendix A).

Form C-4—Sample Notice of Action Taken, Statement of Reasons and Counteroffer

Date_____

Dear Applicant:

Thank you for your application for _____. We are unable to offer you credit on the terms that you requested for the following reason(s):
_____ .

We can, however, offer you credit on the following terms:

_____ .

If this offer is acceptable to you, please notify us within [amount of time] at the following address: _____ .

Our credit decision on your application was based in whole or in part on information obtained in a report from [name, address and [toll-free] telephone number of the consumer reporting agency]. You have a right under the Fair Credit Reporting Act to know the information contained in your credit file at the consumer reporting agency. You also have a right to a free copy of your report from the reporting agency, if you request it no later than 60 days after you receive this notice. In addition, if you find that any information contained in the report you receive is inaccurate or incomplete, you have the right to dispute the matter with the reporting agency.

You should know that the federal Equal Credit Opportunity Act prohibits creditors, such as ourselves, from discriminating against credit applicants on the basis of their race, color, religion, national origin, sex, marital status, age, because they receive income from a public assistance program, or because they may have exercised their rights under the Consumer Credit Protection Act. If you believe there has been discrimination in handling your application you should contact the [name and address of the appropriate federal enforcement agency listed in Appendix A].

Sincerely,

FTC and FRB Model Forms Appx. C.9

Form C-5—Sample Disclosure of Right to Request Specific Reasons for Credit Denial

Date _____

Dear Applicant:

Thank you for applying to us for _____.

After carefully reviewing your application, we are sorry to advise you that we cannot [open an account for you/grant a loan to you/increase your credit limit] at this time.

If you would like a statement of specific reasons why your application was denied, please contact [our credit service manager] shown below within 60 days of the date of this letter. We will provide you with the statement of reasons within 30 days after receiving your request.

    Creditor's Name
    Address
    Telephone number

If we obtained information from a consumer reporting agency as part of our consideration of your application, its name, address, and [toll-free] telephone number is shown below. The reporting agency played no part in our decision and is unable to supply specific reasons why we have denied credit to you. You have a right to a free copy of your report from the reporting agency, if you request it no later than 60 days after you receive this notice. In addition, if you find that any information contained in the report you receive is inaccurate or incomplete, you have the right to dispute the matter with the reporting agency. You can find out about the information contained in your file (if one was used) by contacting:

    Consumer reporting agency's name
    Address
    [Toll-free] Telephone number

Sincerely,

NOTICE

The federal Equal Credit Opportunity Act prohibits creditors from discriminating against credit applicants on the basis of race, color, religion, national origin, sex, marital status, age (provided the applicant has the capacity to enter into a binding contract); because all or part of the applicant's income derives from any public assistance program; or because the applicant has in good faith exercised any right under the Consumer Credit Protection Act. The federal agency that administers compliance with this law concerning this creditor is (name and address as specified by the appropriate agency listed in Appendix A).

| Appendix D | **FTC Official Staff Commentary** |

The Federal Trade Commission has issued a commentary on the Fair Credit Reporting Act. Titled a Statement of General Policy or Interpretation; Commentary on the Fair Credit Reporting Act, it is better known as the FTC Official Staff Commentary (or the Commentary). The authority, purpose and legal effect of the Commentary is set forth at 16 C.F.R. §§ 600.1, 600.2 and the Commentary is reprinted in the Appendix to Part 600.

The important caveat with respect to the FTC Official Staff Commentary is that it predates both the Fair and Accurate Credit Transactions Act of 2003 (FACTA) and the Consumer Credit Reporting Reform Act of 1996 (1996 Reform Act). Both FACTA and the 1996 Reform Act made numerous changes in the FCRA which are not reflected in the FTC Official Staff Commentary. Usually it will be apparent when the language of the FCRA has not changed, or not changed significantly, in which case the Commentary will still be instructive.

There is no indication that the FTC intends to revise the Commentary in light of FACTA and the 1996 Reform Act, especially now that the FTC has significant rulemaking authority under FACTA. As recently as December 2000, the FTC reiterated that "the Commentary will continue to be of use to the public because of its guidance in areas not affected by the 1996 Amendments or included in . . . new interpretations. Therefore, the Commission does not plan to withdraw the Commentary at this time."[1]

It is unclear how much weight the courts will accord the Commentary in light of the rulemaking authority granted to the FTC by the 1999 amendments and FACTA in 2003. The Commentary was issued prior to this rulemaking authority pursuant to FTC rules on administering its enforcement power under the FCRA. 16 C.F.R. subpart H §§ 1.71–1.73. As such, it is an interpretation without the force and effect of statutory provisions, not even a trade regulation or rule. It is "advisory in nature," and provides a "basis for voluntary and simultaneous abandonment of unlawful practices by members of industry." *Id.* at § 1.73(2). It is a guide to FTC enforcement policy.

Although not requiring judicial deference, it may be accorded weight in judicial decision making. It is a policy statement of the federal agency given the primary, though hardly exclusive, enforcement jurisdiction.[2] The weight accorded the Commentary will vary depending on the circumstances of the case, the apparent logic or illogic and reasonableness of the Commentary, and its degree of consistency with the terms and the purpose of the Act itself. By these standards, the Commentary will often be found compelling and other times unpersuasive and even inconsistent with the Act.

The Commentary is not analogous to the Official Staff Commentary to Regulation Z promulgated by the Federal Reserve Board (FRB) pursuant to the Truth in Lending Act. The Truth in Lending Act authorizes FRB rulemaking. 15 U.S.C. § 1604. The FRB rules, its own commentary, and even its own staff's informal opinion letters are binding or, in the appropriate circumstances, entitled to judicial deference. See, for example, Ford Motor Credit Co. v. Milhollin, 444 U.S. 555 (1980).

The amended text of the Commentary is reproduced below.

---

1 65 Fed. Reg. 80804 (Dec. 22, 2000).
2 Yonter v. Aetna Finance Co., 777 F. Supp. 490 (E.D. La. 1991).

List of Subjects in 16 CFR Part 600

Credit, Trade practices.

Pursuant to 15 U.S.C. 1681s and 16 CFR 1.73, the Commission hereby revises 16 CFR part 600 to read as follows:

PART 600—STATEMENTS OF GENERAL POLICY OR INTERPRETATIONS

Sec.

600.1 Authority and purpose.
600.2 Legal effect.

Appendix—Commentary on the Fair Credit Reporting Act.

Authority: 15 U.S.C. 1681s and 16 CFR 1.73.

§ 600.1 Authority and purpose.

(a) *Authority:* This part is issued by the Commission pursuant to the provisions of the Fair Credit Reporting Act. Pub. L. 91-508, approved October 26, 1970. 84 Stat. 1127–36 (15 U.S.C. 1681 *et seq.*).

(b) *Purpose.* The purpose of this part is to clarify and consolidate statements of general policy or interpretations in a commentary in the Appendix to this part. The Commentary will serve as guidance to consumer reporting agencies, their customers, and consumer representatives. The Fair Credit Reporting Act requires that the manner in which consumer reporting agencies provide information be fair and equitable to the consumer with regard to the confidentiality, accuracy, and proper use of such information. The Commentary will enable interested parties to resolve their questions more easily, present a more comprehensive treatment of interpretations and facilitate compliance with the Fair Credit Reporting Act in accordance with Congressional intent.

§ 600.2 Legal effect.

(a) The interpretations in the Commentary are not trade regulation rules or regulations, and, as provided in § 1.73 of the Commission's rules, they do not have the force or effect of statutory provisions.

(b) The regulations of the Commission relating to the administration of the Fair Credit Reporting Act are found in subpart H of 16 CFR part 1 (Sections 1.71–1.73).

Appendix—Commentary on the Fair Credit Reporting Act

Introduction

1. *Official status.* This Commentary contains interpretations of the Federal Trade Commission (Commission) of the Fair Credit Reporting Act (FCRA). It is a guideline intended to clarify how the Commission will construe the FCRA in light of Congressional intent as reflected in the statute and its legislative history. The Commentary does not have the force or effect of regulations or statutory provisions, and its contents may be revised and updated as the Commission considers necessary or appropriate.

2. *Status of previous interpretations.* The Commentary primarily addresses issues discussed in the Commission's earlier formal interpretations of the FCRA (16 CFR 600.1–600.8), which are hereby superseded, in the staff's manual entitled "Compliance With the Fair Credit Reporting Act" (the current edition of which was published in May 1973, and revised in January 1977 and March 1979), and in informal staff opinion letters responding to public requests for interpretations, and it also reflects the results of the Commission's FCRA enforcement program. It is intended to synthesize the Commission's views and give clear advice on important issues. The Commentary sets forth some interpretations that differ from those previously expressed by the Commission or its staff, and is intended to supersede all prior formal Commission interpretations, informal staff opinion letters, and the staff manual cited above.

3. *Statutory references.* Reference to several different provisions of the FCRA is frequently required in order to make a complete analysis of an issue. For various sections and subsections of the FCRA, the Commentary discusses the most important and common overlapping references under the heading "Relation to other (sub)sections."

4. *Issuance of staff interpretations.* The Commission will revise and update the Commentary as it deems necessary, based on the staff's experience in responding to public inquiries about, and enforcing, the FCRA. The Commission welcomes input from interested industry and consumer groups and other public parties on the Commentary and on issues discussed in it. Staff will continue to respond to requests for informal staff interpretations. In proposing revisions of the Commentary, staff will consider and, where appropriate, recommend that the Commentary incorporate issues raised in correspondence and other public contacts, as well as in connection with the Commission's enforcement efforts. Therefore, a party may raise an issue for inclusion in future editions of the Commentary without making any formal submission or request to that effect. However, requests for formal Commission interpretations of the FCRA may also still be made pursuant to the procedures set forth in the Commission's Rules (16 CFR 1.73).

5. *Commentary citations to FCRA.* The Commentary should be used in conjunction with the text of the statute. In some cases, the Commentary includes an abbreviated description of the statute, rather than the full text, as a preamble to discussion of issues pertaining to various sections and subsections. These summary statements of the law should not be used as a substitute for the statutory text.

Section 601—Short Title

"This title may be cited as the Fair Credit Reporting Act."

The Fair Credit Reporting Act (FCRA) is title VI of the Consumer Credit Protection Act, which also includes other Federal statutes relating to consumer credit, such as the Truth in Lending Act (title I), the Equal Credit Opportunity Act (Title VII), and the Fair Debt Collection Practices Act (title VIII).

Section 602—Findings and Purpose

Section 602 recites the Congressional findings regarding the significant role of consumer reporting agencies in the nation's financial system, and states that the basic purpose of the FCRA is to require consumer reporting agencies to adopt reasonable procedures for providing information to credit grantors, insurers, employers and others in a manner that is fair and equitable to the consumer with regard to confidentiality, accuracy, and the proper use of such information.

Section 603—Definitions and Rules of Construction

Section 603(a) states that "definitions and rules of construction set forth in this section are applicable for the purposes of this title."

Section 603(b) defines "person" to mean "any individual, partnership, corporation, trust, estate, cooperative, association, government or governmental subdivision or agency or other entity."

1. Relation to Other Sections

Certain "persons" must comply with the Act. The term "consumer reporting agency" is defined in section 603(f) to include certain "persons." Section 619 subjects any "person" who knowingly and willfully obtains information from a consumer reporting agency on a consumer under false pretenses to criminal sanctions. Requirements relating to report users apply to "persons." Section 606 imposes disclosure obligations on "persons" who obtain investigative reports or cause them to be prepared. Section 615(c) uses the term "person" to denote those subject to disclosure obligations under sections 615(a) and 615(b).

2. Examples

The term "person" includes universities, creditors, collection agencies, insurance companies, private investigators, and employers.

Section 603(c) *defines the term "consumer" to mean "an individual."*

1. Relation to Other Sections

The term "consumer" denotes an individual entitled to the Act's protections. Consumer reports, as defined in section 603(d), are reports about consumers. A "consumer" is entitled to obtain disclosures under section 609 from consumer reporting agencies and to take certain steps that require such agencies to follow procedures in section 611, concerning disputes about the completeness or accuracy of items of information in the consumer's file. Disclosures required under section 606 by one procuring an investigative report must be made to the "consumer" on whom the report is sought. Notifications required by section 615 must be provided to "consumers." A "consumer" is the party entitled to sue for willful noncompliance (section 616) or negligent noncompliance (section 617) with the Act's requirements.

2. General

The definition includes only a natural person. It does not include artificial entities (*e.g.*, partnerships, corporations, trusts, estates, cooperatives, associations) or entities created by statute (*e.g.*, governments, governmental subdivisions or agencies).

Section 603(d) *defines "consumer report" to mean "any written, oral, or other communication of any information by a consumer reporting agency bearing on a consumer's credit worthiness, credit standing, credit capacity, character, general reputation, personal characteristics, or mode of living which is used or expected to be used or collected in whole or in part for the purpose of serving as a factor in establishing the consumer's eligibility for (1) credit or insurance to be used primarily for personal, family, or household purposes, or (2) employment purposes, or (3) other purposes authorized under Section 604"* (with three specific exclusions).

1. Relation to "Consumer Reporting Agency"

To be a "consumer report," the information must be furnished by a "consumer reporting agency" as that term is defined in section 603(f). Conversely, the term "consumer reporting agency" is restricted to persons that regularly engage in assembling or evaluating consumer credit information or other information on consumers for the purpose of furnishing "consumer reports" to third parties. In other words, the terms "consumer reporting agency" in section 603(f) and "consumer report" in section 603 (d) [sic] are mutually dependent and must therefore be construed together. For example, information is not a "consumer report" if the person furnishing the information is clearly not a "consumer reporting agency" (*e.g.*, if the person furnishing the information does not regularly furnish such information for monetary fees or on a cooperative nonprofit basis).

2. Relation to the Applicability of the Act

If a report is not a "consumer report," then the Act does not usually apply to it.[1] For example, because a commercial credit report is not a report on a consumer, it is not a "consumer report". Therefore, the user need not notify the subject of the name and address of the credit bureau when taking adverse action, and the provider need not omit "obsolete" information, as would be required if the FCRA applied.

3. Report Concerning a "Consumer's" Attributes and History

A. *General.* A "consumer report" is a report on a "consumer" to be used for certain purposes involving that "consumer."

B. *Artificial entities.* Reports about corporations, associations, and other collective entities are not consumer reports, and the Act does not apply to them.

C. *Reports on businesses for business purposes.* Reports used to determine the eligibility of a business, rather than a consumer, for certain purposes, are not consumer reports and the FCRA does not apply to them, even if they contain information on individuals, because Congress did not intend for the FCRA to apply to reports used for commercial purposes (see 116 Cong. Rec. 36572 (1970) (Conf. Report on H.R. 15073)).

4. "(C)redit Worthiness, Credit Standing, Credit Capacity, Character, General Reputation, Personal Characteristics, or Mode of Living * * *"

A. *General.* To be a "consumer report," the information must bear on at least one of the seven characteristics listed in this definition.

B. *Credit guides.* Credit guides are listings, furnished by credit bureaus to credit grantors, that rate how well consumers pay their bills. Such guides are a series of "consumer reports," because they contain information which is used for the purpose of serving as a factor in establishing the consumers' eligibility for credit. However, if they are coded (by identification such as social security number, driver's license number, or bank account number) so that the consumer's identity is not disclosed, they are not "consumer reports" until decoded. (See discussion of uncoded credit guides under section 604(3)(A), item 8 *infra*.)

C. *Motor vehicle reports.* Motor vehicle reports are distributed by state motor vehicle departments, generally to insurance companies upon request, and usually reveal a consumer's entire driving record, including arrests for driving offenses. Such reports are consumer reports when they are sold by a Department of Motor Vehicles for insurance underwriting purposes and contain information bearing on the consumer's "personal characteristics," such as arrest information. The Act's legislative history indicates Congress intended the Act to cover mutually beneficial exchanges of information between commercial enterprises rather than between governmental entities. Accordingly, these reports are not consumer reports when provided to other governmental authorities involved in licensing or law enforcement activities. (See discussion titled "State Departments of Motor Vehicles," under section 603(f), item 10 *infra*.)

D. *Consumer lists.* A list of the names of creditworthy individuals, or of individuals on whom credit bureaus have derogatory information, is a series of "consumer reports" because the information bears on credit worthiness.

E. *Public record information.* A report solely of public record information is not a "consumer report" unless that information is provided by a consumer reporting agency, is collected or used for the purposes identified in section 603(d), and bears on at least one of the seven characteristics listed in the definition. Public record information relating to records of arrest, or the institution or disposition of civil or criminal proceedings, bears on one or more of these characteristics.

F. *Name and address.* A report limited solely to the consumer's name and address alone, with no connotations as to credit worthiness or other characteristics, does not constitute a "consumer report," if it does not bear on any of the seven factors.

G. *Rental characteristics.* Reports about rental characteristics (*e.g.*, consumers' evictions, rental payment histories, treatment of premises) are consumer reports, because they relate to character, general reputation, personal characteristics, or mode of living.

5. "(U)sed or Expected to Be Used or Collected in Whole or in Part for the Purpose of Serving as a Factor in Establishing the Consumer's Eligibility * * *"

A. *Law enforcement bulletins.* Bulletins that are limited to a series of descriptions, sometimes accompanied by photographs, of individuals who are being sought by law enforcement authorities for alleged crimes are not a series of "consumer reports" because they have not been collected for use in evaluating consumers for credit, insurance, employment or other consumer purposes, and it cannot reasonably be anticipated they will be used for such purposes.

B. *Directories.* Telephone directories and city directories, to the extent they only provide information regarding name, address and phone number, marital status, home ownership, and number of children, are not "consumer reports," because the information is not used or expected to be used in evaluating consumers for credit, insurance, employment or other purposes and does

---

[1] However, a creditor denying a consumer's application based on a report from a "third party" must give the disclosure required by section 615(b).

not reflect on credit standing, credit worthiness, or any of the other factors. A list of names of individuals with checking accounts is not a series of consumer reports because the information does not bear on credit worthiness or any of the other factors. A trade directory, such as a list of all insurance agents licensed to do business in a state, is not a series of consumer reports because it is commercial information that would be used for commercial purposes.

C. *Use of prior consumer report in preparation.* A report that would not otherwise be a consumer report may be a consumer report, notwithstanding the purpose for which it is furnished, if it includes a prior consumer report or information from consumer report files, because it would contain some information "collected in whole or in part" for consumer reporting purposes. For example, an insurance claims report would be a consumer report if a consumer report (or information from a consumer report) were used to prepare it. (See discussion, *infra*, in item 6-C under this subsection.)

D. *Use of reports for purposes not anticipated by the reporting party.* The question arises whether a report that is not otherwise a consumer report is subject to the FCRA because the recipient subsequently uses the report for a permissible purpose. If the reporting party's procedures are such that it neither knows of nor should reasonably anticipate such use, the report is not a consumer report. If a reporting party has taken reasonable steps to insure that the report is not used for such a purpose, and if it neither knows of, nor can reasonably anticipate such use, the report should not be deemed a consumer report by virtue of uses beyond the reporting party's control. A reporting party might establish that it does not reasonably anticipate such use of the report by requiring the recipient to certify that the report will not be used for one of the purposes listed in section 604. (Such procedure may be compared to the requirement in section 607(a), discussed *infra*, that consumer reporting agencies furnishing consumer reports require that prospective users certify the purposes for which the information is sought and certify that the information will be used for no other purpose.) For example, a claims reporting service could use such a certification to avoid having its insurance claims reports deemed "consumer reports" if the report recipient/insurer were to use the report later for "underwriting purposes" under section 604(3)(C), such as terminating insurance coverage or raising the premium.

6. "(E)stablishing the Consumer's Eligibility for (1) Credit or Insurance to Be Used Primarily for Personal, Family or Household Purposes, or (2) Employment Purposes, or (3) Other Purposes Authorized Under Section 604"

A. *Relation to section 604.* Because section 603(d)(3) refers to "purposes authorized under section 604" (often described as "permissible purposes" of consumer reports), some of which overlap purposes enumerated in section 603 (*e.g.*, 603(d)(1) and 603(d)(2)), sections 603 and 604 must be construed together, to determine what are "consumer reports" and "permissible purposes" under the two sections. See discussion *infra*, under section 604.

B. *Commercial credit or insurance.* A report on a consumer for credit or insurance in connection with a business operated by the consumer is not a "consumer report," and the Act does not apply to it.

C. *Insurance claims reports.* (It is assumed that information in prior consumer reports is not used in claims reports. See discussion, *supra*, in item 5-C under this subsection.) Reports provided to insurers by claims investigation services solely to determine the validity of insurance claims are not consumer reports, because section 604(3)(C) specifically sets forth only underwriting (not claims) as an insurance-related purpose, and section 603(d)(1) deals specifically with eligibility for insurance and no other insurance-related purposes. To construe section 604(3)(E) as including reports furnished in connection with insurance claims would be to disregard the specific language of sections 604(3)(C) and 603(d)(1).

D. *Scope of employment purpose.* A report that is used or is expected to be used or collected in whole or in part in connection with establishing an employee's eligibility for "promotion, reassignment or retention," as well as to evaluate a job applicant, is a consumer report because sections 603(d)(2) and 604(3)(B) use the term "employment purposes," which section 603(h) defines to include these situations.

E. *Bad check lists.* A report indicating that an individual has issued bad checks, provided by printed list or otherwise, to a business for use in determining whether to accept consumers' checks tendered in transactions primarily for personal, family or household purposes, is a consumer report. The information furnished bears on consumers' character, general reputation and personal characteristics, and it is used or expected to be used in connection with business transactions involving consumers.

F. *Tenant screening reports.* A report used to determine whether to rent a residence to a consumer is a consumer report, because it is used for a business transaction that the consumer wishes to enter into for personal, family or household purposes.

7. Exclusions From the Definition of "Consumer Report"

A. *"(Any) reports containing information solely as to transactions or experiences between the consumer and the person making the report;"*—(1) *Examples of Sources.* The exemption applies to reports limited to transactions or experiences between the consumer and the entity making the report (*e.g.*, retail stores, hospitals, present or former employers, banks, mortgage servicing companies, credit unions, or universities).

(2) *Information beyond the reporting entity's own transactions or experiences with the consumer.*

The exemption does not apply to reports by these entities of information beyond their own transactions or experiences with the consumer. An example is a creditor's or an insurance company's report of the reasons it cancelled credit or insurance, based on information from an outside source.

(3) *Opinions Concerning Transactions or Experiences*

The exemption applies to reports that are not limited to the facts, but also include opinions (*e.g.*, use of the term "slow pay" to describe a consumer's transactions with a creditor), as long as the facts underlying the opinions involve only transactions or experiences between the consumer and the reporting entity.

B. *"(A)ny authorization or approval of a specific extension of credit directly or indirectly by the issuer of a credit card or similar device;"*—(1) *General.* The exemption applies to a credit or debit card issuer's written, oral, or electronic communication of its decision whether or not to authorize a charge, in response to a request from a merchant or other party that the consumer has asked to honor the card.

C. *"(A)ny report in which a person who has been requested by a third party to make a specific extension of credit directly or indirectly to the consumer conveys his decision with respect to such request, if the third party advises the consumer of the name and address of the person to whom the request was made and such person makes the disclosures to the consumer required under section 615."*—(1) *General.* The exemption covers retailers' attempts to obtain credit for their individual customers from an outside source (such as a bank or a finance company). The communication by the financial institution of its decision whether to extend credit is not a "consumer report" *if* the retailer informs the customer of the name and address of the financial institution to which the application or contract is offered *and* the financial institution makes the disclosures required by section 615 of the Act. Such disclosures must be made only when there is a denial of, or increase in the charge for, credit or insurance. (See discussion of section 615, item 10, *infra*.)

(2) *Information included in the exemption.*

The exemption is not limited to a simple "yes" or "no" response, but includes the information constituting the basis for the credit denial, because it applies to "any report."

(3) *How third party creditors can insure that the exemption applies.*

Creditors, who are requested by dealers or merchants to make such specific extensions of credit, can assure that communication of their decision to the dealer or merchant will be exempt under this section from the term "consumer report," by having written agreements that require such parties to inform the consumer of the creditor's name and address and by complying with any applicable provisions of section 615.

Section 603(e) defines "investigative consumer report" as "a consumer report or portion thereof in which information on a consumer's character, general reputation, personal characteristics, or mode of living is obtained through personal interviews with neighbors, friends, or associates of the consumer reported on or with others with whom he is acquainted or who may have knowledge concerning any such items of information. However, such information shall not include specific factual information on a consumer's credit record obtained directly from a creditor of the consumer or from a consumer reporting agency when such information was obtained directly from a creditor of the consumer or from the consumer."

1. Relation to Other Sections

The term "investigative consumer report" denotes a subset of "consumer report" for which the Act imposes additional requirements on recipients and consumer reporting agencies. Persons procuring "investigative consumer reports" must make certain disclosures to the consumers who are the subjects of the reports, as required by section 606. Consumer reporting agencies must comply with section 614, when furnishing "investigative consumer reports" containing adverse information that is not a matter of public record. Consumer reporting agencies making disclosure to consumers pursuant to section 609 are not required to disclose "sources of information acquired solely for use in preparing an investigative consumer report and actually used for no other purpose."

2. General

An "investigative consumer report" is a type of "consumer report" that contains information that is both related to a consumer's character, general reputation, personal characteristics or mode of living and obtained by personal interviews with the consumer's neighbors, friends, associates or others.

3. Types of Sources Interviewed

A report consisting of information from any third party concerning the subject's character (reputation, etc.) may be an investigative consumer report because the phrase "obtained through personal interviews * * * with others" includes any source that is a third party interviewee. A report containing interview information obtained solely from the subject is not an "investigative consumer report."

4. Telephone Interviews

A consumer report that contains information on a consumer's "character, general reputation, personal characteristics or mode of living" obtained through telephone interviews with third parties is an "investigative consumer report," because "personal interviews" includes interviews conducted by telephone as well as in person.

5. Identity of Interviewer

A consumer report is an "investigative consumer report" if personal interviews are used to obtain information reported on a consumer's "character, general reputation, personal characteristics or mode of living," regardless of who conducted the interview.

6. Noninvestigative Information in "Investigative Consumer Reports"

An "investigative consumer report" may also contain noninvestigative information, because the definition includes reports, a "portion" of which are investigative reports.

7. Exclusions From "Investigative Consumer Reports"

A report that consists solely of information gathered from observation by one who drives by the consumer's residence is not an "investigative consumer report," because it contains no information from "personal interviews."

Section 603(f) defines "consumer reporting agency" as "any person which, for monetary fees, dues, or on a cooperative nonprofit basis, regularly engages in whole or in part in the practice of assembling or evaluating consumer credit information or other information on consumers for the purpose of furnishing consumer reports to third parties, and which uses any means or facility of interstate commerce for the purpose of preparing or furnishing consumer reports."

1. Relation to Other Sections

A. *Duties imposed on "consumer reporting agencies."* The Act imposes a number of duties on "consumer reporting agencies." They must have permissible purposes to furnish consumer reports (section 604), avoid furnishing obsolete adverse information in certain consumer reports (sections 605, 607(a)), adopt reasonable procedures to assure privacy (section 604, 607(a)), and accuracy (section 607(b)) of consumer reports, provide only limited disclosures to governmental agencies (section 608), provide consumers certain disclosures upon request (sections 609 and 610) at no cost or for a reasonable charge (section 612), follow certain procedures if a consumer disputes the completeness or accuracy of any item of information contained in his file (section 611), and follow certain procedures in reporting public record information for employment purposes or when reporting adverse information other than public record information in investigative consumer reports (sections 613, 614).

B. *Relation to "consumer reports."* The term "consumer reporting agency," as defined in section 603(f), includes certain persons who assemble or evaluate information on individuals for the purpose of furnishing "consumer reports" to third parties. Conversely, section 603(d) defines the term "consumer report" to mean the communication of certain information by a "consumer reporting agency." In other words, the terms "consumer report" in section 603(d) and "consumer reporting agency" as defined in section 603(f) are defined in a mutually dependent manner and must therefore be construed together. For example, a party is not a "consumer reporting agency" if it provides only information that is excepted from the definition of "consumer report" under section 603(d), such as reports limited to the party's own transactions or experiences with a consumer, or credit information on organizations.

2. Isolated Reports

Parties that do not "regularly" engage in assembling or evaluating information for the purpose of furnishing consumer reports to third parties are not consumer reporting agencies. For example, a creditor that furnished information on a consumer to a governmental entity in connection with one of its investigations, would not "regularly" be making such disclosure for a fee or on a cooperative nonprofit basis, and therefore would not become a consumer reporting agency, even if the information exceeded the creditor's transactions or experiences with the consumer.

3. Provision of Credit Report to Report Subject

A consumer report user does not become a consumer reporting agency by regularly giving a copy of the report, or otherwise disclosing it, to the consumer who is the subject of the report, because it is not disclosing the information to a "third party."

4. Employment Agency

An employment agency that routinely obtains information on job applicants from their former employers and furnishes the information to prospective employers is a consumer reporting agency.

5. Information Compiled for Insurance Underwriting

A business that compiles claim payment histories on individuals from insurers and furnishes them to insurance companies for use in underwriting decisions concerning those individuals is a consumer reporting agency.

6. Private Investigators and Detective Agencies

Private investigators and detective agencies that regularly obtain consumer reports and furnish them to clients may thereby become consumer reporting agencies.

7. Collection Agencies and Creditors

Collection agencies and creditors become consumer reporting agencies if they regularly furnish information beyond their transactions or experiences with consumers to third parties for use in connection with consumers' transactions.

8. Joint Users of Consumer Reports

Entities that share consumer reports with others that are jointly involved in decisions for which there are permissible purposes to obtain the reports may be "joint users" rather than consumer reporting agencies. For example, if a lender forwards consumer reports to governmental agencies administering loan guarantee programs (or to other prospective loan insurers or guarantors), or to other parties whose approval is needed before it grants credit, or to another creditor for use in considering a consumer's loan application at the consumer's request, the lender does not become a consumer reporting agency by virtue of such action. An agent or employee that obtains consumer reports does not become a consumer reporting agency by sharing such reports with its principal or employer in connection with the purposes for which the reports were initially obtained.

9. Loan Exchanges

Loan exchanges, which are generally owned and operated on a cooperative basis by consumer finance companies, constitute a mechanism whereby each member furnishes the exchange information concerning the full identity and loan amount of each of its borrowers, and receives information from the exchange concerning the number and types of outstanding loans for each of its applicants. A loan exchange or any other exchange that regularly collects information bearing on decisions to grant consumers credit or insurance for personal, family or household purposes, or employment, is a "consumer reporting agency."

10. State Departments of Motor Vehicles

State motor vehicle departments are "consumer reporting agencies" if they regularly furnish motor vehicle reports containing information bearing on the consumer's "personal characteristics," such as arrest information, to insurance companies for insurance underwriting purposes. (See discussion of motor vehicle reports under section 603(d), item 4c *supra*.)

11. Federal Agencies

The Office of Personnel Management collects and files data concerning current and potential employees of the Federal Government and transmits that information to other government agencies for employment purposes. Because Congress did not intend that the FCRA apply to the Office of Personnel Management and similar federal agencies (see 116 Cong. Rec. 36576 (1970) (remarks of Rep. Brown)), no such agency is a "consumer reporting agency."

12. Credit Application Information

A creditor that provides information from a consumer's application to a credit bureau, for verification as part of the creditor's evaluation process that includes obtaining a report on the consumer from that credit bureau, does not thereby become a "consumer reporting agency," because the creditor does not provide the information for "fees, dues, or on a cooperative non-profit basis," but rather pays the bureau to verify the information when it provides a consumer report on the applicant.

Section 603(g) defines "file," when used in connection with information on any consumer, to mean "all of the information on that consumer recorded and retained by a consumer reporting agency regardless of how the information is stored."

1. Relation to Other Sections

Consumer reporting agencies are required to make disclosures of all information in their "files" to consumers upon request (section 609) and to follow reinvestigation procedures if the consumer disputes the completeness or accuracy of any item of information contained in his "file" (section 611).

2. General

The term "file" denotes all information on the consumer that is recorded and retained by a consumer reporting agency that might be furnished, or has been furnished, in a consumer report on that consumer.

3. Audit Trail

The term "file" does not include an "audit trail" (a list of changes made by a consumer reporting agency to a consumer's credit history record, maintained to detect fraudulent changes to that record), because such information is not furnished in consumer reports or used as a basis for preparing them.

4. Other Information

The term "file" does not include information in billing records or in the consumer relations folder that a consumer reporting agency opens on a consumer who obtains disclosures or files a dispute, if the information has not been used in a consumer report and would not be used in preparing one.

Section 603(h) defines "employment purposes" to mean "a report used for the purpose of evaluating a consumer for employment, promotion, reassignment or retention as an employee."

1. Relation to Other Sections

The term "employment purposes" is used as part of the definition of "consumer reports" (section 603(d)(2)) and as a permissible purpose for the furnishing of consumer reports (section 604(3)(B)). Where an investigative consumer report is to be used for "employment purposes" for which a consumer has not specifically applied, section 606(a)(2) provides that the notice otherwise required by section 606(a)(1) need not be sent. When a consumer reporting agency furnishes public record information in reports "for employment purposes," it must follow the procedure set out in section 613.

2. Security Clearances

A report in connection with security clearances of a government contractor's employees would be for "employment purposes" under this section.

Section 603(i) defines "medical information" to mean "information or records obtained, with the consent of the individual to whom it relates, from licensed physicians or medical practitioners, hospitals, clinics, or other medical or medically related facilities."

1. Relation to Other Sections

Under section 609(a)(1), a consumer reporting agency must, upon the consumer's request and proper identification, disclose the nature and substance of all information in its files on the consumer, except "medical information."

2. Information From Non-medical Sources

Information from non-medical sources such as employers, is not "medical information."

Section 604—Permissible Purposes of Reports

*"A consumer reporting agency may furnish a consumer report under the following circumstances and no other: * * *"*

1. Relation to Section 603

Sections 603(d)(3) and 604 must be construed together to determine what are "permissible purposes," because section 603(d)(3) refers to "purposes authorized under section 604" (often described as "permissible purposes" of consumer reports), and some purposes are enumerated in section 603 (*e.g.*, sections 603(d)(1) and 603(d)(2)). Subsections of sections 603 and 604 that specifically set forth "permissible purposes" relating to credit, insurance and employment, are the only subsections that cover "permissible purposes" relating to those three areas. Section 604(3)(E), a general subsection, is limited to purposes not otherwise addressed in section 604(3) (A)–(D).

A. *Credit.* Sections 603(d)(1)—which defines "consumer report" to include certain reports for the purpose of serving as a factor in establishing the consumer's eligibility for credit or insurance primarily for personal, family, or household purposes—and 604(3)(A) must be read together as fully describing permissible purposes involving credit for obtaining consumer reports. Accordingly, section 604(3)(A) permits the furnishing of a consumer report for use in connection with a credit transaction involving the consumer, primarily for personal, family or household purposes, and involving the extension of credit to, or review or collection of an account of, the consumer.

B. *Insurance.* Sections 603(d)(1) and 604(3)(C) must be read together as describing the only permissible insurance purposes for obtaining consumer reports. Accordingly, section 604(3)(C) permits the furnishing of a consumer report, provided it is for use in connection with the underwriting of insurance involving the consumer, primarily for personal, family, or household purposes.

C. *Employment.* Employment is covered exclusively by sections 603(d)(2) and 604(3)(B), and by section 603(h) (which defines "employment purposes"). Therefore, "permissible purposes" relating to employment include reports used for evaluating a consumer "for employment, promotion, reassignment or retention as an employee."

D. *Other purposes.* "Other purposes" are referred to in section 603(d)(3) and covered by section 604(3)(E), as well as sections 604(1), 604(2) and 604(3)(D) (which contain specific purposes not involving credit, insurance, employment). Permissible purposes relating to section 604(3)(E) are limited to transactions that consumers enter into primarily for personal, family or household purposes (excluding credit, insurance or employment, which are specifically covered by other subsections discussed above). The FCRA does not cover reports furnished for transactions that consumers enter into primarily in connection with businesses they operate (*e.g.*, a consumer's rental of equipment for use in his retail store).

2. Relation to Other Sections

A. *Section 607(a).* Section 607(a) requires consumer reporting agencies to keep information confidential by furnishing consumer reports only for purposes listed under section 604, and to follow specified, reasonable procedures to achieve this end. Section 619 provides criminal sanctions against any person who knowingly and willfully obtains information on a consumer from a consumer reporting agency under false pretenses.

B. *Section 608.* Section 608 allows "consumer reporting agencies" to furnish governmental agencies specified identifying information concerning consumers, notwithstanding the limitations of section 604.

Section 604(1)—A consumer reporting agency may furnish a consumer report "in response to the order of a court having jurisdiction to issue such an order."

1. Subpoena

A subpoena, including a grand jury subpoena, is not an "order of a court" unless signed by a judge.

2. Internal Revenue Service Summons

An I.R.S. summons is an exception to the requirement that an order be signed by a judge before it constitutes an "order of a court" under this section, because a 1976 revision to Federal statutes (26 U.S.C. 7609) specifically requires a consumer reporting agency to furnish a consumer report in response to an I.R.S. summons upon receipt of the designated I.R.S. certificate that the consumer has not filed a timely motion to quash the summons.

Section 604(2)—A consumer reporting agency may furnish a consumer report "in accordance with the written instructions of the consumer to whom it relates."

1. No Other Permissible Purpose Needed

If the report subject furnishes written authorization for a report, that creates a permissible purpose for furnishing the report.

2. Refusal to Furnish Report

The consumer reporting agency may refuse to furnish the report because the statute is permissive, not mandatory. (Requirements that consumer reporting agencies make disclosure to consumers (as contrasted with furnishing reports to users) are discussed under sections 609 and 610, *infra.*)

*Section 604(3)(A)—A consumer reporting agency may issue a consumer report to "a person which it has reason to believe * * * intends to use the information in connection with a credit transaction involving the consumer on whom the information is to be furnished and involving the extension of credit to, or review or collection of an account of, the consumer;"*

1. Reports Sought in Connection with the "Review or Collection of an Account"

A. *Reports for collection.* A collection agency has a permissible purpose under this section to receive a consumer report on a consumer for use in attempting to collect that consumer's debt, regardless of whether that debt is assigned or referred for collection. Similarly, a detective agency or private investigator, attempting to collect a debt owed by a consumer, would have a permissible purpose to obtain a consumer report on that individual for use in collecting that debt. An attorney may obtain a consumer report under this section on a consumer for use in connection with a decision whether to sue that individual to collect a credit account.

B. *Unsolicited reports.* A consumer reporting agency may not send an unsolicited consumer report to the recipient of a previous report on the same consumer, because the recipient will not necessarily have a permissible purpose to receive the unsolicited report.[2] For example, the recipient may have rejected the consumer's application or ceased to do business with the consumer. (See also discussion in section 607, item 2G, *infra.*)

2. Judgment Creditors

A judgment creditor has a permissible purpose to receive a consumer report on the judgment debtor for use in connection with collection of the judgment debt, because it is in the same position as any creditor attempting to collect a debt from a consumer who is the subject of a consumer report.

3. Child Support Debts

A district attorney's office or other child support agency may obtain a consumer report in connection with enforcement of the report subject's child support obligation, established by court (or quasi-judicial administrative) orders, since the agency is acting as or on behalf of the judgment creditor, and is, in effect, collecting a debt. However, a consumer reporting agency may not furnish consumer reports to child support agencies seeking to *establish* paternity or the duty to pay child support.

4. Tax Obligations

A tax collection agency has no general permissible purpose to obtain a consumer report to collect delinquent tax accounts, because this subsection applies only to collection of "credit" accounts. However, if a tax collection agency acquired a tax lien having the same effect as a judgment or obtained a judgment, it would be a judgment creditor and would have a permissible purpose for obtaining a consumer report on the consumer who owed the tax. Similarly, if a consumer taxpayer entered an agreement with a tax collection agency to pay taxes according to some timetable, that agreement would create a debtor-creditor relationship, thereby giving the agency a permissible purpose to obtain a consumer report on that consumer.

5. Information on an Applicant's Spouse

A. *Permissible purpose.* A creditor may request any information concerning an applicant's spouse if that spouse will be permitted to use the account or will be contractually liable upon the account, or the applicant is relying on the spouse's income as a basis for repayment of the credit requested. A creditor may request any information concerning an applicant's spouse if (1) the state law doctrine of necessaries applies to the transaction, or (2) the applicant resides in a community property state, or (3) the property upon which the applicant is relying as a basis for repayment of the credit requested is located in such a state, or (4) the applicant is acting as the agent of the nonapplicant spouse.

B. *Lack of permissible purpose.* If the creditor receives information clearly indicating that the applicant is not acting as the agent of the nonapplicant spouse, and that the applicant is relying only on separate property to repay the credit extended, and that the state law doctrine of necessaries does not apply to the transaction and that the applicant does not reside in a community property state, the creditor does not have a permissible purpose for obtaining a report on a nonapplicant spouse. A permissible purpose for making a consumer report on a nonapplicant spouse can never exist under the FCRA, where Regulation B, issued under the Equal Credit Opportunity Act (12 CFR 202), prohibits the creditor from requesting information on such

---

2 Of course a consumer reporting agency must furnish notifications required by section 611(d), upon the consumer's requests, to prior recipients of reports containing disputed information that is deleted or that is the subject of a dispute statement under section 611(b).

spouse. There is no permissible purpose to obtain a consumer report on a nonapplicant former spouse or on a nonapplicant spouse who has legally separated or otherwise indicated an intent to legally disassociate with the marriage. (This does not preclude reporting a prior joint credit account of former spouses for which the spouse that is the subject of the report is still contractually liable. See discussion in section 607, item 3-D *infra*.)

6. Prescreening

"Prescreening" means the process whereby a consumer reporting agency compiles or edits a list of consumers who meet specific criteria and provides this list to the client or a third party (such as a mailing service) on behalf of the client for use in soliciting these consumers for the client's products or services. The process may also include demographic or other analysis of the consumers on the list (*e.g.*, use of census tract data reflecting real estate values) by the consumer reporting agency or by a third party employed for that purpose (by either the agency or its client) before the list is provided to the consumer reporting agency's client. In such situations, the client's creditworthiness criteria may be provided only to the consumer reporting agency and not to the third party performing the demographic analysis. The consumer reporting agency that performs a "prescreening" service may furnish a client with several different lists of consumers who meet different sets of creditworthiness criteria supplied by the client, who intends to make different credit offers (*e.g.*, various credit limits) to consumers who meet the different criteria.

A prescreened list constitutes a series of consumer reports, because the list conveys the information that each consumer named meets certain criteria for creditworthiness. Prescreening is permissible under the FCRA if the client agrees in advance that each consumer whose name is on the list after prescreening will receive an offer of credit. In these circumstances, a permissible purpose for the prescreening service exists under this section, because of the client's present intent to grant credit to all consumers on the final list, with the result that the information is used "in connection with a credit transaction involving the consumer on whom the information is to be furnished and involving the extension of credit to * * * the consumer."

7. Seller of Property Extending Credit

A seller of property has a permissible purpose under this subsection to obtain a consumer report on a prospective purchaser to whom he is planning to extend credit.

8. Uncoded Credit Guides

A consumer reporting agency may not furnish an uncoded credit guide, because the recipient does not have a permissible purpose to obtain a consumer report on each consumer listed. (As discussed under section 603(d), item 4 *supra*, credit guides are listings that credit bureaus furnish to credit grantors, rating how consumers pay their bills. Such guides are a series of "consumer reports" on the "consumers" listed therein, unless coded so that the consumer's identity is not disclosed.)

9. Liability for Bad Checks

A party attempting to recover the amount due on a bad check is attempting to collect a debt and, therefore, has a permissible purpose to obtain a consumer report on the consumer who wrote it, and on any other consumer who is liable for the amount of that check under applicable state law.

*Section 604(3)(B)—A consumer reporting agency may issue a consumer report to "a person which it has reason to believe * * * intends to use the information for employment purposes;"*

1. Current Employees

An employer may obtain a consumer report on a current employee in connection with an investigation of the disappearance of money from employment premises, because "retention as an employee" is included in the definition of "employment purposes" (section 603(h)).

2. Consumer Reports on Applicants and Non-applicants

An employer may obtain a consumer report for use in evaluating the subject's application for employment but may not obtain a consumer report to evaluate the application of a consumer who is not the subject of the report.

3. Grand Jurors

The fact that grand jurors are usually paid a stipend for their service does not provide a district attorney's office a permissible purpose for obtaining consumer reports on them, because such service is a duty, not "employment."

*Section 604(3)(C)—A consumer reporting agency may issue a consumer report to "a person which it has reason to believe * * * intends to use the information in connection with the underwriting of insurance involving the consumer;"*

1. Underwriting

An insurer may obtain a consumer report to decide whether or not to issue a policy to the consumer, the amount and terms of coverage, the duration of the policy, the rates or fees charged, or whether or not to renew or cancel a policy, because these are all "underwriting" decisions.

2. Claims

An insurer may not obtain a consumer report for the purpose of evaluating a claim (to ascertain its validity or otherwise determine what action should be taken), because permissible purposes relating to insurance are limited by this section to "underwriting" purposes.

*Section 604(3)(D)—A consumer reporting agency may issue a consumer report to "a person which it has reason to believe * * * intends to use the information in connection with a determination of the consumer's eligibility for a license or other benefit granted by a governmental instrumentality required by law to consider an applicant's financial responsibility or status * * *"*

1. Appropriate recipient

Any party charged by law (including a rule or regulation having the force of law) with responsibility for assessing the consumer's eligibility for the benefit (not only the agency directly responsible for administering the benefit) has a permissible purpose to receive a consumer report. For example, a district attorney's office or social services bureau, required by law to consider a consumer's financial status in determining whether that consumer qualifies for welfare benefits, has a permissible purpose to obtain a report on the consumer for that purpose. Similarly, consumer reporting agencies may furnish consumer reports to townships on consumers whose financial status the townships are required by law to consider in determining the consumers' eligibility for assistance, or to professional boards (*e.g.*, bar examiners) required by law to consider such information on applicants for admission to practice.

2. Inappropriate Recipient

Parties not charged with the responsibility of determining a consumer's eligibility for a license or other benefit, for example, a party competing for an FCC radio station construction permit, would not have a permissible purpose to obtain a consumer report on that consumer.

3. Initial or Continuing Benefit

The permissible purpose includes the determination of a consumer's continuing eligibility for a benefit, as well as the evaluation of a consumer's initial application for a benefit. If the governmental body has reason to believe a particular consumer's eligibility is in doubt, or wishes to conduct random checks to confirm eligibility, it has a permissible purpose to receive a consumer report.

*Section 604(3)(E)—A consumer reporting agency may issue a consumer report to "a person which it has reason to believe * * * otherwise has a legitimate business need for the information in connection with a business transaction involving the consumer."*

1. Relation to Other Subsections of Section 604(3)

The issue of whether credit, employment, or insurance provides a permissible purpose is determined exclusively by reference to subsection (A), (B), or (C), respectively.

2. Commercial Transactions

The term "business transaction" in this section means a business transaction with a consumer primarily for personal, family, or household purposes. Business transactions that involve purely commercial purposes are not covered by the FCRA.

3. "Legitimate Business Need"

Under this subsection, a party has a permissible purpose to obtain a consumer report on a consumer for use in connection with some action the consumer takes from which he or she might expect to receive a benefit that is not more specifically covered by subsections (A), (B), or (C). For example, a consumer report may be obtained on a consumer who applies to rent an apartment, offers to pay for goods with a check, applies for a checking account or similar service, seeks to be included in a computer dating service, or who has sought and received over-payments of government benefits that he has refused to return.

4. Litigation

The possibility that a party may be involved in litigation involving a consumer does not provide a permissible purpose for that party to receive a consumer report on such consumer under this subsection, because litigation is not a "business transaction" involving the consumer. Therefore, potential plaintiffs may not always obtain reports on potential defendants to determine whether they are worth suing. The transaction that gives rise to the litigation may or may not provide a permissible purpose. A party seeking to sue on a *credit* account would have a permissible purpose under section 604(3)(A). (That section also permits judgment creditors and lien creditors to obtain consumer reports on judgment debtors or individuals whose property is subject to the lien creditor's lien.) If that transaction is a business transaction involving the consumer, there is a permissible purpose. If the litigation arises from a tort, there is no permissible purpose. Similarly, a consumer report may not be obtained solely for use in discrediting a witness at trial or for locating a witness. This section does not permit consumer reporting agencies to furnish consumer reports for the purpose of locating a person suspected of committing a crime. (As stated in the discussion of section 608 *infra* (item 2), section 608 permits the furnishing of specified, limited identifying information to governmental agencies, notwithstanding the provisions of section 604.)

5. Impermissible Purposes

A consumer reporting agency may not furnish a consumer report to satisfy a requester's curiosity, or for use by a news reporter in preparing a newspaper or magazine article.

6. Agents

A. *General.* An agent[3] of a party with a "permissible purpose" may obtain a consumer report on behalf of his principal, where he is involved in the decision that gives rise to the permissible purpose. Such involvement may include the agent's making a decision (or taking action) for the principal, or assisting the principal in making the decision (*e.g.*, by evaluating information). In these circumstances, the agent is acting on behalf of the principal. In some cases, the agent and principal are referred to as "joint users." See discussion in section 603(f), *supra* (item 8).

B. *Real estate agent.* A real estate agent may obtain a consumer report on behalf of a seller, to evaluate the eligibility as a prospective purchaser of a subject who has expressed an interest in purchasing property from the seller.

C. *Private detective agency.* A private detective agency may obtain a consumer report as agent for its client while investigating a report subject that is a client's prospective employee, or in connection with advising a client concerning a business transaction with the report subject or in attempting to collect a debt owed its client by the subject of the report. In these circumstances, the detective agency is acting on behalf of its client.

D. *Rental clearance agency.* A rental clearance agency that obtains consumer reports to assist owners of residential properties in screening consumers as tenants, has a permissible purpose to obtain the reports, if it uses them in applying the landlord's criteria to approve or disapprove the subjects as tenant applicants. Similarly, an apartment manager investigating applicants for apartment rentals by a landlord may obtain consumer reports on these applicants.

E. *Attorney.* An attorney collecting a debt for a creditor client, including a party suing on a debt or collecting on behalf of a judgment creditor or lien creditor, has a permissible purpose to obtain a consumer report on the debtor to the same extent as the client.

Section 604—General

1. Furnishing of Consumer Reports to Other Consumer Reporting Agencies

A consumer reporting agency may furnish a consumer report to another consumer reporting agency for it to furnish pursuant to a subscriber's request. In these circumstances, one consumer reporting agency is acting on behalf of another.

2. Consumer's Permission not Needed

When permissible purposes exist, parties may obtain, and consumer reporting agencies may furnish, consumer reports without the consumers' permission or over their objection. Similarly, parties may furnish information concerning their transactions with consumers to consumer reporting agencies and others, and consumer reporting agencies may gather information, without consumers' permission.

3. User's Disclosure of Report to Subject Consumer

The FCRA does not prohibit a consumer report user from giving a copy of the report, or otherwise [sic] disclosing it, to the consumer who is the subject of the report.

Section 605—Obsolete Information

*"(a) Except as authorized under subsection (b), no consumer reporting agency may make any consumer report containing any of the following items of information * * *:*

(b) The provisions of subsection (a) are not applicable in the case of any consumer credit report to be used in connection with—

(1) a credit transaction involving, or which may reasonably be expected to involve, a principal amount of $50,000 or more;

(2) the underwriting of life insurance involving, or which may reasonably be expected to involve, a face amount of $50,000 or more; or

(3) the employment of any individual at an annual salary which equals [sic], or which may reasonably be expected to equal [sic] $20,000, or more."

1. General

Section 605(a) provides that most adverse information more than seven years old may not be reported, except in certain circumstances set out in section 605(b). With respect to delinquent accounts, accounts placed for collection, and accounts charged to profit and loss, there are many dates that could be deemed to commence seven year reporting periods. The discussion in subsections (a)(2), (a)(4), and (a)(6) is intended to set forth a clear, workable rule that effectuates Congressional intent.

2. Favorable Information

The Act imposes no time restriction on reporting of information that is not adverse.

3. Retention of Information in Files

Consumer reporting agencies may retain obsolete adverse information and furnish it in reports for purposes that are exempt under subsection (b) (*e.g.*, credit for a principal amount of $50,000 or more).

4. Use of Shorter Periods

The section does not require consumer reporting agencies to report adverse information for the time periods set forth, but only prohibits them from reporting adverse items beyond those time periods.

5. Inapplicability to Users

The section does not limit creditors or others from using adverse information that would be "obsolete" under its terms, because it applies only to reporting by consumer reporting agencies. Similarly, this section does not bar a credi-

---

[3] Of course agents and principals *are* bound by the Act.

tor's reporting such adverse obsolete information concerning its transactions or experiences with a consumer, because the report would not constitute a consumer report.

6. Indicating the Existence of Nonspecified, Obsolete Information

A consumer reporting agency may not furnish a consumer report indicating the existence of obsolete adverse information, even if no specific item is reported. For example, a consumer reporting agency may not communicate the existence of a debt older than seven years by reporting that a credit grantor cannot locate a debtor whose debt was charged off ten years ago.

7. Operative Dates

The times or dates set forth in this section, which relate to the occurrence of events involving adverse information, determine whether the item is obsolete. The date that the consumer reporting agency acquired the adverse information is irrelevant to how long that information may be reported.

Section 605(a)(1)—*"Cases under title 11 of the United States Code or under the Bankruptcy Act that, from the date of entry of the order for relief or the date of adjudication, as the case may be, antedate the report by more than 10 years."*

1. Relation to Other Subsections

The reporting of suits and judgments is governed by subsection (a)(2), the reporting of accounts placed for collection or charged to profit and loss is governed by subsection (a)(4), and the reporting of other delinquent accounts is governed by subsection (a)(6). Any such item, even if discharged in bankruptcy, may be reported separately for the applicable seven year period, while the existence of the bankruptcy filing may be reported for ten years.

2. Wage Earner Plans

Wage earner plans may be reported for ten years, because they are covered by Title 11 of the United States Code.

3. Date for Filing

A voluntary bankruptcy petition may be reported for ten years from the date that it is filed, because the filing of the petition constitutes the entry of an "order for relief" under this subsection, just like a filing under the Bankruptcy Act (11 U.S.C. 301).

Section 605(a)(2)—*"Suits and judgments which, from date of entry, antedate the report by more than seven years or until the governing statute of limitations has expired, whichever is the longer period."*

1. Operative Date

For a suit, the term "date of entry" means the date the suit was initiated. A protracted suit may be reported for more than seven years from the date it was entered, if the governing statute of limitations has not expired. For a judgment, the term "date of entry" means the date the judgment was rendered.

2. Paid Judgments

Paid judgments cannot be reported for more than seven years after the judgment was entered, because payment of the judgment eliminates any "governing statute of limitations" under this subsection that might otherwise lengthen the period.

Section 605(a)(3)—*"Paid tax liens which, from date of payment, antedate the report by more than seven years."*

1. Unpaid Liens

If a tax lien (or other lien) remains unsatisfied, it may be reported as long as it remains filed against the consumer, without limitation, because this subsection addresses only paid tax liens.

Section 605(a)(4)—*"Accounts placed for collection or charged to profit and loss which antedate the report by more than seven years."*

1. Placement for Collection

The term "placed for collection" means internal collection activity by the creditor, as well as placement with an outside collector, whichever occurs first. Sending of the initial past due notices does not constitute placement for collection. Placement for collection occurs when dunning notices or other collection efforts are initiated. The reporting period is not extended by assignment to another entity for further collection, or by a partial or full payment of the account. However, where a borrower brings his delinquent account to date and returns to his regular payment schedule, and later defaults again, a consumer reporting agency may disregard any collection activity with respect to the first delinquency and measure the reporting period from the date the account was placed for collection as a result of the borrower's ultimate default. A consumer's repayment agreement with a collection agency can be treated as a new account that has its own seven year period.

2. Charge to Profit and Loss

The term "charged to profit and loss" means action taken by the creditor to write off the account, and the applicable time period is measured from that event. If an account that was charged off is later paid in part or paid in full by the consumer, the reporting period of seven years from the charge-off is not extended by this subsequent payment.

3. Reporting of a Delinquent Account That is Later Placed for Collection or Charged to Profit and Loss

The fact that an account has been placed for collection or charged to profit and loss may be reported for seven years from the date that either of those events occurs, regardless of the date the account became delinquent. The fact of delinquency may also be reported for seven years from the date the account became delinquent.

Section 605(a)(5)—*"Records of arrest, indictment, or conviction of crime which, from date of disposition, release, or parole, antedate the report by more than seven years."*

1. Records

The term "records" means any information a consumer reporting agency has in its files relating to arrest, indictment or conviction of a crime.

2. Computation of Time Period

The seven year reporting period runs from the date of disposition, release or parole, as applicable. For example, if charges are dismissed at or before trial, or the consumer is acquitted, the date of such dismissal or acquittal is the date of disposition. If the consumer is convicted of a crime and sentenced to confinement, the date of release or placement on parole controls. (Confinement, whether continuing or resulting from revocation of parole, may be reported until seven years after the confinement is terminated.) The sentencing date controls for a convicted consumer whose sentence does not include confinement. The fact that information concerning the arrest, indictment, or conviction of crime is obtained by the reporting agency at a later date from a more recent source (such as a newspaper or interview) does not serve to extend this reporting period.

Section 605(a)(6)—*"Any other adverse item of information which antedates the report by more than seven years."*

1. Relation to Other Subsections

This section applies to all adverse information that is not covered by section 605(a) (1)–(5). For example, a delinquent account that has neither been placed for collection, nor charged to profit and loss, may be reported for seven years from the date of the last regularly scheduled payment. (Accounts placed for collection or charged to profit and loss may be reported for the time periods stated in section 605(a)(4).)

2. Non Tax Liens

Liens (other than paid tax liens) may be reported as long as they remain filed against the consumer or the consumer's property, and remain effective (under any applicable statute of limitations). (See discussion under section 605(a)(3), *supra*.)

Section 606—Disclosure of Investigative Consumer Reports

"(a) A person may not procure or cause to be prepared an investigative consumer report on any consumer unless—

(1) it is clearly and accurately disclosed to the consumer that an investigative consumer report including information as to his character, general reputation, personal characteristics, and mode of

living, whichever are applicable, may be made, and such disclosure (A) is made in a writing mailed, or otherwise delivered, to the consumer, not later than three days after the date on which the report was first requested, and (B) includes a statement informing the consumer of his right to request the additional disclosures provided for under subsection (b) of this section; or

(2) the report is to be used for employment purposes for which the consumer has not specifically applied.

(b) Any person who procures or causes to be prepared an investigative consumer report on any consumer shall, upon written request made by the consumer within a reasonable period of time after receipt by him of the disclosure required by subsection (a)(1), make a complete and accurate disclosure of the nature and scope of the investigation requested. This disclosure shall be made in a writing mailed, or otherwise delivered, to the consumer not later than five days after the date on which the request for such disclosure was received from the consumer or such report was first requested, whichever is the later.

(c) No person may be held liable for any violation of subsection (a) or (b) of this section if he shows by a preponderance of the evidence that at the time of the violation he maintained reasonable procedures to assure compliance with subsection (a) or (b)."

1. Relation to Other Sections

The term "investigative consumer report" is defined at section 603(e) to mean a consumer report, all or a portion of which contains information obtained through personal interviews (in person or by telephone) with persons other than the subject, which information relates to the subject's character, general reputation, personal characteristics or mode of living.

2. Inapplicability to Consumer Reporting Agencies

The section applies only to report users, not consumer reporting agencies. The FCRA does not require consumer reporting agencies to inform consumers that information will be gathered or that reports will be furnished concerning them.

3. Inapplicability to Noninvestigative Consumer Reports

The section does not apply to noninvestigative reports.

4. Exemptions

An employer who orders investigative consumer reports on a current employee who has not applied for a job change need not notify the employee, because the term "employment purposes" is defined to include "promotion, reassignment or retention" and subsection (b) provides that the disclosure requirements do not apply to "employment purposes for which the consumer has not specifically applied."

5. Form and Delivery of Notice

The notice must be in writing and delivered to the consumer. The user may include the disclosure in an application for employment, insurance, or credit, if it is clear and conspicuous and not obscured by other language. A user may send the required notice via first class mail. The notice must be mailed or otherwise delivered to the consumer not later than three days after the report was first requested.

6. Content of Notice of Right to Disclosure

The notice must clearly and accurately disclose that an "investigative consumer report" including information as to the consumer's character, general reputation, personal characteristics and mode of living (whichever are applicable), may be made. The disclosure must also state that an investigative consumer report involves personal interviews with sources such as neighbors, friends, or associates. The notice may include any additional, accurate information about the report, such as the types of interviews that will be conducted. The notice must include a statement informing the consumer of the right to request complete and accurate disclosure of the nature and scope of the investigation.

7. Content of Disclosure of Report

When the consumer requests disclosure of the "nature and scope" of the investigation, such disclosure must include a complete and accurate description of the types of questions asked, the number and types of persons interviewed, and the name and address of the investigating agency. The user need not disclose the names of sources of information, nor must it provide the consumer with a copy of the report. A report user that provides the consumer with a blank copy of the standardized form used to transmit the report from the agency to the user complies with the requirement that it disclose the "nature" of the investigation.

Section 607—Compliance Procedures

"(a) Every consumer reporting agency shall maintain reasonable procedures designed to avoid violations of section 605 and to limit the furnishing of consumer reports to the purposes listed under section 604. These procedures shall require that prospective users of the information identify themselves, certify the purposes for which the information is sought, and certify that the information will be used for no other purpose. Every consumer reporting agency shall make a reasonable effort to verify the identity of a new prospective user and the uses certified by such prospective user prior to furnishing such user a consumer report. No consumer reporting agency may furnish a consumer report to any person if it has reasonable grounds for believing that the consumer report will not be used for a purpose listed in Section 604.

(b) Whenever a consumer reporting agency prepares a consumer report it shall follow reasonable procedures to assure maximum possible accuracy of the information concerning the individual about whom the report relates."

1. Procedures to Avoid Reporting Obsolete Information

A. *General.* A consumer reporting agency should establish procedures with its sources of adverse information that will avoid the risk of reporting obsolete information. For example, the agency should either require a creditor to supply the date an account was placed for collection or charged off, or the agency should use a conservative date for such placement or charge off (such as the date of the last regularly scheduled payment), to be sure of complying with the statute.

B. *Retention of obsolete information for reporting in excepted circumstances.* If a consumer reporting agency retains adverse information in its files that is "obsolete" under section 605(a) (*e.g.*, information about a satisfied judgment that is more than seven years old), so that it may be reported for use in transactions described by section 605(b) (*i.e.*, applications for credit or life insurance for $50,000 or more, or employment at an annual salary of $20,000 or more), it must have procedural safeguards to avoid reporting the information except in those situations. The procedure should require that such obsolete information be released only after an internal decision that its release will not violate section 605.

2. Procedures to Avoid Reporting for Impermissible Purposes

A. *Verification.* A consumer reporting agency should have a system to verify that it is dealing with a legitimate business having a "permissible purpose" for the information reported. What constitutes adequate verification will vary with the circumstances. If the consumer reporting agency is not familiar with the user, appropriate procedures might require an on-site visit to the user's place of business, or a check of the user's references.

B. *Required certification by user.* A consumer reporting agency should adopt procedures that require prospective report users to identify themselves, certify the purpose for which the information is sought, and certify that the information will be used for no other purpose. A consumer reporting agency should determine initially that users have permissible purposes and ascertain what those purposes are. It should obtain a specific, written certification that the recipient will obtain reports for those purposes and no others. The user's certification that the report will be used for no other purposes should expressly prohibit the user from sharing the report or providing it to anyone else, other than the subject of the report or to a joint user having the same purpose. A consumer reporting agency should refuse to provide reports to those refusing to provide such certification.

C. *Blanket or individual certification.* Once the consumer reporting agency obtains a certification from a user (*e.g.*, a creditor) that typically has a permissible purpose for receiving a consumer report, stating that it will use those reports only for specified permissible purposes (*e.g.*, for credit or employment purposes), a certification of purpose need not be furnished for each individual report obtained, provided there is no reason to believe the user may be violating its certification. However, in furnishing reports to users that typically could have both permissible and impermissible purposes for ordering consumer reports (*e.g.*, attorneys and detective agencies), the consumer reporting agency must require the user to provide a separate certification each time it requests a consumer report.

D. *Procedures to avoid recipients' abuse of certification.* When doubt arises concerning any user's compliance with its contractual certification, a consumer reporting agency must take steps to insure compliance, such as requiring a separate, advance certification for each report it furnishes that user, or auditing that user to verify that it is obtaining reports only for permissible purposes. A consumer reporting agency must cease furnishing consumer reports to users who repeatedly request consumer reports for impermissible purposes.

E. *Unauthorized access.* A consumer reporting agency should take several other steps when doubt arises concerning whether a user is obtaining reports for a permissible purpose from a computerized system. If it appears that a third party, not a subscriber, has obtained unauthorized access to the system, the consumer reporting agency should take appropriate steps such as altering authorized users' means of access, such as codes and passwords, and making random checks to ensure that future reports are obtained only for permissible purposes. If a subscriber has inadvertently sought reports for impermissible purposes or its employee has obtained reports without a permissible purpose, it would be appropriate for the consumer reporting agency to alter the subscriber's means of access, and require an individual written certification of the permissible purpose for each report requested or randomly verify such purposes. A consumer reporting agency should refuse to furnish any further reports to a user that repeatedly violates certifications.

F. *Use of computerized systems.* A consumer reporting agency may furnish consumer reports to users via terminals, provided the consumer reporting agency has taken the necessary steps to ensure that the users have a permissible purpose to receive the reports. (The agency would have to record the identity of consumer report recipients for each consumer, to be able to make any disclosures required under section 609(a)(3) or section 611(d)).

G. *Activity reports.* If a consumer reporting agency provides "activity reports" on all customers who have open-end accounts with a credit grantor, it must make certain that the credit grantor always notifies the agency when accounts are closed and paid in full, to avoid furnishing reports on former customers or other customers for whom the credit grantor lacks a permissible purpose. (See also discussion in section 604(3)(A), item 1, *supra*.)

3. Reasonable Procedures to Assure Maximum Possible Accuracy

A. *General.* The section does not require error free consumer reports. If a consumer reporting agency accurately transcribes, stores and communicates consumer information received from a source that it reasonably believes to be reputable, and which is credible on its face, the agency does not violate this section simply by reporting an item of information that turns out to be inaccurate. However, when a consumer reporting agency learns or should reasonably be aware of errors in its reports that may indicate systematic problems (by virtue of information from consumers, report users, from periodic review of its reporting system, or otherwise) it must review its procedures for assuring accuracy. Examples of errors that would require such review are the issuance of a consumer report pertaining entirely to a consumer other than the one on whom a report was requested, and the issuance of a consumer report containing information on two or more consumers (*e.g.*, information that was mixed in the file) in response to a request for a report on only one of those consumers.

B. *Required steps to improve accuracy.* If the agency's review of its procedures reveals, or the agency should reasonably be aware of, steps it can take to improve the accuracy of its reports at a reasonable cost, it must take any such steps. It should correct inaccuracies that come to its attention. A consumer reporting agency must also adopt reasonable procedures to eliminate systematic errors that it knows about, or should reasonably be aware of, resulting from procedures followed by its sources of information. For example, if a particular credit grantor has often furnished a significant amount of erroneous consumer account information, the agency must require the creditor to revise its procedures to correct whatever problems cause the errors or stop reporting information from that creditor.

C. *Use of automatic data processing equipment.* Consumer reporting agencies that use automatic data processing equipment (particularly for long distance transmission of information) should have reasonable procedures to assure that the data is accurately converted into a machine-readable format and not distorted by machine malfunction or transmission failure. Reasonable security procedures must be adopted to minimize the possibility that computerized consumer information will be stolen or altered by either authorized or unauthorized users of the information system.

D. *Reliability of sources.* Whether a consumer reporting agency may rely on the accuracy of information from a source depends on the circumstances. This section does not hold a consumer reporting agency responsible where an item of information that it receives from a source that it reasonably believes to be reputable appears credible on its face, and is transcribed, stored and communicated as provided by that source. Requirements are more stringent where the information furnished appears implausible or inconsistent, or where procedures for furnishing it seem likely to result in inaccuracies, or where the consumer reporting agency has had numerous problems regarding information from a particular source.

E. *Undesignated information in credit transactions.* "Undesignated information" means all credit history information in a married (or formerly married) consumer's file, which was not reported to the consumer reporting agency with a designation indicating that the information relates to either the consumer's joint or individual credit experience. The question arises what is meant by reasonable procedures under this section for treatment of credit history in the file of only one (present or former) spouse (usually the husband) that has not been designated by the procedure in Regulation B, 12 CFR 202.10, which implements the Equal Credit Opportunity Act. (This situation exists only for certain credit history file information compiled before June 1, 1977, and certain accounts opened before that date.) A consumer reporting agency may report information solely in the file of spouse A, when spouse B applies for a separate extension of credit, only if such information relates to accounts for which spouse B was either a user or was contractually liable, or the report recipient has a permissible purpose for a report on spouse A. A consumer reporting agency may not supply all undesignated information from the file of a consumer's spouse in response to a request for a report on the consumer, because some or all of that information may not relate to both spouses. Consumer reporting agencies must honor without charge the request of a married or formerly married individual that undesignated information (that appears only in the files of the individual's present or former spouse) be segregated—*i.e.*, placed in a separate file that is accessible under that individual's name. This procedure insures greater accuracy and protection of the privacy of spouses than does the automatic reporting of undesignated information.

F. *Reporting of credit obligation*—(1) *Past due accounts.* A consumer reporting agency must employ reasonable procedures to keep its file current on past due accounts (*e.g.*, by requiring its creditors to notify the credit bureau when a previously past due account has been paid or discharged in bankruptcy), but its failure to show such activity in particular instances, despite the maintenance of reasonable procedures to keep files current, does not violate this section. For example, a consumer reporting agency that reports accurately in 1985 that as of 1983 the consumer owed a retail store money, without mentioning that the consumer eventually paid the debt, does not violate this section if it was not informed by the store or the consumer of the later payment.

(2) *Significant, verified information.* A consumer reporting agency must report significant, verified information it possesses about an item. For instance, a consumer reporting agency may continue to report a paid account that was previously delinquent, but should also report that the account has been paid. Similarly, a consumer reporting agency may include delinquencies on debts discharged in bankruptcy in consumer reports, but must accurately note the status of the debt (*e.g.*, discharged, voluntarily repaid). Finally, if a reported bankruptcy has been dismissed, that fact should be reported.

(3) *Guarantor obligations.* Personal guarantees for obligations incurred by others (including a corporation) may be included in a consumer report on the individual who is the guarantor. The report should accurately reflect the individual's involvement (*e.g.*, as guarantor of the corporate debt).

4. Effect of Criminal Sanctions

Notwithstanding the fact that section 619 provides criminal sanctions against persons who knowingly and willfully obtain information on a consumer from a consumer reporting agency under false pretenses, a consumer reporting agency must follow reasonable procedures to limit the furnishing of reports to those with permissible purposes.

5. Disclosure of Credit Denial

When reporting that a consumer was denied a benefit (such as credit), a consumer reporting agency need not report the reasons for the denial.

6. Content of Report

A consumer report need not be tailored to the user's needs. It may contain any information that is complete, accurate, and not obsolete on the consumer who is the subject of the report. A consumer report may include an account that was discharged in bankruptcy (as well as the bankruptcy itself), as long as it reports a zero balance due to reflect the fact that the consumer is no longer liable for the discharged debt. A consumer report may include a list of recipients of reports on the consumer who is the subject of the report.

7. Completeness of Reports

Consumer reporting agencies are not required to include all existing derogatory or favorable information about a consumer in their reports. (See, however, discussion in section 611, item 14, *infra*, concerning conveying consumer dispute statements.) However, a consumer reporting agency may not mislead its subscribers as to the completeness of its reports by deleting nonderogatory information and not disclosing its policy of making such deletions.

8. User Notice of Adverse Action Based on a Consumer Report

A consumer reporting agency need not require users of its consumer reports to provide any notice to consumers against whom adverse action is taken based on a consumer report. The FCRA imposes such notice requirements directly on users, under the circumstances set out in section 615.

Section 608—Disclosures to Governmental Agencies

"Notwithstanding the provisions of section 604, a consumer reporting agency may furnish identifying information respecting any consumer limited to his name, address, former addresses, places of employment, or former places of employment, to a governmental agency."

1. Permissible Purpose Necessary for Additional Information

A consumer reporting agency may furnish limited identifying information concerning a consumer to a governmental agency (*e.g.*, an agency seeking a fugitive from justice) even if that agency does not have a "permissible purpose" under section 604 to receive a consumer report. However, a governmental agency must have a permissible purpose in order to obtain information beyond what is authorized by this section.

2. Entities Covered by Section

The term "governmental agency" includes federal, state, county and municipal agencies, and grand juries. Only governmental agencies may obtain disclosures of identifying information under this section.

Section 609—Disclosures to Consumers

"(a) Every consumer reporting agency shall, upon request and proper identification of any consumer, clearly and accurately disclose to the consumer:

(1) The nature and substance of all information (except medical information) in its files on the consumer at the time of the request.

(2) The sources of the information; except that the sources of information acquired solely for use in preparing an investigative consumer report and actually used for no other purpose need not be disclosed: Provided, That in the event an action is brought under this title, such sources shall be available to the plaintiff under appropriate discovery procedures in the court in which the action is brought.

(3) The recipients of any consumer report on the consumer which it has furnished

(A) for employment purposes within the two-year period preceding the request, and

(B) for any other purpose within the six-month period preceding the request.

(b) The requirements of subsection (a) respecting the disclosure of sources of information and the recipients of consumer reports do not apply to information received or consumer reports furnished prior to the effective date of this title except to the extent that the matter involved is contained in the files of the consumer reporting agency on that date."

1. Relation to Other Sections

This section states what consumer reporting agencies must disclose to consumers, upon request and proper identification. Section 610 sets forth the conditions under which those disclosures must be made, and section 612 sets forth the circumstances under which consumer reporting agencies may charge for making such disclosures. The term "file" as used in section 609(a)(1) is defined in section 603(g). The term "investigative consumer report," which is used in section 609(a)(2), is defined in section 603(e). The term "medical information," which is used in section 609(a)(1), is defined in section 603(i).

2. Proper Identification

A consumer reporting agency must take reasonable steps to verify the identity of an individual seeking disclosure under this section.

3. Manner of "Proper Identification"

If a consumer provides sufficient identifying information, the consumer reporting agency cannot insist that the consumer execute a "request for interview" form, or provide the items listed on it, as a prerequisite to disclosure. However, the agency may use a form to identify consumers requesting disclosure if it does not use the form to inhibit disclosure, or to obtain any waiver of the consumers' rights. A consumer reporting agency may provide disclosure by telephone without a written request, if the consumer is properly identified, but may insist on a written request before providing such disclosure.

4. Power of Attorney

A consumer reporting agency may disclose a consumer's file to a third party authorized by the consumer's written power of attorney to obtain the disclosure, if the third party presents adequate identification and fulfills other applicable conditions of disclosure. However, the agency may also disclose the information directly to the consumer.

5. Nature of Disclosure Required

A consumer reporting agency must disclose the nature and substance of all items in the consumer's file, no matter how or where they are stored (*e.g.*, in other offices of the consumer reporting agency). The consumer reporting agency must have personnel trained to explain to the consumer any information furnished in accordance with the Act. Particularly when the file includes coded information that would be meaningless to the consumer, the agency's personnel must assist the consumer to understand the disclosures. Any summary must not mischaracterize the nature of any item of information in the file. The consumer reporting agency is not required to provide a copy of the file, or any other written disclosure, or to read the file verbatim to the consumer or to permit the consumer to examine any information in its files. A consumer reporting agency may choose to usually comply with the FCRA in writing, by providing a copy of the file to the consumer or otherwise.

6. Medical Information

Medical information includes information obtained with the consumer's consent from physicians and medical facilities, but does not include comments on a consumer's health by non-medical personnel. A consumer reporting agency is not required to disclose medical information in its files to consumers, but may do so. Alternatively, a consumer reporting agency may inform consumers that there is medical information in the files concerning them and supply the name of the doctor or other source of the information. Consumer reporting agencies may also disclose such information to a physician of the consumer's choice, upon the consumer's written instructions pursuant to section 604(2).

7. Ancillary Information.*

A consumer reporting agency is not required to disclose information consisting of an audit trail of changes it makes in the consumer's file, rather is a system of analyzing that information for the credit bureau's client. For a fee, the credit bureau applies a statistical "model" to the information in its files and (generally combined with a full credit report) provides the resulting number ("score") to the client. The score does not exist in the file until that function is performed, and is not retained by the credit bureau after it is provided to the bureau's client.

The industry commenters also argued that the disclosure of risk scores would be costly to the credit-granting and credit-reporting industries, and further contended that the benefits to the public were uncertain and (if they existed at all) far outweighed by the costs. Finally, they noted that consumers already have access to information much more significant than a numerical score—the underlying information in the credit file (under Section 609) and a statement of the reasons why any user rejected their credit applications (under the Equal Credit Opportunity Act ("ECOA") and its implementing Regulation B).

The consumer representatives emphasized the quote from Rep. Sullivan on which the Commission had relied in its February 1992 opinion. They pressed the view that it is only fair for consumers to have risk scores if credit bureau users are receiving them, and contended that consumers should not be deprived of disclosure of billing records, or the contents of a consumer relations folder, if the information is not from consumer reports and will not be used in preparing future consumer reports. Such data is not included in the term "information in the files" which must be disclosed to the consumer pursuant to this section. A consumer reporting agency must disclose claims report information only if it has appeared in consumer reports.

8. Information on Other Consumers

The consumer has no right to information in the consumer reporting agency's files on other individuals, because the disclosure must be lim-

---

* *Ed. note*: Amended at 57 Fed. Reg. 4935 (Feb. 11, 1992). The amendment revises the third sentence of comment 7 of section 609 of the commentary. Before amended the third sentence read: "Similarly, a point score that is provided to evaluate the report for its recipient (and/or the scoring system used to calculate the score) need not be disclosed, because the score is not used in preparing future reports." On September 1, 1995, the FTC reversed its position of February 1992, regarding the disclosure of "risk scores," numerical scores generated by the application of a model to the information in a consumer's file, and furnished by the reporting agency to its clients. The FTC now concludes that such scores are not "information in the file" and need not be disclosed to the consumer. This change is effected by another amendment of Comment 7 to section 609 of the commentary, and by a new Comment 12.

The Supplementary Information published along with the amendments at 60 Fed. Reg. 45659, Sept. 1, 1995, follows:

> The industry commenters argued strongly that section 609 does not literally require the disclosure of risk scores. They contended that a credit bureau's risk score is not "information * * * in its files * * * at the time of the request" but

risk scores simply because credit bureaus do not retain them.

Based on the comments, the Commission has decided to reinstate its original position that Section 609 does not require a credit bureau to disclose risk scores because they are not "information . . . in its files on the consumer at the time of the request" by the consumer for file disclosure. Section 603(g) defines the term "file" to mean "all the information on (the) consumer *recorded and retained* by a consumer reporting agency regardless of how the information is stored." (Emphasis added.) In analyzing the application of Section 609 to a risk score, the Commission has considered the process involved in generating a risk score. The comments indicate that a risk score is not "recorded and retained" by the credit bureau; rather it is produced when the bureau applies the scoring model to the actual data in the consumer's credit history and provides the resulting numerical score to its client who pays to have that function performed by the bureau. In addition to not being in the credit bureau "files", the score does not even exist "at the time of the request."

ited to information "on the consumer." However, all information in the files of the consumer making the request must be disclosed, including information about another individual that relates to the consumer (*e.g.*, concerning that individual's dealings with the subject of the consumer report).

9. Disclosure of Sources of Information

Consumer reporting agencies must disclose the sources of information, except for sources of information acquired solely for use in preparing an investigative consumer report and actually used for no other purpose. When it has used information from another consumer reporting agency, the other agency should be reported as a source.

10. Disclosure of Recipients of Consumer Reports

Consumer reporting agencies must maintain records of recipients of prior consumer reports sufficient to enable them to meet the FCRA's requirements that they disclose the identity of recipients of prior consumer reports. A consumer reporting agency that furnishes a consumer report directly to a report user at the request of another consumer reporting agency must disclose the identity of the user that was the ultimate recipient of the report, not the other agency that acted as an intermediary in procuring the report.

11. Disclosure of Recipients of Prescreened Lists

A consumer reporting agency must furnish to a consumer requesting file disclosure the identity of recipients of any prescreened lists that contained the consumer's name when submitted to creditors (or other users) by the consumer reporting agency.

12. Risk Scores.**

A consumer reporting agency is not required to disclose a risk score (or other numerical evalu-

---

** *Ed. Note*: Amended at 60 Fed. Reg. 45659, Sept. 1, 1995. The amendment deletes a reference to risk scoring. A new comment 12, on risk scores, has been added to Section 609. The former commentary included a third sentence which read: "However, a risk score (or other numerical evaluation, however named) that is reported by a consumer reporting agency to a client to assist in evaluating a consumer's eligibility for credit (or other permissible purpose) must be disclosed (along with an explanation of the risk score), because, as indicated in the legislative history, each consumer should have access to all such information regardless of form. [See 116 Cong. Rec. 36572 (1970) (remarks of Rep. Sullivan.)]"

This third sentence was amended by 57 Fed. Reg. 4935 (Feb. 11, 1992).

ation, however named) that is provided to the agency's client (based on an analysis of data on the consumer) but not retained by the agency. Such a score is not information "in (the agency's) files at the time of the request" by the consumer for full disclosure.

Section 610—Conditions of Disclosure

"(a) A consumer reporting agency shall make the disclosures required under section 609 during normal business hours and on reasonable notice.

(b) The disclosures required under section 609 shall be made to the consumer—

(1) in person if he appears in person and furnishes proper identification; or

(2) by telephone if he has made a written request, with proper identification, for telephone disclosure and the toll charge, if any, for the telephone call is prepaid by or charged directly to the consumer.

(c) Any consumer reporting agency shall provide trained personnel to explain to the consumer any information furnished to him pursuant to section 609.

(d) The consumer shall be permitted to be accompanied by one other person of his choosing, who shall furnish reasonable identification. A consumer reporting agency may require the consumer to furnish a written statement granting permission to the consumer reporting agency to discuss the consumer's file in such person's presence.

(e) Except as provided in section 616 and 617, no consumer may bring any action or proceeding in the nature of defamation, invasion of privacy, or negligence with respect to the reporting of information against any consumer reporting agency, any user of information or any person who furnishes information to a consumer reporting agency, based on information disclosed pursuant to section 609, 610, or 615, except as to false information furnished with malice or willful intent to injure such consumers."

1. Time of Disclosure

A consumer reporting agency must make disclosures during normal business hours, upon reasonable notice. However, the consumer reporting agency may waive reasonable notice, and the consumer may agree to disclosure outside of normal business hours. A consumer reporting agency may make in-person disclosure to consumers who have made appointments ahead of other consumers, because the disclosures are only required to be made "on reasonable notice."

2. Extra Conditions Prohibited

A consumer reporting agency may not add conditions not set out in the FCRA as a prerequisite to the required disclosure.

Before that amendment, disclosure of "point scores" or the scoring system used to produce them, was not required because "the score is not used in preparing future reports."

3. Manner of Disclosure

A consumer reporting agency may, with the consumer's actual or implied consent, meet its disclosure obligations by mail, in lieu of the in-person or telephone disclosures specified in the statute.

4. Disclosure in the Presence of Third Parties

When the consumer requests disclosure in a third party's presence, the consumer reporting agency may require that a consumer sign an authorization before such disclosure is made. The consumer may choose the third party to accompany him or her for the disclosure.

5. Expense of Telephone Calls

A consumer reporting agency is not required to pay the telephone charge for a telephone interview with a consumer obtaining disclosure.

6. Qualified Defamation Privilege

The privilege extended by subsection 610(e) does not apply to an action brought by a consumer if the action is based on information not disclosed pursuant to sections 609, 610 or 615. A disclosure to a consumer's representative (*e.g.*, based on the consumer's power of attorney) constitutes "information disclosed pursuant to section 609" and is thus covered by this privilege.

Section 611—Procedure in Case of Disputed Accuracy

"(a) If the completeness or accuracy of any item of information contained in his file is disputed by a consumer, and such dispute is directly conveyed to the consumer reporting agency by the consumer, the consumer reporting agency shall within a reasonable period of time reinvestigate and record the current status of that information unless it has reasonable grounds to believe that the dispute by the consumer is frivolous or irrelevant. If after such reinvestigation such information is found to be inaccurate or can no longer be verified, the consumer reporting agency shall promptly delete such information. The presence of contradictory information in the consumer's file does not in and of itself constitute reasonable grounds for believing the dispute is frivolous or irrelevant.

(b) If the reinvestigation does not resolve the dispute, the consumer may file a brief statement setting forth the nature of the dispute. The consumer reporting agency may limit such statements to not more than one hundred words if it provides the consumer with assistance in writing a clear summary of the dispute.

(c) Whenever a statement of a dispute is filed, unless there is [sic] reasonable grounds to believe that it is frivolous or irrelevant, the consumer reporting agency shall, in any subsequent consumer report containing the information in question, clearly note that it is disputed by the consumer and provide either the consumer's statement or a clear and accurate codification or summary thereof.

(d) Following any deletion of information which is found to be inaccurate or whose accuracy can no longer be verified or any notation as to disputed information, the consumer reporting agency shall, at the request of the consumer, furnish notification that the item has been deleted or the statement, codification or summary pursuant to subsection (b) or (c) to any person specifically designated by the consumer who has within two years prior thereto received a consumer report for employment purposes, or within six months prior thereto received a consumer report for any other purpose, which contained the deleted or disputed information. The consumer reporting agency shall clearly and conspicuously disclose to the consumer his rights to make such a request. Such disclosure shall be made at or prior to the time the information is deleted or the consumer's statement regarding the disputed information is received."

1. Relation to Other Sections

This section sets forth procedures consumer reporting agencies must follow if a consumer conveys a dispute of the completeness or accuracy of any item of information in the consumer's file to the consumer reporting agency. Section 609 provides for disclosures by consumer reporting agencies to consumers, and section 610 sets forth conditions of disclosure. Section 612 permits a consumer reporting agency to impose charges for certain disclosures, including the furnishing of certain information to recipients of prior reports, as provided by section 611(d).

2. Proper Reinvestigation

A consumer reporting agency conducting a reinvestigation must make a good faith effort to determine the accuracy of the disputed item or items. At a minimum, it must check with the original sources or other reliable sources of the disputed information and inform them of the nature of the consumer's dispute. In reinvestigating and attempting to verify a disputed credit transaction, a consumer reporting agency may rely on the accuracy of a creditor's ledger sheets and need not require the creditor to produce documentation such as the actual signed sales slips. Depending on the nature of the dispute, reinvestigation and verification may require more than asking the original source of the disputed information the same question and receiving the same answer. If the original source is contacted for reinvestigation, the consumer reporting agency should at least explain to the source that the original statement has been disputed, state the consumer's position, and then ask whether the source would confirm the information, qualify it, or accept the consumer's explanation.

3. Complaint of Insufficient File, or Lack of File

The FCRA does not require a consumer reporting agency to add new items of information to its file. A consumer reporting agency is not required to create new files on consumers for whom it has no file, nor is it required to add new lines of information about new accounts not reflected in an existing file, because the section permits the consumer to dispute only the completeness or accuracy of particular items of information in the file. If a consumer reporting agency chooses to add lines of information at the consumer's request, it may charge a fee for doing so.

4. Explanation of Extenuating Circumstances

A consumer reporting agency has no duty to reinvestigate, or take any other action under this section, if a consumer merely provides a reason for a failure to pay a debt (*e.g.*, sudden illness or layoff), and does not challenge the accuracy or completeness of the item of information in the file relating to a debt. Most creditors are aware that a variety of circumstances may render consumers unable to repay credit obligations. Although a consumer reporting agency is not required to accept a consumer dispute statement that does not challenge the accuracy or completeness of an item in the consumer's file, it may accept such a statement and may charge a fee for doing so.

5. Reinvestigation of a Debt

A consumer reporting agency must reinvestigate if a consumer conveys to it a dispute concerning the validity or status of a debt, such as whether the debt was owed by the consumer, or whether the debt had subsequently been paid. For example, if a consumer alleges that a judgment reflected in the file as unpaid has been satisfied, or notifies a consumer reporting agency that a past due obligation reflected in the file as unpaid was subsequently paid, the consumer reporting agency must reinvestigate the matter. If a file reflects a debt discharged in bankruptcy without reflecting subsequent reaffirmation and payment of that debt, a consumer may require that the item be reinvestigated.

6. Status of a Debt

The consumer reporting agency must, upon reinvestigation, "record the current status" of the disputed item. This requires inclusion of any information relating to a change in status of an ongoing matter (*e.g.*, that a credit account had been closed, that a debt shown as past due had subsequently been paid or discharged in bankruptcy, or that a debt shown as discharged in bankruptcy was later reaffirmed and/or paid).

7. Dispute Conveyed to Party Other Than the Consumer Reporting Agency

A consumer reporting agency is required to take action under this section only if the consumer directly communicates a dispute to it. It is not required to respond to a dispute of information that the consumer merely conveys to others (*e.g.*, to a source of information). (But see, however, discussion in section 607, item 3A, of consumer reporting agencies' duties to correct errors that come to their attention.)

8. Dispute Conveyed to the Consumer Reporting Agency by a Party Other Than the Consumer

A consumer reporting agency need not reinvestigate a dispute about a consumer's file raised by any third party, because the obligation under the section arises only where an "item of information in his file is disputed by the consumer."

9. Consumer Disclosures and Adverse Action Not Prerequisites to Reinvestigation Duty

A consumer reporting agency's obligation to reinvestigate disputed items is not contingent upon the consumer's having been denied a benefit or having asserted any rights under the FCRA other than disputing items of information.

10. Reasonable Period of Time

A consumer reporting agency is required to reinvestigate and record the current status of disputed information within a reasonable period of time after the consumer conveys the dispute to it. Although consumer reporting agencies are able to reinvestigate most disputes within 30 days, a "reasonable time" for a particular reinvestigation may be shorter or longer depending on the circumstances of the dispute. For example, where the consumer provides documentary evidence (*e.g.*, a certified copy of a court record to show that a judgment has been paid) when submitting the dispute, the creditor may require a shorter time to reinvestigate. On the other hand, where the dispute is more complicated than normal (*e.g.*, the consumer alleges in good faith that a creditor has falsified its report of the consumer's account history because of a personal grudge), the "reasonable time" needed to conduct the reinvestigation may be longer.

11. Frivolous or Irrelevant

The mere presence of contradictory information in the file does not provide the consumer reporting agency "reasonable grounds to believe that the dispute by the consumer is frivolous or irrelevant." A consumer reporting agency must assume a consumer's dispute is bona fide, unless there is evidence to the contrary. Such evidence may constitute receipt of letters from consumers disputing all information in their files without providing any allegations concerning the specific items in the files, or of several letters in similar format that indicate that a particular third party (*e.g.*, a "credit repair" operator) is counselling consumers to dispute all items in their files, regardless of whether the information is known to be accurate. The agency is not required to repeat a reinvestigation that it has previously conducted simply because the consumer reiterates a dispute about the same item of information, unless the consumer provides additional evidence that the item is inaccurate or incomplete, or alleges changed circumstances.

12. Deletion of Accurate Information That has not Been Disputed

The consumer reporting agency is not required to delete accurate information that could not be verified upon reinvestigation, if it has not been "disputed by a consumer." For example, if a creditor deletes adverse information from its files with the result that information could not be reverified if disputed, it is still permissible for a consumer reporting agency to report it (subject to the obsolescence provisions of section 605) until it is disputed.

13. Consumer Dispute Statements on Multiple Items

A consumer who disputes multiple items of information in his file may submit a one hundred word statement as to each disputed item.

14. Conveying Dispute Statements to Recipients of Subsequent Reports.

A consumer reporting agency may not merely tell the recipient of a subsequent report containing disputed information that the consumer's statement is on file but will be provided only if requested, because subsection (c) requires the agency to provide either the statement or "a clear and accurate codification or summary thereof."

Section 612—Charges for Certain Disclosures

"A consumer reporting agency shall make all disclosures pursuant to section 609 and furnish all consumer reports pursuant to section 611(d) without charge to the consumer if, within thirty days after receipt by such consumer of a notification pursuant to section 615 or notification from a debt collection agency affiliated with such consumer reporting agency stating that the consumer's credit rating may be or has been adversely affected, the consumer makes a request under section 609 or 611(d). Otherwise, the consumer reporting agency may impose a reasonable charge on the consumer for making disclosure to such consumer pursuant to section 609, the charge for which shall be indicated to the consumer prior to making disclosure; and for furnishing notifications, statements, summaries, or codifications to persons designated by the consumer pursuant to section 611(d), the charge for which shall be indicated to the consumer prior to furnishing such information and shall not exceed the charge that the consumer reporting agency would impose on each designated recipient for a consumer report except that no charge may be made for notifying such persons of the deletion of information which is found to be inaccurate or which can no longer be verified."

1. Irrelevance of Subsequent Grant of Credit or Reason For Denial

A consumer denied credit because of a consumer report from a consumer reporting agency has the right to a free disclosure from that agency within 30 days of receipt of the section 615(a) notice, even if credit was subsequently granted or the basis of the denial was that the references supplied by the consumer are too few or too new to appear in the credit file.

2. Charge for Reinvestigation Prohibited

This section does not permit consumer reporting agencies to charge for making the reinvestigation or following other procedures required by section 611 (a)–(c).

3. Permissible Charges for Services Requested by Consumers

A consumer reporting agency may charge fees for creating files on consumers at their request, or for other services not required by the FCRA that are requested by consumers.

Section 613—Public Record Information for Employment Purposes

"A consumer reporting agency which furnishes a consumer report for employment purposes and which for that purpose compiles and reports items of information on consumers which are matters of public record and are likely to have an adverse effect upon a consumer's ability to obtain employment shall—
(1) at the time such public record information is reported to the user of such consumer report, notify the consumer of the fact that public record information is being reported by the consumer reporting agency, together with the name and address of the person to whom such information is being reported; or
(2) maintain strict procedures designed to insure that whenever public record information which is likely to have an adverse effect on a consumer's ability to obtain employment is reported it is complete and up to date. For purposes of this paragraph, items of public record relating to arrests, indictments, convictions, suits, tax liens, and outstanding judgments shall be considered up to date if the current public record status of the item at the time of the report is reported."

1. Relation to Other Sections

A consumer reporting agency that complies with section 613(1) must also follow reasonable procedures to assure maximum possible accuracy, as required by section 607(b).

2. Alternate Methods of Compliance

A consumer reporting agency that furnishes public record information for employment purposes must comply with either subsection (1) or (2), but need not comply with both.

3. Information From Another Consumer Reporting Agency

If a consumer reporting agency uses information or reports from other consumer reporting agencies in a report for employment purposes, it must comply with this section.

4. Method of Providing Notice

A consumer reporting agency may use first class mail to provide the notice required by subsection (1).

5. Waiver

The procedures required by this section cannot be waived by the consumer to whom the report relates.

Section 614—Restrictions on Investigative Consumer Reports

"Whenever a consumer reporting agency prepares an investigative consumer report, no adverse information in the consumer report (other than information which is a matter of public record) may be included in a subsequent consumer report unless such adverse information has been verified in the process of making such subsequent consumer report, or the adverse information was received within the three-month period preceding the date the subsequent report is furnished."

Section 615—Requirements on Users of Consumer Reports

"(a) Whenever credit or insurance for personal, family, or household purposes, or employment involving a consumer is denied or the charge for such credit or insurance is increased either wholly or partly because of information contained in a consumer report from a consumer reporting agency, the user of the consumer report shall so advise the consumer against whom such adverse action has been taken and supply the name and address of the consumer reporting agency making the report.

(b) Whenever credit for personal, family, or household purposes involving a consumer is denied or the charge for such credit is increased either wholly or partly because of information obtained from a person other than a consumer reporting agency bearing upon the consumer's credit worthiness, credit standing, credit capacity, character, general reputation, personal characteristics, or mode of living, the user of such information shall, within a reasonable period of time, upon the consumer's written request for the reasons for such adverse action received within 60 days after learning of such adverse action, disclose the nature of the information to the consumer. The user of such information shall clearly and accurately disclose to the consumer his right to make such written request at the time such adverse action is communicated to the consumer.

(c) No person shall be held liable for any violation of this section if he shows by a preponderance of the evidence that at the time of the alleged violation he maintained reasonable procedures to assure compliance with the provisions of subsections (a) and (b)."

1. Relation to Other Sections and Regulation B

Sections 606 and 615 are the only two sections that require users of reports to make disclosures to consumers. Section 606 applies only to users of "investigative consumer reports." Creditors should not confuse compliance with section 615(a), which only requires disclosure of the name and address of the consumer reporting agency, and compliance with the Equal Credit Opportunity Act, 15 U.S.C. 1691 *et seq.* and Regulation B, 12 C.F.R. 202, which require disclosure of the *reasons* for adverse action. Compliance with section 615(a), therefore, does not constitute compliance with Regulation B.

2. Limited Scope of Requirements

The section does not require that creditors disclose their credit criteria or standards or that employees furnish copies of personnel files to former employees. The section does not require that the user provide any kind of advance notification to consumers before a consumer report is obtained. (See section 606 regarding notice of investigative consumer reports.)

3. Method of Disclosure

The disclosures required by this section need not be made in writing. However, users will have evidence that they have taken reasonable steps to comply with this section if they provide written disclosures and retain copies for at least two years, the applicable statute of limitations for most civil liability actions under the FCRA.

4. Adverse Action Based on Direct Information

This section does not require that a user send any notice to a consumer concerning adverse action regarding that consumer that is based neither on information from a consumer reporting agency nor on information from a third party. For example, no disclosures are required concerning adverse action based on information provided by the consumer in an application or based on past experience in direct transactions with the consumer.

5. Creditors Using "Prescreened" Mailing Lists

A creditor is not required to provide notices regarding consumer reporting agencies that prepare mailing lists by "prescreening" because they do not involve consumer requests for credit and credit has not been denied to consumers whose names are deleted from a list furnished to the agency for use in this procedure. See discussion of "prescreening," under section 604(3)(A), item 6, *supra.*

6. Applicability to Users of Motor Vehicle Reports

An insurer that refuses to issue a policy, or charges a higher than normal premium, based on a motor vehicle report is required to comply with subsection (a).

7. Securities and Insurance Transactions

A consumer report user that denies credit to a consumer in connection with a securities transaction must provide the required notice, because the denial is of "credit * * * for personal purposes," unless the consumer engages in such transactions as a business.

8. Denial of Employment

An employer must provide the notice required by subsection (a) to an individual who has applied for employment and has been rejected based on a consumer report. However, an employer is not required to send a notice when it decides not to offer a position to an individual who has not applied for it, because in this case employment is not "denied." (See discussion in section 606, item 4, *supra.*)

9. Adverse Action Involving Credit

A creditor must provide the required notice when it denies the consumer's request for credit (including a rejection based on a scoring system, where a credit report received less than the maximum number of points possible and caused the application to receive an insufficient score), denies the consumer's request for increased credit, grants credit in an amount less than the consumer requested, or raises the charge for credit.

10. Adverse Action Not Involving Credit, Insurance or Employment

The Act does not require that a report user provide any notice to consumers when taking adverse action not relating to credit, insurance or employment. For example, a landlord who refuses to rent an apartment to a consumer based on credit or other information in a consumer report need not provide the notice. Similarly, a party that uses credit or other information in a consumer report as a basis for refusing to accept payment by check need not comply with this section. Checks have historically been treated as cash items, and thus such refusal does not involve a denial of credit, insurance or employment.

11. Adverse Action Based on Non-derogatory Adverse Information

A party taking adverse action concerning credit or insurance or denying employment, "wholly or partly because of information contained in a consumer report," must provide the required notice, even if the information is not derogatory. For example, the user must give the notice if the denial is based wholly or partly on the absence of a file or on the fact that the file contained insufficient references.

12. Name and Address of the Consumer Reporting Agency

The "section 615(a)" notice must include the consumer reporting agency's street address, not just a post office box address.

13. Agency To Be Identified

The consumer report user should provide the name and address of the consumer reporting agency from which it obtained the consumer report, even if that agency obtained all or part of the report from another agency.

14. Denial Based Partly on a Consumer Report

A "section 615(a)" notice must be sent even if the adverse action is based only partly on a consumer report.

15. Denial of Credit Based on Information From "Third Parties"

Subsection (b) imposes requirements on a creditor when it denies (or increases the charge for) credit for personal, family or household purposes involving a consumer, based on information from a "third party" source, which means a source *other* than the consumer reporting agency, the creditor's own files, or the consumer's application (*e.g.*, creditor, employer, landlord, or the public record). Where a creditor denies a consumer's application based on information obtained directly from another lender, even if the lender's name was furnished to the creditor by a consumer reporting agency, the creditor must give a "third party" disclosure.

16. Substance of Required "Third Party" Disclosures

When the adverse action is communicated to the consumer, the creditor must clearly and accurately disclose to the consumer his or her right to make a written request for the disclosure of the nature of the third party information that led to the adverse action. Upon timely receipt of such a request, however, the creditor need disclose only the nature of the information that led to the adverse action (*e.g.*, history of late rent payments or bad checks); it need not identify the source that provided the information or the criteria that led to the adverse action. A creditor may comply with subsection (b) by providing a statement of the nature of the third party information that led to the denial when it notifies the consumer of the denial. A statement of principal, specific reasons for adverse action based on third party information that is sufficient to comply with the requirements of the Equal Credit Opportunity Act (*e.g.*, "unable to verify employment") is sufficient to constitute disclosure of the "nature of the information" under subsection (b).

Section 616—Civil Liability for Willful Noncompliance

Section 616 permits consumers who sue and prove willful noncompliance with the Act to recover actual damages, punitive damages, and the costs of the action, together with reasonable attorney's fees.

Section 617—Civil Liability for Negligent Noncompliance

Section 617 permits consumers who sue and prove negligent noncompliance with the Act to recover actual damages and the costs of the action, together with reasonable attorney's fees.

Section 618—Jurisdiction of Courts; Limitation of Actions

Section 618 provides that any action brought under section 616 or section 617 may be brought in any United States district court or other court of competent jurisdiction. Such suit must be brought within two years from the date on which liability arises, unless a defendant has materially and willfully misrepresented information the Act requires to be disclosed, and the information misrepresented is material to establishment of the defendant's liability. In that event, the action must be brought within two years after the individual discovers the misrepresentation.

Section 619—Obtaining Information Under False Pretense

Section 619 provides criminal sanctions against any person who knowingly and willfully obtains information on a consumer from a consumer reporting agency under false pretenses.

1. Relation to Other Sections

The presence of this provision does not excuse a consumer reporting agency's failure to follow reasonable procedures, as required by section 607(a), to limit the furnishing of consumer reports to the purposes listed under section 604.

Section 620—Unauthorized Disclosures by Officers or Employees

Section 620 provides criminal sanctions against any officer or employee of a consumer reporting agency who knowingly and willfully provides information concerning an individual from the agency's file to a person not authorized to receive it.

Section 621—Administrative Enforcement

This section gives the Federal Trade Commission authority to enforce the Act with respect to consumer reporting agencies, users of reports, and all others, except to the extent that it gives enforcement jurisdiction specifically to some other agency. Those excepted from the Commission's enforcement jurisdiction include certain financial institutions regulated by Federal agencies or boards, Federal credit unions, common carriers subject to acts to regulate commerce, air carriers, and parties subject to the Packers and Stockyards Act, 1921.

1. General

The Commission can use its cease-and-desist power and other procedural, investigative and enforcement powers which it has under the FTC Act to secure compliance, irrespective of commerce or any other jurisdictional tests in the FTC Act.

2. Geographic Coverage

The Commission's authority encompasses the United States, the District of Columbia, the Commonwealth of Puerto Rico, and all United States territories but does not extend to activities outside those areas.

3. Status of Commission Commentary and Staff Interpretations

The FCRA does not give any Federal agency authority to promulgate rules having the force and effect, of statutory provisions. The Commission has issued this Commentary, superseding the eight formal Interpretations of the Act (16 CFR 600.1–600.8), previously issued pursuant to § 1.73 of the Commission's Rules, 16 CFR 1.73. The Commentary does not constitute substantive rules and does not have the force or effect of statutory provisions. It constitutes guidelines to clarify the Act that are advisory in nature and represent the Commission's views as to what particular provisions of the Act mean. Staff opinion letters constitute staff interpretations of the Act's provisions, but do not have the force or effect of statutory provisions and, as provided in § 1.72 of the Commission's Rules, 16 CFR 1.72, do not bind the Commission.

Section 622—Relation to State Laws

"This title does not annul, alter, affect, or exempt any person subject to the provisions of this title from complying with the laws of any State with respect to the collection, distribution, or use of any information on consumers, except to the extent that those laws are inconsistent with any provision of this title, and then only to the extent of the inconsistency."

1. Basic Rule

State law is pre-empted by the FCRA only when compliance with inconsistent state law would result in violation of the FCRA.

2. Examples of Statutes that are not Pre-empted

A state law requirement that an employer provide notice to a consumer before ordering a consumer report, or that a consumer reporting agency must provide the consumer with a written copy of his file, would not be pre-empted, because a party that complies with such provisions would not violate the FCRA.

3. Examples of Statutes that are Pre-empted

A state law authorizing grand juries to compel consumer reporting agencies to provide consumer reports, by means of subpoenas signed by a court clerk, is pre-empted by the FCRA's requirement that such reports be furnished only pursuant to an "order of the court" signed by a judge (section 604(1)), or furnished for other purposes not applicable to grand jury subpoenas (section 604 (2)–(3)), and by section 607(a). A state statute requiring automatic disclosure of a deletion or dispute statement to every person who has previously received a consumer report containing the disputed information, regardless of whether the consumer designates such persons to receive this disclosure, is pre-empted by section 604 of the FCRA, which permits disclosure only for specified, permissible purposes and by section 607(a), which requires consumer reporting agencies to limit the furnishing of consumer reports to purposes listed under section 604. Absent a specific designation by the consumer, the consumer reporting agency has no reason to believe all past recipients would have a present, permissible purpose to receive the reports.

4. Statute Providing Access for Enforcement Purposes

A state "little FCRA" that permits state officials access to a consumer reporting agency's files for the purpose of enforcing that statute just as Federal agencies are permitted access to such files under the FCRA, is not pre-empted by the FCRA.

(Information collection requirements in this appendix approved by the Office of Management and Budget under control number 3084-0091)

The FCRA was enacted October 26, 1970, and became effective April 24, 1971.

Appendix E — Index to Federal Trade Commission Informal Staff Opinion Letters with FCRA Sections

> **Text of FTC Staff Opinion Letters can be found on the CD-Rom accompanying this manual.**

This appendix contains an index listing of the FTC informal staff opinion letters which discuss the Fair Credit Reporting Act. The letters are organized according to which section of the FCRA are addressed. Within each section listing, the letters are listed chronologically by author. The FTC staff stopped issuing these letters in 2001, and according to the FTC website it will no longer issue them exception in "unusual circumstances."[1]

These letters were written by FTC staff in response to written inquiries from consumer reporting agencies, creditors and other users of consumer reports and consumers. The letters are informal; they are not approved by the FTC Commissioners and they are not formal advisory opinions. They are not even interpretations of an FTC regulation, but of the statute itself. As such, they are not entitled to formal deference by a court of law. Nevertheless, the Federal Trade Commission is the primary, though hardly exclusive, federal enforcement agency under the FCRA. Thus, the letters may be viewed as persuasive, but not binding, by the courts.

The staff opinion letters and the FTC Official Staff Commentary, reprinted at Appendix D, *supra*, are related. The FTC Official Staff Commentary is also not a rule or regulation, does not have the force or effect of a statute, and is not necessarily entitled to judicial deference. The weight accorded the Commentary by the courts will depend on the circumstances. *See* the introduction to Appendix D, *supra*. Unlike staff opinion letters, however, the Commentary has been promulgated by the Commission itself and is an official Commission document. In the event of a conflict between the Commentary and informal staff opinion letters, the Commentary should normally prevail. The letters often contain a degree of analysis and discussion missing from the Commentary. Usually the letters will buttress the conclusions of the Commentary, but sometimes they will persuasively support contrary interpretation. The text of the manual is heavily annotated with references to the letters.

Informal staff opinion letters written before May 4, 1990 are superseded by the Commentary.[2] Nevertheless, these earlier letters may still be found to be persuasive and are recommended as a valuable source to anyone considering the scope and applicability of the Act to particular circumstances. Letters written after the Commentary was published in May 1990, may normally be viewed as supplementing the Commentary.

Letters published after 1997 are important for another reason. The Commentary is based on the Fair Credit Reporting Act prior to its amendment by the Consumer Credit Reporting Reform Act of 1996.[3] The Commentary does not reflect the sometimes important changes in the language of the Act and the often extensive additions to the Act embodied in the 1996 Reform Act, but the letters often do. Beginning June 1997, the informal staff opinion letters addressed changes in the law and are especially useful for analysis of FCRA provisions amended by the 1996 Reform Act.

---

1 www.ftc.gov/os/statutes/fcrajump.htm.

2 *See* Introduction to the Supplementary Information published with the Commentary, 55 Fed. Reg. 18804 (May 4, 1990), available on the accompanying CD-Rom.

3 *See* § 1.4.6, supra.

Appx. E   *Fair Credit Reporting*

FTC Opinion Letters can be found on the CD-Rom accompanying this volume.

Sectional Index to FTC Informal Staff Opinion Letters

FCRA Section	15 U.S.C. Section	Section Topic	Relevant FTC Informal Staff Opinion Letters: Respondent (Date)
602	1681	FINDINGS & PURPOSE	Conway (Sept. 11, 1973) Dea (May 1, 1974) Petruccelli (Apr. 9, 1984) Harlow (Apr. 17, 1984) Medine (Mar. 30, 1994)
603	1681a	DEFINITIONS & RULES AND CONSTRUCTION	
603b	1681a	DEFINITION OF "PERSON"	Goldfarb (July 16, 1971) Scholl (Dec. 10, 1976) Goldfarb (July 9, 1980) Isaac (Feb. 23, 1998) Allison
603c	1681a	DEFINITION OF "CONSUMER"	Carson (Mar. 20, 1971)
603d	1681a	DEFINITION OF "CONSUMER REPORT"	Carson (Mar. 20, 1971) Conway (Mar. 30, 1971) Silbergeld (Apr. 1, 1971) Carson (Apr. 8, 1971) Feldman (Apr. 15, 1971) Kahn (Apr. 27, 1971) Feldman (May 5, 1971) Wan (June 2, 1971) Goldfarb (June 16, 1971) Feldman (July 15, 1971) Carson (Sept. 1, 1972) Russell (Jan. 30, 1973) Wan (May 25, 1973) Grimes (July 5, 1973) Wan (July 5, 1973) Grimes (Sept. 5, 1973) Russell (Sept. 26, 1973) Russell (Sept. 27, 1973) Conway (Dec. 3, 1973) Russell (Dec. 3, 1973) Russell (Dec. 3, 1973) Grimes (Jan. 9, 1974) Feldman (Mar. 10, 1974) Peeler (Apr. 15, 1974) Dea (May 1, 1974) Russell (May 15, 1974) Dea (July 18, 1974) Isaac (Sept. 25, 1974) Dea (Oct. 29, 1974) Dea (Mar. 31, 1975) Dea (Apr. 2, 1975) Dea (Sept. 24, 1975) White (Feb. 2, 1976) White (Apr. 9, 1976) Dea (May 20, 1976) White (Nov. 24, 1976) Scholl (Dec. 10, 1976) Peeler (Feb. 18, 1978) Peeler (July 24, 1978) Peeler (Dec. 10, 1978) Reynolds (May 14, 1979)

Index to FTC Letters   Appx. E

FTC Opinion Letters can be found on the CD-Rom accompanying this volume.

FCRA Section	15 U.S.C. Section	Section Topic	**Relevant FTC Informal Staff Opinion Letters: Respondent (Date)**
			Goldfarb (July 9, 1980)
			Muris (Apr. 29, 1982)
			Buffon (June 16, 1983)
			Meyer (June 21, 1983)
			Brinckerhoff (Nov. 23, 1983)
			Grimes (Dec. 9, 1983)
			Brinckerhoff (Dec. 21, 1983)
			Maloney (Mar. 28, 1984)
			Petruccelli (Apr. 9, 1984)
			Grimes (Aug. 3, 1984)
			Brinckerhoff (Feb. 4, 1985)
			Fitzpatrick (Mar. 8, 1985)
			Brinckerhoff (Apr. 23, 1985)
			Brinckerhoff (May 1, 1985)
			Brinckerhoff (June 11, 1985)
			Grimes (Sept. 26, 1985)
			Grimes (Oct. 4, 1985)
			Grimes (Feb. 27, 1986)
			Grimes (Apr. 30, 1986)
			Grimes (Aug. 6, 1986)
			Brinckerhoff (Jan. 28, 1987)
			Brinckerhoff (May 4, 1987)
			Grimes (July 14, 1987)
			Brinckerhoff (Sept. 22, 1987)
			Grimes (Feb. 11, 1988)
			Brinckerhoff (May 31, 1988)
			Noonan (Apr. 25, 1990)
			Noonan (Aug. 22, 1990)
			Grimes (Jan. 22, 1991)
			Grimes (Oct. 7, 1991)
			Grimes (Mar. 4, 1992)
			Grimes (July 7, 1992)
			Grimes (Nov. 24, 1992)
			Grimes (Jan. 4, 1993)
			Grimes and Medine (Mar. 3, 1993)
			Grimes (June 9, 1993)
			Brinckerhoff (Mar. 4, 1994)
			Grimes (June 2, 1994)
			d'Entremont (July 6, 1995)
			d'Entremont (Jan. 1, 1996)
			Isaac (Sept. 26, 1996)
			Haynes (Mar. 2, 1998) Buchman
			Haynes (June 9, 1998) Beaudette
			Brinkerhoff (June 9, 1998) Goeke
			Haynes (June 9, 1998) Islinger
			Haynes (June 11, 1998) Halpern
			Haynes (June 11, 1998) Lewis
			Brinckerhoff (June 12, 1998) Slyter
			Kane (July 9, 1998) Hinkle
			Brinckerhoff (July 10, 1998) Pickett
			Lamb (July 16, 1998) Kelley
			Foster (Aug. 27, 1998) Haner
			Kane (Sept. 9, 1998) Novak
			Smollen (Oct. 27, 1998) Tabler
			Haynes (Sept. 15, 1999) Sum
			Medine (July 26, 2000) Tatelbaum

Appx. E *Fair Credit Reporting*

FTC Opinion Letters can be found on the CD-Rom accompanying this volume.

FCRA Section	**15 U.S.C. Section**	**Section Topic**	**Relevant FTC Informal Staff Opinion Letters: Respondent (Date)**
603e	1681a	DEFINITION OF "INVESTIGATIVE CONSUMER REPORT"	Russell (Dec. 3, 1973) Peeler (Apr. 15, 1974) Dea (May 1, 1974) Dea (Apr. 2, 1975) Dea (Sept. 24, 1975) Peeler (May 5, 1976) Grimes (Dec. 9, 1983) Grimes (Oct. 4, 1985) Fortney (Jan. 30, 1986) Grimes (Oct. 10, 1986) Kane (Aug. 9, 1993) Isaac (Sept. 26, 1996) Kane (July 9, 1998) Hinkle Brinckerhoff (Mar. 25, 1999) Willner Keller (Apr. 5, 1999) Vail Medine (Aug. 31, 1999) Meisinger Brinckerhoff (Oct. 1, 1999) Fischel
603f	1681a	DEFINITION OF "CONSUMER REPORTING AGENCY"	Silbergeld (Apr. 1, 1971) Carson (Apr. 8, 1971) Kahn (Apr. 27, 1971) Goldfarb (Apr. 29, 1971) Feldman (May 5, 1971) Carson (May 21, 1971) Martin (May 26, 1971) Bragg (May 16, 1972) Carson (Sept. 1, 1972) Wan (May 25, 1973) Grimes (July 5, 1973) Grimes (Sept. 5, 1973) Russell (Sept. 27, 1973) Russell (Dec. 3, 1973) Conway (Dec. 3, 1973) Grimes (Jan. 9, 1974) Feldman (Mar. 10, 1974) Dea (May 1, 1974) Russell (May 15, 1974) Dea (July 18, 1974) Feldman (Sept. 5, 1974) Isaac (Sept. 25, 1974) Dea (Oct. 29, 1974) Dea (Feb. 14, 1975) Dea (Mar. 31, 1975) Grimes (May 22, 1975) Grimes (Sept. 11, 1975) White (c. Sept. 1, 1976) White (Nov. 24, 1976) Peeler (Feb. 8, 1978) Peeler (July 24, 1978) Goldfarb (July 9, 1980) Petruccelli (Jan. 27, 1982) Buffon (June 16, 1983) Meyer (June 21, 1983) Brinckerhoff (Oct. 31, 1983) Brinckerhoff (Nov. 10, 1983) Brinckerhoff (Nov. 23, 1983) Grimes (Dec. 9, 1983)

Index to FTC Letters Appx. E

FTC Opinion Letters can be found on the CD-Rom accompanying this volume.

FCRA Section	15 U.S.C. Section	Section Topic	Relevant FTC Informal Staff Opinion Letters: Respondent (Date)
			Maloney (Mar. 28, 1984)
			Petruccelli (Apr. 9, 1984)
			Brinckerhoff (Apr. 23, 1985)
			Grimes (Sept. 26, 1985)
			Grimes (Oct. 4, 1985)
			Fortney (Jan. 30, 1986)
			Fortney (Mar. 10, 1986)
			Grimes (Apr. 30, 1986)
			Fortney (May 2, 1986)
			Grimes (May 13, 1986)
			Grimes (Aug. 6, 1986)
			Grimes (Oct. 24, 1986)
			Grimes (Apr. 17, 1987)
			Brinckerhoff (May 1, 1987)
			Grimes (July 14, 1987)
			Brinckerhoff (Aug. 14, 1987)
			Brinckerhoff (Dec. 30, 1988)
			Nixon (Feb. 9, 1989)
			Grimes (July 7, 1992)
			Grimes and Medine (Mar. 3, 1993)
			Grimes (June 9, 1993)
			Brinckerhoff (Nov. 14, 1994)
			d'Entremont (Jan. 25, 1996)
			Isaac (June 11, 1996)
			Isaac (Sept. 26, 1996)
			Isaac (Dec. 27, 1996)
			Kane (Oct. 27, 1997)
			Brinckerhoff (June 9, 1998)
			Haynes #3 (June 9, 1998)
			Brinckerhoff (June 10, 1998)
			Brinckerhoff (June 12, 1998)
			Kane (Oct. 27, 1997) Cast
			Brinckerhoff (June 9, 1998) Goeke
			Haynes (June 9, 1998) Islinger
			Haynes (June 9, 1998) LeBlanc
			Brinckerhoff (June 10, 1998) Copple
			Brinckerhoff (June 12, 1998) Slyter
			Brinckerhoff (June 26, 1998) Lee
			Brinckerhoff (July 10, 1998) Pickett
			Brinckerhoff (Sept. 9, 1998) Leathers
			Foster (Nov. 20, 1998) Throne
			Keller (Apr. 5, 1999) Vail
			Medine (Aug. 31, 1999) Meisinger
			Haynes (Sept. 15, 1999) Sum
603g	1681a(g)	DEFINITION OF "CONSUMER'S FILE"	Federbush (Mar. 10, 1983)
			Jerison (Aug. 5, 1988)
			Keller (Aug. 1, 2000) Cohan
603h	1681a(h)	DEFINITION OF "EMPLOYMENT PURPOSES"	Maloney (Sept. 4, 1984)
			Grimes (Oct. 4, 1985)
			Grimes (Oct. 23, 1985)
			Brinckerhoff (July 24, 1986)
			Grimes (July 20, 1992)
			d'Entremont (Jan. 25, 1996)
			Isaac (Feb. 23, 1998) Allison
			Kane (Oct. 7, 1998) Solomon
			Kane (Oct. 20, 1998) Greathouse

Appx. E   *Fair Credit Reporting*

FTC Opinion Letters can be found on the CD-Rom accompanying this volume.

FCRA Section	15 U.S.C. Section	Section Topic	Relevant FTC Informal Staff Opinion Letters: Respondent (Date)
603k	1681a(k)	DEFINITION OF "ADVERSE ACTION"	Brinckerhoff (Mar. 3, 1998) Schieber Kane (Oct. 20, 1998) Greathouse Brinckerhoff (Oct. 26, 1998) Hall Smollen (Nov. 5, 1998) Spritz Keller (Apr. 5, 1999) Vail Isaac (Apr. 29, 1999) Gowen Stires (Mar. 1, 2000) Ball Keller (July 14, 2000) Stinneford Berger (June 28, 2001) Latour
603m	1681a(m)	DEFINITION OF "CREDIT OR INSURANCE THAT IS NOT INITIATED BY THE CONSUMER"	Isaac (Apr. 29, 1999) Gowen
603o	1681a(o)	EXCLUDED COMMUNICATIONS	Haynes (June 11, 1998) Basting
603p	1681a(p)	DEFINITION OF "CONSUMER REPORTING AGENCY THAT COMPILES AND MAINTAINS FILES ON CONSUMERS ON A NATIONWIDE BASIS"	Brinckerhoff (June 29, 1999) Cohan

New Section	Old Section	15 U.S.C. Section	Section Topic	Relevant FTC Informal Staff Opinion Letters: Respondent (Date)
604	—	1681b(a)	PERMISSIBLE PURPOSES FOR WHICH AN AGENCY MAY FURNISH A CONSUMER REPORT	Medine (Feb. 11, 1998) Coffey Haynes (Mar. 2, 1998) Buchman
604(a)	604	1681b(a)	PERMISSIBLE PURPOSES—GENERAL	Conway (May 6, 1971) Kirkpatrick (Oct. 27, 1971) Carson (Apr. 13, 1972) Grimes (Sept. 5, 1973) Russell (Dec. 3, 1973) Russell (Dec. 3, 1973) Grimes (Dec. 19, 1973) Grimes (Jan. 9, 1974) Russell (Jan. 21, 1974) Grimes (Oct. 15, 1974) Dea (Oct. 29, 1974) Dea (Apr. 2, 1975) Grimes (Sept. 11, 1975) White (Dec. 22, 1975) Dea (May 20, 1976) White (c. Sept. 1, 1976) Peeler (Aug. 27, 1977) Peeler (Nov. 1, 1977) Peeler (Feb. 8, 1978) Peeler (July 24, 1978) Reynolds (May 14, 1979) Muris (Apr. 29, 1982) Meyer (Oct. 21, 1982) Federbush (Dec. 22, 1982) Meyer (Mar. 22, 1983) Brinckerhoff (Nov. 23, 1983) Grimes (Dec. 9, 1983) Garman (June 17, 1985) Grimes (Aug. 14, 1985) Grimes (Sept. 26, 1985) Grimes (Oct. 23, 1985) Grimes (Oct. 10, 1986)

Index to FTC Letters   Appx. E

FTC Opinion Letters can be found on the CD-Rom accompanying this volume.

New Section	Old Section	15 U.S.C. Section	Section Topic	Relevant FTC Informal Staff Opinion Letters: Respondent (Date)
				Grimes (Oct. 24, 1986)
				Grimes (May 12, 1987)
				Noonan (Jan. 15, 1988)
				Clark (Feb. 22, 1989)
				Noonan (Aug. 22, 1990)
				Grimes (Jan. 22, 1991)
				Brinckerhoff (Nov. 22, 1991)
				Grimes (Mar. 4, 1992)
				Grimes (July 20, 1992)
				Grimes (July 8, 1993)
				Brinckerhoff (Mar. 4, 1994)
				Medine (Mar. 30, 1994)
				Grimes (June 2, 1994)
				d'Entremont (July 6, 1995)
				d'Entremont (Jan. 25, 1996)
604(a)(1)	604(1)	1681b(a)(1)	COURT ORDERS	Dea (Feb. 13, 1974)
				Peeler (Feb. 26, 1979)
				Brinckerhoff (Nov. 4, 1983)
				Brinckerhoff (Apr. 23, 1986)
				Grimes (Aug. 2, 1990)
604(a)(2)	604(2)	1681b(a)(2)	CONSUMER'S WRITTEN INSTRUCTIONS	Martin (June 11, 1971)
				Carson (Apr. 13, 1972)
				Dea (Feb. 13, 1974)
				Dea (Feb. 14, 1975)
				Dea (c. Jan. 1976)
				Peeler (Mar. 23, 1977)
				Peeler (Feb. 8, 1978)
				Peeler (Jan. 8, 1979)
				Peeler (Feb. 26, 1979)
				Oliver (Mar. 23, 1982)
				Petruccelli (Apr. 9, 1984)
				Brinckerhoff (Feb. 5, 1985)
				Grimes (Mar. 7, 1986)
				Brinckerhoff (Sept. 3, 1986)
				Brinckerhoff (Oct. 27, 1987)
				Noonan (Aug. 22, 1990)
				Grimes (July 20, 1992)
				Grimes (Feb. 10, 1994)
				Brinckerhoff (Nov. 14, 1994)
				Brinckerhoff (Oct. 10, 1995)
				Brinckerhoff (June 8, 1999) Shibley
				Keller (Oct. 12, 1999) Landever
				Brinckerhoff (May 24, 2001) Zalenski
604(a)(3)	604(3)	1681b(a)(3)	INTENDED USE	Silbergeld (Apr. 1, 1971)
				Carson (Apr. 13, 1972)
				Russell (Mar. 7, 1974)
				Dea (July 18, 1974)
				Grimes (Sept. 11, 1975)
				Peeler (Jan. 8, 1979)
				Peeler (Feb. 26, 1979)
				Peeler (May 27, 1982)
				Brinckerhoff (Nov. 10, 1983)
				Brinckerhoff (Dec. 21, 1983)
				Brinckerhoff (May 1, 1985)
				Grimes (Oct. 24, 1986)
				Jerison (Feb. 5, 1988)

FTC Opinion Letters can be found on the CD-Rom accompanying this volume.

New Section	Old Section	15 U.S.C. Section	Section Topic	Relevant FTC Informal Staff Opinion Letters: Respondent (Date)
604(a)(3)(A)	604(3)(A)	1681b(a)(3)(A)	CREDIT	Carson (Apr. 29, 1971) Russell (Sept. 26, 1973) Russell (Jan. 11, 1974) Russell (Jan. 21, 1974) Dea (Feb. 13, 1974) Grimes (Oct. 15, 1974) Dea (Nov. 28, 1974) Dea (Feb. 14, 1975) Dea (Apr. 2, 1975) Grimes (Sept. 11, 1975) Goldfarb (Mar. 29, 1976) White (Feb. 18, 1977) Peeler (Aug. 27, 1977) Morris (July 26, 1979) Meyer (Oct. 21, 1982) Meyer (Mar. 22, 1983) Mowery (May 24, 1983) Peeler (Nov. 1, 1983) Fortney (Dec. 2, 1983) Maloney (Mar. 28, 1984) Petruccelli (Apr. 9, 1984) Garman (June 17, 1985) Grimes (Aug. 14, 1985) Brinckerhoff (May 28, 1986) Brinckerhoff (Sept. 3, 1986) Isaac (Oct. 30, 1986) Noonan (Dec. 18, 1986) Grimes (Feb. 10, 1987) Grimes (May 12, 1987) Noonan (Jan. 15, 1988) Grimes (Mar. 18, 1988) Jerison (Dec. 12, 1988) Grimes (Aug. 1, 1990) Brinckerhoff (Nov. 22, 1991) Grimes (Jan. 4, 1993) Grimes (Feb. 17, 1993) Grimes (July 8, 1993) Medine (Mar. 30, 1994) Grimes (June 2, 1994) Brinckerhoff (Nov. 14, 1994) Brinckerhoff (July 7, 1995) Brinckerhoff (July 26, 1995) Brinckerhoff (Oct. 10, 1995) Brinckerhoff (Aug. 5, 1998) Bauchner Foster (Nov. 20, 1998) Throne Isaac (Apr. 29, 1999) Gowen Brinckerhoff (Apr. 30, 1999) Benner Brinckerhoff (July 6, 2000) Long Medine (July 26, 2000) Tatelbaum Winston (June 22, 2001) Banking Agency Counsels

Index to FTC Letters   Appx. E

FTC Opinion Letters can be found on the CD-Rom accompanying this volume.

New Section	Old Section	15 U.S.C. Section	Section Topic	Relevant FTC Informal Staff Opinion Letters: Respondent (Date)
604(a)(3)(B)	604(3)(B)	1681b(a)(3)(B)	EMPLOYMENT	Carson (Apr. 9, 1971) Goldfarb (Apr. 29, 1971) Dea (Feb. 13, 1974) Dea (Apr. 2, 1975) Peeler (Aug. 27, 1977) Brinckerhoff (Oct. 31, 1983) Brinckerhoff (Nov. 17, 1983) Grimes (Dec. 9, 1983) Brinckerhoff (Dec. 21, 1983) Maloney (Sept. 4, 1984) Grimes (Oct. 23, 1985) Brinckerhoff (July 24, 1986) Grimes (May 12, 1987) Grimes (July 20, 1992) Foster (Sept. 2, 1998) Ross Kane (Oct. 20, 1998) Greathouse Brinckerhoff (Aug. 6, 1999) Woolford Keller (Oct. 12, 1999) Landever
604(a)(3)(C)	604(3)(C)	1681b(a)(3)(C)	INSURANCE UNDERWRITING	Russell (Jan. 30, 1973) Feldman (Sept. 5, 1974) Dea (Apr. 2, 1975) Peeler (Aug. 27, 1977) Brinckerhoff (Nov. 23, 1983) Brinckerhoff (Dec. 21, 1983) Grimes (Aug. 3, 1984) Brinckerhoff (July 29, 1985) Brinckerhoff (Mar. 4, 1994) Medine (Mar. 30, 1994) Grimes (June 2, 1994) Haynes (Mar. 2, 1998) Kane (Oct. 20, 1998) Greathouse Brinckerhoff (Feb. 15, 2000) Amason
604(a)(3)(D)	604(3)(D)	1681b(a)(3)(D)	GOVERNMENT BENEFITS	Feldman (Sept. 5, 1974) Dea (Apr. 2, 1975) White (Feb. 18, 1977) Peeler (Aug. 27, 1977) Grimes (Mar. 7, 1986) Brinckerhoff (July 24, 1986) Brinckerhoff (Nov. 22, 1991) d'Entremont (July 6, 1995) Kane (Oct. 20, 1998) Greathouse
604(a)(3)(F)	604(3)(E)	1681b(a)(3)(F)	OTHER LEGITIMATE BUSINESS NEEDS	Russell (Jan. 30, 1973) Grimes (Sept. 5, 1973) Russell (Sept. 26, 1973) Grimes (Jan. 9, 1974) Dea (Feb. 13, 1974) Dea (May 1, 1974) Isaac (Sept. 25, 1974) Dea (Oct. 29, 1974) Dea (Feb. 14, 1975) Dea (Apr. 2, 1975) Goldfarb (Mar. 29, 1976) Scholl (Dec. 10, 1976) White (Feb. 18, 1977)

Appx. E *Fair Credit Reporting*

FTC Opinion Letters can be found on the CD-Rom accompanying this volume.

New Section	Old Section	15 U.S.C. Section	Section Topic	Relevant FTC Informal Staff Opinion Letters: Respondent (Date)
				Peeler (Aug. 27, 1977)
				Morris (July 26, 1979)
				Goldfarb (July 9, 1980)
				Brinckerhoff (Dec. 21, 1983)
				Petruccelli (Apr. 9, 1984)
				Grimes (Aug. 3, 1984)
				Brinckerhoff (Nov. 26, 1984)
				Brinckerhoff (Feb. 5, 1985)
				Brinckerhoff (July 29, 1985)
				Grimes (Aug. 14, 1985)
				Brinckerhoff (Sept. 3, 1986)
				Noonan (Dec. 18, 1986)
				Grimes (May 12, 1987)
				Jerison (Feb. 5, 1988)
				Jerison (Dec. 12, 1988)
				Brinckerhoff (Dec. 30, 1988)
				Clark (Feb. 22, 1989)
				Grimes (Jan. 22, 1991)
				Brinckerhoff (Nov. 22, 1991)
				Grimes (July 20, 1992)
				Grimes (Feb. 17, 1993)
				Grimes (Feb. 10, 1994)
				Brinckerhoff (Mar. 4, 1994)
				d'Entremont (July 6, 1995)
				Medine (Feb. 11, 1998)
				Haynes (Mar. 2, 1998)
				Medine (Feb. 11, 1998) Coffey
				Brinckerhoff (July 16, 1998) Kaiser
				Cosgrove (Oct. 27, 1998) Greenblatt
				Isaac (Apr. 29, 1999) Gowen
				Brinckerhoff (Apr. 30, 1999) Benner
				Brinckerhoff (June 8, 1999) Shibley
				Brinckerhoff (July 6, 2000) Long
				Medine (July 26, 2000) Tatelbaum
604(a)(4–5)	—	1681b(a)(4–5)	USE OF CONSUMER REPORT FOR CHILD SUPPORT PURPOSES	Brinckerhoff (Apr. 30, 1999) Baughn
				Brinckerhoff (Aug. 6, 1999) Woolford
604(b)	—	1681b(b)	CONDITIONS FOR EMPLOYMENT PURPOSES USE	Isaac (Feb. 23, 1998) Allison
				Haynes (June 9, 1998) Beaudette
				Haynes (June 9, 1998) Rosen
				Haynes (June 11, 1998) Lewis
				Haynes (June 12, 1998) Hauxwell
				Brinckerhoff (June 12, 1998) Slyter
				Brinckerhoff (July 10, 1998) Pickett
604(b)(1)	—	1681b(b)(1)	CERTIFICATION FROM USER	Haynes (Dec. 23, 1997) Hahn
				Kammula (July 28, 1998) Kilgo
604(b)(2)	—	1681b(b)(2)	DISCLOSURE TO CONSUMER	Lamb (Oct. 21, 1997) Steer
				Brinckerhoff (Oct. 23, 1997) Solganik
				Haynes (Dec. 18, 1997) Hawkey
				Medine (Feb. 11, 1998) Coffey
				Isaac (June 11, 1998) Brisch
				Haynes (June 12, 1998) Hauxwell
				Brinckerhoff (June 12, 1998) Slyter
				Haynes (Aug. 5, 1998) James
				Brinckerhoff (Sept. 9, 1998) Leathers

Index to FTC Letters   Appx. E

FTC Opinion Letters can be found on the CD-Rom accompanying this volume.

New Section	Old Section	15 U.S.C. Section	Section Topic	Relevant FTC Informal Staff Opinion Letters: Respondent (Date)
				Brinckerhoff (Mar. 25, 1999) Willner
				Brinckerhoff (Oct. 1, 1999) Fischel
604(b)(3)	—	1681b(b)(3)	CONDITIONS ON USE FOR ADVERSE ACTION	Brinckerhoff (June 27, 1997) Weisberg
				Brinckerhoff (Oct. 23, 1997) Solganik
				Haynes (Dec. 18, 1997) Hawkey
				Medine (Feb. 11, 1998) Coffey
				Haynes (June 9, 1998) Rosen
				Isaac (June 11, 1998) Brisch
				Haynes (June 11, 1998) Lewis
				Haynes (July 8, 1998) Hahn
				Kane (July 9, 1998) Hinkle
				Brinckerhoff (Sept. 9, 1998) Leathers
				Kane (Oct. 7, 1998) Solomon
				Brinckerhoff (Mar. 25, 1999) Willner
				Keller (Apr. 5, 1999) Vail
				Medine (Aug. 31, 1999) Meisinger
604(c)(1)	—	1681b(c)(1)	CREDIT OR INSURANCE NOT INITIATED BY CONSUMER	Haynes (Mar. 2, 1998) Buchman

FCRA Section	15 U.S.C. Section	Section Topic	Relevant FTC Informal Staff Opinion Letters: Respondent (Date)
605	1681c	REQUIREMENTS FOR INFORMATION IN REPORT (See also § 607)	Kahn (Apr. 27, 1971)
			Russell (Jan. 30, 1973)
			Conway (Sept. 11, 1973)
			Conway (c. Nov. 15, 1973)
			Russell (Jan. 21, 1974)
			Feldman (Apr. 18, 1974)
			Peeler (May 30, 1974)
			Dea (July 19, 1974)
			Feldman (Aug. 5, 1974)
			Feldman (Dec. 24, 1974)
			Isaac (June 24, 1975)
			Gold (Jan. 26, 1977)
			Rice (Feb. 14, 1977)
			Peeler (Mar. 22, 1977)
			Goldfarb (c. Apr. 30, 1978)
			Peeler (Nov. 7, 1978)
			Peeler (Aug. 8, 1979)
			Peeler (Jan. 23, 1981)
			Oliver (June 10, 1983)
			Peeler (Aug. 9, 1983)
			Peeler (Oct. 21, 1983)
			Brinckerhoff (Nov. 23, 1983)
			Fortney (Nov. 23, 1983)
			Grimes (Dec. 9, 1983)
			Brinckerhoff (Dec. 21, 1983)
			Petruccelli (Feb. 13, 1984)
			Maloney (Mar. 28, 1984)
			Fortney (Aug. 24, 1984)
			Brinckerhoff (Jan. 9, 1985)
			Fitzpatrick (Mar. 8, 1985)
			Brinckerhoff (July 26, 1985)
			Brinckerhoff (July 30, 1985)
			Brinckerhoff (Sept. 17, 1985)

Appx. E *Fair Credit Reporting*

FTC Opinion Letters can be found on the CD-Rom accompanying this volume.

FCRA Section	15 U.S.C. Section	Section Topic	Relevant FTC Informal Staff Opinion Letters: Respondent (Date)
			Grimes (Sept. 24, 1985)
			Brinckerhoff (Sept. 24, 1985)
			Brinckerhoff (c. Oct. 1985)
			Brinckerhoff (Nov. 6, 1985)
			Fortney (Nov. 15, 1985)
			Fitzpatrick (Dec. 16, 1985)
			Grimes (Apr. 11, 1986)
			Childs (Apr. 18, 1986)
			Grimes (Aug. 28, 1986)
			Grimes (Oct. 10, 1986)
			Grimes (Dec. 15, 1986)
			Brinckerhoff (Apr. 30, 1987)
			Brinckerhoff (May 5, 1987)
			Brinckerhoff (May 7, 1987)
			Grimes (May 12, 1987)
			Brinckerhoff (May 28, 1987)
			Brinckerhoff (Sept. 11, 1987)
			Brinckerhoff (Aug. 10, 1988)
			Fitzpatrick (Aug. 26, 1988)
			Grimes (Apr. 28, 1989)
			Grimes (Nov. 24, 1992)
			Brinckerhoff (Mar. 4, 1994)
			Isaac (Mar. 13, 1996)
			Isaac (Dec. 9, 1996)
			Haynes (Apr. 17, 1998) Seaham
			Haynes (June 9, 1998) Rosen*
			Haynes (June 11, 1998) Halpern*
			Brinckerhoff (Aug. 31, 1998) Johnson
			Haynes (Dec. 10, 1998) Nadell
			Brinckerhoff (June 4, 1999) Kosmerl
			Haynes (Sept. 15, 1999) Sum
			Isaac (Nov. 5, 1999) Anonymous
			Brinckerhoff (Dec. 16, 1999) Holland
			Brinckerhoff (Feb. 15, 2000) Amason
606	1681d	DISCLOSURE OF INVESTIGATIVE CONSUMER REPORTS	Grimes (Oct. 23, 1985)
			Grimes (Apr. 30, 1986)
			Grimes (May 12, 1987)
			Haynes (Dec. 18, 1997) Hawkey
			Isaac (Feb. 23, 1998) Allison
			Haynes (June 9, 1998) Beaudette
			Brinckerhoff (July 10, 1998) Pickett
606a	1681d	NOTICE OF INVESTIGATION	Feldman (Mar. 12, 1971)
			Silbergeld (Apr. 15, 1971)
			Feldman (Apr. 15, 1971)
			Carson (June 3, 1971)
			Bragg (Aug. 27, 1971)
			Bragg (Sept. 16, 1971)
			Peeler (May 30, 1974)
			Feldman (Aug. 21, 1974)
			Dea (Dec. 30, 1974)
			Dea (Mar. 31, 1975)
			Dea (Sept. 24, 1975)
			White (Dec. 22, 1975)

* Repealed.

Index to FTC Letters Appx. E

FTC Opinion Letters can be found on the CD-Rom accompanying this volume.

FCRA Section	15 U.S.C. Section	Section Topic	Relevant FTC Informal Staff Opinion Letters: Respondent (Date)
			Petruccelli (Nov. 14, 1983)
			Grimes (Dec. 9, 1983)
			Maloney (Sept. 4, 1984)
			Grimes (Oct. 4, 1985)
			Grimes (Oct. 23, 1985)
			Grimes (Apr. 30, 1986)
			Grimes (Oct. 10, 1986)
			Grimes (May 12, 1987)
			Wilmore (Jan. 18, 1994)
			Isaac (June 11, 1998) Brisch
			Haynes (June 12, 1998) Hauxwell
			Brinckerhoff (Mar. 25, 1999) Willner
606b	1681d	DISCLOSURE OF NATURE AND SCOPE OF INVESTIGATION	Silbergeld (Apr. 15, 1971)
			Feldman (Aug. 21, 1974)
			Dea (Sept. 24, 1975)
			Isaac (June 11, 1998) Brisch
			Brinckerhoff (Mar. 25, 1999) Willner
606c	1681d	REASONABLE PROCEDURES	Conway (May 3, 1971)
			Feeler (Apr. 15, 1974)
			Grimes (Dec. 9, 1983)
607	1681e	COMPLIANCE PROCEDURES (See also §§ 604, 605)	Carson (Apr. 8, 1971)
			Conway (May 6, 1971)
			Russell (Jan. 30, 1973)
			Grimes (Feb. 23, 1973)
			Russell (Sept. 18, 1973)
			Grimes (Jan. 9, 1974)
			Russell (May 15, 1974)
			Feldman (May 30, 1974)
			Feldman (May 31, 1974)
			Dea (July 19, 1974)
			Feldman (Aug. 5, 1974)
			Feldman (Aug. 21, 1974)
			Feldman (Aug. 30, 1974)
			Grimes (Oct. 15, 1974)
			Peeler (Nov. 4, 1974)
			Dea (Nov. 28, 1974)
			Dea (Feb. 14, 1975)
			Dea (Apr. 2, 1975)
			Grimes (May 22, 1975)
			Peeler (Mar. 8, 1976)
			Peeler (Mar. 20, 1977)
			Peeler (Aug. 27, 1977)
			Peeler (Aug. 27, 1977)
			Peeler (Jan. 4, 1978)
			Peeler (July 24, 1978)
			Peeler (Nov. 7, 1978)
			Peeler (Dec. 10, 1978)
			Peeler (Feb. 26, 1979)
			Morris (July 26, 1979)
			Petruccelli (Jan. 27, 1982)
			Federbush (Mar. 10, 1983)
			Meyer (Mar. 22, 1983)
			Peeler (Aug. 9, 1983)
			Peeler (Nov. 1, 1983)
			Brinckerhoff (Nov. 23, 1983)

Appx. E   *Fair Credit Reporting*

FTC Opinion Letters can be found on the CD-Rom accompanying this volume.

FCRA Section	15 U.S.C. Section	Section Topic	Relevant FTC Informal Staff Opinion Letters: Respondent (Date)
			Grimes (Dec. 9, 1983)
			Petruccelli (Feb. 13, 1984)
			Maloney (Mar. 28, 1984)
			Fortney (Aug. 24, 1984)
			Brinckerhoff (Jan. 31, 1985)
			Brinckerhoff (Oct. 29, 1985)
			Grimes (Feb. 27, 1986)
			Grimes (Apr. 30, 1986)
			Brinckerhoff (July 21, 1986)
			Grimes (Oct. 10, 1986)
			Grimes (Mar. 20, 1987)
			Brinckerhoff (Sept. 11, 1987)
			Noonan (Jan. 15, 1988)
			Brinckerhoff (Mar. 8, 1988)
			Grimes (Mar. 8, 1988)
			Grimes (Mar. 4, 1992)
			Grimes (June 2, 1994)
			Brinckerhoff (Apr. 24, 1998) Lovern
			Haynes (June 9, 1998) Beaudette
			Brinckerhoff (June 9, 1998) Goeke
			Haynes (June 9, 1998) LeBlanc
			Haynes (June 9, 1998) Rosen
			Medine (Mar. 22, 1999) Harris
			Brinckerhoff (Apr. 30, 1999) Benner
			Brinckerhoff (June 3, 1999) McCorkell
			Brinckerhoff (June 24, 1999) Watkins
			Keller (Oct. 12, 1999) Landever
608	1681f	DISCLOSURE TO GOVERNMENTAL AGENCIES	Carson (Apr. 13, 1972)
			Feldman (Sept. 5, 1974)
			Grimes (Sept. 11, 1975)
			White (Feb. 18, 1977)
			Morris (July 26, 1979)
			Meyer (Mar. 22, 1983)
			Peeler (Nov. 1, 1983)
			Fortney (Dec. 2, 1983)
			Grimes (Dec. 9, 1983)
			Petruccelli (Apr. 9, 1984)
			Brinckerhoff (Apr. 23, 1986)
			Brinckerhoff (Sept. 22, 1987)
			d'Entremont (Jan. 25, 1996)
609	1681g	DISCLOSURES TO CONSUMERS (See also §§ 610, 612)	Carson (Apr. 8, 1971)
			Conway (May 3, 1971)
			Martin (May 26, 1971)
			Martin (June 11, 1971)
			Carson (Apr. 13, 1972)
			Bragg (May 15, 1972)
			Grimes (Feb. 23, 1973)
			Conway (Sept. 11, 1973)
			Russell (Sept. 18, 1973)
			Grimes (Jan. 9, 1973)
			Peeler (Apr. 15, 1974)
			Russell (May 15, 1974)
			Feldman (May 22, 1974)
			Feldman (May 30, 1974)
			Dea (July 19, 1974)

Index to FTC Letters   Appx. E

FTC Opinion Letters can be found on the CD-Rom accompanying this volume.

FCRA Section	15 U.S.C. Section	Section Topic	Relevant FTC Informal Staff Opinion Letters: Respondent (Date)
			Feldman (Aug. 21, 1974)
			White (Apr. 9, 1976)
			Peeler (Aug. 23, 1976)
			Peeler (Mar. 23, 1977)
			Peeler (Jan. 4, 1978)
			Peeler (Jan. 15, 1979)
			Peeler (Apr. 12, 1979)
			Goldfarb (c. Sept. 1980)
			Meyer (May 3, 1982)
			Federbush (Mar. 10, 1983)
			Brinckerhoff (Nov. 23, 1983)
			Harlow (Apr. 17, 1984)
			Grimes (Oct. 4, 1985)
			Brinckerhoff (Oct. 17, 1985)
			Grimes (Apr. 30, 1986)
			Brinckerhoff (July 22, 1986)
			Grimes (Oct. 8, 1986)
			Grimes (Oct. 10, 1986)
			Grimes (Dec. 15, 1986)
			Brinckerhoff (Aug. 4, 1987)
			Brinckerhoff (Sept. 11, 1987)
			Brinckerhoff (Oct. 27, 1987)
			Jerison (Aug. 3, 1988)
			Jerison (Aug. 5, 1988)
			Fitzpatrick (Dec. 28, 1988)
			Brinckerhoff (May 18, 1989)
			Grimes (Aug. 1, 1994)
			Isaac (July 5, 1995)
			Haynes (June 9, 1998) Beaudette
			Haynes (June 9, 1998) LeBlanc
			Haynes (June 9, 1998) Rosen
			Brinckerhoff (June 26, 1998) Lee
			Haynes (July 8, 1998) Hahn
			Brinckerhoff (Apr. 30, 1999) Benner
			Brinckerhoff (June 30, 2000) Darcy
			Keller (Aug. 1, 2000) Cohan
610	1681h	CONDITIONS OF DISCLOSURE TO CONSUMERS (See also § 609)	Conway (May 3, 1971)
			Carson (Apr. 13, 1972)
			Russell (Sept. 18, 1973)
			Grimes (Jan. 9, 1974)
			Feldman (May 22, 1974)
			Feldman (May 30, 1974)
			Peeler (Mar. 23, 1977)
			Peeler (Apr. 12, 1979)
			Brinckerhoff (Nov. 23, 1983)
			Harlow (Apr. 17, 1984)
			Brinckerhoff (Aug. 29, 1985)
			Grimes (Oct. 8, 1986)
			Grimes (Oct. 10, 1986)
			Grimes (Dec. 15, 1986)
			Brinckerhoff (Aug. 4, 1987)
			Brinckerhoff #1 (Sept. 11, 1987)
			Brinckerhoff #2 (Sept. 11, 1987)
			Brinckerhoff (Oct. 27, 1987)
			Noonan (Mar. 15, 1989)
			Haynes (June 9, 1998) Beaudette

Appx. E *Fair Credit Reporting*

FTC Opinion Letters can be found on the CD-Rom accompanying this volume.

FCRA Section	15 U.S.C. Section	Section Topic	Relevant FTC Informal Staff Opinion Letters: Respondent (Date)
611	1681i	PROCEDURE IN CASE OF DISPUTED ACCURACY (See also § 612)	Conway (May 3, 1971) Russell (Jan. 30, 1973) Conway (Aug. 27, 1973) Grimes (Jan. 9, 1974) Feldman (Apr. 18, 1974) Dea (July 19, 1974) Feldman (Aug. 21, 1974) Feldman (Aug. 30, 1974) Peeler (Mar. 8, 1976) Peeler (c. Apr. 1976) Peeler (Aug. 23, 1976) Peeler (Mar. 22, 1977) Cook (Apr. 22, 1977) Goldfarb (July 20, 1978) Peeler (July 25, 1978) Peeler (Nov. 7, 1978) Federbush (Mar. 10, 1983) Oliver (June 10, 1983) Peeler (Aug. 9, 1983) Brinckerhoff (Oct. 20, 1983) Brinckerhoff (Nov. 23, 1983) Fortney (Dec. 23, 1983) Petruccelli (Feb. 13, 1984) Harlow (Apr. 17, 1984) Maloney (Sept. 4, 1984) Brinckerhoff (Jan. 31, 1985) Brinckerhoff (July 30, 1985) Brinckerhoff (Oct. 17, 1985) Brinckerhoff (Oct. 29, 1985) Grimes (Feb. 27, 1986) Grimes (Apr. 11, 1986) Grimes (Apr. 30, 1986) Brinckerhoff (July 21, 1986) Grimes (July 23, 1986) Brinckerhoff (Jan. 29, 1987) Grimes (Apr. 16, 1987) Brinckerhoff (Aug. 4, 1987) Brinckerhoff (Sept. 22, 1987) Brinckerhoff # 1 (Sept. 15, 1988) Brinckerhoff # 2 (Sept. 15, 1988) Fitzpatrick (Dec. 28, 1988) Brinckerhoff (Apr. 19, 1989) Grimes (Aug. 1, 1994) Isaac (July 15, 1998) Edwards Keller (Aug. 1, 2000) Cohan
612	1681j	CHARGES FOR CERTAIN DISCLOSURES	Feldman (May 30, 1974) Feldman (May 31, 1974) Feldman (Aug. 30, 1974) Peeler (Aug. 23, 1976) Peeler (Mar. 20, 1977) Brinckerhoff (July 30, 1985) Brinckerhoff (Oct. 17, 1985) Grimes (Apr. 30, 1986) Grimes (Oct. 8, 1986) Grimes (Oct. 10, 1986) Grimes (Dec. 15, 1986)

Index to FTC Letters   Appx. E

FTC Opinion Letters can be found on the CD-Rom accompanying this volume.

FCRA Section	15 U.S.C. Section	Section Topic	**Relevant FTC Informal Staff Opinion Letters: Respondent (Date)**
			Brinckerhoff # 1 (Sept. 11, 1987)
			Jerison (Feb. 5, 1988)
			Grimes (Jan. 17, 1989)
			Brinckerhoff (June 26, 1998) Lee
			Keller (Aug. 1, 2000) Cohan
613	1681k	PUBLIC RECORD INFORMATION FOR EMPLOYMENT PURPOSES	Peeler (Mar. 20, 1977)
			Buffon (June 16, 1983)
			Grimes (Dec. 9, 1983)
			Maloney (Sept. 4, 1984)
			Grimes (Oct. 4, 1985)
			Grimes (Apr. 30, 1986)
			Brinckerhoff (July 24, 1986)
			Grimes (Oct. 10, 1986)
			Brinckerhoff (May 31, 1988)
			Brinckerhoff (June 12, 1998) Slyter
			Foster (May 5, 1999) Allan
			Brinckerhoff (Dec. 16, 1999) Holland
614	1681l	RESTRICTIONS ON INVESTIGATIVE CONSUMER REPORTS	Muris (Apr. 29, 1982)
615	1681m	REQUIREMENTS ON USERS OF CONSUMER REPORTS	Carson (Apr. 9, 1971)
			Silbergeld (Apr. 15, 1971)
			Kahn (Apr. 27, 1971)
			Conway (May 3, 1971)
			Feldman (May 5, 1971)
			Carson (May 21, 1971)
			Wan (June 2, 1971)
			Bragg (Dec. 3, 1971)
			Carson (c. Jan. 12, 1973)
			Russell (Jan. 30, 1973)
			Grimes (July 5, 1973)
			Wan (July 5, 1973)
			Russell (Sept. 27, 1973)
			Grimes (Dec. 19, 1973)
			Grimes (Jan. 9, 1974)
			Russell (Jan. 21, 1974)
			Feldman (Apr. 18, 1974)
			Russell (May 15, 1974)
			Feldman (Aug. 30, 1974)
			Feldman (Sept. 5, 1974)
			Dea (Mar. 31, 1975)
			Peeler (c. Apr. 1976)
			Goldfarb (Dec. 6, 1977)
			Peeler (Jan. 4, 1978)
			Peeler (Feb. 8, 1978)
			Peeler (Feb. 18, 1978)
			Peeler (Dec. 10, 1978)
			Reynolds (May 14, 1979)
			Noonan (Jan. 11, 1980)
			Brinckerhoff (Oct. 31, 1983)
			Brinckerhoff (Nov. 10, 1983)
			Maloney (Sept. 4, 1984)
			Brinckerhoff (Dec. 28, 1984)
			Grimes (Oct. 4, 1985)
			Grimes (Apr. 30, 1986)

Appx. E *Fair Credit Reporting*

FTC Opinion Letters can be found on the CD-Rom accompanying this volume.

FCRA Section	15 U.S.C. Section	Section Topic	Relevant FTC Informal Staff Opinion Letters: Respondent (Date)
			Grimes (Oct. 8, 1986)
			Grimes (Oct. 24, 1986)
			Noonan (Jan. 15, 1988)
			Grimes (Jan. 22, 1988)
			Brinckerhoff (Feb. 16, 1989)
			Clark (Feb. 22, 1989)
			Grimes (Feb. 10, 1994)
			Isaac (May 31, 1995)
			Isaac (July 5, 1995)
			Isaac (Nov. 13, 1995)
			Brinckerhoff (May 31, 1996)
			Brinckerhoff (June 27, 1997) Weisberg
			Brinckerhoff (Oct. 23, 1997) Solganik
			Kane (Oct. 27, 1997) Cast
			Haynes (Dec. 18, 1997) Hawkey
			Isaac (Feb. 23, 1998) Allison
			Brinckerhoff (Mar. 3, 1998) Schieber
			Brinckerhoff (July 10, 1998) Pickett
			Kammula (July 28, 1998) Everson
			Brinckerhoff (Oct. 26, 1998) Hall
			Isaac (Nov. 10, 1998) Sheffield
			Haynes (Mar. 17, 1999) Riddle
			Brinckerhoff (June 29, 1999) Cohan
			Brinckerhoff (Feb. 14, 2000) Allan
			Stires (Mar. 1, 2000) Ball
			Keller (July 14, 2000) Stinneford
			Berger (June 28, 2001) Latour
616	1681n	CIVIL LIABILITY FOR WILLFUL NONCOMPLIANCE	Peeler (Aug. 27, 1977)
			Meyer (Oct. 21, 1982)
			Federbush (Mar. 10, 1983)
			Harlow (Apr. 17, 1984)
			Grimes (Apr. 30, 1986)
			Cosgrove (Oct. 27, 1998) Greenblatt
618	1681p	STATUTE OF LIMITATIONS	Kammula (July 28, 1998) Kilgo
619	1681q	OBTAINING INFORMATION UNDER FALSE PRETENSES	Dea (Apr. 2, 1975)
			Peeler (Aug. 27, 1977)
			Meyer (Oct. 21, 1982)
			Peeler (Nov. 1, 1983)
			Grimes (Apr. 30, 1986)
			Grimes (Oct. 10, 1986)
620	1681r	UNAUTHORIZED DISCLOSURE BY OFFICERS OR EMPLOYEES	Feldman (May 22, 1974)
			Grimes (Apr. 30, 1986)
621	1681s	ADMINISTRATIVE ENFORCEMENT	Conway (Mar. 30, 1971)
			Carson (Apr. 8, 1971)
			Wan (May 25, 1973)
			Conway (Sept. 11, 1973)
			Dea (Feb. 14, 1975)
			Federbush (Mar. 10, 1983)
			Peeler (Nov. 1, 1983)
			Petruccelli (Feb. 13, 1984)
			Cosgrove (Oct. 27, 1998) Greenblatt

Index to FTC Letters Appx. E

FTC Opinion Letters can be found on the CD-Rom accompanying this volume.

FCRA Section	15 U.S.C. Section	Section Topic	**Relevant FTC Informal Staff Opinion Letters: Respondent (Date)**
623	1681s-2	FURNISHERS' RESPONSIBILITIES	Lamb (Dec. 23, 1997) Harvey Brinckerhoff (Mar. 10, 1998) Gillespie Lamb (July 17, 1998) Jaffe Medine (Mar. 22, 1999) Harris Brinckerhoff (June 4, 1999) Kosmerl Brinckerhoff (June 24, 1999) Watkins Brinckerhoff (Feb. 15, 2000) Amason Foster (Feb. 15, 2000) Boynton Keller (Aug. 1, 2000) Cohan
624**	1681t	RELATION TO STATE LAWS	Goldfarb (Sept. 9, 1978) Goldfarb (Sept. 20, 1978) Peeler (July 15, 1981) Oliver (June 10, 1983) Brinckerhoff (Nov. 4, 1983) Petruccelli (Feb. 13, 1984) Brinckerhoff (Sept. 11, 1987) Brinckerhoff (Feb. 16, 1989)

** Formerly §§ 622, 623.

Appendix F — Credit Repair Organizations Act

The Credit Repair Organizations Act was passed by Congress as part of the Omnibus Consolidated Appropriations Act of 1996, Pub. L. No. 104-208, § 2451, 110 Stat. 3009 (Sept. 30, 1996).[1] The Act as codified at 15 U.S.C. § 1679 is set out below.

TITLE 15—COMMERCE AND TRADE

* * *

CHAPTER 41—CONSUMER CREDIT PROTECTION

* * *

SUBCHAPTER II-A—CREDIT REPAIR ORGANIZATIONS

15 U.S.C. §
1679.	Findings and purposes
1679a.	Definitions
1679b.	Prohibited practices
1679c.	Disclosures
1679d.	Credit repair organizations contracts
1679e.	Right to cancel contract
1679f.	Noncompliance with this subchapter
1679g.	Civil liability
1679h.	Administrative enforcement
1679i.	Statute of limitations
1679j.	Relation to State law

§ 1679. Findings and purposes

(a) Findings.—The Congress makes the following findings:

(1) Consumers have a vital interest in establishing and maintaining their credit worthiness and credit standing in order to obtain and use credit. As a result, consumers who have experienced credit problems may seek assistance from credit repair organizations which offer to improve the credit standing of such consumers.

(2) Certain advertising and business practices of some companies engaged in the business of credit repair services have worked a financial hardship upon consumers, particularly those of limited economic means and who are inexperienced in credit matters.

(b) Purposes.—The purposes of this subchapter are—

(1) to ensure that prospective buyers of the services of credit repair organizations are provided with the information necessary to make an informed decision regarding the purchase of such services; and

(2) to protect the public from unfair or deceptive advertising and business practices by credit repair organizations.

[Pub. L. No. 90-321, tit. IV, § 402, *as added* Pub. L. No. 104-208, div. A, tit. II, § 2451, 110 Stat. 3009–462 (Sept. 30, 1996)]

§ 1679a. Definitions

For purposes of this subchapter, the following definitions apply:

(1) Consumer.—The term "consumer" means an individual.

(2) Consumer credit transaction.—The term "consumer credit transaction" means any transaction in which credit is offered or extended to an individual for personal, family, or household purposes.

(3) Credit repair organization.—The term "credit repair organization"—

(A) means any person who uses any instrumentality of interstate commerce or the mails to sell, provide, or perform (or represent that such person can or will sell, provide, or perform) any service, in return for the payment of money or other valuable consideration, for the express or implied purpose of—

(i) improving any consumer's credit record, credit history, or credit rating; or

(ii) providing advice or assistance to any consumer with regard to any activity or service described in clause (i); and

(B) does not include—

(i) any nonprofit organization which is exempt from taxation under section 501(c)(3) of Title 26;

(ii) any creditor (as defined in section 1602 of this title),[2] with respect to any consumer, to the extent the creditor is

---

1 Section 413 of the Act states: "This title [subchapter] shall apply after the end of the 6-month period beginning on the date of the enactment of the Credit Repair Organizations Act [Sept. 30, 1996], except with respect to contracts entered into by a credit repair organization before the end of such period."

2 "The term 'creditor' refers only to a person who both (1) regularly extends, whether in connection with loans, sales of property or services, or otherwise, consumer credit which is payable by agreement in more than four installments or for which the payment of a finance charge is or may be required, and (2) is the person to whom the debt arising from the consumer credit transaction is initially payable on the face of the

assisting the consumer to restructure any debt owed by the consumer to the creditor; or

(iii) any depository institution (as that term is defined in section 1813 of Title 12) or any Federal or State credit union (as those terms are defined in section 1752 of Title 12), or any affiliate or subsidiary of such a depository institution or credit union.

(4) **Credit.**—The term "credit" has the meaning given to such term in section 1602(e) of this title.[3]

[Pub. L. No. 90-321, tit. IV, § 403, *as added* Pub. L. No. 104-208, div. A, tit. II, § 2451, 110 Stat. 3009–455 (Sept. 30, 1996)]

§ 1679b. Prohibited practices

(a) **In general.**—No person may—

(1) make any statement, or counsel or advise any consumer to make any statement, which is untrue or misleading (or which, upon the exercise of reasonable care, should be known by the credit repair organization, officer, employee, agent, or other person to be untrue or misleading) with respect to any consumer's credit worthiness, credit standing, or credit capacity to—

(A) any consumer reporting agency (as defined in section 1681a(f) of this title); or

(B) any person—

(i) who has extended credit to the consumer; or

(ii) to whom the consumer has applied or is applying for an extension of credit;

(2) make any statement, or counsel or advise any consumer to make any statement, the intended effect of which is to alter the consumer's identification to prevent the display of the consumer's credit record, history, or rating for the purpose of concealing adverse information that is accurate and not obsolete to—

(A) any consumer reporting agency;

(B) any person—

(i) who has extended credit to the consumer; or

(ii) to whom the consumer has applied or is applying for an extension of credit;

(3) make or use any untrue or misleading representation of the services of the credit repair organization; or

(4) engage, directly or indirectly, in any act, practice, or course of business that constitutes or results in the commission of, or an attempt to commit, a fraud or deception on any person in connection with the offer or sale of the services of the credit repair organization.

(b) **Payment in advance.**—No credit repair organization may charge or receive any money or other valuable consideration for the performance of any service which the credit repair organization has agreed to perform for any consumer before such service is fully performed.

[Pub. L. No. 90-321, tit. IV, § 404, *as added* Pub. L. No. 104-208, div. A, tit. II, § 2451, 110 Stat. 3009–456 (Sept. 30, 1996)]

§ 1679c. Disclosures

(a) **Disclosure Required.**—Any credit repair organization shall provide any consumer with the following written statement before any contract or agreement between the consumer and the credit repair organization is executed:

"Consumer Credit File Rights Under State and Federal Law

"You have a right to dispute inaccurate information in your credit report by contacting the credit bureau directly. However, neither you nor any "credit repair" company or credit repair organization has the right to have accurate, current, and verifiable information removed from your credit report. The credit bureau must remove accurate, negative information from your report only if it is over 7 years old. Bankruptcy information can be reported for 10 years.

"You have a right to obtain a copy of your credit report from a credit bureau. You may be charged a reasonable fee. There is no fee, however, if you have been turned down for credit, employment, insurance, or a rental dwelling because of information in your credit report within the preceding 60 days. The credit bureau must provide someone to help you interpret the information in your credit file. You are entitled to receive a free copy of your credit report if you are unemployed and intend to apply for employment in the next 60 days, if you are a recipient of public welfare assistance, or if you have reason to believe that there is inaccurate information in your credit report due to fraud.

"You have a right to sue a credit repair organization that violates the Credit Repair Organization Act. This law prohibits deceptive practices by credit repair organizations.

"You have the right to cancel your contract with any credit repair organization for any reason within 3 business days from the date you signed it.

"Credit bureaus are required to follow reasonable procedures to ensure that the information they report is accurate. However, mistakes may occur.

"You may, on your own, notify a credit bureau in writing that you dispute the accuracy of information in your credit file. The credit bureau must then reinvestigate and modify or remove inaccurate or incomplete information. The credit bureau may not charge any fee for this service. Any pertinent information and copies of all documents you have concerning an error should be given to the credit bureau.

"If the credit bureau's reinvestigation does not resolve the dispute to your satisfaction, you may send a brief statement to the credit bureau, to be kept in your file, explaining why you think the record is inaccurate. The credit bureau must include a summary of your

---

evidence of indebtedness or, if there is no such evidence of indebtedness, by agreement." 15 U.S.C. § 1602(f).

3 "The term 'credit' means the right granted by a creditor to a debtor to defer payment of debt or to incur debt and defer its payment." 15 U.S.C. § 1602(e).

statement about disputed information with any report it issues about you.

"The Federal Trade Commission regulates credit bureaus and credit repair organizations. For more information contact:

**"The Public Reference Branch
"Federal Trade Commission Washington, D.C. 20580".**

(b) Separate statement requirement.—The written statement required under this section shall be provided as a document which is separate from any written contract or other agreement between the credit repair organization and the consumer or any other written material provided to the consumer.

(c) Retention of compliance records.—

(1) In general.—The credit repair organization shall maintain a copy of the statement signed by the consumer acknowledging receipt of the statement.

(2) Maintenance for 2 years.—The copy of any consumer's statement shall be maintained in the organization's files for 2 years after the date on which the statement is signed by the consumer.

[Pub. L. No. 90-321, tit. IV, § 405, *as added* Pub. L. No. 104-208, div. A, tit. II, § 2451, 110 Stat. 3009–457 (Sept. 30, 1996)]

§ 1679d. Credit repair organizations contracts

(a) Written contracts required.—No services may be provided by any credit repair organization for any consumer—

(1) unless a written and dated contract (for the purchase of such services) which meets the requirements of subsection (b) has been signed by the consumer; or

(2) before the end of the 3-business-day period beginning on the date the contract is signed.

(b) Terms and conditions of contract.—No contract referred to in subsection (a) meets the requirements of this subsection unless such contract includes (in writing)—

(1) the terms and conditions of payment, including the total amount of all payments to be made by the consumer to the credit repair organization or to any other person;

(2) a full and detailed description of the services to be performed by the credit repair organization for the consumer, including—

(A) all guarantees of performance; and

(B) an estimate of—

(i) the date by which the performance of the services (to be performed by the credit repair organization or any other person) will be complete; or

(ii) the length of the period necessary to perform such services;

(3) the credit repair organization's name and principal business address; and

(4) a conspicuous statement in bold face type, in immediate proximity to the space reserved for the consumer's signature on the contract, which reads as follows: "You may cancel this contract without penalty or obligation at any time before midnight of the 3d business day after the date on which you signed the contract. See the attached notice of cancellation form for an explanation of this right."

[Pub. L. No. 90-321, tit. IV, § 406, *as added* Pub. L. No. 104-208, div. A, tit. II, § 2451, 110 Stat. 3009–458 (Sept. 30, 1996)]

§ 1679e. Right to cancel contract

(a) In general.—Any consumer may cancel any contract with any credit repair organization without penalty or obligation by notifying the credit repair organization of the consumer's intention to do so at any time before midnight of the 3d business day which begins after the date on which the contract or agreement between the consumer and the credit repair organization is executed or would, but for this subsection, become enforceable against the parties.

(b) Cancellation form and other information.—Each contract shall be accompanied by a form, in duplicate, which has the heading "Notice of Cancellation" and contains in bold face type the following statement:

"You may cancel this contract, without any penalty or obligation, at any time before midnight of the 3d day which begins after the date the contract is signed by you.

To cancel this contract, mail or deliver a signed, dated copy of this cancellation notice, or any other written notice to [name of credit repair organization] at [address of credit repair organization] before midnight on [date]
I hereby cancel this transaction,
[date]
[purchaser's signature].".

(c) Consumer copy of contract required.—Any consumer who enters into any contract with any credit repair organization shall be given, by the organization—

(1) a copy of the completed contract and the disclosure statement required under section 1679c of this title; and

(2) a copy of any other document the credit repair organization requires the consumer to sign,

at the time the contract or the other document is signed.

[Pub. L. No. 90-321, tit. IV, § 407, *as added* Pub. L. No. 104-208, div. A, tit. II, § 2451, 110 Stat. 3009–459 (Sept. 30, 1996)]

§ 1679f. Noncompliance with this subchapter

(a) Consumer waivers invalid.—Any waiver by any consumer of any protection provided by or any right of the consumer under this subchapter—

(1) shall be treated as void; and

(2) may not be enforced by any Federal or State court or any other person.

(b) Attempt to obtain waiver.—Any attempt by any person to obtain a waiver from any consumer of any protection provided by or any right of the consumer under this subchapter shall be treated as a violation of this subchapter.

(c) Contracts not in compliance.—Any contract for services which does not comply with the applicable provisions of this subchapter—

(1) shall be treated as void; and

(2) may not be enforced by any Federal or State court or any other person.

[Pub. L. No. 90-321, tit. IV, § 408, *as added* Pub. L. No. 104-208, div. A, tit. II, § 2451, 110 Stat. 3009-459 (Sept. 30, 1996)]

§ 1679g. Civil liability

(a) Liability established.—Any person who fails to comply with any provision of this subchapter with respect to any other person shall be liable to such person in an amount equal to the sum of the amounts determined under each of the following paragraphs:

(1) Actual damages.—The greater of—

(A) the amount of any actual damage sustained by such person as a result of such failure; or

(B) any amount paid by the person to the credit repair organization.

(2) Punitive damages

(A) **Individual actions.**—In the case of any action by an individual, such additional amount as the court may allow.

(B) **Class actions.**—In the case of a class action, the sum of—

(i) the aggregate of the amount which the court may allow for each named plaintiff; and

(ii) the aggregate of the amount which the court may allow for each other class member, without regard to any minimum individual recovery.

(3) Attorneys' fees.—In the case of any successful action to enforce any liability under paragraph (1) or (2), the costs of the action, together with reasonable attorneys' fees.

(b) Factors to be considered in awarding punitive damages.—In determining the amount of any liability of any credit repair organization under subsection (a)(2), the court shall consider, among other relevant factors—

(1) the frequency and persistence of noncompliance by the credit repair organization;

(2) the nature of the noncompliance;

(3) the extent to which such noncompliance was intentional; and

(4) in the case of any class action, the number of consumers adversely affected.

[Pub. L. No. 90-321, tit. IV, § 409, *as added* Pub. L. No. 104-208, div. A, tit. II, § 2451, 110 Stat. 3009-459 (Sept. 30, 1996)]

§ 1679h. Administrative enforcement

(a) In general.—Compliance with the requirements imposed under this subchapter with respect to credit repair organizations shall be enforced under the Federal Trade Commission Act by the Federal Trade Commission.

(b) Violations of this subchapter treated as violations of Federal Trade Commission Act.

(1) In general.—For the purpose of the exercise by the Federal Trade Commission of the Commission's functions and powers under the Federal Trade Commission Act, any violation of any requirement or prohibition imposed under this subchapter with respect to credit repair organizations shall constitute an unfair or deceptive act or practice in commerce in violation of section 5(a) of the Federal Trade Commission Act.

(2) Enforcement authority under other law.—All functions and powers of the Federal Trade Commission under the Federal Trade Commission Act shall be available to the Commission to enforce compliance with this subchapter by any person subject to enforcement by the Federal Trade Commission pursuant to this subsection, including the power to enforce the provisions of this subchapter in the same manner as if the violation had been a violation of any Federal Trade Commission trade regulation rule, without regard to whether the credit repair organization—

(A) is engaged in commerce; or

(B) meets any other jurisdictional tests in the Federal Trade Commission Act.

(c) State action for violations

(1) Authority of states.—In addition to such other remedies as are provided under State law, whenever the chief law enforcement officer of a State, or an official or agency designated by a State, has reason to believe that any person has violated or is violating this subchapter, the State—

(A) may bring an action to enjoin such violation;

(B) may bring an action on behalf of its residents to recover damages for which the person is liable to such residents under section 1679g of this title as a result of the violation; and

(C) in the case of any successful action under subparagraph (A) or (B), shall be awarded the costs of the action and reasonable attorney fees as determined by the court.

(2) Rights of commission

(A) **Notice to commission.**—The State shall serve prior written notice of any civil action under paragraph (1) upon the Federal Trade Commission and provide the Commission with a copy of its complaint, except in any case where such prior notice is not feasible, in which case the State shall serve such notice immediately upon instituting such action.

(B) **Intervention.**—The Commission shall have the right—

(i) to intervene in any action referred to in subparagraph (A);

(ii) upon so intervening, to be heard on all matters arising in the action; and

(iii) to file petitions for appeal.

(3) Investigatory powers.—For purposes of bringing any action under this subsection, nothing in this subsection shall prevent the chief law enforcement officer, or an official or agency designated by a State, from exercising the powers conferred on the chief law enforcement officer or such official by the laws of such State to conduct investigations or to administer oaths or affirmations or to compel the attendance of witnesses or the production of documentary and other evidence.

(4) Limitation.—Whenever the Federal Trade Commission has instituted a civil action for violation of this subchapter, no State may, during the pendency of such action, bring an action under this section against any defendant named in the complaint of the Commission for any violation of this subchapter that is alleged in that complaint.

[Pub. L. No. 90-321, tit. IV, § 410, *as added* Pub. L. No. 104-208, div. A, tit. II, § 2451, 110 Stat. 3009–459 (Sept. 30, 1996)]

§ 1679i. Statute of limitations

Any action to enforce any liability under this subchapter may be brought before the later of—

(1) the end of the 5-year period beginning on the date of the occurrence of the violation involved; or

(2) in any case in which any credit repair organization has materially and willfully misrepresented any information which—

(A) the credit repair organization is required, by any provision of this subchapter, to disclose to any consumer; and

(B) is material to the establishment of the credit repair organization's liability to the consumer under this subchapter, the end of the 5-year period beginning on the date of the discovery by the consumer of the misrepresentation.

[Pub. L. No. 90-321, tit. IV, § 411, *as added* Pub. L. No. 104-208, div. A, tit. II, § 2451, 110 Stat. 3009–459 (Sept. 30, 1996)]

§ 1679j. Relation to state law

This subchapter shall not annul, alter, affect, or exempt any person subject to the provisions of this subchapter from complying with any law of any State except to the extent that such law is inconsistent with any provision of this subchapter, and then only to the extent of the inconsistency.

Pub. L. No. 90-321, tit. IV. § 412, *as added* Pub. L. No. 104-208, div. A, tit. II, § 2451, 110 Stat. 3009–459 (Sept. 30, 1996)]

Appendix G Gramm-Leach-Bliley

Congress passed the Gramm-Leach-Bliley Act in 1999 as Pub. L. No. 106-102. Title V of the Act, codified at 15 U.S.C. §§ 6801–6809, addresses consumers' financial privacy by regulating financial institutions' disclosure of consumers' "nonpublic personal information," 15 U.S.C. § 6809(4).

The Act does not primarily regulate the use of consumers' financial information, rather, the Act requires that financial institutions give certain notices to consumers and customers about their use of such information, and provide them with the opportunity to opt out of some, but not all, disclosures of that information.

This appendix reprints the statutory provisions, the regulations issued by the Federal Trade Commission pursuant to the provisions, key portions of other agencies' regulations implementing the Act's information security requirements, and the FTC's model opt-out notice that financial institutions may use to fulfill some of their obligations under the Act.

G.1 Gramm-Leach-Bliley Act

The following is the text of Title V of the Gramm-Leach-Bliley Act, 15 U.S.C. §§ 6801–6809.

TITLE 15—COMMERCE AND TRADE

* * *

CHAPTER 94—PRIVACY

SUBCHAPTER I—DISCLOSURE OF NONPUBLIC PERSONAL INFORMATION

§ 6801.   Protection of nonpublic personal information
§ 6802.   Obligations with respect to disclosures of personal information
§ 6803.   Disclosure of institution privacy policy
§ 6804.   Rulemaking
§ 6805.   Enforcement
§ 6806.   Relation to other provisions
§ 6807.   Relation to State laws

SUBCHAPTER II—FRAUDULENT ACCESS TO FINANCIAL INFORMATION

§ 6808.   Study of information sharing among financial affiliates
§ 6809.   Definitions

TITLE 15—COMMERCE AND TRADE

* * *

CHAPTER 94—PRIVACY

SUBCHAPTER I—DISCLOSURE OF NONPUBLIC PERSONAL INFORMATION

§ 6801. Protection of nonpublic personal information

(a) Privacy obligation policy

It is the policy of the Congress that each financial institution has an affirmative and continuing obligation to respect the privacy of its customers and to protect the security and confidentiality of those customers' nonpublic personal information.

(b) Financial institutions safeguards

In furtherance of the policy in subsection (a) of this section, each agency or authority described in section 6805(a) of this title shall establish appropriate standards for the financial institutions subject to their jurisdiction relating to administrative, technical, and physical safeguards—

(1) to insure the security and confidentiality of customer records and information;

(2) to protect against any anticipated threats or hazards to the security or integrity of such records; and

(3) to protect against unauthorized access to or use of such records or information which could result in substantial harm or inconvenience to any customer.

[Pub. L. No. 106-102, tit. V, § 501, 113 Stat. 1436 (Nov. 12, 1999)]

§ 6802. Obligations with respect to disclosures of personal information

(a) Notice requirements

Except as otherwise provided in this subchapter, a financial institution may not, directly or through any affiliate, disclose to a nonaffiliated third party any nonpublic personal information, unless such financial institution provides or has provided to the consumer a notice that complies with section 6803 of this title.

(b) Opt out

(1) In general

A financial institution may not disclose nonpublic personal information to a nonaffiliated third party unless—

(A) such financial institution clearly and conspicuously discloses to the consumer, in writing or in electronic form or other form permitted by the regulations prescribed under section 6804 of this title, that such information may be disclosed to such third party;

(B) the consumer is given the opportunity, before the time that such information is initially disclosed, to direct that such information not be disclosed to such third party; and

(C) the consumer is given an explanation of how the consumer can exercise that nondisclosure option.

(2) Exception

This subsection shall not prevent a financial institution from providing nonpublic personal information to a nonaffiliated third party to perform services for or functions on behalf of the financial institution, including marketing of the financial institution's own products or services, or financial products or services offered pursuant to joint agreements between two or more financial institutions that comply with the requirements imposed by the regulations prescribed under section 6804 of this title, if the financial institution fully discloses the providing of such information and enters into a contractual agreement with the third party that requires the third party to maintain the confidentiality of such information.

(c) Limits on reuse of information

Except as otherwise provided in this subchapter, a nonaffiliated third party that receives from a financial institution nonpublic personal information under this section shall not, directly or through an affiliate of such receiving third party, disclose such information to any other person that is a nonaffiliated third party of both the financial institution and such receiving third party, unless such disclosure would be lawful if made directly to such other person by the financial institution.

(d) Limitations on the sharing of account number information for marketing purposes

A financial institution shall not disclose, other than to a consumer reporting agency, an account number or similar form of access number or access code for a credit card account, deposit account, or transaction account of a consumer to any nonaffiliated third party for use in telemarketing, direct mail marketing, or other marketing through electronic mail to the consumer.

(e) General exceptions

Subsections (a) and (b) of this section shall not prohibit the disclosure of nonpublic personal information—

(1) as necessary to effect, administer, or enforce a transaction requested or authorized by the consumer, or in connection with—

(A) servicing or processing a financial product or service requested or authorized by the consumer;

(B) maintaining or servicing the consumer's account with the financial institution, or with another entity as part of a private label credit card program or other extension of credit on behalf of such entity; or

(C) a proposed or actual securitization, secondary market sale (including sales of servicing rights), or similar transaction related to a transaction of the consumer;

(2) with the consent or at the direction of the consumer;

(3)(A) to protect the confidentiality or security of the financial institution's records pertaining to the consumer, the service or product, or the transaction therein; (B) to protect against or prevent actual or potential fraud, unauthorized transactions, claims, or other liability; (C) for required institutional risk control, or for resolving customer disputes or inquiries; (D) to persons holding a legal or beneficial interest relating to the consumer; or (E) to persons acting in a fiduciary or representative capacity on behalf of the consumer;

(4) to provide information to insurance rate advisory organizations, guaranty funds or agencies, applicable rating agencies of the financial institution, persons assessing the institution's compliance with industry standards, and the institution's attorneys, accountants, and auditors;

(5) to the extent specifically permitted or required under other provisions of law and in accordance with the Right to Financial Privacy Act of 1978 (12 U.S.C. 3401 et seq.), to law enforcement agencies (including a Federal functional regulator, the Secretary of the Treasury with respect to subchapter II of chapter 53 of title 31, and chapter 2 of title I of Public Law 91-508 (12 U.S.C. 1951–1959), a State insurance authority, or the Federal Trade Commission), self-regulatory organizations, or for an investigation on a matter related to public safety;

(6)(A) to a consumer reporting agency in accordance with the Fair Credit Reporting Act (15 U.S.C. 1681 et seq.), or (B) from a consumer report reported by a consumer reporting agency;

(7) in connection with a proposed or actual sale, merger, transfer, or exchange of all or a portion of a business or operating unit if the disclosure of nonpublic personal information concerns solely consumers of such business or unit; or

(8) to comply with Federal, State, or local laws, rules, and other applicable legal requirements; to comply with a properly authorized civil, criminal, or regulatory investigation or subpoena or summons by Federal, State, or local authorities; or to respond to judicial process or government regulatory authorities having jurisdiction over the financial institution for examination, compliance, or other purposes as authorized by law.

[Pub. L. No. 106-102, tit. V, § 502, 113 Stat. 1437 (Nov. 12, 1999)]

§ 6803. Disclosure of institution privacy policy

(a) Disclosure required

At the time of establishing a customer relationship with a consumer and not less than annually during the continuation of such relationship, a financial institution shall provide a clear and conspicuous disclosure to such consumer, in writing or in electronic form or other form permitted by the regulations prescribed under section 6804 of this title, of such financial institution's policies and practices with respect to—

(1) disclosing nonpublic personal information to affiliates and nonaffiliated third parties, consistent with section 6802 of this title, including the categories of information that may be disclosed;

(2) disclosing nonpublic personal information of persons who have ceased to be customers of the financial institution; and

(3) protecting the nonpublic personal information of consumers. Such disclosures shall be made in accordance with the regulations prescribed under section 6804 of this title.

(b) Information to be included

The disclosure required by subsection (a) of this section shall include—

(1) the policies and practices of the institution with respect to disclosing nonpublic personal information to nonaffiliated third parties, other than agents of the institution, consistent with section 6802 of this title, and including—

(A) the categories of persons to whom the information is or may be disclosed, other than the persons to whom the information may be provided pursuant to section 6802(e) of this title; and

(B) the policies and practices of the institution with respect to disclosing of nonpublic personal information of persons who have ceased to be customers of the financial institution;

(2) the categories of nonpublic personal information that are collected by the financial institution;

(3) the policies that the institution maintains to protect the confidentiality and security of nonpublic personal information in accordance with section 6801 of this title; and

(4) the disclosures required, if any, under section 1681a(d)(2)(A)(iii) of this title.

[Pub. L. No. 106-102, tit. V, § 503, 113 Stat. 1439 (Nov. 12, 1999)]

§ 6804. Rulemaking

(a) Regulatory authority

(1) Rulemaking

The Federal banking agencies, the National Credit Union Administration, the Secretary of the Treasury, the Securities and Exchange Commission, and the Federal Trade Commission shall each prescribe, after consultation as appropriate with representatives of State insurance authorities designated by the National Association of Insurance Commissioners, such regulations as may be necessary to carry out the purposes of this subchapter with respect to the financial institutions subject to their jurisdiction under section 6805 of this title.

(2) Coordination, consistency, and comparability

Each of the agencies and authorities required under paragraph (1) to prescribe regulations shall consult and coordinate with the other such agencies and authorities for the purposes of assuring, to the extent possible, that the regulations prescribed by each such agency and authority are consistent and comparable with the regulations prescribed by the other such agencies and authorities.

(3) Procedures and deadline

Such regulations shall be prescribed in accordance with applicable requirements of title 5 and shall be issued in final form not later than 6 months after November 12, 1999.

(b) Authority to grant exceptions

The regulations prescribed under subsection (a) of this section may include such additional exceptions to subsections (a) through (d) of section 6802 of this title as are deemed consistent with the purposes of this subchapter.

[Pub. L. No. 106-102, tit. V, § 504, 113 Stat. 1439 (Nov. 12, 1999)]

§ 6805. Enforcement

(a) In general

This subchapter and the regulations prescribed thereunder shall be enforced by the Federal functional regulators, the State insurance authorities, and the Federal Trade Commission with respect to financial institutions and other persons subject to their jurisdiction under applicable law, as follows:

(1) Under section 1818 of title 12, in the case of—

(A) national banks, Federal branches and Federal agencies of foreign banks, and any subsidiaries of such entities (except brokers, dealers, persons providing insurance, investment companies, and investment advisers), by the Office of the Comptroller of the Currency;

(B) member banks of the Federal Reserve System (other than national banks), branches and agencies of foreign banks (other than Federal branches, Federal agencies, and insured State branches of foreign banks), commercial lending companies owned or controlled by foreign banks, organizations operating under section 25 or 25A of the Federal Reserve Act (12 U.S.C. 601 et seq., 611 et seq.), and bank holding companies and their nonbank subsidiaries or affiliates (except brokers, dealers, persons providing insurance, investment companies, and investment advisers), by the Board of Governors of the Federal Reserve System;

(C) banks insured by the Federal Deposit Insurance Corporation (other than members of the Federal Reserve System), insured State branches of foreign banks, and any subsidiaries of such entities (except brokers, dealers, persons providing insurance, investment companies, and investment advisers), by the Board of Directors of the Federal Deposit Insurance Corporation; and

(D) savings associations the deposits of which are insured by the Federal Deposit Insurance Corporation, and any subsidiaries of such savings associations (except brokers, dealers, persons providing insurance, investment companies, and investment advisers), by the Director of the Office of Thrift Supervision.

(2) Under the Federal Credit Union Act (12 U.S.C. 1751 et seq.), by the Board of the National Credit Union Administration with respect to any federally insured credit union, and any subsidiaries of such an entity.

(3) Under the Securities Exchange Act of 1934 (15 U.S.C. 78a et seq.), by the Securities and Exchange Commission with respect to any broker or dealer.

(4) Under the Investment Company Act of 1940 (15 U.S.C. 80a-1 et seq.), by the Securities and Exchange Commission with respect to investment companies.

(5) Under the Investment Advisers Act of 1940 (15 U.S.C. 80b-1 et seq.), by the Securities and Exchange Commission with respect to investment advisers registered with the Commission under such Act.

(6) Under State insurance law, in the case of any person engaged in providing insurance, by the applicable State insurance authority of the State in which the person is domiciled, subject to section 6701 of this title.

(7) Under the Federal Trade Commission Act (15 U.S.C. 41 et seq.), by the Federal Trade Commission for any other financial institution or other person that is not subject to the jurisdiction of any agency or authority under paragraphs (1) through (6) of this subsection.

(b) Enforcement of section 6801

(1) In general

Except as provided in paragraph (2), the agencies and authorities described in subsection (a) of this section shall implement the standards prescribed under section 6801(b) of this title in the same manner, to the extent practicable, as standards prescribed pursuant to section 1831p-1(a) of title 12 are implemented pursuant to such section.

(2) Exception

The agencies and authorities described in paragraphs (3), (4), (5), (6), and (7) of subsection (a) of this section shall implement the standards prescribed under section 6801(b) of this title by rule with respect to the financial institutions and other persons subject to their respective jurisdictions under subsection (a) of this section.

(c) Absence of State action

If a State insurance authority fails to adopt regulations to carry out this subchapter, such State shall not be eligible to override, pursuant to section 1831x(g)(2)(B)(iii) of title 12, the insurance customer protection regulations prescribed by a Federal banking agency under section 1831x(a) of title 12.

(d) Definitions

The terms used in subsection (a)(1) of this section that are not defined in this subchapter or otherwise defined in section 1813(s) of title 12 shall have the same meaning as given in section 3101 of title 12.

[Pub. L. No. 106-102, tit. V, § 505, 113 Stat. 1440 (Nov. 12, 1999)]

§ 6806. Relation to other provisions

Except for the amendments made by subsections (a) and (b), nothing in this chapter shall be construed to modify, limit, or supersede the operation of the Fair Credit Reporting Act (15 U.S.C. 1681 et seq.), and no inference shall be drawn on the basis of the provisions of this chapter regarding whether information is transaction or experience information under section 603 of such Act (15 U.S.C. 1681a).

[Pub. L. No. 106-102, tit. V, § 506(c), 113 Stat. 1442 (Nov. 12, 1999)]

§ 6807. Relation to State laws

(a) In general

This subchapter and the amendments made by this subchapter shall not be construed as superseding, altering, or affecting any statute, regulation, order, or interpretation in effect in any State, except to the extent that such statute, regulation, order, or interpretation is inconsistent with the provisions of this subchapter, and then only to the extent of the inconsistency.

(b) Greater protection under State law

For purposes of this section, a State statute, regulation, order, or interpretation is not inconsistent with the provisions of this subchapter if the protection such statute, regulation, order, or interpretation affords any person is greater than the protection provided under this subchapter and the amendments made by this subchapter, as determined by the Federal Trade Commission, after consultation with the agency or authority with jurisdiction under section 6805(a) of this title of either the person that initiated the complaint or that is the subject of the complaint, on its own motion or upon the petition of any interested party.

[Pub. L. No. 106-102, tit. V, § 507, 113 Stat. 1442 (Nov. 12, 1999)]

§ 6808. Study of information sharing among financial affiliates

(a) In general

The Secretary of the Treasury, in conjunction with the Federal functional regulators and the Federal Trade Commission, shall conduct a study of information sharing practices among financial institutions and their affiliates. Such study shall include—

(1) the purposes for the sharing of confidential customer information with affiliates or with nonaffiliated third parties;

(2) the extent and adequacy of security protections for such information;

(3) the potential risks for customer privacy of such sharing of information;

(4) the potential benefits for financial institutions and affiliates of such sharing of information;

(5) the potential benefits for customers of such sharing of information;

(6) the adequacy of existing laws to protect customer privacy;

(7) the adequacy of financial institution privacy policy and privacy rights disclosure under existing law;

(8) the feasibility of different approaches, including opt-out and opt-in, to permit customers to direct that confidential information not be shared with affiliates and nonaffiliated third parties; and

(9) the feasibility of restricting sharing of information for specific uses or of permitting customers to direct the uses for which information may be shared.

(b) Consultation

The Secretary shall consult with representatives of State insurance authorities designated by the National Association of Insurance Commissioners, and also with financial services industry, consumer organizations and privacy groups, and other representatives of the general public, in formulating and conducting the study required by subsection (a) of this section.

(c) Report

On or before January 1, 2002, the Secretary shall submit a report to the Congress containing the findings and conclusions of the study required under subsection (a) of this section, together with such recommendations for legislative or administrative action as may be appropriate.

[Pub. L. No. 106-102, tit. V, § 508, 113 Stat. 1442 (Nov. 12, 1999)]

§ 6809. Definitions

As used in this subchapter:

(1) Federal banking agency

The term "Federal banking agency" has the same meaning as given in section 1813 of title 12.

(2) Federal functional regulator

The term "Federal functional regulator" means—

(A) the Board of Governors of the Federal Reserve System;

(B) the Office of the Comptroller of the Currency;

(C) the Board of Directors of the Federal Deposit Insurance Corporation;

(D) the Director of the Office of Thrift Supervision;

(E) the National Credit Union Administration Board; and

(F) the Securities and Exchange Commission.

(3) Financial institution

(A) In general

The term "financial institution" means any institution the business of which is engaging in financial activities as described in section 1843(k) of title 12.

(B) Persons subject to CFTC regulation

Notwithstanding subparagraph (A), the term "financial institution" does not include any person or entity with respect to any financial activity that is subject to the jurisdiction of the Commodity Futures Trading Commission under the Commodity Exchange Act (7 U.S.C. 1 et seq.).

(C) Farm credit institutions

Notwithstanding subparagraph (A), the term "financial institution" does not include the Federal Agricultural Mortgage Corporation or any entity chartered and operating under the Farm Credit Act of 1971 (12 U.S.C. 2001 et seq.).

(D) Other secondary market institutions

Notwithstanding subparagraph (A), the term "financial institution" does not include institutions chartered by Congress specifically to engage in transactions described in section 6802(e)(1)(C) of this title, as long as such institutions do not sell or transfer nonpublic personal information to a nonaffiliated third party.

(4) Nonpublic personal information

(A) The term "nonpublic personal information" means personally identifiable financial information—

(i) provided by a consumer to a financial institution;

(ii) resulting from any transaction with the consumer or any service performed for the consumer; or

(iii) otherwise obtained by the financial institution.

(B) Such term does not include publicly available information, as such term is defined by the regulations prescribed under section 6804 of this title.

(C) Notwithstanding subparagraph (B), such term—

(i) shall include any list, description, or other grouping of consumers (and publicly available information pertaining to them) that is derived using any nonpublic personal information other than publicly available information; but

(ii) shall not include any list, description, or other grouping of consumers (and publicly available information pertaining to them) that is derived without using any nonpublic personal information.

(5) Nonaffiliated third party

The term "nonaffiliated third party" means any entity that is not an affiliate of, or related by common ownership or affiliated by corporate control with, the financial institution, but does not include a joint employee of such institution.

(6) Affiliate

The term "affiliate" means any company that controls, is controlled by, or is under common control with another company.

(7) Necessary to effect, administer, or enforce

The term "as necessary to effect, administer, or enforce the transaction" means—

(A) the disclosure is required, or is a usual, appropriate, or acceptable method, to carry out the transaction or the product or service business of which the transaction is a part, and record or service or maintain the consumer's account in the ordinary course of providing the financial service or financial product, or to administer or service benefits or claims relating to the transaction or the product or service business of which it is a part, and includes—

(i) providing the consumer or the consumer's agent or broker with a confirmation, statement, or other record of the transaction, or information on the status or value of the financial service or financial product; and

(ii) the accrual or recognition of incentives or bonuses associated with the transaction that are provided by the financial institution or any other party;

(B) the disclosure is required, or is one of the lawful or appropriate methods, to enforce the rights of the financial institution or of other persons engaged in carrying out the financial transaction, or providing the product or service;

(C) the disclosure is required, or is a usual, appropriate, or acceptable method, for insurance underwriting at the consumer's request or for reinsurance purposes, or for any of the following purposes as they relate to a consumer's insurance: Account administration, reporting, investigating, or preventing fraud or material misrepresentation, processing premium payments, processing insurance claims, administering insurance benefits (including utilization review activities), participating in research projects, or as otherwise required or specifically permitted by Federal or State law; or

(D) the disclosure is required, or is a usual, appropriate or acceptable method, in connection with—

(i) the authorization, settlement, billing, processing, clearing, transferring, reconciling, or collection of amounts charged, debited, or otherwise paid using a debit, credit or other payment card, check, or account number, or by other payment means;

(ii) the transfer of receivables, accounts or interests therein; or

(iii) the audit of debit, credit or other payment information.

(8) State insurance authority

The term "State insurance authority" means, in the case of any person engaged in providing insurance, the State insurance authority of the State in which the person is domiciled.

(9) Consumer

The term "consumer" means an individual who obtains, from a financial institution, financial products or services which are to be used primarily for personal, family, or household purposes, and also means the legal representative of such an individual.

(10) Joint agreement

The term "joint agreement" means a formal written contract pursuant to which two or more financial institutions jointly offer, endorse, or sponsor a financial product or service, and as may be further defined in the regulations prescribed under section 6804 of this title.

(11) Customer relationship

The term "time of establishing a customer relationship" shall be defined by the regulations prescribed under section 6804 of this title, and shall, in the case of a financial institution engaged in extending credit directly to consumers to finance purchases of goods or services, mean the time of establishing the credit relationship with the consumer.

[Pub. L. No. 106-102, tit. V, § 509, 113 Stat. 1443 (Nov. 12, 1999)]

G.2 FTC Rules—Selected Provisions

The FTC has issued regulations regarding the privacy provisions of the Gramm-Leach-Bliley Act, which are collectively known as the "Privacy Rule" and which are set forth below. The FTC has also designated standards that institutions must employ to safeguard customer information, collectively known as the "Safeguard Rules," also set forth below.

TITLE 16—COMMERCIAL PRACTICES

CHAPTER I—FEDERAL TRADE COMMISSION

* * *

SUBCHAPTER C—REGULATIONS UNDER SPECIFIC ACTS OF CONGRESS

* * *

PART 313—PRIVACY OF CONSUMER FINANCIAL INFORMATION

16 C.F.R. §

313.1	Purpose and scope.
313.2	Rule of construction.
313.3	Definitions.

SUBPART A—PRIVACY AND OPT OUT NOTICES

313.4	Initial privacy notice to consumers required.
313.5	Annual privacy notice to customers required.
313.6	Information to be included in privacy notices.
313.7	Form of opt out notice to consumers; opt out methods.
313.8	Revised privacy notices.
313.9	Delivering privacy and opt out notices.

SUBPART B—LIMITS ON DISCLOSURES

313.10	Limits on disclosure of non-public personal information to nonaffiliated third parties.
313.11	Limits on redisclosure and reuse of information.
313.12	Limits on sharing account number information for marketing purposes.

SUBPART C—EXCEPTIONS

313.13 Exception to opt out requirements for service providers and joint marketing.
313.14 Exceptions to notice and opt out requirements for processing and servicing transactions.
313.15 Other exceptions to notice and opt out requirements.

SUBPART D—RELATION TO OTHER LAWS; EFFECTIVE DATE

313.16 Protection of Fair Credit Reporting Act.
313.17 Relation to State laws.
313.18 Effective date; transition rule.

Appendix A to Part 313—Sample Clauses

PART 314—STANDARDS FOR SAFEGUARDING CUSTOMER INFORMATION

314.1 Purpose and scope.
314.2 Definitions.
314.3 Standards for safeguarding customer information.
314.4 Elements.
314.5 Effective Date

TITLE 16—COMMERCIAL PRACTICES

CHAPTER I—FEDERAL TRADE COMMISSION

* * *

SUBCHAPTER C—REGULATIONS UNDER SPECIFIC ACTS OF CONGRESS

* * *

PART 313—PRIVACY OF CONSUMER FINANCIAL INFORMATION

§ 313.1 Purpose and scope.

(a) *Purpose.* This part governs the treatment of nonpublic personal information about consumers by the financial institutions listed in paragraph (b) of this section. This part:

(1) Requires a financial institution in specified circumstances to provide notice to customers about its privacy policies and practices;

(2) Describes the conditions under which a financial institution may disclose nonpublic personal information about consumers to nonaffiliated third parties; and

(3) Provides a method for consumers to prevent a financial institution from disclosing that information to most nonaffiliated third parties by "opting out" of that disclosure, subject to the exceptions in §§ 313.13, 313.14, and 313.15.

(b) *Scope.* This part applies only to nonpublic personal information about individuals who obtain financial products or services primarily for personal, family or household purposes from the institutions listed below. This part does not apply to information about companies or about individuals who obtain financial products or services for business, commercial, or agricultural purposes. This part applies to those "financial institutions" and "other persons" over which the Federal Trade Commission ("Commission") has enforcement authority pursuant to Section 505(a)(7) of the Gramm-Leach-Bliley Act. An entity is a "financial institution" if its business is engaging in a financial activity as described in Section 4(k) of the Bank Holding Company Act of 1956, 12 U.S.C. 1843(k), which incorporates by reference activities enumerated by the Federal Reserve Board in 12 CFR 211.5(d) and 12 CFR 225.28. The "financial institutions' subject to the Commission's enforcement authority are those that are not otherwise subject to the enforcement authority of another regulator under Section 505 of the Gramm-Leach-Bliley Act. More specifically, those entities include, but are not limited to, mortgage lenders, "pay day" lenders, finance companies, mortgage brokers, account servicers, check cashers, wire transfers, travel agencies operated in connection with financial services, collection agencies, credit counselors and other financial advisors, tax preparation firms, non-federally insured credit unions, and investment advisors that are not required to register with the Securities and Exchange Commission. They are referred to in this part as "You." The "other persons" to whom this part applies are third parties that are not financial institutions, but that receive nonpublic personal information from financial institutions with whom they are not affiliated. Nothing in this part modifies, limits, or supersedes the standards governing individually identifiable health information promulgated by the Secretary of Health and Human Services under the authority of sections 262 and 264 of the Health Insurance Portability and Accountability Act of 1996, 42 U.S.C. 1320d-1320d-8. Any institution of higher education that complies with the Federal Educational Rights and Privacy Act ("FERPA"), 20 U.S.C. 1232g, and its implementing regulations, 34 CFR part 99, and that is also a financial institution subject to the requirements of this part, shall be deemed to be in compliance with this part if it is in compliance with FERPA.

[65 Fed. Reg. 33677 (May 24, 2000)]

§ 313.2 Rule of construction.

The examples in this part and the sample clauses in Appendix A of this part are not exclusive. Compliance with an example or use of a sample clause, to the extent applicable, constitutes compliance with this part. For non-federally insured credit unions, compliance with an example or use of a sample clause contained in 12 CFR part 716, to the extent applicable, constitutes compliance with this part. For intrastate securities broker-dealers and investment advisors not registered with the Securities and Exchange Commission, compliance with an example or use of a sample clause contained in 17 CFR part 248, to the extent applicable, constitutes compliance with this part.

[65 Fed. Reg. 33677 (May 24, 2000)]

§ 313.3 Definitions.

As used in this part, unless the context requires otherwise:

(a) *Affiliate* means any company that controls, is controlled by, or is under common control with another company.

(b)(1) *Clear and conspicuous* means that a notice is reasonably understandable and designed to call attention to the nature and significance of the information in the notice.

(2) *Examples*—(i) *Reasonably understandable*. You make your notice reasonably understandable if you:

(A) Present the information in the notice in clear, concise sentences, paragraphs, and sections;

(B) Use short explanatory sentences or bullet lists whenever possible;

(C) Use definite, concrete, everyday words and active voice whenever possible;

(D) Avoid multiple negatives;

(E) Avoid legal and highly technical business terminology whenever possible; and

(F) Avoid explanations that are imprecise and readily subject to different interpretations.

(ii) *Designed to call attention*. You design your notice to call attention to the nature and significance of the information in it if you:

(A) Use a plain-language heading to call attention to the notice;

(B) Use a typeface and type size that are easy to read;

(C) Provide wide margins and ample line spacing;

(D) Use boldface or italics for key words; and

(E) In a form that combines your notice with other information, use distinctive type size, style, and graphic devices, such as shading or sidebars, when you combine your notice with other information.

(iii) *Notices on web sites*. If you provide a notice on a web page, you design your notice to call attention to the nature and significance of the information in it if you use text or visual cues to encourage scrolling down the page if necessary to view the entire notice and ensure that other elements on the web site (such as text, graphics, hyperlinks, or sound) do not distract attention from the notice, and you either:

(A) Place the notice on a screen that consumers frequently access, such as a page on which transactions are conducted; or

(B) Place a link on a screen that consumers frequently access, such as a page on which transactions are conducted, that connects directly to the notice and is labeled appropriately to convey the importance, nature and relevance of the notice.

(c) *Collect* means to obtain information that you organize or can retrieve by the name of an individual or by identifying number, symbol, or other identifying particular assigned to the individual, irrespective of the source of the underlying information.

(d) *Company* means any corporation, limited liability company, business trust, general or limited partnership, association, or similar organization.

(e)(1) *Consumer* means an individual who obtains or has obtained a financial product or service from you that is to be used primarily for personal, family, or household purposes, or that individual's legal representative.

(2) *Examples*—(i) An individual who applies to you for credit for personal, family, or household purposes is a consumer of a financial service, regardless of whether the credit is extended.

(ii) An individual who provides nonpublic personal information to you in order to obtain a determination about whether he or she may qualify for a loan to be used primarily for personal, family, or household purposes is a consumer of a financial service, regardless of whether the loan is extended.

(iii) An individual who provides nonpublic personal information to you in connection with obtaining or seeking to obtain financial, investment, or economic advisory services is a consumer, regardless of whether you establish a continuing advisory relationship.

(iv) If you hold ownership or servicing rights to an individual's loan that is used primarily for personal, family, or household purposes, the individual is your consumer, even if you hold those rights in conjunction with one or more other institutions. (The individual is also a consumer with respect to the other financial institutions involved.) An individual who has a loan in which you have ownership or servicing rights is your consumer, even if you, or another institution with those rights, hire an agent to collect on the loan.

(v) An individual who is a consumer of another financial institution is not your consumer solely because you act as agent for, or provide processing or other services to, that financial institution.

(vi) An individual is not your consumer solely because he or she has designated you as trustee for a trust.

(vii) An individual is not your consumer solely because he or she is a beneficiary of a trust for which you are a trustee.

(viii) An individual is not your consumer solely because he or she is a participant or a beneficiary of an employee benefit plan that you sponsor or for which you act as a trustee or fiduciary.

(f) *Consumer reporting agency* has the same meaning as in section 603(f) of the Fair Credit Reporting Act (15 U.S.C. 1681a(f)).

(g) *Control* of a company means:

(1) Ownership, control, or power to vote 25 percent or more of the outstanding shares of any class of voting security of the company, directly or indirectly, or acting through one or more other persons;

(2) Control in any manner over the election of a majority of the directors, trustees, or general partners (or individuals exercising similar functions) of the company; or

(3) The power to exercise, directly or indirectly, a controlling influence over the management or policies of the company.

(h) *Customer* means a consumer who has a customer relationship with you.

(i)(1) *Customer relationship* means a continuing relationship between a consumer and you under which you provide one or more financial products or services to the consumer that are to be used primarily for personal, family, or household purposes.

(2) *Examples*—(i) *Continuing relationship*. A consumer has a continuing relationship with you if the consumer:

(A) Has a credit or investment account with you;

(B) Obtains a loan from you;

(C) Purchases an insurance product from you;

(D) Holds an investment product through you, such as when you act as a custodian for securities or for assets in an Individual Retirement Arrangement;

(E) Enters into an agreement or understanding with you whereby you undertake to arrange or broker a home mortgage loan, or credit to purchase a vehicle, for the consumer;

(F) Enters into a lease of personal property on a non-operating basis with you;

(G) Obtains financial, investment, or economic advisory services from you for a fee;

(H) Becomes your client for the purpose of obtaining tax preparation or credit counseling services from you;

(I) Obtains career counseling while seeking employment with a financial institution or the finance, accounting, or audit department of any company (or while employed by such a financial institution or department of any company);

(J) Is obligated on an account that you purchase from another financial institution, regardless of whether the account is in default when purchased, unless you do not locate the consumer or attempt to collect any amount from the consumer on the account;

(K) Obtains real estate settlement services from you; or

(L) Has a loan for which you own the servicing rights.

(ii) *No continuing relationship.* A consumer does not, however, have a continuing relationship with you if:

(A) The consumer obtains a financial product or service from you only in isolated transactions, such as using your ATM to withdraw cash from an account at another financial institution; purchasing a money order from you; cashing a check with you; or making a wire transfer through you;

(B) You sell the consumer's loan and do not retain the rights to service that loan;

(C) You sell the consumer airline tickets, travel insurance, or traveler's checks in isolated transactions;

(D) The consumer obtains one-time personal or real property appraisal services from you; or

(E) The consumer purchases checks for a personal checking account from you.

(j) *Federal functional regulator* means:

(1) The Board of Governors of the Federal Reserve System;

(2) The Office of the Comptroller of the Currency;

(3) The Board of Directors of the Federal Deposit Insurance Corporation;

(4) The Director of the Office of Thrift Supervision;

(5) The National Credit Union Administration Board; and

(6) The Securities and Exchange Commission.

(k)(1) *Financial institution* means any institution the business of which is engaging in financial activities as described in section 4(k) of the Bank Holding Company Act of 1956 (12 U.S.C. 1843(k)). An institution that is significantly engaged in financial activities is a financial institution.

(2) *Examples of financial institution.* (i) A retailer that extends credit by issuing its own credit card directly to consumers is a financial institution because extending credit is a financial activity listed in 12 CFR 225.28(b)(1) and referenced in section 4(k)(4)(F) of the Bank Holding Company Act and issuing that extension of credit through a proprietary credit card demonstrates that a retailer is significantly engaged in extending credit.

(ii) A personal property or real estate appraiser is a financial institution because real and personal property appraisal is a financial activity listed in 12 CFR 225.28(b)(2)(i) and referenced in section 4(k)(4)(F) of the Bank Holding Company Act.

(iii) An automobile dealership that, as a usual part of its business, leases automobiles on a nonoperating basis for longer than 90 days is a financial institution with respect to its leasing business because leasing personal property on a nonoperating basis where the initial term of the lease is at least 90 days is a financial activity listed in 12 CFR 225.28(b)(3) and referenced in section 4(k)(4)(F) of the Bank Holding Company Act.

(iv) A career counselor that specializes in providing career counseling services to individuals currently employed by or recently displaced from a financial organization, individuals who are seeking employment with a financial organization, or individuals who are currently employed by or seeking placement with the finance, accounting or audit departments of any company is a financial institution because such career counseling activities are financial activities listed in 12 CFR 225.28(b)(9)(iii) and referenced in section 4(k)(4)(F) of the Bank Holding Company Act.

(v) A business that prints and sells checks for consumers, either as its sole business or as one of its product lines, is a financial institution because printing and selling checks is a financial activity that is listed in 12 CFR 225.28(b)(10)(ii) and referenced in section 4(k)(4)(F) of the Bank Holding Company Act.

(vi) A business that regularly wires money to and from consumers is a financial institution because transferring money is a financial activity referenced in section 4(k)(4)(A) of the Bank Holding Company Act and regularly providing that service demonstrates that the business is significantly engaged in that activity.

(vii) A check cashing business is a financial institution because cashing a check is exchanging money, which is a financial activity listed in section 4(k)(4)(A) of the Bank Holding Company Act.

(viii) An accountant or other tax preparation service that is in the business of completing income tax returns is a financial institution because tax preparation services is a financial activity listed in 12 CFR 225.28(b)(6)(vi) and referenced in section 4(k)(4)(G) of the Bank Holding Company Act.

(ix) A business that operates a travel agency in connection with financial services is a financial institution because operating a travel agency in connection with financial services is a financial activity listed in 12 CFR 211.5(d)(15) and referenced in section 4(k)(4)(G) of the Bank Holding Company Act.

(x) An entity that provides real estate settlement services is a financial institution because providing real estate settlement services is a financial activity listed in 12 CFR 225.28(b)(2)(viii) and referenced in section 4(k)(4)(F) of the Bank Holding Company Act.

(xi) A mortgage broker is a financial institution because brokering loans is a financial activity listed in 12 CFR 225.28(b)(1) and referenced in section 4(k)(4)(F) of the Bank Holding Company Act.

(xii) An investment advisory company and a credit counseling service are each financial institutions because providing financial and investment advisory services are financial activities referenced in section 4(k)(4)(C) of the Bank Holding Company Act.

(3) *Financial institution* does not include:

(i) Any person or entity with respect to any financial activity that is subject to the jurisdiction of the Commodity Futures Trading Commission under the Commodity Exchange Act (7 U.S.C. 1 *et seq.*);

(ii) The Federal Agricultural Mortgage Corporation or any entity chartered and operating under the Farm Credit Act of 1971 (12 U.S.C. 2001 *et seq.*); or

(iii) Institutions chartered by Congress specifically to engage in securitizations, secondary market sales (including sales of servicing rights) or similar transactions related to a transaction of a consumer, as long as such institutions do not sell or transfer nonpublic personal information to a nonaffiliated third party other than as permitted by §§ 313.14 and 313.15 of this part.

(iv) Entities that engage in financial activities but that are not significantly engaged in those financial activities.

(4) *Examples of entities that are not significantly engaged in financial activities.* (i) A retailer is not a financial institution if its only means of extending credit are occasional "lay away" and deferred payment plans or accepting payment by means of credit cards issued by others.

(ii) A retailer is not a financial institution merely because it accepts payment in the form of cash, checks, or credit cards that it did not issue.

(iii) A merchant is not a financial institution merely because it allows an individual to "run a tab."

(iv) A grocery store is not a financial institution merely because it allows individuals to whom it sells groceries to cash a check, or write a check for a higher amount than the grocery purchase and obtain cash in return.

(l)(1) *Financial product or service* means any product or service that a financial holding company could offer by engaging in a financial activity under section 4(k) of the Bank Holding Company Act of 1956 (12 U.S.C. 1843(k)).

(2) Financial service includes your evaluation or brokerage of information that you collect in connection with a request or an application from a consumer for a financial product or service.

(m)(1) *Nonaffiliated third party* means any person except:

(i) Your affiliate; or

(ii) A person employed jointly by you and any company that is not your affiliate (but *nonaffiliated third party* includes the other company that jointly employs the person).

(2) *Nonaffiliated third party* includes any company that is an affiliate by virtue of your or your affiliate's direct or indirect ownership or control of the company in conducting merchant banking or investment banking activities of the type described in section 4(k)(4)(H) or insurance company investment activities of the type described in section 4(k)(4)(I) of the Bank Holding Company Act (12 U.S.C. 1843(k)(4)(H) and (I)).

(n)(1) *Nonpublic personal information* means:

(i) Personally identifiable financial information; and

(ii) Any list, description, or other grouping of consumers (and publicly available information pertaining to them) that is derived using any personally identifiable financial information that is not publicly available.

(2) *Nonpublic personal information* does not include:

(i) Publicly available information, except as included on a list described in paragraph (n)(1)(ii) of this section; or

(ii) Any list, description, or other grouping of consumers (and publicly available information pertaining to them) that is derived without using any personally identifiable financial information that is not publicly available.

(3) *Examples of lists*—(i) Nonpublic personal information includes any list of individuals' names and street addresses that is derived in whole or in part using personally identifiable financial information (that is not publicly available), such as account numbers.

(ii) Nonpublic personal information does not include any list of individuals' names and addresses that contains only publicly available information, is not derived, in whole or in part, using personally identifiable financial information that is not publicly available, and is not disclosed in a manner that indicates that any of the individuals on the list is a consumer of a financial institution.

(o)(1) *Personally identifiable financial information* means any information:

(i) A consumer provides to you to obtain a financial product or service from you;

(ii) About a consumer resulting from any transaction involving a financial product or service between you and a consumer; or

(iii) You otherwise obtain about a consumer in connection with providing a financial product or service to that consumer.

(2) *Examples*—(i) *Information included.* Personally identifiable financial information includes:

(A) Information a consumer provides to you on an application to obtain a loan, credit card, or other financial product or service;

(B) Account balance information, payment history, overdraft history, and credit or debit card purchase information;

(C) The fact that an individual is or has been one of your customers or has obtained a financial product or service from you;

(D) Any information about your consumer if it is disclosed in a manner that indicates that the individual is or has been your consumer;

(E) Any information that a consumer provides to you or that you or your agent otherwise obtain in connection with collecting on, or servicing, a credit account;

(F) Any information you collect through an Internet "cookie" (an information collecting device from a web server); and

(G) Information from a consumer report.

(ii) *Information not included.* Personally identifiable financial information does not include:

(A) A list of names and addresses of customers of an entity that is not a financial institution; and

(B) Information that does not identify a consumer, such as aggregate information or blind data that does not contain personal identifiers such as account numbers, names, or addresses.

(p)(1) *Publicly available information* means any information that you have a reasonable basis to believe is lawfully made available to the general public from:

(i) Federal, State, or local government records;

(ii) Widely distributed media; or

(iii) Disclosures to the general public that are required to be made by Federal, State, or local law.

(2) *Reasonable basis.* You have a reasonable basis to believe that information is lawfully made available to the general public if you have taken steps to determine:

(i) That the information is of the type that is available to the general public; and

(ii) Whether an individual can direct that the information not be made available to the general public and, if so, that your consumer has not done so.

(3) *Examples*—(i) *Government records.* Publicly available information in government records includes information in government real estate records and security interest filings.

(ii) *Widely distributed media.* Publicly available information from widely distributed media includes information from a telephone book, a television or radio program, a newspaper, or a web site that is available to the general public on an unrestricted basis. A web site is not restricted merely because an Internet service provider or a site operator requires a fee or a password, so long as access is available to the general public.

(iii) *Reasonable basis*—(A) You have a reasonable basis to believe that mortgage information is lawfully made available to the general public if you have determined that the information is of the type included on the public record in the jurisdiction where the mortgage would be recorded.

(B) You have a reasonable basis to believe that an individual's telephone number is lawfully made available to the general public if you have located the telephone number in the telephone book or the consumer has informed you that the telephone number is not unlisted.

(q) *You* includes each "financial institution" (but excludes any "other person") over which the Commission has enforcement jurisdiction pursuant to section 505(a)(7) of the Gramm-Leach-Bliley Act.

[65 Fed. Reg. 33677 (May 24, 2000)]

Subpart A—Privacy and Opt Out Notices

§ 313.4 Initial privacy notice to consumers required.

(a) *Initial notice requirement.* You must provide a clear and conspicuous notice that accurately reflects your privacy policies and practices to:

(1) *Customer.* An individual who becomes your customer, not later than when you establish a customer relationship, except as provided in paragraph (e) of this section; and

(2) *Consumer.* A consumer, before you disclose any nonpublic personal information about the consumer to any nonaffiliated third party, if you make such a disclosure other than as authorized by §§ 313.14 and 313.15.

(b) *When initial notice to a consumer is not required.* You are not required to provide an initial notice to a consumer under paragraph (a) of this section if:

(1) You do not disclose any nonpublic personal information about the consumer to any nonaffiliated third party, other than as authorized by §§ 313.14 and 313.15; and

(2) You do not have a customer relationship with the consumer.

(c) *When you establish a customer relationship*—(1) *General rule.* You establish a customer relationship when you and the consumer enter into a continuing relationship.

(2) *Special rule for loans.* You establish a customer relationship with a consumer when you originate a loan to the consumer for personal, family, or household purposes. If you subsequently transfer the servicing rights to that loan to another financial institution, the customer relationship transfers with the servicing rights.

(3)(i) *Examples of establishing customer relationship.* You establish a customer relationship when the consumer:

(A) Opens a credit card account with you;

(B) Executes the contract to obtain credit from you or purchase insurance from you;

(C) Agrees to obtain financial, economic, or investment advisory services from you for a fee; or

(D) Becomes your client for the purpose of your providing credit counseling or tax preparation services, or to obtain career counseling while seeking employment with a financial institution or the finance, accounting, or audit department of any company (or while employed by such a company or financial institution);

(E) Provides any personally identifiable financial information to you in an effort to obtain a mortgage loan through you;

(F) Executes the lease for personal property with you;

(G) Is an obligor on an account that you purchased from another financial institution and whom you have located and begun attempting to collect amounts owed on the account; or

(H) Provides you with the information necessary for you to compile and provide access to all of the consumer's on-line financial accounts at your Web site.

(ii) *Examples of loan rule.* You establish a customer relationship with a consumer who obtains a loan for personal, family, or household purposes when you:

(A) Originate the loan to the consumer and retain the servicing rights; or

(B) Purchase the servicing rights to the consumer's loan.

(d) *Existing customers.* When an existing customer obtains a new financial product or service from you that is to be used primarily for personal, family, or household purposes, you satisfy the initial notice requirements of paragraph (a) of this section as follows:

(1) You may provide a revised privacy notice, under § 313.8, that covers the customer's new financial product or service; or

(2) If the initial, revised, or annual notice that you most recently provided to that customer was accurate with respect to the new financial product or service, you do not need to provide a new privacy notice under paragraph (a) of this section.

(e) *Exceptions to allow subsequent delivery of notice.* (1) You may provide the initial notice required by paragraph (a)(1) of this section within a reasonable time after you establish a customer relationship if:

(i) Establishing the customer relationship is not at the customer's election; or

(ii) Providing notice not later than when you establish a customer relationship would substantially delay the customer's transaction and the customer agrees to receive the notice at a later time.

(2) *Examples of exceptions*—(i) *Not at customer's election.* Establishing a customer relationship is not at the customer's election if you acquire a customer's loan, or the servicing rights, from another financial institution and the customer does not have a choice about your acquisition.

(ii) *Substantial delay of customer's transaction.* Providing notice not later than when you establish a customer relationship would substantially delay the customer's transaction when:

(A) You and the individual agree over the telephone to enter into a customer relationship involving prompt delivery of the financial product or service; or

(B) You establish a customer relationship with an individual under a program authorized by Title IV of the Higher Education Act of 1965 (20 U.S.C. 1070 *et seq.*) or similar student loan programs where loan proceeds are disbursed promptly without prior communication between you and the customer.

(iii) *No substantial delay of customer's transaction.* Providing notice not later than when you establish a customer relationship would not substantially delay the customer's transaction when the relationship is initiated in person at your office or through other means by which the customer may view the notice, such as through a web site.

(f) *Delivery.* When you are required to deliver an initial privacy notice by this section, you must deliver it according to § 313.9. If you use a short-form initial notice for non-customers according to § 313.6(d), you may deliver your privacy notice according to § 313.6(d)(3).

[65 Fed. Reg. 33677 (May 24, 2000)]

§ 313.5 Annual privacy notice to customers required.

(a)(1) *General rule.* You must provide a clear and conspicuous notice to customers that accurately reflects your privacy policies and practices not less than annually during the continuation of the customer relationship. Annually means at least once in any period of 12 consecutive months during which that relationship exists. You may define the 12-consecutive-month period, but you must apply it to the customer on a consistent basis.

(2) *Example.* You provide a notice annually if you define the 12-consecutive-month period as a calendar year and provide the annual notice to the customer once in each calendar year following the calendar year in which you provided the initial notice. For example, if a customer opens an account on any day of year 1, you must provide an annual notice to that customer by December 31 of year 2.

(b)(1) *Termination of customer relationship.* You are not required to provide an annual notice to a former customer.

(2) *Examples.* Your customer becomes a former customer when:

(i) In the case of a closed-end loan, the customer pays the loan in full, you charge off the loan, or you sell the loan without retaining servicing rights;

(ii) In the case of a credit card relationship or other open-end credit relationship, you sell the receivables without retaining servicing rights;

(iii) In the case of credit counseling services, the customer has failed to make required payments under a debt management plan, has been notified that the plan is terminated, and you no longer provide any statements or notices to the customer concerning that relationship;

(iv) In the case of mortgage or vehicle loan brokering services, your customer has obtained a loan through you (and you no longer provide any statements or notices to the customer concerning that relationship), or has ceased using your services for such purposes;

(v) In the case of tax preparation services, you have provided and received payment for the service and no longer provide any statements or notices to the customer concerning that relationship;

(vi) In the case of providing real estate settlement services, at the time the customer completes execution of all documents related to the real estate closing, you have received payment, or you have completed all of your responsibilities with respect to the settlement, including filing documents on the public record, whichever is later.

(vii) In cases where there is no definitive time at which the customer relationship has terminated, you have not communicated with the customer about the relationship for a period of 12 consecutive months, other than to provide annual privacy notices or promotional material.

(c) *Special rule for loans.* If you do not have a customer relationship with a consumer under the special rule for loans in § 313.4(c)(2), then you need not provide an annual notice to that consumer under this section.

(d) *Delivery.* When you are required to deliver an annual privacy notice by this section, you must deliver it according to § 313.9.

[65 Fed. Reg. 33677 (May 24, 2000)]

§ 313.6 Information to be included in privacy notices.

(a) *General rule.* The initial, annual, and revised privacy notices that you provide under §§ 313.4, 313.5, and 313.8 must include each of the following items of information that applies to you or to the consumers to whom you send your privacy notice, in addition to any other information you wish to provide:

(1) The categories of nonpublic personal information that you collect;

(2) The categories of nonpublic personal information that you disclose;

(3) The categories of affiliates and nonaffiliated third parties to whom you disclose nonpublic personal information, other than those parties to whom you disclose information under §§ 313.14 and 313.15;

(4) The categories of nonpublic personal information about your former customers that you disclose and the categories of affiliates and nonaffiliated third parties to whom you disclose nonpublic personal information about your former customers, other than those parties to whom you disclose information under §§ 313.14 and 313.15;

(5) If you disclose nonpublic personal information to a nonaffiliated third party under § 313.13 (and no exception under §§ 313.14 or 313.15 applies to that disclosure), a separate statement of the categories of information you disclose and the categories of third parties with whom you have contracted;

(6) An explanation of the consumer's right under § 313.10(a) to opt out of the disclosure of nonpublic personal information to nonaffiliated third parties, including the method(s) by which the consumer may exercise that right at that time;

(7) Any disclosures that you make under section 603(d)(2)(A)(iii) of the Fair Credit Reporting Act (15 U.S.C. 1681a(d)(2)(A)(iii)) (that is, notices regarding the ability to opt out of disclosures of information among affiliates);

(8) Your policies and practices with respect to protecting the confidentiality and security of nonpublic personal information; and

(9) Any disclosure that you make under paragraph (b) of this section.

(b) *Description of nonaffiliated third parties subject to exceptions.* If you disclose nonpublic personal information to third parties as authorized under §§ 313.14 and 313.15, you are not required to list those exceptions in the initial or annual privacy notices required by §§ 313.4 and 313.5. When describing the categories with respect to those parties, you are required to state only that you make disclosures to other nonaffiliated third parties as permitted by law.

(c) *Examples*—(1) *Categories of nonpublic personal information that you collect.* You satisfy the requirement to categorize the nonpublic personal information that you collect if you list the following categories, as applicable:

(i) Information from the consumer;

(ii) Information about the consumer's transactions with you or your affiliates;

(iii) Information about the consumer's transactions with nonaffiliated third parties; and

(iv) Information from a consumer reporting agency.

(2) *Categories of nonpublic personal information you disclose*—(i) You satisfy the requirement to categorize the nonpublic personal information that you disclose if you list the categories

described in paragraph (e)(1) of this section, as applicable, and a few examples to illustrate the types of information in each category.

(ii) If you reserve the right to disclose all of the nonpublic personal information about consumers that you collect, you may simply state that fact without describing the categories or examples of the nonpublic personal information you disclose.

(3) *Categories of affiliates and nonaffiliated third parties to whom you disclose.* You satisfy the requirement to categorize the affiliates and nonaffiliated third parties to whom you disclose nonpublic personal information if you list them using the following categories, as applicable, and a few applicable examples to illustrate the significant types of third parties covered in each category.

(i) Financial service providers, followed by illustrative examples such as mortgage bankers, securities broker-dealers, and insurance agents.

(ii) Non-financial companies, followed by illustrative examples such as retailers, magazine publishers, airlines, and direct marketers; and

(iii) Others, followed by examples such as nonprofit organizations.

(4) *Disclosures under exception for service providers and joint marketers.* If you disclose nonpublic personal information under the exception in § 313.13 to a nonaffiliated third party to market products or services that you offer alone or jointly with another financial institution, you satisfy the disclosure requirement of paragraph (a)(5) of this section if you:

(i) List the categories of nonpublic personal information you disclose, using the same categories and examples you used to meet the requirements of paragraph (a)(2) of this section, as applicable; and

(ii) State whether the third party is:

(A) A service provider that performs marketing services on your behalf or on behalf of you and another financial institution; or

(B) A financial institution with whom you have a joint marketing agreement.

(5) *Simplified notices.* If you do not disclose, and do not wish to reserve the right to disclose, nonpublic personal information about customers or former customers to affiliates or nonaffiliated third parties except as authorized under §§ 313.14 and 313.15, you may simply state that fact, in addition to the information you must provide under paragraphs (a)(1), (a)(8), (a)(9), and (b) of this section.

(6) *Confidentiality and security.* You describe your policies and practices with respect to protecting the confidentiality and security of nonpublic personal information if you do both of the following:

(i) Describe in general terms who is authorized to have access to the information; and

(ii) State whether you have security practices and procedures in place to ensure the confidentiality of the information in accordance with your policy. You are not required to describe technical information about the safeguards you use.

(d) *Short-form initial notice with opt out notice for non-customers*—(1) You may satisfy the initial notice requirements in §§ 313.4(a)(2), 313.7(b), and 313.7(c) for a consumer who is not a customer by providing a short-form initial notice at the same time as you deliver an opt out notice as required in § 313.7.

(2) A short-form initial notice must:

(i) Be clear and conspicuous;

(ii) State that your privacy notice is available upon request; and

(iii) Explain a reasonable means by which the consumer may obtain that notice.

(3) You must deliver your short-form initial notice according to § 313.9. You are not required to deliver your privacy notice with your short-form initial notice. You instead may simply provide the consumer a reasonable means to obtain your privacy notice. If a consumer who receives your short-form notice requests your privacy notice, you must deliver your privacy notice according to § 313.9.

(4) *Examples of obtaining privacy notice.* You provide a reasonable means by which a consumer may obtain a copy of your privacy notice if you:

(i) Provide a toll-free telephone number that the consumer may call to request the notice; or

(ii) For a consumer who conducts business in person at your office, maintain copies of the notice on hand that you provide to the consumer immediately upon request.

(e) *Future disclosures.* Your notice may include:

(1) Categories of nonpublic personal information that you reserve the right to disclose in the future, but do not currently disclose; and

(2) Categories of affiliates or nonaffiliated third parties to whom you reserve the right in the future to disclose, but to whom you do not currently disclose, nonpublic personal information.

(f) *Sample clauses.* Sample clauses illustrating some of the notice content required by this section are included in Appendix A of this part.

[65 Fed. Reg. 33677 (May 24, 2000)]

§ 313.7 Form of opt out notice to consumers; opt out methods.

(a)(1) *Form of opt out notice.* If you are required to provide an opt out notice under § 313.10(a), you must provide a clear and conspicuous notice to each of your consumers that accurately explains the right to opt out under that section. The notice must state:

(i) That you disclose or reserve the right to disclose nonpublic personal information about your consumer to a nonaffiliated third party;

(ii) That the consumer has the right to opt out of that disclosure; and

(iii) A reasonable means by which the consumer may exercise the opt out right.

(2) *Examples*—(i) *Adequate opt out notice.* You provide adequate notice that the consumer can opt out of the disclosure of nonpublic personal information to a nonaffiliated third party if you:

(A) Identify all of the categories of nonpublic personal information that you disclose or reserve the right to disclose, and all of the categories of nonaffiliated third parties to which you disclose the information, as described in § 313.6(a) (2) and (3) and state that the consumer can opt out of the disclosure of that information; and

(B) Identify the financial products or services that the consumer obtains from you, either singly or jointly, to which the opt out direction would apply.

(ii) *Reasonable opt out means.* You provide a reasonable means to exercise an opt out right if you:

(A) Designate check-off boxes in a prominent position on the relevant forms with the opt out notice;

(B) Include a reply form that includes the address to which the form should be mailed; or

(C) Provide an electronic means to opt out, such as a form that can be sent via electronic mail or a process at your web site, if the consumer agrees to the electronic delivery of information; or

(D) Provide a toll-free telephone number that consumers may call to opt out.

(iii) *Unreasonable opt out means.* You do not provide a reasonable means of opting out if:

(A) The only means of opting out is for the consumer to write his or her own letter to exercise that opt out right; or

(B) The only means of opting out as described in any notice subsequent to the initial notice is to use a check-off box that you provided with the initial notice but did not include with the subsequent notice.

(iv) *Specific opt out means.* You may require each consumer to opt out through a specific means, as long as that means is reasonable for that consumer.

(b) *Same form as initial notice permitted.* You may provide the opt out notice together with or on the same written or electronic form as the initial notice you provide in accordance with § 313.4.

(c) *Initial notice required when opt out notice delivered subsequent to initial notice.* If you provide the opt out notice later than required for the initial notice in accordance with § 313.4, you must also include a copy of the initial notice with the opt out notice in writing or, if the consumer agrees, electronically.

(d) *Joint relationships*—(1) If two or more consumers jointly obtain a financial product or service from you, you may provide a single opt out notice, unless one or more of those consumers requests a separate opt out notice. Your opt out notice must explain how you will treat an opt out direction by a joint consumer (as explained in paragraph (d)(5)(ii) of this section).

(2) Any of the joint consumers may exercise the right to opt out. You may either:

(i) Treat an opt out direction by a joint consumer as applying to all of the associated joint consumers; or

(ii) Permit each joint consumer to opt out separately.

(3) If you permit each joint consumer to opt out separately, you must permit one of the joint consumers to opt out on behalf of all of the joint consumers.

(4) You may not require all joint consumers to opt out before you implement any opt out direction.

(5) *Example.* If John and Mary have a joint credit card account with you and arrange for you to send statements to John's address, you may do any of the following, but you must explain in your opt out notice which opt out policy you will follow:

(i) Send a single opt out notice to John's address, but you must accept an opt out direction from either John or Mary.

(ii) Treat an opt out direction by either John or Mary as applying to the entire account. If you do so, and John opts out, you may not require Mary to opt out as well before implementing John's opt out direction.

(iii) Permit John and Mary to make different opt out directions. If you do so,

(A) You must permit John and Mary to opt out for each other;

(B) If both opt out, you must permit both to notify you in a single response (such as on a form or through a telephone call); and

(C) If John opts out and Mary does not, you may only disclose nonpublic personal information about Mary, but not about John and not about John and Mary jointly.

(e) *Time to comply with opt out.* You must comply with a consumer's opt out direction as soon as reasonably practicable after you receive it.

(f) *Continuing right to opt out.* A consumer may exercise the right to opt out at any time.

(g) *Duration of consumer's opt out direction*—(1) A consumer's direction to opt out under this section is effective until the consumer revokes it in writing or, if the consumer agrees, electronically.

(2) When a customer relationship terminates, the customer's opt out direction continues to apply to the nonpublic personal information that you collected during or related to that relationship. If the individual subsequently establishes a new customer relationship with you, the opt out direction that applied to the former relationship does not apply to the new relationship.

(h) *Delivery.* When you are required to deliver an opt out notice by this section, you must deliver it according to § 313.9.

[65 Fed. Reg. 33677 (May 24, 2000)]

§ 313.8 Revised privacy notices.

(a) *General rule.* Except as otherwise authorized in this part, you must not, directly or through any affiliate, disclose any nonpublic personal information about a consumer to a nonaffiliated third party other than as described in the initial notice that you provided to that consumer under § 313.4, unless:

(1) You have provided to the consumer a clear and conspicuous revised notice that accurately describes your policies and practices;

(2) You have provided to the consumer a new opt out notice;

(3) You have given the consumer a reasonable opportunity, before you disclose the information to the nonaffiliated third party, to opt out of the disclosure; and

(4) the consumer does not opt out.

(b) *Examples*—(1) Except as otherwise permitted by §§ 313.13, 313.14, and 313.15, you must provide a revised notice before you:

(i) Disclose a new category of nonpublic personal information to any nonaffiliated third party;

(ii) Disclose nonpublic personal information to a new category of nonaffiliated third party; or

(iii) Disclose nonpublic personal information about a former customer to a nonaffiliated third party if that former customer has not had the opportunity to exercise an opt out right regarding that disclosure.

(2) A revised notice is not required if you disclose nonpublic personal information to a new nonaffiliated third party that you adequately described in your prior notice.

(c) *Delivery.* When you are required to deliver a revised privacy notice by this section, you must deliver it according to § 313.9.

[65 Fed. Reg. 33677 (May 24, 2000)]

§ 313.9 Delivering privacy and opt out notices.

(a) *How to provide notices.* You must provide any privacy notices and opt out notices, including short-form initial notices, that this part requires so that each consumer can reasonably be expected to receive actual notice in writing or, if the consumer agrees, electronically.

(b)(1) *Examples of reasonable expectation of actual notice.* You may reasonably expect that a consumer will receive actual notice if you:

(i) Hand-deliver a printed copy of the notice to the consumer;

(ii) Mail a printed copy of the notice to the last known address of the consumer;

(iii) For the consumer who conducts transactions electronically, clearly and conspicuously post the notice on the electronic site and require the consumer to acknowledge receipt of the notice as a necessary step to obtaining a particular financial product or service;

(iv) For an isolated transaction with the consumer, such as an ATM transaction, post the notice on the ATM screen and require the consumer to acknowledge receipt of the notice as a necessary step to obtaining the particular financial product or service.

(2) *Examples of unreasonable expectation of actual notice.* You may not, however, reasonably expect that a consumer will receive actual notice of your privacy policies and practices if you:

(i) Only post a sign in your branch or office or generally publish advertisements of your privacy policies and practices;

(ii) Send the notice via electronic mail to a consumer who does not obtain a financial product or service from you electronically.

(c) *Annual notices only.* You may reasonably expect that a customer will receive actual notice of your annual privacy notice if:

(1) The customer uses your web site to access financial products and services electronically and agrees to receive notices at the web site and you post your current privacy notice continuously in a clear and conspicuous manner on the web site; or

(2) The customer has requested that you refrain from sending any information regarding the customer relationship, and your current privacy notice remains available to the customer upon request.

(d) *Oral description of notice insufficient.* You may not provide any notice required by this part solely by orally explaining the notice, either in person or over the telephone.

(e) *Retention or accessibility of notices for customers*—(1) For customers only, you must provide the initial notice required by § 313.4(a)(1), the annual notice required by § 313.5(a), and the revised notice required by § 313.8 so that the customer can retain them or obtain them later in writing or, if the customer agrees, electronically.

(2) *Examples of retention or accessibility.* You provide a privacy notice to the customer so that the customer can retain it or obtain it later if you:

(i) Hand-deliver a printed copy of the notice to the customer;

(ii) Mail a printed copy of the notice to the last known address of the customer; or

(iii) Make your current privacy notice available on a web site (or a link to another web site) for the customer who obtains a financial product or service electronically and agrees to receive the notice at the web site.

(f) *Joint notice with other financial institutions.* You may provide a joint notice from you and one or more of your affiliates or other financial institutions, as identified in the notice, as long as the notice is accurate with respect to you and the other institutions.

(g) *Joint relationships.* If two or more consumers jointly obtain a financial product or service from you, you may satisfy the initial, annual, and revised notice requirements of §§ 313.4(a), 313.5(a), and 313.8(a) by providing one notice to those consumers jointly, unless one or more of those consumers requests separate notices.

[65 Fed. Reg. 33677 (May 24, 2000)]

Subpart B—Limits on Disclosures

§ 313.10 Limits on disclosure of non-public personal information to nonaffiliated third parties.

(a)(1) *Conditions for disclosure.* Except as otherwise authorized in this part, you may not, directly or through any affiliate, disclose any nonpublic personal information about a consumer to a nonaffiliated third party unless:

(i) You have provided to the consumer an initial notice as required under § 313.4;

(ii) You have provided to the consumer an opt out notice as required in § 313.7;

(iii) You have given the consumer a reasonable opportunity, before you disclose the information to the nonaffiliated third party, to opt out of the disclosure; and

(iv) The consumer does not opt out.

(2) *Opt out definition.* Opt out means a direction by the consumer that you not disclose nonpublic personal information about that consumer to a nonaffiliated third party, other than as permitted by §§ 313.13, 313.14, and 313.15.

(3) *Examples of reasonable opportunity to opt out.* You provide a consumer with a reasonable opportunity to opt out if:

(i) *By mail.* You mail the notices required in paragraph (a)(1) of this section to the consumer and allow the consumer to opt out by mailing a form, calling a toll-free telephone number, or any other reasonable means within 30 days from the date you mailed the notices.

(ii) *By electronic means.* A customer opens an on-line account with you and agrees to receive the notices required in paragraph (a)(1) of this section electronically, and you allow the customer to opt out by any reasonable means within 30 days after the date that the customer acknowledges receipt of the notices in conjunction with opening the account.

(iii) *Isolated transaction with consumer.* For an isolated transaction, such as the purchase of a money order by a consumer, you provide the consumer with a reasonable opportunity to opt out if you provide the notices required in paragraph (a)(1) of this section at the time of the transaction and request that the consumer decide, as a necessary part of the transaction, whether to opt out before completing the transaction.

(b) *Application of opt out to all consumers and all nonpublic personal information*—(1) You must comply with this section, regardless of whether you and the consumer have established a customer relationship

(2) Unless you comply with this section, you may not, directly or through any affiliate, disclose any nonpublic personal information about a consumer that you have collected, regardless of whether you collected it before or after receiving the direction to opt out from the consumer.

(c) *Partial opt out.* You may allow a consumer to select certain nonpublic personal information or certain nonaffiliated third parties with respect to which the consumer wishes to opt out.

[65 Fed. Reg. 33677 (May 24, 2000)]

§ 313.11 Limits on redisclosure and reuse of information.

(a)(1) *Information you receive under an exception.* If you receive nonpublic personal information from a nonaffiliated financial institution under an exception in § 313.14 or 313.15 of this part, your disclosure and use of that information is limited as follows:

(i) You may disclose the information to the affiliates of the financial institution from which you received the information;

(ii) You may disclose the information to your affiliates, but your affiliates may, in turn, disclose and use the information only to the extent that you may disclose and use the information; and

(iii) You may disclose and use the information pursuant to an exception in § 313.14 or 313.15 in the ordinary course of business to carry out the activity covered by the exception under which you received the information.

(2) *Example.* If you receive a customer list from a nonaffiliated financial institution in order to provide account processing services under the exception in § 313.14(a), you may disclose that information under any exception in § 313.14 or 313.15 in the ordinary course of business in order to provide those services. You could also disclose that information in response to a properly authorized subpoena. You could not disclose that information to a third party for marketing purposes or use that information for your own marketing purposes.

(b)(1) *Information you receive outside of an exception.* If you receive nonpublic personal information from a nonaffiliated financial institution other than under an exception in § 313.14 or 313.15 of this part, you may disclose the information only:

(i) To the affiliates of the financial institution from which you received the information;

(ii) To your affiliates, but your affiliates may, in turn, disclose the information only to the extent that you can disclose the information; and

(iii) To any other person, if the disclosure would be lawful if made directly to that person by the financial institution from which you received the information.

(2) *Example.* If you obtain a customer list from a nonaffiliated financial institution outside of the exceptions in § 313.14 and 313.15:

(i) You may use that list for your own purposes; and

(ii) You may disclose that list to another nonaffiliated third party only if the financial institution from which you purchased the list could have lawfully disclosed the list to that third party. That is, you may disclose the list in accordance with the privacy policy of the financial institution from which you received the list, as limited by the opt out direction of each consumer whose nonpublic personal information you intend to disclose, and you may disclose the list in accordance with an exception in § 313.14 or 313.15, such as to your attorneys or accountants.

(c) *Information you disclose under an exception.* If you disclose nonpublic personal information to a nonaffiliated third party under an exception in § 313.14 or 313.15 of this part, the third party may disclose and use that information only as follows:

(1) The third party may disclose the information to your affiliates;

(2) The third party may disclose the information to its affiliates, but its affiliates may, in turn, disclose and use the information only to the extent that the third party may disclose and use the information; and

(3) The third party may disclose and use the information pursuant to an exception in § 313.14 or 313.15 in the ordinary course of business to carry out the activity covered by the exception under which it received the information.

(d) *Information you disclose outside of an exception.* If you disclose nonpublic personal information to a nonaffiliated third party other than under an exception in § 313.14 or 313.15 of this part, the third party may disclose the information only:

(1) To your affiliates;

(2) To its affiliates, but its affiliates, in turn, may disclose the information only to the extent the third party can disclose the information; and

(3) To any other person, if the disclosure would be lawful if you made it directly to that person.

[65 Fed. Reg. 33677 (May 24, 2000)]

§ 313.12 Limits on sharing account number information for marketing purposes.

(a) *General prohibition on disclosure of account numbers.* You must not, directly or through an affiliate, disclose, other than to a consumer reporting agency, an account number or similar form of access number or access code for a consumer's credit card account, deposit account, or transaction account to any nonaffiliated third party for use in telemarketing, direct mail marketing, or other marketing through electronic mail to the consumer.

(b) *Exceptions.* Paragraph (a) of this section does not apply if you disclose an account number or similar form of access number or access code:

(1) To your agent or service provider solely in order to perform marketing for your own products or services, as long as the agent or service provider is not authorized to directly initiate charges to the account; or

(2) To a participant in a private label credit card program or an affinity or similar program where the participants in the program are identified to the customer when the customer enters into the program.

(c) *Examples*—(1) *Account number.* An account number, or similar form of access number or access code, does not include a number or code in an encrypted form, as long as you do not provide the recipient with a means to decode the number or code.

(2) *Transaction account.* A transaction account is an account other than a deposit account or a credit card account. A transaction account does not include an account to which third parties cannot initiate charges.

[65 Fed. Reg. 33677 (May 24, 2000)]

Subpart C—Exceptions

§ 313.13 Exception to opt out requirements for service providers and joint marketing.

(a) *General rule.* (1) The opt out requirements in §§ 313.7 and 313.10 do not apply when you provide nonpublic personal information to a nonaffiliated third party to perform services for you or functions on your behalf, if you:

(i) Provide the initial notice in accordance with § 313.4; and

(ii) Enter into a contractual agreement with the third party that prohibits the third party from disclosing or using the information other than to carry out the purposes for which you disclosed the information, including use under an exception in § 313.14 or 313.15 in the ordinary course of business to carry out those purposes.

(2) *Example.* If you disclose nonpublic personal information under this section to a financial institution with which you perform joint marketing, your contractual agreement with that institution meets the requirements of paragraph (a)(1)(ii) of this section if it prohibits the institution from disclosing or using the nonpublic personal information except as necessary to carry out the joint marketing or under an exception in § 313.14 or 313.15 in the ordinary course of business to carry out that joint marketing.

(b) *Service may include joint marketing.* The services a nonaffiliated third party performs for you under paragraph (a) of this section may include marketing of your own products or services or marketing of financial products or services offered pursuant to joint agreements between you and one or more financial institutions.

(c) *Definition of joint agreement.* For purposes of this section, joint agreement means a written contract pursuant to which you and one or more financial institutions jointly offer, endorse, or sponsor a financial product or service.

[65 Fed. Reg. 33677 (May 24, 2000)]

§ 313.14 Exceptions to notice and opt out requirements for processing and servicing transactions.

(a) *Exceptions for processing transactions at consumer's request.* The requirements for initial notice in § 313.4(a)(2), for the opt out in §§ 313.7 and 313.10, and for service providers and joint marketing in § 313.13 do not apply if you disclose nonpublic personal information as necessary to effect, administer, or enforce a transaction that a consumer requests or authorizes, or in connection with:

(1) Servicing or processing a financial product or service that a consumer requests or authorizes;

(2) Maintaining or servicing the consumer's account with you, or with another entity as part of a private label credit card program or other extension of credit on behalf of such entity; or

(3) A proposed or actual securitization, secondary market sale (including sales of servicing rights), or similar transaction related to a transaction of the consumer.

(b) *Necessary to effect, administer, or enforce a transaction* means that the disclosure is:

(1) Required, or is one of the lawful or appropriate methods, to enforce your rights or the rights of other persons engaged in carrying out the financial transaction or providing the product or service; or

(2) Required, or is a usual, appropriate or acceptable method:

(i) To carry out the transaction or the product or service business of which the transaction is a part, and record, service, or maintain the consumer's account in the ordinary course of providing the financial service or financial product;

(ii) To administer or service benefits or claims relating to the transaction or the product or service business of which it is a part;

(iii) To provide a confirmation, statement, or other record of the transaction, or information on the status or value of the financial service or financial product to the consumer or the consumer's agent or broker;

(iv) To accrue or recognize incentives or bonuses associated with the transaction that are provided by you or any other party;

(v) To underwrite insurance at the consumer's request or for reinsurance purposes, or for any of the following purposes as they relate to a consumer's insurance: account administration, reporting, investigating, or preventing fraud or material misrepresentation, processing premium payments, processing insurance claims, administering insurance benefits (including utilization review activities), participating in research projects, or as otherwise required or specifically permitted by Federal or State law;

(vi) In connection with:

(A) The authorization, settlement, billing, processing, clearing, transferring, reconciling or collection of amounts charged, debited, or otherwise paid using a debit, credit, or other payment card, check, or account number, or by other payment means;

(B) The transfer of receivables, accounts, or interests therein; or

(C) The audit of debit, credit, or other payment information.

[65 Fed. Reg. 33677 (May 24, 2000)]

§ 313.15 Other exceptions to notice and opt out requirements.

(a) *Exceptions to opt out requirements.* The requirements for initial notice in § 313.4(a)(2), for the opt out in §§ 313.7 and 313.10, and for service providers and joint marketing in § 313.13 do not apply when you disclose nonpublic personal information:

(1) With the consent or at the direction of the consumer, provided that the consumer has not revoked the consent or direction;

(2)(i) To protect the confidentiality or security of your records pertaining to the consumer, service, product, or transaction;

(ii) To protect against or prevent actual or potential fraud, unauthorized transactions, claims, or other liability;

(iii) For required institutional risk control or for resolving consumer disputes or inquiries;

(iv) To persons holding a legal or beneficial interest relating to the consumer; or

(v) To persons acting in a fiduciary or representative capacity on behalf of the consumer;

(3) To provide information to insurance rate advisory organizations, guaranty funds or agencies, agencies that are rating you, persons that are assessing your compliance with industry standards, and your attorneys, accountants, and auditors;

(4) To the extent specifically permitted or required under other provisions of law and in accordance with the Right to Financial Privacy Act of 1978 (12 U.S.C. 3401 *et seq.*), to law enforcement agencies (including a federal functional regulator, the Secretary of the Treasury, with respect to 31 U.S.C. Chapter 53, Subchapter II (Records and Reports on Monetary Instruments and Transactions) and 12 U.S.C. Chapter 21 (Financial Recordkeeping), a State insurance authority, with respect to any person domiciled in that insurance authority's State that is engaged in providing insurance, and the Federal Trade Commission), self-regulatory organizations, or for an investigation on a matter related to public safety;

(5)(i) To a consumer reporting agency in accordance with the Fair Credit Reporting Act (15 U.S.C. 1681 et seq.), or

(ii) From a consumer report reported by a consumer reporting agency;

(6) In connection with a proposed or actual sale, merger, transfer, or exchange of all or a portion of a business or operating unit if the disclosure of nonpublic personal information concerns solely consumers of such business or unit; or

(7)(i) To comply with Federal, State, or local laws, rules and other applicable legal requirements;

(ii) To comply with a properly authorized civil, criminal, or regulatory investigation, or subpoena or summons by Federal, State, or local authorities; or

(iii) To respond to judicial process or government regulatory authorities having jurisdiction over you for examination, compliance, or other purposes as authorized by law.

(b) *Examples of consent and revocation of consent.* (1) A consumer may specifically consent to your disclosure to a nonaffiliated insurance company of the fact that the consumer has applied to you for a mortgage so that the insurance company can offer homeowner's insurance to the consumer.

(2) A consumer may revoke consent by subsequently exercising the right to opt out of future disclosures of nonpublic personal information as permitted under § 313.7(f).

[65 Fed. Reg. 33677 (May 24, 2000)]

Subpart D—Relation to Other Laws; Effective Date

§ 313.16 Protection of Fair Credit Reporting Act.

Nothing in this part shall be construed to modify, limit, or supersede the operation of the Fair Credit Reporting Act (15 U.S.C. 1681 *et seq.*), and no inference shall be drawn on the basis of the provisions of this part regarding whether information is transaction or experience information under section 603 of that Act.

[65 Fed. Reg. 33677 (May 24, 2000)]

§ 313.17 Relation to State laws.

(a) *In general.* This part shall not be construed as superseding, altering, or affecting any statute, regulation, order, or interpretation in effect in any State, except to the extent that such State statute, regulation, order, or interpretation is inconsistent with the provisions of this part, and then only to the extent of the inconsistency.

(b) *Greater protection under State law.* For purposes of this section, a State statute, regulation, order, or interpretation is not inconsistent with the provisions of this part if the protection such statute, regulation, order, or interpretation affords any consumer is greater than the protection provided under this part, as determined by the Commission on its own motion or upon the petition of any interested party, after consultation with the applicable federal functional regulator or other authority.

[65 Fed. Reg. 33677 (May 24, 2000)]

§ 313.18 Effective date; transition rule.

(a) *Effective date*—(1) *General rule.* This part is effective November 13, 2000. In order to provide sufficient time for you to establish policies and systems to comply with the requirements of this part, the Commission has extended the time for compliance with this part until July 1, 2001.

(2) *Exception.* This part is not effective as to any institution that is significantly engaged in activities that the Federal Reserve Board determines, after November 12, 1999, (pursuant to its authority in Section 4(k)(1–3) of the Bank Holding Company Act), are activities that a financial holding company may engage in, until the Commission so determines.

(b)(1) *Notice requirement for consumers who are your customers on the compliance date.* By July 1, 2001, you must have provided an initial notice, as required by § 313.4, to consumers who are your customers on July 1, 2001.

(2) *Example.* You provide an initial notice to consumers who are your customers on July 1, 2001, if, by that date, you have established a system for providing an initial notice to all new customers and have mailed the initial notice to all your existing customers.

(c) *Two-year grandfathering of service agreements.* Until July 1, 2002, a contract that you have entered into with a nonaffiliated third party to perform services for you or functions on your behalf satisfies the provisions of § 313.13(a)(1) of this part, even if the contract does not include a requirement that the third party maintain the confidentiality of nonpublic personal information, as long as you entered into the contract on or before July 1, 2000.

[65 Fed. Reg. 33677 (May 24, 2000)]

Appendix A to Part 313—Sample Clauses

Financial institutions, including a group of financial holding company affiliates that use a common privacy notice, may use the following sample clauses, if the clause is accurate for each institution that uses the notice. (Note that disclosure of certain information, such as assets and income, and information from a consumer reporting agency, may give rise to obligations under the Fair Credit Reporting Act, such as a requirement to permit a consumer to opt out of disclosures to affiliates or designation as a consumer reporting agency if disclosures are made to nonaffiliated third parties.)

A-1—Categories of Information You Collect (All Institutions)

You may use this clause, as applicable, to meet the requirement of § 313.6(a)(1) to describe the categories of nonpublic personal information you collect.

Sample Clause A-1

We collect nonpublic personal information about you from the following sources:

- Information we receive from you on applications or other forms;
- Information about your transactions with us, our affiliates, or others; and
- Information we receive from a consumer reporting agency.

A-2—Categories of Information You Disclose (Institutions That Disclose Outside of the Exceptions)

You may use one of these clauses, as applicable, to meet the requirement of § 313.6(a)(2) to describe the categories of nonpublic personal information you disclose. You may use these clauses if you disclose nonpublic personal information other than as permitted by the exceptions in §§ 313.13, 313.14, and 313.15.

Sample Clause A-2, Alternative 1

We may disclose the following kinds of nonpublic personal information about you:

- Information we receive from you on applications or other forms, such as [*provide illustrative examples, such as "your name, address, social security number, assets, and income"*];
- Information about your transactions with us, our affiliates, or others, such as [*provide illustrative examples, such as "your account balance, payment history, parties to transactions, and credit card usage"*]; and
- Information we receive from a consumer reporting agency, such as [*provide illustrative examples, such as "your creditworthiness and credit history"*].

Sample Clause A-2, Alternative 2

We may disclose all of the information that we collect, as described [*describe location in the notice, such as "above" or "below"*].

A-3—Categories of Information You Disclose and Parties to Whom You Disclose (Institutions That Do Not Disclose Outside of the Exceptions)

You may use this clause, as applicable, to meet the requirements of §§ 313.6(a)(2), (3), and (4) to describe the categories of nonpublic personal information about customers and former customers that you disclose and the categories of affiliates and nonaffiliated third parties to whom you disclose. You may use this clause if you do not disclose nonpublic personal information to any party, other than as permitted by the exceptions in §§ 313.14, and 313.15.

Sample Clause A-3

We do not disclose any nonpublic personal information about our customers or former customers to anyone, except as permitted by law.

A-4—Categories of Parties to Whom You Disclose (Institutions That Disclose Outside of the Exceptions)

You may use this clause, as applicable, to meet the requirement of § 313.6(a)(3) to describe the categories of affiliates and nonaffiliated third parties to whom you disclose nonpublic personal information. You may use this clause if you disclose nonpublic personal information other than as permitted by the exceptions in §§ 313.13, 313.14, and 313.15, as well as when permitted by the exceptions in §§ 313.14, and 313.15.

Sample Clause A-4

We may disclose nonpublic personal information about you to the following types of third parties:

- Financial service providers, such as [*provide illustrative examples, such as "mortgage bankers, securities broker-dealers, and insurance agents"*];
- Non-financial companies, such as [*provide illustrative examples, such as "retailers, direct marketers, airlines, and publishers"*]; and
- Others, such as [*provide illustrative examples, such as "non-profit organizations"*].

We may also disclose nonpublic personal information about you to nonaffiliated third parties as permitted by law.

A-5—Service Provider/Joint Marketing Exception

You may use one of these clauses, as applicable, to meet the requirements of § 313.6(a)(5) related to the exception for service providers and joint marketers in § 313.13. If you disclose nonpublic personal information under this exception, you must describe the categories of nonpublic personal information you disclose and the categories of third parties with whom you have contracted.

Sample Clause A-5, Alternative 1

We may disclose the following information to companies that perform marketing services on our behalf or to other financial institutions with whom we have joint marketing agreements:

- Information we receive from you on applications or other forms, such as [*provide illustrative examples, such as "your name, address, social security number, assets, and income"*];
- Information about your transactions with us, our affiliates, or others, such as [*provide illustrative examples, such as "your account balance, payment history, parties to transactions, and credit card usage"*]; and
- Information we receive from a consumer reporting agency, such as [*provide illustrative examples, such as "your creditworthiness and credit history"*].

Sample Clause A-5, Alternative 2

We may disclose all of the information we collect, as described [*describe location in the notice, such as "above" or "below"*] to companies that perform marketing services on our behalf or to other financial institutions with whom we have joint marketing agreements.

A-6—Explanation of Opt Out Right (Institutions that Disclose Outside of the Exceptions)

You may use this clause, as applicable, to meet the requirement of § 313.6(a)(6) to provide an explanation of the consumer's right to opt out of the disclosure of nonpublic personal information to nonaffiliated third parties, including the method(s) by which the consumer may exercise that right. You may use this clause if you disclose nonpublic personal information other than as permitted by the exceptions in §§ 313.13, 313.14, and 313.15.

Sample Clause A-6

If you prefer that we not disclose nonpublic personal information about you to nonaffiliated third parties, you may opt out of those disclosures, that is, you may direct us not to make those disclosures (other than disclosures permitted by law). If you wish to opt out of disclosures to nonaffiliated third parties, you may [*describe a reasonable means of opting out, such as "call the following toll-free number: (insert number)"*].

A-7—Confidentiality and Security (All Institutions)

You may use this clause, as applicable, to meet the requirement of § 313.6(a)(8) to describe your policies and practices with respect to protecting the confidentiality and security of nonpublic personal information.

Sample Clause A-7

We restrict access to nonpublic personal information about you to [*provide an appropriate description, such as "those employees who need to know that information to provide products or services to you"*]. We maintain physical, electronic, and procedural safeguards that comply with federal regulations to guard your nonpublic personal information.

[65 Fed. Reg. 33677 (May 24, 2000)]

PART 314—STANDARDS FOR SAFEGUARDING CUSTOMER INFORMATION

§ 314.1 Purpose and scope.

(a) *Purpose*. This part, which implements sections 501 and 505(b)(2) of the Gramm-Leach-Bliley Act, sets forth standards for developing, implementing, and maintaining reasonable administrative, technical, and physical safeguards to protect the security, confidentiality, and integrity of customer information.

(b) *Scope*. This part applies to the handling of customer information by all financial institutions over which the Federal Trade Commission ("FTC" or "Commission") has jurisdiction. This part refers to such entities as "you." This part applies to all customer information in your possession, regardless of whether such information pertains to individuals with whom you have a customer relationship, or pertains to the customers of other financial institutions that have provided such information to you.

[67 Fed. Reg. 36493 (May 23, 2002)]

§ 314.2 Definitions.

(a) *In general*. Except as modified by this part or unless the context otherwise requires, the terms used in this part have the same meaning as set forth in the Commission's rule governing the Privacy of Consumer Financial Information, 16 CFR part 313.

(b) Customer information means any record containing nonpublic personal information as defined in 16 CFR 313.3(n), about a customer of a financial institution, whether in paper, electronic, or other form, that is handled or maintained by or on behalf of you or your affiliates.

(c) Information security program means the administrative, technical, or physical safeguards you use to access, collect, distribute, process, protect, store, use, transmit, dispose of, or otherwise handle customer information.

(d) Service provider means any person or entity that receives, maintains, processes, or otherwise is permitted access to customer information through its provision of services directly to a financial institution that is subject to this part.

[67 Fed. Reg. 36493 (May 23, 2002)]

§ 314.3 Standards for safeguarding customer information.

(a) *Information security program*. You shall develop, implement, and maintain a comprehensive information security program that is written in one or more readily accessible parts and contains administrative, technical, and physical safeguards that are appropriate to your size and complexity, the nature and scope of your activities, and the sensitivity of any customer information at issue. Such safeguards shall include the elements set forth in § 314.4 and shall be reasonably designed to achieve the objectives of this part, as set forth in paragraph (b) of this section.

(b) *Objectives*. The objectives of section 501(b) of the Act, and of this part, are to:

(1) Insure the security and confidentiality of customer information;

(2) Protect against any anticipated threats or hazards to the security or integrity of such information; and

(3) Protect against unauthorized access to or use of such information that could result in substantial harm or inconvenience to any customer.

[67 Fed. Reg. 36493 (May 23, 2002)]

§ 314.4 Elements.

In order to develop, implement, and maintain your information security program, you shall:

(a) Designate an employee or employees to coordinate your information security program.

(b) Identify reasonably foreseeable internal and external risks to the security, confidentiality, and integrity of customer information that could result in the unauthorized disclosure, misuse, alteration, destruction or other compromise of such information, and assess the sufficiency of any safeguards in place to control these risks. At a minimum, such a risk assessment should include consideration of risks in each relevant area of your operations, including:

(1) Employee training and management;

(2) Information systems, including network and software design, as well as information processing, storage, transmission and disposal; and

(3) Detecting, preventing and responding to attacks, intrusions, or other systems failures.

(c) Design and implement information safeguards to control the risks you identify through risk assessment, and regularly test or otherwise monitor the effectiveness of the safeguards' key controls, systems, and procedures.

(d) Oversee service providers, by:

(1) Taking reasonable steps to select and retain service providers that are capable of maintaining appropriate safeguards for the customer information at issue; and

(2) Requiring your service providers by contract to implement and maintain such safeguards.

(e) Evaluate and adjust your information security program in light of the results of the testing and monitoring required by paragraph (c) of this section; any material changes to your operations or business arrangements; or any other circumstances that you know or have reason to know may have a material impact on your information security program.

[67 Fed. Reg. 36493 (May 23, 2002)]

§ 314.5 Effective date.

(a) Each financial institution subject to the Commission's jurisdiction must implement an information security program pursuant to this part no later than May 23, 2003.

(b) Two-year grandfathering of service contracts. Until May 24, 2004, a contract you have entered into with a nonaffiliated third party to perform services for you or functions on your behalf satisfies the provisions of § 314.4(d), even if the contract does not include a requirement that the service provider maintain appropriate safeguards, as long as you entered into the contract not later than June 24, 2002.

[67 Fed. Reg. 36493 (May 23, 2002)]

G.3 Banking Agency Regulations

The Act also granted rulemaking authority to other federal agencies that have jurisdiction over the financial institutions covered by the Gramm-Leach-Bliley Act, and those agencies have issued regulations to protect the security of customer information, set forth below according to agency.

G.3.1 Office of the Comptroller of the Currency Regulations

TITLE 12—BANKS AND BANKING

CHAPTER I—COMPTROLLER OF THE CURRENCY, DEPARTMENT OF THE TREASURY

* * *

PART 30—SAFETY AND SOUNDNESS STANDARDS

* * *

12 C.F.R. Appendix B to Part 30—Interagency Guidelines Establishing Information Security Standards

TABLE OF CONTENTS

I. Introduction
  A. Scope
  B. Preservation of Existing Authority
  C. Definitions
II. Standards for Safeguarding Customer Information
  A. Information Security Program
  B. Objectives
III. Development and Implementation of Customer Information Security Program
  A. Involve the Board of Directors
  B. Assess Risk
  C. Manage and Control Risk
  D. Oversee Service Provider Arrangements
  E. Adjust the Program
  F. Report to the Board
  G. Implement the Standards

I. INTRODUCTION

The Interagency Guidelines Establishing Information Security Standards (Guidelines) set forth standards pursuant to section 39 of the Federal Deposit Insurance Act (section 39, codified at 12 U.S.C. 1831p-1), and sections 501 and 505(b), codified at 15 U.S.C. 6801 and 6805(b) of the Gramm-Leach Bliley Act. These Guidelines address standards for developing and implementing administrative, technical, and physical safeguards to protect the security, confidentiality, and integrity of customer information. These Guidelines also address standards with respect to the proper disposal of consumer information, pursuant to sections 621 and 628 of the Fair Credit Reporting Act (15 U.S.C. 1681s and 1681w).

A. *Scope.* The Guidelines apply to customer information maintained by or on behalf of entities over which the OCC has authority. Such entities, referred to as "the bank," are national banks, federal branches and federal agencies of foreign banks, and any subsidiaries of such entities (except brokers, dealers, persons providing insurance, investment companies, and investment advisers). The Guidelines also apply to the proper disposal of consumer information by or on behalf of such entities.

B. *Preservation of Existing Authority.* Neither section 39 nor these Guidelines in any way limit the authority of the OCC to address unsafe or unsound practices, violations of law, unsafe or unsound conditions, or other practices. The OCC may take action under section 39 and these Guidelines independently of, in conjunction with, or in addition to, any other enforcement action available to the OCC.

C. *Definitions.* 1. Except as modified in the Guidelines, or unless the context otherwise requires, the terms used in these Guidelines have the same meanings as set forth in sections 3 and 39 of the Federal Deposit Insurance Act (12 U.S.C. 1813 and 1831p-1).

2. For purposes of the Guidelines, the following definitions apply:

  a. *Board of directors*, in the case of a branch or agency of a foreign bank, means the managing official in charge of the branch or agency.

  b. *Consumer information* means any record about an individual, whether in paper, electronic, or other form, that is a consumer report or is derived from a consumer report and that is maintained or otherwise possessed by or on behalf of the bank for a business purpose. Consumer information also means a compilation of such records. The term does not include any record that does not identify an individual.

    i. *Examples.* (1) *Consumer information* includes:

(A) A consumer report that a bank obtains;

(B) Information from a consumer report that the bank obtains from its affiliate after the consumer has been given a notice and has elected not to opt out of that sharing;

(C) Information from a consumer report that the bank obtains about an individual who applies for but does not receive a loan, including any loan sought by an individual for a business purpose;

(D) Information from a consumer report that the bank obtains about an individual who guarantees a loan (including a loan to a business entity); or

(E) Information from a consumer report that the bank obtains about an employee or prospective employee.

(2) *Consumer information* does not include:

(A) Aggregate information, such as the mean credit score, derived from a group of consumer reports; or

(B) Blind data, such as payment history on accounts that are not personally identifiable, that may be used for developing credit scoring models or for other purposes.

c. *Consumer report* has the same meaning as set forth in the Fair Credit Reporting Act, 15 U.S.C. 1681a(d).

d. *Customer* means any customer of the bank as defined in § 40.3(h) of this chapter.

e. *Customer information* means any record containing nonpublic personal information, as defined in § 40.3(n) of this chapter, about a customer, whether in paper, electronic, or other form, that is maintained by or on behalf of the bank.

f. *Customer information systems* means any methods used to access, collect, store, use, transmit, protect, or dispose of customer information.

g. *Service provider* means any person or entity that maintains, processes, or otherwise is permitted access to customer information or consumer information through its provision of services directly to the bank.

II. STANDARDS FOR INFORMATION SECURITY

A. *Information Security Program.* Each bank shall implement a comprehensive written information security program that includes administrative, technical, and physical safeguards appropriate to the size and complexity of the bank and the nature and scope of its activities. While all parts of the bank are not required to implement a uniform set of policies, all elements of the information security program must be coordinated.

B. *Objectives.* A bank's information security program shall be designed to:

1. Ensure the security and confidentiality of customer information;

2. Protect against any anticipated threats or hazards to the security or integrity of such information;

3. Protect against unauthorized access to or use of such information that could result in substantial harm or inconvenience to any customer; and

4. Ensure the proper disposal of customer information and consumer information.

III. DEVELOPMENT AND IMPLEMENTATION OF INFORMATION SECURITY PROGRAM

A. *Involve the Board of Directors.* The board of directors or an appropriate committee of the board of each bank shall:

1. Approve the bank's written information security program; and

2. Oversee the development, implementation, and maintenance of the bank's information security program, including assigning specific responsibility for its implementation and reviewing reports from management.

B. *Assess Risk.* Each bank shall:

1. Identify reasonably foreseeable internal and external threats that could result in unauthorized disclosure, misuse, alteration, or destruction of customer information or customer information systems.

2. Assess the likelihood and potential damage of these threats, taking into consideration the sensitivity of customer information.

3. Assess the sufficiency of policies, procedures, customer information systems, and other arrangements in place to control risks.

C. *Manage and Control Risk.* Each bank shall:

1. Design its information security program to control the identified risks, commensurate with the sensitivity of the information as well as the complexity and scope of the bank's activities. Each bank must consider whether the following security measures are appropriate for the bank and, if so, adopt those measures the bank concludes are appropriate:

a. Access controls on customer information systems, including controls to authenticate and permit access only to authorized individuals and controls to prevent employees from providing customer information to unauthorized individuals who may seek to obtain this information through fraudulent means.

b. Access restrictions at physical locations containing customer information, such as buildings, computer facilities, and records storage facilities to permit access only to authorized individuals;

c. Encryption of electronic customer information, including while in transit or in storage on networks or systems to which unauthorized individuals may have access;

d. Procedures designed to ensure that customer information system modifications are consistent with the bank's information security program;

e. Dual control procedures, segregation of duties, and employee background checks for employees with responsibilities for or access to customer information;

f. Monitoring systems and procedures to detect actual and attempted attacks on or intrusions into customer information systems;

g. Response programs that specify actions to be taken when the bank suspects or detects that unauthorized individuals have gained access to customer information systems, including appropriate reports to regulatory and law enforcement agencies; and

h. Measures to protect against destruction, loss, or damage of customer information due to potential environmental hazards, such as fire and water damage or technological failures.

2. Train staff to implement the bank's information security program.

3. Regularly test the key controls, systems and procedures of the information security program. The frequency and nature of such tests should be determined by the bank's risk assessment. Tests should be conducted or reviewed by independent third parties or staff independent of those that develop or maintain the security programs.

4. Develop, implement, and maintain, as part of its information security program, appropriate measures to properly dispose of customer information and consumer information in accordance with each of the requirements of this paragraph III.

D. *Oversee Service Provider Arrangements.* Each bank shall:

1. Exercise appropriate due diligence in selecting its service providers;

2. Require its service providers by contract to implement appropriate measures designed to meet the objectives of these Guidelines; and

3. Where indicated by the bank's risk assessment, monitor its service providers to confirm that they have satisfied their obligations as required by section D.2. As part of this monitoring, a bank should review audits, summaries of test results, or other equivalent evaluations of its service providers.

E. *Adjust the Program.* Each bank shall monitor, evaluate, and adjust, as appropriate, the information security program in light of any relevant changes in technology, the sensitivity of its customer information, internal or external threats to information, and the bank's own changing business arrangements, such as mergers and acquisitions, alliances and joint ventures, outsourcing arrangements, and changes to customer information systems.

F. *Report to the Board.* Each bank shall report to its board or an appropriate committee of the board at least annually. This report should describe the overall status of the information security program and the bank's compliance with these Guidelines. The reports should discuss material matters related to its program, addressing issues such as: risk assessment; risk management and control decisions; service provider arrangements; results of testing; security breaches or violations and management's responses; and recommendations for changes in the information security program.

G. *Implement the Standards.* 1. *Effective date.* Each bank must implement an information security program pursuant to these Guidelines by July 1, 2001.

2. *Two-year grandfathering of agreements with service providers.* Until July 1, 2003, a contract that a bank has entered into with a service provider to perform services for it or functions on its behalf satisfies the provisions of section III.D., even if the contract does not include a requirement that the servicer maintain the security and confidentiality of customer information, as long as the bank entered into the contract on or before March 5, 2001.

3. *Effective date for measures relating to the disposal of consumer information.* Each bank must satisfy these Guidelines with respect to the proper disposal of consumer information by July 1, 2005.

4. *Exception for existing agreements with service providers relating to the disposal of consumer information.* Notwithstanding the requirement in paragraph III.G.3., a bank's contracts with its service providers that have access to consumer information and that may dispose of consumer information, entered into before July 1, 2005, must comply with the provisions of the Guidelines relating to the proper disposal of consumer information by July 1, 2006.

SUPPLEMENT A TO APPENDIX B TO PART 30—
INTERAGENCY GUIDANCE ON RESPONSE PROGRAMS
FOR UNAUTHORIZED ACCESS TO CUSTOMER
INFORMATION AND CUSTOMER NOTICE

I. BACKGROUND

This Guidance[1] interprets section 501(b) of the Gramm-Leach-Bliley Act ("GLBA") and the Interagency Guidelines Establishing Information Security Standards (the "Security Guidelines")[2] and describes response programs, including customer notification procedures, that a financial institution should develop and implement to address unauthorized access to or use of customer information that could result in substantial harm or inconvenience to a customer. The scope of, and definitions of terms used in, this Guidance are identical to those of the Security Guidelines. For example, the term "customer information" is the same term used in the Security Guidelines, and means any record containing nonpublic personal information about a customer, whether in paper, electronic, or other form, maintained by or on behalf of the institution.

A. *Interagency Security Guidelines*

Section 501(b) of the GLBA required the Agencies to establish appropriate standards for financial institutions subject to their jurisdiction that include administrative, technical, and physical safeguards, to protect the security and confidentiality of customer information. Accordingly, the Agencies issued Security Guidelines requiring every financial institution to have an information security program designed to:

1. Ensure the security and confidentiality of customer information;

2. Protect against any anticipated threats or hazards to the security or integrity of such information; and

3. Protect against unauthorized access to or use of such information that could result in substantial harm or inconvenience to any customer.

B. *Risk Assessment and Controls*

1. The Security Guidelines direct every financial institution to assess the following risks, among others, when developing its information security program:

a. Reasonably foreseeable internal and external threats that could result in unauthorized disclosure, misuse, alteration, or destruction of customer information or customer information systems;

b. The likelihood and potential damage of threats, taking into consideration the sensitivity of customer information; and

c. The sufficiency of policies, procedures, customer information systems, and other arrangements in place to control risks.[3]

2. Following the assessment of these risks, the Security Guidelines require a financial institution to design a program to address the identified risks. The particular security measures an institution should adopt will depend upon the risks presented by the complexity and scope of its business. At a minimum, the financial institution is required to consider the specific security measures enumerated in the Security Guidelines,[4] and adopt those that are appropriate for the institution, including:

a. Access controls on customer information systems, including controls to authenticate and permit access only to authorized

---

[1] This Guidance is being jointly issued by the Board of Governors of the Federal Reserve System (Board), the Federal Deposit Insurance Corporation (FDIC), the Office of the Comptroller of the Currency (OCC), and the Office of Thrift Supervision (OTS).

[2] 12 CFR part 30, app. B (OCC); 12 CFR part 208, app. D-2 and part 225, app. F (Board); 12 CFR part 364, app. B (FDIC); and 12 CFR part 570, app. B (OTS). The "Interagency Guidelines Establishing Information Security Standards" were formerly known as "The Interagency Guidelines Establishing Standards for Safeguarding Customer Information."

[3] *See* Security Guidelines, III.B.

[4] *See* Security Guidelines, III.C.

individuals and controls to prevent employees from providing customer information to unauthorized individuals who may seek to obtain this information through fraudulent means;

b. Background checks for employees with responsibilities for access to customer information; and

c. Response programs that specify actions to be taken when the financial institution suspects or detects that unauthorized individuals have gained access to customer information systems, including appropriate reports to regulatory and law enforcement agencies.[5]

C. Service Providers

The Security Guidelines direct every financial institution to require its service providers by contract to implement appropriate measures designed to protect against unauthorized access to or use of customer information that could result in substantial harm or inconvenience to any customer.[6]

II. RESPONSE PROGRAM

Millions of Americans, throughout the country, have been victims of identity theft.[7] Identity thieves misuse personal information they obtain from a number of sources, including financial institutions, to perpetrate identity theft. Therefore, financial institutions should take preventative measures to safeguard customer information against attempts to gain unauthorized access to the information. For example, financial institutions should place access controls on customer information systems and conduct background checks for employees who are authorized to access customer information.[8] However, every financial institution should also develop and implement a risk-based response program to address incidents of unauthorized access to customer information in customer information systems[9] that occur nonetheless. A response program should be a key part of an institution's information security program.[10] The program should be appropriate to the size and complexity of the institution and the nature and scope of its activities.

---

5 See Security Guidelines, III.C.
6 See Security Guidelines, II.B. and III.D. Further, the Agencies note that, in addition to contractual obligations to a financial institution, a service provider may be required to implement its own comprehensive information security program in accordance with the Safeguards Rule promulgated by the Federal Trade Commission ("FTC"), 16 CFR part 314.
7 The FTC estimates that nearly 10 million Americans discovered they were victims of some form of identity theft in 2002. See The Federal Trade Commission, Identity Theft Survey Report, (September 2003), available at http://www.ftc.gov/os/2003/09/synovatereport.pdf.
8 Institutions should also conduct background checks of employees to ensure that the institution does not violate 12 U.S.C. 1829, which prohibits an institution from hiring an individual convicted of certain criminal offenses or who is subject to a prohibition order under 12 U.S.C. 1818(e)(6).
9 Under the Guidelines, an institution's customer information systems consist of all of the methods used to access, collect, store, use, transmit, protect, or dispose of customer information, including the systems maintained by its service providers. See Security Guidelines, I.C.2.d (I.C.2.c for OTS).
10 See FFIEC Information Technology Examination Handbook, Information Security Booklet, Dec. 2002 available at http://www.ffiec.gov/ffiecinfobase/html_pages/infosec_book_frame.htm.

In addition, each institution should be able to address incidents of unauthorized access to customer information in customer information systems maintained by its domestic and foreign service providers. Therefore, consistent with the obligations in the Guidelines that relate to these arrangements, and with existing guidance on this topic issued by the Agencies,[11] an institution's contract with its service provider should require the service provider to take appropriate actions to address incidents of unauthorized access to the financial institution's customer information, including notification to the institution as soon as possible of any such incident, to enable the institution to expeditiously implement its response program.

A. Components of a Response Program

1. At a minimum, an institution's response program should contain procedures for the following:

a. Assessing the nature and scope of an incident, and identifying what customer information systems and types of customer information have been accessed or misused;

b. Notifying its primary Federal regulator as soon as possible when the institution becomes aware of an incident involving unauthorized access to or use of sensitive customer information, as defined below;

c. Consistent with the Agencies' Suspicious Activity Report ("SAR") regulations,[12] notifying appropriate law enforcement authorities, in addition to filing a timely SAR in situations involv-

---

Federal Reserve SR 97-32, Sound Practice Guidance for Information Security for Networks, Dec. 4, 1997; OCC Bulletin 2000-14, "Infrastructure Threats—Intrusion Risks" (May 15, 2000), for additional guidance on preventing, detecting, and responding to intrusions into financial institution computer systems.

11 See Federal Reserve SR Ltr. 00-04, Outsourcing of Information and Transaction Processing, Feb. 9, 2000; OCC Bulletin 2001-47, "Third-Party Relationships Risk Management Principles," Nov. 1, 2001; FDIC FIL 68-99, Risk Assessment Tools and Practices for Information System Security, July 7, 1999; OTS Thrift Bulletin 82a, Third Party Arrangements, Sept. 1, 2004.

12 An institution's obligation to file a SAR is set out in the Agencies' SAR regulations and Agency guidance. See 12 CFR 21.11 (national banks, Federal branches and agencies); 12 CFR 208.62 (State member banks); 12 CFR 211.5(k) (Edge and agreement corporations); 12 CFR 211.24(f) (uninsured State branches and agencies of foreign banks); 12 CFR 225.4(f) (bank holding companies and their nonbank subsidiaries); 12 CFR part 353 (State non-member banks); and 12 CFR 563.180 (savings associations). National banks must file SARs in connection with computer intrusions and other computer crimes. See OCC Bulletin 2000-14, "Infrastructure Threats—Intrusion Risks" (May 15, 2000); Advisory Letter 97-9, "Reporting Computer Related Crimes" (November 19, 1997) (general guidance still applicable though instructions for new SAR form published in 65 FR 1229, 1230 (January 7, 2000)). See also Federal Reserve SR 01-11, Identity Theft and Pretext Calling, Apr. 26, 2001; SR 97-28, Guidance Concerning Reporting of Computer Related Crimes by Financial Institutions, Nov. 6, 1997; FDIC FIL 48-2000, Suspicious Activity Reports, July 14, 2000; FIL 47-97, Preparation of Suspicious Activity Reports, May 6, 1997; OTS CEO Memorandum 139, Identity Theft and Pretext Calling, May 4, 2001; CEO Memorandum 126, New Suspicious Activity Report Form, July 5, 2000; http://www.ots.treas.gov/

ing Federal criminal violations requiring immediate attention, such as when a reportable violation is ongoing;

d. Taking appropriate steps to contain and control the incident to prevent further unauthorized access to or use of customer information, for example, by monitoring, freezing, or closing affected accounts, while preserving records and other evidence;[13] and

e. Notifying customers when warranted.

2. Where an incident of unauthorized access to customer information involves customer information systems maintained by an institution's service providers, it is the responsibility of the financial institution to notify the institution's customers and regulator. However, an institution may authorize or contract with its service provider to notify the institution's customers or regulator on its behalf.

III. CUSTOMER NOTICE

Financial institutions have an affirmative duty to protect their customers' information against unauthorized access or use. Notifying customers of a security incident involving the unauthorized access or use of the customer's information in accordance with the standard set forth below is a key part of that duty. Timely notification of customers is important to manage an institution's reputation risk. Effective notice also may reduce an institution's legal risk, assist in maintaining good customer relations, and enable the institution's customers to take steps to protect themselves against the consequences of identity theft. When customer notification is warranted, an institution may not forgo notifying its customers of an incident because the institution believes that it may be potentially embarrassed or inconvenienced by doing so.

A. Standard for Providing Notice

When a financial institution becomes aware of an incident of unauthorized access to sensitive customer information, the institution should conduct a reasonable investigation to promptly determine the likelihood that the information has been or will be misused. If the institution determines that misuse of its information about a customer has occurred or is reasonably possible, it should notify the affected customer as soon as possible. Customer notice may be delayed if an appropriate law enforcement agency determines that notification will interfere with a criminal investigation and provides the institution with a written request for the delay. However, the institution should notify its customers as soon as notification will no longer interfere with the investigation.

1. Sensitive Customer Information

Under the Guidelines, an institution must protect against unauthorized access to or use of customer information that could result in substantial harm or inconvenience to any customer. Substantial harm or inconvenience is most likely to result from improper access to sensitive customer information because this type of information is most likely to be misused, as in the commission of identity theft. For purposes of this Guidance, sensitive customer information means a customer's name, address, or telephone number, in conjunction with the customer's social security number, driver's license number, account number, credit or debit card number, or a personal identification number or password that would permit access to the customer's account. Sensitive customer information also includes any combination of components of customer information that would allow someone to log onto or access the customer's account, such as user name and password or password and account number.

2. Affected Customers

If a financial institution, based upon its investigation, can determine from its logs or other data precisely which customers' information has been improperly accessed, it may limit notification to those customers with regard to whom the institution determines that misuse of their information has occurred or is reasonably possible. However, there may be situations where the institution determines that a group of files has been accessed improperly, but is unable to identify which specific customers' information has been accessed. If the circumstances of the unauthorized access lead the institution to determine that misuse of the information is reasonably possible, it should notify all customers in the group.

B. Content of Customer Notice

1. Customer notice should be given in a clear and conspicuous manner. The notice should describe the incident in general terms and the type of customer information that was the subject of unauthorized access or use. It also should generally describe what the institution has done to protect the customers' information from further unauthorized access. In addition, it should include a telephone number that customers can call for further information and assistance.[14] The notice also should remind customers of the need to remain vigilant over the next twelve to twenty-four months, and to promptly report incidents of suspected identity theft to the institution. The notice should include the following additional items, when appropriate:

a. A recommendation that the customer review account statements and immediately report any suspicious activity to the institution;

b. A description of fraud alerts and an explanation of how the customer may place a fraud alert in the customer's consumer reports to put the customer's creditors on notice that the customer may be a victim of fraud;

c. A recommendation that the customer periodically obtain credit reports from each nationwide credit reporting agency and have information relating to fraudulent transactions deleted;

d. An explanation of how the customer may obtain a credit report free of charge; and

e. Information about the availability of the FTC's online guidance regarding steps a consumer can take to protect against identity theft. The notice should encourage the customer to report any incidents of identity theft to the FTC, and should provide the FTC's Web site address and toll-free telephone number that customers may use to obtain the identity theft guidance and report suspected incidents of identity theft.[15]

BSA (for the latest SAR form and filing instructions required by OTS as of July 1, 2003).

13 See FFIEC Information Technology Examination Handbook, Information Security Booklet, Dec. 2002, pp. 68–74.

14 The institution should, therefore, ensure that it has reasonable policies and procedures in place, including trained personnel, to respond appropriately to customer inquiries and requests for assistance.

15 Currently, the FTC Web site for the ID Theft brochure and the

2. The Agencies encourage financial institutions to notify the nationwide consumer reporting agencies prior to sending notices to a large number of customers that include contact information for the reporting agencies.

C. Delivery of Customer Notice

Customer notice should be delivered in any manner designed to ensure that a customer can reasonably be expected to receive it. For example, the institution may choose to contact all customers affected by telephone or by mail, or by electronic mail for those customers for whom it has a valid e-mail address and who have agreed to receive communications electronically.

[66 Fed. Reg. 8633 (Feb. 1, 2001), *as amended at* 69 Fed. Reg. 77616 (Dec. 28, 2004); 70 Fed. Reg. 15753 (Mar. 29, 2005); 71 Fed. Reg. 5780 (Feb. 3, 2006)]

G.3.2 Federal Reserve System Regulations

TITLE 12—BANKS AND BANKING

* * *

CHAPTER II—FEDERAL RESERVE SYSTEM

SUBCHAPTER A—BOARD OF GOVERNORS OF THE FEDERAL RESERVE SYSTEM

* * *

PART 208—MEMBERSHIP OF STATE BANKING INSTITUTIONS IN THE FEDERAL RESERVE SYSTEM (REGULATION H)

SUBPART A—GENERAL MEMBERSHIP AND BRANCHING REQUIREMENTS

* * *

208.3 Application and conditions for membership in the Federal Reserve System.

* * *

SUBPART I—INTERPRETATIONS

* * *

Appendix D-2 to Part 208   Interagency Guidelines Establishing Information Security Standards

* * *

FTC Hotline phone number are *http://www.consumer.gov/idtheft* and *1-877-IDTHEFT*. The institution may also refer customers to any materials developed pursuant to section 151(b) of the FACT Act (educational materials developed by the FTC to teach the public how to prevent identity theft).

PART 211—INTERNATIONAL BANKING OPERATIONS (REGULATION K)

SUBPART A—INTERNATIONAL OPERATIONS OF U.S. BANKING ORGANIZATIONS

* * *

211.5 Edge and agreement corporations.

* * *

SUBPART B—FOREIGN BANKING ORGANIZATIONS

* * *

211.24 Approval of offices of foreign banks; procedures for applications; standards for approval; representative office activities and standards for approval; preservation of existing authority.

* * *

PART 225—BANK HOLDING COMPANIES AND CHANGE IN BANK CONTROL (REGULATION Y)

REGULATIONS

SUBPART A—GENERAL PROVISIONS

* * *

225.4 Corporate practices.

* * *

CONDITIONS TO ORDERS

* * *

Appendix F to Part 225   Interagency Guidelines Establishing Information Security Standards

---

CHAPTER II—FEDERAL RESERVE SYSTEM

SUBCHAPTER A—BOARD OF GOVERNORS OF THE FEDERAL RESERVE SYSTEM

* * *

PART 208—MEMBERSHIP OF STATE BANKING INSTITUTIONS IN THE FEDERAL RESERVE SYSTEM (REGULATION H)

SUBPART A—GENERAL MEMBERSHIP AND BRANCHING REQUIREMENTS

* * *

12 C.F.R. § 208.3 Application and conditions for membership in the Federal Reserve System.

* * *

(d) *Conditions of membership.* (1) *Safety and soundness.* Each member bank shall at all times conduct its business and exercise its powers with due regard to safety and soundness. Each member bank shall comply with the Interagency Guidelines Establishing Standards for Safety and Soundness prescribed pursuant to section 39 of the FDI Act (12 U.S.C. 1831p-1), set forth in appendix D-1 to this part, and the Interagency Guidelines Establishing Information Security Standards prescribed pursuant to sections 501 and 505 of the Gramm-Leach-Bliley Act (15 U.S.C. 6801 and 6805) and section 216 of the Fair and Accurate Credit Transactions Act of 2003 (15 U.S.C. 1681w), set forth in appendix D-2 to this part.

(2) *General character of bank's business.* A member bank may not, without the permission of the Board, cause or permit any change in the general character of its business or in the scope of the corporate powers it exercises at the time of admission to membership.

(3) *Compliance with conditions of membership.* Each member bank shall comply at all times with this Regulation H (12 CFR part 208) and any other conditions of membership prescribed by the Board.

* * *

[69 Fed. Reg. 77610 (Dec. 28, 2004) (Effective Date: July 1, 2005)]

* * *

SUBPART I—INTERPRETATIONS

* * *

12 C.F.R. Appendix D-2 to Part 208—Interagency Guidelines Establishing Information Security Standards

TABLE OF CONTENTS

I. Introduction
   A. Scope
   B. Preservation of Existing Authority
   C. Definitions
II. Standards for Safeguarding Customer Information
   A. Information Security Program
   B. Objectives
III. Development and Implementation of Customer Information Security Program
   A. Involve the Board of Directors
   B. Assess Risk
   C. Manage and Control Risk
   D. Oversee Service Provider Arrangements
   E. Adjust the Program
   F. Report to the Board
   G. Implement the Standards

I. INTRODUCTION

These Interagency Guidelines Establishing Standards for Safeguarding Customer Information (Guidelines) set forth standards pursuant to sections 501 and 505 of the Gramm-Leach-Bliley Act (15 U.S.C. 6801 and 6805), in the same manner, to the extent practicable, as standards prescribed pursuant to section 39 of the Federal Deposit Insurance Act (12 U.S.C. 1831p-1). These Guidelines address standards for developing and implementing administrative, technical, and physical safeguards to protect the security, confidentiality, and integrity of customer information. These Guidelines also address standards with respect to the proper disposal of consumer information, pursuant to sections 621 and 628 of the Fair Credit Reporting Act (15 U.S.C. 1681s and 1681w).

A. *Scope.* The Guidelines apply to customer information maintained by or on behalf of state member banks (banks) and their nonbank subsidiaries, except for brokers, dealers, persons providing insurance, investment companies, and investment advisors. Pursuant to §§ 211.9 and 211.24 of this chapter, these guidelines also apply to customer information maintained by or on behalf of Edge corporations, agreement corporations, and uninsured state-licensed branches or agencies of a foreign bank. These Guidelines also apply to the proper disposal of consumer information by or on behalf of such entities.

B. *Preservation of Existing Authority.* Neither section 39 nor these Guidelines in any way limit the authority of the Board to address unsafe or unsound practices, violations of law, unsafe or unsound conditions, or other practices. The Board may take action under section 39 and these Guidelines independently of, in conjunction with, or in addition to, any other enforcement action available to the Board.

C. *Definitions.*

1. Except as modified in the Guidelines, or unless the context otherwise requires, the terms used in these Guidelines have the same meanings as set forth in sections 3 and 39 of the Federal Deposit Insurance Act (12 U.S.C. 1813 and 1831p-1).

2. For purposes of the Guidelines, the following definitions apply:

a. *Board of directors,* in the case of a branch or agency of a foreign bank, means the managing official in charge of the branch or agency.

b. *Consumer information* means any record about an individual, whether in paper, electronic, or other form, that is a consumer report or is derived from a consumer report and that is maintained or otherwise possessed by or on behalf of the bank for a business purpose. Consumer information also means a compilation of such records. The term does not include any record that does not identify an individual.

   i. *Examples.* (1) *Consumer information* includes:

(A) A consumer report that a bank obtains;

(B) Information from a consumer report that the bank obtains from its affiliate after the consumer has been given a notice and has elected not to opt out of that sharing;

(C) Information from a consumer report that the bank obtains about an individual who applies for but does not receive a loan, including any loan sought by an individual for a business purpose;

(D) Information from a consumer report that the bank obtains about an individual who guarantees a loan (including a loan to a business entity); or

(E) Information from a consumer report that the bank obtains about an employee or prospective employee.

(2) *Consumer information* does not include:

(A) Aggregate information, such as the mean credit score, derived from a group of consumer reports; or

(B) Blind data, such as payment history on accounts that are not personally identifiable, that may be used for developing credit scoring models or for other purposes.

c. *Consumer report* has the same meaning as set forth in the Fair Credit Reporting Act, 15 U.S.C. 1681a(d).

d. *Customer* means any customer of the bank as defined in § 216.3(h) of this chapter.

e. *Customer information* means any record containing nonpublic personal information, as defined in § 216.3(n) of this chapter, about a customer, whether in paper, electronic, or other form, that is maintained by or on behalf of the bank.

f. *Customer information systems* means any methods used to access, collect, store, use, transmit, protect, or dispose of customer information.

g. *Service provider* means any person or entity that maintains, processes, or otherwise is permitted access to customer information or consumer information through its provision of services directly to the bank.

h. *Subsidiary* means any company controlled by a bank, except a broker, dealer, person providing insurance, investment company, investment advisor, insured depository institution, or subsidiary of an insured depository institution.

II. STANDARDS FOR INFORMATION SECURITY

A. *Information Security Program*. Each bank shall implement a comprehensive written information security program that includes administrative, technical, and physical safeguards appropriate to the size and complexity of the bank and the nature and scope of its activities. While all parts of the bank are not required to implement a uniform set of policies, all elements of the information security program must be coordinated. A bank also shall ensure that each of its subsidiaries is subject to a comprehensive information security program. The bank may fulfill this requirement either by including a subsidiary within the scope of the bank's comprehensive information security program or by causing the subsidiary to implement a separate comprehensive information security program in accordance with the standards and procedures in sections II and III of this appendix that apply to banks.

B. *Objectives*. A bank's information security program shall be designed to:

1. Ensure the security and confidentiality of customer information;

2. Protect against any anticipated threats or hazards to the security or integrity of such information;

3. Protect against unauthorized access to or use of such information that could result in substantial harm or inconvenience to any customer; and

4. Ensure the proper disposal of customer information and consumer information.

III. DEVELOPMENT AND IMPLEMENTATION OF INFORMATION SECURITY PROGRAM

A. *Involve the Board of Directors*. The board of directors or an appropriate committee of the board of each bank shall:

1. Approve the bank's written information security program; and

2. Oversee the development, implementation, and maintenance of the bank's information security program, including assigning specific responsibility for its implementation and reviewing reports from management.

B. *Assess Risk*. Each bank shall:

1. Identify reasonably foreseeable internal and external threats that could result in unauthorized disclosure, misuse, alteration, or destruction of customer information or customer information systems.

2. Assess the likelihood and potential damage of these threats, taking into consideration the sensitivity of customer information.

3. Assess the sufficiency of policies, procedures, customer information systems, and other arrangements in place to control risks.

C. *Manage and Control Risk*. Each bank shall:

1. Design its information security program to control the identified risks, commensurate with the sensitivity of the information as well as the complexity and scope of the bank's activities. Each bank must consider whether the following security measures are appropriate for the bank and, if so, adopt those measures the bank concludes are appropriate:

a. Access controls on customer information systems, including controls to authenticate and permit access only to authorized individuals and controls to prevent employees from providing customer information to unauthorized individuals who may seek to obtain this information through fraudulent means.

b. Access restrictions at physical locations containing customer information, such as buildings, computer facilities, and records storage facilities to permit access only to authorized individuals;

c. Encryption of electronic customer information, including while in transit or in storage on networks or systems to which unauthorized individuals may have access;

d. Procedures designed to ensure that customer information system modifications are consistent with the bank's information security program;

e. Dual control procedures, segregation of duties, and employee background checks for employees with responsibilities for or access to customer information;

f. Monitoring systems and procedures to detect actual and attempted attacks on or intrusions into customer information systems;

g. Response programs that specify actions to be taken when the bank suspects or detects that unauthorized individuals have gained access to customer information systems, including appropriate reports to regulatory and law enforcement agencies; and

h. Measures to protect against destruction, loss, or damage of customer information due to potential environmental hazards, such as fire and water damage or technological failures.

2. Train staff to implement the bank's information security program.

3. Regularly test the key controls, systems and procedures of the information security program. The frequency and nature of such tests should be determined by the bank's risk assessment. Tests

should be conducted or reviewed by independent third parties or staff independent of those that develop or maintain the security programs.

4. Develop, implement, and maintain, as part of its information security program, appropriate measures to properly dispose of customer information and consumer information in accordance with each of the requirements in this paragraph III.

D. *Oversee Service Provider Arrangements.* Each bank shall:

1. Exercise appropriate due diligence in selecting its service providers;

2. Require its service providers by contract to implement appropriate measures designed to meet the objectives of these Guidelines; and

3. Where indicated by the bank's risk assessment, monitor its service providers to confirm that they have satisfied their obligations as required by paragraph D.2. As part of this monitoring, a bank should review audits, summaries of test results, or other equivalent evaluations of its service providers.

E. *Adjust the Program.* Each bank shall monitor, evaluate, and adjust, as appropriate, the information security program in light of any relevant changes in technology, the sensitivity of its customer information, internal or external threats to information, and the bank's own changing business arrangements, such as mergers and acquisitions, alliances and joint ventures, outsourcing arrangements, and changes to customer information systems.

F. *Report to the Board.* Each bank shall report to its board or an appropriate committee of the board at least annually. This report should describe the overall status of the information security program and the bank's compliance with these Guidelines. The reports should discuss material matters related to its program, addressing issues such as: risk assessment; risk management and control decisions; service provider arrangements; results of testing; security breaches or violations and management's responses; and recommendations for changes in the information security program.

G. *Implement the Standards.*

1. *Effective date.* Each bank must implement an information security program pursuant to these Guidelines by July 1, 2001.

2. *Two-year grandfathering of agreements with service providers.* Until July 1, 2003, a contract that a bank has entered into with a service provider to perform services for it or functions on its behalf satisfies the provisions of section III.D., even if the contract does not include a requirement that the servicer maintain the security and confidentiality of customer information, as long as the bank entered into the contract on or before March 5, 2001.

3. *Effective date for measures relating to the disposal of consumer information.* Each bank must satisfy these Guidelines with respect to the proper disposal of consumer information by July 1, 2005.

4. *Exception for existing agreements with service providers relating to the disposal of consumer information.* Notwithstanding the requirement in paragraph III.G.3., a bank's contracts with its service providers that have access to consumer information and that may dispose of consumer information, entered into before July 1, 2005, must comply with the provisions of the Guidelines relating to the proper disposal of consumer information by July 1, 2006.

SUPPLEMENT A TO APPENDIX D-2 TO PART 208 INTERAGENCY GUIDANCE ON RESPONSE PROGRAMS FOR UNAUTHORIZED ACCESS TO CUSTOMER INFORMATION AND CUSTOMER NOTICE

I. BACKGROUND

This Guidance[1] interprets section 501(b) of the Gramm-Leach-Bliley Act ("GLBA") and the Interagency Guidelines Establishing Information Security Standards (the "Security Guidelines")[2] and describes response programs, including customer notification procedures, that a financial institution should develop and implement to address unauthorized access to or use of customer information that could result in substantial harm or inconvenience to a customer. The scope of, and definitions of terms used in, this Guidance are identical to those of the Security Guidelines. For example, the term "customer information" is the same term used in the Security Guidelines, and means any record containing nonpublic personal information about a customer, whether in paper, electronic, or other form, maintained by or on behalf of the institution.

A. *Interagency Security Guidelines*

Section 501(b) of the GLBA required the Agencies to establish appropriate standards for financial institutions subject to their jurisdiction that include administrative, technical, and physical safeguards, to protect the security and confidentiality of customer information. Accordingly the Agencies issued Security Guidelines requiring every financial institution to have an information security program designed to:

1. Ensure the security and confidentiality of customer information;

2. Protect against any anticipated threats or hazards to the security or integrity of such information; and

3. Protect against unauthorized access to or use of such information that could result in substantial harm or inconvenience to any customer.

B. *Risk Assessment and Controls*

1. The Security Guidelines direct every financial institution to assess the following risks, among others, when developing its information security program:

a. Reasonably foreseeable internal and external threats that could result in unauthorized disclosure, misuse, alteration, or destruction of customer information or customer information systems;

b. The likelihood and potential damage of threats, taking into consideration the sensitivity of customer information; and

---

[1] This Guidance is being jointly issued by the Board of Governors of the Federal Reserve System (Board), the Federal Deposit Insurance Corporation (FDIC), the Office of the Comptroller of the Currency (OCC), and the Office of Thrift Supervision (OTS).

[2] 12 CFR part 30, app. B (OCC); 12 CFR part 208, app. D-2 and part 225, app. F (Board); 12 CFR part 364, app. B (FDIC); and 12 CFR part 570, app. B (OTS). The "Interagency Guidelines Establishing Information Security Standards" were formerly known as "The Interagency Guidelines Establishing Standards for Safeguarding Customer Information."

c. The sufficiency of policies, procedures, customer information systems, and other arrangements in place to control risks.[3]

2. Following the assessment of these risks, the Security Guidelines require a financial institution to design a program to address the identified risks. The particular security measures an institution should adopt will depend upon the risks presented by the complexity and scope of its business. At a minimum, the financial institution is required to consider the specific security measures enumerated in the Security Guidelines,[4] and adopt those that are appropriate for the institution, including:

a. Access controls on customer information systems, including controls to authenticate and permit access only to authorized individuals and controls to prevent employees from providing customer information to unauthorized individuals who may seek to obtain this information through fraudulent means;

b. Background checks for employees with responsibilities for access to customer information; and

c. Response programs that specify actions to be taken when the financial institution suspects or detects that unauthorized individuals have gained access to customer information systems, including appropriate reports to regulatory and law enforcement agencies.[5]

C. Service Providers

The Security Guidelines direct every financial institution to require its service providers by contract to implement appropriate measures designed to protect against unauthorized access to or use of customer information that could result in substantial harm or inconvenience to any customer.[6]

II. RESPONSE PROGRAM

Millions of Americans, throughout the country, have been victims of identity theft.[7] Identity thieves misuse personal information they obtain from a number of sources, including financial institutions, to perpetrate identity theft. Therefore, financial institutions should take preventative measures to safeguard customer information against attempts to gain unauthorized access to the information. For example, financial institutions should place access controls on customer information systems and conduct background checks for employees who are authorized to access customer information.[8] However, every financial institution should also develop and implement a risk-based response program to address incidents of unauthorized access to customer information in customer information systems[9] that occur nonetheless. A response program should be a key part of an institution's information security program.[10] The program should be appropriate to the size and complexity of the institution and the nature and scope of its activities.

In addition, each institution should be able to address incidents of unauthorized access to customer information in customer information systems maintained by its domestic and foreign service providers. Therefore, consistent with the obligations in the Guidelines that relate to these arrangements, and with existing guidance on this topic issued by the Agencies,[11] an institution's contract with its service provider should require the service provider to take appropriate actions to address incidents of unauthorized access to the financial institution's customer information, including notification to the institution as soon as possible of any such incident, to enable the institution to expeditiously implement its response program.

A. Components of a Response Program

1. At a minimum, an institution's response program should contain procedures for the following:

a. Assessing the nature and scope of an incident, and identifying what customer information systems and types of customer information have been accessed or misused;

b. Notifying its primary Federal regulator as soon as possible when the institution becomes aware of an incident involving unauthorized access to or use of sensitive customer information, as defined below;

c. Consistent with the Agencies' Suspicious Activity Report ("SAR") regulations,[12] notifying appropriate law enforcement

---

3 See Security Guidelines, III.B.
4 See Security Guidelines, III.C.
5 See Security Guidelines, III.C.
6 See Security Guidelines, II.B. and III.D. Further, the Agencies note that, in addition to contractual obligations to a financial institution, a service provider may be required to implement its own comprehensive information security program in accordance with the Safeguards Rule promulgated by the Federal Trade Commission ("FTC"), 16 CFR part 314.
7 The FTC estimates that nearly 10 million Americans discovered they were victims of some form of identity theft in 2002. See The Federal Trade Commission, Identity Theft Survey Report, (September 2003), available at http://www.ftc.gov/os/2003/09/synovatereport.pdf.
8 Institutions should also conduct background checks of employees to ensure that the institution does not violate 12 U.S.C. 1829, which prohibits an institution from hiring an individual convicted of certain criminal offenses or who is subject to a prohibition order under 12 U.S.C. 1818(e)(6).
9 Under the Guidelines, an institution's customer information systems consist of all of the methods used to access, collect, store, use, transmit, protect, or dispose of customer information, including the systems maintained by its service providers. See Security Guidelines, I.C.2.d (I.C.2.c for OTS).
10 See FFIEC Information Technology Examination Handbook, Information Security Booklet, Dec. 2002 available at http://www.ffiec.gov/ffiecinfobase/html_pages/infosec_book_frame.htm. Federal Reserve SR 97-32, Sound Practice Guidance for Information Security for Networks, Dec. 4, 1997; OCC Bulletin 2000-14, "Infrastructure Threats—Intrusion Risks" (May 15, 2000), for additional guidance on preventing, detecting, and responding to intrusions into financial institution computer systems.
11 See Federal Reserve SR Ltr. 00-04, Outsourcing of Information and Transaction Processing, Feb. 9, 2000; OCC Bulletin 2001-47, "Third-Party Relationships Risk Management Principles," Nov. 1, 2001; FDIC FIL 68-99, Risk Assessment Tools and Practices for Information System Security, July 7, 1999; OTS Thrift Bulletin 82a, Third Party Arrangements, Sept. 1, 2004.
12 An institution's obligation to file a SAR is set out in the Agencies' SAR regulations and Agency guidance. See 12 CFR 21.11 (national banks, Federal branches and agencies); 12 CFR 208.62 (State member banks); 12 CFR 211.5(k) (Edge and agreement corporations); 12 CFR 211.24(f) (uninsured State branches and agencies of foreign banks); 12 CFR 225.4(f) (bank holding companies and their nonbank subsidiaries); 12 CFR part 353 (State non-member banks); and 12 CFR 563.180 (savings associations). National banks must file SARs in connection with

authorities, in addition to filing a timely SAR in situations involving Federal criminal violations requiring immediate attention, such as when a reportable violation is ongoing;

d. Taking appropriate steps to contain and control the incident to prevent further unauthorized access to or use of customer information, for example, by monitoring, freezing, or closing affected accounts, while preserving records and other evidence;[13] and

e. Notifying customers when warranted.

2. Where an incident of unauthorized access to customer information involves customer information systems maintained by an institution's service providers, it is the responsibility of the financial institution to notify the institution's customers and regulator. However, an institution may authorize or contract with its service provider to notify the institution's customers or regulator on its behalf.

III. CUSTOMER NOTICE

Financial institutions have an affirmative duty to protect their customers' information against unauthorized access or use. Notifying customers of a security incident involving the unauthorized access or use of the customer's information in accordance with the standard set forth below is a key part of that duty. Timely notification of customers is important to manage an institution's reputation risk. Effective notice also may reduce an institution's legal risk, assist in maintaining good customer relations, and enable the institution's customers to take steps to protect themselves against the consequences of identity theft. When customer notification is warranted, an institution may not forgo notifying its customers of an incident because the institution believes that it may be potentially embarrassed or inconvenienced by doing so.

A. Standard for Providing Notice

When a financial institution becomes aware of an incident of unauthorized access to sensitive customer information, the institution should conduct a reasonable investigation to promptly determine the likelihood that the information has been or will be misused. If the institution determines that misuse of its information about a customer has occurred or is reasonably possible, it should notify the affected customer as soon as possible. Customer notice may be delayed if an appropriate law enforcement agency determines that notification will interfere with a criminal investigation and provides the institution with a written request for the delay. However, the institution should notify its customers as soon as notification will no longer interfere with the investigation.

1. Sensitive Customer Information

Under the Guidelines, an institution must protect against unauthorized access to or use of customer information that could result in substantial harm or inconvenience to any customer. Substantial harm or inconvenience is most likely to result from improper access to *sensitive customer information* because this type of information is most likely to be misused, as in the commission of identity theft. For purposes of this Guidance, *sensitive customer information* means a customer's name, address, or telephone number, in conjunction with the customer's social security number, driver's license number, account number, credit or debit card number, or a personal identification number or password that would permit access to the customer's account. *Sensitive customer information* also includes any combination of components of customer information that would allow someone to log onto or access the customer's account, such as user name and password or password and account number.

2. Affected Customers

If a financial institution, based upon its investigation, can determine from its logs or other data precisely which customers' information has been improperly accessed, it may limit notification to those customers with regard to whom the institution determines that misuse of their information has occurred or is reasonably possible. However, there may be situations where the institution determines that a group of files has been accessed improperly, but is unable to identify which specific customers' information has been accessed. If the circumstances of the unauthorized access lead the institution to determine that misuse of the information is reasonably possible, it should notify all customers in the group.

B. Content of Customer Notice

1. Customer notice should be given in a clear and conspicuous manner. The notice should describe the incident in general terms and the type of customer information that was the subject of unauthorized access or use. It also should generally describe what the institution has done to protect the customers' information from further unauthorized access. In addition, it should include a telephone number that customers can call for further information and assistance.[14] The notice also should remind customers of the need to remain vigilant over the next twelve to twenty-four months, and to promptly report incidents of suspected identity theft to the institution. The notice should include the following additional items, when appropriate:

a. A recommendation that the customer review account statements and immediately report any suspicious activity to the institution;

---

computer intrusions and other computer crimes. *See* OCC Bulletin 2000-14, "Infrastructure Threats—Intrusion Risks" (May 15, 2000); Advisory Letter 97-9, "Reporting Computer Related Crimes" (November 19, 1997) (general guidance still applicable though instructions for new SAR form published in 65 FR 1229, 1230 (January 7, 2000)). *See also* Federal Reserve SR 01-11, Identity Theft and Pretext Calling, Apr. 26, 2001; SR 97-28, Guidance Concerning Reporting of Computer Related Crimes by Financial Institutions, Nov. 6, 1997; FDIC FIL 48-2000, Suspicious Activity Reports, July 14, 2000; FIL 47-97, Preparation of Suspicious Activity Reports, May 6, 1997; OTS CEO Memorandum 139, Identity Theft and Pretext Calling, May 4, 2001; CEO Memorandum 126, New Suspicious Activity Report Form, July 5, 2000; http://www.ots.treas.gov/BSA (for the latest SAR form and filing instructions required by OTS as of July 1, 2003).

13 *See* FFIEC Information Technology Examination Handbook, Information Security Booklet, Dec. 2002, pp. 68–74.

14 The institution should, therefore, ensure that it has reasonable policies and procedures in place, including trained personnel, to respond appropriately to customer inquiries and requests for assistance.

b. A description of fraud alerts and an explanation of how the customer may place a fraud alert in the customer's consumer reports to put the customer's creditors on notice that the customer may be a victim of fraud;

c. A recommendation that the customer periodically obtain credit reports from each nationwide credit reporting agency and have information relating to fraudulent transactions deleted;

d. An explanation of how the customer may obtain a credit report free of charge; and

e. Information about the availability of the FTC's online guidance regarding steps a consumer can take to protect against identity theft. The notice should encourage the customer to report any incidents of identity theft to the FTC, and should provide the FTC's Web site address and toll-free telephone number that customers may use to obtain the identity theft guidance and report suspected incidents of identity theft.[15]

2. The Agencies encourage financial institutions to notify the nationwide consumer reporting agencies prior to sending notices to a large number of customers that include contact information for the reporting agencies.

C. Delivery of Customer Notice

Customer notice should be delivered in any manner designed to ensure that a customer can reasonably be expected to receive it. For example, the institution may choose to contact all customers affected by telephone or by mail, or by electronic mail for those customers for whom it has a valid e-mail address and who have agreed to receive communications electronically.

[69 Fed. Reg. 77610 (Dec. 28, 2004) (Effective Date: July 1, 2005); 70 Fed. Reg. 15736 (Mar. 29, 2005) (Effective Date: Mar. 29, 2005); 71 Fed. Reg. 5780 (Feb. 3, 2006) (Effective Date: Feb. 3, 2006)]

* * *

PART 211—INTERNATIONAL BANKING OPERATIONS (REGULATION K)

SUBPART A—INTERNATIONAL OPERATIONS OF U.S. BANKING ORGANIZATIONS

* * *

12 C.F.R. § 211.5 Edge and agreement corporations.

* * *

(*l*) *Protection of customer information and consumer information.* An Edge or agreement corporation shall comply with the Interagency Guidelines Establishing Information Security Standards prescribed pursuant to sections 501 and 505 of the Gramm-Leach-Bliley Act (15 U.S.C. 6801 and 6805) and, with respect to

---

15. Currently, the FTC Web site for the ID Theft brochure and the FTC Hotline phone number are *http://www.consumer.gov/idtheft* and 1-877-IDTHEFT. The institution may also refer customers to any materials developed pursuant to section 151(b) of the FACT Act (educational materials developed by the FTC to teach the public how to prevent identity theft).

the proper disposal of consumer information, section 216 of the Fair and Accurate Credit Transactions Act of 2003 (15 U.S.C. 1681w), set forth in appendix D-2 to part 208 of this chapter.

* * *

[69 Fed. Reg. 77610 (Dec. 28, 2004) (Effective Date: July 1, 2005); 71 Fed. Reg. 13936 (Mar. 20, 2006) (Effective Date: Apr. 19, 2006)]

* * *

SUBPART B—FOREIGN BANKING ORGANIZATIONS

* * *

12 C.F.R. § 211.24 Approval of offices of foreign banks; procedures for applications; standards for approval; representative office activities and standards for approval; preservation of existing authority.

* * *

(i) *Protection of customer information and consumer information.* An uninsured state-licensed branch or agency of a foreign bank shall comply with the Interagency Guidelines Establishing Information Security Standards prescribed pursuant to sections 501 and 505 of the Gramm-Leach-Bliley Act (15 U.S.C. 6801 and 6805) and, with respect to the proper disposal of consumer information, section 216 of the Fair and Accurate Credit Transactions Act of 2003 (15 U.S.C. 1681w), set forth in appendix D-2 to part 208 of this chapter.

* * *

[68 Fed. Reg. 25112 (May 9, 2003) (Effective Date: June 9, 2003); 69 Fed. Reg. 77618 (Dec. 28, 2004) (Effective Date: July 1, 2005); 71 Fed. Reg. 13936 (Mar. 20, 2006) (Effective Date: Apr. 19, 2006)]

* * *

PART 225—BANK HOLDING COMPANIES AND CHANGE IN BANK CONTROL (REGULATION Y)

REGULATIONS

SUBPART A—GENERAL PROVISIONS

* * *

12 C.F.R. § 225.4 Corporate practices.

* * *

(h) *Protection of customer information and consumer information.* A bank holding company shall comply with the Interagency Guidelines Establishing Information Security Standards, as set forth in appendix F of this part, prescribed pursuant to sections 501 and 505 of the Gramm-Leach-Bliley Act (15 U.S.C. 6801 and 6805). A bank holding company shall properly dispose of consumer information in accordance with the rules set forth at 16 CFR part 682.

[63 Fed. Reg. 58621 (Nov. 2, 1998) (Effective Date: Nov. 2, 1998); 63 Fed. Reg. 65281 (Nov. 25, 1998) (technical correction); 65 Fed. Reg. 14442 (Mar. 17, 2000) (Effective Date: Mar. 11, 2000); 66 Fed. Reg. 8636 (Feb. 1, 2001) (Effective Date: July 1, 2001); 69 Fed. Reg. 77610 (Dec. 28, 2004) (Effective Date: July 1, 2005); 71 Fed. Reg. 9901 (Feb. 28, 2006) (Effective Date: Mar. 30, 2006)]

* * *

CONDITIONS TO ORDERS

* * *

Appendix F to Part 225—Interagency Guidelines Establishing Information Security Standards

Table of Contents

I. Introduction
  A. Scope
  B. Preservation of Existing Authority
  C. Definitions
II. Standards for Safeguarding Customer Information
  A. Information Security Program
  B. Objectives
III. Development and Implementation of Customer Information Security Program
  A. Involve the Board of Directors
  B. Assess Risk
  C. Manage and Control Risk
  D. Oversee Service Provider Arrangements
  E. Adjust the Program
  F. Report to the Board
  G. Implement the Standards

I. Introduction

These Interagency Guidelines Establishing Information Security Standards (Guidelines) set forth standards pursuant to sections 501 and 505 of the Gramm-Leach-Bliley Act (15 U.S.C. 6801 and 6805). These Guidelines address standards for developing and implementing administrative, technical, and physical safeguards to protect the security, confidentiality, and integrity of customer information.

A. *Scope.* The Guidelines apply to customer information maintained by or on behalf of bank holding companies and their nonbank subsidiaries or affiliates (except brokers, dealers, persons providing insurance, investment companies, and investment advisors), for which the Board has supervisory authority.

B. *Preservation of Existing Authority.* These Guidelines do not in any way limit the authority of the Board to address unsafe or unsound practices, violations of law, unsafe or unsound conditions, or other practices. The Board may take action under these Guidelines independently of, in conjunction with, or in addition to, any other enforcement action available to the Board.

C. *Definitions.* 1. Except as modified in the Guidelines, or unless the context otherwise requires, the terms used in these Guidelines have the same meanings as set forth in sections 3 and 39 of the Federal Deposit Insurance Act (12 U.S.C. 1813 and 1831p-1).

2. For purposes of the Guidelines, the following definitions apply:

  a. *Board of directors,* in the case of a branch or agency of a foreign bank, means the managing official in charge of the branch or agency.

  b. *Customer* means any customer of the bank holding company as defined in § 216.3(h) of this chapter.

  c. *Customer information* means any record containing nonpublic personal information, as defined in § 216.3(n) of this chapter, about a customer, whether in paper, electronic, or other form, that is maintained by or on behalf of the bank holding company.

  d. *Customer information systems* means any methods used to access, collect, store, use, transmit, protect, or dispose of customer information.

  e. *Service provider* means any person or entity that maintains, processes, or otherwise is permitted access to customer information through its provision of services directly to the bank holding company.

  f. *Subsidiary* means any company controlled by a bank holding company, except a broker, dealer, person providing insurance, investment company, investment advisor, insured depository institution, or subsidiary of an insured depository institution.

II. Standards for Safeguarding Customer Information

A. *Information Security Program.* Each bank holding company shall implement a comprehensive written information security program that includes administrative, technical, and physical safeguards appropriate to the size and complexity of the bank holding company and the nature and scope of its activities. While all parts of the bank holding company are not required to implement a uniform set of policies, all elements of the information security program must be coordinated. A bank holding company also shall ensure that each of its subsidiaries is subject to a comprehensive information security program. The bank holding company may fulfill this requirement either by including a subsidiary within the scope of the bank holding company's comprehensive information security program or by causing the subsidiary to implement a separate comprehensive information security program in accordance with the standards and procedures in sections II and III of this appendix that apply to bank holding companies.

B. *Objectives.* A bank holding company's information security program shall be designed to:

1. Ensure the security and confidentiality of customer information;

2. Protect against any anticipated threats or hazards to the security or integrity of such information; and

3. Protect against unauthorized access to or use of such information that could result in substantial harm or inconvenience to any customer.

III. Development and Implementation of Information Security Program

A. *Involve the Board of Directors.* The board of directors or an appropriate committee of the board of each bank holding company shall:

1. Approve the bank holding company's written information security program; and

2. Oversee the development, implementation, and maintenance of the bank holding company's information security program, including assigning specific responsibility for its implementation and reviewing reports from management.

B. *Assess Risk.* Each bank holding company shall:

1. Identify reasonably foreseeable internal and external threats that could result in unauthorized disclosure, misuse, alteration, or destruction of customer information or customer information systems.

2. Assess the likelihood and potential damage of these threats, taking into consideration the sensitivity of customer information.

3. Assess the sufficiency of policies, procedures, customer information systems, and other arrangements in place to control risks.

C. *Manage and Control Risk.* Each bank holding company shall:

1. Design its information security program to control the identified risks, commensurate with the sensitivity of the information as well as the complexity and scope of the bank holding company's activities. Each bank holding company must consider whether the following security measures are appropriate for the bank holding company and, if so, adopt those measures the bank holding company concludes are appropriate:

a. Access controls on customer information systems, including controls to authenticate and permit access only to authorized individuals and controls to prevent employees from providing customer information to unauthorized individuals who may seek to obtain this information through fraudulent means.

b. Access restrictions at physical locations containing customer information, such as buildings, computer facilities, and records storage facilities to permit access only to authorized individuals;

c. Encryption of electronic customer information, including while in transit or in storage on networks or systems to which unauthorized individuals may have access;

d. Procedures designed to ensure that customer information system modifications are consistent with the bank holding company's information security program;

e. Dual control procedures, segregation of duties, and employee background checks for employees with responsibilities for or access to customer information;

f. Monitoring systems and procedures to detect actual and attempted attacks on or intrusions into customer information systems;

g. Response programs that specify actions to be taken when the bank holding company suspects or detects that unauthorized individuals have gained access to customer information systems, including appropriate reports to regulatory and law enforcement agencies; and

h. Measures to protect against destruction, loss, or damage of customer information due to potential environmental hazards, such as fire and water damage or technological failures.

2. Train staff to implement the bank holding company's information security program.

3. Regularly test the key controls, systems and procedures of the information security program. The frequency and nature of such tests should be determined by the bank holding company's risk assessment. Tests should be conducted or reviewed by independent third parties or staff independent of those that develop or maintain the security programs.

D. *Oversee Service Provider Arrangements.* Each bank holding company shall:

1. Exercise appropriate due diligence in selecting its service providers;

2. Require its service providers by contract to implement appropriate measures designed to meet the objectives of these Guidelines; and

3. Where indicated by the bank holding company's risk assessment, monitor its service providers to confirm that they have satisfied their obligations as required by paragraph D.2. As part of this monitoring, a bank holding company should review audits, summaries of test results, or other equivalent evaluations of its service providers.

E. *Adjust the Program.* Each bank holding company shall monitor, evaluate, and adjust, as appropriate, the information security program in light of any relevant changes in technology, the sensitivity of its customer information, internal or external threats to information, and the bank holding company's own changing business arrangements, such as mergers and acquisitions, alliances and joint ventures, outsourcing arrangements, and changes to customer information systems.

F. *Report to the Board.* Each bank holding company shall report to its board or an appropriate committee of the board at least annually. This report should describe the overall status of the information security program and the bank holding company's compliance with these Guidelines. The reports should discuss material matters related to its program, addressing issues such as: risk assessment; risk management and control decisions; service provider arrangements; results of testing; security breaches or violations and management's responses; and recommendations for changes in the information security program.

G. *Implement the Standards.*

1. *Effective date.* Each bank holding company must implement an information security program pursuant to these Guidelines by July 1, 2001.

2. *Two-year grandfathering of agreements with service providers.* Until July 1, 2003, a contract that a bank holding company has entered into with a service provider to perform services for it or functions on its behalf satisfies the provisions of section III.D., even if the contract does not include a requirement that the servicer maintain the security and confidentiality of customer information, as long as the bank holding company entered into the contract on or before March 5, 2001.

Supplement A to Appendix F to Part 225 Interagency Guidance on Response Programs for Unauthorized Access to Customer Information and Customer Notice

I. Background

This Guidance[1] interprets section 501(b) of the Gramm-Leach-Bliley Act ("GLBA") and the Interagency Guidelines Establishing Information Security Standards (the "Security Guidelines")[2] and

---

1 This Guidance is being jointly issued by the Board of Governors of the Federal Reserve System (Board), the Federal Deposit Insurance Corporation (FDIC), the Office of the Comptroller of the Currency (OCC), and the Office of Thrift Supervision (OTS).

2 12 CFR part 30, app. B (OCC); 12 CFR part 208, app. D-2 and part 225, app. F (Board); 12 CFR part 364, app. B (FDIC); and 12 CFR part 570, app. B (OTS). The "Interagency Guidelines Establishing Information Security Standards" were formerly

describes response programs, including customer notification procedures, that a financial institution should develop and implement to address unauthorized access to or use of customer information that could result in substantial harm or inconvenience to a customer. The scope of, and definitions of terms used in, this Guidance are identical to those of the Security Guidelines. For example, the term "customer information" is the same term used in the Security Guidelines, and means any record containing nonpublic personal information about a customer, whether in paper, electronic, or other form, maintained by or on behalf of the institution.

A. Interagency Security Guidelines

Section 501(b) of the GLBA required the Agencies to establish appropriate standards for financial institutions subject to their jurisdiction that include administrative, technical, and physical safeguards, to protect the security and confidentiality of customer information. Accordingly, the Agencies issued Security Guidelines requiring every financial institution to have an information security program designed to:

1. Ensure the security and confidentiality of customer information;

2. Protect against any anticipated threats or hazards to the security or integrity of such information; and

3. Protect against unauthorized access to or use of such information that could result in substantial harm or inconvenience to any customer.

B. Risk Assessment and Controls

1. The Security Guidelines direct every financial institution to assess the following risks, among others, when developing its information security program:

a. Reasonably foreseeable internal and external threats that could result in unauthorized disclosure, misuse, alteration, or destruction of customer information or customer information systems;

b. The likelihood and potential damage of threats, taking into consideration the sensitivity of customer information; and

c. The sufficiency of policies, procedures, customer information systems, and other arrangements in place to control risks.[3]

2. Following the assessment of these risks, the Security Guidelines require a financial institution to design a program to address the identified risks. The particular security measures an institution should adopt will depend upon the risks presented by the complexity and scope of its business. At a minimum, the financial institution is required to consider the specific security measures enumerated in the Security Guidelines,[4] and adopt those that are appropriate for the institution, including:

a. Access controls on customer information systems, including controls to authenticate and permit access only to authorized individuals and controls to prevent employees from providing customer information to unauthorized individuals who may seek to obtain this information through fraudulent means;

b. Background checks for employees with responsibilities for access to customer information; and

c. Response programs that specify actions to be taken when the financial institution suspects or detects that unauthorized individuals have gained access to customer information systems, including appropriate reports to regulatory and law enforcement agencies.[5]

C. Service Providers

The Security Guidelines direct every financial institution to require its service providers by contract to implement appropriate measures designed to protect against unauthorized access to or use of customer information that could result in substantial harm or inconvenience to any customer.[6]

II. Response Program

Millions of Americans throughout the country, have been victims of identity theft.[7] Identity thieves misuse personal information they obtain from a number of sources, including financial institutions, to perpetrate identity theft. Therefore, financial institutions should take preventative measures to safeguard customer information against attempts to gain unauthorized access to the information. For example, financial institutions should place access controls on customer information systems and conduct background checks for employees who are authorized to access customer information.[8] However, every financial institution should also develop and implement a risk-based response program to address incidents of unauthorized access to customer information in customer information systems[9] that occur nonetheless. A response program should be a key part of an institution's information security program.[10] The program should be appropriate to the size and complexity of the institution and the nature and scope of its activities.

---

known as "The Interagency Guidelines Establishing Standards for Safeguarding Customer Information."

3 See Security Guidelines, III.B.

4 See Security Guidelines, III.C.

5 See Security Guidelines, III.C.

6 See Security Guidelines, II.B. and III.D. Further, the Agencies note that, in addition to contractual obligations to a financial institution, a service provider may be required to implement its own comprehensive information security program in accordance with the Safeguards Rule promulgated by the Federal Trade Commission ("FTC"), 16 CFR part 314.

7 The FTC estimates that nearly 10 million Americans discovered they were victims of some form of identity theft in 2002. See The Federal Trade Commission, Identity Theft Survey Report, (September 2003), available at http://www.ftc.gov/os/2003/09/synovatereport.pdf.

8 Institutions should also conduct background checks of employees to ensure that the institution does not violate 12 U.S.C. 1829, which prohibits an institution from hiring an individual convicted of certain criminal offenses or who is subject to a prohibition order under 12 U.S.C. 1818(e)(6).

9 Under the Guidelines, an institution's customer information systems consist of all of the methods used to access, collect, store, use, transmit, protect, or dispose of customer information, including the systems maintained by its service providers. See Security Guidelines, I.C.2.d (I.C.2.c for OTS).

10 See FFIEC Information Technology Examination Handbook, Information Security Booklet, Dec. 2002 available at http://www.ffiec.gov/ffiecinfobase/html_pages/infosec_book_frame.htm. Federal Reserve SR 97-32, Sound Practice Guidance for Information Security for Networks, Dec. 4, 1997; OCC Bulletin 2000-14, "Infrastructure Threats—Intrusion Risks" (May 15, 2000), for additional guidance on preventing, detecting, and responding to intrusions into financial institution computer systems.

In addition, each institution should be able to address incidents of unauthorized access to customer information in customer information systems maintained by its domestic and foreign service providers. Therefore, consistent with the obligations in the Guidelines that relate to these arrangements, and with existing guidance on this topic issued by the Agencies,[11] an institution's contract with its service provider should require the service provider to take appropriate actions to address incidents of unauthorized access to the financial institution's customer information, including notification to the institution as soon as possible of any such incident, to enable the institution to expeditiously implement its response program.

A. Components of a Response Program

1. At a minimum, an institution's response program should contain procedures for the following:

a. Assessing the nature and scope of an incident, and identifying what customer information systems and types of customer information have been accessed or misused;

b. Notifying its primary Federal regulator as soon as possible when the institution becomes aware of an incident involving unauthorized access to or use of *sensitive* customer information, as defined below;

c. Consistent with the Agencies' Suspicious Activity Report ("SAR") regulations,[12] notifying appropriate law enforcement authorities, in addition to filing a timely SAR in situations involving Federal criminal violations requiring immediate attention, such as when a reportable violation is ongoing;

d. Taking appropriate steps to contain and control the incident to prevent further unauthorized access to or use of customer information, for example, by monitoring, freezing, or closing affected accounts, while preserving records and other evidence;[13] and

e. Notifying customers when warranted.

2. Where an incident of unauthorized access to customer information involves customer information systems maintained by an institution's service providers, it is the responsibility of the financial institution to notify the institution's customers and regulator. However, an institution may authorize or contract with its service provider to notify the institution's customers or regulator on its behalf.

III. Customer Notice

Financial institutions have an affirmative duty to protect their customers' information against unauthorized access or use. Notifying customers of a security incident involving the unauthorized access or use of the customer's information in accordance with the standard set forth below is a key part of that duty. Timely notification of customers is important to manage an institution's reputation risk. Effective notice also may reduce an institution's legal risk, assist in maintaining good customer relations, and enable the institution's customers to take steps to protect themselves against the consequences of identity theft. When customer notification is warranted, an institution may not forgo notifying its customers of an incident because the institution believes that it may be potentially embarrassed or inconvenienced by doing so.

A. Standard for Providing Notice

When a financial institution becomes aware of an incident of unauthorized access to sensitive customer information, the institution should conduct a reasonable investigation to promptly determine the likelihood that the information has been or will be misused. If the institution determines that misuse of its information about a customer has occurred or is reasonably possible, it should notify the affected customer as soon as possible. Customer notice may be delayed if an appropriate law enforcement agency determines that notification will interfere with a criminal investigation and provides the institution with a written request for the delay. However, the institution should notify its customers as soon as notification will no longer interfere with the investigation.

1. Sensitive Customer Information

Under the Guidelines, an institution must protect against unauthorized access to or use of customer information that could result in substantial harm or inconvenience to any customer. Substantial harm or inconvenience is most likely to result from improper access to *sensitive customer information* because this type of information is most likely to be misused, as in the commission of identity theft. For purposes of this Guidance, *sensitive customer information* means a customer's name, address, or telephone number, in conjunction with the customer's social security number, driver's license number, account number, credit or debit card number, or a personal identification number or password that would permit access to the customer's account. *Sensitive customer information* also includes any combination of components of

---

11 See Federal Reserve SR Ltr. 00-04, Outsourcing of Information and Transaction Processing, Feb. 9, 2000; OCC Bulletin 2001-47, "Third-Party Relationships Risk Management Principles," Nov. 1, 2001; FDIC FIL 68-99, Risk Assessment Tools and Practices for Information System Security, July 7, 1999; OTS Thrift Bulletin 82a, Third Party Arrangements, Sept. 1, 2004.

12 An institution's obligation to file a SAR is set out in the Agencies' SAR regulations and Agency guidance. See 12 CFR 21.11 (national banks, Federal branches and agencies); 12 CFR 208.62 (State member banks); 12 CFR 211.5(k) (Edge and agreement corporations); 12 CFR 211.24(f) (uninsured State branches and agencies of foreign banks); 12 CFR 225.4(f) (bank holding companies and their nonbank subsidiaries); 12 CFR part 353 (State non-member banks); and 12 CFR 563.180 (savings associations). National banks must file SARs in connection with computer intrusions and other computer crimes. See OCC Bulletin 2000-14, "Infrastructure Threats—Intrusion Risks" (May 15, 2000); Advisory Letter 97-9, "Reporting Computer Related Crimes" (November 19, 1997) (general guidance still applicable though instructions for new SAR form published in 65 FR 1229, 1230 (January 7, 2000)). See also Federal Reserve SR 01-11, Identity Theft and Pretext Calling, Apr. 26, 2001; SR 97-28, Guidance Concerning Reporting of Computer Related Crimes by Financial Institutions, Nov. 6, 1997; FDIC FIL 48-2000, Suspicious Activity Reports, July 14, 2000; FIL 47-97, Preparation of Suspicious Activity Reports, May 6, 1997; OTS CEO Memorandum 139, Identity Theft and Pretext Calling, May 4, 2001; CEO Memorandum 126, New Suspicious Activity Report Form, July 5, 2000; http://www.ots.treas.gov/BSA (for the latest SAR form and filing instructions required by OTS as of July 1, 2003).

13 See FFIEC Information Technology Examination Handbook, Information Security Booklet, Dec. 2002, pp. 68–74.

customer information that would allow someone to log onto or access the customer's account, such as user name and password or password and account number.

2. Affected Customers

If a financial institution, based upon its investigation, can determine from its logs or other data precisely which customers' information has been improperly accessed, it may limit notification to those customers with regard to whom the institution determines that misuse of their information has occurred or is reasonably possible. However, there may be situations where the institution determines that a group of files has been accessed improperly, but is unable to identify which specific customers' information has been accessed. If the circumstances of the unauthorized access lead the institution to determine that misuse of the information is reasonably possible, it should notify all customers in the group.

B. Content of Customer Notice

1. Customer notice should be given in a clear and conspicuous manner. The notice should describe the incident in general terms and the type of customer information that was the subject of unauthorized access or use. It also should generally describe what the institution has done to protect the customers' information from further unauthorized access. In addition, it should include a telephone number that customers can call for further information and assistance.[14] The notice also should remind customers of the need to remain vigilant over the next twelve to twenty-four months, and to promptly report incidents of suspected identity theft to the institution. The notice should include the following additional items, when appropriate:

a. A recommendation that the customer review account statements and immediately report any suspicious activity to the institution;

b. A description of fraud alerts and an explanation of how the customer may place a fraud alert in the customer's consumer reports to put the customer's creditors on notice that the customer may be a victim of fraud;

c. A recommendation that the customer periodically obtain credit reports from each nationwide credit reporting agency and have information relating to fraudulent transactions deleted;

d. An explanation of how the customer may obtain a credit report free of charge; and

e. Information about the availability of the FTC's online guidance regarding steps a consumer can take to protect against identity theft. The notice should encourage the customer to report any incidents of identity theft to the FTC, and should provide the FTC's Web site address and toll-free telephone number that customers may use to obtain the identity theft guidance and report suspected incidents of identity theft.[15]

---

[14] The institution should, therefore, ensure that it has reasonable policies and procedures in place, including trained personnel, to respond appropriately to customer inquiries and requests for assistance.

[15] Currently, the FTC Web site for the ID Theft brochure and the FTC Hotline phone number are *http://www.consumer.gov/idtheft* and 1-877-IDTHEFT. The institution may also refer customers to any materials developed pursuant to section 151(b) of the FACT Act (educational materials developed by the FTC to teach the public how to prevent identity theft).

2. The Agencies encourage financial institutions to notify the nationwide consumer reporting agencies prior to sending notices to a large number of customers that include contact information for the reporting agencies.

C. Delivery of Customer Notice

Customer notice should be delivered in any manner designed to ensure that a customer can reasonably be expected to receive it. For example, the institution may choose to contact all customers affected by telephone or by mail, or by electronic mail for those customers for whom it has a valid e-mail address and who have agreed to receive communications electronically.

[66 Fed. Reg. 8636 (Feb. 1, 2001); 69 Fed. Reg. 77618 (Dec. 28, 2004); 70 Fed. Reg. 15753 (Mar. 29, 2005); 71 Fed. Reg. 5780 (Feb. 3, 2006)]

G.3.3 Federal Deposit Insurance Corporation Regulations

TITLE 12—BANKS AND BANKING

* * *

CHAPTER III—FEDERAL DEPOSIT INSURANCE CORPORATION

* * *

SUBCHAPTER B—REGULATIONS AND STATEMENTS OF GENERAL POLICY

* * *

PART 364—STANDARDS FOR SAFETY AND SOUNDNESS

* * *

364.101 Standards for safety and soundness.

* * *

Appendix B to Part 364   Interagency Guidelines Establishing Information Security Standards

---

CHAPTER III—FEDERAL DEPOSIT INSURANCE CORPORATION

* * *

SUBCHAPTER B—REGULATIONS AND STATEMENTS OF GENERAL POLICY

* * *

PART 364—STANDARDS FOR SAFETY AND SOUNDNESS

* * *

12 C.F.R. § 364.101 Standards for safety and soundness.

(a) *General standards.* The Interagency Guidelines Establishing Standards for Safety and Soundness prescribed pursuant to section 39 of the Federal Deposit Insurance Act (12 U.S.C. 1831p-1), as set forth as appendix A to this part, apply to all insured state nonmember banks and to state-licensed insured branches of foreign banks, that are subject to the provisions of section 39 of the Federal Deposit Insurance Act.

(b) *Interagency Guidelines Establishing Information Security Standards.* The Interagency Guidelines Establishing Information Security Standards prescribed pursuant to section 39 of the Federal Deposit Insurance Act (12 U.S.C. 1831p-1), and sections 501 and 505(b) of the Gramm-Leach-Bliley Act (15 U.S.C. 6801, 6805(b)), and with respect to the proper disposal of consumer information requirements pursuant to section 628 of the Fair Credit Reporting Act (15 U.S.C. 1681w), as set forth in appendix B to this part, apply to all insured state nonmember banks, insured state licensed branches of foreign banks, and any subsidiaries of such entities (except brokers, dealers, persons providing insurance, investment companies, and investment advisers).

[63 Fed. Reg. 55488 (Oct. 15, 1998) (Effective Date: Oct. 15, 1988); 64 Fed. Reg. 66708 (Nov. 29, 1999) (Effective Date: Nov. 29, 1999); 66 Fed. Reg. 8638 (Feb. 1, 2001) (Effective Date: July 1, 2001); 69 Fed. Reg. 77610 (Dec. 28, 2004) (Effective Date: July 1, 2005)]

* * *

12 C.F.R. Appendix B to Part 364—Interagency Guidelines Establishing Information Security Standards

TABLE OF CONTENTS

I. Introduction
  A. Scope
  B. Preservation of Existing Authority
  C. Definitions
II. Standards for Safeguarding Customer Information
  A. Information Security Program
  B. Objectives
III. Development and Implementation of Customer Information Security Program
  A. Involve the Board of Directors
  B. Assess Risk
  C. Manage and Control Risk
  D. Oversee Service Provider Arrangements
  E. Adjust the Program
  F. Report to the Board
  G. Implement the Standards

I. INTRODUCTION

The Interagency Guidelines Establishing Information Security Standards (Guidelines) set forth standards pursuant to section 39 of the Federal Deposit Insurance Act, 12 U.S.C. 1831p-1, and sections 501 and 505(b), 15 U.S.C. 6801 and 6805(b), of the Gramm-Leach-Bliley Act. These Guidelines address standards for developing and implementing administrative, technical, and physical safeguards to protect the security, confidentiality, and integrity of customer information. These Guidelines also address standards with respect to the proper disposal of consumer information pursuant to sections 621 and 628 of the Fair Credit Reporting Act (15 U.S.C. 1681s and 1681w).

A. *Scope.* The Guidelines apply to customer information maintained by or on behalf of, and to the disposal of consumer information by or on behalf of, entities over which the Federal Deposit Insurance Corporation (FDIC) has authority. Such entities, referred to as "the bank" are banks insured by the FDIC (other than members of the Federal Reserve System), insured state branches of foreign banks, and any subsidiaries of such entities (except brokers, dealers, persons providing insurance, investment companies, and investment advisers).

B. *Preservation of Existing Authority.* Neither section 39 nor these Guidelines in any way limit the authority of the FDIC to address unsafe or unsound practices, violations of law, unsafe or unsound conditions, or other practices. The FDIC may take action under section 39 and these Guidelines independently of, in conjunction with, or in addition to, any other enforcement action available to the FDIC.

C. *Definitions.* 1. Except as modified in the Guidelines, or unless the context otherwise requires, the terms used in these Guidelines have the same meanings as set forth in sections 3 and 39 of the Federal Deposit Insurance Act (12 U.S.C. 1813 and 1831p-1).

2. For purposes of the Guidelines, the following definitions apply:

a. *Board of directors,* in the case of a branch or agency of a foreign bank, means the managing official in charge of the branch or agency.

b. *Consumer information* means any record about an individual, whether in paper, electronic, or other form, that is a consumer report or is derived from a consumer report and that is maintained or otherwise possessed by or on behalf of the bank for a business purpose. Consumer information also means a compilation of such records. The term does not include any record that does not personally identify an individual.

i. *Examples:*

(1) *Consumer information* includes:

(A) A consumer report that a bank obtains;

(B) information from a consumer report that the bank obtains from its affiliate after the consumer has been given a notice and has elected not to opt out of that sharing;

(C) information from a consumer report that the bank obtains about an individual who applies for but does not receive a loan, including any loan sought by an individual for a business purpose;

(D) information from a consumer report that the bank obtains about an individual who guarantees a loan (including a loan to a business entity); or

(E) information from a consumer report that the bank obtains about an employee or prospective employee.

(2) *Consumer information* does not include:

(A) aggregate information, such as the mean score, derived from a group of consumer reports; or

(B) blind data, such as payment history on accounts that are not personally identifiable, that may be used for developing credit scoring models or for other purposes.

c. *Consumer report* has the same meaning as set forth in the Fair Credit Reporting Act, 15 U.S.C. 1681a(d).

d. *Customer* means any customer of the bank as defined in § 332.3(h) of this chapter.

e. *Customer information* means any record containing nonpublic personal information, as defined in § 332.3(n) of this chapter, about a customer, whether in paper, electronic, or other form, that is maintained by or on behalf of the bank.

f. *Customer information systems* means any methods used to access, collect, store, use, transmit, protect, or dispose of customer information.

g. *Service provider* means any person or entity that maintains, processes, or otherwise is permitted access to customer information or consumer information through its provision of services directly to the bank.

II. STANDARDS FOR INFORMATION SECURITY

A. *Information Security Program.* Each bank shall implement a comprehensive written information security program that includes administrative, technical, and physical safeguards appropriate to the size and complexity of the bank and the nature and scope of its activities. While all parts of the bank are not required to implement a uniform set of policies, all elements of the information security program must be coordinated.

B. *Objectives.* A bank's information security program shall be designed to:

1. Ensure the security and confidentiality of customer information;

2. Protect against any anticipated threats or hazards to the security or integrity of such information;

3. Protect against unauthorized access to or use of such information that could result in substantial harm or inconvenience to any customer; and

4. Ensure the proper disposal of customer information and consumer information.

III. DEVELOPMENT AND IMPLEMENTATION OF INFORMATION SECURITY PROGRAM

A. *Involve the Board of Directors.* The board of directors or an appropriate committee of the board of each bank shall:

1. Approve the bank's written information security program; and

2. Oversee the development, implementation, and maintenance of the bank's information security program, including assigning specific responsibility for its implementation and reviewing reports from management.

B. *Assess Risk.*

Each bank shall:

1. Identify reasonably foreseeable internal and external threats that could result in unauthorized disclosure, misuse, alteration, or destruction of customer information or customer information systems.

2. Assess the likelihood and potential damage of these threats, taking into consideration the sensitivity of customer information.

3. Assess the sufficiency of policies, procedures, customer information systems, and other arrangements in place to control risks.

C. *Manage and Control Risk.* Each bank shall:

1. Design its information security program to control the identified risks, commensurate with the sensitivity of the information as well as the complexity and scope of the bank's activities. Each bank must consider whether the following security measures are appropriate for the bank and, if so, adopt those measures the bank concludes are appropriate

a. Access controls on customer information systems, including controls to authenticate and permit access only to authorized individuals and controls to prevent employees from providing customer information to unauthorized individuals who may seek to obtain this information through fraudulent means.

b. Access restrictions at physical locations containing customer information, such as buildings, computer facilities, and records storage facilities to permit access only to authorized individuals;

c. Encryption of electronic customer information, including while in transit or in storage on networks or systems to which unauthorized individuals may have access;

d. Procedures designed to ensure that customer information system modifications are consistent with the bank's information security program;

e. Dual control procedures, segregation of duties, and employee background checks for employees with responsibilities for or access to customer information;

f. Monitoring systems and procedures to detect actual and attempted attacks on or intrusions into customer information systems;

g. Response programs that specify actions to be taken when the bank suspects or detects that unauthorized individuals have gained access to customer information systems, including appropriate reports to regulatory and law enforcement agencies; and

h. Measures to protect against destruction, loss, or damage of customer information due to potential environmental hazards, such as fire and water damage or technological failures.

2. Train staff to implement the bank's information security program.

3. Regularly test the key controls, systems and procedures of the information security program. The frequency and nature of such tests should be determined by the bank's risk assessment. Tests should be conducted or reviewed by independent third parties or staff independent of those that develop or maintain the security programs.

4. Develop, implement, and maintain, as part of its information security program, appropriate measures to properly dispose of customer information and consumer information in accordance with each of the requirements of this paragraph III.

D. *Oversee Service Provider Arrangements.* Each bank shall:

1. Exercise appropriate due diligence in selecting its service providers;

2. Require its service providers by contract to implement appropriate measures designed to meet the objectives of these Guidelines; and

3. Where indicated by the bank's risk assessment, monitor its service providers to confirm that they have satisfied their obligations as required by paragraph D.2. As part of this monitoring, a bank should review audits, summaries of test results, or other equivalent evaluations of its service providers.

E. *Adjust the Program.* Each bank shall monitor, evaluate, and adjust, as appropriate, the information security program in light of any relevant changes in technology, the sensitivity of its customer information, internal or external threats to information, and the bank's own changing business arrangements, such as mergers and acquisitions, alliances and joint ventures, outsourcing arrangements, and changes to customer information systems.

F. *Report to the Board.* Each bank shall report to its board or an appropriate committee of the board at least annually. This report should describe the overall status of the information security program and the bank's compliance with these Guidelines. The report, which will vary depending upon the complexity of each bank's program should discuss material matters related to its program, addressing issues such as: risk assessment; risk management and control decisions; service provider arrangements; results of testing; security breaches or violations, and management's responses; and recommendations for changes in the information security program.

G. *Implement the Standards.* 1. *Effective date.* Each bank must implement an information security program pursuant to these Guidelines by July 1, 2001.

2. *Two-year grandfathering of agreements with service providers.* Until July 1, 2003, a contract that a bank has entered into with a service provider to perform services for it or functions on its behalf, satisfies the provisions of paragraph III.D., even if the contract does not include a requirement that the servicer maintain the security and confidentiality of customer information as long as the bank entered into the contract on or before March 5, 2001.

3. *Effective date for measures relating to the disposal of consumer information.* Each bank must satisfy these Guidelines with respect to the proper disposal of consumer information by July 1, 2005.

4. *Exception for existing agreements with service providers relating to the disposal of consumer information.* Notwithstanding the requirement in paragraph III.G.3., a bank's contracts with its service providers that have access to consumer information and that may dispose of consumer information, entered into before July 1, 2005, must comply with the provisions of the Guidelines relating to the proper disposal of consumer information by July 1, 2006.

SUPPLEMENT A TO APPENDIX B TO PART 364 INTERAGENCY GUIDANCE ON RESPONSE PROGRAMS FOR UNAUTHORIZED ACCESS TO CUSTOMER INFORMATION AND CUSTOMER NOTICE

I. BACKGROUND

This Guidance[1] interprets section 501(b) of the Gramm-Leach-Bliley Act ("GLBA") and the Interagency Guidelines Establishing Information Security Standards (the "Security Guidelines")[2] and describes response programs, including customer notification procedures, that a financial institution should develop and implement to address unauthorized access to or use of customer information that could result in substantial harm or inconvenience to a customer. The scope of, and definitions of terms used in, this Guidance are identical to those of the Security Guidelines. For example, the term "customer information" is the same term used in the Security Guidelines, and means any record containing nonpublic personal information about a customer, whether in paper, electronic, or other form, maintained by or on behalf of the institution.

A. Interagency Security Guidelines

Section 501(b) of the GLBA required the Agencies to establish appropriate standards for financial institutions subject to their jurisdiction that include administrative, technical, and physical safeguards, to protect the security and confidentiality of customer information. Accordingly, the Agencies issued Security Guidelines requiring every financial institution to have an information security program designed to:

1. Ensure the security and confidentiality of customer information;

2. Protect against any anticipated threats or hazards to the security or integrity of such information; and

3. Protect against unauthorized access to or use of such information that could result in substantial harm or inconvenience to any customer.

B. Risk Assessment and Controls

1. The Security Guidelines direct every financial institution to assess the following risks, among others, when developing its information security program:

a. Reasonably foreseeable internal and external threats that could result in unauthorized disclosure, misuse, alteration, or destruction of customer information or customer information systems;

b. The likelihood and potential damage of threats, taking into consideration the sensitivity of customer information; and

c. The sufficiency of policies, procedures, customer information systems, and other arrangements in place to control risks.[3]

2. Following the assessment of these risks, the Security Guidelines require a financial institution to design a program to address the identified risks. The particular security measures an institution should adopt will depend upon the risks presented by the complexity and scope of its business. At a minimum, the financial institution is required to consider the specific security measures enumerated in the Security Guidelines,[4] and adopt those that are appropriate for the institution, including:

a. Access controls on customer information systems, including controls to authenticate and permit access only to authorized individuals and controls to prevent employees from providing customer information to unauthorized individuals who may seek to obtain this information through fraudulent means;

b. Background checks for employees with responsibilities for access to customer information; and

---

1 This Guidance is being jointly issued by the Board of Governors of the Federal Reserve System (Board), the Federal Deposit Insurance Corporation (FDIC), the Office of the Comptroller of the Currency (OCC), and the Office of Thrift Supervision (OTS).

2 12 CFR part 30, app. B (OCC); 12 CFR part 208, app. D-2 and part 225, app. F (Board); 12 CFR part 364, app. B (FDIC); and 12 CFR part 570, app. B (OTS). The "Interagency Guidelines Establishing Information Security Standards" were formerly known as "The Interagency Guidelines Establishing Standards for Safeguarding Customer Information."

3 *See* Security Guidelines, III.B.

4 *See* Security Guidelines, III.C.

c. Response programs that specify actions to be taken when the financial institution suspects or detects that unauthorized individuals have gained access to customer information systems, including appropriate reports to regulatory and law enforcement agencies.[5]

C. Service Providers

The Security Guidelines direct every financial institution to require its service providers by contract to implement appropriate measures designed to protect against unauthorized access to or use of customer information that could result in substantial harm or inconvenience to any customer.[6]

II. RESPONSE PROGRAM

Millions of Americans, throughout the country, have been victims of identity theft.[7] Identity thieves misuse personal information they obtain from a number of sources, including financial institutions, to perpetrate identity theft. Therefore, financial institutions should take preventative measures to safeguard customer information against attempts to gain unauthorized access to the information. For example, financial institutions should place access controls on customer information systems and conduct background checks for employees who are authorized to access customer information.[8] However, every financial institution should also develop and implement a risk-based response program to address incidents of unauthorized access to customer information in customer information systems[9] that occur nonetheless. A response program should be a key part of an institution's information security program.[10] The program should be appropriate to the size and complexity of the institution and the nature and scope of its activities.

In addition, each institution should be able to address incidents of unauthorized access to customer information in customer information systems maintained by its domestic and foreign service providers. Therefore, consistent with the obligations in the Guidelines that relate to these arrangements, and with existing guidance on this topic issued by the Agencies,[11] an institution's contract with its service provider should require the service provider to take appropriate actions to address incidents of unauthorized access to the financial institution's customer information, including notification to the institution as soon as possible of any such incident, to enable the institution to expeditiously implement its response program.

A. Components of a Response Program

1. At a minimum, an institution's response program should contain procedures for the following:

a. Assessing the nature and scope of an incident, and identifying what customer information systems and types of customer information have been accessed or misused;

b. Notifying its primary Federal regulator as soon as possible when the institution becomes aware of an incident involving unauthorized access to or use of sensitive customer information, as defined below;

c. Consistent with the Agencies' Suspicious Activity Report ("SAR") regulations,[12] notifying appropriate law enforcement authorities, in addition to filing a timely SAR in situations involving Federal criminal violations requiring immediate attention, such as when a reportable violation is ongoing;

d. Taking appropriate steps to contain and control the incident to prevent further unauthorized access to or use of customer infor-

---

5 See Security Guidelines, III.C.

6 See Security Guidelines, II.B. and III.D. Further, the Agencies note that, in addition to contractual obligations to a financial institution, a service provider may be required to implement its own comprehensive information security program in accordance with the Safeguards Rule promulgated by the Federal Trade Commission ("FTC"), 16 CFR part 314.

7 The FTC estimates that nearly 10 million Americans discovered they were victims of some form of identity theft in 2002. See The Federal Trade Commission, Identity Theft Survey Report, (September 2003), available at http://www.ftc.gov/os/2003/09/synovatereport.pdf.

8 Institutions should also conduct background checks of employees to ensure that the institution does not violate 12 U.S.C. 1829, which prohibits an institution from hiring an individual convicted of certain criminal offenses or who is subject to a prohibition order under 12 U.S.C. 1818(e)(6).

9 Under the Guidelines, an institution's customer information systems consist of all of the methods used to access, collect, store, use, transmit, protect, or dispose of customer information, including the systems maintained by its service providers. See Security Guidelines, I.C.2.d (I.C.2.c for OTS).

10 See FFIEC Information Technology Examination Handbook, Information Security Booklet, Dec. 2002 available at http://www.ffiec.gov/ffiecinfobase/html_pages/infosec_book_frame.htm. Federal Reserve SR 97-32, Sound Practice Guidance for Information Security for Networks, Dec. 4, 1997; OCC Bulletin 2000-14, "Infrastructure Threats—Intrusion Risks" (May 15, 2000), for additional guidance on preventing, detecting, and responding to intrusions into financial institution computer systems.

11 See Federal Reserve SR Ltr. 00-04, Outsourcing of Information and Transaction Processing, Feb. 9, 2000; OCC Bulletin 2001-47, "Third-Party Relationships Risk Management Principles," Nov. 1, 2001 FDIC FIL 68-99, Risk Assessment Tools and Practices for Information System Security, July 7, 1999; OTS Thrift Bulletin 82a, Third Party Arrangements, Sept. 1, 2004.

12 An institution's obligation to file a SAR is set out in the Agencies' SAR regulations and Agency guidance. See 12 CFR 21.11 (national banks, Federal branches and agencies); 12 CFR 208.62 (State member banks); 12 CFR 211.5(k) (Edge and agreement corporations); 12 CFR 211.24(f) (uninsured State branches and agencies of foreign banks); 12 CFR 225.4(f) (bank holding companies and their nonbank subsidiaries); 12 CFR part 353 (State non-member banks); and 12 CFR 563.180 (savings associations) National banks must file SARs in connection with computer intrusions and other computer crimes. See OCC Bulletin 2000-14, "Infrastructure Threats—Intrusion Risks" (May 15, 2000); Advisory Letter 97-9, "Reporting Computer Related Crimes" (November 19, 1997) (general guidance still applicable though instructions for new SAR form published in 65 FR 1229, 1230 (January 7, 2000)). See also Federal Reserve SR 01-11, Identity Theft and Pretext Calling, Apr. 26, 2001; SR 97-28, Guidance Concerning Reporting of Computer Related Crimes by Financial Institutions, Nov. 6, 1997; FDIC FIL 48-2000, Suspicious Activity Reports, July 14, 2000; FIL 47-97, Preparation of Suspicious Activity Reports, May 6, 1997; OTS CEO Memorandum 139, Identity Theft and Pretext Calling, May 4 2001; CEO Memorandum 126, New Suspicious Activity Report Form, July 5, 2000; http://www.ots.treas.gov/BSA (for the latest SAR form and filing instructions required by OTS as of July 1, 2003).

mation, for example, by monitoring, freezing, or closing affected accounts, while preserving records and other evidence;[13] and

e. Notifying customers when warranted.

2. Where an incident of unauthorized access to customer information involves customer information systems maintained by an institution's service providers, it is the responsibility of the financial institution to notify the institution's customers and regulator. However, an institution may authorize or contract with its service provider to notify the institution's customers or regulator on its behalf.

III. CUSTOMER NOTICE

Financial institutions have an affirmative duty to protect their customers' information against unauthorized access or use. Notifying customers of a security incident involving the unauthorized access or use of the customer's information in accordance with the standard set forth below is a key part of that duty. Timely notification of customers is important to manage an institution's reputation risk. Effective notice also may reduce an institution's legal risk, assist in maintaining good customer relations, and enable the institution's customers to take steps to protect themselves against the consequences of identity theft. When customer notification is warranted, an institution may not forgo notifying its customers of an incident because the institution believes that it may be potentially embarrassed or inconvenienced by doing so.

A. Standard for Providing Notice

When a financial institution becomes aware of an incident of unauthorized access to sensitive customer information, the institution should conduct a reasonable investigation to promptly determine the likelihood that the information has been or will be misused. If the institution determines that misuse of its information about a customer has occurred or is reasonably possible, it should notify the affected customer as soon as possible. Customer notice may be delayed if an appropriate law enforcement agency determines that notification will interfere with a criminal investigation and provides the institution with a written request for the delay. However, the institution should notify its customers as soon as notification will no longer interfere with the investigation.

1. Sensitive Customer Information

Under the Guidelines, an institution must protect against unauthorized access to or use of customer information that could result in substantial harm or inconvenience to any customer. Substantial harm or inconvenience is most likely to result from improper access to *sensitive customer information* because this type of information is most likely to be misused, as in the commission of identity theft. For purposes of this Guidance, *sensitive customer information* means a customer's name, address, or telephone number, in conjunction with the customer's social security number, driver's license number, account number, credit or debit card number, or a personal identification number or password that would permit access to the customer's account. *Sensitive customer information* also includes any combination of components of customer information that would allow someone to log onto or access the customer's account, such as user name and password or password and account number.

2. Affected Customers

If a financial institution, based upon its investigation, can determine from its logs or other data precisely which customers' information has been improperly accessed, it may limit notification to those customers with regard to whom the institution determines that misuse of their information has occurred or is reasonably possible. However, there may be situations where the institution determines that a group of files has been accessed improperly, but is unable to identify which specific customers' information has been accessed. If the circumstances of the unauthorized access lead the institution to determine that misuse of the information is reasonably possible, it should notify all customers in the group.

B. Content of Customer Notice

1. Customer notice should be given in a clear and conspicuous manner. The notice should describe the incident in general terms and the type of customer information that was the subject of unauthorized access or use. It also should generally describe what the institution has done to protect the customers' information from further unauthorized access. In addition, it should include a telephone number that customers can call for further information and assistance.[14] The notice also should remind customers of the need to remain vigilant over the next twelve to twenty-four months, and to promptly report incidents of suspected identity theft to the institution. The notice should include the following additional items, when appropriate:

a. A recommendation that the customer review account statements and immediately report any suspicious activity to the institution;

b. A description of fraud alerts and an explanation of how the customer may place a fraud alert in the customer's consumer reports to put the customer's creditors on notice that the customer may be a victim of fraud;

c. A recommendation that the customer periodically obtain credit reports from each nationwide credit reporting agency and have information relating to fraudulent transactions deleted;

d. An explanation of how the customer may obtain a credit report free of charge; and

e. Information about the availability of the FTC's online guidance regarding steps a consumer can take to protect against identity theft. The notice should encourage the customer to report any incidents of identity theft to the FTC, and should provide the FTC's Web site address and toll-free telephone number that customers may use to obtain the identity theft guidance and report suspected incidents of identity theft.[15]

---

13 See FFIEC Information Technology Examination Handbook, Information Security Booklet, Dec. 2002, pp. 68–74.

14 The institution should, therefore, ensure that it has reasonable policies and procedures in place, including trained personnel, to respond appropriately to customer inquiries and requests for assistance.

15 Currently, the FTC Web site for the ID Theft brochure and the FTC Hotline phone number are *http://www.consumer.gov/ idtheft* and 1-877-IDTHEFT. The institution may also refer customers to any materials developed pursuant to section 151(b) of the FACT Act (educational materials developed by the FTC to teach the public how to prevent identity theft).

2. The Agencies encourage financial institutions to notify the nationwide consumer reporting agencies prior to sending notices to a large number of customers that include contact information for the reporting agencies.

C. Delivery of Customer Notice

Customer notice should be delivered in any manner designed to ensure that a customer can reasonably be expected to receive it. For example, the institution may choose to contact all customers affected by telephone or by mail, or by electronic mail for those customers for whom it has a valid e-mail address and who have agreed to receive communications electronically.

[63 Fed. Reg. 55484, 55486 (Oct. 15, 1998) (Effective Date: Oct. 15, 1998); 64 Fed. Reg. 66706 (Nov. 29, 1999) (Effective Date: Nov. 29, 1999); 66 Fed. Reg. 8638 (Feb. 1, 2001) (Effective Date: July 1, 2001); 69 Fed. Reg. 77610 (Dec. 28, 2004) (Effective Date: July 1, 2005); 70 Fed. Reg. 15736 (Mar. 29, 2005) (Effective Date: Mar. 29, 2005); 71 Fed. Reg. 5780 (Feb. 3, 2006) (Effective Date: Feb. 3, 2006)]

G.3.4 Office of Thrift Supervision Regulations

TITLE 12—BANKS AND BANKING

* * *

CHAPTER V—OFFICE OF THRIFT SUPERVISION, DEPARTMENT OF THE TREASURY

* * *

PART 568—SECURITY PROCEDURES

* * *

568.5 Protection of customer information.

* * *

PART 570—SAFETY AND SOUNDNESS GUIDELINES AND COMPLIANCE PROCEDURES

* * *

Appendix B to Part 570   Interagency Guidelines Establishing Information Security Standards

---

CHAPTER V—OFFICE OF THRIFT SUPERVISION, DEPARTMENT OF THE TREASURY

* * *

PART 568—SECURITY PROCEDURES

* * *

12 C.F.R. § 568.5 Protection of customer information.

Savings associations and their subsidiaries (except brokers, dealers, persons providing insurance, investment companies, and investment advisers) must comply with the Interagency Guidelines Establishing Information Security Standards set forth in appendix B to part 570 of this chapter. Supplement A to appendix B to part 570 of this chapter provides interpretive guidance.

[66 Fed. Reg. 8639 (Feb. 1, 2001) (Effective Date: July 1, 2001); 69 Fed. Reg. 77610 (Dec. 28, 2004) (Effective Date: July 1, 2005); 70 Fed. Reg. 15736 (Mar. 29, 2005) (Effective Date: Mar. 29, 2005); 70 Fed. Reg. 32229 (June 2, 2005) (Effective Date: July 1, 2005)]

* * *

PART 570—SAFETY AND SOUNDNESS GUIDELINES AND COMPLIANCE PROCEDURES

* * *

12 C.F.R. Appendix B to Part 570—Interagency Guidelines Establishing Information Security Standards

TABLE OF CONTENTS

I. Introduction
  A. Scope
  B. Preservation of Existing Authority
  C. Definitions
II. Standards for Safeguarding Customer Information
  A. Information Security Program
  B. Objectives
III. Development and Implementation of Customer Information Security Program
  A. Involve the Board of Directors
  B. Assess Risk
  C. Manage and Control Risk
  D. Oversee Service Provider Arrangements
  E. Adjust the Program
  F. Report to the Board
  G. Implement the Standards

I. INTRODUCTION

The Interagency Guidelines Establishing Information Security Standards (Guidelines) set forth standards pursuant to section 39(a) of the Federal Deposit Insurance Act (12 U.S.C. 1831p-1), and sections 501 and 505(b) of the Gramm-Leach-Bliley Act (15 U.S.C. 6801 and 6805(b)). These Guidelines address standards for developing and implementing administrative, technical, and physical safeguards to protect the security, confidentiality, and integrity of customer information. These Guidelines also address standards with respect to the proper disposal of consumer information, pursuant to sections 621 and 628 of the Fair Credit Reporting Act (15 U.S.C. 1681s and 1681w).

A. *Scope.* The Guidelines apply to customer information maintained by or on behalf of entities over which OTS has authority. For purposes of this appendix, these entities are savings associations whose deposits are FDIC-insured and any subsidiaries of such savings associations, except brokers, dealers, persons providing insurance, investment companies, and investment advisers. This appendix refers to such entities as ''you'. These Guidelines also apply to the proper disposal of consumer information by or on behalf of such entities.

B. *Preservation of Existing Authority.* Neither section 39 nor these Guidelines in any way limit OTS's authority to address unsafe or unsound practices, violations of law, unsafe or unsound conditions, or other practices. OTS may take action under section 39 and these Guidelines independently of, in conjunction with, or in addition to, any other enforcement action available to OTS.

C. *Definitions.* 1. Except as modified in the Guidelines, or unless the context otherwise requires, the terms used in these Guidelines have the same meanings as set forth in sections 3 and 39 of the Federal Deposit Insurance Act (12 U.S.C. 1813 and 1831p-1).

2. For purposes of the Guidelines, the following definitions apply:

a. *Consumer information* means any record about an individual, whether in paper, electronic, or other form, that is a consumer report or is derived from a consumer report and that is maintained or otherwise possessed by you or on your behalf for a business purpose. Consumer information also means a compilation of such records. The term does not include any record that does not identify an individual.

i. *Examples.* (1) *Consumer information* includes:

(A) A consumer report that a savings association obtains;

(B) Information from a consumer report that you obtain from your affiliate after the consumer has been given a notice and has elected not to opt out of that sharing;

(C) Information from a consumer report that you obtain about an individual who applies for but does not receive a loan, including any loan sought by an individual for a business purpose;

(D) Information from a consumer report that you obtain about an individual who guarantees a loan (including a loan to a business entity); or

(E) Information from a consumer report that you obtain about an employee or prospective employee.

(2) *Consumer information* does not include:

(A) Aggregate information, such as the mean credit score, derived from a group of consumer reports; or

(B) Blind data, such as payment history on accounts that are not personally identifiable, that may be used for developing credit scoring models or for other purposes.

b. *Consumer report* has the same meaning as set forth in the Fair Credit Reporting Act, 15 U.S.C. 1681a(d).

c. *Customer* means any of your customers as defined in § 573.3(h) of this chapter.

d. *Customer information* means any record containing nonpublic personal information, as defined in § 573.3(n) of this chapter, about a customer, whether in paper, electronic, or other form, that you maintain or that is maintained on your behalf.

e. *Customer information systems* means any methods used to access, collect, store, use, transmit, protect, or dispose of customer information.

f. *Service provider* means any person or entity that maintains, processes, or otherwise is permitted access to customer information or consumer information, through its provision of services directly to you.

II. STANDARDS FOR INFORMATION SECURITY

A. *Information Security Program.* You shall implement a comprehensive written information security program that includes administrative, technical, and physical safeguards appropriate to your size and complexity and the nature and scope of your activities. While all parts of your organization are not required to implement a uniform set of policies, all elements of your information security program must be coordinated.

B. *Objectives.* Your information security program shall be designed to:

1. Ensure the security and confidentiality of customer information;

2. Protect against any anticipated threats or hazards to the security or integrity of such information;

3. Protect against unauthorized access to or use of such information that could result in substantial harm or inconvenience to any customer; and

4. Ensure the proper disposal of customer information and consumer information.

III. DEVELOPMENT AND IMPLEMENTATION OF INFORMATION SECURITY PROGRAM

A. *Involve the Board of Directors.* Your board of directors or an appropriate committee of the board shall:

1. Approve your written information security program; and

2. Oversee the development, implementation, and maintenance of your information security program, including assigning specific responsibility for its implementation and reviewing reports from management.

B. *Assess Risk.* You shall:

1. Identify reasonably foreseeable internal and external threats that could result in unauthorized disclosure, misuse, alteration, or destruction of customer information or customer information systems.

2. Assess the likelihood and potential damage of these threats, taking into consideration the sensitivity of customer information.

3. Assess the sufficiency of policies, procedures, customer information systems, and other arrangements in place to control risks.

C. *Manage and Control Risk.* You shall:

1. Design your information security program to control the identified risks, commensurate with the sensitivity of the information as well as the complexity and scope of your activities. You must consider whether the following security measures are appropriate for you and, if so, adopt those measures you conclude are appropriate:

a. Access controls on customer information systems, including controls to authenticate and permit access only to authorized individuals and controls to prevent employees from providing customer information to unauthorized individuals who may seek to obtain this information through fraudulent means.

b. Access restrictions at physical locations containing customer information, such as buildings, computer facilities, and records storage facilities to permit access only to authorized individuals;

c. Encryption of electronic customer information, including while in transit or in storage on networks or systems to which unauthorized individuals may have access;

d. Procedures designed to ensure that customer information system modifications are consistent with your information security program;

e. Dual control procedures, segregation of duties, and employee background checks for employees with responsibilities for or access to customer information;

f. Monitoring systems and procedures to detect actual and attempted attacks on or intrusions into customer information systems;

g. Response programs that specify actions for you to take when you suspect or detect that unauthorized individuals have gained access to customer information systems, including appropriate reports to regulatory and law enforcement agencies; and

h. Measures to protect against destruction, loss, or damage of customer information due to potential environmental hazards, such as fire and water damage or technological failures.

2. Train staff to implement your information security program.

3. Regularly test the key controls, systems and procedures of the information security program. The frequency and nature of such tests should be determined by your risk assessment. Tests should be conducted or reviewed by independent third parties or staff independent of those that develop or maintain the security programs.

4. Develop, implement, and maintain, as part of your information security program, appropriate measures to properly dispose of customer information and consumer information in accordance with each of the requirements in this paragraph III.

D. *Oversee Service Provider Arrangements.* You shall:

1. Exercise appropriate due diligence in selecting your service providers;

2. Require your service providers by contract to implement appropriate measures designed to meet the objectives of these Guidelines; and

3. Where indicated by your risk assessment, monitor your service providers to confirm that they have satisfied their obligations as required by paragraph D.2. As part of this monitoring, you should review audits, summaries of test results, or other equivalent evaluations of your service providers.

E. *Adjust the Program.* You shall monitor, evaluate, and adjust, as appropriate, the information security program in light of any relevant changes in technology, the sensitivity of your customer information, internal or external threats to information, and your own changing business arrangements, such as mergers and acquisitions, alliances and joint ventures, outsourcing arrangements, and changes to customer information systems.

F. *Report to the Board.* You shall report to your board or an appropriate committee of the board at least annually. This report should describe the overall status of the information security program and your compliance with these Guidelines. The reports should discuss material matters related to your program, addressing issues such as: risk assessment; risk management and control decisions; service provider arrangements; results of testing; security breaches or violations and management's responses; and recommendations for changes in the information security program.

G. *Implement the Standards.* 1. *Effective date.* You must implement an information security program pursuant to these Guidelines by July 1, 2001.

2. *Two-year grandfathering of agreements with service providers.* Until July 1, 2003, a contract that you have entered into with a service provider to perform services for you or functions on your behalf satisfies the provisions of paragraph III.D., even if the contract does not include a requirement that the servicer maintain the security and confidentiality of customer information, as long as you entered into the contract on or before March 5, 2001.

3. *Effective date for measures relating to the disposal of consumer information.* You must satisfy these Guidelines with respect to the proper disposal of consumer information by July 1, 2005.

4. *Exception for existing agreements with service providers relating to the disposal of consumer information.* Notwithstanding the requirement in paragraph III.G.3., your contracts with service providers that have access to consumer information and that may dispose of consumer information, entered into before July 1, 2005, must comply with the provisions of the Guidelines relating to the proper disposal of consumer information by July 1, 2006.

SUPPLEMENT A TO APPENDIX B TO PART 364 INTERAGENCY GUIDANCE ON RESPONSE PROGRAMS FOR UNAUTHORIZED ACCESS TO CUSTOMER INFORMATION AND CUSTOMER NOTICE

I. BACKGROUND

This Guidance[1] interprets section 501(b) of the Gramm-Leach-Bliley Act ("GLBA") and the Interagency Guidelines Establishing Information Security Standards (the "Security Guidelines")[2] and describes response programs, including customer notification procedures, that a financial institution should develop and implement to address unauthorized access to or use of customer information that could result in substantial harm or inconvenience to a customer. The scope of, and definitions of terms used in, this Guidance are identical to those of the Security Guidelines. For example, the term "customer information" is the same term used in the Security Guidelines, and means any record containing nonpublic personal information about a customer, whether in paper, electronic, or other form, maintained by or on behalf of the institution.

A. *Interagency Security Guidelines*

Section 501(b) of the GLBA required the Agencies to establish appropriate standards for financial institutions subject to their jurisdiction that include administrative, technical, and physical safeguards, to protect the security and confidentiality of customer

---

1 This Guidance is being jointly issued by the Board of Governors of the Federal Reserve System (Board), the Federal Deposit Insurance Corporation (FDIC), the Office of the Comptroller of the Currency (OCC), and the Office of Thrift Supervision (OTS).

2 12 CFR part 30, app. B (OCC); 12 CFR part 208, app. D-2 and part 225, app. F (Board); 12 CFR part 364, app. B (FDIC); and 12 CFR part 570, app. B (OTS). The "Interagency Guidelines Establishing Information Security Standards" were formerly known as "The Interagency Guidelines Establishing Standards for Safeguarding Customer Information."

information. Accordingly, the Agencies issued Security Guidelines requiring every financial institution to have an information security program designed to:

1. Ensure the security and confidentiality of customer information;
2. Protect against any anticipated threats or hazards to the security or integrity of such information; and
3. Protect against unauthorized access to or use of such information that could result in substantial harm or inconvenience to any customer.

B. Risk Assessment and Controls

1. The Security Guidelines direct every financial institution to assess the following risks, among others, when developing its information security program:

   a. Reasonably foreseeable internal and external threats that could result in unauthorized disclosure, misuse, alteration, or destruction of customer information or customer information systems;

   b. The likelihood and potential damage of threats, taking into consideration the sensitivity of customer information; and

   c. The sufficiency of policies, procedures, customer information systems, and other arrangements in place to control risks.[3]

2. Following the assessment of these risks, the Security Guidelines require a financial institution to design a program to address the identified risks. The particular security measures an institution should adopt will depend upon the risks presented by the complexity and scope of its business. At a minimum, the financial institution is required to consider the specific security measures enumerated in the Security Guidelines,[4] and adopt those that are appropriate for the institution, including:

   a. Access controls on customer information systems, including controls to authenticate and permit access only to authorized individuals and controls to prevent employees from providing customer information to unauthorized individuals who may seek to obtain this information through fraudulent means;

   b. Background checks for employees with responsibilities for access to customer information; and

   c. Response programs that specify actions to be taken when the financial institution suspects or detects that unauthorized individuals have gained access to customer information systems, including appropriate reports to regulatory and law enforcement agencies.[5]

C. Service Providers

The Security Guidelines direct every financial institution to require its service providers by contract to implement appropriate measures designed to protect against unauthorized access to or use of customer information that could result in substantial harm or inconvenience to any customer.[6]

---

3 See Security Guidelines, III.B.
4 See Security Guidelines, III.C.
5 See Security Guidelines, III.C.
6 See Security Guidelines, II.B. and III.D. Further, the Agencies note that, in addition to contractual obligations to a financial institution, a service provider may be required to implement its own comprehensive information security program in accordance with the Safeguards Rule promulgated by the Federal Trade Commission ("FTC"), 16 CFR part 314.

II. RESPONSE PROGRAM

Millions of Americans, throughout the country, have been victims of identity theft.[7] Identity thieves misuse personal information they obtain from a number of sources, including financial institutions, to perpetrate identity theft. Therefore, financial institutions should take preventative measures to safeguard customer information against attempts to gain unauthorized access to the information. For example, financial institutions should place access controls on customer information systems and conduct background checks for employees who are authorized to access customer information.[8] However, every financial institution should also develop and implement a risk-based response program to address incidents of unauthorized access to customer information in customer information systems[9] that occur nonetheless. A response program should be a key part of an institution's information security program.[10] The program should be appropriate to the size and complexity of the institution and the nature and scope of its activities.

In addition, each institution should be able to address incidents of unauthorized access to customer information in customer information systems maintained by its domestic and foreign service providers. Therefore, consistent with the obligations in the Guidelines that relate to these arrangements, and with existing guidance on this topic issued by the Agencies,[11] an institution's contract with its service provider should require the service provider to take appropriate actions to address incidents of unauthorized access to the financial institution's customer information, including notification to the institution as soon as possible of any such incident, to enable the institution to expeditiously implement its response program.

---

7 The FTC estimates that nearly 10 million Americans discovered they were victims of some form of identity theft in 2002. See The Federal Trade Commission, Identity Theft Survey Report, (September 2003), available at *http://www.ftc.gov/os/2003/09/synovatereport.pdf*.
8 Institutions should also conduct background checks of employees to ensure that the institution does not violate 12 U.S.C. 1829, which prohibits an institution from hiring an individual convicted of certain criminal offenses or who is subject to a prohibition order under 12 U.S.C. 1818(e)(6).
9 Under the Guidelines, an institution's customer information systems consist of all of the methods used to access, collect, store, use, transmit, protect, or dispose of customer information, including the systems maintained by its service providers. See Security Guidelines, I.C.2.d (I.C.2.c for OTS).
10 See FFIEC Information Technology Examination Handbook, Information Security Booklet, Dec. 2002 available at *http://www.ffiec.gov/ffiecinfobase/html_pages/infosec_book_frame.htm*. Federal Reserve SR 97-32, Sound Practice Guidance for Information Security for Networks, Dec. 4, 1997; OCC Bulletin 2000-14, "Infrastructure Threats—Intrusion Risks" (May 15, 2000), for additional guidance on preventing, detecting, and responding to intrusions into financial institution computer systems.
11 See Federal Reserve SR Ltr. 00-04, Outsourcing of Information and Transaction Processing, Feb. 9, 2000; OCC Bulletin 2001-47, "Third-Party Relationships Risk Management Principles," Nov. 1, 2001; FDIC FIL 68-99, Risk Assessment Tools and Practices for Information System Security, July 7, 1999; OTS Thrift Bulletin 82a, Third Party Arrangements, Sept. 1, 2004.

Gramm-Leach-Bliley

A. Components of a Response Program

1. At a minimum, an institution's response program should contain procedures for the following:

a. Assessing the nature and scope of an incident, and identifying what customer information systems and types of customer information have been accessed or misused;

b. Notifying its primary Federal regulator as soon as possible when the institution becomes aware of an incident involving unauthorized access to or use of sensitive customer information, as defined below;

c. Consistent with the Agencies' Suspicious Activity Report ("SAR") regulations,[12] notifying appropriate law enforcement authorities, in addition to filing a timely SAR in situations involving Federal criminal violations requiring immediate attention, such as when a reportable violation is ongoing;

d. Taking appropriate steps to contain and control the incident to prevent further unauthorized access to or use of customer information, for example, by monitoring, freezing, or closing affected accounts, while preserving records and other evidence;[13] and

e. Notifying customers when warranted.

2. Where an incident of unauthorized access to customer information involves customer information systems maintained by an institution's service providers, it is the responsibility of the financial institution to notify the institution's customers and regulator. However, an institution may authorize or contract with its service provider to notify the institution's customers or regulator on its behalf.

III. CUSTOMER NOTICE

Financial institutions have an affirmative duty to protect their customers' information against unauthorized access or use. Notifying customers of a security incident involving the unauthorized access or use of the customer's information in accordance with the standard set forth below is a key part of that duty. Timely notification of customers is important to manage an institution's reputation risk. Effective notice also may reduce an institution's legal risk, assist in maintaining good customer relations, and enable the institution's customers to take steps to protect themselves against the consequences of identity theft. When customer notification is warranted, an institution may not forgo notifying its customers of an incident because the institution believes that it may be potentially embarrassed or inconvenienced by doing so.

A. Standard for Providing Notice

When a financial institution becomes aware of an incident of unauthorized access to sensitive customer information, the institution should conduct a reasonable investigation to promptly determine the likelihood that the information has been or will be misused. If the institution determines that misuse of its information about a customer has occurred or is reasonably possible, it should notify the affected customer as soon as possible. Customer notice may be delayed if an appropriate law enforcement agency determines that notification will interfere with a criminal investigation and provides the institution with a written request for the delay. However, the institution should notify its customers as soon as notification will no longer interfere with the investigation.

1. Sensitive Customer Information

Under the Guidelines, an institution must protect against unauthorized access to or use of customer information that could result in substantial harm or inconvenience to any customer. Substantial harm or inconvenience is most likely to result from improper access to *sensitive customer information* because this type of information is most likely to be misused, as in the commission of identity theft. For purposes of this Guidance, *sensitive customer information* means a customer's name, address, or telephone number, in conjunction with the customer's social security number, driver's license number, account number, credit or debit card number, or a personal identification number or password that would permit access to the customer's account. *Sensitive customer information* also includes any combination of components of customer information that would allow someone to log onto or access the customer's account, such as user name and password or password and account number.

2. Affected Customers

If a financial institution, based upon its investigation, can determine from its logs or other data precisely which customers' information has been improperly accessed, it may limit notification to those customers with regard to whom the institution determines that misuse of their information has occurred or is reasonably possible. However, there may be situations where the institution determines that a group of files has been accessed improperly, but is unable to identify which specific customers' information has been accessed. If the circumstances of the unauthorized access lead the institution to determine that misuse of the information is reasonably possible, it should notify all customers in the group.

---

12 An institution's obligation to file a SAR is set out in the Agencies' SAR regulations and Agency guidance. *See* 12 CFR 21.11 (national banks, Federal branches and agencies); 12 CFR 208.62 (State member banks); 12 CFR 211.5(k) (Edge and agreement corporations); 12 CFR 211.24(f) (uninsured State branches and agencies of foreign banks); 12 CFR 225.4(f) (bank holding companies and their nonbank subsidiaries); 12 CFR part 353 (State non-member banks); and 12 CFR 563.180 (savings associations). National banks must file SARs in connection with computer intrusions and other computer crimes. *See* OCC Bulletin 2000-14, "Infrastructure Threats—Intrusion Risks" (May 15, 2000); Advisory Letter 97-9, "Reporting Computer Related Crimes" (November 19, 1997) (general guidance still applicable though instructions for new SAR form published in 65 FR 1229, 1230 (January 7, 2000)). *See also* Federal Reserve SR 01-11, Identity Theft and Pretext Calling, Apr. 26, 2001; SR 97-28, Guidance Concerning Reporting of Computer Related Crimes by Financial Institutions, Nov. 6, 1997; FDIC FIL 48-2000, Suspicious Activity Reports, July 14, 2000; FIL 47-97, Preparation of Suspicious Activity Reports, May 6, 1997; OTS CEO Memorandum 139, Identity Theft and Pretext Calling, May 4, 2001; CEO Memorandum 126, New Suspicious Activity Report Form, July 5, 2000; http://www.ots.treas.gov/BSA (for the latest SAR form and filing instructions required by OTS as of July 1, 2003).

13 *See* FFIEC Information Technology Examination Handbook, Information Security Booklet, Dec. 2002, pp. 68–74.

B. Content of Customer Notice

1. Customer notice should be given in a clear and conspicuous manner. The notice should describe the incident in general terms and the type of customer information that was the subject of unauthorized access or use. It also should generally describe what the institution has done to protect the customers' information from further unauthorized access. In addition, it should include a telephone number that customers can call for further information and assistance.[14] The notice also should remind customers of the need to remain vigilant over the next twelve to twenty-four months, and to promptly report incidents of suspected identity theft to the institution. The notice should include the following additional items, when appropriate:

   a. A recommendation that the customer review account statements and immediately report any suspicious activity to the institution;

   b. A description of fraud alerts and an explanation of how the customer may place a fraud alert in the customer's consumer reports to put the customer's creditors on notice that the customer may be a victim of fraud;

   c. A recommendation that the customer periodically obtain credit reports from each nationwide credit reporting agency and have information relating to fraudulent transactions deleted;

   d. An explanation of how the customer may obtain a credit report free of charge; and

   e. Information about the availability of the FTC's online guidance regarding steps a consumer can take to protect against identity theft. The notice should encourage the customer to report any incidents of identity theft to the FTC, and should provide the FTC's Web site address and toll-free telephone number that customers may use to obtain the identity theft guidance and report suspected incidents of identity theft.[15]

2. The Agencies encourage financial institutions to notify the nationwide consumer reporting agencies prior to sending notices to a large number of customers that include contact information for the reporting agencies.

C. Delivery of Customer Notice

Customer notice should be delivered in any manner designed to ensure that a customer can reasonably be expected to receive it. For example, the institution may choose to contact all customers affected by telephone or by mail, or by electronic mail for those customers for whom it has a valid e-mail address and who have agreed to receive communications electronically.

[63 Fed. Reg. 55484, 55486 (Oct. 15, 1998) (Effective Date: Oct. 15, 1998); 64 Fed. Reg. 66706 (Nov. 29, 1999) (Effective Date: Nov. 29, 1999); 66 Fed. Reg. 8640 (Feb. 1, 2001) (Effective Date: July 1, 2001); 69 Fed. Reg. 77610 (Dec. 28, 2004) (Effective Date: July 1, 2005); 70 Fed. Reg. 15736 (Mar. 29, 2005) (Effective Date: Mar. 29, 2005); 71 Fed. Reg. 5780 (Feb. 3, 2006) (Effective Date: Feb. 3, 2006)]

G.3.5 National Credit Union Administration Regulations

TITLE 12—BANKS AND BANKING

* * *

CHAPTER VII—NATIONAL CREDIT UNION ADMINISTRATION

SUBCHAPTER A—REGULATIONS AFFECTING CREDIT UNIONS

* * *

PART 748—SECURITY PROGRAM, REPORT OF CRIME AND CATASTROPHIC ACT AND BANK SECRECY ACT COMPLIANCE

748.0 Security program.

* * *

Appendix A to Part 748 Guidelines for Safeguarding Member Information

Appendix B to Part 748 Guidance on Response Programs for Unauthorized Access to Member Information and Member Notice

---

CHAPTER VII—NATIONAL CREDIT UNION ADMINISTRATION

SUBCHAPTER A—REGULATIONS AFFECTING CREDIT UNIONS

* * *

PART 748—SECURITY PROGRAM, REPORT OF CRIME AND CATASTROPHIC ACT AND BANK SECRECY ACT COMPLIANCE

12 C.F.R. § 748.0 Security program.

(a) Each federally insured credit union will develop a written security program within 90 days of the effective date of insurance.

(b) The security program will be designed to:

(1) Protect each credit union office from robberies, burglaries, larcenies, and embezzlement;

(2) Ensure the security and confidentiality of member records, protect against the anticipated threats or hazards to the security or integrity of such records, and protect against unauthorized access

---

14 The institution should, therefore, ensure that it has reasonable policies and procedures in place, including trained personnel, to respond appropriately to customer inquiries and requests for assistance.

15 Currently, the FTC Web site for the ID Theft brochure and the FTC Hotline phone number are *http://www.consumer.gov/idtheft* and 1-877-IDTHEFT. The institution may also refer customers to any materials developed pursuant to section 151(b) of the FACT Act (educational materials developed by the FTC to teach the public how to prevent identity theft).

to or use of such records that could result in substantial harm or serious inconvenience to a member;

(3) Respond to incidents of unauthorized access to or use of member information that could result in substantial harm or serious inconvenience to a member;

(4) Assist in the identification of persons who commit or attempt such actions and crimes, and

(5) Prevent destruction of vital records, as defined in 12 CFR part 749.

(c) Each Federal credit union, as part of its information security program, must properly dispose of any consumer information the Federal credit union maintains or otherwise possesses, as required under § 717.83 of this chapter.

[53 Fed. Reg. 4845 (Feb. 18, 1988) (Effective Date: Feb. 10, 1988); 66 Fed. Reg. 8161 (Jan. 30, 2001) (Effective Date: July 1, 2001); 69 Fed. Reg. 69269 (Nov. 29, 2004) (Effective Date: Dec. 29, 2004); 70 Fed. Reg. 22763 (May 2, 2005) (Effective Date: June 1, 2005)]

* * *

12 C.F.R. Appendix A to Part 748—Guidelines for Safeguarding Member Information

TABLE OF CONTENTS

I. Introduction
  A. Scope
  B. Definitions
II. Guidelines for Safeguarding Member Information
  A. Information Security Program
  B. Objectives
III. Development and Implementation of Member Information Security Program
  A. Involve the Board of Directors
  B. Assess Risk
  C. Manage and Control Risk
  D. Oversee Service Provider Arrangements
  E. Adjust the Program
  F. Report to the Board
  G. Implement the Standards

I. INTRODUCTION

The Guidelines for Safeguarding Member Information (Guidelines) set forth standards pursuant to sections 501 and 505(b), codified at 15 U.S.C. 6801 and 6805(b), of the Gramm-Leach-Bliley Act. These Guidelines provide guidance standards for developing and implementing administrative, technical, and physical safeguards to protect the security, confidentiality, and integrity of member information. These Guidelines also address standards with respect to the proper disposal of consumer information pursuant to sections 621(b) and 628 of the Fair Credit Reporting Act (15 U.S.C. 1681s(b) and 1681w).

A. *Scope.* The Guidelines apply to member information maintained by or on behalf of federally-insured credit unions. Such entities are referred to in this appendix as "the credit union." These Guidelines also apply to the proper disposal of consumer information by such entities.

B. *Definitions.* 1. *In general.* Except as modified in the Guidelines or unless the context otherwise requires, the terms used in these Guidelines have the same meanings as set forth in 12 CFR part 716.

2. For purposes of the Guidelines, the following definitions apply:

a. *Consumer information* means any record about an individual, whether in paper, electronic, or other form, that is a consumer report or is derived from a consumer report and that is maintained or otherwise possessed by or on behalf of the credit union for a business purpose. Consumer information also means a compilation of such records. The term does not include any record that does not identify an individual.

b. *Consumer report* has the same meaning as set forth in the Fair Credit Reporting Act, 15 U.S.C. 1681a(d). The meaning of consumer report is broad and subject to various definitions, conditions and exceptions in the Fair Credit Reporting Act. It includes written or oral communications from a consumer reporting agency to a third party of information used or collected for use in establishing eligibility for credit or insurance used primarily for personal, family or household purposes, and eligibility for employment purposes. Examples include credit reports, bad check lists, and tenant screening reports.

c. *Member* means any member of the credit union as defined in 12 CFR 716.3(n).

d. *Member information* means any records containing nonpublic personal information, as defined in 12 CFR 716.3(q), about a member, whether in paper, electronic, or other form, that is maintained by or on behalf of the credit union.

e. *Member information system* means any method used to access, collect, store, use, transmit, protect, or dispose of member information.

f. *Service provider* means any person or entity that maintains, processes, or otherwise is permitted access to member information through its provision of services directly to the credit union.

II. STANDARDS FOR SAFEGUARDING MEMBER INFORMATION

A. *Information Security Program.* A comprehensive written information security program includes administrative, technical, and physical safeguards appropriate to the size and complexity of the credit union and the nature and scope of its activities. While all parts of the credit union are not required to implement a uniform set of policies, all elements of the information security program must be coordinated.

B. *Objectives.* A credit union's information security program should be designed to: ensure the security and confidentiality of member information; protect against any anticipated threats or hazards to the security or integrity of such information; protect against unauthorized access to or use of such information that could result in substantial harm or inconvenience to any member; and ensure the proper disposal of member information and consumer information. Protecting confidentiality includes honoring members' requests to opt out of disclosures to nonaffiliated third parties, as described in 12 CFR 716.1(a)(3).

III. DEVELOPMENT AND IMPLEMENTATION OF MEMBER INFORMATION SECURITY PROGRAM

A. *Involve the Board of Directors.* The board of directors or an appropriate committee of the board of each credit union should:

1. Approve the credit union's written information security policy and program; and

2. Oversee the development, implementation, and maintenance of the credit union's information security program, including assigning specific responsibility for its implementation and reviewing reports from management.

B. *Assess Risk.* Each credit union should:

1. Identify reasonably foreseeable internal and external threats that could result in unauthorized disclosure, misuse, alteration, or destruction of member information or member information systems;

2. Assess the likelihood and potential damage of these threats, taking into consideration the sensitivity of member information; and

3. Assess the sufficiency of policies, procedures, member information systems, and other arrangements in place to control risks.

C. *Manage and Control Risk.* Each credit union should:

1. Design its information security program to control the identified risks, commensurate with the sensitivity of the information as well as the complexity and scope of the credit union's activities. Each credit union must consider whether the following security measures are appropriate for the credit union and, if so, adopt those measures the credit union concludes are appropriate:

a. Access controls on member information systems, including controls to authenticate and permit access only to authorized individuals and controls to prevent employees from providing member information to unauthorized individuals who may seek to obtain this information through fraudulent means;

b. Access restrictions at physical locations containing member information, such as buildings, computer facilities, and records storage facilities to permit access only to authorized individuals;

c. Encryption of electronic member information, including while in transit or in storage on networks or systems to which unauthorized individuals may have access;

d. Procedures designed to ensure that member information system modifications are consistent with the credit union's information security program;

e. Dual controls procedures, segregation of duties, and employee background checks for employees with responsibilities for or access to member information;

f. Monitoring systems and procedures to detect actual and attempted attacks on or intrusions into member information systems;

g. Response programs that specify actions to be taken when the credit union suspects or detects that unauthorized individuals have gained access to member information systems, including appropriate reports to regulatory and law enforcement agencies; and

h. Measures to protect against destruction, loss, or damage of member information due to potential environmental hazards, such as fire and water damage or technical failures.

2. Train staff to implement the credit union's information security program.

3. Regularly test the key controls, systems and procedures of the information security program. The frequency and nature of such tests should be determined by the credit union's risk assessment. Tests should be conducted or reviewed by independent third parties or staff independent of those that develop or maintain the security programs.

4. Develop, implement, and maintain, as part of its information security program, appropriate measures to properly dispose of member information and consumer information in accordance with the provisions in paragraph III.

D. *Oversee Service Provider Arrangements.* Each credit union should:

1. Exercise appropriate due diligence in selecting its service providers;

2. Require its service providers by contract to implement appropriate measures designed to meet the objectives of these guidelines; and

3. Where indicated by the credit union's risk assessment, monitor its service providers to confirm that they have satisfied their obligations as required by paragraph D.2. As part of this monitoring, a credit union should review audits, summaries of test results, or other equivalent evaluations of its service providers.

E. *Adjust the Program.* Each credit union should monitor, evaluate, and adjust, as appropriate, the information security program in light of any relevant changes in technology, the sensitivity of its member information, internal or external threats to information, and the credit union's own changing business arrangements, such as mergers and acquisitions, alliances and joint ventures, outsourcing arrangements, and changes to member information systems.

F. *Report to the Board.* Each credit union should report to its board or an appropriate committee of the board at least annually. This report should describe the overall status of the information security program and the credit union's compliance with these guidelines. The report should discuss material matters related to its program, addressing issues such as: risk assessment; risk management and control decisions; service provider arrangements; results of testing; security breaches or violations and management's responses; and recommendations for changes in the information security program.

G. *Implement the Standards.*

1. *Effective date.* Each credit union must implement an information security program pursuant to the objectives of these Guidelines by July 1, 2001.

2. *Two-year grandfathering of agreements with service providers.* Until July 1, 2003, a contract that a credit union has entered into with a service provider to perform services for it or functions on its behalf satisfies the provisions of paragraph III.D., even if the contract does not include a requirement that the servicer maintain the security and confidentiality of member information, as long as the credit union entered into the contract on or before March 1, 2001.

3. *Effective date for measures relating to the disposal of consumer information.* Each Federal credit union must properly dispose of consumer information in a manner consistent with these Guidelines by July 1, 2005.

4. *Exception for existing agreements with service providers relating to the disposal of consumer information.* Notwithstanding the requirement in paragraph III.G.3., a Federal credit union's existing contracts with its service providers with regard to any service involving the disposal of consumer information should implement the objectives of these Guidelines by July 1, 2006.

[66 Fed. Reg. 8161 (Jan. 30, 2001) (Effective Date: July 1, 2001); 69 Fed. Reg. 69269 (Nov. 29, 2004) (Effective Date: Dec. 29, 2004)]

Appendix B to Part 748—Guidance on Response Programs for Unauthorized Access to Member Information and Member Notice

I. Background

This Guidance in the form of Appendix B to NCUA's Security Program, Report of Crime and Catastrophic Act and Bank Secrecy Act Compliance regulation,[29] interprets section 501(b) of the Gramm-Leach-Bliley Act ("GLBA") and describes response programs, including member notification procedures, that a federally insured credit union should develop and implement to address unauthorized access to or use of member information that could result in substantial harm or inconvenience to a member. The scope of, and definitions of terms used in, this Guidance are identical to those of Appendix A to Part 748 (Appendix A). For example, the term "member information" is the same term used in Appendix A, and means any record containing nonpublic personal information about a member, whether in paper, electronic, or other form, maintained by or on behalf of the credit union.

A. Security Guidelines

Section 501(b) of the GLBA required the NCUA to establish appropriate standards for credit unions subject to its jurisdiction that include administrative, technical, and physical safeguards to protect the security and confidentiality of member information. Accordingly, the NCUA amended Part 748 of its rules to require credit unions to develop appropriate security programs, and issued Appendix A, reflecting its expectation that every federally insured credit union would develop an information security program designed to:

1. Ensure the security and confidentiality of member information;

2. Protect against any anticipated threats or hazards to the security or integrity of such information; and

3. Protect against unauthorized access to or use of such information that could result in substantial harm or inconvenience to any member.

B. Risk Assessment and Controls

1. Appendix A directs every credit union to assess the following risks, among others, when developing its information security program:

a. Reasonably foreseeable internal and external threats that could result in unauthorized disclosure, misuse, alteration, or destruction of member information or member information systems;

b. The likelihood and potential damage of threats, taking into consideration the sensitivity of member information; and

c. The sufficiency of policies, procedures, member information systems, and other arrangements in place to control risks.[30]

2. Following the assessment of these risks, Appendix A directs a credit union to design a program to address the identified risks.

---

[29] 12 CFR Part 748.
[30] See 12 CFR Part 748, Appendix A, Paragraph III.B.

The particular security measures a credit union should adopt will depend upon the risks presented by the complexity and scope of its business. At a minimum, the credit union should consider the specific security measures enumerated in Appendix A,[31] and adopt those that are appropriate for the credit union, including:

a. Access controls on member information systems, including controls to authenticate and permit access only to authorized individuals and controls to prevent employees from providing member information to unauthorized individuals who may seek to obtain this information through fraudulent means;

b. Background checks for employees with responsibilities for access to member information; and

c. Response programs that specify actions to be taken when the credit union suspects or detects that unauthorized individuals have gained access to member information systems, including appropriate reports to regulatory and law enforcement agencies.[32]

C. Service Providers

Appendix A advises every credit union to require its service providers by contract to implement appropriate measures designed to protect against unauthorized access to or use of member information that could result in substantial harm or inconvenience to any member.[33]

II. Response Program

i. Millions of Americans, throughout the country, have been victims of identity theft.[34] Identity thieves misuse personal information they obtain from a number of sources, including credit unions, to perpetrate identity theft. Therefore, credit unions should take preventative measures to safeguard member information against such attempts to gain unauthorized access to the information. For example, credit unions should place access controls on member information systems and conduct background checks for employees who are authorized to access member information.[35] However, every credit union should also develop and implement a risk-based response program to address incidents of unauthorized access to member information in member information systems that occur nonetheless.[36] A response program should be a key part of a

---

[31] See Appendix A, paragraph III.C.
[32] See Appendix A, Paragraph III.C.
[33] See Appendix A, Paragraph III.B. and III.D. Further, the NCUA notes that, in addition to contractual obligations to a credit union, a service provider may be required to implement its own comprehensive information security program in accordance with the Safeguards Rule promulgated by the Federal Trade Commission ("FTC"), 12 CFR Part 314.
[34] The FTC estimates that nearly 10 million Americans discovered they were victims of some form of identify theft in 2002. *See* The Federal Trade Commission, *Identity Theft Survey Report*, (September 2003), available at *http://www.ftc.gov/os/2003/09synovatereport.pdf*.
[35] Credit unions should also conduct background checks of employees to ensure that the credit union does not violate 12 U.S.C. 1785(d), which prohibits a credit union from hiring an individual convicted of certain criminal offenses or who is subject to a prohibition order under 12 U.S.C. 1786(g).
[36] Under 12 CFR Part 748, Appendix A, a credit union's *member information systems* consists of all of the methods used to access, collect, store, use, transmit, protect, or dispose of member information, including the systems maintained by its service providers. *See* 12 CFR Part 748, Appendix A, Paragraph I.C.2.d.

credit union's information security program.[37] The program should be appropriate to the size and complexity of the credit union and the nature and scope of its activities.

ii. In addition, each credit union should be able to address incidents of unauthorized access to member information in member information systems maintained by its domestic and foreign service providers. Therefore, consistent with the obligations in this Guidance that relate to these arrangements, and with existing guidance on this topic issued by the NCUA,[38] a credit union's contract with its service provider should require the service provider to take appropriate actions to address incidents of unauthorized access to or use of the credit union's member information, including notification of the credit union as soon as possible of any such incident, to enable the institution to expeditiously implement its response program.

A. Components of a Response Program

1. At a minimum, a credit union's response program should contain procedures for the following:

a. Assessing the nature and scope of an incident, and identifying what member information systems and types of member information have been accessed or misused;

b. Notifying the appropriate NCUA Regional Director, and, in the case of state-chartered credit unions, its applicable state supervisory authority, as soon as possible when the credit union becomes aware of an incident involving unauthorized access to or use of sensitive member information as defined below.

c. Consistent with the NCUA's Suspicious Activity Report ("SAR") regulations,[39] notifying appropriate law enforcement authorities, in addition to filing a timely SAR in situations involving Federal criminal violations requiring immediate attention, such as when a reportable violation is ongoing;

d. Taking appropriate steps to contain and control the incident to prevent further unauthorized access to or use of member information, for example, by monitoring, freezing, or closing affected accounts, while preserving records and other evidence;[40] and

e. Notifying members when warranted.

2. Where an incident of unauthorized access to member information involves member information systems maintained by a credit union's service providers, it is the responsibility of the credit union to notify the credit union's members and regulator. However, a credit union may authorize or contract with its service provider to notify the credit union's members or regulators on its behalf.

III. Member Notice

i. Credit unions have an affirmative duty to protect their members' information against unauthorized access or use. Notifying members of a security incident involving the unauthorized access or use of the member's information in accordance with the standard set forth below is a key part of that duty.

ii. Timely notification of members is important to manage a credit union's reputation risk. Effective notice also may reduce a credit union's legal risk, assist in maintaining good member relations, and enable the credit union's members to take steps to protect themselves against the consequences of identity theft. When member notification is warranted, a credit union may not forgo notifying its customers of an incident because the credit union believes that it may be potentially embarrassed or inconvenienced by doing so.

A. Standard for Providing Notice

When a credit union becomes aware of an incident of unauthorized access to sensitive member information, the credit union should conduct a reasonable investigation to promptly determine the likelihood that the information has been or will be misused. If the credit union determines that misuse of its information about a member has occurred or is reasonably possible, it should notify the affected member as soon as possible. Member notice may be delayed if an appropriate law enforcement agency determines that notification will interfere with a criminal investigation and provides the credit union with a written request for the delay. However, the credit union should notify its members as soon as notification will no longer interfere with the investigation.

1. Sensitive Member Information

Under Part 748.0, a credit union must protect against unauthorized access to or use of member information that could result in substantial harm or inconvenience to any member. Substantial harm or inconvenience is most likely to result from improper access to *sensitive member information* because this type of information is most likely to be misused, as in the commission of identity theft.

For purposes of this Guidance, sensitive member information means a member's name, address, or telephone number, in conjunction with the member's social security number, driver's license number, account number, credit or debit card number, or a personal identification number or password that would permit access to the member's account. *Sensitive member information* also includes any combination of components of member information that would allow someone to log onto or access the member's account, such as user name and password or password and account number.

2. Affected Members

If a credit union, based upon its investigation, can determine from its logs or other data precisely which members' information has been improperly accessed, it may limit notification to those members with regard to whom the credit union determines that misuse of their information has occurred or is reasonably possible. However, there may be situations where the credit union determines that a group of files has been accessed improperly, but is unable to identify which specific member's information has been

---

37 *See* FFIEC Information Technology Examination Handbook, Information Security Booklet, (December, 2002), available at *http://www.ffiec.gov/ffiecinfobase/html_pages/ it_01.html#infosec*, for additional guidance on preventing, detecting, and responding to intrusions into financial institution computer systems.

38 *See* FFIEC Information Technology Examination Handbook, Outsourcing Technology Services Booklet, (June 2004), available at *http://www.ffiec.gov/ffiecinfobase/html_pages/it_01.html #outscouring* for additional guidance on managing outsourced relationships.

39 A credit union's obligation to file a SAR is set out in the NCUA's SAR regulations and guidance. *See* 12 CFR Part 748.1(c); NCUA Letter to Credit Unions No. 04-CU-03, Suspicious Activity Reports, March 2004; NCUA Regulatory Alert No. 04-RA-01, The Suspicious Activity Report (SAR) Activity Review—Trends, Tips, & Issues, Issue 6, November 2003, February 2004.

40 *See* FFIEC Information Technology Examination Handbook, Information Security Booklet, (December 2002), pp. 68–74.

accessed. If the circumstances of the unauthorized access lead the credit union to determine that misuse of the information is reasonably possible, it should notify all members in the group.

B. Content of Member Notice

1. Member notice should be given in a clear and conspicuous manner. The notice should describe the incident in general terms and the type of member information that was the subject of unauthorized access or use. It also should generally describe what the credit union has done to protect the members' information from further unauthorized access. In addition, it should include a telephone number that members can call for further information and assistance.[41] The notice also should remind members of the need to remain vigilant over the next twelve to twenty-four months, and to promptly report incidents of suspected identity theft to the credit union. The notice should include the following additional items, when appropriate:

    a. A recommendation that the member review account statements and immediately report any suspicious activity to the credit union;

    b. A description of fraud alerts and an explanation of how the member may place a fraud alert in the member's consumer reports to put the member's creditors on notice that the member may be a victim of fraud;

    c. A recommendation that the member periodically obtain credit reports from each nationwide credit reporting agency and have information relating to fraudulent transactions deleted;

    d. An explanation of how the member may obtain a credit report free of charge; and

    e. Information about the availability of the FTC's online guidance regarding steps a consumer can take to protect against identity theft. The notice should encourage the member to report any incidents of identity theft to the FTC, and should provide the FTC's Web site address and toll-free telephone number that members may use to obtain the identity theft guidance and report suspected incidents of identity theft.[42]

2. NCUA encourages credit unions to notify the nationwide consumer reporting agencies prior to sending notices to a large number of members that include contact information for the reporting agencies.

C. Delivery of Member Notice

Member notice should be delivered in any manner designed to ensure that a member can reasonably be expected to receive it. For example, the credit union may choose to contact all members affected by telephone or by mail, or by electronic mail for those members for whom it has a valid e-mail address and who have agreed to receive communications electronically.

[70 Fed. Reg. 22778 (May 2, 2005)]

---

41 The credit union should, therefore, ensure that it has reasonable policies and procedures in place, including trained personnel, to respond appropriately to member inquiries and requests for assistance.

42 Currently, the FTC Web site for the ID Theft brochure and the FTC Hotline phone number are *http://www.ftc.gov/idtheft* and 1-877-IDTHEFT. The credit union may also refer members to any materials developed pursuant to section 15(1)(b) of the FACT Act (educational materials developed by the FTC to teach the public how to prevent identity theft).

G.4 Sample Opt-Out Notices

This appendix section reprints the sample clauses that the FTC has designated as meeting the opt-out notice requirements of the Gramm-Leach-Bliley Act and its regulations. Regulated institutions do not have to use these clauses, however.

16 C.F.R. Part 313, App. A

Appendix A to Part 313—Sample Clauses

Financial institutions, including a group of financial holding company affiliates that use a common privacy notice, may use the following sample clauses, if the clause is accurate for each institution that uses the notice. (Note that disclosure of certain information, such as assets and income, and information from a consumer reporting agency, may give rise to obligations under the Fair Credit Reporting Act, such as a requirement to permit a consumer to opt out of disclosures to affiliates or designation as a consumer reporting agency if disclosures are made to nonaffiliated third parties.)

A-1—Categories of Information You Collect (All Institutions)

You may use this clause, as applicable, to meet the requirement of § 313.6(a)(1) to describe the categories of nonpublic personal information you collect

Sample Clause A-1

We collect nonpublic personal information about you from the following sources:

- Information we receive from you on applications or other forms;
- Information about your transactions with us, our affiliates, or others; and
- Information we receive from a consumer reporting agency.

A-2—Categories of Information You Disclose (Institutions That Disclose Outside of the Exceptions)

You may use one of these clauses, as applicable, to meet the requirement of § 313.6(a)(2) to describe the categories of nonpublic personal information you disclose. You may use these clauses if you disclose nonpublic personal information other than as permitted by the exceptions in §§ 313.13, 313.14, and 313.15.

Sample Clause A-2, Alternative 1

We may disclose the following kinds of nonpublic personal information about you:

- Information we receive from you on applications or other forms, such as [provide illustrative examples, such as "your name, address, social security number, assets, and income"];
- Information about your transactions with us, our affiliates, or others, such as [provide illustrative examples, such as "your account balance, payment history, parties to transactions, and credit card usage"]; and
- Information we receive from a consumer reporting agency, such as [provide illustrative examples, such as "your creditworthiness and credit history"].

Sample Clause A-2, Alternative 2

We may disclose all of the information that we collect, as described [describe location in the notice, such as "above" or "below"].

A-3—Categories of Information You Disclose and Parties to Whom You Disclose
(Institutions That Do Not Disclose Outside of the Exceptions)

You may use this clause, as applicable, to meet the requirements of §§ 313.6(a)(2), (3), and (4) to describe the categories of nonpublic personal information about customers and former customers that you disclose and the categories of affiliates and non-affiliated third parties to whom you disclose. You may use this clause if you do not disclose nonpublic personal information to any party, other than as permitted by the exceptions in §§ 313.14, and 313.15.

Sample Clause A-3

We do not disclose any nonpublic personal information about our customers or former customers to anyone, except as permitted by law.

A-4—Categories of Parties to Whom You Disclose
(Institutions That Disclose Outside of the Exceptions)

You may use this clause, as applicable, to meet the requirement of § 313.6(a)(3) to describe the categories of affiliates and nonaffiliated third parties to whom you disclose nonpublic personal information. You may use this clause if you disclose nonpublic personal information other than as permitted by the exceptions in §§ 313.13, 313.14, and 313.15, as well as when permitted by the exceptions in §§ 313.14, and 313.15.

Sample Clause A-4

We may disclose nonpublic personal information about you to the following types of third parties:

- Financial service providers, such as [provide illustrative examples, such as "mortgage bankers, securities broker-dealers, and insurance agents"];
- Non-financial companies, such as [provide illustrative examples, such as "retailers, direct marketers, airlines, and publishers"]; and
- Others, such as [provide illustrative examples, such as "non-profit organizations"].

We may also disclose nonpublic personal information about you to nonaffiliated third parties as permitted by law.

A-5—Service Provider/Joint Marketing Exception

You may use one of these clauses, as applicable, to meet the requirements of § 313.6(a)(5) related to the exception for service providers and joint marketers in § 313.13. If you disclose nonpublic personal information under this exception, you must describe the categories of nonpublic personal information you disclose and the categories of third parties with whom you have contracted.

Sample Clause A-5, Alternative 1

We may disclose the following information to companies that perform marketing services on our behalf or to other financial institutions with whom we have joint marketing agreements:

- Information we receive from you on applications or other forms, such as [provide illustrative examples, such as "your name, address, social security number, assets, and income"];
- Information about your transactions with us, our affiliates, or others, such as [provide illustrative examples, such as "your account balance, payment history, parties to transactions, and credit card usage"]; and
- Information we receive from a consumer reporting agency, such as [provide illustrative examples, such as "your credit-worthiness and credit history"].

Sample Clause A-5, Alternative 2

We may disclose all of the information we collect, as described [describe location in the notice, such as "above" or "below"] to companies that perform marketing services on our behalf or to other financial institutions with whom we have joint marketing agreements.

A-6—Explanation of Opt Out Right
(Institutions that Disclose Outside of the Exceptions)

You may use this clause, as applicable, to meet the requirement of § 313.6(a)(6) to provide an explanation of the consumer's right to opt out of the disclosure of nonpublic personal information to nonaffiliated third parties, including the method(s) by which the consumer may exercise that right. You may use this clause if you disclose nonpublic personal information other than as permitted by the exceptions in §§ 313.13, 313.14, and 313.15.

Sample Clause A-6

If you prefer that we not disclose nonpublic personal information about you to nonaffiliated third parties, you may opt out of those disclosures, that is, you may direct us not to make those disclosures (other than disclosures permitted by law). If you wish to opt out of disclosures to nonaffiliated third parties, you may [describe a reasonable means of opting out, such as "call the following toll-free number: (insert number)"].

A-7—Confidentiality and Security (All Institutions)

You may use this clause, as applicable, to meet the requirement of § 313.6(a)(8) to describe your policies and practices with respect to protecting the confidentiality and security of nonpublic personal information.

Sample Clause A-7

We restrict access to nonpublic personal information about you to [provide an appropriate description, such as "those employees who need to know that information to provide products or services to you"]. We maintain physical, electronic, and procedural safeguards that comply with federal regulations to guard your nonpublic personal information.

Appendix H — Summary of State Laws on Consumer Reporting, Identity Theft, Credit Repair, and Security Freezes

H.1 Introduction

This appendix provides a state-by-state analysis of state laws which affect a consumer's credit report. Most states have a state fair credit reporting statute. Over the past several years, a number of states have enacted statutes governing "credit service organizations" or "credit repair organizations," which offer to improve a consumer's credit rating or history for a fee. A few states have other provisions dealing with credit reports, the most common involving the reporting of child support debts. Increasingly, states are enacting laws intended to address the problem of identity theft, including laws that permit consumers to "freeze" or limit access to their credit report. Summaries of these state laws are included in this appendix.

While this appendix is intended to be useful as a general guide, readers are cautioned to refer to the statutory language for detail and context. Note also that this appendix only analyzes the statutory language itself, and does not include judicial interpretations of that language. Furthermore some state provisions have been preempted by the FCRA; we have noted many of these in footnotes, but readers must carefully consider the full effect of federal preemption on each particular application of state law being considered. Many provisions of state credit repair statutes are preempted by the comprehensive Federal Credit Repair Organization Act, and are not detailed in this appendix. *See* § 10.7, *supra*, for discussion of FCRA preemption.

H.2 State-by-State Summaries of Laws on Credit Reports, Identity Theft, and Security Freezes

Alabama

State Identity Theft Statute: Ala. Code §§ 13A-8-190 to 13A-8-201.

Definition of Offense: Identity theft: Obtains, records or accesses identifying information that would aid in accessing financial resources, or obtaining benefits or identifying documents of victim; obtains goods or services by use of victim's identifying information; obtains identifying documents in victim's name. Trafficking in Stolen Identities: Manufactures, sells, purchases, transfers, or possesses with intent to manufacture, sell, etc., for the purpose of committing identity theft, identifying documents or identifying information of another; unauthorized possession of five identifying documents of one person, or identifying documents of five people creates an inference of intent to commit identify theft.

Victim Remedies in Criminal Case: Mandatory restitution. May include any costs incurred by the victim in correcting credit history or credit rating or costs incurred in connection with any civil or administrative proceeding to satisfy any debt, lien, or other obligations resulting from the theft, including lost wages and attorney fees. The court may order restitution for financial loss to any other person or entity that suffers a loss from the violation. Court records must be corrected if there was a conviction under a stolen name, to indicate that victim did not commit the crime. Court should make detailed order for correction of public and private records, which may then be used by victim in a civil proceeding to set aside a judgment, or submitted it to governmental entity or private business to show that accounts, etc. were not those of victim.

Special Record-Clearing Provisions: No specific provisions.

Duties of Private Entities: If consumer presents court order (see above) agency must within thirty days block all information resulting from the ID theft.[1]

Private Right of Action: Civil action against thief for greater of $5000 or treble damages, reasonable attorney fees and costs. Intentional or reckless violation by agency gives consumer cause of action for actual damages, and attorney fees, and for an injunction (reasonable procedures are a defense).

Alaska

Child Support Debts: Alaska Stat. § 25.27.273. Child support enforcement agency may report delinquencies but must immediately report payments if delinquency was reported. May only report the payment history of the obligor.

State Credit Information in Personal Insurance Statute: Alaska Stat. § 21.36.460.

Scope: Credit information used in underwriting or rating consumer for personal insurance coverage of residence or personal property, including private vehicles.

Disclosures: Insurer must disclose in writing (or in same medium

---

[1] Note that the FCRA has its own blocking provision which preempts similar state provisions, but only to the extent of the specific conduct required by the FCRA provision. *See* § 10.7, *supra*.

as application) at time of application that credit information will be obtained and used. If third party used to develop insurance score, must advise consumer that third party will be used. Insurer must notify consumer if it bases adverse action on credit report or insurance score, and advise consumer of procedure for correcting errors in credit report.[2]

Dispute Resolution: Insurer who bases adverse action on credit report or insurance score, must provide consumer with opportunity to request reconsideration.[3] If dispute resolution pursuant to federal FCRA results in corrected credit report, insurer must re-underwrite, using correct information. If refund is due, it should be for lesser of policy period or 12 months. If insurance is denied, and credit history is being disputed, pursuant to FCRA, and consumer notifies insurer, it must re-underwrite without using credit information.

Prohibited Practices: May not use an insurance score based on income, age, sex, address, zip code, census block, ethnic group, religion, marital status or nationality. May use credit information to cancel, deny, underwrite or rate personal insurance only "in combination with other substantive underwriting factors." May not use credit history to determine insurance score, if information obtained more than 90 days before policy issued. May not refuse to renew, or again underwrite or rate at renewal, based in whole or in part on credit report or insurance score. May not take adverse action based on lack of credit history, certain types of credit inquiries, collection accounts with a medical industry code, lack of a credit card or use of particular kind of credit card, credit history that has been adversely affected by former spouse (or current spouse who is party to divorce action).

Other: No relevant provisions.

Arizona

State FCRA Statute: **Ariz. Rev. Stat. Ann. §§ 44-1691 to 44-1697.**

Scope: Definitions similar to the federal law.

Purposes for Which Reports May Be Issued: Similar to federal law, except no authorization for provision to potential investors or servicers, or current insurers, in connection with the evaluation of credit or prepayment risks associated with existing credit obligations. Limited information to government agencies.

Consumer Access and Disclosure: Upon consumer request; all information and sources in addition to all persons receiving information within the last six months.

Disclosures to Consumers By User: Name of the consumer reporting agency, without consumer request.

Restriction on Content of Reports: The number of days an account has been delinquent may not be rounded up by more than four days.[4]

Consumer Disputes: Written notice to the consumer reporting agency. Thirty days to respond.[5] If disputed information inaccurate, must notify consumer and users within past six months, if requested by consumer; if agency denies information is inaccurate, must notify consumer in writing of the basis for its denial, the name and address and telephone number (if reasonably available) of any furnisher contacted; and notice that the consumer may request description of the procedures used in the reinvestigation.

Duties of Furnishers: A furnisher may not round up by more than four days the number of days an account has been delinquent.[6]

Consumer Remedies: No liability if information is correct. Refusal to correct: court costs, damages, and attorney fees. Willful or gross negligence: actual damages, attorney fees, court costs, and punitive damages.

Statute of Limitations: No relevant provisions.

Miscellaneous: A consumer may file a written statement regarding the contents of the consumer's file, and provided the statement is not frivolous or irrelevant, the agency must include the statement in future reports without charge to the consumer. The agency may limit such statements to 100 words if the agency assists the consumer in writing the statement. Intentional violations, obtaining information under false pretenses or knowingly furnishing false information, are misdemeanors.

Child Support Debts: **Ariz. Rev. Stat. Ann. § 25-512.** Child support delinquencies shall be reported to consumer reporting agencies after fifteen days advance notice and opportunity for administrative review.

State Credit Repair Statute: **Ariz. Rev. Stat. Ann. §§ 44-1701 to 44-1712.**

Covered Activities: Improving credit record or obtaining extension of credit, in return for money or other consideration.

Exemptions: Lenders licensed or authorized under federal or Arizona's law; banks and savings associations eligible for FDIC insurance; nonprofit organizations; licensed real estate brokers acting within scope of license; Arizona lawyers acting within scope of law practice; registered securities broker-dealers.

Right to Cancel? Yes (3 days).

Prohibitions: Charging before complete performance, unless organization has posted bond; charging for referring buyer to retail seller for credit on same terms as generally available to public; making or advising false statements to creditors or credit reporting agencies; making false statements about services offered; requiring buyer to waive rights.

Other Substantive Requirements: Disclosures.

Bond: Five percent of the amount of fees charged during the prior 12 months; not less than $5000 or more than $25,000; to be adjusted yearly.

Private Cause of Action: Actual damages, not less than the amount paid by buyer; attorney fees and costs; punitive damages allowed.

State Identity Theft Statute: **Ariz. Rev. Stat. Ann. § 13-2008.**

Definition of Offense: Takes, uses, sells or transfers any personal identifying information of another, without authority, with the intent to obtain or use the other person's identity for any unlawful

---

2 Note that the FCRA preempts state laws regulating the duties of persons who take an adverse action against a consumer based on that consumer's credit report. See § 10.7, *supra*.

3 Note that the FCRA preempts state laws regulating the duties of persons who take an adverse action against a consumer based on that consumer's credit report. See § 10.7, *supra*.

4 Note that for preemption purposes, this provision was not in effect on Sept. 30, 1996, and as it regulates the contents of consumer reports, it may be preempted. See § 10.7, *supra*.

5 This provision was in effect on September 30, 1996, so although it regulates the time allowed for an agency to reinvestigate a dispute, it is not preempted. See § 10.7, *supra*.

6 Most state laws concerning the duties of furnishers are now preempted. See § 10.7, *supra*.

purpose or to cause loss to a person.
Victim Remedies in Criminal Case: No specific provisions.
Special Record-Clearing Provisions: No specific provisions.
Duties of Private Entities: No specific provisions.
Private Right of Action: No specific provisions.

Other State Provisions: Ariz. Rev. Stat. §§ 20-1652 (Reasons for Cancellation) and 20-2102 to 20-2122 (Insurance Information Practices). Arizona's insurance information practices statute, which covers all kinds of personal insurance (life, health and disability, as well as residential and vehicle), requires that if an insurer plans to use an investigative consumer report, it must advise the consumer of the right to be interviewed and to receive a copy of the report. If an adverse action is based on credit-related information, insurer must disclose that the decision was based on a credit report or lack of credit history; source of consumer report, and how to get a copy; a description of up to four factors that were the primary cause for the adverse action.[7] If insurer uses information from consumer reporting agency or insurance support organization, insurer must obtain information as soon as possible; must be before issuing binder or insurance coverage. After 30 days from application, insurer may not deny or terminate based on information in consumer report. Insurer may not use the following kinds of credit history, or knowingly use an insurance score based on them: absence of credit history; collection accounts with a medical industry code; bankruptcy or lien satisfaction more than 7 years old; use of particular kind of credit card.

Arkansas

State FCRA Statute: Ark. Code Ann. §§ 4-93-101 to 4-93-104.

Scope: Consumer credit (employment, insurance, etc. not mentioned).
Purposes for Which Reports May Be Issued: Granting, denying or limiting of consumer credit.
Consumer Access and Disclosures: No relevant provisions.
Disclosures to Consumer by User: If user denies credit, the further extension of existing credit, or an increase in credit limit for personal, family or household purposes, wholly or partly because of information in a credit report, it shall so advise the consumer. Must disclose action taken, name and address of creditor and of consumer reporting agency, and consumer's Social Security number.[8]
Restrictions on Content of Reports: No relevant provisions.
Consumer Disputes: No relevant provisions.
Duties of Furnishers: No relevant provisions.
Consumer Remedies: Any person who fails to provide notification required by this chapter shall be liable to the injured party for actual damages.
Statute of Limitations: No relevant provisions.

Child Support Debts: Ark. Code Ann. § 9-14-209. Child support delinquencies shall be reported to consumer reporting agencies after seven days advance notice to obligor and an opportunity to contest accuracy of the information.

State Credit Repair Statute: Ark. Stat. Ann. §§ 4-91-101 to 4-91-109.

Covered Activities: Improving credit record or obtaining extension of credit, in return for money or other consideration.
Exemptions: Regulated and supervised lenders; mortgage lenders approved by HUD; banks and savings associations eligible for FDIC insurance; credit unions; nonprofit organizations; licensed real estate brokers acting within scope of license; Arkansas lawyers acting within scope of law practice; registered securities broker-dealers; collection agencies acting within scope of license; consumer reporting agencies.
Right to Cancel? Yes (5 days).
Prohibitions: Charging before complete performance, unless organization has posted bond; charging for referring buyer to retail seller for credit on same terms as generally available to public; making or advising false statements to creditors or credit reporting agencies; making false statements about services offered; requiring buyer to waive rights.
Other Substantive Requirements: Disclosures.
Bond: $10,000.
Private Cause of Action: Actual damages, not less than amount paid by buyer; attorney fees and costs; punitive damages allowed.

State Identity Theft Statute: Ark. Code Ann. § 5-37-227.

Definition of Offense: With intent to unlawfully appropriate financial resources of another to his or her own use or to the use of third party, obtains or records without authority identifying information [defined] that would assist in accessing the financial resources of the other, or accesses or attempts to access the financial resources of the other through the use of the identifying information.
Victim Remedies in Criminal Case: No specific provisions.
Special Record-Clearing Provisions: No specific provisions.
Duties of Private Entities: No specific provisions.
Private Right of Action: Violation is a deceptive trade practice, within the meaning of Ark. Code Ann. § 4-88-101.

State Credit Information in Personal Insurance Statute: Ark. Code Ann. §§ 23-67-401 to 23-67-415.

Scope: Use of credit information in personal (i.e., non-commercial) insurance (private vehicle, boat, or recreational vehicle, homeowners, including mobile home, noncommercial fire).
Disclosures: Must disclose to consumer in writing (or same medium as application) at time of application if credit information will be used. In case of adverse action, must explain reasons and provide notification in accordance with federal FCRA (including source of credit report, and dispute resolution procedure).[9]
Dispute Resolution: On consumer's written request, insurer must re-rate or re-underwrite based on corrected consumer report or recalculated credit score. (Not more than once in 12 months.)
Prohibited Practices: May not base adverse action solely on credit information, without "other applicable underwriting factor" independent of credit information and not expressly prohibited; take

---

7 Note that the FCRA preempts state laws regulating the duties of persons who take an adverse action against a consumer based on that consumer's credit report. See § 10.7, *supra*.

8 Note that the FCRA allows the consumer to request that the agency truncate the consumer's Social Security number, and provides that it preempts state law, but only to the extent of the specific conduct required by the FCRA provision. See § 10.7, *supra*.

9 Note that the FCRA preempts state laws regulating the duties of persons who take an adverse action against a consumer based on that consumer's credit report. See § 10.7, *supra*.

adverse action against consumer solely because he or she does not have a credit card. Absence of credit information or inability to calculate credit score must be treated as neutral, unless insurer can show that the absence or inability relates to the risk for insurer. May not use credit score that was calculated using income, gender, address, zip code, ethnic group, religion, marital status or nationality. May not base adverse action on credit report or credit score issued or calculated more than 90 days before date policy issued or renewed. If credit information used, insurer must recalculate score or obtain new report every 36 months. May not count as negative factor medical collection accounts, and certain kinds of credit inquiries.

Other: Insurers who use credit scores must file their scoring models with state Insurance Department.

California

State FCRA Statute: Cal. Civ. Code §§ 1785.1 to 1787.3 (West).

Scope: Detective agencies may be excluded. (*See* § 1785.4)

Purposes for Which Reports May Be Issued: Similar to the federal law, and may be issued for rental of a dwelling and insurance claims settlements. No express authorization, however, for provision to potential investors or servicers, or current insurers, in connection with the evaluation of the credit or repayment risks associated with existing credit obligations. Agencies must match at least three pieces of identifying information in a consumer's file with information provided by proposed retail seller users before providing a report, and retail sellers must certify that they require photo identification from all who apply for credit in person. Agencies must keep a record of the purposes of the report as stated by the user. Consumers must be given the opportunity to opt out of prescreened lists.[10]

Consumer Access and Disclosure: Similar to the federal law, except all information in file must be disclosed. The agency may charge up to an $8 preparation fee. Notice or disclosure is required only to those consumers who have mailing addresses in California. Upon request, agency must disclose all recipients of the report within a twelve month period (or two years, if for employment purposes) § 1785.10(d). For an investigative consumer report, agency must disclose all recipients within three years § 1786.10(c). If a credit score is used the agency must, upon request, disclose the score, the key factors used to determine it, and related information as defined by § 1785.15.1.[11] The agency may charge a reasonable fee to provide this information. If security alert is placed, agency must supply consumer, upon request, with free copy of report at expiration of 90 day alert period. § 1785.11.3. If a consumer provides a copy of a police report dealing with identity theft, the agency must provide monthly credit reports (up to 12) free.

Disclosures to Consumers By User: Similar to the federal law. The user, if requested, may ask the agency to investigate inaccuracies. Insurers, landlords, and employers must inform a consumer of a request for an investigative report no later than three days after the report request. A user for employment purposes must disclose to the consumer before requesting a report, and offer the consumer a free copy of the report. A lender who uses credit scores must disclose the score and the key factors used to determine it to the consumer. The statute prescribes a form of notice to home loan applicants if credit scores are used. A contractual provision that forbids a lender to disclose the credit scores furnished by an agency is void.

Restrictions on Content of Reports:[12] Similar to federal law, and criminal records more than seven years old or where offense pardoned or no conviction obtained. Inquiries resulting from credit transactions not initiated by a consumer. Unlawful detainer (eviction) actions where the defendant is the prevailing party or the action is settled. Medical information reported to creditors or employers without a consumer's consent. Liens or encumbrances, including *lis pendens*, which have a court order with them striking the lien or encumbrance because against the property of a public officer or employee.[13] Must delete from the file any inquiries for credit reports based on applications for credit initiated as a result of identity theft. Cal. Civ. Code § 1785.16.1. Requires certain precautions by users of consumer reports to prevent identity theft (i.e., further checking if applicant's address doesn't agree with address in credit report, or if some information in credit report is blocked because of reported identity theft). Cal. Civ. Code § 1785.20.3.

Consumer Disputes: Similar to the federal law except 30 business days to reinvestigate. In addition, an agency must notify a consumer if information reinserted or the agency refuses to (re)investigate. If a consumer files a police report alleging that consumer's personal identification information is being used without consumer's consent, agency must block any information in consumer's file which consumer alleges appears on report due to illegal usage and must notify furnishers.[14] A creditor may not sell a consumer's debt if the information regarding that debt is blocked pursuant to this section, or if consumer has provided sufficient information to creditor concerning the identity theft. A consumer may place a "security alert" on his or her account, by notifying the reporting agency that the consumer's identity may have been used without consent to fraudulently obtain goods or services.[15] The agency must have a toll-free number, available 24 hours per day, to receive requests for security alerts, and must place an alert in a consumers account within five business days of the request. The agency must notify all who request credit information on a consumer that a security alert is in place. The alert remains in place for 90 days, and may be renewed at the consumer's request. (Cal. Civ. Code

---

10 State laws regarding the use of prescreened reports are preempted. *See* § 10.7, *supra*.

11 Note that the FCRA requires certain disclosures to be made in connection with credit scores, and preempts similar state provisions; however, this California provision was specifically exempted from preemption. *See* § 10.7, *supra*.

12 Most of these various stricter definitions of information which may not under California law be contained in a consumer report were in effect on Sept. 30, 1996, and therefore, although they regulate the contents of consumer reports and might otherwise be, they are not preempted. *See* § 10.7, *supra*.

13 Note that for preemption purposes, this provision was not in effect on Sept. 30, 1996, and therefore may be preempted by 15 U.S.C. § 1681c. *See* § 10.7, *supra*.

14 Note that the FCRA has its own blocking provision which preempts similar state provisions, but only to the extent of the specific conduct required by the FCRA provision. *See* § 10.7, *supra*.

15 Note that the FCRA has its own fraud alert provision which preempts similar state provisions, but only to the extent of the specific conduct required by the FCRA provision. *See* § 10.7, *supra*.

§ 1785.11.1) A consumer may also place a "security freeze" on his or account, which forbids the agency from releasing credit information without the consumer's specific consent, including the use of a "unique identification number" that the agency must assign when it implements the freeze. (Certain exceptions, mainly for tax and law enforcement.) Cal. Civ. Code § 1785.11.2.

Duties of Furnishers: A furnisher of information must investigate disputed information upon notice of dispute by a consumer reporting agency. If a dispute remains after reinvestigation by the consumer reporting agency, the consumer may demand that the furnisher of the information correct the disputed information. A creditor must notify the consumer when first furnishing negative credit information to a consumer reporting agency.[16]

Consumer Remedies: Similar to the federal law; in addition, prevailing plaintiffs get court costs and reasonable attorney fees, and debt collector defendants get reasonable attorney fees for actions brought in bad faith by consumers. Negligence can result in damages for loss of wages and for pain and suffering. A willful violation results in punitive damages of $100 to $5000 per violation. Injunctions and class actions can result in punitive damages. Civil fines of $2500 for willfully obtaining or using a report without a legitimate purpose. A credit card issuer knowingly communicating false information about a cardholder may be liable for three times actual damages, court costs, and attorney fees. Cal. Civ. Code § 1747.70. For statutory violations by reporting agency, with regard to investigative reports: greater of actual damages or (except in case of class action) $10,000, costs and attorney fees. Punitive damages for grossly negligent or willful violations. Cal. Civ. Code § 1786.50. Non-government creditor who fails to comply with provisions regarding disclosure of reasons for credit denial, liable for actual damages, costs and attorney fees, with possible punitive damages up to $10,000 (or in a class action, lesser of $500,000 or 1% of creditor's net worth). Cal. Civ. Code § 1787.3. No liability if creditor acts in accordance with Federal Reserve Board rules, interpretations or approvals.

Statute of Limitations: Two years from violation or time of discovery but, effective July 1, 1998, not more than seven years.

Miscellaneous: The seven year limit for reporting delinquent accounts begins 180 days after delinquency. Reports of bankruptcies under Title 11 must refer to Title 11 of the Bankruptcy Code if that can be ascertained from the agency's source. Adverse information must be reported to a cosigner at the same time as to the consumer reporting agency. Prospective users who intend to extend credit through solicitation by mail must mail the extension of credit to same address as on the solicitation unless user verifies address change by such method as contacting the person solicited. This statute does not affect a consumer's ability to sue agencies, furnishers or users for defamation or invasion of privacy. A federal FCRA action will bar action under this statute for the same act or omission. Cal. Civ. Code § 1786.52.

Child Support Debts: Cal. Civ. Code § 1785.13(g) (West). A consumer reporting agency shall include in its credit reports information about overdue child or spousal support, if the information has been reported or verified by a federal, state or local governmental agency. **Cal. Fam. Code § 4701 (West).** Department of Child Support Services administers a state-wide program for monthly reporting of court-ordered child support obligations to credit reporting agencies. Before initial reporting of obligation or delinquency, department must attempt to contact obligor, and give 30 days to pay or contest the accuracy of the obligation.

State Credit Repair Statute: Cal. Civ. Code §§ 1789.10 to 1789.26 (West).

Covered Activities: Improving credit record or obtaining extension of credit, in return for money or other consideration.

Exemptions: Regulated and supervised lenders; banks and savings associations eligible for FDIC insurance; nonprofit organizations; licensed real estate brokers and proraters acting within scope of license; California lawyers acting within scope of law practice, unless an employee or direct affiliate of credit services organization; registered securities broker-dealers; consumer reporting agencies.

Right to Cancel? Yes (5 days).

Prohibitions: Charging before complete performance; failing to perform services contracted for within 6 months; charging for referring buyer to retail seller for credit on same terms as generally available to public; making or advising false statements to creditors or credit reporting agencies; advising or creating false identity for buyer to obtain new credit record; submitting a buyer's dispute to credit reporting agency without buyer's knowledge; any fraudulent or deceptive practices; making false statements about services offered; requiring buyer to waive rights.

Other Substantive Requirements: Disclosures.

Bond: $100,000.

Private Cause of Action: Injunctive relief; actual damages, not less than amount paid by buyer; attorney fees and costs; punitive damages allowed. Actions available to consumers, consumer credit agencies, or furnishers of credit information.

State Identity Theft Statute: Cal. Penal Code §§ 530.5 to 530.8 (West); Cal. Civ. Code §§ 1798.92 to 1798.97, 1785.11.1 and 1785.11.2, 1785.16(k), 1785.16.1, 1785.16.2, and 1785.20.3 (West).

Definition of Offense: Willfully obtains personal identifying information, [defined] of another person, and uses that information for any unlawful purpose including to obtain, or attempt to obtain, credit, goods, services, or medical information in the name of the other person without the consent.

Victim Remedies in Criminal Case: If person convicted under false name, court record must show that identity theft victim did not commit crime. Person who suspects he or she is victim of identity theft may initiate law enforcement investigation, receive copy of police report, and petition court for expedited determination and certification of factual innocence if identity thief has been charged with crime under victim's name. California Department of Justice must maintain a data base of identity theft victims, accessible to law enforcement, to victims, and to persons authorized by victims. Victim who wishes to be included must submit fingerprints and copy of police report.

Special Record-Clearing Provisions: If a victim of identity theft (defined in Civil Code as unauthorized use of another person's personal identifying information [defined] to obtain credit, goods, services, money, or property) is sued on an obligation resulting

---

16 California law regarding the responsibilities of furnishers of information is explicitly not preempted by federal law. 15 U.S.C. § 1681t(b)(1)(F). **However, while the substantive California statute is not preempted, courts have held that the California law providing a private right of action to enforce that prohibition is preempted.** See § 10.7, *supra*.

from the theft, victim may bring a cross claim alleging identity theft. If victim prevails, he or she is entitled to a judgment stating that the victim is not obligated on the claim, any security interest in the victim's property resulting from the claim is void and unenforceable, and an injunction restraining any collection efforts. Victim may join other claimants, and court may keep continuing jurisdiction for up to ten years, so as to deal with all claims resulting from the identity theft.

Duties of Private Entities: If victim submits copy of police report or DMV report, credit reporting agency must block all information resulting from identity theft, and must notify furnishers of that information;[17] victim has right upon request to free report each month for up to 12 consecutive months. May unblock only if block resulted from fraud by consumer, or if consumer agrees block was erroneous, or if consumer knowingly received goods or services as a result of blocked transaction. Credit reporting agency must maintain 24-hour toll-free number, to allow consumers to report identity thefts, and seek a security alert or security freeze on account and must inform victim of rights under § 1785.16(k). Alert requires agency to inform all users who request information that a security alert is in place. Freeze requires agency to release information only in response to request by the consumer. Agency must delete from file records of any inquiries based on applications for credit initiated as a result of identity theft. Creditor may not sell debt if information about debt is blocked pursuant to this section, or if consumer provides sufficient information to show identity theft.[18] Users of reports must take certain precautions against identity theft, i.e., check further if consumer's address does not agree with that in report, or if some information in credit report is blocked because of reported identity theft. If a security alert is in place, users must take specific precautions before selling goods or extending credit. Consumer may provide a telephone number, and request that he or she be called to confirm identity before any sale or extension of credit.[19] Any person who learns that an application has been made or an account opened in his or her name without authority may provide the person or entity that received the application or opened the account with a copy of a police report and a request for information. The entity must provide the victim or designated law enforcement agency with all relevant records, i.e., type of personal information used, etc.[20] Must be supplied within ten days of report.

Private Right of Action: Against user of credit report who omits required precautions, for actual damages, costs and attorney fees, and, if appropriate, punitive damages up to $30,000. Victim who brings cross-claim against one attempting to collect a debt that resulted from identity theft (see above) is entitled to actual damages, attorney fees and costs, if victim proves that notice was given—including a copy of a police report—to the claimant thirty days before filing the cross-claim. A civil penalty of up to $30,000 if claimant, after being notified of possible identity theft, pursued the claim without diligently investigating the possibility of identity theft. The provisions for cross-claim, etc. do not bar any other cause of action against the thief or anyone who used or possessed the goods, services or property obtained by the theft. Remedies under this section are cumulative to rights and remedies under other laws. Penalty of $100 per day, plus reasonable attorney fees, for entity that fails to provide records to victim or law enforcement within ten days, as required by Penal Code § 530.8. Statute of limitations, 4 years from date when consumer knew, or in the exercise of reasonable diligence should have known, of facts giving rise to cause of action.

Other State Provisions: Cal. Civ. Code § 1785.13(c), (e) (West). If a bankruptcy is reported, the report must specify the chapter of the Bankruptcy Act. If an open-end credit account was closed by the consumer, the report must say so. **Cal. Ins. Code §§ 791.02, 791.04, 791.07 (West)**. The insurance information practices statute, which regulates all use of personal information in insurance, requires an insurer who seeks to use an investigative consumer report to advise the consumer of the right to be interviewed and to receive a copy of the report.

Security Freeze Laws: Cal. Civ. Code §§ 1785.11.2 to 1785.11.6 (West).

Scope: Any consumer.

Procedure: Request in writing by certified mail to consumer reporting agency; supply identification.

Entities covered: Consumer reporting agencies; some exceptions specified.

Duties of covered entities: Upon consumer requests, shall require proper identification of requesting party and provide notice, as specified, of process of placing and temporarily lifting a security freeze; within 10 business days of placing the freeze, shall send a written confirmation of the security freeze to the consumer and a unique personal identification number or password, other than the consumer's Social Security number, to be used for the release of the credit report.

Time periods: For application of freeze: no later than five business days after receiving written request. For written confirmation of the security freeze to the consumer: within 10 business days of placing the freeze. For temporary suspension of freeze: no later than three business days after receiving the request. For written confirmation of changes to file: within 30 days of the change to file.

Procedure for lifting freeze: With request to agency in manner arranged by agency, consumer is to provide: Proper identification; personal identification number or password; notice of time period if a temporary suspension of freeze.

Freeze not applicable to: Existing creditors or specified various government agencies.

Fees: A fee may be charged of no more than ten dollars ($10) for each freeze, removal of the freeze, or temporary lifting of the freeze; not more than $12 for a temporary suspension of a freeze for a specific party. No fee allowed for victim of identity theft.

Enforcement: Civil penalties, no more than $2500, and attorney fees. § 1785.11.19.

---

17 Note that the FCRA has its own blocking provision which preempts similar state provisions, but only to the extent of the specific conduct required by the FCRA provision. See § 10.7, *supra*.

18 Note that the FCRA has its own provision prohibiting the sale or transfer of an identity theft debt and that it preempts state law, but only to the extent of the specific conduct required by the FCRA provision. See § 10.7, *supra*.

19 Note that the FCRA has its own fraud alert provision which imposes duties on users before they extend credit and which preempts similar state provisions, but only to the extent of the specific conduct required by the FCRA provision. See § 10.7, *supra*.

20 Note that the FCRA has its own transaction information provision that may preempt this sort of state provision. See § 10.7, *supra*.

Colorado

State FCRA Statute: Colo. Rev. Stat. §§ 12-14.3-101 to 12.14.3-109.

Scope: Same as the federal law.

Purposes for Which Reports May Be Issued: Same as the federal law, except that use for insurance underwriting requires prior notice to consumer.

Consumer Access and Disclosure: Upon request by consumer: (1) All information in its files; (2) Names of persons requesting reports within previous twelve months; (3) A toll-free number for use in resolving disputes submitted in writing to a consumer reporting agency which operates nationwide. No fee for first report requested by consumer each year;[21] (4) Information as to credit scoring § 12-14.3-104.3.[22] Agency must notify consumer once per year of right to free report, if agency has either (1) received eight credit inquiries on consumer or (2) received a report that would add negative information to consumer's file. The disclosures may be given in a form letter if it advises the consumer of the number and type of events, and includes a notice or separate form by which the consumer may request a free copy of her credit report.

Disclosures to Consumer by User: A person who intends to use credit-scoring information in connection with the underwriting or rating of the insurance must notify the consumer in writing or in the same medium used in the application of insurance.

Restrictions on Content of Reports: Similar to federal law, and criminal records more than seven years old.[23] See § 12-14.3-105.3.

Consumer Disputes: Same as the federal law, but consumer reporting agency must reinvestigate within thirty days and must correct reports within five days after it receives corrections from furnisher.

Duties of Furnishers: No relevant provisions.

Consumer Remedies: Disputes may be submitted to court or binding arbitration after attempt made to resolve with consumer reporting agency under Act's procedures. Willful violations: three times actual damages or $1000 per inaccurate entry disputed by consumer, whichever is greater, reasonable attorney fees and costs. Negligent violations: actual damages or $1000 per inaccurate entry disputed by consumer which affects consumer's creditworthiness, whichever is greater, reasonable attorney fees and costs. If negligent violation does not affect consumer's creditworthiness, minimum damages are limited to $1000 for all inaccurate entries. No liability for negligent violations if corrected within thirty days of notice from consumer. If consumer's file remains uncorrected ten days after entry of any judgment for damages, additional penalty of $1000 per day per inaccurate entry available, until inaccurate entry corrected.

Miscellaneous: Agency shall not provide users with names of others who have requested consumer's file or with the number of other inquiries.[24]

Child Support Debts: Colo. Rev. Stat. § 26-13-116. Child support enforcement agencies may report information on child support debts to consumer reporting agencies. Prior to furnishing such information, an agency must provide to the obligor parent advance notice containing an explanation of the obligor parent's right to contest the accuracy of the information.

State Credit Repair Statute: Colo. Rev. Stat. §§ 12-14.5-101 to 12-14.5-113.

Covered Activities: Improving credit record in return for money or other consideration.

Exemptions: Nonprofit organizations; Colorado lawyers acting within scope of law practice.

Right to Cancel? Yes (5 days).

Prohibitions: Charging before complete performance; making or advising false statements to creditors or credit reporting agencies; making false statements about services offered; advising buyer to request credit agency to verify credit report information, unless buyer states in writing belief and specific basis for belief that such information is inaccurate; requiring buyer to waive rights.

Other Substantive Requirements: Disclosures.

Bond: No relevant provisions.

Private Cause of Action: Actual damages, not less than amount paid by consumer; attorney fees and costs; twice actual damages if finding of willfulness.

State Identity Theft Statute: Colo. Rev. Stat. §§ 18-5-901 to 18-5-905.

Definition of Offense: Obtains by fraud, theft, or other criminal act personal identifying information in order to obtain credit, goods, services, or moneys in consumer's name.

Victim's Remedies in Criminal Case: No specific provision.

Special Record Clearing Provisions: See Consumer Disputes under state FCRA Statute.

Duties of Private Entities: Permanently block reporting of any information included in police report or court order regarding identity theft and inform consumer of block.[25] § 12-14.3-106.5.

Private Right of Action: Right to court action as provided by federal FCRA or right to submit to binding arbitration, § 12-14.3-107. For remedies for failure to block information, see *Consumer Remedies* under state FCRA Statute.

Other State Provisions: Colo. Rev. Stat. § 5-5-111(3). Creditor may not report cosigner's liability to consumer reporting agency without providing notice of right to cure as specified in statute. **Colo. Rev. Stat. Ann. § 10-4-616** regulates the use of credit reports in personal automobile insurance. Applicants and policy holders must be notified if credit information is to be used in underwriting or rating. Upon consumer's request, insurer must explain the "significant characteristics" of the credit information that will impact the insurance score. If adverse action is based on credit information, the insurer must provide notice as required by federal

---

21 Although the FCRA preempts state laws with respect to the frequency of the right to free reports, the Act specifically exempts this Colorado provision from preemption. *See* § 10.7, *supra*.

22 Note that the FCRA requires certain disclosures to be made in connection with credit scores, and generally preempts similar state provisions. However, the Act specifically exempts this Colorado provision from preemption. *See* § 10.7, *supra*.

23 This obsolescence standard was not in effect on Sept. 30, 1996, and therefore it is probably preempted. *See* § 10.7, *supra*.

24 Note that for preemption purposes, this provision was not in effect on Sept. 30, 1996. *See* § 10.7, *supra*.

25 Note that the FCRA has its own blocking provision which preempts similar state provisions, but only to the extent of the specific conduct required by the FCRA provision. *See* § 10.7, *supra*.

FCRA (i.e., source of report, dispute resolution procedure, etc.).[26]

Colo. Rev. Stat. § 6-1-715 restricts use or dissemination of Social Security number. **Colo. Rev. Stat. § 6-1-716** requires owner or licensor of computerized data to notify resident of any unauthorized acquisition of personal information upon discovery of security breach.

Security Freeze Laws: Colo. Rev. Stat. §§ 12-14.3-106.6 to 12-14.3-106.9.

Scope: Any consumer.
Procedure: Request in writing by certified mail to consumer reporting agency; supply identification (defined at § 12-14.3-3-102).
Entities covered: Consumer reporting agencies; some exceptions specified.
Duties of covered entities: Upon supply identification requests, shall require proper identification of requesting party and provide notice, as specified, of process of placing and temporarily lifting a security freeze; within 10 business days of placing the freeze, shall send a written confirmation of the security freeze to the consumer and a unique personal identification number or password, other than the consumer's Social Security number, to be used for the release of the credit report.
Time periods: For application of freeze: no later than five business days after receiving written request. For written confirmation of the security freeze to the consumer: within 10 business days of placing the freeze. For temporary suspension of freeze: no later than three business days after receiving the request. For written confirmation of changes to file: within 30 days of the change to file.
Procedure for lifting freeze: Consumer is to provide with request to agency in manner arranged by agency: Proper identification; personal identification number or password; notice of time period if a temporary suspension of freeze.
Freeze not applicable to: Existing creditors for purposes of review or collection; specified various government agencies; financial agents serving purposes of underwriting, insurance, pension plans, and licensed hospitals.
Fees: No fee allowed for any consumer's first request of freeze. A fee may be charged of no more than ten dollars ($10) for each subsequent request for freeze or removal of the freeze, or temporary lifting of the freeze; not more than $12 for a temporary suspension of a freeze for a specific party.
Enforcement: Consumer has right to arbitration or civil action. § 12-14.3-107. Actual and treble damages, attorney fees, as provided in § 12-14.3-108.

Connecticut

State FCRA Statute: Conn. Gen. Stat. §§ 36a-695 to 36a-699e.

Scope: Credit for personal, family, or household purposes. Does not apply to disclosure made to federal, state, or local government officers or upon court order.
Purposes for Which Reports May Be Issued: Same as federal law, except credit transactions not initiated by the consumer, if the consumer gives agency written notice withholding consent.[27]
Consumer Access and Disclosure: Within five business days of receipt of request by consumer: (1) Nature and substance of all information in its files, including any credit score;[28] and (2) Written summary of consumer's rights under state and federal law in form substantially similar to Conn. Gen. Stat. § 36a-ag.[29] No charge if requested within 60 days after the consumer is notified of adverse action taken by a creditor; otherwise $5 maximum charge for first report each year, $7.50 for subsequent reports.
Disclosures to Consumer by User: No relevant provisions. Before taking adverse action against consumer based on credit report, user must disclose to consumer the name and address of the agency that issued the report.[30]
Restrictions on Content of Reports: No relevant provisions.
Consumer Disputes: An agency must correct an inaccuracy upon proof of error. Procedures are the same as under FCRA, but consumer reporting agency must provide consumer with its toll-free number to use in resolving dispute. If consumer reporting agency fails to meet relevant thirty or forty-five day deadline, disputed information must be deleted.
Duties of Furnishers: No relevant provisions.
Consumer Remedies: Criminal fine; cease and desist order.
Statute of Limitations: No relevant provisions.
Miscellaneous: No relevant provisions.

Child Support Debts: Conn. Gen. Stat. § 52-362d. The Department of Social Services shall report to any participating consumer reporting agency any overdue support in the amount of $1000 or more. Prior to a report, the Department must give the obligor notice and opportunity for a hearing.

State Credit Repair Statute: Conn. Gen. Stat. § 36a-700.

Covered Activities: "Credit clinics" advising or offering to modify adverse entries in credit record or rating in return for fee.
Exemptions: Credit rating agencies; nonprofit organizations; Connecticut lawyers acting within scope of law practice.
Right to Cancel? No.
Prohibitions: Charging before complete performance.
Other Substantive Requirements: Disclosures.
Bond: N/A
Private Cause of Action: A violation is a UDAP violation. Contract voidable.

State Identity Theft Statute: Conn. Gen. Stat. § 53a-129a; Conn. Gen. Stat. § 52-571h.

Definition of Offense: Intentionally, and without authority, obtains personal identifying information of another and uses that information for any unlawful purpose including, but not limited to, obtaining, or attempting to obtain, credit, goods, services or medical

---

26 Note that the FCRA preempts state laws regulating the duties of persons who take an adverse action against a consumer based on that consumer's credit report. See § 10.7, *supra*.

27 State provisions concerning prescreened lists are preempted. See § 10.7, *supra*.

28 Note that the FCRA requires certain disclosures to be made in connection with credit scores, and that provision may preempt similar state provisions. See § 10.7, *supra*.

29 State laws regarding the contents of the summary of federal rights which must be disclosed to consumers are preempted. See § 10.7, *supra*.

30 Note that the FCRA preempts state laws regulating the duties of persons who take an adverse action against a consumer based on that consumer's credit report. See § 10.7, *supra*.

Summary of State Laws on Consumer Reporting   Appx. H.2-DE

information in the name of that person.
Victim Remedies in Criminal Case: No specific provisions.
Special Record-Clearing Provisions: No specific provisions.
Duties of Private Entities: No specific provisions.
Private Right of Action: Person aggrieved by violation of 53a-129a may bring civil action for greater of treble damages or $1000, plus costs and attorney fees.

Other State Provisions: Conn. Gen. Stat. Ann. §§ 38a-976, 38a-982. The Insurance Information and Privacy Act requires an insurer that seeks to use an investigative consumer report to notify the consumer of the right to be interviewed and to receive a copy of the report.

Security Freeze Laws: Conn. Gen. Stat. §§ 36a-701, 36a-701a.

Scope: Any consumer.
Procedure: Request in writing by certified mail to credit rating agency or in other manner authorized by agency; supply identification.
Entities covered: Credit rating agencies; some exceptions specified.
Duties of covered entities: Upon consumer request shall require proper identification of requesting party and provide notice, as specified, of process of placing and temporarily lifting a security freeze; within 10 business days of placing the freeze, shall send a written confirmation of the security freeze to the consumer and a unique personal identification number or password, other than the consumer's Social Security number, to be used for the release of the credit report.
Time periods: For application of freeze: no later than five business days after receiving written request. For written confirmation of the security freeze to the consumer: within 10 business days of placing the freeze. For temporary suspension of freeze: no later than three business days after receiving the request. For written confirmation of changes to file: within 30 days of the change to file.
Procedure for lifting freeze: Consumer is to provide with request to agency in manner arranged by agency: Proper identification; personal identification number or password; notice of time period if a temporary suspension of freeze.
Freeze not applicable to: Existing creditors for purposes of review or collection; specified various government agencies; any person for the purpose of using such credit information to prescreen as provided by the federal Fair Credit Reporting Act; a credit rating agency for the sole purpose of providing a consumer with a copy of his or her credit report upon the consumer's request.
Fees: A fee may be charged of no more than ten dollars ($10) for each freeze, removal of the freeze, or temporary lifting of the freeze; not more than $12 for a temporary suspension of a freeze for a specific party.
Enforcement: None specified.

Delaware

Child Support Debts: Del. Code Ann. tit. 13, § 2217. Information regarding child support delinquencies shall be reported to consumer reporting agencies, provided that the amount of the delinquency is not less than $500 and the obligor is given notice and a period of twenty days to contest the accuracy of the information.

State Credit Repair Statute: Del. Code Ann. tit. 6, §§ 2401 to 2414.

Covered Activities: Improving credit record or obtaining extension of credit, in return for money or other consideration.
Exemptions: Regulated and supervised lenders; mortgage lenders approved by HUD; banks and savings associations eligible for FDIC insurance; credit unions; nonprofit organizations; licensed lenders, public accountants, and real estate brokers acting within scope of license; mortgage brokers not engaged in covered activities; Delaware lawyers acting within scope of law practice; registered securities broker-dealers; consumer reporting agencies.
Right to Cancel? Yes (3 days).
Prohibitions: Charging before complete performance, unless organization has posted bond; charging for referring buyer to retail seller for credit on same terms as generally available to public; making or advising false statements to creditors or credit reporting agencies; making false statements about services offered; fraudulent and deceptive practices; requiring buyer to waive rights.
Other Substantive Requirements: Disclosures.
Bond: $15,000.
Private Cause of Action: Damages, not less than amount paid by buyer; attorney fees and costs; punitive damages allowed; 4-year statute of limitations.

State Identity Theft Statute: Del. Code Ann. tit. 11, § 854.

Definition of Offense: Knowingly or recklessly obtains, produces, possesses, uses, sells, gives or transfers personal identifying information belonging or pertaining to another person without authority and with intent to use the information to commit or facilitate any crime set forth in this title [theft and related offenses], or recklessly obtains, etc. thereby knowingly or recklessly facilitating the use of the information by a third person to commit or facilitate any crime set forth in this title. (Enhanced penalties if victim is age 62 or over.)
Victim Remedies in Criminal Case: Upon conviction, court must order full restitution for monetary loss, including documented loss of wages and reasonable attorney fees, suffered by the victim.
Special Record-Clearing Provisions: No specific provisions.
Duties of Private Entities: No specific provisions.
Private Right of Action: No specific provisions.

Security Freeze Laws: Del. Code Ann. tit. 6, §§ 2201 to 2204.

Scope: Any resident consumer.
Procedure: Request in writing by certified mail or by electronic mail if available (availability required by Jan. 31, 2009) to credit rating agency or in other manner authorized by agency; supply identification.
Entities covered: Credit rating agencies; some exceptions specified.
Duties of covered entities: Upon consumer request shall require proper identification of requesting party and provide notice, as specified, of process of placing and temporarily lifting a security freeze; within 10 business days of placing the freeze, shall send a written confirmation of the security freeze to the consumer and a unique personal identification number or password, other than the consumer's Social Security number, to be used for the release of the credit report.
Time periods: For application of freeze: no later than five business days after receiving written request. For written confirmation of the security freeze to the consumer: within 10 business days of placing the freeze. For temporary suspension of freeze: no later than three business days after receiving the request (within 15 minutes of request by electronic mail or by telephone after Jan. 31, 2009). For

written confirmation of changes to file: within 30 days of the change to file.
Procedure for lifting freeze: Consumer is to provide with request to agency in manner arranged by agency: Proper identification; personal identification number or password; notice of time period if a temporary suspension of freeze.
Freeze not applicable to: Existing creditors for purposes of review or collection; specified various government agencies; any person for the purpose of using such credit information to prescreen as provided by the federal Fair Credit Reporting Act; private collection agency acting under a court order, warrant, or subpoena; companies serving purposes of underwriting, insurance, or extension of credit requested by consumer.
Fees: A fee may be charged of not more than twenty dollars ($20) for each freeze, removal of the freeze, or temporary lifting of the freeze, or for second or more reissue of new personal identification number/password.
Enforcement: Injunctive relief; civil penalties to consumer of up to $1000 per violation plus any damages available under other laws; costs and attorney fees.

District of Columbia

Child Support Debts: **D.C. Code § 46-225**. Support obligations, of $1000 or more, over thirty days past due shall be reported to consumer reporting agencies, provided that the obligor are given thirty days advance notice and an opportunity to contest in writing the accuracy of the information.

State Credit Repair Statute: **D.C. Code §§ 28-4601 to 28-4608.**

Covered Activities: Improving credit record or obtaining extension of credit, in return for money or other consideration.
Exemptions: Regulated and supervised lenders; mortgage lenders approved by HUD; banks and savings associations eligible for FDIC insurance; credit unions; nonprofit organizations; collection agency operators acting within scope of license; D.C. lawyers acting within scope of law practice; registered securities broker-dealers; consumer reporting agencies.
Right to Cancel? Yes (5 days).
Prohibitions: Charging before complete performance, unless organization has posted bond; charging for referring buyer to retail seller for credit on same terms as generally available to public; making or advising false statements to creditors or credit reporting agencies; making false statements about services offered; misuse of word "repair" to suggest ability to immediately correct credit problems; requiring buyer to waive rights.
Other Substantive Requirements: Disclosures.
Bond: $25,000.
Private Cause of Action: Actual damages, not less than amount paid by consumer; attorney fees and costs; punitive damages allowed; 3-year statute of limitations.

Florida

Child Support Debts: **Fla. Stat. § 61.1354**. Information regarding child support delinquencies shall be reported to consumer reporting agencies. Written notice to be given obligor fifteen days in advance, including notice of right to request a hearing to dispute the accuracy of the information. Notice and hearing required only for initial reporting, not for periodic release of updated information.

State Credit Repair Statute: **Fla. Stat. §§ 817.7001 to 817.706.**

Covered Activities: Improving credit record or obtaining extension of credit, in return for money or other consideration.
Exemptions: Lenders authorized under Florida or federal law; mortgage lenders approved by HUD; banks and savings associations eligible for FDIC insurance; credit unions; nonprofit organizations; licensed collection agencies and real estate brokers acting within scope of license; Florida lawyers acting within scope of law practice; registered securities broker-dealers; consumer reporting agencies.
Right to Cancel? Yes (5 days).
Prohibitions: Charging before complete performance, unless organization has posted bond; charging for referring buyer to retail seller for credit on same terms as generally available to public; making or advising false statements to creditors or credit reporting agencies; making false statements about services offered; requiring buyer to waive rights.
Other Substantive Requirements: Disclosures.
Bond: $10,000.
Private Cause of Action: Actual damages, not less than amount paid by consumer; attorney fees and costs; punitive damages allowed.

State Identity Theft Statute: **Fla. Stat. § 817.568**.

Definition of Offense: Willfully and without authorization fraudulently uses or possesses with intent to use, personal identification information of another.
Victim Remedies in Criminal Case: Restitution of out-of-pocket costs, including attorney fees incurred in clearing victim's credit history or credit rating, and costs in any civil or administrative proceeding to satisfy debts, liens or obligations of victim arising from the defendant's actions. Court may issue orders necessary to clear any public record that contains false information given in violation of this section.
Special Record-Clearing Provisions: No specific provisions.
Duties of Private Entities: No specific provisions.
Private Right of Action: No specific provisions.

State Credit Information in Personal Insurance Statute: **Fla. Stat. § 626.9741.**

Scope: Use of credit reports or credit scores for underwriting and rating personal lines motor vehicle and residential insurance.
Disclosure: Insurer must disclose at time of application, in same medium as application, if a credit report or credit score will be requested. If adverse decision based on credit report, insurer must explain reasons, and provide either a free copy of the credit report, or the name, address and toll-free number of the consumer reporting agency.[31]
Dispute Resolution: Insurer must provide means of appeal for applicant whose credit report or credit score was "unduly influenced" by dissolution of marriage, death of a spouse, or temporary loss of employment. Must complete review within ten days, and if it finds that credit information was "unduly influenced" it must

---

31 Note that the FCRA preempts state laws regulating the duties of persons who take an adverse action against a consumer based on that consumer's credit report. *See* § 10.7, *supra.*

exclude credit information or treat it as neutral, whichever is more favorable. Must establish policies to review the credit history of individual who was adversely affected by credit history at time of application or renewal. (Must do this every 2 years, or at request of insured.) May not cancel, non-renew, or require a change in payment plan as a result of this review.

Prohibited Practices: Insurer may not: request credit score based on race, color, religion, marital status, age, gender, income, national origin or place of residence; base an adverse decision solely on credit information, without considering other rating or underwriting factor; treat lack of credit history as negative factor, unless it can show that this relates to risk; base negative decision on collection account with medical industry code, or on certain types of credit inquiries.

Other: Insurer must comply with restrictions of federal FCRA and rules. Insurers must report to Office of Insurance Regulation regarding their use of credit information.

Security Freeze Laws: Fla. Stat. § 501.005.

Scope: Any consumer.

Procedure: Request in writing by certified mail to consumer reporting agency; supply identification.

Entities covered: Consumer reporting agencies; some exceptions specified.

Duties of covered entities: Upon consumer request shall require proper identification of requesting party and provide notice, as specified, of process of placing and temporarily lifting a security freeze; within 10 business days of placing the freeze, shall send a written confirmation of the security freeze to the consumer and a unique personal identification number or password, other than the consumer's Social Security number, to be used for the release of the credit report.

Time periods: For application of freeze: no later than five business days after receiving written request. For written confirmation of the security freeze to the consumer: within 10 business days of placing the freeze. For temporary suspension of freeze: no later than three business days after receiving the request. For written confirmation of changes to file: within 30 days of the change to file.

Procedure for lifting freeze: Consumer is to provide with request to agency in manner arranged by agency: Proper identification; personal identification number or password; notice of time period if a temporary suspension of freeze.

Freeze not applicable to: Existing creditors for purposes of review or collection; specified various government agencies; any person for the purpose of using such credit information to prescreen as provided by the federal Fair Credit Reporting Act; financial agents serving purposes of underwriting, insurance, or extension of credit requested by consumer.

Fees: A fee may be charged of no more than ten dollars ($10) for each freeze, removal of the freeze, or temporary lifting of the freeze, or replacement of identification number. No fee allowed for victim of identity theft or persons 65 years or older.

Enforcement: Actual damages of not less than $100 or more than $1000, costs and attorney fees. Party obtaining information under false pretenses liable to both consumer and credit reporting agency. Punitive damages allowed.

Georgia

State FCRA Statute: Ga. Code Ann. §§ 10-1-392 and 10-1-393(b)(29).

Scope: Covers consumer reporting agencies.

Purposes for Which Reports May Be Issued: No relevant provisions.

Consumer Access and Disclosure: Two free reports per year upon consumer request.[32]

Disclosures to Consumer by User: No relevant provisions.

Restrictions on Content of Reports: No relevant provisions.

Consumer Disputes: No relevant provisions.

Duties of Furnishers: No relevant provisions.

Consumer Remedies: No relevant provisions.

Statute of Limitations: No relevant provisions.

Miscellaneous: Restricts use or dissemination of Social Security number. § 10-1-393.8.

Child Support Debts: Ga. Code Ann. § 19-11-25. The Department of Human Resources shall make available information regarding the amount of overdue support by an absent parent to any consumer reporting agency upon request, if amount of overdue support exceeds $1000, and may do so when the amount is less than $1000. Information will be made available only after notice is sent to the absent parent and the absent parent has been given reasonable opportunity to contest.

State Credit Repair Statute: Ga. Code Ann. § 16-9-59.

Covered Activities: Improving credit record or obtaining extension of credit, in return for money or other consideration.

Exemptions: Lenders authorized under Georgia or federal law; banks and savings associations eligible for FDIC insurance; nonprofit organizations; licensed real estate brokers acting within scope of license; Georgia lawyers acting within scope of law practice; registered securities broker-dealers; consumer reporting agencies.

Right to Cancel? No.

Prohibitions: Owning or operating a credit repair organization.

Other Substantive Requirements: None.

Bond: N/A

Private Cause of Action: None.

State Identity Theft Statute: Ga. Code Ann. §§ 16-9-121 to 16-9-132.

Definition of Offense: Without authorization, and with intent to appropriate financial resources of or cause physical harm to another, obtains or records identifying information, or access or attempts to access financial resources through use of identifying information.

Victim Remedies in Criminal Case: Court may order restitution and may issue any order necessary to correct any public record that contains false information resulting from the actions that resulted in the conviction.

Special Record-Clearing Provisions: No specific provisions.

Duties of Private Entities: No specific provisions.

---

[32] Although the FCRA preempts state laws with respect to the frequency of the right to free reports, the Act specifically exempts this Georgia provision from preemption. See § 10.7, *supra*.

Private Right of Action: Right to court action for business or consumer victim. Individual or class consumer action for general or punitive damages, including treble damages, attorney fees, costs, injunctive relief.

Other: Administrator of Fair Business Practices Act may investigate complaints, with all the powers granted by that Act.

State Credit Information in Personal Insurance statute: Ga. Code Ann. §§ 33-24-90 to 33-24-98.

Scope: Credit information used in underwriting personal insurance (private vehicle, homeowners, including mobile home, and recreational vehicle).

Disclosures: Must disclose at time of application, in writing or same medium as application, if credit report or credit score will be used. If adverse action is based on credit information, insurer must explain reasons and provide notification as required by federal FCRA (source of information, dispute resolution procedure, etc.).[33]

Dispute Resolution: At time of renewal, consumer may request reunderwriting or rerating based on current credit report or credit score—company must warn consumer that this might result in higher or lower rate, or termination or non-renewal. If an item in a credit report is being disputed pursuant to federal FCRA, then during the 45 days after item was placed in dispute, insurer must either not use credit information, or treat credit information as neutral with respect to the disputed item(s).

Prohibited Practices: Insurer may not use insurance score calculated using income, gender, race, address, zip code, ethnic group, religion, marital status or nationality; take adverse action, or base renewal rates solely on credit information without consideration of other underwriting factors; take adverse action because consumer does not have credit card; treat absence of credit information as negative, unless it can show that this relates to risk; take adverse action based on credit report issued or insurance score calculated more than 180 days before date of issuance or renewal of policy; use credit information if it does not obtain updated credit information at least every 36 months. May not consider as negative factor collection accounts with medical industry code, or certain credit inquiries.

Other: Insurer must file scoring models with commissioner of insurance.

Guam

Child Support Debts: Guam Code Ann. tit. 5, § 34130. Child Support Enforcement Office shall report child support arrears to consumer reporting agencies where delinquency is $1000 or more; may report arrears if less. Obligors must be notified prior to release of information and informed that they have ten days to request a meeting with the head of the Child Support Enforcement Office to contest accuracy of information.

Hawaii

Child Support Debts: Haw. Rev. Stat. § 576D-6(6). Information regarding child support delinquencies shall be made available to consumer reporting agencies. Delinquent parents must be given notice and the opportunity to contest accuracy of the information prior to reporting.

State Credit Repair Statute: Haw. Rev. Stat. § 481B-12.

Covered Activities: Modifying credit record in return for money or other consideration.

Exemptions: None.

Right to Cancel? No.

Prohibitions: Charging for referring buyer to retail seller for credit on same terms as generally available to public; making or advising false statements to creditors or credit reporting agencies; making false statements about services offered. The Telemarketing Fraud Prevention Act, Haw. Stat. § 481P-3(2) forbids telemarketers to request a fee to remove derogatory information from or improve a consumer's credit record or credit history, unless the telemarketer provides the consumer with a credit report, from a credit reporting agency, showing that the promised results have been achieved. The report must have been issued at least six months after the results were achieved.

Other Substantive Requirements: None.

Bond: N/A

Private Cause of Action: Violation is UDAP violation.

Identity Theft: Haw. Rev. Stat. §§ 708-839.6 to 708-839.8.

Definition of Offense: 1st degree: makes or causes to be made a transmission of any personal information of another with the intent to facilitate the commission of certain felonies (including murder, kidnapping, extortion) or to commit first degree theft from the person whose information was used, or from another. Second degree: makes or causes to be made, etc. with intent to commit second degree theft. Third degree: same, with intent to commit third degree theft.

Victim Remedies in Criminal Case: No relevant provisions.

Special Record Clearing Provisions: No relevant provisions.

Duties of Private Entities: No relevant provisions.

Private Right of action: No relevant provisions.

Security Freeze Laws: Haw. H.B. No. 1871; Haw. Rev. Stat. §§ 26-__.

Scope: Victim of identity theft (must submit law enforcement complaint or report).

Procedure: Request in writing by certified mail to consumer reporting agency; supply identification.

Entities covered: Consumer reporting agencies; some exceptions specified.

Duties of covered entities: Upon consumer request shall require proper identification of requesting party and provide notice, as specified, of process of placing and temporarily lifting a security freeze; within 10 business days of placing the freeze, shall send a written confirmation of the security freeze to the consumer and a unique personal identification number or password, other than the consumer's Social Security number, to be used for the release of the credit report.

Time periods: For application of freeze: no later than five business days after receiving written request. For written confirmation of the security freeze to the consumer: within 10 business days of placing the freeze. For temporary suspension of freeze: no later than three business days after receiving the request. For written confirmation of changes to file: within 30 days of the change to file.

---

33 Note that the FCRA preempts state laws regulating the duties of persons who take an adverse action against a consumer based on that consumer's credit report. See § 10.7, *supra*.

Procedure for lifting freeze: Consumer is to provide with request to agency in manner arranged by agency: Proper identification; personal identification number or password; notice of time period if a temporary suspension of freeze.

Freeze not applicable to: Existing creditors for purposes of review or collection; specified various government agencies; any person acting under a court order, warrant, or subpoena; any person for the purpose of using such credit information to prescreen as provided by the federal Fair Credit Reporting Act; financial agents serving purposes of underwriting or insurance.

Fees: None specified.

Enforcement: Actual damages or damages not less than $100 or more than $1000. Party obtaining information under false pretenses liable to consumer for greater of actual damages or $1000. Punitive damages allowed. Negligent non-compliance liability is actual damages. Costs and attorney fees.

Idaho

State Credit Repair Statute: Idaho Code Ann. §§ 26-2221 to 26-2251 ("Collection Agencies" statute).

Covered Activities: Credit or debt "counselors," engaging in applying, paying, or prorating creditors or credit counseling for compensation. § 26-2223(6), (7).

Exemptions: Mortgage lenders approved by HUD; banks and savings associations eligible for FDIC insurance; licensed mortgage companies and real estate brokers acting within scope of license; any governmental body; abstract and title companies doing an escrow business; Idaho lawyers acting within scope of law practice.

Right to Cancel? No.

Prohibitions: Deceptive dealings. Only a non-profit organization may be licensed as a credit counselor. § 26-2222(11).

Other Substantive Requirements: N/A

Bond: $15,000.

Private Cause of Action: None.

State Identity Theft Statute: Idaho Code Ann. §§ 18-3126 and 18-3128; §§ 28-51-101 and 28-51-102.

Definition of Offense: Obtain or record personal identifying information of another without authorization, with intent to obtain credit, money, goods or services in the name of that person.

Victim Remedies in Criminal Case: No specific provisions.

Special Record-Clearing Provisions: No specific provisions.

Duties of Private Entities: Credit reporting agency must block information resulting from violation of Idaho Code § 18-3126, and notify furnisher that a block is in place.[34] Agency and furnisher may refuse to block, or rescind, if block is result of misrepresentation by consumer, if consumer agrees block was in error, or if consumer knowingly received goods or services as a result of the blocked transaction.

Private Right of Action: For violation of § 28-51-102 (duties of agency and furnisher) consumer has private right of action for damages, attorney fees, injunction and "other appropriate relief."

---

[34] Note that the FCRA has its own blocking provision which preempts similar state provisions, but only to the extent of the specific conduct required by the FCRA provision. *See* § 10.7, *supra*.

Other State Provisions: Idaho Code Ann. § 41-1843 (effective January 1, 2003). Forbids property or casualty insurers to charge a higher premium, or to cancel, nonrenew or refuse to issue a policy "based primarily upon an individual's credit rating or credit history." The statute applies only to property or casualty insurance (as defined in Idaho Code Ch. 5, title 41) issued primarily for personal, family or household purposes.

Illinois

Child Support Debts: 305 Ill. Comp. Stat. § 5/10-16.4; 750 Ill. Comp. Stat. § 5/706.3. Courts finding obligors owing more than $10,000 or an amount equal to at least three months support obligation shall direct the clerk of the court to make the information available to consumer reporting agencies.

State Credit Repair Statute: 815 Ill. Comp. Stat. §§ 605/1 to 605/16.

Covered Activities: Improving credit record or obtaining extension of credit, in return for money or other consideration.

Exemptions: Persons authorized to make loans or extend credit under Illinois or federal law; HUD-approved lenders; banks, savings and loan associations, and subsidiaries eligible for FDIC or FSLIC insurance; credit unions; nonprofit organizations that do not charge consumer prior to or upon execution of contract; licensed real estate brokers and attorneys; securities broker-dealers; consumer reporting agencies; licensed residential mortgage loan brokers and bankers.

Right to Cancel? Yes (3 days).

Prohibitions: Charging before complete performance, unless organization has posted bond; charging for referring buyer to retail seller for credit on same terms as generally available to public; making or advising consumer to make untrue or misleading statements to credit reporting agencies or creditors; making false statements about services offered; inducing consumers to waive rights.

Other Substantive Requirements: Disclosures.

Bond: $100,000.

Private Cause of Action: Actual damages, punitive damages, attorney fees, and court costs; injunction; violation is also a UDAP violation.

State Identity Theft Statute: 720 Ill. Comp. Stat. § 5/16G-1 to 5/16G-30.

Definition of Offense: Knowingly uses personal identifying document or information of another to fraudulently obtain credit, money, goods, services or other property uses personal information or personal identification document of another with intent to commit felony theft, or any other felony; obtains, records, possesses, transfers, sells or manufactures personal identification information or document with intent to commit, or aid and abet the commission of, a felony; uses, transfers or possesses document making implements to produce false identification or false documents, with knowledge that they will be used to commit a felony. Enhanced penalty if victim age 60 or over, or disabled.

Victim Remedies in Criminal Case: If a crime has been committed under a stolen name, an identity theft victim may petition the court for, or a court may issue of its own motion, a declaration of factual innocence, and may order the relevant records sealed, corrected, or labeled to indicate that the data do not indicate the defendant's true identity. Person who suspects he or she is victim of ID theft may initiate an investigation and cause a police report to be filed.

Special Record-Clearing Provisions: No specific provisions.

Duties of Private Entities: UDAP statute, 815 Ill. Comp. Stat. Ann. § 505/2MM, provides that any person who uses a credit report in connection with an extension of credit, and who receives notice that a police report of identity theft has been filed with a consumer reporting agency, may not extend credit or lend money without taking reasonable steps to confirm consumer's identity and confirm that the application is not the result of identity theft.[35] Credit card issuer who mails a solicitation, and receives a response with a different address, may not issue a card until it takes reasonable steps to confirm consumer's change of address.

Private Right of Action: Thief liable for damages, attorney fees, and costs.

Other State Provisions: Solicitations or applications to sell consumer access to reports or government records must disclose that such records and reports are otherwise available free or for nominal cost. **815 Ill. Comp. Stat. § 505/2B.2**. No person may report adverse information to a credit reporting agency unless the cosigner is notified first that the primary obligor has become delinquent or defaulted, that the cosigner is responsible for payment, and that the cosigner has fifteen days to pay or make arrangements for payment. Violation is an unlawful act and may result in up to $250 in actual damages in addition to attorney fees.[36] **815 Ill. Comp. Stat. § 505/2S**.

State Credit Information in Personal Insurance statute: 215 Ill. Comp. Stat. §§ 157/1 to 157/99.

Scope: Use of credit information in underwriting personal insurance: private passenger vehicle or recreational vehicle, homeowners (including mobile home), noncommercial fire insurance, individually underwritten for personal, family, or household use.

Disclosures: Insurer must disclose at time of application, in writing or in same medium as application, if it will use credit information. If insurer takes adverse action based on credit report, it must explain reasons to consumer, and provide notice as required by FCRA (source of report, dispute resolution procedure, etc.).[37]

Dispute Resolution: At time of renewal consumer may request company to re-underwrite or re-rate based on current credit report. If information in credit report is disputed, pursuant to the federal FCRA and found incorrect, insurer must re-underwrite or re-rate within 30 days after notice. If refund is required it should be for the lesser of policy period or 12 months.

Prohibited Practices: Insurer may not use credit score based on income, gender, address, ethnic group, religion, marital status or nationality; deny, cancel, or non-renew based wholly on credit information without, another applicable underwriting factor independent of credit information; base renewal rates solely on credit information; take adverse action based on lack of credit card; count lack of credit history as a negative factor, unless insurer can show relationship to risk; take adverse action based on credit report issued or credit score calculated more than 90 days before policy was written or renewed; use credit information if it does not recalculate every 36 months based on current credit report; treat as a negative factor collection accounts with a medical industry code, or certain credit inquiries.

Other: Insurer who uses insurance scores must file scoring model with Department of Insurance.

Security Freeze Laws: 815 Ill. Comp. Stat. § 505/2MM.

Scope: Until January 1, 2007, only victims of identity theft (those providing police report); after that date, any consumer.

Procedure: Request in writing by certified mail to consumer reporting agency; supply identification.

Entities covered: Consumer reporting agencies as defined in 15 U.S.C. § 1681a(f); some exceptions specified.

Duties of covered entities: Upon consumer request shall require proper identification of requesting party and provide notice, as specified, of process of placing and temporarily lifting a security freeze; within 10 business days of placing the freeze, shall send a written confirmation of the security freeze to the consumer and a unique personal identification number or password, other than the consumer's Social Security number, to be used for the release of the credit report.

Time periods: For application of freeze: No later than five business days after receiving written request. For written confirmation of the security freeze to the consumer: within 10 business days of placing the freeze. For temporary suspension of freeze: no later than three business days after receiving the request. For written confirmation of changes to file: within 30 days of the change to file.

Procedure for lifting freeze: Consumer is to provide with request to agency in manner arranged by agency: Proper identification; personal identification number or password; notice of time period if a temporary suspension of freeze.

Freeze not applicable to: Existing creditors for activities related to account maintenance, monitoring, credit line increases, and account upgrades and enhancements; specified various government agencies; the use of credit information for the purposes of pre-screening as provided for by the federal Fair Credit Reporting Act.

Fees: A fee may be charged of no more than ten dollars ($10) for each freeze, removal of the freeze, or temporary lifting of the freeze. No fee allowed for victim of identity theft or consumers 65 years of age or older.

Enforcement: UDAP violation.

Indiana

State Credit Repair Statute: Ind. Code §§ 24-5-15-1 to 24-5-15-11.

Covered Activities: Improving credit record or obtaining extension of credit, in return for money or other consideration.

Exemptions: Regulated and supervised lenders; mortgage lenders approved by HUD; banks and savings associations eligible for FDIC insurance; credit unions; nonprofit organizations; licensed real estate brokers acting within scope of license; Indiana lawyers acting within scope of law practice; registered securities broker-

---

35 Note that the FCRA has its own fraud alert provision which imposes duties on users before they extend credit and which preempts similar state provisions, but only to the extent of the specific conduct required by the FCRA provision. *See* § 10.7, *supra*.

36 Most state laws concerning the duties of furnishers are now preempted. *See* § 10.7, *supra*.

37 Note that the FCRA preempts state laws regulating the duties of persons who take an adverse action against a consumer based on that consumer's credit report. *See* § 10.7, *supra*.

dealers; consumer reporting agencies.
Right to Cancel? Yes (3 days).
Prohibitions: Charging before complete performance, unless organization has posted bond; charging for referring buyer to retail seller for credit on same terms as generally available to public; making or advising false statements to creditors or credit reporting agencies; making false statements about services offered; requiring buyer to waive rights.
Other Substantive Requirements: Disclosures.
Bond: $10,000.
Private Cause of Action: Twice actual damages or $1000, whichever is greater, plus attorney fees.

State Identity Theft Statute: Ind. Code §§ 35-38-1-2.5, 35-43-5-1 and 35-43-5-3.5.

Definition of Offense: Knowingly uses or intentionally obtains, possesses, transfers or uses the identifying information of another without authorization, and with intent to harm or defraud another.
Victim Remedies in Criminal Case: During or after sentencing of thief, the court may issue an order describing the person whose credit history may be affected by the crime of deception, with sufficient identifying information to assist another person in correcting the credit history, and stating that the person was the victim of a crime of deception that may have affected the person's credit history. This order may be used to correct the credit history of any person described in the order.
Special Record-Clearing Provisions: No specific provisions.
Duties of Private Entities: No specific provisions.
Private Right of Action: No specific provisions.

State Credit Information in Personal Insurance Statute: Ind. Code §§ 27-2-21-1 to 27-2-21-23.

Scope: Use of credit information in personal insurance, i.e., for personal, family or household use, including accident, theft, liability, including homeowners and vehicle.
Disclosures: Insurer must disclose at time of application, in writing or in same medium as application, if it will use credit information. If insurer takes adverse action based on credit report, it must explain reasons to consumer, and provide notice as required by FCRA (source of report, dispute resolution procedure, etc.).[38]
Dispute Resolution: If information in credit report is disputed, pursuant to the federal FCRA, and found incorrect, insurer must re-underwrite or re-rate within 30 days after notice. If refund is required it should be for the lesser of policy period or 12 months.
Prohibited Practices: Insurer may not use credit score based on income, gender, address, ethnic group, religion, marital status or nationality; deny, cancel, or non-renew based wholly on credit information without, another applicable underwriting factor independent of credit information; base renewal rates solely on credit information; treat consumer's lack of a credit card as a negative factor, treat lack of credit information as a negative factor, unless insurer can show relationship to risk; take adverse action based on credit report issued or credit score calculated more than 90 days before policy was written or renewed; use credit information if it does not recalculate every 36 months based on current credit report; treat as a negative factor collection accounts with a medical industry code, or certain credit inquiries.
Other: Insurer who uses insurance score must file scoring model with department of insurance. Violation is a UDAP.

Iowa

State Credit Repair Statute: Iowa Code §§ 538A.1 to 538A.14.

Covered Activities: Improving credit record in return for money or other consideration.
Exemptions: Regulated and supervised lenders; mortgage lenders approved by HUD; banks and savings associations eligible for FDIC insurance; credit unions; nonprofit organizations; licensed real estate brokers acting within scope of license; Iowa lawyers acting within scope of law practice; registered securities broker-dealers; consumer reporting agencies.
Right to Cancel? Yes (3 days).
Prohibitions: Charging before complete performance, unless organization has posted bond; charging for referring buyer to retail seller for credit on same terms as generally available to public; making or advising false statements to creditors or credit reporting agencies; making false statements about services offered; requiring buyer to waive rights.
Other Substantive Requirements: Disclosures.
Bond: $10,000.
Private Cause of Action: Injunctive relief (10-year statute of limitations). Actual damages, not less than amount paid by buyer; attorney fees and costs; punitive damages allowed (4-year statute of limitations).

State Identity Theft Statute: Iowa Code §§ 714.16B and 715A.8 and 715A.9.

Definition of Offense: With intent to obtain a benefit, fraudulently obtains identifying information of another, and uses or attempts to use it without authorization to obtain credit, property, or services.
Victim Remedies in Criminal Case: No specific provisions.
Special Record-Clearing Provisions: No specific provisions.
Duties of Private Entities: No specific provisions.
Private Right of Action: In addition to other remedies provided by law, person who suffers pecuniary loss from identity theft has civil action for the greater of treble damages or $1000, plus reasonable costs and attorney fees. Violation of this section is also an unlawful practice under § 714.16 (UDAP).

Other State Provisions: Iowa Code § 654.18(4). A mortgagee shall not report that a mortgagor is delinquent on the mortgage if the mortgagor agrees to an alternative non-judicial voluntary foreclosure procedure. The mortgagee may report that an alternative non-judicial voluntary foreclosure procedure was used.[39]

Kansas

State FCRA Statute: Kan. Stat. Ann. §§ 50-701 to 50-722.

Scope: Same as the federal law.
Purposes for Which Reports May Be Issued: Similar to federal law, except no authorization for provision to potential investors or

---

38 Note that the FCRA preempts state laws regulating the duties of persons who take an adverse action against a consumer based on that consumer's credit report. *See* § 10.7, *supra*.

39 Most state laws concerning the duties of furnishers are now preempted. *See* § 10.7, *supra*.

servicers, or current insurers, in connection with evaluation of the credit or repayment risks associated with existing credit obligations.

Consumer Access and Disclosure: Similar to federal law, except agency only required to disclose non-employment report recipients within previous six months.

Disclosures to Consumers By Users: Similar to federal law.

Restrictions on Content of Reports: Similar to federal law except criminal records more than seven years old or bankruptcies more than fourteen years old.[40] Adverse information (except public record information) from investigative consumer reports may not be used in subsequent reports unless it has been verified while preparing the new report or was received within three months.

Consumer Disputes: Agency must investigate within a reasonable time if informed by consumer of dispute. Must delete if information is inaccurate or no longer verifiable. If dispute not resolved, consumer may file statement, up to 100 words, describing the dispute. If information is deleted, consumer may request agency to inform users who obtained reports within two years for employment purposes or six months for other purposes. Agency must inform consumer of this right.

Duties of Furnishers: No relevant provisions.

Consumer Remedies: Civil liability for agencies and users: actual damages plus costs and reasonable attorney fees; punitive damages for willful violations. Criminal penalties also available.

Statute of Limitations: Two years from violation or time of discovery.

Miscellaneous: No relevant provisions.

Child Support Debts: **Kan. Stat. Ann. § 23-4145**. The Secretary of Social and Rehabilitation Services must make available information concerning support arrearages in excess of $1000 owed or assigned to the Secretary or owed to any person who has applied for services, upon the request of a consumer reporting agency. The Secretary may make information concerning smaller arrearages available. Before making this information available, the Secretary must provide advance notice to the obligor.

State Credit Repair Statute: **Kan. Stat. Ann. §§ 50-1101 to 50-1115.**

Covered Activities: Improving credit record or obtaining extension of credit, in return for money or other consideration.

Exemptions: Regulated and supervised lenders; mortgage lenders approved by HUD; banks and savings associations eligible for FDIC insurance; credit unions; person whose primary business is loans secured by liens on realty; loan brokers registered with Kansas commissioner; nonprofit organizations; licensed real estate brokers acting within scope of license; Kansas lawyers acting within scope of law practice; registered securities broker-dealers; consumer reporting agencies.

Right to Cancel? Yes (3 days).

Prohibitions: Charging before complete performance, unless organization has posted bond; charging for referring buyer to retail seller for credit on same terms as generally available to public; making or advising false statements to creditors or credit reporting agencies; making false statements about services offered; fraudulent and deceptive practices; requiring buyer to waive rights.

Other Substantive Requirements: Disclosures.

Bond: $25,000.

Private Cause of Action: Actual damages, not less than amount paid by buyer; attorney fees and costs; punitive damages allowed; a violation is a UDAP violation; 2-year statute of limitations. Injunctive relief.

State Identity Theft Statute: **Kan. Stat. Ann. § 21-4018**.

Definition of Offense: Knowingly and with intent to defraud for economic benefit, obtains, transfers, possesses or uses, or attempts to obtain, transfer, possess or use, an identification document or PIN number of another.

Victim Remedies in Criminal Case: No specific provisions.

Special Record-Clearing Provisions: No specific provisions.

Duties of Private Entities: No specific provisions.

Private Right of Action: No specific provisions.

Security Freeze Laws: **Kan. Stat. Ann. § 50-702.**

Scope: Victims of identity theft, i.e., those having filed reports or complaints with law enforcement agency. Section 50-703 specifies that a consumer reporting agency may furnish a consumer report *only* to users as requested by consumer, existing creditors or specified various government agencies; users related to current or intended extension of credit, or for purposes regarding employment, underwriting of insurance, or any legitimate business need for the information in connection with a business transaction involving the consumer.

Procedure: Request in writing by certified mail to consumer reporting agency; supply identification.

Entities covered: Consumer reporting agencies; some exceptions specified.

Duties of covered entities: Upon consumer request shall require proper identification of requesting party and provide notice, as specified, of process of placing and temporarily lifting a security freeze; within 10 business days of placing the freeze, shall send a written confirmation of the security freeze to the consumer and a unique personal identification number or password, other than the consumer's Social Security number, to be used for the release of the credit report.

Time periods: For application of freeze: no later than five business days after receiving written request. For written confirmation of the security freeze to the consumer: within 10 business days of placing the freeze. For temporary suspension of freeze: no later than three business days after receiving the request. For written confirmation of changes to file: within 30 days of the change to file.

Procedure for lifting freeze: Consumer is to provide with request to agency in manner arranged by agency: Proper identification; personal identification number or password; notice of time period if a temporary suspension of freeze.

Freeze not applicable to: Existing creditors or specified various government agencies; and users related to current or intended extension of credit, collection of debts, resellers of credit information compilations, fraud prevention services, or for purposes regarding employment, underwriting of insurance.

Fees: No fees allowed.

Enforcement: Actual damages, not less than $100 or more than $1000, costs and attorney fees. Punitive damages allowed.

---

40 These two definitions of information which may not be contained under Kansas law in a consumer report were in effect on Sept. 30, 1996, and therefore are not preempted, although they regulate the contents of consumer reports and might otherwise be preempted. See § 10.7, *supra*.

Kentucky

State FCRA Statute: Ky. Rev. Stat. Ann. §§ 367.310 and 367.990(16) (West).

Scope: No relevant provisions.

Purposes for Which Reports May Be Issued: No relevant provisions.

Consumer Access and Disclosures: No relevant provisions.

Disclosures to Consumer by User: No relevant provisions.

Restrictions on Content of Reports: Criminal charge in Kentucky court which did not result in conviction.[41]

Consumer Disputes: No relevant provisions.

Duties of Furnishers: No relevant provisions.

Consumer Remedies: Civil liability: each violation may result in a fine of up to $200.

Statute of Limitations: No relevant provisions.

Miscellaneous: No relevant provisions.

Child Support Debts: Ky. Rev. Stat. Ann. § 205.768 (West). Child support arrearages shall be reported to consumer reporting agencies, provided that advance notice is given to the obligor explaining the methods available to contest the accuracy of the information.

State Identity Theft Statute: Ky. Rev. Stat. Ann. §§ 411.210, 514.160 and 514.170, and 532.034 (West).

Definition of Offense: Theft of identity: Without consent, knowingly possesses or uses identifying information of another to deprive that person of property, obtain benefits to which not entitled, make financial or credit transactions using identity of another, avoid detection, or obtain commercial or political benefit. Trafficking in stolen identities: Manufactures, possesses, transfers, sells or possesses with intent to manufacture, transfer or sell, the personal identity of another for purposes forbidden by theft of identity section. Possession of 5 or more identities is prima facie evidence of possession for trafficking.

Victim Remedies in Criminal Case: Upon conviction, shall pay restitution for financial loss by victim, which may include any costs incurred in correcting credit history, or in any civil or administrative proceeding to satisfy debt or obligation, including lost wages and attorney fees. Victim includes financial institution, insurance company or bonding company that suffers financial loss.

Special Record-Clearing Provisions: No specific provisions.

Duties of Private Entities: No specific provisions.

Private Right of Action: Victim of identity theft or trafficking in stolen identities has cause of action for compensatory and punitive damages. Theft is violation of Consumer Protection Act. Statute of limitations, 5 years.

Other: Attorney General (Financial Integrity Enforcement Division) shall coordinate with the Department of Financial Institutions, the U.S. Secret Service, and the Kentucky Bankers' Association to prepare and disseminate information to prevent identity theft.

Security Freeze Laws: Ky. H.B. No. 54; Ky. Rev. Stat. Ann. §§ 367.___.

Scope: Any consumer.

---

41 This provision was in effect on Sept. 30, 1996, so even if it could be said to be otherwise preempted by 15 U.S.C. § 1681c, it is not preempted. *See* § 10.7, *supra*.

Procedure: Request in writing by certified mail to consumer reporting agency; supply identification.

Entities covered: Consumer reporting agencies; exceptions specified.

Duties of covered entities: Upon consumer request shall require proper identification of requesting party and provide notice, as specified, of process of placing and temporarily lifting a security freeze; within 10 business days of placing the freeze, shall send a written confirmation of the security freeze to the consumer and a unique personal identification number or password, other than the consumer's Social Security number, to be used for the release of the credit report.

Time periods: For application of freeze: no later than five business days after receiving written request. For written confirmation of the security freeze to the consumer or replacement of password: within 10 business days of placing the freeze. For temporary suspension of freeze: no later than three business days after receiving the request. For written confirmation of changes to file: within 30 days of the change to file.

Procedure for lifting freeze: Consumer is to provide with request to agency in manner arranged by agency: Proper identification; personal identification number or password; notice of time period if a temporary suspension of freeze.

Freeze not applicable to: Existing creditors for purposes of review or collection; specified various government agencies; collection agencies pursuing existing debts; any person for the purpose of using such credit information to prescreen as provided by the federal Fair Credit Reporting Act; agents serving purposes of underwriting or insurance; deposit account information or fraud prevention services companies.

Fees: A fee may be charged of no more than ten dollars ($10) for each freeze, removal of the freeze, or temporary lifting of the freeze, or replacement of identification number. Yearly increase allowed based on consumer price index. No fee allowed for victim of identity theft.

Enforcement: Actual damages of not less than $100 or more than $1000. Party obtaining information under false pretenses liable to consumer for greater of actual damages or $1000. Punitive damages allowed. Negligent non-compliance liability is actual damages. Costs and attorney fees.

Louisiana

State FCRA Statute: La. Rev. Stat. Ann. §§ 9:3571.1 and 9:3571.2.

Scope: Consumer's credit-worthiness, credit standing or credit capacity.

Purposes for Which Reports May Be Issued: A motor vehicle dealer may not request or review a report without consumer's written permission in connection with a test drive, a request to test drive, a request for pricing or financing, or negotiations with a consumer, unless consumer has already applied to lease or finance a vehicle.

Consumer Access and Disclosure: Similar to federal law, but must be made within five days of written request and agency only required to disclose non-employment report recipients within previous six months. Agency may charge $8 fee (unless request made within sixty days of adverse action based on consumer report). Amount of fee may increase annually with increases in consumer price index.

Disclosures to Consumer by User: Name and address of credit reporting agency, if adverse action based wholly or partially on report; notice of right to free report.[42]

Restrictions on Content of Reports: No relevant provisions.

Consumer Disputes: Must investigate and correct or update within 45 days of a consumer's written notification of dispute.

Duties of Furnishers: No relevant provisions.

Consumer Remedies: Intentional or negligent violation: actual damages plus reasonable attorney fees, court costs, and other reasonable costs of prosecution.

If denied credit, insurance, or employment on the basis of erroneous or inaccurate information furnished by a credit reporting agency, and the erroneous or inaccurate information was the significant material cause of the denial, and if the credit reporting agency failed to use ordinary care or failed to exercise due diligence in discovering such error (i.e., by not complying with the FCRA, CCPA, or other provision of this section), the credit reporting agency is liable. The consumer is entitled to actual damages in addition to reasonable attorney fees and court costs.

If a person is required to have erroneous or inaccurate information removed from a credit report as a condition to having a credit, insurance, or employment application approved and the erroneous or inaccurate information was a significant material cause of the request for removal, and if the credit reporting agency failed to use ordinary care or failed to exercise due diligence in discovering such error, the credit reporting agency is liable. The consumer is entitled to actual damages in addition to reasonable attorney fees and court costs.

Violations of § 9:3571.2 (requests by motor vehicle dealers before test drive, pricing inquiry or negotiations): civil penalty of up to $2500 per violation.

Statute of Limitations: No relevant provisions.

Miscellaneous: No relevant provisions.

State Credit Repair Statute: La. Rev. Stat. Ann. §§ 9:3573.1 to 9:3573.16.

Covered Activities: Improving credit record in return for money or other consideration.

Exemptions: Regulated and supervised lenders; mortgage lenders, provided the credit repair service is in connection with the loan, and no additional fee is charged approved by HUD; banks and savings associations eligible for FDIC insurance; credit unions; nonprofit organizations; licensed certified public accountants acting within scope of license; Louisiana lawyers acting within scope of law practice; consumer reporting agencies.

Right to Cancel? Yes (5 days).

Prohibitions: Charging before complete performance, unless organization has posted bond; making or advising false statements to creditors or credit reporting agencies; making false statements about services offered; making nonessential requests for credit information from any source where no cost for such information; engaging in fraudulent or deceptive practices; requiring buyer to waive rights. Structure a transaction so as to circumvent the provisions of this act, or violate any provision of the federal Credit Repair Organizations Act.

Other Substantive Requirements: Disclosures.

Bond: $25,000.

Private Cause of Action: Actual damages, no less than amount paid by buyer; costs; attorney fees based on time expended, not on amount of recovery where willful violation, an additional amount twice actual damages. Injunctive relief. 4-year statute of limitations.

State Identity Theft Statute: La. Rev. Stat. Ann. §§ 9:3568, 14:67.16.

Definition of Offense: Intentional use or attempted use of identifying information of another, without authorization, to obtain credit, money, goods, services or anything else of value.

Victim Remedies in Criminal Case: Court may order full restitution to the victim, or any other who suffered financial loss. If defendant is indigent, a payment plan may be ordered. Victim may file police report in victim's place of domicile, or with state department of justice. Investigating officer should make detailed written report: name of victim, type of information misused, etc. and provide a copy to the victim

Special Record-Clearing Provisions: Consumer may place security alert in file, indicating that identity may have been used without consent to fraudulently obtain goods or services in consumer's name. If consumer provides proper identification, alert must be placed within 5 days of request, and will remain in effect for 90 days.[43] Agency must send alert to any person who requests a consumer report on the consumer. Agency that compiles and maintains files on a nationwide basis must have 24-hour toll free telephone number for receiving security alert requests.

Duties of Private Entities: Creditor that grants credit as result of ID theft must provide victim with information (i.e., billing statements, etc.) needed by victim to undo the effects of the crime.[44] Creditor may require from victim a written statement, copy of the police report, proper identification, and request for information. No creditor may be held liable for good faith release of information to provide information about actual or potential violations to other financial institutions, law enforcement, or victims who provide required written materials, or who assist a victim in recovery of funds or rehabilitation of credit. A person who receives information about a security alert, pursuant to § 9:3571.1 shall not extend credit, lend money, etc. until it takes reasonable steps to verify the identity of the consumer.[45] If consumer has included a phone number in the security alert, creditor should contact the consumer using that number.

Private Right of Action: A creditor, potential creditor, credit reporting agency or other entity that violates the provisions governing security alerts, and assistance to victims of identity theft, will be liable to the victim of ID theft for all documented expenses suffered as a result, plus reasonable attorney fees.

---

42 Note that the FCRA preempts state laws regulating the duties of persons who take an adverse action against a consumer based on that consumer's credit report. *See* § 10.7, *supra*.

43 Note that the FCRA has its own fraud alert provision which preempts similar state provisions, but only to the extent of the specific conduct required by the FCRA provision. *See* § 10.7, *supra*.

44 Note that the FCRA has its own transaction information provision that may preempt this sort of state provision. *See* § 10.7, *supra*.

45 Note that the FCRA has its own fraud alert provision which imposes duties on users before they extend credit and which preempts similar state provisions, but only to the extent of the specific conduct required by the FCRA provision. *See* § 10.7, *supra*.

State Credit Information in Personal Insurance statute: **La. Rev. Stat. Ann. §§ 1481 to 1494.**

Scope: Use of credit information for personal insurance, i.e., for personal, family or household use: homeowners (including mobile home), noncommercial fire, motor vehicle and recreational vehicle.
Disclosures: Insurer must disclose at time of application, in writing or same medium as application, that credit information will be used. If adverse action is based on credit information, insurer must explain the reasons, and give notification as required by federal FCRA (source of report, dispute resolution procedure, etc.).[46]
Dispute Resolution: If information in credit report is disputed, pursuant to the federal FCRA and found incorrect, insurer must re-underwrite or re-rate within 30 days after notice. If refund is required it should be for the lesser of policy period or 12 months. Insurer who uses credit information must provide process for consumer to appeal "the underwriting or rating of risks for which credit scoring may be an inappropriate factor."
Prohibited Practices: Insurer may not use credit score based on income, gender, address, ethnic group, religion, marital status or nationality; deny, cancel, or non-renew based wholly on credit information without, another applicable underwriting factor independent of credit information; base renewal rates solely on credit information; treat consumer's lack of a credit card as a negative factor, treat lack of credit information as a negative factor, unless insurer can show relationship to risk; take adverse action based on credit report issued or credit score calculated more than 180 days before policy was written or renewed; use credit information if it does not recalculate every 36 months based on current credit report; treat as a negative factor collection accounts with a medical industry code, or certain credit inquiries.
Other: Insurer must provide reasonable exemptions from the use of credit information for consumer who can show that credit history was "unduly influenced" by medical crisis, death of a spouse, identity theft, the personal guarantee of a business loan, or other catastrophic event as deemed by the commissioner of insurance. Insurers who use insurance scores must file scoring models with department of insurance.

Other State Provisions: La. Rev. Stat. Ann. §§ 51:3071 to 51:3077. Owner or licensor of computerized information must notify resident of any unauthorized acquisition of personal information upon discovery of security breach.

Security Freeze Laws: La. Rev. Stat. Ann. § 9:3571.1(H) to (Y).

Scope: Any consumer.
Procedure: Request in writing by certified mail to consumer reporting agency; supply identification.
Entities covered: Consumer reporting agencies; some exceptions specified.
Duties of covered entities: Upon consumer request shall require proper identification of requesting party and provide notice, as specified, of process of placing and temporarily lifting a security freeze; within 10 business days of placing the freeze, shall send a written confirmation of the security freeze to the consumer and a unique personal identification number or password, other than the consumer's Social Security number, to be used for the release of the credit report.
Time periods: For application of freeze: no later than ten business days after receiving written request. For written confirmation of the security freeze to the consumer: within 10 business days of placing the freeze. For temporary suspension of freeze: no later than three business days after receiving the request. For written confirmation of changes to file: within 30 days of the change to file.
Procedure for lifting freeze: Consumer is to provide with request to agency in manner arranged by agency: Proper identification; personal identification number or password; notice of time period if a temporary suspension of freeze.
Freeze not applicable to: Existing creditors or specified various government agencies; collection agency pursuing an existing debt; agents of entities reviewing existing accounts; the purposes of prescreening as provided by the federal Fair Credit Reporting Act; resellers of compilations of existing credit information; fraud prevention services; and deposit account information service companies.
Fees: A fee may be charged of no more than ten dollars ($10) for each freeze, and $8 for temporary lifting of the freeze. Fees may be increased yearly in accordance with Consumer Price Index. No fee allowed for revocation of the freeze or for victim of identity theft or for persons 62 years or older.
Enforcement: Actual damages, attorney fees, and costs.

Maine

State FCRA Statute: Me. Rev. Stat. Ann. tit. 10, §§ 1311 to 1329 (See also Advisory Rulings of Bureau of Consumer Protection).

Scope: Investigative consumer report includes telephone information. Adverse information is deemed to be any information likely to have a negative effect on the ability of the consumer to obtain credit, credit insurance, employment, benefits, goods or services.
Purposes for Which Reports May Be Issued: Same as the federal law, but reports listing a consumer as having been denied credit where the sole reason for denial was insufficient information for the granting of credit may not be issued, unless report states denial was for that reason.[47]
Consumer Access and Disclosure: The consumer has the right to have medical information given to the licensed physician of his or her choice. Only requires agency to disclose users for non-employment purposes within previous six months. Right to receive copy of file. Maximum charge: Actual costs for second or subsequent report within 12 months,[48] $5, unless a copy is requested within 60 days after an adverse consumer determination, in which case it is free. Public record information is the same as federal law. Must disclose to consumer the substance of public record information provided for employment purposes. Must advise consumer of the procedures adopted by the agency to enable a consumer to correct any inaccurate information.
Disclosures to Consumers By User: Notice of requests for investigative reports must be delivered three business days prior to the investigation.

---

46 Note that the FCRA preempts state laws regulating the duties of persons who take an adverse action against a consumer based on that consumer's credit report. See § 10.7, *supra*.

47 This provision was in effect on Sept. 30, 1996, so even if it could be said to be otherwise preempted by 15 U.S.C. § 1681c, it is not preempted. See § 10.7, *supra*.

48 Although the FCRA preempts state laws with respect to the frequency of the right to free reports, the Act specifically exempts this Maine provision from preemption. See § 10.7, *supra*.

Restrictions on Content of Reports: Reporting information which cannot be verified unless the report also contains attempts to verify. Adverse information in investigative reports which is not reverified or received within previous three months. Reporting that a consumer was denied credit if the sole reason for denial is lack of credit information, unless the report states that denial was for that reason.[49] A debt collector may not disclose an overdue debt for medical expenses of a minor child, unless the debtor is the responsible party according to a court or administrative order (provided that the collector has been informed of the existence of the order), and the responsible party has been notified and given an opportunity to pay.

Consumer Disputes: Agency must reinvestigate within twenty-one days; otherwise similar to federal law.[50] In addition, an agency must retain inaccurate information in a separate folder which can only be used as defenses in a civil action. Immediate notice to a consumer if a dispute is considered "frivolous."[51] If information is found to be inaccurate or unverifiable, agency must notify users who obtained reports for employment purposes within 2 years or other purposes within six months.

Duties of Furnishers: May not furnish information it knows or should know is inaccurate. May not furnish information if it is informed by consumer that information is inaccurate, and information is, in fact, inaccurate. One who regularly furnishes information to consumer reporting agency must notify agency of corrections, if any information supplied is later found to be inaccurate. Must notify agency if consumer disputes the information. Regular furnisher must investigate dispute reported by consumer. (No private right of action for violations of these requirements; enforcement only by administrator.)

Consumer Remedies: Similar to the federal law for willful noncompliance, but treble damages rather than punitive damages. For negligent violations, in addition to actual damages, minimum damages of at least $100 per violation and each report containing inaccurate or irrelevant information which contributed to an adverse consumer decision. Criminal penalties for obtaining information from a consumer reporting agency on false pretenses, or for unauthorized disclosures by agency officers or employees.

Statute of Limitations: Same as the federal law.

Miscellaneous: Investigative reports must be updated every three months. Reports must be in writing and retained in a file for two years for employment purposes, six months for other purposes. (*See* Equifax Services, Inc. v. Cohen, 420 A.2d 189 (Me. 1980).) If a bankruptcy is reported, must indicate which chapter, if known. If bankruptcy withdrawn by consumer before final judgment, agency must report this. If a credit account is voluntarily closed by consumer, agency must report this along when it reports information about the account.

---

49 These provisions were in effect on Sept. 30, 1996, so although they may regulate the time allowed for an agency to reinvestigate a dispute, or the contents of reports, they are not preempted. *See* § 10.7, *supra*.

50 Provision was in effect on Sept. 30, 1996, so although it regulates the time allowed for an agency to reinvestigate a dispute, it is not preempted. *See* § 10.7, *supra*.

51 This provision was in effect on Sept. 30, 1996, so although it regulates the time allowed for part of the reinvestigation process, it is not preempted. *See* § 10.7, *supra*.

Child Support Debts: Me. Rev. Stat. Ann. tit. 10, § 1329. The Department of Human Services, upon the request of a consumer reporting agency, shall make available information regarding the amount of overdue child support owed by any parent. Prior to making the information available to the requesting agency, the Department shall provide the obligor parent with notice of the proposed action. The parent shall be given twenty days prior notice to contest the accuracy of the information. The Department may voluntarily provide this information as well.

State Credit Repair Statute: Me. Rev. Stat. Ann. tit. 9-A, §§ 10-101 to 10-401.

Covered Activities: Improving credit record or obtaining extension of credit, in return for money or other consideration.

Exemptions: Regulated and supervised lenders; nonprofit organizations; licensed real estate brokers acting within scope of license; Maine lawyers acting within scope of law practice; consumer reporting agencies; certain affiliates or employees of supervised lenders; person who performs marketing services for lender, if person not compensated by consumer for credit services; seller of consumer goods, or seller's employee, who performs services in connection with sale or proposed sale, and is not compensated by the consumer for the services.

Right to Cancel? No.

Prohibitions: False and misleading advertising regarding terms and conditions of services offered.

Other Substantive Requirements: Disclosures. Consumer fees to placed in escrow account pending completion of services contracted for; comply with federal statute and rules governing the privacy of consumer financial information.

Bond: $10,000.

Private Cause of Action: Actual damages; attorney fees and costs. Restitution after administrative hearing.

State Identity Theft Statute: Maine Rev. Stat. Ann. title 17-A, § 905-A. See also Me. Rev. Stat. Ann. tit. 17-A, § 354.

Definition of Offense: Misuse of Identification: presents or uses a credit or debit card . . . obtained as a result of fraud or deception; presents or uses an account, credit or billing number that the person is not authorized to use or that was obtained as a result of fraud or deception; presents or uses a form of legal identification that the person is not authorized to use. Definition of theft by deception includes deception as to identity.

Victim Remedies in Criminal Case: No specific provisions.

Special Record-clearing Provisions: No specific provisions.

Duties of Private Entities: No specific provisions.

Private Right of Action: No specific provisions.

Other: No specific provisions.

State Credit Information in Personal Insurance statute: Me. Rev. Stat. Ann. tit. 24-A, §§ 2169-B and 2201 to 2220.

Scope: Use of consumer reports in personal insurance, i.e., individually underwritten for personal, family or household use: private passenger vehicle or recreational vehicle, homeowners, noncommercial fire. § 2169-B. Use of personal information about Maine residents in most insurance transactions (exceptions for workers' comp., medical malpractice, fidelity, suretyship, boiler and machinery, and certain public record information collected for title insurance purposes). §§ 2201 et. seq.

Disclosure: Insurer must disclose at time of application, in writing or in same medium as application, if it will use credit information. If insurer takes adverse action based on credit report, it must explain reasons to consumer, and provide notice as required by state and federal FCRA (source of report, dispute resolution procedure, etc.).[52] § 2169-B. Consumers must be provided with notice of insurer's information practices. § 2206. Insurer that plans to use investigative consumer report must comply with state FCRA, and inform consumer in writing of right to be interviewed. § 2209.

Dispute Resolution: If information in credit report is disputed, pursuant to the federal FCRA and found incorrect, insurer must re-underwrite or re-rate within 30 days after notice. If refund is required it should be for the lesser of policy period or 12 months. § 2169-B. If an insurer receives a written request to amend or correct personal information, based on a consumer report, it must advise consumer of name and address of reporting agency, and of procedure under state FCRA for challenging the information. § 2211.

Prohibited Practices: Insurer may not use credit score based on income, gender, address, ethnic group, religion, marital status or nationality; deny, cancel, or non-renew based wholly on credit information without, another applicable underwriting factor independent of credit information; base renewal rates solely on credit information; take adverse action based on consumer's lack of a credit card, consider the absence of credit information, the inability to calculate a credit score, or the number of credit inquiries, unless insurer can show relationship to risk; take adverse action based on credit report issued or credit score calculated more than 90 days before policy was written or renewed; use credit information if it does not recalculate every 36 months based on current credit report. § 2169-B.

Other: Insurer who uses scores must file scoring model with superintendent. § 2169-B.

Security Freeze Laws: Me. Rev. Stat. Ann. tit. 10, § 1313-C.

Scope: Any consumer as defined in § 1312.
Procedure: Request in writing by certified mail to a consumer reporting agency; supply identification.
Entities covered: Consumer reporting agencies.
Duties of covered entities: Upon consumer request shall require proper identification of requesting party; shall notify of process of placing and temporarily lifting a security freeze, contents of notice as specified to be submitted to state administrator; within 10 business days of placing the freeze, shall send a written confirmation of the security freeze to the consumer and at the same time shall provide the consumer with a unique personal identification number or password, other than the consumer's Social Security number, to be used for release of credit report.
Time periods: For application of freeze: no later than five business days after receiving written request. For written confirmation of the security freeze to the consumer: within ten business days of placing the freeze. For temporary suspension of freeze: no later than three business days after receiving the request.
Procedure for lifting freeze: With request to agency in manner arranged by agency consumer is to provide: Proper identification; personal identification number or password; notice of time period if a temporary suspension of freeze.

Freeze not applicable to: Existing creditors for review or collection purposes or specified various government agencies and use of credit information for prescreening as provided by the federal Fair Credit Reporting Act.
Fees: A fee may be charged of no more than ten dollars ($10) for each freeze, removal of the freeze, or temporary lifting of the freeze; not more than $12 for a temporary suspension of a freeze for a specific party. No fee allowed for victim of identity theft.
Enforcement: Actual damages and attorney fees for negligent noncompliance, also, treble damages for willful violation; specified powers for state administrator, §§ 1322, 1323, 1328.

Maryland

State FCRA Statute: Md. Code Ann., Com. Law §§ 14-1201 to 14-1218 (West); *see also* Md. Code Regs. §§ 09.03.07.01 to 09.03.07.04 (West).

Scope: Similar to federal
Purposes for Which Reports May Be Issued: Similar to federal law, except no authorization for provision to potential investors or servicers, or current insurers, in connection with evaluation of credit or prepayment risks associated with existing credit obligations.
Consumer Access and Disclosure: Upon customer request all information in file except medical information; in addition, an explanation of code or trade language is required. Must provide one free copy per year,[53] may charge up to a $5.00 fee for additional copies. Substance of any public record information reported for employment purposes.
Disclosures to Consumers By User: Same as the federal law. Must inform consumer if an investigative report is being requested. Must disclose to consumer, upon request, the scope of the proposed investigative report.
Restrictions on Content of Reports: Obsolete information: same as federal law except criminal records more than seven years after disposition, release or parole.[54] Adverse information in investigative reports which is not reverified or received within previous three months.[55]
Consumer Disputes: Disputed information must be investigated within thirty days of written notification by a consumer.[56] If found to be inaccurate, the consumer and users must be notified within seven days; if found to be accurate, the consumer must be notified within seven days. Consumer must be notified within seven days if agency considers dispute to be frivolous.
Duties of Furnishers: No relevant provisions.
Consumer Remedies: Actual damages, reasonable attorney fees

---

52 Note that the FCRA preempts state laws regulating the duties of persons who take an adverse action against a consumer based on that consumer's credit report. *See* § 10.7, *supra*.

53 Although the FCRA preempts state laws with respect to the frequency of the right to free reports, the Act specifically exempts this Maryland provision from preemption. *See* § 10.7, *supra*.

54 These two definitions of information which may not be contained under Maryland law in a consumer report were in effect on Sept. 30, 1996, and therefore are not preempted, although they regulate the contents of consumer reports and might otherwise be preempted. *See* § 10.7, *supra*.

55 *Id*.

56 These provisions were in effect on Sept. 30, 1996, so although they regulate the time allowed an agency to reinvestigate the contents of reports, they are not preempted. *See* § 10.7, *supra*.

and costs are available for negligent violations, plus punitive damages for willful violations. Violations made unintentionally and in good faith are not actionable. Criminal penalties for obtaining information from agency under false pretenses, or for unauthorized disclosure by officers or employees of agency.
Statute of Limitations: Same as the federal law.
Miscellaneous: Cannot provide prescreened information if the consumer precludes it in writing.[57]

Child Support Debts: Md. Code Ann., Fam. Law § 10-108.1 (West). Upon request, the Child Support Enforcement Administration shall report child support arrearages of sixty days for longer duration. Written notice and a reasonable opportunity to contest the accuracy of the information must be given to the obligor before the information is reported.

State Credit Repair Statute: Md. Code Ann., Com. Law §§ 14-1901 to 14-1916 (West).

Covered Activities: Improving credit record or obtaining extension of credit, in return for money or other consideration.
Exemptions: Lenders authorized under Maryland or federal law; licensed mortgage lenders, banks and savings associations eligible for FDIC insurance; nonprofit organizations; licensed real estate brokers acting within scope of license; public accountants and Maryland lawyers acting within scope of practice; registered securities broker-dealers; consumer reporting agencies.
Right to Cancel? Yes (3 days).
Prohibitions: Charging before complete performance; charging for referring buyer to retail seller for credit on same terms as generally available to public; making or advising false statements to creditors or credit reporting agencies; making false statements about services offered; assisting in or creating new identity for buyer for credit purposes; unfair and deceptive practices; requiring buyer to waive rights; assists consumer to obtain credit at a rate of interest that, but for federal preemption of state law would be forbidden by title 12.
Other Substantive Requirements: Disclosures.
Bond: Bond required pursuant to title 11, subtitle 3 of Financial Institutions Code. See Md. Fin. Instit. Code § 11-206.
Private Cause of Action: Contract voidable. Where willful non-compliance, thrice amount collected from consumer; attorney fees and costs; punitive damages allowed; 2-year statute of limitations, from date of discovery of misrepresentation; for willful violations, statute of limitations is 2 years from discovery of violation. Where negligent non-compliance, actual damages; attorney fees and costs; 2-year statute of limitations, from date of violation. A violation is a UDAP violation.

State Identity Theft Statute: Md. Code Ann., Crim. § 8-301 (West); Md. Code Regs. § 09.03.07.04; *see also* Md. Code Ann., Govt. § 6-202 (West).

Definition of Offense: Knowingly, willfully, without authority, with fraudulent intent obtain or help another to obtain personal identifying information of another, with intent to obtain any benefit, credit, goods, services or other thing of value in the name of another; or knowingly or willfully assume the identity of another to fraudulently obtain any benefit, etc., or evade payment of debt or legal obligation.

Victim Remedies in Criminal Case: In addition to restitution required by other provisions of criminal code, court may order restitution to victim for reasonable costs incurred including attorney fees, in clearing victims credit history or credit rating, and in connection with any civil or administrative proceeding to satisfy a debt, lien, judgment or other obligation arising form the identity fraud.
Special Record-Clearing Provisions: No specific provisions.
Duties of Private Entities: If a consumer alleges that errors in the credit report result from identity theft, or mixing of the consumer's information with that of another, the complaint is presumed to be accurate and must receive expedited handling. The agency must make an investigation using the consumer's Social Security number. If the presumption of accuracy is rebutted, the consumer must be notified, and advised of the appeal procedures provided by the state fair credit law. If the presumption of accuracy is not rebutted, the agency must delete the information from its files, send written notice to every person designated by the consumer, and advise the consumer of the rights of action provided by the state fair credit reporting law.
Private Right of Action: No specific provisions.
Other: Electronic Transaction Education, Advocacy and Mediation Unit, in the Office of the Attorney General is empowered to investigate and assist in the prosecution of identity fraud, and to provide public education regarding the prevention of identity fraud.

Other State Provisions: Md. Code Ann., Ins. § 27-605 (West). If an insurer takes adverse action on motor vehicle liability policy based in whole or in part on credit report or credit score, it must disclose the name, address, and toll-free number of the credit reporting agency, and consumer's rights under the federal FCRA to a copy of the report, and dispute resolution procedure.[58]

Massachusetts

State FCRA Statute: Mass. Gen. Laws ch. 93, §§ 50 to 68.

Scope: Same as the federal definitions except the consumer report does not include information communicated by the consumer reporting agency on reputation, character, personal characteristics, or mode of living. Issuance of investigative consumer reports requires the prior written permission of the consumer.
Purposes for Which Reports May Be Issued: Similar to federal law, however business transaction use restricted to transactions where a party transfers interest in real or personal property, pays money or renders services, or becomes obligated to do so; and no authorization for provision to potential investors or servicers, or current insurers, in connection with evaluation of credit or prepayment rules associated with existing credit obligations. Consumers must be given the opportunity, via a toll-free telephone number, to opt-out of prescreened lists.[59]
Consumer Access and Disclosure: Similar to the federal law; in addition, upon customer request, contents of all non-medical information in files must be disclosed. Nationwide agencies must provide one free copy per year,[60] $5 from local agencies; subse-

---

57 State law provisions concerning prescreening lists are now preempted. *See* § 10.7, *supra*.

58 Note that the FCRA preempts state laws regulating the duties of persons who take an adverse action against a consumer based on that consumer's credit report. *See* § 10.7, *supra*.

59 State law provisions concerning prescreening lists are now preempted. *See* § 10.7, *supra*.

60 Although the FCRA preempts state laws with respect to the

quent reports $8.

Disclosures to Consumers By User: Same as the federal law.

Restrictions on Content of Reports: Same as federal law except criminal records more than seven years after disposition, release or parole and bankruptcies over fourteen year old.[61]

Consumer Disputes: Similar to federal law, except that the consumer reporting agency must reinvestigate within thirty days and notify the consumer of the results within a further ten days. If agency determines dispute frivolous, it must notify consumer of specific reasons for decision within five days. Agency must delete information found to be inaccurate within three days and must issue corrected reports within fifteen days of request by consumer.[62] In addition, a consumer reporting agency does not have the right to limit the length of the statement filed by the consumer on the dispute.

Duties of Furnishers: Furnishers of information liable from first for failing to establish reasonable procedures to ensure accuracy of information reported, or for reporting information they know or should know is inaccurate. In addition, furnishers must report voluntary account closures and must include consumer disputes and commencement dates of any delinquencies, when reporting delinquencies.[63]

Consumer Remedies: Fine and/or imprisonment for willful introduction of false information into a file for the purpose of either damaging or enhancing a consumer's credit information or for obtaining information from agency under false pretenses, or unauthorized disclosure by agency personnel. Agencies, users and furnishers are liable for actual damages, reasonable attorney fees and costs, plus punitive damages for willful violations. In addition, remedies in relation to negligent noncompliance are specifically nonexclusive. Failure to comply with any provision is a violation of the state deceptive practices statute.

Statute of Limitations: Two years from date of violation or discovery for willful misrepresentation.

Miscellaneous: Adverse information in an investigative report must be reverified or less than three months old to be included on a subsequent report.[64]

Child Support Debts: **Mass. Gen. Laws ch. 93, § 52A.** Child support arrearages in excess of $500 must be reported upon request of consumer reporting agency. Fifteen-day advance notice must be given to obligor parent, who has right to contest accuracy of information before it is reported to agency.

---

frequency of the right to free reports, the Act specifically exempts this Massachusetts provision from preemption. See § 10.7, *supra*.

61 These two definitions of information which may not be contained under Massachusetts law in a consumer report were in effect on Sept. 30, 1996, and therefore are not preempted, although they regulate the contents of consumer reports and might otherwise be preempted. See § 10.7, *supra*.

62 These provisions were in effect on Sept. 30, 1996, so although they regulate the time allowed an agency to reinvestigate a dispute, they are not preempted. See § 10.7, *supra*.

63 Massachusetts law regarding the responsibilities of furnishers of information is explicitly not preempted by federal law. See § 10.7, *supra*.

64 This provision was in effect on Sept. 30, 1996, so even if it could be said to be otherwise preempted by 15 U.S.C. § 1681c, it is not preempted. See § 10.7, *supra*.

State Credit Repair Statute: **Mass. Gen. Laws ch. 93, §§ 68A to 68E.**

Covered Activities: Improving credit record or obtaining extension of credit, in return for money or other consideration.

Exemptions: Regulated and supervised lenders; mortgage lenders approved by HUD; banks eligible for FDIC insurance; credit unions; nonprofit organizations; licensed real estate brokers acting within scope of license; Massachusetts lawyers acting within scope of law practice; registered securities broker-dealers; consumer reporting agencies.

Right to Cancel? Yes (3 days).

Prohibitions: Charging before complete performance, unless organization has posted bond; charging for referring buyer to retail seller for credit on same terms as generally available to public; making or advising false statements to creditors or credit reporting agencies; making false statements about services offered; any act intended to defraud or deceive buyer.

Other Substantive Requirements: Disclosures.

Bond: $10,000.

Private Cause of Action: A violation is a UDAP violation.

State Identity Theft Statute: **Mass. Gen. Laws ch. 266, § 37E.**

Definition of Offense: Poses as another person and uses that persons identifying information without authority to obtain money, credit, goods, or other thing of value, or identifying documents of that person; or obtains identifying information for purpose of posing as that person or enabling another to pose as that person, for purposes listed above.

Victim Remedies in Criminal Case: In addition to any other punishment, court must order restitution for financial loss, which may include costs of correcting credit history and credit rating, civil or administrative proceeding to satisfy debt or other obligation, including lost wages and attorney fees.

Special Record-Clearing Provisions: No specific provisions.

Duties of Private Entities: No specific provisions.

Private Right of Action: No specific provisions.

Other State Provisions: **Mass. Gen. Laws ch. 175I, §§ 2 and 7.** The Insurance Information and Privacy Protection statute requires that insurer who wishes to use investigative consumer report must advise consumer of right to be interviewed, and to receive a copy of report. The report may not include information about the sexual orientation of any person, or about counseling related to AIDS.

Michigan

Child Support Debts: **Mich. Comp. Laws § 552.512.** The office of friend of the court shall report to a consumer reporting agency support information concerning all child support payers with an arrearage of two months or more. Prior to making such information available, the office of friend of the court shall provide twenty-one days advance notice to the payer and a review enabling the payer to object. Any incorrect information reported must be corrected within fourteen days.

State Credit Repair Statute: **Mich. Comp. Laws §§ 445.1821 to 445.1826.**

Covered Activities: Improving credit record, obtaining extension of credit, advising or assisting regarding foreclosure of real estate

mortgage, or serving as intermediary for debtor with creditor with respect to prior debt, in return for money or other consideration.
Exemptions: Lenders licensed or authorized under state law; federal or state chartered banks, credit unions, savings bank, savings and loans, farm credit entities, and subsidiaries; anyone with a state occupational license when engaged in regular course of business; Michigan attorneys acting within scope of law practice who do not engage in business of credit services organization on regular and continuing basis; judicial officer; persons acting under court agency; consumer reporting agencies; licensed debt management businesses; registered investment advisors and securities broker-dealers; non-profit organizations; and finance subsidiaries of manufacturers.
Right to Cancel? No.
Prohibitions: Charging for obtaining extension of credit before closing the loan; charging for services before completing them; charging for referring buyer to retail seller for credit on same terms as generally available to public; making false statements in offer or sale of services; engaging in fraudulent or deceptive act in connection with offer or sale of services; failing to perform agreed services within 90 days; advise buyer to make false statement to creditor or credit reporting agency; remove or assist removal of accurate non-obsolete information; create or assist creation of new identity; submit dispute without buyer's knowledge; provide service without written contract.
Other Substantive Requirements: None.
Bond: N/A
Private Cause of Action: Buyer may sue for injunction, declaratory judgment, actual damages, attorney fees, costs, and punitive damages (4-year statute of limitations). Credit services organization that violates the act is also barred from recovering fees or other charges from buyer.

State Identity Theft Statute: Mich. Comp. Laws §§ 445.61 to 445.69.

Definition of Offense: Obtaining credit, goods, services, money, property, a vital record, medical records or information, or employment with intent to defraud or violate the law or by concealing, withholding, or misrepresenting the person's identity, using or attempting to use the personal identifying information of another person.
Victim Remedies in Criminal Case: No specific provisions.
Special Record-Clearing Provisions: No specific provisions.
Duties of Private Entities: Prohibition against denying credit or public utility service or to reduce the credit limit of consumers solely because the consumer is a victim of identity theft, if there is prior knowledge that the consumer was a victim of identity theft. A violation of this provision is also a UDAP violation.
Private Right of Action: No specific provisions.

Other State Provisions: Mich. Comp. Laws §§ 445.83, 445.271 to 445.273. No creditor may report adverse information about a cosigner without thirty days notice, or if the cosigner makes satisfactory arrangements in response to a notice; prohibits public display of all or more than 4 sequential digits of a consumer's Social Security number and other uses of Social Security number, unless required by state or federal law, rule or regulation, or by court order or rule; and provided by several other exceptions. These provisions are effective January 1, 2006.[65]

---

65 Most state laws concerning duties of furnishers of information are now preempted. *See* § 10.7, *supra*.

Minnesota

State FCRA Statute: Minn. Stat. §§ 13C.001 to 13C.04, 72A.496 to 72A.505 (insurance investigative reports).

Scope: Similar to federal.
Purposes for Which Reports May Be Issued: Same as federal law.
Consumer Access and Disclosures: Detailed requirements for medical information in insurance reports: may be disclosed to named health care provider instead of directly to consumer; if disclosure could create risk of harm to patient or others, must be disclosed only to treating physician. Insurance company must disclose reasons for adverse underwriting decision, including credit scores.[66] Before seeking information, insurer must obtain consumer's written authorization; form must be in plain language, disclose what information is being sought, and authorization must be for a limited time. Agencies must provide one report per year for a charge of not more than three dollars.
Disclosures to Consumer By User: Similar to federal law, however, no one can procure a consumer report for employment purposes without written disclosure to the consumer prior to the preparation of the report; and the disclosure must include a box for the consumer to check to obtain a free copy of the report. This copy must be sent by the agency to the consumer within twenty-four hours of the time it delivers report to the user. If the report requested is an investigative consumer report, must disclose that the report may include information obtained through personal interviews regarding the consumer's character, general reputation, personal characteristics, or mode of living. Disclosure is not required if the report is to be used for employment purposes for which the consumer has not specifically applied, used for an investigation of a current violation of a criminal or civil statute by a current employer, or used for an investigation of employee conduct for which the employer may be liable. Users who request an investigative report for insurance purposes must notify consumer of right to be interviewed during the investigation and the right to request a copy of the report.
Restrictions on Content of Reports: No relevant provisions.
Consumer Disputes: Adverse decisions regarding insurance reports may be appealed to insurance commissioner.
Duties of Furnishers: No relevant provisions.
Consumer Remedies: Actual damages, equitable relief, and costs and disbursements (including costs of investigation and reasonable attorney fees). Violations of insurance information statute treated like violations of government data practices law: actual damages, costs and attorney fees; exemplary damages for willful violation of $100 to $10,000 per violation; injunction also available. Criminal penalties for obtaining data in violation of the insurance statute.
Statute of Limitations: No relevant provisions.
Miscellaneous: No relevant provisions.

State Credit Repair Statute: Minn. Stat. §§ 332.52 to 332.60.

Covered Activities: Improving credit record or obtaining extension of credit, in return for money or other consideration.
Exemptions: Regulated and supervised lenders; banks and savings associations eligible for FDIC insurance; credit unions; nonprofit

---

66 Note that the FCRA preempts state laws regulating the duties of persons who take an adverse action against a consumer based on that consumer's credit report. *See* § 10.7, *supra*.

organizations; prorating agencies, collections agencies, and licensed real estate brokers acting within scope of license; Minnesota lawyers acting within scope of law practice; registered securities broker-dealers; consumer reporting agencies.
Right to Cancel? Yes (5 days).
Prohibitions: Charging before complete performance; charging for referring buyer to retail seller for credit on same terms as generally available to public; making or advising false statements to creditors or credit reporting agencies; making false statements about services offered; requiring buyer to waive rights.
Other Substantive Requirements: Disclosures.
Bond: $10,000.
Private Cause of Action: Actual damages, not less than amount paid by buyer; attorney fees and costs; punitive damages allowed. A violation is a UDAP violation.

State Identity Theft Statute: Minn. Stat. § 609.527.

Definition of Offense: Transfers, possesses or uses an identity not one's own, with the intent to commit, aid or abet any unlawful activity.
Victim Remedies in Criminal Case: Court-ordered restitution available, also eligible for crime victims' compensation under Ch. 611A.
Special Record-Clearing Provisions: No specific provisions.
Duties of Private Entities: No specific provisions.
Private Right of Action: No specific provisions.

State Credit Information in Personal Insurance statute: Minn. Stat. § 72A.20, subd. 36. and 72A.49 to 72A.505.

Scope: Use of credit information for homeowners' or private passenger motor vehicle insurance (§ 72A.20) personal (i.e., not business or professional) insurance transactions involving Minnesota residents (§§ 72A.49 to 72A.505).
Disclosures: Insurer must disclose if credit information will be obtained and used. § 72A.20. Insurer must disclose its information practices to consumer. § 72A.494. Insurer that plans to use investigative consumer report must inform consumer of right to be interviewed and receive copy of report. § 72A.496. If consumer seeks disclosure of credit information that federal law prohibits insurer from disclosing, must advise consumer of name, address and phone number of credit reporting agency that issued report. § 72A.497. If adverse decision is based on credit report, insurer must disclose reasons in writing.[67] § 72A.499.
Prohibited Practices: May not use insurance inquiries or inquiries not instituted by consumer as factor in calculating credit score; use credit information if credit score is adversely impacted or cannot be generated because of absence of credit history; use credit score that incorporates gender, race, nationality, or religion. § 72A.20.
Other: Insurer must provide reasonable underwriting exemptions for consumer whose credit history has been adversely impacted by catastrophic illness or injury, temporary loss of employment, or death of an immediate family member (may require documentation). § 72A.20. Insurers who use credit scores must file scoring methodology, and information that supports its use, with commissioner. § 72A.20. Aggrieved person entitled to civil remedies provided by § 13.08 (data practices statute). §§ 72A.49 to 72A.505.

---

67 Note that the FCRA preempts state laws regulating the duties of persons who take an adverse action against a consumer based on that consumer's credit report. *See* § 10.7, *supra*.

Security Freeze Laws: Minn. Stat. Ann. §§ 13C.016 to 13C.019.
Scope: Any consumer.
Procedure: Request in writing by certified mail or by telephone to consumer reporting agency or in manner approved by agency; supply identification.
Entities covered: Consumer reporting agencies; some exceptions specified.
Duties of covered entities: Upon consumer request shall require proper identification of requesting party and provide notice, as specified, of process of placing and temporarily lifting a security freeze; within 10 business days of placing the freeze, shall send a written confirmation of the security freeze to the consumer and a unique personal identification number or password, other than the consumer's Social Security number, to be used for the release of the credit report.
Time periods: For application of freeze: no later than three business days after receiving written request. For written confirmation of the security freeze to the consumer: within 10 business days of placing the freeze. For temporary suspension of freeze: no later than three business days after receiving the request. For written confirmation of changes to file: within 30 days of the change to file.
Procedure for lifting freeze: Consumer is to provide with request to agency in manner arranged by agency: Proper identification; personal identification number or password; notice of time period if a temporary suspension of freeze.
Freeze not applicable to: Existing creditors for review or collection purposes or specified various government agencies and use of credit information for prescreening as provided by the federal Fair Credit Reporting Act; private collection agency acting under a court order, warrant, or subpoena.
Fees: A fee may be charged of no more than five dollars ($5.00) for each freeze, removal of the freeze, or temporary lifting of the freeze, or, after first reissue, replacement of identification number. No fee allowed for victim of identity theft.
Enforcement: None specified.

Mississippi

Child Support Debts: Miss. Code Ann. § 93-11-69. The Department of Human Services shall make information about child support debts, thirty days or more overdue, available to consumer reporting agencies; fifteen days advance notice and an opportunity to contest the information must be provided to obligors.

State Identity Theft Statute: Miss. Code Ann. § 97-19-85.

Definition of Offense: False statement as to identity, Social Security, credit or debit card number, or other identifying information, with intent to fraudulently obtain goods, services or other thing of value.
Victim Remedies in Criminal Case: Court must order restitution, as provided by § 99-37-1. (General criminal restitution statute.)
Special Record-Clearing Provisions: No specific provisions.
Duties of Private Entities: No specific provisions.
Private Right of Action: No specific provisions.

Missouri

Child Support Debts: Mo. Rev. Stat. § 454.512. State division of child support enforcement shall periodically report all child support arrearages, the noncustodial parent shall be provided notice and a reasonable opportunity to contest such information before it is reported.

State Credit Repair Statute: Mo. Rev. Stat. §§ 407.635 to .644.

Covered Activities: Improving credit record or obtaining extension of credit, in return for money or other consideration.

Exemptions: Regulated and supervised lenders; lenders making loans secured by liens on realty; banks and savings associations eligible for FDIC insurance; credit unions; nonprofit organizations; licensed real estate brokers acting within scope of license; Missouri lawyers acting within scope of law practice; registered securities broker-dealers; consumer reporting agencies.

Right to Cancel? Yes (3 days).

Prohibitions: Charging before complete performance, unless organization has posted bond; charging for referring buyer to retail seller for credit on same terms as generally available to public; making or advising false statements to creditors or credit reporting agencies; making false statements about services offered; requiring buyer to waive rights.

Other Substantive Requirements: Disclosures.

Bond: $10,000.

Private Cause of Action: Damages not less than amount paid by consumer; attorney fees and costs; punitive damages allowed; 4-year statute of limitations. A violation is a UDAP violation.

State Identity Theft Statute: Mo. Rev. Stat. § 570.223.

Definition of Offense: Knowingly and with intent to deceive or defraud, obtains, transfers, possesses or uses, or attempts to obtain, transfer or use, one or more means of identification not lawfully issued for his use.

Victim Remedies in Criminal Case: Court may order restitution to victim, including costs and attorney fees incurred in clearing credit history or credit rating, and in any civil or administrative proceeding to satisfy a debt, lien or other obligation resulting from the identity theft.

Special Record-Clearing Provisions: No specific provisions.

Duties of Private Entities: No specific provisions.

Private Right of Action: No specific provisions.

State Credit Information in Personal Insurance: Mo. Rev. Stat. § 375.918.

Scope: Use of credit reports or credit scores in underwriting new or renewal private automobile or homeowners (including mobile home and renters) insurance.

Disclosures: Insurer must disclose at time of application that if it will use credit information. If adverse action taken, must notify consumer of name of credit agency furnishing report, and rights to copy of report, and dispute procedure.[68]

Dispute Resolution: If consumer requests in writing within 30 days after notice of adverse action, insurer must provide explanation (i.e., what "significant characteristics" or credit history impacted the insurance credit score).[69] Applicant or insured may request reconsideration, based on corrections made to credit report or credit score.

Prohibited Practices: Insurer who uses credit report or insurance credit score in underwriting may not take adverse action based on this, without consideration of other noncredit-related factor. May not take adverse action based on credit information that is subject to dispute, not yet resolved in accordance with FCRA. Insurer may use credit report or score for new or renewal contracts, but may not use it to take adverse action on renewals until the third anniversary of the contract.

Montana

State FCRA Statute: Mont. Code Ann. §§ 31-3-101 to 31-3-153 *See also* Mont. Admin. R. 2.61.301.

Scope: Same as the federal law.

Purposes for Which Reports May Be Issued: Similar to the federal law except no authorization for provision to potential investors or servicers, or current insurers, in connection with evaluation of the credit or prepayment risks associated with existing credit obligations.

Consumer Access and Disclosure: Upon consumer request, the nature and substance of all information, except medical, in its files, and the sources of the information must be disclosed. The request must be written. Response may be over the phone; the consumer pays the toll charge. The agency must notify the consumer if information of public record with an adverse effect on employment has been reported.

Disclosures to Consumers By User: Notice that an investigative report may be requested is required within three days of request, but is not required pursuant to an employment application. If credit is denied or its cost is increased due to information obtained from a person other than an agency, the user must notify the consumer and must disclose the nature of the adverse information if a request is made within sixty days.[70]

Restrictions on Content of Reports: Similar to federal law, except criminal records more than seven years after disposition, release or parole, and bankruptcies over fourteen years old.[71] No adverse information from a prior investigative report unless it is reverified.[72]

Consumer Disputes: False information must be deleted and users must be notified. The consumer must be notified as to which users have the disputed information.

Consumer Remedies: Actual damages, costs and attorney fees, plus punitive damages for willful violations. Civil action for defamation, invasion or privacy or negligence is available against agencies which do not comply with this statute, or wrongfully judge a

---

68 Note that the FCRA preempts state laws regulating the duties of persons who take an adverse action against a consumer based on that consumer's credit report. *See* § 10.7, *supra*.

69 Note that the FCRA requires certain disclosures to be made in connection with credit scores, and generally preempts similar state provisions. However, the Act specifically exempts from preemption laws governing insurers' use of credit scores, which likely saves this provision. *See* § 10.7, *supra*.

70 Note that the FCRA preempts state laws regulating the duties of persons who take an adverse action against a consumer based on that consumer's credit report. *See* § 10.7, *supra*.

71 These two definitions of information which may not be contained under Montana law in a consumer report were in effect on Sept. 30, 1996, and therefore are not preempted, although they regulate the contents of consumer reports and might otherwise be preempted. *See* § 10.7, *supra*.

72 This provision was in effect on Sept. 30, 1996, so even if it could be said to be otherwise preempted by 15 U.S.C. § 1681c, it is not preempted. *See* § 10.7, *supra*.

dispute frivolous or refuse to delete inaccurate information, and against furnishers (except the Department of Public Health and Human Services) who provide misinformation maliciously or with intent to injure. Administrative procedure available for complaints against the Department. Violation of this statute violates the unfair and deceptive practices statute.

Miscellaneous: A credit rating is a property right with full Montana constitutional protection. An agency must maintain a record of all furnishers and users. Credit reporting agencies must warn all furnishers that they are liable to suit if the information they furnish is false, or is furnished with malice or willful intent to injure the consumer. Adverse information in investigative report may not be reused in later report unless it is verified while preparing the new report.

Child Support Debts: **Mont. Code Ann. §§ 40-5-261 and 40-5-262.** The Department of Public Health may make information about child support debts available to consumer reporting agencies; advance notice and an opportunity to contest the information's accuracy must be provided to obligors.

State Identity Theft Statute: **Mont. Code Ann. § 45-6-332.**

Definition of Offense: Purposely or knowingly obtains personal identifying information of another, and uses it without authority for any unlawful purpose, including to obtain credit, goods, services, financial or medical information, in name of another.
Victim Remedies in Criminal Case: May include costs incurred by the victim, including attorney fees, for clearing credit record or credit report, or in any civil or administrative proceeding to satisfy any debt, lien or obligation resulting from defendant's actions.
Special Record-Clearing Provisions: No specific provisions.
Duties of Private Entities: No specific provisions.
Private Right of Action: No specific provisions.

Other State Provisions: **Mont. Code Ann. § 33-18-210(11).** Use of credit history in homeowners' or private automobile insurance. Credit history includes only debt payment history or lack of history—not public information such as bankruptcies, lawsuits, and criminal convictions. May not take adverse action unless: can provide documentation that credit history is correlated with risk; insurer informs consumer of reasons for action, and, if requested provides either copy of report, or name, address and phone number of reporting agency, within ten days of request. **Mont. Code Ann. §§ 33-19-101 to 33-19-409** (insurance information and privacy protections—individual property, casualty, life, health and disability) Insurer that wishes to use investigative consumer report must advise consumer of right to be interviewed and to receive copy of report. § 33-19-205.

Nebraska

State FCRA Statute: **Neb. Rev. Stat. § 20-149.**

Scope: Similar to federal.
Purposes for Which Reports May Be Issued: No relevant provisions.
Consumer Access and Disclosure: A photocopy or typewritten copy of a report or file information is available for a reasonable fee, if disclosure is required by terms of federal FCRA as it existed on August 26, 1983; otherwise, as required by the federal law.
Disclosures to Consumer by User: No relevant provisions.
Restrictions on Content of Reports: No relevant provisions.
Consumer Disputes: No relevant provisions.
Duties of Furnishers: No relevant provisions.
Consumer Remedies: Misdemeanor.
Statute of Limitations: No relevant provisions.
Miscellaneous: No relevant provisions.

State Credit Repair Statute: **Neb. Rev. Stat. §§ 45-801 to 45-814 (Credit Services Organizations).**

Covered Activities: Improving credit record or obtaining extension of credit, in return for money or other consideration.
Exemptions: Regulated and supervised lenders; mortgage lenders approved by HUD; banks and savings associations eligible for FDIC insurance; persons whose primary business is loans secured by liens on realty; credit unions; nonprofit organizations; licensed real estate brokers and collection agencies acting within scope of license; Nebraska lawyers acting within scope of law practice; registered securities broker-dealers; consumer reporting agencies; licensed debt management organizations (see below).
Right to Cancel? Yes (3 days).
Prohibitions: Charging before complete performance of obtaining an extension of credit, or, before performance of any other service, unless organization has posted bond; charging for referring buyer to retail seller for credit on same terms as generally available to public; making or advising false statements to creditors or credit reporting agencies; making false statements about services offered; engaging in unfair and deceptive practices; requiring buyer to waive rights.
Other Substantive Requirements: Disclosures.
Bond: $100,000.
Private Cause of Action: Injunctive relief. Actual damages; attorney fees and costs; a violation is a UDAP violation; 4-year statute of limitations.

State Identity Theft Statute: **Neb. Rev. Stat. § 28-608(1)(d).**

Definition of Offense: Without authorization, and with intent to deceive or harm another, obtains or records personal identification documents [defined] or personal identifying information [defined] and accesses or attempts to access the financial resources of another for the purpose of obtaining credit, money, goods, or any other thing of value.
Victim Remedies in Criminal Case: Restitution.
Special Record-clearing Provisions: No specific provisions.
Duties of Private Entities: No specific provisions.
Private Right of Action: No specific provisions.

Credit Insurance in Personal Insurance Statute: **Neb. Rev. Stat. §§ 44-7701 to 44-7712.**

Scope: Use of credit information in personal insurance, individually underwritten for personal, family or household purposes: private passenger vehicle, recreational vehicle, homeowners (including mobile home), and non-commercial fire.
Disclosures: Insurer must notify consumer at time of application, in writing or in same medium as application, if it intends to use credit information. If adverse action based on credit report, insurer must disclose reasons to consumer, and provide notification as required by federal FCRA (source of report, dispute resolution procedure, etc.).[73]

---

73 Note that the FCRA preempts state laws regulating the duties of

Dispute Resolution: If, after dispute resolution procedure pursuant to federal FCRA information in credit report is found to be incorrect, insurer must, within 30 days after notice, re-underwrite or re-rate based on corrected report. If refund is required, it must be for lesser of policy period or 12 months.

Prohibited Practices: Insurer may not use credit score based on income, gender, address, ethnic group, religion, marital status or nationality; deny, cancel, or non-renew based wholly on credit information without, another applicable underwriting factor independent of credit information; base renewal rates solely on credit information; take adverse action based on lack of credit card; count lack of credit history as a negative factor, unless insurer can show relationship to risk; take adverse action based on credit report issued or credit score calculated more than 90 days before policy was written or renewed; use credit information if it does not recalculate every 36 months based on current credit report; treat as a negative factor collection accounts with a medical industry code, or certain credit inquiries.

Other: Insurer who uses scores must file scoring model with department of insurance.

Nevada

State FCRA Statute: Nev. Rev. Stat. §§ 598C.010 to 598C.200.

Scope: Similar to federal.

Purposes for Which Reports May Be Issued: Same as the federal law. Consumers must be given the opportunity to opt out of prescreened lists.[74]

Consumer Access and Disclosure: Rights under state FCRA. The nature and substance of a report in the files at the time of the request and disclosure of the name of the institutional sources of information. On request, shall provide a readable copy and the name of each person who has received a report within the preceding two years, if for employment purposes, or the preceding six months if for any other purpose.

Disclosures to Consumers By User: A consumer must be notified if adverse action is taken on the basis of a credit report, and the consumer must be given notice of the name and address of the reporting agency and of the right to obtain a copy of the report from the agency.[75]

Restrictions on Content of Reports: Same as federal law except agencies are forbidden to report criminal proceedings over seven years old and medical information.[76]

Consumer Disputes: Within five days after a consumer disputes the accuracy of any information, agency must notify any institutional sources of the information, and must complete reinvestigation within thirty days.[77] If the information is found to be incorrect, the files must be corrected and the consumer notified. No information that was deleted because of an inaccuracy may be reinserted unless reasonable procedures are used to maximize accuracy, and the consumer is notified within five business days after the reinsertion and offered the opportunity to add a brief statement disputing or adding to the information.

Duties of Furnishers: No relevant provisions.

Consumer Remedies: Willful noncompliance: actual damages, punitive damages, costs, and reasonable attorney fees. Negligent noncompliance: actual damages, costs, and reasonable attorney fees.

Statute of Limitations: No relevant provisions.

Miscellaneous: No relevant provisions.

Child Support Debts: Nev. Rev. Stat. § 598C.110. Reports shall include information concerning delinquent child support payments if they are presented in an acceptable format by the welfare division or district attorney.

State Credit Repair Statute: Nev. Rev. Stat. §§ 598.741 to .787.

Covered Activities: Improving credit record or obtaining extension of credit, in return for money or other consideration, unauthorized debt adjustment counseling.

Exemptions: Regulated and supervised lenders; banks and savings associations eligible for FDIC insurance; credit unions; licensed debt adjusters; licensed real estate brokers acting within scope of license; Nevada lawyers acting within scope of law practice; registered securities broker-dealers; consumer reporting agencies.

Right to Cancel? Yes (5 days).

Prohibitions: Charging before complete performance; charging for referring buyer to retail seller for credit on same terms as generally available to public; making or advising false statements to creditors or credit reporting agencies; making false statements about services offered; creating new credit record by use of new identification for buyer; submitting buyer dispute to reporting agency without buyer's knowledge; calling reporting agency by a person falsely identified as the buyer; requiring buyer to waive rights.

Other Substantive Requirements: Disclosures.

Bond: None, but $100,000 security deposit required with regulatory agency.

Private Cause of Action: Actual damages, not less than amount paid by buyer; attorney fees and costs; punitive damages allowed. A violation is a UDAP violation.

State Identity Theft Statute: Nev. Rev. Stat. §§ 41.1345, 205.463 and 205.465.

Definition of Offense: Obtains personal identifying information [very broadly defined] of another, and uses it to harm that person, or for unlawful purpose, including but not limited to obtaining goods, credit, services or other thing of value in that person's name, or to delay or avoid being prosecuted for any unlawful act. Possesses, sells or transfers any document or personal identifying information, for the purpose of establishing a false identity for self or another.

Victim Remedies in Criminal Case: Court must order restitution, including costs and attorney fees incurred in clearing credit record or credit rating, and in any civil or administrative proceeding to satisfy debt or obligation incurred as a result of the identity theft.

---

persons who take an adverse action against a consumer based on that consumer's credit report. See § 10.7, *supra*.

74 State laws concerning prescreened lists are now preempted. See § 10.7, *supra*.

75 Note that the FCRA preempts state laws regulating the duties of persons who take an adverse action against a consumer based on that consumer's credit report. See § 10.7, *supra*.

76 These provisions were in effect on Sept. 30, 1996, so even if they could be said to be otherwise preempted by 15 U.S.C. § 1681c, they are not preempted. See § 10.7, *supra*.

77 This provision was in effect on Sept. 30, 1996, so although it regulates the time allowed an agency for reinvestigation, it is not preempted. See § 10.7, *supra*.

Special Record-Clearing Provisions: No specific provisions.
Duties of Private Entities: No specific provisions.
Private Right of Action: Person injured as proximate result of violation of § 205.463 has private right of action for actual damages, reasonable costs and attorney fees, and such punitive damages as the facts may warrant.

State Credit Information in Personal Insurance statute: Nev. Rev. Stat. §§ 686A.600 to 686A.730.

Scope: Use of credit information in personal insurance, i.e., not commercial, business or surety.
Disclosures: Insurer must notify consumer at time of application, in writing or in same medium as application, if it intends to use credit information. If adverse action based on credit report, insurer must disclose reasons to consumer, and provide notification as required by federal FCRA (source of report, dispute resolution procedure, etc.).[78]
Dispute Resolution: If, after dispute resolution procedure pursuant to federal FCRA information in credit report is found to be incorrect, insurer must, within 30 days after notice, re-underwrite or re-rate based on corrected report. If refund is required, it must be for lesser of policy period or 12 months. At annual renewal, consumer may request re-underwriting or re-rating based on current credit report.
Prohibited Practices: Insurer may not use credit score based on income, gender, address, ethnic group, religion, marital status or nationality; deny, cancel, or non-renew based wholly on credit information without, another applicable underwriting factor independent of credit information; base renewal rates solely on credit information; take adverse action based on lack of credit card; count lack of credit history as a negative factor, unless insurer can show relationship to risk; take adverse action based on credit report issued or credit score calculated more than 90 days before policy was written or renewed; use credit information if it does not recalculate every 36 months based on current credit report; treat as a negative factor collection accounts with a medical industry code, or certain credit inquiries.
Other: No relevant provisions.

Security Freeze Laws: Nev. Rev. Stat. §§ 598C.300 to 598.390.

Scope: Any consumer.
Procedure: Request in writing by certified mail to consumer reporting agency or in manner approved by agency; supply identification.
Entities covered: Consumer reporting agencies; some exceptions specified.
Duties of covered entities: Upon consumer request shall require proper identification of requesting party and provide notice, as specified, of process of placing and temporarily lifting a security freeze; within 10 business days of placing the freeze, shall send a written confirmation of the security freeze to the consumer and a unique personal identification number or password, other than the consumer's Social Security number, to be used for the release of the credit report.
Time periods: For application of freeze: no later than five business days after receiving written request. For written confirmation of the security freeze to the consumer or replacement of identification number: within 10 business days of placing the freeze or request. For revocation or temporary suspension of freeze: no later than three business days after receiving the request. For written confirmation of changes to file: within 30 days of the change to file.
Procedure for lifting freeze: Consumer is to provide with request to agency in manner arranged by agency: Proper identification; personal identification number or password; notice of time period if a temporary suspension of freeze.
Freeze not applicable to: Existing creditors or specified various government agencies; agents of entities having existing business relationship with consumer, relating to pre-employment screening or past employment investigations; licensed collection agency in regard to consumer's account; use of information for the purposes of prescreening pursuant to the Fair Credit Reporting Act; persons requesting the consumer report pursuant to a court order, warrant or subpoena; persons holding a license issued by the Nevada Gaming Commission for purposes relating to any activities conducted pursuant to the license.
Fees: A fee may be charged of no more than fifteen dollars ($15) for each freeze; for removal of the freeze, or temporary lifting of the freeze, not more than $18; for temporary release to specific party, not more than $20. No fees allowed for victim of identity theft. Fees may increase each January based on Consumer Price Index.
Enforcement: Actual damages, costs, and attorney fees.

New Hampshire

State FCRA Statute: N.H. Rev. Stat. Ann. §§ 359-B:1 to 359-B:21.

Scope: Same as the federal law.
Purposes for Which Reports May Be Issued: Similar to federal law except no authorization for provision to potential investors or servicers, or current insurers, in connection with the evaluation of the credit or prepayment risks associated with existing credit obligations. Consumers must be given the opportunity via a toll-free telephone number to opt out of prescreened lists.[79]
Consumer Access and Disclosure: Upon consumer request, an agency must disclose the nature and substance of all information, except medical information, in its files. Consumers must pay a reasonable copy fee.
Disclosures to Consumers By User: Similar to federal law.
Restrictions on Content of Reports: Similar to federal law except bankruptcies over fourteen years old and criminal records more than seven years after date of disposition, release or parole.[80]
Consumer Disputes: Similar to federal law, except that the consumer reporting agency must reinvestigate within thirty days and notify the consumer of the results within a further ten days.[81] Agency must inform consumer of right to request description of procedures used to reinvestigate, including name, address and

---

78 Note that the FCRA preempts state laws regulating the duties of persons who take an adverse action against a consumer based on that consumer's credit report. See § 10.7, *supra*.

79 State laws concerning prescreened lists are now preempted. See § 10.7, *supra*.

80 This provision was in effect on Sept. 30, 1996, so even if it could be said to be otherwise preempted by 15 U.S.C. § 1681c, it is not preempted. See § 10.7, *supra*.

81 This provision was in effect on Sept. 30, 1996, so although it regulates the time allowed an agency for reinvestigation, it is not preempted. See § 10.7, *supra*.

telephone number of person(s) contacted.
Duties of Furnishers: No relevant provisions.
Consumer Remedies: Actual damages, costs and reasonable attorney fees, plus punitive damages for willful violations. Criminal penalties for obtaining information from agency by false pretenses, or for unauthorized disclosures by agency personnel.
Statute of Limitations: Two years from accrual (or from discovery, if delay resulted from willful and material misrepresentations by defendant).
Miscellaneous: Adverse information in investigative reports must be reverified or less than three months old to be included in a subsequent report.[82]

State Credit Repair Statute: N.H. Rev. Stat. Ann. §§ 359-D:1 to 359-D:11.

Covered Activities: Improving credit record or obtaining extension of credit, in return for money or other consideration.
Exemptions: Lenders authorized by N.H. and federal law; banks and savings associations eligible for FDIC insurance; nonprofit organizations; licensed real estate brokers acting within scope of license; N.H. lawyers acting within scope of law practice; registered securities broker-dealers; consumer reporting agencies.
Right to Cancel? Yes (5 days).
Prohibitions: Charging before complete performance, unless organization has posted bond; charging for referring buyer to retail seller for credit on same terms as generally available to public; making or advising false statements to creditors or credit reporting agencies; making false statements about services offered; requiring buyer to waive rights.
Other Substantive Requirements: Disclosures.
Bond: 5% of amount of fees charged during prior 12 months, not less than $5000 or more than $25,000, to be adjusted annually.
Private Cause of Action: Actual damages, not less than amount paid by buyer; attorney fees and costs; punitive damages allowed.

State Identity Theft Statute: N.H. Rev. Stat. Ann. §§ 638:25 to 638:27.

Definition of Offense: Poses as another with intent to defraud to obtain money, credit, goods, services or other thing of value, or confidential information about that person not available to the general public; obtains records or personal identifying information of another with intent to pose as that person or enable another to do so.
Victim Remedies in Criminal Case: Court shall order restitution for victim's economic loss.
Special Record-Clearing Provisions: No specific provisions.
Duties of Private Entities: No specific provisions.
Private Right of Action: No specific provisions.

Other State Provisions: N.H. Rev. Stat. Ann. § 412:15. Use of credit reports, credit histories, and credit scoring models in homeowners and personal motor vehicle insurance must be "based on objective, documented and measurable standards" and used in a manner that "affords appropriate consumer protections, including consumer notice provisions and confidentiality protections." Commissioner shall make rules. Scoring models must be approved by department.

---

82 This provision was in effect on Sept. 30, 1996, so even if it could be said to be otherwise preempted by 15 U.S.C. § 1681c, it is not preempted. *See* § 10.7, *supra*.

Security Freeze Laws: N.H. Rev. Stat. Ann. §§ 359-B:22 to 359-B:29.

Scope: Any consumer.
Procedure: Request in writing by certified mail to consumer reporting agency or in manner approved by agency; supply identification.
Entities covered: Consumer reporting agencies; some exceptions specified.
Duties of covered entities: Upon consumer request shall require proper identification of requesting party and provide notice, as specified, of process of placing and temporarily lifting a security freeze; within 10 business days of placing the freeze, shall send a written confirmation of the security freeze to the consumer and a unique personal identification number or password, other than the consumer's Social Security number, to be used for the release of the credit report.
Time periods: For application of freeze: no later than five business days after receiving written request. For written confirmation of the security freeze to the consumer or replacement of identification number: within 10 business days of placing the freeze or request. For revocation or temporary suspension of freeze: no later than three business days after receiving the request. For written confirmation of changes to file: within 30 days of the change to file.
Procedure for lifting freeze: Consumer is to provide with request to agency in manner arranged by agency: Proper identification; personal identification number or password; notice of time period if a temporary suspension of freeze.
Freeze not applicable to: Existing creditors for purposes of review or collection; specified various government agencies; person acting pursuant to a court order, warrant, or subpoena; use of credit information for prescreening as provided by the federal Fair Credit Reporting Act; use in setting or adjusting an insurance rate or claim or underwriting for insurance purposes.
Fees: A fee may be charged of no more than ten dollars ($10) for each freeze, for removal of the freeze, or temporary lifting of the freeze, or for replacement of identification number. No fees allowed for victim of identity theft.
Enforcement: The greater of $1000 or actual damages.

Security Freeze Laws: N.J. Stat. Ann. § 56:11-46 (West).

Scope: Any consumer.
Procedure: Request in writing by certified or overnight mail or by secure electronic mail connection to consumer reporting agency; supply identification.
Entities covered: Consumer reporting agencies.
Duties of covered entities: Upon consumer request shall require proper identification of requesting party and provide notice, as specified, of process of placing and temporarily lifting a security freeze; within 10 business days of placing the freeze, shall send a written confirmation of the security freeze to the consumer and a unique personal identification number or password, other than the consumer's Social Security number, to be used for the release of the credit report.
Time periods: For application of freeze: no later than five business days after receiving written request. For written confirmation of the security freeze to the consumer: within 5 business days of placing the freeze. For temporary suspension of freeze: no later than three business days after receiving the request. For written confirmation of changes to file: within 30 days of the change to file.

Procedure for lifting freeze: Consumer is to provide with request to agency in writing by certified or overnight mail or by secure electronic mail connection to consumer reporting agency: Proper identification; personal identification number or password; notice of time period if a temporary suspension of freeze.
Freeze not applicable to: Existing creditors for purposes of review or collection; specified various government agencies; use of credit information for prescreening as provided by the federal Fair Credit Reporting Act.
Fees: A fee may be charged of no more than five dollars for removal or temporary lifting of the freeze or issuance of replacement identification number; no fee allowed for freeze request.
Enforcement: Specified actual damages, punitive damages possible; attorney fees. § 56:11-38.

New Jersey

State FCRA Statute: **N.J. Stat. Ann. §§ 56:11-28 to 56:11-41 (West).**

Scope: Similar to federal.
Purposes for Which Reports May Be Issued: Generally same as federal law, but consumers must give prior written consent for the inclusion of medical information in reports used for employment, credit, insurance or direct marketing purposes, and for the preparation of investigative consumer reports.
Consumer Access and Disclosure: Similar to federal law, but must disclose all information in file. Must provide one free report per twelve month period;[83] subsequent reports $8. Must disclose the dates, original payees and amounts of any checks that are the basis for any adverse characterization. Must disclose requests (for purposes other than a credit transaction initiated by the consumer) within one year.
Disclosures to Consumers By User: Prior to requesting an investigative report must disclose precise nature and scope of investigation and consumer's right to a free copy of the report, and must obtain consumer's prior written consent.
Restrictions on Content of Reports: No relevant provisions.
Consumer Disputes: Similar to federal law, except agency must notify consumer written five business days of determination that dispute is frivolous, including the reasons for its decision.
Duties of Furnishers: No relevant provisions.
Consumer Remedies: Negligent violations: actual damages, costs and reasonable attorney fees. Willful violations: actual damages or minimum damages of at least $100 but not more than $1000, punitive damages, costs and reasonable attorney fees. Those who file pleadings in bad faith or to harass liable for prevailing party's attorney fees for responding to that pleading. Criminal penalties for obtaining information from agency under false pretenses.
Statute of Limitations: No relevant provisions.
Miscellaneous: No relevant provisions.

Child Support Debts: **N.J. Stat. Ann. § 2A:17-56.21 (West).** The state Department of Human Services shall report child support arrearages to consumer reporting agencies. The Department must give obligor prior notice and an opportunity to contest the accuracy of the information.

State Identity Theft Statute: **N.J. Stat. Ann. §§ 2C:21-17 to 2C:21-17.5 (West).**

Definition of Offense: Impersonates another or assumes a false identity for purpose of obtaining a pecuniary benefit, or injuring or defrauding another; obtains personal identifying information of another and uses it without authority to fraudulently obtain a pecuniary benefit or services, or avoid the payment of a debt, or avoid criminal prosecution; or assists another person in using the information for these purposes. Possesses, manufactures or distributes items containing personal identification information of another, without authority, with knowledge that one is facilitating a fraud or injury to another.
Victim Remedies in Criminal Case: Restitution. Restitution includes costs incurred in clearing credit history or credit rating, and in any civil or administrative proceeding to satisfy any lien or debt or other obligation resulting from the actions of the thief. Sentencing court shall issue orders necessary to correct any public record that contains false information as a result of the identity theft.
Special Record-Clearing Provisions: At victim's request, or on court's own motion, court may grant an order requiring all consumer reporting agencies doing business in New Jersey to delete any false information resulting from the theft, and give consumer a free copy of the corrected credit report.
Duties of Private Entities: At victim's request, agency must provided corrected report to any person specified by the victim who has received a report within two years for employment purposes, or one year for any other purpose, if the report contained the false information.
Private Right of Action: Anyone who suffers ascertainable loss of money or property may bring action for treble damages, plus costs and attorney fees. (Damages may be awarded to businesses, financial institutions, etc., but any damages to natural persons must be fully satisfied before any payment to businesses, etc.). Standard of proof is preponderance of evidence; civil action may be brought even if criminal case ends in acquittal. (Conviction in criminal case will estop defendant from denying the conduct in a civil action.)

New Mexico

State FCRA Statute: **N.M. Stat. §§ 56-3-1 to 56-3-8.**

Scope: A consumer is any natural person seeking credit for personal, family, or household purposes.
Purposes for Which Reports May Be Issued: Credit reports for the granting of credit. Other bona fide business transactions. Employment purposes. No financial information to non-credit granting government agencies except by court order.
Consumer Access and Disclosure: Upon consumer request, an agency must disclose all information in a credit report or rating.
Disclosures to Consumer by User: No relevant provisions.
Restrictions on Content of Reports: A credit bureau must delete any derogatory data as soon as practical after ascertaining it can no longer be verified. A credit bureau cannot merge specialized information which is applicable only to personnel investigations.[84]

---

83 Although the FCRA preempts state laws with respect to the frequency of the right to free reports, the Act specifically exempts this New Jersey provision from preemption. *See* § 10.7, *supra*.

84 This provision was in effect on Sept. 30, 1996, so even if it could be said to be otherwise preempted by 15 U.S.C. § 1681c, it is not preempted. *See* § 10.7, *supra*.

Criminal records over seven years old, convictions if a full pardon is granted, and arrests and indictments if learned no conviction resulted.[85] Bankruptcies over 14 years.

Consumer Disputes: A credit bureau must give a consumer who is examining credit reports forms on which to designate errors. If disputed, an agency must reinvestigate at no cost to the consumer if the consumer is denied credit. If the consumer is not denied credit, the consumer can be charged up to $5 for the reinvestigation.

Duties of Furnishers: No relevant provisions.

Consumer Remedies: After a credit bureau is given notice of an error, it is liable for any subsequent report which fails to correct the error. It is not liable for damages for an unintentional error prior to receiving notice of its existence. Damages for negligence include actual damages, costs and attorney fees, plus punitive damages for willful violations. Criminal penalties for obtaining information from agency under false pretenses, and for unauthorized disclosures by agency personnel.

Statute of Limitations: No relevant provisions.

Miscellaneous: A credit bureau must require service contracts in which the user certifies that inquiries will be made only for proper purposes; a credit bureau must refuse services to one who will not certify.

Child Support Debts: **N.M. Stat. § 56-3-3**. Child Support Enforcement Division may obtain credit reports for use in locating obligors and enforcing obligations. Division must furnish to credit bureau, on request, the judgment or case number for the obligation for which a report is requested.

State Identity Theft Statute: **N.M. Stat. § 30-16-24.1**.

Definition of Offense: Willfully obtaining, recording or transferring personal identifying information of another, without authority, and with intent to defraud that person or another.

Victim Remedies in Criminal Case: Out-of-pocket costs, plus expenses incurred, including attorney fees, in clearing credit record or credit report, and in civil or administrative proceeding to satisfy any debt, lien or obligation resulting from the theft. Sentencing court shall issue written findings of fact, and make such orders as are necessary to correct a public record that contains misinformation as a result of the theft.

Special Record-Clearing Provisions: No specific provisions.

Duties of Private Entities: No specific provisions.

Private Right of Action: No specific provisions.

New York

State FCRA Statute: **N.Y. Gen. Bus. Law §§ 380 to 380-t (McKinney)**.

Scope: Adverse information is any information that is likely to have a negative effect upon the ability or eligibility of a consumer to obtain credit insurance, employment or other benefits, goods or services, or information responsible for increases in charges for credit or insurance.

Purposes for Which Reports May Be Issued: Similar to the federal law, but explicitly authorize use for residential rentals and does not authorize provision to potential investors or servicers, or current insurers, in connection with evaluation of the credit or prepayment risks associated with existing credit obligations. May not issue reports listing credit denial if the denial is only due to insufficient information.[86]

Consumer Access and Disclosure: Similar to federal law, except that all information in files must be disclosed. Medical information only to be disclosed to physician designated by consumer. An agency must inform a consumer upon any contact of the right to receive a credit report. All consumers denied credit must be notified of the right to receive a report within thirty days at no charge. All requests for reports for employment purposes for two years, for other purposes for six months. If medical information, or reasons for an adverse action based on medical information must be disclosed, it should be disclosed to a physician designated by the consumer.

Disclosures to Consumers By User: Similar to the federal law, except that a consumer must be informed in writing that a credit report may be requested.[87] Upon consumer request, a user must tell a consumer if a credit report is actually used, and the source of the report. For an investigative consumer report, the user must obtain authorization in all situations. An authorization must state that the consumer can request a credit report, and that the user may request a report from the agency and, upon request, will inform a consumer whether it has done so. A consumer must be furnished with the reason for the denial of credit (statute refers to federal Equal Credit Opportunity Act); cannot furnish the report to others without a legitimate business need.

Restrictions on Content of Reports: Similar to the federal law. Judgments over five years old which have been paid. Bankruptcies over fourteen years old. Information known to be incorrect. In addition:[88] information relative to an arrest or criminal charge unless it is still pending or resulted in conviction. Criminal convictions seven years after disposition, release or parole. Information on race, religion, color, or ethnic origin. Drug/alcohol addiction or mental institution confinement information over seven years old. Agencies may not collect or maintain in its files any information related to or derived from a polygraph examination or similar device. For employment purposes only, an agency may report information related to the detention of an individual by a retail establishment if an uncoerced admission of wrongdoing was executed, and the retail establishment notified the individual that it is furnishing information to a reporting agency, and that the individual may dispute the information's completeness or accuracy.

Consumer Disputes: Similar to the federal law. If an item is corrected or can no longer be verified, an agency must mail a corrected copy to the consumer at no charge.

Duties of Furnishers: No relevant provisions.

Consumer Remedies: Actual damages, costs and reasonable attorney fees, plus punitive damages for willful violations. Criminal penalties for obtaining information from agency under false pretenses; for willfully introducing or attempting to introduce false information into file to damage or enhance credit rating; and for unauthorized disclosures by agency personnel.

---

85 These provisions were in effect on Sept. 30, 1996, so even if they could be said to be otherwise preempted by 15 U.S.C. § 1681c, the are not preempted. *See* § 10.7, *supra*.

86 This provision was in effect on Sept. 30, 1996, so even if it could be said to be otherwise preempted by 15 U.S.C. § 1681c, it is not preempted. *See* § 10.7, *supra*.

87 Scott v. Real Estate Finance Group, 183 F.3d 97 (2d Cir. 1999).

88 Even if these provisions could be said to be otherwise preempted by 15 U.S.C. § 1681c, they were in effect on September 30, 1996 and therefore not preempted.

Statute of Limitations: Two years from accrual (or from discovery, if delay results from willful material misrepresentation by defendant).
Miscellaneous: No adverse information may be included within a subsequent investigative consumer report unless it is reverified or less than three months old.[89]

State Credit Repair Statute: N.Y. Gen. Bus. Law §§ 458-a to 458-k (McKinney).

Covered Activities: Improving credit record in return for money or other consideration.
Exemptions: Nonprofit organizations. N.Y. licensed lawyers, rendering services within the scope of their law practice.
Right to Cancel? Yes (3 days).
Prohibitions: Charging before complete performance; charging for referring buyer to retail seller for credit on same terms as generally available to public; making or advising false statements to creditors or credit reporting agencies; making false statements about services offered; misrepresenting ability to obtain credit card for buyer; requiring buyer to waive rights.
Other Substantive Requirements: Disclosures.
Bond: N/A
Private Cause of Action: No more than thrice actual damages and no less than amount paid by buyer; attorney fees. Contract voidable. A violation is UDAP violation.

State Identity Theft Statute: N.Y. Penal Law §§ 190.77 to 190.84 (McKinney). See also N.Y. Gen. Bus. Law § 380-s (McKinney).

Definition of Offense: Identity theft: Knowingly with intent to defraud assumes identity of another, by presenting self as another, or using personal identifying information of that person, with intent to obtain goods, money, services or credit, or cause financial loss to that person or another, or commit a crime. Degree of offense depends on amount of financial loss caused, or seriousness of crime committed. Unlawful possession of personal identification information: Knowingly possesses certain identifying information of another, knowing it is to be used in furtherance of a crime defined by this chapter [larceny]. Degree of crime depends on number of items possessed or accomplices supervised. *See also* Gen. Bus. Law § 380-s, a civil statute which forbids knowingly and with intent to defraud obtaining, transferring, processing using, or attempting to obtain, etc., credit, goods services or anything of value in the name of another person without that person's consent.
Victim Remedies in Criminal Case: No specific provisions.
Special Record-clearing Provisions: No specific provisions.
Duties of Private Entities: No specific provisions.
Private Right of Action: Any person, firm, partnership, or corporation whose knowing and willful violation of § 380-s resulted in the transmission or provision to a credit reporting agency of information that would not otherwise have been transmitted or provided is liable for actual and punitive damages, costs and attorney fees.

Security Freeze Laws: N.Y. Gen. Bus. Law § 380-a(t) (McKinney).

Scope: Any consumer.

---

89 This provision was in effect on September 30, 1996, so even if it could be said to be otherwise preempted by 15 U.S.C. § 1681c, it is not preempted. *See* § 10.7, *supra*.

Procedure: Request in writing by certified or overnight mail to consumer credit reporting agency; supply identification.
Entities covered: Consumer credit reporting agencies.
Duties of covered entities: Upon consumer request shall require proper identification of requesting party and provide notice, as specified, of process of placing and temporarily lifting a security freeze; within 10 business days of placing the freeze, shall send a written confirmation of the security freeze to the consumer and a unique personal identification number or password, other than the consumer's Social Security number, to be used for the release of the credit report. Whether freeze in place or not, credit reports may ONLY be released to: a person whom it has reason to believe intends to use the information (i) in connection with a credit transaction involving the consumer on whom the information is to be furnished and involving the extension of credit to, or review or collection of an account of, the consumer, or (ii) for employment purposes, or (iii) in connection with the underwriting of insurance involving the consumer, or (iv) in connection with a determination of the consumer's eligibility for a license or other benefit granted by a governmental instrumentality required by law to consider an applicant's financial responsibility or status, or (v) to a person in connection with a business transaction involving the consumer where the user has a legitimate business need for such information, or (vi) in connection with the rental or lease of a residence. § 380-b.
Time periods: For application of freeze: no later than five business days after receiving written request (four days after January 1, 2008; three days after January 1, 2009). For written confirmation of the security freeze to the consumer: within 5 business days of placing the freeze. For temporary suspension of freeze: no later than three business days after receiving the request. For written confirmation of changes to file: within 30 days of the change to file.
Procedure for lifting freeze: Consumer is to provide with request to agency in writing by certified or overnight mail or by secure electronic mail connection to consumer reporting agency: Proper identification; personal identification number or password; notice of time period if a temporary suspension of freeze.
Freeze not applicable to: Existing creditors for purposes of review or collection; specified various government agencies; person acting pursuant to a court order, warrant, or subpoena; use of credit information for prescreening as provided by the federal Fair Credit Reporting Act.
Fees: A fee may be charged of no more than five dollars for a second or subsequent request for freeze, removal or temporary lifting of the freeze, or issuance of replacement identification number. No fees allowed identity theft victims.
Enforcement: Fines and injunctions available in actions by Attorney General.

North Carolina

State Credit Repair Statute: N.C. Gen. Stat. §§ 66-220 to 66-226.

Covered Activities: Improving credit record or obtaining extension of credit, in return for money or other consideration.
Exemptions: Banks and savings associations authorized by N.C. or federal law; licensed consumer finance lenders; credit unions; nonprofit organizations; licensed real estate brokers acting within scope of license; N.C. lawyers acting within scope of law practice; registered securities broker-dealers; consumer reporting agencies.
Right to Cancel? Yes (3 days).

Prohibitions: Charging before complete performance; charging for referring buyer to retail seller for credit on same terms as generally available to public; making or advising false statements to creditors or credit reporting agencies; making false statements about services offered; requiring buyer to waive rights.
Other Substantive Requirements: Disclosures.
Bond: $10,000.
Private Cause of Action: Contract voidable with complete refund; attorney fees and any other additional damages. A violation is a UDAP violation.

State Identity Theft Statute: **N.C. Gen. Stat. §§ 14-113.20 to 14-113.23**.

Definition of Offense: Financial identity fraud: Knowingly obtains, possesses or uses personal identifying information of another, without authority, with intent to fraudulently represent self to be that person for purposes of making financial or credit transactions, or avoiding legal consequences. Punishment is enhanced if victim suffers arrest, detention or conviction as a proximate result of the fraud. Trafficking in stolen identities: Sells, transfers or purchases identifying information of another, with intent to commit financial identity fraud, or assist another in doing so.
Victim Remedies in Criminal Case: If person commits a crime under a stolen name, court records shall reflect that ID theft victim did not commit the crime. Restitution includes lost wages, attorney fees or other costs incurred in correcting credit record or in connection with any civil, criminal or administrative proceeding brought against the victim as a result of the theft.
Special Record-Clearing Provisions: No specific provisions.
Duties of Private Entities: No specific provisions.
Private Right of Action: Victim also has a cause of action under § 1-539.2C, the civil theft statute, for greater of treble damages or $5000. This civil action available whether or not criminal prosecution is brought. Thief is liable for damages; injunctive relief; attorney fees.

Other State Provisions: **N.C. Gen. Stat. § 25B-2**. Agency, upon written request by married person, must report both separate credit history of each spouse and history of joint accounts, if any.

State Credit Insurance in Private Insurance statute: **N.C. Gen. Stat. Ann. § 58-36-90. See also N.C. Gen. Stat. §§ 58-39-1 to 58-39-76.**

Scope: Credit reports or credit scores used in non-commercial insurance underwriting (i.e., residential or non-commercial vehicle).
Disclosures: If credit score or credit report is used as basis for adverse action, must notify consumer of factors used in determining credit score; name, address and toll-free phone number of credit bureau that issued report, and notice that consumer has right to challenge information in report.[90] The insurance information and privacy protection statute, N.C. Gen. Stat. §§ 58-39-1 to 58-39-76, requires insurer to disclose their information practices. An insurer who wishes to use investigative consumer report must notify consumer of right to be interviewed and to receive copy of report. § 58-39-40.
Dispute Resolution: If, after dispute procedure provided by federal FCRA, information is found to be inaccurate or incomplete, insurer must, within 30 days of being notified, re-underwrite or re-rate. If a refund is required, it should be for the shorter of 12 months or the actual policy period.
Prohibited Practices: Insurers may not use credit scores as sole reason for terminating existing policy of noncommercial vehicle or residential insurance.

Security Freeze Laws: **N.C. Gen. Stat. § 75-63**.

Scope: Any consumer.
Procedure: Request in writing by certified mail to consumer reporting agency; supply identification.
Entities covered: Consumer reporting agencies; some exceptions specified.
Duties of covered entities: Upon consumer request shall require proper identification of requesting party and provide notice, as specified, of process of placing and temporarily lifting a security freeze; within 10 business days of placing the freeze, shall send a written confirmation of the security freeze to the consumer and a unique personal identification number or password, other than the consumer's Social Security number, to be used for the release of the credit report.
Time periods: For application of freeze: no later than five business days after receiving written request. For written confirmation of the security freeze to the consumer: within 10 business days of placing the freeze. For temporary suspension of freeze: no later than three business days after receiving the request. For written confirmation of changes to file: within 30 days of the change to file.
Procedure for lifting freeze: Consumer is to provide with request to agency in manner arranged by agency: Proper identification; personal identification number or password; notice of time period if a temporary suspension of freeze.
Freeze not applicable to: Existing creditors for purposes of review or collection; specified various government agencies; person acting pursuant to a court order, warrant, or subpoena; use of credit information for prescreening as provided by the federal Fair Credit Reporting Act; use in setting or adjusting an insurance rate or claim or underwriting for insurance purposes; any depository financial institution for checking, savings, and investment accounts.
Fees: A fee may be charged of no more than ten dollars ($10) for each freeze, removal of the freeze, or temporary lifting of the freeze. No fee allowed for victim of identity theft.
Enforcement: UDAP violation.

North Dakota

Child Support Debts: **N.D. Cent. Code § 50-09-08.4**. Enforcement agencies may report past due support amounts provided obligors given notice and a reasonable opportunity to contest the accuracy of the report first.

State Identity Theft Statute: **N.D. Cent. Code § 12.1-23-11**.

Definition of Offense: Uses personal identifying information of another without authority to obtain credit, money, goods, services or anything of value, while representing self to be another or to be acting under that person's authority.
Victim Remedies in Criminal Case: No specific provisions.
Special Record-Clearing Provisions: No specific provisions.
Duties of Private Entities: No specific provisions.

---

90 Note that the FCRA preempts state laws regulating the duties of persons who take an adverse action against a consumer based on that consumer's credit report. *See* § 10.7, *supra*.

Private Right of Action: No specific provisions.

State Credit Information in Private Insurance statute: N.D. Cent. Code §§ 26.1-25.1-01 to 26.1-25.1-11.

Scope: Credit information used in underwriting personal insurance, i.e., policies individually underwritten for personal, family or household purposes.

Disclosures: Insurer must notify consumer at time of application that credit information will be used. Insurer must notify consumer of reasons for adverse action, if based on credit information.[91]

Dispute Resolution: If, after dispute procedure provided by federal FCRA, information is found to be inaccurate or incomplete, insurer must, within 30 days of being notified, re-underwrite or re-rate. If a refund is required, it should be for the shorter of 12 months or the actual policy period.

Prohibited Practices: Insurer may not use an insurance score that is based on income, gender, address, zip code, ethnic group, marital status or nationality; deny, cancel or non-renew based solely on credit information; take adverse action solely because consumer does not have credit card; take adverse action based on credit report unless report is issued or score calculated within one hundred twenty days of date when policy is issued or renewed; use credit information; use credit information if it does not recalculate or obtain updated report at least every 36 months; consider the following as negative factors: inquiries not initiated nor requested by consumer, inquiries relating to insurance coverage, collection accounts with medical industry code, certain multiple lender inquiries (i.e., relating to home mortgage or auto loan).

Other: No relevant provisions.

Ohio

State FCRA Statute: Ohio Rev. Code Ann. §§ 3904.01 to 3904.22 (West).

Scope: Consumer reports used in connection with a life, health or disability insurance transaction.

Purposes for Which Reports May Be Issued: Life, health or disability insurance transactions.

Consumer Access and Disclosures: Authorization to obtain information must be in plain language, in writing, signed by consumer, indicate what information is sought, be dated, and limited to a specific time. Medical information may be provided to a medical professional designated by the consumer. Disclosure requirements do not apply to certain information gathered in connection with or reasonable anticipation of, civil or criminal proceeding involving the consumer.

Disclosures to Consumer By User: Insurance institutions or agents must disclose that a report may be requested and provide a notice of information practices summarizing consumers' rights under Ohio law. No insurance institution, agent or insurance support organization may procure an investigative consumer report in connection with an insurance transaction without informing consumer of their right to be interviewed for the report and to receive a copy of the report. Upon written request, insurance institutions, agents or insurance support organizations must disclose all recorded personal information to consumer and the sources of such information, and must provide a summary of procedures available to request correction, amendment or deletion of such information. Insurance institutions or agents must notify consumer of reasons for adverse underwriting decision and, if requested within ninety business days, the specific items and sources of information that support those reasons.[92]

Restrictions on Content of Reports: No relevant provisions.

Consumer Disputes: Within thirty days of being informed of dispute, must either correct or delete the information or inform the consumer of its refusal, the reasons, and the right to file a statement describing the dispute. If information is changed or deleted, must notify (at request of consumer) users who have received reports within two years. Must notify insurance support organizations which use the information, or which supplied the information.

Duties of Furnishers: Imposes disputed accuracy procedures similar to those imposed upon consumer reporting agencies by federal law upon insurance institutions, agents and insurance support organizations. Also imposes duties similar to federal law upon insurance institutions, agents and insurance support organizations when furnishing information to others.

Consumer Remedies: Actual damages only available for unauthorized disclosure of information to others, equitable relief available to remedy violations of some other provisions. Costs and reasonable attorney fees available to prevailing party. Criminal penalties for obtaining information from agency under false pretenses. Administrative enforcement by commissioner of insurance, who may issue cease and desist orders, suspend or revoke licenses, and impose civil penalties: up to $10,000 or for violations frequent enough to be a general business practice, up to $50,000.

Statute of Limitations: Two years from date violation is or should have been discovered.

Miscellaneous: No relevant provisions.

Child Support Debts: Ohio Rev. Code Ann. §§ 3123.91 to 3123.932 (West). If the court or agency makes a final determination that an obligor is delinquent, it must report this information to at least one consumer reporting agency. If the entire arrearage is paid, the reporting agency may not record the payment until it is confirmed by the child support agency. Any credit reporting agency may request information regarding child support from the child support agency, which may report whether the consumer is obliged to pay child support, the court or agency that issued the order, and whether the order is being administered by the child support agency.

State Credit Repair Statute: Ohio Rev. Code Ann. §§ 4712.01 to 4712.99 (West).

Covered Activities: Improving credit record or obtaining extension of credit, in return for money or other consideration.

Exemptions: Regulated and supervised lenders; mortgage lenders approved by HUD; banks and savings associations eligible for FDIC insurance; credit unions; nonprofit organizations; licensed motor vehicle dealers acting within scope of license; public agencies; colleges or universities; registered mortgage brokers; consumer reporting agencies.

Right to Cancel? Yes (3 days).

---

91 Note that the FCRA preempts state laws regulating the duties of persons who take an adverse action against a consumer based on that consumer's credit report. *See* § 10.7, *supra*.

92 Note that the FCRA preempts state laws regulating the duties of persons who take an adverse action against a consumer based on that consumer's credit report. *See* § 10.7, *supra*.

Prohibitions: Charging before complete performance; charging for referring buyer to retail seller for credit on same terms as generally available to public; making or advising false statements to creditors or credit reporting agencies; making false statements about services offered; submitting disputes to reporting agency without buyer's consent; any fraudulent or deceptive practices; requiring buyer to waive rights.
Other Substantive Requirements: Disclosures.
Bond: $50,000.
Private Cause of Action: Actual damages, not less than amount paid by buyer; attorney fees and costs; punitive damages allowed. A violation is a UDAP violation. Injunctive relief. Statute of limitations, four years.

State Identity Theft Statute: Ohio Rev. Code Ann. § 2913.49 (West).

Definition of Offense: Without authority uses, obtains, or possesses personal identifying information of another with intent to hold self out as the other person, or represent that person's identifying information as their own; creates, obtains, possesses or uses the personal identifying information of another with intent to aid another in violating this section; possesses personal identifying information with another's permission, but uses it with intent to defraud; allows another to use one's personal identifying information with intent to defraud. Degree of crime depends upon value of credit, property, services, or debt involved.
Victim Remedies in Criminal Case: No specific provisions.
Special Record-Clearing Provisions: After filing report of identity theft with police, victim may apply for "identity fraud passport," which may be presented to law enforcement agencies or to creditors.
Duties of Private Entities: No specific provisions.
Private Right of Action: No specific provisions.
Other State Provisions: Ohio Rev. Code Ann. § 1349.19(B) (West). Owner or licensor of computerized data must notify resident of any unauthorized acquisition of personal information upon discovery of security breach.

Oklahoma

State FCRA Statute: Okla. Stat. tit. 24, §§ 81 to 86, 147 to 148.

Scope: Credit rating book or list published to retail or wholesale businesses.
Purposes for Which Reports May Be Issued: Oklahoma law regulates the business of credit rating.
Consumer Access and Disclosure: Similar to federal statute. Before giving an opinion upon any consumer's credit standing to a retail merchant, an agency must mail a copy of the opinion to the consumer.
Disclosures to Consumers By User: Anyone having a rating book or list must show a consumer his/her rating upon request. Similar to federal statute; when a report is requested for employment purposes, consumers must be given the option to receive a copy.
Restrictions on Content of Reports: Tax liens may not be disclosed unless the information is obtained directly from the state tax commission, and the reporting agency uses due diligence in updating the status of the liens.
Consumer Disputes: No relevant provisions.
Duties of Furnishers: No relevant provisions.

Consumer Remedies: Anyone who knowingly publishes a false opinion in a book or list and circulates it to retail or wholesale business concerns is liable for the amount of injuries in addition to exemplary damages, as determined by a jury. Fine for failure to show a consumer rating upon request. Criminal penalties for introducing false information to damage or enhance credit rating, or for willfully circulating false report.
Statute of Limitations: No relevant provisions.
Miscellaneous: No relevant provisions.

State Credit Repair Statute: Okla. Stat. tit. 24, §§ 131 to 148.

Covered Activities: Improving credit record or obtaining extension of credit, in return for money or other consideration.
Exemptions: Regulated and supervised lenders; mortgage lenders approved by HUD; banks and savings associations eligible for FDIC insurance; credit unions; nonprofit organizations; licensed real estate brokers acting within scope of license; Oklahoma lawyers acting within scope of law practice; registered securities broker-dealers; consumer reporting agencies; residential mortgage brokers; insurance companies; persons authorized to file electronic tax returns, who do not receive any compensation for refund anticipation loans.
Right to Cancel? Yes (5 days).
Prohibitions: Charging before complete performance, unless organization has posted bond; charging for referring buyer to retail seller for credit on same terms as generally available to public; making or advising false statements to creditors or credit reporting agencies; making false statements about services offered; requiring buyer to waive rights.
Other Substantive Requirements: Disclosures.
Bond: $10,000.
Private Cause of Action: Actual damages, not less than amount paid by buyer; attorney fees and costs; punitive damages allowed.

State Identity Theft Statute: Okla. Stat. tit. 21, § 1533.1.

Definition of Offense: Willfully and with fraudulent intent obtain the personal identifying information of another with intent to use, sell, or allow another to use or sell it, to obtain or attempt to obtain credit, goods, property or services in the name of another; or offer another the use of one's own personal identifying information for the purpose of obtaining a false identifying document.
Victim Remedies in Criminal Case: No specific provisions.
Special Record-Clearing Provisions: No specific provisions.
Duties of Private Entities: No specific provisions.
Private Right of Action: No specific provisions.

Other State Provisions: Okla. Stat. tit. 24, § 81. Before rating, a consumer agency must attempt to obtain from the person to be rated a statement of assets and liabilities.

Child Support Debts: Okla. Stat. tit. 56, § 240.7. Department of Human Services shall report child support arrearages to consumer reporting agencies. Obligors must be notified prior to the release of the information and be given a reasonable opportunity to contest the accuracy of the information.

State Credit Information in Private Insurance statute: Okla. Stat. tit. 36, §§ 950 to 959.

Scope: Use of credit information in personal insurance, individually underwritten for personal, family or household use: personal vehicle, recreational vehicle, homeowners (including mobile home), and non-commercial fire.

Disclosures: Insurer must notify consumer at time of application, in writing or in same medium as application, if it intends to use credit information. If adverse action based on credit report, insurer must disclose reasons to consumer, and provide notification as required by federal FCRA (source of report, dispute resolution procedure, etc.).[93]

Dispute Resolution: If, after dispute resolution procedure pursuant to federal FCRA, information in credit report is found to be incorrect, insurer must, within 30 days after notice, re-underwrite or re-rate based on corrected report. If refund is required, it must be for lesser of policy period or 12 months.

Prohibited Practices: Insurer may not use credit score based on income, gender, address, ethnic group, religion, marital status or nationality; deny, cancel, or non-renew based wholly on credit information without, another applicable underwriting factor independent of credit information; base renewal rates solely on credit information; take adverse action based on lack of credit card; count lack of credit history as a negative factor, unless insurer can show relationship to risk; take adverse action based on credit report issued or credit score calculated more than 90 days before policy was written or renewed; use credit information if it does not recalculate every 36 months based on current credit report; treat as a negative factor collection accounts with a medical industry code, or certain credit inquiries.

Other: Insurers who use scores must file scoring model with Insurance Department.

Security Freeze Laws: Okla. Stat. tit. 24, §§ 149 to 159.

Scope: Any consumer submitting proper identification.

Procedure: Request in writing by certified mail to consumer reporting agency; supply identification.

Entities covered: Consumer reporting agencies; some exceptions specified.

Duties of covered entities: Upon consumer request shall require proper identification of requesting party and provide notice, as specified, of process of placing and temporarily lifting a security freeze; within 10 business days of placing the freeze, shall send a written confirmation of the security freeze to the consumer and a unique personal identification number or password, other than the consumer's Social Security number, to be used for the release of the credit report.

Time periods: For application of freeze: no later than five business days after receiving written request (10 days before May 1, 2007, if, in good faith, there is an excessive number of requests). For written confirmation of the security freeze to the consumer: within 10 business days of placing the freeze. For temporary suspension of freeze: no later than three business days after receiving the request. For written confirmation of changes to file: within 30 days of the change to file.

Procedure for lifting freeze: Consumer is to provide with request to agency in manner arranged by agency: Proper identification; personal identification number or password; notice of time period if a temporary suspension of freeze.

Freeze not applicable to: Existing creditors for the purposes of review or collection; various government agencies; collection agency acting pursuant to a court order, warrant, or subpoena; use of credit information for prescreening as provided by the federal Fair Credit Reporting Act; and users for purposes regarding underwriting of insurance.

Fees: A fee may be charged of no more than ten dollars ($10) for each freeze, removal of the freeze, or temporary lifting of the freeze. No fee allowed for victim of identity theft, or consumers 65 years or older.

Enforcement: Actual damages, not less than $100 or more than $1000, costs and attorney fees. Punitive damages allowed. Fraudulent or unlawful user is liable for the greater of $1000 or actual damages. Negligent non-compliance liability is actual damages, costs, and attorney fees.

Oregon

Child Support Debts: Or. Rev. Stat. § 25.650. The Department of Justice shall provide information on child support arrearages to consumer reporting agencies, but first both obligor and obligee parents must be notified and given opportunity to contest accuracy of information. Department of Justice shall promptly notify agency when obligor pays off previously reported arrearage.

State Credit Repair Statute: Or. Rev. Stat. §§ 646.380 to 646.396.

Covered Activities: Improving credit record or obtaining extension of credit, in return for money or other consideration.

Exemptions: Regulated and supervised lenders; mortgage lenders approved by HUD; banks and savings associations eligible for FDIC insurance; credit unions; licensed consumer finance lenders; mortgage brokers; nonprofit organizations; licensed real estate brokers acting within scope of license; Oregon lawyers acting within scope of law practice; registered securities broker-dealers; consumer reporting agencies.

Right to Cancel? Yes (3 days).

Prohibitions: Charging before complete performance; charging for referring buyer to retail seller for credit on same terms as generally available to public; making or advising false statements to creditors or credit reporting agencies; making false statements about services offered; requiring buyer to waive rights.

Other Substantive Requirements: Disclosures.

Bond: $25,000.

Private Cause of Action: Contract voidable. A violation is a UDAP violation.

State Identity Theft Statute: Or. Rev. Stat. § 165.800.

Definition of Offense: With intent to deceive or defraud, obtains, possesses, creates, utters, or converts to person's own use the personal identification of another person.

Victim Remedies in Criminal Case: No specific provisions.

Special Record-Clearing Provisions: No specific provisions.

Duties of Private Entities: No specific provisions.

Private Right of Action: No specific provisions.

Pennsylvania

Child Support Debts: 23 Pa. Cons. Stat. Ann. § 4303. State shall report any child support arrearages provided that obligor is given notice and a period of up to twenty days to contest the accuracy of the information.

---

[93] Note that the FCRA preempts state laws regulating the duties of persons who take an adverse action against a consumer based on that consumer's credit report. *See* § 10.7, *supra*.

Appx. H.2-PR *Fair Credit Reporting*

State Credit Repair Statute: 73 Pa. Stat. Ann. §§ 2181 to 2192 (West).

Covered Activities: Improving credit record or obtaining extension of credit, in return for money or other consideration. The statute also has a separate but somewhat overlapping definition of "loan broker," and separate restrictions applicable to them.
Exemptions: Regulated and supervised lenders; banks and savings associations eligible for FDIC insurance; nonprofit organizations; licensed real estate brokers acting within scope of license; Pennsylvania lawyers acting within scope of law practice; registered securities broker-dealers; consumer reporting agencies.
Right to Cancel? Yes (5 days).
Prohibitions: Charging before complete performance, unless organization has posted bond; charging for referring buyer to retail seller for credit on same terms as generally available to public; making or advising false statements to creditors or credit reporting agencies; making false statements about services offered; advertising a guarantee that credit will be obtained; requiring buyer to waive rights.
Other Substantive Requirements: Disclosures.
Bond: 5% of total fees charged in previous 12 months, but not less than $5000 nor more than $25,000. (Amounts adjusted annually.)
Private Cause of Action: Actual damages, not less than amount paid by buyer; attorney fees and costs; punitive damages allowed. A violation is a UDAP violation.

State Identity Theft Statute: 18 Pa. Cons. Stat. § 4120, 42 Pa. Cons. Stat. § 8315, 42 Pa. Cons. Stat. § 9720.1.

Definition of Offense: Possesses or uses identifying information of another without consent to further any unlawful purpose. Enhanced penalty if victim aged 60 or above.
Victim Remedies in Criminal Case: Court may order restitution for all reasonable expenses incurred by or on behalf of the victim to investigate the theft, bring or defend criminal actions related to the theft, correct victim's credit record or negative credit reports resulting from the theft; reasonable expenses include attorney fees, fees or costs imposed by credit bureaus or incurred in private investigations, court costs and filing fees.
Special Record-Clearing Provisions: Police report by victim stating that identifying information has been lost, stolen, or used without permission is prima facie evidence that information was possessed or used without consent.
Duties of Private Entities: No specific provisions.
Private Right of Action: Greater of actual damages or $500. Actual damages include loss of money, reputation or property. Reasonable attorney fees and court costs. Court has discretion to triple the damages.
Other State Provisions: 73 Pa. Stat. Ann. §§ 2301 to 2329 (West). Owner or manager of computerized data must notify resident of any unauthorized acquisition of personal information upon discovery of security breach. Violation is UDAP violation.

Puerto Rico

Child Support Debts: **P.R. Laws Ann. tit. 8, § 528**. Child Support Administration shall report child support arrears to consumer reporting agencies. Obligors must be notified prior to release of information and notified that they have ten days to either pay the debt or challenge the report (with opportunity to present evidence).

State Identity Theft Statute: **P.R. Laws Ann. tit. 33, § 4309.**

Definition of Offense: Impersonation. Fraudulently impersonates or represents another and under this assumed character performs any act not authorized by the person falsely represented, or to the prejudice of that person or a third party.
Victim Remedies in Criminal Case: No specific provisions.
Special Record-Clearing Provisions: No specific provisions.
Duties of Private Entities: No specific provisions.
Private Right of Action: No specific provisions.

Rhode Island

State FCRA Statute: **R.I. Gen. Laws §§ 6-13.1-20 to 6-13.1-27.**

Scope: Same as the federal law.
Purposes for Which Reports May Be Issued: Same as federal law.
Consumer Access and Disclosure: Similar to federal law. Upon consumer request, an agency must disclose within four business days of the request all information in its files that pertains to the consumer at the time of the request. Any charge is not to exceed $8 per report, although the charge may increase with the Consumer Price Index. Must disclose to the consumer that the consumer has the right to request that corrected credit reports be sent to employers within two years, and to any other person within six months, when the agency has corrected information contained in the report.
Disclosures to Consumers By User: A consumer must be notified that a credit report may be requested before a report is requested in connection with an application for credit, employment, or insurance. Otherwise similar to federal law.
Restrictions on Content of Reports: No relevant provisions.
Consumer Disputes: Once a credit bureau receives notice of a dispute, it has thirty calendar days to reinvestigate the status of the information unless it has reason to believe that the dispute is frivolous or irrelevant.[94] If it is inaccurate, it must be deleted promptly. If reinvestigation does not resolve the dispute, the consumer may file a brief summary of the dispute. The bureau must then include that summary or a summary of its own with any subsequent credit report that it issues. The bureau must furnish free of charge a copy of any corrected credit report to the consumer, and if the consumer requests, furnish a copy of the corrected report to any person designated by the consumer who has received a credit report within the past two years, if for employment purposes, or within the past six months for any other purpose.
Duties of Furnishers: No relevant provisions.
Consumer Remedies: Violations constitute a deceptive trade practice for enforcement purposes. Negligent noncompliance: three working days to correct after being notified of the noncompliance or liability for $10 a day for each day in noncompliance in addition to actual damages, costs, and reasonable attorney fees.
Statute of Limitations: No relevant provisions.
Miscellaneous: Agencies must register with the office of the Secretary of State. Consumers have right to furnish a statement concerning any lapse in employment to agency, at no charge, which must be included in agency's file.

---

94 This provision was in effect on Sept. 30, 1996, so although it regulates the time allowed an agency to reinvestigate, it is not preempted. *See* § 10.7, *supra*.

Child Support Debts: **R.I. Gen. Laws §§ 15-25-1 and 15-25-2**. The child support enforcement agency shall inform reporting agencies of child support arrearages, unless it determines release of information inappropriate in a particular case. Obligor must be given ten days prior notice and an opportunity to contest the accuracy of the information. State child support enforcement agency must give consumer ten days notice prior to requesting report, must make report available to consumer, and must use report solely to establish consumer's capacity to make child support payments. Department must "periodically" report to credit reporting agencies if overdue support is paid, or amount of support due is amended.

State Identity Theft Statute: **R.I. Gen. Laws §§ 11-49.1-1 to 11-49.1-5**.

Definition of Offense: Deals primarily with producing, selling or using false ID documents, but also includes knowingly transfers or uses with intent to defraud, without lawful authority, a means of identification of another person with the intent to commit, or to aid or abet, any unlawful activity that constitutes a violation of federal, state or local law.
Victim Remedies in Criminal Case: No specific provisions.
Special Record-Clearing Provisions: No specific provisions.
Duties of Private Entities: No specific provisions.
Private Right of Action: No specific provisions.

State Credit Information in Personal Insurance statute: **R.I. Gen. Laws § 27-6-53**.

Scope: Use of credit rating for homeowners insurance.
Dispute Resolution: At request of customer, must recalculate score every two years, based on updated insurance score. If a credit bureau determines that information is inaccurate, insurer must re-calculate, based on corrected report, within 30 days of receiving notice.
Prohibited Practices: May not decline to insure based on an insurance score, or take adverse action based on worsening of score, unless either the worsening is a result of a bankruptcy, tax lien, garnishment, foreclosure or judgment, or the worsening is confirmed by another insurance score, at least six months after the first.
Other: Insurer who wishes to use insurance scoring must demonstrate the predictive nature of its score to the insurance division.

South Carolina

Child Support Debts: **S.C. Code Ann. § 43-5-585**. Department of Social Services shall inform agencies of child support arrearages greater than $1000. Obligors must be given notice and an opportunity to contest accuracy of the information.

State Identity Theft Statute: **S.C. Code Ann. §§ 16-13-500 to 16-13-530**.

Definition of Offense: With intent to appropriate the financial resources of another for self or a third party, obtains or records identifying information which would assist in accessing financial records of another, or accesses or attempts to access the financial resources of another by use of identifying information.
Victim Remedies in Criminal Case: Court may order restitution pursuant to § 17-25-322 [general criminal restitution statute].
Special Record-Clearing Provisions: No specific provisions.
Duties of Private Entities: No specific provisions.
Private Right of Action: No specific provisions.

Other State Provisions. **S.C. Code Ann. § 38073-740.** All information, explicitly including credit reports, used by insurer in determining premium classification for automobile insurance must be kept on file for three years after date of application, and made available to applicant on request. Copies must be available, if applicant pays copying expense.

South Dakota

Child Support Debts: **S.D. Codified Laws § 28-1-69**. Department of Social Services may provide information on overdue support to consumer reporting agency at request of agency, or in the discretion of the secretary. Must notify obligor of proposed release of information, and the procedure for contesting the accuracy of the information.

State Identity Theft Statute: **S.D. Codified Laws §§ 22-30A-3.1 to 22-30A-3.3**.

Definition of Offense: Obtains, possesses, transfers, uses, attempts to obtain or records identifying information not lawfully issued for that person's use; accesses or attempts to access the financial resources of another through the use of identifying information.
Victim Remedies in Criminal Case: No specific provisions.
Special Record-Clearing Provisions: No specific provisions.
Duties of Private Entities: No specific provisions.
Private Right of Action: No specific provisions.

Security Freeze Laws: **S.D. Codified Laws §§ 54-15-1 to 54-15-16**.

Scope: Identity theft victims submitting valid police report.
Procedure: Request in writing by certified mail to consumer reporting agency; supply identification.
Entities covered: Consumer reporting agencies; some exceptions specified.
Duties of covered entities: Upon consumer request shall require proper identification of requesting party and provide notice, as specified, of process of placing and temporarily lifting a security freeze; within 10 business days of placing the freeze, shall send a written confirmation of the security freeze to the consumer and a unique personal identification number or password, other than the consumer's Social Security number, to be used for the release of the credit report.
Time periods: For application of freeze: no later than five business days after receiving written request. For written confirmation of the security freeze to the consumer: within 10 business days of placing the freeze. For temporary suspension of freeze: no later than three business days after receiving the request. For written confirmation of changes to file: within 30 days of the change to file.
Procedure for lifting freeze: Freeze expires after seven years or earlier. Consumer is to provide with request to agency in manner arranged by agency: Proper identification; personal identification number or password; notice of time period if a temporary suspension of freeze.
Freeze not applicable to: Existing creditors for purposes of review or collection; specified various government agencies; person or entity acting pursuant to a court order, warrant, or subpoena; use of

Tennessee

Child Support Debts: Tenn. Code Ann. § 36-5-106. The Department of Human Services shall report child support arrearages to agencies and also those who are current with their payments. Must provide obligor with notice and an opportunity to contest accuracy of information before release.

State Credit Repair Statute: Tenn. Code Ann. §§ 47-18-1001 to 47-18-1011.

Covered Activities: Improving credit record or obtaining extension of credit, in return for money or other consideration.

Exemptions: Banks and savings associations eligible for FDIC insurance; lenders authorized under Tenn. or federal law; nonprofit organizations; licensed real estate brokers acting within scope of license; Tenn. lawyers acting within scope of law practice; registered securities broker-dealers; consumer reporting agencies.

Right to Cancel? Yes (5 days).

Prohibitions: Charging before complete performance; charging for referring buyer to retail seller for credit on same terms as generally available to public; making or advising false statements to creditors or credit reporting agencies; making false statements about services offered; creating new credit record under different identity; violating Consumer Credit Protection Act; requiring buyer to waive rights.

Other Substantive Requirements: Disclosures.

Bond: $100,000.

Private Cause of Action: Where willful non-compliance, the greater of actual damages or the amount paid by consumer, with punitive damages allowed; where non-compliance due to negligence, actual damages. Contract voidable. 2-year statute of limitations.

State Identity Theft Statute: Tenn. Code Ann. §§ 39-14-150, 39-16-303, 47-18-2101 to 47-18-2106.

Definition of Offense: Knowingly obtains, possesses, buys, or uses, the personal identifying information of another with the intent to commit any unlawful act including, but not limited to, obtaining or attempting to obtain credit, goods, services or medical information in the name of such other person; and without the consent of such other person; or without the lawful authority to obtain, possess, buy or use such identifying information. Also includes offense of "identity theft tracking," to knowingly sell, transfer, give, trade, loan or deliver, or possess with the intent to sell, transfer, give, trade, loan or deliver, the personal identifying information of another with the intent that such information be used by someone else to commit any unlawful act.

Victim Remedies in Criminal Case: No specific provisions.

Special Record-Clearing Provisions: No specific provisions.

Duties of Private Entities: No specific provisions.

Private Right of Action: Private right of action for damages, costs, attorney fees, and "such other relief" as court considers necessary. Treble damages for willful and knowing violation. Declaratory judgment and injunction available. Plaintiff must send copy of complaint to attorney general. Violation of identity theft statute also violates the Consumer Protection Act. 2 year statute of limitations.

Other: Attorney general may sue for violation of this section, seeking restitution for ascertainable loss (plus interest) suffered by consumers, as well as for injunction, asset freeze, civil penalties, court costs, and reasonable expenses of the investigation. Restitution under this section is a set-off against any judgment obtained in private civil action.

Texas

State FCRA Statute: Tex. Fin. Code Ann. §§ 391.001 to 391.002, 392.001 to 392.404 (Vernon).

Scope: Applies to credit reporting bureaus, i.e., persons who assemble or report credit information about individuals, for purposes of furnishing that information to third parties.

Purposes for Which Reports May Be Issued: No relevant provisions.

Consumer Access and Disclosure: All information in agency files must be disclosed to consumer within 45 days.

Disclosures to Consumer by User: No relevant provisions.

Restrictions on Content of Reports: No relevant provisions.

Consumer Disputes: No relevant provisions.

Duties of Furnishers: If consumer disputes the accuracy of a debt being collected by a third party debt collector, consumer shall notify the debt collector. Debt collector must make written record of the dispute, and cease collection efforts until it makes an investigation. Within 30 days debt collector must respond to consumer, admitting or denying accuracy of debt, or stating that it has not has sufficient time to complete investigation. If information is inaccurate, collector must cease collection efforts and, within five days, notify every person who has previously received notice of the debt. If it has not had sufficient time, it must change item as requested by the consumer, send copy of changed report to all persons who received report, and cease collection efforts. If information found accurate, collector may report information and resume collection efforts. Debt collectors may not attempt to collect debt resulting from unauthorized use of credit where notice provided to collector and law enforcement agency. § 392.303.

Consumer Remedies: No liability for bona fide errors which result despite agency maintaining reasonable procedures to avoid errors. Injunctive relief, actual damages, statutory damages of $100 per violation of provisions concerning disputed accuracy, reasonable attorney fees and costs available. Fine of $200 for knowingly furnishing false information about a person's credit record. Remedies are also available under the state deceptive practices statute.

Statute of Limitations: No relevant provisions.

Miscellaneous: Credit bureau must post bond for $10,000 and file copy with secretary of state before doing business in Texas.

Child Support Debts: Tex. Fam. Code Ann. § 231.114 (Vernon). Amount of child support owed and amount paid shall be reported to consumer reporting agencies, after thirty days notice and an opportunity to contest the accuracy of the information is given to the obligor.

State Credit Repair Statute: Tex. Fin. Code Ann. §§ 393.001 to 393.505 (Vernon).

Covered Activities: Improving credit record or obtaining extension of credit, in return for money or other consideration.
Exemptions: Lenders authorized under Texas or federal law; mortgage lenders approved by HUD; banks and savings associations eligible for FDIC insurance; credit unions; nonprofit organizations; licensed real estate brokers and mortgage brokers acting within scope of license; Texas lawyers acting within scope of law practice; registered securities broker-dealers; consumer reporting agencies; persons whose primary business is making loans secured by liens on realty; an authorized e-file provider who negotiates a refund anticipation loan on behalf of a bank, savings bank, savings and loan association or credit union.
Right to Cancel? Yes (3 days).
Prohibitions: Charging before complete performance, unless organization has posted bond; charging for referring buyer to retail seller for credit on same terms as generally available to public; making or advising false statements to creditors or credit reporting agencies; making false statements about services offered; fraudulent or deceptive practices; requiring buyer to waive rights.
Other Substantive Requirements: Disclosures.
Bond: $10,000.
Private Cause of Action: Actual damages, not less than amount paid by buyer; attorney fees and costs; punitive damages allowed. A violation is a UDAP violation. Injunctive relief. 4-year statute of limitations.

State Identity Theft Statute: Tex. Bus. & Com. Code Ann. §§ 48.001 to 48.203 (Vernon).

Definition of Offense: Obtains, uses, transfers, or possesses personal identifying information without consent and with intent to obtain anything of value in other person's name.
Victim Remedies in Criminal Case: None specified.
Special Record-Clearing Provisions: Victim may apply for court order declaring applicant is victim of identity theft and any information as to accounts or transactions affected by offense.
Duties of Private Entities: Maintain reasonable procedures to prevent unlawful use or disclosure of personal information. Adopt appropriate measures for destruction of personal records to be discarded. Must notify residents of any unauthorized acquisition of personal information upon discovery of security breach.
Private Right of Action: Violation is actionable deceptive trade practice.

State Identity Theft Statute: Tex. Penal Code Ann. § 32.51 (Vernon).

Definition of Offense: Obtains, transfers, possesses, or uses identifying information of another without consent and with intent to harm or defraud another.
Victim Remedies in Criminal Case: Court may order restitution, including lost wages and other expenses—except attorney fees—incurred as a result of the offense.
Special Record-Clearing Provisions: No specific provisions.
Duties of Private Entities: No specific provisions.
Private Right of Action: No specific provisions.

Utah

State FCRA Statute: Utah Code Ann. § 70C-7-107.

Scope: Applies to creditors who furnish negative information to credit reporting agencies.
Purposes for Which Reports May Be Issued: No relevant provisions.
Consumer Access and Disclosures: No relevant provisions.
Disclosures to Consumer by User: No relevant provisions.
Restrictions on Content of Reports: No relevant provisions.
Consumer Disputes: No relevant provisions.
Duties of Furnishers: Notice of negative credit report to be sent in writing by mail, or given in person, to last known address within thirty days after transmission of the information to the reporting agency.[95]
Consumer Remedies: Actual damages, court costs, and attorney fees for failure to provide notice of a negative credit report. Punitive damages of no more than twice actual damages for willful violations. Maintenance of reasonable procedures to avoid errors are a defense to liability.
Statute of Limitations: No relevant provisions.
Miscellaneous: No relevant provisions.

State Credit Repair Statute: Utah Code Ann. §§ 13-21-1 to 13-21-9.

Covered Activities: Improving credit record or obtaining extension of credit in return for money or other consideration.
Exemptions: Regulated and supervised lenders for which at least 35% of income is derived from credit transactions; depositary institutions; licensed real estate brokers acting within scope of license; Utah lawyers acting within scope of law practice; registered securities broker-dealers; consumer reporting agencies.
Right to Cancel? Yes (5 days).
Prohibitions: Charging before complete performance; charging for referring buyer to retail seller for credit on same terms as generally available to public; making or advising false statements to creditors or credit reporting agencies; making false statements about services offered; disputing credit report entry without factual basis and without buyer's written statement of belief in entry's inaccuracy; requiring buyer to waive rights.
Other Substantive Requirements: Disclosures.
Bond: $100,000.
Private Cause of Action: Actual damages, not less than amount paid by buyer; attorney fees and costs; punitive damages allowed.

State Identity Theft Statute: Utah Code Ann. §§ 76-6-1101 to 76-6-1104; *see also* § 13-11-4.5.

Definition of Offense: Knowingly or intentionally, without authorization, obtains personal identifying information of another and uses or attempts to use it with fraudulent intent, including to obtain credit, goods, services, other thing of value, or medical information, or employment, in the name of another without consent.
Victim Remedies in Criminal Case: If thief commits a crime under a false name, court must make "appropriate findings" that theft victim did not commit that crime.
Special Record-Clearing Provisions: No specific provisions.

---

95 Most state laws concerning the duties of furnishers of information are preempted. See § 10.7, *supra*.

Duties of Private Entities: No specific provisions.
Private Right of Action: Violation of this section violates the Consumer Protection Act.
Other: Division of Consumer Protection, as well as law enforcement agencies, may investigate violations.

Other State Provisions: Utah Code Ann. § 31A-22-320. Motor vehicle insurers may not use credit report or credit score [defined—does not include driving record or insurance claims history] to determine renewal, non-renewal, termination, eligibility, underwriting or rating, of motor vehicle related insurance, or except in determining initial underwriting, if risk factors other than credit information are also considered, and in determining eligibility for certain discounts. **Utah Code Ann. § 31A-22-1307.** Insurer who uses credit reports in connection with residential dwelling liability insurance must establish and adhere to written procedures which identify the circumstances under which it will request and the purposes for which it will use consumer reports; give prior notice to consumers of the use or possible use; assure compliance with federal FCRA. Must maintain evidence of compliance, and submit it to commissioner upon request.

Security Freeze Laws: Tex. Bus. & Com. Code Ann. §§ 20.034 to 20.13 (Vernon).

Scope: Identity theft victims.
Procedure: Request in writing by certified mail to consumer reporting agency; supply identification.
Entities covered: Consumer reporting agencies (defined § 20.01); some exceptions specified.
Duties of covered entities: Upon consumer request shall require proper identification of requesting party and provide notice, as specified, of process of placing and temporarily lifting a security freeze; within 10 business days of placing the freeze, shall send a written confirmation of the security freeze to the consumer and a unique personal identification number or password, other than the consumer's Social Security number, to be used for the release of the credit report.
Time periods: For application of freeze: no later than five business days after receiving written request. For written confirmation of the security freeze to the consumer: within 10 business days of placing the freeze. For temporary suspension of freeze: no later than three business days after receiving the request. For replacement of identification number: three days from request. For written confirmation of changes to file: within 30 days of the change to file.
Procedure for lifting freeze: Freeze expires after seven years or earlier. Consumer is to provide with request to agency in manner arranged by agency: Proper identification; personal identification number or password; notice of time period if a temporary suspension of freeze.
Freeze not applicable to: Existing creditors for purposes of review or collection; specified various government agencies; use of credit information for prescreening as provided by the federal Fair Credit Reporting Act; fraud prevention service company; a deposit account information service company; reporting agency that only resell compiled credit information.
Fees: A fee may be charged of no more than eight dollars for request of freeze. Fees may be increased yearly in accordance with Consumer Price Index. No other fees specified.
Enforcement: UDAP violation. Arbitration; civil action for actual damages, costs, and attorney fees. Treble damages for willful violation.

Security Freeze Laws: Utah Code Ann. §§ 13-42-202 to 13-42-205.

Scope: Any consumer.
Procedure: Request in writing by certified mail to consumer reporting agency; supply identification.
Entities covered: Consumer reporting agencies (defined in § 13-42-102); some exceptions specified.
Duties of covered entities: Upon consumer request shall require proper identification of requesting party and provide notice, as specified, of process of placing and temporarily lifting a security freeze; within 10 business days of placing the freeze, shall send a written confirmation of the security freeze to the consumer and a unique personal identification number or password, other than the consumer's Social Security number, to be used for the release of the credit report.
Time periods: For application of freeze: no later than five business days after receiving written request. For written confirmation of the security freeze to the consumer: within 10 business days of placing the freeze. For temporary suspension of freeze: no later than three business days after receiving the request. For removal of freeze: no later than three business days after receiving written request or 15 minutes (except for specified disruptions) if request by telephone or by electronic contact method. For replacement of identification number: three days from request. For written confirmation of changes to file: within 30 days of the change to file.
Procedure for lifting freeze: Freeze expires after seven years or earlier. Consumer is to provide with request to agency in manner arranged by agency: Proper identification; personal identification number or password; notice of time period if a temporary suspension of freeze.
Freeze not applicable to: Existing creditors for purposes of review or collection; specified various government agencies; person or entity acting pursuant to a court order, warrant, or subpoena; a fraud prevention service company; a deposit account information service company; reporting agency that only resell compiled credit information.
Fees: A "reasonable" fee may be charged for request of freeze or for temporary suspension. No fees allowed for identity theft victims.
Enforcement: Fines and injunctions through Attorney General action. § 13-42-401.

Vermont

State FCRA Statute: Vt. Stat. Ann. tit. 9, §§ 2480a to 2480g; 06-031-012 Code Vt. R. § 112.

Scope: Same as the federal law.
Purposes for Which Reports May Be Issued: Only purposes consented to by the consumer. No exception made for sharing of information between affiliates.[96]
Consumer Access and Disclosure: All available information including credit score or predictor.[97] Free once per year;[98] $7.50

---

[96] This provision of Vermont law is explicitly not preempted. See § 10.7, *supra*.

[97] Note that the FCRA requires certain disclosures to be made in connection with credit scores, and that provision may preempt similar state provisions. See § 10.7, *supra*.

[98] Although the FCRA preempts state laws with respect to the

maximum for each additional copy. Written summary of consumer's rights under Vermont law. Agencies must be listed in the white and yellow pages under "Credit Reporting Agency."
Disclosures to Consumer by User: No relevant provisions.
Restrictions on Content of Reports: No disclosure without consumer consent. No exception made for sharing of information between affiliates.[99]
Consumer Disputes: Notice to provider of information within five days of consumer dispute; reinvestigation complete within thirty days.[100] May not reinsert disputed information, if deleted, without a separate affirmation from the provider.
Duties of Furnishers: Duties specified where consumer requests security freeze.
Consumer Remedies: Injunctive relief, actual damages or $100, whichever is greater; punitive damages if willful; costs and attorney fees.
Statute of Limitations: No relevant provisions.
Miscellaneous: Victims of identity theft may request security freeze whereby furnisher must not release information unless expressly authorized.

Child Support Debts: **Vt. Stat. Ann. tit. 15, § 793**. Arrearage equal to at least one-quarter of the annual child support obligation may be reported if the obligor is given notice by first class mail or other means likely to give actual notice and given a period not to exceed twenty days to contest the accuracy of the information. Office of child support must immediately report increases or decreases in the account balance of previously reported accounts.

State Identity Theft Statute: **Vt. Stat. Ann. tit. 13, § 2030.**

Definition of Offense: False personation: falsely personates or represents another, and in such character receives money or other property intended to be delivered to the party so personated, with intent to convert the same to his own use.
Victim Remedies in Criminal Case: No specific provisions.
Special Record-clearing Provisions: No specific provisions.
Duties of Private Entities: No specific provisions.
Private Right of Action: No specific provisions.

Security Freeze Laws: **Vt. Stat. Ann. tit. 9, §§ 2480h to 2480j.**

Scope: Any consumer.
Procedure: Request in writing by certified mail to credit reporting agency; supply identification.
Entities covered: Credit reporting agencies (defined in 2480a); some exceptions specified.
Duties of covered entities: Upon consumer request shall require proper identification of requesting party and provide notice of rights, as specified in § 2480b, of process of placing and temporarily lifting a security freeze; within 10 business days of placing the freeze, shall send a written confirmation of the security freeze to the consumer and a unique personal identification number or password, other than the consumer's Social Security number, to be used for the release of the credit report.
Time periods: For application of freeze: no later than five business days after receiving written request. For written confirmation of the security freeze to the consumer: within 10 business days of placing the freeze. For temporary suspension of freeze: no later than three business days after receiving the request. For written confirmation of changes to file: within 30 days of the change to file.
Procedure for lifting freeze: Consumer is to provide with request to agency in manner arranged by agency: Proper identification; personal identification number or password; notice of time period if a temporary suspension of freeze.
Freeze not applicable to: Existing creditors for purposes of review or collection; specified various government agencies; person or entity acting pursuant to a court order, warrant, or subpoena; use of credit information for prescreening as provided by the federal Fair Credit Reporting Act.
Fees: A fee may be charged of no more than ten dollars ($10) for freeze; a fee of five dollars ($5.00) for removal of the freeze, or temporary lifting of the freeze. No fees allowed for victim of identity theft.
Enforcement: Civil action authorized. § 2480b.

Virginia

Child Support Debts: **Va. Code Ann. § 63.2-1940.** Child Support Enforcement Division shall report child support arrears to consumer reporting agencies. Obligors must be notified prior to release of information and given a reasonable opportunity to contest accuracy of information.

State Credit Repair Statute: **Va. Code Ann. §§ 59.1-335.1 to 59.1-335.12.**

Covered Activities: Improving credit record or obtaining extension of credit, in return for money or other consideration.
Exemptions: Lenders authorized under Va. or federal law; banks and savings associations eligible for FDIC insurance; nonprofit organizations; licensed real estate brokers acting within scope of license; Va. lawyers acting within scope of law practice; registered securities broker-dealers; consumer reporting agencies; seller of consumer goods who, in connection with sale of goods, assists consumer in obtaining loan or extension of credit, or extends credit to consumer.
Right to Cancel? Yes (3 days).
Prohibitions: Charging before complete performance; charging for referring buyer to retail seller for credit on same terms as generally available to public; making or advising false statements to creditors or credit reporting agencies; making false statements about services offered; requiring buyer to waive rights.
Other Substantive Requirements: Disclosures.
Bond: 100 times standard fee charged to consumer, not less than $5000 or more than $50,000.
Private Cause of Action: Where willful non-compliance, actual damages and punitive damages allowed. Where non-compliance due to negligence, actual damages. Contract voidable. 2-year statute of limitations. Violation is a UDAP.

State Identity Theft Statute: **Va. Code Ann. §§ 18.2-186.3 through 18.2-186.5.**

Definition of Offense: Without authority and with intent to defraud,

---

[footnotes]

frequency of the right to free reports, the Act specifically exempts this Vermont provision from preemption. *See* § 10.7, *supra*.

99 This provision of Vermont law is explicitly not preempted. *See* § 10.7, *supra*.

100 This provision was in effect on Sept. 30, 1996, so although it regulates the time agency allowed for reinvestigation, it is not preempted. *See* § 10.7, *supra*.

for own use or that of a third person: obtains, records or accesses identifying information not available to the general public, that would assist in accessing financial resources, or obtaining benefits or identification documents of another; obtains goods or services by use of identifying information of another; obtains identification documents in the name of another. Penalty enhanced if victim is arrested or detained.

Victim Remedies in Criminal Case: Court must order restitution, which may include actual expenses incurred in correcting errors in victim's credit report or other identifying information.

Special Record-Clearing Provisions: Any person whose name or identification has been used without authority by another who has been charged or arrested under the stolen name, may petition the court for an order of expungement, pursuant to § 19.2-392.2. Upon receipt of the order, the Attorney General may issue an "Identity Theft Passport."

Duties of Private Entities: If a consumer submits a police report to a consumer reporting agency, the agency shall, within 30 days of receipt of the report, block any information alleged to result from the identity theft.[101] Agency may refuse to block or rescind a block, if it reasonably and in good faith believes that block resulted from fraud, or that consumer knowingly received goods and services as a result of the blocked transaction, or if agency has specific, verifiable reasons to doubt the report. If information is unblocked, consumer must be notified as provided for in federal FCRA. Agency must accept consumer's version, if backed by documentation from source of the item, or from public records.

Private Right of Action: No specific provisions.

Other State Provisions: Va. Code Ann. § 38.2-2114. No insurer or agent shall refuse to renew a policy written to insure an owner-occupied dwelling solely because of credit information contained in a "consumer report," as defined in the federal Fair Credit Reporting Act, 15 U.S.C. § 1681 to 1681x, bearing on a natural person's creditworthiness, credit standing or credit capacity. If credit information is used, in part, as the basis for the nonrenewal, such credit information shall be based on a consumer report procured within 120 days from the effective date of the nonrenewal.

Washington

State FCRA Statute: Wash. Rev. Code §§ 19.182.005 to 19.182.902.

Scope: Similar to federal.

Purposes for Which Reports May Be Issued: Similar to federal law, except no authorization for provision to potential investors or servicers, or current insurers, in connection with evaluation of the credit or prepayment risks associated with existing credit obligations. In addition, if a report is procured for employment purposes, the consumer must be an employee at the time it is procured unless there is written disclosure that the report will be used in consideration for employment, or unless the consumer authorizes.

Consumer Access and Disclosure: All information in file, but only required to reveal medical information to consumer's health care provider. Otherwise similar to federal law. Must provide consumer with summary of rights under Washington FCRA. Must disclose all users who obtained report for employment purposes within two years, or for any other purpose (including a credit transaction not initiated by consumer) within six months. May charge $8 (to be adjusted for CPI) for disclosure of consumer's file, unless consumer has been subject to adverse action within sixty days, in which case disclosure is free.

Disclosures to Consumers By User: Employers must disclose in writing that consumer reports may be used for employment purposes. Prior to any adverse action based on a report, an employer must provide the name, address, and telephone number of the reporting agency; the description of consumer rights under Washington law pertaining to consumer reports for employment purposes; and a reasonable opportunity to respond to any information in a report that is disputed by the consumer.[102] If adverse action is taken by any user, the consumer must be provided with written notice and the name, address, and telephone number of the reporting agency. Verbal notice may be given involving businesses regulated by state utilities and transportation commission, or involving an application for rental or leasing of residential real estate if it does not impair a consumer's ability to obtain a credit report without charge, and the consumer is provided with the name, address, and telephone number of the consumer reporting agency. Must inform consumer of intent to obtain an investigative consumer report. On consumer's request, must disclose the scope of the proposed investigation.

Restrictions on Content of Reports: Same as federal law, except criminal records more than seven years after date of disposition, release or parole.[103] If consumer provides copy of police report regarding identity theft, agency must notify furnisher of information, and block information resulting from the theft.[104]

Consumer Disputes: If the accuracy of an item is disputed by a consumer, the consumer reporting agency must reinvestigate and record the status of the disputed information before the end of thirty business days with no charge.[105] If agency determines the dispute is frivolous it must notify consumer in writing of its reasons within five days. Before the end of five business days after notice of a dispute by the consumer, the agency shall notify any person who provided an item of information in the dispute. If the information is found to be inaccurate, it must be deleted promptly. If reinvestigation does not resolve the dispute, the consumer may file a brief statement of contentions. The agency must inform the consumer of the right to request a corrected notification to all users within six months, and employers within two years; notification must be within thirty days at no charge. If the agency operates on a nationwide basis, it must have a toll free telephone number that

---

101 Note that the FCRA has its own blocking provision which preempts similar state provisions, but only to the extent of the specific conduct required by the FCRA provision. See § 10.7, *supra*.

102 Note that the FCRA preempts state laws regulating the duties of persons who take an adverse action against a consumer based on that consumer's credit report. See § 10.7, *supra*.

103 This provision was in effect on Sept. 30, 1996, so even if it could be said to be otherwise preempted by 15 U.S.C. § 1681c, it is not preempted. See § 10.7, *supra*.

104 Note that the FCRA has its own blocking provision which preempts similar state provisions, but only to the extent of the specific conduct required by the FCRA provision. See § 10.7, *supra*.

105 This provision was in effect on Sept. 30, 1996, so although it regulates the time agency allowed for reinvestigation, it is not preempted. See § 10.7, *supra*.

the consumer can use in case of a dispute.
Duties of Furnishers: No relevant provisions.
Consumer Remedies: Knowingly and willfully obtaining information under false pretenses: fine of up to $5000, imprisonment for up to one year or both. Violation is an unfair or deceptive act in trade or commerce and an unfair method of competition under state deceptive practices statute. Remedies available for negligent violations: actual damages, costs, and reasonable attorney fees. For willful noncompliance: actual damages, $1,000, costs, and reasonable attorney fees.
Statute of Limitations: Two years from violation or time of discovery.
Miscellaneous: Every agency must maintain reasonable procedures to avoid misuse of reports; agencies must require prospective users to identify themselves, to certify the purposes for which information is sought, and to certify that the information will be used for no other purpose. Agencies must also use reasonable efforts to verify the identity of a new user. If an agency has reasonable grounds for believing that a consumer report will not be used for the above purposes then it is prohibited from furnishing the report. May issue consumer's name, address, former addresses, places of employment or former places of employment to a governmental agency. Cannot provide prescreened information if the consumer precludes it in writing.[106]

State Credit Repair Statute: Wash. Rev. Code §§ 19.134.010 to 19.134.900.

Covered Activities: Improving credit record or obtaining extension of credit or preventing or delaying foreclosure, in return for money or other consideration.
Exemptions: Regulated and supervised lenders; mortgage lenders approved by HUD; banks and savings associations eligible for FDIC insurance; credit unions; nonprofit organizations; licensed real estate brokers, collection agencies, and mortgage brokers acting within scope of license; Washington lawyers acting within scope of law practice; registered securities broker-dealers; consumer reporting agencies.
Right to Cancel? Yes (5 days).
Prohibitions: Charging before complete performance, unless organization has posted bond; charging for referring buyer to retail seller for credit on same terms as generally available to public; making or advising false statements to creditors or credit reporting agencies; making false statements about services offered; requiring buyer to waive rights.
Other Substantive Requirements: Disclosures.
Bond: $10,000.
Private Cause of Action: An amount not less than that paid by buyer; attorney fees and costs; punitive damages allowed. A violation is a UDAP violation.

State Identity Theft Statute: Wash. Rev. Code §§ 9.35.001 to 9.35.902, 19.182.160.

Definition of Offense: Uses false statement, or fraudulent or fraudulently obtained document to obtain financial information of another from various sources (financial institution, merchant, etc.). Obtains, possesses, uses or transfers, financial information or means of identification of another with intent to commit, aid or abet any crime. Uses means of identification or financial information of another to solicit undesired mail for purposes of harassing another.
Victim Remedies in Criminal Case: If means of identification or financial information used without authority to commit a crime, court shall issue necessary orders to correct any public record which contains false information resulting from identity theft.
Special Record-Clearing Provisions: An identity theft victim may request that his or her fingerprints be filed, along with a statement about the theft. (Law enforcement agency may charge $5 for this service.) A copy of the statement may be presented to businesses when the victim requests copies of application, etc. records. (See Duties of Private Entities, above.)
Duties of Private Entities: Entity (merchant, financial institution, financial information repository, etc.) that deals with thief must, upon victim's request, provide all relevant transaction and application information.[107] Violation of this section violates the Consumer Protection Act. Credit reporting agency must permanently block information added to credit report as a result of identity theft within thirty days of receiving copy of police report.[108] May unblock only if block resulted from fraud by consumer, or consumer agrees block was erroneous, or consumer knowingly received goods or services as a result of the blocked transaction.
Private Right of Action: Improperly obtaining financial information—greater of $500 or actual damages plus reasonable attorney fees. Identity theft—same, including costs incurred to repair credit record. Identity crime violates the Consumer Protection Act, and these provisions for private action do not limit a victim's ability to seek treble damages under the act.
Other: State has banned the use of Social Security numbers as college ID numbers. Legislative findings note that this was done because identity theft is becoming more common, and widespread use of Social Security numbers facilitates the crime.

State Credit Information in Personal Insurance Statute: Wash. Rev. Code. § 48.19.035.

Scope: Use of credit information in personal insurance rates, premiums, or eligibility.
Disclosures: Must disclose that it may obtain credit information and, if adverse action taken, must disclose in clear and specific language the reasons for adverse action.[109]
Dispute Resolutions: After a FCRA dispute resolution process finding that credit information was incorrect or incomplete, insurer shall rerate and reunderwrite [no time period specified].
Prohibited practices: The absence of credit history or the inability to determine the consumer's credit history, unless the insurer has filed actuarial data segmented by demographic factors in a manner prescribed by the commissioner that demonstrates compliance with § 48.19.020; the number of credit inquiries; credit history or an insurance score based on collection accounts identified with a medical industry code; the initial purchase or finance of a vehicle

---

106 State law provisions concerning prescreening lists are now preempted. See § 10.7, *supra*.

107 Note that the FCRA has its own transaction information provision that may preempt this sort of state provision. See § 10.7, *supra*.

108 Note that the FCRA has its own blocking provision which preempts similar state provisions, but only to the extent of the specific conduct required by the FCRA provision. See § 10.7, *supra*.

109 Note that the FCRA preempts state laws regulating the duties of persons who take an adverse action against a consumer based on that consumer's credit report. See § 10.7, *supra*.

or house that adds a new loan to the consumer's existing credit history; the consumer's use of a particular type of credit card, charge card, or debit card; or the consumer's total available line of credit; however, an insurer may consider the total amount of outstanding debt in relation to the total available line of credit.
Other: Insurers who use credit scores must file their rates and rating plans with state Insurance Commissioner.

Security Freeze Laws: **Wash. Rev. Code §§ 19.182.170 to 19.182.210.**

Scope: Identity theft victims submitting valid police report.
Procedure: Request in writing by certified mail to consumer reporting agency; supply identification.
Entities covered: Consumer reporting agencies (defined § 19.182.010); some exceptions specified.
Duties of covered entities: Upon consumer request shall require proper identification of requesting party and provide notice, as specified, of process of placing and temporarily lifting a security freeze; within 10 business days of placing the freeze, shall send a written confirmation of the security freeze to the consumer and a unique personal identification number or password, other than the consumer's Social Security number, to be used for the release of the credit report.
Time periods: For application of freeze: no later than five business days after receiving written request. For written confirmation of the security freeze to the consumer: within 10 business days of placing the freeze. For temporary suspension of freeze: no later than three business days after receiving the request. For written confirmation of changes to file: within 30 days of the change to file.
Procedure for lifting freeze: Freeze expires after seven years or earlier upon consumer request. Consumer is to provide with request to agency in manner arranged by agency: Proper identification; personal identification number or password; notice of time period if a temporary suspension of freeze.
Freeze not applicable to: Existing creditors for purposes of review or collection; specified various government agencies; private collection agency acting pursuant to a court order, warrant, or subpoena; use of credit information for prescreening as provided by the federal Fair Credit Reporting Act.
Fees: No fees specified.
Enforcement: UDAP violation. Civil action for actual damages, costs, and attorney fees. Punitive damages allowed for willful violation. § 19.182.150.

West Virginia

Child Support Debts: **W. Va. Code § 48-18-121**. Those in arrears for child support payments must be provided procedural due process, including notice and a reasonable opportunity to contest accuracy of information, prior to state reporting such arrearages to consumer reporting agencies. State child support enforcement agency must give consumer ten days notice prior to requesting report and must use report solely to establish consumer's capacity to make child support payments.

State Credit Repair Statute: **W. Va. Code §§ 46A-6C-1 to 46A-6C-12.**

Covered Activities: Improving credit record or obtaining extension of credit, in return for money or other consideration.

Exemptions: Regulated and supervised lenders; lenders making loans secured by liens on realty; banks and savings associations eligible for FDIC insurance; credit unions; nonprofit organizations; public accountants and licensed real estate brokers acting within scope of license; W. Va. lawyers acting within scope of law practice; registered securities broker-dealers; consumer reporting agencies.
Right to Cancel? Yes (10 days).
Prohibitions: Charging before complete performance, unless organization has posted bond; charging for referring buyer to retail seller for credit on same terms as generally available to public; making or advising false statements to creditors or credit reporting agencies; making false statements about services offered; unfair and deceptive acts; requiring buyer to waive rights.
Other Substantive Requirements: Disclosures.
Bond: $15,000.
Private Cause of Action: An amount not less than that paid by buyer; attorney fees and costs; punitive damages allowed. A violation is a UDAP violation.

State Identity Theft Statute: **W. Va. Code § 61-3-54**.

Definition of Offense: Knowingly takes the name or other identifying information of another, without authority, in order to fraudulently represent self as that person, for purpose of making financial or credit transactions in that person's name.
Victim Remedies in Criminal Case: No specific provisions.
Special Record-Clearing Provisions: No specific provisions.
Duties of Private Entities: No specific provisions.
Private Right of Action: No specific provisions.

Wisconsin

Child Support Debts: **Wis. Stat. § 49.22(11)**. Department of Public Assistance shall report child support arrearages, but must give twenty business days prior notice to obligor and disclose methods available to contest accuracy of information. Department must report any errors or payments within thirty days and reporting agency must correct consumer files within thirty days.

State Credit Repair Statute: **Wis. Stat. §§ 422.501 to 422.506**

Covered Activities: Improving credit record or obtaining extension of credit, in return for money or other consideration.
Exemptions: Regulated and supervised lenders; banks and savings associations eligible for FDIC insurance; nonprofit organizations; licensed real estate brokers, adjustment service companies, mortgage bankers, loan originators, or mortgage brokers acting within scope of license; Wisconsin lawyers acting within scope of law practice; registered securities broker-dealers; consumer reporting agencies.
Right to Cancel? Yes (5 days).
Prohibitions: Charging for referring buyer to retail seller for credit on same terms as generally available to public; making or advising false statements to creditors or credit reporting agencies; making false statements about services offered; requiring buyer to waive rights.
Other Substantive Requirements: Disclosures.
Bond: $25,000.
Private Cause of Action: A violation is a UDAP violation.

State Identity Theft Statute: **Wis. Stat. §§ 943.201 and 895.80**.

Definition of Offense: Uses or attempts to use any personal identifying information or personal identification document of another, without authorization, to obtain credit, goods, money, services or anything of value by misrepresenting self as that other person, or as acting with that person's authority.
Victim Remedies in Criminal Case: No specific provisions.
Special Record-Clearing Provisions: No specific provisions.
Duties of Private Entities: No specific provisions.
Private Right of Action: Civil action for treble damages, plus all reasonable costs of investigation and litigation. Criminal conviction not a prerequisite.

Other State Provisions: Wis. Stat. §§ 186.53, 214.507, 215.26(8)(a)(3), 224.26. A customer, loan applicant or credit applicant of a bank, credit union, savings and loan or other banking institution may request a free copy of any written credit report on them held by the institution, for which a fee was imposed.

Security Freeze Laws: Wis. Stat. § 100.54.

Scope: Any consumer.
Procedure: Request in writing by certified mail to consumer reporting agency or in manner approved by agency; supply identification.
Entities covered: Consumer reporting agencies; some exceptions specified.
Duties of covered entities: Upon consumer request shall require proper identification of requesting party and provide notice, as specified, of process of placing and temporarily lifting a security freeze; within 10 business days of placing the freeze, shall send a written confirmation of the security freeze to the consumer and a unique personal identification number or password, other than the consumer's Social Security number, to be used for the release of the credit report.
Time periods: For application of freeze: no later than five business days after receiving written request. For written confirmation of the security freeze to the consumer: within 10 business days of placing the freeze. For temporary suspension of freeze: no later than three business days after receiving the request. For written confirmation of changes to file: within 30 days of the change to file.

Procedure for lifting freeze: Consumer is to provide with request to agency in manner arranged by agency: Proper identification; personal identification number or password; notice of time period if a temporary suspension of freeze.
Freeze not applicable to: Existing creditors for purposes of review or collection; specified various government agencies; person or entity acting pursuant to a court order, warrant, or subpoena; use of credit information for prescreening as provided by the federal Fair Credit Reporting Act; use for employment purposes or for setting or adjusting an insurance rate or claim or underwriting for insurance purposes.
Fees: A fee may be charged of no more than ten dollars ($10) for each freeze, removal of the freeze, or temporary lifting of the freeze. No fee allowed for victim of identity theft.
Enforcement: Person in violation liable for actual damages, costs, and attorney fees. Consumer acting under false pretenses liable for the greater of actual damages or $1000.

Wyoming

State Identity Theft Statute: Wyo. Stat. Ann. §§ 1-1-128 and 6-3-901.

Definition of Offense: Willfully obtains personal identifying information of another and uses it without authority for any unlawful purpose, including to obtain money, credit, goods, services or medical information in the name of the other person.
Victim Remedies in Criminal Case: May include any costs incurred by victim, including attorney fees, in clearing credit rating or credit history, or in any civil or administrative proceeding to satisfy debt, lien or other obligation resulting from the theft. If thief commits another crime under victim's name, court records shall reflect that victim did not commit that crime.
Special Record-Clearing Provisions: No specific provisions.
Duties of Private Entities: No specific provisions.
Private Right of Action: Civil action for damages, costs and attorney fees. Injunction may also be available. Criminal conviction not a prerequisite.

Appendix I Sample Credit Reports and Industry Forms

Appendix I.1 contains sample credit reports from the three major nationwide consumers reporting agencies—Equifax, Experian and TransUnion. These sample reports are illustrative only, and are subject to modification. Sample credit reports are available for viewing on the websites of these CRAs.[1]

Appendix I.2 contains a Universal Data Form (UDF). The UDF is used by furnishers to update and correct or delete information about a consumer. The UDF was designed by the industry and may be used with the major CRAs. The form may be filled out manually or an automated version (AUDF) may be communicated electronically. If an attorney is seeking to have a furnisher of information change information previously provided to a CRA, the UDF is one important instrument to consider.[2]

Appendix I.3 contains a sample Consumer Dispute Verification (CDV) Form. The CDV is used by CRAs to report disputes to a furnisher. In addition, the furnisher is supposed to fill in relevant portions of the form following reinvestigation. The form may be sent manually or, as in the case of the sample, an automated version (ACDV) may be communicated electronically.

1 www.equifax.com; www.experian.com; www.transunion.com.
2 *See* § 8.2.18, *supra*.

I.1 Sample Credit Reports

I.1.1 *Equifax*

Appx. I.1.1 *Fair Credit Reporting*

EQUIFAX
CREDIT FILE : May 17, 2005

SAMPLE CREDIT FILE

Confirmation # 5556677722

Personal Identification Information: This section includes your name, current and previous addresses, and any other identifying information reported by your creditors.

Please address all future correspondence to:
www.investigate.equifax.com
Equifax Information Services LLC
P.O. Box 740256, Atlanta, GA 30348
Phone (800)685-1111 M-F 9:00am to 5:00pm in your time zone

Name On File: Mark Allen Customer
Social Security #: 123 - 45 - 6789   Date of Birth: November 8, 1964
Current Address: 123 Main St., Metairie, LA 70005
Previous Address(es): RR 4 Box 27, Sulphur Springs, LA 70726
Last Reported Employment: Owner, Ace Garden Supply

In order to speak with a Customer Service Representative regarding the specific information in this credit file, you must call **WITHIN 60 DAYS** of the date of this credit file **AND** have a copy of this credit file along with the confirmation number.

Public Record Information - This section includes public records obtained from local, state and federal courts.
Bankruptcy filed 06/2000; Eastern district of LA.; Case or I.D. # 0015458; Type - Personal; Filer - Individual; Current Disposition - Discharged CH-7

Collection Agency Information - This section includes accounts that credit grantors have placed for collection with a collection agency.
Blue Tiger Collection Agency, Inc. (555) 703-0020; Collection Reported; Assigned 07/1988; Client -First Bank Colo; Amount $1,831; Status as of 09/1998-In Bankruptcy; Balance; as of 09/1998 -$0; Individual Account; Account # - 98105444; ADDITIONAL INFORMATION - Bankruptcy Chapter 7

Credit Account Information
For your security, the last 4 digits of account number(s) have been replaced by an *. This section includes open and closed accounts reported by credit grantors.

Department Store

Account Number ❶	❷ Date Opened	High Credit ❸	Credit Limit ❹	❺ Scheduled Paymnt Amount	Terms Duration ❺	Terms Frequency ❻	Activity Description ❽	Mnths Revd ❼	Creditor Classification ❾	Date Closed
52910720642⑩*	10/1997	$795		$23		Monthly		76		
Items As of ⑩	Amount Past Due	⑫ Actual Last Paymt Amount				⑯ Date of Last Activity	⑲ Deferred Pay Start Date	Charge Off Amount	⓴ Balloon Pay Amount	㉑ Balloon Pay Date
02/2004	$774	01/2004				02/2004				

Current Status - Pays As Agreed; Type of Account - Revolving; Type of Loan - Credit Card; Whose Account - Individual Account

Finance Company   Phone: (800)555-9200

Account Number	Date Opened	High Credit	Credit Limit	Scheduled Paymnt Amount	Terms Duration	Terms Frequency	Activity Description	Mnths Revd	Creditor Classification
2483*	02/1995	$36,381			47 Months	Monthly		76	
Items As of	Balance	Date of Last Paymt	Amount Past Due	Actual Paymnt Amount		Date of Last Activity	Date Maj. Del. 1st Rptd	Charge Off Amount	Deferred Pay Start Date	Balloon Pay Amount	Balloon Pay Date
06/1999	$0					03/1999					

Current Status - Pays As Agreed; Type of Account - Installment; Whose Account - Individual Account; ADDITIONAL INFORMATION - Account Paid/Zero Balance; Auto

㉓ Account History with Status Codes	10/1998	08/1998	06/1998	05/1998	04/1998	03/1998	02/1998	01/1998	12/1997	11/1997	08/1997	07/1997
	2	2	3	4	3	2	1	2	2	2	2	2

Inquiries that display to companies (may impact your credit score). This section lists companies that requested your credit file. Credit grantors may view these requests when evaluating your credit worthiness. Employment inquiries do not impact your credit score.

Company Information	Inquiry Date(s)
Auto Finance	11/2003
Car Dealer	11/2003

Inquiries that do not display to companies (do not impact your score). This section includes inquiries which display only to you and are not considered when evaluating your credit worthiness. Examples of this inquiry type include a pre-approved offer of credit, insurance, or periodic account review by an existing creditor.

Company Information - Prefix Descriptions:
PRM - Inquiries with this prefix indicate that only your name and address were given to a credit grantor so they can provide you a firm offer of credit or insurance. (PRM inquiries remain for twelve months.)
AM or AR - Inquiries with these prefixes indicate a periodic review of your credit history by one of your creditors.
    (AM and AR inquiries remain for twelve months.)
Equifax or EFX - Inquiries with these prefixes indicate Equifax's activity in response to your contact with us for a copy of your credit file or a research request.
ND - Inquiries with this prefix are general inquiries that do not display to credit grantors. (ND inquiries remain for twelve months.)

Company Information	Inquiry Date(s)				
Equifax	03/2004	02/2004			
PRM-Financial	02/2004	11/2003			
AR-Credit	12/2003	11/2003	10/2003	09/2003	07/2003	05/2003

Copyright 2006 Equifax Inc.

Account Column Title Descriptions

❶ The account number reported by credit grantor
❷ The date that the credit grantor opened the account
❸ The highest amount charged
❹ The highest amount permitted
❺ The number of installments or payments
❻ The scheduled time between payments
❼ The number of months reviewed
❽ The most recent account activity
❾ The type of company reporting the account
❿ The month and year of the last account update
⓫ The total amount owed as of the date reported
⓬ The amount past due as of the date reported
⓭ The date of last payment
⓮ The actual amount of last payment
⓯ The requested amount of last payment
⓰ The date of the last account activity
⓱ The date the 1st major delinquency was reported
⓲ The amount charged off by creditor
⓳ The 1st payment due date for deferred loans
⓴ The amount of final balloon payment
㉑ The date of final balloon payment
㉒ The date the account was closed
㉓ *Account Status Code Descriptions*

1 : 30-59 days past due
2 : 60-89 days past due
3 : 90-119 days past due
4 : 120-149 days past due
5 : 150-179 days past due
6 : 180 or more days past due
G : Collection Account
H : Foreclosure
J : Voluntary Surrender
K : Repossession
L : Charge Off

Sample Credit Reports and Industry Forms

Appx. I.1.1

Commonly Asked Questions About Credit Files

Q. How can I correct a mistake in my credit file?
A. Complete the Research Request form and give details of the information you believe is incorrect. We will then check with the credit grantor, collection agency or public record source to see if any error has been reported. Information that cannot be verified will be removed from your file. If you and a credit grantor disagree on any information, you will need to resolve the dispute directly with the credit grantor who is the source of the information in question.

Q. Why doesn't my credit information from Equifax match that of Experian and TransUnion?
A. Credit information providers do not share your credit data with each other. As a result, updates made to your Equifax credit file may not be reflected on reports from Experian and TransUnion. You will need to contact the other credit reporting agencies directly to correct any inaccurate information. Contact information is provided below:

    TransUnion, PO Box 1000, Chester, PA 19022 Phone: (800) 888-4213

    Experian, P.O. Box 9530 Allen, TX 75013 Phone: (888) 397-3742

Q. If I do have credit problems, is there someplace where I can get advice and assistance?
A. Yes, there are a number of organizations that offer assistance. For example, the Consumer Credit Counseling Service (CCCS) is a non-profit organization that offers free or low-cost financial counseling to help people solve their financial problems. CCCS can help you analyze your situation and work with you to develop solutions. There are more than 600 CCCS offices throughout the country. Call 1 (800) 388-2227 for the telephone number of the office nearest you.

Q. Once the fraud alert is added to my credit file, who will contact me to verify if an application is legitimate?
A. When the credit grantor accesses your credit file, they should contact you as a part of their credit application approval process.

Facts You Should Know

• Payment history on your credit file is supplied by credit grantors with whom you have credit. This includes both open accounts and accounts that have already been closed. Payment in full does not remove your payment history. The length of time information remains in your credit file is shown below:
    Collection Accounts: Remain for 7 years.
    Credit Accounts: Accounts paid as agreed remain for up to 10 years. Accounts not paid as agreed remain for 7 years.
    (The time periods listed above are measured from the date in your credit file shown in the "date of last activity" field accompanying the particular credit or collection account.)
    Public Records: Remain for 7 years from the date filed, except:
        • Bankruptcy-Chapters 7 and 11 remain 10 years from the date filed.
        • Bankruptcy-Chapter 13 dismissed or no disposition rendered remain 10 years from the date filed.
        • Unpaid tax liens remain indefinitely.
        • Paid tax liens remain for up to 7 years from the date released.

    New York State Residents Only: Satisfied judgments remain 5 years from the date filed; paid collections remain 5 years from the "date of last activity".
    California State Residents Only: Unpaid tax liens remain 10 years from the date filed.

• Many companies market consumer products and services by mail. Millions of people take advantage of these direct marketing opportunities because it is a convenient way to shop. If you prefer to reduce the number of direct marketing mailings, you can write to: Direct Marketing Association, Mail Preference Service, P.O. Box 9008, Farmingdale, NY 11735-9008. To request that your name be removed from Direct Marketing Association member lists, include your complete name, full address and signature.

• Name, address, and Social Security number information may be provided to businesses that have a legitimate need to locate or identify a consumer.

• To protect your information from misuse, you should monitor any change in mail receipt patterns. Ensure that documents containing personal data or account numbers are destroyed or made illegible before disposing of them. Do not preprint checks or other documents with unique identifiers such as your driver's license or Social Security number. Never give out your account number or identifying information on phone calls in which you did not initiate the contact.

• To have a fraud alert removed from your credit file, identification information, such as, a copy of your driver's license or utility bill reflecting your current address along with a copy of your Social Security card must be provided.

Notice: Dispute Review Process and Your Rights:
Upon receipt of your dispute, we first review and consider the relevant information you have submitted regarding the nature of your dispute. If that review does not resolve your dispute and further investigation is required, notification of your dispute, including the relevant information you submitted, is provided to the source that furnished the disputed information. The source reviews the information provided, conducts an investigation with respect to the disputed information, and reports the results back to us. The credit reporting agency then makes deletions or changes to your credit file as appropriate based on the results of the reinvestigation. The name and address and, if reasonably available, the phone number of the furnisher(s) of information contacted while processing your dispute(s) is shown under the Results of Your Investigation section on the cover letter that accompanies the copy of your revised credit file.

If you still disagree with an item after it has been verified, you may send to us a brief statement, not to exceed 100 words (200 words for Maine residents) explaining the nature of your disagreement. Your statement will become part of your credit file and will be disclosed each time your credit file is accessed.

If the reinvestigation results in a change to or deletion of the information you are concerned about, or you submit a statement in accordance with the preceding paragraph, you have the right to request that we send your revised credit file to any company that received your credit file in the past 6 months for any purpose (12 months for California, Colorado, Maryland, New Jersey and New York residents) or in the past two years for employment purposes.

The FBI has named identity theft as the fastest growing crime in America.
Protect yourself with Equifax Credit Watch TM, a service that monitors your credit file every business day and notifies you within 24 hours of any activity. To order, go to: **www.creditwatch.equifax.com**

Copyright 2006 Equifax Inc.

EQUIFAX

Appx. I.1.2 *Fair Credit Reporting*

I.1.2 Experian

Please note that this report is a sample only and is subject to change.

Sample Credit Report   Page 1 of 4

experian

Online Personal Credit Report from Experian for

Experian credit report prepared for
JOHN Q CONSUMER
Your report number is
1562064065
Report date:
01/24/2005

Index:
- Potentially negative items
- Accounts in good standing
- Requests for your credit history
- Personal information
- Important message from Experian
- Contact us

Experian collects and organizes information about you and your credit history from public records, your creditors and other reliable sources. Experian makes your credit history available to your current and prospective creditors, employers and others as allowed by law, which can expedite your ability to obtain credit and can make offers of credit available to you. We do not grant or deny credit; each credit grantor makes that decision based on its own guidelines.

Potentially Negative Items

back to top

Public Records

Credit grantors may carefully review the items listed below when they check your credit history. Please note that the account information connected with some public records, such as bankruptcy, also may appear with your credit items listed later in this report.

MAIN COUNTY CLERK

Address:	Identification Number:	Plaintiff:
123 MAINTOWN S BUFFALO , NY 10000	1	ANY COMMISSIONER O.

Status:		Status Details:
Civil claim paid.		This item was verified and updated on 06-2001.

Date Filed:	Claim Amount:	
10/15/2000	$200	
Date Resolved:	Liability Amount:	
01/04/2001	NA	
Responsibility:		
INDIVIDUAL		

Credit Items

For your protection, the last few digits of your account numbers do not display.

ABCD BANKS

Address:	Account Number:	
100 CENTER RD BUFFALO, NY 10000 (555) 555-5555	1000000....	

Status: Paid/Past due 60 days.

Date Opened:	Type:	Credit Limit/Original Amount:
10/1997	Installment	$523
Reported Since:	Terms:	High Balance:
11/1997	12 Months	NA
Date of Status:	Monthly Payment:	Recent Balance:
01/1999	$0	$0 as of 01/1999
Last Reported:	Responsibility:	Recent Payment:
01/1999	Individual	$0

Account History:
60 days as of 12-1998
30 days as of 11-1998

MAIN COLL AGENCIES

Address: PO BOX 123 ANYTOWN, PA 10000 (555) 555-5555	**Account Number:** 0123456789	**Original Creditor:** TELEVISE CABLE COMM.

Status: Collection account. $95 past due as of 4-2000.

Date Opened: 01/2000	**Type:** Installment	**Credit Limit/Original Amount:** $95
Reported Since: 04/2000	**Terms:** NA	**High Balance:** NA
Date of Status: 04/2000	**Monthly Payment:** $0	**Recent Balance:** $95 as of 04/2000
Last Reported: 04/2000	**Responsibility:** Individual	**Recent Payment:** $0

Your statement: ITEM DISPUTED BY CONSUMER

Account History:
Collection as of 4-2000

Accounts in Good Standing

back to top

AUTOMOBILE AUTO FINANCE

Address: 100 MAIN ST E SMALLTOWN, MD 90001 (555) 555-5555	**Account Number:** 12345678998....	

Status: Open/Never late.

Date Opened: 01/2000	**Type:** Installment	**Credit Limit/Original Amount:** $10,355
Reported Since: 01/2000	**Terms:** 65 Months	**High Balance:** NA
Date of Status: 08/2001	**Monthly Payment:** $210	**Recent Balance:** $7,984 as of 08/2001
Last Reported: 08/2001	**Responsibility:** Individual	**Recent Payment:** $0

MAIN

Address: PO BOX 1234 FORT LAUDERDALE, FL 10009	**Account Number:** 1234567899876	

Status: Closed/Never late.

Date Opened: 03/1991	**Type:** Revolving	**Credit Limit/Original Amount:** NA
Reported Since: 03/1991	**Terms:** 1 Months	**High Balance:** $3,228
Date of Status: 08/2000	**Monthly Payment:** $0	**Recent Balance:** $0 /paid as of 08/2000
Last Reported: 08/2000	**Responsibility:** Individual	**Recent Payment:** $0

Your statement:
Account closed at consumer's request

Requests for Your Credit History

Requests Viewed By Others

We make your credit history available to your current and prospective creditors and employers as allowed by law. Personal data about you may be made available to companies whose products and services may interest you.

The section below lists all who have requested in the recent past to review your credit history as a result of actions involving you, such as the completion of a credit application or the transfer of an account to a collection agency, mortgage or loan application, etc. Creditors may view these requests when evaluating your creditworthiness.

HOMESALE REALTY CO

Address:
2000 S MAINROAD BLVD STE
ANYTOWN CA 11111
(555) 555-5555

Date of Request:
07/16/2001

Comments:
Real estate loan on behalf of 1000 COPRORATE COMPANY. This inquiry is scheduled to continue on record until 8-2003.

ABC BANK

Address:
PO BOX 100
BUFFALO NY 10000
(555) 555-5555

Date of Request:
02/23/2001

Comments:
Permissible purpose. This inquiry is scheduled to continue on record until 3-2003.

ANYTOWN FUNDING INC

Address:
100 W MAIN AVE STE 100
INTOWN CA 10000
(555) 555-5555

Date of Request:
07/25/2000

Comments:
Permissible purpose. This inquiry is scheduled to continue on record until 8-2002.

Requests Viewed Only By You

The section below lists all who have a permissible purpose by law and have requested in the recent past to review your information. You may not have initiated these requests, so you may not recognize each source. We offer information about you to those with a permissible purpose, for example, to:

- other creditors who want to offer you preapproved credit;
- an employer who wishes to extend an offer of employment;
- a potential investor in assessing the risk of a current obligation;
- Experian or other credit reporting agencies to process a report for you;
- your existing creditors to monitor your credit activity (date listed may reflect only the most recent request).

We report these requests **only to you** as a record of activities. We **do not** provide this information to other creditors who evaluate your creditworthiness.

MAIN BANK USA

Address:
1 MAIN CTR AA 11
BUFFALO NY 10000

Date of Request:
08/10/2001

MAINTOWN BANK

Address:
PO BOX 100
MAINTOWNS DE 10000
(555) 555-5555

Date of Request:
08/05/2001

ANYTOWN DATA CORPS

Address:
2000 S MAINTOWN BLVD STE
INTOWN CO 11111
(555) 555-5555

Date of Request:
07/16/2001

Sample Credit Reports and Industry Forms   **Appx. I.1.2**

Sample Credit Report

Personal Information

The following information is reported to us by you, your creditors and other sources. Each source may report your personal information differently, which may result in variations of your name, address, Social Security number, etc. As part of our fraud-prevention program, a notice with additional information may appear. As a security precaution, the Social Security number that you used to obtain this report is not displayed. The Geographical Code shown with each address identifies the state, county, census tract, block group and Metropolitan Statistical Area associated with each address.

Names:
JOHN Q CONSUMER
JONATHON Q CONSUMER
J Q CONSUMER

Social Security number variations:
999999999

Year of birth:
1954

Employers:
ABCDE ENGINEERING CORP

Telephone numbers:
(555) 555 5555 Residential

Address: 123 MAIN STREET
ANYTOWN, MD 90001-9999
Type of Residence: Multifamily
Geographical Code: 0-156510-31-8840

Address: 555 SIMPLE PLACE
ANYTOWN, MD 90002-7777
Type of Residence: Single family
Geographical Code: 0-176510-33-8840

Address: 999 HIGH DRIVE APT 15B
ANYTOWN, MD 90003-5555
Type of Residence: Apartment complex
Geographical Code: 0-156510-31-8840

Your Personal Statement

No general personal statements appear on your report.

Important Message From Experian   back to top

By law, we cannot disclose certain medical information (relating to physical, mental, or behavioral health or condition). Although we do not generally collect such information, it could appear in the name of a data furnisher (i.e., "Cancer Center") that reports your payment history to us. If so, those names display in your report, but in reports to others they display only as MEDICAL PAYMENT DATA. Consumer statements included on your report at your request that contain medical information are disclosed to others.

Contacting Us   back to top

Contact address and phone number for your area will display here.

©Experian 2006. All rights reserved.
Experian and the Experian marks herein are service marks or registered trademarks of Experian.

I.1.3 TransUnion

Note: This report example is only an illustration of the type of information provided on a TransUnion Personal Credit Report. The information in the report example does not reflect a particular or personal situation. You must order your TransUnion Personal Credit Report to obtain information that pertains to your personal situation. The sample TransUnion Personal Credit Report, TransUnion and the "T" logo are registered or unregistered copyrighted works, service marks or trademarks of TransUnion L.L.C. All Rights Reserved.

Sample Credit Reports and Industry Forms Appx. I.1.3

Consumer Credit Reports - View Single Bureau Credit Report

| home | privacy | learning center | help | member login |

Single Credit Report
The **Single Credit Report** is a snapshot of your credit history according to one major credit bureau.

Find out what personal information the credit bureaus have in your file.

- Make sure your name, address, and employer are accurate and up-to-date.
- Watch out for incorrect addresses—this may be a sign that an identity thief has redirected your mail to a false address.

Name: Sample Link Report **Date of Birth:** 03/17/1950
Address Information:

	Street Address	Date Reported:
Current:	123 NE FLAT TER MIAMI, FL 331333217	06/24/1999
Previous:	2222 ONE DR MIAMI BEACH, FL 33141	08/16/1998

Employers:

	Employer Name:	Street Address:
Current:	LARRY'S BARBER SHOP	3026 South Higue San Luis Obispo

Understand your credit file with an easy-to-read summary of your report.

- See all of your essential credit report information at-a-glance.
- Watch out for inaccuracies that could negatively impact your credit standing.

Account Distribution

Account Type	Count	Balance($)	Payment($)
Real Estate	1	106400	1130
Revolving	2	1773	25
Installment	1	15050	250
Other	0	0	0
Collection	1	5432	5432
Total	5	128655	6837

Public Records: 4 **Open Accounts:** 4 **Closed Accounts:** 1

Get detailed information about all of your loans and credit card accounts.

- Is the account open or closed?
- What is your monthly payment?
- What is your total balance?
- What is your maximum limit?
- Have you ever had any late payments?
- Make sure the information is accurate and up-to-date.
- Watch out for accounts that are not familiar—these could be accounts that were opened fraudulently in your name.

MORTGAGE COMPANY INC
Account: 123**** **Acct Type:** Real estate
Date Opened: 06/XX/1999 **Balance:** $99153
Date Reported: 06/30/1999 **High Balance:** $106400
Past Due: **Account Condition:** Open
Remarks:
Payment Status: Current. This account is in good standing.
Payment History:

CUR	CUR	CUR	CUR	30	60	CUR	CUR	CUR	CUR	CUR	CUR
Aug 2000	Sep	Oct	Nov	Dec	Jan 2001	Feb	Mar	Apr	May	Jun	Jul	Aug

Discover who's been looking at your credit report.

Consumer Credit Reports - View Single Bureau Credit Report

- Make sure you've authorized all of the inquiries.
- Watch out for names of companies that are not familiar—if you haven't authorized the inquiry, it may be a sign of fraud.
- **Note:** When you personally check your credit report with TrueCredit.com, the inquiry that is recorded *will not* adversely affect your credit standing.

Creditor Name	Date of Inquiry
LENDER	05/11/1999
MORTGAGE SUPPORT	03/12/1999
BIG BANK	10/21/1997
CREDIT COMPANY	05/25/1999
CREDIT CARD COMPANY	08/12/1997

Get contact information for all of your creditors.

- Use the addresses and phone numbers to contact them in case you identify issues that need to be resolved.

Creditor Name	Address	Phone
BANK CREDIT CARD	123 NEW LINDEN HILL WILMINGTON, DE 19808	BY MAIL ONLY
CREDIT CARD CO	PO BOX 123456 FORT LAUDERDALE, FL	
HOME LOAN LENDER	123 BEACH DRIVE MIAMI CITY, FL 33314	555-1234

home | learning center | privacy | help | member login | terms of use | about | sitemap

TrueCredit features TransUnion data for all complimentary credit scores as well as fraud-watch emails.
TrueCredit is a wholly owned subsidiary of TransUnion.
© Copyright 1998-2006 TrueCredit. All Rights Reserved.

Sample Credit Reports and Industry Forms   **Appx. I.2**

I.2 Universal Data Form

UNIVERSAL DATA FORM

This form has been approved for reporting or updating account information.

General Help (F1)

☐ New   ☐ Change   If Change makes trade current, is previous delinquent history to be deleted? ☐ Yes ☐ No
☐ Delete (By checking Delete, tradeline will be removed)
(Do not include security passwords with codes below.)

Subscriber Name: _____   EXPERIAN Subscriber Code: _____
Subscriber Address: _____   EQUIFAX Subscriber Code: _____
_____   TRANS UNION Subscriber Code: _____

CONSUMER INFORMATION

Surname	First	Middle Name	Suffix	SSN: - -	DOB

Current Address	City	State	Zip Code -

Previous Address	City	State	Zip Code -

Current Employer Name	Occupation	City	State

Co-Applicant Information

Surname	First	Middle Name	Suffix	SSN: - -	DOB

Address (if different)	City	State	Zip Code -

Employer Name	Occupation	City	State

CURRENT HISTORICAL ACCOUNT INFORMATION

Account Number	Present Status				24-Month Payment History	Type Acct/MOP
	Date Open	Date	Balance	Past Due	☐ MOP History	
	/ /	/ /				
MetroStatusCode / Orig. or Credit Limit Amt. / Terms/Amount / Date Last Pay	Maximum Delinquency			Status		ECOA

		Date	Amt.*	MOP	Closed Date	CCC	CII	SCC
	/	/ /	/ /		/ /			

Type of Loan	High Credit	First Delinquency			Historical Status					
		Date	P & L Amount	MOP	No. Mos.	30	60	90	120	150	180
		/ /									

*Must be present when reporting a charge off or repossession.   ☐ Automated   ☐ Manual

When you sign this form, you certify that your computer and/or manual records have been adjusted to reflect any changes made.

Reason for deletion or status change from adverse to favorable:

Authorized Signature: _____   Date: / /

Please Print Name: _____   Telephone: ( ) -   EXT.

Appx. I.3 *Fair Credit Reporting*

I.3 Automated Consumer Dispute Verification Form

Sample Automated Consumer Dispute Verification Form[1]

Return this dispute response to:
ICRA - exp affiliated
123 Street New Town, NY 12603--
FAX # -
Account Number 37012345678
Subscriber Code DF Credit/dfcreditexp

Date : 05-19-2006
Control # 9070605040
DNR Date 06-10-2006
Response Date 05-19-2006

Please check the SAME box for each identification item appearing on the CDV which is identical to your records; or provide differing information in the shaded area.

		SAME	
Name/Gen Code John Q Consumer / ---		☐	**Name/Gen Code** - Quentin - / ---
Address 123 Main St, atlanta GA 30328--		☑	**Address** -, -- ---
Prev Name/Prev Gen Code --- / ---		☐	**Prev Name/Prev Gen Code** --- / ---
Prev Address 8946 S Water St, Chicago IL 60601--		☐	**Prev Address** 525 W Belmont St, Chicago IL 60657--
SSN 909122242		☑	**SSN** -
DOB 04-15-1965		☑	**DOB** -
Telephone Number 4045251212		☐	**Telephone Number** 4048325454
2nd Prev Addr -, -- ---			

Consumer States/Comments:
Dispute Code 1: 24:Claims account closed by consumer. Verify Compliance Condition Code, Account Status, Date Closed, and Payment Rating.
Dispute Code 2:
FCRA Relevant Information:
Account paid in full and closed on 5/4/06. Check number 7682

Please write clearly and report changed information in the shaded box directly below where it is currently reported.

Verified as Reported ☐   Change Data as Shown ☑   Delete Account ☐   Delete due to Fraud ☐

Acct Status	Pay Rate	MOP	Cond/Cumm Status	Date Opened	Balance	Amt Past Due	High Cr/Org	Credit limit	Org Chg Off Amt
11	0	-	-	02-05-1999	14386	-	68000	-	-
13	0				0	0			

Acct Type	Portf Type	Terms Dur	Freq	Date of Account Information	Date Closed	Date of Last Pymnt	Sch Pymnt	ECOA	Status Date (EXP only)	FCRA DOFD
6D	I	-	-	04-15-2006	-	04-15-2006	734	1	-	-
-				05-19-2006	05-09-2006	05-09-2006	-		-	-

CCC	SCC	CII	Orig Cr Name	Orig Cr Class	Spec Pymnt Ind	Deferred Start Date	Balloon Date	Balloon Amt
-	-	-	-	-	-	-	-	-

Accounts History

0	0	0	0	0	0	0	0	0	0	1	0	0	0	0	0	0	1	0	0	0	0	0	0
0	0	0	0	0	0	1	0	0	0	0	0	0	0	0	0	0	0	0	0	0	0	0	0
0	0	0	0	0	1	0	0	0	0	0	0	0	0	0	0	0	0	0	0	0	0	0	0
0	0	1	0	0	0	0	0	0	0	0	0												
0	0	0	0	0	0	0	0	0	0	1	0	0	0	0	0	1	0	0	0	0	0	0	0
0	0	0	0	0	0	1	0	0	0	0	0	0	0	0	0	0	0	0	0	0	0	0	0
0	0	0	0	0	0	1	0	0	0	0	0	0	0	0	0	0	0	0	0	0	0	0	0
0	0	1	0	0	0	0	0	0	0														

Agency ID	Sec Mktg Agency Acct #	Mortgage ID
-	-	-
-	-	-

Actual Pymnt	Portfolio Indicator	Prchsd from/Sold to
900	-	-

Remarks : -

DF Contact # : 9723903912

Authorized Name _____   **Tel #** _____

When you sign this form, you certify that you have verified the accuracy of the entire item in compliance with all legal requirements, and your computer and/or manual records will be adjusted to reflect changes noted above.

© 2006 Online Data Exchange LLC

---

[1] Source: Consumer Data Industry Association, as reprinted in Federal Trade Commission and Federal Reserve Board, "Report to Congress on the Fair Credit Reporting Act Dispute Process," Appendix C (August 2006).

Appendix J Sample Pleadings and Other Litigation Documents

J.1 Introduction

This appendix contains several sample FCRA-related pleadings and case excerpts. These include four sample complaints (J.2.1–J.2.4); three sample sets of interrogatories (J.3.1–J.3.3); two sample requests for production of documents (J.4.1 and J.4.2); two sample requests for admissions (J.5.1 and J.5.2); and two sample notices of deposition (J.6.1 and J.6.2). Also included is a sample confidentiality order (J.7). For trial practice, this appendix includes sample jury instructions and a sample closing argument (J.8.1–J.8.4). Finally, this appendix includes model language to be used in settlements over debt litigation designed to address credit reporting consequences (J.9.2 and J.9.3).

These sample pleadings have been drafted and supplied by experienced attorneys who litigate FCRA and other consumer law cases. Additional sample pleadings can be found on the CD-Rom included at the end of this manual and in the Consumer Law Pleadings series. Nearly all these samples are from actual cases, but they must be reviewed and adapted by practitioners. Not only do courts have their own rules and customs, but what may be appropriate for one case may not be appropriate for another. These materials are provided as a starting point for ideas and may be useful in the initiation and prosecution of an individual case. Practitioners are encouraged to use and build upon these sample pleadings. Practitioners should also be cognizant of any changes in law that may affect the applicability of these pleadings to specific cases.

The four complaints vary in terms of defendants and causes of action. The first complaint involves claims against a furnisher of information and a credit reporting agency. It includes claims that the furnisher and the credit reporting agency failed to properly reinvestigate disputed information pursuant to 15 U.S.C. § 1681s-2(b) and 15 U.S.C. § 1681i.

The second complaint involves claims against an insurance company that is a user of credit reports. This complaint includes allegations that the user obtained credit reports of consumers without a permissible purpose under the FCRA. The user obtained the credit reports of household members of applicants for insurance; however, these household members had not consented nor had they themselves applied for insurance.

The third sample complaint involves claims against a credit reporting agency in a "mixed file" case. This complaint alleges that the credit reporting agency included bankruptcy and other derogatory information in the plaintiff's file that belonged to another consumer and that the agency refused to correct this inaccurate reporting or conduct a reasonable investigation after the plaintiff disputed the errors.

The fourth sample complaint involves class action claims against a tenant screening bureau, which is a specialty consumer reporting agency, over inaccurate consumer reports. This complaint alleges that the agency, among other things, failed to maintain reasonable procedures to ensure maximum possible accuracy.

The sample sets of interrogatories, requests for production of documents, requests for admissions and notices of deposition cover a broad range of fair credit reporting issues, including impermissible access to credit reports, failure to reinvestigate disputed information and credit scoring. These discovery pleadings also relate to some of the claims contained in the sample complaints. Additional discovery pleadings are contained on the companion CD-Rom.

FCRA litigation frequently involves overly broad claims of confidentiality by consumer reporting agencies, users, and furnishers. The sample confidentiality order requires that a party seeking confidentiality clearly and precisely document the need for secrecy. Sample motions opposing an over-broad protective order are included on the CD-Rom.

Experienced practitioners must always be prepared for the possibility that their FCRA claims will be put before a jury. This appendix thus includes a sample closing argument and sample jury instructions. As stated earlier, practitioners must use these materials as educational tools and modify their arguments and instructions for the jury as appropriate. Additional jury instructions can be found on the CD-Rom.

Finally, there is no better time to clear up a consumer's credit record than when settling a lawsuit with a creditor that has furnished negative information on the consumer. Failure of a settlement to protect a client's credit record will probably mean that the consumer will be plagued by a bad credit record for at least seven years. As a matter of routine, practitioners should demand that all credit settlements include a provision specifying exactly what the creditor should and should not report to a consumer reporting agency. Sample language which may be adapted and included in settlement agreements is included in this appendix. Practitioners are advised to consult the discussion and practical suggestions about using such language in the text of this volume at § 12.6.4, *supra*.

J.2 Complaints

J.2.1 Complaint—Failure to Reinvestigate

IN THE UNITED STATES DISTRICT COURT
FOR THE EASTERN DISTRICT OF VIRGINIA
Richmond Division

[PLAINTIFF], Plaintiff v. EQUIFAX INFORMATION SERVICES, L.L.C. and MBNA AMERICA BANK, N.A., Defendants	)))))) CIVIL NO.))))

COMPLAINT

COMES NOW the Plaintiff, [PLAINTIFF], (hereafter collectively the "Plaintiff") by counsel, and for her complaint against the Defendants, alleges as follows:

PRELIMINARY STATEMENT

1. This is an action for actual, statutory and punitive damages, costs and attorney's fees brought pursuant to 15 U.S.C. § 1681 *et seq.* (Federal Fair Credit Reporting Act), 15 U.S.C. § 1666 (Federal Fair Credit Billing Act), and for the common law tort of defamation.

JURISDICTION

2. The jurisdiction of this Court is conferred by 15 U.S.C. § 1681(p) and 28 U.S.C. 1367.

3. The Plaintiff is a natural person and resident of the State of Virginia. She is a "consumer" as defined by 15 U.S.C. § 1681a(c).

4. Upon information and belief, EQUIFAX INFORMATION SERVICES, L.L.C ("Equifax") is a corporation incorporated under the laws of the State of Georgia authorized to do business in the State of Virginia through its registered offices at 11 South 12th Street, Richmond, Virginia.

5. Upon information and belief, Equifax is a "consumer reporting agency," as defined in 15 U.S.C. § 1681(f). Upon information and belief, Equifax is regularly engaged in the business of assembling, evaluating, and disbursing information concerning consumers for the purpose of furnishing consumer reports, as defined in 15 U.S.C. § 1681(d) to third parties.

6. Upon information and belief, Equifax disburses such consumer reports to third parties under contract for monetary compensation.

7. Upon information and belief, MBNA AMERICA BANK, N.A. ("MBNA") is a national bank, authorized to do business in the State of Virginia, as a consumer credit card lender.

8. In January, 2001, Plaintiff received a statement from Defendant, MBNA, (Exhibit "A") showing an outstanding balance of $17,210.69 (the "MBNA statement") on an account held by her estranged husband for which she was not liable.

9. In March, 2001, Plaintiff requested and received a copy of the credit file of the Plaintiff compiled and maintained by Equifax (Exhibit "B") (the "Equifax credit report").

10. Within the Equifax credit report, Equifax reported that Plaintiff had opened and was responsible for the credit account, which account was still outstanding and had a derogatory payment history (the "MBNA representation").

11. The MBNA representation was false. Plaintiff had never applied for or obtained any credit from MBNA.

12. In or about March, 2001, Plaintiff, through her attorney, contacted MBNA disputing the MBNA representation and requested further information regarding same (Exhibit "C"). Plaintiff's attorney notified MBNA that the account was opened by her estranged husband prior to their marriage and that Plaintiff was only an authorized user of the account. Plaintiff's attorney demanded proof from MBNA showing that Plaintiff was co-signor and suggested that MBNA had mistakenly tied the MBNA account to the Plaintiff.

13. MBNA did not respond to Plaintiff's dispute letter.

14. A copy of the correspondence was also forwarded to Defendant, Equifax, requesting that Equifax verify and delete the erroneous MBNA representation from her credit file. On or about March 27, 2001, Equifax responded by letter dated March 27, 2001 and attached hereto as Exhibit "D" (the "March 27, 2001 Equifax letter").

15. Upon the Plaintiff's request for verification and deletion, and in accordance with its standard procedures, Equifax did not evaluate or consider any of Plaintiff's information, claims or evidence and did not make any attempt to substantially or reasonably verify the MBNA representation.

16. In the alternative to the allegation that Equifax failed to contact MBNA, it is alleged that Equifax did forward some notice of the dispute to MBNA and MBNA failed to conduct a lawful investigation.

FIRST CLAIM FOR RELIEF AGAINST EQUIFAX

17. The Plaintiff realleges and incorporates paragraphs 1 through 16 above as if fully set out herein.

18. Equifax violated 15 U.S.C. § 1681e(b) by failing to establish or to follow reasonable procedures to assure maximum possible accuracy in the preparation of the credit report and credit files it published and maintains concerning the Plaintiff.

19. As a result of this conduct, action and inaction of Equifax, the Plaintiff suffered damage by loss of credit, loss of the ability to purchase and benefit from a credit, the mental and emotional pain and anguish and the humiliation and embarrassment of credit denials.

20. Equifax's conduct, action and inaction was willful, rendering it liable for punitive damages in an amount to be determined by the Court pursuant to 15 U.S.C. § 1681n. In the alternative, it was negligent, entitling the Plaintiff to recover under 15 U.S.C. 1681o.

21. The Plaintiff is entitled to recover costs and attorney's fees from Equifax in an amount to be determined by the Court pursuant to 15 U.S.C. § 1681n and/or § 1681o.

SECOND CLAIM FOR RELIEF AGAINST EQUIFAX

22. Plaintiff realleges and incorporates paragraphs 1 through 21 above as if fully set out herein.

23. Equifax violated 15 U.S.C. § 1681i on multiple occasions by failing to delete inaccurate information in the Plaintiff's credit file after receiving actual notice of such inaccuracies; by failing to conduct a lawful reinvestigation; by failing to forward all relevant information to MBNA; by failing to maintain reasonable procedures with which to filter and verify disputed information in the Plaintiff's credit file; and by relying upon verification from a source it has reason to know is unreliable.

24. As a result of this conduct, action and inaction of Equifax, the Plaintiff suffered damage by loss of credit; loss of the ability to purchase and benefit from credit; and the mental and emotional pain, anguish, humiliation, and embarrassment of credit denials.

25. Equifax's conduct, action and inaction was willful, rendering it liable for actual or statutory damages, and punitive damages in an amount to be determined by the Court pursuant to 15 U.S.C. § 1681n. In the alternative, it was negligent entitling the Plaintiff to recover actual damages under 15 U.S.C. § 1681o.

26. The Plaintiff is entitled to recover costs and attorney's fees from Equifax in an amount to be determined by the Court pursuant to 15 U.S.C. § 1681n and/or 1681o.

FIRST CLAIM FROM RELIEF AGAINST MBNA

26. Plaintiff realleges and incorporates paragraphs 1 through 26 above as if fully set out herein.

27. MBNA published the MBNA representations to Equifax and through Equifax to all of Plaintiff's potential lenders on multiple occasions, including but not limited to the MBNA response to Equifax published just prior to March 27, 2001 and which formed the basis of the Equifax letters (the "Defamation").

28. The Defamation was willful and with malice. MBNA did not have any reasonable basis to believe that the Plaintiff was responsible for the account reported in the MBNA representation. It also had substantial evidence by which to have verified that the Plaintiff was not the person who had applied and contracted for the credit. MBNA willfully determined to follow procedures which did not review, confirm or verify the identity of persons to whom it lent money. Further, even if MBNA would attempt to plead ignorance prior to January, 2001, it had all of the evidence and information with which to confirm and recognize the Plaintiff had not signed its credit application and was not obligated upon the MBNA account after the events previously alleged in this complaint.

29. As a result of this conduct, action and inaction of MBNA, the Plaintiff suffered damage by loss of credit; loss of the ability to purchase and benefit from credit; and the mental and emotional pain, anguish, humiliation, and embarrassment of credit denials.

30. The Defamation, conduct and actions of MBNA were willful, deliberate, intentional and/or with reckless disregard for the interests and rights of Plaintiff such as to justify an award of punitive damages against MBNA in an amount to be determined by the Court.

SECOND CLAIM FOR RELIEF AGAINST MBNA

31. Plaintiff realleges and incorporates paragraphs 1 through 30 above as if fully set out herein.

32. MBNA violated the Fair Credit Reporting Act, 15 U.S.C. § 1681s-2(b) by continuing to the MBNA representation within Plaintiff's credit file with Equifax without also including a notation that this debt was disputed; by failing to fully and properly investigate the Plaintiff's dispute of the MBNA representation; by failing to review all relevant information regarding same; by failing to accurately respond to Equifax; by failing to correctly report results of an accurate investigation to every other credit reporting agency; and by failing to permanently and lawfully correct its own internal records to prevent the re-reporting of the MBNA Representations to the consumer reporting agencies.

33. As a result of this conduct, action and inaction of MBNA, the Plaintiff suffered damage by loss of credit; loss of the ability to purchase and benefit from credit; and the mental and emotional pain, anguish, humiliation, and embarrassment of credit denials.

34. MBNA's conduct, action and inaction was willful, rendering it liable for actual or statutory, and punitive damages in an amount to be determined by the Court pursuant to 15 U.S.C. § 1681n. In the alternative, it was negligent entitling the Plaintiff to recover actual damages under 15 U.S.C. 1681o.

35. The Plaintiff is entitled to recover costs and attorney's fees from MBNA in an amount to be determined by the Court pursuant to 15 U.S.C. § 1681n and § 1681o.

THIRD CLAIM FOR RELIEF AGAINST MBNA

36. Plaintiff realleges and incorporates paragraphs 1 through 35 above as if fully set out herein.

37. MBNA violated the Federal Fair Credit Billing Act, 15 U.S.C. § 1666 ("FCBA") by its refusal and failure to respond to Plaintiff's written dispute letter mailed by her attorney within sixty (60) days of receipt of Exhibit "A" and for its failure to conduct a lawful investigation of Plaintiff's dispute.

38. As a result of MBNA's violation of the FCBA, MBNA is liable to Plaintiff for her actual and statutory damages and for her attorneys fees and cost pursuant to 15 U.S.C. § 1640.

WHEREFORE, Your Plaintiff demands judgment for compensatory and punitive damages against Defendants, jointly and severally; for her attorneys fees and costs; for pre-judgment and post-judgment interest at the legal rate, and such other relief the Court does deem just, equitable and proper.

TRIAL BY JURY IS DEMANDED.

[PLAINTIFF],
By _____
Of Counsel

J.2.2 Complaint—Impermissible Purposes

UNITED STATES DISTRICT COURT
NORTHERN DISTRICT OF _____
_____ DIVISION

TOM SMITH and JULIE SMITH, Plaintiffs,	)))
v.	) COMPLAINT) CIVIL ACTION NO.
XXX INSURANCE COMPANY, Defendant	))))

COMPLAINT AND JURY DEMAND

Plaintiffs Tom Smith and Julie Smith, on behalf of themselves, state as follows

INTRODUCTION

1. This is a consumer class action under the Fair Credit Reporting Act, 15 U.S.C. § 1681a et seq. In the process of underwriting applications for insurance, defendant XXX Insurance Company ("XXX") customarily obtains without consent credit reports of people other than the applicant for insurance. XXX's practice is prohibited by § 1681b of the Fair Credit Reporting Act. In this action, plaintiffs seek money damages as provided under the Act as a result of XXX's conduct.

PARTIES, JURISDICTION AND VENUE

2. Plaintiff Tom Smith is a citizen of the State of _____ and a resident of _____. At all relevant times, he has been over the age of 21 years.

3. Plaintiff Julie Smith is a citizen of the State of _____ and a resident of _____ County. Julie Smith is the mother of Tom Smith.

4. Defendant XXX is a foreign insurance company registered with the _____ Secretary of State and authorized to transact business in the State of _____. Its address as listed with the Secretary of State is 111111 Blueberry Road, Suite 000, Meadowbrook, _____, 60609. Its registered agent for service of process is _____.

5. This Court has jurisdiction over the subject matter of this lawsuit pursuant to 15 U.S.C. §§ 1681p. Venue is proper in this Court pursuant to 15 U.S.C. §§ 1391(b

FACTUAL BACKGROUND

6. On or about December 1, 2001, Julie Smith applied to XXX for a homeowner's insurance policy. The application was taken over the telephone by an XXX agent located in _____, _____.

7. Julie Smith informed the agent that she was the sole applicant for the insurance and was the sole owner of the home which she sought to insure.

8. As part of the application process, XXX's agent requested, and Julie Smith provided, the social security numbers of her two adult children who would be residing in the home, including the social security number for her son Tom Smith.

9. After receiving Tom Smith's social security number, XXX obtained Tom Smith's credit report from CRA, L.L.C., ("CRA") a credit reporting agency.

10. XXX's avowed purpose in obtaining the credit report of Tom Smith was to use it in the underwriting of an application for homeowner's insurance.

11. XXX, in fact, reviewed Tom Smith's credit report in the underwriting of Julie Smith's application for homeowner's insurance.

12. XXX denied Julie Smith's application for homeowner's insurance.

13. XXX's denial of Julie Smith's application for homeowner's insurance was based in whole or in part on its review of Tom Smith's credit report.

14. XXX never received permission from Tom Smith to obtain his credit report. Tom Smith never applied for homeowner's insurance from XXX. XXX never made Tom Smith a firm offer of insurance in connection with obtaining Tom Smith's credit report.

15. XXX did not have a permissible purpose under the Fair Credit Reporting Act, 15 U.S.C. § 1681b, to obtain Tom Smith's credit report.

16. The fact that XXX obtained his credit report caused actual damage to Tom Smith.

17. Following denial of Julie Smith's application, XXX did not notify either Julie Smith or Tom Smith that Tom Smith's credit report had been obtained from CRA, that her application for insurance had been denied based upon the contents of her son's credit report, that a free copy of his credit report could be obtained from CRA, or that the accuracy or completeness of any information in the credit report could be disputed.

18. During the course of underwriting applications for homeowner's insurance, XXX has a practice of obtaining credit reports of individuals who are not applying for the insurance, but who reside in the home to be insured.

COUNT I
WILLFUL WRONGFUL PROCUREMENT OF CREDIT REPORT

19. Under the Fair Credit Reporting Act, 15 U.S.C. § 1681a et seq., a consumer reporting agency is prohibited from furnishing a consumer report to a person who lacks a permissible purpose. The permissible purposes allowed by the Act are set forth in 15 U.S.C. § 1681b.

20. Under 15 U.S.C. § 1681b(3)(C), an insurance company such as XXX has a permissible purpose to obtain a credit report when it "intends to use the information in connection with the underwriting of insurance involving the consumer." The scope of this permissible purpose, however, is restricted to obtaining the credit report of the person applying for the insurance being underwritten. The section does not permit an insurer to obtain credit reports of persons who are not the consumer applying for the insurance being underwritten.

21. 15 U.S.C. § 1681b(c) governs situations where an insurer requests a credit report in connection with an insurance transaction that is not initiated by the consumer whose credit report the insurer seeks to obtain. Under the section, a credit reporting agency can properly release the nonapplicant's credit report only if the nonapplicant authorizes the credit reporting agency to do so or the transaction involved consists of a firm offer of insurance.

22. Under 15 U.S.C. § 1681b(f), a person is prohibited from obtaining a credit report on a consumer unless the person has a permissible purpose for procuring the report and certifies that purpose to the consumer reporting agency.

23. An insurer which obtains a credit report on a person who has not initiated an insurance transaction by applying for insurance violates 15 U.S.C. § 1681b(f) unless the person has authorized release of the credit report or a firm offer of insurance is made to the person.

24. During the course of underwriting insurance, XXX has a pattern and practice of obtaining consumer reports from credit reporting agencies of people other than the consumer applying for such insurance without obtaining their consent or making a firm offer of insurance to them.

25. XXX's pattern and practice of obtaining consumer reports relating to people other than the consumer applying for insurance violates the Fair Credit Reporting Act, in particular 15 U.S.C. § 1681b(f). XXX has no permissible purpose in obtaining the credit reports of such people.

26. Consistent with its pattern and practice, XXX wrongfully obtained the credit report of Tom Smith during the process of underwriting the insurance application submitted by Julie Smith. XXX had no permissible purpose under 15 U.S.C. § 1681b for obtaining the credit report of Tom Smith.

27. The entities from which XXX obtains credit reports of nonapplicants in connection with its underwriting activities, including specifically CRA are "consumer reporting agencies" within the meaning of the Fair Credit Reporting Act.

28. The credit reports that XXX obtains of nonapplicants in connection with its underwriting activities, including specifically the credit report it obtained relating to Tom Smith, are "consumer reports" within the meaning of the Fair Credit Reporting Act.

29. In connection with its practice of obtaining credit reports of people other than the consumer applying for insurance, XXX acts willfully, knowingly, and in conscious disregard for the rights of such persons under the Fair Credit Reporting Act. Consistent with its practice, XXX acted willfully, knowingly, and in conscious disregard of the rights of Tom Smith in obtaining his credit report from CRA.

30. In connection with its practice, XXX customarily certifies to the credit reporting agency that it is requesting the credit report for the purpose of underwriting an application for insurance when, in fact, the person whose credit report is being requested has not applied for insurance. Accordingly, pursuant to its practice, XXX obtains credit reports of nonapplicants through false pretenses within the meaning of 15 U.S.C. § 1681n(b).

31. As a result of XXX's willful practice of violating the Fair Credit Reporting Act, XXX is liable under 15 U.S.C. § 1681n for punitive damages in an amount sufficient to deter XXX from engaging in this kind of illegal practice in the future.

32. As a result of XXX's willful practice of violating the Fair Credit Reporting Act, XXX is liable under 15 U.S.C. § 1681n for the costs of bringing this action as well as reasonable attorney's fees.

WHEREFORE, plaintiffs request the following relief:

(a) a judicial declaration that XXX's practice of obtaining credit reports of nonapplicants in connection with the underwriting of insurance applications violates the Fair Credit Reporting Act;

(b) an award of statutory damages to plaintiff in an amount to be determined at trial;

(c) an award of punitive damages as provided by the Fair Credit Reporting Act;

(d) an award of the costs of bringing this action and reasonable attorney's fees;

(e) such other and further relief as deemed just and appropriate by the Court.

JURY DEMAND

Plaintiffs demand trial by jury on all issues so triable.

[Attorneys for Plaintiff]

J.2.3 Complaint*Mixed File*

IN THE UNITED STATES DISTRICT COURT
FOR THE DISTRICT OF NEW MEXICO

```
_____  )
[PLAINTIFF],           )
              Plaintiff, )
                       )
v.                     )
                       )
EQUIFAX CREDIT         )
INFORMATION SERVICES,  )
INC.,                  )
              Defendants. )
_____  )
```

AMENDED COMPLAINT FOR DAMAGES AND DEMAND FOR JURY TRIAL

1. Plaintiff [Plaintiff]'s consumer credit report contains a bankruptcy and negative credit entries for another person. She provided to Defendants irrefutable proof that the bankruptcy and these derogatory accounts belong to another [Name] with a different social security number. Nevertheless, Defendants obstinately refuse to correct their damaging and inaccurate credit reporting and refuse to undertake a genuine and reasonable reinvestigation into [Plaintiff]'s dispute.

Jurisdiction and Venue

2. This Court has jurisdiction under the Fair Credit Reporting Act ("FCRA"), 15 U.S.C. § 1681p, and under 28 U.S.C. §§ 1331 and 1337, and it has supplemental jurisdiction over the state claims under 28 U.S.C. § 1367. The events took place in this District.

Parties

3. Plaintiff [Plaintiff] resides in [City], New Mexico. She is a "consumer" as defined by FCRA, 15 U.S.C. § 1681a(c), and as defined by the New Mexico Credit Bureaus Act ("CBA"), NMSA 1978 § 56-3-1.

4. Defendant Equifax Credit Information Services, Inc. is a foreign corporation which is a "consumer reporting agency" as defined by the FCRA, 15 U.S.C. § 1681a(f) and a "credit bureau" as defined by the CBA, NMSA 1978 § 56-3-1. Equifax assembles or evaluates consumer credit information or other information on consumers for the purpose of furnishing consumer reports to third parties. It uses means of interstate commerce for the purpose of preparing or furnishing consumer reports.

Facts

5. In the summer of 2003, [Plaintiff]'s son applied for financing to buy his first home. [Plaintiff] applied to be a co-buyer on her son's loan so that he could qualify for lower payments.

6. In the process [Plaintiff] discovered that Equifax was reporting that she had filed for bankruptcy and was delinquent on several accounts. These negative entries drastically reduced her credit worthiness and credit score.

7. The two other national credit reporting agencies, Trans Union, L.L.C., and Experian Information Solutions, Inc., did not report this negative information.

8. [Plaintiff] discovered that another [Plaintiff's Name]—[Name]—had declared bankruptcy and defaulted on accounts.

9. In the summer of 2003, [Plaintiff] contacted Equifax and told Equifax that it was reporting another person's bankruptcy and delinquent accounts on her credit report. She requested that Equifax reinvestigate and correct her credit report.

10. One account that [Plaintiff] specifically disputed involved a Discover credit card. This credit card belonged to [Name]. Equifax was reporting the Discover credit card account as "included in bankruptcy."

11. Beginning in June, 2003, [Plaintiff] provided Equifax with the social security number of [Name], to prove the bankruptcy and the negative accounts did not belong to her. She provided Equifax with a copy of her social security card, a copy of a pay stub from her job as a teacher at Moriarty High School and a copy of her driver's license. She provided a copy of these documents numerous times to different people at Equifax, at Equifax's request.

12. In a letter dated July 15, 2003, [Plaintiff] told Equifax:

> I have signed a purchase agreement to purchase a home and I am under a time deadline, so your prompt attention would be greatly appreciated.

13. On July 30, 2003, in response to [Plaintiff]'s disputes, Equifax added [Plaintiff]'s social security number to the credit file it maintained on [Name]. It also provided [Plaintiff] with a copy of [Name]'s credit report.

14. [Plaintiff] and her son missed an opportunity to buy the first house that they selected for purchase because Equifax had not yet deleted the inaccurate entries listed on [Plaintiff]'s report.

15. In a letter dated August 8, 2003, [Plaintiff] again told Equifax why it was crucial that it correct its inaccurate reporting.

> Please take care of this matter as quickly as possible. I have been trying to take care of my credit file with Equifax since May. Like I stated in my last letter, I have signed a purchase agreement for a home and my credit report has caused problems for me in attaining financing. Your prompt attention would be greatly appreciated.

16. [Plaintiff] provided documentary proof to Equifax from the United States District Court for New Mexico, Bankruptcy Division. These documents showed that she had never filed bankruptcy but that [Name] had.

17. In a letter faxed to Equifax during the week of August 11, 2003, [Plaintiff] again told Equifax why it was crucial that it promptly correct its inaccurate reporting.

> Sonya, I have been trying to clear my credit file with Equifax since May. I have send in letters, verifications (drivers license, pay stubs, social security number etc.) and this matter still isn't cleared up. I am hoping you can take care of this matter ASAP. Please give me a call at [phone number] when you have received this fax and have cleared it from my file. The underwriter for the home is just waiting to have this cleared, so we can sign the paperwork and closed the purchase of our home by this Friday. Thank you Sonya!

18. [Plaintiff] and her son scheduled to close the mortgage loan in August, 2003. They had to cancel the closing because Equifax still had not removed the bankruptcy and delinquent accounts from [Plaintiff]'s credit report.

19. On August 22, 2003, [Plaintiff]'s son closed his mortgage loan without the benefit of having [Plaintiff] listed as a co-buyer, because [Plaintiff]'s credit score was still so bad that it would be better for him to close by himself than with his mother as co-buyer.

20. On September 5, 2003, Equifax reported the results of its reinvestigation into [Plaintiff]'s disputes. It reported to [Plaintiff] that it had "reviewed the bankruptcy information" and "verified that this item belongs to you." It also reported that it had "researched the credit account" concerning the Discover credit card and had "verified that this item belongs to you." It did not note that [Plaintiff] disputed the Discover account.

21. On September 18, 2003, Equifax again reported to [Plaintiff] that it had reinvestigated the bankruptcy and Discover credit card account reported on her credit report. Again it stated that it had "verified that [the items] belongs to you." It did not note that [Plaintiff] disputed the Discover account.

22. Equifax continued to report the bankruptcy and the Discover credit card account—listing the status of the account as "included in bankruptcy"—on [Plaintiff]'s credit report.

23. In a letter dated October 9, 2003, [Plaintiff] again disputed the inaccurate information that Equifax continued to report. She again asked Equifax to remove the bankruptcy and the Discover credit card account. [Plaintiff] again provided Equifax with a copy of her social security card and driver's license to show that the bankruptcy and the Discover credit card account belonged to [Name], a different person with a different social security number.

24. On November 6, 2003, Equifax again reported to [Plaintiff] that it had "reviewed the bankruptcy information" and "verified that this item belongs to you." Equifax also reported that it had "researched the credit account" concerning the Discover credit card and had "verified that this item belongs to you." Also, Equifax reported that "[a]dditional information has been provided" by Discover concerning the credit card account.

25. Equifax continued to report the bankruptcy and the Discover credit card account on [Plaintiff]'s credit report. Equifax now reported the Discover credit card account as a "charged off account" instead of "included in bankruptcy." It did not note that [Plaintiff] disputed the account.

26. [Plaintiff] applied for a Wells Fargo credit card. In a letter dated November 26, 2003, Wells Fargo stated that it was

> unable to approve your application at this time for the following reason(s): CONSUMER HAS A BANKRUPTCY ON HIS/HER CREDIT BUREAU.

Wells Fargo stated that it had obtained this information from Equifax.

27. In a letter dated April 2, 2004, [Plaintiff] again disputed the inaccurate information and asked Equifax to remove the bankruptcy and the Discover credit card account. She again told Equifax that it had merged onto her report the bankruptcy and the Discover credit card account for [Name], a different person with a different social security number. Plaintiff provided Equifax with the separate

social security numbers for herself and [Name]. She again provided Equifax with documents from the bankruptcy court that showed the bankruptcy belonged to [Name].

28. In a form letter dated April 9, 2004, Discover stated:

> We have investigated your recent inquiry. Our records indicate that the above referenced account is correctly reporting under your name as stated in the credit bureau report.

29. On April 29, 2004, Equifax reported to [Plaintiff] that it had finally deleted the bankruptcy from her credit report. However, Equifax refused to delete the Discover credit card account. Equifax reported that it had "researched the credit account" concerning the Discover credit card and had "verified that this item has been reportedly correctly" and "verified that this item belongs to you."

30. Equifax resumed reporting the Discover credit card account as "included in bankruptcy." It did not note that [Plaintiff] disputed the account.

31. Upon information and belief, Equifax failed to provide Discover with all relevant information provided by [Plaintiff].

32. Equifax failed to review and consider all relevant information submitted by [Plaintiff] with her repeated disputes.

33. Equifax failed to conduct a genuine and reasonable reinvestigation in response to [Plaintiff]'s repeated disputes concerning the Discover credit card account.

34. Equifax persisted in reporting information that it knew or should have known to be inaccurate and damaging.

35. If Equifax had conducted a genuine and reasonable reinvestigation into [Plaintiff]'s disputes, it would have removed the bankruptcy and negative accounts belonging to [Name]. [Plaintiff] could have participated in the loan to purchase a home for her son. The loan would have been at a lower Annual Percentage Rate, with lower monthly payments.

36. Furthermore, due to Equifax's failures, the mortgage company required a higher down payment and required other additional costs be paid at closing. [Plaintiff] gave her son money to cover these higher costs caused by her inability to be a co-buyer on the loan. She borrowed some of this money, accruing finance charges.

37. [Plaintiff] suffered actual damages, including:
   a. damage to her credit rating;
   b. lost opportunities to enter into consumer credit transactions, including the opportunity to be a co-buyer for her son;
   c. higher down payment and other additional costs for her son's loan;
   d. incurring finance charges on the money she borrowed to pay for these higher costs;
   e. denial of credit; and
   f. lost time, aggravation, inconvenience, embarrassment and frustration.

First Claim for Relief: FCRA Violations by Equifax

38. Equifax failed to maintain reasonable procedures to ensure the maximum possible accuracy of the consumer credit information it reported concerning [Plaintiff].

39. Equifax failed to review and consider all relevant information submitted by [Plaintiff], including unrebutted information; failed to provide Discover and other merchants with all relevant information provided by [Plaintiff]; failed to conduct a genuine and reasonable reinvestigation in response to [Plaintiff]'s repeated disputes; persisted in reporting information that it knew or should have known to be inaccurate and damaging; and failed to delete inaccurate information from the credit report.

40. Equifax's actions were willful, or, in the alternative, negligent violations of the FCRA.

41. [Plaintiff] is entitled to actual damages, punitive damages, costs and reasonable attorney fees.

Second Claim for Relief: CBA Violations by Equifax

42. Equifax's actions violated the CBA, including but not limited to NMSA 1978 § 56-3-2.

43. Equifax's actions were willful, or, in the alternative, negligent violations of the CBA.

44. [Plaintiff] is entitled to actual damages, punitive damages, costs and reasonable attorney fees.

Request for Relief

[Plaintiff] prays that this Honorable Court:

A. Enjoin Defendants from reporting the Discover credit card account and any reference to bankruptcy on [Plaintiff]'s credit report;

B. Award actual damages;

C. Award punitive damages;

D. Award costs and reasonable attorney fees;

E. Award any further relief this Court deems just. Respectfully submitted,

J.2.4 Complaint—Accuracy; Specialty Reporting Agency

UNITED STATES DISTRICT COURT
SOUTHERN DISTRICT OF NEW YORK

[PLAINTIFF], individually and on behalf of all others similarly situated, Plaintiff, and [PLAINTIFF-INTERVENOR-APPLICANT], individually and on behalf of all others similarly situated, Plaintiff-Intervenor-Applicant,

v.

FIRST AMERICAN REGISTRY, INC., Defendant,

[No.] (LAK)

CLASS ACTION COMPLAINT

Plaintiff [PLAINTIFF] (hereafter "[Plaintiff]") and Plaintiff-Intervenor-Applicant [PLAINTIFF-INTERVENOR-APPLICANT] (hereafter "[Plaintiff-Intervenor-Applicant]") (collectively hereafter "Plaintiffs") by their attorneys Fishman & Neil, LLP, Locks Law Firm, PLLC, and the AARP Foundation, as and for their complaint against the defendant FIRST AMERICAN REGISTRY, INC. (hereafter "Defendant" or "FAR") allege, upon information and belief, except those allegations which directly relate to each plaintiff him or herself which are alleged upon personal knowledge, as follows:

PRELIMINARY STATEMENT

1. This is an action for declaratory and injunctive relief and money damages brought pursuant to 15 U.S.C. § 1681, *et seq.* ("Fair Credit Reporting Act" or "FCRA"), the New York Fair Credit Reporting Act (General Business Law Art. 25, §§ 380, *et seq.*) ("NYFCRA"), and New York Deceptive Practices Act (General Business Law §§ 349) brought by plaintiffs on behalf of themselves and all others similarly situated.

2. At issue in this litigation is the wholesale failure of FAR, a tenant screening bureau, as well as a credit reporting agency within the meaning of the federal and state laws, to comply with those laws' requirements that the consumer reports it produces are accurate, complete and not misleading. Instead, FAR compiles records of the initiation of landlord/tenant cases brought in the New York Housing Court (and possibly other courts as discovery may demonstrate) but it fails to update such information periodically to reflect dispositions or further proceedings in the cases. FAR markets and sells this information to landlords who use it to screen potential tenants. As a consequence of FAR's failure to ensure that the information is—as required by law—accurate and not misleading, individuals, like the plaintiffs herein, can be denied the opportunity to obtain housing. FAR's actions and omissions have been undertaken in utter disregard for its clear and unequivocal legal obligations to ensure that its reports are complete, accurate and not misleading. Unless restrained and enjoined, FAR's practices will continue to harm consumers.

PARTIES

3. [Plaintiff] is a natural person over the age of eighteen years residing in the County of Kings, City and State of New York. [Plaintiff] is a "consumer" within the meaning of 15 U.S.C. § 1681a(c) and GBL § 380-a(b).

4. [Plaintiff-Intervenor-Applicant] is a natural person over the age of eighteen years residing in the County, City and State of New York. [Plaintiff-Intervenor-Applicant] is a "consumer" within the meaning of 15 U.S.C. § 1681a(c) and GBL § 380-a(b).

5. Defendant First American Registry is a Nevada corporation whose principal place of business is located at 11140 Rockville Pike, Rockville, Maryland. The defendant regularly does business in the County, City and State of New York.

JURISDICTION AND VENUE

6. This Court possesses original jurisdiction of this matter pursuant to 28 U.S.C. § 1331 insofar as the plaintiffs bring claims arising under the FCRA, and it possesses supplemental jurisdiction over the asserted state law claims pursuant to 28 U.S.C. § 1367.

7. Venue is proper in this District pursuant to 28 U.S.C. § 1391(b), insofar as the acts and transactions that give rise to this action occurred, in substantial part, in this District. Venue is also proper in this District since the Defendant can be found in, has agents in and/or transacts business in this District.

CLASS ALLEGATIONS

8. This action is brought as, and may properly be maintained as, a class action pursuant to Rule 23(b)(2) of the Federal Rules of Civil Procedure. Plaintiffs bring this action on behalf of themselves and all members of a class (the "Class"), consisting of all persons who are listed, or who were listed, from the three years prior to the initiation of this action up to and including the present day, in Defendant's National Registry Check database as a tenant, occupant, respondent, defendant or other similar categorization in a proceeding commenced in the Civil Court of the City of New York, Housing Part. Excluded from the Class is Defendant, any entity in which Defendant has a controlling interest, and any of its subsidiaries, affiliates, and officers, directors, employees and agents as well as any person or entity who is named in any such proceeding as a landlord.[1]

9. The requirements of Rule 23(a) and 23(b)(2) of the Federal Rules of Civil Procedure are met in that:

a. Rule 23(a)(1) Numerosity—The Class for whose benefit this action is brought is so numerous that joinder of all class members is impracticable. Plaintiffs believe that there are at least hundreds of thousands of members of the Class, as described above, although the exact number and identities of individual class members are presently unknown, and can only be ascertained through appropriate discovery.

b. Rule 23(a)(2) Commonality—There are no individual issues in this case. All of the legal and factual issues in this class action are common to each proposed class member; including:

  i. Whether FAR is a credit reporting agency within the meaning of the FCRA and the NYFCRA?

  ii. Whether FAR has maintained consumer records with respect to proceedings in the Civil Court of the City of New York, Housing Part, and, if so, whether FAR has failed, and continues to fail, to maintain policies and procedures for ensuring that those records periodically updated?

  iii. Whether FAR has prepared, and today continues to prepare, consumer reports for sale or provision to third-parties concerning proceedings in the Civil Court of City of New York, Housing Part, without maintaining policies and procedures for ensuring that those reports are accurate, complete and not misleading?

  iv. Whether FAR's actions have violated, and continue to violate, 15 U.S.C. § 1681e(b), and/or subsections (a)(3) and (e) of New York General Business Law § 380-j and New York General Business Law § 380-k?

  v. Whether FAR's actions have violated, and continue to violate GBL Section 349?

  vi. Whether FAR's alleged violations of law have been negligent and/or willful?

  vii. Whether plaintiffs and the Class are entitled to declaratory or injunctive relief as a result of FAR's alleged violations of law?

  viii. Whether plaintiffs and the Class are entitled to punitive damages as a result of FAR's alleged violations of law?

c. Rule 23(a)(3) Typicality—Plaintiffs' claims are typical of the proposed class members' claims inasmuch as all such claims

---

[1] This proposed class definition is provisional and may be adapted, as appropriate, upon discovery, including, but not limited to, discovery as to whether Defendant's violations of law, as set forth hereinafter, have also affected its records as to consumers in courts other than the Civil Court of the City of New York, Housing Part.

arise out of FAR's alleged failure to maintain its database within proscriptions required by federal and state law.

d. Rule 23(a)(4) Adequacy of Representation—Plaintiffs can and will fairly and adequately represent and protect the interests of the proposed class. Plaintiffs have no interests antagonistic to the interests of the other members of the Class. Plaintiffs are committed to the vigorous prosecution of this action and have retained competent counsel with substantial experience in representing tenants in the New York City Housing Court, class actions and consumer litigation, including actions brought under the FCRA and the NYFCRA. Accordingly, plaintiffs are adequate representatives of the Class and will fairly and adequately protect the interests of the Class.

10. Without the representation provided by plaintiffs, and without this action proceeding on a class-wide basis, Defendant will not change its wrongful conduct and ongoing practices and virtually no proposed class member would be able to obtain the relief sought herein because the claims are unknown to most consumers, and, even if known, are cost prohibitive to pursue because of the burden and expense of showing the systematic and regular nature of Defendant's failure to comply with applicable law.

10a. Rule 23(b)(2)—Certification is appropriate under Rule 23(b)(2) of the Federal Rules of Civil Procedure because defendants have acted on grounds generally applicable to the proposed classes, thereby making appropriate final injunctive relief or corresponding declaratory relief with respect to the class as a whole. Plaintiffs seek to obtain declaratory and injunctive relief requiring FAR to implement company policies designed to prevent the wrongful activities described herein and for whatever further equitable relief the Court deems appropriate to remedy the wrongful actions that have already taken place.

FACTUAL ALLEGATIONS

11. FAR represented itself as "the nation's largest and most experienced information management company, providing the multi-family housing industry with risk management expertise for resident screening of applicants. *See* www.residentscreening.com/6about_main.html (current as of 2/5/04). Among the services it sells is prospective tenant screening, pursuant to which it offers, for a fee, immediate internet access to The National Registry Check, our comprehensive proprietary database of over 33 million landlord/tenant eviction court records." *Id.* In other words, it sells information about potential residential tenants to landlords and real estate management companies that is based upon court records. According to Defendant, by using National Registry Check, a landlord can:

> Search the nation's largest database of over 33 million landlord/tenant court records involving suits filed for eviction, failure to pay rent, and property damage. Discover your applicant's past lease performance and avoid inviting tenancy problems in the future. The National Registry Check is the most powerful tool available today to predict which applicants will pay their rent—and those who won't.

www.residentscreening.com/1prod_main.html (Current as 2/5/04). The National Registry Check database is, according to FAR, used "over 17,000" times a day. www.residentscreening.com/1prod_natl_reg_check_more.html (Current as of 2/5/04).

12. FAR unequivocally represents that its National Registry Check court records database is "fast accurate and complete," www.residentscreening.com/1prod_natl_reg_check.html (Current as of 2/5/04), and, indeed, that the "database is updated every day, every hour and every minute via court record downloading, landlord supplied payment information and subscriber inquiries." www.residentscreening.com/1prod_natl_reg_check_more.html (Current as of 2/5/04) (emphasis supplied).

13. FAR further represented that: "All records are collected and maintained in strict compliance with the Federal Fair Credit Reporting Act and are continually, systematically audited for accuracy." *Id.* (Current as of 2/5/04) (emphasis supplied). As this public representation acknowledges, and also as a result of other proceedings that have involved FAR, defendant knows, and for all relevant time periods has known, of its responsibilities requiring compliance with the FCRA.

14. The resident screening reports prepared and sold by FAR are "consumer reports" as defined by both the FCRA, 15 U.S.C. § 1681a(d), and the NYFCRA, GBL § 380-a(c). Thus, FAR is a "consumer reporting agency" within the meaning of FCRA, 15 U.S.C. § 1681a(f), and the NYFCRA, GBL § 380-a(e).

15. One of the court sources from which FAR has obtained, and today continues to obtain, court records for inclusion in its National Registry Check database is the New York City Housing Court (the "Housing Court"). Pursuant to an agreement with the New York Unified Court System ("UCS"), FAR paid $34,000.00 to the UCS for the purchase of information about court proceedings filed with the Housing Court for the period of April 1, 2002 to March 31, 2003. FAR's National Registry Check database contains information about tens, if not hundreds, of thousands of New York City Housing Court proceedings which it purchased from UCS.

16. Notwithstanding its express representations as to its database's accuracy and completeness, FAR does not, as a routine policy and practice, in preparing consumer reports, request, purchase, or obtain copies of any actual documents filed in the Housing Court in connection with any proceeding before it.

17. FAR's routine data collection policy, practice and procedure employed in preparing consumer reports does not include sending any employee, agent or representative to the office of any clerk of the Housing Court, or any other location maintained by the UCS, to view any court files or documents filed with that court.

18. In preparing consumer reports FAR's routine policy and practice has been, and today continues to be, only to obtain, from UCS, information about the initial filing of Housing Court proceedings. In doing so, FAR has not had, and today does not have, a policy to obtain, or a practice of obtaining, updated information to include in the National Registry Check database about Housing Court proceedings beyond the initial filing. Nor has FAR had, and today it does not have, a procedure whereby it periodically re-evaluates its database to determine whether information it maintains concerning Housing Court proceedings has become obsolete or misleading. When FAR has prepared consumer reports about Housing Court proceedings for its customers, and today when it continues to prepare such reports, it had, and today has, no policy to obtain, or practice of obtaining, updated or current information.

19. UCS has made available to FAR, and continues to make available to FAR, updated information about the current status of court proceedings FAR has previously purchased, yet, FAR itself

has had, and today continues to have, no routine practice or policy to incorporate this updated information into its database when preparing consumer reports. As a result, the updated information provided by the UCS has not been, and today is not, regularly or routinely incorporated into the consumer reports FAR has provided or continues to provide to its customers. As a further result, the actual and accurate status of thousands, of ongoing Housing Court proceedings has not been, and is not, reflected in the National Registry Check database.

20. Further, also as a result of FAR's failure to update its National Registry Check database about proceedings beyond initial filings in Housing Court, the database has contained, and today continues to contain, numerous proceedings that were dismissed, discontinued, abandoned or withdrawn, and the database has failed to, and today continues to fail to, reflect such dispositions.

21. Instead, it is only when FAR receives a dispute from a consumer challenging the accuracy or misleading nature of an initial FAR report that it takes steps to incorporate updated information into the National Registry Check database. By that time, however, an inaccurate and misleading report has already been provided by FAR to a third party. Since, in numerous instances, a FAR report is the sole basis used by prospective landlords in making an adverse determination about the application submitted by a prospective tenant, the harm has already occurred, or, similar harms will continue to occur in the future, unless FAR's practices are enjoined and rectified.

22. The circumstances of [Plaintiff] are typical of how FAR's practices impact consumers whose credit reports FAR handles.

23. In 1996, [Plaintiff] resided on the top floor in a rent stabilized apartment located at 310 East 83d St., New York, New York. The monthly rent was $649.00.

24. For many months during his tenancy, a leak in the roof of the building caused water to enter through the ceiling and into [Plaintiff]'s apartment, causing damage to his property and diminishing the value of the apartment.

25. [Plaintiff] repeatedly requested that the landlord repair the leak. [Plaintiff] further requested that the landlord afford him a reasonable rent abatement of the monthly rent based upon the diminished value of the apartment.

26. The landlord failed and refused to make the repairs or agree to any rent abatement.

27. [Plaintiff] consulted counsel and was advised to withhold his rent in order to compel the landlord to make the needed repairs. Accordingly, [Plaintiff] withheld his monthly rent for November and December 1996, in the total amount of $1,298.14.

28. The landlord continued to refuse to make the needed repairs or agree to a rent abatement.

29. Instead, on or about December 13, 1996 the landlord commenced a summary nonpayment proceeding against [Plaintiff] in the Housing Court pursuant to the New York Real Property Actions and Proceeding Law alleging that [Plaintiff] owed $1,298.14 in rent arrears. *Koppelman v. White*, Civil Court New York County, (Index No. L&T 118370/96)(the "eviction proceeding") In its petition the landlord requested that the court issue both a money judgment against [Plaintiff] in the amount of $1298.14, as well as a possessory judgment directing his eviction from the apartment.

30. On or about December 24, 1996 [Plaintiff] appeared in the eviction proceeding by serving and filing a written answer to the petition. In his answer [Plaintiff] denied the landlord's allegations and asserted a counterclaim alleging that the landlord had breached the warranty of habitability. (New York Real Property Law § 235-b)

31. On January 2, 1997, the first time the eviction proceeding appeared on the court calendar, it was dismissed by the court based upon the landlord's failure to appear to prosecute the proceeding.

32. The landlord did not commence a new proceeding against [Plaintiff] seeking the rent claimed in the petition. The landlord never obtained a judgment against [Plaintiff] in the eviction proceeding or in any other proceeding.

33. The landlord never obtained a determination, of any nature, from any Court, that it was entitled to either a money judgment or a possessory judgment against [Plaintiff] or directing or authorizing the eviction from his apartment.

34. Instead of prosecuting the eviction proceeding, the landlord agreed to repair [Plaintiff]'s apartment. In addition, the landlord consented to a reasonable rent abatement to [Plaintiff] based upon the presence of defective conditions in his apartment.

35. In or about August 2001, having left the apartment on East 83d Street, and while residing in a small, non-rent regulated apartment in Brooklyn, New York with his infant son and his son's mother, [Plaintiff] submitted an application to Eiges & Eiges Management Co. d/b/a Plaza Management, ("Eiges") the management company for a different landlord, to rent a larger rent stabilized apartment in a different residential building in Brooklyn. [Plaintiff]'s name was added to a waiting list for a vacancy in the building.

36. In or about April, 2002, [Plaintiff]'s application for the apartment was reached by Eiges and he was considered for a rent stabilized apartment that was larger and less expensive than the apartment in which he was residing.

37. On or about April 29, 2002, Eiges contacted FAR and requested that it supply a "Registry Check" in connection with [Plaintiff]'s application for the new apartment.

38. On or about April 29, 2002, FAR provided to Eiges a "tenant registry" consumer report pertaining to [Plaintiff]. This report contained information about the eviction proceeding that had been brought against [Plaintiff] in December 1996.

39. The information contained in the consumer report identified the name of the "plaintiff" [sic] as Joseph B. Koppelman, the "defendant" [sic] as [Plaintiff], the index number for the proceeding, and the "Court" as "Manhattan" in "New York" County.

40. The report described the "status" of the proceeding simply as "Case Filed," even though it had been dismissed over five years earlier. Under the heading "Claim$" the report stated 1298 (indicating that the "plaintiff's" money claim against the "defendant" in the proceeding was $1298.00) even though the claim had been dismissed over five years earlier.

41. The report further described the proceeding as having been commenced in "12/96" and that the "Case-Type" was "nonpayment."

42. The report contained no information whatsoever about the ultimate outcome of the proceeding, including the fact that it had been dismissed in early January 1997, even though FAR knew, or reasonably should have known, and easily could have determined, the actual closed and dismissed status of the proceeding.

43. The consumer report FAR prepared and provided to Eiges was both materially inaccurate, incomplete and misleading because it described the status of the proceeding simply as "Case Filed," over five years after it had been dismissed.

44. The report was a "consumer report" or a "credit report" within the meaning and definition of 15 U.S.C. § 1681a(d) and NYFCRA § 380-a(c).

45. Shortly after FAR provided the report, Eiges prepared and sent an "adverse action notice" to [Plaintiff] advising him that his application to rent the apartment was denied.

46. The sole reason stated by Eiges in the notice in making this determination was information about [Plaintiff] contained in the consumer report produced by FAR.

47. FAR never advised Eiges that the proceeding involving [Plaintiff] that was referenced in the report had been dismissed, much less dismissed for want of prosecution.

48. Following receipt of the adverse action notice from Eiges, [Plaintiff] wrote a letter to FAR, dated May 7, 2002, requesting a copy of the report that it had issued to Eiges. At no time prior to making this request did FAR provide [Plaintiff] with a copy of the report it had issued to Eiges.

49. In response, [Plaintiff] received a copy of the FAR report, dated May 30, 2002, annexed as Exhibit A hereto.

50. After receipt of the report [Plaintiff] wrote to FAR advising that he "dispute[d] the accuracy, completeness and propriety" of the report and he demanded that it refrain from any further issuance of a report pertaining to him which contained "inaccurate, incomplete, stale, or otherwise inappropriate records."

51. In response to [Plaintiff]'s letter, [Name], who identified herself as FAR's Manager of Consumer Relations, wrote a letter to [Plaintiff] dated July 16, 2002 marked "Confidential."

52. Ms. Johnson advised that the defendant had "completed the reinvestigation of the disputed items concerning your report." Ms. Johnson further wrote that "the case you disputed was removed in accordance with New York law, which provides that public record information can exist [sic] for no more than 5 years."

53. By that time however, the apartment [Plaintiff] sought to rent had been rented to someone else and [Plaintiff] was harmed to his financial detriment by FAR's actions by being unable to obtain the apartment.

54. The circumstances of [Plaintiff-Intervenor-Applicant] are typical of how FAR's practices impact consumers whose credit reports FAR handles.

55. Since 1999, [Plaintiff-Intervenor-Applicant] resided in Apartment 1A at a building located at 1608 Amsterdam Avenue, New York, New York.

56. In February 2005, the landlord commenced a summary nonpayment proceeding against [Plaintiff-Intervenor-Applicant] and her husband in the Housing Court pursuant to the New York Real Property Actions and Proceeding Law alleging rent arrears (the "eviction proceeding").

57. On or about March 22, 2005, [Plaintiff-Intervenor-Applicant] appeared in court regarding the eviction proceeding, where the landlord's lawyer advised her that the landlord wished to discontinue the action.

58. On the same day, she, the landlord's attorney and the landlord signed a stipulation of discontinuance, and upon her information and belief, the stipulation was then filed with the Court.

59. In the summer of 2004, [Plaintiff-Intervenor-Applicant] applied with West Harlem Group Assistance ("West Harlem"), the landlord of a building at 625 Lennox Avenue, New York, New York to rent an apartment there. [Plaintiff-Intervenor-Applicant]'s name was added to a waiting list for a vacancy in the building.

60. In or about June 2005, [Plaintiff-Intervenor-Applicant]'s application for the apartment was reached by West Harlem and she was considered for a rent stabilized apartment that was larger than the apartment in which she was residing.

61. On or about August 10, 2005, West Harlem contacted FAR and requested that it supply a "Registry Check" report in connection with [Plaintiff-Intervenor-Applicant]'s application for the new apartment.

62. On or about August 10, 2005, FAR provided to West Harlem a "tenant registry" consumer report pertaining to [Plaintiff-Intervenor-Applicant]. This report contained information about the eviction proceeding that had been brought against [Plaintiff-Intervenor-Applicant] in February 2005.

63. The report described the "status" of the proceeding simply as "Case Filed," even though it had been discontinued four or five months earlier.

64. The report contained no information whatsoever about the ultimate outcome of the proceeding, including the fact that it had been discontinued in March 2005, even though FAR knew, or reasonably should have known, and easily could have determined, the actual closed and dismissed status of the proceeding.

65. The consumer report FAR prepared and provided to West Harlem was both materially inaccurate, incomplete and misleading because it described the status of the proceeding simply as "Case Filed," approximately four to five months after it had been discontinued.

66. The report was a "consumer report" or a "credit report" within the meaning and definition of 15 U.S.C. § 1681a(d) and NYFCRA § 380-a(c).

AS AND FOR A FIRST CAUSE OF ACTION
(For Violation of the FCRA, 15 U.S.C. § 1681e(b))

67. Plaintiffs repeat and reallege each paragraph set forth above in paragraphs 1-66 as if fully set forth herein.

68. 15 U.S.C. § 1681e(b) provides:

> Whenever a consumer reporting agency prepares a consumer report it shall follow reasonable procedures to assure maximum possible accuracy of the information concerning the individual about whom the report relates.

69. As previously set forth herein, when preparing consumer reports, including those of plaintiffs and of the Class herein, FAR has lacked, and today continues to lack, any reasonable procedures to assure the maximum possible accuracy of the information concerning the individuals about whom the reports relate. Accordingly, FAR's activities have violated, and today continue to violate, 15 U.S.C. § 1681e(b).

70. As a result of its knowledge of its responsibilities under the FCRA, FAR's failure to comply with § 1681e(b) as to plaintiffs and the Class has been intentional and willful, or, at the very least, negligent.

71. As set forth hereinbefore, as a result of FAR's violation of § 1681e(b), plaintiff [Plaintiff] was economically harmed to his detriment and is entitled either to actual damages in an amount to be shown according to proof, or alternatively and together with Plaintiff [Plaintiff-Intervenor-Applicant], to damages in amount of not less than $100 or more than $1,000 pursuant to 15 U.S.C. § 1681n, as well as the other relief set forth below.

72. In order to punish such conduct by FAR, and to deter FAR and others from engaging in similar practices hereafter, Plaintiffs and the Class are entitled to an award of punitive damages, pursuant to 15 U.S.C. § 1681n, to be distributed to Plaintiffs and the Class in the manner directed by the Court, as well as the other relief as set forth below. In addition, the Plaintiffs and the Class are entitled an award of statutory attorney's fees pursuant to 15 U.S.C. § 1681n and/or 1681o.

AS AND FOR A SECOND CAUSE OF ACTION
(For Violation of the NYFCRA, General Business Law §§ 380-j and 380-k)

73. Plaintiffs repeat and reallege each allegation set forth in paragraphs 1-73, above, as if fully set forth herein.

74. Section 380-j(a), of the New York General Business Law provides that:

> No consumer reporting agency shall report or maintain in the file on a consumer, information:
>
> . . .
>
> (3) which it has reason to know is inaccurate.

75. Section 380-j(e) of the New York General Business Law, in turn, provides:

> Whenever a consumer reporting agency prepares a consumer report it shall follow reasonable procedures to assure maximum possible accuracy of the information concerning the individual about whom the report relates.

76. Section 380-k of the New York General Business Law, in turn, provides:

> Every consumer or reporting agency shall maintain reasonable procedures designed to avoid violations of sections three hundred eighty-b and three hundred eighty-j of this article. . . .

77. As previously set forth herein, in maintaining its National Credit Registry database, FAR knew or reasonably shown have known, and today knows or reasonably should know, that its entries as to proceedings in Housing Court were materially inaccurate and misleading. Accordingly, FAR's activities have violated, and continue to violate, GBL §§ 380-j(a) and 380-k.

78. In addition, or in the alternative, as previously set forth herein, when preparing consumer reports, including those of Plaintiffs and the Class herein, FAR has lacked, and today continues to lack, any reasonable procedures to assure the maximum possible accuracy of the information concerning the individuals about whom the reports relate. Accordingly, FAR's activities have violated, and today continue to violate, GBL §§ 380-j(e) and 380-k.

79. As a result of its knowledge of its responsibilities under the FCRA, FAR's failure to comply with GBL § 380-j as to Plaintiffs and the Class has been intentional and willful, or, at the very least, negligent.

80. As set forth hereinbefore, as a result of FAR's violation of GBL §§ 380-j and 380-k, plaintiff [Plaintiff] was economically harmed to his detriment, and he is entitled to an award of actual damages in an amount to be shown according to proof pursuant to GBL §§ 380-l and/or 380-m, as well as other the relief set forth below.

81. FAR's continuing and ongoing failure to comply with GBL § 380-j, will, unless restrained and enjoined, cause similar harms to other consumers and members of the Class herein, and, accordingly, plaintiffs and the Class are entitled to declaratory and injunctive relief, as set forth below.

82. In order to punish such conduct by FAR, and to deter FAR and others from engaging in similar practices hereafter, plaintiffs and the Class are entitled to an award of punitive damages, under GBL § 380-l, to be distributed to plaintiffs and the Class in the manner directed by the Court, as well as the other relief as set forth below.

83. The plaintiffs and the Class are entitled to an award of statutory attorney's fees pursuant to GBL § 380-l.

AS AND FOR A THIRD CAUSE OF ACTION
(For Violation of New York General Business Law § 349)

84. Plaintiffs repeat and reallege each allegation set forth in paragraphs 1-84, above, as if fully set forth herein.

85. GBL § 349 proscribes "[d]eceptive acts or practices in the conduct of any business, trade or commerce or in the furnishing of any service in this state."

86. GBL § 349 provides that "any person who has been injured by reason of any violation of [their respective] section[s] may bring an action in his own name to enjoin such unlawful act or practice" as well as to obtain actual damages, or fifty dollars, whichever is greater.

87. As set forth hereinbefore, FAR has engaged in deceptive acts and practices and false advertising within the meaning of GBL § 349, namely, engaging in a practice of making available for sale to the public information as a credit reporting agency and also representing to the public that its database is continually updated and is fast, accurate and complete.

88. By virtue of the harmful results of its activities, FAR's actions, as set forth hereinbefore, have caused both consumer injury and harm to the public interest.

89. As set forth hereinbefore, as a result of FAR's violation of GBL § 349, plaintiff [Plaintiff] was economically harmed to his detriment, and is entitled either to actual damages in an amount to be shown according to proof, or alternatively and together with Plaintiff [Plaintiff-Intervenor-Applicant], to damages in amount of $50 pursuant to GBL § 349(h), whichever is greater, as well as the other relief set forth below.

90. FAR's continuing and ongoing failure to comply with GBL § 349 will, unless restrained and enjoined, cause similar harm to other consumers and members of the Class herein, and, accordingly, Plaintiffs and the Class are entitled to declaratory and injunctive relief, as set forth below.

91. In order to punish such conduct by FAR, and to deter FAR and others from engaging in similar practices hereafter, Plaintiffs and the Class are entitled to an award of punitive damages to be distributed to Plaintiffs and the Class in the manner directed by the Court, as well as the other relief as set forth below. In addition, the Plaintiffs and the Class are entitled an award of statutory attorney's fees pursuant to GBL §§ 349(h).

WHEREFORE, Plaintiffs, [Plaintiff] and [Plaintiff-Intervenor-Applicant], on behalf of themselves and the Class, prays for this Court to issue an order against Defendant as follows:

a. Certifying this case as a class action and certifying the named plaintiffs herein to be adequate class representatives and their counsel to be adequate class counsel;
b. Entering a judgment pursuant to 28 U.S.C. § 2201 declaring that acts and practices of Defendant complained of herein violate the FCRA and the NYFCRA;
c. Entering a permanent injunction enjoining Defendant, and its agents and employees, from continuing to prepare and sell credit reports to third parties that do not comply with GBL § 380-j(e), and ordering Defendant to adopt and enforce policies and procedures to ensure future compliance with this law;
d. Entering a permanent injunction enjoining Defendant, and its agents and employees, from continuing to report, or maintain in files, on consumers information relating to proceedings in New York City Housing Court that is not current, updated, complete and accurate, and ordering Defendant to adopt and enforce policies and procedures to ensure future compliance with this law;
e. Entering a permanent injunction enjoining Defendant, and its agents and employees, from continuing to engage in practices that violate Sections 349 and 350 of the New York General Business Law;
f. Entering a judgment, on behalf of plaintiff [Plaintiff], for actual damages proved at trial, or in the alternative, on behalf of [Plaintiff] and [Plaintiff-Intervenor-Applicant] either for damages in an amount not less than $100 and not more than $1,000, under 15 U.S.C. 1681n or for damages of $50, under GBL §§ 349(h) and 350-e(3) ;
g. Entering a judgment, on behalf of plaintiffs and the Class, for punitive damages, in an amount to be determined following evidence at trial, to be distributed to plaintiffs and the Class in a manner directed by the Court;
h. Entering a judgment awarding plaintiffs the costs of this action, including the fees and costs of experts, disbursements, together with attorneys fees; and
i. Awarding such other and further relief as the Court finds necessary and proper.

JURY DEMAND

Plaintiffs demand a trial by jury on all issues so triable.
Dated: New York, New York

Respectfully submitted,
[Attorneys for the Plaintiff and Plaintiff-Intervenor-Applicant]

J.3 Sample Interrogatories

J.3.1 Interrogatories—Reinvestigation (to CRA)

UNITED STATES DISTRICT COURT IN AND FOR THE DISTRICT OF _____

_____)
      Plaintiff,)
)
v.   )
)
TRANS UNION, ET AL)
_____)

**INTERROGATORIES
TO DEFENDANT, CORP.**

To: XYX CORP.
 through its attorneys of record:

PLEASE TAKE NOTICE that you are hereby notified and required to respond to the following Interrogatories and produce the requested information to Plaintiff herein, through his attorney of record, _____, within thirty (30) days from service hereof in accordance with the provisions of Rule 33, et. seq., of the Federal Rules of Civil Procedure.

You are further placed on notice that these requests are deemed continuing, requiring supplemental responses thereto in the event requested information changes or otherwise becomes known, if not currently known after proper inquiry, or otherwise becomes available which would require amendment or supplementation of your responses in order that they would be proper and truthful, become known to you.

INSTRUCTIONS

In answering these requests, please furnish all information which is available to you, including, without limitation, all information in the possession of your attorneys, accountants, affiliates, auditors, agents, employees, officers, directors, shareholders, contractors, or other personnel, and not merely such information as is in your possession.

If you cannot respond to any of the following requests in full, after exercising due diligence to secure information to do so, please so state, and respond to the extent possible, specifying all reasons why you are unable or unwilling to respond to the remainder, stating whatever information you have concerning the unproduced information, and what efforts you made to secure information sufficient to allow you to respond fully to the particular request.

Although one or more of the following requests may not appear to be applicable to or directed to you, please respond to each and every one of them to the extent that you are able to provide any response thereto whether such response consists of information within your own knowledge or what you have obtained from others. However, for every response in which you include information received from others, please provide the name, any known address, and any known phone number of the person from whom you so received such information. And, in every such instance please state that you cannot verify such of your own personal knowledge, identifying particularly the information for which you cannot vouch. Further, these requests contain words or phrases which require you to refer to the "Definitions" section of this document provided herein below.

Unless otherwise stated, each request pertains to the time period beginning January, 2000, through the present date. Thus, your responses should be fully answered as they pertain to information, recordings or information within that time frame. Further, each request should identify the appropriate time frame, if your response requires same.

DEFINITIONS

1. "You" includes XYX Corp., the company, entity, institution, agency, subsidiary(ies), parent corporation(s) and/or any of its branches, departments, employees, agents, contractual affiliates, or otherwise connected by legal relationship, in the broadest sense. "You" includes any of your sister companies or related entities and their connected companies, whether or not separately incorporated. You may also be referenced herein simply as "XYZ"

2. "Document(s)" shall mean and include any printed, typewritten, handwritten or otherwise recorded matter of whatever character, including specifically, but not exclusively, and without limiting the generality of the foregoing, letters, diaries, desk and other calendars memoranda, telegrams, posters, cables, reports, charts, statistics, envelopes, studies, newspapers, news reports, business records, book of account(s) or other books, ledgers, balance sheets, journals, personal records, personal notes, any piece of paper, parchment, or other materials similarly used with anything written, typed printed, stamped, engraved, embossed, or impressed upon it, accountants statements, accounting records of any kind, bank statements, minutes of meetings or other minutes, labels, graphics, notes of meetings or conversations or other notes, catalogues, written agreements, checks, announcements, statements, receipts, returns invoices, bills, warranties, advertisements, guarantees, summaries, pamphlets, prospectuses, bulletins, magazines, publications, photographs, work-sheets, computer printouts, telex transmissions or receipts, teletypes, telefaxes, file folders or other folders, tape recordings, and any original or non-identical (whether different from the original by reason of any notation made on such copies or otherwise), carbon, photostatic or photograph copies of such materials. The term "documents" shall also mean and include every other recording of, or means of recording on any tangible form, any form of information, data, communication, or representation, including but not limited to, microfilm, microfiche, any records stored on any form of computer software, audio or video tapes or discs, digitally recorded disks or diskettes, or any other medium whatsoever.

For each "document" responsive to any request withheld from production by you on the ground of any privilege, please state:
 (a) the nature of the document (e.g., letter, memorandum, contract, etc.);
 (b) the author or sender of the document;
 (c) the recipient of the document;
 (d) the date the document was authored, sent, and/or received; and
 (e) the reason such document is allegedly privileged

3. "Audit Trail" means complete, detailed listings of each and every alteration, deletion, inquiry into, modification or other change to the credit report or profile as maintained in recorded form, in the broadest sense, by "you." The listing should include the identity, address, employer and title of the person(s) taking the action, the identity, address, employer and title of the person(s) authorizing the action, a detailed explanation of the action taken, the date of the action, the means used to effect such action, the location of origin of the action and the reason the action was taken. The term "audit trail" also includes the definition provided for the phrase in the FederBush, Federal Trade Commission and Formal Staff Opinion Letter, March 10, 1983.

4. "Data" means the physical symbols in the broadest sense that represent information, regardless of whether the information is oral, written or otherwise recorded.

5. "Data field" means any single or group of character(s), number(s), symbol(s) or other identifiable mark(s) maintained in a permanent or temporary recording which represent, in any way, an item or collection of information. "Data field" includes all types of data whether maintained in integer, real, character or Boolean format.

6. "Database" or "databank" means any grouping or collection of data field(s) maintained, in any format or order, in any permanent or temporary recorded form.

7. "Computer" means any and all programmable electronic devices or apparatuses, including hardware, software, and other databanks, that can store, retrieve, access, update, combine, rearrange, print, read, process or otherwise alter data whether such data maintained in that device or at some other location. The term "computer" includes any an all magnetic recording or systems, systems operating on or maintaining data in digital, analog, or hybrid format, or other mechanical devices, or other devices capable of maintaining writings or recording, of any kind, in condensed format, and includes any disk, tape, recording, or other informational source, regardless of its physical dimension or size.

8. "Identify" means that you should state:
 (a) any and all names, legal, trade or assumed;
 (b) all addresses used;
 (c) all telephone and telefax numbers used; and, if applicable:
 (d) brand, make, manufacturer's name, address, phone number and the manufacturer's relationship to any and all Defendants in the above captioned action; and
 (e) employer's name, address, phone number and the employer's relationship to any and all Defendants in the above captioned action.

9. "Explain" mean to elucidate, make plain or understandable, to give the reason for or cause of, and to show the logical development or relationships thereof.

10. "Describe" means to represent or give an account of in words.

11. "Plaintiff" refers to _____.

12. "Other Defendant[s]" mean any Defendants(s) in the above entitled and captioned action except you, jointly or separately.

13. "Program" means the following: (1) a plan for solving a problem; (2) to devise a plan for solving a problem; (3) a computer routine (i.e., a set of instructions arranged in proper sequence to cause a computer to perform a particular process); (4) to write a computer routine.

14. "Header record" means a machine readable record at the beginning of a file containing data identifying the file and data used in file control.

INTERROGATORIES

INTERROGATORY NO. 1

Please state the full name, present address, employer, title and occupation of all persons providing information and documents responsive to these requests.

ANSWER:

INTERROGATORY NO. 2

Please identify all individuals known to you or your attorney who are witnesses to the events described in plaintiff's complaint or to any event which is the subject of any defense you have raised to this lawsuit. For each such person, please provide a brief summary of facts to which each might or could testify. Also for each such person, please state the following:
  (a) Please state whether each such person is affiliated with, or related to, or employed by any party (or its agents, servants, officers, or employees) to this lawsuit;
  (b) If any of the persons so listed in response to this interrogatory do not fit the characterization in subpart A above, please describe the nature of their involvement in this lawsuit;
  (c) Please explain and describe your understanding of their knowledge of such facts.

ANSWER:

INTERROGATORY NO. 3

Please list, explain and describe documents known to you or believed by you to exist concerning any of the events described in plaintiff's complaint or concerning any of the events which are the subject[s] of any defense[s] you have raised to this lawsuit.

ANSWER:

INTERROGATORY NO. 4

Please identify each expert witness, whether your employee or otherwise, that you believe may have formed any opinion or consulted with you about the facts or basis of this lawsuit or any defense or allegation you have raised in this lawsuit.

ANSWER:

INTERROGATORY NO. 5

Please identify all individuals known to you or your attorney who are not witnesses, but who you have reason to believe have knowledge pertinent to the events at issues as alleged in plaintiff's complaint, and provide a brief summary of the *facts* to which each such person could testify. For each person, please state the following:
  (a) Please state whether each such person is affiliated with, or related to, or employed by any party (or its agents, servants, officers, or employees) to this lawsuit;
  (b) If any of the persons so listed in response to this interrogatory do not fit the characterization in subpart A above, please describe the nature of their involvement in this lawsuit;
  (c) Please explain and describe your understanding of their knowledge of such facts.

ANSWER:

INTERROGATORY NO. 6

Please state whether any of the individuals listed in the answers to the preceding interrogatories have given any statement[s] to you and, if so, please identify the individual giving the statement, identify the individual to whom the statement was given, the date of the statement, and whether or not the statement was written or recorded and, if it was written or recorded, identify the individual presently in possession of it.

ANSWER:

INTERROGATORY NO. 7

Please list each exhibit which you may attempt to introduce as evidence at the trial of this case, or which has been used or referred to by any expert witness on your behalf [as called for in interrogatory no. 4].

ANSWER:

INTERROGATORY NO. 8

For each paragraph of plaintiff's complaint for which you deny the allegations, please explain and describe any facts which you believe may support each denial.

ANSWER:

INTERROGATORY NO. 9

Please explain and describe when, how and under what circumstances you archive, retain or capture consumer credit data in any file bearing any of plaintiff's personal identifiers. List the dates of each such archived data report wherein any personal information about plaintiff or attributed to any of plaintiff's personal identifiers, including the date such data was captured, retained and/or archived, who has possession of those reports, the manner in which the reports are maintained, and the retention policy[ies] regarding those reports. Please explain and describe each category and type of data field in each such report or recording.

ANSWER:

INTERROGATORY NO. 10

Please state whether you have authorized by each of your co-defendants/credit reporting agencies to report account data about your alleged customers on and by way of any or all of their credit reporting systems and affiliate networks during the years, 1998, 1999, 2000, 2001, 2002, 2003. If so, state whether you authorized each of your co-defendants/credit reporting agencies to report your credit data about plaintiff on and by way of any or all of their credit reporting systems and affiliate networks during the years, 1998, 1999, 2000 2001, 2002, 2003. Please list each co-defendants/credit reporting agencies separately and indicate your answers. Please explain and describe the terms of your authority and all reciprocal duties and obligations arising between you and your co-defendants/credit reporting agencies.

ANSWER:

INTERROGATORY NO. 11

Please state your net income for the preceding twenty-four (24) quarters.

ANSWER:

INTERROGATORY NO. 12

Please state the dates and exact content of each of your reportings, which bore any of plaintiff's personal identifiers, which you made to any person which contained any of the disputed account[s] data or account[s] reportings, as identified in plaintiff's complaint. Please fully identify the recipient.

ANSWER:

INTERROGATORY NO. 13

Please explain and describe any disputes you received from plaintiff or from any other source which concerned or pertained to plaintiff. Please explain and describe what actions you took as a result of the dispute and the disposition of your actions in connection with each contact or communication.

ANSWER:

INTERROGATORY NO. 14

Please explain and describe the audit trail of your records regarding credit reportings you made in connection with each disputed account, as identified in plaintiff's complaint.

ANSWER:

INTERROGATORY NO. 15

Please list, explain and describe each and every code contained in each of your computerized records which you have produced. For each such code, please also explain and describe, in detail, the purpose of such code, the content of such action, the duration of such action, and the reason you permitted such action or entry.

ANSWER:

INTERROGATORY NO. 16

Please list, explain and describe each and every the header record which you reported to the credit reporting agencies in connection with each account bearing your subscriber name on plaintiff's credit reports as issued by the credit reporting agencies and as already produced to you in this lawsuit.

ANSWER:

INTERROGATORY NO. 17

Please list, explain and describe each and every contact or communication you received from your co-defendants which, in any way, referenced plaintiff. This request would include any GEIS [General Electric Information Services]-based and E-Oscar communications, UDFs, AUDFs, CDVs, ACDVs, tape transfers, system to system transfers, phone calls and other means of communication.

ANSWER:

INTERROGATORY NO. 18

For each credit reporting you issued to any third person in the two years preceding the filing of this lawsuit and since the filing of this lawsuit, please list, explain and describe, in the greatest detail you are able, each and every negative item of data appearing in the reporting and how you sought the reported item to be factored in the credit scores generated and issued about plaintiff.

ANSWER:

INTERROGATORY NO. 19

If you deny your credit reportings about plaintiff, as complained of in his lawsuit, were false, please explain and describe, in the greatest degree of detail, what facts you believe exist to support your belief and identify any witnesses who you believe will support or testify in support of your belief.

ANSWER:

INTERROGATORY NO. 20

Did you authorize the co-defendants/credit reporting agencies to re-report to other users of credit data [subscribers] the credit data you reported to them?

ANSWER:

INTERROGATORY NO. 21

Please list, explain and describe your reinvestigation activities in response to each of plaintiff's disputes. Please identify each of your employees involved in each notice, transaction or event, as well as any supervising employee overseeing such each notice, transaction or event.

ANSWER:

INTERROGATORY NO. 22

For each employee witness or proposed expert witness which you may call as a witness as trial, please list each and every lawsuit in which each respective person has published a such a written or otherwise recorded report, proposed expert report, affidavit, deposition testimony and/or trial testimony, and explain and describe the nature of the employee witness's or proposed expert witness's testimony and the complete caption, including court name and location, of the case where such a written or otherwise recorded report was rendered, where the proposed expert report was rendered, where the affidavit was filed or exchanged, where deposition testimony and/or trial testimony was taken.

ANSWER:

INTERROGATORY NO. 23

Does any account exist in your records bearing a party listing a social security number of _____? If so, please state the account number associated with any consumer listing a social security number of _____ and fully identify each responsible party on such account, the account number and the complete set of Metro Tape data fields you have reported about such an account since its inception. Similarly, please explain and describe all facts known to you as to whether you have received notice of any fraud alerts or other report flags or alerts in connected with the a social security number of _____.

ANSWER:

INTERROGATORY NO. 24

Does any account exist in your records bearing a party listing a name of "_____," and/or any of the following address(es): "_____" and "_____?" If so, please state the account number associated with the consumer[s] shown as responsible parties and fully identify each responsible party on such account, the account number and the complete set of Metro Tape data fields you have reported about such an account since its inception. Similarly, please explain and describe all facts known to you as to whether you have received notice of any fraud alerts or other report flags or alerts in connected with the name "_____," or any of the following address(es): "_____" and "_____."

ANSWER:

Respectfully submitted:

[Attorney]

J.3.2 Interrogatories—Impermissible Purpose

UNITED STATES DISTRICT COURT
DISTRICT OF NEW JERSEY

```
_____
                           )
ALLAN R. CONSUMER,         )
              Plaintiff,   )
                           )
v.                         )
                           )
TRANS UNION, L.L.C. and    )
COLLEGIATE FUNDING         )
SERVICES,                  )
              Defendants,  )
_____)
```

FIRST SET OF INTERROGATORIES TO DEFENDANT, TRANS UNION, L.L.C.

PLEASE TAKE NOTICE that the Defendant, Trans Union, L.L.C. is hereby notified and required to respond to the following Interrogatories propounded by plaintiff herein, through his counsel of record, **within thirty (30) days** from April 29, 2002 in accordance with the provisions of Rule 33 of the Federal Rules of Civil Procedure.

You are further placed on notice that these Interrogatories are deemed continuing, requiring supplemental responses thereto in the event requested information becomes known or available to you which would require amendment or supplementation of your responses in order that they be proper and truthful.

INSTRUCTIONS

In answering these Interrogatories, please furnish all information which is available to you, including, without limitation, all information in the possession of your attorneys, accountants, affiliates, auditors, agents, employees, officers, directors, shareholders, members, contractors, or other personnel, and not merely such information as is in your possession.

If you cannot respond to any of the following Interrogatories in full, after exercising due diligence to secure information to do so, please so state, and respond to the extent possible, specifying all reasons why you are unable or unwilling to respond to the remainder, stating whatever information you have concerning the unproduced information, and what efforts you made to secure information sufficient to allow you to respond fully to the particular Interrogatory.

Although one or more of the following Interrogatories may not appear to be applicable to or directed to you, please respond to each and every one of them to the extent that you are able to provide any response thereto whether such response consists of information within your own knowledge or what you have obtained from others. However, for every response in which you include information received from others, please provide the name, any known address, and any known phone number of the person from whom you so received such information. And, in every such instance please state that you cannot verify such of your own personal knowledge, identifying particularly the information for which you cannot vouch. Further, these Interrogatories contain words or phrases which require you to refer to the "Definitions" section of this document provided herein below.

Unless otherwise stated, each Interrogatory pertains to the time period beginning January, 1, 1995, through the present date. Thus, your responses should be fully answered as they pertain to information within that time frame. Further, each Interrogatory should identify the appropriate time frame, if your response requires same.

DEFINITIONS

1. "**You**," "**Your**" or "**TU**" means Trans Union, L.L.C., the company, entity, institution, agency, subsidiary(ies), parent corporation(s), predecessors and/or any of its branches, departments, employees, agents, contractual affiliates, or otherwise connected by legal relationship, in the broadest sense. "You" or "TU" also includes any of your sister companies, affiliate credit bureaus, service bureaus, or related entities, and their connected companies, whether or not separately incorporated.

2. "**Document(s)**" shall mean and include any printed, typewritten, handwritten or otherwise recorded matter of whatever character, including specifically, but not exclusively, and without limiting the generality of the foregoing, letters, diaries, desk and other calendars, memoranda, telegrams, posters, cables, reports, charts, statistics, envelopes, studies, newspapers, news reports, business records, book of account(s) or other books, ledgers, balance sheets, journals, personal records, personal notes, any piece of paper, parchment, or other materials similarly used with anything written, typed, printed, stamped, engraved, embossed, or impressed upon it, accountants statements, accounting records of any kind, bank statements, minutes of meetings or other minutes, labels, graphics, notes of meetings or conversations or other notes, catalogues, written agreements, checks, announcements, statements, receipts, returns invoices, bills, warranties, advertisements, guarantees, summaries, pamphlets, prospectuses, bulletins, magazines, publications, photographs, work-sheets, computer printouts, telex transmissions or receipts, teletypes, telefaxes, file folders or other folders, tape recordings, and any original or non-identical (whether different from the original by reason of any notation made on such copies or otherwise), carbon, photostatic or photograph copies of such materials. The term "**documents**" shall also mean and include every other recording of, or means of recording on any tangible form, any form of information, data, communication, or representation, including but not limited to, microfilm, microfiche, any records stored on any form of computer software, audio or video tapes or discs, digitally recorded disks or diskettes, or any other medium whatsoever.

For each "**document**" responsive to any request withheld from production by you on the ground of any privilege, please state:
  (a) the nature of the document (e.g., letter, memorandum, contract, etc.);
  (b) the author or sender of the document;
  (c) the recipient of the document;
  (d) the date the document was authored, sent, and/or received; and
  (e) the reason such document is allegedly privileged.

3. "**Data**" means the physical symbols in the broadest sense, that represent information, regardless of whether the information is oral, written or otherwise recorded.

4. "**Hardware**" means the physical components of a computer or any device capable of maintaining recorded data.

5. "**Software**" means the entire set of computer programs, procedures, documentation, or other recorded instructions which guide a mechanical device or human in the operation of the computer or mechanical device.

6. "**Computer**" means any and all programmable electronic devices or apparatuses, including hardware, software, and other databanks, that can store, retrieve, access, update, combine, rearrange, print, read, process or otherwise alter data whether such data maintained in that device or at some other location. The term "**computer**" includes any and all magnetic recordings or systems, systems operating on or maintaining data in digital, analog, or hybrid format, or other mechanical devices, or other devices capable of maintaining writings or recordings, of any kind, in condensed format, and includes any disk, tape, recording, or other informational source, regardless of its physical dimension or size.

7. "**Identify**" means that you should state:
   (a) any and all names, legal, trade or assumed;
   (b) all addresses used;
   (c) all telephone and tele-fax numbers used; and, if applicable:
   (d) brand, make, manufacturer's name, address, phone number and the manufacturer's relationship to any and all defendants in the above captioned action; and
   (e) employer's name, address, phone number and the employer's relationship to any and all defendants in the above captioned action.

8. "**Person(s)**" means any human being, sole proprietorship, limited partnership, partnership, association, group of human beings, other legal or de facto entity, or corporation, of whatever kind.

9. "**Explain**" means to elucidate, make plain or understandable, to give the reason for or cause of, and to show the logical development or relationships thereof.

10. "**Describe**" means to represent or give an account of in words.

11. "**User**" means any person or computer which interacts with a different computer.

12. "**Consumer Credit Database**" is intended to mean the entire TU consumer credit network (also commonly known as "CRONUS"), including but not limited to text file mode, file purge, file reorganization mode, all operator preamble, identification and password modes, and all other single or overlaying programs, applications and/or systems, and does include, but is not limited to, the main operating system.

13. "**Program**" means the following: (1) a plan for solving a problem, addressing an issue or achieving a goal; (2) to devise a plan for solving a problem, addressing an issue or achieving a goal; (3) a computer routine (i.e., a set of instructions arranged in proper sequence to cause a computer to perform a particular process); (4) to write a computer routine.

14. "**FCRA**" means the Fair Credit Reporting Act, 15 U.S.C. § 1681 et seq., as amended.

15. "**Consumer Report**" is intended to have the same meaning as the term is defined under the FCRA.

16. "**Consumer Reporting Agency**" is intended to have the same meaning as the term is defined under the FCRA.

17. "**CFS**" means the Defendant, Collegiate Funding Services, L.L.C. the company, entity, institution, agency, subsidiary(ies), parent corporation(s), predecessors and/or any of its branches, departments, employees, agents, contractual affiliates, or otherwise connected by legal relationship, in the broadest sense.

INTERROGATORIES

INTERROGATORY NO. 1:
Identify the names, addresses, and telephone numbers of all persons who have personal knowledge of any of the facts, events, or matters that are alleged in plaintiff's Complaint and your Answers and defenses thereto and describe and explain your understanding of the matters on which the persons named have knowledge and the nature and extent of that knowledge.

ANSWER:

INTERROGATORY NO. 2:
Identify all correspondence or communications or documents that refer or relate to any correspondence or communications between you and any other defendant in this action, relating or referring to the facts, acts, events, or matters alleged in plaintiff's Complaint or your Answers and/or defenses thereto.

ANSWER:

INTERROGATORY NO. 3:
Identify each person whom you may call as an expert witness at trial including name, business address, and telephone number, and the substance of the facts and opinions to which the expert may testify, and summarize the grounds for each opinion.

ANSWER:

INTERROGATORY NO. 4:
Identify any and all of your policies and procedures designed to ensure that a person (such as CFS) to whom you provide consumer credit information does not obtain or receive information for which a "permissible purpose" as listed in § 1681b of the FCRA is required without a permissible purpose, including but not limited to those policies and procedures which were in effect in 1999.

ANSWER:

INTERROGATORY NO. 5:
With regard to your relationship with CFS, provide the following:
   A. State when CFS initially made request or application with TU for service, including the nature of that request and whether a written application for service was submitted to you in connection with said request and identify the location and content of all documents memorializing or containing said request or application.
   B. Describe in detail the investigation and/or inquiry in which TU engaged once it received a request from CFS for service with TU, whether or not said request was made via a written application for service, including TU's investigation into CFS's identity and its intended and stated uses of each type of information or data it was seeking to access from TU. In addition, identify the normal and customary process which TU undertakes to investigate and either approve or disapprove an application or request for membership or service, and specifically identify the process which was taken with regard to the approval of CFS's application or request for service or membership. Finally, identify and describe the location and content of any documents memorializing, recording, discussing or pertaining to said investigation.
   C. State when CFS initially became a customer or subscriber of TU and identify the nature and extent of each and every

service CFS initially and subsequently gained access to as offered by TU, including but not limited the nature and extent of each service to which CFS has or has had access to which service allows it access to your consumer credit database. In addition, identify and describe the location and content of any documents memorializing, discussing or describing all of said services.

D. Describe in detail all documents, data or information you have provided CFS with respect to its use of your services and its access to your consumer credit database, including when each of said documents, data or information was provided to CFS and the manner in which it was provided.

E. Describe in detail all training and/or education you have provided to CFS and/or its employees, representatives or agents with respect to its use of your service and its access to your consumer credit database, including the dates, times and location of said training or education, the identity of the person or persons who provided said training and/or education, the identity of all persons who attended any of said education or training sessions and identify and describe the location and content of all documents describing, memorializing or related to said training.

F. State whether you have ever received any other complaints or notices of dispute relating to CFS's use of your service and its access to your consumer credit database (including any complaint that CFS obtained a consumer report or accessed a person's consumer file without having a permissible purpose as described under § 1681b of the FCRA, including the name of the complainant, the date of the complaint or dispute, whether said complaint or dispute was in writing, the nature of the complaint or dispute and the disposition of the complaint or dispute. In addition, identify and describe the location and content of any documents related to said complaints or disputes.

ANSWER:

INTERROGATORY NO. 6:

If any document that is or would have been responsive to plaintiff's First Requests for Production of Documents to you was destroyed, lost, mislaid, or otherwise missing, identify the document, state the date of and reason for its destruction, and identify all persons having knowledge of its contents and/or the reason for its destruction.

ANSWER:

INTERROGATORY NO. 7:

If any document responsive to plaintiff's First Requests for Production of Documents to you is withheld from production, identify each such document by date, title, subject matter, length and the request to which it is potentially responsive and state the reason for withholding production, and identify each person to whom the document was sent, shown, or made accessible, or to whom it was explained.

ANSWER:

INTERROGATORY NO. 8:

With respect to the information and data you furnished to CFS in July of 1999 regarding plaintiff, provide the following information:
A. The date the request for information was transmitted to you by CFS and the manner via which that request was transmitted, including but not limited to identification of the computer hardware and software or other medium via which that request was made or transmitted and its location. In addition, identify and describe the location and content of any documents memorializing or pertaining to said request.
B. The date you received the request for information from CFS and the manner via which that request was received, including but not limited to identification of the computer hardware and software or other medium via which said request was received and its location and the permissible purpose, if any, which CFS articulated to TU when it made said request. In addition, identify and describe the location and content of any documents memorializing or pertaining to your receipt of said request.
C. The date you furnished to CFS the information or data it was requesting; the nature and content of said information and/or data; and the manner via which said information and data was transmitted to CFS including but not limited to identification of computer hardware and software or other medium used and its location. In addition, identify and describe the location and content of any documents memorializing or pertaining to your furnishing of said information to CFS.
D. The identity of the CFS employee who sought and obtained the plaintiffs' consumer reports. In addition, identify and describe the location and content of any documents memorializing said person's identity.

ANSWER:

INTERROGATORY NO. 9:

With respect to any information and data you have furnished to CFS other than in July of 1999 regarding plaintiff, provide the following information:
A. The date the request for information was transmitted to you by CFS and the manner via which that request was transmitted, including but not limited to identification of the computer hardware and software or other medium via which that request was made or transmitted and its location. In addition, identify and describe the location and content of any documents memorializing or pertaining to said request.
B. The date you received the request for information from CFS and the manner via which that request was received, including but not limited to identification of the computer hardware and software or other medium via which said request was received and its location and the permissible purpose, if any, which CFS articulated to TU when it made said request. In addition, identify and describe the location and content of any documents memorializing or pertaining to your receipt of said request.
C. The date you furnished to CFS the information or data it was requesting; the nature and content of said information and/or data; and the manner via which said information and data was transmitted to CFS including but not limited to identification of computer hardware and software or other medium used and its location. In addition, identify and describe the location and content of any documents memorializing or pertaining to your furnishing of said information to CFS.
D. The identity of the CFS employee who sought and obtained the plaintiffs' consumer reports. In addition, identify and describe the location and content of any documents memorializing said person's identity.

ANSWER:

INTERROGATORY NO. 10:

Identify any and all complaints, investigations, inquiries, administrative proceedings, and civil or criminal actions made or brought against you, or in which you were involved, since January 1, 1995, as instituted by any person, entity, or governments agency or representative relating to (in the broadest sense) related to your providing any information to any person wherein it was alleged that a permissible purpose as required by § 1681b of the FCRA was necessary and did not exist at the time you furnished information regarding a consumer to said person.

ANSWER:

INTERROGATORY NO. 11:

Identify all documents, communications and correspondence you have received from, transmitted to, or exchanged with the plaintiff and/or any other defendant to this action, either before or since the filing of the Complaint, including all communications directed to you by CFS regarding this matter.

ANSWER:

INTERROGATORY NO. 12:

Identify all persons from whom you have received statements, as statement is defined in Federal Rule 26(b)(3).

ANSWER:

INTERROGATORY NO. 13:

With respect to the following affirmative defenses raised in your Answer to plaintiff's Complaint, provide each and every fact on which each defense is based; identify all persons from whom information was obtained in support of TU's assertion of each affirmative defense; and, identify the location and content of all documents on which CFS relies in support of each affirmative defense:
  a. First Affirmative Defense.
  b. Second Affirmative Defense.
  c. Third Affirmative Defense.
  d. Fourth Affirmative Defense.
  e. Fifth Affirmative Defense. With respect to this defense, specifically identify the "third parties" referenced therein.
  f. Sixth Affirmative Defense.
  g. Seventh Affirmative Defense.
  h. Tenth Affirmative Defense.

ANSWER:

INTERROGATORY NO. 14:

Describe in detail each step in the step-by-step process by which you process requests by persons (such as CFS) for information of the nature furnished to CFS regarding plaintiff in July of 1999 and with respect to each step of said process, describe the approximate *average*, *maximum*, and *minimum* quantities of time it takes you to complete each step in said process.

ANSWER:

INTERROGATORY NO. 15:

Identify any and all persons who you consulted with and/or provided you any information contemplated and/or utilized during the process of responding to any and all written discovery (in whatever form) propounded to you by plaintiff, including these interrogatories and the requests for production of documents served herewith.

ANSWER:

[Attorney for Plaintiff]

J.3.3 Interrogatories—Reinvestigation (to Furnisher)

JOE CONSUMER'S FIRST INTERROGATORIES TO ZIPODEEDODA FINANCE COMPANY

1. *INTERROGATORY:* Identify by name, publisher, publisher's address, vendor and vendor's address, any commercial software which you use to maintain, bill, collect, or report any information relating to your consumer accounts or application information relating to your consumer accounts.

ANSWER:

2. *INTERROGATORY:* Please provide the dates of each and every communication Zipodeedoda Finance Company had with the Consumer or any other party to this lawsuit concerning any of the facts or allegations described in this lawsuit or any pleading you have filed or may file, identify the persons with whom you communicated, and explain and describe the contents of your communications.

ANSWER:

3. *INTERROGATORY:* Please state the names, home addresses and telephone numbers of each and every person having knowledge of facts or having formed any opinions relating to any or all of the incidents which are the basis of this lawsuit, any allegation made in this lawsuit, any defense raised in this lawsuit, the cause of any alleged incident underlying this lawsuit or damages claimed in this lawsuit, or relating to any of the damages incurred by Consumer including any of your employees who, in any way, handled or supervised any matters in connection with Consumer's disputes to you, your credit reportings about Consumer, and any of your communications with Consumer or any credit reporting agency regarding Consumer.

ANSWER:

4. *INTERROGATORY:* Please state the full name, address and telephone number, qualifications and present employment, of each and every person whom you expect to or may call as an expert witness at the trial of this matter, including any alleged employee experts under Federal Rule of Civil Procedure Rule 26, the subject matter on which each such expert is expected to testify, the substance of the facts and opinions to which each such expert is expected to testify, a summary of the grounds for each opinion expected to be expressed by such expert, and the identification of any document, writing, publication, treatise, book and/or other tangible source, upon which such expert may have relied, or is expected to rely, in the formation of any such opinion.

ANSWER:

5. *INTERROGATORY:* Please identify the date, recipient, and content (as recorded by Metro or Metro 2 data) of occurrence during the preceding five years in which you reported credit data

regarding Consumer. If you have reported such data, state whether such reportings were made pursuant to an express or written authorization by you for the relevant consumer reporting agency to report that data.

ANSWER:

6. ***INTERROGATORY:*** Identify by name, home address, telephone number, social security number, and date of birth each individual employed by Zipodeedoda Finance Company in preceding 5 years who supervised reinvestigations of credit data reported to any consumer reporting agency for you. Include in your answer a description of the individual's job title and the dates of employment of the individual.

ANSWER:

7. ***INTERROGATORY:*** In light of the allegations, please identify each credit reporting which relating to Consumer you contend was inaccurate.

ANSWER:

8. ***INTERROGATORY:*** In light of the allegations, please identify each incident where you erroneously verified credit information relating to Consumer which should not have been verified.

ANSWER:

9. ***INTERROGATORY:*** In light of the allegations, please identify each action taken by you in verifying the credit information relating to Consumer which was NOT taken intentionally with full knowledge of your obligations and Consumer's rights under the Fair Credit Reporting Act.

ANSWER:

10. ***INTERROGATORY:*** Explain in detail Zipodeedoda Finance Company's procedures for reinvestigating consumer disputes of your account and consumer credit data forwarded by the national consumer reporting agencies for Zipodeedoda Finance Company's response.

ANSWER:

11. ***INTERROGATORY:*** Please explain and describe Zipodeedoda Finance Company specific allocation, in percentages or dollar amounts, of Zipodeedoda Finance Company's resources committed to reinvestigation of consumer disputes in each of the preceding five years.

ANSWER:

12. ***INTERROGATORY:*** Please describe the amount per dispute which you have budgeted to resolve credit reporting disputes from consumers.

ANSWER:

13. ***INTERROGATORY:*** Please describe the pay scale, any incentive, bonus, or other factors affecting compensation for the person(s) who conducted or supervised any credit reporting dispute relating to Consumer.

ANSWER:

14. ***INTERROGATORY:*** Please explain and describe Zipodeedoda Finance Company's actions to assess or identify the risks and potential for harm to consumers arising from inaccurate credit reporting by you.

ANSWER:

15. ***INTERROGATORY:*** Please explain and describe Zipodeedoda Finance Company's specific projects, initiatives, or programs during the preceding five years, to reduce potential harm to consumers arising out of inaccurate credit reporting by you.

ANSWER:

16. ***INTERROGATORY:*** Describe every step taken by you to investigate Consumer's dispute of your account and consumer credit data which was reported to the national consumer reporting agencies—including the identity, home address, telephone number, social security number and date of birth of witnesses interviewed and persons conducting the investigation; documents requested and reviewed, communications with the national consumer reporting agencies, description of any computer systems queried or other investigative means employed. Please include reference to the manner in which the data in this case was investigated, Zipodeedoda Finance Company's understanding as to how it continued to be placed in Consumer's credit files and reports and whether Zipodeedoda Finance Company took any steps to have that information removed or altered so as to prevent said data from being incorrectly attributed to Consumer.

ANSWER:

17. ***INTERROGATORY:*** Describe in detail any policies, procedures, or practices which have been in place at any time during the preceding five years concerning the renumbering of accounts which have been acquired, sold, assigned, referred for collection, marked as uncollectible, marked as fraudulent, or previously reinvestigated. Include in your description the manner in which you notify credit reporting agencies of the renumbering.

ANSWER:

18. ***INTERROGATORY:*** Identify each document which Zipodeedoda Finance Company claims was executed by Consumer in order to initiate, consummate, or fulfill any transaction with you.

ANSWER:

19. ***INTERROGATORY:*** Identify the date, time, manner, purpose and individual's responsible for each incident in which Zipodeedoda Finance Company obtained access to Consumer's consumer credit or any consumer report associated with social security number at any time during the preceding 5 years.

ANSWER:

20. ***INTERROGATORY:*** Identify the true creditor of any account which Zipodeedoda Finance Company reported in association with Consumer's personal identifiers—including but not limited to the holder of the account or securitization trust which owned the credit obligation—and the nature of any relationship between Zipodeedoda Finance Company and that creditor.

ANSWER:

21. ***INTERROGATORY:*** Identify by description, author, date of creation any documents which have been requested by Consumer, but which have been withheld on the basis of trade secret, confidentiality or privilege.

ANSWER:

22. *INTERROGATORY:* Identify—including Case number, venue, parties, amount of any settlement or judgment paid by Zipodeedoda Finance Company—every lawsuit in which you were alleged to have improperly reported or reinvestigated credit reporting data relating to a consumer report.

Respectfully Submitted,

J.4 Sample Requests for Production

J.4.1 Request for Production of Documents (to Furnisher)

IN THE UNITED STATES DISTRICT COURT
FOR THE EASTERN DISTRICT OF PENNSYLVANIA

```
_____  )
                       )
                       )
          Plaintiff    )
                       )
v.                     )  Civil Action No.
                       )
[defendants]           )
            Defendants )
_____  )
```

PLAINTIFF'S REQUEST FOR PRODUCTION OF DOCUMENTS TO DEFENDANT [FURNISHER NAME]

Plaintiff, [Name], pursuant to Rules 26 and 34 of the Federal Rules of Civil Procedure, hereby serves upon Defendant [Name], the following Requests for Production of Documents. Defendant shall produce the requested documents for inspection and copying at the offices of Francis & Mailman, P.C., Land Title Building, 19th Floor, 100 South Broad Street, Philadelphia, PA 19110, within 30 days of receipt of this Request.

DEFINITIONS AND INSTRUCTIONS

The following definitions and instructions shall apply to Plaintiff's requests for production:

1. "Document" is used in the broadest sense contemplated by Federal Rule of Civil Procedure 34, and includes, but is not limited to, the following items: agreements; drafts; communications; correspondence; telegrams; cables; facsimiles; memoranda; records; books; financial statements; summaries of records or notes of personal conversations or interviews; diaries; calendars; forecasts; statistical statements; accountants work papers; graphs; charts; maps; diagrams; blue prints; tables; indexes; pictures; recordings; tapes; microfilm; charge clips; accounts; analytical records; minutes or records of meetings or conferences; reports and/or summaries of investigations; opinions or reports of consultants; appraisals; reports and/or summaries of negotiations; brochures; pamphlets; circulars; trade letters; press releases; contracts; stenographic, handwritten or any other notes; projections; working papers; federal and state income tax returns; checks, front and back; check stubs or receipts; shipping documents; manifests; invoice vouchers; computer printouts and computer disks and tapes; and tape data sheets or data processing cards or disks or any other written, recorded, transcribed, punched, taped, filmed or graphic matters; however produced or reproduced.

2. "Communication" includes every manner of transmitting or receiving facts spoken by one person and from one person to another person, information, opinions, or thoughts, whether orally, by documents, writing, or copy thereof, or otherwise, including, but not limited to, words transmitted by telephone, radio, or any method of voice recording.

3. The word "Person" means any natural or artificial person, including business entities and other legal entities.

4. "You" includes [NAME OF DEFENDANT] personally, your company, entity, institution, agency, subsidiary (ies), parent corporation(s) and/or any of its branches, departments, employees, agents, contractual affiliates, or otherwise connected by legal relationship, in the broadest sense. You may also be referenced herein simply as "[Abbreviation of Defendant's Name]." "You" refers to you, your agents, servants and/or employees, and in the instance of Defendant corporations or other business entities, "you" refers to the person or entity designated to these interrogatories as well as any person, agent, servant and/employee who acted on behalf of the Defendant at any time and in connection with answering these interrogatories.

5. The word "Plaintiff" refers to the person named in the caption above who instituted this action.

6. The "FCRA" refers to the Federal Fair Credit Reporting Act, codified at 15 U.S.C. §§ 1681–1681t.

7. The term "Plaintiff's Credit Report" refers to the report or reports on Plaintiff's credit history compiled by Trans Union, L.L.C., Experian Information Solutions, Inc., CBA Information Services, Equifax Credit Information Services, Inc., and any credit reporting agency to whom you have furnished, reported or otherwise communicated any credit information concerning the Plaintiff and referred to in Plaintiff's Complaint.

8. "And" or "or" shall be construed conjunctively or disjunctively as necessary to make the requests inclusive rather than exclusive. The use of the word "including" shall be construed to mean "without limitation."

9. Reference to the singular in any of these requests shall also include a reference to the plural, and reference to the plural shall include a reference to the singular.

10. "Related to" or "relating to" shall mean directly or indirectly supporting, evidencing, describing, mentioning, referring to, contradicting, comprising or concerning.

11. "Audit Trail" means a complete, detailed listing of each addition, deletion, modification, or other change to the credit account or account profile as maintained in recorded form, in the broadest sense, by "you." The listing should include the identity, address, employer and title of the person(s) taking the action, the identity, address, employer and title of the person(s) authorizing the action, a detailed explanation of the action taken, the date of the action, the means used to effect such action, the location of origin of the action and the reason the action was taken.

12. "Data" means the physical symbols in the broadest sense, that represent information, regardless of whether the information is oral, written or otherwise recorded.

13. "Data field" means any single or group of character(s), number(s), symbol(s) or other identifiable mark(s) maintained in a permanent or temporary recording which represent, in any way, an

item or collection of information. "Data field" includes all types of data whether maintained in integer, real, character or boolean format.

14. "Database" or "databank" means any grouping or collection of data fields maintained, in any format or order, in any permanent or temporary recorded form.

15. "Hardware" means the physical components of a computer or any device capable of maintaining recorded data.

16. "Software" means the entire set of computer programs, procedures, documentation, or other recorded instructions which guide a mechanical device or human in the operation of the computer or mechanical device.

17. "Computer" means any and all programmable electronic devices or apparatuses, including hardware, software, and other databanks, that can store, retrieve, access, update, combine, rearrange, print, read, process or otherwise alter data whether such data maintained in that device or at some other location. The term "computer" includes any and all magnetic recordings or systems, systems operating on or maintaining data in digital, analog, or hybrid format, or other mechanical devices, or other devices capable of maintaining writings or recordings, of any kind, in condensed format, and includes any disk, tape, recording, or other informational source, regardless of its physical dimension or size.

18. "Personal Identifiers" means a person's name or social security number or other unique data which identifies or is associated with a particular person.

19. "Credit Furnisher" means any person or business entity, including you, which has provided, communicated, furnished or reported any credit information concerning the Plaintiff.

20. The documents requests herein shall be produced as they are kept in the usual course of business or shall be organized and labeled according to the number of the document request.

21. The duty to produce documents shall not be limited or affected by the fact that the same document is available through another source. All documents should be produced which are not subject to an objection and are known by, possessed or controlled by, or available to Plaintiff or any of Plaintiff's attorneys, consultants, representatives, employees, officers, directors, partners, or other agents.

22. In the event you assert any form of objection or privilege as a ground for not answering a document production request or any part of a request, set forth the legal grounds and facts upon which the objection or privilege is based. If the objection relates to only part of the document, the balance of the document production should be answered in full. With respect to any document which is withheld on a claim of privilege, Plaintiff shall provide, at the time its responses are due hereunder, a statement setting forth as to each such document the following information:

(1) the name(s) of the sender(s) of the document;

(2) the name(s) of the author(s) of the document;

(3) the name(s) of the person(s) to whom the document or copies were sent;

(4) the date of the document;

(5) a brief description of the nature and subject matter of the document; and

(6) the nature of the privilege or the authority which is claimed to give rise to it.

23. Notwithstanding the assertion of an objection, any purportedly privileged document containing non-privileged matter must be disclosed, with the purportedly privileged portion redacted. All such documents should be held separately and retained intact subject to and pending a ruling by the Court as to the claimed privilege.

24. If any documents requested have been destroyed, lost, mislaid, or are otherwise missing, please so state, specifying for each document or thing:

(1) the type of document;

(2) a description of the nature and contents of the document;

(3) the identity of the author;

(4) the circumstances under which it ceased to exist;

(5) the identity of all Person(s) having knowledge of the circumstances under which it ceased to exist; and

(6) the identity of all Person(s) who had knowledge of the contents.

25. This request for production of documents is deemed to be continuing. Should you obtain any other documents or information which would supplement or modify the documents or information supplied by you in response to this request, you are directed, pursuant to Federal Rule of Civil Procedure 26(e), to give timely notice of such documents and information and to furnish the additional documents or information to Plaintiff without delay.

REQUEST FOR PRODUCTION OF DOCUMENTS

1. Please produce any and all investigative reports prepared or obtained which in any way reference Plaintiff, the events alleged in the Complaint, Plaintiff's Social Security number, Plaintiff's true identity or any allegations or defenses asserted in this action.

2. Please produce any and all written or recorded statements prepared or obtained which in any way reference Plaintiff, Plaintiff's Social Security number, Plaintiff's true identity or any allegations or defenses asserted in this action.

3. Please identify and produce a copy of each and every document referencing communications between you and any of the other Defendants in this action, and any of the credit furnishers referenced in Plaintiff's Complaint, which in any way references Plaintiff, Plaintiff's Social Security numbers or other identifiers, or any allegation or defense asserted in this action.

4. Please provide a copy of each liability policy issued to you which may cover your alleged liability in this suit, including declaration page and/or all endorsements.

5. Please produce all documents referring or relating to any communications, including but not limited to, credit reports, Consumer Dispute Verification(s) (CDV or ACDV) forms, METRO tapes or telephone investigation logs, between you and any other Defendant in this action, as well as any other credit furnishers referenced in Plaintiff's Complaint, which refer or relate to the Plaintiff, Plaintiff's Social Security number, any of Plaintiff's account numbers and/or Plaintiff's personal identifiers:

6. Please produce all documents sent to Plaintiff by you.

7. Please produce all documents sent to you by Plaintiff.

8. Please produce all documents relating or referring to any communications between you and Plaintiff.

9. Please produce all of your documents, subscriber contracts, manuals or other recorded data, concerning your relationships with any of the credit furnishers referenced in Plaintiff's Complaint.

10. Please produce copies of all of your quarterly profit and loss statements for the past three (3) years.

11. Please produce copies of all of your current balance sheets and financial statements.

12. Please produce copies of your income tax returns for the past three (3) years.

13. Please produce all credit report(s) which bear any identifier(s) associated with Plaintiff for the last three (3) years.

14. Please produce all documents evidencing, constituting or including data concerning notification of any allegation that any account bearing Plaintiff's personal identifiers had been created by application fraud or had been used by a person not authorized to use or possess Plaintiff's personal identification.

15. Please produce any documents sent by you to any other person or entity concerning the Plaintiff within the past five (5) years.

16. Please produce any documents sent to you or received by you concerning the Plaintiff within the past five (5) years.

17. Please produce all documents evidencing or including data concerning the names, addresses, telephone numbers, current employers and current whereabouts of each and every one of your employees who has communicated with the Plaintiff.

18. Please provide a complete audit trail of any document(s), data bases, credit files, computer(s), or other data held by you which, in any degree, address or discuss the Plaintiff, or any one of the Plaintiff's personal identifiers.

19. Please produce all documents which constitute consumer dispute verification (CDV) forms or notices, correspondence with any consumer reporting agency or creditor or subscriber or data deletion forms which contain any one of Plaintiff's personal identifiers.

20. Please produce all documents constituting your entire credit file(s), collection file(s) and fraud investigation file(s), which in any way references Plaintiff, Plaintiff's personal identifiers or any of the account numbers associated with Plaintiff's identifiers.

21. Please produce all documents which contain any data about complaints, assessments, audits, reports or studies of the frequency of credit application fraud or identity fraud in your credit operations.

22. Please produce all documents which evidence, constitute and/or address your means, methods or abilities to correctly identify whether a tradeline or former address has been previously reported as incorrect.

23. Please produce copies of all documents evidencing telephone messages, log books or your other regularly maintained records which contain information about communications between you and Plaintiff.

24. Please produce all policy manuals, procedure manuals or other documents which address your policies, practices or procedures in the investigation or reinvestigation of credit data which is disputed as inaccurate by a consumer.

25. Please produce all policy manuals, procedure manuals or other documents, which address your policies, practices or procedures in correcting, updating, modifying and/or deleting or suppressing credit data or historical address data which is disputed as inaccurate.

26. Please produce copies of any and all telephone reinvestigation forms which in any way reference Plaintiff, Plaintiff's social security number or any allegation or defense asserted in this action.

27. Please produce the original of all data tapes (metro tapes) transmitted to you by any subscriber or affiliate which pertains to Plaintiff or which references Plaintiff's social security number.

28. Please produce for inspection and copying all documents which you will or may use as exhibits in the trial of this case.

29. Please produce all archived prints (whether stored digitally or in hard copy) of all consumer disclosures made in response to the Plaintiff's requests.

30. Please produce all archived prints (whether stored digitally or in hard copy) of all internal disclosures generated as a result of the Plaintiff's dispute of accuracy in Plaintiff's credit file.

31. Please produce all archived prints of verification responses, if any, from any of the credit furnishers referenced in Plaintiff's Complaint (whether stored digitally or in hard copy) pertaining to Plaintiff.

32. Please produce all archived prints of Plaintiff's corrected credit report reflecting the results of your reinvestigation of Plaintiff's disputes (whether digitally stored or in hard copy).

33. Please produce a copy of your entire database on the Plaintiff (i.e., all screens) including but not limited to:

a) "consumer personal information" screens;

b) "consumer address information" screens;

c) "address information" screens;

d) "public record detail" screens;

e) "dispute verification menu" screens; and

f) "ACDV records" screens.

34. Please produce an organizational chart for the Defendant.

35. Please produce all exhibits which you intend to introduce at trial.

36. Please produce copies of all papers, records and documents referred to in Plaintiff's First Set of Interrogatories Directed to Defendant.

37. Please produce all documents that are referenced in Defendant's Initial Disclosures.

38. Please produce any and all documents or computer screens which set forth or demonstrate all of the account information that you are currently reporting about the Plaintiff.

BY: _____

[Attorneys for Plaintiff]

J.4.2 Request for Production of Documents (to CRA)[2]

IN THE UNITED STATES DISTRICT COURT
FOR THE DISTRICT OF _____

```
_____ )
[PLAINTIFF],          )
            Plaintiff )
                      )
v.                    )
                      ) CIVIL NO.
EXPERIAN INFORMATION  )
SOLUTIONS, INC.,      )
            Defendant.)
_____ )
```

PLAINTIFF'S REQUEST FOR PRODUCTION OF DOCUMENTS

Pursuant to the Federal Rules of Civil Procedure, and the Local Rules for the Eastern District of Virginia, Plaintiff, by counsel, propounds the following Request for Production of Documents to Defendant, EXPERIAN INFORMATION SOLUTIONS, INC., to be answered under oath within the time prescribed by the Federal Rules of Civil Procedure and the Local Rules of the United States District Court for the Eastern District of Virginia.

REQUEST FOR PRODUCTION OF DOCUMENTS

PLEASE TAKE NOTICE, that pursuant to F.R.C.P. 34, the plaintiff, by counsel, requests that you produce in ORIGINAL form for the purposes of inspection, copying and/or testing, the documents described below. Such documents are to be produced at the offices of plaintiff's counsel within the time prescribed by the Federal Rules of Civil Procedure.

1. All materials used by you since 2002 which pertain to and/or describe your consumer dispute procedures under 15 U.S.C. Section 1681i.

2. The original file(s), including all original documents placed therein, maintained by you, pertaining to the plaintiff.

3. All documents identified in or regarding any of your answers to the interrogatories propounded by the plaintiff.

4. All documents regarding the plaintiff.

5. Your annual report and financial statements for fiscal and/or calendar years 2002, 2003, 2004 and 2005.

6 All documents you intend to introduce at trial.

7. A complete copy of all information in the Plaintiff's file as of the date of this request.

8. A complete copy of any documents relating to any requests or responses to requests for reinvestigation of any information reported in the plaintiff's consumer report B including but not limited to any CDVs, ACDVs AUDs, responses, universal data forms, notes, screens, logs, internal memoranda, correspondence or supporting documentation.

9. A complete copy of any communications B including but not limited to any supporting documentation, specific requests for information, instructions, notes, screens, logs, policies, or legal requirements B relating to the plaintiff or any reinvestigation of any information contained in the plaintiff's consumer report.

10. Any other documents prepared, sent or received by you in the course of conducting any reinvestigation regarding the plaintiff's consumer report.

11. Any computerized data relating to the plaintiff or any reinvestigation of any trade-line appearing on the plaintiff's consumer report.

12. Any historical, archived or electronic record of any Metro Tape Data which was the subject of a reinvestigation relating to the plaintiff.

13. Any listing, concordance, of definition of any codes, response codes, shorthand, or abbreviations appearing in any of the preceding documents.

14. Any codes or response codes used by you in the course of documenting or conducting any reinvestigation relating to the plaintiff.

15. Your Indicating Manual.

16. Your trade set detail.

17. Any history search summary screens relating the plaintiff.

18. Any other document prepared in the course of any reinvestigation of any credit information relating to the plaintiff.

19. Any agreement under which any furnisher who reported information subject to reinvestigation by the plaintiff, reported, accessed, or furnished credit information to you.

20. Any schedule of consideration incentives under which any furnisher who reported information subject to reinvestigation by the plaintiff, reported or furnished credit information to you.

21. Any manuals, bulletins, or other documents created or published by you addressing the prevalence or consequences of identity theft.

22. Any manuals, bulletins, or other documents created or published by you identifying steps taken by you to reduce harmful consequences to consumers of identity theft.

23. Any list generated by you B and specifically by any writing department within your organization—of manuals or guides produced or published by or within your organization.

24. Any name scan or snapshot prepared in association with the plaintiff or any of the plaintiff's personal identifiers, from January 1, 2004 through the present.

25. Any archived records of actions taken by your Consumer Relations Center in relation to the plaintiff or any of the plaintiff's personal identifiers.

26. Any on-line combine log relating to the plaintiff.

27. Business rules relating to the subject selection procedure and/or any documents which contain them.

28. Copies of the plaintiff's consumer reports provided to any of your subscribers.

29. Subscriber agreements for any of your subscribers who have received the plaintiff's consumer report.

30. Terminal audit trails as of the date of access of the plaintiff's consumer report by any of your subscribers who have received the plaintiff's consumer report since January 1, 2003.

31. Any description of the matching algorithm used to correlate specific credit information to a specific individual for the purpose of assembling a consumer report.

32. Any description of the merging algorithm used to correlate specific credit information to a specific individual for the purpose of future assembly of consumer reports.

---

[2] *Editorial Note*: This set is very comprehensive and contains far more requests than are usually appropriate. Select from these requests—do not use them all.

33. Any complaints (civil, regulatory, or administrative) served upon you which involved cases of mismerged or mixed credit files.

34. Any judgments, final orders, or settlements (civil, regulatory, or administrative) relating to any complaints served upon you which involved cases of mismerged or mixed credit files.

35. Any reports to administrative agencies, regulatory agencies, shareholders or corporate officers reflecting overall incidents or assessment of known problems of mismerged or mixed credit reports.

36. Any manuals, bulletins, or instructions for remedying or otherwise rendering accurate, mismerged or mixed credit reports.

37. Any complaints (civil, regulatory, or administrative) served upon you which involved cases involving theft of identity or fraud.

38. Any judgments, final orders, or settlements (civil, regulatory, or administrative) involving theft of identity or fraud.

39. Any reports to regulatory agencies, shareholders or corporate officers reflecting overall incidents or assessment of known problems of identity theft or fraud.

40. Any manuals, bulletins, or instructions for remedying or otherwise rendering accurate, consumer reports which contain information resulting from theft of identity or fraud.

41. Any manuals, bulletins, or instructions for preventing the improper appearance of credit information resulting from theft of identity or fraud in consumer reports.

42. Any manuals, memoranda, bulletins or other documents instructing your employees or agents as to the requirements of 15 U.S.C. § 1681i.

43. Any manuals, memoranda, bulletins or other documents instructing your employees or agents as to your policy regarding reinvestigation.

44. Any manuals, memoranda, bulletins or other documents instructing your employees or agents as to the manner in which reinvestigation are to be conducted.

45. Any cost/benefit analysis regarding expenditures necessary for compliance with 15 U.S.C. § 1681i or the reinvestigation of disputed credit information.

46. Any cost/benefit analysis regarding expenditures necessary for cost of defending cases of disputed credit information versus compliance with 15 U.S.C. § 1681i or the reinvestigation of disputed credit information.

47. Any budgets or projections prepared within the preceding five years, allocating resources or expenditures to the conducting of reinvestigation under 15 U.S.C. § 1681i.

48. Any programs under which any of your employees are provided any bonus, pay, or other incentive relating to reinvestigations of consumer disputes.

49. Any manuals, bulletins or notices provided to furnishers of credit information, describing their contractual or statutory duties relating to the reinvestigation of inaccurate or incomplete credit information.

50. Transcripts of any deposition given by any witness to be offered by you at trial.

51. Transcripts of any deposition given by any witness to be offered by you as a corporate designee pursuant to Rule 30(b)(6).

52. Transcripts of any deposition given by any individual identified by you in your disclosures given pursuant to rule 26(a).

53. Any shareholder reports or management reports of current or past litigation.

54. Any and all correspondence, documents or other recordings between you (including your attorneys) and any other defendant in this action, or their attorneys relating to this action.

55. Any internal report, memoranda, or document assessing liability in this case.

56. All documents evidencing telephone messages, log books or other regularly maintained records by you which contain information about communications between you and the plaintiff or any defendant in this action.

57. All work papers, notes, and documents in the file of any expert witness who is expected to testify on your behalf, or in the file of the expert who has written a report which is or will be relied upon, in whole or in part, by a testifying expert, on your behalf.

58. All expert reports which have been prepared in connection with this lawsuit or the incident giving rise to this lawsuit, if the expert is expected to or may testify in this case.

59. Please produce any and all policy manuals, procedure manuals, or other documents, which address your policies, practices or procedures in the investigation or reinvestigation of credit data which is disputed as inaccurate upon the consumer's allegation that the creditor misplacing responsibility for its account on the consumer.

60. Please produce your statistics compiled on an annual basis regarding the number of disputes you received complaining or disputing inaccurate data allegedly reported by your subscribers.

61. Please produce any and all policy manuals, procedure manuals, or other recordings or documents of any kind, which address any or all of your policies, practices or procedures in insuring the maximum possible accuracy of data posted, maintained or disseminated by you.

62. Please produce any and all policy manuals, procedure manuals, or other documents, which address your policies, practices or procedures in insuring the post-reinvestigation accuracy of data maintained or disseminated by you.

63. Please produce each and every archived report you maintain regarding plaintiff or any of his personal identifiers. This request *includes* the full set of scans available regarding any data file which you or any of your affiliates have caused to be merged into plaintiff's consumer credit reports or disclosures.

64. Please produce any and all policy manuals, procedure manuals, or other documents, which are training manuals for your employees, in the following areas: consumer relations, disputes, reinvestigation, delete mechanisms, suppression functions and deletion functions.

65. Please produce any and all policy manuals, procedure manuals, or other documents, which are consumer relations manuals for your employees and/or consumer credit database system.

66. Please produce each and every dispute resolution log or report you generated regarding plaintiff or any of his personal identifiers.

67. Please produce your data file maintenance manuals and any decoding manuals used to interpret the various items of data appearing on the dispute resolution log or report.

68. Please produce any and all of your CDVs, ACDVs, and UDFs which bear any of the personal identifiers of plaintiff, as well as the complete log of all reinvestigation activities in any file, report or other record bearing any of plaintiff's personal identifiers.

69. Please produce any and all of your documents discussing any of the following programs:

a) Archival of consumer reports and other data maintained;

b) On-line maintenance and storage of consumer reports accessed by subscribers and you;

c) On-line maintenance, storage, archival process and microfiche process of consumer reports captured due to maintenance activity;

d) Weighing of variables considered in assessing matches of files returned in the search process; and

e) Generation and dissemination of summary profiles, derogatory data flags, credit scores and adverse action codes/denial codes.

70. Please produce all internal remark and notation screen prints in your consumer credit database showing any information regarding plaintiff or any of his personal identifiers.

71. Please produce your documents discussing the Metro Tape Format and the Metro Tape 2 Format.

72. Please produce your documents discussing research or studies by Associated Credit Bureaus [ACB], CDIA or other third parties concerning the accuracy of data contained in your consumer credit database.

73. Please produce any and all policy manuals, procedure manuals, or other documents, which address the minimal amount and type of information required of any consumer disputing any item of information on a consumer report, in order to cause you to initiate your correction, update, modification and/or deletion of the disputed data.

74. Please produce your policy manuals, procedure manuals, or other documents, which address instructions or directions, provided by your company to any subscriber, with regard to the means, methods and guidelines for communicating corrections of credit data to you.

75. Please produce any and all policy manuals, procedure manuals, or other documents, which address instructions or directions, provided by your company to any subscriber, with regard to application processing and inquiry formatting from the subscriber to you.

76. Please produce your policy manuals, procedure manuals, or other documents, which address any of the following programs:

a) any credit scoring models used by you;

b) required input and match system used for generating consumer disclosures, as opposed to the input and match system provided for use by your subscribers;

c) scorecard development programs used in your credit scoring models.

77. Please produce copies of any and all credit reports generated and/or issued by you concerning the Plaintiff or which bear any of his personal identifiers. This request includes all archived data reports, archived reports, current, on-line reports, off-line reports, and a report consisting of the current state of your consumer credit database storing the credit data which you believe is attributable to the Plaintiff or which bear any of his personal identifiers. In connection therewith, please identify the recipient(s) of each document.

78. Please provide a complete audit trail of any document(s), computer(s), or other data held by you which, in any degree, address or discuss the Plaintiff, any of his personal identifiers and/or any of the data identified, as false, by the Plaintiff in this action.

79. Please provide copies of your subscriber contracts with any of the other defendants which were in effect in the two year period preceding the date of the filing of this lawsuit.

80. Please produce any and all policy manuals, procedure manuals, or documents, which address, explain and describe each and every inquiry search algorithms, including data formats, available to your various subscribers.

81. Please produce any and all policy manuals, procedure manuals, or other documents, which address the particular architecture of your archived credit data report system, credit data archival system, credit data microfiche system, or other system which electronically captures the state of a consumer's file(s) at a given point in time. This includes the periodic electronic capture of the state of the entire consumer credit database.

82. Please produce any and all policy manuals, procedure manuals, or other documents, which address, explain and describe each and every design and/or configuration of each and every search/inquiry algorithms/programs for your consumer credit database.

83. Please produce copies of any and all correspondence, documents or other recordings from you, or your attorneys, to any other defendant in this action, or their attorneys.

84. Please produce copies of any and all correspondence, documents or other recordings to you, or to your attorneys, from any other defendant in this action, or their attorneys.

85. Please produce copies of all of the internal notations made by your employees regarding contacts with plaintiff, his attorneys, or any other defendant in this lawsuit, with regard to plaintiff, any of his personal identifiers and/or the disputed account[s].

86. Please produce copies of any and all documents bearing credit scoring assessments in connection with any report or data bearing Plaintiff's name or any of his personal identifiers.

87. Please produce copies of the current credit report(s) of Plaintiff, as maintained by you.

88. Please produce copies of any and all telephone reinvestigation forms and/or message books which in any way references Plaintiff or any allegation or defense asserted in this action.

89. Please produce copies of any and all documents which contain any data concerning a security assessment, audit, report or study of your consumer credit database and/or credit reporting terminal system(s) in the years: 2000, 2001, 2002, 2003, 2004, 2005 and/or 2006.

90. Please produce copies of any and all documents which contain any data concerning any Electronic Data Processing [EDP] assessment, audit, report or study of your consumer credit database and/or credit reporting terminal system(s) in the years: 2000, 2001, 2002, 2003, 2004, 2005 and/or 2006.

91. Please produce copies of any and all documents which contain any data concerning a search [inquiry] algorithm [formats] assessment, audit, report or study of your consumer credit database and/or credit reporting terminal system(s) in the years: 2000, 2001, 2002, 2003, 2004, 2005 and/or 2006.

92. Please produce copies of any and all documents which contain any data about complaints, assessments, audits, reports or studies of improperly posted data made to your consumer credit database and/or credit reporting terminal system(s), in the years: 2000, 2001, 2002, 2003, 2004, 2005 and/or 2006.

93. Please produce copies of any and all documents which provides explanations and descriptions about the various coded or encrypted data appearing on consumer reports, scratchpad notes, archival recordation identification codes, record identification codes and employee identification codes.

94. Please produce copies of any and all documents which contain any data about reliability assessments, audits, reports or studies of consumer credit data provided to you by your subscribers, or any grouping of subscribers, in the years: 2000, 2001, 2002, 2003, 2004, 2005 and/or 2006.

95. Please produce copies of any and all documents which contain any data about and/or constitute a listing, explanation and description of your consumer dispute codes.

96. Please produce copies of any and all documents which contain any data about internal, self audits or external audits of the accuracy of credit data you maintain and disseminate, in the years: 2000, 2001, 2002, 2003, 2004, 2005 and/or 2006

97. Please produce copies of any and all documents which contain any data about internal, self audits or external audits of your dispute process, reinvestigation and dispute resolution procedures and mechanisms, in the years: 2000, 2001, 2002, 2003, 2004, 2005 and/or 2006.

98. Please produce any and all work papers, notes, and documents in the file of any expert witness who is expected to testify, or in the file of the expert who has written a report which is or will be relied upon, in whole or in part, by a testifying expert.

99. Please produce any and all expert reports which have been prepared in connection with this lawsuit or the incident giving rise to this lawsuit, if the expert is expected to or may testify in this cause.

100. Please produce any and all expert reports that were or will be relied upon, in whole or in part, or which were produced by any expert retained or engaged by you.

101. Please produce copies of any statements you have taken or received from any third person in any way connected with the allegations contained in this lawsuit.

102. Please produce any and all documents which contain data listing or otherwise identifying each of your operators or other employees, their corresponding office descriptions and numbers, and their corresponding badge and identification numbers, who communicated with either or both Plaintiff, any person concerning any account, dispute, report, or other document(s) made subject of and/or requested in any of the foregoing requests by Plaintiff to you.

103. Please produce a copy of each and every screen and file in your consumer credit database which in any way references plaintiff and/or his personal identifiers.

104. Please produce any document which you have provided, maintained or received which explains the automated scans of EXPERIAN credit reports or which explains the method by which a credit score is calculated from an EXPERIAN credit file.

[PLAINTIFF],

By _____
    Of Counsel

J.5 Sample Requests for Admissions

J.5.1 Sample Requests for Admissions (to Furnisher)

IN THE UNITED STATES DISTRICT COURT
FOR THE EASTERN DISTRICT OF PENNSYLVANIA

```
_____  )
Plaintiff,               )
                Plaintiff )
                         )
v.                       ) Civil Action No.
                         )
[Furnisher]              )
                Defendant )
_____  )
```

PLAINTIFF'S REQUESTS FOR ADMISSIONS TO DEFENDANT [FURNISHER]

I. DEFINITIONS AND INSTRUCTIONS

Plaintiff incorporates in these Requests for Admissions those Instructions and Definitions set forth in Plaintiff's First Set Of Interrogatories and Requests for Production of Documents directed to Defendant FURNISHER.

Additionally, the account[s] listed in paragraph [13] of plaintiff's Complaint will be [collectively] referred to as the "Account[s]."

II. REQUESTS FOR ADMISSIONS

Pursuant to Rule 36 of The Federal Rules of Civil Procedure, plaintiff requests defendant to admit or deny the truth of the following for the purposes of this action only:

1. Defendant [FURNISHER] is a "furnisher of information" as that term is described in the Fair Credit Reporting Act ("FCRA"), 15 U.S.C. § 1681s-2.

2. Defendant [FURNISHER] is a "person" as that term is defined in the Fair Credit Reporting Act ("FCRA"), 15 U.S.C. § 1681a.

3. Defendant has published the Account[s] to Trans Union, L.L.C. ("Trans Union"), Experian Information Solutions, Inc. ("Experian"), CBA Information Services (CBA), and Equifax Credit Information Solutions ("Equifax") within the two-year period prior to the filing of this action.

4. Defendant has published the Account[s] as belonging to the plaintiff.

5. The information that defendant has published about the Account[s] is adverse credit information that negatively reflects upon plaintiff's credit history.

6. Defendant has reported that plaintiff made late payments on the Account[s].

7. Defendant has reported that plaintiff was in default on the Account[s] at one or more times.

8. Defendant has reported that plaintiff was delinquent on the Account[s] at one or more times.

9. Defendant has reported that the Account[s] was placed into collection.

10. The Account[s] do[es] not belong to the plaintiff.

11. The Account[s] belong[s] to a person other than the plaintiff.

12. At the current time, defendant does not know if the Account[s] belong[s] to the plaintiff.

13. At the current time, defendant is unable to determine if the Account[s] belong[s] to the plaintiff.

14. Defendant has not yet determined whether the Account[s] belong[s] to the plaintiff.

15. Defendant is still investigating whether the Account[s] belong[s] to the plaintiff.

16. Defendant was notified by Trans Union that plaintiff had disputed the information about the Account[s] with Trans Union on or about the following dates: [September 23, 2004, October 31, 2004 and November 13, 2004].

17. Defendant received one or more CDV form(s) from Trans Union regarding the plaintiff and the Account[s] on or around the following dates: [September of 2004, October of 2004, November of 2004, December of 2004, October of 2004, November of 2004 and December of 2004].

18. Defendant did not receive any documents from Trans Union regarding plaintiff's disputes other than a CDV form.

19. In response to the CDV forms that it received from Trans Union, defendant conducted an investigation of plaintiff's dispute within thirty (30) days of its receipt of the CDV form(s).

20. Defendant was notified by Experian that plaintiff had disputed information about the Account[s] with Experian on or about these dates: [August 28, 2004, October 4, 2004, November 2, 2004 and November 13, 2004].

21. Defendant received one or more CDV form(s) from Experian regarding the plaintiff and the Account[s] on or around the following dates: [August of 2004, September of 2004, October of 2004, November of 2004, December of 2004, October of 2005 and November of 2005].

22. Defendant did not receive any documents from Experian regarding plaintiff's disputes other than a CDV form.

23. In response to the CDV forms that it received from Experian, defendant conducted an investigation of plaintiff's dispute within thirty (30) days of its receipt of the CDV form(s).

24. Defendant was notified by CBA that plaintiff had disputed information about the Account[s] with CBA on or about these dates: [August 28, 2004, October 4, 2004, November 2, 2004, November 13, 2004, October 19, 2005, October 25, 2005 and November of 2005].

25. Defendant received CDV form(s) from CBA regarding the plaintiff and the Account[s] on or around the following dates: [August of 2004, September of 2004, October of 2004, November of 2004, December of 2004, October of 2005 and November of 2005].

26. Defendant did not receive any documents from CBA regarding plaintiff's disputes other than CDV form(s).

27. In response to the CDV forms that it received from CBA, defendant conducted an investigation of plaintiff's dispute within thirty (30) days of its receipt of the CDV form(s).

28. Defendant was notified by Equifax that plaintiff had disputed information about the Account[s] with Equifax on or about these dates: [September 1 2004, October 21 2004, November 13 2004, December of 2004 and January of 2005].

29. Defendant received one or more CDV form(s) from Equifax regarding the plaintiff and the Account[s] on or around the following dates: [September of 2004, October of 2004, November of 2004, December of 2004, January of 2005 and February of 2005].

Defendant did not receive any documents from Equifax regarding plaintiff's disputes other than CDV form(s).

30. In response to the CDV forms that it received from Equifax, defendant conducted an investigation of plaintiff's dispute within thirty (30) days of its receipt of the CDV form(s).

31. In or around [August of 2004 through October of 2004], plaintiff sent correspondence directly to defendant disputing the accuracy of the information defendant was reporting about the Account[s].

32. Plaintiff orally disputed his credit information concerning the Account[s] by telephoning defendant.

33. Defendant does not know whether plaintiff orally disputed his credit information by telephoning defendant.

34. In response to plaintiff's oral disputes, employees from defendant conducted an investigation of plaintiff's dispute.

38. The employees of defendant who participated in investigating plaintiff's disputes and completing CDV forms verified the information that defendant had reported about the Account[s].

39. Defendant's employees sent Trans Union CDV forms that indicated that defendant had conducted an investigation and verified the information about the Account[s] as accurate.

40. Defendant's employees sent Experian CDV forms that indicated that defendant had conducted an investigation and verified the information about the Account[s] as accurate.

41. Defendant's employees sent CBA CDV forms that indicated that defendant had conducted an investigation and verified the information about the Account[s] as accurate.

42. Defendant's employees sent Equifax CDV forms that indicated that defendant had conducted an investigation and verified the information about the Account[s] as accurate.

48. No employee from defendant ever telephoned the plaintiff to verify or question the accuracy of plaintiff's disputes.

49. No employee from defendant ever contacted the plaintiff in any way to verify the accuracy of plaintiff's disputes.

51. No employee from defendant who participated in investigating plaintiff's disputes ever sent any written correspondence to any credit reporting agency other than a CDV form to verify the accuracy of the information that it had reported about the Account[s].

52. No employee from defendant who participated in investigating plaintiff's disputes ever sent any written correspondence to any other person or party other than a credit reporting agency to verify the accuracy of the information that defendant had reported about the Account[s].

53. As part of their job duties, the employees who participated in investigating plaintiff's disputes were required to perform a certain number of investigations within a specified time period as established by defendant.

54. As part of their job duties, the employees who participated in investigating plaintiff's disputes were required to perform a certain number of investigations of consumer disputes per hour as established by defendant.

61. Defendant has written procedures regarding the investigation of consumer credit report disputes.

62. Defendant has written procedures to assure the compliance with and avoid violation of 15 U.S.C. § 1681s-2.

63. Defendant did not remove the Account[s] from plaintiff's credit file within thirty days (30) after being notified by Trans Union that plaintiff disputed information being reported about the Account[s].

64. Defendant did not remove the Account[s] from plaintiff's credit file within thirty days (30) after being notified by Experian that plaintiff disputed information being reported about the Account[s].

65. Defendant did not remove the Account[s] from plaintiff's credit file within thirty days (30) after being notified by CBA that plaintiff disputed information being reported about the Account[s].

66. Defendant did not remove the Account[s] from plaintiff's credit file within thirty days (30) after being notified by Equifax that plaintiff disputed information being reported about the Account[s].

67. Defendant has failed to remove the Account[s] and has continued to report the Account[s] as belonging to the plaintiff.

71. Defendant has posted account information and data for other persons to plaintiff's credit files.

78. At no time during the course of defendant's investigation in this matter did any employee of the defendant ever conduct any handwriting analysis.

79. At no time during the course of defendant's investigation in this matter did any employee of the defendant ever request that plaintiff provide documents corroborating plaintiff's disputes.

80. At no time during the course of defendant's investigation(s) did any employee of the defendant ever examine any of the contracts or credit applications creating plaintiff's alleged obligations on the Account[s].

81. At no point during the course of any of its investigations did any employee of defendant examine any records of the Account[s].

82. None of defendant's employees have ever telephoned any representatives of the credit reporting agencies which have reported the Account[s].

BY: _____
[Attorneys for Plaintiff]

J.5.2 Sample Requests for Admissions (to CRA)

PLAINTIFF'S FIRST REQUESTS FOR ADMISSION TO [CONSUMER REPORTING AGENCY 1]

For purposes of these requests the following definitions apply:

- [Consumer Reporting Agency 1 Alias] means [Consumer Reporting Agency 1].
- *Account 1* means the information relating to a ******* account, as disputed by Plaintiff and which was identified in the complaint in this matter.
- *FCRA* means the Fair Credit Reporting Act, 15 U.S.C. 1681, *et. seq.*
- *FDCPA* means the Fair Debt Collection Practices Act, 15 U.S.C. 1692 *et. seq.*
- *Consumer Report* has the same meaning as defined under the FCRA.
- *Inaccurate* means "patently incorrect" or when it is "misleading in such a way and to such an extent that it can be expected to have an adverse effect."

1. **ADMIT:** [Consumer Reporting Agency 1 Alias] is a "consumer reporting agency" as defined in FCRA.

RESPONSE:

2. **ADMIT:** [Consumer Reporting Agency 1 Alias] has published consumer reports regarding Plaintiff to third parties.

RESPONSE:

3. **ADMIT:** [Consumer Reporting Agency 1] has published consumer reports regarding Plaintiff to third parties containing information about Account 1.

RESPONSE:

4. **ADMIT:** Plaintiff disputed the accuracy of the information that [Consumer Reporting Agency 1 Alias] was reporting about Account 1.

RESPONSE:

5. **ADMIT:** [Consumer Reporting Agency 1 Alias] received Plaintiff's dispute of the information about Account 1.

RESPONSE:

6. **ADMIT:** The document attached hereto as Exhibit A is a true and correct copy of Plaintiff's dispute of Account 1

RESPONSE:

7. **ADMIT:** [Consumer Reporting Agency 1] did not remove the information about Account 1 from Plaintiff's consumer file in response to Plaintiff's dispute.

RESPONSE:

8. **ADMIT:** [Consumer Reporting Agency 1 Alias] published consumer reports regarding Plaintiff on each of the dates set forth in the inquiry section of each consumer disclosures which [Consumer Reporting Agency 1 Alias] provided to Plaintiff.

RESPONSE:

9. **ADMIT:** [Consumer Reporting Agency 1 Alias] published consumer reports regarding Plaintiff to each of the entities identified in the inquiry section of each consumer disclosures which [Consumer Reporting Agency 1 Alias] provided to Plaintiff.

RESPONSE:

10. **ADMIT:** The attached Exhibit B is a true and accurate copy of a consumer disclosure provided to Plaintiff by [Consumer Reporting Agency 1 Alias].

RESPONSE:

11. **ADMIT:** Exhibit A accurately reflects the dates on which and persons to whom [Consumer Reporting Agency 1 Alias] published consumer reports regarding Plaintiff.

RESPONSE:

12. **ADMIT:** [Consumer Reporting Agency 1 Alias] has published information about Account 1 after Plaintiff disputed Account 1.

RESPONSE:

13. **ADMIT:** At this time [Consumer Reporting Agency 1 Alias], has removed the information regarding Account 1 from Plaintiff's consumer file.

RESPONSE:

14. **ADMIT:** Each consumer report published by [Consumer Reporting Agency 1 Alias] after the time that Plaintiff disputed Account 1 through September 12, 2006 contained the information

about Account 1 that Plaintiff had disputed.

RESPONSE:

15. **ADMIT:** Each consumer report published by [Consumer Reporting Agency 1 Alias] between the time that Plaintiff disputed Account 1 and the time that [Consumer Reporting Agency 1 Alias] removed the item from Plaintiff's consumer file contained the information about Account 1 that Plaintiff had disputed.

RESPONSE:

16. **ADMIT:** The information about that [Consumer Reporting Agency 1 Alias] has published about Account 1 inaccurate.

RESPONSE:

17. **ADMIT:** The Account 1 information published by [Consumer Reporting Agency 1 Alias] is untrue.

RESPONSE:

18. **ADMIT:** [Consumer Reporting Agency 1] does not currently know whether Account 1 information published by [Consumer Reporting Agency 1 Alias] was inaccurate.

RESPONSE:

19. **ADMIT:** [Consumer Reporting Agency 1] does not currently know whether Account 1 information published by [Consumer Reporting Agency 1 Alias] was untrue.

RESPONSE:

20. **ADMIT:** Following Plaintiff's dispute, [Consumer Reporting Agency 1] intended that the information relating to Account 1 remain on the report.

RESPONSE:

21. **ADMIT:** Following Plaintiff's dispute, [Consumer Reporting Agency 1]'s representative followed [Consumer Reporting Agency 1]'s policies, procedures, and practices when that representative determined that the information relating to Account 1 should remain in Plaintiff's file.

RESPONSE:

22. **ADMIT:** Following Plaintiff's dispute, [Consumer Reporting Agency 1]'s policies, procedures, and practices operated as intended when [Consumer Reporting Agency 1] determined that the information relating to Account 1 should remain in Plaintiff's file.

RESPONSE:

23. **ADMIT:** No employee from [Consumer Reporting Agency 1 Alias] who participated in investigating the dispute of Account 1 ever sent any written correspondence or documents to any other person or party to verify the accuracy of the information that [Consumer Reporting Agency 1 Alias] had reported about Account 1.

RESPONSE:

24. **ADMIT:** [Consumer Reporting Agency 1 Alias] made a mistake when it allowed information about Account 1 to remain in Plaintiff's consumer file.

RESPONSE:

25. **ADMIT:** [Consumer Reporting Agency 1 Alias] is sorry that it allowed information about Account 1 to remain in Plaintiff's consumer file.

RESPONSE:

26. **ADMIT:** No employee from [Consumer Reporting Agency 1 Alias] who participated in investigating Plaintiff's disputes of Account 1 ever obtained or reviewed any additional documents other than Plaintiff's dispute, and the CDV or ACDV form from the furnisher of the information regarding Account 1 in evaluating the veracity of Plaintiff's dispute.

RESPONSE:

27. **ADMIT:** At no time during the course of Defendant's investigations in this matter did any employee of the [Consumer Reporting Agency 1 Alias] ever telephone Plaintiff to verify or acquire additional information.

RESPONSE:

28. **ADMIT:** At no time during the course of Defendant's investigations in this matter did any employee of the [Consumer Reporting Agency 1 Alias] ever send written correspondence to the Plaintiff to request additional information or verify Plaintiff's disputes.

RESPONSE:

29. **ADMIT:** At no time during the course of Defendant's investigation of Account 1 did any employee of the [Consumer Reporting Agency 1 Alias] ever contact (orally or in writing) any third party (other than sending a CDV or ACDV form) to evaluate, verify or request additional information concerning Plaintiff's dispute(s).

RESPONSE:

30. **ADMIT:** At no time during the course of Defendant's investigation in this matter did any employee of the [Consumer Reporting Agency 1 Alias] ever request that Plaintiff provide additional documents corroborating Plaintiff's dispute of Account 1.

RESPONSE:

31. **ADMIT:** At no time during the course of Defendant's investigation in this matter did any employee of the [Consumer Reporting Agency 1 Alias] ever request that the furnisher of the information about Account 1 provide additional documents supporting the information which it reported regarding Account 1.

RESPONSE:

32. **ADMIT:** In performing its investigations of Plaintiff's dispute of Account 1, [Consumer Reporting Agency 1 Alias]'s employee(s) never considered any of the contracts, account histories, cancelled checks, payment receipts or credit applications creating Plaintiff's alleged obligations underlying Account 1.

RESPONSE:

33. **ADMIT:** [Consumer Reporting Agency 1 Alias]'s employee(s) have never telephoned any representative of the furnisher that provided information about Account 1.

RESPONSE:

34. **ADMIT:** As part of their job duties, the employee(s) who participated in investigating Plaintiff's disputes of Account 1 were

required to perform a certain number of investigations within a specified time period as established by [Consumer Reporting Agency 1 Alias].

RESPONSE:

35. **ADMIT:** Following Plaintiff's dispute of Account 1, [Consumer Reporting Agency 1] prepared consumer reports relating to Plaintiff using the information about Account 1.

RESPONSE:

36. **ADMIT:** Following Plaintiff's dispute of Account 1, [Consumer Reporting Agency 1] published consumer reports relating to Plaintiff which were prepared using information about Account 1

RESPONSE:

37. **ADMIT:** Following Plaintiff's dispute of Account 1, [Consumer Reporting Agency 1] published consumer reports containing information about Account 1.

RESPONSE:

J.6 Sample Notices of Deposition

J.6.1 Sample Notice of Deposition (to Furnisher)—Fed. R. Civ. P. 30(b)(6)

UNITED STATES DISTRICT COURT
IN THE EASTERN DISTRICT OF MICHIGAN
SOUTHERN DIVISION

DAVID CONSUMER,	)
Plaintiff	) Case No.
	)
v.	) Hon.
	)
	) **JURY TRIAL**
TRANSPERIAN, CAPITAL	) **DEMANDED**
BANK OF AMERICA,	)
Defendants	)

NOTICE OF DEPOSITION

Take notice, that the Plaintiff will take stenographic depositions of the following entities or individuals. All deponents must bring all documents listed in the accompanying subpoenas and any attachments, and present the originals of these documents for inspection and copying at the deposition.

1. Capital Bank of America
TIME:
PLACE:

Please note that pursuant to F.R.Civ.P. 30(b)(6), this corporate deponents must designate an individual to testify as to the following matters:

a. All allegations of fact stated in the complaint in this lawsuit.
b. All affirmative defenses asserted by the deponent.
c. Whether or not Deponent's credit reportings to the major credit reporting agencies relating to Plaintiff were accurate and verifiable.
d. Whether or not Plaintiff owes or ever owed money to Deponent.
e. The policies, procedures and practices put in place by the Deponent to insure that the reinvestigations initiated by Plaintiff would result in accurate credit reportings relating to Plaintiff.
f. The definition of "accurate" and "verifiable" as those terms are used in Deponent's reinvestigation process.
g. The net worth of the deponent.
h. The annual revenue of the deponent.
i. The net income of the deponent.
j. The nature and content of any records maintained by the deponent—including archived copies and recorded conversations—relating to the reinvestigation of any trade lines appearing on Plaintiff's credit report.
k. The number of reinvestigations of credit disputes handled by the deponent on an annual basis and economic resources attributable to those reinvestigations.
l. The existence and content of any reports or documents assessing the accuracy or reliability of credit reporting submitted by any furnisher of credit information whose credit data the subject matter of this litigation including any reports to the credit reporting agencies regarding the accuracy and reliability of those reportings.
m. Any quotas or productivity targets for the deponent's reinvestigators of credit disputes.
n. Amount paid to and training provided to the employees responsible for reinvestigating disputed credit reportings made by the Deponent.
o. The documents and informational resources available to the Deponent's employees who are responsible for reinvestigating disputed credit reportings made by the deponent.
p. The budgetary allocation of resources of the deponent to reinvestigations of credit reporting disputes.
q. The existence, nature, and content of any training provided to your employees or agents conducting reinvestigations.
r. The nature, purpose, and means by which requests for reinvestigation are received and by which response may be made.
s. The identity, content, and number of computer systems used to maintain data on consumers, their accounts, collections or applications and the access given to each of those systems.
t. Scope of deponent's employees' authority to correct credit reporting errors.
u. The existence and content of any policy or procedure for handling credit reporting reinvestigations.
v. The documents which are regularly maintained by the deponent relative to any reinvestigation or credit reporting, and the content of those documents relative to the Plaintiff.
w. The identity of any known witnesses to the allegations of fact stated in the complaint or the affirmative defenses asserted by the deponent.
x. The authenticity of any documents identified in any of the disclosures, pleadings, or discovery responses.
y. The identity and expert credentials of any of the deponent's employees or witnesses.
z. Identity of an person participating in the negotiations of the transaction underlying this law suit or events surrounding it.
aa. Any communications between the deponent and the Plaintiff relating to the reinvestigation of any credit reporting relating to Plaintiff.
bb. Any releases or waivers signed by the Plaintiff.
cc. Any insurance or bonding carried by the Deponent.

dd. Any exhibits to be produced at trial.

ee. Any other acts by the deponent which might serve as a basis for amendment or supplementation of the complaint.

ff. Whether or not the Plaintiff is a consumer as defined by the Fair Credit Reporting Act, 15 U.S.C. §§ 1681 *et seq* ("FCRA") at § 1681a(c).

gg. The existence of, date of and receipt of any credit applications from the Plaintiff.

hh. The existence and content of any policies or procedures in place to assure the true identity of any individuals to whom credit is extended.

ii. Whether or not the Deponent regularly furnishes credit information to any credit reporting agencies.

jj. The manner in which the Deponent reports or otherwise furnishes credit information to credit reporting agencies.

kk. The procedures in place at the Deponent to insure that false or inaccurate information is not reported on any consumer's credit report or to any credit reporting agency.

ll. Whether or not the Deponent has reported credit information relating to any of Plaintiff's personal identifiers including but not limited to name, address and social security number.

mm. The time, place, manner, and content of any reporting of credit information relating to any of Plaintiff's personal identifiers including but not limited to name, address and social security number.

nn. The format of the Deponent's credit reportings [e.g.] Metro or Metro II format.

oo. The content of each available data field or segment reported relating to any of Plaintiff's personal identifiers including but not limited to name, address and social security number.

pp. The capability of the Deponent's computer to reproduce records of past credit reportings to consumer reporting agencies.

qq. The policy, practice, and procedure relating to incomplete reporting of the available data fields or segments reported to credit reporting agencies.

rr. Whether or not Plaintiff disputed any credit information, supplied by the Deponent, which reportings related to any of Plaintiff's personal identifiers including but not limited to name, address and social security number.

ss. Whether or not the Deponent received notice from any consumer reporting agency that Plaintiff disputed any credit information, supplied by the Deponent, which reportings related to any of Plaintiff's personal identifiers including but not limited to name, address and social security number.

tt. The time and form in which such dispute was received, and the identity of any persons reviewing or acting on it.

uu. The time, place, and manner in which any actions were taken in response to any such notice.

vv. The steps and measures that were taken in the course of reinvestigating any credit information supplied by the Deponent, which credit information related to any of Plaintiff's personal identifiers including but not limited to name, address and social security number.

ww. The content of any information which was used in order to reinvestigate any credit reporting dispute by Plaintiff's of credit information supplied by the Deponent.

xx. The identity, home address, and phone number of any individual who participated in or supervised any reinvestigation of a credit reporting dispute by Plaintiff's of credit information supplied by the Deponent.

yy. Any steps which were taken to insure that credit reporting information relating to any of Plaintiff's personal identifiers including but not limited to name, address and social security number did not appear on Plaintiff's credit report.

zz. Any remedial steps taken by the Deponent to insure that its trade line did not appear on the credit report of Plaintiff.

aaa. The type and number of matching personal identifiers required by the Deponent's credit reinvestigators in order to confirm or verify the identity of an individual who has submitted a reinvestigation of credit information supplied by the Deponent.

bbb. The existence and nature of the legal relationship between the Deponent and any consumer reporting agencies to which it reports credit information.

ccc. Any conditions under which the Deponent has agreed to make its data available to the any consumer reporting agency to which it reports credit information.

ddd. Whether or not the deponent's actions in relation to its reporting of credit data relating to the Plaintiff was willful.

eee. Whether or not the Deponent willfully failed in its duties to properly reinvestigate credit disputes sent by the Plaintiff to consumer reporting agencies.

fff. Whether or not the Deponent's actions in reinvestigation its credit reporting relating to the Plaintiff was willful.

ggg. The motive and intent of the Deponent's actions in relation to its reporting an reinvestigation of the credit information relating to Plaintiff's personal identifiers.

hhh. Whether or not the account bearing the Deponent's name at issue in this case was opened by or is otherwise the legal responsibility of the Plaintiff.

iii. The existence and location of any documents establishing or tending to establish the responsible party or debtor on the account at issue in this case relating to the Deponent.

jjj. Amount paid to and training provided to the employees responsible for verifying disputed credit reportings made by the Deponent.

kkk. The time, place, and permissible purpose of any access or use of Plaintiff's credit report.

All deponents must bring all documents listed in the accompanying subpoenas and any attachments, and present the originals of these documents for inspection and copying at the deposition.

Respectfully Submitted,

[Attorney For David Consumer]

Schedule A
Items to Bring to Deposition

I. Copies of any credit report relating to or mentioning David Consumer, [Street], [City], LA 59876 including any printouts of electronically stored copy of such reports.

II. Copies of any credit report relating to or mentioning Social Security Number 999-99-9999.

III. Any application for credit submitted by David Consumer.

IV. Any application for credit submitted by any person using Social Security Number 999-99-9999.

V. Any document advising David Consumer of an approval or denial of credit.

VI. Any document advising David Consumer that a credit decisions was adversely affected by any information contained within David Consumer's credit report.

VII. Any memorandum, letter, or other document evaluating the credit-worthiness of David Consumer.

VIII. Any risk factors, credit assessments, and credit scores relating to Social Security Number David Consumer.

IX. Any risk factors, credit assessments, and credit scores relating to Social Security Number 999-99-9999.

X. Any other document upon which any credit decision was made in relation to David Consumer.

XI. Any other document relating to any credit decision made in relation to David Consumer.

XII. Any requests for explanations of any credit information derived from David Consumer's credit report.

XIII. Any policies, procedures, or practices relating to the resolution of credit reporting disputes.

XIV. The personnel file of any person performing any form of credit reporting dispute resolution or reinvestigation in relation to Plaintiff.

XV. Originals of any other document requested previously in discovery.

J.6.2 Sample Notice of Deposition (to Furnisher)—Video Deposition

UNITED STATES DISTRICT COURT
WESTERN DISTRICT OF WASHINGTON
AT SEATTLE

John Consumer and Judy Consumer,	)))
Plaintiffs,	))
v.	)))
Collectech Systems, Inc. and Experian Information Solutions, Inc.,	))))
Defendants.	))

PLAINTIFF'S FRCP 30(B)(6) NOTICE OF VIDEOTAPED DEPOSITION OF COLLECTECH SYSTEMS INC

TO: Collectech Systems, Inc., Defendant
AND TO: Defendant's Counsel,
AND TO: All Counsel of Record

Please take notice that pursuant to CR 30(b)(6) the testimony of Collectech Systems, Inc. ("Collectech") will be taken upon oral examination at the instance and request of the plaintiffs in the above-entitled and numbered action, pursuant to the Federal Rules of Civil Procedure, before a notary public at the offices of [Attorney], [Address], *or at such other place of business to be provided by Collectech upon reasonable notice*, on May 29, 2002. Said oral examination is to be subject to continuance or adjournment from time to time or place-to-place until completed. Collectech shall designate one or more officers, agents or other persons who shall consent to testify on behalf of this defendant with respect to the following matters, on which examination is requested:

1. The facts supporting all COLLECTECH's defenses to plaintiffs' claims.
2. All facts and circumstances relating to the furnishing of credit information by COLLECTECH to all credit reporting agencies to which it reports including, but not limited to, Trans Union Corporation, Trans Union L.L.C. (Trans Union), Equifax Credit Information Services, Inc. (Equifax), Experian Information Solutions, Inc. (Experian) and all affiliates of Trans Union, Equifax and Experian, including, but not limited to the facts and circumstances as follows:
   a. The manner and format in which credit information is reported to each credit reporting agency by COLLECTECH;
   b. All agreements, oral, written or those resulting from custom and practice between COLLECTECH and each credit reporting agency regarding the manner in which COLLECTECH reports information to each credit reporting agency;
   c. All media and/or formats by which COLLECTECH reports credit information to credit reporting agencies;
3. All communication or any document referencing any communication between COLLECTECH and any entity that had any ownership interest in the debt that COLLECTECH was attempting to collect from plaintiffs that references either plaintiff or their personal identifiers;
4. All facts and circumstances relating to communications or contacts between plaintiffs and COLLECTECH (and/or any of its affiliated companies) related to the alleged debt COLLECTECH was attempting to collect from plaintiffs;
5. Any and all communications or contacts with regard to any personal and/or credit information bearing, or listing in connection therewith, any or all of the personal identifiers of Plaintiff(s), by and between you and Trans Union, Equifax, Experian and any affiliate of Trans Union, Equifax and Experian;
6. All facts and circumstances relating to the notification of COLLECTECH by Trans Union, Equifax, Experian and any affiliate of Trains Union, Equifax and Experian of any dispute by plaintiffs with regard to any account;
7. The corporate or company structure of COLLECTECH and all its affiliates, all parent companies, all affiliates of said parent company and all entities that in any manner created, maintained and investigated the collection account(s) allegedly owed by plaintiffs;
8. All facts and circumstances relating to the relationship between COLLECTECH and any entity for which it attempted to collect the alleged debt from either plaintiff;
9. The entity or entities from whom COLLECTECH bought or received the assignment of the alleged debt that it was attempting to collect from plaintiffs;
10. The amount paid by COLLECTECH to purchase the alleged debt it was attempting to collect from plaintiffs;
11. All facts and circumstances relating to the investigation by COLLECTECH of plaintiff's claim including the information as follows:
   a. Who conducted each part of the investigation;
   b. Who was contacted during the investigation;
   c. Each act constituting the investigation(s);
   d. When each act constituting the investigation was performed;
   e. Each document related to the investigation;
   f. Each document consulted or reviewed by defendant in its investigation;

g. Who created each entry on each document related to the investigation;

h. Where each document connected with the investigation is maintained by COLLECTECH and who is the custodian of the document;

12. What the date of last payment on the collection account COLLECTECH was attempting to collect from plaintiffs;

13. The name, creator and characteristics of any software used to maintain records related to any account maintained by COLLECTECH with plaintiff's personal identifiers;

14. All lawsuits filed against COLLECTECH since 1998 alleging violation of the Fair Debt Collection Practices Act or the Fair Credit Reporting Act including their subject matter and terms of their resolution.

15. All complaints filed against COLLECTECH with the Federal Trade Commission related to its practices since 1998.

16. COLLECTECH's use of the METRO 2 format to provide credit data to any consumer reporting agency;

17. How COLLECTECH's practices with regard to plaintiff conform or do not conform with the Credit Reporting Resources Guide published by Associated Credit Bureaus, Inc. and specifically, section 10 of that title attached as Exhibit 1.

18. The fields used by the METRO 2 format for determining the obsolescence period as provided in 15 U.S.C. 1681c;

19. The reporting of all fields in METRO 2 format relating to plaintiff John Consumer including Base Segment, Field number 7, Base Segment, Field number 9, Base Segment, Field number 10, Base Segment, Field number 17A, Base Segment, Field number 24 and Base Segment, Field number 25.

20. All efforts used by COLLECTECH to comply with the obsolescence period in reporting credit data to Experian, Trans Union and Equifax.

Respectfully submitted,
Attorney for Plaintiffs

J.7 Sample Confidentiality Order

UNITED STATES DISTRICT COURT
FOR THE DISTRICT IN YOUR STATE

```
_____ )
CONSUMER,                )
               Plaintiff, )
                         )
v.                       )
                         )
UNKNOWN FINANCIAL        )
SERVICES INC.,           )
              Defendant. )
_____ )
```

PLAINTIFF'S PROPOSED CONFIDENTIALITY ORDER

1. If any motions, briefs, deposition transcripts, or other material to be produced or filed with the Court incorporate documents or information sought to be maintained as confidential, the party filing such papers shall designate such materials or portions as "CONFIDENTIAL" and shall file them with the clerk under seal; provided, that a copy of such filing having the confidential information deleted may be made part of the public record.

2. If some document is to be marked "CONFIDENTIAL," the party so designating the information confidential shall provide an affidavit stating:

a. Precisely what information is designated confidential;

b. the specific reason the information is being designated confidential;

c. the exact harm to the defendant if the information is not kept confidential;

d. a sworn statement that the information is not available to anyone outside the defendant and has never been provided to any credit bureau or member of the Association of Credit Bureaus, Inc., the Federal Trace Commission, any state agencies, subscribers, auditors or separate companies;

e. a sworn statement that each employee who has access to the information is compelled as a condition of employment to sign a document prohibiting disclosure of the information to be made confidential in this action;

f. a sworn statement that the document sought to be made confidential has never been made part of a public record;

g. a sworn statement that no former employee of the party seeking confidentiality has ever had access to the information and then gone to work for any other collection agency;

h. a disclosure of the number of employees who have access to the information sought to be made confidential;

i. a copy of the form nondisclosure agreement signed by each employee with access to the information; and

j. if the information sought to be made confidential relates to software or a method, whether the software is still in use and a patent for the method or software has ever been applied for by anyone.

An example of an acceptable form of this affidavit is attached hereto as Appendix A and a separate affidavit must be completed for every document for which confidentiality is sought. A copy of each affidavit shall be provided to plaintiff's counsel with all documents for which confidentiality is sought.

3. If the producing party is to mark a document "Confidential," it must number consecutively (or Bates stamp) all documents it provides in discovery including the document the producing party seeks to maintain as confidential.

4. All documents, transcripts, or other materials subject to this Order and all information derived from them shall not be used by any person for any business, commercial competitive purposes or for any purpose whatsoever other than solely for the preparation and trial of this action in accordance with the provisions of this Order.

5. Except with the prior written consent of the individual or entity asserting confidential treatment, no information may be disclosed except to the Court and:

a. parties to this litigation;

b. counsel of record and employees of counsel who are assigned to this case;

c. fact witnesses;

d. experts retained for this case;

e. consultants; and

f. current temporary employees of counsel of record.

6. Nothing set forth herein prohibits the use at trial and deposition of any information designated as "Confidential."

7. Any party may at any time object to the designation of any information as "Confidential." Should the producing party and the objecting party be unable to resolve informally any such objection, the producing party through counsel may submit such dispute to the Court for resolution within five (5) business days, excluding Saturdays, Sundays, and court holidays, after receiving written notice from the objecting party that the parties are unable to resolve the dispute. If the producing party does not submit the dispute to the Court within that time, the confidential information will no longer remain confidential. However, until the Court resolves the dispute, the disputed information shall be treated as confidential.

8. Within sixty (60) days after final termination of this litigation, and upon the written request by the party who designated the materials confidential, all documents, transcripts, or other materials afforded confidential treatment pursuant to this Stipulation and Order, including any extracts, summaries, or compilations taken from them; but excluding any materials which in the good faith judgment of counsel are work product materials, shall be returned to the individual or entity having produced or furnished the same at the expense of the party requesting return of the documents.

9. Nothing in this Order affects the rights of any party with respect to its own documents or to information obtained or developed independently of documents, transcripts, and materials afforded confidential treatment pursuant to this Order.

10. Nothing in this Order pertains to making any settlement agreement confidential.

11. If confidential information submitted in accordance with this Stipulation and Order is disclosed to any person other than in the manner authorized by this order, the party responsible for the disclosure must immediately bring all pertinent facts relating to the disclosure to the attention of the party asserting confidential treatment and, without prejudice to other rights and remedies of the party asserting confidential treatment, make every effort to prevent further disclosure by the responsible party or by the person who was the recipient of such information

ORDER

IT IS SO ORDERED.

[Date]
UNITED STATES DISTRICT COURT JUDGE

APPENDIX A

I swear under penalty of perjury to the following information.

1. I am over 18 years of age and I am competent to testify.

2. I am employed by [name of defendant] as [job description]. I am authorized to make the following representations on behalf of [name of defendant]. The defendant seeks to mark a document and information confidential. The document has been Bates stamped by the defendant [number] which is [description of document (e.g. defendant's feasibility study of the Washington market)] and has been conspicuously marked "CONFIDENTIAL" on the front.

3. The information to be protected _____ does not relate to a method and/or software; _____ does relate to a method and/or software (check one).

   a. (If it relates to a method and/or software) a patent has _____, has not _____(check one) been applied for by the party seeking confidentiality.

   b. (If a patent has been applied for) the application is [application number], a patent number [patent number] was issued. Patent(s) for this software or method were applied for in the following countries: [list countries].

4. The specific reason the information/document is confidential is that: [explain reason in detail].

5. The significant harm to the defendant, if disclosed, would be: [explain harm in detail].

6. The defendant safeguards the information contained in the document stamped [Bates number] by: [list each way the secrecy of the information is maintained].

7. Neither the document nor any of the information in the document is available to anyone outside [the party seeking confidentiality] and has never been provided to the Federal Trade Commission, any state agency, any subscriber, any separate company, or any auditor.

8. No former employee of [the party seeking confidentiality] has ever had access to this document and then left the employ of [the party seeking confidentiality] and gone to work for any other defendant to this action.

9. Each employee who works for [the party seeking confidentiality] and who has access to [the document] is required, as a condition of employment, to sign a document prohibiting disclosure of the information to be marked confidential.

10. The number of employees with access to this information is [number of employees].

11. The information the defendant asserts as confidential has never been made part of the public record and has never been produced in discovery without a confidentiality agreement.

12. A copy of the nondisclosure agreement signed by each employee with access to the information is attached hereto.

13. The purpose of this document being marked as confidential is that if [party seeking confidentiality's] competitors were to obtain the information, it would cause severe financial damage to [party seeking confidentiality].

This affidavit signed in [city], [state].

[Name]
[Position]

Witnessed By: [Notary]

J.8 Sample Litigation Documents

J.8.1 Sample Closing Argument

IN THE UNITED STATES DISTRICT COURT
FOR THE DISTRICT OF OREGON

```
_____ )
[PLAINTIFF]              )
               Plaintiff ) [NO.]
                         )
v.                       ) [Date]
                         )
                         ) [City],[State]
TRANS UNION              )
              Defendant  )
_____ )
```

TRANSCRIPT OF JURY TRIAL
BEFORE THE HONORABLE JOHN JELDERKS
UNITED STATES DISTRICT COURT MAGISTRATE

APPEARANCES

FOR THE PLAINTIFFS: [Attorney for Plaintiff]
Attorney at Law

FOR THE DEFENDANTS: [Attorneys for Defendants]
Attorneys at Law

COURT REPORTER: [Court Reporter]

([Date])

EXCERPT OF PROCEEDINGS

(Open court; jury present :)

[ATTORNEY FOR PLAINTIFF]: Thank you, Your Honor. Thank you, lady and gentlemen, for serving on the jury. We appreciate your attention throughout the case. I know some of it has been tedious. There has been a lot of documents, a lot of figures. That's the type of case this is. When I first addressed you, I told you it is a case about [Plaintiff] and the case about credit reports. That's the consumer side. Then on the other side you have the credit reporting agency.

We have Trans Union, one of the biggest credit reporting agencies in the country, headquartered in Chicago, offices around the world, as you have heard paid approximately $200 million a year in their credit reporting business, a company with immense power over people's lives. Credit reports are used everywhere. They are tied to get a loan, to buy a car, to get a loan for a house, used by employers for prescreening and landlords for prescreening, insurance companies to determine your insurance rates.

Trans Union's power to report is really the power to destroy, to control a life. You heard what happened to [Plaintiff]. She almost didn't get her house but through her own work, her hard work and the work of [Name] she did. It is a case about corporate irresponsibility.

The evidence clearly showed that Trans Union doesn't care about the law. It either doesn't tell their people, the people that are in the trenches doing the work, what the law is. They admitted—[Name] admitted that she didn't know important provisions in the law, provisions governing the re-investigation.

We had seen multiple violations of the Fair Credit Reporting Act. I am going to get into more of the details. There is nine. Some of them were violated 15, 18 times. We have seen destruction of documents, important documents that could have helped resolve these matters. It is not just about [Plaintiff]. This is a Trans Union system that affects 200 million consumers.

Now, [Plaintiff] has been disputing her credit report since 1996. You saw all the records, dozens of contacts, paper going back and forth, doesn't get a clean credit report, doesn't get an accurate credit report. She files a lawsuit. Still Trans Union won't give her an accurate credit report. She has never had an accurate Trans Union credit report.

We are asking you to enforce the law. It is a Fair Credit Reporting Act case. That's your job to enforce the law. The Fair Credit Reporting Act allows for a civil action such as this. That's one of the primary ways this law is enforced, through people like you saying: You need to stop breaking the law. You need to comply with the law. It is for the benefit of everyone. All consumers.

Now, the law sets a very high standard for the credit reporting agencies, as it should because of the importance of credit reports. They must follow reasonable procedures to assure maximum possible accuracy. I know you have heard that phrase before because it is a linchpin. There are many other provisions of the Act, but that's one of the broadest.

We saw here there was not maximum possible accuracy. There was never accuracy for [Plaintiff]. The other very important provision of the law that this case is about is the re-investigation provision. A consumer can dispute an item on their credit report. That's the only chance that a consumer has to affect their credit report.

It is all in Trans Union's control except for the right that Congress gave consumers to dispute, and with the dispute comes a responsibility, a very important responsibility of Trans Union to re-investigate that dispute and to do it according to the law. The evidence shows that Trans Union ignores that right, ignores that responsibility. And the result, inaccurate credit reports.

Now, you have heard the facts. I'm not going to go through them in detail, but I just want to highlight some of what we heard, the long, sad story of [Plaintiff]'s plight. And, again, we don't need to go into detail. I'm not going to read any of the exhibits. Remember, it starts in 1996 when she sends her first dispute letter to Trans Union telling them: Don't mix me up with [Name].

And then it is full of bad items. 1999, she sees her credit report and all the Upton things are on it, about 15 items. None of that should be there. None of that is hers. Where is the accuracy? Where are the procedures? She has told them already she is not [Name]. But when she really needs the credit, 1999, she needs a mortgage, the credit report is full of inaccuracies. She does what the law allows. She files a dispute, and they ignore it.

Then we look at her file. It is hard to read, but I know you have seen it before. This is one from February. So this is Trans Union's file at this time, she is also known as Judith she told them. It has got February of 1999. It has got—Upton directly, contrary to what the wrong address.

It is full of all these bad debts. I am not going to show you all of them again. I think you know most of them. There is 15 of them. Things charged off as bad debt. None of that should be there. It is all wrong, and they have already been notified it is wrong. And that's what makes it even worse. Not just are they issuing false credit reports, but she continues to tell them that they are issuing false credit reports. And they won't fix them.

She is seeking her mortgage. She needs to get this resolved. If we move onto the March 8th, she sends the package March 8th, her letter. This is urgent. It needs immediate attention. She explains, again, she is not [Name]. She gives them proof, [Name]' Social Security card. That is rare to get someone else's Social Security card.

You saw the letter from [Name]. She said: I'm not using your number. Here is my Social Security number. We are different. She gets that. She sends it. She tells Trans Union: Just check with the credit grantors. Have them look at who applied for the credit. You are going to see it is not me.

They don't use this information. She sends them her utility bill, her Social Security number and card, her driver's license. Trans Union has said on the stand we did not use this information. We did not send it to the furnishers. We didn't even know we were supposed to. The directors, the president, the vice president, the legal counsel. This is a sophisticated corporation. They have been in this business almost 40 years. They know the Fair Credit Reporting Act. They know they are governed by it, but they don't even bother to make sure that people who are supposed to follow the law, the people that actually implement the law, know it.

So what happens is Trans Union either doesn't know the law, or they ignore the law, or they have a system that simply violates the law as we will see.

Moving on, she includes all the 1996 information. She has kept the records. She wants Trans Union to know she has been through it all before. Trans Union doesn't even have this. They have admitted this stuff is useful. This is important. This would help resolve disputes. But their system destroys documents after 30 months even though information on your credit report stays on forever and at least seven years. Seven years, if it is adverse, but other information stays on forever. So the 30-month policy makes no sense.

Let's move on to the next one. She calls Trans Union. She calls Trans Union. They tell her Texaco is verified. Gulf is verified. CitiBank is verified. They are not her accounts. She contacts those creditors, starts calling them. The only reason those come off is because of her work. Some of the creditors don't respond. But the ones that are verified, she calls them. She gets the letters. She does the work Trans Union is supposed to do.

But she is not making 200 million a year. That's not her job to re-investigate. It is their job. It is Trans Union's job. It is their legal responsibility, but they don't do that.

Providian. This is a great example. They re-investigate Providian. Now, we are in march. TransUnion has admitted that when they got their March package—her March package, they knew that she wasn't [Name]. They said so. At that point they considered it a mixed file. They know she is mixed. Mixed means it is wrong, shouldn't be mixed.

They know she is not [Name]. So we are in March here. So they send out a request to Providian, the one time—the only time that they actually told the creditor she claims this account belongs to [Name]. That re-investigation is pretty close to being valid, to being substantial, adequate. But even when they know she is not [Name], when Providian comes back with the information that says it is under the name [Name], we have got a match here, Trans Union says she is not Judith Upton. Providian comes back and says the account is under [Name], they leave it on.

I mean they ignore the information they have. That's a violation. We will go into the law, but they have to use the information they have. They don't use it. So Providian stays on.

We look at the next page and you—let's move back. By the way, though, you still have other accounts that aren't hers. You have got GTE. We will talk about that. She disputed that three times, and they didn't investigate it. Still on.

If we move to the next one, Bank of America, according to Trans Union's investigation, Bank of America has been verified. But [Plaintiff] has a letter. She has contacted Bank of America. She is giving them the same information that she is giving to Trans Union but Bank of America sends her a letter saying: We will tell the credit report agencies that's not your account. She faxes it. This was her cover letter. She faxed the letter.

So Bank of America comes off. Trans Union's re-investigation fails. [Plaintiff]'s re-investigation succeeds. The only way it comes off, she faxes the Bank of America letter.

Move on to the next one. Move on about a month. She is still disputing it. April 16th. She sends in many letters she has gotten from creditors, including a letter from Mervyn's. This says: No late pays on this account or Scott's account. We will talk about that more. But just remember the evidence showed they fixed it for [Plaintiff's Spouse]'s account. They didn't fix it for [Plaintiff]'s account. They accepted the letter as valid, but they didn't act on it for her.

Lets move on to the next one. She is angry because of the phone call. She sends this letter. You heard [Name] talk about it. You heard [Plaintiff] talk about. [Plaintiff] said: They wouldn't talk to us on a speaker phone even though this is my mortgage broker. They treated me like a debtor, like someone who doesn't pay their bills. Who was at fault? It was Trans Union. But they are treating [Plaintiff] like she did something wrong, like she is a deadbeat. [Name]. They are rude to [Name]. There is no reason for that. They are supposed to be responsive disputes. They are rude to the people.

[Name] and [Plaintiff] is angry about it. She has already gone over her deadline for her mortgage. So she writes this letter and says: You know, what do I have to do? She says—a very important line: I have done everything you have told me to do and still it is wrong. She is frustrated.

The question here is right after this letter comes into Trans Union, the 19th. I think they may it came in on the 20th, but right around that time, the next day or the 21st, they fix Scott's late pays. They delete those from his credit report but not [Plaintiff].

They get the angry letter from [Plaintiff]. They don't fix the credit report, although they have accepted the Mervynls letter as valid. Now, we go to April 27th and Key Bank is re-inserted. Things aren't necessarily getting better. In some ways they are getting worse. They put the Key Bank account—[Name] is still on there. I mean, again, they have accepted that she is not [Name]. They have acknowledged that. They are treating it as a mixed file.

What does that mean they are treating it as a mixed file? It means nothing. They put on a do not confuse statement. Think about that. It says: Do not confuse with people of similar identification, something to that effect. Don't confuse this consumer with somebody else.

What they are putting on the credit report, which they have acknowledged, is that [Plaintiff] is also known as [Name]. So they know she is not [Name], but they are telling the financial world that she is [Name].

The do not confuse statement is essentially do not confuse [Plaintiff]/[Name] with anybody else. It has no purpose. Do they do anything else about it being misfiled except use a code? We will talk about the codes.

Then we go to July 2000. [Name]'s name is still on the credit report. The Texaco account has come back as a collection. But, again, they know she is not Upton. But they continue to lie and tell people she is. We go, again, to October 2001. We are now five years after she has told them that she is not [Name], and they are still telling people she is [Name].

Now, we are over two years over the 1999 dispute, two and a half years when they acknowledged she is not [Name], but they are still lying.

She has filed a lawsuit. She got exasperated. She ends up trying to file a lawsuit to try to get an accurate credit report because all her work doesn't succeed. This is a year and a half after the lawsuit. Nothing seems to change their false reporting.

Now, Judge Jelderks will instruct you about many provisions of the Fair Credit Reporting Act because in this case we have alleged that Trans Union violated nine separate provisions. This isn't a case of one mistake here, one oversight there. Nine separate provisions have been violated.

The judge will tell you that the purpose of the Fair Credit Reporting Act is to govern credit reporting agencies so we can meet the needs for commerce for consumer credit. This is commerce. This is the economy we are talking about. These credit reports are the linchpin of the banking system. You saw that when I first showed you the findings by Congress that credit is essential to the function of our banking system. We know it is essential to our economy. It is important to business.

When there is a false credit report everybody gets hurt. In [Plaintiff]'s situation, think of what happens. There is no sale. The seller gets hurt. The buyer get hurts. The mortgage company gets hurt. Everybody involved in the transaction gets hurt. It is not just [Plaintiff]. This hurts business and every consumer who is subject to this system.

The first provision of the Fair Credit Reporting Act is to ensure maximum possible accuracy. It is a very high standard because of the importance of credit reports. What is the proof? What evidence did you see? Just about everything in this case [Plaintiff] is disputing since 1996, never getting an accurate credit report. Is that maximum possible accuracy? Obviously not. But actually [Name] said this is the maximum possible accuracy that can be afforded under Trans Union's system.

That's their system. This is the maximum. That's not maximum possible accuracy. That's a system that is minimum possible accuracy.

The next provision the Court will instruct you about is that the Fair Credit Reporting Act requires if there is a dispute, Trans Union must re-investigate and complete the re-investigation within 30 days.

I'm simplifying this language and these instructions as you remember the language of the Fair Credit Reporting Act is much longer and a little more complicated. Did Trans Union re-investigate within 30 days? Did they even re-investigate at all? Not the GTE dispute. Again, if it was one mistake, it was one oversight, that might be understandable. But she disputed it three times.

Did they re-investigate the Mervyn's within 30 days and fix it? They re-investigated it. They had the document. They didn't fix it within 30 days. Even the February 19th disputes, those weren't fixed within 30 days. They completed their investigation on March 22d. They make excuses. You heard a lot of excuses because they won't accept responsibility. They won't accept the obligation that they have under the law. They are making $200 million a year. They sure have a responsibility to make that money legally, but they are making it illegally.

The third provision is that Trans Union is required to review and consider all relevant information received from the consumer regarding the dispute.

The evidence, and I'll go into more, is that they violated this provision about 20 times. All 15 disputes in February, they did not use the information that she provided in March. We have Providian, FCNB, Mervynls, the later disputes, they didn't consider all her information. They admitted it. They admitted it. They just disregarded the law.

The fourth provision that they must begin their re-investigation within five days of the dispute. You heard [Name], when I asked about the Providian dispute was received on March 12th with that package, the only thing they did with that March 8th package was start an investigation of Providian. But they didn't start it within five days. She admitted they started it on March 22. Their own records show that, ten days later. They don't even start the re-investigation on time.

That provision also requires that when they do a re-investigation, that they provide all relevant information to the furnisher. That's a linchpin, again, of this act. They can't just contact the furnisher and say: Not minor, inaccurate. If they have more relevant information, they have to tell the creditor. And they don't. They don't use the information they have.

In fact, after three months any information that they have—three to six months—I want to try to be accurate. She wasn't sure. Talked about archiving. After three to six months, information is just archived. That might not be so bad if the operator then looked in the archive to see what the information was about.

When I asked [Name]: Does the operator look at the archive, she said no. That's their system. So after three months information is essentially gone. After 30 months it is destroyed.

The other provision is they must provide the furnisher of the disputed information all relevant information received between the 5th day of the dispute and the 30th day of the dispute. Remember, we talked about this a lot. If there is a pending investigation, then the consumer sends in more information. They have to use it, again. That's going to be very common. If you are going to dispute something, maybe you don't have all the records. Maybe you are waiting for a letter. You dispute it because you want to get the re-investigation going, then you get some document and you send it in because it validates your dispute or it assists in your re-investigation. Exactly what [Plaintiff] did.

She sent in her February disputes. She wanted to get those started. She didn't have all the Upton information with her. It was old. It was in a box somewhere. She dug it out. She sends it in. All her re-investigations are still open. They don't use it, and they don't furnish it. They totally disregard that provision of the law.

They are required to promptly delete her correct information. You saw that. If they find it is incorrect. They didn't do that with the Mervyn's account. Certainly with the [Name] AKA they didn't do that. They would delete it and put it back and kept it on. They knew it was wrong.

Trans Union is required to have procedures to prevent the re-appearance of deleted information. The Court will instruct you that this re-appearance issue—we saw accounts from 1996 that came back in 1999. The Court will instruct you that you shouldn't make an award for any damages that were occasioned by that simply because of statute of limitations issues.

We are not talking about the 1996 re-appearance, although that shouldn't be on her credit report just because that's wrong. That's still a violation under 181681EB. The fact that information is on there still violates the reasonable procedures provision, but we did have re-appearances in 1999. Deleted information. Key Bank came back. The Texaco account that was deleted came back as a collection. They violated that provision.

Next one, they have to give notice of re-insertion. If an account has been previously deleted and it is re-inserted, what Congress said must happen is you have got to notify the consumer. You can't just put something back that you took off. You have got to notify the consumer you are re-inserting it.

So Trans Union sends this letter. I know it is hard to read. This is the notification, April 27th, that we are putting the information back on. I'm not sure of the exhibit number. Exhibit 31. You can look at it if you want. The key here is the Act requires when you send that notice, you have to put the address and phone of the furnisher of the information, if it is reasonably available.

I asked [Name] yesterday: Was the address and phone number of Key Bank, the source of the information, reasonably available? She said: Yes, it was. It is not anywhere in that letter. We talked about that letter. That letter is a form letter. The only thing they change—you can look through it. But there is no address. There is no phone. It simply says: Key Bank has been re-inserted. That's a form that she said—the only thing they change on that form is who it is going to and what account it is about.

Okay. So their form letter is inadequate. This is a systematic violation. Their form letter doesn't even meet the law. Every time they give a notice of re-insertion to anybody it is a violation. That's carelessness. That's just disregard of the law. You make a form letter that doesn't comply. The law is being broken every day because you heard there is approximately 2 million disputes a year.

[Plaintiff] suffered from this. It might seem minor, but she is trying to call all these creditors. You saw all the notes she had it from Key Bank. She had to call Tigard and some warehouse somewhere. It is a big company. You try to call. You are not immediately going to get the person in charge of the credit reporting. That's why Congress said: Give the consumer a number, an address, so they can contact somebody if they want to dispute this or work on it. They didn't give her that. So she had to go through much more work to try to contact Trans Union—to try to contact Key Bank.

They are required to provide results of the re-investigation. This is No. 9. Provide results of the re-investigation, written results, within five days of when they complete the re-investigation. [Plaintiff] testified that she did not get a written summary of the results of her February 19th disputes.

You might remember what she got was results of the Bank of America re-investigation. Now, Trans Union pointed out the credit report itself had the accounts that were still left. So in a way they are saying that's the results because you have got the new credit report. But the law says you should get written notice of the results of re-investigation.

You saw how they did it in 1996. Remember, they had that long list of all the accounts, and it said deleted or verified as accurate. That's how it is supposed to be done. That's how they do it normally because then a consumer can quickly see what happened on each account. They didn't do that for [Plaintiff] in 1999.

Now, there is two claims in this case. Claim 1, that Trans Union negligently failed to comply with the Fair Credit Reporting Act and all those provisions we mentioned. [Plaintiff]'s claim No. 2 is that Trans Union willfully failed to comply with the Fair Credit Reporting Act. On the verdict form those are going to be your first two questions: Did Trans Union negligently fail to comply? And then No. 2: Did they willfully fail to comply?

Let me explain to you what the Court is going to instruct you about what negligently means and what willfully means.

Negligence, the standard is what would a reasonable person do or—what a reasonable person would do under the circumstances that existed. It is the standard we use in any kind of regular negligence case. What's reasonable under the circumstances? Now, Trans Union certainly issuing false credit report after false credit report. Failing to fix. Putting [Name]'s name on and knowing it is wrong. I won't go through all the evidence. They did not act reasonably under the circumstances. They violated nine separate provisions of the Fair Credit Reporting Act multiple times. So it is not simple negligence. It is willfulness.

The Court will instruct that an act is done willfully if it is done knowingly and intentionally or with a conscious disregard for the rights of others. A conscious disregard for rights. In this case, the rights are those rights that are given to every consumer under the Fair Credit Reporting Act. You heard there is a conscious disregard for the consumer's rights, particularly under the re-investigation procedure.

Trans Union just ignores those rights. They either don't have their people know what those rights are so they can't comply with them or they don't follow. They disregard.

Let's look at why this is clearly a case of willful violations and not just negligence as Trans Union completely ignores the key provisions of the re-investigation section. Again, they must consider all the relevant information from the consumer. They have got that information. In this case they got relevant information on March 8th. They were saying to [Plaintiff]: But you didn't tell us in February that you were mixed with [Name]. You didn't tell us in February that you had previous disputes.

Well, one thing is they knew that already because she had disputed it before. But they destroyed the records. So if they had knowledge, they destroyed it.

But they were complaining she hadn't told them that. So she did tell them. She got her old records out and she sent them in on March 8th, just saying what they needed in this trial. They never told [Plaintiff], of course, that they needed that.

She understood. She wasn't getting action. She could see her mortgage was not going to make it. So she sent them the relevant information, the information that they agreed would be useful, and they ignored it. I mean that's a clear violation. The law requires that they review and consider all of that, and they ignored it.

Then they knew it was a mixed file. Right at that point they have admitted it was a mixed file. She was not [Name], but they continued to act as if that didn't matter. They might as well have shredded her March 8th package along with all the other documents because they didn't use it.

She has 15 pending disputes at that time. You heard those re-investigations were not completed. They started at some point after February 19th, hopefully within five days. We didn't look into that, but they started some time in February. They were still pending, and the law requires they consider that information. They didn't use that information in the pending re-investigations at all, not one. Not one out of 15.

Did they use that information? That's 15 violations right there. If they used that information and used it properly, they would have taken all those accounts off. That's what they wanted. That's what she needed. That's what the law required. But they didn't use it at all.

Again, not just consider—not only do they have to consider and review it, but they must provide it to the furnisher. Now, we are in that section, you know, where you supplement your dispute. She sent that in between the 5th day and the 30th day. So not only were they required to review it and consider it, they were required to send it to key bank, Bank of America, AVCO, Gulf state, CitiBank, Texaco, on and on, 15 different creditors should have received that information. Those creditors then would have known about the mix with [Plaintiff] and would have responded appropriately.

They didn't provide that information to any of them, not to one. Now, [Plaintiff] provided it on her own. I think at this point she knows that Trans Union is not doing their job. She has got to do it. She learned that in 1996. You heard their dispute manager. She didn't even know they are supposed to do this. Their dispute department manager doesn't even know the essential procedure for re-investigation under the Fair Credit Reporting Act. What kind of company would have their people that are doing it not even know what they are supposed to do? I mean that is blatant, conscious disregard of the law.

What they do know, they don't do it properly. We saw that.

During trial and [Plaintiff]'s case you heard what happened. You heard about all the bad credit reports or attempts to fix it, the inability to get it fixed. You saw her side, what happened.

But when we saw Trans Union's case, we saw why it happened. We saw inside this company. You were lucky and privileged because you are on this jury. Because this case was brought by [Plaintiff] who stood up and said they shouldn't get away with breaking the law. They hurt me. Their system is bad. This is a violation.

She took a stand for everyone, for all consumers, and brought this case. Because she did Trans Union came up here, and we saw why they violated this law, because they don't care about it. They don't know it. They ignore it. We saw that. It was shocking. It was shocking when [Name] admitted she didn't know the provisions of the law that she is required to execute.

It is a system designed to fail. Even when they do the re-investigation, the system won't work. You heard that the dispute goes out from one department and then it comes back in another department and the other department doesn't even know what the dispute is or the essentials. You heard [Name] testify that Providian, the one case where they told the furnisher that she claims she is not [Name], the response came back, the account is Judith Upton, it gets verified. She said probably because the operator that received the response didn't know that she was being mixed with [Name]. What kind of system is that? It is a system designed to fail. To separate that kind of information is to not use that kind of information.

When the receiving person doesn't know what the dispute is, the system won't work. That's their system, and it is not just [Plaintiff]. That's what was so important about the evidence and [Name]'s testimony. This isn't a case of [Plaintiff]. It is a case of their system that affects 200 million people. That's what is really sad. That's why you have got to do something.

This reliance on the Social Security number, I mean, first off, why does it matter? They admitted in March she is not [Name]. So when the account comes in and it says [Name] they say: But we are looking at the Social Security number. But you already agreed and admitted they are mixed. Again, it is the operator and the system that doesn't make any sense.

Also, relying on the Social Security number as just the essence of a match despite things being wrong, [Name] even agreed that because of the prevalence of identity theft and fraud and using a false Social Security number that system increases the possibility of mistakes.

They need to check more identifiers. Trans Union admits Social Security fraud is rampant. We saw the figures, 500,000 complaints for Trans Union in 1996. You saw that chart of Mr. Hendricks. It is a ramping up. It started at 30,000 in the early '90s. It is to 500,000 by 1997; '99, 7- or 800,000. Today, maybe over a million. So it is reckless to rely on Social Security number when they are not reliable, and they knew anyway she wasn't Judith Upton.

You heard Mr. Hendricks' testimony, Trans Union has been aware of these problems, aware of mixed files, aware of identity theft. What did we see? They are not doing anything to fix their system. They are aware of these problems. They ignore them. That's intentional violations. You know a problem exists, you won't fix it, so the credit reports continue to be inaccurate.

GTE, another evidence of willfulness. The GTE dispute, she disputed February 4th They ignored that entire dispute. They said that wasn't specific enough. But her complaint was—her complaint didn't have any specificity. They re-investigated. But the February 4th they didn't investigate.

You heard [Name] talk about the kind of quality we expected from the people at Trans Union. She ignored that.

The February 19th dispute, GTE, by [Plaintiff], they ignore it. The March package, the GTE dispute, they ignore it. If it happened once, I grant you maybe it is an oversight. But three times? To ignore it over and over again? That's disregard of their obligation under the law.

Now we have the AKA of [Name]. They put it on her credit report. It is wrong. They know it is wrong. This is, again, why their admission that on March 8th they knew it was a mixed file is so important, and it is so obvious because she gave them the information on March 8th that it was a mixed file and she wasn't Upton. They knew it. They admitted that. But they put Upton on anyway. I mean they take it off for a couple of weeks, but they put it back on. They know it is false, and they put it back on.

She has proved to them that she is not Judith Upton, and they are telling the creditors that she is. They should be telling the creditors she is not. But they are telling the creditors she is [Name] when they know that is wrong. It is simply a lie. They are selling a lie. They are selling those credit reports with information that they know is false, and they won't stop, not for two more years. They are continuing to do it through 2001.

Trans Union lied. They lied there. They lied to [Name]. You heard [Name] testify in that April 19th phone conversation. They said you need a date form. Trans Union said you need a date form. You heard [Name] say the form, she doesn't have that. That's what the banks use. That's what the companies use to report into Trans Union. That's a data processing form. All a consumer has to do is send in a dispute. They have to send in a dispute saying which account is disputed and why they are disputing it.

But Trans Union is lying. Crystal, she is saying you need this, we can't help you. It is your problem. Get me the date form. Otherwise, I don't want to talk to you. And she wouldn't talk to her. Even though she was authorized to.

You didn't see any Trans Union employees—there are a couple of high level employees—but you didn't see any employee that worked on this file. No one came into court and said that anything that [Plaintiff] or [Name] said was inaccurate.

Next thing. They verify accounts under Judith [Name]'s name. Again, I have already gone through that. They knew she wasn't [Name], but the information came in under a different name and they verified it. They knew she wasn't [Name] by March 8th, but they verified disputes after that date that were under [Name]. It only came off because of [Plaintiff]'s work. She is doing their job. She is doing the re-investigation. They are making 200 million a year.

827

Next item is this refusal to fix Mervyn's. Again, the letter comes in. It says that Scott and Judy Thomas' account should have no late payments. Comes in on April 16th. On April 19th [Plaintiff] writes her angry letter. She is upset. She is frustrated. She complains about Trans Union's process, not fixing and then they fix only Scott's and not Judy's. That's evidence of malice. That's evidence of intent to harm [Plaintiff]. They try to give excuses.

You heard [Name] say, well, no, the April 16th letters came in, and there were other disputes in there. When I asked her, show me the other disputes that came in April 16th. She couldn't. I asked her: So [Plaintiff's Spouse] and [Plaintiff] disputes on April 16th should have been handled the same. She said yes. But they weren't handled the same. No, not after [Plaintiff] wrote a letter complaining to Trans Union.

Re-inserting accounts that were deleted. Again, that's a violation. This information is inaccurate. They know the Texaco account is wrong. They deleted it in 1999. They put it back on. It is a collection account now. There was no evidence of any method to keep that from coming back. Accounts are often sent to collection. Bad accounts are what go to collection. Bad accounts, negative entries are what hurts you.

All the times that you have got an account that is on your credit report, they delete it. Well, that creditor is trying to get the money. Well, somebody opened that account. They send it to collection. Then when the collection agency reports on it, it is back on your credit report.

We could see it was the same account. We could see Texaco was reported. Texaco was reported as the original creditor, and the account number was virtually the same. It had a MKM on there. I don't work on the credit reporting business. I could see it was the same account. [Plaintiff] could see it was the same account. Trans Union knew it was the same account, but they put it back on.

There is conscious disregard of consumer rights. There is so many violations that we can't even name them all. But Trans Union admitted that they didn't start re-investigations within five days. They didn't complete them within 30 days. Their system is to archive information after three months and after 30 months to destroy it.

Let's talk about the codes a little bit. You heard a lot about the codes. That's what they punch in. So when a consumer sends in a dispute, they punch in 01 if it is not mine. If it is a mixed file, you get an 02 code. That's not mine; do not confuse the person with similar identification.

It is so much easier, and [Name] admitted it is quicker and easier to use the code. That's why they do it. Yes, it is cheaper. It is faster. Use the code. There is more profit if you just punch a button than if you follow the law and provide all the relevant information to the furnisher. Consider all the relevant information.

That takes a little more time. So that costs more money. So that means less profit. So they are just going to punch the code. You saw they punched that code. 01 for virtually all her disputes. That's not even the right code. After they know it is a mixed file, it should be 02, which is still inadequate.

But I showed that excerpt for Providian. They didn't use the 02 code. Remember at the very end I showed the FCNB re-investigation. In April, a month after they know she is a mixed file, they are using the 01 code.

If you can get those re-investigations done quick, those operators, they can meet their quota. They have got to do nine an hour. They can pump in that code. Maybe they can do 15 an hour. Maybe 20. Maybe they can get those incentives and those awards. [Name] commented that for workers, these are really important to them. Our lowly workers, they can get to dress casual. So those workers want to get those awards, and they will use the fast way that Trans Union says they can. They will use the easy way, not the legal way.

It is a system designed to minimize inaccuracy. They testified that when there is more than one dispute, they won't update the credit report until all the disputes are completed. This is very important. Think about that. You have got this dispute. Let's say you have five. You dispute them all on day one. Okay. On day five one of the furnishers—let's say they get the dispute out quickly. Let's say they get the re-investigation out on day five. On day ten it comes back, delete.

So account No. 1 should be deleted on the tenth day. They are waiting for the other responses. They won't fix account one until all the responses are in and the process is completed. That's 30 days. You saw it. They don't take less than 30 days. They usually take more. So even though they have got in evidence that account one should be deleted on day ten, they are going to continue to send out credit reports with account one not fixed until the 30th day. That's minimizing the accuracy because for the next 20 days there is going to be false credit reports.

When someone disputes it, that person is disputing on day one. Usually when someone disputes it is because they are seeking a loan. They are seeking credit. They are seeking a job. They want to fix an error. They shouldn't have to wait 30 days. That's a system designed to maximum inaccuracy. They are going to put out false credit report for another 20 days under my scenario. That's what happened with [Plaintiff].

Trans Union simply broke the law. That's why you are here. That's why this case was brought, to enforce the law. Trans Union doesn't care. It ignores its legal responsibility. These days we need to hold corporations responsible. No more irresponsibility, breaking the law. You need to comply with the law. You have the power to enforce that law.

Congress told Trans Union the standard it needs to meet, and you can hold them to that standard. We talked about destruction of documents, but it wasn't just documents over 30 days old. There were CDVs that were destroyed. There were some accounts that were automated CDVs. But even the automated CDVs, there was that information that came in, narrative information that came in. Where is that? Why isn't it in a computer. It is automated. They destroyed that. They destroyed the hard paper CDVs. Even documents within two years they destroyed so we didn't see that evidence. The less evidence, the less chance someone will have to sue and succeed.

Now, [Plaintiff] kept good records so she has got the evidence, but Trans Union doesn't keep the evidence. That helps them to fight these kind of lawsuits. Trans Union is making $200 million a year breaking the law. It is corporate greed. It is corporate irresponsibility. It is time to put a stop to it. How many consumers have been hurt by Trans Union's misconduct? How many have had false credit reports?

Again, we see it is not [Plaintiff]; it is their system. They disregard the law. They have a system that doesn't work. [Name] testified—I read parts of her deposition—I know it is not always very important and you might not have heard every word, but she testified that they followed the standard procedures for handling [Plaintiff]'s disputes, the standard procedure. This is how everybody is treated.

Damages. Let me talk a little bit about damages. What happened to [Plaintiff] shouldn't happen to anyone. Everyone has got rights under this act, and they need to be respected. There are two types of damages that you can consider: Actual, which are also we have known as compensatory to [Plaintiff] for her damages and her injuries, and punitive damages.

The Fair Credit Reporting Act allows actual damages which include nonmonetary losses. Congress understood that a bad credit report doesn't simply cause financial loss. It causes damage to reputation. It causes mental anguish, distress. It causes embarrassment, humiliation. I will go through the list.

So the law is very broad. It allows all different types of damages. [Plaintiff] here didn't suffer a major financial loss because of her own work. She couldn't afford to. She couldn't afford to lose that $5,000 deposit. So she worked and worked and worked and got that house.

The only reason she doesn't have big losses financially is because of her, not because of Trans Union, but she has other damages. Congress says those can be award to her. Judge Jelderks will instruct you on the different elements of damages to be considered. They include denial of credit. Loss of opportunity to obtain credit. Damage to reputation. Financial loss. Mental anguish. Anxiety. Humiliation.

I'll be putting some of those up here so we can talk in more detail, and he will instruct you that for you to award damages, you need only find that the damage that—that the violation was a substantial factor in causing the damage. It doesn't have to be the only cause. As long as it is a substantial factor, their violation is a substantial factor in causing damage, then you can award damages.

You heard a lot about [Plaintiff]'s damages. You heard from her about the stress, the frustration, the anxiety she went through dealing with all these problems. She had to contact all these creditors, and it wasn't easy. The only reason she had to contact those creditors is because Trans Union put this false information on her credit report. Remember that. She didn't have CitiBank on there. She didn't have Texaco on there. She wouldn't need to call them. She wouldn't need to go through all that work and sometimes very stressful work. The risk of losing the mortgage. You heard about those damages.

[Name] testified, too, about damages. She said she thought [Plaintiff] would have a heart attack. You heard [Plaintiff] testify how she would be in tears. You heard Dr. Beaman's testimony. Dr. Beaman said she was under a lot of stress, April 1999. Yes, it got to the point where [Plaintiff] went to a doctor. She had some other conditions. She had hypertension. She had hyperlipidemia. She went to a doctor and said: I'm under a lot of stress.

He testified that that stress aggravates those conditions. I think we all know that high blood pressure, stress makes it worse. Hypertension is high blood pressure. The doctor is saying this stress aggravated her existing conditions.

Now, the Court will instruct you that you cannot award damages based on events before May 26th, 1998. That is simply that under the law the date she filed the complaint, which was in May of 2000, you go back two years. You heard about things from 1996. So she gets damages from that.

That was simply to put this case in perspective so you would know that Trans Union knew about the Upton mix-up in 1996, to help you better look at their conduct in 1999. Because if you are on notice of a problem, you obviously have more responsibility to fix it than if you are not. So the 1996 information came in just so you could see the history.

Damages you can just go back to May, 1998. So we're looking at about the last four years. I just wanted to—

[ATTORNEY FOR DEFENDANTS]: Your Honor, can I request that counsel put this where I can see it.

THE COURT: Feel free to move over to one of the chairs on the far side.

[ATTORNEY FOR DEFENDANTS]: Thank you, Your Honor.

[ATTORNEY FOR PLAINTIFF]: Denial of credit, that's our first category the Court will instruct you on. And the mortgage. She couldn't get her mortgage when she needed it. That's her main problem, denial of credit. But she is getting bad credits reports going out. They are going out. They are going to people. Not getting offer for credits. She testified she doesn't have confidence in the credit reporting system. She knows at this time she can't go in and get credit. So she has got denial of credit.

Mortgage opportunity. Just call it opportunity. Reputation. It is very important, reputation, because that's what your credit report is. Your credit report is your financial reputation. Right there on that piece of paper that's what people see. Anybody you want to get credit from, you are going to get the credit report.

You saw her credit report went out to various businesses, retailers, banks. You saw her credit report went to insurance companies, GEICO, Allstate. They assess credit reports, too, in determining their insurance rates. So her credit report goes out to the business world. But another thing is her reputation in her world, her world being a realtor in [City] because she was buying this house. She was working for VIP Real Estate. Her boss knew, because they were the brokers on it. And then this other company she ended up going to work for, they were the realtor for the seller.

Then there is a woman, [Name]. All these other people, they know [Plaintiff]. She is a realtor. She is trying to sell houses. She can't even get credit to buy her own house. That damages her reputation in her own business. Her job is helping people buy houses or sell houses, one of the biggest financial decisions anyone ever makes.

She also refers people to lenders, as realtors often do so they can get the financing for the home. In her world in [City], in that small town, they know that she can't even get her own loan. Who is going to refer a client to her? It is a small town. You heard her. There is like one WalMart. It is a nice town, but it is small. Word gets around. That's the environment she is in. Her reputation gets damaged and her profession, her career is damaged.

She said that she noticed her boss—I think it was Jerri Riddell—treated her differently when she learned about those credit reports. She said she is in a room full of people and she feels inferior. She knows it is not deserved. It is not hers, but it is real. She can't get a mortgage. She is not the same person. She is not thought of the same way. A reputation, that's really important. It is important to everybody to have a good reputation.

Next category, mental anguish. That's pretty much a legal term. I think everybody considers that stress. Anxiety. The judge will talk about anxiety. Lawyers often use the words "mental anguish," and she had that. She had that over and over again and you heard about it. Almost every contact with Trans Union was stressful because it wasn't helping. Trans Union was not very nice about it.

Stress about her mortgage. Stress about losing her down payment. Stress every time she contacted Trans Union. Stress every time she saw an incorrect credit report, which was virtually every credit report, going on now for four years. And it will continue. She continues to have stress. She has no confidence in Trans Union's credit reporting system. Why should she? She has seen it fail for her. So she continues to have stress.

She is not confident she can go in and get an accurate credit report. It continues and it will continue. Stress from dealing with the creditors, trying to clean it up. Some creditors are nice; some creditors weren't so nice. But, again, she wouldn't have been talking to them at all if Trans Union hadn't put the false information on her credit report.

You heard [Name] testify she thought she would have a heart attack. Tears. [Plaintiff] mentioned she went home in tears. Other days she had information. Some new phone numbers gave her a reason to keep plugging away. She worked on this all the time. Month after month. Month after month, stress. Goes to the doctor. Then it becomes years.

After this lawsuit, she is still getting bad credit reports. Now we are four years we are talking about. I know it is hard to put numbers on these type of damages. It is up to you to decide amounts. We will talk a little bit more about some ideas that we might suggest. But that's part of your job as a jury to award a fair amount of damages, but don't let Trans Union get away with this. They hurt her. She should get fair damages for what they did.

Loss of self-esteem. You heard her talk about that. Self-esteem. She didn't have that. She felt inferior. Loss of financial independence. She doesn't want to have to rely on her husband. She is a businesswoman. Always has been independent. She always had good credit before this.

Mixing confidential information. Her information was mixed with [Name] so information went out. It wasn't hers. Information went out about her to people she wasn't dealing with. You saw Providian and other companies got her credit report. It wasn't hers that they were dealing with. That causes stress. Now that's her privacy. That causes stress. She knows her private information is going out where it shouldn't. It is being sold by Trans Union. Remember that, they are not giving that information away, that false information. They are selling it.

Hours spent fixing. I think I skipped one here. Well, under the mental anguish you got her health. It affected her health. You heard Dr. Beaman's testimony. It aggravated her high blood pressure, her hyperlipidemia. I guess we can call it work. Work to fix. All the time, all those letters. You saw the documents. I think it was 15 exhibits. I think they are Nos. 43 to 55, which are all the communications to AVCO, Bank of America, CitiBank, Emporium, Key Bank, Texaco, Providian. It just goes on and on and on. They are all in this.

All that work, all that time writing back to Trans Union, getting responses from Trans Union. All that work. Let's move on. The credit report only got better because of her work. Remember that, not because of Trans Union's system.

Now, next area of damages—I will move that over a little bit. Next area I want to talk about is punitive damages. Congress allowed recovery of punitive damages under the Fair Credit Reporting Act. It did it for a reason, because credit reports were so important. Not every federal law allows recovery of punitive damages. Most consumer protection laws don't in the federal system.

The Fair Credit Reporting Act is one of few that does because credit reports are so important. Remember, I showed you those findings of Congress and talked about credit reporting agencies have grave responsibilities to exercise their credit reports to make sure those credit reports are accurate. Grave responsibilities.

So that's why you can consider punitive damages. This is a case you need to award punitive damages because for a big company like Trans Union, that's the only language they understand. That's the only thing that is going to get them to change.

Nine provisions violated repeated times. Blatant disregard of the law. They are breaking the law. Don't let them get away with it. Punish people. That's our system. If someone breaks the law, they should be punished. That's the American system of justice. They broke the law. They should be punished. It is just that simple. You can be the prosecutor. That's your responsibility.

The Court will instruct you on the burden of proof. This is a legal term. [Plaintiff] has the burden of proof. She has to prove her case. The evidence shows she has proved her case. She has proved negligent non-compliance with the Act. She has proved willful non-compliance with the Act.

They admitted they ignored the law. They either don't know it or don't follow it. [Name] admitted that. All [Plaintiff] has to do is prove that it is more likely than not that the greater weight of the evidence proves her violations. We are not in criminal court here. It is not beyond a reasonable doubt. It is just greater weight of the evidence.

Think of it like a scale. You have got a scale, two sides of the scale. All the plaintiff has to do is tip it to her side. As long as the greater weight of the evidence proves these violations, she should win. It is like 51 percent or maybe 50.1 percent, just the greater weight of the evidence. That's the standard. It is a civil action, so the standard is only a preponderance. That's very important.

She has had overwhelming evidence. Maybe beyond a reasonable doubt. But you don't even need to think about that. So it is only preponderance.

Now, the Court will instruct you that the purpose of punitive damages is to punish the defendant, to deter the defendant and others from committing similar acts in the future. So there is three aspects. Let's talk about each one.

The first one, punish Trans Union. Yes, punish Trans Union. They broke the law. They should be punished. You are not going to let them get away with that. You are not going to let them get away with disregarding the Fair Credit Reporting Act. You must punish them for their violations of the law, their system that disregards the law, their continuing violations.

Again, how many people have suffered under this system? How many bad credit reports? They have been aware of this problem for years. They haven't fixed it. In fact, they just don't fix it. They just go on. It is cheaper, it is faster, it is more profitable to continue the system where they don't re-investigate properly or they don't have procedures to assure maximum possible accuracy. So that deserves punishment.

You heard [Name] say they get about a million requests a day, inquiries for credit reports. Maybe they are not all for credit reports. But a million a day. I think that is requesting information from Trans Union. So they are selling 300 million. 400 million credit reports a year and making $200 million doing it. They shouldn't get away with profiting when they are breaking the law. That's not just. That's injustice. That's an injustice to everyone. You know to enforce that law. Don't let them take home those ill-gotten gains. Take something away. We will go through some numbers. They are a rich company. They are worth almost half a billion dollars. They have accumulated that money breaking the law.

Second, and this is very important, you can punish them—excuse me. You cannot just punish them. You can award damages to deter them from doing this in the future. That's more important in a lot of ways. Sure, they should be punished. That's our system. You break the law, you are punished, but you can prevent them from doing it in the future, hopefully, if you punish them severely enough. We all know that.

A mild punishment people don't change. A severe punishment, people change. You can make them change. You can make them follow the law and protect every consumer, but you can only do it by awarding punitive damages in a number that will affect them. It is a big company. A couple hundred thousand dollars is nothing to them. It is like pennies to anyone else. So you are going to have to get a number that is going to get the attention of Chicago in the board room. Because if you don't award punitive damages, why will they change? They will walk out of here and go: Hey, we don't have to change. The jury didn't punish us. The jury didn't say we were breaking the law. That's why punitive damages are in here. That's the enforcement a prosecutor in a criminal case can enforce with a fine or people going to jail. Under the Fair Credit Reporting Act the only way you can enforce is with punitive damages. That's your tool. That's the power you have. And that's our jury system.

Third, not just to deter Trans Union from this kind of conduct but to deter others. You take your responsibility seriously. I know you do. You can do some good by awarding punitive damages. The other credit reporting agencies will hear that, and they will be on notice, too. They better do it right. You will send a message to the whole industry that they have got to comply with the law. You will be helping everybody. It is really a chance to do some real good. That's the civil justice system. It is unique in the world. It is the best.

You hear complaints about juries sometimes. You are the jury now. You have seen the evidence. So you can decide. You can make them obey the law and benefit everyone.

Now, the Court, again, is going to instruct you no damages prior to May, 1998. So it is real simple. You are just talking about the last four years. That's what we're talking about. You punish them for their conduct from then, May, 1998, through the present, all the false credit reports from that time she has gotten. Everybody you have seen. Their disregard of the law. Don't let that interfere. That's a line we draw. You have got four years. You punish them for what they did. You punish them for what they are doing. You punish them to keep them from doing it any more.

You tell them that they have to obey the law. We all do. We live under the rule of law. We all must obey it. No one should profit from breaking the law.

Now, Judge Jelderks will instruct you in considering the amount of punitive damages you should look at four things: The purpose of the Fair Credit Reporting Act. We have already talked about that. The purpose is to make sure we have an efficient commercial system, an efficient banking system, because our whole system depends on credit. The purpose of the Fair Credit Reporting Act is to make credit reporting agencies meet a high standard so that system functions so people get the credit they deserve so the reputation is preserved so there is accuracy.

The nature of Trans Union's conduct, we talked about that. That's the other thing you are going to consider in setting the amount, the nature of Trans Union's reprehensible conduct. They are not following the law. They didn't even try. They don't even tell the people who are taking the actions what it is in some cases. You heard that. That's corporate irresponsibility.

The other factor you need to look at is Trans Union's income, a very important factor, because it takes a very different penalty to affect different people. You look at that net worth. Their income is 234 million in 1999, the year the second set of disputes started. I think it was 181 in 2000. 167 million—about 200 million a year if you average it out. That's after paying all salary and expenses. That's their income after taxes. That's not gross. That's net. After they paid all their bills, they have paid all their people, that's the income they made.

Okay. Let's look at that. So they are making 200 million a year. They are not following the law. 200 million, okay, you go back to 1998, under the Court's instructions, and let's look at the last four years. So you have 200 million times four. Approximately they make 800 million over these four years. They shouldn't keep all that money. It is time to hold them accountable for their illegal conduct. We also have a net worth here, worth, 396, I think, is the number. 396.

So what they have done over time, they have accumulated assets of almost 400 million for not following the law. You need a verdict, a punitive verdict, that is going to get the attention of the boardroom up in Chicago. If you give something small, they are going to have middle management write a check. Nothing is going to change. You need to get their attention. We need them to change. They can't get away with breaking the law. They can't follow it. That's your job. That's your responsibility, your power to tell them to stop.

If nothing changes, how many more people are going to get hurt? How many consumers are subject to this system? 200 million subject to this system. How many false credit reports? How much damage to economy, business, to people's reputations, to people's livelihood, people's peace of mind?

I talked about everyone is hurt. Everyone in the transaction is hurt if the credit report is bad. The landlord is hurt if the tenant doesn't get the apartment. The tenant is hurt. The bank is hurt. The seller is hurt. The lender is hurt. The car dealer is hurt. Everybody is hurt by these false credit reports, not just the consumer. Trans Union has refused to accept the responsibility placed on it by Congress. It doesn't care about the law. You have seen the evidence. The evidence clearly showed that. Most of it is from Trans Union's own people.

Trans Union has immense power. The power to report is the power to destroy. They have got their CEOs and CFOs and board of directors and lawyers up there in their skyscraper in Chicago. You can't touch them. The average person, [Plaintiff], she tries. You can't touch them. You can't get through to them. The only time the average person can make a big company like this change, to make a big company like this obey the law is right now: You, the power of the jury.

That's our great system. That's why they hate courts so much. They hate jury trials because they know now there is a level playing field. We can't hide behind all our wealth and power. Eight people are going to decide, and this is your only opportunity. You have that power now, only now. You won't have it when you leave this jury room and you go back to your normal lives. You will be the average person. You won't have the power to make them change. So take advantage of that opportunity.

You are the prosecutor. There is no prosecutor here. There is no district attorney here. There is one on the sixth floor, but you are the district attorney now. You are the prosecutor. You are the person who will enforce the law to make sure that there is justice. That's our system.

It is a unique opportunity for you to do something positive to benefit everybody and to turn the tide on this corporate irresponsibility. Tell one company, one big company: You are going to stop. We are going to make you stop. We have seen too much of that. We have seen too much corporate irresponsibility. You have seen it in this courtroom. It is time to say no more. You can do that.

800 million. What about 1 percent? 2 percent? It is really a small number. What's 1 percent. 1 percent is 8 million. 2 percent, 16 million. You can go on. 24 million. It sounds like a big number 8 million, 16 million. Some of you probably think, well, hey juries they give these numbers, and they seem too, too big. But look who you are dealing. $800 million.

Let's say you have a criminal, a fraudulent person does some nasty business, and they make $100,000. All right. A person makes $100,000 doing an illegal business. Okay. What's 1 percent of that? $1,000. It is nothing. I mean that's what you got to look at. I don't think anybody here would think if someone did an illegal business and made $100,000, if I penalize them $1,000 that would be too high. It only works in relation to what they are making.

So 8 million, 1 percent, that's not too high. That's like 1,000 for someone who made $100,000 for breaking the law. It is up to you. You have the power and you make the decision as to what is an appropriate amount of punitive damages.

Now, compensatory damages. Let's look back at the denial of credit, reputation, mental anguish, health, all the time working to fix it. It is harder to put numbers on these. You should give a fair amount. Don't let Trans Union get away with what they have done. It is so hard. Mental anguish, four years, $50,000, $100,000. What provides peace of mind? What price is your health? $25,000 for health problems? Work to fix all that aggravation, all that time? I don't know. I'm throwing numbers for you to consider. You decide.

Reputation. It is so hard to put a price on your reputation, your good name. It is hard to know. 10, 50, $100,000. What's your reputation worth? It is worth a lot because your good name is what you have. Yes, I agree the last couple of years her credit reputation has gone down. She broke her ankle. You heard about that. She didn't pay her bills on time—she paid them on time. We are not blaming that on Trans Union, but she continues to be called [Name].

She continues to have her reputation damaged. She continues to have false items on credit reports. Denial of credit. Mortgage opportunity. What's that worth? Lost opportunities, not being able to get credit? 25,000. I don't know. You can add them up.

Whether it is $100,000, $200,000, $300,000, that's for you to decide. We just ask that you give her a fair amount. Give her an adequate amount. Let Trans Union know that they hurt somebody; that they have to pay.

You will get a verdict form. This probably isn't warmed up yet. You will get the verdict form. You will look at it. The first question is: Has [Plaintiff] proved by a preponderance of the evidence that Trans Union negligently failed to comply with the Fair Credit Reporting Act?

Second, has she proved that they willfully failed to comply? I ask that you answer yes. Yes, they negligently failed to comply. Yes, they willfully failed to comply.

The evidence leads to no other conclusion. Just a preponderance; just more likely than not. That's all you have to look at. Do we have more evidence of willfulness than not? It is clear with these repeated, multiple violations, their own admission that they don't follow the law.

Then it goes on to damages. I have given you some numbers there, but I just want you to take your responsibility seriously. Realize that you can do some good; that you can enforce the law; that you can protect everybody; that you at least try to stop this company from breaking the law and punish them. You have the power to do justice, enforce the law and tell Trans Union that they can't get away with breaking it.

Thank you.

(End of requested excerpt of proceedings.)

I certify, by signing below that the foregoing is a correct transcript of the recorded proceedings in the above-entitled cause. A transcript without signature is not certified.

_____   _____
[Name]   DATE
Official Court Reporter

J.8.2 Jury Instructions—Reinvestigation

THE COURT: Ladies and gentlemen, now that you have heard the evidence and argument of counsel, it becomes my responsibility to instruct you on the law applicable to this case. I give a general charge in all civil cases, and then after I give a general charge, I will instruct you on the substantive law that governs this case.

On the assumption all you of you aren't so gifted you can remember verbatim what the substantive law is, you will have a copy of that to take back in the jury room, and I will give you further guidance as we go along.

You aren't to single out any one of my instructions as being controlling, but you are to consider them as a whole. And irrespective of any thoughts that you might have as to what the law ought to be, it would be a violation of your oath if you disregarded what The Court had to say and applied some law that you thought would be more appropriate.

You have been chosen as jurors, and you took an oath that you would try the issues that have been raised by the pleadings and the evidence, and the public expects you to do your duty without bias or prejudice and to render justice in the case between these litigants.

Also, under our system all entities that appear in a court of law are entitled to be treated equally, and it doesn't make any difference whether it is a corporation that is organized in Delaware or Virginia, or it is an individual against a corporation or an individual against a partnership. They are all entitled to the same even-handed justice at the hands of a jury.

The burden is on the plaintiff in a civil action such as this to prove every essential element of her claim by a preponderance of the evidence. Now, preponderance of the evidence is a quantitative concept. All of you have seen the blind lady holding the scales of justice. As she holds those scales they are always in perfect balance. And whenever someone has the burden of proving something by preponderance of the evidence, it means that they have, their evidence tilts that perfect balance every so slightly in their favor. And that is a preponderance.

There are generally speaking two types of evidence from which a jury may properly find the truth as to the facts of the case. One is direct evidence, such as the testimony of an eye witness. And the other is independent or circumstantial evidence, which is the proof of a chain of circumstances pointing to the existence or nonexistence of certain facts. As a general rule, the law makes no distinction between direct and circumstantial evidence. And, ladies and gentlemen, bear in mind that the system recognizes that the eight of you bring to the jury box your accumulated common sense of a lifetime, and we expect you to use your common sense in reaching a decision in this case, just as you do on a daily basis in making other important decisions.

Exhibits are considered direct forms of evidence. Arguments and statements of counsel are not evidence, unless the attorneys enter into a stipulation, and if they enter into a stipulation you can accept that stipulation as a fact in the case.

From time to time in their arguments the lawyers may have stated what law was applicable to the case. If what they made reference to differs from what The Court said, disregard what they had to say altogether and literally apply the law as stated by The Court. Also, the lawyers from time to time may have made reference to what the witnesses testified to. If their recollection differs from yours, then ignore entirely what they said and make your own determination. But we have so much confidence in the jury system that we rely a hundred percent upon you to make a determination of the facts in the case.

You as jurors are the sole judges of the credibility of the witnesses and the weight that their testimony deserves. You may be guided by the appearance and conduct of the witness or by the manner in which the witness testifies, or by the character of the testimony given. You should carefully scrutinize all the testimony, the circumstances under which each witness has testified, and every matter in evidence which tends to show whether a witness is worthy of belief. Consider each witness' intelligence, motive, and state of mind and demeanor and manner while on the stand. Consider the witness' ability to observe the matter to which the witness testifies, and whether the witness impresses you as having an accurate recollection of these matters. Consider, also, any relation each witness may bear to each side of the case, the manner in which each witness might be affected by your verdict, and the extent to which, if at all, each witness is either supported or contradicted by other evidence in the case.

Inconsistencies or discrepancies in the testimony of a witness or between the testimony of different witnesses may or may not cause you to discredit such testimony. Two or more persons witnessing an incident or transaction may see or hear it differently. And innocent misrecollection, like failure of recollection, is not an uncommon experience. In weighing the effect of the discrepancy, always consider whether it pertains to matters of importance or an unimportant detail and whether the discrepancy results from innocent error or intentional falsehood. After making up your own judgment, you will give the testimony of each witness such weight, if any, as you think it deserves.

On occasion it was suggested that a witness may have given a prior inconsistent statement when the witness' deposition was taken in a prior situation. If such is shown, it could be considered for purposes of impeaching the witness' testimony. Before discounting a witness' testimony for this reason you ought to consider whether the inconsistency was of a minor, insignificant nature, or something material to the case.

A verdict cannot be based upon surmise, speculation, or sympathy for either party, but must be based solely upon the evidence and the instructions of The Court.

Now, that concludes my general charge, and while you breathe a collective sigh of relief I will take a drink of water, and then I will instruct you on the substantive law.

The plaintiff, [Plaintiff], is suing the defendant, MBNA America Bank, N.A., for damages alleging that the defendant negligently and willfully violated the Fair Credit Reporting Act, 15 U.S.C. section 1681. The plaintiff claims that the defendant violated the Fair Credit Reporting Act because she claims that after receiving notice from three credit reporting agencies that the plaintiff was disputing the identity and balance of an MBNA account. The defendant failed to review all of the information provided by the credit reporting agencies, failed to investigate the plaintiff's disputes, and failed to report back to the agencies the result its investigation. The defendant denies that it violated any provision of the Fair Credit Reporting Act. The defendant claims that it reviewed all of the information provided by the credit reporting agencies, investigated the plaintiff's disputes, and reported back to the these agencies the results of an investigation. The plaintiff claims first, that the defendant negligently failed to comply with the Fair Credit Reporting Act in failing to review all of the information provided by Experian, Equifax and TransUnion; failing to conduct a reasonable investigation of her disputes, and failing to accurately report back to these agencies the result of its investigation. To establish her claim that the defendant negligently failed to comply with the Fair Credit Reporting Act the plaintiff must establish the following elements by a preponderance of the evidence: One, that the defendant negligently failed to, A, conduct an investigation with respect to the disputed information B, review all relevant information provided by the consumer reporting agencies; or C, report the results of the investigation to the consumer reporting agencies; and two, that the plaintiff was damaged; and three, that the negligence of the defendant proximately caused the damage suffered by the plaintiff.

Your verdict will be for the defendant if you find that the plaintiff fails to establish any one of the three elements.

Negligence as used in these instructions means the failure to do something which a reasonably prudent person would do, or the doing of something which a reasonably prudent person would not do under the circumstances which you find existed in this case.

It is for you to decide what a reasonably prudent person would do or not do under the circumstances as they existed in this case. In other words, you must determine whether the defendant's investigation of the disputed information was reasonable. The term "proximate cause" as used in these instructions means that there must be a connection between the conduct of the defendant that the plaintiff claims was negligent and the damage complained of by the plaintiff, and that the act that is claimed to have produced the damage was a natural and probable result of the negligent conduct of the defendant.

If your verdict is for the plaintiff on the claim of negligent non compliance, then your duty is to determine the amount of money that reasonably, fairly, and adequately compensates her for the damage that you decide resulted from the defendant's failure to comply. Whether the element of damages has been proved by the plaintiff is for you to decide based upon evidence and not upon speculation, guess or conjecture. Damages for embarrassment, humiliation and mental anguish will not be presumed to have occurred, but the plaintiff must prove that they did occur, and the plaintiff, while it is not obligated to prove it with mathematical precision, they must give you sufficient raw material so that you can make an intelligent estimate of it. And, also, the burden is on the plaintiff to mitigate her damages, and if you feel that any evidence shows that she had an opportunity to lessen those damages and she didn't take advantage of it, then you can take that into consideration, also.

The plaintiff's second claim is that the defendant willfully failed to comply with the Fair Credit Reporting Act in failing to review all of the information provided by Experian, Equifax and TransUnion. Failing to investigate her disputes and failing to report back to these agencies the result of its investigation to establish her claim that the defendant willfully failed to comply with the Fair Credit Reporting Act the plaintiff must establish the following elements by a preponderance of the evidence. Bear in mind we are now talking about willfully doing something, whereas the first claim was negligently doing something. That the defendant willfully failed to, A, conduct an investigation with respect to the disputed information; B, review all relevant information provided by the computer reporting agencies; or C, report the results of the investigation to the consumer reporting agency. If the plaintiff fails to prove one of these three, A, B or C, you should find your verdict for the defendant.

The term "willfully" as used in these instructions means that the defendant knowingly and intentionally committed an act in conscious disregard for the rights of the consumer and not by mistake or accident or other innocent reason. A showing of malice or evil motive is not required to prove willfulness. MBNA was required to conduct a reasonable investigation. Factors to be considered in determining whether MBNA has conducted a reasonable investigation include whether the consumer has alerted MBNA that its information may be unreliable; and two, the cost of verifying the accuracy of the information versus the possible harm of reporting inaccurate information. The standard for such an investigation is what a reasonably prudent person would do under the circumstances. And evaluating the reasonableness of MBNA's investigation involves weighing the potential harm from inaccuracy against the burden of safeguarding such inaccuracy. The damage that [Plaintiff] may recover for MBNA's alleged failure to investigate a claim of inaccuracy of the record or to report the results of its investigation may not include any damages that were caused by the inaccuracy of the information itself.

Damages to be recoverable are limited to those, if any, arising from a willful or negligent failure to conduct any investigation or to report the results. Damages recoverable for willful noncompliance with the Fair Credit Reporting Act are two kinds. First, there are damages that are actually suffered by reason of the wrong complained of. Second, there are punitive damages, which means damages over and above the actual damages, if any, suffered by the plaintiff. These are damages that may be awarded by you in your discretion for the purpose of punishing the defendant for the wrong done. Punitive damages also serve as an example to others not to engage in such conduct. If you find that MBNA willfully failed to follow reasonable procedures in its investigation of the plaintiff's dispute, you must award her the actual damage she sustained as a result of the defendant's failure. If you find that MBNA willfully failed to follow reasonable procedures in its investigation, and also find that the plaintiff suffered no actual damage or actual damages of less than a hundred dollars, then you must award the plaintiff at least a hundred dollars, but not more than one thousand dollars.

If you as a juror further find that the acts or omissions of the defendant that proximately caused the actual injury or damage to the plaintiff were willfully done, then you may, if in the exercise of your discretion, you unanimously chose to do so, add to the award of actual damages such amount as you shall unanimously agree to be proper as punitive damages. Whether or not to make any award punitive damages in addition to actual damages is a matter exclusively within your province.

You should bear in mind not only the conditions under which and the purpose for which the law permits an award of punitive damages to be made, but also the requirement of the law that the amount of such punitive damages must be fixed with calm discretion and sound reason, and must never be either awarded or fixed in amount because of any sympathy, bias or prejudice with respect to any party. You may consider the defendant's net worth in connection with punitive damages, and I believe their net worth at 12/31/01 was 7.7 million. And also under the law there should be a rational relationship between punitive damages, if you elect to award any, and the plaintiff's actual damages.

The Fair Credit Reporting Act is not required, does not require that credit card account records, including original applications, be kept in any particular form; however, the law does prohibit MBNA from maintaining its record in such manner as to consciously avoid knowing that information it is reporting is accurate.

A corporation may act only through natural persons as its agents or employees, and in general any agent or employee of a corporation may bind the corporation by his acts and declarations made while acting within the scope of his authority delegated to him by the corporation, or within the scope of his duties as an employee of the corporation.

If a corporation has established a standard of procedure for the accomplishment of an act, it is relevant to proving that it acted in a specific instance in conformance with that standard of procedure. And here again, you have heard evidence that everybody is getting electronic now days, and it is up to you to decide whether that is a reasonable way to conduct your business or not.

Now, that concludes my substantive charge.

[ATTORNEY FOR DEFENDANT]: May we approach?

BENCH CONFERENCE

[ATTORNEY FOR PLAINTIFF]: It is 7.7 billion.

THE COURT: Did I say million? I meant billion.

[ATTORNEY FOR DEFENDANT]: I think on instruction number 12 you said "accurate" instead of "inaccurate."

THE COURT: Okay.

[ATTORNEY FOR DEFENDANT]: And you had something that was not here, not printed, but you put in something, if the "plaintiff," sounded like "the defendant," had failed to prove. If you will instruct the plaintiff has the burden on everything.

THE COURT: I told them that the plaintiff failed to prove.

IN OPEN COURT

THE COURT: On my instruction number 12, ladies and gentlemen—you will have a copy of it—counsel tells me that I used the word "reporting is accurate," and it should have been "inaccurate." You will have it in printed form.

Isn't that your complaint, counsel?

[ATTORNEY FOR DEFENDANT]: Yes, Your Honor.

THE COURT: All right.

Your first order of business when you go back in your room is to select a foreperson. It is that individual's responsibility to preside over your deliberations and see that each juror is given full opportunity to express their views and participate in your verdict. The verdict must ultimately be unanimous. The foreperson's vote counts no more than any other. You will have in addition to the charge a verdict form. It says, we, the jury, unanimously find as follows. Did the defendant MBNA negligently fail to comply with the reporting act? It has, yes, no. If you answer yes, proceed to question two. If the answer is no, proceed to question three. And then, did the defendant's conduct proximately cause plaintiff's damage? If yes, you plug in a number. And then you would go to whether MBNA willfully failed to comply with the Fair Credit Act. And then you have the same sort of questions after that.

Now, from time to time during the course of your deliberations you may need to communicate with The Court. If you do, Mr. Winn will be sitting outside the jury room. Knock on the door and he will come in. And if you have a question, that should be in writing and signed by the foreperson. If it's something I can help you with, I will bring you back in and give you further guidance. Also, after you have reached a verdict, the foreperson has to sign it and date it. Knock on the door and let Mr. Winn know you have reached a verdict. I will bring you back in and receive it and send you home. I leave it up to jurors to determine their work hours after they start deliberating, but I will tell you now that if you haven't reached a verdict by 6:30 or 7:00 I will send you home for the evening because they close down here at night, and I don't want you to freeze up there in the jury room.

Everyone remain seated while the jury departs. And see that you take your handouts with you because you will now need those.

I will get you the instructions back in due course.

(Jury withdrew)

THE COURT: Before you put anything else on the record, let me warn you that I am about to go into some arrangements, and I would hate to mistake you for one of the defendants in the case. So do you have anything further to put on the record, [ATTORNEY FOR PLAINTIFF]?

[ATTORNEY FOR PLAINTIFF]: No, Your Honor.

THE COURT: [ATTORNEY FOR DEFENDANT].

[ATTORNEY FOR PLAINTIFF]: Although I didn't do it.

THE COURT: All right.

[ATTORNEY FOR DEFENDANT]: No, Your Honor, just so the record is clear that I was complaining about a minor mistake, that my main objections to the instructions were preserved.

THE COURT: Right. And you renew those for purposes of the record.

[ATTORNEY FOR DEFENDANT]: Right.

THE COURT: All right, fine.

Recess court for five minutes, and just leave your things in place, counsel. They don't need to be displaced.

Tell them we are ready to proceed with the arraignment.

(Recess)

THE COURT: Counsel, I have a question from the jury. What is the total amount of the outstanding credit debt in dispute as of 1/21/03? That is a simple question. What is the number? But what is the last dun you got from the parasitic outfit that buys this kind of paper?

[ATTORNEY FOR PLAINTIFF]: $20,300.

THE COURT: Okay. Is your client being dunned for that by whoever bought the paper?

[ATTORNEY FOR PLAINTIFF]: Yes.

THE COURT: Huh?

[ATTORNEY FOR PLAINTIFF]: Yes.

THE COURT: Okay. Bring the jury in. I will tell them the number is—

[ATTORNEY FOR DEFENDANT]: I want to object to answering that question.

THE COURT: Fine. Your objection is now a matter of record.

[ATTORNEY FOR DEFENDANT]: This is not a collection action. We don't even own the debt. So obviously if they are going to use that number for something, it would be to do a quotient verdict on something that is irrelevant.

THE COURT: That is fine.

[ATTORNEY FOR DEFENDANT]: I object to answering the question.

(Jury took its place in the well of the court)

THE COURT: Who is the foreperson? All right. Fine.

I have your question. What is the total amount of the outstanding credit debt in dispute as of 1/21/03? That figure is $20,300. But let me tell you the MBNA sold that to one of these outfits that pays a certain sum, and then I guess they are the ones that take over, sort of a parasitic way. You pay a small sum for it, and then you try to collect the whole thing. But, bear in mind any action that is brought against her, she has defenses to it, that they still have to prove that she is liable for it on the account. That would be the burden of the purchaser of the paper for MBNA. Does that answer your question?

THE FOREPERSON: Yes.

THE COURT: Right.

Because they are doing their own collecting work. If they think somebody owes it, they get to sell it to one of these discounts, and then that outfit goes after them.

A JUROR: Thank you.

THE COURT: Okay.

(Jury withdrew)

[ATTORNEY FOR PLAINTIFF], put any dissatisfaction that you have to The Court's instructions on the record, if you like.

[ATTORNEY FOR PLAINTIFF]: We do not have any objection.

THE COURT: All right.

[ATTORNEY FOR DEFENDANT], do you want to renew yours?

[ATTORNEY FOR DEFENDANT]: I would renew the one I made before they were brought in. And then I would add that I object to the general explanation of things being beyond the scope of this case.

THE COURT: All right. Fine.

Adjourn court awaiting furthered word from the jury.

(A recess was taken)

(Jury took its place in the jury box)

THE CLERK: Mr. Foreperson, has the jury reached a verdict in this matter?

THE FOREPERSON: Yes, we have.

THE CLERK: Please hand it to the Marshal.

THE COURT: Publish the verdict.

THE CLERK: [Plaintiff], plaintiff, versus MBNA America Bank, N.A., defendant. Civil action number [No.]. Verdict form. We, the jury, unanimously find as follows:

Number one, did the defendant, MBNA, negligently fail to comply with the Fair Credit Reporting Act?

Yes.

Number two. Did the defendant's conduct proximately cause the plaintiff to suffer damage?

Yes.

If yes, what amount of actual damage did the plaintiff suffer? $90,000.300.

THE COURT: $90,300.

THE CLERK: 90,300.

Number three. Did the defendant fail to comply with the Fair Credit Reporting Act?

No.

Number four. Do you find that punitive damages are warranted under these facts?

No.

Signed by the foreperson, [Jury Foreperson], January 21st, 2003.

Ladies and gentlemen, was this your unanimous verdict?

THE COURT: Any motion while the jury is in the box?

[ATTORNEY FOR DEFENDANT]: Would you pole the jury?

THE COURT: Pole the jury.

THE CLERK: Ladies and gentlemen of the jury, if this was your verdict, please respond by saying "yes."

Juror number two, [Juror 2].

A JUROR: Yes.

THE CLERK: Juror number 3, [Juror 3]?

A JUROR: Yes.

THE CLERK: Juror number 6, [Juror 6]?

A JUROR: Yes.

THE COURT: Juror number 8, [Juror 8]?

A JUROR: Yes.

THE COURT: Juror number 10, [Juror 10]?

A JUROR: Yes.

THE COURT: Juror number 17 [Juror 17]?

A JUROR: Yes.

THE COURT: Juror number 20, [Juror 20]?

A JUROR: Yes.

THE COURT: Juror number 24, [Juror 24]?

A JUROR: Yes.

THE COURT: Ladies and gentlemen, that completes your assignment, but before I discharge you I want to express The Court's appreciation for your services, and also commend you for the conscientious manner in which you accepted your responsibilities and discharged them.

[Jury Foreperson], I want to single you out for special thanks, because you accepted the added responsibility of being foreperson, and you kept your forces together and deliberating until such time as they reached a verdict.

Leave all of your handouts in the jury room. My staff will see they are put in a shredder and, that will be the end of them.

Thank you for your services, and now that you have some experience under your belt, don't beg off if you get notified that I need more jurors in the future. All right.

Everyone remain seated while the jury departs.

Thank you for a job well done.

(Jury withdrew)

THE COURT: Judgment will be entered on the verdict. I want to thank counsel for your cooperation and helping to expedite the case so that the jury had it presented in a reasonable period of time and you didn't convert it in to a marathon sort of operation.

J.8.3 Jury Instructions—Mixed File

[PLAINTIFF] v. TRANS UNION L.C.C.

[Action No.]

JURY INSTRUCTIONS

[Date]

Members of the jury, you have now heard all the evidence in this case and it is now your duty to decide the facts and reach your decision.

I will tell you the law which you must follow in reaching your decision. Although you may think the law is, or should be different, you are bound by your oath to apply the law that I give to you.

Your decision must be based solely on the evidence. Do not allow bias, prejudice or sympathy to influence you. The evidence consists of the testimony of the witnesses, the exhibits you will have in the jury room and the facts to which the parties have agreed.

As I have earlier advised you, the comments of the attorneys are not evidence. If your recollection of the evidence differs from that of the attorneys, rely upon your own memory.

You are the judges of whether the witnesses were telling the truth when they testified. In considering the testimony of any witness, you may take into account:

(1) The opportunity and ability of the witness to see or hear or know the things testified to;
(2) The witness' memory;
(3) The witness' manner while testifying;
(4) The witness' interest in the outcome of the case and any bias or prejudice;
(5) Whether other evidence contradicted the witness' testimony;
(6) The reasonableness of the witness' testimony in light of all evidence; and
(7) Any other factors that bear on believability.

You should not decide a fact merely by counting the number of witnesses or exhibits. The testimony of one witness whom you believe is enough to prove any fact in dispute.

In evaluating the evidence, you may consider the power of each side to produce evidence. If weaker and less satisfactory evidence is offered by either party when it appears to you that stronger and more satisfactory evidence was within the power of that party to produce, the evidence offered should be viewed with distrust.

Evidence may be direct or circumstantial. Direct evidence is direct proof of a fact, such as testimony by a witness about what the witness personally saw or heard or did. Circumstantial evidence is proof of one or more facts from which you could find another fact. You should consider both kinds of evidence. The law makes no distinction between the weight to be given to either direct or circumstantial evidence. It is for you to decide how much weight to give to any evidence.

Experts may give opinions on those subjects in which they have special skills, knowledge, experience, training or education. You should consider each expert opinion in evidence and give it whatever weight it deserves. Remember, you decide all the facts. If, in reaching an opinion, you find that an expert relied on certain facts, and you decide that any of those facts were not true, then you are free to disregard the opinion.

Defendant Trans Union is a corporation. Corporations can only act through their officers, agents, or employees. Here, you are to consider any actions by Trans Union employees or agents as the actions of Trans Union.

All persons are equal before the law, and corporations, whether large or small, are entitled to the same fair and conscientious consideration by you as any other persons.

Plaintiff [Plaintiff] must prove her claims by a preponderance of the evidence. "Preponderance of the evidence" means the greater weight of evidence. It is such evidence that, when weighed with that opposed to it, has more convincing force and is more probably true and accurate. If the evidence on that claim appears to be equally balanced, or if you cannot say upon which side it weighs more heavily, you must resolve that question against plaintiff upon whom the burden of proof rests.

This case arises under the fair credit reporting act. One purpose of this Act is to require that credit reporting agencies adopt reasonable procedures for meeting the needs of commerce for consumer credit in a manner which is fair and equitable to the consumer, with regard to the confidentiality, accuracy, relevancy, and proper utilization of such information in accordance with the requirements of the law.

Plaintiff [Plaintiff] is a "consumer" entitled to the protection and benefits of the fair credit reporting act, and defendant Trans Union is a credit reporting agency. The Act allows consumers to recover damages for negligent or willful violations of the Fair Credit Reporting Act committed up to two years before a lawsuit is filed.

Plaintiff [Plaintiff] filed her lawsuit on May 26, 2000 therefore, defendant Trans Union is liable only for violations of the Fair Credit Reporting Act, if any, committed from August 18, 1998, to the present. You have heard evidence about events occurring *before* May 26, 1998, only to help you better understand the events and conduct of the parties from that date to the present.

Plaintiff [Plaintiff] contends that Trans Union violated one or more of the following nine requirements of the Fair Credit Reporting Act:

1. The Fair Credit Reporting Act requires credit reporting agencies like defendant Trans Union to maintain reasonable procedures to assure maximum possible accuracy of credit information concerning the individual about whom the reports relate.

2. The Fair Credit Reporting Act requires that if a consumer disputes the completeness or accuracy of any item of information contained in their file and notifies the agency directly of such dispute, the agency shall reinvestigate free of charge and record the current status of the disputed information, or delete the item from the file within 30 days from the date the agency receives notice of the dispute.

3. The Fair Credit Reporting Act requires a credit reporting agency to review and consider all relevant information submitted by the consumer in conducting any reinvestigation of disputed information.

4. The Fair Credit Reporting Act requires that within five business days of receiving a consumer's notice of a dispute, the credit reporting agency shall provide notification of the dispute to the business which provided the disputed information and shall include all relevant information regarding the dispute that the agency has received from the consumer.

5. The Fair Credit Reporting Act requires that a credit reporting agency shall promptly provide to the business which provided the disputed information all relevant information regarding the dispute that is received by the agency from the consumer between the 5th day and the 30th day after receiving notice of the dispute.

6. The Fair Credit Reporting Act requires that if after any reinvestigation information is found to be inaccurate or incomplete or cannot be verified, the credit reporting agency shall promptly delete the information from the consumer's file or modify the information, as appropriate, based on the results of the reinvestigation.

7. The Fair Credit Reporting Act requires a credit reporting agency to maintain reasonable procedures designed to prevent the reappearance in a consumer's file or in consumer reports on that consumer, of information that has been deleted pursuant to reinvestigation. This section of statute does not apply to information that was deleted in 1996.

8. The Fair Credit Reporting Act requires that a credit reporting agency provide notice to the consumer if any information that has been deleted pursuant to a reinvestigation is reinserted in the file. Notice must be in writing no later than five business days after the reinsertion. A notice must include the business name and address of any furnisher of information contacted and the telephone number of such furnisher, if reasonably available, or of any furnisher of information that contacted the credit reporting agency, in connection with the reinsertion of such information.

9. The Fair Credit Reporting Act requires that a credit reporting agency provide written notice to the consumer of the results of a reinvestigation not later than five business days after the completion of a reinvestigation. As part of or in addition to that notice the credit reporting agency shall provide to the consumer in writing a consumer report that is based upon the consumer's file as that file is revised as a result of the reinvestigation.

Plaintiff contends that defendant Trans Union *negligently* or *willfully* failed to comply with the fair credit reporting act. I will define these terms for you.

Negligence is failing to do something that a reasonably prudent person would do, or doing something that a reasonably prudent person would not do, under the circumstances that existed.

An act is done willfully if it is done knowingly and intentionally, or is committed with a conscious disregard for the rights of others.

Defendant Trans Union denies that it negligently or willfully failed to comply with any requirements of the Fair Credit Reporting Act.

I instruct you that the law does not require defendant Trans Union to produce error-free credit reports. Instead, in order to prevail on her claim for money damages, [Plaintiff] must prove by a preponderance of the evidence:

(1) That there were errors in one or more of her credit reports;

(2) That the errors resulted from a violation of one or more of the nine requirements of the Fair Credit Reporting Act listed above;

(3) That the violation or violations of the Act resulted from the negligence or willfulness of defendant Trans Union; and

(4) That she suffered damages as a result of the negligence or willfulness of defendant Trans Union.

If you find that the plaintiff has proven that defendant Trans Union negligently or willfully violated the Fair Credit Reporting Act, you must then determine the damages, if any, to which she is entitled. However, you should not infer that the plaintiff is entitled to recover damages merely because I am instructing you on the elements of damages. My instructions on damages do not reflect in any way whether I believe the plaintiff should or should not win this case. It is exclusively your function to decide upon liability, and I am instructing you on damages only so that you will have guidance in the event you decide that the plaintiff is entitled to recover.

If you find that defendant Trans Union negligently or willfully violated the Fair Credit Reporting Act, and that as a result [Plaintiff] suffered damages, then your duty is to determine the amount of money which reasonably, fairly, and adequately compensates her for the actual damage that you decide was caused by the defendant's failure to comply with the Act.

In order to recover damages, plaintiff must establish that defendant's violation of the Fair Credit Reporting Act was the "legal cause" of her injuries. The term "legal cause" requires that the conduct of defendant Trans Union which plaintiff claims violated the Fair Credit Reporting Act must have been a substantial factor in causing the injury complained of by the plaintiff, and that the injury must have been either a direct result or a natural and probable consequence of the conduct of the defendant. A substantial factor is an important or material factor and not one that is insignificant. The elements of damages which you may consider are: financial loss, denial of credit, loss of opportunity, damage to reputation, mental anguish, embarrassment, humiliation, anxiety and depression.

Which, if any, of those elements of damages has been proven by Plaintiff is for you to decide, based upon evidence and not upon speculation, guess or conjecture. The amount of money to be awarded for certain of these elements of damages, such as mental anguish, cannot be proved in a precise dollar amount. The law leaves the determination of such amount to your sound judgment

In determining the amount of actual damages to award to Plaintiff [Plaintiff], if any, I remind you that you have heard testimony and evidence about events that occurred before May 26, 1998. No damages can be awarded based on events which occurred before May 26, 1998. You are permitted to examine those earlier events for the limited purpose of placing the relevant events in perspective and to evaluate events after August 18, 1998.

If you find that defendant Trans Union *willfully* failed to comply with a requirement of the Fair Credit Reporting Act, you may, but are not required to, award punitive damages. The purposes of punitive damages are to punish a defendant and to deter a defendant and others from committing similar acts in the future.

Plaintiff has the burden of proving willful noncompliance by a preponderance of the evidence. In determining the amount of punitive damages to award, if any, you may consider the purpose of the Fair Credit Reporting Act, the nature of the defendant's conduct, and the defendant's income and net worth.

If you find that punitive damages are appropriate, you must use reason in setting the amount. Punitive damages, if any, should be in an amount sufficient to fulfill their purposes, but should not reflect bias, prejudice or sympathy toward any party.

Your decision must be based on the considered judgment of each of you. All of you must agree with the decision.

You must talk with one another with the idea of reaching an agreement, if you can do so based on your own judgment. You must each decide the case for yourself. Do not reach a decision until you have impartially considered the evidence in the case with your fellow jurors. Do not hesitate to re-examine your views or change your mind if you become convinced you are wrong, but do not change your mind about the effect or credibility of the evidence solely because your fellow jurors disagree with you, or because you want to reach a unanimous decision.

When you go to the jury room, select a presiding juror. The presiding juror shall preside over the deliberations, but has no greater voice than any other juror.

A verdict form has been prepared for your use. This form will be with you in the jury room and, when you have reached a unanimous agreement as to your verdict, the presiding juror should fill in, date and sign the form to state the verdict upon which you unanimously agree. You will then return your verdict to the courtroom.

If it becomes necessary during your deliberations to communicate with the court, you may send a note by a bailiff, signed by your presiding juror, or by one or more members of the jury.

J.8.4 Jury Instructions—Impermissible Purpose

UNITED STATES DISTRICT COURT
DISTRICT OF CONNECTICUT

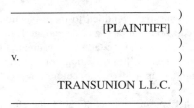

PLAINTIFF'S PROPOSED JURY INSTRUCTIONS

Plaintiff notes that the defendant's proposals misstate the facts of this case and the applicable law. For instance, this case is NOT limited to the Zale account as Trans Union contends (Def. Descr. of Defenses at 2, Instr. D-7); Trans Union is NOT entitled to rely upon the accuracy of any information reported to it once it learns of a dispute, as here. (Instr. D-4)

BACKGROUND AND PURPOSE OF FCRA

PLAINTIFF'S PROPOSED INSTRUCTION NO. 1

In 1970, the Congress of the United States passed a law known as the Fair Credit Reporting Act. Congress passed the law because it found "There is a need to insure that consumer reporting agencies exercise their grave responsibilities with fairness, impartiality, and with respect for the consumer's right to privacy." 15 U.S.C. § 1681.

"Congress enacted the FCRA in 1970 to promote efficiency in the Nation's banking system and to protect consumer privacy. As relevant here, the Act seeks to accomplish those goals by requiring credit reporting agencies to maintain 'reasonable procedures' designed 'to assure maximum possible accuracy of the information' contained in credit reports and to 'limit the furnishing of [such reports] to' certain statutorily enumerated purposes." *TRW Inc. v. Andrews*, 534 U.S. 19, 122 S. Ct. 441, 444 (2001) (citations omitted).

PLAINTIFF'S PROPOSED INSTRUCTION NO. 2

The focus of the FCRA is to ensure the confidentiality and accuracy of the information collected by consumer reporting agencies (commonly referred to as credit bureaus). *St. Paul Guardian Ins. Co. v. Johnson*, 884 F.2d 881, 885 n.3 (5th Cir. 1989)

> [W]ith the trend toward computerization of billings and the establishment of all sorts of computerized data banks, the individual is in great danger of having his life and character reduced to impersonal "blips" and key-punch holes in a stolid and unthinking machine which can literally ruin his reputation without cause, and make him unemployable or uninsurable, as well as deny him the opportunity to obtain a mortgage to buy a home. We are not nearly as much concerned over the possible mistaken turn-down of a consumer for a luxury item as we are over the possible destruction of his good name without his knowledge and without reason. * * * [A]s Shakespeare said, the loss of one's good name is beyond price and makes one poor indeed.

Bryant v. TRW, Inc., 689 F.2d 72, 79 (6th Cir. 1982) (quoting 116 Cong. Rec. 36570 (1970)) (emphasis added).

"Compliance with the consumer disclosure, reinvestigation and correction provisions of the statute is fundamental to achievement of Congress' goal of assuring 'maximum possible accuracy' in consumer reports." *In re Equifax*, 96 FTC 1045, 1066 (1980), *rev'd in part on other grounds*, 678 F.2d 1047, 1052 (11th Cir. 1982) (whether procedures followed posed an unreasonable risk of producing error).

PLAINTIFF'S PROPOSED INSTRUCTION NO. 3

Before 1996, Congress required a credit bureau, such as Trans Union, to conduct a reasonable investigation when it received a dispute from a consumer that information on her report was wrong. In 1996, Congress amended the Fair Credit Reporting Act to impose more specific standards for a credit bureau's investigation of consumer disputes, as well as to require, for the first time, those who furnished information to cooperate in the investigation. (The information furnished by each creditor is referred to as a "tradeline" in credit bureau jargon.) Amendments to § 1681i of the FCRA, and new § 1681s-2(b), Pub.L.No. 104-208, 110 Stat. 3009 [1996] (eff. September 30, 1997)

PLAINTIFF'S PROPOSED INSTRUCTION NO. 4

In 1996, Congress set up a dispute system requiring credit bureaus to notify the creditors who furnished the disputed information to increase the credit bureaus' ability to prepare correct credit reports, because a furnisher that realizes its report is wrong must notify the other credit bureaus. Trans Union must "implement an automated system through which furnishers of information to that consumer reporting agency may report the results of a reinvestigation" to other such consumer reporting agencies. § 1681i(a)(5)(D). In addition, Congress set up the notification system so that the furnisher could meet its own statutory obligation to report credit information accurately. Finally, Congress set up the notification system so that the consumer could have some remedy if the furnisher's investigation was so inadequate that the error stayed on her report.

PLAINTIFF'S CLAIMS

PLAINTIFF'S PROPOSED INSTRUCTION NO. 5

Certain facts have been established conclusively, which means that plaintiff does not need to prove them and you must accept them as true. Those facts are:

[SEE STIPULATION OF UNCONTESTED FACTS IN THE PARTIES' Amended Joint Trial Memorandum, or answer to proposed amended complaint]

Fed. R. Civ. P. 8(d); *Meschino v. N. Am. Drager, Inc.*, 841 F.2d 429, 436-36 (1st Cir. 1988) (admission in answer precludes having to prove the allegation); Weinstein's Federal Evidence (2d) § 201.35 at p. 201-85.

PLAINTIFF'S PROPOSED INSTRUCTION NO. 6

Trans Union did not comply with the notification requirements of § 1681i(a)(2)(A) as amended in 1996. I have ruled as a matter of law that Trans Union's noncompliance with the notification requirements is negligent. One who does not meet the standard of conduct established by a statute, or by the courts, is negligent as a matter of law. Restatement (Torts), Second § 285; Black's Law Dict. 1057 (7th ed. 1999). Negligence is "conduct which falls below the standard of what a reasonably prudent person would do under similar circumstances judged at the time of the conduct at issue." *Fane v. Zimmer*, 927 F.2d 124 n.3 (2d Cir. 1991).

It is up to you to decide whether Trans Union's conduct also was willful, using factors I will tell you about in a few minutes. Trans Union violated several subsections of 1681i(a)(2) which require notice to the creditor that furnished the information. *First*, subsection (A) required Trans Union to notify the furnisher of the consumer's dispute within five days of its receipt of the dispute. Trans Union did not notify the furnisher of *any* of the four disputed accounts within five days. Instead, pursuant to its own internal procedures, Trans Union forwarded plaintiff's dispute from Pennsylvania to its California office instead of undergoing the timely investigation process mandated by Congress (ordinarily done by a written or electronic Consumer Dispute Verification form or Automated Consumer Dispute Verification form.)

Second, subsection (A) mandates that the five-day notice be provided "at the address and in the manner established with the person." Trans Union deleted three of the accounts without contacting the furnishers as mandated by Congress.

Third, subsection (A) mandates that the notice "shall include all relevant information regarding the dispute that the agency has received from the consumer." Trans Union did not provide any information to three of the furnishers.

PLAINTIFF'S PROPOSED INSTRUCTION NO. 7

I have also ruled as a matter of law that Trans Union was negligent because it did not comply with § 1681i (a)(5) as amended in 1996. Once again, it is up to you to decide whether Trans Union's failure to comply was willful.

Here is how Trans Union did not comply. Trans Union deleted (or cloaked) three of the disputed accounts without contacting the furnishers as mandated by Congress. Trans Union did not determine whether the deleted accounts were fraudulent before deleting them. Subsection (a)(8), as amended, allows deletion only "after any reinvestigation *under paragraph (1)*" except for the safe harbor provision. (Emphasis added reflecting amended language.) § 1681i(a)(8), captioned "Expedited dispute resolution" provides that if the item is deleted within three business days of receipt of the consumer's dispute, the consumer reporting agency need not notify the furnisher. Trans Union did not take advantage of this "safe harbor" which would have excused it from contacting the furnishers. Congress wanted to be sure its procedures were adopted and followed by the consumer reporting agencies, not flouted.

PLAINTIFF'S PROPOSED INSTRUCTION NO. 8

Another requirement adopted in 1996 [§ 1681i(a)(6)(B) (iii)–(v)] is that when Trans Union provides a written notice of the results of its reinvestigation, it must include certain notices. One of those notices is of the consumer's right to obtain a description of the procedure used to determine the accuracy and completeness of the disputed information, including identification of any furnisher contacted (business name, address and telephone number). You must decide whether Trans Union gave the required notices effectively, so that a consumer would notice them. If you find that the notices were not given effectively, you must decide whether Trans Union acted intentionally or negligently.

Russell v. Equifax A.R.S., 74 F.3d 30, 35 (2d Cir. 1996):

> "Congress intended that such [FDCPA] notice be clearly conveyed. See *Swanson v. Southern Or. Credit Serv., Inc.*, 869 F.2d 1222, 1225 (9th Cir. 1988) (per curiam). Here the initial February notice failed to convey the validation information effectively. We recognize there are many cunning ways to circumvent § 1692g under cover of technical compliance, see *Miller v. Payco-General Am. Credits, Inc.*, 943 F.2d 482, 485 (4th Cir. 1991), but purported compliance with the form of the statute should not be given sanction at the expense of the substance of the Act."

PLAINTIFF'S PROPOSED INSTRUCTION NO. 9

The Fair Credit Reporting Act mandates that, whenever a credit bureau prepares a consumer report, it shall follow reasonable procedures to assure maximum possible accuracy of the information concerning the individual about whom the report relates.

Once a creditor is on notice of a dispute, it cannot blindly rely on what a creditor is reporting. It is in a state of "heightened alert," so to speak, and must take extra care to make sure the report it prepares about an individual is accurate as to that individual.

Section 1681e(b); *Cushman v. Trans Union Corp.*, 115 F.3d 220, 224-25 (3d Cir. 1997) (perfunctory investigation improper once a claimed inaccuracy is pinpointed; must go beyond original source); *Henson v. CSC Credit Services & Trans Union Corp.*, 29 F.3d 280, 286 (7th Cir. 1994) (must go beyond original source where there is a possibility that information unreliable); *Podell v. Citicorp Diners Club, Inc. & Trans Union Corp.*, 112 F.3d 98, 104-05 (2d Cir. 1997) (Trans Union acted properly because it received confirming reports from creditors shortly after the creditors' had requested removal, and removed once contacted by the consumer); *Philbin v. Trans Union Corp.*, 101 F.3d 957, 970 (3d Cir. 1996) (confusing father/son files); *Barron v. Trans Union Corp.*, 82 F. Supp. 2d 1288, 1299 (M.D. Ala. 2000) (failure to adequately reinvestigate); *Cousin v. Trans Union Corp.*, 246 F.3d 359, 368 (5th Cir. 2001); *Zala v. Trans Union, L.L.C.*, 2001 U.S. Dist LEXIS 549 *25-26 (N. D. Tex. Jan. 17, 2001) (refusing to dismiss punitive damage claim for willful violations of reinvestigation obligations). See also the long-established standards set in *Bryant v. TRW, Inc.*, 689 F.2d 72, 79 (6th Cir. 1982) (two phone calls to the creditors insufficient); *Dynes v. TRW Credit Data*, 652 F.2d 35-36 (9th Cir. 1981) (single effort to investigate inadequate); *Swoager v. Credit Bureau*, 608 F. Supp. 972, 976 (D.C. Fla. 1985) (merely reporting whatever information a creditor furnished not reasonable).

You must decide whether Trans Union applied reasonable procedures to assure maximum possible accuracy, and to exclude information about the impostor from her report, once Trans Union was informed of plaintiff's problems with an identity thief. If you find that Trans Union did not meet this standard, you have automatically found that Trans Union was negligent. Then you must determine whether Trans Union acted willfully.

PLAINTIFF'S PROPOSED INSTRUCTION NO. 10

Congress requires that a disputed item be deleted if it is wrong or if the furnisher does not respond in a timely fashion to the credit bureau's inquiry. § 1682i(a)(5)(A). Trans Union uses a system of "cloaking" the tradeline instead of deleting it. Trans Union told [Plaintiff] that three of the disputed tradelines had been deleted. You must decide whether telling a consumer that a tradeline had been deleted when it had merely been cloaked was a misrepresentation.

PLAINTIFF'S PROPOSED INSTRUCTION NO. 11

To protect the confidentiality of the consumer's private financial information, the Act expressly limits the circumstances under which a credit reporting agency may disclose a consumer's credit information to certain enumerated "permissible purposes" and allows for "no other" disclosure of the consumer's private financial information.

The Act states the "permissible purposes" for which a consumer report may be obtained. With regard to the facts of this case, the only possible purposes for which someone could obtain information from [Plaintiff]'s credit report are

EITHER to use the information in connection with a credit transaction involving the consumer on whom the information is to be furnished AND the credit transaction involves the extension of credit to, or review or collection of an account of [Plaintiff], § 1681b(1)(3)(A);

OR otherwise had a legitimate business need for the information in connection with a business transaction that was initiated by [Plaintiff]. § 1681b(a)(3)(F).

You must decide whether Trans Union disclosed [Plaintiff]'s credit report to someone that had no permissible purpose to receive it.

If you decide that Trans Union did disclose [Plaintiff]'s report to someone that had no permissible purpose, that disclosure is negligence as a matter of law. You must go on to decide whether the disclosure was willful.

Russell v. Shelter Financial Services, 604 F. Supp. 201, 203 (W.D. Mo. 1984) (defendant's burden to prove request for consumer's information proper).

PLAINTIFF'S PROPOSED INSTRUCTION NO. 12

The Fair Credit Reporting Act imposes certain responsibilities on credit bureaus. One is to conduct a reasonable investigation of any disputes conveyed to them by a consumer. As a matter of law, Trans Union did not conduct a reasonable investigation because it did not contact the creditors or comply with the time limits for investigation set by Congress. You must decide whether Trans

Union's failure to conduct a reasonable investigation was willful. I have already ruled it was negligent.

15 U.S.C. § 1681i

PLAINTIFF'S PROPOSED INSTRUCTION NO. 13

Once plaintiff has shown there are inaccuracies in her report, the *burden of proof* shifts to Trans Union to prove it adopted and maintained reasonable procedures to investigate her disputes, or reasonable procedures to assure the maximum possible accuracy of her credit reports. The burden is allocated to Trans Union because information as to a defendant's procedures and whether they were followed is, of course, exclusively within the defendant's knowledge and control.

Guimond v. Trans Union Credit Information Co., 45 F.3d 1329 (9th Cir. 1995); Lendino v. Trans Union Credit Information Co., 970 F.2d 1110, 1111-12 (2d Cir. 1992); Stewart v. Credit Bureau, Inc., 734 F.2d 47, 52 (D.C. Cir. 1984); Parker v. Parker, 124 F. Supp. 2d 1216 (N.D. Ala. 2000); Natale v. TRW, Inc., 1999 U.S. Dist. LEXIS 3882 (N.D. Cal. 1999).

COMPENSATORY DAMAGES

PLAINTIFF'S PROPOSED INSTRUCTION NO. 14

The Act specifically permits you to award damages to the plaintiff for either willful or negligent noncompliance with the Act by defendant.

15 U.S.C. §§ 1681n, 1682o

PLAINTIFF'S PROPOSED INSTRUCTION NO. 15

If you find that Trans Union violated the Act and [Plaintiff] was harmed by such violation, then you may award compensatory damages for:

Out-of-pocket expenses
Fischl v. GMAC, 708 F.2d 143, 151 (5th Cir. 1983).
Humiliation.
Casella v. Equifax Credit Information Serv., 56 F.3d 469, 474 (2d Cir. 1995); *Guimond v. Trans Union Credit Corporation*, 45 F.3d 1329, 1333 (9th Cir. 1995); *Fischl v. GMAC*, 708 F.2d 143 (5th Cir. 1983); *Jones v. Credit Bureau of Huntington*, 399 S.E.2d 694, 699 (W. Va. 1990) (surveying cases)
Mental Distress.
Guimond v. Trans Union Credit Corporation, 45 F.3d 1329, 1333 (9th Cir. 1995); *Fischl v. GMAC*, 708 F.2d 143 (5th Cir. 1983); *Jones v. Credit Bureau of Huntington*, 399 S.E.2d 694, 699 (W. Va. 1990); *Johnson v. Dept. of Treasury, I.R.S.*, 700 F.2d 971, 977 (5th Cir. 1983).
Emotional Distress.
Casella v. Equifax Credit Information Serv., 56 F.3d 469, 474 (2d Cir. 1995); *Dalton v. Capital Assoc.*, 257 F.3d 409, 418-19 (4th Cir. 2001); *Guimond v. Trans Union Credit Corporation*, 45 F.3d 1329, 1333 (9th Cir. 1995); *Bryant v. TRW, Inc.*, 487 F. Supp. 1234, 1238-39 (D. Mich. 1980), *aff'd*, 689 F.2d 72 (6th Cir. 1982); *Johnson v. Dept. of Treasury, I.R.S.*, 700 F.2d 971, 977 (5th Cir. 1983).
Injury to Plaintiff's Reputation.
Dalton v. Capital Assoc., 257 F.3d 409, 418019 (4th Cir. 2001); *Jones v. Credit Bureau of Huntington, Inc.*, 399 S.E.2d 694, 699 (W. Va. 1990); *Fischl v. GMAC*, 708 F.2d 143, 151 (5th Cir. 1983).
Injury to Plaintiff's Credit Rating
Jones v. Credit Bureau of Huntington, Inc., 399 S.E.2d 694, 699 (W. Va. 1990); *Fischl v. GMAC*, 708 F.2d 143, 151 (5th Cir. 1983).
Anxiety
Bryant v. TRW, Inc., 487 F. Supp. 1234, 1238-39 (D. Mich. 1980), *aff'd*, 689 F.2d 72 (6th Cir. 1982)
Embarrassment
Bryant v. TRW, Inc., 487 F. Supp. 1234, 1238-39 (D. Mich. 1980), *aff'd*, 689 F.2d 72 (6th Cir. 1982)
Frustration
Millstone v. O'Hanlon Reports, Inc., 529 F.2d 829, 834-35 (8th Cir. 1976)
Being accused of owing a debt which one does not owe
Cox v. Sears, Roebuck & Co., 647 A.2d 454, 464 (N.J. 1994); *Sorge v. Transworld Systems, Inc.*, Civil No. 3:94CV71 (JBA) (D. Conn. Sept. 19, 1996)
Harm to plaintiff's interest in privacy
TRW's Reply Brief in *TRW Inc. v. Andrews*, __ U.S. __, No. 00-1045, citing Restatement (Second) of Torts sec. 652H (1977).[3]

PLAINTIFF'S PROPOSED INSTRUCTION NO. 16

There is no fixed standard or measure in the case of intangible items such as anxiety, humiliation, embarrassment, mental anguish and emotional distress. You must determine a fair and adequate award for these items, both the distress and embarrassment to date and any continuing distress, using your judgment and experience in the affairs of the world after considering all the facts and circumstances presented during the trial of this case. A person may recover for emotional distress based on his own subjective testimony about his feelings. He does not have to introduce medical or other testimony.

Smith v. Law Office of Mitchell N. Kay, 124 B.R. 182, 187-88 (D. Del. 1990); *Johnson v. Dept. of Treasury, I.R.S.*, 700 F.2d 971, 985 n. 39 (5th Cir. 1983); *Bryant v. TRW, Inc.*, 487 F. Supp. 1234, 1239 n. 7 (E.D. Mich. 1980), *aff'd*, 689 F.2d 72 (6th Cir. 1982); *Jones v. Credit Bureau of Huntington, Inc.*, 399 S.E.2d 694, 699 fn. 5 (1990); *Giordano v. Giordano*, 39 Conn. App. 183, 207-08, 664 A.2d 1136 (1995); *Oakes v. New England Dairies, Inc.*, 219 Conn. 1, 13, 591 A.2d 1261 (1991); *Berry v. Loiseau*, 223 Conn. 786, 811, 614 A.2d 414 (1992).

PLAINTIFF'S PROPOSED INSTRUCTION NO. 17

If you find there were no actual damages, you must award at least nominal damages.

Guccione v. Hustler Magazine, Inc., 800 F.2d 298, 303 (2d Cir. 1986); *Auwood v. Harry Brandt Booking Office, Inc.*, 647 F. Supp. 1551, 1553 (D. Conn. 1986); *Boule v. Hulton*, 138 F. Supp. 2d 491, 506 (S.D.N.Y. 2001); *Beckford v. Irvin*, 49 F. Supp. 2d 170 (W.D.N.Y. 1999); *Russell v. Shelter Fin. Services*, 604 F. Supp. 201, 203 (W.D. Mo. 1984); *Creem v. Cicero*, 12 Conn. App. 607, 610-11, 533 A.2d 234 (1987) ($100 nominal damages); *Patalano v. Chabot*, 139 Conn. 356, 362, 94 A.2d 15 (1952) ($25 nominal damages).

PLAINTIFF'S PROPOSED INSTRUCTION NO. 18

Denial of credit to [Plaintiff] is not necessary in order for you to

---

3 "[I]t is hornbook law that an individual may recover damages not only for emotional distress and pecuniary harm resulting from an invasion of privacy, but also for the 'harm to his interest in privacy resulting from the invasion.'" Reply Brief of Petitioner, p. 19.

award actual or punitive damages under the Act.

Casella v. Equifax Credit Information Serv., 56 F.3d 469 (2d Cir. 1995); *Guimond v. Trans Union Credit Corporation*, 45 F.3d 1329, 1333 (9th Cir. 1995); *McMillan v. Associates Financial Services, Inc.*, 2001 US Dist LEXIS 17973 (D. Conn. Oct. 19, 2001)

PUNITIVE DAMAGES[4]

PLAINTIFF'S PROPOSED INSTRUCTION NO. 19

The FCRA allows the consumer to recover statutory damages of not less than $100 and not more than $1,000, plus punitive damages, costs and attorney's fees statutory when "any person" "*willfully* fails to comply with any requirement imposed" by the FCRA. 15 U.S.C. § 1681n.[5] In *Casella v. Equifax Credit Information Serv.*, 56 F.3d 469, 476 (2d Cir. 1995), the Second Circuit defined the FCRA standard as "conscious disregard" *or* "deliberate and purposeful action."

Philbin v. Trans Union, 101 F.3d 957, 970 (3d Cir. 1996) (multiple notice of dispute sufficient to support punitive damages); *Collins v. Retail Credit Co.*, 410 F. Supp. 924, 932, 933-34 (E.D. Mich. 1976) (haphazard procedures showed indifference to accuracy); *Dalton v. Capital Associated Industries, Inc.*, 257 F.3d 409, 418 (4th Cir. 2001) (defendant was on notice of error but disregarded it). See also *Nitti v. Credit Bureau of Rochester, Inc.*, 84 Misc. 2d 277, 375 N.Y.S.2d 817, 821 (1975) (defendant's "routine method of conducting business was in complete disregard of the requirements of the [FCRA]"). In *Nitti*, the court aptly commented:

> It was this very kind of contumacious conduct that Congress sought to correct. It recognized that to do so, it might be necessary to cause, and, if need be, to coerce a change in the defendant's operations in order to make it comply with the law. Congress intended to make it expensive for the defendant not to comply. This was the purpose of assessing, without limitation, punitive damages. As one commentator has observed, "Deterrent awards should be large enough to remove any financial incentive to violate the statute." (Comment, *Punitive Damages Under Federal Statutes: A Functional Analysis*, 60 Cal. L. Rev. 191, 223)

Id. at 822.

PLAINTIFF'S PROPOSED INSTRUCTION NO. 20

Malice or evil motive need not be found in order to award punitive damages, but Trans Union' violation must have been willful.

15 U.S.C. § 1681n; *Casella v. Equifax Credit Information Serv.*, 56 F.3d 469, 476 (2d Cir. 1995); *Bakker v. McKinnon*, 152 F.3d 1007, 1011-12 (8th Cir. 1998); *Cushman v. Trans Union Corp.*, 115 F.3d 220, 224-25 (3d Cir. 1997); *Yohay v. City of Alexandria Employees Credit Union, Inc.*, 827 F.2d 967, 972 (4th Cir. 1987); *Fischl v. GMAC*, 708 F.2d 143, 151 (5th Cir. 1983).

PLAINTIFF'S PROPOSED INSTRUCTION NO. 21

One of the things you may consider is that this is not the first time Trans Union has failed to meet the reinvestigation standards set by Congress in 1996, or by the courts before the 1996 amendments. There are more than five published appeals court decisions confirming that Trans Union failed to meet reinvestigation standards, and several lower court rulings as well. For instance, a year ago, in Thomas v. Trans Union, a jury found that Trans Union repeatedly failed to protect [Plaintiff] from use of her credit by Judy Upton, where the first names and year of birth were the same and the social security numbers were one digit difference.[6] (Copy attached for purposes of judicial notice of public records.) In 1992, both the Federal Trade Commission and the Connecticut Attorney General obtained consent orders from Trans Union requiring it to improve its system to prevent merging files with similar identifying information. (Copy attached for purposes of judicial notice of public records.)

Guimond v. Trans Union Credit Corporation, 45 F.3d 1329, 1333 (9th Cir. 1995) (reappearance of disputed information); *Cushman v. Trans Union Corp.*, 115 F.3d 220, 224-25 (3d Cir. 1997) (perfunctory investigation improper once a claimed inaccuracy is pinpointed; must go beyond original source); *Henson v. CSC Credit Services & Trans Union Corp.*, 29 F.3d 280, 286 (7th Cir. 1994) (must go beyond original source where there is a possibility that information unreliable); *Podell v. Citicorp Diners Club, Inc. & Trans Union Corp.*, 112 F.3d 98, 104-05 (2d Cir. 1997) (Trans Union acted properly because it received confirming reports from creditors shortly after the creditors' had requested removal, and removed once contacted by the consumer); *Philbin v. Trans Union Corp.*, 101 F.3d 957, 970 (3d Cir. 1996) (confusing father/son files); *Barron v. Trans Union Corp.*, 82 F. Supp. 2d 1288, 1299 (M.D. Ala. 2000) (failure to adequately reinvestigate); *Cousin v. Trans Union Corp.*, 246 F.3d 359, 368 (5th Cir. 2001); *Zala v. Trans Union, L.L.C.*, 2001 U.S. Dist LEXIS 549 *25-26 (N. D. Tex. Jan. 17, 2001) (refusing to dismiss punitive damage claim for willful violations of reinvestigation obligations). See also the long-established standards set in *Bryant v. TRW, Inc.*, 689 F.2d 72, 79 (6th Cir. 1982) (two phone calls to the creditors insufficient); *Dynes v. TRW Credit Data*, 652 F.2d 35-36 (9th Cir. 1981) (single effort to investigate inadequate); *Swoager v. Credit Bureau*, 608 F. Supp. 972, 976 (D.C. Fla. 1985) (merely reporting whatever information a creditor furnished not reasonable). See also *In re MIB, Inc.*, 101 FTC 415, 423 (1983) (FTC ordered the credit reporting agency to include as part of such reinvestigation a reasonable effort to contact original sources); *In re Credit Data Northwest*, 86 FTC 389, 396 (1975) (FTC ordered a credit reporting agency to "request[] examination by the creditor, where rel-

---

4 In federal court, all damage issues, including punitive damages, are to be decided by the jury. *Feltner v. Columbia Pictures Television, Inc.*, 523 U.S. 340, 348, 118 S. Ct. 1279 (1998); *Kobs v. Arrow Service Bureau, Inc.*, 134 F.3d 893 (7th Cir. 1998); *McGuire v. Russell Miller, Inc.*, 1 F.3d 1306 (2d Cir. 1993); *Kampa v. White Consolidated Inc.*, 115 F.3d 585, 586 (8th Cir. 1997).

5 In contrast, Congress used "knowingly and willfully" in §§ 1681q and 1681r; "materially and willfully" in § 1681p; "malice or willful intent to injure" in § 1681h(e).

6 This Court can take judicial notice of newspaper articles. Fed. R. Civ. P. 201(f); *Cheshire Mortgage Serv. Inc. v. Montes*, 223 Conn. 80, 123 n.9, 612 A.2d 1130 (1992); See also *Peters v. Delaware River Port Authority*, 16 F.3d 1346, 1356–57 (3d Cir. 1994)(appellate court may take judicial notice of newspaper articles). One such article on the Thomas case is attached.

evant, of any original documentation relating to the dispute in addition to its own records).

PLAINTIFF'S PROPOSED INSTRUCTION NO. 22

Alternative "willful misrepresentation or concealment" standard. You may also award punitive damages if you find that Trans Union willfully misrepresented or concealed information from the consumer.

Long before the 1996 FCRA amendments, beginning with *Stevenson v. TRW Inc.*, 987 F.2d 288, 294 (5th Cir. 1993), courts have ruled that punitive damages are called for when a credit bureau willfully misrepresents or conceals information. *Parker v. Parker*, 124 F. Supp. 2d 1216, 1225-26 (M.D. Ala. 2000) (surveying case law).

PLAINTIFF'S PROPOSED INSTRUCTION NO. 23

Because the procedures used by Trans Union to investigate did not comply with its obligations under the FCRA, I direct you to find that the procedures were willful.

Carroll v. Exxon Co., U.S.A., 434 F. Supp. 557, 561 (E.D. La. 1977).

You may award punitive damages if you find that the defendant was on notice of the error and then disregarded it. Dalton v. Capital Associated Industries, Inc., 257 F.3d 409, 418 (4th Cir. 2001)

PLAINTIFF'S PROPOSED INSTRUCTION NO. 24

If you find that Trans Union did not correct an admitted error in Plaintiff's credit file, then its conduct was in reckless disregard of its legal duties owed to the Plaintiff to correct errors and entitles Plaintiff to an award of punitive damages.

Nitti v. Credit Bureau of Rochester, Inc., 84 Misc. 2d 277, 375 N.Y.S.2d 817 (1975); *Sayers v. GMAC*, 522 F. Supp. 835, 842 (D. Mo. 1981).

PLAINTIFF'S PROPOSED INSTRUCTION NO. 25

Trans Union has willfully violated the FCRA, and you may award punitive damages if you find that it did not properly train its employee and have the employee's work checked by a second person.

Jones v. Credit Bureau of Huntington, Inc., 399 S.E.2d 694, 700 (W. Va. 1990); 15 U.S.C. § 1681-1681t.

PLAINTIFF'S PROPOSED INSTRUCTION NO. 26

Upon a finding that Trans Union willfully failed to follow reasonable procedures in its investigation of [Plaintiff]'s claim that the accounts appearing on his credit reports were not hers, or willfully distributed her credit report without a permissible purpose, you must award her actual damages in whatever amount you choose. If you have not awarded her any actual damages, or have awarded her less than $100 in actual damages, then you must award her at least $100 but not more than $1,000.

15 U.S.C. § 1681n(a) (1)(A)

PLAINTIFF'S PROPOSED INSTRUCTION NO. 27

Willful has been defined to be voluntary or conscious acts. There is no requirement that you find that Trans Union knew it was violating the Fair Credit Reporting Act, or intended to violate the Act, but merely that Trans Union intended its conduct, and its intentional acts were with reckless disregard of whether its conduct violated the Act.

§ 1681n(a); *Jones v. Credit Bureau of Huntington, Inc.*, 399 S.E.2d 694, 702 n.8 (W. Va. 1990) (voluntary or conscious acts). If it intended to take any step which violated the Act, the defendant acted intentionally. *Rutnya v. Collection Accounts Terminal, Inc.*, 478 F. Supp. 980, 982 (N.D. Ill. 1979) ("Defendant here obviously intended the conduct which violated the Act in respect to the return address, but it simply failed to acquaint itself with the pertinent law"); *Johnson v. Associates Fin. Inc.*, 369 F. Supp. 1121, 1125 (S.D. Ill. 1974) ("While defendant may have acted in good faith, its acts were, nevertheless, intentionally done and not by mistake"); *Nitti v. Credit Bureau of Rochester, Inc.*, 84 Misc. 2d 277, 375 N.Y.S.2d 817, 821 (1975) (defendant's acts were "deliberate and purposeful"; its "routine method of conducting business was in complete disregard of the requirements of the [FCRA]").

PLAINTIFF'S PROPOSED INSTRUCTION NO. 28

If Trans Union' formal reinvestigation policy is in contravention of consumers' rights to a complete and accurate credit report, [or in conscious disregard of whether the reinvestigation policy contravened those rights], you must find that Trans Union acted willfully and you may award punitive damages.

Cushman v. Trans Union Corp., 115 F.3d 220, 227 (3d Cir. 1997); *Transworld Airlines v. Thurston*, 469 US 111, 105 S. Ct. 613 (1985); *Yohay v. City of Alexandria Employees Credit Union, Inc.*, 827 F.2d 967 (4th Cir. 1987).

PLAINTIFF'S PROPOSED INSTRUCTION NO. 29

In awarding punitive damages under the Fair Credit Reporting Act, you may award punitive damages even if you believe Plaintiff proved no actual damages or just nominal actual damages.

15 U.S.C. § 1681n; *Cush-Crawford v. Adchem Corp.*, 271 F.3d 352 (2d Cir. 2001); *Casella v. Equifax Credit Information Serv.*, 56 F.3d 469, 476 (2d Cir. 1995); *Bakker v. McKinnon*, 152 F.3d 1007, 1013 (8th Cir. 1998); *Guimond v. Trans Union Corp.*, 45 F.3d 1329, 1333 (9th Cir. 1995).

PLAINTIFF'S PROPOSED INSTRUCTION NO. 30

If you choose to award punitive damages, you should award punitive damages which, in your judgment, are necessary or appropriate, in light of the factors provided to you.

Jones v. Credit Bureau of Huntington, Inc., 399 S.E.2d 694, 702 (W. Va. 1990).

PLAINTIFF'S PROPOSED INSTRUCTION NO. 31

In determining whether to award punitive damages, you may consider the following factors:

The remedial purpose of the Act;
The harm(s) to consumer intended to be avoided or corrected by the Act;
The manner in which the defendant conducted its business;
The manner in which agency dealt with plaintiff; and
The defendant's income and net worth.

Fury Imports, Inc. v. Shakespeare Co., 554 F.2d 1376, 1389 (5th Cir. 1977; *Continental Trend Resources v. OXY USA Inc.*, 44 F.3d 1465, 1476 (10th Cir. 1995); *Dunn v. HOVIC*, 1 F.3d 1371, 1380 (3d Cir. 1993);); *Jones v. Credit Bureau of Huntington, Inc.*, 399 S.E.2d 694, 702 (W. Va. 1990); *Nitti v. Credit Bureau of Rochester, Inc.*, 84 Misc. 2d 277, 375 N.Y.S.2d 817, 821 (1975); 15 U.S.C. 1681n.

PLAINTIFF'S PROPOSED INSTRUCTION NO. 32

In determining the amount of any award of exemplary damages you may also consider the following factors;

The reprehensibility of defendant's acts

The harm to other consumers that might have been caused by Trans Union' failure to have adequate investigation procedures

The profitability of defendant's conduct

The wealth of the defendant

The amount needed to punish the defendant, to affect Trans Union' future conduct and to deter the defendant and others like it from violating the FCRA.

TXO Prod. Corp. v. Alliance Resources Corp., 509 U.S. 443, 460-61 (1993); *Jones v. Credit Bureau of Huntington, Inc.,* 399 S.E.2d 694, 702, 704 (W. Va. 1990); *Pinner v. Schmidt,* 805 F.2d 1258 (5th Cir. 1986); *Collins v. Retail Credit Co.,* 410 F. Supp. 924 (D. Mich. 1976).

PLAINTIFF'S PROPOSED INSTRUCTION NO. 33

In awarding punitive damages under the Fair Credit Reporting Act, you should consider an award which would be adequate to affect defendant's future conduct.

PLAINTIFF'S PROPOSED INSTRUCTION NO. 34

Each act by defendant which did not comply with its obligations under the FCRA is a separate and distinct tort, and you may award compensatory and punitive damages for each event.

Hyde v. Hibernia Nat. Bank in Jefferson Parish, 861 F.2d 446, 450 (5th Cir. 1988).

PLAINTIFF'S PROPOSED INSTRUCTION NO. 35

In summary then: The Fair Credit Reporting Act required that Trans Union follow reasonable procedures in its investigation of [Plaintiff]'s claim that the accounts appearing on her credit report did not belong to her, and prohibited Trans Union from disclosing information from her credit report except for certain listed purposes. If you find that Trans Union was negligent in following the requirements of the law, you should award [Plaintiff] the actual damages sustained by her because of such negligence. If you find Trans Union willfully or recklessly did not follow the requirements of the law, [Plaintiff] is entitled the greater of either her actual damages or up to $1,000 in statutory damages. You may also award punitive damages in an amount sufficient to give Trans Union an incentive to follow the law in the future and as a warning to others by way of example.

J.9 Sample Settlement Language to Address Credit Reporting

J.9.1 Introduction

Two alternative settlement provisions are provided below. The first requires the creditor to withdraw the entire report of the disputed debt. This withdrawal is sometimes referred to as a "hard delete." The credit record will then be altogether silent about the debt and will not even provide a basis for another creditor, interested in the creditworthiness of the consumer, to inquire further. This is often the simplest solution for the consumer and the safest.

The second alternative permits reporting of the debt, but requires the creditor to take steps to avoid having unfavorable information about the debt included in any credit report. The consumer may benefit from this approach, especially if the consumer report contains only information which suggests good consumer experience with credit management. For the second alternative to be successful, the settlement provisions must carefully delineate what information cannot be furnished to an agency because it might be construed unfavorably to the client. The model language found at J.9.3 *infra*, suggests some possibilities. Even so, there is always the risk that even the limited information reported, though accurate in a narrow sense, will permit another creditor using the report to fill in the gaps incorrectly or to draw its own negative inferences. For example, if there was a dispute, a creditor might suppose there was a default as well.

J.9.2 Alternative I: Deleting All Mention of the Debt

The following is proposed settlement language that would require the creditor to request deletion of all reference to a disputed debt in a consumer's credit reporting file where complete deletion is preferable to amendment of the information:

It is further agreed that [name of creditor] shall take all steps necessary to ensure that no credit report or credit reference that is unfavorable or that may be construed unfavorably to [name of consumer] shall be made by it or by any consumer reporting agency with regard to any debts or claims as between [creditor] and [consumer]. Without limiting the effect of the foregoing obligation, [creditor] shall also within ten days hereof send notice [in writing or electronically or both] [in the form attached hereto as Appendix A], to each consumer reporting agency to which the creditor has reported any information about [consumer], deleting from their files all references to the [alleged] debt which is the subject of this settlement agreement. To that end, [creditor] shall submit a [Metro II form coded with "DA" (delete account)] [and/or] [a Universal Data Form with the "Delete Tradeline" option box checked] to each consumer reporting agency to which the creditor has reported any information about the consumer. Prior to any execution of any release of claims by [consumer], [creditor] shall submit to counsel for [consumer] clear and complete copies of these forms (with [creditor's] subscriber/password code redacted if [creditor] chooses) and proof that [creditor] has submitted these forms. Each required "Universal Data Form" or the equivalent must contain [creditor's] certification that it has modified its internal records so that the information to be deleted is not re-reported. In the event Plaintiffs discover, more than 45 days following [creditor's] submission of the [Metro II form][Universal Data form]as described, that any consumer reporting agency still reports the alleged debt, [consumer] may notify [creditor] in writing, and [creditor] will within ten business days re-submit a request for deletion of all reference to the debt.

[Creditor] shall adjust its relevant internal records in a manner that will permanently reflect the agreed-upon status of the debt. [Creditor] agrees to take all steps necessary or appropriate to prevent the re-reporting of any information about the [alleged] debt. In the event any such information is re-reported to any consumer reporting agency, [creditor] agrees to take all steps necessary or appropriate to ensure that the re-reported information is deleted from the files of every consumer reporting agency to which the information was re-reported. Further, should a consumer reporting agency ever notify [creditor] that [consumer] is disputing the tradeline, [creditor] will not verify the tradeline or will confirm that the tradeline should be deleted; in such an event, [creditor] will also submit to counsel for [consumer], within forty-five days after receiving the notification of the dispute from the consumer reporting agency, clear and complete copies of the notification of the dispute and any and all forms (including electronic forms) by which it responds to such notification (with [creditor's] subscriber/password code redacted if [creditor] chooses). [Creditor] further agrees that it will not assign, hypothecate, or transfer the [alleged] debt to another creditor, a collection agency, or any other third party,[7] and that it will not alter the account number or otherwise relabel the account. The parties agree that time is of the essence of this contract. This release shall not extend to the obligations created by this Agreement or to any claim or cause of action based in whole or in part upon a communication to a consumer reporting agency after the date of this agreement.[8]

J.9.3 Alterative II: Correcting the Status of an Account, But Retaining Information About the Account

The following is proposed settlement language that would require the creditor to request correction of a disputed credit account, but would leave the account listed in the consumer's credit reporting file. This option is recommended only when there is a significant benefit to the client of maintaining information about the account, for it is far more likely to raise post-settlement problems.

It is further agreed that [creditor] shall take all steps necessary to ensure that no credit report or credit reference that is unfavorable or that may be construed unfavorably to [consumer] shall be made by it or by any consumer reporting agency with regard to any debts or claims as between [creditor] and [consumer]. Without limiting the foregoing obligation, the [creditor] shall, within ten days hereof, send written or electronic notice of the current status of the debt which is the subject of this settlement agreement to each consumer reporting agency to which the creditor has reported any information about [consumer], such notice to be in a form [approved by counsel for consumer] [or, attached hereto as Appendix A], and shall cause the deletion of all information that is unfavorable or may be construed unfavorably to [name of consumer]. For this purpose, the parties agree that the current status of the debt is [describe]. [Creditor] shall submit a [Metro II form coded with [describe codes]] [and/or] [a Universal Data Form [describe marks to be made on Form]] to each credit reporting agency to which the creditor has reported any information about the consumer. Prior to any execution of any release of claims by [consumer], [creditor]

shall submit to counsel for [consumer] clear and complete copies of these forms (with [creditor's] subscriber/password code redacted if [creditor] chooses) and proof that [creditor] has submitted these forms. In the event Plaintiffs discover, more than 45 days following [creditor's] submission of the [Metro II form][Universal Data form]as described, that any consumer reporting agency still reports the [alleged] debt other than as described above, [consumer] may notify [creditor] in writing, and [creditor] will within ten business days re-submit a request for reporting of the [alleged] debt. as described above. Furthermore, should a consumer reporting agency ever notify [creditor] that [consumer] is disputing the [alleged] debt, [creditor[will re-report the [alleged] debt only as described above; in such an event, [creditor] will also submit to counsel for [consumer], within forty-five days after receiving the notification of the dispute from the consumer reporting agency, clear and complete copies of the notification of the dispute and any and all forms (including electronic forms) by which it responds to such notification (with [creditor's] subscriber password code redacted if [creditor] chooses).

Creditor shall further refrain from reporting any information that is unfavorable or may be construed unfavorably to [consumer] about said debt, so long as [consumer] remains in compliance with [specify any paragraphs of the settlement that deal with future payments].

[Creditor] shall adjust its relevant internal records in a manner that will permanently reflect the agreed-upon status of the debt. [Creditor] agrees to take all steps necessary or appropriate to prevent the re-reporting of any information about the debt that is inconsistent with the current status of the debt or the payment history from the date of this settlement agreement. In the event any such information is re-reported to any consumer reporting agency, [creditor] agrees to take all steps necessary or appropriate to ensure that the re-reported information is deleted from the files of every consumer reporting agency to which the information was re-reported. [Creditor] further agrees that it will not assign, hypothecate, or transfer the [alleged] debt to another creditor, a collection agency, or any other third party,[9] and that it will not alter the account number or otherwise relabel the account. The parties agree that time is of the essence of this contract. This release shall not extend to the obligations created by this Agreement or to any claim or cause of action based in whole or in part upon a communication to a consumer reporting agency after the date of this agreement.[10]

If [creditor] receives inquiries about said debt from anyone not a party to this settlement agreement, [creditor] will report only the current status of the debt as described above and the payment history from the date of this settlement. [Creditor] shall not provide, directly or indirectly, any information regarding the status of the debt before the date of this settlement, including [delinquencies] [repossessions] [deficiencies] [judgments] [foreclosures] [collection efforts].

---

7 The consumer may also want to include a paragraph in the settlement agreement in which the creditor certifies that it has not already assigned, hypothecated, or transferred the debt.

8 This language is advisable in light of the lower court opinion that was reversed in Young v. Equifax Credit Information Servs., Inc., 294 F.3d 631 (5th Cir. 2002).

9 The consumer may also want to include a paragraph in the settlement agreement in which the creditor certifies that it has not already assigned, hypothecated, or transferred the debt.

10 This language is advisable in light of the lower court opinion that was reversed in Young v. Equifax Credit Information Servs., Inc., 294 F.3d 631 (5th Cir. 2002).

Appendix K Government Enforcement Orders

K.1 Introduction

This appendix summarizes the enforcement orders found on the companion CD-Rom that have been secured by law enforcement agencies against credit reporting agencies (CRAs), resellers, users, furnishers, and identity thieves. The major enforcement orders against the three largest consumer reporting agencies are reprinted on the CD-Rom, as well as important examples of the other categories of enforcement orders.

The remedies specified in the orders are binding on the defendants, and they provide evidence of reasonable procedures which may be expected of all consumer reporting agencies. For these reasons, they should be useful to most practitioners who are litigating complaints under the Fair Credit Reporting Act.

Important Note: Virtually all of these enforcement orders pre-date the FACTA amendments, and a number of them even pre-date the Consumer Credit Reporting Reform Act of 1996 and the Credit Repair Organizations Act.

K.2 Orders Against Experian (Formerly TRW)

FTC v. TRW, Inc., 784 F. Supp. 361 (N.D. Tex. 1991) (consent order), *amended by* (N.D. Tex. Jan. 14, 1993) (agreed order amending consent order). This FTC enforcement action brought against TRW [now Experian] resulted from widespread dissatisfaction with the accuracy of reported information and apparent systematic FCRA compliance difficulties. The resulting federal court consent order prohibits Experian from engaging in a series of practices that were the source of many consumer complaints: mixed files, failing to detect logical errors, failing to obtain full identifying information on consumers, failing to tell furnishers the nature of a consumer's dispute, failing to give credit to consumer documentation concerning a dispute, and otherwise failing to conduct proper reinvestigations. TRW also agrees to attempt to keep information from re-appearing in a file after it has been deleted as inaccurate, and to provide risk scores. The order also includes TRW responsibilities when selling information to a broker intending to resell it. Later, the FTC agreement was amended to address TRW practices when creating lists of consumers for targeted telemarketing efforts and for direct mailing campaigns.

TRW Inc. v. Morales, Civil Action No. 3-91-1340-H (N.D. Tex. Dec. 10, 1991) (consent order). This is an enforcement action brought against TRW [now Experian] by a large group of state attorneys general as a result of widespread dissatisfaction with the accuracy of reported information and apparent systematic FCRA compliance difficulties. The resulting consent order is similar to the consent order between TRW and the FTC, described in the prior paragraph. The consent order was entered into with the attorneys general of the following states: Alabama, Arkansas, California, Connecticut, Delaware, Florida, Idaho, Illinois, Louisiana, Michigan, Missouri, Nevada, New Hampshire, New Mexico, New York, Ohio, Pennsylvania, Rhode Island, and Texas.

U.S. v. Experian Information Solutions, Inc., CA 3-00CV0056-L (N.D. Tex. Jan. 12, 2000) (consent decree). This is an FTC proceeding against Experian (with similar proceedings against Equifax and Trans Union) for failing to adequately provide telephone access for consumer inquiries. The action ended with an agreement that Experian pay a $1 million fine and enter into a consent decree to insure future telephone access for consumers.

K.3 Equifax

In re Equifax, Inc., 96 F.T.C. 1045 (1980) (opinion and final order), *rev'd in part*, 678 F.2d 1047 (11th Cir. 1982). Just a few years after enactment of the FCRA, the FTC initiated a major, protracted enforcement action against Equifax, then known as Retail Credit Company. A voluminous record resulted in an FTC order addressing a wide variety of improper, commonplace practices. Parts of the final order concerning internal incentive plans for employees and offices were set aside upon appeal, but the rest of the FTC adjudication remains in place. The FTC opinion and order dealt with such practices as the CRA's failure to fully disclose to consumers the contents of their files, including claim reports, the CRA discouraging consumers from receiving disclosures over the phone or in-person, misrepresenting the identity of CRA investigators, and obtaining unauthorized medical information.

In re Equifax Credit Information Services, Inc. (June 22, 1992) (agreement of assurances with attorneys general). This agreement is similar to *TRW Inc. v. Morales*, described in Appx. K.2, *supra*, and is entered into between Equifax and the attorneys general of Alabama, Arkansas, California, Connecticut, Florida, Idaho, Illinois, Michigan, Minnesota, Missouri, Nevada, New Mexico, New York, Ohio, Pennsylvania, Texas, Utah, and Washington on credit reporting practices.

In the Matter of Equifax Credit Information Services, Inc., 61 Fed. Reg. 15484 (Apr. 8, 1996) (consent order). Another wide-ranging FTC investigation resulted in a consent order addressing a litany of common abuses ranging from mixing the files of different consumers, failing to delete inaccurate information, and failing to present deleted information from reappearing in consumer reports, to general failures in reducing inaccuracies and prescreening practices. The order also covers a requirement that the agency adopt reasonable procedures to assure permissible use, guarantee adequate disclosures to consumers, prevent impermissible information from being reported to users, and conduct proper reinvestigations. Monitoring and recordkeeping requirements were also included.

FTC Enforcement Orders can be found on the CD-Rom accompanying this manual.

In the Matter of Equifax Credit Information Services, Inc., 60 Fed. Reg. 9842 (Feb. 22, 1995) (analysis of proposed consent order to aid public comment). This document is an FTC analysis of the consent order with Equifax described in the prior paragraph.

In the Matter of Equifax Credit Information Services, Inc. (Vt. Super. Ct., Wash. Cty. Jan. 2000) (assurance of discontinuance). The State of Vermont obtained an Assurance of Discontinuance from Equifax requiring Equifax to implement specific procedures to assure that only those with permissible purposes are provided consumer reports, which prevents any businesses from obtaining reports for impermissible purposes and prevents individual employees of those businesses from wrongly using their employer's access to a reporting agency. While Vermont, unlike most states, requires a consumer's consent before a user may obtain a report, the procedures agreed to by Equifax in Vermont may bear upon what is reasonable conduct elsewhere.

U.S. v. Equifax Credit Information Services, Inc., CA 1:00-CV-0087 (N.D. Ga. Jan. 12, 2000) (consent decree). The FTC proceeded against the big three nationwide reporting agencies for failing to provide adequate telephone access for consumer inquiries. This is the resulting consent decree involving Equifax, which agreed to pay a fine of $500,000 and improve telephone access for consumers.

U.S. v. Equifax Credit Information Services, Inc., C.A. # 1:00-CV-0087-MHS (N.D. Ga. July 29, 2003) (joint motion for modification of consent decree). Equifax agreed to pay $250,000 to settle FTC charges that its rate of blocked-calls and its hold times violated provisions of the 2000 FTC consent decree described in the prior paragraph concerning Equifax not having sufficient personnel available to answer the toll-free phone number provided on consumers' credit reports. Equifax failed to meet the specific performance standards in the consent decree for blocked calls and hold times for certain periods in 2001.

K.4 Trans Union

In re Trans Union Credit Information Co., 102 F.T.C. 1109 (1983) (consent order). An FTC investigation that addressed, among other issues, the provision of reports to detective agencies and government agencies, the delayed deletion of obsolete credit account information, the premature deletion of non-derogatory information, the disclosure of file information to consumers, and reinvestigation of disputed information. The order covers reasonable procedures regarding furnishing reports to investigators and government agencies, not providing users obsolete information, noting consumer disputes, not purging recent positive data, conducting proper reinvestigations, and developing computer systems to insure accuracy, monitoring, and record-keeping.

Alabama v. Trans Union Corp., Civil Action No. 92C 7101 (N.D. Ill. Oct. 26, 1992) (consent order). This order, obtained by seventeen state attorneys general, deals with procedures to avoid mixed and duplicate files and other data errors, to ensure maximum accuracy, to require information identifying consumers, and to require furnishers to use a standardized form to furnish data to the CRA. Other provisions deal with disclosures to consumers of the content of their files, reinvestigations, procedures ensuring that deleted incorrect information not reappear, and prescreening.

In the Matter of Trans Union Corp., 118 F.T.C. 821 (1994) (FTC decision and final order). The FTC ordered Trans Union to change its practice with regard to the compilation of targeted marketing lists. Trans Union appealed, and *In Trans Union Corp. v. FTC*, 81 F.3d 228 (D.C. Cir. 1996), the matter was remanded to the FTC for a factual determination as to whether information in specialized mailing lists compiled by Trans Union would or could be used to determine credit eligibility. The issue is whether target marketing lists, such as used for sweepstake promotions, mail order catalogues, and other solicitations, involve credit worthiness. The court disagreed with the FTC's finding that the targeted mailing list provided by Trans Union were consumer reports under the Act, both because an issue of material fact was not considered in the summary proceeding before the Commission and because the court did not accept as a matter of logic and interpretation a clear distinction between identifying information and information collected for use as a factor in determining credit eligibility. A First Amendment challenge to the FTC injunction was commented upon sympathetically, but left undecided. The court opinion should be consulted on those issues. On the other hand, other parts of the FTC opinion were generally endorsed by the court.

In the Matter of Trans Union Corp, F.T.C. Dkt. # 9255 (July 31, 1998) (FTC initial decision). At trial on remand, an FTC Administrative Law Judge (ALJ) reconsidered Trans Union's target marketing practices in light of the U.S. Court of Appeals decision. The ALJ ruled that Trans Union's target marketing lists are consumer reports, based on consumer credit data, and ordered Trans Union to stop selling the lists except for the prescreening purposes permitted by the FCRA. The ALJ opinion offers considerable insight into the practices of Trans Union and some useful findings about credit scoring and the direct mail industry.

In the Matter of Trans Union Corp., F.T.C. Dkt # 9255 (Feb. 10, 2000) (FTC decision and final order). Trans Union appealed the ALJ decision to the full Commission. The Commission's ruling, reprinted in part also concluded that Trans Union's target marketing lists are consumer reports wrongly disclosed to users without a permissible purpose. Although some identifying information on which the lists are based, such as name, address and Social Security number, does not meet the definition of consumer report, other information such as age and the fact that a person has a relationship with a creditor, does. The Commission also disposed of First Amendment challenges. The Commission's ruling was upheld in all particulars in *Trans Union Corp. v. Fed. Trade Comm'n*, 245 F.3d 809 (D.C. Cir. 2001).

U.S. v. Trans Union, L.L.C., CA 00C 0235 (N.D. Ill. Jan. 12, 2000) (consent decree). The FTC proceeded against all three of the big nationwide reporting agencies for failing to provide adequate telephone access for consumer inquiries. The resulting consent decree against Trans Union provides for a $1 million fine and requires improvement in consumer's phone access to the CRA.

K.5 ChoicePoint

U.S. v. ChoicePoint, Inc., CA 1 06-CV-0198 (N.D. Ga. Jan. 30, 2006) (stipulated final judgment), *reprinted at* www.ftc.gov/os/caselist/choicepoint/choicepoint.htm. Choicepoint in 2005 acknowledged that the personal financial records of more than 163,000 consumers in its database had been compromised. The

FTC's complaint alleged that the CRA did not have reasonable procedures to screen prospective subscribers to verify their identity and to make sure they had a permissible use for the information. Some subscribers had commercial mail drops as addresses or in other ways indicated a high likelihood that they were not real businesses or did not have a permissible purpose. The FTC also alleged Choicepoint misrepresented the secureness of its privacy practices. The stipulated final judgment requires ChoicePoint to pay $10 million in civil penalties and $5 million for consumer redress. It bars the company from furnishing consumer reports to people who do not have a permissible purpose and requires the company to maintain reasonable procedures to ensure that consumer reports are provided only to those with a permissible purpose, including the verification of the user's identity. It must also maintain a comprehensive information security program to protect the security, confidentiality, and integrity of its data.

K.6 Resellers of Consumer Reports

FTC Analysis of Proposed Consent Order with Inter-Fact, 57 Fed. Reg. 38684 (Aug. 26, 1992). This FTC analysis accompanied the publication of the proposed consent agreement with Inter-Fact, a reseller of consumer reports. The consent order is described in the next paragraph.

In the Matter of Inter-Fact, Inc., 58 Fed. Reg. 26788 (May 5, 1993) (consent order). Known in the trade as resellers, "information brokers," or "superbureaus," some agencies act as middlemen between large consumer reporting agencies like Experian and users. They buy information from reporting agencies and sell it to users such as attorneys, private detectives, and employers. Often information brokers cared little about the requirements of the FCRA and the agencies from which the information was purchased did not concern themselves with the practices of these brokers. As a result, a segment of the industry grew in which personal information was distributed and used without the knowledge of the consumers and without honoring consumer protections. The Consumer Credit Reporting Reform Act of 1996 included provisions specifically applicable to superbureaus, or resellers, which incorporate some of the terms of prior FTC orders, such as this decision and order. The order sets forth detailed requirements for information brokers, primarily delineating controls resellers should exercise over who may be provided the resold information, in particular information provided to an insurance company that intends to use the information for purposes other than underwriting insurance involving the consumer on whom the report is furnished. In addition, the reseller is required to notify the consumer whenever a consumer report is furnished for employment purposes and contains information that may adversely affect the consumer's ability to obtain employment.

In the Matter of First American Real Estate Solutions, L.L.C., F.T.C. File No. 95 23267 (F.T.C. 1998) (complaint). The FTC alleged that this CRA, which merged information from the three major national credit bureaus and then resold that information, failed to reinvestigate disputed information, failed to correct consumer files when errors were made apparent, and failed to indicate the consumer's dispute of the information in the file. The FTC also alleged the reseller failed to institute reasonable procedures to prevent the re-insertion of previously deleted information.

In the Matter of First American Real Estate Solutions, L.L.C., 63 Fed. Reg. 59566 (Nov 4, 1998) (FTC analysis of proposed consent order). The FTC produced this analysis to aid public comment of the order resulting from the complaint described in the prior paragraph.

In the Matter of First American Real Estate Solutions, L.L.C., F.T.C. File No. 95 23267 (1999) (consent order). This order, resulting from the complaint detailed above, is significant because it addresses the role of resellers when consumers dispute the accuracy of information reported by a reseller. The order is analyzed in the document described in the prior paragraph.

United States v. Far West Credit, Inc., Civ. No. 2:06-CV-00041 (D. Utah Jan. 12, 2006) (consent decree), *available at* www.ftc.gov/os/caselist/0423185/060113farwestcreditconsentdecree.pdf. The FTC complaint alleged this reseller of consumer reports did not follow reasonable procedures to assure the accuracy of the information in the consumer reports it sold to mortgage companies. When information it purchased from nationwide CRAs was insufficient, it accepted documentation from the consumer or other interested party on behalf of the consumer, such as the mortgage broker or originator, purporting to show sources of credit and credit status with businesses that do not report to the nationwide credit bureaus, and merged it into the other information it had purchased. This led to origination of FHA loans that subsequently defaulted. It agreed to implement reasonable procedures to assure the maximum possible accuracy of its information, to pay $120,000, and to follow certain record keeping and reporting requirements to allow compliance monitoring.

K.7 Users of Consumer Reports

FTC v. Citigroup, Inc., C.A. No. 010CV-0606 (N.D. Ga. Sept. 18, 2002) (stipulation of settlement), *available at* www.ftc.gov/opa/2002/09/associates.htm. The FTC alleged that Associates First Capital Corporation and Associates Corporation of North America (both acquired by Citigroup) had used consumer reports for the impermissible purpose of soliciting consumers for loans beyond the loan amount for which the report was originally obtained. The lawsuit, which focused primarily on other deceptive marketing and abusive lending practices, resulted in a settlement of $240 million in redress to consumers and extensive provisions limiting the lenders' practices.

In the Matter of Quicken Loans, Inc., F.T.C. Dkt. # 9304 (Dec. 30, 2002) (consent order). The FTC obtained this order against a user of a credit report that allegedly failed to provide adverse action notices pursuant to the FCRA. The consent agreement requires Quicken Loans to provide to applicants the FCRA adverse action notice whenever it takes any adverse action with respect to an application for credit, either in whole or in part because of information contained in a credit report.

U.S. v. AT&T Corp., Civ. No. 022-3159 (N.D.N.J. Sept. 9, 2004) (consent decree), *reprinted at* www.ftc.gov/opa/2004/09/sprintatt.htm; *U.S. v. Sprint Corp.*, Civ. No. 022-3160 (N.D. Fla. Sept. 9, 2004) (consent decree), *reprinted at* www.ftc.gov/opa/2004/09/sprintatt.htm. The FTC charged Sprint and AT&T with using consumers' credit reports to deny telephone service and to place restrictions on consumers' service, without providing complete adverse action notices required under the FCRA and ECOA. Sprint sometimes failed to provide any notice at all. Under the consent decrees, Sprint agreed to a civil penalty of over a million dollars and AT&T agreed to pay $365,000. The decrees barred both companies from failing to comply with adverse action notice requirements and included recordkeeping and monitoring requirements.

K.8 Furnishers

U.S. v. Performance Capital Management, Inc., F.T.C. File No. 982 3542 (C.D. Cal. Aug. 24, 2000) (consent decree), *reprinted at* www.ftc.gov/opa/2000/08/performance.htm. The FTC alleged that a debt buyer furnished CRAs with inaccurate delinquency dates, using more recent dates instead of the date the debt was first delinquent, failed to reinvestigate consumer disputes referred by CRAs, and failed to notify CRAs when consumers disputed collection accounts with the debt buyer. The debt buyer agreed to cease these practices and immediately delete information in CRA files where account records no longer exist for a disputed debt. This case is significant both for its indication of problems debt buyers may face complying with the FCRA and for the FTC's view that a reasonable reinvestigation requires inspection of the original account records, with the furnisher having to admit it cannot verify a debt where such records do not exist. If the debt buyer does not have those records, it must seek them from the creditor selling them the debt.

U.S. v. DC Credit Services, Inc., C.A. No. 02-5115 (D.C. Cal. June 27, 2002) (consent decree). The FTC alleged a debt collection agency violated the FCRA by furnishing information to a CRA when it consciously avoided knowing that the information was inaccurate, for failing to notify a CRA promptly that previously-furnished information was incomplete or inaccurate, even after making such a determination, for furnishing adverse information to CRAs without disclosing that the consumer had disputed the information, and for falsely reporting the date of delinquency of a debt as a later date than when it first became delinquent. The debt collector agreed to pay $300,000 in civil penalties, to notify CRAs to delete all adverse information previously provided for the past seven years, and only to re-report information after a determination that it is accurate and reportable.

U.S. v. NCO Group, Inc., F.T.C. File No. 922-3012 (E.D. Pa. May 12, 2004) (consent decree). This is an FTC action against a debt collector that furnishes information to credit reporting agencies. The debt collection agency allegedly reported dates of delinquency to credit reporting agencies that were later than the month and year of the commencement of the delinquency, in violation of the FCRA. The consent decree enjoins the debt collection agency from reporting a date of delinquency later than allowed under the FCRA and it is required to implement a program for five years to monitor complaints received regarding the accuracy of information it furnishes to credit reporting agencies.

K.9 Identity Thief

FTC v. a Minor (C.D. Cal. 2003) (stipulated final judgment and order for permanent injunction and other equitable relief). This order is against an identity thief who allegedly used hijacked corporate logos and deceptive spam to con consumers out of credit card numbers and other financial data. The FTC alleged that the scam, called "phishing," had the thief posing as America Online and sending consumers e-mail messages claiming that there had been a problem with the billing of their AOL account. The e-mail warned consumers that if they did not update their billing information, they risked losing their AOL accounts and Internet access. The message directed consumers to click on a hyperlink in the body of the e-mail to connect to the "AOL Billing Center," an AOL look-alike web page that directed consumers to enter credit card numbers they had used for charges on their AOL account. It then asked consumers to enter numbers from a new card to correct the problem. The phony AOL web page also asked for consumers' names, mothers' maiden names, billing addresses, Social Security numbers, bank routing numbers, credit limits, personal identification numbers, and AOL screen names and passwords. The FTC charged the defendant's practices were deceptive and unfair, in violation of the FTC Act. In addition, the FTC alleged that the defendant's practices violated provisions of the Gramm-Leach-Bliley Act designed to protect the privacy of consumers' sensitive financial information. The stipulated judgment and permanent injunction bars the defendant from future violations of the FTC Act and the Gramm-Leach-Bliley Act. It also bars the defendant from sending spam in the future.

Appendix L Consumer Guides to Credit Reporting and Credit Scores (Appropriate for General Distribution)

This appendix contains two consumer guides on credit reports and credit scores. The first guide summarizes for consumers their basic rights under the Fair Credit Reporting Act. The second guide provides information to consumer regarding credit scores.

There are many self-help steps that a consumer may take to assure that his or her credit reports and credit scores are accurate, and to protect against identity theft. The guides in this appendix are intended to inform consumers about what they may do on their own to protect their credit histories and credit scores. Permission is hereby granted to duplicate these guides for the purpose of making them available to consumers who may be concerned about their credit reports.

Consumers will also find helpful the FCRA's *General Summary of Consumer Rights* and *Summary of Consumer Identity Theft Rights*, which are reprinted at Appendix C.2 and C.3, *supra*.

What You Should Know About Your Credit Report

If you have ever applied for a credit card, a personal loan, insurance, or a job, there is probably a company keeping a credit file or credit report about you. This file contains information about where you live and work, how you pay your bills, or whether you have been sued, arrested, or have filed for bankruptcy.

Companies that gather and sell this information are called "Consumer Reporting Agencies" or "Credit Bureaus." The information sold by Consumer Reporting Agencies to creditors, employers, insurers, and other businesses is called a "credit report."

Here are answers to some common questions about credit reports, consumer reporting agencies, and credit scores.

Can I obtain free copies of my credit reports?

Yes. Due to a recent change in the law, you can get a free copy of your credit report once every 12 months from each of the three big nationwide Consumer Reporting Agencies. By September 1, 2005, everyone in the country will have this right.

How do I order my free annual report?

The three nationwide Consumer Reporting Agencies have set up one central website, toll-free telephone number, and mailing address through which you can order your free annual report. To order:

- Log on www.annualcreditreport.com;
- Call 877-322-8228; or
- Complete the Annual Credit Report Request Form and mail it to:

  Annual Credit Report Request Service
  P.O. Box 105281
  Atlanta, GA 30348-5281.

You can print the form at www.ftc.gov/credit.

Do not contact the three nationwide Consumer Reporting Agencies individually for your free annual report. They are only providing free annual credit reports through the three centralized sources listed above.

You may order your free annual reports from each of the three nationwide Consumer Reporting Agencies at the same time, or you can order from only one or two.

The three major national credit bureaus are:

Equifax
800-685-1111
www.equifax.com

Experian
888-EXPERIAN
(888-397-3742)
www.experian.com

Trans Union
800-916-8800
www.transunion.com

What information do I have to provide to get my free report?

You need to provide your name, address, Social Security number, and date of birth. If you have moved in the last two years, you may have to provide your previous address. To maintain the security of your file, each nationwide Consumer Reporting Agency may ask you for some information that only you would know, like the amount of your monthly mortgage payment. Each agency may ask you for different information.

The website, www.annualcreditreport.com, is the only authorized source for your free annual credit report from the three nationwide Consumer Reporting Agencies. The website, www.annualcreditreport.com, and the nationwide Consumer Reporting Agencies will not call you or send you an e-mail asking for your personal information. If you get a telephone call or an e-mail or see a pop-up ad claiming it's from www.annualcreditreport.com or any of the three nationwide Consumer Reporting Agencies, do not reply or click on any link in the message—it's probably a scam. Forward any e-mail that claims to be from www.annualcreditreport.com or any of the three Consumer Reporting Agencies to the FTC's database of deceptive spam at spam@uce.gov.

Can I obtain other free credit reports?

Yes, in certain circumstances. If your application was denied because of information furnished by the Consumer Reporting Agency, and if you request a copy of your credit report within 60 days of receiving the denial notice, you are entitled to the information without charge. You are also entitled to one free report once in any 12 month period, if you certify in writing that you:

- Are unemployed and intend to apply for a job in the next 60 days;
- Are receiving public welfare assistance; or
- Believe that your report is wrong due to fraud.

If you don't meet one of these requirements, the Consumer Reporting Agency may charge a fee, currently up to $9.50 for a copy of your report. In some states, Consumer Reporting Agencies are required to provide consumers a free report or a report at a reduced fee.

Why should I order my credit report?

It is a good idea to check your report regularly, even when you are not experiencing problems. The information in your report affects your credit score and whether you can get a loan—and how much you will have to pay to borrow money. It is also helpful to make sure the information is accurate, complete, and up-to-date before you apply for a loan for a major purchase like a house or car, buy insurance, or apply for a job. Ordering your report can also help you guard against identity theft. That's when someone uses your personal information—like your name, your Social Security number, or your credit card number—to commit fraud.

What do I do if the information is inaccurate or incomplete?

In 1970, Congress created the Fair Credit Reporting Act (FCRA) to protect consumers when dealing with Consumer Reporting Agencies. Under the FCRA, both the Consumer Reporting Agency and the information provider have responsibilities for correcting inaccurate or incomplete information in your report. To protect your rights, contact both the Consumer Reporting Agency and the provider of information, including lenders, collection agencies or other businesses.

First, tell the Consumer Reporting Agency *in writing* what information you believe is inaccurate. Be as specific as possible. The Consumer Reporting Agency must investigate the items in question—usually within 30 days—unless they consider your dispute frivolous. They must also forward all relevant data you provide about the dispute to the information provider. After the information provider receives notice of a dispute from the Consumer Reporting Agency, it must investigate, review all relevant information provided by the Consumer Reporting Agency, and report the results to the Consumer Reporting Agency. If the information provider finds the disputed information to be inaccurate, it must notify all nationwide Consumer Reporting Agencies so that they can correct this information in your file. (Job applicants can have corrected reports sent to anyone who received a copy during the past two years.)

When the investigation is complete, the Consumer Reporting Agency must give you the written results and a free copy of your report if the dispute results in a change. (This free report does not count as your annual free report.) If an item is changed or deleted, the Consumer Reporting Agency cannot put the disputed information back in your file unless the information provider verifies that it is accurate and complete. The Consumer Reporting Agency also must send you written notice that includes the name, address, and phone number of the information provider.

What can I do if the Consumer Reporting Agency or information provider refuses to correct the information I dispute?

If an investigation doesn't resolve your dispute with the Consumer Reporting Agency, you can ask that a statement of the dispute be included in your file and in future reports. You also can ask the Consumer Reporting Agency to provide your statement to anyone who received a copy of your report in the recent past. You will probably have to pay a fee for this service.

If you tell the information provider that you dispute an item, a notice of your dispute must be included any time the information provider reports the item to a Consumer Reporting Agency.

How long can a Consumer Reporting Agency report bad information?

A Consumer Reporting Agency can report most accurate negative information for seven (7) years and bankruptcy information for ten (10) years. However, there is no time limit on reporting information about criminal convictions.

Who else can get a copy of my credit report?

Only people with a legitimate business need, as recognized by the Fair Credit Reporting Act, can look at your report without your permission. For example, a company is allowed to get your report if you apply for credit, insurance, employment, or to rent an apartment.

A Consumer Reporting Agency may not give information about you to your employer, or to a prospective employer, without your consent, unless you are being investigated for suspected misconduct, compliance with federal, state or local laws, or preexisting written policies of your employer.

What if I think a Consumer Reporting Agency has violated my rights under the law?

You may wish to seek the advice of an attorney about bringing a private lawsuit. You should also consider contacting the Federal Trade Commission (FTC). Although the FTC cannot act as your lawyer in private disputes, information about your experiences and concerns is important to the enforcement of the Fair Credit Reporting Act. To file a complaint or to get free information on consumer issues, visit www.ftc.gov or call toll-free, 1-877-FTC-HELP (1-877-382-4357); TTY: 1-866-653-4261. The FTC enters Internet, telemarketing, identity theft, and other fraud-related complaints into Consumer Sentinel, a secure, on-line database available to hundreds of civil and criminal law enforcement agencies in the U.S. and abroad.

States may also enforce the FCRA, and many states have their own consumer reporting laws. In some cases, you may have more rights under state law. For more information, contact your state or local consumer protection agency or your state Attorney General.

Publications and Websites

Publications:

- National Consumer Law Center, Fair Credit Reporting (6th ed. 2006).
- National Consumer Law Center Guide to Surviving Debt (2006 ed.).
- Call 617-542-9595 or visit www.consumerlaw.org for more information about NCLC publications.

Websites:

Consumer Federation of America
202-387-6121
www.consumerfed.org

Consumers Union
www.consumersunion.org

U.S. PIRG
(202) 546-9707
www.uspirg.org

Understanding Credit Scores

For years, creditors have been using credit scoring systems to determine whether a consumer is a good risk for credit cards and auto loans. More recently, credit scoring has been used to help creditors evaluate a consumer's ability to repay home mortgage loans and whether to charge deposits for utility services. Many auto and home insurance companies use special credit scores to decided whether to issue a policy and for how much.

Here's how credit scoring works in helping decide who gets credit—and why.

What is credit scoring?

Information about consumers and their credit experiences, such as bill-paying histories, numbers and types of accounts, collection actions, outstanding debt, and the age of accounts, is collected from a consumer's credit application and credit report. Using a statistical program, creditors compare this information to the credit performance of consumers with similar profiles. A credit scoring system awards points for each factor that helps predict who is most likely to repay a debt. A total number of points—a credit score—helps predict how creditworthy a consumer is, that is, how likely it is that a consumer will repay a loan and make the payments when due. The most popular type of credit score is usually between 300 and 850. A higher number is considered a better score.

How is a credit scoring model developed?

A creditor selects a random sample of its customers, or a sample of similar customers if their sample is not large enough, and analyzes it statistically to identify characteristics that relate to creditworthiness. Each of these factors is assigned a weight based on how strong a predictor it is of credit risk. Each creditor may use its own credit scoring model, different scoring models for different types of credit, or a generic model developed by a credit scoring company.

Under the Equal Credit Opportunity Act, a credit scoring system may not use certain characteristics like—race, sex, marital status, national origin, or religion—as factors. However, creditors are allowed to use age in properly designed scoring systems. Any scoring system that includes age must give equal or better treatment to elderly applicants.

What can consumers do to improve credit scores?

Credit scoring models are complex and often vary among creditors and for different types of credit. Only the creditor can explain what might improve a score under the particular model used to evaluate a credit application.

Scoring models generally evaluate the following types of information:

- *Payment history*. It is likely that a score will be affected negatively for late payments, accounts referred to collections, or bankruptcies.
- *Amount of outstanding debt*. Many scoring models evaluate the amount of debt compared to credit limits. Debt amounts that are close to the credit limit will likely have a negative effect on a score.
- *Length of credit history*. Generally, scoring models give more points the longer a consumer's credit track record is. An insufficient credit history may have an effect on a score, but that can be offset by other factors, such as timely payments and low balances.
- *Recent applications for credit*. Many scoring models consider whether a consumer has applied for credit recently by looking at "inquiries" on the credit report. A lot of inquires can negatively affect a score. However, not all inquiries are counted. Inquiries by creditors who are monitoring an account or looking at credit reports to make "prescreened" credit offers are not counted. Credit inquiries made by consumers of their own credit records aren't included either. Some creditors and credit bureaus claim that they do not even consider inquiries. Others claim that a lot of inquiries will have only a small impact on a credit score.
- *Number and types of credit accounts*. Although it is generally good to have established credit accounts, too many credit card accounts may have a negative effect on a score. In addition, many models consider the type of credit accounts and give more points to what they consider a healthy "mix." Under some scoring models, loans from finance companies may negatively affect a credit score.

Scoring models may be based on more than just information in a credit report. For example, the model may consider information from a credit application as well as information about jobs or occupations, length of employment, and homeownership.

To improve a credit score under most models, it is best to concentrate on paying bills on time, paying down outstanding balances, and not taking on new debt. It's likely to take some time to improve a score significantly. Errors involving negative information should be disputed. (See NCLC Consumer Guide, "What You Should Know About Your Credit Report."[1])

How reliable is the credit scoring system?

Although a credit scoring system may seem arbitrary or impersonal, it can help make decisions faster, more accurately, and more impartially than individual judgment when it is properly designed. And many creditors design their systems so that in marginal cases, applicants whose scores are not high enough to pass easily or are low enough to fail absolutely are referred to a credit manager who decides whether the company or lender will extend credit. This may allow for discussion and negotiation between the credit manager and the consumer.

On the other hand, credit scoring does have some flaws. Credit scoring is only as good as the information in the credit report—garbage in, garbage out—and credit reports are notorious for containing errors. Credit scoring programs often cannot generate a score if the consumer has no recent activity on an account, usually within the last six months. This can be a problem for seniors who have paid off all their loans and do not use credit cards. Lack of a score can mean denial of credit or auto or homeowner's insurance. Finally, there are serious concerns that credit scoring disproportionately hurts certain minority groups.

What happens if a consumer is denied credit or does not get the terms she wants?

If a consumer is denied credit, the Equal Credit Opportunity Act[2] requires that the creditor give a notice that tells the consumer

---

1 Available at www.consumerlaw.org/action_agenda/seniors_initiative/information.shtml. *See generally* National Consumer Law Center, Fair Credit Reporting (6th ed. 2006); National Consumer Law Center, Guide to Surviving Debt (2006 ed.).

2 15 U.S.C. §§ 1691–1691f.

the specific reasons that the application was rejected or the fact that the consumer has the right to learn these reasons. Indefinite and vague reasons for denial are illegal. Acceptable reasons include: "Your income was low" or "You haven't been employed long enough." Unacceptable reasons include: "You didn't meet our minimum standards" or "You didn't receive enough points on our credit scoring system."

Sometimes consumers are denied credit because of information from a credit report. If so, the Fair Credit Reporting Act requires the creditor to give out the name, address and phone number of the credit reporting agency that supplied the information. Consumers should contact that agency to find out what the report said. This information is free if requested within 60 days of the credit denial. (See NCLC Consumer Guide, "What You Should Know About Your Credit Report" and NCLC Consumer Guide, "The Truth About Credit Reports."[3]) The credit reporting agency can tell consumers what is in their reports, but only the creditor can tell them why applications were denied.

If a consumer has been denied credit, or did not get the rate or credit terms he wanted, he should ask the creditor if a credit scoring system was used. If so, a consumer should ask what characteristics or factors were used in that system, and the best ways to improve the application. If the consumer is offered credit, she should ask whether she got the best rate and terms available and, if not, why. Asking about the best rate is very important. If the consumer is not offered the best rate available because of inaccuracies in the credit report, it is important to dispute the inaccurate information.

How to Obtain Credit Scores?

Until 2004, federal law did not require the disclosure of credit scores to consumers. This was changed by the Fair and Accurate Credit Transactions Act (FACTA) of 2003,[4] which amended the Fair Credit Reporting Act (FCRA)[5] to require disclosures of credit scores. This became effective on December 1, 2004. Now, upon request, and for a fee that is to be determined by the FTC, credit reporting agencies must disclose the following:

- A consumer's current credit score or most recent score that was calculated by the credit reporting agency relating to the extension of credit.
- A statement indicating that the information and credit scoring model may be different than the credit score used by the lender.
- The range of credit scores of the model used to generate the credit score.
- The key factors that adversely affected the consumer's credit score, listed in order of impact. The agency cannot list more than four (4) key factors, unless one of the factors is the number of inquiries, in which case that factor must be included.
- The date on which the credit score was created.
- The name of the provider of the credit score or the credit file used to generate the credit score.[6]

The new law also requires mortgage lenders who use credit scores in connection with an application for residential real estate secured credit to provide, free of charge, the consumer's credit score and associated key factors.[7]

More Information from the Federal Trade Commission (FTC)

The FTC works for the consumer to prevent fraudulent, deceptive and unfair business practices in the marketplace and to provide information to help consumers spot, stop and avoid them. To file a complaint or to get free information on consumer issues, visit www.ftc.gov or call toll-free, 1-877-FTC-HELP (1-877-382-4357); TTY: 1-866-653-4261. The FTC enters Internet, telemarketing, identity theft and other fraud-related complaints into Consumer Sentinel, a secure, on-line database available to hundreds of civil and criminal law enforcement agencies in the U.S. and abroad.

Publications and Websites

Publications:

- National Consumer Law Center, Fair Credit Reporting (6th ed. 2006).
- National Consumer Law Center Guide to Surviving Debt (2006 ed.).
- Call 617-542-9595 or visit www.consumerlaw.org for more information about NCLC publications.

Websites:

Consumer Federation of America
202-387-6121
www.consumerfed.org

Consumers Union
www.consumersunion.org

U.S. PIRG
202-546-9707
www.uspirg.org

---

3 Available at www.consumerlaw.org/action_agenda/seniors_initiative/information.shtml.
4 Pub. L. No. 108-159 (2003).
5 15 U.S.C. §§ 1681–1681x.
6 15 U.S.C. § 1681g(f).
7 15 U.S.C. § 1681g(g)(1).

Appendix M **Fair Credit Reporting Related Websites**

Government Web Sites

Free Annual Credit Report Centralized Source: www.annualcreditreport.com

Federal Trade Commission: www.ftc.gov

State Attorneys General: www.naag.org/ag/full_ag_table.php

Secretaries of State: www.nass.org/sos/sos.html

Federal legislative information: thomas.loc.gov

Consumer Reporting Agencies and other Industry Sites

Equifax: www.equifax.com

Experian: www.experian.com

TransUnion: www.transunion.com

Fair Isaac: www.myfico.com (consumer site)
  www.fairisaac.com

Choicepoint: www.choicetrust.com (consumer site)
  www.choicepoint.com

Consumer Data Industry Association (CDIA) www.cdiaonline.com

Consumer Advocacy Organizations

National Consumer Law Center: www.consumerlaw.org

National Association of Consumer Advocates: www.naca.net

Consumers Union: www.consumersunion.org

Consumer Federation of America: www.consumerfed.org

U.S. Public Interest Research Group: www.uspirg.org

Consumer Action: www.consumer-action.org

Electronic Privacy Information Center: www.epic.org

Privacy Rights Clearinghouse: www.privacyrights.org

Trial Lawyers for Public Justice: www.tlpj.org

Resources

FTC Identity Theft site: www.consumer.gov/idtheft

Appx. M *Fair Credit Reporting*

Identity Theft Resource Center: www.idtheftcenter.org

Identity Theft Prevention and Survival: www.identitytheft.org

My Fair Credit: www.myfaircredit.com

Credit Scoring Site: www.creditscoring.com

Privacy Times: www.privacytimes.com

General Consumer Information

Consumer World: www.consumerworld.com (non-commercial site that catalogs over 1500 useful consumer resources)

www.consumeraffairs.com (links to consumer-related sites)

Federal Consumer Information Center: www.pueblo.gsa.gov

Index

ACCIDENT REPORTING BUREAUS
see also DRIVING RECORDS
FCRA, application, 2.7.8

ACCOMMODATION PARTIES
see COSIGNERS

ACCOUNTANTS
see also TAX PREPARATION SERVICES
GLB Act, application, 16.4.1.2

ACCOUNT NUMBERS
see also CREDIT ACCOUNTS; FINANCIAL INFORMATION; FINANCIAL SERVICES
data brokers, "pretexting" to obtain, 16.4.2.3
sharing for marketing purposes, 16.4.1.8
truncation for identity theft protection, 9.2.5.1

ACCOUNTS
see also ACCOUNT NUMBERS
bank accounts, *see* FINANCIAL SERVICES
credit accounts, *see* CREDIT ACCOUNTS

ACCURACY
see also INACCURATE INFORMATION
agency liability, 4.1.1, 4.4
affiliate information sharing, 6.4.5
bankruptcy reporting, 4.4.6.9
billing errors, *see* BILLING ERRORS
credit scores, 14.8
definition, 4.2
duty to report accurately, 6.4.2
FTC study, 4.1.3.2
furnisher liability, 6.4.1, 6.4.4, 6.5.1
investigative consumer reports, 13.6.1
management policies discouraging, 4.4.6.1
Metro 2 Format, 6.3.3.2, 6.3.3.7, 6.4.2
missing information, 4.3.2, 4.4.6.8, 12.6.9, 14.8.3.3
public record information, 4.4.6.4
reinvestigations, *see* REINVESTIGATIONS
reseller liability, 4.4.4
standards
   affiliate information sharing, 6.4.5
   applies to report not later explanation, 4.2.2
   FTC Staff Commentary, Appx. D
   furnishers of information, 6.4
   legislative history, 1.4.2, 1.4.3, 1.4.6, 1.4.9.2, 4.1.2
   reasonable procedures, 4.4.4, 4.4.5, 4.4.6
   reinvestigations, 4.5.3
   reporting agencies, 4.4.5
   resellers, 4.4.4

ACTIONS
see also DISCOVERY; JURY TRIALS; LEGAL PROCEEDINGS; LITIGATION; PLEADINGS
burden of proof, *see* BURDEN OF PROOF
case selection, 11.3
civil rights, *see* CIVIL RIGHTS ACTIONS
class actions, *see* CLASS ACTIONS
collection suits, *see* COLLECTION SUITS
credit repair violations
   CROA violations, 15.2.8.2
   state law violations, 15.3.6
   telemarketing statutes, 15.4
damages, *see* DAMAGES
defamation, *see* DEFAMATION
defenses, *see* DEFENSES
evidence, *see* EVIDENCE
FCRA violations, *see* FCRA CLAIMS
FTC civil actions, 11.16.2.1
identity theft, 12.6.6
invasion of privacy, *see* INVASION OF PRIVACY
jurisdiction, *see* JURISDICTION
liability, *see* LIABILITY
libel, *see* DEFAMATION
limitations, *see* STATUTE OF LIMITATIONS
negligence, *see* NEGLIGENCE
parties, *see* PARTIES
reporting, *see* PUBLIC RECORD INFORMATION
RESPA violations, 10.3
state law, *see* STATE CLAIMS
successful action, defined, 11.14.1

ACTIVE MILITARY ALERTS
see MILITARY DUTY ALERTS

ACTS
see STATUTES

ACTUAL DAMAGES
see DAMAGES, ACTUAL

ADDRESS VERIFICATION SYSTEMS (AVS)
FCRA, application, 2.3.4.2.1

ADDRESSES
consumers
   changes resulting in mismatched files, 4.3.3.6
   discrepancies, notice to user, 8.5.3, 9.2.5.2
furnishers of information, error notification, 6.4.4
investigating agencies, disclosure, 13.4.1.6
Medical Information Bureau, 3.4.2.3
major credit bureaus, 3.4.2.2
update reports, consumer report status, 2.3.4.2.1

ADMINISTRATIVE ORDERS
child support enforcement, permissible use, 7.2.3.4
FCRA enforcement, 11.16.1, 11.16.2, Appx. K

ADMINISTRATIVE SUMMONS OR SUBPOENAS
consumer reports, obtaining, 7.2.1

ADOPTION AGENCIES
see also GOVERNMENT AGENCIES
FCRA, application, 2.3.6.6, 2.5.2

ADVERSE ACTION
account reviews, 8.2.6.4.3.9
affiliates, by, 3.3.1.6
check-writing denial, status, 8.2.6.4.7.2
consumer-initiated transactions, 8.2.6.4.7.1
consumer report, basis, 7.1.9
   free report, 3.3.6
cosigner's credit history, 8.2.7.4.3
credit card authorizations, 2.4.5
credit denial
   consumer reports, use, 7.2.3.2
   definition, 8.2.6.4.3.3
   reasons, disclosure, 8.2.6.2.1
counteroffer acceptance, status, 8.2.6.4.3.5
definition, 8.2.6.4.3
ECOA obligations
   notice requirements, 8.2.6.6, Appx. C.9
   reasons for action, 8.2.6.2.1
   record retention, 11.6.4
employment report, disclosures prior to, 3.3.1.4, 7.2.4.3.3
   employee misconduct exemption, 7.2.4.5, 13.2.4.2
FTC interpretations, Appx. D
government benefits and licenses, 8.2.6.4.6
impermissible purpose situations, 7.1.9
information other than consumer report, 3.3.1.5, 8.2.7
insurance purposes, 7.2.5
investigative reports, 13.4.1.6
lease denial, status, 8.2.6.4.7.3, 8.2.7.2
notice, see ADVERSE ACTION NOTICE
prescreening exclusion, 8.2.6.4.3.8
price quotes, status, 8.2.6.4.3.6
property sale, 8.2.6.4.7.4
reasons for, disclosure, 8.2.6.2.1
reporting by creditor, status as consumer report, 2.7.2
risk-based pricing, 8.2.6.4.3.4, 8.2.8, 14.7.3
state law preemption, 10.7
third party credit requests, 2.4.6
third party information, 8.2.7

ADVERSE ACTION NOTICE
see also ADVERSE ACTION
accepted counteroffers, 8.2.6.4.3.5
account reviews, 8.2.6.4.3.9
affiliate information sharing, 3.3.1.6, 8.2.7.5
   enforcement of right, 8.2.7.5.2
check-writing denial, 8.2.6.4.7.1, 8.2.6.4.7.2
consumer-initiated transactions, 8.2.6.4.7.1
content, 8.2.6.2
cosigners, 8.2.6.4.3.7, 8.2.7.4.3
ECOA notice
   comparison with FCRA notice, 8.2.6.6
   model form, Appx. C.9
   record retention, 11.6.4
employee misconduct investigations, 7.2.4.5, 13.2.4.2
   time, 8.2.6.4.4.2

employment reports, 7.2.3.4.4, 8.2.6.4.4
   contents, 8.2.6.2.5
   time, 8.2.6.4.4.3
enforcement of notice right, 8.2.6.5
entitlement to notice, 8.2.6.4
failure to send, 10.2.5.2, 11.10.2.2
government benefits, time, 8.2.6.4.6
importance, 8.2.6.1
information other than consumer report, 8.2.7
   contents, 8.2.7.1
   time and manner, 8.2.7.3
insurance purposes, 7.2.5
   time, 8.2.6.4.5
investment opportunities, 8.2.6.4.7.1
lease denial, 8.2.6.4.7.1, 8.2.6.4.7.3, 8.2.7.2, 12.7.3
manner of giving notice, 8.2.6.3
nature of, 8.2.6.1
prescreening offers, 8.2.6.4.3.8
price quotes, 8.2.6.4.3.6
risk-based pricing, 8.2.6.4.3.4, 8.2.8, 14.7.3
sale of property, 8.2.6.4.7.1, 8.2.6.4.7.4
third party information use, 8.2.7

ADVERSE INFORMATION
affiliate sharing, 3.3.1.6
checks as basis for, identification, 3.5.5
concealment
   identity alteration, 15.2.7.3
   misstatements, 15.2.7.2
consumer reporting agency obligations
   investigative reports, 13.6.2
   obsolete information, see OBSOLETE INFORMATION
cosigners, 5.6.2, 5.6.3
credit record, protecting when settling disputes, 12.6.4
credit repair organizations, concealing, 15.2.7.2
deletion before obsolete, 5.2.2.2
disputed debts, 6.5.3
ECOA restrictions, 5.5.2, 6.11, 12.4.8
explanations, 4.8.3
financial institutions, reporting by, 6.9, 8.2.10
fraudulent, blocking, 9.2.4
home mortgages, guidelines, 12.7.2
identifying information as, 7.2.10.2
inaccurate, see INACCURATE INFORMATION
investigative reports, verification, 13.6.2.3
management policies encouraging, 4.4.6.1
notice
   cosigners, 5.6.3
   financial institutions, 6.9
   model notices, Appx. C.8
   public record information, 8.2.20
   state law, 5.6.3
   student loans, 12.4.5
obsolete information, see OBSOLETE INFORMATION
other than consumer report, 3.3.1.5, 8.2.7
public record information, see PUBLIC RECORD INFORMATION
servicemembers, 5.5.1
source, disclosure, 3.3.1.5, 3.3.1.6
student loans, 12.4.5
theft-related debts, blocking, 9.2.4
third party, obtaining from, 3.3.1.5, 8.2.7
updating, 4.4.6.8.4
use, see ADVERSE ACTION
verification, reasonable procedures, 10.2.2.1.2

ADVERSE USE
see ADVERSE ACTION

ADVERTISEMENTS
credit repair, 15.2.2.2.3, 15.2.2.7
  fraud or deception, 15.2.7.5
  services, 15.2.7.4

AFFILIATE SHARING OF INFORMATION
see also AFFILIATES
accuracy standards, 6.4.5
adverse action, notice, 3.3.1.6, 8.2.7.5
consumer opt-out rights, 2.4.3.2
  marketing purposes, 2.4.3.2.3, 8.2.18.2.1.1
  notice to consumer, 2.4.3.2.2, 8.2.18
  third party information, 2.4.3.2.2, 8.2.18.2.1.2
disputed debts, 6.4.5
FCRA application, 2.4.3, 6.2.2.1
financial institutions, 8.2.18.2.2, 16.4.1.5.2
legislative history, 1.4.6
marketing information, 2.4.3.2.3, 8.2.18.2.1.1
medical information, 5.4.1.4
notice to consumers
  adverse action, 3.3.1.6, 8.2.7.5
  marketing information sharing, 2.4.3.2.3, 8.2.18.2.1.1
  use of information, 2.4.3.2.2, 8.2.18
state law preemption, 2.4.3.2.4, 10.7.6

AFFILIATES
adverse action, 3.3.1.6, 8.2.7.5
debt collectors affiliated with reporting agencies, 3.3.6
defined, 16.4.1.5.2
disputing debts with, 6.4.5
information sharing, see AFFILIATE SHARING OF INFORMATION
nationwide reporting agencies, reinvestigation, 4.5.2.3

AGE
reports containing, consumer report status, 2.3.4.2.1

AGENCIES
adoption, see ADOPTION AGENCIES
child support, see CHILD SUPPORT ENFORCEMENT AGENCIES
credit reporting, see CONSUMER REPORTING AGENCIES
federal, see FEDERAL AGENCIES
government, generally, see GOVERNMENT AGENCIES
law enforcement, see LAW ENFORCEMENT AGENCIES
local government, see LOCAL GOVERNMENT AGENCIES
state, see STATE AGENCIES
welfare, see WELFARE AGENCIES

AGENTS
consumer reports, obtaining, 7.1.6
  power of attorney, 3.4.4

AGREEMENTS
see also CONTRACTS
arbitration agreements, see ARBITRATION AGREEMENTS
repayment plans, see REPAYMENT AGREEMENTS
settlement of disputes, see SETTLEMENT

ALERTS
see also IDENTITY THEFT
active military service, see MILITARY DUTY ALERTS
fraud alerts, see FRAUD ALERTS

ALIMONY
see also CHILD SUPPORT; DIVORCE PROCEEDINGS
consumer reports, use, 7.4.2, 12.2.4

ALTERNATIVE CREDIT BUREAUS
see also CONSUMER REPORTING AGENCIES; SPECIALTY AGENCIES
credit scoring, 14.9.1
FCRA, application, 2.7.10

APARTMENT LEASES
see RESIDENTIAL LEASES

APARTMENT MANAGERS
consumer reports, obtaining, 7.1.6

ARBITRATION CLAUSES
enforceability, 11.9
  credit repair organizations, 15.2.8.4

ARRESTS
see PUBLIC RECORD INFORMATION

ASSIGNEES
CROA, application, 15.2.2.6, 15.2.2.2.4

ASSOCIATED CREDIT BUREAUS, INC.
see CONSUMER DATA INDUSTRY ASSOCIATION, INC. (CDIA)

ATTORNEY FEES AND COSTS
CROA claims, 15.2.8.5.1
FCRA claims
  bad faith, 11.1, 11.14.1
  establishing, 11.1
  liability for, 11.14.1
  maximizing awards, 11.14.3
  prevailing party, 11.1, 11.14.1
  right to, 11.1
  standards, 11.14.2
federal fee shifting standards, 11.14.2.2
lodestar approach, 11.14.2.2
published awards, quick reference, 11.15
Rule 68, 11.14.5
settled cases, 11.14.4
settlement agreements, breach, 12.6.4.3
successful action, 11.14.1
tort claims, 11.14.3

ATTORNEYS
consumer files
  power of attorney disclosures, 3.4.4
  reinvestigation requests, 4.5.2.2
consumer reports
  certification of permissible use, 7.5.2.2
  impermissible use, 7.4.4
  obtaining, 7.1.6, 7.2.1, 11.6.3.6
  permissible user, 7.2.3.4
  prospective clients, 7.4.4
CROA, application, 15.2.2.5
  credit repair organization status, 15.2.2.4, 15.2.2.5
FCRA, application, 2.7.7
fees, see ATTORNEY FEES AND COSTS
practice aids, see PRACTICE AIDS
subpoenas issued by, court order status, 7.2.1, 11.6.3.6

AUDIT TRAIL
consumer files, disclosure, 3.5.8

AUTHORIZED USERS
reporting of debts, 5.6.2

AUTOMATED CONSUMER DISPUTE VERIFICATIONS (ACDVs)
see also CONSUMER DISPUTE VERIFICATION (CDV) FORM
electronic processing of, 4.5.6.1, 6.10.1
reinvestigation notice, 4.5.4.2, 6.10.3
reinvestigation results, 6.10.6.4
sample form, Appx. I.3

AUTOMATED REINVESTIGATION SYSTEM
nationwide reporting agencies, 4.6.3, 6.10.1
  use by furnishers, 6.10.6.2, 6.10.6.4

AUTOMATED UNIVERSAL DATA FORMS (AUDFs)
see also UNIVERSAL DATA FORM
e-OSCAR processing system, 4.5.6.1, 6.10.1

AUTOMOBILE DEALERS
see also DEALER PAPER
credit repair laws, application
  CROA, 15.2.2.7
  state law, 15.3.4
disclosure obligations, 8.2.7.4.1
GLB Act, application, 16.4.1.2

AUTOMOBILE INSURANCE
see INSURANCE

AUTOMOBILE LEASES
see also PERSONAL PROPERTY LEASES
blemished credit record, impact, 12.7.1
fraud lists, 12.7.7
return of car, advertised rewards, bad debt list exemption, 12.2.3

AUTOMOBILE LOANS
blemished credit record, impact, 12.7.1

BAD CHECK LISTS
see CHECK CASHING LISTS

BAD DEBT LISTS
see also CONSUMER LISTS
publication, 12.2.3

BAD DEBTS
see CHARGED-OFF ACCOUNTS; DELINQUENT ACCOUNTS

BAD DRIVING LISTS
see also CONSUMER LISTS
specialized agencies, 3.2.4

BANKING REGULATORS
credit unions, see NATIONAL CREDIT UNION ADMINISTRATION
FCRA regulatory powers, 1.3.3.1, 11.16.1, 11.16.2.3
  text of regulations, Appx. B.3
federal savings banks, see OFFICE OF THRIFT SUPERVISION (OTS)
FRB, see FEDERAL RESERVE BOARD (FRB)
GLB Act regulatory and enforcement powers, 16.4.1.1, 16.4.1.10
national banks, see OFFICE OF COMPTROLLER OF THE CURRENCY (OCC)
state-chartered banks, see FEDERAL DEPOSIT INSURANCE CORPORATION

BANKRUPTCY
advantages, 12.6.8
cosigner, reporting, 5.6.2
discharge
  failure to report, 4.3.2.4, 4.4.6.9.2
  reporting, time limit, 12.7.2
Metro 2 Format reporting, 6.3.3.12
mortgage applications, impact, 12.7.2
reporting
  discharged debts, 4.3.2.4, 4.4.6.9.2
  erroneous, 4.4.6.9.3
  other issues, 4.4.6.9.4
  time limits, 5.2.3.7, 12.7.2
risk scoring, 14.2.2.3
spouses, 4.4.6.9.3
stay violations, 10.3
student loans, impact, 12.6.5, 12.7.8
updating files after, 4.3.2.4
utility services, effect, 12.7.4

BANKS
see also CREDITORS; FINANCIAL INSTITUTIONS
accounts
  see also FINANCIAL SERVICES
  pretexting, 11.16.2.1, 16.4.2.3
  number sharing, 16.4.1.8
CROA exemption, 15.2.2.3.4
financial information, see FINANCIAL INFORMATION
GLB Act, application, 16.4.1
regulatory authorities, see BANKING REGULATORS

BENEFITS
see GOVERNMENT BENEFITS; INSURANCE BENEFITS

BILLING ERRORS
see also CREDIT DISPUTES; DISPUTED INFORMATION
claims re, 10.3
definition, 5.3.4
FCBA, regulation, 5.3.4
home mortgages, 5.3.5
notification address, 6.4.4
open-end credit, 5.3.4

BOUNCED CHECKS
see DISHONORED CHECKS

BROKERS
data brokers, see DATA BROKERS
information brokers, see RESELLERS
loan brokers, see LOAN BROKERS
real estate brokers, see REAL ESTATE AGENTS

BULK SALES
consumer files, 7.1.7

BULLETINS
see LAW ENFORCEMENT BULLETINS

BURDEN OF PROOF
see also EVIDENCE
FCRA violations
  actual damages, 11.10.2.1
  attorney fees, 11.14.2.2
  negligence, 10.2.2.4, 10.2.5.2
  punitive damages, 11.12.1.1
  reasonable procedure violations, 4.4.5.1.2
  reasonable procedures as defense, 10.2.5.2

BURDEN OF PROOF (*cont.*)
FCRA violations (*cont.*)
  willful noncompliance, 11.12.1.2
tort claims, 10.4.6

BUSINESS CREDIT
see also COMMERCIAL TRANSACTIONS; CREDIT
consumer reports
  impermissible use, 7.1.9
  permissible use, 7.2.3.1.3
FCRA, application, 2.3.6.2, 2.3.6.3.1
reports for, *see* COMMERCIAL REPORTS

BUSINESS DEBTS
collection, consumer report, use, 7.2.3.1.3

BUSINESS INSURANCE
see also INSURANCE
consumer reports, use, 7.2.5

BUSINESS PURPOSES
see BUSINESS CREDIT; COMMERCIAL TRANSACTIONS

BUSINESS REPORTS
see COMMERCIAL REPORTS

BUSINESS TRANSACTIONS
see also BUSINESSES
commercial purposes, *see* COMMERCIAL TRANSACTIONS
consumer report, permissible purpose, 2.3.6.8, 7.2.8.2
  eligibility determination, necessity, 7.2.8.2.2.2
  initiated by consumer, 7.2.8.2.3
  legitimate business need, 7.2.8.2.4
definition, 7.2.8.2.2.1

BUSINESSES
see also CORPORATIONS; PARTNERSHIPS; SOLE PROPRIETORSHIPS
affiliated, *see* AFFILIATES
credit for, *see* BUSINESS CREDIT
FCRA, application, 2.3.3.3, 2.3.6.2, 2.3.6.8, 2.3.6.3.1, 7.2.8
insurance, *see* BUSINESS INSURANCE
legitimate need for information, consumer report use
  account review, 7.2.8.3
  impermissible use, 7.4.9
  insurance benefit issuance, 2.3.6.5.2
  permissible use, 2.3.6.8, 7.2.8
  transactions initiated by consumer, 7.2.8.2.4
reports on, *see* COMMERCIAL REPORTS
transactions
  commercial purpose, *see* COMMERCIAL TRANSACTIONS
  involving consumers, *see* BUSINESS TRANSACTIONS

CASE LAW
unreported cases, 1.1.3

CDIA
see CONSUMER DATA INDUSTRY ASSOCIATION, INC. (CDIA)

CDV
see CONSUMER DISPUTE VERIFICATION (CDV) FORM

CERTIFICATION
see also VERIFICATION
consumer reports, permissible use
  blanket certification, 4.9.1
  child support purposes, 7.2.9
  counterterrorism, 7.2.10.5

electronic communication, 7.5.4
employment reports, 7.2.4.3
generally, 7.5.2
obsolete information, 5.2.5.4
resellers, 2.6.3.3, 10.2.3
violations, 10.2.5.1
investigative reports, 13.4.1.5, 10.2.5.3
reinsertion of information, 4.7.3

CHARGED-OFF ACCOUNTS
see also DELINQUENT ACCOUNTS
date of charge-off, duty to provide, 5.2.3.3.3
nature of charge-offs, 5.2.3.3.2
reporting restrictions, 5.2.3.3

CHARGES
see FEES

CHECK APPROVAL COMPANIES
see also CONSUMER REPORTING AGENCIES; SPECIALTY AGENCIES
FCRA, application, 2.3.6.3.2
GLB Act, application, 16.4.1.2
identity theft, blocking of information, 9.2.4.1
lists issued by, *see* CHECK CASHING LISTS
nationwide agencies, 2.6.2

CHECK CASHING LISTS
see also CHECK APPROVAL COMPANIES; CONSUMER LISTS
adverse use, notice, 8.2.6.4.7.1, 8.2.6.4.7.2
blemished credit record, implications, 12.7.7
coding requirement, 12.7.7
consumer report status, 2.3.4.1, 2.3.6.3.2
publication, 12.2.3

CHECK CASHING REPORTS
see CHECK CASHING LISTS

CHECK GUARANTEE BUSINESSES
see CHECK APPROVAL COMPANIES; CHECK CASHING LISTS

CHECKS
see also CHECK APPROVAL COMPANIES; CHECK CASHING LISTS
adverse characterizations, identification disclosure, 3.5.5
credit, status as, 7.2.3.1.2
payment by
  consumer report, permissible use, 2.3.6.8, 7.2.3.1.2, 7.2.8.2.2.1
  denial, notice requirements, 8.2.6.4.7.2
returned checks, *see* DISHONORED CHECKS

CHEXSYSTEMS
see CHECK APPROVAL COMPANIES

CHILD CUSTODY
see CHILD SUPPORT; DIVORCE PROCEEDINGS

CHILD SUPPORT
see also DIVORCE PROCEEDINGS
consumer report
  impermissible uses, 12.2.4
  permissible uses, 2.3.6.9, 7.2.9, 7.4.2
enforcement, *see* CHILD SUPPORT ENFORCEMENT AGENCIES
overdue, inclusion in consumer report, 5.7.1, 7.4.2

CHILD SUPPORT ENFORCEMENT AGENCIES
see also CHILD SUPPORT
computer linkups with reporting agencies, 7.5.4
consumer reports, permissible users, 7.2.3.4, 7.4.2
determination of support levels, 2.3.6.9, 7.2.9
disclosure notice, 8.2.19
   content and nature, 8.2.19.1
   enforcement of right, 8.2.19.3
   time and manner, 8.2.19.2
reporting of debts, 5.7.1, 7.4.2

CHILDREN'S ONLINE PRIVACY PROTECTION ACT
scope, 16.4.2.1

CHOICEPOINT
see DATA BROKERS

CITY DIRECTORIES
consumer report status, 2.3.4.2.1, 2.3.5.3

CIVIL RIGHTS ACTIONS
credit reporting abuses, 10.3
privacy from governmental intrusion, 16.2

CIVIL SUITS
see ACTIONS; COLLECTION SUITS; LITIGATION

CLASS ACTIONS
credit repair violations, 15.2.8.6
credit reporting violations, 11.2.2

CLEARINGHOUSE NUMBERS
see also SARGENT SHRIVER NATIONAL CENTER ON POVERTY LAW
documents and unpublished cases, 1.1.3

CLUE
see DATA BROKERS

CODED LISTS
see also CONSUMER LISTS
bad debt lists, 12.2.3
check cashing lists, 12.7.7
consumer report status, 2.3.3.2, 7.3.2.3, 12.2.2

CODING SCHEMES
check cashing lists, 12.7.7
medical furnisher information, 5.4.1.3

COLLECTION AGENCIES
see DEBT COLLECTORS

COLLECTION SUITS
see also CREDITORS
consumer reports, use, 12.2.4
court orders covering reporting issues, 12.6.4.5
reporting limitations, 5.2.3.4
settlement, resolving reporting issues, 12.6.4

COLLEGE PLACEMENT OFFICES
FCRA, application, 2.7.6

COMMERCIAL REPORTS
consumer report status, 2.3.3.3, 2.3.5.2, 2.3.5.4, 2.3.6.2
false pretenses, obtaining under, 7.7.4
litigation, use, 7.4.4

COMMERCIAL TRANSACTIONS
see also BUSINESS TRANSACTIONS
consumer reports, impermissible use, discovering, 7.1.9
credit transactions, see BUSINESS CREDIT
FCRA, application, 2.3.6.2, 2.3.6.3.1, 7.2.3.1.3, 7.2.8.2.2.1
insurance transactions, see BUSINESS INSURANCE
reports in connection with, see COMMERCIAL REPORTS

COMMON LAW
privacy protections, 16.3, 16.5
torts, see TORT CLAIMS

COMPANIES
affiliated, see AFFILIATES
businesses, see BUSINESSES
check approval companies, see CHECK APPROVAL COMPANIES
consumer reporting companies, see CONSUMER REPORTING AGENCIES
corporations, see CORPORATIONS
credit reporting companies, see CONSUMER REPORTING AGENCIES
tenant screening, see TENANT SCREENING COMPANIES

COMPLAINTS
see also PLEADINGS
credit disputes, complaint address, 6.4.4, 12.6.2.3
FTC Identity Theft Hotline, 12.6.6
FTC referral program, 11.16.2.1

COMPUTER DATING SERVICES
see DATING SERVICES

COMPUTER ERRORS
see also ELECTRONIC COMMUNICATION
consumer files
   data retrieval, 4.4.6.7
   mismerged files, 4.3.3, 4.4.6.5
   legislative response, 1.4.3
   transcription errors, 4.4.6.7
Metro 2 Format, 6.3.3.7

COMPUTER FRAUD AND ABUSE ACT
see also COMPUTER FRAUD LAWS
claims under, 10.3
criminal sanctions, 11.16.3
financial information, protections, 16.4.2.1

COMPUTER FRAUD LAWS
credit reporting, application, 11.16.3
federal statute, see COMPUTER FRAUD AND ABUSE ACT
financial information, protections, 16.4.2.1

COMPUTER HOOKUPS
see ELECTRONIC COMMUNICATION

CONDITIONAL PRIVILEGE
defense to tort action, 10.5.2, 10.5.4

CONFIDENTIALITY
see also PRIVACY
consumer files, legislative history, 1.4.2, 1.4.3
credit score calculations, 14.5.4
discovery requests and, 11.6.3.4
   sample order, Appx. J.7
financial information, 16.5
investigative reports, sources, 13.4.2.3, 13.4.3
Metro 2 Format, 6.3.3.1
purpose of FCRA, 7.1.1

CONSENT
see also WAIVER
consumer reports
  consumer's, effect, 7.2.2
  employment reports, requirement, 7.2.4.3.2, 13.5.1
  insurance report, business purpose, 7.2.5
  medical information, inclusion, 5.4.1.2
employee agency communications, 2.4.4.2.5
FCRA disclosures
  form of disclosure, 3.6.1, 3.6.2
  presence of another person, 3.6.2

CONSOLIDATION SERVICES
see RESELLERS

CONSUMER
see CONSUMERS

CONSUMER CREDIT INFORMATION
see CONSUMER REPORTS

CONSUMER CREDIT PROTECTION ACT (CCPA)
see also EQUAL CREDIT OPPORTUNITY ACT (ECOA); FAIR CREDIT BILLING ACT (FCBA); FAIR CREDIT REPORTING ACT (FCRA); FAIR DEBT COLLECTION PRACTICES ACT (FDCPA)
rights under, exercise, discrimination, 5.5.2, 6.11, 12.4.8

CONSUMER CREDIT TRANSACTIONS
see CREDIT TRANSACTIONS

CONSUMER DATA INDUSTRY ASSOCIATION, INC. (CDIA)
E-OSCAR, creation, 6.10.1
Metro 2, creation, 6.3.1
professional liability insurance, 11.6.3.7
website, 6.3.2

CONSUMER DISPUTE VERIFICATION (CDV) FORM
electronic (ACDV) communication, 6.10.6.4
  on-line processing system, 6.10.1
Metro 2 alternative, circumstances, 6.3.2
notification of furnisher, 6.10.3
problems with, 6.10.1, 6.10.3

CONSUMER DISPUTES
see CREDIT DISPUTES; DISPUTED INFORMATION

CONSUMER FILES
see also CONSUMER REPORTING AGENCIES; CREDIT RECORD
access rights, 3.3
  adverse action, 3.3.6
  affiliated debt collector communications, 3.3.6
  contents of disclosure, 3.5
  credit repair organizations, disclosure, 15.2.3
  credit scores, 3.3.4, 3.5.2
  fee payment, 3.3.9
  fraud, 3.3.5
  free annual disclosure, 3.3.2, 3.4.2.1
  identity theft, 3.3.5
  mechanics of exercising, 3.4
  representative of consumer, 3.4.4
  time limits, 3.3.9.3
  users, from, 3.3.1
additional information
  consumer rights, 4.8, 12.6.9
  updated information, 4.4.6.8.4, 4.4.6.8.5
adverse information, *see* ADVERSE INFORMATION
alerts, 4.8.2, 9.2.2
  active military duty, *see* MILITARY DUTY ALERTS
  fraud alerts, *see* FRAUD ALERTS
audit trail, 3.5.8
authorized users, 5.6.2
bankruptcy, effect, 12.6.8
big three credit bureaus, 3.2.3, 3.4.1
building by reporting agency, 4.3.3.2
bulk sales, 7.1.7
business reports, commingling, 2.3.5.4
cleaning up, 12.6
computer access, 7.5.4
consumer report distinguished, 2.3.1.2
contents, 3.2
  disclosure, *see* DISCLOSURE
  nationwide agencies, 3.2.3.2, 3.4.1
  obsolete information, *see* OBSOLETE INFORMATION
  restrictions, 3.2.2
  specialized agencies, 3.2.4
  third party's information, 3.5.7, 4.3.3.1
corrections
  automated reinvestigation system, 4.6.3, 6.10.6.2, 6.10.6.4
  expedited dispute resolution, 4.5.5.2, 12.6.2.2
  following reinvestigations, 4.6.2
  monitoring, 4.6.3, 4.7.1, 12.6.4.7
credit limits, missing, 4.3.2.3, 14.8.3.2
credit scores, *see* CREDIT SCORES
dating of information, 5.2.5.3
defined, 3.2.2, 5.6.1
deletion of information
  agency rights, 5.2.2.2
  expedited dispute resolution, 4.5.5.2, 12.6.2.2
  following reinvestgation, 4.6.2
  obsolete information, *see* OBSOLETE INFORMATION
  reinsertion, *see* REINSERTION OF INFORMATION
  reporting, 4.9.1
  soft-deletes, 4.6.2, 4.7.1, 12.6.4.3
disclosure requests, *see* CONSUMER REPORTS, obtaining
disclosure distinguished from consumer report, 4.4.3
disclosure rights, 3.3, 3.5, 13.4.3
disclosure violations, 10.2.2.8
disputed information
  cleaning up after resolution, 12.6.4.6
  cloaking, 4.6.2
  correction, 4.6.2, 6.5.4, 12.6.4.5
  expedited dispute resolution, 4.5.5.2
  missing accounts, 4.4.6.8.2, 12.6.9
  monitoring after resolution, 12.6.4.7
  notation on file, 4.6.1, 4.8.1, 4.8.2, 6.6, 8.5.4, 12.4.7
  past users, notification, 4.9, 8.5.4
  public record information, 12.6.3
  reinsertion after deletion, *see* REINSERTION OF INFORMATION
  reinvestigation, *see* REINVESTIGATIONS
  removal, 12.6.4.1
  soft-deletes, 4.6.2, 4.7.1, 12.6.4.3
employment agencies, 2.4.4.2.5
errors, *see* INACCURATE INFORMATION
examining
  importance of, 3.1
  mechanics of, 3.4
  practice tips, 3.7
  right to, 3.3, 3.5

CONSUMER FILES (*cont.*)
explanations, inclusion, 4.8.3
favorable information, 5.2.2.1, 5.2.2.2
identifying information
   altering to confuse reporting agency, 12.5.5, 15.2.7.3
   furnishing to government agencies, 7.2.10.2
   theft of, *see* IDENTITY THEFT
illogical files, 4.4.6.2
inaccurate, *see* INACCURATE INFORMATION
incomplete files, 12.6.9
inconsistencies, 4.4.6.2
information collected, purpose, 2.3.5
insurance purposes, segregation, 12.7.5
investigative report materials, 3.2.1
medical information, *see* MEDICAL INFORMATION
mismerged files, 4.3.3, 4.4.6.5
missing accounts, adding, 4.4.6.8.2, 4.8.4, 12.6.9
nationwide agencies, 3.2.3
negative information, *see* ADVERSE INFORMATION
new files or information, 4.4.6.8.2, 4.8.4, 12.5.9
obsolete information, *see* OBSOLETE INFORMATION
prescreened inquiries, *see* PRESCREENED REPORTS
prior use, effect, 2.3.5.2
public record information, *see* PUBLIC RECORD INFORMATION
reinsertion of information, *see* REINSERTION OF INFORMATION
reinvestigation of information, *see* REINVESTIGATIONS
repayment schedules, reporting, 12.6.7.3
reports on, *see* CONSUMER REPORTS
retrieval errors, 4.3.4, 4.4.6.7
sales between agencies, 2.3.1, 7.1.7
segregation techniques, 12.5.5, 15.2.7.3
   insurance purposes, 12.7.5
settled disputes, 12.6.4
   monitoring file, 12.6.4.7
sources of information
   see also FURNISHERS OF INFORMATION
   disclosure, 3.5.3
   inaccurate sources, 4.4.6.3
   nationwide agencies, 3.2.3.2
specialized agencies, 3.2.4
spouses
   ECOA requirements, 5.6.1, 12.6.9
   FCRA restrictions, 5.6.1
standards, legislative history, 1.4.2
statement of dispute, inclusion, 4.6.1, 4.8.1, 8.5.4, 12.4.7
supplementing information, 12.6.9
tenant screening companies, 12.7.3
third party information in, 3.5.7, 4.3.3.1
transcription errors, 4.4.6.7
updating, 4.4.6.8.4, 4.4.6.8.5
   after dispute settlement, 12.6.4.6, 12.6.4.7
   furnishers, 6.5
variation, 3.4.1
withdrawing information, 12.6.4.1

CONSUMER LISTS
address updates, 2.3.4.2.1
bad debts, *see* BAD DEBT LISTS
blemished record, implications, 12.7.7
check cashing, *see* CHECK CASHING LISTS
coded lists, *see* CODED LISTS
consumer report status, 2.3.3.2, 2.3.4.2.3, 2.3.4.2.4, 7.3.2, 7.3.3
credit guides, *see* CREDIT GUIDES
FCRA, application, 2.3.3.2, 2.3.4.2.3, 2.3.4.2.4, 7.3.2.1, 7.3.3
fraud lists, use by banks, 12.7.7
identifying information, consumer report status, 2.3.4.2.1, 7.2.10.2
impermissible use, 7.4.8
insurance claims, *see* INSURANCE CLAIM LISTS
judgment debtors, 12.2.3
law enforcement agencies, *see* LAW ENFORCEMENT BULLETINS
mailing lists, *see* MAILING LISTS
permissible uses, 7.3
prescreened, *see* PRESCREENED REPORTS
skip tracing, 2.3.6.3.2
specialized lists, 3.2.4
targeted marketing, *see* TARGETED MARKETING LISTS
trade directories, *see* TRADE DIRECTORIES
trigger lists, *see* TRIGGER LISTS

CONSUMER REPORTING AGENCIES
see also CREDIT BUREAUS; INSPECTION BUREAUS; RESELLERS
accident reporting bureaus, status, 2.7.8
account numbers, information sharing, 16.4.1.8
accuracy standards, 4.1.1
   see also INACCURATE INFORMATION
address discrepancies, monitoring, 8.5.3.1, 9.2.5.2
affiliated collection agencies, 3.3.6
agents, status, 7.1.6
alternative agencies, *see* ALTERNATIVE CREDIT BUREAUS
assemble information, 2.5.3.2
attorneys, status, 2.7.7
bad debt lists, publication, 12.2.3
big three, *see* NATIONWIDE REPORTING AGENCIES
business reporting, 2.3.6.2
check approval companies, status, 2.3.6.3.2, 2.6.2.2
   see also CHECK APPROVAL COMPANIES
collection agencies, status, 2.7.3
college placement offices, status, 2.7.6
complaint referral from FTC, 11.16.2.1
computer fraud, liability, 11.16.3
consumer reports
   see also CONSUMER REPORTS
   discretion to provide, 7.1.2, 7.1.6, 7.2.2
   interdependence, 2.3.2, 2.5.1
   refusal to provide, 4.3.6, 7.1.2, 11.6.3.6
   requests, response time, 3.3.9.3
consumer's guide, Appx. L
consumer's written instructions, effect, 7.2.2
cooperative loan exchanges, status, 2.5.4
credit bureau collection departments, status, 2.7.3
credit bureaus, status, 2.7.1
credit header information, disclosure, 2.3.4.2.2
credit repair organizations
   dealing with, 15.1.1, 15.2.1
   misstatements by, 15.2.7.2
credit scores
   credit risk scores, 14.2.2.1
   disclosure requirements, 3.3.4, 14.4.1
creditors, receipt of information, *see* CONSUMER REPORTS
creditors, status, 2.5.4, 2.7.2
creditors, supply of information, *see* FURNISHERS OF INFORMATION
data brokers, status, 2.7.4

CONSUMER REPORTING AGENCIES (cont.)
definition, 2.1.1, 2.5
detective agencies, status, 2.7.5
disclosure obligations, 10.2.2.8, 13.4.3
   consumer assistance, 3.6.3
   file information, 3.3, 3.5
   office hours, 3.6.2
discovery, informal, 11.6.2
disputed information
   see also REINVESTIGATIONS
   deletion, 4.5.2.1, 4.5.3.1, 4.5.5.2, 4.6.2
   expedited dispute resolution, 4.5.5.2, 12.6.2.2
   FCRA claims re, 10.2.2.2
   formal dispute process, 6.10
   notice to furnisher, 6.10.3
   reporting restrictions, 5.3.2.1
electronic communications, 6.3.1, 7.5.4
   Metro 2 Format, 6.3.2, 6.3.3
   see also METRO 2 FORMAT
electronic processing systems, 4.5.6.1, 6.10.1
employees
   criminal liability, 7.6, 11.16.3
   disclosure assistance, 3.6.3
   dispute processing, procedures, 4.5.6.2
   reasonable procedures, following, 4.4.5.1.5
employers, status, 2.7.5
employment agencies, status, 2.3.6.4.2, 2.7.5
employment purpose information, see EMPLOYMENT REPORTS
Equifax, see EQUIFAX
errors
   see also INACCURATE INFORMATION
   duty to correct, 4.5.2.2
   mismatched files, 4.3.3, 4.4.6.5
   prevalence, 4.1.3
   retrieval errors, 4.3.4, 4.4.6.5, 4.4.6.7
   transcription errors, 4.4.6.7
evaluation of information, 2.5.3.2
exclusions, 2.5.5, 2.5.6
examples, 2.7
Experian, see EXPERIAN (TRW)
FBI security clearances, 7.2.10.4
FCRA, application, 2.1.1, 2.5
FCRA rights notice, provision 8.2.2.2
   employment purposes, 7.2.4.4
FCRA violations
   civil actions, see FCRA CLAIMS
   civil penalties, 11.16.2.1
   criminal sanctions, 11.16.3
   disclosure violations, 10.2.2.8
   generally, 7.5.1
   impermissible reports, 7.5.1, 7.6, 10.2.2.4
   improper handling of disputes, 10.2.2.2
   inaccurate reports, 10.2.2.1
   investigative reports, 10.2.2.6
   liability, 10.2.1
   medical information, 10.2.2.5
   negligent non-compliance, 10.2.1
   obsolete reports, 10.2.2.3
   per se UDAP violation, 10.6.2
   public record information, 10.2.2.7
   reasonable procedures, failure to maintain, 7.5.1, 10.2.2.1.2
   testers, use, 11.6.2
federal agencies, status, 2.5.6
fees, see FEES
files, see CONSUMER FILES
financial institution status, 2.3.4.2.2
FTC Staff Commentary, Appx. D
FTC complaint referral, 11.16.2.1
FTC enforcement orders, Appx. K
furnishers of information to, see FURNISHERS OF INFORMATION
furnishing of information by, see CONSUMER REPORTS
GLB Act, application, 2.3.4.2.2, 16.4.1.2, 16.4.1.5.3, 16.4.1.8
government agencies, status, 2.5.6, 2.5.7
identification requests, 7.5.3
identity theft
   alerts, implementation, 9.2.2
   blocking of information, 9.2.4.1, 12.6.6.1
   notice of refusal to block, 8.2.16
inaccurate information, see INACCURATE INFORMATION
independent contractors, status, 2.5.4
information collected by, see CONSUMER FILES
information furnished by, see CONSUMER REPORTS; INVESTIGATIVE CONSUMER REPORTS
information furnished to, see FURNISHERS OF INFORMATION
inquiries, reporting, 2.3.4.2.4
inspection bureaus, status, 2.7.1
   see also INSPECTION BUREAUS
insurance claim compilers, status, 2.7.8
insurance claim exchanges, status, 2.3.6.5.2
investigative reports
   see also INVESTIGATIVE CONSUMER REPORTS
   disclosure obligations, 13.4.3
   FCRA claims, 10.2.2.6
   preparation, 13.1
joint lenders or users, status, 2.4.6, 2.5.5
liability, see under LIABILITY
limited qualified immunity, 10.4
loan companies, status, 2.7.2
local government agencies, status, 2.5.7
management policies, improper, 4.4.6.1
medical information agencies, status, 2.6.2.2
   see also MEDICAL INFORMATION AGENCIES
medical information, see MEDICAL INFORMATION
missing accounts, obligations, 4.4.6.8.2, 4.8.4, 12.6.9
misstatements to, 15.2.7.2
motor vehicle departments (state), status, 2.5.7, 2.7.8
nationwide agencies, see NATIONWIDE REPORTING AGENCIES
notice obligations
   address discrepancies, 8.5.3, 9.2.5.2
   corrections following reinvestigation, 4.6.2
   employment reports, 4.4.7.2, 10.2.2.7
   expedited dispute resolution, 4.5.5.2
   fraud alerts, 8.2.15, 9.2.2.3.3
   frivolous disputes, 8.2.14
   identity theft block refusal, 8.2.16
   inaccurate information received, 6.4.2
   prescreening opt-out, 7.3.4.4
   public record information, 4.4.7.2, 8.2.20
   reinsertion of information, 4.7.4, 8.2.13
   reinvestigation request, 4.5.4.2, 6.10.3
   reinvestigation results, 4.6.1, 6.10.6.2, 8.2.12
notice of dispute, receipt, 8.3
obsolete information, see OBSOLETE INFORMATION
overview, 1.2.2

CONSUMER REPORTING AGENCIES (*cont.*)
police departments, status, 2.7.8
prescreening, *see* PRESCREENED REPORTS
public record information, reporting, 4.4.7, 8.2.20
qualified immunity, 10.4
reasonable procedures, *see* REASONABLE PROCEDURES
record retention, 11.6.4
   request records, 7.5.5
refusal to issue report, 4.3.6
   impermissible purpose, 7.1.2
refusal to provide report to litigant, 11.6.3.6
regulation, 1.3.1
regularly engages, 2.5.3.1
reinsertion of deleted information, 4.7
   certification from furnisher, 4.7.3
   notice, 4.7.4
   standards, 4.7.2
reinvestigation of information, *see* REINVESTIGATIONS
reports, *see* CONSUMER REPORTS
resellers, status, 2.6.3.2
security procedures, 4.4.6.7
sheriff's departments, status, 2.7.8
social service agencies, status, 2.5.2
specialized agencies, 2.6.2, 3.2.4
state agencies, status, 2.5.7
state law, application, 10.6.1
   federal preemption, 10.7.5.3, 10.7.9.2
statements of dispute, obligations, 4.6.1
student loan defaults, report receipt, 12.4.5
suits against, 11.2.3
Summary of Consumer Rights, provision, 8.2.2.2
telephone companies, status, 2.7.9
tenant screening companies, status, 2.6.2.2
   see also TENANT SCREENING COMPANIES
terminology, use, 1.2.1
TransUnion, *see* TRANSUNION
trigger lists, 2.3.4.2.4
trucker database services, status, 2.6.4
TRW, *see* EXPERIAN (TRW)
types, 2.6, 2.7
UDAP violations, 10.6.2
Universal Data Form, *see* UNIVERSAL DATA FORM
unsolicited reports, 7.1.2
unverifiable information, reporting, 4.2.5
updating procedures, 4.4.6.8.4, 4.4.6.8.5

CONSUMER REPORTS
see also CONSUMER REPORTING AGENCIES; CONSUMER FILES; CREDIT BUREAUS
access, *see* CONSUMER REPORTS, obtaining
accuracy concerns
   see also INACCURATE INFORMATION
   FCRA intent to combat, 4.1.2
   FTC to study, 4.1.3.2
   prevalence of inaccurate reports, 4.1.3
active military alerts, 9.2.2.4
additional information, 12.6.9
administrative summons, 7.2.1
adverse information, *see* ADVERSE INFORMATION
adverse use, *see* ADVERSE ACTION
affiliate information sharing, status, 2.4.3
agents, obtaining, 7.1.6
bankruptcy, special procedures, 4.4.6.9.2
between agencies, 7.1.7

blemished, implications, 12.7
business reports, status, 2.3.3.3, 2.3.5.2, 2.3.5.4, 2.3.6.2
check cashing lists, status, 2.3.6.3.2
child support debts, inclusion, 5.7.1, 7.4.2
city directories, status, 2.3.5.3
closed accounts, voluntary, 6.8
coded lists, status, 2.3.3.2, 7.3.2.3
commercial reports, status, 2.3.3.3, 2.3.5.2, 2.3.5.4, 2.3.6.2
confidentiality, 7.1.1
consent of consumer
   business purposes, 7.2.5
   employment purposes, 7.2.4.3.2, 13.5.1
   medical information, 5.4.1.2
   written instructions, 7.2.2
consumer lists, status, 7.3.2, 7.3.3
consumer reporting agencies, interdependence, 2.3.2, 2.5.1
consumer's file, distinguished, 2.3.1.2, 4.4.3
consumer's guide, Appx. L
contents, restrictions, 5.1, 5.2.2.1
   obsolete information, *see* OBSOLETE INFORMATION
continuing reports, 7.5.2.3
copies, *see* CONSUMER REPORTS, obtaining
corrections
   disputed debts, 4.6.2, 12.6.4.7
   notification of previous users, 4.9
cosigners, 5.6.2
court orders, 7.2.1
credit card accounts, 5.3.4
credit card authorizations, status, 2.4.5
credit headers, status, 2.3.4.2.1
credit purposes, 2.3.6.3
credit scores, *see* CREDIT SCORES
definition, 2.1.1, 2.3
denial of credit, *see* ADVERSE ACTION
disclosure distinguished, 4.4.3
disclosure re, *see* DISCLOSURE
disposal regulations, 9.2.5.3
disputed information
   notation, 4.6.1, 4.8.1, 4.8.2, 8.5.4, 12.4.7
   notice to past users, 4.9
   restrictions, 5.3
distinguished from consumer's file, 2.3.1.2
distinguished from file disclosure, 4.4.3
driving records, status, 2.3.4.1, 2.5.7
electronic communication, 7.5.4
employment reports
   see also EMPLOYMENT REPORTS
   status as consumer report, 2.3.6.4, 2.4.4, 7.2.4.5
erroneous information, *see* INACCURATE INFORMATION
evidentiary issues, 11.6.3.5
examining
   assistance from reporting agency, 3.6.3
   first considerations, 12.6.1
   mechanics of obtaining, 3.4
   practice tips, 3.7
exemptions, 2.4
   employee misconduct investigations, 7.2.4.5
explanation from consumer
   giving to creditor, 12.6.9
   inclusion, 4.8.3
false pretenses, obtaining under, 7.2.2, 7.7.3, 7.7.4, 10.2.5.1, 11.16.3
FACTA amendments
   application, 5.4.1.3
   key provisions, 1.4.9.2

CONSUMER REPORTS (*cont.*)
  favorable information, 5.2.2.1
  FBI access, 1.4.8, 7.2.1, 7.2.10.4
  FCRA enforcement authorities, subpoenas, 7.2.1
  FCRA scope, 2.1.1, 2.3, 2.4
  fees, 3.3.9.2
    see also CONSUMER REPORTS, free reports
  file, distinguished, 2.3.1
  first-hand experience, 2.4.2
  follow-up reports, 7.5.2.3
  form, 3.6
  fraud alerts, 9.2.2.2, 9.2.2.3.3
  fraudulent information, blocking, 9.2.4
  free reports
    adverse action, 3.3.6
    affiliated debt collector communications, 3.3.6
    annual free reports, 3.3.2, 3.3.5, 3.4.2.1, 10.7.8
    fraud, 3.3.5
    "free" reports that are not free, 3.3.3
    identity theft, 3.3.5, 9.2.2.2, 9.2.2.3.3
    provision, time, 3.3.9.3
    requesting, 3.4.2.1, Appx. C.1
    state law rights, 3.3.8, 10.7.8
    unemployed or public assistance recipients, 3.3.7
  FTC Staff Commentary, Appx. D
  FTC subpoenas, 7.2.1
  GLB Act exemption, 2.3.4.2.2, 16.4.1.5.3
  governmental use, 12.7.9
  grand jury subpoenas, 7.2.1
  guarantors, 5.6.2
  home mortgages, use, 7.2.7, 12.7.2
  identifiable person, necessity, 2.3.3
  identifying information, status, 7.2.10.2
  identity theft, *see* IDENTITY THEFT
  impermissible purposes, *see* IMPERMISSIBLE PURPOSES
  inaccurate, *see* INACCURATE INFORMATION
  incomplete, 4.3.2.2, 4.3.2.3, 4.4.6.8, 12.6.9
  information about another, 5.6
  information based on interviews, 5.4.2
  information gathered for, *see* CONSUMER FILES
  insurance reports
    see also INSURANCE REPORTS
    status as consumer report, 2.3.6.5, 2.7.8
  intended purpose, effect, 2.3.5
  investigative reports, *see* INVESTIGATIVE CONSUMER REPORTS
  IRS summons, 7.2.1
  joint accounts, 7.4.6.4
  law enforcement bulletins, status, 2.3.5.3
  law enforcement requests, 7.2.1, 7.2.10.4
  legislative history, 2.3.6.1, 2.3.6.2
  lists of consumers, status, 7.3.2, 7.3.4.2
  medical information, inclusion, 5.4.1.2
  military personnel, 5.5.1
    active military alerts, 9.2.2.4
  misidentification, 4.3.3, 4.3.4
    see also IDENTITY THEFT
  misleading, 4.2.3, 5.2.2.2
  neutral information, 5.2.2.1
  notice requirements, *see* NOTICE
  obsolete information, *see* OBSOLETE INFORMATION
  obtaining
    agency time response, 3.3.9.3
    consumer's representative, 3.4.4
    contents of report, 3.5
    deciding from which agency, 3.4.1
    examining report, 3.7
    fee payment, 3.3.9
    form of report, 3.6
    free reports, *see* CONSUMER REPORTS, free reports
    identification, 3.4.3
    mechanics of obtaining, 3.4
    model form, Appx. C.1
    requesting a report, 3.4.2
    subpoenas, 11.6.3.6
    unreasonable preconditions, 3.4.5
    users, from, 3.3.1
  open-end account customers, 5.3.4
  overview of industry, 1.2.2
  permissible purposes, *see* PERMISSIBLE PURPOSES
  personal interviews, restrictions, 5.4.2
  prescreened reports, *see* PRESCREENED REPORTS
  previous recipients or inquiries
    activity reports, 2.3.4.2.4
    disclosure to consumer, 5.2.3.8, 7.5.5
    prescreened lists, disclosure, 5.2.3.8
    record retention, 7.5.5
  prior report, partial use, 2.3.5.2
  protective bulletins, status, 7.3.3
  public record information, status, 2.3.4.2.1
  reading, 3.7.2.3, 12.6.1
  refusal by agency to provide report, 4.3.6
    impermissible purpose, 7.1.2
  release
    agent of user, 7.1.5
    between agencies, 7.1.7
    discovering impermissible use, 7.1.9
    FCRA violations, 7.5.1
    impermissible purpose, effect, 7.1.8
    impermissible purposes, *see* IMPERMISSIBLE PURPOSES
    objection, effect, 7.1.2
    permissible purpose only, 7.1.4
    permissible purposes, *see* PERMISSIBLE PURPOSES
    reasonable procedures, *see* REASONABLE PROCEDURES
    refusal, 4.3.6, 7.1.2
    restrictions, 7.1.2
    written instructions of consumer, 7.2.2
  request records, disclosure
    prescreened inquiries, 5.2.3.8
    record retention, 7.5.5
    trigger lists, 2.3.4.2.4
  requests for, *see* CONSUMER REPORTS, obtaining
  resellers, *see* RESELLERS
  restriction on information in, 5.1, 5.2.2.1
    obsolete information, *see* OBSOLETE INFORMATION
  sample reports, Appx. I.1
  scope, 2.3, 2.3.6.1
  servicemembers, 5.5.1
  settlement negotiations
    impermissible purpose, 7.4.4
    issues, resolving, 12.6.4
  snapshot in time, 3.7.2.1
  spouses of consumers, restrictions, 5.6.1, 7.4.6
  state law preemption, 5.7.2, 10.7
  state law restrictions, 5.7
  state law summaries, Appx. H
  statement of dispute, inclusion, 4.6.1, 4.8.1.2, 8.5.4, 12.4.7
  statutory exemptions, 2.4

CONSUMER REPORTS (cont.)
subpoenas
  attorneys, 11.6.3.6
  court orders, 7.2.1
  enforcement authorities, 7.2.10.3
targeted marketing lists, 7.3.2.4
technically accurate, 4.2.3
telephone directories, status, 2.3.5.3
tenant reports, status, 2.3.6.3.3
terminology, use, 1.2.1
third party credit requests, exemption, 2.4.6
tort claims, 10.4, 10.5
trimerger reports, 11.6.2
understanding, assistance to consumers, 3.6.3
unfavorable, policies encouraging, 4.4.6.1
unsolicited, restrictions, 7.1.2
unverifiable information, 4.2.5
updated information only, 4.4.6.8.4, 4.4.6.8.5
use
  actual use, 2.3.5.2, 7.1.9
  adverse use, *see* ADVERSE ACTION
  business purposes, effect, 2.3.5.4, 2.3.6.2
  disclosure, *see* DISCLOSURE; NOTICE
  expected use, 2.3.5.3
  impermissible, *see* IMPERMISSIBLE PURPOSES
  landlords, 12.7.3
  permissible purpose only, 7.1.4
  permissible uses, *see* PERMISSIBLE PURPOSES
  prior use, 2.3.5.2
  reasonable procedures, *see* REASONABLE PROCEDURES
  restrictions, 7.1.2
  utilities, 12.7.4
users, *see* USERS OF REPORTS
variations
  between agencies, 3.4.1
  between consumer and users, 3.7.2.2

CONSUMER RIGHTS SUMMARY
see SUMMARY OF CONSUMER RIGHTS

CONSUMER TRANSACTIONS
see also CONSUMERS; CREDIT TRANSACTIONS
family purposes, *see* FAMILY PURPOSE TRANSACTIONS
household purposes, *see* HOUSEHOLD PURPOSE TRANSACTIONS
legitimate business need for information, 2.3.6.8, 7.2.8.2
personal purposes, *see* PERSONAL PURPOSE TRANSACTIONS

CONSUMERS
see also CONSUMER TRANSACTIONS
business transactions involving, 2.3.6.8, 7.2.8.2
  initiated by consumer, 7.2.8.2.3
consumer reports, obtaining
  mechanisms of, 3.4
  rights, 3.3
credit record, *see* CREDIT RECORD
credit reporting rights, generally, 1.3.1
debts, *see* DEBTS
definition, 2.2, 2.3.3
  CROA, 15.2.2.2.4
  GLB Act, 16.4.1.3
disclosure rights, *see* DISCLOSURE; NOTICE
disputing debts, *see* CREDIT DISPUTES; REINVESTIGATIONS
FCRA, application, 2.2

FCRA rights summary, *see* SUMMARY OF CONSUMER RIGHTS
files on, *see* CONSUMER FILES
GLB Act, application, 16.4.1.3
guides to credit reporting, Appx. L
identification
  see also IDENTIFYING INFORMATION
  alteration, 15.2.7.3
  consumer report, obtaining, 3.4.3
identity theft, *see* IDENTITY THEFT
information on, *see* CONSUMER REPORTS; INFORMATION ON CONSUMERS
medical information, *see* MEDICAL INFORMATION
power of attorney, 3.4.4
reinvestigation requests, *see* REINVESTIGATIONS
sole proprietorships, status, 2.3.3.3
spouses, *see* SPOUSES
summary of rights, *see* SUMMARY OF CONSUMER RIGHTS

CONTRACTS
credit repair organizations
  arbitration clauses, 15.2.8.4
  disclosure requirements, 15.2.3
  required terms, 15.2.4
  state regulation, 15.3
  void contracts, 15.2.8.1, 15.3.6

CONVICTIONS
see PUBLIC RECORD INFORMATION

COOPERATIVE LOAN EXCHANGES
FCRA, application, 2.5.4

CORPORATIONS
see also BUSINESSES
affiliated, *see* AFFILIATES
credit applications, *see* BUSINESS CREDIT
employees, reports on, *see* EMPLOYMENT REPORTS
FCRA, application, 2.3.3.3
reports on, *see* COMMERCIAL REPORTS

COSIGNERS
adverse action notice, 8.2.6.4.3.7, 8.2.7.4.3
adverse information reporting, 5.6.2, 5.6.3
business credit, consumer report, use, 7.2.3.1.3

COSTS
see ATTORNEY FEES AND COSTS

COUNTERCLAIMS
FCRA claims, to, 11.8

COUNTERTERRORISM
see also NATIONAL SECURITY; SECURITY CLEARANCES
permissible purpose, 7.2.10.5
  FBI access, 7.2.10.4

COURT ORDERS
see also COURTS; PUBLIC RECORD INFORMATION
attorney-issued subpoenas, status, 7.2.1, 11.6.3.6
consumer reports, permissible purpose, 7.2.1, 7.4.5, 11.6.3.6
disputed debts
  reporting issues, 12.6.4.5
  settlement approval, 12.6.4.4
grand jury subpoenas, status, 7.2.1
law enforcement agencies, consumer report requirement, 7.2.1

COURT RECORDS
see PUBLIC RECORD INFORMATION

COURTS
credit reporting claims, selection, 11.4
federal, *see* FEDERAL COURTS
jurisdiction, *see* JURISDICTION
orders, *see* COURT ORDERS
state, *see* STATE COURTS

CREDIT
see also CREDIT TRANSACTIONS
accounts, *see* CREDIT ACCOUNTS
adverse action, *see* ADVERSE ACTION
applications for, *see* CREDIT APPLICATIONS
business credit, *see* BUSINESS CREDIT
cards, *see* CREDIT CARDS
checks, status, 7.2.3.1.2
consumer reports, permissible uses, 7.2.3
    collections, 7.2.3.4
    extension of credit, 7.2.3.2
    generally, 7.2.3.1
    prescreened reports, 7.3.4
    review of accounts, 7.2.3.3, 7.2.8.3
    risk assessment, 2.3.6.7, 7.2.7
definition, 2.3.6.3.1, 7.2.3.1.2, 8.2.6.4.3.2
    CROA, 15.2.2.2.4
denial
    see also ADVERSE ACTION
    consumer reports, use, 7.2.3.2
    definition, 8.2.6.4.3.3
    reasons, disclosure, 8.2.6.2.1
disputes, *see* CREDIT DISPUTES
extension
    see also CREDIT TRANSACTIONS
    consumer report, permissible use, 7.2.3.2
FCBA, application, 5.3.4
FCRA, application, 2.3.6.3
information, *see* CONSUMER REPORTS
offers, *see* CREDIT OFFERS
public utility credit, *see* PUBLIC UTILITY CREDIT
purposes, prescreened reports, 7.3.4.1
reporting agencies, *see* CONSUMER REPORTING AGENCIES
residential leases, status, 8.2.7.2
risk-based pricing, 14.7.3
    notice requirements, 8.2.6.4.3.4

CREDIT ACCOUNTS
see also CREDIT CARDS; OPEN-END CREDIT
account numbers, information sharing, 16.4.1.8
applications for, *see* CREDIT APPLICATIONS
authorized users, reporting restrictions, 5.6.2
billing errors, *see* BILLING ERRORS
charged-off, *see* CHARGED-OFF ACCOUNTS
closed voluntarily, reporting, 6.8
delinquent, *see* DELINQUENT ACCOUNTS
disputes, *see* CREDIT DISPUTES
missing from consumer file, adding, 4.4.6.8.2, 4.8.4, 12.6.9
new accounts, establishing, 12.5.4
permissible purposes
    account reviews, 7.2.3.3, 7.2.8.3
    collections, 7.2.3.4
    risk assessment, 2.3.6.7, 7.2.7
placed for collection, *see* COLLECTION SUITS; DEBT COLLECTORS
review by creditor, 7.2.3.3, 7.2.8.3
    adverse action notice, 8.2.6.4.3.9
spouses, designation, 12.6.9

CREDIT APPLICATIONS
see also CREDIT TRANSACTIONS
automated underwriting systems, 14.2.2.4
home mortgages, 12.7.2
misstatements, 15.2.7.2
rejection *see* ADVERSE ACTION; CREDIT, denial
scoring systems, 14.2.2.4

CREDIT BUREAUS
see also CONSUMER REPORTING AGENCIES; NATION-WIDE REPORTING AGENCIES
alternative bureaus, *see* ALTERNATIVE CREDIT BUREAUS
collection departments, FCRA application, 2.7.3
Equifax, *see* EQUIFAX
examples, 2.7.1
Experian, *see* EXPERIAN (TRW)
files, *see* CONSUMER FILES
overview, 1.2.2
reports, *see* CONSUMER REPORTS
terminology, use, 1.2.1
TransUnion, *see* TRANSUNION
TRW, *see* EXPERIAN (TRW)

CREDIT CARDS
see also CREDIT ACCOUNTS
authorized users, 5.6.2, 12.7.6
billing errors, 5.3.4
blemished credit record, implications, 12.7.6
disputed amounts, 5.3.4, 12.4.2
FCBA, application, 5.3.4, 12.4.2
identity theft prevention
    see also IDENTITY THEFT
    guidelines, 9.2.6
    number truncation, 9.2.5.1
immigrants, 12.8
issuers, use of credit scores, 14.3
limits, importance to credit scores, 14.8.3.2
number truncation, 9.2.5.1
obtaining, 12.7.6
secured credit cards, 12.7.6
state law preemption, 10.7.9.6
transaction authorizations, FCRA, application, 2.4.5
using to build credit history, 12.5.4

CREDIT CLINICS
see CREDIT REPAIR ORGANIZATIONS

CREDIT COUNSELORS
contacting, 12.6.7.3
CROA, application, 15.2.2.2.1, 15.2.2.2.3
repair organizations, *see* CREDIT REPAIR ORGANIZATIONS
use to improve credit record, 12.5.2

CREDIT DISPUTES
see also DISPUTED INFORMATION
agency obligations, 4.5, 12.6.2.2
billing errors, *see* BILLING ERRORS
collection of disputed debts, 5.3.3
complaint address, 6.4.4, 12.6.2.3
court orders covering reporting issues, 12.6.4.5
credit card accounts, 5.3.4, 12.4.2
credit scores and, 14.8.2
dealing directly with creditor, 6.5.2, 6.10.1, 12.6.2.3
expedited dispute resolution, 4.5.5.2, 12.6.2.2
FCBA, application, 5.3.4
FCRA violations, 10.2.2.2

CREDIT DISPUTES (*cont.*)
frivolous disputes, 4.5.2.4
  notice of frivolous dispute, 8.2.14
furnishers
  address to notify, effect, 6.4.4
  notice of inaccuracies, 6.5.2, 6.10.1, 12.6.2.3
  notice of formal dispute, 4.5.4.2, 6.10.3
  obligations, 4.5.4, 6.5.2, 6.10.4, 12.6.2.2
  reporting restrictions, 6.4.4, 6.5.3
home equity loans and mortgages, 12.4.4
inaccurate information, 6.5.2
  correcting, 4.5.2.2, 6.5.4, 12.6.2
  formal dispute process, 4.5, 6.10
  notification address, 6.4.4
investigations into, *see* REINVESTIGATIONS
irrelevant disputes, 4.5.2.4, 8.2.14
litigation aids, 12.6.4
notation of dispute
  by consumer, 4.6.1, 4.8.1, 8.5.4, 12.4.7
  by furnisher, 4.8.2, 6.6
notice of dispute, 4.5.2, 12.6.2.1
  identity theft, Appx. C.4
open-end credit, 5.3.4
procedures
  disputing with agency, 4.5, 6.10, 12.6.2.1, 12.6.2.2
  disputing with creditor, 6.5.2, 6.10.1, 12.6.2.3
  disputing with reseller, 4.5.2.3, 6.13
  failure to properly follow, 10.2.2.2
  formal process, *see* REINVESTIGATIONS
reporting of disputed information, restrictions, 5.3
settlement
  breach of agreement, 12.6.4.3
  cleaning up file after, 12.6.4.6
  court approval, 12.6.4.4
  monitoring file after, 12.6.4.7
  negotiating, 12.6.4.2
  resolving credit reporting issues, 12.6.4.1
  selecting correct language, 12.6.4.3, Appx. J.9
statement of dispute, 4.6.1
telephone charges, 12.4.3
utility charges, 12.4.3
withholding payment, effect, 12.4

CREDIT FILES
see CONSUMER FILES

CREDIT GUIDES
see also CONSUMER LISTS
prohibition, 7.3.2.2
  coded guide exception, 7.3.2.3

CREDIT HEADER INFORMATION
consumer report status, 2.3.4.2.1
GLB Act, disclosure restrictions, 2.3.4.2.2, 16.4.1.10
FCRA, application, 2.3.4.2.1

CREDIT HISTORY
see CREDIT RECORD

CREDIT INFORMATION
see CONSUMER REPORTS; CREDIT RECORD; FINANCIAL INFORMATION; INFORMATION ON CONSUMERS

CREDIT LIMITS
furnishers, failure to report, 4.3.2.3, 14.8.3.2
importance to credit score, 14.8.3.2

CREDIT OFFERS
"firm offers," 7.3.4.3
prescreened lists, 7.3.4

CREDIT PURPOSES
see also CREDIT TRANSACTIONS
prescreening, 7.3.4.1

CREDIT RATING
see CREDIT RECORD; CREDIT SCORES

CREDIT RECORD
see also CONSUMER FILES
blemished records
  automobile loans and leases, impact, 12.7.1
  banking and check cashing, impact, 12.7.7
  coping with, 12.7
  credit card applications, impact, 12.7.6
  explaining with additional information, 12.6.9
  first considerations, 12.6.1
  home mortgages, impact, 12.7.2
  identifying, 12.6.1
  improving, right way, 12.6
  improving, wrong way, 12.5
  insurance, impact, 12.7.5
  repair agencies, *see* CREDIT REPAIR ORGANIZATIONS
  residential leases, impact, 12.7.3
  spouses, impact, 12.2.5
  student loans and grants, impact, 12.7.8
  utility service, impact, 12.7.4
bankruptcy, impact, 12.6.8
building, 12.5.4
contents, *see* CONSUMER FILES
court orders, 12.6.4.5
disputing, *see* CREDIT DISPUTES; REINVESTIGATIONS
ECOA, application, 5.6.1, 7.4.6.2, 12.2.5, 12.6.9
examining, *see* CREDIT REPORTS
financially troubled consumers, 12.1
first considerations, 12.6.1
identity theft, 12.6.6
immigrants, 12.8
impermissible purposes, *see* IMPERMISSIBLE PURPOSES
inaccurate, *see* INACCURATE INFORMATION
incomplete, providing additional information, 12.6.9
insufficient
  adding missing accounts, 4.4.6.8.2, 4.8.4, 12.6.9
  establishing new accounts, 12.5.4
joint accounts, 5.6, 7.4.6.4
publication in the community, 12.2.2, 12.2.3
rating, *see* CREDIT SCORES
recent delinquencies, removing, 12.6.7
repair agencies, *see* CREDIT REPAIR ORGANIZATIONS
self-help, Ch. 12
settlement negotiations, protecting, 12.6.4
  sample language, Appx. J.9
spouses
  ECOA reporting requirements, 5.6.1, 12.6.9
  effect on consumer, 7.4.6.1, 12.2.5
  explanation to creditor, 12.6.9
  requests to consider, 12.6.9
  use by creditor, 7.4.6, 12.2.5
student loan defaults, 12.6.5
threats to damage, 12.3
withholding of payments, effect, 12.4

CREDIT REPAIR ORGANIZATIONS
ancillary services, status as, 15.2.2.4
attorneys, status as, 15.2.2.5
cancellation rights, 15.2.4
contract terms, 15.2.4
   arbitration clauses, 15.2.8.4
   noncomplying contracts void, 15.2.8.1
   three-day right to cancel, 15.2.5
CROA
   application, 15.2.2
   violations, 15.2.8, 15.2.10
debt collectors, status as, 15.2.2.6
defined, 15.2.2.2
   exemptions, 15.2.2.3
disclosure requirements, 15.2.3
federal law, see CREDIT REPAIR ORGANIZATIONS ACT (CROA)
fees, 15.2.2.2.2
   advance payment, 15.2.6, 15.3.5
   state law requirements, 15.3.4.2
fraud and deception, 15.2.7.5
FTC Telemarketing Rule, application, 15.4.1
non-profit organizations, 15.2.2.3.2
overview, 15.1
   credit repair laws, 15.1.2, 15.1.3, 15.2.1
   nature of credit repair organizations, 15.1.1
misrepresentations regarding services, 15.2.7.4
misstatements to reporting agencies or creditors, 15.2.7.2
regulation, 15.2
reinvestigation requests, 4.5.2.2
state law, see STATE CREDIT SERVICES (REPAIR) STATUTES
suits against, 15.2.8
   class actions, 15.2.8.6
   damages, 15.2.8.5
   jurisdiction, 15.2.8.7
   jury trials, 15.2.8.10
   standing, 15.2.8.2
   state law violations, 15.3.6
   statute of limitations, 15.2.8.9
Telephone Consumer Protection Act, application, 15.4.2
wrong way to improve credit record, 12.5.1

CREDIT REPAIR ORGANIZATIONS ACT (CROA)
see also CREDIT REPAIR ORGANIZATIONS
advance payments, prohibition, 15.2.6
ancillary services, application, 15.2.2.4
attorneys, application, 15.2.2.5
contract terms, 15.2.4
   arbitration clauses, validity, 15.2.8.4
   cancellation right, 15.2.5
debt collectors, application, 15.2.2.6
deceptive practices, prohibition, 15.2.7
definitions
   credit repair organization, 15.2.2.2
   other definitions, 15.2.2.2.4
disclosure requirements, 15.2.3
enforcement
   federal and state agencies, 15.2.10
   private enforcement, 15.2.8
exemptions, 15.2.2.3
overview, 15.1.2, 15.2.1
private remedies, 15.2.8
   damages, 15.2.8.5

voiding of contract, 15.2.8.1
prohibited practices, 15.2.7
scope, 15.2.2
   surprising reach, 15.1.3
state law relationship, 15.2.9
violations, 15.2.8
   damages formula, 15.2.8.5.1
   liability, 15.2.8.3
   pleading, 15.2.8.8
   statute of limitations, 15.2.8.9
text, Appx. F

CREDIT REPORTING
see also CONSUMER REPORTING AGENCIES; CONSUMER REPORTS
consumer guides, Appx. L
current developments, 1.1.4
federal legislation, see FAIR CREDIT REPORTING ACT (FCRA)
legislative history, see LEGISLATIVE HISTORY OF FCRA
overview, 1.2
   industry overview, 1.2.2
regulation, 1.3.1
state law summaries, Appx. H
   see also STATE CREDIT REPORTING STATUTES
terminology and convention, 1.2.1

CREDIT REPORTING AGENCIES
see CONSUMER REPORTING AGENCIES; CREDIT BUREAUS

CREDIT REPORTING RESOURCES GUIDE
Metro 2 manual, 6.3.2

CREDIT REPORTS
see also CONSUMER REPORTS
terminology, use, 1.2.1

CREDIT SCORES
see also CREDIT RECORD
accuracy concerns, 14.8
   account type, 14.8.3.6
   disputed debts, 14.8.2
   duplicate accounts, 14.8.3.5
   inaccurate information, 14.8.1, 14.8.3
   lack of validation and re-validation, 14.8.4
   lender misuse, 14.8.5
   missing credit limits, 14.8.3.2
   obsolete information, 14.8.3.7
   unreported information, 14.8.3.3
actual damages calculations, use, 11.10.2.2
automated underwriting systems, 14.2.2.4
basics of, 14.2.1
calculations, 14.5
   black box, 14.5.1
   confidentiality, 14.5.4
   FICO scores, 14.5.2
   Freddie Mac, 14.5.3
consumer's guide, Appx. L
credit applications, 14.2.2.4
credit reporting agencies, 14.2.2.1
custom versus generic, 14.2.2.2
definition, 14.2.3
   ECOA, 14.2.3.2
   FCRA, 14.2.3.1

CREDIT SCORES (cont.)
disclosure, 3.3.4, 3.5.2, 14.4
   FCRA requirements, 14.4.1
   notice accompanying, 8.2.4, 8.2.5
   obtaining, 14.4.2
   preemption of state law, 10.7.7
discrimination, 14.9
   disparate impact, 14.9.1
   growing credit score gap, 14.9.2
FICO scores, 14.2.2.1, 14.5.2
fraud alerts, 9.2.2.3.3
improving
   additional advice, 14.6.2
   industry advice, 14.6.1
   organizations assisting, see CREDIT REPAIR ORGANIZATIONS
   re-scoring, 14.6.3
   ways to improve, 12.6
insurance scores, 14.10
missing information, 14.8.3.3
   credit limits, 4.3.2.3, 14.8.3.2
models
   "alternative" models, 14.9.1
   development, 14.2.2.1
   misuse by creditors, 14.8.5
   notice of model used, 8.2.4, 8.2.5
   validation, 14.8.4
mortgage lenders, use, 3.3.1.3, 14.4.1
   mortgage scoring notice, 8.2.5
notice of preparation and scoring model, 8.2.3
   enforcement of notice right, 8.2.4.3
   entitlement, 8.2.4.2, 8.2.5.2
   mortgage transactions, 8.2.5
   nature and content, 8.2.3.1
objective standard, 6.3.3.2
obtaining, 14.4.2
overview, 14.1
policy concerns, 14.7
   lack of flexibility, 14.7.2
   lack of transparency, 14.7.1
   risk-based pricing, 14.7.3
risk scores, 14.2.2.1
specialty scores, 14.2.2.3
student loan deferments, effect, 14.8.3.4
variations, 3.4.1
   actual score, 14.4.3
   types of scores, 14.2.2
widespread use, 14.3

CREDIT SELLERS
information on consumers, see CONSUMER REPORTS

CREDIT SERVICES ORGANIZATIONS
see CREDIT REPAIR ORGANIZATIONS

CREDIT SOLICITATIONS
see CREDIT OFFERS

CREDIT TRANSACTIONS
see also CREDIT APPLICATIONS
accepted counteroffers, 8.2.6.4.3.5
adverse action, see ADVERSE ACTION
commercial transactions, see BUSINESS CREDIT
consumer reports
   see also CONSUMER REPORTS
   obsolete information, 5.2.4
   permissible use, 7.2.3
   spouses, 7.4.6.2
credit scores, use, 14.3
defined, 7.2.3.1.2
   CROA, 15.2.2.2.4
ECOA, application, 5.5.2, 6.11, 12.4.8
FCRA, application, 2.3.6.3
information concerning, see CONSUMER REPORTS
residential lease, status, 8.2.7.2

CREDIT UNIONS
see also FINANCIAL INSTITUTIONS
CROA exemption, 15.2.2.3.4

CREDITORS
see also FURNISHERS OF INFORMATION
account reviews, 7.2.3.3, 7.2.8.3
   adverse action notice, 8.2.6.4.3.9
address for error complaints, 6.4.4, 12.6.2.3
affiliates, see AFFILIATES
billing errors, see BILLING ERRORS
consumer reports, permissible use, 2.3.6, 7.2.3, 7.2.7, 7.2.8.3, 12.2.4
credit card transactions, 2.4.5
credit limits, failure to report, 4.3.2.3, 14.8.3.2
credit reporting agency status, 2.7.2
credit scoring systems, misuse, 14.8.5
CROA, application, 15.2.2.3.3
dealer paper sales, notice obligations, 8.2.7.4.1
dealing directly with, 6.5.2, 6.10.1, 12.6.2.3
definition, 15.2.2.3.3
disputed debts, see CREDIT DISPUTES; DISPUTED INFORMATION
ECOA, application, 2.4.5, 2.4.6, 5.5.2, 12.4.8
FCRA, application, 2.3.6.3, 2.5.4, 2.7.2, 6.2.2.2
first-hand experience, 2.4.2, 2.5.4
   direct selling of information, 6.2.2.2
friendly, use as testers, 11.6.2
FTC Staff Commentary, Appx. D
identity theft, red flag guidelines, 9.2.6
inaccurate information, see INACCURATE INFORMATION
information obtained from non-reporting agency, 2.3.2, 3.3.1.5, 8.2.7
information obtained from reporting agency, see CONSUMER REPORTS
information supply to reporting agency, see FURNISHERS OF INFORMATION
joint lenders, FCRA, application, 2.4.6, 2.5.5
judgment creditors, see JUDGMENT CREDITORS
landlords, status, 13.3.3
law suits, see COLLECTION SUITS
medical information restrictions, 5.4.1.5
misstatements to, 15.2.7.2
mortgage lenders, see HOME MORTGAGES
negotiating repayment plans with, 12.6.7.3
non-furnishing of information, 4.3.2.2, 4.3.2.3, 14.8.3.2, 14.8.3.3
notice obligations
   adverse action, 2.4.5, 2.4.6, 8.2.6, 8.2.7
   affiliate information sharing, 8.2.18
   disputes, 4.8.2, 6.6
   risk-based pricing, 8.2.8
prospective creditors, alerting to unreported history, 12.6.9
record retention, 11.6.4
third party credit requests, 2.4.6
threats to report debt, 12.3

CREDITORS (cont.)
tort liability, 10.4, 10.5
use of consumer reports, see USERS OF REPORTS

CRIMINAL CONVICTIONS
see CRIMINAL RECORDS; PUBLIC RECORD INFORMATION

CRIMINAL OFFENSES
alleged criminals lists, see LAW ENFORCEMENT BULLETINS
arrests, see PUBLIC RECORD INFORMATION
Computer Fraud and Abuse Act, 16.4.2.1
convictions, see CRIMINAL RECORDS; PUBLIC RECORD INFORMATION
FCRA violations, 11.16.3
Financial Information Privacy Act, 16.4.2.2
Identity Theft and Assumption Deterrence Act, 9.3
indictments, see PUBLIC RECORD INFORMATION
investigations, consumer reports, use, 7.4.5
prosecutions, see PROSECUTIONS

CRIMINAL RECORDS
see also CRIMINAL OFFENSES; PUBLIC RECORD INFORMATION
reporting limitations, 5.2.3.6

DAC SERVICES
see TRUCKER DATABASE SERVICES

DAMAGES
see also ATTORNEY FEES AND COSTS
actual, see DAMAGES, ACTUAL
class actions, 11.2.2
CROA claims, 15.2.8.5
FCRA claims, 11.1–11.4
multiple, see DAMAGES, MULTIPLE
nominal, see DAMAGES, NOMINAL
published awards, quick reference, 11.15
punitive, see DAMAGES, PUNITIVE
reasonable procedures claims, 4.4.5.3
reinvestigations, failure to comply, 6.10.2
state claims
  credit repair, 15.3.6
  credit reporting, 11.1
statutory, see DAMAGES, STATUTORY
Telephone Consumer Protection Act, 15.4.2

DAMAGES, ACTUAL
see also DAMAGES
class actions, 11.2.2
CROA violations, 15.2.8.5.2
definition, 11.10.2.1
FCRA violations
  furnishers, 6.10.2
  generally, 11.10.2.1
  intangible damages, 11.10.2.3
  mitigation, 11.10.2.1
  negligent violations, 11.1
  pecuniary loss, 11.10.2.2
nominal damages alternative, 11.10.2.4
punitive damages prerequisite, 11.12.1.3
tort claims, 11.1, 11.10.2.1

DAMAGES, MULTIPLE
see also DAMAGES
credit reporting claims, 11.1, 11.11

DAMAGES, NOMINAL
recovering, 11.10.2.4

DAMAGES, PUNITIVE
see also DAMAGES
class actions, 11.2.2
CROA violations, 15 2.8.5.3
FCRA violations
  actual damages, no need, 11.12.1.3
  amount, determination, 11.12.2
  determination by judge or jury, 11.12.3
  purpose, 11.12.1.1
  prerequisites, 11.12.1
  willful noncompliance, 11.1, 11.12.1.1, 11.12.1.2
financial standing of defendant, discovery, 11.6.3
jury trials, 11.7
obsolete information reporting, 5.2.5.1
tort claims, 11.1, 11.12.1.1

DAMAGES, STATUTORY
see also DAMAGES
credit reporting violations
  FBI provision, 7.2.10.4
  FCRA claims, 11.11
  state law claims, 11 11

DATABASE SERVICES
see DATA BROKERS

DATA BROKERS
see also SPECIALTY AGENCIES
employment-related, 2 7.5
FCRA, application, 2.7.4
file contents, 3.2.4
FTC enforcement order, Appx. K.5
obtaining reports from 3.4.2.3
"pretexting" to obtain financial information, 16.4.2.3
public record information, 4.3.2.5.1
retail services, 2.7.11
sources of information. 2.7.4, 3.2.4
trucker services, 2.6.4

DATA COMMUNICATION
electronic, see ELECTRONIC COMMUNICATION
reasonable procedures, 4.4.6.7
universal form, see UNIVERSAL DATA FORM

DATA MANAGEMENT COMPANIES
use by creditors, 6.3.1

DATING SERVICES
consumer report, permissible use, 2.3.6.8, 7.2.8.2.2.1

DEALER PAPER
see also AUTOMOBILE DEALERS
sales, disclosure requirements, 8.2.7.4.1

DEALERS
see AUTOMOBILE DEALERS; CREDITORS; MERCHANTS

DEBIT CARDS
credit card alternative, 12.7.6
identity theft prevention guidelines, 9.2.6
state law preemption, 10.7.9.6

DEBT COLLECTION IMPROVEMENT ACT
reporting of federal government debts, 12.4.5

DEBT COLLECTORS
see also COLLECTION SUITS
accounts placed with, reporting, 5.2.3.3
   creditor's delinquency date, using, 5.2.3.3.6
   re-aging of delinquency date, 5.2.3.3.5, 6.7
affiliated collectors, communications giving rise to free report, 3.3.6
bad debt lists, publication, 12.2.3
consumer reports, permissible user, 7.2.3.4
CROA, application, 15.2.2.4, 15.2.2.6
disputed debts, reporting and collection restrictions, 5.3.3
false threats or information, 12.3
FCRA, application, 2.7.3
FDCPA requirements, 12.4.6
identity theft information, obligations, 9.2.3.2
Metro 2 Format, use, 6.3.3.8
re-aging of accounts, 5.2.3.3.5, 6.7
   creditor's delinquency date to be used, 5.2.3.3.6
state law restrictions, federal preemption, 10.7.9.5
threats to report debt, 12.3
validation notice, 12.4.6

DEBT COUNSELORS
see CREDIT COUNSELORS

DEBT ELIMINATION COMPANIES
wrong way to improve credit record, 12.5.2

DEBTS
bad debts
   charged-off to, see CHARGED-OFF ACCOUNTS
   lists, see BAD DEBT LISTS
bankruptcy discharge, see BANKRUPTCY
delinquent, see DELINQUENT ACCOUNTS
discharging through bankruptcy, 5.2.3.7, 12.6.8
disputed debts, see CREDIT DISPUTES; DISPUTED INFORMATION
elimination companies, 12.5.2
payment, priorities, 12.5.3
purchasers of debt, see ASSIGNEES
new debt, taking on to improve credit record, 12.5.4, 12.6.7.2
repayment, effect on reporting limitations, 5.2.3.3
repayment plans, 12.6.7.3
theft-related, blocking, 9.2.4

DECEPTIVE ACTS OR PRACTICES
CROA prohibitions, 15.2.7
   pleading violations, 15.2.8.8
state laws, see UNFAIR OR DECEPTIVE ACTS OR PRACTICES (UDAP)

DECLARATORY JUDGMENT ACT (DJA)
FCRA violations, application, 11.13

DECLARATORY RELIEF
FCRA violations, 11.13

DEFAMATION
see also TORT CLAIMS
actual damages, 11.10.2.1
conditional privilege defense, 10.5.2
elements of claim, 10.5.2
false reports, 10.5.2
FCRA qualified immunity, 10.4
inaccurate reports, 10.5.2

DEFENSES
conditional privilege, 10.5.2

defamation claims, 10.5.2
disputed debts, see CREDIT DISPUTES
FCRA claims, 11.8
GLB Act as, 16.4.1.11
impermissible reports, 10.2.2.4
mitigation, 11.10.2.1
notice violations, 10.2.5.2
obsolete reports, 10.2.2.3
reasonable procedures, 13.4.4, 10.2.5.2, 10.2.5.3
student loans, raising, 12.4.5, 12.6.5
technical accuracy, 4.2.3

DEFINITIONS
accuracy, 4.2.1
active duty military consumer, 9.2.2.4
actual damages, 11.10.2.1
adverse action, 8.2.6.4.3.1
affiliate, 16.4.1.5.2
assemble, 2.5.3.2
assure, 10.2.2.1.2
billing error, 5.3.4
business transaction, 7.2.8.2.2.1
consumer, 2.2, 15.2.2.2.4, 16.4.1.3
consumer credit transaction, 15.2.2.2.4
consumer report, 2.1.1, 2.3
consumer reporting agency, 2.1.1, 2.5.1
credit, 2.3.6.3.1, 7.2.3.1.2, 8.2.6.4.3.2, 15.2.2.2.4
credit repair organization, 15.2.2.2
credit score, 14.2.3
creditor, 15.2.2.3.3
customer relationship, 16.4.1.3
denial, 8.2.6.4.3.3
employment purposes, 2.3.6.4.1, 7.2.4.2
evaluate, 2.5.3.2
file, 3.2.2, 5.6.1
financial institution, 16.4.1.2
furnisher of information, 2.1.2, 6.2.1
governmental agency, 7.2.10.2
identity theft report, 9.2.2.3.2
investigation, 4.5.3.1
investigative consumer report, 13.2
malice, 10.4.6
medical information, 5.4.1.1, 10.2.2.5
negligence, 10.2.1
nonpublic personal information, 16.4.1.1
person, 2.5.2, 13.4.1.1
personal, family, or household purpose, 2.3.6.3.1
privacy, 10.5.3
red flag, 9.2.6
regularly engages, 2.5.3
reseller, 2.6.3.2
user, 2.1.2, 7.1.2, 7.1.4

DELINQUENT ACCOUNTS
see also COLLECTION SUITS
bringing up-to-date, 12.6.7
   payments on old accounts, 12.5.3
   student loans, 12.7.8
charged-off to bad debts, see CHARGED-OFF ACCOUNTS
date of delinquency to be furnished, 5.2.3.3.3, 6.7
   debt collectors must use creditor's date, 5.2.3.3.6
   re-aging by debt collectors, 5.2.3.3.5, 6.7
discharging in bankruptcy, 12.6.8
importance of resolving issues, 12.6.4.1

References are to sections

DELINQUENT ACCOUNTS (*cont.*)
reporting limitations
    obsolete information, 5.2.3.2
    sent for collection or charged-off, 5.2.3.3

DENIAL
see ADVERSE ACTION

DEPARTMENT OF HOUSING AND URBAN DEVELOPMENT (HUD)
insured home mortgages, *see* FEDERAL HOUSING ADMINISTRATION (FHA)

DEPOSITORY INSTITUTIONS
see also BANKS; FINANCIAL INSTITUTIONS
CROA exemption, 15.2.2.3.4

DETECTIVE AGENCIES
consumer reports
    certification of permissible use, 7.5.2.2
    obtaining, 7.1.6
    use, 7.4.5
electronic communication with reporting agencies, 7.5.4
FCRA, application, 2.7.5
identifying information, obtaining, 7.2.10.2
investigative consumer reports, preparation, 13.1.1

DIRECTORIES
city, *see* CITY DIRECTORIES
telephone, *see* TELEPHONE DIRECTORIES
trade, *see* TRADE DIRECTORIES

DISCLOSURE
see also NOTICE
adverse action
    employment report, 7.2.4.3.3, 7.2.4.5, 13.2.4.2
    information used, 3.3.6
    legislative history, 1.4.7
affiliate information sharing, 2.4.3.2.2, 16.4.1.5.2
audit trail, 3.5.8
checks, dishonored, 3.5.5
consumer files
    all information, 3.5.1
    cleaning up after a dispute, 12.6.4.6
    check identification, 3.5.5
    contents of disclosure, 3.5
    differences in information, 3.4.1
    distinguished from consumer report, 4.4.3
    fee, upon payment, 3.3.9
    form, 3.6
    free annual reports, 3.3.2, 3.3.8, 3.4.2.1, 10.7.8
    free reports, other circumstances, 3.3.5–3.3.8
    mechanics of obtaining, 3.4
    model form, Appx. C.1
    oral disclosure, 3.6.2
    other persons in consumer's file, 3.5.7
    practice tips, 3.7
    previously reported information, 3.5.6
    right to, 3.3
    scope, 3.5
    sources, 3.5.3, 13.4.2.3
    time limits, 3.3.9.3
    unreasonable preconditions, 3.4.5
    written disclosure, 3.6.1
consumer reporting agencies
    assistance to consumers, 3.6.3
    disputed information, notification rights, 4.9.2
    location, 3.6.2
    public record information, 8.2.20
consumer reports
    adverse action, 3.3.6, 7.2.4.3.3
    affiliated debt collector communications, 3.3.6
    contents by users, 3.3.1
    distinguished from file disclosure, 4.4.3
    employment reports, 7.2.4.3.3, 7.2.4.4
    previously reported information, 3.5.6
    use for counterterrorism purposes, 3.5.4.2, 7.2.10.4, 7.2.10.5
    users, 3.5.4, 3.7.3
consumer rights summary, 3.5.1, 8.2.2.2
    employment reports, 7.2.4.3.3, 7.2.4.4
credit card rejections, 2.4.5
credit header information, 2.3.4.2.2
credit repair organizations, 15.2.3
credit scores, 3.3.4, 3.5.2, 14.4
    mortgage transactions, 3.3.1.3, 14.4.1
    preemption of state law, 10.7.7
disputed information, right to request notification, 4.9.2
electronic disclosure, 3.6.1
employment agency files, 2.4.4.2.5
employment reports
    employee misconduct, 7.2.4.5, 8.2.6.4.4.2, 13.2.4.2
    prior to adverse action, 7.2.4.3.3, 8.2.6.4.4
    prior to information request, 7.2.4.3.2
    Summary of Consumer Rights, 7.2.4.3.3, 7.2.4.4
FBI, consumer report access by, 3.5.4.2, 7.2.10.4
FCRA rights, 3.5.1, 8.2.2
    employment reports, 7.2.4.3.3, 7.2.4.4
federal agencies, debtor information, 5.5.3, 8.2.11
financial institutions
    consumer opt-out rights, 16.4.1.7
    privacy notice, 16.4.1.6
    restrictions, 16.4.1
form of disclosure, 3.6
FTC Staff Commentary, Appx. D
GLB Act restrictions, 16.4.1
    exempt disclosures, 16.4.1.5
    opt-out rights, 16.4.1.7
identification of consumer, 3.4.3, 3.6.2
in-person disclosures, 3.6.2
investigative consumer reports
    additional disclosures, 13.4.2
    nature of report, 13.4.3
    reasonable procedures defense, 13.4.4
    requests for report, 13.4.1
    rights, 13.4.1.3
    sources, 13.4.2.3
    time, 13.4.2.4
    waiver of rights, 13.4.5
mail disclosures, 3.6.1
misrepresentations, limitations, 11.5.2
nonpublic personal information, 2.3.4.2.2, 16.4.1.4
obtaining, 3.4
power of attorney requests, 3.4.4
presence of another person at disclosure, 3.6.2
prescreening lists, 5.2.3.8, 8.2.9, 10.2.5.4
qualified immunity, 10.4.3
reading disclosures, 3.7.2.3
resellers, 2.6.3.3
security clearance usage, 3.5.4.2
sources of information, 3.5.3, 13.4.2.3

DISCLOSURE (*cont.*)
state law requirements, 8.2.23
   federal preemption, 10.7.7
telephone disclosures, 3.6.2
tenant screening reports, 12.7.3
third party credit rejections, 2.4.6
users receiving reports, 3.5.4, 3.7.3
   FBI exception, 3.5.4.2, 7.2.10.4

DISCOVERY
see also ACTIONS; LITIGATION
attorney fee rates, 11.14.3
company information about defendants, 11.6.3.3
confidentiality agreements re, 11.6.3.4
consumer reports
   admissibility groundwork, 11.6.3.5
   determination of use, 7.1.9, 7.4.4
   subpoena, 11.6.3.6
credit scores, 14.5.4
electronic discovery, 11.6.3.2
formal discovery, 11.6.3
generally, 11.6.1, 11.6.3.1
informal discovery, 11.6.2
insurance coverage, 11.6.3.7
investigative consumer reports, sources, 13.4.2.3, 13.4.3
protective orders, 11.6.3.4
   sample order, Appx. J.7
reinvestigation procedures, 4.5.6.3
sample interrogatories, Appx. J.3
sample notices of deposition, Appx. J.6
sample requests for admissions, Appx. J.5
sample requests for production, Appx. J.4

DISCRIMINATION
credit scores, 14.9
ECOA protections, 5.5.2, 6.11, 12.4.8
medical information, based on, 5.4.1.5.1

DISHONORED CHECKS
consumer report, permissible use, 7.2.3.4
Metro 2 Format reporting, 6.3.3.11

DISPUTED INFORMATION
see also CREDIT DISPUTES
credit scores and, 14.8.2
dealing directly with creditor, 6.5.2, 6.10.1, 12.6.2.3
   notification address, 6.4.4
deletion, 4.5.2.1, 4.5.3.1, 4.5.5.2, 4.6.2, 5.3.2.1
expedited dispute resolution, 4.5.5.2, 12.6.2.2
formal dispute process, *see* REINVESTIGATIONS
frivolous or irrelevant disputes, 4.5.2.4
   notice of frivolous dispute, 8.2.14
home mortgages, 5.3.5
   open-end lines of credit, 5.3.4
notation on file
   by consumer, 4.6.1, 4.8.1, 8.5.4, 12.4.7
   by furnisher, 4.8.2, 6.6
notice to reporting agency, 4.5.2, 12.6.2.1
   identity theft, Appx. C.4
reinvestigations
   see also REINVESTIGATIONS
   agency responsibilities, 4.5.1, 4.5.2.1
   correction or deletion following, 4.6.2
   deletion alternative, 4.5.2.1, 4.5.3.1, 4.5.5.2
   expedited resolution, 4.5.5.2, 12.6.2.2

failure to properly handle, 10.2.2.2
furnisher responsibilities, 4.5.4, 6.5.2, 6.10
resellers, 6.13
notice of dispute, 6.10.3
notice to past users, 4.9, 8.5.4
reporting restrictions, 5.3
   consumer reporting agencies, 5.3.2.1
   credit cards, 5.3.4
   debt collectors, 5.3.3
   FCBA restrictions, 5.3.4
   FCRA restrictions, 5.3.2
   FDCPA restrictions, 5.3.3
   furnishers, 5.3.2.2, 6.4.4
   open-end accounts, 5.3.4
   RESPA restrictions, 5.3.5
   TIL restrictions, 5.3.4

DISTRESS
see EMOTIONAL DISTRESS

DIVORCE PROCEEDINGS
see also ALIMONY; CHILD SUPPORT
consumer reports, use, 7.4.2, 7.4.4, 12.2.4
spousal reporting, effect on, 5.6.1

DOCTORS
see FURNISHERS OF INFORMATION; MEDICAL INFORMATION

DRIVER PRIVACY PROTECTION ACT
privacy protections, 16.2

DRIVING RECORDS
see also ACCIDENT REPORTING BUREAUS
bad driving lists, 3.2.4
FCRA, application, 2.3.4.1, 2.5.7

E-OSCAR
electronic data processing system, 4.5.6.1, 6.10.1

ELECTRONIC COMMUNICATION
see also COMPUTER ERRORS; DATA COMMUNICATION
adverse action notice, 8.2.6.3.2
computer fraud law, application, 11.16.3
consumer reports, 3.6.1, 7.5.4
discovery, 11.6.3.2
e-OSCAR, *see* E-OSCAR
furnishing of information, 6.3.1
   Metro 2 Format, *see* METRO 2 FORMAT
privacy protections, 16.4.2.1
reasonable procedures, 4.4.6.7, 7.5.4
reinvestigation of disputed information
   ACDV, 4.5.4.2, 4.5.6.1, 6.10.3
   e-OSCAR processing system, 4.5.6.1, 6.10.1
   notice to furnisher, 4.5.4.2, 6.10.3
   processing of disputes, 4.5.6
   results, 6.10.6.2, 6.10.6.4
transmission, 7.2.2

ELECTRONIC COMMUNICATIONS PRIVACY ACT
scope, 16.4.2.1

ELECTRONIC DATA SYSTEMS, INC.
data management services, 6.3.1

EMOTIONAL DISTRESS
damages for, 11.10.2.3

EMPLOYEES
see also EMPLOYMENT PURPOSES
consumer reporting agencies
  criminal liability, 7.6, 11.16.3
  disclosure assistance, 3.6.3
  dispute processing, procedures, 4.5.6.2
  reasonable procedures, following, 4.4.5.1.5
FCRA violations, employer liability, 7.7.5
misconduct investigations, 2.4.4.1, 7.2.4.5, 8.2.6.4.4.2, 8.2.17.2.2, 13.2.4.2, 13.5.1
reports on, see EMPLOYMENT REPORTS

EMPLOYERS
see also EMPLOYMENT PURPOSES; FURNISHERS OF INFORMATION
adverse action notice, 3.3.1.4, 7.2.4.3.3, 8.2.6.4.4
  contents, 8.2.6.2.5
consumer reports, 7.2.4
  see also EMPLOYMENT REPORTS
  authorization, 7.2.4.3.2
  certification, 7.2.4.3
  disclosure requirements, 3.3.1.4, 7.2.4.3, 8.2.6.2.5, 8.2.6.4.4, 8.2.17
  employee misconduct exemption, 2.4.4.1, 7.2.4.5, 8.2.6.4.4.2, 8.2.17.2.2, 13.2.4.2
  impermissible purpose, vicarious liability, 7:7.5
  notice prior to use, 7.2.4.3, 8.2.17
  permissible use, 7.2.4.2
  Summary of Consumer Rights, providing, 7.2.4.3.3, 7.2.4.4
FCRA, application, 2.3.6.4, 2.7.5, 7.2.4.2
former employers, provision of information, 7.2.4.2

EMPLOYMENT
adverse action, see ADVERSE ACTION
agencies, see EMPLOYMENT AGENCIES
denial, see ADVERSE ACTION
purposes, see EMPLOYMENT PURPOSES
reports, see EMPLOYMENT REPORTS

EMPLOYMENT AGENCIES
FCRA, application, 2.3.6.4.2, 2.4.4.2, 2.7.5
  adverse action notice, 8.2.6.4.4.3
investigative reports
  certification to agency, 13.4.1.5
  exclusions, 2.4.4.2.2

EMPLOYMENT PURPOSES
certification of authorization, 7.2.4.3, 13.3.2
credit scores, use, 14.3
definition, 2.3.6.4, 7.2.4.2
FCRA, application, 2.3.6.4
FTC Staff Commentary, Appx. D
investigative reports, 13.3.2, 13.4.1.5
jurors, reports on, status, 7.2.4.2
licenses, status, 7.2.4.2
permissible purpose, 2.3.6.4, 7.2.4.2
public record information, 4.4.7, 8.2.20, 10.2.2.7
relatives, impermissible purpose, 7.2.4.2, 12.2.5
reports, see EMPLOYMENT REPORTS
security clearances, 2.3.6.4, 3.5.4.2, 4.4.7.4, 7.2.4.2, 8.2.6.4.4.3
workers' compensation claims, status, 7.2.4.2

EMPLOYMENT-RELATED COMPANIES
consumer reporting agency status, 2.7.5
employment agencies, see EMPLOYMENT AGENCIES

inspection bureaus, see INSPECTION BUREAUS

EMPLOYMENT REPORTS
see also CONSUMER REPORTS; EMPLOYMENT PURPOSES
adverse action notice, 3.3.1.4, 7.2.4.3.3, 8.2.6.4.4
  contents, 8.2.6.2.5
  truckers, 8.2.6.4.4.3
authorization from consumer, 7.2.4.3.2, 13.5.1
  employee misconduct exemption, 13.5.1
  truckers, 8.2.17.2.3
certification, 7.2.4.3, 13.3.2
consumer report status, 2.3.6.4
  exemptions, 2.4.4
disclosure, 3.3.1.4, 7.2.4.3.3
  truckers, 8.2.17.2.3
FACTA amendment provisions, 1.4.9.2, 2.4.4.1
FCRA exemptions
  employee misconduct investigations, 2.4.4.1, 7.2.4.5, 8.2.6.4.4.2, 8.2.1.7.2.2, 13.2.4.2
  employment agency communications, 2.3.6.4.2, 2.4.4.2
FTC Staff Commentary, Appx. D
investigative, see INVESTIGATIVE CONSUMER REPORTS
medical information, inclusion, 5.4.1.2
national security exemptions, 3.5.4.2, 4.4.7.4, 8.2.6.4.4.3
nationwide agencies, 2.6.2
notice obligations
  prior to adverse action, 3.3.1.4, 7.2.4.3.3, 8.2.6.2.5, 8.2.6.4.4
  prior to information request, 7.2.4.3.2, 8.2.17
  public record information, 4.4.7.2, 8.2.20
obsolete information, 5.2.4
obtaining by consumer, 3.4.2.3
overview, 7.2.4.1
permissible use, 7.2.4.2
public record information, protections, 4.4.7, 8.2.20, 10.2.2.7
spouses and relatives restrictions, 7.2.4.2
Summary of Consumer Rights, inclusion, 7.2.4.4
trucker database services, 2.6.4
  adverse action notice, 8.2.6.4.4.3
  employment use notice, 8.2.17.2.3
use notice, 7.2.4.3.2, 8.2.17
workers' compensation
  lists at specialized agencies, 3.2.4
  use for claims, 7.2.4.2

E-OSCAR
electronic data processing system, 4.5.6.1, 6.10.1

EQUAL CREDIT OPPORTUNITY ACT (ECOA)
see also CONSUMER CREDIT PROTECTION ACT (CCPA)
adverse action notices
  comparison with FCRA notice, 8.2.6.6
  model form, Appx. C.9
  record retention, 11.6.4
claims under, 10.3
codes, use in Metro 2 Format, 6.3.3.3
credit discrimination, prohibition, 5.5.2, 6.11, 12.4.8
credit score definition in Regulation B, 14.2.3.2
disputed debts, application, 6.5.3
federal agency interpretations, 1.1.3
furnishers of information, application, 5.5.2, 6.11, 12.4.8
identity theft suits under, 12.6.6
insufficient credit history, application, 12.6.9
spouses, reporting requirements, 5.6.1, 7.4.6.2, 12.2.5, 12.6.9

References are to sections

EQUIFAX
see also CONSUMER REPORTING AGENCIES; CREDIT BUREAUS; NATIONWIDE REPORTING AGENCIES
consumer disputes, processing, 4.5.6.2
consumer files, 3.2.3
   contents, 3.2.3.2
   sources of information, 3.2.3.3
contact information, 3.4.2.2
credit scores
   BEACON score, 14.2.2.1
   obtaining, 14.4.2
FCRA, application, 2.7.1
   special provisions, 2.6.1
FTC enforcement orders, Appx. K.3
investigative consumer reports, specialization, 13.1.1
liability insurance, 11.6.3.7
overview, 1.2.2
sample credit report, Appx. I.1.1

EQUITABLE RELIEF
FCRA violations, 11.13

ERRORS
see also ACCURACY; INACCURATE INFORMATION
billing errors, see BILLING ERRORS
consumer files, see INACCURATE INFORMATION
disputing, see CREDIT DISPUTES
Metro 2 Format, 6.3.3.7

EVIDENCE
see also BURDEN OF PROOF
consumer reports, use as, 7.4.4, 11.6.3.5
damages
   intangible damages, 11.10.2.3.2
   pecuniary loss, 11.10.2.2
denial based on erroneous information, 11.10.2.2
reasonable procedures, non-utilization, 4.4.5.2.2
willfulness, 11.12.1.2

EXPERIAN (TRW)
see also CONSUMER REPORTING AGENCIES; CREDIT BUREAUS; NATIONWIDE REPORTING AGENCIES
consumer disputes, processing, 4.5.6.2
consumer files, 3.2.3
   contents, 3.2.3.2
   sources of information, 3.2.3.3
contact information, 3.4.2.2
credit scores
   Experian/Fair Isaac score, 14.2.2.1
   obtaining, 14.4.2
FCRA, application, 2.7.1
   special provisions, 2.6.1
FTC enforcement orders, Appx. K.2
liability insurance, 11.6.3.7
overview, 1.2.2
sample credit report, Appx. I.1.2

EXPLANATIONS
see also STATEMENT OF DISPUTE
adverse information, 4.8.3
blemished credit records, 12.6.9
consumer file, inclusion, 4.8.3
creditors, provision, 4.2.2

FAIR AND ACCURATE CREDIT TRANSACTIONS ACT (FACTA)
FCRA, amending, 1.4.9
   FTC circumvention rule, 2.6.1.3
   key provisions, 1.4.9.2
   legislative history, 1.4.9.1
   privacy protections, 16.6
   regulations under, 1.3.3.1, 1.4.9.2

FAIR CREDIT BILLING ACT (FCBA)
see also CONSUMER CREDIT PROTECTION ACT (CCPA)
billing errors, application, 5.3.4
claims under, 10.3
credit card charges, application, 12.4.2
credit scores, conflicts with dispute mechanisms, 14.8.2
disputed information, reporting restrictions, 5.3.4, 6.5.3

FAIR CREDIT REPORTING ACT (FCRA)
see also CONSUMER CREDIT PROTECTION ACT (CCPA); CONSUMER REPORTING AGENCIES; CONSUMER FILES; CONSUMER REPORTS; FAIR AND ACCURATE CREDIT TRANSACTIONS ACT (FACTA)
actions under, see FCRA CLAIMS
administrative enforcement, 11.16.1, 11.16.2
affiliate exemption, 2.4.3
application
   business reports, 2.3.6.2
   consumer reporting agencies, 2.5, 2.6
   consumer reports, 2.3, 2.4
   consumers, 2.2
   furnishers of information, 6.2
   generally, 1.3.1, 2.1
   investigative consumer reports, 13.2
   resellers, 2.6.3
compliance
   FTC Staff Commentary, Appx. D
   reasonable procedures, 5.2.5
computer fraud law, application, 11.16.3
consumer guides, Appx. L
credit scores
   conflicts with dispute mechanisms, 14.8.2
   definition, 14.2.3.1
   disclosure requirements, 14.4.1
criminal enforcement, 11.16.3
cross-reference table, section numbers, Appx. A.1
disputed information, reporting restrictions, 5.3.2
ECOA notice obligations, comparison, 8.2.6.6
enforcement
   administrative, 11.16.1, 11.16.2
   consumer reports, subpoena, 7.2.1
   criminal enforcement, 11.16.3
   FTC enforcement, 11.16.2, Appx. K
   furnisher duties, 6.1.2, 6.10.1, 6.10.2
   private enforcement, 6.10.1, 6.10.2, 11.14.2.1, 11.14.2.2, 11.16.2.1
   sample orders, Appx. K
   state enforcement, 11.16.4
exemptions, 2.4
FACTA amendments, see FAIR AND ACCURATE CREDIT TRANSACTIONS ACT (FACTA)
federal agency interpretations, 1.3.3
FTC interpretations
   authority, 1.3.3.1, 11.16.2.3
   Official Staff Commentary, 1.3.3.2, 11.16.2.3, Appx. D
   opinion letters, 1.3.3.2, 11.16.2.3, Appx. E
FTC jurisdiction, 11.16.2.1
   sample enforcement orders, Appx. K
GLB Act impact, 16.4.1.9

FAIR CREDIT REPORTING ACT (FCRA) (cont.)
identity theft provisions, see IDENTITY THEFT
legislative history, see LEGISLATIVE HISTORY OF FCRA
limited qualified immunity, 6.12, 10.4
litigation use, 1.3.2
   see also FCRA CLAIMS
medical information, reporting restrictions, 5.4.1
NCLC manual, using, 1.1
   updates, 1.1.4
overview, 1.3.1
preemption of state law, see PREEMPTION OF STATE LAW
privacy protections, 7.1.1, 16.1
published awards, quick reference, 11.15
purpose, 1.3.1, 7.1.1
recent developments, 1.1.4
regulations, see REGULATIONS (FCRA)
rights under
   Summary of Rights, see SUMMARY OF CONSUMER RIGHTS
   waiver, 7.2.2
scope, Ch. 2
state enforcement, 11.16.4
terminology, 1.2.1
text of Act, Appx. A.2
user notice, 7.1.5, 8.5.2
   model form, Appx. C.6
utilization, 1.3.2
violations
   actual damages, 11.10.2
   attorney fees and costs, 11.14
   civil suits, 10.2
   consumer reporting agencies, 7.5.1
   continuing violations, 11.5.1
   criminal penalties, 11.16.3
   declaratory relief, 11.13
   defenses, see DEFENSES
   false pretenses, 7.2.2, 7.7.3
   injunctive relief, 11.13
   investigation, 7.2.10.3
   knowing non-compliance, 7.7.2
   liability, 7.7, 11.2.3
   limitations, 11.5.1
   negligent, 10.2.1
   obsolete information, 5.2.5.1
   private remedies, 11.1
   punitive damages, 11.12
   reasonable procedures, failure to maintain, 7.5.1, 5.2.5.1
   state enforcement, 11.16.4
   statutory damages, 11.11
   systematic practices, 11.2.2
   testers, 11.6.2
   uncertified use, 7.7.2
   unfair or deceptive practice, as, 10.6.2, 11.16.1
   vicarious liability, 7.7.5
   willful noncompliance, 11.11, 11.12.1.1, 11.12.1.2
weaknesses, 1.3.2

FAIR DEBT COLLECTION PRACTICES ACT (FDCPA)
see also CONSUMER CREDIT PROTECTION ACT (CCPA)
bad debt lists, restrictions, 12.2.3
claims under, 10.3
disputed debts, restrictions, 5.3.3, 6.5.3
federal agency interpretations, 1.1.3

FAIR ISAAC & CO. (FICO)
see also CREDIT SCORES
credit risk scores, 14.2.2.1
   variations, 14.4.3
obtaining credit score from, 14.4.2
scorecards, 14.5.2.2
scoring factors, 14.5.2.1

FALSE INFORMATION
see also INACCURATE INFORMATION
credit repair organizations, 15.2.7.2
debt collectors, 12.3
tort liability, 10.4.6

FALSE PRETENSES
see also FRAUD
consumer reports, obtaining under
   civil liability, 7.7.3, 10.2.5.1
   criminal liability, 7.7.4, 11.16.3
   impermissible purpose, 7.7.3, 7.7.4
   testers, 11.6.2
   written permission, 7.2.2

FALSE THREATS
see also THREATS
debt collectors, 12.3
investigative consumer report, 13.4.1.2

FAMILY LAW PROCEEDINGS
see CHILD SUPPORT; DIVORCE PROCEEDINGS; PATERNITY PROCEEDINGS

FAMILY PURPOSE TRANSACTIONS
see also CONSUMER TRANSACTIONS
consumer report, permissible purpose, 2.3.6.1, 7.2.3.1.3
   business transactions, 7.2.8.2.2.1
defined, 2.3.6.3.1

FANNIE MAE
see FEDERAL NATIONAL MORTGAGE ASSOCIATION (FANNIE MAE)

FARMERS HOME ADMINISTRATION (FmHA)
see RURAL HOUSING SERVICE (RHS)

FCRA CLAIMS
see also FAIR CREDIT REPORTING ACT (FCRA); LITIGATION
actual damages, 11.10.2
arbitration agreements, effect, 11.9
attorney fees and costs, 11.14
blocking of reports by agency due to, 5.5.2
case selection, 11.3
class actions, 11.2.2
consumer reporting agencies, 10.2.2
court selection, 11.4
defenses and counterclaims, 11.8
disclosure violations, 10.2.2.8
discovery, see DISCOVERY
discrimination based on, 5.5.2
disputes, improper handling 10.2.2.2
FTC actions, 11.16.2.1
furnishers of information, 6.1.2, 6.10.2, 10.2.4
   statute of limitations, 6.10.7
identity theft, 9.5, 12.6.6
illegally obtained reports, 10.2.5.1
impermissible purposes, 10.2.2.4
inaccurate reports, 10.2.2.1

FCRA CLAIMS (*cont.*)
injunctive relief, 11.13
interest on judgments, 11.14.6
investigative reports, 10.2.2.6, 10.2.5.3
jury trials, 11.7, Appx. J.8
liability insurance, 11.6.3.7
limitations, 11.5.1
medical information, 10.2.2.5
negligent noncompliance, 10.2.1
notice violations, 10.2.5.2
obsolete reports, 10.2.2.3
parties, 11.2
pleadings, *see* PLEADINGS
prescreening violations, 10.2.5.4
private remedies, 11.1
public record information, 10.2.2.7
published awards, quick reference, 11.15
punitive damages, 11.12
reasonable procedures violations
    damages, 4.4.5.3
    determining reasonableness, 4.4.5.1
    proof issues, 4.4.5.2
reinvestigations, improper handling, 10.2.2.2
removal to federal court, 11.4.5
resellers, 10.2.3
sample documents, Appx. J
state enforcement actions, 11.16.4
statute of limitations, 11.5.1
   reinvestigation provisions, 6.10.7
statutory damages, 11.11
superbureaus, 10.2.3
users, 10.2.5
utilization, 1.3.2
willful noncompliance, 11.11, 11.12.1.1

FEDERAL AGENCIES
see also GOVERNMENT AGENCIES
counterterrorism purposes, consumer reports, access, 7.2.10.5
employment reports
   adverse notice exemption, 8.2.6.4.4.3
   adverse public information exemption, 4.4.7.4
   disclosure exemption, 3.5.4.2
FBI, *see* FEDERAL BUREAU OF INVESTIGATIONS (FBI)
FCRA, application, 2.5.6
FCRA enforcement agencies, 11.16.1
   consumer reports, subpoena powers, 7.2.10.3
   regulations and interpretations, 1.3.3
   furnishing of information, 5.5.3, 6.2.1, 8.2.11, 12.4.5
   student loans, 12.4.5
IRS, *see* INTERNAL REVENUE SERVICE (IRS)
privacy protections, 2.5.6, 16.2

FEDERAL BUREAU OF INVESTIGATIONS (FBI)
see also FEDERAL AGENCIES; GOVERNMENT AGENCIES; LAW ENFORCEMENT AGENCIES
consumer reports, obtaining, 7.2.1, 7.2.10.4
   special legislation, 1.4.8, 1.4.10
FCRA, application, 2.5.6
USA PATRIOT Act, application, 1.4.8

FEDERAL CONSUMER CREDIT PROTECTION ACT
see CONSUMER CREDIT PROTECTION ACT (CCPA)

FEDERAL COURTS
FCRA claims
   jurisdiction, 11.4.1
   removal from state court, 11.4.5
   selection of court, 11.4.4
state claims, pendent jurisdiction, 11.4.2

FEDERAL DEPOSIT INSURANCE CORPORATION
FCRA, enforcement powers, 11.16.1
FCRA regulatory authority, 1.3.3.1, 11.16.2.3
   text of regulations, Appx. B.3.3
GLB Act, regulatory and enforcement authority, 16.4.1.1, 16.4.1.10
   text of regulations, Appx. G.3.3

FEDERAL HOME LOAN BANK BOARD
see OFFICE OF THRIFT SUPERVISION (OTS)

FEDERAL HOME LOAN MORTGAGE CORPORATION (FREDDIE MAC)
automated underwriting system, 14.2.2.4, 14.5.3
underwriting guidelines, 12.7.2, 14.7.2

FEDERAL HOUSING ADMINISTRATION (FHA)
joint lender exemption, 2.5.5
underwriting guidelines, 12.7.2

FEDERAL NATIONAL MORTGAGE ASSOCIATION (FANNIE MAE)
automated underwriting system, 14.2.2.4
underwriting guidelines, 12.7.2, 14.7.2

FEDERAL PREEMPTION
see PREEMPTION OF STATE LAW

FEDERAL RESERVE BOARD (FRB)
FCRA
   enforcement powers, 11.16.1
   interpretations, 1.3.3.1, 11.16.2.3
FCRA regulations
   authority, 1.3.3.1, 11.16.2.3
   negative information model notice, 6.9
   text, Appx. B.2, Appx. B.3.2
GLB Act regulatory and enforcement powers, 16.4.1.1, 16.4.1.10
   text of regulations, Appx. G.3.2

FEDERAL TRADE COMMISSION (FTC)
accuracy study, 4.1.3.2
complaint referral program, 11.16.2.1
consent decrees, 11.16.2.1, Appx. K
consumer reports, subpoenas, 7.2.1, 7.2.10.3
CROA, enforcement responsibilities, 15.2.10
ECOA model forms, Appx. C.9
FCRA
   advisory opinions, 1.3.3.2, 11.16.2.3, Appx. E
   civil actions, 11.16.2.1, 11.16.2.2
   enforcement against furnishers, 11.16.2.2. Appx. K.8
   enforcement powers, 11.16.1, 11.16.2, Appx. K
   Official Staff Commentary, 1.3.3.2, 11.16.2.3, Appx. D
   public interest only, 11.16.2.1
   regulatory authority, 1.3.3.1, 11.16.2.3
   Summary of Rights, *see* SUMMARY OF CONSUMER RIGHTS
FCRA regulations
   authority, 1.3.3.1, 11.16.2.3
   FACTA amendment provisions, 1.4.9.2
   model forms, Appx. C
   text, Appx. B.1
GLB Act, regulatory and enforcement authority, 16.4.1.1, 16.4.1.10

FEDERAL TRADE COMMISSION (FTC) *(cont.)*
identity theft complaint department, 12.6.6
   Identity Theft Hotline, 12.6.6
model forms
   ECOA adverse action, Appx. C.9
   FTC Identity Theft Affidavit, Appx. C.4
   negative information, notices, Appx. C.8
   Notice of Responsibilities of Furnishers, Appx. C.5
   Notice of User Responsibilities, Appx. C.6
   opt-out notices, C.7
   request for annual file disclosure, Appx. C.1
   Summary of Identity Theft Rights, Appx. C.3
   Summary of Consumer Rights, Appx. C.2
nationwide reporting agencies, circumvention rule, 2.6.1.3
opinion letters, 11.16.2.3, Appx. E
Privacy Rule, *see* PRIVACY RULE (FTC)
Safeguard Rules, 16.4.1.10
Telemarketing Rule, *see* TELEMARKETING RULE (FTC)
unfair or deceptive practices, standards, 16.4.2.3

FEES
credit repair organizations, 15.2.2.2.2, 15.3.4.2
   advance payments, 15.2.6, 15.3.5
credit scores, 14.4.1
disputed reports, notification of past users, 4.9.3
file disclosures, 3.3.9
   free annual reports, 3.3.2, 10.7.8
   free reports, other circumstances, 3.3.5–3.3.8
   maximum charge, 3.3.9.2
   state restrictions, 3.3.8, 10.7.8
new information, addition to file, 4.8.4
reinvestigations, 4.5.2.1
statements of dispute, 4.8.1.1

FICO SCORES
see CREDIT SCORES; FAIR ISAAC & CO. (FICO)

FILES
see CONSUMER FILES

FINANCE COMPANIES
see FINANCIAL INSTITUTIONS; LOAN COMPANIES

FINANCIAL ADVISORS
credit repair organization status, 15.2.2.4

FINANCIAL INFORMATION
see also INFORMATION ON CONSUMERS
common law privacy protections, 16.3, 16.5
nonpublic personal information, *see* NONPUBLIC PERSONAL INFORMATION
"pretexting" to obtain, 16.4.2.3
statutory privacy protections, 16.4
   Computer Fraud and Abuse Act, 16.4.2.1
   Financial Information Privacy Act, 16.4.2.2
   FTC Act, 16.4.2.3
   Gramm-Leach-Bliley Act, 16.4.1
   state law, 16.4.2.4

FINANCIAL INFORMATION PRIVACY ACT
overview, 16.4.2.2

FINANCIAL INSTITUTIONS
see also BANKS; CREDIT UNIONS; LOAN COMPANIES
account number sharing, 16.4.1.8
affiliate information sharing, 8.2.18, 2.2, 16.4.1.5.2
CROA, application, 15.2.2.3.4
customer relationships, 16.4.1.3
dealer paper purchases, disclosure obligations, 8.2.7.4.1
defined, 16.4.1.2
FCRA, administrative enforcement, 11.16.1
GLB Act, application, 2.3.4.2.2, 16.4.1.2
GLB exempt disclosures, 16.4.1.5
GLB opt-out rights, 15.4.1.7
GLB privacy notice, 16.4.1.6
identity theft, red flag guidelines, 9.2.6
information security program, 16.4.1.10
negative information, reporting notice, 6.9, 8.2.10
nonpublic personal information, disclosure restrictions, 2.3.4.2.2, 16.4.1.4
   exempt disclosures, 16.4.1.5
privacy protections
   common law, 16.3, 16.5
   governmental intrusion, 16.2
   Gramm-Leach-Bliley Act, 16.4.1
   Safeguard Rules, 16.4.1.10
   statutory protections, 16.4
   tort claims, 16.3
regulatory authorities, *see* BANKING REGULATORS
services provided by, *see* FINANCIAL SERVICES

FINANCIAL RESOURCES
information pretexting, 11.16.2.1, 16.4.2.3

FINANCIAL SERVICES
account information, pretexting, 11.16.2.1
account number sharing, 16.4.1.8
consumer report, permissible use, 2.3.6.8, 7.2.8.2.2.1
blemished credit record, implications, 12.7.7
fraud lists, 12.7.7
immigrants, 12.8
provision, FCRA, application, 2.3.6.8

FORECLOSURES
prior, impact on mortgage applications, 12.7.2
rescue scams, credit repair laws, application, 15.3.2

FORMS
ECOA adverse action forms, Appx. C.9
FTC model forms, Appx. C

FORUM
FCRA claims
   removal, 11.4.5
   selection, 11.4.4

FRAUD
see also FALSE PRETENSES
alerts, *see* FRAUD ALERTS
credit repair organizations, 15.2.7.5
   pleading, 15.2.8.8
file segregation as, 12.5.5
free consumer report, 3.3.5
identity theft, *see* IDENTITY THEFT
notice of rights, 8.2.3
prevention, database services, 2.7.11
protection notices, 8.2.24
specialized fraud lists, 3.2.4, 12.7.7

FRAUD ALERTS
see also FRAUD; IDENTITY THEFT
effect, 9.2.2.5
extended fraud alerts, 9.2.2.3
   effect, 9.2.2.3.3
   identity theft report, 9.2.2.3.2

FRAUD ALERTS (cont.)
FCRA provisions, overview, 9.2.2.1.1
free consumer report, entitlement, 3.3.5, 8.2.15.1, 9.2.2.2, 9.2.2.3.3
initial fraud alerts, 9.2.2.2
notice of free consumer report, 8.2.15, 9.2.2.2, 9.2.2.3.3
    enforcement of notice rights, 8.2.15.3
    nature and contents, 8.2.15.1
    time and manner, 8.2.15.2
"one-call" alerts, 9.2.2.2
placing on file, 4.8.2, 9.2.2.2, 9.2.2.3.1, 12.6.6.2
proof of identity, necessity, 9.2.2.1.2

FREDDIE MAC
see FEDERAL HOME LOAN MORTGAGE CORPORATION (FREDDIE MAC)

FRIVOLOUS DISPUTES
see also DISPUTED INFORMATION
agency obligations, 4.5.2.4
notice of frivolous dispute, 8.2.14

FTC
see FEDERAL TRADE COMMISSION (FTC)

FURNISHERS OF INFORMATION
see also CREDITORS
accuracy standards, 6.4
    affiliate information sharing, 6.4.5
    duty to correct and update, 6.5
    enforcement, 6.4.1, 6.10.1
    general duty, 6.4.2
    guidelines and regulations, 6.4.3
    liability, 6.4.1, 6.4.4, 6.5, 6.10.2, 6.12
    Metro 2 Format, 6.3.3.2, 6.4.2
    state law, 10.7
address for error complaints, 6.4.4
adverse information, *see* ADVERSE INFORMATION
affiliate sharing of information, 6.2.2.1, 6.4.5
bankruptcy reporting, 4.4.6.9.2
child support debts, 5.7.1
closed accounts, reporting, 6.8
contacting regarding errors, 6.4.4
cosigner obligations, 5.6.2, 5.6.3
credit limits, failure to report, 14.8.3.2
date of delinquency, furnishing, 6.7
debt collectors, *see* DEBT COLLECTORS
defined, 2.1.2, 6.2.1
delinquencies, reporting limitations, 6.7, 5.2.3.3
direct selling of information, 6.2.2.2
discrimination, 5.5.2, 6.11, 12.4.8
disputed information
    billing errors, 5.3.4, 10.3
    correcting and updating, 6.5, 6.10.5
    direct notification, 6.5.2, 6.10.1, 12.6.2.3
    formal dispute notification, 4.5.4.2, 6.10.3
    notation of dispute, 4.8.2, 6.6
    reinvestigation involvement, 4.5.4.2, 6.10
    reporting restrictions, 5.3.2.2
    student loans, 12.4.5
    withdrawal of information, 12.6.4.1
duty to correct and update, 6.5
duty to report accurately, 6.4.2
    consumer enforcement, 6.10.1
ECOA restrictions, 5.5.2, 6.11, 10.3, 12.4.8
electronic provision of information, 6.3.1

Metro 2 Format, *see* METRO 2 FORMAT
    reinvestigation results, 6.10.6.4
failure to report information, 4.3.2.2
    credit limits, 4.3.2.3, 14.8.3.2
    favorable information, 14.8.3.3
    intentional withholding, 4.3.2.3, 14.8.3.3
FCRA
    application, 2.1.2, 6.2.1
    claims against, 6.10.2, 6.10.7, 10.2.4
    enforcement of duties, 6.1.2, 6.4.1, 6.10.1
    FTC enforcement, 11.16.2.2
    notice of obligations, 6.2.1, 8.4.1, Appx. C.5
    state enforcement, 11.16.4.2
federal agencies, 5.5.3, 8.2.11
financial institutions *see* FINANCIAL INSTITUTIONS
FTC enforcement powers, 11.16.2.2
    sample enforcement order, Appx. K.8
generally, 1.3.1, 6.2.1
identity theft information, obligations, 6.4.2, 6.14, 9.2.4.2
inaccurate information, 4.3.2, 4.4.6.3
    address to contact, 6.4.4
    billing errors, 5.3.4, 10.3
    correcting, 6.5, 6.10.5
    disputing, 6.5.2, 6.10
    liability, 6.4.1, 6.4.4, 6.5, 6.10.1, 10.2.4
    provision, 4.3.2.1
integrity standards, 6.4.3
legislative history, 1.4.6, 6.1.1
liability
    accuracy standards, 6.4.1, 6.5.1, 10.2.4
    consumer enforcement, 6.10.1, 10.2.4
    ECOA, 10.3
    FCBA, 10.3
    FCRA, 10.2.4
    FDCPA, 10.3
    limited qualified immunity, 10.4
    other federal statutes, 10.3
    reinvestigation, 6.10.2, 10.2.4.2
    RESPA, 10.3
    tort claims, 6.12, 10.4
manual reporting, 6.3.2
medical information, 5.4.1.3
nationwide bureaus, to, 3.2.3.3
non-reporting agencies, to, 10.4.5
notice obligations
    disputed information, 4.8.2, 6.6
    negative information by financial institutions, 6.9
    voluntarily closed accounts, 6.8
notice of FCRA obligations, 6.2.1, 8.4.1
    Summary of Responsibilities, FTC model form, Appx. C.5
notice, to, other notices, 8.4.2
    notice of dispute, 4.8.2, 6.6, 6.10.3
objective standard, 6.3.3.2
overview, 6.1.1
personal interviews, 5.4.2
qualified immunity, 6.12, 10.4
reinsertion of information, certification, 4.7.3
reinvestigations
    conducting, 6.5.2, 6.10.4
    deletion or correction after, 6.10.5
    liability, 6.10.2
    notification of dispute, 6.10.3
    reporting of results, 6.10.6

FURNISHERS OF INFORMATION (cont.)
state law restrictions, 5.7
    federal preemption, 5.7.2, 6.2.2.3, 10.7.5.2, 10.7.9.4
tort liability, 6.12, 10.4.5
UDAP violations, 10.6.2
Universal Data Form, use, 6.3.2, 6.5.4
updating information, 6.5
withholding of information, 4.3.2.3, 14.8.3.3

GOSSIP
consumer report users, 12.2.2
legislative response, 1.4.3

GOVERNMENT AGENCIES
see also FEDERAL AGENCIES; LOCAL GOVERNMENT
    AGENCIES; STATE AGENCIES
adverse action notice
    government benefits, 8.2.6.4.6
    security clearance exemption, 8.2.6.4.4.3
child support, *see* CHILD SUPPORT ENFORCEMENT
    AGENCIES
consumer reports
    child support purposes, 12.3.6.9, 7.2.9, 7.4.2
    counterterrorism purposes, 7.2.10.5
    disclosure notice, 12.4.5
    license approval, 2.3.6.6, 7.2.6
    obtaining, 7.2.10.2, 7.2.10.4, 12.2.4
    permissible use, 7.2.3.4, 7.2.6, 7.2.9, 7.2.10, 12.7.9
    public assistance eligibility, 2.3.6.6, 7.2.6, 12.7.9
    tax collection, 7.4.3
defined, 7.2.10.2
disclosure exemptions
    counterterrorism, 7.2.10.5
    security clearances, 3.5.4.2
FBI, *see* FEDERAL BUREAU OF INVESTIGATIONS (FBI)
FCRA application
    federal, 2.5.6
    generally, 2.3.6.6, 2.5.2
    joint-use exception, 2.5.5
    state and local, 2.5.7
furnishing of information, 6.2.1
    federal agencies, 5.5.3, 8.2.11, 12.4.5
GLB Act enforcement, 16.4.1.10
identifying information, obtaining, 7.2.10.2
law enforcement, *see* LAW ENFORCEMENT AGENCIES
loan guarantee programs
    FCRA, application, 2.5.5
    reporting of defaults, 12.4.5
    student loans, *see* STUDENT LOANS
privacy protections, 2.5.6, 16.2
security clearance usage, disclosure, 3.5.4.2
social service agencies, *see* ADOPTION AGENCIES;
    WELFARE AGENCIES

GOVERNMENT BENEFITS
see also WELFARE AGENCIES
eligibility
    adverse action notice, 8.2.6.4.6
    permissible use, 2.3.6.6, 7.2.6, 12.7.9
impermissible use, 7.1.9
overpayments, permissible use, 2.3.6.8, 7.2.8.2.2.1

GOVERNMENT LICENSES
see LICENSES

GRAMM-LEACH-BLILEY (GLB) ACT
account number sharing restrictions, 16.4.1.8
application, 16.4.1.2, 16.4.1.3
banking agency regulations, Appx. G.3
consumer reporting agencies, application, 2.3.4.2.2
credit headers, disclosure restrictions, 2.3.4.2.2
enforcement, 16.4.1.10
    no private right of action, 16.4.1.11
exempt disclosures, 16.4.1.5
    affiliates, 16.4.1.5.2
    categories, 16.4.1.5.3
    redisclosure and reuse restrictions, 16.4.1.5.4
FCRA, impact on, 16.4.1.9
FTC rules, Appx. G.2
implementation, 16.4.1.10
notice requirements, 16.4.1.6
opt-out rights, 16.4.1.7
    exemptions, 16.4.1.5.3
    exercise, 16.4.1.7.3
    generally, 16.4.1.7.1
    notice, 16.4.1.7.2
    sample notices, Appx. G.4
overview, 16.4.1.1
preemption of state law, 16.4.1.12
privacy protections, 16.1
regulations, 16.4.1.1
    Privacy Rule, *see* PRIVACY RULE (FTC)
    Safeguard Rules, 16.4.1.10
    text, Appx. G.2
scope
    consumers, 16.4.1.3
    customers, 16.4.1.3
    exemptions, 16.4.1.6
    financial institutions, 16.4.1.2
    information, 16.4.1.4
text, selected provisions, Appx. G.1
violation as UDAP violation, 16.4.1.11
weaknesses, 16.4.1.13, 16.6

GRAND JURY
governmental agency status, 7.2.10.2
subpoenas, consumer report, permissible purpose, 7.2.1

GUARANTORS
see COSIGNERS

HEALTH CARE INFORMATION
see MEDICAL INFORMATION

HIGHER EDUCATION ACT
student loan defaults, application, 5.2.3.9, 12.6.5

HOME EQUITY LOANS
see HOME MORTGAGES

HOME FINDERS
credit repair laws, application, 15.3.2

HOME IMPROVEMENT CONTRACTORS
credit repair laws, application, 15.3.4

HOME MORTGAGES
applying for, 12.7.2
bankruptcy, effect on eligibility, 12.6.8
blemished report, implications, 12.7.2
consumer explanations, consideration, 12.6.9
credit reports, *see* RESIDENTIAL MORTGAGE CREDIT
    REPORTS

HOME MORTGAGES (*cont.*)
credit scores, disclosure, 3.3.1.3, 14.4.1
   mortgage scoring notice, 8.2.5
disputed charges, qualified written request, 12.4.4
disputed information, reporting restrictions, 5.3
   open-end accounts, 5.3.4
   RESPA restrictions, 5.3.5
Fannie Mae and Freddie Mac standards, 12.7.2
government-insured, joint lender exemption, 2.5.5
open-end lines of credit, 5.3.4
pre-approval, 12.7.2
RESPA, application, 5.3.5, 12.4.4
risk assessment, 2.3.6.7, 7.2.7
   credit scores, disclosure, 14.4.1
varying standards amongst lenders, 12.7.2

HOME SAVERS
credit repair laws, application, 15.3.2

HOUSEHOLD PURPOSE TRANSACTIONS
see also CONSUMER TRANSACTIONS
consumer report, permissible purpose, 2.3.6.3.1, 7.2.3.1.3
   business transactions, 7.2.8.2.2.1
defined, 2.3.6.3.1

HUD-MORTGAGES
see FEDERAL HOUSING ADMINISTRATION (FHA)

IDENTIFICATION
see also VERIFICATION
alerts, necessary to issue, 9.2.2.1.2
concealment, 15.2.7.3
consumer reports
   consumer, 3.4.3, 3.6.2
   person accompanying consumer, 3.6.2
   users, 7.5.2
identity theft victims, access to information, 9.2.3.1
immigrants, 12.8
reasonable procedures, 4.4.6.5
theft of, *see* IDENTITY THEFT

IDENTIFYING INFORMATION
see also CREDIT HEADER INFORMATION
altering to confuse reporting agency, 12.5.5, 15.2.7.3
checks, adverse characterizations, 3.5.5
consumer files, examining, 3.7.1
consumer list, status as consumer report, 2.3.4.2.1, 7.2.10.2
governmental agencies, obtaining, 7.2.10.2
medical information furnishers, 5.4.1.3
private investigators, obtaining, 7.4.5
reporting, consumer report status, 2.3.4.2.1
Social Security numbers, 9.2.5.1

IDENTITY THEFT
access to information after, 9.2.3
alerts
   active military service, *see* MILITARY DUTY ALERTS
   fraud alerts, *see* FRAUD ALERTS
blocking of fraudulent information, 9.2.4
   agency responsibilities, 9.2.4.1
   furnisher responsibilities, 9.2.4.2
   refusal to block notice, 8.2.16
credit record, coping with, 12.6.6
   cleaning up after, 12.6.6.1
   heading off new problems, 12.6.6.2
criminal offence, 9.3
debt collectors, obligations, 9.2.3.2

FACTA
   key provisions, 1.4.9.2, 9.2.1
   legislative history, 1.4.9.1, 9.2.1
FCRA provisions, 9.2
   access to information, 9.2.3
   alerts, 9.2.2
   blocking of information, 9.2.4
   claims under, 9.5
   overview, 9.2.1
   prevention of theft, 9.2.5
filing suit, 12.6.6
free consumer report, 3.3.5
FTC, complaints to, 12.6.6
   FTC hotline, 12.6.6
FTC enforcement orders, Appx. K.9
FTC ID Theft Affidavit, Appx. C.4
furnisher responsibilities, 6.4.2, 6.14
Identity Theft and Assumption Deterrence Act, 9.3
identity theft report, 9.2.2.3.2
mismerged files aggravate problem, 4.3.3.7, 4.3.5
overview, 4.3.5, 12.1
notifying reporting agencies
   alerts, 9.2.2
   FTC ID Theft Affidavit, Appx. C.4
preventing, 9.2.5
   address discrepancies, 9.2.5.2
   credit card number truncation, 9.2.5.1
   disposal of consumer information, 9.2.5.3
   reasonable procedures, 4.4.6.6
   red flag guidelines, 9.2.6
   Social Security number truncation, 9.2.5.1
prevention programs, 9.2.6
   reasonable procedures, 4.4.6.6
protection notices, 8.2.24
   address discrepancy, 8.5.3, 9.2.5.2
   alerts, 9.2.2
rectifying by filing suit, 9.5
red flag guidelines, 9.2.6
security freezes, state law, Appx. H
state law, 9.4, 10.6.3
   federal preemption, 10.7.5.5
   summaries, Appx. H
steps to correct, 12.6.6
summary of rights notice, 8.2.3, 9.2.2.5
   model form, Appx. C.3
tort claims, 16.3
   federal preemption, 10.7.5.5
transactional information, access to, 9.2.3.1

IDENTITY THEFT AND ASSUMPTION DETERRENCE ACT
overview, 9.3

IMMIGRATION MATTERS
credit issues for immigrants, 12.8
consumer reports, use, 12.2.4

IMMUNITY
see LIABILITY; QUALIFIED IMMUNITY

IMPERMISSIBLE PURPOSES
see also PERMISSIBLE PURPOSES
alimony, 7.4.2, 12.2.4
anything not permissible, 7.4.1
bad debt lists, 12.2.3
business credit, 7.2.3.1.3

IMPERSMISSIBLE PURPOSES (*cont.*)
child custody, 12.2.4
child support, 7.4.2, 12.2.4
consumer's objection, obtaining despite, 7.1.2
criminal liability, 11.16.3
curiosity, 12.2.2
discovering, 7.1.9
divorce proceedings, 7.4.2, 12.2.4
FCRA claims, 10.2.2.4
generally, 7.4.1, 12.2.1
immigration matters, 12.2.4
insurance claims, 7.2.5, 7.4.7
investigators, 7.4.5
liability, 7.5.1, 7.6, 7.7, 10.2.2.4
litigation, 7.4.4, 12.2.4
marketing research, 7.4.8
obtaining for, 2.3.5.3
other uses, 7.4.9
paternity proceedings, 7.4.2
prescreening, 7.3.2.4, 7.3.4.1
preventative procedures, 7.5
prosecutions, 7.4.4, 12.2.4
publication in community, 12.2.2
relatives, 7.4.6.3, 12.2.5
spouses, 7.4.6.3, 12.2.5
tax collection, 7.4.3
testers, restrictions, 11.6.2
third parties, 7.4.6.1, 12.2.5
use, effect on status, 7.1.8
use for, 2.3.5.1, 2.3.6.2, 7.1.4, 10.2.5.1
vicarious liability, 7.7.5

INACCURATE INFORMATION
see also ACCURACY; CREDIT DISPUTES; FALSE INFORMATION
address to contact, 6.4.4
agency refusal to supply report as, 4.3.6
avoiding through reasonable procedures, *see* REASONABLE PROCEDURES
bankruptcy reporting, 4.3.2.4, 4.4.6.9
consumer identification, 4.4.6.5
  identity theft, *see* IDENTITY THEFT
consumer reports, 10.2.2.1
  agency liability, 4.4, 10.2.2.1.2
  examining for, 3.7.2.4, 12.6.1
  prevalence, 4.1.3
correcting, 12.6.2
  automated reinvestigation system, 4.6.3, 6.10.6.2, 6.10.6.4
  creditor, 6.5
  disputing information, 12.6.2.1, 12.6.2.2
  importance, 12.6.4.1
  mismerged files, 4.3.3.8
  reporting agency, 4.5.2.2, 4.6
  soft-deletes, 4.6.2, 4.7.1, 12.6.4.3
  Universal Data Form, 6.5.4
credit repair organizations, 15.2.7.2
credit scores, effect, 14.8
data retrieval errors, 4.4.6.7
defamation claims, 10.5.2
disputing, *see* CREDIT DISPUTES; REINVESTIGATIONS
explaining
  by agency, 4.2.2
  by consumer, 12.6.9
FCRA claims

consumer reporting agencies, 10.2.2.1
furnishers of information, 10.2.4
file retrieval errors, 4.3.4, 4.4.6.5
FTC study, 4.1.3.2
furnishers, 4.3.2
  address to correct, 6.4.4
  liability, 6.4.2, 6.4.4, 6.5, 10.2.4
  notice to furnisher, 6.4.2
  prohibition, 6.4.2
  provision, 4.3.2.1, 4.4.6.3
  reinvestigations, 6.5.2
identification errors, 4.3.3, 4.3.4, 4.4.6.5
  identity theft, *see* IDENTITY THEFT
incomplete information, 4.3.2.2, 4.3.2.3, 12.6.9, 14.8.3.3
  consumer offers of new information, 4.8.4
  credit limits, 4.3.2.3, 14.8.3.2
  existing accounts, 4.4.6.8.3
  new accounts, 4.4.6.3.2
  reasonable procedures, 4.4.6.8
legislative history, 1.4.3, 4.1.2
liability
  furnishers, 6.4.4
  limited qualified immunity, 10.4
  reporting agencies, 4.4
  resellers, 4.4.4
management policies encouraging, 4.4.6.1
mismerged files, 4.3.3, 4.4.6.5
missing accounts, 4.3.2.2, 4.4.6.8.2, 4.8.4, 12.6.9
obsolete information, 4.4.6.8, 5.2.2.2
overview, 4.1
prevalence, 4.1.3
public record information, 4.3.2.5, 4.3.3.4
reasonable procedures to avoid, *see* REASONABLE PROCEDURES
reinsertion after deletion, *see* REINSERTION OF INFORMATION
reinvestigation, *see* REINVESTIGATIONS
resellers, 4.4.4
state law preemption, 10.7
statement of dispute, 4.6.1, 4.8.1, 8.5.4, 12.4.7
subscriber inquiries resulting in, 4.3.3.5
technically accurate information as, 4.2.3, 4.4.6.8.3
third parties, information on as, 4.2.4
transcription errors, 4.4.6.7
tort claims, 10.4, 10.5
types of inaccurate information, 4.3
unverifiable information as, 4.2.5

INDEMNIFICATION
impleading a third party, 11.8

INDEPENDENT CONTRACTORS
consumer reports, obtaining, 2.5.4, 7.1.6
FCRA, application, 2.5.4, 2.5.5

INDICTMENTS
see PUBLIC RECORD INFORMATION

INDIVIDUALS
see CONSUMERS; PERSONS

INFORMATION BROKERS
see RESELLERS

INFORMATION DATABASES
see DATA BROKERS

INFORMATION   *Fair Credit Reporting*

References are to sections

INFORMATION FURNISHERS
see FURNISHERS OF INFORMATION

INFORMATION ON CONSUMERS
see also CONSUMER FILES; CONSUMER LISTS; CONSUMER REPORTS
adverse, see ADVERSE INFORMATION
assemble, definition, 2.5.3.2
business need, 2.3.6.8
business purposes, 2.3.6.2
collection purpose, 2.3.5.4
communication by other than agency, 2.3.2, 3.3.1.5
confidentiality, 16.5
consumer reporting agencies, see CONSUMER FILES
consumer reports, see CONSUMER REPORTS
credit header information, see CREDIT HEADER INFORMATION
credit purposes, 2.3.6.3
direct selling of information, 6.2.2.2
disposal regulations, 9.2.5.3
disputed information, see DISPUTED INFORMATION
employment purposes, 2.3.6.4.1
expected use, 2.3.5.3
evaluate, definition, 2.5.3.2
false, see FALSE INFORMATION; INACCURATE INFORMATION
false pretenses, obtaining by, 7.2.2, 7.7.3, 7.7.4, 10.2.5.1
favorable information, 5.2.2.1, 5.2.2.2
   unreported, 4.3.2.3, 12.6.9, 14.8.3.3
FBI access, 1.4.8, 7.2.10.4
FCRA, scope, Ch. 2
Financial Information Privacy Act, 16.4.2.2
first-hand experience, 2.4.2, 2.5.4, 6.2.2.2
fraudulent, blocking, 9.2.4
furnishing, see FURNISHERS OF INFORMATION
GLB Act, application, 2.3.4.2.2, 16.4.1
identifying information, see IDENTIFYING INFORMATION
identity theft related, see IDENTITY THEFT
inaccurate, see INACCURATE INFORMATION
joint users, sharing, 2.4.6, 2.5.5
legislative history, 1.4.3
nationwide bureaus, 3.2.3.3
non consumer reports, improper use, 2.1.1
nonpublic personal information, see NONPUBLIC PERSONAL INFORMATION
not consumer-specific, FCRA, application, 2.3.4.1
personally identifiable financial information, 16.4.1.4
pretexting, 11.16.2.1, 16.4.2.3
previously reported, 3.5.6
privacy protections
   common law protections, 16.3, 16.5
   governmental intrusion, 16.2
   identity theft, see IDENTITY THEFT
   overview, 16.1
   statutory protections, 16.4, 16.6
   tort claims, 16.3
public record information, see PUBLIC RECORD INFORMATION
purpose, 2.3.5, 2.3.6
release for impermissible purpose, 7.1.8
reporting
   see also CONSUMER REPORTING AGENCIES; CONSUMER REPORTS
   regularly engages in, 2.5.3.1

third parties, to, 2.5.4
sources
   see also FURNISHERS OF INFORMATION
   data brokers, 2.7.4
   disclosure, 3.5.3, 13.4.2.3
   inaccurate sources, 4.4.6.3
   nationwide agencies, 3.2.3.3
   specialized agencies, 3.2.4
spousal information, 5.6.1, 7.4.6
suppliers, tort liability, 10.4.5
unverifiable information, 4.2.5

INJUNCTIVE RELIEF
credit reporting violations, 11.13

INJURIES
see DAMAGES; DAMAGES, ACTUAL

INQUIRY ACTIVITY
record retention, 7.5.5
reporting on
   consumer report status, 2.3.4.2.4
   consumer requests, 7.5.5, 5.2.3.8
   prescreened lists, 5.2.3.8
   trigger lists, 2.3.4.2.4

INSPECTION BUREAUS
see also CONSUMER REPORTING AGENCIES; INVESTIGATIVE CONSUMER REPORTS
disclosure obligations, 13.4.3
FCRA claims, 10.2.2.6
FCRA, application, 2.7.1
investigative reports, preparation, 13.1
   insurance reports, 13.3.1

INSURANCE
adverse action, see ADVERSE ACTION
benefits, see INSURANCE BENEFITS
business insurance, see BUSINESS INSURANCE
claims, see INSURANCE CLAIM EXCHANGES; INSURANCE CLAIM LISTS; INSURANCE CLAIMS
companies, see INSURANCE COMPANIES
coverage, see INSURANCE COVERAGE
denial, see ADVERSE ACTION
liability insurance, see LIABILITY INSURANCE
life insurance, see LIFE INSURANCE
marketing lists, see PRESCREENED REPORTS
purposes, see INSURANCE PURPOSES
reports, see INSURANCE REPORTS
underwriting, see INSURANCE UNDERWRITING

INSURANCE BENEFITS
FCRA, application, 2.3.6.5.2
issuance, status as business transaction, 2.3.6.5.2

INSURANCE CLAIM EXCHANGES
see also INSURANCE CLAIMS
FCRA, application, 2.3.6.5.2
nationwide agencies, 2.6.2

INSURANCE CLAIM LISTS
see also CONSUMER LISTS; INSURANCE CLAIMS
compilers, FCRA, application, 2.7.8

INSURANCE CLAIMS
exchanges, see INSURANCE CLAIM EXCHANGES
lists, see INSURANCE CLAIM LISTS
reports, 2.3.6.5.2, 7.2.5, 7.4.7, 12.7.5

INSURANCE COMPANIES
see also FURNISHERS OF INFORMATION
FCRA, application, 2.3.6.5, 2.5.4
information requests, see INSURANCE REPORTS
notice obligations, 7.2.5, 8.2.6.4.5

INSURANCE COVERAGE
FCRA liability, 11.6.3.7

INSURANCE PURPOSES
blemished credit record
  impact on relatives, 12.2.5
  implications, 12.7.5
credit scores, use, 14.3, 14.10
FCRA, application, 2.3.6.5
impermissible purposes, 7.4.7
investigative reports, 13.3.1
medical information, 12.7.5
permissible purposes, 7.2.5, 7.2.7
prescreening, 7.3.4
reports for, see INSURANCE REPORTS
underwriting purposes, see INSURANCE UNDERWRITING

INSURANCE REPORTS
see also CONSUMER REPORTS
adverse action notice, 8.2.6.4.5
blemished reports, implications, 12.7.5
claims reports, 2.3.6.5.2, 7.2.5, 7.4.7, 12.7.5
consumer report, status, 2.3.6.5, 2.7.8, 7.4.7
FTC Staff Commentary, Appx. D
investigative, see INVESTIGATIVE CONSUMER REPORTS
medical information, inclusion, 5.4.1.2
  furnisher identification, 5.4.1.3
permissible purposes, 7.2.5
preparation by inspection bureaus, 13.3.1
underwriting reports, 2.3.6.5.1, 7.2.5, 12.7.5

INSURANCE UNDERWRITING
adverse action notice, 8.2.6.4.5
blemished credit record, implications, 12.7.5
consumer report, permissible use, 7.2.5, 7.2.7, 12.7.5
credit risks, 7.2.7
credit scores, 14.3, 14.10
described, 7.2.5
FCRA, application, 2.3.6.5.1
medical information, 12.7.5
obsolete information, using, 5.2.4

INTEREST RATES
adverse rates, notice requirements
  accepted counteroffers, 8.2.6.4.3.5
  price quotes, 8.2.6.4.3.6
  risk-based pricing, 8.2.6.3.4
blemished credit record, impact
  car loans, 12.7.1
  home mortgages, 12.7.2
risk-based pricing, 14.7.3
  notice requirements, 8.2.6.3.4, 8.2.8

INTER-FACT
see RESELLERS

INTERNAL REVENUE SERVICE (IRS)
see also FEDERAL AGENCIES; GOVERNMENT AGENCIES
consumer reports
  administrative summons, 7.2.1, 7.4.3
  impermissible use, 7.4.3
  permissible user, 7.2.3.4

INTERNET
see ELECTRONIC COMMUNICATION; WEB RESOURCES

INTERVIEWS
see PERSONAL INTERVIEWS

INVASION OF PRIVACY
see also PRIVACY; TORT CLAIMS
check cashing lists as, 12.7.7
common law tort
  elements of claim, 10.5.3
  overview, 16.3
FCRA qualified immunity, 6.12, 10.4, 10.5.3, 16.3
federal agencies, 2.5.6
identity theft, see IDENTITY THEFT

INVESTIGATING AGENCIES
see CONSUMER REPORTING AGENCIES; DETECTIVE AGENCIES; INSPECTION BUREAUS

INVESTIGATIONS
consumers, see INVESTIGATIVE CONSUMER REPORTS
disputes, see REINVESTIGATIONS
employee misconduct, 2.4.4.1, 7.2.4.5, 8.2.6.4.4.2, 13.2.4.2

INVESTIGATIVE CONSUMER REPORTS
see also CONSUMER REPORTING AGENCIES; CONSUMER REPORTS
additional obligations, 13.1.2
adverse action based on, 13.4.1.6
contents, 13.2.3
copy to consumer, 13.4.2.2
definition, 13.2
  exclusions, 13.2.4
described, 13.1.1
disclosure requirements, 13.4
  additional disclosures, 13.4.2, 13.5.2
  address of reporting agency, 13.4.1.6
  form of disclosure, 13.4.2.4
  nature of report, 13.4.3
  reasonable procedures defense, 13.4.4
  request for report, 13.4.1
  user certification, 13.4.1.5
  violations, 10.2.5.3
  waiver of rights, 13.4.5
distinguished from consumer report, 3.2.1
employment agencies, 2.4.4.2.2
employment purposes, 2.3.6.4.2, 13.3.2
  employee consent, 13.5.1
  employee misconduct exemption, 2.4.4.1, 7.2.4.5, 13.2.4.2
false threats, 13.4.1.2
FCRA definition, 13.2
FCRA violations
  reporting agencies, 10.2.2.6
  users, 10.2.5.3
FTC Staff Commentary, Appx. D
identifying investigator, 13.4.3
inspection bureaus, see INSPECTION BUREAUS
insurance purposes, 13.3.1
notice
  adverse action, 13.4.1.7
  user request, 13.4.1
  utilization of notices, 13.5
permissible purposes, 13.3.4

INVESTIGATIVE CONSUMER REPORTS (cont.)
personal interviews
　confirmation of information, 13.6.2.2
　requirement, 13.2.3
　status as, 5.4.2
procedures, 13.6
public record searches, status, 13.3.1
reinvestigation, 13.5.2
re-use, 13.6.2.4
sources of information
　confidentiality, 13.4.2.3, 13.4.3
　notice of potential discovery of identity, 13.4.3
state laws, 13.7
stoppage of investigation, 13.5.1, 13.5.2
subject matter, 13.2.2
tenant screening purposes, 13.3.3
updating, 13.5.2
user certification, 10.2.5.3, 13.4.1.2, 13.4.1.5
verification
　adverse information based on public records, 13.6.2.3
　personal interviews, 13.6.2.2
　reverification of information, 13.6.2.4

INVESTIGATORS
see DETECTIVE AGENCIES

INVESTMENTS
adverse action notice, 8.2.6.4.7.1
consumer reports, permissible use, 2.3.6.3.1, 7.2.3.1.3, 7.2.8.2.2.1

IRRELEVANT DISPUTES
see also DISPUTED INFORMATION
agency obligations, 4.5.2.4
notice of irrelevant dispute, 8.2.14

IRRELEVANT INFORMATION
see also INFORMATION ON CONSUMERS
legislative response, 1.4.3

JOINT ACCOUNTS
see also CREDIT ACCOUNTS; SPOUSES
consumer reports, 5.6, 7.4.6.4
ECOA reporting requirements, 5.6.1

JOINT LENDERS
consumer reporting agency status, 2.4.6, 2.5.5
third party information, sharing, 2.4.6

JUDGMENT CREDITORS
see also CREDITORS
consumer reports, permissible use, 7.2.3.4

JUDGMENT DEBTORS
lists for locating, 12.2.3

JUDGMENTS
see also PUBLIC RECORD INFORMATION
discharged through bankruptcy, reporting, 5.2.3.7
reporting limitations, 5.2.3.4

JURISDICTION
CROA claims, 15.2.8.7
FCRA claims
　court selection, 11.4.1
　personal jurisdiction, 11.2.3, 11.4.3
FTC enforcement powers, 11.16.2.1
state claims
　pendent jurisdiction, 11.4.2
　removal to federal court, 11.4.5

JURORS
see also JURY TRIALS
reports on, FCRA application, 7.2.4.2, 7.4.4

JURY TRIALS
see also JURORS
CROA claims, 15.2.8.10
punitive damages, determination, 11.7, 11.12.3
right to, 11.7
sample closing argument, Appx. J.8.1
sample instructions to jury, Appx. J.8.2–Appx. J.8.4

LAND CONTRACTS
adverse action notice, 8.2.6.4.7.4
FCRA, application, 7.2.8.2.2.1

LANDLORD REPORTING COMPANIES
see TENANT SCREENING COMPANIES

LANDLORDS
see also FURNISHERS OF INFORMATION; USERS OF INFORMATION
creditor status, 13.3.3
FCRA application, 2.3.6.8, 7.2.8.2.2.1
　joint-use exception, 2.5.5
tenant reports
　notice of adverse use, 8.2.7.2
　prior landlords, investigative status, 13.3.3
　use, 2.3.6.3.3, 12.7.3

LANGUAGE
dispute settlements, 12.6.4.3

LAW ENFORCEMENT AGENCIES
see also GOVERNMENT AGENCIES
consumer reports
　court order requirement, 7.2.1
　impermissible use, 7.4.5
　permissible use, 7.2.6, 7.2.10.4
FBI, see FEDERAL BUREAU OF INVESTIGATIONS (FBI)
identity theft reports, 9.2.2.3.1
lists used by, see LAW ENFORCEMENT BULLETINS
police departments, see POLICE DEPARTMENTS
sheriff's departments, see SHERIFF'S DEPARTMENTS

LAW ENFORCEMENT BULLETINS
see also LAW ENFORCEMENT AGENCIES
consumer report status, 2.3.5.3
FCRA, application, 7.3.3

LAWSUITS
see ACTIONS; COLLECTION SUITS; LITIGATION

LAWYERS
see ATTORNEYS; FURNISHERS OF INFORMATION

LEASES
automobile, see AUTOMOBILE LEASES
credit transaction status, 8.2.7.2
denial, notice obligations, 8.2.6.4.7.3
permissible uses, 2.3.6.8, 7.2.8.2.2.1
personal property leases, see PERSONAL PROPERTY LEASES
residential leases, see RESIDENTIAL LEASES

LEGAL PROCEEDINGS
see also ACTIONS; LITIGATION
bad debts published pursuant to, 12.2.3

LEGISLATIVE HISTORY OF FCRA
see also FAIR CREDIT REPORTING ACT (FCRA)
conference committee bill, 1.4.4
confidentiality, 7.1.1
Consumer Credit Reporting Reform Act of 1996, 1.4.6
early amendments, 1.4.5
early history, 1.4.2
FACTA amendments, 1.4.9.1
FCRA, 1.4
insurance purposes, 2.3.6.5.1
intent, 2.3.6.2, 4.1.2
introduction, 1.4.1
1997 and 1999 amendments, 1.4.7
passage of FCRA, 1.4.4
qualified immunity, 10.4.1
recent amendments, 1.4.10
Senate Bill 823, 1.4.3
USA PATRIOT Act, 1.4.8

LENDERS
see CREDITORS; JOINT LENDERS

LIABILITY
"any person," 11.1
consumer reporting agencies
  computer fraud laws, 11.16.3
  employees, 7.6
  FCRA violations, 10.2.1, 11.16
  impermissible reports, 7.6, 10.2.2.4
  improper handling of disputes, 10.2.2.2
  inaccurate reports, 4.4, 10.2.2.1.2
  inadequate procedures, 4.4.5.1, 10.2.2.1.2
  insurance coverage, 11.6.3.7
  limited qualified immunity, 10.4
  obsolete information, 10.2.2.3
  officers or employees, 7.6
  public record information, 10.2.2.7
credit repair fraud, 15.2.7.5, 15.2.8.3
defenses, see DEFENSES
FCRA violations
  attorney fees and costs, 11.14.1
  civil liability, generally, 10.2.1
  criminal penalties, 11.16.3
  furnishers of information, 6.5, 6.10.2, 10.2.4
  insurance coverage, 11.6.3.7
  reporting agencies, 10.2.2
  users, 10.2.5
  vicarious liability, 7.7.5
furnishers of information
  accuracy standards, 6.5, 10.2.4.1
  inaccurate information, 6.4.4
  limited qualified immunity, 10.4
  reinvestigation, 6.10.2, 10.2.4.2
identity theft, 9.3, 12.6.6
inaccurate information
  furnishers, 6.4.4
  limited qualified immunity, 10.4
  no strict liability, 4.4.5.1.1
  reporting agencies, 4.4
  resellers, 4.4.4
insurance coverage, 11.6.3.7
legislative history, 1.4.3
limitation periods, see STATUTE OF LIMITATIONS
qualified immunity, see QUALIFIED IMMUNITY
resellers, 4.4.4

users
  FCRA violations, 10.2.1, 10.2.5
  illegally obtained reports, 10.2.5.1
  impermissible purposes, 7.7, 10.2.5.1
  investigative report violations, 10.2.5.3
  notices, failure to provide, 10.2.5.2
  prescreening lists, 10.2.5.4

LIABILITY INSURANCE
consumer reporting agencies, 11.6.3.7

LIBEL
see DEFAMATION

LICENSES
see also STATE LICENSING BOARDS
adverse actions, notice obligations, 8.2.6.4.6
consumer report, permissible use, 7.2.4.2, 7.2.6
eligibility, FCRA application, 2.3.6.6, 7.2.4.2
employment purpose, inclusion, 7.2.4.2

LIENS
see also PUBLIC RECORD INFORMATION
reporting limitations, 5.2.3.5
tax liens, see TAX LIENS

LIFE INSURANCE
see also INSURANCE PURPOSES; INSURANCE UNDERWRITING
obsolete information, reporting exemption, 5.2.4

LIMITATIONS
see STATUTE OF LIMITATIONS; TIME LIMITS

LISTS
see CONSUMER LISTS

LITIGATION
see also ACTIONS; DISCOVERY; JURY TRIALS; LEGAL PROCEEDINGS; PLEADINGS
consumer reports
  evidentiary issues, 11.5.3.5
  impermissible use, 7.2.8.2.2.1, 7.4.4, 12.2.4
  permissible use, 7.2.3.4
  subpoena, 11.6.3.6
criminal, see PROSECUTIONS
FCRA, see FCRA CLAIMS

LITIGATION AIDS
see PRACTICE AIDS

LOAN BROKERS
adverse action, disclosure requirements, 8.2.7.4.2
credit services organization status, 15.3.2
joint-use exception, 2.5.5

LOAN COMPANIES
see also FINANCIAL INSTITUTIONS
consumer reporting agency status, 2.7.2

LOAN EXCHANGES
FCRA, application, 2.5.4

LOAN GUARANTY AGENCIES
FCRA, application, 2.5.5
student loan reporting, 12.6.5

LOANS
see also CREDIT; DEBTS
car loans, see AUTOMOBILE LOANS
home equity, see HOME MORTGAGES

LOANS (cont.)
interest rates, *see* INTEREST RATES
special purpose assistance, *see* SPECIAL CREDIT ASSISTANCE PROGRAMS
student loans, *see* STUDENT LOANS
taking on to improve credit record, 12.5.4, 12.6.7.2

LOCAL GOVERNMENT AGENCIES
see also GOVERNMENT AGENCIES
FCRA, application, 2.5.7

LOCATION
see ADDRESSES

LODESTAR FORMULA
attorney fee awards, application, 11.14.2.2

MAIL DISCLOSURES
consent, 3.6.1

MAILING LISTS
FCRA, application, 7.3.3
prescreened, *see* PRESCREENED REPORTS

MALICE
see also WILLFUL INTENT
defamation claims, 10.5.2
definition, 10.4.6
invasion of privacy claims, 10.5.3
negligence claims, 10.5.4
tort liability, 10.4.6

MARKETING LISTS
see PRESCREENED REPORTS; TARGETED MARKETING LISTS

MARKETING RESEARCH
account number information sharing, 16.4.1.8
affiliate information sharing, 8.2.18.2.1.1
consumer reports
   impermissible use, 7.4.8
   permissible use, *see* PRESCREENED REPORTS
target lists, *see* TARGETED MARKETING LISTS

MEDICAL INFORMATION
affiliate sharing, 5.4.1.4
clearing house, *see* MEDICAL INFORMATION BUREAU (MIB)
consent requirement, 5.4.1.2
creditor discrimination, restrictions, 5.4.1.5
defined, 5.4.1.1, 10.2.2.5
FACTA amendment protections, 1.4.9.2, 5.4.1.1
FCRA claims, 10.2.2.5
FCRA restrictions, 5.4.1
financial medical information, 5.4.1.5.3
furnishers of
   see also FURNISHERS OF INFORMATION
   identifying information, restrictions on reporting, 5.4.1.3
insurance implications, 12.7.5
re-disclosure, 5.4.1.2
reporting agencies, *see* MEDICAL INFORMATION AGENCIES
special purpose credit assistance, use, 5.4.1.5.4

MEDICAL INFORMATION AGENCIES
see also CONSUMER REPORTING AGENCIES; MEDICAL INFORMATION
FCRA application, 2.6.2.1
FCRA violations, 10.2.2.5

file contents, 3.2.4
MIB, *see* MEDICAL INFORMATION BUREAU (MIB)
nationwide agencies, 2.6.2
obtaining reports from, 3.4.2.3

MEDICAL INFORMATION BUREAU (MIB)
see also MEDICAL INFORMATION AGENCIES
contact information, 3.4.2.3
file contents, 3.2.4
specialized information collection, 2.6.2.2, 3.2.4

MEDICARE
see GOVERNMENT BENEFITS

MERCHANTS
see also CREDITORS
check cashing lists, adverse use, 8.2.6.4.7.1, 8.2.6.4.7.2
credit card authorizations, 2.4.5
credit repair laws, application
   CROA, 15.2.2.7
   state law, 15.3.4
database services, 2.7.11
GLB Act, application, 16.4.1.2
third party credit requests, 2.4.6, 2.5.5

METRO 2 FORMAT
accuracy standards, 6.3.3.2, 6.4.2
associated consumers segment, 6.3.3.4
base segment, 6.3.3.3
bankruptcy and, 6.3.3.12
closed accounts, 6.8
common errors, 6.3.3.7
date of first delinquency, 6.7
debt collectors and, 6.3.3.8
dishonored checks and, 6.3.3.11
disputes, noting, 6.6
objective standard, 6.3.3.2
other specialized segments, 6.3.3.6
overview, 6.3.3.1
standard automated data reporting format, 6.3.1, 6.3.2
student loans and, 6.3.3.9
transfers of accounts segment, 6.3.3.5
utility bills and, 6.3.3.10

MILITARY DUTY ALERTS
see also IDENTITY THEFT
effect, 9.2.2.4, 9.2.2.5
FCRA provisions, overview, 9.2.2.1.1
proof of identity, necessity, 9.2.2.1.2
use by consumers, 4.8.2

MILITARY PERSONNEL
identity theft prevention, *see* MILITARY DUTY ALERTS
special protections, 5.5.1

MISLEADING INFORMATION
see INACCURATE INFORMATION

MISREPRESENTATION
see also FALSE PRETENSES
actions, limitations, 11.5.2
credit repair organizations
   creditworthiness, 15.2.7.2
   pleading, 15.2.8.8
   services, 15.2.7.4

MOBILE HOME LEASES
see RESIDENTIAL LEASES

MORTGAGE SCORING NOTICE
see also CREDIT SCORES
contents, 8.2.5.1
    credit score information, 8.2.5.1.2
    home loans, 8.2.5.1.3
enforcement of notice right, 8.2.5.3
entitlement, 3.3.1.3, 8.2.5.2, 14.4.1

MORTGAGES
see HOME MORTGAGES

MOTOR VEHICLE DEPARTMENTS (STATE)
FCRA, application, 2.5.7, 2.7.8

MOTOR VEHICLE REPORTS
consumer report status, 2.5.7

MULTIPLE DAMAGES
see DAMAGES, MULTIPLE

NAMES
theft of identity, see IDENTITY THEFT

NATIONAL CLEARINGHOUSE FOR LEGAL SERVICES
see SARGENT SHRIVER NATIONAL CENTER ON POVERTY LAW

NATIONAL CONSUMER LAW CENTER (NCLC)
fair credit reporting manual, using, 1.1
    scope of FCRA, 2.1
    structure of manual, 1.1.2
    terminology, 1.2.1
    updates, 1.1.4
website, 1.1.3

NATIONAL CREDIT UNION ADMINISTRATION
FCRA enforcement, 11.16.1
FCRA regulatory authority, 1.3.3.1, 11.16.2.3
    text of regulations, Appx. B.3.5
GLB Act, regulatory and enforcement authority, 16.4.1.1, 16.4.1.10
    text of regulations, Appx. G.3.5

NATIONAL DATA RETRIEVAL, INC (NDR)
see DATA BROKERS

NATIONAL SECURITY
special provisions relating to, 1.4.8, 1.4.10
    adverse notice exemption, 8.2.6.4.4.3
    adverse public record reporting exemption, 4.4.7.4
    disclosure exemption, 3.5.4.2, 7.2.10.4, 7.2.10.5
    permissible purposes, 7.2.10.4, 7.2.10.5

NATIONWIDE REPORTING AGENCIES
see also CONSUMER REPORTING AGENCIES; CREDIT BUREAUS
affiliates of, reinvestigations, 4.5.2.3
consumer files, 3.2.3
    contents, 3.2.3.2
    fraud alerts, 9.2.2
    military duty alerts, 9.2.2.4
    obtaining disclosure, 3.4
    right to disclosure, 3.3
    sources of information, 3.2.3.3
    variations, 3.4.1
contact information, 3.4.2.2, 3.4.2.3
credit risk scores, 14.2.2.1
    disclosure requirements, 14.4.1
    obtaining from, 14.4.2

    variation between, 3.4.1, 14.4.3
defined, 2.6.1.1
e-OSCAR processing system, 4.5.6.1, 6.10.1
Equifax, see EQUIFAX
Experian, see EXPERIAN (TRW)
FTC circumvention rule, 2.6.1.3
fraud alerts
    extended fraud alerts, implementation, 9.2.2.3.3
    initial fraud alerts, implementation, 9.2.2.2
free reports
    annual free report, 3.3.2, 3.4.2.1, 10.7.8
    fraud alert, 3.3.5
    "free" reports that are not free, 3.3.3
    identity theft, 3.3.5
    requesting, 3.4.2
identity theft, obligations
    alerts, 9.2.2
    blocking of information, 9.2.4.1
prescreening opt-out notification system, 7.3.4.4
reinvestigations
    automated reinvestigation system, 4.6.3, 6.10.6.2, 6.10.6.4
    deposing as to procedures, 4.5.6.3
    electronic dispute processing, 4.5.6, 6.10.1
    results, reporting to, 5.10.6.2, 6.10.6.4
responsibilities, 2.6.1.2
sample reports, Appx. I.1
specialty agencies, 2.6.2
    see also SPECIALTY AGENCIES
    check writing, see CHECK APPROVAL COMPANIES
    contact information, 3.4.2.3
    defined, 2.6.2.1
    files, 3.2.4
    obtaining reports from, 3.4.2.3
    medical information, see MEDICAL INFORMATION AGENCIES
    tenant screening, see TENANT SCREENING AGENCIES
    types, 2.6.2.2
toll-free number, disclosure, 3.4.2.2, 3.4.2.3
TransUnion, see TRANSUNION

NECESSARIES
state law doctrine, 5.6.1, 7.4.6.2

NEGATIVE INFORMATION
see ADVERSE INFORMATION

NEGLIGENCE
conditional privilege defense, 10.5.4
definition, 10.2.1
dispute procedures, failure to follow, 10.2.2.2
elements of claim, 10.5.4
FCRA qualified immunity, 6.12, 10.4
FCRA violations
    liability, 10.2.1
    limitations, 11.5.1
impermissible reports, 10.2.2.4
inaccurate reports, 10.2.2.1
investigative reports, disclosure, 10.2.5.3
notice violations, 10.2.5.2
obsolete information reporting, 5.2.5.1, 10.2.2.3
prescreening violations, 10.2.5.4
reasonable procedures
    accuracy assurance, 10.2.2.1.2
    failure to follow, evidence, 5.2.5.1
    impermissible reports, 10.2.2.4

NEGLIGENCE (*cont.*)
reasonable procedures (*cont.*)
  obsolete information, 10.2.2.3
  reseller obligations, 10.2.3
tort actions, *see* TORT CLAIMS

NOMINAL DAMAGES
see DAMAGES, NOMINAL

NON-PROFIT ORGANIZATIONS
CROA exemption, 15.2.2.3.2

NONPUBLIC PERSONAL INFORMATION
see also PRIVACY
data brokers, "pretexting" to obtain, 16.4.2.3
defined, 16.4.1.1
GLB disclosure restrictions, 2.3.4.2.2, 16.4.1.4
  exempt disclosures, 16.4.1.5

NON-SUFFICIENT FUNDS
see DISHONORED CHECKS

NOTICE
see also DISCLOSURE
adverse action
  ECOA notice, Appx. C.9
  FCRA notice, *see* ADVERSE ACTION NOTICE
adverse information, reporting
  financial institutions, 6.9
  model form, Appx. C.8
  public record information, 4.4.7.2, 8.2.20
  state law, 5.6.3
affiliate information sharing, 3.3.1.6, 8.2.7.5, 8.2.18
child support debts
  government agencies, 7.2.9, 8.2.19
  reporting, 5.7.1
consumer files
  deletion of disputed information, 4.5.5.2
  deletion of favorable information, 5.2.2.1
  inaccuracy, statement of dispute, 4.6.1
  reinsertion of deleted information, 4.7.4
consumer reporting agencies, obligations
  corrections following reinvestigation, 4.6.2
  employment reports, 4.4.7.2, 10.2.2.7
  expedited dispute resolution, 4.5.5.2
  fraud alerts, 8.2.15, 9.2.2.3.3
  frivolous disputes, 8.2.14
  identity theft block refusal, 8.2.16
  inaccurate information received, 6.4.2
  past user notification, consumer rights, 4.9.2
  public record information, 4.4.7.2, 8.2.20
  prescreening opt-out, 7.3.4.4
  reinsertion of information, 4.7.4, 8.2.13
  reinvestigation request, 4.5.4.2, 6.10.3
  reinvestigation results, 4.6.1, 6.10.6.2, 8.2.12
consumer reporting agencies, to, 8.3
  fraud alerts, 9.2.2
  inaccurate information, 8.3
  reinvestigation request, 4.5.2.5
consumer report requests
  child support enforcement agencies, 7.2.9
  employment reports, 7.2.4.3.2
consumers, to, 8.2
  adverse action notice, 8.2.6
  adverse information use, 8.2.7
  affiliate sharing notice, 8.2.18
  child support use notice, 8.2.19
  credit score notice, 8.2.4
  employment use notice, 8.2.17
  expedited dispute resolution, 4.5.5.2
  FCRA rights notice, 8.2.2
  fraud alert notice, 8.2.15
  frivolous dispute, 8.2.14
  governmental agency reporting notice, 8.2.11
  ID theft information, blockage refusal, 8.2.16
  ID theft rights notice, 8.2.3
  investigative report notice, 8.2.21
  mortgage scoring notice, 8.2.5
  negative information reporting notice, 8.2.10
  other notices, 8.2.24
  overview, 8.2.1
  past user notification, rights, 4.9.2
  prescreening opt-out notice, 8.2.22
  prescreening use notice, 8.2.9
  public record information for employment purposes, 4.4.7.2, 8.2.20
  reinsertion notice, 4.7.4, 8.2.13
  reinvestigation results notice, 4.6.1, 8.2.12
  risk-based pricing notice, 8.2.8
  state law requirements, 8.2.23
cosigners
  adverse action, 8.2.6.4.3.7, 8.2.7.4.3
  adverse information, state law, 5.6.3
credit score notice, accompanying disclosure of score, 8.2.4
  mortgage scoring notice, 8.2.5
dealer paper purchases, 8.2.7.4.1
debt collectors, validation notice, 12.4.6
dispute notices, 8.1
  CDV or "611" notice, 6.10.3
  reinvestigation requests, to furnisher, 4.5.4.2, 6.10.3
  reinvestigations, requesting, 4.5.2.5, 6.10.2, 8.3, 12.6.2.1
  resellers, 6.13
  settlement, 12.6.4.3
  statement in file, 4.6.1
ECOA
  comparison with FCRA notice, 8.2.6.6
  model form, Appx. C.9
  record retention, 11.6.4
employee misconduct investigations, 7.2.4.5, 8.2.6.4.4.3, 13.2.4.2
employment agency files, right to disclosure, 2.4.4.2.5
employment reports
  adverse action, 8.2.6.2.5, 8.2.6.4.4
  adverse public record information, 4.4.7.2, 8.2.20
  intention to request, 7.2.4.3.2, 8.2.17
FCRA rights, *see* SUMMARY OF CONSUMER RIGHTS
FCRA violations, user liability, 10.2.5.2
federal agency reporting notice, 5.5.3, 8.2.11
  content, 8.2.11.2
  time and manner, 8.2.11.3
financial institutions, by
  affiliate information sharing, 8.2.18.2.2
  negative information reporting, 6.9, 8.2.10
  opt-out notice, 16.4.1.7.2
  privacy notice, 8.2.18.2.2, 16.4.1.6
fraud alert notice, 8.2.15, 9.2.2.3.3
frivolous dispute, 8.2.14
furnishers of information, obligations
  disputed information, 4.8.2, 6.6
  negative information by financial institutions, 6.9

NOTICE (*cont.*)
  furnishers of information, obligations (*cont.*)
    voluntarily closed accounts, 6.8
  furnishers of information, to, 8.4
    blocking of fraudulent information, 9.2.4.2
    disputed debts directly, 6.5.2, 6.10.1, 12.6.2.3
    FCRA obligations, 6.2.1, 8.4.1, Appx. C.5
    inaccurate information reporting, 6.4.2, 12.6.2.3
    other notices, 8.4.2
    reinvestigation requests, 4.5.4.2, 6.10.3, 12.6.2.2
  GLB Act requirements, 16.4.1.6
    opt-out notice, 16.4.1.7.2
    privacy notice, 16.4.1.6
  government agencies
    child support purposes, 7.2.9, 8.2.19
    government benefits, adverse action, 8.2.6.4.6
  identity theft
    block refusal notice, 8.2.16
    blocking of information, 9.2.4.2
    protection notices, 8.2.24, 9.2.2
    summary of rights, *see* SUMMARY OF CONSUMER IDENTITY THEFT RIGHTS
  insurance reports, adverse action, 8.2.6.4.5
  investigative consumer reports, 13.4.1, 8.2.21
    contents, 13.4.1.3
    form, 13.4.1.3
    right to disclosure, 13.4.1.3
    sources, potential discovery of identity, 13.5.2
    time, 13.4.1.2
    user requests, 13.4.1, 8.2.21
  mortgage scoring notice, *see* MORTGAGE SCORING NOTICE
  prescreened reports, adverse action, 8.2.6.4.3.8
  prescreening opt-out notice, 8.2.22
    content, 8.2.22.1
    enforcement of rights, 8.2.22.3
    time and manner, 8.2.22.2
  prescreening use notice, 7.3.4.4, 8.2.9
    contents, 8.2.9.1
    enforcement of rights, 8.2.9.3
    time and manner, 8.2.9.2
  public record information for employment purposes, 4.4.7.2, 8.2.20
    claims re, 10.2.2.7
  reasonable procedures defense, 10.2.5.2, 13.4.4
  reinsertion, 4.7.4, 8.2.13
  reinvestigations
    denials, 8.2.14
    investigative sources, 13.5.2
    past users, 4.9
    nationwide reporting agencies, 6.10.6.2
    resellers, 6.13
    results, 6.10.6, 8.2.12
    requests, 4.5.2.5, 4.5.4.2, 6.10.3
  risk-based pricing, 8.2.6.4.3.4, 8.2.8, 14.7.3
  state law requirements, 8.2.23
  status notices, 8.1
  student loan defaults, 12.4.5
  summary of FCRA rights, *see* SUMMARY OF CONSUMER RIGHTS
  summary of identity theft rights, *see* SUMMARY OF CONSUMER IDENTITY THEFT RIGHTS
  truckers
    adverse action notice, 8.2.6.4.4.3
    employment use notice, 8.2.17.2.3
  users of reports, obligations
    adverse action, *see* ADVERSE ACTION NOTICE
    employment reports, 8.2.17
    investigative reports, 13.4.1.2
    reasonable procedures, 10.2.5.2
    risk-based pricing, 8.2.6.4.3.4
    violations, 10.2.5.2
  users of reports, to, 8.5
    address discrepancy, 8.5.3, 9.2.5.2
    disputed information, 4.6.1, 4.8.1, 4.8.2, 8.5.4, 12.4.7
    FCRA responsibilities, 7.1.5, 8.5.2
    FCRA violations, 10.2.5.2
    overview, 8.5.1
    past users, 4.9, 8.5.4

NSF CHECKS
see DISHONORED CHECKS

OBSOLETE INFORMATION
see also CONSUMER FILES; INFORMATION ON CONSUMERS
agency liability, 10.2.2.3
dating, 5.2.5.3
deletion, 5.2.2.2, 5.2.5.3
existence, reporting, 5.2.2.3
favorable information, 5.2.2.1
  deletion from file, 5.2.2.2
  effect on credit scores, 14.8.3.7
FCRA claims, 10.2.2.3
FTC Staff Commentary Appx. D
inaccurate information as, 5.2.2.2
investigative consumer reports, 13.6.1, 13.6.2.4
reasonable procedures, 5.2.5
reliance on, 5.2.2.3
reporting exemptions, 5.2.4, 5.2.5.4
reporting restrictions, 5.2
  adverse items, 5.2.3
  existence of information, 5.2.2.3
  general principles, 5.2.2
  judgments, 5.2.3.4
  overview, 5.2.1
  structure of FCRA, 5.2.3.1
retention, 5.2.1, 5.2.3, 5.2.4, 5.2.5.4
standards, legislative history, 1.4.2
state law preemption, 5.2.6
verification, 5.2.4

OFFENSES
see CRIMINAL OFFENSES

OFFERS OF CREDIT
see CREDIT OFFERS

OFFICE OF COMPTROLLER OF THE CURRENCY (OCC)
FCRA enforcement responsibilities, 11.16.1
FCRA regulatory authority, 1.3.3.1, 11.16.2.3
  text of regulations, Appx. B.3.1
GLB Act, regulatory and enforcement authority, 16.4.1.1., 16.4.1.10
  text of regulations, Appx. G.3.1

OFFICE OF PERSONNEL MANAGEMENT
FCRA application, 2.5.6

OFFICE OF THRIFT SUPERVISION (OTS)
FCRA enforcement responsibilities, 11.16.1

OFFICE OF THRIFT SUPERVISION (OTS) *(cont.)*
FCRA regulatory authority, 1.3.3.1, 11.16.2.3
   text of regulations, Appx. B.3.4
GLB Act, regulatory and enforcement authority, 16.4.1.1, 16.4.1.10
   text of regulations, Appx. G.3.4

OFFICIAL STAFF COMMENTARY (FTC)
see also FEDERAL TRADE COMMISSION (FTC)
FCRA
   status and weight, 1.3.3.2, 11.16.2.3
   text, Appx. D

OPEN-END CREDIT
see also CREDIT ACCOUNTS
account review, 7.2.3.3
credit cards, *see* CREDIT CARDS
disputed information, reporting restrictions, 5.3.4

OPT-OUT RIGHTS
affiliate sharing of information, 2.4.3.2
nonpublic personal information disclosure, 16.4.1.7
   exemptions, 16.4.1.5.3
   sample notices, Appx. G.4
prescreened lists, 7.3.4.4
   notice, 8.2.22, Appx. C.7

ORAL COMMUNICATIONS
adverse action notice, 8.2.6.3.2
consumer file disclosure, 3.6.2
consumer reporting agency assistance to consumers, 3.6.3

PARTIES
credit reporting claims
   class actions, 11.2.2
   defendants, 11.2.3
   plaintiffs, 11.2.1

PARTNERSHIPS
see also BUSINESSES
credit applications, *see* BUSINESS CREDIT
FCRA, application, 2.3.3.3
reports on, *see* COMMERCIAL REPORTS

PATERNITY PROCEEDINGS
see also CHILD SUPPORT ENFORCEMENT AGENCIES
consumer reports, use, 7.4.2

PATRIOT ACT
see USA PATRIOT ACT

PEOPLE SEARCH SERVICES
consumer report status, 2.3.4.2.1

PENDENT JURISDICTION
see also JURISDICTION
FCRA actions, 11.4.2

PERMISSIBLE PURPOSES
see also IMPERMISSIBLE PURPOSES
account reviews, 2.3.6.8, 7.2.3.3, 7.2.8.3
agents, 7.1.6
business transaction initiated by consumer, 2.3.6.8, 7.2.8.2
certification, *see* CERTIFICATION
check cashing lists, 2.3.6.3.2
child support, 2.3.6.9, 2.7.9
consumer lists, 7.3
consumer's permission, 7.2.2
counterintelligence, 7.2.10.4
counterterrorism, 7.2.10.4, 7.2.10.5
court order, 7.2.1
credit transactions, 2.3.6.3, 7.2.3
debt collection purposes, 2.3.6.3, 7.2.3.4
employment agencies, 2.4.4.2
employment purposes, 2.3.6.4, 7.2.4.2
expected use, 2.3.5.3
FBI purposes, 7.2.10.4
generally, 2.3.5.1, 2.3.6.1, Ch. 7
government agencies, 2.3.6.9, 7.2.9, 2.7.10
government licenses, 2.3.6.6, 7.2.6
information collected for, 2.3.5
insurance purposes, 2.3.6.5, 7.2.5
legitimate business need, 2.3.6.8, 7.2.8
medical information, 5.4.1.5.3, 5.4.1.5.4
original purpose, 2.3.5.4
personal credit, 2.3.6.3
prescreening lists, 7.3.1, 7.4.8
prospective clients, 7.4.4
public assistance eligibility, 2.3.6.6, 7.2.6, 12.7.9
requirement for release, 7.1.2
risk assessment, 2.3.6.7, 7.2.7
skip tracing, 2.3.6.3, 7.2.3.4
spouses, 7.4.6.2, 12.6.9
tenant reports, 2.3.6.3.3
terrorism protection, 7.2.10.4
third parties, 7.4.6
use only for, 7.1.4
verification, 7.5.1
waiver of rights, 7.2.2

PERSONAL CREDIT
see also CREDIT
consumer report, permissible purpose, 2.3.6.3.1, 7.2.3.1.3
defined, 2.3.6.3.1

PERSONAL INFORMATION
credit header information, *see* CREDIT HEADER INFORMATION
nonpublic personal information, *see* NONPUBLIC PERSONAL INFORMATION
privacy concerns, *see* PRIVACY

PERSONAL INTERVIEWS
consumer reports, information from, restrictions, 5.4.2
investigative consumer reports
   confirmation, 13.6.2.2
   contents, 13.2.3
   reinvestigation, 13.5.2
   requirement, 13.2.3

PERSONAL JURISDICTION
see also JURISDICTION
FCRA actions, 11.2.3

PERSONAL PROPERTY LEASES
see also AUTOMOBILE LEASES; LEASES
adverse action notice, 8.2.6.4.7.3
consumer report, permissible purpose, 2.3.6.8, 7.2.8.2.2.1

PERSONAL PURPOSE TRANSACTIONS
see also CONSUMER TRANSACTIONS
consumer report, permissible purpose, 2.3.6.3.1, 7.2.3.1.3
   business transactions, 7.2.8.2.2.1
   insurance report, 7.2.5
defined, 2.3.6.3.1

PERSONAL REPRESENTATIVES
see POWER OF ATTORNEY

PERSONNEL
see EMPLOYEES

PERSONS
see also CONSUMERS; CONSUMER REPORTING AGENCIES
"any person," liability, 11.1
definition, 2.5.2, 13.4.1.1

PLEADINGS
see also FCRA CLAIMS
credit repair violations, 15.2.8.8, 15.3.6
sample complaints, Appx. J.2

POINT SCORES
see CREDIT SCORES

POLICE DEPARTMENTS
see also LAW ENFORCEMENT AGENCIES
FCRA, application, 2.7.8

POWER OF ATTORNEY
see also ATTORNEYS
consumer files, disclosure requests, 3.4.4

PRACTICE AIDS
consumer report, examining, 3.7
court orders covering reporting issues, 12.6.4.5
discovery, see DISCOVERY
FCRA, utilization, 1.3.2
FCRA claims, see FCRA CLAIMS
follow-up after dispute resolution, 12.6.4.6, 12.6.4.7
generally, 11.6.1
guides to credit reporting, Appx. L
insurance coverage, 11.6.3.7
jury trials, Appx. J.8
pleadings, see PLEADINGS
reasonable procedures, establishing, 4.4.5.1.3
record retention, 11.6.4
reinsertion cases, 8.2.13.5.2
reinvestigation requests, 4.5.2.5
reinvestigation suits, 6.10.1, 6.10.2, 10.2.4.2
sample documents, Appx. J
settlement, generally, see SETTLEMENT
settling non-FCRA litigation, 12.6.4
  negotiating credit reporting issues, 12.6.4.2
subpoenas, 11.6.3.6
web resources, see WEB RESOURCES

PREEMPTION OF STATE LAW
affiliate information sharing, 2.4.3.2.4, 10.7.6
child support debt reporting, 5.7.1
consumer reporting agencies, 10.7.5.3, 10.7.8, 10.7.9.2
cosigner reporting, 5.6.3
credit or debit cards, 10.7.9.6
credit repair laws, 15.2.9, 15.3.8
credit scores
  disclosure, 10.7.7, 14.4.1
  insurance scores, 14.10
debt collection, 10.7.9.5
disclosures, 10.7.7
  credit report fees, 3.3.8, 3.3.9.2, 10.7.8
explicit preemption, 10.7.3
  affiliate information sharing, 10.7.6
    conduct, 10.7.9

disclosures, 10.7.7
identity theft, 10.7.3
subject matter, 10.7.4, 10.7.5
FACTA amendments
  key provisions, 1.4.9.2
  legislative history, 1.4.9.1
field preemption, 10.7.1
furnishers of information, 5.7.2, 6.2.2.3, 10.7.5.2, 10.7.9.4
  medical information, 5.4.1.3
generally, 5.7.2, 10.7
Gramm-Leach-Bliley Act, 16.4.1.12
identity theft, 9.2.4.1, 9.2.5.2, 10.7.5.5
inconsistent state laws, 10.7.2
pre-FACTA case law, 10.7.3.3
similarity to FCRA, 10.7.4.4
state obsolescence laws, 5.2.6
statutory claims, 10.7.4.2, 10.7.4.3
tort claims, 10.4.1, 10.7.4.2, 10.7.4.3
trigger, 10.7.4.5
users of information, 10.7.5.4, 10.7.9.3

PRESCREENED REPORTS
see also CONSUMER LISTS
account number information, 16.4.1.8
active duty military, exclusion, 9.2.2.4
adverse action notice, 8.2.6.4.3.8
consumer report status, 2.3.4.2.3, 7.3.4.2
described, 2.3.4.2.3, 5.2.3.8, 7.3.4.1, 7.3.4.2
disclosure requirements, 5.2.3.8, 8.2.9, 10.2.5.4
exclusion requests, 7.3.4.4
FCRA application, 2.3.4.2.3, 7.3.4
"firm offer" of credit or insurance, 7.3.4.3
fraud alert consumers, exclusion, 9.2.2.3.3
misuse, 10.2.5.4
notification system for consumers, 7.3.4.4
"opt out" rights, 7.3.4.4
  notice, 8.2.22, Appx. C.7
permissible purposes, 7.3.1, 7.3.4.1, 7.3.4.3
record of inquiries, time period, 5.2.3.8
state law preemption, 10.7
target marketing
  form of, 7.3.2.4
  legislative response, 1.4.6
users
  differentiation from report users, 7.1.9
  FCRA violations, 10.2.5.4
  notice requirements, 8.2.9

PRIVACY
see also CONFIDENTIALITY
Children's Online Privacy Protection Act, 16.4.2.1
common law protections, 16.3, 16.5
Computer Fraud and Abuse Act, 16.4.2.1
data brokers, concerns, 2.7.4
definition, 10.5.3
Electronic Communications Privacy Act, 16.4.2.1
FCRA purpose, 1.4.1, 7.1.1
financial information, 16.4.1
  FTC rule, see PRIVACY RULE (FTC)
  Safeguard Rules, 16.4.1.10
GLB notice, 16.4.1.6
governmental intrusion, 16.2
legislative response, 1.4.3, 1.4.6
overview, 16.1

PRIVACY (cont.)
statutory protections
  computers and the Internet, 16.4.2.1
  FCRA, 7.1.1, 16.1
  Financial Information Privacy Act, 16.4.2.2
  FTC Act, 16.4.2.3
  Gramm-Leach-Bliley (GLB) Act, 16.4.1
  interests impeding, 16.6
  state law, 16.4.2.4
  Telecommunications Act, 16.4.2.1
tort claims, *see* INVASION OF PRIVACY

PRIVACY ACT
federal agencies, protections, 2.5.6, 16.2

PRIVACY RULE (FTC)
see also GRAMM-LEACH-BLILEY (GLB) ACT
account number sharing, 16.4.1.8
customer relationship, 16.4.1.3
exempt disclosures, 16.4.1.5
financial institutions, 16.4.1.2
notice requirements, 16.4.1.6
opt-out notices, 16.4.1.7.2
opt-out rights, exercise, 16.4.1.7.3
rulemaking authority, 16.4.1.2
Safeguard Rules, 16.4.1.10
selected provisions, Appx. G.2

PRIVATE INVESTIGATORS
see DETECTIVE AGENCIES

PRIVILEGE
see CONDITIONAL PRIVILEGE

PROOF
see BURDEN OF PROOF; EVIDENCE

PROPERTY MANAGERS
consumer reporting agency status, 13.3.3
consumer reports, obtaining, 7.1.6

PROPERTY SALES
adverse action notice, 8.2.6.4.7.4
FCRA, application, 7.2.8.2.2.1

PROPERTY SETTLEMENTS
see DIVORCE PROCEEDINGS

PROSECUTIONS
see also CRIMINAL OFFENSES
consumer reports, use, 7.4.4, 7.4.5, 12.2.4
FCRA violations, 11.16.3
identity theft, 12.6.6

PROTECTIVE BULLETINS
see also LAW ENFORCEMENT BULLETINS
FCRA, application, 7.3.3

PROTECTIVE ORDERS
discovery requests, 11.6.3.4
  sample order, Appx. J.7

PUBLIC AGENCIES
see GOVERNMENT AGENCIES

PUBLIC ASSISTANCE RECIPIENTS
see also GOVERNMENT BENEFITS
consumer file disclosure, free reports, 3.3.7

PUBLIC RECORD INFORMATION
clearing up blemished report, 12.6.3

consumer report status, 2.3.4.2.1
consumer reporting agencies
  collection, 4.3.2.5.1, 4.3.3.4
  employment purposes, 4.4.7, 8.2.20
  FCRA violations, liability, 10.2.2.7
  notice requirements, 4.4.7.2
  reasonable procedures, 4.4.6.4
  specialty agencies, 2.7.1
  strict procedures, 4.4.7.3
employment reports, 4.4.7
  FCRA violations, 10.2.2.7
  notice, 4.4.7.2, 8.2.20
  strict procedures, 4.4.7.3
FTC Staff Commentary, Appx. D
inaccurate reports, 4.3.2.5, 4.4.6.4
  employment reports, 4.4.7.3
  mixed information, 4.3.3.4
reporting limitations
  criminal records, 5.2.3.6
  judgments, 5.2.3.4
  suits, 5.2.3.3.1, 5.2.3.4
  tax liens, 5.2.3.5
searches by inspection bureaus, 13.3.1
up-to-date, 4.4.7.3

PUBLIC UTILITY CREDIT
see also UTILITY SERVICES
Metro 2 Format reporting, 6.3.3.10

PUBLIC WELFARE RECIPIENTS
see PUBLIC ASSISTANCE RECIPIENTS

PUBLICATION
bad debt lists, 12.2.3
credit record, 12.2.2

PUNITIVE DAMAGES
see DAMAGES, PUNITIVE

QUALIFIED IMMUNITY
application, 10.4.2, 10.4.4
disclosure prerequisite, 10.4.3
exceptions, 10.4.6
information to nonreporting agency, 10.4.5
legislative history, 10.4.1
overview, 10.4.1
tort liability, 6.12, 10.4, 16.3

RACKETEERING INFLUENCED AND CORRUPT ORGANIZATIONS ACT (RICO)
credit repair organizations, application, 15.3
credit reporting abuses, application, 10.3

REAL ESTATE AGENTS
consumer reports, obtaining, 7.1.6

REAL ESTATE SETTLEMENT PROCEDURES ACT (RESPA)
claims under, 10.3
reporting restrictions, 5.3.5, 6.5.3
qualified written request, 12.4.4

REAL PROPERTY LEASES
see RESIDENTIAL LEASES

REAL PROPERTY SALES
see LAND CONTRACTS

REASONABLE PROCEDURES
see also CONSUMER REPORTING AGENCIES; CONSUMER REPORTS
accuracy assurance, 4.4.5, 10.2.2.1.2
availability and minimal burden of corrective measures, 4.4.5.1.3
balancing test, 4.4.5.1.2, 4.5.3.2
bankruptcy reporting, 4.4.6.9
consumer identification, 4.4.6.5, 4.4.6.6
consumer reporting agencies
   accuracy, 4.4.5, 10.2.2.1.2
   permissible purposes, 7.5.1, 10.2.2.4
   reinsertion of information, 4.7.2
   specific problems, 4.4.6
data communication, 4.4.6.7
defense, as, 10.2.5.2, 10.2.5.3
discovery, 11.6.3.1
electronic communication of reports, 7.5.4
employee access to files, 7.6
employees must follow established procedures, 4.4.5.1.5
employment reports, public record information, 4.4.7.3
   national security exemption, 4.4.7.4
factors bearing on, 4.4.5.1.4
FCRA claims, 10.2.2.1.2
   damages, 4.4.5.3
   determining reasonableness, 4.4.5.1
   no strict liability, 4.4.5.1.1
   proof issues, 4.4.5.2
FCRA purpose, 1.3.1
FTC Staff Commentary, Appx. D
identity theft prevention, 4.4.6.6
   after alerts, 9.2.2.5
illogical files, 4.4.6.2
impermissible purposes, avoiding, 7.5.1, 10.2.2.4
inaccurate sources, 4.4.6.3
incomplete information, 4.4.6.8
internal inconsistencies, 4.4.6.2
investigative reports
   disclosure obligations, 13.4.4, 10.2.5.3
   preparation, 13.6.1
management policies discouraging, 4.4.6.1
mismerged information, 4.4.6.5
missing accounts
   consumer offers of new information, 4.8.4
   existing accounts, 4.4.6.8.3
   new accounts, 4.4.6.8.2
notice violations, 10.2.5.2
obsolete information, 4.4.6.8, 5.2.5, 10.2.2.3
   legal standard, 5.2.5.2
proof issues, 4.4.5.2
public record information, 4.4.6.4
   employment reports, strict procedures, 4.4.7.3
   national security exemption, 4.4.7.4
reinsertion of information, 4.7.2
reinvestigations, 4.5.2.2, 4.5.3, 6.10.4
resellers, 4.4.4, 10.2.3
retention of request records, 7.5.5
sources of information, 4.4.6.3
specific procedures, 4.4.6
standards, 4.4.5.1.2, 5.2.5.2
systematic violations, 11.2.2
transcription, 4.4.6.7
updating procedures, 4.4.6.8.4, 4.4.6.8.5
user identification and certification
   blanket certifications, 7.5.2.2
   continuing reports, 7.5.2.3
   employment purposes, 7.2.4.3
   follow-up reports, 7.5.2.3
   investigative consumer reports, 13.4.1.5, 10.2.5.3
   nature of certification, 7.5.2.1
verification procedures, 7.5.3
violations, 7.5.1

RECORDS
consumer reporting agencies, obligations, 7.5.5. 11.6.4
consumer reports, users, 7.5.5
credit record, *see* CREDIT RECORD
criminal records, *see* CRIMINAL RECORDS; PUBLIC RECORD INFORMATION
public, *see* PUBLIC RECORD INFORMATION

REGULATIONS (ECOA)
credit score definition, 14.2.3.2

REGULATIONS (GLBA)
Privacy Rule, *see* PRIVACY RULE (FTC)
rulemaking authority, 16.4.1.1, 16.4.1.10

REGULATIONS (FCRA)
identity theft prevention
   disposal of consumer information, 9.2.5.3
   red flag guidelines, 9.2.6
FTC trade regulation rules, 11.16.2.3
furnisher accuracy and integrity, 6.4.3
generally, 1.3.3.1, 11.16.2.3
legislative history, 1.4.7, 1.4.9.2
text, Appx. B

REINSERTION OF INFORMATION
agency obligations, 4.7.2
breach of settlement, 12.6.4.3
failure to handle properly, FCRA claims, 8.2.13.5, 10.2.2.2
furnisher certification, 4.7.3
legislative history, 1.4.6, 4.7.1
notice to consumer, 4.7.4, 8.2.13
   claims re, 8.2.13.5
   enforcement of rights, 8.2.13.4
   nature and content, 8.2.13.2
   time and manner, 8.2.13.3
overview, 4.7.1
soft-deleted information, 4.6.2, 4.7.1
what constitutes reinsertion, 8.2.13.5.1

REINVESTIGATIONS
see also REVERIFICATION
agency obligations, 4.5.1, 4.5.2.1
   affiliated agencies, 4.5.2.3
   corrections, 4.6.2, 6.10.5
   expedited dispute resolution, 4.5.5.2, 12.6.2.2
   liability, 10.2.2.2
   nationwide agencies, 6.10.1, 6.10.6.2, 6.10.6.4
   notice to furnisher, 4.5.4.2
   response time, 4.5.5
automated reinvestigation system, 4.6.3, 6.10.1
   use by furnishers, 6.10.6.2, 6.10.6.4
consumer requests, 4.5.2
   direct requests, 4.5.2.2
   expedited dispute resolution, 4.5.5.2, 12.6.2.2
   frivolous requests, 4.5.2.4, 8.2.14
   practical tips, 4.5.2.5

REINVESTIGATIONS (cont.)
correction or deletion after, 4.6.2, 6.10.5
   following-up, 4.6.3
deadline for response, 4.5.5
deletion alternative, 4.5.2.1, 4.5.3.1, 4.5.5.2
electronic processing, 4.5.6
   e-OSCAR, 4.5.6.1
entitlement, 4.5.2.1
expedited dispute resolution, 4.5.5.2, 12.6.2.2
failure to handle properly, FCRA claims
   actual damages calculations, 11.10.2.2
   consumer reporting agency, 10.2.2.2
   furnisher of information, 6.10.2, 10.2.4.2
   practice tip, 6.10.1
fees, 4.5.2.1
formal dispute process, 4.5, 6.10
frivolous disputes, 4.5.2.4, 8.2.14
furnisher obligations
   conducting, 6.5.2, 6.10.4
   consumer enforcement, 6.10.1
   involvement, 4.5.4, 6.10.3, 6.10.4
   liability, 6.5, 6.10.1, 6.10.2, 10.2.4.2
   unverifiable information, 6.10.5
investigative reports, 13.5.2, 13.6.2.4
nature of, 4.5.3
notation of dispute, 4.6.1, 4.8.1, 8.5.4, 12.4.7
notification
   consumer, 4.6.1, 6.10.6.2
   electronic, 6.10.1, 6.10.6.4
   furnishers, 4.5.4.2, 6.10.3
   previous users, 4.9, 8.5.4.1
   results, 4.6.1, 6.10.6
on-line processing system, 6.10.1
overview, 4.5.1
private enforcement, 6.10.1, 6.10.2
   statute of limitations, 6.10.7
reasonable investigation standard, 4.5.3, 6.10.4
resellers, 2.6.3.3, 4.5.2.3, 6.13
results notice
   electronic, 6.10.6.4
   enforcement of rights, 8.2.12.4
   nationwide agencies, 6.10.6.2, 6.10.6.4
   nature and content, 8.2.12.2
   reporting agency, 6.10.6.1
   time and manner, 8.2.12.3
state law preemption, 10.7
statement of dispute, filing after, 4.6.1, 4.8.1, 8.5.4, 12.4.7
third party requests, 4.5.2.2
time limits, 6.10.6.3
unreasonable preconditions, 4.5.2.1

RELATIVES
see also SPOUSES
blemished credit records, implications, 12.2.5
consumer reports, restrictions on use, 7.2.4.2, 7.4.6.3

REMOVAL
see JURISDICTION

RENT-TO-OWN TRANSACTIONS
see PERSONAL PROPERTY LEASES

RENTAL AGREEMENTS
see RESIDENTIAL LEASES

RENTAL AGENCIES
consumer report, permissible use, 7.1.6

RENTAL APPLICATIONS
consumer report, permissible use, 2.3.6.3.3, 2.3.6.8, 7.2.8.2.2.1
denial, adverse action notice, 8.2.6.4.7.3, 8.2.7.2

RENTAL CLEARANCE AGENCIES
see TENANT SCREENING COMPANIES

RENTAL SCREENING REPORTS
see TENANT REPORTS

RENTERS
see TENANTS

REPAYMENT AGREEMENTS
negotiating, 12.6.7.3
reporting limitations, effect, 5.2.3.3

REPORTERS
consumer reports, impermissible use, 7.4.9

REPORTS
business, *see* COMMERCIAL REPORTS
consumers, *see* CONSUMER REPORTS; INVESTIGATIVE CONSUMER REPORTS
credit, *see* CONSUMER REPORTS
employment purposes, *see* EMPLOYMENT REPORTS
identity theft reports, 9.2.2.3.2
inquiry activity, *see* INQUIRY ACTIVITY
insurance purposes, *see* INSURANCE REPORTS
investigative reports, *see* INVESTIGATIVE CONSUMER REPORTS
prescreened, *see* PRESCREENED REPORTS
residential mortgage, *see* RESIDENTIAL MORTGAGE CREDIT REPORTS
tenant screening, *see* TENANT REPORTS

REPRESENTATIVES
consumer reports, obtaining, 3.4.4, 7.1.6

RESEARCH
see MARKETING RESEARCH

RESEARCH AIDS
see CASE LAW; WEB RESOURCES

RESELLERS
see also CONSUMER REPORTING AGENCIES
certifications, 2.6.3.3, 10.2.3
consumer reporting agency status, 2.6.3.2
data brokers, status, 2.7.4
defined, 2.6.3.2
duties, 2.6.3.3
FCRA, application, 2.6.3
FCRA violations, 10.2.3
FTC enforcement order, Appx. K.6
identity theft, blocking of information, 9.2.4.1
inaccurate information, liability, 4.4.4
nationwide reporting agency provisions, exclusion, 2.6.1.1
overview, 2.3.6.1
permissible purpose requirement, 7.1.2
reasonable procedures, 4.4.4
reinvestigation requirements, 4.5.2.3, 6.13
trimerger reports, 11.6.2
verification, 10.2.3

RESIDENTIAL LEASES
see also LANDLORDS; TENANTS

RESIDENTIAL LEASES (cont.)
blemished credit record, implications, 12.7.3
credit transaction status, 8.2.7.2
denial, notice requirements, 8.2.6.4.7.3, 8.2.7.2
FCRA, application, 2.3.6.3.3, 2.3.6.8, 7.2.8.2.2.1
reports re, see TENANT REPORTS

RESIDENTIAL MORTGAGE CREDIT REPORTS
see also HOME MORTGAGES
credit scores, disclosure, 3.3.1.3, 14.4.1
   mortgage scoring notice, 8.2.5
disputed information
   open-end accounts, 5.3.4
   RESPA restrictions, 5.3.5
use by lenders, 12.7.2

RETAILERS
see CREDITORS; MERCHANTS

RETURNED CHECKS
see DISHONORED CHECKS

REVERIFICATION
see also REINVESTIGATIONS; VERIFICATION
investigative reports, subsequent reports, 13.6.2.4

RICO
see RACKETEERING INFLUENCED AND CORRUPT ORGANIZATIONS ACT (RICO)

RIGHT TO FINANCIAL PRIVACY ACT
privacy from governmental intrusion, 16.2

RIGHT TO PRIVACY
see PRIVACY

RISK-BASED PRICING
credit scores and, 14.7.3
notice requirements, 8.2.6.4.3.4, 8.2.8
   enforcement of rights, 8.2.8.4
   nature and content, 8.2.8.2
   time and manner, 8.2.8.3

RISK SCORES
see CREDIT SCORES

RULE 68 OFFERS
attorney fee considerations, 11.14.5

RURAL HOUSING SERVICE (RHS)
joint lender exemption, 2.5.5
underwriting guidelines, 12.7.2

SAFEGUARD RULES
financial information, 16.4.1.10

SALES
consumer files, 7.1.7
property sales, 8.2.6.4.7.4
resellers of information, see RESELLERS

SARGENT SHRIVER NATIONAL CENTER ON POVERTY LAW
see also CLEARINGHOUSE NUMBERS
documents, obtaining, 1.1.3

SCAN
see CHECK APPROVAL COMPANIES

SCHOLARSHIP LOCATION SERVICES
credit services organization status, 15.3.2

SECRETARY OF AGRICULTURE
FCRA enforcement, 11.16.1

SECRETARY OF TRANSPORTATION
FCRA enforcement, 11.16.1

SECURED CREDIT CARDS
see also CREDIT CARDS
described, 12.7.6

SECURITIES AND EXCHANGE COMMISSION (SEC)
FCRA, regulatory authority, 1.3.3.1, 11.16.2.3
   text of regulations, Appx. B.3.6
GLB Act, regulatory and enforcement authority, 16.4.1.1, 16.4.1.10

SECURITIES TRANSACTIONS
see INVESTMENTS

SECURITY AGREEMENTS
see DEALER PAPER

SECURITY CLEARANCES
adverse notice exemption, 4.4.7.4, 8.2.6.4.4.3
disclosure exemption, 3.5.4.2
employment purpose status, 2.3.6.4, 7.2.4.2

SECURITY PROCEDURES
consumer reporting agencies, 4.4.6.7

SELF-EMPLOYMENT
see INDEPENDENT CONTRACTORS; SOLE PROPRIETORSHIPS

SELLERS
see MERCHANTS

SERVICEMEMBERS
see MILITARY PERSONNEL

SETTLEMENT
see also LITIGATION
attorney fee awards, 11.14.4
breach of settlement agreement, 12.6.4.3
consumer reports, use, 7.4.4
credit record, protecting, 1.3.2, 12.6.4
   sample settlement language, Appx. J.9
credit disputes
   cleaning up file after, 12.6.4.6
   court approval, 12.6.4.4
   credit rating, protecting, 12.6.4.1
   monitoring file after, 12.6.4.7
   negotiating reporting issues, 12.6.4.2
   selecting correct language, 12.6.4.3, Appx. J.9
debt settlement companies, 12.5.2
delinquent accounts, repayment plans, 12.6.7.3
FTC consent decrees, 11.16.2.1
insurance liability coverage, 11.6.3.7
Rule 68 offers, 11.14.5

SHERIFF'S DEPARTMENTS
see also LAW ENFORCEMENT AGENCIES
FCRA, application, 2.7.8

SKIP TRACING
consumer reports, permissible purpose, 2.3.6.3, 7.2.3.4, 7.4.5

SOCIAL SECURITY NUMBERS
see also IDENTIFYING INFORMATION
truncation to prevent identity theft, 9.2.5.1

SOCIAL SERVICE AGENCIES
see ADOPTION AGENCIES; CHILD SUPPORT ENFORCEMENT AGENCIES; GOVERNMENT AGENCIES; WELFARE AGENCIES

SOLDIERS AND SAILOR'S CIVIL RELIEF ACT
military personnel protections, 5.5.1

SOLE PROPRIETORSHIPS
see also BUSINESSES
consumer reports, permissible purpose, 7.2.3.1.3
credit applications, see BUSINESS CREDIT
FCRA, application, 2.3.3.3

SOURCES OF INFORMATION
see also FURNISHERS OF INFORMATION
data brokers, 2.7.4
disclosure, 3.5.3, 13.4.2.3
inaccurate sources, 4.4.6.3
public record information, see PUBLIC RECORD INFORMATION
nationwide agencies, 3.2.3.3
specialized agencies, 3.2.4

SPECIAL CREDIT ASSISTANCE PROGRAMS
medical information, use, 5.4.1.5.4

SPECIALTY AGENCIES
see also CONSUMER REPORTING AGENCIES
check writing, see CHECK APPROVAL COMPANIES
consumer files, 3.2.4
consumer reports, obtaining from, 3.4.2.3
contact information, 3.4.2.3
data brokers, see DATA BROKERS
defined, 2.6.2.1
medical information, see MEDICAL INFORMATION AGENCIES
tenant screening, see TENANT SCREENING AGENCIES
types, 2.6.2.2

SPOUSES
consumer reports
  bankruptcy notations, 4.4.6.9.3
  ECOA requirements, 5.6.1, 7.4.6.2, 12.2.5. 12.6.9
  FCRA requirements, 5.6.1, 7.4.6, 12.2.5
  permissible purposes, 7.4.6.2
  separate files, 5.6.1
credit record, application to consumer, 5.6.1, 7.4.6, 12.2.5, 12.6.9
doctrine of necessaries, 5.6.1, 7.4.6.2
utility services, 12.7.4

STANDARDS
accuracy
  consumer reports, 4.4.5.1
  FTC Staff Commentary, Appx. D
  furnishers, see under FURNISHERS OF INFORMATION
  legislative history, 1.4.2, 1.4.3, 1.4.6, 1.4.9.2
legislative history, 1.4.2
home mortgages, 12.7.2
reasonable procedures, 4.4.5.1.2, 5.2.5.2
  reinsertion of deleted information, 4.7.2

STANDING
credit repair organizations, suits against, 15.2.8.2

STATE AGENCIES
see also GOVERNMENT AGENCIES
child support purposes, permissible users, 7.2.9
see also CHILD SUPPORT ENFORCEMENT AGENCIES
FCRA
  application, 2.5.7
  enforcement agencies, see STATE ENFORCEMENT
privacy protections, 16.2

STATE CLAIMS
damages
  generally, 11.1
  nominal damages, 11.10.2.4
  statutory damages, 11.11
federal preemption, see PREEMPTION OF STATE LAWS
generally, 10.6.1
identity theft, 10.6.3
injunctive relief, 11.13
jury trials, 11.7
limitations, 11.5.2
pendent jurisdiction, 11.4.2
private remedies, 11.1
removal to federal court, 11.4.5
supplemental jurisdiction, 11.4.2
unfair and deceptive practices, 10.6.2

STATE COURTS
FCRA claims
  jurisdiction, 11.4.1
  removal to federal court, 11.4.5
  selection of court, 11.4.4

STATE CREDIT REPAIR STATUTES
see STATE CREDIT SERVICES (REPAIR) STATUTES

STATE CREDIT REPORTING STATUTES
see also STATE LAW
claims under, see STATE CLAIMS
furnishing of information, 5.7.2
generally, 10.6.1
investigative reports
  disclosure, 13.4.1.3
  insurance purposes, 13.3.1
  landlord and tenant purposes, 13.3.3
preemption, see PREEMPTION OF STATE LAW
summary, Appx. H

STATE CREDIT SERVICES (REPAIR) STATUTES
see also CREDIT REPAIR ORGANIZATIONS; STATE LAW
federal preemption, 15.2.9, 15.3.8
overview, 15.1.2, 15.3.1
private causes of action, 15.3.6
remedies, 15.3.7
retailers, application, 15.3.4
scope
  coverage, 15.3.2
  exemptions, 15.3.3
  surprising reach, 15.1.3
substantive prohibitions, 15.3.5
summaries, Appx. H

STATE ENFORCEMENT
child support, see CHILD SUPPORT ENFORCEMENT AGENCIES
CROA, 15.2.10
FCRA
  generally, 11.16.4.1
  information furnishers, 11.16.4.2
  investigator powers, 11.16.4.4

STATE ENFORCEMENT (cont.)
FCRA (cont.)
  limitations, 11.16.4.5
  notification of federal regulators, 11.16.4.3

STATE LAW
claims under, *see* STATE CLAIMS
consumer file disclosure, fees, 3.3.8, 3.3.9.2, 10.7.8
consumer reporting restrictions, 5.7
  child support debts, 5.7.1
  cosigners, 5.6.3
  generally, 5.7.2
  summaries, Appx. H
credit repair statutes, *see* STATE CREDIT SERVICES (REPAIR) STATUTES
credit reporting statutes, *see* STATE CREDIT REPORTING STATUTES
deceptive practices statutes, 10.6.2
disclosure requirements, 8.2.23
federal preemption, *see* PREEMPTION OF STATE LAW
furnishers of information, 6.2.2.3
identity theft
  generally, 9.4
  suits under, 9.5, 12.6.6
  summaries, Appx. H
insurance scores, 14.10
investigative reports, 13.7
necessaries doctrine, 7.4.6.2, 7.6.1
privacy protections, 16.4.2.4
  governmental intrusion, 16.2
summaries, Appx. H
telemarketing, 15.1.2
utility services, 12.7.4

STATE LICENSING BOARDS
see also LICENSES
consumer report
  adverse action notice, 8.2.6.4.6
  permissible use, 7.2.4.2

STATEMENT OF DISPUTE
see also DISPUTED INFORMATION; EXPLANATIONS
consumer rights, 4.6.1, 4.8.1, 8.5.4, 12.4.7
enforcement of rights, 8.5.4.3
improper handling by agency, 10.2.2.2
investigative consumer reports, 13.5.2
nature and content, 8.5.4.1
overview, 4.8.1.1
time and manner, 4.8.1.2, 8.5.4.2

STATUTE OF LIMITATIONS
CROA violations, 15.2.8.9
FCRA violations, 11.5.1
  reinvestigation provisions, 6.10.7
state claims, 11.5.2
suits and judgments, effect on reporting limitations, 5.2.3.4
tort claims, 11.5.2

STATUTES
CCPA, *see* CONSUMER CREDIT PROTECTION ACT (CCPA)
CROA, *see* CREDIT REPAIR ORGANIZATIONS ACT (CROA)
ECOA, *see* EQUAL CREDIT OPPORTUNITY ACT (ECOA)
FACTA, *see* FAIR AND ACCURATE CREDIT TRANSACTIONS ACT (FACTA)
FCBA, *see* FAIR CREDIT BILLING ACT (FCBA)
FCRA, *see* FAIR CREDIT REPORTING ACT (FCRA)
FDCPA, *see* FAIR DEBT COLLECTION PRACTICES ACT (FDCPA)
GLB, *see* GRAMM-LEACH-BLILEY (GLB) ACT
Higher Education Act, *see* HIGHER EDUCATION ACT
Privacy Act, *see* PRIVACY ACT
RESPA, *see* REAL ESTATE SETTLEMENT PROCEDURES ACT (RESPA)
soldiers, *see* SOLDIERS AND SAILOR'S CIVIL RELIEF ACT
state, *see* STATE CREDIT REPORTING STATUTES; STATE LAW
telemarketing, *see* TELEMARKETING AND CONSUMER FRAUD ABUSE PREVENTION ACT
UDAP, *see* UNFAIR OR DECEPTIVE ACTS OR PRACTICES (UDAP)

STATUTORY DAMAGES
see DAMAGES, STATUTORY

STUDENT LOANS
blemished credit record, implications, 12.7.8
defaults
  clearing up, 12.6.5, 12.7.8
  reporting, 5.2.3.9, 12.4.5, 12.6.5
defenses, raising, 12.4.5, 12.6.5
deferments, effect on credit scores, 14.8.3.4
Higher Education Act, application, 5.2.3.9, 12.6.5
joint lender exemption, application, 2.5.5
Metro 2 Format reporting, 6.3.3.9
reporting limitations, 5.2.3.9

SUBPOENAS
consumer reports, obtaining by, 7.2.1, 7.2.10.3, 11.6.3.6

SUITS
see ACTIONS; COLLECTION SUITS; LEGAL PROCEEDINGS; PUBLIC RECORD INFORMATION

SUMMARY OF CONSUMER RIGHTS
contents, 8.2.2.1
disclosure inclusion, 3.5.1, 8.2.2.2
  employment reports, 7.2.4.3.3, 7.2.4.4
enforcement of notice rights, 8.2.2.3
entitlement, 8.2.2.2
model form, Appx. C.2
state law, preemption by FCRA, 10.7

SUMMARY OF CONSUMER IDENTITY THEFT RIGHTS
contents, 8.2.3.1
enforcement of notice rights, 8.2.3.3
entitlement, 8.2.3.2, 9.2.2.5
model form, Appx. C.3

SUMMARY OF RESPONSIBILITIES OF FURNISHERS
model form, Appx. C.5
requirement to provide, 6.2.1, 8.4.1

SUMMARY OF USER RESPONSIBILITIES
model form, Appx. C.6
requirement to provide, 7.1.5, 8.5.2

SUPERBUREAUS
see RESELLERS

SURETIES
see COSIGNERS

TARGETED MARKETING LISTS
see also PRESCREENED REPORTS

TARGETED MARKETING LISTS (cont.)
FCRA, application, 2.3.4.2.3, 7.3.2.4, 7.3.3
   legislative history, 1.4.6
FCRA violations, 10.2.5.4
impermissible purpose, 7.3.2.4
permissible purpose, 7.1.9, 7.3.2.4, 7.3.4

TAX COLLECTION
see also INTERNAL REVENUE SERVICE (IRS)
consumer reports, use, 7.4.3

TAX LIENS
see also PUBLIC RECORD INFORMATION
consumer report, permissible purpose, 7.4.3
reporting limitations, 5.2.3.5

TAX PREPARATION SERVICES
credit services organization status, 15.3.2
GLB Act, application, 16.4.1.2

TELECHECK
see CHECK APPROVAL COMPANIES

TELECOMMUNICATIONS ACT
privacy protections, 16.4.2.1

TELEMARKETING
credit card offers, 12.7.6
federal statute, see TELEMARKETING AND CONSUMER FRAUD ABUSE PREVENTION ACT
FTC rule, see TELEMARKETING RULE (FTC)
state law, 15.1.2
Telephone Consumer Protection Act, application, 15.4.2

TELEMARKETING AND CONSUMER FRAUD ABUSE PREVENTION ACT
FTC rule, see TELEMARKETING RULE (FTC)
overview, 15.4.1

TELEMARKETING RULE (FTC)
see also FEDERAL TRADE COMMISSION (FTC); TELEMARKETING
credit repair agencies
   application, 15.1.2, 15.4.1
   enforcement against, 15.2.10
overview, 15.4.1
violations, 15.4.1

TELEPHONE
companies, see TELEPHONE COMPANIES
directories, see TELEPHONE DIRECTORIES
disclosures via, 3.6.2
services, see TELEPHONE COMPANIES

TELEPHONE COMPANIES
disputed charges, 12.4.3
FCRA application, 2.7.9

TELEPHONE CONSUMER PROTECTION ACT
credit repair clinics, application, 15.1.2, 15.4.2
overview, 15.4.2

TELEPHONE DIRECTORIES
consumer report status, 2.3.4.2.1, 2.3.5.3
FCRA, application, 7.3.3

TELETYPE HOOKUPS
see ELECTRONIC COMMUNICATION

TENANT REPORTS
adverse use, notice, 8.2.6.4.7.3, 8.2.7.2
blemished report, implications, 12.7.3, 12.7.7
consumer report status, 2.3.4.1, 2.3.6.3.3
financially troubled consumer, 12.7.9
FTC Staff Commentary, Appx. D
inaccuracy, 12.7.3
investigative consumer report, status, 13.3.3
obtaining by consumer, 3.4.2.3
permissible use, 2.3.6.3.3, 2.3.6.8, 7.2.8.2.2.1
   agents, 7.1.6
rental payment subsidies, 7.2.6, 12.7.9
use by landlords, 12.7.3

TENANT SCREENING COMPANIES
see also CONSUMER REPORTING AGENCIES
contact information, 3.4.2.3
FCRA, application, 2.3.6.3.3, 2.6.2
identification, 12.7.3
reports by, see TENANT REPORTS
nationwide agencies, 2.6.2

TENANTS
see also LANDLORDS; RESIDENTIAL LEASES
denial of lease, notice, 8.2.6.4.7.3, 8.2.7.2
reports regarding, see TENANT REPORTS

TERRORISM
counterterrorism, consumer report access, 7.2.10.5
   FBI access, 7.2.10.4

TESTERS
FCRA violations, use, 11.6.2

THEFT
see FRAUD; IDENTITY THEFT

THIRD PARTIES
creditors, obtaining information from non-reporting agencies, 2.3.2, 3.3.15, 8.2.7
FCRA claims, 11.8
information on in consumer's file, 3.5.7, 4.2.4, 4.3.3.1
reinvestigation requests, 4.5.2.2
relatives, see RELATIVES
requests for credit for consumer, 2.4.6, 2.5.5
reporting to, consumer report status, 2.5.4
reports on, impermissible purpose, 7.4.6.1, 12.2.5
spouses, see SPOUSES

THREATS
false threats
   debt collectors, 12.3
   investigative consumer report, 13.4.1.2
reporting debt to credit bureau, 12.3

TIME LIMITS
see also STATUTE OF LIMITATIONS
active military duty alerts, 9.2.2.4
adverse information reporting, 5.2.1, 5.2.3, 6.7, 12.6.4.1
   bankruptcies, 5.2.3.7, 12.6.8
   criminal records, 5.2.3.6
   delinquent accounts, 5.2.3.2, 5.2.3.3, 12.6.4.1
   exemptions, 5.2.4
   judgments, 5.2.3.4
   obsolete information, 5.2.1, 5.2.2.1, 5.2.3
   public record information, 5.2.3.4–5.2.3.6
   repayment agreements, effect, 5.2.3.3
   student loans, 5.2.3.9
   suits, 5.2.3.4
   tax liens, 5.2.3.5

References are to sections

TIME LIMITS (*cont.*)
consumer file disclosure, 3.3.9.3
investigative consumer reports
   disclosure, 13.4.2.4
   notice of investigation, 13.4.1.2
fraud alerts
   extended alerts, 9.2.2.3.1
   initial alerts, 9.2.2.2
reinvestigations, 6.10.6.3

TORT CLAIMS
advantages, 10.5.1
appropriation, 16.3
attorney fees, 11.14.3
conditional privilege defense, 10.5.2, 10.5.4
consumer reporting issues, 10.4, 10.5
defamation, *see* DEFAMATION
false light, 16.3
FCRA preemption, 10.4.1, 10.7.4.2, 10.7.4.3
furnishing inaccurate information, 6.12, 10.4, 10.5
inaccurate information, 10.4
intrusion, 16.3
invasion of privacy, *see* INVASION OF PRIVACY
limitations, 11.5.2
malice, 10.4.6
negligence, *see* NEGLIGENCE
public disclosure, 16.3
punitive damages, 11.12.1.1
qualified immunity, 6.12, 10.4
   see also QUALIFIED IMMUNITY
utilizing, 6.12
willful intent, 10.4.6

TRADE DIRECTORIES
FCRA, application, 7.3.3
   consumer report status, 2.3.5.3

TRADE EXPERIENCE
exchanging, FCRA exemption, 2.4.2

TRANSCRIPTION ERRORS
see also INACCURATE INFORMATION
consumer files, 4.4.6.7

TRANSFERS
see SALES

TRANSUNION
see also CONSUMER REPORTING AGENCIES; CREDIT BUREAUS; NATIONWIDE REPORTING AGENCIES
consumer disputes, processing, 4.5.6.2
consumer files, 3.2.3
   contents, 3.2.3.2
   sources of information, 3.2.3.3
contact information, 3.4.2.2
credit scores
   FICO risk score, 14.2.2.1
   obtaining, 14.4.2
FCRA, application, 2.7.1
   special provisions, 2.6.1
FTC enforcement orders, Appx. K.4
liability insurance, 11.6.3.7
overview, 1.2.2
sample credit report, Appx. I.1.3

TRIALS
see ACTIONS; DISCOVERY; JURY TRIALS; LITIGATION; WITNESSES

TRIGGER LISTS
see also ACCOUNT ACTIVITY; PRESCREENED REPORTS
consumer report status, 2.3.4.2.4

TRUCKER DATABASE SERVICES
employment reports, 2.6.4
   adverse action notice, 8.2.6.4.4.3
   employment use notice, 8.2.17.2.3
FCRA, application, 2.6.4

TRUTH IN LENDING ACT
credit card protections, 5.3.4, 12.4.2

TRW
see EXPERIAN (TRW)

UNEMPLOYED PERSONS
consumer file disclosure, free reports, 3.3.7

UNFAIR OR DECEPTIVE ACTS OR PRACTICES (UDAP)
actions, forum, 11.4.5
credit repair organizations, 15.3.6, 15.4.1
FCRA violations, 10.6.2, 11.16.1
FTC Act, 16.4.2.3
injunctive relief, 11.13
limitations, 11.5.2
nominal damages, 11.10.2.4
non-FCRA violations, 10.6.2
state law, 10.6.2
statutory damages, 11.11
waiver of rights, 13.4.5

UNIVERSAL DATA FORM
electronic processing system, 3.4.6.1, 6.10.1
sample form, Appx. I.2
use by creditors, 6.3.2
   correcting inaccuracies, 6.5.4

USA PATRIOT ACT
effect on privacy, 16.2
FBI access to credit information, 1.4.8, 1.4.10

USERS OF REPORTS
see also CONSUMER REPORTS
adverse action, *see* ADVERSE ACTION
alerts
   active military duty, 9.2.2.4
   duties, 9.2.2.5
   fraud alerts, 9.2.2.2, 9.2.2.3.3
certification, 7.5.1, 7.5.2, 13.4.1.5
computer fraud, liability, 11.16.3
corrected information, notification, 4.6.3, 4.9
definition, 2.1.2, 7.1.2, 7.1.4
disclosure, 3.5.4, 3.7.3
   FBI exemption, 3.5.4.2, 7.2.10.4
disputed information, notification, 4.6.1, 4.8.1, 4.8.2, 8.5.4, 12.4.7
past users, 4.9
employers, *see* EMPLOYERS
false pretenses, 7.7.3, 7.7.4, 10.2.5.1
FBI, 3.5.4.2, 7.2.1, 7.2.10.4
FCRA application, 2.1.2
FCRA requirements, notice to user, 7.1.5, 8.5.2
   FTC model form, Appx. C.6

USERS OF REPORTS (cont.)
FCRA violations
   defenses, 10.2.5.2
   liability, 7.7, 10.2.5
FTC enforcement orders, Appx. K.7
gossip, 12.2.2
identification, 7.5.1, 7.5.2
inquiries leading to mixed files, 4.3.3.5
inquiries, records of, retention, 7.5.5
   prescreened inquiries, 5.2.3.8
investigative reports
   certification, 13.4.1.5
   claims against, 10.2.5.3
   notice of request, 13.4.1.2
joint users, 2.4.6, 2.5.5
landlords, *see* LANDLORDS
liability, *see under* LIABILITY
medical information, 5.4.1
notice obligations
   adverse action, *see* ADVERSE ACTION NOTICE
   employment reports, 8.2.17
   investigative reports, 13.4.1.2
   reasonable procedures, 10.2.5.2
   risk-based pricing, 8.2.6.4.3.4
   violations, 10.2.5.2
notice to, 8.5
   address discrepancy, 8.5.3, 9.2.5.2
   corrected information, 4.9, 8.5.4
   disputed information, 4.6.1, 4.8.1, 4.8.2, 8.5.4, 12.4.7
   duties under FCRA, 7.1.5, 8.5.2, Appx. C.6
past users, updated reports, 4.6.3, 4.9
permissible purposes only, 7.1.4
   see also PERMISSIBLE PURPOSES
   violations, 10.2.5.1
prescreening lists
   claims re, 10.2.5.4
   differentiation, 7.1.8
providing report to consumer, 3.3.1
regulation, 1.3.1
restrictions, 7.1.2
state law, federal preemption, 10.7.5.4, 10.7.9.3
Summary of Responsibilities, FTC model form, Appx. C.6
verification of, 7.5.1, 7.5.2
written permission, 7.2.2

UTILITY SERVICES
see also PUBLIC UTILITY CREDIT
blemished credit record, implications, 12.7.4
disputed charges, 12.4.3

VENUE
removal to federal court, 11.4.5

VERIFICATION
see also CERTIFICATION; IDENTIFICATION; REINVESTIGATIONS
adverse information, reasonable procedures, 10.2.2.1.2

consumer files, information, 4.2.5
consumer identity, 3.4.3, 3.6.2, 9.2.2.1.2
consumer reports, users, 7.5.3, 5.2.5.4
delinquent debts, 12.4.6
disputed information, 12.6.4.1, 12.6.4.7
investigative consumer reports, information
   personal interviews, 13.6.2.2
   public record information, 13.6.2.3
   re-use, 13.6.2.4
obsolete information, 5.2.4
obsolete information exemption, 5.2.5.4
public record information, 13.6.2.3
reasonable procedures, 7.5.3
resellers, 10.2.3
reverification, 13.6.2.4

VETERANS ADMINISTRATION (VA)
joint lender exemption, 2.5.5
underwriting guidelines, 12.7.2

WAIVER
see also CONSENT
consumer reports, written permission, effect, 7.2.2
credit repair contracts, statutory provisions, 15.2.8.1
investigative reports, rights, 13.4.5

WEB RESOURCES
CDIA, 6.3.2
fair credit reporting, related websites, Appx. M
NCLC, 1.1.3
Sargent Shriver National Center on Poverty Law, 1.1.3
unreported cases, 1.1.3

WELFARE AGENCIES
see also GOVERNMENT AGENCIES; GOVERNMENT BENEFITS
consumer reports, permissible users, 7.2.6, 12.7.9
FCRA, application, 2.3.6.6

WELFARE RECIPIENTS
consumer file disclosure, free reports, 3.3.7

WILLFUL INTENT
see also MALICE
FCRA noncompliance, 11.11, 11.12.1.1
invasion of privacy claims, 10.5.3
misrepresentation, limitations, 11.5.2
proving, 11.12.1.2
punitive damages, 11.1, 11.12.1.1
tort liability, 10.4.6

WITNESSES
see also EVIDENCE; JURY TRIALS
consumer reports re, impermissible purpose, 7.4.4

WORKERS' COMPENSATION CLAIMS
consumer reports, use, 7.2.4.2
lists at specialized agencies, 3.2.4

Quick Reference to the Consumer Credit and Sales Legal Practice Series

References are to sections in *all* manuals in NCLC's Consumer Credit and Sales Legal Practice Series. References followed by "S" appear only in a Supplement.

> Readers should also consider another search option available at *www.consumerlaw.org/keyword*. There, users can search all seventeen NCLC manuals for a case name, party name, statutory or regulatory citation, or *any* other word, phrase, or combination of terms. The search engine provides the title, page number and context of every occurrence of that word or phrase within each of the NCLC manuals. Further search instructions and tips are provided on the web site.

The Quick Reference to the Consumer Credit and Sales Legal Practice Series pinpoints where to find specific topics analyzed in the NCLC manuals. References are to individual manual or supplement sections. For more information on these volumes, see *What Your Library Should Contain* at the beginning of this volume, or go to www.consumerlaw.org.

This Quick Reference is a speedy means to locate key terms in the appropriate NCLC manual. More detailed indexes are found at the end of the individual NCLC volumes. Both the detailed contents pages and the detailed indexes for each manual are also available on NCLC's web site, www.consumerlaw.org.

NCLC *strongly recommends*, when searching for PLEADINGS on a particular subject, that users refer to the *Index Guide* accompanying *Consumer Law Pleadings on CD-Rom*, and *not* to this *Quick Reference*. Another option is to search for pleadings directly on the *Consumer Law Pleadings* CD-Rom or on the *Consumer Law in a Box* CD-Rom, using the finding tools that are provided on the CD-Roms themselves.

The finding tools found on *Consumer Law in a Box* are also an effective means to find statutes, regulations, agency interpretations, legislative history, and other primary source material found on NCLC's CD-Roms. Other search options are detailed in *Finding Aids and Search Tips*, *supra*.

Abbreviations

AUS	=	Access to Utility Service (3d ed. 2004 and 2006 Supp.)
Auto	=	Automobile Fraud (2d ed. 2003 and 2006 Supp.)
Arbit	=	Consumer Arbitration Agreements (4th ed. 2004 and 2006 Supp.)
CBPL	=	Consumer Banking and Payments Law (3d ed. 2005 and 2006 Supp.)
Bankr	=	Consumer Bankruptcy Law and Practice (8th ed. 2006)
CCA	=	Consumer Class Actions (6th ed. 2006)
CLP	=	Consumer Law Pleadings, Numbers One Through Twelve (2006)
COC	=	The Cost of Credit (3d ed. 2005 and 2006 Supp.)
CD	=	Credit Discrimination (4th ed. 2005 and 2006 Supp.)
FCR	=	Fair Credit Reporting (6th ed. 2006)
FDC	=	Fair Debt Collection (5th ed. 2004 and 2006 Supp.)
Fore	=	Foreclosures (2005 and 2006 Supp.)
Repo	=	Repossessions (6th ed. 2005 and 2006 Supp.)
Stud	=	Student Loan Law (3d ed. 2006)
TIL	=	Truth in Lending (5th ed. 2003 and 2006 Supp.)
UDAP	=	Unfair and Deceptive Acts and Practices (6th ed. 2004 and 2006 Supp.)
Warr	=	Consumer Warranty Law (3d ed. 2006)

Quick Reference to the Consumer Credit and Sales Legal Practice Series

References are to sections in *all* manuals in NCLC's Consumer Credit and Sales Legal Practice Series

Abandonment of Apartment Building in Bankruptcy—Bankr § 17.8.2
Abbreviations Commonly Used by Debt Collectors—FDC App G.4
Abuse of Process—UDAP § 5.1.1.4; FDC § 10.6
Acceleration—COC §§ 5.6.2, 5.7.1; Repo § 4.1
Accessions—Repo § 3.5.3.2
Accord and Satisfaction—CBPL §§ 2.7, 9.3.1
Account Aggregation—CBPL § 3.12
Accountants—UDAP § 5.12.8
Accrediting Agencies, Student Loans—Stud § 9.4.1.2
Accurate Information in Consumer Reports—FCR Ch. 4
ACH—*See* NACHA
Actual Damages—*See* Damages
Actuarial Rebates—COC § 5.6.3.4
Adhesion Contracts—UDAP § 5.2.3
Adjustable Rate Mortgages—TIL § 4.6.4; COC § 4.3.6
Administration of Lawsuit, Class Action—CCA Ch 13
Admissibility of Other Bad Acts—Auto § 9.8.1
Admissions, Requests for—CCA § 7.1.3; Repo App E.5; Fore App. I.2.3; CLP; COC App L; FDC App I.3; Auto App F.1.4
Advertisements as Warranties—Warr § 3.2.2.5
Advertising Credit Terms—TIL §§ 5.4, 10.4
Affordability Programs, Utilities—AUS Ch 9, App F
After-Acquired Property—Repo § 3.4.5.2
Age Discrimination re Credit—CD § 3.4.2
Airbags—AF §§ 2.8S, 6.3bS
Airline Fare Advertising—UDAP §§ 2.5, 5.4.13.1
Alteration of Checks—CBPL § 2.3.1.4
Alimony Discharged in Bankruptcy—Bankr § 14.4.3.5
Alimony, Protected Source under ECOA—CD §§ 3.4.1, 5.5.5.3
Alternative Dispute Mechanisms—Arbit; FDC § 15.4
American Arbitration Association—Arbit App B.1
Americans With Disabilities Act—CD § 1.6
Amortization Explained—COC § 4.3.1
Amortization Negative—COC § 4.3.1.2
Amount Financed—TIL § 4.6.2
Annual Percentage Rate—TIL §§ 4.6.4, 5.6.9; COC § 4.4
Answer and Counterclaims—Repo Apps D.1, D.2; Fore App. I.2; COC App L; CLP
Antecedent Debt Clauses—Repo § 3.9
Anti-Competitive Conduct as UDAP Violation—UDAP § 4.10
Anti-Deficiency Statutes—Repo § 12.6.3
Apartment Buildings Abandoned in Bankruptcy—Bankr § 17.8.2
Apartment Leases—Bankr § 12.9; UDAP §§ 2.2.6, 5.5.2
Appeal of Order Requiring Arbitration—Arbit § 9.5
Applications for Credit—CD § 5.4
Appraisal Fraud—COC § 11.5.6
Appraisals, Right to a Copy—CD § 10.11
APR—*See* Annual Percentage Rate
Arbitration—Arbit; Bankr § 13.3.2.5; COC § 10.6.11; FDC § 15.4; TIL § 7.7; Warr § 13.4
Arbitration and Class Actions—Arbit § 9.4; CCA Ch 2;
Arbitration & Collection Actions – Arbit Ch. 11
Arbitration Fees—Arbit § 5.4
As Is—Warr Ch 5; Auto § 7.8.2
Assignee Liability—UDAP § 6.6; TIL § 7.3
Assignment of Tax Refunds—COC § 7.5.4
Assistance for the Payment of Utility Service—AUS Ch 16
Assisted Living Facilities—UDAP § 5.11.4
Assistive Device Lemon Laws—Warr Ch 16
ATM Cards—CBPL Ch 3
ATM Machines, Bank Liability for Robberies at—CBPL § 3.5.4
ATM Machine Payments—CBPL Ch 3
ATM Machines, Access for Disabled—CBPL Ch 8
Attorney as Debt Collector—FDC §§ 4.2.7, 11.5.3

Attorney Fees—TIL § 8.9; Bankr Ch 15; Auto §§ 5.8.4, 9.12; CD § 11.7.6; FCR § 11.14; FDC §§ 6.8, 11.2.5, 11.3.5; UDAP § 8.8; Warr §§ 2.7.6, 10.7
Attorney Fees, Class Actions—CCA Ch 15, App E
Attorney Fees for Creditors—COC § 7.3.3; FDC § 15.2
Attorney Fees, Pleadings—Auto App L; FDC App K
Attorney General Enforcement—UDAP Ch 10
Attorneys Liable Under FDCPA—FDC §§ 4.2.7, 4.6.3
Attorneys Liable Under UDAP—UDAP §§ 2.3.9, 5.12.1
Auctions—Repo §§ 10.7.2, 10.10.6; Auto §§ 2.5.4, 2.6.4
Authorization to Represent—CCA App E
Authorization to Sue—CCA § 1.2.4
Automated Clearing House for Electronic Transfer—CBPL Ch3
Automatic Stay—Bankr Ch 9
Automobile Accessories—UDAP § 5.4.11
Automobile Auctions—*See* Auctions
Automobile Dealer Files—UDAP § 5.4.2
Automobile Dealer Licensing—Auto § 6.4, Appx. F
Automobile Dealers, Bonding Requirement—Auto § 9.13.4, App C
Automobile Dealers, Registration with Auction—Auto Appx. E.3
Automobile Fraud—Auto
Automobile Insurance, Force-Placed—*See* Force-Placed Auto Insurance
Automobile Leases, Article 9 Coverage—Repo § 14.2.1
Automobile Leases, Default and Early Termination—TIL Ch 10; UDAP § 5.4.8.3; Repo § 14.2
Automobile Leases, Misrepresentation—UDAP § 5.4.8
Automobile Leases, Odometer Rollbacks—Auto §§ 4.6.6.5, 5.2.6
Automobile Leases, Sublease Scams—UDAP § 5.4.10
Automobile Leases, Unconscionability—UDAP § 5.4.8.5
Automobile Manufacturers, List—Warr App N
Automobile Pawn Transactions—Bankr § 11.9; COC § 7.5.2.3; Repo § 3.5.5
Automobile Rentals—UDAP § 5.4.9
Automobile Repairs—Warr Ch 19; UDAP § 5.4.1
Automobile Repossession—*See* Repossessions
Automobile Safety Inspection Laws—Warr § 15.4.6
Automobile Sales—Warr Chs 14, 15; UDAP §§ 5.4.2, 5.4.6, 5.4.7
Automobile Service—Warr § 19.8; UDAP § 5.3.5
Automobile Sublease Scams—UDAP § 5.4.10
Automobile, Theft Prevention, Federal Statutes & Regulations—Auto App B.2
Automobile Title—Auto §§ 2.3, 2.4, Apps. D, E; UDAP § 5.4.5; Warr § 15.2
Automobile Valuation—Bankr § 11.2.2.3.2
Automobile Yo-Yo Abuses—UDAP § 5.4.5; Repo § 4.5; TIL §§ 4.4.5, 4.4.6
Bad Checks—FDC §§ 5.6.4, 15.3
Bail (i.e. replevin)—Repo Ch 5
Bait and Switch—UDAP § 4.6.1
Balloon Payments—COC § 4.6.2, Ch 5; TIL § 2.2.4.2.2
Bank Accounts, Attachment—FDC Ch 12, CBPL § 4.2
Bank Accounts, Closing—CBPL § 2.6.3
Bank Account Garnishment—CBPL § 4.2, FDC Ch 12
Bank Accounts, Joint—FDC § 12.7
Bank Accounts, Set-Off—FDC § 12.6.7, CBPL § 4.3
Bank Fees—CBPL § 4.5
Bank Accounts, Unfair Practices—UDAP §§ 4.4.9, 5.1.10
Bankruptcy Abuse Prevention and Consumer Protection Act—Bankr; Stud § 7.2.2
Bankruptcy and Debt Collection—FDC §§ 2.2, 9.10; Bankr § 9.4.3
Bankruptcy and Security Interests—Repo Ch 8
Bankruptcy and Utility Service—AUS §§ 4.5, 12.1; Bankr § 9.8
Bankruptcy, Claims Against Landlords in—Bankr § 17.8

Quick Reference to the Consumer Credit and Sales Legal Practice Series

References are to sections in *all* manuals in NCLC's Consumer Credit and Sales Legal Practice Series

Bankruptcy, Claims Against Creditors, Merchants in—Bankr Ch 17; UDAP § 6.8
Bankruptcy Code, Text—Bankr App A
Bankruptcy, Consumer Reports of—FCR Chs 4, §§ 5.2.3.7, 12.6.8
Bankruptcy Court as Litigation Forum—Bankr Ch 13
Bankruptcy Discharge of Student Loans—Stud Ch 7
Bankruptcy Forms—Bankr Apps D, E, G
Bankruptcy Petition Preparers—Bankr § 15.6
Benefit Overpayments and Bankruptcy—Bankr § 14.5.5.4
Bibliography—Bankr
Billing Errors—FDC § 5.7; Fore § 5.2.2
Billing Error Procedures, Credit Cards—CBPL § 6.5; TIL § 5.8
Bill Stuffers—Arbit § 3.8
Binding Arbitration—Arbit
Blanket Security Interests—Repo § 3.4.5.2.2
Bond, Claims Against Seller's—UDAP § 6.8; Auto § 9.13.4, App C
Bonding Statutes—Auto App C
Book-of-the-Month Clubs—UDAP § 5.8.5
Bounced Checks—CBPL § 2.5
Bounce Loans—TIL § 3.9.3.3, COC § 7.5.6
Breach of Contract—UDAP § 5.2.5
Breach of the Peace and Repossession—Repo § 6.4
Breach of Warranties—Warr; UDAP § 5.2.7.1
Briefs, Class Action—CCA Ch 9
Broker Fees—COC §§ 7.4.2, 11.5.4
Brokers, Auto—UDAP § 5.4.10
Brokers, Loan—*See* Loan Brokers
Brokers, Real Estate—*See* Real Estate Brokers
Budget Payment Plans—AUS § 6.4
Burglar Alarm Systems—UDAP § 5.6.2
Business Credit, Discrimination re—CD § 2.2.6.4
Business Opportunities—UDAP §§ 2.2.9.2, 5.13.1
Buy Here, Pay Here Car Sales—UDAP § 5.4.6.13
Buy Rate—UDAP § 5.4.7.6
Buying Clubs—UDAP § 5.10.6
Calculating Interest Rates—COC Ch 4
Campground Resort Memberships—UDAP §§ 2.2.8, 5.10.5
Cancellation Rights—TIL Ch 6; UDAP §§ 5.2.6, 5.8.2, 9.5
Cardholders' Defenses—TIL § 5.9.5
Carfax—Auto § 2.3.2, Appx. E.2
Cars—*See* Automobile
Case Selection—CCA § 1.2
Case Summaries, FDCPA—FDC App L
Cash Discounts—TIL § 5.9.6.4
Cashier's Checks—CBPL § Ch 5
Chapter 7 Bankruptcy—Bankr Ch 3
Chapter 11 Bankruptcy—Bankr §§ 6.3.4, 17.7
Chapter 12 Bankruptcy—Bankr Ch 16
Chapter 13 Bankruptcy—Bankr Ch 4
Charge Cards—TIL § 5.2.4.2
Charitable Contributions—Bankr § 1.1.2.6
Charitable Solicitations—UDAP § 5.13.5
Check 21—CBPL §§ 2.2, 2.4, App B
Check Advancement Loans—*See* Payday Loans
Check Approval Companies—FCR § 2.6.2.2
Check Cards—CBPL § 4.1.4.2
Check Cashing Services—UDAP §§ 5.1.10
Check Cashing Regulation—CBPL § 1.14
Check Guarantee Companies—FDC § 4.2.3
Checklist, Automobile Fraud Litigation—Auto § 1.4
Checklist, Debt Collection—FDC App G
Checklist, Truth in Lending—TIL §§ 1.6, 3.11
Checklist, Usury—COC § 1.6
Checks—CBPL Ch 2

Checks, Bad—FDC §§ 5.6.4, 15.3, CBPL § 2.5
Checks, Preauthorized Draft—UDAP §§ 5.1.10, CBPL § 2.3.5
Child Support, Credit Reports—FCR § 7.4.2
Child Support Discharged in Bankruptcy—Bankr § 14.4.3.5
Children in Household, Discrimination Based On—CD § 3.5.1
Choice of Laws—COC § 9.2.9; Repo § 2.6
Churning Repossession Schemes—Repo § 10.11
Civil Rights Act—CD § 1.5
Class Actions Fairness Act of 2005—CCA § 2.4, 11.5, 11.6
Class Actions—CCA; Auto § 9.7, App H; FCR § 11.2.2; FDC §§ 6.2.1.3, 6.3.5, 6.6; TIL §§ 6.9.9, 8.8; UDAP § 8.5
Class Actions and Arbitration—Arbit § 9.4; CCA Ch 2
Class Actions and Diversity Jurisdiction—CCA §§ 2.3, 2.4
Class Actions Guidelines for Settlement, NACA—CCA App D
Class Actions in Bankruptcy Court—Bankr §§ 13.7, 17.4.2
Class Actions, Removal to Federal Court—CCA § 2.5
Class Certification Motions, Sample—CCA App N; CLP
Class Definitions—CCA Ch 3
Class Notices—CCA Ch 10, App Q
Client Authorization to Represent—CCA App E
Client Authorization to Sue—CCA § 1.2.4
Client Contacts with Other Parties—CCA §§ 1.2.6, 5.3
Client Handout on Bankruptcy—Bankr App K
Client Handout on Credit Discrimination—CD App I
Client Handout on Credit Reporting—FCR App L
Client Interview Checklist, Bankruptcy—Bankr App F
Client Interview Checklist, Debt Collection Harassment—FDC App G
Client Interview Sheet, Warranties—Warr App I
Client Retainer Forms, Sample—CLP
Closed-End Auto Leases—TIL Ch 10; Repo § 14.2
Closed-End Credit—TIL Ch 4
Closed School Discharge—Stud § 6.2
Closing Arguments, Sample—Auto App I
Coercive Sales Techniques—UDAP § 4.8
Collateral—Repo
Collection Fees—FDC § 15.2; Stud § 4.4
Collection of Student Loans—Stud Ch 4
College Transcripts and Bankruptcy—Bankr §§ 9.4.3, 14.5.5.2
Collision Damage Waiver (CDW)—UDAP § 5.4.9
Common Law Contract Defenses—UDAP § 9.5
Common Law Fraud, Misrepresentation—Warr § 11.4; UDAP § 9.6.3; Auto Ch 7
Common Law Right to Utility Service—AUS § 3.1
Common Law Violations and Credit Reporting—FCR § 10.4
Common Law Warranties—Warr § 19.4
Communications to Client from Other Attorney—CCA § 5.3; FDC § 5.3.3
Community Reinvestment Act—CD § 1.9
Compensating Balances—COC § 7.4.4
Complaint Drafting, Class Actions—CCA Ch 4
Complaints—Arbit App C; Auto App G; CD App G; CCA App F; COC App L; FCR App J.2; FDC App H; Repo Apps D.3, D.4; Fore App I; Warr App K; TIL Apps D, E; CLP
Compound Interest—COC § 4.6.1
Computers, Sale of—UDAP § 5.7.6
Condominiums—UDAP § 5.5.4.5
Condominium Warranties—Warr Ch 18
Consignment—Repo § 9.6.3.3
Consolidation Loan—Stud § 8.2
Conspiracy in Odometer Case—Auto § 4.7
Constitutionality of Arbitration Agreement—Arbit Ch 8
Contract Formation of Arbitration Agreement—Arbit Ch 3
Constructive Strict Foreclosure—Repo §§ 10.5.2, 12.5

Quick Reference to the Consumer Credit and Sales Legal Practice Series

References are to sections in *all* manuals in NCLC's Consumer Credit and Sales Legal Practice Series

Consumer Class Actions—CCA
Consumer Complaints to Government Agencies—UDAP § 9.8
Consumer Credit Reporting Reform Act of 1996—FCR § 1.4.6
Consumer Guide to Credit Reporting—FCR App L
Consumer Leasing Act—TIL Ch 10, App I.1
Consumer Recovery Funds—Auto § 9.13.5
Consumer Reporting Agencies—FCR
Consumer Reporting Agencies, Enforcement Agreements—FCR App K
Consumer Reports, Disputing—FCR Ch 4
Consumer Reports, Keeping Credit Disputes Out of—FCR § 12.4
Consumer Reports for Business Transactions—FCR §§ 2.3.6.2, 2.3.6.8, 7.2.8
Consumer Reports for Employment Purposes—FCR §§ 2.3.6.4, 7.2.4
Consumer Reports for Government Benefits—FCR §§ 2.3.6.6, 7.2.6
Consumer Reports for Insurance Purposes—FCR §§ 2.3.6.5, 7.2.5
Consumer Reports from Non-Reporting Agencies—FCR § 8.2.18
Consumer/Seller Liability under Odometer Act—Auto § 4.8.13
Contests—UDAP §§ 4.6.6, 5.13.4
Contract Defenses—UDAP § 9.5
Contractual Misrepresentations—UDAP § 5.2.4
Cooling Off Periods—*See* Cancellation
Correspondence Schools—Stud Ch 9
Cosigners—Bankr § 9.4.4; CD § 5.4; Repo § 12.9; TIL §§ 2.2.2.2, 8.2; UDAP § 5.1.1.2.9
Counseling the Debtor—Bankr Ch 6
Coupon Settlement, Class Actions—CCA § 11.6
Cramming—AUS § 2.7.5
Credit Abuses—COC; UDAP §§ 2.2.1, 5.1
Credit Accident and Health Insurance—COC § 8.3.1.3; TIL §§ 3.7.9, 3.9.4
Credit Balances—TIL § 5.6; UDAP § 5.1.9.4
Credit Card Finders—UDAP § 5.1.9.2
Credit Card Issuers, Raising Seller-Related Claims Against—UDAP § 6.6, TIL § 5.9.5; CBPL § 6.4
Credit Card Issuer's Security Interest in Goods Purchased—Repo § 3.6
Credit Card Surcharges—TIL § 5.9.6.4
Credit Card Unauthorized Use—TIL § 5.9.4
Credit Cards—TIL Ch 5; CBPL Ch 6; UDAP § 5.1; FDC § 4.2.3
Credit Cards, Reporting Services for Lost—UDAP § 5.1.5.5
Credit Charges—COC Ch 5; UDAP § 5.1.6
Credit Denial, Notice—CD § 10.5; FCR § 8.2.6
Credit Disability Insurance—COC §§ 8.3.1.3, 8.5.2.3; Fore § 4.13; TIL §§ 3.7.9, 3.9.4
Credit Evaluation—CD §§ 6.2, 6.3
Credit File, Disputing and Right to See—FCR Chs 3, 4
Credit Insurance—COC Ch 8; TIL §§ 3.7.9, 3.9.4; Repo § 4.4; UDAP § 5.3.10
Credit Life Insurance—COC §§ 8.3.1.2, 8.5.3.1.2; TIL §§ 3.7.9, 3.9.4
Credit Math—COC Ch 4
Credit Property Insurance—COC §§ 8.3.1.5, 8.5.3.1.4, 8.5.3.4, 8.5.4.4; TIL §§ 3.9.4.4, 3.9.4.6, 4.9.8
Credit Rating, Injury to—FCR § 1110.2.3; FDC §§ 5.5.2.9, 8.3.8; UDAP § 8.3.3.6
Credit Regulation, History of—COC Ch 2
Credit Repair Organizations—FCR Ch 15; UDAP § 5.1.2.2
Credit Reporting Agencies, Contacting—FCR Ch. 3
Credit Reporting Sample Forms—FCR App I
Credit Reports—FCR; TIL § 5.9.4.5
Credit Reports, Affiliate Sharing—FCR §§ 2.4.3, 3.3.1.5, 8.2.18

Credit Reports, Furnishers of Information Obligations—FCR Ch 6
Credit Reports, Keeping Credit Disputes Out of—FCR § 12.4
Credit Reports from Non-Reporting Agencies—FCR § 8.2.18
Credit Scams—UDAP §§ 5.1.2; 5.1.3; 5.1.8
Credit Scoring—CD § 6.4; FCR Ch. 14
Credit Terms—COC; UDAP § 5.1.5; 5.1.7
Creditor Remedies—FDC Chs 12, 13, 15; UDAP § 5.1.1; 5.1.1
Creditors, Types of—COC Chs 2, 9
Creditors Filing Bankruptcy—Bankr Ch 17
Creditworthiness—Bankr § 6.2.2.3
Criminal Prosecution Threats—FDC § 15.3
Cross-Collateral—Repo § 3.7.2
Cross Metering, Utility Service—AUS § 5.2
Cruise Line Port Charges—UDAP § 5.4.13.2
Cure of Default—Repo §§ 4.8, 13.2.4.4
Cy Pres—CCA § 11.7
Daily Accrual Accounting—COC § 4.6.8
Damages—FDC §§ 2.5.2, 6.3, Ch 10; FCR Ch 11; Repo Ch 13; TIL Ch 8; UDAP § 8.3; Warr §§ 10.3–10.5
Damage to Credit Rating—UDAP § 8.3.3.6
Dance Studios—UDAP § 5.10.4
Daubert Doctrine—Warr § 13.8.4
Dealer's Only Auto Auctions—Repo § 10.10.6
Debit Cards—CBPL Ch 3
Debt Cancellation Agreements—TIL §§ 3.7.10, 3.9.4.7
Debt Collection—FDC; UDAP §§ 2.2.2, 5.1.1
Debt Collection and Bankruptcy—FDC § 2.2.5
Debt Collection by Arbitration—FDC § 15.4; Arbit Ch. 11
Debt Collection Case Preparation—FDC Ch 2
Debt Collection Procedures Act—FDC § 13.2.1.1
Debt Collectors—FDC § 1.2, Ch 4
Debt Collector's Common Abbreviations—FDC App G.4
Debt Harassment, How to Stop—FDC § 2.3
Debtor in Possession under Chapter 12—Bankr § 16.3
Debt Pooling—FDC § 1.5.5
Deceit—Warr § 11.4; UDAP § 9.6.3
Deception—UDAP § 4.2; FDC § 5.5
Deceptive Practices Statutes—*See* UDAP
Deceptive Pricing—UDAP § 4.6.3
Defamation—FDC § 10.5; FCR § 10.5.2
Deeds-in-Lieu of Foreclosure- – Fore § 2.4.5
Defamatory Use of Mail—FDC § 9.1
Default—Repo Ch 4
Default Insurance—TIL § 3.7.7
Defective Automobile Title—Auto
Defenses as Grounds for Nonpayment—Repo § 4.6
Defenses to Credit Card Charges—CBPL § 6.4; TIL § 5.9.5; UDAP § 6.6
Deferment of Student Loan—Stud § 3.2
Deferral Charges—COC § 4.8.2
Deferred Payment Plans—AUS § 6.6
Deficiency Actions—Repo Ch 12, App C.1
Deficiency Judgments—Fore § 10.3
Delay—UDAP § 4.9.2
Delaying Tactics, Opposing—CCA Ch 6
Delinquency Charges—*See* Late Charges
Deliverable Fuels—AUS § 1.6
Demonstrator Vehicles—Auto §§ 1.4.8, 2.1.6
Denial of Credit, Notice—FCR § 8.2.6
Department of Housing and Urban Development (HUD)—CD § 12.3.1, App D; Fore Chs 2, 4, § 3.2
Department of Motor Vehicles—Auto Appx. D
Deposit, Consumer's Right to Return When Seller Files Bankruptcy—Bankr § 17.5

Quick Reference to the Consumer Credit and Sales Legal Practice Series

References are to sections in *all* manuals in NCLC's Consumer Credit and Sales Legal Practice Series

Depositions in Class Actions—CCA § 7.1.2.4, Ch 8
Deposition Notice, Sample—CLP
Deposition Questions, Sample—Auto § 9.5.5; CLP
Deposition Questions and Answers, Sample—CLP
Depository Creditors—COC Ch 2; FDC Ch 12
Deregulation of Utilities—AUS Ch 1
Detinue—Repo Ch 5
Digital Divide—CD § 3.8.2
Direct Deposits—CBPL Ch 10
Disabilities, Discrimination Based On—CD § 3.5.2
Disability Discharge—Stud § 6.6
Disabled Access to ATM machines—CBPL Ch 8
Discharge in Bankruptcy—Bankr Ch 14
Discharge of Indebtedness Income—Fore § 10.7.3
Discharging Student Loan Obligations—Stud Ch 6, § 7.2.3
Disclaimers, Warranties—Warr Ch 5
Disclosure and UDAP—UDAP § 4.2.14
Disclosure of Credit Terms—TIL
Disconnection of Utility Service—AUS Chs 11, 12
Discovery—Auto § 9.5, App H; *see also* Interrogatories; Document Requests
Discovery, Arbitration—Arbit § 9.1, App D
Discovery, Class Actions—CCA Ch 7, App H
Discovery, Motions to Compel—CCA Apps I, J
Discrimination in Collection Tactics—FDC § 9.8
Discrimination re Credit—CD
Disposition of Repo Collateral—Repo Chs 9, 10
Dispute Resolution Mechanisms—Warr §§ 2.8, 14.2.9
Disputing Information in Consumer Report—FCR Ch. 4
Document Preparation Fees—TIL § 3.9.6; UDAP § 5.4.3.8
Document Production Requests, Sample—Arbit App D; Auto App F; CCA App H; CD App H; FDC App I.2; Repo Apps E.2; Fore App. I.2.3; TIL App F.3; Warr App L.3; CLP
Document Requests, Sample Objection to—CCA App M
D'Oench, Duhme Doctrine—COC § 10.7; Repo § 12.10; Fore § 4.10; UDAP § 6.7.5
Door-to-Door Sales—UDAP § 5.8.2
Dragnet Clauses—Repo § 3.9
Driver Privacy Protection Act—Auto § 2.2.4, App A.2
Driver's Licenses and Bankruptcy—Bankr §§ 14.5.4, 14.5.5.1
Drunk Driving Debts in Bankruptcy—Bankr § 14.4.3.9
Due on Sale Clauses—Fore § 4.5.5
Due Process—Fore § 3.1.2.2, 4.4
Dunning, How to Stop with Sample Letters—FDC § 2.3
Duress—UDAP § 9.5.12; AUS § 6.1.9
Duty of Good Faith and Fair Dealing—COC § 12.8
Early Termination Penalties in Auto Leases—TIL § 10.5
Earned Income Tax Credit—Bankr § 2.5.5
EBT—CBPL Ch 8
E-Commerce, Jurisdiction—COC § 9.2.9.4
Educational Loans—*See* Student Loans
EFT 99—CBPL Ch 10
Election of Remedy Statutes—Repo § 12.4
Electric Service—AUS § 1.2.2; UDAP § 5.6.9
Electric Industry Restructuring—AUS § 1.4
Electronic Banking—CBPL Ch 3; FDC § 12.6.6
Electronic Benefit Transfers—CBPL Ch 8
Electronic Check Conversion—CBPL Ch 3
Electronic Credit Transactions—COC § 9.2.10
Electronic Disclosure—TIL §§ 4.2.9, 5.3.6, 9.3.9; UDAP § 4.2.14.3.9
Electronic Fund Transfers—CBPL Chs 3, 10
Electronic Repossession—Repo § 6.6
Electronic Check Representment—CBPL Ch 2
Electronic Signatures and Records—CBPL Ch 11
Electronic Transaction Fraud—UDAP § 5.9.4; CBPL Ch 3
Electronic Transfer Account (ETA)—CBPL Ch 10
Employer Bankruptcy—Bankr § 17.7.12
Employment Agencies—UDAP § 5.13.2
Encyclopedia Sales—UDAP § 5.7.1
Endorsements—UDAP § 4.7.7
Energy Savings Claims—UDAP § 5.6.7
Enforceability of Arbitration Clause—Arbit
Equal Credit Opportunity Act—CD; AUS § 3.7.2
Equal Credit Opportunity Act Regulations—CD App B
E-Sign—CBPL Ch 11; COC § 9.2.10, 11.3.1.8a
ETAs (Electronic Transfer Accounts)—CBPL Ch 10
Ethnic Discrimination—CD § 3.3.3
Evictions—AUS § 12.4; UDAP § 5.5.2.10; FDC § 1.5.2
Evidence Spoilation—Warr § 13.2.5
Evidentiary Issues in Automobile Litigation—Auto § 9.8
Exempt Benefits and Bankruptcy—Bankr § 10.2.2.11
Exempting Interest Rates—COC Ch 3
Exemption Laws, Liberal Construction—FDC § 12.2
Exemption Planning—Bankr § 10.4.1
Exemptions, Benefits, Earnings, Due Process Protections—FDC Ch 12
Expert Inspection—Warr § 13.6.1
Experts, Attorney Fee Award for—UDAP § 8.8.7.3
Expert Witnesses—FDC § 2.4.14; Warr § 13.8
Expert Witnesses, Sample Questions—Auto App I
Exportation of Interest Rates—COC Ch 3
Express Warranties—Warr Ch 3
Expressio Unius Est Exclusio Alterius—COC § 9.3.1.2
Extended Warranties—*See* Service Contracts
Extortionate Collection—FDC § 9.5
FACT Act—FCR
FACT Act Regulations—FCR Appx. B
Fair Credit Billing Act—CBPL § 6.5; TIL § 5.8; FCR § 12.4.2.; AUS § 11.3.5
Fair Credit Reporting Act—FCR; FDC § 9.6
Fair Debt Collection Practices Act—FDC Chs 3–7, Apps A, B, L
Fair Housing Act—CD
Fair Housing Act Regulations—CD App D
False Certification Discharge—Stud § 6.3
False Pretenses, Obtaining Consumer Reports—FCR § 7.7
Family Expense Laws—FDC § 14.6; CD § 9.3
Farm Reorganizations, Bankruptcy—Bankr Ch 16
Farmworker Camps—UDAP §§ 2.2.7, 5.5.4
Faxes, Junk—UDAP § 5.9.2.2
Federal Agency Collection Actions—FDC Ch 13
Federal Arbitration Act—Arbit Ch 2, App A
Federal Benefit Payments, Electronic—CBPL Ch 10
Federal Civil Rights Acts—CD; AUS § 3.7.1
Federal Direct Deposit of Benefits—CBPL Ch 10
Federal Direct Student Loans—Stud
Federal Energy Regulatory Commission (FERC)—AUS § 1.2.2.2
Federal False Claims Act—UDAP § 9.4.13
Federal Family Education Loans—Stud
Federal Preemption—FDC §§ 2.2, 6.14; UDAP § 2.5
Federal Preemption of State Usury Laws—COC Ch 3
Federal Racketeering Statute—*See* RICO
Federal Reserve Board—*See* FRB
Federal Trade Commission—*See* FTC
Fees—TIL § 3.7; COC § 7.2.1; FDC § 15.2
FHA Mortgage Foreclosure—Fore Ch 3
Fiduciary Duty—COC §§ 8.7.2, 12.9
Fifth Amendment Privilege—Auto § 9.8.6.7

911

Quick Reference to the Consumer Credit and Sales Legal Practice Series

References are to sections in *all* manuals in NCLC's Consumer Credit and Sales Legal Practice Series

Filed Rate Doctrine—UDAP § 5.6.10.1
Film Developing Packages—UDAP § 5.7.10
Finance Charge—TIL Ch 3; COC § 4.4
Finance Charges, Hidden—COC Ch 7; TIL § 3.10
Finance Companies—COC Ch 2; UDAP §§ 2.2.1, 5.1.5
Flipping—COC § 6.1; UDAP § 5.1.5
Flipping of Property—COC 11.5.6
Flood Damage to Vehicle—Auto § 2.1.3
Food Advertising—UDAP § 5.11.2
Food Stamps, Electronic Payment—CBPL Ch 8
Forbearance of Student Loans—Stud § 3.3
Forbearance Plans, Mortgage Loans—Fore § 2.3.4.3
Force-Placed Auto Insurance—UDAP § 5.3.11; COC § 8.3.1.4; TIL § 3.9.4.4.2
Foreclosure—Fore
Foreclosure, False Threat—Repo Ch 6
Foreclosure, Government-Held Mortgages—Fore Ch 3
Foreclosure, Preventing Through Bankruptcy—Bankr Ch 9, §§ 10.4.2.6.4, 11.5, 11.6; Fore Ch 7
Foreclosure, Preventing Through Refinancing—COC § 6.5; Fore § 2.11.2
Foreclosure, Preventing Through Rescission—TIL Ch 6; Fore § 4.8.4.1
Foreclosure, Preventing Through Workouts—Fore Ch 2
Foreclosure, Rescue Scams—Fore § 4.8.2.5, ch 11S; TIL §§ 6.8.5S, 9.2.5.6S, 9.2.6.3.8S
Foreclosure, Setting Aside—Fore § 10.1
Foreclosure, Summary of State Laws—Fore App C
Foreclosures and UDAP—UDAP § 5.1.1.5; Fore § 4.8.1
Forged Signatures, Indorsements—CBPL § 2.3.1.3
Franchises—UDAP §§ 2.2.9.2, 5.13.1
Fraud—UDAP; Warr § 11.4
Fraud and Arbitration—Arbit Ch 4
FRB Official Staff Commentary on Reg. B—CD App C
FRB Official Staff Commentary on Reg. M—TIL App I.3
FRB Official Staff Commentary on Reg. Z—TIL App C
Free Offers—UDAP § 4.6.4
Freezer Meats—UDAP § 5.7.2
FTC (Federal Trade Commission)—UDAP
FTC Act, No Private Action Under—UDAP § 9.1
FTC Cooling Off Period Rule—UDAP § 5.8.2, App B.3
FTC Credit Practices Rule—Repo § 3.4.2; UDAP § 5.1.1.2, App B.1; FDC § 8.4.2
FTC Debt Collection Law—FDC Ch 8
FTC FCR Enforcement Actions—FCR App K
FTC FCR Official Staff Commentary—FCR App D
FTC FDCPA Official Staff Commentary—FDC § 3.2.6, App C
FTC Funeral Rule—UDAP § 5.11.5, App B.5
FTC Holder Rule—UDAP § 6.6, App B.2
FTC Mail or Telephone Order Merchandise Rule—UDAP § 5.8.1.1, App B.4
FTC Staff Letters on FCR—FCR App E
FTC Staff Letters on FDCPA—FDC § 3.2.5, App B
FTC Telemarketing Sales Rule—UDAP App D.2.1
FTC Telephone and Dispute Resolution Rule—UDAP App D.2.2
FTC Used Car Rule—UDAP § 5.4.3.2, App B.6; Warr § 15.8, App D
Funds Availability—CBPL § 9.4
Funerals—UDAP § 5.11.5
Furniture Sales—UDAP § 5.7.3
Future Advance Clauses—Repo § 3.9
Future Service Contracts—UDAP § 5.10
GAP Insurance—TIL §§ 3.7.10, 3.9.4.7
Garnishment—FDC § 5.5.7, Ch 12, App D

Garnishment of Bank Account—CBPL § 4.2
Garnishment to Repay Student Loans—Stud § 5.3, App B.1.3
Gas Service—AUS § 1.2.1; UDAP § 5.6.9
Gasoline, Price Gouging—UDAP § 5.6.8.5
Gift Cards—UDAP § 5.1.10.6S
Government Benefits—FCR §§ 2.3.6.6, 7.2.6
Government Checks—CBPL Ch 9
Government Collection Practices—FDC Ch 13; Stud Ch 4
GPS Devices—UDAP § 5.4.9.5S
Gramm-Leach-Bliley Act—COC §§ 3.9, 8.4.1.5.2; FCR § 16.4.1
Gray Market Sales—Auto § 1.4.11; Warr § 14.7
Guaranteed Student Loans—Stud
Guarantees—UDAP § 5.2.7.3
Guarantors—*See* Cosigners
Handguns—UDAP § 5.7.9
Handicapped, Discrimination Against—CD § 3.5.2
Handouts for Client—*See* Client Handouts
Health Care Bills—FDC Ch 14; Bankr § 6.2.2.4.1
Health Care Plans, Misrepresentations—UDAP § 5.11.6
Health Care Treatment, Discrimination In—CD § 2.2.2.6
Health Cures, Misrepresentations—UDAP § 5.11
Health Spas—UDAP § 5.10.3
Hearing Aids—UDAP § 5.11.1
Heating Fuel—AUS §§ 1.2, 1.6; UDAP § 5.6.8
HELC—TIL § 5.11
Hidden Interest—COC Ch 7; TIL § 3.10
High Cost Loans, State Laws—COC Ch 7
High Pressure Sales—UDAP § 4.8
Hill-Burton Act Compliance—UDAP § 5.11.5
Holder in Due Course—UDAP § 6.6; COC §§ 10.6.1
Home Builders—UDAP § 5.5.5.2
Home Equity Lines of Credit—TIL § 5.11
Home Equity Loans—TIL Ch 9
Home Foreclosure—*See* Foreclosure
Home Heating Fuel—AUS §§ 1.2, 1.6; UDAP § 5.6.8
Home Improvement Practices—TIL § 6.5.3; UDAP § 5.6.1; Warr § 19.7, Apps I.3, K.4
Home Mortgage Disclosure Act—CD § 4.4.5
Home Mortgage, Rescission of—TIL Ch 6, App E.3
Home Owners' Loan Act—COC § 3.5
Home Owners Warranty Program—UDAP § 5.5.5.2
Home Ownership & Equity Protection Act—TIL Ch 9, App E.4; Fore § 4.8.5
Homes and UDAP—UDAP §§ 2.2.5, 5.5.5
Homes, Warranties—Warr Ch. 18
Homestead Exemptions, Bankruptcy—Bankr § 10.2.2.2
Horizontal Privity—Warr § 6.3
Hospital Bills—FDC Ch 14
House Warranties—Warr Ch 18
Household Goods, Bankruptcy Exemption—Bankr §§ 10.2.2.4, 10.4.2.4
Household Goods Security Interest—Repo § 3.4; UDAP §§ 5.1.1.2; 5.1.1.5; TIL § 4.6.7
Household Goods Security Interest, Credit Property Insurance on—COC § 8.5.4.4
Houses and UDAP—UDAP §§ 2.2.5, 5.5
HOW Program—UDAP § 5.5.5.5.2
HUD—*See* Department of Housing and Urban Development
Identity Theft—FCR Ch. 9
Illegal Conduct—UDAP §§ 4.3.9, 9.5.8
Illegality as Contract Defense—UDAP § 9.5.8
Immigrant Consultants, Deceptive Practices—UDAP § 5.12.2
Immigrant Status, Discrimination Based On—CD § 3.3.3.3
Implied Warranties—Warr Ch 4

Quick Reference to the Consumer Credit and Sales Legal Practice Series
References are to sections in *all* manuals in NCLC's Consumer Credit and Sales Legal Practice Series

Improvident Extension of Credit—UDAP § 5.1.4
Incomplete Information in Consumer Reports—FCR Ch 4
Inconvenient Venue—*See* Venue
Indian Tribal Law, Bankruptcy Exemptions—Bankr § 10.2.3.1
Industrial Loan Laws—COC Ch 2
Infancy—*See* Minority
Infliction of Emotional Distress—FDC § 10.2
In Forma Pauperis Filings in Bankruptcy—Bankr §§ 13.6, 17.6
Informal Dispute Resolution—Warr § 2.8
Injunctions—UDAP § 8.6; FDC §§ 6.12, 12.6.2, 13.3
Insecurity Clauses—Repo § 4.1.6
Inspection by Experts—Warr § 13.6.1
Installment Sales Laws—COC §§ 2.3.3.4, 9.3.1.1
Insurance and Arbitration—Arbit § 2.3.3
Insurance and UDAP—UDAP §§ 2.3.1, 5.3
Insurance Consumer Reports—FCR §§ 2.3.6.5, 2.6.8, 7.2.5
Insurance, Credit—COC Ch 8; TIL §§ 3.7.9, 3.9.4; UDAP § 5.3.10
Insurance, Illusory Coverage—UDAP § 5.3.6
Insurance Packing—COC § 8.5.4; UDAP § 5.3.12
Insurance Redlining—CD § 7.3
Insurance, Refusal to Pay Claim—UDAP § 5.3.3
Intentional Infliction of Emotional Distress—FDC § 10.2
Intentional Interference with Employment Relationships—FDC § 10.4
Interest Calculations—COC §§ 4.2, 4.3
Interest, Hidden—COC Ch 7; TIL § 3.10
Interest Rates, Federal Preemption of—COC Ch 3
Interference with Employment Relationships—FDC § 10.4
Interim Bankruptcy Rules – Bankr App B
International Driving Permits- – UDAP § 5.4.13.5S
International Money Orders and Wires—CBPL Ch 5
Internet Banking—CBPL Ch 3
Internet, Fraudulent Schemes—UDAP § 5.9
Internet, Invasion of Privacy—UDAP § 4.11
Internet Service Providers—UDAP § 5.6.10.7
Interrogatories—Arbit App D; Auto App F; CCA App E; CD App H; COC App L; FCR App J.3; FDC App I.1; Repo App E; Fore Apps I.2.3, I.3.4, I.3.5; Warr App L; TIL App F.2; CLP
Interstate Banking and Rate Exportation—COC § 3.4.5
Intervenor Funding—AUS § 9.5
Interview Checklist for Debt Collection—FDC App G
Interview Form, Bankruptcy—Bankr App F
Interview Form for Clients, Warranties—Warr App I
Invasion of Privacy—FCR §§ 10.5.3, 16.3; FDC § 10.3
Investigative Reports—FCR Ch 13
Investments—UDAP §§ 2.2.9, 5.13
Involuntary Bankruptcy Cases—Bankr §§ 13.8, 16.1.2
JAMS—Arbit App B.3
Joint Bank Accounts, Seizure—FDC § 12.7
Joint Checking Accounts—CBPL §§ 2.6.3, 4.2, 4.3
Judicial Liens, Avoiding in Bankruptcy—Bankr § 10.4.2.3
Jury, Disclosure to, that Damages Will Be Trebled—UDAP § 8.4.2.8; Auto § 9.9.7
Jury Instructions, Sample—CCA Ch 14; Auto App G.6S; FDC App J.2; FCR App J.8; TIL App G
Jury Trial, Class Action—CCA Ch 14
Jury Trial, Preparing FDCPA Case—FDC § 2.5.7
Land Installment Sales Contract (aka "Contract for Deed")- – Fore § 4.12
Land Sales—UDAP §§ 2.2.5, 5.5.4.7
Land Trusts—TIL §§ 2.2.1.1, 2.4.3
Landlord Evictions—FDC § 1.5.2.2
Landlord's Removal of Evicted Tenant's Property—Repo § 15.7.4; FDC § 1.5.2.4

Landlord's Requested Disconnection of Utility Service—AUS § 12.4
Landlord's Termination of Utility Service—AUS Ch 4
Landlord-Tenant—Bankr §§ 12.9, 17.8; UDAP §§ 2.2.6, 5.5.2; FDC § 1.5.2
Landownership, Utility Service Conditioned on—AUS Ch 4
Late Charges—COC §§ 4.8, 7.2.4; TIL §§ 3.9.3, 4.7.7; UDAP §§ 5.1.1.2.8; 5.1.6
Late Charges, Utility Bills—AUS §§ 6.2, 6.3
Late Posting of Payments and Interest Calculation—COC § 4.6.3.5
Law, Unauthorized Practice of—FDC §§ 4.2.7.7.3, 11.5; Bankr § 15.6
Lawyer—*See* Attorney
Layaway Plans—UDAP § 4.9.1
Lease-Back of Home—COC § 7.5.2.1; TIL § 6.2.4.1
Leases—Repo Ch 14; TIL § 2.2.4.2, Ch 10; UDAP §§ 2.2.6, 5.4.8, 5.5.2; Warr Ch 21; Auto §§ 4.6.2.3, 4.6.6.5, 5.2.6; Bankr § 12.9; CD § 2.2.2.2; COC § 7.5.3; *see also* Rent to Own
Lease Terms for Residence—UDAP §§ 5.5.2.2, 5.5.2.3
Leased Vehicle Damages—Auto § 9.10.1.2
Legal Rights, Misrepresentation of—UDAP § 5.2.8
Lemon Cars Being Resold—Auto §§ 1.4.6, 2.1.5, 2.4.5.5, 6.3, App C; Warr § 15.7.3; UDAP § 5.4.6.7
Lemon Laws—Warr § 14.2, App F
Lender Liability—UDAP Ch 6
Letter to Debt Collector, Sample—FDC § 2.3
Liability of Agents, Principals, Owners—UDAP Ch 6; FDC § 2.8
Licenses to Drive and Bankruptcy—Bankr § 14.5.5.1
Liens—Repo Ch 15
Life Care Homes—UDAP § 5.11.3
Life Insurance, Excessive Premiums for—UDAP § 5.3.9
Lifeline Assistance Programs—AUS § 2.3.2
LIHEAP—AUS Ch 7, App D
Limitation of Remedies Clauses—Warr Ch 9
Live Check Solicitations- – UDAP § 5.1.10.5S
Living Trusts—UDAP § 5.12.3
Loan Brokers—UDAP §§ 2.2.1, 5.1.3; COC § 7.3.2
Loan Flipping—*See* Flipping
Loan Rehabilitation—Stud § 8.4
Loans, High Cost—COC Ch7
Long Arm Jurisdiction—COC § 9.2.9.6; UDAP § 7.6.2
Loss Mitigation, Foreclosures—Fore Ch 2
Lost Checks—CBPL §§ 2.8, 9.2
Lost Credit Card Reporting Services—UDAP § 5.1.5.5
Low Balling—UDAP § 4.6.5
Low Income Home Energy Assistance Program—AUS Ch 7, App D
Magazine Sales—UDAP § 5.7.1
Magnuson-Moss Warranty Act—Warr Ch 2, Apps A, B; Auto § 8.2.5
Magnuson-Moss Warranty Act Relation to Federal Arbitration Act—Arbit § 5.2.2, App G
Mail Fraud—UDAP § 9.2.4; FDC § 9.1
Mail Order Sales—UDAP § 5.8.1
Malicious Prosecution—FDC § 10.6.2
Managed Care, Misrepresentations—UDAP § 5.11.6
Manufacturer Rebates—UDAP § 4.6.3
Marital Status Discrimination—CD § 3.4.1
Mass Action—CCA § 2.4.5
Master Metering—AUS § 5.5
Math, Credit—COC Ch 4
McCarran-Ferguson Act—Arbit § 2.3.3; COC § 8.5.2.7; TIL § 2.4.9.5
Means Testing—Bankr
Mechanical Breakdown Insurance—*See* Service Contracts

Quick Reference to the Consumer Credit and Sales Legal Practice Series

References are to sections in *all* manuals in NCLC's Consumer Credit and Sales Legal Practice Series

Mediation—Auto § 9.11.1.3
Medical—*See* Health Care
Mental Anguish Damages—FDC §§ 2.5, 6.3, 10.2
Mental Incompetence—UDAP § 9.5.7.3
Meter Tampering—AUS Ch 5
Migrant Farmworker Camps—UDAP §§ 2.2.7, 5.5.4
Mileage Disclosure—Auto §§ 2.4.5.8, 4.6.6
Military Personnel and Credit Protection—FDC § 9.12; FCR § 5.5.1; Repo § 6.3.5.1; Fore § 4.7
Mini-FTC Laws—*See* UDAP
Minority—UDAP § 9.5.7
Misrepresentation—UDAP § 4.2; Warr § 11.4; Auto § 8.4
Mistaken Undercharges, Utility Bills—AUS § 5.1.2
Mobile Home Defects—Warr § 17.1.3
Mobile Home Foreclosure—Fore Ch 8
Mobile Home Parks—UDAP §§ 2.2.6, 5.5.1
Mobile Homes, Federal Statutes—Warr App C
Mobile Homes and Interstate Rate Deregulation—COC Ch 3
Mobile Homes and Repossession—Repo §§ 2.4.1, 3.5, 4.8.3, 5.2, 6.3.3, 7.1
Mobile Homes, Sale by Consumer—Repo § 9.6.3
Mobile Homes and UDAP—UDAP §§ 2.2.5, 5.4.12
Mobile Homes, Utility Service—AUS § 5.6
Mobile Homes, Warranties—Warr Ch 17
Model Pleadings—*See* Complaints, Interrogatories, Document Requests, etc.
Modification of Mortgage Loans—Fore § 2.3.4.6
Money Orders—CBPL Ch 5
Moratorium on Foreclosures—Fore § 2.13.1
Mortgage Assistance Scams—UDAP § 5.1.2.1; Fore § 4.8.2.5
Mortgage Assistance, State Programs—Fore § 2.11.3
Mortgage Electronic Registration System (MERS)—Fore § 4.3.4.3
Mortgage Fees—TIL § 3.9.6; COC Ch 7
Mortgage Loans—UDAP § 5.1.5
Mortgage Servicers—Fore § 2.2.5.3, Chs 4AS, 5
Mortgage Servicing, Summary of State Laws—Fore App E
Most Favored Lender—COC § 3.4.3
Motion in Limine, Sample—Auto App I; FDC App J.5
Motions for Class Certification—*See* Class Certification Motions
Motor Homes—Warr § 14.8.5
Motor Vehicle Information and Cost Savings Act—Auto Chs 4, 5, App A.1
Motor Vehicle Installment Sales Act—COC § 2.3.3.5; Repo § 2.2
Multiple Damages—UDAP § 8.4.2; Auto § 5.8.1
Municipal Utilities (MUNIs)—AUS §§ 1.5, 12.2
NACA Class Actions Guidelines for Settlement—CCA App D
NACHA—CBPL Ch 3
National Arbitration Forum—Arbit App B.2, App H
National Origin Discrimination—CD § 3.3.3
"Nationwide" Reporting Agencies—FCR § 2.6.1
Native Americans and Repossession—Repo § 6.3.5.2
Natural Disasters—Fore § 2.13
Necessities Laws—FDC § 14.6; CD § 9.3
Negative Equity—COC § 11.6.3
Negative Option Plans—UDAP § 5.8.5
Negligence—Warr Ch 12; FCR § 10.5.4; FDC §§ 10.2, 10.7
Negotiations, Class Actions—CCA Ch 11
New Car Lemon Laws—Warr § 14.2, App F
New Cars, Sales—Warr Ch 14; UDAP § 5.4.7
New Cars, Undisclosed Damage to—Auto §§ 1.4.5, 6.2.3
New House Warranties—Warr Ch 18
900 Numbers—UDAP §§ 5.9.3, 6.10, Apps D, E
Nonattorney Legal Service Providers, Deceptive Practices—UDAP § 5.12.2

Nondisclosure and UDAP—UDAP § 4.2.14
Non-English Speaking—UDAP § 5.2.1
Nonfiling Insurance—COC § 8.5.4.5
Nonpayment of Loans, When Excused—Repo § 4.6
Non-Signatories Rights and Obligations—Arbit §§ 6.3, 6.4
Notario Fraud—UDAP § 5.12.2
Notice Consumer Deducting Damages From Outstanding Balance—*See* Warr App J.3
Notice of Rescission—*See* Rescission Notice
Notice of Revocation—Warr App J.2
Notice to Class—CCA Ch 10
Notice to Quit, Deceptive—UDAP § 5.5.2.9
Not Sufficient Funds (NSF) Checks—CBPL § 2.5
Nursing Homes, Deceptive Practices—UDAP § 5.11.3
Obsolete Information in Consumer Reports—FCR § 5.2
Odometers—Auto; Warr § 15.7.2; UDAP § 5.4.6.5
Odometer Tampering—Auto §§ 4.3, 4.4
Offer of Judgment—FDC § 2.4.13; CCA § 6.3.2
Official Bankruptcy Forms—Bankr App D
Oil, Home Heating—AUS § 1.6; UDAP § 5.6.8
On-Line Fraud—UDAP § 5.9.4
On-Line Disclosures—UDAP § 4.2.14.3.9
On Us Checks—CBPL § 1.3.1.4
Open-End Credit—TIL Ch 5; COC § 2.3.2.3
Open-End Credit, Spurious—TIL § 5.2.3
Opening Statement, Sample—Auto App I
Outdated Information in Consumer Reports—FCR § 5.2
Overcharges by Creditor in Bankruptcy—Bankr § 13.4.3.3
Pain and Suffering Damages—FDC § 2.5; UDAP § 8.3.3.9
Paralegals, Attorney Fees for—UDAP §§ 8.6.11.6, 8.8.7.2
Parol Evidence—UDAP § 4.2.15.3; Warr § 3.7
Partial Prepayment—COC § 8.2
Pattern and Practice Evidence—Auto § 9.8
Payroll Cards—CBPL Ch 7
Pawnbrokers—COC §§ 2.3.3.9, 7.5.2.3; UDAP § 5.1.1.5.5
Payday Loans—COC § 7.5.5, App L
Payment Holidays for Interest-Bearing Loans—COC § 4.8.3
Payment Packing—COC § 11.6.4
Payment Plans, Utility Bills—AUS Ch 6
Pay Phones—AUS § 2.6
Pensions in Bankruptcy—Bankr §§ 2.5.2, 10.2.2.11
Percentage of Income Payment Plans—AUS § 9.2.3
Perkins Loans—Stud
Personal Injury Suits—UDAP § 2.2.11
Personal Property Seized with Repo—Repo Ch 7
Pest Control Services—UDAP § 5.6.3
Petroleum Products, Price Gouging—UDAP § 5.6.8.5
Photoprocessing Packages—UDAP § 5.7.10
Plain English—UDAP § 5.2.2
Pleadings—*See* Complaints, Interrogatories, Document Requests, etc.
Point of Sale (POS) Electronic Transfers—CBPL Ch 3
Points—COC §§ 4.7, 6.4.1.3, 7.2.1, 8.3.1.2; TIL § 3.7.5
Postal Money Order—CBPL Ch 5
Postdated Checks—CBPL § 2.6.1
Preauthorized Drafts—CBPL § 2.3.5
Precomputed Interest—COC § 4.5
Precut Housing—UDAP § 5.5.5.8
Preemption of State Usury Laws—COC Ch 3
Preemption and State Chartered Banks—COC Ch3
Preexisting Debt Clauses—Repo § 3.9
Prepayment—TIL § 4.7.6; COC Ch 5
Prepayment Penalties—COC § 5.8
Prescreening Lists—FCR § 7.3
Preservation of Documents, Class Actions—CCA § 5.2

Quick Reference to the Consumer Credit and Sales Legal Practice Series

References are to sections in *all* manuals in NCLC's Consumer Credit and Sales Legal Practice Series

Price Gouging in an Emergency—UDAP § 4.3.11
Pricing—UDAP § 4.6
Privacy, Invasion of—FCR §§ 10.5.3, 16.3; FDC § 10.3
Privacy, Restrictions on Use of Consumer Reports—FCR § Ch 7, § 12.2
Private Mortgage Insurance (PMI)—COC § 8.3.2.1; UDAP § 5.3.13
Private Sale of Collateral—Repo § 10.5.7
Privity—Warr Ch 6; UDAP § 4.2.15.3
Prizes—UDAP § 5.13.4
Procedural Unconscionability—Warr § 11.2; COC § 12.7
Proceeds—Repo § 3.3.2
Progress Payments—COC § 4.9
Propane—AUS § 1.6; UDAP § 5.6.8
Property Flipping—COC § 11.5.6; Fore § 4.8.2.3
Protective Orders—CCA § 5.2, App K
Public Assistance Status, Discrimination Based on—CD § 3.4.3
Public Housing, UDAP Coverage—UDAP §§ 2.3.3.3, 2.3.6
Public Housing, Utility Service—AUS Ch 8
Public Records—FCR
Public Sale of Collateral—Repo § 10.7
Public Utilities—AUS
Public Utility Credit—TIL § 2.4.6
Punitive Damages—Auto § 7.10; CD § 11.7.4; FCR § 11.12; FDC § 2.6, Ch 10; UDAP § 8.4.3
Punitive Damages & Arbitration—-Arb § 9.6S
Pyramid Sales—UDAP § 5.13.3
Pyramiding Late Charges—COC § 7.2.4.3; AUS § 6.2.6
Qualified Written Request—Fore App A
Race Discrimination re Credit—CD § 3.3.1
Racketeering Statute—*See* RICO
Reachback Periods—Bankr § 6.5.3.4
Reaffirmations and Bankruptcy—Bankr § 14.5.2
Real Estate—UDAP §§ 2.2.5, 5.5.5
Real Estate Settlement Procedures Act—-*See* RESPA
Real Estate Tax Abatement Laws—Fore App G
Real Party in Interest—Fore § 4.3.4
Reassembled Cars from Parts—Auto §§ 1.4.3, 2.1.4; UDAP § 5.4.6.6
Rebates from Manufacturer—UDAP § 4.6.3.2; TIL § 3.7.5.2
Rebates of Interest—COC Ch 5, §§ 6.3, 6.4; TIL §§ 2.7, 3.7.2.2
Recoupment Claims—TIL §§ 6.3.3, 7.2.5; Bankr § 13.3.2.4
Redemption and Repo—Repo § 9.3
Redemption, Foreclosures—Fore §§ 4.2.6, 10.2
Redlining—CD §§ 7.1, 7.2
Referral Sales—UDAP § 5.8.3
Refinancings—COC Ch 6; Repo § 3.8; TIL § 4.9; UDAP § 5.1.5
Refund Anticipation Loans—COC § 7.5.4
Refunds—UDAP § 5.2.6
Regulation B, Text—CD App B
Regulation E—CBPL Ch 3, App D
Regulation M, Text—TIL App I.2
Regulation Z, Text—TIL App B
Regulation CC—CBPL § 9.4
Regulation DD—CBPL § 4.5
Rejection—Warr Ch 8
Reliance—TIL §§ 8.5.4.2, 8.5.5.7; UDAP § 4.2.12
Religious Discrimination re Credit—CD § 3.3.2
Remittances—UDAP § 5.1.10.4S
Rent and Bankruptcy—Bankr §§ 12.9, 14.5.5.3, 17.8
Rent to Own—UDAP § 5.7.4; Bankr § 11.8; COC § 7.5.3; Repo § 14.3
Rent, Utility Service—AUS Chs 4, 8
Rental Cars—UDAP § 5.4.9; Auto § 2.4.5.6
Rental Housing, Substandard—UDAP §§ 5.5.2.4, 5.5.2.5

Repairs—UDAP § 4.9.7
Repairs, Automobile—Warr § 19.8; UDAP § 5.4.1
Repayment Plan for Student Loans—Stud § 8.3
Replevin—Repo Ch 5
Reporting Agencies—FCR
Repossessions—Repo; UDAP § 5.1.1.5; FDC § 4.2.5
Repossessions, Stopping—Bankr Ch 9
Resale of Utility Service—AUS §§ 5.5, 5.6
Rescission—TIL Ch 6, App E.3; Auto § 7.11; Fore § 4.8.4.1; UDAP §§ 8.7, 9.5.2
Rescission by Recoupment—TIL § 6.3.3
Rescission Notice, Sample—TIL App D
Resisting Repossession, Liability for—Repo § 6.2.4.3
RESPA—COC § 12.2.2; Fore §§ 2.2.4.6, 2.2.5.3, Ch 5; TIL §§ 4.1.1, 4.3.4
Retail Installment Sales Acts (RISA)—COC § 2.3.3.5; Repo § 2.5.2
Retail Sellers—COC §§ 2.3.1.3.2, 9.2.3.2
Retaliation for Exercise of TIL, CCPA Rights—CD § 3.4.4
Retroactive Statutes—UDAP § 7.4; COC § 9.3.2
Reverse Metering—AUS § 5.1
Reverse Mortgages—Fore § 4.8.2.6.2
Reverse Redlining—CD §§ 8.2, 8.3
Review of Arbitration Decision—Arbit Ch 10
Revised Uniform Arbitration Act – Arbit Ch. 10
Revocation of Acceptance—Warr Ch 8
Revolving Repossessions—Repo § 10.11
RHS—*See* Rural Housing Service
RICO—UDAP §§ 9.2, 9.3, App C.1.1; COC § 12.6; FDC § 9.5; Auto § 8.5
Right to Cure Default—Repo § 4.8, App B; Bankr § 11.6.2
Right to See Consumer Reports—FCR § 3.3
Right to Utility Service—AUS Ch 3
RISA—COC § 2.3.3.5; Repo § 2.5.2
Rooker Feldman—FDC § 7.6.4
RTO Contracts—*See* Rent to Own
Rule of 78—COC § 5.6.3.3; TIL § 3.7.2.2.3; Repo § 11.3.2.2.2
Rural Electric Cooperatives (RECs)—AUS §§ 1.5, 12.2
RHS—*See* Rural Housing Service
Rural Housing Service—Fore § 2.7.3
Rustproofing—UDAP § 5.4.3.3
Safety—UDAP § 4.7.4
Sale and Lease-Back—COC § 7.5.2.1; TIL § 6.2.5
Sale of Collateral—Repo Ch 10
Salvage Auctions—Auto § 2.6.4.2
Salvage Vehicles, Sale of—Auto §§ 1.4.3, 2.1.4, 2.4.5.4, 6.2.1; Warr § 15.7.4
Salvaged Parts—UDAP § 5.4.6.6
Sample Answer and Counterclaims—*See* Answer and Counterclaims
Sample Attorney Fee Pleadings—*See* Attorney Fee Pleadings
Sample Client Retainer Forms— *See* Client Retainer Forms
Sample Closing Arguments—*See* Closing Arguments
Sample Complaints—*See* Complaints
Sample Deposition Questions—*See* Deposition Questions
Sample Discovery—*See* Interrogatories; Document Requests
Sample Document Production Requests—*See* Document Production Requests
Sample Forms, Bankruptcy—*See* Bankruptcy Forms
Sample Interrogatories—*See* Interrogatories
Sample Jury Instructions—*See* Jury Instructions
Sample Motion in Limine—*See* Motion in Limine Auto App I; FDC App J.5
Sample Motions for Class Certification—*See* Class Certification Motions

915

Quick Reference to the Consumer Credit and Sales Legal Practice Series

References are to sections in *all* manuals in NCLC's Consumer Credit and Sales Legal Practice Series

Sample Notice for Rescission—*See* Rescission Notice
Sample Notice of Deposition—*See* Deposition Notice
Sample Notice of Revocation—*See* Notice of Revocation
Sample Objection to Document Requests—*See* Document Requests, Sample Objection to
Sample Opening and Closing Statement—*See* Opening Statement; Closing Argument
Sample Pleadings—*See* Complaint, Interrogatories, Document Requests, etc.
Sample Requests for Admissions—*See* Admission Requests
Sample Trial Brief—*See* Trial Brief
Sample Trial Documents—*See* Trial Documents
Sample Voir Dire—*See* Voir Dire
School-Related Defenses to Student Loans—Stud § 9.6
Schools, Vocational—Stud Ch 9
Scope of Arbitration Agreement—Arbit Ch 6
Scrip Settlements, Class Actions—CCA § 11.6; CLP
Second Mortgage, Rescission of—TIL Ch 6
Secret Warranties—UDAP § 5.4.7.10.2; Warr § 14.5.3.2
Securities Law—UDAP § 9.4.10
Securitization of Consumer Paper—COC § 2.4.2
Security Deposits, Consumer's Rights to Reform Where Seller in Bankruptcy—Bankr § 17.8.4
Security Deposits, Tenant's—UDAP §§ 5.5.2.2, 5.5.2.3; FDC § 1.5.2.5
Security Deposits, Utility § 3.7
Security Interest Charges—TIL § 3.9
Security Interests—Repo Ch 3; TIL § 4.6.7
Security Interests, Avoiding in Bankruptcy—Bankr § 10.4.2.4, Ch 11
Security Systems—UDAP § 5.6.2
Seizure of Collateral—Repo
Self-Help Repossession—Repo Ch 6
Service Contracts—Warr Ch 20, App G; UDAP §§ 5.2.7.2, 5.4.3.5; Auto §§ 2.5.10, 2.6.2.11
Service Contracts, When Hidden Interest—COC §§ 7.2.3, 7.3.1; TIL § 3.6.5
Servicemembers Civil Relief Act—FDC § 9.12; FCR 5.5.1; Repo 6.3.5.1
Servicer Abuses—Fore Ch 5
Services and Warranties—Warr Ch 19
Set Off, Banker's—CBPL Ch 4.3
Set-Offs—TIL §§ 5.9.3, 8.4; FDC § 12.6.7
Settlement, Auto Case—Auto § 9.11; Warr § 13.7
Settlement, Class Actions—CCA Chs 11, 12, Apps R, S, T
Settlement, Class Actions, Objections—CCA § 12.10, App U
Settlement, Individual Prior to Class Action—CCA § 1.2
Settlements and Consumer Reports—FCR § 12.6.4
Sewer Service—AUS § 1.2.3
Sex Discrimination re Credit—CD § 3.3.4
Sexual Orientation, Discrimination Based On—CD § 3.7
Shell Homes—UDAP § 5.5.5.8
Single Document Rule—COC § 11.6.8
Slamming, Telephone Service—AUS § 2.7.5.1; UDAP § 5.6.11
Small Loan Laws—COC § 2.3.3.2
Smart Cards—CBPL § Ch 7
Social Security Benefit Offset to Repay Student Loan—Stud § 5.4
Social Security Payments, Electronic—CBPL Ch 10
Soldiers' and Sailors' Civil Relief Act—*See* Servicemembers' Civil Relief Act
Spendthrift Trusts in Bankruptcy—Bankr § 2.5.2
Spoilation of Evidence—Warr § 13.2.5
Spot Delivery of Automobiles—UDAP § 5.4.5; Repo § 4.5; TIL §§ 4.4.5, 4.4.6; COC § 11.6.5

Spouses, Consumer Reports on—FCR § 5.6.1
Spreader Clauses—TIL § 4.6.7.6
Spurious Open-End Credit—TIL § 5.2.3
Stafford Loans—Stud
Standard Form Contracts, Unfair—UDAP § 5.2.3
State Arbitration Law—Arbit Ch 2
State Bonding Laws—Auto App C
State Chartered Banks and Preemption—COC Ch 3
State Cosigner Statutes—Repo § 12.9.6.2
State Credit Discrimination Laws—CD § 1.6, App E
State Credit Repair Laws—FCR App H
State Credit Reporting Laws—FCR § 10.6, App H
State Debt Collection Statutes—FDC § 11.2, App E
State Foreclosure Laws—Fore App C
State High Cost Loan Laws—COC Ch 7
State Home Improvement Statutes and Regs—Warr § 19.7.4
State Leasing Disclosure Statutes—TIL § 10.5.2.2
State Lemon Buyback Disclosure Laws—Auto App C
State Lemon Laws—Warr § 14.2, App F
State Lending Statutes—COC App A
State 900 Number Laws—UDAP App E
State Odometer Statutes—Auto App C
State Real Estate Tax Abatement Laws—Fore App G
State RICO Statutes—UDAP § 9.3, App C.2
State Right to Cure, Reinstate and Redeem Statutes—Repo App B
State Salvage Laws—Auto App C
State Service Contract Laws—Warr App G
State Telemarketing Laws—UDAP App E
State TIL Laws—TIL § 2.6
State Title Transfer Laws—Auto § 6.5, App C
State UDAP Statutes—UDAP App A
State Usury Statutes—COC App A
Statute of Limitations—TIL § 7.2
Statute of Limitations as Consumer Defense to Collection Action—Repo § 12.7
Statutory Damages—TIL § 8.6; FDC §§ 6.4, 11.2; Repo § 13.2; UDAP § 8.4.1
Statutory Liens—Repo Ch 15
Statutory Liens, Avoiding in Bankruptcy—Bankr § 10.4.2.6.3
Staying Foreclosure—Bankr Ch 9
Stolen Checks—CBPL §§ 2.8, 9.2
Stolen Vehicles—Auto §§ 1.4.10, 2.1.7, 8.2.2
Stop Payment on Checks, Credit and Debit Cards—CBPL §§ 2.6.2, 6.4, Ch3
Storage of Evicted Tenant's Property—Repo § 15.7.4; UDAP § 5.5.2.5
Stored Value Cards—CBPL Ch 7, App F
Straight Bankruptcy—Bankr Ch 3
Strict Liability in Tort—Warr Ch 12
Student Loan Collection Abuse—Stud Ch 4
Student Loan Repayment Plans—Stud Ch 8
Student Loan Regulations—Stud App B
Student Loans—Bankr § 14.4.3.8; FCR § 12.6.5; Stud; TIL § 2.4.5
Student Loans and Bankruptcy—Stud Ch 7
Student Loans, Reinstating Eligibility—Stud Ch 8
Summary Judgment Briefs, Sample—FDC App J.1; CLP
Surety for Consumer Debtor—Repo § 12.9
Surety Liability for Seller's Actions—Auto § 9.13.4
Survey Evidence—FDC § 2.9.3
Surveys, Use in Litigation—CCA § 7.1.2.2.3
Target Marketing Lists—FCR § 7.3.4
Tax Abatement Laws, State Property, Summaries—Fore App G
Tax Collections—FDC §§ 4.2.8S, 13.2
Tax Consequences, Bankruptcy Discharge—Bankr § 14.6

Quick Reference to the Consumer Credit and Sales Legal Practice Series

References are to sections in *all* manuals in NCLC's Consumer Credit and Sales Legal Practice Series

Tax Form 1099-C—CCA § 12.5.2.3.6
Tax Implications of Damage Award—CCA § 12.5.2.3
Tax Implications to Client of Attorney Fees—CCA § 15.5
Tax Intercept—Bankr § 9.4.3
Tax Liens—Fore Ch 9
Tax Refund Intercepts—Stud § 5.2; FDC § 13.2
Tax Refunds—COC § 7.5.4
Tax Refunds in Bankruptcy—Bankr § 2.5.5
Tax Sales—Fore Ch 9
Taxis, Undisclosed Sale of—Auto § 2.4.5.6
Telechecks—UDAP §§ 5.1.10
Telecommunications Act of 1996—AUS Ch 2, App C
Telemarketing, Payment—CBPL §§ 2.3.5, 3.8
Telemarketing Fraud—UDAP § 5.9; FCR § 15.4
Telemarketing Fraud, Federal Statutes—UDAP App D
Telephone Cards, Prepaid—CBPL Ch 7
Telephone Companies as Credit Reporting Agencies—FCR § 2.7.9
Telephone Harassment—FDC § 9.3
Telephone Inside Wiring Maintenance Agreements—UDAP §§ 5.2.7.2, 5.6.10
Telephone Rates, Service—AUS Ch 2, App C
Telephone Service Contracts—UDAP §§ 5.2.7.2, 5.6.10
Telephone Slamming—AUS § 2.7.5.1; UDAP § 5.6.10
Teller's Checks—CBPL Ch 5
Tenant Approval Companies—FCR §§ 2.6.2.2, 3.2.4
Tenant Ownership in Chapter 7 Liquidation—Bankr § 17.8.2
Tenant's Property Removed with Eviction—Repo § 15.7.4
Tenant's Rights When Landlord Files Bankruptcy—Bankr § 17.8; AUS § 4.5
Termination of Utility Service—AUS Chs 11, 12
Termite Control Services—UDAP § 5.6.3
Testers, Fair Housing—CD §§ 4.4.4, 11.2.2
Theft at ATM Machines, Bank Liability—CBPL § 3.5.4
Theft of Identity—FCR § 9.2
Third Party Liability Issues—AUS §§ 11.4, 11.5
Threats of Criminal Prosecution—FDC § 15.3
Tie-In Sale Between Mobile Home and Park Space—UDAP § 5.5.1.2
TIL—*See* Truth in Lending
Time Shares—UDAP § 5.5.5.10
Tire Identification—Auto § 2.2.3
Title, Automobile—Auto §§ 2.3, 2.4, Ch 3, Apps. D, E; UDAP § 5.4.5; Warr § 15.4.4
Tobacco—UDAP § 5.11.7
Tort Liability—FDC Ch 12
Tort Liability, Strict—Warr Ch 12
Tort Remedies, Unlawful Disconnections—AUS § 11.7.2
Tort Remedies, Wrongful Repossessions—Repo § 13.6
Towing—UDAP § 5.4.1.8; Repo Ch 15
Trade-in Cars—UDAP § 5.4.4.4
Trade Schools—Stud Ch 9; UDAP § 5.10.7
Trading Posts—UDAP § 5.1.1.5.5
Transcripts and Bankruptcy—Bankr § 14.5.5.2
Traveler's Checks—CBPL Ch 5, UDAP § 2.2.1.3
Travel Fraud—UDAP § 5.4.13
Treble Damages—UDAP § 8.4.2
Trebled, Disclosure to Jury that Damages Will Be—UDAP § 8.4.2.7.3
Trial Brief, Sample—FDC App J.4
Trial Documents, Sample—*See* Auto App I; FDC App J; Warr App M
Trustees in Bankruptcy—Bankr §§ 2.6, 2.7, 16.4.1, 17.7
Truth in Lending—TIL; COC §§ 2.3.4, 4.4.1; FDC § 9.4
Truth in Mileage Act—Auto Chs 3, 4, 5
Truth in Savings—CBPL § 4.5

Tuition Recovery Funds—Stud § 9.8
Typing Services—Bankr § 15.6
UCC Article 2—Warr
UCC Article 2 and Comments Reprinted—Warr App E
UCC Article 2A—Repo §§ 2.5.1.1, 14.1.3.1; Warr Ch 21, App E.5; UDAP § 5.4.8 5
UCC Articles 3 and 4—CBPL Chs 1, 2, App A
UCC Article 9—Repo
UCC Article 9, Revised—Repo App A
UCC Article 9 and Comments Reprinted—Repo App A
UDAP—UDAP; AUS § 1.7.2; Auto § 8.4; COC §§ 8.5.2.6, 12.5; FDC § 11.3; FCR § 10.6.2; Repo §§ 2.5.3.1, 13.4.3; Warr § 11.1
Unauthorized Card Use—TIL § 5.9.4
Unauthorized Practice of Law—FDC §§ 4.2.7.7, 5.6.2, 11.5; Bankr § 15.6; UDAP § 5.12.2
Unauthorized Use of Checks, Credit and Debit Cards—CBPL §§ 2.3, 3.3, 6.3
Unauthorized Use of Utility Service—AUS § 5.3
Unavailability of Advertised Items—UDAP § 4.6.2
Unconscionability—Warr §§ 11.2, 21.2.6; COC §§ 8.7.5, 12.7; UDAP §§ 4.4, 5.4.6.5; Auto § 8.7
Unconscionability of Arbitration Clauses—Arbit §§ 4.2, 4.3, 4.4
Unearned Interest—COC Ch 5
Unemployment Insurance—COC § 8.3.1.4
Unfair Insurance Practices Statutes—UDAP § 5.3; COC § 8.4.1.4
Unfair Practices Statutes—*See* UDAP
Unfairness—UDAP § 4.3
Uniform Arbitration Act – Arbit. Ch. 10
Uniform Commercial Code—*See* UCC
United States Trustee—Bankr §§ 2.7, 17.7.2
Universal Telephone Service—AUS Ch 2
Unlicensed Activities—COC § 9.2.4.5
Unpaid Refund Discharge of Student Loan—Stud § 6.4
Unsolicited Credit Cards—TIL § 5.9.2
Unsolicited Goods—UDAP § 5.8.4; FDC § 9.2
Unsubstantiated Claims—UDAP § 4.5
Used as New—UDAP § 4.9.4
Used Car Lemon Laws—Warr § 15.4.5
Used Car Rule—Warr § 15.8, App D; UDAP § 5.4.6.2, App B.6
Used Cars—Auto; Warr Ch 15, App K.3, App L.4; UDAP § 5.4.6
Used Cars, Assembled from Salvaged Parts—Auto §§ 1.4.3, 2.1.4
Used Cars, Financing—COC § 11.6
Used Cars, Undisclosed Sale of Wrecked Cars—Auto §§ 1.4.4, 2.1.4
Users of Consumer and Credit Reports—FCR Ch 7
Usury, Trying a Case—COC Ch 10
Utilities—AUS; CD §§ 2.2.2.3, 2.2.6.2; TIL § 2.4.6; UDAP §§ 2.3.2, 5.6.9
Utilities and Bankruptcy—AUS §§ 4.5, 12.1; Bankr § 9.8
Utilities as Credit Reporting Agencies—FCR § 2.7.9
Utility Commission Regulation—AUS § 1.3, App A
Utility Service Terminated by a Landlord—AUS § 12.4
Utility Subsidies in Subsidized Housing—AUS Ch 8
Utility Termination, Remedies—AUS § 11.7; UDAP § 5.6.9.1; FDC § 1.5.6
Utility Terminations, Stopping—AUS Chs 11, 12; Bankr Ch 9
VA Mortgage Foreclosures and Workouts—Fore §§ 2.7.2, 3.3
Variable Rate Disclosures—TIL § 4.8
Variable Rates, Calculation—COC § 4.3.6
Vehicle Identification Number—Auto § 2.2.4
Venue, Inconvenient—FDC §§ 6.12.2, 8.3.7, 10.6.3, 11.7; UDAP § 5.1.1.4
Vertical Privity—Warr § 6.2

Quick Reference to the Consumer Credit and Sales Legal Practice Series

References are to sections in *all* manuals in NCLC's Consumer Credit and Sales Legal Practice Series

Vocational Schools—Stud Ch 9
Voir Dire, Sample Questions—FDC App J.2
Voluntary Payment Doctrine—UDAP § 4.2.15.5; COC § 10.6.5
Wage Earner Plans—Bankr Ch 4
Wage Garnishment—FDC Ch 12, App D
Waiver of Default—Repo § 4.3
Waiver of Right to Enforce Arbitration Clause—Arbit Ch 7
Wage Garnishment of Student Loans—Stud § 5.3, App B.1.3
Warehouseman's Lien—Repo § 15.7.4
Warranties—Warr; Auto § 8.2; UDAP § 5.2.7
Warranties, Secret—Warr § 14.5.3.2; UDAP § 5.4.7.10.2
Warranty Disclaimers—Warr Ch 5
Warranty of Habitability, Utility Service—AUS § 4.4.1
Water Quality Improvement Systems—UDAP § 5.6.5
Water Service—AUS § 1.2.3, App I; UDAP § 5.6.11
Weatherization Assistance—AUS Ch 10
Web Sites, Consumer Advocacy—UDAP § 1.3
Welfare Benefits, Bankruptcy—Bankr §§ 10.2.2.11, 14.5.5

Welfare Benefits, Credit Discrimination—CD §§ 3.4.3, 5.5.2.5
Welfare Benefits, Credit Reporting—FCR §§ 2.3.6.6, 7.2.2
Welfare Benefits, Exemptions—FDC § 12.5
"Wheelchair" Lemon Laws—Warr Ch 16a
Wire Fraud—UDAP § 9.2.4.4
Wires—CBPL Ch 5
Withholding Credit Payments—Repo § 4.6.3; Warr § 8.5
Women's Business Ownership Act of 1988—CD § 1.3.2.4
Workers Compensation and Bankruptcy—Bankr § 10.2.2.1
Workout Agreements—TIL § 4.9.7
Workout Agreements, Foreclosures—Fore Ch 2
Wraparound Mortgages—COC § 7.4.3
Writ of Replevin—Repo Ch 5
Yield Spread Premiums—CD § 8.4; COC §§ 4.7.2, 7.3.2, 11.2.1.4.3, 11.2.2.6; UDAP §§ 5.1.3.3, 5.4.3.4
Yo-Yo Delivery of Automobiles—UDAP § 5.4.5; Repo § 4.5; TIL §§ 4.4.5, 4.4.6; COC § 11.2.2.5; CD § 10.4.2

NOTES

NOTES

NOTES

NOTES

NOTES

NOTES

NOTES

NOTES

About the Companion CD-Rom

CD-Rom Supersedes All Prior CD-Roms

This CD-Rom supersedes the CD-Roms accompanying *Fair Credit Reporting* (5th ed. 2002) and its supplement. Discard all prior CD-Roms. This 2006 CD-Rom contains everything found on the earlier CDs and contains much additional material.

What Is on the CD-Rom

For a detailed listing of the CD's contents, see the CD-Rom Contents section on page xxxvii of this book. Highlights and new additions include:

- The Fair Credit Reporting Act, including amendments made by FACTA, plus a redlined version of the FCRA, FACTA and its legislative history, FACTA regulations and supplemental Federal Register material, and an FTC report under FACTA;
- The Consumer Repair Organizations Act, sections of Gramm-Leach-Bliley, and summaries of state credit reporting and identity theft laws;
- Over 40 sample complaints, over 40 discovery requests and discovery documents, sample deposition transcripts, and other pleadings;
- Trial transcripts from an identity theft case, plaintiff's direct testimony on damages, closing arguments, jury instructions, over 30 briefs and memos, FTC amicus briefs, and other trial documents;
- A universal data form, FTC model credit reporting forms updated for FACTA compliance, sample credit reports, explanations of credit reports, summary of rights, sample contracts between credit bureau and retailers, and other forms;
- The full text of *all* FTC Staff Opinion Letters on the FCRA with a sectional index and the FTC Official Staff Commentary;
- Over 20 enforcement orders against the major reporting agencies and others; and
- Consumer's guide to credit reporting, an FRB report on accuracy in credit reporting, and numerous other consumer education brochures.

How to Use the CD-Rom

The CD's pop-up menu quickly allows you to use the CD—just place the CD into its drive and click on the "Start NCLC CD" button that will pop up in the middle of the screen. You can also access the CD by clicking on a desktop icon that you can create using the pop-up menu.[1] For detailed installation instructions, see *One-Time Installation* below.

All the CD-Rom's information is available in PDF (Acrobat) format, making the information:

- Highly readable (identical to the printed pages in the book);
- Easily navigated (with bookmarks, "buttons," and Internet-style forward and backward searches);
- Easy to locate with keyword searches and other quick-search techniques across the whole CD-Rom; and
- Easy to paste into a word processor.

While much of the material is also found on the CD-Rom in word processing format, we strongly recommend you use the material in PDF format—not only because it is easiest to use, contains the most features, and includes more material, but also because you can easily switch back to a word processing format when you prefer.

Acrobat Reader 5.0.5 and 7.0.7 come free of charge with the CD-Rom. **We strongly recommend that new Acrobat users read the Acrobat tutorial on the Home Page. It takes two minutes and will really pay off.**

How to Find Documents in Word Processing Format

Most pleadings and other practice aids are also available in Microsoft Word format to make them more easily adaptable for individual use. (Current versions of WordPerfect are able to convert the Word documents upon opening them.) The CD-Rom offers several ways to find those word processing documents. One option is simply to browse to the

---

1 Alternatively, click on the D:\Start.pdf file on "My Computer" or open that file in Acrobat—always assuming "D:" is the CD-Rom drive on your computer.

folder on the CD-Rom containing all the word processing files and open the desired document from your standard word processing program, such as Word or WordPerfect. All word processing documents are in the D:\WP_Files folder, if "D:" is the CD-Rom drive,[2] and are further organized by book title. Documents that appear in the book are named after the corresponding appendix; other documents have descriptive file names.

Another option is to navigate the CD in PDF format, and, when a particular document is on the screen, click on the corresponding bookmark for the "Word version of . . ." This will automatically run Word, WordPerfect for Windows, or *any other word processor* that is associated with the ".DOC" extension, and then open the word processing file that corresponds to the Acrobat document.[3]

Important Information Before Opening the CD-Rom Package

Before opening the CD-Rom package, please read this information. Opening the package constitutes acceptance of the following described terms. In addition, the *book* is not returnable once the seal to the *CD-Rom* has been broken.

The CD-Rom is copyrighted and all rights are reserved by the National Consumer Law Center, Inc. No copyright is claimed to the text of statutes, regulations, excerpts from court opinions, or any part of an original work prepared by a United States Government employee.

You may not commercially distribute the CD-Rom or otherwise reproduce, publish, distribute or use the disk in any manner that may infringe on any copyright or other proprietary right of the National Consumer Law Center. Nor may you otherwise transfer the CD-Rom or this agreement to any other party unless that party agrees to accept the terms and conditions of this agreement. You may use the CD-Rom on only one computer and by one user at a time.

The CD-Rom is warranted to be free of defects in materials and faulty workmanship under normal use for a period of ninety days after purchase. If a defect is discovered in the CD-Rom during this warranty period, a replacement disk can be obtained at no charge by sending the defective disk, postage prepaid, with information identifying the purchaser, to National Consumer Law Center, Publications Department, 77 Summer Street, 10th Floor, Boston, MA 02110. After the ninety-day period, a replacement will be available on the same terms, but will also require a $20 prepayment.

The National Consumer Law Center makes no other warranty or representation, either express or implied, with respect to this disk, its quality, performance, merchantability, or fitness for a particular purpose. In no event will the National Consumer Law Center be liable for direct, indirect, special, incidental, or consequential damages arising out of the use or inability to use the disk. The exclusion of implied warranties is not effective in some states, and thus this exclusion may not apply to you.

System Requirements

Use of this CD-Rom requires a Windows-based PC with a CD-Rom drive. (Macintosh users report success using NCLC CDs, but the CD has been tested only on Windows-based PCs.) The CD-Rom's features are optimized with Acrobat Reader 5 or later. Acrobat Reader versions 5.0.5 and 7.0.7 are included free on this CD-Rom, and either will work with this CD-Rom as long as it is compatible with your version of Windows. Acrobat Reader 5 is compatible with Windows 95/98/Me/NT/2000/XP, while Acrobat Reader 7.0.7 is compatible with Windows 98SE/Me/NT/2000/XP. If you already have Acrobat Reader 6.0, we *highly* recommend you install the 6.0.1 update from the Adobe web site at www.adobe.com because a bug in version 6.0 interferes with optimum use of this CD-Rom. The Microsoft Word versions of pleadings and practice aids can be used with any reasonably current word processor (1995 or later).

One-Time Installation

When the CD-Rom is inserted in its drive, a menu will pop up automatically. (Please be patient if you have a slow CD-Rom drive; this will only take a few moments.) If you do not already have Acrobat Reader 5 or later, first click the "Install Acrobat Reader" button. Do not reboot, but then click on the "Make Shortcut Icon" button. (You need not make another shortcut icon if you already have done so for another NCLC CD.) Then reboot and follow the *How to Use the CD-Rom* instructions above.

[*Note*: If the pop-up menu fails to appear, go to "My Computer," right-click "D:" if that is the CD-Rom drive, and select "Open." Then double-click on "Read_Me.txt" for alternate installation and use instructions.]

---

2 The CD-Rom drive could be any letter following "D:" depending on your computer's configuration.

3 For instructions on how to associate WordPerfect to the ".DOC" extension, go to the CD-Rom's home page and click on "How to Use/Help," then "Word Files."